Handbook of
Marketing Research

Handbook of
Marketing Research

ROBERT FERBER   *Editor-in-Chief*

Research Professor of Economics and Marketing
Director, Survey Research Laboratory
University of Illinois
Urbana, Illinois

McGRAW-HILL BOOK COMPANY

New York   St. Louis   San Francisco   Düsseldorf   Johannesburg
Kuala Lumpur   London   Mexico   Montreal   New Delhi
Panama   Rio de Janeiro   Singapore
Sydney   Toronto

Library of Congress Cataloging in Publication Data

Ferber, Robert, date.
    Handbook of marketing research.

    Includes bibliographies.
    1. Marketing research—Handbooks, manuals, etc.
I. Title.
HF5415.2.F419   658.8′3   73-12967
ISBN 0-07-020462-4

567890 KPKP 79

*The editors for this book were W. Hodson Mogan and George Ryan,
the designer was Naomi Auerbach, and its production
was supervised by George E. Oechsner.   It was set in Caledonia
by Monotype Composition Co., Inc.*

It was printed and bound by The Kingsport Press.

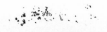

Contributors

ALVIN A. ACHENBAUM   *J. Walter Thompson Company, New York, New York*

ARNOLD E. AMSTUTZ   *Decision Technology, Incorporated; Sloan School of Management, Massachusetts Institute of Technology, Cambridge, Massachusetts*

LEE ANDREWS   *Consultant, New York, New York*

WILLIAM APPLEBAUM   *Nova University, Fort Lauderdale, Florida*

SEYMOUR BANKS   *Leo Burnett, Inc., Chicago, Illinois*

BRUCE M. BARE   *Arthur D. Little, Inc., Cambridge, Massachusetts*

FRANK M. BASS   *Krannert Graduate School of Industrial Administration, Purdue University, Lafayette, Indiana*

JOSEPH C. BEVIS   *Consultant, Stuart, Florida*

A. B. BLANKENSHIP   *Bowling Green State University, Bowling Green, Ohio*

PHILIP J. BOURQUE   *School of Business Administration, University of Washington, Seattle, Washington*

HARPER W. BOYD, JR.   *Graduate School of Business, Stanford University, Stanford, California*

STEUART HENDERSON BRITT   *Graduate School of Management, Northwestern University, Evanston, Illinois*

LOUIS P. BUCKLIN   *Institute of Business and Economic Research, University of California, Berkeley, California*

JAMES M. CARMAN   *Graduate School of Business Administration, University of California, Berkeley, California*

HENRY J. CLAYCAMP   *International Harvester Co., Chicago, Illinois*

ARNOLD CORBIN   *Graduate School of Business Administration, New York University, New York, New York*

v

A. GRAEME CRANCH *Russell International Marketing Services Ltd., London, England*

C. MERLE CRAWFORD *Graduate School of Business Administration, University of Michigan, Ann Arbor, Michigan*

IRVING CRESPI *The Gallup Organization, Inc., Princeton, New Jersey*

RICHARD D. CRISP *Richard D. Crisp and Associates, Inc., Pasadena, California*

HARRY DAVIS *Graduate School of Business, University of Chicago, Chicago, Illinois*

RALPH L. DAY *Graduate School of Business, Indiana University, Bloomington, Indiana*

CORNELIUS DuBOIS *Consultant; Advertising Research Foundation, Inc., New York, New York*

S. WATSON DUNN *Department of Advertising, University of Illinois, Urbana, Illinois*

SOL DUTKA *Audits and Surveys Company, New York, New York*

PAUL L. ERDOS *Erdos and Morgan, Inc., New York, New York*

CHARLES W. FARIS *The Boston Consulting Group, Inc., Boston, Massachusetts*

JOHN U. FARLEY *Graduate School of Business, Columbia University, New York, New York*

GEORGE FISK *Department of Marketing, Syracuse University, Syracuse, New York*

RONALD E. FRANK *Department of Marketing, University of Pennsylvania, Philadelphia, Pennsylvania*

LESTER R. FRANKEL *Audits and Surveys Company, New York, New York*

MARTIN R. FRANKEL *Graduate School of Business, University of Chicago, Chicago, Illinois*

DENNIS H. GENSCH *Graduate School of Business Administration, Carnegie-Mellon University, Pittsburgh, Pennsylvania*

LAWRENCE D. GIBSON *General Mills, Inc., Minneapolis, Minnesota*

HOWARD L. GREEN *Howard L. Green & Associates, Inc., Bloomfield Hills, Michigan*

PAUL E. GREEN *Wharton School, University of Pennsylvania, Philadelphia, Pennsylvania*

MARSHALL G. GREENBERG *National Analysts, Inc., Philadelphia, Pennsylvania*

EDWIN C. GREIF *Department of Business Administration, University of Vermont, Burlington, Vermont*

DAVID K. HARDIN *Market Facts, Inc., Chicago, Illinois*

MATTHEW HAUCK *Survey Research Laboratory, University of Illinois, Urbana, Illinois*

GEORGE B. HEGEMAN *Arthur D. Little, Inc., Cambridge, Massachusetts*

PETER L. HENDERSON *Marketing Economics Division, U.S. Department of Agriculture, Washington, D.C.*

MELVIN J. HINICH *Carnegie-Mellon University, Pittsburgh, Pennsylvania*

SIDNEY HOLLANDER, JR. *Sidney Hollander Associates, Baltimore, Maryland*

WILLIAM S. HOOFNAGLE *Marketing Economics Division, U.S. Department of Agriculture, Washington, D.C.*

G. DAVID HUGHES *School of Business Administration, University of North Carolina, Chapel Hill, North Carolina*

RIKUMA ITO *College of Business and Administration, University of Detroit, Detroit, Michigan*

ROGER M. JOHNSON *Roger Johnson & Associates, Inc., Pasadena, California*

HAROLD H. KASSARJIAN *Graduate School of Business Administration, University of California, Los Angeles, California*

ROBERT F. KELLY *Commerce and Business Administration, University of British Columbia, Vancouver, Canada*

WILLIAM R. KING *Graduate School of Business, University of Pittsburgh, Pittsburgh, Pennsylvania*

WILLIAM LAZER *Graduate School of Business Administration, Michigan State University, East Lansing, Michigan*

LAWRENCE C. LOCKLEY, (Deceased) *University of Santa Clara, Santa Clara, California*

WILLIAM F. MASSY *Graduate School of Business, Stanford University, Stanford, California*

CHARLES S. MAYER *Faculty of Administrative Studies, York University, Downsview, Ontario, Canada*

ROBERT L. McLAUGHLIN *Scovill Manufacturing Company, Waterbury, Connecticut*

DAVID B. MONTGOMERY *Graduate School of Business, Stanford University, Stanford, California*

WILLIAM M. MORGENROTH *College of Business Administration, University of South Carolina, Columbia, South Carolina*

JOHN MORRIS *Consultant, Clinton, New York*

DONALD G. MORRISON *Graduate School of Business, Columbia University, New York, New York*

WILLIAM F. O'DELL *Consultant, Charlottesville, Virginia*

KRISTIAN S. PALDA *School of Business, Queen's University, Kingston, Ontario, Canada*

LEONARD J. PARSONS *Graduate School of Business, Indiana University, Bloomington, Indiana*

STANLEY L. PAYNE *Survey Research Consultant, Breckenridge, Colorado*

ROBERT W. PRATT, JR. *General Electric Company, Louisville, Kentucky*

LAWRENCE SALZMAN *Consultant, New York, New York*

KYOHEI SASAKI *Consultant, East Orange, New Jersey*

DAN E. SCHENDEL *Krannert Graduate School of Industrial Administration, Purdue University, Lafayette, Indiana*

CLARK SCHILLER *Time Magazine, New York, New York*

THOMAS T. SEMON *BMD Consultants, New York, New York*

PAUL B. SHEATSLEY *National Opinion Research Center, University of Chicago, Chicago, Illinois*

JAGDISH N. SHETH *Department of Business Administration, University of Illinois, Urbana, Illinois*

PHILIP S. SIDEL *Social Science Information Center, University of Pittsburgh, Pittsburgh, Pennsylvania*

ALVIN J. SILK *Sloan School of Management, Massachusetts Institute of Technology, Cambridge, Massachusetts*

J. TAYLOR SIMS *College of Business Administration, University of South Carolina, Columbia, South Carolina*

R. CLAY SPROWLS *Graduate School of Business Administration, University of California, Los Angeles, California*

CHANNING STOWELL III *Corporate Market Information Services, The Pillsbury Company, Minneapolis, Minnesota*

SEYMOUR SUDMAN *Survey Research Laboratory, University of Illinois, Urbana, Illinois*

GORDON D. THOMAS *Faculty of Commerce, University of Manitoba, Winnipeg, Canada*

DONALD L. THOMPSON *Slippery Rock State College, Slippery Rock, Pennsylvania*

DONALD S. TULL *School of Business Administration, University of Oregon, Eugene, Oregon*

KENNETH P. UHL *Department of Business Administration, University of Illinois, Urbana, Illinois*

M. VENKATESAN *School of Business Administration, University of Iowa, Iowa City, Iowa*

KEN WARWICK *Grey Advertising, New York, New York*

CHESTER R. WASSON *School of Business, Northern Illinois University, DeKalb, Illinois*

WILLIAM D. WELLS *Graduate School of Business, University of Chicago, Chicago, Illinois*

ROBERT L. WINKLER *Graduate School of Business, Indiana University, Bloomington, Indiana*

ROBERT G. WYCKHAM *Simon Fraser University, British Columbia, Canada*

CHARLES YANG *Hakuhodo Incorporated, Tokyo, Japan*

Contents

Section II. TECHNIQUES

Part A. Research Design

Part B. Surveys

Part C. Sample Design

Part D. Statistical Inference

Index follows Section IV

Preface

The purpose of this handbook is to provide a basic reference source of marketing research methods and applications for the user of marketing research. The need for such a handbook is highlighted by the growing scope and diversity of the field. This expansion has been so rapid that by now it is hard to determine where marketing ends and such other subjects as applied mathematics, sociology, psychology, and operational research begin.

The fact is that, on the one hand, the scope of marketing research has broadened to include essentially the study of marketing distribution institutions and behavior within a sociopolitical as well as a business framework. At the same time, the methods used in marketing research have expanded to include a wide variety of approaches from such diverse fields as mathematics, sociology, psychology, and engineering in addition to the more closely associated fields of economics and statistics.

Yet a third aspect is the growing importance of marketing, and of marketing research, in a world where production is becoming increasingly efficient, with the consequence that marketing and distribution begin to replace production as the chief bottlenecks to economic and social progress.

The result of these developments is that marketing research is being used on an ever-increasing scale and is tending to employ methods that are increasingly varied and sophisticated. No longer is it possible for one person to be well versed in the entire range of marketing research methods. On the contrary, specialists, evolving in various branches of marketing research, have barely enough time to keep up with the developments in their own subject areas and can have only passing acquaintance with other methods and approaches. In addition, there are the marketing research generalists who may have a little knowledge of many different methods but who know none of them well enough to use them without outside consultation. These generalists are usually marketing research administrators and marketing executives, who fulfill a valuable function in helping to focus different approaches on a single problem. Still a third group are the clients of marketing research, who are principally marketing and management executives in business or government. They have only a limited familiarity with marketing research and more often than not have no real background in the subject. They seldom know the range of marketing research methods or how one goes about dealing with a particular marketing problem.

This handbook is directed primarily at the latter two groups. It seeks to provide them with information on virtually all the principal methods used in marketing research, and also to indicate, in the last section, how one may go about solving a wide variety of marketing problems. The first section of the book, containing the present chapter and nine others, provides general introductory material on marketing research, focusing on its historical, functional, and operational aspects. This section also discusses such questions as the use and communication of marketing research findings, the role of ethics in marketing research, and the use of marketing research contractors.

The second and third sections of the book cover the principal techniques of marketing research, Section II dealing with quantitative methods and Section III focusing on behavioral science techniques. Each chapter begins with a brief explanation of the technique. The chapter then deals with how the technique is used, operating problems, and examples of its use, and usually concludes with a comparison of the advantages and limitations of that particular technique relative to alternative approaches. Most chapters also contain a list of selected references or a bibliography for those who are interested in exploring particular techniques at greater length.

The last section of the book covers principal areas of application in six major branches of marketing. Here, in contrast to the preceding sections, each chapter deals with a particular type of marketing problem, discussing various techniques for handling the problem, giving illustrations of their use, and indicating the pros and cons of each approach.

For purposes of presentation, it is generally assumed that the reader's knowledge of mathematics does not exceed college algebra, the rudiments of differential calculus, and such statistics as learned in an elementary course in statistics. He is also viewed not to be a specialist in any of the behavioral sciences. It is assumed, however, that he has a very general knowledge of these areas, such as is obtained in a broad social science survey course.

For these reasons, the chapters on methodology frequently present the material at two levels. The first part of the chapter discusses the content in a nontechnical way, whereas the second part, which may be an appendix, describes the same material in more rigorous fashion for the advanced reader. Even in these parts, however, no attempt is made to cover all aspects of the subject as deeply as might be desired by a specialist in that technique. Rather, the aim is to explain the salient point, with the references indicating where more complete coverage may be obtained.

The preparation of a volume of this sort entailed the generous cooperation of a number of individuals. In particular, the outline and structure of the volume was guided by an advisory committee that consisted of Paul Green, David Hardin, Herbert Krugman, William Massy, Tom Semon, and Robert Buzzell. Their counsel and advice in the development of the volume and in commenting on drafts of particular chapters were invaluable.

I would also like to thank the authors of the individual chapters for their willingness to devote the time and effort to preparing their materials and for their frequent collaboration with other authors to fit material more closely to the desired format. The ultimate responsibility, however, is that of the editor-in-chief. All decisions regarding the nature of this book were made by him, and he should be blamed for any errors or shortcomings that may be found.

Robert Ferber

Section One

Introduction

Chapter 1

History and Development
of Marketing Research

LAWRENCE C. LOCKLEY* *Formerly Professor of Marketing, University of Santa Clara, Santa Clara, California*

THE DEVELOPMENT OF MARKETING RESEARCH

The practice of informal marketing research is old. Even the children of Israel sent interviewers out to sample the market and the produce of Canaan. Probably before that, young women tried to foresee their matrimonial prospects by repeating, as they pulled petals from daisies, "He loves me, he loves me not." For business or personal reasons, people have wanted to foresee the future so they could plan more intelligently.

Probably the first instance of using information from direct observation of business affairs in various locations was provided by the Fugger family. In 1380, Johann Fugger left his native Swabian village of Graben to settle in Augsburg, where he engaged in the international sale of textiles.[1] Family members settled in strategic capitals, moving into finance, trade, manufacturing, and mining. They helped finance the rulers of the western European countries and dominated international finance until the mid-seventeenth century.

The interest to us results from their practice of exchanging detailed letters on trade conditions and finance in the localities of their branches so that all partners could base their decisions on current knowledge of changing conditions of supply and demand for money and goods. There was probably no thought of pioneering in the development of a new method for directing business. Nevertheless, the Fugger family—through its cohesiveness—was able to

---

* Deceased.
[1] *Encyclopedia of the Social Sciences*, New York: Macmillan, 1948.

provide one of the essentials of marketing research, that is, the collection of market data from the field to reinforce judgment on business problems.

Another example of the inherent reaching for broad-based market facts is Daniel Defoe's *A Tour through the Whole Island of Great Britain,* published in the 1720s.[2] Defoe's *Tour* was a careful inventory of the business and economic resources of England and Scotland, indicating what economic activity was under way in each location. With slow and uncomfortable transportation, an almost complete lack of background economic data, and limitations imposed by a single viewpoint, it is certain that much information in the *Tour* was approximate. Yet its availability to businessmen added much to merchants' ability to make business decisions. The *Tour's* nine editions are evidence of its value.

There is no reason to suppose that firms other than the Fugger family organization did not acquaint their members with trade conditions at distant points. Nor can we overlook a considerable number of journals of travelers which contained comments on business conditions. We can justly draw the conclusion that there was a need for the collection, analysis, and dissemination of commercial information. Originally, business was largely local; the need for business information from distant parts was small. But after the impact of the industrial revolution's early phases, pressure for information on which to base marketing decisions must have increased.

BEGINNINGS IN THE UNITED STATES

The first evidence of more formalized marketing research techniques in the United States came from attempts to forecast elections.

"*The Harrisburg Pennsylvanian* of July 24, 1824, printed a report of a straw vote taken at Wilmington, Delaware, 'without Discrimination of Parties.' In this poll, Andrew Jackson received 335 votes; John Quincy Adams, 169; Henry Clay, 19; and William H. Crawford, 9."[3]

"Again during the same summer, the *Raleigh Star* canvassed North Carolina political meetings 'at which the sense of the people was taken.' "[4]

Though these instances were not marketing research, they used some marketing research tools in preliminary form. That two newspapers chose to try forms of "straw vote counting" at so near the same time suggests that this form of political forecasting may have been more widely used than present and available data can establish.

More by accident than foresight, N. W. Ayer & Son applied marketing research to marketing and advertising problems. In 1879, in attempting to fit a proposed advertising schedule to the needs of the Nichols-Shepard Company, manufacturers of agricultural machinery, the agency wired state officials and publishers throughout the country requesting information on expected grain production. As a result, the agency was able to construct a crude but formal market survey by states and counties.[5] This attempt to construct a market survey is probably the first real instance of marketing research in the United States.

[2] Now most conveniently available in Everyman's Library, London: Dent, 1962.

[3] Although in the straw vote the three candidates were arrayed in the same order as in the popular balloting, the accuracy of the division of votes was lacking.

[4] George Gallup and Saul F. Rae, *The Pulse of Democracy,* New York: Simon & Schuster, 1940, p. 35.

[5] Ralph M. Hower, *The History of an Advertising Agency,* Cambridge, Mass.: Harvard University Press, 1939.

The next known instance of marketing research is provided by E. I. du Pont de Nemours & Co. Today at Du Pont, a companywide service division, the Trade Analysis Division, makes monthly analyses of salesmen's call reports. According to the needs of each selling department or division, salesmen are asked to estimate the total sales volume for the product they sell, report any new products or processes discussed, estimate future sales, and so forth. A company with a large number of customers in many manufacturing classifications can soon accumulate considerable knowledge about its markets and the development of products and processes in its fields.

Some documentary evidence indicates early use of the systematic analysis of salesmen's call reports at Du Pont. George H. Kerr wrote:

> Mr. Haskell authorized the first "Trade Report." This comprehensive survey of each customer and each prospective customer was, at first, an outrage to the salesman, the bane of his career. But Trade Reports produced sales—and bred other salesmen necessary to service multiplying customers. The sales force of one in 1892—Mr. Patterson himself—grew to 65 in 1902. Sales first doubled, then tripled, and within the same period had quadrupled. Mr. Patterson's conquest of the explosives market was well nigh complete.[6]

The *History of the Explosives Industry in America* provides further corroboration: "At this time (1903) George H. Kerr was assigned the task of organizing a trade record bureau, which became a very important source of information for the sales division."[7]

How much earlier what is now called trade analysis was carried on we cannot be sure. Mr. Ernst S. Erickson, Jr., assigned to marketing research at Du Pont, writes, "I can recall Luther Reed (for many years Director of the Trade Analysis Division) telling us of earlier, perhaps as early as 1880, informal attempts to organize the information sent in from the field by sales agents."[8] As manager of Du Pont's central Marketing Research Division, I heard Luther Reed make this statement at several company meetings and add the fact that the federal judge, presiding over the monopoly trial which forced Du Pont to dispose of Hercules Powder Company and Atlas Company, had commented in his decision that no company could have acquired such intimate knowledge of the explosives industry and explosives markets without resorting to commercial espionage!

The development of marketing research techniques was inconsistent. It will become increasingly apparent that people in various parts of the United States were venturing into aspects of marketing research without the knowledge of others. In 1895, Professor Harlow Gale of the University of Minnesota took the next step forward and sent a questionnaire to advertising practitioners.[9] It will be instructive to see what may be the first academic questionnaire on marketing research:

[6] George H. Kerr, *Du Pont Romance,* Wilmington, Del.: Du Pont Printing Division, 1938, p. 107.

[7] Van Gelder & Schlatter, *History of the Explosives Industry in America,* New York: Columbia University Press, 1927, p. 615.

[8] From a personal letter dated October 4, 1968 from Mr. Erickson to the present writer.

[9] Privately published under the title of *On the Psychology of Advertising* in 1900; at least one copy of this pamphlet has been preserved in the Library of the University of Minnesota, from which the present writer obtained a photographic copy.

University of Minnesota
Question Blank No. 3 in Experimental Psychology.
For the Study of Advertising.

At the University of Minnesota we are making a psychological investigation of advertisements. It is an entirely new field for psychological work and one of great and increasing importance. It is our aim to find the mental processes which go on in the minds of the customers from the time they see an advertisement until they have purchased the article advertised. To get down to the bottom of our subject and make our work successful, we need the aid of experienced advertisers, and to that end, we have sent out this circular with the following questions and will be greatly indebted to you if you will send us your answers to them. Please return answers to H. Gale, University of Minnesota.

Advertisements seem to have two aims, viz: 1. To attract attention. 2. To induce to buy.

If you have any corrections to make with this they will be gladly received. We have classified the chief ways of advertising into four groups, viz:

1. Magazines and periodicals.
2. Newspapers and handbills or posters.
3. Show windows.
4. Painted signs and placards.

Do you know of any other ways of advertising?

What are the best ways you have found in your experience for attracting attention under these four ways of advertising?

Please name them in order of their importance from best to poorest.

Give your reasons why each way of attracting attention does attract attention.

What are the best ways you have found in your experience for inducing people to buy? (e.g., constant reiteration of firm or article, add figure prices, leaders, testimonials, prizes, use of superlatives, argument, plain statements, etc.)

Please name them in the order of their importance from best to poorest.

Give your reasons why each way of inducing people to buy does induce them to buy.

Two hundred questionnaires were sent, mostly to business firms in St. Paul and Minneapolis. Professor Gale writes: "Tho only some twenty were answered and returned, yet they gave us many valuable corrections and additions from their experience." The businessman who, today, studies Gale's questionnaire will wonder what the 20 respondents had to say, because 78 years later we are still trying to find clues to some of his questions.

After his questionnaire, Gale conducted several experiments among his students, and on the basis of the questionnaire returns and the results of his observations of his student subjects, he wrote a pamphlet entitled *On the Psychology of Advertising* (1900). Though the contribution may seem small today, Gale introduced the concept of the mail questionnaire to several advertising men and may have hastened the application of marketing research in the field of advertising.

A second academic psychologist picked up the torch:

Walter Dill Scott, who had established a psychological laboratory at Northwestern University in 1900, was more successful than Gale in convincing advertising men that the application of psychological principles had practical value. Addressing the Agate Club of Chicago at its annual banquet in December, 1901, he obtained enthusiastic support for the idea that something could be done to make the practice of advertising more scientific. Scott agreed to prepare a series of articles and to do experimental research on a consulting basis for members of the Agate Club.

The articles written by Walter Dill Scott were published in *Mahin's Magazine*, beginning in April, 1902 and appearing in each monthly issue until May, 1904.

The first twelve of these articles were revised by Scott, and published in book form in November, 1903, under the title, *The Theory of Advertising*. Additional research and the articles which appeared in 1903 and 1904 were ultimately included in Scott's book entitled *The Psychology of Advertising*, published in 1908.[10]

THE 1910s AND 1920s

We have been discussing the sporadic use of various aspects of marketing research. In the decade following the publication of Scott's work, several people and institutions undertook to develop what must undeniably be regarded as marketing research. There is no one person who "invented" marketing research or who first applied its techniques. We have seen that aspects of marketing research techniques were used sporadically for nearly a century. As the art of packaging grew and brands developed, the need for marketing research increased. Marketing research made major advances from approximately 1910 to 1920.

First mentioned is J. George Frederick.[11] In 1903 he was offered a job with Lord & Thomas, one of the more prominent Chicago advertising agencies, because of articles he had been writing for *Printers' Ink*, the leading trade journal for advertising and marketing of which he became editor in 1907. In 1911, he resigned his editorship to devote full time to his marketing research firm, called The Business Bourse, but he continued in the publishing business editing *Advertising & Selling* as a sideline. Frederick reported that his was the first organization in the United States to maintain a group of interviewers in strategic spots in the country. The flow of the early work of The Business Bourse is hard to describe because much of it was proprietary and thus never available for general examination and much of it was ephemeral. Besides consultation and specific research projects, his firm supplied annual marketing data maps.

A parallel development was the establishment of the Bureau of Business Research by the Harvard Business School, with Selden O. Martin as first director. The idea grew out of a discussion between Dean Edwin F. Gay and A. W. Shaw, then temporarily at the Harvard Business School. The first study undertaken was on operating expenses of retail shoe stores. During the first summer, Professor Cherington and Mr. Stoner did fieldwork and found additional information was needed before they could determine these expenses. Many shoe retailers kept no accounts, and of those who did, no two kept them similarly. Consequently a standard classification of accounts was next set up, with the help and advice of retailers in the shoe business, shoe manufacturers, and accountants. Using that standard classification, Dr. Martin went out into the field and, during the next year, obtained figures from about 130 shoe stores, the results being published in the bureau's first bulletin.

Undertaken in the spring of 1914 was a similar study of operating expenses in retail grocery stores.[12] Although this was not its only field of interest, determining common figures of operating costs became one of the major contribu-

[10] From Frank G. Coolsen, "Pioneers in the Development of Advertising," *The Journal of Marketing*, vol. 12, no. 1, pp. 83–84. Information concerning the contribution of Walter Dill Scott was obtained by Dr. Coolsen in a personal interview June 5, 1942.

[11] Information on J. George Frederick comes from reasonably extensive correspondence with him in May and June of 1945 and from material sent to the present writer from his files.

[12] Excerpt from a letter written to the present author by Dr. Melvin T. Copeland, June 20, 1945.

tions of Harvard's Bureau of Business Research. For many years it held a contract with the National Retail Drygoods Association (which later changed its name to the National Retail Merchants Association) to prepare annual studies of operating expenses in department and specialty stores.

So firmly established was the importance of this field that when, sometime before 1918, Northwestern University's School of Commerce instituted a Bureau of Business Research under the direction of Horace Secrist, most of the bureau's emphasis was on operating figures of various classifications of retailers.[13]

Another "first" for the year 1911 was accomplished by R. O. Eastman, then advertising manager of the Kellogg Company in Battle Creek, Michigan. Working through the National Association of Advertising Managers (now the Association of National Advertisers), he undertook a postcard survey to determine which magazines were read by different classifications of people. As far as we know, this was the first readership survey. Results were so enlightening that Eastman arranged to have Kellogg Company salesmen interview people, off season, with a more elaborate questionnaire. He became so thoroughly involved in this subject that, after some time with Fuller & Smith, the Cleveland advertising agency, he began (in 1916) devoting his entire time to administering a market research organization.

To bring in enough income, Eastman solicited various kinds of research assignments. Because of his background in readership surveys, his first clients were magazines.

His first industrial client, in 1917, was the General Electric Company, which wanted to estimate the marketing value of the trade name Mazda. After the first postcard survey, Eastman relied entirely on interviewers and gradually decreased the numbers of people interviewed. The last industrial survey he conducted, before developing his firm into a service organization for publications, included a national sample of only 167 respondents, though each interview was exceedingly detailed.[14]

Because the field developed gradually, with contributions by many individuals, there is no real primacy in marketing research. Another major contributor was Charles Coolidge Parlin, previously the high school principal in a Wisconsin town, who began work for The Curtis Publishing Company in 1911. No advertising medium had marketing information. The Boston manager of Curtis' advertising department, a former student of Parlin's, obtained permission from Curtis to hire Parlin as a research manager, and he chose the name "commercial research" to designate his field of activity. At that time, many believed that the term *research* was too grandiloquent for a business service. As a result, Parlin called his service Commercial Research, while Frederick named his firm The Business Bourse. Others went to considerable lengths to avoid using a term that would have alienated many businessmen.

The Curtis Publishing Company's headquarters were in Philadelphia, as was the office of Cyrus H. K. Curtis, the company's head. So uncertain of the values of marketing research was the company's management that Parlin was kept in the Boston office.

According to S. R. Latshaw, who initially supervised his work, Parlin was asked to make a study of agricultural implements and their marketing problems, which required about six months to complete.[15] The company had just

---

[13] According to a letter to the present writer from Professor Richard M. Clewett, chairman of the department of marketing, Northwestern University, October 15, 1968.

[14] Based on a letter from R. O. Eastman to the writer written May 28, 1945.

[15] Based on a letter from S. R. Latshaw to the writer dated April 14, 1945.

acquired *The Country Gentleman,* a small farm publication.   On completing the study, the space salesman did not know what to do with it.

The second assignment is best described by Parlin:[16]

> Following this (the implement study) a year was spent studying the wholesale and retail distributive system of the textile industry.   An important phase of this study was the study of department stores in which, for the first time, a rudimentary census of distribution was attempted.   I personally visited every important department store in every one of the 100 largest cities in the United States and attempted, through conversation with the proprietors and others well informed, to place a valuation on the volume of business done by each department store and each of the wholesale houses operating in these cities in the textile field.   In this report, for the first time, a distinction was made between convenience goods and shopping lines, and the differences in character between men and women shoppers were stated.

It required many years for the company's space salesmen to reach an agreement that would allow them to use Parlin's research reports by themselves. As a result, Parlin traveled incessantly, making presentations to important advertisers and advertising agencies and being a featured speaker at annual conventions of many trade associations.

One of the most curious aspects of the introduction of marketing research to The Curtis Publishing Company is that while Parlin was still at the company's Boston office, Cyrus H. K. Curtis hired a researcher to supply him with needed information.   John C. Rink, a 1903 graduate of Boston University, was hired as a sales auditor by Curtis after Rink had had about ten years of experience in statistical work.   He worked for Curtis from 1914 to 1919, when he moved to N. W. Ayer & Son, the large Philadelphia advertising agency.   By this time Parlin's work was well established, and Rink remained in charge of the Ayer marketing department's special library until his death in 1950.[17]

Long before such information was available from any other source, Parlin produced market data books giving county information as well as books on various trades.   His most successful work, published annually for many years, was *Sales Opportunities,* a small book presenting population maps for most of the country's large cities.   It showed the population density by areas and the population divided by the four income quartiles.

Parlin created a division with eight staff specialists, two field supervisors, a group of about twenty tabulators, and a similar number of chartists.   At one time, he maintained a part-time interviewing force of about 1,200 people.[18]

After the stabilization of Parlin's division and its location in Philadelphia, many people regarded it as one of the leading marketing research organizations.   Its maintenance under satisfactory budgets and Parlin's continuous guidance from 1911 till his retirement in 1938 gave the Division of Commercial Research the opportunity to develop research standards and adapt to new methods of marketing research as they developed.   Nevertheless, S. R. Latshaw believed that Parlin's services had been used too much for direct selling and that he had not been given enough scope to develop marketing research.[19]

---

[16] Excerpted from a letter sent by Parlin dated January 6, 1938 answering an inquiry about the beginnings of marketing research at The Curtis Publishing Company.

[17] According to a letter from Mr. Theodore Whittelsey, Jr., personnel director of N. W. Ayer & Son, written to the present author on September 16, 1968.

[18] The present writer was one of the staff specialists for seven years and was well acquainted with the organization, the publications, and the assignments of the Commercial Research Division.

[19] *Ibid.*

After the establishment of marketing research at The Curtis Publishing Company, events moved rapidly.   In 1918, Frederick published *Business Research and Statistics*.   The following year, Dr. C. S. Duncan, then assistant professor at the University of Chicago, published *Commercial Research: An Outline of Working Principles*.   Though Duncan's book is over fifty years old, it somewhat reflects the growth of marketing research in that parts of it still seem current.

The degree to which individual firms were developing marketing research in the period immediately after 1911 cannot now be determined except by the accidental location of clippings and records long buried in files.   Little attention has been given to the contribution of *The Chicago Tribune*.   Yet in 1916 this newspaper published a substantial pamphlet entitled *Winning a Great Market on Facts* to promote the use of the *Tribune's* Merchandising Service Department.   Typical of material available to advertisers, space buyers, and advertising agencies, the pamphlet shows interview forms with retailers, maps of neighborhoods indicating the rental value of dwellings by block, and the number of residential vacancies by block.   The city of Chicago was divided into 48 units for detailed analysis.   Reproduced, completed interview forms cover such points as occupation, shopping sources by types of merchandise, buying motives, reliance on advertising, and sales practices of retailers.   On the right-hand side of the questionnaire page is a rating column in which the interviewer was to qualify each answer with the following code:

V = Voluntary   S = Suggestion   P = Prejudiced
A = Answered   F = Facetious   ? = Doubt

Each questionnaire form is dated, the earliest date among the few reproduced forms being February 19, 1913.

Correspondence with *The Chicago Tribune* has suggested that the newspaper's records do not indicate when this type of research was started.   Clearly *The Chicago Tribune* had, in 1913, well-developed plans for the analysis of Chicago's consumer market, a questionnaire prepared with considerable skill, and a group of trained interviewers.   Of this much we can be certain from the questionnaire and the maps in the pamphlet.   *The Chicago Tribune* may be one of the unrecognized pioneers in the field of marketing research.

The Commercial Research Division of The Curtis Publishing Company remained in Boston until 1915 and was then moved to the company's Philadelphia headquarters.[20]

After 1915, manufacturing establishments and advertising media began to establish marketing research divisions.   In June 1915, the U.S. Rubber Company established a Department of Commercial Research with Dr. Paul H. Nystrom in charge.   Nystrom wrote, "the suggestion to have market research or commercial research as it was called, carried on in the U.S. Rubber Company was first made to that Company by C. C. Parlin, then in charge of Commercial Research for The Curtis Publishing Company.   It was he also who recommended me to begin the work in that Company."[21]

Dr. Louis D. H. Weld, largely inspired by Parlin's work for Curtis Publishing, became manager of the Commercial Research Department for Swift & Company.[22]   As you will recall, R. O. Eastman established a research department for Fuller & Smith, the Cleveland advertising agency, in 1916.

[20] From a speech by Charles Coolidge Parlin before the Philadelphia Chapter of the American Marketing Association, June 5, 1936, honoring the twenty-fifth anniversary of the establishment of the division.

[21] Letter to the present author from Dr. Paul H. Nystrom, May 14, 1945.

[22] Letter from Dr. L. D. H. Weld to the present author, April 17, 1945.

Perhaps the best summary of the growth of marketing research may be presented through the early history of the Research Group, a study group under The Advertising Club of New York. *The Advertising Club News*[23] reports:

> Starting auspiciously its career for the season, the Research Group held a lunch on Thursday, October 23, 1924, which overflowed all reservations made for it. Nearly 100 diners came to listen to the first talk on research. J. George Frederick, research authority, of The Business Bourse, explained for the Committee what the Research Group planned to do. It will hold a series of lunches for the special study of New York as a market, and after the close of the year will take up other research subjects of general interest and profit.

Frederick was chairman of this group from its organization in 1924 through 1928.

An early list of the Research Group's regular members indicates the growth of marketing research facilities in the period from 1920 to 1925:[24]

Norris Brisco, New York University
Fred Wood, International Magazine Co.
J. A. Hayes, Crowell Publishing Co.
Daniel Starch, American Association of Advertising Agencies
Lewis Hovey, New York University
Henry Bruere, Metropolitan Life Insurance Co.
David Grimes, David Grimes, Inc. (Jersey City, N.J.)
Alex. Sclater, Great Neck, Long Island
W. A. Berridge, Metropolitan Life Insurance Co.
Ernest Bradford, Tanners' Council
Stanley J. Clark, Joseph Richards Co.
G. E. Conkling, McGraw-Hill Publishing Co.
Walter Emery, U.S. Rubber Co.
F. M. Feiker, Soc. for Electrical Development
Wm. A. Fitzgerald, National Retail Dry Goods Assoc.
Chester A. Haring, Barton, Durstine & Osborne, Inc.
H. B. Holtz, Economist Group
Wilford I. King, National Bureau of Economic Research
Edmund E. Lincoln, Western Electric Co.
L. J. McCarthy, International Magazine Co.
E. M. West, Blackman Company
Percival White, marketing counselor
L. Guerin, Mgr., Market Analysis Department, Hyatt Roller Bearing Co. (Newark, N.J.)
L. E. McGivins, *The News*
T. F. Hickey, *The News*
C. C. Parlin, The Curtis Publishing Company (Philadelphia, Pa.)
Paul H. Nystrom, Assoc. Merchandising Corp.
Edw. H. Krehbiel, The Gorham Company
Frederick C. Kendall, *Advertising & Selling Fortnightly*
Paul T. Cherington, J. Walter Thompson Co.
Ralph Starr Butler, General Foods
J. R. Hayes, Burroughs Adding Machine Co.
J. George Frederick, Chairman, *The Business Bourse*
   In addition, Street & Finney, a publisher of magazines, and Frank Seaman, Inc., Frank Presbrey Company, George Batten Company, and Erwin, Wasey & Co., advertising agencies, were mentioned, but specific names were not included for them. It will be noticed that media, advertising agencies, trade associations,

---

[23] The clipping in the files of the present writer does not carry the date of the issue, but it is presumably a weekly issue soon after the date of the meeting reported.

[24] A list supplied by J. George Frederick with a letter dated June 14, 1945.

and manufacturers dominate the list of members. These were in or near New York City. In Boston, Philadelphia, Chicago, Cleveland, Cincinnati, and Detroit, companies and service organizations were undertaking marketing research activity and doing so with more and more assurance of methodology.

To the mid-1920s, marketing research was conducted with little backing from general statistics except what could be located in the decennial population censuses and the periodic censuses of agriculture and manufacturing. In October 1926, the Domestic Commerce Division of the U.S. Department of Commerce, under the chairmanship of J. Walter Drake, Assistant Secretary of Commerce, scheduled a conference to discuss possible services the Department of Commerce could perform for marketing research. A committee of well-known and well-qualified marketing research men discussed the question and reported their belief that a national census of distribution was badly needed. The conference adopted the subcommittee's report. As the result of pressures generated by this conference, the first Census of Distribution was taken in 1929, and now the Census of Business is taken regularly and covers retailing, wholesaling, and the field of service industries. This basic material has produced many background publications of use to marketing research.

The difficulty of learning when specific courses were added to collegiate curricula makes it almost impossible to give a collective account of the service of our business schools in developing marketing research methodology and standards. We can, however, get some idea of the early incidence of marketing research courses by looking at available textbooks.

C. S. Duncan's *Commercial Research* was first copyrighted in 1919 and was apparently reprinted. It may be assumed, therefore, that even this early there was some attention to marketing research in the colleges.   J. George Frederick's *Business Research and Statistics,* published in 1920, was available for text use at the same time, though it is more likely that the audience for Frederick's book was business-oriented. Z. Clark Dickinson wrote *Industrial and Commercial Research,* published by the University of Michigan at Ann Arbor in 1928. Nothing is known of the use of this volume. In 1929, Ronald Press published *Marketing Investigations* by William J. Reilly, marketing professor at the University of Texas and formerly on the research staff of Procter & Gamble Company.

In 1921, Percival White's *Market Analysis* was published by McGraw-Hill. This was the first book on marketing research to go through a series of editions and printings and may be regarded as the first textbook which retained popularity over several years.   Through Walther Printing House in Philadelphia, Frank R. Coutant and J. Russell Doubman published *Simplified Market Research,* which is believed to have had only one printing.

In 1937 *The Technique of Marketing Research* appeared under the sponsorship of the American Marketing Association. It was written cooperatively by an editorial committee made up of Ferdinand C. Wheeler, chairman; Robert N. King of Batton, Barton, Durstine and Osborn; Pauline Arnold, Market Research Corporation of America; Louis Bader, New York University; Alfred T. Falk, Advertising Federation of America; Paul L. Lazarsfeld, University of Newark; J. George Frederick, The Business Bourse; Thomas S. Holden, F. W. Dodge Corporation; and E. P. H. James, National Broadcasting Company. This volume went through several printings and enjoyed wide popularity.

In the same year, *Market Research and Analysis,* by Lyndon O. Brown, was published by The Ronald Press Company. This book went through three different editions, with many printings, and constituted one of the more popular college textbooks used in the field of marketing research. After the publication of Brown's text, other texts entered the market in a rather steady flow, providing ample text material on which to base college teaching of marketing research. We can say that marketing research was infrequently presented in business schools before 1930 and infrequently omitted after 1937.

The development of one aspect of marketing research is, briefly, a history of the field's technological growth. Marketing research requires formulation of problems; location of information sources; obtaining of information by inquiry, observation, or inference; tabulation and analysis; and presentation of research results in a way which helps management make wiser marketing decisions. Knowledge of all these aspects of marketing research can be acquired through experience. A research operator with little technical background can become competent in these tasks if he will observe, reflect upon, and draw conclusions from his experience.

ROLE OF SAMPLING

Essentially, marketing research is based on analyzing data from individual consumers, retailers, manufacturers, or other appropriate classifications. Each grouping of these cases, interviews, or observations is expected to reflect some characteristic of the entire group. If these subgroups or samples do, in fact, reflect some characteristic of the entire group, marketing research is possible; if they do not, all other marketing research techniques become meaningless and marketing research becomes impossible. In an important way, the growth of the sampling concept reflects the significance of the growth of marketing research. It is interesting to look briefly at the changes in sampling concepts as a way of appraising the maturity of marketing research.

When most moderately large bodies of data were first being collected by those doing marketing research or attitude studies, the data were frequently the result of mail questionnaires or inquiries. A sample was regarded as entirely satisfactory if the percentage distribution of responses was unchanged by the addition to the tabulation of successive increments of tabulated data, a method worked out in considerable detail.[25] This type of stabilization test fell into discredit when the *Literary Digest* presidential poll, validated by this method, presented election forecasts for the 1936 presidential election that underforecasted Franklin Roosevelt's vote by 19 percent.[26]

It had become clear that any form of sample validation by stabilization could not avoid persistent bias in the selection of individuals. Therefore the quota system of selection gradually became popular. It is important to remember that, until some time toward the mid-1930s, much of the introductory course work in statistics went little farther than describing the various kinds of averages, calculation of seasonal variation and of secular trend, sample correlation, the construction of index numbers, and—of course—the giving of instructions on neatness in chart making. Methods of sample design straggled in and straggled out. For a long time many people were still relying on sample stabilization despite the fact that most analysts had moved on to other methods of sample selection and validation.

---

[25] See Lyndon O. Brown, *Market Research and Analysis*, New York: Ronald, 1937, pp. 312–319.

[26] Frederick Mosteller, Herbert Hyman, Philip J. McCarthy, Eli S. Marks, and David B. Truman, *The Pre-Election Polls of 1948*, New York: Social Science Research Council, 1949, p. 10.

One of the best statements on the nature of the quota method of sample construction was that produced by the National Opinion Research Center in July 1946.[27]

> In the quota-control method, which is used by the National Opinion Research Center and many other research organizations, the degree of accuracy or representativeness achieved depends primarily upon the careful stratification of the sample drawn from the population universe. Stratification is effected by the use of "control factors"; the type and number of controls used to determine the representativeness of the sample.
>
> Three types of control factors are at the disposal of the statistician to obtain a photographically accurate reproduction of the population universe. Distinctions among the three types play a real part in the choice and results of the control factors applied in quota-controlled sampling and are important in the decisions as to the degree of stratification to be required.
>
> 1. Impersonal factors do not relate to the individual directly, and are (at least theoretically) subject to personal choice. These are the geographic distribution of the population, not only as far as the different parts of the country are concerned, but also rural-urban variations.
>
> 2. Personal, unchangeable factors, such as age, sex, race, are attributes of the individual beyond his control.
>
> 3. Personal, changeable factors are such attributes as education, occupation, religion, political preference, and standard-of-living level. These are not as strictly personal as race or sex, because to a considerable extent they are subject to the individual's discretion. A man can move from a medium-size town in the South to a farm in the Northwest, simultaneously changing his occupation from that of a mechanic to a farm proprietor; he can change his political affiliation from the Democratic to the Republican party; he can take a course at an agricultural college but he cannot change his sex, age, or race.
>
> NORC's social cross-section of the civilian adult population is controlled by *geographic* distribution of the population (regional and rural-urban), and by *sex, color, and standard-of-living* level. The *age* variable is partially controlled by assignment of age quotas under and over 40 years of age.
>
> Variables are controlled by the proportions reported by the 1940 census; NORC's control factors are objective in that they are not subject to individual and personal determination by members of the interviewing staff.

The application of several controls by an interviewer inevitably produces biases. If one of the controls is religious preference, then the sample should have the same percentage distribution of religious affiliation as the population. It would be easy for an interviewer to reproduce this percentage distribution if that were the only requirement. But perhaps sex, occupation, and income level are additional controls. It becomes virtually impossible for an interviewer to mesh several controls into an operation at once, and the sample's forced similarity with the population becomes distorted.

In the early and middle 1930s statistical training began to improve greatly in the colleges, especially in England. Technical preparation in this country improved and quota sampling—or some approach to quota sampling—was under heavy attack. Two concepts rapidly emerged. The first was that bias could be decreased or eliminated if individual persons or cases were chosen randomly—that is, with a table of random numbers or by some method of drawing from an urn, thus preventing any human bias from intruding. The other concept was that areas could be chosen randomly and that they could

[27] National Opinion Research Center, *How NORC Builds Its Cross-Section*, University of Denver, July 1946, pp. 1–2.

provide the basis for a suitable sample.[28]   Blocks were numbered in various cities, and a sample of these blocks was selected randomly.   But examination showed that many blocks were the sites of commercial establishments, institutions, or parks, or that they were vacant.   There appeared to be little similarity between recent census information on the city populations concerned, but the method apparently provided an excellent sample of land use.   During the latter part of the 1940s much thinking on sampling coalesced and the so-called probability sample emerged—a sample in which the selection of all respondents or cases was by random methods.   This sample is susceptible to tests for size and extent of sampling error.   Its one great drawback is that it is hard to administer in the field and requires close and expensive supervision.   Increasingly, however, probability samples are being tested against known facts about the populations under study.   Yet theoretically, the probability sample answers many questions that have arisen on the problems of sampling.[29]

During the 1960s, interest has turned to Bayesian sampling, with its greater emphasis on subjective probabilities.

Marketing research has been, if we accept a little oversimplification, an organized field of activity for 50 years.   Survey design is still not entirely satisfactory, as is true of various other techniques used in marketing research, but the progress made thus far has been very considerable.

The changes in techniques and methods of dealing with problems in the last few years have been dramatic, and the entire emphasis of marketing research has been shifting with the advent of such new concepts as marketing information systems, computers, and the expansion of the scope of marketing research to deal with social problems.   Since these topics take us into the present, they are covered in the following chapters.   To conclude this chapter, it can be said with certainty that marketing research will continue to have to adapt itself to changing problems, changing techniques, and a changing environment.

[28] Philip M. Hauser and Morris H. Hansen, "On Sampling in Market Surveys," *Journal of Marketing*, vol. 9, no. 1, pp. 26–31.
[29] Morris H. Hansen and William N. Hurwitz, "Dependable Samples for Market Surveys," *Journal of Marketing*, vol. 14, no. 3, pp. 363–372.

Chapter 2

The Functions of
Marketing Research

GEORGE FISK   *Department of Marketing, Syracuse University, Syracuse, New York*

Marketing research serves two major functions: it provides information for decision making and it develops new knowledge. The purpose of this chapter is to show how these functions are applied and to indicate potential applications under the broadened concept of marketing that is now gaining acceptance.

Aid in Decision Making

Decisions can be subdivided into elements about which the decision maker seeks additional information. The discussion here will be organized around the role of marketing research in furnishing information about the following decision elements:

1. Alternative courses of action. Long-range actions are termed strategic because they affect the entire marketing program. Short-range actions are termed tactical because they focus on a few elements of a particular action.

2. States of nature. Events that affect the outcomes associated with a particular course of action.

3. Payoffs. The spectrum of outcomes associated with a particular course of action.

4. Probabilities. The likelihood that a particular state of nature will prevail and that a particular outcome will result from a decision maker's choice of alternatives.

5. Payoff matrix or table. A tabular arrangement of alternatives, states of nature, payoffs, and probabilities associated with each of the outcomes.

6. Expected value outcome. Sum of payoffs associated with an alternative

and weighted by their probability of occurrence. The decision maker chooses the alternative yielding the most desirable (that is, maximum or minimum or optimal combination) expected value.

In the real world every action has multiple consequences, so that payoff tables which focus only on direct and desired outcomes are inadequate to assess second-order side effects which may be important. Models more complicated than a payoff matrix are ordinarily required to explain and predict the spectrum of desirable and undesirable outcomes. Payoff tables are useful for tactical decisions involving a single element of a marketing program, such as choosing among varying levels of sales or advertising effort under a limited number of foreseeable states of nature.

Developing New Knowledge

Commercial research is aimed primarily at solving current problems, basic research at finding new ways to solve old problems and the discovery of new knowledge. Commercial research workers often improve methods by learning from experience, just as specialists do in any field of endeavor. Sometimes they stumble on new explanations or "theories" that can be tested in subsequent work.

For example, an advertising researcher might seek to learn of the consequences of T.V. on such advertising effects as "attention, interest, desire, and purchase" under a variety of circumstances. His findings might lead to the conclusion that these effects were conditioned and cumulative. To test his hypothesis, he would conduct another study, perhaps of a group of children as they progressed into adolescence, to determine differences between other characteristics of heavy versus light T.V. exposure. If he succeeded in linking several hypotheses together, he would have the rudiments of a theory.

Understandably the task of developing new knowledge rests largely in the hands of research institutes and academic investigators who are not required to provide immediate answers for operating problems. Many developments in scaling and measurement theory, mathematical model building, social class and reference group theory, and methods of demand and market segmentation analysis have been adapted to commercial research after being initiated by academic research workers. On the other hand, unexplainable findings by the research worker engaged in practical research forces academic and research institute personnel to search for improved theories and measurement methods. The role of nonprofit research organizations will be examined in a later section.

MARKETING RESEARCH FUNCTIONS IN BUSINESS

Business executives take risks to attain company objectives. They need information to choose rather than shift or eliminate risks. The value of information, however, varies sharply according to the magnitude of the risk. While the importance of a decision to the individual firm cannot be estimated from the absolute size of the risk, this conventional perspective is useful and will be followed here.

Marketing Research in Large Firms

Top corporate officers spend more time making strategic decisions than do middle- or lower-level managers. Strategic marketing research consists of producing information for deciding on major elements of total marketing programs, whereas tactical research on choices among alternatives answers questions about day-to-day operations. Although marketing research in most firms continues to stress tactical applications, an increasing number of large firms have established long-range planning departments to encourage heavier emphasis on strategic planning.

Table 1 shows system relationships among desired information output, analytical process, and inputs. Outputs are of three kinds: demand analyses to detect marketing opportunities, marketing resource deployment decisions to match the firm's offer to opportunities, and states of nature which affect the results produced by deploying resources. Information outputs in the first column of Table 1 are formally identical to elements of a payoff matrix. Marketing research converts raw data into information for decision making or elaboration of knowledge, so corresponding to each output (column 1) is a set of analytical processes (column 2) performed on the raw data inputs (column 3).

Table 2 shows the extent to which business firms reported the use of marketing research in each of five functional applications surveyed by the Conference Board. Almost all reporting firms used marketing research to study markets. Strategic research on corporate growth and development was reported by 97 percent, although only 93 percent of consumer firms used research for this purpose. Long-range planning applications are gaining adherents rapidly, but these statistics do not imply that all firms use research with equal frequency or to the same extent. Many firms that failed to respond to this survey may not use research at all.

Most of the applications reported stress tactical decision aids such as product planning, advertising, and sales. In consumer goods firms, product research centers on what is sometimes called human factors engineering, which is intended to emphasize functional use characteristics that make products easier for users to manipulate or consume. Extrinsic differentiation studies dealing with style, packaging, and product image are also used to a greater degree among consumer products than among industrial goods to make products more appealing in competition with rival products.

Among tactical problems solved by marketing research, allocation problems probably receive most emphasis by commercial researchers in advertising, sales, and physical distribution. Sales analysis and inventory problems are well suited to solution by quantitative model building. These kinds of problems are being increasingly solved by routine computer programs instead of research staff on an individual custom study. While recognition of the impossibility of global optimization is growing, the number of firms using routine methods for solving repetitive problems lags. This lag may be due to ignorance of the uses and limitations of quantitative methods and inertia and failure to recognize that for large firms, suboptimal allocations for promotion and physical distribution can provide solutions superior to the largely intuitive decisions that have been customary for decades.

A third class of tactical problems for which marketing research is used by large firms consists of adaptive response to change. Changing marketing opportunities, changing competition, and changing government policy continuously affect responses of large firms to their environment. When decisions are based on continuous marketing intelligence reports, choices may be better informed. Nevertheless, research on adaptive response to change probably produces most of the unneeded information directed to marketing managers.

Information overload has become an increasing problem partly because executives are obliged to respond to more varied challenges now than in the past, but the problem could be mitigated by improving theories of change to provide means to reduce the number of influences considered. Inundation of the executive suite with irrelevant reports is to some extent due to the failure

TABLE 1 Marketing Information Systems: Information Requirements, Types of Study and Raw Data Analyzed to Aid in Tactical Decision Making in Business

Information output	Analytical process	Raw data input

1. Market opportunity (payoff income)
  a. Identify unmet wants to be gratified
  b. Market target identification
	a. Image and behavioral studies
	b. Potential markets:
	    demographic gravity models
	    size and location
	    market segmentation
		a. Motivation of consumers and buyers
		b. Consumer preferences, expectations, buying intentions

c. Present consumption and use	c. Market share analysis by:
	    Consumer panel sample
	    Retail store audits
	    Wholesale shipments
	    Brand switching models
		c. Shopping patterns by age, income, social class, etc.
		Product and brand purchase quantities and prices, store patronage, functional product used by age, income, social class, etc.

d. Desired market position	d. Sales trend analysis by: product, territory, method of distribution	d. Aggregate firm and industry sales by geographic location, city size, etc.

2. Marketing resource deployment (alternatives)
  a. Product planning
	a. Product studies:
	    New product tests
	    Product improvement tests
	    Packaging test and panels
	    Design and style studies
	    Sales forecast
	    Break-even analysis
		a. User response to functional features, style, design, performance, price, and ancillary service after sale
		New-product acceptance rate
		Old-product sales decay rates

b. Promotion	b. Media analysis:
	    Audience measurement
	    Copy testing message content
	    Media effectiveness/cost
	    Message effectiveness/cost
		b. Readership, circulation, viewing, listening, tuning, eye tracking, recall
		Copy, program scenario preferences, attention, interest, motivation, image, message recall, purchase of product or brand advertised

TABLE 1 Marketing Information Systems (Continued)

Information output	Analytical process	Raw data input
c. Price	c. Price studies: Product-line price Competitive price/quantity Promotional pricing	c. Price paid at retail, wholesale, and industrial transaction—competitive bids Price/quality perception studies
d. Physical distribution	d. Logistics: Stock turnover—warehouse flow Origin and destination Location	d. Cost of handling, order filling, inventory flows Order assembling, cost per ton mile, routing Order processing time-motion Dealer attitudes, display, terms of sale, franchising. Breadth and depth of stock assortments
e. Channels of distribution	e. Channel network analysis	e. Inquiries Invoices, orders, dealer manufacturer contracts
3. States of nature a. Competition b. Invention and change	a. Environmental studies b. Methods of marketing rivalry, game theory, simulation	a. Social costs, social benefits b. Entry and exit rates from industry Rival firm product, price, promotion, physical distribution, and channel tactics
c. Business cycle	c. Technology transfer, diffusion models	c. Acceptance of innovation, imitation, and adaptation
d. Business cycle	d. Business cycle forecasting	d. Incomes, profits, sales, contracts, expenditure distributions, shipments, employment
	e. Institutional analysis	e. Qualitative decisions and change in business practices: collusion, competitive bidding, etc.

of top corporate managers to specify what information they need to make strategic as well as tactical decisions.

Marketing Research in Small Firms

Marketing research serves the same purposes in small firms as it does in large ones. However, for a small firm the costs of research, compared with the value of the information produced, are higher than for a large firm, thus limiting the frequency of its use. Consequently, research is more likely to be used for strategic entry decisions, such as what business to enter or where to locate a store, than for tactical surveillance of environmental change or resources allocation decisions. Since they cannot attain economies of scale in spreading research costs over many units of output, small businessmen must learn to do research for themselves or hire consultants to do it for them. Although outside consultants may take longer to learn the firm's problems, they bring a breadth

TABLE 2   Proportion of Firms Engaged in Marketing Research

Engaged in research on	Total companies	Manufacturing consumer products (percent)	Manufacturing industrial products (percent)	Nonmanufacturing companies (percent)
1. Markets......................	99	100	99	100
2. Sales.........................	99	100	99	100
3. Corporate growth and development.................	97	93	98	97
4. Products.....................	96	100	96	91
5. Advertising..................	93	98	91	94
Number of companies reporting.....	237	61	141	35

SOURCE: *The Role and Organization of Marketing Research*, Experiences in Marketing Management, no. 20, New York: National Industrial Conference Board, 1969, p. 5.

of experience in solving problems that most small businessmen cannot duplicate.

Whether small businessmen do their own research or hire consultants, the functions performed are determined by the characteristics of the business. Among the most common questions to be answered are the following:

1. Where does an unsatisfied demand for what I am capable of offering exist?

2. How do I cultivate demand by using marketing instruments—offer of a product or service, price, promotion, and customer availability?

3. What major social and environmental forces are most favorable to or imperil survival of my business?

Small business handbooks often stress the need to carefully match services offered to marketing opportunity. The mere existence of an unsatisfied demand segment offers no assurance of survival if a small businessman fails to study the demand characteristics of his potential market. For example, the availability of a large unsatisfied demand for television and appliance repair does not guarantee that customers will flock to an appliance repair center. Particularly in affluent suburban neighborhoods, repairs must be made in the home, because the time costs of traveling to repair centers may limit the number of customers willing to travel to a central city location.

To illustrate, an army technician, seeking to establish himself in civilian life, approached housewives in supermarkets and men waiting for service in local filling stations with the question, "What do you want most that you can't find around here?" The desire for guaranteed repair services, mentioned by several customer prospects, led him to query still other area residents about the kinds of repairs that were most unsatisfactory. He started an electronics repair center in which high-fidelity and television components were tested and repairs were guaranteed. As his business expanded, he added a distributorship for quality lines not carried in discount houses and established a reputation for "selling what we service." Although his research was limited to an initial probing of the nature of unsatisfied demand, observation of his market led him to detect marketing opportunities for additional product lines.

The cultivation of demand through the use of marketing instruments can be studied experimentally. Small businessmen need to know how effective different marketing instruments are in converting prospects to customers. To get this information, they can conduct experimental and observational studies combining variations in one or two critical variables with sales records. For example, postcards to different classes of customers with different merchandise or price offers can be mailed with varying frequencies and coded for mail or telephone return inquiry.

Few small businessmen can devote much time to experimental design, but nearly all have ample opportunities to use sales records for studies of relationships between elements of an offer and results. When nonsales or returns result from a particular combination of marketing inputs, these too can be analyzed to discover which combinations yielded the most or least effective marketing program. Since efficient use of resources depends on such knowledge, marketing research can be used to produce the Horatio Alger success effect for determined small enterprisers.

Monitoring the business environment by regular reading of business literature can also enable a small businessman to ward off foreseeable consequences of changes affecting his business. For example, one shoe repairman, on learning that his neighborhood was about to be subjected to urban renewal, immediately started a site search for a new store. Fortunately, highway construction programs gave him a choice of three shopping center sites. His ambitious wife stationed herself at each of these and, on the advice of a local university professor who gave them a randomized block observation pattern to use in selecting observation periods, counted daily traffic. Equipped with shopping center rental figures before construction was completed, the couple moved to the same area that they intuitively chose based on their knowledge of the community but at a rental lower than the developer offered because they were able to demonstrate to him differences in the drawing power of traffic-generating highways leading to other centers under construction.

Small businessmen who keep track of population movements, income changes, and methods of distribution used by manufacturers are not as likely to be surprised by market changes as those who do not.

MARKETING RESEARCH IN NONPROFIT INSTITUTIONS

Additions to knowledge improve measurement techniques and increase the accuracy of predicting outcomes when marketing managers combine marketing instruments under risky conditions. Basic research consists of investigations that improve measurement and prediction but do not have commercial objectives.   In applied research the investigator seeks practical use of knowledge, but in basic research the purpose is to gain fuller knowledge of the subject.

Foremost among institutions conducting basic research are the Associated University Bureaus of Business and Economic Research and the Marketing Science Institute at Harvard University.   These agencies examine aggregate marketing and social and economic phenomena, and they also conduct studies analyzing the consequences of public policy on marketing.

Applied Research Functions

Applied research as distinguished from consulting may be fixed by the criterion of benefit to a segment of society rather than to a firm or its stockholders. Among nonprofit agencies applied research tends to focus on industries and economic regions or on historical-institutional analyses of technological change.

Well-known examples of applied research include the *Quarterly Survey of Change in Consumer Attitudes and Inclinations to Buy Durable Goods,* conducted by the Survey Research Center at the University of Michigan.   It attempts to explain and predict changes in consumers' demand for automobiles and other durables.

Longitudinal surveys over time take many other forms.   Wholesale and retail operating ratios compiled by trade associations are used to control and improve current performance of the firms contributing to the financial support of these associations.   Historical studies, such as one of Macy's Department Stores,[1] trace institutional change over several generations, putting critical choice points into historical perspective.   Even long-range planning simulations based on internal company records and environmental variables search for trends, structural interdependencies among market prices, productivity, and technological advance.   Such multifunctional studies tend to contribute to other research functions, such as theory building and social policy formulation, sometimes by design but more often by accident.

Social Policy Research

The functions that nonprofit research institutes should perform are extensions of work they do now.   In a visionary analysis, Rensis Likert, then of the Institute for Social Research at the University of Michigan, says that

> the social sciences are now at a stage of development in which it is essential that there be encouraged the formation and support of institutions capable of:
> Conducting social science research in ways that supplement but do not replace the existing resources for research
> Pursuing major problems over a span of many years until they are resolved
> Getting basic information on a scale appropriate to the problems they are asked to comprehend
> Dealing with social sciences in their natural complexity without necessary restrictions to disciplinary boundaries
> Treating in an integrated way the full spectrum of research from methodological innovation, to basic theory development, to experiments and demonstrations in applications of the results[2]

Likert's rationale for this view is clearly expressed in the same report:

[1] Ralph M. Hower, *History of Macy's of New York, 1859–1919,* Cambridge, Mass.: Harvard University Press, 1967.

[2] *ISR: A Report on Recent Activities,* Ann Arbor, Mich.: University of Michigan, 1968, p. 5.

... the conditions are right to sustain a significant change in the role of the social sciences in human affairs. With riots in our cities, ... with quandaries about how to end international wars and how to prevent new ones, with persistent poverty in the presence of plenty, with a shortage of talent in a world full of underdeveloped talent—with such conditions pressing upon us there can be no doubt about the need for whatever help the social sciences can offer.[3]

Luck has questioned whether concern over phenomena outside the marketplace does not in fact broaden the concept of marketing too far because they do not meet the criterion of "the ultimate purchase-and-sale of a product or service."[4]

While admitting that focus on processes which result in a market transaction "is in line with the widely understood meaning of the term and has the virtues of clarity, closure, and comfort," Kotler and Levy maintain that such a viewpoint is too limited because it denies marketing expertise to rapidly growing institutional sectors and because "business marketing per se will forgo the enrichment that comes from examining the same processes practiced in other contexts."[5] In accordance with the broadened concept identified by Kotler and Levy, Julian Simon pointed out that increasing the amount of family planning in less developed countries is basically a marketing job requiring opinion studies of receptivity to family planning information, word-of-mouth communication flow analyses, and experimental studies of alternative motivation appeals in presenting contraceptive products. Simon points out yet another case of rediscovering the wheel in which family planners attempted to discover for themselves promotional techniques already developed by marketers and advertisers.[6] Simon's example underscores the social importance and relevance of the Kotler-Levy demand-service concept of marketing as compared to the transaction view.

Marketing research is already being used to some extent to perform the social functions recommended by Likert, Kotler and Levy, and Simon. For example, Bruce has examined the ecological structure of retail institutions. By using behavioral science constructs, he furnishes useful guidelines for planning urban facilities, including spatial distribution of stores and services.[7] Case studies by the National Planning Association of marketing as a machine for economic development and simulation studies by Galbraith and Holton[8] and by Griggs[9] point to macrosystemic analyses as a methodology for shaping the contours of economic and social progress. In addition, such multifunctional studies contribute to the development of new theories and measurement techniques.

---

[3] Ibid., p. 4.

[4] David J. Luck, "Broadening the Concept of Marketing Too Far," *Journal of Marketing*, vol. 33, July 1969, p. 54.

[5] Philip Kotler and Sidney J. Levy, "A New Form of Marketing Myopia: Rejoinder to Professor Luck," *Journal of Marketing*, vol. 33, July 1969, pp. 55–56.

[6] Julian Simon, "Marketing Research: A Huge Marketing Research Task—Birth Control," *Journal of Marketing Research*, vol. 5, no. 1, pp. 21–27, February 1968.

[7] Grady D. Bruce, "The Ecological Structure of Retail Institutions," *Journal of Marketing Research*, vol. 6, February 1969, pp. 48–53.

[8] John K. Galbraith, Richard H. Holton et al., *Marketing Efficiency in Puerto Rico*, Cambridge, Mass.: Harvard University Press, 1955.

[9] John E. Griggs, *Evaluating Marketing Change, An Application of Systems Theory*, East Lansing, Mich.: Michigan State University, Graduate School of Business Administration, 1970.

FUNCTIONS OF MARKETING RESEARCH IN GOVERNMENT

Government marketing research serves the following functions:
1. The data bank function
2. Technology transfer and utilization
3. Economic development studies
4. Assessment of public policy impact
5. Planning

The Data Bank Function

Government data collection provides at best a clouded crystal ball because no agency knows in advance exactly who will use the information it collects or for what purpose. Yet without the censuses of business, manufactures, transportation, housing, and population, many decisions would be predicated on guesses rather than on hard data. Despite waste and underutilization, data banks offer a wide variety of statistical aids.

Periodic user conferences and specific requests addressed to government have aided in focusing more closely on user needs. Only if users of government statistics make their specific needs known can the statistical agencies of federal and state governments collect the desired information. However, data such as the Consumers' Price Index maintained by the Bureau of Labor Statistics are already used for applications ranging from wage negotiations to econometric model building.

Technology Transfer and Utilization

Constant surveillance of new inventions and processes produced by federal and other public agencies can yield commercially salable products. Computerized key-word scrutiny of government publications such as *Nuclear Science Abstracts* and *Space Technology Abstract Reports* (STAR) also gives advance notice of possible developments. Government research consists mainly of presenting new alternatives, but special-purpose market potential analyses or interindustry effects of these developments are intermittently studied by the Technology Utilization Division of NASA or the Agricultural Marketing Service of the U.S. Department of Agriculture. While government agencies have accepted responsibility for technology transfer research, little has been written on the role of government in this area.[10]

Economic Development Studies

The United States government established in 1968 the Federal Advisory Council on Regional Economic Development to alleviate regional economic distress through a more systematic allocation of available federal, state, and local resources.[11] Studies of potential markets for the human and natural resources of Appalachia, the Ozarks, and the four corners area of Arizona, New Mexico, Utah, and Colorado are mandated under the jurisdiction of this Council. Economic development studies of regional resources, such as the Delaware River Valley, are also conducted by a regional planning authority.

Urban market development analyses are supervised by the Department of

---

[10] Samuel I. Doctors, *The Role of Federal Agencies in Technology Transfer*, Cambridge, Mass.: MIT, 1969.

[11] *Federal Advisory Council on Regional Economic Development Initial Meeting Report*, U.S. Department of Commerce, October 1968.

Housing and Urban Development, which has sponsored studies of the retail structure of decaying central business districts. The Economic Research Service of the U.S. Department of Agriculture publishes agricultural marketing studies to assist in the development of particular agricultural industries. Similarly, the Export Expansion Program of the U.S. Department of Commerce is aimed at economic development for industries seeking to increase United States exports in international trade.

International and multinational organizations conduct marketing research to discover overseas markets. For example, the Organization for Economic Cooperation and Development issues the OECD *Observer* which reports on current trade and market developments among participating nations. Occasionally, in-depth studies of market demands for a particular commodity or by a particular nation are examined in the *Observer* or in OECD research reports.

Assessment of Public Policy Impact

Market share studies and studies of complementary and substitute products have been used in antitrust cases by the Department of Justice and the Federal Trade Commission in Sherman, Clayton, and Federal Trade Commission Act cases. The Bureau of Labor Statistics collects consumption statistics that are used in writing labor legislation. Food consumption and nutrition studies are conducted by the Agricultural Marketing Service, and pricing studies are conducted by the Department of Agriculture for use in subsidy legislation.

Many other types of marketing channel studies and studies of agricultural efficiency are used by agencies of the federal government, these studies being sometimes prepared by the faculty of land-grant agricultural colleges. Crop forecasts and commodity flow analyses are used to improve regulation of common carriers and marketing efficiency of state and federal agencies dealing with commodity surpluses.

In the private sector, defendants in antitrust and Robinson-Patman price discrimination cases have conducted studies to demonstrate the absence of monopoly or price discrimination based on differences in costs of selling to different customers. Business firms use policy analyses to buttress causes they advocate as well as to defend themselves from government law-enforcement agencies.

Firms promoting protective tariff legislation have sought to measure the effect of sheltered foreign competition or domestic market share in steel, textiles, and electronics. Multinational rivalry and international trade agreements are sometimes studied by the Bureau of Foreign and Domestic Commerce on behalf of small export traders to determine the attitudes of foreign governments to American export marketing programs.

Despite these and other studies by government and private business, the systematic study of public policy impact is still relatively limited. This is an area in which more extensive work will prove increasingly rewarding as the role of government in multinational trade promotion expands.

Planning

Long-range government programs require market and technological forecasts. The government has the power to obtain data needed in planning such private programs as capital investment and new ventures. Three major groups of publications are also issued from time to time to aid in long-range planning by business and by the federal government.

1. Long-term economic growth analysis. Historical statistics and long-term

economic growth studies are published by the Bureau of the Census. These examine such time series as total output, input, productivity, and population.[12] Such studies are useful to government and business planners concerned with investment in new plant, the career development of personnel, and revenue forecasting.

2. Input-output structure of the United States economy. Studies of economic sectors providing inputs to meet intermediate and final demands were first made in 1958. A sequel described the structure of the United States economy in 1963.[13] Input-output studies identify existing derived demands, provide estimates of growth, and aid in allocating marketing effort according to marketing opportunities defined by the sector demands or outputs. Input-output studies have gained in usage among public planning agencies concerned with manpower training as well as with administrative groups charged with regional or public utility planning. (See Section IV, Part D, Chapter 3 for a more detailed discussion of this method.)

National income accounting is used for shorter-range planning. National income components are reported quarterly and annually by the Office of Business Economics of the U.S. Department of Commerce in a variety of technical and popular media. Their frequent and easily accessible publications permit regionally oriented governments to plan tax receipts and expenditures, and their use by local businessmen for potential market planning is equally feasible.

3. United States industrial outlook. Each year the Business Defense Service Administration publishes a forecast of the sales and market outlook for industries for which statistics are collected in the *Survey of Current Business*.[14] Trade specialists examine shifts in the structure of demand, thus providing benchmark data against which to compare planned business performance for the coming year.

Many government research memoranda are for internal agency planning purposes and are not widely distributed. For example, massive planning programs requiring demand analysis include urban transportation planning for passengers and freight, highway-use planning, land-use planning, shopping center location and facilities planning, and national aviation system planning. These are often contracted studies conducted by major research organizations, such as the Stanford Research Institute or the Syracuse University Policy Research Institute.

Technological forecasting, still an infant discipline, is used by research contractors working for the government, such as the RAND Corporation and the Systems Development Corporation. Data inputs include a variety of statistics from government and private sources. Other types of forecasting and "futurology" are attempted as a means for providing federal and state governments with contingency estimates of events which could affect planned actions.

As the role of planning in government expands to deal with an increasingly complex world, technological forecasting and other futuristic skills will doubtless improve. The National Planning Association and the World Future Society number among their membership technicians in government agencies whose official publications already reflect improvement in the planning arts.

[12] For example, *Long Term Economic Growth 1860–1965*, Bureau of the Census, U.S. Government Printing Office, October 1966.

[13] *Input Output Structure of the U.S. Economy*, 1963, Office of Business Economics, U.S. Department of Commerce, 1969, 3 vols.

[14] *U.S. Industrial Outlook, 1970*, Business Defense Service Administration, U.S. Government Printing Office, 1969.

POTENTIAL FUNCTIONS OF MARKETING RESEARCH

Three major potential functions of marketing research that exist in relatively primitive form have become operationally reasonable as a result of plummeting computer costs. Use has been limited to date because management lacks familiarity with the benefits as well as the techniques and because the generation of quantitatively oriented managers now emerging from business schools has not yet had sufficient impact on top management. These potential functions are:
1. Planning research
2. Intelligence systems for total channel system coordination and control
3. Public utility status for research

1. Planning Research. Rapid changes in the business environment and the growing necessity to make large capital and organizational commitments before results can be produced have made long-range planning more important to sustained growth and business profit. Techniques for extending the planning horizon are gaining in sophistication in response to market demands for such development. Among the techniques available are scenario writing and simulation, technological forecasting, quantitative total systems model building, and even Delphian methods employing independent judgments of seasoned executives. By using information retroactively to test the effectiveness of outputs from an earlier period in forecasting the present, the usefulness of planning models and projections has been enhanced.

Although long-range planning is still more widespread as a phrase than a practice, improvements in data bases and planning models and pressures for accuracy are driving top management to invest heavily in the development of this art. Whereas marketing plans were seldom longer than one or two years in the precomputer era, five- and even ten-year planning horizons are no longer regarded as visionary. As marketing research moves out of the backroom fire-fighting operation and into the boardroom task of defining company mission and goals, it becomes more useful for a second function relating to long-range planning. This task is total channel systems coordination.

2. Marketing Intelligence Systems for Total Channel Coordination and Control. The processing of data synchronized with marketing processes by devices in direct communication with central processing units during the time that marketing activities occur makes possible closer coordination of geographically separated units of a firm's physical distribution network, as is covered in further detail in Section IV, Part D, Chapter 4. Whereas many decisions about ill-structured marketing problems were attempted by computer and found deficient, physical distribution decisions are often near optimal or at least satisfactory for logistic problems when computerized. However, most marketing decisions require interaction between a decision maker and an array of different types of information. For these, on-line real-time computations will become increasingly feasible for aiding the decision maker to coordinate marketing inputs which cannot be effectively blended by relying on quantitative solutions.

The existence of closed-circuit television, videophone and remote-access computer terminals through which decision makers can query central computers has extended the range of management. Many firms are now designing intelligence networks to provide managers with the kinds of data needed to make daily operating decisions. Marketing research is a fundamental source of such data, and there are indications that the research function is being slowly transformed into the broader function of providing intelligence for planning, directing, coordinating, and controlling marketing activities. Thus what was a well-bounded staff marketing department function promises to evolve into a corporate activity which will affect business strategy as well as tactics.

Recent developments in centralizing channel command through vertically integrated marketing channels, therefore, pose new challenges to marketing research. Large firms, such as Goodrich and Singer that are integrated forward from manufacturing into retail distribution or backwards such as A&P and Sears Roebuck, already have vertical marketing organizations for which optimal combinations of channel units are sought.

Franchise operations and retail voluntary chains are forms of limited vertical integration by contract that require the same kinds of coordination and control. However, since command power is diffuse in voluntary associations, these organizations cannot centrally direct operations as much. As the organizational design of voluntary channel association improves, their managers will demand more accurate and faster delivery of marketing research information for decision making. Daily records of sales, competitive prices, advertising volume, deals, expressions of buyer interest, back orders, and other statistics will have to be examined in order to coordinate the use of marketing instruments.

This calls for on-line real-time marketing intelligence systems. The marketing executive of the near future may well stare at a wall of continuously changing cathode tube displays of planning and operating variables about which he queries his computer whenever a control limit is signaled on one of the screens. Reaction time, now measured in weeks and months, may well be reduced to minutes and hours—even for coordinating total channel distribution systems.

Long after computer hardware has improved beyond today's technology, it is highly probable that marketing research will still depend on careful observation and recording by human agents—and, of course, the responsibility for interpreting and evaluating the data will be the responsibility of the research consultant and analyst.

3. Public Utility Status for Research. In an information-rich society, the person without equal information is underprivileged. Although computers, television, and other electronic aids have reduced costs, many small firms are not able to maintain an effective competitive information level. Since radically heterogeneous demands and supplies are constantly changing, small firms require access to market information to gain knowledge which gives them power to compete. If they cannot secure economies of scale in producing their own information, they will inevitably diminish in number, learn how to pool their resources, or secure substantially greater assistance from government than has been thus far offered in the history of any enterprise economy. The implications for independent business survival and antitrust enforcement are profound.

By converting marketing research to public status and giving free access to any legitimate marketing inquiry, governments can serve both the household consumer and small business. The so-called consumer-education movement for inner-city residents is one step in this direction. However, a vast increase in on-the-job training in the use of information by householders and business is needed to develop the necessary skills.

Substantial reduction in costs of producing and distributing research findings is also needed. While home computer consoles and desk-size computers promise to lower information costs, people still have to learn how to use information in the same way public utilities have taught consumers of their products how to use electricity, telephone, and heating services. An apocryphal tale shows how small information users may view the level of information ascribed to big business and to God. An executive unable to stump his new-generation computer finally typed into his console the question: "Does God exist?" A brief second later his cathode ray tube displayed the answer, "He does now."

In reality information is only an aid to decision makers. They must understand what use will be made of it before it is collected.

BIBLIOGRAPHY

Articles

Adler, Lee, "Phasing Research into the Marketing Plan," *Harvard Business Review*, May–June 1960, pp. 113–122.

Keane, John G., "Some Observations on Marketing Research in Top Management Decision Making," *Journal of Marketing*, vol. 33, October 1969, pp. 10–15.

Kotler, Philip, "New Mathematics for Marketing Planning," *New Ideas for Successful Marketing, Proceedings of the American Marketing Association*, 1966, 507–528.

Newman, Joseph W., "Put Research into Marketing Decisions," *Harvard Business Review*, March–April 1962, pp. 105–112.

Roberts, Harry V., "The Role of Research in Marketing Management," *Journal of Marketing*, vol. 22, July 1957, pp. 21–32.

Starr, Martin K., "Management Science and Marketing Science," *Management Science*, vol. 10, April 1964, pp. 557–573.

Books

Donnelly, James H., and John M. Ivancevich, *Analysis for Marketing Decisions*, Homewood, Ill.: Irwin, 1970.

Green, Paul E., and Ronald E. Frank, *A Manager's Guide to Marketing Research*, New York: Wiley, 1967.

Heidingsfield, Myron S., and Frank Eby, Jr., *Marketing and Business Research*, New York: Holt, 1962.

Montgomery, David B., and Glen L. Urban, *Management Science in Marketing*, Englewood Cliffs, N.J.: Prentice Hall, 1969.

Myers, James H., and Richard R. Mead, *The Management of Marketing Research*, Scranton, Pa.: International Textbook, 1969.

Periodicals

Journal of Advertising Research, published quarterly by the Advertising Research Foundation, 3 East 54 St., New York, N.Y. 10022.

Journal of Marketing, Published quarterly by the American Marketing Association, 230 N. Michigan Ave., Chicago, Ill. 60601.

Journal of the Marketing Research Society, published quarterly by the Market Research Society (of England), 39 Hertford St., London W1Y8EP, England.

Journal of Marketing Research, published quarterly by the American Marketing Association, 230 North Michigan Ave., Chicago, Ill. 60601.

Marketing Information Guide Monthly Annotated Bibliography, U.S. Department of Commerce, Business and Defense Services Administration, Supt. of Documents, U.S. Government Printing Office, Washington, D.C.

Operational Research Quarterly, published for the Operational Research Society by Pergamon Press, Headington Hill Hall, Oxford, England.

Chapter 3

Marketing Information Systems

KENNETH P. UHL *Department of Business Administration, University of Illinois at Urbana-Champaign, Illinois*

The focus of this chapter is on marketing information systems. The primary questions to be considered are:

1. What is a marketing information system, and what are its objectives?

2. Are marketing information systems a replacement for marketing research?

3. What are the major parts and crucial dimensions of marketing information systems?

4. How should marketing information systems be organized and where should they fit in a company?

WHAT IS A MARKETING INFORMATION SYSTEM?

A definition that describes the concept of a marketing information system is:

> A structured, interacting complex of persons, machines, and procedures designed to generate an orderly flow of pertinent information, collected from both intra- and extra-firm sources, for use as the basis for decision-making in specified responsibility areas of marketing management [21].

This definition suggests the interdependence of the activities associated with the assembly, processing, and communication of marketing information. Just as the myriad activities can be viewed as subsystems within a marketing information system, in a larger context a marketing information system can be one of the several subsystems in a firm's total information system [26].

Figure 1 symbolizes a marketing information system, the major activities within it, and its relationships to the firm and the environment. The illustrated information system, as shown in the concentric circles, is composed of three subsystems: current awareness, in-depth crisis, and unanticipated information (which are defined and discussed in more detail later in this chapter).

The marketing information system is composed of and is dependent on the activities shown in the three outlying concentric rings. For example, models and model building, including simulation models, are used to formulate problems, to provide analysis, and to seek answers through all three subsystems. The next outlying concentric ring suggests that the model-building activities require data—data inputs which must be stored, retrieved, transmitted, and discarded. Finally, the outside ring shows many of the information assembly

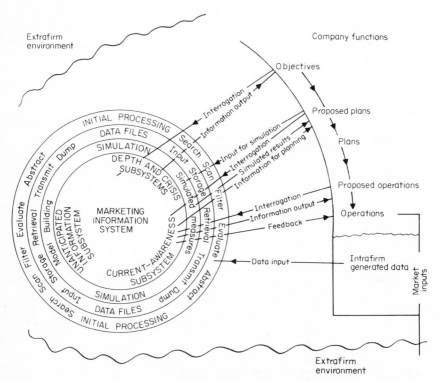

Fig. 1.   Marketing information system.

activities, the major ones being searching, scanning, filtering, evaluating, and abstracting.

The marketing information system interfaces with the company's major functions: setting objectives, establishing plans, and operating the firm [27]. The straight lines between objectives and the information system indicate that management interrogates and gets information about proposed objectives from the system. At the next level, management gets information for planning and also uses the information system to simulate the outcomes of proposed plans. A similar arrangement is indicated for operations. In a continuing process, the system assembles and processes data on firm and market results and the environment and provides managers with information feedback.

Finally, the terms *marketing information system* and *computer system* are *not* synonymous. A marketing information system may make use of computer facilities, but a computer system is not an information system. A study of information systems is focused on how the organization communicates and processes information to maximize the effectiveness of management and to further the objectives of the organization [22].

OBJECTIVES OF MARKETING INFORMATION SYSTEMS

The fundamental objective of a marketing information system is to help managers make better decisions. To accomplish this, information systems must assemble, process, and communicate information that is used by managers to reduce uncertainty. The solution appears to lie with the creation of user-oriented systems which provide managers with information when they need it. These two notions, user orientation and information, provide key insights into the objectives of information systems.

User Orientation

A user-oriented system is not simply one that provides user-managers with all the information they may think they want. Examinations of operating systems [1] have suggested that:

1. Most systems suffer more from an overabundance of irrelevant information than from a lack of relevant information. This overabundance results in managers being burdened with information overload, both through the number of communications received and the redundancy within the communications. Such an overloaded system is not user-oriented. More consideration of data evaluation and aggregation is needed.

2. Most user-managers initially need help to know which information will help them to make better decisions. The system designer and information user, each left on his own, tend to oversupply and overask in order to be safe rather than sorry. To know which information helps reduce uncertainty, users *and* suppliers must be jointly aware of the decisions that *should* be made, and they must have models of them.

3. It is *not* enough to provide managers with information. User-managers, because of the complexity of decision processes, often need help in formulating decision rules or in performance feedback so they can gain experience and learn. User-oriented systems help provide this.

4. User-managers must understand their information system. It is a *mistake* to provide user-managers with only output information and assure them they need to know nothing about the system. Involvement helps users to understand their system and to make their views a part of the system. This, in turn, helps them to evaluate, control, and make the system more *adaptive* to their dynamic decision-making situations.[1]

Information

Relevance is a major criterion for including information in a system. Many information specialists, in fact, consider information as data which are relevant; that is, relevant information is a redundant term. To be relevant, data must:

1. Be different under available alternatives
2. Provide users with insight into their problems
3. Be reflected in some differences in the decisions made [12]

In other words, information is reduction of uncertainty. For example, data

---

[1] Readers wishing to explore adaptation and stability in systems should see [7].

about last week's sales are relevant to a sales manager to the extent that they (1) reflect differences that could have influenced his decisions, (2) help him foresee the future (the past is beyond influence), and (3) bear on his future decisions.

Not all relevant data (information) should be part of a system. "Indeed, the fundamental question . . . may well be when to stop collecting data and developing the model and when to produce a recommendation for action" [18]. When the expected *cost* of information exceeds the expected *value* of that information in terms of reduction of decision errors, the information should *not* be obtained. This also provides a rule for selecting among alternative items of information. The particular information set that is expected to yield the largest excess of value (largest reduction in decision errors) over the accompanying cost should be selected for inclusion in the system.

The costs of various information can be approximated. Values or benefits, in contrast, must ultimately be related to results arising from manager-users' decisions.[2] These benefits, while difficult to measure, are largely a function of:

1. The degree of uncertainty regarding the outcome of alternative courses of action

2. The economic consequences of *not* choosing the alternative which would lead to the "best" outcome

3. The amount by which the information, if obtained, is expected to reduce the initial uncertainty

ARE MARKETING INFORMATION SYSTEMS A REPLACEMENT FOR MARKETING RESEARCH?

The answer to this question is partly dependent on semantics. This statement, however, is not made merely to dismiss all substantive questions.

A frequently used definition of marketing research is "the systematic gathering, recording, and analyzing of data about problems relating to the marketing of goods and services" [5]. When marketing research means all this, as it does in this handbook, it can hardly be said that marketing information systems are a replacement for marketing research. A comparison of the two definitions also suggests that the objectives of both are essentially the same.

This being the situation, why should marketing information systems be developing? The general explanation seems to be that in practice, in many companies, the breadth of what has been called marketing research has fallen far short of the definition. In turn, management has been disappointed in marketing research.

The essence of the criticisms appears to be that marketing research has too frequently (1) produced data which were not relevant, (2) been concerned with research on nonrecurrent problems while it has virtually ignored current awareness information, and (3) failed to provide sufficient payoff-relevant marketing information.

These shortcomings arise largely because marketing research has been principally a series of independent, uncoordinated activities scattered throughout the complaining companies.

Marketing information systems are being viewed as the supplanters of unsatisfactory marketing research because they promise the very features that were not available through poor marketing research: *integrated, analytic, systematic approaches which will identify, assemble, process, and communicate*

---

[2] For a good discussion of attaching values to information, see [19].

payoff-relevant marketing information to decision makers. The hope is that marketing information systems will serve to identify, establish, and integrate the various subfunctions so managers can work under the marketing concept.

THE MAJOR PARTS AND CRUCIAL DIMENSIONS OF MARKETING INFORMATION SYSTEMS

There is no one unique marketing information system that will serve all companies. Each management has unique information requirements because of its unique perspective on its environment and its company, along with a unique order of priorities and styles of management [13]. Furthermore, successful systems are a matter of evolution. Therefore in this handbook marketing information systems are discussed in terms of typical subsystems and their general dimensions.

The most obvious and also one of the fundamental aspects of existing marketing information systems is that they are composed of subsystems. Also, they typically have been built one subsystem at a time and have been managed in terms of subsystems. There are usually two or three major subsystems in mature systems and, despite wide variation in titles, the same two subsystems are commonly found in most marketing information systems.

One subsystem is usually designed to handle continuing current-awareness information. A second one usually handles in-depth information on special problems and areas of immediate, high-priority concern to users. Many companies have had the activities performed by this subsystem which has been available for years from their marketing research groups. When a third major subsystem is present, it tends to handle information and situations which do not fit into the other two subsystems but which seem to warrant attention [16]. Each of these three types of subsystems and their more crucial dimensions will be examined in some detail.

Current-Awareness Subsystems

Continuing flows of information for managers can be provided through a current-awareness information subsystem. A descriptive title frequently used for this kind of system is *selective dissemination subsystem.* Such subsystems can provide periodic (daily or otherwise) reports of company sales by products and by territories, total annual sales to date, comparative past sales data, and future forecasted values. They can also indicate changes in market share, competitive activities, and a host of other past and present information as well as estimates of future developments in internal matters, competition, and the environment.

This type of subsystem is usually computer-based and virtually requires that a firm have access to extensive and meaningful sources and supplies (banks) of data. Furthermore, a firm must be able to analyze, synthesize, match, and transfer information as managers need it. The more crucial dimensions of current-awareness subsystems are (1) information recency and aggregation levels, (2) computer systems' analytical sophistication and authority, and (3) transfer mechanisms.

Information Recency and Aggregation. Current-awareness information can be no better than the data available in various sources or banks. Therefore, their constant feeding and care are of prime concern. Data sources are maintained by individual user companies and by commercial information companies. Generally, individual firms safeguard their own sales and costs and other internally generated data within their own data banks. Market data and other external and environmental data may be purchased from one or more outside sources or banks.

Aggregation refers to the detail in which data are available in a system. Data can vary from individual customer or product files, which record each transaction as it occurs, to massive aggregate files, which record measurements such as industry sales and market shares.

Data files are most useful when maintained in detailed time sequences, with new inputs maintained along with (not replaced or combined with) existing data. Such disaggregated files provide immediate advantages in that they allow data to be assembled, reshuffled, and, in general, to be more adaptive in many different ways than more aggregate files. Second, such disaggregated data files make information systems far more adaptive to future needs. If data files are initially aggregated to meet only first-stage system needs, later-stage system development, in response to managers' greater needs, may require complete file redevelopment. Such revisions are costly and, furthermore, aggregated data files may not be convertible [6].

Unfortunately, the more disaggregated the data files, the more costly they are to maintain as a data base. Therefore management must consider the cost of disaggregate data files against their present and probable future use.

Recency refers to the lapse of time between the occurrence of an event and the time at which it is reported in an information system. Data can be collected, analyzed, and transmitted periodically in batches of varying sizes (and aggregation levels) and time periods, or individual transactions can be noted and immediately transmitted and used without any batching. The latter, live-operation information is often called on-line, real-time (OLRT) information [Section II, Part G, Chapter 2]. *On-line* means compiling information instantaneously as events occur and maintaining instant access to the data in computer core. *Real-time* means managers use the information to control operations within the short or instantaneous period.

Many airlines use OLRT passenger reservation systems. With American Airlines' SABRE program, for example, each reservation request is transmitted directly to a computer and is either rejected or confirmed, with the "space available" figure in the memory unit adjusted accordingly. Another illustration is afforded by Bank of America, which keeps customers' balances OLRT. In both situations decisions are made in view of the knowledge of current conditions. The benefits from such systems are obvious. Other OLRT systems are used to control inventories, various facets of manufacturing operations, chemical process operations, and other reservation systems.

At present, the practicality of OLRT handling of masses of marketing information is questionable. There is the problem of the state of the art, both in terms of hardware and software. Costly computers with large storage capacities and random-access capabilities are required. Programming costs are also very high because systems must be sufficiently flexible to handle dynamic marketing situations.

To be practical, OLRT systems must provide sufficient benefits in the form of better decisions to justify the added costs as compared with batch-processing information systems. Three major factors currently limit the marketing benefits obtainable through the use of OLRT information. First, only incomplete parts of the total necessary decision information can be available in most open marketing system situations. Consequently, most of the real-time advantages are lost as decision makers wait for batched information. Second, most marketing *operations* are set up on a batch basis, so there is little advantage in reacting on an individual activity basis. The final customers, for example, may buy individual units, but channel orders, shipments, inventories, payments, and most other marketing operations are more economically handled on a batch basis.

Finally, there is little need to make decisions faster than a firm can respond [25]. For example, if shoes can be shipped to Dubuque only once a day, there is little point in making numerous decisions throughout the day. Instead, information should be batched until the one time at which the best decision can be made. In conclusion, the appropriate information recency in a situation depends on management's proposed use of the information along with consideration of the costs associated with various batch periods.[3]

Computer Systems.   The typical current-awareness system has at its center a computer system. A computer is essential for rapid analysis, storage, and retrieval of information. The role of computers varies among current-awareness systems. Their relationships, however, can be described fairly well in terms of *analytical sophistication* and *computer authority.*

The degree of *analytical sophistication* of a computer system refers to the complexity of its models or structures. At the first level, a computer only identifies a specific file or record, retrieves it, and displays its information (this often presents horrendous problems). At the next level, a computer gathers data from one or more files and produces a subtotal or total. At the third level of sophistication, the computer is programmed to perform simple arithmetic operations such as computing differences and averages. The fourth level involves the computer in aggregating data by various classification schemes.

The fifth level introduces more complex analyses such as statistical best estimates, trend estimates, and analyses of variance. At the sixth level, the computer is programmed to "learn"; that is, to modify values of parameters and structures of models based on data inputs. At the most advanced level of analytical sophistication, simulation models are used in sufficient magnitude and detail to represent the real world. This permits management to test various combinations of variables in simulated environments [6].

The types of decisions a computer system is programmed to make without further man review or intervention determines its *authority* in a current-awareness system. At the elementary level, a computer is granted the authority only to store and retrieve certain information from designated locations. At the second level, the computer reviews (checks) the reasonableness of each file or record. The computer at the third level performs analyses on records and refers exceptions to managers for additional review.

At the fourth stage, the additional review noted at the third level is programmed for the computer and a *recommendation* for action is reported by the computer. At the fifth level, the computer is programmed to take *action* on all but the exceptional cases (as defined by managers) reported at the prior level. The final level of authority exists when the computer is programmed to predict. Involvement is greater here than at the prior levels in that predictions are used in future planning and commitments and not just in current activities [6].

Transfer Mechanisms.   In current-awareness information systems, a major matchmaking (adaptability) mechanism between data sources and manager-users is interest profiles of the managers. Individual managers (with the aid of information specialists) are responsible for describing the decisions they make and their optimal information sets. Furthermore, managers' interest profiles are changed over time in response to the actual information they use. These

---

[3] Situations where OLRT systems may be desirable are described in Section I, Part G, Chapter 2.

collective interest profiles are used to help determine what data will be collected and stored, how they will be analyzed, and which information will be disseminated to individual managers [10, 24]. These relationships are illustrated in Figure 2.

Data selection for inputs is of great concern since irrelevant or inaccurate data increase costs and overload users without providing payoffs. Payoffs can accrue only when decision makers receive and use information. Two of the complicating factors are (1) the continuing inflow of new data (some of which is from unstable processes) into data banks and (2) the changing needs of man-

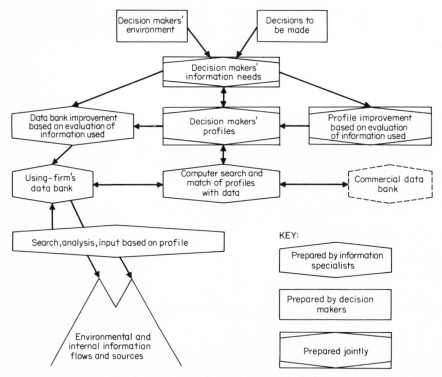

Fig. 2.   Selective dissemination subsystem.

agers. The objective is to construct a sufficiently adaptable linkage through which relevant data can be selected and matched to decision makers.

The types of final communication linkage vary from those where managers directly interrogate the computer to those where the managers never interrogate it but instead look to information specialists who provide the linkage. With the first type of linkage, the managers must have very complete knowledge of the system, its contents, the forms in which the data outputs are available, and the language needed to communicate with the computer. In the second type of situation, managers need only a general understanding of the system and the available types and forms of information. Direct interrogation of data banks by managers will become increasingly common as more conventional communication languages and more advanced remote terminals become available [11].

In-Depth and Crisis Information Subsystems

In-depth and crisis information on special problems or on areas of immediate, high-priority interest to decision makers can be provided by a subsystem called a *retrospective search subsystem.* A company's current-awareness system, for example, may indicate deteriorating sales and profits for a major product line but may not provide insight into the causes and needed corrections. A retrospective search subsystem in such situations should be able to provide decision makers with detailed information and possible solutions to such special problems.

A situation faced by a brewery provides a case in point. The brewery bought a small but popular regional brewery. For about 14 months its current-awareness system indicated that market share and profit patterns were remaining constant. Suddenly, the current-awareness system reported declines in market shares followed by, at first, small declines in sales which were followed by larger losses in each of the following three months. Although management did get an early warning of trouble, it could not determine what caused the losses. The causes were finally ferreted out, but only after considerable in-depth research and information furnished through their retrospective search subsystem.

Structural Problem. The successes of in-depth and crisis information subsystems are conditioned by the availability of flexible organizational structures capable of adapting to unique problems which present severe time constraints and often seem to occur at inappropriate times. Consequently, the highly structured, extensively staffed, routinized, and computer-centered organizations which serve well in current-awareness subsystems are particularly inappropriate for in-depth and crisis information subsystems.[4]

The concept of temporary organizations, originally advocated by Bennis, appears to be a promising structure to provide the needed flexibility. Instead of bureaucracy, temporary, specialized task forces are assembled to handle specific, unique problems as they are identified [8]. As new and unique problems are encountered, new groups, uniquely qualified for the task, are assembled, and upon solution the task forces are dissolved.

These problem-oriented task forces are composed of "relative strangers" with diverse skills appropriate to each situation. The task force used by the brewery, for example, was composed of a brewmaster, a market planning expert, a regional sales manager, and an advertising research specialist, and it was coordinated by a marketing research specialist. This diverse group was assembled because a preliminary investigation showed increased dissatisfaction with the taste of the beer among formerly loyal customers.

Under this concept, which still needs more testing, the administrators of the subsystem serve as "linking pins" among task forces, their special skills being (1) research—to help identify problems, (2) mediation—to get the best efforts from each task force, and (3) communication—both to help secure cooperation and ongoing adoption of task forces and their solutions.

In some respects, the temporary organization concept has received considerable testing and use. Over the years many companies have maintained only small in-house marketing research groups and have hired specific consulting groups, because of their expertise, to examine various problems. In these sit-

---

[4] This does not suggest that data banks and computers are of no use. In fact, retrospective search subsystems are strengthened when data banks can be searched for information on similar problems and their solutions and when problems can be simulated on computers.

uations the consultants assembled the specialists, and a person within the hiring company served as the linking pin. The temporary organization made primary use of internal experts with supplementary help only when key insiders were not available.

Incidental Information Subsystems

Incidental and unsolicited information normally will not flow through either of the two subsystems discussed to this point. Those subsystems handle identified types and sources of information, or information for crisis or special problems. Some companies are developing *unsolicited information subsystems.*

These subsystems are unique both in terms of inputs and outputs. The *input* side is present to facilitate the collection, analysis, and synthesis of unsolicited, unanticipated, and incidental data which appear to warrant the attention of managers. In a sense, it is like a giant jigsaw puzzle assembly.

The *output* side concerns the communication to managers of what was unsolicited and incidental information. The output side also provides the information specialists a means of bringing managers together with unusual and unsolicited but relevant data which now can enter the system.

An illustration should help clarify and define the nature of unsolicited or incidental information. In this case a series of seemingly unrelated incidents provided the information. A draftsman for a writing instrument manufacturer received a complimentary sample of a Japanese-built sign pen. He used it, told a few close associates about it, and ordered a half-dozen of each of five colors. Later he reordered three dozen of each color. Almost simultaneously, two representatives of the same writing instrument company noted a Japanese-built sign pen in a few artist supply stores. One of them purchased a dozen for use around his home and office. About two months prior to these events a buyer in the purchasing department of the writing instrument company had heard about some new materials being used in the construction of writing instruments. He had no need for them and was not interested.

Less than one year after these seemingly unrelated events had occurred, the Japanese sign pen came to the unmistakable attention of the executives of the writing instrument company. Some of their pen lines were down in sales by as much as 12 percent due to broad market acceptance of the Japanese sign pen. The incidents experienced by a company draftsman, two salesmen, and a buyer provided a nucleus of incidental unsought information. Unfortunately, these particles of information were not treated as useful marketing information and their importance was not realized until it was too late.

Two major problems confront firms wishing to build and use this third type of marketing information subsystem. First, key personnel are often in contact with relevant data but neither recognize it as valuable nor collect and transmit it to appropriate places in their organizations. These failures are due largely to problems of selective exposure, perception, and retention.

The second problem is that key personnel do not know *where* and *how* to transmit the data; and prospective users do not know it is even available, let alone *where* it is to be found. These two problems are somewhat common to all information situations, but they are particularly oppressive to this subsystem because of the apparently incidental (that is, inconsequential) nature of the data.

Successful management of unsought and incidental information evolves around (1) the human element and (2) the organizational aspects [4].

The Human Element. Identification and training of key information people are the first requirement. These should be people who have considerable contact with sources where needed data can be found. Salesmen, for example, are exposed to the general market, including both buyers and the salesmen who sell to competitors. These key people need to know how to search for and handle data. They must be *aware* of the need for broad exposure, critical perception, and data retention.

The second requirement is that key people be encouraged to seek and transmit data discoveries. When transmitters are subject to ridicule or find personal gains by holding back, few data flow [4].

Organizational Aspects. A special framework is required. Basically, a structural framework should strive to (1) optimize securers' knowledge of what to do with secured data, (2) optimize the knowledge of decision makers as to the existence of information, (3) reduce the probability of information biases and distortions, (4) provide means whereby the data can be evaluated and related to company needs, and (5) reduce to the optimum the time required for relevant data to be initially secured, transmitted, analyzed, synthesized, and made available to decision makers [4].

A centralized control office appears to be virtually mandatory for accomplishing the preceding tasks. With one central office, securers know where to send data; at least they know there is only one receiver. Manager-users also know there is only *one* source, so they do not search among numerous units. Consequently, less time is wasted between securing and using the information. Direct handling also reduces distortions resulting from multiple transmitting, analysis, condensation, and so forth. Finally, the only way to fit jigsaw puzzle parts together and to know what parts are missing is to have a central staging and assembling location.

Subsystems do *not* exist and operate as separate information activities. They are managed as integrated analytic systems to discern, supply, and communicate needed marketing information to decision makers.

THE ORGANIZATION AND LOCATION OF MARKETING INFORMATION SYSTEMS WITHIN COMPANIES

It is not enough to say that marketing information systems are composed of and managed by subsystems. More specifically, the following question must be considered: Should there be one centralized marketing information system, or should there be a multiple number of independent divisional systems? Also, should marketing information systems be directed and controlled by marketing management or by nonmarketing management, perhaps as one subsystem with a companywide management information system?

In some companies, the overall organizational alignments are so distinctly and completely centralized or decentralized that marketing information system alignments obviously must fit the same patterns. In other companies, where some activities are centralized and others are not, the most advantageous alignment is often far from being clear. In this latter case, one centralized marketing information system is used mainly because (1) it minimizes duplication of personnel, space, and equipment; (2) it is more likely to permit full-time employment of a few extremely competent specialists; and (3) it facilitates companywide decision making. On the other hand, if information problems for regional, product, or customer divisions are radically different or if corporate staff is unacquainted with individual regions, product lines, or customers, divisional information systems may be advantageous.

The question of where marketing information systems should be located within companywide organizations has received very little attention. However, a basic question that should be considered is this: Should such systems (whether centralized or decentralized) be under the jurisdiction of marketing managers or under other personnel?

If marketing information systems follow the location patterns of marketing research offices, far more than half of them will report to marketing managers [23].

Prescriptive advice indicates that if information activities are limited to sales and marketing information, the information office should report to a marketing manager. The major explanation has been that such an information office works primarily with and for persons in the marketing division and, accordingly, it functions best in that division. When its activities are more inclusive and the office serves other parts of the company (finance, production, etc.), it should report to top-level nonmarketing management [17].

Several criteria which have been used to determine the placement of marketing research departments within companies also appear appropriate when marketing information systems are being considered. They should be located to provide (1) freedom from the influence of those whom their work affects, (2) maximum efficiency of operations, and (3) cooperation and support of managers to whom they report [17].

Organizational considerations will receive more attention in the following chapter. To date, the real-world experience with the organization of marketing information systems is scanty because, in general, attempts to integrate them are in their infancy.

SUMMARY

This chapter has dealt with marketing information systems and their relationship to marketing research. Marketing research, using the broadest definition, can perhaps be considered almost the equivalent of marketing information systems. However, marketing research as frequently practiced has not lived up to the popular definition. In turn, the systems' analytic approach is emerging as a reflection of the changing conceptual view of the payoffs available from marketing information.

Because of differences in managements, environments, and a host of other considerations, there does not appear to be any unique information system that will serve all companies. The most fundamental concept is that information systems need to be adaptive to users' dynamic environments. The most obvious dimensions are that information systems are composed of subsystems, usually two or three.

One subsystem is typically designed to provide current-awareness information and normally has at its center a computer system. A second subsystem provides in-depth and crisis information. This one typically evolves out of and is more akin to the marketing research function in the firm. A third subsystem, when present, typically handles information and situations which do not fit into the other two subsystems.[5]

REFERENCES

1. Ackoff, Russell L., "Management Misinformation Systems," *Management Science,* vol. 14, no. 4, pp. B-147–B-156, December 1967.
2. Albaum, Gerald, "Horizontal Information Flow: An Exploratory Study," *Journal of Academy of Management,* March 1964.

[5] For an illustration, see [2].

3. ———, "Information Flows and Decentralized Decision Making in Marketing," *California Management Review*, Summer 1967, pp. 59–70.
4. ———, "The Hidden Crisis in Information Transmission," *Pittsburgh Business Review*, vol. 33, no. 7, p. 2, July 1963.
5. Alexander, Ralph S., *Marketing Definitions*, Chicago: American Marketing Association, Committee on Definitions, 1963, pp. 16–17.
6. Amstutz, Arnold E., "The Marketing Executive and Management Information Systems," in R. Hass, ed., *Science, Technology and Marketing*, Chicago: American Marketing Association, 1966, pp. 69–86.
7. Ashby, Ross, *Design for a Brain*, New York: Wiley, 1960, pp. 44–70.
8. Bennis, W., "Changing Organizations," *The Journal of Applied Behavioral Science*, July–August–September 1966, pp. 247–262.
9. Cox, Donald, and Robert Good, "How to Build a Marketing Information System," *Harvard Business Review*, May–June 1967, pp. 145–154.
10. Craven, D. W., "Information Systems for Technology Transfer," in R. Hass, ed., *Science, Technology and Marketing*, American Marketing Association, 1966, pp. 47–60.
11. Diebold, John, "What's Ahead in Information Technology," *Harvard Business Review*, September–October 1965, pp. 76–82.
12. Feltham, Gerald A., "The Value of Information," *The Accounting Review*, October 1968, pp. 684–696.
13. Heany, Donald F., *Development of Information Systems; What Management Needs to Know*, New York: Ronald, 1968.
14. Hein, Leonard W., "The Management Account and the Integrated Information System," *Management Accounting*, June 1968, pp. 34–38.
15. Kostetsky, Oleh, "Decision Making, Information Systems, and the Role of the Systems Analyst," *Management Science*, October 1966, pp. C-17–C-20.
16. Liston, D., Jr., "Information Systems: What They Do, How They Work," *Machine Design*, July 21, 1966, pp. 190–197.
17. "Marketing Business and Commercial Research in Industry," *Studies in Business Policy 72*, New York: National Industrial Conference Board, 1955.
18. Morris, William T., *Management Science In Action*, Homewood, Ill.: Irwin, 1963, p. 113.
19. Rappaport, Alfred, "Sensitivity Analysis in Decision Making," *The Accounting Review*, July 1967, pp. 441–456.
20. Rhind, Ridley, "Management Information Systems," *Business Horizons*, June 1968, pp. 37–46.
21. Smith, S., R. Brien, and J. Stafford, ed., *Readings in Marketing Information Systems*, Boston: Houghton Mifflin, 1968, p. 7.
22. *The Use of Computers in Business Organizations*, Reading, Mass.: Addison-Wesley, 1966.
23. Twedt, D. W., ed., *A Survey of Marketing Research: Organization, Functions, Budgets, Compensation*, Chicago: American Marketing Association, 1963.
24. Uhl, Kenneth P., "Marketing Information Systems and Subsystems," in Robert L. King, ed., *Marketing and the New Science of Planning*, Chicago: American Marketing Association, 1968, pp. 163–168.
25. ———, and Bertram Schoner, *Marketing Research: Information Systems and Decision Making*, New York: Wiley, 1969.
26. Woods, Richard S., "Some Dimensions of Integrated Systems," *Accounting Review*, July 1964, pp. 598–614.
27. Zannetos, Zenon S., "Toward Intelligent Management Information Systems," *Industrial Management Review*, Spring 1968, pp. 21–38.

Chapter 4

Marketing
Decision Information Systems:
Some Design Considerations

DAVID B. MONTGOMERY   *Graduate School of Business, Stanford University, Stanford, California*

> The modern age has a false sense of superiority
> because of the great mass of data at its disposal.
> But the valid criterion of distinction is rather
> the extent to which man knows how to form
> and master the material at his command.
> GOETHE (1749–1832)

A major problem with marketing information systems has been the tendency to view them merely as systems for the generation, storage, and retrieval of vast volumes of data. All too often models and statistical methods have been overlooked in the design of a marketing information system, and yet they are necessary if the full potential of the new information technology is to be harnessed for management use. Models and statistical methods provide the information system with the capacity to digest, analyze, and interpret data.

An overemphasis on data generation, storage, and retrieval carries with it the grave danger that the manager will suffer a data overload and receive little help in decision making. Proper system design must provide for a balanced growth of all aspects of the marketing information system to provide decision-relevant information to marketing management. To emphasize this need for a balanced, decision-relevant system development, the system envisaged in this chapter will be referred to as a marketing decision information system.

The purposes of this chapter are to:

1. Outline the components that are required in a marketing decision information system

2. Establish the necessity for a balanced development of the system components

3. Present design considerations in developing these components

4. Suggest certain organizational considerations that have been found to be important to successful system development

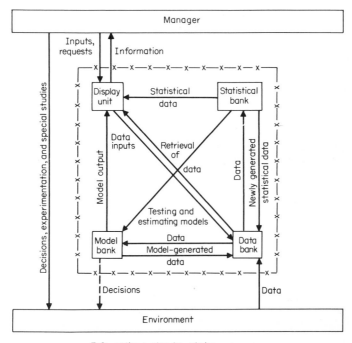

Fig. 1.   Decision-information system structure. *(Adapted from [29].)*

THE MARKETING DECISION INFORMATION SYSTEM

Four components comprise the major subsystems in a marketing decision information system (MDIS): (1) a data bank, (2) a model bank, (3) a measurement statistics bank, and (4) a man-system communications capability.[1]   The MDIS interacts with two external elements, the user and the environment. The latter includes everything (both internal and external to the firm) which affects the firm's marketing activities.   A diagram of the system components and their interactions is given in Figure 1.

The data bank provides the MDIS with the capacity to store, retrieve, manipulate, and transform data.   Though the manager or user will have use for retrieval of raw data from the system, for decision purposes he will gen-

[1] This structure was first proposed in [29] and was elaborated on in [31].

erally want to process the data in some manner.   For example, he may require sales summaries or market share information, which involve further processing of the raw data stored in the system.

The model bank includes various marketing models for use in planning and controlling the firm's marketing activities—for example, sales effort allocation models, advertising budgeting models, and simulation models.   Model-based analysis provides input to the management planning and control process, but a manager or user generally intervenes between the model analysis and company actions.   However, in certain special cases the models may be delegated authority to make routine decisions, as in the case of inventory reorder systems and Amstutz's [4] stock market model.

The measurement statistics bank provides the system with the capacity for statistical data analysis, such as multiple regression, cluster analysis, factor analysis, and multidimensional scaling.   These statistical techniques are considered in more detail in other chapters of this handbook.   Besides data analysis, the measurement statistics bank should contain procedures for obtaining and analyzing subjective marketing judgments—for example, applications of statistical decision theory and forecasts of competitors' promotional activities.

The man-system communications capability, which operates through the display unit, provides a two-way link between the user and the system.   It is a vital system component since meaningful communication is necessary if the MDIS is to be utilized.

Interaction between System Components.   A few illustrations should establish the highly interdependent nature of the system components.   This high degree of interaction between the system components requires that a coordinated system development be undertaken if the MDIS is to be used to full advantage.

One of the most important interdependencies is that between the model bank and the data which are retained in the data bank.   Data are generally desirable for purposes of model formulation, discriminating between alternative models of the same phenomenon, estimation of model parameters, and model testing. The latter purpose is often a key one in gaining management's confidence in a marketing model.

At any point in time, the use of data in developing and using a firm's marketing models is constrained by the data which are available.   Though the firm may, of course, elect to gather additional cross-sectional data, data related to the dynamics of the marketplace are generated over time, often with considerable time periods between observations.   If important pieces of data relating to market dynamics are missing because of their never having been collected or the fact that the firm has discarded them, then model development and estimation must rely heavily on judgment until appropriate data develop over time.   Model testing will have to await the generation of the data.   Consequently, decisions made today on what data to obtain and retain in the data bank have long-run implications for the firm's development and use of marketing models.

Two examples from the author's experience will illustrate the point.   The first relates to the formation of a multifirm marketing information system in the pharmaceutical industry.   This system is designed to measure the impact of competitive market communications.   Commercial data sources have existed for some time.   Since past usage of the data tended to be for short-run market assessment, old data have been discarded.   As a result, monthly data were only available for the past two years, which seriously limited the data base on which the multifirm marketing information system could formulate and test dynamic measurement models.   This forced the effort toward more complex and expensive measurement methods. The second example is from a research study on a drug product for the international division of a large United States drug firm. In this international market as well, much valuable data, such as competitive sales calls on doctors, had been discarded by the commercial data supplier. Thus again, invaluable raw material for model development was lost because its potential use in model development was not foreseen by the data supplier.

These are not isolated examples. It is painful to contemplate the enormous volume of potentially useful data which has been discarded by users and suppliers alike. The MDIS design implication seems clear. If a firm expects to become involved in data-based marketing models at any time in the next five years, it must begin immediately to assess the directions its modeling efforts will take and the data requirements to support these efforts. This assessment should then have an impact on decisions of what data to obtain and retain in the data bank.

Further examples of how models interact with the data bank may be found in the work of Madansky [23] and Little and Lodish [21]. Madansky describes a situation in which a client wanted a computer-based system to organize the vast volume of data it collected and purchased. The goal was to provide decision-relevant information. As a first step, a decision model was structured based on data which were either available or readily obtainable. The model analysis identified further data requirements and specified the form of the data required for analysis. The latter suggested a change in the data collection procedure which would render the data directly compatible with the model. In Madansky's words, "we have gone from a decision model to a data bank organization scheme for the client." The Little and Lodish MEDIAC media selection model utilizes only single media exposures and paired duplications. Hence the model specifies the data collection scheme—for example, no data are required on triplications, quadruplications, etc.

The measurement statistics bank and the man-system communications capability also interact with the other system components. The ability to estimate and test marketing models is provided by the measurement statistics bank. Since the model bank will probably contain nonlinear, dynamic models, the measurement statistics bank must be designed to contain procedures which will support these models. Furthermore, the nature of the display capability will have design implications for the other components. The use of remote terminals which allow interactive operation in the MDIS will have a very significant impact. For a discussion of the use of remote, on-line terminals in marketing, see Section II, Part G, Chapter 2.

THE DATA BANK

The data bank involves two primary aspects: (1) the data and (2) computer-based and manual systems for data storage, retrieval, manipulation, and transformation.

The Data. Though an extensive discussion of appropriate data for the data bank is outside the scope of this chapter, it should be noted that careful consideration must be given to specification of what data will be maintained within the system, particularly as it affects future activities in marketing models.

Examples of data categories which might be maintained in the data bank are given in Table 1. Although the table is far from exhaustive, it does illustrate some of the basic types of market data which might be maintained within the system. For example, the collection and maintenance of competitive mar-

TABLE 1   Data Categories: Consumer Goods Company

I. Internal corporate records
    A. Financial and cost data by product and time period
    B. Internal report data
        1. Salesman's call reports
        2. Marketing-mix data by product, time period, and market
        3. Sales performance information on previously implemented new products
        4. Life-cycle information on line products
        5. Copy and format data on company advertisements
    C. Judgmental inputs
        1. Judgmental forecasts by product, time, and forecaster
        2. Estimates of market sensitivity to company and competitive marketing activities
II. External data
    A. Secondary sources
        1. Government data (e.g., population demographic data by zip coded area)
        2. Commercial data (e.g., MRCA panel data, Nielsen store audits, BRI data)
        3. Freight rate data
    B. Primary data
        1. Test-market information
        2. Market experiments
        3. Market structure analysis
        4. Competitive marketing activity
        5. Advertising performance measures (e.g., Schwerin, Gallup-Robinson, Starch)

ket activity data (II. B. 4 in Table 1) will be increasingly important as better models are developed to assess the impact of competitive activities. Many of the data categories will subsequently be related to each other to gain understanding of market response. Thus, the data file on copy and format in company advertisements (I. B. 5 in Table 1) may be related to advertising performance measures (II. B. 5) to learn systematically how the market is responding to these characteristics of ads. Cox and Good [8] report that one large consumer goods company is doing precisely that, while Diamond [9] has developed an on-line model called ADFORS which utilizes the results of such analysis.

Freight rate data (II. A. 3 in Table 1) will support the development of distribution applications within the MDIS. Western Electric has found that such a data base, made accessible on a computer system, enables the company to perform, in a matter of hours, rate analyses and studies which formerly took months.

A key data bank design issue is the level of aggregation (level of detail) in which to maintain the data. In general, data should be stored in disaggregated form, that is, in its most elemental form. For example, salesmen's call reports might be maintained in a disaggregated form, providing such details as person visited, place of visit, time of visit, sales aids used, and so forth. An aggregated form for this data might be the annual call frequency of a salesman on a particular account. The goal of maintaining disaggregated data is, of course, to provide future flexibility. If data are maintained only in aggregate form, the possibility of organizing them in a different way for future but at present unknown purposes is sacrificed. The importance of this flexibility is illustrated in Amstutz's [4] discussion of his computerized portfolio selection system when he states, "If initial data files had been structured to maintain data at the level of aggregation required when the system was begun, many operations of the present system would be precluded by data limitations." In a survey of marketing information system developments in the late 1960s, Amstutz [5] found a trend toward lower levels of data aggregation, that is, toward maintaining data in more disaggregated form.

Systems for Processing the Data. The processing systems in the data bank should be able to perform the following basic operations:

1. *Data preprocessing.* This involves the ability to clean and edit data.
2. *File creation, reorganization, and deletion.*
3. *File maintenance and updating.*
4. *Information retrieval.*
5. *Logical operations on data.* This will prove useful when a file is being prepared for statistical analysis.
6. *Data transformation.* The ability to perform arithmetic operations on data is crucial to simple analysis, such as computation of market shares, as well as to more complex statistical analysis.
7. *Report generation.* The system should be able to generate reports readily in nearly any desired format.

Frank and Massy [13] have reported on a useful batch processing system for performing these basic operations on consumer panel data. Miller's [27] DATANAL system provides a very general, flexible data handling capability for time-sharing systems.

Modularity and Flexibility. Two key design issues in the data bank processing systems development are modularity and flexibility. Since the data bank, and indeed the entire MDIS, will be an evolving system, it is vital that the system be readily adaptable to changes in the data and in the operations to be performed on the data. Modularity or compartmentalization of the processing operations will help minimize problems involved in adapting the processing systems to future requirements.

Flexibility may be achieved by developing a variety of general commands which may be used to retrieve and manipulate data. These general commands may then be called to operate on the data, whatever the data file may be. Development of these general commands, which are not specific to a particular data file, greatly reduces the problems which result when a file is altered by additions, deletions, or reorganization. An example of an operational data handling system using such general commands is the DATANAL system developed by Miller [27].

System Administration. The data bank should maintain information on who used which data for what purposes. This should provide information on which to base decisions regarding which data should be kept in high-speed computer storage and, further, which data should be phased out of the system. Thus the data bank should gather information appropriate to adapting itself to meet the needs of its users better and to developing specifications for the storage of disaggregated data. Similarly, the system should accumulate information on the frequency and duration of use of the data bank processing functions as well as the procedures incorporated in the measurement statistics and model banks. This will provide the raw material for decisions on the allocation of system improvement efforts.

Security Systems. The data bank must have security systems which ensure that the system and the data are protected. At the system level it is necessary to prevent a user from inadvertently altering or destroying one of the system programs. Such user-generated accidents are both costly and frustrating. There is also a clear need for data security systems both vertically and hori-

zontally in the firm.   The problem is one of who may have access to what.
For example, a branch manager might have access to data relative to his
branch, a regional manager to data for his region, and the marketing vice president to national data.   In effect, the system should allow users access to data
on a "need-to-know" basis.   This can be accomplished by assigning to each
user an identification code or password which specifies the data to which he
may have access.

There is an obvious need for bottom-up security.   Thus individuals at a
given organizational level should not have access to certain types of information
relative to a higher level in the firm.   But there may also be a need for top-
down security, for there may be data which should not be conveniently accessible to managers at higher organizational levels.   For example, Amstutz [2]
reports a case of a sales vice president spending too much time worrying about
sales results in individual territories.   In this case he was able to access detailed
territorial information very readily, and this capability distracted him from his
primary task—overall market planning.

Horizontal security systems are also required.   For example, the firm may
not want the branch manager in Boston to have access to data relative to the
San Francisco branch.   As Ackoff [1] has noted, organizational harmony and
efficiency are not necessarily enhanced by allowing managers access to one
another's data files.   As with vertical security systems, horizontal systems may
be implemented by means of user identification codes.

Access to the Data Bank.   Data in the data bank must be readily accessible
to the manager.   Rapid, accurate access will enable the manager to be more
thorough in his market analyses.   In some circumstances, such as a situation in
which the firm needs to react quickly to a competitive move in some market,
ready access to data will render data-based analysis feasible.

Perhaps the most convenient system for providing the manager access to the
data bank is via remote terminals which provide the opportunity for man-system
interaction.   The notion of interactive systems is explored more fully in Section
II, Part G, Chapter 2.   However, at this point it should be noted that interactive operations will enable the manager to "data browse."   That is, it will
allow him to explore a wide variety of marketing data in rapid succession.   This
should help him spot emerging problems not yet sufficiently severe to have
come to management's attention through the firm's customary channels.

As an example, consider IBM's information system.   Branch offices are connected to a data base in White Plains, New York, via remote consoles.   The
data base contains information files on such items as sales plans, sales, financial
results, orders, customers, and products.   Now suppose a regional manager has
noticed that new orders are down for the current month.   He may then instruct the system to present an analysis by district.   If this shows two districts
below plan, he might then ask for a breakdown by metropolitan branch offices
in those two districts.   The readout on the terminal might show that four
branch offices are down.   To find out why, the manager may then ask the system to present a report on installation activities for each of these branches.
When that report indicates exceptionally high installation activities, he may
then assume that this has distracted from sales time.   He then decides whether
or not to adopt a counterstrategy, and if so, what kind.

All this analysis can be done in a few minutes using the remote terminal
located in the manager's office.   The rapid, convenient system response enables
the manager to pursue the analysis of the problem while it is current.   The
manager's thought processes need not be interrupted for hours or perhaps days
while a secretary or assistant ferrets out the desired data.

THE MODEL BANK

The model bank should contain models for use in understanding market behavior, diagnosis of factors underlying market results, control of marketing operations, and planning of marketing strategy. Some examples of potential models would be brand switching models [26], total market simulations models [3], and new-product planning models [7, 17, 39]. Detailed discussion of marketing models may be found in [29, 30]. In this section consideration will be given to some design aspects for the model bank and to emerging trends in market modeling.

Model Bank Design. The model bank should contain a multiplicity of models which vary according to their level of detail (or aggregation) and number and type of control variables. At the highest level of aggregation might be a model reflecting the market response to dollar expenditures on elements in the marketing mix, such as price, personal sales effort, advertising, and special promotions. At the other extreme would be microanalytic simulation models [3].

Having a variety of models available which vary in detail and control variables provides flexibility in response to any given problem situation. Thus the manager may choose an analysis appropriate to his perception of the cost/benefits situation in any specific case. For example, the SPRINTER consumer product model has three levels of detail [39]. The first is a simple representation of the process of new-product diffusion. The second adds control variables (price and advertising). The third adds several more control variables and provides a more detailed representation of the buying process. In any given situation the manager may select the level of detail and number of control variables he deems appropriate.

Though more detail is generally useful, the financial and time costs of both model operation and analysis of the model results increase rapidly as detail is increased. For example, in the SPRINTER model, level 1 costs 10 percent as much to operate as level 3, while level 2 costs 20 percent as much as level 3 [39].

It may prove advantageous to have several alternative models at a given level of detail, since different managers may have different requirements because of variations in their areas of responsibility and decision styles. The model bank may ultimately have multiple models available at each combination of level of detail and number of control variables to service the decision needs of the firm's various marketing managers. This reinforces the important point that the model bank's development, like all aspects of the MDIS, must be an evolutionary, adaptive process that adjusts to the managers' varied and changing needs.

The models in the model bank should be designed for compatible usage. That is, they should, insofar as is possible, be consistent with one another. One advantage of simpler, less detailed models is the ability to evaluate a large number of alternatives. However, they in turn suffer from having ignored many potentially relevant phenomena. The compatible use of models takes advantage of the strengths of both the simple and the more complex models. The simple models may be used to explore a wide range of alternatives and to choose one or several which seem promising. More detailed models may then be called on to assess this smaller set of alternatives.

For example, a simple aggregate model such as ADBUDG [20] might be used to specify an annual budget. Then a media allocation model such as MEDIAC [21] might be used to develop a good media schedule for expending that budget. Finally, the best media schedule might be submitted to a microanalytic simulation to obtain detailed purchase and attitude response results. The results of the simulation may in turn indicate a need for a reevaluation of one of the earlier analyses. Furthermore, it will provide control guidelines for evaluating results once the policy is implemented. Such compatible use of models is an effective method for taking advantage of the strengths of various model types.

Trends in Marketing Models. Several new developments are supporting the model bank concept. First, there is the emergence of a problem-centered rather than technique-centered approach to marketing models. Much early work in marketing models could be characterized as techniques looking for problems. Marketing relevance was often sacrificed to achieve formulations which would satisfy the requirements of given solution techniques. The rush to formulate the media selection problem as a linear program is a case in point.

Marketing problems are now beginning to dominate techniques in the formulation of marketing models. Maturing experience in the structuring of marketing models, the realization that successful implementation and use depend on this approach, and steady progress in management science and operations research in developing methods for solving more realistic and complex problems have all spurred this trend. Although optimization techniques are improving, the recent trend in marketing is to nonalgorithmic techniques, such as heuristic programming and simulation, because these techniques are more capable of a rich representation of the interdependent and dynamic nature of marketing problems. Efforts are being expended to achieve good solutions to relevant problems rather than optimal solutions to the wrong problems.

The growing availability of data for estimating and testing models is fostering the emergence of more realistic, detailed, and valid model structures. The trend toward realistic market response representation is further enhanced by a tendency to include more behavioral phenomena, more variables, nonlinear response functions, and stochastic elements in marketing models.

A significant model trend, emerging as a result of the development of time-shared computers, is that toward interactive models. An interactive model operating on a time-shared computer system provides a decision maker with the capacity to quickly and efficiently explore the implications of how judgments relate to given problems. Examples are discussed in Section II, Part G, Chapter 2.

A major development trend is toward inclusion of dynamic market effects. A model that encompasses the dynamic aspects of markets is the adaptive modeling work of Little, who proposed a model for adjusting the advertising budget in the face of a changing environment via a series of continuing market experiments, the results of which are used to update the budget decision [19]. Distributed lag models are increasingly being used to measure dynamic effects [24].

Another trend is toward building models considering competitive effects. This will involve a significant interaction with the data bank since the development of competitive models must be supported by data bank capabilities which provide for the systematic monitoring and storing of competitive market data for use in developing, validating, and using these competitive models. Given this trend, it would seem important for firms to consider initiating a program of competitive data generation that will match their future model intentions.

THE MEASUREMENT STATISTICS BANK

The measurement statistics bank provides the basis for measurement and estimation as well as methods for testing response functions and models. Both data-based and judgment-based methods should be incorporated in the measurement statistics bank. For example, this bank should provide procedures for estimating the demand elasticities of marketing variables based on data in the data bank. It should also provide for making judgmental assessments, such as the likelihood that a competitor will lower price and the reference life cycle of a new product. For testing response functions and models, the measurement statistics bank should encompass techniques for assessing the adequacy of a postulated model or function in the light of empirical evidence.

Methods of Measurement. The methods which should be incorporated into the measurement statistics bank fall into two categories: data-based and judgment-based. Some representative examples are given in Table 2. Although the examples are not exhaustive, they illustrate the nature of this kind of bank.

TABLE 2   Methods in the Measurement Statistics Bank

I. Data-based methods
   A. Analysis of variance and other parametric procedures
   B. Multivariate procedures
      1. Regression analysis
      2. Discriminant analysis
      3. Factor analysis
      4. Cluster analysis
   C. Nonparametric statistics
      1. Cross-classification
      2. Goodness-of-fit measures
      3. Rank-order measures
      4. Nonparametric analysis of variance and multivariate procedures
   D. Time series analysis
   E. Numeric estimation techniques
   F. Nonmetric scaling
II. Judgment-based methods
   A. Decision theory program
   B. Methods for obtaining judgmental assessments
   C. Bayesian multivariate analysis

Data-based Methods. Analysis of variance and other classical parametric procedures are helpful in analyzing the results of market experiments and exploring marketing data for useful relationships. Market experiments are increasingly useful in assessing the nature of market response to marketing policies. In particular, the emergence of adaptive marketing models, making use of continuing market experiments, will make these statistical procedures increasingly relevant to marketing managers.

Multivariate methods are useful in measuring and testing the multiple factor relationships which exist in marketing. Historical data from the data bank will generally serve as input to these procedures. Perhaps the most widely used of these techniques is regression analysis, which finds many uses in estimating and testing market response functions. Since realistic representation of market response generally requires nonlinear response functions, the measurement statistics bank should include techniques for nonlinear regression.

Multivariate methods have many practical uses in marketing and therefore ought to be included in the measurement statistics bank. For instance, discriminant analysis may be used to identify the attributes which distinguish innovators and early adopters of new products from noninnovators [34]. Latent product attributes may be identified by using factor analysis [32].

Cluster analysis has been used to characterize consumer response to opinion leadership questions [28] and to select markets for test marketing [16].

Data often do not satisfy the measurement assumptions of the parametric techniques. In such cases the nonparametric statistics subsystem will be particularly useful. Tests to determine "goodness of fit" should be included to assess the descriptive adequacy of models or distributions.

Procedures for time series analysis are necessary for applications involving market dynamics. For example, spectral analysis may be a useful technique for the analysis of market simulations [18] or the measurement of seasonal patterns [33].

Numeric estimation procedures should be included to enable the MDIS to estimate and test models which involve complex estimation equations. See [26] for some brand switching models which require numeric estimation. The capacity for numeric estimation is extremely important in that it enables the MDIS to handle realistic marketing models that are intractable in terms of analytical estimation methods. These methods will be closely related to the techniques required to implement nonlinear regression.

Nonmetric scaling techniques are useful in assessing customer perceptions of a set of competing brands. They may also be used to identify potential new-product opportunities and to develop market communications [35, 36].

Judgment-based Methods. Statistical decision theory is perhaps the best known example of a judgment-based method of analysis for marketing. Applications have been proposed for a wide variety of problems including advertising [14] and pricing [15]. One of the major barriers to widespread management use of this technique has been the burdensome amount of calculation required in problems of meaningful size. This barrier may be greatly reduced by developing computer programs, most likely on time-shared computers, to perform the necessary calculations. These programs will ask the manager or user the questions that must be answered for analysis to proceed and will report the analysis results in a convenient format for management use. Some steps have already been taken to develop such systems. (See [11] and [37].) When decision theory techniques are readily available to marketing managers, it is safe to predict increasingly widespread use.

The importance of judgmental inputs to marketing analysis can perhaps best be illustrated by two examples. The first is the competitive bidding work done by Franz Edelman and his colleagues at RCA [11]. They formulated a simple model of the competitive bidding situation which required three types of input from management:

1. The likelihood that a competitor will bid each of several possible prices
2. The likelihood that RCA will win the contract if RCA bids a price of X and the competitor bids a price of Y
3. The value to RCA of winning the contract at any given price X

The model then takes these management judgments and combines them to indicate which bid price RCA should use to gain the greatest expected reward. This model was tested in seven actual bidding situations. The test required management to supply the preceding judgments to the model. The managers then submitted the actual bid using their customary methods. Independently, the model used the judgments to recommend a bid. However, in the test cases, the model's bid price was not used as the bid price. Rather, it was determined in order to assess what would have happened if the model bid had been submitted.

The results proved extremely interesting. RCA won only three of the seven bids using its standard bidding procedure. In the three cases in which the managers' bids won, the RCA bid was an average of 5.5 percent below the next lowest competitive bid. If the bid recommended by the model analysis had been submitted, RCA would have won all seven contracts, and the bids would have averaged only 2.1 percent below the lowest competitive bid. Hence RCA would have been substantially better off had they been using the model to make their bids.

This example illustrates several important points. First, the issue is not one of men versus models but rather one of men using unaided judgment versus men plus models that help to organize their judgments and to derive consistent conclusions from these judgments. Second, this case indicates that managers can indeed provide useful judgmental inputs about the components of a decision problem. Finally, the RCA bidding example demonstrates that a model-based analysis can help to assemble management judgments and derive decision-relevant conclusions from them.

The second example relates to a company that shall be called Chain Store. One problem faced by Chain Store's management was which items to feature at what prices in their weekly ads so as to generate store traffic, sales, and profits. In addition, decisions were required on how much advertising space to allocate to each of the items featured in the ad. A simple model was developed representing the store managers' understanding of how the market would respond to the advertised items and their respective prices as well as to the amount of ad space devoted to each item. The model thus represented a general statement of the managers' notion of how the controllable marketing activities related to measures of performance. To use the model to plan the weekly ad for a given store, that store manager would supply a variety of judgmental inputs concerning market response in that specific instance. The model was programmed on a time-share computer facility and used by the store managers to test a variety of promotional plans and assumptions about market response. Thus the model was used for planning weekly promotions, and excellent results were reported.[2] The consultant who helped develop the model attributes its success to the managers' ability to provide meaningful judgmental inputs to this simple model. As in the RCA case, the model simply helped the managers to integrate their judgments about a variety of phenomena and to draw proper conclusions from them.

The measurement statistics bank should provide procedures for systematic monitoring, evaluation, and improvement of the judgmental inputs provided by individuals in the firm. Monitoring and evaluation will help identify particularly valuable sources of judgmental inputs to the market planning process. For example, monitoring and evaluating judgmental inputs to site location problems for a chain store revealed that the best source of judgment seemed to be the operations vice president rather than personnel on the real estate staff. Clearly the firm would want to give his judgments greater weight in similar future decisions. In addition, the firm would also know more about what it was losing should he subsequently resign.

The monitoring and evaluation process also provides the raw material for improving performance. First, feedback may be provided to the individuals concerned, which should give them the opportunity to improve over time. Second, the system itself may learn to adjust the judgments of given individuals for systematic bias.

Such a system has been developed for a manufacturer of electronic components.[3] The company needed to develop better methods for short-run sales

---

[2] Personal communication from the consultant who helped develop the model.

[3] This work is reported as a case study entitled *Litz Instruments,* copyrighted by Stanford University. The case and the approach were developed by Henry Claycamp.

forecasting since production to inventory was extremely expensive and yet sales depended heavily on delivery. Since the company's salesmen had the most direct customer contact, it was felt that they could provide useful information for forecast purposes.

Accordingly, salesmen were asked to report on a product-by-product, customer-by-customer basis their subjective assessment of how likely they were to achieve a given sale within 30, 60, and 90 days. Each salesman's forecasting performance was monitored to adjust his current predictions based on his past performance. When the adjusted inputs were aggregated by product across all salesmen, the firm had a short-run sales forecast for use in production planning.

These examples demonstrate that judgmental inputs are being used successfully in systematic market analysis. However, much work remains to be done on procedures for obtaining good subjective estimates. Winkler has made an interesting beginning in the area of using experts and group judgments as well as techniques for providing managers with incentives to supply their best judgments [40, 41].

Finally, the measurement statistics bank should ultimately contain Bayesian multivariate procedures which should be of use in combining data-based analysis with management judgment.

Design Considerations for the Measurement Statistics Bank. Computerized statistical analysis and the widespread availability of program packages for performing such analysis carry with them a danger of misuse. Every effort should be made to guard against such misuse of the proposed measurement statistics bank.

As a case in point, consider the application of regression analysis made by a consultant to a large aircraft company. The problem was forecasting the company's manpower requirements. The consultant, using time series data, developed a forecasting function for each department [10]. Unfortunately, he was evidently unfamiliar with the assumptions and theory underlying this analysis technique. He ignored the autocorrelation in his time series data despite ample evidence of its presence. This error caused him to recommend a departmental reduction of hundreds of men, even though proper application of his technique would have indicated a much smaller reduction [22].

Unfortunately, such abuses of technique are not rare. Consequently, the measurement statistics bank itself should warn the user of potential pitfalls and recommend appropriate tests and courses of action. Though this will not eliminate abuse, it should at least help to minimize naïve use of statistical methods.

Sometimes it will be possible for the system to get the user out of trouble automatically. For example, Miller's DATANAL contains an on-line statistical package that automatically performs a Fisher exact test when the user has specified a chi-square contingency analysis and he has insufficient data [27].

As a final design note, the techniques incorporated in the measurement statistics bank should have an option to have the computations performed in double-precision arithmetic. This will help minimize round-off problems which can be serious in applications of multivariate techniques [37].[4]

---

[4] An excellent source of information and programs relevant to a firm's measurement statistics bank is the Computer Applications Section of the *Journal of Marketing Research*. Besides discussions of techniques for analysis, this section also provides abstracts of computer programs available for performing a wide variety of statistical analyses.

THE USER-SYSTEM INTERFACE

The user-system interface or display capability is the point of direct contact between the user and the system. If the system is to be utilized effectively, care must be taken to provide for convenient, efficient user-system interaction.

Although batch processing operations will continue to play an important role, the advent of the time-shared computer has made possible closely coupled man-system interaction in problem solving. Since the use of such on-line systems is the subject of Section II, Part G, Chapter 2, further discussion of the user-system interface will be deferred to that chapter.

ORGANIZING FOR MDIS

Successful development and implementation of an MDIS (marketing decision information system) require considerable attention to organizational aspects of system development. Some of the major issues to consider are:

1. Top-management support
2. Evolutionary system development
3. Involvement of line marketing managers in system development
4. Composition of the system development team
5. Provision for convenient system use by marketing managers

Certain aspects of these issues will be discussed in turn.

Top-management Support. The design, development, and implementation of a marketing decision information system are a long-term and often costly undertaking. Substantial amounts of energy and resources are required to bring such a system to successful fruition. In view of the level and time span of the resource commitment implied by system development, there must be strong, unequivocal top-management support if the system is to command the required resources and cooperation.

System development will require the cooperation of rather diverse groups within the firm, particularly the active cooperation of marketing managers. However, marketing managers are often rather wary of computers, mathematical models, and such. The system development team must demonstrate to these managers that the system is designed to assist them, not replace them. Strong top-management support for system development will help the development team gain the attention and cooperation of marketing managers.

A case in point occurred at an in-house executive seminar on management science in marketing conducted by the author and several of his colleagues for a large consumer goods manufacturer. The seminar was attended by many of the top marketing executives in this company. At the end of the final day, the senior vice president summed up the seminar with a statement to the effect that those attending would be badly mistaken if they thought they could return to their offices and simply forget about applying the content of the seminar to their own problems. In no uncertain terms he indicated this was the way the company was headed; and if those attending wanted to grow with the company, they had better get aboard this effort. Since then this company has been one of the most progressive in applying the new information technology to marketing.

System Evolution. Successful systems require evolution, not revolution. The system should be viewed as a dynamic development effort that can grow with and adapt to changing management needs. Large-scale, once-and-for-all system efforts are practically always doomed to failure. They inevitably exhaust the available resources and management's patience long before the systems actually work. Even if the development team does make them function properly, chances are that the system will tend to overwhelm management in terms of its complexity and comprehensiveness.

A far better development strategy is to let the system and the users (managers) develop together in mutual interaction. This mutual development will also tend to yield useful intermediate systems and results providing evidence that the development effort will indeed pay off.

Line Marketing Involvement. Applications of marketing models and other aspects of the MDIS in the past few years have made it abundantly clear that line marketing managers must become involved in system development. In many instances which the author has seen, this notion of line involvement has come as something of a surprise to the managers concerned. They somehow thought that system development could be successfully achieved by hiring a staff of technical wizards or consultants and sending them off to a corner with instructions to report back when the system was ready. It has been the rare case where such an approach worked. Fortunately, when the need for their direct involvement in system development is pointed out, most line managers seem willing and able to provide useful inputs to the development effort.

Why doesn't the wizards-in-a-corner approach seem to work? First, development of an MDIS should begin with a reassessment of the decision and information requirements of the marketing organization. Ignoring this step and plunging ahead with system development will tend to cast past mistakes in concrete. The process of reassessment clearly requires participation of line marketing managers if the resultant design is to meet their decision needs. In addition, when line managers become participants in the system evolution, it becomes "their" system and not one imposed on them by a staff group. The fact that evolution of the system has been in response to their decision needs will markedly enhance their utilization of it.

System Development Team. The interdependencies between the system components in an MDIS have significant implications for staffing the system development team. The functions performed by the different system components have generally been in the purview of a variety of organizational units within the firm. That is, the operations research staff has generally been in charge of model development (model bank); the market research staff has been responsible for data collection (data bank) and methods for data analysis (measurement statistics bank); and the computer systems group has generally had responsibility for maintaining computer-based data files and computer programs for their manipulation (data bank) as well as systems for generating management reports (one aspect of the man-system interface).

The system development team should be composed of representatives from all three areas—operations research, market research, and computer systems— to avoid an unbalanced system growth. For example, if the MDIS is viewed as merely a data storage and retrieval system with perhaps some associated report generation and statistical capability (recall that this view has been all too prevalent in the past), the system development team is likely to consist only of representatives from computer systems and marketing research. Such a team is unlikely to be cognizant of the requirements of future model development efforts and is likely to make data and system design decisions which will not serve the future model development needs of the firm. As noted before, the team should also have representation from line marketing management.

Convenient System Use. If the system is to achieve widespread utilization by marketing management, provision must be made for its convenient use. On the hardware side this will probably imply access to both time sharing and remote batch hardware. The former will provide instant access to the system as well as a capacity for interactive operation. Remote batch hardware will provide convenient access to a central computer from distant locations. This will allow many locations in the firm to have convenient, economical access to batch operations. Without a remote batch capability, many units in the firm which will use the MDIS could experience rather significant time delays as the input and output are being physically transported to and from the computer.

On the software side, convenient management use implies that the system must speak management's language and not vice versa. The software must be well documented and must provide the user with instructional details sufficient to make appropriate use of the system. This is an area that will witness considerable development during the 1970s.

One way to achieve management access to the MDIS without requiring the manager to become a technical specialist is to provide a human buffer to act as an interface between the MDIS and the user. IBM has found such an arrangement useful in its advanced information system (AIS). In AIS, information specialists are trained to operate terminals and display devices. They also have an in-depth knowledge of the contents of data and information files in the system. These specialists are located centrally and act in much the same way as a librarian would. When a call is received requesting information, the information specialist determines the specifics, obtains the answer in the most efficient manner, and suggests additional data which might pertain to the subject. The caller may receive his answer via a terminal in his office or by more conventional methods such as the mail, depending on how soon he needs the information.

A related concept is used in the PROMENADE interactive graphic computer system developed by the Stanford Research Institute for statistical analysis of data [6]. The PROMENADE system envisions a data analysis team composed of an operator who knows how to make the computer system work, a statistical consultant, and a subject matter analyst. In this case the latter is buffered from both the computer and the technical details of the statistics. In some systems, especially large scale, complex ones, human buffers should greatly enhance utilization.

As a final point it should be noted that the system development team should have its own computer programming capability and convenient access to hardware and software both internal and external to the firm. Without such provision, there will be many stumbling blocks to system development and utilization. Even with pre-MDIS systems, computer usage in marketing has often been accompanied by complaints about the service rendered by the corporate computer staff. Perhaps this should not be too surprising considering that most corporate computer staffs grew out of accounting-type applications. Consequently, large-scale, routine data processing applications, such as billings, payrolls, and orders, have generally taken precedence over other applications, much to the frustration of marketing personnel. To assure reasonable service in developing the MDIS, the system development team should be free to seek outside suppliers for computer usage should these outside sources prove to be the best choice. It is hoped that this will also tend to teach the marketing concept to corporate computer groups.

SYSTEM AND DATA GERIATRICS

An important, yet often neglected area in the design and implementation of a marketing information and decision system is that of phasing out obsolete systems and data. While the explicit criteria which should be used are likely to be industry specific, there are some general considerations which should be given attention.

The problem of phasing out systems and data represents the extreme case of the trade-off between storage costs and access costs. In general, the lower the storage costs, the greater the access costs, and vice versa. Access costs include the financial and time costs involved in retrieving and using systems and data. Further, they should reflect the opportunity costs of not performing analysis due to inconvenience of use or perhaps even impossibility of use given the time scale for a particular decision. The extreme case, of course, is that of phasing out systems and data, which has a zero storage cost but access becomes impossible.

The operating system in an MDIS should accumulate information relative to usage of various systems components—for example, particular data manipulation commands, statistical programs, or models. These data should then provide raw material to help in deciding whether to retain a particular system in high-speed but costly storage, to relegate it to less convenient but more economical storage, or to delete the system altogether. Some systems, such as annual budgeting programs, will experience only occasional use but require rapid, convenient access when they are in use. Such a system clearly should be stored in a low-cost mode until it is ready for use. The operating system in an MDIS should be made cognizant of these periodic but recurrent needs and should provide a signal to the system operators to remind them to have the program in question available in a convenient mode when it is needed.

When it comes to phasing data out of an MDIS, there seem to be many more examples of firms destroying information which they later need than there are of firms saving too much. Recall the examples in the discussion of the interdependencies between components in an MDIS. In a word, most organizations seem to be particularly adept at prematurely destroying their own history. Yet this history is often a key input in the development and testing of models and in helping the organization to learn correctly from experience. The latter, of course, conditions future judgment. While there no doubt is some upper limit on how long data should be maintained, the useful life of much market-related data has generally been greatly underestimated by most companies.

There should be periodic review of both systems and data. While no precise guidelines exist, a useful starting point would be an annual review. The review should be performed by the same type of interdisciplinary committee which was suggested for designing the system, for the same reasons as were given in the previous section.

Finally, it should be noted that thorough documentation must be maintained. If this is not done, there is little point in maintaining data and systems, as they will be of little use.

CONCLUSION

The marketing decision information system was presented as an interacting set of components consisting of a data bank, a model bank, a measurement statistics bank, and a display capability. Design considerations were presented for each of the system components except display, which will be treated in Section II, Part G, Chapter 2. Certain organizational aspects were also considered. The overriding issue in the discussion has been the need for a balanced, evolutionary development of all system components.

REFERENCES

1. Ackoff, Russell L., "Management Misinformation Systems," *Management Science*, vol. 14, December 1967, pp. 147–156.
2. Amstutz, Arnold E., "A Basic Market Oriented Information System," Cambridge, Mass.: Sloan School of Management Working Paper, M.I.T., 1968, pp. 307–368.
3. ———, *Computer Simulation of Competitive Market Response*, Cambridge, Mass.: M.I.T., 1967.
4. ———, "The Computer—New Partner in Investment Management," in Harry Stern, ed., "Information Systems in Management Science," *Management Science*, vol. 15, October 1968, pp. 91–99.
5. ———, "Market-Oriented Management Systems: The Current Status," *Journal of Marketing Research*, vol. 6, November 1969, pp. 481–496.
6. Ball, Geoffry H., and David J. Hall, "Some Implications of Interactive Graphic Computer Systems for Data Analysis and Statistics," *Technometrics*, vol. 12, February 1970, pp. 17–31.
7. Claycamp, Henry J., and Lucien E. Liddy, "Prediction of New Product Performance: An Analytical Approach," *Journal of Marketing Research*, vol. 6, November 1969, pp. 414–420.
8. Cox, Donald F., and Robert E. Good, "How to Build a Marketing Information System," *Harvard Business Review*, vol. 45, May–June 1967, pp. 145–154.
9. Diamond, Daniel S., "Quantitative Approach to Magazine Advertisement Format," *Journal of Marketing Research*, vol. 5, November 1968, pp. 376–387.
10. Drui, Albert B., "The Use of Regression Equations to Predict Manpower Requirements," *Management Science*, vol. 9, July 1963, pp. 669–677.
11. Edelman, F., "Art and Science of Competitive Bidding," *Harvard Business Review*, vol. 33, July–August 1965, pp. 53–66.
12. Frank, Ronald E., and William F. Massy, "Innovation and Brand Choice: The Folger's Invasion," in Stephen A. Greyser, ed., *Toward Scientific Marketing*, Chicago, Ill.: American Marketing Association, 1963, pp. 96–107.
13. ———, "Computer Programs for the Analysis of Consumer Panel Data," *Journal of Marketing Research*, vol. 5, May 1968, pp. 210–217.
14. Green, Paul E. "Bayesian Decision Theory in Advertising," *Journal of Advertising Research*, vol. 2, December 1962, pp. 33–42.
15. ———, "Bayesian Decision Theory in Pricing Strategy," *Journal of Marketing*, vol. 27, January 1963, pp. 5–15.
16. Green, Paul E., R. E. Frank, and P. J. Robinson, "Cluster Analysis in Test Market Selection," *Management Science*, vol. 13, April 1967, pp. 387–400.
17. Herniter, Jerome D., and Victor J. Cook, "Nommad: Normative Models of Market Acceptance Determination," Management Science Institute Working Paper p-43-5, Philadelphia: M.S.I., 1967.
18. Kiviat, P. J., and G. S. Fishman, "The Analysis of Simulation-Generated Time Series," *Management Science*, vol. 13, March 1967, pp. 555–557.
19. Little, John D. C., "A Model of Adaptive Control of Promotional Spending," *Operations Research*, vol. 14, November–December 1966, pp. 175–197.
20. ———, "Models and Managers: The Concept of a Decision Calculus," *Management Science: Applications*, April 1970.
21. Little, John D. C., and Leonard M. Lodish, "A Media Planning Calculus," *Operations Research*, vol. 17, January–February 1969, no. 1, pp. 1–35.
22. Livingstone, J. Leslie, and David B. Montgomery, "The Use of Regression Equations to Predict Manpower Requirements: Critical Comments," *Management Science*, vol. 12, March 1966, pp. 616–618.
23. Madansky, Albert, "Models, Games and Data Banks: Implications for Data Collection," in Keith Cox and Ben Enis, eds., *A New Measure of Responsibility for Marketing*, American Marketing Association Proceedings, June 1968, pp. 236–238.
24. Massy, William F., and R. E. Frank, "Short Term Price Dealing Effects in Selected Market Segments," *Journal of Marketing Research*, vol. 2, May 1965, pp. 171–185.

25. ———, ———, and R. M. Lodahl, *Purchasing Behavior and Personal Attributes*, Philadelphia: University of Pennsylvania Press, 1968.

26. ———, David B. Montgomery, and Donald G. Morrison, *Stochastic Models of Buying Behavior*, Cambridge, Mass.: M.I.T., 1970.

27. Miller, James R., "DATANAL: An Interpretive Language for On-Line Analysis of Empirical Data," Sloan School of Management Working Paper, Cambridge, Mass.: M.I.T., 1967, pp. 275–367.

28. Montgomery, David B., and Alvin J. Silk, "Patterns of Overlap in Opinion Leadership and Interest for Selected Categories of Purchasing Activity," *Proceedings of the 1969 A.M.A. Educators Conference*, Chicago: American Marketing Association, 1970.

29. ———, and Glen L. Urban, *Management Science in Marketing*, Englewood Cliffs, N.J.: Prentice-Hall, 1969.

30. ———, and ———, *Applications of Management Science in Marketing*, Englewood Cliffs, N.J.: Prentice-Hall, 1970.

31. ———, and ———, "Marketing Decision-Information Systems: An Emerging View," *Journal of Marketing Research*, vol. 7, May 1970.

32. Mukhergee, Bishwa Nath, "A Factor Analysis of Some Qualitative Attributes of Coffee," *Journal of Advertising Research*, vol. 5, March 1965, pp. 35–38.

33. Nerlove, Marc, "Spectral Analysis of Seasonal Adjustment Procedures," *Econometrica*, vol. 32, July 1964, pp. 241–286.

34. Robertson, Thomas S., and James N. Kennedy, "Prediction of Consumer Innovators: Applications of Multiple Discriminant Analysis," *Journal of Marketing Research*, vol. 5, February 1968, pp. 64–69.

35. Silk, Alvin J., "Preference and Perception Measures in New Product Development: An Exposition and Review," *Industrial Management Review*, vol. 11, Fall 1969, pp. 21–37.

36. Stefflre, V., "Market Structure Studies: New Products for Old Markets and New Markets (Foreign) for Old Products," in F. Bass, C. King, and E. Pessemier, eds., *Applications of the Sciences in Marketing Management*, New York: Wiley, 1968.

37. Trozzi, Mark Allen, "A Computer Based Teaching and Operational Aid for Applications of Statistical Decision Theory," unpublished M.S. thesis, Cambridge, Mass.: Sloan School of Management, M.I.T., 1967.

38. Urban, Glen L., "A New Product Analysis and Decision Model," *Management Science*, vol. 14, April 1968, pp. 490–517.

39. ———, "SPRINTER mod III: A Model for the Analysis of New Frequently Purchased Consumer Products," Cambridge, Mass.: Sloan School of Management Working Paper 364-69, M.I.T., 1969.

40. Winkler, Robert L., "The Consensus of Subjective Probability Distributions," *Management Science*, vol. 15, October 1968, pp. 61–75.

41. ———, "The Quantification of Judgment: Some Methodological Suggestions," *Journal of the American Statistical Association*, vol. 62, 1967, pp. 1105–1120.

42. Zellner, Arnold, and H. Thornber, "Computational Accuracy and Estimation of Simultaneous Equation Econometric Models," *Econometrica*, vol. 34, July 1966, pp. 727–729.

Chapter 5

Organization of
the Marketing Research Function

RICHARD D. CRISP   *Richard D. Crisp and Associates, Inc., Pasadena, California*

This chapter deals with the approaches that have proved to be most productive in fitting the marketing research function into a firm's organizational structure.   The firm may be a manufacturer; a service organization, such as a bank or insurance company; a trade association; or some other entity.

The first point in considering organizational aspects of marketing research is that there is no single, easy, or "cookbook" answer to the question, How should we organize for marketing research?   A single answer is impossible for at least two reasons.   The first, obviously, is that organizations differ in the relative importance of the marketing research function as well as in the scale and complexity of their activities.   Marketing research organization must be custom-tailored to the firm's informational requirements.

The second reason is less obvious.   Experience has demonstrated that within any single firm the organization of the marketing research function is almost certain to exhibit dynamism and to move through progressive changes as time passes.   What is appropriate as an organizational approach to establishing a new, specialized, and differentiated function in a company is unlikely to be an acceptable solution to the organizational requirements of the same firm at a point in time five or ten years later.

THREE APPROACHES TO THE FIRST ORGANIZATIONAL DECISION

The first organizational decision that must be made in a firm that has decided to introduce a differentiated marketing research function involves selecting one of three basic directions or approaches.

First, the company may decide to assign responsibility for marketing research to a formalized department. Such a department might be defined as consisting of one or more individuals who have *full-time* responsibility for marketing research. They have no other major operational responsibilities. Second, the company may make marketing research the *part-time* responsibility of a line or staff executive who *does* have other major responsibilities. Third, it can choose some other manner of assigning responsibility for marketing research, such as assigning responsibility to someone outside the organization. The latter may be to a specialized, outside service organization in the marketing research field. Another possibility may involve assigning responsibility to an individual consultant, perhaps drawn from academic circles.

These three approaches are listed in descending order of cost. To illustrate, consider the full-time versus part-time employment of individuals of equal ability, experience, and compensation. Full-time assignment would obviously commit more dollars to the marketing research function than would part-time utilization of the same caliber of individual.

There is a direct relationship between the use of marketing research as a specialized, differentiated function and company size measured in terms of annual volume. To illustrate, consider the population of manufacturers. Classify as "small" those manufacturers whose annual volume is below $25 million, as "medium" those with sales in the $25 to $100 million range, and as "large" those whose annual volume exceeds $100 million. Full-time assignment of responsibility for marketing research exists in from one-fifth to one-quarter of all "small" firms, in two-thirds or more of medium-sized firms, and in nine-tenths or more of the organizations whose sales exceed $100 million annually.

Similarly, the use of part-time assignment of responsibility declines as sales volume increases. That approach is found in somewhat more than half the small firms, in about one-quarter of the medium-sized firms, and in less than five percent of the large ones.

DEFINITION OF A DEPARTMENT

Studies on marketing research organization distinguish between companies with marketing research departments and those in which one individual is assigned full-time responsibility for marketing research. Provided that the individual in question is qualified to handle the broad range of activities that constitute marketing research today, this is a distinction without significance.

The assumption of qualifications is a reasonable one in a company's first full-time research director. What company would knowingly assign responsibility to someone lacking qualifications? That individual will be of at least middle-management stature and caliber. He will be supported by secretarial assistance. Such an individual may choose to build a department within his company, or he may instead choose to confine his own activities to the planning of research and assign execution to external service facilities. This is a purely philosophical decision which is not necessarily related either to the competence with which the function is exercised or to the volume of expenditures involved.

ECONOMICS OF NEW MARKETING RESEARCH DEPARTMENTS

A survey by Dik Warren Twedt for the American Marketing Association[1] disclosed that from 1948 through 1968 new marketing research departments were

[1] Dik Warren Twedt, *1968 Survey of Marketing Research*, Chicago: American Marketing Association, 1968, p. 21.

established at an accelerating rate. Marketing research is an "expense" or "cost" type of activity and operates within a cost-conscious business environment. The continuing growth in the number of new departments established over the 20-year span cited makes it clear that, in the experience of most companies, the cost of setting up and maintaining such a department is less than the value to decision makers of the information it generates. A closer look at the economics of such a decision is helpful in understanding this.

To illustrate, assume the company in question has an annual volume of about $50 million. If the company chooses to rely on average figures developed by surveys, it may decide to budget its department in the first year at the median expenditure rate of one-tenth of 1 percent of sales. (Half the companies covered by each of the surveys in this field spent a higher proportion of sales than that figure, while the other half spent at that or a lower rate.) We are considering a hypothetical budget in the first year of about $50,000.

In considering such a proposed $50,000 expenditure, two points are worth emphasizing. First, not all of the $50,000 would represent new or additional or incremental costs to the company. On the contrary, there would be some significant offsets. Before marketing research responsibility is consolidated as a discrete, specialized function, parts of the marketing research task are typically scattered among different individuals in different departments. In many cases, a company is overdue for specialization before the opportunity is recognized. The company is often in the position of paying the price of a fully effective staff agency without securing the benefits of specialized attention.

The second point is that even though the full $50,000 is included in the budget for a fiscal year, the actual first-year expenditure will be considerably lower in all probability. The company's first task, following a decision to specialize, is to find and employ a fully qualified marketing research specialist. Such individuals are in short supply, partly as a result of the expanded number of new departments. It takes time to find such a man. After he is located and hired, it will take him time to develop and recommend such other expenditures and commitments as he feels are necessary and appropriate.

There is one further aspect of the decision to establish a new department. Readily available research makes it clear that most companies with volume at or above $50 million have found investing in a specialized marketing research department to be profitable. Among the companies with such departments, there are almost certainly one or more competitive firms.

With the development of management information systems, there has been a broadening of the information gathering and processing role of marketing research departments. This has led some writers to describe such departments as marketing intelligence departments, using *intelligence* in the military sense of the term. The function of such departments is to provide company decision makers with information to aid and guide their major decisions.

Combine the preceding two paragraphs and the key decision of whether to establish a new department becomes a somewhat different one. The question management faces is this: If our major competitors are basing their decisions on marketing information gathered and interpreted by specialists, can we risk operating without similar specialized knowledge and skill? The decision to establish a distinct marketing research function has been weighed and affirmatively made by many, many firms, as the Twedt survey demonstrates. Any company considering the establishment of a new department today may safely rely on the combined experience of those firms. Viewed in this light, the key decision becomes not "whether" but "how."

PLACING THE FUNCTION WITHIN THE COMPANY

Where should the marketing research function be positioned within an existing organizational structure? Again, no hard and fast rules can be laid down. However, guidance in answering that question is provided by considering the nature of the function and the responsibilities of the individual to whom it is assigned.

The individual who heads a marketing research department usually has marketing research director (or manager) as his title. Just what type of job is he called on to fill? It is helpful to recognize that *he is primarily a specialist in the development, analysis, interpretation, and management of marketing information.*

Computers have greatly shortened the time interval between the development of a marketing problem, management awareness of the existence of that problem, and the date when an action decision must be made on constructive steps to solve it. To maximize contribution to a firm's marketing effectiveness, the marketing research function should be placed as close as possible to the point at which major marketing decisions are made. This is usually accomplished by making it a staff function, accountable to the company's chief marketing executive.

In any well-managed company, the chief marketing executive is a member of the top-management team. He has primary responsibility for the myriad activities and functions necessary to accomplish marketing objectives. His top-management responsibility, however, is divisional rather than general. He is concerned with part rather than all of the company's activities.

Some experts feel that marketing research can make an even greater contribution if it is positioned so that the director reports to a *general* management executive. Such an individual is concerned with the total scope of the company's activities and is likely to have the title of executive vice president or president. This organizational role is satisfactorily filled in many companies where marketing research has been a specialized, discrete activity for many years. In other words, this is a form of "promotion" which sometimes occurs when the responsibilities of the marketing research function are broadened over time. Initially—and this is why the newly established function has been emphasized to this point—marketing research can usually make its greatest immediate contribution when the director is a member of the marketing-management team reporting to the chief marketing executive. That puts the information-supplying function where the decision-making responsibility is.

INTERNAL-EXTERNAL DIVISION OF WORK

There are a variety of approaches to organizing marketing research as an internal, departmentalized function. One of two contrasting directions which might be chosen has already been suggested. It involves dividing the marketing research work load among internal people, on the staff of the department, and outside service organizations or facilities.

Some companies maintain extremely large marketing research departments and do virtually all their own marketing research, including actual fieldwork and interviewing. Procter & Gamble is a notable example. Other companies prefer a small, talented core of key people whose efforts are supplemented on a when-and-as-needed basis by outside service organizations.

As the other chapters in Section I will also point out, the marketing research universe is populated by a large number of various types of independent organizations, in business to perform either all or portions of the marketing research function for other (client) firms. These range from the very large, full-service marketing research agency qualified to handle a major assignment, from planning through delivery of the final report and recommendations, to smaller firms that specialize in doing part of the total task. The latter category includes firms specializing in interviewing or other types of fieldwork, in conducting store audit studies as part of test market activities or new product programs, etc.

The marketing research director responsible for an established department and function must appraise for his company the alternative costs and benefits associated with operating a lean internal department versus staffing specialists to handle specific types of research activities. Periodically, previously arrived at decisions must be reviewed in the light of changing work load requirements.

The economic aspects of this decision tend to be of primary importance. An individual with qualifications and experience in any specific functional specialty within the marketing research spectrum tends to have a "going market price" in the employment market. That price is unchanged whether he is employed by a research agency or a manufacturing or other organization. The key questions concern the effective utilization of that individual's time and skills. How much work does a particular organization have for such a specialist? What other related or unrelated activities can he or she be expected to assume within the department, when not engaged in the specialty?

AN EXAMPLE OF FUNCTIONAL SPECIALIZATION

Before World War II, one of America's largest food marketers had a very small marketing research department which consisted of a research director, an assistant, and two secretarial-clerical people. When the department's budget and responsibilities were increased after the war, there was an initial attempt to find and hire two or three broadly experienced marketing research men. These would have been, in effect, generalists—capable of handling almost any specific assignment in the marketing research field.

The initial search was unsuccessful for two reasons. First, a very limited number of such generalists were available. Second, those who were available had their choice of jobs as the number one man in any of several newly established departments. Reconsidering their recruiting task, the research director and his assistant decided to reorganize the department on the basis of functional specialization. A major advantage of this approach was that it in effect simplified the marketing research job by subdividing it into smaller components. An adequately educated applicant could then be taught within a rather limited period how to do a specific type of marketing research work satisfactorily.

Four specialists were added to the departmental staff. One was engaged exclusively in analyzing data based on salesmen's activities and sales volume—by products, customer types, geographic areas, etc. A second spent all his time working with purchased syndicated services supplied by the A. C. Nielsen Company and the Market Research Corporation of America. (Such services are discussed in Section II, Part B, Chapter 10.) A third specialist worked exclusively on consumer-acceptance product tests of existing and proposed new products. This involved work with one outside firm that specialized in in-home product testing among a mail panel of households. In addition, relatively small-scale product placements for preliminary consumer acceptance testing were conducted. The fieldwork involved in the latter activity was farmed out to an agency specializing in interviewing and fieldwork. The fourth individual brought a psychological background to focus on attitude and opinion surveys—planning, conducting, analyzing, and reporting such studies.

As time passed, this department continued to expand. The caliber of the specialists responsible for specific functional activities was continuously upgraded, partly through company-sponsored educational activities. Other specialized functions were added to the departmental skill bank. Operations research specialists were introduced to permit more effective utilization of increasingly important quantitative techniques and to integrate activities with the company's computer capability. Behavioral scientists were added to utilize the many innovations flowing from those disciplines.

The present organization of this department is interesting as an illustration of the continuing evolutionary process present in much marketing research organizational development. As sales volume moved up toward the billion-dollar level, the company found it necessary to reorganize into nine or ten product- or market-type divisions. Each division was headed by a general manager, and each included several marketing directors—one for each major subdivision of products involved. Within each division there was also a marketing research director reporting to the divisional general manager.

At this point, the company's marketing research function had come full circle. Each divisional marketing research director was a broadly experienced generalist. Each worked closely with the specialists within the marketing research department. That department had become a *corporate* staff unit, serving all divisions as well as corporate management informational needs. Within the marketing research department, one individual had primary responsibility for service to each division, working closely with the divisional marketing research director. But note that he worked *with*, not *for*, the divisional research director.

The corporate vice president in charge of marketing services, formerly the company's marketing research director, is responsible for marketing research and supervises the many specialists who work within the department. He is also responsible for quality control of the marketing research function. An increasing proportion of his time tends to be spent working closely with other marketing executives, especially at the higher levels in the organization.

The contribution of this activity to the company's total marketing research productivity lies in the early identification of problems to which research can be profitably applied and in directing the attention of the divisional marketing research directors to such problems. Subsequent comments in this chapter will expand on this particular role of a marketing research director.

THE SHORTAGE OF EXPERIENCED MARKETING RESEARCH GENERALISTS

As noted earlier, there was a great shortage of experienced marketing research practitioners immediately following World War II. That shortage was due in part to the explosive expansion of the function at that time. Considering the long time interval since that date and the continuing expansion in the number of marketing research departments operative within industry, one might logically expect any such shortage to have been overcome long ago. However, it is an ever-present fact of marketing life today that the shortage still exists and is likely to extend into the predictable future. The explanation of this fact has important organizational implications.

To an increasing extent, the marketing research department has been perceived by management as an ideal training ground and first-job for potential marketing managers. The topflight applicants recruited from college campuses by many marketing departments were placed in research positions for two to four years' experience. This period of internship provided them with exposure to a wide variety of different aspects of the company's marketing program, activities, and problems. They were then promoted out of research into positions in brand management or other marketing-management areas. Only a minority of those entering marketing research have chosen to make a career commitment to it and to stay in the field over a period of ten years or more.

Many of those who did make a career commitment to marketing research have found the financial rewards of entrepreneurship attractive. They have established independent marketing research agencies. As a consequence, a relatively large proportion of America's most experienced marketing research specialists are today employed by (and typically owners of) service and consulting organizations in the field.

Another vocational direction which has proved attractive to career specialists in marketing research has been the role of marketing research director in a large advertising agency. Such agencies conduct extensive research themselves for the information and guidance of their creative teams in developing marketing plans and recommendations. They also provide counsel and assistance to client research departments in the formulation, planning, and execution of major research assignments. When a client organization has no internal research capability, it is not unusual to find the advertising agency called on to function as a de facto extension of the client organization in the marketing research area.

THE ROLE OF ADVERTISING AGENCY RESEARCH

The marketing research function within advertising agencies deserves additional attention in considering the alternative approaches to organizing the marketing research function. Advertisers with substantial advertising budgets whose agencies offer marketing research as part of the service package should be considered as one approach to the provision of a marketing research capability. This approach is particularly appropriate for the relatively small company with a research requirement perceived to be intermittent rather than continuous.

Substantial research, particularly by the National Industrial Conference Board, indicates that marketing research directors in organized departments do not tend to rely heavily on the research capabilities of their advertising agencies. The approach of companies lacking a formal research function, however, might well take a different tack. On the positive side, it should be recognized that many outstandingly competent and experienced marketing research executives are on the payrolls of advertising agencies, particularly the larger ones. On the negative side, the primary service of an advertising agency's research department is to the agency itself. Research conducted for clients may suffer from a conflict of priorities if the agency itself requires the same talents as the client research is utilizing at the same time. Further, if the research involves anything approaching an evaluation of the competence or effectiveness of the advertising itself, the agency research department is an obviously poor choice as a research facility for executing the assignment.

CENTRAL STAFF VERSUS DIVISIONAL ASSIGNMENT

In the increasingly large-scale, diversified firms that make up a large and growing proportion of American industry today, a high degree of decentralization of operations is often found. This poses an organizational problem: Should the marketing research function be operated at the headquarters location and level as part of the responsibility of the corporate staff; or should separate marketing research departments be maintained within major individual decentralized divisions? This is a difficult question to answer. The shortage of generalists mentioned earlier is one influence on this decision. Obviously finding a large number of qualified research specialists to direct the function within each division is a formidable recruiting task.

The most popular resolution of this dilemma is for the central staff to include a highly qualified marketing research function, available as needed to counsel with and reinforce the divisional research functions. Those functions, with the constant availability of broadly experienced specialists on the corporate staff as a resource, need not be staffed with such experienced (and therefore expensive) people.

Some companies have found a compromise solution to the central-versus-divisional assignment to be the best approach. An example is provided by FMC Corporation. The divisions of this large and diversified firm are grouped, and responsibility for each of several different groups of divisions is assigned to an executive vice president. His staff includes highly competent marketing research specialists. These specialists are much closer to the divisional level than they would be if they were moved up to the corporate staff. They can, therefore, provide the divisions within the group with more readily available service than would otherwise be possible. The need to duplicate the function in individual divisions is eliminated. (Some specific functions—for example, sales analysis and sales forecasting—are often performed at the divisional level by individuals trained and supervised by the marketing research department, which is on the staff of the executive vice president responsible for the group of divisions.)

One of the advantages of the approach just discussed is that it permits a degree of uniformity and consistency of operation of the marketing research function that is often difficult, if not impossible, to achieve through individual, quasi-independent departments in each division. This advantage is of increasing importance since there is greater reliance on written marketing plans. Such plans must be integrated for different divisions within a group and must, therefore, be prepared uniformly for all divisions. Further, the increasing importance of management information systems places a premium on the increased uniformity inherent in this approach.

THE SYSTEMS APPROACH

One of the significant relatively recent developments affecting the organization of marketing research activities has been the adoption by an increasing number of companies of the "systems approach" to management in general and to marketing management in particular. Briefly, the systems approach views marketing as a total process consisting of many different elements that must be closely coordinated and integrated. There are several variations on this theme which are being experimentally explored. Some of them involve a relatively heavy emphasis on operations research techniques and approaches and other mathematically related management tools. Often there is a high degree of association between the computer and the marketing decision maker in companies exploring this approach.

The question of whether operations research should be part of and subordinate to marketing research or vice versa is one which tends to be answered differently by specialists in the two disciplines. The location of primary responsibility for data processing within an organization is a key consideration. If that responsibility is assigned, as it often is, to the financial management group within the company, it is extremely unlikely to make the contributions which would otherwise be possible to the improvement of marketing-management decision making.

In a book written more than a quarter of a century ago and covering the subject of this chapter among other topics, I pointed out that if the data processing responsibility were assigned to the financial-management function, separate provision for marketing-management informational needs was essential. The financial manager and the marketing management need different kinds of information developed in different ways and on different timing cycles. Some things don't change—and this point is one of them. It is still true.

As noted in the preceding chapter, an additional concept which enters into organizational thinking about marketing research has been developing management interest in management information systems. A substantial amount of quantitative information from internal sources relevant to management decisions is generated as a natural by-product of the order-processing function. Marketing research often adds depth and meaning to that information by analyzing and interpreting it. Marketing research also secures additional information from external sources. That information typically reflects industry and competitive volume, market shares, variations in performance by territory, etc. By a natural extension of the systems approach to information flowing from both internal and external sources, it has become apparent that carefully integrated management information systems can be developed that make available much of the input needed for improved decision making with a minimum of delay. The computer is, of course, at the heart of such a development.

A fully effective management information system to guide marketing decisions is unlikely to be developed without the active and continuing participation of marketing research specialists. The explanation for this is found in the need to evaluate the quality of data developed externally. Only the marketing research specialist is likely to have the competence to conduct such an evaluation.

SUBDIVISION OF MARKETING RESEARCH FUNCTION

A company which has had a long and successful experience with marketing research as a specialized function tends to apply it to an ever-expanding range of decision areas. Often those areas involve major functions other than marketing. Mergers and acquisitions, for example, and some major line extension and diversification decisions are typically the responsibility of general management rather than of divisional management executives.

It is not unusual to find that in such a situation the marketing research function "moves upstairs" and reports to a general management executive—for example, the executive vice president or president. When this occurs, it is not unusual to find that a subdivision of the marketing research function is desirable. This subdivision typically leaves a splinter marketing research function reporting to the chief marketing executive, while the major executives within the marketing research group move to the higher organizational level. The function remaining in the marketing division primarily concerns continuing (and important) analyses of current operating data—salesmen's activities, sales performance, etc. When a major nonrecurring problem arises, the resources and capabilities available at the general management level are consulted.

A LOOK AHEAD

Organizations in the years ahead are likely to change at an accelerating rate to keep pace with and respond to modifications of their environments and competitive conditions. What changes seem likely to occur in the organization of the marketing research function?

A key word in answering that question is *integration*. In its early days, marketing research was often something of a floating function. It was called in on specific assignments and projects as the need for research or the potential for a research contribution was perceived. Note that the perception in question was then rarely that of the best-qualified individual—the marketing research specialist. Instead, it tended to be the perceptions of line marketing executives who determined when and to what problems research was applied. Over the last decade or two, there has been great progress toward integration of research into an expanded and increasingly important marketing function, as this chapter has indicated. That integration is likely to be even greater in the future than it has been in the past.

The computer represents a management tool of potentially great power. Its possible contributions to improved decision making by marketing managers are tremendous. Unfortunately, the contribution of the computer to marketing-management decision making has so far been disappointing. Certainly the future will see the computer making increasing contributions to the decision-making process in marketing. It will be called on to combine data from the company's own records (internal data) with information from external sources dealing with trends in market size, competitive activities, etc. The marketing research man and function will be increasingly involved in an interface with computer specialists, as noted in Section II, Part G, Chapter 2.

Two other trends affecting the composition of the research function should be mentioned. One is the increasing reliance on operations research and other mathematical approaches, including simulation, model building, and so forth. Research men will have to continue their education to keep abreast of developments in this field. The other is the increasing contribution of the behavioral sciences to an understanding of consumer marketing actions and reactions. Attention to psychographic rather than demographic details in market segmentation in the future will require more continuing education by marketing research specialists, this time in psychological and behavioral areas rather than mathematical fields.

The computer will make possible the shortening of the traditional organizational structure by reducing the number of levels of marketing managers needed for on-the-spot supervision of field sales activities. Computerization of sales records will permit monitoring of performance far more rapidly at a centralized location. This trend seems likely to increase both the importance and the responsibilities of marketing research men in the future.

Chapter 6

Marketing Research Expenditures, Budgets, and Controls

A. B. BLANKENSHIP   *Bowling Green State University, Bowling Green, Ohio*

Organization is only one of the first steps in the successful functioning of the marketing research department. The department must also be functional: it must plan and control the expenditure of research funds and effort in a way that will maximize contribution to the company. Specifically, this planning and control includes dollars, time, and quality of the research output.

If properly carried out, this functional direction and control of research effort provides an integrating force for the department. It places any single research study in perspective to the total group effort. It relates dollars, time, and quality to the total research plan, interrelates elements within the plan, and provides an effective model within which these elements can be properly executed.

Control ensures that work is performed on schedule and within cost limits. It provides direction to departmental efforts and enables the department to be effective. Specific project control means that any one project is considered a unit of administration and will not get lost in the shuffle of departmental activity. In short, control provides a driving mechanism for the effective execution of research.

This chapter is aimed primarily at research control in the research department of the manufacturer, the advertising medium, and the advertising agency —firms which contract some or all of their marketing research work. Most of the following applies whether the firm does its own fieldwork and processing or whether it depends on outside suppliers.

The present chapter discusses expenditures, budgets, and controls, first examining department budgets, what they are, and how they are determined.

Then it considers what project budgets are and how they are determined. Finally, budget and project controls are discussed.

ANNUAL BUDGETS

An annual research budget is a plan or schedule showing how money will be spent for research over the next year. It typically includes cost estimates for particular projects and time estimates of when each study will occur during the year. Typically this budget is coincident with the company's fiscal year and becomes part of the total company budget.

If marketing research within the firm is the vehicle for obtaining and interpreting information to aid marketing planning and decisions, then it makes sense to plan research that relates to such needs. Thus the market research department budget is an important tool for ensuring carefully planned research —not merely research quickly designed to put out marketing fires.

Companies have good fiscal reasons for insisting on a research budget. From the research manager's viewpoint, there's an even better reason. It ensures that the research plan will meet the needs of the marketing program as well as requiring those in marketing to consider their research needs on a planned basis. Finally, it means that top management, at least on an annual basis, must evaluate the past and probable future role of research in the total company operation.

Requirements of the Annual Research Budget. It is difficult to plan research for a year in advance. In its often frenetic environment, marketing and marketing research plans are subject to constant change and revision.

So the first requirement of the annual research budget is that it must knowingly be very "blue sky." It is not, and cannot be, a precise prediction about the organization's needs. This does not reduce its value; in fact, the very process of assembling the plan and budget means that thinking about the future is required of the research manager.

This very characteristic of marketing (and therefore of research) also means that the annual research plan and budget must be flexible. They cannot possibly be adhered to rigidly. As the marketing demand requires, the research budget may have to be shifted from one type of study to another to meet exigencies.

For example, several years ago the manufacturer of a brand of personal deodorants had a line of creams and roll-ons. Though it was common knowledge that he and some of his competitors were "working" on a spray deodorant, there was no hint that anyone was close to an immediate breakthrough. The research plan and budget for the next year did not anticipate any of the competition test marketing a spray.

Yet that is exactly what happened, and the manufacturer consequently had to change his research (and marketing) plans almost at once. Tracking studies were introduced in the competitor's test markets to check the brand's performance. Samples of the new product were obtained for consumer product testing. Studies were made to determine the degree to which the new spray was cutting into the company's sales. Various kinds of research had to be undertaken for which there was no provision in the original annual research plan and budget.

Centralized versus Decentralized Research Department Budgets. With a centralized research budget, the total research budget is administered within the research department. The research manager has prepared and integrated all the pieces of the budget, and these are now departmental funds awaiting authorization to be spent.

With the decentralized budget, each piece of the research budget is a portion of some other group's budget. In a brand-oriented company, for instance, the research budget for a brand would fall within the brand manager's budget, in which it would be only one part. In a divisionalized company with a centralized research function, divisional research budgets might well be a portion of the division's budget, rather than all divisional research budgets being combined into a centralized research budget.

General Foods, Ltd., works this way. The research budget falls within the total marketing budget for each brand. Jell-O research is budgeted within the Jell-O marketing budget.

There are advantages to each. In the centralized budget, one of the greatest advantages to research management is that the status of the research department is enhanced. The centralized budget places control for research spending—and therefore direction—where it ought to be, that is, with the research manager. Another advantage is that it makes it easy to see what the company is spending in total for research. This enables top management to evaluate research spending more readily, that is, to compare it with similar spending in other related firms and to consider whether it is getting proper value for the funds being spent.

With a centralized budget, there is a greater opportunity for the research decision to be made in the research department. Direction of research is more likely to remain with the research manager if *his* funds are being allocated and spent. Finally, there is less chance—after budget approval—that management will trim research spending to shift funds into other areas. If the research budget is an integrated whole, as are other budgets, then it becomes a little less likely that management will actually chop dollars. In the decentralized budget, however, it does not appear so difficult; the manager is merely shifting, not chopping. Only a psychological difference, to be sure, but a real one nonetheless.

With the decentralized budget there are also advantages. One is that there may be higher acceptance of research. If the brand, division, or other operating unit sees research funds being allocated and spent from its own funds, then it may take research more seriously. Similarly, the research user is more likely to see that research for which he is paying is really useful in his marketing activities. If it is the research department's money, he may be willing to do a study "for the fun of it;" if it is his own money, he will want to be sure that the results can be applied in the marketplace.

Usually—but not always—the budget's centralization or decentralization will follow the way that research itself is set up within the firm. If there are divisional research units, these will typically have their own budgets. However, if there is a centralized department, the chances are good that there will be a centralized research budget.

Elements within the Research Budget. Categories of the research budget are often determined by the *company's* accounting system. The categories listed here are those considered to be *ideal*, but they may not fit into the company's scheme.

The following tabulation shows these categories. Basically, the costs are divided into *fixed* or *internal* costs, and *variable* or *external* costs. (*Fixed* and *internal* are not quite synonymous, and neither are *variable* and *external*, but they will still be used that way here.)

EXPENSE CATEGORIES WITHIN A RESEARCH BUDGET

Fixed or Internal Costs	*Variable or External Costs*
Salaries	Subscriptions
Space	Facilities
Supplies	Projects
Memberships	Market studies
Publications	Consumer product tests
Travel and entertainment	Advertising copy tests
Depreciated costs	Attitude and image studies
Miscellaneous costs	Experimental studies

Variable or external costs are those that rise with the activity level and typically involve spending *outside* the department, in the form of contracts with outside suppliers. One way to categorize such spending is shown here: subscriptions, facilities, and projects. With subscriptions and facilities there is usually a flat charge, so no financial controls are required once the basic contract has been signed. A subscription is the purchase of a continuing service, such as retail store audits offered by A. C. Nielsen Company. These are contracted on a long-term basis at a flat rate; once authorized, they literally become a fixed cost, even though considered here as variable. A service, on the other hand, is a facility awaiting use as the buyer requires it. Audience Studies, Inc., offers a theater-type commercial testing facility, which is contracted at a fixed rate.

The individual research project is the truly variable cost. This is a custom-built study and must be individually costed. Later sections of this chapter discuss the individual project in further detail. The major point here is that *this* sort of project is one on which costs *may* get out of line. It is this sort of study, in particular, that requires the buyer's attention and control.

The project section of the budget is typically classified by types. The groups listed in the preceding tabulation include some of the major forms of marketing studies, but there is nothing sacrosanct about this list. The demand and needs of the particular company and marketing research groups will dictate the categories. Often, too, there is another element in the annual budget not listed here. The variable costs, in particular, may be broken down by brand in a multibrand firm in which each brand is a profit center.

How the Budget Is Prepared and Approved. In preparing the research budget, the first step is to examine last year's budget. This will not only provide the approximate total level of operation but also strongly indicate the dollar level of some categories.

The second step is to consider this year's needs. These needs will primarily affect external spending, which is typically the largest portion of the budget. To determine these needs, the marketing research manager must know the marketing plans, which requires conversation with brand management and study of any plans or other related documents available. After understanding roughly what these plans are—including possible new product introductions or product alterations—the research manager then begins to "get a fix" on the kinds of research projects required for the brand during the coming year. At the same time, he should review with brand management the needs for subscriptions and services so these can be added.

Once these plans are known and discussions with brand management have been held, the research manager can start to estimate costs of the proposed studies. The project costs can be summarized, along with facilities and subscriptions, for a total of external costs.

Now each area of costs should be compared with budget and spending for the year before, to see how they compare. Are any large rises or drops warranted? What about the total dollar level? The research manager must assure himself that all looks well before he proceeds with the next step.

He is then ready to recheck with his users and translate what their proposed studies mean in dollar terms. Between them they must determine where the budget looks overallotted and where too skimpy and revise accordingly.

Then internal department requirements must be added. Salaries, for instance, will almost certainly rise; expected salary increases must be planned and identified by person and time period to arrive at the year's total. Space is usually a figure which comes out of accounting and will likely remain constant unless the company moves or the research department plans a major change in activity level. Supplies, too, can usually be taken from last year's figures.

Memberships are an important cost in the typical research department, for many of its workers regard themselves as professionals and will want to retain memberships in the American Marketing Association and perhaps in more specialized groups as well. Usually this, too, is fairly constant from one year to another.

Professional staff members also like to read professional publications, and the department itself may want to subscribe to journals it believes important, either from a professional or a business point of view. Once again, after this fund has been established, it will usually remain fairly constant. If the department maintains a library for its own use or that of the firm, this amount could be sizable.

The third step in budget preparation is examination of the total research spending proposed against that for last year and comparison of the change with the rate of change in sales projected for the coming year. In general, the rate of change for research should not be too different from the rate of change for sales, but of course, this is only a very rough guide; there are many factors that could be responsible for the two changing at different rates.

Finally, a check should be made on the constancy of outside research costs. Some suppliers should be consulted to determine whether they see any upward shift, and if so, how much. Subscriptions and service costs should be checked, and then, if necessary, adjustments made in the figures.

There is—in the well-run and profitable firm—one last budget element not yet considered and not shown on our list of budget elements simply because it is not standard. This is a fund for *experimental research*, which is devoted to study of research techniques. While generally such funds are at the discretion of the research manager, in practice they are wisely devoted to study of some of the major research tools used by the firm. If the company spends more on consumer product testing than on any other kind of research, basic research of an experimental nature might be applied to such tools. If a company, on the other hand, concentrates on commercial testing, its budget should be spent in such an area.

The point is, however, that the company that is truly progressive in its research thinking will provide such a budget. This is the time—during budget formulation—when the research manager should put in his request for funds, and, as with the rest of his budget, he must have a sound plan for its spending.

If all homework has been done well, getting approval is usually little more than a formality. The budget is reviewed with the manager's superior and documentation is ready if needed. About the only complication one can run into at this point is if the superior knows something the manager doesn't. But this is unlikely with regard to marketing plans—if the manager has done his homework. If he knows something about company plans that might affect the research budget (such as an effort to show a higher rate of earnings), then the research manager should be informed of this before getting into any of the details of planning the budget.

The research manager should know how to present his budget. Typically, his superior will not be interested in the myriad details unless the research manager finds himself in trouble during the discussion and many questions are raised. Usually it is sufficient to present the total budget and show how it is broken down among the major elements and among the brands (if there is a brand breakdown).

The superior's stress on total budget should not be too surprising, since he likely has some percentage of forecasted sales in mind for the research budget. The new research manager may find this a curious yardstick; he is likely to think that need determines the budget. However, the manager's superior knows that he must balance all the budgets under his jurisdiction into some preset total in order to show a reasonable profit for his operation. While this may be an arbitrary way to set a total budget, the budget will be modified should unusual research needs arise.

How Management Predetermines the Research Budget. The marketing research manager, well armed with arguments for the company needs, sees his superior for approval of his budget. But before he even gets a hearing, the manager should also know a little about how management has already set some range within which the marketing research budget should fall.

Management does this—necessarily—by reviewing the historical pattern of spending for various activities. If profits and sales have been maintained for some time with particular spending patterns, management will probably continue these patterns. More specifically, if profitable sales growth has been maintained with marketing research spending at 0.5 percent of sales, then this figure will be used as a rough guide—against predictions of the new year's sales—for marketing research spending.

There is the occasional company, however, which gears marketing research spending not as a percentage of sales but as a percentage of advertising. This tends to be true of those firms that regard their advertising spending as the key to all their marketing efforts. It includes firms such as beverage companies, toiletries firms, and cigarette manufacturers.

How This Predetermined Need Should Be Modified. The basic concept of the percentage method makes good sense. Marketing management, along with other management, must have some fairly simple system of arriving at budgets consistent with overall company planning.

However, the marketing research needs for a particular year may be well under or over the stringencies of a percentage. The informed market research manager will not only know what his budget on a percentage basis is likely to be, but he should also be fully prepared to argue for more or less than the percentaged amount according to the needs that he sees.

On the plus side, this might include, for instance, the planned introduction of one or more products or the planned increase in advertising expenditure for a particular brand. On the minus side, this could include the decision to "milk" a brand (meaning that the firm has decided the brand is going no place and that it should eliminate as many marketing costs as possible to maximize profits while the brand dies).

Essentially, it is the responsibility of the marketing research manager to defend a budget which starts with some percentage allocation (whether on sales, advertising, or some other base), modified by his knowledge of what the firm's marketing plans are for the next fiscal period.

Controlling the Annual Research Budget. The budget is meaningless if controls are not applied constantly to ensure that it is being followed (although, as mentioned earlier, the budget—with management approval—should be modified according to circumstances and needs). If there is no control, the budget may as well never have been prepared.

Control requires that the manager watch his spending, in each category, against what was provided in the budget. Usually this control should be on a running basis so that the manager can guard against exceeding his level of spending for any category at any period of time.

The accounting department typically provides quarterly reports on spending according to the preset categories. This method is a sound one in companies operating with a small margin, where rapid and accurate accounting statements necessarily are periodically produced and distributed for business survival.

But in most firms review of the accounting statement against the budget is usually not too satisfactory as a method of control. Accounting summaries are typically slow; they arrive so far after the fact that they are not a warning at all but merely a report of where things have been overspent or underspent. Sometimes too, the accounting figures contain inaccuracies that the manager recognizes could not possibly be correct; when this occurs, much time is spent tracing them. Often too, the accounting department records do not show the appropriate categories for control purposes in the research department.

The research department is able to set up its own control devices on a rather simple basis, especially for outside spending, which represents the bulk of the typical department's expenditures. The research department need only have one of its secretaries maintain spending records for a limited number of accounts: supplies, memberships, publication, travel expenses, research firm spending, and other spending.

As supplies are drawn from a central pool or purchased from the outside, the costs can readily be entered, periodically summarized, and compared with the budget for the period. Professional memberships can be handled similarly. As bills are processed for payment by the firm or as staff members are reimbursed by the firm for such memberships, the necessary entry can be made in the ledger. Publication costs can be handled in the same manner.

As department members spend travel and entertainment funds and bring in their receipts for expense accounts, all that is necessary is that the appropriate secretary record the total amount of the bill in a ledger and cumulate the expense spending of that type in the final column of the book. In this way, there is immediately a current total of the category for the year. On another page, the same secretary can record spending with research firms for custom projects. As these are authorized (not as bills are received, since this will be too late), an entry should be made and again total results accumulated. There should be a separate page of entries for each type of custom project, and by brand, if this is the way the budget has been set up.

One exception is recording of dollars committed to research projects. If it has been agreed between buyer and supplier that a project will not be billed until the new fiscal year, then, regardless of when the project is authorized, it should be entered only in the new fiscal year. Warning: since most projects are priced with a clause of "plus or minus 10 percent" (or some other percentage), it is important to make the entries at the maximum price quoted, then correct downward if any savings result when the bill arrives. (It would be dangerous to enter any but the top figure, for the manager might unluckily find himself with a series of studies all running at the maximum, and his budget would be overspent.) Other miscellaneous bills can be handled the same way.

If the research department maintains its own checks on budget spending, these records should, to complete the picture, be summarized monthly—or at least quarterly—in order to compare spending in each category with the budget. Without this last step there is no control.

THE SPECIFIC RESEARCH PROJECT

In the typical marketing research department, project expenditures represent the largest single portion of the budget. Project planning and control therefore become a significant consideration in this whole area of budgeting and control.

The Research Plan. The first step in handling a research project is to plan it, the second is to cost it. The research plan is the design of the research study. The quotation is the quoted price for the study.

There are several steps in developing a research plan. One is a statement of the marketing objectives. The marketing problem or program must be defined, and the marketing decision or decisions on which the research is to cast light must be specified.

The second element of the research plan is a statement of the research objectives. This spells out the kinds of research information needed to contribute to solution of the marketing problem. If the study is one of tracking in a test market, then measurements such as brand awareness, awareness and playback of the advertising, brand trial, and brand repurchase will all be pertinent, along with measurement of the purchase cycle.

The third element of the research plan is the research approach, both in general, and, insofar as possible at the planning stage of a new study, in detail. The nature of the questionnaire—if a questionnaire study—should be outlined, at least in terms of subject matter if not in actual construction. The definition of the population must be specified, together with a description of the sampling method and sample size. The broad nature of tabulation should also be described.

In some manufacturer's research departments, all details of the research plan are developed by department staff members; then prices are obtained from one or more outside research firms for handling of the study. In other firms, only the broad definition of the problem is provided by the research department member, who then turns to one or more outside research firms to obtain proposals on how the study should be designed and what it will cost.

Which system is superior is debatable. It can be argued that members of the advertiser's research staff must be generalists, prepared to tackle almost any kind of marketing problem, and that it is better to consult specialists skilled in designing a study aimed at answering a particular kind of marketing problem. On the other hand, in at least one department which followed this method, brand management referred to department members as mere "order takers" who had no skills of their own other than soliciting proposals from research firms. Yet some of the larger users of research operate in this manner; also, in the smaller research department, because of limited manpower and skills, there is no choice but to work in this way.

Research Cost Quotation. From the preceding steps, the research house provides a cost quotation. This cost is typically quoted as "plus or minus 10 percent" since there are so many intangibles in the custom-tailored research project.   The research house quotation will also typically contain a time schedule, another aspect of control that the usual purchaser must watch.

Sometimes the research buyer will decide to get more than a single cost quotation to be sure that he is getting a reasonable price.   On the other hand, other research buyers deal almost exclusively with a single supplier, rarely getting a competitive estimate unless they feel that a price is out of line.   The merits of these and other methods of working with the supplier are discussed in Section I, Chapter 10 of this handbook.

Budgetary Controls.   The first step in maintaining control over a research project is to assign each project a number; this number becomes the identifying device for everything connected with that study.   The research manager should see that a project file is established at a central location in his department and that information files about each project be placed within that file.

The first internal operation in control is obtaining or providing an internal *research authorization.*   Depending on how the particular system is set up, this form may require only the research manager's signature on a form with all the descriptive elements of the study: study title, study nature, sample size, sample design, tabulation specifications, price, and research firm being authorized to proceed.   More often, however, the signature of people outside the research department is also required.   This seems sensible, for it means that either brand management or general management is agreeing, rather than leaving the decision *only* to the research manager, that a particular study should be conducted.

Before the research manager obtains these outside signatures, he has a little homework to do.   He should first be certain that there is enough money left in the particular budget category to proceed with this study.   After this, obtaining the necessary signatures is little more than a formality.

The sequence now is to provide the selected research firm with an external *research authorization.*   Depending on the buyer's practice, this may take the informal form of a letter describing the study and stating its cost.   Or the firm may have a form regularly used for this purpose; some firms, for instance, simply have a duplicate copy of the internal research authorization form which is given to the research firm.   In rare cases—and it is usually only for research subscription purposes—the selling firm has a contract that the buyer is asked to sign.   (For one such procedure, see Section I, Chapter 10.)

The good research manager stresses proper use of these forms because it is the start of his control.   In one case a research manager refused to pay extra costs on a study because, although these had been orally requested by one of the people within the buyer's research department, the research firm had never sought to amend the authorization form to include the changes.

Time Control.   Time control is absolutely essential for a department with a heavy volume of research projects.   Some sort of system for maintaining time control is the only way that projects will be kept on schedule.   And the manager will find himself in trouble with his "customers"—those in the company for whom the research is intended—if deadlines are missed.

There are two basic methods the manager can use.   One is a periodic written summary on the status of each project.   The other is a personal meeting with those in the department involved in which they review, project by project, where each one stands.   Which method is better?   Probably one that combines both, for then the written report can be reviewed and points which are not clear can be explained.

How frequently should the meetings be held? This depends on the size of the department and how busy it is. A small department, with a relatively light load, may not need a review more than once a month. A large department, with many projects running simultaneously, may need weekly reviews.

Departments that deal with few suppliers but give them a large volume of work sometimes set up meetings with the suppliers to review the status of each of the many jobs. One Canadian company dealing primarily with a single research house holds Monday morning review meetings at which research house representatives tell the department manager and his team of project directors the precise status of each assignment. This has the effect of spotting possible trouble jobs early and applying pressure while there is still an opportunity to meet the deadline.

Quality Control. Unless the buyer takes steps to ensure quality control, he may not obtain quality work. It is the responsibility of the buyer—as well as of the seller—to see that quality is maintained. The two areas where quality is most likely to slip are fieldwork (interviewing) and coding.

Fieldwork quality has two main dimensions: quality of sampling and quality of interviewing. On sampling, the buyer has a right—and should use it—to know the rate of completions. The greater the number of incompletions (not at homes, refusals, breakoffs after the start of interviewing), the lower the sampling quality is likely to be. If it is a probability study, then, if no weighting is to be provided for not-at-homes, records on attempted callbacks and completions must be obtained if sample quality is to be maintained.

Quality of the interviewing has two subfacets: one is assurance that the work was honestly done and the other is that the quality of the work is high. The usual method used by the research firm to check honesty is to verify some percentage of its interviews on a given study. This is done by telephone calls or postcard checks. With these, the respondent is typically asked whether he was interviewed; but then, if the validation is carefully performed, there will be some additional questions. Usually, key questions are repeated—questions such as brand used and the like, for which answers would be unlikely to change from one day to the next. The intention is to see whether the person replying is consistent.

What about the quality of the fieldwork? Unless the research manager can be present at every interview, he will never really know. But one clever research firm devised a scheme of having every one of its field interviews recorded on a tape recorder carried by the interviewer. The interviewer never knows when her work will be checked by means of the recorder, so the step, in and of itself, probably has added to the field quality. In another case a research firm carefully examines the first day's returns of all fieldwork so that it can point out any errors that are being made. This too undoubtedly helps interviewing quality, but it doesn't *measure* quality, which is what the research manager really needs. (For methods of evaluating quality of fieldwork, see Section II, Part B, Chapters 5 and 7.)

Most buyers do *not* measure field quality. It is either too expensive or too difficult to do so. One buyer sends people from his office—unannounced in advance—to accompany field personnel in selected spots around the country.

Coding is the other chief aspect of research quality that needs control and is discussed in more detail in Section II, Part B, Chapter 9. The research buyer should make sure that the research supplier *is* using some method of quality control for this important aspect of the work. To be sure, in these computer days, coding is necessary only for open-ended questions, but open-ended questions are and will remain an important part of marketing research surveys.   One method of quality control is to require a supervisor to check a sample of each coder's work and to keep records on error incidence.   The buyer should determine whether this or some other method is used, and if so, what standards are maintained and how.

A few major buyers of marketing research are establishing their own systems of quality-control checking of their suppliers.   General Foods is one of these, and perhaps the easiest way to report what they are doing is to reproduce a memorandum written internally at General Foods outlining the system.

GF SUPPLIER EVALUATIONS AND VALIDATION PROCEDURES

A yearly evaluation of all of the marketing research companies who do work for General Foods is considered an important part of the General Foods research quality-control program.

The following eleven areas are covered in a personal visit to each supplying company and the findings are written into a confidential report.   This report is sent to all people at GF who buy research.

1. A brief summary of the marketing research experience history and qualifications of the principals of each company as well as relevant information on the people who are responsible for all functions in the administration of a GF study.

2. A summary of the standard questionnaire development practices including design, layout and use of pre-testing.

3. Relevant information on field instructions—method of transmission, detail and clarity.

4. A summary on sampling—what is their standard sampling procedure when sampling is not included in the job specifications.   (Stated procedure is checked against GF validation results.)

5. Pertinent information on training, briefing and supervision of field interviewers.   Review of field training materials.   (Materials provided by the supplier for review are kept on file in Corporate for reference by any interested GF personnel.)

6. Some analysis of check-in procedures—methods, numbering of questionnaires and use of call record forms.

7. Relevant facts on editing—who does it, how is it done, use of written editing instructions, what checks are used.

8. A brief summary of coding procedure—who does it?   Use of written codes and coding instructions.   What checks are used?

9. Summary information on punching and cleaning—who does it?   What kind of verification?   Use of written cleaning instructions.   How are corrections made?   What checks are made on outside key punch suppliers, if any are used?   What checks are made on inside key punching?

10. A short analysis of tabulation.   Who does it?   What checks are made on outside tabulation forms?   Who writes the tab specifications?   Are marginals and cross tabs available?   Are extra runs available?

11. A limited evaluation of reports.   These are briefly analyzed as to form, style, statistical presentation, summaries, etc.

A comparative validation of the supplier's validating is also done.   (GF validates all studies done by outside suppliers and maintains a permanent validating staff in its Corporate Marketing Research Services Department.)   The general validation procedure followed by each company is reported as well as how well each company complies with GF procedure—the most important factor being time.   Names and phone numbers must reach GF as soon as possible after a study is completed to obtain reliable validation results.

Standard GF validation procedure of outside suppliers' work requires that a full interviewer's field kit with sampling instructions and all respondents' names and phone numbers be sent to GF within two weeks of completion of the study.   Then a 25% validation of each interviewer's work for each day of interviewing is done on all studies.   GF validation results are compared with the supplier's results and action, where necessary, is recommended to the GF research project director and the supplier.

At the conclusion of each evaluative visit the principals are told the areas which the evaluator feels are weak. Suggestions are sometimes made as to how areas could be altered or improved. A brief overall summary of supplier, based on the aforementioned eleven areas, rounds out the annual supplier evaluation report.

General Control through Communication between Buyer and Supplier. As the research project proceeds, the buyer or supplier may comunicate with the other to relay information on how things are going or on changes in specifications, schedules, and so forth. It is important that the research manager have written confirmation of all decisions reached during the course of the job. He may use the letter as the permanent record, in which case he will either write the supplier or ask that the supplier write him. But a somewhat easier way— simply because it can become a standardized matter—is to have the supplier prepare call reports, just as the advertising agency does. Each discussion on a project is written up and summarized in the form of a terse, accurate statement. This gives either party—the research manager or the supplier—an opportunity not only to have a permanent record but also to disagree quickly if the report states something he does not accept.

Reporting to Management on Progress. The research manager should keep his own customers of research well informed on the status of their projects. Recommended are monthly written reports on the status of each project. This will largely take the form of a summary of timing along with a statement of any problems that may be occurring on the project. (These are fortunately rare; but when they happen, the "customer" should be among the first to know.)

Reporting to Management on Results. Logically, communication with management must go far beyond mere status reports, and it does. The next chapter considers how the research department communicates research findings to management.

BIBLIOGRAPHY

Blankenship, A. B., and Doyle, J. B., *Marketing Research Management*, New York: American Management Association, 1965, chaps. 6 and 7.

Parker, K. R., "Organizing an Industrial Marketing Research Study," Talk before Sixth Regional Industrial Marketing Research Conference, New York: American Marketing Association, May 5, 1961.

Rice, J. F., "Project Scheduling and Control," Thirteenth Annual Marketing Conference, National Industrial Conference Board, October 20, 1965.

Chapter 7

The Communication
of Your Research Findings

STEUART HENDERSON BRITT   *Graduate School of Management, Northwestern University, Evanston, Illinois*

To communicate your research findings effectively, should you make an oral report, a written report, or both?

One advantage of an oral report is that you can perceive some of the reactions of your listeners; and if it seems desirable, you can modify later parts of your presentation. And both you and your audience may learn some things if there is a give-and-take discussion.

But unless a written report is forthcoming, people may think of questions without being able to get answers quickly and accurately. Should you present this written report and then follow it with an oral report—or the other way around, an oral and then a written report?

The first combination—written and then oral report—has the advantage of giving people an opportunity to read and think about your material prior to its discussion. The second combination—oral and then written report—has the advantage of providing information that can be consulted at any time.

In any case, some type of written report, even though brief, is essential. That is why the entire focus of this chapter is on the written report—to help you to think carefully about five things:

1. You, the *sender* of your message
2. The *receivers* of your message
3. Your *message*
4. The *channels* for your message
5. The *feedback* you need

YOU, THE SENDER OF YOUR MESSAGE

The most remarkable thing about any report you write is *you*. And your written report is the "lifeline" between you and those to whom your writing is addressed. The combination of *you* and *your report* is your message.

If you do not make yourself clear to your readers, it is because you have not thought out what you are trying to say. And good style means *clean, clear thinking*—which usually comes only after lots of trial and error and thinking and rethinking.

Bernard DeVoto is supposed to have pointed out that the best reason for putting anything down on paper is so that one may then change it. Whether he said this or not is unimportant. What *is* important is that no matter what you put down on paper the first time, it nearly always needs changing—and so does what you get down on paper as a revision of what you wrote the first time, and so on.

Or do you honestly believe that what you get down on paper the first time is really very good?

You may argue, "Why should a research report be well-written? Isn't it enough to be 'scientific' without trying to be 'literary'?"

There are two answers. The first one is that good writing will increase the chances that what you have written will be understood and considered important. The second answer is that good writing invites your readers to read what you have written and even encourages them to read your next report.

Scriboskepsis. From now on, how about practicing *scriboskepsis?* If you think there is no such word, you are right—or you were right just now. There now is such a word as *scriboskepsis*, because you just read it three times in the present paragraph.

If *omphaloskepsis* means meditation while gazing at one's own navel (which is what it does mean), why not *scriboskepsis*, which would mean meditation while gazing at one's own writing?

Remember too that everything you write has your "tone of voice," whether you intended this or not. This tone of voice reflects how you feel about your material and about your audience. Your tone can be dull and complicated or the reverse. The choice is up to you.

Do you remember the very last report you wrote? Yes, the last one will do just as well as any other. Get it out and look at it carefully. Now meditate while gazing at it.

No, not just the cover. The *inside* of the report. Keep looking through it and contemplating it; and see if you have really written what you are perfectly capable of writing.

Questions for You to Answer. Here are some questions for you to answer about your last report:

1. Did you think out what you wanted to say *before* you started to write; or were you thinking it out for the first time as you wrote?

2. Did you consider *more than one way* of writing your report? If not, why not?

Halt! Don't read on yet—not until you have answered the two questions above.

THE RECEIVERS OF YOUR MESSAGE

You do not have to and should not try to write like everybody else. Your language is your own.

But wait.   Is it *your* language?   You will be a more effective communicator if you keep in mind the language of your reader.   He is the receiver of your message, *not you.*   And almost everyone in your reading audience spends a lot of time reading reports of various kinds; but a lot of this time is wasted because the reader has to hack his way through a jungle of verbiage.

In such creative fields as music, literature, sculpture, and painting, truly great ideas have been developed by men and women whose compelling drive was to make or develop something that pleased *them.*   However, in the world of business writing there is no excuse for writing just to please yourself. There is only one audience to be pleased: the person or persons to whom your writing is primarily addressed.

Before even one line of writing is produced, you ought to be absolutely and completely clear to whom you are writing and why you are writing to that person or persons.   You need lots of reflection on what you select to say.

You run two real risks if you use "lingo" instead of "language."

The first risk is use of a word or phrase so familiar that you think your readers understand it the same way you do when actually they do not.   As an example, the phrase *penetration study* is a familiar one; but are you certain that the ideas you associate with a penetration study are precisely the same as for other marketing men?

The second danger is use of a word or phrase meaningful to researchers but without as much significance to other marketing people.   Such words or phrases run all the way from A to Z—from *apperception* to the *Zeigarnik effect.*

If you write a research report for brand managers and for copywriters about a commercial, your *style* of reporting should be quite similar for both groups —not "creative" for the creative people and "businesslike" for the brand managers—but *what you report* to the two groups might be somewhat different. For the creative group you might emphasize the quantitative aspects and include materials of special value to them.

However, if you send a research document to creative people or to brand managers written as if for researchers only, it probably will be perceived as a frightening number of pages of grandiloquent graphs and terrifying tables and thus will not be read at all.

Just remember that your readers know less about your particular research than you do but that they do not want to know *everything.*

Questions for You to Answer.   Now once more as to your last report, here are some more questions:

1. Do you know who were supposed to be the *receivers* of your message?
2. Did you think about *them* in writing your message?
3. Did you, so far as feasible, take *their* point of view?
4. Were you just trying to express your own thoughts, or were you really communicating to *them?*
5. Did you prepare them *in advance* for your message, before it arrived in writing?

Once more, halt!   Stop and answer the above questions before you read on.

YOUR MESSAGE ITSELF

Let us get one thing clear about the message.   It is a great deal more than punctuation, spelling, abbreviations, and capitalizations.

Those are matters of mechanics; and an efficient secretary ought to be able quietly to correct your mechanical errors.   But that is a bit sneaky—great big brain like you depending on some gal to make you look good.

You really should know a good deal about the mechanics of writing. Once upon a time you did a lot of reading about the "facts of life," and later on more reading to learn the facts of statistics. You wanted to master the techniques of lovemaking and then of graph-making.

Well, how about mastering the mechanics of writing? There is a sizable and respectable list of articles and books on readable writing that *can* be helpful.

"They *can* be helpful?" Yes, if you will do something more than just look at the list. That would be about as useful as developing muscular tone by reading your setting-up exercises.

The Title of Your Report. Obviously the title of your report must be accurate. But it does not have to be dull. It should be descriptive or attention-getting —or both, if possible.

Compare the outside of your report with the outside of a package. Your report has a title and the package has a title (usually a brand name). The hope of the manufacturer of the report (you) and of the manufacturer of the package should be the same—that someone will *want* to open it.

Questions for You to Answer. How about the following questions:

1. What was your communication *really about?*
2. Was its purpose *indicated in the title?*
3. Was your title *interest-arousing?*

Taking into account your last report, what are your answers to these questions?

Your Purpose. Your *real purpose* in writing a research report should be a sincere desire to communicate to someone else (or perhaps several people) information that might be useful to him (or them).

This means that you are obligated to learn as much as you can about *why* the information you are providing is needed or wanted *before* you try to provide it. You then can write intelligently about why you did what you did, how you did it, and what you learned.

Questions for You to Answer. Are you sure you know the answers to these?

1. What was the *real purpose* of your communication?
2. Was there *more than one purpose?* If so, did you keep these purposes distinct?
3. Did your communication *achieve your purpose or purposes?*

As before, stop now and answer these questions about your last report.

Your Plan of Organization. There is no such thing as *the* way to write up your research. You probably have your own individual ways of expressing yourself.

Even so, there are advantages to laying out a plan of organization *before* you start to write. Although your plan probably will change as you write, especially after your first draft, you still need a plan. This is a formal outline, one that provides a clear and logical sequence for what you want to communicate.

This outline or plan helps you to write logically and sensibly; even more important, it helps your readers to understand you.

Prepare a list of main headings, and under each heading indicate probable subheadings. Following is one possible plan of organization for a report, although, of course, not the only one:

1. *Problem.* This is a concise statement of the specific question or questions asked, and the reasons for asking them.
2. *Method.* An explanation of the design of your research is needed—for instance, your sample, control methods, and techniques of measurement.

3. *Results.*   You need to present enough data to justify your conclusions, but not necessarily every last bit of data.

4. *Discussion.*   Your discussion of your results, perhaps including comparisons with other studies, should be relevant to the original problem.

5. *Conclusions.*   Your conclusions are *not* the same as your results; instead, they flow from the results. The main consideration is the application of the findings to the problem at hand, the one that was set forth at the beginning of the report.

On certain reports you may want to put your conclusions *first*. Every research report has its own logical arrangement; this depends on your problem, your findings, and especially your audience.

Questions for You to Answer.   For each of the topics or headings in your plan of organization:

1. *Were related ideas grouped together?*

2. Could the receivers of your communication easily understand the *relationships of your ideas?*

Stop and answer these questions for your last report.

Your Language.   The writing of words, sentences, and paragraphs that communicate what you want them to communicate is *hard work.* And it takes *time.*

Red Smith once pointed out that there was nothing at all to writing his daily newspaper sports column—all that a writer needs to do is to stare at a blank sheet of paper until little drops of blood break out on his forehead!

Similarly, the process of writing an advertisement consists of a blank sheet of paper confronting a "lonely man at his typewriter" who "has to have the wit and wisdom, vitality and courage to interpret 1,001 impressions, facts, and fancies into a clear, lucid commercial message."[1]

The writing of a research report is difficult too, although not nearly as difficult as the writing of a newspaper column or an advertisement. After all, you, the research writer, already have something before you, something tangible to report and discuss. And yet with this head start, how many research reports ever represent great writing?

Researcher Influences.   Perhaps you have been influenced too much by the kinds of research reports written by other researchers.

And the likelihood of most researchers becoming great writers is of about the same order as that of most writers becoming great researchers. The researcher is primarily a gatherer of information rather than a skilled wordsmith. By contrast, the writer is a man "overpowered by words, sentences, rhythms. . . . Language haunts him. Words, sentences, rhythms are not things to him; they are presences."[2]

Professorial Influences.   There is an additional consideration. If you do not write well, is it possible that your writing ability was "spoiled" by going to college? Did the process of getting a degree damage your writing psyche?

"By the evidence of their writing, a very high fraction of American professors today are, if not illiterate, at least boorish in their literary manners. Their writing lacks style, grace, or conviction. It is pompous and redundant. Its diction is undiscriminating when not absurd." Thus wrote a man who knows

---

[1] Richard Holznecht, Director of Advertising and Public Relations, Parker Pen Company, 1962.

[2] John Ciardi, "On Writing and Bad Writing," *Saturday Review,* vol. 45, December 15, 1962, pp. 10–12.

—John E. Burchard, former Dean of the School of Humanities of the Massachusetts Institute of Technology.[3]

Says the gifted and unabashed editor-in-chief of *Commentary*: ". . . Even if one . . . asks for a piece of exposition whose virtues include clarity, economy, coherence, and grace, one is hard put to find it even among . . . professors of English, let alone professors of economics or sociology."[4]

As to the textbook manuscripts that reach him, the editor for a leading book company commented: "A shocking number of them would find hard sledding in a freshman composition course."[5]

The point is that much of your own early writing was done to meet the demands of your teachers and professors, many of whom do not know how to write effectively.   Over many years you wrote quite a number of reports and papers, most of which were marked by people who themselves are not good writers.   But they expected you to write like *them*, and it was your job to please them.

Terminology.   The readers of your reports are busy people, and very few of them can balance a research report, a cup of coffee, and a dictionary at one time.   Most of them have never had specialized courses in statistics.   Most of them cannot speedily visualize a regression equation, and almost none of them ever has considered the relative merits (if any) of a skewed distribution.

And why should they?   That is not their job.   Their mission is to make use of the information provided in your reports.

Why should a package designer be expected to understand what is meant by a coefficient of correlation unless it is explained to him, any more than a research man should understand the benday process?   Why should a copywriter be expected to know the difference between a Latin square and chi square any more than a research man should be expected to know the difference between Baskerville and Bodoni?   Why should an account executive or an advertising manager necessarily be familiar with the details of area-probability sampling any more than a researcher would necessarily be familiar with the details of advertising budgeting?

This does *not* imply that there should be any "talking down" of technical terms in your research report.   Your readers, after all, are far from mentally retarded.   But you will be more easily understood if you will provide just a brief word of explanation of any special words or phrases.   If technical terms or mathematical formulas are used, oftentimes it is important to explain them briefly on first usage.   If you write about dichotomization or a tetrachoric coefficient of correlation, you might add a sentence or so just to "clue" some of your readers what these terms mean.

A second possibility is to do this the other way around—that is, after the explanatory phrase or sentence to add the technical term or phrase and then to use the technical term freely in the remainder of your report.

A third possibility is to avoid the technical term and simply to use a more common word or phrase which carries essentially the same meaning.

You need to decide which of these three ways is the best for each report you write.

[3] "Will Education Pass the Test?" *Chicago Sun-Times*, April 21, 1966, sec. 2, pp. 1–3.

[4] Norman Podhoretz, "In Defense of Editing," *Harper's Magazine*, vol. 231, October 1965, pp. 143–147.

[5] Henry F. Thoma, "Good Morning, Professor, Want to Write a Textbook?" *College English*, vol. 19, November 1957, pp. 45–50.

Gobbledygook. By all means, guard against gobbledygook. This is a loathsome verbal disease by no means limited to bureaucrats. According to Bergen and Cornelia Evans, gobbledygook combines the idea of "the self-important, indignant, incomprehensible gobbling of a turkey-cock with the idea of a sticky and loathsome mush into which the unhappy listener or reader sinks with a bubbling cry."[6]

Of the hundreds of examples that might be given from the writings of researchers, consider the following gem from a well-known senior research executive:

> The use of the analytical techniques of the behavioral sciences will gradually revolutionize the communication arts by predicating their practice upon a body of demonstrably general principles which will be readily available to creative people for increasing their knowledge of consumer response to advertising communication.

And here is an example of a junior researcher also writing nonsense:

> Inspection of the curves shows that at the outset an unusually high level of arousal was generated, which was rapidly dissipated; this unusual phenomenon suggests that an investigation of the tension-building and tension-reduction process in terms of its rapid and slow phases and its relation to memory should shed some light on the meaningfulness-recall relationship.

Why do so many researchers consider their own writing profound just because their language is complicated, cumbersome, and confounding—instead of being clear, simple, and concise? So many examples of abominable writing abound among certain researchers that we might do well to invent a new research concept, to be known from now on as the "Mercedes-Benz factorial line of communication."

Length of Report and Length of Words. Long-windedness seems to be in style. Many a researcher seems to have a greater feeling of accomplishment if he has written a report of over a hundred pages than a short report of only ten pages.

Yet neither the long nor the short possesses virtue merely because it is long or short. The value is in what is communicated. Both *Hamlet* and *The Origin of Species* consist of thousands of words each, whereas Lincoln's Gettysburg Address is only 268 words and Winston Churchill's famous "blood, sweat, and tears" speech only 667.

No, it is neither length nor brevity that matters. It is how much length was necessary. Either the short or the long report, or for that matter the medium-length report, can be couched in such words that the reader's reading is difficult—to put it bluntly, *tough.*

Yet errors of *too long* a report far exceed the number of instances of *too short* a report. One of Parkinson's laws is: "Work expands so as to fill the time available for its completion." And a corollary law for you might be the following: "Your language expands so as to fill the time you have available for paperwork."[7]

As to number of words, if it is possible to cut out a word, cut it out. The fewer the words that can be made to convey an idea, the clearer and more powerful that idea.

[6] Bergen Evans and Cornelia Evans, *The Dictionary of Contemporary Language,* New York: Random House, 1957, p. 204.

[7] Rudolph Flesch, "Why Business Can't Write," *Advertising Age,* vol. 38, June 29, 1966, p. 102.

The World War II slogan "Is this trip necessary?" might be changed with reference to writing to read "Is this word necessary?" Even better, "Is this paragraph necessary?" Better still, "Is this section necessary?"

Consider the words of a former member of Churchill's War Cabinet discussing the tendency to use words too carelessly and too copiously: "Rather let a man take his rest in the shade of the tree in hot weather than turn it into paper which keeps him in the office late at night, when he ought to be breathing some of God's air, and confining himself to reading some of God's English."[8]

Are you one of the many researchers involved in sesquipedalianisms, that is, the use of long words when in reality shorter words would convey your meaning better? If you are, ponder the following advice:

> Never fear big long words.
> Big long words name little things.
> All big things have little names.
> Such as life and death, peace and war.
> Or dawn, day, night, hope, love, home.
> Learn to use little words in a big way.
> It is hard to do but they say what you mean.
> When you don't know what you mean, use big words.
> That often fools little people.[9]

Questions for You to Answer. Ask yourself:

1. Were your *ideas actually there in the report,* or were you merely hinting at them?

2. Did you always *come directly to the point*?

3. Did you use words and phrases that are *easily understood by your readers*? For your last report, what are your answers to these questions?

THE CHANNELS FOR YOUR MESSAGE

Take just one more good, long look now at your last report. Yes, the same one will still do.

This was *your* channel of communication, and sometimes the only one, between you and some of your readers. Therefore, read again your summary or headnote, then your opening paragraph, and finally your headings and subheadings.

Summary or Headnote. You need either a brief summary or else a headnote at the very beginning of almost every report—preferably on paper of a different color than the rest of your report.

Your *summary* should state the problem, the method, the results, and the conclusions. There may be reports for which a *headnote* is more suitable, with no statement of the results and conclusions but with just enough information as to what your report is about to whet the appetite of your readers.

Think carefully about your primary audience and their interests and then decide whether to write a summary or a headnote. Be sure to indicate how the reading of your report might benefit your readers, and do this in less than 300 words (better still, less than 200 words).

Opening Paragraph. Get the attention of your readers in your very opening

---

[8] Viscount Chandos, "Pray, Don't Call It English," *Columbia Journal of World Business,* vol. 1, Fall 1965, pp. 137–141.

[9] Arthur Kudner, in a letter to his son.

sentence and in your opening paragraph. How easy it is to say this, and how difficult to do!

Getting your readers' attention is more than just the writing of a clever lead sentence and paragraph. It is a matter instead of saying something so interesting and inviting that your readers *want* to read further.

Because every member of your reading audience never has enough hours in any day to read everything that he is supposed to read, your opening paragraph must provide him with some "nourishment" or food for thought. You may want to use the technique of answering in the very first paragraph the questions of who, what, where, when, and why.

Just as the best package on a shelf gets potential purchasers to respond to its symbolic cry, "Take me home! Take me home!" your report should get potential readers to respond to its symbolic cry, "Read me! Read me!"

Main Headings and Subheadings. Usually you need several main headings in your report, and often subheadings also. This is to help your readers to know what they are going to read about next.

Your major topics can be center headings, centered on the page. Your subtopics can be side headings, probably placed at the left side of the typed page.

Final Touches. By now your report has been written and rewritten until you believe that it says for you what you want it to say. And you have run out of time or energy or both.

But just take a few minutes, and:

1. Be sure that your *pages are numbered.*

2. Make sure also that you have *a table of contents* at the beginning (except for reports of only a few pages) with the page numbers given.

3. Check once more to make sure that *sources for all data* have been cited, and cited correctly.

4. When your report comes back in supposedly final typed form, check it carefully for *typographical errors.*

5. Finally, never, never, never throw away any *early draft of your report* until your report is in final form.

The real task is for *you* to study your report in exactly the same way that a conscientious editor would (or should). With a ruthlessly close study of your manuscript, the deficiencies that you will discover will not be just of *form* but of *substance* also.

> Under the editorial microscope things that were not visible to the naked eye ... suddenly make an unexpected appearance. One sentence does not logically follow from the next; the paragraph on page 8 only makes sense if it is transposed to page 6 and stitched in with a clever transition to cover the seam. ...[10]

The person who should make the changes is *you.* And you can do two things that will help you to spot what needs to be changed or rewritten:

1. *Read your report aloud.* Yes—read it aloud. Do not be embarrassed. If you are, it is better for you to be embarrassed privately by yourself than to think of your embarrassment at what your readers might say about your report and about you.

2. *Give your report to someone else to read, preferably not another researcher.* What you want to find out is whether someone else who is intelligent but not necessarily an expert on research understands your report without

[10] Norman Podhoretz, op. cit., p. 145.

laborious concentration. You also want to learn from him what improvements in your writing he can suggest.

Written or Oral Reports. One more point—"talking" your report to some of your potential audience may at times be more efficient than just writing. If you decide to do this, your written report can then sometimes be shorter than otherwise.

Your main job is to *communicate*, however that may best be accomplished.

Questions for You to Answer. Now ask yourself:

1. Did you use the *channels of communication best suited* to what you wanted to communicate?

2. Does your communication *need to be explained orally* in addition to being presented in written form?

THE FEEDBACK YOU NEED

The content of your report is your most important consideration. But *your content and your way of expressing the content* are inseparable.

You are obligated, therefore, to try to find out at the appropriate time what your readers thought about your report—*both* as to content and as to form. Or did they think about your report at all? You must get some feedback from them.

And get some feedback from yourself, too. Many a person trying to write "sees only what he intended to write. . . . *He never sees what he has actually written.*"[11]

Feedback information can help you in planning future research as to its *content* and in preparing the best *form* of expression. Both your content and form are important. If either is inadequate, you have failed to meet your objectives of effective communication.

Feedback criticisms can help you to learn about your possible errors of *omission* and of *commission*, so that you can plan to avoid such errors in the future. However, for feedback information to be useful to you in future studies, you will have to train yourself not to be overly sensitive or defensive about criticisms; and this is not easy.

Questions for You to Answer. You can write better research reports in the future if you will answer the following questions:

1. Did you really try to get some *feedback* from others about your report—both as to content and as to form?

2. What specifically did you *learn*?

3. Was what you wrote *helpful* to anyone? If so, what was helpful? If not, why was your report not helpful?

4. If your report was not well received, do you *blame your readers or yourself*?

YES, YOU CAN WRITE

Now that you have (we hope) been prodded and pushed in this chapter, do not be like a turtle and take refuge by pulling your head into your shell, emitting nothing. But do not be like an octopus either and squirm slowly about, emitting impenetrable ink.

Yes, you *can* write. And if you will work at it and really write clearly, all

[11] John Ciardi, op. cit., p. 12.

your superiors and inferiors and even your peers will bow down before you in undying gratitude.

BIBLIOGRAPHY

Brown, Leland, *Effective Business Report Writing*, 2d ed., Englewood Cliffs, N.J.: Prentice-Hall, 1963.

Callihan, E. L., *Grammar for Journalists*, New York: Ronald, 1957.

Chandos, Viscount, "Pray, Don't Call It English," *Columbia Journal of World Business*, vol. 1, Fall 1965, pp. 137–141.

Cox, Sidney, *Indirection for Those Who Want to Write*, New York: Knopf, 1947; Viking, 1962.

Fielden, John S., "For Better Business Writing," *Harvard Business Review*, vol. 43, January–February 1965, pp. 164–172.

———, "What Do You Mean I Can't Write?" *Harvard Business Review*, vol. 42, May–June 1964, pp. 144–152.

Flesch, Rudolf, *How to Write, Speak, and Think More Effectively*, New York: Harper and Row, 1960.

———, *The ABC of Style: A Guide to Plain English*, New York: Harper and Row, 1964.

Gallagher, William J., *Report Writing for Management*, Reading, Mass.: Addison-Wesley, 1969.

Hayakawa, S. I., ed., *The Use and Misuse of Language*, New York: Fawcett, 1967.

Johnson, Thomas P., *Analytical Writing: A Handbook for Business and Technical Writers*, New York: Harper and Row, 1966.

Klein, Lawrence R., "The Professional Journal—Writing Without Fun or Profit," *Business and Society*, vol. 2, Spring 1962, pp. 31–36.

Lambuth, David, et al., *The Golden Book on Writing*, New York: Viking Press, 1963.

McCrimmon, James M., *Writing With a Purpose*, Boston, Mass.: Houghton Mifflin, 1963.

Menzel, Donald H., Howard Mumford Jones, and Lyle G. Boyd, *Writing a Technical Paper*, New York: McGraw-Hill, 1961.

Perlmutter, Jerome H., *A Practical Guide to Effective Writing*, New York: Random House, 1965.

Pugh, Griffith Thompson, *Guide to Research Writing*, 2d ed., Boston: Houghton Mifflin, 1963.

Reiter, Michael J., "Reports That Communicate," *Management Services*, vol. 4, January 1967, pp. 27–36.

Shurter, Robert L., Peter J. Williamson, and Wayne G. Broehl, *Business Research and Report Writing*, New York: McGraw-Hill, 1965.

Strunk, William Jr., and E. B. White, *The Elements of Style*, New York: Macmillan, 1959.

Tichy, H. J., *Effective Writing: For Engineers—Managers—Scientists*, New York: Wiley, 1966.

Turabian, Kate L., *A Manual for Writers of Term Papers, Theses, and Dissertations*, Chicago: University of Chicago Press, 1955.

Turnbull, Arthur T., and Russell M. Baird, *The Graphics of Communication*, New York: Holt, 1964.

Turner, Rufus P., *Technical Writer's and Editor's Stylebook*, Indianapolis: Sams, 1964.

Tuttle, Robert B., and C. A. Brown, *Writing Useful Reports*, New York: Appleton-Century-Crofts, 1956.

Woodford, F. Peter, "Sounder Thinking through Clearer Writing," *Science*, vol. 156, May 12, 1967, pp. 743–745.

Chapter 8

Uses of Research Findings

DONALD L. THOMPSON *Slippery Rock State College, Slippery Rock, Pennsylvania*

Marketing research, by definition, has no use other than to support decision making. It does this by helping to identify and solve problems where the distributive processes are a necessary consideration. Clearly, business firms are the principal users of marketing research. But, it is a mistake to assume that only business firms have markets. Educational and charitable institutions, hospitals, government agencies, and even religious organizations all, to a lesser or greater extent, must meet the test of market acceptance for their products.

BUSINESS USES

In a free-enterprise economy, it is hard to think of a business firm proceeding totally ignorant of the state of its market. The very act of setting a price forces such consideration. But, it cannot be denied that some firms use very little formal marketing research. Many of these are small in size and owner-controlled and -operated.

Among larger firms, the use of marketing research is very likely to emerge as a function of the degree of competition. An example might be the firm producing a specialized, highly technical product, protected by patents and setting prices largely on the basis of cost plus some acceptable rate of return. Such a firm might grow to a considerable size and yet undertake little formal investigation of its markets and how they operate.

The use of marketing research also appears to vary with the firm's position within the distribution channel. Manufacturers seem to be most interested in data on their markets, possibly because size and middlemen so often serve to insulate their decision centers from their customers. Retailers, on the other hand, tend to ignore the inherent advantages of being the last agency in the channel—in direct contact with the consumer. Many reasons may be advanced for this: possibly marketing research is a luxury they can't afford, that merchandise well bought is really "sold," that attention to other, more immediate activities must take precedence, that retail stores don't attract research-oriented personnel, etc.

Wholesalers probably don't use marketing research as much as they should, especially those handling a wide range of products. The tendencies for wholesalers to specialize and to develop medium-size firms, however, make it difficult to come to a really firm conclusion in this respect if they lead in the direction of informally conducted marketing research. Thus, if they are more prone to formalize or otherwise identify their research activities, manufacturers' use of marketing research may be overstated in comparison with that of wholesalers and retailers.

In the discussion of uses of marketing research which follows, it should be remembered that business firms are separately treated for purposes of analysis, primarily to give organization to this chapter. While businesses differ in significant ways from, say, church or government agencies, in many respects they face common marketing problems. We give primary treatment to business uses of marketing research and then discuss the problems of nonbusiness uses within the general framework already provided. Finally, separate consideration is given to using marketing research in legal proceedings.

In the following discussion, the reader may feel that a disproportionate amount of attention is given to the use of marketing research in making decisions affecting consumer rather than industrial products. This is not intended to downgrade the use of marketing research in industrial marketing. Instead, it is felt that there are considerable advantages to looking on industrial purchasers as consumers in general, without special consideration to their buying motives. They may be less concerned with nonrational considerations than other types of consumers, but this does not mean that research into industrial markets should assume away the effect of such factors as advertising, personal selling, sales promotion, and so forth. The marketing, customer-oriented approach intelligently supported by marketing research can profitably be applied to all types of marketing situations.

Setting Prices. One of the most important uses of marketing research is to help firms price their products. In this respect, the key planning concept is *price elasticity of demand,* that is, the effect on sales of changes in price. It is a mistake to assume that marketing research designed to support price decisions is obtained only through consumer surveys. Commonly overlooked are data in the firm's internal records on product sales and prices. Often these can be obtained as an inexpensive by-product of the firm's need to account for its operations.

In using such information, the problem exists that sales are affected by factors other than price. Thus one must also take account of the likely effect of changes in the other elements of the firm's and its competitors' market offers, shifts in consumer demand, and changes in the general level of economic activity.

In using survey data to set prices, the danger exists that the conditions under which the research was conducted may differ materially from the conditions existing at the time of sale. The respondent in her living room may be affected by entirely different influences than those that affect her in the supermarket. Additionally, in the case of self-reported data, it is often difficult for a consumer to analyze his or her own feelings and reactions to products and prices.   If properly controlled, simulated shopping and in-store experiments can overcome some of the difficulties encountered in using marketing research to help set prices.

Designing Products and Packages.   Marketing research, in many different ways, can help the firm design its products and packages.   It helps define the general climate in which the firm obtains acceptance of its existing products and in which new products will be evaluated.   Key information with respect to existing products includes definition of uses to which products are put (sometimes quite different from the primary uses for which they were designed), experience in using the product, product features liked and disliked and for what reasons, carryover effects of the image of other products in the line, and similar evaluation of competitors' offerings.

In evaluating the market for future products, marketing research can help by showing the current stage of the firm's products in the product life cycle (are they in the introductory, maturing, or declining phases?), by documenting needs not met by existing products, and by evaluating the adequacy of the present product line.   Marketing research can be of material assistance to the firm's research and development department in deciding on potentially fruitful avenues of investigation and in evaluating the economic possibilities of ongoing product research.   Documented lack of marketability can help the firm avoid expensive scientific and engineering studies or serve to truncate efforts apparently not leading in a profitable direction.   In this respect, market tests are an important research tool.

The field of packaging research is one which in recent years has grown to vast proportions.   It not only concerns the physical aspects of containers but also the psychological considerations attached to the way consumers react to packages.   Experimentation and in-depth probing of consumer reactions to shape, size, design, and color are frequently undertaken.   Extensive research may even support the design of packages for industrial products or the containers received by wholesalers and retailers.

Selecting Channels of Distribution.   The channel decision is one made infrequently, and when made, it is usually from a limited number of alternatives.   Yet, the costs of various channels differ materially, and a critical consideration must be the way consumers react to the prices they pay and the services they receive in return.   Central in this respect is the varying degree of control producers enjoy under different types of channel configurations.   An often overlooked aspect of channel research is to consider middlemen external to the firm as customers, motivated not by the utility of the product itself but by the profits they may obtain through handling it.

Designing Promotional Programs.   *Promotion* here refers to advertising, personal selling, and sales promotion.   Marketing research is a critical consideration in obtaining satisfactory answers to the three fundamental problems of advertising: How much to spend?   On what?   And with what consequences?   Yet, none of the three can be resolved independently of the other two.   In fixing the budget, some idea must be obtained about the effect at the margin of spending an additional dollar on advertising versus other forms of sales promotion.

Clearly, one must have some idea about how customers react to all dimensions of the firm's market offer, in context and in combination.   In practice, media research is often partially delegated to an advertising agency or marketing research consultant external to the firm.   And substantial amounts of marketing research are undertaken by mass media in support of their own sales efforts.

As a general rule, firms probably pay insufficient attention to marketing research in support of personal selling activities. Sorely needed is basic research into personal selling, the psychological demands it makes on the salesman, and the impact it makes on the prospect. Better understanding of the sales process, in turn, leads to a better solution of the problems of territorial division, establishment of quotas, bases for compensation, and development of methods for motivating, supervising, and evaluating salesmen.

Inasmuch as sales promotion efforts make their impact directly at the store level, research into their effectiveness involves direct contact with the customer market. But given the many factors which can affect response to sales promotion efforts, a research design which involves something more than the collection of sales figures is usually desirable.

Locating Retail Outlets.   Marketing research helps solve the two basic problems of store location: choice of the area in which to locate and choice of a specific site. There is considerable evidence to support the view that consumers' purchasing decisions are importantly affected by their images of retail outlets. Image studies further suggest that while a store may be located on the basis of objective considerations, it is evaluated by consumers in subjective terms. Marketing research supporting retail location decisions thus should not only involve study of market potential, accessibility, and the effect of competition but should also focus on the extent to which consumers take account of these factors in their patronage decisions, as discussed in Section III, Part E, Chapter 1.

Selling or Promotional Support.   A common use of marketing research is to support selling or promotional efforts. The validity of much of this research is open to question, especially when the findings are generated by the interested party. Regardless of this fact, backing up sales claims with research findings is for many companies an effective promotional technique.

Making Physical Distribution Decisions.   Marketing research is frequently the basis for making physical distribution decisions which can have an important long-range effect on the firm's cost structure. If the location of retail outlets is affected by marketing considerations, the location of warehouses, wholesale distribution points, and even manufacturing plants is also affected.

Aiding Credit Management.   The credit manager can use marketing research both in setting general policy and in making specific decisions. In a general vein, marketing research can help identify trends in credit seeking and payment and help predict probable reactions to credit solicitation and collection efforts. More specifically, marketing research can be the source of customer profiles which then may be related to propensities to seek credit, preferences for certain types of credit plans, and the likelihood of repayment.

Defining Costs of Distribution.   Marketing research can suggest bases on which distribution cost studies may be developed. For example, marketing research may suggest that from a decision-making standpoint it is meaningful to analyze distribution costs along the following lines: distribution channel, type of customer, type of market served, location of customer, size of order, frequency of purchases, and so forth.

Coordinating Functional Efforts.   A major problem faced by business firms is the profitable coordination of the finance, marketing, and production managers and their departments. Marketing research facilitates their cooperation in many ways. First, marketing research helps define the objective to which the firm's resources are committed. Common agreement on this objective then permits the various functional managers to develop plans that will coordinate efforts at all levels within the organization.

Second, it is inevitable that conflicts will develop among the functional managers. Marketing research can help resolve such conflicts in favor of the firm rather than in favor of individual departments. It is hoped that this will help avoid suboptimization. This does not mean that differences of opinion must always be resolved in favor of the marketing manager. But it does mean that objective market considerations should normally take precedence over subjectively defined departmental programs which are inconsistent with them.

Finally, some measure of how well the market is served emerges as the acid test of how well the firm's organizational structure is working. It is one thing to desire to serve customers, but it is another to develop the organization to carry out this lofty and easily adopted objective. Marketing research thus can be a valuable source of information on how well the firm can coordinate the separate efforts of its functional managers in terms of service to the customer. Customers are remarkably insensitive to the problems of the separate functional managers—their interest is in how well the firm as a whole serves them.

Evaluating Prospects for Merger or Partial Acquisition. Recent years have seen mergers and partial acquisitions increasingly used to strengthen or diversify corporate structure. In such instances, fixing a valuation on firms to be acquired is a critical factor, especially when recognition must be given to the value of goodwill (which in some cases conceivably could be negative). Marketing research has been used to supply an objective basis for such valuation.

Forecasting and Planning Uses. Rarely is marketing research undertaken for its historical value; almost always the interest is in forecasting and planning. Even though most of the uses already discussed involve situations in which the ability to anticipate the future is critical, it is useful at this point to highlight the role that marketing research plays in this respect. Marketing research helps identify problems before they arise, to anticipate desires before they are apparent. Often business firms cannot wait until something is so obvious that it represents a sure thing. The length of the lead times required for corporate planning and action means that those who succeed are those who make the best guesses about the future and who have committed their resources while things are still in the probable stage. Marketing research is an important source of such probabilities.

NONBUSINESS USES

Obviously any distinction between business and nonbusiness uses of marketing research is arbitrary. This section discusses certain special cases in which marketing research is used for purposes other than to support business decisions. A nonbusiness situation is one in which the key concern is not profit but some other consideration. Government agencies, for example, are involved in both business and nonbusiness situations: purchasing as contrasted with the payment of welfare. Our next focus is not on whether a firm or organization is a business but on those uses of marketing research which are fundamentally nonbusiness in nature.

Allocating Public Resources. Presently, at least in the United States, it can be argued that the market concept has been extended to the distribution of public resources, and that research on this market frequently serves to *directly* determine the distribution pattern. In this sense, the national censuses may be regarded as a type of marketing research conducted by the federal government. For example, distribution of federal and state tax monies is often on the basis of official population counts, even to the point that a political unit may gamble on covering the cost of a special (interim) census if the feeling is that it is not being given credit for the actual rate at which population might have grown beyond official estimates. Direct distributions based on demographic and economic data include gasoline, liquor, and cigarette taxes and school aid payments to the states.

Supporting Cost-Benefits Analysis. Cost-benefits analysis is to the government agency what the marketing audit is to the business firm. Here the concern is with less direct use by government of marketing research data than is the immediately preceding case. The first step is for government to estimate its revenues. By looking on its services in terms of the benefits provided, government presumably is in a position to evaluate alternative programs and to justify the ones offered for the revenue level anticipated. Even though government does not have to "sell" its programs (in the short run), ascertaining the reactions of consumers to the services provided still constitutes a valid use of marketing research. As in the business situations described previously, marketing research by government helps identify and solve problems, helps choose among alternatives.

Planning and Administering Educational Programs. Even though government is a major provider of education, academic institutions at all levels need marketing research of various types. The examples which could be cited are many: a school district utilizes a public opinion poll to analyze the prospects that its bond issue will pass, a university obtains data on alumni to help plan its annual giving drive, a teacher obtains the reactions of a class to his course, and so forth.

Analyzing Political Campaigns. Increasingly, marketing research is being used to analyze the impact of political campaigns. And, there is some evidence to indicate that political polls in themselves can affect voting decisions, even to the point that charges of poll rigging have been made by candidates in some elections.

Analyzing the Role of Religion. Declining church attendance in the United States has produced a desire on the part of church leaders to explore the nature of the market for their services. A great deal of such information is collected informally and passed upward. A more formal use of marketing research in this respect is illustrated by the five-year study by the Danforth Foundation of the campus ministry.[1] The heart of this study is a survey of some 12,000 campus and parish ministers in six Protestant denominations.

Distributing Foundation Wealth. Directors of nonprofit foundations, in soliciting requests for support, are obtaining research data on the state of the market for their products. Furthermore, major foundations often go to considerable lengths to identify problem areas and to estimate the impact attached to various funding alternatives and patterns of support.

Supporting Economic Analysis. Marketing research facilitates analysis of the state of the economy and the progress of the business cycle and is essential to the welfare economist concerned with the manner in which a society's material output is distributed. In the former vein, especially significant is the work of the Survey Research Center of the University of Michigan in attempting to evaluate the climate of consumer expectations.

Developing Other Disciplines. Marketing research has contributed significantly to other disciplines. Marketing applications have considerably ex-

[1] Kenneth W. Underwood, *The Church, The University and Social Policy*, Middletown, Conn.: Wesleyan University Press, 1969.

tended knowledge about survey research and facilitated its application to a great variety of situations. Investigation of the materialistic base of our society has also helped conceptually and empirically to fill out the theoretical skeletons of sociology, social psychology, cultural anthropology, economics, geography, and so forth. The techniques and concepts of marketing research are proving relevant to all those who are formally and objectively interested in the study of contemporary society and its materialistic base.

Aiding Community Planning. Marketing research is of no small help to those involved, individually or collectively, in community planning, which can take many forms—from areawide to neighborhood programs. Not all who use marketing research for planning purposes are necessarily planners. A retail merchants association, for example, may seek to determine the hours at which patrons would most like to shop. Or a real estate developer may try to find the most desired location for a new regional shopping center.

Aiding Community Action Programs. There has been far too little use to date of marketing research as a basis for developing, administering, and evaluating community action programs. Massive problems exist in defining the problems of the ghetto area as perceived by the residents themselves. For example, very little attempt has been made to uncover the attitudes of ghetto area residents to commercial and business establishments, which in times of civil disorder seem to bear the brunt of the attack. Furthermore, despite several sophisticated attempts to do so, the basic question "Do the poor pay more?" has yet to be satisfactorily answered.

LEGAL USES

The legal uses of marketing research stem from two types of actions: those involving government and those which result from private disputes. Government intervention in a free-enterprise economy is purportedly on behalf of the consumer. In some cases, government intervention is direct—for example, when the issue is allegedly deceptive labeling or advertising. Indirect intervention focuses on the structure and climate of competition—for example, when the Justice Department opposes a merger. Private disputes with marketing overtones can take many forms: from cases involving resale price maintenance to those concerning trademark infringement.

While marketing research can be an important source of factual information, in such cases the decision still depends on the weight given to the evidence and the manner in which the law is applied. Furthermore, antitrust law often requires not proof but instead the determination of whether there was a "likelihood" of deception, a "substantial" lessening of competition, a "tendency" toward monopoly, etc.

In commercial disputes and antitrust cases it is relatively easy for either side to introduce marketing research findings in support of its position. In commercial actions where damages are involved, marketing research may play a major role in fixing the extent to which the aggrieved party has suffered injury. On the other hand, documenting the extent of injury is usually not a primary consideration in antitrust cases. Marketing research data, under such circumstances, constitute the facts from which inferences are made.

There are so many cases in which distributive processes are a significant consideration that it is hard to even categorize the legal uses of marketing research. Discussed here are only the major types of actions in which marketing research is commonly introduced and in which such research is usually given some weight in the final decision.

Price Fixing. Approximately two-thirds of the antitrust cases handled by the

Justice Department concern price fixing.   Data on prices are usually obtained from the records of the firms involved.   Frequently offered as evidence are price lists, records of price movement over time, standardized methods for calculating or lists of transportation charges, rosters of representatives to trade associations or other industry meetings, and internal correspondence relating to price administration.   Sometimes primary data are presented to the government as, for example, the eleven sealed bids which were received by the United States Army Corps of Engineers offering 6,000 barrels of cement at the identical price of $3.28654 per barrel.[2]

Price fixing cases require more than merely proving to a reasonable man's satisfaction that prices were not set independently.   Additionally, the adverse effects of price fixing must be shown, often through extensive inferences from limited data.   However, proving price fixing is not always an easy matter.   Often one is dealing with extremely subtle forms of collusion, for example, the "phase of the moon" cyclic rotation uncovered in the 1960 electrical equipment industry price fixing cases.   Thus the government is often in the position of trying to prove conspiracy by circumstantial evidence.

Price Discrimination.   Price discrimination actions stem principally from the Robinson-Patman Amendment to Section 2 of the Clayton Act.   The government's case usually rests on relatively limited data showing allegedly discriminatory instances where different prices were charged for the same quantities of goods of like grade and quality.   Any extensive use of marketing research in such cases is usually by the defendant in an effort to prove that the price differentials resulted from differences in cost or represented efforts made in good faith to meet competition (two allowable exceptions under the law).

Cost justification defenses, which traditionally have failed more than they succeeded, involve extensive analysis of distribution costs (which in some cases has proceeded to the extent of accounting for cost differentials amounting to but a few thousandths of a cent per unit).   Attempts to document good faith frequently involve the introduction of affidavits collected at the time of sale (attesting that the recipient indeed had received a bona fide lower offer), and the introduction of testimony by customers on the effects of the action in question.

It is hard to determine how judges will react when a significant portion of the facts are established by marketing research.   Generally reactions are variable and sometimes appear quite arbitrary (for these and other reasons reversals on appeal are not uncommon).

Mergers and Partial Acquisitions.   The following comments from the famous Brown Shoe opinion help pinpoint, from a legal standpoint, the way courts look on marketing research data in merger and other antitrust cases:

> Both the Federal Trade Commission and the courts have, in the light of Congress' expressed intent, recognized the relevance and importance of economic data that places any merger under consideration within an industry framework almost inevitably unique in every case.   Statistics reflecting the shares of the market controlled by the industry leaders and the parties to the merger are, of course, the primary index of market power; but only a further examination of the particular market—its structure, history, and probable future—can provide the appropriate setting for judging the probable anticompetitive effect of the merger.[3]

[2] *Aetna Portland Cement Co. v. Federal Trade Commission,* 157 F. 2d 533, 576-7, revised, 333 U.S. 683.

[3] *Brown Shoe Co., Inc. v. U.S.,* 370 U.S. 294, 322 n. 38; 82 S. Ct. 1502, 1522 n. 38.

Clearly, the findings of marketing research are needed to carry out the court's stated intent. While simple statistics on the percentage distribution of the market are most frequently cited in merger opinions (and presumably carry the heaviest weight in the decision), the amount of data introduced by either or both sides is at times awesome. For example, in rendering a decision on the possible anticompetitive effects of Du Pont's acquisition of 23 percent of General Motors' common stock, the court was presented with some 3,000 pages consisting largely of the testimony of expert witnesses augmented by "numerous charts and tables received as exhibits."[4]

But in merger and other antitrust cases, the data can lead only so far. Analyses of and inferences from the data are critical. In effect, the court must look ahead and evaluate the twin effects of the merger on industry structure and performance (an alternative approach is to assume that the latter is a function of the former). In this respect, final decisions in important cases frequently rest on little more than trend analysis and inferences from relatively straightforward data, usually figures on the market shares recast in terms of the proposed or actual merger. Sophisticated expert witnesses "proving" their points by advanced statistical and mathematical analyses often have little or no weight attached to their testimony. The traditional basis for decision has not gone unchallenged. For example, in a dissenting opinion Justice Douglas argued, "Our choice must be made on the basis not of abstractions but of the realities of modern industrial life."[5]

False and Misleading Advertising. Regulation of advertising and labeling is governed by Section 5 of the Federal Trade Commission Act (except the advertising of foods, drugs, cosmetics, and therapeutic devices, which is covered by the Food, Drug, and Cosmetic Act of 1938, as amended). Covered are representations in all media. It does not have to be shown that persons were actually misled or deceived[6] nor in what proportions. Instead, the government must show only that there existed a capacity or tendency to deceive, taking into account the probable effect on "that vast multitude which includes the ignorant, the unthinking and the credulous."[7] In practice, this requires the court to evaluate everything from the claims of a correspondence course to determination of what the words "safe and harmless" really mean, and in contexts often inherently unfamiliar to the average judge. But the focus which the law directs to "tendency" or "capacity" leads in this direction and away from extensive documentation of the effects of the advertisements in question.

If survey or other data were used to measure an advertisement's tendency to mislead, would it be sufficient to show one person misled? Five percent of those exposed? Ten percent? Drawing the line between what is deceptive and what is nondeceptive is still a matter of judgment. In practice, decisions in such cases are usually far less affected by marketing research data than by whatever inferences and reactions result from the court's exposure to the actual advertisement.

Trademark Infringement. In trademark infringement cases it is necessary for the plaintiff to convince the court that his trademark tends to be confused with that of an allegedly infringing competitor. Marketing research may be

---

[4] *U.S. v. E. I. du Pont de Nemours & Co. et al.*, 366 U.S. 316, 320.

[5] *Standard Oil Company of California, et al. v. U.S.*, 337 U.S. 293, 320.

[6] *American Life and Accident Insurance Co. v. Federal Trade Commission*, 255 F. 2d 289.

[7] *Florence Mfg. Co. v. J. C. Dowd and Co.*, 178 F. 73, 75.

used to document such a contention, but historically it has been difficult to get courts to accept such data. Technically survey data are hearsay, although both parties may agree not to enter a challenge on that basis and thus open the way for introduction of such data. And, even if admitted, there is no reason why survey research findings should be given any weight in the final decision. As is the case with false and misleading advertising, the likelihood of confusion is still mainly determined by the court's own reaction.[8]

Resale Price Maintenance. It is up to brand owners to prove that Fair Trade prices are being violated. Evidence supporting such a contention must be collected by the brand owner, commonly by employing commercial shoppers who act in an undercover manner. Data so collected have not always been accepted without challenge. For example, in one case it was charged that the shoppers of the alleged violator were more insistent than the shoppers of the brand owner in trying to obtain discounts from list prices in the process of collecting data.[9]

Quasijudicial Hearings. Technically speaking, hearings of such public bodies as the Federal Trade Commission and the Interstate Commerce Commission are quasijudicial in nature. However, strict adherence to adversary trial procedure is often difficult. One reason is that the rules of evidence rigidly interpreted could serve to exclude almost all survey data and thus materially interfere with the establishment of the facts of the case. And, the nature of the complaint being heard frequently poses problems. For example, consider the following brief transcript from the famous FTC "sandpaper" hearings:

> Mr. Downs (the FTC attorney): Let the record show that Mr. Rote has applied the Rapid Shave to the sandpaper and he is now wiping it off his hand.
> Q: Is that the stroke you would use on your face, Mr. Rote?
> A: Not at all.
> Q: Is that heavier than you would use on your face?
> A: Yes, sir.
> Q: Will you now apply as much pressure as you can in an attempt to shave off this rough surface of this sandpaper?
> A: Yes, sir [complying].
> Mr. Downs: Let the record show that Mr. Rote used both hands on it.[10]

While such proceedings may have a courtroom atmosphere, they do not always follow strict legal procedure. As mentioned, the laws of evidence may be less stringently applied. This means that marketing research findings, including survey data and testimony of expert witnesses, are more likely to be allowed and may receive more weight than in a court of law. But the decisions of such hearings are still subject to judicial review on appeal.

Within present space limitations it is possible to detail only the most important types of legal actions in which marketing research findings are of importance. It is not possible to cite all the special circumstances which affect the admissibility of such findings or the weight given to them.

---

[8] In rare cases, judges have collected their own data, although not on a very scientific basis. See *LaTouraine Coffee Co., Inc. v. Lorraine Coffee Co., Inc., et al.,* 157 F. 2d 115, 120; and *Triangle Publications, Inc., v. Rohrlich et al.,* 167 F. 2d 969, 976.

[9] *Victor Fischel and Co., Inc. v. R. H. Macy and Co.,* Sup. Ct., New York County, Special and Trial Term, part V, index no. 6636165.

[10] Daniel Seligman, "The FTC Presents the Great Sandpaper Shave," *Fortune,* vol. 70, December 1964, p. 192.

BIBLIOGRAPHY

Brown, Lyndon O., and Leland L. Belk, *Marketing Research and Analysis*, 4th ed., New York: Ronald, 1969, pp. 3–34.

Ferber, Robert, Donald F. Blankertz, and Sidney Hollander, Jr., *Marketing Research*, New York: Ronald, 1964, pp. 19–38.

Green, Paul E., and Donald S. Tull, *Research for Marketing Decisions*, Englewood Cliffs, N.J.: Prentice-Hall, 1966, pp. 1–31.

Rigby, Paul H., *Conceptual Foundations of Business Research*, New York: Wiley, 1965, pp. 37–71.

Thompson, Donald L., "Survey Data as Evidence in Trademark Infringement Cases," *Journal of Marketing Research*, vol. 2, February 1965, pp. 64–73.

Wasson, Chester R., *Research Analysis for Marketing Decision*, New York: Appleton-Century-Crofts, 1965, pp. 246–268.

Werner, Ray O., "Marketing and the United States Supreme Court, 1965–1968," *Journal of Marketing*, vol. 33, January 1969, pp. 16–23.

Chapter 9

Ethics in Marketing Research

SIDNEY HOLLANDER, JR. *Sidney Hollander Associates, Baltimore, Maryland*

INTRODUCTION

Scope of Discussion. "Ethics in Marketing Research" covers a wide range of topics, some in common with other agency-client relationships, some arising from the special nature of the structure and methods of the research industry. Included in the first category are such questions as:

Should a research agency publicize its clientele?

What steps must it take to safeguard client confidentiality?

What use should a client make of agency proposals?

Should an agency accept competing accounts?

Should an agency become the client's partisan or advocate?

The second category of questions reflects the fact that most marketing research involves questionnaires administered by telephone, by face-to-face interviewing, or by mail. This raises questions of responsibility to those interviewed:

To what extent does the survey respondent have a right to know who is asking the questions?

What protection should the public have against invasion of privacy on the part of interviewers?

Is it permissible to mislead or deceive respondents in presenting questions?

How can the respondent be protected against giving information that can be used to his detriment?

In this second category, too, are operational questions arising from the peculiar structure of the interviewing mechanism as it has evolved to the present:

How can fieldwork standards be maintained against price competition?

How can field organizations and their interviewers protect themselves against unreasonable demands or exploitation by their clientele?

How can research agencies be protected against interviewer cheating and other malfeasance?

As with most questions of ethics, business or otherwise, the law provides a background and sets limits on conduct. However, important day-to-day questions of ethics are extralegal. In marketing research, we have codes of ethics issued by several trade and professional organizations (appended for reference at the end of this chapter). Scrutiny of these codes indicates that, although necessarily couched in generalities, they constitute a reasonably explicit guide to conduct for certain aspects of the subject, notably in confidentiality for both client and interview respondent. However, they are silent on some crucial business and public relations questions such as those just cited.

Except for these codes and the law itself, no one can say with authority what constitutes ethical conduct in so diversified a field involving so many relationships. In what follows we try to show application of existing codes and, beyond them, to present problems arising under prevalent standards or practices. Evaluation or possible improvement will be discussed not from the standpoint of any segment of the industry, nor on the assumption that "more" ethics is necessarily better, but rather as a search for ways in which standards of ethical conduct can be used to facilitate accurate and efficient operation with due consideration of all interests, including the public's.

Source of Interest. Within this broad scope, concern for ethics consists of four spheres of interest.

General Business. Marketing research is primarily a business activity, and it is generally businessmen and women who contract for it as buyers and sellers. Business interest and business precedents govern ethical relationships in such matters as promotion, negotiation, conflict of interest, and selection of resources. Bribery, whether overt or in the form of undue entertainment and gifts for the purpose of securing a contract, would appear to be governed by the same considerations in marketing research as in any other field, whether advertising, construction, or industrial purchasing.

Contractual Relations. Most marketing research activity involves transfer of services from one organization to another: client management may contract with a research agency, a research agency with a field organization, and any of these with a data processing service. Even the individual interviewer is regarded for most purposes as an independent contractor, not an employee.

Such relationships are normally governed explicitly or implicitly by contract. A research company makes a proposal with specifications which, when accepted, governs the scope and conduct of the work. A field organization receives a request for a certain number of interviews to be obtained under designated conditions at given rates which, when accepted, serves as a contract.

As with many contracts, they are not always to be followed to the letter. For example, it is common for clients to request bills tailored to make the payment fit a budget category which best suits them but imprecisely describes the task. Other contract bending is done by mutual consent for expediency or out of motives of simple justice: if the interview is longer than specified, the number of callbacks may be reduced; a research agency may lower its fee if the task turns out to be simpler than expected; or the client may voluntarily increase the payment to prevent the agency from incurring a loss.

Ethical considerations arise in cost-plus arrangements, which is the way much contract fieldwork is arranged. What constitutes a "cost" may sometimes depend on a particular system of record keeping. Also, there are questions that can be classified under "expense-account ethics," involving such petty questions as whether mileage expense must be defined as the shortest way rather than the actual or quickest; whether the individual or agency performing a service should collect for meals or transportation allowed but not used; or whether expenses which benefit more than one client should be billed to each. There seems to be no reason why answers to such questions should be different for marketing research than for other contractual relations.

Public Interest. Marketing research, like other industries, has broad obligations in dealing with the general public. Foremost is the question of confidentiality and anonymity of the survey respondent. This topic is central in the ethical codes of all industry segments and occupies most discussion of ethics within the industry. But there are more subtle collateral questions of public interest, such as the invasion of privacy inherent in all interviewing, the balance of satisfaction versus inconvenience for the respondent in any survey, and the circumstances under which survey results may be socially useful or antisocial.

Scientific Implications. More tangential is the relationship of marketing research to science. As an application of several disciplines rather than a science itself, marketing research evidences a close relationship between the business and academic communities. Many leading practitioners have worked in both areas at different times or divide their time between the two. Scientific interests are served by development of methodology in the conduct of research work through systematic testing and in dissemination of findings through publications and meetings among colleagues in the field. In research practice, science is not always served by using the most elaborate methods in all studies, since not every problem requires such precision; but it is in the interest of science to provide accurate description of what was done and how it was done.

As discussed later, such methodological reporting is of prime ethical importance when results are used for purposes of advocacy. However, ethics may vary depending on whether the research is an audience measurement study designed to influence potential advertisers, an opinion survey for legislative advocacy, or land-use analysis for zoning or planning applications.

APPLICATION OF GENERAL BUSINESS ETHICS

There is no need here to recapitulate principles of business ethics, still less of ethics in general. Nevertheless, it is useful to catalog some major applications that apply to marketing research.

Honesty. In research, as in other business, ethics begins with simple honesty in dealing with people. This means honesty with respect to handling money and property (for instance, in accounting for materials to be used in a survey) as well as truthfulness in reporting, such as number of callbacks attempted or the exact definition of readership used in measuring the size of an audience.

Legality. Ethics implies obedience to law. One pays employment taxes on interviewers even though in other contexts they are regarded as independent contractors. On the other hand, research is no different from other fields in which laws are ignored when they apply in only the most technical sense. For example, researchers may not feel obligated to seek out the application of every tax or licensing requirement when merely placing a test product in the home or every aspect of communications law applicable to recording telephone conversations when testing a questionnaire.

Value. Ethics requires one to vend a useful product. An ethical problem confronts the researcher who is asked to accept an assignment which he believes will not serve the client's expressed purpose. However, it may be regarded as ethical in research, as in the legal profession, to undertake an assignment which in the opinion of the practitioner will not yield the desired result if the client is so informed in advance and nevertheless wishes to proceed.

Conditions of Production. It is ethical to see that employees are adequately compensated and that working conditions are safe. In marketing research, this question is most likely to arise in connection with interviewers who, by the nature of their work, are vulnerable to financial exploitation and who find that personal interviewing is becoming increasingly hazardous in some areas.

Increasingly too, business ethics is concerned with environmental pollution. Several researchers have applied this concept to what they regard as the "natural resource" of interview respondents. In this opinion, questionnaire designs, interviewer personalities, and conditions of the interview which antagonize the public are as guilty as those who despoil forests or contaminate rivers.

Responsibility of Initiative. In a completely ethical system, one does not wait to be called but assumes affirmative responsibility for maintaining conditions which meet the standards he sets. As individuals and through organizations, many researchers are taking the initiative in seeing that interviewers are paid promptly, that interviews are unobtrusive and pleasant, that anonymity is respected, and that findings are reported scrupulously.

CLIENT RELATIONSHIPS

Research users contract for work with a research agency of some kind, described in detail in the following chapter. The agency may be a general practitioner of research, a supplier of a syndicated service (audience measurement or store audit), or a specialized agency such as a field or data processing service. Some ethical problems are common to several or all types.

Confidentiality. Any actual or prospective client who approaches or uses a service organization has a right to expect that what he reveals to them as a consequence of this relationship is confidential. Although not covered by professional status like that afforded to lawyers and accountants, the researcher resembles the category of consultants, such as management or personnel specialists, the nature of whose service requires that they become aware of client secrets. It can be said categorically that none of this can be revealed without the client's authorization (except under legal duress).

The temptation to disclose usually comes about either through involvement in small talk and gossip or by a desire to impress a prospective client with what an agency has done for others. A fringe benefit for many researchers is the interest attached to their work, and the desire to enhance one's ego may usually be satisfied by camouflage which permits discussion of the point without revealing the client. This rule is incumbent not only on agency principals and professionals, but, for obvious reasons, applies to all personnel including clerical. In well-run research agencies, even custodial personnel take conscious pride in concealing test products from areas frequented by visitors and in methods for disposing of questionnaires and other materials which may yield clues to what is being done for whom.

For the agency representative seeking new business, camouflage usually permits describing a relevant situation without breach of confidence. There is difference of opinion on whether it is ethical to mention a client's name, even without indicating the service performed. To some extent, this depends on the type of agency. A field interviewing service may be justified in doing so, because simply to have obtained interviews does not disclose much about a client's business; for a more specialized service, however, such as an agency which performs tachistoscopic package research or pretesting of TV commercials, a mere listing of names might provide more clues to competition than is proper. Therefore some agencies will not publicize their list of clients without permission.

Less clear is the ethical responsibility of the client as a beneficiary of indiscretion. On one hand, it may be argued that he is entitled to all he can get—indeed, that with increasing emphasis on industrial espionage, he is failing his company if he does not do so. The other viewpoint is that one who solicits or even accepts intelligence unethically given is complicit as a receiver. Regardless, it seems clear that a sophisticated client is likely to disqualify one who betrays another's confidence on the practical ground that if he tells the secrets of one, he will tell those of another.

Bids and Proposals. Some research services do not lend themselves to bids and proposals. Many syndicated services are sold from standardized price lists, usually replete with options and discounts.

Local field interviewing services operate on cost-plus-percentage, but other kinds of service are negotiated or are subject to bid or proposal. As in any business, it is unfair to request an elaborate proposal from a firm that is not being seriously considered for the job simply to satisfy a corporate purchasing requirement.

One practice that is universally regarded as unethical is to have one supplier bid on another's specifications or to appropriate ideas from one proposal to include in the assignment given to another bidder. Of course, a client may develop his own specifications and request bids on them, but he is not justified in appropriating one bidder's idea for another's price.

Indeed, a reputable researcher does not bid on specifications he knows were obtained from another firm. This is because in many problem-solving proposals the research firm is often in the anomalous position of having to give away its highest skill—research design—in order to sell the operating and analytical services which produce income. Therefore, to appropriate the design and request bids on its specifications is like asking a house advertising agency to carry out ideas obtained from competitive agency presentations or asking a low-priced architect to execute the design, submitted in competition, of a higher priced one.

While this is typically the case in problem-solving proposals, the same may also apply to ideas which are more mechanical or procedural in nature yet for which the proposer should receive benefit, such as an ingenious method for finding eligible respondents or a more efficient means of data collection. One way to permit the client to utilize all such ideas without ethical transgression is to pay for proposals and thus obtain the right to use their ideas. Developmental costs are usually so small a portion of the entire research undertaking and the principle is so logical that one may wonder why it is seldom put into practice.

Restrictions. Regardless whether the job is negotiated or competitively bid, there are ethical considerations governing who is eligible to do the work. Again, with syndicated services there is no problem; they are generally open to all subscribers except when a client is willing to pay for exclusive rights to a particular category. In other instances, there are two considerations that might restrict the propriety of handling a project: bias and conflict. The first occurs when an agency has an interest in the outcome. For example, there is evident possibility for bias if an advertising agency's research department is given the task of evaluating campaign results, and many an agency researcher finds himself cross-pressured between his obligation for good research and his employer's best interest.

The conflict situation occurs when a research agency working for one company is asked to work for a competitor. If the projects are specific and unrelated, there may be no conflict. In fact, there are situations where to refuse an assignment on grounds of conflict might be a greater breach of confidence than accepting business from a competitor without comment.

Apart from syndicated services, research assignments tend to be on a project basis, so research agencies usually have looser ties to their clients than advertising agencies do. Hence research firms working on a project basis usually have no compunction about serving competing clients, even at the same time. It is obligatory, therefore, for the researcher to separate in his mind his general stock of information about methodology and subject matter, which constitutes his personal competence, from specifics which are the confidential property of clients he has served. This is analogous to the ethics of job changes, under which an employee is free to carry all he has added to his personal skills to a new employer but must abandon detailed knowledge.

The project basis of operation facilitates this. Even so, conflicts may arise when the researcher is so deeply involved in the development of a product, package, or advertising theme that he could not work for a competitor without having his loyalty to one or the other compromised. He might have to hold back in the second assignment to protect the use made of his work by the first; or, alternatively, he might unwittingly use his knowledge of the first to help the second counter it.

Sometimes the research agency is on a retainer relationship, meaning that it cannot accept assignments from a competitor unless it is acceptable to both clients. In such cases, the second prospect might not want the retainer client even to know he was interested in research, in which case there is an ethical question whether the inquiry should be reported. Is there a professional obligation to treat all inquiries confidentially, or does the retainer relationship obligate a practitioner to report the inquiry as a matter of trade intelligence? If the second client is willing to have the request made, it should be reported to the first. However, the content of neither assignment should be revealed to the other client.

Sometimes the possibility of conflict is resolved in advance by the nature of a retainer. For example, a department store engaged a research firm on an exclusive basis to evaluate potential for proposed branch sites but left it free to accept other kinds of consumer studies from competitors. Moreover, the understanding was that as soon as the store made its site selection, the agency would be free to work for any other retailer even on that subject.

Disputes. As in any contractual relationship, disputes may occur over conformity to specifications, quality, timing, or cost of research. One source of disagreement, even in the face of explicit proposals, is the fact that the agency preparing the proposal is technique- and task-oriented while the client is use- and result-oriented. This difference is widely cited as a cause of poor communication between researchers and users. For this reason, experienced research agencies seek to learn as much as possible about end-use of the data by reviewing the problem in its entirety and providing specifications in terms of results, not efforts.

Nevertheless, work may be done according to specifications and still fall short of the client's expectation. Under such circumstances, it is presumed that the contractor is entitled to payment, however grudging; but the client may not be willing to pay.   As in other industries, where disputes occur the outcome often depends on the circumstances.   Some aggrieved clients pay as a means of dismissal; sometimes they withhold until sued, knowing that most creditors prefer to settle out of court.   Lawsuits are not unknown in the industry; arbitration has also been used, but rarely.   Such instances underscore the need for both parties to explore the problem to be solved and understand how research will be used before commitment to the project is made.

FIELD INTERVIEWING

One type of contractual relationship requires separate discussion because of the distinctive problems it presents.   The interviewing function, carried out largely by housewives on an intermittent and part-time basis, presents a cottage-industry structure virtually unique in the highly organized and controlled world of modern marketing.

This anomalous structure arises from need, most of it intermittent, at specified times and widely diversified places.   Some interviewers perform repetitive services, but most fieldwork is for custom projects.   Few work directly for the client or user of information.   Sometimes they are engaged by central agencies which maintain contact and control with interviewers throughout the country; most often they are engaged and directed by local supervisors, many of whom work out of their homes.

Validation.   One set of ethical problems arises from the loose organization of fieldwork, because it is so difficult to check and evaluate interviewer performance.   Except for central location telephone interviewing which can be monitored, the field interviewer is largely on her own.

It is usually considered a client prerogative to validate interviews, which means the ultimate user of the data can check on the research agency and the agency, in turn, on the field contractor.   There is also logic in assigning the verification function to a neutral organization, and contract specialists exist. One trade association has also established a validation service intended to build up performance records on individual interviewers, but the movement has not made much progress to date.

Unfortunately, in seeking control over quality, most attention has been given to simple verification—making sure that the interviewer made the call and spoke to the designated individual, rather than taking the trouble to go further and gain insight into the quality of the interview, the feasibility of the task, and the adequacy of training.   This is an ethical matter, in part because some students of fieldwork operations believe that much of the difficulty in fieldwork is caused by cumbersome interviews, complicated or poorly written instructions, tight deadlines, and inadequate instructions.   Consequently, client responsibilities are overlooked if the only check is on the interviewer's mere presence.   Further, it is alleged that much validation is conducted in such a way as to undermine the morale of the interviewer and the confidence of the respondent public.   One association [14] has developed a manual on validation procedures which takes these factors into consideration.

Pirating.   Since most interviewers have no steady employment and are free to accept or refuse jobs from any research organization or local supervisor, there exists the possibility of pirating.   A local supervisor performs a valuable function simply by having access to able and willing interviewers.   Her clients, often research agencies, may engage her to conduct projects in the course of which interviewers become known to them.   Thus, they are in a position to make direct overtures in the future.

Since access to the interviewers, and sometimes their training as well, is a proprietary asset of the field agency, it is unethical for its client to circumvent the contact without assent. Even if there is no supervisory function to be performed, ethical users will usually arrange to go through the initial supervisory contact in reaching local interviewers, perhaps paying a recruiting fee rather than a supervisory one.

As with most ethical principles, there are borderline instances. For example, if the client decides to recruit on his own through public means, such as newspaper advertising, most researchers would agree that he is entitled to recognize and engage interviewers he met through a supervisor if they respond to his ad independently.

Payment. It should be superfluous to state that bills should be paid in full and on time. However, local supervisors and interviewers complain that they are often victimized in this respect; that an agency will request special treatment requiring extra expense and then renege at the time of payment, or arbitrarily reduce bills submitted in good faith, or—more rarely—fail to pay at all. This seems to come about because some agencies operate on too small a margin, are undercapitalized, and will accept work involving large-scale interviewing at a low markup. Squeezed between low budgets and tight deadlines, they will cut corners, knowing that field personnel have no practical way to compel payment. Some agencies, in turn, claim that interviewers or local agencies pad their bills and that the only practical way to curb this is to cut some bills arbitrarily, perhaps to comply with an average cost of other markets.

Even where there is no question of the amount, local field agencies and small research firms may pay interviewers only after they receive payment from the client. Since client companies tend to pay research bills, like other bills for merchandise and service which carry no discount, on a 30-day basis or longer, the interviewer often waits as long as six or eight weeks for payment. Thus the individual interviewer often carries the burden of financing the project for the variety of functionaries upstream, including the ultimate client. To date, the industry has shown little disposition to change this anomalous situation.

QUALITY

Besides quality control in fieldwork, discussed from a methodological point of view in Section II, Part B, Chapter 8, there are ethical implications in the way work is designed and executed.

Design. Marketing research has been plagued almost from its inception by preoccupation with technique to the exclusion of utilization. This is partly because of the nature of the individuals attracted to the field, partly because of its multidisciplinary origins, and partly because in a gadget-minded economy practitioners sometimes find it easier to sell—and clients find it more agreeable to buy—an ingenious method than to develop a rigorous line of reasoning between data to be obtained and action to be taken. Thus technique sometimes appears as an end in itself.

As in the medical profession, so in marketing research techniques tend to rise and fall in popularity as new discoveries are made and old ones are discredited and then rediscovered. Like his medical counterpart, the research practitioner must decide whether to administer the newest discovery or stick to more conservative treatment, sometimes in the face of demands by a client who has read glamorous accounts of an innovation but nothing of its limitations. Or, conversely, the practitioner may believe that he has no mastery of a technique needed to deal with a problem and must decide whether to disqualify himself or use some other approach.

This raises the question whether the research practitioner is bound to advise what is best for the client, regardless of self-interest, which is often regarded as the mark of a true profession. However, it is difficult to classify marketing research as a profession, since it has no formal standards for entry and no legal recognition. Further, there is no restriction on advertising and promotion as in true professions. Therefore, occasional rhetoric to the contrary, marketing research is a business in which each negotiating party acts in self-interest—including the self-interest that some researchers find in advising clients professionally.

Despite the lack of a recognized professional requirement, there remains a trade ethic more difficult to define that is implied in all business relationships in which a buyer puts his trust in the seller's expertise. In this, the research practitioner may be no different from the butcher, the auto mechanic, or the appliance salesclerk who is free to promote what and how he will but whose role often changes in response to the question "What do you recommend?" There is good reason to argue that a practitioner is bound to place a client's interest ahead of his own when he feels he is trusted, but otherwise he may assume that the research buyer is able to decide what is best and to purchase accordingly. Thus, relationships may vary among clients and research agencies, with the latter acting sometimes as vendor, sometimes as professional.

The question of competitive versus negotiated proposals is relevant to this point. When a firm must bid against others, it is natural to push its own specialty, if it has one, or to provide technical embellishment for a proposal in the hope of differentiating it from competition. On the other hand, if negotiations are conducted with a single firm, it is likely to give unqualified attention to solving the client's problem rather than to making a successful bid. Professionalism in this sense can be encouraged in some instances by replacing the proposal with purchase of consultation from a firm which can then feel free to recommend that no research be conducted or that it should be conducted by another firm with appropriate expertise.

Description. As in many other fields, quality in marketing research relates not only to design but also to execution. There are numerous opportunities for quality controls, from interviewing through processing, which differentiate high-quality from inferior work. However, except for repetitive studies like those of syndicated services, it is seldom known which controls are worth the cost of application in a given situation. There is therefore a subjective element in designating quality standards, and sometimes a competitive element as well.

It is almost literally true that there are no good or bad marketing research techniques—only appropriate and inappropriate ones. It will be observed that codes of ethics in the field do not specify what is standard research practice since this depends on the circumstances and purposes of the study. But all codes require a clear statement of methodology. Hence questions of ethics are resolved by providing full disclosure of what is to be done or what has been done, leaving judgment on merit to the reader or user.

Frequently, even statements of method do not suffice to describe quality. For one thing, it is as possible to obfuscate quality with too much description as with too little. Further, terminology is not precise or uniform. An area probability sample, for instance, does not indicate a fixed proportion of initially designated respondents and almost never includes true representation of inner-city slum dwellers. A representative sample of retailers in a store audit necessarily excludes units of chains which refuse to cooperate.

Similarly, statements of method and evaluation tend to ignore error of the nonsampling variety because it is generally impossible to measure. And even sampling error is, with commendable exceptions, stated as though the sample were truly random and unclustered, which is practically never the case in face-to-face interviewing. Even a simple specification like number of interview callbacks is imprecise, since there is no simple way to report the extent to which attempts were varied by time of day or day of week to complete interviews with difficult-to-reach respondents.

The situation is not likely to improve greatly under present conditions because research on quality controls is usually ad hoc and difficult to generalize. Furthermore, much of what is known is not made public. Under the circumstances, what to disclose and how remains a matter of judgment, based largely on who the audience is likely to be. The ethical challenge is "Will the reader come away with an understanding of what was done and with a fair impression of the accuracy and limitations of the findings?"

THE INTERVIEW RESPONDENT

To the extent that marketing research depends on interviews, the survey respondent is, as stated earlier, a natural resource which must be protected against exploitation if the industry is to survive. At a time of growing concern with consumer rights and public interest, the industry must be increasingly conscious of public attitudes toward the interview and measures of protection for publics interviewed.

Ethical considerations may be grouped into two major headings: those concerned with obtaining the interview and those for protecting the respondent after the interview has been obtained.

Approach. At an elemental level of ethics is the question of sheer inconvenience and imposition on those we seek to interview. To what extent does the survey interviewer invade privacy, disturb the respondent, take up his time? That respondents are free to refuse is not a satisfactory answer if they are brought to the door or roused to answer telephones; nor is the right to skip replies to troublesome questions much consolation to the person who regrets having answered them after the fact.

On the other hand, there is much evidence that most people approached enjoy an opportunity to give their opinions to a respectful listener, perhaps sensing that this represents a form of playback giving recognition to the individual in a largely impersonal society.

Thus, respondent gratification as well as respondent convenience are primary considerations if we are to expect the public to answer our questions. To work with representative samples, the industry must have access to respondents of all kinds, yet this accessibility is already curtailed. As stated, commercial samples seldom include accurate representation from inner-city slums. Similarly, many apartment buildings are closed to interviewers; unlisted telephones are unavailable for telephone surveys except through the more cumbersome means of random digit dialing.

Even more severe in its implications is the fact that some entire communities restrict interviewing, generally included under local antisolicitation ordinances. Spokesmen for marketing research oppose such prohibitions, of course, but some do not oppose licensing interviewers if rates are not punitive, especially if it will serve to differentiate the legitimate interview from sales solicitation. Indeed, field agencies often notify local police and Better Business

Bureaus of each survey undertaken so that householders may check credentials of those who ring doorbells or telephones. Some agencies routinely hand or mail a notice to each survey respondent, thanking him for the interview and indicating the essential differences between a survey and a sales call.

This distinction is further supported by the direct sales solicitation industry, whose code of ethics, in turn, prohibits any approach which suggests that the salesman is "making a survey." The extent of this abuse is indicated by a 1963 survey of nearly four thousand adults, showing that 27 percent of a national probability sample had at some time been approached for a survey interview by someone who, in fact, was trying to sell something. And a large national research organization reported that half of its 747 interviewers polled in a survey said that some respondents reported within the year 1969 an attempt by a salesman to pose as an interviewer. Half also answered yes to the question, "Have you ever been refused an interview because the respondent thought you were trying to sell him or her something?"

While codes uniformly proscribe selling under the guise of interviewing, there is no accepted standard of honesty within the interview itself. No existing code so much as mentions the subject, although as of this writing one has it under review. Following the pattern of much academic psychological research, some of which depends on ingenious deception of experimental subjects, survey researchers have used many different disguises when necessary to obtain the interview.

Granted that most marketing research surveys depend on respondent naïveté and would fail of their purpose if respondents were fully informed, there are varying degrees of deception. These range from inevitable vagueness in presenting the subject matter when requesting an interview to outright falsification; for example, offering a selection of nonexistent premiums in order to conduct a realistic concept test without the expense of making items under consideration.

There is no consensus among researchers on where to draw the line. At one extreme is the view, rarely advocated, that ethics compels complete disclosure of purpose when a respondent is asked for the interview, even if this means the end of most survey research as we know it. At the other extreme are those who condone any white lie if no harm results to the respondent. The question is sometimes resolved by telling nothing but the truth, rather than the whole truth. In practical terms, this means using general phrases such as, "We're making a survey about what housewives think of different products," without biasing the result by indicating at the outset which products or brands are the subjects of inquiry.

When validity of results so often depends on concealing the purpose of a survey, the respondent has no way to judge whether cooperation is in his interest. It would therefore seem to be an ethical requirement that those who answer in good faith be protected against testifying to their detriment. Thus, for instance, a retailer who agrees to answer questions about his product lines should have confidence that the survey is being conducted for a manufacturer and not by another retailer whose competitive position would be unwittingly enhanced by willing respondents.

In short, if researchers reserve the privilege of a concealed approach, they must assume ethical responsibility for the questions: "Will anything detrimental to the respondent occur as a result of his willingness to respond?" and "If this respondent did know the purpose, would he still be inclined to answer?"

Anonymity. If codes are silent on the subject of honesty toward respondents in the course of gaining an interview, they are unanimous and emphatic on protection of anonymity afterwards. It is unethical by any standard to divulge the content of any interview so that it can be traced to a given respondent.

Like other simple principles of this kind, the declaration of anonymity requires interpretation for particular situations. First of all, it is never taken to mean anonymity from the research agency for possible callback. As indicated earlier, respondents are automatically subject to verification calls. In panel or longitudinal studies, they are also subject to reinterview. It is also common for a broad and brief survey to be conducted to screen individuals for an intensive follow-up interview.

In some purportedly anonymous mail surveys, questionnaires are precoded to permit subsequent classification according to source of names or respondent characteristics or merely as a convenience to permit follow-up of nonresponse without waste of mailing to those who have already replied. The one-way mirror and the concealed tape recorder also yield more information to the researcher than the respondent knows he is giving when he consents to reply. Such practices are not covered by existing codes as long as the information so obtained is used only for research purposes. However, the ethical issue is often raised and the acts condemned on the grounds that they are essentially deceptive even if no abuse of information occurs. More pragmatically, it is argued that if the industry permits such practices, the fact will eventually become known to the respondent public which will thereupon tend to refuse interviews.

Another aspect of the anonymity stricture involves those who see the results. Obviously, interviewers themselves are privy to individual replies, as are those in the research organization who process questionnaires. Like their counterparts in law and accounting firms, they are impressed with the requirement of confidentiality as part of their job training. A borderline case arises when a client requests original questionnaires from a research agency that has compiled the data. Some research firms take the position that original interviews are a research tool and that only composite findings belong to the client. Others hold that all work paid for by the client is his property but take steps to delete identifying information such as respondents' names and addresses before yielding them. Another position is taken by those who will yield complete interviews to a fellow member of the research fraternity on a client staff but not to management executives.

All these policies have the same end—to protect respondent anonymity; but they represent different degrees of confidence in clients versus degrees of caution in protecting respondents. In some cases the decision may vary with the type of survey. If results are to indicate sales potential such that individual respondents have indicated receptivity to purchase, they represent a greater temptation for sales follow-up and therefore may be guarded more closely than if replies merely give attitudes toward a company, its products, or its advertising.

A question is sometimes raised whether it is ethical to disclose that a person was interviewed at all, while respecting confidentiality of what he said. As already indicated, a client is generally assumed to have the right to verify interviews if he wishes. Similarly, in studies of closed populations, such as a club membership or a trade study, it can be important in assessing results to know which individuals or firms are represented in the replies, although to reveal this necessitates taking extra precautions in reporting results to insure that specific replies cannot be traced to individual respondents.

A special case occurs in studies for use in legal cases, such as a survey of trademark identification for use in an infringement suit or a study of retail practices in antitrust proceedings.   Legal ethics are quite different from survey research ethics and, unless notified to the contrary, lawyers will expect to take depositions or even subpoena respondents whose answers make them potentially favorable witnesses.   In at least one instance, a lawyer interested in evidence of trademark confusion designed a survey and shopped around in several cities for interviewing firms willing to violate the ethics of the field. Where he failed, he engaged individuals previously unacquainted with interviewing procedures who thus had no way of knowing the ethical implications of what they were doing.

This instance shows dramatically that there is no way to enforce ethics of anonymity among those who will not voluntarily respect it.   On the contrary, the law has a right to subpoena questionnaires, interviewers, and even respondents, so there is a question of survey researchers' ethical responsibility in the face of legal action which does not recognize the interview as privileged.   A few survey researchers, like their medical and journalist counterparts, have indicated willingness to face contempt charges rather than reveal contents of individual interviews, but to date none has been put to that test.

Where identification of individual opinion or experience is needed for legal evidence, for testimonial advertising, or even for the benign purpose of locating dissatisfied customers to rectify complaints, ethical conflict can be avoided simply by an open approach in the name of the client.   Since no ethical code questions the right of acknowledged solicitation, information can be openly sought and used if requested in the name of a law firm seeking evidence or a seller checking his customers.   Only when information is sought for "research" or as part of "a survey" is anonymity an ethical obligation.

USE

In an age of increasing technological specialization, we can no longer rely on an informed general public to pass judgment on the uses of invention.   There is less disposition than in decades past to say that science and technology are neutral and conscienceless servants of an abstract public will.   Increasingly, the medical researcher will be held accountable for his drugs and the physicist for his nuclear weapons.

If ethics dictate that an individual survey respondent should not be asked to supply information to be used against his best interest, does not the same apply to the general public?   Is research to be used, by exploiting their weaknesses, to the detriment of consumers who reply to questionnaires?   While similar questions are increasingly directed at the entire marketing system, researchers have a more immediate responsibility because they reserve the right to work behind a screen when soliciting cooperation in answering survey questions.   As stated previously, it is ethically untenable to reward such response with exploitation.   Practically, if the public senses that such is the consequence of replying, doors will refuse to open and researchers will have lost their indispensable natural resource.   Such refusal has long been advocated by some labor unions in resisting employee attitude surveys which they feel may be used to their detriment.

Interpretation of this ethical principle inevitably reflects one's outlook on the function of the marketing system generally.   If a survey is conducted to see whether the consumer is willing to pay a higher price for some commodity, the consumer advocate will say it smacks of exploitation; but perhaps the price would rise in the absence of such information, so by conducting the survey there is as much chance of holding the price down as raising it. In any case, the aggressive marketer will say that in a competitive system he is entitled to get all he can and that competition will bring the price down if it gets too high. The same conflicting viewpoints apply to studies for determining whether consumers can distinguish high quality from low or for ascertaining which product attributes to emphasize in advertising. It is more difficult to justify the social utility of studies to determine which package of given contents looks largest or which size of units within the package encourages greatest consumption, yet such aims are within the legitimate scope of competitive marketing activity. What appears as exploitation to some may be regarded by others as merely the give and take of the marketplace.

Regardless of individual decision in such ethical matters, the research industry is in a uniquely responsible position to interpret public attitudes toward the marketing system and to anticipate discontent as it occurs in a rapidly changing consumer outlook. As one practitioner has observed, in performing its feedback function, research can serve as the conscience of marketing.

A special case of ethical responsibility occurs when research findings are used for advocacy of a position. This may occur in the public sector, as when research findings are used in zoning, antitrust, trademark infringement, or deception hearings; or in private advocacy, as in measurement of the size and quality of an audience reached by an advertising medium for use in sales solicitation. Here the researcher is in a category with other types of expert witnesses, from psychiatrists to structural engineers, in seeking an ethical middle ground between the requirements of abstract truth and responsibility for one's client under an advocacy system of law or of business competition.

All codes of ethics insist that the researcher take responsibility for his findings and for the way they are used, at least to the extent that they are made public. At the same time, there is nothing against presenting findings in the best light for the client when this can be done without distortion and without withholding information. For example, a summary of findings might be presented with age or income combinations that help to prove the client's case, provided that all detail is shown in the methodology which permits other combinations to be requested by the adversary.

Similarly, one would not select an interviewing medium, sample design, or eligibility criterion merely to favor the client's case. When such a selection is made for sound operational reasons, it should be properly described, including any anticipated biasing effects on results. Clearly this is a matter of judgment and conscience. For example, if it is decided to interview by telephone for reasons of speed, economy, and sample dispersion, a statement of method should clearly indicate how omission of nontelephone homes and unlisted telephones might be expected to affect findings; however, a summary of results might merely state that "a telephone survey shows. . . ."

In short, when findings are used in advocacy situations, the researcher is justified in stating his client's case positively while at the same time providing the opposition with the basis for challenge if it wishes.

However, where there is no designated opposition, as in an advertisement claiming public acceptance of a product, the researcher has full responsibility for stating the findings in simple and unbiased terms which do not rely on the rebuttal of adversary procedures. His client has the option of saying nothing if facts do not provide sufficient support for the position claimed. This ethical position is necessary to prevent such obvious deceptions of an earlier era in research history when brand use was studied immediately after distribution of free samples or blind-taste-test results were reported in situations in which the client's product was distributed in greater frequency than that of his competitors.

All codes make the research agency responsible for statements made in its name, but one association recently added an amendment to place further responsibility on the researcher: he must reserve right of approval of statements based on his findings whether or not his name is used and he must take steps to correct misimpression if statements are released without his approval. These requirements prevent circumvention of ethical conduct which sometimes occurs simply by a client's neglect of his obligation to consult his specialist. Under this interpretation, the research organization is no longer dependent on the client's willingness to act ethically but is given full responsibility for published use of his data.

To oblige the research firm to disclaim misleading use of its findings removes an incentive for its client to publish findings without clearance. Still, in practice, the research agency is usually at a disadvantage in gaining attention for its disclaimer of a message that has already appeared in an advertisement or press release. Even with the greatest skill, an attempt to impugn another's statement may backfire and could be regarded as mudslinging which brings no credit to either the well-intentioned firm or the industry.

Action is more difficult still for the employed researcher when he sees his findings misused, either through biased reporting in an advocacy situation or in exploitation of the buying public. If his registered objections are ignored or overruled, how long and how far should he press until he feels impelled to resign and perhaps even expose? In business as with government and other organizations, there are no accepted rules to indicate how far the conscience is sheltered by institutional anonymity and at what point the individual must assume responsibility for his own acts.

REFERENCES

1. Arnold, Rome G., "The Interview in Jeopardy," *Public Opinion Quarterly*, vol. 28, no. 1, Spring 1964.
2. Baxter, Richard, "An Inquiry into the Misuse of the Survey Technique by Sales Solicitors," *Public Opinion Quarterly*, vol. 28, no. 1, Spring 1964.
3. Biel, Alexander, "Abuses of Survey Research Techniques: The Phoney Interview," *Public Opinion Quarterly*, vol. 31, no. 2, Summer 1967.
4. Bogart, Leo, ed., *Current Controversies in Marketing Research*, Chicago: Markham Publishing Co., 1969.
5. ————, "The Marketer as a Radical," American Marketing Association, *Annual Meeting Proceedings*, June 1968.
6. Carlson, Robert O., "The Issue of Privacy in Public Opinion Research," *Public Opinion Quarterly*, vol. 31, no. 1, Spring 1967.
7. Case, Peter, "Catching Interviewer Errors: ARF's FACT Service," American Statistical Association, Annual Meeting, December 1970.
8. Crawford, C. Merle, "Attitudes of Marketing Executives toward Ethics in Marketing Research," *Journal of Marketing*, vol. 34, no. 2, April 1970.
9. Ferber, Robert, Donald F. Blankertz, and Sidney Hollander, Jr., *Marketing Research*, New York: Ronald, 1964, chap. 20.
10. Hartmann, Elizabeth L., H. Lawrence Isaacson, and Cynthia M. Jurgell, "Public Reaction to Public Opinion Surveying," *Public Opinion Quarterly*, vol. 32, no. 2, Summer 1968.
11. Hollander, Sidney, Jr., "Should the AMA Encourage Arbitration of Trade Disputes?" *Journal of Marketing Research*, vol. 2, no. 4, November 1965.
12. Kelman, Herbert C., "The Human Use of Human Subjects," *A Time to Speak*, San Francisco: Jossey-Bass, 1968, Chap. 8.

13. Kornhauser, Arthur, "Are Public Opinion Polls Fair to Organized Labor?" *Public Opinion Quarterly,* vol. 12, no. 3, Fall 1948.
14. Manfield, Manuel N., *Standards Committee Study of Validation Practices,* American Association of Public Opinion Research, April 1968.
15. Thomas, Mary, unpublished manuscript, Cambridge, Mass.: Department of Social Relations, Harvard University, May 1970.

Exhibit 1

Code of Ethics
for the Marketing Research Association

IN CONSIDERATION of my membership in the Marketing Research Association and its goal of improving survey practices at all levels of market research, I, the undersigned, do pledge:

1. To maintain high standards of competence and integrity in marketing research as further outlined in the MRA Recommended Procedures.
2. To exercise all reasonable care to observe the best standards of objectivity and accuracy in the development, processing, and referral of marketing research information.
3. To protect the anonymity of respondents and hold as privileged and confidential all facts or opinions of a specific nature concerning any individual respondent, within the limits of a particular study.
4. To not refer to my membership in this organization as proof of competence.

For Research Practitioners and Field Supervisors

5. To thoroughly instruct and supervise all interviewers under my charge in accordance with Clients' specifications.
6. To keep in confidence all research data or other information obtained for clients, as well as processes and techniques of research considered confidential by clients.
7. To observe the right of ownership and hold as confidential all materials received from and/or developed for clients.
8. To make available to clients at the conclusion of an assignment such detail on research methods and techniques as may reasonably be required by the client, providing this does not violate the confidence of respondents or other clients.
9. To reject all assignments which would be inconsistent with the aforementioned principles.
10. To avoid any activity purported to be Marketing Research, but which has as its real purpose the sale of merchandise or services to all or part of the respondents.

For Users of Marketing Research

11. To encourage the observance of the aforementioned principles among research contractors and field service organizations.
12. To exercise all diligence to insure the operation of research programs consistent with the aforementioned principles.

Exhibit 2

Code of Professional Ethics and Practices*

We, the members of the American Association for Public Opinion Research, subscribe to the principles expressed in the following code. Our goal is to support sound practice in the profession of public opinion research. (By public opinion research we mean studies in which the principal source of information about individual beliefs, preferences, and behavior is a report given by the individual himself.)

We pledge ourselves to maintain high standards of scientific competence and integrity in our work, and in our relations both with our clients and with the general public. We further pledge ourselves to reject all tasks or assignments which would be inconsistent with the principles of this code.

THE CODE

I. *Principles of Professional Practice in the Conduct of Our Work*

    A. We shall exercise due care in gathering and processing data, taking all reasonable steps to assure the accuracy of results.

    B. We shall exercise due care in the development of research designs and in the analysis of data.

        1. We shall employ only research tools and methods of analysis which, in our professional judgment, are well suited to the research problem at hand.

        2. We shall not select research tools and methods of analysis because of their special capacity to yield a desired conclusion.

        3. We shall not knowingly make interpretations of research results, nor shall we tacitly permit interpretations, which are inconsistent with the data available.

        4. We shall not knowingly imply that interpretations should be accorded greater confidence than the data actually warrant.

    C. We shall describe our findings and methods accurately and in appropriate detail in all research reports.

II. *Principles of Professional Responsibility in Our Dealings with People*

    A. The Public:

        1. We shall protect the anonymity of every respondent. We shall hold as privileged and confidential all information which tends to identify the respondent.

        2. We shall cooperate with legally authorized representatives of the public by describing the methods used in our studies.

        3. We shall maintain the right to approve release of our findings, whether or not ascribed to us. When misinterpretation appears, we shall publicly disclose what is required to correct it, notwithstanding our obligation for client confidentiality in all other respects.

    B. Clients or Sponsors:

        1. We shall hold confidential all information obtained about the client's general business affairs and about the findings of research conducted for the client, except when the dissemination of such information is expressly authorized.

        2. We shall be mindful of the limitations of our techniques and facilities and shall accept only those research assignments which can be accomplished within these limitations.

    C. The Profession:

        1. We shall not cite our membership in the Association as evidence of professional competence, since the Association does not so certify any persons or organizations.

        2. We recognize our responsibility to contribute to the science of public opinion research and to disseminate as freely as possible the ideas and findings which emerge from our research.

* Offprint from *The Public Opinion Quarterly*, Volume 24, Fall 1960.

Exhibit 3

Marketing Research Code of Ethics

The American Marketing Association, in furtherance of its central objective of the advancement of science in marketing and in recognition of its obligation to the public, has established these principles of ethical practice of marketing research for the guidance of its members. In an increasingly complex society, marketing management is more and more dependent upon marketing information intelligently and systematically obtained. The consumer is the source of much of this information. Seeking the cooperation of the consumer in the development of information, marketing management must acknowledge its obligation to protect the public from misrepresentation and exploitation under the guise of research.

Similarly the research practitioner has an obligation to the discipline he practices and to those who provide support for his practice—an obligation to adhere to basic and commonly accepted standards of scientific investigation as they apply to the domain of marketing research.

It is the intent of this code to define ethical standards required of marketing research in satisfying these obligations.

Adherence to this code will assure the users of marketing research that the research was done in accordance with acceptable ethical practices. Those engaged in research will find in this code an affirmation of sound and honest basic principles which have developed over the years as the profession has grown. The field interviewers who are the point of contact between the profession and the consumer will also find guidance in fulfilling their vitally important role.

For Research Users, Practitioners and Interviewers

1. No individual or organization will undertake any activity which is directly or indirectly represented to be marketing research, but which has as its real purpose the attempted sale of merchandise or services to some or all of the respondents interviewed in the course of the research.

2. If a respondent has been led to believe, directly or indirectly, that he is participating in a marketing research survey and that his anonymity will be protected, his name shall not be made known to anyone outside the research organization or research department, or used for other than research purposes.

For Research Practitioners

1. There will be no intentional or deliberate misrepresentation of research methods or results. An adequate description of methods employed will be made available upon request to the sponsor of the research. Evidence that field work has been completed according to specifications will, upon request, be made available to buyers of research.

2. The identity of the survey sponsor and/or the ultimate client for whom a survey is being done will be held in confidence at all times, unless this identity is to be revealed as part of the research design. Research information shall be held in confidence by the research organization or department and not used for personal gain or made available to any outside party unless the client specifically authorizes such release.

3. A research organization shall not undertake marketing studies for competitive clients when such studies would jeopardize the confidential nature of client-agency relationships.

For Users of Marketing Research

1. A user of research shall not knowingly disseminate conclusions from a given research project or service that are inconsistent with or not warranted by the data.

2. To the extent that there is involved in a research project a unique design involving techniques, approaches or concepts not commonly available to research practitioners, the prospective user of research shall not solicit such a design from

one practitioner and deliver it to another for execution without the approval of the design originator.

For Field Interviewers

1. Research assignments and materials received, as well as information obtained from respondents, shall be held in confidence by the interviewer and revealed to no one except the research organization conducting the marketing study.

2. No information gained through a marketing research activity shall be used directly or indirectly, for the personal gain or advantage of the interviewer.

3. Interviews shall be conducted in strict accordance with specifications and instructions received.

4. An interviewer shall not carry out two or more interviewing assignments simultaneously unless authorized by all contractors or employers concerned.

Members of the American Marketing Association will be expected to conduct themselves in accordance with the provisions of this Code in all of their marketing research activities.

Exhibit 4

The following "position papers" were developed by the Ethics Committee of the Market Research Council during 1967–1968 and were adopted by an overwhelming vote of the membership as official positions of the Market Research Council in July 1968.

These papers are intended as a first step, not a final step—the thought being that additional papers on other subjects may be added in the future or that these papers may be amended as future developments might warrant.

The Respondent's Right to Privacy

The goodwill and cooperation of the public are necessary to successful public opinion and market research. Actions by researchers which tend to dilute or dissipate these resources do a disservice both to the research profession and to the public.

By its very nature, research must in some measure invade the privacy of respondents. The ringing of a respondent's doorbell or his telephone is an intrusion. If he agrees to participate in a study, his private world of attitudes, knowledge, and behavior is further invaded.

Researchers should recognize that the public has no obligation to cooperate in a study. Overly long interviews and subject matter which causes discomfort or apprehension serve to reduce respondent cooperation. When such interviews cannot be avoided, efforts should be made to explain the reasons to the respondent and to mitigate his anxieties to the extent possible.

One of the greatest invasions of the privacy of respondents is through the use of research techniques such as hidden microphones and cameras. When such a research technique has been used, a respondent should be told and, if the respondent requests it, any portion of the interview that serves to identify the respondent should be deleted.

Even after the respondent has been interviewed, his privacy is endangered while his interview is being coded, processed, and analyzed. Research agencies have the same responsibility as other professional groups to take all reasonable steps to insure that employees with access to these data observe the canons of good taste and discretion in handling this information.

Since public opinion and market researchers must infringe on the privacy of the public at several stages of the research process, it is unlikely that any set of rules or code of ethics can prevent abuses by unscrupulous or careless researchers, even though such abuses are inexcusable. The best hope of maintaining an

attitude of goodwill and cooperation among the public will depend on researchers':
1. Being constantly mindful of the problem.
2. Keeping in mind the recommendations above.
3. Doing everything in their power to inform the public of the benefits of market and opinion research.

Maintaining Respondent Anonymity

Good and accurate research requires obtaining honest and frank expressions of opinions and beliefs. Respondents are more likely (a) to participate in a survey and (b) to speak honestly and frankly if they believe that they will remain anonymous and will not be called to account for their expressed opinions or stated behaviour. For this reason, every researcher should do everything in his power to protect the anonymity of the people he interviews unless he obtains their permission to reveal their names.

This does not preclude follow-up contacts for further research or for verification purposes. However, if there seems to be a reasonable possibility that there will be contacts for any other purposes, it is incumbent on the researcher to warn the respondent of this possibility.

The researcher should be willing to make reasonable efforts to provide evidence on the authenticity of the interviews he has made, providing this does not subject the respondents to harassment.

Disclosure or Release of Survey Results

Implicit in the nature of surveys is the fact that they purport to reflect the opinions or behaviour of the population under study. It is the obligation of the researcher to present survey results in such a manner that they do not give a distorted or biased picture of his findings. The client also has this same obligation in reporting survey findings. When others report his findings, the researcher has an additional responsibility to make all reasonable effort to see that they, likewise, present the results impartially.

It is not incumbent on the researcher to insist on an "all-or-nothing" policy in the release of his findings. Only part of the results may be released provided this part does not give a distorted picture of the subject matter it covers.

If the client misuses, misstates, or distorts a survey finding, the researcher should release such other findings and information about how the data were obtained as will put it in proper perspective. Client-researcher agreement prior to release would minimize misunderstandings in this respect.

Any release of findings should include appropriate information about objectives, sample, research techniques, the name of the research organization, etc. that will be helpful in evaluating the results.

Buyer-Seller Relationships

A successful marketing research study is a joint operation involving a research company and its client. It requires mutual respect and confidence between the two parties and imposes certain obligations on each of them.

The buyer of research services has the right to make sure that the work he has contracted for meets all the specifications. He has the right to examine all operations of the research company to see that they are being carried out in the manner agreed upon. However, in doing so he should respect the research company's obligations to the public in matters of anonymity and invasion of respondents' privacy.

The buyer should recognize that the research company is a professional organization engaged in collecting marketing and/or opinion data. The buyer should not, therefore, ask or expect the research company to violate any of the suggested rules of procedure covered elsewhere in this statement. The buyer should not publicly identify the research agency in any release of findings, implying the endorsement of the research agency without prior agreement from the agency.

It is understood that in seeking a research agency the buyer may request proposals from more than one research company. However, generating ideas and planning research designs to solve specific problems are an important part of the services a research agency offers. The buyer, therefore, should not (1) lift ideas from one proposal and give them to another research agency or (2) ask for a proposal from a company which he knows has little or no chance of obtaining his business, unless he so informs them in advance. Soliciting bids for the purpose of obtaining free ideas which will be turned over to another bidder, or for purely technical compliance with a company's policy of obtaining competitive bids, does a disservice to the research firms involved, reflects on the integrity of the client company, and generally lessens the professional level of the research profession.

Kickbacks, rebates, and other "inducements" similarly destroy the professional character of research and should not be solicited, offered, or agreed to.

The research agency has the obligation to express, as they become apparent, any reservations about the usefulness of the proposed research in solving the client's problem. The agency also has the obligation, of course, to do the study contracted for in the manner agreed on. No additional questions designed for another purpose should be included in interviews done for a client without the client's knowledge and consent.

Unless otherwise agreed on by the seller and the buyer, the study report and the compiled tabulated data on which it is based are the property of the buyer. No by-product information should be sold to another buyer unless express permission is obtained from the original buyer.

In the course of conducting research, the researcher may become privy to confidential information relating to the client company. The researcher should not reveal any of this material to any outsider at any time.

Information to Be Included in the Research Firm's Report

Every research project differs from all others. So will every research report. All reports should nonetheless contain specific references to the following items:
1. The objectives of the study (including statement of hypotheses).
2. The name of the organization for which the study is made and the name of the organization that conducted it.
3. Dates the survey was in the field and date of submission of final report.
4. A copy of the full interview questionnaire, including all cards and visual aids used in the interview; alternatively, exact question wording, sequence of questions, etc.
5. Description of the universe(s) studied.
6. Description of the number and types of people studied:
   a. Number of people (or other units)
   b. Means of their selection
   c. If sample, method of sample selection
   d. Adequacy of sample representativeness and size
   e. Percentage of original sample contacted (number and type of call-backs)
   f. Range of tolerance
   g. Number of cases for category breakouts
   h. Weighting and estimating procedures used

Where trend data are being reported and the methodology or question wording has been changed, these changes should be so noted.

On request—clients and other parties with legitimate interests may request and should expect to receive from the research firm the following:
   a. Statistical and/or field methods of interview verification (and percentage of interviews verified)
   b. Available data re validation of interview techniques
   c. Interviewing instructions
   d. Explanation of scoring or index number devices

Chapter 10

Use of Marketing
Research Contractors

LAWRENCE D. GIBSON   *General Mills, Inc., Minneapolis, Minnesota*

Most marketing research departments use outside contractors to develop the bulk of their data. The company researcher concentrates on assisting marketing in problem definition before projects are undertaken and in data analysis at project completion. Although project management may be controlled by the client, most operating details are handled by the supplier.

There is great variation in the performance of suppliers, and frequently clients are disappointed, for example, when reports are late, findings are not clear, or costs seem excessive. Often suppliers feel that they have been treated unfairly. Projects are poorly defined; operating decisions are abruptly changed. Unforeseeable problems arise. Despite hard work, their efforts may not be appreciated and their profit margins may vanish.

Detailed project work with suppliers is often avoided by client researchers. To many, this area of research seems less glamorous and exciting than meetings with advertising agency or senior marketing management. And the problems continue to recur with distressing regularity. Yet good working relationships with research contractors are essential to the success of the client marketing research department. Competent, surprise-free project management is extremely valuable and requires concentrated client effort.

The purpose of this chapter is to discuss certain ways of looking at the client-supplier relationship and certain operating procedures which have proved useful, that is, useful in reducing client disappointment, in improving the supplier's lot, and, one hopes, in increasing the profitability of the marketing research investment.

Simple rules can improve the working relationship significantly. These involve the client buyer's as well as the supplier's acceptance of obligations. Failure to do so may result in some temporary advantage for one or the other but will inevitably cause the relationship to deteriorate.

CLIENT OBLIGATIONS

The client must realize that the supplier has to make a profit if he is to stay in business. Excessive demands for client service, unexpected technical requirements, and, very commonly, indecision and abrupt changes in project direction increase costs—costs which ultimately the client must pay. Obvious as this may be, clients frequently act as if payment of such costs is a reasonable subsidy from supplier to client.

The client owes the supplier and himself a full and open statement of the problem, explication of constraints in time and money, and any other insights that may help the supplier anticipate costs and problems. Anything less means that the supplier runs unreasonable profit risks and the client runs unreasonable risks of project failure.

The supplier needs client counsel as the project proceeds. Problems frequently develop that could not have been anticipated. An interviewing supervisor may become ill, a computer may go down, or public disturbances may occur in an interviewing area. In such situations, the client must help the supplier by reviewing alternative solutions to the problem and by jointly determining the best available alternative action.

Finally, the client has an obligation with respect to new or different study designs which a supplier may develop. This obligation is particularly awkward, since general knowledge seems so desirable and is so traditional in academic circles. Yet the different insights into and ways of looking at problems developed by a given supplier may be his stock in trade. Freely giving supplier A's ideas to supplier B or "shopping" for cheaper ways to implement A's idea may make it unprofitable and thus impossible for supplier A to continue developing new approaches that are so badly needed. And, whether supplier B's "improvements" and/or "efficiencies" are solid gains for the client is frequently questionable.

SUPPLIER OBLIGATIONS

A supplier must promise practicable results. In selling research services, the temptation is very great to promise somewhat more, to stretch the truth, to appear ingenuous. Unfortunately, the overpromises are quickly discovered, with permanent damage to any long-term relationship.

The supplier must also do precisely what he has promised—certainly no less, perhaps a little more. Attempts to bypass agreed-on procedures and to conceal such attempts are not uncommon—particularly when the buyer has unfairly jeopardized the supplier's profit margins. However, if the client is experienced, such deceptions will ultimately be discovered.

When practical problems arise, the supplier must invite the client's help in their solution. If the client is to be helpful, the supplier must open all project details to client study. Only the supplier and the client openly working together can decide the best course of action when changes seem desirable or when it proves impossible to fulfill the original project commitments.

TYPES OF RELATIONSHIPS

Most relationships between clients and research suppliers are of one of two forms. Long-term continuing contracts are used by suppliers of syndicated media and product-movement data. These relationships arise from data requirements shared by many clients who have a willingness to standardize in order either to cut costs or receive more data.

These relationships have tended to work well. Locating suppliers is simple since only a limited number of suppliers tend to dominate supply of specific kinds of data. Negotiations are relatively straightforward. Suppliers have specific contract terms and tend to be firm in price negotiations. Most operating problems have been successfully worked out over the years.

Problems in this relationship relate to inflexibility. Clients often see their continuing-data suppliers as unwilling to adapt to meet specific client requirements. The supplier feels that he is unable to modify data without agreement among several of his clients—and this of course can be quite difficult.

Ad hoc project relationships are used for most individual studies and present the greatest difficulties. In principle, the problems seem solvable. The client should specify his problem and his requirements. The supplier should be specific in his proposal and pricing. After final negotiations, the work should be performed as agreed on.

In practice, this procedure frequently breaks down. Each project tends to have unique features, and these provide opportunities for misunderstanding. Client and supplier seldom specify all project details. Unexpected events occur, and the client or supplier may fail to abide by his basic obligations.

The ad hoc nature of the relationship does little to lessen the impact of such problems. For example, it may make it difficult for the client research representative to secure more money for a project which has run into trouble or make it difficult to recover the cost differential on the next project by voluntarily accepting a higher charge. Similarly, the supplier cannot be content to accept added costs and reduced profits from a given project, hoping that he will make it up next time. This is especially true if he believes that the added costs were beyond his control.

The implication of competitive bidding (or at least comparison) by constantly seeking many proposals subtly affects the supplier's proposals. He may find himself decreasing such visible proposal elements as time and money by reducing the quality of less visible elements—sample design, number of sampling points, interviewer training, and so forth.

When a buyer secures proposals from several research firms for an ad hoc project and selects one for the job, he generates nonreimbursable costs for the unsuccessful firm. In turn, this may force a supplier who sells to such a buyer to raise prices to cover the costs of unsuccessful proposals. Alternatively, he may refuse to invest time and effort in proposal preparation for such a client.

In other words, the relationship itself may contribute to instability, and it may not integrate client and supplier interest. Thus, contradictory though it may seem, ad hoc relationships work best when they are honored in form but violated in substance. When the client explicitly or implicitly assures the supplier some volume of work, the climate in which there can be sound resolution of practical operating problems is created. Unfortunately, the informality of such assurances sometimes works to the supplier's disadvantage.

Other types of relationships for nonsyndicated services are being explored by many clients. These include consulting fees, profit guarantees, and research agency relationships. Each is designed to guarantee the supplier a profit and a more stable relationship to secure his total commitment to the client's long-term interest.

Under certain special conditions, quite different relationships have been designed and successfully used. Some years ago, a client embarked on a major continuing advertising research program. Technically, the project was demanding. Between twenty and thirty thousand long, complex interviews were to be conducted each year and analyzed by a unique method. Politically, it was complex. The project was managed by the client plus representatives from his five different advertising agencies. Strategically, it was important. This was the first attempt to routinely control this sensitive function, and it had been approved by the highest level of the client organization.

After agreement on the project specifications, discussions about the supplier's profit were held. The annual cost and profit margin was specified and defined, subject to audit. While the project was to be budgeted annually, the supplier was not given a formal contract.

Largely because of these arrangements, the relationship has continued for seven years, with productive results for the client and the supplier. Profit and prestige made the research extremely desirable to the supplier. There was no way profits could be improved. The supplier was forced to do everything possible to strengthen the study technically, to help the client use the data, and to assist in the resolution of political problems. Any failure to perform could immediately jeopardize the relationship. Such experimentation in the forms of relationship is commendable and should be encouraged.

CONDUCTING A PROJECT

The first step in conducting a project is problem definition. While the process of problem definition is outside the scope of this chapter, its importance cannot be overestimated. Only when the problem is defined, the facts to be gathered are specified, and the relationship between facts and the problem is clear does the project have a reasonable chance of success. Most project failures can ultimately be traced to insufficient thought during problem definition.

Problem definition cannot be delegated outside the company. The client researcher is peculiarly positioned to clarify the problem openly and thoroughly with his marketing management. An outside researcher can sometimes help the process, but primary responsibility must be accepted internally.

A significant element of problem definition is setting time and cost constraints. To some researchers, these specifications have seemed in conflict with their role as purchasing agent. "If the outside supplier knows how much a client is willing to pay, he may not develop the lowest-cost proposal." This client attitude is wasteful and shortsighted at best.

The traditional purchasing-agent attitude toward price assumes that a completely standardized item is being purchased. Under these circumstances, price competition should be encouraged and the lowest possible price should be sought. But a marketing research project is seldom, if ever, completely standardized or specified. Frequently, the buyer is not even aware of all the details of sample design and execution, interviewer training and validation, and data reduction and processing. This makes the bidding process irrational.

There are only two ways in which research can be designed. The client may specify what data he needs and the level of accuracy required. This permits the outside firm to design to the specifications with whatever costs result. Or the client may specify how much time and money he is willing to spend for the data. The outside firm can then develop the most accurate possible data for the fixed cost. However, there is no way for the research firm to simultaneously optimize data accuracy and minimize project costs.

Formal decision analysis may be used by the client to determine the value of the information to him. With the appropriate model, the risks and profitability of the alternative marketing decisions can be analyzed to determine the value of perfect information and of sample information. However, so far we know how to use this procedure in only a limited number of cases, and unless the models have already been programmed, the procedure can be quite cumbersome.

Most often the client must set time and cost constraints by judgment. His judgment process will, one hopes, parallel decision analysis by focusing on risks and profitability of alternative marketing actions and risk reduction derived from additional data. But the issues must be faced; appropriate time and cost constraints must be agreed on; and these decisions must be communicated to the outside research firm.

One research firm has adopted a very useful alternative in this area. Instead of giving specific quotations, this supplier provides cost formulas for each project. The formulas show the relationship between key elements of design (sample size, number of treatments, and so on) and the final costs. This permits the client researcher to make his own decisions on design elements and to set his own cost.

Often, thorough problem definition will dictate the appropriate research design. What data are needed may be obvious; and with time and costs set, the supplier's proposal preparation can be straightforward. In other cases, the problem may be so new or unusual that considerable creativity may be required from the supplier. Here, proposal preparation may require several meetings before a final design can be set.

If the outside supplier is new to the client, operating procedures and research standards should also be specified. How will the questionnaire be approved? Will the field instructions be subject to approval? Does the client plan field trips? Will the final report be subject to review and rewriting? Such details may seem obvious to a particular client but may be quite new to a new supplier.

Similarly, client research standards may be new to the supplier. What, if any, interviewing validation is expected? What quality control is expected in data processing? Is key punching to be verified? What level of inconsistent codes may be cleaned in the computer? Again, early client specification can eliminate serious subsequent misunderstandings.

The form shown in Exhibit 1 has proved useful to at least one client in summarizing this material. Notice the emphasis on problem definition, the specification of time and cost, and the routine copies for appropriate people.

SELECTING THE SUPPLIER

Frequently, the problem definition, taken together with previous experience, will suggest the appropriate supplier to the client researcher. Where this fit between past experience and the current problem is good, there should be no standard requirement for alternative proposals.

On the other hand, it may be necessary to consider several suppliers for a project. Here, trade contacts can be especially helpful. Review of supplier presentations at trade meetings may help locate potential suppliers. Finally, simple visibility as a research buyer will attract prospective suppliers.

In any event, the client researcher will find that each supplier has special areas of expertise and that no single supplier will be able to handle all his problems. Industrial research projects frequently require technical background in the subject area. Also, a limited number of key contacts may be essential

Control Number: _____

GENERAL MILLS, INC.
MARKETING RESEARCH PROBLEM DEFINITION

Product (s): _____

Date: _____ _____

Title: _____

To: _____
(Research Agency Proj. Director/
Mgr. Test Mkt. Res. & Special Analyses)

cc: Mktg. Res. Dir. - GP (2-1 cc Att. to MR:4)
Originator - (2)

From: _____
(Marketing Research Manager)

1. Problem & Background

2. Decision Involved

3. Critical Information Considered

4. Criteria for Interpretation Considered

Exhibit 1.   General Mills, Inc., marketing research problem definition.

to the project. Accordingly, industrial research firms tend to develop special backgrounds in particular trades.

Consumer research suppliers specialize in syndicated services or in ad hoc projects. Though suppliers of syndicated services have made attempts to branch out into project work, these attempts have usually failed. Some ad hoc project suppliers specialize in formal projects with expertise in experimental design, sample design, and tight operational controls. Others concentrate on less formal investigations with the personal creativity of the key individuals in the firm being their special stock in trade. But few consumer research suppliers are competent in both formal and informal areas.

Some clients find the use of approved supplier lists helpful. Formal approval of a supplier encourages continuity of the relationship. In turn, the client can take the time and effort to thoroughly investigate the outside firm. However, these systems can be cumbersome, the approvals can quickly become outdated, and the system may discourage new suppliers.

A personal visit to the supplier's office can be useful for explaining fully the nature of the project. It also provides an opportunity for discussion with the proposed project director, field supervisor, data reduction supervisor, and statistician. This gives the client a much deeper understanding of the outside firm's capabilities.

After formal proposals have been received, they must be thoroughly reviewed. This process frequently suggests the need for additional discussions about project details. The newer the problem or the supplier, the greater is the need for these discussions.

A recurring problem during negotiations is responsibility for errors in estimating yields of qualified respondents. Whenever respondents must be specially qualified, a certain proportion of the initial field contacts will be wasted on unqualified respondents and the supplier must make some prediction of his yield of qualified respondents. The cost implication of errors in estimating are seldom serious when qualified respondents are a significant portion of the population. If a yield of 40 percent is estimated and the actual proportion is found to be 35 percent, the effect on supplier costs is nominal. However, when qualified respondents are few, the effect can be disastrous. For example, if the estimate is a 6 percent yield but only 3 percent of the contacts prove to be qualified respondents, the supplier may find his field costs 25 to 50 percent over the budget.

Previous studies using the same respondent qualification may provide evidence to resolve this problem; but when a new qualification is used for the first time, a financial risk is incurred and must be accepted either by the client or by the supplier. A few clients demand that their suppliers accept this risk. Most feel, however, that since the definition is theirs, they have a better basis for the estimate than the supplier. Thus they make the estimate and accept the risk of error.

Final supplier selection is often straightforward once these steps have been taken. One supplier will seem to understand the problem better or will uniquely possess certain vital technical capabilities.

When the choice is not clear, more detailed examination must be made of the project requirements and the capabilities of the various alternative suppliers. The special requirements of trade knowledge, heavy fieldwork, or complex analysis should be listed out. Then each supplier's strengths and weaknesses on each project characteristic should be rated. Such an analysis may suggest ways in which a supplier's weaknesses can be buttressed with in-house skills or those of other consultants.

Recommendations from the supplier's other clients will occasionally be helpful. However, individual client operations and expectations differ sharply, and the same supplier may be highly regarded by one client and poorly rated by others. Such discussions should be detailed and focus on the specific skills, strengths, and weaknesses of the supplier.

A simple decision on the basis of different quotations is seldom justified. When two suppliers' quotations differ dramatically and inexplicably, at least two of the three interested parties do not understand something. One supplier is including cost-generating components not included by the other. Intelligent evaluation of the two quotations requires that the client know exactly what components have been included or excluded from each quotation.

Project Number__________

MARKETING RESEARCH PROJECT PROPOSAL AND EXPENDITURE APPROVAL

Requested By:__________ cc: Dir Mktg Res; Dir-Cons Res; Interview Supv — Originator - (2)

Title:__________ Product(s):

Date:__________ Control #:

1. Problem and Background

2. Decision Involved

3. Method and Design

4. Criteria for Interpretation

5. Mktg Res Budget: $_____ Est Proj Exp ± $500: $_____ Balance $_____
6. Individual who must finally approve recommended action:__________
7. Report to be delivered by__/__/__ if authorized by__/__/__ and test materials shipped by__/__/__.

_____ Time & Cost (Supplier/Proj Dir) Commitments were Confirmed By	Proposal Submitted By (Mktg Res Mgr)	Proposal Authorized By * (Attach MR#2 & See Below)

ROUTE TO:	RECOMMEND APPROVAL OF RESEARCH EXPENDITURE		
	Initials	Date	REMARKS (Attach note if more space is needed)
Product Manager	____	__/__/__	
Marketing Manager	____	__/__/__	
Director of Marketing	____	__/__/__	
	____	__/__/__	
Coord of Mktg Budget	Research Expenditure Approved By ** _____		Date_____
Originator - - Mktg Res Dept			

When Project Expense Amounts to:	**Research Expenditure Must be Approved by - -	*Problem & Design Must be Authorized by - -
$1,499 or less	Product Manager	Mktg Res Dir-GP/Corp
$1,500 to $9,999	Marketing Manager	Mktg Res Dir-GP/Corp
$10,000 to $24,999	Director of Marketing	Mktg Res Dir-GP/Corp
Over $25,000	VP Adv & Mktg Serv/Gen'l. Mgr.	Director of Mktg Res

Exhibit 2. Marketing research project proposal and expenditure approval.

Formal written authorization of the project internally and externally is essential. The risk of misunderstanding is too great to skip this step. The forms shown in Exhibit 2 have been useful in ensuring precise communication of project objectives, methodology, and commitments to all parties concerned.

OPERATING THE PROJECT

At the start of a project, it is good practice to review again the study objectives and design with operating personnel of the outside firm. The degree of client participation desired, the standards for the research, and particularly the decision-making authority of specific individuals of the client and research firms should also be specified.

As planning proceeds, detailed breakdowns of time and cost will become available and can be specified on such forms as those shown in Exhibits 3 and 4. It is then simple to follow project progress by periodic contacts to check whether steps have been accomplished according to plan and whether costs are developing as anticipated.

Discovering project problems as they develop permits flexibility in overcoming the problems. If the field mailing is three days late or if field cutoff must be extended, it may be possible to provide extra coders to make up the time— if the delay is spotted immediately.

If delays do force a postponement in the final report or presentation, this postponement is most acceptable when announced early. A two-day postponement can be quite serious if announced two days before a formal presentation. The same postponement might have been unimportant if announced three weeks earlier.

Field materials should be meticulously reviewed and approved. Questionnaires, field instructions, and especially respondent stimulus materials deserve very careful study. All the data collected will be a resultant of these materials, and there is seldom a way to correct the data for mistakes in the original materials.

Client field trips during the project can be useful. They can deepen the client's understanding of project findings, particularly in the case of group interviews. Also, they can provide special insight into the operation of the outside researcher. A field briefing session in which the client observes messy stacks of papers and materials in the supervisor's living room, hears the supervisor say, "Read the instructions, honey. Any question? Thanks," after which all interviewers leave, is an experience not easily forgotten. The contrast is

---

(To be attached to departmental file copy of the MR #4)

MARKETING RESEARCH PROJECT BUDGET ESTIMATE

Project Title:

Project Number:

Total Budget Estimate

Account Number	Expense Description	Expense	Amount of Invoice	
001	a. Research House	$____	$____	$____
	b. JFBRC	$____	$____	$____
002	Interviewing (incl labor & Misc. Costs)	$____	$____	$____
003	Product (incl. shipping)	$____	$____	$____

Exhibit 3.   Marketing research project budget estimate.

Project Control Number _____

PROJECT MASTER CONTROL FORM

Project Title: Date:

                                                   Product:

Client in Marketing: Project #:

Supplier: Contact: Phone #:

Special Remarks:

For Ref.	Working Days	Function	Orig. Date	Rev.	Rev.	Rev.	Date Completed
a	_____	☆ Request Received	____	____	____	____	_____
b	_____	☆MR#2-Problem Defin. to Supplier with Requir., 2 copies of MR#3 & MR#3a	____	____	____	____	_____
c	_____	☆MR#3-Project Proposal from Supplier	____	____	____	____	_____
d	_____	☆MR#4-Project Approval sent to Mktg.	____	____	____	____	_____
e	_____	☆MR#4-Project Approval returned	____	____	____	____	_____
f	_____	☆Ltr. of Authorization to Supplier	____	____	____	____	_____
g	_____	☆Field Work Start	____	____	____	____	_____
h	_____	☆Field Work Close	____	____	____	____	_____
i	_____	☆Preliminary Report to Marketing	____	____	____	____	_____
j	_____	Rough Draft of Final Report & Oral Presentation ‚from Supplier	____	____	____	____	_____
k	_____	☆Preliminary Report to Marketing	____	____	____	____	_____
l	_____	☆Final Written Report from Supplier	____	____	____	____	_____
m	_____	☆Cover Letter (cc to D.D.) & Final Report to Marketing	____	____	____	____	_____
n	_____	☆Oral Presentation (if requested)	____	____	____	____	_____
—	_____	_____	____	____	____	____	_____
—	_____	_____	____	____	____	____	_____

☆ If any of these functions are delayed causing a:

1. Time Change--The pink "Notice of Exception" is required to be completed and forwarded.

2. Time & Cost Change--MR#6 is required to be completed, forwarded and returned with approval signature.

Exhibit 4.   Project master control form.

particularly striking with those supervisors who operate in a very businesslike fashion, allowing time for the interviewers to study the materials, leading detailed discussion of the implications of the instructions, conducting sample interviews, and specifying how problems should be handled.

Prior review and approval of data reduction plans frequently eliminate costly and embarrassing reprocessing delays. Open-end coding, weighting plans, and final table layouts are the key areas for study.

Finally, the client researcher should schedule time for review of written reports, tabulations, and formal presentations before their submission to marketing management. This provides an opportunity for clarification and modification of the material to improve the likelihood of total client acceptance of the project. Obviously, this review should not be used to censor the supplier.

Ref.	Date	Reason for Change in Schedule

*   *   *   *   *

Project Invoice Payment Summary		Estimated Project Expense:			
Date	Supplier	Invoice #	Inv. Date	Amount	Balance

Exhibit 4.   Project master control form. (Continued)

Where legitimate disagreements develop on the findings or their interpretation, the supplier should be encouraged to inform the client of his opinions, but in some less formal way than the report itself. Cover letters or final personal interviews are frequently used for this purpose.

Frequently, modification in the original design or plan may seem appropriate or prove necessary during the conduct of the project. This is when the detailed planning and control pays off. Only when objectives and plans were thorough and specific, the client has carefully monitored project progress, and decision-making authority was specified can the changes be intelligently considered and the correct decisions made. After changes are agreed on, they should be confirmed in writing.

PROJECT EVALUATION

No project should be considered complete without formal evaluation of the supplier's performance. This reduces the likelihood of repeating problems that occurred. It provides specific guidance on how to work with the supplier, helps define his area of specialization, and, if necessary, documents a decision not to reemploy him.

Traditionally, quality control of the fieldwork has been the important part of supplier evaluation. In the field, interviewers receive little direct supervision, and opportunities for sloppy or even fraudulent work are obvious. Although there is considerable evidence to suggest that most interviewers are conscientious and honest, concern about fieldwork remains prevalent.

Availability of long-distance WATS lines has simplified quality control of the fieldwork. After a supplier has provided the questionnaires, identified by interviewer, it is easy to draw a sample and conduct a short follow-up interview using several questions from the original questionnaire. The answers can then be checked for consistency and appropriate reports prepared. Generally, it is good practice to supply the research firm with complete copies of this validation material.

In evaluating results of validation, two points must be remembered. First, total consistency between the original and validation interviews is not possible. Even so factual a question as respondent's age will not always be the same on the follow-up. After all, one week after the original interview, 2 percent of respondents are one year older. Not only time but simply using the different interviewing medium can cause considerable difference in response—especially to attitudinal questions.

Second, field validation should not be associated with a punitive client attitude. Such an attitude offends the conscientious research supplier and is seldom rationally justified. Significant levels of sloppy or dishonest fieldwork usually result from client or supplier errors. It is when instructions are poorly written and difficult to understand that they are not followed. It is when questionnaires are long and redundant that interviewers shorten the interview and simply fill in "obvious" answers. It is when quotas are excessive that respondent qualifications are ignored.

Less quality-control attention has traditionally been paid to data reduction. It has been assumed that the data, once received, were appropriately coded, keypunched, and computer-processed. However, this area is coming under increasing study, with evidence that it may justify as much concern as the fieldwork itself.

Finally, the client researcher should have a form on which his overall appraisal of the supplier's work can be recorded and communicated to the supplier. Exhibit 5 is a form which is simple and easy to use and also provides coverage of the project's key aspects.

Analysis of these reports defines the supplier's strengths and weaknesses, shows where he must be watched and helped, and documents where he can be relied on. It may even be desirable to prepare summary image profiles such as those shown in Figure 1.

SUMMARY

Good supplier-client relations are essential to a successful research department. Such relations require that the client adopt a constructive viewpoint and do his share of the project preparation as well as participate in the actual operation of the project.

The levels of control and degree of client involvement suggested in this chapter may seem excessive to some researchers. There are some projects so simple, so repetitive, or so well understood that the procedures are unnecessary. It is true that frequently projects do "luck out." But client researchers have traditionally erred on the side of loose control, and they have been correctly blamed for the distressing frequency with which projects go awry. If only one project in five goes more smoothly or only one each year avoids disaster, the use of these procedures on all projects will have been justified.

An additional benefit of detailed client involvement is the client's deeper understanding of the substantive findings of the research. If he has been involved, he may be able to answer questions immediately that would otherwise have taken days. He should be able to avoid misinterpretation of the findings by those less knowledgeable than himself. He will be able to provide much better judgment to the application of the study findings.

Finally, repeated client involvement will deepen the client's understanding of a basic aspect of his chosen profession.

Project Control Number _____

SUPPLIER EVALUATION FORM - Surveys   Date:

Supplier: Project:
Project Description:
                                         Project #

(Evaluate each item below and mark with "X". See Implement. Sect. as needed.)	Distinguished Himself	Okay	Source of Concern	Doesn't Apply
1. Marketing Insight				
2. Fundamental Design				
3. Questionnaire Construction . .				
4. Field Supervision				
5. Tab Design				
6. Analysis.				
7. Report Organization				
8. Quality of Report Writing . . .				
9. Quality of Presentation Materials				
10. Personal Presentation				
11. Delivery Time				
12. Cost Estimate				

Explain Items checked as "Distinguished Himself" and "Source of Concern" (use reference numbers).

Signature: _____

Title: _____

Distribution
  Supplier
  File - G. Plant
  Report - with letter of transmittal to Marketing Research Director
  Report - with letter of transmittal to L. D. Gibson

Exhibit 5. Supplier evaluation form—surveys.

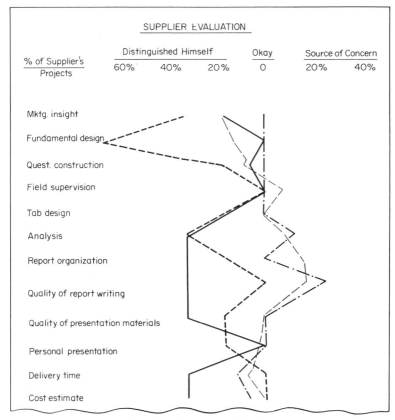

Fig. 1.   Supplier evaluation.

BIBLIOGRAPHY

Buell, Victor, "When and How to Use Marketing Research Agencies," and "How to Work with Marketing Research Agencies," *Handbook of Modern Marketing,* New York: McGraw-Hill, 1970.

Clay, Reg, and John Parfitt, "Buying Research From Only One Agency," *ADMAP,* September 1970.

Manfield, Mannie, "Status of Validation in Survey Research," in Leo Bogart, ed., *Current Controversies in Marketing Research,* Chicago: Markham Publishing Co., 1969.

McBurney, William J., Jr.: "Market Research and the Consultant," *American Marketing Association Proceedings,* June 1965.

"Using Marketing Consultants and Research Agencies," Studies in Business Policy, no. 120, *The Conference Board,* 1966.

Williams, Robert J., "Make-or-Buy Decision for the Research Director," *American Marketing Association Proceedings,* June 1969.

Section Two
Techniques

Part A

Research Design

Chapter 1

Problem Delineation

WILLIAM F. O'DELL *Consultant, Charlottesville, Virginia*

Delineating a marketing problem is basically a very simple thing. Ask a few elementary questions, and the answers, whether yes or no, dictate further actions.

Of course the implementation may not be so simple, but let's start with a list of these elementary questions:

1. Have the marketing alternatives been clearly stated, and at some point is there agreement on them among the decision makers?

2. Is there agreement on the basis for selecting one alternative over the others; in other words, have acceptable criteria been developed?

3. Would a "wrong" decision have serious profit consequences?

4. Is there serious disagreement among the decision makers on which alternative to adopt?

If the answers to all four questions are yes, marketing research information is needed to reduce the chances of making the wrong decision. If the answers to the latter two questions are no, little or no information is required. It's that simple, and it makes no difference whether you are a marketing researcher or the marketing decision maker.

Problem definition becomes sticky in most business situations because both marketing and marketing research planners often flounder in answering the first two questions. The decision alternatives are not well defined. Often the "correct" decision is not placed on the discussion table in the form of a possible course of action. Even when all the decision choices are listed with clarity, the basis for selecting one rather than another is not agreed on. In such instances, uncertainty and disagreement among the decision makers continue despite the gathering of vast amounts of marketing research data. Unfortunately, this condition frequently leads to a faulty decision.

How can intelligent problem delineation enhance the chances of making the "right" marketing decision? How can this initial, but vital, phase of the decision-making process be approached so that the chances of a more profitable decision are heightened? Let us explore the subject somewhat more thoroughly, starting with an understanding of the role of information in marketing decisions. This is an area that must be thoroughly understood by the marketing researcher and the marketing decision maker alike.

All information or data, regardless of size, shape, or form, are of two basic types: *environmental* and *actionable*. The former can be defined as information that aids the decision makers in *formulating* possible courses of marketing action. Such information can be encountered by chance, or through the systematic gathering of data in a highly sophisticated fashion. In either event, it helps describe the marketing *environment* in which an industry, company, product class, or brand exists. Actionable data, on the other hand, are sought only after the marketing-decision alternatives have been formulated.

ENVIRONMENTAL INFORMATION

If the company has well-defined marketing goals or objectives, environmental information tells how well it is doing and whether any change should be considered. The information aids in locating specific actions to be contemplated and placed on the table for discussion. An example will help.

A certain company has recently introduced a new product and it has stated its marketing objective in terms of desired minimum sales by the end of a given period, say one year. Data obtained from some syndicated research service reveal sales to be far short of that required sales goal. These sales data are *environmental* in nature. They describe a situation. The information does not tell what to do, but the need for *some* action becomes obvious. This, after all, is what a problem really is: a situation that calls for a change, a condition that is unsatisfactory and suggests correction. Environmental information, then, reveals such situations—conditions that need correction or present opportunities. It also may provide clues to the *external* reasons (for example, competitive sales trends, broad economic factors) for the situation.

In the preceding example, the impending failure to reach the stated sales goal was revealed by environmental data. Certainly something must be done; but what step to take is not readily apparent. Many possible courses of action are suggested by this revelation of inadequate sales. Of course the company could reexamine and perhaps alter the objective. If not that, it could drop the brand. It could continue the product, but modify it in some way. It could increase the marketing support, or change the price. The list of possible actions is unending. But the *environmental* data per se do not tell what to do. That responsibility is reserved for *actionable* data.

Here is a great opportunity for the marketing researcher to be creative—not so much in the development of innovative research techniques as in the occasion to develop environmental data that will reveal new situations not known or perceived by the marketing people. Creative market segmentation, meaningful imagery data, new product uses, buyer motivations, cognitive dissonance, and competitive-product acceptance are but a few of the opportunities for the marketing researcher to develop new environmental data that will lead the marketing decision makers to new marketing horizons, to previously unthought-of marketing alternatives. In many firms, this role of the researcher is paramount. Its vital contribution cannot be understated, for marketing creativity is often closely related to the researcher's innovativeness.

If the marketer can readily differentiate between environmental and actionable data, he has already learned something about the precision of such data. Environmental information need *not* be highly precise. It merely uncovers a situation and perhaps suggests *possible* ways of correcting it. This is why clinical motivational research data are often viewed as environmental in nature. The data result not from *measurement* but from research, which need not be precise to be useful. Thus, motivational information of this type contributes largely to the creativity so essential to successful marketing. Motivational research reveals new courses of possible action that have not been considered and that perhaps have not even been thought of. Normally, the findings uncovered by clinical motivational researchers are not supported by quantification from systematically or scientifically drawn population samples. And the nature of the interview often results in information obtained in a wide variety of interviewing techniques, precluding meaningful quantification. Moreover, motivational research findings are often nothing more than one or two interviewers' limited interpretations of respondent comments—often subject to the interviewers' bias.

None of these conditions detracts from valid use of such information. But such research does not tell the decision maker what to do; it simply poses some possible action choices. New action ideas are suggested. Creativity is stimulated. Dormant ideas are brought to life. Innovation becomes a reality. And all of this happens because some type of environmental data or information has been obtained—in one way or another.

So a significant phase in this entire area of problem delineation consists of recognizing the differences between environmental and actionable information. It is important that both the marketing decision maker and the researcher grasp this differentiation, for it aids considerably in determining the moves the marketer should take. If only environmental data have been obtained, the next step would most likely be development of the alternative courses of action for marketing. In many instances, however, additional environmental data are sought because the full picture was not initially presented. The additional data, it is assumed, will enable the marketing staff to prepare a more complete list of the decision choices for consideration.

Is there any rule that will aid the decision maker in recognizing environmental data? Yes. If the information is sought or comes to light prior to the formation of the marketing alternatives, it is environmental. But if the marketing choices have already been formulated and if data are being sought specifically to aid in selecting the "most profitable" alternative, then such information is actionable. Understanding this role of information or data is the first phase of problem delineation. Such an understanding tells the decision maker whether a problem exists—whether a change or adjustment is needed.

If the marketer knows that the problem is in the environmental stage, any definition of the problem would state that the next move is the posing of possible marketing alternatives. Creativity, speculation, innovativeness, and other such approaches stemming from one's imagination come into play so that all meaningful decision choices are on the decision maker's table.

ACTIONABLE INFORMATION

Once the alternative actions have been agreed on, the next stage is selecting the "most profitable" option. The problem delineator must fully recognize where he is in the decision-making process. Is there a complete understanding of the basis on which the decision will be made? Do the marketing people realize that selecting one alternative over others involves a prediction—a fore-cast that the one course of action opted will result in greater benefits than the others under consideration?

The understanding of the information function is essential to meaningful problem delineation. Disagreement among marketers on which course to adopt is a manifestation of uncertainty. Obviously, if there were no uncertainty, everyone would agree on which action to take, and there would be no decision problem. However, when decision makers disagree, some type of information is often needed to reduce uncertainty and the risk of making the "wrong" decision. This stage of the problem calls for a comprehensive understanding of actionable data.

At this point, the so-called Bayesian approach is useful. As the decision makers assess the alternatives, subjective "prior probabilities" are placed on each of the outcomes under consideration. These probabilities are stated on the basis of the information available at the time of the discussion, together with the experience and judgment of those involved in making the decision. In most instances, however, prior probabilities do not reach the table in such a formalized manner. Either there is agreement on what to do, or there is not —with varying levels of intensity of disagreement.

In general, the more serious the profit consequences of a "wrong" decision and the higher the level of disagreement among the decision makers, the greater the need for *actionable* data. The purpose of gathering such information is to aid in reducing uncertainty and the chances of making an unprofit-able decision.

DECISION CRITERIA

To the person charged with the responsibility of problem delineation, one thing must be unmistakably clear: The reasons for disagreement must be identified. Does the argument center on which of the alternatives to select? Or, as is often the case, does a debate occur because there is no clear statement regarding the *basis* on which the decision is to be made? To illustrate, let's assume that the issue is whether to commercialize a particular product. On what basis will the decision be made? Of course it involves a prediction, but a prediction of what? Profits, undoubtedly, because marketing decisions are usually based on maximization of expected long-run profits. But this need for prediction of profitability does not always lend itself to precise measurements in advance of the decision itself.

The problem delineator at this stage must recognize that some acceptable criterion is to be determined so that the decision makers themselves can at least agree on the basis on which the action is to be taken. If profitability over a given period is to be the criterion, it is necessary to predict sales so that total revenue can be forecast. From this prediction, the relative profitability of the two possible actions—to commercialize the product or not—can be assessed.

As mentioned earlier, it is seldom feasible to predict profits in a highly precise fashion. Nor does time always permit this. Is there some other criterion assumed or known to be highly correlated with profits? If so, the marketing research effort should be directed toward gathering the "substitute" data. For example, would consumer attitudes be an acceptable criterion? Can marketers assume a sufficient relationship between attitudes and actual purchase to risk using attitudinal data? These are issues in problem delineation—and marketing management and marketing research management must resolve them jointly.

MARKETING-FINANCE DECISIONS

Whether to introduce a new product is a decision involving alternative uses of corporate funds. If the product were not commercialized, the funds would be utilized in some other manner—in marketing or elsewhere. If they are not used in marketing, the forecast is that the funds will be more profitable if used in some manner other than in support of the new product. In other words, management must seek to maximize the return on investment.

These are *financial* decisions, and in a very real sense. But they have strong marketing overtones. If anything, such decisions are a blend of marketing and finance, and it behooves the problem delineator to recognize that the marketer should not abdicate his responsibility merely because a prediction of profits is involved. This is where the finance and accounting people, along with the marketing management and marketing research staff, join forces and work out a plan that will enable them to predict which of, say, two marketing alternatives—to introduce the product or not—should be adopted.

To say that profit will be the criterion is not enough. What levels of profit are required? What sales figure will produce that profit—at what selling price —when coupled with a given level of marketing investment? It follows that the *marketing research* responsibility is to design a study that will enable management to predict sales with the necessary degree of precision, keeping the profit consequences of a wrong decision in mind. How this measurement of predicted sales is to be obtained depends to a great extent on the experience and ingenuity of the researcher, coupled with the research facilities available to him. But this fact remains: A decision that involves alternative uses of corporate funds requires a sales prediction, so that revenue and profits resulting from the contemplated actions can be computed.

With consumer goods, sales predictions are often feasible through research facilities available to the researcher. Syndicated services and special household and store panels are already set up by research organizations. The joint use of these facilities by marketers reduces the user-cost to a reasonable figure, given the need for highly precise data when making marketing decisions that embrace the alternative uses of the company's financial resources. The industrial marketer faces a more difficult problem in that he seldom can place a new product on a simulation run. He cannot test-market the item because the cost precludes producing it in advance of full-scale marketing. Therefore he looks for criteria closely correlated to sales. One criterion might be stated intentions to buy among a sample of industrial prospects and customers, hardly a precise prediction of sales but perhaps sufficient for making the decision.

The worth of a particular decision criterion must be weighed in light of alternative criteria. Some measurement, assumed to be imprecise, may be the best available. The industrial marketer, in employing a non-sales criterion, is not too dissimilar from the consumer-goods marketer who must fall back on attitudinal information as a substitute for sales when time or other practical limitations are encountered.

Selection of appropriate criteria for the decision is one of the most crucial areas for the problem delineator. Does he really need a sales prediction (plus estimated revenue and profits) as the basis for making the decision? He probably does if the decision choices involve alternative uses of financial resources. However, the so-called pure marketing decision (with no financial overtones) rarely requires prediction of profits, although it is implicit that the "best" decision will always have a strong positive effect on profits.

"PURE" MARKETING DECISIONS

Let us look at a few *pure* marketing decisions. First, why are they called "pure"? Simply because no other business function is involved. Moreover, the cost of implementing any one decision is identical to the cost of implementing each of the other alternatives. For example, the cost of using advertising theme A or B is identical. Whether to allocate a portion of a fixed advertising budget to one medium or another costs the marketer the same amount of advertising money. (The cost of spending a million dollars in either television or newspapers is the same.) Whether to alter the formula of a product can be an identical cost decision, if the altered formula would cost virtually the same as the formula currently used. Of course, one could argue that the production or research and development people would enter the decision-making arena, and they might. But essentially, a product-change decision is a marketing decision—often an identical-cost marketing decision.

How does all this affect the type of decision criteria to be selected? If the objective is to maximize expected long-run profits, why not be interested just as much in sales, revenue, and profits as the criteria for the identical-cost decision as in decisions involving the alternative uses of corporate funds? There is one basic answer: no interest in predicting revenue. You can settle for some other criterion. In other words, in choosing between theme A and theme B, the *precise* effect on profits of using one theme over the other need not be predicted. It is essential only to determine which of the two themes is "better." It is not even necessary to know how much better (assuming there is complete agreement on the two themes as alternative courses of action). If one theme is "5 percent better," *and if only two themes are under consideration*, it matters not whether one is 5 rather than 25 percent better. Only the more effective one will be used, regardless of how much more effective it is.

Of course, what is meant by "better" becomes a critical issue for the problem delineator. In essence, the issue centers around the selection of the decision criterion—whether it be theme selection or any other identical-cost decision. On what basis will the decision be made? What should be the decision criterion?

The answer is closely related to the marketing objectives. What, for example, is the advertising expected to achieve? Of course the advertising goal is to increase profits, but this goal is usually too vague for most advertising efforts. To increase sales is an expected assignment of advertising, but in many, if not most, situations, advertising is assigned the task of achieving something short of actual sales—something that will affect a sales increase. For example, the advertising may be expected to create a given level of brand awareness, to change the attitude of nonusers toward the brand, to recruit new users, to broaden the scope of usage, to increase the flow of traffic into a dealer's place of business. The decision criterion, then, should relate to advertising's goals and be evaluated accordingly.

A list of possible criteria is infinite, but some of the more common measures are:

Awareness
Attitude
Stated intention to buy
Consumer purchase probabilities
Stated likes and dislikes
Recall, aided and unaided

Traffic flow
Coupon redemption
Simulated purchases
Sales
Readership-listenership-viewership
Circulation—sets-in-use

Data gathered to satisfy any of the criteria will rarely lead to a precise prediction of sales. There is a wide gap between attitude and purchase, and an even wider gulf between awareness and purchase. But any of the preceding criteria are appropriate for many decision choices when the cost of one marketing alternative is the same as others under consideration.

Problem definition for the marketing researcher, then, centers around data requirements. He faces two main issues: the nature of the data to be sought, and the required level of precision and reliability. To resolve these issues requires knowledge of the *marketing* decisions in the offing: making certain the alternatives are well defined, the profit consequences established, the practical limitations of data collection recognized, and the criteria for the decision agreed on. Any marketing researcher, in an attempt to define the problem, must equate his own activities with those of the marketer. They are inseparable in the sense that the researcher is expected to contribute to the efficiency of the marketing decision.

STUDY DESIGN

The researcher's definition of the problem will be an outgrowth of how well he resolves the preceding two issues. If he has established the nature and accuracy of the data to be collected, he now faces the task of determining *how* he will obtain the necessary information. "Defining the problem" could embrace a full statement of the study design. He has departed from the marketer, and now assumes the sole responsibility for determining how he can gather the required data at minimum cost. Any statement of the problem must describe how he plans to gather the data, and why this data collection method is appropriate. He has turned technician.

To this point, he has been engrossed in the marketing decision, talking with the decision makers about the marketing alternatives, decision criteria, profit consequences of the wrong decision, and levels of agreement among the decision makers. But this is past. He now devotes himself to his own discipline. The problem is one of drawing on his vast array of tools and techniques, of combining them so that meaningful and acceptable data emerge.

The marketing researcher, interestingly enough, is now in the same position as the marketer for whom he is conducting the study: he must develop his own alternative courses of action, but they are *research* alternatives. Moreover, he must designate appropriate criteria for the selection of these research choices in methodology. These decisions are under the researcher's control. They follow those made jointly with the marketer for whom the data are being collected. The marketer plans, states goals, develops marketing strategy, and works out marketing alternatives to achieve the goals. In so doing, he draws on the marketing researcher to provide him with necessary data. From the researcher's vantage point, any definition of the problem combines these marketing alternative courses of action with the need for data. This definition is a statement that should be supported by the marketing decision maker because he is part of it. However, if the data collection issues have progressed to the stage where only technical considerations remain, the researcher's statement of the problem stresses the relative efficiency of data collection and processing alternatives.

No one general rule governs problem definition. The researcher soon learns he must know precisely where he is in the total decision-making process—whether he is in the environmental stage where marketing alternatives have not yet been finally formulated, or in the actionable phase where data are sought so that the risk of a wrong decision is lessened. It matters not whether the decisions embrace marketing strategy with possible serious profit consequences, or pure marketing decisions which are sometimes narrow in scope. Is it a *marketing* problem, or is it a *marketing research* problem? If the researcher is confident of the answer to this question, he is well along in problem definition.

SUMMARY

The marketing researcher must become actively engaged in the discussion of the marketing problem if he is to employ his research techniques and tools efficiently. To design a study without full and complete knowledge of how the information is to be used risks the gathering of wholly inadequate information for the task at hand. But the more serious result is that a wrong decision is more likely to be made.

BIBLIOGRAPHY

Alderson, Wroe, and Paul E. Green, *Planning and Problem Solving in Marketing,* Homewood, Ill.: Irwin, 1964.

Buzzell, Robert D., *Mathematical Models and Marketing Management,* Boston: Harvard University Graduate School of Business Administration, Division of Research, 1964.

Halbert, Michael, *Meaning and Sources of Marketing Theory,* New York: McGraw-Hill, 1965.

Juster, F. Thomas, "Consumer Buying Intentions and Purchase Probability," *National Bureau of Economic Research, Occasional Paper 99,* New York: Columbia University Press, 1966.

Kepner, Charles H., and Benjamin Tregoe, *The Rational Manager,* New York: McGraw-Hill, 1965.

Kotler, Philip, *Marketing Management: Analysis, Planning and Control,* Englewood Cliffs, N.J.: Prentice-Hall, 1967.

Maier, Norman R. F., *Problem Solving Discussions and Conferences,* New York: McGraw-Hill, 1963.

Morris, William T., *Management Science in Action,* Homewood, Ill.: Irwin, 1963.

National Bureau of Economic Research, *The Quality and Economic Significations of Anticipations Data,* Princeton, N.J.: Princeton University Press, 1960.

O'Dell, William F., *The Marketing Decision,* New York: American Management Association, 1968.

Part A

Research Design

Chapter 2

Use and Appraisal
of Existing Information

CHESTER R. WASSON   *School of Business, Northern Illinois University, Dekalb, Illinois*

Existing information provides the foundation of all well-conducted research and constitutes a large part of the structure of subsequent analysis. The sole factual basis for problem formulation must be information that can illuminate the situation. The nature of already-available information tends to shape the research design and define the nature of any additional data to be collected. Most of the analysis and interpretation of any new information must usually lean heavily on available information for its meaning.

Such information comes in many forms and from varied sources: the large volume of myriad kinds of basic statistical information collected and published by federal, state, and local governmental bodies; other statistics published or otherwise made available by private and commercial organizations; special studies of many kinds undertaken by public, academic, and private organizations; the accumulated but unpublished experience of observant individuals in favorable positions; and the concepts and other theoretical structures which condense the research knowledge of various social and behavioral disciplines.

At times, a "good enough" decision can be reached by reorganization and reanalysis of these existing data, provided they are skillfully reanalyzed and reinterpreted. Such reinterpretation and appraisal are always wise because the data have been produced in a different context of time, place, and problem and are thus normally not in exactly the right form for a specific new use, nor always completely valid in the new context.

USING EXISTING INFORMATION IN PROBLEM FORMULATION

Existing information of some kind is the only possible basis for situation analysis which leads to problem formulation, as noted in the preceding chapter. Since the acuteness of that formulation depends on the quality, quantity, and nature of already-known data, the eventual efficiency and value of the research itself depend on the quality of the search for such data at this initial stage and the accuracy of the appraisal of their meaning for the problem being studied. An incomplete search or a misinterpretation of either the relevance or the meaning of existing information leads to wasted research and often to costly "wrong" decisions.

One obvious failure was the multimillion-dollar loss experienced by two American food processors who introduced quality dehydrated soups in 1962. The introduction was predicated on repeating the European sales success of one of the brands, and the decision was bolstered by apparently extensive product research in the American market. Unfortunately, that research disregarded the knowledge of at least one of these firms about the American use of soup—as a light emergency meal, largely for children. Moreover, available data on the two dehydrated brands already on the market indicated that neither brand was used primarily for soup, but rather mostly as a convenient dry flavoring for gravies and snack foods. Although the latter use meant modestly satisfactory sales for the two existing main brands, it did not presage a market of the intended size or one for gourmet quality. Consequently, a go-ahead was evidently based on a favorable finding about the mixes as soup bases and on the production of some flavors unsuitable for nonsoup uses.

The information initially available to the soup companies came from commercial consumer-diary operations and special surveys, but not all available information is so highly structured. Some of the more valuable sources may be general knowledge about industry practices and about behavioral concepts and theories.

A drug firm's research director used both these information sources in formulating a requested study into what had seemed a problem in salesmen recruitment and selection. When regional sales supervisors asked for headquarters help on how to choose a successful salesman, the sales manager confessed to the research director that he, too, would like an answer. He had tried all conventional answers, such as analysis of the personal backgrounds of good and poor salesmen, but had found no difference.

The research director started by reviewing his knowledge of industry hiring practices. All new salesmen, he knew, were pharmacology graduates because their knowledge of the pharmacopeia was considered important. He remembered that many of these graduates had originally hoped to enter medical school but could not make it. Since their sales jobs required working directly with physicians and instructing them in using the firm's pharmaceuticals, he reasoned that their past histories could create a feeling of inferiority in the detail situation. He then decided that the problem might be the interpersonal relationship in this situation, and accordingly hired psychologists to travel with a sample of salesmen and to observe what happened in the detail situation and in other personal contacts—for example, with receptionists and distributors. The resulting analyses led to development of a successful professional training program—not a change in the selection procedure.

The initial search for useful data inevitably yields a mixed haul of the irrelevant and the relevant in varying degrees of pertinence and quality. Accurate problem formulation involves sifting out the really irrelevant and systematically classifying and analyzing the data that seem to bear on the problem. One useful way of systematizing the process is first to group the available information by the marketing-mix aspect to which each item applies, that is, product, pricing, distribution, logistics, promotion, and consumer attitudes. Then, for insight into the problem being considered, each item should be labeled according to one of three value classifications: *negative* information, *positive* information, and *zero* information. The classifications are defined as follows:

Negative information indicates that the information need does not lie in a specific area or direction, but indicates no other specific direction in which the answer may lie. For instance, an analyst, studying possible oil-field uses for a temperature-control device, learned from oil-field distributors that they did not make the purchase decision, but he could not learn from them who did.

Positive information indicates a specific direction or market segment likely to yield part of a useful answer. A brewery concerned about its relatively low share in one major market discovered from sales analysis that its distribution was relatively weak in an important part of that market, indicating a need to study why its product was not stocked on the retail shelves in that market.

Zero information is seemingly related knowledge which furnishes no guidance of any sort, negative, or positive, in formulating the problem or in designing or analyzing the study.

Such a systematic classification of the data, arranged in tabular form, can do much to indicate the nature of the additional research which might be conducted. It will also help to point out any contradictions in what is assumed to be known, and to aid in focusing on the points needing closest appraisal. Thus it helps to determine the best research design.

EXISTING DATA AND RESEARCH DESIGN

Generally, the purpose of any research design is to fill gaps in existing knowledge. That design therefore tends to be a corollary of the analysis of available information. If the gaps are too wide and too many, the initial research must necessarily be exploratory, so that the researcher can define the problem more clearly before conducting anything highly structured in nature. By contrast, sometimes a skilled analytical reorganization of available information gives an answer good enough for decision making. A major chemical firm found that a few days in its own library, studying competitors' known plans and the past history of prices and costs of other plastics, enabled it to decide that production of a new synthetic resin was unlikely to be profitable.

More usually, the most readily available data may not yield an answer, but the known existence of other easily available information suggests looking at the alternative problem formulation which will proceed to use these less expensive data first. This was true for a study for a mail-order firm whose women's sportswear buyer wanted to know why his items were selling less well than other women's apparel sales indicated they should be. Discussion with the buyer indicated four areas of ignorance, suggesting four different hypotheses:

1. The specific merchandise items might not fit the market defined by the firm's clientele.

2. The market itself might be very limited.

3. The firm's clientele might be the wrong market for this type of item.

4. The assumption on how well such items "should" sell relative to others was wrong.

Discussion also revealed an important source of information, however, which convinced the analyst to look first at the third hypothesis because of the ready availability of information. That information was the buyer's own running sales record of individual items by size. Since the firm's size range for sportswear was narrower than that for dresses, and the same information was available for dresses, a simple comparison was made of these two pieces of data. When the comparison revealed that sportswear sales clustered in the smaller sizes and dress sales in the larger, more data on sales distribution by geographic region and by size of city were obtained from the order flow. All finally supported the hypothesis that the customers were not typical buyers of sportswear; it thus eliminated any need to conduct the much more expensive studies necessary to test the other hypotheses.

Commonly, of course, we must go beyond readily available information to collect new information from some kind of sample. Even then, the most efficient sampling scheme depends on maximum use of available information in its design and interpretation.

USE OF AVAILABLE INFORMATION IN SAMPLE DESIGN

Pure textbook probability-sampling designs are never really attainable in marketing studies, and are necessary only when there are no existing estimates of the outcome and no knowledge of the patterns of likely responses among respondents. At any other time, they may be inefficient because they require more responses than would otherwise be needed, and they result in greater sampling variability than when known social, economic, and market-structure patterns are used to stratify or otherwise limit the sample taken. Existing information may be used either to form a prior probability estimate, to be modified by Bayesian calculations on a very small sample, or to structure the sampling design and decrease the variability of sample results.

Use of Prior Probabilities

The use of prior probability estimates and of Bayes' theorem to modify them by succeeding small samples has grown in favor with the realization that characteristics of the market we measure change by the time we carry out the plans based on the measurement. Consequently, no matter how meticulous the research, the results are never really representative of the situation that will obtain when they are put to use. Fortunately, high degrees of precision are seldom, if ever, needed for correct decision. It is thus possible to use available knowledge to make a prior probability estimate, then to sharpen this to a better posterior analysis with extremely small samples—sometimes as few as a couple of score of responses—if they are taken from the market segment for which the action is planned. (See the next chapter for further discussion of this point, and also Chapter 3 of Part C of this section.)

The information used to arrive at a prior probability estimate cannot normally meet the conditions for comparability required by traditional statistical tests because of the uniqueness of any marketing decision situation, but they need not do so. However, such an estimate should never be a purely arbitrary number, but should be based on a reasoned judgment that the information arises out of circumstances analogous to those under consideration.

For example, suppose a firm is considering the introduction of a new frozen food entrée and wishes to get consumer reaction to the concept. Since the item is new, the executives have no prior information about the probability distribution of previous such introductions of this item, which is what traditional statistical techniques require. But they can easily find information on tests and even actual sales results of several other frozen food items considered to have similar appeal, and they can perhaps locate some data on the use of similar items in other forms in home dinners. From these findings they can construct an estimated probability distribution. Buttressed by such a probability estimate, they may choose to test a sample as small as 25 respondents known to be representative of the target market segment and get a result usable for decision purposes.[1] In choosing such a small sample, they have also used another kind of existing information, that is, knowledge about the general structure of the market.

Use of Market-Structure Knowledge to Lower Sampling Variability

No product is universally accepted. Both the degree and the nature of the acceptance are governed by known cultural consumption patterns based on social class, family or industry structure, regional or other geographic considerations, and other known market-segmenting forces. The range of response within any one such cultural or economic segment tends to be very limited. Since the sample size needed for any given level of precision is a function of variation of possible response within the sample set, a sample consciously stratified by factors known to be related to market response drastically reduces the required sample size, and thus the expense, while increasing the usability of the results. Gaining such efficiency through stratification, however, requires more than mere routine application of traditional forms of stratification. It involves a good working knowledge of cultural consumption patterns and careful analysis of their relevance to the problem being investigated.

As in the use of existing data, stratification is not a mechanical process; it must be grounded in a careful evaluation of some kind of knowledge or estimate of the relationship between the factor on which the sample subdivision is based and the kind of marketing action expected. The basis of stratification should always reflect information which justifies the assumption that reactions within any one stratum may vary substantially less than in the universe as a whole. Far too many studies, for example, use income level as a stratifying measure. Yet, there is abundant evidence that income is no longer a valid measure of social class for the bulk of the population. A primary element in social class is occupation, and consumer expenditure studies clearly show that the spending pattern is much more uniform within an occupational class, even across incomes lines, than in the population as a whole or within any one income class chosen without regard to occupation.[2] Neither can any direct or indirect measure of social class be used indiscriminately. Consumption of some products depends more on position within a given social class than on the class,[3] and some products are used without relation to class considerations of any kind. Much the same would be true of any other widely used basis of stratification. In other words, stratification is valid only when based on carefully evaluated knowledge or estimates and thorough analysis of the implications of this knowledge relevant to the specific problem.

[1] For a more complete discussion of the use of Bayesian estimates, see Chester R. Wasson, *Understanding Quantitative Analysis,* New York: Appleton-Century-Crofts, 1969, pp. 72–104.

[2] Chester R. Wasson, "Is It Time to Quit Thinking in Terms of Income Class?" *Journal of Marketing,* April 1969.

[3] Richard P. Coleman, "The Significance of Social Stratification in Selling," in Martin L. Bell (ed.), *Proceedings of the 43rd National Conference of the American Marketing Association, December 1960, Chicago,* American Marketing Association, 1961.

Stratification in sampling design can utilize existing knowledge in several ways. It can be direct, indirect, serial (to take account of continuous directional variation), inferential, or analytical.

Direct stratification involves choosing respondents or respondent areas in some specified proportion or disproportion according to sharply defined, measurable, or observable characteristics of the individual or area. This simple basis is feasible if the stratifying element is as observable as the respondent's sex or general age level or the number of employees in the establishment. It is not very useful, however, for many kinds of stratifying factors, for example, national descent, religion, politics, and occupation. In such cases, the tendency is to use some form of indirect stratification.

Indirect stratification uses known relationships between some easily identified characteristic (such as neighborhood) and the actual relationships on which stratification is sought. Thus, the preponderant number of residents in a single city block tend to belong to one social class, so that block statistics can be used to identify strata and to proportion them.

Serialized samples may be a stratification device whenever the basis is some characteristic that varies little within a given small location (either in geography or in a file), although it differs continuously in some linear manner. The access convenience of a given shopping center can be perceived as such a characteristic, varying in direct relationship to the travel time from the center. Studies of shopping patterns should thus be stratified by carefully proportioning respondents according to time required to travel in each major direction along commonly used transportation routes.

Some forms of stratification must rest on *inferential* assumptions. Some kinds of market behavior, for example, may derive from the respondent's ancestral background. This is often true for matters of diet. Initial letters of last names are probably clustered relative to national origin, although the exact nature of this clustering is not always clear. If such origins might be important and a name list is the sample basis, it may prove wise to spread the sample over the alphabet.

Finally, *analytical stratification* may be required to take account of every usable stratifying factor, either because of difficulties in identifying characteristics before interviews or because the factors are too numerous. It is often worthwhile to stratify the analysis and reweight the results according to previously known proportions.

All stratification forms clearly involve careful evaluation of the significance and utility of a given factor in developing an adequate research design. In this respect, the use of existing knowledge to stratify the sample is like all other uses of existing knowledge: it requires a careful prior assessment of the quality and utility of the existing knowledge for the specific purpose.

EVALUATION OF AVAILABLE INFORMATION

No data should be used without careful evaluation, but available data require even closer scrutiny than information gathered specifically for the purpose intended, because such data have not been so assembled. As a result, there may be unsuspected, substantial divergences between the most useful form of classification and the available one. The definitions of categories chosen may not be apropos for their intended use. The quality of the data collection process may have been poorer than desired or slanted because of some personal intent or time and place of collection. Even the origin of the data demands careful perusal.

Ten sets of questions should always be asked about any readily available data:

1. *How do we know?* Are the data real—or just a compilation of horse-back guesses? If somewhere in between, how were the data collected, in what time period, under what conditions, and for what purpose? How does the original purpose parallel the purpose now intended? If not exactly parallel, how does this disparity change the significance?

2. *How are the units and concepts defined?* Do these definitions fit the need in mind? If not, what adjustments can be made to align the compilations with our own information needs? (Even such simple, seemingly objective terms as "family," "house," "consumer," "manufacturer," and "automobile" can have varying definitions. For example, in measuring market share for automobiles, is a pickup truck [sometimes the only family vehicle] defined as passenger car or truck? Are sport cars that are specially equipped for race-tracks included, and what about dragsters?)

3. *Are the data classifications clear for our purpose,* or are they mixed, containing some irrelevant or contradictory data? (As just noted, "income class" is a highly mixed classification in terms of consumption patterns, containing identifiable social groups with disparate standards of expenditure even when the definition of income is both clear and realistic.)

4. *Do any of the categories omit substantial items of major significance for our intended use?* (For example, items such as imputed opportunity costs in money or effort that are real for our purposes but unaccounted for.)

5. *What is the degree of directness of the measurement?* Are the assumed relationships between attributes measured and the phenomena they are supposed to represent valid either originally or in terms of the intended use? (Many kinds of psychological tests of personality, for example, rest on paper-and-pencil choices that can be faked, or, for some individuals, they may measure something other than labeled. Even when validated for a given purpose, such as diagnosis of types of psychosis, they may be irrelevant for studying normal consumer-purchase choices or for classifying salesmen.)

6. *How complete are the data?* What is the possible significance of any omissions, relative to our need?

7. *Considering the objectives, what is the real degree of accuracy of the figures used,* their level of significance, and the quality of their measurement for that particular use?

8. *What effect could the passage of time between their collection and use have on the scale or significance of the measurements?*

9. *Who collected the information, under what authority, and for what purpose?* How well equipped were they to do the job, and could any element of personal interest or lack of skill have biased the results?

10. *Is this the latest information on this subject from this or any other source?*[4]

KINDS AND SOURCES OF AVAILABLE INFORMATION

Although much of the available data is recorded, some is simply experience data stored in the minds of observant individuals. Either recorded or experience data may be found within the firm or may be external.

---

[4] Adapted from Chester R. Wasson, *Understanding Quantitative Analysis,* op. cit., chap. 2, "Measurement, Its Problems, Complications, and Pitfalls." By permission. For a more extended discussion of the meaning of numbers, see pp. 1–8 therein.

Experience Data

Much valuable business information consists of impressions stored, organized, and interpreted by observant executives, salesmen, dealers, customers, and others in the trade. Such stored impressions and conclusions are sometimes the only dependable answer to certain kinds of questions. For instance, a buyer for a retail organization can frequently furnish a more definitive and reliable answer regarding the best price target for familiar consumer items than can any research short of elaborate and time-consuming sales tests. His conclusions represent the observed actions of thousands of customers in actual purchase situations. Because his information is the result of a multitude of real experiences, one interview with him may be enough to obtain a valid answer. However, when using such experience data, one should be certain that the conclusion expressed actually arises from carefully observed experience and not from unsupported bias, and that its meaning has not been distorted by the observer's own preconceptions and personal attitudes. Even when the conclusion is the result of observation, that observation was informal and lacked scientific controls.

In any organization, many employees, especially the salesmen, store impressions well worth retrieval if carefully evaluated and analyzed. For example, nearly all basic information helpful to one industrial-components manufacturer in uncovering a new market that later produced $1 million in annual sales was collected in interviews with six of its own manufacturer's representatives. Even the executives who pose a problem for research already have much of the information needed to understand the problem, and they themselves may indicate a possible solution when their knowledge is subjected to impartial external analysis.

Of course, special care must be taken in separating unsupported opinion from observed market action when dealing with such experience data. All the evaluation rules are important, but in particular, we need to ask, "How does he know?"

Recorded Internal Data

By far the most directly applicable recorded data are likely to be in the routine business records every organization must maintain. Any estimate of the potentials for a firm's normal business, for example, nearly always starts, and often ends, with a special analysis of the internal sales records. The new customers a firm can hope to attract are generally similar to its established clientele.

Every organization generates many kinds of data in the normal management of its affairs. At least the identity and location of its principal immediate customers are available from invoice records. Once we identify these customers and/or their locations, we can learn a great deal more from industrial directories, census data, and other information sources. Merely spotting customer locations on a map reveals much to an experienced analyst. The nature of buyers of a mail-order firm's garden tractor line was defined by one analyst from a simple locational study of the buyers, supported by his own knowledge, derived from census and other sources, of the character of the rural population in areas where orders originated. In another firm, the analysis of the customers' industrial classifications revealed a major industrial market still largely untapped.

Usually, such available internal information must be reorganized and re-analyzed in a different form from that in which it was gathered, in order to reveal needed answers. This is especially true of routine accounting information, particularly cost data. The classifications of various expenditures useful for normal operating-control purposes are nearly always incorrect when applied without adjustment to marketing plan decisions. Quite often also, such important information categories as imputed opportunity costs should be added. In one firm, for example, executives were told that the firm could save a half-million dollars a year by dropping its charge-account service which costs customers nothing, and requiring customers to use its other credit system of time payments, which yields a carrying charge. The suggestion was based on the accounting controls which allocated this half-million-dollar cost to the charge service on a customer-account basis. Careful recheck and analysis indicated that on an opportunity cost basis, nothing would be saved.

As already noted, interpretation of such internal recorded data requires use of external available data. Indeed, by far the greatest volume of information used in research comes from the vast body of external published and private statistics and special studies. The organization and analysis of these data depend, in turn, almost entirely on access to another type of available information—the distilled research results of the academic world as summarized in the theories and relationships observed in the economic, behavioral, and social sciences.

EXTERNALLY AVAILABLE RECORDED INFORMATION

Published Statistics

Modern mass-market planning is thoroughly dependent on the huge mass of available published statistics. The most voluminous and most basic source is the great body of official statistics produced by the federal government and its agencies and, to a lesser extent, by state and local governments. Many of the convenient compendiums of data published by private organizations are derived in whole or in part from these governmental data.

The census is the best known of such governmental compilations, but many people are unaware of the variety of census statistics and the wealth of subject matter and detail they provide. Published tabulations from each of the several regular censuses occupy long shelves in the library, and the U.S. Census Bureau makes available both special tabulations and computer tapes of raw data at nominal fees (as long as the material does not disclose individual information). Besides the general complete enumerations, the Bureau produces interim estimates of many kinds. It also publishes a quarterly *Bureau of Census Catalog*, cumulated annually, giving complete information on both preliminary and final reports on all censuses, lists of data files (computer tapes and punchcards), and available unpublished material.

The regularly conducted censuses include:

> *Decennial Census of Population.* The population count for states, counties, all incorporated population centers, minor civil divisions, unincorporated places of 1,000 or more population, and standard metropolitan statistical areas. Population characteristics by sex, marital status, age, color or race, and relationship to the head of the household. General social and economic characteristics: nativity or parentage, state and nation of birth, mobility, education, number of families and their composition, employment status, occupation, income, and other subjects classified by age, color, and other characteristics, with added information on families, age by single years, occupation, and industry. Various cross-tabulations under special subject reports (33 of them in the 1960 census), and information on population and housing by census tracts within each of the 180 metropolitan area tracts in the United States.

Decennial Census of Housing.   Data collected simultaneously with the decennial population census.   Information on tenure, color, vacancy status, population per occupied housing unit, number of rooms, type of structure, housing condition and plumbing facilities, financial characteristics, and other subjects by states, counties, urbanized areas, standard metropolitan statistical areas, and places of 1,000 or more people.   Housing also analyzed in terms of city blocks for all metropolitan centers of 50,000 or more people plus some 200 other places.

Quinquennial Census of Agriculture.   Data, by states and, in some instances, by smaller areas, on farms, farm acreage, crops, sources of income, population, production, and expenditures.   Usually conducted in the fourth and ninth year of each decade.

Census of Transportation.   (Approximately quinquennial; 1963 and 1967 latest available.)   Includes a national travel survey, analyzing travel in terms of transportation, purpose, duration, origin and destination, size of party, lodgings used, socioeconomic factors of travelers.   Also includes a Truck Inventory and Use Survey, a Shipper Group series of reports, and a Commodity Group series.

Census of Business.   (Approximately quinquennial; 1963 and 1967, latest.)   Broken down into Retail Trade, Wholesale Trade, and Selected Services, by states, standard metropolitan statistical areas, counties and cities, and kind of business.

Census of Manufactures.   (Approximately quinquennial, 1963 and 1967.)   Data by industry and by location—by states, counties, standard metropolitan statistical areas, and cities with 10,000 or more residents.   Details on size of establishments, legal form of organization, products shipped and consumed, payrolls, employment, capital expenditure, inventories, value added by manufacture, and other elements.

Census of Mineral Industries.   (1963 and 1967.)   Data, by states and nine geographic regions, on size of establishments, type of organization, employment and related statistics, type of operation, fuels, electric energy, and selected supplies used, power equipment and water use, product shipped, and other subjects.

Census of Commercial Fisheries.   (1967)

Census of Governments.   (1967)   Number of governmental units and public school districts by state, and local governments by county.   Most of the data are by state, county, and selected cities, with data on employment, elected officials, finances, taxable property values, and other items.

Voluminous as the census reports are, they constitute a minor fraction of the highly usable information issued by federal governmental agencies.   Every major governmental body and commission generates statistics and special reports of many kinds, all of them listed in the cumulative catalog of government documents available in every major library.   Five federal organizations generate statistical compilations of wide utility:

Department of Agriculture.   Issues several regular monthly reports and special studies, and three major annual volumes: *Agricultural Statistics, Crop Production,* and *Crop Values.*

Department of Commerce.   Besides the many publications of the Census Bureau (including two on imports and exports), publishes the monthly *Survey of Current Business,* containing over 2,000 updated statistical series, and covering general business indicators, commodity prices, and statistics on construction and real estate, domestic trade, employment, population, finance, international transactions, transportation, communications and other subjects.

Department of Labor. Publishes the *Monthly Labor Review,* containing statistics on employment; wages; labor turnover; retail, wholesale, and commodity price indexes; and other current labor-related statistics. Also conducts and publishes periodic detailed studies of family expenditure patterns to update the budget used as the basis for its Consumer Price Index.

Department of Health, Education, and Welfare. Publishes the monthly *Vital Statistics Report* and an annual summary, *Vital Statistics in the United States,* containing series on births, deaths, marriages, and other data related to health. Also publishes an annual *Digest of Educational Statistics.*

Federal Reserve System. Issues the monthly *Federal Reserve Bulletin,* containing statistics on banking, money rates, security markets, finance of all kinds (government, business, real estate, and consumer), flow of funds, savings, national product and income department store sales, and international trade and finance.

Congress, too, originates many kinds of data in the course of its hearings and investigations. Executive messages are also the medium for many kinds of statistics.

In general, the quality with which data are gathered for the regular statistical series and agency studies is of the best, and the categories are defined carefully so that the user can easily evaluate their utility for his purposes. But political considerations occasionally distort the statistical purity of some classifications, as in the definition of a few of the standard metropolitan statistical areas (SMSAs). Local pride has apparently resulted in the separation of the Orange County segment of the Los Angeles area into a separate Anaheim–Santa Ana–Garden Grove SMSA, and something similar has caused the Census Bureau to separate the Northern New Jersey communities, within sight of Manhattan's towers, from the Greater New York area. (However, the New Jersey suburbs are still included in the consolidated New York–New Jersey metropolitan data.)

Not all official statistics, however, share the care in expression and the validity of the routine series. Governmental bodies of all sorts seem to have a rule that a request for a figure is to be answered, not with an "I don't know," but with whatever can be dredged up, however tenuous its basis. Often an executive, wishing to strengthen a legislative request, may ask for some specific statistic to be produced overnight, and his subordinates oblige with something. A widely quoted figure on the national cost of air pollution apparently originated from such a situation. After searching every possible source, subordinates uncovered only a single quantitative study—one done for the city of Pittsburgh early in the century. Having nothing better or more recent, they simply made a horseback projection to a national figure, which was printed in a message to Congress. As suggested earlier, "How do you know?" must always be asked of every figure.

Many private organizations also generate primary statistics. Most trade associations conduct statistical operations on subjects important to their members, and some of their findings are published. Trade publications gather and publish many series of considerable value in conjunction with their news and promotional activities. Many governmental series, in fact, use these private series. Other organizations compile and digest various official data, converting them into more convenient form. Among the most useful of these private compilations are:

Rand McNally Commercial Atlas and Marketing Guide. (Rand McNally & Company, Chicago, annual, with monthly supplements.) A single-volume world atlas with both statistics and maps. Contains population figures for over 60,000

United States localities, and about 40 statistical items for every county in the nation.

Sales Management Survey of Buying Power. (Bills Brothers Publishing Company, New York, annual.) Contains *Sales Management* estimates of numbers of people and of households, income, and retail sales in nine categories, for cities, counties, metropolitan areas and the country as a whole, together with *Sales Management* indexes of relative buying power and sales activity for each area.

Editor & Publisher Market Guide. (Editor & Publisher, New York, annual.) Standardized surveys of over 1,500 daily newspaper markets, with statistics on transportation, population, automobile registrations, housing, banks, principal industries, utilities, number of wage earners, average weekly wages and principal paydays, and various kinds of retail statistics.

The development of computer data banks is beginning to improve greatly the availability and utility of much of this mass of statistics and render it more readily usable in desired cross-tabulations.

With these, as with all other data, we need to investigate their relevance as compiled for our specific need. For example, the utility of *Sales Management's* buying-power indexes will vary greatly for different sales operations.

Published Research Studies

Governmental, academic, and even private organizations conduct research of many kinds which is reported in periodical literature and in special reports, such as bulletins. The results reported are often sufficiently relevant to be applicable to some need of our own. Even more often, they furnish suggestions valuable in designing research and in defining the problem more sharply.

The American Marketing Association has developed a series of research bibliographies covering much of this material, and periodically updates them. Locating such studies and articles is facilitated by the various cumulative indexes to periodical and other literature which every library maintains. As with all other data, we must separate fact from mere opinion and evaluate the quality of the work, particularly the published studies by organizations with a publicity ax to grind. Even the latter, however, may pass the most rigid evaluations.

Unpublished but Available Studies

Several organizations gather regular series of marketing statistics for private sale and use at appropriate subscription prices—such statistics as broadcast program ratings, merchandise movement at retail, consumer-purchase diaries, and similar materials.

ACADEMIC KNOWLEDGE

The most valuable available information is the organized research knowledge condensed and generalized into the concepts and principles of economic, social, and behavioral science. These furnish necessary guidance in terms of the data's relevance for solving various research problems, and they help determine the kinds of relationships worth investigating. The purely empirical collection of data without reference to a theoretical framework always wastes time and frequently fails to provide a right answer. The lack of focus in such principles often keeps us from perceiving the existence of sought-for relationships in the data presented. One typical example is that of a young market analyst who spent two months trying to find factors associated with the location of customers of a specialized retail service. He tried to relate his mapped concentration of customers to every conceivable kind of census information without perceiving any associated relationships. Finally, an older analyst, with less industry experience but with a more fundamental social science background, looked over his work and suggested that one certain kind of information be reviewed. After a few hours of computation, a relationship was discovered which proved, on a subsequent promotional test, to be very close.

Research is the process of gathering and organizing information *relevant* to a given problem and analyzing the results in terms of one or more *expected frameworks* of relationships. We decide in advance what kinds of information would be relevant on the basis of some kind of conceptual framework we believe in, whether that framework is conscious or unconscious, naïve or informed. We relate those factors and results according to some framework which we think may hold an answer. The most useful concepts for classifying our data are those which extensive past research in the learned disciplines has tested. The most revealing relationships are usually those which these disciplines have validated as basic to human behavior. Unfortunately, the guidance that such concepts and principles can furnish is not always followed. The neglect is unnecessary. The major concepts and principles of value for business decisions are few in number and easily comprehended. When thoroughly understood, they are also comparatively easy to apply.

SUMMARY

Every aspect of research planning, execution, and interpretation involves using and evaluating already available information. Problem formulation and the sharpness of its focus are completely dependent on existing information and its use. What is already known reveals the gaps in our knowledge, and the ready availability of other information often tends to influence the initial direction of research design. Any efficient sample design maximizes the use of existing information in developing prior probability estimates and/or sample stratification based on knowledge about the probable structure of responses. Such stratification can be direct, indirect, serial, inferential, or analytical in nature, but should never be arbitrary or perfunctory.

All information used in research planning and analysis needs thorough evaluation especially readily available data because they usually have been gathered to meet a different information need at a much earlier time. Such evaluation should be based on at least 10 questions:

1. How do we know?
2. How are the units and concepts defined, and do the definitions meet our objective for use of the data?
3. Are the classifications clean for our purpose?
4. Is the category coverage complete for our use?
5. How directly were the attributes measured?
6. How complete are the data for our purpose?
7. How accurate and significant are the numbers in the context of our use of them?
8. How has the significance of the data been affected by the passage of time?
9. Who collected the information, for what purpose, and how well did he do it?
10. Is this the latest information on the subject?

Existing information may be recorded or unrecorded, either internal to the organization or external. A significant quantity consists of the unrecorded experience and conclusions of observant individuals, both inside the firm and outside. All firms generate, in the routine conduct of business, a substantial amount of recorded data which are very relevant when reorganized and analyzed in the context of the problem studied. External recorded information consists of both published and unpublished material. The published material includes quantities of statistical series and special studies gathered under government auspices and supplemented by trade associations and private businesses. Periodical literature of both the academic and business worlds carries reports on special studies of many kinds. Finally, the academic literature outlines major concepts and principles of human behavior helpful in discerning the most useful kinds of information and the types of relationships to investigate.

APPENDIX

Published Materials: Where to Start Your Search

THE REFERENCE LIBRARIES. Every major library has a reference department staffed with reference librarians trained to help readers find needed materials.

Additionally, every major city and most large universities have a library which has been designated as a government depository, and which therefore receives a copy of every official governmental document. Every library of any consequence also subscribes to most of the finding guides listed here and the principal directories of wide interest. The United States Department of Commerce maintains field offices in 33 major cities, each with its own reference library.

A BASIC ITEM FOR YOUR DESK. *The Statistical Abstract of the United States,* published every September by the Bureau of the Census. Also available in a paperback edition on newstands, under the title *The U.S. Book of Facts, Statistics, and Information* (Simon & Schuster, Essandess Special Editions). Contains nearly 1,300 tables from the most widely used governmental and private statistical series, including some not published elsewhere, under 32 subject headings, and a standard metropolitan statistical area section. Extremely useful as to the information included, but also a sampling of what is available and a guide to other sources. The guide to each subject section lists the principal sources for the kinds of information in that section, and an appendix contains a 52-page classified bibliography of statistical sources, governmental and private. It is thus a basic finding guide as well as an excellent compendium.

OTHER USEFUL FEDERAL COMPENDIUMS OF STATISTICS. *City and County Data Book.* Contains 144 items of statistical data for each county in the United States, 133 items for each of the 224 standard metropolitan statistical areas, and 148 items for each of the 683 incorporated cities having 25,000 or more people in 1960.

Historical Statistics of the United States, Colonial Times to 1957. More than 8,000 statistical series covering periods from 1610 to 1957, documented as to original sources, and thoroughly indexed.

Historical Statistics of the United States, Colonial Times to 1957, Corrections to 1962 and Revisions.

Other Basic Finding Guides to Statistical and Other Collected Information

Monthly Catalog of U.S. Government Publications, Government Printing Office.
Bureau of the Census Catalog, quarterly, U.S. Bureau of the Census.
Statistical Services of the U.S. Government, Bureau of the Budget.
How and Where to Look it Up, Robert W. Murphey, New York: McGraw-Hill.

Indexes to Periodical Literature

The following volumes will be found in most libraries.
Business Periodical Index

Reader's Guide to Periodical Literature.   Covers mainly general-interest, popular publications.

Industrial Arts Index
Agriculture Index
Engineering Index
The Bulletin of the Public Affairs Information Service.   Lists the latest books, pamphlets, government publications, reports of private and public agencies, and periodicals on economic and social conditions, public administration, and international relations.

Index to The New York Times
Wall Street Journal Index
Sociological Abstracts
Psychological Abstracts.   Indexed abstracts of professional articles on psychology.
Executive's Guide to Information Sources, Detroit: Gale Research Co.

Directories to Trade Associations

Directory of National Trade and Professional Associations in the United States, Washington: Potomac Books.
Encyclopedia of Associations, Detroit: Gale Research Co.

Other Useful Directories

Guide to American Directories, New York: McGraw-Hill.
Reference Book of Dun & Bradstreet.   Available only to subscribers
Thomas Register of American Manufacturers
Research Centers Directory, Detroit: Gale Research Co.

Information on Periodicals, Advertising Rates, and Related Facts

Standard Rate and Data Service, Skokie, Ill.: Standard Rate and Data Service.   A series of periodical publications listing information needed in preparing and placing information in print and broadcast media, plus market information on the media.
N. W. Ayer & Son's Directory of Newspapers and Periodicals, Philadelphia: N. W. Ayer.   Listing of newspapers and periodicals published in the United States, Canada, Panama, and the Philippines.
Ulrich's Periodical Directory, New York: Bowker.   An international directory of periodicals, categorized by subject matter.

Finding Guide on Recent Research

Advertising Age Market Data Issue, published in April or May of each year, Chicago: Advertising Publications.   A list of hundreds of privately published compilations of data and studies offered by media, trade associations, and other sources, most of them available without charge.

Summaries of Behavioral Concepts and Principles Applicable to Marketing

Steuart Henderson Britt, *Consumer Behavior and the Behavioral Sciences,* New York: Wiley, 1966.   A relatively exhaustive collection of excerpted readings on managerial economics, sociology and anthropology, and psychology.

Chester R. Wasson, Frederick D. Sturdivant, and David H. McConaughy, *Competition and Human Behavior,* New York: Appleton-Century-Crofts, 1968.   A concise summary of the principal contributions applicable to marketing and their significance for competitive decisions, from managerial economics, sociology and anthropology, psychology, and political science.

James E. Myers and William H. Reynolds, *Consumer Behavior and Market Management,* Boston: Houghton Mifflin, 1967.   An excellent summary of the major research findings in psychology, social psychology, and sociology as they apply to marketing management.

Part A

Research Design

Chapter 3

Assessing the Value of Additional Information

DONALD S. TULL *School of Business Administration, University of Oregon, Eugene, Oregon*

Someone has observed that "grace is given of God but knowledge is bought in the market." He might have added that decision makers have a persistent need for both.

It is apparent that decisions can be made only after the persons concerned have concluded that no more information will be sought. The normative base for such a decision is a weighing of the potential value and the cost of the information being considered. It is this assessment of value versus the cost of additional information that is the concern of this chapter.

Our approach to the problem of assessment is Bayesian in nature. A brief review is provided of the basic propositions and procedures in conducting the extensive form of Bayesian analysis of the expected value of information (EVI). The chapter then derives the general relationship of EVI and its determinants for problems in "venture analysis" form.

AN EXAMPLE OF A DECISION PROBLEM ON OBTAINING ADDITIONAL INFORMATION

Suppose you are the marketing manager of a company that has developed a new product. A decision to introduce or not to introduce it is needed. A survey of consumers to determine their degree of acceptance of the product is being considered prior to making the decision on its introduction.

A convenient way to structure and to present information available for making decisions of this type is to use a conditional payoff table. Table 1 is

TABLE 1   New-Product Commercialization: Conditional Payoff

	States			
	S_1 — Optimistic market share $\geq 10\%$		S_2 — Pessimistic market share $< 10\%$	
Action	$P(S_1)$	Payoff	$P(S_2)$	Payoff
A_1 — Introduce	0.60	$6.0 M	0.40	− $4.0 M
A_2 — Do not introduce	0.60	0.0	0.40	0.0

such a table.   It shows the alternative actions being considered, the possible consequences in terms of payoff of each act, and the probability that each consequence will occur.

This is an example of a *venture analysis* problem in which one "go" action is being considered.   The "no-go" action is assumed to have payoffs of zero. When reference is made to the venture analysis form of problem hereafter, it should be understood to mean a two-action problem in which one of the actions has payoffs of zero.

The venture analysis form of problem is a highly convenient one with which to work, and it is commonly encountered in practice.   It is the simplest form of problem to analyze and yet it illustrates fully the method of analysis applicable to more complex problem formulations.   In addition, derivation of the general relationship between EVI and its determinants for this type of problem can be made.

Estimated payoffs for the market shares that the product may capture are shown in Table 1.   Market shares have been divided into two possible ranges, or *states of nature*.   In the example, it is estimated that the average payoff for a market share greater than, or equal to, 10 percent (state 1) is $6.0 million.   Conversely, if the market share is less than 10 percent (state 2), payoff (loss) is estimated to average −$4.0 million.

The subjective probability of each state's occurring is .60 for the "optimistic" state and .40 for the "pessimistic" state.   If no additional information is obtained, and if management makes the decision on the basis of expected monetary value (EMV), the decision will be to introduce the product (act A_1). The prior EMV of act A_1, which will be written as EMV_0, is

$$EMV_0 = P(S_1)V_1 + P(S_2)V_2$$
$$= (0.60)(\$6.0 \text{ M}) + (0.40)(-\$4.0 \text{ M}) = \$2.0 \text{ M} \quad (1)$$

The EMV of A_2 is, of course, zero.   The algebraic sum of the EMVs of the two acts is therefore equal to EMV_0.   In this problem, $EMV_0 = \$2.0$ M.

In the marketing manager's judgment, the survey, if conducted, would have a likelihood of .85 of correctly identifying S_1, but a likelihood of only .70 of correctly identifying S_2.   These likelihoods are shown in Table 2.

The manager is aware that respondents generally have a favorable bias when asked about new products.   He therefore believes there is a greater chance of concluding incorrectly that the true state is S_1 than there is of wrongly concluding that S_2 is the true state.   If we let the research indication I_1 designate S_1 and, similarly, research indication I_2 designate S_2, the probability of receiving an I_1 indication when S_2 is the true state is .30 and, similarly, the probability of receiving an I_2 indication when S_1 is the true state is .15. The probabilities for receiving correct indications for S_1 and S_2, respectively, are .85 and .70.

It is estimated that the survey will take three months to conduct and cost $100,000, inclusive of expected opportunity losses from delaying the introduction.

Should the survey be conducted?

PAYOFFS, STATES OF NATURE, AND SUBJECTIVE PROBABILITIES

A discussion of some of the concepts used in the residual payoff table just presented is appropriate before considering whether the survey should be conducted.

Payoffs

Payoffs may be expressed in whatever units the decision maker decides are most useful. To a political candidate it may be votes, and to a union organizer it may be numbers of members. In our problem, it will be dollars.

TABLE 2   New-Product Commercialization Likelihoods: Identification of States — $P(I_i|S_j)$

Research indication I_i	State of nature — S_j S_1	S_2
	$P(I_i|S_1)$	$P(I_i|S_2)$
I_1	0.85	0.30
I_2	0.15	0.70
Total	1.00	1.00

Let us assume that the dollars of estimated payoff may be transformed linearly into utilities over the full range of payoffs. As a practical matter, such an assumption is more likely to be true for a large company than for a small one.[1]

Monetary payoffs are most usefully estimated in terms of the present value of future net cash flows. In preparing payoff estimates, therefore, one estimates net cash flow for each action for each future period (quarter, year) included in the analysis of the venture. These cash flows are then discounted back to the present, using an appropriate discount rate. The sum of the discounted cash flows for each action constitutes the estimated payoff for that action.[2]

States of Nature

States of nature result from sets of environmental conditions which determine the possible consequences of each alternative act. A market share of ≥ 10 percent or < 10 percent is the result of many environmental variables; the degree of consumer acceptance, competitive actions, and incomes are examples of such variables.

[1] See Raiffa [7], chap. 4, or Fellner [2, chap. 3], for a discussion of the procedures to follow when this assumption is inappropriate.

[2] See Green and Tull [4, chap. 2].

It is implicitly assumed that other states can be usefully subsumed within the ones used in structuring a problem. The two-state formulation may not be a realistic one for some problems. A third state is included in an expanded version of the example in a later section of the chapter.

Subjective Probabilities

The basic probability theorems are reviewed in the next section. *Personal* probabilities are a measure of one's degree of belief concerning an event. If an executive believes strongly that a new product will be successful if introduced, he is assigning a high personal probability to its success. He may or may not express this probability as a number.

It is an everyday occurrence to hear (and to use) such phrases as "the chances are good," "the risk is low," "we can't miss on this one," and so on. It is also not uncommon to hear such comments as, "We have at least an 80 percent chance of breaking even by the third year" and "The chances are about 50:50 that the board will approve it." Whether expressed verbally or numerically, a probability assessment has been made and is being stated.

The term *subjective* probability will be reserved here to mean a personal probability that is both expressed numerically and is *consistent*. A consistent set of probabilities, when applied to a betting situation, is one in which an opponent cannot obtain a "straddle"; he cannot choose his bets in such a way that he will lose money regardless of the outcome.

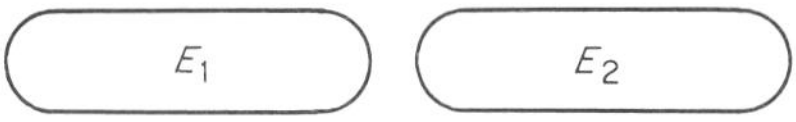

Fig. 1. Diagram of two mutually exclusive events.

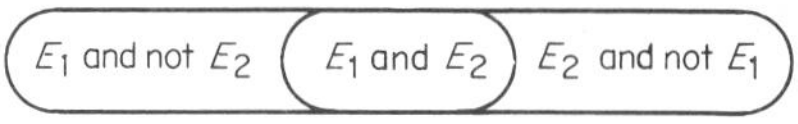

Fig. 2. Diagram of two nonmutually exclusive events.

In the illustrative problem, the marketing manager believes that there is a 60 percent chance that the product, if introduced, would get a market share of at least 10 percent. Correspondingly, he believes there is a 40 percent chance that the share of the market captured would be less than 10 percent.

PROBABILITY THEOREMS

A brief review of the basic probability theorems may be useful here. If we let the event E be the occurrence of subevents E_1 or E_2, it will be recalled that we may write

$$P(E_1 \text{ or } E_2) = P(E_1) + P(E_2) \tag{2a}$$

in which "or" is interpreted as "E_1 or E_2, or both E_1 and E_2." This formula is valid only for mutually exclusive events. This is illustrated in Figure 1. Figure 2 illustrates the general case in which the events are *not* mutually exclusive. For this situation we may write

$$P(E_1 \text{ or } E_2) = P(E_1) + P(E_2) - P(E_1 \text{ and } E_2) \tag{2b}$$

where "and" means "both E_1 and E_2." A variation of this theorem is

$$P(E_1) = P(E_1 \text{ and } E_2) + P(E_1 \text{ and not } E_2) \tag{2c}$$

For events that are independent, the multiplication theorem may be written for the joint occurrence of two events, or

$$P(E_1 \text{ and } E_2) = P(E_1) \cdot P(E_2) \tag{2d}$$

Where dependence can exist between the two events, the theorem must be written as

$$P(E_1 \text{ and } E_2) = P(E_1 | E_2) \cdot P(E_2) \tag{2e}$$

or, reversing the order,

$$P(E_1 \text{ and } E_2) = P(E_2 | E_1) \cdot P(E_1) \tag{2f}$$

where $P(E_1 | E_2)$ is read as "the probability of event E_1, given that event E_2 already exists" and is known as a *conditional* probability. $P(E_1 \text{ and } E_2)$ is known as a *joint* probability.

Bayes' Theorem

By utilizing Equations $(2c)$ and $(2e)$ and using the notation of our problem, we may derive Bayes' theorem. For the two-state case, the theorem is as follows[3]:

$$P(S_1 | I_1) = \frac{P(I_1 | S_1) \cdot P(S_1)}{P(I_1 | S_1) \cdot P(S_1) + P(I_1 | S_2) \cdot P(S_2)} \tag{3a}$$

This theorem permits *revision* of our earlier unconditional probability, $P(S_1)$, to the conditional probability, $P(S_1 | I_1)$, given that the I_1 indication is obtained from the reserach project.

Stated in terms of the example, the theorem allows us to answer the question, "If I now think there is a 60 percent probability that we would get at least a 10 percent market share if we introduced the product, *and* if we were to conduct a research project that would have an 80 percent probability of correctly identifying whether there would be a market share of at least 10 percent, *and* if the results of the project were to indicate that the share would be at least 10 percent, what is the *revised* probability of getting a market share of at least 10 percent?" The theorem also permits obtaining a revised probability of getting a minimum market share of 10 percent even though the results of the research indicate that such a high share will not be obtained.

This revision of the unconditional to the conditional probabilities of the occurrence of each state allows us to determine what the EMV of the venture would be if the additional information that could be provided by the research project were obtained: it permits us to determine EMV_1.

[3] From Equation $(2c)$ and $(2e)$, we may write the following:

$$P(I_1) = P(S_1 \text{ and } I_1) + P(S_2 \text{ and } I_1) \tag{3b}$$
$$P(S_1 | I_1) = P(S_1 \text{ and } I_1)/P(I_1) \tag{3c}$$
$$P(S_1 \text{ and } I_1) = P(I_1 | S_1) \cdot P(S_1) \tag{3d}$$
$$P(S_2 \text{ and } I_1) = P(I_1 | S_2) \cdot P(S_2) \tag{3e}$$

The derivation may then be made by

a. using $(3c)$, $P(S_1 | I_1) = P(S_1 \text{ and } I_1)/P(I_1)$
b. substituting $(3d)$, $P(S_1 | I_1) = P(I_1 | S_1) \cdot P(S_1)/P(I_1)$
c. substituting $(3b)$,

$$P(S_1 | I_1) = \frac{P(I_1 | S_1) \cdot P(S_1)}{P(S_1 \text{ and } I_1) + P(S_2 \text{ and } I_1)}$$

d. substituting $(3d)$ and $(3e)$,

$$P(S_1 | I_1) = \frac{P(I_1 | S_1) \cdot P(S_1)}{P(I_1 | S_1) \cdot P(S_1) + P(I_1 | S_2) \cdot P(S_2)}$$

DETERMINATION OF THE EXPECTED VALUE OF INFORMATION (EVI)

EVI may be thought of as the amount the EMV_0 would increase if the information were obtained; that is,

$$EVI = EMV_1 - EMV_0 \tag{4a}$$

This expected *value* of the information should be compared with the estimated *cost* of obtaining it (ECI). The *net expected value of information* (NEVI) may be defined as

$$NEVI = EVI - ECI \tag{4b}$$

The decision rule which will be used for deciding whether a project should be rejected or not is as follows:
A research project should be considered further only when NEVI > 0.
EVI may be calculated by following the steps described below.
1. Prepare a conditional payoff table showing the relevant states, actions, the unconditional probability assigned to each state, and the payoff for each action-state pair.
The estimates of these values for our example are given in Table 1.
2. Estimate the conditional probability of each research indication given each state of nature, or $P(I_i|S_j)$.
The conditional probability estimates for the example are shown in Table 2.
At this point, all the judgments required to calculate EVI have been made. The rest of the procedure involves calculation only.
3. Calculate the joint probabilities of research indication and state of nature, using Equation (2e):

$$P(S_j \text{ and } I_i) = P(S_j) \cdot P(I_i|S_j) \tag{5a}$$

These calculations for our example are given in Table 3.

TABLE 3   Product-Commercialization Example: Joint Probabilities $P(S_j$ and $I_i)$ and Marginal Probabilities $P(I_i)$

Research indication	$P(S_1 \text{ and } I_i)$	$P(S_2 \text{ and } I_i)$	$P(I_i)$
I_1	$0.60 \times 0.85 = 0.51$	$0.40 \times 0.30 = 0.12$	0.63
I_2	$0.60 \times 0.15 = 0.09$	$0.40 \times 0.70 = 0.28$	0.37
Total	$P(S_1) = 0.60$	$P(S_2) = 0.40$	1.00

4. Calculate the probability of each research indication, $P(I_i)$, by using Equation (2c):

$$P(I_i) = \sum_{i=1}^{n} (S_j \text{ and } I_i) \tag{5b}$$

These summations are also shown in Table 3.
5. Calculate the revised probability $P(S_j|I_i)$ using Bayes' theorem, Equation (3a). The calculations for the four revised probabilities involved in the example are shown in Table 4.

6. Calculate the revised expected monetary value:

$$EMV_1 = \sum_{j=1}^{k} P(S_j|I_i) \cdot P(I_i) V_{kj} \qquad (5c)$$

where the intermediate EMV's ≥ 0.

TABLE 4   Product-Commercialization Example: Revised Probabilities —
$P(S_j|I_i)$

State of nature	$P(S_j|I_1)$	$P(S_j|I_2)$
S_1	$0.51/0.63 = 0.810$	$0.09/0.37 = 0.243$
S_2	$0.12/0.63 = 0.190$	$0.28/0.37 = 0.757$
Total	1.000	1.000

The calculation of the revised expected monetary value can be shown either in a table or in a decision tree. The decision tree, the better of the two for illustration, is used here.

The decision tree for the example is given in Figure 3. The two strategies of CONDUCT SURVEY and DO NOT CONDUCT SURVEY are shown as the two main branches. The fork from which they come is shown as a square to indicate that it is a *decision* fork. The forks shown as circles represent *chance* forks; that is, forks at which chance determines which of the branches will be followed.

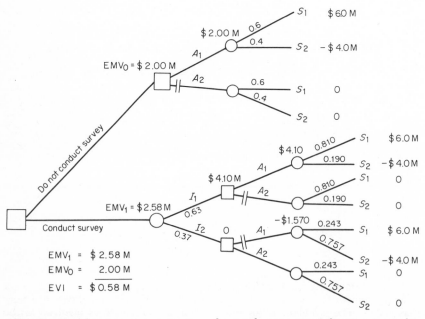

Fig. 3.   Decision tree: two-state case of a product commercialization example.

The making of any decision, by whatever procedure, requires predicting the consequences of each action and then choosing the action that is considered to have the "best" consequence. The decision tree illustrates every possible consequence of each alternative action.

At each branch after the chance forks, a probability of selection must be shown. These probabilities are those whose methods of calculation were described earlier. A payoff (consequence) must also be provided at the end of each branch.

In reading Figure 3, suppose we go out the CONDUCT SURVEY branch to the first chance fork, and then up the I_1 branch to the decision fork. At this point, we may determine the expected value of the venture conditional on having conducted the research project and the result being I_1 (that S_1 is the true state).

We may make this evaluation easily. If the A_1 (INTRODUCE) branch is looked at first, the expected value may be determined by multiplying the probability of S_1's occurring times its payoff (.810 × $6 M), and adding the product of the probability of S_2 and its payoff (.190 × − $4 M). The resulting conditional expected payoff is $4.10 M.

Choosing the A_2 (DO NOT INTRODUCE) branch will of course result in a zero payoff regardless of state. Since the A_1 action results in the higher expected value when I_1 is the research result, we will choose it and reject A_2. The rejection of the A_2 action is shown by its being blocked off with the two perpendicular lines through the branch.

A similar evaluation can be made of the venture given an I_2 result of the research. Not very surprisingly, the best action to be taken with an I_2 research indication is A_2. The payoff will of course be zero. The expected loss associated with the A_1 branch requires rejection of that action; the branch is accordingly blocked off with the perpendicular lines.

We are now in a position to evaluate the expected monetary value of the venture after research (EMV$_1$). We may do this by multiplying the conditional expected payoff given an I_1 indication times the probability of getting an I_1 indication ($4.10 × 0.63), performing a similar calculation for the I_2 branch (which in this case will be zero because the payoff is zero), and summing the two. The resulting EMV$_1$ is $2.58 M.

The only remaining step in determining the expected value of the research information is:

7. Subtract the prior EMV from the revised EMV as in Equation (4a).

This is the extensive form of Bayesian analysis of EVI. It has also been called the "averaging out and folding back" method.

We see from Figure 3 that the EVI is $0.58 M or $580,000. NEVI is then $480,000 (EVI of $580,000 − ECI of $100,000), and so a research project is indicated.

It has been rather troublesome to reach that conclusion, however, and we are still not through. Suppose a survey of a larger sample is suggested that will cost $200,000 but will give likelihoods of $P(I_1|S_1) = P(I_2|S_2) = 0.85$. Should this survey be conducted instead of the less expensive one? What about the likelihood–cost combinations of still other research designs?

We shall return to this question later.

Expected Value of Perfect Information (EVPI)

Since EVI is the difference between revised and prior EMVs, its maximum value will occur when the information identifies the true state with certainty. EVPI, the expected value of perfect information, is this maximum value and is found by taking the difference of the revised and prior EMVs, the revised EMV being calculated under the assumptions that (1) the research outcome will occur with the same prior probability as the occurrence of the state $P(S_1) = P(I_1)$, $P(S_2) = P(I_2)$, and (2) a research indication always correctly identifies the state.

Referring to our example, it will be recalled that the probability assigned of realizing a market share of $\geq$ 10 percent is $0.60[P(S_1) = 0.60]$, and the probability of a market share of < 10 percent is 0.40 $[P(S_2) = 0.40]$. If the information we get is perfect, we could expect that the probability of the occurrence of indications I_1 and I_2 would also be 0.60 and 0.40, respectively. Further, $P(S_1|I_1) = P(S_2|I_2) = 1.0$, since we are assuming the survey gives perfect information about the states of nature.

It will be recognized immediately that, given perfect information, the new product should not be introduced if the research outcome is I_2. The only possible result would be an estimated residual negative payoff of \$4.0 M.

We may now calculate the EVPI.

$$EVI_1 = P(S_1)V_1 + P(S_2)\cdot V_2 = (0.60)\cdot\$6.0\text{ M} + 0 = \qquad \$3.60\text{ M}$$
$$EVI_0 = P(S_1)V_1 + P(S_2)\cdot V_2 = (0.60)\cdot\$6.0\text{ M} + (0.40)(-4.0\text{ M}) = \$2.00\text{ M}$$
$$EVPI = \qquad\quad - P(S_2)\cdot V_2 = \qquad\qquad\qquad\qquad\qquad\qquad \$1.60\text{ M}$$

In our example, therefore, we could afford to spend as much as \$1.60 M if we could be assured our information would be perfect.

Note that $EVPI = -P(S_2)V_2 = |P(S_2)V_2|$. For two-action–two-state venture analysis problems, the general case is

$$EVPI = |P(S_2)V_2| \tag{6}$$

This of course presupposes that S_2 is the designation for the state with the negative payoff.

RELATIONSHIP OF EVI AND ITS DETERMINANTS FOR TWO-ACTION– TWO-STATE VENTURE ANALYSIS PROBLEMS

From the analysis to determine EVI, just completed, it seems reasonable to suspect that a functional relationship for EVI exists. Such proves to be the case. For two-action–two-state venture analysis problems, the relationship turns out to be

$$EVI = |P(S_2)V_2| - P(I_1|S_2)\cdot|P(S_2)V_2| - P(I_2|S_1)P(S_1)V_1 \tag{7a}$$

If we consider this decisional problem as a test of the null hypothesis, "H_0: the true state of nature is S_2," the error probabilities may be termed

$$P(I_1|S_2) = \text{Probability of type I error} = \alpha$$
$$P(I_2|S_1) - \text{Probability of type II error} = \beta$$

As has already been shown,

$$|P(S_2)V_2)| = EVPI$$

and so we may rewrite Equation (7a) as

$$EVI = EVPI - \alpha|P(S_2)V_2| - \beta\cdot P(S_1)V_1 \tag{7b}$$

This equation has considerable intuitive appeal. It indicates that EVI is the remaining expected value after the expected costs of the two possible kinds of errors are subtracted from EVPI.

In the example,

$$\alpha = P(I_1 | S_2) = 0.30$$
$$\beta = P(I_2 | S_1) = 0.15$$

Substituting the other values in Equation ($7b$) gives an expected value of information of

$$
\begin{aligned}
EVI &= EVPI - \alpha |P(S_2)V_2| - \beta \cdot P(S_1)V_1 \\
&= \$1.60 \text{ M} - 0.30|0.40(-4.0)| - 0.15(0.60)\ \$6.0 \text{ M} \\
&= \$1.60 - 0.48 - 0.54 \\
&= \$-0.58 \text{ M}
\end{aligned}
$$

It will be observed that the value for EVI is the same as that obtained from the extensive form used earlier (Figure 3).

We may now quickly answer the question of whether we would be better off to choose a survey design that gives likelihoods of $P(I_1|S_1) = P(I_2|S_2) = 0.85$ but would cost \$200,000 instead of \$100,000. In such a design, $\alpha = \beta = 0.15$, and so

$$
\begin{aligned}
EVI &= \$1.60 \text{ M} - .15|0.40(-4.0)| - .15\ (0.60)\ \$6.0 \text{ M} \\
&= \$1.60 - 0.24 - 0.54 \\
&= \$0.820 \text{ M} = \$820,000
\end{aligned}
$$

The net expected value of information is therefore \$620,000, or \$140,000 more than that of the design first considered. Clearly an expected-value decision maker will prefer the second design to the first.

Two-Action–Three-State Problems

Thus far, we have dealt with problems structured into "optimistic" and "pessimistic" states. The decision maker may feel this is an unnatural division of consequences; he may be accustomed to making decisions based on what he believes to be the "most probable" consequence tempered by the likelihood of a pessimistic result and supported by the possibility of an optimistic one. Thus, in our example, it may be more meaningful to think of a 7.0 to 12.0 percent market share as being most probable with > 12.0 percent as being optimistic and < 7.0 percent as pessimistic. Corresponding payoffs may be estimated and prior probabilities assigned for each. Table 5 is an example of a conditional payoff table that might result.

The prior probabilities in Table 5, $\{P(S_j) = 0.20, 0.50, 0.30\}$, were chosen to conform reasonably closely to those in the two-state formulation, $\{P(S_j) = 0.60, 0.40\}$. The payoffs have also been selected so that the EMV_0s for both formulations of the example will be the same.

TABLE 5   New-Product Commercialization: Conditioned Residual Payoff

Alternatives	S_1 — Optimistic $MS > 12\%$		S_2 — Most probable $7\% \leq MS \leq 12\%$		S_3 — Pessimistic $MS < 7\%$	
	$P(S_1)$	Payoff	$P(S_2)$	Payoff	$P(S_3)$	Payoff
A_1 — introduce	0.20	\$8.0 M	0.50	\$2.0 M	0.30	−\$2.0 M
A_2 — do not introduce	0.20	0	0.50	0	0.30	0

Similarly, the likelihoods given in Table 6 are also approximations of those in the two-state example.

TABLE 6   New-Product Commercialization: Likelihoods of Identification of States — $P(I_1|S_1)$

Research indication I_i	State of nature — S		
	S_1 $P(I_i|S_1)$	S_2 $P(I_i|S_2)$	S_3 $P(I_i|S_3)$
I_1	0.85	0.10	0.10
I_2	0.10	0.75	0.20
I_3	0.05	0.15	0.70
Total	1.00	1.00	1.00

Some obvious questions arise concerning the EVI under the two formulations. Is it the same? Given the options considered before, the $100,000, $\alpha = .30$, $\beta = 0.15$ survey versus the $200,000, $\alpha = \beta = 0.15$ survey, would we still choose the latter?

The first of these questions will be answered by determining EVI, using the extensive form of analysis. The answer to the second question will be deferred until we have established the functional relationship for EVI, in the two-action–three-state case.

Extensive Analysis of Two-Action–Three-State Problems

The extensive analysis of three-state problems is analogous to that used for two-state formulations. One must determine the joint probabilities, $P(S_j$ and $I_i)$, and revised probabilities, $P(S_j|I_i)$. These calculations are made in Tables 7 and 8, respectively. The decision tree is then formed, and the "averaging out and folding back" procedure completed. The decision tree for our problem is shown in Figure 4.

As shown in Figure 4, the EVI is $0.19 M, substantially less than the $0.58 M in the two-state example. Three factors account for this decrease: the reduction in possible loss (from −$4.0 M to −$2.0 M), the lowering of the probability of loss (from 0.40 to 0.30), and the additional information implicit in the more detailed structuring.

Functional Relationship for EVI in Two-Action–Three-State Venture Analysis Problems

For a two-state–three-action problem in venture analysis form, the expression for EVI becomes

$$EVI = EVPI - \alpha|P(S_3)V_3| - \beta_1 P(S_1)V_1 - \beta_2 P(S_2)V_2 \qquad (8)$$

where $\alpha = 1 - P(I_3|S_3)$
$\beta_1 = P(I_3|S_1)$
$\beta_2 = P(I_3|S_2)$

It is apparent that this is an extension of the two-state case. The same interpretation of EVPI applies and is arrived at by the same reasoning as used for the two-state case; the notation has now been changed to show the pessimistic state as S_3, however (Table 5), and so $EVPI = |P(S_3)V_3|$.

TABLE 7   Product-Commercialization Example: Joint Probabilities — $P(S_j$ and $I_i)$

Research indication	$P(S_1$ and $I_i)$	$P(S_2$ and $I_i)$	$P(S_3$ and $I_i)$	$P(I_i)$
I_1	$0.20 \times 0.85 = 0.170$	$0.50 \times 0.10 = 0.050$	$0.30 \times 0.10 = 0.030$	0.250
I_2	$0.20 \times 0.10 = 0.020$	$0.50 \times 0.75 = 0.375$	$0.30 \times 0.20 = 0.060$	0.455
I_3	$0.20 \times 0.05 = 0.010$	$0.50 \times 0.15 = 0.075$	$0.30 \times 0.70 = 0.210$	0.295
Total	$P(S_1) = 0.200$	$P(S_2) = 0.500$	$P(S_3) = 0.300$	1.000

TABLE 8   Product-Commercialization Example: Revised Probabilities — $P(S_j|I_i)$

State of nature	$P(S_j|I_1)$	$P(S_j|I_2)$	$P(S_j|I_3)$
S_1	$0.170/0.250 = 0.680$	$0.020/0.455 = 0.044$	$0.010/0.295 = 0.034$
S_2	$0.050/0.250 = 0.200$	$0.375/0.455 = 0.824$	$0.075/0.295 = 0.254$
S_3	$0.030/0.250 = 0.120$	$0.060/0.455 = 0.132$	$0.210/0.295 = 0.712$
Total	1.000	1.000	1.000

In the three-state example, the error probabilities were given (Table 6) as

$$\alpha = (1 - 0.70) = 0.30$$
$$\beta_1 = 0.05$$
$$\beta_2 = 0.15$$

Reference to Table 5 to obtain the prior probabilities and conditional payoffs allows us to solve for EVI, using Equation (8). The resulting value is

$$EVI = |0.30 (-\$2.0 \text{ M})| - 0.15|0\$30 (-\$2.0 \text{ M})|$$
$$- 0\$05 (0.20) \$8.0 \text{ M} - 0.15 (0.50) \$2.0$$
$$= \$0.60 - 0.09 - \$0.08 - \$0.15$$
$$= \$0.28 \text{ M} = \$280,000$$

It may be seen that the NEVI is lower for this design ($280,000 − $200,000 = $80,000) than for the initial one ($190,000 − $100,000 = $90,000). The additional increment of expected value of $90,000 is less than the estimated cost to obtain it. The EMVer would therefore prefer the first design.

ASSESSMENT OF EVI IN SEQUENTIAL-STAGE VERSUS FIXED-STAGE RESEARCH DESIGNS

To this point, the discussion has been conducted as if the only option available in acquiring information from a research project is to use a fixed-stage design. In practice, we know that sequential-stage designs are often used: a pilot study may be made to determine whether a full-scale project should be undertaken; a survey may be required next year depending upon the outcome of the one now being contemplated; a larger sample may need to be taken, conditional on the results of the research using the sample size now being considered; and so forth.

The methods described in this chapter for assessing the expected value of information are applicable to sequential-stage as well as to fixed-stage designs. We simply apply them sequentially to each stage.   Although the application is not difficult, it will be worthwhile to read about assessing EVI in sequential-stage designs before trying it for the first time.   A good explanation is given in Schlaifer [10].

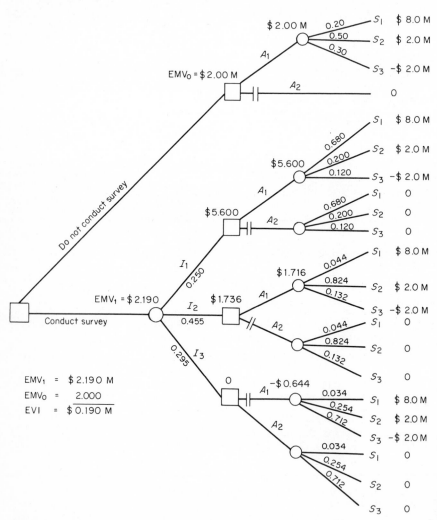

Fig. 4.   Decision tree: three-state case of a product commercialization example.

SUMMARY

This chapter has been concerned with an assessment of the value of additional information in making marketing decisions.

The chapter first reviewed some of the basic notions of Bayesian analysis, elementary probability theory, and developed Bayes' theorem.   A two-action—

two-state example, using the extensive form of analysis, was then worked through. The functional relationship of EVI with EVPI, the error likelihoods, and the payoffs for each state were then derived for two-state venture analysis problems. The two-action–three-state formulation was considered. The extensive form of analysis was first illustrated and the functional relationship for EVI and its determinants was developed for problems in venture analysis form.

For problems that have structures other than two-action–two- or three-state, the extensive form of analysis must be used.

REFERENCES

1. Bass, Frank M., "Marketing Research Expenditures—A Decision Model," *Journal of Business,* vol. 36, January 1963, pp. 77–90.
2. Fellner, William, *Probability and Profit,* Homewood, Ill.: Irwin, 1965.
3. Green, Paul E., "Uncertainty, Information, and Marketing Decisions," in Wroe Alderson, Reavis Cox, and Stanley J. Shapiro (eds.), *Theory in Marketing,* Homewood, Ill.: Irwin, pp. 333–354.
4. ——— and Donald S. Tull, *Research for Marketing Decisions,* Englewood Cliffs, N.J.: Prentice-Hall, 1970.
5. Hirshleifer, Jack, "The Bayesian Approach to Statistical Decision: An Exposition," *Journal of Business,* vol. 34, October 1961, pp. 471–489.
6. Mayer, Charles, "Integrating Non-Sampling Error Assessment into Research Design," in Robert L. King (ed.), *Marketing and the New Science of Planning,* Chicago: American Marketing Association, 1968, pp. 184–192.
7. Raiffa, Howard, *Decision Analysis,* Reading, Mass.: Addison-Wesley, 1968.
8. Roberts, Harry V., "Bayesian Statistics in Marketing," *Journal of Marketing,* vol. 27, January 1963, pp. 1–4.
9. Savage, Leonard J., *The Foundations of Statistics,* New York: Wiley, 1954.
10. Schlaifer, Robert, *Analysis of Decisions under Uncertainty,* New York: McGraw-Hill, 1969.
11. von Neumann, John, and Oskar Morgenstern, *The Theory of Games and Economic Behavior,* Princeton, N.J.: Princeton University Press, 1947.

Part A

Research Design

Chapter 4

Planning Research Strategy

ARNOLD CORBIN and **SOL DUTKA** *New York University, Graduate School of Business Administration, New York, New York and Audits and Surveys Company, New York, New York*

This chapter is concerned with the planning of research strategy primarily in the "macro" sense of programming it within the total company frame of reference, and only secondarily in the "micro" sense, that is, with regard to a particular research project.

The reason for this relative emphasis on the global aspects of the function is twofold. In the first place, it is not covered in detail elsewhere in this volume. Secondly, the opportunities for improving the deployment of marketing research resources as a key contribution to the achievement of a company's strategic goals and objectives, particularly those in the marketing end of the business, are far broader in scope and potential payout than those involved in the execution of any single research project.

This task of developing a unified systems approach to the effective planning of research strategy will be undertaken by first discussing some of the problems and difficulties in current research planning—in other words, "*What is.*" With this as a base, a number of normative points will be developed which will serve as the foundational elements in the proposed system, that is, "*What should be,*" for both the company research function and for specific research projects.

Before getting into the substance of the matter, let us first clarify a few terminological points and establish an appropriate frame of reference for discussing research strategy.

Throughout the chapter reference will be made to *corporate marketing research.* Hence, it is important to spell out clearly what we have in mind with the term *corporate.* It may convey at least two distinct connotations. In the broader sense, and the basic one in which it is used in this chapter unless otherwise indicated, it embraces marketing research activities performed throughout the entire company, including subsidiaries, divisions, and other organizational subunits. In the narrower sense, it refers only to the research activities undertaken by people at the corporate or staff level of a firm that is organized on a divisionalized basis.

The distinction between research conducted at the corporate level of a multidivisional company and that conducted within its divisions or other subunits is essentially one of degree rather than kind. In effect, the same principles apply at all levels, although the research done at the top, staff level may sometimes be broader in scope, particularly with respect to environmental factors affecting the company as a whole. A further distinction may also be valid: Those who do research at the top level may be given the additional responsibility of providing basic objectives and guidelines to research echelons lower down in the organizational hierarchy.

RELATIONSHIP OF GOALS AND OBJECTIVES TO RESEARCH STRATEGY AND FUNCTIONS

A corporation's general goals and objectives determine its corporate marketing research strategy. Just as corporate goals and objectives are both long- and short-term, so, too, is corporate marketing research strategy, which more directly concerns itself with the *marketing* goals and objectives defined by the corporation.

Broadly speaking, corporate marketing research strategy contributes to these marketing goals by means of the following overlapping functions:

Control. This provides corporations with measures of feedback on the marketplace itself and their companies' specific performance within the marketplace in relation to corporate marketing goals and objectives.

Development. Corporate marketing research utilizes developmental research to provide the company with an organized method for seeking out new corporate opportunities or directions.

These interlocking functions are carried out by means of the more formal marketing research tools and techniques.

The extent to which a company utilizes these resources in the pursuit of its goals and objectives is prescribed by the resources it allocates to this function. Essentially, a company's marketing research strategy should be an optimization of its corporate and marketing goals and the resources it allocates to its corporate marketing research functions. These resources consist of:

1. The corporate goals and objectives themselves
2. The company's marketing goals and objectives
3. The dollar resources it can allocate within this framework
4. The manpower capabilities it has, or can retain
5. Other facilities it can bring to bear, for example, computer capabilities
6. The corporate climate, that is, the organizational structure and environment within a company in which marketing decisions are made

Figure 1 outlines the functions of corporate marketing research as it operates within the framework of corporate marketing goals. In this diagram as well are the elements or tactics of marketing research by which these strategies are achieved.

As indicated previously, the functions of marketing research can most generally be separated into areas of *developmental* and *control* concerns. The developmental area includes the research and developmental processes which mediate between the possibilities offered by the state of technology and customer needs to bring new consumer and industrial products or services to the marketplace.   Marketing research operates in three major spheres in this area of development: in *concept testing*—designed to assay the feasibility of an idea; in *product testing*—to measure the extent to which the suggestions of the concept tests are realized in the product; and in *test marketing*—to determine if the market is ready and willing to accept the new product as readily as the company's marketing and profit goals require.

The second part of the development process concerns tracking those char-

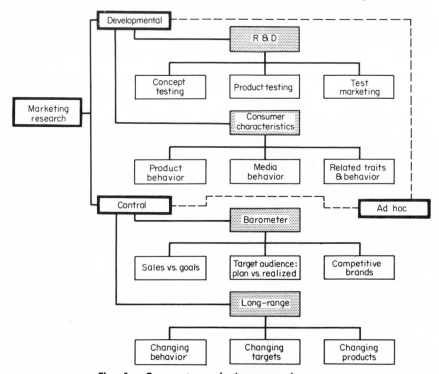

Fig. 1.   Corporate marketing research strategy.

acteristics of the customer that imply changing needs and desires which could be satisfied by new-product development.   In fact, this segment of effort often feeds suggestions into the product-engineering and design sections of R&D laboratories.

While the development area focuses on the future and is concerned with bringing the company into tomorrow's world as smoothly and as profitably as possible, the control function concentrates more on making sure that the *present* does not get out of hand.   The control concern has two major subsections into which the marketing research operations are organized: *barometric measurements*—to gauge the corporation's progress toward the achievement of marketing and communication goals; and *long-range monitoring*—to examine changes in markets, consumer behavior, and needs insofar as these changes can affect the company's current product mix and stance.

As may be noted in Figure 1, ad hoc research—to investigate specific problems uncovered either by any of the barometric checks or through other sources—is positioned with a dotted-line relationship to both developmental and control research to indicate that it may be effectively employed in either or both of these two principal types of activity.

These two areas are of course not independent. Separating the control function from the developmental one is a convenient way to separate these two major types of research, although the same personnel will often perform one function or the other. For example, the appearance of an aerosol dispenser in a field previously committed to liquid formulations may be discovered in one of the barometric checks and trigger an ad hoc study to investigate the relative appeals of the two formulations. This study is already part of the developmental process in that its findings will give direction to the design of a new product, if management decides that such a product probably will be a viable one.

Development and control, thus, are two functions which appear quite similar and really differ only in terms of emphasis. In the developmental area, one of the spheres of concern is the investigation of consumer characteristics, including *product behavior, media behavior,* and *related traits and behavior.* Control's *long-range* assignment covers much the same areas—changing targets, and changing products. In the first sphere, development focuses on new product areas as they may be affected by changes in life-style, product use, and preference. In the latter area, control deals with similar concerns, but they tend to be directed to the products the company is now manufacturing and marketing, and so serve as distant, early-warning signals of imminent changes.

There is one area of change which can be monitored by either of these two main functions; that is, the changes in the environment that may affect the company's operations. The clues through which the signals of such change may be detected are not easily predetermined since the change may make itself felt in a number of ways. To cite some examples common today: (1) The current concern with environmental pollution has affected the kinds of containers used by bottlers of beverages (soft drinks and beer)—aluminum versus steel cans, returnable versus nonreturnable bottle. And (2) the change in eating habits of the American public—particularly the young—from formal dining to informal, snack type foods has made it difficult for established hot drinks to survive and easy for cold soft drinks to flourish.

It is moot as to which function (control or development) would have discovered these changes first, but both would certainly play a role in finding and diagnosing them and in providing suggestions for solutions to the accompanying problems.

There is, finally, one area of the development function, not yet discussed, that concerns the problems of acquisitions—what kinds of product lines should be sought, whether they fit the company's objectives, and how effective they might be toward enhancing the corporation's growth and development. Regular barometric data on the sales of a corporation's products would, for example, provide data on its distribution by type of outlet. The potential "fit" and effectiveness of a contemplated acquisition could then be determined by examining the degree of overlap of the candidate firm's product line and the corporation's existing product line. High distribution overlap would indicate that the company under consideration might, all other things equal, be a better candidate for acquisition than a company whose product line shows low overlap.

By way of example, a company in the toiletry and cosmetic field was recently interested in acquiring another firm whose product line complemented its own. One of the anticipated benefits was that it could use its already-existing sales force to distribute the products of the acquired company as well and, in effect, do away with operating two independent sales forces after the acquisition.

A relatively simple retail-distribution study, conducted prior to the final negotiations, revealed that the retail-distribution patterns of both companies overlapped only slightly. The acquiring company, as part of its corporate distribution strategy, had set up its distribution patterns to distribute mostly in those areas outside of major metropolitan centers and in the smaller cities. Its marketing strategy was designed so that its product line would dominate the cosmetic and toiletry counters in these particular outlets—in contrast to being just another brand distributed alongside of more powerful competitors in the major cities.

The firm which the company was thinking of acquiring, on the other hand, had for years used television advertising in major metropolitan areas and had set up its distribution accordingly. Thus, the potential saving to be effected by the elimination of one sales force would not come about.

Both the areas just mentioned—environmental analysis and corporate development (acquisitions)—represent examples of the ways in which progressive companies are enlarging the scope of deployment of the corporate marketing research function. They illustrate the macro use of research strategy to serve the fact-finding needs which flow from the ever-widening dimensions of corporate concern in today's dynamic business world. In such companies, the research function is not narrowly confined, in a microsense, to specific marketing projects. Quite the contrary—in the macro sense in which we have been discussing it, research strategy may be effectively deployed to aid and improve decision making within company functions other than strictly marketing, for example, environmental analysis and corporate development, as already cited.

PRESENT STATUS OF RESEARCH STRATEGY

Although companies obviously show substantial differences in the way their marketing research resources are strategically deployed, we might venture a few generalizations which characterize quite a number of companies today.

The main criticism which might be leveled at current use of research is its narrow boundaries in terms of *time span, scope* of activities, and *techniques.*

In the first place, research tends to be preoccupied with maintaining the momentum of the present: doing more of what is already being done, putting out "fires," responding to emergency requests for studies; in other words, concentrating on urgent, day-to-day operational projects. Relatively little time is devoted to integrating current activities with a long-range strategic research plan for optimizing its potential contributions to the achievement of corporate goals and objectives. The strategic "forest" is being lost while excessive attention is accorded the tactical "trees." The emphasis tends to be more on "doing the thing *right*" than on asking, "Are we doing the *right* thing?"

A typical corporate research budget reinforces this conclusion concerning the obsessive concern with "today" at the expense of "what we might do tomorrow." A certain company manufactures health and beauty aid products having a total sales volume of over $100 million and an advertising budget of $15 million. Its total budget for market research is $275,000. Of this amount, $200,000 (or 73 percent) is spent on only one kind of barometric research, that is, sales data on its own and its competitors' products.

If the setting of goals and the direction of efforts to achieve these goals make any sense, then the allocation of budget to measure the rate of goal fulfillment also makes sense. But the failure to allocate funds to the other control as well as to the developmental research functions is dangerous in an age when change, at an ever-increasing rate, is dominant. One characteristic of this acceleration of change is, in the words of Toffler, that the turnover of things in our lives grows ever more frantic [10, p. 64].[1]

The *scope* of research in many companies also tends to become excessively narrow in at least two senses. In the first sense, researchers often concentrate more on collecting isolated "facts," or bits and pieces of information, than on building an integrated body of knowledge relevant to the broad, long-range problems and strategic decisions facing management. One of the ironies of the large investment made by so many companies in marketing research is that the results of this effort do not become part of a systematic body of knowledge which can be useful to the company in judging the viability of "new" ideas. This "data bank," which could serve as a valuable first screening for the evaluation of suggestions, can be expected to come closer to reality as computer storage and information-seeking algorithms become both more sophisticated and more available.

In the second sense, the bulk of the specialized individual studies is preoccupied with solutions to ad hoc crises, or with providing barometric feedback measurements on the marketplace and the position of the company's entries in it. They tend to focus more on the *descriptive*—the "what *is*"—than on the *creative*—the "what *could* be."[2]

Admittedly, the developmental R&D type of research which seeks to discover unsatisfied needs—the so-called holes in the market—is much harder to do, but it can reveal potentially much more rewarding opportunities for quantum leaps forward in market penetration, sales, and earnings growth. Unfortunately, it often receives too small a share of total marketing research resources; the scales of the balance are likely to tip heavily in favor of the more "applied" type of ad hoc and measurement-oriented research. Perhaps, if the wider perspective of the total system for planning research strategy presented in this chapter is adopted, this imbalance in the deployment of research efforts may be redressed and a more effective mix achieved.

Finally, there is a concomitant tendency for researchers to look *inward* too much toward refining the elegance of their techniques, and to look *outward* too little toward providing useful inputs to the solution of managerial problems or toward discovering new opportunities in the marketplace. Too many research workers seek ways to bend the problem to the technique of the day rather than to view solution of the problem as their research goal. These myopic "love affairs" with new techniques often isolate ivory-tower research specialists from the main stream of management, thus creating a gulf which militates against the development of an effective corporate research strategy. It should be added quickly, however, that all too often management encourages this tendency by its compartmentalization of research and by its failure to recognize the research role as part of corporate marketing strategy.

---

[1] The rest of the paragraph is also of some interest. "We face a rising flood of throw-away items, impermanent architecture, mobile and modular products, rented goods and commodities designed for almost instant death. From all these directions, strong pressures converge toward the same end: the inescapable ephemeralization of the non-thing relationship."

[2] ". . . to be creative, research must be predictive . . ." [7, p. 118].

A System Approach for Planning Research Strategy

What is a viable approach to dealing with some of the difficulties just mentioned? The solution may well lie in establishing a total, long-range strategic plan for the company, for each of its organizational components, and for its principal products and markets. As Adler recommended some time ago: "This program would be used to guide the design of individual studies so that they not only contribute knowledge for the short term but also contribute to the evolution of a unified body of information needed to implement the marketing concept over the long term" [1, p. 115].

In designing such a *research* plan, the developmental steps should be integrated with those applicable to the strategic *marketing* plan, which, in turn, should be tied to, and flow from, the strategic *business* plan for the company as a whole and for each of its major components.

The planning process should embrace certain steps. Specifically, the planner should:[3]

1. Formulate specific long-term marketing objectives, based upon long-term corporate objectives.

2. Spell out in detail the policies and programs required to achieve the marketing objectives.

3. Identify roadblocks in the way of attaining objectives and specify where further information or research is needed.

4. Define what and how marketing research can contribute to the discovery of unsatisfied needs, to problem solving, and to information gathering.

5. Get inputs and commitments from all members of the marketing team re objectives, strategies, plans, and programs.

6. Formulate a priority order and a timetable for the research projects agreed on by the team.

7. Allocate the necessary funds, personnel, and facilities for implementing the research program according to the weights decided by the team.

8. Include provisions for checkpoints and yardsticks for measurement, feedback, control, analysis of variations from plan, and plan revision during the implementation process, in order to "close the loop" on the system.

Some Underlying Concepts

There are a number of underlying concepts and premises upon which the success of planning an effective overall research strategy is predicated. Two, in particular, are worthy of detailed treatment here. They are (1) the team approach, and (2) "allocation-by-objective."

The Team Approach

Based upon the experience of companies that have been most successful at it, the most effective planning occurs when all the principal "resource owners" and functional managers do the *planning*, as well as the *running*, of a business, a marketing operation, a marketing research function, or even a specific project, *as a team*. The key concepts that underwrite successful planning and implementation are *involvement* and *commitment*. One sure way to condemn a plan, and the planning process, to failure is to delegate the entire planning job to a single "planner" who designs the plan in "splendid isolation" and then leaves its implementation to others.

---

[3] Loc. cit., as modified and expanded by the authors of this chapter.

To be effective, planning should be a team activity. This principle applies equally at all echelons in the organization, although the composition of the teams obviously changes as one moves down the ladder. Thus, at the top, members of the *business* team would typically include representatives of the marketing, manufacturing, R&D, and finance functions. Members of the *marketing* team would embrace managers of the sales, advertising, sales promotion, marketing research, and product-planning functions, with the marketing manager acting as "prime mover." When there are product or brand managers, they may also serve as prime movers of teams concerned with the welfare of their particular products.

The principle which should be strongly emphasized is that the marketing *research* manager should be a regular, fully accredited member of the *marketing* team. This implies that he should be considered not only as a *research specialist* who can make useful inputs to the information base for planning, but also as a *marketing generalist* who can contribute to the decision making of the marketing team in formulating objectives, strategies, and action programs with respect to products and markets, within the framework of overall corporate goals and objectives.

Such recognition of the marketing research man as a fully equal member of the marketing team, along with his peers in the other marketing functions, will go far to alleviate his principal source of frustration. In an unpublished study conducted by C. Theodore Smith of the American Telephone & Telegraph Company for The Conference Board, he polled 66 members of the Board's Council of Marketing Research Directors about their problems in dealing with their management associates. His findings indicated that the single thing that bothered researchers most and that occurred most frequently was: "Not thinking of the researcher as a full member of the team."

Far more effective research planning will result if the research manager is regarded as a marketing man as well as a researcher. (This, of course, implies that he should possess the necessary credentials and competence to be so regarded.) If he is accorded this status and does participate in the running and the decision making of the marketing operation, he can gain a truly first-hand appreciation of what is going on in the marketplace, with customers and their marketing people, with customers' customers, and so on down the line. Operating at these grass-roots levels, he will be stimulated to generate his own research projects to meet the needs of the operation as he detects them, based upon his own first-hand evidence, instead of waiting solely for second-hand requests from others. His role in initiating research thus changes from a *passive* one to an *active* one. He thereby gains a greater insight into research needs and opportunities and can therefore plan and program research activities with greater realism and effectiveness on a longer-range time-scale and within a broader frame of reference.

This normative approach to planning research is in strong contrast to the present situation in many companies where marketing research is managed "by crisis" rather than by objective, and where it is set up as purely staff activity "on the 39th floor" to which marketing executives address their "Request for Research" forms and hope that someone sometime will get around to working on them.

Allocation-by-Objective

In planning the allocation of market research resources, companies tend to budget such funds on what may be called a "natural" classification basis, to use a parallel expression from the lexicon of accounting. This type of classification simply *describes* the activities of services for which funds are expended, for example, syndicated audit and panel services (retail and consumer), advertising research services, public relations indexes, surveys, and so on.

Although this "natural" classification may be satisfactory for certain purposes, it is not so useful as a so-called functional classification in planning research programs and tying them into the company's objectives. In other words, research resources should be directed and programmed toward the accomplishment of specific marketing and product/market targets. This concept of budgeting research efforts might be called *allocation-by-objective*, to coin a phrase.

To cite an example, consider this product/market matrix (shown in Figure 2):

In many companies, the bulk of marketing and marketing research resources (time, money, people, and facilities) are concentrated within box A: selling more of the firm's current line to its present customers. Yet, this myopic and excessive preoccupation with the present is unaffordable if companies are to survive and grow. More resources must be positioned against box B (new markets for present products), box C (new products for present markets), and box D (new products for new markets). However, unless a conscious planning effort is programmed to achieve this better balance of resource allocation against product/market objectives, it will not occur. In other words, such a system of allocation-by-objective might help redress the present imbalance in the programming of research efforts in many companies and focus them in proper proportions against logical business objectives, in contrast to simply classifying them by type of supplier or kind of technique.

		MARKETS	
		Present	New
P R O D U C T S	Present	A Sales	B Market development
	New	C Product development	D Diversification

Fig. 2.   The product/market matrix.

CRITERIA FOR SELECTING MARKETING RESEARCH STRATEGY FOR SPECIFIC PROJECTS

The selection of a specific marketing research design can be evaluated in several ways. One standard evaluative procedure is to consider the alternative designs in terms of their cost/precision relationships. This relationship is phrased either as: Which design offers the *desired precision at minimum cost?* Or, which design offers *maximum precision at a fixed, preset cost?*

In actual practice, most commercial research projects are too often of the latter type. Companies set budgets before they set objectives. Thus, they perhaps unwittingly constrain the research design to a fixed budget regardless of the precision necessary for the company's decision making, thereby involving considerably more money.

In the preceding chapter, Tull used applications of decision theory in assessing the value of additional research information in decision making applied to new-product introductions and their expected payoffs. Variations of these techniques can also be used to evaluate the effectiveness of a company's overall marketing R&D function and as a means of choosing among alternative product areas for the allocation of R&D funds, both marketing and technical.

These might be accomplished in either of two ways. Consider Table 1. The cells in this table are an enumeration of the events which may occur when a test procedure is confronted by reality. The test hypothesis concerning a new product, a new process, or a new marketing program is that the new way is no better than the old. Data are then collected and used to test the tenability of the hypothesis. Now, the test hypothesis may be true, with (say) a likelihood of P. The likelihood that it is false is, then, $1 - P$. The sample data may lead us to conclude, correctly, that the hypothesis is true when it really is, or that it is false when it really is false. Or, these data may lead us to the wrong conclusions.

The test design will give us specific assessments of the probabilities that we will make wrong (or correct) decisions on the basis of the test data. Thus, if the test hypothesis is *really false*, there is a chance, β, that we will accept the hypothesis as true. If the hypothesis is *really true*, the chance that sample data will lead us to say that the hypothesis is false is α.

TABLE I   Hypothesis, Truth, and Consequences: A Decision Matrix

Sample says hypothesis is:	Item	Hypothesis* is really	
		True (Prob. = P)	False (Prob. = $1 - P$)
True	Decision Likelihood Return	Correct $1 - \alpha$ $A_0 - C_R$	Wrong β (type II error) $A_0 - C_R$
False	Decision Likelihood Return	Wrong α (type I error) $A_0 - C_c - C_R$	Correct $1 - \beta$ $\dfrac{\mu_1}{\mu_0} A_0 - C_c - C_R$

* Hypothesis: The new product's brand share is less than, or equal to, the value μ_0.

The decision chosen in each of the cells may lead to certain economic consequences. If we accept our test hypothesis (the northwest cell), we stay with existing products and our return continues at A_0, less the cost of research, C_R. A wrong decision (a type I error) leads to changing to the new product which is really no better than the current one; it also leads to the cost, C_c, of converting all procedures to market the new product, and the resulting return is $A_0 - C_c - C_R$.

If we make the decision in the southeast cell, we have returns which are affected by the new product's degree of superiority. If μ_1 is the new brand share and μ_0 the current one, $(\mu_1/\mu_0)A_0 - C_c - C_R$ represents the net return of the new program.

A good corporate R&D program should produce a relatively high proportion of successful products. The fraction $(1 - P)$ is a measure of a company's success with new-product introductions over time. The expected payoff $E(P)$ and $P(C)$, the probability that research testing procedures will yield correct conclusions, are the end-measure of the effectiveness of the combined R&D and test procedures. These can be derived as follows:

$$P(C) = P(1 - \alpha) + (1 - P)(1 - \beta)$$

This provides the research designer with a measurement of the effectiveness of his suggested procedure. Effectiveness in this case is defined simply as the likelihood of arriving at a correct decision. On the other hand, the expected value of the payoff $E(P)$, defined below, can translate not only research decisions but also relative contributions of new-product alternatives to profit.

The payoff is:

$$E(P) = P(1 - \alpha)(A_0 - C_R) + (1 - P) \beta (A_0 - C_R)$$
$$+ P\alpha (A_0 - C_e - C_R) + (1 - P)(1 - \beta)$$
$$\{(\mu_1/\mu_0)(A_0 - C_e - C_R)\}$$

A second way of looking at the model is to view all R&D and testing as one process, with the payouts in the several cells viewed as totals including *all* the testing and development supported by the company during some fixed period, say one year. The assignment of an appropriate value P to the variables in each cell provides the basis for evaluating the entire process from concept testing through market testing as a unified system whose ultimate aim is to maintain the company's viability and growth.

SUMMARY

This chapter has attempted to deal with the problem of planning research strategy at two levels: (1) the macro—for the company as a whole, and (2) the micro—for specific research projects. The macro approach was presented as a generalization of the micro approach for single projects.

With respect to corporate strategy, we first discussed some of the principal weaknesses and difficulties in current research planning ("what is"), particularly its narrow boundaries in terms of time span, scope, and techniques. In this connection, a distinction was drawn between two major categories of research: (1) *control*, which emphasizes the *present* (barometric measurement), and (2) *developmental*, which emphasizes the *future* (discovery of opportunities for new products, services, markets, uses, and so on, based upon changing technology and customer needs).

After some of the main problems and limitations of the current situation were detailed, a normative systems approach for planning research strategy was presented. Two underlying concepts which help to implement the proposed systems approach effectively were then developed; that is, the team approach and allocation-by-objective.

The remaining portion of the chapter dealt with some criteria for selecting marketing research strategy for specific projects, particularly in terms of the cost/precision relationships of alternative designs.

REFERENCES

1. Adler, L., "Phasing Research into the Marketing Plan," *Harvard Business Review*, May–June 1960.
2. Chernoff, H., and L. E. Moses, *Elementary Decision Theory*, New York: Wiley, 1959.
3. Keane, J. G., "Some Observations on Marketing Research in Top Management Decision Making," *Journal of Marketing*, vol. 34, October 1969.
4. Koestler, A., *The Act of Creation*, New York: Macmillan, 1964.
5. Myers, J. H., and A. Sanli, "Management Control of Marketing Research," *Journal of Marketing Research*, vol. 6, August 1969.

6. Newman, J. W., "Put Research into Marketing Decisions," *Harvard Business Review*, vol. 40, March–April 1962.
7. Politz, A., "Science and Truth in Marketing Research," *Harvard Business Review*, vol. 35, January–February 1957.
8. Raiffa, H., *Decision Analysis, Introductory Lectures on Choices Under Uncertainty*, Reading Mass.: Addison-Wesley, 1968.
9. Schlaifer, R., *Probability and Statistics for Business Decisions*, New York: McGraw-Hill, 1959.
10. Toffler, A., *Future Shock*, New York: Random House, 1971.
11. Webb, E. J., D. T. Campbell, R. D. Schwartz, and L. Sechrest, *Unobtrusive Measures: Non-Reactive Research in Social Sciences*, Chicago: Rand McNally, 1966.

Part A

Research Design

Chapter 5

Planning for Data Processing and Data Storage

CHANNING STOWELL, III *Corporate Market Information Services, The Pillsbury Company, Minneapolis, Minnesota*

When data processing and data storage are to play a major role in a market research project, planning for their application is an integral part of the project's research design. Previous chapters have discussed some of the considerations involved in this planning. This chapter presents the subject in its entirety.

The purpose here, however, is not to instruct the reader in data processing, but to aid him in understanding how to plan for its use. Its objectives are (1) to define what is meant by planning for data processing and data storage, and (2) to explain the methodology by which it is done.

The planning procedure presented here takes a "systems" approach. Planning for data processing and data storage is viewed as the basic design of a system of functions necessary to convert the project's data into the desired information.

The chapter's initial section defines the objectives for this planning and describes its end-product. Systems and data processing concepts required to do this planning are reviewed in the second section. A concluding section focuses on the details of the planning process. Examples are used throughout to illustrate the points discussed.

THE OBJECTIVE OF PLANNING FOR DATA PROCESSING AND DATA STORAGE

The objective of planning for data processing and storage is to explicitly define and document the project's requirements for data processing. To do this, planning involves two major activities, performed sequentially during the project's research design:

1. Evaluation of the data processing necessary in each research strategy alternative (including estimation of the resources required).

2. Specification, once the project's strategy has been formulated, of the "plan" whereby the data processing can be implemented

The documented plan resulting from the second activity represents an initial design or "macrospecification" of an information system. These macrospecifications consist of (1) the *functional* characteristics of the system to produce the information required by the project; and (2) a calendar and dollar budget defining the resource allocations necessary to design, develop, and implement the system.

The remainder of this chapter section provides an explanation of these documents and presents a condensed example of their contents.

System Specifications. The preliminary system design contains the following parts:

1. A flow-chart representation of the *functional* structure of the system. This indicates each of the major processing and storage functions (and their interrelationship) required to generate the project's information. It also identifies the man-machine interaction for controlling information generation.

2. A definition of each of the functions shown on the flow chart. Each function's description outlines the input and output data and the transformations to be performed. Any mathematical techniques or logic operations to be included are explained.

3. A description of each major data file shown in the system flow chart. In this description, the basic source for each file and its contents are defined.

Calendar and Dollar Budget. This document outlines the timetable and estimated allocations of resources necessary to design, develop, and implement the system (see "Systems Concepts," the next major chapter section). It indicates the major milestones to be achieved, the date of each, and an estimate of the necessary resources.

In addition to dollars, resources that are budgeted are (1) manpower (system analysts and programmers); and (2) equipment (processing and data conversion).

Example. Throughout the chapter, an example of a system that was part of a market research project will be used to clarify the concepts presented. The project concerned measuring population attitudes toward, and awareness of, several products and product characteristics. Data were to be collected by telephone survey over an extended period. Data processing and storage were to be used to record responses to telephoned questionnaires and to generate attitude and awareness measures for different population segments. Important dimensions for analysis were time, geography, and demography.

This system was structured as follows:

1. The macrospecifications flow chart is shown in Figure 1.

2. Each of the functions shown is briefly described as follows:

CONVERSION. The completed questionnaires, which will be on optical scanning forms, are converted by an optical scanner into magtape records. Mutilated or folded questionnaires will not be processed. Input is questionnaire forms; output is magnetic-tape files.

FILE UPDATE.   The questionnaire records on the magtape will be edited for appropriate character placement and logic of responses and then will be placed on the questionnaire master file.   Input is questionnaire magtape records; outputs are on updated questionnaire master file and error records.

RETRIEVAL.   Retrieval will permit subsets of the respondent population to be isolated from the questionnaire master file by any combination of the following:

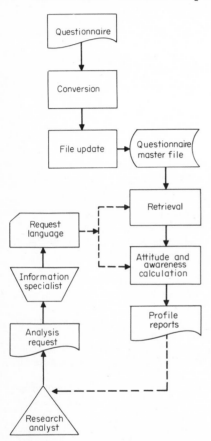

a. Geography
    (1) Region
    (2) State
    (3) City
    (4) County
b. Demography
    (1) Age
    (2) Sex
    (3) Race
    (4) Family size
    (5) Income
    (6) Occupation
    (7) Education
c. Date of response
d. Attitude toward product attribute(s)
e. Awareness of product(s)
f. Awareness of product attribute(s)

Input is the questionnaire master file and a Boolean request language.[1]   Output is the questionnaire's work file which contains the questionnaires requested.

ATTITUDE AND AWARENESS CALCULATION.   This function will calculate the percentage of a retrieved market segment having a cash attitude and awareness of each product and product attribute. A derived attitude score for each product will also be determined.[2] Input is a retrieved work file.

Fig. 1.   Macrospecification flow chart.

Output is attitude and awareness measures for the population and attitude scores by product.

PROFILE REPORTS.   These reports will display tabularly and/or graphically the "profiles" of attitudes and awareness levels for the different

---

[1] The Boolean request language specifies the criteria for retrieval of questionnaires through "and/or" logic.   It permits the isolation of various combinations of respondent geography, demography, and responses, for example, all females between 20 and 30 years of age, single, living in New York City, who are "aware" of Vote toothpaste.

[2] The technique used for computation of derived attitude is the proprietary information of Decision Technology, Inc.

population subsets. When calculated, the derived attitudes will also be displayed. The inputs for these reports are the attitude and awareness calculations.

3. The questionnaire master data file's description was basically the following: This file (probably on disk) is built by FILE UPDATE from returned questionnaire records on magtape. There is one record for each returned questionnaire. Each record contains codes describing the following:

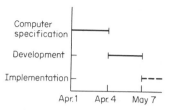

Fig. 2. Project schedule.

a. Respondent's demography and geographic location
b. The date of response
c. Answers to each question

4. The schedule and budget shown was:
a. Overall schedule (see Figure 2)
b. Overall budget
   (1) Computer specification

Analyst/Programmer A	(2 man-weeks)	$ 500
Analyst/Programmer B	(2 man-weeks)	500
Coordinator A	(0.5 man-week)	200
Total cost		**$1,200**

   (2) Development

Analyst/Programmer A	(3 man-weeks)	$ 750
Analyst/Programmer B	(3 man-weeks)	750
Programmer A	(3 man-weeks)	450
Coordinator A	(0.5 man-week)	200
Computer	(5 hours)	500
Total cost		**$2,650**

   (3) Implementation (per month)

Programmer A	(1 man-week)	$ 500
Coordinator A	(0.5 man-week)	150
Computer	(5 hours)	500
Optical scanning (assuming 10,000 questionnaires per month)	(4 hours)	200
Total monthly cost		**$1,350**

c. Milestone schedule for computer specification (see Figure 3)

SYSTEMS CONCEPTS

This section reviews basic systems concepts that are prerequisites for understanding the approach to planning presented in this chapter. These concepts are (1) the systems perspective; (2) the systems design, development, and implementation process which occurs after planning; and (3) sources of resources for system design, development, and implementation.

The Systems Perspective

The systems perspective implies that the planner initially views the application of data processing and data storage to his project as the complete set of in-

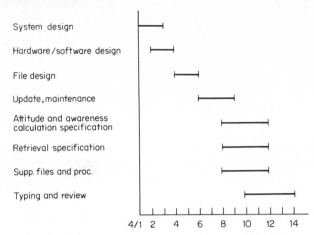

Fig. 3.   Milestone schedule for computer specification.

terrelated functions necessary to transform data into the information desired. Two concepts here are important:

1.   Functions—transformations and storage of data—are the concern at this time, not *computers, programs,* or *data files.*

2.   The *complete* set of functions—the system—is initially viewed, not isolated parts.

"System" in this context refers only to the functions; it does not pertain to the hardware (computer equipment) or the software (programs).

Figure 4 is a simplified diagram of the basic system functions which may be present in an information system.   They represent, exhaustively, the operations which have to be performed to transform the data.   All of these functions may not be required in a given application.   Any of them may appear more than once.   The necessity of each is considered during the planning.

These functions are:

Data Conversion.   This is the translation of source information (a returned questionnaire, a bill of lading, an invoice, a panel diary) into a form which can be "read" by a computer.   Most frequently, this procedure involves keypunching cards directly from the documents or from manually coded versions of them.   However, as illustrated in the example in the first section, it is possible to go directly from a document to a machine-readable storage device. This trend will continue with the development of key to tape (and to disk) and optical character-recognition devices.   In eliminating keypunching cards, this equipment produces significant savings by reducing errors and processing time.

Preprocessing.   Preprocessing involves the "editing"—error checking—of the converted data and the transformation of those data into the data file record structure.   The edited and transformed data are placed into the data file.

To use the example of the system already discussed, the preprocessor (called FILE UPDATE) did the following with each record for a returned questionnaire: It checked to see that the questionnaire's demography was "logical," that is, that no one was both male and female or lived in two or more cities.   The presence of appropriate alphabetic and/or numeric characters where required was also tested. Once tested, each record (a questionnaire on tape) was placed on the Questionnaire Master File.

Another example of preprocessing occurs with panel diary data. Input diary records on cards or tape are checked for proper product and geographic codes before being inserted into a work file for processing.

Data Storage. This refers to the inclusion of data records in machine-readable data files. A data file is the repository of information remaining in the system for analysis and display.

A computer does not have "room" in its internal "core" memory to store at one time all the data records to be analyzed. A data file is the means by which all this information is stored. The file's data are still available for analysis, several records at a time. The file might be thought of as a "book." The computer cannot absorb more than two or three "pages" at a time but must eventually look at each one. Therefore, the book—the data file—is made available to the computer, which can look at a few pages (the records) at a time.

The *medium* of a file is also important. Data records may be stored on punched cards, magnetic tape, or on a magnetic disk (or drum). All information is in a coded form that is meaningful to the computer. The medium used and the record structure are prime determinants of the speed at which a system can process data.

In the example, the main data file was on a magnetic disk. Temporary data files were magnetic tapes from the optical scanner. The basic record structure was at the level of a returned questionnaire. There was one record on file for each questionnaire. Each file record represents a single purchase transaction for a family.

MRCA panel data is another good example of data files. These coded purchase records for the panel members may be on punched cards or on tape. In either event, a record's contents and structure remain the same. This is the storage *medium.*

Data Retrieval. Retrieval is the process that isolates or extracts from a complete data file only the data required for analysis and information display. This process improves processing efficiency by reducing the amount of data that must be "read" to produce specific information. In small-scale systems it is often not required. A manual retrieval is often performed through selection of appropriate "physical" file units (decks of cards, reels of magtape, disk units).

In the questionnaire system, retrieval extracted only those returned questionnaires of interest for analysis. The system could retrieve the questionnaires which satisfied any combination of dates, demography, and geography. Thus, a file of 50,000 questionnaires could rapidly be reduced to one of 1,000 or fewer records (the entire file could still be used).

Manual retrieval for individual time periods could have been done had the questionnaires for each month been stored on separate reels of magnetic tape. Then, when a certain month was required, the proper reel or reels of tape could have been used.

When cross-tabulations involving aggregations across several dimensions are to be used, it is far simpler and cheaper to let

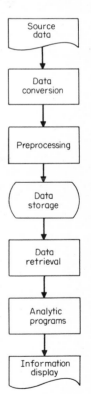

Fig. 4. Basic system functions.

the computer do the work of choosing the required data than to separate data onto individual files.

Analytic Programs. These are commonly referred to as algorithms, statistical routines, or models. They are the computational programs which manipulate data in a prespecified manner. They range in sophistication from the simple arithmetic operations to complex predictive and simulation models.

The example's system involved nothing more complex than the computation of the percentage of a defined respondent population with certain awarenesses of, and/or attitudes toward, products. Its calculation also computed an attitude "score" for each product among population subsets. Another analytic function could have been added to identify "exceptions": products in different segments with lower-than-average awareness or with declining trends in awareness.

Information Display. The information display function "formats" (arranges) the information calculated in the analytic functions onto an output medium—report paper, most often. Alphabetic descriptions of the report, rows, and columns are usually inserted. Most simple tabulations combine the analytic function with information display. In many instances, this is possible with the system's parameter language which controls both calculations and display.

This was the case in the attitude and awareness system. The Boolean request language specified both the population subjects for the calculation and the alphabetic descriptions and positioning for the report. A graph rather than a tabular report could have been requested for display from the same calculations.

The Systems Design, Development, and Implementation Process

The objective of the planning under discussion is to produce the preliminary specifications of an information system and estimates of the resource requirements to implement this data processing. Although this chapter is not intended as a discussion of "classical" computer system design, the elements of the process by which the macrospecifications are implemented into a system should be understood if resource requirements are to be properly estimated. This process brings into existence the data processing system whose objectives were specified during planning.

The stages in this process, shown in Figure 5, are computer-oriented system specification, system development, and system implementation. The first stage sets more precise, technical objectives for the data processing. The second establishes hardware and software configurations to meet those objectives. The final stage interfaces the system with the rest of the project to generate the desired information.

Examples for this part of the chapter are inappropriate in a discussion of planning. They would be too technical and at a level of detail not required for successful planning.

Computer-oriented System Specification. This stage is the classical systems design. Its objective is to provide the detailed technical design and documentation of the system. This documentation enables programmers and other systems personnel to implement the system which was broadly defined in the macrospecifications.

It must be noted that it is not until this stage, *after planning*, that the decision on the computer equipment and software is made.

The document produced will fully explain hardware and software configuration; data files; program structures; and data collection and processing procedures.

The hardware/software configurations can be explained by two flow charts.

One identifies the computer hardware necessary; the other, each program that will be required.

Each major file is explained in terms of its contents, organization, and structure. Record layouts (the internal file configuration of a record) and field explanations (the code structures to be used in each record) are provided.

Each program is explicitly defined by explanations of purpose; input files; output files and/or report formats; processing steps; and detailed flow chart of processing logic.

The resource quantities needed for this stage will vary with system complexity. The primary resources are systems analysts. However, the market researcher is involved to explain any models or algorithms necessary and to ensure that the system defined in these microspecifications meets the original objectives of the macrospecifications.

These microspecifications are prepared in the following order:

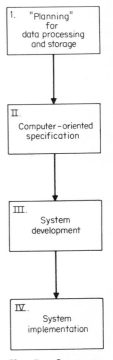

1. Detailed functional design
2. Hardware and software components
3. Major files
4. Programs and procedures necessary to create, update, and maintain the files
5. Analytic programs
6. Retrieval programs
7. Supplementary files and data collection procedures

Throughout this stage, frequent reviews of the design are necessary to ensure that the detailed system is being designed according to original objectives. The systems perspective provides the means to evaluate the implications of a file or program design on the other parts. This stage serves to reduce the cost of the data processing from both a dollar and a time basis by explicating these interrelationships before programming begins.

System Development. This stage involves the actual programming, testing, and validation of the system. The principal resources required are programmers (and existing programs) and the computer (and/or other data processing equipment). The product of this stage is an operating system meeting the requirements outlined in the computer-oriented specifications (and originally in the macrospecifications). This stage brings into existence the programs and files for each of the major portions of the system.

Fig. 5. Stages to system implementation.

The tasks necessary to develop each program are sequenced as follows:

1. Communication of program requirements (via specifications and, when necessary, personal discussion)
2. Flow-charting
3. Coding
4. Testing ("debugging")
5. Validation

The market researcher and the systems analyst must review the resultant output of the major analytic programs to ensure that their goals are being achieved. When mathematical models are involved, the market researcher should be responsible for their validation (a program may function perfectly and the model may still not be valid).

Before this phase is completed, the entire system is validated—a dry run is made to see that it generates the required information within the time and budget constraints. All individual parts must be "connected" into the complete system. The system's ability to transform the data into required information can thus be tested.

System Implementation. This final stage focuses on the utilization of the system to produce the information desired. Operating personnel and the data processing equipment must be scheduled. The system must be operationally interfaced with the project's other activities. Procedures must be established to monitor both this interface and the information output of the system, and thus to identify needed modifications.

The major resources involved here are the market research project staff, the processing equipment, and the support personnel. As system modifications are needed, system analysts and programmers will be required.

Assessment of Data Processing Resource Alternatives

Before the data processing and data storage requirements of different strategy alternatives can be evaluated, the planner should be familiar with the availability of resources to design, develop, and implement the system. Here again, the resources needed are of two major types: personnel (programmers and analysts) and equipment (computer hardware and software). The planner must assess the availability of these two resources both "in-house" and "out-of-house" but need not concern himself at a low level of detail.

The author's bias is toward the use of in-house resources whenever possible. However, there are many situations where such resources are either unavailable or inadequate, particularly when time is a major project constraint.

With regard to personnel, different sources should be assessed as to their quantity; quality (experience, background, level of competence); schedule of availability; and cost.

In ascertaining the availability of different computer systems (or computer hardware and software configurations), the planner should evaluate each system in terms of:

Core (internal memory) size
Input devices (tapes, disks, card readers) and their speed
Output devices (printers, tapes, disks, card punches) and speed
Software operating system and programming languages
Operating costs—rate structure
Compatibility with other computer systems
Operating procedures
  program testing
  production
Turnaround time
Schedule of availability

Programmers and analysts can be found in several sources other than a company's internal systems or information service staff. Consultant firms, software houses, service bureaus, and free-lance programmers are among these sources.

Besides in-house computer systems, numerous data processing service bureaus provide computer equipment rentals. Banks, universities, and corporations also sell computer time on their equipment. Consulting firms and software houses will often have their own equipment.

There are consulting firms which perform the entire planning, design, development, and operation of the system. Consultants and software houses may also be engaged to do the detail system design and development and operation (on other equipment or on that of the employing company). Market research contractors can often provide these resources. Software packages (groups of programs for specific functions) are also available.

In-house and out-of-house resources can be employed effectively in a variety of combinations. The important aspect of this problem is that the market researcher know the characteristics and different suppliers of the resources that will have to be applied. During planning, it is not necessary to get deeply involved with the details of programming and computer equipment.

THE PLANNING PROCESS

This section presents the steps in the planning process that are necessary to evaluate alternatives and to arrive at a final system macro design. These steps, depicted in Figure 6, are:

1. Determination of information objectives
2. Determination of analytic requirements
3. Evaluation of data sources
4. Selection of system
5. Preliminary system design
   a. File
   b. Analytic functions

Steps 1 through 3 are necessary to evaluate alternatives for data processing. Step 4 represents the selection of a system design in conjunction with the project's strategy formulation. Documentation of that system is done in step 5.

Besides pointing out the considerations involved in each step, this section will describe the estimation of schedules and costs.

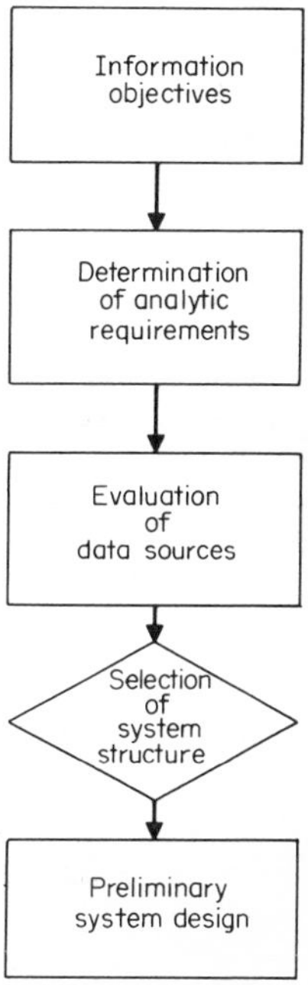

Fig. 6. Planning process for data processing and data storage.

Determination of Information Objectives

This first step in planning occurs during the project's problem specification, which must provide the conceptual framework for the problem. As strategy alternatives are formulated, the measures ("statistics") desired must be explicitly defined. The problem should be structured into its major elements and the relationships among the elements defined.

Again, to refer back to the attitude and awareness project, the basic information objective was to report measured and predicted attitude and awareness levels of the market and its segments. An attempt was being made to identify the effects of different media and the content strategies which would be applied geographically and over time.

Measured and predicted attitude and awareness levels were to be generated for market segments identified by demography, geography, and media habits. The effect of time also had to be reported.

This first step, although seemingly obvious, is the one most often overlooked. It is this step that sets the direction and boundaries for the rest of the planning effort. Without clear objectives, the planning process, indeed the entire project, is doomed to insignificant results.

Determination of Analytic Requirements

Once the information objectives for each alternative have been defined, the market research staff must determine, for each alternative, which analytic technique or techniques can provide the measures specified in these objectives.

The resource requirements for each of the three steps leading to implementation must be approximated at this stage. On the basis of these estimates and the project's budget constraints, some system alternatives can be eliminated.

It was at this stage in the questionnaire-project example that predicted measures for levels of attitude and awareness were eliminated. Because of time constraints, building a model was infeasible. The rest of the system could not be delayed for this effort. Instead, model development was to be a parallel effort with the system's implementation.

Evaluation of Data Sources

With the analytic requirements defined, the availability of data for the various techniques must be considered. To do this, the data objectives must first be specified in terms of measures to be collected, historical perspective, and information recency.

The measures to be collected are those data necessary to generate the information specified in the information objectives. If dollar market share is to be reported for a product, that product's dollar sales and the total sales of the product category must be included. Dimensions needed in classifying the data are also important. Demography, geography, time, and product category are typical dimensions.

The example used previously required measures of attitude based on a semantic differential scale. Top-of-mind brand awareness also had to be collected. Responses needed to be classified by demography, geography, brand name, and media habits.

Historical perspective means the prior time series data which may be required. The value and utility of models and/or tabulations may increase if historical information is available. The information objectives and the analytic requirements set previously will govern the choice of historical perspective.

The attitude and awareness survey did not require prior data but would use the first survey to initiate the analysis.

Information recency refers to the lag between the time at which an event occurs and the time at which data about that event are entered into the data file. The acceptance level will vary from project to project. In our example, a maximum of three days from survey completion to report preparation was allowed.

When the necessary historical perspective and information recency have been specified, the resource requirements for designing, developing, and implementing the primary data file from different sources can be estimated. These estimates must be made in terms of the system which is necessary to transform source data into the file. The estimates should cover each of the three succeeding stages in the system design, development, and implementation process.

Selection of the System

Once the analytic requirements have been determined and the data sources evaluated, a decision can be made on the overall system's macro design. The resource requirements of the alternative structures of analytic functions and data sources can be evaluated. The planner must consider the costs of these requirements on the basis of the resources that will be available and the implications of the alternative structures on the rest of the project activities. This decision is based on elementary cost-benefit analysis of the alternatives. The costs can be approximated during the planning process. The benefits must be assessed with respect to the entire project's research design and are not confined only to data processing and storage.

The principal criterion for selecting the system must be its ability to meet the project's original information objectives. Cost *alone* is not a major factor.

Because of the critical time constraints in the attitude and awareness project, the decision was made to eliminate from the questionnaire questions relating to media habits. It was thought that their inclusion would make the questionnaire too long for proper administration. Approximate measures of these habits could be obtained from published data relating media to population demography and geography. Trial questions relating to these habits would be developed in the system implementation.

Preliminary System Design

The final effort in this process is devoted to outlining the functional requirements for the system selected. These requirements center around the two major system parts: data files and analytic programs.

Data Files. Each major file's purpose and source should be defined. An estimate of its size in terms of number and size of individual records must be given. The file's contents, records structure, and organization must also be explained.

These primary data files should be "disaggregate." That is, data should be stored at its lowest level of capture—for example, by individual invoice-line items, individual responses to each question in a survey, each purchase for each person in a panel, rather than as combined statistics at a summary level. The outline specifies for each file the record structure in terms of:

1. Account descriptors: information about each specific source (for example, demographic codes for panel members, trade class, area, address for retail accounts). In the example, the descriptor was the demographics of the respondent.

2. Transaction descriptors: pertinent data regarding the event of collection (for example, invoice data and warehouse number, interviewer code, area code). Date of survey and interviewer number were used in the questionnaire example.

3. Transaction data: the actual information codes (for example, invoice line items, answers to questionnaire). The answers to each question were the transaction data in the example presented.

Analytic Programs. The design of the analytic functions occurs after files have been specified. These outlines describe in detail the output or reports required and the mathematical techniques to be employed. The input files necessary for each function are defined. If a data retrieval function is needed, its characteristics are specified at this time.

An important objective of this design is to minimize the number of programs. This is achieved by allowing for maximum external control over the output of the function. That is, a single function which can be parameterized to produce many different report formats, rather than separate functions for each format, can be designed.

This generalization was achieved in the present example system by formatting reports via the request language. The appropriate label descriptions to be used on the reports were included in this language.

Estimating Resource Requirements

There are no universal rules of thumb for resource estimation. Factors influencing such estimates change with individual situations. The important rule is to prepare budget and schedule estimates in conjunction with personnel responsible for the system's implementation.

The principal method used is that of subdividing the total project into as fine a level of separate tasks as possible. This can be done by first dividing the process into the three major stages: design, development, and implementation. Each of these stages can then be separated by activity, and each activity by its component tasks.

Two principal resource estimates, programming time and computer time, are so common that they must be presented in detail.

Programming Time. The programming activity for each program, as pointed out earlier, consists of analysis of program function, flow-charting, coding, testing and "debugging," and validation. Such a division makes it easier to prepare, with systems personnel, estimates of the amount of both calendar time and man-time that will be necessary during development.

Computer Time. Once files and records have been defined, an estimate is needed of how long it will take a computer to "read" an individual record (or block of records by dividing the computer's input speed into the records size). The number of records to be read multiplied by this read time becomes the basic component of other estimates.

When the data processing output cannot be prepared simultaneously with input, the output time must be added to the input figure. The estimate is prepared on the same basis: the output record size is divided by the machine's output rate. When input and output operations can be performed simultaneously with input, the output time must be added to the input figure. The estimate is prepared on the same basis: the output record size is divided by the machine's output rate. When input and output operations can be performed simultaneously but the output requires the greater time, this output time becomes the estimate. If the time for computation is greater than that for input and output, the computation time governs the estimate.

This estimated processing time for a single "run" multiplied by the number of runs in a period yields the estimated total computer time for the period. Man-time for programming and computer time can be converted to dollars via a rate per unit of time.

In the example system's FILE UPDATE, it was assumed that 10,000 questionnaires would be processed each month. It was estimated that the computer being used could read approximately 30,000 of these records per hour. Since the output of these records could be performed simultaneously with the input and required less time, it was estimated that update would require one-third hour per month. At $100 an hour for the computer, the cost amounted to $33 a month. The required calculation routines could input 50,000 records per hour. Calculations required only one minute, but report printing (output) took approximately 20 minutes because of the printer's slower speed.

It is important to note the dependence of calendar time (schedule) on man-time (budget). Implicit in a calendar schedule is the allocation of resources to a specific period. Failure to recognize this requirement will lead to unrealistic schedules.

CONCLUSION

This chapter has discussed planning for data processing and data storage as a preliminary step in the design of a system. The objective of this procedure is to determine the data processing implications of the strategy alternatives, to evaluate these implications, and to document the data processing requirements of the chosen system. The chapter has attempted to acquaint the reader with a systems approach to planning, not the technical details of data processing. Prerequisites for this process, explained earlier, are:

Determination of what constitutes a system

The steps required to design, develop, and implement the system

The alternative suppliers of resources for each step

Without this background knowledge, successful planning cannot be accomplished.

The last section of the chapter delineated the steps in the process that accomplish the objectives of the planning. Methods used in each step were explained.

The planning process begins with clear definition of information objectives and alternatives. The succeeding step involves identifying the alternatives for satisfying those objectives and the costs of each alternative. Once an alternative has been chosen, the final phase of the planning defines and documents the data processing requirements and the strategy (budget and schedule) for system implementation.

BIBLIOGRAPHY

Amstutz, A. E., "The Marketing Executive and Management Information Systems," Working Paper 213–66, Cambridge, Mass.: M.I.T., Alfred P. Sloan School of Management, 1966.

Colbert, D. A., *Data Processing Concepts,* New York: McGraw-Hill, 1968.

Computer Simulation of Competitive Market Response, chaps. 2, 5, 13, and 15, Cambridge, Mass.: M.I.T., 1967.

Data Processing Digest, monthly.

Dearden, J., and F. W. McFarlan, *Management and Information Systems,* Homewood, Ill.: Irwin, 1966.

Donald, A. G., *Management: Information & Systems,* Oxford, England: Pergamon, 1967.

EDP Analyzer.

Gregory, R. H., and R. L. Van Horn, *Automatic Data Processing Systems,* Belmont, Calif.: Wadsworth, 1963.

Hugo, St. J. I., *Marketing and the Computer,* New York: Pergamon, 1967.

Montgomery, D. B., "Computer Applications in Market Research," Working Paper 212–66, Cambridge, Mass.: M.I.T., Alfred P. Sloan School of Management, 1966.

Rosove, P. E., *Developing Computer-based Information Systems,* New York: Wiley, 1967.

Sales Management, monthly.

Sisson, R. L., and Corning, R. G., *A Manager's Guide to Computer Processing,* New York: Wiley, 1967.

Chapter 1

Survey Design

PAUL B. SHEATSLEY *National Opinion Research Center, University of Chicago, Chicago, Illinois*

The term *survey* in marketing or public opinion research generally refers to a planned effort to collect needed data from a representative sample of the relevant population. Preceding chapters have suggested that the survey is not necessarily the answer to all information problems. Secondary analysis of existing materials may often serve almost as well. In many cases, the value of the new information may hardly be worth the cost of collecting and tabulating it. Yet there is no doubt that surveys, when properly conducted, offer a reasonably quick, inexpensive, efficient, and accurate means of ascertaining the characteristics, knowledge, attitudes, and behavior of almost any population of interest.

Indeed, surveys have so many advantages that they are in some danger of overuse. In the United States, a mere 1,500 interviews can accurately reflect the views of 120 million adults within a few percentage points. Even smaller samples can provide fairly reliable guides to popular attitudes and behavior. The survey is infinitely flexible. If one is interested in only a certain segment of the population—for example, teen-agers, owners of motorboats, housewives of a certain age—the survey can be focused on just that particular group. The American public has shown itself to be remarkably good-humored about cooperating with survey interviewers, and they can ask almost any question, and as many questions, as the surveyor may wish to include in the interview. Though the tabulated responses to each questionnaire item are of interest, the value of the collected data goes far beyond that. Properly analyzed, the data can be manipulated in many ways so that the researcher can look at intergroup differences, examine the effects of independent variables such as income or family size, or even predict future behavior. It is small wonder, then, that the use of surveys has proliferated since their feasibility and accuracy were first demonstrated 40 years ago.

On the other hand, it may be no exaggeration to say that the greater number of surveys conducted today are a waste of time and money. Many are simply bad surveys. Samples are biased; questions are poorly phrased; interviewers are not properly instructed and supervised; and results are misinterpreted. Such surveys are worse than none at all because the sponsor may be misled into a costly error. Even well-planned and neatly executed surveys may be useless if, as often happens, their results come too late to be of value or are converted into a bulky report which no one has time to read.

One must distinguish between the design of surveys and their execution, processing, and analysis. Survey design refers to the planning of a study: the necessary decisions regarding the population to be sampled, the size and nature of the sample, the means of data collection, and the development of the questionnaire or other field instruments. Although a well-designed survey may be poorly executed or inadequately analyzed, a poorly designed survey can rarely be redeemed by high-quality data collection or insightful analysis. Once the survey is consigned to the field, its design is set; it is too late to change any of the elements. This inexorable fact dictates the importance of survey design—of thinking through in advance the purpose of the survey and of devising the most appropriate procedures to produce the relevant information in the most efficient manner. This chapter touches only lightly on problems of actual data collection, field supervision, coding, data processing, and analysis. Rather, it addresses itself to the considerations that must enter into survey planning and design.

LEVEL OF EFFORT: TIME AND COST

The most important considerations affecting survey design are the available time and resources, for of course neither is unlimited. There is always a trade-off between these two factors and the amount and quality of data collected. Let us consider two extreme examples.

Management is prepared to spend $100,000 or more on a survey of the male cosmetics market. It wants to know such things as how many males use what kinds of cosmetics how often. Who are these males in terms of age, income, region of the country? What are their attitudes toward cosmetics? What gratifications do they receive from their use? Who are the nonusers? Why do they not use cosmetics? What might be done to persuade them to use cosmetics? What would be the probable reaction to several new cosmetic products for males that the company is considering introducing? Management understands that this research effort will take some time, but it needs a report, with recommendations, within nine months.

With these specifications, the researcher can answer most of his problems of survey design. He will need a national probability sample of males, and since management wants fairly precise estimates and also a look at population subgroups, the sample should be large enough for these purposes—probably at least 1,500 cases, or 2,000 if he can afford them. The researcher will have to determine where to set the minimum age: 18? 16? 14? He will need personal interviews with the men in their homes. (Incidentally, might men talk more readily to male interviewers than to the usual female interviewers on this subject? He will have to think about that.)

Since management wants much information, the interview will probably be a long one, perhaps an hour or more. And since men may not know their motivations in this area or may be reluctant to state them, the researcher must come up with a pretty sophisticated questionnaire, one that includes some open-ended questions and perhaps a personality test to be self-administered during the interview. And so on . . .

Now consider another situation in another firm. It is Friday, just after lunch. The poor researcher is informed that management needs some data by Monday noon on women's preferences on two proposed advertisements. The firm can spend $500 for this information. Again, most of the researcher's problems of survey design are already solved. National surveys, probability samples, one-hour interviews go out the window. He will have to contact a local field supervisor who can persuade three or four interviewers to work over the weekend. They will have to go wherever women can be found most easily for a brief interview. The researcher will need to set some kind of quotas: make certain that the interviewers work in some poor neighborhoods and not just in middle-class areas, and that they do not interview too many younger women and not enough older women. He can hand-tabulate the data Monday morning, and with luck he will have maybe 200 interviews that will provide some sort of answer to the question.

Note that either survey can be performed well or poorly. The first researcher may design an ineffective questionnaire that fails to meet management objectives; he may overspend his budget, misinterpret his findings, and so on. His seemingly ample budget and generous time limit do not ensure a good study. Similarly, the small budget and short deadline imposed on the second researcher do not necessarily indicate a poor survey. The design may be quite appropriate for the problem involved, and if the interviewers are properly instructed and do their job well, the data will probably be useful. Given the level of effort specified, it is the best he can do.

Most research problems, of course, fall between these two extremes. Management has a vague problem, would like to "conduct a survey," wants it done cheaply (naturally) and quickly (naturally). What can research do and how much will it cost? Since surveys can be designed at almost any level, the researcher, before he can answer those questions, must try to gain some notion of the cost and time parameters. It would be a futile exercise to design a $100,000 study if management can spend only a fraction of that amount on the project. On the other hand, management may be receptive to a variety of proposals, at various degrees of effort, depending on what results the researcher believes can be achieved for each expenditure level.

Note that if the cosmetics company could budget only $25,000 for its proposed survey, instead of $100,000, this decision would not in itself preclude a survey. One could still be conducted, but on a less elaborate scale. The scope of the questioning and probably the sample size would have to be reduced; the sample design would have to be less rigorous; the questions might have to be "piggybacked" on some other ongoing national survey instead of being administered as an independent interview, and so forth. Data could still be collected in the most efficient manner for the level of support provided. But management should be forewarned that the information collected for $25,000 will be both much less complete and subject to more error than that of a survey with four times the budget.

SURVEY PURPOSES AND SURVEY DESIGN

The purposes of surveys can be as diverse as the range of problems which create a need for them. Once the parameters of time and cost have been specified, the fundamental aspects of survey design will be dictated by the study's purpose.

A basic distinction exists between what have been called *qualitative* research and *quantitative* research. The former type of survey implies a haphazard or loosely structured sample; a relatively small number of cases; an informal interview consisting mostly of open-ended questions and probes and taped or recorded verbatim by the interviewer; and a nonstatistical approach to the data either by "eye-balling" the recorded materials or by classifying each case on one or more dimensions on the basis of a global evaluation of its record. Such an approach is useful when the survey's purpose is to gain insight into possible motivations for people's attitudes or behavior; when not enough is known about the subject to compose a more structured questionnaire and the researcher is looking for clues to how people view the problem; or when the researcher wants to get an idea of the possible range of attitudes and behavior without caring much at this point about their distribution in a particular population.

Quantitative research, on the other hand, seeks to count or quantify the data and normally applies some statistical form of analysis. Quantification of the data suggests a large and representative sample, so that the results will accurately reflect the characteristics of the population being surveyed within a particular margin of error, and so that analysis will reveal whether apparent differences are statistically significant. This in turn implies a standardized questionnaire with mostly precoded, rather than open-ended questions, since a large number of interviewers will be needed to collect a large number of interviews and no interviewer can be left to invent her own question wordings and probes, and since it is not possible to study individually each of several hundred or several thousand interviews. This type of survey is obviously appropriate and even necessary when the purpose is to collect data from a sample which can then be generalized to the total population under study.

There are, of course, gradations between the two prototypes. In the earlier example, the quick weekend survey of preferences between two advertisements was quantitative in the sense that the results were tabulated and some effort was made to make the sample as representative as possible, even though no statistical analysis was applied and no effort was made to estimate sampling error. Similarly, in a basically qualitative survey, there may be rough attempts to achieve a representative sample and to estimate from the data the approximate proportions of the general population that exhibit certain characteristics, even though the findings are never put through a computer or even systematically tabulated. Even in a large-scale statistical survey, respondents may be asked to "comment" or to explain their replies, and their responses may be handled qualitatively.

A distinction somewhat parallel to that between qualitative and quantitative research is exemplified by another dimension along which surveys can be classified. One can distinguish among an exploratory survey, a pilot survey or pretest, and a full-scale survey. Although an exploratory survey will often be qualitative in nature and a full-scale survey will normally be quantitative, this need not necessarily be the case. Sometimes the three survey types will be separate aspects of a single research assignment. The researcher in the cosmetics industry, used as an earlier example, might decide that he needs a better understanding of the whole subject of men's cosmetics and therefore might conduct some exploratory interviews himself or have professional interviewers do the job for him. On the basis of these data, he might decide, before going into the full survey, to conduct a pilot study, of perhaps 100 interviews in a single city, to serve as a pretest of his questionnaire and field procedures.

As the name implies, the pilot study is intended to point the way for a larger, more definitive study.   In some cases, however, it may serve the equally valuable purpose of showing the researcher that he is on the wrong track or that his original goals are unlikely to be achieved and that investment in the intended final study is therefore unwise.

The aims and objectives of the survey will also enable the researcher to decide whether he is dealing with a descriptive or an explanatory survey.   A descriptive survey is designed to answer the question, "What are the facts?" Examples: What is the sponsor's share of a certain segment of the market? Which of two proposed package designs do consumers prefer?   Who does the shopping for a particular product?   An explanatory (or analytical) survey is mainly addressed to the question, "Why are the facts as they are?"   Examples: Why is the sponsor's share of the market decreasing?   Why isn't the product purchased by more young people?   Why do people prefer one advertisement to another?

Whether the survey is to be descriptive or explanatory has implications for the survey design.   Offhand, the task of description might seem to be easier, and in fact it is, since describing a situation is usually easier than explaining it.   On the other hand, a survey aimed at "just getting the facts" implies a need for precise, standardized measures of those facts and a large and representative sample from which the facts may accurately be adduced.

An explanatory survey, on the other hand, assumes by definition that the basic facts are known.   Since there is no need for establishing them, there is less need for their precise measurement and for a large and representative sample.   The researcher will instead attempt to measure all the possible explanatory variables that might account for the situation under study.   His options remain large.   He might attempt a qualitative, exploratory study in which he would search for explanations in a series of informal interviews, or he might design a large-scale study in which he would search for explanatory relationships by means of multiple-regression analysis or other statistical techniques from computer-generated data.

Another typology of surveys lies along the time dimension.   At one extreme, we have the single survey addressed to a particular problem at a given point in time.   It is designed to describe or to explain the situation at that time, and it may never be repeated.   At the other extreme are trend surveys designed to measure facts over time.   They may comprise an endless series, in which the same basic facts are collected monthly, quarterly, or annually, or they may be of shorter duration.   By definition, trend surveys imply quantitative methods and large and comparable samples, since the purpose is to measure change with some degree of accuracy.   They also suggest the importance of using the same measures and the same data collection methods, for any alteration in these elements would obscure the trend.

Other types of survey along this dimension are the controlled experiment, or before-after comparison, and the panel survey (the latter covered in much more detail in Sec. II, Part B, Chap. 10).   In the before-after type of study, one measures the effects on people's attitudes or behavior of some innovation—say, a new or changed product or a new advertising campaign.   One interviews a sample of people before the innovation is introduced and then repeats many of the same questions at a certain later time to see what changes have occurred. Because any observed changes may have been due to factors other than the innovation itself, a control group is usually recommended.   A comparable group is given the same before-and-after interviews in a comparable city in which the innovation was not introduced.   The effect of the innovation then is the difference between the amount of change registered in the two samples.

Less rigorous forms of the before-after study often dispense with the control group and try to account for extraneous variables through internal analysis, or they measure the "after" group on an equivalent sample rather than reinterview the same individuals.   Such methods naturally produce less rigorous conclusions.

The panel survey is similar to the trend survey in that it seeks to measure change over a long or indefinite period of time.   It differs in that the same individuals serve as respondents, at least for an extended period before they are phased out and new panelists are introduced.   Thus, a representative sample of families might be recruited to a panel and asked to keep daily or weekly records of certain categories of expenditures, products purchased or other activities. Premiums are commonly paid to induce cooperation.

Panels are subject to three possible difficulties.   One is selective recruitment, since poorly educated, low-income people are less likely to cooperate than the middle class.   Another is attrition, as panelists die, move, change their circumstances, or stop cooperating.   A third is "panel effect," in which the panelists may become self-conscious about their role and, even unconsciously, subtly alter their behavior or reporting to reflect what they think is a "correct" response.   Rotation of panelists can partially overcome these latter two difficulties, however, and patient instruction and inducement can achieve an adequate sample of the less well-educated.

SAMPLE DESIGN

A basic problem in survey design is the size, nature, and method of sample selection.   The survey sample should be representative of the relevant universe or population, so the researcher's first question, in designing his sample, is: Exactly whose opinions and/or behavior are we trying to measure?   Sometimes the answer to this question is obvious: the civilian, noninstitutionalized population of the United States, married women aged 18 to 65 in Kansas City, and so on.   But more often the question is thought-provoking and agreement may not come easily.

One major consideration is the geographical boundaries of the universe.   At one extreme, the survey might be restricted to a single community or even a particular neighborhood within the community.   At the other extreme, the universe might be nationwide or even cross-national.   Thus, an international corporation might be interested in studying its "image" in each of the twelve countries in which it operates.   Between these extremes are many other possibilities. One might decide, for example, on a nationwide survey but exclude the rural areas or all places with less than 50,000 population.   If the product is distributed only regionally, one would probably survey only the region in which it is marketed.   Or, by some standard of judgment, one might pick any of various combinations of particular cities or metropolitan areas.

Shaping this type of decision is the statistical (and economic) fact that it usually takes as many cases, observations, or interviews to achieve a given level of sampling precision in a single city as it does in all the United States.   Thus, a sample of 500 interviews in Chicago will be representative of that city's population to the same extent as a national sample of 500 will be representative of the entire nation's population.   It follows that a local or regional survey will normally take about as long and cost about as much as a national survey if both are drawn to the same specifications. Indeed, the local or regional survey may cost more because many research companies have national samples already drawn and national field staffs already located, whereas, in a particular locality, the sample may have to be drawn from scratch and the interviewers newly recruited and trained. It also follows from the same statistical fact that if one wants to conduct a six-city survey and look at each city separately, one is in effect conducting six separate surveys and needs a total sample six times the size deemed adequate for a single city. On the other hand, if one does not want to make intercity comparisons but merely wants to pool the data from six cities, one needs no more cases to represent the six-city area than to represent a single city.

Aside from the geographical boundaries of the universe from which the sample is to be selected, the researcher must consider the appropriate demographic characteristics. Depending on the survey's purpose, one might study only men or only women. Frequently the relevant universe is age-bounded. The age span may be very wide, such as 18 to 65, or very narrow, such as 21 to 29. Income, education, or occupation may be a relevant consideration. Perhaps the survey should be restricted to those families earning more than $15,000, or to high school graduates, or to blue-collar workers. Sometimes the relevant universe is defined by race or ethnicity. For example, one may want to study the Negro market or the opinions of the Italian community.

The sample may be designed to any of these specifications, with interviewers in the field screening prospective survey respondents for the appropriate characteristics. Obviously, the more narrow the specifications and the more "hidden" the characteristics, the more difficult and more expensive the survey becomes. Screening for men or women is simple because about half the population is of each sex and the characteristic is easily recognizable. But screening for a particular income or occupation group is much more difficult—first, because only a small fraction of the total population may qualify for the group, and second, because the characteristic cannot be readily recognized. The interviewer must ask each family she approaches whether its members are of the appropriate income or occupational category. For characteristics covered by United States census data, some of this difficulty can be eased. If the population of interest is a high-income group, for example, the researcher can oversample in tracts with a high median income and undersample in the poorer areas.

Beyond this, the researcher may be interested in a population whose characteristics are even harder to define or locate. He may, for example, wish to survey the opinions or behavior of "community leaders" or "key influentials." How does one define a community leader or a key influential? Or he may be interested in talking with owners of stereo equipment or with mothers of children under age two. How does one draw a sample of such individuals? Such problems, like almost all problems of survey design, are amenable to solution, or at least can be made manageable with an appropriate investment of time and cost.

"Community leaders" might be defined by their role positions, for example—top city officials, business and labor leaders, clergy, minority group leaders, and so forth—or files of newspapers scanned to see which local names appear with greatest regularity. To sample "key influentials," one must first ask, "Influential in what?" because few people are influential in all areas. Having defined the term for purposes of the survey, a good sample of such individuals might be identified through a "snowball" method. Here, a sample of the general public is interviewed and asked a question such as, "Who would you say knows the most about this matter around here? Whose opinions would you especially respect?" Names collected by this means can be pooled as a sample of "influentials," or each person might be weighted by the number of times he was named in the original survey. Owners of stereo equipment or mothers of children under age two can perhaps be located from lists (of purchasers or birth records) or, again, they can be screened for.

SAMPLING METHODS

Sampling methods can range from the most simplistic to the most elaborate, again depending on the purpose and budget of the survey. The most simplistic can be described as haphazard or convenience sampling. It consists simply of interviewing the most readily available persons. They may be friends, relatives, or fellow workers, or they may be people sitting in parks, shopping at a supermarket, or passing a given street corner.

This method is not at all scientific, and the results cannot be generalized to any other population and may be grossly misleading. One can only deplore, for instance, the frequent headlining of "surveys" based on catch-as-catch-can samples conducted by newspaper reporters. Nevertheless, haphazard sampling is often useful, especially when the researcher wants to try out a particular question wording or series of questions, or when he is interested merely in obtaining a range of responses from a variety of people. These haphazard interviews may be enough to convince him that a particular approach does not work, that most people do not understand one of his questions, or, alternatively, that he is on the right track.

A more refined type of sampling is the quota method. Since one of the weaknesses of haphazard sampling is that only available people are reached and the people available at any particular location tend to have similar characteristics, the imposition of quotas can ensure the proper inclusion of harder-to-get types. In a simple type of quota design, an interviewer might be assigned to contact 10 men and 10 women, with half of each sex to be under age 35 and half to be over that age. With these controls, the interviewer will probably soon fill her quota of older women and thereafter will pass them up, while deliberately seeking out younger men, for example, who are probably harder to find for interviews. The researcher is assured by the quota that he will not receive too many cases of one type and not enough of others.

Setting quotas may be simple, as in the preceding case, or quite complex. The nature and number of quota controls again depend on the survey's purpose and budget. In sampling the general public, the normal practice is to assign interviewers to particular geographical areas and then to give them quotas for age, sex, and some measure of socioeconomic status, such as income, rent, or value of home. One might add a racial control to be sure that enough Negroes are interviewed, or one might control on still other variables. The more variables that are controlled and the more rigid these controls (five or six age groups, for example, instead of two or three), the more closely the final sample will conform to these known characteristics. On the other hand, a complex network of quotas may confront the interviewer with a difficult or impossible task and raise interviewing costs very quickly. One can picture an interviewer searching endlessly for an upper-income woman over age 65 in a ghetto area.

Most of the usual quota categories are demographic variables. Aside from the fact that such characteristics as sex, age, and socioeconomic status powerfully influence a person's attitudes and behavior, there are two reasons for this. First, such data are readily available from the United States census. For a particular survey, one might want to assign quotas based on the amount of car driving a person does or on the religious group to which he belongs. But there are no good data on such variables, especially on a local basis, and thus there is no criterion for setting the quotas in order to assure a representative sample. The second reason is that such variables as age, sex, and socioeconomic status are easily observed or ascertained. To use quotas on some hidden characteristic may involve one screening question or a series of them, which some persons may resent.

Though quota controls are normally used to ensure a representative sample, they may sometimes be applied for a very different purpose. Let us assume the researcher is most interested in a particular group which is rare in the papulation. If his sample is representative, it may yield him only 20 cases of this type; he would like at least 50 for purposes of his analysis. He may then impose an additional quota designed to produce this increase. If the interviewer, after filling her other quotas, is short of this one, she must screen additional people until she fulfills this particular quota requirement.

Although quota controls are commonly employed in survey sampling, this sampling method still has many weaknesses. For one thing, the problem of availability remains a plaguing one. An interviewer may easily fill her quotas of women of various ages, but her sample may be heavily biased because she has found no working women at home to interview. Her sample may be further biased by the fact that if someone expressed reluctance to be interviewed or claimed to be busy, she made no attempt to persuade or call back but simply went to the next house where someone was more likely to be available and interested. A further difficulty with quota controls is the natural tendency of interviewers to seek pleasant experiences and avoid unpleasant ones. If left to her own devices, the interviewer may avoid "foreign" or "slum" areas, upper-story flats, or people who look hostile, busy, or uninformed, and deliberately or subconsciously seek out middle-class areas, ground-floor apartments, people whose name on the doorplate is not "strange," or those she has some reason to believe will be interested in the survey.

Because quota samples still have the basic characteristic of "convenience" samples, they can be defended only on pragmatic and not on scientific grounds. Statistical tests based on probability-sampling theory do not properly apply to quota samples because not every element in the universe has a known probability of being selected for the sample. When time and resources permit and when accurate projections to the universe are important, the researcher will usually opt for some form of probability sampling. With such a sample, he will know the error limits of his data, and he can confidently apply statistical methods of estimation and inference.

Probability sampling normally refers to the unbiased selection of sample cases in some statistically random manner, for example, by means of a table of random numbers or by the selection of every nth name from a complete list. But, since people are not numbered or completely listed, the researcher turns to what is called area probability sampling when he wishes to sample the general public.

In area probability sampling, as the name implies, the researcher first samples areas and then samples individuals or households within those areas. The sampling is thus done in stages. To sample the population of a city, the first stage might be to go to the national census block data and systematically select a sample of the city's blocks, with probability of selection proportionate to the block's population. The second stage would be to have interviewers list the address of every dwelling unit on the selected blocks and to assign every nth dwelling unit for interview after a random start. If a sample of individuals were required, there would be a third stage in which the interviewer might enumerate all adults in the household in order of age and then select one of them for interview by means of random number. With this method, every adult living in the city would have had a known chance of selection for the sample and the characteristics of the sample could accurately be projected to the total population with a known degree of probable error, depending on the sample size.

In practice, probability sampling of humans falls short of theory, mainly because the designated individuals are not always available and cooperative. In quota sampling, such people are freely substituted for until the quotas are met, but any substitution violates the theory on which probability sampling is based. Thus, in probability sampling, interviewers must keep calling back when they have found no one at home or have called at an inconvenient time, and intensive efforts must be made to overcome lack of interest, suspicion, or even outright hostility in the designated respondent. These efforts, together with the preliminary listings of dwelling units, normally take considerable time and cost a good deal of money; yet they are essential. A probability sample in which only 60 percent of the assigned cases have been completed can be subject to severe bias, since the 40 percent who are "hard to get" may have quite different characteristics. In certain circumstances and with certain populations, it is possible to obtain completion rates of 90 percent or more. Generally, 80 percent is regarded as acceptable; anything below 75 percent may be viewed with suspicion.

For some populations, lists do exist; where they do, the researcher will save himself time and expense by applying probability-sampling methods directly to the list. There are directories of many kinds, lists of organization members, and so forth. In sampling from lists, however, the researcher must beware of two possible dangers. First, the list may not provide a complete sampling frame. The American Medical Association directory is an excellent sampling frame for physicians, for example, because approximately 95 percent of M.D.'s belong to the association. The telephone directory, on the other hand, is not a good frame for many purposes because 20 percent or more of the households may not be included. They consist of families that have unlisted phones, have no telephones, or can be reached only through a central number like an apartment-house switchboard.

The other danger in sampling from lists is that they are frequently outdated. Few lists are continuously updated. Lists published in one year were usually compiled the year before. Since about 20 percent of the nation's households move every year, and many people die, marry and change their names, or prove unlocatable, there is a good deal of attrition in any list as much as two years old. . Of equal importance, such a list will not include the names of people who have become eligible for listing since the roster was first compiled.

SAMPLE SIZE

Statistical theory can provide estimates of sampling error for various sample sizes. These estimates are based on probability theory which assumes simple random sampling; they do not apply to non-probability samples, nor to multistage area probability samples. They are nevertheless useful to the researcher in that they demonstrate the effects of increasing sample size on the variance of the survey estimates and may serve as a rough rule of thumb.

A striking feature of tables based on such probability estimates is the rapidity with which sampling variance is reduced when additional cases are added to small samples, and the relative inflexibility of the variance when additional cases are added to samples that are already large. If the probability of a particular characteristic in a population is .50, theory tells us that 19 times out of 20 a random sample will not deviate from .50 by more than twice the standard error. Twice the standard error of a sample of 100 in this case is 10, so the observed percentage in a sample of this size will, 95 percent of the time, range from 40 to 60. If we double the sample size to 200, the probable error is reduced from 10 percentage points to about 7, so that we have narrowed the range to the interval 43 to 57. If we boost the sample size to 500, the probable error drops to 4.4 percentage points. If we increase it to 1,500, error falls to 2.6. The probable error of a random sample of 2,500 cases is 2 percentage points, but even if we double this sample size to 5,000, it is only reduced to 1.4.

These numbers suggest that the optimum sample size for most surveys will be between 200 or 300 cases and about 2,000 cases. Samples of fewer than 200 will usually be useful only in exploratory research; samples of more than 2,000 generally achieve only small increments in precision in return for large expenditure of resources. But note that the estimates of error refer to the total sample size, whereas the researcher may be particularly interested in one or more specific subgroups of the total. The sampling error for any subgroup will depend on the size of that subgroup and not on the size of the total sample. Thus, in looking at the characteristics of the users of three rival brands of product, no one of which accounts for more than 30 percent of the market, the probable error for these three subsamples individually will be considerably higher than for the sample as a whole. It is for this reason that when the survey's purpose is to develop profiles of the readers of eight or ten national magazines, for example, the total sample size may exceed 5,000 cases.

Often, the need for increased numbers of a particular subgroup can be served without enlarging the total sample by means of some sort of oversampling of the desired group. Thus, if one were especially interested in upper-income households, one might oversample blocks with high median income and thus increase their frequency in the overall sample. A consequence of such oversampling, of course, is that final data for the total sample must be weighted to restore the natural distribution of the population.

DATA COLLECTION

Though most surveys collect the desired data directly from the respondent by some form of questioning, one should not overlook other methods. The very act of questioning a respondent may have undesirable and unexpected effects, and his answers may be subject to distortions and errors caused by faulty memory, a desire to enhance prestige, distraction, poor motivation, lack of understanding, and many other possible deterrents to a frank, accurate response. Alternatives to questioning are observation of behavior and the use of records of one kind or another. Systematic observation and recording of shoppers' behavior in the natural setting of a store may tell more about their actual behavior than the shoppers themselves can or will reveal during a subsequent interview. Similarly, a comparative analysis of sales records may suggest explanations of behavior which would be hard to elicit in a personal interview situation.

The major disadvantage of personal observation is the difficulty of obtaining a probability sample of the kind of behavior under study. Another drawback is the distinct possibility that the observer may selectively record or misinterpret what he sees or hears. Observation is more generally suited to exploratory research. Analysis of records is often unsatisfactory because the records are incomplete or because there is no way of relating them to possible explanatory variables.

Despite all the possible errors and biases in direct questioning of respondents, this method of data collection is by far the most frequent in survey research. The advantages are many. Questioning can be standardized so that all respondents react to the same stimulus. There are means of obtaining representative samples of individuals to whom the questions can be addressed. There is evidence that people can, within limits, report fairly accurately and truthfully about their attitudes, opinions, level of knowledge, behavior, expectations, and beliefs; and the skillful researcher can organize his questionnaire to increase their ability to do so. It is perhaps only stating the obvious to say that for many kinds of information, the respondent himself is the only, or the best, source. What is more natural than to ask him? The most frequent forms of data collection, therefore, are the mail questionnaire, the telephone interview, and the personal or face-to-face interview.

The appropriateness of using a mail questionnaire depends on two considerations: the availability of a good list and the prospects of an adequate response. This chapter has already discussed the possible disadvantages of sampling from lists. They are often incomplete or outdated, and either defect can produce biased data. Reference has also been made to the importance of achieving high completion rates in probability samples. Many mail surveys produce response rates of only 20, 30, or 40 percent, and the responses are likely to be highly unrepresentative of the total. Mail surveys are most effective with relatively small, special-interest groups, such as subscribers to specialized magazines, employees of a particular company, or members of an organization, when the survey deals with their particular concern. Mail surveys are usually ineffective if the group is large and amorphous and if the survey's subject is of little interest.

Response rates to mail surveys can be improved by various methods. A letter from a prestigious individual or organization urging cooperation, assurances of anonymity, a clear statement of the purpose and utility of the survey will all help. At least two follow-up mailings should be addressed to nonrespondents at suitable intervals, stressing the importance of their cooperation, and some tangible inducement may be offered as a reward. If response rates remain below acceptability, intensive efforts are usually made to obtain returns from a subsample of the nonresponders to determine to what extent these individuals may be different from those who responded. Night-letter telegrams or personal phone calls will usually produce a sizable response from this subsample.

The great advantage of mail questionnaires is their economy. Though their development, formatting, and printing and the processing of the data may cost as much as, or even more than, other types of surveys, the costs of data collection are enormously reduced because no interviewers need be paid or supervised. But, aside from the problem of inducing an adequate response, the mail questionnaire has other disadvantages. For example, one never knows just who filled it out. The family member to whom it was addressed may have handed it to someone else, or questions which should have been answered by an individual may have been decided by family consensus. Moreover, the respondent can read through the entire questionnaire before he answers the first question. His awareness of subsequent questions may very markedly affect his responses to the earlier ones.

Still another difficulty is that the researcher cannot test the respondent's information level. Rather than answer "Don't know" to a particular question, the respondent may choose to look up the answer or ask someone else. Finally, the quality of data obtained from mail surveys is usually below the level provided by personal interviews. Without an interviewer to guide him, the respondent to a mail questionnaire will often skip questions, misunderstand instructions, answer in vague or irrelevant terms, or misinterpret a question's intent.

Telephone surveys offer something of a compromise between mail questionnaires and personal interviews. The problems of mail surveys just mentioned are mostly eliminated since the interviewer can ensure that she has the proper respondent, see that every question is understood and answered, and probe inadequate responses. Much higher response rates are usually obtained with less effort because the interviewer is there to persuade, answer questions, and counter objections. Costs of data collection by telephone are much higher than by mail because interviewers must be paid and supervised, but they are much lower than the costs of personal interviews because interviewers can work out of their homes instead of traveling to distant parts of the city.

The basic disadvantage of telephone interviews is, obviously, that the sample is restricted to persons who can be reached by phone. Sometimes this is no disadvantage at all as, for example, when one wants to telephone a sample of businessmen or professionals in their offices. For such a survey, the telephone is probably an ideal data collection instrument. But if as much as 30 percent or more of the population under study cannot be reached by phone, either because of unlisted numbers or lack of service, the data collected may be subject to serious bias. Means of dealing with this problem are discussed in a later chapter of this part.

It is commonly supposed that telephone interviews must be severely restricted in length, though this is not always the case as noted in the chapter just cited. It has been found that if the survey is directed to a special-interest group and the questioning deals with that special interest, if an advance letter describes the survey and warns of the impending call, and if the call is made long-distance person-to-person, interviews lasting as long as an hour can be conducted without resistance. On the other hand, when one is calling members of the general public locally and without advance notice, the questioning may have to be more brief. Telephone interviews are inappropriate, of course, when one wishes to present visual materials to the respondent or when it is important for the interviewer to rate various aspects of the respondent's behavior or observe particulars about the respondent's place of residence.

The personal interview is usually the preferred method of data collection if the budget permits. Face-to-face interviewing has most of the advantages of telephone interviewing, plus many others as well. Interviewers can visit homes that are unreachable by telephone. By her physical presence, the interviewer can help achieve a high completion rate by tracking down hard-to-find respondents, by exercising personal charm or flattery on doubtful or suspicious persons, and by projecting an air of "You're really going to enjoy the interview."

The interviewer can also use visual as well as auditory clues to determine when a respondent has not understood a question or appears to be less than candid in his reply. She can ask the respondent to perform certain tasks as part of the interview: rank a series of show cards, fill out a brief test form, or play a variety of "games," such as placing counters on a board to indicate how she allocates her time among different activities or how she would spend a windfall of dollars. The interviewer can even ask (and usually receive) the respondent's permission to inspect the medicine chest or grocery shelves to determine the presence or absence of a particular product or to take a rough inventory.

A personal interview is usually required when the questionnaire is a long one. If the subject of the interview is at all interesting to the respondent, if the questionnaire is skillfully devised and the interviewer well trained, respondents will normally not object to spending an hour or even two expressing their opinions or answering questions about themselves. They will seldom take this amount of time to fill out a mail questionnaire or to be engaged in telephone conversation.

Good personal interviewing is expensive [see Chapter 5 of this part]. Interviewers are usually paid by the hour for all hours worked, including all time spent in study or training, in editing their work and filling out reports, and in traveling to and from their assigned area. In an area probability sample, they may spend four or five hours attempting to obtain a single half-hour interview, because of travel time and call-backs. The quality of training and supervision of interviewers varies from excellent to poor, and the researcher will do well to check the qualifications and references of the agency he selects to perform his field services. Means of doing this are discussed in Sec. I, Chap. 10.

There are still other methods of data collection, however. One is the self-administered questionnaire which the respondent fills out in the interviewer's presence. This instrument is frequently used to collect data from groups of people: a preselected audience, students in a classroom, or employees in an office or factory. This approach has a particular set of advantages [see Chapter 6 of this part.] Another is the diary method, in which the respondent is asked to record certain activities or expenditures over a period of time, is personally persuaded to participate, is instructed on how to fill out the form, and is asked to mail the diary in at the end of the period. Or the interviewer might call back to pick up the diary, at the same time inspecting it for errors or missing data.

THE SURVEY QUESTIONNAIRE

Like his choice of sampling method and means of data collection, the researcher's selection of questionnaire design will reflect the survey's purposes and the resources available for it. In an exploratory survey in which the researcher himself will do all or most of the interviewing, the questionnaire may be only a rough interview guide, perhaps a piece of paper on which he has jotted down the six or eight major topics he wants the respondent to discuss. The actual questions he can improvise. In any quantitative survey, however, the results of which are to be tabulated and perhaps analyzed statistically, the questionnaire must be standardized. It can be a simple one-page form or a complicated document of 32 pages or more, but it must be standardized.

The reasons for standardization are fairly obvious. If the answers are to be tabulated, it is assumed that they have equal meaning, and to have equal meaning each response must be a reaction to the same stimulus. If interviewers were free to vary the wording and order of the questions on the questionnaire as seemed best to them under the circumstances, all comparability would be lost and the meaning of the tabulated responses would be most equivocal. There are many examples in the survey literature of marked differences in results which can be produced by seemingly minor changes in question wording or order.

The need for standardization has consequences for questionnaire design in that once the questionnaire is set, the researcher is powerless to change it. If he has omitted an important dimension, if some of the questions cannot be understood by respondents or turn out to be seriously biased, it is too late to repair matters. The careful researcher therefore will make every effort to design the most efficient set of questions to meet his research objectives and will try to phrase and order them so as to elicit the most complete and accurate information possible.

In devising the questionnaire content, the researcher will usually start by listing the basic objectives of the survey, the types of information he wants to obtain, and the particular variables which he believes might explain or help him understand them. Only when these have been agreed on and clarified does he start formulating specific questions. Though it may seem simpler to start by writing the actual questions, one can formulate an infinite number of questions and word them in an infinite number of ways, and still fail to elicit the desired information. Without a clear understanding of just what information is needed, there is little basis for choosing one possible question over another. When the questionnaire is finally developed, the researcher should be able to explain just what purpose each item serves and how he intends to use it in his analysis.

An early and basic decision in the actual formulation of the questions is the form of response desired. There are open-ended questions in which the respondent is asked to volunteer his own reply, with no suggestions from the researcher or interviewer. There are multiple-choice questions in which the respondent is asked to choose among two or more alternatives. The response may also be in the form of a rank-ordering of items or of marking a number or letter on a scale.

Open-ended questions offer many advantages. They let the respondent answer in his own terms, within his own frame of reference. Closed questions unfairly restrict respondents at times and may force them into an unfamiliar or unacceptable frame of reference. On the other hand, open-ended questions are subject to more interviewer variation than closed ones are, responses often come in different dimensions which cannot be combined, and it is costly and time-consuming to code large amounts of verbatim material. Therefore, the researcher will usually try to close as many of his questions as possible and use open-ended items only sparingly for strategic purposes.

Although the art of writing survey questions may seem simple, every experienced researcher knows that it is full of pitfalls. The first draft of any questionnaire will likely have many of the following defects: Certain words will be unfamiliar to some respondents, others will be ambiguous; some questions will be too long or too complicated for the respondent to understand, others will seem repetitious or silly; some will be biased or loaded in that they do not allow for all viewpoints or lead the respondent to a particular answer; the order of the questions will seem illogical or biased. Many defects of this kind can be spotted by clients, colleagues, and experienced field people, but the true test can only be a series of pretest interviews with actual respondents. If the survey is important enough and a great deal is invested in it, several pretests of successive questionnaire drafts are strongly advised.

The researcher must also consider the format or layout of the questionnaire, for this concerns the interviewers and also the coders or keypunchers. If the instrument appears crowded or cluttered, if there is insufficient space to record replies, or if the interviewer's instructions are not clear, this factor will affect the quality of the data and increase the likelihood of error; in mail surveys, it can cut response sharply, as discussed in Chapter 3 of this part.

Once his questionnaire goes into the field, the survey design is set and the researcher is helpless to change it. He cannot then alter his sampling instructions or recall his questionnaires to insert another idea; hence the importance of all decisions he has made in the design stage. If he is wise and lucky, he will—through his selection of sampling method, sample size, means of data collection, and questionnaire development—have designed a survey that will fulfill the specified purpose within the cost and time budget available to him.

BIBLIOGRAPHY

Backstrom, Charles H., *Survey Research,* Handbooks for Research in Political Behavior, Evanston, Ill.: Northwestern University Press, 1963.

Blalock, Hubert J., *An Introduction to Social Research,* Englewood Cliffs, N.J.: Prentice-Hall, 1970.

Blankenship, Albert B. (ed.), *How to Conduct Consumer and Opinion Research: The Sample Survey in Operation,* New York: Harper & Row, 1946.

Hyman, Herbert H., *Survey Design and Analysis: Principles, Cases and Procedures,* Chicago: Free Press, 1955.

Moser, C., *Survey Methods in Social Investigation,* London: Heinemann, 1958.

Oppenheim, A. N., *Questionnaire Design and Attitude Measurement,* New York: Basic Books, 1966.

Parten, Mildred, *Surveys, Polls and Samples,* New York: Harper & Row, 1950.

Selltiz, Claire, et al., *Research Methods in Social Relations,* rev. ed., one vol., New York: Holt-Dryden, 1959.

Shannon, Lyle W., et al., *A Community Self-Survey System: Part 1: The Interview Schedule; Part 2: The Survey Director's Manual; Part 3: Manual for Training Local Residents as Interviewers; Part 4: Manual for Training Coders and Code Book for the Interview Schedule,* Iowa City: Urban Community Research Center, 1968.

Stephan, Frederick R., *Sampling Opinions: An Analysis of Survey Procedure,* New York: Wiley, 1958.

Tufte, Edward R. (ed.), *The Quantitative Analysis of Social Problems,* Reading, Mass.: Addison-Wesley, 1970.

U.S. Executive Office of the President, Bureau of the Budget, *Household Survey Manual, 1969,* Washington: Government Printing Office, 1970.

Young, Pauline V., *Scientific Social Surveys and Research: An Introduction to the Background, Content Methods, and Analysis of Social Studies,* 4th ed., Englewood Cliffs, N.J.: Prentice-Hall, 1966.

Part B

Surveys

Chapter 2

Data Collection Methods: Personal Interviews

CHARLES S. MAYER *Faculty of Administrative Studies, York University, Downsview, Ontario, Canada*

Personal interviews are certainly the most common way of gathering data in marketing research. They are also, on a cost-per-interview basis, the most expensive way. This chapter examines the nature of personal interviews, conditions under which they should be used, and their potential pitfalls.

Kahn and Cannell [9] define the survey interview as "a two-person conversation, initiated by the interviewer for the specific purpose of obtaining research-relevant information, and focused by him on content specified by [the] research objectives." Bingham et al. [1] define the interview as "basically a communications system." Both these definitions will increase our understanding of personal interviewing.

What differentiates the personal interview from any other kind is the interviewer's physical presence during the interview. All the strengths and weaknesses of the personal interview method can be attributed to this one factor.

Characteristics of Interviewers

To understand the nature of the personal interview method requires a description of the interviewers. Although generalizations are often dangerous, the term "motley crew" as applied to interviewers is probably quite accurate.

Interviewing, especially for one firm, tends to be a sporadic requirement. Accordingly, interviewers are hired for specific jobs on a part-time basis, and are usually treated as independent contractors. A firm with a personal interviewing requirement may hire individual interviewers, or may work through local supervisors who have several interviewers working for them.   Research firms in a particular area will often use the same pool of "trained" interviewers. The interviewers themselves are usually female, often married, and available only at certain times.   Few of these women make a career of interviewing. Rather, they view it as part-time employment and the income derived therefrom as supplementary.   Means of recruiting and training interviewers are discussed in Chapter 5 of this part.

Motivations for interviewing vary.   However, it is safe to say that income earned through interviewing is only part of the motivation.   This is especially true since interviewers are traditionally underpaid for the job's skill requirements.

THE NATURE OF PERSONAL INTERVIEWS

The various methods of data collection may be compared on the following set of criteria.   In this chapter, only the characteristics of the personal interview will be considered.   Other methods are presented in later chapters.

Flexibility.   The personal interview is the most flexible method of data collection.   The interviewer's physical presence enables the researcher to use various forms of interaction between the interviewer and the respondent.   The most common interaction is that the interviewer asks questions of the respondent, following a structured format or questionnaire, and records the respondent's answers on the questionnaire.   However, the questions asked may be unstructured, or the interviewer may hand the questionnaire to the respondent to fill out, or may even ask the respondent to mail the questionnaire to the research agency at a later date.   Answers may also be tape-recorded during the interview.

The degree of flexibility within the personal interview is limited only by the researcher's imagination and the interviewer's training.   The interviewer can use all sorts of visual or mechanical aids, displays, or other props during the interview; for example, she may hand the respondent a "barometer" scale, or ask him to sort a set of cards into piles or to smell or taste certain products. Such participative methods, in addition to gathering information, help to retain respondent interest during the session.

Motivation.   The interviewer's mere presence is useful in motivating the respondent to cooperate.   Richardson et al. [14] identify *altruism* (the desire to help one's fellow man), *emotional satisfaction* (gained from the opportunity to express opinions), and *intellectual satisfaction* (resulting from discussing a stimulating topic) as the three forces that stimulate the respondent to cooperate.   Kahn and Cannell [8] use the concepts of *extrinsic* and *intrinsic motivation* to express somewhat similar ideas.   The former refers to the respondent's desire somehow to influence the interviewer (or, through the interviewer, a manufacturer, in regard to the characteristics of some product, package, or advertisement), while the latter refers to the opportunity afforded by the interview to talk about topics of interest.   The skillful interviewer will take advantage of these several means of respondent "rewards" to obtain cooperation.

Respondent motivation is most obvious in the cooperation rate.   However, it can also increase the accuracy of reporting.   Especially in cases in which information may not be immediately accessible or where obtaining it may require the use of records, the motivating effect of the interviewer can become important.

Anonymity.   Most surveys guarantee the respondent's anonymity.   This anonymity refers to the nondisclosure, on an individual basis, of information supplied by the respondent. However, another form of anonymity can also be formulated—*psychological anonymity*. The very presence of the interviewer, which is so helpful in motivating the respondent, precludes the possibility of this type of anonymity. Respondents will be less likely to admit to socially unacceptable behavior in the face-to-face situation of a personal interview than in the psychologically protected medium of the self-administered questionnaire.

Interview Length. Personal interviews can be substantially longer than interviews using other methods of data collection. The interviewer, through detecting the respondent's impatience, reassuring him of the survey's importance, and generally maintaining his interest, can steer him through lengthy surveys. Personal interviews lasting over an hour are not uncommon. Since interviews of such length are difficult to administer by any other method, the interviewer must be credited with the ability to complete longer and more difficult interviews than are possible, for example, by telephone.

Time Dimensions. The interviewer calls on a potential respondent at a unique point in time. Depending on this time, the respondent may be away from home, busy, or willing to grant an interview. Though the interview can be postponed to a more convenient time, respondents are usually reluctant to ask the interviewer to return later. Thus, the interviewer's presence at a specified period puts time-dimension constraints on the interview. Careful planning of attempted calls can alleviate the problems posed by these constraints.

Response Rate. The highest potential response rate can be obtained through the personal interview. This is true because of two interacting phenomena. First, the personal interview seems to have the highest respondent motivation. Second, the researcher has full control over the number of times the interviewer revisits potential respondents who are difficult to contact. Although several waves of call-backs are expensive, they can increase response rate. Response rates of between 65 and 85 percent can be achieved in studies requiring an original call and two call-backs.

Required Speed of Response. Certain information requested in the interview may not be immediately available to the respondent. Had he more time before answering, he might check with records or more knowledgeable members of the household. However, the interviewer's actual presence requires an immediate response. Though such a response will be given, it may be less carefully thought out or documented than it might otherwise be.

Scheduling Requirements. The personal interview survey has the longest and most complicated scheduling requirements. Once the field director is notified about the location of the sampling points and the number of interviews required in each, he must alert his interviewers about the future survey. Even when he has field staff scattered throughout the country, some recruiting, selection, and training may be needed. It may also be necessary to select a few new sampling points if staff cannot be found to cover those originally chosen.

The next task is to distribute the materials physically, usually by mail. If the study is not particularly complex or unique, instructions may accompany the materials. Otherwise, personal briefing sessions must be scheduled.

Once the actual interviewing starts, tight controls must be maintained to ensure that the interviewers are following their schedules so that potential problems with response rates or meeting deadlines can be foreseen.

So many problems with personal interviews can arise in the field and elsewhere that Sudman [15] suggests that an additional 25 percent should be allowed when estimating the time requirements for studies lasting a year or longer, and even higher percentages on shorter studies.

Speed of Completion. The scheduling and timing requirements of personal interview surveys are the chief reasons why this method of data collection is the slowest.

Credibility of Sponsorship. The legitimacy of an interview can be most credibly established in the personal interview. The fact that a respectable "stranger" is able to certify his sponsor and his authorization for the survey through an identification card, a printed questionnaire, and professional deportment, helps to reassure a respondent that the survey's purpose is not other than it seems. Should the interviewer encounter any resistance, he can also explain the purpose of the survey and the need for information from this particular respondent.

Respondent Identification. Besides presenting himself in person to the respondent, the interviewer can also uniquely identify the respondent because of the face-to-face nature of personal interviewing.

Elaboration. If the respondent has trouble understanding certain questions or phrases, the interviewer can attempt to elaborate on them. Such elaboration, however, must be made carefully since it may change the meaning of the question. The dangers of elaboration will be discussed later.

Getting Complete Responses. The interviewer can judge whether a question has been answered satisfactorily before proceeding to the next one. If the answer is incomplete or ambiguous, he can probe for more detail. On the other hand, if the answer is sufficient, he can stop the respondent from digressing and redirect him to the questionnaire's objectives. The interviewer controls the information flow from the respondent by asking specific questions and by deciding when to terminate one topic and introduce the next.

Controlling the Order of Presentation. In some surveys, such as those in which both unaided and aided recall questions are posed, it is essential that the planned order of presentation be maintained. In all others, a uniform order of presentation is desirable. The interviewer can fully control the order of questions asked of the respondent.

Observation. Besides communicating with the respondent, the interviewer can also observe his actions. For example, his facial expression during a description may be as meaningful as the words used. Observation can also take the place of some questions. For example, respondents are often categorized as belonging to a social class, age group, or race through observation. And, in the extreme, observation can be the essence of the survey.

Respondent Training. Being interviewed is a new role for most respondents. They do not know how to behave in this role. Part of the interviewer's job is to teach them how to act as respondents. It should be emphasized that "teaching" here does not refer to providing hints on how questions should be answered, but merely to making the respondents efficient and comfortable in their new role. Such teaching must be very subtle, and it requires skill. It does, however, contribute to the successful completion of the interview.

Assumptions about Respondents. Of all interview methods, the personal interview assumes the least about the respondents. For example, although literacy must be assumed in a self-administered questionnaire, such is not the case in the personal interview. The presence of an interviewer who is verbally communicating with the respondent, who is willing to "train" him in his new role, and who can elaborate on the survey ensures that the personal interview makes the least demands on the respondent.

Cost. Since an interviewer must be physically present, personal interviews are more expensive than other methods of data collection. However, actual *interviewing* time is only a fraction of the cost of personal interviewing. Sudman [15] reports that from 30 to 40 percent of the interviewer's time is devoted to interviewing itself. The interviewer spends time in *learning* the specific requirements of the survey, *traveling* to the designated areas, *locating* the required households, *identifying* the desired respondent, *asking* questions, *recording* the answers, and *submitting* the completed work. Many of the attempts to contact potential respondents may be unsuccessful. The travel costs, moreover, must include transportation expenses as well as interviewer time.

Geographic Spread of the Sample. Since travel from respondent to respondent is a critical cost factor with personal interviews, sampling plans usually call for some degree of clustering. The most common form of sampling used in conjunction with personal interviewing is the area probability sample discussed in Sec. II, Part C, Chap. 2.

Sampling-Frame Requirements. With other methods of data collection, sample selection depends on the existence of some form of sampling frame. The interviewer's presence makes such frame requirements minimal for personal interviewing. As long as the sampling frame can be geographically identified (for example, by blocks or land tracts), the interviewer can combine frame listing and sample selection into a single operation. For some sample designs, the interviewer can also combine screening for certain attributes with selection. For example, the interviewer can determine whether the respondent meets certain quota requirements before administering the interview.

The absence of a sampling-list requirement means that personal interviews can be based on more current and relevant sample frames than either telephone or mail interviews.

Control. Control over interviewers is both costly and difficult. Interviewers work in the field by themselves. Attempts at control, such as verification and traveling supervisors, are expensive, of questionable value, and may actually interfere with the interviewing itself. As Chapter 5 of this part shows, proper recruiting, selection, training, and motivation are the most effective methods of interviewer control.

Instrument Error. The interviewer may be said to take the measurements required in survey research. As a survey instrument, he has the opportunity to insert error that is specifically attributable to him. The consideration of the extent and potential magnitude of such errors will be the subject of the next section.

THE INSTRUMENT CONCEPT

If we look at personal interviewing as a system of communication between the researcher and the respondent, we can identify the interviewer, in conjunction with the questionnaire, as the system's measuring instrument. The systems concept permits us to think of this communication as dependent on the occurrence of a chain of events, the quality of the communication being determined by the weakest link in the chain. It might as well be recognized that this weakest link is usually the personal interviewer. Krueger [10], referring to errors that can be introduced by the interviewer, said, "The interviewer, no matter how well-trained, will always be a leaky receptacle in which to carry questions to the respondents and carry back answers." This "leak," commonly referred to as *interviewer bias*, will be the subject of this section.

Treating the personal interviewer, plus the questionnaire, as the measuring instrument permits us to include various concepts of instrumentation in the discussion. Among them are validity, reliability, sensitivity, selectivity, contamination, feedback, and noise.

Validity. The term *validity* refers to whether an instrument measures what it is designed to measure.   In marketing research, the whole concept of validity is not definitive, since empirical tests are seldom available.   For cases in which they are available, the results are discouraging.   For example, Ferber [4], in studying the reporting of savings accounts through personal interviews, found substantial errors resulting from underreporting.   Lansing et al. [11] found similar results.   In these studies, information on the amounts kept in savings accounts was available from institutional sources as well as from the survey respondents, and comparisons could thus be made.   These are known as tests of *convergent validity*, validity being ascribed if the measurements from two different sources tend to converge.

In most situations, however, such information is not available, and thus validity measures must be restricted to *face validity*.   Face validity refers to whether the answers seem to give what the questions purport to measure. Clearly, measures of face validity are weak and may not even be worthy of the designation of measurement.

The tests of validity, although manifestations of symptoms, do not explain causes, however.   Though tests of convergent validity can be assumed to demonstrate often substantial *biases* (differences between the measurements and what they purport to measure), the source of these biases needs further exploration.

Reliability.   An instrument is said to be *reliable* if repeated measurements, made on the same object, are stable.   In the interview setting, reliability would be present if similar interview results were obtained from the same respondents by, for example, an interviewer and a supervisor.

The difference between reliability and validity should be emphasized.   If an instrument has a consistent error, or bias, it can be highly reliable without being valid.   On the other hand, a measuring instrument that is valid, but unreliable, will, in the long run, measure what it purports to measure.   However, individual measurements may be far from the "true" value.

Sensitivity.   A measuring instrument is *sensitive* if it can discriminate between similar but different entities.   For each instrument, there are limits on the power of discrimination.   Attempting to make too fine distinctions will cause an instrument to become unreliable.   Conversely, reliability can be increased by reducing sensitivity.   For example, interviewers will be able to estimate household income far more reliably if the sensitivity requirements are met with a three-point scale than with a seven-point scale.

Sensitivity, reliability, and validity are useful concepts in considering the efficacy of a measuring instrument, but they are symptomatic rather than diagnostic.   The concepts of *selectivity, contamination, feedback*, and *noise* will permit diagnosis.

Selectivity.   The interviewer as a measuring instrument is selective in several ways.   First, the interviewer plays a role in respondent selection.   If he chooses the wrong respondent either by mistake or because of greater ease of contact, he can introduce error into the measurement.

Second, the interviewer acts as a selective filter in hearing and recording the respondent's answers.   If some of the message the respondent is attempting to transmit is filtered out by the interviewer, or if the interviewer introduces a new question before the respondent has had the opportunity to transmit his whole answer, the communication will be imperfect.

Contamination.   Filtering of responses can be particularly dangerous when it occurs together with contamination.   The interviewer, as the measuring instrument, can contaminate the measurement by introducing his own ideas into the communication system.   For example, by using leading probes and then selectively recording responses, he can substantially change the message content. Moreover, he may do so subconsciously. Rice [13], for example, found that a prohibitionist interviewer was more likely to obtain responses from derelict men that blamed drink for their plight than was a socialist interviewer, who seemed to get more frequent responses indicting the industrial state.

It is commonly held that the interviewer should create a neutral and permissive environment in which the respondent can state his opinions. Whenever the interviewer destroys the neutrality of the environment by offering his opinions, using leading probes or intonation, or showing a certain facial expression or even appearance, she will contaminate the measurement.

Feedback.   As Kahn and Cannell [9] argue, interviewing is more than the interviewer's posing a set of questions and the respondent's giving a set of answers. The third element in this sequence is a *sanctioning statement* or sign, improvised by the interviewer to tell the respondent whether he has met the requirements of each question, and if not, to indicate the direction in which additional response is required.

Through the sanctioning statement, the interviewer provides feedback to the respondent about his response adequacy. Especially when combined with the selective-filter concept mentioned earlier, this feedback can be the source of substantial bias. Hildum and Brown [6] show, for example, that using the affirmative sanctioning statement "Good" can bias survey results.

Noise.   The interviewer, as a measuring instrument, has another way of introducing errors into the communication system—through measuring noise instead of messages. For example, the interviewer could fabricate answers, or ask only key questions and fill in the rest of the questionnaire by inference. He could also improvise questions, change the question order, or make errors in recording.

Though all these deviations are contrary to good interviewing practice, they occur. Their minimization is the goal of interviewer selection, training, and control, as discussed in Chapter 5 of this part.

In summary, this section has shown that results obtained through personal interviews may to some extent be invalid, unreliable, and insensitive. The prime reason is that the interviewer, as the measuring instrument in the communication system afforded by personal interviews, may be selective, may contaminate the message, may generate feedback for the respondent, and may measure noise. Nevertheless, recognition of the potential weaknesses of personal interviews should not discourage the researcher from using them. Rather, it will permit him to use them more appropriately. This is particularly true when one recognizes that the other methods of data collection also suffer from similar, and sometimes more severe, limitations.

When to Use Personal Interviews

In some surveys, personal interviewing is the only means of gathering data; in others, it is inappropriate; and in still others, it is one of several alternatives. For example, if observation, unstructured questioning, or visual or mechanical props are an integral part of the survey design, then personal interviewing is the only means available. Similarly, if the survey is long or difficult and a high response rate is required, personal interviewing may be necessary. On the other hand, if a survey must be completed in a short time, if information is required from several members in the family, or if the geographic scatter of respondents is very extensive, personal interviews may not be advisable.

In instances in which personal interviews are one of several alternatives, decisions should be made on a cost-benefit basis. The benefit of the survey is measured through the value of information [Sec. II, Part A, Chap. 3]. An analysis of the information's value will yield both a budget constraint and specific tolerance requirements.

Personal interviews tend to be the most expensive on a cost-per-interview basis. However, the cost-per-interview concept is faulty in terms of making cost comparisons. The amount of information yielded per dollar is far more relevant where information is defined as the inverse of total error. And, in many instances, a small number of personal interviews will yield more information than a large survey conducted by other means.

Pitfalls of Personal Interviews

The major pitfall of personal interviews is the assumption that this method of data collection is very accurate. As the preceding sections have argued, such interviews may be invalid, unreliable, and insensitive for several reasons. The most basic reason is that the interviewers may not follow instructions through their lack of either training or motivation. Interviewers can influence results given by respondents in many ways. The purpose of recruiting, selection, training, and control [Chapter 5 of this part] is to minimize such influence.

REFERENCES

1. Bingham, W., et al., *How to Interview*, 4th rev. ed., New York: Harper & Row, 1959.
2. Boyd, Harper W., Jr., and Ralph Westfall, "Interviewer Bias Revisited," *Journal of Marketing Research*, vol. 2, February 1965, pp. 58–63.
3. Durbin, J., and A. Stuart, "Differences in Response Rates of Experienced and Inexperienced Interviewers," *Journal of the Royal Statistical Society*, vol. 114, part III, 1951, pp. 164–206.
4. Ferber, R., *The Reliability of Consumer Reports of Financial Assets and Debts*, Urbana: University of Illinois, Bureau of Economic and Business Research, 1966.
5. Hauck, M., and S. Steinkamp, *Survey Reliability and Interviewer Competence*, Urbana: University of Illinois, Bureau of Economic and Business Research, 1964.
6. Hildum, D., and R. W. Brown, "Verbal Reinforcement and Interviewer Bias," *Journal of Abnormal Psychology*, vol. 53, July 1956, pp. 108–111.
7. Hyman, Herbert H., et al., *Interviewing in Social Research*, Chicago: The University of Chicago Press, 1954.
8. Kahn, Robert L., and Charles F. Cannell, *The Dynamics of Interviewing*, New York: Wiley, 1957.
9. Kahn, Robert L., and Charles F. Cannell, in Gardner Lindzey and Elliot Aronson (eds.), *The Handbook of Social Psychology*, 2d ed., vol. II, *Research Methods*, Reading, Mass.: Addison-Wesley, 1968.
10. Krueger, Lester E., "The Big Noise in the System," *Journal of Advertising Research*, vol. 5, June 1965, pp. 56–57.
11. Lansing, J., et al., *An Investigation of Response Error*, Urbana: University of Illinois, Bureau of Economic and Business Research, 1961.
12. Mayer, C. S., *Interviewing Costs in Survey Research*, Ann Arbor: University of Michigan, Bureau of Business Research, 1964.
13. Rice, S. A., "Contagious Bias in the Interview: A Methodological Note," *American Journal of Sociology*, vol. 35, November 1929.
14. Richardson, S. A., et al., *Interviewing*, New York: Basic Books, 1965.
15. Sudman, S., *Reducing the Cost of Surveys*, Chicago: Aldine, 1967.

Surveys

Chapter 3

Data Collection Methods: Mail Surveys

PAUL L. ERDOS   *Erdos and Morgan, Inc., New York, New York*

Mail surveys are conducted by mailing out self-administered questionnaires. The basic distinction between this and other types of survey is the fact that in surveying by mail, there is no personal interviewer to ask the questions and guide the respondent. This creates important differences in survey design, questionnaire construction, and various other aspects of data collection operations.

In planning a survey, the researcher must decide which data collection method is to be used, as noted in Chapter 1 of this part. He must choose among several possible techniques, such as personal interviews, telephone interviews, and mail surveys. He must decide which method is most appropriate and applicable to the particular problem at hand, can achieve the most complete and most reliable results, and will best fit the available budget and time requirements.

In many situations, the mail survey method has advantages, while in other cases, it would be either inappropriate or infeasible.

ADVANTAGES AND DISADVANTAGES

The major advantages of mail surveys may be summarized by the following points:

Wider distribution. The mailman has no difficulty in reaching people scattered all over the country, or those located in rural districts or small towns. It is therefore unnecessary to look for "representative" cities, counties, or states.

We can cover the universe without introducing the complications inherent in clustering.

Less distribution bias. The mails show no favoritism for a certain neighborhood, type of family, or type of individual. With the personal interview, reluctance to work in "bad" neighborhoods may cause underrepresentation of poor families or those of a specific racial, national, or occupational background. The individual sought may be working, in a hospital, on a business trip, or vacationing in Acapulco, but sooner or later the mail survey (especially if it includes follow-up mailings) will find him.

No interviewer bias. The Bureau of the Census has changed its data collection method from personal interviews to mail surveys in censuses because it believes that a census by mail produces "better results, including a shortening of the period for collecting the data and more reliable answers supplied directly by respondents instead of through a more or less inhibiting intermediary, the enumerator [5]." Mail surveys avoid not only the bias attributable to the interviewer but also the inhibiting factor of another person's presence; the average person does not wish to appear prejudiced, stupid, poor, or boastful to the interviewer.

Furthermore, the respondent's anonymity and the confidential handling of his answers can be made clear in the letter accompanying the questionnaire, while the same respondent facing the personal interviewer or answering questions on his home or office telephone must be aware that his name and identity can be connected with his answers.

Better likelihood of thoughtful reply. If a person decides to answer a mail questionnaire, he will do it at his leisure and not when the interviewer happens to call on the phone or in person. He will have a chance to give it such thought as is needed, and he can seek help from another family member on subjects for which such help is required.

Time-saving. By sending out a single mailing by air, a nationwide survey of a large sample distributed all over the United States can be completed in two weeks. (Usually this mailing will yield about 90 percent of all the returns which would come in if the survey were kept open longer.) It is often impossible to obtain the results in two weeks by personal interview. The time-saving can be even more pronounced in international surveys.

Centralized control. Mail surveys can be conducted from one office, with built-in checks and controls for every phase of the operation. On a major personal interview survey, hundreds of interviewers must be instructed, supervised, and checked, with special controls by region, state, or city.

Cost saving. Low overall costs result in more flexibility per dollar spent. Not only is the interviewer's time costly, but his training, briefing, supervision, and checking are all expensive items. The combined costs of a mailing piece, postage, and incentives offered to respondents are usually considerably less. Because of this great difference in expense, on any given budget one can afford to produce a larger number of completed questionnaires by using the mail method.

The major shortcomings of the mail survey method may also be summarized in a few points:

Usable mailing lists sometimes are unavailable. If no acceptable list is available and the cost of creating one is prohibitive, the research *cannot* be done by mail. As shown later, existing lists may be unacceptable because of incompleteness or bias.

The subject matter or nature of the research may require the presence of a specially trained interviewer. In some types of research (for example, psychological motivation, medical case histories), the questioning may be the key to the whole project, and it may have to be done by a psychologist, a physician, or some other specially trained professional person.   In the case of in-depth interviews, for which the information required from respondents cannot be structured, it is often impossible to construct a questionnaire.

The questionnaire is too long.   In general, a questionnaire longer than six or eight pages should be administered by a well-trained interviewer who can maintain the respondent's interest.   Everything else being equal, when the questionnaire becomes too long, the percentage of response falls off sharply. There are cases in which respondents are willing to complete 20-page questionnaires.   These, however, usually concern the special interest or hobby of the group surveyed.

The questionnaire is too difficult.   It may not be possible to conduct a mail survey (and sometimes any other survey) if the questions and answers are too time-consuming and complicated, or require too much concentration, checking of documents, or consultation with other people.

The information required is confidential.   If a company has a strict rule that its sales or purchasing figures are confidential, no survey will succeed in obtaining them.   A person may feel the same way about some aspects of his or her private life.

The respondent is not the addressee.   It can happen that a wife fills out a questionnaire addressed to her husband, or that an assistant or a secretary completes a form for her employer.   To check on the size of such pass-along respondent groups, one may end the questionnaire with a simple question: "Are you the person to whom the envelope containing this questionnaire was addressed? Yes ☐ No ☐."

The time available is not enough to conduct a mail survey.   If the researcher needs the answers in 48 hours, the job cannot be done by mail.

The problem of nonrespondents must be faced in connection with every type of data gathering, whether it be personal interviews, telephone interviews, or mail surveys, and will be discussed later.

MAILING LISTS—SAMPLING NOTE

To conduct a mail survey, we must have a mailing list.   For most research projects, it is advisable to have the names and addresses in the sample on cards.

Card lists have many advantages.   It may be possible to include available information (demographic data, SIC numbers, and so on) on these cards. With the help of a matching key number on the list cards and questionnaires, information on the cards can be transferred to the replies or, in the case of punched cards, directly to the tabulating cards punched from the completed questionnaires.   Card lists can facilitate all handling and checking of counts. They can save time and reduce error in the case of follow-up mailings: the respondents' list cards can be pulled (preferably daily) from the mailing deck and the follow-up mailing sent to nonrespondents still outstanding on the closing date of the first wave.

The following are some types of mailing lists frequently used in market research: city directories, telephone directories, records published by federal, state, and municipal governments, lists and rating books published by such firms as Dun & Bradstreet and the Credit Rating Bureau, business directories (Poor's, Thomas', and so on), membership lists of associations and organizations, publication subscription lists, and a large variety of lists sold by mailing-list houses.

The researcher should always try to obtain lists that include the names of individuals, not just the names of companies or institutions with their job titles, because the percentage of return is higher when the mailing is addressed to specific persons.

Lists may contain a variety of so-called frame biases. Here are some of them:

1. The frame which is sampled may include the names of people who do not belong in it or may omit those of persons who should be listed.

2. The list may be too old to be reliable.

3. All or part of the list may have been used for surveys or promotional or sales efforts which can bias the research at hand.

4. There may be a duplication of names within the list.

The researcher must carefully check the nature and origin of his lists to avoid any such biases.

The sampling rules described in Sec. II, Part C, Chap. 1–3 apply to mail surveys, as they do to all other types of research.

For many mail surveys, a systematic sample is usually considered adequate. It involves using every nth name in the list. If the list consists of 7,000 names and a sample of 1,000 is needed, the systematic sample would comprise every seventh name on the list.

One thing to avoid, especially in the case of published lists or of lists purchased from list houses, is starting with the first name and continuing with an obvious interval, such as every tenth name or every name at the top of a page in a directory. There is a chance that others have used the list in the same way, which may make the sample less responsive or less representative.

To avoid problems of this kind, some researchers prefer the more lengthy system of numbering the names in the universe and using a table of random numbers for selection. A compromise is to employ systematic sampling, using as the starting place a name selected by taking a number from a table of random numbers.

It is often easy to make mistakes by not following sampling instructions. It is good practice to check the sample against some known distribution of the universe, such as state of residence. This procedure will not guarantee a good sample but may help to catch some obvious mistakes.

PILOT STUDIES

Pilot studies (or pretests) can serve many purposes, such as testing the quality of the mailing list, checking the percentage of returns, and measuring the relative effectiveness of various techniques in producing high-percentage returns. The effect of using advance mailings, incentives, and various types of follow-up efforts can be tested. Pilot studies are also helpful in discovering the occurrence of bias resulting from the wording of letters and questionnaires and in establishing how well the questions are understood and answered. Finally, they are useful in checking, or refining, a cost estimate.

Each pilot study must be based on a random sample of the population surveyed. Obviously, a biased sample would be as wrong for the test as for the main mailing.

If we want to measure more than one variable with a test, for example, if we want to measure the relative effectiveness of using an advance postcard and of offering a 25-cent incentive, the correct procedure is to divide the test names into random subsamples. Each of these should test only one variable or a known combination of variables, while all other elements of the mailing remain constant. For example, the subsamples can be labeled (1) no advance post-card, no incentive, (2) postcard, no incentive, (3) incentive, no postcard, and (4) postcard and incentive. Each of these subsamples must represent separate random samples of the universe and must be based on a large-enough mailing for a meaningful measurement of the specific element being tested.

If the pilot study results do not warrant any major changes in the questionnaire, the total time loss due to such a study need not be more than 15 or 16 days, and the returns from the pilot test can be included in the main survey.

QUESTIONNAIRE CONSTRUCTION

Questionnaire construction is an essential part of any survey, but it must be done with more painstaking care for mail surveys than for any other data-gathering method. This is necessary because no interviewer will be present to answer questions or prevent any misunderstanding. A mail survey questionnaire, in its clarity, must perform both these functions itself.

There is another important difference between questionnaires for mail surveys and those administered by an interviewer: The mail survey questionnaire has to "sell" itself. There is no particular pressure on the recipient of a mail questionnaire to fill it in. Therefore, the appearance and contents of the form itself must encourage the respondent to start doing so, and it must hold his interest until he has completed it.

1. *Completeness and Relevance.* Once the returns are in, it is too late to realize that the answers are not very meaningful without an analysis by income, occupation, or some other vitally important variable which was not included in the questionnaire.

It is helpful to start by listing all possible subjects we want to ask about and then paring this list to the essential items. Next, we can use the same procedure within each subject by listing the largest number of questions which might be asked in connection with that subject, and then omitting the ones which are not absolutely relevant or necessary.

2. *The "Short and Easy" Look.* No matter how good the accompanying letter or how attractive the incentive, a forbidding questionnaire containing too many pages of small type will draw very few replies. "Easy looks" for a questionnaire involve the following points:

In general, the shorter and smaller the questionnaire, the easier it looks.

Rule of thumb: the fewer the pages, the higher the percent of return. Normally, a six-page questionnaire of 8½- x 11-inch size is considered the upper limit in length. There is, of course, a strong interrelation between size and number of pages: often a monarch size or somewhat smaller four-pager will draw as good a response as a full-size two-pager.

Illustrations should be used *only* when they can help clarify or shorten questions. Illustrated questionnaires look too much like advertisements and may very easily be considered as such when the addressee opens the envelope.

Because of its resemblance to advertising mail, colored stock should be avoided.

The paper used should be pleasant to look at, substantial enough to handle, nonporous enough to be printed on both sides without showing through, light enough to fit within the planned weight of the mailing piece, suitable for writing on with pen or pencil, and hardy enough to withstand some wear and tear in tabulating.

The questionnaire should look professional but not slick. This precludes mimeographing it, but ordinarily there is no need for the most expensive kind of paper or printing. The choice is usually between letterpress and offset printing from Varityped copy or a typed original. If the questionnaire is longer than one page, it should always be printed on both sides of the paper. This reduces weight and simplifies the tasks of both the respondent and the tabulator. A four-page questionnaire should be a folded sheet, to be opened and read like a newspaper. A six-page questionnaire can have the same format, with the extra page glued or stapled in.

The layout should give the impression of a neat, printed page which is both easy to read and simple to fill out. The page should never be overcrowded; it should have reasonable margins and sufficient white space to separate solidly printed blocks; use of the sometimes unavoidable tabular form (multiple columns of boxes) should be minimized.

It must be made explicitly clear to the respondent where to *check* the answer and where to *write in* numbers or words. The simple, graphic way of indicating this is by using boxes for check questions and rules (lines) for open-end questions. In using boxes or rules, it is very important to be certain that each *obviously* belongs to one item only.

It is also important that the space allowed for each answer (whether indicated by a box or a rule) always appears consistently on the same side of the question or of the suggested answer. The right side is preferable because the respondent must read the question and the suggested answers before he can check or otherwise indicate his reply.

Check-boxes should be vertically aligned wherever possible (which not only helps respondents and tabulators, but also enhances the questionnaire's appearance). Dotted lines or "leaders" guide the respondent in putting his check in the appropriate box.

It is rather discouraging to a respondent to discover that the questions run up to number 68. On all but the shortest questionnaires, therefore, it is advisable to group questions into sections by subject matter and start the numbering with question 1 within each section.

3. *Questions Which Respondents Will Be Willing and Able to Answer.* The general appearance of the questionnaire may be innocent enough to induce the respondent to take out his pencil; but if he finds that the questions are too involved and too difficult to answer, he will not continue.

Here are some pitfalls to avoid:

The respondent may stop answering if he feels that the questions do not apply to him. It is not advisable to ask an engineer about the company's media-selection problems or a sales manager about the engineering or chemical processes used by his firm. In general, the answers to questions concerning the respondent himself or his own job will be more reliable than his replies about the affairs of other people.

Even if the question is addressed to the right person, the answer should not require too much thinking or checking. One cannot ask an engineer to do an entire calculating job, or the sales manager to look up all his sales records of five years ago.

Strain on memory must be avoided. There is no point in asking anyone how much he spent on gas five years ago. Even if he should answer, the reply would hardly be reliable.

As mentioned earlier, some business firms have rules against revealing certain information, and some individuals have similar feelings about their private affairs. If there is any question on the likelihood of meeting this form of resistance, pilot studies should be conducted to test various phrasings and to establish the maximum amount of information that one can reasonably expect to receive.

A personal interviewer will not ask the respondent to answer questions which obviously do not apply to him. Similarly, the mail questionnaire should direct the respondent to skip any inapplicable question, section, or page.

One of the main reasons a respondent answers a questionnaire is the importance he attaches to the survey. If the questions look unimportant or frivolous, the researcher will lose some of his most intelligent respondents. One must be sparing in the use of humor.

4. *Interest and Importance.* Some of the most common mistakes in questionnaire construction occur because the researcher and the respondent are not interested in the same things. The personal characteristics and ownership data of its subscribers may be vitally important to the survey's sponsor. At the same time, few things are more boring to Mr. or Mrs. John Doe than answering dozens of questions on demographics or on brands of household items.

There are several ways to reconcile these differences in interest. One is careful wording of the letter of transmittal, which largely functions to motivate the respondent to answer. Another is a good introductory question, or set of questions, which will get the respondent started. A third is nimble sectionalizing and phrasing, in an effort to make the subject matter seem more interesting.

Often a bridge can be built between the letter of transmittal and the questionnaire by a carefully constructed title, which can also serve the survey's purpose by (a) appealing to the respondent's ego ("Survey among Top Executives"); (b) underlining the importance of the research ("Nationwide Survey among Top Executives"); (c) recalling the tie between the sponsor and the respondent ("Survey among Wall Street Journal Subscribers"); or (d) emphasizing a subject which interests the reader ("Study of Imported Cars"). Of course the title must appeal to all members of the sample. The last example works well *only* if the sample consists of owners of imported cars.

An introductory question can be very helpful. It must be on a subject that is of obvious interest to respondents. If the proposed questionnaire does not have such a question, it may be worth the space to insert one just to get the respondent started.

To keep the respondent interested, it is important to be as brief as possible and to use language which he will understand. Every business and trade has its own vocabulary, and it is difficult for each group to remember that the rest of the world is not necessarily acquainted with the jargon of an industry or a profession; for example, "ethical brands" or "EDP" may mean nothing to the respondent.

5. *Bias.* There are many possible biases which the researcher must avoid. Sample distortion can introduce a bias as can a nonrepresentative return. Further problems can be caused by a faulty letter of transmittal.

Even the title of the questionnaire may bias returns, as can questionnaire construction and specific questions. It is impossible to make general rules to prevent all biases; they hide under an infinite variety of disguises. However, here are a few general rules:

In a competitive survey, the questionnaire (or letter) should never divulge the identity of the sponsoring company if it is one of the contestants. A questionnaire from General Electric, so identified, cannot be expected to elicit unbiased answers on the comparative merits of G.E. and Westinghouse appliances.

If the subject of the questionnaire may appeal only to a limited segment of the sample, care should be taken to obtain a very high percentage of return, and to check nonrespondents if possible. A good method is to bury the subject of interest in the middle of a diversified questionnaire.

No question should lead (bias) the answers in any direction. It is not reasonable to ask, "In which magazine do you prefer to read about foreign affairs?" when one of the multiple-choice answers is *Foreign Affairs.* In a questionnaire on labor relations, the answers can be quite different, depending on whether we ask questions about "scabs and strike breakers" or about "people who continue working at a struck plant."

The lack of a filter question can often bias a respondent's answer. "How many cars do you own?" is a very biased beginning for a questionnaire mailed to the general public on the subject of cars. The proper start is:

> Do you now own a car? . . . Yes □ No □
> (If "No," skip to Q. X)
> If "Yes," how many cars do you now own? _____

Without this precaution, some nonowners may not return the questionnaire or, even worse, may feel that they have to give a positive answer, such as listing a car they *used* to own.

Bias can be introduced by fatigue when a large number of items are listed in a check question. In short lists (two or three items) where the respondent can see the names at a glance, the order of names seems to cause no significant difference. But when a larger number of items are listed, they should be rotated, or at least reversed in order on a random half of the questionnaires.

A question may embarrass the respondent and result in a biased answer or a "No answer." Occasionally, this is unavoidable. However, the problem can often be minimized by introducing a section of the questionnaire with a note emphasizing that the answers will be used only for statistical purposes.

When examples are given to instruct the respondent, great care must be taken that the examples themselves do not introduce a bias.

Even the order of questions may bias some answers.

6. *Questions Eliciting Clear, Precise Answers.* One of the most frustrating experiences a researcher can suffer is to look over a set of tabulations and realize they are meaningless because some of or all the respondents misunderstood a question or answered it in such varying ways that their responses cannot be combined. Questions and instructions must be clear enough to eliminate the possibility of such confusion.

Any question about size, amount, distance, time-lapse, and similar measurements should be asked with reference to a unit of measure. The answer to the question, "When did you move to your present home?" could be, "In 1961," "Six years ago," "When my wife died," "A short while ago," "Years ago," "When I was a child," or some other vague response.

Here are two good ways of asking this question:

> In what year did you move to your present home?   In 19_____.
> or
> How many years ago did you move to your present home?
> _____ years ago.

Ambiguity can often be eliminated by examples. Consider the question, "What is your occupation?" First, this is a very poor question because the answer can be "Retailing," "President," "Lawyer," "Sales," or another designation. The answers will be more precise and therefore more useful if there are separate questions on the respondent's line of business or profession and on his title and position, with examples showing the type of answers desired for each question.

An excellent device for clarifying meaning is to organize the questions into sections that keep the respondent in well-defined frames of reference. This should be true of both subject and time. All questions on travel should be grouped in one section, questions on car ownership in another, and so forth. Similarly, questions about last week's activities and those of the past two years should be grouped whenever possible by the period of time involved.

7. *Open-end versus Check Questions.* It is often very difficult to decide whether to use the open-end or the check (or closed-end) question form to elicit the desired information. Though it is clear that in most cases the check question is more readily answered and much cheaper to tabulate, it can have several drawbacks. Often the researcher has no way of knowing what the answers to his question will be and therefore cannot list them. What is worse, he may *think* he knows and be wrong, in which case he may never discover that he *was* wrong.

One can have an open-end line, "Other," following the checklist. However, this is only of limited help in establishing the comparative importance of an answer because a large percentage of people who would check a reason (or brand, or magazine, or some other item) when reminded of it through a listing would not remember it or might not bother writing it down as an "Other."

Another difficulty is the bias that a checklist can introduce. Plain laziness may induce a respondent to check something listed instead of thinking of a more specific or precise answer.

Open-end questions are often used in mail surveys, but their success will depend on the nature of the question, the interest of the subject matter to the respondent, and the literacy and education of the group surveyed.

8. *Questionnaire Construction.* Even though a questionnaire may seem unbiased, precise, interesting, and easy enough to be answered, it should still be examined from the viewpoint of data processing. Is there any possible improvement in layout, structuring, or wording that would make data processing more accurate, less costly, or both, without impairing the quality of the questionnaire? The answer is usually yes.

Precoding is the easiest way to facilitate fast and accurate punching operations. It is advisable to precode most questionnaires used for personal interviews. In the author's experience, it is not usually advantageous to precode mailed questionnaires. There is more printing and less available space on the precoded questionnaire, which makes it appear more difficult to read and answer. With proper layout, one can achieve results very similar to precoding, and this "proper" layout will help the respondent as much as the keypunch operator.

Here are a few final remarks on questionnaire construction:

The tone of the questionnaire should always be as polite as precision of language and brevity will permit. In any case, the last page should always end with a thank-you note.

Once the questionnaire is written, it is always good practice to run off a few (or few dozen) copies and to have the researcher or a personal interviewer hand them to people whose characteristics are similar to those of the members in the sample. The recipients are requested to fill out the questionnaire, and are afterward asked about any difficulties they may have encountered. A pilot mailing is usually the final check on questionnaire construction.

The questionnaire should be folded to fit the reply envelope, which in turn must fit inside the outer envelope. After it has been folded, the title of the first page should be on top.

Figure 1 shows page 4 of a survey conducted in 1969 among a systematic sample of the subscribers to *Natural History* magazine. It was mailed under the publication's name, with a 25-cent coin incentive. A reminder postcard was sent out three days after the questionnaire mailing. Completed returns represented 80 percent of the 3,000 mailing. The reproduced page illustrates the following points described previously:

Page 4

ABOUT YOU AND YOUR FAMILY (Confidential information, for the statistical analysis of previous data.)

1. Are you: .... Male? ☐   Female? ☐

   Married? ☐   Single? ☐   Widowed, separated, divorced? ☐

2. Please enter the number of household members in each age group below, including yourself:

   Males: Under 18 _____   Females: Under 18 _____
          18 and over_____   18 and over_____

3. Are you the head of the household? .... Yes ☐   No ☐

4. Please check your age group and the highest level of schooling you reached. (If you are not the head of the household, please also check his or her age and education.)

Age:	Self	Head of Household (If not yourself)	Education:	Self	Head of Household (If not yourself)
Under 18 ... ☐	☐		Grade school .... ☐	☐	
18 - 24 .... ☐	☐		High school .... ☐	☐	
25 - 34 .... ☐	☐		Attended college....... ☐	☐	
35 - 49 .... ☐	☐		Graduated from college ☐	☐	
			Post-graduate study ... ☐	☐	
50 - 64 .... ☐	☐				
65 or over .. ☐	☐				

5. In what type of business, industry or service is your company or employer engaged? (Please be specific: e.g., steel manufacturing, education, textile wholesale, state government, hardware retailing, etc.) If you do not work for an employer, please give your occupation or profession:

   _____

6. What is your title or position? (e.g., partner, president, foreman, doctor, teacher, etc.)

   _____

7. Do you live in a house or an apartment? .... A house ☐   An apartment ☐

   a. Do you or members of your household own it, or rent it? .... Own it ☐   Rent it ☐

8. In addition to your permanent residence, do you own or have you rented during the past 12 months a summer home or apartment?   Own ☐   Rent ☐   Neither ☐

9. Please check the estimated total household income before taxes in 19XX (Please include income from all household members and from all sources, including bonuses, dividends, rentals, etc.)

   Under $5,000 ☐ $ 7,500-$ 9,999 ☐ $15,000-$19,999 ☐ $25,000-$49,999 ☐
   $5,000-$7,499 ☐ $10,000-$14,999 ☐ $20,000-$24,999 ☐ $50,000 or over ☐

   THANK YOU FOR YOUR HELP.

Fig. 1.   Page of a 1969 *Natural History* survey.

1. The "easy-looking" questionnaire was offset-printed from copy typed with a carbon-ribbon electric typewriter.

2. The page has nine questions but does not look crowded because of the layout.

3. Tabular setups (questions 4 and 9) are minimized, as are the open-end questions (2, 5, and 6).

4. Questions 2, 5, and 6 also indicate by means of lines that write-in answers are needed, while all other questions have boxes for check answers.

5. The boxes are properly spaced and aligned, and leaders are provided where needed.

6. The questionnaire is sectionalized, and page 4 starts with a new section and a new question 1.

7. Reference is made to the confidential nature of the replies and to their intended use for statistical analysis.

8. The examples in question 6 include both "president" and "foreman" to avoid bias.

9. Questions 5 and 6 are very explicit, to avoid ambiguity.

10. Questions 3 and 4 are ordered consecutively because they include questions about the household head, and questions 7 and 8, because they are on the subject of residence.

11. Questions 5 and 6 are open-end questions because a list might bias some answers.

12. The layout makes the questionnaire quite easy to keypunch.

Figure 2 shows page 1 of a four-page questionnaire mailed in 1969 to a sample of college students. It was sent out with a letter from the research organization, a 25-cent coin incentive was used, and a reminder postcard was mailed three days after the questionnaire mailing. Completed returns were received from 68.3 percent of the students in the sample.

This page illustrates (besides several points already shown in Figure 1):

1. The use of a title

2. An introductory question

3. The use of a filter question (question 2) which allows the respondent to skip those questions (questions 2a–e) which do not apply to him

4. Proper layouts for make and brand questions.

TECHNIQUES FOR INCREASING RESPONSE RATES

Many tests have shown that *advance notice* can increase the percentage of returns. Some such notices that have proven successful are a preliminary postcard, letter, or telephone call, or in the case of surveys among subscribers, a notice in the publication. The purpose of any type of advance notice is to announce the survey before the arrival of the questionnaire and thereby to assure it a better reception.

The *letter* accompanying the questionnaire should have the format and appearance of a personal communication; it is more effective if it has a matching personalization and corresponding signature. It should express, or at least imply, the importance of the research project and of the addressee's participation. It should indicate that completing the questionnaire will take only a short time and that it can be answered easily. The letter should also note that a stamped reply envelope is enclosed and that the answers will be anonymous or confidential, and finally, it should express the sender's appreciation. On some surveys, it may be useful to explain how the addressee was selected and how the survey may benefit him or his profession. If an incentive is used, it should be described.

The letter should always be truthful (for example, keyed questionnaires should not be called anonymous), and its style and tone should be acceptable to the group of people surveyed, and it should be as brief as possible.

Incentives are needed whenever the questionnaire's subject matter is not of sufficient interest or the sender's prestige is not impressive enough to induce a high percentage of the sample to complete and return the questionnaire. The incentive must be effective in increasing the percentage of return and do so without biasing the responses or their distribution.   Furthermore, it must be small and light enough to be mailed easily and inexpensively, and its cost must fit the available research budget.

Incentives are either mailed with the questionnaire or promised as a gift to those answering it and then sent to the respondents after they have returned their questionnaires.   The first method is more effective but also more costly.

NATIONAL SURVEY OF COLLEGE MEN

1. What are your reactions to the recent confrontations, building takeovers, etc., which have been happening on college campuses? (Please check the statement that comes closest to your point of view—or write your own.)

   They are completely destructive and unjustified .... ☐

   There is some justification, but students have overreacted in most cases.. ☐

   There is at least as much to be said for as against the student actions ..... ☐

   The students have been right most of the time .... ☐

   Any comments? _____

   _____

   _____

2. Do you have your own car at college? .... Yes ☐   No ☐

   If "Yes," please complete the following information:

Make and Model (Ford Mustang, Chevrolet Impala, Dodge Charger, etc.)	Model year	How purchased	
		New	Used
		☐	☐

   a. Is this car registered in your name? .... Yes ☐   No ☐

   b. Who paid for its purchase? .... I did ☐   Parents did ☐   We both did ☐

   c. Who decided on the make and model? ..... I did ☐   Parents did ☐   Did it together ☐

   d. If you needed a battery, spark plugs or tires, who would decide on the brand, you or your parents? .... I would ☐   Parents would ☐

   e. Have you actually had occasion to replace any of these items? .... Yes ☐   No ☐

   If "Yes," please check which of them you replaced and write the name of the brand you bought.

Item	Bought	Brand
Battery	☐	_____
Spark plug(s)	☐	_____
Tire(s).	☐	_____

3. Do you have a motorcycle, motor bike or motor scooter at college? .... Yes ☐   No ☐

4. Do you plan to acquire one in the next 12 months? .... Yes ☐   No ☐

Fig. 2.   First page of a 1969 questionnaire mailed to college students.

Researchers have used many different premiums (incentives) for surveys. Possible premiums include trading stamps, unused postage stamps, packages of stamps for collectors, tie clips, pennies (both American and foreign), books, pencils, pens, and similar items.

In general, money seems to be the most effective and least biasing incentive, the easiest to provide and mail, and useful to *all* recipients.   Quarters and dollar bills are incentives often used in the United States.   In most surveys, such incentives will increase the number of returns very significantly, often by 50 percent or more.

An essential point to remember in using incentives in general, and money in particular, is that they are not intended to be a payment or even a reward, but only an attention getter and a token of appreciation, of thanks.

The primary purpose of *follow-up mailings* is to reduce the percentage of nonrespondents and thereby make the survey more representative. Regardless of how high the percentage of response to the first mailing, a follow-up mailing will nearly always produce several additional returns.

Some of the most common types of follow-up mailing are:

The reminder postcard. This is often effective. It contains a brief reminder of the questionnaire mailed previously, is usually sent out three to five days after the first mailing, and is addressed to the entire sample.

The second wave. This mailing will contain another copy of the questionnaire and a reply envelope. The accompanying letter will expand the theme of the reminder postcard. The researcher must decide whether to use an incentive, and if so, whether to use the one already offered or a different one. If the questionnaires of the main mailing were keyed and if enough time is available, the second wave can be mailed to nonrespondents when the returns from the first wave start petering out.

The third wave. This mailing, if used, must squeeze out of the sample a few more percentage points worth of responses. Mailed to nonrespondents from the previous waves and using one or more of the following approaches, it may emphasize the importance of receiving an answer from every member of the sample; repeat or increase the incentive; stress the urgency of completing the survey; mention the percentage of response already received; and possibly ask the respondents to answer only certain key questions. It usually contains another copy of the questionnaire.

The fourth and subsequent waves (if any). Reminders may be sent out by mail or by wire, or they may consist of telephone or personal interviews.

THE NONRESPONDENT PROBLEM

It is nearly impossible to achieve a 100 percent response, and this is true regardless of what data-gathering methods are used.

The research methods committee of the American Marketing Association found that: "Even with several attempts at contact it is seldom possible (for personal interviewers) to reach and interview 90 per cent, usually not more than 85 per cent, often as little as 75 or 80 per cent" [2].

The Advertising Research Foundation recommends an 80 percent or better response on mail surveys, which brings the rate of nonresponse into line with the rate of substitution in well-conducted personal interview studies. In both this country and abroad, numerous mail surveys achieve better than 80 percent returns every year. However, the last few percentage points of an 80 percent response are by far the most costly to achieve, and often the researcher may feel that, for his purposes, the additional representativeness gained is not worth the additional cost.

Actually, no level of response is automatically "sufficient"; its acceptability must be judged in each case by the nature of the survey and the goals and standards set by the researcher for a particular project.

The importance of nonresponse can be simply stated: It may destroy the randomness of the sample and thereby the representativeness and reliability of the survey. It should be part of the survey design to decide how high a percentage of nonresponse can be tolerated, and what, if anything, should be done about it. The researcher can choose from among several procedures:

He can take a chance on assuming that the nonrespondents will not be different in any significant way from the respondents, or that the differences will be so small that they will not significantly affect the results.

He may feel that while the returns to the first mailing are not representative of the sample, the last wave or a combination of the last waves of returns are representative of all nonrespondents to the first mailing. In this case, he will weight the final nonresponse by the replies to the follow-up mailings.

Another method would be to establish trends from the results of several waves and to weight the nonresponse by continuing these trends.

The survey design may call for analyzing a random sample of nonrespondents and, if necessary, weighting all nonresponses according to the results of this procedure.

Several statistical methods have been devised for eliminating, or at least reducing, the nonrespondent bias. To attain the required precision at a minimum cost, Hansen and Hurwitz [4] developed a double sampling procedure which formulates how to determine the number of mail questionnaires to send out and the number of personal interviews to conduct in following up nonresponses to the mail questionnaire. The Swedish researcher Tore Dalenius [3] developed a special design of the Hansen-Hurwitz scheme aimed at the "hard to contact" segment of the sample. Rex V. Brown [1] developed a technique called "Credence Decomposition," which relies on splitting out the various sources of error, including nonresponse, to which a research estimate may be subject.

DATA PROCESSING

Most data processing operations are the same for mail surveys as for surveys using other methods of data collection. However, the researcher must bear in mind that no personal interviewer is present when the mail questionnaires are filled out. He must therefore be certain that all the answers are consistent. This requires careful editing, coding, and consistency checking.

Editing is essential in all survey work, but it is particularly important in mail surveys. Without the help of an interviewer, respondents may misread instructions, give imprecise answers, and send back incomplete returns. Careful questionnaire construction, pretesting, and pilot surveys should reduce these flaws to a minimum, but the editing process will always be important for maximizing the questionnaire's usefulness.

Editing has four main purposes:

1. To improve the accuracy and clarity of answers to specific questions.

2. To eliminate inconsistent, incorrect, or imprecise replies.

3. To reduce "No answers" or incomplete replies to some questions with the help of information found elsewhere on the questionnaire.

4. To make entries clear, consistently uniform, and comprehensible to coders and keypunch operators.

Coding and tabulating are discussed elsewhere in this handbook. However, for the reasons just mentioned, the researcher, when processing mail surveys, should be very careful with regard to test tabulations, code construction, and the supervision of coders. He must always consider the specific problems connected with mail response. For example, if he needs test tabulations as an aid in code construction, it is essential that the questionnaires selected for test tabulating represent a random sample of all returns, and not only of those replies of the first day or two.   Early returns may be heavily overbalanced with respondents who live nearby and with the kind of people who return questionnaires at once.

CONCLUSIONS

A very large part of the market research both in the United States and abroad is done by means of mail surveys.   Many of these surveys leave much to be desired from the point of view of their accuracy and professionalism.   For a mail survey to be acceptable, it must be based on an adequate mailing list, use proper sampling procedures, avoid biasing the answers by anything contained in the letter or the questionnaire, and finally, achieve a very high rate of response or take other steps to eliminate or reduce nonrespondent bias.   Special care must also be given to the data processing operations.

All these considerations bring us back to one of the opening remarks of this chapter.   Part of the survey design is the choice of the data collection method. One of the methods is the mail survey.   The appropriateness of the mail survey method should be considered, compared with that of other data collection techniques, and properly evaluated.   If chosen as the most suitable method, it should be carefully planned and properly executed, preferably by researchers with experience in this field.

The principles and procedures described in this chapter are discussed in more detail (including the results of tests and case histories) in the author's book *Professional Mail Surveys* (McGraw-Hill, 1970).

REFERENCES

1. Brown, Rex V., "Research Appraisal in Confusion—Where Can the User Turn?" Paper delivered at American Marketing Association Summer Conference, Philadelphia, June 18, 1968.
2. Cohen, Reuben, Samuel Richmond, J. Stevens Stock, and Thomas T. Semon, "Sampling in Marketing Research," *Marketing Research Techniques Series*, no. 3, American Marketing Association, 1958, p. 9.
3. Dalenius, Tore, "The Treatment of the Nonresponse Problem," *Journal of Advertising Research*, September 1961, pp. 1–7.
4. Hansen, Morris H., and William N. Hurwitz, "The Problem of Non-Response in Sample Surveys," *Journal of The American Statistical Association*, December 1946, pp. 517–519.   Also: Hansen, Morris H., W. N. Hurwitz, and W. G. Madow, *Sample Survey Methods and Theory*, vol. 1, New York: Wiley, 1953, pp. 473–474.
5. U.S. Department of Commerce, Bureau of the Census: "Planning Notes for 1970 Decennial Census," no. 1, Washington: Government Printing Office, March 17, 1966, p. 2.   Also: U.S. Department of Commerce, Bureau of the Census: *Effects of Interviewers and Crew Leaders*, Series ER 60, no. 7, 1968, pp. 1–91.

Part B

Surveys

Chapter 4

Data Collection Methods: Telephone Surveys

STANLEY L. PAYNE   *Survey Research Consultant, Breckenridge, Colorado*

Interviews by telephone are satisfactory, efficient, and economical for a wide range of survey purposes—so much so that many market researchers make a practice of asking themselves with each survey whether they can possibly conduct it entirely or in part by telephone, and whether they can compensate for the limitations this method may impose. Only if their answers are negative do they consider other methods.

This chapter discusses the several limitations of the telephone method, suggesting how some of them can be overcome or adjusted for; the many advantages of this method; examples of its varied applications and adaptations; selection of samples from telephone directories and other sources, as well as sampling pitfalls to avoid; telephone questionnaire design; telephone interviewing etiquette; and telephone interviewer selection.

LIMITATIONS OF TELEPHONE SURVEYS

Several serious limitations of the telephone survey method have been encountered. Most can be ameliorated or even eliminated. Some of them are also present in other data collection methods. Sometimes a combination of survey methods is needed. Many researchers, aware of the problems, accept the telephone method as adequate for most of their marketing research purposes even without correction of the limitations.

Incomplete Universe. Not everybody has a telephone. This has been the main drawback of the telephone method, at least historically. The ill-fated *Literary Digest* election poll of 1936 was so disastrously wrong largely because it was based on telephone-subscriber samples, which did not include lower-income people in proper proportions. To the extent that it is important to have all sections of the population fairly represented in a marketing survey, differential rates of telephone "ownership" remain a serious obstacle.

Population subgroups, many of them overlapping or duplicating, that are underrepresented as telephone subscribers include lowest-income people, slum dwellers, tenement dwellers with shared hall telephones, ethnic groups, recent arrivals, poor credit risks, tenant farmers, Southerners, and others. Some types of people who do have telephones may also be overlooked or underrepresented in a sample of "residence" telephones, for example, business proprietors who live behind their shops but list their only telephones under business names, and apartment or hotel dwellers whose telephones are reached only through a common switchboard. Also, in samples of separate individuals as distinct from representatives of entire households, members of large families may have less chance than those in small families of being interviewed.

Over the years, however, a much higher telephone saturation has developed so that in areas covered by some telephone directories, well over 95 percent of all households now have telephones. The telephone company has records of the number of trunk lines (or residence main stations) in each directory area—or perhaps better yet, the researcher can count the number of residence listings in a sample of directory columns or pages for comparison with updated census household counts for approximating the proportion of all dwelling units with listed telephones.

Furthermore, some of the preceding types of people with less than their share of telephones may be such unlikely potential consumers of particular products or services that their underrepresentation may be considered an advantage. The ideal matching of the limited telephone universe to a product would be in a survey on attachments for telephones.

Also, the types who seldom have telephones are commonly shorted in other survey methods anyway, since they are disinclined to answer mail questionnaires and since interviewers often hesitate to enter their neighborhoods. When included in a sample design, such people often contribute more heavily to the nonresponse rate than to the subject matter under investigation.

An obvious way to include residents of areas with few telephones is to sample those areas separately and to interview there in person. Another combination method, more elaborate and exact, is to draw the entire sample from other sources, such as address listings, and to interview by telephone the large number who have telephones and the remainder in person.

Another technique useful in making a rough adjustment of a telephone-number sample is simply to ask respondents the location of the dwelling nearest theirs with a telephone, or to determine this later from a street-address telephone directory. The nearest dwelling unit with a telephone should be counted in only one direction, of course, such as consistently in the direction of the next higher address or apartment number. Weights are then assigned to the completed interviews according to how many dwelling units away the next telephones are: if next door, as is most common, the interview weight is 1; if the second door away, the weight is 2; if the third dwelling unit away, the weight is 3, and so on. Such simple adjustment is based on the hopeful assumption that respondents with telephones are like their neighbors without telephones. Similarly, individuals interviewed one to a family can be assigned weights in proportion to the number of family members determined during the interview.

One way or another, incomplete telephone saturation need not itself preclude the use of telephone interviewing. Although there are many techniques for compensating or adjusting telephone samples, the most common practice is to accept the telephone universe as is and to report the results as "based on a telephone-owner sample." Much satisfactory, useful, and worthwhile information can be obtained without equal coverage of all parts of the population.

Unlisted Telephone Numbers. A growing practice among some telephone subscribers is to refuse to list their names in telephone directories, personally giving out their numbers only to selected people. This effectively removes them from telephone directory samples and, to the extent that they may be alike, may cause their types to be insufficiently represented in telephone surveys. Surprisingly, perhaps, unlisted numbers have been much more common in proportion to total telephones in lower-income than in upper-income areas.

Major reasons for unlisted telephone numbers seem to be avoiding disclosure of telephone ownership and escaping unwanted calls. Among such nuisance calls, unlisted telephone subscribers may include survey interviews and, in particular, sham "survey" sales solicitations. Nevertheless, their ideas need to be represented in legitimate surveys, and they themselves are sometimes interested in the subject matter of a particular interview. It can well be argued that efforts should be made to include them despite their aloofness.

An indirect sampling technique, described later in this chapter, provides a means of sampling telephone numbers for all types of subscribers, listed and unlisted, in representative proportions.

Directory Obsolescence. At time of issue, telephone directories are models of accuracy, which cannot be said of many other listings. Also, when a subscriber moves into the locality and if his former number has not been reissued, an intercept message gives his new number. However, as new telephone numbers are assigned and a telephone directory ages, it becomes less and less complete in its coverage, there being up to 20 percent turnover of numbers within a year.

Recent incomers to the directory area are not included. Yet, for many research purposes, they are the mobile types who may be the most rewarding to interview. Many techniques of listing recent move-ins have been used to obtain their names and addresses, from which the Directory Assistance (formerly "Information") operator can provide telephone numbers. Among such listing methods are lists of other recent utility hook-ups, canvasses of new real estate developments and new apartment houses, realtors' lists, Welcome Wagon hostess lists, and so on. Again, the indirect sampling technique, described later, can be used for a current sampling of all telephone numbers.

Need for Props. Some market research surveys require visual aids, packages, products, or other props for reference or use during, or in connection with, the interviews. Such requirements may well be the most obvious and overriding reasons for rejecting the telephone survey method in particular instances.

Open-minded ingenuity, however, has often found ways of converting personal interview studies to the telephone method by accomplishing the desired effect with substitute props, separate delivery of product, or replacement of a visual aid by an audio aid. A most clever substitution is treating the telephone dial itself as a 10-point rating scale, from the "1" for extreme like to the "0" for total dislike. A seven-point or nine-point scale usually presented on a card may be approximated by two oral questions: the "like or dislike?" idea, followed by the "how much?" intensity type of question. A four- or five-point buying-intention question can be almost as readily comprehended orally as visually: "Would you definitely buy it, probably buy it, probably not buy it, or definitely not buy it?" with "No opinion" accepted as a mid-scale value.

For appraisals of a food product, personal visits can be made initially to leave the samples and make appointments for telephone follow-up interviews after home trial. As high as 97 percent of the follow-up interviews have been completed in such studies, and the original placements have often been easier to make because homemakers could be told that there would be no personal follow-up. Packages, products, or visual aids can also be mailed in advance of telephone interviews. In a brand-name survey among purchasing agents, the buyers were asked to write down a new brand name as it was spelled to them during the telephone interview. They thus constructed their own visual aids.

Interview Length. It was once thought that telephone interviews had to be kept very brief. After an interview has started, it is probably easier for a bored or hurried respondent to hang up the telephone than to slam the door on a personal interviewer. However, telephone interviews requiring as much as 25 or 30 minutes and including as many as 60 questions have now become commonplace, and some hour-long interviews have been successfully completed by telephone. When called later for verification purposes, respondents typically estimate that the telephone interviews took less than half the time actually spent.

The need for interesting questions on interesting subjects is magnified in telephone surveys. Personal interviews of several hours have been conducted on some relatively uninteresting subjects; they probably could not have been made by telephone. Very few marketing research interviews need be that long or that deadly, however. The telephone method seldom need be ruled out because of interview length. A careful look might better be taken at the questionnaire to judge whether its inordinate length is justified.

Shorter Comments. It has been demonstrated that open-end questions may not be answered in as great detail over the telephone as in person. To some extent, that brevity could be a reaction to which the interviewer contributes. Writing out a verbatim reply of as few as 15 or 20 words creates what may seem to both participants an interminable hiatus in the conversation. The interviewer may therefore attempt to edit down the comment to fewer words in haste to proceed to the next question. The same situation occurs with open-end answers in personal interviews but is a lesser problem there because the respondent can observe the interviewer writing, whereas, over the telephone, nothing can be seen or heard to be happening.

It is good interviewing practice in either case, but is almost essential in telephone interviewing, that the interviewer fill in the conversation gap in some way—perhaps merely by saying, while writing: "I am writing down in your own words, 'I liked the taste and flavor of that pie because it was unusually tart without being too sour, if you know what I mean.' Please go on."

One small, offsetting advantage in telephone interviewing is that the interviewer is usually in a more comfortable writing position in the office or her own home than when interviewing in person.

Even with the preceding precautions and offsetting advantage, the telephone method may produce shorter answers than the personal method. That circumstance nevertheless is not necessarily so great a problem as word counts might suggest. Most of the extended verbiage in longer statements consists of elaboration, repetition, and rephrasing of a few dominant themes. Even in-depth probing may not increase the number of basic ideas by more than 20 percent over the number originally expressed—unless the interviewer (mistakenly) offers suggestions.

Differences in answers to check-box questions between personal and telephone surveys have been found to be comparatively trivial.

Other Telephone Survey Limitations.   Several other shortcomings may be less obvious and less important than the previous limitations.

One problem is the lack of observational material in the telephone interview. Race, ethnic origin, age, physical condition, type of dwelling, socioeconomic status, and other factors are examples of classifications which cannot be seen. Even the respondent's sex is occasionally contradicted by the voice, and it is embarrassing to ask for a child's mother only to be told that the childish person speaking is the mature lady of the house.   Some of these background items are not too difficult to convert to question form; others are more touchy to ask about.   Particularly, it may seem unpleasant to start an interview with questions designed to screen out certain types, as in eliminating persons over 55 years of age.   A characteristic like socioeconomic status may have to be approached by the occupation and education route—and may be the better for it.   Some of the classifying questions will be discussed later in this chapter under "Telephone Questionnaire Design."

Related to the preceding limitation is a lack of behavioral cues in the telephone interview: grins, winks, puzzled frowns, raised eyebrows, gestures of impatience, affirming or negating motions by either participant are missed by the other.   Although such cues from the interviewer may better go unobserved by the respondent, the respondent's acts are often useful in correctly understanding his words.   Little can be done about this limitation other than suggesting that, in cases of doubt, the interviewer might carefully seek confirmation without influence: "You say that you believe it writes under water."

Multiple listings of telephones present an opposite problem to that of unlisted numbers—the possible overrepresentation of some types of people in a telephone survey.   Multiple listings are of two types.   The first is most common among professional and business men who have both office and residence telephones.   A technique for reducing their double opportunity of inclusion is discussed in the "Sampling for Telephone Surveys" section of this chapter.

The second type of multiple listing is the rapidly growing duplicate listings of two telephones in the same dwelling unit, as when the parents and the children have separate numbers or when two or more of their names are listed for the same number.   When extra listings of the same family appear on successive lines of the directory, it is simple enough in sampling to ignore all but the first. When the listings under the surname are widely separated alphabetically by other first names or initials, the duplication is not so readily noticed.

The indirect sampling technique, discussed later, eliminates the oversampling of homes of the type having multiple listing of the same number, but it does not avoid the oversampling of the type having more than one number.   The latter problem can be countered by asking in every interview whether any other telephone numbers are listed for members of that household and weighting down to one-half and one-third the interviews with those having two and three telephone numbers.   Although the latter solution is sound, the question is wasted in most interviews.   In actual practice, the technique is seldom, if ever, used, and the possibility of overrepresentation is accepted.

ADVANTAGES OF TELEPHONE SURVEYS

The telephone survey method has several apparent advantages over other methods as well as other plus features not so evident.   Some attributes are not always used to full advantage.   This section discusses not only the special values of this method but also some means of exploiting them further.

Economy.   The most obvious advantage of the telephone survey method is its cost saving in comparison with personal, house-to-house interviewing. Elimination of time spent in travel and in locating respondents accounts for the greatest saving, of course, but the difference between mileage costs and telephone charges may also be considerable. Generally, the shorter the actual interview time relative to the other time factors, the greater the economy of the telephone method. The real differences in costs must be estimated for a particular survey, and they depend on such factors as subject matter, interview length, distances between interviews, call-back requirements, listing technique, supervisor and training time, rates of pay, mileages, and tolls, versus telephone charges and related expenses, and interviewer home locations. Seldom, however, do the data collection costs of the telephone survey exceed two-thirds of the comparable costs of the personal survey.

Differences in costs between telephone and mail surveys are not so one-sided. Depending primarily on mail response rates, one or the other may prove more economical, since the mailing cost per return for a 10 percent mail response is essentially five times that for a 50 percent mail response.

Compared with personal interviews, telephone call-backs to reach people not initially at home are almost cost-free. Therefore, less need may exist to provide for substitutions within the sample, so that fewer listings need be drawn.

An economy which should be undertaken more often is that of drawing the telephone numbers centrally so that interviewers may concentrate on interviewing. It is feasible in the central sampling approach also to make separate listings for the different exchanges within a directory area so that assignments may be tailored to the different interviewers' locations, thus avoiding unnecessary message-unit charges.

Before the introduction of Wide Area Telephone Service (WATS), long-distance telephoning had sometimes proven economical in national or regional surveys in which respondents were widely scattered or were otherwise difficult to reach in person. WATS, offered by the telephone company regionally or nationally, makes long-distance telephoning even more competitive with other survey methods. Indeed, interviewing nationally from one location over WATS lines may often be cheaper than interviewing the same national sample by local telephones from individual interviewer homes scattered around the country—selection, training, and all other costs taken into account. It is unlikely that installation of WATS lines would pay for a single small national survey, but some marketing research departments or firms conducting many national surveys find savings in Wide Area Telephone Service.

Speed and Efficiency. All these conclusions on the economy and cost savings of the telephone method apply also to its relative speed and time-savings and to its greater efficiency. More interviews can be done by telephone than in person within a limited time period—say, three hours—and more hours of the day can be productive. In the short interval between the dinner hour and bedtime, for example, an interviewer may think it foolish to drive back 30 miles to obtain another personal interview. By telephone, however, she may readily make half-a-dozen interviews that evening at greater distances.

The principle of utilizing interviewer time most efficiently leads to a special call-placing technique for long-distance, person-to-person calls: The interviewer at the outset gives the operator a series of names and telephone numbers, requesting that as she completes each interview, the operator place the next call. In utilizing this method, arrangements should be made in advance with the telephone company since there may be delays during periods of high traffic volume.

Special Universes. Although the telephone method may sometimes be faulted for not completely covering the general public universe, there are many classifications of people who all have telephones. Doctors, lawyers, and most other professional people, automobile dealers, electric contractors, movers, and most other business firms have 100 percent telephone saturation. Moreover, it is important to them that their numbers be listed. The classified telephone directory, therefore, is usually one of the best available source listings for such types. The chief precaution in preparing to draw samples from the yellow pages is to eliminate double and multiple listings of the same person or business.

The classified telephone directory and telephone calls can be used to reach samples representative of full universes of certain types of persons not listed there at all. For example, purchasing agents of television service companies can be contacted by drawing a sample of such companies, calling them, and asking to speak to "the person responsible for buying your television repair parts." Such approaches to buyers and other company executives have delivered telephone interview completions as high as 94 percent with no substitutions.

Unreachable People. In towns which enforce Green River ordinances against interviewers (that is, ordinances that prohibit door-to-door survey interviewers), treating them like door-to-door salesmen, personal interviews are impossible and telephone interviews enjoy more than an advantage—almost a monopoly. Other towns which prohibit door-to-door canvassing in the evening and on weekends also present problems which can be overcome by using the telephone approach. Similarly, residents of locked-door apartment houses are shielded from personal interviewers unless reached by telephone for admittance or appointment. They may better be interviewed by telephone. One caution: If many such interviews are to be conducted in a concentrated area, it may be wise to clear with local authorities.

Imperativeness. Rightly or not, the telephone tends to command greater attention than the doorbell or other direct means of confrontation. People will answer the telephone under home conditions when they would not open the door to an interviewer, let alone invite her in. Easier access by telephone carries over into many business situations as well. The same switchboard operator-receptionist who informs an interviewer in the company lobby that all interviewing is taboo may readily connect a telephone interviewer with the purchasing agent. Long-distance calling brings a high degree of urgency and insistence into reaching the desired respondent.

When the interviewer can give assurance that the telephone interview will take only a short time, such as four or five minutes, the request may more readily be granted. In one notable instance concerning a brief survey on mouth washes, telephone calls for office appointments were made to doctors and dentists. A suggestion was also made that, instead, the interviews could be conducted here and now over the telephone. Two-fifths of the busy respondents elected to answer the questions by telephone.

Uniformity. As for individual interviewer effects on results, the telephone interview is midway between the zero effect of the mail questionnaire and the pronounced effect of the personal interview. Ideally, as little of the interviewer as possible should go into the recorded responses. Uniformity in interviewing is considered desirable, that is, the questions should be asked in a standardized way, as in all stimulus-reaction research.

In the telephone method, the respondent's only impression of the interviewer is that conveyed by voice.   Clothes, personal characteristics, mannerisms, and similar things are all masked.   Bias introduced by interviewers over the telephone should generally be less than in the personal interview.

Another minor advantage may be that with the telephone approach, the respondent does not see the questionnaire and is less likely to be scared off by its apparent bulk or length.   Probably more important, respondents cannot peek at any of the coming questions, as may occur in personal interviews.

Frankness.   Another little-explored aspect of telephone interviews is that of comparatively honest reporting.   Completed methodological research suggests that respondents may reply with greater candor to personal questions asked on the telephone than to the same questions asked in person.   For example, substantially more women have admitted in telephone interviews that they sometimes drink alcoholic beverages than have admitted doing so when facing interviewers or returning mail questionnaires.

Privacy.   Mail questionnaires may be open to view and comment by several family members, as may indeed be the intent of the research.   In cases where individual opinions are desired, however, there can be no assurance that a mail form has not been checked over and contributed to by more than one person.   In fact, there is no guarantee that the wife has not filled in her husband's questionnaire.

Personal interviewers are instructed not to interview respondents in the presence of other people, but that instruction is sometimes practically impossible to observe.   Not infrequently the interviewer has the choice between letting someone else sit in and not being granted the interview at all.

Telephone calls, on the other hand, are commonly considered private.   Participation by other household members is minimized.   At least the interviewer's side of the conversation is not overheard by others.   The relative privacy of the telephone method may help to explain the more candid replies to personal questions it produces.   Also, the shorter answers to open-end questions may in part result from the respondent's attempt to keep the subject matter private at his end of the line.

Control.   Any desired degree of control over the interviewing can be imposed with the telephone method.   At one extreme, interviewers may be permitted to make the calls, unsupervised, from their homes at their own hours, and even to draw their own samples.   At the other extreme, they may be required to work in a central office at prescribed hours using predesignated samples, and every word may be monitored by a supervisor.   From the respondents' standpoint, there need be no detectable differences between the two widely different interviewing situations, so even the strictest supervision need not inhibit answers.   Supervision of a personal interview injects a third party into the scene, and therefore does not really tell much about how two-party interviews go.

The extreme of complete monitoring (listening in on every call or assigning a supervisor to every interviewer) is not very practical.   Rather, the system may use a supervisor for every five or six interviewers with the option of cutting in on any of them at any time without awareness of either party to the interview; the supervisor may instead simply cock her ear to one or another interviewer's side of the conversation, or she may plug in the device called a "watch-case receiver" by the telephone company.   Listening in may be done at will or governed by rigid quality-control sampling procedures.

Through central-office supervision, not only the exact wording of questions but even talking speeds and voice inflections of the different interviewers can be brought closer to desired uniformity.   Self-created problems of various interviewers can be corrected.   In effect, advanced training can be carried on while production continues.

Since the WATS system usually operates from a central office, it permits close supervisory control even of national surveys.   Of course, the same may be true for other long-distance calling done from a central location.

Another possibility with the telephone survey method is full control of the sample.   A strictly designed sampling pattern can be imposed on the interviewers and observance of that pattern can readily be verified.   The detailed sample itself can be drawn in a central office, which is not always feasible in door-to-door interviewing.

Clerical verification that the interviews have been made can be established by an ingenious procedure.   From a sample centrally drawn, only the telephone numbers are given to the interviewer.   As part of each interview, she asks for the respondent's name or for the name under which that telephone is listed.   A clerk later verifies that the number and name correspond.   This procedure works on the theory that without making the call, the interviewer would have had to scan the entire alphabetical telephone directory to discover the name for that number.   It does not, however, constitute full validation that all questions were asked.   When random numbers are drawn, much the same name-checking procedure can be used against the directory.   Even if names of respondents (not necessarily subscribers) are accepted and long runs of common names (Jones, Smith, and so on) are not checked, a quick matching of surnames and telephone numbers can verify 75 percent or more of the interviews.

Complete Automation.   In prospect is the ultimate in efficiency, uniformity, privacy, and control—fully automated telephone surveys by computer!   The computer dials telephone numbers on a prearranged sampling basis; the questions are asked by a tape recording; respondents are told to indicate their answers by dialing 1 for "Yes," 2 for "No," and so on; those dialings are directed into the computer for tabulation.   That method, well within range today, may be in effect by time of publication of this book.

TELEPHONE SURVEY APPLICATIONS

For many years, telephone interviews were used almost solely for ratings at first of radio and then of television programs.   They are obviously well suited for that "coincidental rating" purpose because they can reach into so many homes within the span of a broadcast.   All that the brief interviews have to cover is: "Was your set turned on when the phone rang?   To what channel?"

As the advantages in telephone surveys have become better recognized and their limitations taken more fully into account, they have come to be used for almost all survey purposes, and more and more frequently.   The only marketing research approaches not yet in general use by telephone are observational studies and group interviews, but both are possible through picture phones, speaker phones, and conference hookups.   Even when the telephone is not the prime survey method, it often is a useful adjunct.   In this section, then, applications of the telephone beyond its original survey use for coincidental ratings are discussed.   Applications are classified into three dimensions: scope, population types, and subject matter.

Scope.   The telephone has been used:

1.   As the sole instrument for the conduct of entire surveys

2.   As one of two or three methods used in combination to obtain answers from different types of people determined in advance

3.   As the basic method of interviewing all who can be covered by tele-

phone, castoffs (such as nonsubscribers or refusers) then being approached by other means

4. As the means of approaching the castoffs from other methods (those for whom interviews were not completed)

5. As the basic method of making follow-up interviews with persons originally contacted by other methods

6. To make appointments for personal interviews

7. To locate difficult-to-find people for personal interviews

8. For alerting prospects to expect a forthcoming mail questionnaire

9. To remind them to return the mail questionnaire

10. To fill in missing information or to clarify questionnaires obtained by any method

11. To validate personal or telephone interviews.

Probably the most common uses of the telephone are (1) conducting entire surveys and (11) validating interviews. Some of the types of entire surveys, as well as combinations (2), (3), (4), and (5), are described under the later subheadings "Population Types" and "Subject Matter." Some aspects of validating (11) are covered under the section "Telephone Interviewing Etiquette."

The use of the telephone to arrange for personal interviews (6) is best reserved for a few special situations because it may have a serious drawback. Some researchers argue that people will more readily consent to be interviewed when approached in person than when reached by telephone; it is easier to say no over the telephone than face-to-face. They contend that although substitutes may be found, the more willing people are then more than ever overrepresented in the survey. In contacting many business and professional people, it may be better, although more costly, to take a chance on finding them in than to request appointments. Where doors are found closed, however, as with topmost executives or locked-door apartment houses, the appointment approach is likely to raise the proportion of completed personal interviews. For best results, considerable lead time between calls and appointments may have to be allowed for some executives.

Locating types of hard-to-find people for personal interviews (7) is economical by telephone only in somewhat extreme needle-in-a-haystack cases. The telephone search creates the need for name-and-address personal interviewing, which is much more expensive than door-to-door interviewing. Once a person is located by telephone, the interviewer must travel to that address and find that person at home. The problem is one of trade-offs—at which point does it become less expensive to make telephone calls and name-and-address interviews than to hunt qualified respondents door-to-door for immediate interviews? It certainly is not less expensive to telephone when there is a qualified person at every fifth address (1 in 15 or 16 people). Probably it is, when the ratio is 1 person for every 10 addresses. Possibly it is, when the ratio is 1 in every 15 addresses, which a search for mothers of infants might approximate. In that example, however, it might almost be a defensible personal approach in place of canvassing door-to-door to ask the whereabouts of the nearest qualified person and skip to her address, at less cost than a telephone search. Of course, both these methods of personal search involve quotas instead of probability samples.

The remaining applications of the telephone in surveys, (8), (9), and (10), are self-evident and seem to require no special admonitions.

Population Types.   The most frequently intended subgroup for marketing research surveys by telephone can be described as the "lady-of-the-house" universe, a term seldom seen in reports but deliberately chosen here to indicate the inclusion of housewives *and* employed homemakers in proper proportions. Appropriate representation of employed female heads requires evening and/or weekend interviewing and call-backs.

The "lady-of-the-house" is interviewed for any of three reasons—as the spokesman for the household, as the probable cook and purchasing agent, or as a representative of female adults. Despite her possible employment, she is still the most likely family member to be found at home.

Next in frequency as the telephone survey target is probably a universe of individuals in the telephone population—all adults, all persons over 16 years of age, all persons from 13 to 65, or a similar group. Such surveys may be based on a systematic method of selecting certain persons from households of different sizes. Because of possible interaction, it is unusual to interview every family member or everyone who happens to be home at the time of the call. That, of course, does not preclude asking some one person *about* all other members of the family, as in a coincidental survey that may ask which family members are watching a program.

Male heads of families are also sometimes the indicated universe for a telephone survey. Because of their employment, the telephone may be much more efficient than the personal interview. Other closely allied types, such as car owners, may be interviewed. Or a survey may be directed at retirees, pensioners, and widows, or at teen-agers, since teen-age boys and young men are the most difficult of family members to find at home for personal interviews.

Population types not readily identifiable over the telephone—at least not without initially asking embarrassing questions, such as on race or ethnic origin—are not likely candidates for separate telephone surveys unless they live in concentrations within certain telephone-exchange areas.

As indicated earlier, the classified telephone directory furnishes excellent listings of some occupational types and gives a means of accessing others not directly listed there. Telephone interviews may also be the preferred means of covering those universes of occupations—if the subject matter is of interest to them and if the questionnaire is of reasonable length from their standpoint.

Subject Matter. The telephone method has been employed in almost every type of marketing survey—from conception of products and services through test marketing and national introduction to continuing measurement of awareness, buying intention, trial and usage, purchase, repurchase, package reactions, product shortages, and displacement of former products. It has been used in surveys of advertising awareness, message recall, and coupon redemptions, for copy testing and radio and television program ratings, in brand-profile and corporate image research, and in name-reaction tests. Telephone interviews have been conducted with dealers to check distribution and obtain sales data. They have even been employed to obtain evidence in trademark litigation. The wide variety of research problems for which the telephone method has been used is illustrated next.

In a brand and advertising awareness survey series, three waves of telephone interviews were carried out at different stages of the campaign. Three samples of telephone numbers were drawn from alphabetical telephone directories and quotas of individuals were established by sex and age so that comparability could be maintained from wave to wave.

Full-price purchasers and coupon-redeeming purchasers of a test-market product were found by telephone screening large samples drawn from alphabetical telephone directories. They were questioned during the same calls about reasons for buying, appraisals of the product and its packaging, intentions to repurchase, and so forth.

In a home-use test, (1) preliminary personal interviews were used to screen out unqualified households, obtain background information, learn current and past usage of similar products, place the test products, and leave questionnaires and return envelopes for individual family members; (2) 82 percent mailed in their questionnaires; and (3) 97 percent of the homemakers were successfully interviewed in follow-up telephone calls. Thus, this test used all three basic survey methods.

In a persistence test, an experimental product was similarly placed with qualified households and they either telephoned in or were telephoned every two weeks over a six-month period for reorders. On some reordering calls and either on the homemaker's dropping out or at the end of the test, she was reinterviewed by telephone.

In a service usage survey, an area probability sample was drawn; all eligible household members with telephones were interviewed by telephone, and two additional telephone call-backs were made if necessary. Households without telephones were sent mail questionnaires and if necessary, follow-up mailings. Nonrespondents by telephone or by mail were followed up in person.

Dummy magazines containing test and control advertisements and control articles were left with a sample of magazine readers. Telephone interviews two days later determined recall of the test advertisements, messages, and themes.

Car purchasers whose names were obtained from recent license registrations were interviewed by telephone on their reactions to certain accessories and optional equipment items. Credit-card gasoline purchasers at tollway service stations were later interviewed by telephone in their home cities about gasoline service, food service, and restroom facilities. Another sample of credit-card holders were asked their reactions to possible changes in card-issuing and credit-collecting procedures.

In one city, 94 percent of the interviews attempted with responsible persons in the 600 largest companies were successfully completed. The questionnaire dealt with the use of marketing research in those companies.

Advertising agency images have been obtained from advertising managers by telephone. Motel convention facilities have been rated over the telephone in some detail by manufacturers, dealers, and other convention goers after returning to their desks. A census of certain types of electronic data processing equipment has been conducted by telephone.

In a national survey, long-distance calls were placed to a sample of companies known to use a certain type of equipment. For each company, both the purchasing agent and the design engineer were interviewed to determine which function exercised more control over brand buying decisions for that equipment. Calls were placed person-to-person by titles, since the names of the eligible individuals were not known in advance.

For a trademark litigation case concerning the brand name of an industrial product, purchasing agents in a sample of companies using such products were interviewed. Respondents were requested to write down the brand name under investigation and then to list other brand names they associated with it and the name of its probable manufacturer.

Dermatologists, selected from a national directory, were telephoned for a short interview about a contact dermatitis. They were asked what causal factors they found for this allergy and what treatments they used for it. Similarly, general practitioners and internal-medicine men have been queried about their use of enzyme therapy.

From the widely scattered examples just given, the general applicability of the telephone survey method can readily be recognized.

SAMPLING FOR TELEPHONE SURVEYS

The basic concepts and general principles observed in other sampling apply also to sampling for telephone surveys. Many of the samples, as may be seen from the preceding section, are indeed the same samples that would be drawn for surveys made by other methods. Other telephone survey samples, however, have special features to be observed and possible traps to be avoided.

Telephone Directory Sampling. Drawing a proper sample from an alphabetical telephone directory is not the simple, straightforward process that it is often assumed to be. Calling the first number in every column or haphazardly sticking a pin in each page is not a suitable way of producing statistically random samples.

First, telephone-directory area boundaries seldom coincide with city limits or metropolitan area definitions. Parts of two or more directories may have to be used to approximate the desired survey area. Entire exchange areas (three-digit prefixes) may have to be excluded. At the other extreme, sometimes the survey area may include just a small section of a city involving only one or two exchanges. Usually, a reasonably satisfactory approximation of exchange areas to the desired area can be made; but if exact agreement is required, street addresses may be used to further eliminate telephone numbers drawn outside of the survey limits in the overlapping exchanges. Another possibility is to draw the sample from street-address telephone directories, but their leasing costs have to be considered.

When drawing regional or national samples from telephone directories, it may be preferable to use telephone-directory areas as primary sampling units instead of the usual political boundaries. For national samples, it is well to know that the central offices of most telephone-operating companies have more or less complete libraries of telephone directories of other locations which may be used for sampling purposes. It is possible also to procure out-of-town directories through the business office, and some research firms continually ask their interviewers to supply them with local directories as they are issued.

Most sampling done from alphabetical telephone directories is systematic rather than random. For example, a sample of residence subscribers may be designated as the tenth number listed in the third column of each even-numbered page, provided it is a residence listing that does not duplicate an earlier one. A slotted overlay may be applied to the page, sample numbers appearing in the slots. Or, the edges of all pages may be marked at one time, the mark on each page being used to indicate a telephone number in the outside column or in the other columns by extension.

Several important considerations are illustrated in the first example in the preceding paragraph. Notice that it is not the first or last number in the column that is to be taken—because those easy numbers are likely to be overworked in surveys and in other applications. It may now be advisable to avoid the tenth number to prevent its overuse.

Notice, too, that no provision is made for substituting by dropping down the column. If the tenth number is a business or professional listing, no substitute draw is to be made for that number. If substitutions were permitted, then "Amerio, Ambrose," whose name might immediately follow many columns of

"American" companies, would be in everyone's sample. If a lawyer's office is listed on the tenth line and his home on the eleventh line, that latter line cannot be used; otherwise, lawyers' homes would have double the chance of getting into the sample that laymen's homes have.

Further, only the first listing for a duplicated number or address should be taken. For example, if the tenth line lists a child of "Affluent, John," who is listed at the same address on the ninth line, neither the tenth line nor the ninth line is drawn from the sample whether they have the same or different telephone numbers. If the first "Affluent" at that address had been listed on the tenth line, that telephone number would have been drawn for the sample.

The suggested procedures reduce the possibility of overrepresenting families with multiple listings. It should be pointed out that the no-substitution and nonduplicating rules are made not simply to exclude the particular professional or business man's home or the particular multiple-telephone home but to equalize the chances for inclusion of all multitelephone homes with all single-telephone homes. The "Amerio" example merely highlights the possibility of overexposure.

Elimination of columns or pages because of the ban on substitutions means that more columns or pages must be looked at. For example, assume that 100 telephone numbers are to be drawn from a directory in which listings start on page 19 and end on page 258, a total of 240 pages of listings. A random start might be made at the thirteenth listing in the second column of page 19, to be followed by the thirteenth listing in the second column of all odd-numbered pages, a total of 120 listings. Elimination of nonresidence, duplicate, and, say, exchange UR 2 (not in the telephone survey area) listings might produce 104 eligible numbers, from which 4 could be eliminated randomly. If only 97 eligible numbers result from the first sampling, 3 additional ones can be drawn from another starting point.

When only a few exchange areas are eligible from a large directory, judgment may dictate full coverage of those exchanges in selected columns instead of the preceding nth listing procedure. For example, if the only eligible exchanges are 455, 456, and 533 in a 64-exchange directory, the sample might call for listing all numbers having any of those three-digit prefixes in the first column of all page numbers ending in 5 or 8, provided they are for residences, and then interviewing all of, or a subsample from, that sample of listings.

If quota samples are to be drawn from within an alphabetical directory sample or if limited survey time necessitates substitutions for no-answer calls, busy signals, not-at-home individuals, or other reasons, it becomes expedient to draw an oversample of original telephone numbers. The sample draw may require two or three times the final number of interviews. Except for the added size, however, the same procedures should be followed, including the no-substitution rule (the just-mentioned substitutions for uncompleted calls do not come within this rule).

When oversamples are drawn and because not all numbers may be used, it is essential to ensure randomness in the order in which the numbers are called. Otherwise, possibly no surnames in the directory beyond, say, "S" might be reached. Randomness may be achieved by using a separate card for each number and thoroughly shuffling the cards before calling starts. If different exchanges are to be given to different interviewers, the cards may first be sorted by exchanges before all cards for all exchanges given to one interviewer are shuffled together. The only problem remaining then is to make sure that some interviewers do not finish more than their share of the calls in their exchanges, causing other interviewers to short their exchange areas by having to cut off their interviewing early to maintain desired sample proportionalities.

Various other ways of sampling from alphabetical directories have been used and are acceptable as long as they incorporate the basic sampling principles and do not violate the no-substitution and nonduplicating rules.

Indirect Sampling Technique.   A technique for sampling telephone numbers independently of directories has an important special advantage and a few drawbacks.   It amounts to drawing samples of "possible" numbers at random or on a systematic basis without regard to actual listings.

For an example of a systematic indirect sample, assume that the first (lowest three-digit prefix) telephone exchange in the survey area is 455, that many blocks of 1000 numbers are unassigned, that a sampling interval of 259 is indicated, and that a random start is to be made at 0123.   The first 16 numbers to be drawn would then be:

455-0123	455-1159	456-5195	533-0231
455-0382	455-1418	456-5454	533-0490
455-0641	455-1677	456-5713	533-0749
455-0900	455-1936	456-5972	533-1008

In the 455 exchange, the 0-thousand and 1-thousand blocks of numbers, and in the 456 exchange the 5-thousand block, contain the only numbers assigned, while the 0-thousand block starts the third exchange—533 prefix.   The sample of numbers is drawn in this fashion: $0123 + 259 = 0382$; $0382 + 259 = 0641$; ... ; $1936 + 259 = 195$ or 5195; ... ; $5972 + 259 = 231$ or 0231, and so on.

If required, instead of a systematic sample, a random sample of four-digit numbers may be drawn from a table of random numbers and applied to the assigned thousand blocks within the exchange areas.   When information is unavailable on which thousand or hundred blocks are unassigned, the proportion of dialings made to dead numbers may be as high as 20 percent.

The indirect sampling technique has the advantage of providing equal chance for inclusion of all currently assigned numbers.   Being timeless, it is always up to date.   Because it does not depend on subscriber choice, it includes unlisted numbers.   Since each telephone number has the same chance of inclusion, it corrects for duplicate listings of the same number (although not for two or more lines in a single household).

The disadvantage of this technique lies in its inevitable wastage of calls. Not all numbers in an active thousand block are assigned.   In a residence sample, unwanted calls must be made to nonresidence numbers.   If an entire exchange is known to have no residences, it may be excluded as in any method of residence sampling.   The wastage requires an overdraw of sample numbers, which therefore should be shuffled into a random calling order, as was recommended for oversampling in directory samples.

In this technique, no names can be attached to telephone numbers given to the interviewers, but the simple verification described earlier can be invoked. That is, as part of each interview the interviewer can ask for the name under which the telephone number is listed, and agreement of that name and number can be checked in the alphabetical directory.

TELEPHONE QUESTIONNAIRE DESIGN

Little about the telephone survey method calls for questionnaire design different from that of the personal survey method.   The same fundamentals of understandability and freedom from bias apply.   Some features of telephone questionnaires do merit special emphasis or slightly different treatment, however.

Pretesting.   Telephone questionnaires depend as fully on pretesting as do other questionnaires, and may be subject to even greater improvement because monitoring can pick up subtle nuances which might otherwise be overlooked by pretest interviewers. Two such situations were discovered by listening in on a pretest of recruiting interviews for a consumer panel. Homemakers, somehow divining that the interviewers were young, single girls, made remarks such as, "When you have a family of your own . . ."; their conversations also seemed to be somewhat inhibited by a few interviewer names that were difficult to understand and pronounce. To improve rapport, interviewers were consequently asked to introduce themselves by aliases in the form of "Mrs. Sally Jones."

Another advantage of telephone questionnaires when pretesting is that under such close supervision, word changes and other experiments can be made at will from one interview to the next. The pretest form itself need not be so structured as it must be for pretests in person.

Screening. In the telephone method, it is impossible to eliminate ineligible persons through observation, meaning that some personal questions may have to be asked at the outset instead of at the end of the interview. Careful attention should be given to the wording of such questions, softening them as much as possible. For example, in a telephone survey intended to include people from 13 to 64 years of age and with special age quotas for teen-agers, the first questions after the brief introduction were worded thus:

> "First, though, which does your own age come nearest to—20 years, 30, 40, 50, 60, or 70 years?" If 20 years, "Are you in the age group 20 to 24, 17 to 19, 13 to 16, or are you younger than 13?"

The more detailed second question is reasonable to ask of young people, who are not very sensitive about disclosing their ages. Persons who at first answered, "Around 70 years," and youngsters under 13 years were not interviewed further.

Multiple-Choice Questions. Many questions offering more than four or five stated alternatives, which requires handing the respondent a card during a personal interview, do not lend themselves very well to telephone interviews. Some, such as the age example just given and the ratings questions reported earlier, can be converted to readily comprehended oral forms. Others less adaptable to oral presentation may have to be foregone or revised into sets of successive questions.

Free-Answer Questions. Because of the shorter answers recorded for open-end questions asked by telephone, it may be advisable to include as few such free-answer questions as possible. This does not necessarily mean ignoring the ideas that emerge from such questions. Rather, answers obtained to them in the pretesting may well serve as guides for constructing check-box questions, which often prove more useful.

Two-Way Questions. The telephone interview's forte is the relatively simple check-box question, with only two or three alternatives and with the no-opinion possibility stated or merely allowed for by an extra check-box. The telephone approach need not alter the formulation of such direct questions from the face-to-face approach.

TELEPHONE INTERVIEWING ETIQUETTE

Telephone surveys can have a major effect on the public relations of marketing research—probably greater than that of other survey methods. Partly because the telephone interview is an imperious intruder, partly because it is relatively impersonal, partly because of increasing volume, partly because of sham surveys, and partly because of legitimate inquiries that are thought to be sales calls, most of the criticisms are directed at telephone surveys. Mail questionnaires may be discarded, and face-to-face interviewers may be regarded as individuals. The telephone survey is the most likely target for criticism as a "survey."

It therefore behooves marketing researchers to be especially circumspect in conducting telephone surveys. Under the following three subheadings, some examples illustrating reasonable considerateness in telephone interviewing are discussed. In addition, the local telephone company may offer instruction in effective telephone practices.

Interviewing Hours. Telephone companies, concerned with their own customer relations as well as with their subscribers' public relations, commonly restrict interviewing hours on their telephone surveys to those causing the least inconvenience to respondents. The interviewing hours permitted by one telephone company are: 9:00 A.M. to 11:30 A.M., 1:00 P.M. to 4:30 P.M., and 6:30 P.M. to 9:30 P.M. on weekdays; none after 4:30 P.M. on Saturdays; and none on Sundays. Although this schedule may seem unduly restrictive, especially to interviewers who have found Sunday evenings good for interviewing men, many surveys are successfully conducted during those hours.

Obviously, in national surveys made from central offices, interviewing hours should be adjusted to the time zones being called.

Introduction. The interview's introduction is its most crucial part, and much attention has been given to developing standardized approaches. Courtesy requires giving one's own name, a rationale for the interview, and an idea of its length (unless very short), as well as asking permission. The introduction need not be long nor, usually, mention sponsorship, anonymity, tabulation, and other purposes, as used to be considered necessary. Although permission is asked, it may usually be taken for granted, so that the interviewer then plunges directly into the first question: "First, though, . . ." A typical introduction incorporating the essentials might run like this:

"Hello! I'm [interviewer's name] of [firm name]. I am conducting some interviews about automobile advertising and would like to learn some of your ideas if you have about 10 minutes and haven't been surveyed too often lately."

At first glance, the last part of this introduction may seem to beg for a turndown, but it has actually proven quite disarming. Also, even immediate turndowns can set the stage for call-backs at a better time. Such an introduction is at least worth a try in the pretest interviews.

Validations. More surveys are validated by telephone than are originally conducted by telephone because this validation method is often used with personal interviews as well. Many marketing researchers have expressed concern that inept and callous validation procedures may be harmful to the public's view of surveys in general.

To dispose of one occasional criticism, validating calls should of course observe the same restrictions on hours (locally and in other time zones) that are placed on the original interviews.

The major criticism of some validating is that it amounts to a cross-examination, making a respondent defend an interviewer against a supervisor who apparently does not trust his own employees. Instead of creating the impression of calling to check on the interviewer, the supervisor can just as easily call to clarify an entry or two. In one recommended procedure, the supervisor affirms that she has the questionnaire form "for the interview which you so kindly gave our Mrs. Jones when she visited you at your home last Wednesday, but there are a couple of questions for which the answers aren't as clearly shown as they might be. Your interview is so important to us that I am calling to make sure of those answers."

To acquaint both interviewers and respondents with the possibility of such calls, it is advisable in the original questionnaire to ask for identifying information in a question like this: "May I please have your name and telephone number in case my supervisor needs to call you about the interview?"

It should be mentioned that some research organizations, relying fully on the trustworthiness of their interviewers, ordinarily do not validate their work. The more common practice is to validate some set fraction of every interviewer's completed assignment and the entire assignment of any whose work comes under suspicion.

TELEPHONE INTERVIEWER SELECTION

In general, the same friendly, resourceful, dependable, unobtrusive, intelligent paragons sought out as personal interviewers are also the persons needed for telephone interviewing, but other desirable attributes may be considered too.

Of course, the telephone voice is all-important in this type of work. Some women's voices, otherwise pleasant enough, are relatively difficult to hear clearly over the telephone. Others are clear enough but may sound childish. Borderline voices which are hard to distinguish as male or female may sometimes inhibit respondent answers. Therefore, it is obviously important to talk to telephone survey applicants on the telephone as well as in person.

The independent interviewer who conducts her personal interviews at will or makes her telephone interviews from her home at her own convenience must be a self-starter. That personality ingredient is most elusive, very difficult to predict, and a major factor in interviewer success. Until tests are devised to measure it, the recruiter must depend on evidence of past experience in interviewing, selling, and similar occupations.

On the other hand, the central-office telephone interviewer is a 9:00 to 4:30, or 1:00 to 9:30, kind of person who need not be such a self-starter but is rather like other office workers. She must be willing to work under close supervision and to conform even in minor details.

Some types of capable people are available for at-home telephone interviewing who cannot do personal interviewing. For pleasant, trained voices, former telephone operators tied down with small children are one category. Shut-ins, such as paraplegics, find this one of the few jobs open to them.

One last point—the recruiter of at-home telephone interviewers should ensure that they have single-party lines and also determine the free-call areas available to them.

SUMMARY

Although the telephone survey method has noteworthy limitations—less-than-universal telephone ownership, directory obsolescence, unlisted numbers, dependence on voice, brevity, and similar qualifications—these problems can sometimes be moderated or overcome. The advantages of economy, speed, uniformity, and control, as well as accessibility of difficult-to-reach respondents, may counterbalance the limitations. A market researcher may well accept the limitations in order to obtain the advantages of telephone interviewing.

The span of telephone applications has grown to be almost all-encompassing. The only research techniques not tried as yet are observational studies and group interviewing. The telephone has been used as the sole method, as one of many different combinations of methods, and for validating interviews made by any method. A great variety of respondent universes, including, perhaps, some surprising occupations, have been designated for this method. Subjects covered by the telephone survey have ranged as far and wide as those covered by any other method.

Sampling for telephone surveys is best not left to interviewers but should be done as a separate operation. It is not a casual process but a function requiring some exacting steps, especially when telephone directories are the source. The sample may have to be tailored to fit the universe, or vice versa. Business listings and multiple listings must be treated consistently and not substituted. Oversampling may be necessary in certain situations. Randomization of systematically drawn samples may be required. Sampling of random numbers has some advantages and disadvantages compared with sampling from directory listings.

Design of telephone questionnaires generally takes into consideration the same fundamentals as design of personal interview forms, changes being more in degree than in kind. Pretesting, for example, may be even more worthwhile for telephone questionnaires. Considerateness in telephone interviewing calls for particular emphasis on suitable calling hours, adequate introductions, and responsible validating procedures. The interviewer's telephone voice is extremely important.

For any marketing research when the telephone-subscriber universe may be acceptable, the possibility of conducting the survey by this method should always be evaluated as a possible alternative to face-to-face interviewing. Even if the telephone-owner universe is inadequate, the possibility of conducting a substantial part of the interviews by telephone should be considered.

BIBLIOGRAPHY

Cooper, Sanford L., "Random Sampling by Telephone—An Improved Method," *Journal of Marketing Research,* vol. 1, November 1964.

Glasser, G. J., and G. D. Metzger, "Random Digit Dialing as a Method of Telephone Sampling," *Journal of Marketing Research,* vol. 9, February 1972.

Hochstim, Joseph R., "Alternatives to Personal Interviewing," *Public Opinion Quarterly,* vol. 29, Winter 1963.

——, "A Critical Comparison of Three Strategies of Collecting Data from Households," *Journal of the American Statistical Association,* vol. 62, September 1967.

Oakes, Ralph H., "Difference in Responsiveness in Telephone vs. Personal Interviews," *Journal of Marketing,* vol. 18, October 1954.

Payne, Stanley L., "Some Advantages of Telephone Surveys," *Journal of Marketing,* vol. 20, January 1956.

——, "Combination of Survey Methods," *Journal of Marketing Research,* vol. 1, May 1964.

Schmiedeskamp, Jay W., "Reinterviews by Telephone," *Journal of Marketing,* vol. 26, January 1962.

Sudman, Seymour, *Reducing the Cost of Surveys,* Chicago: Aldine, 1967.

Troldahl, Verling C., and Roy E. Carter, Jr., "Random Selection of Respondents in Phone Surveys," *Journal of Marketing Research,* vol. 1, May 1964.

Wales, H. G., and Robert Ferber, *A Basic Bibliography on Marketing Research,* Chicago: American Marketing Association, 1974.

Part B

Surveys

Chapter 5

Interviewers:
Recruiting, Selecting,
Training, and Supervising

LEE ANDREWS *Consultant, New York, New York*

At first it seems strangely inconsistent that, in as erudite a field as marketing research, collection of the actual data on which reports are based and decisions made is entrusted to persons with little research training or experience. Other sections of this handbook discuss sample design, mathematical formulas for setting samples, behavioral study and techniques for constructing questionnaires, and other ways in which the academic training offered in most of our major colleges is used. It may seem amazing, therefore, that the data are collected by interviewers who are not required to have any particular scholastic status.

But, considering the matter further, one will realize that the purpose of marketing research is, for the most part, the accumulation of information about people's habits and preferences. This information can best be gathered by those experienced in using the products being studied. They should have a baccalaureate in the techniques of living. If the subject under discussion is a detergent, for example, the person best qualified to discuss it is the housewife who uses one daily, not a Ph.D. in chemistry!

So we have a profession open to the public at large, to those whose background is as varied as possible and who have the kind of personality that gets along well with other people.

There are certain characteristics that determine good interviewer prospects. Although it is possible to train persons without all these qualities, those who have them will certainly learn skill in the field sooner and more effectively.

SELECTION OF INTERVIEWERS

Native Characteristic. *Good health* is essential! Field interviewing is a tiring job, and an interviewer is likely to be on her feet much of the day, walking from house to house or office to office. The incessant repetition of battling resistance and establishing rapport is exhausting in itself. Sometimes there are cumbersome or heavy displays to carry, tape recorders to haul from car to respondent, and other such impedimenta. Strong feet, steady nerves, and sensitivities as invulnerable as possible are interviewer essentials. Interviewers should be of prime age, that is, over 18 if they are to be taken seriously and under 55 for health stamina.

Interviewers should be *extroverts*. They should enjoy contact with the public and have no qualms about talking with people to whom they have not been formally introduced. In fact, the better they like it, the happier the whole experience will be. The person who withdraws from strangers would not only be miserable as an interviewer, but also ineffective. People respond to those whom they instinctively feel want to talk to them.

Interviewers should present a *favorable personal appearance.* There is no need, let us hasten to say, for beauty-contest winners, but a pleasant personality, coupled with good, tailored grooming, is essential. Any physical defect is likely to call the respondent's attention to itself and away from the subject under discussion. Clothing should be practical, not extreme or high style. Excessive costume or any other kind of jewelry is not only in poor taste, but may be unsafe to wear in bad neighborhoods. Comfortable walking shoes are an obvious must. The first impression that an interviewer makes may determine whether or not an interview is granted. Since clothes are the first thing seen, they are more important in this work than in many other professions.

There is opportunity in marketing research for both *male* and *female interviewers.* The selection criterion of personnel for the field requires, among other attributes, matching of interviewer to respondent. Women do better gathering information from other women, and men from other men (in most cases). On household products, when the female head of the house is interviewed in her own home, a male interviewer has difficulty gaining admittance. He is immediately assumed to be selling magazine subscriptions or brushes, or, for other reasons, his intentions are suspect—frequently the parlor curtain is pulled aside and an unexpected visitor scrutinized before the door is opened. An unknown man's chances of being received are slim. On the other hand, if an evening call is being made on the man of the house, there may well be a curt refusal of admittance to the attractive young lady when Mrs. Respondent opens the door. Similarly, in this era of continued sex inequality in business, a personable man may well be ushered into the executive's presence by an otherwise vigilant secretary, whereas the woman interviewer may have difficulty gaining entrance. So each to his kind, but inasmuch as more surveys are done with housewives in the home than with men at home or executives, women have a better chance of employment than men.

Race, Nationality, Color. The same criteria apply here as with sex distinctions. Blacks do better with black respondents, and whites with white. Of course, individuals with mixed racial characteristics may do as well with one race of respondents as another. Knowledge of the native language of any group existing in quantity in one's interview area is very valuable. Many housewives are first-generation Americans, and ability to speak to them in the language of their national origin usually gains instant acceptance into their homes, and will result in a much fuller interview. A bilingual interviewer must, of course, translate replies back into English on the questionnaire form, so obviously, she herself must be proficient in English.

Finally, the interviewer's *attitude* must be pleasant and informal (without being "fresh"), cheerful (without being flippant or facetious), and generally suggest the kind of person one would want to meet. From the respondent's standpoint, an interview is a sort of social occasion and should be made as pleasant as possible.

Among *other essentials* is availability for work at unusual hours such as in the evening and on weekends and holidays. Accessibility to, if not ownership of, an auto is also essential for nonurban assignments.

Finally, *frequent contact with strangers* is the best possible experience for an interviewer. Such contact may have been through selling, demonstrating, teaching, club work, and other activities. The more contact a person has had with the public, the fewer personal phobias she will have to combat when she goes forth, questionnaire in hand.

RECRUITMENT OF PERSONNEL

How does one find these gems of humanity?

One may look first to certain occupations: housewives, teachers, actors, artists, writers, people working for academic degrees—in general, those who can make their own schedules or whose work schedules are flexible.

Most research companies receive frequent, unsolicited applications for work. Field interviewers are constantly performing a public relations job for the research profession!

"Someone from your company came to interview me the other day. I'd like to do this sort of work. . . ." Here is evidence of the sort of aggressiveness necessary if an interviewer is to be invited into homes. The people who *volunteer* are often of the desirable caliber.

An interviewer will frequently *refer a friend*. Since every interviewer knows what is required in the job, such referrals are likely to be good prospects.

Unsolicited applicants, however, do not always provide sufficient personnel, since interviewing, for many people, is only a temporary occupation. So most field directors are constantly searching for recruits.

Help-wanted advertisements may be run in the classified columns of daily, or better yet, weekly newspapers. It is important to mention in such ads that the work is not full-time but on an on-call basis, paid by the hour or the interview.

College employment agencies may refer graduate students whose training makes them particularly qualified. Undergraduates, with ever-changing schedules and often an unworkmanlike attitude, are not usually desirable personnel. Even the marketing student, for whom such work would be valuable per se, is questionable material.

State or commercial employment agencies are not so likely to be good sources of personnel as the other means listed since their applicants usually want full-time, permanent jobs.

Other less fruitful sources are schools, urban leagues, the Girl Scouts, radio or T.V. stations, chambers of commerce, or any organization likely to be in touch with part-time personnel of fairly high caliber.

These are the most obvious sources for interviewers. But if one remembers the job's requirements as outlined in this chapter, one will doubtless identify other people who may be excellent in this work.

BASIC TRAINING FOR THE FIELD

Let us assume that we have assembled some people who meet the qualifications just outlined. We have interviewed, appraised, and tested them. They have filled out whatever application forms we have devised, from simply entering name, address, phone number, age, education, experience, time available, and similar facts on a blank index card to laboriously writing answers to questions on fully structured forms. They are ready, willing, and eager to start—but they don't know the first thing about the work. They may have read a book or two on interviewing, or had a college course on marketing research. They may have been regaled by exaggerated anecdotes from interviewers in the field, or they may have worked for a somewhat similar, but really different, company or bureau. However, they all must be basically trained for market research.

Text books have been published by many research companies for their own personnel. These manuals cover some general training, and some special techniques suitable for the issuing company only.[1]

Training classes, given by most research companies, may range from a few hours to a week in time and vary in degree of detail. Usually some slight background is given: the place of marketing in today's economy; the place of research in today's marketing; and the function of the interviewer. Then very detailed instruction is given on types of surveys, data collection, responsibilities, and matters for interviewers to avoid. Test work is usually given to reinforce the instructions. Method and amount of compensation are described.

Training in the field is provided by many, but not all, research companies. They customarily send an interviewer with a supervisor on the first assignment —the supervisor conducts the first interview while the trainee observes. The neophyte conducts the second interview while the supervisor observes and then corrects her pupil outside afterward. On the third call and thereafter, the new interviewer calls alone, but the supervisor looks the questionnaire over very carefully each time. This continues until the supervisor feels sure that her trainee is well launched. If such a personal training system is not used, the interviewer is given solitary test work which is carefully evaluated to aid her.

Content of the training is too long and detailed to cover completely in this chapter. Furthermore, it will vary with individual companies. For the majority, it may be described under the following headings:

Types of surveys
    Consumer market studies   Copy tests
    Product and package tests   Audit and store-observation jobs
    Attitude studies   Dealer and executive studies
    Readership surveys   Motivation studies
    Media studies
Techniques used
    Checklists   Focus depth interviews
    Open-end questions   Unstructured interviews
    Diaries   Mechanical recording
    Panels

[1] The Marketing Research Trade Association publishes a manual, *Asking Questions,* which is sufficiently general to be applicable to the work of any research user. It may be ordered for $1.00 from the Association, P.O. Box 1415, Grand Central Post Office, New York, N.Y. 10017.

Methods used

Personal interviews in the home or office	Telephone
	Mail
Street or public place interception	Mechanical recording

WORKING PROCEDURE

The interviewer's procedure in the United States usually follows this plan (in England and some other countries, field work is done by staff employees). After the questionnaire has been perfected and the sample planned, those interviewers with the most suitable background and geographic location are contacted by telephone, wire, or letter. The study and their part in it are described, and they are invited to participate. As independent workers, they may refuse. If they accept and are in the same city where a briefing is scheduled, their attendance is required at a designated time and place for specific training. If they live in another city, the work is mailed to them with full instructions on sampling, materials, deadline, and all other necessary facts. At a briefing session, the questionnaire is discussed in detail and, usually, test interviews are conducted. If the work is to be done in another city where there is a local supervisor, he or she selects the local interviewers and holds a briefing session.

Interviewers usually work alone. It is essential that they be familiar with their city, and a car is often advisable. Should any question of location or procedure arise, they are to contact their supervisor for instructions. The first few interviews or the first several days' work is usually checked by the supervisor. A careful observance of quota must be maintained constantly, and, needless to say, all data must be recorded legibly and in the proper place on the form. Interviewing is usually recorded with a medium-hard lead (#2) pencil. The interviewer should check each interview thoroughly before delivering it to the local supervisor.

Here are a few "do's and don'ts" usually given to interviewers:

DO's.

1. Always carry proper identification.

2. Interview strangers, not friends, unless specifically told to interview people you know.

3. Sell yourself to the respondent—make her like you!

4. Conduct the interview in a relaxed, friendly way. Remember that you set the tempo and, in a way, are your respondent's hostess even though you are in her home.

5. Read the questions, word for word, exactly as written.

6. Follow the order of questions on the questionnaire.

7. Give the respondent plenty of time to think each question through.

8. Record replies verbatim except when otherwise instructed, or when the length of the reply prevents doing so.

9. Make your entries accurate and legible.

10. Unless otherwise instructed, record unsolicited comments that pertain to the subject matter.

11. While on the premises, check your interviews for completeness and legibility.

12. Start early in the day while people are still at home.

13. Meet your deadline . . . beat it if possible.

DON'Ts.

1. Don't ever compromise with quality. If you can't complete an assignment, notify your supervisor, but don't rush interviews.

2. Don't let personal problems interfere with your work.

3. Don't deviate from a business attitude while calling on your respondents. Don't accept alcoholic drinks.

4. Don't do anything but the survey at hand. Don't try to combine one survey with another, or with sales or other activities.

5. Don't take anyone with you when you interview.

6. Don't deviate from prescribed sampling in order to seek "good" respondents. Don't reuse the same respondents.

7. Don't interpret questions. If they are not understood, reread them, and ask the respondent to interpret them herself.

8. Don't concentrate your interviews in one or two neighborhoods unless told to do so. Don't work near your own home.

9. Don't allow the respondent to read over your shoulder. Don't ever let her read the questionnaire or the responses you have recorded unless specifically instructed to do so.

10. Don't ever begin work unless fully equipped.

As an interviewer becomes more experienced, she will perfect her manner of approach and her own way of meeting people. At the beginning, the point to stress is getting into the questionnaire as quickly as possible and not giving the respondent a chance to interview the interviewer by asking why she is chosen, the purpose of the study, and so on. Since there is considerable house-to-house convassing, it is often advisable for the interviewer to explain that she is not selling anything, but only wants to obtain opinions. It is important that the interviewer have an identification card and any other credentials possible.

Night work and bad neighborhoods are required by some studies, and the local supervisor must meet these problems according to the specifics of the particular study at hand. In some cases, interviewers work in pairs. Sometimes arrangements may be made with a local church or social service organization to bring respondents to a central place. These are real field problems, but can generally be solved. If there is no solution for a particular area, the problem should be reported to the research company and possibly a substitute area can be arranged. Although most research companies carry workmen's compensation insurance, nobody wants to invoke it.

Interviewers' compensation is calculated either by the interview or by the hour, usually figured portal to portal. The going rate, as of July 1973, was $2.00 to $2.50 per hour for daytime, weekday work on the average check questionnaire. Evening and weekend work pays about 12 percent more. All out-of-pocket expenses are covered. For executive and depth interviews, the rate is higher—sometimes as much as $5.00 per hour. In some states where interviewers are classed as employees, the unemployment and disability benefit insurances apply. In other states, they are considered independent contractors.

Interviewing is frequently a *temporary function.* Because of its casual, on-call basis with no guarantees of regularity and, hence, of income, many people who usually earn considerably more will take on the work between other jobs or while waiting for a niche in their chosen careers. They must therefore be trained for a short period of availability, a nuisance for the supervisor.

Industrial interviewing is in a class by itself. Here the work is usually in depth: a highly trained technical man is sent to interview others in sessions that may take hours and that require background information on a particular subject. This sort of industrial interviewing pays a minimum of $50.00 per day, plus expenses. Specific interviewer training is often omitted since content supersedes form, and the interview is usually submitted in the form of a lengthy report.

Interviewer Bias. A major pitfall in data collection by personal interview is interviewer bias. Everyone is different and, to some extent, looks at the world through glasses of a different color. Using several interviewers on a study helps to resolve these differences, but all interviewers should still be warned against the following sources of bias:

Voice inflection that implies the interviewer's own approval or disapproval of an attitude.

Disdain for respondent, that is, a conscious or unconscious supercilious attitude of the interviewer, which may be shown by overdressing in a poor neighborhood, riding in an expensive or chauffeur-driven car, or even actually asserting superiority in words.

Suggesting or *implying an answer* to an open-end question.

Conversation about the interviewer's *own problems.*

The interviewer's voluntary expression of *her opinion* about the product or question involved.

In short, if the interviewer thinks of herself merely as an activated pencil, to record and further to probe but not to influence, much bias will be eliminated.

THE SUPERVISOR'S ROLE

Briefly, the role of the supervisor is primarily to see that the work is done conscientiously according to instructions and delivered on time. Actually, it involves many functions: guide, philosopher, teacher, big sister, friend—and wet nurse. A supervisor's job is likely to continue around the clock, and it requires the utmost tact combined with a knowledge of research. Categorically, a supervisor's work should include:

1. Gathering and training interviewers on fundamentals of interviewing, including application forms
2. Alerting and briefing interviewers for a particular job
3. Allocating territory, in some cases requiring map work of a fairly detailed nature
4. Carefully studying first day's work, and correcting errors
5. Editing all work
6. Validating some of reports (10 percent—or whatever percentage is required)
7. Keeping careful production records
8. Reviewing time sheets
9. Rendering a detailed bill for the work

The functions are much the same whether the supervisor is a full-time employee of the research company or an independent functionary working in another city. But besides the functions listed, the supervisor is really conducting her own business, and should have an employer's number (issued by the state). She should also have sufficient capital to pay her interviewers promptly, even though she herself has not been paid. She should have a separate office, or a room in her home set aside for this work, and have such business facilities as letterhead, bill head, business cards, and so forth. Most important, she should have either a telephone-answering service or someone on whom she can depend to answer her telephone in her absence.

In some of the larger cities, local supervisors have fully staffed and equipped, centrally located offices.   In other places, it is a "kitchen-table" operation.   It is the volume of work that determines whether a supervisor can afford the rent and upkeep of an office, or whether she works at home, spasmodically as the need arises.   The functions are the same.

The supervisor usually bills her services on a cost-plus basis, which varies from 25 percent of the interviewer compensation up—in some cases up to 50 percent.   The average in the larger cities is 30 percent.   Expenses are usually billed at exact cost.   In a few cases the supervisor works on a per-hour basis, but because of the nature of the work, hours are difficult to determine: telephone calls from the field may come in at any time, and the supervisor is rare indeed who keeps accurate records of the amount of time involved.

Maintaining production records is essential.   A supervisor must be able to report to her superior at any time on the number of completed interviews; the number delivered to the client or, for a supervisor working in a research company, to the project director; and the number still outstanding and their completion date.   When work is mailed or sent express to another city, the date and method of sending must be on the production sheet.   For carrier delivery, the receipt number should be listed.

To be sure that everything has been done properly, the supervisor *validates* a certain percentage of the interviews.   Usually she does so by telephone, randomly selecting the required percentage of interviews to be validated from each interviewer's work.   The respondents are telephoned, primarily to make sure that the interview was made, and also to ask certain key questions from the questionnaire to be sure that the interviewer's notations are accurate.   If the respondent has no telephone, validation is done by letter or card, enclosing a postage-paid return card on which the respondent is asked to say whether the interview was conducted, when, and what she recalls of the subject matter.

If no name is recorded on the interview form, as sometimes happens on street interviews in the interest of speed, the supervisor, unknown to the interviewer, will observe her at work.   Although it is to be assumed that all interviewers are honest and trustworthy, cases of falsifying interviews are known; for the sake of her own reputation, no supervisor will deliver work that has not been checked.

Similarly, *time sheets* must be checked for accuracy.   If several interviewers work without knowledge of one another and handle comparable assignments, their time records should be similar, barring unusual incidents.   There have been cases of time and expense padding, and the alert supervisor will find and rectify such irregularities.

Central-location telephone interviewing permits closer supervision than most other work does, for with several interviewers working from one office, the supervisor, sitting at the switchboard, can listen in to various conversations and be assured that all goes well.   When there is no such arrangement, interviewers work from their own homes and bill any telephone charges on their time sheets.   Usually a detailed form is provided for recording the result of each dialing: no answer, busy, no qualified respondent, language barrier, and so on, or interview completed.

Interviewer evaluation is the final part of the supervisor's job.   From her editing of the work and her validation, she must be able to evaluate each worker in order to know, among other things, whether, and for what type of job, to use her next.   Some of the points on which an interviewer may be evaluated are:

Punctuality in delivering work
Legibility
Adherence to sampling pattern

Completion of work exactly as assigned
Field costs
Attitude toward work
Punctuality at briefing
Neatness
Quality of work

Other points will arise according to the specifics of the job. Some companies give each interviewer a work rating with each check, hoping that deficiencies will thus be eliminated and quality improved.

SUMMARY

The foregoing pages have attempted to describe procedures for selecting, recruiting, training, and supervising marketing research field work as currently handled in the United States. Some native and acquired qualities of interviewers were identified, and methods were suggested for finding and training workers, including in some detail both plus and minus ratings of their performance. Various types of surveys and the techniques and methods for their conduct were listed. Finally, the functions and responsibilities of good supervision were described.

It is hoped that this information will prove of interest and value to directors and buyers of research. As the research profession has grown, the chasm between the ivory-towered designers of research and those who actually put their designs into practice has widened. In the belief that the best generals were once privates, the suggestion is made that every buyer of research spend a little time in the field learning first-hand the many practical problems that arise. Such understanding, which can be gained only by personal experience, will not only increase rapport with field workers, but will stabilize any flights of theory by good common sense.

BIBLIOGRAPHY

Atkinson, Jean, A Handbook for Interviewers, London: Her Majesty's Stationery Office, 1968.
Brown, Lyndon O., and Leland L. Beik, Marketing Research and Analysis, 4th ed., New York: Ronald, 1969.
Richardson, Stephen A., Barbara Dorenwend, and David Klein, Interviewing, Its Forms and Functions, New York: Basic Books, 1965.
Roberts, Ann, Ann's Survey Girls, Phoenix, Ariz.: Southwest Publishing Company, 1965.

Chapter 6

Group Interviewing

WILLIAM D. WELLS *Graduate School of Business, University of Chicago, Chicago, Illinois*

Group interviewing—interviewing people in groups rather than individually—entered the marketing research scene shortly after World War II as part of "motivation research" [3]. Like most motivation research techniques, it was instantly condemned by the conservative research establishment as "unscientific" and therefore untrustworthy. It has prospered nonetheless, and today in many marketing research organizations, group interviews are nearly as common as interviews done by the traditional survey questionnaire.

Group interviewing has proved so durable because it has some important assets that allow it to compete effectively with other ways of getting information. Some of these assets are undiluted virtues; some are not.

One asset is that group interview studies can be, and often are, fast and cheap. A three- or four-interview study can be conducted, analyzed, and reported in less than a week in an emergency, and at a cost much lower than that of most other ways of learning about attitudes and behavior. This means that an efficient group-interviewing facility can be extremely valuable when time and cost constraints are severe. It also means that group interviews will sometimes be employed when a more expensive, more time-consuming method would be more appropriate—the research equivalent of Gresham's law.

A second, related advantage is that the group interview is a superb mechanism for generating hypotheses when little is known. Even when time and funds are ample for the most painstaking research, the researcher must get some background somewhere before he can cope with a problem in any useful way. When other information sources are sparse or lacking, or when the researcher needs immediate, personal contact with the subject matter to spark his own thought, group interviews are highly productive idea breeders.

third important advantage is that the group method drastically reduces the distance between the respondent who produces research information and the client who uses it.[1] In a typical large-scale survey, the respondent talks to an overworked and undertrained field interviewer who cannot possibly fully appreciate the client's problems or the context of the research. The field interviewer's version of what the respondent said goes to a coder who is similarly in the dark. The coder's work goes to an assistant analyst who does further injustice to the data, next through an analyst to a supervisor, then maybe to someone who knows what the study is about. With so many chances to lose information and add noise, it is not surprising that clients who order surveys sometimes get mostly what they do not want.

In a group interview study, on the other hand, the number of interviews is so small and the time consumed is so short that the client can participate in most or all of the interviews himself, either by providing feedback to the interviewer on the relevance of the material being produced, or by asking questions himself as the interview unfolds. Besides its obvious feedback value, client participation promotes acceptance of the research by the person who counts most. As a true participant, the client can see with his own eyes and hear with his own ears. Once the study is completed, nothing makes a finding more compelling than the memory of having been there, actively involved, when it emerged.

Some researchers feel that clients, like unruly children, must be protected from their own impulses—in this case, their impulse to influence the course and nature of the research. When that assertion is true, a group interview study is probably not a good idea.

A fourth advantage of the group interview technique is its flexibility. Survey interviewers work from a rigid question schedule. A good group interviewer works from a list of topics—listening, thinking, probing, exploring, framing hunches and ideas as he proceeds. He also "listens with the third ear," trying to achieve a grasp and an intuitive understanding of what is being said. He looks at the respondents, watches posture, listens to voice tone, and tries to decide when respondents are "putting him on." He is not an automatic, mechanical, wind-up question asker, as survey interviewers necessarily and properly are.

A fifth advantage of the group interview, an advantage shared with the individual depth interview, is its ability to handle contingencies. Much of consumer behavior is "if . . . and . . . otherwise." "If it is one of the three brands I sometimes use *and* it is on sale, I buy it; *otherwise*, I buy my regular brand." "*If* the day is hot *and* I have to serve the whole neighborhood, I make bug juice; *otherwise*, I give them soda or Coke." "*If* I know that we're going to take a long trip with a lot of high-speed driving *and* the tires are getting a little worn, I replace them; *otherwise*, I leave them on until I trade in the car." Single survey questions can obtain all these elements separately; but unless the relationships are already fairly well known, it is hard to design questions that pick up those contingencies that link the events.

A sixth advantage is that group interview respondents stimulate one another. One respondent's remarks may lead another to pursue a line of thinking he would not have followed in an individual interview. A bold respondent may

---

[1] Hereafter "client" means anyone who uses the information the interviews produce. He may be a client in the usual sense. He may also be another investigator who will use the results of group interviews as a basis for further research. Or he may be the investigator himself.

encourage a less outgoing one to voice feelings and opinions that he never would have revealed had someone else not had the courage to express them first.

Finally, a group interview study has an important advantage over the standard questionnaire study in that the findings emerge in a form that most clients fully understand. The typical survey report is a thicket of percentages. Unless the client has the researcher's eye for numerals, he is apt to find a percentage-ridden report arid and impersonal. The typical group interview report (like the typical individual depth-interview report) is crammed with real people. Instead of mysterious symbols and dull tables, there are direct quotations in which believable people give their views at length and in their own words. For many clients, this is the texture of the world.

These advantages—speed, relatively modest cost, ready production of hypotheses and ideas, direct connection between respondent and client, flexibility, sensitivity to contingencies, intragroup stimulation and comfortable results— make the group interview a formidable contender when research-method decisions must be made. Each of these advantages carries a penalty, but none should be ignored.

PREPARATION

Understanding the Problem. Although it seems almost too obvious, it is probably worth emphasizing that the value of a group interview study depends to a very great extent on the interviewer's appreciation of the client's problems. Before doing anything else, the interviewer talks to the client. He finds out what the client already knows or thinks he knows and what he thinks he wants to know.

This step is exceedingly important because the group interviewer does not normally have his questioning route prescribed. He must hunt for answers in the interview like a hound following a scent. If the interviewer doesn't recognize the wisp of an answer, that trail may never be taken.

For this reason, the term *interviewer* used in this chapter has a somewhat different connotation from the term *interviewer* in the preceding and later chapters. Here, the interviewer is not only skilled at interviewing but also very well aware of the purpose and objectives of the research. He is the client's proxy. He does what he thinks the client would do if the client had the time, inclination, and skill to do it.

The Questions. Once the client's problems are understood, it is helpful to cast them into a set of questions—not questions to be asked of the respondents, but rather, questions to be asked of the research results. For example:

What do dog owners think about their dogs? Do they regard them as animals or as members of the family? Do dogs have "personalities"? If so, what are the major types? How do dog owners decide what form of food to buy? What part does the dog play in evaluating a food? What roles do children play? Is price important? Under what circumstances and in what way? How do dog owners select a specific brand? Do they think they should buy a variety, or do they think they should be consistent? Why? What dogfood advertising can respondents remember? What is their reaction to this advertising?

This detailed set of questions has two purposes. It ensures that both client and interviewer have thought about what they really want to know, and it ensures agreement on specific objectives before the study begins. Though this sort of preparation is obviously desirable in any study, it is especially important in group interview research because a group study does not normally have its scope and objectives specified by a preset questionnaire.

The Outline.   Once the questions to be answered by the research have been established, the interviewer can prepare a topic outline.   Instead of a specific set of questions to be asked in a predetermined order, the group interviewer uses a set of notes on major issues, a set of cues to help ensure that all important points are covered.   Novice interviewers often feel uncomfortable with so skimpy a guide because they feel the need to ask questions continuously, and they fear they will not be able to frame just the right question at just the right time.   Experienced interviewers know that it is far more important to listen and react perceptively to what respondents are saying than to emit a volley of questions, regardless of how elegantly they are phrased.   The novice interviewer should remember that all his respondents have had many years of practice at giving sensible answers to stupid questions, and he should not be afraid of asking some himself.   Sometimes a fumbling, stumbling question will elicit a long, detailed, and interesting response because the respondent has adapted the question to his own purposes and can therefore use it as a lead-in to say what he has on his mind.

Recruiting Groups.   Group interviewing is now so common that field supervisors anywhere in the country can recruit groups to fit almost any specifications.   Their sources include their own staffs or interviewers, their interviewers' acquaintances, local organizations whose members participate in return for contributions to the organization treasury, and as a last (expensive) resort, telephone or door-to-door recruiting.

When recruiting respondents, it is usually helpful to provide for both homogeneity and contrast within specific groups.   In marketing research, homogeneity is particularly desirable with respect to social class and stage in the family life cycle.   Consumers occupying different stages of the life cycle have such different needs and problems, such different resources, such different sets of experiences and perceptions of reality that they sometimes have difficulty communicating with one another.   Especially in conversations about shopping and homemaking, younger, less experienced women are apt to defer to the veterans.   When social classes are mixed, the more literate and articulate middle-class respondents may suppress participation by lower-class interviewees who feel unlearned.   When the topic is personal, it is usually unwise to mix the sexes.

With this homogeneity, it is often helpful to provide for a spark to be struck by contrasting opinions.   One of the best ways to produce contrast is to be certain each group includes both users and nonusers of the client's brand.   (This keeps the client interested too.)   If the product carries no social stigma, it is also useful to include within the same group both users and nonusers of the product class.   But if the product does have social connotations—for example, if nonusers of instant coffee think users are lazy, or if buyers of big life insurance policies think nonbuyers are selfish—mixing users and nonusers may soft-pedal some important ideas.

Group Size.   Small groups are inefficient because they provide less than the maximum number of respondent hours per hour of interviewer time.   Very small groups lose the mutual stimulation among respondents that makes the group setting unique.   When groups are too large, they are difficult to manage, and in very large groups, less forward but potentially valuable respondents hesitate to speak.   The ideal group size will depend somewhat on the physical accommodations (for example, the number of chairs that will fit around the table) and on the interviewer's personal style. Most physical accommodations and most interviewers are amenable to groups of six to ten.

It is a good idea to overrecruit. Group interviewing requires appearance by designated individuals in a specific place at a preset time. When an emergency occurs (baby-sitters didn't show up, friends dropped in, the weather got bad, the car wouldn't start), any one of these individuals is likely to decide that personal concerns are more important than market research.

Friends? When respondents are recruited from neighborhoods or organizations, at least some of them will know one another fairly well before the interview begins. Some interviewers object to this because they believe that discussions among friends produce unreal homogeneity of opinion. Some feel that friends may converse with one another, leaving others out, or that respondents are less than candid in the presence of people they see every day. Other interviewers feel that the naturalness and ease of conversation among acquaintances make an interview among friends dramatically more productive. The assets and liabilities of allowing friends to participate in the same group almost balance out.

Sites. Group interviews can be conducted in the client's office building, in some more "neutral" setting (a research supplier's office, a school, a motel), or in respondents' homes.

Conducting the interviews at the client's home base strongly increases the probability that the client will attend, and for this reason alone it is frequently a good idea. In addition, home-base interviewing greatly simplifies the mechanics of setting up tape recorders, motion picture projectors, samples, and props. On the other hand, home-base interviewing—assuming home base is downtown—makes recruiting of certain types of respondents exceedingly difficult. Also, it always reveals the client's identity, with all the biases which this implies.

"Neutral site" interviewing usually incurs out-of-pocket costs for transportation and room rental, reduces the probability the client will participate, and requires transport and setup of equipment in a strange place. In return, it facilitates recruiting some respondents and conceals the client's identity.

Interviewing in respondents' homes makes it relatively easy to recruit interviewees who will not go downtown. It also provides a setting that the respondents find friendly and familiar and gives both client and interviewer the opportunity to see how a wide variety of consumers live. This latter opportunity can be especially enlightening to a client who would not otherwise see the inside of an inexpensive home.

But in-home interviewing has its dangers. It is easy to get lost on the way to the interview site, especially in a strange town, especially at night, and especially in bad weather. At least once during an in-home interview the doorbell (or telephone) will ring. The hostess will leap up, trip over the microphone cord, rush to the door, and conduct a breathless conversation in tones loud enough to disrupt the interview but soft enough to ensure its continuation.

Equipment. Most interviews are tape-recorded for later listening or transcription. Even in this sensitive age, respondents rarely object to this procedure. When the machine is treated routinely, its obvious presence has no notable effect on the conversation. Respondents forget it is there.

The problems posed by tape recorders are mostly mechanical. When a second interview is recorded over the first by mistake, the first one is erased. Extraneous sounds, easily ignored by the ear during the interview, can make large portions of the recording unintelligible.

Mechanical problems multiply when interviewing is conducted out of town.

Airline baggage handlers seem to have a union rule requiring tape recorders to be broken. Rented recorders stop in the middle of the interview. When interviews are conducted outside the United States, for example, in Canada, the United States Customs may decide—against all reason—that tape-recorded group interviews are "artistic productions." Then trouble knows no end. To all these hazards, the airlines' attempt to protect their planes from hijackers has added still another: the magnetic fields generated by weapon-detection devices will erase magnetic tapes.

Sound motion-picture projectors are cumbersome, obstreperous, and not easily repaired in the field. Different makes and models are threaded differently. When films are to be used, it is most important that projection equipment, especially if rented, be tested beforehand, and that someone be available who knows what to do when the lights go out.

Some organizations specializing in group interviewing have comfortably appointed rooms in which clients can watch and listen to group interviews from behind a one-way screen. The advantage of such a facility is that clients can talk, laugh, smoke, sleep, or make telephone calls without disturbing the moderator or group.

But the one-way vision room has two disadvantages that deserve some thought. First, by removing the client from the group, it prevents the client participation that is so often fruitful. Second, because it is deceptive, it violates the implicit contract between researcher and respondent. Social psychologists have already found that even well-intended deception can lead to outrage [2]. It would be prudent to think carefully before repeating that discipline's mistakes.

Number of Interviews. By questionnaire survey standards, the number of interviews in a typical group study is ridiculously small. When the study is limited to "middle-aged, middle-income homemakers," reports are often written after three or four sessions, and it is a rare study indeed that requires more than eleven or twelve. From the first interview on an unfamiliar topic, the analyst invariably learns a great deal. The second interview produces much more, but not all of it is new. Usually by the third session, and certainly by the fourth, most of what is said has been said several times before, and it is obvious that little is to be gained from continuing.

Exceptions to this general rule occur when there are important regional effects and when the investigation is intended to cover respondents who differ in age, sex, and social class. Then it is essential that each segment be represented, even though some of the material may appear again and again.

THE INTERVIEW

Styles. As group interviewing has developed under different practitioners, interviewing styles have diverged along a continuum that runs from nondirective at one extreme to directive at the other. At the nondirective extreme, the interviewer (frequently called a "moderator," to emphasize his nondirective role) participates only enough to start the conversation and prevent it from wandering too far from topics of interest to the client. The emphasis is on the group, on the dynamics of group interaction, and on the latent significance of what is said. Thus, in describing the "group depth interview," Goldman [1] writes:

> The moderator guides the discussion, keeping it within fruitful bounds, but rarely participates in it himself. When he can lead a group member to ask a question of a group, the moderator will not question them himself.

The rationale for encouraging spontaneous interchange among group members is that this sort of discussion may reveal important material that would not have emerged in response to direct questioning. The approach is based on the notion that people, allowed to be spontaneous in a nonevaluative, nonthreatening environment, will reveal much about themselves that they would otherwise hide. It even is sometimes asserted by those who advocate the nondirective approach that the dynamics of an in-depth group interview will let respondents reveal things of which they themselves were previously unaware. In the Freudian tradition, the search is at least in part for the "real," as opposed to the obvious and overt reasons why.

At the directive extreme, the interviewer maintains control of the discussion, does most of the questioning himself, and terminates the group's verbal interchanges unless they are clearly on the issue. In this style, the effort is to keep the discussion orderly, follow a predetermined sequence of topics, and explore each topic one at a time. No attempt is made to generate group cohesion or to plumb the unconscious.

Nondirective in-depth group interviewing is well described in the Goldman article [1]. The material that follows is biased toward the directive style.

Arrangement of Respondents.   It sometimes makes a difference where respondents sit. Since those directly across from the interviewer have the most eye contact, they tend to participate more than others, and respondents immediately to the interviewer's right or left are likely to participate less. It is therefore often helpful to seat the least talkative respondents opposite the interviewer when possible, and to place the most talkative on the sides.

Some interviewers prefer that respondents be labeled so that they can be called by name. Others prefer the relative anonymity of a conversation in which names are not used. This decision is best left to the interviewer to make on the basis of his personal style.

Opening the Interview.   The interviewer's initial remarks define the ground rules and set the tone. In an interview to be conducted according to the directive style, the opening comments might be as follows:

"Today we are going to be talking about a topic that I think you will find interesting and that I'm sure you all know a lot about, and that is shortening [or cigarettes, or tea, or doctors, or whatever]. First I'd like to find out something about when you use shortening, what you use it for, how you use it and so on. Then I'd like to find out something about what you think of different forms of shortening, then different brands. Finally, we're going to be talking about some advertising for shortening that you may have seen, and we'll look at some shortening commercials and talk about them.

"First I have a couple of requests. One is that you speak up and only one person speak at a time. We're tape-recording this, and if someone speaks very softly, or if two or three conversations are going at once, we can't hear it later. The other thing is, please say exactly what you think. We're just as interested in negative comments as positive ones, and in fact, the negative comments are sometimes the most useful.

"One thing more. We're not making a radio commercial or a television commercial here, so don't look for the hidden camera. Say exactly what you think, because that's what we want to know.

"Now, to get started, perhaps it would be best to go around the table one at a time. I'd like to know something about your families—how many children you have, how old they are, what variety they are, and what your husband does for a living."

These opening comments have special purposes. The first is to give the respondents some idea of the scope of the interview and the topics to be covered. This tells them not only what to expect but also approximately what the boundaries are.

The comments about the tape recorder are intended to make note of the machine in a routine way and set the stage for later requests from the interviewer to speak up or to stop sideline conversations. Such requests are often necessary if a good recording is to be made.

The comment about radio and television commercials is useful because most respondents will have seen commercials that portray real or role-played interviews, and if they assume that a commercial is in progress, they will be self-consciously "on stage."

The tactic of starting the interview by proceeding around the table and asking about family serves several ends. It ensures that every respondent will speak at least once—and on a topic that he is certain to know very well. It acquaints the respondents with one another. It puts relevant information about family composition and social class on the tape. And, by giving the interviewer an opportunity to speak briefly with each respondent at the outset, it allows him to show he is interested in more than skeletal replies. Immediately, if a respondent answers sparsely, the interviewer can pose a question or two, probing for information beyond that which is explicit in the question itself. For instance, the interviewer may ask, "How many of the children are living at home?" "Any grandchildren yet?" "I believe you said your husband works for the telephone company. What does he do?" This sort of light probing helps set the stage for what will happen later.

Tracking. If the interview is to follow the directive style, the interviewer then embarks on a topic and endeavors to keep the interview on that topic until it is covered to his satisfaction. For instance, an interview on shortening might open with a general question on the purposes for which shortening is used. That topic would then be pursued until the interviewer believes he has obtained all the information he needs or thinks he can get on that topic from that group.

During the opening stage, the danger is that the interview will digress in seven different directions, because comments on the first topic are virtually certain to contain material on other subjects also of great interest. Even though it is tempting to follow one or more of these other topics while the trial is hot, the practice of tracking requires that these interesting, off-the-immediate-topic clues be filed away mentally and that the immediate topic be maintained as the conversation focus. After the first topic is exhausted, the second is taken up, and so on until all topics have been covered.

Tracking produces a more or less orderly set of interviews in which all subjects are discussed in much the same sequence. It provides some assurance that all topics of interest will in fact be covered, and, as shown later, it provides a framework for a thorough and speedy report.

In the opinion of interviewers who prefer the nondirective style, tracking imposes far too much order and discipline on the respondents. The nondirective interviewer prefers to let topics emerge spontaneously and to foster dynamic, highly involved group interaction in the hope of obtaining material that would not be available in everyday, face-to-face contacts.

Nondirective interviewers often employ techniques derived from sensitivity training and group psychotherapy to further draw out the group. For instance, they sometimes use marathon sessions lasting far into the evening or through much of a day. They may use projective stimuli, like inkblots, pictures, or designs. Or they may assign roles and ask respondents to act out spontaneous dramas that center on the topic under study. All these practices foster respondent involvement, but they tangle the record and make an already difficult analysis problem that much more complicated.

Pacing. In a directive interview, a specific set of topics (and any other obviously relevant issues that emerge unexpectedly) must be covered within a fixed period of time. Most respondents want to know in advance about how long the interview will last and usually make their plans according to what they are told. The interviewer must therefore pace the session so that an interesting subject does not crowd out other equally interesting topics to be covered toward the end. Pacing an interview is much like writing an essay examination. The interviewer must assign an implicit weight to each question and move on, even if not entirely finished, when the question has taken as much time as it is worth. Like the ideal examination, the ideal interview ends at the bell.

One of the advantages of conducting a series of group interviews with continuous feedback from the client is that different interviews can be paced differently. If a topic has already been well covered in previous interviews, the interviewer need only assure himself, by a series of comparatively brief questions and answers, that the opinions of the present group are much like those he has already heard in detail. He can then move on to examine matters that have not been thoroughly discussed before.

Balancing Participation. In the ideal group interview, all respondents contribute everything they know that is relevant to the topic. This means that the interviewer must encourage the less forward respondent who might otherwise sit back and say little or nothing. It also means that a dominant individual or a small, dominant subgroup cannot be permitted to suppress others' contributions. Participation can be balanced by asking direct questions, by asking for further comment from respondents who seem hesitant about expressing their opinions, by calling on respondents who look as though they are about to speak, and, when the issue is especially important, talking to each group member in turn, progressing systematically around the table. Participation will never be absolutely uniform, but it is important that those who have something to say be given every opportunity.

Pest Control. Group interviews are susceptible to two species of pests. One is the genuine expert who knows so much about the subject matter that other group members hesitate to express their own opinions: the ex-dental technician in discussions about dental care, the dietician involved in a food-product discussion, the man with a lifetime hobby of rebuilding cars in an interview on motor oil. Experts can usually be eliminated in advance, provided that the recruiter is forewarned to ask the appropriate screening questions. Even then, an occasional expert will seep through.

The other species of pest is the all-purpose expert who knows everything about everything, from the amount of preservative per ounce of dry cereal to the effects of television on the moral development of children. Pests of this species give their opinions as established fact and attempt to inflict their viewpoints on everyone else in the room.

The genuine expert can sometimes be induced to withhold his opinions at least until other group members have had their chance. If he enters into the spirit of the investigation, he will let others talk just to learn what they think. If not, there is little the interviewer can do except ensure that another expert of the same type does not crop up in the next interview.

The pseudo expert can often be controlled by maneuvers showing that the interviewer is interested in what all group members have to say. The interviewer can cut him (or her) off in mid-phrase, ask pointedly if there are others who want to express an opinion, avoid eye contact with the pest, look bored, study the ceiling while the pest is speaking, pretend to have a severe headache, change the subject abruptly the second the pest has stopped talking, or display other signs of fatigue. Most pests can be controlled by such tactics but, alas, a few cannot. When an uncontrollable pest appears and has his (or her) way, the only consolation is that some group interviews are better than others. In most states, it is illegal for a civilian to use Mace.

Who Is a Good Interviewer?   Almost anyone can learn the mechanics of directive interviewing. It helps to start by watching someone who knows how and to listen to one's own tapes, second-guessing what could have been said or done to make the interview more productive.

It is not easy, however, to acquire the background that enables the skilled interviewer to direct the conversation toward relevant talk and away from chatter that is unrelated to the client's problems. Even when the research questions are outlined in advance, it still takes a command of the specific problem and a fairly close acquaintance with marketing problems in general to know when to probe and when to stop.

Nondirective interviewing is a somewhat different matter. Here clinical training, or at least an intimate acquaintance with the clinical approach, is a great help, as is a contemplative, introspective, openly receptive frame of mind. The ideal nondirective interviewer is somewhat like an animate inkblot.

When the topic is delicate, it is always a good idea to have an interviewer of the same sex as the respondents. When the topic is impersonal, the sex of the interviewer does not matter much, except that young, attractive female interviewers sometimes have trouble keeping young male respondents on the track. Adult males often find it difficult to interview adolescent girls, who usually giggle or sulk. Anyone can experience problems when interviewing adolescent boys.

Report Preparation.   Reports of group interview studies have followed several quite different patterns depending on the time and cost constraints of the study, the investigator's personal style, and the client's needs and tastes. At one extreme, when time and cost limitations are severe, the interviewer can prepare a brief, impressionistic summary of the principal findings, depending mainly on his own memory. When the interviews are intended to evaluate a new product idea or a new copy concept and when the outcome is so obvious that it needs little support or documentation, this kind of reporting may be enough. Especially when the client has been present and participating, and when the respondents' reactions can lead to only one conclusion, it may be undesirable to report more than the minutes of the meetings.

At the other extreme, the analyst listens and relistens carefully to the tapes, copying down pregnant segments, fitting the respondents' reactions into a more general scheme derived from his understanding of the history and present status of the problem and his own model of human nature. In this kind of report, the respondents' manifest reactions make roughly the same contribution to the final report as the patient's free associations make to a psychoanalyst's case report. When the reporter is sagacious, imaginative, discerning, and skillful, reports in this tradition are rich, stimulating, novel, creative, and fascinating—and infuriating to anyone who is not prepared to take the analyst at his word.

A method between these two extremes—one designed to preserve the most significant interview material more or less intact and still allow for imaginative interpretation—is technically known as the "Scissor and Sort" or "Long Couch, Short Hallway" technique. The first step in this procedure is to have all the interviews transcribed. Although this step may seem costly and time-consuming (typing a moderately long interview takes about a day), investment is more than repaid in the efficiencies a typed transcript brings to report preparation. Typing services in most large cities provide quick protocols at moderate fees. If the interviewer has encouraged respondents to speak up and talk singly and if there are not too many telephone bells, boat whistles, fire sirens, or jet overflights, the protocols will be reasonably accurate.

The next step is to edit, code, and bracket the interview segments that will form the muscle of the report. Respondents do not usually speak perfect prose. They hem and haw, back up, skip words and phrases, and sometimes forget what they were about to say in mid-sentence. In the editing process, much of this verbal meandering (which the typist will faithfully reproduce) can be deleted, leaving a comparatively readable script. The degree of editing is a matter of judgment. On one hand, it is important to make reports as readable as possible, or they will not be read. On the other hand, it is essential to preserve as much as one can of the flavor and texture of the respondents' remarks, including bad English, clumsy attempts at description, and obvious confusion when confusion is what occurred. In many instances, the chief value of the report will be its presentation of what the respondents had to say in the respondents' own words.

The next step is to bracket those transcript segments that are relevant to the problem and to code the bracketed material by subject matter. A bracket may enclose an interchange among the interviewer and one or more respondents covering part of a page, the bottom of one page and the top of the next, or several pages—as long as the bracketed material has some common subject core. The coding, written longhand in the margin, is simply the analyst's notes to himself on what the bracketed segment is about and where in the report it might fit.

The next step is to cut each interview apart, bracket by bracket, and to staple or tape together the segments that extend over several pages. The segments are then sorted by topic (a long couch or a short hallway will do), and the material is ready for the final step.

The last step is writing the supporting and connective tissue. This material usually starts with an introduction describing the study's purpose, the major questions the investigator sought to answer, the size and structure of the sample, and the major features of the group interview technique. Many reports then go on to a two- or three-page summary of the results, and conclude with the main body of the findings.

If the respondents' conversations have been well segmented and sorted, preparing the main body of the report is not difficult. The first major topic is introduced; the first set of interview segments is placed into the report as a series of exhibits, and the segments are summarized and discussed. Single-spacing the quotations and double-spacing the discussion provide a varied format that is easy to follow.

Subsequent sections have the same pattern, that is, introduction, exhibits, discussion, the major difference being that later discussions point out relationships with material that has appeared before.

This method of report preparation preserves the most relevant sections of each interview, and presents the interview material in an organized, coherent framework. It makes the reader's task easy and provides the analyst with an opportunity to highlight relationships, interpret where interpretation is needed, and point out implications. In a practiced analyst's hands, it does not require an unreasonable amount of time.

TRAPS

Seduction. The group interview is nearly the world's worst instrument for producing hard data like share-of-market percentages, brand-switching turn-over tables, and media-reach and frequency figures. No one sets out to use group interviews for such purposes, but the sense of immediacy and conviction one gets from listening to real consumers describe and defend their activities and preferences can lead the unwary investigator into thinking that his samples are larger and more representative than they actually are.

For a quick grasp of broad trends, where an error of 5, 10, or even 20 per-cent may not lead the investigator too far astray, and for a reading of reactions that are apt to be much the same from one segment of the population to another, three to five group interviews may be all the decision maker needs. But when every percentage point counts or when reactions are likely to vary greatly from one population subgroup to another, seduction by vivid anecdote is an ever-present danger. It is little help to say, "All group interview studies should be followed up by carefully designed, precisely executed, large-scale survey research." Maybe they should be, but they won't.

Taste. The technology of taste tests is now well developed. Among the factors that influence the perceived taste of a beverage or food are the taster's orientation to the product, the perceived reactions of others, physical properties of the environment (such as light, heat, and smoke), the product's physical condition (including temperature and freshness), and the order in which sam-ples are served. When group interviews concern foods or beverages, it is tempting to have the respondents taste some samples at the end of the inter-view to see how they will react. Then, all the variables that are well controlled in the taste-testing laboratory will affect the group-interview taste test in un-knowable ways.

Newness. Group interviews are frequently used to screen new-product ideas. If the new product is a minor variation on something with which re-spondents are already familiar, group interviews will show how the new-product concept, as presented, is perceived. But if the new product is so truly innovative that it falls outside the respondents' range of experience or if accep-tance of the new product requires a change in mores (for example, miniskirts), the group interview filter will likely screen the product out. Evaluation by means of group interviews is essentially conservative. It favors ideas that are easy to explain and understand and, therefore, not very new. It works against radical, but maybe highly profitable, change.

Order Effects. When concepts, products, or advertisements are presented to groups for evaluation, each judgment is certain to be influenced by previous judgments. If group members have been highly critical of one thing, they are apt to compensate by being overly uncritical of the next. Order effects occur in individual interviews too, but they are accentuated by the sentiment and cohesiveness that develop in groups, and they can be powerful enough to over-balance everything else.

Delicate Topics. Since group interviews are more "public" than individual interviews, it might seem at first that they are inappropriate for discussing mat-ters generally considered personal. Experience has shown, however, that group interview respondents are surprisingly open in their remarks on their attitudes toward, and use of, contraceptives, deodorants, laxatives, sanitary napkins, liquor, and drugs.   If the group leader is unembarrassed and if he (or she) can establish an atmosphere of trust, groups will discuss with surprising frankness many matters that are not usually mentioned in public.

Compared with individual depth interviews, group interviews focus more on shared experiences and less on personal and individual ones.   When the topic is delicate, that is doubly true.   This characteristic of group interviews has led some investigators to conclude that studies of delicate topics should always include at least some individual interviews.   It has led others to argue that since advertising and marketing must operate at the shared-experience level rather than at the individual level anyway, the less deep, less personal material produced by the group interview is about as deep and personal as one should go.

One Final Trap.   When concepts, products, or advertisements are presented for evaluation, group members will assume that the material being evaluated is the interviewer's.   Therefore, if a friendly atmosphere has been established, respondents will hesitate to be frankly critical unless the interviewer has emphasized that negative reactions are just as valued as positive ones.   Obviously, the interviewer must not only say that he is interested in negative comments; he must also show that he means it.

HOW CAN ANYTHING SO BAD BE GOOD?

Group interviewing violates most of the accepted canons of survey research. Samples are invariably small and never selected by probability methods. Questions are not asked the same way each time.   Responses are not independent.   Some respondents inflict their opinions on others; some contribute little or nothing at all.   Results are difficult or impossible to quantify and are not grist for the statistical mill.   Conclusions depend on the analyst's interpretive skill.   The investigator can easily influence the results.

With these glaring defects, why have group interviews been so widely used? Why have skeptical clients, who tried them only to see what they were like, come back for more?   As noted earlier, part of the answer is that group interviews are fast and cheap.   When decisions must be made and resources are limited, the alternative to a group interview study may well be no study at all. But a more important, less thoroughly understood part of the answer is that *any* way of gathering information is a series of compromises.   The group interview is the product of one selection of compromises; the traditional survey interview is the product of another.   What traditional survey research gains in sample size, standardization, and quantification, it loses in lack of contact between respondent and client, rigidity, elasped time, and high cost.   Too often it also produces elegantly quantified "results" that neither investigator nor client really understands.

CONCLUDING COMMENT

Since most of this chapter has emphasized how interesting group interviews are and how useful they can be, it is appropriate to close by recapitulating and reemphasizing what has already been said about the dangers of using group interviews to the exclusion of other techniques.

Group interviews cannot be conducted with large samples of the population, and sampling techniques that ensure representativeness cannot be employed. One must therefore assume that whatever is being investigated is so uniformly distributed that it does not matter much where one dips into the population or that crude attempts at stratification—such as prescreening respondents on education and age—will pick up all of the variation that is really important. Both these assumptions are questionable and, at times, very wrong.

Group interview respondents are not independent. In a four-interview study with 32 respondents, the degrees of freedom are 3, not 31—one less than the number of independent observations. It is therefore deceptive as well as tedious to count the pros and cons on an issue and subject the proportions to statistical test. By the same token, group interview data are not amenable to analysis by the powerful and extremely helpful multivariate statistical techniques discussed in other chapters in this handbook.

The group leader can, does, and should influence the results. A moderator with the wrong bias can therefore make the findings wrong. Similarly, as in the analytic study of any qualitative material, the analysis and interpretation of group interview material are strongly influenced by the analyst's view of the world—so much so that the usefulness of a group interview study may depend as much on the analyst's insight and creativity as on what the respondents say. Bad analyst: bad report.

For these reasons and because of the ever-present danger of falling into one or more of the six traps described earlier, the conservative course is to use group interviews as a preliminary step to generate hypotheses for more rigorous investigation later on.

When that second step cannot be taken, as sometimes it cannot, the user of group interview material should weigh the risks just described.

REFERENCES

1. Goldman, Alfred E., "The Group Depth Interview," *Journal of Marketing*, vol. 26, July 1962, pp. 61–68.
2. Seeman, Julius, "Deception in Psychological Research," *American Psychologist*, vol. 24, November 1969, pp. 1025–1028.
3. Smith, George H., *Motivation Research in Advertising and Marketing*, New York: McGraw-Hill, 1954.

Surveys

Chapter 7

Planning Field Operations

MATHEW HAUCK *Survey Research Laboratory, University of Illinois at Urbana-Champaign, Illniois*

Plans for field operations will be determined primarily by the method of data collection used. Regardless of the approach, however, all planning involves some common elements, such as time schedules, budgets, personnel, and expected results (quantity and quality).

This chapter will first review these common elements and then, for each method of data collection, discuss its specific planning requirements. The last part of the chapter will look at bias as it relates to planning field operations. Identification of the sources of biases will be followed by a discussion on avoiding biases or, if they cannot be avoided, on how to detect and correct them.

PREPARING FOR FIELD OPERATIONS

A study can be completed by a specified date and within the budget if care is taken in planning before the study goes into the field. Studies that fail to meet the target date or exceed the budget are usually those for which planning is slipshod or nonexistent.

Also often overlooked are the number and skills of personnel required to stay within the time schedule and budget. In addition, an estimate is needed of the expected results and the quality of the data necessary for the analysis.

Time Schedule. A target date for the completion of data collection is sometimes set without reviewing the schedule to determine whether it is realistic and obtainable. When preparing for field work, it is important to estimate the number of days needed for each phase and also to select starting and completion dates for each phase. As one would expect, some phases overlap in time. A good example of overlapping is the time necessary for sampling. For some studies, the sample can be obtained from lists and is not related to the rest of the field time schedule; the sample lists need only be ready in time for interviewer training and assignments. For other studies, sampling work is directly related to the field and must be provided for in the time schedule, either as a separate screening operation or in combination with the interviewing, as is done for quota sampling. Interviewing forms and procedures sometimes cannot be established until the details of the sampling plan are known. Frequently, sampling materials must be completed before any field assignments are made.

Table 1 and Exhibit 1 are examples of a detailed time schedule for a personal interview study. If any phase of the field work is subcontracted to another organization or to an interviewing service, or if sampling is part of the field work, the time necessary for these additional phases should be allowed.

TABLE 1   Field Time Schedule

Phase of the study	Starting date	Completion date	Number of days	Number of days to completion
Draft pretest questionnaire	Jan. 10	Jan. 26	16	132
Select pretest sample	Jan. 23	Jan. 25	3	132
Select pretest interviewers	Jan. 10	Jan. 15	5	143
Prepare pretest training material	Jan. 20	Jan. 26	6	132
Train pretest interviewers	Jan. 27	Jan. 28	2	130
Pretest interviewing	Jan. 29	Feb. 5	7	123
Evaluate pretest results	Feb. 6	Feb. 20	14	109
Finalize all forms and procedures including printing of questionnaire	Feb. 21	Mar. 5	14	95
Select interviewers	Feb. 6	Feb. 28	22	102
Prepare training material	Feb. 26	Mar. 5	7	96
Train interviewers	Mar. 6	Mar. 10	4	91
Interviewing	Mar. 11	Apr. 22	42	49
Cleanup in field	Apr. 23	May 6	14	35
Interviewer verification	Mar. 14	Apr. 31	47	40
Office cleanup	May 7	May 28	21	14
Final field report	May 29	June 12	14	0

Some phases frequently tend to be underestimated in the planning stage. In particular, final approval and printing of the questionnaire, selection of interviewers, evaluation of the pretest, and cleanup in the field are likely to take more time than anticipated.

Enough time should be allowed for in the schedule to adjust for unforeseen contingencies. Delays caused by rail strikes, weather conditions, civil disturbances, catastrophes, and other possible blockades should be anticipated in a general sense, so that if they do occur, the study can still be completed on schedule. If, on the other hand, they do not arise, the study will be finished ahead of schedule, a delightful occurrence.

An added advantage of preparing a detailed time schedule is that it forces one to make decisions on the overall study design. Details often overlooked are brought to attention. For this reason, details on the study design should accompany the time schedule.

Budget. Many of the points on time schedules are also applicable to the preparation of budgets, such as:

recognizing the need for a detailed breakdown of the budget into categories

taking care in estimating for specific categories which tend to be under-estimated

building extra money into the budget for unforeseen contingencies

having the budget reviewed (if not prepared) by those responsible for the work

bringing to light details in the study design which may have been overlooked

In these and other respects, the time schedule and the budget are inexorably interrelated. They should be worked out together, for changes made in one often require changes in the other.

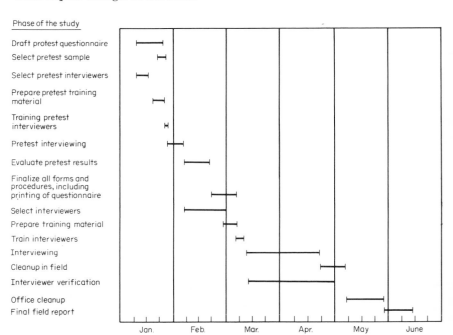

Exhibit 1.   Field time schedule flow diagram.

Following is a list of cost categories that need to be budgeted for a personal interview study:

Office wages and salaries   Field supervisors or interviewing services
Materials and supplies   Interviewers' compensation
Postage   Reproduction of questionnaires and other field
Telephone   forms

Each of these categories may be further separated by stage of data collection, such as:

Pretest   Final field reports
Selection and hiring of interviewers   Data collection
Interviewer training

For each of these categories, it is valuable to have a detailed description of what to include and how to calculate it; for example, how to figure interviewer compensation.

This latter category merits special attention because it is usually the major expense item in field operations and various aspects of it are easily overlooked. In particular, it includes all money to be paid to interviewers for the data collection, such as hourly rates, pre-interview rates, and expenses. Its budget can be calculated in several ways. Whether one is paying by the completed interview or by the hour, the following information will be needed:

1. Number of interviews
2. Number of interviewers
3. Geographic scope of study (Chicago standard metropolitan statistical area, State of Illinois, nationwide, and so on)
4. Approximate length of time for each interview
5. Approximate length of time for training interviewers (including home-study time and practice interviews)
6. Average distance from interviewer's home to training session
7. Average distance from interviewer's home to assigned housing units
8. Average time required for listing housing units and locating and contacting respondents
9. Average time needed for editing each interview

In calculating the interviewer's *time,* the following elements should be considered:

1. Home study before training session
2. Travel time to and from training session, time at session
3. Practice interviews and home-study time after training session
4. Preparation of advance letters and assignments
5. Travel time to sample area (one or more trips)
6. Locating and contacting sample members
7. Interviewing sample members
8. Travel time from sample area (one or more trips)
9. Editing, completing forms and mailing
10. Travel time to and from debriefing session, time at session

Besides the time, the following *expenses* should be considered:

1. Mileage at a fixed rate per mile
2. Public transportation
3. Tolls and parking
4. Meals if necessary
5. Lodging if necessary

With this information the cost per interview can be calculated, regardless of whether paying by the hour or by the interview,[1] and then multiplied by the number of interviews needed, to arrive at the total cost for this category.

It is worth keeping in mind that in preparing budgets, one often spends as much time calculating costs of small items as of large ones. Even so, for better cost control it is best to break down the larger items into their smallest components.[2]

Personnel.   A carefully prepared field budget and time schedule may not be met without adequate personnel who possess the skills needed to carry out the plans for the study. The responsibility for the specific aspects of field work should be clearly assigned and understood. Not completing studies on time or exceeding budgets can most often be traced back to the fact that no one person was assigned responsibility for the various parts of the study.

In most survey organizations, one person has the overall responsibility of

[1] Further discussion on compensating interviewers by the hour or by the interview is presented in the subsection "Personal Interviews."
[2] Sudman [5] has a more detailed discussion on reducing survey costs.

selecting field personnel. Previous experience with these personnel is the best guide in selecting those who will finish the study on time and within the budget. Skilled people therefore not only must be selected, but they also need to be clearly informed of what is expected of them.

Expected results. The number of interviews expected for a study is often the only target set for quantity. For greater control, it is also advisable to estimate the number of expected refusals, noncontacts, and other noninterview categories. These categories could take the form shown in Table 2. Though shown at the bottom, the ratios are usually estimated first (on the basis of past experience and, if possible, a pretest) and then used for deriving the figures in the body of the table.

If the study covers several geographic areas, the totals may be further subdivided into regions, supervisors, or other meaningful control categories. Past

TABLE 2   Study Results Expected*

1. Total eligible respondents   _____

   1.1 Interviews   _____

   1.2. Refusals   _____

   1.3. Noncontacts (assumed eligible)   _____

   1.4. Other (specify) _____   _____

2. Total ineligible respondents   _____

   2.1. Moved   _____

   2.2. Other (specify) _____   _____

3. Total sample   _____

Response rate $(1.1 \div 1)$ ____%

Refusal rate $(1.2) \div (1.1 + 1.2)$ ____%

Contact rate $((1 - 1.3) \div 1)$ ____%

Eligibility rate $(1 \div 3)$ ____%

* Additional columns for the actual results may be added to this table for immediate comparison with the original expectations.

experience with the categories or with similar studies can be useful in creating these strata. For some studies, the pretest, if large and representative enough, may be used to project more accurate estimates of the study's results.

Before the study goes into the field, the supervisor, the interviewing service, or others responsible for reaching these goals should have an opportunity to evaluate the expectations to be certain they are as realistic as possible.

In planning for the field work, preparing the IBM code for the questionnaire is often a prerequisite for establishing the standards of quality needed for the completed interviews. These standards should be spelled out. It is not enough to stipulate that there should be no unexplained blanks and that the data have to be codable and useable for analysis. Following are some questions that can assist in specifying quality criteria:

1. How complete should each questionnaire be? What degree of incompleteness will be acceptable for the analysis?

2. What questions are crucial for the analysis, and for which ones must data be obtained?

3. For open-ended questions, what sort of answers (dimensionality) are needed for the analysis?

4. What procedures are needed to verify that the interviews were conducted, that the person identified was interviewed, that the questions were asked, and that the answers recorded by the interviewer were those given by the respondent?[3]

5. What plans are needed for checking completed interviews when they are received? Will the checking be done more efficiently and accurately in the field section or in a separate section, such as a "control desk" attached to the data reduction staff, where the work can be checked by a third party?

A decision on what to do if quality does not meet expectations should be part of the field preparation. The final action will depend on the specific circumstances, but it is useful to have some tentative plans.

The main value in setting up quality standards early in a study is that it helps spot areas where problems may exist. Steps can then be taken to avert them. Interviewers can be given more detailed training on crucial questions or on what may be expected from open-ended ones.

CARRYING OUT THE FIELD PLANS

Even when the plans for field work are carefully prepared, progress during the study needs to be watched.

Will the study be completed by the target date?

Will it be within the budget?

Will the expected number of interviews be obtained?

Will the quality of the data be adequate for the analysis?

Maintaining the Time Schedule. Besides preparing the overall time schedule (Table 1), it is advantageous to separate the data collection aspects into weekly expectations. Other elements of the time schedule may also benefit from setting such expectations.

The number of interviews expected each week should be related to the time schedule. For example, on a study for which the field work should take six weeks and a total of 1,500 interviews are needed, the following tabulation may be prepared. The tabulation also has provisions for the actual weekly and cumulative results as received.

EXPECTED AND ACTUAL NUMBER OF INTERVIEWS

Week ending	Weekly Expected	Weekly Actual	Cumulative Expected	Cumulative Actual
May 7	200	———	200	———
May 14	300	———	500	———
May 21	400	———	900	———
May 28	300	———	1,200	———
June 5	200	———	1,400	———
June 12	100	———	1,500	———

[3] For more details related to validation, see the next chapter.

The same type of breakdown can be used for refusals, noncontacts, and so forth, if enough information is known to make reasonably accurate estimates. During the study, the schedule should be checked weekly to determine whether it is being maintained. This can be done by filling in the results on the tabulation, thereby having immediate feedback. For studies where the field work is subcontracted, progress reports should be obtained weekly.

If the study is on, or ahead of, the planned time schedule, the researcher can have some degree of confidence that the deadline date will be met, assuming that the remaining time schedule is realistic. On the other hand, if the study falls behind the schedule, there are at least three possibilities:

1. The problem is only temporary, and the study will be back on schedule by the next week or so.

2. The problem causing the delay will clear up, but the study will go beyond the target date by the amount of time it is now lagging.

3. The problem will probably become worse, and the study will run far beyond the present target date.

For most studies, the last assumption is the most realistic. Once it is clear that a study is not on schedule, positive steps must be taken to correct the problem. The most risky assumption is that the situation will improve; it seldom does.

When it has been determined that the target date cannot be reached with the present field operation, reasons need to be identified and a decision reached on what should be done. The researcher has numerous options, such as to:

—Do nothing, and let the study exceed the time schedule and possibly the budget.

—Establish a new time schedule based on present results.

—Hire new interviewers or retrain the old interviewers.

—Change the sample design or the study design.

Cost Control. In practice, studies are not always completed within their budgets. Changes in the study design, a careless time schedule, or other factors may be the cause of excess costs.

One method of keeping within the budget is to project what expenditures may be cumulative by the week for the main budget categories, as indicated in Table 3. Actual expenditures, on a weekly basis, can then be compared to the budget expectations. For the control to be effective, a system must be organized so the expenditure information can be kept accurately and totaled quickly. For example, Mayer [4] shows how interviewer costs can be controlled by computer methods.

If the original budget has been carefully set up and the expenditures carefully recorded, comparisons of actual weekly costs to the weekly estimates will be reliable indicators of whether the budget is realistic or not. If actual weekly costs begin to exceed the estimates, immediate action should be taken either to cut back on the study's scope or to obtain additional financial support to cover the extra costs.

At the end of any study, it is valuable to record the actual costs compared with the budget, so that future budgets can be prepared more accurately.

Quality Control. To maintain the quality standards set for the study, prompt editing of the first interview reports received from each interviewer is essential. Poor-quality work needs to be detected early and corrected quickly. A sample of each interviewer's completed interviews also should be validated. (These topics are covered in greater detail in the next chapter.)

TABLE 3 Expected and Actual Study Costs (cumulative weekly)

Category	May 7		May 14		May 21		May 28		June 5		June 12	
	Ex-pected	Actual	Ex-pected	Actual	Ex-pected	Actual	Ex-pected	Actual	Ex-pected	Actual	Ex-pected	Actual
Pretest												
Selecting and training interviewers												
Data collection												
Total												

PLANNING FIELD OPERATIONS FOR SPECIFIC DATA COLLECTION METHODS

This section will cover only those parts of a field study that differ according to whether personal interviews, telephone, mail, or observation were used to obtain the data.

Personal Interviews. The use of interviewers is the primary distinction of this method. At the planning stage, sufficient time and money should be allocated to the selection, training, and supervision of the interviewers.

First, interviewers must be located and hired. For many studies, insufficient time is allotted to this activity, especially if the study requires interviewers with special capabilities (for example, those who can do depth interviewing, work unusual hours, and so on). Generating applicant inquiries, sending application forms, evaluating applicants, conducting employment interviews, checking references, and selecting field staff cannot be done overnight.

Next, the selected interviewers must be trained. Because the researcher himself is thoroughly familiar with all parts of the study, he may not allot enough time for this. He may feel that since the questionnaire and instructions are so clear, anyone can follow them. This is an erroneous assumption. The pretest results can be used to indicate the necessary training, including study time before the training session and practice interviews afterward, as well as time at the session. Since, on most studies, the interviewers work independently of the researcher, training should be such that each interviewer conducts her field work in a way comparable to that of the other interviewers.

Once the study is underway, there should be a constant check to determine whether the study is progressing according to plans. If the interviewing phase falls behind schedule, it may be necessary either to stimulate the present interviewers to greater productivity (possibly through bonuses), to hire additional interviewers, or to cut back on some parts of the study so it can be completed on schedule.

The quality of the data obtained on the personal interview also requires special attention during the planning stage. Completed interviews need to be checked and interviewers either retrained or dropped if the quality of their work does not meet minimum standards.

One topic not often considered in planning personal interview surveys is the method of interviewer compensation—hourly or by the interview. The more traditional method has been by the hour, because paying by the interview may lead to:

1. The interviewer's rushing the interview and not taking enough time to establish or maintain rapport with the respondent, thereby reducing the opportunity to obtain complete and carefully considered answers.

2. Falsification of interviews, if the interviewer thinks her work will not be verified. Even if she knows it will, the temptation to falsify may be too great because compensation depends on the completed interview.

3. Failure to ask all the questions or to probe answers fully.

One study [3] has indicated, however, that, with adequate control, paying by the interview can have some advantages:

1. Interviewers may earn more since they have a tendency to plan their work and be more efficient.

2. The target date is more likely to be reached.

3. The quality may be higher, especially when interviewers are paid only for acceptable, completed interviews.

4. There are fewer administrative details in filling out and processing time and expense sheets.

Therefore, paying by the personal interview rather than by the hour should be considered.

The success of field work can often be attributed to the competence of the supervisors used. Previous experience with the supervisor (or interviewing service) is the best guide. If new supervisors are used, their capability should be verified by questioning some of their other clients.

A good supervisor is a rarity and can often mean the difference between success and failure of the field work. If in doubt about a supervisor's capability, she should *not* be used.

Telephone Interviews. As with personal interview surveys, great care is needed in planning for the selection, training, and supervision of telephone interviewers. However, if the telephoning is being done from a central location, there is the added advantage of close control. Problems related to the time schedule or to the quality of the interviews can be spotted early and corrected quickly.

If a telephone study does not reach its target-completion date, the delay can usually be attributed to one or more of the following:

1. Locating the telephone numbers took longer than anticipated.
2. Respondents could not be reached, and unplanned follow-up calls were necessary.
3. The interviews took longer than originally anticipated.
4. More time was needed for editing the completed telephone interviews.
5. Interviewers were lost because of problems with, or complexity in, the questionnaire or study design.

From a budgetary viewpoint, the cost of the calls themselves should not be overlooked, especially if direct tie lines or WATS lines are not available. In some cities, a so-called cal-pack can be obtained; for a set charge, it provides for an unlimited number of calls in a certain geographic area for a specified period.

As with personal interviews, paying the telephone interviewers by the completed interview rather than by the hour is not only feasible but can lead to greater control in keeping within the budget and in reaching the target-completion date.

Mail. Of all data collection methods, mail is often most likely to meet a time schedule and to stay within the budget because there are fewer outside influences, such as interviewers, supervisors, and so on. However, mail questionnaire surveys may fail to meet the target date and cost more than expected because of overestimation of appeal of the mail approach.

The time schedule should still be prepared, separating the overall time into the phases involved, such as:

1. Drafting the questionnaire
2. Pretesting
3. Questionnaire finalization and reproduction
4. First mailing
5. Second or third mailing if used
6. Check of nonrespondents
7. Data collection from a subsample of nonrespondents

Past experience is the best guide for setting a realistic time schedule. A person conducting a mail questionnaire study for the first time often overlooks such details as allowing enough time for perfecting the questionnaire and reproducing it; having enough postage, envelopes, and other necessities; and having personnel available for collating, stuffing, stamping, addressing, sealing, and sending out the questionnaire.

If these, as well as other details, are well thought out, the only reason why a mail study may not be completed on schedule is a change in the study design during the study. This may be due to an inadequate pretest, causing the need for an additional mailing to nonrespondents or even telephone or personal interviews to counteract the unexpectedly low response rate.

Observation (Human or Mechanical). Plans for field operation of observation surveys will be directly related to their complexity and the personnel or equipment used. If field personnel are utilized, the same points covered in planning personal interview surveys are applicable. The use of mechanical equipment, such as counters, timers, cameras, or other photographic equipment, may add to the planning problem. The cost of the equipment, and its setup time as well as its maintenance, should be included in the budget.

Such equipment, if fragile, may also be subject to breakdowns or improper functioning, thus affecting the time schedule as well as creating unforeseen costs.

CONTROLLING NONSAMPLING ERRORS

In planning field operations, errors other than sampling need to be considered if valid survey data are to be obtained. This section will first review the possible sources of these response and nonresponse errors and then discuss ways to avoid them when planning the field work. The last part will review ways of detecting bias after the study is underway and methods of correcting for the bias that is uncovered.

Sources of Bias. There are four main sources of bias: the questionnaire, the interviewer, the respondents, and the nonrespondents. Although they overlap considerably, each will be reviewed separately.

The questionnaire, being the instrument by which information is transmitted from the respondent to the researcher, is the primary source of bias in surveys. The length of the questionnaire, the wording and layout of each question, the answer categories, space for written answers, and instructions to interviewers or respondents can all lead to biased results.

Since interviewers are used for personal and telephone surveys, another source of bias is interjected. Not only what the interviewer says (or does not say) but how she looks or behaves can influence the data being obtained. On personal interview surveys, who is to say what the interviewer is asking? She may or may not be reading the question exactly as it is worded, or she may not have even asked the question. If the respondent asked the interviewer to explain the question, what did the interviewer say?

When the interviewer records the respondent's answer, is it what the respondent said, only part of what he said, or merely the interviewer's interpretation? The interviewer can have a great deal of influence on all phases of the interview situation, and she is one of the main sources of bias. Boyd and Westfall [1] conclude that recent research in this area is sparse and does little to increase existing knowledge.

There are numerous areas where respondent bias may enter the survey picture. If the subject of the study is of no particular interest or if the respondent is strongly against the topic, he may refuse to answer some questions, distort his answers, or possibly refuse the entire interview. Even when he is interested in the topic, there is no assurance that unbiased data will be obtained; in fact, the respondent may even embellish his answers.

At the time of the interview, the respondent may or may not be receptive to the session regardless of the topic. He may have just had an argument with his employer or his wife or just returned from work tired and irritable. If he does permit the interview, biased answers may possibly be given.

Bias may also be introduced by the respondent if he does not understand the question or does not know the answer. Regardless of the handling of such questions, biased answers (or no answers) will be the result.

For most surveys, there are usually some questions which the respondent will be sensitive about answering. These questions may also lead to incorrect answers or outright refusals to answer.

Another source of potential bias is the nonrespondents. Noncontacts and refusals can create a lack of representation of all members of the population under study. They may be attributed to several causes: poor sample design, the interviewers' inadequate training, the study's subject matter or poor design, or many others.

Avoiding Bias. Awareness of potential sources of bias certainly aids in planning field operations, and steps can and should be taken to avoid these errors.[4] This section will cover ways of averting bias when the questionnaire is being prepared, when interviewers are being selected and trained, and during the supervision of the interviewers. Bias can also be avoided by planning callbacks for nonrespondents and by scrutinizing the time schedule and budget to ensure that they are really in line with the study design.

To avoid bias related to the questionnaire, the questions should be understandable to the respondent, the respondent should know the answer (an obvious but often overlooked element of questionnaire design), and sensitive questions should either be worded so as not to be offensive to the respondent or perhaps dropped. These points apply regardless of whether the survey is by personal interview, a telephone study, or conducted by mail. In addition, the instructions on the questionnaire to both the respondent and the interviewer should be comprehensive and precise.

Even when thorough care is taken in designing the questionnaire, it is not until the pretest that it can be determined whether the instrument will do what the researcher thinks it will do. Debriefing sessions with the pretest interviewers is a good method of identifying the problems. If the study is being conducted by mail, it sometimes proves useful to recontact some respondents by telephone to discuss what problems they may have had in completing the questionnaire.

Errors related to interviewers can be avoided, or at least reduced, by selecting more competent interviewers and by giving them more complete and thorough training [as covered in Chapter 5 of this part]. Suffice it to say here that if little attention is given to interviewer hiring and training, errors in survey data are certain to result.

Close interviewer supervision is also essential if nonsampling errors are to be avoided. At this point, the field operation depends on the work of the supervisors, which is why those who are highly qualified should be sought and used.

To avoid bias related to nonrespondents, plans should be made early in the field operation, on both noncontact call-back procedures and reassignment of refusals to other interviewers. Ideally, it would be better if each interviewer were sufficiently trained so that her contact rate would be high and her refusal rate low. In practice, however, some interviewers inevitably have high noncontact or refusal rates. Besides a plan for retraining these interviewers, there should be an alternate plan for further contacts with the nonrespondents

[4] Even though bias should be avoided, if it is built into the study design, it may be of value in answering particular survey problems [6].

and for reworking the refusals. Especially competent interviewers should be used for this troubleshooting work.

As stated earlier in this chapter, the importance of a good time schedule and budget cannot be overemphasized. If the time schedule cannot be maintained, errors often result. Similarly, costs that exceed the budget may lead to a reduction of not only quantity but also quality.

Detecting Bias. Even though every effort may have been made to avoid response and nonresponse errors before a study goes into the field, procedures are still needed for detecting errors that occur during data collection. First are the procedures for checking the quality of the completed interviews to see that they maintain standards set at the planning phase. Second are the validation procedures for detecting falsified interviews or parts of interviews. Third is the comparison of the results of each question by each interviewer with the totals for each question for all interviewers. Procedures for detecting such biases are reviewed in the next chapter.

Correcting for Bias. If errors are detected in a survey, there are numerous ways to correct for them. First, if the errors are observed early enough, changes can be made to reduce or eliminate them. Poor interviewers may be either retrained or dropped, new instructions on different ways of handling parts of the interview or questionnaire can be sent to the interviewing service, the supervisors, or directly to the interviewers. A change may be made in the sample design. The interviewers' "introduction" to the respondents may be leading to a high refusal rate. Possibly advance letters or telephone calls to the respondents are needed before the interviewer attempts the interviews.

Rather than change the design or procedures, some follow-up work may be necessary to eliminate the errors. The respondent may be either completely reinterviewed or only partially reinterviewed on the specific questions causing the errors. This reinterview may be included in the verification telephone call, thus eliminating the need for a second personal contact.

Low contact and high refusal rates may be corrected by reassigning them to good troubleshooting interviewers.

Once the study is completed, if some information is known about the respondents, the data obtained about them can be weighted to account for the nonrespondents.

SUMMARY

The field operations of a survey can be conducted efficiently, accurately, and economically if care is taken at all phases of the operation. From preparing for data collection through carrying out the field operation, the researcher should ask where errors may exist and how these errors can be corrected.

REFERENCES

1. Boyd, Harper W., Jr., and Ralph Westfall, "Interviewer Bias Once More Revisited," *Journal of Marketing Research*, vol. 7, May 1970, pp. 249–253.
2. Ferber, Robert, and Hugh Wales, *Marketing Research Bibliography*, Chicago: American Marketing Association, 1964, pp. 6–8, 31–34, 156–158.
3. Hauck, Mathew, "Interviewer Compensation on Consumer Surveys," *Commentary, Journal of the Marketing Research Society*, Summer 1964, pp. 15–18.
4. Mayer, Charles S., "A Computer System for Controlling Interviewer Costs," *Journal of Marketing Research*, vol. 5, August 1968, pp. 312–318.
5. Sudman, Seymour, *Reducing the Costs of Surveys*, Chicago: Aldine, 1968.
6. Tortolani, Roy, "Introducing Bias Intentionally into Survey Techniques," *Journal of Marketing Research*, vol. 2, February 1965, pp. 51–55.

Part B

Surveys

Chapter 8

Quality Control

CHARLES S. MAYER *Faculty of Administrative Studies, York University, Downsview, Ontario, Canada*

The concept of quality control comes to marketing research from the field of production. There, quality control attempts to limit to acceptable levels the number of "failures" or "defects" that may be generated by a process. As applied to marketing research, however, the analogy of defects has great limitations from both a conceptual and a measurement point of view. Thus, the first task in this chapter will be to define the concept of research quality.

The dictionary defines quality as: "Any characteristic which may make an object good or bad, commendable or reprehensible; the degree of excellence which a thing possesses." From this definition it can be surmised that quality in research must have something to do with goodness or excellence. However, this semantic exercise does not resolve the problem, since *goodness* or *excellence* are just as vague as *quality*. To get an idea of what these terms might mean in research, they should be considered in context.

Marketing research is not conducted for its own sake, but rather to help managers make better decisions. The contribution of research to decision making, and hence its goodness or excellence, can be measured in two ways—by its relevancy and by its accuracy. That research should be relevant to the marketing problem seems a truism. Yet the number of unused research reports on corporate shelves testifies that relevancy is not automatically guaranteed. For the present discussion, however, the criterion of relevancy is outside the domain of quality control.

The second measure of research excellence or quality, accuracy, refers to freedom from error. The difference between reliability and accuracy (validity) is an important one. Reliability refers to reproducibility only. If process is reliable, it will respond to the same stimuli in the same way on repeated trials. However, although these reponses may be very similar, that is, may demonstrate little variability, they may all be inaccurate. Quality control generally concerns controlling the variation of a process and hence its reliability when the real issue should be process accuracy.

Kish [11] has defined "accuracy" in operational terms as the inverse of total error. Total error comprises a host of error sources, including both sampling and nonsampling errors. Their identification and control will be the subject of this chapter.

Any one research result has a finite but unknown amount of error associated with it; in other words, it differs from the unknown "true" value by a fixed amount. But, since the magnitude of the error is unknown, the best that can be done is to control the process which generated the result to keep the error within acceptable limits. These limits must be supplied by the user of the research. Given his requirements, quality control attempts to regulate the process in order to deliver, on the average, acceptable results. The significance of the term *on the average* is that the quality control of a process is probabilistic. Any single result may fall outside acceptable limits even though the process is under control. However, the probability of such a happening is known and can be adjusted by control procedures.

Quality as a Relative Concept. A perfectly accurate result is not feasible in marketing research. Accordingly, the goal of quality control is not to eliminate error, but to keep it within acceptable limits. The determination of such limits is made on the basis of costs relative to benefits. Generally, the more stringent the accuracy requirements for a study, the more it will cost. The more sensitive a decision is to the research inputs, the greater the need for accuracy.

Determining the required level of accuracy is one of the unresolved problems in marketing research. Under the classical statistical approach, required accuracy emerges from a rule of thumb with little empirical justification, such as the 95 or 99 percent level of confidence. Under the Bayesian approach [Sec. II, Part A, Chap. 3], value of information emerges after some rather heroic assumptions about the availability of a payoff matrix and expressed prior probabilities. The practitioner is left with few practical tools for objectively determining the required level of accuracy. The problem is further complicated by the numerous sources of error that may affect accuracy. Quality control attempts to operate on each source separately, whereas the user's concern is with total accuracy. The comments in this section will do little to alleviate this problem. Rather, the concern will be with how, once a required level of accuracy or quality is specified, the researcher can formulate procedures and controls for its delivery.

Identification of Error Sources. Both sampling and nonsampling errors contribute to total error. Sampling errors refer to errors associated with sample selection. These include frame error, selection error, and random-sampling error. Nonsampling errors include nonresponse error, response error, "instrument" error, data-reduction error, and data processing error. Each of these will reduce survey quality, and their control will be the topic of various sections in this chapter.

A survey sample is drawn from a sampling frame. If this frame does not include all elements of the defined population or if it includes some elements more than once, a frame error will occur. Any estimates made on the basis of a sample drawn from a nonrepresentative frame will be nonrepresentative.

The way a sample is selected from the frame may also affect total error. If each element in the frame has a known and non-zero probability of selection, then selection is a probability process and has no selection error. If, however, elements in the frame can be selected on an uncontrolled, non-probabilistic basis, there will be a selection error.

Any estimate based on a sample will also exhibit the well-known random-sampling error. Since the nature and control of sampling errors are discussed later in greater detail [Sec. II, Part C, Chap. 2], they are merely identified here as contributors to total error.

Nonresponse error occurs if certain members of the selected sample do not provide information either because they cannot be contacted or because they refuse to give information. Response error occurs if the respondent gives the wrong response to a question. The concept of wrongness implies certain criteria. A response would be classified as "wrong" if it did not correspond to the facts of the situation. Wrongness has nothing to do with the researcher's preference for a particular response. Respondents may give the wrong answer because they do not wish to reveal the truth, because of communication problems, or because they cannot remember the facts but feel obliged to respond. An incomplete answer may also be considered wrong, although what is reported is accurate, if it does not contain sufficient detail to be operationally useful.

Instrument errors refer to those introduced by the measuring instrument in the survey process. For personal or telephone interviews, the measuring instrument is the questionnaire as administered by the interviewer. For self-administered questionnaires, the instrument is the questionnaire itself. Instrument errors occur if the measurement is made on other than the desired respondent, if the manner in which the measurement is made influences the response, or if the response is not recorded accurately or in sufficient detail.

After the data have been collected, they are subjected to data reduction (editing and coding) and are processed to give the required tabulations. Errors can be introduced in both the reduction and the processing stage.

This list of potential error sources identifies marketing research as a very fragile, error-prone process. Moreover, the errors are often cumulative. For example, an undetected error introduced in either the interviewing or the coding stage will pass through all the subsequent stages.

Though some errors may be offsetting in the aggregate, their impact on accuracy may still be important. For example, if keypunching errors are assumed to be random, their effect on the aggregate may not be great. However, if detailed cross-classifications are attempted, even such random errors may significantly affect accuracy; and accuracy is the measure of quality adopted in this chapter.

Design and Implementation. Quality can be imparted to a study through both design and implementation. For example, the design of the sampling plan for a survey will have definite quality implications. The way that interviewers implement the sampling plan will have similar implications.

From the user's point of view, there is no difference between quality due to design and that due to implementation; from the researcher's viewpoint, however, there are significant differences. Increases in quality through design are usually accompanied by increases in cost. Accordingly, the level of quality imparted through design must be justified on a cost-benefit basis which, as has already been stated, is very difficult.

The cost of control to ensure implementation, on the other hand, does not vary greatly with the design. Such control may take two forms. First, it may be a screening operation which attempts to eliminate the "defective" items (for example, fabricated interviews) from the legitimate interviews after their completion.   Second, it may take the form of preventive measures at potential problem points—for example, training interviewers to ask certain questions that conform to the original design.   Screening and eliminating faulty items are obviously costly and can create havoc with survey schedules.   Prevention, on the other hand, not only reduces the need for screening, but also eliminates potential problems.

Quality through design and through implementation also differs in time dimensions.   Since design characteristics relate to a whole study or sometimes to a mode of operation, changes are made only occasionally.   For example, the number of required call-backs, a design specification, might be prescribed at the start of each survey.   It is unlikely, however, that keypunch-verification procedures would be changed even that frequently.   Control of implementation, on the other hand, must be continuous if it is to be effective.

Although quality introduced through design is at least as important as quality through implementation, the term *quality control* usually refers only to implementation.   The reason is that there are no universally accepted design standards in research.   For example, the choice between open- and closed-end questions seems largely a matter of opinion or style.   The choice among postcard, telephone, or in-person validation is open to debate; and whether questionnaires are better coded entirely by one coder or in sections by specialists is a moot question.   In the absence of standards, quality through design also lacks objective measurement.   The only approach open to evaluate such quality is to rely on rather subjective checklists, such as suggested by Mayer [13].

Note that measurement difficulties have nothing to do with relative importance.   Quality imparted by design should not be underestimated.   No amount of control in implementation can remove design faults.   However, in the absence of unequivocal criteria that identify errors of design, quality control techniques cannot be applied.

Quality through implementation, on the other hand, is far more amenable to measurement, and hence to control.   For example, how well the keypunching operation was performed can be measured through the punching-error rate; whether an interview was conducted through validation; and coding accuracy through verification.   Since there can be no control without measurement, and since only the quality of implementation lends itself to measurement, quality control in marketing research refers to implementation only.

STATISTICAL QUALITY CONTROL

Statistical quality control can be applied at several stages of the marketing research process.   For example, the work of interviewers, coders, and keypunchers can be controlled through statistical inspection.

The basic tenet of statistical quality control is that any process exhibits some variation because of a complex of causes not readily identifiable.   Such variation is known as the "normal" or "random" variation of the process.   A process may also exhibit relatively large variation that can be identified with separate unique causes, such as differences among interviewers, coders, or keypunchers.   Statistical quality control operates through a set of control limits defined in a manner such that random variations are ignored but larger variations due to unique causes are detected.   These control limits should attempt to balance the cost of inspection and removal of errors against the potential costs that could be incurred if the system were out of control (produced defective work), and the trouble remained undetected.

The reason why such quality control is termed *statistical* is that decisions on the quality of the process are based on samples taken from that process. In marketing research, judgments about the work of interviewers, editors, coders, and keypunchers are made on the basis of samples of their work.

Acceptance Sampling. The quality of work performed by an interviewer, say, is determined through acceptance sampling. The work is accepted or rejected on the basis of inspecting (validating) a sample from it. If the sample fails to meet standards, all of that interviewer's work is rejected and either discarded or redone.

Since such screening is based on samples, two types of errors can be committed. First, work that is deemed of acceptable quality level (AQL) may be rejected on the basis of a sample. Rejecting acceptable work is known as a Type I error, and the risk of making such an error as an α-risk. Conversely, work that is below standards, that is, has a higher percentage of defectives than tolerable (lot tolerance percent defective, or LTPD), may be accepted on the basis of a sample. Accepting work that is below acceptable standards is known as Type II error, and the risk of doing so as a β-risk. Both Type I and Type II errors can be controlled through statistical design. Given an AQL, α, LTPD, and β, the statistician's role is to design a quality control system that will satisfy these at the least cost. Specifying these parameters is the role of the users of the research.

The α- and β-risks are not independent of each other. A system that, for a given sample size, has a low α-risk will have a relatively high β-risk. The α- and β-risks requirements are met through sample-size adjustments, which have obvious cost implications.

In marketing research, quality control systems tend to be biased toward Type I errors for several reasons. First, since the cost of a Type II error is implicit, it seems more expensive to err in the Type I direction than in the Type II direction. Second, often the supplier of research information and the user have an agent-client relationship. The costs of α-risks are borne by the supplier, and those of β-risks, by the user. For this reason, α- and β-risks are also known as *producer's risks* and *consumer's risks*. As long as users do not insist on the reduction of β-risks, or are unwilling to pay for the reduction, research suppliers will naturally attempt to reduce α-risks.

Third, in some instances, it is difficult to prove that an aspect of research is indeed faulty and, hence, that a Type II error has in fact occurred. If a subsequent field validation yields discrepancies from the original interview, it could be that the facts have changed, that the respondent altered his answer, that the validation is incorrect, or that the original interview is incorrect. Isolating the true condition can be costly and at times impossible.

Control Charts. If the statistical control system is implemented by people without a high degree of statistical sophistication, a vehicle known as a *control chart* may be useful. Its essential features are a process average and upper and lower control limits.

There are two ways that these limits may be established. First, by observing a system's output, say the work of a group of coders, the "normal" variation and process average can be determined. Then, using probability theory and establishing the desired risks in screening, the appropriate control limits can be established. As an alternative, management might decide, on the basis of the rest of the information-generating process, what an acceptable average outgoing quality level (AOQL) would be, and adjust the system so that it would deliver this level.

Such adjustments can take two forms. First, the inherent variation of the process can be reduced. Among coders, for example, additional training, better codebooks, or an improved working environment may reduce coder-induced variation. The inherent variation can also be reduced by 100 percent *inspection* and *correction* of work judged, on the basis of samples, to be outside control limits. In this way, the average outgoing quality level, that is, the highest number of defects that will, on the average, be found after inspection, can be controlled.

Although control charts can control for averages of variables, ranges of measurements, or number of defects, attribute charts, such as percent-defective or error-fraction charts, are most useful for marketing research. For the development of such charts, the reader is referred to Carson [3]. An example should suffice here.

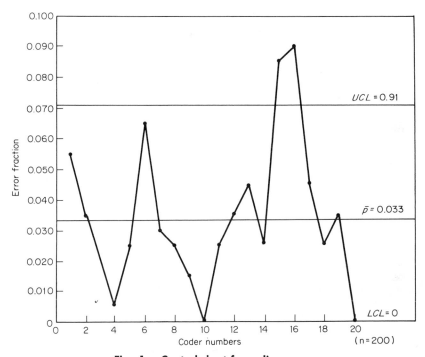

Fig. 1.   Control chart for coding errors.

Suppose that a sample of 200 questionnaires is taken from each of 20 coders. From the data for all coders, the mean and the variance of the error-fraction can be determined. These would be used to establish the control limits for an attribute chart, as shown in Figure 1.

Coders 15 and 16 would appear to need additional training or replacement, according to the figure. Note, however, that a control chart, like any other analytic technique operating on historical data, can identify deviations from the norm but cannot unequivocally determine their cause.

Note also that the information contained in Figure 1 could also be given as a rule of thumb. In this instance, ". . . if the error-fraction in the work of any coder on a sample of 200 questionnaires exceeds .071, 100 percent inspection of his work plus retraining or release are indicated." Such blanket rules, however, do not provide information so clearly and desirably as control charts do.   Moreover, control charts present permanent visual records from which trends, or other patterns, can be observed.   For these reasons, control charts are preferable to rules of thumb.

Sequential Sampling.   With single samples, a substantial sample size is required before the error-fraction can be estimated with any degree of certainty. An alternative to large, single samples is repeated, sequential, smaller samples. Sequential samples are less expensive and quite practicable in most research situations.   With sequential sampling, a small sample is drawn initially, and on its basis, a decision is made whether to accept or reject the work or to continue sampling.   Additional samples are drawn until an accept or reject decision can be made.

An example of a sequential sampling plan is given graphically in Figure 2.

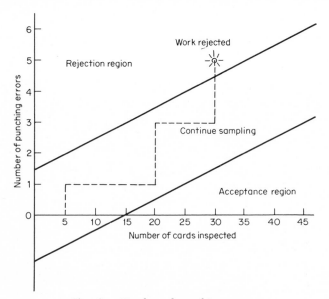

Fig. 2.   Number of punching errors.

In the plan shown, a minimum sample of 15 cards must be inspected in order to judge the work.   If no errors are found, the work is accepted.   If the errors at any time rise to a number on or above the rejection line, the work is rejected; if their number falls on or below the acceptance line, the work is accepted.   Until one of these events occurs, sampling is continued.

Sequential sampling plans are most efficient if additional samples can be drawn without great cost.   Since such is the case with most quality control operations in marketing research, sequential plans are in common use.   As with single-sampling plans, an AQL, α, LTPD, and β are required to set up a sequential sampling plan.   For detailed procedures on setting up a sequential plan, the reader is referred to Duncan [5].

The Need for Feedback.   An essential phase of any quality control system is feedback.   Only through feedback can future errors be prevented, through either eliminating or adjusting error-producing elements in the process.   For example, if some interviewers are not following their routing maps in an area probability sample according to instructions, either the instructions must be improved or the interviewers must be trained further in sampling procedures. With appropriate feedback, preventive measures for future errors can be taken. Without it, quality can be maintained only through continuous elimination of faulty work. Obviously, the latter is more expensive.

Feedback is not only for those who implement a design, but also for those responsible for specifying it. For example, if a large number of interviewers are not asking a specific question as worded because they feel the respondent might be offended, all interviewers should be apprised of this, as should the questionnaire designer. It is assumed that in future questionnaires, the designer will want to avoid questions considered embarrassing by the interviewers.

The time dimension associated with feedback is almost as important as the feedback itself. If interviewers, for example, are not asking a question correctly, the sooner they are informed of this the better. Accordingly, the efficacy of a feedback system must be evaluated both by its ability to detect errors and the speed with which it can initiate corrective action.

FIELD OPERATIONS

Quality control is most crucial and also most difficult with field operations. Even if the problem of quality of design is set aside, controling quality of implementation presents grave difficulties. This is because of the nature of the interviewing job and the many potential ways an interviewer can introduce errors into a survey. For the purpose of this chapter, only quality control of personal interviews will be considered. The justification for this is that personal interviews present the greatest leeway for deviation, that the interviewer effects are most pronounced in personal interviewing, and that the greatest number of surveys rely on personal interviews.

Interview Effects. An examination of the interviewing process quickly reveals why quality control is absolutely essential. The interviewer works alone, for relatively low pay and usually under time pressure. He operates with little direct supervision and often inadequate training, collecting information whose use he may not appreciate. It is not surprising that interviewers are tempted to cut corners; and such corner-cutting will by necessity erode survey quality.

The most common way that interviewers can affect survey quality is through the outright fabrication of interviews. In practice, interviewers contaminate research quality in many other, more subtle ways [Chapters 5 and 7 of this section]. For example, survey quality will be affected if the interviewer does not implement the sampling plan exactly as instructed, thereby selecting the wrong respondent. Nonresponse, either through noncontact or refusal, can also be affected by interviewers; and interviewers can sway responses through the way they motivate, interact with, influence, and question the respondent. Furthermore, they can be selective in what they hear and record on the questionnaire. Changes in the survey vehicle, through the omission of some questions or alteration in the order or wording of questions, also erode quality.

The mere listing of all these potential error sources indicates that verifying that an interview was really conducted falls very short of anything that might be considered quality control. Yet, this is all that is normally done.

Validation. Validation in this context refers to a second contact with a sample of respondents during which the fact that an interview was conducted is established. Usually, some of the questions asked on the original questionnaire are asked again to check on the consistency of response.

Validation may be done by postcard, telephone, or in person; by a supervisor, the home office, the client, or an independent third party. The method of validation will naturally affect the amount of control that can be achieved. For example, sending postcards to 10 percent of the sample on relatively small surveys is unlikely to detect anything but the grossest amount of cheating. Personal validation by a supervisor (provided she is actually trying to detect errors) is probably the most effective way. Telephone validation falls somewhere in between.

The effectiveness of the validating technique is roughly proportional to its cost. Therefore, technique selection must be justified on a cost-benefit basis; and, as has been suggested, this is very difficult.

Was the Interview Conducted? Determinating whether the interview was conducted is clearly an easier task than reconstructing the procedures used and checking the consistency of responses. Partially for this reason, then, interviewer-performance checking has concentrated on the validation of contact. However, confirming contact cannot be equated to quality. Validation of content, besides being more difficult, is also less actionable. For example, the same question(s) asked during the interview and subsequent validation may elicit different answers because of differences in skill between the interviewer and the validator, true changes in the respondent's perceptions occasioned by elapsed time between the initial interview and the validation, or different responses prompted by the sequence of questions in the interview and the validation (seldom is a whole questionnaire repeated during validation).

The nature and method of validation used depend greatly on the researcher's model of the interviewer. If the interviewer's honesty is in question, then validation to determine whether the interview was conducted is appropriate. However, as Crespi [4] stated,

> . . . this prevailing moral interpretation (of the need for validation) is shortsighted in that it engenders a narrow moralistic approach to difficulties which are fundamentally technical and only incidentally moral. What is termed 'cheating' is most constructively regarded as . . . a problem of interviewers' morale and the factors that make or break that morale.

For example, if interviewers feel that certain questions may offend the respondent, they are not likely to ask such questions. It is not through any moral shortcomings of the interviewers that this occurs. Rather, the questionnaire designer has created conditions that reduced interviewer morale.

Under the morale approach, more emphasis is placed on preventing demoralization, thereby reducing the need for massive inspection through validation. And, as suggested earlier, prevention of defects is both less costly and more easily scheduled than inspection and removal of them after the fact.

Nevertheless, even under the morale approach, careful and thorough validation is absolutely essential for recognizing when a field force is demoralized and taking corrective action. If handled properly, validation can have a morale-building effect on the field force. It signals to them that their work is sufficiently important for the researcher to take the necessary steps to ensure that the work is correct. Such steps should include feedback to the interviewers on how they can improve their techniques on future studies.

Statistical Analyses of Interviewer Performance. As well as physically validating interviewer performance in the field, statistical tests on the consistency of interviewer reporting can detect quality-eroding deviation. Namais [16] describes the use of the Mosteller-Tukey binominal probability paper for detecting interviewer deviations by graphical means. Benson [1] discusses two statistical techniques for isolating interviewer-related variations. Using only a calculator, a paired-comparison matrix of performance differences can be obtained, which helps to identify deviant interviewers. If the available data base is large, the same technique can also be implemented on the computer. Using the computer, Benson [i] suggests an alternative technique to paired-comparisons, a multiple-regression procedure for calculating the variance in interviewer performance.

As is true for all statistical analyses on historical data, interviewer-performance analyses cannot detect the cause for interviewer variation. They can merely identify potential problems for more thorough subsequent field checks.

Quality Rating of Interviewers.   Validation is essentially redoing some of the interviews.   Statistical analysis attempts to establish norms among interviewers and identify deviations.   In addition, the quality of fieldwork can be rated on a set of predetermined criteria.   Such quality ratings rely on some sort of checklist, either implicit or explicit, which strives to identify and weight various quality-producing features in interviews.

For a telephone interview, for example, Eastlack and Assael [7] used the following criteria of interviewer performance:

Number of refusals
Number of call-backs which failed to locate the respondent
Number of interviews partially complete
Number of completed interviews
Average interviews per hour
Number of times per week questionnaires must be returned for editing
Subjective interviewer ratings by the supervisor

A quality control report based on these factors was produced. Initially, it showed high variability among interviewers, a productivity of 1.10 to 1.25 interviews per hour, and refusal rates varying between 25 and 35 percent. As control procedures began to weed out several interviewers, variability among interviewers and variability over time for given interviewers began to decrease, refusals dropped to an average of 20 percent, and the average productivity rose to 1.80 interviews per hour. These are clear improvements in quality *on the criteria selected for control.*

In personal interviews, quality ratings are most often made by supervisors. Ratings tend to be subjective and are frequently based on the supervisor's intuition.   However, supervisors can be assigned specific criteria on which to base quality ratings.   For example, adherence to sampling plan, completeness of the questionnaire (if it is available to the supervisor), refusal rates, productivity, and promptness of completion, as well as the discrepancies found during validation, might form part of the list.   The problem, however, is to get different supervisors to rate interviewers on the same criteria in the same way.

On such criteria as promptness in returning work, productivity, and refusal rates, quality can also be controlled effectively by well-organized checking-in procedures in the field office.

Editors or coders may also be asked to give a quality rating for interviewers. Again, such ratings often suffer from subjectivity and lack of explicitness of the rating criteria.   Sudman [22] reports two attempts to make these quality ratings more objective.   The Bureau of the Census assigns a specific code for missing answers.   Study results then include a special tabulation to show the number of missing answers per interviewer. Dividing by the number of interviews gives a ratio of missing answers per interview. Although this ratio measures only one aspect of interviewer error, it does so clearly and at very little additional cost.

The National Opinion Research Center uses a more detailed method. Coders are supplied with error sheets on which they note the following types of interviewer error:

Type of error	Error weight
1. Answer missing	3
2. Irrelevant or circular answer	3
3. Lack of sufficient detail	2
4. "Don't know," with no probe	2
5. Dangling probe	1
6. Multiple codes in error	1
7. Superfluous question asked	1

Though this list does not exhaust all interviewing errors, it does include all errors that a coder could spot. Although the evidence is inconclusive, Sudman [22] reports high correlation between coder quality ratings and more thorough quality ratings by trained field supervisors.

Quality ratings have traditionally suffered from subjectivity introduced by the rater. Such subjectivity can be lessened by explaining the criteria over which control will be exercised and assigning relative weights to each. Obviously, not all quality-producing factors can be spelled out as criteria. Nevertheless, quality ratings, when performed and reported back to the interviewer, have been effective in increasing the quality of interviews, at least on the criteria explained for control.

An interviewer's quality rating on any one study may be thought of as a single sample of all his potential work. As quality ratings are performed for interviewers over several studies, it is essential to record the results of these ratings on one control form, thereby increasing the sample size and permitting the observation of trends. Though such cumulation is complicated by the variation of difficulty among studies and by differences among raters, these problems can be overcome. In a sense, each new quality rating may be viewed as an additional input in a sequential sampling plan. Without the sequence, the results of a single quality rating are likely to be inconclusive.

Error Detection by Editors.   Editing is a process designed to detect and eliminate error through the inspection, correction, and modification of information submitted on questionnaires. It is the interface between field operations and data reduction. As such, it can provide feedback to the field as well as simplify subsequent coding.

One type of error a trained editor can detect is fabrication of information. Fictitious interviews can be detected through apparent inconsistencies within a questionnaire, consistencies in responses obtained by one interviewer, or responses at variance with known facts.

Apart from detecting dishonest work, editing attempts to detect and correct information obtained or recorded in error. Though editors may correct minor typographic errors, major problems should be returned to the interviewer. The frequency of such questionnaire returns to the field is a measure in itself of field quality.

Although editing is performed primarily to prepare information on the questionnaires for subsequent coding, it can play a significant role in improving and controlling field quality. Organizing work so that individual interviewers can be identified and providing adequate feedback are the only requirements for bringing this control into operation.

MATERIALS HANDLING

The quality of a survey can be affected not only by errors introduced in interviewing, data reduction, and data processing, but also by inadequate controls on materials handling. For example, the quality imparted through sample design may be compromised if part of the work is lost during coding or if some data are punched twice.

Quality control of the work flow starts when materials are sent to interviewers, carries through a checking-in procedure when the work is returned, and ensures, through control forms and check-totals, that the same number of documents leave a particular stage as came into it (or that differences are accounted for).

There is nothing very sophisticated about materials-handling controls. Without them, however, especially in larger studies for which the work may be scheduled in batches to permit overlapping of the various functions of coding, keypunching, and machine cleaning, serious omissions or duplications might occur.

DATA REDUCTION

Once the data have been collected, they go through a process termed *data reduction*, in which the data on individual questionnaires are prepared for mechanical processing. Two distinct steps can be identified in this process: editing and coding.

Editing. Editing has already been identified as the process whereby materials are prepared for subsequent coding. It is not always performed as a separate step from coding, but can still be thought of as a separate function. If correct data are changed in the editing process, quality will suffer.

Since editing is a highly subjective process, the training and qualifications of the editors, plus the instructions they receive, are the only controls on quality. Since coding follows editing, most editing errors are detected during coding. For this reason, editing is not usually verified. To identify editing errors, coders should be able to distinguish the work of editors from that of interviewers. It is standard practice for editors not to erase anything on the original document. Rather, they make changes by crossing out or transferring data, using a distinctly colored pencil.

Nordbotten [17] reports an experiment in which a sample of questionnaires was edited thoroughly, while the rest received only superficial editing. His conclusion was that the increase in accuracy gained from a thorough and expensive edit is small.

Therefore, it might be argued that editing is performed more to facilitate subsequent coding than as a means of quality control. An important role of editing, however, is providing feedback to the field. The quality implications of such feedback have already been discussed.

Coding. Information can be changed and certainly will be lost during coding. Coding is the process whereby responses on the questionnaire are assigned to specific categories, and symbols (usually numbers) are assigned to identify them with the categories. Information is lost in the sense that each response, especially to open-ended questions, is unique. In the assignment process, this uniqueness disappears.

Quality of information can be affected in coding in two ways: through selection of the codes used, and through coding errors. Various techniques for building codes are discussed in the following chapter. It should suffice to say here that codes should not be too general, and that the items falling in the "All other" category should be minimized.

Coding Errors. A coding error occurs if two independently assigned codes are in disagreement. There may be two sources for such disagreement—the code and the coders. If the code categories are poorly defined, overlapping, ambiguous, or not mutually exhaustive, coders may disagree because there is no clear, correct category for some of the responses. On the other hand, because of differences in training, personality, or care exercised, one coder may assign a response to one category while a second coder may assign it to another.

Working on the assumption that errors in a code seem to produce random disagreements, whereas coder errors produce systematic disagreements, Funkhouser and Parker [10] suggest a control technique that not only detects disagreements but assigns the cause of such disagreements either to the code or the coders.

The error rate of coders can be affected by such factors as training, format of the codebooks, environment (for example, lighting, noise level), supervision, coding procedures, and caliber of the coders. All these factors will have an effect on the reliability of the coding process. For example, Woodward and Franzen [24] report a study in which coding reliability was markedly improved through coder training and instruction.

The average outgoing quality level of coding can also be controlled through acceptance sampling. A sample of each coder's work is verified, that is, recoded, on a continuous basis, and if the error rate in a coder's work is higher than acceptable (higher than the lot tolerance percent defective, or LTPD), all of that coder's work is redone. The coder is either retrained or released. Since additional samples of each coder's work are drawn through time, the appropriate design is a sequential sampling plan.

Two requirements of an effective control system are early detection of error and rapid feedback for correcting future potential errors. Early detection in coding is achieved through initially taking larger samples of each coder's work, so that coding errors through misunderstanding can be rapidly discovered. But, unlike sequential sampling, the decision is never made to accept all future work of a coder. Coding must be checked continuously. An efficient plan, however, will select samples of coders' work on a basis that reflects their error rate *on this study.*

To deliver useful feedback to coders, the work of each coder must be identifiable. This is usually done through a batch-control form showing who coded and verified each batch of questionnaires.

Quality control charts can also be kept on each coder through time. Although such charts will suffer from aggregation problems if studies of different complexity levels are mixed, these problems can be avoided through relatively simple standardizing procedures. The process to be kept "in control" is the coders, and control charts over time will signal developing trends. Without the charts, unfavorable trends will be treated as random variation for a far longer period.

DATA PROCESSING

After the coding has been completed, the next stages in research are converting the codes into machine-readable form, machine "cleaning" or editing, and tabulation of results.

It is not uncommon in marketing research to find some of these functions performed by an outside specialist, such as a tabulation house or computer service center. Such specialists usually maintain their own quality control systems. Nevertheless, a researcher would be lax in merely accepting data that have been processed outside as "in control." Either first-hand experience with the supplier's quality control system *on this study* or independent quality control checks seem to be a prerequisite for accepting work performed by an outside agent.

Quality control in data processing is similar to that in manufacturing operations; entities such as raw materials, machines, and operators can be identified. Raw materials in this case are the work coming from data reduction, or keypunching; the machines are keypunches, computers, or other mechanical devices, such as counter-sorters; and operators are required to run them. Errors can be introduced by each of these sources separately, or through the interaction of any of them. For example, a particular operator may be more likely to make errors on one type of device than another. To have effective quality control, both the presence and the cause of defective work must be established.

Conversion into Machine-readable Form. After the data have been coded, they must be converted into machine-readable form. A wide variety of equipment is used both for the conversion and for later processing. The processing machine will dictate how the data are converted.

Errors can be introduced by the data's format prior to conversion, by the machine itself, and by the operators. Machine-caused errors occur if the character produced by the machine differs from the key activated by the operator. Since the most commonly used equipment for conversion into machine-readable form is key-activated unit-record cardpunches (keypunches), they will receive the major attention here. It is also possible, however, to make the conversion on keypunched paper tape, key-driven magnetic-tape recorders, mark-sensed cards or paper, or via optical scanning devices.

The machine-error rate is a function of the equipment used, its age, and its condition. Some machines have built-in machine-error checking devices, such as parity-checking. This involves adding an extra "bit" of information to each keyed character, so that it is composed of an even or odd number of bits. If a machine malfunction results in having created an improper number of bits, this will be detected automatically, and the operator so warned. Though internal checking devices can detect machine errors, most keypunches do not have such features. Their accuracy, however, is excellent, provided they are maintained properly. Preventive maintenance, combined with frequent testing, will minimize machine errors. Residual errors can be detected during verification.

An automatic checking device for both punching and machine accuracy can be used if the absolute accuracy of a piece of information, such as the identification code, is of paramount importance. A self-checking digit can be tagged to the end of the identification code, based on an arithmetic manipulation of all other digits in this code. Prior to data processing, a derived digit is compared to the self-checking digit to ascertain punching accuracy.

Usually, keypunching error detection is performed on a complementary piece of equipment known as a verifier. It has the same physical appearance as the keypunch, but instead of punching a unit-record, it senses whether the keyed character is the same as the record punched into the card it is reading. The information from the source-document is keyed into the verifier, and discrepancies between the already-punched cards and the keyed information are identified for later correction.

An alternative to using a verifier is to punch a second set of cards from the source-documents, and to compare it to the initial set either mechanically or visually.

Verification, using either a verifier or some alternative method, results in detecting all disagreements between the initial entries and the reentries for checking purposes. As such, verification will confound errors caused by machine, source-document, and operator.

Machine-caused errors are generally very low. Errors caused by source-documents are difficult to separate from operator errors, since there is a high degree of interaction between the two. Certainly the layout and legibility of the source-document will affect the operator-error rate. However, the format and layout of the source-document, prepared by coders, will also have an effect on the coder-error rate. Since these error rates generally move in opposite directions, the source-document is at best a compromise, which reflects coding- and punching-error rates as well as costs.

Verification will generate an important index for quality control, the fraction of disagreements between independently keyed entries. Since such disagreements can be interpreted as defects, the application of statistical quality control is most appropriate. In particular, acceptance sampling and control charts seem germane.

It is not uncommon to find 100 percent verification of punched documents in marketing research. Since the cost of setting up and implementing a sampling plan may be higher than the marginal cost of 100 percent verification, such a procedure may be justified for smaller surveys. For larger surveys, however, involving several thousand documents, acceptance sampling is appropriate.

As with all acceptance sampling plans, an AQL, α, LTPD, and β are necessary to construct the specifications of a plan. Provided that 100 percent error correction occurs, a desired AQL can be maintained.

Quality is imparted to the conversion process through operator caliber, training, and experience, the working environment, clarity of the source-document, and the equipment used. AQL can be controlled through acceptance sampling. It is strictly an economic decision as to how much quality is built into the conversion process through such preventive measures as training or equipment maintenance, and how much through screening out defective entries. Defective items must not only be detected, but also corrected through reference to the original source-document. Consequently, the source-documents must be available and filed in such a way as to permit easy access.

Error detection and correction are an important phase of quality control. The identification and feedback to the error-producing elements are also important, so that future errors can be prevented. To fulfill this function, the work of individual keypunchers must be fully traceable. Also, since the keypunchers are the "processes" to be kept under control, control charts of error-fractions by keypunchers should be maintained over time.

Machine Cleaning or Editing of Data. By the time data are presented for computer analysis, they must be perfectly clean, that is, they must show no entries which the computer is not programmed to handle. Logical inconsistencies must also be removed.

Any such irregularities that have passed through coding and keypunching can be removed mechanically and sometimes automatically. The type of equipment used will have a significant effect on the extensiveness of the cleaning. If data processing is to be performed on unit-record equipment, such as collators, sorters, printers, and summary punches, only the most rudimentary cleaning can be done. This equipment can detect illegal or multiple punches and sequencing errors, and can do simple logical-consistency checks. To perform a more complex edit, a reasonably large computer is normally needed, since editing programs usually require a considerable amount of core storage and magnetic tape and/or some direct-access device.

From a quality control point of view, two aspects of machine cleaning are important: how extensive the cleaning is, and how detected errors are corrected. To specify the requirements of an editing program, the researcher must supply the systems analyst with such details as the editing criteria, procedures to be followed on detection of an error, and control totals. Using this information, an editing program is written and tested. Testing the program with dummy data contrived by the programmer can be very unsatisfactory, for many potential errors may be missed.

What happens to detected errors is of major importance to subsequent quality. If errors are printed out to be corrected manually through reference to source-documents, there is no great danger of quality deterioration, since corections are made only when legitimate. In fact, such a procedure can also provide insights into the effectiveness of quality control at the prior stages of coding and data preparation. However, manual correction of errors is both costly and time-consuming. For this reason, procedures are available not only for the automatic detection of errors but also for their automatic correction.

Automatic correction is a very dangerous process. First, it must be recognized that errors are not really "corrected," but rather, inconsistent or missing data are replaced by data, usually inferred from the rest of the data, which will satisfy the editing criteria. For example, if the data show that a family has only one car, but if the year, make, and model of two cars are given, the number of cars could automatically be changed to two. Automatic correction might also take the format of placing all illegal punches into the "No answer" category.

The only justification for automatic error correction is when the error rate is so low that the costs of manual correction are not warranted. Whether this is the case can be determined by designing the cleaning program in such a way that the unmodified data and a tally of all corrections are kept. Without such a tally, the user has no way of knowing how many corrections were made and, hence, the quality of the results.

Tabulations. After the data have passed through machine cleaning, they are ready for tabulation. How they are tabulated, and to what analyses they are subjected, are critical to research relevancy. However, as discussed in this chapter's introduction, relevancy is outside the domain of quality control. The only concern here will be whether the tables really say what they appear to say; that is, do they accurately portray the data from which they were prepared? The equipment on which the tabulations were made will have a significant effect on error potentials. For example, tables prepared on counter sorters are subject to operator errors both in recording the counts and in identifying the variables appropriately. Computer-produced tables, although not affected by the small foibles of human operators, are susceptible to substantial and continuous errors through programming flaws, the most common one being the wrong mating of identifiers and data.

The quality of computer-produced results hinges largely on the quality control procedures used in the computer department. Proper identification of programs, tapes, and disks will prevent many potential errors. Programming procedures which require control totals will further reduce errors.

Quality control of tabulations operates through inspection. First, tables can be inspected for face validity by an "expert," usually the project director. If the expert is knowledgeable about the information contained in the tables, he can detect gross errors immediately. An alternative to expertise is the availability of historical data from other sources against which some of the tables can be checked. Finally, and most specifically, the information generated in the tables can be compared to check-totals or marginal counts obtained during keypunching or machine cleaning. If there are only a few tables, such comparisons can be done manually; for more massive tabulations, the same equipment that produced the tables can also compare the actual and the expected totals.

A BALANCED QUALITY CONTROL SYSTEM

This chapter has shown how quality control can be applied to interviewers, editors, coders, keypunchers, and data processing. For each of these, quality control was applied to implementation only, even though the quality that can be imparted to a study through design is at least as important as the quality of implementation.

There is a great temptation in research to exercise very stringent quality controls on some processes simply because measurement is relatively inexpensive and simple. The common practice of 100 percent verification of keypunching is an example. Other aspects, such as field control, receive far less attention.

Quality control should be concerned with reducing total error in the research process. This goal is complicated by several factors. First, the costs of control, as well as the potential errors introduced at each stage, are different. Second, the measurement of the contribution of quality control at each stage is difficult. Third, the same result can be achieved through different control procedures. For example, coder errors can be detected either through verification or through machine cleaning.

Nevertheless, if rational decisions are to be made on how much to spend on quality control relative to other quality-producing features, such as design, and if allocation decisions for quality control dollars must be made at various research stages, the costs and benefits of quality control at each stage must be known. When the research process is viewed as a single result-producing system, the greatest value can be obtained when costs and benefits are balanced throughout the system.

REFERENCES

1. Benson, Purnell H., "A Paired Comparison Approach to Evaluating Interviewer Performance," *Journal of Marketing Research*, vol. 6, February 1969, pp. 66–70.
2. Brandon, Dick H., *Management Standards for Data Processing*, Princeton, N.J.: Van Nostrand, 1963.
3. Carson, Gordon B., *Production Handbook*, New York: Ronald, 1959, chap. 8.
4. Crespi, Leo, "The Cheater Problem in Polling," *Public Opinion Quarterly*, Winter 1945–1946, pp. 431–445.

5. Duncan, A. J., *Quality Control and Industrial Statistics*, Homewood, Ill.: Irwin, 1955.

6. Dutka, Solomon, "The Application of Statistical Quality Control to the Field Work of Audits and Surveys," *Marketing's Role in Scientific Management*, Chicago: American Marketing Association, 1957, pp. 483–491.

7. Eastlack, J. O., and H. Assael, "Better Telephone Surveys through Centralized Interviewing," *Journal of Advertising Research*, vol. 9, March 1966, pp. 2–7.

8. Feldman, J., H. Hyman, and C. Hart, "A Field Study of Interviewer Effect on the Quality of Survey Data," *Public Opinion Quarterly*, vol. 15, Winter 1951–1952, pp. 743–761.

9. Freund, R. J., and H. O. Hartley, "A Procedure for Automatic Data Editing," *Journal of the American Statistical Association*, vol. 62, June 1967, pp. 341–352.

10. Funkhouser, G., and E. B. Parker, "Analyzing Coding Reliability: The Random-Systematic Error Coefficient," *Public Opinion Quarterly*, vol. 32, Spring 1968, pp. 122–128.

11. Kish, Leslie, *Survey Sampling*, New York: Wiley, 1965.

12. Manfield, M. N., "The Status of Validation in Survey Research," in L. Bogart (ed.), *Current Controversies in Marketing Research*, Chicago: Markham Publishing Co., 1969, pp. 61–85.

13. Mayer, C. S., "Evaluating the Quality of Marketing Research Contractors," *Journal of Marketing Research*, vol. 4, May 1967, pp. 134–141.

14. Mayer, C. S., "A Computer Control System for Field Interviewers," *Journal of Marketing Research*, vol. 5, August 1968, pp. 312–318.

15. Minton, George, "Inspection and Correction of Error in Data Processing," *Journal of the American Statistical Association*, vol. 64, December 1969, pp. 1264–1265.

16. Namais, Jean, "Measuring Variation in Interviewer Performance," *Journal of Advertising Research*, vol. 9, March 1966, pp. 8–12.

17. Nordbotten, S., "The Efficiency of Automatic Detection and Correction of Errors in Individual Observations as Compared with Other Means for Improving the Quality of Statistics," *Proceedings of the 35th Session of the International Statistical Institute*, Belgrade, Yugoslavia, September 1965, pp. 417–441.

18. Orlicky, Joseph, *The Successful Computer System*, New York: McGraw-Hill, 1969.

19. O'Reagan, R. T., "Relative Costs of Computerized Error Inspection Plans," *Journal of the American Statistical Association*, vol. 64, December 1969, pp. 1245–1255.

20. Pritzker, L., J. Ogus, and M. H. Hanan, "Computer Editing Methods—Some Application and Results," *Proceedings of the 35th Session of the International Statistical Institute*, Belgrade, Yugoslavia, September 1965, pp. 442–465.

21. Stuart, W. J., "Computer Editing of Survey Data—Five Years of Experience in BLS Manpower Surveys," *Journal of the American Statistical Association*, vol. 61, June 1966, pp. 375–383.

22. Sudman, Seymour, *Reducing the Cost of Surveys*, Chicago: Aldine, 1967, chap. 8.

23. Szameitat, K., and H. J. Zindler, "The Reduction of Errors in Statistics by Automatic Corrections," *Proceedings of the 35th Session of the International Statistical Institute*, Belgrade, Yugoslavia, September 1965, pp. 395–417.

24. Woodward, J. L., and R. Franzen, "A Study of Coding Reliability," *Public Opinion Quarterly*, vol. 12, Summer 1948, pp. 253–277.

Surveys

Chapter 9

Coding

PHILIP S. SIDEL *Social Science Information Center, University of Pittsburgh, Pittsburgh, Pennsylvania*

WHY CODE SURVEY DATA?

Surveys are taken to describe or compare groups of people. Each individual in the group, each respondent, has a unique, complex set of characteristics and attitudes and his own distinct way of expressing himself in response to our questions. To analyze these very heterogeneous responses, we must classify them into a limited number of categories or scores. The symbols used to represent these categories or scores are called *codes*, and the procedure of classifying responses and entering the codes on the questionnaire or on another form is called *coding*.

Over the years, researchers have developed rules and procedures which facilitate the coding operation and the subsequent operations of tabulating and analyzing the data. These conventions pertain to the development of sets of categories ("code construction") and to the editing of the raw data as well as to the coding operation itself. They will be the focus of our discussion in this chapter. Since very little is absolute and there is much room for innovation in code construction and coding, the most important part of the following sections will be the explanation of why the various procedures and conventions have developed as they have.

In order to discuss the many problems and issues to be decided in respect to coding, the questionnaire design and code construction stages will be taken up first, and then the more technical stage of actual coding. Finally, ways to control and improve accuracy and reliability will be described. At several points, the impact of our technology will be discussed—transcription of data onto machine-readable media, the impact of computers on the forms of codes used, and the possibilities of using computers to assist in, or perform, coding in the future.

SETTING UP CODES

Structured and Open-ended Questions

In large surveys, relatively little classification of responses is done at the coding stage. Most of the questions are typically *structured*. That is, the response categories are established before the data collection stage and are printed right on the questionnaire. Usually this results in a multiple-choice kind of question. For example, the respondent might be asked, "What is your religion—Catholic? Protestant? Jewish? Some other religion? No religion?" Such questions are useful when the researcher knows (from previous research, pretests, or on theoretical grounds) what information he wants, and the respondent's frame of reference is not of particular interest. Here the respondent himself does the classifying—he chooses the category into which his response is to be coded.

In contrast to the structured item is the *open-ended* question where the respondent's answer is recorded in his own words, later to be categorized by the coder and qualitatively analyzed by the analyst. Many open-ended questions are of the short-answer type: "What is your religious preference?" Many others, however, are designed to elicit lengthy statements about the respondent's attitudes, feelings, opinions, and perceptions. For instance, "Tell me about your religion."

Although responses to structured questions are always classified into code categories at the time the questionnaire is filled out, sometimes open-end responses to unstructured questions are also classified in the field. Of course, here it is the interviewer rather than the respondent or the office coder who does the classifying.[1] In fact, questionnaires are sometimes designed so that the interviewer records the full response to an open-ended question *and* classifies the respondent into pertinent categories on the basis of that response.

Some questionnaires are wholly or partially *precoded*. This means that the response categories to structured items are accompanied by corresponding numeric codes.[2] Instead of just checking the response category, the respondent or interviewer circles or checks its corresponding code. Often the card column in which each item is to be punched is also printed on the questionnaire, so that after a minimal edit for completeness and consistency, the coded responses can be punched directly from the questionnaire.

For systematic analysis, classificatory schema must be established, and if not done when the questionnaire is being designed, it must be done at a later point.

---

[1] A comparison of the results of such field coding with results from office coding of verbatim records of responses is described in Stember and Hyman [10]. Statistical evidence of bias affecting classification by interviewers appeared in field coding of level-of-information questions and in field coding by inexperienced interviewers. Hypotheses of biases due to interviewers having prejudicial expectations regarding respondents or to interviewers' own attitudes on the questions being coded were rejected.

[2] Others, such as Stember and Hyman [10] and Payne [8] use the word "precoded" simply to mean field classification by checking or circling a response category— whether or not the codes to be punched are indicated. The distinction is minor, since classification has long been the primary part of coding.

Developing Codes

Code construction is something of an art, and the final categories will reflect the tastes and interests of the individual researcher. Nevertheless, certain procedures and principles help ensure that the code will at least be usable and logical. One helpful procedure is to list a sample (usually 50 or 100) of the separate responses. Some researchers prefer to make these lists on cards, one response to each card; then the cards can be sorted into categories. Sometimes punched cards and machine listings can be used. The purpose of this operation is to get a manageable, visible array of the responses to group and sort into categories. The final list from which categories are to be defined should have only one entry or line for each different response; if an answer occurred more than once, a count of the occurrences should be indicated.

It may not be desirable to pattern the final code on the way the responses fall into groups. Theoretical criteria ("relevance to the study") may override natural groupings. What is important is that each response clearly fits into one category or another. It is essential to include categories for responses that do *not* show up in the sample. If no one gives a certain answer, it may be important to show this fact. For example, when respondents were asked, "Where do you buy your groceries?" no one mentioned a particular grocery store; it is as important to make allowance for that store in the code as it is to include others like it that were mentioned.

Advantages of Extensive Codes and Empirical Codes

Since every researcher will have his own way of grouping responses to measure what he sees as theoretically meaningful dimensions of the variable, it is wise to use an *extensive* code for general-purpose studies. An extensive code is one that includes a separate category and code for every distinguishably different response. Some examples of extensive codes are the Census Bureau codes for occupation and industry [12, 13] and the extensive code for religions used by Michigan's Survey Research Center in some of its studies.[3] These codes do practically no grouping. Grouping or collapsing of categories can easily be done at the time of analysis, using one of many computer programs available. This means that each analyst who works on the data can use the classification which best suits his theoretical orientation and practical needs. If the grouping he first tries proves inadequate in one way or another, he can regroup without having to go back to the original questionnaire.[4]

The late Ralph Bisco [2] coined the term *empirical coding* for the technique of collecting and coding numerical data (such as age, income, hours spent in an activity, and so on) in full, original, numeric form. The numerical value of the code then corresponds with the specific magnitude of the quantity being measured. The code represents an interval scale which can effectively be used

---

[3] These and several other useful extensive codes will be found in the codebooks for the Election Studies and other studies archived by the Inter-University Consortium for Political Research [2a].

[4] In both the Census Occupations Code [12, 13] and the extensive SRC code of religions, a simple grouping is obtained by reading just the digit at the extreme left of the code. In this way, broad distinctions are preserved and are retrievable if an analyst wishes to use them. One warning must be made in regard to use of these codes. Vague, general responses are difficult to code on a scale of many specific categories. Some general categories, such as "Laborer, exact job not specified," are also needed if responses are not uniformly specific.

in correlation and other parametric statistical analyses.   On the other hand, as with the extensive codes just described, grouping into wider intervals for cross-tabulation and similar operations can be done at any time during the analysis.

In empirical coding as in other extensive coding, the researcher must decide upon the degree of specificity to which he wants to code.   Codes cannot be more specific than most of the responses being coded.   In addition to a general "No information" code, it may be desirable to set up codes for each general category for which specific information is lacking.   For instance, a two-digit age code might include:

$$1 = \text{under 20, exact age not given}$$
$$2 = \text{20 to 29, exact age not given}$$
$$3 = \ldots, \text{and so on}$$

The Primary Rule of Code Construction—"All-inclusive and Mutually Exclusive"

Whether one is setting up a detailed, extensive code or a simple, unidimensional variable, certain rules must be followed.   The most important of these is: The categories must be *all-inclusive* and *mutually exclusive*.   Making a classification all-inclusive is not difficult; it is commonly achieved by adding the categories "Other," "No information," and (where applicable) "None" to the major substantive categories enumerated.

The rule that categories should be mutually exclusive is most often violated when more than one dimension is embodied in a single code.   For example, a naïve researcher might come up with the following code taken directly from responses to the question: "Where do you buy most of your groceries?"

1. At the supermarket
2. At the neighborhood grocery store
3. Outside the neighborhood
4. Several different places, varies, no single place
5. No information; don't know

In this and many similar cases, the difficulty can be resolved by substructuring the response categories to find the dimensions involved, then making a separate new variable for each dimension.   Here we find two dimensions— location of the store and type of store.   They could be coded as two variables as follows:

Location where groceries are bought:
1. Local neighborhood
2. Outside neighborhood
3. At different places, sometimes in neighborhood, sometimes outside
4. Location not indicated; no answer
5. Does not apply; doesn't buy groceries

Type of store where groceries are bought:
1. Supermarket
2. Small grocery store
3. Other (farmers' market, specialty shops and so forth)
4. Various places of different types
5. Type of store not indicated
6. Does not apply; doesn't buy groceries

If most respondents gave information on both dimensions of this question, some very interesting findings might result from examining how the two dimensions are interrelated.   A useful typology might be constructed from these two variables.[5] Unfortunately, it is probable that in response to a question of this type, most respondents would give information only on one dimension or another. Few would give a detailed answer from which measures on both dimensions could be derived.[6]

One other situation in which the "all-inclusive" and/or the "mutually exclusive" rules are frequently broken is in collapsing or grouping categories. When collapsing categories, it is essential to be explicit about which responses are included in each final category. Furthermore, it should be perfectly unambiguous in which category any given responses should be placed. This point can best be illustrated by the following examples of correct and incorrect codes for "Age last birthday."

	An incorrect code	Two correct codes	
	(A)	*(B)*	*(C)*
	1 to 10	0 to 9	Under 1 yr.
	10 to 20	10 to 19	1 to 10
	20 to 30	20 to 29	11 to 20
	30 to 40	30 to 39	21 to 30
	40 to 50	40 to 49	31 to 40
	50 to 60	50 to 59	41 to 50
	60 or over	60 or over	51 to 60
	no information	no information	over 60
			no information

In this code there is no category for infants under one year old. A second problem is in classifying people who are exactly 10 years old, 20 years old, 30, 40, 50, or 60—any such response could be coded in either of two categories.

These codes are both correct. There is no ambiguity about the category in which each score is to be placed.

Note that in a true continuous variable, the response is always rounded when it is given, and may be further rounded in coding. The rounding rule should be explicit. In this example, age is rounded to the respondent's last birthday. The only ambiguity would be in the case of respondents interviewed on their birthday anniversaries. Almost any consistent procedure would suffice for these infrequent cases. (This topic of rounding and the more general problem of specificity in coding are discussed in the earlier section, "Advantages of Extensive Codes and Empirical Codes.")

Choosing Breakpoints

Aside from the requirement that categories be unambiguous (mutually exclusive) and all-inclusive, there are few, if any, absolute rules about choosing breakpoints for scales. In collapsing or grouping scores from a continuous or

---

[5] The general procedures of substructuring and reconstructing typologies for clarification of dimensions involved are described in Barton [1].

[6] Problems of this sort are even more prevalent in analyzing people's reasons for their attitudes and behavior. See Lazarsfeld [6] and Gaudet [3] for descriptions of these problems and ways of coping with them.

unit-interval scale into a small number of categories, the following kinds of questions must be decided by the researcher:

1. Into how many categories should the variable be cast?

2. Should the final categories be equal-interval, or should they be so constructed that each category has (approximately) the same number of cases, thus forming a sort of standardized variable, or should some combination of these approaches be used?

3. Should the extreme categories be "open" (for example, "under 10," "60 or over") to include a wide range of extreme scores in relatively few categories, or should every interval be of a fixed, clearly defined length? Use of the fixed intervals and defined upper and lower values, even for the extreme of the scales, will enable the researcher to do later statistical operations on the variable. The value for every case can be the midpoint of its category.

4. On some variables, responses tend to cluster at certain points on the scale. For instance, estimates of percentages tend to cluster on numbers divisible by 10 or by 5. It is desirable from a statistical standpoint that these clusters fall as much as possible on the midpoints of the categories. However, ease of coding and general usage generally dictate that the values at which these clusters occur will be selected as upper or lower limits for the categories.

These decisions are difficult to make and very crucial when the raw data (the actual numbers or scores) are not being retained. When the only information retained is a collapsed scale, the one scale has to be used for all subsequent analysis—contingency tables and correlational analysis alike. The form of scale most useful for one type of approach may not be very helpful for another. Therefore, if costs permit, the data should be retained in their original and most complete form. From these, grouped variables can be created as needed.

Card Layout Conventions

It is important to review some of the more formal rules, conventions, and procedures of code construction. The requirement that codes be all-inclusive and mutually exclusive is the only absolute rule of code construction and coding. Other rules are only conventions useful with today's technological tools. The key assumption behind these conventions is that one is coding data onto tab cards for input to a computer. This is the prevailing current practice. As Janda [5] points out, the technology of tomorrow may make the rules and procedures of today obsolete. It is up to the individual to adapt his procedures to take advantage of developing tools and techniques. He is best able to do this by having a clear view of what he wants to learn from the data and understanding the reasons for each rule or convention recommended to him. Here are some coding conventions used currently:

1. Use only one punch per column. Most computer programs will not accept cards that have been multiple-punched. In fact, many of the newest card readers cannot read multiple-punched cards. Therefore, today we *spread,* or spray, multiple-response variables. That is, a separate column is assigned each of the multiple-response categories. If the response is not checked, a zero is punched in the column. Again, past justification for multiple punching within columns has been the practicality of this coding layout for counter-sorter tabulation. It is highly impractical for most computer analysis.

2. Use only numeric codes. If the ten codes (0 through 9) are not sufficient, do not hesitate to use a second column (00 through 99). Strictly numeric codes are acceptable input to virtually any computer and to any analytic

program or package. Furthermore, tab cards and computer tapes are a very minor portion of any survey's cost. The only justification for trying to squeeze codes into fewer columns is to restrict a small survey to one card per case so it can be tabulated on a counter sorter or similar unit-record machine.

3. The field for a variable may consist of a single column or a set of two or more columns, but no more than one variable may be assigned to a single column.

4. Use standard codes for "No information." Insofar as possible, one should use the same code throughout the study for each kind of "No information." For instance, one organization follows the rule that for any code of seven or fewer substantive categories, a "Don't know" will be coded 8, a "No answer" will be coded 9, and a "Does not apply" will be coded 0. That leaves the codes 1 through 7 available for substantive codes. This kind of procedure facilitates coding and subsequent processing.

In addition to these conventions, general coding instructions should include clear-cut rules governing such matters as the color and type of pencil to be used and the way the codes should be written, for instance, the symbols to enter for blank or reject, for zero so it will be distinguishable from the letter "O," and so on. Such conventions facilitate control of data processing and avoid errors due to illegibility or ambiguity of entries.

Codebook and Coding Instructions

There is some confusion about just what a codebook is. The term sometimes refers to the list of code categories and the responses that go into them—the list that is prepared for the coders—which may be denoted as the initial codebook. In other instances, it refers to the list of code categories and their frequencies. This list is primarily for the use of analysts in their subsequent processing of the data and may be denoted as the final codebook. This codebook is often produced on the computer. Sometimes it is stored on magnetic tape or in some other machine-readable form so that extra copies can be printed as needed.

The initial codebook is usually accompanied by a set of general instructions to the coder. These instructions cover standard procedures that apply to all the coding to be done: the locations and forms in which the codes are to be written; standard rules about editing; handling "No answers," "Don't knows," and answers that don't fit into any of the regular categories; procedure in coding ambiguous, hard-to-classify responses; and administrative procedures. The codebook itself contains the codes and a full description of what responses go into which code on all the open-end (free answer) questions. Codes for precoded questions usually are not included, since they appear directly on each questionnaire. Figure 1 shows an example of (part of) a code as it might appear in an initial codebook, to be used for classifying responses.

The final codebook is for analysts rather than coders. It should contain enough information to define what was included in each category of an item, but it may contain fewer examples. Strictly procedural information may also be omitted. On many surveys, the final codebook also contains the response frequency on each of the categories. Figure 2 shows the final codebook entry for the question illustrated in Figure 1.

In addition to an initial codebook, the coder should be provided a set of general instructions covering rules that apply to all items and procedures to be followed throughout the editing and coding operations. It is to those procedures and the operations themselves, viewed from the standpoint of the project director or supervisor, that our attention now turns.

POSTINTERVIEW EDITING AND CODING

Administrative Procedures

A major job for the director or supervisor is controlling the questionnaires or other data documents and their systematic flow through the sequential steps of data processing. This is especially important because of the necessary confidentiality of the data. Each completed questionnaire, as it is received, should be assigned a sequential number and logged in on a list under that

---

QUESTION 16.   "IF YOU HAD AN EXTRA FEW HOURS A WEEK, WHAT WOULD BE YOUR FIRST CHOICE OF HOW TO SPEND IT?"

Cols. 29–30

01—Community service or civic activities or organizations:
This is a fairly restricted category for those who would do volunteer work or would participate in explicitly service or civic activities. Include those who would work for community service organizations or who mention specifically the community service program of a multipurpose organization (such as the organizations listed in 03). Community service organizations include: March of Dimes; Red Cross (note—taking RC courses, such as First Aid, is *not* included here . . . see code 08); Heart Fund; Community Chest; PTA; Welcome Wagon; USO; Hospital Volunteer; Volunteer Fire Department.

02—Political activities or organizations:
Campaign or work for a candidate or a party; Join a political movement; Work for peace; Environmental action.

03—Other types of organizations (community service programs not specified):
Include here: Churches and religious organizations; Economic and occupational organizations (trade unions, coops, credit unions, etc.); Patriotic and veterans' organizations (Amer. Legion, VFW, DAR, AMVETS, DAV, etc.); Lodges, Fraternal organizations, & Ethnic organizations (Masons, Knights of Columbus, Elks, Shriners, Eastern Star, B'nai B'rith, Daughters of Scotia, Rotary, Kiwanis, Lions, Order of Hibernians, NAACP, Polish Falcons, etc.).

04—Personal contact with friends:
Visiting; Correspondence; "Just Gabbing"; Helping friend; etc.   Informal discussions.

Fig. 1.   Example of (part of) a page from an initial codebook. *(Adapted from R. K. Merton's "Study of Craftown and Hilltown," unpublished codebook, 1946.)*

number. It is often useful to write or stamp that sequential number on the questionnaire and use it for the case identification (ID). The questionnaires are then divided into work packs—each containing an equal number (say, 50 or 10) of sequentially numbered questionnaires. A list should be kept with each work pack, indicating what questionnaires are included and what processing has been completed on the pack. A separate list containing the same information for all packs should be kept by the supervisor.

In coding, there will inevitably be classification and editing problems on which arbitrary decisions must be made. It is important that these decisions be centralized; coders should take all questions to one supervisor who makes all the decisions and records them in a log book. This ensures consistency in the results and greatly simplifies the subsequent work of processing and analyzing the data. The record of problems brought up and decisions made should be complete; this is important for consistency and makes it possible for decisions to be changed and corrections made with minimum difficulty.

Although this log of work completed and actions taken facilitates correction of errors all the way back to the beginning of the job, a long, retroactive correction process is always agonizing. Every effort should be made to get the

---

QUESTION 16. "IF YOU HAD AN EXTRA FEW HOURS A WEEK, WHAT WOULD BE YOUR FIRST CHOICE OF HOW TO SPEND IT?"

Card 1: Cols. 29–30

Code Response Category	Freq.	Percent
01—Community service or civic activities or organizations........ Volunteer work with service organizations (Red Cross, PTA, Hospital Volunteers, etc.) or community service programs of more general organizations.	34	5
02—Political activities or organizations..................................... Includes work in political movements as well as political parties and campaigns.	3	0
03—Other organizational activities................................. General activities of church, economic, patriotic, fraternal, and ethnic organizations.	20	3
04—Personal contact with friends...................................... Includes talk and informal discussions.	56	8
05—Family-oriented activities; activities with/for family..........	13	2
06—Home-oriented activities...................................... Activities specifically for improvement of home and home life, including cooking and housework.	97	13
07—Extra work for income...	2	0
08—Self-improvement; education; studying................................	8	1
09—Recreation (unspecific): enjoyment; having good time........	15	2
10—Hobbies: arts; crafts; collections........................... Not specifically for home or family.	86	12
11—Participatory sports, games, and recreation...................	47	6
12—Reading (or pleasure; not studying).............................	40	5
13—Audience activities: Watch TV, plays, ball games, etc........	122	17
14—Rest; Sleep; Relax; "Nothing"......................................	149	20
15—Other: (Drink; Annoy others; Contemplate)......................	4	1
16—Don't know..	30	4
17—No one thing; different things; no first choice....................	3	0
18—No answer; refused to answer.....................................	10	1

Fig. 2.   Example of a page from a final or analyst's codebook. (*Adapted from R. K. Merton's "Study of Craftown and Hilltown," unpublished codebook, 1946.*)

job going correctly in the very first stages, even if it means sacrifice of early productivity.   Early checks and early corrections are essential.   No matter how carefully coders are trained and instructed, each will inevitably get off on the wrong track in handling one question or another.

The major purpose of many of the administrative operations recommended is the maintenance of high accuracy.   Since quality control is not limited to the coding phase but is conducted at nearly all stages and is aimed at many kinds of errors, it is treated in a separate section near the end of this chapter.

Editing

An important task usually done by the coder is editing.   Editing consists of making corrections in the entries on the original document so the final coded data represent the best possible picture of the facts or of the respondent's attitudes. A few examples will clarify what editing is.

1.   The respondent has checked two answers on an item where only one response was to be checked.   The editor resolves this by selecting one of the checked responses, or another, intermediate response, as the right one, or by coding "No information" for the item.   The rules governing his decision have been clearly specified to him in advance as part of his coding and editing instructions.

2.   The answers given by the respondent are logically inconsistent with one another.   The editor must determine which response (if either) is "correct" and make the other response consistent.

3.   The respondent checked one category in a structured item, but his comments and qualifications, written in the margin, indicate that he does not really belong in that category.   His response is edited to whichever category best fits his qualified response.

Editing instructions should be complete and specific, covering the form of the edit, for example, use of a different colored pencil to distinguish edits from changes made by a respondent or an interviewer, as well as general decision-making rules.

Another task the coder is often requested to do is flagging responses which might be of use in subsequent qualitative analysis.   Typically, the coder is given the criteria for selecting responses of interest; as he encounters them, he enters the case and item numbers on appropriate lists.   Later, the researcher will review them and use the relevant parts of those responses that he has selected.

Coding Forms

One decision must be made at an early stage: On what form should the codes be entered?   Three choices are possible here: (1) The codes can be entered on, and subsequently punched from, the questionnaire itself; (2) a special coding sheet (or sheets) can be drawn up for the job and keyed into the questionnaire; or (3) a standard sheet with 80 spaces for each of the 80 columns of the tab card can be used, each sheet accommodating codes for one or more "cards" of data.

When using the questionnaire itself for the coding form, the card layout must be developed before the questionnaire is printed.   The card and column numbers are printed on the questionnaire near the item to be coded into that column.   The coder simply enters the code in a space provided next to the printed number for the column into which the code will be punched.   Usually, it is best for all codes to be entered in a reserved space on the right-hand margin of the page.   However, Figure 3 is an illustration of a very well-designed questionnaire on which the coder enters codes in spaces on the left-hand margin, and the precoded items can be keypunched directly from the indicated entries in the body of the questionnaire.   Even on the typical, mimeographed questionnaire of the low-budget survey, some items—such as batteries of items in checklist form—can usually be keypunched directly from the original answer, with no entry to be made by the coder beyond necessary editing.

The second kind of coding form, the specially designed coding sheet, is illustrated in Figure 4.   The coder has, right on the coding sheet, some identification of which questionnaire item is to be coded into a given card and column.   It may even be feasible to put on the code sheet mnemonics for the code categories on some items.   This tends to routinize the coding of open-ended items, thus improving efficiency and reducing certain kinds of errors (though perhaps inducing others). Usually, it is possible to set up a sheet for coding two or more cards of data, or the same card for several cases, as in Figure 4. However, if mnemonics for codes are also printed on the code sheet,

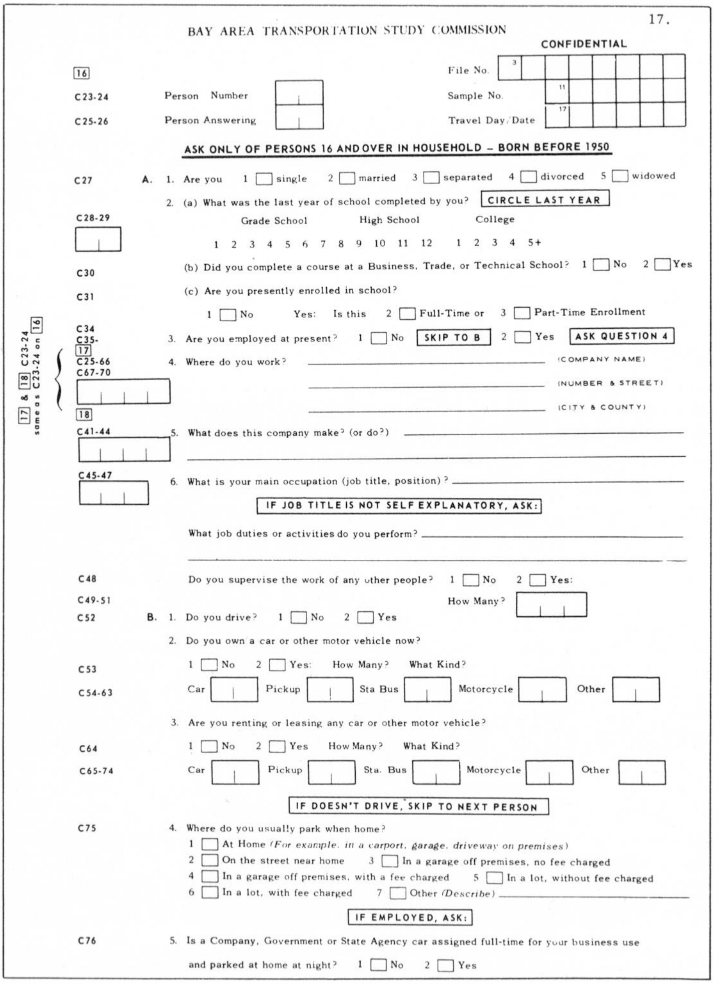
17.

BAY AREA TRANSPORTATION STUDY COMMISSION

CONFIDENTIAL

16 | File No. 3

C23-24 Person Number | Sample No. 11

C25-26 Person Answering | Travel Day/Date 17

ASK ONLY OF PERSONS 16 AND OVER IN HOUSEHOLD – BORN BEFORE 1950

C27 A. 1. Are you 1 ☐ single 2 ☐ married 3 ☐ separated 4 ☐ divorced 5 ☐ widowed

2. (a) What was the last year of school completed by you? CIRCLE LAST YEAR

C28-29 Grade School High School College

1 2 3 4 5 6 7 8 9 10 11 12 1 2 3 4 5+

C30 (b) Did you complete a course at a Business, Trade, or Technical School? 1 ☐ No 2 ☐ Yes

C31 (c) Are you presently enrolled in school?

1 ☐ No Yes: Is this 2 ☐ Full-Time or 3 ☐ Part-Time Enrollment

C34 C35- 17 3. Are you employed at present? 1 ☐ No SKIP TO B 2 ☐ Yes ASK QUESTION 4

17 & 18 C23-24 same as C23-24 on 16

C25-66 C67-70 4. Where do you work? ________ (COMPANY NAME) ________ (NUMBER & STREET) ________ (CITY & COUNTY)

18

C41-44 5. What does this company make? (or do?) ________

C45-47 6. What is your main occupation (job title, position)? ________

IF JOB TITLE IS NOT SELF EXPLANATORY, ASK:

What job duties or activities do you perform? ________

C48 Do you supervise the work of any other people? 1 ☐ No 2 ☐ Yes:

C49-51 How Many?

C52 B. 1. Do you drive? 1 ☐ No 2 ☐ Yes

2. Do you own a car or other motor vehicle now?

C53 1 ☐ No 2 ☐ Yes: How Many? What Kind?

C54-63 Car Pickup Sta Bus Motorcycle Other

3. Are you renting or leasing any car or other motor vehicle?

C64 1 ☐ No 2 ☐ Yes How Many? What Kind?

C65-74 Car Pickup Sta. Bus Motorcycle Other

IF DOESN'T DRIVE, SKIP TO NEXT PERSON

C75 4. Where do you usually park when home?
1 ☐ At Home (*For example, in a carport, garage, driveway on premises*)
2 ☐ On the street near home 3 ☐ In a garage off premises, no fee charged
4 ☐ In a garage off premises, with a fee charged 5 ☐ In a lot, without fee charged
6 ☐ In a lot, with fee charged 7 ☐ Other (*Describe*) ________

IF EMPLOYED, ASK:

C76 5. Is a Company, Government or State Agency car assigned full-time for your business use and parked at home at night? 1 ☐ No 2 ☐ Yes

Fig. 3. Illustration of a combination questionnaire and coding form. *(Bay Area Transportation Study Commission.)*

it may not be possible to get more than 80 columns of data on a single code sheet. Special code sheets facilitate independent double coding as a checking procedure since the coding verifier simply codes on a separate copy of the form, and the two copies are afterward compared item by item.

Standard, 80-column coding forms are often used very successfully. There may be difficulties with entering the codes in the proper spaces for the columns in which they are to be punched; however, to experienced coders this is no

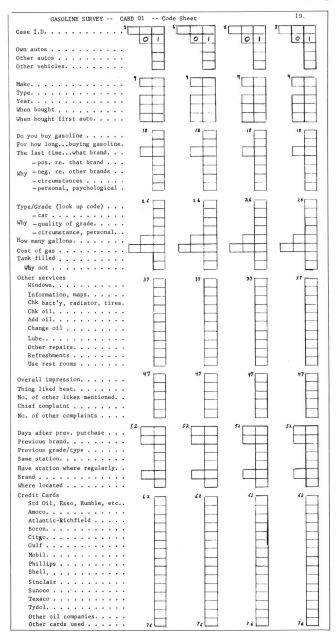

Fig. 4.   A custom-designed coding form for a survey of gasoline-buying habits.

real problem, and such errors are very few.   This type of standard form can be designed so that the codes for many cards (frequently 20 to 30) can be entered on a single sheet.

Generally, it is worthwhile to set up the questionnaire in such a way that the keypuncher can punch directly from the questionnaire itself if it consists, to any great extent, of precoded items.   This should be checked out beforehand with the keypunch operator or supervisor.

Transcription of Codes onto Machine-readable Media

Many of the decisions made during the coding process are based on the requirements of one or another transcription procedure.   The most common such procedure is keypunching the codes onto tab cards, and most of the coding rules described here were established on the assumption that the data would be processed in this way.

Production rates on keypunching vary, but for rough planning, an estimate of about 100 cards (80 punched columns per card) per hour is realistic. Punching on a fairly difficult job with much paper handling or poor writing will reduce the estimate; an easy, straightforward job with little or no paper handling will progress at a much faster rate.   Of course, these estimates will not apply for an unskilled keypuncher or a complex job where the keypuncher must change operations frequently.

Estimates of time to do a job should be doubled if keypunching will be fully verified.   The verifying machine is like a keypunch, and the operator goes through virtually the same motions as were made on the original keypunching. However, the verifying machine simply checks the holes already in the card, instead of punching holes.   If the hole punched does not match the key struck at any point, a red light comes on.   If rechecking at that point indicates that the card truly was mispunched, a small notch is cut in the edge of the card to indicate the error.   Machine verification only checks and improves the accuracy of keypunching.   Coding errors are not affected by this procedure. Ways of controlling coding accuracy and overall accuracy will be discussed later.

A good keypuncher typically makes very few errors, and verification is a very expensive procedure for the slight increase in accuracy it affords.   Therefore, project directors often dispense with keypunch verification and count on the card-cleaning procedure (to be described later) for correction of the few keypunch errors.   Full verification is typically used only where the keypuncher is inexperienced, or where accurate keypunching was particularly difficult. Sometimes partial verification (say, the first 200 cards punched on a job and a small sample of those punched thereafter) is used to ascertain that the punch-error rate was indeed within acceptable limits.   Often, verification is skipped altogether.

In addition to keypunching, there are a number of electronic and other methods of transcribing codes onto cards, tapes, or other media.   One of the most elaborate is FOSDIC (Foto-Electric Sensing Device for Input to Computers), designed for, and used by, the Bureau of Census.   (See Figure 5). This device senses black spots made in little circles (in lieu of X marks) directly on the interview schedule.   For most purposes, however, it still requires too much work and expense to design the interview schedule and get all the little circles in precisely the right position.

A more generalized form to be read by a photoelectric scanner for "automatic" punching is the sheet designed for input into an optical scanner, such

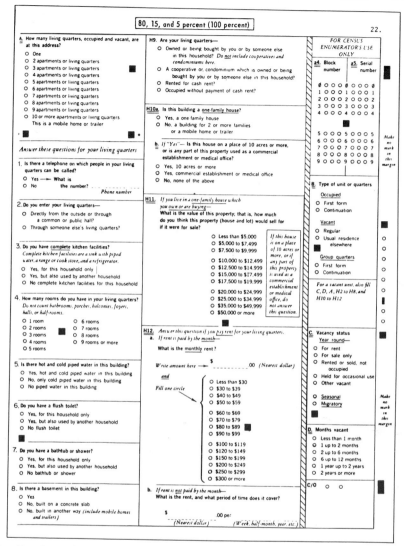

Fig. 5. Example of a FOSDIC census schedule. (*U.S. Bureau of the Census, Washington:* Sample Schedule for 1970 Census of Population and Housing.)

as the IBM 1230, which senses the marks and punches corresponding holes on a tab card. See Figure 6. Readers may be familiar with these forms as the score sheets for IQ and other psychological tests. These forms are particularly appropriate for large batteries of multiple-choice items, but they can be adapted for almost any questionnaire.

Several problems arise in using optical scanning sheets in survey research, and so far their use has been fairly limited. One problem is the high probability of error in associating a code with an indicated response, then marking the proper row and column for that code on that item on a separate sheet.

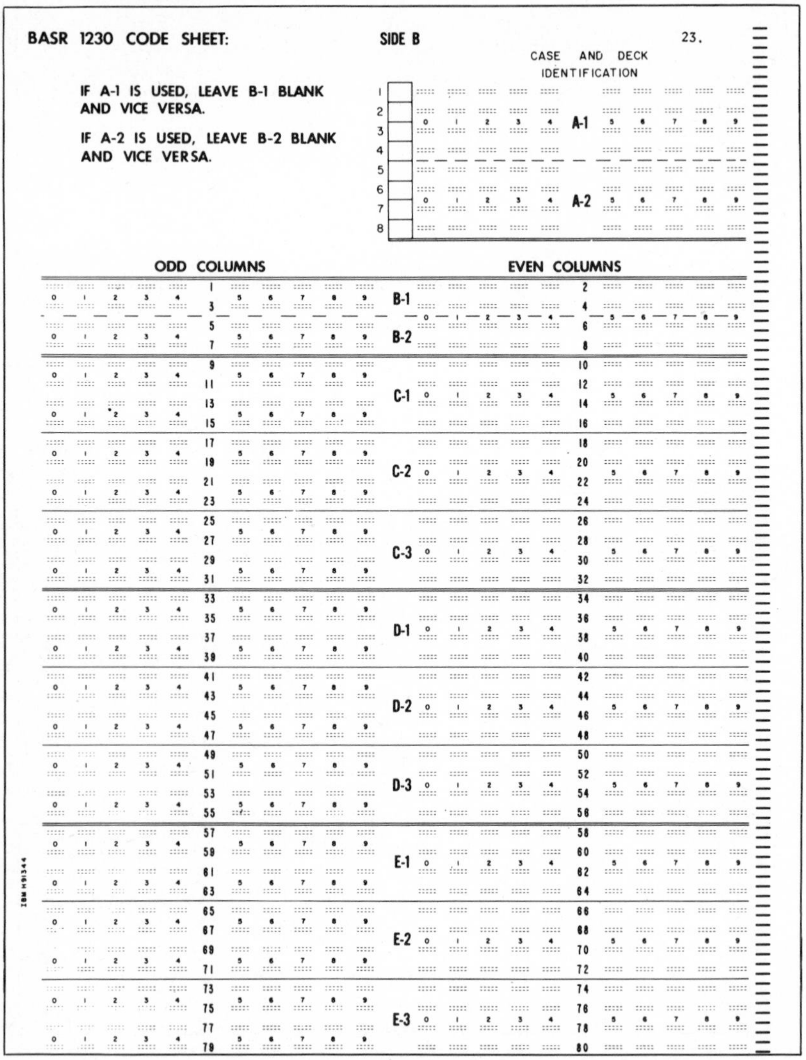

Fig. 6.   A code sheet for the IBM 1230 Optical Scanner and Punch. *(Columbia University, Bureau of Applied Social Research, (BASR), New York, 1966.)*

This is difficult to do accurately at a desk under good conditions, and virtually impossible under field conditions. Time saved in keypunching is paid for in slower and less accurate coding. Special mark-sensing forms imprinted with the questions and response categories to show which spaces are to be marked for which responses provide a way around that problem. These forms (like the FOSDIC census schedules) can be used directly in the field by the interviewer, or even by the respondent in a self-administered survey. However, such custom-designed mark-sensing forms are usually prohibitively expensive.

After the form comes into the office, only a relatively fast editing review is needed before the questionnaire is fed into the optical scanning machine. These machines can be programmed to flag certain kinds of inconsistencies, illegal entries, and ambiguities, such as poor erasures. To date, the reliability and flexibility of standard optical scanning equipment have been below the acceptability level for many survey practitioners. However, both electronic and mechanical hardware are being constantly improved to meet customer demand.

Electrographic mark-sensing is similar to photoelectric mark-sensing, but there are a number of technical differences. One is that a special electrographic pencil must be used for the coding. Typically, the marks are made directly on tab cards or on other kinds of card stock. (See Figure 7.) Then the marks are "sensed" and the codes are electromechanically transferred into punches on tab cards. For a number of years, the government's Current Population Survey has gathered labor-force data, housing information, and other demographic data on mark-sense cards. They are especially useful for gathering small numbers of items on a large and/or on a recurrent basis. The processing equipment was, for a long time, slower and less flexible, but more reliable, than optical-sensing equipment.

Both optical sensing and electrographic sensing can be most useful in dealing with short, standardized surveys with all precoded data. For other types of survey, the more pedestrian procedures—collecting, editing, and coding,

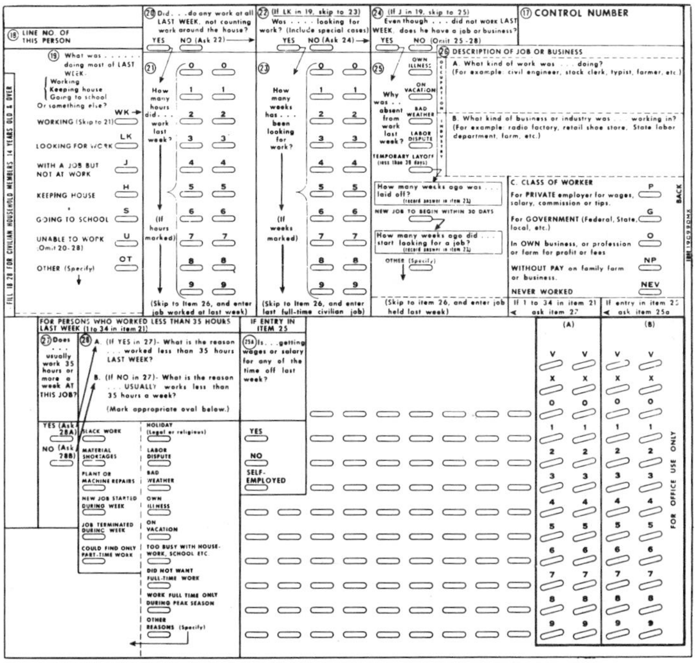
(18) LINE NO. OF THIS PERSON
FILL 18-28 FOR CIVILIAN HOUSEHOLD MEMBERS 14 YEARS OLD & OVER
(19) What was . . . . . . doing most of LAST WEEK- Working, Keeping house, Going to school, Or something else?
WORKING (Skip to 21) WK
LOOKING FOR WORK LK
WITH A JOB BUT NOT AT WORK J
KEEPING HOUSE H
GOING TO SCHOOL S
UNABLE TO WORK (Omit 20-28) U
OTHER (Specify) OT
(20) Did . . . do any work at all LAST WEEK, not counting work around the house? YES NO (Ask 22)
(21) How many hours did . . . work last week? (If hours marked)
(Skip to Item 26, and enter job worked at last week)
(22) (If LK in 19, skip to 23) Was . . . . looking for work? (Include special cases) YES NO (Ask 24)
(23) How many weeks has . . . been looking for work? (If weeks marked)
(Skip to Item 26, and enter last full-time civilian job)
(24) (If J in 19, skip to 25) Even though . . . did not work LAST WEEK, does he have a job or business? YES NO (Omit 25-28)
(25) Why was . . . absent from work last week? OWN ILLNESS ON VACATION BAD WEATHER LABOR DISPUTE TEMPORARY LAYOFF (less than 30 days)
How many weeks ago was . . . laid off? (record answer in item 21)
NEW JOB TO BEGIN WITHIN 30 DAYS
How many weeks ago did . . . start looking for a job? (record answer in item 21)
OTHER (Specify)
(Skip to item 26, and enter job held last week)
(17) CONTROL NUMBER
(26) DESCRIPTION OF JOB OR BUSINESS
OCCUPATION
A. What kind of work was . . . doing? (For example: civil engineer, stock clerk, typist, farmer, etc.)
INDUSTRY
B. What kind of business or industry was . . . working in? (For example: radio factory, retail shoe store, State labor department, farm, etc.)
C. CLASS OF WORKER
For PRIVATE employer for wages, salary, commission or tips. P
For GOVERNMENT (Federal, State, local, etc.) G
In OWN business, or profession or farm for profit or fees O
WITHOUT PAY on family farm or business. NP
NEVER WORKED NEV
BACK
If 1 to 34 in item 21 ask item 27
If entry in item 25 ask item 25a
FOR PERSONS WHO WORKED LESS THAN 35 HOURS LAST WEEK (1 to 34 in item 21)
(27) Does . . . usually work 35 hours or more a week AT THIS JOB?
YES (Ask 28A)
NO (Ask 28B)
(28) A. (If YES in 27)- What is the reason . . . worked less than 35 hours LAST WEEK?
B. (If NO in 27)- What is the reason . . . USUALLY works less than 35 hours a week?
(Mark appropriate oval below.)
SLACK WORK
MATERIAL SHORTAGES
PLANT OR MACHINE REPAIRS
NEW JOB STARTED DURING WEEK
JOB TERMINATED DURING WEEK
COULD FIND ONLY PART-TIME WORK
HOLIDAY (Legal or religious)
LABOR DISPUTE
BAD WEATHER
OWN ILLNESS
ON VACATION
TOO BUSY WITH HOUSEWORK, SCHOOL ETC.
DID NOT WANT FULL-TIME WORK
WORK FULL TIME ONLY DURING PEAK SEASON
OTHER REASONS (Specify)
IF ENTRY IN ITEM 25
(25A) Is . . . getting wages or salary for any of the time off last week?
YES
NO
SELF-EMPLOYED
(A) (B)
V X O 1 2 3 4 5 6 7 8 9
FOR OFFICE USE ONLY

Fig. 7. An electrographic mark-sensing card for field-coding population survey data in machine-readable form. *(U.S. Bureau of the Census, Washington:* Current Population Survey, 1960.)

then keypunching the data—will probably serve better. Today, most key-punch operations produce punched cards, but there are keyboard-type machines for transcribing the coded data directly onto other media, such as magnetic tapes and paper tapes.

The rationale of such procedures as optical scanning and mark-sensing is to minimize the number and magnitude of intermediary human operations between the respondent's expression of his attitude or behavior and the final, coded representation of it that is tallied by the computer. Machines are faster, more accurate, and more economical coders and code processors than we humans. However, as indicated in the preceding paragraphs, it is only in limited kinds of situations that transcription of codes to cards or tape can be automated. To date, no machine has been designed to distinguish the full and complex range of signals and symbols (spoken or written) used in communicating information. Data must be put into special, machine-readable form, and usually that must be a separate step from the coding operation.

A similar rationale lies behind efforts to computerize the coding operation itself, and developments in this line are similarly limited. The basic idea is to transcribe the full text responses into machine-readable form (in alphanumeric code), and to program the computer to search this text for terms and phrases listed in a codebook or "dictionary." The output can be an encoded summary of the individual record or a statistical tabulation of the contents of the entire set of records.

One of the best-known programs for such analysis is the Harvard General Inquirer [11] and its successor, Inquirer 11 [7]. Using extensive dictionaries and special syntax signals within the text that gets read into the machine, the program can identify, record, and tally categories of references to various concepts.

Another development in this line is computer-aided coding of short-answer types of open-ended data. A good illustration of this approach is the computer coding of data punched directly from nineteenth-century census schedules.[7]

QUALITY CONTROL

The project director and his coding supervisor have two major responsibilities for the quality of coding. First, the accuracy (validity and reliability) of the coding must be as high as possible. The error rate[8] must be kept down to acceptable levels on all parts of the job. Second, the approximate extent of the coding error must be known. Unless the second requirement is met, it is impossible to say whether the first has been met.

Certain procedures are extremely useful (if not essential) in maintaining and measuring coding quality. The first consists of *early checks* on the coders' work. The supervisor and the director should work very closely with the coders as they begin each new part of the coding job. The coders should be watched as they work, so that misunderstandings can be caught immediately and corrected. Before the end of the first day of coding, it is useful to hold a

---

[7] This procedure of computer coding data punched free-form from census schedules is described in some detail by Glasco [4].

[8] Error rate on an item is the number of times it was miscoded, divided by the total number of times it was coded, that is, the number of cases. The error rate is estimated by careful double coding and resolution of discrepancies on a sample of questionnaires. There is an overall error rate which is the mean of the error rates for each of the items.

review session, going over the instructions which have been changed or which were not clearly understood by all the coders at the outset. Such review sessions are useful periodically during the coding of a survey, but the early ones are most critical and valuable.

As noted earlier, it is very important to keep complete records (a journal or log) of all the problems and questions that come up, indicating the dispositions made of them. This log should be used to update coding instructions. It will also be useful in eventual documentation of what the codes actually mean.

The first few questionnaires coded by each coder should be 100 percent checked by the project director or supervisor. After that, the best routine checking procedure is independent double coding of the questionnaires. To assure that the checking will be independent, the checker recodes the item on a separate code sheet without looking at the codes given by the original coder. After a pack is double-coded, the supervisor resolves any discrepancies found, corrects all errors, and tabulates (by coder, by item) each error in coding or checking.

The running tally on coding errors discovered (as a ratio of codes checked) provides a measure of the error rate—an indication of further training needed, additional checks to be made, and general accuracy of the job.

Independent double coding is expensive. Therefore, it usually is done on only a sample of each coder's work. A number of considerations enter into the sample design used, but *simplicity* of design should be most important, especially if the coding supervisor has not had long experience in that role. Other considerations are the level of tolerance acceptable and the relative difficulty of individual items. Different items can be checked at different rates, but it is usually too complex to have more than two rates. The sampling rate for an item can be changed (lowered, it is hoped, as the coding progresses and becomes more standardized and reliable), but such changes should be infrequent for administrative simplicity. If a coder's work on a given item falls below tolerance level, his coding on that item should be 100 percent checked until the supervisor is certain that he has learned what he previously misunderstood or until he is consistently coding the item well above the minimum tolerable level of accuracy.

If error rates are generally and persistently high, the director must consider changing the codes or getting new coders who understand the codes better. If intelligent coders are consistently unable to make the same judgment, more often than not the code itself needs reworking.

Sometimes the conceptualization of the codes is faulty and a complete new code is needed. More often, a more explicit definition of the code categories will bring greater reliability. This can take the form of examples. Elaboration of interpretations and assumptions to be made from indirect or incomplete responses can also be useful. Finally, it is very important to specify when a case should be coded "No answer" (NA) due to insufficient information in the response.

The double-coding procedure is an excellent way to maintain the quality of coding. However, even if every item is 100 percent double-coded, the quality will not be perfect; additional checks must be made at several points. A major further quality check is *card cleaning.*

In this procedure, the cards for each case are checked (on the computer or on multiple passes through card-processing machines) for "out-of-field" punches or for response patterns that are internally inconsistent. Card cleaning will show up errors that occurred in keypunching, in interviewing, or in the respondent's memory, as well as coding errors.

Cases with illegal or illogical punch patterns are identified (the card is printed out, or it is dropped into an "error" pocket), cards with errors are matched against the original document, and necessary corrections are made.

Card cleaning should be the first step after the coded data have been put on a machine-readable medium such as cards or tape. Those who begin analysis before card cleaning is completed must anticipate that if changes are extensive, they may have to revise findings based on the "uncleaned" data. However, preliminary frequency distributions are often a useful first step in the card-cleaning process. They allow one to identify columns which contain illegal (out-of-field) punches.

Although the researcher's critical attitude toward the data must continue throughout his analysis, the card-cleaning stage is the last formal opportunity to check and improve the quality of the data. Everything possible should be done at this stage to ensure that the final data going into the analysis are accurate representations of the responses on the questionnaires. This does not mean that every code should be rechecked. That would be impractical. It does mean that a well-planned series of logical tests should be run on the data, and the results of those tests used to track down as many errors as possible, both systematic and random.

The first check is to make certain that all cards for every case are present and properly identified by card number and case number. Usually this is done by a match-merge procedure. Matching serialized case identification (ID) numbers on cards and merging the cards for each case used to be done on a unit-record machine, the collator. Now the computer is used to create a sorted, matched-merged file on tape or on another storage medium. For IDs with too many or too few cards for the case, or improperly numbered cards, the computer program lists or punches the cards in a separate file. The researcher examines this file and resolves all the errors and discrepancies. Finally, the corrected cards are match-merged into the file with the other cases, and the entire file is rechecked to be sure that all cases and cards are in order. See Figure 8 for an example of a correctly match-merged deck.

For those studies in which match-merging is impossible or inappropriate (for instance, where there are varying numbers of cards in the cases, or where not all cards have the same ID fields), the researcher must design appropriate checks to ascertain that all the data are present, properly identified and in the proper order for card cleaning and for analysis. Often a specially written computer program is the best tool for this purpose. However, a number of general-purpose analytic and cleaning programs are flexible enough to handle a wide variety of input formats. Frequently, these programs can be used to perform all the checks necessary even when the structure of the data is highly unusual.

As soon as all the cases are in order and have the proper IDs (or even earlier, in some instances), one should run preliminary "marginals" or column-by-column frequency distributions. These will be useful in planning the analysis and also in setting up logical checks on the data. Columns which show frequencies for out-of-field punches will have to be checked, and incorrectly punched or coded cases will have to be pulled.

The idea is to set up a logical condition that defines a consistency to be checked for. It may be simple, like "PUNCH 7, 8 ØR 9 IN CARD 02, CØL 57," or it may be complex, like "PUNCH 0 ØR 9 IN CARD 01, CØL 22, AND NØT PUNCH 3 ØR 4 in CARD 02, CØL 8." Pull (or identify and print out) all cases that do not meet that logical condition. Pulled cases are then checked against the code sheets and the original questionnaire. Decisions are made about what corrections (if any) should be made. Sometimes a specific decision is made for each and every case. Sometimes, after checking some of the cases, a general decision is reached about the whole set of cases with a particular inconsistency. Finally, each card to be corrected is deleted from the file, and a corrected card is inserted in its place.

With computer programs, the analyst can check for a wider and more complex list of inconsistencies than was formerly possible. He can check improbable conditions as well as clearly unacceptable ones. In this card-cleaning stage, he can correct any systematic coding errors that he knows or suspects were made in the course of the job. Suppose, for instance, that halfway

---

Case ID	Card number
001	01
001	02
001	03
.	
.	
.	
001	m
002	01
002	02
.	
.	
.	
002	m
.	
.	
.	
n	01
n	02
.	
.	
.	
n	m

NOTE: Although case and card numbers are typically arranged in ascending sequence, any consistent order is acceptable. The major point is that the card numbers must be in the *same* order within each case.

Fig. 8.   Order of cards in a match-merged deck of _n_ cases, _m_ cards per case.

through the coding job, a researcher discovers that several coders have been coding documentaries as "News programs" on a question about favorite television programs. The documentaries should be classified as a separate category. At card-cleaning time, it is possible to select and list by ID number all those cases which were coded before the miscoding was discovered and which were coded "News programs" on the "Favorite television program" question. The questionnaires for those cases can then be examined, and the cards can be corrected for those that should have been coded "Documentaries." Card cleaning, then, consists of five major kinds of checks:

1. Checks for out-of-field punches.

2. Checks that the questionnaire instructions were properly followed—for instance, checks on the consistency between punches on screener items and punches for "Does not apply" on subsequent items.

3. Checks for internal inconsistency—for instance, physicians who have no graduate education; car-owning households that don't buy gasoline; or other improbable but not impossible conditions. Questionnaires with a great many improbable conditions must be evaluated. The responses may have been falsified, or the respondent may be from a different population than the one under study.

4. Checks on consistency of responses to pairs of items that represent the same question asked in a different way (or sometimes in the same way). Sometimes such pairs of items are purposely built into a questionnaire to check a respondent's reliability. It is essential, of course, that such discrepancies be coded as they occur and not be "made consistent." On the other hand, it is useful to look over the whole questionnaire of the inconsistent respondent to evaluate the validity and probable reliability of his other responses.

5. Checks on specific codes and/or cases on which coding errors are suspected to have occurred.

After the cards are pulled on the basis of these checks, the analyst should compare the card against the code sheet and against the original questionnaire. He must determine if an error was made and its source. Some typical sources of error are:

Failure to write clearly, for example, a zero written to look like a 6.

Keypuncher accidently struck the wrong key for that column.

Code was punched into the wrong column (often meaning a number of adjacent columns have the wrong entries).

Code was entered on wrong location on code sheet (may affect several items).

Item was simply miscoded.

It is useful to keep a tally of the kinds of errors found and who made them. The tally may indicate at some point that a direct check should be done on some portion of the job before calling the card cleaning complete.

The procedures described here are not a guaranteed path to accurately, reliably coded data. They will, however, prevent many of the fiascos that can occur when the coding operation (or any other research phase) is left to "take care of itself."[9]

Perhaps the best way to prepare oneself to manage the coding operation of a survey is to spend some time working in, or carefully observing, the coding office of an established survey organization. Such apprenticeship has been a standard part of the training of many survey researchers, and can be very valuable. Knowledge of the elements involved—as presented here—can alert the observer on what to look for, and will accelerate his learning.

REFERENCES

1. Barton, A. H., "The Concept of Property Space in Social Research," in Paul F. Lazarsfeld and Morris Rosenberg (eds.), *The Language of Social Research,* Glencoe, Ill.: Free Press, 1955.

[9] The strong possibility of such fiascos is well described in Julian A. Roth's "Hired Hand Research" [9]. Aside from the sheer problem of misunderstood instructions, there is the problem of coders taking easy, deviant ways around difficult portions of their task. Roth suggests that the best way to avoid this sort of error is to involve people who will work on the study, the coders, for instance, right from the planning stage rather than use them as "hired hands." Anyone embarking on research that will require a staff to accomplish the job should read Roth's warning.

2. Bisco, R. L., Memo to ICPR members on "Policies and Standards for Coding Data," from Inter-University Consortium for Political Research, Technical Service Division, undated (ca. 1967).

2a. Campbell, Angus, et al., *1960 Election Study*, Ann Arbor, Mich.: University of Michigan, Survey Research Center. Also, *1966 Election Study*.

3. Gaudet, H., "A Model for Assessing Changes in Voting Intention," in Paul Lazarsfeld and Morris Rosenberg (eds.), *The Language of Social Research*, Glencoe, Ill.: Free Press, 1955.

4. Glasco, L. A., "Computerizing the Manuscript Census," *Historical Methods Newsletter*, vol. III, December 1969 and March 1970.

5. Janda, K., *Data Processing Applications to Political Research*, 2d ed., Evanston, Ill.: Northwestern University Press, 1969.

6. Lazarsfeld, P. F., "The Art of Asking Why," *National Marketing Review*, vol. I, no. 1, 1935.

7. Miller, J. P. (ed.), *INQUIRER II Programmer's Guide*, St. Louis, Mo.: Washington University Computing Facilities, 1970.

8. Payne, S., *The Art of Asking Questions*, Princeton, N.J.: Princeton University Press, 1951.

9. Roth, J. A., "Hired Hand Research," *American Sociologist*, vol. 1, August 1966.

10. Stember, H., and H. Hyman, "Interviewer Effects in the Classification of Responses," *Public Opinion Quarterly*, vol. 13, Winter 1949.

11. Stone, P. J., D. C. Dunphy, M. S. Smith, and D. M. Ogilvie, *The General Inquirer: A Computer Approach to Content Analysis*, Cambridge, Mass.: M.I.T., 1966.

12. U.S. Bureau of the Census, *1950 Census of Population: Alphabetical Index of Occupations and Industries*, rev. ed., Washington: Government Printing Office, 1950.

13. U.S. Bureau of the Census, *1950 Census of Population: Classified Index of Occupations and Industries*, Washington: Government Printing Office, 1950.

Surveys

Chapter 10

Consumer Panels

JAMES M. CARMAN *Graduate School of Business Administration, University of California, Berkeley, California*

As a body of marketing knowledge has developed over the years, interest in the study of marketing dynamics has increased. The ability to construct and empirically to study static models of market behavior has led to the realization that, for greater understanding, it is desirable to measure and analyze change in marketing variables by studying the time path of the behavior and attitudes of both buyers and sellers. Such study is known as *longitudinal analysis*.

The primary design considerations in planning longitudinal analyses involve two factors: level of aggregation and sample continuity. A somewhat oversimplified choice of these primary design possibilities follows:
A. Level of aggregation
    1. Aggregate behavior or attitudes
    2. Individual behavior or attitudes
B. Sample design
    1. Independent samples
    2. Dependent or overlapping samples
    3. Repeated measurement of the same sample

The panel design is one in which individual behavior or attitudes are studied by repeated measurement of the variables of interest obtained from a single sample of respondents. Thus, the panel design consists of choices A2/B3 just given.

Though individual respondents could be real persons or firms, buyers or sellers, or neither, the chief interest in, and use of, the panel design in marketing research is for the study of ultimate consumers. In this chapter, when it is not possible to be completely general, the focus will be on this application.

The dependent or overlapping samples mentioned earlier include several different and useful designs which, although not panels, deserve mention. One such design would ask different questions of the same respondents. For example, a study to predict marital compatibility may investigate couples both before and after marriage but may not ask any "before" questions in the second interview.

A second design in this category would compare matched samples of respondents at different stages but at one point in time; for example, a child development study that asks the same questions of children of different ages.

A cohort design is sometimes used to describe classification A1/B2 mentioned earlier, but this designation is ambiguous and should be avoided. *A cohort is any respondent matched with, or replacing, another specified respondent with the same characteristics.* As will be learned later, replacement of respondents on a quota basis is usually required in the panel design. The difference between cohorts in the panel and in the cohort design as previously defined is one of intent. In the panel design, respondents are replaced as infrequently as possible; in the cohort design, replacement is frequent and planned. Where conditioning bias is considered a serious problem, a cohort replacement plan may be made part of a panel design.

One other word in the definition of a panel design requires elaboration: *repeated.* Some experimental panel studies view time conceptually in discrete terms, that is, base observation, first stimulus, second observation at a specific point in time, second stimulus, third observation at a specific point in time, and so on. In other words, time is purposely broken into discrete units by using equal intervals between observations and stimuli. Other panel studies are particularly interested in the rates of change of variables through time and, hence, are concerned with time increments, Δt. In attitude studies, it is usually assumed that attitudes are subject to rapid and frequent change and that the design's goal is *continuous* measurement. One problem of design discussed later is how operationally to approximate continuous measurement through time.

APPLICATION OF PANEL DESIGN IN MARKETING RESEARCH

The panel design in marketing research grew out of Lazarsfeld's work in the late 1930s. The interruption of World War II delayed commercial application of the design until the late 1940s. Few panels have had a life span as long as 10 years. Because panel research is expensive and difficult to administer, the best-known national panels have been syndicated, the output being sold to a rather large number of clients. The building and maintenance of staff for field work, data processing, and administration require first-rate research management and a high fixed cost which is best spread over many users.

Another type of syndicated marketing research service (often called a panel even when it is not) consists of consumer juries which act as omnibus permanent samples. Any client may ask the jury questions with reasonably short lead time and little recruitment cost. However, to be a true panel, the same questions must be repeated to study change through time in the same respondents.

Purchase Panels

Two true consumer panels which have long and rich histories are the *Chicago Tribune* panel and that of the Market Research Corporation of America (MRCA). Both these panels exist for the purpose of recording changes in consumers' behavior through time; specifically, purchases of nondurable consumer products. The latter is nationwide, whereas the former covers only the Chicago market area. In both cases, purchases of frequently bought nondurables are recorded in writing in carefully designed, self-administered diaries which are mailed weekly to participants. A similar panel is operated in the United Kingdom by the Audits and Surveys Company.

The MRCA panel is a nonrandom sample of 7,500 homes selected to match closely the key demographic characteristics of the total United States population. Panel members receive a small compensation administered through a point system, which is useful in motivating accurate and complete reporting.

Recorded information includes the product, brand, type or variety, quantity purchased, price, store where purchased, presence of a special price or promotion, and similar matters of importance to marketers. Key demographic data on each family are also collected at the time of recruitment. Panels are kept "representative" of the population through continuous programs of recruitment and months of careful training.

The following kinds of information can be obtained from continuous consumer-purchase panels.

Product Movement. This is continuous measurement of the sales and market share of one brand and of its competitors by geographic region, retail price, type of retail outlet, and package variant. All this information, that is, the basic product-movement information required by a firm, can be provided by consumer panels, store-audit panels, or warehouse-withdrawal data. The difference, of course, is from whom the data are collected: consumer, retailer, or distributor. Panel data will provide information on retail-transaction size, transaction price, reported "deal" information, and purchase frequency. Store-audit and withdrawal data will provide additional information on display and price. Furthermore, the reliability of these other sources is often greater if only the aggregate movement statistics or only the net change in movement is required.

The unique advantage of the panel design is that it permits measurement of both net and gross change (or turnover) of customers to and from a product. Turnover analysis permits one to answer questions about the number of new-product triers, number of repeat purchasers, and number of buyers who switched to competing brands. Because the subject is in a natural environment, any experimenter effect should be minimized.

Obviously, one must interview consumers on a regular and frequent basis to obtain such information. Here, the panel has the unique advantage, compared with repeated samples, of minimizing the effects of sampling error and consistent bias in this process of measuring change. There is an economic advantage as well. Once recruitment and training have been completed, the cost per interview will be less than for a new sample.

Constructing a Demand Profile. Both statically and dynamically, panel data on purchases yield more data on demand characteristics than do alternative sources. A demographic description of customers and potential customers, heavy users and light users, is possible. Similarly, the characteristics of brand-loyal customers and nonloyal customers can be constructed. The characteristics and destination of lost customers can likewise be determined. This kind of information is invaluable in determining both marketing strategies and tactics. Store-audit and warehouse-withdrawal data are of little use for this purpose.

The importance of the dynamics of competitive and market activity deserves emphasis in this context. Shifts in brand share may stem from shifts in consumer life-style characteristics or from shifts in competitors' marketing activities. If one is to respond to these shifts, it is important to know how and why they have occurred. Only then can the appropriate marketing strategy and tactics be designed. Consumer-panel data provide this information.

Determining Relative Importance of Store Type. This information is also obtainable from audit and withdrawal data. However, these sources are restricted, by definition, to particular channels, whereas panel data should provide unbiased sales distribution in all types of outlets.

A Vehicle for Before-After Experimental Design. Consumer panels often provide all the requirements for a before-after experimental design [7]. The variable under study may be purchases, other behavior, or even an attitude. If any ongoing, commercial purchase panel is measuring the experimental variable, it may be unnecessary to set up a special one.

A panel will not provide evidence of causal factors unless the design is restricted to that of a true experiment. Two additional elements of design are then required:

1. The stimuli between observations must be induced by the experimenter.

2. Other possible causes of change must be identified and controlled.

In this section, these two restrictions are not assumed.

The stimuli in marketing research would usually be some marketing factor, such as a special promotion, an advertising campaign, or a price change. If a control group is required, another geographic area may, if one is careful, serve this purpose. Thus, panel data are often a valuable tool in evaluating test markets.

Audience Panels

The A. C. Nielsen Company provides data on television audiences in the United States as well as in Canada, Germany, Ireland, and Japan. Other companies supply similar services for radio and television in this country and others. Most of these audience research services use the continuous panel design.

Nielsen offers both a national Television Index and a local Station Index. For local television in 220 markets, a weekly diary is used, not unlike that used for product purchases. However, unlike the act of purchasing, television viewing can be continuous in time rather than a discrete event. Thus, the recording instrument in an audience panel must be equipped to record behavior almost continuously. Both conventional diaries and personal interviews with recall have proven unsatisfactory for this purpose. Spot interviewing by telephone is also used, but generally not in a panel design.

The instrument developed for continuous audience measurement is an electronic device called the Audimeter which is wired to the television receiver. The Audimeter records on an internal tape the time (by minute) the set is on or off and the channel to which it is tuned. Each week the panel member receives a new tape cassette by mail. When the panel member removes the used cassette from the Audimeter, she also receives two coins from the machine—thus ensuring rapid replacement and, it is hoped, rapid mailing of the previous week's record. Processing the taped information into completed reports is almost totally automated.

Note that this technique constitutes a panel of television sets and not a panel of people. To convert from one to the other, that is, to collect information on audience composition as well as on tuned-in receivers, requires using a diary in which the audience composition is recorded at 15-minute intervals. Nielsen has extensively developed electronic devices designed to improve the accuracy of these diary records. Respondents are also compensated for participating.

Households taking part remain on the panel for extended periods. However, the data on audiences are recorded by a single household for no more than 30 weeks per year.

Clients for these services are networks, individual stations, advertisers, advertising agencies, and program producers. Although some of these groups clearly are interested in audience composition and an exact count of the number of persons viewing, many marketing and media-selection decisions can be made simply by knowing the set information obtained from the Audimeter. Panel households' demographic characteristics are known, and audience reports can be broken down by these characteristics. Overlapping audience data are useful in media selection. Minute-by-minute audience ratings are valuable if one is buying spot commercials. Since time period and program content will often determine which household members are viewing, for these purposes a panel of T.V. sets is a satisfactory substitute for a panel of people.

Attitude Panels

Panels established to measure changes in attitudes through time are subject to more methodological problems than those established to record behavior. Some panels, of course, measure both. One well-documented example of attitude data currently being collected in a panel design is information on consumer attitudes on the economic outlook. The University of Michigan Index of Consumer Sentiment is constructed from six attitude questions on confidence in the economy and future expectations. These questions have been asked from two to four times per year since 1952. However, only in recent years have they been asked of a panel.

The panel design has been used more regularly by the Census Bureau, which has collected data on household purchase anticipations since 1959. Currently, a national sample, composed of approximately 11,500 households, is interviewed for six consecutive quarters, with one-sixth of the sample replaced each quarter. This Consumer Buying Expectations Survey asks panel members to evaluate the probability that they will make specific major-purchase decisions, such as to purchase a new car, during the next 12 months. The development of the probability scale shown to respondents has been the subject of considerable research. Aggregate results of each section of the survey are published quarterly by the Census Bureau. Relatively few series are broken down by characteristics of panel members. These series have been used as predictors of consumers' durable purchases.

Other Panels

A few large companies have maintained sizable panels for their personal use. The General Electric Company operates a national consumer panel that studies changes by means of a permanent core of questions on purchase behavior, plans, and attitudes on consumer durables. The panel also provides a service of one-time or short-term surveys to G.E.'s operating departments. Thus, the cost-sharing feature is still evident.

The description of these long-lived national panels should not suggest that the panel design is appropriate only for collecting high-volume, national statistics such as those on product movement. On the contrary, the panel design's unique feature is its ability to study dynamic movements in variables. Most often, such studies are planned around the before-after experimental design discussed earlier. Quasi experiments of this type seldom call for national samples. Many require only two waves, with one application of the stimulus.

Others study repeated applications of stimuli for periods ranging from three months to one year. These short-term, special-purpose panels far outnumber the national panels and offer the greatest potential of this design for marketing research.

THE DESIGN AND ADMINISTRATION OF CONSUMER PANELS

Sample Design. The sample selected for a panel, regardless of the situation, will almost inevitably result in a mixture of a probability and a quota design. Most sampling plans call for rather detailed stratification on the basis of key demographics, such as area, urban or rural, life cycle, or family structure. The specification of the hypotheses for stratification is important, for the researcher should anticipate replacing half his original sample before he obtains any usable data. With such an expectation, the plan for sample replacement is as important as the plan for sample selection. So much replacement is needed because any longitudinal study requires much work by respondents. Either initially or after a few waves, many of those initially recruited will be unwilling or unable to give the required time to the project. (Errors associated with replacement will be discussed shortly.)

After strata have been determined, an initial probability sample will be preferable to an initial quota sample. Since error of other kinds is to be anticipated, special efforts should be made to avoid error in defining the sampling frame and in selecting the initial sample. Those efforts suggest the use of an initial probability design. Initial replacement within strata might also be made by probability means, but the administrative efficiency of such a procedure will probably be low. Time constraints will start to become serious, travel bills will increase rapidly, recruiter morale will fall sharply. In the end, substitution of an initial probability sample will appear much like filling quotas within each stratum.

Bias Created by Initial Refusals. Deviations from random selection of panel participants may occur because selected families refuse to cooperate either at the time of recruitment, shortly after recruitment, or at some time later in the panel's life. Insofar as the families which refuse to participate at any of these three stages differ from the overall population, they create bias in the panel. Mortality at the first two stages will be discussed in this section; the next section will discuss mortality at the third stage.

As in any survey, the extent to which respondents refuse to cooperate reflects the efficiency of the recruitment operation, the prestige of the institution directing the study, and the nature of the task. In a panel, the success of training, the rate of compensation, and the frequency of reporting also affect early mortality. Thus, one cannot conclude that every panel inevitably faces a specific high-refusal and early-dropout rate.

However, the literature suggests some consistency in refusal and early-mortality rates. The range in initial refusals in 12 panel studies, disregarding preselected subjects who cannot be located (which should be the same for a panel as for any other survey), was 15 to 80 percent of those initially contacted. The median and mode of this distribution are approximately 40 percent (see [1], [4], [8], [5]).

In almost all panels, mortality is very high during the first three waves, but levels off at a reasonably constant *rate* thereafter. The analysis of the 12 panel studies yielded a range, for second-stage mortality, of 8 to 26 percent of initial contacts. The median was 12 percent and the mode 10 percent. Second-stage mortality is probably a function of the contact interval between waves. Intervals of one to three weeks appear to yield lower second-stage mortality than do shorter or longer intervals.

Initial cooperation can be secured through the same techniques used in any survey, for example, introductory letters and well-trained interviewers. However, the trade-off between first- and second-stage mortality is somewhat more subtle. Most second-stage mortality occurs among people who want to be congenial with the interviewer but who change their minds when released from this social pressure. This means that subjects recruited by a hard sell often become early dropouts. Since a dropout is far more harmful and costly to the panel than an initial refusal, there is a payoff in training interviewers to be less aggressive than they normally might be in the single-survey technique. Similarly, close contact with, and training of, subjects for at least three waves seem a worthwhile investment for the project's success.

Bias Created by Subsequent Mortality.   Third-stage mortality represents those persons who drop out after the first few waves. Beyond this point, most panels maintain fairly stable membership; most mortality stems from natural causes, such as death, hospitalization, and relocation. If the design permits following families who move away from the area or "resting" members in a split panel design, this steady-state mortality may be no more than 1 percent per month. In other situations, 2 percent per month is a better figure for planning.

An underlying connecting thread through the literature on panel mortality suggests that aside from natural causes and relocation, panel mortality can be attributed to some manifestations of a single cause—interest. The prospective member must resolve a personal time-allocation problem before deciding to join or to continue in a panel. The personal characteristics correlating with mortality all can be related to the interest factor [4].

In a variety of different panels in which the topic has been shopping behavior, for example, dropouts have been participants with small food budgets, nonusers of the test products, unsystematic shoppers, and those who expressed a disinterest in shopping. On the other hand, interest may sometimes have a reverse effect. In all studies of reporting on time savings deposits, respondents with large deposits are less cooperative than those with small deposits [8].

Life-cycle influences on mortality likewise can usually be traced to interest. Where the subject has been family-oriented in regard to purchases, nonconjugal households and two-person families are poor risks. Were automobiles the subject, the life-cycle influence would not be the same.

In general, busy households are often dropouts. In various panels, working wives, wives with many community activities, mobiles, renters, and those with high "other-directed" scores have been a major source of dropouts. However, in one panel on food shopping, busy mothers with many small children remained active because the interest factor was more important than the "busy" factor [4].

Mortality has often been associated with low education. The intercorrelation of education with age, income, and difficulty of the respondent's tasks makes this relationship somewhat more involved. Similarly, both extremes of the income scale are correlated with high mortality for reasons that relate to education, interest, and opportunity cost.

However, all these factors fundamentally point in the same direction. A household's propensity to join and remain in a panel varies widely, and this variation is a function of the relationship between the panel and the householders' attitudes and ways of life. The panel represents a household's long-term investment in return for, at best, a very nominal financial reward. The panelist, then, is one who finds the project related to her own interest, hence

important. Her motivation, not the financial incentive, sustains her activities.
The task required of her is not simple. For her to continue to cooperate, she
must feel that her participation is important.

Bias Created through Conditioning. Conditioning bias is defined as the bias
in a response created by the appearance of the topic of the question, or the
question itself, on previous waves of the panel. Several different types of conditioning effects may cause changes in panel responses—not all of them bad.

1. Exaggeration or lying of any kind on early waves may later give way to
more truthful answers, and hence to changes.

2. The conditioning effect may cause subjects to improve the accuracy of
their answers or strengthen their attitudes. This learning will result in changes
on subsequent waves.

3. Subjects with no defined attitude on a topic under study may, from repeated questioning, be sufficiently motivated to formulate a clear position, thus
becoming atypical of the universe they supposedly represent. In purchase
panels, this "expert bias" is revealed by respondents' becoming more careful
shoppers than they would otherwise be.

4. As subjects answer the same batteries of questions repeatedly, they may
tire, remember their responses from the previous wave, and repeat them—even
though a real change has occurred.

The quality improvements in conditioning types 1 and 2 will usually be
achieved by the third wave, which for long panels is the suggested duration of
the training period. Whether types 3 and 4 occur depends on the characteristics of each particular panel. When questions require recall about behavior,
such as purchases, in the interval between waves, the "bounded recall" technique has been shown to yield more accurate responses than any other type of
survey technique. In this technique, the respondent is given her answers on
the previous wave. The result is improved accuracy on the previous responses
and an elimination of double reporting.

The learning effect of type 3 will be present most critically if the panel asks
attitude questions. Where shopping behavior is under study, the panel may
cause respondents to be more careful shoppers than otherwise. On factual
questions, "Don't know" responses can be expected to decline over the life of
the panel. For attitudes, subjects will form firm attitudes if the questioning
continually calls attention to particular brands or topics which the subject
thinks about only with regard to the panel. However, if the subject discusses
the topic regularly outside the panel, conditioning may be slight indeed. In
short, panel membership "professionalizes" respondents. They become better
informed and more critical; they solidify their opinions and are better able to
verbalize them.

The "freezing" effect of conditioning type 4 will exist if the same questions
are asked repeatedly, unless the interval between waves is longer than one
month. The problem is most severe for difficult questions and attitude questions when this interval is two weeks or less.

Panel Administration. The previous sections emphasize that recruiting and
training respondents are administrative functions which are never complete.
The recruitment of new panel members has three purposes:

1. Replacement of dropout respondents
2. Replacement of respondents on some systematic basis to reduce conditioning
3. Replacement of respondents to reflect changes in the quota characteristics of panelists

Recruitment procedures for panels are not greatly different from those for any survey design.   Advance letters will help obtain cooperation.   In some panels, the respondents themselves can help by finding other persons interested in participating.

Training is another matter.   If the same instruments are to be used throughout the panel, it is critical that respondents use the instrument correctly and efficiently.   A training session should be employed at the beginning of each of the first two waves as a minimum.   After that, responses of new panelists should be coded separately until it is clear that they are completing all forms correctly and that no systematic differences exist between the responses of old and new panel members.

This need for continuous recruitment, training, and general communication with panel members requires that administrative time be allocated for these purposes throughout the panel's life, not only at its beginning.   Similarly, incentive schemes to reduce mortality require administrative time.

Compensation to panel participants will help to reduce mortality.   However, within a wide range of amounts and techniques, the effect on mortality will be slight.   Respondents who decide to drop out have reasons which cannot be overcome with increased compensation.   Further, "buying off" panel members may create increased and nonrandom differences in reporting accuracy before and after the payoff.

Establishing rapport through noneconomic compensation is more important and less costly than monetary payment.   It is essential to make the respondent feel she is part of a group with a worthwhile purpose to which her contribution is appreciated.   Often the panel can become a social group itself.   Such things as Christmas cards, newsletters, publicity, a recipe exchange, and a birthday flower have all been used successfully.   Clearly, some economic and noneconomic compensation schemes may bias response.   It is important to appraise the potential bias connected with any contemplated technique.

Statements similar to those just mentioned can be made about reporting as well as about mortality.   Fatigue and boredom will decrease the accuracy and completeness of reporting.   Compensation will help to overcome fatigue, but rapport and noneconomic rewards will probably be even more helpful.

One way to establish rapport is by occasional personal visits or telephone calls.   Such techniques cannot be used every week—perhaps not every month; their effectiveness will decrease with repetition.   They usually represent negative rather than positive motivation; and the man-hours required make them expensive.   However, most panel experience indicates that follow-ups help in minimizing panel mortality, particularly if personal contact fits into the natural panel design.

The form of honorarium used in panel research varies to some extent with the kind of study.   Generally, direct monetary payment should be avoided: it is expensive, has lower marginal effectiveness than more sophisticated schemes, and makes it too easy for the respondent to compute an hourly rate of pay.

A better approach is the use of a system of compensation in "points" that are convertible to merchandise.   The advantage of a point system is that it permits compensation incentive to draw attention to certain sections of the response procedure at particular periods in time.   Thus, an extra task can be added in one period simply by offering additional points for completion of the extra work.

Merchandise, purchased at wholesale, is often a good incentive because respondents perceive a retail-price value.   However, merchandise is more difficult to administer and deliver, harder to make useful to the respondent, and less flexible than a point system since it cannot be subdivided.   All these disadvantages are overcome by trading stamps, but this medium may create a new source of bias.

Just as there are unique aspects of recruiting and training for panels, there are unique features of editing and coding. These features are associated with the volume of data collected and the similarity of the information from wave to wave: respondents are the same, interviewers are the same, collection forms are usually the same or similar. Thus, although the volume of data expands the complexity of editing and coding, the opportunity for systemization and automation is likewise expanded. A few examples will show the investigator where to direct his attention.

First, personnel can become extremely familiar with some aspect of the data. In some studies, it may be best to take advantage of familiarity with certain questions and certain sections of the codebook; in others, it is best to familiarize editors and coders with the responses of specific panel members. In both cases, increased productivity through learning may be anticipated.

Second, efficiencies can be achieved in computer editing and data cleaning. Reasonably sophisticated contingency checks can be built into cleaning routines because their continued use over the panel's life will justify their construction cost. Also, because so much information is obtained about a respondent, the opportunity to construct contingency checks is increased.

Third, the volume and constancy of the data make possible the use of electronic devices in preparing data for the computer. The Audimeter for use in audience panels, described earlier, is one such device. Optical scanning of questionnaires is a reality today in some limited cases. Almost any panel with more than three waves can now efficiently use devices, such as the optical mark reader, to transfer coded questionnaires directly to tape without keypunching.

Measurement of Error in Panel Research. This discussion on bias and precision suggests that it is particularly desirable in a panel design to seek some quantitative measures of validity and reliability. Algebraically, the mean square error ($MSE_{\bar{x}}$) for a panel may be written as

$$MSE_{\bar{x}t} = \sigma_{\bar{x}}^2 + b_D^2 + b_{Rt}^2 + b_{Mt}^2 + b_{Nt}^2 + b_{Ct}^2 \tag{1}$$

where

$\sigma2/x$ is the sampling variance of the mean
$b_i{}^2$ is the measure of bias from the ith cause
$b_i = (E[\bar{x}] - \mu)$, the difference between the expected value of the sample mean and the true mean, which can be accounted for by the ith bias
t is time, since some panel bias will differ from wave to wave
D is design or sampling-frame error
R is error that stems from initial selection and replacement
M is error that stems from mortality
N is nonresponse error
C is error from conditioning

Besides the large number of terms in this expression, their magnitude varies greatly with the subject and design of each study. The previous sections qualitatively discuss each source of error. The literature provides hints about the qauntitative magnitude of some of these [1, 4, 8, 15, 17, 19]. The investigator need not assume that no useful measures exist. Biases D, R, and N may be estimated from the experience in single-interview surveys with similar subjects. Biases M and C are more uniquely related to the panel design. Where serious error is expected, the design should be altered or a control group should be used as a means for measuring error.

Panel Costs. The cost function for a panel study has the general form:

$$C = f_1 T + f_2 N[f_3(X_F) + f_4(W X_V) + f_5(T) + f_6(T)] \tag{2}$$

where

C is total cost
T is total time period of the panel
N is sample size to be maintained
X_F is quantity of information collected that is not a function of time
X_V is quantity of information collected which is a function of time
W is number of waves
f_1 is general fixed administrative costs per unit of time
f_2 is scale function reflecting decreasing marginal cost per subject
f_3 is collection and variable editing and coding cost for information asked only once; approximately constant
f_4 is collection and variable editing and coding cost per wave of variable information; should decline because of favorable learning effect
f_5 is cost of sample maintenance and replacement
f_6 is cost of incentives per subject per unit of time; approximately constant

A minimum-cost design is not easy to discuss in general terms for several reasons, not all of which are obvious from Equation (2). Cost functions f_1, f_3, f_5, and f_6 all increase with sample size; f_1 and f_6 will be essentially linear, whereas f_3 and f_5 should be concave from below. Offsetting these increasing costs are learning and scale economies reflected in f_2 and f_4.

More difficult to reflect in a general cost function is the detrimental effect on cooperation, and hence on cost, of heavy workloads (X_F and particularly X_V), of a large number of waves without retirement (W), and of short intervals between waves (T/W).

TECHNIQUES FOR ANALYSIS OF PANEL DATA

A panel design is used to determine the nature and extent of change in study variables between discrete points in time. Analysis of these changes is complex. This discussion is necessarily brief and restricted to changes in a single variable. The analyst is urged to consult the chapters in Sec. II, Parts E and F, of this handbook and also certain end-of-chapter references [6, 9, 11, 12, 13, 14, 19].

Much of the early literature on panel analysis deals only with the two-time period case. However, the advantage of longitudinal analysis lies in its ability to study the *path* of change in a variable through time.

The following joint discussion of the two-period case and the case of more than two periods will be divided by the level of measurement provided in the data: nominal, ordinal, and interval measurements.

Nominal Data. Nominal data may have two (dichotomous) or more levels or states. Although the exposition is somewhat clearer in the former case, four states will be considered here; and dichotomies may be seen as more obvious and simple.

The analysis centers around a two-dimensional array of the data known as a *turnover table*, which is the primary analytical device of panel analysis. The one used as an example here concerns brand switching among four different brands between just two waves of a panel.

TABLE 1   Turnover Table of Number of Purchasers

Previous brand purchase, t_0	Current brand purchase, t_1				
	A	B	C	D	Total
A	240	50	40	20	350
B	40	230	55	25	350
C	45	20	120	20	205
D	30	15	15	135	195
Total	355	315	230	200	$1,100 = N$
Net change	5	(35)	25	5	
Turnover	225	205	195	125	750

One can derive several useful descriptive statistics from the turnover table:

$$\text{Net change (NC)} = \text{gains} - \text{losses} \tag{3}$$
$$NC_A = 115 - 110 = 5$$
$$\text{Turnover} = \text{gains} + \text{losses} \tag{4}$$
$$\text{Turnover}_A = 115 + 110 = 225$$
$$\text{Gross turnover (GTO)} = (\text{turnover}/N) \times 100 \tag{5}$$
$$= (750/1100) \times 100 = 71.4\%$$

Net turnover for

$$\text{Brand A (NTO}_A) = (NC_A/N_{A0}) \times 100$$
$$= (5/350) \times 100 = 1.43\% \tag{6}$$

This percentage can be positive or negative. One may also be interested in the percentage loyal to a brand.

$$\text{Percent loyals}_A = (\text{loyals}_A/N_{A0}) \times 100 \tag{7}$$
$$= (240/350) \times 100 = 68.6\%$$

Note that percent net turnover plus percent loyals do not total 100.

One other related descriptive statistic may be useful in communicating the change in a particular brand.

Index of net turnover

$$\text{in A (INTO}_A) = [\text{net change/turnover}] \times 100$$
$$= [(115 - 110)/(115 + 110)] \times 100 \tag{8}$$
$$= 2.22\%$$

The index of net turnover is very similar to the most simple test of the null hypothesis that NTO = 0. It is a chi-square test, known as McNemar's test [7].

$$\chi^2 = (|\text{net change}| - 1)^2/\text{turnover} \tag{9}$$

When one wants to describe the changes in all brands, the denominator of net turnover is more appropriately the total sample size, and the numerator should measure the changes from one state to and from a single other state (brand). Thus,

Net turnover (NTO) in A with reference to B
is percentage of net gain or loss by brand A to brand B
$= [(\text{gain}_{BA} - \text{loss}_{AB})/N] \, 100$
$= [(40 - 50)/1,100] \, 100$
$= -.909\%$
It is often useful to describe total net turnover between brands in this way
by constructing a *net turnover matrix* showing this ratio for all brands.   In
general, the entries are:

$$NTO_{ij} = [(\text{gain}_{ji} - \text{loss}_{ij})/N] \, 100 \qquad (10)$$

This matrix is shown in Table 2.   For ease in reading, the brands are listed
in order of increasing magnitude in net turnover.   Note that all principal
diagonal elements are zero and that the matrix is symmetrical but with opposite sign.

TABLE 2   Net Turnover Matrix for Data in Table 1

Previous brand purchase, t_0	Current brand purchase, t_1				Total
	C	D	A	B	
C	0	−0.454	−0.454	+3.18	+2.272
D	+0.454	0	−0.909	+0.909	+0.454
A	+0.454	+0.909	0	−0.909	+0.454
B	−3.18	−0.909	+0.909	0	−3.18
Total	−2.272	−0.454	−0.454	+3.18	

Another approach to the analysis of panel data is to treat them as a Markov
process.   To do so assumes that the analyst is ready to accept that the process
and the data conform to the Markov assumptions and that the observations are
usable for the construction of empirically determined transition probabilities.[1]
If so, the turnover table is quickly converted to a transition matrix, as shown
in Table 3.
From the table, the proportion of purchasers loyal to a brand or lost to each
of the other brands can now be read directly and need not be calculated as in
the raw turnover table.
Yet a third approach to the analysis of panel data is similar to and makes
less restrictive assumptions than the Markov approach but still contains implicit
assumptions not present in the turnover-table approach [6].   This approach
assumes the process is a continuous one and calculates *transition rates* from
one state to another.   If the rate of transition of buyers from brand A is desig-

---

[1] See [13].   The asumptions are:
1.   Intervals between purchases are constant or unimportant.
2.   Respondents in the sample are homogeneous with regard to their brand-choice
process and their initial purchase probabilities.
3.   Stationarity of the purchase process is either assumed or is being tested with
the data.
4.   Brand choice is independent of past purchases (zero-order) or affected only by
the last purchase (first-order Markov).
5.   The size of the purchase by an individual consumer is constant or unimportant.
6.   Purchases are not being made for multiple uses or users.

TABLE 3   Turnover of Brand Purchases in Proportions

Previous brand purchase, t_0	Current brand purchase, t_0					
	A	B	C	D	Total	N
A	0.686	0.143	0.114	0.057	1.00	350
B	0.114	0.658	0.157	0.071	1.00	350
C	0.219	0.098	0.585	0.098	1.00	205
D	0.154	0.077	0.077	0.692	1.00	195
Total						1,100

nated as q_{AX} and the number of original buyers of brand A who remain at time t as $N_{At}{}^0$, then the rate of change can be seen as:

$$\frac{d N_{At}{}^0}{dt} = -q_{AX} N_{At}{}^0$$

$$\frac{d N_{At}{}^0}{N_{At}{}^0} = -q_{AX} dt \tag{11}$$

Integrating from $= 0$ to t,

$$\int_0^t \frac{d N_{At}{}^0}{N_{At}{}^0} = \int_0^t -q_{AX} dt$$

$$\ln \frac{N_{At}{}^0}{N_{A0}{}^0} = -q_{AX} t$$

$$q_{AX} = -\frac{1}{t} \ln \frac{N_{At}{}^0}{N_{A0}{}^0} \tag{12}$$

For brand A in the example, if we assume one month between waves,

$$q_{AX} = -\frac{1}{1} \ln \frac{240}{350} = 0.377$$

the rate at which brand A is losing customers as it approaches some equilibrium market share.

Note that the assumption of a continuous and constant rate of change leads to a different answer from the one given in Table 3. Here one can observe that the probability of an A customer's switching is .314, or 31.4 percent. This is not to say that either the raw turnover approach, the transition probability approach, or the transition rate approach should always be preferred over the other two. Descriptive statistics are meant to communicate. The latter two approaches suggest projectability under rather specific conditions. Whether they are useful depends on the characteristics of the particular panel under study.

One major condition suggested by both the Markov and the flow-rate approach is that the process is in equilibrium; that transition probabilities will remain the same from wave to wave; and that net turnover will decline toward zero. Statistical tests for this and similar properties may be found in the literature on Markov processes and brand switching. In most marketing panels, however, one is usually more concerned with observing *changes in transition rate* than with testing for equilibrium.

On the other hand, when one has a panel with K waves, the Markov and velocity models are more appealing, first, because the sheer volume of data makes the wave-to-wave approach unsatisfactory, and second, the entire motivation for longitudinal analysis lies in its ability to study the *process* of change. Thus, notions of Markov order, change in transition rate, and equilibrium are central to the analysis of panel data. Presented here are only the more basic descriptive statistics. Although it is somewhat frightening to consider all the information which may be extracted from K-1 turnover tables for each stratum of the sample, the analyst may expect rich and substantive inference to flow from the techniques suggested here.

Ordinal Data. Assume that the brands in Table 1 are ranks with $D > C > B > A$. Shifts from t_0 to t_1 to the lower triangle represent increases in magnitude, and shifts to the upper triangle represent decreases in magnitude. (There is no change among those on the principal diagonal.) From this crude categorization comes the most basic index of directional trend (IDT).

$$IDT = \frac{\text{total up} - \text{total down}}{\text{total up} + \text{total down}} \times 100 \tag{13}$$
$$= \frac{165 - 210}{165 + 210} \times 100$$
$$= -14.7\%$$

McNemar's test, Equation (9), is applicable.

A slightly more powerful approach, using all information about rank differences, can be obtained from the net turnover matrix (Equation (10)) like the one shown in Table 3. A turnover table of ordered data shows:

Perfect consistency if its NTO matrix has only positive signs on one side of the principal diagonal.

Consistency if its NTO matrix has only positive and zero entries on one side of the principal diagonal.

Inconsistency if its NTO matrix has both positive and negative signs on one side of the principal diagonal.

Interval Measurement. If the variables under study are interval measurements, then the approaches to analysis are not unique to panels but encompass the entire subject of multivariate statistical analysis of time series data [Sec. II, Parts E and F]. One may also investigate the work on the application of differential equations to the analysis of change in the velocity of social variables.

For two-wave panels, the elementary test for the sum of the differences in paired comparisons applies. One may also want to use tests for differences in the second moment between waves to uncover conditioning.

For three or more wave panels, increasing application of simultaneous equation techniques is now found in social sciences other than economics [2, 5, 16, 18]. The most powerful contribution so far is the technique of analysis of *cross-lagged correlations*.

SUMMARY

Unless restricted to a laboratory environment, a panel survey is a considerable task. It commits one to a lengthy field operation which is expensive in terms of both fixed and variable costs. Although one need not recruit a new sample for each wave, the costs associated with maintenance of the original sample will be significant and important to the reliability and validity of the study.

In this chapter, a panel study has been defined and several examples of panels have been cited to convey to the reader the technique's power in describing and helping to explain the process of change. It must be emphasized that a panel is not an experiment but can often be transformed into a quasi experiment if some measure of exposure to stimuli between waves can be constructed.

Next, the chapter dealt with the chief sources of bias characteristic of the panel design: initial refusals, subsequent mortality, and conditioning. These were then related to techniques for panel administration, total error, and panel costs.

The last section described special techniques for analysis of panel data with particular emphasis on nominal data. Techniques for the analysis of panel data with ordinal and measurement data will be discussed later [Sec. II, Parts E and F].

REFERENCES

1. Allison, Harry, C. J. Zwick, and Ayers Brinser, "Recruiting and Maintaining a Consumer Panel," *Journal of Marketing*, April 1958, pp. 377–390.
2. Blalock, H. M. Jr., and A. B. Blalock (eds.), *Methodology in Social Research*, New York: McGraw-Hill, 1968.
3. Boyd, H. W., Jr., and R. L. Westfall, *An Evaluation of Continuous Consumer Panels as a Source of Marketing Information*, Chicago: American Marketing Association, 1960. A general introduction.
4. Bucklin, Louis P., and James M. Carman, *The Design of Consumer Research Panels: Conception and Administration of the Berkeley Food Panel*, Berkeley: University of California, Institute of Business and Economic Research, 1967.
5. Campbell, D. T., and J. C. Stanley, "Experimental and Quasi-experimental Designs for Research on Teaching," in N. L. Gage (ed.), *Handbook of Research On Teaching*, Chicago: Rand McNally, 1963.
6. Coleman, James S., *Introduction to Mathematical Sociology*, New York: Free Press, 1964. On more advanced techniques of data analysis.
7. Edwards, Allen L., *Experimental Design in Psychological Research*, New York: Holt, 1950.
8. Ferber, Robert, *The Reliability of Consumer Reports of Financial Assets and Debts*, Urbana: University of Illinois, Bureau of Economic and Business Research, 1966.
9. Goodman, Leo A., "Statistical Methods for Analyzing Processes of Change," *American Journal of Sociology*, 1962, pp. 57–78.
10. Granbois, Donald H., James F. Engel, Francesco M. Nicosia, Robert W. Pratt, Jr., and Alan R. Andreasen, "Longitudinal Analysis," *Proceedings of the American Marketing Association*, September 1965, pp. 203–275.
11. Lazarsfeld, Paul F., and Robert K. Merton, "Friendship as a Social Process: A Substantive and Methodological Analysis," in Monroe Berge, Theodore Able, and Charles H. Page (eds.), *Freedom and Control in Modern Society*, New York: Van Nostrand, 1954, pp. 21–54. One approach to analysis of nominal data.
12. Massy, William F., David B. Montgomery, and Donald G. Morrison, *Stochastic Models of Consumer Behavior*, Cambridge, Mass.: M.I.T., 1970, chap. 4. An excellent summary of tests of hypothesis for Markov processes.
13. Montgomery, David B., and Glen L. Urban, *Management Science in Marketing*, Englewood Cliffs, N.J.: Prentice-Hall, pp. 53–93. On stochastic modeling of consumer response.
14. Morrison, Donald G., "Testing Brand Switching Models," *Journal of Marketing Research*, November 1966, pp. 401–409.
15. Quackenbush, G. G., and J. D. Shaffer, *Collecting Food Purchase Data by Con-*

sumer Panel. Methodological Report on the MSU Consumer Panel, 1951–1958. Michigan State Agricultural Experiment Station, Technical Bulletin 279, 1960.

16. Sandell, R. G., "Note on Choosing Between Competing Interpretations of Cross-lagged Panel Correlations," *Psychological Bulletin,* vol. 75, 1971, pp. 367–368.

17. Sudman, Seymour, "On the Accuracy of Recording of Consumer Panels," *Journal of Marketing Research,* May 1964, pp. 14–20, and August 1964, pp. 69–88. Helpful in designing forms.

18. Yee, A. H., and N. L. Gage, "Techniques for Estimating The Source and Direction of Causal Influence in Panel Data," *Psychological Bulletin,* vol. 70, 1968, pp. 115–126.

19. Zeisel, Hans, *Say It With Figures,* New York: Harper & Row, 1957, chap. 10. Old but very clearly written.

Part C

Sample Design

Chapter 1

Basic Concepts

THOMAS T. SEMON *BMD Consultants, New York, New York*

DEFINITION AND RATIONALE

Sample: A small part of anything, designed to show the style, quality, and nature of the whole (dictionary definition).

In marketing research, the "whole" is a totality of market elements (persons, households, firms) or marketing actions (such as purchases). Whatever the nature of the elements, statisticians call the whole to be sampled "population." Except in rare cases, we must be content with measurement or description of a sample, rather than of the whole population, for reasons of both cost and time. The sample description or measurement entails sampling errors, but the whole group or population is usually too large or diffuse to be measured in its entirety. Although the sampling process introduces a possibility of error that can generally not be disproved, even fairly crude sampling provides results considered more reliable than guesswork.

QUALITY CRITERIA

The purpose of a sample is to approximate the measurement or description of the whole population well enough for the intentions of the information user. A *good* sample permits generalization from its findings within acceptable limits of doubt. An *efficient* sample is a good sample for which costs (of design and execution combined) are minimized.

These criteria appear simple and straightforward but are very difficult to apply. It is often hard even to establish what limits of doubt are "acceptable" in the eventual use of the information. More importantly, the limits of doubt that apply to sample-based measurements can usually not be reliably ascertained. These difficulties, often overlooked or poorly understood by both research practitioners and research users, bar any simple, objective way of assessing a sample's quality. Checking for biases in design and execution (biases that usually defy quantification and often detection too) and computing a probable range of sampling error other than bias are usually all that can be done. Without foolproof objective assessment of quality, the sample design itself becomes both the major determinant and the major indicator of quality. Avoiding error that would transcend acceptable limits of doubt is the major task of the sample design.

One aspect of design is the specification of skills needed for execution. A theoretically very good design will produce poor results if its demands exceed the training or capabilities of the available field staff. To be good in practice, the design must include the instructions and skill-level definitions it requires in the field, or must be simplified to permit execution by the staff available.

ERRORS DUE TO SAMPLING

All errors due to sampling fall into two classes: *inaccuracies* and *imprecision*. Inaccuracies or biases are actual nonrandom errors. Imprecision is a statistical likelihood of random error which can be computed or estimated. The usual statements of "sampling error" or "confidence limits" relate only to imprecision and indicate nothing whatever about the size or direction of inaccuracies that may be present.

There are, naturally, many inaccuracies that can enter survey results outside the sampling process: misunderstandings between respondent and interviewer, misrecording of answers, coding and editing errors, computer programming errors, to note a few. Within the sampling process, inaccuracies are differences between two populations: the population for which information is needed (the target population) and the one that was actually sampled.

These differences can arise for various reasons: use of inaccurate or obsolete statistics (without built-in correction procedures) as a basis for the sample; use of a design that excludes, slights, or favors some population units over others; and incomplete or incorrect execution of the sample design in the field. The first two are sometimes unavoidable, and their effects can sometimes be predicted or allowed for; the last also is often unavoidable, but its effect is difficult to allow for.

Further discussion of errors must be carried on within the framework of the two major sample-design classes. Both the importance of the two error types and the means to minimize error differ sharply between these classes.

CLASSES OF SAMPLE DESIGN

There are essentially two ways of obtaining a sample: devise a mechanism that will *draw* a sample from the population as it exists; or *build up* a sample out of individual units so that their total mirrors some important characteristics of the population. The first might be called *natural* sampling, the second *synthetic*. The terms are not invidious. A poorly conceived and executed "natural" sample will almost certainly be less reliable than a well-executed "synthetic" design.

The natural design is often called *probability sampling* because of a widespread belief that such samples permit the application of probability theory to compute likely magnitudes of error, or deviation from the true (population-wide) results. This belief is based on correct theory, but in populations studied in marketing, probability samples often cannot be correctly drawn in actual practice. The practical difficulties in designing and applying the sampling mechanism introduce unknown biases potentially far greater than the random error whose magnitude can be theoretically computed. In these cases, the probability computation of sampling error (imprecision) becomes a largely irrelevant and potentially misleading exercise. A good example of this situation is a probability sample of households with inadequate nonresponse corrections—a common occurrence.

The term *natural sample* is not in common use, and the standard terminology distinguishes only *probability* and *judgment* samples. Yet there are samples that do not comfortably fit into that dichotomy. Two examples follow. In both cases, chances are good that the designers and users will call them probability samples in commercial marketing research.

Example 1. Blocks are selected in a primary sampling unit with probability proportional to size. The criterion of size is the United States Census Block Statistics of 1970. This selection criterion calls for constant-size clusters. The design achieves this goal by assigning each block a sampling rate inversely proportional to its size.

This is a natural sample; in fact, it is a good probability design—but not of the target population. It is a sample of the population living in blocks that were inhabited in 1970. In many cities, the design's failure to include blocks whose 1970 population was zero (which had zero opportunity of being selected on a proportional-to-size basis) is a serious bias. Although this example is a natural sample, it is an incomplete one, drawn from an incorrectly defined population frame.

Example 2. With blocks selected as in example 1, each block is assigned an equal number of interviews (instead of a sampling rate). No matter how good the selection of blocks, this frequently used hybrid design is not a natural sample because it is not drawn by any random or systematic-ratio method from any population as it now exists.

The first example shows a potentially serious bias; the second has the same bias, and prejudges the population distribution on the basis of obsolete data, a further bias within the blocks. Since the original bias can also be considered a prejudgment of population distribution, why is example 1 still a natural sample and example 2 not? The difference lies in the mechanism for selecting the ultimate households within the block. In example 1, this mechanism automatically reflects the population being sampled; in example 2, it is fixed in size, incapable of reflecting what may have changed. It is worth noting that many commercially used probability samples provided by research contractors strongly resemble example 2.

Sampling theory, based on probability theory, was originally developed and applied for use in biological, agricultural, and other physical science research and in assembly-line quality control. In these fields, the elements to be sampled are often arranged in some manner that is known, observable, or reliably predictable. The physical arrangement of the population to be sampled is important: Unless all the elements can be identified, they cannot be sampled randomly in such a way that each element has a known chance of selection— the necessary criterion for a probability sample, and a very different thing from haphazard selection.

The ideal population for sampling is the one for which a complete list of all elements is available—about the only case where a pure random sample can actually be practical. A department store's survey of charge-account customers' attitudes and preferences is an example.   In industrial marketing, customers, known prospects, and subscribers to relevant trade publications may be listed populations.   A list of individual units that make up the population is the ideal sampling frame.   The term *frame* refers to any descriptive physical arrangement that can be used for drawing a sample.   For natural samples, a frame is indispensable.   If no list is available, or if available lists are judged too unreliable or incomplete, some other frame must be used, or the list corrected.   This correction can sometimes be accomplished on a sample basis.   If no list at all is available, the frame will consist of some mutually exclusive grouping of individual units such that (1) a list of the groupings exists or can be made, and (2) the list of all groupings includes all units in the population.

These group or cluster frames are especially important in consumer surveys. For the population at large, no reliable lists are available.   A target population entitled "All Households in the Cleveland Standard Metropolitan Statistical Area [SMSA]" is conceptually simple, yet it is not a frame from which a sample can be drawn, because there is no list.   But there are maps showing all streets in the area, all uniquely identified by name or number; and since every household must have a street address, a frame of "All Blocks (or street segments) in the Cleveland SMSA" encompasses the entire household population and forms a suitable frame.

AREA AND CLUSTER SAMPLING; MULTISTAGE SAMPLES

The result of using a frame that defines groups or clusters of population elements, rather than the elements themselves, is a sample which is no longer a direct one-step operation, but a *two-stage* sample.   Samples of the consumer population on a regional or national basis may use three or more stages.   The first-stage frame, for instance, might be a list of the 3,000-plus counties in the United States.   Minor civil divisions within counties might be the second stage, blocks or enumeration districts within minor civil divisions the third, occupied dwellings within blocks or districts the fourth, and individuals within households the fifth.

Another characteristic of this sample type is that it uses *clusters* (unless each block selected is used for only one interview), and that the clusters are defined as *areas*.   Area and cluster samples need not be probability samples.   Clusters can be defined in whatever terms are practical.   For a survey of the office-equipment market, for example, the target population was defined as all functional departments (such as accounting, sales, and personnel) in certain industries.   No list of such departments was (or is) available.

For this survey, a large sample of business establishments was drawn from available lists, and the departments existing in these establishments were ascertained by telephone interviews.   The resulting list of departments in the sample establishments was then used as a frame for drawing the sample.   In large establishments, two or three departments were usually drawn, so that the business establishment became in effect a cluster and the probability of a department's being sampled was known.

More important than the non-area cluster, the preceding example illustrates a technique known as *double sampling*, which is conceptually similar to two-stage sampling.   In double sampling, the final sample is drawn not directly from the total population, but from a large sample of the population.   That large sample may also provide data for stratification not available for the entire population, or a base for correcting the original list.

The most usual form of cluster sampling, however, is to select small geographic areas, and then to make each of those areas the ultimate sampling stage by interviewing all units—households, businesses, or whatever the target population is—found in it.

The reason for cluster sampling is economy in field interviewing through reduction of travel between interviews. The economy can be substantial, but it is offset to some extent by reduced sampling efficiency: because units located in close proximity to one another often tend to have important similarities, a cluster sample with a given number of interviews reflects less diversity in the population than an unclustered sample of equal size. The phenomenon is known as intra-cluster correlation. In studying households or individuals, the trend of the past two decades toward uniform-tract housing developments, larger multiple dwellings, and retirement communities has aggravated the effect of intra-cluster correlation and reduced the attractiveness of cluster sampling in many cases.

A useful variant of cluster sampling is the use of "exploded clusters" in which a predetermined proportion of all units in the cluster are drawn into the sample, identified in advance on a systematic or random-number basis. This is a widely used practical compromise, retaining much of the economy of whole-cluster sampling while reducing the influence of intra-cluster correlation.

SELECTION OF INDIVIDUAL SAMPLING UNITS

Selection of the actual units to be studied is the last step in sampling. In theory, if the formulas of probability theory are expected to apply, this selection should be made at random. This can be done by use of random-number tables if the population is listed. In a large sample, however, using random-number tables can be a laborious process (unless done by computer), and in many cases, there is no advance listing available, so that random selection is often not practical.

The most widely used substitute for random selection is systematic selection —proceeding through the population frame and selecting every nth unit passed, r being the sampling interval determined by dividing the sample size into the population size. Theoretically, the first unit selected should be determined by a random number not larger than r; in practice, the first unit is usually drawn at $\frac{1}{2}(r+1)$, the average of such random numbers.

There has been much argument whether systematic selection is better or worse than random selection. It is simpler to use in most cases. It affords an automatic stratification along the dimension that controls the sampling path, clearly superior to random selection for small samples; the sampling path might be clockwise around the block, or straight down a list arranged by date, size, alphabet, or account number. Systematic sampling does carry the danger of periodicity error; it occurs if there is an inherent systematic pattern in the population frame along the sampling path, and if r matches this pattern or has a factor in common with it.

The classic case of periodicity occurs in urban or suburban blocks of two-story, two-family homes. If r is an even number, the sample will consist either wholly of first-floor dwellers or wholly of second-floor dwellers. Since the second-floor dwelling is usually occupied by the owner and is usually the larger dwelling, such selection is a biased one.

Another potential bias in systematic sampling is that next-door neighbors are hardly ever interviewed. This reduces intra-cluster correlation, but it could nevertheless be an important bias for attitude and opinion studies. The problem can be avoided by minor modifications of r that consist of superimposing a repetitive second pattern, such as $+1$, -1, 0; even so simple a variation will usually suffice to avoid bias of periodicity. For example, with $r = 6$, a modified systematic pattern, using the $+1$, -1, 0, would yield a selection pattern:

Original pattern ($r = 6$, start at 4)	Modification pattern	Modified pattern
4	+1	5
10	−1	9
16	0	16
22	+1	23
28	−1	27
34	0	34

Systematic samples are statistically more efficient, that is, they have lower imprecision for a given size than pure random samples, but the difference is usually negligible—and difficult to compute, in any case.

VARIANCE AND SAMPLING ERROR

Variance in several guises assumes the role of either villain or hero in sampling. In the population itself, the variance of a measure is the average of squared deviations (of all elements in the population) from the average measure. That variance is neither good nor bad; it is merely a fact, but it does determine the sample size needed to achieve any given degree of precision.

Variance of a sample mean, on the other hand, is a villain—its square root is the standard error of estimate, often called sampling error, the measure of imprecision. It is essentially equal to the variance in the population divided by the sample size. It should be minimized.

(It is worth noting that there is no such thing as a variance or standard error of a sample; errors and variances always refer to one specific measure and are different for different results from the same sample. It is assumed that in the absence of other qualification, we always refer to the error of the most important result, the critical variable being studied. It is quite possible with two samples, A and B, for sample A to yield a lower error on one variable and for sample B to yield a lower error on another.)

In cluster sampling, the role is reversed. Variance is desirable within the cluster—because high intra-cluster variance means low intra-cluster correlation, and only a slow decline in marginal efficiency for interviews beyond the first one in a cluster. Clusters, therefore, should be designed to be as heterogeneous as possible—a prescription that often makes stratification difficult.

The use of the term *sampling error* to denote the square root of the variance of a sample mean is theoretically sound, since it is a measure of potential error because of being based on a sample. In practice, the term is often misinterpreted to include *all* errors incurred in the sampling process. As already noted, the statistically determined standard error is an indicator only of imprecision and tells nothing about potentially more serious inaccuracies or biases.

STRATIFICATION

One way to reduce the variance of a sample measure is to increase the sample size; other things equal, the standard error of estimate (the square root of the variance of the sample mean) decreases in inverse ratio to the square root of any increase in sample size so that, if sample B is nine times as large as sample A from the same population, its mean will have a standard error one-third that of the sample A mean. This is a reliable but costly way to improve precision. A more practical way in many cases is to reduce the variance of the population being sampled.

To understand how this is possible (after all, isn't the population something that just *is*, not subject to change?), consider how variance builds up within the population. If the population were divided into smaller subpopulations ("strata") according to some available criterion, its total variance (which we cannot change) consists of (1) the total variance *within* all the strata, (2) plus the total variance *between* the strata.

Suppose that each stratum is considered as a separate population, separately sampled, and that the results are separately projected and then combined for an estimate of the total population. The variance *among* strata has then been eliminated from the sampling process; we are no longer drawing a sample of a population that contains these several strata. By subdividing the population, stratification reduces the variance reflected in the sample measures as standard error. Differences between strata do not enter the sampling process.

Efficient use of stratification depends on finding practical stratification criteria such that variance *among* strata is relatively high and variance *within* strata relatively low. (Note that what is desirable for clusters—internal heterogeneity—is undesirable for efficient stratum definition.)

In a survey of the potential market for college-level home-study courses, the nature of the appeals of such courses for different prospect groups was of major interest. It was hypothesized that these appeals or motivations differ sharply between life-cycle groups but may be fairly limited within such groups. Accordingly, separate samples were drawn for different strata: college dropouts under 25, housewives with grown children, men in low-level management positions without college degrees, and several others. The hypothesis proved to be correct, and the results obtained were far more reliable and informative than they could have been from any unstratified sample including these varied groupings.

This illustration seems ambiguous in that it does not relate directly to a measurable improvement in precision in a quantitative measure, but appears to be a simple exercise of marketing common sense requiring no statistical reasoning or expertise whatever. It merely confirms that statistical considerations are not esoteric abstractions, nor are they necessarily tied to numerical treatment or results.

THE ERROR OF A SAMPLE SURVEY RESULT

What the research user generally wants to know is *overall error*, which is the square root of the *mean square error*. The mean square error is (1) the sampling variance (indicating imprecision), plus (2) the square of the bias (indicating inaccuracy). This simple definition is a major frustration of research users and analysts. The sampling variance can be computed or estimated fairly easily, but the bias is almost always unknown and generally not estimable.

It is important to note that the overall error as defined is an absolute quantity, not identified as positive or negative, since it is merely the square root of a square. Sampling variance, by definition a random error, can naturally take either a plus or minus sign with equal probability. On the other hand, bias is always tendential in one direction or the other. Interestingly enough, the direction of the bias can often be guessed quite reliably; but its size eludes determination.

One approach to gauging the size of the bias is regression analysis. If the variable being measured is known to correlate highly with one or a set of known population parameters, an estimate of bias can be derived from the ascertainable differences between the sample results and the known population. Two cautions are in order: Unless the correlation is very high, the error of estimate may be large enough to make the analysis a pointless exercise; in many cases, direct comparison of sample results and population statistics is unrealistic because of obsolescence and, more importantly, differences in definitions, interviewer instructions, context, and questionnaire wording. This latter caution is especially important in the case of complex subjects, such as income, or any subjective answers, such as attitudes or opinions. It is less of a problem with simple concepts, such as age, home ownership, and certain family characteristics.

IMPRECISION, CONFIDENCE LIMITS, STATISTICAL POWER

Imprecision is defined as the potential error inherent in the process of using a sample rather than the whole population. Statistically, it is called the standard deviation of the mean (or of a proportion), and usually designated by the letter s or σ. It is a measure of random error, equally likely to occur in either direction; it is stated in terms of a confidence range for most purposes, for example, "There is a 95 percent probability that the mean of this sample will lie within ±4.7 of the mean of all possible samples," the latter being the mean of the population being sampled.

For purposes of both design and analysis of research, the desired confidence limits should be set by the ultimate user of the survey results, or should reflect his conservatism or gambling spirit—not that of the researcher. The use of the 95 percent confidence level is traditional but not always sound. After all, most business decision makers are accustomed to relying on information whose odds of being right are more in the area of 2:1 (67 percent) than 19:1 (95 percent).

Imprecision is a serious source of potential error in small samples, in samples of populations in which the critical variable being measured has a very wide range of values, unevenly distributed, and in quantitative measurement used for projection to the population.

Small samples cannot reliably reflect small changes or small differences, or test which is the better of two marketing alternatives unless the difference is great.

In advertising copy testing, samples of 120 interviews were long used as a standard by some major agencies. The author demonstrated the inadequacy of that sample size by the following method: From a standard random-number table, 100 pairs of samples were drawn, each sample containing 120 random digits. The incidence of 6s and 7s was tabulated in each sample—two digits out of ten, so that the expected incidence should average 20 percent over all samples, and the expected difference between the two samples of a pair should be zero. Of the 100 pairs, 96 showed differences within the 95 percent confidence limits, very close to expectation.

In the second pair of each sample, the number of 8s was added to the number of 6s and 7s, so that the expected measure in those samples was now 30 percent. Applying the same test as before to each pair, testing whether the difference between the two samples was beyond the 95 percent tolerance limit from zero, 39 of the 100 pairs tested out as "not significantly different from zero"—meaning that 39 times out of 100, a population difference of 10 percentage points (between 20 percent and 30 percent) was not evident in sample pairs of 120 each. Only 61 of the 100 would have led to the correct conclusion at the .05 significance level.[1] Betting on a coin toss will prove to be right 50 percent of the time, so the use of tests like these is no great improvement over chance—and a difference between 20 percent and 30 percent in advertising effectiveness is very substantial.

This example, illustrating the danger of small-sample surveys, refers to the frequently overlooked concept of *statistical power*, which is vital to correct determination of sample size. Many textbooks ignore this concept, which is presented in a useful way in [3]. In the absence of power analysis, a crude but effective rule-of-thumb approach to determination of sample size consists of asking whether the conclusions would be different if some negligible number of responses—say half a dozen—were reversed. If such a change would affect the conclusion, the sample is probably too small for the purpose. This is strictly a pragmatic, nonstatistical rule which appeals to some decision makers.

In small samples, imprecision becomes great enough to be a real danger when relying on any one sample. For this reason, good synthetic sample design (where controls inhibit the workings of random variability) may be a safer decision base than probability samples if the sample size is small.

Imprecision is a greater concern in the estimation of quantities than of proportions. Simplistically, this is easy to see since proportions are always circumscribed by the absolute maximum range from 0 to 100 percent, whereas averages and quantities are not.

A survey of business establishments, stratified by industry type, was conducted to ascertain the use of desk calculators. In analyzing the results for the insurance industry, it was found that over half the calculators in the insurance stratum sample were accounted for by one respondent, a very large company's headquarters. If by chance this establishment had not been included in the sample, the projections for the insurance industry would have been less than half the actual result (which, incidentally, was too high).

This example illustrates several points. One, the error in the sample is not a bias, since the selection process did not favor or disfavor selection of this one very large unit; it is the result—and an example—of imprecision, a concept of *potential* error, concluding in *actual* error in a given sample.

The error could have been avoided by advance estimation of heterogeneity in the stratum. Chances are that expert prior judgment would have indicated a very wide range in machine inventories between the smallest and largest firms in the insurance field. A minor branch office might have only one desk calculator; a top underwriter's central office, including claims, adjustments, and actuarial departments, might have hundreds. The standard error in a stratum that includes these extremes is bound to be very high, requiring a very large sample. The practical solution is to use size stratification within the industry, possibly even to the extent of not just sampling the few extremely large firms, but including all of them in the study together with a sample of the smaller firms. In this way, heterogeneity within the stratum is reduced sharply, and the precision of sample averages is improved. Each substratum, of course, is then projected separately, since the sampling fractions are different.

Even if knowledge of the size range within a stratum is sketchy, it should be used; in sample design, a little information is not dangerous—it is better than nothing. It is preferable to substratify on the suspicion of excessive vari-

---

[1] The results of this experiment were actually better than expected: the power of this particular test is only .50, substantially below the observed .61.

ability, and then find the substratification was not really needed, than to assume it is not needed. The extra cost is negligible; the danger of ill effects is slight; and the potential for improved precision is substantial.

REPLICATED SAMPLES

A special sample design that has potentially important advantages in experimental studies, and in studies in which error definitions are of particular importance, is offered by the use of interpenetrating subsamples, usually called *replicated* samples. It consists, very simply, of the division of what otherwise would be a single sample into several *random* subsamples. In cases where bias may arise from a controllable procedure (question sequence, interviewer bias, editor bias), each subsample can be wholly handled in one way—assigned to one interviewer or editor, or using one questionnaire sequence. A fairly simple variance analysis, comparing variance within and among subsamples, can detect the presence of bias and its importance, again provided that the subsamples were randomly selected from the total sample. If this important precaution is observed, replicated sampling can be used to advantage even within synthetic sample designs.

Aside from its experimental advantages, replicated sampling offers simplified ways of estimating sampling variance at least approximately, an advantage less important when computer variance programs are available than when variance computation is done manually.

Replicated samples are generally costlier to execute in the field if interviews are conducted in person, and they are more complex to administer. Tabulating costs are also higher than for equivalent single samples. In many types of work, though—developmental research, various kinds of controlled experiments, and in much attitude and opinion work—the analytic advantages of replicated sampling can far outweigh the extra cost and trouble.

INACCURACY

Since inaccuracies in sampling are not a phenomenon arising by chance in predictable ranges, statistical theory is of no help in gauging the accuracy of sample results. Inaccuracy in sampling has different origins in natural and synthetic samples, namely:

Class of sample	Source of inaccuracy
Natural (probability)	Failure to correct obsolete or incomplete frame
	Failure to interview all selected sample elements (nonresponse)
Synthetic	Use of obsolete or incorrect control statistics
	Inconsistencies of definition between control statistics and survey data

Inaccuracy is a particularly vexing problem in probability samples, in part because they are widely regarded as the scientific method in sampling and therefore have a good deal of prestige value. Any researcher today can buy a perfectly good probability sample *design* for the United States population from several sources—but very few research organizations are capable of executing the design properly, and very few research users are willing to pay the considerable premium that correct execution requires, at least where personal in-home interviewing is called for.

In correctly designed probability samples, the use of obsolete statistics for stratification or cluster selection does not introduce inaccuracy, since all sample-selection steps are described in terms of sampling rates, not numerical assignments. As a result, the final sample (except for nonresponse) should reflect what is actually there,[2] not what was expected.

The characteristics of a sample, as obtained from a survey, should not be expected to check closely with available statistics. In most cases, there are good reasons why differences should be found, such as:

1. The available statistics are obsolete.

2. The definitions used and the wording or context of the question may not be the same that were used in collecting available statistics; hence, responses may differ.

3. Nonresponse in a sample survey may be higher than in census or other large-scale statistical compilations.

The same cautions apply in even greater degree to results on record from earlier studies of the same population. Strictly speaking, the problem of definitions is not really a sampling component, but it frequently affects the appraisal of sampling accuracy. Comparison with available data is subject to the same caution widely disregarded throughout research analysis: The amount of suspicion that attaches to a finding should be independent of the prior assumption about what that finding would be. If a sample's income distribution agrees closely with available income statistics, that result should be investigated just as critically as if there were wide disagreement.

SAMPLE SIZE

Sample size in no way affects inaccuracy, but, other things equal, imprecision diminishes in inverse proportion to the square root of the sample size. In terms of added precision, the marginal utility of larger sample sizes diminishes rapidly—to cut imprecision in half requires quadrupling the sample size—and there is no marginal utility at all with respect to inaccuracy. As a result, imprecision has perforce been used as the criterion for setting sample size. For a given desired maximum imprecision, the required sample size, as noted earlier, is determined through statistical power analysis.

Setting the desired maximum imprecision has been generally quite arbitrary, even when it reflects management's risk style. A more rational approach to setting sample-size requirements is to use Bayesian statistics, a procedure which forces formalizing prior implicit assumptions as to risks, payoffs, and information value. Although the approach still relies largely on an imprecision criterion and tends to ignore bias because it is mathematically intractable, it is a major step forward in the practical, management-oriented design of research.

CHOICE OF SAMPLE DESIGN

In most populations, the researcher has a choice between natural and synthetic sample designs. The choice between them depends on several factors:

---

[2] In practice, this ideal is hardly ever achieved, and even fairly sophisticated designs may unwittingly fail to include population segments of special characteristics amounting to as much as 15 percent of the population. Of course, chances are that even larger segments may be excluded in synthetic designs; exclusion in these cases means exclusion from the population being sampled.

Cost. If correctly designed and executed, probability samples tend to be more costly—sometimes much more so—than other sample designs. Exceptions are found in populations where nonresponse is not a major problem (among some membership groups, and some commercial/industrial populations whose members are readily found at their known address, with interviews that elicit a low refusal rate). The cost disadvantage of probability sampling is most pronounced where interviews must be made in person.

Accuracy. The choice between design classes is partially a function of the amount of prior knowledge available and the confidence in that knowledge.

A three-year-old study of corporate image for company W had shown that some individual characteristics and general attitudes were correlated with the company image. The image was far better among both labor and business executives than among housewives (an important customer group), professionals and students, and white-collar workers. Company W had enough confidence in these findings to conduct the follow-up survey three years later with a quota sample, controlling the important occupational distribution as well as age and education, located in the same markets as the original study.

With less confidence in the continued validity of the observed relationship, the company might have decided to conduct a probability-sample follow-up survey. The occupational groupings could not even have been used for stratification except by means of a lengthy and costly double-sampling operation—since there are no usable occupational lists and since occupations do not cluster reliably on an area basis. Except for nonresponse bias, the results would probably have been more accurate than the quota sample if the prior information was obsolete (or based on a spurious analysis); the probability sample might have been less precise than the quota sample because it allowed the important occupational variable to vary randomly without control, hence contributing to sampling variance.

Where prior knowledge is scant, a probability sample with adequate nonresponse correction provisions should yield results more accurate than nonprobability samples. That is theoretically a sound rule. In the few cases where side-by-side comparisons have been made, the results of the two designs have been quite similar, but the experiments have been, and probably will remain, too few to be conclusive.

Use of Results. Where the survey results are to be used as legal evidence, or otherwise to buttress a position or enhance an image, probability samples have a major public relations advantage quite apart from their intrinsic merits: they are after all the only sample type based on recognized scientific theory. For surveys designed to sell media to advertisers, to be published under foundation or academic auspices, or to be used in other highly publicized and exposed ways, the prestige value of probability sampling is real and may exceed its actual cost premium.

It should be added that there is no watchdog over the use of the term *probability sample;* almost anyone can claim the term for a survey without submitting any proof of its veracity. One exception is the Advertising Research Foundation, which sets standards for probability samples in studies it publishes or approves.

Size of Sample. Where samples are small, probability samples are a risky investment, as stated earlier. The possibilities for distribution control on a limited number of variables offered by quota sampling, for instance, at least provide a priori assurance that certain gross errors will not accidentally occur in the one sample to which the researcher is usually restricted. The fact that probability samples of that size will average out correctly is cold comfort if the one actually drawn happens to be freakish.

Importance of Comparability between Studies. Where the major purpose of studies at different points in time is to trace change rather than establish very reliable measures of magnitude, quota samples with area control—a synthetic design—are preferable to probability samples because they offer greater opportunity for eliminating random errors that can prevent correct reflection of small changes in time. The importance of this point is best shown by the fact that the sampling error of the difference between two sample means or proportions is substantially greater (about 40 percent, in most cases) than the sampling error for either sample alone. Power analysis to determine needed sample sizes for given precision often indicates the need for near-astronomical sample sizes to measure small differences reliably. The reduction of random variation between the samples thus becomes a very important practical need.

REFERENCES

1. Cochran, W. G., *Sampling Techniques*, 2d ed., New York: Wiley, 1963.
2. Hansen, M. H., W. N. Hurwitz, and W. G. Madow, *Sample Survey Methods and Theory*, New York: Wiley, 1953.
3. Johnson and Smith (eds.), *New Developments in Survey Sampling*, New York: Wiley, 1969.
4. Kish, L., *Survey Sampling*, New York: Wiley, 1965.
5. McCarthy, P. J., *Replication—An Approach to the Analysis of Data from Complex Surveys*, series 2, no. 14, Washington: National Center of Health Statistics, 1966.
6. Stephen, F. F., and P. J. McCarthy, *Sampling Opinions: An Analysis of Survey Procedure*, New York: Wiley, 1958.

Sample Design

Chapter 2

Probability Sampling

MARTIN R. FRANKEL and **LESTER R. FRANKEL** *Graduate School of Business, University of Chicago, Chicago, Illinois, and Audits and Surveys Company, New York, New York*

When probability sampling was first introduced as an essential tool in market research, it was accepted with great reluctance. This type of sampling, though scientifically sound, was believed to impose so many restrictions on the actual designation of a sample that, after a short period of use, it would be discarded in favor of the then more economical method of quota sampling.

The demise of probability sampling in marketing research did not occur because market researchers discovered that this type of sampling is less costly than it had originally appeared. In selecting a probability sample, it is necessary to adhere to a single basic principle. With this limitation, one has complete freedom to select samples that will be compatible with the many practical operating conditions present in collecting data. In addition, probability samples, unlike quota, judgment, or haphazard samples, may be used as the basis for objective statistical inferences about the population from which the sample was selected. These inferences, which usually take the form of confidence limits or significance tests, are valid only if the sample is a probability sample.

These two factors—flexibility of sample-selection procedures and the ability to make valid statistical probabilistic statements about the reliability of sample estimates—have made probability sampling a practical tool in marketing research.

The object of sample design is to specify the particular probability sampling procedure that will attain the greatest precision in the survey findings within fixed administrative and cost conditions.

Choosing a particular sample design involves more than simply choosing a sample size. Questions of stratification, clustering and number of stages, and other details must be dealt with.   As we shall see later, a particular sample design requiring 500 interviews may be more precise than a higher-cost sample involving 1,000 interviews.

Before considering some of the many options available in formulating a specific sample design, we briefly review some of the basic definitions and concepts associated with probability sampling.

BASIC DEFINITION OF PROBABILITY SAMPLING

1. *Probability sampling:* the process of selecting elements or groups of elements from a well-defined population by a procedure which gives each element in the population a calculable non-zero probability of inclusion in the sample.

The phrase "element or group of elements" designates the unit of sampling. Thus, in selecting a sample of households in a certain city, the element or unit of sampling might be the individual household, or it might be a group of four consecutive households.   It should be pointed out that the element of sampling need not necessarily be the unit of analysis.   Sometimes a sample of households is selected and the analysis is based on the individuals living in these households.

The phrase "calculable non-zero probability of inclusion" means that every element in the population has some chance of being included in the sample and that the probability of its inclusion can be determined.   At one time, it was thought that the selection probability had to be known in advance by the sampling statistician.   This is not true.   In many marketing surveys, a household is selected; and after the household is contacted, one individual is randomly chosen for an interview.   The probability of selecting this individual depends on family size, which is known only after household contact at the field level.

OTHER CONCEPTS AND DEFINITIONS

2. *Sample frame:* either an explicit listing of all elements in the population or a structure convertible to an explicit list when necessary.

3. *Sample design:* a set of rules completely describing how each population element is given its chance of inclusion in the sample.

4. *Sample estimate:* a value computed from the sample and used to estimate a parameter or value defined in the *population*.   For example, the mean of a sample is generally used as an estimate of the true mean value of the entire population.

5. *Distribution of the sample estimate:* the hypothetical frequency distribution of sample estimates that would result if, for a fixed design, the sample-selection process were repeated a great many times.

6. *Standard error of the sample estimate:* a measure of the variation of the sample estimate about its mean value.   It is the standard deviation of the *sample estimate's distribution*.

7. *Bias of the sample estimate:* the difference between the mean value of the sample estimate's distribution and the "true" value of the parameter being estimated.

8. *Simple random sample of elements size* n: a sample selected by a design that gives each element in the population an equal chance of being included in the sample, and in addition, gives each possible set of n distinct elements in the population an equal chance of being the sample actually selected.

ROLE OF THE SIMPLE RANDOM SAMPLE

The simple random-sample design is only one of many possible designs that satisfy the criterion required for probability sampling. The theoretical simplicities associated with simple random samples and the widespread exposition of its theory in introductory texts have tended to lead many survey practitioners to the mistaken conclusion that all probability samples can be treated, for the purposes of analysis and inference, as if they were simple random samples.

With this particular sample design, the sample mean, $\bar{y}$, is an unbiased estimate of the population mean, $\bar{Y}$. The standard error of the sample estimate, $\bar{y}$, can be expressed in terms of the sample size n and the N population values $Y_1, Y_2, \ldots, Y_N$.[1]

Population mean

$$\bar{Y} = \frac{1}{N} \sum_{i=1}^{N} Y_i \tag{1}$$

Sample mean

$$\bar{y} = \frac{1}{n} \sum_{i=1}^{n} y_i \tag{2}$$

Expected value of the sample mean $E(\bar{y}) = \bar{Y}$
Standard error (S.E.) of the sample mean

$$\text{S.E.} (\bar{y}) = \sqrt{\left[1 - \frac{n}{N}\right] \frac{S_y^2}{n}} \tag{3}$$

where the unit variance of variate Y is

$$S_y^2 = \frac{\sum_{i=1}^{N} (Y_i - \bar{Y})^2}{N - 1} \tag{4}$$

and the term $(1 - \frac{n}{N})$ is known as the finite population correction (f.p.c). Since $0 < n \leqslant N$, the f.p.c. is always between 0 and 1. It may be interpreted as expressing the reduction in the sampling variability due to the finite size (N) of the population.

If the mean in question is a percentage or proportion, the formula for the standard error of the sample mean is somewhat simplified. Then we have

Population mean (proportion) $= P$ $\qquad\qquad$ (1a)
Sample mean (proportion) $= p$ $\qquad\qquad$ (2a)

Standard error of the sample mean (proportion)

$$\text{S.E.} (p) = \sqrt{\left[1 - \frac{n}{N}\right] \frac{S_p^2}{n}} \tag{3a}$$

where $S_p^2 = \left(\frac{N}{N-1}\right) P(1 - P)$. $\qquad\qquad$ (4a)

[1] The notation follows that used in the current sampling literature. Population values and parameters are denoted by capital letters, sample values and estimates by lower-case letters. For a given variate, the values associated with the N population elements are written $Y_1, \ldots, Y_N$. Thus Y_3 would be the variate value associated with the third population element. The population mean is written $\bar{Y} = \sum_{i=1}^{N} Y_i$. The variate values associated with the n sample elements are written $y_1, \ldots, y_n$. Note that the ith sample element is not necessarily the ith population element.

A simple random sample is a *measurable* sample, that is, the standard error of the sample estimate can be estimated from the sample itself. This estimate of standard error S.E. $(\bar{y})$ is written as s.e. $(\bar{y})$ and is computed as

$$\text{s.e. } (\bar{y}) = \sqrt{\left[1 - \frac{n}{N}\right]\frac{s_y^2}{n}} \tag{5}$$

where

$$s_y^2 = \frac{\sum_{i=1}^{n}(y_i - \bar{y})^2}{n - 1}. \tag{6}$$

In the case of a proportion, we have

$$\text{s.e. } (p) = \sqrt{\left[1 - \frac{n}{N}\right]\frac{s_p^2}{n}} \tag{5a}$$

where $s_p^2 = \left(\dfrac{N}{N-1}\right)p\,(1 - p).$ (6a)

It cannot be stressed too often that the preceding formulas apply *only* to simple random-sample designs and not in general. The fact is that most probability samples encountered in actual survey work are not simple random samples and should not be treated as such. However, this type of sample does have value in developing more complex designs. The simple random sample is easy to deal with theoretically and is a basis for comparison with other sample designs. This comparison may be made through using two related measures: *design effect* and *effective sample size*.

Suppose that our interest lies in estimating a population value B. This might be a percentage, a mean, a total, a correlation coefficient, a regression coefficient, or some other value. If VAR (b) is defined as the variance (standard error squared) of our sample estimate of B under a particular design, and if VARSRS (b) is equal to the variance of the sample estimate of B when a simple random sample (SRS) of the same size is used, then the design effect (DEFF) of the estimate b for that particular design is

$$\text{DEFF } (b) = \frac{\text{VAR } (b)}{\text{VARSRS } (b)} \tag{7}$$

Alternatively, if the size of our sample selected under a particular design is M, we may ask what size of simple random sample would give us the *same variance* of our estimate as that in the design we are using. This effective sample size may be expressed as

$$M \text{ (effective)} = M/\text{DEFF } (b) \tag{8}$$

For example, suppose a survey was conducted to estimate the proportion of housewives in the United States population who have purchased a certain product within the past month. After selecting, say, a multistage clustered sample of size 1,000, we might find that the sample estimate of this proportion was $p = .20$ (20 percent) and, after elaborate computations, that the variance of this sample estimate was VAR $(b) = .00064$.

If we had used a simple random sample of size 1,000, the variance of the estimate would have been approximately VARSRS $(p) = .00016$, from Formula (5).

Then, from Formula (7), DEFF $(b) = .00064/.00016 = 4.0$, and from Formula (8), M (effective) $= 1000/4.0 = 250$.

We might be tempted to say that the efficiency of the design used is 25 percent. However, we have neglected to take into account that the multistage clustered sample and the hypothetical simple random sample would have very different *costs* per sample element. To arrive at a more realistic measure of efficiency, we would have to multiply DEFF by the ratio of the cost per element, under the design being evaluated, to the cost per element using a simple random sample. In designing efficient samples, this is the value to minimize.

THE PROBLEM OF SAMPLE DESIGN

The actual sample design will depend on many different factors. In theory, a mathematical model might conceivably be developed which would indicate the unique optimal sample design for a given set of survey objectives and available resources. In certain rather restrictive situations (for example, where the objective is the estimate of a single population parameter and where the costs can be expressed as a single fixed cost plus an equal marginal cost per sample observation), this has been done.

However, in practice the objective of a sample survey rarely is to obtain an estimate of a single variate for a single population group. In almost all marketing surveys, many factors (such as advertising awareness, brand purchase, brand consumption, and attitude) are estimated for the total market as well as for various segments of the market (for example, demographic and psychological groupings). Even if we could specify, a priori, each desired estimate, it would be even more difficult to describe the relative importance of each, as would be necessary for an optimization model.

Also, cost functions under various designs are not often linear in the number of sample observations, and therefore they may be difficult to specify in exact component terms. Thus, the formulation of a complete, exact optimization model would often cost more than the survey budget itself.

Although it may be impossible to select the one sample design which is optimal, samples can still be designed that come close to this optimal point.

The remainder of this chapter outlines the basic principles and various alternatives available to the statistician in designing a probability sample. These alternatives are presented as six basic and distinct decision points, each of which must be faced at least once. After these decisions have been made, the overall sample size can be specified. This specification must take each of the decisions into account since each one plays a role in determining the overall design effect or the effective M that the sample size will produce.

SIX DECISION POINTS OF SAMPLE DESIGN

The six decisions on sample design are based on the following alternatives:
1. Stratified or unstratified
2. Single stage or multistage
3. Clustered or unclustered (elements)
4. Equal probability (EPSEM) or unequal probability
5. One-phase or two-phase (double) sampling
6. Simple random selection or systematic selection

Stratified or Unstratified Sampling

Stratified sampling occurs when we divide the original population into mutually exclusive and mutually exhaustive subpopulations or strata and select separate and independent samples within each of the strata. Stratified sampling was first proposed as a method of improving the sample estimate of a total population parameter when some homogeneity (with respect to the parameter of interest) exists within the strata.

Thus, suppose the selection of a sample of drugstores in a city is required to estimate the mean number of prescriptions filled per store in a given month. A listing of all stores is available and the number of pharmacists regularly employed in each retail outlet is indicated. Strata would be created by first sorting all stores into groups defined by the number of pharmacists employed. After this, a random sample of stores is selected from each stratum. Estimates of the mean number of prescriptions filled per store are obtained for each stratum and the overall estimate of the mean is made by obtaining a weighted average of the strata means.

If we let N represent the number of elements in the population, H, the number of strata, and N_h, the number of population elements in the hth stratum, we have

$$N = \sum_{h=1}^{H} N_h \tag{9}$$

In terms of population values, the mean value of variate Y within each stratum is

$$\overline{Y}_h = \frac{1}{N_h} \sum_{i=1}^{N_h} Y_{hi} \tag{10}$$

where Y_{hi} is the variate value of the ith element in the hth stratum.

The means value over the entire population is

$$\overline{Y} = \frac{1}{N} \sum_{h=1}^{H} \sum_{i=1}^{N_h} Y_{hi} = \frac{1}{N} \sum_{h=1}^{H} N_h \overline{Y}_h = \sum_{h=1}^{H} W_h \overline{Y}_h \tag{11}$$

where $W_h = \dfrac{N_h}{N}$. $\tag{12}$

W_h, the proportion of population elements in the hth stratum, is usually called the stratum weight.

If we took a simple random-element sample (SRS) of size n_h within each stratum, our sample estimate of $\overline{Y}$ would be

$$\overline{y}_{st} = \sum_{h=1}^{H} W_h \overline{y}_h \tag{13}$$

where y_h is the sample mean within the hth stratum,

$$\overline{y}_h = \frac{1}{n_h} \sum_{i=1}^{n_h} y_{hi} \tag{14}$$

The standard error of the (stratified) weighted estimate $\overline{y}_{st}$ is

$$\text{S.E.} \, (\overline{y}_{st}) = \sqrt{\sum_{h=1}^{H} W_h{}^2 \, [\text{S.E.} \, (\overline{y}_h)]^2} \tag{15}$$

When the selection within strata is by simple random elements (SRS), we have:

$$\text{S.E. } (\bar{y}_h) = \sqrt{\left(1 - \frac{n_h}{N_h}\right)\frac{S_h{}^2}{n_h}} \qquad (16)$$

where $S_h{}^2 = \sum_{i=1}^{N_h}(Y_{hi} - \bar{Y}_h)^2/(N_h - 1)$ \qquad (17)

We can make a sample estimate of S.E. $(\bar{y}_{st})$ by substituting sample values in Equations (15), (16), and (17).

When (SRS) is used within strata for a given total sample size, the precision of our estimate $\bar{y}_{st}$ is maximum (that is, S.E. $(\bar{y}_{st})$ is minimum) when the H sampling fractions $(f_h = n_h/N_h)$ are proportional to the S_h; that is:

$$f_h = \frac{n_h}{N_h} \propto S_h; \qquad h = 1, \ldots, H \qquad (18)$$

If the cost per sample observation within the hth stratum is C_h, and if C_h is not the same for all strata, the maximum precision per unit cost occurs when the sample fractions are proportional to S_h and inversely proportioned to $\sqrt{C_h}$.

$$f_h = \frac{n_h}{N_h} \propto \frac{S_h}{\sqrt{C_h}}; \qquad h = 1, \ldots, H \qquad (19)$$

When applying Formulas (18) and (19), it sometimes turns out that the sampling fraction f_h comes out to be greater than 1. If this occurs, f_h is set equal to one and $n_h = N_h$. There will then be no sampling in the hth stratum. For the remaining strata, a new n and a new N are established where $n(\text{new}) = n(\text{old}) - n_h$ and $N(\text{new}) = N(\text{old}) - N_h$.

In some market research situations, it is often possible to design samples which are highly efficient because they have been stratified and optimally allocated among the various strata using these or similar formulas. For example, suppose we were designing a sample to estimate the average year-end inventory (in thousands of dollars) for a certain class of retail outlet. The population consists of 100,000 retail outlets. If the overall population mean $\bar{Y}$ were 4.1773 with $S_y{}^2 = 1250.57$, we would expect that a random sample of size $n = 1,000$ taken to estimate $\bar{Y}$ would have a standard error of 1.113, according to Formula (3).

However, suppose we were able to divide this population of retail outlets into the seven strata indicated below:

Size of establishment (number of employees)	Stratum (h)	Number of establishments (N_h)	Variance of inventories ($S_h{}^2$)
Less than 5	1	50,000	0.25
5–9	2	23,000	2.89
10–14	3	20,000	72.25
15–19	4	5,300	1,225.00
20–49	5	1,500	9,025.00
50–99	6	80	28,900.00
100 or more	7	120	40,000.00
Total	All	100,000	1,250.57

With the information contained in this table, a stratified sample with optimum allocation can be designed. Assuming that the sampling and interviewing costs are constant among all seven strata, the allocation of the 1,000 stores, according to Formula (18), would be achieved when $n_1 = 42$, $n_2 = 65$, $n_3 = 284$, $n_4 = 309$, $n_5 = 238$, $n_6 = 22$, $n_7 = 40$.

By Formula (15), the expected standard error of the estimate of the mean is .1819. The design effect (7) for this design is DEFF $= (.1819)^2/(1.113)^2 = .0267$. The effective sample size, Formula (8), is $1000/.0267 = 37,453$.

In this rather extreme example, we find that using "optimal allocation" (that is, choosing n_h's according to Formulas (18) and (19)) produces enormous gains in precision for the estimate of an average.

However, we must remember that the costs of designating the strata, creating a separate frame for each stratum, and preparing the estimates may be quite expensive.

In addition, in many general-type surveys for which the specified areas of interest cannot be formulated in advance, it is impossible to specify which particular kinds of estimates will turn out to be of prime importance. Hence, the one ideal type of stratification cannot be formulated.

This should not deter us from using a stratified design for other purposes. Stratification can be used to ensure that the sample has an adequate number of cases in various subclasses that we might want to examine separately. Stratification schemes, which include the four United States census regions (Northeast, South, Central, and West) as well as degree of urbanization, are normally used in most cross-section samples because they are not costly to implement and probably do result in somewhat more efficient samples, although the exact gain in efficiency cannot always be specified in advance.

In such situations, proportionate allocation is often used, which means that the same sampling fraction is used in all strata. If each of the strata is of equal size, then proportionate allocation will result in equal-size samples from each strata (equal allocation).

Proportionate allocation results in self-weighting sample estimates of the mean. In this case, the sample estimate of the population mean is

$$\bar{y}_{\text{prop}} = \frac{1}{n}\sum_{h=1}^{H}\sum_{i=1}^{n_h} y_{hi} \tag{20}$$

However, the stratum weights W_h must be used in computing the standard error.

Stratification may also be used when partially complete frames exist. Since each stratum is sampled separately, a different frame may be used in each stratum.

Single-stage or Multistage Sampling

As previously stated, the basic principle of probability sampling is that each element in the population has a nonzero and calculable chance of being included in the sample. To ensure this condition, a frame is necessary. A frame is a list (explicit) or a structure which can be turned into a list (implicit) of all the elements in the population. Multistage sampling is usually employed in situations for which explicit frames do not exist at all, or do not exist in a desirable form. Multistage sampling allows the selection of probability samples when the construction of an explicit frame of the ultimate sampling units is either impossible or too costly. Thus, most national cross-section samples of the United States population are selected this way because a complete up-to-date list of all individuals in the population does not exist. Aside from its advantages in the selection process, multistage sampling is also used because of its many administrative and cost advantages in controlling the field and interviewing processes.

A multistage sample of all households in the United States could be selected as follows:

1. Obtain a list of all counties in the nation (frame for stage 1).
2. Select a sample of counties and designate the probability of the ith county coming into the sample as PC_i.
3. Within each county selected at stage 1, divide the land area into segments. In cities, use blocks, and in rural areas, construct definable areas from maps (frame for stage 2).
4. Select a sample of areas within each selected county and designate the probability of the jth area in the ith county coming into the sample as PA_{ij}.
5. Within each selected block, have the interviewers list all households (frame for stage 3).
6. Select a sample of households within each selected block and designate the probability that the kth household in the jth area in the ith county will come into the sample as PH_{ijk}.

The preceding is a simplified version of a national probability sample. It should be noted that (1) there are three stages of sampling; (2) three different frames are used; (3) three different types of sampling elements are used; (4) the probabilities of selection of each element drawn into the sample are known at each stage. The probability that the ultimate element of sampling, the household, will come into the sample is the product of probabilities of inclusion at each stage.

Thus, consider a particular household in the sample. The probability that this household (the kth household within the jth area of the ith county) will be included is equal to PC_i (the probability of the county of residence coming into the sample) $\times$ PA_{ij} (the probability of the particular block in the selected county coming into the sample) $\times$ PH_{ijk} (the probability of the household in the selected block coming into the sample).

Clustered or Unclustered

In selecting a probability sample, a frame must be used. The frame is made up of sampling elements and the statistician selects elements from the frame. Thus, if a sample of households were to be selected from a city and a city directory is available which lists all the households in geographic sequence, each household would be considered a sampling element and a sample of individual households could be selected.

From the viewpoint of field costs, this type of sample is often not efficient. The interviewer would conduct an interview in one household and then he or she would have to travel some distance to contact the second household, and so on. It would be more convenient from the field-interviewing standpoint if someone had systematically gone through the directory and had circled groups of, say, five adjacent households. Then, instead of selecting a sample of a certain number of single households, one-fifth as many groups of five households would be selected.

With either method, the same size sample in terms of number of households would be obtained. Clearly, this second sample could be interviewed at a lower field cost than the same size sample of individual households.

This latter type of sample is known as a *clustered* sample. Here the sample elements are not single units but groups of units. Each unit is identified with one and only one cluster in the sample-selection process, and the probability that a unit will be selected is the same as that the cluster in which it is located will be selected.

Estimates made from a clustered sample are usually less precise than those made from a simple random sample of equal size. That is, the design effects (DEFF) from clustered samples are usually greater than 1; and, correspondingly, M (effective) is usually less than M (actual sample size). This may be interpreted as resulting from a tendency toward homogeneity within clusters. That is, two elements within the same cluster tend to be more alike than two elements selected completely at random from the population.

This homogeneity is usually measured by the intraclass correlation (Rho) and is defined in the following manner.

Suppose we have a total of N elements partitioned into A clusters, each of size B. Thus, $A \times B = N$. If we let $Y_{\alpha\beta}$ stand for the value associated with the βth element, β going from 1 to B, within the αth cluster, going from 1 to A, then:

$$\text{Rho} = \frac{\dfrac{A-1}{A} S_a{}^2 - \dfrac{1}{B} S_b{}^2}{\dfrac{N-1}{N} S^2}$$

where $\overline{Y}_\alpha = \dfrac{1}{B} \displaystyle\sum_{\beta=1}^{B} Y_{\alpha\beta}$,

$$S_a{}^2 = \frac{1}{A-1} \sum_{\alpha=1}^{A} (\overline{Y}_\alpha - \overline{Y})^2 \tag{21}$$

$$S_b{}^2 = \frac{1}{A(B-1)} \sum_{\alpha=1}^{A} \sum_{\beta=1}^{B} (Y_{\alpha\beta} - \overline{Y}_\alpha)^2 \tag{22}$$

S is the variance of the element values (Equation 4). S_a and S_b are known as the "between-cluster variance" and the "within-cluster variance" components, respectively.

When a sample of a of the A clusters, each of size B, is selected by simple random sampling (that is, if a cluster is selected, all of its elements are included in the sample), the sample mean $\overline{y}_c l$ and its sampling error S.E. $(\overline{y}_c l)$ are:

$$\overline{y}_c l = \frac{1}{aB} \sum_{\alpha=1}^{a} \sum_{\beta=1}^{B} y_{\alpha\beta} \tag{23}$$

and

$$\text{S.E. } (\overline{y}_c l) = \sqrt{\left(1 - \frac{a}{A}\right) \frac{S_a^2}{a}} \tag{24}$$

The measure of the intraclass correlation (Rho) is useful in designing samples because it can be employed to express the design effect of a cluster sample when the clusters are of equal size B and are selected by simple random sampling.

$$\text{DEFF}(\overline{y}_c l) = [1 + (B - 1)\text{Rho}] \tag{25}$$

If $B = 1$, then we have a simple random sample of elements, and DEFF $= 1$.

(Rho) is almost always positive in marketing studies, and as the cluster size increases, the DEFF increases.

So far, we have assumed that all clusters are of equal size, that the selection is done in one stage by simple random sampling of clusters, and that no stratification is used. None of these conditions is necessary. Often, stratified multistage samples of clusters are used. In many practical sample situations, natural clusters of equal size do not exist, and constructing such clusters for sampling would be too costly. Valid probability samples still may be selected with clusters of unequal size. When clusters are not of equal size, the sample mean is known as a *ratio* mean since the sample size, the sum of the cluster sizes in the sample, is no longer a fixed number but a random variable.

If we let x_α denote the size of the αth cluster in our sample and y_α denote the sum of the x_α values of the variate Y in this cluster, then the ratio mean from a sample of a out of A clusters is written as

$$\overline{y}_r = \frac{y}{x} = \frac{\displaystyle\sum_{\alpha=1}^{a} y_\alpha}{\displaystyle\sum_{\alpha=1}^{a} x_\alpha} \tag{26}$$

The standard error of this ratio mean estimate is estimated by

$$\text{s.e.}(y_r) = \sqrt{(a)\left(1 - \frac{a}{A}\right)\left(\frac{1}{x}\right)^2 \left[\text{var}(\overline{y}_\alpha) + (\overline{y}_r)^2 \text{var}(x_\alpha) - 2y_r \text{cov}(\overline{y}_\alpha, x_\alpha) \right]} \tag{27}$$

Here

$$x = \sum_{\alpha=1}^{a} x_\alpha,$$
$$\text{var}(x_\alpha) = \frac{1}{a - 1} \sum_{\alpha=1}^{a} (x_\alpha - x/a)^2 \tag{28}$$

and

$$\text{cov}(y_\alpha, x_\alpha) = \frac{1}{a - 1} \sum_{\alpha=1}^{a} (y_\alpha - y/a)(x_\alpha - x/a) \tag{29}$$

The formulas for y and var (y_α) are given by Formula (28) by replacing x by y.

Most probability samples that are not selected directly from explicit frames of individual elements, as well as those in which data are collected by personal interview, are clustered samples. The cost involved in creating an explicit frame (prelisting) and the costs associated with interviewer recruiting, training, and travel make it more efficient to use clustered samples.

The reader is reminded that when clustering is used, the design effect DEFF is almost always greater than 1. Thus, using the usual formulas (SRS) for estimating standard errors will yield understatements of the true standard error of the estimate.

Equal Probability or Unequal Probability

The decision to select a sample with equal probability for each element in the population or unequal probabilities for different elements is always a difficult one.

Unequal probability of selecting often tends to simplify the selection procedure. It allows better control over sample size, and, in some cases, particularly in stratified sampling, it yields an allocation that tends to improve the sample estimates. However, when obtaining estimates from a sample in which the elements are given different selection probabilities, it is necessary that each observation be weighted prior to analysis. In general, if the probability of selection of the ith sample element is p_i, its contribution to a sample estimate (that is, weight) should be proportional to $1/p_i$.

Of course, if all p_i's are the same (equal probabilities), each sample case will have the same weight in the sample estimates.

As sample analysis procedures become more computerized, one of the basic problems inherent in selecting samples with unequal probabilities is disappearing. However, many of the theoretical problems associated with making statistical inferences from sample to population are still unsolved.

When multistage sampling is used, it is possible, and often desirable, to select sampling units at two or more stages with unequal probabilities and still end up with a final sample in which each element has an equal chance of appearing in the sample. This procedure is frequently used in clustered samples in which the sample units at a particular stage are of unequal size, and it is desirable from the standpoint of practicality as well as from a theoretical viewpoint to end up with clusters of approximately equal size.

A very common procedure is to select sampling units at the first stage with probabilities proportional to their estimated sizes, and then, within each of the selected units, to select next-stage units with probabilities inversely proportioned to their estimated size. The procedure tends to select larger units more often than smaller ones in the first stage, but compensates by selecting a smaller fraction within these larger units at the second stage.

One-Phase or Two-Phase (Double) Sampling

In survey sampling, the procedures known as *screening, subsampling,* and *split sampling* are special cases of the more general technique of two-phase, or double, sampling.

Double sampling or *two-phase sampling* occurs when a sample is selected; some information is collected from all the elements in the original sample (first phase); and additional information is collected from a subsample (second phase) of the original sample. Double sampling may be extended beyond two phases to three or more phases. The different phases may occur simultaneously or at different times.

In its widest application, double sampling is used when no frame is readily available for selecting the ultimate sampling units but when the elements of this frame are contained within the elements of a broader frame. For example, suppose a sample must be selected of households in a certain town that consume breakfast cereal. A frame for all households may be available (from a city directory) and although the cereal-consuming households are contained within the set of all households, they are not specifically identified.

In a simple two-phase operation, a sample of all households is selected, and each household is screened to determine whether it is a consumer of breakfast cereal.   If a particular household is a nonuser, the interview can be either terminated or continued to obtain demographic data, depending on the study's objectives.   The user households in the sample would be asked a series of questions relating to the different aspects of use, demographic data, and whatever other information is required to satisfy the survey's goals.

It is often desirable to ascertain the characteristics of the nonusers as well as of the users.   Once the characteristics of the total sample are known, it may be possible to use poststratification based on demographic distribution in preparing the sample estimates.   If the incidence of product usage is very low, demographic characteristics of the nonusers need not be obtained from all nonuser households in the sample, but a subsample of nonusers may be selected. The use of an X-ing pattern on the main questionnaire enables the interviewer to know, by means of X marks placed in advance on selected questionnaires, which households are to be subsampled and maintains the sample's probability framework.

It is often relatively easy to extend a two-phase sample to a three-phase sample in order to obtain gains in sampling efficiency.   For example, in the preceding illustration it is known (or can be safely assumed) that cereal consumption rises as size of household increases and that if stratification were to be used, larger households should be sampled more intensively than smaller ones.   In actual operations, the third phase would be introduced after, in the second phase, a household was established as a user.   The size of household would be determined, and then, through a series of X-ing patterns, different subsampling rates would be set, depending on household size.

Split sampling, another form of double sampling, is used when the amount of interviewing time required to obtain all the information desired is too long for a satisfactory interview.   In this case, certain designated questions in the questionnaire are administered to, say, one-half the respondents, and other designated questions are administered to the other half.

The technique of two-phase sampling is used with great advantage in store audits where certain products can be found in outlets of various types but not in all outlets of a given type.   Take, for example, camera film.   This product may be found in all camera stores, in some stationery stores, in some grocery stores, in some variety stores, in most drugstores, and so on.   Let us assume that camera film is sold in 20 percent of the outlets in a given area.   A sample of 100 outlets yielding only 20 with the product line would be highly inefficient.   To improve the efficiency of the audit, *two* surveys are conducted.   The first, usually referred to as a distribution study, is conducted with a relatively large sample.   By means of this study, the outlets carrying the product are identified without the necessity of using highly trained auditors.   Calls need be made only on those outlets that carry the product.   In selecting the particular outlets to be audited, stratification and optimum-allocation procedures may be employed.

In some cases, for example when screening is used, double sampling is necessary.   In other cases, it may be optimal.   The decision whether to use it is determined by examining the expected gain from using the information obtained in the first study.   If the cost of the preliminary study is less than the expected gain in the more intensive study, two-phase sampling should be used.

In general, the gain in efficiency in double sampling will occur if the final sample does make use of disproportionate allocation, that is, where some strata are sampled more intensely than others.

Simple Random Selection or Systematic Selection

The basic definition of probability sampling requires that a procedure be used for selecting a sample that gives each element in the population a calculable non-zero probability of inclusion in the sample. Although all of the designs previously discussed adhere to this principle, no mention has been made of the actual mechanical process of selecting the sample. For the selection of elements, the statistician has two basic methods.

The first method is known as simple random sampling (without replacement). In this type of sampling, every element in the population has an equal chance of being included and, in addition, each equal-sized set of distinct elements in the population has an equal chance of selection. Perhaps the simplest way to select such a sample is to use a table of random numbers, as also noted in the preceding chapter. Such a table contains rows and columns of digits ranging from 0 through 9, the particular digit at each cell in the table having been selected by a random process. Each row can represent a number, the maximum being determined by the number of columns being used. Thus, to represent numbers 000 to 999, three columns are used.

To use random numbers to select a sample of elements from a frame, the elements must first be numbered. Then the statistician turns to the table of random numbers, using as many columns as necessary to include the highest numbered element. He examines the first number in the table; this identifies the first element in the frame to be included in the sample. He then proceeds to the next number to identify the second sampled element, and continues this process until he has selected the given size sample. If in the process a number has been repeated, the statistician ignores that number and proceeds to the next random number.

With this type of sampling, each element in the frame has the same chance of being included in the sample. If, from a frame of 2,000 elements, 100 were selected through the use of the table of random numbers, each element in the frame would have 1 chance in 20 of coming into the sample. Since no restrictions have been imposed, it is possible but unlikely that the sample would consist of the first 100 elements in the frame. There is no assurance against this happening.

Because of the possibility of obtaining seemingly unrepresentative samples and also because of the labor involved in using a table of random numbers, another approach is often used. This is known as *systematic* sampling. If it were desired to select a sample of 100 elements out of 2,000, the sampling interval, 2,000 divided by 100 = 20, is first computed. A random number between 1 and 20 is selected, and starting with the number, every twentieth element is included in the sample. By using this type of selection, every element in the population has an equal chance of being included. However, this is a restricted type of selection: for example, if element number 47 were selected in the sample, the probability that, say, element 48 will be included is zero.

This type of restriction tends to spread the sample elements equally throughout the frame and has great intuitive appeal. However, by using this plan, one cannot get a true estimate of the variance of the estimate from the sample by itself. This type of sample is a clustered one of 100 elements per cluster, with a single cluster selected out of 20 possible clusters.

ESTIMATION OF SAMPLING ERRORS

As was indicated at the beginning of this chapter, one of the major reasons for using probability samples is the ability to make a statistical inference about a *population* from the *sample observations*. This inference is usually based on the assumption that a population estimate, computed from a probability sample, follows a normal frequency distribution, with the mean value of this distribution close to the actual population value.

In previous sections, we have cited, for several types of sample designs, formulas appropriate for estimating the standard error when the sample estimate is an average, such as a mean, a proportion, or a ratio. For more complex sample designs, analytical formulas for the estimates of the standard errors of these averages are available. However, they often involve a great deal of computation. When we estimate more complex population parameters (for example, correlation coefficients, regression coefficients, and so on) from samples, the formulas required to estimate the standard errors therein may not exist at all, and if they do, they require enormous amounts of computation. Because of this complexity, market researchers usually do not attempt to compute standard errors, or if they do, they tend to use the formulas appropriate for simple random sampling and thus usually understate the standard errors of their estimates.

In such cases, where the computation of standard errors is complex and costly, reasonably good estimates of standard errors can often be made by using the technique of replicated (interpenetrating) sample designs, or by the more recently developed "repeated replication" techniques.

Replicated (interpenetrating) sampling is accomplished as follows:
1. Assume that a total sample of size n is desired.
2. Choose a sample design that will yield samples of size (n/k), for some $k \geqslant 2$.
3. Select k samples with this design.
4. Compute the estimate b, of the population parameter B using data from all k samples taken together.
5. Compute the same estimate for each of the k samples separately $(b_1, \ldots, b_k)$.
6. Estimate s.e.(b) by the formula:

$$\text{s.e.}(b) = \sqrt{\left[1 - \frac{n}{N}\right]\frac{s_{bi}^2}{k}} \tag{30}$$

where
$$S_{bi}^2 = \frac{\sum_{i=1}^{k}(b_i - \bar{b})^2}{k - 1}$$

The number of replications or interpenetrations, k, may be chosen to be as small as 2, or as large as n. In practice, k is usually between 4 and 25.

When replicated (interpenetrating) sampling was first suggested, many practitioners believed that because of the ease of computing estimates of standard errors, all probability samples should be designed in this manner. However, this method is not without drawbacks. For a given total sample size n, as k, the number of replications, is increased, the degree to which the sample can be stratified decreases. This leads to samples with large design effects. In addition, as the number of replications increases, the *bias* of the estimate of standard error (30) tends to increase for the more complex population estimates. On the other hand, as k decreases, the precision of the estimate of the standard error (30) decreases (that is, the variability of the estimate of standard error increases). This decrease is the result of the decrease in the "degrees of freedom" $(k - 1)$ in Formula (30).

Very recently a group of techniques, which might be called repeated ("pseudo") replication methods, has been developed which does away with this bias-precision trade-off. These repeated replication techniques use replicated designs with $k = 2$. However, instead of estimating the standard error by Formula (30), m pseudo replicates are formed by selecting primary sampling units from both of the $k = 2$ original replicates. The selection of these pseudo replicates is done in a way that preserves the complexity of the original sample design. Estimates of the standard error are made by contrasting these pseudo replicates. In this way the estimate bias is kept small (since $k = 2$), and the precision of the estimate is increased through the use of m repetitions.

A recent study[1] has indicated that among these repeated replication techniques, the method of balanced repeated replication (BRR) is "optimal" in the sense that standard errors computed by BRR best satisfy the following approximation:

$$\frac{\text{sample estimate} - E(\text{sample estimate})}{\text{BRR estimate of standard error}} \simeq t_{(H)}$$

That is, the distribution of the sample estimate minus its expected value, divided by its BRR estimate of standard error, is approximately distributed as student's t with degree of freedom H. The sample estimate may be a mean, a proportion, a simple or partial correlation coefficient, or a simple or multiple-regression coefficient.

The value of this finding is that standard, normal inference procedures can be used with clustered and stratified samples. Prior to this study, these techniques were thought proper only for simple random samples.

The reader who wishes to use BRR techniques for estimating standard errors will find a complete description of the method in the article "Balanced Repeated Replications for Standard Errors."[2]

CONCLUSION

Despite its rigid basis with respect to the probability of selection of elements, a great deal of flexibility is inherent in the application and use of probability sampling. No fixed probability sample design is optimum for all surveys because no two sample surveys are alike. They differ with respect to the goals and objectives, to the types of questioning procedures to be used, to the amount and nature of human resources necessary for its execution at the field-interviewing level, and finally, to the funds available for the survey.

With the many variations of probability sampling now available and with other variations that may be introduced, the sampling statistician is in an excellent position to design samples that are practical and efficient.

BIBLIOGRAPHY

Practical Applications

Deming, W. E., *Sample Design in Business Research*, New York: Wiley, 1960.
Hansen, M. H., W. N. Hurwitz, and W. G. Madow, *Sample Survey Methods and Theory*, vol. 1, New York: Wiley, 1953.

[1] M. R. Frankel, *Inference from Survey Samples*, Ann Arbor: Institute for Social Research, University of Michigan, 1971.
[2] L. Kish and M. R. Frankel, in *Journal of the American Statistical Association*, vol. 65, December 1970, pp. 1071–1094.

Kish, L., *Survey Sampling*, New York: Wiley, 1965.

Kish, L., M. Frankel, and N. Van Eck, *SEPP: Sampling Error Program Package*, Ann Arbor: Institute for Social Research, University of Michigan, 1972.

Yates, F., *Sampling Methods for Censuses and Surveys*, 3d ed., London: Griffin, 1960.

Mathematical Theory

Cochran, W. G., *Sampling Techniques*, 2d ed., New York: Wiley, 1963.

Raj, D., *Sampling Theory*, New York: McGraw-Hill, 1968.

Elementary Theory

Stuart, A., *Basic Ideas of Scientific Sampling*, Griffin's Statistical Monographs and Courses, no. 4, London: Griffin, 1962.

Part C

Sample Design

Chapter 3

Bayesian Framework for Sample Design

SEYMOUR SUDMAN   *Survey Research Laboratory, University of Illinois at Urbana-Champaign, Illinois*

INTRODUCTION

Recent developments in Bayesian statistics have helped to clarify some of the more perplexing problems faced in designing a sample. This chapter will discuss three such sample design problems and contrast the Bayesian solutions with those suggested by classical statistical methods. The text discussion, mainly nonmathematical, will be developed primarily by using examples.

The design problems to be discussed are:

1. How large a sample should be selected; or how much money should be spent to obtain sample information; or, basically, is any sampling required?

2. What level of cooperation from sample respondents is required; or how much money should be spent to achieve a given cooperation level; or, basically, can any sample be considered adequate if less than full cooperation is obtained?

3. If prior information (in different amounts) is available about the different strata of the population to be sampled, how does this affect an optimum sampling design?

The first of these problems is by far the most difficult and important.

HOW LARGE SHOULD THE SAMPLE BE?

The basic factors determining the value of additional information have been given in Sec. II, Part A, Chap. 3. In summary, they are:

The current degree of uncertainty

Alternative decisions or actions based on information

The gains or losses connected with each possible decision

If there were no cost for obtaining additional information, the entire population would be sampled. In the real world, however, information is never free. There are direct costs of purchasing information from either surveys or other outside sources, and often hidden costs in time spent evaluating such information or in deferring a decision until the information is gathered.

Information is like other economic goods; it has decreasing marginal utility. The less we know about anything, the more useful the new information will be. The same optimizing principle used for other economic goods is used when purchasing information. The purchase of additional information continues until its marginal value equals the marginal cost. Since marginal costs of information remain roughly constant, there will come a time when we would not pay for additional information. This is why the researcher does not continue to collect information until he is completely certain, even if it were possible to do so.

The statement of the principle is only the start of the problem of determining optimum sample costs for new information. Methods must be found for estimating both the marginal value and the cost of sample information.

Direct costs of obtaining sample information are obtained from past experience or by asking for bids from research organizations. In the following examples, only these direct costs will be considered. Indirect costs due to time delays are far more difficult to quantify, but may be far more critical. An important illustration of this is found in the introduction and marketing of new products. For many such products, time is crucial. If the product is successful, its greatest profitability will come in the early months of its life before competitive products have been introduced on the market. For this reason, many new products are rushed on the market before any or much market research is done. This need not be irrational behavior (although often it turns out to be a mistake). The decision to market without testing implies that the decision maker thinks the time costs of research are greater than the value of any new information.

The problems in determining the value of information are even greater. Although most of the debate between Bayesian and classical statisticians has been on the issue of the manager's current degree of uncertainty or prior judgments, this is not seen here as the worst of the difficulties. Through a proper series of questions, it is possible to obtain a reasonably good estimate of the decision maker's prior judgments. That these judgments exist is evident to any researcher who has presented the same research findings to two different managers and had the findings interpreted in two different ways. The Bayesian approach does not create prior judgments; it formally attempts to surface them so they may be examined for logical errors. Nor is there any assumption that the prior judgments of different decision makers are equally valid. In the business world, some firms and managers are consistently more successful than others, although they may have access to the same information sources.

VALUE OF DECISIONS

The greatest difficulty in determining the value of information is in determining the gains or losses connected with the possible decisions. The problem becomes increasingly challenging as one moves from the profit to the nonprofit sector of the economy and from the present into the future. Nevertheless, decisions must still be made, although it is impossible to describe the formal decision process.

Here are four examples, arranged in increasing order of uncertainty, about the value of alternative decisions. Only for the first example is it possible to describe a formal Bayesian procedure for estimating the value of new information. (This example will be used subsequently.)

Example 1: The marketing manager of a large food-manufacturing firm must decide whether to market a new gourmet product. He is told by his accountants that the fixed costs of introducing this product are $2.9 million for marketing, advertising, and the adaptations required in current production facilities. Also, it is estimated that there will be an expected unit-profit margin of 30 cents per package after unit production and marketing costs are covered. Assume, for simplicity, that the marketing manager must ultimately decide whether to market this product. His decision will depend on his predictions about the product's life and its sales curve during this life. Thus, if he believes that the company can sell 10 million units the first year because of the product's novelty but nothing thereafter, the value of the decision to market would be:

$$V_{\text{market}} = .30(10,000,000) - 2,900,000 = \$100,000$$
$$V_{\text{do not market}} = 0 \text{ (nothing ventured, nothing gained)}$$

If he believes that 10 million units (or any other quantity) can be sold annually during the next 10 years, he can compute the present value of his firm's discounted income stream, using the interest rate of alternative investments. In general, however, he will be uncertain about his product's future, since he will not be able to predict coming market changes and, particularly, the introduction of new, competitive brands.

The crucial periods he must consider are the early years of his new product. Uncertainty about the distant future will probably cause him to use a discount rate two or three times larger than the current interest rate for nearly all products. His expectations for a period of longer than about 10 years will be discounted to a present value so small that it may usually be ignored when he makes his decision. On the other hand, he cannot ignore his uncertainty about the near future. Suppose he must choose between a novelty item that will have a high profit the first year but a very indefinite future beyond that, and another product whose first year's sales will be smaller but whose future sales are reasonably certain for five or six years. His choice should be based on the present value of the discounted income streams of the two products. Generally, the product with the reasonably certain future would be preferred unless the novelty item's profits in the first year would probably be greater than the sum of the discounted profits of the other product.

Example 2: The Value of a Public Relations Program for a Utility. Since the rate of return on investments is regulated for utilities by public regulatory bodies that ultimately reflect public attitudes toward these utilities, all utility companies conduct vigorous programs to keep everyone happy. Presumably, many utilities view these activities very much as they view their insurance programs, that is, as a reasonable cost incurred to prevent large potential losses. A utility must decide each year how much to allocate for public relations activities. In practice, this decision is probably made using the previous year's expenditures as a base, with additional funds allocated if any special problems are foreseen.

Underlying this process, however, is an implicit evaluation that the decision to spend x dollars when the state of public opinion is S results in a discounted income stream of I dollars. The utility must be careful not to spend too much money on public relations, since eventually public opinion might be negatively affected if people should feel the utility is spending too much of its money to influence them.

Example 3: Public Policy Issues. How much should the federal government spend for cancer research next year, how much for welfare programs, how much for defense activities? These decisions require an evaluation of how valuable cures for cancer might be, what the value to society of reducing social ills is, or, most fundamentally, what value can be placed on human life. Stated thus baldly, many people would argue that it is impossible to answer these questions, and yet these decisions are made continuously at both legislative and executive levels. To simplify the process, the decisions are made in many stages. First, overall decisions are made on the proportion of the gross national product to allocate to the public sector of the economy. Then, within the public sector, funds are allocated to major areas such as defense and welfare, and the allocation process continues until funds are allocated at the lower levels to very specific projects. Even then, the directors of these projects must make decisions on fund allocations based on value judgments. Of course, the values of alternative decisions also depend on the state of the world. During periods of world tension, defense spending takes an increased portion of public funds. As a cure for cancer becomes ever more probable, funds for cancer research will be increased by transferring money from somewhere else.

Since it is so difficult to determine the value of decisions, mistakes are made frequently, or substantial disagreements arise about the value of certain decisions. Many public health officials believed that too much money was allocated for research in poliomyelitis during the 1950s, since so few people were affected, but the decision was based on public opinion at the time. The value of landing men on the moon has also been questioned. What must be stressed is that decisions are made even when there are disagreements about their value.

Example 4: Basic Research. After the National Science Foundation has been allocated funds by Congress, which believes that basic research increases the nation's general welfare, it must decide how to allocate its funds to different areas of basic research. Though it is not possible to put a value on basic research (typically, scientists, when asked about its value, reply, "What's the value of a new-born baby?"), the decision is made by considering all basic research to be of roughly equal value. This does not mean that all proposals are treated equally. Value judgments are made about the researcher and his probability of success based on past performance, so that fund allocations may be based primarily on judgments about the researcher, rather than about the research.

THE VALUE OF INFORMATION

If we limit ourselves to a situation, such as a new-product introduction, where we can specify the value connected with each possible decision as well as the current degree of uncertainty, it should be possible to compute the value of additional information. If prior probabilities and cost functions are expressed complexly, then the value of information cannot be expressed simply but may still be estimated, using high-speed electronic computers to do the necessary integration.

It is possible to express the value of information relatively simply and to estimate optimum sample sizes and costs if the cost function for the new product is linear and if the decision maker's prior judgments can be expressed in the form of a normal distribution. This is not a trivial case. For many decisions, the manager's prior distribution will be either roughly normal or so loose that a normal distribution fits as well as more complex distributions. Let us assume in our example that the marketing manager's prior distribution is normal. A way of testing this assumption is to compute the consequences of the manager's prior distributions and present these results to him. If they do not agree with his judgment, then the normality assumption was not warranted.

The value of information is calculated using the table of the unit normal loss integral, first given by Schlaifer [6] and reprinted here as Appendix Table 1. The use of this table is best illustrated by continuing our example.

Example 1 (cont.): To specify a normal distribution, one must give its mean and standard deviation, or more generally, any two points on the distribution. The marketing manager has given the mean of the distribution when he estimates that 10 million units will be sold the first year. He is then asked how certain he is of this estimate. If he answers that he is 90 percent certain that at least 9 million will be sold, then he has specified the standard deviation of his prior normal distribution as being equal to 780,000 units. (Readers who have difficulty in verifying this statement should consult a statistics book that discusses the unit normal integral.) The prior standard deviation will be designated by v (not to be confused with V for value), the prior variance by v^2, and the prior mean by $\bar{X}_p$.

The formula for a slightly more general case than the example follows. It contains two acts, both with linear cost curves.

Let the value of act $1 = V_1 = Xk_1 - C_1$,
and the value of act $2 = V_2 = Xk_2 - C_2$,
where k_1 is the unit profit from act 1,
k_2 is the unit profit from act 2,
C_1 is the fixed cost of act 1,
C_2 is the fixed cost of act 2.
Define $k_t = k_1 - k_2$

The break-even value $X_b = \dfrac{c_1 - c_2}{k_1 - k_2}$

Then, the loss due to uncertainty, or the value of perfect information, is $L = k_t v G(D)$, where G is the unit normal loss integral and

$$D = \frac{|X_b - \bar{X}_p|}{v}$$

What is the maximum amount that the marketing manager would pay for information about future sales of his company's new gourmet food? His break-even point is $X_b = \dfrac{2,900,000 - 0}{.30 - 0} = 9,666,667$ units. Note that the decision not to market is merely a special instance of the more general case in which the choice is between two marketing actions. Since

$$\bar{X}_p = 10,000,000 \text{ and } v = 780,000$$

$$D = \frac{10,000,000 - 9,666,667}{780,000} = .427$$

and, from Appendix Table 1 (pp. 2-259 and 2-260), $G(.427) = .22$, then

$$L = (.30)[(780,000)](.22) = \$51,500$$

The proof of this formula is given by Schlaifer [6]. The formula mathematically expresses the three factors previously discussed as related to the value of new sample information. The current degree of uncertainty is expressed by v. The gain or loss connected with each possible decision is expressed by k_t, and the effect of the uncertainty on the decision is expressed by $G(D)$. Note that as D becomes larger, $G(D)$ becomes smaller. The greater the difference between the break-even point and the prior mean, the larger D becomes and the smaller $G(D)$. Also D depends on v. As v becomes smaller, $G(D)$ becomes larger and the lower the loss due to uncertainty.

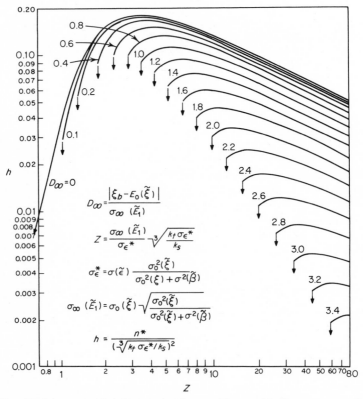

Fig. 1.   Optimum sample size: two-action problems with linear costs. *(Reproduced with permission from [6, p. 712].)*

OPTIMUM SAMPLE SIZE FOR NEW SAMPLE INFORMATION

Since we now have a way of expressing the value of sample information, there is only one other factor to consider in deciding how large to make our sample—the cost of sampling. This cost consists of two parts, fixed and variable. The fixed costs are important in deciding whether to sample at all, and the variable costs determine how large the sample should be after the decision is made to sample.

The sample size for which the marginal decrease in uncertainty just equals the marginal cost is not easily described in uncertainty, but the above Figure 1, taken from Schlaifer, enables one to determine the optimum sample size after some calculations. One must know the values of two parameters, D and Z, to find a value h on the chart. D has already been defined as

$$D = \frac{X_b - \bar{X}_p}{v}$$

Z *is* defined as

$$\frac{v}{\sigma} \sqrt[3]{\frac{k_t \sigma}{k_s}}$$

where k_s = the variable cost of sampling

$k_t = k_1 - k_2$ as defined earlier, and

σ = the standard deviation among individuals in the population, measuring the marginal information of a single observation

Since all these factors are assumed known before any sample is selected, the value of σ must be estimated from past experience with similar products or from a pilot test.

Once h is read from the chart, the optimum sample size n^* is found from the equation

$$n^* = h \left(\sqrt[3]{\frac{k_t \sigma}{k_s}} \right)^2$$

Example 1 (cont.): Continuing the normal distribution example, suppose the fixed cost of sampling is $1,000 and the variable cost is $10 per case. Assuming for the moment that additional information should be obtained, how large should the sample be? We know that $D = .427$. Suppose that, based on past experience, we estimate $\sigma = 6,000,000$ units. Then,

$$Z = \frac{780,000}{6,000,000} \sqrt[3]{\frac{(.30)(6,000,000)}{10}} = (.13)(56.50) = 7.3$$

and from Figure 1, $h = .135$, so

$$n^* = .135(56.50)^2 = 431$$

There is one additional step: determining whether any sample is justified. If it is, then the total cost of the sampling will be less than the reduction in the loss due to uncertainty. Here the total cost of the optimum sample of 431 cases is $1,000 + 10(431) = $5,310$.

To compute the gain in information due to sampling, the posterior standard deviation must be computed. This can be done most easily by translating the manager's prior distribution into an equivalent sample size. To do this, recall that for a sample of n independent observations,

$$\sigma_X = \frac{\sigma}{\sqrt{n}}$$

Rearranging the terms to solve for n,

$$n = \left(\frac{\sigma}{v} \right)^2$$

For the example,

$$n = \left(\frac{6,000,000}{780,000} \right)^2 = 59$$

That is, the manager's prior distribution is equivalent to his having earlier selected a sample of size 59 and observed the results. If a sample of 431 cases is then selected and combined with his earlier prior distribution, he will have the equivalent of 490 independent observations and the new posterior standard deviation

$$v' = \frac{6{,}000{,}000}{\sqrt{490}} = 271{,}000$$

Now, $D = \dfrac{|10{,}000{,}000 - 9{,}666{,}667|}{271{,}000} = 1.23,$

and $G\ (1.23) = .053,$
and $L = (.30)\ (.053)\ (271{,}000) = \$4{,}300.$
The reduction in the loss due to uncertainty $= 51{,}500 - 4{,}300 = \$47{,}200,$ which is far more than the cost of sampling, so sampling is justified.

All this analysis has occurred before any sample was selected. Now suppose the sample was actually selected and the *sample* estimate of consumption was 9,600,000 per year. The posterior estimate of consumption is

$$\bar{x}_p' = \frac{59\ (10{,}000{,}000) + 431\ (9{,}600{,}000)}{490} = 9{,}648{,}000$$

These sample results require renewed consideration of whether additional sampling is required. Note that as a result of the sample, the marketing manager would change his decision if he had to make it immediately. He would now decide not to market the new gourmet product since his posterior expectation is below the break-even point. Since he is also nearer the break-even point, he should now recompute L.

$$L = (.30)\ (271{,}000)(.36)$$

since D is now $\dfrac{|9{,}648{,}000 - 9{,}666{,}667|}{271{,}000} = .069,$ and $G(D) = .36,$ and $L =$ \$29,300.

Again, an optimum new sample size should be computed. Now,

$$Z = \frac{271{,}000}{6{,}000{,}000}\ (56.50) = 2.55$$

From Figure 1, $h = .18$ and $n^{\circ} = .18\ (56.50)^2 = 575.$
Assuming there are no additional fixed costs of sampling, this additional sample will cost \$5,750. Before sampling, we expect that our new v'' will equal $\dfrac{6{,}000{,}000}{\sqrt{1{,}065}} = 184{,}000,$

and our new D will equal $\dfrac{|9{,}648{,}000 - 9{,}666{,}667|}{184{,}000} = .10,$
and our new $L = (.30)\ (184{,}000)\ (.35) = \$19{,}300.$
The reduction in loss due to uncertainty is \$10,000, a little more than the cost of the sampling, so the additional sampling should be done. This does not mean that the initial sample was too small. It was the correct size based on prior judgments at that time. The additional sample was required because the first sample, surprisingly, brought us closer to the break-even point. If the sample results had confirmed the prior judgment, then no new sample would have been required. If the sample results, on the other hand, produced an

estimate larger than the prior estimate of consumption, the posterior estimate would have been even further from the break-even point and the initial sample would have been too large, although by then it would have been too late to do anything about it.

One might feel from this discussion that a sequential sampling plan might be employed, where the decision to sample another unit would be made only after examining the sample selected to date. Though such procedures are feasible for production-line sampling, they are not administratively feasible for survey work conducted simultaneously in many locations.

This example, although oversimplified, does suggest the process for determining an optimum sample when costs of alternative decisions are clearly specified. Perhaps the least realistic assumption made is that it is possible to estimate precisely the product's future use through sample surveys. Problems with the reliability of attitudes toward products not yet on the market are considerable, but discussion of these problems is deferred to a later chapter [Sec. IV, Part B, Chap. 2].

STRATIFIED SAMPLING

Both of the two other problems discussed in the introduction, level of cooperation and optimum sampling design, are subclasses of the more general problem of an optimum design for a stratified sample with prior probabilities. This more general problem will be discussed first, using the same examples as illustrations.

In many cases, particularly in industrial marketing, it is possible to divide the population into subgroups that samplers usually call *strata*. The basic property of these subgroups is that they differ from one another in one of the three major factors that determine an optimum sampling plan.

1. *Variance within the Subgroup on Parameters of Interest.* The total population variance is a sum of the variances of the subgroups of that population. There may, or may not, be substantial differences in these subgroup variances. When sampling firms or institutions, the sample designer often relates variances to the firm's size, either as expressed in some dollar measure of activity or in number of employees. Differences among the variances in strata of human populations are far smaller and may frequently be ignored, except when the parameter is highly related to income. Thus, if an attempt was being made to measure total annual expenditures for home repairs and improvements, the sample of homes would first be stratified by some measure of value of the home, since substantially more variability in expenditures on repairs and improvements would be expected in high-cost homes than in middle- or low-cost homes.

2. *Cost of Data Gathering.* There may well be differential costs for obtaining information from the strata of the population. These costs arise from the methods of obtaining information and from the availability of the strata members. If it is possible to use mail questionnaires for some strata while personal interviews are required for the rest, costs will differ substantially, with the mail strata costing far less. Or, if the households or individuals in some strata are much harder to locate or less willing to cooperate, the costs in these strata will be higher.

3. *Prior Information about Strata.* Based either on earlier research or his own experience, the decision maker may have substantial information about some of the strata while knowing very little about the others. Thus, the value of sample information varies for him by stratum.

Optimum Stratified Sampling

The three factors all influence the design for an optimum stratified sample. Those strata with larger variances should be sampled more heavily than those with small variances. Strata for which data gathering is cheap should be sampled more heavily than those for which it is expensive. Finally, strata about which the decision maker knows little should be sampled more heavily than strata about which he knows a great deal. Ericson [1] has shown that it is possible to select an optimum sample subject to the conditions that the total sampling cost is C and the decision maker's prior estimates of strata means are independently and normally distributed.

Following his notation, let

π_i = proportion of the population in the ith stratum,

c_i = cost per case in the ith stratum,

σ_i^2 = population variance in the ith stratum,

v_i^2 = the decision maker's prior variance in the ith stratum.

If B_i is defined as $\sigma_i\sqrt{c_i}/\pi_i v_i^2$ and the strata are numbered so that $B_0 > B_1 > B_2 \ldots B_k$, where $B_0 = \infty$, then the solution consists of sampling the subset of strata so that the optimum sample sizes, for C included in I_r, are

$$n_i = 0 \qquad i \leq r$$

$$n_i = \frac{\pi_i \sigma_i}{\sqrt{c_i}} \left[\frac{C + \sum_{j=r+1}^{L} \frac{c_j \sigma_j^2}{v_j^2}}{\sum_{j=r+1}^{L} \pi_j \sigma_j \sqrt{c_j}} \right] - \frac{\sigma_i^2}{v_i^2} \qquad i > r$$

where $r = 0,1,2,\ldots,h-1$ is found by

$$I_r = \{C | C_r \leq C \leq C_{r-1}\}$$

and

$$C_r = B_{r+1} \sum_{i=r+1}^{L} \pi_i \sigma_i \sqrt{c_i} - \sum_{i=r+1}^{L} \frac{c_i \sigma_i^2}{v_i^2}$$

$$C_{-1} = \infty$$

This formidable formula may sometimes be simplified if the terms are identical for all strata. Thus, if the population variances are equal or roughly equal in the different strata, they do not affect the optimum allocation, and similarly if costs or prior expectations are equal in the different strata.

This formula simplifies, if all the prior expectations in the different strata are equal, to the Neyman allocation formulas for stratified samples used by classical statisticians. The next example, however, illustrates a problem that cannot be handled formally by classical statistical methods. If one has no prior beliefs about the noncooperators in a sample survey, then there is no way to determine an acceptable rate of noncooperation; and theoretically, any noncooperation could lead to the rejection of all sample results. In practice, a cooperation level of less than 100 percent is deemed acceptable, based on past experience. Thus, implicitly, a Bayesian method has been adopted.

Example 5: Optimum Sampling for Nonresponse. Suppose, now, that for the food product of example 1 a pilot study costing $1,000 is being planned. For this survey, taste tests and reactions to different package designs are required, so only personal interviewing will be used. From past experience, it is known that not all selected households are equally available and cooperative. Theoretically, it is possible to obtain an interview from everyone if sufficient efforts are made or incentives offered to the respondent. Many respondents who refuse to be interviewed initially would cooperate if offered $10, $50, $100, or more. This example illustrates why such an incentive is not used.

It may be known from past experience that there are three main classes of respondents. The easy 60 percent, such as unemployed housewives, retired people, or households in rural areas, cost $16 per case to complete. The more difficult 20 percent, such as employed men or households in large cities, cost $25 per completed case, and the "impossible" 20 percent cost $400 each. The parameters are summarized in Table 1.

TABLE 1 Stratum Values for Bayesian Computations

Stratum	Cost C	Percent of population π	σ^2	v^2	B
1 Impossible	400	0.2	100	25	40
2 Difficult	25	0.2	100	25	10
3 Easy	16	0.6	100	25	2.67

$$C_0 = 40\,[40 + 10 + 24] - \frac{100}{25}\,[400 + 25 + 16]$$

$$= \$1,196$$

$$C_1 = 10\,[34] - 4\,(41) = \$176$$

Since C_0 is larger than $1,000, no sample will be drawn from the "impossible" stratum, but only from the other two strata. It is for this reason that survey researchers usually do not attempt to convert the "impossible" cases. Unless one suspects them of having a much greater variability than the remaining 80 percent of the sample, the value of information they provide does not pay for the cost.

The problem now remains to optimize the sample from the two remaining strata. This is done just as before. Now, however, since the cost differences between the two strata are small, there is little difference between the optimum sampling design and a proportional design, as shown in Table 2. Here, many samplers would choose the proportional design since it is self-weighting and avoids the need for special weighting in the processing of results. This reduces processing costs, as well as the possibility of mistakes. As a rule of thumb, it

TABLE 2 Stratum Sample Sizes for Optimum and Proportional Sampling

Stratum	Optimum n	Optimum $(v^2)'$	Proportional n	Proportional $(v^2)'$
1	0	25.00	0	25.00
2	10	7.14	14	5.56
3	47	1.96	41	2.22
Total sample	57	1.99	55	2.02

is sometimes suggested that disproportionate sampling be avoided unless the ratio of costs between strata exceeds three.

Optimum Stratified Sampling When Cost, Variance, and Prior Information Differ by Stratum

The final example presents an industrial marketing problem in which the marketing manager has differential information by stratum, and unit sampling costs and variances also differ by stratum. It is assumed, however, that fixed sampling costs do not vary from stratum to stratum. For most sampling applications, this is a reasonable assumption since fixed costs are usually due to the overall sample design and not to any particular stratum. Ericson [2] has extended his previous work to cover the case in which fixed costs vary from stratum to stratum, so this assumption is unnecessary.

Example 6: Hypothetical Industrial Research Example. Suppose that a manufacturer of a new fabricated steel widget has grouped 10,000 potential customers into four strata by size. Although he does not know the variances in each stratum as he plans a survey, he is reasonably certain that they are highly correlated to size of previous purchases of fabricated steel products. He also has differential knowledge by stratum, based on salesmen's reports and other informal contacts, that he is willing to express as prior variances from independent, normal distributions.

He has decided to spend $25,000 (excluding fixed costs) to conduct a survey. Since each case costs $25, his decision implies a final sample size of 1,000 cases.

This information is summarized in Table 3.

TABLE 3 Hypothetical Example of Factors Related to Optimum Sampling of Customers for New Product

Stratum	Number of firms (1)	π_i (2)	Total previous steel purchases (000) (3)	σ_i^2/v_i^2 (4)
1	100	0.01	$ 5,000	100
2	500	0.05	2,500	50
3	2,400	0.24	1,500	15
4	7,000	0.70	1,000	10
	10,000	1.00	$10,000	175

From these data, it is possible to determine an optimum sample allocation by assuming that $\pi_i\sigma_i = Km_i$ where, here, the measure of size is total previous steel purchases. If no strata are omitted, it is unnecessary to know or estimate K since it would cancel out in the formulas for computing optimum samples. A brief explanation is required for the σ_i^2/v_i^2 terms.

Earlier, this discussion ignored the finite correction factor and called this term "the equivalent sample based on prior information." This is still true for strata 3 and 4 in the example in which the numbers 15 and 10 may be considered as indicating that the prior information is the equivalent of samples of size 15 and 10 in these two strata. In the first two strata, however, the finite correction factor must be considered. Thus the ratio σ_i^2/v_i^2 is the equivalent of $n/(1-f)$.

APPENDIX TABLE 1 Unit Normal Loss Integral $G(u) = P'_N(u) - u\,P_N(\bar{u} > u)$

u	.00	.01	.02	.03	.04	.05	.06	.07	.08	.09
.0	.3989	.3940	.3890	.3841	.3793	.3744	.3697	.3649	.3602	.3556
.1	.3509	.3464	.3418	.3373	.3328	.3284	.3240	.3197	.3154	.3111
.2	.3069	.3027	.2986	.2944	.2904	.2863	.2824	.2784	.2745	.2706
.3	.2668	.2630	.2592	.2555	.2518	.2481	.2445	.2409	.2374	.2339
.4	.2304	.2270	.2236	.2203	.2169	.2137	.2104	.2072	.2040	.2009
.5	.1978	.1947	.1917	.1887	.1857	.1828	.1799	.1771	.1742	.1714
.6	.1687	.1659	.1633	.1606	.1580	.1554	.1528	.1503	.1478	.1453
.7	.1429	.1405	.1381	.1358	.1334	.1312	.1289	.1267	.1245	.1223
.8	.1202	.1181	.1160	.1140	.1120	.1100	.1080	.1061	.1042	.1023
.9	.1004	.09860	.09680	.09503	.09328	.09156	.08986	.08654	0.8654	.08491
1.0	.08332	.08174	.08019	.07866	.07716	.07568	.07422	.07279	.07138	.06999
1.1	.06862	.06727	.06595	.06465	.06336	.06210	.06086	.05964	.05844	.05726
1.2	.05610	.05496	.05384	.05274	.05165	.05059	.04954	.04851	.04750	.04650
1.3	.04553	.04457	.04363	.04270	.04179	.04090	.04002	.03916	.03831	.03748
1.4	.03667	.03587	.03508	.03431	.03356	.03281	.03208	.03137	.03067	.02998
1.5	.02931	.02865	.02800	.02736	.02674	.02612	.02552	.02494	.02436	.02380
1.6	.02324	.02270	.02217	.02165	.02114	.02064	.02015	.01967	.01920	.01874
1.7	.01829	.01785	.01742	.01699	.01658	.01617	.01578	.01539	.01501	.01464
1.8	.01428	.01392	.01357	.01323	.01290	.01257	.01226	.01195	.01164	.01134
1.9	.01105	.01077	.01049	.01022	$.0^{2}9957$	$.0^{2}9698$	$.0^{2}9445$	$.0^{2}9198$	$.0^{2}8957$	$.0^{2}8721$
2.0	$.0^{2}8491$	$.0^{2}8266$	$.0^{2}8046$	$.0^{2}7832$	$.0^{2}7623$	$.0^{2}7418$	$.0^{2}7219$	$.0^{2}7024$	$.0^{2}6835$	$.0^{2}6649$
2.1	$.0^{2}6468$	$.0^{2}6292$	$.0^{2}6120$	$.0^{2}5952$	$.0^{2}5788$	$.0^{2}5628$	$.0^{2}5472$	$.0^{2}5320$	$.0^{2}5172$	$.0^{2}5028$
2.2	$.0^{2}4887$	$.0^{2}4750$	$.0^{2}4616$	$.0^{2}4486$	$.0^{2}4358$	$.0^{2}4235$	$.0^{2}4114$	$.0^{2}3996$	$.0^{2}3882$	$.0^{2}3770$
2.3	$.0^{2}3662$	$.0^{2}3556$	$.0^{2}3453$	$.0^{2}3352$	$.0^{2}3255$	$.0^{2}3159$	$.0^{2}3067$	$.0^{2}2977$	$.0^{2}2889$	$.0^{2}2804$
2.4	$.0^{2}2720$	$.0^{2}2640$	$.0^{2}2561$	$.0^{2}2484$	$.0^{2}2410$	$.0^{2}2337$	$.0^{2}2267$	$.0^{2}2199$	$.0^{2}2132$	$.0^{2}2067$

APPENDIX TABLE 1 Unit Normal Loss Integral $G(u) = P_N(u) - u\,P_N(u > u)$ (Continued)

u	.00	.01	.02	.03	.04	.05	.06	.07	.08	.09
2.5	$.0^2 2004$	$.0^2 1943$	$.0^2 1883$	$.0^2 1826$	$.0^2 1769$	$.0^2 1715$	$.0^2 1662$	$.0^2 1610$	$.0^2 1560$	$.0^2 1511$
2.6	$.0^2 1464$	$.0^2 1418$	$.0^2 1373$	$.0^2 1330$	$.0^2 1288$	$.0^2 1247$	$.0^2 1207$	$.0^2 1169$	$.0^2 1132$	$.0^2 1095$
2.7	$.0^2 1060$	$.0^2 1026$	$.0^3 9928$	$.0^3 9607$	$.0^3 9295$	$.0^3 8992$	$.0^3 8699$	$.0^3 8414$	$.0^3 8138$	$.0^3 7870$
2.8	$.0^3 7611$	$.0^3 7359$	$.0^3 7115$	$.0^3 6879$	$.0^3 6650$	$.0^3 6428$	$.0^3 6213$	$.0^3 6004$	$.0^3 5802$	$.0^3 5606$
2.9	$.0^3 5417$	$.0^3 5233$	$.0^3 5055$	$.0^3 4883$	$.0^3 4716$	$.0^3 4555$	$.0^3 4398$	$.0^3 4247$	$.0^3 4101$	$.0^3 3959$
3.0	$.0^3 3822$	$.0^3 3689$	$.0^3 3560$	$.0^3 3436$	$.0^3 3316$	$.0^3 3199$	$.0^3 3087$	$.0^3 2978$	$.0^3 2873$	$.0^3 2771$
3.1	$.0^3 2673$	$.0^3 2577$	$.0^3 2485$	$.0^3 2396$	$.0^3 2311$	$.0^3 2227$	$.0^3 2147$	$.0^3 2070$	$.0^3 1995$	$.0^3 1922$
3.2	$.0^3 1852$	$.0^3 1785$	$.0^3 1720$	$.0^3 1657$	$.0^3 1596$	$.0^3 1537$	$.0^3 1480$	$.0^3 1426$	$.0^3 1373$	$.0^3 1322$
3.3	$.0^3 1273$	$.0^3 1225$	$.0^3 1179$	$.0^3 1135$	$.0^3 1093$	$.0^3 1051$	$.0^3 1012$	$.0^4 9734$	$.0^4 9365$	$.0^4 9009$
3.4	$.0^4 8666$	$.0^4 8335$	$.0^4 8016$	$.0^4 7709$	$.0^4 7413$	$.0^4 7127$	$.0^4 6852$	$.0^4 6587$	$.0^4 6331$	$.0^4 6085$
3.5	$.0^4 5848$	$.0^4 5620$	$.0^4 5400$	$.0^4 5188$	$.0^4 4984$	$.0^4 4788$	$.0^4 4599$	$.0^4 4417$	$.0^4 4242$	$.0^4 4073$
3.6	$.0^4 3911$	$.0^4 3755$	$.0^4 3605$	$.0^4 3460$	$.0^4 3321$	$.0^4 3188$	$.0^4 3059$	$.0^4 2935$	$.0^4 2816$	$.0^4 2702$
3.7	$.0^4 2592$	$.0^4 2486$	$.0^4 2385$	$.0^4 2287$	$.0^4 2193$	$.0^4 2103$	$.0^4 2016$	$.0^4 1933$	$.0^4 1853$	$.0^4 1776$
3.8	$.0^4 1702$	$.0^4 1632$	$.0^4 1563$	$.0^4 1498$	$.0^4 1435$	$.0^4 1375$	$.0^4 1317$	$.0^4 1262$	$.0^4 1208$	$.0^4 1157$
3.9	$.0^4 1108$	$.0^4 1061$	$.0^4 1016$	$.0^5 9723$	$.0^5 9296$	$.0^5 8908$	$.0^5 8525$	$.0^5 8158$	$.0^5 7806$	$.0^5 7469$
4.0	$.0^5 7145$	$.0^5 6835$	$.0^5 6538$	$.0^5 6253$	$.0^5 5980$	$.0^5 5718$	$.0^5 5468$	$.0^5 5227$	$.0^5 4997$	$.0^5 4777$
4.1	$.0^5 4566$	$.0^5 4364$	$.0^5 4170$	$.0^5 3985$	$.0^5 3807$	$.0^5 3637$	$.0^5 3475$	$.0^5 3319$	$.0^5 3170$	$.0^5 3027$
4.2	$.0^5 2891$	$.0^5 2760$	$.0^5 2635$	$.0^5 2516$	$.0^5 2402$	$.0^5 2292$	$.0^5 2188$	$.0^5 2088$	$.0^5 1992$	$.0^5 1901$
4.3	$.0^5 1814$	$.0^5 1730$	$.0^5 1650$	$.0^5 1574$	$.0^5 1501$	$.0^5 1431$	$.0^5 1365$	$.0^5 1301$	$.0^5 1241$	$.0^5 1183$
4.4	$.0^5 1127$	$.0^5 1074$	$.0^5 1024$	$.0^6 9756$	$.0^6 9296$	$.0^6 8857$	$.0^6 8437$	$.0^6 8037$	$.0^6 7655$	$.0^6 7290$
4.5	$.0^6 6942$	$.0^6 6610$	$.0^6 6294$	$.0^6 5992$	$.0^6 5704$	$.0^6 5429$	$.0^6 5167$	$.0^6 4917$	$.0^6 4679$	$.0^6 4452$
4.6	$.0^6 4236$	$.0^6 4029$	$.0^6 3833$	$.0^6 3645$	$.0^6 3467$	$.0^6 3297$	$.0^6 3135$	$.0^6 2981$	$.0^6 2834$	$.0^6 2694$
4.7	$.0^6 2560$	$.0^6 2433$	$.0^6 2313$	$.0^6 2197$	$.0^6 2088$	$.0^6 1984$	$.0^6 1884$	$.0^6 1790$	$.0^6 1700$	$.0^6 1615$
4.8	$.0^6 1533$	$.0^6 1456$	$.0^6 1382$	$.0^6 1312$	$.0^6 1246$	$.0^6 1182$	$.0^6 1122$	$.0^6 1065$	$.0^6 1011$	$.0^7 9588$
4.9	$.0^7 9096$	$.0^7 8629$	$.0^7 8185$	$.0^7 7763$	$.0^7 7362$	$.0^7 6982$	$.0^7 6620$	$.0^7 6276$	$.0^7 5950$	$.0^7 5640$

$$G(-u) = u + G(u)$$

Examples: $G(3.57) = .0^4 4417 = .00004417$
$G(-3.57) = 3.57004417$

source: These tables of unit normal loss function appear in *Probability and Statistics for Business Decisions*, by Robert Schlaifer, published by the McGraw-Hill Book Company in 1959. They are reproduced here by specific permission of the publisher and the President and Fellows of Harvard College.

Solving for n, one finds that

$$n = \frac{N\sigma_i^2/v_i^2}{N + \sigma_i^2/v_i^2}$$

In the example, the equivalent n in the first stratum is $100^2/200 = 50$, and the equivalent n in the second stratum is $500 \times 50/550 = 45$.
Using the formula for optimum n_i, we first compute

$$n_1 = 5,000\left[\frac{1,000 + 175}{10,000}\right] - 100 = 488$$

This means that we take all 100 firms from the first stratum. Then, based on a total remaining sample of 900:

$$n_2 = 2500\left[\frac{500 + 75}{5000}\right] - 50 = 438$$
$$n_3 = 1500\,(.195) - 15 = 277$$
$$n_4 = 1000\,(.195) - 10 = 185$$

SUGGESTED REFERENCES

The examples given in this chapter should enable the reader to see the usefulness of Bayesian procedures, both for determining optimum sample sizes and in the design of efficient samples. Since space limits prevent a full mathematical treatment of the examples given here, the interested reader is directed to the original sources listed in the references.

REFERENCES

1. Ericson, W. A., "Optimum Stratified Sampling Using Prior Information," *Journal of the American Statistical Association*, vol. 60, September 1965, pp. 750–771.
2. Ericson, W. A., "Optimum Allocations in Stratified and Multistage Samples Using Prior Information," *Journal of the American Statistical Association*, vol. 63, September 1968, pp. 964–983.
3. Green, Paul, and Donald Tull, *Research for Marketing Decisions*, Englewood Cliffs, N.J.: Prentice-Hall, 1970.
4. Raiffa, Howard, and Robert Schlaifer, *Applied Statistical Decision Theory*, Boston: Harvard University, Graduate School of Business Administration, 1961.
5. Roberts, Harry, *Statistical Inference and Decision*, Chicago: University of Chicago, Graduate School of Business, 1966–1967, chaps. 9, 10. (Multilith)
6. Schlaifer, Robert, *Probability and Statistics for Business Decisions*, New York: McGraw-Hill, 1959.

Statistical Inference

Chapter 1

Parameter Estimation

KYOHEI SASAKI *Consultant, East Orange, New Jersey*

INTRODUCTION

We live in a world of uncertainty. Every day we form opinions, draw conclusions, and make decisions. We are often not sure we are right, since we often act on the basis of incomplete (or erroneous) information about the problem under consideration. The concern of statistics is to help define and collect information to reduce the risk of a wrong decision. The method of collecting statistical data and using incomplete information to draw conclusions about reality is called *statistical inference*. The ultimate objective of statistical inference is to determine and use information as a guide for making decisions under uncertainty; thus, statistical inference is of primary concern to decision makers.

Hence, this introductory overview will clarify the meaning of decision making under uncertainty, then the meaning and role of statistical inference in decision making under uncertainty. Subsequent sections will discuss the two major approaches to statistical inference, classical and Bayesian statistics, with focus on the estimation of parameters. The other aspect of statistical inference, the testing of hypotheses, is covered only briefly here, since it is the subject of the next chapter.

DECISION MAKING UNDER UNCERTAINTY

Meaning of Decision Making under Uncertainty

To understand the meaning of decision making under uncertainty, let us consider the following illustration.

A manufacturing company is thinking of producing a new product, but is uncertain whether there is a potential market for it. The company must decide whether to produce this new product. The situation may be summarized as shown in Table 1a.

TABLE 1a Possible Decisions (or Actions)

Action: a_i / State of Nature: S_i	S_1: Potential market for the product	S_2: No potential market for the product
Produce the new product (a_1)	Correct	Wrong
Do not produce the new product (a_2)	Wrong	Correct

This table shows two possible market conditions: potential market and no potential market. Before the company manufactures a new product, it is not certain which condition will prevail. If there is a market for the product, the right decision is to manufacture it; if there is no market for the new product, the company should not produce it. If there is no market for the new product and the firm does manufacture it, losses will be incurred. If there is a market and the company does not manufacture the new product, it has made an incorrect decision and will not gain any profit. If there is no market and it does not manufacture the new product, the company has made the right decision and will not incur any losses (or profit).

This means that for each situation (each one of the states of nature), there is one right decision to make and one right action to take; a correct decision (or action) will result in profit or negative profit (or losses), and an incorrect decision will result in losses or negative profits.

Let us indicate the consequences of the actions in terms of profit. We assume that the true consequences of each action are given in Table 1b.

TABLE 1b Payoffs of Decisions Given Alternative States of Nature (Actual Profits)

Action: a_i / State of nature: S_i	S_1: Potential market for the product	S_2: No potential market for the product
Produce the new product (a_1)	$100	$-50
Do not produce the new product (a_2)	0	0

Table 1b may also be expressed in terms of opportunity losses, as in Table 1c. The opportunity loss here is the profit forgone by not taking the right action; it

TABLE 1c Consequences of Decisions: Table 1b Expressed in Opportunity Losses (L_i)

Action: a_i / State of nature: S_1	S_1: Potential market for the product	S_2: No potential market for the product
Produce the new product (a_1)	$L_1 = 0$	$L_3 = \$50 > 0$
Do not produce the new product (a_2)	$L_2 = \$100 > 0$	$L_4 = 0$

represents the difference between the profit actually realized and the greater profit that could have been obtained. Thus, the forgone profit is zero when the right action is taken.

Further, let us look at the following example. Suppose that a large retailer is considering the purchase of several lots of watermelon, each lot containing 100 melons. According to past experience, the percentages of underripe and overripe melons were either 0.3, 0.4, 0.7, or 0.8. The retailer will make a net profit of $0.30 per melon sold. However, he will lose $0.20 if the melon is either overripe or underripe. The possible decisions and the consequences of the actions (decisions) are shown in Table 2a. The profits for this table were computed as follows.

If the lot contains 30 percent defectives, he can make a profit of $0.30 $\times$ 10,000 $\times$ 0.7 $-$ $0.20 $\times$ 10,000 $\times$ 0.3 = $1,500 by buying the lot.

Similarly, if a lot contains 40, 70, or 80 percent defectives, the profits are computed as follows:

$$\$0.30 \times 10,000 \times 0.6 - \$0.20 \times 10,000 \times 0.4 = \$1,000$$
$$\$0.30 \times 10,000 \times 0.3 - \$0.20 \times 10,000 \times 0.7 = -\$500$$
$$\$0.30 \times 10,000 \times 0.2 - \$0.20 \times 10,000 \times 0.8 = -\$1,000$$

These are shown in 2a.

TABLE 2a   Payoff Matrix (Profit)

State of nature Action: a_i	S_1: 0.3	S_2: 0.4	S_3: 0.7	S_4: 0.8
To buy (action a_1)	$1,500	$1,000	$-$500	$-$1,000
Not to buy (action a_2)	$0	$0	$0	$0

When Table 2a is expressed in terms of opportunity loss, the result is shown in Table 2b.

TABLE 2b   Opportunity Loss of Table 2a

State of nature Action: a_i	S_1: 0.3	S_2: 0.4	S_3: 0.7	S_4: 0.8
To buy (action a_1)	$0	$0	$500	$1,000
Not to buy (action a_2)	$1,500	$1,000	$0	$0

Given the preceding payoff matrix, there are several criteria (or methods) available to determine the optimum action. Before these are discussed, more general computations of profit, opportunity loss, and break-even point will be shown.

Opportunity Loss and Break-even Point

Profit Function.   In the preceding example, more generally the profit function can be computed as follows.

Let p be the fraction defective. Then, the profit K from purchasing the lot is

$$K = \$0.30 \times 10,000\,(1 - p) - \$0.20 \times 10,000p = \$3,000 - \$5,000p$$

This is the profit equation (function) for purchasing the lot. If the retailer does not purchase the lot, there cannot be any profit, and therefore, $K = 0$. Thus, if purchase is identified as action a_1 and nonpurchase as action a_2, the profit can be expressed as follows:

For a_1: $K_1 = \$3,000 - \$5,000p$

For a_2: $K_2 = 0 + 0p$

These linear equations are plotted in Figure 1. When $p = 0.3$, 0.4, 0.7, and 0.8, note that the profit for taking actions a_1 and a_2 are the same as given in Table 2a.

Break-even Point. The point where profit from taking actions a_1 and a_2 is equal is the break-even point, and the profit at this point is the break-even value. Hence, the break-even value occurs where the two equations intersect. Algebraically,

$$3,000 - 5,000p = 0 + 0p$$

Hence, the break-even point $p = 0.6$. When p is smaller than 0.6, there is a positive profit. When it reaches 0.6, profit becomes zero. After it exceeds 0.6, the profit becomes negative. Hence, where p is greater than 0.6, losses will be incurred from purchasing the lot. In general, if the profit function of a_1 and a_2 is expressed as $K_1 = A_1 + B_1\,p$ and $K_2 = A_2 + B_2\,p$ respectively, the break-even point can be obtained as follows. The break-even point occurs at K_1 and K_2. Hence, $A_1 + B_1p = A_2 + B_2p$, and

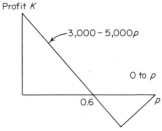

Profit K

3,000 − 5,000p

0 to p

0.6

p

Fig. 1.   Profit function for melon example.

$$p = \frac{A_2 - A_1}{B_1 - B_2} = P_0$$

where p_0 is the break-even point.

Opportunity Loss. The preceding can also be expressed in terms of opportunity loss, which was defined earlier as the profit forgone by not taking the right action.

When $0 \le p \le 0.6$, the optimum action is a_1 because it will result in the greatest profit $(3,000 - 5,000p)$, and no profit is forgone. Hence, the opportunity loss is zero for taking action a_1. If, however, action a_2 is taken in this situation, there will be zero profit $(0 + 0p)$; hence, the profit forgone, or the opportunity loss, is $(3,000 - 5,000p) - (0 + 0p) = 3,000 - 5,000p$.

If $0.6 \le p \le 1$, a_2 is the optimal action because it will bring about the greatest profit $(0 + 0p) = 0$ and no profit is forgone. Thus, the opportunity loss is zero. In this situation, if action a_1 is taken, there will be a loss or negative profit of $(3,000 - 5,000p)$. Hence, the profit forgone, or the opportunity loss, is $0 + 0p - (3,000 - 5,000p) = 5,000p - 3,000$.

These points are summarized in Table 3. Values of p are listed in the first column, and the corresponding opportunity losses are computed and entered for action a_1 and a_2. These opportunity losses are shown by the shaded area in

TABLE 3   Opportunity Loss Functions

Value of p	a_1	a_2
$0 \leq p \leq 0.6$	0	$3,000 - 5,000p = 5,000\,(0.6 - p)$
$0.6 < p \leq 1$	$5,000p - 3,000 = 5,000\,(p - 0.6)$	0

Figure 1.   In general, given the profit functions for a_1 and a_2 shown earlier, the opportunity loss function can be obtained as follows.

For a_1: $K_2 - K_1$ $p \geq p_0$
              0 $p \leq p_0$

For a_2: $K_1 - K_2$ $p < p_0$
              0 $p > p_0$

Criteria for Optimum Actions without Sampling

We have defined decision making under uncertainty and have developed the concept of a payoff matrix.   Given the payoff matrix, there are various ways of finding an optimum action under the situation of uncertainty.   Some involve sampling and others do not.   Some of the important criteria without sampling are minimax, maximin, the Hurwicz, and Bayesian.   Also, there are two important methods of finding an optimum action when sample data are available—classical statistical inference and Bayesian statistics.   After discussing the various criteria without sampling, we shall examine classical statistical inference and Bayesian statistics in the following section.

Minimax Criterion.   In this case, the payoff matrix is expressed in terms of opportunity losses or disutilities for all possible actions, and the decision maker expects the worst possible outcomes or consequences, that is, the greatest losses or disutilities, and selects the strategy yielding the smallest loss or disutility.   To clarify this, let us consider the example in Table 1c.

Given these data, what action should a decision maker take?   If he decides to use the minimax strategy or decision rule, he will reason as follows:

If he takes action a_1, the worst that can happen (maximum loss) is a loss of \$50.   If he takes action a_2, the worst that can happen is a loss of \$100.   Thus, if a decision maker behaves in accordance with the minimax principle, his optimum decision rule is to take action a_1.

Maximin Criterion.   In this case, the payoff matrix is expressed in terms of profit or utility.   Consider, for instance, Table 1b.   Using this criterion, the decision maker expects the worst possible outcome (or consequences) and selects the action or strategy that will yield the greatest profit (or utility) among the worst possible profits (or utilities).   In the example in Table 1b, if he takes action a_1, the worst that can happen (minimum profit) is −\$50.   If he takes action a_2, the worst that can happen is \$0 profit.   Thus the strategy that will yield the greatest profit among the worst possible profits is action a_2.

Hurwicz Criterion.   Leonid Hurwicz suggested that the weighted average of the minimum and maximum payoffs be employed to select the best or optimum strategy.   Suppose we have the payoff matrix shown in Table 2a.   The minimum payoff for strategy a_1 is −\$1,000 and the maximum payoff is \$1,500.   Hence, if we weighted the minimum payoff by 3/4 and the maximum by 1/4, the Hurwicz criterion would evaluate strategy a_1 at

$$3/4(-\$1,000) + 1/4(\$1,500) = -\$375$$

Similarly, this criterion would evaluate strategy a_2 at

$$3/4(\$0) + 1/4(\$0) = \$0$$

By the Hurwicz criterion, the decision maker should therefore select strategy a_2.

In applying this criterion, weights are designed to reflect the decision maker's subjective opinion.

Bayesian Criterion.   Bayesian theory assumes that the decision maker subjectively establishes probabilities for the state of nature. Bayesians interpret probability as a measure of personal belief in a particular statement. They state that it is quite reasonable to say that "the odds are 8 to 2 that the Yankees will win the World Series" or that "the chances are 9 to 1 that Mr. Smith will be elected president of company A."

This probability is different from the objective probability which is the relative frequency in a repeated process, for example, $p = s/n$, where n is the total number of outcomes and s is the number of favorable outcomes. The objective probability is applicable only to an event which can be repeated over and over under the same conditions, such as tossing a coin. Subjective probability is a priori information about the state of nature and may come from general theoretical considerations or the results of previous experiments.[1] It is called prior probability.

Given the subjective probability for the state of nature, it is possible for the decision maker to compute the expected (weighted average) loss (profit) and select the strategy having the smallest expected (or average) loss (highest expected profit). This is called the Bayesian method of selecting optimum action. To clarify this, consider the example in Table 2b.

Suppose that on the basis of past experience, the decision maker assigns the subjective probabilities to the states of nature as shown in Table 4.

TABLE 4   Prior (Subjective) Probabilities

Percent defective	Prior (subjective) probabilities
0.3	0.6
0.4	0.2
0.7	0.1
0.8	0.1

Then, the weighted average of the opportunity loss or the expected opportunity loss can be computed as follows.

The expected loss for taking action a_2 is

$$0.6(\$1,500) + 0.2(\$1,000) + 0.1(\$0) + 0.1(\$0) = \$1,100$$

The expected loss for taking action a_1 is

$$0.6(\$0) + 0.2(\$0) + 0.1(\$500) + 0.1(\$1,000) = \$150$$

---

[1] For a detailed discussion of subjective probability, see Kyohei Sasaki, *Statistics for Modern Business Decision Making*, Belmont, Calif.: Wadsworth, 1968, pp. 52–54.

Since the expected loss for taking action a_1 is smaller than that for a_2, the decision maker will take action a_1. Thus, a_1 is the optimum action.

CLASSICAL THEORY OF ESTIMATION OF POPULATION PARAMETERS

In testing hypotheses, it is assumed that the decision maker has some a priori knowledge about the state of nature. However, frequently the decision maker has no such information. Hence, in determining the appropriate action, he must infer the state of nature on the basis of sample information. This is called the estimation of population parameters.

There are two methods of estimating parameters—*point* estimates and *interval* estimates. This section discusses both methods as applied to a population mean.

Point Estimate

The sample mean, $\bar{x}$, is called the point estimate of the population mean μ, since a particular number is specified as an estimate of μ.

For example, suppose a gasoline company is interested in knowing the average consumption of gasoline per family in a city. Assume that a random sample of size 100 is drawn with a sample mean of 18 gallons. The statistician of the company will infer that the true average consumption of gasoline per family is 18 gallons; this is the point estimate.

Confidence Interval Estimate

It would be highly optimistic to suppose that an estimate based on a sample mean is exactly equal to the population mean. Hence, an interval estimate is used. For example, the first step in determining a confidence estimate of the population's mean consumption of gasoline per family in the preceding example is to compute the sample mean, 18 gallons. Then, after suitable statistical manipulation, the statement is made that there is a 95 percent probability that the interval between 15 to 21 gallons contains the true mean. This is called an interval estimate. It is determined by two numbers, 15 gallons and 21 gallons.

An interval estimate is a range determined by two figures calculated on the basis of data provided by a sample, and is expected to contain the true value of the population parameter with a given degree of confidence. To clarify the nature of the interval estimate, the concept of the sampling distribution of means will be briefly reviewed.

Sampling Distribution of Means. Suppose a sample of size n is drawn with replacement from a population with unknown mean μ but known standard deviation σ. There are many possible sample means, all of which are normally distributed around the population mean μ with the standard deviation of these sample means, the standard error, equal to $\sigma/\sqrt{n} = \sigma_{\bar{x}}$.

Now let us take 1.96 standard errors, or $1.96\sigma_{\bar{x}}$ on both sides of the population mean μ. Since this range includes 95 percent of the area under the normal distribution, 95 percent of all possible sample means will fall in this range, provided that the sample means are normally distributed.

Next add and subtract $1.96\sigma_{\bar{x}}$ from each sample mean. Then, 95 percent of these intervals will contain the true (unknown) population mean μ. This can be easily seen if we consider sample mean A in Figure 2. If $1.96\sigma_{\bar{x}}$ is added to and subtracted from this mean, the interval will contain the population mean. However, if one adds $1.96\sigma_{\bar{x}}$ to, and subtracts $1.96\sigma_{\bar{x}}$ from, sample mean D, the interval will not contain the population mean μ. Thus, if any interval is to contain the population mean μ, the corresponding sample mean must fall within the prescribed range $(\mu - 1.96\sigma_{\bar{x}})$ to $(\mu + 1.96\sigma_{\bar{x}})$.

If we denote all the possible sample means by x, then all the possible intervals can be expressed as $x \pm 1.96\sigma_{\bar{x}}$. The implication that 95 percent of the intervals of all the possible sample means contain the population mean μ can be expressed mathematically by

$$P(\bar{x} - 1.96\sigma_{\bar{x}} < \mu < \bar{x} + 1.96\sigma_{\bar{x}}) = 0.95 \tag{1}$$

In actual practice, however, only one sample is selected. Hence, it is not known whether the interval will contain the population mean μ, and we have to rely on the law of probability, as previously described.

Confidence Interval When σ Is Known. Suppose that a gasoline company statistician wants to estimate the average consumption of gasoline per family in a city. He will use the following procedures.

First he will draw a sample of size, say, 100, and compute a sample mean $\bar{x}$. Let us assume $x = 18$ gallons. Second, he computes the standard error of the

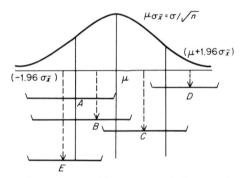

Fig. 2.   Alternative confidence intervals for sample means.

sampling distribution of means. Assume that the population standard deviation σ is given, say $\sigma = 3$ gallons. Then, the standard error is $\sigma_{\bar{x}} = \dfrac{3}{\sqrt{100}} = 0.3$ gallons. Third, the preceding data are fitted into the following formula.

$$P(\bar{x} - 1.96\sigma_{\bar{x}} < \mu < \bar{x} + 1.96\sigma_{\bar{x}}) = 0.95 \tag{2}$$

using a confidence interval of 95 percent.

(Notice that Equations (1) and (2) are different. In (1), $\bar{x}$ is a random variable, whereas, in (2), x is a particular value which $\bar{x}$ will take. Therefore, P in (2) is not to be interpreted as the same P in (1). It is called the confidence coefficient, which will be explained subsequently.)

Hence,

$$P[18 - 1.96(0.3) < \mu < 18 + 1.96(0.3)] = 0.95$$

Therefore,

$$P(17.4 < \mu < 18.6) = 0.95$$

This is read as follows: With the confidence coefficient of 95, the interval 17.4 to 18.6 gallons contains the population mean. The conclusion is that since, in 95 percent of the cases, the intervals of all the possible sample means will contain the population mean, it is very likely that this particular interval contains the population mean.

Confidence Interval When σ Is Unknown. In the preceding example, σ was assumed given. Frequently, however, σ is unknown. In that case, σ must be estimated by a sample. Therefore the following procedures are used.

First, we draw a sample of size n, say $n = 101$. Second, compute the sample mean, $\bar{x}$, say 18.4. Third, compute the sample standard deviation, s, say 3.4 gallons.

Then, the estimate of the standard error $\sigma_{\bar{x}}$ is $3.4/\sqrt{100 - 1}$; that is, $\sigma_{\bar{x}} = 3.4/\sqrt{101 - 1} = .0.34$.

If the size of the sample is large, $(\bar{x} - \mu)/s\sqrt{(n - 1)}$ is approximately normally distributed. Thus, these data can be substituted in Equation (2) as follows:

$$P[\bar{x} - 1.96 \times s/\sqrt{(n - 1)} < \mu < \bar{x} + 1.06 \times s/\sqrt{(n - 1)}] = 0.95$$

Hence, $[P18 - 1.96(0.34) < 18 < 1.96(0.34)] = 0.95$.
Hence, $P(17.3 < \mu < 18.7) = 0.95$.

This is read as follows: With a confidence coefficient of 95, the interval 17.3 to 18.7 gallons contains the population mean. Since in 95 percent of all cases, the intervals of all the possible sample means will contain the population mean, it is very likely that this particular interval does contain the population mean.

It was so far assumed that the size of the sample was large. If this condition is not satisfied, we use $t = (x - \mu)/s\sqrt{(n - 1)}$ instead of z, and the t distribution must be used for the interval estimate. With a confidence coefficient of 95 percent, the preceding formula becomes:

$$P[\bar{x} - t_{0.025} \times s/\sqrt{(n - 1)} < \mu < \bar{x} + t_{0.025} \times s/\sqrt{(n - 1)}] = 0.95$$

Suppose $n = 10$ and $s = 3.4$. We obtain the following:

$$P\{18 - 2.262[3.4/\sqrt{(10 - 1)}] < \mu < 18 + 2.262[3.4/\sqrt{(10 - 1)}]\} = 0.95$$
$$P = (18 - 2.55 < \mu < 18 + 2.55) = 0.95$$

Therefore,

$$P(15.4 < \mu < 20.5) = 0.95$$

Estimation of Population Proportion

So far, the estimation of the population mean has been discussed. Frequently, however, a decision maker is interested in estimating population proportions. For instance, the manager of a firm may have to decide whether to buy a lot of machinery parts. Suppose that if the percentage of defective parts is less than 0.3, he is interested in buying the lot; otherwise, the optimum action is not to buy. He must therefore estimate the population proportion. To do so, he must have an understanding of the sampling distribution of the proportion of defective parts when a sample of size n is drawn from the respective population.

It is cited without proof that if a sample of size n is drawn with replacement from a population divided into attributes (or classes) in the ratio of p and q, the expected value and the variance of the proportion are p and $(pq)/n$, respectively. If the sample size is large, the sampling distribution of p approaches a normal distribution.

If p is unknown, the sample estimate of a proportion of successes, $\hat{p}$, is used in estimating $(pq)/n$. That is,

$$s_{\hat{p}} = \sqrt{\frac{\hat{p}(1-\hat{p})}{n}}$$

where $s_{\hat{p}}$ denotes the sample estimate of the $\sqrt{(pq)/n}$. Given this theorem, the confidence interval estimate of the population proportion can be obtained in exactly the same fashion as that used for the population mean.

Example. Suppose a company manager is considering purchasing a lot of 2,000 photographic flash bulbs. If the proportion of defectives is less than 70 percent, he will decide to buy the lot. A sample of size 100 flash bulbs is selected at random and the sample proportion is found to be 0.60. He must find 95 percent confidence limits for the proportion of defectives of all the flash bulbs in this lot.

Solution: The 95 percent confidence intervals for the population proportion p are:

$$\hat{p} \pm 1.96\, s_{\hat{p}} = \hat{p} \pm 1.96 \sqrt{\frac{\hat{p}(1-\hat{p})}{n}}$$

$$= 0.60 \pm 1.96 \sqrt{\frac{(0.6)(0.4)}{100}}$$

$$= 0.60 \pm 0.096$$

Therefore, $\qquad P(0.504 < p < 0.6) = 0.95$

Since the proportion of defective bulbs is estimated to be less than 0.7 (though just barely), the appropriate action is to buy the lot.

BAYESIAN DECISION THEORY AND ESTIMATION OF POPULATION PARAMETERS

This section will examine the Bayesian method of estimating population parameters. Before doing so, it will discuss the Bayesian method of finding optimum action, given sample data.

Bayesian Decision Theory with Binomial Sampling

In a previous section, Bayesian decision theory without sampling was discussed. In that case no samples were involved. If, in addition to the prior information on the state of nature, information from a sample is available on the state of nature, these two pieces of information must be combined to determine the optimum action.

With sample data, the prior probability can be modified by computing the *posterior* probability, which then replaces the prior probability to find the new expected loss. The action associated with the smallest loss is the optimum action. Consequently, a method of finding the posterior probability, given a prior probability and sample information, must be determined.

Posterior Probability. The posterior probability is the conditional probability of the occurrence of the state of nature, given the sample information. Suppose the state of nature and a sample outcome are denoted by S_1 and O_i. Then, $P(S_1)$ is the prior probability and $P(S_1|O_i)$ is the posterior probability of the state of nature, given an outcome O_i; it is a conditional probability. Hence, by the definition of conditional probability,[2]

$$P(S_1|O_i) = P(S_1 \cap O_i)/P(O_i)$$

[2] Those not familiar with conditional probability should see [11] or [12].

Since

$$P(S_1 \cap O_i) = P(S_1) \times P(O_i|S_1), \quad P(S_1|O_i) = P(S_1) \times P(O_i|S_1)/P(O_i)$$

This is called Bayes' theorem. To illustrate, let us consider the watermelon example given earlier in this chapter.

A large produce retailer has the opportunity of purchasing an early shipment of 100 lots of watermelons. Each lot contains 100 melons. The retailer will make a net profit of $0.30 per melon sold. Conversely, he will lose $0.20 per underripe or overripe melon. His experience with previous shipments reveals that the distribution of overripe and underripe melons is as already shown in Table 4.

Let us modify this example as follows: Suppose the produce retailer is allowed to take a random sample of size three and that one under- or overripe melon is found in this sample. Should he purchase the shipment? Assume no cost of sampling involved. To solve this problem, the posterior probabilities must first be computed from the prior probabilities and the outcome of the experiment. The calculations are shown in Table 5.

TABLE 5   Derivation of Posterior Probabilities

State of nature	Prior probability	Likelihood	Joint probability	Posterior probability
0.3	0.6	$P(1|0.3) = 0.441$	$P(0.3 \cap 1) = 0.2646$	$P(0.3|1) = 0.6972$
0.4	0.2	$P(1|0.4) = 0.432$	$P(0.4 \cap 1) = 0.0864$	$P(0.4|1) = 0.2277$
0.7	0.1	$P(1|0.7) = 0.189$	$P(0.7 \cap 1) = 0.0189$	$P(0.7|1) = 0.9498$
0.8	0.1	$P(1|0.8) = 0.096$	$P(0.8 \cap 1) = 0.0096$	$P(0.8|1) = 0.0253$
Total	1.0		$P(1) = 0.3795$	1.0

The first and second columns need no explanation. The third column is called the likelihood and represents the probability of getting outcome 1, if a sample of size three is drawn from a population having elements divided into two attributes (for instance, melons in good or poor condition) in certain ratios, and is obtained from the binomial distribution table. According to the theory of the binomial distribution, when a sample of size n is drawn with replacement from a population divided into two attributes, p and q, the probability of obtaining r successes (for instance, r poor melons) is given as follows:

$$\binom{n}{r} p^r q^{n-r} = \frac{n!}{r!(n-r)!} p^r q^{n-r}$$

where n represents sample size, p and q $(= 1 - p)$ represent the probability of successes (melons in poor condition) and failures (melons in good condition), respectively. These probabilities are given in Table 5.

In this formula, the likelihood is $P(O_i|S_1)$. When $O_i = 1$ and $S_1 = 0.3$, $P(O_i|S_1) = P(1|0.3) = 0.441$, as shown in Table 5.

The fourth column represents the joint probability and is the product of the second and third columns, as can be demonstrated by Bayes' formula:

$$P(S_1 \cap O_i) = P(S_1) \times P(O_i|S_1)$$

In this example, when $S_1 = 0.3$ and $O_i = 1$, $P(0.3|1) = P(0.3 \cap 1)/P(1)$ $= P(0.3)$. $P(1|0.3)/P(1) = (0.6 \times 0.441)/P(1) = 0.2646/P(1)$. Hence, if $P(1)$ can be found, $P(0.3|1)$ can be derived. This $P(1)$ can be obtained by taking the sum of the joint probabilities given in the fourth column. That is,

$$P(1) = 0.3795$$

Thus, $P(0.3|1) = P(0.3 \cap 1)/P(1) = 0.2646/0.3795 = 0.6972$. Similarly, we can compute $P(0.4|1)$, $P(0.7|1)$, and $P(0.8|1)$ as shown in the last column.

Expected Opportunity Losses and the Optimum Action. Given these posterior probabilities and the opportunity losses shown in Table 2b, the expected losses for taking actions a_1 (to buy) and a_2 (not to buy) can be computed as follows:
For a_1: $\$0(0.6972) + \$0(0.2277) + \$500(0.9498) + \$1000(0.0253)$
$\quad = \$50.2$.
For a_2: $\$1,500(0.6972) + \$1,000(0.2277) + \$0(0.9498) + \$0(0.0253)$
$\quad = \$1273.52$.

Since the expected loss for a_1 is smaller than that for a_2, action a_1, or to buy, is the optimum action.

Bayesian Estimate

Without Sampling. The example just given was concerned with finding the optimum action, given the probability distribution of the state of nature. In both cases, optimum actions were nonnumerical (purchase or nonpurchase). Frequently, however, the decision maker is interested in estimating the proportion of such attributes (for instance, the proportion of poor-quality watermelon) in the population. A wrong guess (either an over- or underestimate) will result in a loss. Suppose the loss due to a wrong estimate is proportional to $(a - S)^2$, where S is the state of nature and a is an estimated value of S.

This is a problem of estimation without sampling. It will be stated without proof that if the loss function is quadratic, that is, if $L = (a - S)^2$, the optimum action (estimation) is $E(S)$, the mean of the random variables, S.[3]

Example. To clarify this, consider the melon example once again. The states of nature and their probability distribution are reproduced here:

Percent defective (p)	Prior (subjective) probability $P(p)$
0.3	0.6
0.4	0.2
0.7	0.1
0.8	0.1

Suppose that the loss due to a wrong estimate is $L = (\hat{p} - p)^2$ where p is the state of nature and $\hat{p}$ is the estimate of P. Then, the optimum estimate is computed as:

$$E(p) = 0.3 \times 0.6 + 0.4 \times 0.2 + 0.7 \times 0.1 + 0.8 \times 0.1 = 0.41.$$

[3] If the loss function is not quadratic, this is not the case. For instance, if $L = |a - S|$, the optimum estimate is the median. In decision theory, we usually assume that the loss function is quadratic.

With Binomial Sampling. This estimate was made without sampling. Now, suppose a random sample of size n, say, x_1, x_2, x_3, $\ldots$, x_n, is drawn from a population with the following probability distribution:

$$f(x|p) = p^x(1-p)^{1-x}$$

where $x = 0$ or 1 and $0 \leq p \leq 1$.

Suppose the loss due to a wrong estimate is $L = (p - p)^2$ and the prior probability distribution is rectangular, that is, $g(p) = 1$. Then, it can be given without proof that the optimum estimate is

$$\hat{p} = \frac{r+1}{n+2}$$

where r is the number of successes (defectives) in n trials.

Example. Suppose that a retailer is interested in estimating the fraction p of watermelons in poor condition in a lot of 100. Let us assume that the loss resulting from a wrong estimate of p is $\$1,000(\hat{p} - p)^2$, where $\hat{p}$ is the estimate of p. In estimating p, assume that the retailer has no prior information about p, and so assumes a rectangular distribution. Suppose he takes a random sample of size three and obtains one overripe watermelon. What is the optimum estimate of p?

Using the preceding formula,[4] we obtain:

$$\hat{p} = \frac{r+1}{n+2} = \frac{1+1}{3+2} = 0.4$$

Bayesian Decision Theory with Normal and Other Sampling

So far, it has been assumed that the state of nature is discrete and that sampling is from a population divided into two attributes in the ratio of p to q. This assumption can be qualified to assume that both prior probability and the population from which a sample is drawn are normally distributed. The case in point is when the state of nature consists of population means and both the prior probability distribution of these states of nature and each population are normally distributed. To clarify this, consider the following example.

A pharmaceutical firm extracts a certain vitamin from a liquid raw material purchased in 1,000-gallon batches. The amount of this vitamin per gallon, taken at random from the batch, is approximately normally distributed with a mean μ and a standard deviation of three ounces per gallon. The mean ounces of vitamin per gallon varies from batch to batch. Past records indicate that the means of previous batches are normally distributed with a mean of 18 ounces and a variance of 36 ounces, that is, $N(18,36)$. The firm uses a process which extracts the vitamin content from the raw material with 100 percent perfection. The profit margin obtained from selling this extracted vitamin is a linear function of the form:

$$\$K = -30 + 3x$$

where x is the ounces of vitamin per gallon.

Before the firm decides whether to purchase a new batch of this raw material, it has a chemist draw nine test tubes of material from a batch. The material was found to contain, on the average, 15 ounces of vitamin per gallon of liquid raw material. Should the firm buy the batch or not?

[4] Note that this formula (or theorem) is based on the assumption that the loss function is quadratic (see footnote 3).

In this example, we can identify two types of normal distributions, as follows:

Population distribution from which the sample is drawn:

$$N(\mu,\sigma^2) = N(\mu,3^2) \tag{3}$$

The population has unknown mean μ and variance $\sigma^2 = 3^2$.

Prior distribution of population mean:

$$N(\mu_0,\sigma_0) = N(18,6^2) \tag{4}$$

That is, the prior distribution of the states of nature (population mean, M) is normally distributed with the mean $\mu_0 = 18$ and variance $\sigma_0{}^2 = 6^2$.

Sampling Distribution of Mean. From a theorem on the sampling distribution of means, we know that when we draw a sample of size n from a population with a mean μ and a variance σ^2, the sampling distribution of means is normally distributed with mean μ and a variance, σ^2/n, that is:

$$N(\mu,\sigma^2/n) \tag{5}$$

Thus, in this example, we have

$$N(\mu,\sigma^2/n) = N(\mu,3^2/9)$$

Posterior Distribution. From the preceding distributions, a posterior probability distribution can be derived. Given the posterior probability distribution and the loss matrix computed from the profit function, the optimum action can be determined. This chapter will merely give the posterior distribution[5] without proof and compare it with the classical confidence interval estimate.

The following theorem is stated without proof:

Let us assume a population to be $N(\mu,\sigma^2)$ and the (prior) probability distribution of these unknown μ to be $N(\mu_0,\sigma_0{}^2)$. Suppose we draw a sample of size n with replacement from this population $N(\mu,\sigma^2)$ and find that the sample mean is $\bar{x}$. Then, the posterior probability distribution of the unknown μ given $\bar{x}$ is normally distributed with the following μ_1 and $\sigma_1{}^2$:

$$\mu_1 = \frac{n\bar{x}/\sigma^2 + \mu_0/\sigma_0}{n/\sigma^2 + 1/\sigma_0{}^2} \tag{6}$$

$$\sigma_1{}^2 = \frac{\sigma_0{}^2\sigma^2}{\sigma_0{}^2 + \sigma^2/n} \tag{7}$$

where x represents the sample mean and the rest of the notation is as explained earlier.

Using the example given earlier, we can compute the posterior distribution as follows:

$$\mu_1 = \frac{nx/\sigma^2 + \mu_0/\sigma_0{}^2}{n/\sigma^2 + 1/\sigma_0{}^2}$$

$$= \frac{(9 \times 15)/3^2 + 18/6^2}{9/3^2 + 1/6^2} = 15.1$$

$$\sigma_1 = \frac{\sigma_0{}^2\sigma^2/n}{\sigma_0{}^2 + \sigma^2/n} = \frac{6^2 \times 3^2/9}{6^2 + 3^2/9} = \frac{36}{37} = 0.99$$

Note that the posterior mean, μ, is the weighted average of the sample mean, $\bar{x}$ and the prior population mean, μ_0, with the weights being the reciprocals of

---

[5] Those interested in finding an optimum action should see [11] or [12].

variances of the two distributions respectively. Thus, the greater the variance, the smaller the precision, and hence, the smaller the weight. Conversely, the smaller the variance, the greater the weight.

For instance, if there is little prior information on the state of nature, the value of the prior variance would be extremely large. Thus, suppose $\sigma_0 \to \sigma$. Then, $1/\sigma_0^2 \to 0$. Hence, from Equation (6), $\mu_1 = \bar{x}$. This means that when there is little prior information on the state of nature, the posterior mean will be dominated by the sample evidence. Similarly, as $\sigma_0 \to \sigma$, $1/\sigma_0 \to 0$ and hence, from Equation (7), $\sigma_1^2 = \sigma^2/n$. Therefore, when there is little information on the prior distribution of μ, the posterior distribution approaches a normal distribution of μ with mean $\bar{x}$ and variance σ^2/n.

This shows that when there is little prior information on the states of nature, the classical interval estimate will coincide with that of the Bayesian posterior distribution. The classical confidence interval estimate therefore can be interpreted as the central area of the posterior probability distribution.

Classical and Bayesian Statistics

Earlier, it was stated that in deriving an optimum decision rule, classical statistics measures the risk of wrong decision in terms of error probabilities. On the other hand, in finding an optimum action, Bayesian statistics measures the risk using error probabilities, loss, and prior probability. Consequently, from a Bayesian viewpoint, classical statistics apparently ignores the loss function and the prior probability in evaluating the optimum action. However, if classical statistics are carefully examined, it will be noticed that it implicitly takes these factors into account. To clarify this, recall the following.

In determining an optimum decision rule, the classical school first determines an α value and then selects a decision rule that will minimize the value of p. Determining an α value, however, requires some idea about the loss function and the prior probability of the state of nature.

For instance, if the loss from taking a wrong action is felt to be great when the null hypothesis is true, one will attempt to make the value of α smaller; and if the loss from taking a wrong action is felt to be great when the alternative hypothesis is true, one will tend to increase the value of α. If the possibility of occurrence of the null hypothesis is felt to be greater than that of the alternative hypothesis, one will tend to make the α value smaller; the converse is likely if the probability of occurrence of the null hypothesis is felt to be smaller than that of the alternative hypothesis.

This shows that the classical school implicitly takes loss and prior probability into account. The contribution of the Bayesian decision theory is that it takes these factors into consideration explicitly.[6]

REFERENCES

Introductory Materials

1. Bierman, H., et al., *Quantitative Analysis for Business Decision*, Homewood, Ill.: Irwin, 1965, chaps. 7–9 and 12–14.
2. Chernoff, H., and L. Moses, *Elementary Decision Theory*, New York: Wiley, 1959.

[6] I am grateful to the publisher of my *Statistics for Modern Business Decision Making* and my *Introductory Statistics for Business Decision Making Under Uncertainty*, Wadsworth Publishing Company, Inc., for permission to use material from them to develop this chapter.

3. Clelland, R., et al., *Basic Statistics with Business Applications*, New York: Wiley, 1966, chaps. 15 and 16.
4. Hadley, G., *Introduction to Probability and Statistical Decision Theory*, San Francisco: Holden-Day, 1967, chaps. 8 and 9.
5. Hirshleifer, J., "The Bayesian Approach to Statistical Decision, an Exposition." *Journal of Business*, vol. 34, October 1961, pp. 471–489.
6. Machol, R. E., et al., *Recent Development in Information and Decision Process*, New York: Macmillan, 1962.
7. Peters, W., S. Peters, and G. W. Summers, *Statistical Analysis for Business Decision*, Englewood Cliffs, N.J.: Prentice-Hall, 1968, chaps. 10 and 11.
8. Pratt, J. H., "Bayesian Interpretation of Standard Inference Statement," *Journal of the Royal Statistical Society*, B. 27, 1967, pp. 169–203.
9. Pratt, J., H. Raiffa, and R. Schlaifer, "The Foundations of Decision Under Uncertainty: An Elementary Exposition," *Journal of the American Statistical Association*, vol. 59, June 1964, pp. 353–375.
10. Raiffa, H., *Decision Analysis, Introductory Lecture on Choices under Uncertainty*, Reading, Mass.: Addison-Wesley, 1968, chaps. 6 and 8.
11. Sasaki, K., *Statistics for Modern Business Decision Making*, Belmont, Calif.: Wadsworth, 1968.
12. Sasaki, K., *Introductory Statistics for Decision Making Under Uncertainty*, Belmont, Calif.: Wadsworth, chaps. 7, 8, 10, and 11. (In press)
13. Schlaifer, R., *Probability and Statistics for Business Decision*, New York: McGraw-Hill, 1959.
14. Schlaifer, R., *Analysis of Decision Under Uncertainty*, New York: McGraw-Hill, 1967.
15. Schmitt, S. A., *Measuring Uncertainty, an Elementary Introduction to Bayesian Statistics*, Reading, Mass.: Addison-Wesley, 1969, chaps. 6 and 8.
16. Spurr, W., and C. Bonini, *Statistical Analysis for Business Decision*, Homewood, Ill.: Irwin, 1969, chaps. 9 and 10.
17. Wonnacott, T., and R. Wonnacott, *Introductory Statistics*, New York: Wiley, 1969, chap. 15.

Advanced Materials

18. Aoki, M., *Optimization of Stochastic System*, New York: Academic, 1967.
19. Ferguson, T. S., *Mathematical Statistics, A Decision Theoretical Approach*, New York: Academic, 1967.
20. Lindley, D. V., *Introduction to Probability Theory from a Bayesian Viewpoint*, Part I, *Probability*, and Part II, *Inference*, Cambridge, England: Cambridge University Press, 1965.
21. Martin, J. J., *Bayesian Decision Problems and Markow Chains*, New York: Wiley, 1967.
22. Mood, A., and F. A. Graybill, *Introduction to the Theory of Statistics*, New York: McGraw-Hill, 1963.
23. Pratt, J., H. Raiffa, and R. Schlaifer, *Introduction to Statistical Decision Theory*, New York: McGraw-Hill, 1965.
24. Raiffa, H., and R. Schlaifer, *Applied Statistical Decision Theory*, Cambridge, Mass.: Harvard University Press, 1966.
25. Savage, Leonard J., *The Foundations of Statistics*, New York: Wiley, 1954.
26. Weiss, Leonard, *Statistical Decision Theory*, New York: McGraw-Hill, 1961.

Statistical Inference

Chapter 2

Statistical Inference

R. CLAY SPROWLS *Graduate School of Business Administration, University of California, Los Angeles, California*

Many business decisions are formulated on the basis of aggregates and the properties of these aggregates. This is especially true in market research where knowledge of a total (readership or viewership) or a percentage of a total (market share) is the basis for a decision. Thinking in terms of such aggregates rather than of individuals is fundamental to many practical decision situations.

The aggregate of all conceivable observations of some kind is a statistical population. The observations which in the aggregate form such a population may be measurements (number of packages purchased) or merely the designation of the presence or absence of a certain characteristic (buy or not buy). The population may consist of measurements of a single characteristic (univariate) which may be continuous (as when it results from measurement) or discrete (as when it results from counting). Multiple observations may be made to form a set of observations in pairs (bivariate) or in more than two characteristics (multivariate). Populations may be further classified as finite (limited number of possible observations) or infinite (unlimited).

The general nature of a statistical population is determined by the character of the observations of which it is composed. If the exact nature of the population—the mathematical formula or the numerical values of its parameters—is known, everything about the population is known. Rarely is this the case. Very often, however, one can make a hypothesis about the population. The hypothesis may be based upon general knowledge or earlier experiment and observation of the same problem, or be merely an a priori speculation.

Judgment about the validity of the hypothesis may need to be based on only a part of the existing data or on data from a sample of the population. One reason samples are used is that measuring the total population in its entirety is too costly. Because the decision about the validity of the hypothesis is dependent on incomplete information, it is subject to error; therefore, any inference about some population property or characteristic is an uncertain inference. The validity of the hypothesis is judged not in the sense of "proving" it, but merely in terms of judging the sample to be more consistent with one hypothesis than another, or of accepting a hypothesis as being correct as long as the data cannot disprove it.

Statistical inference is a method of judging the validity of a statistical hypothesis about a statistical population based upon a sample. It provides a theory of uncertain inference that takes account of the randomness of sample observations and stochastic happenings. It is a method of induction based upon probability theory so that the uncertainty of the inference can be measured, that is, the risks of making incorrect inferences can be stated. Allowing for the laws of chance as they affect individuals, statistical inference permits generalization from sample observations to the population characteristics and a choice from among alternative hypotheses in a manner that minimizes the risks of error.

Certain assumptions are needed for the valid application of statistical inference. Sometimes the assumptions concern the basic mathematical form of the population itself; for example, it may be assumed that the totality of all measurements follows a normal distribution. Sometimes it is about a parameter value, for example, that the variance is finite. At all times the assumptions include a statement about the method of selecting the sample, for example, that the individuals in the sample are random, independent drawings from the population. Each application of statistical inference is based upon a set of very specific assumptions.

The two standard subdivisions of statistical inference are estimation (the preceding chapter) and tests of hypotheses. Hypotheses in marketing research may come from a speculation about a marketing phenomenon, the economics of the situation, or other considerations. Examples of hypotheses are that women are more attracted to a certain form of advertising than men, that a particular product will penetrate 25 percent of the market, that there is no difference between the sales of two types of product packaging. When the hypothesis can be translated into a statement about a population distribution, it becomes a statistical hypothesis. The procedure which specifies how a sample is to be selected and examined so that the sample result may be used to accept or reject the hypothesis is called a test of the hypothesis.

This chapter will examine a number of simple statistical hypotheses and their corresponding tests. The decision rule for accepting or rejecting a hypothesis will be developed as well as an explanation of the errors that can occur. Decision rules are not infallible. Hypotheses which are actually true may be rejected; hypotheses which are actually false may be accepted. The probability that these errors will occur is an important part of the statistical test. The basic ideas developed in this chapter regarding tests that apply to percentage problems are also appropriate to the next chapter, on nonparametric statistics.

TEST OF HYPOTHESIS ON A PROPORTION

A market research firm is undertaking a direct mail promotion of a product with a $10 profit margin. The firm desires to conduct a small mailing test before embarking on a full-scale promotion. A quality advertising brochure costs $0.90 and postage is $0.10, so the total direct mail cost is $1.00 per unit. The product must sell to 10 percent of those solicited to break even on the promotion. More than 10 percent sales will generate a profit.

This situation fits a classical test of a hypothesis specifying the value of P in a dichotomous population. A brochure recipient either buys or does not buy the product; P is the percentage or proportion of those in the population who do buy. The basic statistical hypothesis to be tested is that 10 percent of the market will buy the product from a direct mail promotion. An alternative hypothesis for this problem may be that the proportion of buyers is more than 10 percent. (Two other alternative hypotheses will be discussed later.) The statistical test is a procedure whereby a sample of customers is mailed a brochure and the sample result is used to accept one or the other hypothesis. Acceptance of the basic hypothesis leads to a decision to abandon any further direct mail marketing. Acceptance of the alternative hypothesis is a signal to proceed with full-scale marketing effort.

Decision Errors. The sample might lead to the rejection of the hypothesis that 10 percent of the market will buy the product when, in fact, this is actually true. Or, the sample might lead to the acceptance of the hypothesis that more than 10 percent will buy when, in fact, this is actually false. These errors are given standard names and symbols, as shown in Table 1. Rejection of the basic hypothesis (or acceptance of the alternative) when, in fact, it is correct is an error of the first kind, or a Type I error, and its probability of occurrence is designated by the Greek letter alpha (α). Acceptance of the basic hypothesis when, in fact, it is false is an error of the second kind, or a Type II error, and its probability of occurrence is designated by the Greek letter beta (β).

TABLE 1   Decision Alternatives

Decision	Hypothesis actually true	
	Basic	Alternative
Accept basic	O.K. $1 - \alpha$	Error II β
Accept alternative	Error I α	O.K. $1 - \beta$

Direct mail test costs

Action	$H_0: P_0 = .1$ Break-even or loss	$H_1: P_1 > .1$ Profitable
Abandon project Full-scale marketing	O.K. Out-of-pocket cost	Lost opportunity cost O.K.

Translated into the context of the direct mail problem, the alpha error is the error of proceeding with a large volume mailing when the market is at best at a "break-even" position (10 percent sales). The beta error is the error of not going ahead with a large volume mailing when the market is actually in a profitable (more than 10 percent) sales state. Alpha is the probability that the test may incur a large out-of-pocket cost. Beta is the probability of losing a profitable opportunity.

Both of these are costly errors. Market managers would most likely prefer to have the probability of being wrong very small. The ideal situation is to have both probabilities zero, but this is attainable only if the true value of the proportion of sales is known. Since this is not known and only sample evidence is available, some probability of making each error exists and must be dealt with. The statistical test procedure permits an exact measurement of these probabilities and their control at levels that are reasonable to the problem. The various ideas presented in the preceding sections may be formalized as follows.

Basic hypothesis: $P_0 = .10$ (10 percent sales).

Alternative hypothesis: $P_1 > .10$ (more than 10 percent sales).

The marketing research manager decides that he can invest $100 in direct mail costs of a pilot mailing. This means that he will mail 100 advertising brochures to a random sample of 100 customers in the market area. (Methods of selecting random samples are covered in Sec. II, Part C, of this handbook.)

The marketing manager in charge of the project weights the Type I error very heavily, wishing to avoid the potentially large out-of-pocket costs that would result from going ahead with a volume mailing when the market is not favorable. He therefore sets alpha at a very low level of 0.01.

The sample test statistic can vary from 0 to 100 sales. Large sample sales (for example, 15, 20, or larger) are more consistent with the alternative hypothesis than with the basis hypothesis.

The *critical region* is defined as sample values sufficiently far from P_0 that they are very unlikely to occur in the sample by chance if P_0 is correct. "Very unlikely" is defined by the level of significance (α) which is selected by the manager to be 0.01.

The critical region may be determined from a table of probabilities of the *binomial distribution*. This probability distribution describes the probability of X sample occurrences in a sample of n observations from a population with P percent in one category.

Probability computations are not shown here but are adapted from a large table [3]. With alpha set at 0.01, the critical region is 18 or more sales in the sample. This value is selected because the probability of 18 or more sales in a sample of 100 from a population with exactly 10 percent customers is 0.010.

Critical region: If 18 or more sample sales occur, accept $P > 0.10$ and proceed to volume mailing.

The critical region defines the decision rule to follow in assessing the sample results. It is based upon a predetermined selection of the *level of significance* for the test or the probability of making a Type I error. This critical region is one-sided, that is, all of the values that reject the basic hypothesis are to one side of the expected number of sales. This is because the alternative hypothesis states that the value of P is one-sided, that is, only P-values greater than 10 percent are to be considered.

SUMMARY OF TEST STEPS

The preceding example may be summarized in terms of a series of test steps which may then be used in further examples. The steps are:

1. State the experimental or testing goal.
2. Select the basic (null) and alternative hypotheses.
3. Choose a value of α, after assessing the risks of both Type I and Type II errors.
4. Identify the standard test statistic.

5. Select the standard probability distribution for that sample statistic.

6. Select the sample size (to be discussed later).

7. Compute the critical region of the test statistic.

8. Select, measure, and assess the sample results by stating a statistical conclusion.

9. State the experimental conclusion for the sample.

These steps are illustrated with a different statement of the same marketing problem.

One-sided Test, "Less than" Alternative.   Another market research manager might look at the same problem differently.   He might reason that the basic hypothesis is 10 percent sales in the market but that the alternative is less than 10 percent.   According to this reasoning, if the basic hypothesis is accepted, the large volume mailing will be made.   If the alternative is accepted, the whole project will be dropped.

The differences between this statement and the previous example are how the basic hypothesis is interpreted and what values of P are to be included under the alternative hypothesis.   These decisions affect the critical region because now very small sample values are more consistent with the alternative hypothesis.   The critical region is one-sided but at the lower end of the scale of sample values.   This test may follow the test steps outlined previously.

1. The experimental goal is to decide whether to undertake a volume direct mail campaign based upon a pilot sample.

2. Basic hypothesis: $P_0 = 0.10$.

   Alternative hypothesis: $P_1 < 0.10$.

3. The value of alpha is set by the manager at 0.01.

4. The number of sales in the sample is the test statistic.

5. Binomial probabilities are taken from published tables [3].

6. A sample size of 100 is again selected, based upon the $100 cost of the pilot.

7. The critical region is now three or fewer sales.   The probability of three or fewer sales in a sample of 100 from a population characterized by 10 percent sales is exactly 0.008, which is approximately 0.01.

8. A sample with three or fewer sales will lead to rejection of the basic hypothesis in favor of the alternative.

9. A sample with three or fewer sales will lead to a rejection of the large volume mailing in favor of acceptance of project termination.

Two-sided Test, "Not Equal to" Alternative.   A third market manager might view this project in another way.   He states the basic hypothesis as 10 percent sales.   However, he argues that the alternative hypothesis should include values of P both greater and less than 10 percent.   If P is not 10 percent, he wishes to know whether rejection is because the market is very much worse than break-even or very much better.   This is a two-sided test because very small sample values are consistent with the "less than" alternative and very large values are consistent with the "more than" alternative.

1. The experimental goal is the same.

2. Basic hypothesis: $P_0 = 0.10$.

   Alternative hypothesis: $P_1 \neq 0.10$ (both less than and greater than 0.10).

3. The value of α is set at 0.01.   This is now divided equally between the lower and upper critical regions so that 0.005 is the probability for small, and 0.005 the probability for large, values of $P = 0.10$.

4. The test statistic is the number of sample sales.

5. Binomial probabilities are taken from published tables [3].

6. A sample of 100 is again selected.

7. The critical region is now 2 or fewer sales (exact probability 0.002) and 19 or more sales (exact probability 0.0046).

8. Therefore, 2 or fewer sales or 19 or more sales lead to the rejection of the basic hypothesis in favor of the alternative.

9. *a.* Two or fewer sales definitely lead to abandoning the project.

b. Conversely, 19 or more sales definitely lead to the volume mailing.

c. A range of 3 to 18 sales definitely accepts the basic hypothesis but the decision depends upon the promoter's judgment. He may decide that acceptance of 10 percent is good enough to go ahead, bad enough to stop, or uncertain enough to take another trial run.

These examples cover the three standard alternative hypotheses ("less than," "greater than," and "not equal to") that arise in many situations. The procedure illustrated has rather wide applicability. Step 6, selecting the sample size, was accomplished in each example only on the basis of the $100 cost of the pilot sample which would support 100 observations. Moreover, setting a low value of α (0.01) to control errors of the first kind does not take into account errors of the second kind and the values of β. Planning a sample size should explicitly account for both errors I and II and their probabilities of occurrence.

ASSESSING ERRORS OF THE SECOND KIND

An error of the second kind is the acceptance of the basic hypothesis when, in fact, the alternative hypothesis is true. The probability of this error is designated by β. For the first example ("greater than" alternative), the critical region is 18 or more occurrences. This makes 17 or fewer occurrences the region of acceptance for the basic hypothesis. Beta is the probability that the sample result will be 17 or fewer occurrences for a value of P_1 under the alternative hypothesis. Since the alternative hypothesis is stated merely as an inequality $(P_1 > 0.10)$, β has no one single value. For each P_1 there is a value of β. Thus, β is a function. It may be computed by finding the probability of 17 or fewer occurrences in a sample of 100 for different values of P_1 greater than 0.10 in a table of binomial probabilities [3]. The function values of β are called an *operating characteristic curve* or OC curve. The OC curve for the test, with 100 observations and the "greater than" alternative, is shown in Table 2.

One point on this curve is set by the value of P_0 and α. Given the sample size, the other points then follow. In this problem, for example, if the true proportion of purchasers is as high as 15 percent, the chances are about 3 in 4 (0.763) that the basic hypothesis will be accepted and the project will be terminated. If the proportion of buyers is as large as 20 percent, the probability of project termination is still 14 in 100. In other words, β values may be very high, even for values of P_1 that are far from P_0.

Changing the value of α will have some, but little, effect on β. The curve will be slightly lowered. The sample size is the key to controlling β. The ideal shape for the OC curve with a "greater than" alternative is shown in Figure 1. Both α and β are zero. This curve may be realized only with a 100 percent sample and no errors of measurement in the sample result. For sample sizes less than 100 percent, the curve begins to bend slightly around P_0 and α and β take on values greater than zero.

PLANNING THE SAMPLE SIZE

Planning sample size is a matter of selecting the desired OC curve and finding the number of observations that matches it. In practice, the selection is based upon two points on the OC curve. One point is the value of P_0 and its asso-

TABLE 2 Operating Characteristic Curve*

Value of P (percent)	$\beta = Pr(\text{Acc } H_0)$
10 $(P_0 = 0.10)$	$0.990 = 1 = \alpha$
11	0.976
12	0.949
13	0.906
14	0.844
15	0.763
16	0.668
17	0.390
18	0.290
19	0.207
20	0.141
21	0.092
22	0.058
.	.
.	.
.	.
25	0.003

$* n = 100; \alpha = 0.01; \text{Acc } H_0 \text{ of } X \leq 17;$
$\text{Rej } H_0 \text{ if } X \geq 18.$

ciated value of α. The other point is a critical value of P_1 and its associated value of β. The closer this critical value of P_1 is to P_0, for given values of α and β, the larger the sample size.

The selection of P_1 depends upon the practical effect of accepting the basic hypothesis when that value of P_1 is actually true. The significance of this effect depends upon the nature of the testing situation and how the researcher feels about it. An example is given for the "greater than" alternative which was first posed in this chapter.

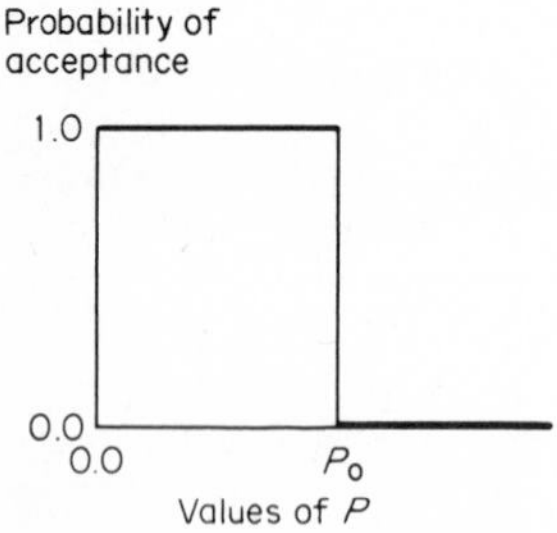

Probability of acceptance

Fig. 1. Ideal OC curve for a "greater than" alternative.

The basic hypothesis remains the same. At a 10 percent level of sales, the market manager wishes a very small probability α of proceeding with a large market test. He also reasons that if sales are as large as 15 percent, he will generate a 50 percent profit on the direct mail costs. For each 100 units mailed, 15 are sold at $10 profit each for a gross profit of $150. The 10 units cost $100 to mail. The potential profit is $50 or 50 percent.

He does not wish to miss this opportunity. At the 0.15 value of P_1, he sets a very small value of $\beta = 0.01$. The improvement to 15 percent sales over the break-even 10 percent figure is a practical significant difference. The point on the OC curve defined by this selection is a value of $P_1 = 0.15$ and $\beta = 0.01$. These are summarized below:

$$H_0 : P_0 = 0.10 \qquad \alpha = 0.01$$
$$H_1 : P_1 = 0.15 \qquad \beta = 0.01$$

What value of n will make the OC curve pass through these two points? This value may be found by trial and error in the table of binomial probabilities [3]. Trial and error selections are shown in Table 3. Sample sizes of 200 and 400 are much too small. A sample of 1,000 is a little too large. A sample of 950 controls both α and β at the desired levels on the OC curve.

TABLE 3   Trial and Error Selection of Sample Size for Operating Characteristic Curve*

n	Critical region	Value for $P_1 = 0.15$ (binomial probabilities)	Sample size
200	$X \geq 31$	0.55, too large	Too small
400	$X \geq 55$	0.223, too large	Too small
1,000	$X \geq 123$	0.00636, too small	Too large
950	$X \geq 118$	0.01017, correct	Correct

* $P_0 = 0.10$; $\alpha = 0.01$; $P_1 = 0.15$; $\beta = 0.01$.

Therefore, a sample of 950 mailing pieces is to be used in the test. The cost of the promotion is $950. The sampling plan is approximately a $1,000 project, less any reduced cost from a price break on printing 950 brochures and bulk mail rates.

If this is too expensive a promotion, the sample size can always be lowered. The effect is to change the OC curve so that at $P_1 = 0.15$, β will be larger than 0.01. It may be calculated for any sample size. The point is that a high protection against error (or very small probabilities) is paid for through sample size. Lower protection can be bought for small samples.

The same principles apply to "less than" and "not equal to" alternative hypotheses. They will not be illustrated here. The two-sided alternative provides protection against large and small values of P_1, both of which may be specified in advance on the basis of a practical judgment about a significant difference. The result may be two different sample sizes, one for the lower and one for the upper value. Then, some sort of compromise must be made for a final single value of n.

ASSESSING SAMPLE RESULTS

Now suppose that the 950 pieces are mailed and 115 orders are received. This sample result accepts the basic hypothesis and the large marketing effort is abandoned. The total cost of the pilot is $950. The 115 orders yield $1,150 of revenue, or a $200 profit on direct costs.

This result may cause the market manager to have second thoughts about the whole sampling plan. He might ask the following question: What is the probability of 115 or more orders in a sample of 950 if only 10 percent of the market are true buyers? The probability (from three percent) is 0.02. This is very close to α. In fact, if at the planning stage the decision had been to select $\alpha = 0.05$, a very common level, this sample result would have definitely pointed to the large marketing effort.

When sample results are close to the boundary of the critical region, the tendency is to weigh the problem of setting α again. Business judgment must be brought to bear here. That judgment might say, "Go ahead," since the sample result is close to the borderline of the critical region and the costs of not going ahead with the mass marketing effort are very large if a profitable market is missed.

This can be a dangerous argument. Changing the value of α after the fact can always lead to the acceptance of the hypothesis when the sample indicates rejection, and to the rejection of the hypothesis when the sample indicates acceptance. The value of α can always be raised to reject and lowered to accept. This is neither good statistical practice nor good scientific method. Exercising judgments of this kind cannot be absolutely ruled out. The decision maker should realize what he is doing and how he may be changing probability levels. After the fact, setting of α is a potentially dangerous procedure.

OTHER TESTS OF HYPOTHESES

Hypothesis testing has been illustrated in the previous sections with regard to a population that is finite (but very large), discrete (buy or not buy), and univariate (a single measurement). Statistical inference treats other populations as well and provides standard testing procedures. These procedures will follow the same steps as illustrated, but the test statistic and probability distribution will differ. Some examples of common hypotheses and their tests will be summarized very briefly here.

1. The population mean μ is equal to a specified number and the population standard deviation σ is known. For a sample of n observations, the sample mean is $\bar{X}$. The test statistic is $z = (\bar{X} - \mu)/(\sigma/\sqrt{n})$. Assume z has a normal distribution with mean 0 and variance 1.

2. The population mean is equal to a specified number, but the standard deviation σ is not known and must be measured by the sample standard deviation s. The test statistic is $t = (\bar{X} - \mu)/(s/\sqrt{n})$. If the population is a normal distribution and if the hypothesis is true, the statistic t has a $t(n-1)$ distribution.

3. The population variance σ^2 is equal to a specified number. If the population is normal and the population variance does have that value, the test statistic $\chi^2/df = s^2/\sigma^2$ follows the $\chi^2/df(n-1)$ distribution.

4. The variances of two normally distributed populations are equal. The test statistic $F = s_1^2/s_2^2$ follows the $F(n_1 - 1, n_2 - 1)$ distribution.

5. The means of two populations are equal. The populations have the same σ and their value is known. The test statistic

$$z = \frac{\bar{X}_1 - \bar{X}_2}{\sqrt{\sigma_1^2/n_1 + \sigma_2^2/n_2}}$$

is normal if the populations are normal, and approximately normal if n_1 and n_2 are large.

6. The means of two populations are equal and σ is unknown but equal in the two populations. The test statistic is

$$t = \frac{\bar{X}_1 - \bar{X}_2}{s_p \sqrt{1/n_1 + 1/n_2}}$$

where s_p^2 is a pooled estimate of σ^2.

$$s_p{}^2 = \frac{(n_1 - 1)s_1{}^2 + (n_2 - 1)s_2{}^2}{n_1 + n_2 - 2}$$

Hypothesis testing extends to more than the observations. Analysis of variance treats the problem of several sample means, as illustrated in Chapter 10 of the next part. Hypothesis testing with several sample proportions is illustrated in the next section.

EXTENSION TO SEVERAL PROPORTIONS

Hypothesis testing may be extended to several sample proportions. As an example, suppose that the sales promotion covers several different market areas. One question that may be asked is whether some market areas are better than others. A properly designed sample can be used to test this hypothesis. An illustration is given using the same basic marketing problem as in the previous sections.

While testing the overall reaction to the direct mail marketing (10 percent response or better), the research director decides to test different area response rates as well. Since the market divides itself into five different areas quite naturally, he allocates one-fifth, or 190, of the total sample of each of the five areas during the random-sample selection. The sample responses will be used to test whether the area response rates are different.

The basic statistical hypothesis to be tested is that the area rates are all equal (no differences) or that 20 percent (0.20) of the total orders will come from each area. The alternative hypothesis is that the rates are not all equal but vary from one area to another. The model for testing which of these hypotheses is correct is based upon the observed and expected frequencies of occurrence in the sample using the chi-square probability distribution. Assumed data for the sample result of 115 sales (see the previous section) and computations are shown in Table 4.

TABLE 4   Testing for Equality of Several Proportions

Area i	Proportion P_i	Expected E_i	Observed O_i	$O_i - E_i$	$(O_i - E_i)^2$	$(O_i - E_i)^2/E_i$
1	0.2	23	18	−5	25	1.09
2	0.2	23	19	−4	16	0.70
3	0.2	23	24	+1	1	0.04
4	0.2	23	29	+6	36	1.57
5	0.2	23	25	+2	4	0.17
Total	1.0	115	115	0	—	$\chi^2 = 3.57$

$K - 1 = $ d.f; $\alpha = 0.05$; $\chi^2(0.05, 4) = 9.49$.

A measure of the differences between the observed and expected frequencies if the basic hypothesis (equal percentages) is true is the sum of ratios of the square of the difference between the observed and expected frequency divided by the expected frequency. In this example, the expected number of sales in each area under the basic hypothesis is 23 (0.2 times 115). For each area, the square of the difference between the observed and expected frequency is divided by the expected number. The sum of these ratios is a value of chi-square.

Should all observed frequencies equal their respective expected frequencies, the value of chi-square will be zero because the differences will all be zero. To the extent that the observed and expected frequencies differ, the value of chi-square will be greater than zero. How large an observed chi-square can be before the basic hypothesis is rejected is based upon a probability analysis, as illustrated in the earlier examples. The complete test procedure is summarized below, according to the model steps outlined earlier.

1. The experimental goal is to decide whether the response rate to the direct mail campaign differs from one area to another.
2. Basic hypothesis: $P_i = 0.20$ for all areas.
   Alternative hypothesis: $P_i \neq 0.20$ for all areas.
3. A value of alpha is set at 0.05 by the manager.
4. The test statistic is the chi-square measure of difference between observed and expected frequencies.
5. The appropriate probability distribution is the chi-square distribution for which probabilities are tabled in [1]. The parameter is the degrees of freedom, which in this case is one less than the number of areas (k), or four.
6. A sample of 115 sales is assumed to be the result of the direct mail test.
7. The critical region, that is, the value of chi-square for 4 degrees of freedom which is exceeded by a probability 0.05 if the basic hypothesis is true is $\chi^2(0.05,4) = 9.49$.
8. A sample with a chi-square measure greater than 9.49 will lead to the rejection of the basic hypothesis in favor of the alternative.
9. A sample with a chi-square greater than 9.49 is evidence that the market areas are not equal but have different response rates to the direct mail promotion.

The observed sample of chi-square is 3.57. The sample result accepts the hypothesis of *no difference* among the response rates in the five different market areas. The differences between the observed and the expected values are well within the limits of chance as defined by the alpha value of 0.05.

PLANNING THE SAMPLE SIZE

The sample of 115 is used in the test of market-area response rates only because it is the assumed result of the overall test of market response with respect to the 10 percent standard. This sample size may or may not meet the requirements for a planned sample that effectively discriminates among the five market areas according to management decisions about the criteria for describing markets as different.

The decision to accept the basic hypothesis that the market areas are the same could be wrong. The market areas might well be different, with the sample not detecting the differences because it is too small. One measure of the ability of a sample to detect differences is the *power* or the probability of detecting departures from the basic hypothesis. (The power is related to β and the OC curve, because power $= 1 - \beta$. It is merely another way of looking at errors in testing hypotheses.) The sample size for a specific power may be computed for chi-square tests of this kind.

A measure of the difference between the P_i (basic hypothesis) and the P_i (alternative hypothesis), which is approximately distributed according to the noncentral chi-square distribution with $k - 1$ degrees of freedom, is

$$\lambda = n \sum_{i=1}^{k} \frac{(p_i - P_i)^2}{P_i}$$

This equation may be reduced to

$$\lambda = n\left(\sum_{i=1}^{k} \frac{p_i^2}{P_i} - 1\right)$$

and solved directly for n,

$$n = \frac{\lambda}{\sum_{i=1}^{k} \dfrac{p_i^2}{P_i} - 1}$$

The denominator is determined from the p_i and P_i. Tables of λ values for selected values of alpha, power, and degrees of freedom are published [2].

An illustration is given in Table 5. The basic hypothesis is that the area response rates (P_i) are equal. The alternative hypothesis is a statement about the rates (p_i) that would define "different" marketing areas. This is a marketing management decision. Rates that differ as much as 5 percent from the equal distribution are worth detecting.

TABLE 5   Sample Size Calculation in Chi-Square Tests

Area i	Basic hypothesis P_i	Alternative hypothesis P_i	p_i^2	p_i^2/P_i
1	0.20	0.25	0.0625	0.3125
2	0.20	0.20	0.0400	0.2000
3	0.20	0.15	0.0225	0.1125
4	0.20	0.25	0.0625	0.3125
5	0.20	0.15	0.0225	0.1125
Total	1.00	1.00	—	1.0500

An alpha of 0.05 is selected for the risk of making an error of the first kind—deciding that the areas are different when, in fact, they are equal. A power of 0.90 is selected for the probability of detecting that the areas are different when, in fact, they are different. For 4 degrees of freedom, alpha $= 0.05$ and power $= 0.90$, $\lambda = 15.405$ [2]. Substituting in the equation for n,

$$n = \frac{15.045}{1.05 - 1.00} = 308$$

In other words, approximately 300 *orders* are needed to detect differences as specified by the alternative hypothesis with a power of 0.90.

This is approximately three times as many orders as are generated by the market test with 950 mailings. A total mailing of 3,000 would be needed to test for differences among the market areas, or three times the sample size determined for the gross test of the overall 10 percent response rate. Should the test for equality in the five market areas be the more important, this sample size would direct the market research, and the test of the overall response rate would be oversampled with respect to its specifications.

Market research very often involves several questions or attributes in one survey. To plan the sample, the most important aspect must be selected and planned for in the sample size. For some attributes, the sample sizes may be too small and the probability risks higher than one might like. Other attributes may be oversampled with the probability risks smaller than needed. A compromise is worked out among them, based upon the most important aspect of the survey.

Perhaps, in these examples, 950 is correct because it is the basis of the go-ahead decision for a large project which is more important at this point than refining market area responses.

DECISION THEORY

The classical tests of hypotheses discussed in the previous sections include statements about basic (or null) and alternative hypotheses, errors of the first and second kind, level of significance (*alpha*), OC curve (*beta*) or power function, probability distributions for the sample statistics, and decision rules based upon a critical region that is defined by the probability *alpha*. Sample sizes may be calculated by specifying the operating characteristic curve or the power function desired. Although decision theory was discussed in earlier chapters in this handbook, a simple example based upon the marketing situation used in classical testing will be reviewed here.

The classical test is based upon values of alpha and beta (or power). Their selection somehow implicitly takes into account the seriousness of the two kinds of errors that can occur. If rejecting the null hypothesis when it is correct (Error I) is very serious (costly or damaging), then alpha should be made small. However, Error II may also be serious, so that beta should be small. The classical testing situation controls both probabilities of error through the selection of the sample size.

Decision theory focuses less upon hypotheses than upon actions to be taken and the consequences of the actions, that is, upon the payoffs that accrue to each action under each testing state. A payoff table with two actions and three states is shown in Table 6.

TABLE 6   A Payoff Table with Two Actions

State (P)	Action	
	A_1: Go ahead	A_2: Terminate project*
<0.10	Loss	0
$=0.10$	Break-even	0
>0.10	Profit	0

* Payoffs assume no opportunity costs or alternative revenues.

One action, A_1, is to go ahead with the project. If the true proportion of buyers is less than 10 percent, the promotion loses money. If the proportion is exactly 10 percent, it is a break-even promotion. If the promotion is more than 10 percent, the payoff is a profit. The extent of the loss or the profit depends upon the exact value of P, which is not known.

The other action, A_2, is to terminate the project. The payoffs are recorded as zero for each state because the complications of opportunity costs or alternative revenues that would accrue from applying the resources available to another project are not considered, although they can be put into the analysis and should be in a more extended discussion.

The decision theorist does not necessarily accept the whole range of parameter values for the two hypotheses as relevant. He exercises judgment and knowledge of the marketing situation to select specific values of the market reaction. To make the example simple, only three such values are used in Table 7. These are 5, 10, and 15 percent.

TABLE 7   Market Research Director's Decision Table*

| State (P) | Prior probability | A_1: Go ahead | | | A_2: Terminate |
		Revenue	Profit	Weighted profit	
0.05	0.2	50	−50	−10	0
0.10	0.5	100	0	0	0
0.20	0.3	200	100	30	0
		Exp. value		$+20	$0

Decision: Definite go-ahead.

* $n = 100$, total cost = \$100; profit = \$10 per item.

For each state (value of P), the exact dollar profit or loss may be computed. The market test will be with 100 direct mail pieces at a cost of \$1 each or a total cost of \$100. If the market response is 5 percent, the total revenue from the five sales is \$50 and the loss on the promotion is \$50. Break-even and \$100 profits are computed for the 10 and 15 percent response rates.

The market researcher is not certain which state is correct. It is his judgment that their probabilities are 0.2, 0.5, and 0.3 respectively. These *prior probabilities* are an expression of a prior state of knowledge about the unknown parameter. The classical statistician objects to such probabilities being attached to parameters because he deems them not to be random variables. However, decision theorists find such statements useful in formalizing their beliefs.

Each payoff is weighted by its prior probability. This is headed "Weighted profit" in the table. The sum of the weighted profits is the expected value of the action. The expected value of A_1, to go ahead, is \$20; the expected value of A_2, to terminate the project, is zero. The manager selects action A_1, to go ahead with the market test because the expected payoff from that action is greater than from A_2.

The company controller might look at the market-test situation with less optimism than the research director. His prior probabilities for the three response rates might take the values shown in Table 8. His judgment is that the loss-state prior probability is 0.3 and the profit-state prior probability is 0.2. The expected value of the market decision A_1 is now a profit of only \$5. Although this is larger than the expected value of A_2, his decision is that the test is of doubtful value and should be terminated. Now, the conflict between the controller and the research director must be resolved on other grounds.

The analysis according to decision theory is based upon:

a. A payoff-profit table for each action and each state

b. Prior probabilities of the given states

Then, the choice of an action is based upon the expected values of the consequences of taking each action, with the selection awarded to the action with the maximum expected profit. The analysis incorporates explicit use of economic costs and payoffs in evaluating the worth of actions and subjective prior

TABLE 8   Controller's Decision Table

| State (P) | Prior probability | A_1: Go ahead | | | A_2: Terminate |
		Revenue	Profit	Weighted profit	
0.05	0.3	50	−50	−15	0
0.10	0.5	100	0	0	0
0.15	0.2	150	100	20	0
		Exp. value		$+5	$0

Decision: Marginal profit and doubtful experiment.

probabilities for the different states to arrive at a best procedure for any situation.

BAYES' THEOREM FOR POSTERIORI PROBABILITIES

The market research director and the controller differ in their evaluation of the market research test situation. The difference reflects their judgments about the prior probabilities of the market response rates. One way to resolve the difference is to take a sample and use the sample result as data with which to revise the prior probabilities. Since even the controller's evaluation is a small expected profit, the decision is made to go ahead with the 100-item test in order to gather more evidence.

Suppose that in the sample of 100, 18 individuals accept the offer. This is an 18 percent response. It provides information about the market response that can be used to change the prior probabilities. The analysis for the controller's judgment is shown in Table 9. The computation of posterior probabilities is done in the following manner.

TABLE 9   Posterior Probability Calculations for Controller
(N = 100; X = 18)

State	Prior probability	Likelihood	Joint probability	Posteriori probability
0.05	0.3	0.0	0.00	0.00
0.10	0.5	0.012	0.0060	0.29
0.15	0.2	0.074	0.0148	0.71
	1.0		0.0208	1.00

Decision table

| State (P) | Posteriori probability | A_1: Go ahead | | A_2: Terminate |
		Profit	Weighted average	
0.05	0.00	−50	$0	$0
0.10	0.29	0	0	0
0.15	0.71	100	71	0
	1.00	Exp. value	$71	$0

The conditional probability or *likelihood* of the sample result is evaluated by the binomial probability distribution for each sample result [3]. Thus, the probability that a true market response rate of 5 percent will give a sample result of 18 in 100 is .00. The probability of the sample result if the true state of the market is 15 percent is .074.

Each of these probabilities is multiplied by the probability of each state as assessed before the sample is drawn, that is, by the prior probability, to form a *joint probability*. Each of these joint probabilities is then divided by their sum to obtain the posterior distribution. In this example, the posterior distribution is considerably changed from the prior distribution.

The revised or posterior distribution probabilities are now used in the decision analysis, as shown in the lower part of Table 9. The expected value of action A_1 is now a definite profit. The sample evidence is enough to change the controller's decision from doubtful to a definite go-ahead.

The posterior distribution computation and the expected value analysis for the market research director's prior distribution are shown in Table 10. His earlier judgments and decision are reinforced by the sample results.

TABLE 10   Posterior Analysis for Research Director

State (P)	Prior probability	Likelihood	Joint probability	Posteriori probability
0.05	0.2	0.00	0.00	0.00
0.10	0.5	0.012	0.006	0.18
0.20	0.3	0.091	0.027	0.82
	1.0		0.033	1.00

Decision table

State	Posteriori probabilities	A_1: Go ahead		A_2: Terminate
		Profit	Weighted average	
0.05	0.00	−50	$0	$0
0.10	0.18	0	0	0
0.20	0.82	100	82	0
	1.00	Exp. value	$82	$0

SUMMARY

The classical method of testing statistical hypotheses has been illustrated for a parameter that is the proportion or percentage of occurrences in a dichotomous population. The binomial distribution is the appropriate probability distribution for hypotheses about a single proportion. The chi-square distribution is appropriate for hypotheses about several proportions. In each case, the specifications necessary to compute the sample size were given.

Similar methods apply to a wide variety of practical problems that involve other sample variables such as means, variances, regression, and correlation coefficients, and nonparametric statistics. Probability distributions such as the normal, t, F, and Poisson, as well as special distributions for ranks, runs, and other measures are applied to the computation of alpha, beta, power, and sample size.

The details of applying these probability distributions to hypotheses about other variables are given in most standard books on statistical methods. The ideas and steps illustrated here can serve as a model with which to approach different sampling problems in order to formulate the hypotheses, select the appropriate probability distribution, and apply it to the computation of alpha, beta, power, decision rule, and sample size.

Decision theory and the application of Bayes' theorem to the revision of prior probabilities have been illustrated here with only the simplest examples. The methods can be extended to particular prior distributions, such as the normal distribution; to more complex cost and revenue functions that include opportunity costs for alternative uses of economic resources; and to the selection of the optimal sample size that is based upon balancing the improvement in expected payoff from an increased sample size against the increased cost of sampling. These subjects are covered in the references cited in this chapter as well as in other chapters of this handbook.

REFERENCES

1. Dixon, W. J., and F. J. Massey, Jr., *Introduction to Statistical Analysis,* 3d ed., New York: McGraw-Hill, 1969.
2. Fix, Evelyn, *Tables of Non-Central* χ^2, Berkeley: University of California Publications in Statistics, vol. 1, no. 2, 1949.
3. Harvard University, *Tables of the Cumulative Binomial Probability Distribution,* Cambridge, Mass.: Harvard University Press, 1955.
4. Patnaik, P. B., "The Non-Central χ^2- and F-Distributions and Their Applications," *Biometrika,* June 1949, p. 202.
5. Raiffa, Howard, *Decision Analysis: Lectures on Making Decisions Under Uncertainty,* Reading, Mass.: Addison-Wesley, 1969.
6. Schlaifer, Robert, *Analysis of Decisions Under Uncertainty,* New York: McGraw-Hill, 1969.

Statistical Inference

Chapter 3

Nonparametric Statistics[1]

JOHN MORRIS   *Consultant, Clinton, New York*

Parameters are whatever we can measure in a population. The average weight of all male chimpanzees is a parameter (where all male chimps are the population). The range of family incomes in Slumsville is a parameter (where families in Slumsville are the population). A *parametric test* assumes that parameters like these exist, and are meaningful. A *t*-test, for example, is based upon a comparison of the averages (or means) of two samples. Naturally, the *t*-test makes no sense when the averages are not meaningful. Consider a survey of family incomes within a restricted area of Chicago. It might show 19 families with incomes under $5,000 per year, and one family with an income of $100,000 per year. If we were to take the average income of these 20 families, we would find that the "average" family was making nearly $10,000 per year—but nobody's income is anywhere near this figure! For data like this, we would prefer to use the *median* (the income of the middle family, which would be close to $5,000), rather than the mean or average.

Pathological data (of which this is only a very mild example) frequently occur in marketing research, and we need statistical tests which are designed to deal with them. Such tests are often called *nonparametric tests,* which simply means that fewer assumptions are made about the way in which the population parameters are distributed. Several hundred such tests have been developed during the past 30 years, of which a few of the best known and most popular will be described here.[2]

[1] The research upon which this chapter is based was completed under the sponsorship of the Computer Institute for Social Science Research, Michigan State University, East Lansing, Mich.

[2] For further information, see Siegel's *Nonparametric Statistics* [9], which, in spite of many errors, remains the most readable source of information about such tests.

When should a nonparametric test be used, rather than a parametric test? Here are some examples, typical of the sort that might be met in marketing research.

1. We have a questionnaire, which asks the respondents to assign a number, ranging from 0 ("dislike intensely") to 9 ("like very much"), to a dozen proposed new package designs. These subjective preferences will vary in meaning from one person to the next. In addition, they probably won't be normally distributed in the population, that is, they will not form a neat, bell-shaped curve, with most responses clustering around the middle. Instead, they are likely to cluster around two extreme positions, with very few people responding in a neutral fashion to the packages.

2. Sometimes the responses to a survey are given in terms of names (called "nominal" data), which cannot be treated like numbers at all. We ask, "In what part of the country would you prefer to live, if you had to move?" The replies will be names of areas—Midwest, Northwest, Pacific Coast, and so on—rather than numbers. For nominal data, nonparametric tests *must* be used. There are no other alternatives.

3. With appalling frequency, questionnaires are sent back only partially completed. People refuse to answer some of the questions. Nonparametric tests are designed to take missing data in stride, and to make whatever adjustments are needed to extract the maximum of information from the data that are available.

4. A test of sales performance is being attempted, but the data base is found to be extremely small. Some offices have a sales force consisting of only four or five people. Can statistical tests be applied to very small samples like these? Nonparametric tests are intended to provide results even for very small samples, where approximations (such as the chi-square tests) are so inaccurate as to be useless.

5. As the example on family income showed, many statistics are not neatly distributed in the population. The output of a new and untried questionnaire may very well show even more pathological results, which are badly skewed, or which show many unexpected irregularities. Nonparametric tests are intended to deal with such data.

Anyone who has worked at marketing research can unearth other examples like these, in which the data simply do not fit the traditional mathematical models. Nonparametric statistics should be familiar to every worker in marketing research, enabling him to turn apparently useless data into useful, marketable output.

TYPES OF DATA

We may classify data into three general types.[3]

Nominal data consist of names, such as the names of products, firms, persons, or groups. Even though a number may be used, it is simply a means of identification.

Ordinal data consist of responses which can be arranged in a given order. One response is higher or lower on the scale than another response. A list of consumer preferences will often constitute an ordinal measure, since some products are more strongly preferred (are higher in the preference scale) than others.

Ordinal data are often given as *ranks*. When data are ranked, the first or

---

[3] Coombs [1] gives a much more exhaustive breakdown of data into types.

lowest may be given the number 1, the second the number 2, and so on, up to the last or highest.

Interval data are numbers which measure the quantity of something, such as weight, distance, and cost. Interval data will not greatly concern us in this chapter, because interval data usually qualify for the more restrictive parametric tests, which are described elsewhere.

For convenience, we may consider still another classification, *dichotomous data*. Such data have only two values, such as true-false, yes-no, male-female. They might also represent pairs of numbers, such as 0-1 (or any other pair of numbers). All types of dichotomous data get the same statistical treatment, which is why they are classified together here.

DICHOTOMOUS DATA

A telephone survey is made in which the first question is, "Do you own a dog?" The replies are either yes or no (or no answer, which is classified as missing data). Another question asks, "How many children do you have?" Here the replies give numbers of children, but for the purpose of this test they have been classified into two groups, zero (meaning "no children") or one (meaning "have children"). These are examples of *dichotomous* data, since there are only two values for each of the variables.

Here are examples of a few of the nonparametric tests that might be used with such data:

The Binomial Test. In a national survey, about one-tenth of all families in the population are found to watch a T.V. show, "The Zombie Hour." We now want to identify those communities in which the proportion is *significantly* greater or less than one-tenth. For this purpose, we may use the binomial test, which estimates the probability that a given sample of dichotomous data departs significantly from some preassigned proportion.

One of the samples consists of 19 responses from a high-income area. One person says that he watches "The Zombie Hour," whereas the other 18 say that they do not. This is less than the national average, but we want to know whether it is *significantly* less. That is, we would like to know the probability that we could obtain a sample like this simply "by chance," if we selected 19 people at random from the general population.

The following formula gives the required probability. Let N be the total number of persons in the sample, and let x be the number of "yes" responses. Let P be the hypothetical proportion (one-tenth) and let Q be $1 - P$ (nine-tenths). The probability that the given response occurred by chance is:

$$p = \sum_{i=0}^{x} \binom{N}{i} P^i Q^{N-i}$$

This instructs us to compute the sum, letting i equal 0, 1, 2, ..., x, of $P^i Q^{N-i}$ times the binomial coefficient of N and i, that is, the number of combinations of N things taken i at a time; tables of the binomial coefficient are given in Siegel [9] and elsewhere.

In the example, we calculate as follows. For $i = 0, \binom{N}{i} = 1$. This is multiplied by $P^0 Q^{19}$. Next, we find that for $i = 1, \binom{N}{i} - N = 19$. This is multiplied by $P^1 Q^{18}$ and added to the first product. The sum of the two products represents the exact probability that we might have found a sample with zero "yes" responses, and with one "yes" response, respectively. They are 0.135 and 0.300. Added together, they give 0.435, the probability that this sample, or one which is more unlikely, might have occurred simply by chance. Since this probability is not very low, it cannot be said with any assurance whether people in this particular area are as likely to watch the T.V. show as people in the population as a whole.

The Sign Test. We have a new T.V. commercial, which some critics have found to be extremely annoying. We wish to determine whether the effect of the commercial is to produce *more* or *less* favorable attitudes toward the sponsor's product, Bowser Bergers. We administer a questionnaire to a panel of 23 people, which enables us to obtain a rating of their attitudes toward the product. Then we show them the commercial, and administer the questionnaire again. We score the pairs of questionnaires as follows: For every person whose rating of the product *increased*, we record a plus sign. For everyone whose rating *decreased*, we record a minus. Those whose ratings remained the same are given a zero and excluded from this particular evaluation.

In the example, 4 people increased their ratings of the product, and 12 people decreased their ratings. This indicates that the commercial may have had a somewhat unfavorable effect, but we do not yet know whether these changes might not have simply occurred by chance. To evaluate the probability that this result might have been simply due to random changes in the ratings, we apply the same formula that was used for the binomial test. Since we are counting only the pluses and minuses (not the zeros), N will be 16, and x will be 4. If the changes were purely random, then half would go up and half would go down, so that P and Q will each be equal to one-half. Letting i equal 0, 1, 2, 3, and 4, in the previous formula, we add the probabilities, 0.00001, 0.00046, 0.0056, 0.035, and 0.121, giving a total sum of 0.162. This indicates that it is somewhat unlikely that the sample occurred simply by chance, and that the commercial might be having a detrimental effect upon the product.

The One-Sample Runs Test. Several nonparametric tests are based upon the number of *runs*, or continuous sequences of similar responses. One of these, based on "runs up and down," may be used to determine the likelihood that a market trend will continue in an upward, or a downward, direction. Another, somewhat simpler, runs test will be illustrated here.

A national chain of commercial photographers, Snappy Photos, operates a booth at the county fair. A salesman at the booth explains to potential customers that they have won a "free" portrait, and offers them an opportunity to sign a contract for six annual sittings. The customer may then reply with a yes or no. We believe that there is some interaction between the customers, so that if one person says "Yes," the next person is also likely to say "Yes," and conversely.

To test this hypothesis, we use the one-sample runs test. In one of the samples, the sequence of "yes" and "no" responses is as follows: NNNNYYNNN YYYYNNNNNNNN, where Y and N represent "yes" and "no," respectively. We now count the number of runs. There are three sequences of "no" responses, and two sequences of "yes" responses, in this sample, for a total of five runs. There are 6 positive and 15 negative responses altogether. Use of the appropriate formula, or consultation of applicable tables, indicates that the probability of this number of runs is 0.014. This low a probability indicates that it is quite likely that the customers *were* influenced by the responses of the persons ahead of them in line.

The McNemar Test.   McNemar's test for the significance of changes may be applied to before-and-after situations, as when a group of subjects is asked to express their opinions of a product before and after an experimental promotion. A 2×2 table is formed as follows:

Initial preference	*Later preference*	
	X	Y
X	A	B
Y	C	D

A contains the number of subjects who preferred product X before and after the promotion; B, those who initially preferred X but later preferred Y; C, those who initially preferred Y but later preferred X; and D, those who preferred Y both before and after. Cells B and C, then, represent the number of subjects who changed their minds, presumably because of the promotion.

We have, for example, introduced a new frozen fish product into a limited number of local markets. This contains extra ingredients providing a different flavor from that of earlier products, which produces an initially unfavorable response. However, through extensive advertising in local papers, we attempt to explain that the new product is really superior to its predecessors. Through surveys of each market, we obtain tables like that just shown. One such table is given here:

Initial preference	*Later preference*	
	Yes	No
Yes	2	5
No	3	17

The crucial cells in this table are B and C. We first obtain a value for chi-square through the use of the following formula:

$$\chi^2 = \frac{(|B - C| - 1)^2}{B + C}$$

where the expression $|B - C|$ means the "absolute value" of the difference (obtained by taking either $B - C$ or $C - B$, whichever is positive). Substituting the values from the table into the formula, we obtain a value for chi-square of $1/8 = 0.1250$. Using a standard chi-square table at one degree of freedom, we find that the probability of obtaining a chi-square value at least this large is 0.72367. We should thus conclude that the ad campaign has had no measurable effect in this market, since this result could easily have occurred by chance.

The Fisher Test.   One of the items on a questionnaire indicates the sex of the respondent; another item indicates whether this person makes the decision concerning the purchase of major appliances. There appears to be some tendency for women to make this decision, and we wish to determine the probability that this tendency might be due solely to chance.

If the sample is sufficiently large, the chi-square test may be satisfactory, particularly if the correction for continuity is used. But if the sample is very small, the chi-square test may become quite inaccurate, giving probabilities that are grossly overestimated or underestimated.

For such small samples, the Fisher exact probability formula may be used. First, the data are cast into a 2 × 2 table as follows:

Chooses major appliance?

Sex	Yes	No
M	7	18
F	12	4

Using the method of computation described by Siegel [9, p. 97], we find that the probability of this result is 0.0040. This shows that the sample distribution is unlikely to have happened by chance, and we may conclude that women are significantly more likely to choose a major appliance than are men.

NOMINAL DATA

Nominal data consist of names. Even a number is a "name," if it is used only as an identification code (such as a license plate or a social security number). Nominal data cannot be subjected to any mathematical manipulations, other than comparing (to determine whether two names are the same) and counting. It would make no sense to add together two license-plate numbers, or to divide one social security number by another. In marketing research, the data often consist of names, including the names of people, products, producers, cities, types of transportation, and so on.

The various chi-square tests (described elsewhere in this handbook) can be applied to nominal data when the samples are sufficiently large. The chi-square statistic, however, is only an approximation to the exact probability, and this approximation becomes very poor when the sample size is small. This section will mention some applications of the chi-square test to nominal data, together with some techniques for evaluating the appropriate probability in very small samples.

The One-Sample Chi-Square Test. A consumer panel, consisting of 12 people, has been asked to indicate their preferences among three package designs, all of which contain the same quantity of breakfast food, but for which the package dimensions differ. Of the 12 panel members, 4 prefer package A, 7 prefer package B, and 1 prefers package C. This would appear to give the edge to package B, but how significant are these results? What is the probability that this particular distribution of choices might have occurred by chance? The panel is certainly a very small one, but is there any statistical justification for concluding that it is *too* small?

To find out what the probability of our null hypothesis is, we use the one-sample chi-square test. First, we determine the *expected value* for each of the preferences. If each person were merely picking one package at random, we might expect that the preferences would be equally distributed among the various options. On the average, 4 persons out of the 12 might be expected to choose each of the three packages. The number 4, then, is the expected value for each choice.

We then subtract this expected value from the *actual* number who chose each option, and square this difference. This gives three figures: $(4 - 4)^2 = 0$; $(7 - 4)^2 = 9$; and $(1 - 4)^2 = 9$. Each of these is now divided by the expected value, giving $0/4 = 0$; $9/4$; and $9/4$. These are added, giving $18/4 = 4.5$. This value is chi-square.

Now we must determine how likely it is that this large a chi-square might have occurred by chance, in the sense that panel members were simply choosing packages at random. This probability might be determined by consulting the chi-square tables found in Siegel [9] (or any standard statistical text), at $3 - 1 = 2$ degrees of freedom. Using a computer program for this purpose, we can determine the probability as 0.1054, which means that the results are not significant even at the 10 percent level.

On the other hand, this probability is low enough to suggest that the apparent preference for package B *might not* be merely an accident. But it would be quite unwise to risk any serious investment in results which are as tentative as these. In addition, we should note that the expected cell values are small, which means that the chi-square value is likely to be inflated. This would give us even more reason to look with suspicion at the apparently strong preference for package B.

One-Sample Exact Probabilities. As an alternative procedure, when our sample size is small, we may determine the exact probability that a particular distribution might have occurred by chance. Computation of exact probabilities is described in standard texts on probability, but the method requires computer techniques to be feasible for any extensive use, and it will not be described in detail here. In general, we would form *all possible* distributions of our data into various categories, and count the number of possible distributions which are equally likely, or more unlikely, than the distribution of responses that we have observed. We then divide this by the number of *possible* distributions, to obtain the likelihood that our observed distribution happened by chance. For the example on package preference, this exact probability is 0.1151, which is somewhat higher than the probability determined by the chi-square test. Apparently, the value of chi-square *was* inflated, because of the small expected values.

Other examples show even greater discrepancies between the probabilities estimated by the chi-square test and the exact probabilities. Thanks to the greater power achieved through the use of computer-based techniques, we can extract useful information from very small samples.

The Chi-Square Test for k Samples. Chi-square tests are described elsewhere in this handbook. Here we will be concerned only with those cases in which the chi-square test cannot be used because of small expected values.

Exact Probabilities for k Samples. Three types of lawn mower are marketed through retailers in various cities, and we wish to determine whether the differences in the distribution of sales among individual retailers are great enough to be significant. In one city, there are two retailers, A and B. In August, A reports sales as follows: three of type 1, one of type 2, and three of type 3. During the same month, B reports that he has sold seven of type 1, two of type 2, and one of type 3. Clearly, there are differences in the distribution of sales between these two outlets, but we wish to know how likely it is that this difference might be due entirely to chance.

Our first step is to set up these results in the form of a table:

Retailer	Type of mower		
	1	2	3
A	3	1	3
B	7	2	1

We may now, if we wish, compute chi-square for this table, obtaining a value of 2.4812, which carries a probability of 0.2892 at two degrees of freedom (through the use of a computer program). The cell values are small, however, and we suspect that chi-square may be inflated.

Computation of the exact probability proceeds in a manner analogous to the method used in the Fisher Exact Test [12, pp. 96–104]. All possible distributions of the data into the six cells are considered. Those distributions which are equally likely, or less likely, than the given distribution are counted. This count is divided by the total number of possible distributions, and the resulting figure is the exact probability of obtaining such a distribution, or one which is less probable. Using a computer program for this purpose, we obtain an exact probability of 0.3318. Notice that this is considerably higher than the probability which was estimated by the chi-square test, indicating that the chi-square value is considerably inflated when the sample size is this small.

This high a probability would imply the possibility that the differences between these two dealers were due simply to chance, and that we would not be justified in regarding them as two different types of outlet, on the basis of the data that we have.

ORDINAL DATA

In marketing research, we very frequently deal with data which can be arranged in a meaningful *order*. We can say that item A is "greater than" item B, item B is "greater than" item C, and infer from this that item A is "greater than" item C ("greater than" is in quotes to indicate that it may be taken in the broadest possible sense). Two or more items might be equal, or tied for a given position. Ordinal data cannot, however, be subjected to such mathematical operations as multiplication and division, because the result will not be meaningful.

When we are dealing with preferences, for example, a person may be able to say that he likes A better than B, but he will find it very difficult to say that he likes A "twice as much" as B, in the sense that he would exchange one A for two Bs. Preferences must usually be given special statistical treatment, to avoid subjecting them to mathematical operations which are not meaningful for ordinal data. (Techniques for the more rigorous quantification of preferences are described in texts on game theory, statistical decision theory, and systems analysis.)

Quite frequently, ordinal data appear in the form of *ranks*. Typically, we give the number 1 to the lowest-ranking item, the number 2 to the next-lowest, and so on. When two items are tied, in these tests they are given the average of the ranks for which they are tied.

The Wilcoxon Tests. Wilcoxon devised two important tests which bear his name. The "signed ranks" test is applied to matched pairs, such as before-and-after tests, to determine whether there is a significant difference between the samples. When we speak of "matched pairs," we mean that every subject in one sample is matched to a subject in the second sample, and vice versa. Ideally, the two members of each pair are exactly alike in every respect except for the condition we are attempting to manipulate. Any differences which we locate, then, may be ascribed to this condition.

A given company, for example, wishes to determine whether employee attitudes might not be improved by a series of weekly assemblies at which it presents films and lectures dealing with the company and its products. Employees are tested before and after the series of programs, and their questionnaires are coded to permit identification of the particular respondent. One of the questions concerns the quality of the company's thermostats, one of many products which it manufactures. It wishes to find out whether employee attitudes toward this product have improved.

To obtain the Wilcoxon statistic, we first subtract each employee's *pretest* score (his rating of the thermostats before the lectures) from his *posttest* score (his rating of them after the lectures). Suppose that for 12 employees we obtain the following set of differences: -7, -4, 0, 2, 0, -6, -12, 3, 4, 0, 1, 4. Our next step is to exclude those with zero difference (who showed no change), and substitute the *ranks* of the remaining differences. The smallest difference is given rank 1, the next-smallest is given rank 2, and so on. These ranks are as follows: 8, 5, *x*, 2, *x*, 7, 9, 3, 5, *x*, 1, 5. (Note that three persons are tied for ranks 4, 5, and 6, and are therefore given the average of the three ranks, which is 5.)

Now we add together the ranks for those persons that originally showed a negative difference, and the ranks for those that showed a positive difference. This gives us two sums, 29 and 16. We choose the *smaller* of these two sums, which becomes the Wilcoxon T statistic. Finally, we may determine the probability of a T of 16, for a sample of nine persons (the three persons who showed no difference being excluded).

The probability is determined by counting the number of possible samples which have a T equal to, or larger than, the T found in the sample, and dividing this figure by the number of possible samples. This is best done with the aid of a computer, and the method will not be described in detail here. Siegel reproduces a very accurate approximation formula which may be used when a computer is not available [9, p. 79, formula 5.5], and he also includes a table of exact values [table G].

Using the approximation formula, we find that the probability associated with the sample in our example is 0.2206, while a computer evaluation of the exact probability gives 0.2480. This is the probability that the *apparent* change in direction (toward lower scores) might have occurred by chance—if, for example, the employees had simply marked their questionnaires at random. The probability here is obviously too high to exclude this possibility, and we cannot conclude that the lectures have had any negative effect.

The Mann-Whitney Test. A second version of the Wilcoxon test, which was revised and extended by Mann and Whitney, compares the scores of two groups to determine the probability that both groups come from identical populations.

Consider the following example. Salesmen for the Acme Blotter Company are to be compared to determine whether those in group A are significantly more or less productive than those in group B. Because two or three of the men have made very large individual sales which greatly inflate their group's mean scores, we prefer not to use a parametric test, such as the *t*-test. Using the Mann-Whitney test, we proceed as follows. Imagine the men labeled "A" or "B" according to their groups, ranging upward from the least productive salesman on the left to the most productive man on the right. Suppose that this produces the order ABBAABBAB. Now we begin with the left-most B salesman, and count the number of A men to his right; there are three of them. Go to the next B salesman, who also has three A men on his right. The next has only one on his right, and similarly for the fourth B man. The fifth B salesman has no man to his right.

Adding up these numbers, we have a total of eight, which we will call *U*. This is the Mann-Whitney statistic, on the basis of which we may estimate the probability that there is no difference between the populations from which the two groups were drawn (two-tailed test), or that the population represented by the B group was no higher than that represented by the A group (one-tailed test).

The significance of this value of U may be estimated by consulting table J in Siegel [9]. Exact computation (using a computer program developed by Uleman) gives a value of 0.7302 for the two-tailed test, or 0.3651 for the one-tailed test. These probabilities are much too high to exclude the possibility that the apparent difference between the two groups of salesmen was due only to chance.

The computer program that determines these probabilities is interesting as an example of the way in which many nonparametric measures are evaluated. The program simply forms all possible orderings of the data, ranging from that in which all the As are on the left (AAAABBBBB) to that in which all the Bs are on the left (BBBBBAAAA). It finds a value for U for each of these orderings, and counts the number of orderings for which U is greater than or equal to the U of the original data. These may be considered more "skewed" or "unusual" than the original. The program then divides this number by the number of *possible* orderings, obtaining a value for P, the probability that the original distribution of scores might have occurred by chance.

Although a method such as this may seem extraordinarily simple, it is this very simplicity that makes nonparametric tests applicable to such a wide range of data.

RANK CORRELATION COEFFICIENTS

The concept of *correlation* is a familiar one, and correlations are widely used to show the degree of similarity or difference between two measures. The type of correlation most frequently used is the Pearson product-moment coefficient of correlation. But this type of correlation makes several rather strong assumptions concerning the data, and if these assumptions are not met, the resulting correlation may not be valid. Specifically, if some of the measurements are very large in comparison with the bulk of the others (as in measures of family income), the Pearson correlation may not be valid. Again, if a graph of the data shows two or more peaks (as when answers to a questionnaire are grouped at the high and low ends of a scale, with few answers in between), the usual types of correlation may be inaccurate.

To overcome these limitations of the Pearson correlation, many other types of correlation coefficient have been proposed. To illustrate the methods involved in computing these nonparametric measures of correlation, the Spearman ranks correlation coefficient (*rho*) will be described here, primarily because of the ease with which it can be implemented on the computer when used in conjunction with an effective ranking routine.

The Spearman Rank Correlation Coefficient. This corrects for some of the shortcomings just listed by substituting *ranks* for the observed values of the data. For each variable, we substitute the number 1 for the lowest observed value, the number 2 for the next-lowest, and so on, up to the highest value. When two or more observations are tied, we substitute the average of all ranks for which they are tied.

When this transformation has been made, computation of the Spearman *rho* may be performed in exactly the same way as that of the Pearson *r*. The actual computation is somewhat simpler, because the sum of the ranks is known in advance, and the following formula may be used:

$$\rho = (A + B - \Sigma\, d^2)/(2\sqrt{AB})$$

where

$$A = 1/12 \ ((N^3 - N) - \Sigma \ (t^3 - t))$$

t is the number of ties at any given level, over all ties in the first variable
B is the same formula applied to the second variable
$\Sigma \ d^2$ is the sum of squares of all differences between the first and second variables
N is the number of pairs of observations

These computations may be clarified through the following example. We wish to determine the relationship between expenditures on advertising and gross sales during five one-week periods. The cost of the ads (to the nearest thousand dollars) and corresponding gross sales figures are:

Ads	Sales
10	31
15	45
4	45
10	19
9	17

Next, we substitute the ranks within each column, find the differences between these ranks (d), and square the differences:

Ads	Sales	d	d^2
3.5	3	0.5	0.25
5	4.5	0.5	0.25
1	4.5	3.5	12.25
3.5	2	1.5	2.25
2	1	1.0	1.00

$$\Sigma \ d^2 = 16.00$$

Each of the variables contains one set of ties. In the first variable, two subjects are tied for the third and fourth ranks, and they receive a rank of 3.5. In the second variable, two subjects are tied for the fourth and fifth ranks, and they get a rank of 4.5. We compute A and B, using the formula above, with $t = 2$ (that is, there is one set of ties, and two observations are tied), and A and B will be equal. Thus $A = B = 1/12 \ [(125 - 5) - (8 - 2)] = 9.5$.

Substituting in the formula for *rho*, we find a correlation of 0.1579. A computer-based calculation of the probability of this correlation gives a figure of 0.4. This is the likelihood that a positive correlation as high as this might occur by chance.

Calculation of these probabilities, like that of the Mann-Whitney test above, is very simple in concept, although it becomes tedious without the aid of the computer or reference to tables, for example, table Q in Siegel [9]. We simply form all possible distributions of ranks in the two samples, calculate *rho* for each of these, and count the number of distributions for which *rho* is equal to, or larger than, the *rho* found in the sample. We divide this number by the total number of possible distributions, and obtain the probability that the *rho* we have observed might have occurred by chance.

Like the Pearson correlation coefficient, the Spearman coefficient will vary in significance, depending on the size of the sample. The significance of the two coefficients, however, is not the same, and it would be a mistake to assume that a *rho* of 0.4 has the same significance as a Pearson *r* of 0.4.

FURTHER NONPARAMETRIC TESTS

Siegel presents a convenient listing of some of the major nonparametric tests, most of which are similar in concept and application to the tests described here. Walsh [12] gives a much more comprehensive coverage, describing a great variety of tests in extremely condensed form.

In addition to the general types of test described in this chapter, many forms of analysis of variance are nonparametric in orientation when they are based on ranks or on the median (rather than the mean). They are discussed in Part E, Chapter 10 of this section.

Scaling procedures, which attempt to locate an underlying scale or system of measurement in nonparametric fashion, are described in Torgerson [10] and in Coombs [1].

Related to these are a wide variety of methods for locating patterns and trends in various types of data. These are primarily methods which depend upon lengthy computer programs for their effective use. Torgerson and Coombs both give some introduction to the general concepts involved.

REFERENCES

1. Coombs, Clyde H., *A Theory of Data,* New York: Wiley, 1964.
2. Freeman, G. H., and J. H. Halton, "Exact Probabilities for k × 1 Tables," *Biometrika,* vol. 31, 1951, pp. 141–149.
3. Goodman, Leo A., "Kolmogorov-Smirnov Tests for Psychological Research," *Psychological Bulletin,* vol. 51, March 1954, pp. 160–168.
3a. Kraft, C. H., and C. van Eeden, *A Nonparametric Introduction to Statistics,* New York: Macmillan, 1968.
3b. Langley, Russell, *Practical Statistics Simply Explained,* New York: Dover Publications, 1971.
4. Massey, F. J., Jr., "Distribution Table for the Deviation Between Two Sample Cumulatives," *Annals of Mathematical Statistics,* vol. 23, September 1952, pp. 435–441.
5. Morris, John, "Nonparametric Statistical System," *Behavioral Science,* vol. 13, May 1968, pp. 262–263.
6. Morris, John, "Nonparametric Statistics on the Computer," *Journal of Marketing Research,* February 1969.
7. Morris, John, "Computation of the Kolmogorov-Smirnov Statistics," *Behavioral Science,* vol. 14, September 1969.
7a. Noether, G. E., *Elements of Nonparametric Statistics,* New York: Wiley, 1967.
8. Savage, I. Richard, "Nonparametric Statistics," *Journal of the American Statistical Association,* vol. 52, September 1957, pp. 331–344.
9. Siegal, Sidney, *Nonparametric Statistics for the Behavioral Sciences,* New York: McGraw-Hill, 1956.
10. Torgerson, Warren S., *Theory and Methods of Scaling,* New York: Wiley, 1968.
11. Uleman, J. S., "The Mann-Whitney U Test with Small Samples and Many Ties," *Psychological Bulletin,* February 1969.
12. Walsh, John E., *Handbook of Nonparametric Statistics,* Princeton, N.J.: Van Nostrand, 1962 (vol. I), 1965 (vol. II).
13. Wilson, Kellogg V., "A Distribution-Free Test of Analysis of Variance Hypotheses," *Psychological Bulletin,* vol. 53, January 1956, pp. 96–101.

Statistical Analysis of Relationships

Chapter 1

Trend Fitting and Other Approaches

RIKUMA ITO *College of Business and Administration, University of Detroit, Detroit, Michigan.*

In Part D of Section II, various statistical tests were discussed. As was indicated, these tests are used primarily to test the presence or absence of relationships among variables.

The ten chapters in Part E present quantitative models that define functional relations between a variable of interest and a set of other variables. Part E also considers a number of statistical methods that may be used to estimate the parameters of a model. A major use of this type of analysis is in forecasting the future behavior of the variable being studied, often called the *dependent variable,* on the basis of its observed relationships with other variables, frequently called *independent* or *explanatory variable* (*s*).

The analytical framework of relationships is diverse, using different techniques with varying degrees of complexity. It ranges from a simple, linear trend equation to stochastic multiple-regression analysis and to simultaneous dynamic models. Trend models are discussed in this chapter; others are described in later chapters. Particularly, this chapter discusses a variety of methods of trend fitting, with special emphasis on the least-squares method. It also explains the use of trend analysis as a forecasting device and the difference between trend analysis and regression analysis, as well as the general problems involved in the analysis of relationships.

GENERAL PROBLEMS ENCOUNTERED IN ANALYSIS OF RELATIONSHIPS

Two classes of problems are particularly pronounced in a statistical analysis of relationships among variables: One is the choice of variables and the specification of a form of relation; the other concerns the assumptions on the disturbances (or random components) of the specified model.

The first step in studying association among variables is to determine what variables are to be included in a model. The variables are generally chosen on the basis of either a priori theory that describes the existence of relations among them in logical terms or on past experience. Thus, a simple consumption function includes consumption expenditures as the dependent variable and disposable income as a key explanatory variable, since economic theory supports the hypothesis that income is a major determinant of consumption.

Sometimes the problem of singling out the independent (or dependent) variable is not so simple. The relation between price and quantity in a free market, for instance, is simultaneously, not unidirectionally, determined. Therefore, there is difficulty in selecting the independent (likewise, dependent) variable. A usual procedure is to treat them both as endogenous, and their relation is estimated simultaneously. In trend analysis of a time series, however, the selection of variables presents little difficulty. Unlike a regression model of sophisticated nature, a trend equation is formulated on the premise that the passage of time alone influences the variation in the variable under investigation. Then time naturally becomes the independent variable.

Once relevant variables have been decided upon, the next step is to specify the mathematical forms of functional relationships, for example, linear, logarithmic, exponential, polynomial of higher degree, and so on. A priori theory is of little help here. The mathematical forms should be determined largely by the researcher himself, applying such criteria as goodness of fit and agreement of the signs of coefficients with a priori expectations, and at the same time considering the statistical property of parameter estimation. Some of the more commonly used mathematical forms of trend equations are linear, exponential, and the Gompertz growth curve.

It is commonly assumed that the successive values of disturbance are independent. That is,

$$E(\epsilon_t \cdot \epsilon_{t-1}) = 0$$

in a model of the following form:

$$Y_t = \alpha + \beta X_t + \epsilon_t$$

where Y is the dependent variable, X the independent variable, and ϵ_t the random component.

The assumption of independence of the disturbances over time may not be met often in marketing problems that tend to exhibit serial correlation in residuals. If the assumption is not satisfied, estimates of the standard errors will be biased, and the interval estimates of parameters and tests of significance will be invalidated.

This problem is serious in studying relations among variables. Methods of testing for, and reducing, serial correlations are available; they will be discussed in later chapters.

INTRODUCTORY REMARKS ON TREND ANALYSIS

Four Principal Components of a Time Series

Nothing remains constant in a dynamically moving world. Change is observed everywhere. Marketing and economic variables are not immune to this phenomenon. For example, retail sales increased approximately 200 percent between 1957 and 1969 (in current prices). The gross national product has maintained an annual growth rate of about 3 percent since 1790.

This change pattern is of great interest to businessmen, the consuming public, and public authorities. Thus a marketing manager may be interested in the time behavior of retail sales; a consumer may be interested in the growth of disposable income through time; and the government may be concerned with the time rate of change in the propensity to consume.

The conventional approach to the analysis of business and economic time series decomposes the forces operating in these time series into four types of movements: (1) secular trend, (2) seasonal variations, (3) cyclical oscillations, and (4) irregular or random movements.

The secular trend is a gradual, smooth, persistent movement over a long period. This long-term pattern of growth or decay is thought to occur mainly because of population changes and technological improvement.

Seasonal variations are short-run movements that follow much the same pattern year after year. Weather and custom are two of the most important factors accountable for these types of fluctuations. Cyclical oscillations are wave-like movements around trend with a duration of longer than seasonal to shorter than trend, of about 16 months to as much as 20 or more years. The time duration and amplitude of cyclical fluctuations vary considerably from one cycle to another.

This component of time series is often referred to as the business cycle in economic literature. There is no unified, simple explanation for the cause of the cycle. Business cycles are regarded as the result of diversified factors, including mass psychological forces, misreadings of business conditions, and the like.

Irregular movements are erratic variations that show no repetitive pattern and are totally unpredictable. Their causes are attributed to such chance factors as strikes, wars, pestilences, and accidents.

Time Series Model

The conventional time series model accepts the hypothesis that the operative forces in a time series can be divided into the four principal components just listed, and then assumes that the importance of each factor can be separated and measured with time as the only independent variable. The model is laden with somewhat tenuous assumptions.

First, the assumption of decomposability of the underlying forces is hardly acceptable, because they are interdependent more than independent, and a fine distinction among them is, in practice, very difficult, if not impossible, to draw. Second, the implicit assumption that the passage of time alone can explain the movements of a time series is naïve. Time may be considered one of many factors responsible for variations in time series, but it can never be the only one. If these assumptions are satisfied, however, the classical model becomes a powerful analytical tool both in predicting the future pattern and in studying the nature of a series.

There are two forms of the time series model: the additive form and the multiplicative form. The additive model is expressed as

$$O = T + S + C + I$$

and the multiplicative model is written as

$$O = T \cdot S \cdot C \cdot I$$

where O is the original time series, and T, S, C, and I stand for values of trend, seasonal, cyclical, and irregular components, respectively. In the additive model, all values are expressed in terms of absolute units; in the multiplicative model, T and O are expressed in absolute units, and others are in terms of relatives or percentages. Both models are discussed further in the next chapter.

Secular Trend Analysis: Its Purposes and Uses

As previously stated, a secular trend is a component force which influences the long-run, continuous, underlying movement of a time series. This long-run movement requires careful analysis. Suppose the sales of a certain corporation have shown a 10 percent increase per annum over the last 10 years. The question may arise whether the realized growth rate is satisfactory or whether this growth pattern is in line with the industry's trend. Furthermore, it is desirable to know what factors have affected the upward shift of sales over time. An analysis of trend will provide an approximate answer to these questions.

Thus, one purpose of fitting trends is to secure a better understanding of the historical growth or decline of a time series. Another purpose is to eliminate the trend component from the original data so that the cyclical and seasonal fluctuations may be clarified.

Trend analysis is also used for long-term prediction. A long-range forecast is essential in making decisions on almost every phase of business operation. It is particularly crucial in deciding on capacity expansion, development of new products and new markets, and adoption of improved technology. It is also needed in planning capital requirements and in selecting portfolio mix for investment in stocks.

The projection of trends into the future rests on the assumption that the forces affecting the past pattern will continue to operate. If this assumption is not justified, the trend equation will be of little use as a forecasting device. Therefore, trend analysis yields a most useful and reliable result when the growth or decline of time series is steady and smooth and when the effects of other components are kept at a minimum.

Some Considerations in Trend Analysis

The first important consideration in trend analysis is the choice of time periods and their duration. Since trend is by definition a long-run movement, the selected period should be as long as possible. Unless it is long enough, preferably 20 years or longer, there is a danger that the trend may not be revealed because of the effect of short-run fluctuations. It is also advisable that each end period in the series be in the same phase of the business cycle and that various phases of the cycle represent the series about evenly. This is required for a reliable estimate of a trend coefficient.

When units of economic time series are in dollars, conversion of the current price series into constant prices should also be considered. The conversion is usually done by use of a suitable price index or implicit deflator. In this way, the derived trend line reflects the real growth pattern, apart from price changes.

METHODS OF MEASURING SECULAR TRENDS

A trend is a function relating a variable quantity, denoted by Y, to a time variable, X, that is,

$$Y = f(X)$$

The problem here is finding a specific functional relation between Y and X and then estimating the parameters of the function.

Among the varied forms of trend relations corresponding to different modes of growth, a linear trend model is most widely accepted. The linear trend equation is popular because most business and economic time series are in fact linear in their long-run growth trend, so a straight-line trend may satisfactorily approximate many nonlinear trend relations. Simplicity in equational forms and ease in computation are also reasons for its wide acceptance.

A simple linear (or arithmetic) straight-line trend is described by the equation

$$Y_c = a + bX$$

where Y_c is the trend value or calculated value of the variable of interest, Y; X is the time unit; and a and b are parameters to be estimated.

The time unit is usually one year, one half-year, one quarter, or one month; but in trend analysis, the one-year unit is conventionally used.

A linear trend may be fitted to a series by any of the following methods:
1. Graphic freehand method
2. Semiaverage method
3. Method of least squares
4. Method of selected points
5. Method of moving averages

The first three are discussed in this section; the selected points method will be introduced in the section "Nonlinear Trends"; and the fifth method will be described in the section "Moving Averages and Exponential Smoothing."

Freehand Method. The freehand method, the simplest way of fitting a trend, involves plotting the data on a graph and drawing a straight line through the plotted data by inspection in such a way that the deviations of observed values above and below the line are about equal. Once the trend line is determined by observation, a trend equation can be obtained easily. This is done by selecting two points on the trend line and reading their values from the chart.

Suppose, for example, that we selected two points, say, those of the first and last periods and found their values on the line. Then the value for the first period (where X is zero) becomes the value of the Y intercept, that is, a. The difference between the values of the two periods divided by the number of periods is the value of b for the equation, which is the average change in Y per unit of time, or the slope of the trend.

Figure 1 and Table 1 show a fit of a straight-line trend, by inspection, to United States personal consumption expenditures on durables from 1956 through 1968. The trend was drawn through the plotted data in such a fashion that the deviations above and below the line were, by observation, approximately equal. A trend line may be drawn with the aid of a transparent ruler or other measuring device. By inspection,
$a = 3.2$
$b = (7.7 - 3.2)/12 = .375$
Thus,
$Y_c = 3.2 + .375$ Origin: July 1, 1956
                                          X: one-year unit

This graphic method has an advantage of simplicity compared with other methods, but it depends largely on the researcher's subjective judgment. This lack of objective criterion is a serious limitation of the freehand method. Yet the method often proves helpful as a preliminary to more refined methods by giving a quick idea concerning the shape of a trend curve to be fitted.

Semiaverage Method. The procedure of measuring a trend by means of the semiaverage method is as follows: The data are first divided into two equal parts, the arithmetic means for each part are computed, and a straight line

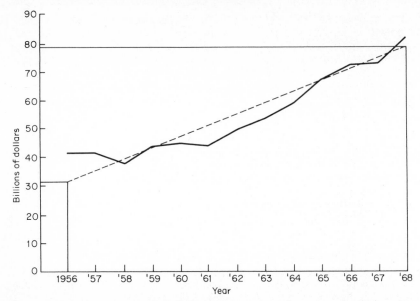

Fig. 1.   United States personal consumption expenditures on durables, 1956–1968 (billions of dollars: 1958 prices).

going through these two means is drawn, taking the semiaverages as the trend values for the middle year of each segment series.   This line represents the semiaverage trend line.   This method is illustrated in Table 2.

Since there are six observations in the series, each segment will include three years.   The mean for each half is:

$$\bar{X}_1 = (6.8 + 7.3 + 7.7)/3 = 21.8/3 = 7.3$$
$$\bar{X}_2 = (8.2 + 8.7 + 9.1)/3 = 26.0/3 = 8.7$$

Since the semiaverages of 7.3 and 8.7 are taken as the trend values for 1964 and 1967, respectively, the trend line is obtained by drawing a straight line through these two points (1, 7.3) and (4, 8.7).   It is shown graphically in Figure 2.

TABLE 1   United States Personal Consumption Expenditures on Durables, 1956–1968 (billions of dollars: 1958 prices)

Year	Expenditures	Year	Expenditures
1956	41.0	1963	53.7
1957	41.5	1964	59.0
1958	37.9	1965	66.6
1959	43.7	1966	71.7
1960	44.9	1967	72.8
1961	43.9	1968	80.7
1962	49.2		

SOURCE: U.S. Department of Commerce, Office of Business Economics.

TABLE 2   Disposable Personal Income per Family in the United States, 1963–1968
(Units in thousands of dollars)

Year	X	Y	Semitotal	Semiaverage
1963	0	6.8		
1964	1	7.3	21.8	7.3
1965	2	7.7		
1966	3	8.2		
1967	4	8.7	26.0	8.7
1968	5	9.1		

SOURCE: *Life Insurance Fact Book*, 1969, p. 28.

The trend equation for the series is then determined by solving the following two equations for constants a and b:

$$7.3 = a + b \tag{1}$$
$$8.7 = a + 4b \tag{2}$$

Multiplying Equation (1) by 4 and subtracting the result from Equation (2), we have

$$a = 6.83$$

Substituting

$$a = 6.83$$

into any of the above equations yields

$$b = 0.47$$

Thus, the trend equation is

$$Y_c = 6.83 + 0.47X \qquad \text{Origin: July 1, 1963}$$
$$X: \text{ one-year unit}$$

The trend value for each year can be obtained by substituting the value of X for the year into this trend equation. For example, disposable family income for 1965 will be estimated by substituting $X = 2$ in the equation, that is,

$$Y_{\hat{c}1965} = 6.83 + (0.47)(2)$$
$$= 6.83 + 0.94 = 7.77$$

When the number of periods is uneven, the series cannot be divided equally. In this case, the series can be separated in any one of the following ways:

1. Omit the value of the middle period so that the number of periods is even.
2. Add either the one-half value or the total value of the middle period to the total sum of each part.
3. Divide the series unevenly.

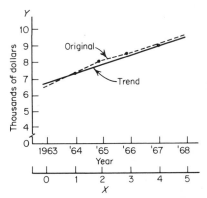

Fig. 2.   **Disposable personal income in the United States, 1963–1968 (units in thousands of dollars).**

The semiaverage method is relatively simple, but it may be influenced by an extreme value of the series in the process of computing the semiaverages. If an extreme value is present, it is advisable to omit it. Otherwise, the trend equation may not describe the long-run movement of the series because of possible distortion of parameter estimates by the extreme value.

Least-Squares Method. The least-squares method is the most widely used method of fitting a trend. This method yields a trend line with the following mathematical properties:

1. The sum of the deviations of observed values from the computed or trend values is equal to zero, that is,

$$\Sigma(Y - Y_c) = 0$$

where Y is the observed value and Y_c is the computed or trend value.

2. The sum of the squares of these deviations is least, that is,

$$\Sigma(Y - Y_c)^2 = \text{minimum}$$

The name "least squares" is derived from this property.

The method of least squares can be applied to simple linear, logarithmic linear, or nonlinear trend fits.

A linear trend equation is written as

$$Y_c = a + bX \tag{3}$$

To estimate the constants a and b of the equation, the following set of equations is solved simultaneously:

$$\Sigma Y = na + b\Sigma X \tag{4}$$
$$\Sigma XY = a\Sigma X + b\Sigma X^2 \tag{5}$$

where n is the number of periods in the series.

These equations are known as the normal equations. The formulas for a and b are, then,

$$a = (\Sigma Y)/n = b(\Sigma X)/n \tag{6}$$
$$= \bar{Y} - b\bar{X}$$
$$b = (n\Sigma XY - \Sigma X\Sigma Y)/(n\Sigma X^2 - (\Sigma X)^2) \tag{7}$$

The formulas for a and b can be simplified by choosing the middle point of the time series as the origin. Then the value of X for the middle period becomes the mean of the time variable X, and X is now measured as a deviation from its mean. Since the sum of X is zero in this case, the normal equations are simplified to:

$$\Sigma Y = na \tag{8}$$
$$\Sigma XY = b\Sigma X^2 \tag{9}$$

or

$$a = \Sigma Y/n \tag{10}$$
$$b = \Sigma XY/\Sigma X^2 \tag{11}$$

Not only is a now the value of Y at the origin, but it is also the mean of the Y values.

The general procedure of fitting a trend by the least-squares method is as follows:

1. Locate the middle period of the series (in the example in Table 3, it is 1962), call it the origin, and assign it an X value of zero. Since X is a time-unit variable and is measured in terms of deviation units from the

TABLE 3   Disposable Personal Income per Family in the United States, 1956–1968
(In thousands of dollars)

(1) Year	(2) Y	(3) X	(4) X^2	(5) $X \cdot Y$	(6) Y_c
1956	5.4	−6	36	−32.4	5.02
1957	5.6	−5	25	−28.0	5.33
1958	5.9	−4	16	−22.8	5.64
1959	5.9	−3	9	−17.7	5.95
1960	6.1	−2	4	−12.2	6.25
1961	6.3	−1	1	− 6.3	6.56
1962	6.5	0	0	0	6.87
1963	6.8	1	1	6.8	7.18
1964	7.3	2	4	14.6	7.49
1965	7.7	3	9	23.1	7.79
1966	8.2	4	16	32.1	8.10
1967	8.7	5	25	43.5	8.41
1968	9.1	6	36	54.6	8.72
	$\Sigma Y = 89.3$	$\Sigma X = 0$	$\Sigma X = 182$	$\Sigma XY = 56.0$	89.31

SOURCE: *Life Insurance Fact Book*, 1969, p. 28.

origin, assign an X value of −1 to the year 1961, −2 to 1960, −3 to 1959, +1 to 1963, +2 to 1964, and so on.

2. Compute ΣY, ΣXY, and ΣX^2.
3. Substitute the totals ΣY, ΣXY, and ΣX^2 in the formulas $a = \Sigma Y/n$ and $b = \Sigma XY/\Sigma X^2$ to find the values of a and b of the trend equation $Y_c = a + bX$.   For our example,

$$a = \Sigma Y/n = 89.3/13 = 6.87$$
$$b = \Sigma XY/\Sigma X^2 = 56.0/182.0 = 0.308$$

The trend equation is

$$Y_c = 6.87 + 0.308X$$

Origin: July 1, 1962
X: One-year units

Note that the origin and time units are specified along with the trend equation.   Here the quantity 6.87 is the estimated value of Y at the origin, or when X is zero.   The quantity 0.308 represents the average amount of change in Y per unit of time.   It is the slope of the trend line.

4. Take any two values of X, compute the trend values for these periods by substituting them in the trend equation, plot the trend values obtained on the chart, and draw a straight line through them.   (See Figure 3.) This straight line is the trend line.
5. To project the trend into the future, substitute the X value for the future year in question in the trend equation, and solve it.   The result is the value of Y_c.

For example, suppose we want the trend value of disposable family income for 1975.   Since the X value for 1975 is 13, the projected value Y_c will be

$$Y_{c1975} = 6.87 + (0.308)(13)$$
$$= 6.87 + 4.004$$
$$= 10.874$$

There is a difference in assigning values to time units between an even number of periods and an odd number of periods in a time series so that $\Sigma X = 0$. In the previous example, we had an odd number of periods, so we could use the numbering system ... $-2, -1, 0, 1, 2, \ldots$, for the X variable. This type of numbering system is not, however, applicable to an even number of time periods. There are two common ways of numbering the X variable in the case of an even number of periods so that $\Sigma X = 0$. These are illustrated in Table 4.

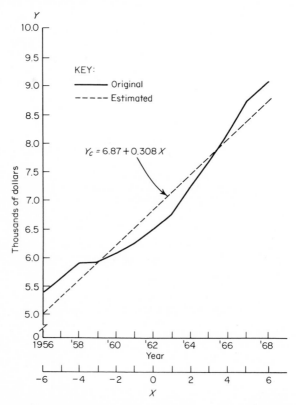

Fig. 3. Disposable personal income per family in the United States, 1956–1968 (units in thousands of dollars).

The origin in that example should be placed between 1964 and 1965. Obviously, we cannot use the numbering system of $-3, -2, -1, 1, 2, 3$, because there are two units between -1 and 1 while the difference between 1 and 2, 2 and 3, and so on, is one unit. Hence, we use the numbering method in column (2) of part A of Table 4. Now the X units are half-year and the origin is January 1, 1965. The procedure for obtaining the trend equation is the same as in the odd-number case, that is:

$$a = \Sigma Y/n = 113.9/8 = 14.24$$
$$b = \Sigma XY/\Sigma X^2 = 94.7/168 = 0.5637 \qquad \text{Origin: January 1, 1965}$$
$$Y_c = 14.24 + 0.5637X \qquad\qquad X: \text{Half-year units}$$

TABLE 4   Life Insurance in Force per Family in the United States, 1951–1968
(In thousands of dollars)

(1) Year	(2) X	(3) Y	(4) X^2	(5) $X \cdot Y$	(5) Yc
		A. Half-year time units			
1961	−7	10.8	49	−75.6	10.29
1962	−5	11.4	25	−57.0	11.42
1963	−3	12.2	9	−36.6	12.55
1964	−1	13.3	1	−13.3	13.68
1965	1	14.7	1	14.7	14.80
1966	3	15.9	9	47.7	15.93
1967	5	17.2	25	86.0	17.06
1968	7	18.4	49	128.8	18.18
		$\Sigma Y = 113.9$	$\Sigma X^2 = 168$	$\Sigma XY = 94.7$	113.91
		B. Yearly time units			
1961	−3.5	10.8	12.25	−37.80	10.29
1962	−2.5	11.4	6.25	−28.50	11.42
1963	−1.5	12.2	2.25	−18.30	12.55
1964	−0.5	13.3	0.25	−6.65	13.68
1965	0.5	14.7	0.25	7.35	14.80
1966	1.5	15.9	2.25	23.85	15.93
1967	2.5	17.2	6.25	43.00	17.06
1968	3.5	18.4	12.25	64.40	18.18
		$\Sigma Y = 113.9$	$\Sigma X^2 = 42.00$	$\Sigma XY = 47.35$	113.91

SOURCE: *Life Insurance Fact Book*, 1969, p. 28.

If we want one-year units for X, we simply multiply the X values by one-half. Then the X values will be −2.5, −1.5, −0.5, 0.5, 1.5, 2.5 and so on, and the time units for X will become one year. This way of numbering the time variable involves fractions, which make the computation of a trend a little cumbersome, as shown in part B of Table 4.

The value of the Y intercept is not affected by the change in numbering X, but the value for b becomes

$$b = \Sigma XY/\Sigma X^2 = 47.35/42 = 1.1274$$

The trend equation is:

$$Y_c = 14.24 + 1.1274X$$

Origin: January 1, 1965
X: Half-year units

LOGARITHMIC LINEAR TREND OR SIMPLE EXPONENTIAL TREND

A simple exponential trend equation is written as

$$Y_c = ab^x \tag{12}$$

By transforming Equation (12) into logarithms, we obtain a logarithmic linear equation

$$\log Y_c = \log a + (\log b) X \tag{13}$$

This is a linear function of X and appears as a straight line on a semilogarithmic chart. The exponential function is employed when we believe in constancy of a relative rate of change rather than an absolute amount of change of time series. Thus, when a company's sales are believed to increase by a constant rate over time, an exponential trend should be fitted to the data.

In applying the method of least squares to Equation (13), we derive the estimates of the constants, $\log a$ and $\log b$, that make the sum of the squared deviations of the logarithmic Y values from the trends at a minimum; that is,

$$\Sigma(\log Y - \log Y_c)^2 = \text{minimum}$$

The normal equations are then:

$$\Sigma \log Y = n \cdot (\log a) + (\log b) \Sigma X \tag{14}$$
$$\Sigma X \cdot (\log Y) = (\log a) \cdot \Sigma X + (\log b) \cdot \Sigma X^2 \tag{15}$$

If the origin is selected at the middle of the series such that

$$\Sigma X = 0$$

the formulas for the two constants become:

$$\log a = (\Sigma \log Y)/n \tag{16}$$
$$\log b = (\Sigma X \cdot (\log Y))/\Sigma X^2 \tag{17}$$

As an example, Table 5 illustrates the computation of a logarithmic trend in life insurance in force per family. From Table 5, we find

$$\Sigma \log Y = 13.8946$$
$$\Sigma X^2 = 182$$
$$n = 13$$

TABLE 5   Life Insurance in Force per Family in the United States, 1956–1968
(In thousands of dollars)

(1) Year	(2) Y	(3) X	(4) X²	(5) log Y	(6) X·(log Y)	(7) log Yc	(8) Yc
1956	7.5	−6	36	.8751	−5.2506	0.87758	7.5
1957	8.3	−5	25	.9191	−4.5955	0.90945	8.1
1958	8.8	−4	16	.9445	−3.7780	0.94132	8.7
1959	9.5	−3	9	.9777	−2.9331	0.97319	9.4
1960	10.2	−2	4	1.0086	−2.0172	1.00506	10.1
1961	10.8	−1	1	1.0334	−1.0334	1.03930	10.9
1962	11.4	0	0	1.0569	0	1.06880	11.7
1963	12.2	1	1	1.0864	1.0864	1.10067	12.6
1964	13.3	2	4	1.1239	2.2478	1.13254	13.6
1965	14.7	3	9	1.1673	3.5019	1.16441	14.6
1966	15.9	4	16	1.2014	4.8056	1.19628	15.7
1967	17.2	5	25	1.2355	6.1775	1.22815	16.9
1968	18.4	6	36	1.2648	7.5888	1.26002	18.2
	158.2		182	13.8946	5.8002		158.0

SOURCE: *Life Insurance Fact Book*, 1969, p. 28.

and

$$\Sigma X \cdot (\log Y) = 5.8002$$

The trend equation is:

$$\log Y_c = 1.0688 + 0.03187X \qquad \text{Origin: July 1, 1962}$$
$$X: \text{One-year unit}$$

The computed trend and the original data are shown graphically in Figure 4.

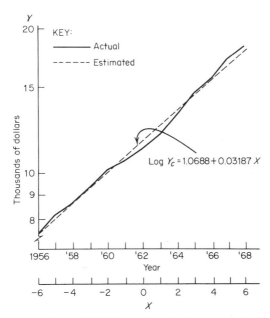

Fig. 4.   Estimated and actual life insurance in force per family, 1956–1968.

To estimate the trend value for, say, 1965, we first substitute the value of X for the year in the trend equation and get

$$\log Y_{c1965} = 1.0688 + 0.03187(3)$$
$$= 1.1644$$

Taking the antilogarithm of 1.1644, we obtain a trend value of 14.6 for 1965.

The trend equation in log form can be converted to an exponential trend equation in natural numbers.   Thus, the trend equation in our example can be written as

$$Y_c = 11.7 \, (1.076)^X$$

The quantity 11.7 is the trend value at the origin, that is, at 1962 when $X = 0$, and the value of 1.076, that is, the value of b, is the ratio of the trend value of each year to that of the preceding year.   If we subtract 1 from the b value and express it as a percentage, the result is the constant rate of change in Y per unit of X.   For our example, the average increase in the life insurance per family at a constant rate is 7.6 percent per annum.

NONLINEAR TRENDS

The linear trend—both arithmetic and geometric straight-line—characterizes most business and economic time series and contains the desirable property that its slope is constant. However, some series may not be adequately described by a straight-line trend. This section discusses briefly other types of trend, such as a second-degree parabolic trend and a special growth curve called the Gompertz curve.

Second-Degree Parabolic Trend. The second-degree parabolic trend is represented by the equation

$$Y_c = a + bX + cX^2$$

where a = the value of Y_c at the origin, that is, when $X = 0$
b = the slope of the curve at the origin
c = the rate of change in the slope per unit of change of X

Applying the least-squares method to the parabolic function, three normal equations are derived:

$$\Sigma Y = na + b\Sigma X + c\Sigma X^2$$
$$\Sigma XY = a\Sigma X + b\Sigma X^2 + c\Sigma X^3$$
$$\Sigma X^2Y = a\Sigma X^2 + b\Sigma X^3 + c\Sigma X^4$$

If the origin is set at the middle of the series so that $\Sigma X = 0$, the formulas for the constants are:

$$a = (\Sigma Y - c\Sigma X^2)/n$$
$$b = \Sigma XY/\Sigma X^2$$
$$c = [n\Sigma X^2Y - (\Sigma X^2)(\Sigma Y)]/[n\Sigma X^4 - (\Sigma X^2)^2]$$

As an example, such a trend is fitted to the hypothetical sales data in Table 6. We obtain

$$b = \Sigma XY/\Sigma X^2 = 18.5/60 = 0.3083$$
$$c = (n\Sigma X^2Y - \Sigma X^2\Sigma Y)/[n\Sigma X^4 - (\Sigma X^2)^2]$$
$$= [9(297.1) - (60)(42.7)]/[9(708) - (60)^2]$$
$$= 0.0404$$
$$a = (\Sigma Y - c\Sigma X^2)/n$$
$$= [42.7 - (0.0404)(60)]/9$$
$$= 4.475$$

TABLE 6   Sales of S & R Company, 1959–1965

(1) Year	(2) X	(3) Y	(4) X^2	(5) $X \cdot Y$	(6) X^2Y	(7) X^4	(8) Yc
1957	−4	3.8	16	−15.2	60.8	256	3.898
1958	−3	3.9	9	−11.7	35.1	81	3.914
1959	−2	4.2	4	−8.4	16.8	16	4.020
1960	−1	4.3	1	−4.3	4.3	1	4.207
1961	0	4.4	0	0	0	0	4.475
1962	1	4.7	1	4.7	4.7	1	4.824
1963	2	5.2	4	10.4	20.8	16	5.253
1964	3	5.8	9	17.4	52.2	81	5.764
1965	4	6.4	16	25.6	102.4	256	6.355
		42.7	60	18.5	297.1	708	42.710

The trend equation can be written as

$$Y_c = 4.475 + 0.3083X + 0.0404\,X^2$$

Origin: July 1, 1961
X: One-year units

The value 4.475 is the trend value at the origin, that is, 1961; 0.3083 is the slope of the trend curve at this point; and 0.0404 shows the extent of curvature. The positive values of b and c indicate that the trend curve is upward convex to the origin, as shown in Figure 5.

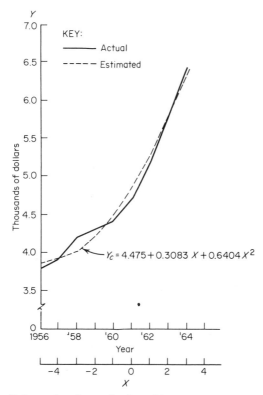

Fig. 5.   Estimated and actual sales of S & R Company, 1959–1965.

The usefulness of the parabolic trend as a forecasting tool is somewhat restricted because of its explosive nature at the limit. That is, as X gets larger, the trend value will approach an extreme value depending upon the sign and magnitude of the coefficient estimate of X^2.

Special Growth Curves. Growth curves are a special type of nonlinear trend function. They are used mainly for describing a biological growth pattern or a learning process. Also, they are appropriate for depicting the long-run growth behavior of a new product since the product typically shows slow growth in the early stage of introduction into the market, then rapid growth as it is accepted by the market at large, and finally a tapering off with maturity or as it reaches a saturation point.

Typical growth curves are modified exponential, Gompertz, logistic, and learning functions.   All these functions produce an elongated S-shaped curve. The Gompertz curve is derived by the equation

$$Y_c = Ca^{R^X}$$

where $C = $ growth at maturity

$a = $ proportion of initial growth

and R is assumed to lie between 0 and 1 and may be considered as a measure of the rate of growth.

To estimate the values of the constants c, a, and R, we first transform the exponential Gompertz into logarithmic form:

$$\log Y_c = \log C + (\log a) (R^X)$$

The simplest way of fitting the growth curve is the method of selected points. The procedure is as follows:

1.   Divide the series into three (or more) even parts.
2.   Compute geometric means for each segment.
3.   Draw a curve that passes through these mean points.

The formulas for the constants may be written

$$\log a = \Delta_1(R - 1)/[(R^n - 1)^2]$$
$$\log R = (\Delta_2/\Delta_1)/k$$
$$\log c = 1/k[S_1 - (R^n - 1/R - 1) \log a]$$

where $k = $ number of observations in each third

$\Delta_1 = S_2 - S_1$

$\Delta_2 = S_3 - S_2$

$S_1 = $ sum of observed values, log Y, in first third

$S_2 = $ sum of observed values, log Y, in second third

$S_3 = $ sum of observed values, log Y, in last third

CHANGING THE TIME UNIT

A trend equation is often desired in monthly or quarterly terms.   Such an equation may be derived either by fitting a trend curve directly to the original monthly or quarterly data or by converting a trend equation based on annual data into a monthly or quarterly equation through a simple conversion technique.   The latter approach is simple and avoids the computational complexity involved in the former method.   This is illustrated by using the derived trend equation for disposable personal income per family in the previous section. The equation was

$$Y_c = 6.87 + 0.308X \qquad\qquad (i)$$
$$\text{Origin: July 1, 1962}$$
$$X: \text{One-year units}$$

Suppose we wish to transform this annual trend equation into a monthly equation.   To carry out the transformation, we divide the value for a by 12 and b by 144.   That is,

$$Y_c = 6.87/12 + 0.308/24X$$
$$= 0.5725 + 0.01283X \qquad\qquad (ii)$$

Now the time unit for X is one month, the origin is July 1, 1962, and Y is the monthly total.   Equation (ii) is a technically correct form of the monthly equation, but requires adjustment of the origin because it should be placed at the midpoint of the series. We can shift the origin from July 1, 1962, to July 15, 1962, by substituting 0.5 for X in Equation (ii), and we obtain:

$$Y_c = 0.57892 + 0.01283X$$

Origin: July 15, 1962
X: One-month units

MOVING AVERAGES AND EXPONENTIAL SMOOTHING

A trend equation enables us to project time series into the future. However, its primary use is in long-term forecasting, and its usefulness in routine short-run forecasts is somewhat restricted. Furthermore, a trend model is relatively inefficient in predicting short-run movements of sales and inventory when compared with other techniques, such as the method of moving averages and exponential smoothing.

Moving Averages. Prediction concerns the values that some variables will take at a certain future time. Since future values are not known and cannot be predicted with certainty, these values may be considered as a random variable generated by a stochastic process. Let this random variable be denoted by X. Then the value of X at time t can be written as

$$X_t = \theta + \epsilon_t \tag{18}$$

where θ is the expected value of X, and ε is a stochastic disturbance with zero expectation and constant variance.

Equation (18) implies that the process generating the observed values is constant and that a specific observed value at time t is, on the average, deviant from the constant value θ by a random effect, ε. The forecasting problem is then to estimate the expected value of X. The procedure for estimating θ is obviously to use the past observed values.

The method of moving averages uses the most recent observations for the estimate. Specifically, let us denote by $\hat{X}_{t+1}$ the estimate of a certain economic variable, say sales, in period $t + 1$. According to a moving average, $\hat{X}_{t+1}$ is obtained by dividing the sum of recent period observed values by the number of periods, that is,

$$\hat{X}_{t+1} = (X_t + X_{t-1} + \ldots + X_{t-k+1})/k$$

$$= (1/k) \sum_{j=0}^{k-1} X_{t-j} \tag{19}$$

where k is the number of observations.

A simple algebraic manipulation allows us to simplify Equation (19) to:

$$\hat{X}_{t+1} = \hat{X}_{t+i-1} + (X_t - X_{t-k})/k \tag{20}$$

As is shown, a moving average implicitly assigns weight one to the recent k period observed values, and weight zero to the earlier periods. Therefore, the choice of k determines the rate of response to a change of the process in this forecasting system. Thus, a large k implies a stable underlying process which in turn needs a slow adjustment in the system, whereas a small k is required when the process is changing rather rapidly.

The moving average method is simple computationally and useful in predicting a smoothly changing series. However, a difficulty with the moving average is that data for the most recent k periods must be available.

Exponential Smoothing. Exponential smoothing is a simple procedure for computing an average in which weights for past observations are exponentially declining according to their age. It is a special kind of weighted moving average that resolves the above-mentioned difficulty with the simple moving average. Exponential smoothing requires only the current observation and the previous estimate for predicting the future behavioral pattern of the series. The basic equation for exponential smoothing is

$$S_t(X) = \alpha X_t + (1 - \alpha)S_{t-1}(X) \tag{21}$$

where $S(X)$ is the smoothed value of X or the estimate of θ and α is the smoothing constant whose value lies between 0 and 1. It can be shown that the smoothed value is a linear function of all past observations, the weight of which decreases geometrically with age. This is made clearer if Equation (21) is rewritten in the original form; that is,

$$S_t(X) = \alpha X_t + \alpha(1 - \alpha)X_{t-1} + \alpha(1 - \alpha)^2 X_{t-2}$$
$$+ \alpha(1 - \alpha)^3 X_{t-3} + \ldots + \alpha(1 - \alpha)^n X_{t-n}$$
$$+ \ldots + (1 - \alpha)^t X_0 \tag{22}$$

If the value of α is 0.4, the weights assigned are 0.4 to the current observation and 0.16, 0.064, 0.0256, 0.01024, and so on, to the successive previous observations. Since the sum of weights equals one, the weighted average by exponential smoothing is unbiased and, consequently, its forecasting scheme produces an unbiased estimate of θ.

Exponential smoothing is more efficient than a moving average in that it requires less computing and fewer observations. It also has the relative advantage of flexibility in its response to a change in the process behavior. If the time pattern of the series is shifting drastically, the only thing required for a quick response to the change is to increase the numerical value of the smoothing constant. On the other hand, if the change takes place rather slowly, a smaller value of the smoothing constant is needed.

SUMMARY

Methods of measuring linear secular trends for a time series have been discussed in this chapter with special emphasis on the least-squares method. Logarithmic linear trend and nonlinear trend functions, along with moving averages and exponential smoothing techniques, have also been described.

The main emphasis has been on the use of a time series model in forecasting the long-run movement of economic and business variables and on the application of this trend analysis to marketing (or marketing research) problems. The importance of obtaining efficient forecasts of future values is widely recognized for optimal planning and decision making. For example, correct demand forecasts of products (existing or newly introduced) are crucial for optimally planning the course of actions for the company and minimizing possible risks involved in the choice of an appropriate strategy. A time series model such as that presented here provides a basis for optimal prediction over the short run (via moving averages and exponential smoothing methods) or over longer periods (via secular trend analysis).

REFERENCES

1. Box, George P., and G. M. Jenkins, *Time Series Analysis: Forecasting and Control*, San Francisco: Holden-Day, 1970.

2. Brown, R. G., *Smoothing, Forecasting and Prediction of Discrete Time Series,* Englewood Cliffs, N.J.: Prentice-Hall, 1962.
3. Clelland, R. C., F. Brown, J. deCani, J. Bursk, D. Murry, *Basic Statistics with Business Applications,* New York: Wiley, 1966.
4. Cox, D. R., "Prediction by Exponentially Weighted Moving Averages and Related Methods," *Journal of the Royal Statistical Society,* vol. 23, 1961.
5. Croxton, F. E., D. Cowden, and S. Klein, *Applied General Statistics,* 3d ed., Englewood Cliffs, N.J.: Prentice-Hall, 1967.
6. Ferber, R., and P. J. Verdoorn, *Research Methods in Economics and Business,* New York: Macmillan, 1962.
7. Grenander, U., and M. Rosenblatt, *Statistical Analysis of Stationary Time Series,* New York: Wiley, 1957.
8. Hadley, G., *Introduction to Business Statistics,* San Francisco: Holden-Day, 1968.
9. Neiswanger, W. A., *Elementary Statistical Methods,* New York: MacMillan, 1956.
10. Winters, P. R., "Forecasting Sales by Exponentially Weighted Moving Averages," *Management Science,* 1960.

Part E

Statistical Analysis of Relationships

Chapter 2

Time Series Analysis

LAWRENCE SALZMAN *Consultant, New York, New York*

HISTORY

The concept of a time series, that is, a measurement of the change, development, or level of something over time, is as old as recorded history. One of the earlier papers on this subject which showed great vision and insight was written by Warren M. Persons over 50 years ago as the lead article for the first issue of the *Review of Economics and Statistics* [15]. He clearly perceived that an economic phenomenon is of consequence only as a relative event. As he stated, "Only by a comparison of items over a period of time can one sense the meaning. . . . The meaning of fundamental statistics can be sensed only by a comparison over time of fluctuations occurring in continuous and homogeneous series" [15, p. 7].

In the nineteenth century, Augustin Cournot, the French economist, recognized the existence of secular or long-term movements in economic phenomena. In 1860, another Frenchman, Clement Juglar, published *Des Crises Commerciales*, a treatise on the business cycle. The English economist and mathematician William Stanley Jevons developed, although he did not originate, the idea of seasonal variations, attempting to show their regularity and to quantify their amplitudes [11, p. vii].

It was assumed early in the study of time series that periodic observations of economic levels of activity were the amalgam of various forces sometimes working in concert and at other times in opposition. With remarkable clarity, Persons outlined the model for a decomposed time series in the article mentioned earlier. His working hypothesis is still the basic concept. He wrote [15, p. 8]:

It is essential . . . that at the outset of this study there should be a clear-cut definition of the assumptions which we have made concerning the nature of the fluctuations found in time series. A preliminary survey . . . has led to the following working hypothesis, namely that each series is a composite consisting of four types of fluctuations. The four types are:
    1.   A long-term tendency or secular trend . . .;
    2.   A wave-like or cyclical movement superimposed upon the secular trend . . . their rise and fall constituting the business cycle;
    3.   A seasonal movement within the year with a characteristic shape for each series;
    4.   Residual variations. . . .

Researchers realized that it is the underlying movements that are of real concern, that is, trend and cycle. The effort, therefore, was to eliminate the other components from the raw data and work only with trend and cycle. Logically, this demanded an estimate not only of the seasonal factors for past data, but also of future seasonal variations. With these forecasted seasonals, as new data became available, they could be adjusted and compared not only with the same months of previous years, but equally as well with the rest of the series.

Persons turned his attention to this problem of isolating and quantifying seasonal variations. He concluded that the study of these movements should be based on the percentage changes from one month to the next, calling them link relatives [15, p. 22]. Modifications to the link-relative method were introduced after Persons's initial writing. The basic approach, however, remained popular for many years.[1]

Others were active by the early 1920s in developing various approaches to isolating, quantifying, and forecasting seasonal variations. Two main problems, as seen by these analysts, were that the methods in use did not adjust properly for isolated extremes and cycles and that the methods themselves required too many time-consuming computational steps. The time factor was particularly important in two subtle ways. First, since much time was needed, much money was necessary if these analysts were to produce results except for a few laboratory cases. Second, long delays were experienced between the event and the availability of comprehensive results.[2]

The first comprehensive book dealing specifically with seasonal variations, written by Simon Kuznets, appeared in 1933 [11, especially pp. 27–30].[3] In a 1941 article, H. C. Barton, Jr., described a method he was using to isolate and adjust for seasonal variations [1]. He spoke in terms of "preliminary seasonal factors" and outlined a series of steps which begin with a 12-month smoothing. His is a direct descendant of the Kuznets technique. These concepts appear later in this chapter when the X-11 variant of the Census Method II Seasonal Adjustment Program is described.

The earliest methods attempted to isolate and describe an "average seasonal variation" for each of the 12 months in the year. It was evident, however, that "we do not live at the average." Even Persons noted, "Although we wish to ascertain if a systematic variation exists it is not accurate to think of seasonal

---

[1] For an extensive discussion of the link-relative method, see Day [4].

[2] See, for instance, Falkner [5], Hall [6], and King [9]. The first of these articles reviews other methods of the day before presenting an approach which reduces the computational steps.

[3] The Federal Reserve Board described its method in an earlier article. See Joy Aryness and Thomas Woodlief, "The Use of Moving Averages in the Measurement of Seasonal Variations," *Journal of the American Statistical Association*, Sept. 1928.

variations . . . as being exactly the same the year after [15, p. 19]." Kuznets [11, pp. 29–30] discusses this problem in detail, stating, ". . . whenever the behavior of the series necessitated it, average seasonal indexes were established for rather short periods." In other words, relative to the "evolving seasonal" now in use where the seasonal factors change slightly each year for a given month, Kuznets developed a series of "average seasonals" over the length of a time series.

Another question given a good deal of thought was (and still is), what is the "best" period for which to collect data? Persons' observations are as current today as when he wrote [15, pp. 18f.],

> The week appears to be too short an interval for the measurement of seasonal variations. . . . Days are certainly too short. . . . We must be just as careful not to choose too short a period for measuring seasonal variation as to choose too long a period. The month has been adopted here as the most satisfactory unit.

During the decade of the 1920s, much work was done and many articles were published regarding the isolation of, and adjustment for, seasonal variations. In the 1930s as the Depression deepened, economists and statisticians turned to other problems. In the 1940s, first World War II and then the recovery period drew the attention of most. During that score of years, however, work continued on the application of developed techniques at the National Bureau of Economic Research and the Federal Reserve Board.

Not until the early 1950s did a new, major effort develop to upgrade the methods for analysis of seasonal and other variations in a time series. The arrival of the computer completely solved the problem of laborious effort in time-consuming computations. This development was combined with the talent and imagination of Julius Shiskin and Harry Eisenpress. Their work led to the techniques in use today, which were introduced in 1955 with the release of Census Method II, a fully automated, computerized approach to the isolation and analysis of the components outlined many years earlier by Warren Persons.

THE MULTIPLICATIVE MODEL

Each observation in a time series is thought of as Y_{ij}, where $i = 1, \ldots, n$ for n years of data, and $j = 1, \ldots, 12$ for monthly data. If we assume the first observation in a series to be January, its subscript i,j would be 1,1. The first 1 identifies it as being from the first year of data and the second 1 signifies a January observation. Similarly, the July observation for the fourth year of data, for example, would have the subscript 4,7. In this manner, the single equation for the model describes a two-dimensional matrix of data with n rows and 12 columns. If the model were describing quarterly data, then $j = 1, \ldots, 4$.

Each Y_{ij} is thought of as the combination of the four basic components outlined by Persons [15].[4] They are:

1. T_{ij}: that part of the Y_{ij} which is the result of a long-term or secular trend.

2. C_{ij}: that part which develops a cyclical component consisting of recurring oscillations of unequal amplitude and period.

---

[4] The above equation is a multiplicative model, i.e., the four components are multiplied to obtain a Y_{ij}. Under certain conditions an additive model is used. This is of the form $Y_{ij} = T_{ij} + C_{ij} + S_{ij} + I_{ij}$. Each type is discussed in the chapter.

3. S_{ij}: a factor which accounts for a seasonal variation or intrayear pattern which repeats itself exactly or in an evolving manner from year to year.

4. I_{ij}: a movement which forms an irregular or residual variation.

Each of these components has a unique time frame. The secular trend will move in one direction for 10, 20, or more years. The cyclical factor will have a period from 2 or 3 years to as many as 10 to 12 years. If sufficient data are available, more than one cyclical swing will emerge in a series. The seasonal fluctuations, by definition, have a period of one year. The irregular component has dynamic, short-lived perturbations from one to five or six months' duration.

On a month-to-month basis, the influence of the trend factor is very slight. Its prime feature is its cumulation month after month, moving in a single direction for many years. Therefore, over the long term,[5] the secular trend component will dominate the other three factors. Normally, if data for a given series were plotted for a decade or score of years, a long-term trend would be obvious even to the casual observer.

On a month-to-month basis, the influence of the cyclical factor is not too great either, although of greater significance than the trend component. The cyclical forces will be cumulative also, usually dominating the trend for the period of a half-cycle. Since the time frame of the cycle is less than that of the trend, the cycle will dominate the trend in the shorter term, with the trend dominating the cycle in the long term.

The seasonal influence, for most series, will dominate cycle and trend for perhaps a few months. Because of the nature of the seasonal component, it will more or less cancel itself out over a 12-month period.

The irregular factor is the most dynamic of the four components in the very short run, one to three or four months, for many time series. In a single month, it is quite normal for the irregular variations to dominate a series. The component's behavior, however, is erratic and usually it begins to cancel itself out in two or three months. Therefore, within a three- to five-month period, it often cancels itself either completely or in part.[6]

Irregular movements are not necessarily random. The analyst will often know the reason for an unusually high or low level of activity. Anticipation of a price rise may induce buyers to move their purchase dates forward to avoid the increase. This would induce a short spurt followed by a decline. A dock-workers' strike would drastically reduce imports and exports for the period of the dispute. As soon as it was settled, there would be a catching-up period during which more than normal levels of cargo would be handled until shippers and importers balanced their flows. Unusual heat or cold, precipitation, or dry weather can cause an irregular variation at any time of the year. A specific irregular movement that is not only known but quantified and adjusted for is the trading-day variation discussed in detail later in the chapter.

When the researcher approaches the problem of analyzing a time series, he should determine first the "stage of maturity" of his series. Under special circumstances, this domination and counterdomination of the component parts may not hold. Thus, consider the introduction of a new product. If there is a latent market for the new item, such as when black-and-white television sets were introduced commercially, sales (and production) are increasingly brisk. In the "takeoff" phase, the secular trend may very well dominate the other components, even in the short run. This initial period may last for several years.

---

[5] In most series 10 or more years would be considered the long term.

[6] In the real world 3 to 5 months can seem to be a long time to wait to see if a movement is irregular before making a decision. More on this later in the chapter.

Figure 1 shows the rapid rise in production of television sets beginning in 1947, the takeoff lasting until 1950.

Eventually, however, the product enters a "mature" phase. At this second development stage, the "normal" relationships among the factors return. Data from most time series include a period of maturity, which may last for generations. An example is the total production of raw steel, which has had a

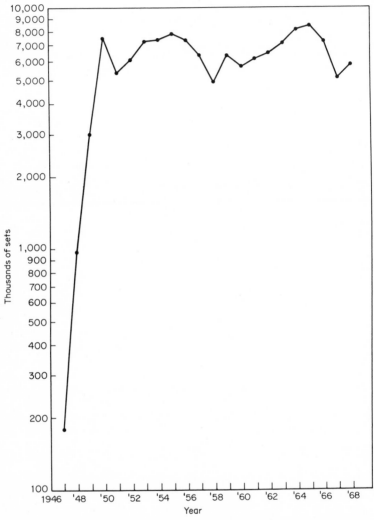

Fig. 1.   Annual production of black and white television sets (in thousands).
(SOURCES: *U.S. Bureau of the Census, Washington:* Historical Statistics of the United States, Colonial Times to 1957, 1960, p. 491, for the years 1947–1956; Historical Statistics of the United States—Continuation to 1962 and Revisions, 1965, p. 68, for the years 1957–1962; Statistical Abstract of the United States, 1969, 90th ed., 1969, p. 749; ibid., 89th ed., 1968, p. 753; ibid., 87th ed., 1966, p. 804; ibid., 86th ed., 1965, p. 815, for the years 1963–1968.)

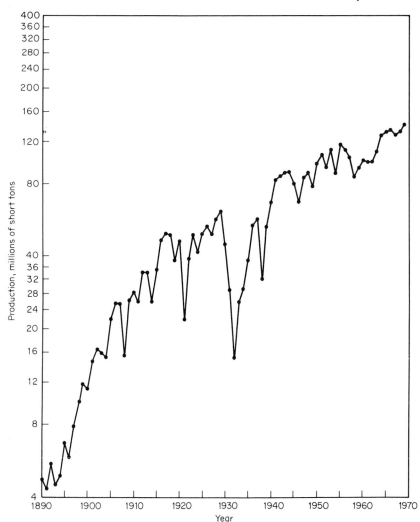

Fig. 2.   Annual steel production (millions of short tons). (SOURCES: *U.S. Bureau of the Census, Washington:* Historical Statistics of the United States—Continuation to 1962 and Revisions, *1965, p. 136 (figures multiplied by 1.12 to convert to short tons), for the years 1890–1938. U.S. Department of Commerce, Office of Business Economics, Washington:* Business Statistics—A Supplement to the Survey of Current Business, *1967 ed., p. 159, for the years 1939–1966;* Survey of Current Business, *February 1970, p. S-32, for the years 1967–1969.*)

slowly increasing long-term trend for years with cyclical movements of both minor and major proportions.   Figure 2 pictures steel production beginning in 1890.   The cycles are pronounced and outline periods of expansion and recession.   The secular growth, however, is very evident.

A third development stage would be a period of "secular stagnation."   This would be indicated by a market that is not growing.   The trend factor for such a series would not influence the curve at all and would show no dominance even in the long run. It is fairly difficult to give an example of this in the United States because of the situation produced by the rising per capita income multiplied by the rising population. This combination ensures a rising secular trend for any item in constant relative demand. The maintenance of a balance between rising population and income and declining demand, resulting in no absolute growth and no decline, is not too common. However, production of

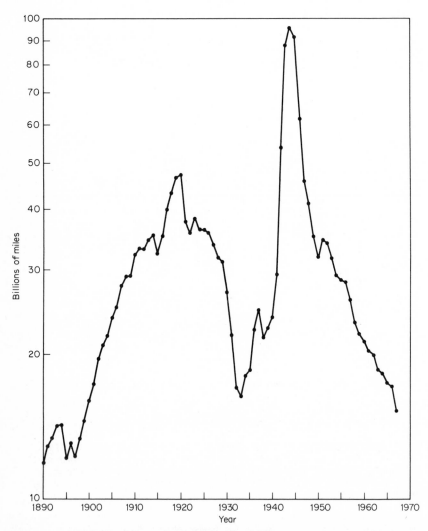

Fig. 3.   Annual railroad passenger-miles (in billions).   (SOURCES: *U.S. Bureau of the Census, Washington:* Historical Statistics of the United States, Colonial Times to 1957, *1960, p. 430, for the years 1890–1957;* Historical Statistics of the United States—Continuation to 1962 and Revisions, *1965, p. 61, for the years 1958–1962;* Statistical Abstract of the United States, *1969, p. 559, and 1968, p. 562, for the years 1967–1969.*)

black-and-white television sets, used as an example to show a takeoff period, appears to fit this balance of forces which produce secular stagnation, beginning in 1950. The data *would* have an upward trend, if production of color television sets were added to the series. (There is no reason to expect a series to go through the development stages in order.)

A fourth stage of development may also be thought of. It would be the reverse of the second, or mature, stage. In other words, this would be the slow decline in absolute overall demand within a market. It would have all the characteristics and relative relationships of the mature market except that the change in the trend factor would be negative.[7] An example of this phase is the post-World War II passenger miles traveled on the nation's railroads. The airlines, in combination with the automobile, have slowly garnered the travel market. Figure 3 shows railroad passenger miles beginning in 1890. Here we see the many years of secular growth culminating in 1944. The cycles are dynamic, but the change in trend is clear.

A fifth and final stage of development would be the rapid decline and "death" of a market. If data were available, production of horse-drawn carriages from about 1910 to 1920 would show this phase of a time series. Other examples would be production of wood-burning stoves, high button shoes, spats, and so on.

The components of a decomposed time series can be viewed graphically to illustrate the individual factors and their combination. The data for Figure 4 were obtained by analysis of the time series, Retail Sales, Durable Goods Stores, Total,[8] through the use of the X-11 variant of the Census Method II Seasonal Adjustment [computer] Program [24]. The Census Method II approach does not separate trend and cycle. It develops a factor called the final trend cycle. The trend in Figure 4a was arrived at by fitting a first-order exponential curve to the final trend cycle. The cycle in Figure 4b was obtained by taking the ratio of trend cycle to trend for each observation.[9] The seasonal variations in Figure 4c and the irregular series in 4d are from tables D10 and D13 respectively from computer output of Census Method II, X-11.

Thus, each of the four component parts can be viewed individually and seen to contain the characteristics just discussed. The secular trend rises approximately threefold during the 22.5-year period beginning in January 1947. The cyclical component winds its way above and below the trend, rising during prosperity and falling during recession.[10]

Decomposition of the trend cycle into its two distinct parts is accomplished

---

[7] The first difference, or ΔT, which is $T_{ij} - T_{i,j-1}$ would be negative.

[8] *Business Statistics*, 1967 edition, for 1947–1960 data; *Survey of Current Business*, vol. 48, no. 11, November 1968, for 1961–1967; *Survey of Current Business*, vol. 49, nos. 1 and 9, January and September 1969, for 1968–June 1969; all publications of the U.S. Department of Commerce.

[9] Salzman [16]. Chapters 4 and 5 contain the method, analysis, and FORTRAN computer programs to perform the statistical computations.

[10] The historical dates for the peak, the beginning of a recession, the trough, and the beginning of an expansion (end of a recession) are those designated by the National Bureau of Economic Research (NBER). The NBER has recorded for the period World War II to the middle of 1969 four recessions: (1) November 1948 to October 1949; (2) July 1953 to August 1954; (3) July 1957 to April 1958; and (4) May 1960 to February 1961. Other periods showing minor downward or level movements have been referred to as "mini-recessions" and/or "subcycles." Sometimes, however, specific events which have economic consequences lasting for several months appear as recessions. Thus, many series show a dip during the steel strike of 1959 which lasted for four months during the second half of the year.

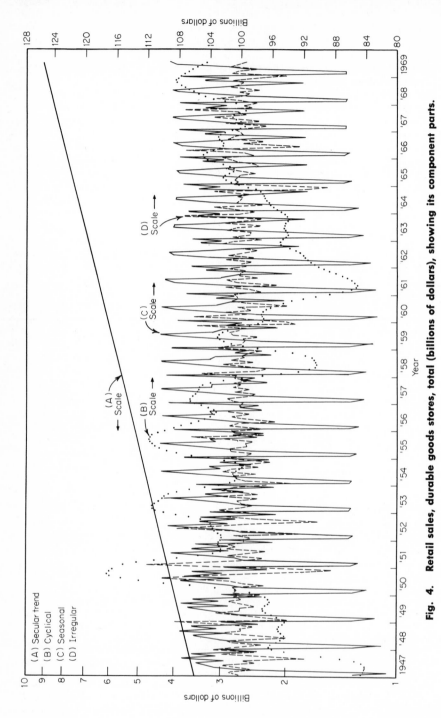

Fig. 4. Retail sales, durable goods stores, total (billions of dollars), showing its component parts.

through the use of the statistical tools just discussed. Choosing the specific tools, it should be realized, is a subjective process. If we choose to fit a curve other than the one selected, we would have results different from those pictured in Figures 4a and 4b. The analyst should not have such strong preconceived ideas as to the nature of the results to mold his choice of "tools," thereby forcing the expected.

The seasonal index, Figure 4c, traces a similar but evolving path from year to year. The data which are the source for Figure 4c show that August and September, for example, have changed 8 to 10 percent over the 22-year span, thus moving from above- to below-average months. January and February, on the other hand, are traditionally poor months for retail sales of durable goods and have not changed their relative position significantly over the years.

Most economic time series contain seasonal variations of significant proportion. A few, such as Standard & Poor's 500 Stock Index, have been judged not to vary significantly because of seasonal factors.[11]

The irregular component, Figure 4d, has perturbations above and below the mean value.[12] The changes in direction occur several times each year at different times from one year to the next. This is to be expected because of the time frame and nature of the irregular movements.

Figure 5 is a representation of the data as each component, in turn, is reintroduced into the trend. At first we see only the long-term movement, Figure 5a. It is the same as the secular trend in Figure 4a. The trend is multiplied by the cyclical component resulting in the movement shown in Figure 5b. This is the final trend cycle, Table D12 in the X-11 computer output. The trend cycle is multiplied next by the irregular factors, giving us the final seasonally adjusted series, Figure 5c, Table D11 in the X-11 computer output. The last step to return to the original data is to multiply by the seasonal factors. The original data are graphed in Figure 5d.[13]

With the return of each successive factor, the curve takes on the additional features of the factor. The trend is undisturbed in its majestic simplicity when viewed alone. The cycle introduces the movements we associate with the ebbs and flows of business: the recession, the "mini-recession," the "rolling readjustment," and the other terms dreamed up by economists and politicians.[14] The irregular vibrations introduce reverse and accented movements within the trend cycle each year. The seasonal fluctuations complete the picture, returning us to a series that may appear, on occasion, to "move in all directions at the same time."

It is only the perspective of time, usually, that allows us to perceive the underlying movements (trend cycle) of a series. These movements are the determinants of policy. Thus, the businessman will increase or decrease inventory during the year because of seasonal fluctuations. However, policy pronouncements of major consequence in business (and government) dealing with

[11] The Bureau of the Census in its publication *BCD* (Business Conditions Digest), a recognized authority in the application of adjustments for seasonal variations, states that this series does not appear to contain seasonal movement. See [26, p. 74].

[12] Table 2 indicates the mean is 99.9.

[13] Table B1 in the X-11 computer output. Notice that the trend is multiplied first by the cycle, then by the irregular, and lastly by the seasonal. The equation is normally written with the irregular factor last. In practice, however, the seasonal is the first component to be isolated in "final" form and therefore the last to be put back.

[14] President Truman once remarked that the difference between a recession and depression is: A recession is when your neighbor loses his job; a depression is when you lose yours.

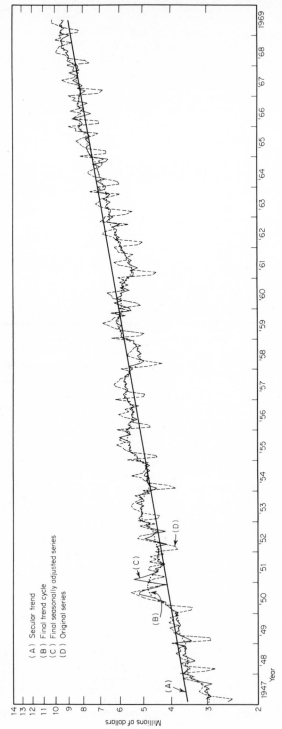

Fig. 5. Retail sales, durable goods stores, total, showing combination of component parts.

(A) Secular trend
(B) Final trend cycle
(C) Final seasonally adjusted series
(D) Original series

Millions of dollars

Year

the state of the economy are those concerned with the trend cycle. Monetary policy formed by the Board of Governors of the Federal Reserve System and fiscal policy developed by the Executive branch of the federal government aim toward promoting or modifying movements in the trend-cycle component of the gross national product (GNP).

Since the money managers are charged with making these vital decisions which affect us all, and since their human limitations are those of the rest of the population, they are in the unenviable position of normally having to act with relatively little knowledge, almost no perspective in time, and much conjecture.[15]

The multiplicative model of the form $Y_{ij} = T_{ij} \times C_{ij} \times S_{ij} \times I_{ij}$ has been used more extensively and has proven to be more effective and reliable than the additive model $Y_{ij} = T_{ij} + C_{ij} + S_{ij} + I_{ij}$ described elsewhere in this chapter. The reason is that the relationship among economic variables tends to be relative rather than absolute.

A time series will be in dollars, tons, passenger miles, or whatever quantity is being measured. In the multiplicative model, the sign can be attached to only one of the four basic factors. It would be meaningless, for instance, to have two or more of the components in dollars. If this were done, it would imply dollars raised to a power. Obviously, the concept "dollar" has an exponent of 1.

One factor, trend, is given the sign (dollars, tons, or whatever) and the other three, cycle, seasonal, and irregular, are developed as index or unsigned numbers. This can be viewed in Figure 4. Only Figure 4a is signed; for the specific series shown here, retail sales of durable goods, in billions of dollars. Figures 4b, c, and d are index values with bases of 1.000 (or 100.0, as in the computer printout discussed later in the chapter).

The multiplicative model would develop the same adjustment factors (indexed components: cycle, seasonal, and irregular) for two economic establishments which perform identical functions under identical conditions, the one difference being that one is twice the size of the other. This difference in size would be reflected in the single signed component, the trend. This feature (index numbers as adjustment factors) allows the analyst to compare all seasonal adjustments no matter what the trend sign may be. This feature is unique to the multiplicative adjustment.

Why, if the multiplicative model has these advantages, would one want to use the additive model? The reason is that the multiplicative adjustment has limitations. To perform the multiplicative adjustment, the analyst must have a series with *all* positive observations. If there were a negative datum in a series, it would require either one or three negative signs associated with the four components in order to be able to regenerate the original point. There is no basis for knowing how many or where these negative signs should be placed. Therefore, it is impossible to perform a multiplicative adjustment if there is a negative observation in a series. Similarly, zero observations would also prevent the use of the multiplicative model.

We can think of a time series as consisting of three time periods: past, present, and future. It is the purpose of analysis to see (1) where we have been; (2) where we are; and (3) what path we will follow. When we think of these three segments or periods of a series and our interest in each, we are really trying to isolate the basic or underlying movements, that is, the first and second of Persons' "four types of fluctuations": long-term trend and business cycle.

---

[15] To paraphrase Winston Churchill, time series analysis and forecasting are half science and all art.

Ideally, if we could remove the other components, seasonal and irregular, from the historical data, we would clearly see "where we have been." Also, we should have a good idea of "where we are" relative to "where we have been." The problem develops in the analysis of the future position, or "what path we will follow." The future, unfortunately, is not deterministic. Future events greatly depend on exogenous past and future developments.

This does not mean that attempts to forecast are pointless. It does mean that the analyst or forecaster must clearly and qualitatively at least list his assumptions as to future decisions or, more precisely, list those exogenous forces which will affect the movement of the series under analysis. It is hoped that he will not only list these exogenous or outside variables, but will quantify them as well. In this manner the researcher is better able to isolate the causes of future fluctuations. He will, consequently, understand more fully the problems in making a forecast at a later date because he will be able to test his earlier hypothesis as to causes and effect.

Time series analysis is concerned primarily with the isolation, study, and forecast of the component parts of a series without regard to outside or exogenous variables. The approach to the decomposition of these component parts from a set of "continuous and homogeneous" data and the forecasting of the seasonal fluctuations is the principal focus of this chapter. Forecasting the trend and cycle independently or as a single component is explored elsewhere.[16]

CENSUS METHOD II

Background

Before the work of Shiskin and Eisenpress [21], adjusting a series for seasonal variations was a laborious task taking many man-hours of hand calculations and highly subject to human error. A great deal of professional talent had to be expended on performing the statistical manipulations, thereby limiting the supply of economists and statisticians for collecting and preparing data as well as analyzing results.

The National Bureau of Economic Research and the Federal Reserve System were maintaining and updating seasonal adjustments for roughly a thousand series. Each organization had been a pioneer in the development of technique and analysis. Where appropriate and possible, moving seasonals were calculated and used. However, computational limitations at the time led to greater use of stable seasonal factors than is currently practiced. Even a thousand series, by today's standards, represented relatively few. With the foregoing restraints on productivity, summary information on the general characteristics of series under analysis was greatly limited and even nonexistent [14, p. 15].

In the early 1950s, with the birth of the computer industry, a tool was available for the first time which could raise the productivity of the statistician-economist several fold. At this time, Julius Shiskin, then at the Bureau of the Census, working with Harry Eisenpress, produced an automated approach to the adjustment of seasonal variations in economic time series. The first computer program developed by Shiskin, Census Method I [18], introduced in 1954, was programmed by the late Edward Lober and was "an adaptation and elaboration of the familiar ratio-to-moving-average method at its most advanced stage of development" [21, p. 416; also 1; 2, pp. 43–55; 3, pp. 320–363; 13, pp. 360–375; 32, pp. 580–586]. Use of this program in adjusting series for

[16] See Sec. II, Part E, Chaps. 1 and 6, and Part F, Chap. 4.

seasonal variations quickly pointed to the need for modifications. The improved computer program for the Univac I was dubbed Census Method II. It followed the general procedure of Census Method I, taking greater advantage of the computational speed of computers by using more sophisticated techniques and providing additional information about each series[17] [18, pp. 416–427].

The general approach to the isolation of the factors from the basic model, $Y_{ij} = T_{ij} \times C_{ij} \times S_{ij} \times I_{ij}$, by the Census method begins by developing a centered, 12-month moving average of the original data.[18] A 12-month smoothing is chosen because it represents a one-year period. If the series is smoothed or averaged over this period, it should result in a series relatively free from factors which tend to cancel themselves out during the period. Both seasonal and irregular variations fall into this category. Thus, the resulting series is made up primarily of trend and cycle.

The next step is to divide each observation in the original series by its corresponding point in the preliminary estimate of the trend-cycle curve. This isolates a series consisting mainly of seasonal and irregular fluctuations.

$$\frac{T_{ij} \times C_{ij} \times S_{ij} \times I_{ij}}{T_{ij} \times C_{ij}} = S_{ij} \times I_{ij}$$

In turn, each column, which consists of data over a span of years for a single month of this preliminary seasonal-irregular series, is smoothed by a weighted moving average. This provides a series consisting of preliminary estimates of the seasonal factor. These seasonals are adjusted to make the monthly average for a year equal 100.0; that is, the sum of the 12 seasonals for a year is set to be approximately 1,200. The adjusted preliminary seasonal factors are divided into their corresponding original observations, providing a preliminary seasonally adjusted series.

$$\frac{T_{ij} \times C_{ij} \times S_{ij} \times I_{ij}}{S_{ij}} = T_{ij} \times C_{ij} \times I_{ij}$$

Census Method II develops a preliminary trend cycle by applying a weighted moving average to the preliminary seasonally adjusted series.[19] From this point the method goes through a series of iterations, testing and smoothing for highly irregular values in an effort to develop better estimates of the various components. This ensures the relative stability of seasonal factors. The

[17] For a step-by-step description of Census Method II, see [16, pp. 223–230]. For a step-by-step description of the X-11 Variant, see [24].

[18] A centered 12-month moving average is achieved by weighting the first observation 1/2, each of the next 11 observations 1, and the thirteenth observation 1/2. Sum the 13 items and divide by 12. This gives a smoothed seventh observation. For a smoothed eighth point, begin by weighting the second point 1/2, the next 11 by 1, and the next by 1/2. Continue as for the first smoothing. Continue iterating, point by point, until the end of the series. This is the same as performing a 12-month smoothing followed by a 2-month smoothing. The centered 12-month smoothing "loses" 6 observations at each end of the series. The "centering" feature ensures that the smoothed observations have the same time position as the original data. A simple 12-month smoothing would develop a series that had points which fell "between" months rather than "on" months, i.e., from the fifteenth of one month to the fifteenth of the next rather than from the first to last day of each month.

[19] The earlier versions of Census Method II through the X-10 revision use a 15-term weighted moving average called a Spencer smoothing. For a full explanation of the derivation and use of this moving average, see [16, pp. 74–87].

smoothed series is extended also to time periods for which original observations are available. This leads to a series of smoothed ratios which constitute the final seasonal adjustment factors. These factors are estimated one year ahead "by adding to the seasonal factor for the end year, one-half the trend between the factor for that year and the preceding year. If X_n = seasonal adjustment factor for year n, then X_{n+1} is estimated by the equation $X_{n+1} = (3X_n - X_{n-1})/2$."

A noteworthy point is that this formula for projecting the seasonal does not give an average value, but rather, a marginal value.

Once the seasonal factors are developed, they are divided into the original data, giving a final seasonally adjusted series. This is then smoothed by a weighted moving average to eliminate the irregular variations and isolate a final trend-cycle series of data. This final trend-cycle series is divided into the final seasonally adjusted series, isolating a series of irregular variations.

$$\frac{T_{ij} \times C_{ij} \times I_{ij}}{T_{ij} \times C_{ij}} = I_{ij}$$

The development of more accurate estimates of the components through a series of iterations loses nothing in the original data since the final seasonal factors are divided into the original data. Therefore, any error in the estimate of one component must appear as a compensating error in one or more of the other factors.

Census Method II was introduced in December 1955. Between that time and November 1960, more than 10,000 time series were adjusted for seasonal and other variations at the Bureau of the Census. Besides the original version of Census Method II on a UNIVAC computer, the method was programmed for various IBM computers. Also, five private business organizations had set up facilities to process time series data for a fee [14, p. 81]. In just five years with the computerized versions of Census Method II, more data were analyzed for seasonal and other variations than had been analyzed in the previous 35 years. With this expanding wealth of experience and resultant knowledge, modifications and variations of the original version were constantly being developed.

Two specific problems with Census Method II were its difficulty in handling extreme seasonal-irregular $(S_{ij} \times I_{ij})$ ratios[20] and its apparently excessive reliance on end points where the extension of series for smoothing routines seemed necessary.[21] In 1960, Census Method II, X-3, was released. It incorporated changes in technique from the original Census Method II program which were designed to rectify these problems.[22]

[20] An "extreme" ratio would be one that fell outside a prescribed statistical limit, for example, 2 standard deviations from the mean.

[21] If a series were not extended a given number of periods before a smoothing, end points would be "lost." Specifically, in order to end with as many points as begun with, a series is extended by the span of the smoothing minus one, divided by two. Therefore, a seven-term smoothing demands an extension of 3 terms in the series in order not to "lose" end points. Not to lose any points in the smoothing would demand an extension at each end of the series. Normally a smoothing is an odd number of terms so that time positions are not displaced.

[22] "First, extreme seasonal-irregular ratios are replaced by the average of the two preceding and the two following ratios. When the extreme ratio falls at the end of the series, it is replaced by the average of the three preceding ratios. When the extreme ratio falls one position before the end, it is replaced by the average of the two preceding ratios and the end ratio. A similar procedure is followed for extremes

In late 1961, two more computer programs for decomposing time series were released by the Bureau: Census Method II, X-9 and X-10. Changes in each dealt basically with smoothing end points and substituting for extreme values [25]. Another problem with the original version was that as additional data were added to a series, and the longer series readjusted and new seasonal factors produced, large changes sometimes occurred in the seasonals, including those from the beginning of the series. This disconcerting feature was modified to a degree by the revisions in the X-9 and X-10 versions. In general, the revised methods gave approximately the same results as before for most series and superior results for series with greater irregularity [14, p. 83].

X-11 Variant

In October 1965, the X-11 variant of Census Method II replaced the X-9 and X-10 versions as the standard program used at the Bureau of the Census for time series decomposition and analysis. The program encompasses three new aspects. First, changes from the earlier versions improve the basic approach. Second, important, completely new additions to the program increase the scope of the adjustment and analysis. And third, the analyst employing the program is able to control its operation through selecting various options from a single control card. Consequently, the program can decompose a series in numerous ways, allowing the very efficient testing of many possibilities if necessary.

Changes from Earlier Versions. Prior to the release of X-11, the Census method employed a weighted 15-term average for smoothing a seasonally adjusted series in order to eliminate the irregular fluctuations. In the X-11, the span of the weighted moving average is automatically chosen, depending on a preliminary estimate of the amplitude of the irregular variations in a series vis-à-vis the amplitude of the trend-cycle variations.[23] This relationship is known as the $\bar{I}/\bar{C}$ ratio. The smoother the series, the less smoothing power necessary to eliminate the irregular component. Therefore, if this preliminary estimate of the $\bar{I}/\bar{C}$ ratio is less than 1.00, a 9-term Henderson smoothing is employed [16, pp. 88–98; 12, p. 54]. If the ratio falls between 1.00 and 3.49, a 13-term Henderson smoothing is applied. The 13-term smoothing has approximately the same smoothing power as the 15-term Spencer smoothing, with the advantage of one less point "lost" at each end of the smoothing. If the preliminary $\bar{I}/\bar{C}$ ratio is greater than 3.49, a 23-term Henderson smoothing is used. The reasoning is that if the irregular is so large compared to the trend cycle, more smoothing is necessary despite the loss of more end points [24, pp. 3–4].

Smoothing, or "taking a moving average," is an average technique. There are unweighted smoothings where each observation is given an equal weight (assumed to be 1.0) and weighted smoothings where each point is assigned a

---

falling at the beginning of the series. Second, in order to compute the moving averages which measure the seasonal factors for the first and last years of each series, ratios are required for additional years preceding and following the actual period covered by the data. Where the average month-to-month change in the irregular factor is 2.00 or more the average of the first *four* available ratios is used as the estimated value for each of the three years preceding the period covered by the series. The estimated ratios for three years following the actual period of the series are computer in a similar manner [20, p. 561]."

[23] The user also has the option, from the control card, of specifying the span of the smoothing that the program selects.

specific weight for each specific iteration in the smoothing. An unweighted two-month smoothing, for instance, would add two consecutive observations in a time series and divide by 2.0 to obtain a smoothed point. The resultant smoothed point would be positioned, in the time frame, "between" the two unsmoothed observations. An unweighted three-month smoothing would add three consecutive points and divide by 3.0 to obtain a smoothed point which would fall on the middle observation. Longer smoothings average over longer periods. Therefore, the greater span of the unweighted smoothing, the more "averaging power" it has and the smoother the resultant series.

An even-span smoothing, that is, two-, four-, six-month spans, develops data which fall between the unsmoothed data. An even-span smoothing followed by another even-span smoothing "recenters" the data on their original time positions. This is true for both unweighted and weighted smoothings. An odd-term smoothing does not shift the time position of the resultant data.

A technique used to obtain smoothed data for the lost end points is to assume sufficient observations before and past the available data so the smoothing can begin with a smoothed point in the time position of the first actual observation. These theoretical data are developed by averaging end points and assuming these averages as the extended data or projecting the end points in a specified manner. The former approach has been used for Spencer weighted 15-term smoothings in Census Method II, the original through the X-10 versions. The latter approach is used in the X-11 variant when Henderson variable-span, weighted moving averages are employed.

A change was made also in the columnar smoothing of the seasonal-irregular $(S_{ij} \times I_{ij})$ ratios which estimate the final seasonal factors. Where in the X-9 version a 3×3- or 3×5-term smoothing[24] was employed depending on the value of I, the X-11 uses only the 3×5-term smoothing. This helps to reduce further the revisions in seasonal factors when additional data are added to the series.

A third change in the X-11 concerns the isolation, weighting, and replacement of values which are considered extreme. In previous versions, preliminary estimates of the seasonal adjustment factors and the standard deviation of the irregular variations were computed. Preliminary $S_{ij} \times I_{ij}$ values which fell two or more standard deviations beyond the estimates of the seasonals were designated to be extreme and given a weight of zero. All other data were given a weight of 1.0. (See footnote 21 for replacement procedure of zero-weighted $S_{ij} \times I_{ij}$ values in earlier programs except in the original.) The X-11 replaces this "all or nothing" weighting procedure with a graduated scheme where the program uses declining weights from 1.0 to 0.0 for extremes with deviations from 1.5 to 2.5 sigmas. Those data outside of 2.5 standard deviations receive a weight of zero. The selection of 1.5 and 2.5 sigmas as the "weighting band" is the default option. That is, the analyst has the option of specifying the lower and upper limits on the control card. If he does not, the program automatically uses these limits.

The span of data in the preliminary irregular that is used to establish the standard deviation has been modified also in the X-11 version. This technique modifies the original series instead of the $S_{ij} \times I_{ij}$ ratios. Therefore, the effect of the extremes on the trend cycle is taken into account. Also, the different approach to developing standard deviations of the irregular component and the graduated weighting of extremes greatly reduces the revisions of seasonal fac-

---

[24] A three-term smoothing followed by another three-term smoothing or a five-term smoothing followed by a three-term smoothing.

tors for earlier years when additional data are added to the series for re-evaluation [24, pp. 2–5].[25]

Additions.

Trading-Day Adjustment. In many monthly economic time series, trading-day variations are a significant source of month-to-month fluctuations. These variations are caused in part by the shift in the number of days of the week found in a given month from one year to the next. January always contains 31 days. However, for example, January 1969 had five Wednesdays, Thursdays, and Fridays, and January 1970 contained five Thursdays, Fridays, and Saturdays. *Ceteris paribus,* if Saturday activity is significantly different from Wednesday activity for a series under analysis, January 1969 results would be different from January 1970 results. Over the years, relatively large differences can be observed because of this calendar shift from year to year.

November 1969 is a good example of the trading-day phenomenon. It had five Saturdays and Sundays. For a series measuring an activity which takes place only on weekdays, the month would have no more activity than a 28-day February, again *ceteris paribus*. The similarity of results from two such dissimilar months would have been caused strictly by trading- or working-day variations.[26]

A cursory look at a calendar shows that if a month has "extra" days, whatever they may be, the following non-28-day month will contain extra days which follow in order those from the previous month. In other words, November 1969 had an extra or fifth Saturday and Sunday. December 1969 had an extra Monday, Tuesday, and Wednesday, and January 1970 had five Thursdays, Fridays, and Saturdays. Therefore, this trading-day variation canceled itself within a few months.

Thinking back to Persons' original four component parts, we see that this variation falls clearly in the residual or irregular component. If it could be isolated and adjusted, the apparent degree of irregularity of the series would be reduced. This is exactly what is done in the X-11 version, and it represents a major addition to the Census Method approach. The program uses a regression technique where data are developed on the basis of the irregular component series and the number of extra days in each month for which data are available. The program has a built-in calendar which determines these extra days for the data period for each series [23; 16, pp. 41–72].

Additive Model. The foregoing has dealt with the multiplicative model for time series decomposition. As mentioned earlier, a model can be written where the components are added together to sum to the original observation (Y_{ij}). This is of the form $Y_{ij} = T_{ij} + C_{ij} + S_{ij} + I_{ij}$.[27]

The two methods parallel each other except that where the multiplicative approach uses multiplication and division, the additive method uses addition

[25] This approach to the replacement of extreme values is a modification of the method developed at the Bureau of Labor Statistics and employed in its computer program for time series decomposition and analysis called "The BLS Seasonal Factor Method" [28].

[26] Trading- or working-day variations should not be confused with "length-of-month" or "between-month" variation which refers to the variation in the total number of days in each month. This varies from month to month, but is constant from one year to the next, except for February which has a 4-year cycle.

[27] For a step-by-step description of the multiplicative and additive approaches in the X-11 to time series decomposition, see [24, pp. 7–20]. This is an excellent description and comparison for both clarity and organization.

and subtraction. In the isolation of a preliminary estimate of the seasonal-irregular curve, the additive method begins in the same way as the multiplicative approach—with a centered 12-month smoothing of the original series. This gives an estimate of the trend-cycle curve. This trend cycle is then *subtracted* from the original data, month by month, leaving $S_{ij} + I_{ij}$.

$$T_{ij} + C_{ij} + S_{ij} + I_{ij} - (T_{ij} + C_{ij}) = S_{ij} + I_{ij}$$

To isolate a preliminary series of S_{ij} factors in the multiplicative and additive approaches, a weighted smoothing is applied to each of the 12 columns of monthly data of the seasonal-irregular values. Whereas, in the former method, the S_{ij} factors isolated by this technique were adjusted to sum approximately to 12.0 for any 12-month period, in the additive approach they are adjusted to sum to zero for the same time span. This is accomplished in each method with a centered 12-term smoothing of the preliminary S_{ij} factors. In the multiplicative case, these smoothed seasonal values are divided into the preliminary S_{ij} factors. In the latter method, they are subtracted.

Both methods determine extreme I_{ij} values in the same manner [24, p. 9]. Then, similar adjustments are made to the seasonal-irregulars which were isolated by the first two steps just described to correct for extreme I_{ij} values. This adjusted set of seasonal-irregulars is resmoothed, column by column, to isolate a new set of preliminary monthly seasonal factors. This new series of S_{ij} values is readjusted as described so that they sum to approximately 12.0 in the multiplicative decomposition, or 0.0 in the additive method, for any 12-month period. To obtain an estimate of a preliminary seasonally adjusted series, these S_{ij} factors are subtracted from the original observations in the additive approach:

$$T_{ij} + C_{ij} + S_{ij} + I_{ij} - S_{ij} = T_{ij} + C_{ij} + I_{ij}$$

To eliminate the I_{ij}, both methods use the same technique, variable-span Henderson weighted moving averages, 9-, 13-, or 23-term depending on the level of the $\overline{I}/\overline{C}$ ratio. The irregular factor is isolated in the additive approach by subtracting the $T_{ij} + C_{ij}$ from the seasonally adjusted series.

$$T_{ij} + C_{ij} + I_{ij} - (T_{ij} + C_{ij}) = I_{ij}$$

The trading-day adjustment performed in the X-11 is available to both multiplicative and additive decompositions. The approaches are similar in that a least-squares estimate determines the seven daily coefficients. The difference is that the seven weights in the multiplicative model are established to sum to 7.0, and those in the additive model to sum to 0.0.

Once the seven daily weights are computed, the monthly trading-day adjustment factor in the multiplicative model is determined by

$$M_i = \frac{b_1 X_{1i} + b_2 X_{2i} + \ldots + b_7 X_{7i}}{N_i}$$

where M_i is the trading-day adjustment factor for month i

b_j is one of the seven daily weights; $j = 1, \ldots, 7$

X_{ji} is the number of times a day of the week appears in month i

N_i is the total number of days in month i

The weights of the first 28 days of the month sum to 28.0. Add to this the weights of the remaining days of the month and divide by the number of total days in the month to determine the trading-day adjustment factor M_i for a multiplicative adjustment.

If we assume $I_{ij} = I'_{ij} \times D_{ij}$ where D_{ij} is the trading-day adjustment factor for the ijth month and I'_{ij} is the residual, to adjust a series for trading-day variations in the multiplicative model, divide Y_{ij} by M_{ij}:

$$\frac{T_{ij} \times C_{ij} \times S_{ij} \times I'_{ij} \times D_{ij}}{M_{ij}} = T_{ij} \times C_{ij} \times S_{ij} \times I'_{ij}$$

This assumes that $M_{ij} = D_{ij}$. In other words, the estimate of the trading-day variation is "perfect."

The monthly trading-day adjustment factor for the additive approach is calculated in a similar manner. The absolute or additive adjustment has an advantage over the multiplicative approach. Specifically, there are no restrictions on the magnitude of the data, that is, a series may contain positive, negative, and zero observations. The multiplicative adjustment is operative on series with positive data only.[28]

Another difference is that each component in the additive model is in the same unit as the original series. If the data Y_{ij} are in dollars, T_{ij}, C_{ij}, S_{ij}, I'_{ij}, and D_{ij} are each in dollars. Consequently, adjustment factors from one series cannot be compared directly to those from another series unless both have the same unit.[29]

Summary Measures. In earlier versions of Census Method II, the average, without regard to sign, of the percentage changes of O (original); CI (seasonally adjusted); I (irregular); C (trend cycle); and S (seasonal) were computed for a one-month span. This gave a measure of the average monthly amplitude of each of the factors. The X-11 version expands this to include percentage changes without regard to sign for P (prior adjustment); TD (trading-day adjustment); and MCD (final seasonally adjusted series smoothed by a moving average, using the months for cyclical dominance (MCD) as the span), and gives these measures for one- to seven-month spans, nine-, eleven-, and twelve-month spans. This allows the analyst to see the magnitude of the average percentage change without regard to sign of the components over lengthening time spans.

In earlier versions of the Census method, ratios of the one-month span of the previously mentioned variables were provided. These gave the relative amplitude of one variable compared to another. The X-11 version has modified this table to give the "relative contributions of components to variance in original series." For the same assortment of monthly spans as in this table, the analyst can see the relative or percentage contribution of each component.

The $\overline{I}/\overline{C}$ ratio, that is, the average change in the irregular component compared to the average change in the trend cycle, which gives a measure of the

---

[28] A series with negative and/or zero data can often be transformed into a series with only positive data by summing or cumulating the series. This transform is accomplished by adding the first observation to the second to arrive at a transformed second point. Add this "new" second point to the third for a cumulative third observation, and so on. This will produce a final transformed observation which is the sum of the data from the original series. The disadvantage of employing this method before decomposing a series using the multiplicative model is that it "smooths" the series and the relative change from point to point is greatly reduced.

[29] If the additive adjustment must be used, or if it is felt to be more appropriate for other reasons, the analyst may transform the seasonal factors into relative terms (index numbers). A necessary condition for this transform is that the long-term trend (T_{ij}) has an upward or positive slope [17]. This transform may be useful if it is necessary to develop, compare, and use seasonal factors for many items where one or more have some zero or negative values.

number of months for the trend cycle to dominate the irregular, has been expanded in the X-11 to include spans from one to twelve months.

X-11 VARIANT OF THE SEASONAL ADJUSTMENT PROGRAM

Each series to be analyzed by this computer program must consist of a minimum of 36 consecutive monthly observations, with a maximum of 360 months or 30 years of data. Data can have as many as six places, with the decimal point falling at any desired position except to the left of the first of a six-place number.

Either the multiplicative or additive adjustment may be chosen for a specific series. In running the program, as many series of data as desired may be sequentially analyzed. For each series, either seasonal adjustment may be performed or only the summary measures developed from the inputted data. In the second case, it is assumed that the inputs are seasonally adjusted. The routine checks for residual or unadjusted-for seasonality and trading-day variations and develops the relevant summary measures.

Three different sets of printed tables can be requested—a "standard printout" of 17 to 27 tables per series, depending on the other chosen options; all the tables in the standard printout plus an additional dozen; and a "full printout" consisting of 44 to 59 tables. The full printout gives tables with data at each step of the adjustment. Three options are available also as to the charts produced for a series. The analyst may want to suppress the printing of the charts completely; obtain a set of "standard charts" consisting of the trend cycle and 12 seasonal factors; or receive "all charts," which include the former plus several others.

The next option is available with the multiplicative decomposition only. The analyst may provide seven daily weights for an a priori adjustment for trading-day variations, that is, before adjustment for seasonal and other variations. This option allows the analyst to quantify his subjective value judgment with reference to trading-day variations. An example of its use might be where a series to be adjusted consists of data developed from activity occurring only from Monday through Friday. Weights of 1.000 might be entered for the five weekdays and zero for the weekend. The program proportions the seven weights to sum to 7.000. Program output will provide t-tests for these exogenous weights combined with the weights derived by regression to determine if they are significantly different from weights of 1.000 or from the prior weights at the 1 percent level. This allows the analyst to determine the usefulness of the prior exogenous weights.

When a prior and/or endogenously developed trading-day adjustment is specified in the multiplicative routine, the length-of-month, that is, the number of days in the month regardless of what days they are, can be included as part of the seasonal factors or in the trading-day factors. If the length-of-month is included in the seasonal factors, the more commonly used option, "divisors used in the construction of monthly weights from daily weights are 31.0, 30.0, and 28.25 for 31- and 30-day months and February, respectively" [24, p. 51]. Notice the February weight is the "average" February weight, that is, $(3 \times 28 + 29)/4$. Therefore, the monthly trading-day adjustment factor for a non-leap year February is not 1.000 as might be expected, but 99.1; $(28.00/28.25)$. If the length-of-month is included as a part of the monthly trading-day factors, 30.4375 is used as the divisor for all months.

The next option has to do with the trading-day adjustment itself. It can be excluded entirely from the analysis; developed and printed but not used to adjust the series; developed, printed, and always used as an adjustment factor; or developed, printed, and used in the first iteration, but not in the second unless it explains a significant variation on the basis of an F-test. The last of these is most powerful because the routine makes the value judgment based on the statistical significance of the trading-day adjustment.

If the analyst chooses one of the options which produces the trading-day adjustment factors, a further option is available as to the starting date of the data used for computing these factors. A multiple-regression technique based on the irregular factors is employed in computing the trading-day adjustment. This technique develops coefficients which represent the "center of gravity" of the data, that is, coefficients which minimize the sum of squares of the actual from the theoretical data. If, as is not uncommon, trading-day variations in a series evolve over the time span of the data, the trading-day adjustments will represent the "best average" adjustments. However, are we most interested in this "best average" adjustment? Quite often not, because we live "at the margin," not "at the average." If it is judged most important to have the "best" adjustment for the forecasted year,[30] it might be advisable to *not* use the first few years of data for this calculation. Normally, 8 to 10 years are sufficient for developing trading-day factors that are reliable. If 15 or more years of data are available, it is advisable to calculate one adjustment using all data and one using only the last 10 years. If there is a significant difference, the analyst must make some value judgment decisions.

When the trading-day adjustment option is chosen, the analyst can specify a "sigma limit for excluding extreme (irregular) values" from the computation. If no value is specified, the program has the default option of excluding irregular values beyond a standard deviation of 2.5. This sigma limit is usually adequate for removing undue influences upon the computation by "extreme" irregular variations. If the data are highly irregular, the analyst may wish to use a sigma value less than 2.5. This would eliminate more data from the trading-day analysis. If, on the other hand, the data are relatively free from irregular fluctuations, a value greater than 2.5 may be desirable. On the initial pass of a series through the program, it is probably best to use the default option.

If the analyst thinks necessary, he can introduce an exogenous adjustment factor for each month of data of a series. This option might be used to adjust for a specific event, such as Easter or extreme weather, which "distorted" one or more months of data in a series. However, it is difficult, if not impossible, to know what effect an a priori adjustment will have on the subsequent analysis. In the multiplicative adjustment, these factors are divided into the original data. They are subtracted from the data in the additive adjustment.

In the multiplicative routine, the adjustment factors are stated as percentages. The analyst enters a figure which he believes represents the percentage of original observation to "what it should have been." That is, if it is thought that exceptionally bad weather in a particular month reduced activity 5 percent, then 95 would be entered. If activity increased 5 percent in a specific month by some ad hoc factor, then 105 would be used as the adjustment.

The adjustment factors for each calendar year must average 100. If they do not, "then the level of the prior adjusted series will be different from that of the original series for that year [27]." Also, the factors must average 100 for each calendar month. Otherwise they will contain seasonal variations which will

---

[30] The program projects the monthly trading-day adjustment and seasonal factors 12 periods (months) into the future.

show up in the final seasonal factors developed by the X-11 program. In the additive model, these adjustment factors should average 0.0 for each calendar year and each calendar month for the reasons just described.

The next option available to the user allows the specification of the sigma limits for graduating the weights of extreme irregular values. If the default option is used (no limits specified explicitly), the program automatically gives full weight (1.0) to those values which fall within 1.5 standard deviations (lower limit) from 1.0 in the multiplicative program or 0.0 in the additive version. Irregular values beyond the upper limit (the default upper limit is 2.5 sigmas) are given a weight of 0.0. Irregular values falling between these two limits are assigned linearly declining weights from 1.0 to 0.0. The analyst has the option of overriding either one or both of these limits with values from 0.1 to 9.9.

In practice, this option should be explicitly used only when the data under analysis are felt to be exceptionally irregular or exceptionally smooth. In the former (highly irregular), the limits might be lowered so that more values farther from the mean would be reduced in importance. In the latter case, the limits might be raised so the influence of fewer values are reduced in the development of seasonal and trend-cycle components.

In general, it takes much experience and insight to use this and other options to their best advantage. The early runs of a series should, in most cases, be analyzed using the default options, with the exception of the trading-day analysis.

The next option allows the analyst to specify for each month the smoothing that the program will employ when isolating the seasonal factor from the seasonal-irregular component. The default option employs a 3×3 moving average for the first estimate in each part and a 3×5 smoothing for the second estimate. If a specific smoothing is chosen to override the default for a given month, it is used for both the first and second estimates. Available smoothings are a 3-, 3×3-, 3×5-, or 3×9-term and average of all values for the month (for a stable seasonal factor).

The analyst can select a 9-, 13-, or 23-term Henderson weighted smoothing for isolating the irregular component from the seasonally adjusted series. The default option is to allow the program to select on the basis of a preliminary relationship between the irregular and trend-cycle component ($\bar{I}/\bar{C}$). In general, the greater the relative irregularity, the more smoothing power needed. This is automatic with the default option. Therefore, this option should be used only if the analyst wants to apply one of the Henderson smoothings.

The final option permits the analyst to perform a special adjustment of a preliminary estimate of the seasonally adjusted series to correct for extremes produced by prolonged strikes or other similar, irregular, ad hoc occurrences. This adjustment is designed to reduce the effect of these major distorting influences, but it might influence also the peaks or troughs of dynamic business cycles.

CASE STUDY: A MONTHLY TIME SERIES

Chosen for analysis are data for the time series on Retail Sales, Nondurable Goods Stores, Total. Figure 6, the first page of computer printout from Census Method II, X-11, identifies the series and the options chosen. Table 1 is a printout of the original time series data to be analyzed. A cursory look shows one feature clearly, that is, the growth of retail sales in nondurable goods

```
                    X-11 SEASONAL ADJUSTMENT PROGRAM
                       U. S. BUREAU OF THE CENSUS
                  ECONOMIC RESEARCH AND ANALYSIS DIVISIO
                          NOVEMBER 1, 1968

THE X-11 PROGRAM IS DIVIDED INTO SEVEN MAJOR PARTS-
     PART     DESCRIPTION
     A.  PRIOR ADJUSTMENTS, IF ANY
     B.  PRELIMINARY ESTIMATES OF IRREGULAR COMPONENT WEIGHTS
         AND REGRESSION TRADING DAY FACTORS
     C.  FINAL ESTIMATES OF ABOVE
     D.  FINAL ESTIMATES OF SEASONAL, TREND-CYCLE AND IRREGULAR COMPONENTS
     E.  ANALYTICAL TABLES
     F.  SUMMARY MEASURES
     G.  CHARTS
TABLES ARE IDENTIFIED BY THEIR PART LETTER AND SEQUENCE WITHIN THE PART. A GIVEN TABLE HAS THE SAME
IDENTIFICATION IN THE STANDARD, LONG AND FULL PRINTOUTS. THE SAME NUMBER IS GIVEN TO CORRESPONDING
TABLES IN PARTS B, C AND D. THUS, TABLES B10., C10. AND D10. ARE ALL TABLES OF SEASONAL FACTORS.
WHERE NO CORRESPONDING TABLE EXISTS THE SEQUENCE NO. IS NOT USED IN THE PART. THUS, BB. AND DB. ARE
TABLES OF UNMODIFIED SI RATIOS BUT THERE IS NO CB.

                              THIS SERIES RUN OCTOBER 1969
SERIES TITLE-  RETAIL SALES, NONDURABLE GOODS STORES, TOTAL (BILLIONS OF DOLLARS)   SERIES NO. RSNG
                     PERIOD COVERED-  1/47 TO  6/69
               TYPE OF RUN - MULTIPLICATIVE SEASONAL ADJUSTMENT.
                     STANDARD PRINTOUT. STANDARD CHARTS.
TRADING DAY REGRESSION COMPUTED STARTING 1947 EXCLUDING IRREGULAR VALUES OUTSIDE 2.5-SIGMA LIMITS.
          TRADING DAY REGRESSION ESTIMATES APPLIED STARTING 1947 IF SIGNIFICANT.
          SIGMA LIMITS FOR GRADUATING EXTREME VALUES ARE 1.5 AND 2.5
```

Fig. 6. X-11 seasonal adjustment computer program; identification and options chosen.

stores during the 20-plus years since 1947. The last column on the right, titled TOT (total), shows that not since 1949 have sales for a full year been less than the previous year.

Note that data for the first six months of 1969 are less than half those for the full year 1968. A month-by-month check of these six months reveals that in each month, the 1969 sales are greater than those in the previous year. This would indicate that more sales are made in the second half of the year than in the first half. The seasonal factors isolated from these data should show this phenomenon. Further supporting evidence may be seen in the next-to-bottom row of the printout, labeled AVGE (average). The first half of the year has averaged 47.8 percent of the annual retail sales of nondurable goods stores since 1947.

The Trading-Day Adjustment

The first component isolated in its final form is the trading-day adjustment. Table 2 contains the daily (combined) weights developed through the trading-

TABLE 1   Retail Sales, Nondurable Goods Stores, Total Original Series

```
           OCTOBER 1969 RETAIL SALES, NONDURABLE GOODS STORES      (BILLIONS OF DOLLARS)   P. 1, SERIES RSNG
B 1. ORIGINAL SERIES
  YEAR   JAN     FEB     MAR     APR     MAY     JUN     JUL     AUG     SEP     OCT     NOV     DEC       TOT
  1947  6.124   5.774   6.830   6.800   7.187   6.727   6.644   6.981   7.236   7.658   7.634   9.269    84.864
  1948  6.953   6.381   7.515   7.316   7.523   7.440   7.344   7.188   7.658   8.106   7.727   9.580    90.731
  1949  6.794   6.361   7.255   7.679   7.243   7.222   6.891   7.040   7.534   7.592   7.603   9.586    88.800
  1950  6.571   6.337   7.434   7.417   7.536   7.529   7.671   7.843   8.118   7.931   8.115   10.436   92.938
  1951  7.874   7.361   8.656   7.938   8.370   8.406   7.936   8.394   8.473   8.969   9.008   10.684  102.069
  1952  7.910   7.749   8.450   8.674   8.981   8.560   8.622   8.892   8.811   9.552   9.340   11.542  107.083
  1953  8.453   7.841   8.838   8.877   9.120   8.962   8.872   8.856   8.949   9.500   9.086   11.370  108.724
  1954  8.352   7.878   8.641   9.234   9.096   9.075   9.237   8.885   9.170   9.685   9.615   12.124  110.962
  1955  8.665   8.139   9.142   9.785   9.488   9.475   9.541   9.501   9.465   10.121  10.212  12.938  116.872
  1956  9.037   8.776   10.298  9.537   10.311  10.526  9.809   10.448  10.352  10.614  11.002  13.208  123.918
  1957  9.769   9.144   10.243  10.678  11.022  10.840  10.815  11.510  10.776  11.355  11.631  13.868  131.651
  1958  10.483  9.502   10.698  11.012  11.737  11.013  11.153  11.639  11.246  11.981  11.696  14.784  136.944
  1959  11.106  10.034  11.360  11.381  12.168  11.886  11.917  11.820  11.868  12.682  12.141  15.442  143.805
  1960  11.238  10.620  11.613  12.859  12.163  12.315  12.306  12.215  12.303  12.654  12.593  16.090  148.969
  1961  11.171  10.595  12.474  11.991  12.535  12.709  12.294  12.629  12.791  12.734  13.156  16.611  151.690
  1962  11.845  11.074  12.918  12.980  13.417  13.496  12.827  13.621  13.284  13.606  14.198  17.403  160.669
  1963  12.581  11.669  13.296  13.554  14.016  13.727  13.592  14.499  13.307  13.965  14.560  17.973  166.739
  1964  13.167  12.680  13.811  13.882  14.873  14.587  14.808  14.833  14.487  15.547  14.979  19.623  177.277
  1965  13.962  12.987  14.261  15.525  15.660  15.448  16.047  15.525  15.634  16.637  16.751  21.505  189.942
  1966  15.084  14.248  16.090  17.088  16.677  17.157  17.150  17.097  17.188  17.281  17.730  22.865  205.655
  1967  15.533  14.832  17.428  16.859  17.611  18.200  17.441  17.887  18.023  17.379  20.558  24.411  213.636
  1968  16.577  16.327  18.133  18.468  19.368  19.059  18.846  20.027  18.312  19.379  20.558  24.411  229.465
  1969  17.902  16.599  18.733  19.072  20.553  19.418  ******  ******  ******  ******  ******  ******  112.277

  AVGE  10.746  10.126  11.483  11.679  12.028  11.903  11.444  11.695  11.608  12.051  12.182  15.223
        TABLE TOTAL- 3195.652          MEAN- 11.836          STD. DEVIATION-  3.838
```

day regression; a t-test for each; an F-test for the regression; and other statistical data.

The second column contains the "prior weight[s]," in this case assumed to be 1.000 for each day because no exogenous weights were introduced. Column (1), the combined weights, is the sum of columns (2) and (3). These are the daily weights which are used to develop monthly trading-day adjustment factors. Column (5) contains t factors for the combined weights indicating whether a significant difference from 1.000 exists for each. Column (6) contains t factors for the combined weights indicating whether a significant difference exists from the prior weights for each. Since the prior weights in this example are all assumed to be 1.000, columns (5) and (6) are the same.

The interpretation of t determines whether a daily weight is significantly different from a specified value. If it differs significantly from that value, in this case 1.000, we can conclude that its use will, in fact, adjust for trading-day

TABLE 2   Retail Sales, Nondurable Goods Stores, Total Final Trading-Day Regression

```
              OCTOBER 1969 RETAIL SALES, NONDURABLE GOODS STORES      (BILLIONS OF DOLLARS)    P. 3, SERIES RSNG
  C15.  FINAL   TRADING DAY REGRESSION
                 COMBINED       PRIOR      REGRESSION    ST.ERROR         T             T
                  WEIGHT        WEIGHT       COEFF.     (COMB.WT.)        (1)        (PRIOR WT.)
       MONDAY     0.868         1.000        -0.132       0.033        -4.033*        -4.033**
       TUESDAY    1.006         1.000         0.006       0.033         0.173          0.173
       WEDNESDAY  0.841         1.000        -0.159       0.033        -4.813*        -4.813**
       THURSDAY   1.069         1.000         0.069       0.033         2.124          2.124
       FRIDAY     1.363         1.000         0.363       0.033        10.997*        10.997**
       SATURDAY   1.408         1.000         0.408       0.033        12.225*        12.225**
       SUNDAY     0.445         1.000        -0.555       0.033       -16.688*       -16.688**
                *   COMBINED WT. SIGNIFICANTLY DIFFERENT FROM 1 AT 1 PER CENT LEVEL
                **  COMBINED WT. SIGNIFICANTLY DIFFERENT FROM PRIOR WEIGHT AT 1 PER CENT LEVEL

                SOURCE OF       SUM OF      DGRS.OF        MEAN
                VARIANCE       SQUARES      FREEDOM       SQUARE         F

                REGRESSION      45.645        6.          7.608      212.473***
                ERROR            8.701      243.           0.036
                TOTAL           54.346      249.
                *** RESIDUAL TRADING DAY VARIATION PRESENT AT THE 1 PER CENT LEVEL

       STANDARD ERRORS OF TRADING DAY ADJUSTMENT FACTORS DERIVED FROM REGRESSION COEFFICIENTS
                31-DAY MONTHS-       0.10
                30-DAY MONTHS-       0.11
                29-DAY MONTHS-       0.11
                28-DAY MONTHS-        .00
```

variations. An F-test determines the significance level of the regression. The program has a built-in table of significance levels for the t- and F-tests.[31] "If the computed t-ratios are greater than the tabled 1 percent level . . . messages of significance are printed. . . . If the computed F-ratio is greater than the tabled 1 percent level . . . a message that significant trading-day variation is present is printed [24, p. 12]." Five of the seven t-ratios and the F-ratio in Table 2 are judged to be significant and are marked with asterisks.

Table 3 presents the monthly adjustment factors and the daily weights developed from the regression coefficients. The daily weights have been forced to sum to 7.000 by adding 1.000 to each. These adjusted coefficients are printed as C16A. The seven daily weights will always sum to 7.000 by design because, over the span of seven consecutive days, the trading-day variations (and therefore the adjustment) by definition will cancel itself.

To develop a monthly adjustment factor from the daily weights, sum them for the days in the month and divide by the total number of days in the month. The adjustment factor estimated for March 1970, for instance, shown as 97.8 in Table 3, is calculated as follows:

[31] For a table of t- and F-ratios at the 5 and 1 percent confidence levels, see [16, p. 50]. For an extensive discussion of estimating trading-day variations, see [23].

28.000	sum of the weights for the first 28 days of the month
0.445	29th day, a Sunday
0.868	30th day, a Monday
1.006	31st day, a Tuesday
30.319	

$$\frac{30.319}{31} = 0.978$$

The forecasted trading-day adjustment factors one year ahead are for adjusting data available subsequent to the computer analysis. These newly adjusted data can be compared to the adjusted historical data more easily because short-

TABLE 3   Retail Sales, Nondurable Goods Stores, Total Trading-Day Adjustment Factors Derived from Regression Coefficients

```
              OCTOBER 1969 RETAIL SALES, NONDURABLE GOODS STORES      (BILLIONS OF DOLLARS)   P. 4, SERIES RSNG
C16. TRADING DAY ADJUSTMENT FACTORS DERIVED FROM REGRESSION COEFFICIENTS
C16A. REGRESSION COEFFICIENTS - MON     TUE      WED     THUR     FRI      SAT      SUN
                              0.868    1.006    0.841    1.069    1.363    1.408    0.445
C16B. REGRESSION TRADING DAY ADJUSTMENT FACTORS
  YEAR    JAN    FEB    MAR    APR    MAY    JUN    JUL    AUG    SEP    OCT    NOV    DEC    AVGE
  1947   100.9   99.1   99.1   99.5  102.7   97.7   99.7  100.7   99.6  100.9   99.5   99.1   99.9
  1948   102.7  100.7   99.1  101.4   99.1   99.5  102.7   97.8   99.7  100.7   99.6  100.9  100.3
  1949    99.1   99.1   99.1  102.6   97.8   99.7  100.7   99.1  101.4   99.1   99.5  102.7  100.0
  1950    97.8   99.1  100.9   99.5   99.1  101.4   99.1   99.7  102.6   97.8   99.7  100.7   99.8
  1951    99.1   99.1  102.7   97.7   99.7  102.6   97.8  100.9   99.5   99.1  101.4   99.1   99.9
  1952    99.7  103.9   99.1   99.5  102.7   97.7   99.7  100.7   99.6  100.9   99.5   99.1  100.2
  1953   102.7   99.1   97.8   99.7  100.7   99.6  100.9   99.1   99.5  102.7   97.7   99.7   99.9
  1954   100.7   99.1   99.1  101.4   99.1   99.5  102.7   97.8   99.7  100.7   99.6  100.9  100.0
  1955    99.1   99.1   99.7  102.6   97.8   99.7  100.7   99.1  101.4   99.1   99.5  102.7  100.0
  1956    97.8  102.1  102.7   97.7   99.7  102.6   97.8  100.9   99.5   99.1  101.4   99.1  100.0
  1957    99.7   99.1  100.7   99.6  100.9   99.5   99.1  102.7   97.7   99.7  102.6   97.8   99.9
  1958   100.9   99.1   99.1   99.5  102.7   97.7   99.7  100.7   99.6  100.9   99.5   99.1   99.9
  1959   102.7   99.1   97.8   99.7  100.7   99.6  100.9   99.1   99.5  102.7   97.7   99.7   99.9
  1960   100.7  102.2   99.7  102.6   97.8   99.7  100.7   99.1  101.4   99.1   99.5  102.7  100.4
  1961    97.8   99.1  100.9   99.5   99.1  101.4   99.1   99.7  102.6   97.8   99.7  100.7   99.8
  1962    99.1   99.1  102.7   97.7   99.7  102.6   97.8  100.9   99.5   99.1  101.4   99.1   99.9
  1963    99.7   99.1  100.7   99.6  100.9   99.5   99.1  102.7   97.7   99.7  102.6   97.8   99.9
  1964   100.9  104.1   97.8   99.7  100.7   99.6  100.9   99.1   99.5  102.7   97.7   99.7  100.2
  1965   100.7   99.1   99.7  101.4   99.1   99.5  102.7   97.8   99.7  100.7   99.6  100.9  100.0
  1966    99.1   99.1   99.7  102.6   97.8   99.7  100.7   99.1  101.4   99.1   99.5  102.7  100.0
  1967    97.8   99.1   99.1  100.9   99.7  101.4   99.1   99.7  102.6   97.8   99.7  100.7   99.8
  1968    99.1  102.9  100.7   99.6  100.9   99.5   99.1  102.7   97.7   99.7  102.6   97.8  100.2
  1969   100.9   99.1   99.1   99.5  102.7   97.7 ****** ****** ****** ****** ****** ******   99.8

           TABLE TOTAL-   27000.4
C16C. REGRESSION TRADING DAY ADJUSTMENT FACTORS, ONE YEAR AHEAD
  YEAR    JAN    FEB    MAR    APR    MAY    JUN    JUL    AUG    SEP    OCT    NOV    DEC    AVGE
  1969 ****** ****** ****** ****** ****** ******   99.7  100.7   99.6  100.9   99.5   99.1   99.9
  1970  102.7   99.1   97.8   99.7  100.7   99.6 ****** ****** ****** ****** ****** ******   99.9
```

term movements would be removed and underlying, longer-term cyclical movements would be more easily discerned. If more than 12 months' projection of the trading-day factors is desired, it is a simple matter to use the method just described either by hand or by extension of the X-11 computer program.

If prior trading-day adjustment factors had been used in our example, another table similar to Table 3 would be printed by the program. It would contain the trading-day adjustment factors developed from the combined weights, that is, those introduced exogenously added to those developed by the regression analysis. This table would be labeled by the program as C18.

Table 4 shows the original data after adjustment by these trading-day factors. To arrive at the adjusted observation for January 1947, for instance:

$$\frac{T_{ij} \times C_{ij} \times S_{ij} \times TD_{ij} \times I'_{ij}}{TD_{ij}} = T_{ij} \times C_{ij} \times S_{ij} \times I'_{ij}$$

$$I_{ij} = TD_{ij} \times I'_{ij}$$

$$i = 47 \qquad j = 1$$

$$\frac{6.124}{1.009} = 6.070$$

TABLE 4 Retail Sales, Nondurable Goods Stores, Total Adjusted Original Series (Adjusted by Trading-Day Adjustment Factors)

```
                 OCTOBER 1969 RETAIL SALES, NONDURABLE GOODS STORES          (BILLIONS OF DOLLARS)    P. 7, SERIES RSNG
C19.      ADJUSTED* ORIGINAL SERIES
         *ADJUSTED BY...TRADING DAY ADJUSTMENT FACTORS DERIVED FROM REGRESSION COEFFICIENTS
   YEAR     JAN     FEB     MAR     APR     MAY     JUN     JUL     AUG     SEP     OCT     NOV     DEC        TOT
   1947    6.070   5.826   6.892   6.835   6.997   6.885   6.662   6.933   7.267   7.591   7.672   9.355      84.984
   1948    6.769   6.337   7.585   7.212   7.591   7.478   7.150   7.350   7.681   8.050   7.760   9.496      90.460
   1949    6.856   6.418   7.275   7.487   7.406   7.244   6.843   7.106   7.427   7.661   7.642   9.333      88.696
   1950    6.719   6.394   7.369   7.453   7.606   7.422   7.741   7.864   7.915   8.109   8.139  10.364      93.095
   1951    7.997   7.427   8.427   8.124   8.393   8.195   8.114   8.321   8.515   9.052   8.880  10.781     102.177
   1952    7.932   7.455   8.527   8.719   8.744   8.761   8.645   8.830   8.848   9.469   9.386  11.649     106.965
   1953    8.230   7.911   9.037   8.904   9.057   9.000   8.794   8.936   8.995   9.249   9.299  11.401     108.813
   1954    8.294   7.948   8.721   9.103   9.179   9.122   8.993   9.054   9.198   9.618   9.656  12.018     110.903
   1955    8.744   8.212   9.167   9.540   9.701   9.504   9.475   9.589   9.725  10.213  10.265  12.596     116.730
   1956    9.240   8.596  10.026   9.761  10.339  10.262  10.029  10.357  10.403  10.713  10.846  13.328     123.900
   1957    9.796   9.226  10.172  10.723  10.926  10.893  10.916  11.206  11.029  11.386  11.339  14.180     131.791
   1958   10.391   9.587  10.795  11.059  11.427  11.271  11.183  11.558  11.294  11.876  11.753  14.922     137.127
   1959   10.813  10.124  11.615  11.415  12.084  11.936  11.813  11.927  11.929  12.347  12.426  15.484     143.913
   1960   11.160  10.393  11.645  12.537  12.436  12.352  12.221  12.329  12.128  12.769  12.658  15.665     148.292
   1961   11.422  10.690  12.365  12.050  12.652  12.528  12.406  12.663  12.470  13.020  13.196  16.496     151.958
   1962   11.955  11.173  12.577  13.284  13.454  13.158  13.115  13.502  13.349  13.733  13.996  17.561     160.857
   1963   12.615  11.773  13.204  13.611  13.894  13.794  13.719  14.116  13.619  14.003  14.195  18.377     166.920
   1964   13.052  12.181  14.121  13.924  14.770  14.649  14.679  14.968  14.562  15.136  15.330  19.676     177.047
   1965   13.865  13.103  14.394  15.304  15.802  15.528  15.623  15.874  15.681  16.522  16.822  21.317     189.835
   1966   15.221  14.375  16.134  16.660  17.052  17.209  17.031  17.256  16.944  17.438  17.821  22.261     205.401
   1967   15.882  14.966  17.276  16.942  17.775  17.941  17.599  17.936  17.571  17.960  18.717  23.426     213.996
   1968   16.731  15.867  18.007  18.546  19.199  19.153  19.021  19.498  18.741  19.432  20.043  24.960     229.198
   1969   17.746  16.747  18.903  19.170  20.010  19.873 *******  ******* ******* ******* ******* *******    112.450

  AVGE   10.759  10.118  11.488  11.668  12.021  11.920  11.444  11.690  11.604  12.061  12.175  15.211
            TABLE TOTAL-  3195.478         MEAN-   11.835              STD. DEVIATION-    3.832
```

TD_{ij} is the trading-day variation and I'_{ij} the residual irregular. Since this is a multiplicative adjustment, the factors are divided into the original data to correct for a variation. In the additive model, the adjustments would be subtracted.[32]

The Seasonal Adjustment

The second component to be isolated in its final form is the seasonal factor. Table 5 shows the computer output of these data, printed after being multiplied by 100.0 so that variations from 100.0 can be thought of in percentage terms. A seasonal factor of 100.0 indicates no effect by the factor for the specified period (month). A monthly adjustment factor greater than 100.0 indicates a positive influence by the factor for the period, that is, the level of activity for the specified period, because of the factor's influence, is somewhat higher than it would have been if the factor were 100.0.

TABLE 5 Retail Sales, Nondurable Goods Stores, Total Final Seasonal Factors

```
                 OCTOBER 1969 RETAIL SALES, NONDURABLE GOODS STORES          (BILLIONS OF DOLLARS)    P.10, SERIES RSNG
D10.  FINAL    SEASONAL FACTORS
   YEAR     JAN     FEB     MAR     APR     MAY     JUN     JUL     AUG     SEP     OCT     NOV     DEC       AVGE
   1947    90.8    85.5    99.5    98.1   100.1    98.1    94.4    97.4   100.9   105.0   103.4   126.5     100.0
   1948    90.9    85.7    99.5    98.1   100.1    98.0    94.6    97.5   100.7   105.0   103.3   126.4     100.0
   1949    91.1    85.9    99.3    98.2    99.9    97.9    95.0    97.7   100.4   105.0   103.1   126.5     100.0
   1950    91.4    86.2    98.8    98.2    99.7    97.9    95.4    97.9   100.0   104.8   103.0   126.6     100.0
   1951    91.4    86.4    98.3    98.5    99.6    98.0    96.0    98.2    99.6   104.5   102.9   126.5     100.0
   1952    91.5    86.6    97.7    98.7    99.6    98.2    96.5    98.3    99.3   104.1   103.0   126.6     100.0
   1953    91.6    86.6    97.1    98.8    99.8    98.5    96.9    98.4    99.1   103.7   103.0   126.6     100.0
   1954    91.7    86.5    96.5    98.9   100.0    98.8    97.2    98.6    99.1   103.3   103.0   126.6     100.0
   1955    91.9    86.3    95.9    98.9   100.2    99.0    97.4    99.0    99.1   103.2   102.8   126.7     100.0
   1956    92.0    86.1    95.7    98.7   100.5    99.1    97.7    99.4    99.0   102.6   102.5   126.7     100.0
   1957    92.1    85.9    95.7    98.5   100.7    99.2    97.9    99.7    99.0   102.5   102.3   126.8     100.0
   1958    92.1    85.7    95.8    98.1   100.8    99.4    98.2    99.9    99.7   102.3   102.1   126.9     100.0
   1959    92.1    85.6    95.9    97.8   100.9    99.5    98.3   100.0    98.5   102.1   102.1   127.1     100.0
   1960    92.0    85.6    96.1    97.7   101.0    99.5    98.4   100.0    98.3   101.9   102.2   127.4     100.0
   1961    91.9    85.5    96.1    97.8   101.1    99.5    98.4   100.0    98.1   101.5   102.3   127.9     100.0
   1962    91.8    85.5    96.1    98.0   101.0    99.4    98.5   100.0    97.9   101.1   102.3   128.3     100.0
   1963    91.7    85.6    96.0    98.2   101.0    99.4    98.6   100.1    97.8   100.8   102.3   128.7     100.0
   1964    91.5    85.5    95.9    98.3   100.9    99.5    98.7   100.1    97.7   100.5   102.4   129.0     100.0
   1965    91.4    85.5    95.9    98.4   100.8    99.8    98.8   100.1    97.7   100.4   102.5   129.0     100.0
   1966    91.2    85.5    95.9    98.3   100.7   100.0    98.9   100.2    97.7   100.2   102.6   128.8     100.0
   1967    91.0    85.5    96.0    98.2   100.7    99.9   100.0    98.9   100.1    97.7   100.1   102.7   128.7     100.0
   1968    90.9    85.5    96.1    98.1   100.7   100.6    98.9   100.1    97.7   100.0   102.8   128.5     100.0
   1969    90.9    85.5    96.1    98.0   100.6   100.6 *******  ******* ******* ******* ******* *******     95.3

            TABLE TOTAL-  26971.4           MEAN-    99.9              STD. DEVIATION-    9.4
D10A.  SEASONAL FACTORS, ONE YEAR AHEAD
   YEAR     JAN     FEB     MAR     APR     MAY     JUN     JUL     AUG     SEP     OCT     NOV     DEC       AVGE
   1969  ******* ******* ******* ******* ******* *******    98.9   100.1    97.7   100.0   102.8   128.5     104.7
   1970    90.9    85.5    96.1    98.0   100.6   100.8 *******  ******* ******* ******* ******* *******     95.3
```

[32] For discussion and another example of using trading-day adjustments, see [16], pp. 41–72].

By definition, the seasonal factors tend to cancel over a 12-month period, since the method of decomposition employed by the X-11 computer program allows for a monthly seasonal factor to change slowly over time. If a set of stable seasonal factors were employed, that is, if each month's adjustment factor remains constant over time, any 12 consecutive monthly factors would cancel themselves exactly. This would be accomplished by proportioning the 12 factors to sum to 1,200.0, making the average adjustment for any 12-month period 100.0. Table 5 shows the "evolving seasonal." October 1947, for example, has an adjustment factor of 105.0. This changes gradually over the 22 years to 100.0 in 1968 and is forecasted to remain the same in 1969.

The number of days in a month varies from 28 to 31. Each month, excluding February, always has the same number of days. Other things equal, we would assume that activity in a 31-day month would be greater than in a 30- or 28-day month. The X-11 computer program has the option of including the adjustment for length-of-month in either the seasonal or trading-day factor. Usually the length-of-month is left as part of the seasonal adjustment and the program has this as the default option. We have used this default option in the analysis; consequently, the length-of-month is taken into account in the seasonal factors. This, no doubt, is an important reason why February is the poorest month for retail sales of nondurable goods stores, as indicated by the seasonal factors in Table 5. There are other reasons, such as the generally poorer weather for shopping in February than in other months, and January's traditionally being a month for post-Christmas sales of nondurable goods. However, February's having an average 10 percent fewer shopping days is certainly significant.

The strong influence of seasonal variations can be seen with the large factor for December (Table 5), preceded by a considerably smaller adjustment in November and followed by a still smaller adjustment in January. Clearly, the Christmas shopping season gives a dynamic thrust to nondurable retail sales in December.

The Seasonally Adjusted Series

With the isolation of the final seasonal adjustment factors, it is possible to develop a time series which is the original series adjusted for trading-day and seasonal variations. To obtain a final seasonally adjusted series, the program divides each adjusted monthly observation in Table 4 by the corresponding seasonal adjustment factor in Table 5, producing the data in Table 6.

$$\frac{T_{ij} \times C_{ij} \times S_{ij} \times I'_{ij}}{S_{ij}} = T_{ij} \times C_{ij} \times I'_{ij}$$

Figure 7 pictures the final seasonally adjusted series (Table 6) and the original data (Table 1). The annual pattern of lower sales in the first three months of the year, followed by slight seasonal influences for the next eight, and ending with a very strong December becomes clear. Minor variations from this pattern caused by irregular movements can be observed. With removal of these trading-day and seasonal fluctuations, the underlying trend-cycle movements become more apparent. This is the objective: to observe cyclical behavior and long-term growth or decay of economic activity. Two or more series may have highly related cyclical activity. If their respective seasonal and trading-day patterns are dissimilar and if these components are not removed, it may be difficult to uncover the important relationships among the data.

To adjust a month's data which develop after the X-11 run, multiply the

TABLE 6   Retail Sales, Nondurable Goods Stores, Total Final Seasonally Adjusted Series

OCTOBER 1969 RETAIL SALES, NONDURABLE GOODS STORES   (BILLIONS OF DOLLARS)   P.11, SERIES RSNG

D11. FINAL SEASONALLY ADJUSTED SERIES

YEAR	JAN	FEB	MAR	APR	MAY	JUN	JUL	AUG	SEP	OCT	NOV	DEC	TOT
1947	6.685	6.812	6.927	6.968	6.987	7.016	7.056	7.120	7.201	7.232	7.419	7.397	84.820
1948	7.446	7.393	7.624	7.350	7.586	7.631	7.559	7.538	7.624	7.669	7.513	7.514	90.446
1949	7.525	7.469	7.326	7.625	7.412	7.397	7.207	7.270	7.396	7.294	7.411	7.381	88.712
1950	7.367	7.419	7.455	7.586	7.627	7.580	8.115	8.030	7.912	7.737	7.900	8.200	92.928
1951	8.696	8.592	8.572	8.251	8.426	8.359	8.456	8.473	8.551	8.663	8.631	8.522	102.190
1952	8.670	8.606	8.725	8.838	8.777	8.921	8.962	8.984	8.912	9.095	9.113	9.205	106.808
1953	8.985	9.140	9.305	9.011	9.078	9.138	9.079	9.084	9.077	9.918	9.025	9.003	108.843
1954	9.042	9.193	9.042	9.207	9.179	9.235	9.256	9.187	9.278	9.314	9.370	9.493	110.796
1955	9.516	9.521	9.558	9.646	9.678	9.601	9.724	9.688	9.814	9.930	9.987	9.945	116.608
1956	10.041	9.984	10.481	9.889	10.290	10.359	10.264	10.420	10.503	10.440	10.580	10.522	123.772
1957	10.634	10.745	10.634	10.892	10.855	10.978	11.145	11.237	11.155	11.111	11.086	11.186	131.657
1958	11.283	11.183	11.272	11.283	11.339	11.339	11.390	11.566	11.445	11.607	11.506	11.759	136.973
1959	11.746	11.825	12.107	11.666	11.973	11.994	12.016	11.927	12.116	12.088	12.170	12.182	143.808
1960	12.130	12.143	12.123	12.828	12.309	12.409	12.418	12.334	12.340	12.536	12.386	12.291	148.246
1961	12.427	12.501	12.863	12.321	12.517	12.589	12.603	12.667	12.711	12.825	12.902	12.902	151.827
1962	13.024	13.066	13.087	13.559	13.315	13.232	13.312	13.498	13.631	13.578	13.678	13.683	160.663
1963	13.760	13.775	13.750	13.862	13.761	13.879	13.912	14.099	13.926	13.887	13.875	14.275	166.760
1964	14.259	14.249	14.719	14.161	14.644	14.718	14.869	14.948	14.902	15.056	14.974	15.256	176.755
1965	15.178	15.333	15.006	15.557	15.685	15.564	15.807	15.851	16.055	16.463	16.419	16.527	189.447
1966	16.698	16.819	16.818	16.952	16.939	17.204	17.212	17.227	17.346	17.398	17.368	17.227	205.259
1967	17.447	17.499	17.992	17.250	17.647	17.871	17.799	17.916	17.992	17.948	18.228	18.208	213.798
1968	18.397	18.548	18.745	18.904	19.066	19.032	19.238	19.477	19.184	19.427	19.505	19.417	228.941
1969	19.519	19.582	19.675	19.556	19.882	19.732	*******	*******	*******	*******	*******	*******	117.946
AVGE	11.760	11.800	11.905	11.877	11.955	11.990	11.700	11.752	11.776	11.828	11.866	11.916	

TABLE TOTAL- 3197.978   MEAN- 11.844   STD. DEVIATION- 3.644

forecasted trading-day and seasonal factors for the month, as found in Tables 3 and 5. Next, divide the result of this multiplication into the month's data. This adjusts the observation for the variations of these two components.

$$\frac{Y_{ij}}{TD_{ij} \times S_{ij}} = T_{ij} \times C_{ij} \times I'_{ij}$$

After providing the analyst with a seasonally adjusted series, the X-11 performs a Henderson weighted moving average which smooths the data, eliminating the irregular component (I'). Figure 8 is a graph of the data.

If the analyst is interested in adding additional observations to the trend cycle, he must first adjust raw data for trading-day and seasonal variations. Using the final seasonally adjusted series with the additional new points, it is a simple matter, with a computer, to reapply the desired length of Henderson smoothing to the lengthened series. Resmoothed end points will be different, the degree of change being dependent on the newly available data and their degree of displacement from forecasted points in the previous smoothing. Normally, however, changes are not large.[33]

"Unexplained" Residuals: The Irregular Component

The time series decomposition has isolated and adjusted for trading-day and seasonal factors and smoothed the final seasonally adjusted series to eliminate irregular variations leaving the trend-cycle component. If we divide the final seasonally adjusted series, month by month, by the corresponding months of the trend-cycle component, we develop a series of residual irregulars (I'_{ij}).

$$\frac{T_{ij} \times C_{ij} \times I'_{ij}}{T_{ij} \times C_{ij}} = I'_{ij}$$

Table 7 is the series of residual irregulars isolated from the data under analysis. We may now ask: Is there serial correlation in this series of "unexplained" residuals? In other words, does the irregular series contain some factor not accounted for by the decomposition?

The Durbin-Watson statistic is designed to make the test for the possible

[33] For a FORTRAN computer program to perform a Henderson smoothing, see [16, pp. 96–98].

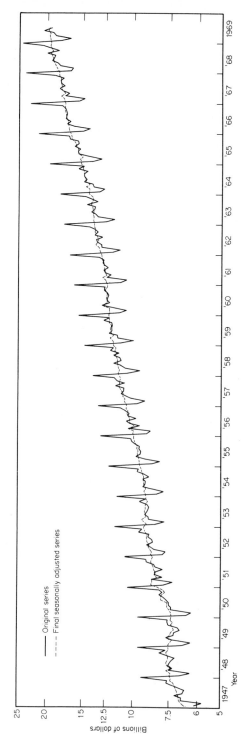

Fig. 7. Retail sales, nondurable goods stores, total (billions of dollars).

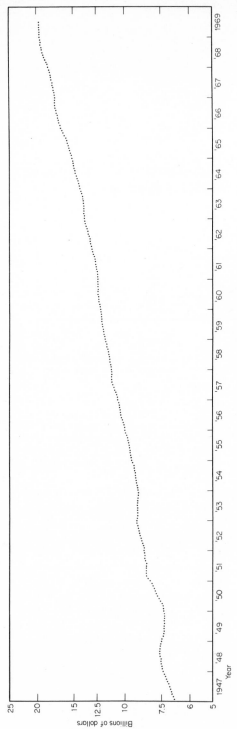

Fig. 8. Retail sales, nondurable goods stores, total—final trend cycle.

TABLE 7   Retail Sales, Nondurable Goods Stores, Total Final Irregular Series

D13. FINAL IRREGULAR SERIES	JAN	FEB	MAR	APR	MAY	JUN	JUL	AUG	SEP	OCT	NOV	DEC	S.D.
1947	98.7	99.8	100.7	100.5	100.0	99.8	99.7	99.8	100.0	99.4	101.1	100.0	0.6
1948	100.1	98.8	101.5	97.5	100.4	100.7	99.6	99.2	100.4	101.1	99.3	99.8	1.0
1949	100.5	100.2	98.7	103.1	100.5	100.7	98.3	99.2	100.9	99.4	100.8	100.1	1.2
1950	99.6	99.9	99.7	100.5	99.8	97.9	103.7	101.7	99.5	96.5	97.5	99.9	1.8
1951	104.5	102.2	101.3	97.5	99.8	99.1	100.0	99.8	100.1	101.0	100.4	98.9	1.7
1952	100.4	99.3	100.1	100.7	99.3	100.4	100.4	100.1	98.8	100.3	100.1	101.0	0.6
1953	98.5	100.4	102.4	99.2	100.0	100.6	100.0	100.2	100.4	98.9	100.2	99.9	0.9
1954	100.1	101.3	99.2	100.6	99.9	100.3	100.3	99.3	100.0	99.9	99.9	100.5	0.6
1955	100.2	99.7	99.7	100.4	100.5	99.4	100.2	99.3	100.0	100.5	100.5	99.5	0.4
1956	99.9	98.8	103.2	96.8	100.2	100.4	99.1	100.2	100.6	99.5	100.5	99.4	1.4
1957	100.0	100.6	98.9	100.5	99.3	99.7	100.6	101.0	100.0	99.6	99.3	100.1	0.6
1958	100.7	99.6	100.1	99.9	100.1	99.7	99.8	100.9	99.4	100.3	98.9	100.6	0.6
1959	100.0	100.2	102.2	98.2	100.4	100.3	100.2	99.1	100.4	99.9	100.4	100.2	0.9
1960	99.6	99.4	98.9	104.2	99.7	100.3	100.3	99.6	99.7	101.3	100.0	99.2	1.4
1961	100.1	100.6	103.3	98.7	100.0	100.0	100.4	100.0	99.8	100.1	100.2	99.7	1.0
1962	100.2	100.0	99.8	102.9	100.6	99.4	99.5	100.2	100.6	99.7	100.1	99.8	0.9
1963	100.2	100.1	99.8	100.4	99.5	100.2	100.2	101.3	99.8	99.1	98.5	100.7	0.7
1964	100.0	99.2	101.8	97.3	99.9	99.8	100.3	100.3	99.6	100.3	99.3	100.7	1.0
1965	99.6	100.0	97.3	100.3	100.6	99.3	100.1	99.6	100.0	101.5	100.1	99.9	1.0
1966	100.2	100.3	99.7	100.0	99.5	100.5	100.1	99.8	100.2	100.3	99.9	99.3	0.3
1967	100.1	100.1	102.6	98.0	99.8	100.6	99.8	100.1	100.1	99.4	100.4	99.6	1.0
1968	99.9	99.9	100.1	100.2	100.3	99.5	100.0	100.8	98.9	99.9	100.0	99.4	0.5
1969	99.8	100.0	100.3	99.6	101.1	100.3	*******	*******	*******	*******	*******	*******	0.5
S.D.	1.1	0.7	1.6	1.8	0.5	0.6	0.9	0.7	0.5	1.0	0.8	0.5	

OCTOBER 1969 RETAIL SALES, NONDURABLE GOODS STORES   (BILLIONS OF DOLLARS)   P.13, SERIES RSNG

TABLE TOTAL— 27007.6   MEAN— 100.0   STD. DEVIATION— 1.0

existence of serial correlation. Normally, it is employed to test the unexplained residuals from a least-squares regression using the formula:

$$d = \frac{\sum_{t=2}^{n}(d_t - d_{t-1})^2}{\sum_{t=1}^{n} d_t^2} \tag{1}$$

where d_t is the residual for observation t with n observations.

When using this test on the series of irregulars I'_{ij} developed from the decomposition, a modification must be introduced. In the above formula, d_t is a residual from an estimate $(Y_t - \hat{Y}_t)$. The irregular series is *not* a set of residuals consistent with the above definition.

We are interested in testing whether the differences of the I'_{ij} from 100.0 (1.000) are serially correlated. The formula becomes:

$$d = \frac{\sum_{t=2}^{n}[(I'_t - 100.0) - (I'_{t-1} - 100.0)]^2}{\sum_{t=1}^{n}(I'_t - 100.0)^2}$$

where I'_t is the I'_{ij}th point in the irregular series. The data are from $t = 1,$ ..., n in chronological order where $t = 1$ corresponds to $i = 1; j = 1;$ and so on. This can be simplified to:

$$d = \frac{\sum_{t=2}^{n}(I'_t - I'_{t-1})^2}{\sum_{t=1}^{n}(I'_t - 100.0)^2}$$

When the data from the irregular series in Table 7 are introduced into this formula, the Durbin-Watson statistic is:

$$d = \frac{621.0}{267.0} = 2.33$$

Comparing this statistic with a table of Durbin-Watson statistics leads to the conclusion that there is no positive serial correlation in the irregular series' residuals from 100.0.

The test for negative serial correlation is made by calculating $4 - d$ (in our example, 1.67) and comparing it with the same table of Durbin-Watson statistics, using the test criteria as discussed in the appropriate material.[34]   At the 5 percent probability level, we can state that no positive or negative serial correlation exists in the irregular component of our test data.

Summary Measures

The last table in the printout is a compendium of measures of the basic components and relationships among them.   Table 8 pictures these "summary measures" for the data under analysis.

The top block of data gives the "average percent change without regard to sign" over various spans in months.[35]   The identifications at the top of each column label the data sources for "average percent change(s) without regard to sign."   In order, left to right, $B1$, $D11$, and so on, refer to the specific tables from which the percent changes are developed.   The letters under each table number are identified as:

O: original series
CI: final seasonally adjusted series
I: final irregular series
C: final trend cycle
S: final seasonal factors
P: prior monthly adjustment factors
TD: trading-day adjustment factors[36]
MCD: months-for-cyclical-dominance moving average
MOD.CI: modified seasonally adjusted series
MOD.I: modified irregular series

The original series for retail sales of nondurable goods stores has an average change without regard to sign of roughly 10 percent for spans of from 1 to 11 months.   This drops to just over 5 percent for a 12-month interval.   It appears that within periods of less than a year, the series is dominated by seasonal factors.   Only in the 12-month span when the seasonal factor is not present (to a significant degree) does the change correspond roughly to that found in the seasonally adjusted series.   The seasonally adjusted series (CI) has a slowly increasing change as the span of months increases.   This is consistent with the concept of the trend and cycle components, that is, slowly and steadily increasing their significance and dominance of a series as the time span increases. The trend-cycle component (C) shows this same pattern; a slowly increasing percentage change as the span in months increases.

---

[34] For a discussion of this statistical measure and the appropriate tables, see [16], pp. 158–162].   This test is *not* a part of the X-11 computer program.   The formula reverts to Equation (1) for an additive decomposition because differences of I'_t from 0.0 are calculated ($d_t = I'_t$).

[35] Notice that 8- and 10-month spans are omitted.   The reason for these omissions in each of the 3 two-dimensional blocks of data in the table is that it was felt to be more important to have the data on a single page of output and maintain the spacing between the parts of the table than include these additional data.

[36] The asterisk refers to the note at the bottom of the table which identifies which choice was made as far as the length-of-month adjustment.   In this example the length of month was accounted for in the seasonal variations.   For a brief discussion of these summary measures, see [19].

TABLE 8   Retail Sales, Nondurable Goods Stores, Total Summary Measures

```
                OCTOBER 1969 RETAIL SALES, NONDURABLE GOODS STORES        (BILLIONS OF DOLLARS)    P.21, SERIES USNG
F 2. SUMMARY MEASURES
     AVERAGE PER CENT CHANGE WITHOUT REGARD TO SIGN OVER INDICATED SPAN
     SPAN
       IN     B1     D11    D13    D12    D10     A2     C18    F1              F1     F2     F3
     MONTHS    O     CI      I      C      S      P     TD*    MCD            MOD.O  MOD.CI  MOD.I
        1     8.15   1.15   1.04   0.44   7.19    0.0   2.12   0.57           8.01   0.91   0.77
        2     9.62   1.37   1.05   0.87   8.77    0.0   1.90   0.99           9.63   1.17   0.76
        3    10.51   1.71   1.01   1.31  10.02    0.0   1.22   1.41          10.61   1.51   0.73
        4    10.83   2.03   0.98   1.74  10.07    0.0   2.05   1.81          10.89   1.89   0.68
        5    10.24   2.41   0.94   2.17   9.53    0.0   1.72   2.22          10.27   2.28   0.67
        6     9.85   2.77   0.98   2.60   9.09    0.0   1.35   2.45           9.89   2.68   0.73
        7    10.46   3.15   0.95   3.03   9.35    0.0   2.07   3.06          10.45   3.07   0.65
        9    11.26   3.99   1.03   3.88  10.18    0.0   1.09   3.89          11.27   3.94   0.73
       11     9.90   4.78   0.90   4.72   7.72    0.0   1.53   4.70           9.80   4.74   0.65
       12     5.39   5.24   1.09   5.13   0.16    0.0   1.58   5.10           5.29   5.17   0.76

     RELATIVE CONTRIBUTIONS OF COMPONENTS TO VARIANCE IN ORIGINAL SERIES
     SPAN
       IN     D13    D12    D10     A2     C18                   RATIO
     MONTHS    I      C      S      P     TD*    TOTAL          (X100)
        1     1.90   0.33  89.97    0.0   7.80   100.00         86.69
        2     1.34   0.93  93.36    0.0   4.38   100.00         89.01
        3     0.98   1.63  95.97    0.0   1.41   100.00         94.68
        4     0.88   2.76  92.53    0.0   3.83   100.00         93.45
        5     0.88   4.75  91.40    0.0   2.98   100.00         94.68
        6     1.04   7.34  89.64    0.0   1.98   100.00         95.07
        7     0.89   9.02  85.89    0.0   4.20   100.00         93.06
        9     0.87  12.46  85.69    0.0   0.99   100.00         95.55
       11     0.94  26.24  70.07    0.0   2.75   100.00         86.64
       12     3.92  87.72   0.08    0.0   8.28   100.00        103.31

     AVERAGE DURATION OF RUN       CI      I      C     MCD
                                  1.79   1.46  24.45   3.38

     I/C RATIO FOR MONTHS SPAN
                     1      2      3      4      5      6      7      8      9      10     11     12
                    2.39   1.20   0.77   0.56   0.43   0.38   0.31   0.29   0.26   0.24   0.19   0.21

     MONTHS FOR CYCLICAL DOMINANCE    3

     AVERAGE PER CENT CHANGE WITH REGARD TO SIGN AND STANDARD DEVIATION OVER INDICATED SPAN
     SPAN                      B1            D13           D12           D10           D11           F1
       IN                      O                           C                           CI            MCD
     MONTHS  AVGE    S.D.   AVGE   S.D.   AVGE   S.D.   AVGE   S.D.   AVGE   S.D.   AVGE   S.D.
        1    1.19   12.03   0.02   1.51   0.40   0.31   0.74   11.51   0.42   1.57   0.40   0.62
        2    1.91   13.58   0.02   1.49   0.80   0.62   1.05   13.14   0.82   1.58   0.80   0.99
        3    2.24   13.84   0.02   1.53   1.20   0.91   1.01   13.56   1.22   1.89   1.20   1.30
        4    2.61   13.72   0.02   1.46   1.60   1.19   0.95   13.16   1.62   2.00   1.61   1.47
        5    2.86   13.33   0.02   1.35   2.01   1.45   0.81  12.78    2.03   2.07   2.01   1.64
        6    3.23   13.17   0.02   1.34   2.42   1.70   0.76   12.48   2.43   2.33   2.42   1.82
        7    3.77   13.23   0.02   1.40   2.83   1.93   0.87   12.35   2.84   2.44   2.82   2.04
        9    4.78   14.77   0.02   1.45   3.65   2.38   1.07   14.00   3.66   2.85   3.64   2.48
       11    5.44   14.57   0.01   1.31   4.47   2.76   0.88   13.35   4.48   3.15   4.46   2.86
       12    4.92    4.06   0.02   1.60   4.88   2.92   0.00    0.20   4.89   3.42   4.87   3.03

     * (TRADING DAY ADJUSTMENT FACTORS WITHOUT LENGTH OF MONTH ADJUSTMENT)
```

The seasonal factor (S) has the greatest average change for a one-month span of any component. It dominates the direction of the series in the short run for the test series. This clearly indicates how important it is to be able to adjust for seasonal variations. Without this adjustment, it would be almost impossible to know the underlying cyclical and trend movements for almost one year, at least. The prior adjustment (P) is zero from month to month because this option was not used in the example. The changes in the MCD series are similar to those of the trend-cycle component because the MCD smoothing helps to remove the irregular variations from the final seasonally adjusted series, as does the Henderson smoothing.

The next block of data gives the "relative contributions of components to variance in [the] original series." Here we see that for our test series, the seasonal factor completely dominates the other components for spans from 1 to 11 months. Only in a 12-month period when the seasonal variations negate themselves are they dominated by the trend cycle. The increasing importance of the trend cycle over a larger and larger span is also illustrated quite clearly.

The next line of data shows the "average duration of run" for several of the components. These data are read as the average number of months a specific component moves in a positive or negative direction before changing direction, that is, the span of months before the first difference goes from plus to minus or vice versa. If there is no change between two months, a change in the same direction as the preceding change is assumed.

Those factors that contain the irregular variations have a short average duration of run because of the nature of the irregular factor. The trend cycle for the series under analysis has an average duration of run of just over two years (24.45 months). This is a fairly long span and indicates a "well-behaved" series.

The $\bar{I}/\bar{C}$ ratios for spans of from 1 to 12 months are printed on the next line of output. These show the average change without regard to sign of the irregular component divided by the average change without regard to sign of the trend-cycle component for the indicated spans. The irregular factor moves dynamically in a given direction for short spans, by definition and by observation as shown in the average duration of run. The trend-cycle factor cumulates slowly in one direction for longer average spans than the irregular. Usually, except for series with relatively little unexplained movement, the irregular factor will dominate the trend cycle for spans of one, two, or more months. However, except in "ill-behaved" series, the trend cycle will usually dominate the irregular component after spans of three to six months.

When the average change of the trend cycle for a specific span of months is greater than the average change of the irregular for the same span, the $\bar{I}/\bar{C}$ ratio is less than 1.00. For such a span, the trend cycle dominates the irregular. A movement in a specific direction in a time series for a span of months for which the $\bar{I}/\bar{C}$ ratio is less than 1.00 is interpreted as probably a trend-cycle movement and not an irregular movement. In economic analysis and decision making, the importance of knowing the minimum span of months to wait before stating with relative confidence that a movement is a trend cycle or a cyclical movement is self-evident.

In the example shown (Table 8), the $\bar{I}/\bar{C}$ ratio falls below 1.00 for a three-month span. This minimum span for an $\bar{I}/\bar{C}$ of less than 1.00 is known as the "months for cyclical dominance," or MCD span. The $\bar{I}/\bar{C}$ spans are developed by dividing the "average percent change without regard to sign" of each $\bar{I}$ factor by the corresponding $\bar{C}$ factor found in the top block of Table 8.

The bottom block of Table 8 gives the "average percent change *with* regard to sign and standard deviation" for the original series (O) and various components and combinations thereof. Here too, the cumulating phenomenon of the trend-cycle component can be observed.

Charts

After the development of the foregoing data, four groups of charts are produced at the option of the analyst. The first group contains two series; the final seasonally adjusted series and the final trend cycle. The data are plotted on a semilogarithmic scale selected from six possible choices, depending on the relation of the largest observation to the smallest.

Figure 9 pictures the first and last parts of the printout of this chart for our sample series. To identify the series being plotted, the chart notes the table numbers which were data sources.

The second chart, actually a series of 12 charts, one for each month, contains plots of the final, unmodified seasonal-irregular ratios (SI); final SI ratios modified for extremes; and final seasonal factors. Each month's chart uses the same arithmetic scale and contains a given month's data for the available years. The analyst has options of selecting shorter or longer spans for each month's smoothing than those automatically provided as the default options.

Figure 10 is the January chart developed from the data under analysis. Most of the data for each January appear "well-behaved." January 1951, however, is far removed from the relative position of previous and following years. Under these circumstances, the program judges the large displacement of this point to be irregular and the modified ratio is adjusted to be coincident with the final seasonal factor. The analyst in this manner has a graphical tool for analyzing SI ratios and their adjustments.

The third chart is the same as the second set of 12 monthly charts except

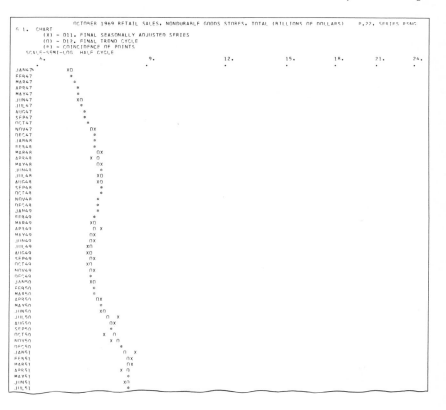

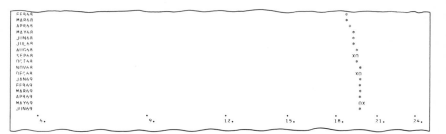

Fig. 9.   Retail sales, nondurable goods stores, total—Chart G1.

that the three series are plotted chronologically, month by month, on a single chart for the entire period of available data. The last chart plots, month by month, the final irregular series and the final modified irregular series. An arithmetic scale is used and the tables supplying the data are identified at the top of the chart.

X-11Q: A VERSION FOR QUARTERLY DATA

At approximately the time the Bureau of the Census released the X-11 for analysis of monthly data, it introduced a version for the analysis of quarterly data. This computer program was designated Census Method II, X-11Q. The program is designed to seasonally adjust quarterly economic data, facilitating the decomposition of time series previously analyzed by adaptation of the data to the monthly seasonal adjustment programs.

The monthly and quarterly versions of Census Method II are essentially the same. Differences relate to various options and smoothings. The quarterly program, X-11Q, is a simpler analysis because the trading-day and prior adjustments are not included. Besides, where a choice is available in the monthly program as to the term of the moving averages used for estimating the seasonal

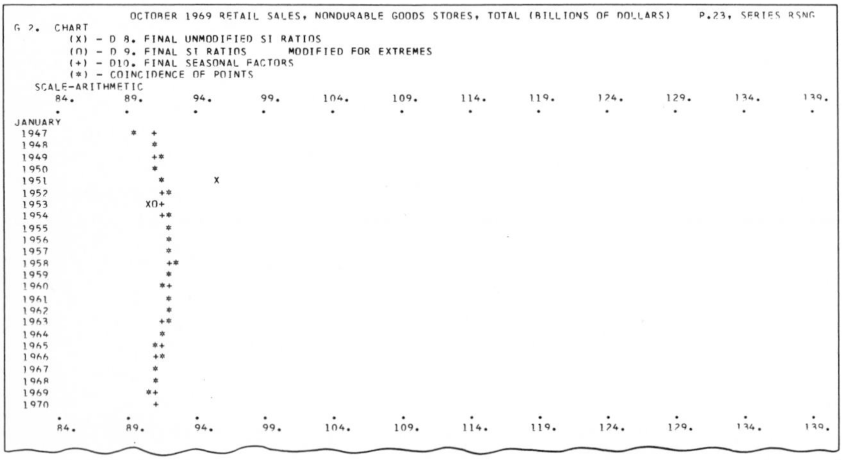

```
                      OCTOBER 1969 RETAIL SALES, NONDURABLE GOODS STORES, TOTAL (BILLIONS OF DOLLARS)     P.23, SERIES RSNG
G 2.  CHART
          (X) - D 8. FINAL UNMODIFIED SI RATIOS
          (0) - D 9. FINAL SI RATIOS        MODIFIED FOR EXTREMES
          (+) - D10. FINAL SEASONAL FACTORS
          (*) - COINCIDENCE OF POINTS
SCALE-ARITHMETIC
        84.       89.       94.       99.      104.      109.      114.      119.      124.      129.      134.      139.
         .         .         .         .         .         .         .         .         .         .         .         .
JANUARY
  1947          * +
  1948          *
  1949          +*
  1950          *
  1951          *       X
  1952          +*
  1953          X0+
  1954          +*
  1955          *
  1956          *
  1957          *
  1958          +*
  1959          *
  1960          *+
  1961          *+
  1962          *
  1963          +*
  1964          *
  1965          *+
  1966          +*
  1967          *
  1968          *
  1969          *+
  1970          +
         .         .         .         .         .         .         .         .         .         .         .         .
        84.       89.       94.       99.      104.      109.      114.      119.      124.      129.      134.      139.
```

Fig. 10.   Retail sales, nondurable goods stores, total—Chart G2.   January.

and trend-cycle components, no choice is given in the quarterly version. Instead, a specific smoothing is used for the seasonal and another for the trend cycle. The X-11Q performs either a multiplicative or an additive adjustment and can accept seasonally adjusted data as input when only summary measures are desired.

The step-by-step procedure in the quarterly version parallels that of the monthly program, with the following differences:

1. There is no part A because no prior adjustment of the data is permitted by the program.

2. No provision is made for adjustment of trading-day variations.

3. Centered 4-term smoothings are used rather than centered 12-term smoothings for a first approximation of the trend cycle in each iteration and for forcing seasonal factors for an annual period to sum to 4.000 (12.000 in the monthly version).

4. No option is available for specifying other than a 3×5-term smoothing for developing final seasonal factors.

5. The estimates of the trend-cycle component other than the ones mentioned earlier are developed by using a weighted five-term Henderson smoothing. The monthly program employs a 13-term Henderson moving average ex-

cept possibly for the estimate of the final trend cycle where the span of the Henderson smoothing is chosen on the basis of a preliminary estimate of the $\bar{I}/\bar{C}$ ratio.

6. When chosen as an option, the adjustment of a preliminary estimate of the trend cycle for strikes replaces extreme values with an average of the value times its weight and the nearest full-weighted values on both sides. End points judged by the program to be extreme are replaced by an average of the extreme value times its weight and the nearest full-weighted value.

7. Summary measures are developed for one- to four-quarter spans. Prior adjustment factors (P) and trading-day factors (TD) are omitted from the summary table as these options are not available in the X-11Q. The span in quarters of the first $\bar{I}/\bar{C}$ ratio less than 1.00 is designated the "quarters for cyclical dominance," or QCD, span [27, pp. 79–81].

SUMMARY

Review and Conclusions

Modern approaches to time series decomposition and analysis began more than 50 years ago with the work of Warren Persons. His basic model and many of his original concepts are pertinent to this day. With the coming of the computer age combined with the work of Shiskin and Eisenpress, extensive study of vast numbers of time series and modification of methods led to rapid advances in methodology, techniques, and computational speeds.

Various computerized statistical techniques have been used to seasonally adjust economic time series. It is the ratio-to-moving-average method, evolving through the development of Census Method II and the Bureau of Labor Statistics Seasonal Factor Method computer programs, culminating with the X-11 variant of Census Method II released in late 1965, that has been employed most widely in government and business for the decomposition and analysis of the component parts of economic time series. The discussion and computer output in this chapter have centered on this ratio-to-moving-average technique.

The Census Method II programs in general and the X-11 variants, with their many options, in particular allow the analyst the widest choice of any current method in decomposing and analyzing time series and forecasting several of the components. Also, the Census method has stood the test of time. In retrospect, its isolation and forecast of the seasonal and trading-day components in many and varied series have proven reliable and accurate. The United States Department of Commerce, many foreign governments, and commercial establishments are using the X-11 and X-11Q decomposition computer programs for forecasting and analyzing the component parts of time series. Econometric models of the United States, such as the Wharton model, use data adjusted for seasonal and trading-day variations as input rather than attempt these adjustments within the solution of the model. In conclusion, refinements to the Census method are inevitable.

The X-11 and X-11Q variants are currently the most widely used programs and are regarded as reliable techniques for isolating, analyzing, and forecasting component parts of an economic time series.

Availability of Computer Programs

The X-11 and X-11Q programs are written in FORTRAN IV and are run at the Bureau of the Census on a UNIVAC 1107 computer. The FORTRAN IV used in both programs is limited to those features of the language which are common to the 1107 FORTRAN as described in the "UNIVAC 1107 FORTRAN Reference Manual U-3569" and the IBM 7090 FORTRAN as described in "Form C28-6390-1, IBM 7090/7094 IBSYS Operating System, Version 13, FORTRAN IV Language." Since the release of the programs in 1965, FORTRAN IV versions for the IBM S/360 have also been made available by the Bureau. These require a minimum configuration of an IBM 360/40 with a core storage of 256k and an operating system with a level G FORTRAN compiler. The X-11 program contains about 2,500 FORTRAN source statements, and the X-11Q about 1,400 statements.

The X-11 program consists of a main program and 13 separately assembled subprograms. The largest of these contains approximately 500 FORTRAN source statements. The entire program and all intermediate results remain in core memory throughout the computations. The X-11Q program consists of a main program and 13 subroutines, the largest of which contains roughly 400 FORTRAN statements.

Copies of the source decks for these programs are available from the Census Bureau at cost. Information on obtaining the programs and their exact price may be obtained from the Bureau of the Census, Washington, D.C.

Seasonal Adjustments Using Dummy Variables

When constructing a quarterly or monthly econometric model, the analyst has the choice of using seasonally adjusted data as input or making the adjustment within the framework of the model.[37] One approach is to introduce dummy variables to account for seasonal variations in those equations requiring them. With quarterly data, it would be necessary to establish three variables giving the following for a typical linear relationship:

$$Y_t = a + b_1 S_{1t} + b_2 S_{2t} + b_3 S_{3t} + cX_t + U_t$$

where Y_t is the dependent variable for time t
a is the intercept term
S_{it} is the seasonal correction variable, $i = 1, \ldots, 3$
X_t is the independent variable
U_t is the random disturbance

It is not possible to establish four dummy variables, one for each quarter, because under this condition the matrix would be singular and could not be solved [7, 22]. In general, if n levels are to be distinguished in a regression, $n - 1$ dummy variables are designated.

The constant term (a) in the above equation would contain the seasonal adjustment for that quarter where $S_{it} = 0$; $i = 1, 2, 3$. In other words, the coefficients for these dummy variables would be solved for initially and the variables would be treated as exogenous when the multiequation econometric model was solved.[38]

Each seasonal adjustment variable (S_{it}) would be 1 in a specific quarter each year and zero in the other three quarters. All three dummy variables would be zero in one of the four quarters. The quarters would be differentiated as follows:

---

[37] Some econometric models are annual systems where the problem of seasonal variations does not arise.

[38] In a single equation model they would be endogenous.

S_{1t}	S_{2t}	S_{3t}	
1	0	0	for first-quarter adjustment
0	1	0	for second-quarter adjustment
0	0	1	for third-quarter adjustment
0	0	0	for fourth-quarter adjustment

In the solution where these variables are exogenous, the constant term (a) can be thought of as taking on four possible values, one for each quarter where each value encompasses an adjustment for seasonal variations for the specific quarter.

An advantage of this method of adjustment for seasonal variations is that the degrees of freedom lost in making the adjustment can be taken into account. Specifically, a quarterly model would lose three degrees of freedom, one for each variable S_{it}; $i = 1, \ldots, 3$. These variables are not specific to any single variable in an equation. "They are attached to equations and represent a synthesis of seasonal influences of all the variables appearing in the equation" [10, pp. 40–44].

The seasonal adjustments developed using this dummy variable approach are stable and additive. Stable seasonality is not generally a "good" assumption. In fact, much of the developmental effort in creating seasonal adjustments over the years has been to produce "evolving" seasonal correction factors, as developed in the Census Method II approach. Also, an additive adjustment is considered to be less desirable than a multiplicative relationship where data allow the latter. Study has shown that seasonal variations tend to be relative rather than absolute.

Time series analysis as a tool for isolating seasonal adjustment factors, however, has the weakness of leaving doubt as to whether "too little" or "too much" has been accounted for, quantitatively speaking. In other words, has there been an over- or undercorrection for seasonal variations causing possibly a "correction" or elimination of movements caused by other phenomena?

Spectral analysis is another statistical technique that has been applied extensively to the problem of isolating and forecasting seasonal variations. It is discussed in a later chapter.

REFERENCES

1. Barton, H. C., Jr., "Adjustment for Seasonal Variations," *Federal Reserve Bulletin*, vol. 27, 1941.
2. Burns, A. F., and W. C. Mitchell, *Measuring Business Cycles*, New York: National Bureau of Economic Research, 1946, pp. 43–55.
3. Croxton, R. E., and D. J. Cowden, *Applied General Statistics*, 2d ed., New York: Prentice-Hall, 1955, pp. 320–363.
4. Day, E. E., *Statistical Analysis*, chap. XVIII, New York: Macmillan, 1925.
5. Falkner, H. D., "The Measurement of Seasonal Variation," *Journal of the American Statistical Association*, vol. 19, June 1924.
6. Hall, L. W., "Seasonal Variation as a Relative of Secular Trend," *Journal of the American Statistical Association*, vol. 19, June 1924.
7. Johnston, J., *Econometric Methods*, New York: McGraw-Hill, 1963.
8. Joy, A., and W. Thomas, "The Use of Moving Averages in the Measurement of Seasonal Variations," *Journal of the American Statistical Association*, vol. 23, September 1928.
9. King, W. I., "An Improved Method for Measuring the Seasonal Factor," *Journal of the American Statistical Association*, September 1924.

10. Klein, L. R., F. J. Ball, A. Hazelwood, and P. Vandome, *An Econometric Model of the United Kingdom*, Oxford, England: Blackwell, 1961, pp. 40–44.
11. Kuznets, S., *Seasonal Variations in Industry and Trade*, New York: National Bureau of Economic Research, 1933.
12. Macaulay, F. R., *The Smoothing of Time Series*, New York: National Bureau of Economic Research, 1931.
13. Mills, F. C., *Statistical Methods*, New York: Holt, 1955, pp. 360–375.
14. Organization for Economic Cooperation and Development, "Seasonal Adjustment on Electronic Computers," *Report and Proceedings of an International Conference, sponsored by the Organization for European Economic Cooperation*, November 1960, pp. 15, 81, and 83.
15. Persons, W. M., "Indices of Business Conditions," *Review of Economics and Statistics*, January 1919.
16. Salzman, L., *Computerized Economic Analysis*, New York: McGraw-Hill, 1968, chaps. 4 and 5.
17. Salzman, L., "A Direct Application of Seasonal Adjustment Factors to Forecasting," *1969 Proceedings of the Business and Economic Statistics Section*, Washington: American Statistical Association, 1970, pp. 27–72, 74–87.
18. Shiskin, J., "Seasonal Computations on Univac," *American Statistician*, February 1955.
19. Shiskin, J., "How Accurate?", *American Statistician*, October 1960.
20. Shiskin, J., "Electronic Computers and Business Indicators," in Geoffrey Moore (ed.), *Business Cycle Indicators*, vol. 1, chap. 17, Princeton, N.J.: Princeton University Press for the National Bureau of Economic Research, 1961.
21. Shiskin, J., and H. Eisenpress, "Seasonal Adjustment by Electronic Computer Methods," *Journal of the American Statistical Association*, December 1957.
22. Suits, D. B., "Use of Dummy Variables in Regression Equations," *Journal of the American Statistical Association*, vol. 52, December 1957.
23. U.S. Bureau of the Census, "Estimating Trading-day Variation in Monthly Economic Time Series," Technical Paper no. 12, Washington: Government Printing Office, 1965.
24. U.S. Bureau of the Census, "The X-11 Variant of the Census Method II Seasonal Adjustment Program," Technical Paper no. 15, rev., February 1967, Washington: Government Printing Office, 1965.
25. U.S. Bureau of the Census, "Summary Description of X-9 and X-10 Versions of the Census Method II Seasonal Adjustment Program," *Business Cycle Developments*, U.S. Department of Commerce, September 1963.
26. U.S. Bureau of the Census, *Business Conditions Digest*, Series ES1, no. 69-1, U.S. Department of Commerce, January 1969, p. 74.
27. U.S. Bureau of the Census, "X-11 Information for the User," *Papers prepared for the Seminar on Seasonal Adjustments of the National Association of Business Economists*, Philadelphia: Pa.: U.S. Department of Commerce, March 10, 1969.
28. U.S. Bureau of Labor Statistics, "The BLS Seasonal Factor Method (1966)," U.S. Department of Labor, May 1966, pp. 12–13.
29. U.S. Office of Business Economics, *Business Statistics*, Washington: Department of Commerce, 1967.
30. U.S. Office of Business Economics, *Survey of Current Business*, November 1968.
31. U.S. Office of Business Economics, *Survey of Current Business*, January and September, 1969, for 1968–June 1969.
32. Wallis, W. A., and H. V. Roberts, *Statistics: A New Approach*, Glencoe, Ill.: Glencoe Press, 1956, pp. 580–586.

Part E

Statistical Analysis of Relationships

Chapter 3

Time Series versus Cross-Section Analysis

KRISTIAN S. PALDA *Claremont Graduate School, Claremont, California*

INTRODUCTION

It is more than 10 years since Ferber and Verdoorn made the discussion of cross-section and time series approaches for marketing research problems one of the anchors of their well-known text [3]. Nevertheless, their masterful treatment of these two basic kinds of research analysis remains the most systematic and comprehensive to be found in the literature. Anybody who wishes to inform himself about cross-section and time series analysis at greater length is advised to turn to the relevant chapters in that source.

The scope of this chapter requires a very condensed treatment, so the main accent will be put on the probable differences in answers to market-measurement questions depending on whether time series information or cross-section information is drawn upon. Stress will also be laid on the insufficiency of one approach alone and on the effectiveness of using data which possess both a time and a cross-section character. The context within which the discussion will proceed will be largely that of a single equation demand model whose parameters are to be estimated by least-squares regression—one of the most common ways of deriving quantitative structural estimates of demand for a product in market research. This implies also that attention will be paid only to nonexperimental observational data.

The plan of the chapter is set out accordingly:

1. A general model of demand for a firm's product, in which demand determinants are sectioned into those controllable and those not controllable by the firm.

2. Classification of demand variables into predominantly time series, predominantly cross section, and mixed.
3. Time series observations
    a. Aspects of data collection.
    b. Typical problems tackled with the use of such data, such as estimation of the influence of noncontrollable demand determinants upon industry-wide demand and the building of sales forecasts.
    c. Difficulties encountered and means to overcome them.
4. Cross-section observations
    a, b, and c as under point 3.
5. Difference in estimates yielded by the two kinds of data and their theoretical explanation.
6. Time series of cross sections—the ideal body of observations to use in demand estimation.

GENERAL MODEL

The predominant task of the marketing research function is to provide marketing and top management with as complete a picture of the structure and characteristics of the market in which the firm operates (or intends to operate) as possible. The most convenient and, indeed, the operationally useful way to present this information is in the form of a market model, in which the quantitative relationship between the firm's sales and various demand-determining influences is numerically specified.

The most general way in which to present such a model would be to state that the firm's brand sales are a function of those present and past demand determinants that are at least partly under the control of the firm and of those which are not, such as:

$$
\begin{aligned}
s_{i,t} = (m_{i,A,t},\ m_{k,B,t},\ \ldots &\qquad,\ m_{i,Z,t}; \\
m_{i,A,t-1},\ \ldots &\qquad,\ m_{i,Z,t-1}; \\
\cdot \\
\cdot \\
\cdot \\
m_{i,A,t-k},\ \ldots &\qquad,\ m_{i,Z,t-k}; \\
r_{j,A,t},\ \ldots &\qquad,\ r_{j,Z,t}; \\
\cdot \\
\cdot \\
\cdot \\
r_{1,A,t-k},\ \ldots &\qquad,\ r_{1,Z,t-k}; \\
z_{m,t},\ \ldots &\qquad,\ z_{n,t}; \\
\cdot \\
\cdot \\
\cdot \\
z_{m,t-k},\ \ldots &\qquad,\ z_{n,t-k})
\end{aligned}
\tag{1}
$$

CLASSIFICATION OF DEMAND VARIABLES

This somewhat formidable-looking equation is actually a compact expression of a set of relationships familiar to all marketers. The actual demand (unit sales) for the firm's brand i at time t is specified as being dependent upon the firm's marketing actions A to Z during the current period *and* during the preceding periods $(t-1)$ to $(t-k)$; upon the marketing actions A to Z of rivals r_j to r_l

during the same periods; and, finally, upon autonomous environmental variables, the z's, that originate outside the industry. The latter two groups are largely beyond the control of the firm.

Such a classification of variables can be useful on three counts: (1) it distinguishes between changes in demand variables which were caused by, or call for, vigorous marketing action, and changes in those which—not being subject to the firm's action—require a more or less passive adjustment; (2) to a large extent, "controllable" and "noncontrollable" demand determinants are synonymous with "proper-to-the-firm" and "industry-wide" influences, a condition which leads to a fairly natural division between approaches to demand estimation; (3) the classification also focuses attention on those demand variables which are "competitive" in character, that is, which are in a sense jointly and sometimes simultaneously determined by the firm *and* its rivals. In that sense, the model could be written in a condensed fashion as:

$$s_{i,t} = x_{i,t} \cdot I_t \tag{2}$$

where x is market share and I is industry sales.

Confronted with the task of estimating such complex demand relationships, the market researcher will frequently decompose the model in the fashion of Equation (2) into an industry component and a market-share component, and then estimate the relevant relationships for each of them separately.

Consider the industry component first. Two quite distinct views of industry (product) demand can be taken. The first, which might be called the *time series perspective,* regards industry demand as being influenced by such aggregate (macro) variables as total consumer expenditures, housing starts, stocks of inventories, or variables which are the same for all buyers, such as prices or tax schedules. Because of their aggregate nature (or because of their invariance to all buyers), changes in these variables can be observed only over successive time periods. Therefore, the method which aims to extract estimates of demand relationships from these data is called time series analysis.

The second, *cross-section,* view of industry demand sees it as shaped by differences between levels of demand determinants among individual buyers or buyer groups. As an example, disposable income, in conjunction with purchases, is ascertained for each household (or its liquid assets holdings, life-cycle stage, and so on). The variations over each variable occur here among the individual components of the buying universe at a single point in time. The variables themselves are often of a micro character (disposable income of a household rather than of a group or of the total population).

In concise form, the linear time series model of industry demand is written as:

$$I_t = \alpha + \beta z_t \tag{3}$$

where z stands for all the environmental variables.

In this demand model, the assumption is that over the specified period of years (which may include a forecasting horizon), the form and parameters (α, β) of the equation do not change.[1]

The cross-section case assumes that Equation (4)

$$c_i = \gamma + \delta a_i \tag{4}$$

[1] Or that they change in a specified manner, for instance,
$$I_t = \alpha + d_t + \beta_t$$
where d is a dummy variable indicating a shift in the intercept when it is "activated."

applies without change to all the buyers, that is, that the parameters γ and δ do not change from one buyer to another.[2]   But note that the dependent variable is no longer industry demand, but rather that of an individual buyer, c_i. In order to get to the industry demand concept, the individual buyer's demands have to be aggregated, thus:

$$I_t = \Sigma_i c_i \tag{5}$$

From the foregoing brief discussion, it can be inferred that a demand analyst can draw upon data that are predominantly observations on time series variables (those that are the same for all potential buyers at one point in time, or are aggregates) and cross-section variables (those that vary from one buying unit to another but change only very slowly with time—such as demographic characteristics).   Obviously, however, there is a third class: mixed variables (such as buying-unit income), comprising those variables that vary both with time and from one buying unit to another.   This class of variables will be discussed later.

Consider, now, the market-share (or brand) component.   It is necessary to understand this factor so that the industry (product) demand can be properly apportioned.   Here the main influence is exerted by the competitive forces (r) and the firm's own marketing actions (m).   On this micro level, a distinction can again be made between relatively aggregate and relatively disaggregate data, this distinction then carrying over into time series and cross-section variables.   Thus

$$x_{i,t} = g\left(\frac{m_{i,A,t}}{\frac{1}{l}\sum_{j}^{l} r_{j,A,t}}, \ldots, \frac{m_{i,Z,t}}{\frac{1}{l}\sum_{j}^{l} r_{j,Z,t}} \right) \tag{6}$$

states that the market share of brand i depends upon the ratios of the levels of marketing efforts A to Z (such as price, promotional outlay, and distribution density) of firm i to the suitably weighted mean levels of similar marketing efforts by rivals in the *whole market* at time t.

This is a time series approach for modeling the market-share component. Dropping the subscript t and adding the subscript p to stand for sales territory, we can conceive of the firm's demand as being susceptible to estimation from cross-sectional data gathered in the firm's individual submarkets p to q:

$$x_i = g\left(\frac{m_{i,A,p}}{\frac{1}{l}\sum_{j}^{l} r_{j,A,p}}, \ldots, \frac{m_{i,Z,q}}{\frac{1}{l}\sum_{j}^{l} r_{j,Z,p}} \right) \tag{7}$$

(With a single seller in the market, the model simplifies drastically.)

Here the variables used in time series and cross-section analysis are not as conceptually different as on the industry level; furthermore, it is apparent that a mixed time-series cross-section model might not be too exacting of data collection:

$$x_{i,t} = g\left(\frac{m_{i,A,p,t}}{\frac{1}{l}\sum_{j}^{l} r_{j,A,p,t}}, \ldots, \frac{m_{i,Z,q,t}}{\frac{1}{l}\sum_{j}^{l} r_{j,Z,q,t}} \right) \tag{7a}$$

[2] Again, by putting in a dummy variable to stand for, say, the buyer's regional location, variation in a specified manner can be allowed without violating the substance of this statement.

TIME SERIES ANALYSIS

The kind of data (and thus the type of analysis) used to estimate the demand for the firm's brand depends on the urgency of the particular questions asked of the demand model and on the availability of such data, as well as upon the difficulties typically encountered in this analysis.

Aspects of Data Collection

It is probably safe to state that, in general, time series observations are less costly to amass than cross-sectional ones. If they derive from aggregates, they are often found in secondary data sources, such as national income and expenditure accounts, state and local government statistics, such trade publications as *Sales Management* and *Advertising Age,* or in the company's own sales records.[3]

Types of Problems

On the industry (or total market) level, the demand component will often be subject to seasonal and cyclical variations. An estimate of such effects is probably the first and most obvious task of time series analysis. A fuller account of methods isolating the seasonal and cyclical elements is rendered in the preceding chapter.

Other general categories of demand questions typically tackled with the help of time series analysis are those concerning structural change over time, sales forecasting (on both the industry and the brand level), price-quantity relations, lagged market response—and any and all for which no cross-section or mixed data are available. A few illustrations follow.

Structural change designates any sudden and permanent change in a given relationship. Where, for instance, there was a positive correlation between two variables, there is now a negative one. (Naturally, this need not be a consequence of a changed relationship between the two observed variables, but between the first and the emergence of a third *unobserved* variable, the latter strongly correlated with the second.) This change can be detected only by studying movements over time either by a simple graphic comparison or by the so-called Chow test [13]. Figure 1 shows how sales of a patent medicine correlated positively with expenditures on medical care from 1929 to the 1941–1945 period, and negatively from 1941–1945 to 1960. The sharp break is very apparent; it was not possible to find a reason for this structural change.

Unless the observation period is short (say, a month or a quarter) and the change in the underlying demand structure fast-paced, it is almost impossible to detect structural shift as it occurs. Careful study of the pattern of regression residuals may sometimes provide a clue that a shift is underway.

For short-term (say over a time horizon up to two years) *sales forecasts,* particularly of the industry component of the firm's demand, a time-series analysis approach is indispensable. First of all, cyclical and seasonal movements must be taken into account. Then, more sophisticated, but still "mechanistic," extrapolation techniques, such as exponential smoothing, must obviously utilize time series data [2]. More practically, there is little danger— over a brief time span—that the relationships between cross-section variables (such as age distribution among buyers or regional population densities) will change. Therefore they can be safely ignored and the less expensive time series statistics utilized.

If the product, because of the industry's competitiveness or its collusion, car-

---

[3] For a brief but excellent discussion of marketing information sources, see [4].

ries a uniform price throughout the market, the classical *price-quantity relationship*, which is often of central interest, cannot be assessed except from readings over time. Frequently, however, the impact of price (or, for that matter, of many other market "action" variables) occurs with a lag, and this phenomenon then calls for use of time series information.

$$I_t = \alpha - \beta p_t - \beta\lambda p_{t-1} - \beta\lambda^2 p_{t-2} - \ldots \qquad 0 < \lambda < 1 \tag{8}$$

Equation (8) is an example of the reaction of industry sales to a price change over several periods, the distributed lag being a declining geometric function of time.

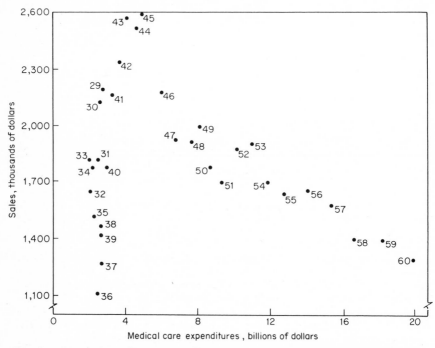

Fig. 1. Correlation of patent medicine sales with medical-care expenditures. Data from Lydia Pinkham Company 1920–1960. (SOURCE: *[8, p. 65].*)

Imposing the distributed lag form upon a regression equation in order to estimate such a delayed market response to a change in one of the demand determinants offers certain advantages. Let us write Equation (8) as lagged by one period

$$I_{t-1} = \alpha - \beta p_{t-1} - \beta\lambda p_{t-2} - \ldots \tag{8a}$$

If we now multiply the equation by λ and add the result to (8a), we obtain

$$I_t = \alpha(1 - \lambda) - \beta p_t - \lambda I_{t-1} \tag{8b}$$

Instead of having to include a potentially large number of mutually correlated price variables, we now have only two variables on the right-hand side of the equation. Nevertheless, this so-called Koyck transformation may exact other penalties and should be used very cautiously [7].

Even a well-designed experimental attempt to derive price-quantity relationships by varying price over several sales territories is bound to yield biased answers if a distributed lag is operating and if the experiment is carried out over too short a period of time [19].

Cautionary Remarks on Using Time Series Analysis

Apart from the isolation of periodic swings and other patterns[4] and exponential smoothing, time series analysis is almost wholly synonymous with least-squares regression. Thus, the assessment of the possible weaknesses of estimates yielded by such an analysis starts with the confrontation of the assumptions underlying the least-squares model with the characteristics of the time series observations used.

Since the chapter on spectral analysis (Sec. II, Part E, Chap. 4) outlines in detail these assumptions, we need only state that the condition most frequently violated by the use of such data is that of successive independence (nonautocorrelation) of error terms. Autocorrelation among residuals (estimated error terms) reduces the efficiency of the least-squares estimates. In economic time series, in which serial correlation is almost always positive, this results in an underestimate of the standard error of residuals and leads to the tendency to reject more often than should be the case the hypothesis that regression coefficients are equal to zero.

Effects of chance disturbances (for example, wars) or variables omitted from the regression equation (perhaps an upsurge of imports) tend to persist through several data-collection periods; another reason for autocorrelation is that methods of collecting observations incorporate elements of smoothing which spread disturbances over neighboring periods. Modern econometrics texts discuss a host of methods to cope with the autocorrelation problem, such as first differencing or correcting with the autocorrelation coefficient.[5] Nevertheless, autocorrelation remains a typical symptom of time series regressions, whereas cross-section estimates are generally not affected by it.

Another black mark against time series data is their typical brevity, which leads often to collinearity among the variables employed in the regression demand model. Twenty to thirty annual or semiannual observations over time is considered an already large sample, owing both to difficulties of getting data over such long periods and to the danger of structural change within the demand relationships if such a long, or a longer, time span is scanned. Since the two most important aggregate demand variables, price and total disposable income, move in the same direction, they will show a typically large correlation (collinear relationship). Collinearity among data is a troublesome though partially remediable phenomenon endemic to time series regressions [15].

CROSS-SECTION ANALYSIS

Aspects of Data Collection

Most of the cross-section data used to estimate the structure of industry demand and some of the data useful to the assessment of brand demand characteristics are generated by surveys. Two large problem areas face all surveys: the statistical problems inherent in the selection of a sample yielding unbiased estimates at bearable cost, and the difficulties of getting accurate information out of the

---

[4] A technique of growing popularity to decompose time series is spectral analysis. For a good introduction, see the next chapter; also [17].

[5] For a particularly good introductory review of such methods, see [5].

selected sample (response error). As a rule, cross-section information is more expensive than simple usage of secondary sources with aggregate data. (The exception, already mentioned, is the use of company sales records if they are kept across territories, groups of customers, or other small strata of the sales universe.) On the other hand, a detailed insight into market characteristics is rarely available without recourse to such information.

Cross-section data are also the result of experimentation, an expensive but sometimes inevitable probing of the market, details of which are discussed elsewhere in this handbook. Consumer panels and store audits, although normally classified under the heading of cross-section data, are really sources of time-section (or mixed) observations and will be discussed separately.

Types of Problems

Roughly speaking, cross-section information is employed for three major purposes. They are (1) to obtain estimates of quantitative relationships between market (industry) demand and various levels of attributes of buyer units, the most important of which are income, assets, family size, and expectations; (2) to assess the outcome of competitive differentials (price, promotion, quality); and (3) to evaluate the significance of variables whose impact is not easily aggregated, such as attitudes, images, or preference.

Since cross-section observations are almost always abundant (indeed, this is perhaps their chief advantage), their statistical analysis is not cramped by the existence of insufficiently large samples, a situation common with time series data.

Cautionary Remarks on Using Cross-Section Analysis

Although analysis of variance is a frequently employed method of examining survey or experimental data, regression is more powerful in that it estimates the shape of market demand curves. Thus cross-section analysis will be viewed—parallel to time series analysis—in the context of regression. The question is: What assumptions of the least-squares regression model are most likely to be violated when cross-section data are used? The typical answer is that such data will likely give rise to heteroskedasticity in the error terms, that is, differing variances with different levels of the independent variables. If the variance of the residuals (observed error terms) is not the same at every level of the independent variables (say, for instance, that with increasing income levels, one observes a larger variability of consumer durable expenditures), regression estimates decrease in efficiency. This is similar to the effects of autocorrelation in time series.

Repairs can be made by suitable weighting with the help of the suspected culprit variable, or by a logarithmic or square-root transformation of the variables. Nevertheless, when there are many determining variables in the regression—normally the case with cross-section data—it is extremely tedious to find out which of them are causing the nonhomogeneity of variance among error terms.

DIFFERENCES IN ESTIMATES FROM TIME SERIES AND CROSS-SECTIONS

The central problem arising from least-squares regressions using time series and cross-sectional data is that the results are rarely in accord. Thus a regression of expenditure upon income will yield a different elasticity estimate, depending upon whether the observations are taken from United States quarterly data from 1950 to 1970, or from Bureau of Labor Statistics surveys undertaken in

1961 and 1972.   Similarly, one would expect to get different estimates of the advertising elasticity of demand from a firm's quarterly data on sales and advertising and from its sales district data taken at one point in time.   The detection of such differences and their explanation provide, however, a necessary starting point for the upgrading of the general demand model and also indicate the degree of urgency to acquire additional data.

An example from an economic study illustrates one of the many possible ways of comparing time series and cross-section regression results [12].   One of the questions to be resolved by that study was whether a relationship exists between a country's economic growth (as measured by per capita gross national

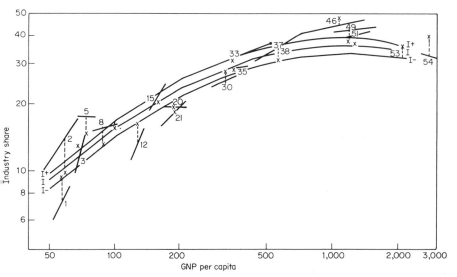

Fig. 2.   Relations between economic growth and national output. 1, Nigeria; 2, Burma; 3, Pakistan; 5, India; 8, Thailand; 12, Korea; 15, Brazil; 20, Turkey; 21, Philippines; 30, Mexico; 33, Japan; 35, Spain; 37, Argentina; 38, Italy; 46, Germany; 49, France; 51, United Kingdom; 53, Canada; 54, United States.   (SOURCE: *[12, Fig. 1b].*)

product (GNP)) and the share of the total output (GNP) accounted for by industry (manufacturing and construction).

The large-country (over 15 million population) sample consisted of 19 countries, each observed over the 1950–1963 period.   A regression with pooled data (that is, 14 observations for each country) yielded a slope which is curvilinear in logarithms of industry share on per capita GNP.   Log-linear regressions were then run for each country and the results were graphically superimposed, as in Figure 2.   The log-linear slopes are drawn only over the range of observations for each country.   An interquartile range (designated as I^+, I^-) forms a band around the pooled-data slope.

Here it is apparent that the intertemporal and intercountry patterns are very similar.   The median time series elasticity is 0.32, and the cross-section elasticity, taken at the sample mean, is 0.37.   Furthermore, by running separate cross-country regressions for 1952, 1956, and 1960, it was determined that the slopes (and their standard errors) remained stable.

The incidence of such useful overlap between time series and cross-section results is rare. Table 1, with results from a well-known Swedish study, shows a pattern in which time series estimates of income elasticities are higher than cross-sectional estimates. Similarly, automobile time-series income elasticities are higher than cross-sectional ones [18].

TABLE 1   Income-expenditure Elasticities from Household-Survey and Aggregate Time Series Data in Sweden

Item	Workers and employees (1933 survey)	Aggregate for Sweden (1921–1939 yearly data)
Butter and margarine	0.25	0.60
Butter	0.40	0.55 (tentative)
Cheese	0.35	0.50 (tentative)
Eggs	0.50	0.60 or 0.70
Meat and pork	0.25	0.30
Pork	0.10	0.30
Flour	−0.50	−0.55
Sugar	0.25	0.30

SOURCE: H. Wold, *Demand Analysis*, New York: Wiley, 1963, p. 22, Table 1.6.3.

Yet, in theory, it is agreed in the literature that higher elasticities will, in general, be found in cross-section estimates, because such estimates reflect long-run, "full-adjustment" behavior, whereas time series estimates refer to fluctuations around long-run equilibrium values.

How can these different estimates be reconciled and how can they be explained, once they have been detected?[6]

The key to understanding such differences is the classification of demand variables into time series, cross-section, and mixed variables (as discussed early in this chapter) and their influence on the error term.

Let us again write the industry part of the firm's demand model as

$$c_{i,t} = \alpha + \beta y_{i,t} + \gamma p_t + \delta n_i + u_{i,t} \tag{9}$$

$$I_t = \sum_i c_{i,t}$$

and specify that $c_{i,t}$ is expenditure of household i at time t on the product in question, $y_{i,t}$ is the household's disposable income during period t, p_t the price that all households face at the given time, n_i the household's size, and $u_{i,t}$ the random disturbance at time t.

The disturbance is composed of three terms,

$$u_{i,t} = s_i + v_t + w_{i,t} \tag{10}$$

reflecting the behavior of variables omitted from the model—time series (v_t), cross section (s_i), and mixed $(w_{i,t})$.

[6] The most extensive discussion of statistical tests to determine significant differences between time series and cross-section estimates based on the same body of data is in Kuh [6, chaps. 5 and 6]. For those with a taste for econometrics, this book offers the standard classical treatment of time series cross-section differences.

The least-squares regression model assumes that on the whole, the error term, which summarizes the behavior of such omitted variables, will behave in a purely random, or nonsystematic, fashion. In this way, it will not be correlated either with any of the determining variables or with itself over time. Picture now cross-section data, derived from survey information, with which to estimate Equation (9). The income variable is specified to be of a mixed kind, meaning that it changes both among households and over time. (By contrast, family size (n) changes over families and only very slowly over time.) The implication, therefore, is that the change in income from the last to the current period (positive or negative, small or large) matters to the household. This amounts to specifying the influence of the income variable as

$$\beta_1 y_{i,t} + \beta_2 \Delta y_{i,t} = y_{i,t} - y_{i,t-1}$$

The cross-section information we have does not give us, however, an observation on the household's previous period's income and we cannot respecify the model accordingly. This builds a systematic element into $w_{i,t}$, the error term associated with mixed omitted variables.[7]

A similar reasoning holds for time series information. As an example, let us write the market-share part of the firm's demand model as

$$x_{i,t} = A + B(\bar{p}_i - p)_t + C(a_i - \bar{a})_{t-1} + Dw_i + e_{i,t} \tag{11}$$

where $x_{i,t}$, the market share of firm i, depends on the difference between the price of its brand and the average market price at time t, on a similar difference between its advertising and that of its rivals during the preceding period, and on the index of distribution pressure w of all firms in the industry. This index could be considered as a cross-section variable. Its exclusion (which is to be expected) from time series information may again lead to serious misspecification of the model and the injection of systematic influence into the random-error term.

The basic conflict between cross-section and time-series regression estimates based on observations over similar variables is due to the omission of different variables from each. Thus, if there is a conflict between estimates derived from time series regressions and cross-section regressions based on similar variables, the chief explanation lies in the omission of variables—different ones in each of them—and the consequent introduction of systematic influence upon the error term.[8] The nonrandomness of the error term's behavior introduces bias into the estimates and leads to their differences.

A graphic illustration of the effect of a left-out variable is shown in Figure 3. Unfortunately, the illustration pertains only to the case of a cross-section variable omitted from a cross-section model. The income-expenditure relation shifts and changes slope depending on the age of the household head. Had this variable been omitted from the cross-sectionally specified model

$$c_i = f(y, \text{ age of head}) \tag{12}$$

it is obvious that quite a different relationship would have been obtained.

The somewhat ad hoc explanations why cross-section estimates should be higher or lower than those derived from time series can be replaced by a uni-

---

[7] Provided, it must be added, that the omitted variable $\Delta y_{i,t}$ is correlated with the included variable $y_{i,t}$—as we would expect here.

[8] The fact that time series variables are typically "aggregates" will also inject a difference into the estimates.

fied treatment of this problem based on the so-called misspecification bias analysis developed by econometricians and applied to the cross-section, time series issue [23].

The chief result of this analysis shows that the bias in the estimates of coefficients of included variables in a misspecified cross section, where the left-out variables are of a time series or mixed character, is composed of a *product* of two terms: (1) the value of the regression coefficients of the excluded variables *had they been included* in the regression, and (2) the correlation coefficient, *r*, between the excluded and the included variables. With suitable rephrasing, this result also holds for misspecified time series regression.

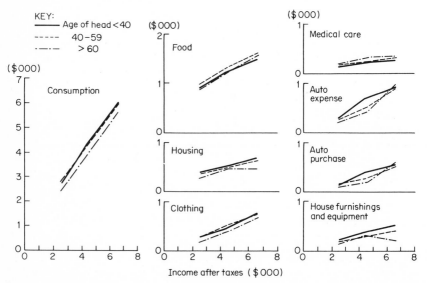

Fig. 3. Income slopes by age of family head for selected values of other family characteristics. Observations are restricted to white employee families of two, three, or four persons with cash assets less than $2,000.

TIME SERIES OF CROSS-SECTIONS

Obviously, the only type of data thoroughly satisfactory for use in the statistical analysis of demand are observations on individual buyers or firms (or other demand determinants) over *time*. Such data can be designated as time series of cross sections or, more simply, *moving cross sections*. Only with the help of such data can we encompass all three classes of variables: time-related, cross-sectional, and mixed.

On the buyer side, we have panels (both industrial and consumer) and store audits to provide us with such data; company sales-district or customer records are the second major information source on customer characteristics and competitive action. The increasing flow of such information does not make it unrealistic for marketing management to insist upon demand studies fully based on the demand model specified in Equation (1).

The use of moving cross-sections does not, however, automatically ensure the elimination of bias due to cross-section or time series misspecification.[9] A simple method of preventing its frequent occurrence is the employment of dummy variables.

Consider industry demand, $I_t = \sum_i c_{i,t}$, first. Let us say that it is a linear function of household income, lagged income, relative price (relative to the consumer price index), and household homeownership:

$$c_{i,t} = \alpha + \beta_i y_{i,t} + \beta_2 y_{i,t-1} + \beta_3 \left(\frac{p}{c_{p1}}\right)_t + \beta_4 H + u_{i,t} \tag{13}$$

Yet probably a large number of household-specific attributes (cross-sectional characteristics) are omitted from the specification, and the total effect may not be random. Similarly, a large number of time-related variables will be left out.

If a dummy variable for each household and a dummy variable for each time period are now added to the equation, their coefficients will "soak up" these unspecified influences and leave us with "clean" estimates of slopes of those variables which we consider to be of greater interest.

Thus Equation (13) would be rewritten as

$$c_{i,t} = \alpha + \beta_1 y_{i,t} + \beta_2 y_{i,t-1} + \beta_3 \left(\frac{p}{c_{p1}}\right)_t + \beta_4 H_{i,t} + \sum_i \gamma_i + \sum_t \delta l_t \tag{13a}$$

where γ and δ are the coefficients of the household-specific and time-specific dummies.

Frequently, however, it is not possible to carry a dummy variable for each household for, if we have many households, the staggering number of determining variables would be impossible to handle even by a large computer. We can then turn to a so-called covariance regression which is the exact equivalent of a regression analysis employing dummy variables.[10]

Similarly, when estimating the market-share portion of the total demand expression, if the data are observed over territories, over competitors, and over time, the regression equation should be specified along somewhat the same lines:

$$x_{i,t} = A + \sum_A^Z B\, m_{i,t} + \sum_A^Z \sum_j^l Cr_{j,t} + \sum_j^l Dd_j + \sum_t^u El_t \tag{14}$$

$$+ \sum_A^Z B\, m_{i,t-1} + \sum_A^Z \sum_j^l Cr_{j,t-1}$$

$$\vdots$$

$$+ \sum_A^Z B\, m_{i,t-k} + \sum_A^Z \sum_j^l Cr_{j,t-k}$$

A to Z signify marketing actions (price, advertising, distribution pressure,

---

[9] Simultaneous equation bias has not been discussed, since it is outside the scope of this chapter.

[10] A good illustration of covariance regression is in [10].

and so on) on the part of the firm, m, and on the part of rivals, r_j to r_l; the d's stand for dummies specific to rivals, j to l; t stands for dummies activated during specified periods t to u. There are also lagged terms written on the second and last lines of the equation to express the market's delayed reactions to changes in relevant stimuli.

Similar models are already in active use in finance (where they are used to explain investment behavior) [6, 21]; market-share equations have been estimated based on such time series of cross-sections but not, as yet, using the dummy variable approach to eliminate possible specification bias. The potential payoff is attractive.

REFERENCES

Books

1. Balestra, P., *The Demand for Natural Gas in the United States*, Amsterdam: North Holland, 1967, chap. 5.
2. Brown, R. G., *Smoothing, Forecasting and Prediction*, Englewood Cliffs, N.J.: Prentice-Hall, 1963.
3. Ferber, Robert, and P. J. Verdoorn, *Research Methods in Economics and Business*, New York: Macmillan, 1962, chaps. 4–9.
4. Green, P. E., and D. S. Tull, *Research for Marketing Decisions*, Englewood Cliffs, N.J.: Prentice-Hall, 1966.
5. Kane, Edward J., *Economic Statistics and Econometrics*, New York: Harper & Row, 1968, pp. 359–373.
6. Kuh, Edwin, *Capital Stock Growth: A Micro-Econometric Approach*, Amsterdam: North Holland, 1963, chaps. 5 and 6.
7. Nerlove, Mark, *Distributed Lags and Demand Analysis*, Agricultural Handbook no. 141, U.S. Department of Agriculture, 1957.
8. Palda, K. S., *The Measurement of Cumulative Advertising Effects*, Englewood Cliffs, N.J.: Prentice-Hall, 1963.
9. Palda, K. S., *Economic Analysis for Marketing Decisions*, Englewood Cliffs, N.J.: Prentice-Hall, 1969, chap. 4.
10. Schipper, L., *Consumer Discretionary Behavior*, Amsterdam: North Holland, 1964, chaps. 1 and 2.
11. Wold, H., *Demand Analysis*, New York: Wiley, 1963, chaps. 1, 14, and 15.

Journal Articles and Other Material

12. Chenery, H. B., and L. Taylor, "Development Patterns: Among Countries and Over Time," *Review of Economics and Statistics*, vol. 47, November 1965.
13. Chow, G. C., "Tests of Equality between Sets of Coefficients in Two Linear Regressions," *Econometrica*, vol. 28, July 1960.
14. Crockett, J., and I. Friend, "A Complete Set of Consumer Demand Relationships," in I. Friend and R. Jones (eds.), *Consumption and Saving*, Philadelphia: University of Pennsylvania Press, 1966.
15. Farrar, D. E., and R. R. Glauber, "Multicollinearity in Regression Analysis," *Review of Economics and Statistics*, vol. 49, February 1967.
16. Grunfeld, Y., "The Interpretation of Cross Section Estimates in a Dynamic Model," *Econometrica*, vol. 30, 1962.
17. Harkness, J. P., "A Spectral-Analytic Test of the Long-Swing Hypothesis in Canada," *Review of Economics and Statistics*, vol. 50, November 1968.
18. Houthakker, H. S., and J. Haldi, "Household Investment in Automobiles: An Intertemporal Cross-Section Analysis" in I. Friend and R. Jones (eds.), *Consumption and Saving*, vol. 1, Philadelphia: University of Pennsylvania Press, 1960, pp. 175–224.
19. Jessen, R. J., "A Switch-Over Experimental Design to Measure Advertising Effect," *Journal of Advertising Research*, vol. 1, March 1961.

20. Kuh, E., and J. Meyer, "How Extraneous Are Extraneous Estimates?" *Review of Economics and Statistics,* vol. 47, 1965.
21. Lambin, J. J., "Measuring the Profitability of Advertising: An Empirical Study," *Journal of Industrial Economics,* 1969.
22. Liviatan, N., "Estimates of Distributed Lag Consumption Functions from Cross Section Data," *Review of Economics and Statistics,* vol. 47, February 1965.
23. Simon, J. L., and D. J. Aigner, "Cross-Section versus Time-Series Estimates: A Specification Bias Analysis," Systems Formulation, Methodology, and Policy Workshop Paper 6801 of the Social Systems Research Institute, University of Wisconsin, June 1968.
24. Theil, H., "On the Use of Incomplete Prior Information in Regression Analysis," *Journal of the American Statistical Association,* vol. 56, 1965.

Statistical Analysis of Relationships

Chapter 4

Spectral Analysis

JOHN U. FARLEY *Graduate School of Business, Columbia University, New York, New York*

MELVIN J. HINICH *Carnegie-Mellon University, Pittsburgh, Pennsylvania*

Cycles abound in marketing time series. Industry and firm sales almost always involve some cyclical behavior over time—seasonal patterns, relationships between sales and business cycles, or rhythmic sales patterns over the month, the week, or even the day [3]. Besides these regular, repetitive, and well-known cyclical phenomena, there are some more subtle questions related to cycles. Some sales patterns (like certain consumer durables) move with the business cycle, whereas others are countercyclical (like certain construction patterns). Advertising cycles may lead or lag sales cycles, depending on the decision rules used in timing expenditures. Some cyclical patterns are complexly interrelated (as with the corn and hog sales and price cycles), and others may or may not even exist (as in the case of hypothesized, decades-long, sales cycles in certain construction industries).

Time series are usually attacked statistically with techniques like those described in the last chapter. These techniques deal with cycles as well as with a variety of other time series phenomena. Time series may also be analyzed with most of the other techniques described in Part E—regression, correlation, index numbers, and so on. All of these are very useful, but there is a statistical technique, called *spectral analysis*, that is especially tailored to handle analysis of cycles in time series. This section discusses the theory behind spectral analysis, and then presents an application to a pair of related marketing time series.

CYCLES IN MARKETING TIME SERIES

The notion of a cycle, regardless of its source, is usually thought of in terms of sinusoidal functions, as shown in Figure 1. Sinusoidals are cyclical functions that repeat the same pattern over and over as they move along the horizontal axis. Sinusoidals are characterized by two features: (1) the period, or time required to complete one full swing through the cycle, and (2) the importance or strength of the cycle, measured by the height above the horizontal axis at the highest point. The functions themselves are usually modeled as sines and cosines, which have the same shape but differ in the point at which they cross the horizontal axis.

Time series analysis is much richer when this analogy to sine and cosine waves is exploited. For example, a seasonal pattern may involve sinusoidals with known periods (12 months, say), and values of sines and cosines can be used as independent variables in regressions to estimate the importance (amplitudes) of these cycles. These same regressions can be used for seasonal adjustment, both by computing seasonal adjustment factors and by replacing the

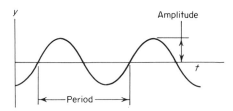

Fig. 1.   A cycle as a sinusoidal function.

original data series with residuals about the regression line, now free of the worrisome cyclical components.

Ad hoc use of sinusoidals with known periods is very useful, but it does not fully exploit the potential for two reasons:

1. The periods of the cyclical components in a marketing time series are often irregular. For example, the particular month, week, or day on which a movable holiday like Easter falls may cause seasonal patterns to vary slightly; the periods of longer business cycles are often so irregular that even detecting turning points is a major task for the time.series analyst. In both cases, specification of the exact period of the sinusoidals for regression analysis may be difficult.

2. There is usually uncertainty about which sinusoidals are present in a series. A procedure is needed for seeking cyclical components or combinations of components which occur in any given series.

Both these problems may be attacked with spectral analysis, a set of techniques specially designed to capitalize on the analogy of sinusoidals to cyclical phenomena in statistical series.

AUTOCOVARIANCES AND STATIONARITY

A fundamental ingredient of all time series analysis is the notion of autocovariance—the covariance of a given observation in a time series with its neighbors

1, 2, . . . , k positions to its right and left in the same series. For observations τ positions apart, the autocovariance is defined as

$$C(t, \tau) = E[X(t) - \mu(t)][X(t + \tau) - \mu(t + \tau)] \tag{1}$$

which depends on both the time period, t, and the lag or distance between the two points, τ.

The definition in Equation (1) leads to some real practical difficulties unless other restrictions are imposed. Since $\mu(t)$ depends on time, repeated, simultaneous observations on the series are required to estimate $\mu(t)$. However, if μ were "stationary," this equation could be simplified. Stationarity means that the expected value of any observation, neglecting sinusoidal components, is the same; that is, for all t

$$E[X(t)] = \mu$$

In particular, no trend components are permissible—a formidable requirement, but one which can often be achieved through transformation of even raw series which flagrantly violate the assumption. The importance of stationarity is that the mean, μ, can replace $\mu(t)$ for all observations in Equation (1).

An ordinary homoskedasticity assumption—variance stationarity or $E[X(t) - \mu]^2 = \sigma^2$ for all t—is similarly required, and can also be achieved with basic and well-known transformations in most cases.

With these assumptions, the definition of the autocovariances in Equation (1) simplifies to:

$$C(t, \tau) = E[X(t) - \mu][X(t + \tau) - \mu] \tag{2}$$

because μ is independent of t by assumption. But the autocovariance still depends on time (t), so another critical property is required; the autocovariance must be independent of the particular time period. That is, it must depend only on distance between itself and its neighbors' τ positions on either side. This is dictated by the statistical necessity of building up a sample of repetitions of the same basic behavior of the series over time. (If a given set of autocovariances occurs only once and then changes, this amounts to a sample with one observation.) A computing formula for the autocovariance for a given lag, τ, then follows from summing over t and estimating the stationary μ with $\bar{X}$, the arithmetic mean:

$$\hat{C}(t) = \frac{1}{n - \tau} \sum_{t=1}^{n-\tau} [X(t) - \bar{X}][X(t + \tau) - \bar{X}] \tag{3}$$

Notice that $\hat{C}(0)$, the zero-lag autocovariance, is really the estimate of the covariance of the time series with itself and is the ordinary variance of the series—a fact central to spectral analysis.

The computing formula reflects a very troublesome facet of time series analysis—a large number of observations are required to analyze long movements (long lags involving large τ). The number of lags, τ, for which autocovariances can be reasonably computed is much smaller than the number of data points, because the number of elements in each estimate decreases as τ becomes large and the estimates become noisy.

In practice, it is reasonable to compute no more than $n/5$ autocovariances, where n is the sample size. For example, if a 15-year building cycle is hypothesized, at least 75 years of observations of an annual construction series meeting the stationarity assumptions are necessary—truly formidable data requirements.

HOW SPECTRAL ANALYSIS WORKS

The following example [2] illustrates how spectral analysis works. Suppose an observed time series is composed of cosine waves of different periods plus a random-error term which is serially uncorrelated and has mean zero:

$$X(t) = a_1 \cos(2\pi f_1 t) + \ldots + a_m \cos(2\pi f_m t) + \epsilon_t \tag{4}$$

(Cosines alone, rather than a mixture of sines and cosines, are used to keep the algebra manageable.) The f_i's are the frequencies of the cosine terms and are the reciprocals of the periods—for example, a yearly cycle involves a period of 12 months and hence a frequency of $1/12$. The a_i's are the amplitudes of each component. The series is clearly stationary and has mean zero.

Using the formula for autocovariances in Equation (3),

$$\hat{C}(\tau) = \frac{1}{n-\tau} \sum_{t=0}^{n-\tau} \left\{ \sum_{i=1}^{m} \sum_{j=1}^{m} a_i \cos(2\pi f_i t) \, a_j \cos[2\pi f_j (t+\tau)] + \epsilon_t \epsilon_{t+\tau} \right\} \tag{5}$$

Allowing the sample size to become large as it stretches into the future, four characteristics of Equation (5) are useful: (1) For large samples, the estimated value of any autocovariance converges to the true value; (2) all the terms multiplying sinusoidal terms times the error term drop out because $E(\epsilon_t) = 0$ for all t; (3) sinusoidal functions at different frequencies are orthogonal, so all terms involving multiplications of elements of cycles of different frequencies drop out; (4) $E(\epsilon_t \epsilon_{t+\tau}) = 0$ for all $\tau \neq 0$ and σ_ϵ^2 for $\tau = 0$ by assumption. As n becomes large, then,

$$C(\tau) = \frac{1}{2} \sum_{i=1}^{m} a_i^2 \cos(2\pi f_i \tau) \qquad \text{for all } \tau \neq 0 \tag{6}$$

As mentioned earlier, if $\tau = 0$, Equation (6) is the ordinary variance of the series in Equation (4). The squared error of ε, σ_ε^2, remains for this case only. Because $\cos(0) = 1$, $\cos(2\pi f_i 0) = 1$ for all frequencies and

$$C(0) = \sigma_x^2 = \frac{1}{2} \sum_{i=1}^{m} a_i^2 + \sigma_\epsilon^2 \tag{7}$$

For large samples, then, the variance of the series (4) has been decomposed into components of two types: (1) the squared amplitudes of the sinusoidal components that originally made up the series, and (2) the variance of the additive error term. If the variance of the error term is large relative to the overall variance, the sinusoidal terms are unimportant and the weights are small. If the series is a precise set of sinusoidals, the variance is composed entirely of the squared weights of sinusoidals.

Relationship (7) reflects the spirit of spectral analysis—decomposing the overall variance of a stationary time series into a set of components attributable on the one hand to various important cyclical components and on the other to a random component. The random component plays the same role in spectral analysis as it does in regression, factor analysis, and so on; it is the variance of the series unexplained by the statistical model.

FOURIER ANALYSIS AND THE SPECTRUM

Spectral analysis is done by performing Fourier analyses on estimated auto-covariances of stationary time series. With Fourier analysis, any empirical series or mathematical function can be approximated by a sum of sine and cosine terms with different periods and amplitudes. Like any such technique, the approximation is better if the functions used for approximation behave much like the data-generating process; Fourier series approximation of cycles in time series thus has considerable intuitive appeal. The approximation assumes, in effect, that the series is made up of sinusoidals, as in Equation (4). Fourier transforms of weighted autocovariances transform the analysis from autocovariances in the time domain to densities or contributions of cycles of various frequencies in the frequency domain.

The *power spectrum*, the result of the transformation, expresses the overall variance of a series as a function of the frequencies of various sinusoidal components. If there are substantial peaks in the spectrum, analogous to large values of the a_i in Equation (7), sinusoidals of that frequency contribute measurably to the series. If there are no substantial cyclical components, the spectrum is flat, meaning that no cycle in the series contributes strongly to the variance. In spectral jargon, this is "white noise"—randomly distributed, serially uncorrelated disturbances.

The idea of applying Fourier analysis to cyclic economic series is quite old, but several solutions to practical problems associated with spectral decomposition of variance are relatively new. For example, straightforward application of Fourier analysis to a set of autocovariances estimated from a short series produces wobbly and uninterpretable results. Various schemes to weight raw observations and autocovariances have been developed which make estimated values of the power spectrum more interpretable and their statistical properties more desirable. One set of weights for the autocovariances is the "spectral window," a term which comes up in connection with all discussion of spectra [3, 4].

AN APPLICATION OF SPECTRAL ANALYSIS

To illustrate the use of spectral analysis on a type of data frequently used in marketing research, spectral analyses were done on two monthly series—one the series of national automobile registrations for a European country from 1956 to 1965, and the other series the factory sales (excluding a special product), during the same period, of a firm with a significant domestic market share. The first series comes from public documents and the second from the firm's sales records. The analysis stresses those matters important to study of marketing time series—which frequencies are present in each of the series, how these components affect the series, how the series should be adjusted for further analysis, and how the two series are interrelated.

"Filtering" Data

The plots of the two raw data series (Figure 2) give an impression of complex cyclical movement about some kind of trend line. The latter means that the assumption of mean stationarity is violated. Statistical procedures may or may not be robust with regard to violations of this type; unfortunately, spectral analysis is sensitive to this violation—an important reason for some dissatisfaction with the technique. The sensitivity follows from the weighting procedures developed to deal with the finite record length and the uncertainty as to the exact cyclical components present in the series. Computational routines view a trend as a small piece of a cycle of extremely long duration. Since the trend usually explains a substantial portion of the overall variance, the contribution of this very-low-frequency term to the spectrum is enormous relative to other components, and the estimates of the importance of these other components are smudged out by weighting procedures used to make the spectral estimates stable. The offending trend must be removed, but the method of removal is quite important for further analysis of the adjusted data.

The spectral term for such adjustment is *filtering*, because the adjustment procedures process the series to remove or filter out undesirable characteristics

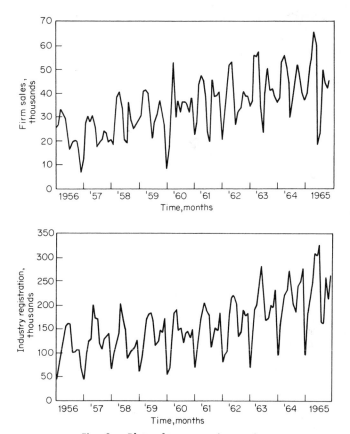

Fig. 2.   Plots of two raw time series.

while passing through other components with as little distortion as possible. Behavior of various filtering procedures (in Fourier terminology, the "transfer function" of the filter) is very important, and mechanical data adjustment, particularly with various moving average techniques, can have substantial impact on other elements of both a raw series and the spectrum. Of course, the appropriate filter also depends on the goals of the analysis. The higher frequencies are important in this case and the trend is undesirable, so a very-narrow-band filter is needed—one which removes the trend with minimum effect on the higher frequencies. A filter with desirable properties, if the trend is linear and additive, is a simple regression on t. The actual equations for the two series are:

$$\text{Firm sales: } x_1(t) = 21.5 + 0.2104t \qquad R^2 = 0.392$$
$$(S_b = 0.0241)$$
$$\text{Industry registrations: } x_2(t) = 93.25 + 1.008t \qquad R^2 = 0.412 \qquad (8)$$
$$(S_b = 0.1197)$$

The linearity assumption is important, as many standard time-series adjustment procedures model trend, cyclical components, and error terms multiplicitively. (This problem is discussed later in connection with the bispectrum.) The linearity assumption is reasonable, as the same regressions fitted to logarithms of the raw observations have coefficients of determination of 0.290 and 0.285, respectively. Range tests on the first 24 and last 24 observations in each series indicate no heteroskedasticity, so the variance stationarity assumption is reasonable.

Spectra of the Individual Series

The first task is to examine the spectra of the two detrended series, that is, of the residuals about the trend lines in Equation (8). Given 120 observations, it is reasonable to compute no more than 24 autocovariances, meaning in turn that it is possible to examine the importance of sinusoidal components of only 25 different periods, ranging from two months (the shortest cycle which can be analyzed with data collected monthly) to extremely long waves (approaching infinite lengths). The estimated power spectra for the two detrended series are shown in Table 1. Interpretation involves looking for peaks in these spectral estimates that can reasonably be explained in terms of what the analyst knows about the market he is studying.

Both series clearly contain strong peaks at 12 months, meaning that an annual cycle, probably part of a strong seasonal pattern, is present in both series. It is important to notice that frequencies next to important peaks are contaminated so that they also appear to be important. The spectral values of neighbors (9.6 months and 16 months) are probably examples of such contamination by the strong 12-month cycle. Trends appear as large values of low-frequency terms in the spectra; Table 1 shows that the spectrum of the firm data has very small values for these terms, whereas the suspiciously large terms related to long periods in the industry data deserve closer examination.

In addition to the seasonal peak, both series have large peaks at six months and smaller peaks at periods which are harmonics of the 12- and 6-month cycles. Harmonics are certain cycles which might be induced by a strong effect of another cycle if the latter enters the generating process nonlinearly—for example, if it were multiplied against the trend rather than added to fit. These harmonics have periods of 4, 3, and 2.4 and 2 months, respectively.

These results suggest two further areas for analysis:

1. A model is needed of the interaction of the various cyclical components found in the spectra of the two series. Unsatisfactory explanations of the presence of harmonics in spectra have been a source of dissatisfaction with the technique, but bispectral analysis may be useful in resolving these problems.

2. Relationships between the series, such as the lead-lag structure, might be studied. Cross-spectral analysis is useful for this purpose.

The Cross-Spectrum and the Relationship between the Two Series

The frequency patterns of the two series are quite similar, and both series deal with aspects of the same market. This means that the series are closely related to each other. Cross-spectral analysis can be used to analyze these relationships in a very sensitive and disaggregated way. Cross-spectral analysis looks at the interrelationships of cyclical components of a given frequency in each of the series (as in Figure 3). It can uniquely answer two questions about these interrelationships:

1. To what extent are components of various frequencies important in the makeup of both series? That is, are the spectra really similar, component by component? The ratio of the peaks of the two amplitudes (B/A in Figure 3) is a rough measure of this type of relationship, and can be computed separately for each frequency.

TABLE 1   Spectral Densities of Detrended Series

Period of cycle (months)	Estimated power spectrum	
	Firm shipments	Industry registrations
∞	6.84	1078.34
48.00	13.42	661.40
24.00	16.99	201.93
16.00	33.84	1101.83
12.00	55.74	2448.14
9.60	30.83	1190.22
8.00	20.33	222.31
6.85	78.12	1464.78
6.00	142.62	2889.35
5.33	64.73	1153.88
4.80	19.42	53.28
4.36	25.73	199.84
4.00	25.46	408.26
3.69	16.50	273.84
3.42	10.29	131.78
3.20	9.46	233.68
3.00	15.80	372.70
2.82	12.80	187.67
2.66	8.71	78.66
2.52	6.70	340.52
2.40	3.54	638.04
2.28	2.07	276.97
2.18	6.67	30.09
2.08	5.85	144.73
2.00	2.71	301.48

2. If a given frequency is important, do the cycles occur simultaneously with respect to time, or is there a lag (or phase shift) between the components of two series at that frequency? Such a lag is shown in Figure 3. Again, these shifts may be quite different for different frequencies.

The advantages of cross-spectral analysis over autocorrelation are clear for both purposes. In the time domain, cross-autocorrelation coefficients can be calculated between the series for different lag values and that lag value chosen which maximizes this correlation (in this case, when the firm's sales are lagged one month

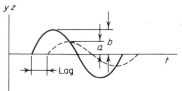

Fig. 3.   Components of a given frequency in two series.

behind industry sales). The analyst is then forced to assume that the entire process generating the firm's sales lags one month behind the process generating the market data. Suppose, however, that the seasonals for the two series coincide (the lag is zero) but that a substantial lead or lag exists between the six-month components. Cross-spectral techniques allow the analyst to look at each cyclical component separately. It is very much like simple regression of a given frequency component in one series on the same frequency component in another.

There are three statistical measures involved in cross-spectral analysis:

1. *Coherency:* essentially the correlation between the components of the two series which are attributable to a given frequency.
2. *Gain:* essentially the regression coefficient by which the value of the frequency component in one series is multiplied to produce the same component of the other.
3. *Phase shift:* length of the time period that a given frequency component leads or lags the same component in the other series.

For the two series studied here, these statistics (Table 2) indicate very high coherency for 12- and 6-month cycles, again with some contamination at neighboring frequencies. The other harmonic frequencies also have larger than average coherencies. The only other coherency greater than 0.7 is at the period of 3.42, which has such small spectral values for each series (Table 1) that the coherency is probably a statistical accident.

TABLE 2   Results of Cross-spectral Analysis between Firm Sales and Industry Registrations

Period of cycle (months)	Coherency	Gain	Lead of sales over shipments (radians)
∞	0.635	0.064	−0.294
48.00	0.366	0.086	−0.519
24.00	0.338	0.169	−1.244
16.00	0.787	0.155	1.047
12.00	0.915	0.144	1.007
9.60	0.799	0.144	0.987
8.00	0.403	0.192	0.807
6.85	0.888	0.218	0.930
6.00	0.963	0.218	0.934
5.33	0.883	0.223	0.933
4.80	0.535	0.442	1.250
4.36	0.198	0.160	−0.588
4.00	0.244	0.123	−0.253
3.69	0.195	0.108	−1.293
3.42	0.719	0.237	1.389
3.20	0.483	0.139	0.500
3.00	0.619	0.162	0.114
2.82	0.199	0.117	0.376
2.66	0.311	0.186	−0.797
2.52	0.189	0.061	−0.229
2.40	0.325	0.042	0.221
2.28	0.151	0.034	0.391
2.18	0.203	0.212	0.684
2.08	0.082	0.058	0.824
2.00	0.023	0.014	1.464

The phase statistics indicate that shipments lag sales by about seven weeks in the 12-month cycle and that the component lags about three weeks in the 6-month cycle. Notice that these are in fact different lags for each component. There are some well-known phase and gain patterns which correspond to well-known lag structures (simple delay or distributed lag, for example), but the results in Table 2 do not correspond to these patterns [5].

Bispectra and Nonlinear Relationships among Cycles

The patterns of the individual spectra in Table 1 provide a clue that the two- and six-month cycles enter the relationship nonadditively, inducing the harmonic values at 4, 3, and 2.4 months. Alternatively, the higher harmonics may be present in their own right. The bispectrum, useful for discriminating between these two cases, is somewhat analogous to the skewness in classical statistics. It indicates whether a lower frequency induces some or all of the higher frequencies nonlinearly—multiplicatively, for example. The theory of bispectra is beyond this discussion [6], but computation for a few important points is feasible for the detrended data in both series. These calculations show highly significant nonlinear interactions among the 12-, 6-, 4-, and 3-month cyclical components in each of the detrended series. This is useful both for modeling purposes and for choosing among a variety of seasonal adjustment procedures.

Spectra of Seasonally Adjusted Data

On the basis of the bispectrum, the method of link relatives was chosen to deseasonalize the series. This nonlinear seasonal adjustment procedure divides the series by a seasonal index in deseasonalization. The spectra of the two deseasonalized series are shown in Table 3. The spectrum of the firm's sales data is flat—that is, linear detrending and the multiplicative deseasonalization has reduced the residuals to random error or "white noise." The spectrum of industry registrations is not so well-behaved. Substantial power at the low frequencies indicates a long-period cycle remains. This has also been observed in this series for another time period and in other economic series [1]. This very subtle long movement, apparently related to employment and per capita income series, is identified by the spectrum as both present and important. For some reason, firm sales are immune to this influence.

USES OF SPECTRAL ANALYSIS

Spectral analysis is a time series technique useful for analyzing cyclical components in series. Reasons for using spectral analysis include:

1. When the analyst has prior knowledge that certain cyclical components are present in a series, spectral analysis ascertains their relative importance.

2. When the analyst is uncertain about which cyclical components are present, the spectrum identifies important cycles in the data. A flat spectrum indicates no important cycles, whereas peaks in the spectrum indicate the presence of strong cycles.

3. The lead and lag structure between two series can be studied with the cross-spectrum, even when different structures occur at different frequencies.

4. The effect of various adjustment procedures—detrending and deseasonalizing, for example—can be studied. One question is whether the residual series has been reduced serially uncorrelated, random error, or whether some important components remain in an adjusted series. Undesirable side effects of adjustment procedures can also be determined in terms of spectral peaks or phase shifts induced by the adjustment procedure [7].

5. The bispectrum helps model building and sensible choice among data adjustment procedures by seeking nonlinear relationships among cyclical phenomena in a data-generating process.

6. Cross-spectral analysis of two series may suggest models for forecasting one series with another which leads it. Comparing empirical phase and gain patterns with known patterns implied by various mathematical relationships between series [5] may suggest models for forecasting or for econometric analysis.

TABLE 3   Spectral Density Estimates for Detrended, Seasonally Adjusted Data

Period of cycle (months)	Estimated power spectrum	
	Seasonally adjusted firm shipments	Seasonally adjusted industry registrations
∞	0.036	3.975
48.00	0.070	2.398
24.00	0.095	0.954
16.00	0.110	0.747
12.00	0.093	0.680
9.00	0.058	0.531
8.00	0.079	0.255
6.85	0.079	0.255
6.00	0.059	0.159
5.33	0.047	0.466
4.80	0.068	0.419
4.36	0.084	0.338
4.00	0.074	0.384
3.69	0.057	0.378
3.42	0.036	0.290
3.20	0.027	0.316
3.00	0.033	0.405
2.82	0.034	0.379
2.67	0.030	0.179
2.53	0.027	0.103
2.49	0.023	0.074
2.29	0.009	0.088
2.18	0.004	0.098
2.08	0.021	0.207
2.00	0.018	0.312

Problems facing these applications are, however, important. Properties of the estimates are virtually all asymptotic and the stationarity assumptions are often critical. Since most marketing series are quite short, statistical testing methodology, when available, is often clumsy. Further, spectral analysis does not itself adjust series, and must be combined with other techniques, such as regression. In concert with these other techniques, however, spectral analysis provides a very efficient and powerful tool for analysis of cycles in time series.

REFERENCES

1. Brandes, O. E., J. U. Farley, M. J. Hinich, and U. Zackrisson, "The Time Domain and Frequency Domain in Time Series Analysis," *Journal of Swedish Economics,* May 1968, pp. 25–42.

2. Brown, R. G., *Smoothing, Forecasting and Prediction,* Englewood Cliffs, N.J.: Prentice-Hall, 1962, pp. 393–401.
3. Granger, C. W., *Spectral Analysis of Economic Time Series,* Princeton, N.J.: Princeton University Press, 1964.
4. Hannan, E. J., *Time Series Analysis,* London: Methuen, 1960.
5. Jenkins, G. M., "Some Examples of and Comments on Spectral Analysis," *Proceedings of the IBM Computing Symposium on Statistics,* White Plains, N.Y.: International Business Machines.
6. McDonald, G. J. F., *The Bispectra of Atmosphere Pressure Records,* White Plains, N.Y.: International Business Machines.
7. Nerlove, M., "Spectral Analysis of Seasonal Adjustment Procedures," *Econometrica,* vol. 32, October 1964, pp. 241–286.

Statistical Analysis of Relationships

Chapter 5

Correlation and Regression Methods

HENRY J. CLAYCAMP *N. W. Ayer and Son, New York, New York*

Correlation and regression techniques are statistical analysis tools that are particularly useful in quantifying relationships between a single dependent (criterion) variable and one or more independent (predictor) variables. Because of their flexibility and ease of use, correlation and regression methods are relevant to a wide range of marketing research problems.

The purpose of this chapter is to provide an introduction to correlation and regression analysis. The first section will present a brief discussion of basic concepts and measures with major emphasis on the analysis of linear relationships between two variables. The second section deals with correlation and regression analysis of multivariate statistical relationships, that is, relationships among three or more variables. The final section focuses on the critical assumptions involved in regression analysis as they relate to the major applications in marketing research.

BASIC CONCEPTS

Correlation and regression are closely related concepts. The more general term *correlation analysis* refers to the *extent* or *degree* of statistical association among two or more variables. The term *regression analysis* refers to the *nature* of the statistical dependence, that is, the regression of a single criterion (dependent) variable upon one or more independent variables.

The basic measures produced by regression techniques are of two types:

1. The parameter values of a mathematical model—called a regression equation—that can be used to calculate expected values of the dependent variable as a function of specific independent variable values.

2. Measures of the deviations, or variance, between the original and the expected values of the dependent variable.

Correlation techniques, on the other hand, produce standardized summary statistics to measure the goodness-of-fit of the regression equation to the data as well as to analyze the relative strength of statistical relationships among alternative combinations of variables.

The following example illustrates these basic concepts in the analysis of linear relations between two variables, that is, in *simple correlation* and *simple regression* analysis.

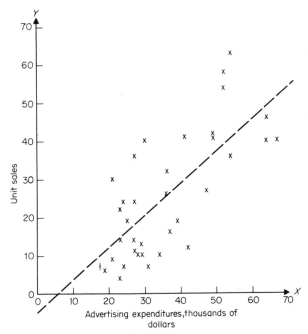

Fig. 1.   Relation of retail sales to advertising expenditures for 35 market areas.

Simple Regression

Suppose we wish to develop a linear mathematical model of the statistical relationship exhibited by the data in Figure 1 in order to calculate expected values of Y, conditional upon given values of X. For purposes of discussion, let us assume that the data have been drawn from 35 market areas and that

Y = retail sales of a consumer product (in thousands of units/time period)
X = advertising expenditures (in thousands of dollars/time period)

Thus, we wish to calculate values of the parameters (a) and (b_{yx}) for an equation

$$Y_c = a + b_{yx} X$$

where
a = expected values of sales at $X = 0$
b_{xy} = average change in sales per unit change in advertising expenditures
Y_c = calculated value of Y, given X

such that the deviations between the original observations and calculated values of the dependent variable measured by the following formula are at a minimum

$$\sigma_{y_c}{}^2 = \sum_{i=1}^{N} \frac{(Y_i - Y_c)^2}{N}$$

where

Y_i = value of sales in the ith market area

N = number of market areas

The equation $Y_c = a + b_{yx}X$ is known as the *simple regression equation of Y on X*. The slope parameter b_{yx}, *called the coefficient of gross regression of Y on X*, defines the gross change in Y associated with a one-unit change in X.

The statistic $\sigma_{y_c}{}^2$ is known as the *residual or unexplained variance*. It is a measure of the variation in the dependent variable *not* associated with, or explained by, variations in the independent variable.

The square root of the residual variance, denoted by the symbol (σ_{y_c}), is called the *standard deviation of regression*.

Although trial-and-error methods and graphical analysis[1] could be used to select values of a and b_{yx} for a line which depicts the average linear relationship between the variables, the problem can be solved mathematically using the method of ordinary least squares.

Ordinary least-squares regression analysis produces values of the intercept and slope for a regression line such that the residual variance $\sigma_{y_c}{}^2$ is minimized

and the sum of vertical deviations—$\sum_{i=1}^{N}(Y_i - Y_c)$—is equal to zero. Conse-

quently, values of Y_c calculated from a least-squares regression equation are estimates of the *conditional arithmetic mean* of Y. The residual variance $(\sigma_{y_c}{}^2)$ and standard deviation of regression (σ_{y_c}) measure the dispersion about the regression line, and are directly analogous to the total sample variance $(\sigma_y{}^2)$ and sample standard deviation (σ_{y_c}) which measure the dispersion about the sample mean Y,

where

$\sigma_y{}^2$ = sample variance

$$= \sum_{i=1}^{N} \frac{(Y_i - Y)^2}{N}$$

σ_y = sample standard deviation = $\sqrt{\sigma_y{}^2}$

$\bar{Y}$ = arithmetic mean = $\sum_{i=1}^{N} \frac{Y_i}{N}$

The least-squares coefficient of gross regression is defined as follows:[2]

$$b_{yx} = \frac{\text{covariance } (y, x)}{\text{variance } (x)} = \frac{\sigma_{yx}}{\sigma_x{}^2}$$

where $\sigma_{yx} = \sum_{i=1}^{N} \frac{(Y_i - \bar{Y})(X_i - \bar{X})}{N}$

---

[1] For a complete discussion of graphical regression analysis, see [4, pp. 370–379].

[2] The least-squares formulas are obtained by setting the partial derivative of $\sum_{i=1}^{N} \frac{[Y_i - (a + b_{yx}X)]^2}{N}$, with respect to a and b_{yx} equal to zero. Readers with a working knowledge of differential calculus are encouraged to derive the above formulas as an exercise.

Once the value of b_{yx} has been calculated, it can be substituted into the following formula to determine the least-squares estimate of the intercept,

$$a = \bar{Y} - b_{yx} \bar{X}$$

Table 1 shows the sample means, variances, standard deviations, and the covariance calculated[3] from the original data plotted in Figure 1. The follow-

TABLE 1   **Sample Statistics Entering into a Simple Regression Problem**

Statistic	Y	X
Mean	$\bar{Y} = \sum\limits_{i=1}^{N} \dfrac{Y_i}{N}$ $= \dfrac{878}{35}$ $= 25.086$	$\bar{X} = \sum\limits_{i=1}^{N} \dfrac{X_i}{N}$ $= \dfrac{1242}{35}$ $= 35.486$
Variance	$\sigma_y^2 = \sum\limits_{i=1}^{N} \dfrac{(Y_i - \bar{Y})^2}{N}$ $= \dfrac{8800.687}{35}$ $= 251.448$	$\sigma_x^2 = \sum\limits_{i=1}^{N} \dfrac{(X_i - \bar{X})^2}{N}$ $= \dfrac{6336.716}{35}$ $= 181.049$
Standard deviation	$\sigma_y = \sqrt{\sum\limits_{i=1}^{N} \dfrac{(Y_i - \bar{Y})^2}{N}}$ $= \sqrt{251.448}$ $= 15.857$	$\sigma_x = \sqrt{\sum\limits_{i=1}^{N} \dfrac{(X_i - \bar{X})^2}{N}}$ $= \sqrt{181.0492}$ $= 13.455$
Covariance	$\sigma_{yx} = \sum\limits_{i=1}^{N} \dfrac{(Y_i - \bar{Y})(X_i - \bar{X})}{N}$ $= \dfrac{5371.524}{35}$ $= 153.472$	

ing calculations show the values of the least-squares regression coefficients determined from the statistics in Table 1.

$$b_{yx} = \frac{153.472}{181.049} = 0.8476$$
$$a = 25.086 - (0.848)(35.486) = -4.994$$

Thus, the least-squares regression equation for the data in Figure 1 can be written

$$Y_c = -4.994 + 0.848X$$

The gross regression coefficient indicates that on average, sales increase by 848 units for each $1,000 increase in advertising expenditures, while the value

---

[3] All the calculations shown in this chapter have been performed on a computer. Short-cut formulas for manual calculation of regression and correlation statistics are given in most basic textbooks on the subject, for example, [1], [3], and [6].

of the intercept, a, indicates that the expected value of sales, given $X = 0$, is -4.994.

The straight line running from the lower left to the upper right corner of Figure 1 corresponds to the least-squares regression line calculated here.

The sum of the squared vertical deviations between the original sales observations and the line of regression is 4247.332 (calculations not shown). Hence, the residual variance, that is, the variation in Y *not* associated with variations in X, and the standard deviation of regression for the previous example, are:

$$\sigma_{y_c}^2 = \sum_{i=1}^{N} \frac{(Y_i - Y_c)^2}{N} = \frac{4247.332}{35} = 121.352$$

$$\sigma_{y_c} = 11.02$$

Thus, if the sales observations are normally distributed about the line of regression, one would expect to find approximately 68 percent of the sample data points within $Y_c \pm 11.02$.

Note also that $\sigma_{y_c}^2$ is approximately one-half the value of σ_y^2 shown in Table 1. Hence, the regression equation "explains" approximately one-half of the total sales variation for the 35 sample points.

Simple Correlation

The coefficient of simple correlation, denoted by the symbol r, measures the linear association between two variables. For two variables Y and X, it is defined:

$$r_{yx} = \frac{\text{covariance } (y, x)}{\sqrt{\text{variance } (Y)} \sqrt{\text{variance } X}} = \frac{\sigma_{yx}}{\sigma_y \sigma_x}$$

Since the covariance can be positive or negative and its maximum absolute value is exactly equal to the product of $\sigma_y \sigma_x$, the simple correlation coefficient can take any value between ± 1.0.

The value of $+1.0$ for r_{yx} indicates perfect positive correlation between the variables; in other words, all the data points lie on a straight line having a positive slope. A value of -1.0 means that all the points lie on a straight line having a negative slope. If two variables are statistically independent, that is, variations in Y are totally unrelated to variations in X, r_{yx} is zero.

Although the simple correlation coefficient is the most widely cited measure of association between two variables, r_{yx}^2, the *coefficient of simple determination,* is more easily interpreted. It measures the proportion of the variance in the dependent variables that is associated with, or "explained by," the independent variable. Thus,

$$r_{yx}^2 = \frac{\sigma_y^2 - \sigma_{y_c}^2}{\sigma_y^2} = 1 - \frac{\sigma_{y_c}^2}{\sigma_y}$$

where

$\sigma_y^2 = $ total variance of y

$\sigma_{y_c}^2 = $ residual, or unexplained variance

It should be clear that r_{yx}^2 is a summary measure of the goodness-of-fit of the regression equation to the data, and that this measure is not influenced by the original measurement units of the variables.

For example, the simple determination coefficient for the illustration just discussed shows that the regression equation accounts for slightly more than 50 percent of the total sales variation.

$$r_{yx}^2 = 1 - \frac{121.352}{251.448} = 0.5174$$

The corresponding simple correlation coefficient is

$$r_{yx} = \sqrt{r_{yx}^2} = \sqrt{0.5174} = 0.72$$

The preceding examples show that the least-squares estimates of a and b_{yx} maximize the value of r_{yx}^2. It is also apparent that the coefficient of simple correlation and the coefficient of gross regression are related in the following way.

$$r_{yx} = b_{yx}\frac{\sigma_x}{\sigma_y} \qquad \text{or} \qquad b_{yx} = r_{yx}\frac{\sigma_y}{\sigma_x}$$

MULTIVARIATE ANALYSIS

To this point, the discussion has concentrated on simple correlation and simple regression analysis to develop a clear understanding of the basic concepts. Unfortunately, few problems in marketing research involve only two variables. Far more common is the situation where analyses are desired of the association between an important criterion variable and several independent variables. Such problems require the use of multiple-correlation and multiple-regression methods.

In order to illustrate the use of correlation and regression methods in the analysis of multivariate relationships, we will add a second independent variable (Z)—median disposable income per household—to the hypothetical example discussed in the preceding section.

Multiple Regression

The general form of the model used in analysis of linear regression of a single criterion variable Y upon two independent variables X and Z is:

$$Y_c = a + b_{yx.z}X + b_{yz.x}Z$$

where
a = expected value of Y, at $X = Z = 0$
$b_{yx.z}$ = change in Y per unit change in X, with Z held constant
$b_{yz.x}$ = change in Y per unit change in Z, with X held constant
Y_c = expected value of Y, given X and Z

As in the bivariate case, the objective of multiple-regression analysis is to determine values of the parameters $b_{yx.z}$ and $b_{yz.x}$ such that the residual variance (σ_{yc}^2) is minimized.

The parameters $b_{yx.z}$ and $b_{yz.x}$ are known as the *net regression coefficients* for Y on X and Y on Z. The relationship between net and gross regression coefficients can be seen from the least-squares formula for $b_{yx.z}$ and $b_{yz.x}$:

$$b_{yx.z} = \frac{\sigma_y}{\sigma_x}\left[\frac{r_{yx} - r_{yz}r_{xz}}{1 - r_{xz}^2}\right] \qquad b_{yz.x} = \frac{\sigma_y}{\sigma_z}\left[\frac{r_{yz} - r_{yx}r_{xz}}{1 - r_{xz}^2}\right]$$

Note that when the two independent variables are orthogonal (where $r_{xz} = 0$), the net regression coefficients are exactly equal to the gross regression coefficients.

For example, when $r_{xz} = 0$,

$$b_{yx.z} = \frac{\sigma_y}{\sigma_x}\left[\frac{r_{yx} - r_{yz}(0)}{1 - 0}\right] = \frac{\sigma_y}{\sigma_x}r_{yx} = b_{yx}$$

However, when collinearity exists between the independent variables (that is, when $r_{xz} \neq 0$), adjustments must be made for the correlation between Y and Z, and X and Z to obtain an estimate of the net regression of Y on X.

Also note that perfect collinearity ($r_{xz} = 1.0$) between the independent variables makes it impossible to estimate the values of net regression coefficients, since the denominator of the term inside the brackets is zero.

Thus, the net regression coefficient $b_{yx.z}$ is a measure of the regression of Y on X, when the effects of Z have been held constant; and $b_{yz.x}$ is a measure of the regression of Y on Z when the effects of X have been held constant.

The following calculations show the values of the simple correlation coefficients and the net regression coefficients determined from the data plotted in Figure 1 and observations of median disposable income per household (Z) for each of the 35 hypothetical market areas,

where $Z = 8.438$ (measured in \$000)

      $\sigma_z = 3.070$

$$r_{yx} = 0.719 \qquad r_{yz} = 0.521 \qquad r_{xz} = 0.147$$

$$
\begin{aligned}
b_{yx.z} &= \frac{\sigma_y}{\sigma_x}\left[\frac{r_{yx} - r_{yz}r_{xz}}{1 - r_{xz}^2}\right] \\
&= \frac{15.857}{13.455}\left[\frac{0.719 - (0.521)(0.147)}{1 - (0.147)^2}\right] \\
&= 0.774
\end{aligned}
$$

$$
\begin{aligned}
b_{yz.x} &= \frac{\sigma_y}{\sigma_x}\left[\frac{r_{yz} - r_{yx}r_{xz}}{1 - r_{xz}^2}\right] \\
&= \frac{15.857}{3.070}\left[\frac{0.521 - (0.719)(0.147)}{1 - (0.147)^2}\right] \\
&= 2.192
\end{aligned}
$$

Given the above values of the net regression coefficients, the least-squares estimate of the intercept is determined by the equation

$$
\begin{aligned}
a &= \bar{Y} - b_{yx.z}\bar{X} - b_{yz.x}Z \\
&= 25.08 - 0.774(35.48) - 2.192(8.44) \\
&= -20.892
\end{aligned}
$$

Thus, the multiple-regression equation for sales on advertising and income is

$$Y_c = -20.892 + 0.774(X) + 2.192(Z)$$

The value of $b_{yx.z}$ indicates that on average, sales increase by 774 units for each \$1,000 increase in advertising expenditures when income is held constant. The value of $b_{yz.x}$ indicates that the average increase in sales is 2,192 units per \$1,000 increase in household income when advertising expenditures are held constant.

It is important to emphasize that the magnitudes of these net regression coefficients do *not* indicate the relative importance of X and Z in accounting for the variations in Y.[4] In order to compare the relative importance of the inde-

---

[4] Detailed discussions of beta weights and their interpretation are found in [4, pp. 363–370].

pendent variables, it is necessary to standardize the regression coefficients by putting them on a common base. Standardized coefficients (called beta weights and denoted by the symbol β) are calculated as follows:

$$\beta_{yx} = \frac{\sigma_x}{\sigma_y} b_{yx.z} = \left[\frac{r_{yx} - r_{yz}r_{xz}}{1 - r_{xz}{}^2} \right]$$

$$\beta_{yz} = \frac{\sigma_z}{\sigma_y} b_{yz.x} = \left[\frac{r_{yz} - r_{yx}r_{xz}}{1 - r_{xz}{}^2} \right]$$

The calculated β weights for the present example show that, despite the fact that $b_{yz.x} > b_{yx.z}$, advertising expenditures are relatively more important than income in determining the variation in the sample observations of sales, that is,

$$\beta_{yx} = 0.656 > \beta_{yz} = 0.424$$

The sum of the squared deviations between the original sales observations and the estimated values produced by the multiple-regression equation is 2695.877 (calculations not shown). Therefore the residual variance and standard deviation of regression are

$$\sigma_{y_c}{}^2 = \sum_{i=1}^{N} \frac{(Y_i - Y_c)^2}{N} = \frac{2695.877}{35} = 77.025$$

$$\sigma_{y_c} = \sqrt{77.025} = 8.8$$

Note that inclusion of income in the relationship has resulted in a substantial decrease in the unexplained variance from that found in the simple regression analysis, from 121.352 to 77.025.

Multiple Correlation Analysis

The coefficient of multiple determination (denoted by the symbol R^2) and the coefficient of multiple correlation (R) are the basic measures of statistical association between a single dependent variable and two or more independent variables.

The coefficient of multiple determination measures the proportion of the dependent variable variance that is associated with, or explained by, the combined effects of the independent variables, that is,

$$R^2_{y.xz} = \frac{\sigma_y{}^2 - \sigma_{y_c}{}^2}{\sigma_y{}^2} = 1 - \frac{\sigma_{y_c}{}^2}{\sigma_y{}^2}$$

The following calculation shows that the two variables X and Z in the example account for nearly 70 percent of the variation of sales for the sample.

$$R^2_{y.xz} = 1 - \frac{77.025}{251.448} = 0.6939$$

The multiple correlation coefficient (that is, the square root of $R^2_{y.xz}$) for the example is

$$R_{y.xz} = \sqrt{0.6939} = 0.83$$

Thus the inclusion of the independent variable income (Z) in the regression equation results in an increase of the explained variation from $r_{yx}{}^2 = 0.519$ to

$R_{y.xz}^2 = 0.694$.   Note that this increase is less than the value of $r_{yz}{}^2$ (where $r_{yz}{}^2 = (0.521)^2 = 0.271$).   In other words,

$$R_{y.xz}^2 - r_{yx}{}^2 < r_{yz}{}^2$$
$$0.694 - 0.519 < 0.271$$
$$0.175 < 0.271$$

The relationship between the multiple and simple determination coefficients can be seen in the following formula for $R_{y.xz}^2$:

$$R_{y.xz}^2 = \frac{r_{yx}{}^2 + r_{yz}{}^2 - 2r_{yx}r_{yz}r_{xz}}{1 - r_{xz}{}^2}$$
$$= \frac{(0.719)^2 + (0.521)^2 - 2(0.719)(0.521)(0.147)}{1 - (0.147)^2}$$
$$= 0.694$$

Thus, it should be clear that $R_{y.xz}^2$ equals the sum of the simple determination coefficients $r_{yx}{}^2$ and $r_{yz}{}^2$ *only* in the special case of zero correlation between the two independent variables, that is, if r_{xz} is zero.

Partial Correlation Analysis

Two types of statistics without direct analogs in simple correlation analyses are used to measure the relative importance of each independent variable in a multivariate relationship.

Partial determination coefficients measure the association between the dependent variable and a given independent variable with the effects of additional variables held constant.   For example, the partial determination coefficients for Y and Z, and Y and X, are given by the equations

$$r_{yz.x}^2 = \frac{R_{y.xz}^2 - r_{yx}{}^2}{1 - r_{yx}{}^2}$$
$$= \frac{0.694 - 0.519}{1 - 0.519} = 0.364$$
$$r_{yx.z}^2 = \frac{R_{y.xz}^2 - r_{yz}{}^2}{1 - r_{yz}{}^2}$$
$$= \frac{0.694 - 0.271}{1 - 0.271} = 0.580$$

These calculations show that 36.4 percent of the sales variation that is *not* explained by advertising is accounted for by income variations.   Similarly, 58 percent of the sales variation *not* explained by income is accounted for by advertising-expenditure variations.

Note that the partial determination coefficients *cannot* be added to obtain the value of $R_{y.xz}^2$, since the denominators of the two formulas are not the same.

Partial correlation coefficients can be calculated by taking the square root of the partial determination coefficients.   Partial correlation coefficients can also be determined directly from simple correlation coefficients, using the formulas

$$r_{yz.x} = \frac{r_{yz} - r_{yx}r_{xz}}{\sqrt{1 - r_{yx}{}^2}\sqrt{1 - r_{xz}{}^2}}$$

$$r_{yx.z} = \frac{r_{yx} - r_{yz}r_{xz}}{\sqrt{1 - r_{yz}{}^2}\sqrt{1 - r_{xz}{}^2}}$$

Partial determination statistics are particularly useful in evaluating the net effect of adding alternative independent variables to a multiple-regression analysis.

GUIDELINES TO APPLICATION

The discussion to this point has been limited to measures describing the statistical association existing in a given body of data. However, we are rarely interested in sample statistics per se. The ultimate goal in nearly every regression application is (1) to obtain valid inferences about the nature of the causal or structural relationship between the variables in the population; and/or (2) to make accurate forecasts of the dependent variable.

In structural analysis, the primary objective is to obtain unbiased and efficient estimates of the true population parameters. In strictly forecasting applications where the dependent and independent variables may or may not be causally linked, the objective is to develop an equation that will yield unbiased and efficient (that is, minimum-error) forecasts of specific dependent variable values.

The term *unbiased* implies that the expected value of the regression estimates obtained in a large number of samples is exactly equal to the population parameter, whereas the term *efficient* refers to the sampling variability (for example, to the values of σ_a and $\sigma_{b_{yx}}$). An efficient estimator has the minimum possible sampling error for a given sample size and a monotonically decreasing error as the sample size is increased.[5]

Both types of application require careful consideration of the following assumptions that underlie linear regression analysis.[6]

Basic Assumptions

ASSUMPTION 1: *The true relationship between the dependent and independent variables is, in fact, linear.* For example, in order to draw inferences about the true relationship between sales and advertising from the simple regression on the data shown in Figure 1, it must be assumed that the population relationship is

$$Y = A + BX + \mu$$

where
$A =$ expected sales at $X = 0$
$B =$ effect of advertising on sales
$\mu =$ error $=$ composite effect of excluded variables and/or measurement errors in sales

Given this assumption, the intercept and slope of the simple regression equation—a and b_{yx}—can be interpreted as sample estimates of the population parameters A and B. Similarly, the regression residuals $(Y_i - Y_c)$ are estimates of the error term (μ_i) corresponding to the ith observation of Y.

Thus, the values of Y_c calculated from the regression equation can be regarded as forecasts of the true value of Y corresponding to a given value of X, and as independent of measurement errors and the influence of excluded variables.

---

[5] See [5, pp. 16–17] and [7, p. 47].
[6] Excellent discussions of assumptions of regression are found in [5] and [7].

Moreover, the residual variance, $\sigma_{y_c}{}^2$, when adjusted for degrees of freedom, provides an estimate of the true variance of Y about the population regression line, that is

$$\hat{\sigma}^2 = \text{estimate of population regression variance}$$

$$= \sum_{i=1}^{N} \frac{(Y_i - Y_c)^2}{N - M}$$

where

$N = $ number of observations

$M = $ number of parameters in the regression

$N - M = $ number of degrees of freedom

ASSUMPTION 2: *The independent variables are free of measurement errors.* This assumption is, of course, implicit in the statement that the v's are attributable to the composite effects of excluded variables and/or measurement errors in the dependent variable.

The remaining four assumptions deal with the characteristics of the error terms.

ASSUMPTION 3: *The μ's are randomly distributed with an expected value of zero.*

ASSUMPTION 4: *The μ's are uncorrelated with the independent variables.*

ASSUMPTION 5: *The μ's are statistically independent, that is, $rv_iv_j = 0$ (where $i \neq j$).*

ASSUMPTION 6: *The variance of the error terms is uniform, that is, homoskedastic, for all values of the independent variables.*

The relative importance of these six assumptions depends to a large extent upon the objectives of the analysis. Assumptions 1 through 4 are particularly significant in structural analyses, since violations lead to biased, and in some cases inefficient, estimates of the true regression parameters. For example, it can be shown that violations of assumption 2 result in a bias toward zero in the value of the regression coefficient, that is, $E[\,|b_{yx}|\,] < |B|$.

Assumption 5 is frequently violated by economic time-series data, since many variables tend to have similar seasonal, cyclical, and growth characteristics. Although autocorrelation of the error terms—a violation of assumption 5—does not lead to biased regression coefficients, it does result in a bias toward zero in the estimate of the variance of the regression coefficients and the forecast variance. Hence, significance tests and confidence intervals for the regression coefficients and forecasts are also biased.

Although violations of assumption 6, the requirement of homoskedastic error variance, do not produce biased regression coefficients, they do result in a loss of efficiency.

Violations of assumptions 5 and 6 also lead to inefficient forecasts of population values of the dependent variable.

Unfortunately, since the true relationship and error terms are never known, there is no way to guarantee compliance with the cited requirements. Once the regression has been run, however, tests can be made of the residuals' homoskedasticity, autocorrelation, and correlation with the independent variables.[7] A simple plot of the regression residuals against each independent variable will also reveal the nature of the nonlinearities, if any, that exist in the sample data.

[7] See [2, pp. 177–200].

Although evidence of critical assumption violations in the sample data does not prove that the model is incorrectly specified, it casts serious doubts upon the validity of inferences and forecasts based on the regression results.

Forecasting

Generation of forecast values of the dependent variable is a simple matter once the parameters of the regression equation have been estimated. However, serious mistakes are frequently made in calculating the expected error of a specific forecast and the sampling error associated with a given regression equation. Unfortunately, the standard deviation of regression σ_{y_c} is often confused with the standard error of the regression line $\sigma_{\bar{y}_c}$ and/or the standard error of the forecast σ_{y_i}. The simple regression example discussed earlier can be used to illustrate differences among these statistics.

For example, it will be recalled that the simple regression equation

$$y_c = a + b_{yx}X$$

where
$$a = -4.994$$
$$b_{yx} = 0.884$$
reduced the total variance of Y from $\sigma_y{}^2 = 251.448$ to $\sigma_{y_c}{}^2 = 121.352$.

Thus, given the regression analysis, $\hat{\sigma}_u{}^2$ and $\hat{\sigma}_u$ provide the following estimates of the population variance of Y_i about $\bar{Y}$, and the population standard deviation

$$\hat{\sigma}_u{}^2 = \sum_{i=1}^{N} \frac{(Y_i - Y_c)^2}{N - M} = \frac{4247.332}{33} = 128.707$$

$$\hat{\sigma}_u = \sqrt{128.707} = 11.348$$

However, the regression equation just shown is only one of many possible *sample* estimates of the true regression line. Since Y, which determines the elevation of the regression line, and b_{yx}, which determines the slope of the line, are subject to sampling error, both must be considered in calculating the total sampling variance and standard error for the regression equation.

For example, the sampling variance and standard error of the mean and b_{yx} are defined by the formulas

$$\sigma_{\bar{y}}{}^2 = \text{sampling variance of } \bar{Y}$$
$$= \frac{\hat{\sigma}_u{}^2}{N}$$
$$\sigma_{\bar{y}} = \text{standard error of } \bar{Y}$$
$$= \sqrt{\frac{\hat{\sigma}_u{}^2}{N}}$$
$$\sigma_{b_{yx}}{}^2 = \text{sampling variance of } b_{yx}$$
$$= \frac{\sigma_y{}^2}{\sigma_x{}^2} = \frac{\hat{\sigma}_u{}^2}{N\sigma_x{}^2}$$
$$\sigma_{b_{yx}} = \text{standard error of } b_{yx}$$
$$= \sqrt{\frac{\sigma_y{}^2}{\sigma_x{}^2}}$$

The total sampling variance and standard error of the regression equation are given by

$$\sigma_{y_c}^2 = \text{sampling variance of } \hat{Y}_c$$
$$= \sigma_{\hat{y}}^2 + \sigma_{b_{yx}}^2 x^2$$
$$= \frac{\hat{\sigma}_u^2}{N} + \frac{\hat{\sigma}_u^2 x^2}{N\sigma_x^2}$$
$$= \frac{\hat{\sigma}_u^2}{N}\left(1 + \frac{x^2}{\sigma_x^2}\right)$$

$$\sigma_{y_c} = \text{standard error of } \hat{Y}_c$$
$$= \sqrt{\frac{\hat{\sigma}_u^2}{N}\left(1 + \frac{x^2}{\sigma_x^2}\right)}$$

where $x^2 = (X_i - \bar{X})^2$.

Note that values of $\sigma_{\hat{y}_c}^2$ depend upon the values of X^2. At $X_i = \bar{X}$, the second term on the right of the equation is zero and $\sigma_{\hat{y}_c}^2$ is exactly equal to $\sigma_{\hat{y}}^2$. The logic of this result should be clear since the sampling error of b_{yx} need not be considered at the point defined by $(\bar{Y}, \bar{X})$. However, the importance of $\sigma_{b_{yx}}^2$ increases as the difference between X_i and $\bar{X}$ grows large.

In order to calculate the expected error associated with a *specific* forecast, it is necessary to add $\hat{\sigma}_u^2$ (the variance associated with a specific value of Y_i) to the total sampling variance for the regression equation. For example, the total sampling variance and standard error of the forecast where $X_i = 55.5$ is given by

$$\sigma_{\hat{y}_i}^2 = \text{sampling variance of the forecast}$$
$$= \hat{\sigma}_u^2 + \sigma_{\hat{y}_c}^2 + \sigma_b^2 X^2$$
$$= \hat{\sigma}_u + \left[\frac{\hat{\sigma}^2}{N}\left(1 + \frac{x^2}{\sigma_x^2}\right)\right]$$
$$= 128.707 + \left[\frac{128.707}{35}\left(1 + \frac{(55.5-35.5)^2}{181.049}\right)\right]$$
$$= 140.509$$
$$\sigma_{\hat{y}_i} = \text{standard error of the forecast}$$
$$= \sqrt{140.509}$$
$$= 11.90$$

Thus the specific forecast $\hat{Y}_i$ and 95 percent confidence interval at $X_i = 55.5$ is

$$\hat{Y}_i = -4.994 + .884\,(X_i) \pm 1.96\sigma_{\hat{y}_i}$$
$$= -4.994 + 0.884\,(55.5) \pm 1.96\,(11.90)$$
$$= 44.068 \pm 23.324$$

It should be clear from the preceding discussion why great care must be exercised in making forecasts beyond the range of sample observations. For example, the minimum value of $\sigma_{\hat{y}_i} = 11.50$ occurs at the point $(\bar{Y}, \bar{X})$, whereas at $X = 155.5$, $\sigma_{y_c} = 20.60$.

Thus, the forecast and 95 percent confidence interval at $X = 155.5$ is

$$\hat{Y}_i = -4.994 + 0.884(155.5) \pm 1.96(20.60)$$
$$= 132.46 \pm 40.38$$

Parameter Estimation versus Exploratory Analyses

The use of regression techniques to estimate the parameters of a model that has been specified on the basis of a priori judgment must be clearly distinguished from the use of regression and correlation techniques to explore relationships present in a given body of sample data. Failure to do so often results in serious errors.

For example, inexperienced users frequently make repeated regression runs, trying out different combinations of variables and data transformations in search of a regression equation that yields an R^2 close to 1.0. While this is an appropriate and oft-times highly informative exploratory technique, it must be recognized that the final "model" has been derived from the sample data and that statistical significance tests of the regression and correlation statistics are meaningless. Thus, it is essential to validate such models on new sample data that have not been "massaged" before attempting to draw inferences about population parameters and forecast values.

If, however, the model has been specified on the basis of a priori reasoning—without consulting the sample data—it constitutes an explicit hypothesis about the structure of the true relationship; standard statistical inference procedures can therefore be applied to establish significance levels for the sample regression and correlation statistics and confidence intervals for the population parameters. (This, of course, assumes that probability sampling has been used.)

Statistical Association versus Correlation

The foregoing discussion is closely related to the distinction between statistical association and causation. Although regression and correlation techniques—as well as other statistical procedures—may provide evidence in support of a hypothesis of causation, they cannot be used to *prove* causation.

For example, suppose that we state the hypothesis that variations in unit sales are caused by variations in the advertising expenditures for the hypothetical product discussed earlier. From the simple regression analysis, we learned that the equation

$$\text{Sales } Y = -4.994 + 0.848 \text{ (advertising expenditures } X)$$

"explains" slightly more than 50 percent of the variation in sales ($r_{yx}^2 = 0.519$). Note, however, that a regression of advertising expenditures on sales yields

$$r_{xy}^2 = \frac{\sigma_{xy}^2}{\sigma_y^2 \, \sigma_x^2} = 0.519$$

Thus, the same correlation results are obtained even though the "causation" is reversed.

It must also be recognized that highly significant regression and correlation statistics may be obtained in a given analysis when no causal links actually exist between the dependent and independent variables. For example, there is undoubtedly a high correlation between the number of passenger miles traveled in space vehicles and the consumption of birth-control pills over the past ten years. Yet few people would argue that the concomitant variation of the two variables is proof of a causal relationship.

The sampling process itself can also produce spuriously correlated observations that are simply due to chance even though the variables are not causally linked.

Thus, the researcher must rely upon theory and judgment in specifying causal models and the test of reasonableness when interpreting the meaning of regression and correlation results.

REFERENCES

1. Croxton, Fredrick E., and Dudley J. Cowden, *Applied General Statistics*, New York: Prentice-Hall, 1955.
2. Dixson, Wilfrid J., and Frank J. Massey, Jr., *Introduction to Statistical Analysis*, New York: McGraw-Hill, 1957.
3. Ezekiel, Mordecai, and Carl A. Fox, *Methods of Correlation and Regression Analyses*, New York: Wiley, 1959.
4. Ferber, Robert, and P. J. Verdoorn, *Research Methods in Economics and Business*, New York: Macmillan, 1962.
5. Johnston, J., *Econometric Methods*, New York: McGraw-Hill, 1960.
6. Spurr, William A., and Charles P. Bonini, *Statistical Analysis for Business Decisions*, Homewood, Ill.: Irwin, 1967.
7. Valvanis, Stefan, *Econometrics*, New York: McGraw-Hill, 1959.

Statistical Analysis of Relationships

Chapter 6

Bayesian Regression Methods

ROBERT L. WINKLER   *Graduate School of Business, Indiana University, Bloomington, Indiana*

INTRODUCTION

In the "classical," or "sampling theory," approach to statistics, inferences about an unknown parameter in a statistical model should be based solely on sample information. For instance, if a random sample of 100 consumers yields 20 persons who have purchased a certain brand during the past month, then the sample proportion, 0.20, is taken as an estimate of the parameter p, the proportion of consumers in the entire population of interest who purchased the given brand during the past month. Classical statisticians generally follow the frequency interpretation of probability, in which the probability of an event is interpreted as the relative frequency of occurrence of the event in a long series of trials. Followers of the frequency view claim that a population parameter, such as p, μ, or σ^2, has a certain fixed value which may be unknown, and that it is meaningless to talk of the probability that the parameter equals some number; either it does or it does not.

In contrast to the classical viewpoint, the Bayesian approach to statistics admits the inclusion of prior information concerning the parameters of interest. Such information, whether it represents the results of a previous sample or whether it is entirely of a subjective nature, is included in the formal statistical model. The term *Bayesian* is used to describe this approach because the mechanism used to combine prior information and sample information is Bayes' theorem. Many Bayesian statisticians subscribe to the subjective interpretation of probability, in which the probability of an event is interpreted in terms of a person's degree of belief about that event. The subjectivist argues that there is generally some information other than sample information available about an unknown parameter, and this information should be expressed in probabilistic terms and included in the formal statistical model. The classical statistician may consider such information in a highly informal manner (for instance, in the way he sets up his model); the Bayesian includes it in the formal analysis.

In real-world problems in marketing and other areas, the objective is often to make a decision on the basis of imperfect information about some unknown parameter. For instance, in a decision regarding the introduction of a new product, the relevant parameter of interest may be p, the proportion of consumers who will purchase the product each month, or μ, the mean sales of the product per month. A market survey will provide some information about p or μ. Surely there is more information available, perhaps in the form of sales records of similar products or simply in the form of subjective judgments of a marketing manager, based on his experience with various new products in the past. The Bayesian approach includes all such information in the formal statistical model for making a decision under uncertainty. Here, the uncertainty in the problem refers to p or μ. Even if the objective is merely predicting the market share or mean sales instead of making a decision regarding the product, the Bayesian approach is useful because it enables the statistician to include all relevant information in making his prediction.

The use of Bayes' theorem to revise probabilities in the light of new information is a key feature of the Bayesian approach to inferential and decision-making problems. If the unknown parameter of interest is denoted by θ and the new information is denoted by z, then Bayes' theorem is given by

$$P(\theta|z) = \frac{P(\theta)\,P(z|\theta)}{\Sigma P(\theta)P(z|\theta)}$$

if θ is taken to be discrete and

$$f(\theta|z) = \frac{f(\theta)\,f(z|\theta)}{\int f(\theta)f(z|\theta)d\theta}$$

if θ is continuous, where the sum or integral in the denominator is taken over all possible values of θ. The probability $P(\theta)$ [the density function $f(\theta)$] represents the prior distribution of θ, which reflects the prior information concerning θ. The probability $P(\theta|z)$ [the density function $f(\theta|z)$] represents the posterior distribution of θ, which reflects the state of information about θ after the new information is observed. Of course, the terms *prior* and *posterior* are relative terms. If, after the application of Bayes' theorem, more new information is obtained, the posterior distribution, determined after the previous set of new information was obtained, is now the prior distribution relative to the current set of new information. The final input to Bayes' theorem, $P(z|\theta)$ or $f(z|\theta)$, is the likelihood function, reflecting the likelihood of the new information z, conditional on the various possible values of θ. Since the new information is generally in the form of sample information, the classical statistician bases many of his inferences on the likelihood function. The Bayesian, on the other hand, combines the likelihood function and the prior distribution to form the posterior distribution and bases his inferences (and decisions) on this posterior distribution.

For a simple illustration, consider $\theta = p$, the market share of a particular new brand, and suppose that a marketing manager decides that p is either .1 or .2. On the basis of his prior information, he assesses his prior probabilities to be $P(p = .1) = .30$ and $P(p = .2) = .70$. This implies that the prior odds in favor of $p = .2$ are 7 to 3.   He then observes a random sample of 20 consumers who purchase the product, and five of them state that they would definitely purchase this brand if it becomes available.   Using Bayes' theorem, his posterior probabilities are

$$P(p = .1 | z) = \frac{P(p = .1)P(z | p = .1)}{P(p = .1)P(z | p = .1) + P(p = .2)P(z | p = .2)}$$
$$= \frac{(.3)(.0319)}{(.3)(.0319) + (.7)(.1746)} = .073$$

and

$$P(p = .2 | z) = \frac{P(p = .2)P(z | p = .2)}{P(p = .1)P(z | p = .1) + P(p = .2)P(z | p = .2)}$$
$$= \frac{(.7)(.1746)}{(.3)(.0319) + (.7)(.1746)} = .927$$

The likelihoods $P(z | p = .1)$ and $P(z | p = .2)$ are found from the binomial distribution.   For a sample of size 20 from a stationary and independent dichotomous process (assuming that each person states either that he will or will not purchase the given brand), the distribution of r, the number of persons who state that they will buy the brand, is a binomial distribution.   If $p = .1$, the binomial probability that $r = 5$ is .0319; if $p = .2$, it is .1746.   Note that the observed sample greatly increases the probability that $p = .2$ and decreases the probability that $p = .1$.   If the marketing manager simply wants an estimate of p, he could just take the mean of the posterior distribution, which is $E(p) = (.1)(.073) + (.2)(.927) = .1927$.   If he wants to compare the hypotheses $p = .1$ and $p = .2$, he could consider the odds ratio.   The posterior odds in favor of $p = .2$ are $.927/.073 = 12.7$.   By means of comparison, a classical statistician would consider the sample mean, .25, as an estimate, and he would look at the likelihood ratio, $.1746/.0319 = 5.5$, in order to compare the two hypotheses.

The assumption that p can take on only the values .1 and .2 is obviously a simplification.   It would be much more realistic to take p as a continuous variable.   In particular, suppose that the marketing manager's prior distribution for p is a beta distribution with parameters $r' = 2$ and $n' = 10$.   This distribution is illustrated in Figure 1.[1]   On the basis of a sample of $r = 5$ "successes" (persons who say that they will buy the brand) in $n = 20$ trials, the application of Bayes' theorem results in a posterior beta distribution with parameters $r'' = r' +$

---

[1] A beta distribution with parameters r' and n' has a density function of the form

$$f(p | r', n') = \frac{(n' - 1)!}{(r' - 1)!(n' - r' - 1)!} p^{r'-1}(1 - p)^{n'-r'-1}$$

for $0 \leq p \leq 1$, where $n' > r' > 0$.   In this situation, the beta distribution is a particularly convenient prior distribution because it simplifies the determination of the posterior distribution; in Bayesian terminology, the beta distribution is a *natural-conjugate* distribution (see [15]).   Natural-conjugate distributions not only simplify the application of Bayes' theorem; they also can be interpreted in terms of "equivalent sample information."   In the example, for instance, the beta prior distribution with $r' = 2$ and $n' = 10$ implies that the marketing manager's prior information about p, the market share, is roughly equivalent to the information contained in a sample of 10 consumers, with 2 purchasing the brand in question.

$r = 7$ and $n'' = n' + n = 30$.[2]   This posterior distribution is also graphed in Figure 1; comparison with the prior distribution shows how the new information changes the distribution.

This introductory section has briefly presented the Bayesian approach to problems of statistical inference and decision and compared it with the classical approach.   For more extensive discussions, see [11], [13], [14], [15], [18], [19], and [21]; for marketing applications, see [4], [5], [6], [7], [16], and [17].[3] In the previous chapter, the classical approach to a specific class of problems, those of regression and correlation, was presented.   In the rest of this chapter, the Bayesian approach to regression problems will be considered.

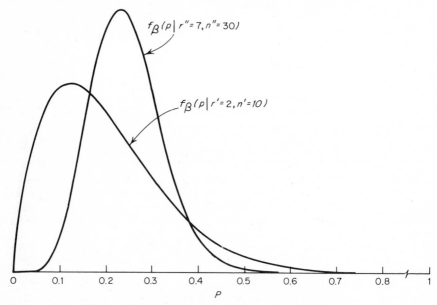

$f_\beta(p \mid r'' = 7, n'' = 30)$

$f_\beta(p \mid r' = 2, n' = 10)$

Fig. 1.   Hypothetical prior and posterior distributions.

THE BAYESIAN APPROACH TO REGRESSION

In a regression problem, the statistician wants to predict the value of a particular variable (generally called the dependent variable), given the values of a number of other variables (called the independent variables).   That is, he wants to take advantage of the relationship among the variables; any information he can obtain about this relationship should improve the predictability of the model.   The Bayesian uses prior information in regression problems in both an informal and a formal sense.   Informally, prior information is used to construct the regression model.   First of all, the statistician must decide which variables should be included in the model as independent variables.   In most real-world situations, one can think of hundreds of variables that bear some

[2] Throughout this chapter, single primes denote parameters of the prior distribution and double primes denote parameters of the posterior distribution.

[3] For general discussions of applications of quantitative models in marketing, see [2], [3], and [12].

relationship to the dependent variable of interest. For instance, the dependent variable may be the mean sales of a particular item, which can be affected by pricing decisions regarding that item and all other items considered competitive; amount and type of advertising and other promotional activities; legislation, such as tax laws; personal income and numerous other factors involving consumers; and so on. If every single variable which bears any relationship to the dependent variable is included in the regression model, it will be very difficult to handle. The computations may be burdensome, and, more important, the interpretation of the model may be obscured by the relationships among the various independent variables. This is, of course, a problem in mathematical modeling in general: including enough variables to make the model realistic but not so many as to make it unmanageable.

Once the variables are chosen, the next question concerns the form of the model. Can the relationship best be expressed in terms of a linear model, a polynomial model of order greater than one, a multiplicative model, an exponential model, a logarithmic model, or some other model (perhaps even a combination of some of those mentioned)? The choice of a model is generally made on the basis of prior information, which may include knowledge of similar situations in which different models have been compared. As in the choice of variables, the selection of a model represents a balance between realism and manageability. The linear model is perhaps the easiest to deal with, and it has been studied quite extensively both from a theoretical and an applied standpoint, so it is the most commonly encountered type. Of course, even if the chosen model is nonlinear, it may be possible to convert it to a linear one by a transformation or to approximate it by using, say, a piecewise linear model. Detailed discussions of model building, transformations, and so on, may be found in the econometrics literature. (See, for example, [1], [8], [9], and [10].)

Although it is possible to use more than one model in any given situation and to compare their performance for future reference, the model-building process is basically an informal procedure. Prior information is used informally—by classicists and Bayesians alike. Once the model is determined, however, the two approaches differ. The classical statistician uses sample information alone to estimate the unknown parameters of the regression model, whereas the Bayesian formally incorporates additional prior information in the form of prior distributions for these parameters and then combines this information with the sample information to determine posterior distributions for the parameters. His inferences are then based on the joint posterior distribution of the unknown regression parameters. The classical statistician may go so far as to impose constraints on the parameters (for example, the constraint that a certain regression coefficient must be positive), but he will not express his prior information about the parameters in probabilistic form, as does the Bayesian.

To understand this procedure, consider a simple linear regression with just one independent variable:

$$Y = \beta_1 + \beta_2 X + \epsilon$$

For instance, Y might be monthly sales of a certain product and X might be the monthly advertising budget for the product. Suppose that the marketing manager believes that his best sales estimate, given no advertising at all, would be \$50,000. He might take this as the mean of his prior distribution of β_1, since β_1 is the Y-intercept (the predicted value of Y, given that $X = 0$). After further contemplation, he might decide that his prior distribution of β_1 is, say, a normal distribution with mean \$50,000 and standard deviation \$10,000.

Considering β_2, suppose that he feels that, on the average, each additional dollar spent on advertising increases sales by \$10. His prior distribution of β_2 might be, for example, a normal distribution with mean 10 and standard deviation 3. This implies that he assesses a probability of approximately .95 that β_2 is between 4 and 16. Of course, his prior distributions need not be normal distributions in general, although for the linear model presented in the next section, it will be particularly convenient if the joint distribution of the regression coefficients is a normal distribution.

Once the joint prior distribution of the unknown parameters of the regression model (linear or otherwise) is assessed, it can be combined with any available sample information via Bayes' theorem to determine a joint posterior distribution of the parameters. This posterior distribution can then be used to find point estimates or interval estimates for the parameters. The marginal posterior distributions of the parameters can be found, and their means can be taken as point estimates of the parameters. Furthermore, posterior interval estimates can be determined from these distributions, and hypotheses of interest may be investigated. Considering the marketing manager's problem, one might be interested in the hypothesis that $\beta_2 > 5$. To find out how likely this hypothesis is under the posterior distribution, simply find $P(\beta_2 > 5)$. From the prior distribution given in the example (a normal distribution with mean 10 and standard deviation 3), $P(\beta_2 > 5) = .9525$. Of course, this probability would likely change when the posterior distribution following a sample is used instead of the prior distribution.

In most applications, the primary objective of the regression model is to determine a predictive equation for the dependent variable. Given values for the independent variables and given the joint posterior distribution of the regression coefficients, a probability distribution can be determined for the dependent variable. For instance, in the example involving sales as a linear function of advertising, a probability distribution of sales can be determined for any given level of advertising, and this distribution will reflect the uncertainty about the regression parameters β_1 and β_2. Clearly, since the prediction equation is linear, the expected value of Y (sales) is

$$E(Y \mid X) = E(\beta_1) + XE(\beta_2) + E(\epsilon)$$

and the variance of Y is

$$V(Y \mid X) = V(\beta_1) + X^2 \, V(\beta_2) + 2X \operatorname{cov}(\beta_1, \beta_2) + V(\epsilon)$$

Of course, the exact form of the distribution of Y depends on the form of the joint posterior distribution of β_1 and β_2.

In summary, both the classicist and the Bayesian may use prior information in an informal manner to select independent variables and choose the form of the regression model. In addition, the Bayesian formally includes further prior information once the model is specified by assessing a joint prior distribution for the parameters of the model. This prior distribution can then be combined with sample information to find a joint posterior distribution for the parameters. The posterior distribution may be used to determine point and interval estimates or to test hypotheses involving the parameters; it may also be used to determine a probability distribution for the dependent variable of interest, given values of the independent variables.

Everything in this section has been presented in general terms; in the next section, the Bayesian approach to regression is considered under specific distributional assumptions.

BAYESIAN REGRESSION UNDER NORMALITY ASSUMPTIONS

The linear regression model is commonly stated in the following form:

$$Y = \beta_1 + \beta_2 X_2 + \beta_3 X_3 + \beta_4 X_4 + \ldots + \beta_K X_K + \epsilon$$

where Y is the dependent variable, the X_i's are the $(K - 1)$ independent variables, and ϵ is an error term. Furthermore, if successive observations are made (with the same or different values for the independent variables), the successive error terms are assumed to be independent, each normally distributed with mean zero and variance one. This assumption of normally distributed errors is a distributional assumption (such assumptions were not considered in the general discussion of the previous section). If the values of the regression parameters $\beta_1, \beta_2, \ldots, \beta_K$, the values of the independent variables, and the variance of the error term σ^2 are known, then the dependent variable Y is normally distributed with mean $\beta_1 + \beta_2 X_2 + \beta_3 X_3 + \ldots + \beta_K X_K$ and variance σ^2. Usually, the objective is to predict Y, given values for the X's, so the values of the independent variables can be taken to be known. However, the regression coefficients $\beta_1, \beta_2, \ldots, \beta_K$ and the error variance σ^2 are not known in general.

To simplify the notion, it is convenient to introduce a dummy variable, X_1, which always takes on the value 1. The linear regression model can then be written in the form

$$Y = \sum_{j=1}^{K} \beta_j X_j + \epsilon$$

If a sample of size n is taken, with the ith observation represented by the $(K + 1)$-tuple $(Y_i, X_{1i}, X_{2i}, \ldots, X_{Ki})$, then the results can be represented by a system of n equations.

$$Y_i = \sum_{j=1}^{K} \beta_j X_{ji} + \epsilon_i, \qquad i = 1, \ldots, n$$

This system of equations can be written in matrix notation,

$$\mathbf{Y} = \mathbf{X}\beta + \epsilon$$

where $\mathbf{Y}$ and ϵ are $n \times 1$ column vectors, $\mathbf{X}$ is an $n \times K$ matrix, and β is a $K \times 1$ column vector:

$$
\mathbf{Y} = \begin{vmatrix} Y_1 \\ Y_2 \\ \cdot \\ \cdot \\ \cdot \\ Y_n \end{vmatrix}, \quad
\mathbf{X} = \begin{vmatrix} X_{11} & X_{21} & \ldots & X_{K1} \\ X_{12} & X_{22} & \ldots & X_{K2} \\ \cdot & \cdot & \cdot & \cdot \\ \cdot & \cdot & \cdot & \cdot \\ \cdot & \cdot & \cdot & \cdot \\ X_{1n} & X_{2n} & & X_{Kn} \end{vmatrix}, \quad
\beta = \begin{vmatrix} \beta_1 \\ \beta_2 \\ \cdot \\ \cdot \\ \cdot \\ \beta_K \end{vmatrix}, \quad
\epsilon = \begin{vmatrix} \epsilon_1 \\ \epsilon_2 \\ \cdot \\ \cdot \\ \cdot \\ \epsilon_n \end{vmatrix}
$$

Throughout this chapter, vectors and matrices are denoted by boldface letters.

The distribution of Y_i, given the X_{ji}'s and given values of the regression co-efficients and the error variance, is a normal distribution with mean $\sum_{j=1}^{K} \beta_j X_{ji}$ and variance σ^2:

$$f(Y_i | X_{1i}, \ldots, X_{Ki}, \beta_1, \ldots, \beta_K, \delta^2) = \delta^{-1}(2\pi)^{-1/2} e^{-\frac{(Y_i - \Sigma \beta_j X_{ji})^2}{2\delta^2}}$$

The likelihood of the entire sample, given the values of the independent variables, the regression coefficients, and the error variance, is the product of n such density functions:

$$f(\mathbf{Y} | \mathbf{X}, \beta, \delta^2) = \delta^{-n}(2\pi)^{-n/2} e^{-\frac{\sum_i (Y_i - \sum_j \beta_j X_{ji})^2}{2\sigma^2}}$$

The usual classical estimator of β, which is a least-squares estimator and is also a maximum-likelihood estimator under the normality assumption, is

$$\mathbf{b} = (\mathbf{X}^t \mathbf{X})^{-1} \mathbf{X}^t \mathbf{Y}$$

provided that the $K \times K$ matrix $\mathbf{X}^t\mathbf{X}$ has an inverse, where the superscript t denotes the transpose of a matrix.

The Bayesian approach to problems of statistical inference and decision involves the assessment of a prior distribution on the unknown parameters of the model. In the linear regression model, these parameters are $\beta_1, \beta_2, \ldots, \beta_K$, and σ^2. To simplify the analysis, it shall be assumed that the error variance σ^2 is known. There is no restriction on the joint distribution of the K regression coefficients, but the analysis is quite difficult unless the distribution is a member of the natural-conjugate family of distributions. In Bayesian analysis, the use of natural-conjugate distributions greatly simplifies the application of Bayes' theorem (see [15] and footnote 1). In the example in the first section of this chapter, the beta distribution was a natural-conjugate distribution, and the determination of the posterior distribution was a simple matter of addition, $r'' = r' + \mathrm{r}$ and $n'' = n' + n$. Particularly in situations involving several variables, the use of natural-conjugate distributions, although not required by the Bayesian approach, is virtually a necessity to avoid mathematical complexities. For the linear regression model presented here, the family of natural-conjugate distributions is the family of multivariate normal distributions. Thus, it will be assumed that the joint distribution of the regression coefficients is multivariate normal with mean vector

$$\mathbf{b}' = \begin{vmatrix} E'(\beta_1) \\ E'(\beta_2) \\ \cdot \\ \cdot \\ \cdot \\ E'(\beta_K) \end{vmatrix} = \begin{vmatrix} b_1' \\ b_2' \\ \cdot \\ \cdot \\ \cdot \\ b_K' \end{vmatrix}$$

and variance-covariance matrix

$$\Sigma' = \begin{vmatrix} V'(\beta_1) & \mathrm{cov}'(\beta_1,\beta_2) & \cdots & \mathrm{cov}'(\beta_1,\beta_K) \\ \mathrm{cov}'(\beta_1,\beta_2) & V'(\beta_2) & \cdot & \cdot & \cdot \\ \cdot & \cdot & \cdot & \cdot \\ \cdot & \cdot & \cdot & \cdot \\ \cdot & \cdot & \cdot & \cdot \\ \mathrm{cov}'(\beta_1,\beta_K) & \cdot & \cdot & \cdot & V'(\beta_K) \end{vmatrix}.$$

The elements on the diagonal of Σ' are the variances of the K regression coefficients and the off-diagonal terms are covariances between pairs of coefficients.

The combination of this multivariate normal prior distribution with the information of a sample of size n results in a posterior distribution for β which is another multivariate normal distribution with mean vector $\mathbf{b}''$ and variance-covariance matrix Σ'', where

$$\Sigma'' = [(\Sigma')^{-1} + \sigma^{-2}(\mathbf{X}^t\mathbf{X})]^{-1}$$

and

$$\mathbf{b}'' = \Sigma''[(\Sigma')^{-1}\mathbf{b}' + \sigma^{-2}(\mathbf{X}^t\mathbf{X})\mathbf{b}]$$

Before continuing with the discussion of the linear regression model, it should prove useful to consider a simple example to illustrate the process of determining a posterior distribution for the regression coefficients. Suppose that you are interested in predicting monthly family expenditures on food, using the family's yearly income as a dependent variable. Let Y represent monthly family expenditures on food (in dollars), and let $X_2 = $ (yearly income $- \$10,000)/1,000$. Thus, X_2 represents income, expressed in thousands of dollars, above or below $\$10,000$. This transformation simplifies the calculations somewhat. In practice, other independent variables, such as size of family, would probably be included in the model. The example is limited to one independent variable so that the concepts being illustrated are not obscured by computational problems. For most real-world applications involving several variables, it is necessary to use a high-speed computer; conceptually, however, such problems are no different than the simple example given here.

The linear regression model in this case is

$$Y = \beta_1 X_1 + \beta_2 X_2 + \epsilon$$

Suppose that you know (perhaps from previous studies on family expenditures) that $\sigma^2 = 400$. Moreover, you decide that your prior judgments regarding β_1 are reasonably well represented by a bivariate normal distribution with $E'(\beta_1) = 120$, $E'(\beta_2) = 10$, $V'(\beta_1) = 100$, $V'(\beta_2) = 25$, and $\mathrm{cov}'(\beta_1,\beta_2) = -10$. That is, your marginal distribution for β_1 is a normal distribution with mean 120 and standard deviation 10; for families with incomes of $\$10,000$ ($X_2 = 0$), you judge the average monthly expenditures on food to be $\$120$, and you assess a probability of .95 that the mean expenditures will be between $\$100$ and $\$140$. Your marginal distribution for β_2 is a normal distribution with mean 10 and standard deviation 5; on the average, you expect each increase of $\$1,000$ in yearly family income to result in a $\$10$ increase in monthly food expenditures, and you assess a probability of .95 that the mean increase will be between \$0 and \$20. It is reasonably easy to give an intuitive interpretation of the marginal distributions of β_1 and β_2. The final parameter of the joint prior distribution, $\text{cov}(\beta_1,\beta_2)$, is more difficult to interpret; hopefully, past results of similar studies will provide some information about covariances such as these.

In matrix form, your prior distribution for

$$\beta = \begin{bmatrix} \beta_1 \\ \beta_2 \end{bmatrix}$$

is a bivariate normal distribution with mean

$$\mathbf{b}' = \begin{bmatrix} 120 \\ 10 \end{bmatrix}$$

and variance-covariance matrix

$$\Sigma' = \begin{bmatrix} 100 & -10 \\ -10 & 25 \end{bmatrix}$$

Next, suppose that you take a random sample of $n = 9$ families, with the following results (I represents yearly income):

Y	I	X_2
130	10,000	0
140	12,000	2
120	9,000	−1
160	15,000	5
160	14,000	4
100	8,000	−2
150	12,000	2
140	11,000	1
130	11,000	1

In matrix form,

$$\mathbf{Y} = \begin{bmatrix} 130 \\ 140 \\ 120 \\ 160 \\ 160 \\ 100 \\ 150 \\ 140 \\ 130 \end{bmatrix} \quad \text{and} \quad \mathbf{X} = \begin{bmatrix} 1 & 0 \\ 1 & 2 \\ 1 & -1 \\ 1 & 5 \\ 1 & 4 \\ 1 & -2 \\ 1 & 2 \\ 1 & 1 \\ 1 & 1 \end{bmatrix},$$

so that

$$\mathbf{X'X} = \begin{bmatrix} 9 & 12 \\ 12 & 56 \end{bmatrix}, \quad (\mathbf{X'X})^{-1} = \begin{bmatrix} .15556 & -.03333 \\ -.03333 & .02500 \end{bmatrix},$$

$$\text{and} \quad \mathbf{X'Y} = \begin{bmatrix} 1230 \\ 1970 \end{bmatrix}$$

The classical estimate of β is

$$\mathbf{b} = (\mathbf{X'X})^{-1}\,\mathbf{X'Y} = \begin{bmatrix} 125.67 \\ 8.25 \end{bmatrix}$$

Application of Bayes' theorem yields

$$\Sigma'' = [(\Sigma')^{-1} + \sigma^{-2}(\mathbf{X'X})]^{-1}$$

$$= \left\{ \begin{bmatrix} 25/2400 & 10/2400 \\ 10/2400 & 100/2400 \end{bmatrix} + \begin{bmatrix} 9/400 & 12/400 \\ 12/400 & 56/400 \end{bmatrix} \right\}^{-1}$$

$$= \begin{bmatrix} 79/2400 & 82/2400 \\ 82/2400 & 436/2400 \end{bmatrix}^{-1} = \begin{bmatrix} 37.7489 & -7.0996 \\ -7.0996 & 6.8398 \end{bmatrix}$$

and

$$\mathbf{b''} = \Sigma''[(\Sigma')^{-1}\,\mathbf{b'} + \sigma^{-2}(\mathbf{X'X})\mathbf{b}]$$

$$= \begin{bmatrix} 37.7489 & -7.0996 \\ -7.0996 & 6.8398 \end{bmatrix} \times$$

$$\left\{ \begin{bmatrix} 25/2400 & 10/2400 \\ 10/2400 & 100/2400 \end{bmatrix}\begin{bmatrix} 120 \\ 10 \end{bmatrix} + \begin{bmatrix} 9/400 & 12/400 \\ 12/400 & 56/400 \end{bmatrix}\begin{bmatrix} 125.67 \\ 8.25 \end{bmatrix} \right\} = \begin{bmatrix} 123.37 \\ 8.95 \end{bmatrix}$$

Therefore, the posterior distribution of β is a bivariate normal distribution with $E''(\beta_1) = 123.37$, $E''(\beta_2) = 8.95$, $V''(\beta_1) = 37.75$, $V''(\beta_2) = 6.84$, and $\text{cov}''(\beta_1,\beta_2) = -7.10$. The sample information has increased the mean of β_1 from 120 to 123.37 (the sample estimate of β_1 was 125.67) and decreased the mean of β_2 from 10 to 8.95 (the sample estimate of β_2 was 8.25). In general, Bayes' theorem yields posterior means which lie between prior means and sample means. Also, note that $V(\beta_1)$ is reduced from 100 to 37.75 and $V(\beta_2)$ is reduced from 25 to 6.84. In most cases, posterior variances of parameters in Bayesian studies are less than the corresponding prior variances, which is reasonable since additional information should reduce the uncertainty and hence reduce the variance.

At this point, consider the general Bayesian framework for regression problems once again. The objective is to make a prediction about Y, given values of the independent variables, and this prediction is in the form of an entire probability distribution, called the predictive distribution of Y. This is different from the likelihood of Y, which is conditional on the values of both the independent variables *and* the regression coefficients. That is, the likelihood is calculated with the β_j's fixed; the predictive distribution takes into account the uncertainty about the β_j's as represented by their joint posterior distribution. From the model, $Y = \sum_{j=1}^{K} \beta_j X_j + \varepsilon$, and the posterior distribution of β is taken to be multivariate normal with mean vector

$$\mathbf{b}'' = \begin{vmatrix} b_1'' \\ b_2'' \\ \cdot \\ \cdot \\ \cdot \\ b_K'' \end{vmatrix}$$

and variance-covariance matrix

$$\Sigma'' = \begin{vmatrix} V''(\beta_1) & \mathrm{cov}''(\beta_1, \beta_2) & \cdots & \mathrm{cov}''(\beta_1, \beta_K) \\ \mathrm{cov}''(\beta_1, \beta_2) & V''(\beta_2) & \cdots & \mathrm{cov}''(\beta_2, \beta_K) \\ \cdot & \cdot & \cdot & \cdot \\ \cdot & \cdot & \cdot & \cdot \\ \cdot & \cdot & \cdot & \cdot \\ \mathrm{cov}''(\beta_1, \beta_K) & \mathrm{cov}''(\beta_2, \beta_K) & \cdots & V''(\beta_K) \end{vmatrix}$$

A linear combination of normally distributed random variables is itself normally distributed, so Y is normally distributed with mean

$$E(Y \mid \mathbf{X}) = E\left(\sum_{j=1}^{K} \beta_j X_j + \epsilon \right) = \sum_{j=1}^{K} X_j E''(\beta_j) + 0$$

$$= \sum_{j=1}^{K} b_j'' X_j$$

and variance

$$V(Y \mid \mathbf{X}) = V\left(\sum_{j=1}^{K} \beta_j X_j + \epsilon \right) = V\left(\sum_{j=1}^{K} \beta_j X_j \right) + \sigma^2$$

$$= \sum_{j=1}^{K} X_j^2 \, V''(\beta_j) + \sum_{i=1}^{K} \sum_{\substack{j=1 \\ i \neq j}}^{K} X_i X_j \mathrm{cov}''(\beta_i, \beta_j) + \sigma^2$$

In the example, suppose that the yearly income of a particular family is \$11,500, so that $X_2 = 1.5$. The predictive distribution for Y, monthly expenditures on food, is a normal distribution with mean

$$E(Y \mid \mathbf{X}) = X_1 E''(\beta_1) + X_2 E''(\beta_2) = (1)(123.37) + (1.5)(8.95)$$
$$= 136.80$$

and variance

$$V(Y|\mathbf{X}) = X_1{}^2\,V'''(\beta_1) + X_2{}^2\,V''(\beta_2) + 2X_1X_2\mathrm{Cov}''(\beta_1,\beta_2) + \sigma^2$$
$$= (1)^2(37.75) + (1.5)^2(6.84) + 2(1)(1.5)(-7.10) + 400$$
$$= 431.84$$

Note that $V(Y|\mathbf{X})$ is larger than the error variance, since the variability of the predicted Y is due not only to error variance, but also to uncertainty concerning the regression coefficients. Using the predictive distribution, you could determine a single point to predict Y, which in this case would be the mean, 136.80. You could also find predictive intervals for Y; for instance, a 68 percent predictive interval for Y is $(136.80 - \sqrt{431.84},\ 136.80 + \sqrt{431.84})$, or $(116.02,\ 157.58)$. Finally, if you were interested, say, in the hypotheses that $Y > 120$ and $Y \leq 120$, you could determine the posterior odds ratio, $P(Y > 120)/P(Y \leq 120) = .79/.21 = 3.76$.

It has been assumed in this section that the error variance σ^2 is known. If it is not known, it must be included as an unknown parameter of the model, and the prior distribution is then a joint distribution of β_1, β_2, ..., β_K, and σ^2. This joint distribution can be factored into two terms, the marginal distribution of σ^2 and the conditional distribution of β given σ^2. The latter distribution is taken to be multivariate normal with mean $\mathbf{b}'$ and variance-covariance matrix Σ', just as in the case of known error variance. The distribution of σ^2 is transformed to a distribution of σ^{-2}, which is taken to be a gamma-2 distribution. The product of these two distributions is a $(K + 1)$-variate distribution known as the normal-gamma distribution. Finally, it should be noted that the marginal distribution of β is a multivariate student distribution and the predictive distribution of Y (given values of the X_js) is a univariate student distribution; this is analogous to the simple univariate normal situation, in which the distribution of the mean μ when the variance is not known is a univariate student, or t, distribution. For a discussion of this model, see [15] and [22].

At any rate, when the error variance of the regression model is unknown, no conceptual difficulty is presented for the Bayesian, but the assessment of prior distributions and the computational aspects of the problem become more complex. Similarly, the model becomes more complex if the assumption of a linear model, the assumption of normally distributed errors, or the assumption of a multivariate normal prior distribution is violated. Linear models in regression analysis have found wide applicability in the past, and the assumption of a normally distributed error term may be justified on the basis that the error term can be thought of as a sum of many different errors and that the central limit theorem can be invoked. These assumptions are generally also made in classical regression analysis. The assumption of a multivariate normal prior distribution for β is uniquely a Bayesian assumption. Unless the prior information indicates that the marginal distributions of some of the regression coefficients are quite skewed or have "fat tails," the multivariate normal distribution should provide a reasonable fit to the prior information. As noted earlier, it is not necessary that the prior distribution be multivariate normal, but it is convenient because this is the natural-conjugate family for the normal linear regression model.

BAYESIAN REGRESSION WITH DIFFUSE PRIOR DISTRIBUTIONS

Although the Bayesian wants to include any relevant prior information in the formal analysis, there are some situations in which he has very little such information. In other words, his prior distribution for the unknown parameters is relatively "flat" or "diffuse." The term *diffuse* is a relative term; when someone's prior distribution is said to be diffuse, the prior distribution need not be perfectly flat, or uniform, but only flat in relation to the likelihood function. In Figure 2, the prior distribution is clearly not perfectly flat, but it *is* flat relative to the likelihood function. It is convenient to think of a prior distribution as being diffuse when it is "swamped" by the sample information, as represented by the likelihood function. According to Bayes' theorem, the posterior distribution is proportional to the product of the prior distribution and the likelihood.

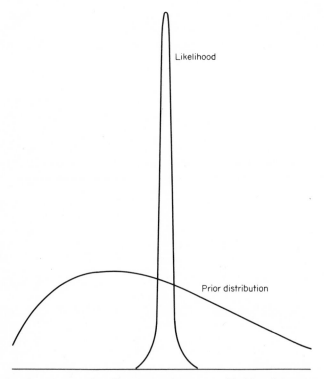

Fig. 2.   A prior distribution in relation to a likelihood function.

If the prior distribution is diffuse, or "gentle," in comparison to the likelihood function, then the posterior distribution will depend almost solely on the likelihood function. In such a situation, it is convenient to approximate the prior distribution with a uniform distribution. This simplifies the analysis, and it is a good approximation to the actual prior distribution for the purposes of the Bayesian analysis.

In the normal linear regression model with known error variance, discussed in the previous section, the most convenient choice of a prior distribution to represent a diffuse state of information is a distribution with a constant density function for all values of $\beta_1, \beta_2, \ldots,$ and β_K. Since these parameters can take on any real numbers as values, the area under this density function is infinite and the distribution is improper. However, the application of Bayes' theorem to incorporate sample information results in a proper posterior density function; the improper diffuse prior distribution is intuitively reasonable and creates no difficulties with respect to the determination of the posterior distribution.

In terms of the notation of the previous section, the improper diffuse prior distribution of β corresponds to an improper multivariate normal distribution with

$$(\Sigma')^{-1} = \begin{vmatrix} 0 & 0 & . & . & . & 0 \\ 0 & 0 & . & . & . & 0 \\ & . & . & . & & \\ & . & . & . & . & \\ & . & . & . & . & \\ 0 & 0 & . & . & . & 0 \end{vmatrix}$$

Essentially, this means that the elements of the variance-covariance matrix Σ are infinite, which is why the distribution is improper. Interestingly, the prior mean $\mathbf{b}'$ is irrelevant, since it drops out in the process of finding the posterior distribution:

$$\Sigma'' = [(\Sigma')^{-1} + \sigma^{-2}(\mathbf{X}^t\mathbf{X})]^{-1} = \sigma^2(\mathbf{X}^t\mathbf{X})^{-1}$$

and

$$\begin{aligned} \mathbf{b}'' &= \Sigma''[(\Sigma')^{-1}\mathbf{b}' + \sigma^{-2}(\mathbf{X}^t\mathbf{X})\mathbf{b}] \\ &= \sigma^2(\mathbf{X}^t\mathbf{X})^{-1}[\sigma^{-2}(\mathbf{X}^t\mathbf{X})\,\mathbf{b}] \\ &= \sigma^2\,\sigma^{-2}(\mathbf{X}^t\mathbf{X})^{-1}\,(\mathbf{X}^t\mathbf{X})\,\mathbf{b} \\ &= \mathbf{b} \end{aligned}$$

Thus, the posterior distribution of β is multivariate normal with mean $\mathbf{b}$ and variance covariance matrix $\sigma^2(\mathbf{X}^t\mathbf{X})^{-1}$.

Bayesian results under a diffuse prior distribution, inasmuch as they are based only on the sample information, may be compared with the corresponding classical results. Often the numerical results are virtually identical, but the interpretation is still quite different. In the regression model with an improper diffuse prior distribution, the mean of the posterior distribution of β is equal to $\mathbf{b}$, the usual classical estimator of β which is a least-squares estimator and is a maximum-likelihood estimator under the normality assumption. Furthermore, the posterior variance-covariance matrix of β is identical to the variance-covariance matrix of the sampling distribution of $\mathbf{b}$, although the interpretation is entirely different. The former gives variance and covariance terms involving the regression coefficients, *given* the sample result $\mathbf{b}$. The latter gives variance and covariance terms involving the sample result $\mathbf{b}$, given the values of the regression coefficients. If the classical statistician wanted to predict Y, given

values of the independent variables, his prediction would be $\sum_{j=1}^{K} b_j X_j$, which

is equal to the mean of the predictive distribution of Y when the prior distribution is diffuse.

In the example from the previous section involving family expenditures on food and family income, suppose that the prior distribution of β is diffuse. The posterior distribution is then a bivariate normal distribution with mean vector

$$\mathbf{b}'' = \mathbf{b} = \begin{bmatrix} 125.67 \\ 8.25 \end{bmatrix}$$

and variance-covariance matrix

$$\Sigma'' = \sigma^2(\mathbf{X}^t\mathbf{X})^{-1} = \begin{bmatrix} 62.2222 & -13.3333 \\ -13.3333 & 10.0000 \end{bmatrix}$$

Thus, the marginal distribution of β_1 is a normal distribution with mean $E''(\beta_1) = 125.67$ and variance $V''(\beta_1) = 62.2222$. The marginal distribution of β_2 is a normal distribution with mean $E''(\beta_2) = 8.25$ and variance $V''(\beta_2) = 10.0$. These marginal distributions can be used to determine point and interval estimates or to investigate hypotheses concerning the regression coefficients.

If the yearly income of a certain family is \$13,000, so that $X_2 = 3$, then the predictive distribution for Y, monthly expenditures on food, is a normal distribution with mean

$$E(Y \mid \mathbf{X}) = X_1E''(\beta_1) + X_2E''(\beta_2) = (1)(125.67) + (3)(8.25)$$
$$= 150.42$$

and variance

$$V(Y \mid \mathbf{X}) = X_1{}^2V''(\beta_1) + X_2{}^2V''(\beta_2) + 2X_1X_2\mathrm{cov}''(\beta_1,\beta_2) + \sigma^2$$
$$= (1)^2(62.2222) + (3)^2(10.0) + 2(1)(3)(-13.3333) + 400$$
$$= 472.22$$

Under a diffuse prior distribution, then, the results of Bayesian and classical regression analysis are similar numerically, although they are interpreted differently. The classical statistician refuses to make a probability statement about the unknown vector of parameters β. Instead, he determines an estimate of β from the sample and measures the accuracy of the procedure by considering the standard error of the estimate. Using this estimate and standard error, he can find interval estimates and test hypotheses concerning the regression parameters or concerning a predicted value of the dependent variable Y. The Bayesian summarizes his information about β in terms of an entire probability distribution of β. The entire posterior distribution represents an inferential statement, and from this distribution other inferences (point estimates, interval estimates, odds ratios for hypotheses) can be determined if so desired. Similarly, the Bayesian prediction of Y is expressed in terms of an entire predictive distribution, and if a single-point prediction is wanted, the mean of the distribution can be used.

Because they simplify the analysis and because they yield results that can be compared to classical results, diffuse prior distributions are used quite frequently in Bayesian analysis. They are useful when the state of prior information is actually diffuse, and they are often helpful in supplementary analyses if the Bayesian is interested in the sample information by itself. In any problem in which there is relevant prior information, however, the Bayesian should formally include this information in his primary statistical analysis.

SUMMARY

In summary, both the Bayesian and the classical approaches to regression problems involve the informal utilization of prior information in the choice of variables, selection of a model, and so on. The Bayesian approach goes one step further by formally introducing prior information in the form of a prior distribution of the parameters of the regression model. The prior distribution is then combined with sample information to form the posterior distribution of the parameters, and inferences and decisions regarding the parameters are based on this posterior distribution. Furthermore, the distribution of the parameters can be used to find a probability distribution for the dependent variable, given values of the independent variables. This distribution is called a predictive distribution, and it is used to make inferences in the form of predictions concerning the dependent variable.

The Bayesian model places no restrictions on the form of the prior distribution of the regression parameters, but the analysis is greatly simplified if this distribution is a member of the relevant natural-conjugate family. For the linear regression model with normally distributed error terms and known error variance, this means that the prior distribution of the vector of regression coefficients should be multivariate normal. The application of Bayes' theorem then results in a posterior distribution which is also multivariate normal, and the predictive distribution for the dependent variable is univariate normal. Perhaps the most serious problem in applying this Bayesian regression model is the assessment of a prior distribution. Unless the prior information is in the form of previous sample results, it may be difficult to express it in terms of a joint probability distribution. The most reasonable approach seems to be to consider the marginal distribution of each regression coefficient separately, leaving only the problem of the assessment of the covariances between pairs of coefficients. The assessment of prior distributions may be difficult in the univariate case (see [20]), and the difficulties are greatly increased in the multivariate case.

If there is very little prior information available, the choice of a prior distribution is easy, for a diffuse distribution may be used as an approximation to the actual prior distribution. The posterior distribution will then depend almost entirely on the sample information, as reflected in the likelihood function. In the normal linear regression model, the posterior mean of the vector of regression coefficients is identical to the usual classical estimator of this vector of coefficients if the prior distribution is taken to be an improper diffuse multivariate normal distribution. In general, Bayesian results under a diffuse prior distribution are similar numerically to classical results, although the interpretation is quite different.

Because of difficulties in the choice of a suitable prior distribution and because Bayesian regression methods are not widely known, there have been relatively few real-world applications of the Bayesian approach to regression problems. This is unfortunate, for the Bayesian approach provides a useful framework to formally combine prior information and sample information concerning the parameters of interest, thus enabling the analyst to utilize all available information in making inferences and decisions. More research is needed on the practical problems involved in the application of Bayesian procedures, both for regression models and for other statistical models.

REFERENCES

1. Christ, C. F., *Econometric Models and Methods,* New York: Wiley, 1966.
2. Frank, R. E., and P. E. Green, *Quantitative Methods in Marketing,* Englewood Cliffs, N.J.: Prentice-Hall, 1967.
3. Frank, R., A. A. Kuehn, and W. Massy, *Quantitative Techniques in Marketing Analysis,* Homewood, Ill.: Irwin, 1962.
4. Frederick, D. G., "An Industrial Pricing Decision Using Bayesian Multivariate Analysis," *Journal of Marketing Research,* vol. 8, May 1971, pp. 199–203.
5. Green, P. E., "Bayesian Decision Theory in Advertising," *Journal of Advertising Research,* vol. 2, December 1962, pp. 33–41.
6. Green, P. E., "Bayesian Decision Theory in Pricing Strategy," *Journal of Marketing,* vol. 27, January 1963, pp. 5–14.
7. Green, P. E., and D. S. Tull, *Research for Marketing Decisions,* Englewood Cliffs, N.J.: Prentice-Hall, 1966.
8. Goldberger, A. S., *Econometric Theory,* New York: Wiley, 1968.
9. Johnston, J., *Econometric Methods,* New York: McGraw-Hill, 1963.
10. Klein, L. R., *An Introduction to Econometrics,* Englewood Cliffs, N.J.: Prentice-Hall, 1962.
11. Lindley, D. V., *Introduction to Probability and Statistics from a Bayesian Viewpoint,* 2 vols., Cambridge, England: Cambridge University Press, 1965.
12. Montgomery, D. B., and G. L. Urban, *Management Science in Marketing,* Englewood Cliffs, N.J.: Prentice-Hall, 1969.
13. Pratt, J. W., H. Raiffa, and R. Schlaifer, *Introduction to Statistical Decision Theory,* New York: McGraw-Hill, 1965.
14. Raiffa, H., *Decision Analysis,* Reading, Mass.: Addison-Wesley, 1968.
15. Raiffa, H., and R. Schlaifer, *Applied Statistical Decision Theory,* Boston: Harvard University, Graduate School of Business Administration, 1961.
16. Reinmuth, J. E., and M. D. Geurts, "A Bayesian Approach to Forecasting the Effects of Atypical Situations," *Journal of Marketing Research,* vol. 9, August 1972, pp. 292–297.
17. Roberts, H. V., "Bayesian Statistics in Marketing," *Journal of Marketing,* vol. 27, January 1963, pp. 1–4.
18. Schlaifer, R., *Probability and Statistics for Business Decisions,* New York: McGraw-Hill, 1959.
19. Schlaifer, R., *Analysis of Decisions Under Uncertainty,* New York: McGraw-Hill, 1969.
20. Winkler, R. L., "The Assessment of Prior Distributions in Bayesian Analysis," *Journal of the American Statistical Association,* vol. 62, September 1967, pp. 776–800.
21. Winkler, R. L., *An Introduction to Bayesian Inference and Decision,* New York: Holt, 1972.
22. Zellner, A., *An Introduction to Bayesian Inference in Econometrics,* New York: Wiley, 1971.

Part E

Statistical Analysis of Relationships

Chapter 7

Regression Methods With Simultaneous Equations

FRANK M. BASS *Krannert Graduate School of Industrial Administration, Purdue University, Lafayette, Indiana*

LEONARD J. PARSONS *Graduate School of Business, Indiana University, Bloomington, Indiana*

INTRODUCTION

Unlike single-equation regression methods, simultaneous-equation methods recognize simultaneous, or two-way, causation among certain variables. Thus, for example, it may be possible to estimate the parameters in systems of relationships in which it is hypothesized that advertising influences sales but is also influenced by sales. The explicit formulation of models with two-way causation can be critical if the purpose of the analysis is to infer the influence of marketing-decision variables upon sales in time series data.

This chapter is concerned with the problems imposed by the additional complexities of the simultaneous-equation models. One of these problems is that of *identifying* the individual relationships in the system. The chapter will therefore discuss and compare alternative estimation methods, including two-stage least squares, limited information, and least-variance ratio; k-class estimators; three-stage least squares; and full-information maximum-likelihood methods.

Simultaneous-equation regression both permits and requires tests of hypotheses over and above tests which are conventionally associated with single-equation regression. Testing concepts and methods are explored in this chapter. Finally, a few examples in which simultaneous-equation regression has been applied to marketing problems are discussed.

Structural and Reduced-Form Equations

Often, marketing theory specifies the existence of a system of linear relationships or equations. Because each of these equations expresses some aspect of the behavior of an individual or sector in describing the structure of the market mechanism, the relationships are called *structural equations*. A hypothetical marketing model for a product might be represented by the following three structural equations:

$$S_t = \beta_{12}D_t + \beta_{13}A_t + \gamma_{11}S_{t-1} + (0)A_{t-1} + \gamma_{13}P_t + \gamma_{14} + u_{1,t} \qquad (1a)$$
$$D_t = (0)S_t + \beta_{23}A_t + \gamma_{21}S_{t-1} + (0)A_{t-1} + (0)P_t + \gamma_{24} + u_{2,t} \qquad (1b)$$
$$A_t = \beta_{31}S_t + (0)D_t + (0)S_{t-1} + \gamma_{32}A_{t-1} + \gamma_{33}P_t + \gamma_{34} + u_{3,t} \qquad (1c)$$

where S is logarithm of sales
$\quad\quad\ \ A$ is logarithm of advertising
$\quad\quad\ \ D$ is logarithm of distribution
$\quad\quad\ \ P$ is logarithm of price
$\quad\quad\ \ u_{i,t}$ is random disturbances

We have adopted the conventional normalization rule which assumes that in the ith structural equation, the coefficient of the ith endogenous variable is equal to one.

The variables in the model are classified as endogenous (S, D, A) or exogenous (P), depending on whether their values are or are not intended to be explained by the model. Lagged endogenous variables (S_{t-1}, A_{t-1}) which occur in dynamic models are statistically similar to exogenous variables and are correspondingly grouped with the exogenous variables as predetermined variables. The current endogenous variables (S_t, D_t, A_t) are jointly dependent variables.

When the number of equations is equal to the number of endogenous variables, the equation system is said to be complete. Completeness is a necessary condition that allows the endogenous variables to be expressed in terms of the predetermined variables and disturbances. When this is possible, the endogenous variables are said to be determined jointly or simultaneously by the predetermined variables and the disturbances, giving rise to the expression "simultaneous-equation models" for such systems.

This logically equivalent system of equations into which the original structural equations may be transformed is called the *reduced form*. A given reduced-form equation contains only one endogenous variable. In our example:

$$S_t = \alpha_{11}S_{t-1} + \alpha_{12}A_{t-1} + \alpha_{13}P_t + \alpha_{14} + w_{1,t} \qquad (2a)$$
$$D_t = \alpha_{21}S_{t-1} + \alpha_{22}A_{t-1} + \alpha_{23}P_t + \alpha_{24} + w_{2,t} \qquad (2b)$$
$$A_t = \alpha_{31}S_{t-1} + \alpha_{32}A_{t-1} + \alpha_{33}P_t + \alpha_{34} + w_{3,t} \qquad (2c)$$

The reduced-form parameters can be expressed in terms of the structural parameters.

The marketing interpretation of the structural equations is simpler and more direct than that of the reduced form. On the other hand, the reduced form expresses the explicit dependence of the dependent variables on the predetermined variables and disturbances. The reduced form is closer to the standard linear model than the structural form since a reduced-form equation has only independent variables and a random-disturbance term on the right side of the equation.

IDENTIFICATION

The ability to express the parameters of the reduced form as explicit functions of the parameters of the structural form, or conversely, to express the structural parameters as explicit functions of the reduced-form parameters, is unfortunately not automatic and, indeed, is sometimes impossible. Determination of whether there is a one-to-one correspondence between the reduced-form parameters and the structural parameters is called the *identification* problem. Identification is logically prior to estimation.

To make clear what this means in marketing terms, let us investigate the issues involved in statistically determining a demand curve.[1] There is general agreement that not only are sales influenced by advertising, but also that advertising is influenced by sales. Advertising decision rules, whether rigid or flexible, certainly take sales into account. Consider the situation in which a firm employs the decision rule to budget advertising as a fraction of sales. Two equations are required for specification of the market mechanism. The first relationship is the demand function which specifies how the quantity demanded, S, is affected by a firm's advertising expenditures, A. Second is the advertising

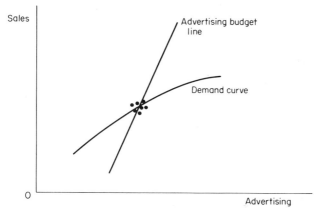

Fig. 1.   Stable advertising and demand curves.

function which expresses how advertising decisions are influenced by demand for the product.

These two hypothetical relationships are drawn in Figure 1, along with the observations available to the market researcher. If the two curves do not shift over time but maintain their present positions, and if our theoretical model corresponds closely to the facts so that other external marketing factors have minimal effect, then our observed data will be densely clustered around the intersection of the two curves. This scatter of points does not provide any information about the shape of either curve and so it is said that neither curve is identified.

A more frequent situation occurs when the demand curve shifts while the firm's advertising budgeting practices remain rigid. In such cases, there will be a series of different intersection points, but they will merely trace out the advertising budget line (Figure 2). One danger lies in mistaking the advertising-budget line for the demand curve. In this example, the advertising-budget line is identified, whereas the demand curve is not.

Both curves can be identified only when both curves shift over time. The observations available from such a process may bear no resemblance to either

[1] The material in this section follows Baumol [2].

curve (Figure 3). The fact that a plot of the observations reveals a long and narrow dispersion is not in itself sufficient to assure that the observed dependence expresses one of the relationships. Both curves could shift simultaneously, with the result that the observations would lie along the path of their point of intersection.

How may the researcher, in principle, test whether the relationships he is seeking are identifiable? A sufficient condition for identification of the two

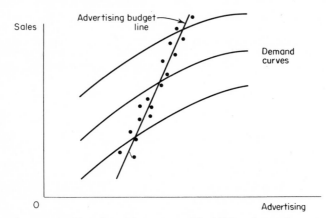

Fig. 2.   Stable advertising curve with shifting demand curve.

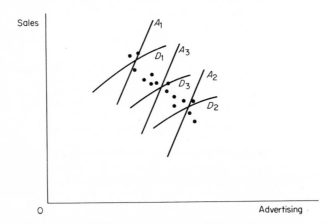

Fig. 3.   Shifting advertising and demand curves.

relationships is that some distinguishable factors influencing advertising leave demand unchanged and that some distinguishable factors affecting demand do not influence advertising.

To evaluate whether an equation is sufficiently distinctive from the others in its system, we examine the a priori information available. There are several types of a priori information. Two structural parameters may be known (or assumed) to be equal, or to sum to a known constant, or to have a known ratio. The covariance between two structural disturbances might be known to be zero. The focus here will be on the most important of these a priori restrictions, the one that tells which variables are absent in a particular equation. For example, in Equation ($1a$), there is the a priori restriction that lagged advertising does not enter the equation, that is, its coefficient (γ_{12}) is zero.

We may use the following rule, called the *order condition* for identifiability, to assist us. For the ith equation in a model consisting of G linear equations to be identified, the equation must exclude at least $G - 1$ of the variables contained in that model (that is, their coefficients are zero). Although, logically, an equation may satisfy this rule yet remain unidentified, pragmatically any equation fulfilling this rule may be considered identified. In our system (Equations $1a$, $1b$, and $1c$), there are three equations, so $G = 3$. Thus, a minimum of $G - 1 = 2$ coefficients are required to be zero in order to achieve identification. In the first equation, only one coefficient (γ_{12}) is zero. Therefore the first equation is said to be underidentified. Three coefficients (β_{21}, γ_{22}, γ_{23}) are zero in the second equation and this equation is said to be overidentified. In the last equation, exactly two coefficients (β_{33}, γ_{31}) are missing, so it is said to be just identified.

A more rigorous rule, called the *rank condition* for identifiability, is sometimes used. For the ith equation in a modeling consisting of G linear equations to be identified, an array, which is formed by taking the array of all coefficients in the model and then removing all columns of coefficients corresponding to non-zero coefficients in the ith equation as well as the row of coefficients of the ith equation, must have at least one nonzero determinant of $G - 1$ rows and columns. The array of all coefficients in our example is:

S_t	D_t	A_t	S_{t-1}	A_{t-1}	P_t	1	
-1	β_{12}	β_{13}	γ_{11}	0	γ_{13}	γ_{14}	($3a$)
0	-1	β_{23}	γ_{21}	0	0	γ_{24}	($3b$)
β_{31}	0	-1	0	γ_{32}	γ_{33}	γ_{34}	($3c$)

Thus, for the third equation, the relevant array of coefficients is

$$\begin{vmatrix} \beta_{12} & \gamma_{11} \\ -1 & \gamma_{21} \end{vmatrix} \tag{4}$$

If its determinant, $\beta_{12}\gamma_{21} + \gamma_{11}$, is nonzero, then the third equation is identified. Since the true values of the structural parameters are unknown, estimates of the structural parameters may be used to test the hypothesis that the relevant determinant is zero. However, the researcher is usually safe to use only the order condition and to neglect the rank condition.

If the identifiability condition is met, the researcher may then proceed to estimate the parameters in his model. There are alternative techniques for this estimation. Two-stage least squares, limited information and least-variance ratio, k-class estimators, three-stage least squares, and full-information, maximum-likelihood methods will be discussed and compared.

BACKGROUND TO SIMULTANEOUS-EQUATION REGRESSION

Assumptions

The various simultaneous-equation estimation methods are predicated on certain assumptions. The assumptions determine what can be said about the estimates produced by a particular technique, especially with regard to three basic criteria—bias, consistency, and efficiency.[2]

We assume that the model is linear and that the determinant of the matrix of coefficients of the endogenous variables is not zero. The same assumptions required in conventional single-equation regression are required of each of the reduced-form equations. The column vectors of observations on the predetermined variables must be linearly independent so that no one of these vectors can be expressed as a linear combination of the other vectors.

The random-disturbance element in each equation in each time period must be uncorrelated with the disturbance in other time periods, although correlation is permitted between the disturbance in one equation and the disturbances in other equations. The disturbances should be distributed with zero mean, and the covariance matrix of the disturbances in the different equations should have a determinant which is not zero. Frequently, we will use the additional supposition that the disturbances are normally distributed.

The predetermined variables will be exogenous, although this restriction will frequently be relaxed to permit the inclusion of lagged endogenous variables. The argument is that since the values of lagged endogenous variables represent events which have already occurred, they are predetermined for the current period. Recalling that identification precedes estimation, the structural equation to be estimated must be identified.

As we describe the various simultaneous-equation regression methods, we will specify the assumptions necessary for derivation of their estimators. But why is there this proliferation of methods? Why not simply apply ordinary least squares of each equation in the structural form individually?

Ordinary Least Squares

The ordinary least-squares method may be applied to each equation in a model. However, if there is more than one endogenous variable in an equation, as is usual, the estimators for parameters of this relationship will be biased and inconsistent. This is because no matter which endogenous variable is chosen as the dependent variable, the remaining endogenous variables will be correlated with the disturbance term.

Let us return to our sales-advertising example. Figure 4 shows the observations resulting from both curves constantly shifting as a consequence of minor random occurrences. The least-squares line fitted to the observations is a poor representation of the demand curve.

REDUCED-FORM ESTIMATION

Indirect Least Squares

Although the ordinary least-squares method should not be applied to estimating the parameters of the structural equations, the method may be used to estimate the parameters of the reduced-form equations, since each of these equations contains only one stochastic variable. A stochastic variable is a variable determined directly or indirectly by chance. The disturbance is determined by chance alone, whereas the endogenous variable is determined by the exogenous variables and by the random disturbance.

If the structural system is just identified, the estimates of the structural parameters can be derived from the estimated reduced-form parameters. Al-

---

[2] See, for example, Chapter 2 of Part D of this section.

though, under our assumptions, the reduced-form estimators will be best linear, unbiased estimators, this property does not hold, in general, under transformation, so that the derived structural estimators are biased.   If the structural disturbances are normally distributed, the reduced-form disturbances are also normally distributed.   The least-squares estimators of the reduced-form parameters will be maximum-likelihood estimators, as will the derived structural parameters, since this property does hold under transformation.

In modeling marketing situations, the researcher often specifies overidentified equations to which the indirect least-squares method cannot be applied.   This chapter will now consider several methods that are available for estimating the parameters of an overidentified structural equation.

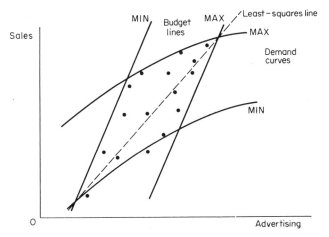

Fig. 4.   Random shifts in advertising and demand curves.

STRUCTURAL-FORM ESTIMATION: SINGLE-EQUATION METHODS

Two-Stage Least Squares

As noted previously, the ordinary least-squares method produces inconsistent estimators of the structural parameters in a simultaneous-equation model because the endogenous variables are jointly dependent on the random disturbances.   This dependency is made explicit in the reduced form.   Notice that if the researcher knows the true value for the reduced-form disturbances for each observation he has on the endogenous variables, he could remove these stochastic portions from them and have left a nonrandom variable.   Let us rewrite Equation (1c) accordingly:

$$A_t = \beta_{31}(S_t - w_{1,t}) + \gamma_{32}A_{t-1} + \gamma_{33}P_t + \gamma_{34} + u_{3,t} + \beta_{31}w_{1,t} \qquad (5a)$$
$$A_t = \beta_{31}(S_t - w_{1,t}) + \gamma_{32}A_{t-1} + \gamma_{33}P_t + \gamma_{34} + v_{3,t} \qquad (5b)$$

where $v_{3,t} = u_{3,t} + \beta_{31}w_{1,t}$.

Ordinarily least squares can now be legitimately used to estimate β_{31}, since the new equation contains only one random variable.   Although we cannot determine the true values of $w_{1,t}$, we can use the residuals $(w_{1,t})$ generated by least-squares regression on the first reduced-form equation to estimate these values.

Theil and Basmann independently devised the two-stage least-squares method. In the equation we wish to estimate, we choose the endogenous variable we want to be the dependent variable. The first stage consists of computing the least-squares estimates of the reduced-form equations for the other jointly dependent variables in the equation. After calculating the values of these jointly dependent variables in the equation, substitute these calculated values in place of the observed data. The second stage consists of computing the least-squares regression for the selected dependent variable on other variables in the equation to be estimated, using these calculated values of the remaining jointly dependent variables and the observed values of the predetermined variables. The resultant two-stage least-squares estimates are consistent. Thus, in the first stage, the parameters of Equation $(2a)$ may be estimated and

$$\hat{S}_t - \hat{w}_{1t} = \hat{\alpha}_{11} S_{t-1} + \hat{\alpha}_{12} A_{t-1} + \hat{\alpha}_{13} P_t + \hat{\alpha}_{14}$$

Substituting this into Equation $(5b)$, we have

$$A_t = \beta_{31}(\hat{S}_t - \hat{w}_t) + \gamma_{32} A_{t-1} + \gamma_{33} P_t + \gamma_{34} + \hat{v}_{3,t} \qquad (5c)$$

where $\hat{v}_{3,t} = u_{3,t} + \beta_{31}\hat{w}_{1t}$.
Then, β_{31}, γ_{32}, γ_{33}, and γ_{34} can be estimated from a regression (the second-stage regression) on the regression model:

$$A_t = \beta_{31} \hat{S}_t + \gamma_{32} A_{t-1} + \gamma_{33} P_t + \gamma_{34} + u_{3,t} \qquad (5d)$$

If a structural equation is just identified, as is the case for Equation $(1c)$, the two-stage least-squares estimates will be the same as those produced by the direct least-squares solution.

Limited Information and Least-Variance Ratio

The limited-information method and the least-variance ratio method provide the same consistent estimators of the parameters of a single just-identified or overidentified structural equation. These methods employ only the a priori restrictions for the equation being estimated. Our model building is eased by the fact that it is not necessary to specify the exact form of the remaining equations in the system, or whether they are identified, or even the number of these equations; only the variables that enter these equations need be specified. In making these relaxing assumptions, we lose some efficiency in our estimators.

To apply the least-variance-ratio principle, we will adopt our usual assumptions plus the assumption that the disturbances are normally distributed. Both lagged endogenous and exogenous variables may be in the equation. Ideally, we would like our equation to contain only one current endogenous variable so that we might apply the least-squares method and get maximum-likelihood estimators for the parameters in the equation. This may be accomplished by defining a single composite endogenous variable to represent the entire current endogenous section of the equation. In equation $(1b)$, we could define the following composite endogenous variable (CEV):

$$\text{CEV}_t = D_t - \beta_{23}A_t \qquad (6)$$

and rewrite the equation as

$$\text{CEV}_t = \gamma_{21}S_{t-1} + u_{2,t} \qquad (7)$$

Ordinarily least squares would now be appropriate for estimating the coefficients of the exogenous variables in this redefined equation. Unfortunately, this does not tell how to estimate the coefficients of endogenous variables, for example, β_{23}, which, moreover, are necessary to find the values of the composite endogenous variable so that the above regression can be performed.

Our a priori restrictions state that the coefficients of some of the predetermined variables are zero $(\gamma_{22} = \gamma_{23} = 0)$. Consequently, computation of the regression of the composite endogenous variable on all the predetermined variables in the system (S_{t-1}, A_{t-1}, P_t), using an infinite sample, should provide estimates which are equal to zero for these restricted variables. Although we cannot find a set of values for the endogenous coefficients which will permit these estimators to be exactly zero in an overidentified equation because of sampling variation, we can try to minimize the weight of the theoretically excluded variables in our regression equation. We select the coefficient values of the endogenous variables so that the theoretically excluded predetermined variables contribute minimal additional explanation of the variation of the composite endogenous variable in our regression equation. This is done by making the sum of the squared residuals of the composite endogenous variable from its regression on the predetermined variables in the equation as close as possible to the sum of the squared residuals of the composite variable from its regression on all the predetermined variables in the system. That is, we would like the variance ratio, 1, as close to one as possible.

$$1 = \frac{\text{sum of squared residuals of the composite endogenous variable from its regression on the predetermined variables in the equation}}{\text{sum of squared residuals of the composite endogenous variable from its regression on the predetermined variables in the system}} \tag{8}$$

To accomplish this, we minimize 1 with respect to the coefficients of the endogenous variables by differentiating. This minimization provides the estimators for these coefficients which are needed to calculate the least-squares estimates of the coefficients of the predetermined variables.

K-Class

Theil [8] has suggested a general family of estimators known as the k-class estimators. Each member of the family is described by a particular value of the scalar k. Ordinary and two-stage least-squares estimators belong to the k-class and possess values of k equal to 0 and 1, respectively. The limited-information estimator is also a member, with k being equal to the smallest root 1, in its determinantal equation (not shown). If k is such that it converges in probability to one, the k-class estimator is consistent. (Note that for ordinary least squares, k stays at 0 and thus does not converge to 1 as the sample size is increased.)

STRUCTURAL-FORM ESTIMATION: SYSTEMS METHODS

The methods considered thus far have dealt with individual structural equations in a model. In discussing them, this chapter has neglected much of the information available about other equations in the system. Let us now explore several methods for simultaneously estimating the parameters of all the identified structural equations in a model. These full-information methods should increase the efficiency of estimation.

Three-Stage Least Squares

Zellner and Theil [8] invented the three-stage least-squares method in order to be able to estimate an entire structure subject to all the identifying restrictions simultaneously. The first stages merely involve using two-stage least squares to estimate each structural equation of the model, subject only to the identifying restrictions on that equation. The estimated structural coefficients can then be used to provide estimates of the residuals in each structural equation and, in turn, these residuals can be used to get an estimate of the variance-covariance matrix of the structural disturbances. The third stage uses the estimated variance-covariance matrix and the identifying restrictions on all the coefficients in the model to determine the coefficients of all the equations simultaneously by means of Aitken's generalized least-squares method [5].

Under our regular assumptions, Zellner and Theil show that the three-stage least-squares estimator is consistent and asymptotically normal. Moreover, this estimator is asymptotically more efficient than two-stage least squares for any structural equation in a model that has both (1) overidentifying restrictions on its other equations and (2) a nondiagonal covariance matrix of disturbances. If either or both of these conditions fail to hold, then the three-stage least-squares estimator is identical to the two-stage method.

Full-Information Maximum Likelihood

The full-information maximum-likelihood method extends the application of the maximum-likelihood principle to the joint conditional distributions of two or more jointly dependent variables, given the values of a set of predetermined variables. Besides our regular assumptions, we will also assume that the disturbances are normally distributed and that the nonstochastic variables may be predetermined.

The first step in this method is to transform the structural equations into the corresponding reduced-form equations. Here is the procedure: Recall that the reduced form expresses the joint conditional distributions of each of the jointly dependent variables given the values of the predetermined variables. Rewrite the reduced form so that each equation has its disturbance term on its left side, and has on the right its dependent variable minus a linear function of the predetermined variables with unknown parameters. Replace each disturbance term in the joint normal distribution of all the disturbances by its value from the reduced form. Restate each of the reduced-form parameters in this expression in terms of the structural parameters to yield the likelihood function of the structural parameters given observations on the dependent and predetermined variables. Finally, maximize this likelihood function with respect to the structural parameters, subject to a priori restrictions.

RELATIVE MERITS OF STRUCTURAL-FORM ESTIMATION METHODS

What are the relative merits of the various methods? For estimation of structural parameters, ordinary least squares (OLS) is biased and inconsistent, but has minimum variance. Two-stage least squares (2SLS), limited-information maximum-likelihood (LIML), full-information maximum-likelihood (FIML), and three-stage least squares (3SLS) are consistent; LIML, FIML, and 3LS are asymptotically normal. If normally distributed disturbances are assumed, then among the systems methods, FIML and 3SLS are asymptotically efficient and among the single-equation methods, 2SLS and LIML are asymptotically efficient, compared with consistent estimators using the same a priori information. These results are summarized in Table 1.

What method should be selected? Theoretically, we should choose the consistent estimator with the minimum asymptotic variance. However, this criterion, based on desirable asymptotic properties, is often irrelevant to marketing practitioners who must work with small sample sizes. Econometricians have conjectured about the relative merits of each method by drawing upon the available information provided by Monte Carlo experiments involving small sample cases.

Theoretically, the best method for structural estimation is FIML; however, this method has not often been used because of the computational effort involved. Moreover, the optimal properties of this estimator are very sensitive to the correct specification of the model. This latter drawback is very serious, given the current state of marketing theory. Still, if a priori information on the

TABLE 1   Summary of the Properties of Structural Estimators

Estimator	Properties Usual assumptions (lagged endogenous variables permitted; disturbances serially independent but not necessarily normal)	Properties Usual assumptions
Ordinary least squares	Inconsistent in general; small variance	
Indirect least squares[1]	Consistent	
Instrumental variables[1]	Consistent; asymptotically normal; approximate covariance matrix available	Asymptotically efficient
Two-stage least squares[1]	Consistent; asymptotic covariance	Asymptotically efficient
K-class	Consistent if plim $(K - 1) = 0$	
Three-stage least squares[2]	Consistent; same as two-stage least squares if covariance matrix of disturbances is diagonal	Asymptotically efficient
Full information[2]	Consistent; asymptotically normal	Asymptotically efficient

[1] The four estimators marked 1 in the table are identical in the case of a just-identified equation.

[2] If the entire model is just identified, then all six estimators marked 2 or 3 in the table are identical for the model.

[3] Compared to other estimators using the same incomplete a priori information.

SOURCE: C. F. Christ, *Econometric Models and Methods*, New York: Wiley, 1966, p. 466, Table 12.1.

disturbance covariance matrix is available, then FIML should be used. Otherwise, econometricians seem to favor 3SLS. Often, computational costs restrict us to single-equation methods. Econometricians have tentatively ranked the main single-equation methods as follows: 2SLS, first; LIML, second; and OLS, third. Recall that the 3SLS and 2SLS estimators are identical except in a special case. Consequently, the two-stage least-squares method should be the one most frequently applied to simultaneous-equation models in marketing.

APPRAISAL OF SIMULTANEOUS-EQUATION MODELS AND ESTIMATES

Although we have followed convention and chosen to discuss estimation procedures first, model testing has an even higher priority than estimation. If we know that a model is correct and are uncertain only about the values of its parameters, then our attention should properly be focused on estimation. Unfortunately, in marketing we seldom have great confidence in our models. It is for this reason that testing should take precedence over estimation. Estimation is warranted only after a model has been tested and found to be consistent with the evidence. The concept of the predictive test is especially useful when applied to simultaneous-equation regression models. Under this concept, the premises of a theory (that is, the model and premises about the parameters) are used to deduce implications about the data.

Concept of the Predictive Test

Since tests of theories utilizing well-established principles of scientific methodology are notably sparse in statistical studies in economics and marketing, it may not be inappropriate to discuss them briefly here. It is important to note at the outset that no empirical test can prove that a theory is true. A theory may be shown to be in good agreement with the empirical evidence, but since it is not possible to test all the infinitely many alternative theories, some of which may agree equally well with the data, the failure of a particular theory to be rejected is far from conclusive proof that it is true. It is for this reason that it is especially important to develop tests which are not easily satisfied. Unsuccessful predictions can, in principle, be conclusive with respect to the truth of a theory. It is necessary, however, to examine carefully the underlying statistical assumptions and background conditions regardless of the outcome of the test.

The concept of the predictive test within the framework of simultaneous-equation regression has been cogently established in theoretical and empirical studies by Basmann.

In addition to a system of structural relations, an explanatory marketing model is comprised of theoretical marketing premises and justifiable factual statements of initial conditions. A set of prediction statements that attribute definite probabilities to specified observable marketing events is deduced from the model. Since the model can be discredited by unsuccessful predictions, close attention must be given to substantiating assertions that external influences are negligible during the historical period analyzed.

The theoretical marketing premises are a priori restrictions not incorporated in the estimation method. The predictive test involves comparing the numerical estimates with this set of premises: Suppose that in our marketing model for a product [Equations $(1a)$, $(1b)$, and $(1c)$], we know a priori that the magnitude of the advertising elasticity parameter (β_{13}) must lie in a finite range between 0.5 and 0.8 with positive sign. If the numerical estimate of this parameter turns out to be negative and the probability of this event's occurring is small, then we must reject the hypothesis that our explanatory marketing model is true.

Discussion about the origins of premises is not meant to be an argument defending them as self-evident. Any argument about the a priori plausibility of these marketing premises is purposeless. The outcome of the predictive test can, in principle, settle the argument. Rather, the background and rationale for the premises are provided to aid in understanding the present interpretation of the premises and to assist researchers in formulating and testing alternative premises. The fact that the premises have not been falsified suggests that even sharper restrictions might have been placed on the underlying postulates. From the viewpoint of improving and sharpening theories of marketing processes, this may be the primary significance of a successful predictive test.

A statement of initial conditions is a combination of three statements. One statement specifies the observed values of the exogenous variable explicitly included in the structural relations of the model. Another specifies the statistical distribution of the random disturbances explicitly included in the structural relations. In addition, one statement asserts that relevant external conditions stay approximately constant during the historical period under consideration.

The predictive test of an explanatory marketing model is implemented by specification of an observable event (the critical region for the test) which has a very small probability of occurring if the conjunction of initial conditions and economic premises is true. Occurrence of this theoretically improbable event implies that at least one, and maybe only one, of the assumptions about the initial conditions and marketing premises is discredited.

It is important to note that a forecast and a prediction are not synonymous. Important and pragmatic statements about future occurrences can often be made without deducing these statements from initial conditions with the aid of a model. Naïve, nonexplanatory models frequently yield good forecasts. A forecast is an extrapolation from statistical parameter estimates obtained in one historical period to observations generated in another historical period. Tidal and astronomical computations are still carried out as they were by the Babylonians. Newton's physical theories help provide the basis for an understanding of why these techniques work, and for a long time traditional calculations were more accurate than those based on the best theoretical principles. Although, as a matter of interest, we shall often develop a forecast from the model to be tested, it is not the basis for accepting or rejecting the model.

In addition to a predictive test developed from premises about the structural parameters, additional predictive tests are sometimes useful. One is an identifiability test for equations which are overidentified. Since there can be only one true parameter value for those structural parameters which are overidentified, as in Equation ($1b$), it will be necessary to test the hypothesis that the separate and distinct estimates of the same parameter disagree because of chance.

If the model is dynamic, as in the example presented earlier in this chapter, lagged values of endogenous variables appear as elements in the set of predetermined variables. The dynamic stability of the model must therefore be tested. If it can be shown that the parameter estimates are such that the model will diverge (explode) as time goes on, then such a model cannot represent reality. In the present example, Equations ($1a$) and ($2a$) are first-order difference equations. In order to show dynamic stability, it is necessary to demonstrate that if the exogenous variables are constant, these equations will converge. The requirement for stability in this case is that $|\hat{\alpha}_{11}| < 1$.

Since the form and nature of tests of identifiability and dynamic stability vary from model to model, it is not possible to specify general methods of constructing these tests. Since predictive tests can, in principle, prove conclusively that a model is false, it is important to conduct predictive tests before proceeding to estimation. Estimates may vary with the estimation technique used, and in some instances (underidentification), estimation may not even be possible. Confidence in a model is enhanced and knowledge is gained, however, if the model satisfies the predictive tests to which it is put. The failure to discredit a model is not proof that the model is true, but then, there is no way to prove this conclusively.

Other Nonpredictive Tests

The various nonpredictive tests—tests on coefficients, residuals, and so on—which might be performed on an ordinary single linear equation are equally applicable to a reduced-form equation. Most of these tests may also be applied to the structural equations and their residuals, although substantial modification of the test may be required. The Durbin-Watson test is inappropriate for serial correlation of the disturbances in dynamic and/or structural models, but this test may be modified and applied in some special cases. Difficulties arise primarily from the fact that we often do not know the exact, finite distributions of parameters in a structural model.

MARKETING APPLICATIONS

Bass [9] was the first marketing researcher to apply the concept of predictive testing to a simultaneous-equation model. This empirical analysis focused on the influence of advertising on the sale of cigarettes. By going to a system of equations, he was able to model not only the influence of advertising on sales, but also the influence of sales on advertising. In that study, the four equations were

$$y_{1t} = \beta_1 y_{3t} + \beta_2 y_{4t} + \gamma_1 x_{1t} + \gamma_2 x_{2t} + \gamma_3 + u_{1t} \tag{6a}$$
$$y_{2t} = \beta_3 y_{3t} + \beta_4 y_{4t} + \gamma_4 x_{1t} + \gamma_5 x_{2t} + \gamma_6 + u_{2t} \tag{6b}$$
$$y_{1t} = \beta_5 y_{2t} + \beta_6 y_{3t} + \gamma_7 + u_{3t} \tag{6c}$$
$$y_{2t} = \beta_7 y_{1t} + \beta_8 y_{4t} + \gamma_8 + u_{4t} \tag{6d}$$

where y_{1t} is logarithm of sales of filter cigarettes (number of cigarettes) divided by population over age 20

y_{2t} is logarithm of sales of nonfilter cigarettes (number of cigarettes) divided by population over age 20

y_{3t} is logarithm of advertising dollars for filter cigarettes divided by population over age 20 divided by advertising price index

y_{4t} is logarithm of advertising dollars for nonfilter cigarettes divided by population over age 20 divided by consumer price index

x_{1t} is logarithm of disposable personal income divided by population over age 20 divided by consumer price index

x_{2t} is logarithm of price per package of nonfilter cigarettes divided by consumer price index

Equations (6a) and (6b) represent the demand equations and are intended to reflect the influence of advertising on sales, and the last two equations reflect the influence of sales on advertising. The model was tested along with premises about the structural parameters. Although the first two equations are underidentified, the premises that $\beta_2 = -\beta_1$, $\beta_3 = -\beta_4$, $0.5 \leq \beta_1 \leq 0.6$, $0.2 \leq \beta_4 \leq 0.3$ were found, on the basis of a predictive test, to be in good agreement with the data. Since, in this case, the coefficients are elasticities, there is evidence to support the theory that the advertising elasticity for filter cigarettes is roughly twice that for nonfilter cigarettes.

Extending this development, Bass and Parsons [10] studied a product that belongs to the general class of frequently purchased products sold predominantly in supermarkets. Besides the sales-advertising interaction for one brand, the sales and advertising for the brand's competition were described through several additional equations. The managerial implications of this study were explored in Parsons and Bass [12]. Since the statistical model was dynamic, the resultant optimization plan was multiperiod in character. The implied optimal strategy was compared with the actual strategy used by the firm.

Farley [11] developed a five-equation model of the Jamaican distribution structure. The five jointly dependent variables in his system are index of distribution, sales, proportion of retailers contacted directly by importers and manufacturers, average number of wholesalers calling on retailers for product-class group, and index of depth of brand stocking. The structural parameters of the model were estimated by four alternative methods—ordinary least squares, two-stage least squares, limited-information maximum-likelihood, and full-information maximum-likelihood.

SUMMARY

The simultaneous interaction or multidimensional causation among certain variables in the marketing mix occurs frequently. To correctly model these situations when they arise requires a system of equations. This chapter has concerned itself *first*, with the problems imposed by the additional complexities of simultaneous-equations models; *second*, with the choice between alternative estimation methods; *third*, with the tests of hypotheses associated with simultaneous-equation regression; and *fourth*, with the application of this methodology to marketing problems.

The major problem in simultaneous-equation models was shown to be that of identifying the individual relationships. This problem must be dealt with prior to estimation. Alternative methods of estimation were summarized by drawing on the work of leading econometricians and mathematical economists. Two-stage least squares was judged to be the method with most general application to marketing. The concept of the predictive test was then introduced.

Finally, current applications of this approach to marketing were reviewed. The ability of simultaneous-equation regression to model complex marketing problems has been demonstrated, suggesting more applications in the future.

REFERENCES

Books

1. Basmann, R. L., *Lectures in Quantitative Economics,* unpublished manuscript, Lafayette, Ind.: Purdue University, 1965.
2. Baumol, W. J., *Economic Theory and Operations Analysis,* Englewood Cliffs, N.J.: Prentice-Hall, 1965.
3. Christ, C. F., *Econometric Models and Methods,* New York: Wiley, 1966.
4. Fisher, F. M., *The Identification Problem in Econometrics,* New York: McGraw-Hill, 1966.
5. Goldberger, A. S., *Econometric Theory,* New York: Wiley, 1964.
6. Johnston, J., *Econometric Methods,* New York: McGraw-Hill, 1963.
7. Malinvaud, E., *Statistical Methods of Econometrics,* Chicago: Rand McNally, 1966.
8. Theil, H., *Lectures on Econometrics,* unpublished manuscript, Chicago: The University of Chicago, Center for Mathematical Studies in Business and Economics, 1966.

Marketing Articles

9. Bass, F. M., "A Simultaneous-Equation Regression Study of Advertising and Sales—Analysis of Cigarette Data," *Journal of Marketing Research,* vol. 6, August 1969.
10. Bass, F. M., and L. J. Parsons, "Simultaneous-Equation Regression Analysis of Sales and Advertising," *Applied Economics,* vol. 1, May 1969.
11. Farley, J. U., "Estimating Structural Parameters of Marketing Systems: Theory and Application," in Reed Moyer (ed.), *Changing Marketing Systems, Winter Conference Proceedings,* Chicago: American Marketing Association, 1967.
12. Parsons, L. J., and F. M. Bass, "Optimal Advertising Expenditure Implications of a Simultaneous-Equation Regression Analysis," *Institute for Research in the Behavioral, Economic, and Management Sciences,* Institute paper no. 234, Lafayette, Ind.: Purdue University, Krannert Graduate School of Industrial Administration, 1969.

Statistical Analysis of Relationships

Chapter 8

Discriminant Analysis

DONALD G. MORRISON *Graduate School of Business, Columbia University, New York, New York*

INTRODUCTION

The objective of discriminant analysis is very simple. On the basis of a set of independent variables, we wish to classify individuals or objects into one of two or more mutually exclusive and exhaustive categories or classes. For example, basing our decision on an individual's income, occupation, home ownership, and so forth, we wish to classify him as either a good or bad credit risk. In another case, we may wish to classify someone as an early trier, a late trier, or a non-trier of a newly marketed consumer product. We might also want to classify automobile owners as loyal to nationally advertised or cut-rate gasoline.

When the analysis is finished, three questions need to be answered. How well did we classify the individuals? Which variables were most effective in discriminating among the different classes? How can the answers to the first two questions be used to help set and implement marketing plans? This last point is important because one can often do a study and get excellent classification, identify the variables that do the discriminating, and yet have very little idea as to how these results can be used.

The technical aspects of discriminant analysis can be explained very easily. Essentially, there is a simple "scoring system" that assigns a "score" to each individual or object. This score is a weighted average of the individual's numerical values of his independent variables (for example, age, income, education). On the basis of this score, the individual is assigned to the "most likely" category. Suppose an individual is 30 years old, has an annual income of $10,000, and has 16 years of formal education. Let b_1, b_2, and b_3 be the weights attached to the independent variables of age, income, and education. Then this individual's score would be

$$z = b_1(30) + b_2(10{,}000) + b_3(16)$$

This value of z could be (say) a credit score or rating. This numerical value of z can then be transformed into the probability that the individual is a good credit risk.

If certain assumptions (to be discussed later) are true, this simple linear scoring rule can be shown to be the best scoring rule. The numerical values and signs of the b's indicate the importance of the independent variables in their ability to discriminate among the different classes of individuals.

The mathematical details will be very similar to those of multiple regression. The discriminant coefficients, the b's, will be analogous to the regression coefficients. However, instead of explaining variance of the dependent variable as is done in regression, the object of the discriminant function will be to correctly classify as many individuals as possible. In summary, the discriminant function is a simple linear scoring rule (which has certain optimal properties) that generates scores for individuals; these scores are then used to assign the individuals to one of two or more mutually exclusive and exhaustive categories.

DESCRIPTION OF LINEAR DISCRIMINANT ANALYSIS

For expository purposes, this discussion will be limited to classification into two groups; later, some comments will be made on n-group discriminant analysis:
For notation, let

X_{ji} = the ith individual's value of the jth independent variable
b_j = the discriminant coefficient for the jth variable
Z_i = the ith individual's discriminant score
$z_{\text{crit.}}$ = the critical value for the discriminant score

A Linear Classification Procedure

Suppose we let each individual's discriminant score Z_i be a linear function of the independent variables. That is:

$$Z_i = b_0 + b_1 X_{1i} + b_2 X_{2i} + \ldots + b_n X_{ni}$$

The classification procedure is:
If $Z_i > z_{\text{crit.}}$, classify individual i as belonging to group I.
If $Z_i < z_{\text{crit.}}$, classify individual i as belonging to group II.
The classification boundary will then be the locus of points where

$$b_0 + b_1 X_{1i} + \ldots + b_n X_{ni} = z_{\text{crit.}}$$

When n (the number of independent variables) $= 2$, we have a straight-line classification boundary. Every individual on one side of the line is classified as group I; on the other side, everyone is classified as belonging to group II. When $n = 3$, the classification boundary is a two-dimensional plane in 3 space, and in general the classification boundary is an $n - 1$ dimensional hyperplane in n space.

Advantages of a Linear Classification Procedure

The particularly simple form of the linear discriminant function allows a very clear interpretation of the effect of each of the independent variables. Suppose the independent variable X_1 is income, and the classification procedure is that, if $Z_i > z_{crit.}$, the individual is classified as a good risk. This means the higher the value of Z_i, the more likely the individual is a good credit risk. If the sign of b_1 is positive, then higher income implies a better credit risk, and the larger the magnitude of b_1 the more important variable X_1 is in discriminating between group I and group II individuals. Clearly, if $b_1 = 0$, X_1 has no effect.

If we had a more complex discriminant function, we could not isolate the effect of each variable so easily. Suppose we had a nonlinear discriminant function, say,

$$Z' = a + bX_i + cX_i^2 + dY_i + eY_i^2 + fX_iY_i$$

The effect on Z_i' of increasing X_i by one unit depends on the value of X, b, c, f, and even the value of Y.

Therefore, for interpretation reasons a linear discriminant function is highly desirable. This leads to the following question.

When Is a Linear Classification Procedure Valid?

The technical details of this section may be found in a very mathematical form in Anderson [1] and in a more condensed form in Morrison [14]. However, the essence of these details can be verbalized very easily. A linear classification procedure is optimal if the spreads (variance) of the independent variables (the X's) in group I are the same as the spreads in group II. In more technical terms, the covariance matrices of group I and group II are equal. We also assume that the variables are normally distributed.

Morrison [14] also gives a brief example of the type of nonlinear classification region that can arise when this assumption of equal covariance is not true. In general, most empirical situations have groups with reasonably similar covariance matrices. This fact, coupled with the ease of interpretation of a linear function, makes linear discriminant analysis an appropriate technique in most cases.

This completes our brief overview of the technique of two-group discriminant analysis. The multiple-group discriminant analysis is very similar.

N-Group Discriminant Analysis

In n-group discriminant analysis a discriminant function is formed for each pair of groups. If there were five groups, we would have $5!/3!2! = 10$ pairs of groups, and hence 10 discriminant functions. The b values for each function tell which variables are important for discriminating between that particular pair of groups. The z score for each discriminant function tells in which of those two groups the individual is more likely to belong. Here, use is made of the transitivity of the relation "more likely than," for example, if group II is more likely than group I and group III is more likely than group II, then group III is also more likely than group I; thus, all necessary comparisons are made and the individual is assigned to the most likely of all the groups.

Hence, multiple-group discriminant analysis is just like two-group discriminant analysis; the multiple groups are merely examined two at a time. Massy [12] gives an empirical study which uses a five-group discriminant analysis.

STATISTICAL SIGNIFICANCE

Distance between Groups

One of the standard quantities that appear on the output of a discriminant analysis is a distance measure, the Mahalanobis D^2 statistic, between the two groups.[1] After a transformation, this D^2 statistic becomes an F statistic. This F statistic is then used to see if the two groups are *statistically* different from each other. In fact, this test is merely the multidimensional analog of the familiar t test for the statistical significance of the difference between one sample mean $\bar{x}_1$ and another sample mean $\bar{x}_2$. The D^2 (or transformed F) statistic tests the difference between the n-dimensional mean vector $\bar{x}_1$ for group I and the corresponding n-dimensional mean vector $\bar{x}_2$ for group II. However, the statistical significance per se of the D^2 statistic means very little.

Suppose the two groups are significantly different at the 0.1 level. With large enough sample sizes, $\bar{x}_1$ could be virtually identical to $\bar{x}_2$, and we would still have statistical significance. In short, the D^2 statistic (or any of its transformed statistics) suffers the same drawbacks of all classical tests of hypotheses. The statistical significance of the D^2 statistic is a very poor indicator of the efficacy with which the independent variables can discriminate between group I individuals and those that belong to group II.

PERCENT CORRECTLY CLASSIFIED

A Bias in Many Canned Programs

One common source of misinterpretation of discriminant analysis results comes from the way in which most of the "canned" computer programs construct the classification table (sometimes called the confusion matrix). The computer will print out the following table.

		Classified		
		Group I	Group II	
Actual	Group I	n_{11}	n_{12}	$n_{1.}$
	Group II	n_{21}	n_{22}	$n_{2.}$
		$n_{.1}$	$n_{.2}$	n

The entry n_{ij} is the number of individuals that are actually in group i and were classified as belonging to group j. Then $(n_{11} + n_{22})/n$ is the proportion

---

[1] The Mahalanobis D^2 statistic can be thought of as a generalized distance between two groups, where each group is characterized by the same set of n variables, and where it is assumed that the variance-covariance structure is identical for both groups. Each group can be further characterized by its n-dimensional mean vector. In the special case where all n variables are mutually independent, D^2 is merely the square of the usual Euclidean distance between the two mean vectors, where the orthogonal coordinate system is normalized by the standard deviation of each variable. If the variables are collinear, the coordinate axes are also rotated so that the cosine of the angle between the two axes is equal to the correlation between the two variables associated with these axes.

Let μ_1 be the mean vector for group I and μ_2 be the mean vector for group II. If V is the common covariance matrix then the Mahalanobis D^2 statistic is

$$(\mu_1 - \mu_2)V^{-1}(\mu_1 - \mu_2)'$$

of individuals that were correctly classified. However, the typical canned program uses all n observations to calculate the discriminant function. Bias occurs because the program attempts to maximize the percent correctly classified *in the sample*. Hence, we are fitting the discriminant function to that *particular* set of data. When the sample sizes are small and the number of independent variables is sizable, this upward bias can be very large.

In multiple regression, there is a correction factor (involving sample size and number of independent variables) that can be used to "adjust" the R^2 statistic, that is, to eliminate the upward bias in R^2 caused by getting the best fit for the particular set of data used. In multiple-discriminant analysis there is no simple analytical technique for adjusting the percent correctly classified. Frank, Massy, and Morrison [7] give a detailed discussion of the upward biases that can occur in classification tables constructed using all the data. One method of avoiding this bias is to fit a discriminant function to part of the data, and then use this function to classify the remaining individuals. It is the classification table for these latter individuals that will now be discussed.

The Percent Correctly Classified by Chance

Suppose a researcher is interested in determining the socioeconomic variables that distinguish adopters from nonadopters of a new product. His "fresh" second half of the split sample contains 30 adopters and 70 nonadopters. He applies his discriminant function obtained in the first half of the split sample to this second half, and he gets 70 percent correct classifications. He then says: "By chance I could get 70 percent correct classifications; therefore my discriminant function is not effective in separating adopters from nonadopters." Notice that the chance model has not been explicitly stated. The remainder of this section will develop a more appropriate chance model; this model will show that this hypothetical researcher is being overly pessimistic in a statistical sense.

Assume that there exists a population which consists of only two types of individuals: type I and type II. Let p be the proportion of the population that is type I, and $1 - p$ the proportion that is type II. If the variables (age, income, and so on) actually have no effect on discriminating I's from II's, we can expect to get a proportion p correctly classified *if we classify everyone as type I*. Hence, *if $p < \frac{1}{2}$*, we would classify everyone as type II.

Our hypothetical researcher wishes to identify adopters. However, since there are only 30 percent adopters and 70 percent nonadopters in his sample, he is "bucking the pure chance odds" if he classifies an individual as an adopter. This is true because any individual has an a priori probability of .7 of being a nonadopter and only a .3 probability of being an adopter. But what if the researcher says: "I want to try to identify the adopters, I believe my discriminant function has some merit, and therefore I am going to classify 30 percent of the individuals as adopters." Given this outlook, what is the appropriate chance model?

Let p be the true proportion of type I individuals,

α be the proportion classified as type I.

Then the probability of an individual's being classified correctly is

$P(\text{correct}) = P(\text{correct} \mid \text{classified type I}) P(\text{classified type I})$
$\qquad\qquad + P(\text{correct} \mid \text{classified type II}) P(\text{classified type II})$

$$P(\text{correct}) = p\alpha + (1 - p)(1 - \alpha) \qquad (1)$$

For our researcher, $p = \alpha = 0.3$. Hence the chance proportion correctly classified is $(0.3)^2 + (0.7)^2 = 0.58$. *Note that when $p = 0.5$ (that is, two groups of equal size), P(correct) = .50 regardless of the value of α.*[2]

$$C_{\text{pro}} = \alpha^2 + (1 - \alpha)^2 \tag{2}$$

where $\alpha =$ the proportion of individuals in group I
       $1 - \alpha =$ the proportion of individuals in group II

The researcher who thought, "By chance I could get 70 percent correct," was using the maximum chance criterion

$$C_{\text{max}} = \max(\alpha, 1 - \alpha) \tag{3}$$

where $\max(\alpha, 1 - \alpha)$ is read, "the larger of α or $1 - \alpha$." For example, $\max(0.3, 0.7) = .7$.

Situations Where C_{pro} and C_{max} Should Be Used

If the sole objective of the discriminant analysis is to maximize the percent correctly classified, then clearly C_{max} is the appropriate chance criterion. If the discriminant function cannot do better than C_{max}, it is wiser to disregard it, and merely to classify everyone as belonging to the larger of the two groups.

Obviously, this is rarely the case in a marketing research study. Usually, a discriminant analysis is run because someone wishes to try to correctly identify members of *both* groups. As we have seen, the discriminant function bucks the odds by classifying an individual in the smaller group. The chance criterion should take this into account. Therefore, in most situations, C_{pro} should be used.

Recall that all our discussion on chance models applies to the individuals who were not used in calculating the discriminant function. If the individuals were used in this calculation, then some upward adjustment must be made on C_{pro} or C_{max}. Frank, Massy, and Morrison [7] give methods for estimating these biases.

DISCRIMINANT ANALYSIS AND MULTIPLE REGRESSION

An Analogy with Regression

Perhaps an analogy with regression will clarify these concepts. We have all read articles in which the author says he has found "significant" relations; however, he has "explained" only 4 percent of the variance. That is, $R^2 = 0.04$, but since the sample size is large, this sample R^2 is statistically significantly different from zero. In discriminant analysis, the percent correctly classified is somewhat analogous to the magnitude of the R^2. One tells how well we classified the individual, the other how much variance we explained. The statistical significance of the R^2 is analogous to the statistical significance of the D^2 statistic. Clearly, with a large enough sample size, in discriminant analysis we could classify 52 percent correctly (when chance was 50 percent) and yet have a statistically significant difference (distance) between the two groups.

---

[2] A generalization of Equation (1) for N groups with n_i individuals in group i, $i = 1, \ldots, N$, is found in Mosteller and Bush [15]. This is an excellent article, worthwhile reading for any one who works with discriminant analysis or any other classification techniques. These more general results will be necessary for multiple-discriminant analysis when the number of groups (or types) is greater than two.

Equivalence of Regression Coefficients

Another technically interesting similarity with regression exists. A multiple-regression program can be used to obtain discriminant coefficients. Let the individuals in group I have a value of 1 as their dependent variable; similarly, let group II individuals have 0 as their dependent variable. Then a least-squares fit of a linear regression function to the resulting data will yield a vector of regression coefficients that are proportional to the discriminant coefficients. See Ladd [11] for a proof of this fact.

INTERPRETING A DISCRIMINANT ANALYSIS

When the results of a discriminant analysis are obtained, there are some basic questions to ask:
1. Which independent variables are good discriminators?
2. How well do these independent variables do in discriminating among the two groups?
3. What decision rule should be used for classifying individuals?

This chapter has already touched on the first two questions; the third obviously involves economic considerations. More complete answers to these questions require a synopsis of the theoretical derivation of the discriminant function. The mathematical details of this derivation may be found in Anderson [1, chap. 6].

Deriving the Discriminant Function

Suppose we look at individual i and observe his values of the n independent variables. That is, we see

$$\mathbf{x}_i = (x_{1i}, x_{2i}, \ldots, x_{ni})$$

Let $P(I) =$ the unconditional (prior) probability that an individual belongs to group I.

$P(I \mid \mathbf{x}_i) =$ the conditional (posterior) probability that an individual belongs to group I given we have observed $\mathbf{x}_i$.

$l(\mathbf{x}_i \mid I) =$ the likelihood that an individual has the vector of values $\mathbf{x}_i$, given that he belongs to group I.

Analogous definitions hold for group II. From Bayes' theorem we have

$$\frac{P(I \mid \mathbf{x}_i)}{P(II \mid \mathbf{x}_i)} = \frac{l(\mathbf{x}_i \mid I)}{l(\mathbf{x}_i \mid II)} \cdot \frac{P(I)}{P(II)}$$

Or, in words,

Posterior odds = likelihood ratio × prior odds   (4)

The classification procedure will then be: If the odds are strongly enough in favor of group I, classify the individual as belonging to group I. (If the odds were 3 to 1 in favor of group I, this would mean a probability of 0.75 that the individual belongs to group I.)

We may also use the logarithm of the odds as a criterion. For example, odds greater than 1 (a probability greater than 0.5) is equivalent to the logarithm of the odds being greater than 0. We may write Equation (4) as

$$\log (\text{posterior odds}) = \log(\text{L.R.}) + \log(\text{prior odds}) \tag{5}$$

If the assumptions of normality and equal covariance matrices discussed earlier are true, the logarithm of the likelihood ratio is of the form[3]

$$\log(\text{L.R.}) = b_0 + b_1 X_1 + \cdots + b_n X_n \qquad (6)$$

This is the discriminant function. When the two groups are of equal size, the prior probabilities are equal for each group. The prior odds are then 1, and the posterior odds are merely the likelihood ratio. When the prior odds are different from 1, then

$$\log(\text{post. odds}) = b_0 + b_1 X_{1i} + \cdots + b_n X_{ni} + \log(\text{prior odds})$$

However, since the prior odds do not contain any of the independent variables, this quantity is a constant and the discriminant function is

$$b_0' + b_1 X_{1i} + \cdots + b_n X_{ni}$$

where

$$b_0' = b_0 + \log(\text{prior odds}) \qquad (7)$$

An understanding of the above nonmathematical material is sufficient to be able to answer our three basic questions.

Bayesian Discriminant Analysis

The reader familiar with Bayesian statistics will note the Bayesian "flavor" of the final discriminant function. Prior knowledge (odds) on group membership has been updated by sample information (the likelihood function contains all the sample information) to give posterior knowledge on group membership. Some controversy may arise if the prior probabilities of group membership are "subjective," but no one would argue with the methodology.

A certain type of Bayesian discriminant analysis would be very similar to Bayesian multiple regression [see Sec. II, Part E, Chap. 6]. Prior distributions would be put on the discriminant coefficients and these distributions would be updated by the sample data. Since the discriminant coefficients also can be obtained by using a dummy dependent-variable multiple regression, the techniques and interpretations used in Bayesian regression can be carried over to discriminant analysis. However, in practice the prior knowledge on the coefficients will be so diffuse that the sample information will swamp the prior infor-

---

[3] This result can be derived very easily if we use matrix notation. The multivariate normal likelihood function is of the form

$$l(\mathbf{x}\,|\,) = \text{constant } x \exp[-1/2(\mathbf{x} - \mu_{\text{I}}) V^{-1} (\mathbf{x} - \mu_{\text{I}})]$$

where μ_{I} is the mean vector for group I and V is the common variance-covariance matrix. A similar expression holds for $l(\mathbf{x}\,|\,\text{II})$. Then the likelihood ratio is

$$\frac{l(\mathbf{x}\,|\,\text{I})}{l(\mathbf{x}\,|\,\text{II})} = \exp[-1/2(\mathbf{x} - \mu_{\text{I}}) V^{-1} (\mathbf{x} - \mu_{\text{I}}) - 1/2(\mathbf{x} - \mu_{\text{II}}) V^{-1} (\mathbf{x} - \mu_{\text{II}})']$$

Collecting terms and taking the natural logarithm gives

$$\log(\text{L.R.}) = \mathbf{x}' V^{-1}(\mu_{\text{I}} - \mu_{\text{II}}) - 1/2(\mu_{\text{I}} + \mu_{\text{II}})' V^{-1}(\mu_{\text{I}} - \mu_{\text{II}})$$

The second term is merely a constant and the $n \times 1$ vector $V^{-1}(\mu_{\text{I}} - \mu_{\text{II}})$ is the vector of discriminant coefficients.

mation and the classical solutions arrived at with the likelihood ratio will be numerically very close to any Bayesian solution.

A full-blown Bayesian analysis would deal directly with the likelihood functions for each group. The normality assumption would still be needed (or more precisely, some specified form for the distribution of the independent variables), but the assumption of equality of the covariance matrices could be dropped. An expression for the posterior probabilities of group members could then be developed.[4]

Determining the Effect of the Independent Variables

The sign and magnitude of the b_j's determine the effect of the independent variables X_j. The magnitude of the coefficient b_j in the discriminant function,

$$Z_i = b_0 + b_1 X_{1i} + \cdots + b_j X_{ji} + \cdots + b_n X_{ni}$$

is clearly going to be influenced by the scale that we use for X_j. Suppose X_j is family income. A change of X_j from \$6,000 to \$7,000 will have the same effect on Z_i whether X_j is scaled in dollars or thousands of dollars. Therefore, if X_j is measured in thousands of dollars, b_j will be 1,000 times larger than if the units of X_j are in dollars. However, if we normalize (divide) each variable by its standard deviation, the original units become irrelevant. As the units are scaled by a factor k, the standard deviation is also scaled by the same factor k. That is, if the standard deviation of X_j is σ_j, the standard deviation of kX_j is $k\sigma_j$. Then, since $X_j/\sigma_j = kX_j/k\sigma_j$, we do not have to worry about the scale of X_j.

Let b_j^* be the discriminant coefficient that results when the standardized variables $X_j^* = X_j/\sigma_j$ are used. Suppose $|b_j^*| > |b_k^*|$. We can then say that variable X_j is a better discriminator between group I and group II than variable X_k. A unit change in X_j^* has more effect on Z_i than a unit change in X_k^*, and the more a variable affects Z_i, the better it discriminates. We are justified in normalizing our variables by their standard deviations, since we are discriminating on the basis of the *statistical* distance between the two groups, and statistical distances are measured in units of standard deviations. (See Morrison [13] for a detailed discussion of *distance* concepts.)

If the discriminant analysis is run with nonstandardized variables, it is extremely easy to obtain b_j^* from b_j. We have seen that

$$b_j X_j = b_j^* X_j^* = b_j^* \frac{X_j}{\sigma_j}$$

Hence,

$$b_j^* = b_j \sigma_j \tag{8}$$

Recall that the sign of b_j^* (which is, of course, the same as the sign of b_j) determines the direction of the effect of X_j. If b_j^* is positive, as X_j increases Z_i increases, and the larger Z_i, the more likely it is that individual i belongs to group I.

We want to obtain the best possible estimates b_j. As in all statistical estimation, the larger the sample size (assuming the sample is representative), the better the estimates. Suppose we have 900 individuals in group I and only 100

---

[4] The whole subject is fairly complex—both mathematically and from an interpretation viewpoint. Massy, in an unpublished working paper for the Stanford Graduate School of Business, presented a formal discussion of Bayesian discriminant analysis.

individuals in group II.   If we use only 100 of the group I individuals in calculating the discriminant function, then the prior probability of an individual belonging to group I is 0.5.   But if we use all 900 members of group I, this prior probability becomes 0.9.   Does this affect any of the b_j's of interest?   No. Recall from Equation (7) that the prior probabilities only affect b_0 and have no effect on $b_1, b_2, \ldots, b_n$.   Therefore, in determining which variables are the best discriminators, we should use all the data.   (By this we mean all the individuals, and not necessarily all available independent variables.   As in any multivariate technique, if X_j and X_k are highly correlated, they are measuring almost the same thing.   The coefficients b_j and b_k will then be unstable and hard to interpret.)

The fact that we should use all the data in calculating the b_j's is not a surprising result; in fact, it is intuitively quite obvious.   However, in assessing how well the discriminant function discriminates, we may not want to use all the data.

Using Variables That Have No Natural Scales

Dummy variables as independent variables in a discriminant analysis present no special problems.   Of course, the normality assumption is not met, but then the optimality of a linear discriminant function is not very sensitive to the normality of the data (the linearity is much more sensitive to the equality of the covariance matrices).   As we have seen from the section on standardized discriminant coefficients, these coefficients are not affected by a linear transformation of the raw data.   Hence, our dummy variables can be scaled 0, 1, or 1, 2, or 0, 10, or anything else.   It is often more convenient to use 0, 1 coding.

The interpretation of the discriminant coefficient is then exactly the same as for any other variable.   Suppose we code the sex variable as $0 =$ male, $1 =$ female.   If the discriminant score is, say, a credit rating and persons with higher scores are better credit risks, then a positive discriminant coefficient implies women are better credit risks, and vice versa.

A problem does arise when a variable has more than two categories and has no natural rank-order scaling.   Let us assume that religion is one of the variables being used.   We could code Protestant $= 1$, Catholic $= 2$, and Jewish $= 3$, but the discriminant coefficient would be hard to interpret unless we could say that (with respect to discriminating among the groups) a Catholic was "half-way" between a Protestant and a Jew.   In this case, it would be better to form three separate dummy variables: Protestant, non-Protestant; Catholic, non-Catholic; and Jewish, non-Jewish.   If these three categories are exhaustive, only two should be used; otherwise, the sample covariance matrix will be singular and hence it will be impossible to form the discriminant function.   In general, if we have n dichotomous variables that are exhaustive, only $n - 1$ of them can be used.

A single variable like occupation is almost impossible to use.   We may be able to identify 15 or so distinct types of work, but constructing a relevant scale may not be possible.   We must not only rank order the data, we must also imply that the width of the intervals has meaning.   In short, we must assume interval-scale data.   That is, any variable X can be transformed to a new variable $Y = a + bX$, where a and b are arbitrary constants, without affecting the analysis.   The standardized coefficients b_j^* will remain unaffected by these linear transformations of the data.   Some of the other multivariate methods, for example, some cluster-analysis techniques, do not require such strict assumptions about the scale of the independent variables.

The problem with variables like race, religion, occupation, attitude, and so on, has nothing to do with the technical aspects of discriminant analysis. If scales appropriate to these variables and relevant to the differences among groups can be constructed, then these variables will work perfectly well in discriminant analysis. Often, clever uses of multiple dummy variables can alleviate some scaling problems.

How Well Do the Variables Discriminate?

In order to answer this question, it is necessary to use the classification table and an appropriate chance criterion. Throughout this discussion, we will assume that we either have "fresh" data or have adjusted for the "fitting the discriminant function to data" bias. The real question of how to use the data arises when the two groups are of greatly unequal size.

We saw from Equation (5) that when the two groups are of equal size, the likelihood ratio (which contains all the sample information) completely determines the discriminant function. However, when the prior probabilities are unequal, this influences the classification procedure. If the groups are greatly unequal, we see that the term log (prior odds) can completely dominate the term log (L.R.). In this case, we cannot determine how well the independent variables discriminate. We would obtain the clearest picture if the prior odds were equal and hence did not affect the classification.

Assume that we were attempting to discriminate adopters from nonadopters of a new product. If we had a sample of 1,000 people, a result such as 50 adopters and 950 nonadopters would not be unusual. If we attempted to classify all 1,000 of these individuals, we might end up with a classification table something like this:

		Classified		
		I	II	
Actual	I	7	43	50
	II	13	937	950
		20	980	1,000

Here we classified 944 (or 94.4 percent) of the individuals correctly. The proportional chance criterion is (see Equation (2))

$$C_{pro} = (0.05)^2 + (0.95)^2 = 0.907$$

However, given that we classified 98 percent as belonging to group II, we should have gotten

$$(0.98)(0.95) + (0.02)(0.05) = 0.932,$$

or 93.2 percent correctly classified.

The maximum chance criterion is, of course,

$$C_{max} = 0.95$$

Therefore, our 94.4 percent correct classification is not too impressive. However, of the 20 individuals that we classified as belonging to group I, we got 7 correct. This is 35 percent against a chance percentage of 5. This latter result is fairly impressive.

Now let us change the hypothetical classification slightly.

Classified

		I	II	
	I	1	49	50
Actual				
	II	9	941	950
		10	990	1,000

In this case, we still classified slightly over 94 percent correctly; however, we only got 1 out of 10 correct for group I classifications.

In summary, when one group is much larger than the other, almost all the individuals are classified into the larger group. This means a large number will be automatically correctly classified. When we allow the posterior odds to classify the individuals—see Equation (4)—we usually get even fewer classified as belonging to the smaller group than actually belong to this group. We are often more interested in this smaller group, and classification tables like the two just given are not the best way to assess the discrimination power of the independent variables.

One possibility is to rank all 1,000 individuals by their Z values and classify the 50 highest as belonging to group I. This assures that a sufficient number will be classified as group I. We now can see how well we classified these individuals.

Another method would be to randomly divide the 950 group II individuals into 19 groups, each with 50 members. We could construct 19 classification tables; the same 50 group I members and the 19 different group II's. We could then see how well we did on the average.

This procedure has the advantage that the chance model is unambiguously 50 percent. Also, working with 50 percent chance models makes interpretation easier. It is clear that correctly classifying 75 percent when chance is 50 percent is a good classification. (Of the 50 percent by which we could improve "chance," we got half, or 25 percent.) When the sample sizes were 50 and 950, the proportional chance criterion was 90 percent.

Suppose we again obtain half of that remaining after "chance" and classify 95 percent correctly. This could happen by doing well with group I individuals, or by merely classifying everyone as group II. The interpretation is just not so clear.

In summary, it can be said that:

1. When the groups are of greatly unequal size, it may be difficult to interpret the classification table.

2. Regardless of the total sample size, the "effective" sample size (for determining how well we can discriminate) is governed by the *smaller* of the two groups.

This latter point is particularly relevant in the planning stages of a research project.   A large total sample size is of little comfort without a sufficient number of individuals in each group.

The Classification Decision

The previous two sections dealt with the questions of which variables are good discriminators and how well they discriminate.   However, if the discriminant function is to be used to classify individuals, then clearly the costs of misclassification must enter into the decision.

As before, let

$P(\mathrm{I}|\mathbf{x}_i)$ = the posterior probability that an individual belongs to group I, given that we observed his vector of independent variables $\mathbf{x}_i$.

$P(\mathrm{II}|\mathbf{x}_i)$ = analogous definition for group II.

C_{21} = the opportunity cost of classifying an individual as belonging to group II when he actually belongs to group I.

C_{12} = the opportunity cost of classifying an individual as belonging to group I when he actually belongs to group II.

Any rational cost structure would have $C_{11} = C_{22} = 0$.

If we classify individual i as belonging to group I, then the expected opportunity cost is

$$K_i(\mathrm{I}) = P(\mathrm{II}|\mathbf{x}_i)C_{21}$$

Similarly, if we classify him as belonging to group II, the expected opportunity cost is

$$K_i(\mathrm{II}) = P(\mathrm{I}|\mathbf{x}_i)C_{12}$$

The classification procedure becomes: If $K_i(\mathrm{I}) < K_i(\mathrm{II})$, we classify individual i as belonging to group I, and vice versa.

By the same reasoning we used in examining the effect of prior probabilities on the discriminant function, it is clear that C_{12} and C_{21} only affect the b_0 term of the discriminant function (or equivalently, it merely changes the z_{crit} value).

Let the logarithm of the likelihood ratio—see Equation (6)—be

$$\log(\mathrm{L.R.}) = b_0 + b_1 X_{1i} + b_2 X_{2i} + \cdots + b_n X_{ni}$$

The classification rule is:
Classify individual i as group I if

$$b_0 + b_1 X_{1i} + b_2 X_{2i} + \cdots + b_n X_{ni} > \log k \qquad (9a)$$

Classify individual i as group II if

$$b_0 + b_1 X_{1i} + b_2 X_{2i} + \cdots + b_n X_{ni} < \log k \qquad (9b)$$

where

$$k = \frac{P(\mathrm{II})C_{21}}{P(\mathrm{I})C_{21}} \qquad (10)$$

In a real application, the difficult problem will be obtaining good estimates for the opportunity costs C_{12} and C_{21}.

IMPLEMENTATION OF THE RESULTS

One of the first successful business applications of discriminant analysis was in credit selection (see [3]).   Good credit risks were separated from poor credit risks on the basis of demographic and socioeconomic variables. On the credit application, the individual fills in information on these very same demographic and socioeconomic variables. Hence, the discriminant function can be applied directly to his application. The classification procedure, Equations (9a) and (9b), is then used to determine whether or not the applicant is to be given credit.

A major problem with this type of project is in obtaining representative past data. Chances are that the company only has data on individuals that it accepted as good credit risks. Of these already-screened individuals, some were actually good credit risks, others were not. However, this sample is not representative of the applicants that are now applying for credit. In other words, the discriminant function for past data may not be the best for discriminating among the current individuals.

In general, we want the sample from which we calculate the discriminant function to be as representative as possible of the future individuals whom we will be attempting to classify. In the credit-selection case, this means that all applicants should be given credit, and then the discriminant function will be calculated from the results of this sample (which, it is hoped, is representative of future credit applicants). Of course, there is always the problem that the past discriminant function is out of date. Time or the competitive situation has changed the environment enough to make the old results inapplicable. But at least in the area of credit selection, the variables used for discrimination were operational; the independent variables were used in the decision making. This is not always the case.

Suppose that a researcher is able to discriminate adopters from nonadopters of a new product on the basis of demographic characteristics. If the product is sold through supermarkets and advertised in the mass media, it may be very difficult to direct in-store displays and advertisements specifically at the likely adopters. However, if cents-off coupons are sent through the mail, it may be relatively easy to direct this mailing to the more likely adopters. If a discriminant analysis is to be considered as a decision-making aid (as opposed to a strictly research-oriented study), management should have a clear idea how the results will be implemented before the project is undertaken.

When the independent variables are obtained by personal interviews, there is a whole new set of problems. Ferber discusses these problems in some detail [6, pp. 251–259]. It may be particularly hard to get comparability across interviewers.

High degrees of collinearity (high correlations) among independent variables should be avoided. The resulting discriminant coefficients will be very unstable and it will be more difficult to interpret the contribution of each independent variable. Hence, if two independent variables are highly correlated (say $r = .95$) only one of these variables should be included in the analysis. Otherwise, the variances of the b's (the discriminant coefficients) will be unnecessarily large. The chapter on multiple regression goes into more detail on the problems of collinearity. All that is said there clearly applies to discriminant analysis.

DISCRIMINANT ANALYSIS IN MARKETING

Linear discriminant analysis has been used quite extensively in marketing. Some of the topics investigated include the use of demographic and psychological factors in identifying Ford and Chevrolet buyers [4]; variables that determine early adopters of new fashions [10]; the question of whether new-product buyers, as a group, can be identified [16]; the difference between people who save money in commercial banks and those saving at savings and loan associations [2]; consumer behavior toward new products or brands [8] and [17]; brand loyalty and the amount of searching that is done [5]; the development of a checklist of properties that separates successful new products from those that fail [6]; and the relation between demographic variables and favorite radio station [12]. This list, although far from exhaustive, is sufficient to illustrate the types of problems that are amenable to discriminant analysis.

It is worth noting that some of the cited studies contain some methodological errors, particularly in the areas of validation and chance criterion. In reading any report and evaluating the results, the reader should look for invalid procedures which could cause spuriously impressive results. This caveat holds for all empirical studies, not just those using discriminant analysis. However, it is fair to say that discriminant analysis studies have more than their fair share of methodological errors. The way that most of the "canned" computer programs for discriminant analysis have been written (in particular, they usually have no validation provisions) has contributed to these errors.

DISCUSSION

Perhaps a good way to summarize this discussion is to present a checklist of things to consider.

1.   A linear discriminant function is only appropriate when the covariance matrices of the groups are equal (or nearly equal).

2.   The D^2 statistic (which may be transformed to an F statistic) only tests the statistical significance of the difference between the groups. Recall the effect of the sample size on statistical significance.

3.   Beware of the upward bias that results from classifying the same individuals who were used to calculate the discriminant function.

4.   Be aware of the different chance models that can result when the groups are of different sizes. Also, remember that great inequality in the sizes of groups makes the interpretation of the classification table difficult.

5.   The "effective" sample size is really governed by the smaller group.

6.   Be sure that the discriminant coefficients have been normalized by the standard deviations of the independent variables.

7.   In forming the classification decision, be sure that prior probabilities and opportunity costs of misclassification have been taken into account.

8.   The independent variables used for discrimination must be operational.

All the above points apply to multiple-discriminant analysis; that is, when individuals are classified into more than two groups. The only major difference is that it is not as easy to assess the effect of the independent variables in discriminating among the groups. For example, variable j might be the best discriminator for group I and group II, but variable k does the best job between group II and group III. But strictly speaking, all eight points also apply to discriminant analysis for more than two groups.

REFERENCES

1. Anderson, T. W., *Introduction to Multivariate Statistical Analysis,* New York: Wiley, 1958.
2. Claycamp, H. J., "Characteristics of Owners of Thrift Deposits in Commercial Banks and Savings and Loan Associations," *Journal of Marketing Research,* vol. 2, May 1965, pp. 163–170.
3. Durand, D., "Risk Elements in Consumer Installment Financing," New York: National Bureau of Economic Research, 1941.

4. Evans, F. B., "Psychological and Objective Factors in the Prediction of Brand Choice: Ford versus Chevrolet," *Journal of Business*, vol. 32, October 1959, pp. 340–369.
5. Farley, J. U., " 'Brand Loyalty' and the Economics of Information," *Journal of Business*, vol. 37, October 1964, pp. 370–381.
6. Ferber, R., *The Reliability of Consumer Reports of Financial Assets*, Studies in Consumer Savings, no. 6, Urbana: University of Illinois, Bureau of Economic and Business Research, 1966.
7. Frank, R. E., W. F. Massy, and D. G. Morrison, "Bias in Multiple Discriminant Analysis," *Journal of Marketing Research*, vol. 2, August 1965, pp. 250–258.
8. Frank, R. E., W. F. Massy, and D. G. Morrison, "The Determinants of Innovative Behavior with Respect to a Branded, Frequently Purchased Food Product," in L. George Smith (ed.), *Reflections on Progress in Marketing*, Chicago: American Marketing Association, 1965, pp. 312–323.
9. Freimer, M., and L. S. Simon, "The Evaluation of Potential New Product Alternatives," *Management Science*, vol. 13, February 1967, pp. B279–B292.
10. King, C. W., "The Innovator in the Fashion Adoption Process," in L. George Smith (ed.), *Reflections on Progress in Marketing*, Chicago: American Marketing Association, 1965, pp. 324–339.
11. Ladd, G. W., "Linear Probability Functions and Discriminant Functions," *Econometrica*, vol. 34, October 1966, pp. 873–885.
12. Massy, W. F., "On Methods: Discriminant Analysis of Audience Characteristics," *Journal of Advertising Research*, vol. 5, March 1965, pp. 39–48.
13. Morrison, D. G., "Measurement Problems in Cluster Analysis," *Management Science*, vol. 13, August 1967, pp. B775–B780.
14. Morrison, D. G., "On the Interpretation of Discriminant Analysis," *Journal of Marketing Research*, vol. 6, May 1969, pp. 156–163.
15. Mosteller, F., and R. R. Bush, "Selective Quantitative Techniques," in Lindsey (ed.), *Handbook of Social Psychology*, vol. I, New York: Addison-Wesley, 1954.
16. Pessemier, E. A., P. C. Burger, and D. J. Tigert, "Can New Product Buyers be Identified?" *Journal of Marketing Research*, vol. 4, November 1967, pp. 349–354.
17. Robertson, T. S., and J. N. Kennedy, "Prediction of Consumer Innovators: Application of Multiple Discriminant Analysis," *Journal of Marketing Research*, vol. 5, February 1968, pp. 64–69.

Part E

Statistical Analysis of Relationships

Chapter 9

Factor Analysis[1]

WILLIAM D. WELLS *Graduate School of Business, University of Chicago, Chicago, Illinois*

JAGDISH N. SHETH *Department of Business Administration, University of Illinois at Urbana-Champaign, Illinois*

When it works well, factor analysis helps the investigator make sense of large bodies of intertwined data. When it works unusually well, it also points to interesting relationships that might not have been obvious from examination of the input data alone.

In marketing research, factor analysis can be useful in four ways. First (but not necessarily most important), it can point out the latent—that is, underlying, not directly observed—dimensions that account for the relationships among product preferences or other kinds of ratings obtained in market studies. For example, suppose one has no idea of the dimensions consumers use when choosing among types of liquor. If respondents are asked to rate several liquor types (Scotch, gin, rum, bourbon, vodka, and so on) according to preference, a factor analysis may reveal some salient characteristics of liquors that underlie the relative preferences. These characteristics might turn out to be sensory attributes, such as degree of sweetness, bouquet, or intoxicative potency. They might be intangible attributes, such as stereotyped product images. Or they might be identified as some mixture of both. The results, whatever they are,

[1] The authors wish to express their great appreciation for comments on early drafts of this chapter made by Harry Roberts and Douglas Tigert of the Graduate School of Business, University of Chicago. For the occupational data used in the first part of the chapter, we are indebted to Douglas Tigert.

will not dictate infallible marketing policy.   But they will probably be of some help to the marketer who is trying to organize his thinking.

The second way in which factor analysis can be helpful is by pointing out relationships among observed values that were there all the time but not easy to see.   For example, a factor analysis of cosmetic use once suggested that hair spray is more closely associated with face cosmetics, such as eye shadow and lipstick, than with other products women use specifically for their hair.   It also showed that hair spray, eye shadow, and lipstick belong in a group of purchases and activities that include the number of movies attended in the past month.   This grouping pointed to a dimension of consumer behavior that seemed to be worth intensive follow-up research.   It also suggested some immediate applications: a lipstick instead of a comb as a hair-spray premium; movie themes, or movie-related prizes, as sales promotions for face cosmetics.   In the long run, the latent dimension and the unforeseen relationship are perhaps of more value than the specific immediate application, but on an exceptionally good day one can have all three.

Third, factor analysis is useful when data must be condensed and simplified. Suppose, for example, that some television commercials have been rated on 50 or 60 rating scales, and that the problem is to present these ratings to a decision maker who does not have three weeks to study them.   If several of the scales, or several groups of scales, are heavily correlated with one another because they are in fact redundant, factor analysis will summarize the information in them and make the whole set easier to handle.   It is this use of factor analysis that comes in handiest when the marketing vice-president says, "Don't give me 10 pages of numbers.   Just give me the main results."

Finally, and related to the third use, the factor analysis can be employed as one step in empirical clustering of products, media, stimuli, or people.   In the previous example, for instance, an additional outcome might be the clustering of a large number of commercials into a smaller number of useful, meaningful, and possibly nonobvious types.

WHAT IS FACTOR ANALYSIS?

Factor analysis is a multivariate statistical technique that addresses itself to the study of interrelationships among a total set of observed variables.   Unlike multiple regression, in which one variable is explicitly considered the criterion (dependent) variable and all others as the predictor (independent) variables, all the variables in factor analysis are considered simultaneously.   In a sense, each of the observed variables is considered as a dependent variable that is a function of some underlying, latent, and hypothetical set of factors.   Conversely, one can look at each factor as a dependent variable that is a function of the observed variables.

Several methods of factor analysis are available, and these several methods do not necessarily give the same results.   In this sense, factor analysis is indeed a *set of techniques* rather than a single, unique method.

VOCABULARY

Factor analysis has some specialized concepts and terminology.   A *factor* is an underlying dimension that "accounts for" several observed variables.   For example, consider the following tabulation of all the possible intercorrelations among nine variables:

TABLE 1 Correlation Coefficients among Nine Variables (decimals omitted)

Variable	Correlations among variables								
	1	*2*	*3*	*4*	*5*	*6*	*7*	*8*	*9*
1. Author, fiction		76	48	20	08	25	05	28	18
2. Author, children's books	76		47	19	07	25	10	30	21
3. Newspaper reporter	48	47		22	13	22	09	31	26
4. Computer programmer	20	19	22		42	53	00	20	33
5. Bookkeeper	08	07	13	42		36	−01	09	18
6. College math teacher	25	25	22	53	36		08	31	33
7. Nurse	05	10	09	00	−01	08		45	34
8. Doctor	28	30	31	20	09	31	45		48
9. Laboratory technician	18	21	26	33	18	33	34	48	

In this illustration, the variables are ratings of nine occupations by a large sample of 850 homemakers. On a five-point scale, each respondent rated each occupation in terms of how well she thought she would do in it if she had the opportunity to build a career in that field. The entry "76" in row 1, column 2, means that homemakers who thought they would do well in occupation 1 (author, fiction) also tended to say they would do well in occupation 2 (author, children's books). The entry "20" in row 1, column 4, means that homemakers who thought they would do well as a fiction author had a much weaker tendency to say they would do well as a computer programmer (occupation 4).

It is obvious from inspection alone that variables 1, 2, and 3 have something in common that they do not share with the other variables. It is also obvious that variables 4, 5, and 6 form a second group, and that 7, 8, and 9 form a third. This sort of pattern in raw data leads to the inference that one underlying dimension—one factor—accounts for variables 1, 2, and 3; that a second factor accounts for 4, 5, and 6; and that a third accounts for 7, 8, and 9.

Real data do not usually come this neatly dressed. The patterns in real data are not generally so striking as in this example, contrived for clarity of exposition. The data are real, but they were especially selected so as to make the relationship between the raw data and the factor solution intuitively obvious. A more realistic example will be given later.

A factor analysis performed by one of the most commonly used methods (principal-components analysis with varimax rotation) produced the following solution, shown in Table 2.[2]

The entries in columns A, B, and C are the *factor loadings*. They show how closely the nine variables are related to each of the three underlying factors, and they are the key to understanding what the factors mean. For instance, the heavy loadings of "Author, fiction," "Author, children's books," and "Newspaper reporter" on factor A indicate that it represents an underlying general interest in things literary and verbal. Factor B evidently represents interest in figures. And factor C represents interest in the medical field. The minus signs

[2] For computational techniques, see Harman [4].

in front of the entries in column C do not affect the interpretation of the factor. In fact, as a matter of convenience, it is customary to "reflect" (change *all*) the signs of a factor on which the highest loadings are negative. As long as all the signs in a column are changed, it is the absolute size of the loadings, rather than the signs, that count.

The h^2 (*communality*) column shows how much of each variable is accounted for by the three underlying factors taken together. A large communality figure means that not much of the variable is left over after whatever the factors represent is taken into consideration. A small communality figure means that the factors taken together do not account for much of whatever the variable is all about.

The *sum of squares*, or *eigenvalue*, indicates the relative importance of each factor in accounting for the particular set of variables being analyzed. It is

TABLE 2   Factor Loadings on Nine Variables (decimals omitted)

Variable	Loadings on factors			h^2 (communality)
	A	B	C	
1. Author, fiction	90	08	−05	82
2. Author, children's books	89	07	−10	80
3. Newspaper reporter	69	15	−17	53
4. Computer programmer	14	81	−08	69
5. Bookkeeper	−01	76	03	57
6. College math teacher	20	73	−20	62
7. Nurse	−02	−13	−83	70
8. Doctor	28	14	−77	69
9. Laboratory technician	13	36	−68	61
Sum of squares (eigenvalue)	223	197	183	603

sometimes implied, mistakenly, that the eigenvalue indicates importance in some more abstract sense, for example, the relative importance of each factor in influencing choice, or the relative dominance of each factor in the respondent's world. Not so. The eigenvalue refers to one particular set of variables (and one specific solution method) and can easily be changed by changing either the method or the mix of variables.

The entry at the far right of the eigenvalue row (603, in Table 2) is the total sum of squares. Dividing it by the number of variables (603/9 = about .067) provides an index of how well this particular solution accounts for what all the variables taken together represent. If the variables are all very different from each other, this index will be low. If they fall into one or more highly redundant groups, and if the extracted factors account for all the groups, the index will approach unity.

DECISIONS, DECISIONS

As noted earlier, the name *factor analysis* is applied to a variety of procedures. Although the mathematical analysis is pretty much the same, the procedures provide a large number of options to the analyst to suit the method to his purposes. Unfortunately, the results from these options vary considerably, and there is no sure guide as to which options are "right." The trick is to pick the combination of options that best does the job at hand. Among the options on which the analyst must decide are the following:

Correlation, Covariance, or Cross-Products Matrix? Although it is most common to factor-analyze a matrix of correlations, as in the illustration given earlier, that choice is not mandatory. Since a correlation coefficient is derived from standard scores in which the averages of all variables are set equal to zero and the variances equal to one, factor analysis of correlations loses two of the three types of information contained in a data matrix, namely, the levels and dispersions of variables. In some cases, it may be desirable to retain one or both of these types of information in analyzing data. In such cases, a covariance matrix (only means being set equal to zero, but variance not being standardized) or cross-products (unstandardized data matrix) may be appropriate as input to factor analysis.

Generally, if the units of measurement are disparate among observed variables (as, for example, between income and education), it is advisable to standardize the data and hence use a matrix of correlations. By the same token, if the units of measurement are identical or very similar across variables, and if individual differences are expected, it may be better to factor-analyze a matrix of covariances or cross-products so as not to lose the information contained in the means and standard deviations. For example, in the illustration just given, if some of the occupations had received very high average ratings and some had received relatively low average ratings, or if there had been much more disagreement about some occupations than others, our use of a correlation matrix as a starting point would have erased this possibly useful information. *Moral:* The most widely used factor-analytic procedures ignore level differences and dispersion differences among input variables. If these differences are important to the investigator, alternative procedures are available and must be followed.[3]

What Goes into the Diagonal of the Correlation Matrix? If the researcher chooses the option of using a matrix of correlations as the input to factor analysis, he must decide on one more option: What value should be put in the diagonal of the matrix—the diagonal that represents correlation of a variable with itself? The various options and their consequences are discussed in Harman [4].

For many marketing research purposes, the best choice seems to be 1 (unity). This choice usually produces clear, intuitively appealing solutions, and it is now so much in vogue that it is the standard option employed in many of the most widely used canned computer programs.

Rotation. Another substantive option is the derivation of "new" factors from the initial results by the methods of rotation. As a very rough analogy, rotation is something like staining a microscope slide. Just as different stains reveal different structures in the tissue, different rotations reveal different structures in the data, even though in both cases all the structures are always actually there.

Different rotations give results that appear to be entirely different. From a statistical point of view, all results are equal, none superior or inferior to others; but from the standpoint of making sense of the results of factor analysis, selecting the right rotation is extremely important.

[3] For further information on this point, see Nunnally [6].

An illustration of the effects of rotation is shown in Table 3. The "unrotated factor-loading matrix"—shown here for the nine-variable occupation problem—is the first output of any factor analysis. A glance at the unrotated factor loadings will show that the pattern is not at all clear. In the matrix to the right, the factors have been rotated by the varimax method, a procedure that produces, within each factor, as many high loadings and as many low loadings as possible.

TABLE 3   Comparison of Unrotated and Rotated Factor Solutions (decimals omitted)

Variable	Loadings on unrotated factors				Loadings on rotated factors			
	A	B	C	h^2	A	B	C	h^2
1. Author, fiction	68	−52	31	82	90	08	−05	82
2. Author, children's books	69	−51	26	80	89	07	−01	80
3. Newspaper reporter	63	−32	16	53	69	15	−17	53
4. Computer programmer	58	53	27	69	14	81	−08	69
5. Bookkeeper	38	59	29	57	−02	76	03	57
6. College math teacher	63	44	16	62	20	73	−20	62
7. Nurse	33	−04	−77	70	−02	−13	−83	70
8. Doctor	65	−04	−52	69	28	13	−77	69
9. Laboratory technician	62	22	−42	61	13	36	−68	61
Sum of squares (eigenvalue)	312	151	139	602	223	197	183	602

Note that the communality for each variable remains the same regardless of rotation. This is another way of saying that the rotated factors, taken together, account for exactly the same amount of each variable as the unrotated factors do. It is just that the weight of each variable on each factor is now redistributed.

The eigenvalues have changed, since they are the sums of the squares of the loadings. In the unrotated matrix, one factor (factor A) dominates the picture. In the rotated matrix, the loadings have shifted so that the eigenvalues are now more nearly equal. Had the input variables been different—for instance, had variables 4, 5, and 6 also been literary occupations—the relative sizes of the eigenvalues in the rotated solution would have shifted to reflect the greater weight of literary activities in the altered variable mix.

When to Stop Factoring. When a large, unorganized set of variables is factored, as is often done in marketing research, the analysis will extract the largest and most interesting combinations of variables first and then proceed to smaller combinations. For example, in an analysis of grocery-product use, the first factor extracted was a group of food and laundry products that appeared upon examination to be products consumed in quantity by large, middle-income families. The next factor consisted of products used for wrapping and preserving food. The next was a group of foods used heavily by relatively low-income families, and the next was a group of products that are supposed to germproof and deodorize the home. All these product groups were interesting and meaningful, but as the analysis proceeded, the groups became smaller and less understandable until finally they each consisted of only one of the remaining products.

Carrying an analysis too far has two penalties. It is exceedingly wasteful of

TABLE 4   Correlation Matrix of 30 Magazines (decimals omitted)

Variable description	Var. no.	1	2	3	4	5	6	7	8	9	10	11	12	13
Bus. Week	1		19	31	30	33	23	12	09	07	24	04	09	04
Life	2	19		14	31	27	10	10	38	35	21	08	08	07
New Yorker	3	31	14		23	26	16	36	08	09	20	00	17	00
Time	4	30	31	23		25	15	12	18	16	25	08	13	02
Newsweek	5	33	27	26	25		29	18	23	15	09	18	15	02
U.S. News & World Report	6	23	10	16	15	29		15	18	11	16	05	13	−01
Sat. Review	7	12	10	36	12	18	15		13	14	10	−00	22	−01
Look	8	09	38	08	18	23	18	13		39	04	16	13	06
Sat. Ev. Post	9	07	35	09	16	15	11	14	39		05	16	12	−01
Forbes	10	24	06	20	25	09	16	10	04	05		−00	14	−01
Argosy	11	04	21	00	08	18	05	−00	16	16	−00		02	12
Atl. Monthly	12	09	08	17	13	15	13	22	13	12	14	02		−02
Car & Driver	13	04	07	00	02	02	−01	−01	06	−01	−01	12	−02	
Field & Stream	14	08	11	01	09	12	04	−01	16	15	03	27	04	05
Farm Journal	15	−05	−04	−08	−05	−01	10	02	01	−01	−02	−01	−03	−04
Fortune	16	29	12	33	34	14	15	12	06	08	25	04	15	02
Harper's	17	08	08	27	07	13	07	19	10	08	09	−01	08	06
Mech. Illus.	18	07	16	01	06	10	02	−00	14	11	08	18	01	27
Pop. Mech.	19	09	09	02	07	12	04	09	14	09	05	17	02	20
Pop. Science	20	11	13	04	05	11	03	08	13	11	03	12	−02	19
Outdoor Life	21	03	06	01	02	06	02	01	11	10	02	22	02	04
Prog. Farmer	22	−06	−03	−07	−06	−07	03	06	−06	01	−03	00	−02	−05
Reader's Digest	23	11	16	03	08	20	09	03	16	20	11	13	03	−11
Road & Track	24	03	10	03	01	02	−04	04	04	04	−01	13	01	55
Sci. Amer.	25	19	06	19	10	11	05	25	05	03	08	04	12	03
Succ. Farming	26	−06	−06	−07	−08	01	05	01	01	−01	−03	05	−02	−06
Sports Afield	27	02	11	02	05	10	03	−00	13	12	−01	18	02	06
True	28	04	16	02	12	11	02	−00	19	18	01	41	01	06
Hot Rod	29	−01	01	−01	−04	01	−03	−01	07	02	−03	16	00	35
Motor Trend	30	04	05	02	03	05	−02	03	10	03	−04	20	05	45

computer time, and it obscures the meaning of the findings because it affects the rotation adversely. When many factors are involved in varimax rotation, the tendency is to produce rotated factors that have very high loadings on a very few variables. This produces fragments. On the other hand, if very few factors are rotated, the tendency is to have moderate to low loadings on quite a few variables, so no meaningful interpretation is possible. To return to the microscope analogy, choosing the number of factors to be extracted is something like focusing. Too high or too low an adjustment will obscure a structure that is obvious when the adjustment is just right.

Four "stopping" criteria may be employed. When the analyst already knows how many factors he wants to get out, he can have the analysis stopped after the desired number of factors have been extracted. In marketing research, this situation is rare. Second, if he has a clear idea in advance about how much of each variable the factors can explain (also a rare privilege in marketing research), he can stop when that criterion is reached. Most commonly, however, if he does not know very much about his data to begin with, he will want to keep factoring until factors get small and meaningless.

Two criteria for "small and meaningless" are often used. If, after a certain number of factors have been extracted, the eigenvalue of the next factor drops to a sharply lower level, the factor with the low eigenvalue may be discarded and factoring may be stopped. Second, when all factors whose eigenvalues are greater than unity have been extracted, the factoring may be stopped.

The reader who has come this far will know why critics of factor analysis have insisted that it is a branch of theology rather than a properly objective scientific method. What to correlate, the type of data input, the entries in the diagonal, the type of rotation used, and the stopping criterion are all decisions

14	15	16	17	18	19	20	21	22	23	24	25	26	27	28	29	30
08	−05	29	08	07	09	11	03	−06	11	03	19	−06	02	04	−01	04
11	−04	12	08	16	09	13	06	−03	16	10	06	−06	11	16	01	05
01	−08	33	27	01	02	04	01	−07	03	03	19	−07	02	02	−01	02
09	−05	34	07	07	07	06	02	−06	18	01	10	−08	05	12	−04	03
12	−01	14	13	10	12	11	06	−06	20	02	11	01	10	11	01	05
04	10	15	07	02	04	03	02	03	19	−04	05	05	03	02	−03	−02
−01	02	12	19	−00	09	08	01	06	03	04	25	01	−00	−00	−01	03
16	00	06	10	14	14	13	11	−06	16	04	05	01	13	19	07	10
15	−01	08	08	11	09	11	10	01	20	04	03	−01	12	18	02	03
03	−02	25	09	08	05	03	02	−03	11	−01	08	−03	−01	01	−03	−04
27	−01	04	−01	18	17	12	22	00	13	13	04	05	18	41	16	20
04	−03	15	38	01	02	−02	02	−02	03	01	12	−02	02	01	00	05
05	−04	02	06	27	20	19	04	−05	−11	55	−03	−06	06	06	35	47
	09	01	−01	22	26	12	59	06	03	13	04	08	56	28	09	11
09		−05	−04	−01	01	−03	06	34	07	−05	−02	58	09	00	−04	−01
01	−05		24	06	04	03	01	−00	05	04	13	−06	00	07	00	01
−01	−04	24		−02	−05	−04	−03	01	−04	07	11	−04	00	02	00	03
22	−01	06	−02		56	46	20	00	07	24	09	−02	20	18	25	31
26	01	04	−05	56		58	23	01	06	19	07	−01	21	17	22	28
12	−03	03	−04	46	58		13	−02	10	16	09	−04	13	15	17	24
59	06	01	−03	20	23	13		08	03	11	04	07	47	26	05	13
06	34	−00	01	00	01	−02	08		02	−03	−02	13	06	−04	−01	−01
03	07	05	−04	07	06	10	03	02		−10	03	08	04	14	−09	−04
13	−05	04	07	24	19	16	11	−03	−10		13	−05	12	12	36	49
04	−02	13	11	09	07	09	04	−02	03	13		−02	05	06	05	09
08	58	−06	−04	−02	−01	−04	07	13	08	−05	−02		15	02	−03	01
56	09	00	00	20	21	13	47	06	04	12	05	15		23	18	14
28	00	07	02	18	17	15	26	−04	14	12	06	02	23		10	13
09	−04	00	00	25	22	17	05	−01	−08	36	05	−03	08	10		54
11	−01	01	03	31	28	24	13	−01	−04	49	09	01	14	13	54	

the analyst must make. The decisions create numerous combinations, and are not easy or automatic. Along with the data, they determine the results.

A Realistic Example. As noted earlier, the nine-variable example that employed occupation ratings was deliberately simplified to facilitate an intuitive understanding of the terms and procedures. A more realistic example will now be presented—more realistic in the sense that it employs more variables, and also in the sense that the pattern in the input variables is not so self-evident as it was in the case of the occupation ratings. In this example, the data consist of correlations in reported reading of 30 magazines by a large sample of 980 adult males. The fact that variable *Business Week* correlates 19 with *Life* and 31 with *The New Yorker* says that *Business Week* and *The New Yorker* have more in common than do *Business Week* and *Life*, at least in this sample. Note that the correlations are not very distinct from one another, and therefore, eyeballing the matrix does not show any obvious simple groups. When the relationships are as complex and as numerous as these (and this is a simple and small matrix compared to some that are generated in marketing research), factor analysis will help sort them out.

This matrix of correlations was factor-analyzed by the principal-components method in which ones were placed in the diagonal.

The first output of the factor analysis looked like that shown in Table 5.

The columns represent the factors. The items being analyzed are listed down the side. The entries in the columns are the factor loadings, the correlation between each item and the factor. This is an unrotated matrix and, as usual, its meaning is not clear.

The matrix in Table 6 is the product of a varimax rotation. The rotation has clarified the factors, and they can now be interpreted as shown in the table.

TABLE 5 Principal Components Factor Loadings (decimals omitted)

Variable description	Variable number	Factor 1	2	3	4	5	6	7	8	9	10	Communality
Bus. Week	1	35	43	-12	04	06	-28	-33	17	15	00	56
Life	2	45	26	07	-27	16	33	-03	-05	21	-28	61
New Yorker	3	30	51	-21	19	-19	-13	04	17	00	-11	52
Time	4	37	45	-04	-12	05	-08	-32	-20	05	-21	55
Newsweek	5	43	38	05	-03	12	05	-10	33	11	32	58
U.S. News & World Report	6	24	37	11	15	23	00	-12	14	18	47	57
Sat. Review	7	25	36	-10	32	-03	04	41	32	-01	-20	61
Look	8	45	18	15	-20	16	41	18	-05	22	-02	58
Sat. Ev. Post	9	39	20	20	-23	12	38	23	-16	14	-21	58
Forbes	10	20	36	-07	08	01	-31	-22	-37	-05	04	47
Argosy	11	45	-13	19	-18	-07	23	-19	10	-49	05	64
Atl. Monthly	12	21	35	-10	23	-24	18	35	-25	-14	36	65
Car & Driver	13	37	-38	-46	17	04	19	-21	-05	17	01	63
Field & Stream	14	50	-21	46	-02	-43	-14	-04	00	18	04	75
Farm Journal	15	-02	-09	49	63	32	09	-11	-06	-01	-08	77
Fortune	16	29	44	-17	14	-12	-19	-25	-32	-15	-16	58
Harper's	17	17	35	-21	29	-32	22	28	-27	-13	19	63
Mech. Illus.	18	57	-31	-09	-06	24	-29	18	-16	-04	02	63
Pop. Mech.	19	57	-30	-03	-04	26	-40	31	-08	-04	06	75
Pop. Science	20	50	-23	-10	-10	36	-36	33	-01	-05	-01	69
Outdoor Life	21	43	-24	43	-00	-44	-19	01	01	13	01	67
Prog. Farmer	22	-03	-08	30	44	13	00	07	-24	04	-30	46
Reader's Digest	23	21	25	29	-16	40	02	-09	02	-23	13	45
Road & Track	24	42	-37	-41	19	-09	21	-18	02	11	-10	63
Sci. Amer.	25	26	18	-16	22	-10	-12	11	45	-22	-35	58
Succ. Farming	26	-01	-11	48	54	25	12	-13	06	-10	04	63
Sports Afield	27	44	-23	43	05	-39	-10	-01	05	22	03	64
True	28	45	-11	24	-22	-13	15	-12	03	-52	-05	65
Hot Rod	29	36	-41	36	15	04	18	-12	00	-05	09	51
Motor Trend	30	48	-42	-37	21	04	16	-13	03	-01	06	65
Eigenvalues		413	292	225	169	150	144	125	106	101	100	1825

TABLE 6 Rotated Factor Matrix (decimals omitted)

Variable description	Variable number	Factor 1	2	3	4	5	6*	7	8	9*	10	Communality
Bus. Week	1	05	51	06	-10	02	03	-15	26	-06	43	56
Life	2	07	20	04	-06	73	01	-09	08	09	10	61
New Yorker	3	00	37	04	-11	05	-05	21	53	-07	19	52
Time	4	-00	65	02	-06	31	-01	-07	07	08	12	55
Newsweek	5	03	10	09	-09	20	04	05	20	11	68	59
U.S. News & World Report	6	-03	12	00	12	07	03	14	-02	-06	72	57
Sat. Review	7	-04	-03	-03	09	17	09	26	69	-11	10	61
Look	8	06	-05	09	-01	71	09	13	00	08	20	58
Sat. Ev. Post	9	-05	03	07	03	74	08	11	03	10	-01	58
Forbes	10	-07	64	-00	02	-06	12	15	-07	-03	09	47
Argosy	11	17	00	17	-01	12	04	01	01	75	07	64
Atl. Monthly	12	-02	08	02	-02	07	02	78	07	03	13	65
Car & Driver	13	78	04	01	-04	04	10	-02	-04	-06	01	63
Field & Stream	14	05	04	84	04	09	10	-00	-02	14	04	75
Farm Journal	15	-01	-03	05	87	-02	-02	-04	-02	-00	09	77
Fortune	16	03	72	-02	-00	01	-01	19	14	07	-03	58
Harper's	17	08	15	-01	-03	07	-09	75	15	-02	-01	63
Mech. Illus.	18	26	10	15	-01	09	72	-01	-03	09	-01	63
Pop. Mech.	19	16	03	19	00	03	82	00	04	05	05	75
Pop. Science	20	12	00	03	-04	09	81	-07	10	04	05	69
Outdoor Life	21	02	01	80	04	01	13	01	01	13	-02	67
Prog. Farmer	22	-04	07	07	61	07	05	02	03	-13	-25	47
Reader's Digest	23	-24	12	-14	15	21	18	-07	-08	36	34	45
Road & Track	24	77	03	10	-03	06	04	-01	10	01	-07	63
Sci. Amer.	25	07	08	01	-00	-05	06	-04	74	14	-01	58
Succ. Farming	26	-01	-11	07	75	-08	-06	-03	-01	12	17	63
Sports Afield	27	08	-03	78	10	-08	08	-00	01	07	06	64
True	28	06	05	23	-03	13	10	02	04	75	-06	65
Hot Rod	29	68	-07	-01	-01	-04	16	05	-03	13	01	51
Motor Trend	30	77	-03	05	03	01	20	04	04	12	04	65
Sums of squares		250	190	215	178	188	206	145	152	147	154	1823

* The signs in variables 6 and 9 have been reflected as an aid to interpretation.

2-467

Factor 1 has high loadings on *Car and Driver, Road & Track, Motor Trend,* and *Hot Rod.* This means that respondents who say they read *Car and Driver* also tend to say they read the other magazines that load high on factor 1. In other words, these four magazines form a group based on some degree of common audience.

Factor 2 has relatively high loadings on *Fortune, Forbes, Time,* and *Business Week.* Again, the interpretation is that magazines in this group have more audience overlap with one another than with magazines that load high on other factors. The inference is that they, like the first group, represent some common core of interests.

Factor 3 has high loadings on *Field and Stream, Outdoor Life,* and *Sports Afield.* Factor 4 has high loadings on *Farm Journal, Successful Farming,* and *Progressive Farmer.* Thus, one can proceed through the whole matrix, factor by factor, looking for high loadings to determine what the various factors "mean."

The Meaning of Loading. Note that all the magazines have a loading of some size on every factor, and that for any one factor, the loadings of a few magazines are large while the loadings of the other magazines are small. This result is exactly what a varimax rotation is intended to achieve. Other rotation systems, designed to achieve other outcomes, would have produced a different configuration from the same unrotated matrix. The loadings portray the degree to which the individual items (magazines, in this case) represent the factor as a whole. Thus, *Fortune* and *Forbes* serve better than *Business Week* as representatives of the underlying, latent dimension signified by factor 2. If the high-loaded items on a factor are thought of as a group, the highest-loaded items are the best instances of whatever it is that holds the group together. In the present example, the cement that glues the groups is presumably editorial content that makes magazines within groups appealing to somewhat the same group of readers.

Note that *Reader's Digest* does not have a high loading on any of the factors. Instead, its positive loadings are divided among the news group (factor 10) best typified by *U.S. News* and *Newsweek,* a "general reading" group (factor 5, *Life, Look, Saturday Evening Post*), a men's fiction group (factor 9, *Argosy* and *True*) and factor 4, a group of farm magazines. This result implies that *Reader's Digest* has an appeal that spreads broadly through readers of at least four magazine types. *Reader's Digest* also has small negative loadings on the sports-car factor (factor 1). This finding shows that *Reader's Digest's* broad appeal is not unlimited—that, in fact, men who are heavy readers of the magazine type represented by *Motor Trend* tend *not* to read *Reader's Digest.*

Communality. The column to the far right of the matrix, after factor 10, shows the degree to which the factors account for, or explain, each of the variables. Thus, the factors extracted in this analysis account for the reported readership of *Life* somewhat better than for the reported readership of *Business Week,* and they account for *Outdoor Life* better than for *Progressive Farmer* or *Reader's Digest.* The size of the communality is a useful index to how much of the variable is in a sense "left over" after what it has in common with other variables has been accounted for. The comparatively low communality of *Reader's Digest,* for example, shows that it has relatively little in common with the other magazines included in this analysis, whereas the relatively high loadings of *Field and Stream* and *Farm Journal* show that they have much in common with the magazine groups, *taken as groups,* that the factors represent.

Factor Scores. Most factor-analysis computer programs compute factor scores for each respondent on each factor. The factor score represents the degree to which each *respondent* gets high scores on the *group* of items that load high on each factor. For instance, let us assume that readership of the magazines in Table 6 was reported by each respondent on a six-category scale ranging from "Never read" to "Read four issues out of the last four." The computer would determine each respondent's score on factor 1 by averaging his reported reading of each magazine, weighted by the magazine's loading on factor 1. Thus, since *Car and Driver, Road & Track, Motor Trend,* and *Hot Rod* have high loadings on factor 1, each respondent's factor score on factor 1 would be determined largely by his reading of these magazines. If he were a heavy reader of these magazines, he would have a high score on this factor; if he were a light (or non-) reader of them, his score on factor 1 would be low.

Similarly, since *Time, Forbes,* and *Fortune* have high loadings on factor 2, each respondent's factor score on factor 2 would be determined largely by his reading of this set of magazines, so avid *Time, Forbes,* and *Fortune* readers would get high factor 2 scores. Light or non-readers of these magazines would get low factor 2 scores, and so on.

Factor scores have a variety of uses. Because they can be cross-tabulated with other variables, they can help explain what the factors mean. For instance, if the interpretation of factors 1 and 2 above were not already obvious, some insight into their meaning could be obtained by cross-tabulating respondents' factor scores on these factors with other variables, like age and occupation. This procedure would show that respondents who score high on factor 1 are significantly younger than respondents who score high on factor 2, and that respondents who score high on factor 2 have professional and managerial occupations, whereas respondents who score high on factor 1 tend to be blue-collar workers.

This aid to interpretation would of course have been unnecessary in the magazine example, but it can sometimes be a great help. In the cosmetics study mentioned earlier, for example, the underlying differences between two groups of cosmetics became obvious when it was found that one group was used primarily by younger women while the other group was used by more mature women. In another study, the distinction between two groups of grocery items was clarified when it was found that one group was heavily used by middle-income families while the other group was heavily used by low-income families. These relationships were obvious once the factor scores had pointed them out, but without the factor scores as a guide through the tangle of correlations between products and demographic variables, it was hard to know where to look.

Since factor scores represent combinations of items, they can facilitate comparisons among groups of items as groups. For example, the availability of factor scores makes it possible to say what types of T.V. programs are viewed by readers of what types of magazines, or what types of recreational interests go with what types of taste in clothes.

Finally, factor scores can be treated as if they were raw scores to perform any of a number of multivariate analyses. These include multiple regression, multiple-discriminant analysis and clustering.

COMMENTS ON Q ANALYSIS

The analysis just described is *R-type* factor analysis, by far the most common. In *R* analysis, high correlations occur when respondents who score high on variable 1 also score high on variable 2, and respondents who score low on variable 1 also score low on variable 2.   Factors emerge when there are (relatively) high correlations within groups of *variables.*

In Q analysis, the correlations are computed between pairs of respondents instead of pairs of variables.   High correlations occur when respondent 1's pattern of responses *on all the variables* is much like respondent 2's pattern of responses.   Factors emerge when there are relatively high correlations within groups of *people.*

Q analysis is useful when the object is to sort people into groups based on their simultaneous responses to all the variables.   It is therefore being increasingly employed in market-segmentation studies.

Two difficulties with Q analysis have limited its use to date.   Currently available Q-analysis computer programs do not handle even moderately large samples of respondents easily, and reliability tests have suggested that Q factors are disappointingly unstable from sample to sample.   It seems reasonable to expect that these problems will be overcome or at least better understood as time goes by, and that Q analysis or one of its mathematical relatives will become a standard and important market research technique.[4]

DIFFICULTIES, PROBLEMS, AND CAUTIONS

Cost.   A factor analysis of even moderate size requires a prodigious amount of number crunching.   Before the advent of computers, factor-analytic studies employing 50 or more variables were almost never attempted, and even much smaller studies required so many hours of labor on a hand calculator that they were seldom replicated, checked for reliability, or even examined for arithmetic errors.   Perhaps it was the heroic amount of effort required that led some of the early analysts to believe that their work had revealed the Truth.

Although computerized factor analysis is now much faster and much easier, it is still not costless.   The cost of an R analysis increases roughly linearly with the number of respondents, and it increases much faster than linearly with the number of variables.   The cost of a Q analysis is extremely sensitive to the number of respondents.   Large analyses are liable to be expensive, and adding variables to an already large analysis is apt to increase the cost far faster than it increases value.

Reliability.   Like any other statistical procedure, a factor analysis starts with a set of imperfect data.   When the data change because of changes in the sample, changes in data-gathering procedures, or any of the numerous kinds of measurement errors, the results of the analysis will change too.   The results of any single analysis are therefore *always* less than perfectly dependable.

This problem is especially pernicious because the results of a single-factor analysis usually look plausible.   In fact, they sometimes look so plausible that the analyst is tempted to say to himself, "What's interesting about this?   I knew it all the time."   (He didn't.)

It is important to emphasize that plausibility is no guarantee of validity or even stability.   A factor analysis of randomly generated data will seem to make some sense when stared at long enough and hopefully enough [1].   A factor solution computed from one randomly selected half of the respondents may seem to be an obvious representation of reality until it is placed beside a somewhat different, but equally plausible, solution computed from the remaining respondents.   The moral is: Do the analysis at least twice.   As a minimum, divide the respondents into two groups at random by means of a random-

---

[4] For more on Q analysis, see Stevenson [9] and Schlinger [8].

number table and check one group against the other. When different samples produce similar results, confidence increases.

The sampling problem extends to the set of variables used in the analysis. It should be obvious that a dimension cannot emerge from a factor analysis unless at least two variables are in the analysis to represent it. It is perhaps less obvious that putting variables in and taking them out will influence the patterns formed by other variables. If some variables are added that have a strong relationship with some variables that would otherwise have formed a factor, the factor may break into two parts, one with high loadings on the new and some of the old variables, the other with high loadings on only the old.

Judgment. It has been said that sending data out to be factor-analyzed is much like sending suits to the cleaners—you don't have to know anything about what was done to the suits or the data as long as they come back clean and free from wrinkles. It should be clear by now that the problem is not that simple. The user of factor analysis makes decisions that determine how the analysis will come out, or else the decisions are made for him. Even with a given set of decisions, different findings will come from different groups of respondents, different ways of obtaining data, and different mixes of variables.

All this is highly disconcerting to anyone who needs to believe that the results of any one factor analysis will be Revealed Universal Truth Forever Enduring, and it has sometimes led to disappointment and even indignant rejection of the method [3].

If, on the other hand, factor analysis is regarded as one of several fairly complicated tools that may help unsnarl badly tangled data, the user is much less liable to feel cheated when he tries to line up the results of a factor analysis against the real world. When it works well, factor analysis helps the investigator make sense of large bodies of intertwined data. When it works unusually well, it also points out some interesting relationships that might not have been obvious from examination of the input data alone. And that's what makes all the work worthwhile.

REFERENCES

1. Armstrong, J. S., and P. Soelberg, "On the Interpretation of Factor Analysis," *Psychological Bulletin,* vol. 70, 1968, pp. 361–364.
2. Cattell, R. B. (ed.), *Handbook of Multivariate Experimental Psychology,* Chicago: Rand McNally, 1966.
3. Ehrenberg, A. S. C., "On Methods: The Factor Analytic Search for Program Types," *Journal of Advertising Research,* vol. 8, March 1968, pp. 55–70.
4. Harman, H., *Modern Factor Analysis,* 2d ed., Chicago: The University of Chicago Press, 1967.
5. Horst, P., *Factor Analysis of Data Matrices,* New York: Holt, 1965.
6. Nunnally, J. C., *Psychometric Theory,* New York: McGraw-Hill, 1967.
7. Ramond, C. K., "Factor Analysis: When to Use it," in A. Shuchman (ed.), *Scientific Decision Making in Business,* New York: Holt, 1963.
8. Schlinger, M. J., "On Methods: Cues on Q-Technique," *Journal of Advertising Research,* vol. 9, September 1969, pp. 53–60.
9. Stevenson, W., *The Study of Behavior,* Chicago: The University of Chicago Press, 1953.

Statistical Analysis of Relationships

Chapter 10

Experimental Design and Control

SEYMOUR BANKS   *Leo Burnett, Inc., Chicago, Illinois*

INTRODUCTION

The chief characteristic of modern experimentation is its reliance upon administrative and analytical procedures to "control" undesired variables.   Under this system, one uses procedures which allow him to eliminate the effects of non-desired variation from his test data by statistical procedures, rather than by means of literally physical control.   The most notable part of the administrative aspects of experimentation is that called experimental design; its statistical partner is the analysis of variance.

Before we go further, let us introduce some useful terms:

> *Treatments:* the marketing alternatives whose effects the researcher is primarily concerned with—package designs, various display devices, advertising themes or budgets, and so on.
> *Test units:* the individuals or organizations whose responses to the experimental treatments yield the data of the experiment.
> *"Other" variables:* the nonexperimental or classification factors that affect the response of test units during the experiment.   There are two kinds: those the researcher can identify and measure; and the remainder, whose effect is evaluated by experimental error.

The heart of experimental design is the identification, prior to field operations, of factors which might affect the response of test units to experimental treatments and the use of that information in the test structure.   Experimental design is analogous to stratification in that it ensures the use of each experimental treatment within all classifications of test units, and vice versa.   However, the ultimate allocation of treatments to test units must be made by means of some randomizing device.

The combination of sound experimental design and random allocation of treatments to test units will prevent systematic (even if unconscious) bias in favor of any particular experimental treatment over its rivals and increase the sensitivity of the experimentation by reducing the size of the experimental error [2, chap. 4]; [13, chap. 3].

Before plunging into a discussion of particular experimental designs, this chapter will outline a conceptual framework or procedure for choosing among alternative designs. The viewpoint is simply that designs should be chosen on purely utilitarian bases, depending on the researcher's needs and the resources at his disposal as well as on the nature of the test units he will be working with, including their normal pattern of variation.

For this, we need some ideas derived from work on the economic design of surveys [16, chap. 8]; [14, chaps. 6–9]. Kish [16] points out that a preferred sample design will have a smaller cost-per-unit variance or smaller variance-per-unit cost than alternative designs. Costs which vary with the nature of the sampling design are the preparation of sampling frames; travel time between respondents; training of fieldworkers in sampling per se; and the process of computing variances of sample estimates. The influence of different designs on sample variance is shown by the fact that the variance of stratified, nonclustered samples is typically less than that of pure random sampling, while the variance of clustered samples is greater than those of pure random sampling. Thus, if clustered samples are chosen for a particular survey, it is because the expected cost saving from reducing interviewer travel time outweighs the expected increase in variance. Stratification procedures also are examined in terms of cost versus variance reduction.

Of course, one can make good estimates of cost components and contributions of various universe components to sample variance only after one has had actual field experience. Nevertheless, these concepts (of which only the briefest mentions are given here) should lead would-be experimenters to the proper issues to investigate as they go about the process of choosing a design: variance and cost.

One point requires elucidation. Because of the nature of the analysis of variance, the principal statistical technique for analyzing data from experiments, experimental data are most frequently absolutes rather than relative, for example, units or dollars sold per test unit per data period rather than market shares. Hence, test units treated alike by an experimenter vary in absolute levels of "response" because of size, season, day of the week, and so on, as well as in competitive activity. The art of experimental design is exactly the same as the art of stratification: to select criteria of classification in such a way that one maximizes variance among strata and minimizes variation within. The choice of these criteria must be pragmatic, arising from experience and informed judgment. If nothing else is available for classifying test units and hence for designing marketing experiments, first choice as the basic design factor should be size of stores, markets, regions as measured by relevant and available data (such as actual past sales); retail sales of a particular type of business, number of check-outs or employees, population, automobile registrations; or some similar factor.

A major cost consideration in marketing experiments is the time required to conduct a study. One of the best experimental designs in terms of reducing experimental variance is the Latin square design which rotates all treatments among all test units. However, this design takes much longer to run than other designs.   The researcher must therefore decide whether it is better for his particular needs to pay the cost in time required for the Latin square design or to pay in money for the increase in numbers of test units to achieve the same experimental error.

Another area of consideration in designing experiments is the extent of the data required.   It is important to ask whether one is interested only in estimating the effects of his treatments or whether he also wants to determine whether different types of test units respond differently to given treatments (in the statistical jargon which the reader may be acquainted with, these levels of data are referred to as *main effects* and *interactions*).   It may be that the analyst is more interested in one treatment than another, or interested in some interactions and not in others.   If so, he can design his experiment so as to maximize precision for a given quantity of resources or obtain the desired data for minimum cost and effort.

One of the most commonly accepted shibboleths is that unless one varies only one thing at a time, it will be impossible to infer causality.   This chapter will show that there is no difference in the logic underlying experiments with one set of treatments and one or more sets of classification variables and that underlying experiments with two or more sets of treatments.

Finally, there are situations in which it is either physically impossible or experimentally difficult to test all treatments within a given stratum of test units.   For example, one may wish to evaluate eight flavor blends, but he finds that people become confused, sated, or bored if they taste more than four in a single taste session.   The designs which cope with such difficulties are known as *incomplete* designs; however, they are constructed to offer the researcher the complete set of comparisons he requires.

To sum up this discussion, it should be pointed out that the choice of design should be based upon rather straightforward considerations: the nature and complexity of the variables for which estimates are desired; the source and extent of variation among test units treated alike by the analyst; the resources, including time, available to him; and, finally, limitations on the number of particular types of test units or on their ability to respond to a number of treatments.

If the basic question is the choice of one consumer media mix versus others, the choice of optimum media advertising level, the optimum mix of consumer advertising and sales promotion/merchandising, and so on, then the appropriate test unit is a territory or market.   If the basic issue is one that operates at the store level—price, display devices, effect of shelf space or number of facings, package sizes, and the like on sales—then the appropriate test unit is a store. Similarly, there are certain problems where people are the appropriate unit. The universes of markets, stores, and people differ in size and variance.   Therefore, the choice of experimental design might well vary with the nature of the issue under investigation and the choice of appropriate test units.

The following discussion will attempt to elucidate the characteristics of various types of design so that the researcher will be able to consider their appropriateness for the various situations he encounters.   But neither these designs nor the substantially more complete range found in textbooks on experimental design represents the alternatives from which one must select.

CONTROL OF ONE "OTHER" VARIABLE

The simplest experimental design is the completely randomized one which assigns treatments to test units entirely by a chance process—any number of treatments can be tested and any number of test units allocated to each treatment. However, this design is seldom, if ever, used in marketing experiments because it implies that the test units either are approximately equal in size and responsiveness or that they are so numerous that the resulting experimental error will be small.

Therefore, let us begin our discussion of experimental design with *randomized blocks*, a technique which seeks to control a single "other" variable. In this design, test units are classified into groups or strata on the basis of some predetermined "other" variable. Some of the "other" variables which can be controlled in this fashion are store size or location; market shares possessed by the test brand or its major competitor; per capita or per household consumption levels for a product class; and city size or territory location.

The experimental procedure consists of dividing possible test units into groups on the basis of the "other" variable most significant for the marketing problem at issue and then applying all treatments to the test units within each group. In the analysis of the data, the results are separated into two major categories, differences between treatments and differences within treatments.[1]

The differences between treatments is unaffected by the "other" variable because each treatment has been used at all levels of this variable. The data indicating variation of results among test units receiving a given treatment may be subdivided into three separate subcategories: that due to the varying levels or types of the "other" variable; that due to the interaction of treatments and this variable; and that due to experimental error. Similarly, it is possible to measure the effect of the "other" variable unaffected by variations in treatment effectiveness since all treatments are used at all levels of the "other" variable.

The randomized block design is very flexible since it can accommodate any number of treatments and any number of test units per treatment. If one uses more than one test unit for each combination of treatment and the "other" factor, he can also measure the degree of interaction between experimental treatments and the "other" variable. The term *interaction* here refers to a situation where the effect of a particular treatment is not constant across all "other" variable levels.

Let us illustrate the concepts discussed so far by analyzing two sets of hypothetical data. First, we will deal with the simplest case—one test unit per treatment for each level of "other" variable.

The problem is the effect of the number of package facings upon sales of salt. The influence of store size on salt sales is essentially irrelevant to the experiment's purpose but this influence is controlled by the experimental design and analytical process in order that the assignment of displays to stores may avoid biasing the results or generating unduly large estimates of experimental error. (See [7] and [10] for real experiments on the effect of shelf space on sales; [10] uses a more complicated design.)

Let us express the data from Table 1 in algebraic terms before discussing their analysis. The process will also serve to present some of the assumptions underlying the analysis of variance. (See [2, chaps. 3, 4]; [20, chaps. 1–4, 7, 9]; and [24, chaps. 2, 3, 5].)

$$X_{ij} = \mu + \alpha_i + \beta_j + \varepsilon_{ij} \tag{1}$$

---

[1] This remark is based upon the assumption that the relevant data are the differences between treatments, not their absolute values. For most situations, information on the size of differences in effect between experimental treatments will suffice to answer the marketing questions involved. This is fortunate because it is much easier to evaluate such differences or changes than to estimate absolute levels of response to marketing or advertising variables.

where X_{ij}, the figure shown in any cell of Table 1, is derived from the sum of four quantities:

μ = the overall mean

α = the effect of treatment i (numbers of facings)

β = the effect of block j (store size)

ε_{ij} = an error term. This is regarded as being drawn at random for a nor- mally distributed population with zero mean and standard deviation, σ

ε_{ij} is a very important statistic since it will be used to test the significance of the variation found among the data on treatment and store-size effects.

Instead of trying to work with Equation (1) in the form shown, let us adapt it to a form suitable for a desk calculator.

1. Correction term for overall mean, $C = \Sigma(X_{ij})^2/ij$
2. Total sum of squares $= \Sigma(X_{ij})^2 - C$

The whole concept lying behind the analysis of variance is the partition of the total variation of the experimental data into separate segments, each asso-

TABLE 1 Units of Packaged Salt Sold during January 1969 from One, Two, and Three Package-Facing Displays among Stores Classified by Size

Number of package facings on shelf	Store size		Total
	Large	Small	
One	73	25	98
Two	103	45	148
Three	115	58	173
Total	291	128	419

ciated with some aspect of the design or the underlying variability of the system.

In the remainder of this chapter, a dot notation will be used: the substitution of a dot for a letter in the subscript of a term will indicate summation over the corresponding variable.

3. Total sum of squares for treatments $= \Sigma(X_{i.})^2/j - C$
4. Total sum of squares for blocks $= \Sigma(X.j)^2/^2i - C$
5. Error = total SS − treatment and block SS

In terms of the data in Table 1, the steps are as follows:

Correction term $= (419)^2/6 = 29{,}260.17$

Total sum of squares $= (73)^2 + (25)^2 + \ldots + (58)^2 - C = 5{,}916.83$

Total treatment SS $= \frac{1}{2}[98^2 + 148^2 + 173^2] - C = 1{,}458.33$

Total blocks SS $= \frac{1}{3}[291^2 + 128^2] - C = 4{,}428.17$

Error $= 5{,}916.83 - (1{,}458.33 + 4{,}428.17) = 30.33$

These results are shown in Table 2, along with their associated degrees of free- dom. These degrees are, respectively, $i - 1$, $j - 1$, and $[(ij - 1) - (i - 1) - (j - 1)]$.

The mean square entries merely consist of the sums of squares divided by their respective degrees of freedom. Now we have three estimates of variance, one derived from the treatments, one derived from the blocks or store sizes, and one based upon experimental error. The appropriate test of the null hypothesis that either one of the first two variance estimates differs from the third only through chance sampling fluctuation is

$$F = \frac{j\sigma_t^2 + \sigma_e^2}{\sigma_e^2} \quad \text{and} \quad F = \frac{i\sigma_b^2 + \sigma_e^2}{\sigma_e^2} \tag{2}$$

where σ_t^2, σ_b^2, and σ_e^2 stand for the mean squares for treatment, block, and error, respectively. Thus, if σ_t^2 or σ_b^2 were zero, as would be the case if there were no treatment or block effects, then the expected value of F would be unity.

In practice, tabled values of the F distribution are evaluated in terms of two numbers of degrees of freedom: one associated with the numerator of the ratio —a treatment or block mean square; the other, with the denominator. Such tables conventionally assign their columns to the greater mean square (in almost all instances, this is a treatment or block mean square) while the rows correspond to the smaller.

TABLE 2   Analysis of Variance of Packaged Salt Sales

Source of variation	Sum of squares	Degrees of freedom	Mean square	F
Displays	1,458.33	2	729.22	48.0*
Store size	4,428.17	1	4,428.2	291.3†
Error	30.33	2	15.2	
Total	5,916.83			

* Significant at the 5 percent level of significance.
† Significant at the 1 percent level of significance.

In our example, the F ratios for the displays and store sizes are 48.0 and 291.3, respectively. Although these F ratios are very much larger than 1 because of the very small numbers of degrees of freedom involved, the treatment effect was statistically significant only at the 5 percent level of confidence. The tabled $F_{.01}$ value (for 2,2 degrees of freedom) is 99.

Our discussion of this hypothetical experiment is interrupted here to point out that if one had used a completely randomized design—that is, had assigned these displays to stores as diversified in salt sales as these entirely by chance without previously stratifying them by size—he would have required over 300 stores to obtain an error as small as the randomized block design produced with six stores [6, pp. 112–114].

It is nice to know that the displays differ significantly in their sales effectiveness, but this knowledge should be the beginning of our analysis rather than the end. Our fundamental interest is not in there being significant variations among treatment means or block means but in determining which means really differ from others of the same type. A number of procedures might be used to test simultaneously all comparisons among means, differing slightly in their properties [20, chap. 3]; [22, chap. 10]; [24, chap. 3]; we shall suggest Tukey's. It is conservative and has the property that all tests of differences between pairs of means have levels of significance which do not exceed α, where α is the prespecified level of confidence, usually 1 or 5 percent.

The pair-wise differences between the three displays in terms of row mean minus column means are:

	2	3
1	25.0	37.5
2		12.5

To evaluate such pair-wise differences of treatment means, we need the Tukey statistic

$$k = k^* \sqrt{\frac{\text{experimental error}}{n}} \tag{3}$$

where k^* is read from a table of the upper points of the Studentized range at the desired level of risk, and n is the number of test units involved in generating the treatment means.

The k^* values are found at the intersection of the appropriate column and row of the tabled values in the upper points of the Studentized range; the column corresponds to the number of treatments and the row corresponds to the number of degrees of freedom for error ([2], [22], and [24] offer such tables). For three treatments and two degrees of freedom for error, $k^*_{.05} = 8.33$ and $k^*_{.01} = 19.02$; therefore $k^*_{.05} = 8.33 \sqrt{\dfrac{15.2}{2}} = 23.0$ and $k_{.01} = 52.4$.

Thus it can be said that if one had previously set 5 percent as his criterion level of significance, he would be able to report that both multiunit facing conditions generated significantly greater sales results than a single-unit facing; however, the lead of the three-package display over the two-unit display was not statistically significant.[2]

Two points should be noted. The choice of the proper level of statistical significance to use in evaluating experimental results should not rest upon convention or arbitrary choices but should be based upon the economics and risk aspects of the problem under investigation [2, chap. 10]; [13, chaps. 2, 9]. Also, the choice of a criterion level of statistical significance must be made in advance of the analysis; it should be part of the planning phase when one is deciding upon the number of test units to be assigned to each treatment.

Interaction between Treatments and "Other" Variable

One may often suspect that the effect of various treatments depends upon the circumstances of their use. There are many such situations: in the shelf-facing experiment just discussed, the effect of increased shelf facings may well differ in larger and smaller stores (the careful reader has no doubt noticed that, in Table 1, the amounts of increase for two and three facings over that produced by one were greater in the large stores than in the small ones); sales response to advertising expenditures for a brand may well depend upon the strength or quality of its distributor force or per capita consumption of the product category, and so on. Technically, the interdependence of two variables is known as interaction.

In order to detect and measure such interactions, it is necessary to have two or more test units per treatment–"other" variable combination. If the experi-

---

[2] When treatments differ quantitatively it is possible to fit regression equations to the results, thus deriving a mathematical model of the response mechanism. See [22, chap. 15] for a discussion of curve fitting by use of Fisher's orthogonal polynomial procedure.

ment on the effect of the number of shelf facings on sales of packaged salt had been expanded so that there were two stores for each cell of Table 1, the results might be those shown in Table 3.

TABLE 3   Units of Packaged Salt Sold during January 1969 from One, Two, and Three Package-Facing Displays among Stores Classified by Size

| Package facings on shelf | Store size | | Total |
	Large	Small	
One	73	25	
	68	33	
	—	—	
	141	58	199
Two	103	35	
	95	45	
	—	—	
	198	80	278
Three	115	39	
	125	44	
	—	—	
	240	83	323
Total	579	221	800

The analysis of variance shown previously must be modified slightly to take into consideration the fact that the data of the experiment fall into two parts: Some of the data arise from stores treated alike by the researcher while others arise from situations directly manipulated or chosen differently. For example, in the upper left-hand corner of Table 3, we have 73- and 68-unit sales of packaged salt from two large stores, each using single-unit facings; the difference between those two results is an estimate of the underlying variability in the consumer-store population involved. The differences between the two-store subtotals, say between 141 and 198 or between 141 and 58, on the other hand, were caused by the researcher's variation of treatments or "other" conditions, in this case, store size. Thus we shall first subdivide the variation of the data of Table 3 about their overall mean: variation within subclasses, which provides our estimate of experimental error; and variation between subclasses. The latter will be further subdivided into treatment, store size, and interaction sums of squares.

Incidentally, we shall refer to the treatment and store size as main effects; interaction terms are indicated by convention as treatment times store size because the number of degrees of freedom of an interaction term is the product of the numbers of degrees of freedom of the main effects involved.

1. Correction term for overall mean $C = \Sigma(X_{ijk})^2/ijk$
2. Total sum of squares $= \Sigma(X_{ijk})^2 - C$
3. Sum of squares for subclasses $= \dfrac{1}{k}\Sigma(X_{ij\cdot})^2 - C$
4. Sum of squares for treatments $= \dfrac{1}{jk}\Sigma(X_i\ldots)^2 - C$

5. Sum of squares for store sizes $= \dfrac{1}{ik}(\Sigma X_{\cdot j \cdot})^2 - C$

6. Sum of squares for interaction $= (3) - [(4) + (5)]$

7. Sum of squares for error $= \displaystyle\sum_{ij}\left[\sum_k (X_{ijk})^2 - (X_{ij\cdot})^2\right]$

7. Sum of squares for error $= (3) - (2)$

In terms of our data:

$C = (800)^2/3 \cdot 2 \cdot 2 = 53{,}333.33$

Total sum of squares
$$= (73)^2 + (68)^2 + \ldots + (44)^2 - 53{,}333.33 = 13{,}524.67$$
Sum of squares for subclasses
$$= \tfrac{1}{2}(141^2 + 198^2 + \ldots + 83^2) - C = 13{,}335.67$$
Sum of squares for treatments $= \tfrac{1}{4}(199^2 + \ldots + 323^2) - C = 1{,}970.17$

Sum of squares for store sizes $= \tfrac{1}{6}(579^2 + 221^2) - C = 10{,}680.33$

Sum of squares for interaction
$$= 13{,}335.67 - (1970.17 + 10{,}680.33) = 685.17$$
Direct estimate of sum of squares for error
$$= [73^2 + 68^2 - \tfrac{1}{2}(141)^2 + \ldots + 39^2 + 44^2 - \tfrac{1}{2}(83)^2] = 189.00$$
Indirect estimate of sum of squares for error
$$= 13{,}524.67 - 13{,}335.67 = 189.00$$

We have shown both the direct and indirect procedures for calculation of the sum of squares for error both as an arithmetic check and as a further demonstration of the variance partitioning process. Let us now put the results of these calculations into Table 4.

TABLE 4   Analysis of Variance of Packaged Salt Sales

Source of variation	Sum of squares	Degrees of freedom	Mean square	F
Displays	1,970.17	2	985.1	31.3*
Store sizes	10,680.33	1	10,680.3	339.1*
Displays × store sizes	685.17	2	342.1	10.9†
Error	189.00	6	31.5	

* Significant at the 1 percent level of confidence.

† Significant at the 5 percent level of confidence.

The significant interaction between the displays and store size arises from there being different patterns of response to the various treatments in the two sizes of store. Thus, the average marginal increases in units of salt sold with increased facings by store size are:

Number of facings	Large stores	Small stores
2 versus 1	28.5	11.0
3 versus 2	21.0	1.5

Another way of describing significant interactions is to say that they arise when the results in the various treatment–"other" variable cells *cannot* be estimated from the simple addition of the average results for the corresponding treatment and "other" variable levels. In such cases, one must temper the interpretation of apparently significant treatment effects because there is clearly no one treatment effect. The overall treatment averages may well fit none of the data for various levels of the "other" variable.

Another consideration in cases of significant interactions arises from the nature of the process by which the particular treatments and "other" variable levels were selected. The model of the randomized block data expressed by Equation (1) assumes that all variates are fixed except for a single random-error term, that is, no sampling is involved and no population generalizations are to be drawn from the data at hand. This type of model is referred to as Model I or the fixed model. However, the experimenter may regard either or both treatment and block effects as samples drawn from a normal population. For example, if the particular sets of stores used in this experiment were drawn by random sampling from two strata, each containing a larger number of such stores, the size effect of 59.7 units found in Table 3 ([579–221]/6) is a sample value rather than a constant. In circumstances like that, the researcher may wish to estimate both the store-size effect and its sampling variation. A similar question might arise with regard to a treatment effect.

We have referred to the situation in which both treatment and block effects are regarded as constant, as in the Model I case. By convention, if both main effects are regarded as variables whose average and variance are to be estimated, we have a Model II situation; and, finally, if one main effect is a constant and the other is a variable, we have a Model III experiment. These situations are also known as fixed, random, and mixed-effect, respectively.

There are no differences in the process of calculating sums of squares, degrees of freedom, or mean squares for all three models. Differences, stemming from the experiment's purpose, affect the interpretation of F tests when an interaction term is found to be statistically significant.

The F test requires the variances used in the numerator and denominator to be identical in structure except for one component of variance corresponding to the null hypothesis under test. If we assume that we have a mixed model and there is a significant interaction, the appropriate denominator for the treatment effect is not the error variance but the interaction variance [2, chap. 7]; [22, chap. 10–1]; [24, chap. 5]. When we redo the F test of the treatment effect in Table 4, we find the new F ratio to be 2.9, not even significant at the 25 percent level of significance.

Thus we find that the interpretation of the results of this experiment depends on the experimenter's original conception of the types of data to be obtained. If he has regarded both effects as constants, he will have shown that both are significant and interactive. If the treatment effect is regarded as constant but the store effect is a variable, he will have found that the treatment effect was not statistically significant but he will be able to estimate the variance of the store effect.[3]

In this perhaps overlong discussion, we have dealt with two major areas: concepts of experimental design and the analysis of variance. Subsequent sections will be shorter since we concentrate much more on experimental designs.

ASSUMPTIONS OF THE ANALYSIS OF VARIANCE

It is not enough to know how to carry out the arithmetical procedures of the analysis of variance. One must also ask whether the analysis is valid, that is, whether the data do not violate the assumptions underlying the analysis of variance and its decision rules. Researchers have found that the procedure is quite robust—in other words, that its results make sense even when there are

---

[3] The references cited in the preceding paragraph describe the procedures for estimating the components of variance of main effect and interaction terms.

departures from the strict observance of its technical requirements. However, under such circumstances, one should be conservative in selection of criterion values of significance, say by using 1 percent values for 5 percent confidence levels, since the great danger is in imputing causal effects where none exist [2, pp. 72–77]; [6, chap. 3]; [22, chap. 11]. The basic assumptions are:

1. Both the concepts of experimental design and the assumptions of the analysis of variance require that treatments be assigned to test units at random; by this we mean the use of some randomizing device rather than some haphazard allocation device.

2. The appropriate data are quantitative in nature and are normally distributed. Market research often generates or uses other types of data—nominal or ordinal data whose results are expressed in percentages or ranks. To handle such situations, one can use either transformations which change the scale of measurement or nonparametric techniques. Percentage data—recallers per sample or brand switchers per panel—depart from the requirements of the analysis of variance on two criteria: they are distributed binomially rather than normally; and their variance is proportional to the mean or population value, rather than being independent of it. The recommended transformation for percentage data is to the angle whose sine is the square root of the proportion or percentage; this is known as the arcsin transformation ([2], [22], and [24] offer tables of the arcsin transformation). Nonparametric procedures applicable to rank-order data have been developed by Kruskal and Wallis for one-way analyses of variance [23, pp. 184–193], and by Friedman for two-way analyses [23, pp. 166–172].

3. The model of analysis of variance requires additivity of effects with constant variance within groups of test units. Nonadditivity of effects is the greatest challenge to the assumptions of the analysis of variance—such a situation arises when main effects are formed by a multiplicative process, or when a test unit has come from a population different from that under investigation. Typically, one copes with such problems by converting the data to logarithms. Tests of homogeneity of variance within treatment groups should always precede the use of the analysis of variance [2, pp. 73–75]; [22, pp. 285–289]. If there are substantial differences among the within-group variances, one can either try the use of transformations, such as the square root transformation; or, if necessary, divide the data into groups of similar variance and analyze each group separately.

4. Finally, one should be aware of the fact that substantial variation in cell frequencies—numbers of test units per treatment—causes correlations among classification variables; hence, analytical procedures must be adapted to cope with this problem [19]; [22, pp. 268–274, 375–391].

CONTROL OF TWO "OTHER" VARIABLES

It is a simple step from controlling one "other" variable via experimental design to controlling two. The latter is done by the use of perhaps the most widely known of all experimental designs, the Latin square. Visualize a table made up of rows based on one "other" variable, such as store size, and columns based upon a second "other" variable, such as ownership type or average household income within the trading area. Treatments are assigned to cells at random, subject to the restriction that each treatment can appear only once in each row and each column. Because this design requires n columns and n rows for n treatments, n^2 test units are demanded. Hence its name: the Latin square. Conventionally, a Latin square is described in terms of its number of rows and columns.   To illustrate, Table 5 shows a 3 × 3 Latin square used in a test of promotional expenditures in promoting the sales of fluid milk [5].

TABLE 5   3 × 3 Latin Square for Three Levels of Milk Promotion

Time period	Chattanooga	Knoxville	Rochester
1	A	B	C
2	C	A	B
3	B	C	A

Treatments: A = Normal promotion (approximately 2 cents per capita annually).
B = Medium promotion (approximately 17 cents per capita annually).
C = Heavy promotion (approximately 32 cents per capita annually).

With this design, each expenditure level appears in all three markets. Therefore, sales at all promotional levels are subjected to whatever peculiarities of milk consumption are associated with each of the markets.   Also, each expenditure level was in effect during each six-month time period; thus all expenditure levels were tested in both high-consumption and low-consumption seasons.   This design guarded against the possibility that one level of promotion expenditure would gain an advantage in the experiment because it happened to be used when milk consumption was at a peak, or would suffer because of being used in periods of low consumption.

During the actual test, the design shown in Table 5 was further refined, as will be discussed later.

The model for a Latin square experiment (with fixed effects) is:

$$X_{ijk} = \mu + \alpha_i + \beta_j + \gamma_k + \epsilon_{ijk, \ i, \ j, \ k=1 \ \dots \ n} \tag{4}$$

where μ = population mean
α = treatment effect
β = row effect
γ = column effect
ϵ = error, which is assumed normally distributed with zero mean and unit standard deviation

The basic Latin square experiment uses one test unit per cell and one Latin square per experiment, relying upon the assumption of no interactions between the row and column "other" variables and the treatments.   Under these conditions, the appropriate analysis of variance partitions the total variance and numbers of degrees of freedom into treatment, row, column effects, and experimental error, as shown in Table 6.

The notation used here uses dots to indicate processes of summarization. X_{ijk} refers to a particular entry found in treatment i, row j, and column k, with treatment totals as $X_{i..}$; row totals as $X_{.j.}$; column totals as $X_{..k}$ and the overall total as $X_{...}$.

There are many situations when the researcher will find it useful or necessary to elaborate on the basic Latin square design by partial or complete repetition (the technical term is replication) of the original design.   First of all, the basic Latin square controls the order of using each treatment; that is, each treatment is used first, second, and so on, an equal number of times across all test units.   However, one square cannot control for all sequences of use or all

TABLE 6   Analysis of n × n Latin Square Design

Rows		*a.* Data columns			
	1		2 ...	n	Total
1					$\sum X_{.1.}$
2					$\sum X_{.2.}$
n				$\sum X \ldots_n$	$\sum\sum X_{.n.}$
Total	$\sum X_{..1}$		$\sum X_{..2} \ldots$	$\sum X \ldots_n$	$\sum\sum X \ldots$
Treatment total: $A = \sum X_{1..}$,	$B = \sum X_{2..} \ldots$		$N = \sum X_{n..}$		

b. Sums of squares

1. Correction term: $C = (\sum\sum X_{...})^2/n$
2. Total sum of squares $= \sum\sum\sum(X_{ijk})^2 - C$
3. Sum of squares for rows $= \dfrac{1}{n}\sum_j(\sum X_{.j.})^2 - C$
4. Sum of squares for columns $= \dfrac{1}{n}\sum_k(\sum X_{..k})^2 - C$
5. Sum of squares for treatments $= \dfrac{1}{n}\sum_i(\sum X_{i..})^2 - C$
6. Sum of squares for error $= (2) - (3) - (4) - (5)$

c. Degrees of freedom *(df)*

Rows	$n-1$
Columns	$n-1$
Treatments	$n-1$
Error	$n^2 - 3n + 2$
Total	$n^2 - 1$

combinations of one level of a variable with all other pairs of levels of the other two variables. For example, in Table 5, although each treatment is used once first, second, and third, A was followed by C twice and never by B. Similarly, B is preceded by C twice but never by A.

An example of an experimental design which balances pair and trio sequences of usage for a 3 × 3 Latin square is given in Table 7. This is also known as a double changeover design since the treatment sequence is reversed in the second square.

TABLE 7   Controlled Sequence of Exposure to Treatments in 3 × 3 Latin Squares

	Replicate I			*Replicate II*		
	Test units or subjects					
Market size	1	2	3	4	5	6
X	A	B	C	A	B	C
Y	B	C	A	C	A	B
Z	C	A	B	B	C	A

A very important modification of the Latin square design arises when treatments are rotated through test units, as in the case of the milk-promotion experiment mentioned earlier, and when one wishes to measure possible carryover effects; that is, the effect which treatments exert on subsequent periods [6, pp. 127–142].

For both controlling and measuring carryover effect, one needs the Table 8 type of design, illustrated by the one used for the milk-promotion experiment [5].

TABLE 8   Experimental Design Used to Measure Both Direct and Carryover Effects of Fluid Milk Promotions

Time period	*Square I*			*Square II*		
	Chatta-nooga	Knoxville	Rochester	Clarksburg	Sioux Falls	Neosho Valley
1	A	B	C	A	B	C
2	B(a)	C(b)	A(c)	C(a)	A(b)	B(c)
3	C(b)	A(c)	B(a)	B(c)	C(a)	A(b)
4	C(c)	A(a)	B(b)	B(b)	C(c)	A(a)

Capital letters represent direct effects of treatments; lower-case letters in parentheses represent carryover effects.

It can be seen that Table 8 is the same as Table 7 except for repetition of the last treatment for an additional period. The addition of the fourth period increases the precision of the estimate of the carryover effects. In this experiment, because the exact length of the carryover influence was not known, promotion for each six-month time period was concentrated in its first three months. Thus, although the analytical technique concerned itself only with carryover from one period to the next, nine months were allowed for the dissipation of the carryover influence.

Analysis of the experimental data revealed significant direct and carryover effects of the promotion expenditures; in fact, the carryover effects of the medium and heavy promotional levels were two-thirds as great as their direct effect, as shown in Table 9.

TABLE 9   Incremental Effects of Increased Promotion on Fluid Milk Sales in Six Markets, March 1963—February 1965

(Data are increases in 1,000 pounds per day over normal promotion)

Effect	*Promotion level*	
	Medium	Heavy
Direct	8*	10†
Carryover	5*	7*
Combined effect	13†	17†

* Significant at 5 percent level.[1]
† Significant at 1 percent level.
[1] Detailed descriptions of analytical procedures applicable to changeover designs can be found in Banks [2, Chap. 6] and Henderson, Hind, and Brown [15].

The critical question in dealing with treatments of substantially differing costs is not whether the results are statistically significant but whether the experimental improvements are economically justified. It was found in this case that both levels of stepped-up promotion expenditures generated such substantial increases in milk sales that the increase in returns to farmers exceeded the cost of the extra promotion effort. However, the 15-cents-per-capita effort (the medium promotion) was better than the heavy-promotion level, since it generated almost twice as many extra dollars of profit yet cost slightly more than half as much.

Largely for the sake of logical completeness, let us point out that an experimental design exists for the control of three "other" variables, known as the Greco-Latin square. In this design, a pair of letters, one Latin and one Greek, is assigned at random to each cell of a square subject to the following restrictions: as before, the Latin letters appear once in each row and each column; the Greek letters appear once in each row, once in each column, and once with each Latin letter. Examples of 3 × 3 and 4 × 4 Greco-Latin squares are:

A α	B β	C γ
B γ	C α	A β
C β	A γ	B α

A α	B γ	C δ	D β
B β	A δ	D γ	C α
C γ	D α	A β	B δ
D δ	C β	B α	A γ

FACTORIAL EXPERIMENTS: TESTING TWO OR MORE SETS OF TREATMENTS SIMULTANEOUSLY

The distinction in the preceding section between treatments and "other" variables is arbitrary. Actually, in such situations a researcher deliberately chose both a set of treatments and a set or two of "other" variables for the sake of the resulting data themselves and the interpretation or generalizations to be drawn from them. Both types of conditions are described as *main effects;* another term used in the statistical literature to describe these is *factor;* the described experimental designs used treatment factors and classification factors. Exactly the same research concepts and procedures are used in experiments involving two or more treatment factors and in those with only one treatment factor and one or more classification factors. Where differences exist, they stem from the fact that, whereas one quite willingly assumes no interaction exists between treatment and classification factors, the reverse expectation usually applies to various treatment factors. Therefore, experiments involving two or more treatment factors—here referred to as factorial experiments—usually are designed to measure at least some of the interactions among the factors.

Factorial experiments are advantageous because one learns a great deal about experimental variables. He can analyze the significance among levels (the various alternative forms or amounts tested) of each treatment factor as before, and he will also know whether he can generalize his findings, since he will have evidence on what happens when two or more such variables operate in combination.

The dimensions of a factorial experiment are indicated by the number of factors and the number of levels of each factor; for example, in a 2 × 4 × 5 factorial experiment, there are three factors having two, four, and five levels, respectively.   It can be seen that as the number of factors or the number of levels within factors increases, the number of treatment combinations rises rather rapidly.

Before discussing experimental designs useful for large numbers of treatment combinations, let us outline the analysis of an hypothetical $2 \times 3 \times 2$ factorial experiment on canned sweet potatoes.

Factor A represents use of sales notices for the brand on supermarket shopping cars: some versus none.

Factor B represents reductions of shelf price: 0, 1 cent, 2 cents.

Factor C represents use of coupons good for 5 cents on purchase of related item: yes or no.

It was decided to apply each treatment combination to 2 different stores, making 24 stores in all.   Finally, because the stores were heterogeneous in size, the decision was made to apply the treatment combinations to stores by means of a completely randomized design, and to express the results not in their original form but in terms of units per $1,000 of store grocery sales.[4] The data are shown in Table 10.

TABLE 10   Sales of Canned Sweet Potatoes under Three Types of Promotional Effort

(Units per $1,000 grocery sales from two stores)

Shopping-cart notice	Related-item coupon						Subtotal
	Yes			No			
	Price reduction			Price reduction			
	0	−1	−2	0	−1	−2	
Yes	36	38	40	40	42	44	240
No	12	20	30	8	16	33	119
Subtotal	48	58	70	48	58	77	359

Before these data can be analyzed, Table 10 must be collapsed into three two-way tables, as shown in Table 11.

By using Table 11 to calculate the sum of squares of subclasses, the analysis of variance table (Table 12) is obtained.

In examining an analysis of variance table, one should start with the bottom and work upward—from the interaction terms to the main effects.   One can see that only one of the four interaction terms, A × B, has an F ratio greater than one; however, it is below the criterion level of significance.   With the problem of significant interaction terms not an issue, we can point out that both the shopping-cart notices and the shelf-price reductions had significant effects on canned sweet potato sales, with the shopping-cart notices actually much

[4] This use of item sales as a ratio of total departmental or store sales is a very simple and useful form of covariance.   Covariance is a statistical procedure, based upon regression analysis, which is used to adjust treatment effects and experimental error on the basis of measurement of environmental conditions.   (See [2, chap. 5]; [15]; [22, chap. 14].)   Floyd and Stout [9] illustrate the use of a multiple-regression model using discrete dummy variables in order to remove the effect of unplanned changes in their experimental situation from adversely affecting their estimates of error.

TABLE 11   Collapsed Form of Table 10

Shopping-cart notice	10a. Shopping-cart notice by price reduction: AB				10b. Shopping-cart notice by coupon: AC			
	0	−1	−2	Total		Yes	No	Total
Yes	76	80	84	240	Yes	114	126	240
No	20	36	63	119	No	62	57	119
Subtotal	96	116	147	359	Subtotal	176	183	359

	10c. Price reduction by coupon: BC			
	0	−1	−2	Total
Coupon				
Yes	48	58	70	176
No	48	58	77	183
Subtotal	96	116	147	359

TABLE 12   Analysis of Variance of Canned Sweet Potato Sales

Source of variation	Sum of squares	Degrees of freedom	Mean square	F
Main effects				
A: Shopping-cart notices	610.0417	1	610.0417	38.63*
B: Price reductions	165.0834	1	82.5417	5.23†
C: Coupons	2.0417	1	2.0417	0.13
1st-order interactions				
A × B	79.0833	2	38.0416	2.41
A × C	12.0416	1	12.0416	0.76
B × C	4.0833	2	2.0416	0.13
2d-order interaction				
A × B × C	4.0834	2	2.0416	0.13
Experimental error (within cell)	189.5000	12	15.7916	
Total	1,065.9584	23		

* Significant at the 1 percent level.
† Significant at the 5 percent level.

more influential than the price reductions. The use of coupons good only on related items had no effect on canned sweet potato sales.

It can be seen that this single experiment permitted the analyst not merely to evaluate each of the main effects simultaneously but also to indicate whether responses to these various experimental variables were independent or not. The data make clear that store coupons consistently had no effect whether they were used with shopping-cart notices or with shelf-price reductions. Also, although the results are merely suggestive but not definitive, it looks as though the combination of shopping-cart notices and price reductions was more effective than might be surmised from the effect of each acting alone.

To comment upon the virtues of factorial experiments in another way, let us point out that had this experiment been run as three separate tests, each with eight stores, the experimental error for the price-reduction test would have had five degrees of freedom, and its 5.23 F ratio would not have been considered significant at the 5 percent level. More important, no information on the interactions would have been available.

Thus, factorial experiments often increase the number of degrees of freedom for error. Hence, they improve the sensitivity of the overall experiment; also, they measure and evaluate interaction terms.

As noted earlier, the number of treatment combinations for a factorial experiment can become quite large. However, if one can assume that higher-order interactions (those arising from several factors simultaneously) are relatively small compared to main effects and lower-order interactions (those arising from factors interacting only a few at a time), only a small fraction of the complete set need be included in an experiment. Thus, one can economize in expense, and research is made feasible where homogeneous groups of test units are limited or where wearout occurs among test subjects. There is a cost—the confounding (or comingling) of the effect of higher-order interactions with main effects and the lower-order interactions. (See [6, chaps. 6–8] and [8, chap. 7] for principles underlying the use of confounded designs.)

Another advantage of confounding is that it permits one to conduct fairly wide-ranging experiments involving many different treatment combinations even though the test units have relatively few homogeneous test units per stratum. Such designs are particularly useful in experiments with human beings where the researcher fears that sensitivity or motivation may drop off if the subject participates more than a few times. The disadvantage of experimental designs which use confounding is that often their analysis is much more complicated than analysis of similar designs without confounding.

INCOMPLETE BLOCK DESIGNS

The preceding two paragraphs provide a bridge to a group of designs where a block or group of test units will receive fewer than the complete set of treatments or treatment combinations. Very often, need for such designs arises in taste and preference testing where subjects have increasing difficulty in making meaningful choices as the number of choices rises. For this purpose, it is quite common to use a general class of designs known as balanced incomplete blocks —a block is usually a trial by an individual test subject. In these designs, any pair of treatments appears together equally often within some blocks; hence the same standard error may be applied to every pair of treatments. Also, the statistical analysis is facilitated, since each treatment total is adjusted in a single operation for all the blocks in which the treatment appears.

Let us illustrate a balanced incomplete block design with Table 13, which shows nine treatments, tested in groups of threes.

TABLE 13   Balanced Design for Nine Treatments in Blocks of Three Units

Blocks				Blocks				Blocks				Blocks			
(1)	1	2	3	(4)	1	4	7	(7)	1	8	6	(10)	1	5	9
(2)	4	5	6	(5)	2	5	8	(8)	4	2	9	(11)	7	2	6
(3)	7	8	9	(6)	3	6	9	(9)	7	5	3	(12)	4	8	3

Every pair of treatments can be found to occur once, and only once, in the same block over the complete design. For example, treatment 1 occupies the same block with 2 and 3 in the first group of three blocks, with 4 and 7 in the second, 6 and 8 in the third, and 5 and 9 in the fourth. Note that each treatment occurs once and only once in each group of three blocks; hence, each group of three blocks may be considered a replicate of the desired set of comparisons.

Four major categories of balanced incomplete block designs are of interest. The type shown in Table 13 is known as a lattice design. In such designs, k^2 treatments are arranged in blocks of size k, where k is a prime number. Also, the blocks can be grouped into separate replicates.

However, there are cases when it is not possible to form complete replicates from the blocks available. Let k, as before, equal the number of test units per block; let t be the number of treatments, and b the number of blocks; then $r = bk/t$. If r is not an integer, we have a situation where the blocks cannot be grouped into separate replicates. Designs which operate under these conditions are known as incomplete block designs.

It is possible to lay out balanced lattice designs in such a way that each pair of treatments will occur together an equal number of times in both the same row and the same column. Such designs are known as quasi-Latin or lattice squares. One such example is shown in Table 14.

TABLE 14   Balanced Design for Nine Treatments in Four Lattice Squares

Replication I				*Replication II*				*Replication III*				*Replication IV*			
Row	Column			Row	Column			Row	Column			Row	Column		
	(1)	(2)	(3)		(4)	(5)	(6)		(7)	(8)	(9)		(10)	(11)	(12)
(1)	1	2	3	(4)	1	4	7	(7)	1	6	8	(10)	1	9	5
(2)	4	5	6	(5)	2	5	8	(8)	9	2	4	(11)	6	2	7
(3)	7	8	9	(6)	3	6	9	(9)	5	7	3	(12)	8	4	3

Analogously, it is possible to take balanced incomplete block designs and rework them into the equivalent Latin square set of restrictions. For example, seven treatments tested in blocks of three test units could be arranged as shown in Table 15.

TABLE 15   Balanced Design for Seven Treatments in an Incomplete Latin Square

Row	Column (block)						
	(1)	(2)	(3)	(4)	(5)	(6)	(7)
(1)	1	2	3	4	5	6	7
(2)	2	3	4	5	6	7	1
(3)	4	5	6	7	1	2	3

Because this design could represent the first three rows of a 7×7 Latin square, it has been called an incomplete Latin square; but it is also known as a Youden square after its originator, W. J. Youden.

Cochran and Cox list a substantial number of balanced incomplete block designs—in most plans, the blocks contain six or fewer units [6, pp. 390–394]. They subdivide the plans into five types:

Type I: Designs arranged in replications
Type II: Designs arranged in groups of replications
Type III: Designs not arranged in replications or groups of replications
Type IV: Designs where the number of treatments equals the number of blocks
Type V: Small experiments

Analysis of Variance for Balanced Incomplete Block Designs

Since all treatments do not appear in the same block of balanced incomplete block designs (using this term in its broadest sense), treatment effects are partially confounded with block effects and vice versa. Although the primary purpose of the experiment is to obtain estimates of treatment effects free of block effects, we go about this in a roundabout fashion. First, we find block effects unbiased by treatment effects, and then we use those findings to adjust the treatment effects. The adjusted treatment totals utilize both intrablock and interblock information.

The following experiment deals with $t = 6$ treatments arranged in blocks of size $k = 3$. For balance, 10 blocks are required but they cannot be arranged in distinct replications although each treatment is tested $r = 5$ times. It will be seen that each treatment is paired with each of the other treatments in a common block $\lambda = 2$ times [24, pp. 486–489].

Subjects were assigned at random to each of the 10 three-picture sequences. Within each sequence, the order in which the pictures were shown was independently randomized. The scores shown in Table 16 are readings on a 15-point preference scale (let us ignore, for the purposes of this analysis, the fact that such data may not meet the interval-scale requirements of the analysis of variance).

TABLE 16   Preference Scores for Six Advertising Illustrations

(Illustrations identified by letter, scores by number)

Subject	Scores			Total	Subject	Scores			Total
1	A3,	B 4,	E 9	16	6	B 4,	C 7,	D 6	17
2	A6,	B 5,	F11	22	7	B 5,	C 8,	E11	24
3	A5,	C 9,	D 9	23	8	B 8,	D 8,	D12	28
4	A8,	C10,	F13	31	9	C10,	E13,	F12	35
5	A7,	D10,	E14	31	10	D10,	E15,	F14	39

The first step in the analysis is given in the two left-hand columns of Table 17 in which T_i represents the sum of the five scores given to treatment i. B_i is the sum of the r blocks in which treatment i appears.

TABLE 17   Work Table for Adjusting Treatment Means

Illustration	T_i	B_i	$Q_i = 3T_i - B_i$	$W_i = 3T_i - 5B_i + 2G$
A	29	123	−36	4
B	26	107	−29	75
C	44	130	2	14
D	43	138	−9	−29
E	62	145	41	−7
F	62	155	31	−57
Total	266	798	0	0

The quantity Q_i provides an intrablock estimate of treatment effects, where $Q_i = kT_i - B_i$. Similarly, W_i is an estimate of the block effects in which treatment i appears. In general, for balanced incomplete block designs,

$$W_i = (t - k)T_i - (t - 1)B_i + (k - 1)G$$

One other element is required before we launch upon the analysis of variance of these data for blocks adjusted for treatment effects—the efficiency of this type of incomplete block design relative to a complete randomized block design: $E = t(k - 1)/k(t - 1)$. In our example, $E = 6(2)/3(5)$, or 0.8.

TABLE 18   Computation of Sums of Squares

Total	$= \sum X^2 - G^2/rt$	$= 311.47$	
Treatments (unadj.)	$= \sum(T_i^2)/r - G^2/rt$	$= 239.47$	
Blocks (adjusted)	$= \sum(B_j^2)/k + \sum(Q_i^2)/(k^2rE) - \sum(T_i^2)/r - \sum G^2/rt = 65.78$		
Intrablock error	$= \sum X^2 - \sum(B_j^2)* - \sum(Q_i^2)/k^2rE = 6.22$		

* The block B_j here refers to the original block totals of Table 16, not the adjusted block totals B_i of Table 17.

The calculations are shown in Table 18. Incidentally, it is possible to check these calculations, taking advantage of the tautology:

SS(blocks unadjusted for treatments) + SS(treatments adjusted for blocks)
    = SS(blocks adjusted for treatments) + SS(treatments unadjusted for blocks).

SS blocks unadjusted for treatments $= \sum(B_j)^2/k - G^2/rt = 170.14$
SS treatments adjusted for blocks $= \sum(Q_i)^2/k^2rE$ $= 135.11$
Thus $170.14 + 135.11$ $= 65.78 + 239.47$ $= 305.25$

In Table 19, E_b refers to the between-blocks error and E_e to the intrablock error term—the experimental error.

TABLE 19   Summary of Analysis of Variance, Unadjusted Treatments

Source	Sum of squares	Degree of freedom	Mean square
Treatments (unadjusted)	239.47	$(t - 1) = 5$	
Blocks (adjusted)	65.78	$(b - 1) = 9$	$7.31 = E_b$
Intrablock error	6.22	$(tr - t - b + 1) = 15$	$0.42 = E_e$
Total		$(tr - 1) = 29$	

Next, the treatment means must be adjusted to remove the effect of confounding treatment and block effect. There are two methods of adjusting treatment totals: one, T_i', based upon intra- as well as interblock information, and the other, T_i'', based solely on intrablock information.

$$T_i' = T_i + \mu W_i \qquad \text{where } \mu = \frac{(b - 1)(E_b - E_e)}{t(k - 1)(b - 1)E_b + (t - k)(b - t)E_e}$$

$$T_i'' = \frac{Q_i}{kE} + \frac{G}{t}$$

In our situation, $\mu = 0.078$.

The two sets of adjusted treatment totals are shown in Table 20. It can be seen that these two methods give almost identical results, the biggest difference being 0.6 for illustration B.

Table 20   Adjusted Illustration Total Scores

Illustration	T'_i	T''_i
A	29.31	29.33
B	31.85	32.25
C	45.09	45.17
D	40.74	40.58
E	61.45	61.42
F	57.55	57.25

Given the adjusted treatment totals, the sum of squares for adjusted treatments can be calculated exactly as for the unadjusted treatments except that the former is based upon the T'_i or T''_i. The sum of squares for treatments adjusted for blocks is 173.52; the corresponding mean square is 34.70.

Finally, the overall estimate of experimental error which adjusts the intrablock error must be calculated by adding the contribution for interblock variation.

$$E'_e = E_e[1 + (t - k)\mu] = 0.52$$

If the mean square for adjusted treatments is divided by the new estimate of experimental error, the result is an F ratio of 66.7, which is highly significant ($F_{.01}5, 15 = 4.56$).

The analysis of variance of balanced incomplete designs differs according to the nature of the design, the number of replications, and the restrictions. Table 21 summarizes the preliminary analyses of variance for several designs.

PARTIALLY BALANCED DESIGNS

Although a balanced design can be constructed with any number of treatments and with any number of units per block, the minimum number of replications may be too large for practical use. By eliminating or compromising the complete symmetry of the balanced designs, designs can be developed that offer the researcher substantially greater flexibility in the number of replicates.

Because of the lack of symmetry of partially balanced, incomplete block design, some pairs of treatments occur together within blocks more frequently than others. Thus, for each treatment, all other treatments can be sorted into groups, called associates, on the basis of the frequency in which they occur together in common blocks. The analyst can turn this fact into an advantage by designing his experiment so that the pairs of treatments of greatest significance appear together most frequently. (See [6, chaps. 10–13] and [24, chap. 9] for further discussion.)

DESIGNS WITH REPEATED MEASUREMENTS FROM TEST UNITS

In the preceding discussion, on a number of occasions a test unit was asked to respond to two or more different treatments over time. Except in the case of the double changeover design, an implicit assumption was made that there was

TABLE 21   Breakdowns of Degrees of Freedom, Preliminary Analyses of Variance, and Various Balanced Incomplete Block Designs

Source of variation	Simple lattice	Lattice squares	Replicated incomplete blocks	Youden squares
Replications	k	$r-1$	$r-1$	$k-1$
Treatments, unadjusted	k^2-1	k^2-1	$t-1$	$t-1$
Blocks (adjusted), within replications	k^2-1		$b-r$	$t-1$
Rows (adjusted)		$r(k-1)$		
Columns (adjusted)		$r(k-1)$		
Intrablock error	$(k-1)(k^2-1)$	$(k-1)(rk-r-k+1)$	$rt-t-b+1$	$(k-2)(t-1)$
Total	k_2+k^2-1	rk^2-1	$rt-1$	$kt-1$

no carryover effect or correlation of responses. However, this assumption should always be suspect, particularly when the test units are human beings who have voluntarily participated in experiments.[5]

When using human test subjects, one experiments and obtains repeated measures from each individual. That fact should be considered in the analysis because such observations are correlated and dependent, rather than independent, as required by the assumptions underlying the analysis of variance [24, chaps. 4 and 7]. A generalized form of the analysis of variance for such repeated measurement experiments involving n people and k treatments is shown in Table 22.

TABLE 22   Summary of Analysis of Repeated Measure Experiments Involving n Subjects, Each Being Tested on k Treatments

Source of variation	Degrees of freedom
Between people	$n - 1$
Within people	$n(k - 1)$
Treatments	$k - 1$
Residual or experimental error	$(n - 1)(k - 1)$
Total	$kn - 1$

Let us illustrate the appropriate procedure for analyzing such a situation with a portion of the data taken from a home-consumption test of three formulations of a food product, whose identity was disguised by calling it "butter," during a free-choice period following a warm-up period [23]. Both the spreads had been enriched, but one had also received a food coloring to visually indicate its enrichment; the other was the same color as the regular product. The data are in Table 23.

Table 24 gives the results of the analysis of variance of these "butter"-consumption data—note that only the significance of the within-family data is tested, since the error term is appropriate only for that use.

Obviously, one should go on to test the significance of the various means. In the complete analysis of this study [2], it was pointed out that the highly significant variation among the spreads was due primarily to the preference for the enriched "butter"; although there was more demand for the dark spread, its lead over the regular version was not statistically significant.

The procedure used with the data from Table 23 is applicable to single-factor experimentation. As we move into multiple-factor experimentation with repeated measures from subjects, the analysis must take account of those facts. One of the most interesting developments in the application of experimentation in marketing is the establishment of split- or double-CATV cable systems [1 and 15]. Since the data of these experiments come from diaries, the data analysis must take into consideration the intercorrelation of purchases of given

[5] Obviously all market research experiments derive their data from the behavior of human beings. The distinction we wish to draw is between (1) experiments where people know they are being used as experimental subjects and the data come directly from them as individuals, and (2) those experiments where it is hoped that people will remain unaware of changes in their marketing environment and the data are aggregates of behavior by unidentified purchasers.

TABLE 23   Units of Butters Selected During Free-Choice Period

Family	Dark	Enriched	Regular	Family total
1	4	6	3	13
2	5	9	2	16
3	9	12	10	31
4	10	15	5	30
5	3	6	2	11
Butter total	31	48	22	101

Correction term $= (101)^2/3.5 = 680.07$
$(1) = \sum(X_{ij})^2 = 4^2 + 5^2 + \ldots 2^2 = 895.00$
$(2) = \sum(X_{.j})^2/_i = (31^2 + 48^2 + 22^2)/5 = 749.80$
$(3) = \sum(X_{i.})^2/_j = (13^2 + 16^2 + \ldots 11^2)/3 = 802.33$

Sum of squares between families $= (3) - C = 122.26$
Sum of squares within families $= (1) - (3) = 92.67$
Sum of squares for butters $= (2) - C = 69.73$
Sum of squares for error $= (1) - (2) - (3) + C = 22.94$
Total sum of squares $= (1) - C = 214.93$

TABLE 24   Analysis of Variance of Free-Choice Selection of Butters

Source of variation	Sum of squares		Degrees of freedom		Mean square	F
Between families	122.26		4			
Within families	92.67		10			
Butters		69.73		2	34.86	12.15**
Error		22.94		8	2.87	
Total	214.93		14			

brands in a commodity field over time [3]. Tables 25 and 26 sketch two such designs: the first of these is from a two-factor experiment where respondents were exposed to treatment combinations involving repeated measures on one factor; the second shows a three-factor experiment with repeated measurements on two factors.

TABLE 25   Summary of Analysis of Variance of Experiment on Factors A and B, Involving Repeated Measures on Factor B

(n subjects per level of A, p levels of A, and q levels of B)

Source of variation	Degrees of freedom
Between subjects:	$np - 1$:
A	$p - 1$
Subjects within groups	$p(n - 1)$
Within subjects:	$np(q - 1)$:
B	$q - 1$
AB	$(p - 1)(q - 1)$
B × subjects within groups	$p(n - 1)(q - 1)$

TABLE 26 Summary of Analysis of Variance of Experiment on Factors A, B, and C, with Repeated Measures on Factors B and C

(n subjects per level of A; p, q, and r levels of A, B, and C, respectively)

Source of variation	Degrees of freedom
Between subjects:	$np - 1$:
A	$p - 1$
Subjects within groups	$p(n - 1)$
Within subjects:	$np(qr - 1)$:
B	$q - 1$
AB	$(p - 1)(q - 1)$
B × subjects within groups	$p(n - 1)(q - 1)$
C	$r - 1$
AC	$(p - 1)(r - 1)$
C × subjects within groups	$p(n - 1)(r - 1)$
BC	$(q - 1)(r - 1)$
ABC	$(p - 1)(q - 1)(r - 1)$
BC × subjects within groups	$p(n - 1)(q - 1)(r - 1)$

In both these multiple-factor experiments, the nature of the components of the mean square terms is such that there are several experimental error terms; therefore the researcher must use the appropriate error term in testing the significance of his treatment main effect and interactions. The summary analyses of variances have been laid out in such a way that the subject-within-group variance term which provides an error variance follows the main effect or interaction terms for which it is the appropriate divisor—assuming a fixed model [24, chap. 7].

REFERENCES

1. Adler, J., and A. A. Kuehn, "How Advertising Works in Market Experiments," *Proceedings, 15th Annual Conference, Advertising Research Foundation,* Oct. 14, 1969.
2. Banks, S., *Experimentation in Marketing,* New York: McGraw-Hill, 1965.
3. Banks, S., "Analysis of Ad Lab Data," *1969 Proceedings, American Statistical Association, Business and Economic Statistics Section,* pp. 111–112.
4. Campbell, D. T., and J. Stanley, "Experimental and Quasi-experimental Designs for Research on Teaching," in N. L. Gage (ed.), *Handbook on Research on Teaching,* Chicago: Rand McNally, 1963, chap. 5.
5. Clement, W. E., P. L. Henderson, and C. P. Eley, *The Effect of Different Levels of Promotional Expenditures on Sales of Fluid Milk,* ERS-259, Washington: U.S. Department of Agriculture, Economic Research Service, 1965.
6. Cochran, W., and G. Cox, *Experimental Designs,* 2d ed., New York: Wiley, 1957.
7. Cox, K. K., "The Effect of Shelf Space upon Sales of Branded Products," *Journal of Marketing Research,* vol. 7, February 1970, pp. 55–58.
8. Fisher, R. A., *The Design of Experiments,* 5th ed., New York: Hafner, 1949.
9. Floyd, T. E., and R. G. Stout, "Measuring Small Changes in a Market Variable," *Journal of Marketing Research,* vol. 7, February 1970, pp. 114–116.
10. Frank, R., and W. F. Massy, "Shelf Position and Space Effects on Sales," *Journal of Marketing Research,* vol. 7, February 1970, pp. 59–66.
11. Friedman, Milton, "The Use of Ranks to Avoid the Assumption of Normality Implicit in the Analysis of Variance," *Journal of the American Statistical Association,* vol. 32, December 1937.

12. Gibbons, Jean D., *Nonparametric Statistical Inference,* New York: McGraw-Hill, 1971.

13. Green, P., and D. Tull, *Research for Marketing Decisions,* 2d ed., Englewood Cliffs, N.J.: Prentice-Hall, 1970.

14. Hansen, M., W. N. Hurwitz, and W. G. Madow, *Sample Survey Methods and Theory,* New York: Wiley, 1953, vol. I.

15. Henderson, P. L., J. F. Hind, and S. E. Brown, "Sales Effects of Two Campaign Themes," *Journal of Advertising Research,* vol. 1, December 1961, reprinted in R. L. Day and L. J. Parsons (eds.), *Marketing Models: Quantitative Applications,* Scranton, Pa: International Textbook, 1971.

16. Kish, L., *Survey Sampling,* New York: Wiley, 1965.

17. Kruskal, W. H., and W. A. Wallis, "Use of Ranks in One-criterion Analysis of Variance," *Journal of the American Statistical Association,* vol. 47, December 1952, errata vol. 48, December 1953, pp. 907–911.

18. Mayer, C. S., "Establishing and Maintaining Balanced Panels in a CATV Test Laboratory," *1969 Proceedings, American Statistical Association, Business and Economic Statistics Section.*

19. Overall, J. E., and D. K. Siegel, "Concerning Least Squares Analysis of Experimental Data," *Psychological Bulletin,* vol. 72, November 1969.

20. Scheffe, H., *The Analysis of Variance,* New York: Wiley, 1959. The most thorough mathematical discussion of the theory of the analysis of variance.

21. Spiegel, S., *Nonparametric Statistics,* New York: McGraw-Hill, 1956.

22. Snedecor, G. W., and W. G. Cochran, *Statistical Methods,* 6th ed., Ames: The Iowa State University Press, 1967.

23. Welch, A. C., "The Development of Advertising Copy," in A. B. Blandenship (ed.), *How to Conduct Consumer and Opinion Research,* New York: Harper & Row, 1946. Summarized in Banks [2, pp. 89–96].

24. Winer, B. J., *Statistical Principles in Experimental Design,* New York: McGraw-Hill, 1962.

Part F
Model Building

Chapter 1

Model Building in Marketing: An Overview

WILLIAM F. MASSY *Graduate School of Business, Stanford University, Stanford, California*

INTRODUCTION

The techniques of marketing research are bringing more and more information to bear on the processes of marketing planning, decision making, and control. As described in this handbook, we are learning to obtain better information from more adequate samples of respondents, to use secondary source materials more effectively, and to integrate the corporation's internal data with marketing research results through the medium of the marketing information system. We are improving our methods for evaluating and analyzing such data by invoking the tools of multivariate statistics and econometrics.

But the very success of the methods of marketing research and its related disciplines has raised the possibility, if not yet the fact, that the volume and complexity of available data may act as deterrents to its effective use by management. In Kotler's words, "Making decisions must be made in the context of insufficient information about processes that are dynamic, lagged, stochastic, interactive, and downright difficult." By themselves, more data can go only so far in alleviating these difficulties. Means must be found to integrate the data with theoretical and judgmental inputs, often in the context of particular management decisions, in order to provide meaningful representations of these "dynamic, lagged, stochastic, interactive and downright difficult" processes. These representations are called *models*. The marketing profession has a large stake in their development and effective use.

In our context, Webster's Dictionary defines the word "model" as a pattern of something to be made, a representation of a thing. We are all familiar with the use of physical models as aids in the design of automobiles, aircraft, and the like. Engineers use working models or prototypes to help them test hypotheses or solve problems that are too complex to tackle by other methods. In computer design, one machine may be programmed to serve as a model of another machine, as yet unbuilt.

In marketing, models usually take the form of representations of markets or market processes. For instance, many models of consumer decision making, brand choice and market penetration, and sales response to the firm's advertising, price, or promotional inputs have been constructed. Other models provide representations of advertising reach and frequency—and the accumulation and duplication of audiences. Models describing how retailers respond to manufacturers' promotional offers and how salesmen react to alternative compensation plans have been proposed. Problems of store and warehouse location, development of new product lines, and even investment in new marketing research activities have been attacked by model builders in recent years. Some of these models are designed only to describe the relevant processes, others provide forecasts of future events, and still others attempt to supply formal decision rules to help management make plans and allocate marketing resources.

Most of the modeling with which marketing people are likely to come into contact is aimed at improving the planning and decision-making activities of their firm's marketing management. That will also be the focus of this chapter. Nevertheless, it is important to recognize that the same principles, and often the same techniques, can be used to make better marketing decisions in the social arena. Models are being proposed as aids to the understanding of market structures so that better decisions can be made in antitrust and similar areas. Cost-benefit analysis (a form of modeling) is being applied to a number of proposals for consumer-protection legislation. These activities are being supported by some substantial investments in marketing research by social agencies.

The advantages of formal marketing models stem directly from the complexity of the marketing environment. Powerful techniques must be brought to bear if hard problems are to be solved. Although, in the past, the process of management intuition has done well enough in the making of marketing decisions, few would doubt that improvements are possible. Yet the very complexity of the task has had a retarding effect upon the progress of model building in marketing. Models are no panacea, and many of the promises made by early practitioners have proved to be without merit. In spite of some excellent pioneering work in the 1950s and early 1960s, it seems fair to say that the practical application of formal marketing models has begun to be significant only in the past few years. This advance has been aided tremendously by the increasing availability of relatively inexpensive computer resources, especially time-shared computer systems.

This chapter will describe some of the approaches that are emerging in the art of market modeling. It will attempt to provide a classification of the various kinds of marketing models, and to give some examples of each. (More detailed consideration of specific models can be found in the other chapters in Part F of Section II and elsewhere in the book.) Finally, some of the approaches to judging the validity of models will be reviewed.

THE LANGUAGES OF MODELING

When we speak of models, we usually think of mathematics, and indeed, most of the models used in marketing are in some sense mathematical. However, mathematics is really just the *language* in which the process or thing being modeled happens to be represented.   Although certain languages are more convenient for some types of representation than others (as will soon be clear), it is important not to confuse form and substance.   This is particularly true in marketing, where many criticisms of models and model builders seem to be directed toward the language of mathematics rather than toward the underlying activity of analyzing and trying to understand marketing processes.

Models can be constructed in a variety of languages.   The following paragraphs will contrast the representation of a single market process in the form of a prose model, a mathematical model, and a logical flow model.[1]

Prose Models.   Everyone has constructed simple models of human or marketing behavior, using only "everyday English" as the language of representation.   For example, the sales manager for a certain firm might describe a competitor's reaction to a price cut by saying, "If I cut my price, my competitor will cut his by an equal amount."   When pressed, he may give a more detailed description of his reactions: for example, the prose model in part *a* of Figure 1.

Whereas the one-sentence model is easy to grasp, more complicated formulations like the many-sentence model in the figure may be rather cumbersome.   It may be difficult to keep all their important characteristics and conditions in mind when attempting to draw conclusions or make predictions.   Yet the prose model meets the basic requirements for a model of a marketing process: It provides a representation of the relevant aspects of the behavior under consideration and can be used for decision-making purposes.

Mathematical Models.   Based on the sales manager's verbal statements, the mathematically inclined marketing analyst might build a model like that described in part *b* of Figure 1.   The everyday English of the prose model is still used in the definition of the variables, but the relations between the variables are described in the language of mathematics.

The mathematical model provides considerable economy and precision in the representation of the relationships between the variables.   (The degree of economy becomes more and more important as the model becomes larger and more complex.)   Models expressed in a mathematical language can be subjected to a variety of powerful analysis techniques, for example, algebraic manipulation and calculus, as well as programmed on a computer.   On the negative side, the mathematical language is not so widely known or so thoroughly understood by decision makers as is everyday English.   This means that the model builder must often be prepared to build two models of the same process: one in mathematical terms, to be used for analysis and prediction, and another in everyday English, to provide the commonsense explanation needed by the decision maker.

Logical Flow Models.   The third model of Figure 1 is also based on the sales manager's prose statements.   It is expressed directly in the language of computers and computer programmers.   The logical flow language is most effective when the model represents a process involving many discrete questions and alternative paths, rather than relatively continuous relations between variables that are easily expressed in mathematical notation.   It is also more easily understood by nontechnical people, thus putting a smaller translation burden on the model builder.   However, it is much harder to apply analytical (as opposed to computational) techniques to logical flow models.

Both the mathematical and logical flow representations are examples of what may be called *formal models*.   That is, these models are precise and unambigu-

---

[1] Adapted from [35], with permission.

Prose Model (a)	Given that my competitor is operating at or above his break-even point with a price equal to mine, then: If I cut my price, my competitor will cut his to match mine providing that the price cut is likely to be permanent and the competitor can break even at my new price. If I do not cut my price, my competitor will not cut his either. If I cut my price and if the price cut is not likely to be permanent, my competitor will watch price and volume but will do nothing now. If I cut my price and if the price cut is likely to be permanent and my competitor cannot break-even at my new price, he will cut his price down to his break-even point.
Mathematical Model (b)	$$P_{c,t+1} = (1-K) \cdot P_{c,t} + K \cdot \max\left[P_{a,t+1}, \frac{F_c}{Q_{c,t}} + V_c \right]$$ for cases where $\quad P_{c,t} = P_{a,t} \geq \dfrac{F_c}{Q_{c,t}} + V_c$ where $\quad t$ = current week (month, etc.) $\quad t+1$ = next week $\quad P_a$ = my price $\quad P_c$ = competitor's price $\quad Q_c$ = competitor's sales (in units) $\quad F_c$ = competitor's fixed costs $\quad V_c$ = competitor's variable cost per unit $\quad K$ = a "dummy" variable, taking value: $\qquad 0$ if my price is not cut in a "permanent" way $\qquad I$ if my price is cut in a "permanent" way A term like max (x, y) is read " the larger of x and y." The symbol $\geq$ is read "greater than or equal to."

Fig. 1.   Three models of a competitor's reaction to Firm A's price cut.

ous compared to the more intuitive prose model. Many marketing models are couched in a combination of the mathematical and logical flow languages. The model builder should feel free to switch back and forth between the two methods of representation as long as his objective is to produce a model that is "computable" only.[2]   (A model is computable if the rules and calculations embodied in it can be followed without ambiguity, for example, by a clerk or a computer.)   If he plans to rely heavily upon analytical procedures, however, he must usually represent the process in a mathematical language.

   [2] For an example of a large-scale model involving both types of representation, see [3].

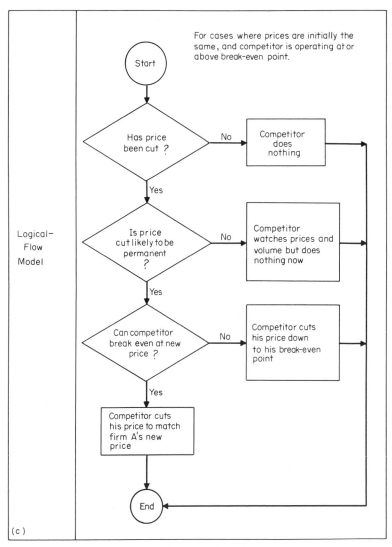

Fig. 1.   (Continued).

MODELS AND TECHNIQUES

Having built a model, we are faced with the desirability of doing something useful with it.   This may involve performing the computations implied by the model to make predictions about future events.   Sometimes these predictions will be made many times, each with a different set of inputs to the model. (For instance, the researcher may use the model to predict market shares for a variety of different levels of advertising weight.)   Mathematical or computational optimization procedures like the differential calculus or linear programming may be used to find the set of inputs that best achieves a given objective. Alternatively, mathematical or computational techniques may be used to explore the characteristics of the process represented by the model, so that the model builder may better understand it and perhaps suggest improvements in the structure of the process.

Management science techniques like computer simulation, sensitivity analysis, and optimization are all methods that can be applied to a model of a marketing process or entity. However, they should not be confused with the model itself.

For example, the early linear-programming models for advertising-media selection were justly criticized for providing inadequate representations of media characteristics, such as exposure value, audience accumulation and duplication, and cost discounts. Thus linear programming got a bad name in certain circles. But the technique itself was not at fault. It is just a mathematical procedure for finding the constrained maximum (or minimum) of a linear function. As such, it is neutral with respect to the media-selection problem, or indeed to any real-world problem.

The fault lay with the model builders who developed an oversimplified representation of media characteristics. Rather than being guided by the salient characteristics of the real-world process (where "salient" is ultimately defined by the decision makers who must use the model), they limited themselves to a narrow class of representations that seemed to be required by a particular optimizing technique. Without implying censure of the pioneering individuals involved in this work, one might say that the approach appears to have put the cart before the horse.[3]

To demonstrate that linear programming may in fact be a useful optimizing device even in the media-selection problem (but with an entirely different model), the recent work of Charnes, Cooper, et al. [8] on goal programming can be cited. Approaches involving heuristic rather than linear programming have been reported by Moran [39] and Little and Lodish [29].

Another kind of confusion can also be found in discussions of marketing models. It stems from the fact that most models are based in some way upon empirical data. Often, models of marketing processes contain unknown constants (usually called parameters) that must be estimated from data. Therefore, some statistical or econometric technique must be used to derive the estimates. (Regression analysis is probably the most widely used of such techniques.) The statistical technique is separate from the model, and should not be confused with it. Thus, although we often speak of "regression models" or "econometric models" of marketing processes, we really mean the class of models whose parameters are efficiently estimated by these techniques. It is possible to point to "good" and "bad" models of the same process, both of which incorporate parameters estimated by a given statistical technique.

TYPES OF MODELS

Models can be classified in a variety of ways [7, 15, 22]. This section will consider some technical characteristics that are particularly relevant for describing marketing models. The dimensions are: (1) micro-macro; (2) static-dynamic; and (3) deterministic-probabilistic.

Micro or Macro Models. Some models include explicit representations of the behavior of individual consumers, retailers, salesmen, or the like. Others are concerned only with aggregates of such behavior; for instance, with the total purchases of all customers of a given type or in a given territory. These two types of models are called *micro* and *macro*, respectively. (The terms *dis-*

[3] For more discussion of this type of problem, see [24].

aggregative and *aggregative* models are also used.)   Both are very useful in marketing.

Micro models have the advantage of allowing very detailed representations of a wide variety of behaviors. For example, Claycamp and Amstutz [10] report a simulation of physicians' drug-choice behavior which includes representations of awareness and attitude change, media exposure, detailing and responses to detailing, and even word-of-mouth processes. Such models have great flexibility and can utilize a broad range of empirical data and managerial judgments.[4] (Getting such judgments is made easier by the fact that micro models are often expressed in the logical flow language.) Many micro models of market processes have been built and tested.

Macro models of behavior sacrifice detail for simplicity and comprehensiveness. Instead of providing a detailed representation of the drug-choice behavior of many different types of doctors, a macro model might "explain" the behavior in terms of a single equation relating drug-prescription shares for all doctors to the total amount of advertising and detailing for each brand. Many macro models are known as *econometric models,* which are the subject of Chapter 4 [Sec. II, Part F].

Static or Dynamic Models.   A model is static or dynamic, depending upon whether time is explicitly included in it.[5]

Static models relate the level of a dependent variable to the levels of one or more explanatory variables, with all variables defined at a given point in time. The method of *comparative statics,* in which the effects of different levels of the independent variable are compared by means of a static model, is powerful and well used.

Dynamic models generalize these elements to include a representation of how the dependent variable in the model gets from one static level to another, given a change in the independent variables. Thus, dynamic models are concerned with the process of change, not just with the final results that will be achieved after equilibrium is established.

Dynamic models can be richer and more powerful than static models, but at the cost of being more complex and having more stringent data requirements. Both types of models have great relevance to marketing.[6]

Deterministic or Probabilistic Models.   Another important distinction among models is whether or not they take explicit account of the uncertainty that is nearly always present in the market process being modeled. The model of competitive-pricing behavior presented in Figure 1 is an example of a deterministic model. Given a certain condition (for example, "Has price been cut? No"), the model gives a deterministic prediction of the outcome ("Competition does nothing"). A probabilistic version of the same model might look this way:

> Has our price been cut?
> If not, then the competitor will do nothing 8 times out of 10 (probability = .8), but will cut his price unilaterally 2 times out of 10 (probability = .2), and so on.

In this case, the introduction of the probabilistic component allows for the possibility that factors external to the model may affect the competitor's pricing decision. That is, our uncertainty about his action is introduced explicitly.

Although many have argued about whether human behavior (or the world in

[4] For an excellent discussion of micro modeling, see [41].

[5] The importance of this distinction is well documented in the economics literature, for example, in [46].

[6] For an example of a situation where both types of models have been applied to the same behavior, compare [11] with [32].

general) is ultimately probabilistic, this is a moot point so far as model building in marketing is concerned. We can never hope to know enough or put a sufficiently fine level of detail into our models to remove all uncertainty, even if this should be theoretically possible.

Probably the most compelling reason for including uncertainty explicitly in marketing models is that it often affects decision making. If we know that new product A is slightly more likely to succeed than product B (on an average or expected value basis) but that A is by far the riskier, we just might decide in favor of B. A model that ignored the risk factor would not catch this difference. Another example of the importance of an explicit representation of uncertainty involves the value of information. If we know that 53 of 100 respondents in a blind taste test preferred product A, is this difference "good enough" for decision-making purposes? How much more information would be obtained from another 100 respondents, and how much would this information be worth?

Questions like these abound in marketing, and models aimed at answering them must be probabilistic. On the other hand, the inclusion of probabilistic elements can complicate a model tremendously. It is better to have a manageable deterministic model than an unmanageable probabilistic one.

Problems of uncertainty are best handled within the framework of what has come to be called *decision analysis,* discussed in several previous chapters. This is an application of Bayesian decision theory, which has attracted considerable interest among marketing experts. It will be discussed in the next section of this chapter.

Models not normally considered to be applications of decision theory can also be interpreted in the Bayesian way. In fact, the author believes that Bayesian statistical procedures should be substituted for classical ones wherever possible when empirical data are being analyzed for model-building purposes.[7] Even where programs for implementing the Bayesian machinery are not readily available, Bayesian interpretations can often be applied to classical methods like regression analysis and confidence interval estimation, as shown earlier [Sec. II, Part E, Chap. 7].

A second reason for developing probabilistic models is that they often provide a convenient way of representing complex behavioral processes. Some good examples of this capability are found in the area of brand choice, where the so-called stochastic models have held sway for some time.[8] (The well-known Markov and linear learning models—to be discussed later—are in this class.) In addition, many of the micro simulation models of behavior considered earlier contain stochastic components, and so do some of the normative models to be discussed a few pages on.

These statements should not be interpreted to mean that *all* marketing models should be probabilistic, or that probabilistic components should permeate all parts of any model. Most models involving uncertainty are reduced to a "certainty-equivalent" basis, for example, by the taking of expected values, somewhere along the line. Often it is appropriate to think in certainty-equivalent terms all through a given model; in this case, the model looks like a deterministic one; that is, probability notions are not introduced explicitly, though uncertainty has implicitly been considered. Moreover, deterministic

---

[7] For an excellent discussion of the difference between Bayesian and classical statistical inference, and a justification of the Bayesian point of view, see [45].

[8] *Stochastic* is a synonym of *probabilistic.* For a comprehensive treatment of brand-choice models, see [34].

models are often useful as approximations to more complex probabilistic models. Many very useful marketing models are deterministic in structure. The same is true of many (if not most) models in economics, the behavioral sciences, and physical sciences and engineering.

MODELING OBJECTIVES

Models may be constructed for a variety of purposes. There are models whose sole purpose is to add to general scientific knowledge, and others which seek to aid in solving specific decision problems. (This chapter is concerned mostly with the latter type.) Marketing decision models may be classified according to the type of decisions to which they are designed to contribute, for example, pricing or advertising.

The objectives of modeling may also be defined in terms of how the model is expected to help the decision maker. This approach is useful because it gives the model builder and the model user explicit guidance about what to expect from the model. The following hierarchy of types will be discussed here: (1) taxonomic models, (2) descriptive or explanatory models, (3) predictive models, and (4) normative models.

Taxonomic Models. One of the first tasks of any science is to develop procedures for classifying events, entities, or data. (This and the previous discussion on types of models can be interpreted as an exercise in taxonomic modeling of the modeling field.) Marketing is no exception. Verbal models of the taxonomic type abound in the marketing literature. Classifications of industries, commodities, and marketing institutions are taxonomic models. McCarthy's well-known "Four P's" represent a taxonomy of the set of marketing management's decision variables.[9] Alderson's functionalism falls into the same category [2].

These models help us to think about marketing problems. If well done, a taxonomy allows the researcher to (1) examine individual classes of events or entities separately, thus achieving important simplifications and improvements in the research, modeling, or decision process; and (2) compare these different classes with an eye to explaining differences in structure, or creating new classes in "empty" spaces in the hierarchy.

Market Segmentation. Taxonomic models can also be formal, that is, based on mathematical or statistical procedures. Probably the best-known problem in this category is that of defining meaningful market segments. Formally, the question is one of grouping possible buyers according to some measure of potential or response to promotional activities [12]. Rather than directing its marking efforts to an undifferentiated mass market, the firm hopes through segmentation to develop a taxonomy of buyers that will allow it to focus its resources where they will do the most good. From the standpoint of technique, the problem is one of finding an optimal way to group households or industrial customers into a manageable number of distinct classes, such that within-class differences are minimal and between-class differences are as large as possible.

Brands or even product categories may also be grouped by taxonomic methods. Knowledge of which brands or products are consumed by the same customers, or for the same purpose, can be a helpful input to the segmentation process. Or brands can be grouped according to their attributes, either technical or as perceived by users. A variant on this approach is to try to determine the group membership of a new product or brand on the basis of knowledge

---

[9] The "Four P's" are product, price, promotion, and place. See [37, chap. 2].

about and preferences for its attributes [49]. (Studies of this kind often go beyond purely taxonomic questions to examine customer response to the promotional appeals associated with the brand.)

Certain statistical techniques have come to be associated with taxonomic models, particularly in the area of market segmentation. They are factor analysis, cluster analysis (often called numerical taxonomy), and multivariate scaling. These techniques are discussed elsewhere in this volume.

Marketing Information Systems.   Another and increasingly important application of taxonomic models in marketing is in the classification of data. As more and more marketing data are stored for later use by management, the problems of file organization and efficient retrieval become increasingly significant. This trend is being accelerated by the development of computer-based information systems, particularly on-line interactive systems, as discussed in Chapter 5 of Section I.

Efficient file organization requires a detailed hierarchical classification of data. This is often called an information structure [26]. The information structure is not necessarily imposed directly by the data. Rather, the system designer must determine what attributes of each set of data are important, how the attributes of different sets relate to one another, and how attributes and data items can best be grouped into a meaningful information structure. The problem is analogous to that of grouping customers into meaningful market segments. It is a problem of taxonomic modeling. Probably the best-known examples of models for file organization are the Dewey Decimal System and the Library of Congress classification system.[10]

To date, the line of research most directly concerned with information structures has been systems analysis. The techniques developed here are most useful in building models that represent the decision-making process in which the information is to be employed as well as the inherent characteristics of the data themselves.[11] Simulation has been widely used to evaluate the characteristics of specific representations of information structures. Formal methods for defining such structures in the first place have been far less common, though the use of cluster analysis has at least been proposed [6].

Descriptive-Explanatory Models.   Models are often constructed to describe or explain some phenomenon. In marketing, the most extensive use of descriptive-explanatory models has been in the area of consumer behavior, though they are not limited to this area.

Descriptive-explanatory models may be termed *theoretical* or *empirical,* depending on the degree to which they incorporate empirical data for parameter estimation or testing. Francesco Nicosia's model of consumer behavior is a good example of the theoretical variety [40]. In effect, it sets up a series of detailed hypotheses about the ways in which consumers process information and make decisions. Amstutz's model of competitive market response is of the same general type, though he has been able to move toward empirical estimation and verification [3]. Many similar models can be found in the marketing and communications literature.

Another group of models of consumer behavior attempts to explain differences in buying patterns among households or household groups on the basis of summary information about the group members. Such models are often couched in so-called English, with characteristics inferred from cross-tabulation

---

[10] An earlier paper used the term *librarian* to describe taxonomic models for information retrieval. See [31].

[11] For an excellent presentation of applied methods, see [20].

studies of empirical data [51]. (For example, it might turn out that high-income families consume 20 percent more of a certain product on average than do low-income families.) Other models are mathematical in character. Their parameters are estimated and their efficacy is tested by the methods of correlation and regression, analysis of variance, or multiple-discriminant analysis.[12] (In the example just given, a correlation study might report that the correlation coefficient between income and product usage is 0.35, which might be statistically significant at the 90 percent level.)

A descriptive-explanatory model may help to solve a particular decision problem, make a general contribution to knowledge, or both. It may suggest hypotheses for future research, help to determine what data should be collected and from whom, facilitate the interpretation of taxonomic model results, or simply aid researchers or managers in understanding complex, interactive markets or marketing processes. If relevant to the problem at hand, such understanding will, it is assumed, improve decisions even though the thought process by which this improvement occurs cannot be objectively defined.

Predictive Models. As the name implies, models of this type are constructed for the purpose of predicting future events. They are designed to be operational in the sense of providing a direct, explicit input to the marketing decision process rather than of making a general contribution to knowledge as descriptive-explanatory models do. (The meaning of "direct, explicit input" will become clear in the examples which follow.) Of course, models do not always meet their creators' objectives. Some predictive models fail to contribute directly to decision making and so end up being interpreted as descriptive-explanatory models. Some descriptive-explanatory models can be upgraded to predictive models with only a little extra effort.

The foregoing suggests that predictive models are "better" than descriptive-explanatory ones. It should be noted, however, that this chapter is concerned more with models intended to provide direct inputs to the management decision process than with general models or theories as used in the broad range of scientific inquiry. Although prediction is of crucial importance in science (it is usually the ultimate test of a theory's veracity), it is generally viewed as supporting the *explanatory powers* of a model rather than as an end in itself. Thus the distinction between descriptive-explanatory and predictive models is fuzzier in basic science than in models aimed at improving specific management decisions, where operational considerations are paramount.

Symbolically, the predictive model provides a representation (usually formal) of the function:

Outcome $= f$ (decision variables and environmental variables)

where the decision variables are those under the control of the firm (for example, advertising, price) and the environmental variables are those which, while uncontrollable, may be forecast by the firm to improve its overall prediction of outcomes.

There are two general classes of predictive models: (1) unconditional or forecasting models; and (2) conditional or structural models. In the former, the decision variables are left out of the prediction procedure, whereas, in the latter, they are explicitly modeled.

Forecasting Models. Unconditional prediction models are designed to take account of the persistence exhibited by many marketing processes over time. Information about the time path of the process during the recent past is used to make extrapolations into the future. These models are widely used in sales

---

[12] For a representative study of this type, see [33].

forecasting. Exponential smoothing models can often provide viable short-term sales forecasts on a product-by-product or area-by-area basis. These forecasts are obtained by forming a weighted average of the actual value of sales for the previous period and the value predicted for that period: that is,

forecast at $t = \alpha$ (actual sales at $t - 1$) $+ (1 - \alpha)$ (predicted sales for $t - 1$)

where α is a smoothing constant. It is also possible to build time-trend and seasonal factors into exponential smoothing models [48, chap. 4].

Long-term sales forecasts are often obtained from some kind of model based on the analysis of time series data. It is frequently desirable to attempt to predict sales (or market potential) as a function of independent variables like aggregate income, population, and so on, which may in turn be predicted by time series methods. Time-trend terms, for example, the idea of a constant percent rate of growth, are also widely used in long-run forecasting models. Multiple regression is commonly employed to estimate the parameters of such models.

Most of the stochastic models for purchase timing and brand choice also fall into the unconditional prediction class, that is, they rely on persistence of behavior or behavior patterns. On the brand-switching side, the best-known models are the Markov model and the linear learning model. In the Markov model, the probability that a household will purchase a particular brand at time t is assumed to depend only on the brand purchased at $t - 1$. (The likelihood of buying brand A, given a previous purchase of B, is written $Pr\ (A\,|\,B)$; it is called the *transition probability* of A from B.) The linear learning model extends the assumptions of the Markov model so that the probability of buying brand A at t depends on all the household's previous brand choices, with the most recent purchases exerting the greatest influence.

The assumptions built into these models are similar in concept to those of the exponential smoothing type of short-term forecasting model. Similar examples could be given with respect to models for purchase timing.[13]

Structural Models. Conditional prediction models (also called structural models) evaluate the effects of controllable or decision variables. They answer "what if" questions, for example, "What will happen to sales if I cut my price?" These models usually represent specific aspects of marketing behavior. The interaction between the variables should be carefully considered, alternative model forms thoroughly tested, and so on. Considerable attention is usually focused on problems of estimating parameters from the data and integrating empirical results with management judgment. It is here that the methods of econometrics become highly important for marketing.

There are many examples of structural modeling in marketing. One of the best known is probably Agostini's model for predicting audience duplication as a function of the particular set of print media employed in an advertising schedule [1]. Although it might be argued that Agostini's work is an exercise in curve fitting rather than modeling, later work has shown that his approach can be grounded in some reasonable assumptions about audience behavior [13]. At any rate, it is conditionally predictive and highly operational.

The general class of models for evaluating sales response to advertising has been reviewed by Palda [43]. Some specific models that have been reported in the literature are (1) Palda's model for measuring the cumulative effects of advertising for Lydia Pinkham's Vegetable Compound [42]; (2) Frank and Massy's model for evaluating the short-term effects of relative price, dealing,

---

[13] A comprehensive review of brand-choice and purchase-timing models will be found in [33].

and advertising for a convenience product [16]; and (3) Bass's simultaneous-equation model for the effects of advertising on cigarette sales [5]. All these models include evaluations of results in terms of a management decision problem. In principle, there is no reason why the same methods cannot be applied to personal selling, but the work in this area to date has been rather sparse.[14]

Models for brand switching and purchase timing can also be made into conditional predictors. For example, Telser has proposed that the transition probabilities of a Markov brand-switching model be made functions of price and promotional variables [50]. It is theoretically possible to make the parameter of an exponential purchase-timing model a function of marketing decision variables [33, chap. 11]. Kuehn and Rohloff use the linear learning model as a basis for explicitly evaluating the effects of consumer deals [25].

Often a number of models like the ones discussed here are combined into a more general model and analyzed by simulation. Such simulations can be highly operational and useful. As mentioned earlier, Claycamp and Amstutz report a large-scale simulation of doctor's drug choices, where advertising, direct mail, detailing, and other marketing inputs by drug firms are explicitly considered [10]. Forrester describes numerous large- and small-scale simulations for structural analysis [14]. Many small-scale marketing simulations have been constructed and used successfully by business firms but not reported in the literature.

Normative Models. The last class of models deals with normative questions like "what should be," as opposed to the "what would be if . . ." questions addressed by predictive models. The objective of the normative model can be summarized symbolically as:

to maximize (or minimize)
outcome $= f$ (decision variables and environmental variables)
with respect to the decision variables (perhaps with constraints).

In practice, it is usually necessary to introduce the intermediate step of defining the values to be associated with each outcome. This is particularly important if several different types of outcomes are to be considered. Symbolically, the procedure is:

to maximize (or minimize)
value $= f$ [outcome (1), outcome (2), . . .]
where outcome (1) $= g$ (decision variables and environmental variables)
outcome (2) $= h$ (decision variables and environmental variables, and so on)
with respect to the decision variables (perhaps with constraints).

The normative model as a whole represents the decision process of the manager whom it is aimed at helping. The function f models his value system. (For instance, he may consider current contribution to profit to be twice as important as increases in market share.) The functions g and h are conditional predictive models representing the relations between marketing inputs and outcomes. (Every normative model requires that one or more conditional predictive models be embedded in it.[15]) The constraints in the problem define the set of values for the decision variables deemed to be admissible by the decision maker. (For instance, the company's policies might preclude a price less than that of a certain major competitor.)

---

[14] Some personal-selling effects models, as well as models for other marketing decision variables, are reported in [21], [38], and [47].

[15] The relations between predictive and normative models are further explored in [31] and [36].

Formal normative models can be classified in terms of (1) whether they make use of enumerative, algorithmic (for example, linear programming), or heuristic optimization methods; and (2) whether uncertainty with respect to predicted outcomes is explicitly considered. We shall consider the most-populated cells of this grid.

Decision Analysis Models.   These models are built to handle uncertainty. The well-known "decision tree" models of Bayesian decision theory fall into this class. They are enumerative in character, as all admissible alternatives are evaluated. But there is no inherent reason why other optimization techniques cannot be used, and in fact they sometimes are. (The models are usually always Bayesian, however.) The effect of uncertainty on the value function, and the value of uncertainty reduction, that is, of increasing information, are important facets of decision analysis models.

Paul Green's early work with Bayesian marketing models showed how decision tree analysis and subjective probabilities could be used to augment traditional sources of marketing research data [17, 18, 19]. Little's model for adaptive control of promotional spending is also of the decision analysis type [27]. At the other end of the spectrum of complexity, the DEMON model for new-product evaluation is essentially a decision analysis that makes use of a network-based optimization algorithm [8]. Other examples are given in connection with discussions of decision theory and Bayesian analysis [see Sec. II, Part A, Chaps. 3 and 4].

Algorithmic and Heuristic Models.   When the set of admissible decision alternatives is too large for optimization by enumeration, some kind of organized search procedure must be invoked. Sometimes this procedure is formal, such as when mathematical programming or formal heuristics are used. Most models embodying formal search procedures that have been built in marketing so far have employed deterministic or certainty-equivalent (that is, expected value), objective functions.

An *algorithm* is a set of rules which, if followed faithfully, will always find the best decision alternative in a finite number of steps. The techniques of linear, quadratic, and integer programming are algorithms. (A linear program finds the maximum of a linear function of many decision variables, subject to constraints on the values of the variables. Quadratic and integer programs do the same thing in cases where the objective function involves the squares or cross-products of the decision variables, or where the decision variables must be integer values.) Dynamic programming provides an algorithm for maximizing a set of decisions over time, where the choice of strategy in one period affects the available options or probable outcomes in another period. These methods are often referenced under the general heading of "mathematical programming."

A *heuristic* is a set of rules which generally enables one to find a good strategy, though not necessarily the best one. Heuristics may be formal, in the sense that the rules are unambiguously defined and may be carried out by a clerk or a computer. Or they may be informal or intuitive, for example, the highly personal "rules of thumb" used by a particular decision maker. (The term *heuristic program* generally refers to a set of formal heuristic rules.) Heuristics usually are more flexible and require much less computation than algorithms, though at the cost of finding only a "good," rather than the "best," decision alternative.

The best-known marketing models using formal search procedures are the advertising media-selection models. Linear programming was used in the early models.[16] Extensions to piecewise linear programming were soon forthcoming, and were followed by suggestions for the use of quadratic and integer programming [52]. The idea of *goal programming,* in which the objective is to minimize deviations between the characteristics of the schedule and a whole series of specific goals stated by the media planner, has recently been proposed [8]. (These goals were usually included as constraints, in earlier models.) Heuristic programming has been applied to the media-selection problem by Little and Lodish [29] and as reported by Moran [39]. It is interesting to note that the heuristic methods described by Little and Lodish are intended to be an approximation to a dynamic programming approach to media selection proposed by the same authors [28].

Various models for setting advertising budgets, price levels, and personal-selling levels have also been proposed. Most deterministic ones are based on classical economics allocation theory [44]. Methods of differential calculus rather than those of mathematical programming are used to find the optimum for these models.

Many other normative models for various classes of marketing problems have been proposed. Both linear and heuristic programming have been used to determine warehouse locations [24]. More recently, a dynamic warehouse-location model has been proposed [4]. Dynamic programming has also been suggested as a method for optimizing a Markov model for the effects of salesmen's time allocations on demand [30]. The reader may consult the general references at the end of this chapter for a comprehensive review of these and other efforts.

APPROACHES TO MODEL VALIDATION

The practical significance of a model depends on (1) the degree to which it represents those aspects of the thing, structure, or process it is intended to represent; and (2) the degree to which these aspects are relevant to the purposes of its sponsor. Although these criteria are obviously related, they are not identical. A model rarely can provide an accurate representation of *all* aspects of a thing or process, so one can build useless models that do very well on attributes that are largely irrelevant for decision-making purposes. Similarly, many very useful models provide inadequate representations of many, if not most, aspects of the thing or process under study—only those attributes that are critical for a particular decision being modeled effectively. Thus, there is no absolute standard on which to judge a model's adequacy. Models cannot be judged in isolation from the purposes for which they are constructed, nor can they be effectively built without reference to some clearly stated objective.

The *validity* of a model is hard to determine, even where clear objectives have been established. One way of meeting this problem is to say that a model which is believed by management is a "valid" model. There is more than a grain of truth to this assertion, as belief is the prerequisite to use of a model, and use is the hallmark of success. Moreover, the manager is the person ultimately responsible for the decision, so his degree of belief should be controlling.[17]

But this point of view leaves many unsatisfied. Model builders would like

---

[16] These models were discussed earlier in this chapter. There are many reports in the literature, most of which are cited in [21], [38], and [47].

[17] For a discussion of degree of belief and its effect on implementation, see [31].

to have some objective measures of a model's validity. Moreover, as model builders they should be prepared to give the manager some guidance about how to judge models, and this requirement would seem to imply some kind of objective criteria.

Some general criteria for validity have indeed been formulated. One such structure is outlined in the following paragraphs.[18]

Tests of Viability. The model should "work," in the sense that answers can be computed. In behavioral modeling, that is, in descriptive and predictive modeling, this means that empirical data can in fact be used to estimate critical parameters, for example, that problems of collinearity do not destroy the estimates, that predictions can be obtained from a simulation, and so on. In normative modeling, viability requires that the system is properly determined, that the algorithms or heuristics work satisfactorily, and the like. Viability is a weak but absolutely necessary criterion for model validity.

Tests of Stability. The answers generated by the model should not fluctuate wildly over time or with changes in the input data. For example, a dynamic simulation model should not generate explosive oscillations. A mathematical or heuristic programming model should not produce tremendous changes in the recommended policy, given small shifts in the values or constraints of the model. This criterion can be interpreted as a form of reliability testing.

Tests of Consistency. The model should be more or less consistent with the real-world process that is being represented. This has been said to mean (1) that the assumptions of the model agree with known facts or with the decision maker's prior beliefs; and (2) that the model has internal consistency or "deductive veracity [7, p. 52]." After the model has been constructed, sensitivity analyses may be performed to see whether its output varies in a reasonable way, given inputs of the type that could be expected in the real world. (This is a more stringent type of stability testing.) Consistency tests are aimed at establishing face validity.

Duplication of Historical Conditions. Models of market processes should be able more or less to reproduce the relevant aspects of historical real-world conditions, provided that the inputs to the model are comparable to those actually in existence during the period under study. (When the model is normative in character, this and the following test should be performed on the objective function or predictive part of the model.) Many models may be validated statistically by means of goodness-of-fit tests. The strongest form of this test occurs when the model is applied to data that were not used to suggest its structure or estimate its parameters. A weaker but still useful form uses the same data for estimation and validation. An example is the use of the multiple correlation coefficient in regression analysis as a measure of validity.

Prediction of Future Conditions. Probably the ultimate test of a model is its ability to predict the future. This kind of test ensures that the data were not implicitly used to formulate the model's structure. Moreover, it places the model in the kind of situation in which it will have to perform for decision-making purposes.

Predictive testing must be applied carefully. There is often the question, "How good a prediction is good enough?" (This question also applies to tests on historical data.) Uncertainty about exogenous events and feedbacks between the output of the model and resulting actions aimed at changing the course of events also cause difficulties of interpretation. For example, many models yield probability distributions rather than point estimates. The results

---

[18] The hierarchy of tests is given by Amstutz [3, pp. 380–383].

of a few test cases may be insufficient to prove or disprove the model's adequacy. Or the model might predict a decline in market share if the status quo is maintained, thereby leading management to increase its advertising budget, which would then negate the prediction given by the model. Nevertheless, tests of prediction should be performed where possible, even though this procedure may mean deliberately maintaining the status quo for purposes of the experiment.

SUMMARY

This chapter has reviewed some of the salient considerations involved in the construction and validation of marketing models. Some of the general advantages of the model-building approach were discussed. Then attention was given to (1) the languages of modeling, including prose models, mathematical models, and logical flow models; (2) the differences between models and mathematical or statistical techniques; (3) types of models, namely, micro versus macro models, static versus dynamic models, and deterministic versus probabilistic models; (4) modeling objectives, in terms of taxonomic models, descriptive or explanatory models, predictive models, and normative models; and (5) approaches to the validation of models.

The footnotes provide references to some of the important modeling efforts that have been reported in the marketing literature. Additional material on many of these models can be found in the other chapters of this volume.

The application of modeling to marketing decision problems is growing rapidly. Many models are still in the basic research stage, though a growing number of them have been used in actual decision situations. Although the results have not always been favorable, there is little doubt that models will become indispensable tools of marketing research and marketing management.

REFERENCES

1. Agostini, M. M., "How to Estimate Unduplicated Audiences," *Journal of Advertising Research*, vol. 1, March 1961.
2. Alderson, W., *Marketing Behavior and Executive Action*, Homewood, Ill.: Irwin, 1957.
3. Amstutz, A. E., *Computer Simulation of Competitive Market Response*, Cambridge, Mass.: M.I.T., 1967.
4. Ballou, R. A., "Dynamic Warehouse Location Analysis," *Journal of Marketing Research*, vol. 5, August 1968.
5. Bass, F. M., "Simultaneous-Equation Regression Study of Advertising and Sales-Analysis of Cigarette Data," *Journal of Marketing Research*, vol. 6, August 1969.
6. Bonner, R., "On Some Clustering Techniques," *IBM Journal of Research and Development*, vol. 8, January 1964.
7. Buzzell, R. D., *Mathematical Models and Marketing Management*, Boston: Harvard University, Graduate School of Business Administration, Division of Research, 1964, pp. 13–31.
8. Charnes, A., W. W. Cooper, J. K. Devoe, and D. B. Learner, "Demon, Mark II: An Extremal Equation Approach to New Product Marketing," *Management Science*, vol. 14, July 1968.
9. Charnes, A., W. W. Cooper, J. K. Devoe, D. B. Learner, and W. Reinecke, "A Goal Programming Model for Media Planning," *Management Science*, vol. 14, April 1968.
10. Claycamp, H. J., and A. E. Amstutz, "Simulation Techniques in the Analysis of Marketing Strategy," in Frank M. Bass, Charles W. King, and Edgar A. Pessemier (eds.), *Applications of the Sciences in Marketing Management*, New York: Wiley, 1968.

11. Claycamp, H. J., and L. E. Liddy, "Prediction of New Product Performance: An Analytical Approach," *Journal of Marketing Research*, vol. 6, November 1969.
12. Claycamp, H. J., and William F. Massy, "A Theory of Market Segmentation," *Journal of Marketing Research*, vol. 5, November 1968.
13. Claycamp, H. J., and C. W. McClelland, "On Methods: Estimating Reach and the Magic of K," *Journal of Advertising Research*, vol. 8, June 1968.
14. Forrester, J. W., *Industrial Dynamics*, Cambridge, Mass.: M.I.T., 1961.
15. Frank, R. E., A. A. Kuehn, and W. F. Massy (eds.), *Quantitative Techniques in Marketing Analysis*, Homewood, Ill.: Irwin, 1962, pp. 106–114.
16. Frank, R. E., and W. F. Massy, "Effects of Short-Term Promotional Strategy in Selected Market Segments," in Patrick J. Robinson (ed.), *Promotional Decisions Using Mathematical Models*, Boston: Allyn and Bacon, 1967.
17. Green, P. E., "Bayesian Decision Theory in Advertising," *Journal of Advertising Research*, vol. 2, December 1962.
18. Green, P. E., "Bayesian Decision Theory in Pricing Strategy," *Journal of Marketing*, vol. 27, January 1963.
19. Green, P. E., and D. Tull, *Research for Marketing Decisions*, Englewood Cliffs, N.J.: Prentice-Hall, 1970.
20. Hare, V. C., *Systems Analysis: A Diagnostic Approach*, New York: Harcourt, Brace & World, 1967.
21. King, W. R., *Quantitative Analysis for Marketing Management*, New York: McGraw-Hill, 1967.
22. Kotler, P., "The Use of Mathematical Models in Marketing," *Journal of Marketing*, vol. 27, October 1963.
23. Kotler, P., *Marketing Management*, Englewood Cliffs, N.J.: Prentice-Hall, 1967.
24. Kuehn, A. A., and M. J. Hamburger, "A Heuristic Program for Locating Warehouses," in Ronald E. Frank, Alfred A. Kuehn, and William F. Massy (eds.), *Quantitative Techniques in Marketing Analysis*, Homewood, Ill.: Irwin, 1962.
25. Kuehn, A. A., and A. Rohloff, "Consumer Response to Promotions," in Patrick J. Robinson (ed.), *Promotional Decisions Using Mathematical Models*, Boston: Allyn and Bacon, 1967.
26. Lefkovitz, D., *File Structures for On-Line Systems*, New York: Spartan Books, 1969, p. 43.
27. Little, J. D. C., "A Model for Adaptive Control of Promotional Spending," *Operations Research*, vol. 14, August 1965.
28. Little, J. D. C., and L. M. Lodish, "A Media Selection Model and Its Optimization by Dynamic Programming," *Industrial Management Review*, vol. 8, Fall 1966.
29. Little, J. D. C., and L. M. Lodish, "A Media Selection Calculus," *Operations Research*, vol. 17, January–February, 1969.
30. Lodish, L. M., D. B. Montgomery, and Frederick E. Webster, Jr., "A Dynamic Sales Call Policy Model," presented at the joint meeting of TIMS and ORSA in San Francisco, May 1–3, 1968.
31. Massy, W. F., "Information and the Marketing Manager: A Systems Analysis," *Proceedings of the Paul D. Converse Awards Symposium of the University of Illinois*, April 1967. Reprinted in *Computer Operations*, October 1968.
32. Massy, W. F., "Forecasting the Demand for a New Convenience Product," *Journal of Marketing Research*, vol. 6, November 1969.
33. Massy, W. F., R. E. Frank, and T. M. Lodahl, Jr., *Purchasing Behavior and Personal Attributes*, Philadelphia: University of Pennsylvania Press, 1968.
34. Massy, W. F., D. B. Montgomery, and D. M. Morrison, *Stochastic Models of Buying Behavior*, Cambridge, Mass.: M.I.T., 1970.
35. Massy, W. F., and Jim D. Savvas, "Logical Flow Models for Marketing Analysis," *Journal of Marketing*, vol. 28, January 1964.
36. Massy, W. F., and F. E. Webster, Jr., "Model-Building in Marketing Research," *Journal of Marketing Research*, vol. 1, May 1964.
37. McCarthy, E. J., *Basic Marketing: A Managerial Approach*, rev. ed., Homewood, Ill.: Irwin, 1964.

38. Montgomery, D. B., and G. L. Urban, *Management Science in Marketing*, Englewood Cliffs, N.J.: Prentice-Hall, 1969.
39. Moran, W. T., "Practical Media Models—What Must They Look Like?" *Proceedings of the 8th Annual Conference, Advertising Research Foundation*, New York, 1962.
40. Nicosia, F. M., *Consumer Decision Processes: Marketing and Advertising Implications*, Englewood Cliffs, N.J.: Prentice-Hall, 1966.
41. Orcutt, G. H., M. Greenberger, J. Korbel, and A. M. Rivlin, "A Stochastic Microanalytic Model of a Socioeconomic System," in R. E. Frank, A. A. Kuehn, and W. F. Massy (eds.), *Quantitative Techniques in Marketing Analysis*, Homewood, Ill.: Irwin, 1962.
42. Palda, K. S., *The Measurement of Cumulative Advertising Effects*, Englewood Cliffs, N.J.: Prentice-Hall, 1964.
43. Palda, K. S., "The Hypothesis of a Hierarchy of Effects: A Partial Evaluation," *Journal of Marketing Research*, vol. 3, February 1966.
44. Palda, K. S., *Economic Analysis for Marketing Decisions*, Englewood Cliffs, N.J.: Prentice-Hall, 1969.
45. Pratt, J. W., H. Raiffa, and R. Schlaifer, *Introduction to Statistical Decision Theory*, New York: McGraw-Hill, 1965.
46. Samuelson, P. A., *Foundations of Economic Analysis*, Cambridge, Mass.: Harvard University Press, 1955.
47. Simon, L., and M. Freimer, *Analytical Marketing*, New York: Harcourt, Brace & World, 1970.
48. Springer, C. H., R. E. Herlihy, and R. I. Beggs, *Advanced Models and Methods, Mathematics for Management Series*, vol 2, Homewood: Ill.: Irwin, 1965.
49. Stefflre, V., "Market Structure Studies: New Products for Old Markets and New Markets (Foreign) for Old Products," in Frank M. Bass, Charles W. King, and Edgar A. Pessemier (eds.), *Applications of the Sciences in Marketing Management*, New York: Wiley, 1968.
50. Telser, L. G., "The Demand for Branded Goods as Estimated from Consumer Panel Data," *Review of Economics and Statistics*, vol. 44, August 1962.
51. Zaltman, G., *Marketing: Contributions from the Behavioral Sciences*, New York: Harcourt, Brace & World, 1966.
52. Zangwill, W. I., "Media Selection by Decision Programming," *Journal of Advertising Research*, vol. 5, September 1965.

Model Building

Chapter 2

Simulation: Methods and Applications

WILLIAM M. MORGENROTH   *College of Business Administration, University of South Carolina, Columbia, South Carolina*

J. TAYLOR SIMS   *College of Business Administration, University of South Carolina, Columbia, South Carolina*

THE NATURE OF SIMULATION

Introduction

The complexity of many marketing problems prohibits their representation by standard mathematical models. A promising method of handling these complex problems is through simulation [42, p. 237].

Simulation can be identified with a growing family of models used in marketing. Each has its own purposes, strengths, and weaknesses, with all sharing the common goal of serving as structures of theory for analysis. Simulation models may represent either a descriptive or decision-oriented process. Descriptive processes include communicative, explanatory, predictive, and behavioral models. Decision processes include optimization and heuristic models. Quantitative models, in contrast, include linear and nonlinear models, static and dynamic models, and deterministic and stochastic models [42, p. 224]. These quantitative models are discussed elsewhere in this handbook and are well referenced. However, certain differences between them and simulation models will be noted in this chapter.

Definitions and Concepts

A simulation of a system or an organism is the operation of a model or simulator which is a representation of the system or organism. The model is amenable to manipulations which would be impossible, too expensive or impractical to perform on the entity it portrays. The operation of a model can be studied and, from it, properties concerning the behavior of the actual system or sub-system can be inferred [49].

The main characteristics of simulation involve a general method of studying the behavior of a real system or phenomenon; they usually provide the user with features that enable him to (1) devise a model or set of mathematical and logical relations which represents the system's essential features, and (2) carry out step-by-step computations with those relations that imitate the manner in which the real system might perform. Typically, the real system is subject to chance elements, and this susceptibility leads to the inclusion of probabilistic characteristics in the model. In systems of complexity, a high-speed digital computer may be programmed to carry out the sequence of computations. Also, a simulation may involve both a computer and persons imitating certain human functions in a system.

An important advantage of simulation is that the system can be studied under a wide range of conditions which might be expensive or impossible to apply directly to the real system. "Simulation is an important tool of a great variety of problems, particularly where ordinary mathematical solution is not possible, or where intangibles or human judgment are involved. . . ." [35, pp. 243–244].

Purposes and Uses

Distinction between the purposes and uses of simulation should be briefly explained. Uses, or the methods of operation and the areas of application, are discussed in the chapter's later sections. Purpose deals with the end in mind, the values or objectives to be attained. Descriptions of the various purposes of simulation follow, written primarily from the standpoint of marketing decisions, although usages stem from the physical and social sciences.

Behind the primary comprehensive purpose of being a useful tool for decision making in the realm of models, simulation has specific areas of excellence. "Simulation techniques have been adopted primarily because the complexity of the relationships under analysis appeared intractable to more familiar approaches, such as direct observation, logical reasoning, or mathematics" [54].

Clarification of Concepts and Their Interrelationships. One specific purpose of simulation is the clarification of concepts. To the extent that the model simulates reality, it tries "to identify some major dimension of administrative behavior . . . and how such dimensions might be related to a variety of other measurable characteristics of people" [29, p. 124]. One such concept is that the sequencing of variables may be the vital ingredient, and is a variable itself [47, pp. 17–36].

Concepts are clarified and identified through study. Scrutinizing the internal relationships and interactions of a firm, a system, an industry, or a market can develop insights. Ultimately, the effects of experimental variables within the model, be they in the categories of informational changes, environmental changes, or organizational changes, may thus be measured and evaluated. In simulation we can specify not only the outcomes of decisions, as in classical analysis, but also in what order they can be considered [36, pp. 75–76]. Again sequence is a consideration. Simulation not only identifies the concepts; it permits and, it is hoped, requires structuring their proper relationships.

Reduction of Time, Space, Cost. A reason for using simulation is that it can provide major savings of time, space, and money. Simulation can avoid distortion of the real world that real experiments may produce. It permits manipulation of the time dimension by accelerating, delaying, or recycling without any effect on the real world. Rarely can the real experiment be performed as quickly or as inexpensively as simulation can be done. Space, like time, can be telescoped or extended to introduce situations without risk to the experimenter and at a fraction of the cost.

Computer Adaptability and Mathematical Treatment.   Oddly enough, simulation gets along in the real world because of its symbiosis with both types of computers. Continuous flows, as in a process, require the analog computer [58, p. 4], and discrete systems, exemplifying product rather than process, utilize digital computers. The *analog computer* in essence is a *simulation* of the process it measures. The mathematical treatment of the two computer systems briefly covers calculus and rough measurements in the analog system, whereas the digital system is merely a highly accurate series of split-second additions.

However, although simulation often includes sophisticated mathematics,

> Many simulation processes are relatively free from complex mathematics, making them more widely comprehensible than other more complex systems of formal mathematical analysis. The lack of dependency upon complex mathematical analysis not only has the advantage of making simulation comprehensible to the mathematically unsophisticated, but it can also be used in studying situations where mathematical methods capable of considering all of the desired factors are not available [17, p. 13].

Optimum Decision Making.   At the substantive level, simulation studies have focused both on analysis of general classes of phenomena and on development of detailed models and normative solutions [53, pp. 1, 4; 59]. Where a simulation of a series of limited alternatives aims to find the optimal or best solution, a search technique is justified. In searching systematically among limited alternatives, the investigator tends to minimize the number of steps. Where a large number of alternatives are present, the investigator may be satisfied with an approximation of the optimal.

Search techniques are useful with both mathematical and simulation techniques in striving toward the optimum [58, pp. 516–530]. In other words, rather than evaluate a large series of alternatives, the simulation, to be practical, must find a procedure minimizing the time and alternatives simulated. This procedure approximates optimization and approaches normative decision making.

Testing Variables.   In a simulation model, the variables may be either exogenous or endogenous. Exogenous variables, which are independent of the model system, are inputs that act on the system. They serve as casual variables in the experiment. Endogenous variables are the output of the system, that is, the results generated within the system by interaction with static variables. The static variables describe the state of the system at one point in time, thus maintaining an internal consistency with the operating characteristics inherent therein [49, pp. 10, 11].

The nature of the parameters and functional relationships identified in a simulation model are also extremely important. The parameters define the specific levels of the simulated system. The functional relationships prescribe the interaction of the variables with the system's components. Involving the operating characteristics of the system with the identities, they generate behavior within the system.

As a replication device, simulation permits marketing to more effectively use experimentation prior to application in the real market or to real market testing.

The simulated experiment provides for evaluating the effects of different variables, such as alternate prices, different promotion mixes, varying channel strategies, or any combination of these. Latin square designs, other experimental designs, and factor analysis can be used to test the variables separately or in consort. Both endogenous and exogenous variables may be introduced and tested.

Balderston and Hoggett simulated an experiment by constructing a general system of the dynamics of the Northwest lumber market. They examined the effects of changes in the availability and cost of information on the survival and efficiency of participating firms [5, p. 73]. The experimental variables were the availability and cost of information. Other studies measure the internal interactions of a firm, a system, a market, or an industry. The effects of experimental variables in the form of organizational, environmental, and/or informational changes can be measured and evaluated.

Simulation permits the system to operate in such a way that a whole year's transactions can be run through under close scrutiny. "Goods" flow through the system from factory to mixing point, to warehouse, to customer. Transportation and operating costs are incurred just as in real life, permitting the testing of various schemes for developing better distribution methods and achieving lower operating costs. Different cost trends relating to the alternative distribution arrangements are compared, leading ultimately to a plan of distribution at lowest cost [60, p. 66].

Teaching and Research. Ralph Day, in developing his SAMPLES (Simulated Action of Market Populations in Laboratory Experiments and Surveys), had as an objective "a powerful and flexible teaching tool" [20, p. 7] to explain the research process and methods, with simulated appearance, errors, and biases, that would approximate the real world. Data analysis and data interpretation would be real and would provide additional training. The methods would include fictitious consumer surveys and panels providing for cross-section and longitudinal analysis. Day believes simulation could be helpful in "statistics courses . . . to provide data for application and evaluation for multivariate statistical techniques" [20, p. 12].

The marketing game has been developed to teach the dynamics of the marketplace to businessmen and other students. The M.I.T. game permits students to develop integrated marketing programs in detail, with their performance being measured after their decisions. Such games stimulate student empathy and provide opportunities both to test quantitative knowledge and tools and to develop an insight into the complex interrelationships of the market and an overview of the arena [28, 36, and 37].

The extent to which learning occurs in gaming is not readily discernible. The learning depends in part on the care with which the specific goals of the game are built into it, in part on the mental processes of the participants. In each area, simulation methods may help teach both teacher and pupil: they appear to have a significant role in "sharpening our formulation concerning mental processes and phenomena . . . illumination and verification . . . specifying the nature of these processes in such complete detail that a computer is able to solve problems by following the sequence of steps programed into the machine" [32, p. 25].

Besides the training values, simulators can serve as research devices on problems of roles of customer change, on market enlargement, and on improving behavior roles heuristically [36, pp. 75–84].

Other Purposes. Other specific purposes of simulation include the valuation of perfect information, partially reliable information, survey information, inter-game comparisons, and the development of a basic method of comparing models of different natures, for example, mathematical, stochastic, heuristic, and so on. Even the interaction of mathematical and nonmathematical elements of a model, a system, or a theory can be measured via simulation.

DESIGN AND CONSTRUCTION

Design

Model Formulation. The concept of abstraction is extremely important in formulating simulation models. Abstraction permits generalization and "... highlights those things that are important for a specific purpose and suppresses the attributes which are unimportant" [49, p. 4]. Models should be simple enough for manipulation and understanding by those who would use them, representative enough in the total range of their possible implications, and complex enough to accurately represent the system under study [10, p. 31].

Simulation models can be used when analytical-solution techniques to a marketing problem are not readily available or when the performance of model components cannot be predicted with certainty. Processing the simulation model involves monitoring the changes of state of the modeled system. Outcomes result from random occurrences related to the nondeterministic performances of system components [46, pp. 148–149]. With each run of the model, a different set of random occurrences and events would be expected. In sum, the simulation model is not solved but is run a sufficient number of times to generate some measure of expected performance [46].

Data Sources. Two types of data are normally required for simulation experiments:

Historical data for estimating parameters, the behavior of variables, and relationships

A data-recording system to record data at their source and update records

In considering kinds of historical data required, the experimenter must determine data requirements for estimating:

1. The parameters of the system, for example, population parameters of random variables, cost figures, maximum queue length, and storage limitations
2. The behavior of system variables, for example, probability distributions of random variables
3. The overall interaction of system components, for example, internal dependencies among components, external influences, and computational abstractions

Collection of historical data is by far the greatest input problem of simulation studies. Complete data are often not available. When they are not, the simulator is forced to approximate, use similar data from a related process, or transform data from a different process into workable form [46, p. 148].

Although not a trivial matter in complex systems, a data-recording system is less of a problem than the collection of historical data. For operational purposes, it can be designed and incorporated as an integral part of the simulator.

Sampling and Design. Parameter estimation can be made from data sources mentioned in the previous paragraphs. Since the large size of these data often prohibits their total use, some randomization process is required to assure that the simulation sample is representative. These sample data might be used to determine any or all of the following:

The type of distribution of random variables

Distribution parameters, for example, estimating within desired confidence intervals such parameters as the mean, variance, and range

Interactions among components of the system

Efficient statistical design improves the interpretation of data gathered from simulation experiments. For the present purposes, the more important aspects of experimental design are:

1. *Problem definition.* The problem statement should include, among other things, the hypotheses to be tested.

2. *Choice of variables.* The more important variables should be identified in terms of their interactions and effects on the modeled system.

3. *Factor levels.* The levels of each factor in the experiment should be designated along with a determination whether the factors are "fixed" or "random."

4. *Extraneous variable control and classification.* Extraneous variation should be controlled where possible. For those variables that cannot be rigidly controlled, a broad classification scheme may be developed to aid in identifying causation.

5. *Specification of the method of analysis.* The method might be analysis of variance, multiple regression, or some other appropriate technique.

Although these and other methods will be discussed in the section on applications, it should be noted here that the data analysis method should be specified at the time of design.

Model Validation. The simulator should make every attempt to validate his model before constructing a computer program or other system for the model. One cannot expect a simulation to be an exact representation of the physical system being studied. It should be verified, however, that the system's more important characteristics are included in the model and that its relationships portray the actual behavior of the modeled system as closely as possible. Mize and Cox [46, p. 155] suggest certain useful guidelines in this respect:

1. *Accurate reproduction of past data.* All simulations should be able to reproduce underlying probability distributions with a high degree of accuracy. Also, at this stage it should be reaffirmed that the data used were in the proper form.

2. *Validity testing.* The model's behavior should be noted by pretesting. For example, certain results should never be negative, others should follow specific time paths, and so on.

3. *Checking for omissions and deletions.* A final check should be made to determine if significant factors have been omitted.

In summary, it is extremely important to ascertain that the pertinent system components have been defined and the relationships among components properly determined.

Construction

Operational Procedures. Most simulation models require several runs to achieve normal operations. For example, a waiting-line model in which arrivals are simulated according to some probability distribution may have an empty space for its first arrival. This certainly could not be considered typical of the overall system. Normal arrival conditions may not be attained until after several runs.

The problem is to develop a good set of starting conditions. On how to do this, one writer states:

There can be no general theory of how to do this but the technique most favorable is to invent starting conditions and allow the simulation to proceed for some time and take the final conditions as the initial conditions of the genuine run. This raises the question of how long to make the preliminary run and again no definite answers are possible. A general requirement is that the longest cycle in the plant should have been executed at least 3 or 4 times before transient abnormal behavior induced by non-sensible starting conditions can be expected to have died away [64, p. 176].

It is too much to expect any starting system to be perfect. After several runs, however, the system should have reached an acceptable level of stability.

Another important operating procedure involves the use of some type of time-flow mechanism. Since most simulations are concerned with time, the simulation program must be constructed so that it can move the model through simulated time, causing events to occur in the proper sequence with proper time intervals between successive occurrences. This can be a complex problem in the use of computerized models.

Two basic mechanisms are available for simulating the flow of time: the uniform-increment method and the variable-increment method [46, p. 158]. With the uniform-increment method, the model is constructed so that it proceeds through time in equal increments. A master clock is included for control, and the simulation usually begins at time zero. With passing increments and events, a bookkeeping operation is performed and appropriate logic tests are made. All interrelational reactions among model components are noted and values are computed. The master clock then advances by the proper increment, and the process is repeated.

The variable-increment method moves the simulation through time in uneven increments. Again a master clock is used, with the simulation beginning at time zero. Event results are noted and the master clock is updated to the time of the next-earliest event occurrence. This process is repeated throughout the simulation's total run.

Validation. If a simulation model can closely approximate results from the real-world system, it has validity. If a computer model is used, the first thing that should be done in validation is to "debug" the program. Logic loops and communication links between the main program and any subroutines should be checked very carefully to certify proper program functioning. Early runs of the model may expose weaknesses that initial validation efforts failed to find.

Data Analysis

Statistical Tests. Simulation data have been analyzed using analysis of variance [8 and 10]. However, the use of this statistical technique has been criticized [15, p. 92]. The problem is that analysis of variance can be employed with success only if separate sequences of random numbers are used for each set of operation rules. This procedure forces the simulator to forfeit a unique advantage of simulated experimentation—the ability to test different alternatives under identical conditions. Alternative analysis methods involve ranking procedures and multiple comparisons [14, p. 47]. These methods have been justified in that numerous simulations have as their main objective the comparison of alternative operational rules that result in the best system performance.

Interest has also been expressed in the use of spectral analysis as a method of interpreting simulation data. This type of analysis is considered appropriate because simulation output data are often autocorrelated. Since nonindependence of experimental outcomes violates one of the underlying assumptions of analysis of variance, spectral analysis provides a means by which these data may be analyzed and interpreted [25].

Interpretation of Results.   The uncertainties concerning proper methods of simulation data analysis carry over into interpretation.   It is often difficult to generalize from the results of a particular simulation study.   Thus:

> When one constructs a model of a hypothetical organization, intended to be representative of a large class of organizations, the evaluation must be entirely subjective.   The evaluation is not aided by imprecision in the definition of the class of organizations to which inference is intended, nor by inadequate description of the characteristics of the model.   The investigator must enlist support for the credibility of his model, either by argument or demonstration, before attempting the presentation of substantive results.   If the credibility of the model is allowed to depend upon the intuitive acceptability of results one can prove only the obvious and the model is essentially useless [14].

It is clear that methodological questions about simulation design and evaluation must be examined closely for possible insights into their answers.   Only when these answers have been found will general application of simulation be possible.

Simulation Languages

Several simulation languages have been developed to take advantage of the common features of simulation models.   These programs greatly simplify the process of programming the model in computer language.

Two widely used simulation languages are GPSS [22, p. 22] and SIMSCRIPT [40].   Others include GASP [45, p. 28], DYNAMO [39 and 55], and SIMULA [18, p. 671].   Among these languages, SIMSCRIPT is considered the most flexible but has the drawback of requiring an in-depth knowledge of FORTRAN.   GPSS can be learned quickly with no prior knowledge of programming, but is less flexible and slower in execution than SIMSCRIPT [63, p. 723].   In terms of general output, neither SIMSCRIPT nor GPSS has shown superiority over the other.   Less is known of the other languages because of their relatively infrequent usage.

TYPES AND APPLICATIONS

Types of Models

Kotler suggests six types of simulation models useful in marketing; they may be categorized as either small or large scale [40, pp. 238–241].   The three small-scale models are enterprise, marketing mix, and competitive response.   The large-scale models are total market, distribution, and comprehensive (total marketing system).

Small Scale.   The enterprise model simulates the information and decision systems in a firm operating on the flows of money, men, materials, and machines.   It is used to find better information and decision rules to improve the flows.

Carnegie-Mellon University developed one behavioral approach, incorporating actual and theoretical behavior rules into decision and information systems [17].   Sales are considered an independent variable in this and the Jay Forrester model.   Forrester studied delays in the information system and facility coordination in the decision systems and their effect on the timing of sales [26].

Bonini's enterprise model treats sales as an output of market factors, salesmen, and a random variable. He did not use most of the mix elements, including advertising, product characteristics, and competitive interactions [7].

Competitor reactions and interactions are detailed in competitor response models. Oligopoly models show reactions of firms to their competitors' price changes [47, pp. 17–26]. A duopoly model, wherein a firm predicts its costs, profits, market demand, and competitor response to various marketing plans as a means of evaluating those plans, has been developed in a simulation of the container-industry duopoly: the Continental Can Company versus the American Can Company [17, pp. 83–97].

The third small-scale type works on correct proportions of the marketing mix or submix sets. Business games, such as the UCLA (University of California, Los Angeles) game, the Carnegie Tech Management Game, and the M.I.T. Marketing Game, are prime examples of simulations involving the interactions of decisions affecting elements of the marketing mix [13; 37, pp. 83–102]. One study, not a game, has evaluated empirical activities for a grocery chain in its marketing-mix decisions [65].

Large Scale. Guy Orcutt has developed a simulation model of the United States economy which analyzes the interactions between and within households, firms, financial institutions, and other decision-making units. The model includes a simulation of 10,000 hypothetical customers who are subjected to the effects of alternate marketing mixes. The sample is representative of the nation's total population and parallels its demographic structure [52].

The Pitt-Amstam Market Simulator, developed by William Kehl [36, pp. 75–84], uses as input data the buyer characteristics of 300 retailers in a model wherein wholesale branch-sales managers compete with one another in managing their personnel. The Simulator is used for training branch managers who, besides performing their departmental duties, must become aware of the other facets of marketing management.

The Simulmatics Corporation developed another sample universe of almost 3,000 hypothetical individuals resembling the United States population in demographic structure. Each computer run represents a year in which the people are exposed to specific media schedules. Evaluation of the schedules is done by tabulating the characteristics of the people exposed [61].

Distribution models cover simulated behavior of various forms of different levels in the marketing channels. Balderston and Hoggatt's model of the West Coast lumber industry was used primarily to measure the resulting efficiency of various firms with changes in the cost and availability of information [54].

The Cohen model of the shoe, leather, and hide industry simulated purchasing and price behavior by firms at various levels and compared computer output with the industry's actual behavior in sales and prices over time [12].

Gerson and Maffei developed a physical-distribution model simulating alternate routes for a superorganization of 10 factories, 40 warehouses, and 4,000 customers, comparing the costs of each route [27, pp. 62–69].

Models may include firms, channels, competitors, the economy, and the customers in a comprehensive simulation. Kotler developed such a model to test marketing strategies as well as basic strategies with various market segments. He simulated two rival firms introducing new products simultaneously with 13 different strategies. He was able to test competing strategies at different stages in the product life cycle [41, pp. 104–119].

Functional Applications

Pricing. Pricing is one of the most complex decisions faced by businessmen. Because of the complexity of this task, many executives have been forced to develop rules of thumb, or heuristics, for determining prices. Heuristic programming models are based on these so-called rules of thumb and are used to simulate the actual decision criteria in the solution to a price-setting problem. If the model accurately replicates the executive's pricing policies and predicts well, it can be used to examine the effects of different pricing strategies.

Cyert, March, and Moore followed the heuristic process in developing a descriptive model of pricing behavior in a department store [17, pp. 128–148]. The heuristic procedure involved two general goals: a sales objective and a markup objective. These goals followed the reasoning that "the department expects (and is expected by the firm) to achieve an annual sales objective" and "the department attempts to realize a specified average mark-up on the goods sold [17, p. 129]." Three different pricing situations were recognized as relative to the basic organizational goals: *normal, sale,* and *markdown* pricing. "The first two situations occur at regularly planned times. The third is a contingent situation, produced by failure or anticipated failure with respect to organizational goals. In each pricing situation the basic procedure is the same, the application of a mark-up to a cost to determine an appropriate price [17, p. 137]."

A standard industry margin was used to determine regular prices in the model. The normal pricing heuristic was based on an argument between competitors to establish similar initial prices. Sale pricing was resorted to on those occasions when the sales-volume goal was not being achieved.

With these general policy constraints, a flow diagram and a mathematical model were constructed to describe the complete heuristic process. A markdown procedure for pricing was initiated in cases where sale pricing did not achieve the sales-volume goal [17, pp. 140–145].

In the test for validity, the models predicted to the penny 188 of 197 normal prices, 36 of 58 sale prices, and 140 of 159 markdown prices. Thus, the tests tend to support the model as a good description of the actual procedure used in that particular department store.

Morgenroth developed another heuristic model describing the pricing procedure followed by a firm in an oligopolistic industry [47, pp. 17–27]. In the model, price increases by competitors are followed if the district sales office agrees. Figure 1 illustrated the pricing-decision process. Major wholesaler prices are watched (box 1) for any disruptive activity. If the price does not change, no further action is taken other than to return to box 1 and continue watching. If there is a price change, one proceeds to box 3, which differentiates the direction of the price move and divides the model into two basic sequences: upward or downward.

If the price increases, it is followed if the district sales office concludes that the increase is the proper decision (boxes 3, 4, and 5). Even when the district sales office says no to the price increase, higher authority, represented by the decision maker in box 6, can raise the price by overruling the district sales office if he feels that competitors will increase their prices. If not, a holding period is initiated (box 7) for 24 hours. At the end of that time, price may be increased if competitors' prices rise.

If the prices do not increase, a return is made to box 1 and watching is initiated once again. If the initial competitive price decreases, the decision procedure is again triggered, utilizing the lower half of the model. The district sales office is contacted (boxes 8 and 13), competitive sales are observed (box 9), a waiting period is enforced (box 14), and steps are taken to block any spreading of the price cut (boxes 15, 10, 11, and 12). Tests of Morgenroth's model closely simulated 31 actual pricing decisions, indicating a close approximation of the pricing procedure used by the company.

Promotion.   Promotion in marketing encompasses communication procedures related to product characteristics and appeals that are directed toward consumers. Three subcategories of promotion may be identified: (1) *media advertising,* involving the use of one or a combination of radio, television, direct mail, outdoor, or newspaper communications; (2) *point-of-sale promotion,* in-

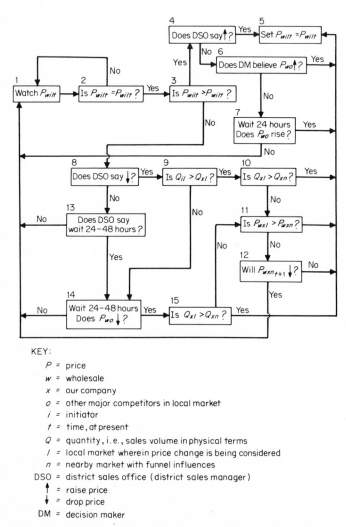

KEY:

P = price
w = wholesale
x = our company
o = other major competitors in local market
i = initiator
t = time, at present
Q = quantity, i.e., sales volume in physical terms
l = local market wherein price change is being considered
n = nearby market with funnel influences
DSO = district sales office (district sales manager)
↑ = raise price
↓ = drop price
DM = decision maker

Fig. 1. Heuristic model of the pricing process in an oligopolistic industry. (source: W. M. Morgenroth, *"A Method for Understanding Price Determinants,"* Journal of Marketing Research, *August 1964, p. 19.*)

cluding consumer-information flow through use of brochures, broadsides, placards, and displays at point of sale; (3) *selling presentations,* including person-to-person communication from sellers to potential buyers. Simulation models of all these subcategories of promotion have been developed.

Two well-known simulation models of media advertising are the Computer Assessment of Media (CAM) model developed by the London Press Exchange and the media-mix model of the Simulmatics Corporation [9 and 61].

The CAM model simulates the process by which television and magazine advertisements reach consumers. Through use of the model, steps in the communication process are described and quantitative values are assigned to the various stages.

As a base, viewing data in four-week periods are provided by Television Audience Measurement, Ltd. (TAM). These data are converted into probabilities of television viewing for a yearly period. Magazine data are provided by the National Readership Survey (NRS). A pairing process is then used to link the two sources of data. The TAM and NRS sample members are paired off on the basis of demographic characteristics, with the NRS sample member assigned the viewing pattern of his TAM counterpart.

After this has been accomplished, a target sample for a message is selected and evaluated. For each type of media, a perception value is then determined that attempts to measure the impact of a particular advertisement on the viewer.

The users of CAM hypothesized that certain times during the week may be more suitable for T.V. commercials. The same advertisement may also have more prestige and influence when it appears in one publication rather than in another. To allow for these effects, selectivity weight factors are used. Impact weight factors are then applied to determine the advertisement's effectiveness on viewers.

The simulation's primary purpose is to describe how a promotional campaign affects the defined market target. The measure used in this determination is called the "Probability of Receiving an Impression" (PRI) and is computed as the adjusted probability of seeing a particular magazine times its perceived impact.

The use of the PRI measure makes it possible to obtain an impression distribution. By applying a series of weights to the impression distribution, one number can be produced as the model's entire output. The single value from the model is the schedule-effectiveness value. This value is the criterion used for choosing among schedules.

A major criticism of the CAM simulation has been leveled by Jones:

> The main broad criticism is that CAM gives a measure of effectiveness, but in what terms? The media planner is suddenly thrust from circumstances in which he uses his rather limited but understandable measurements of effectiveness into a new space age dimension which he cannot relate in any way to this traditional measurement. In making these criticisms, however, it becomes increasingly obvious that CAM is a model of the future. Most of the assumptions can be validated or modified by research [34, p. 109].

The Simulmatics Corporation has proposed a microanalytic simulation approach to media scheduling [61]. Its computer-based model contains detailed information on 2,994 imaginary individuals more than four years of age. The computerized sample is balanced to the United States by demographic characteristics, and each individual is described by his social characteristics and media habits.

As an example, one can follow through the Simulmatics simulation evaluation program for television. For this, an initial probability of an individual's being exposed to a particular program at a given time is used. This probability is derived from actual audience data if available. If not, multiple-regression analysis is used to estimate the exposure probability of a particular show, based on relative viewing variables, such as show type, time of day, network, and station coverage.

The initial exposure probability is factored by functions representing habit, show saturation, formation in T.V. viewing, and show competition. Separate results on various medium exposures are maintained throughout the simulation. The final report is in the form of summary statistics relative to the media scheduling problem.

Amstutz has developed a comprehensive heuristic model of point-of-sale promotion activity and effects along with supporting probability functions for use in computer simulation. Figure 2 summarizes the activities that may lead to alternative consumer experiences and responses at the point of sale [2].

The consumer's explicit decision to shop, illustrated at the top of Figure 2, is based on a perceived need function involving attitude and awareness of products and response to various stimuli.

According to Amstutz, the consumer's perceived need for all brands is established before he makes any explicit decision to shop [2, p. 209]. Given the decision to shop, the consumer goes to the retailer that ranks highest on his attitude-preference scale. Having entered the chosen store, the consumer must determine whether the favored brand is being carried. If the first-choice brand is not in stock, the consumer may move on to another store or consider other brands carried by the favored retailer. This decision outcome is based on the consumer's relative preference for brand and retailer. If brand preference is stronger than retailer preference, the consumer will go to another store. If the converse is true, other brands will be considered.

Once consumer exposure to a brand in a particular retail outlet is established, it is necessary to determine the exposure level (if any) to point-of-sale promotion in support of that brand. If exposure is achieved, the consumers' assimilation of and response to selling effort effected by retail salesmen are then determined similarly.

If a purchase is made, the point-of-sale activity is terminated. If not, the process continues until all potential reactions and responses to available brands have been exhausted.

The third subcategory of promotion involves personal selling. Several simulations in this area have been developed, especially in estimating sales response to selling effort. Amstutz examined in detail the interaction between salesman, product, and customer to provide insight into the number and type of salesmen a firm should employ.

Stokes and Mintz utilized a Monte Carlo queuing model to determine the number of clerks to assign to a floor in a department store [62, p. 388–393]. An interesting example of a simulation approach dealing with the service aspect of personal selling is given by Hespas [31, pp. 160–166]. Utilizing data on the distribution of customer-service expectations, the distribution of service calls, and the distribution of service-time requirements, the researchers developed a simulation which helped identify a satisfactory combination of call-scheduling rules and size of the service staff. The simulation also helped determine future service needs by providing a criterion for identifying the best operating method for various future levels of machines in the field.

Product.   There are at least four stages which can be considered in the new-product decision process: search, screening, evaluation, and implementation. The simulation example in this section deals with the preliminary search and evaluation policy for a firm, given certain basic inputs. The model was developed by Pessemier as part of a comprehensive analysis on new-product decisions [53, chap. 2].

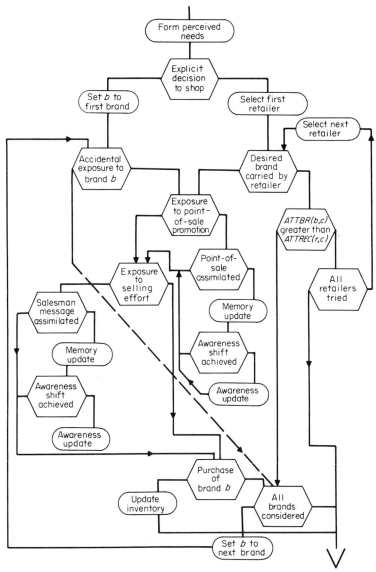

Fig. 2.   Heuristic model of consumer point-of-sale activity. (source: *A. E. Amstutz,* Computer Simulation of Competitive Market Response, *Cambridge, Mass.: MIT, 1967, p. 209.*)

The inputs to Pessemier's simulation are developed from managerial policy decisions and forecasts. Five input areas are identified:

1. Specification of the largest capital investment and the longest economic life which can reasonably be associated with new-product proposals in a specific area

2. Investigation to determine how homogeneous new-product proposals would be with respect to the expected timing of cash flows, and a subsequent categorization based on these findings

3. An estimate of the percentage of all new-product proposals which will fall within a particular category and the distribution of total-earnings cash-flow outcomes

4. Computation of the rate of return from each potential outcome to determine if minimum-return standards are met for the product's continuance

5. An estimate of the expected cost and number of proposals resulting from each alternative search plan

Figure 3 summarizes the simulation run utilizing these input data. A Monte Carlo simulation (explained in the next subsection) is used to generate a distribution of return on investment to searching in each area i with search policy j

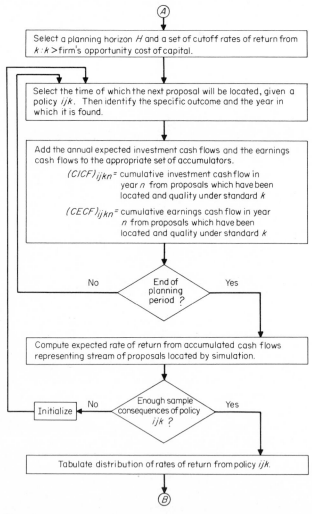

Fig. 3.   Flow diagram for selecting an optimal or near-optimal new-product search and evaluation policy. (SOURCE: *E. A. Pessemier,* New-Product Decisions: An Analytical Approach, *New York: McGraw-Hill, 1966, pp. 69–70.*)

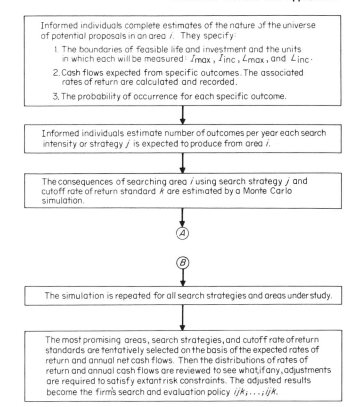

Informed individuals complete estimates of the nature of the universe of potential proposals in an area i. They specify:

    1. The boundaries of feasible life and investment and the units in which each will be measured: I_{max}, I_{inc}, L_{max}, and L_{inc}.

    2. Cash flows expected from specific outcomes. The associated rates of return are calculated and recorded.

    3. The probability of occurrence for each specific outcome.

Informed individuals estimate number of outcomes per year each search intensity or strategy j is expected to produce from area i.

The consequences of searching area i using search strategy j and cutoff rate of return standard k are estimated by a Monte Carlo simulation.

(A)

(B)

The simulation is repeated for all search strategies and areas under study.

The most promising areas, search strategies, and cutoff rate of return standards are tentatively selected on the basis of the expected rates of return and annual net cash flows. Then the distributions of rates of return and annual cash flows are reviewed to see what, if any, adjustments are required to satisfy extant risk constraints. The adjusted results become the firm's search and evaluation policy $ijk; \ldots; ijk$.

Fig. 3. (Continued).

and cutoff return criterion k. The simulation is then repeated for all search strategies and areas under study. The next phase of the simulation selects the best combination of search area, strategy, and cutoff return on the basis of expected return on investment and risk as measured by the standard deviation of return for the area-strategy-cutoff combination. The final output yields the best search and preliminary evaluation policy for the firm, given the inputs to the model. The reader is referred to the original source [53] for a detailed accounting of the model.

Physical Distribution

How Many Servicemen? The first illustrative simulation to be presented involves servicing. With the aid of a Monte Carlo simulation, a queuing problem involving randomly distributed arrival and service times will be constructed and analyzed. Monte Carlo simulation is a means of approximating business and other problems wherein events occur in accordance with assigned or computed probabilities [30; 57, chap. 13]. In this example, a table of random numbers will be used in connection with a continuous probability distribution.

The problem involves a multiline retailer who operates a warehouse for the local distribution of houseware products to his various branch outlets. Only authorized branch sales managers can receive the products and then only with proper certification. Ten sales managers have the proper certification and use the warehouse facility. These sales managers have indicated to the warehouse manager that a serious waiting-line problem exists that is tying up much of their valuable time. The warehouse manager is certain the problem can be solved by adding additional servicemen to the two he currently employs. He wishes to know how many servicemen should be added to give the most efficient service relative to cost.

For a one-month period, the operation of the warehouse was observed for a one-hour span each day. These observation periods were scheduled randomly to get a representative cross-section of distribution activities. The following data were collected.

1. Average time between sales-manager visits: 10 min.
2. Total number of visits during the month: 200
3. Minutes waited for service and number of instances:

20 minutes	20
25 minutes	40
30 minutes	60
35 minutes	80
Total service requests	200

Additional data were collected by dividing the observation time into 10-minute intervals and recording the number of sales managers arriving during these periods. It was found that a 100 percent chance existed for the arrival of one or more sales managers during any given 10-minute observation period.

Tabulations at the end of the observation period yielded the following data:

A. Percentage distribution of service times
$$20/200 = 10\% \quad (20 \text{ minutes})$$
$$40/200 = 20\% \quad (25 \text{ minutes})$$
$$60/200 = 30\% \quad (30 \text{ minutes})$$
$$80/200 = 40\% \quad (35 \text{ minutes})$$

B. Weighed average of service times
$$10\% \times 20 \text{ minutes} = 2.0 \text{ minutes}$$
$$20\% \times 25 \text{ minutes} = 5.0 \text{ minutes}$$
$$30\% \times 30 \text{ minutes} = 9.0 \text{ minutes}$$
$$40\% \times 35 \text{ minutes} = 14.0 \text{ minutes}$$

C. Average service time............30.0 minutes

With these data, the warehouse manager can simulate the operation of his distribution point, utilizing a table of random digits [56].

The first task is to simulate the arrivals of sales managers at the warehouse. Although these arrivals are random, it is known that there is a 100 percent probability that at least one manager will arrive within any 10-minute observation period. Since there are ten digits (0, 1, 2, 3, 4, 5, 6, 7, 8, 9) representing 100 percent probability of an arrival, any one of these numbers can be selected to represent the randomly occurring arrivals. For purposes of this problem, let us use 6.

Having determined the randomization process for approximating the number of arrivals per period, we must now go through a different list of 10-digit random numbers for each simulated period. The number of 6's that are found in each sequence of numbers will represent the number of sales managers arriving during that period. For illustration, a total of 15 simulated 10-minute periods are used. Reading the rows of random digits from left to right and utilizing the first 20 columns, the following arrival rates can be simulated:

Digits	Number of 6's appearing
1009732533	0
3754204805	0
0842268953	1
9901902529	0
1280799970	0
6606574717	3
3106010805	1
8526977602	2
6357332135	1
7379645753	1
9852017767	1
1180505431	0
8345299634	1
8868540200	1
9959467348	1

The number of 6's found in each 10-digit random number represents the number of sales managers arriving at the warehouse during 15 periods of 10 minutes each. The results for all 15 simulation periods are shown in Table 1.

TABLE 1   Simulated Arrivals for 15 Ten-Minute Periods

Ten-minute periods	Simulated arrivals	Service time for each (minutes)
1	0	
2	0	
3	1	35
4	0	
5	0	
6	3	35, 30, 25
7	1	20
8	2	35, 30
9	1	35
10	1	35
11	1	30
12	0	
13	1	25
14	1	35
15	1	35

The corresponding servicing times are also shown in the table opposite each simulated arrival. These servicing times were calculated from the percentage distribution of service times using the following data:

Servicing time	Percent of time
20 minutes	10%
25 minutes	20%
30 minutes	30%
35 minutes	40%

With the use of the random-number table, the simulated servicing times can be analyzed in the following sequence:

1. Let 0 represent the probability of a service time of 20 minutes.
2. Let 1 and 2 represent the probabilities of a service time of 25 minutes.
3. Let 3, 4, and 5 represent the probabilities of a service time of 30 minutes.
4. Let 6, 7, 8, and 9 represent the probabilities of a service time of 35 minutes.

The logic of this method is clear. The use of 0 to represent the probability of a service time of 20 minutes parallels the .1 probability of this service time's occurring, since the digit 0 has a 1-in-10 chance of occurring. Because there are 2 chances in 10 of getting either a 1 or 2, they represent in combination a .2 probability. The use of 3, 4, and 5 in combination represent a .3 probability, and 6, 7, 8, and 9 represent a .4 probability of occurrence. To simulate the service times, the table of random numbers must once again be used. In this way, servicing times are assigned in accordance with the preceding probability criteria.

The basic input data of sales-manager arrival and servicing times completed, the warehouse manager is now ready to determine the optimum number of warehouse servicemen. The primary objective is to minimize the total cost of warehouse operation plus the cost of lost time by waiting sales managers.

The servicing rule followed by the warehouse is first-come, first-served. The facility opens for business at 9:00 A.M., with uninterrupted operations until a 1:00 P.M. lunch break. Operations are resumed at 2:00 P.M. and continue until 6:00 P.M. each weekday.

From previous data observed by the warehouse manager, the following additional assumptions are made relative to the arrival routine:
1. If there is one arrival, it will be assumed to occur at the beginning of the 10-minute period.
2. If there are two arrivals, one will be assumed to arrive at the beginning of the 10-minute period and the other at the beginning of the fourth minute during the period.
3. If there are three arrivals, one will be assumed to arrive at the beginning of the 10-minute period, the second at the beginning of the fourth minute, and the third at the beginning of the sixth minute.

The first arrival in the simulation (Figure 4) is at 9:20 A.M. The second is at 9:50 A.M.; the third is at 9:54, and so on. The solid lines in Figure 4 indicate service in operation; the broken lines, waiting times.

Counting the total minutes of waiting time yields 410 minutes, with an average waiting time per arrival of $410/13 = 31.54$ minutes. The warehouse servicemen are paid $3 an hour, and the branch-office sales managers are paid $5 an hour. If the average time between arrivals is 10 minutes, the cumulative number of visits by sales managers must be equal to 48 trips per day (8 hours per day $\times$ 6 trips per hour). The total waiting time is the product of the average waiting time and the number of daily trips, $31.54 \times 48 = 1513.92$ minutes, or 25.23 hours of lost time daily.

The sales manager's pay of $5 an hour times the daily lost time (25.23 hours) yields a daily cost of lost time of $25.23 \times \$5 = \$126.15$. The daily cost of the warehouse servicemen is 8 hours $\times$ $3 $\times$ 2 men = $48. The sum of these two costs is the total cost of operating the warehouse per day under present servicing conditions.

Cost of sales manager's lost time	$126.15
Wages of warehouse servicemen	48.00
Total cost per day (2 servicemen)	$174.15

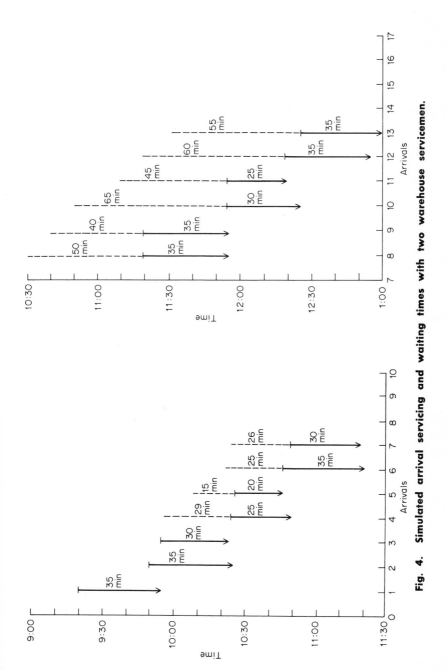

Fig. 4. Simulated arrival servicing and waiting times with two warehouse servicemen.

2-537

What, then, is the optimum number of servicemen to assign to the warehouse? To solve this problem, the operating system must now be simulated with an additional number of warehouse servicemen. This has been done in Figure 5, using three servicemen instead of the two illustrated in Figure 4.

The total time lost waiting with three servicemen is 63 minutes. The computed lost time per arrival in this case (63/13) is 4.85 minutes lost per arrival. With 48 daily arrivals, the total lost time is 48 × 4.85, or 232.80 minutes, which is equivalent to about 4 hours per day.

Cost of sales manager's lost time (4 × $5) = $20
Wages of warehouse servicemen (8 × $3 × 3) =   <u>72</u>

Total cost per day (3 servicemen) $92

Thus, a reduction in costs can clearly be obtained by adding a third serviceman. But is this the optimum number to employ under current arrival and servicing conditions? The answer can be obtained by simulating servicing times and costs with four salesmen. No lost time by sales managers would be incurred, but the wages of four servicemen would total $96 (8 × $3 × 4). Therefore, the use of three servicemen is optimum under current conditions, since the costs incurred in this case are $4 less than those incurred using four servicemen.

Other Examples. Kuehn and Hamburger have developed a heuristic program for ascertaining the optimum number and location of warehouses [43, pp. 361–368], the objective being to minimize distribution costs. The primary function of the Kuehn-Hamburger program is to locate warehouses one at a time until an optimum number are reached and further additions would increase total distribution costs. A "bump and shift" routine scans the list of potential warehouse sites, yielding an output decision on whether to activate or eliminate specific sites. The criteria for these decisions are as follows [43, p. 647]:

1. Eliminate those warehouses which have become uneconomical as a result of subsequent placement of warehouses. Each customer formerly serviced by a newly closed warehouse will now be supplied by that remaining warehouse which can perform the service at the lowest cost.

2. Evaluate the economics of shifting each remaining warehouse to another potential site whose local concentration of demand is now serviced by that warehouse.

The inputs required by the program include factory locations, potential warehouse sites, specific characteristics of each site, shipping costs between factories, potential warehouses and customers, expected sales volume for each customer, operating costs of each warehouse, and opportunity costs associated with shipping delays.

An alternate approach for warehouse-location determination has been developed by Feldman, Lehrer, and Ray [24, pp. 670–684]. Their procedure involves the analysis of all possible warehouse locations, dropping one by one until no further cost reduction can be obtained. At the same time, they preserve the current location patterns that minimize cost.

Cooper has discussed the feasibility of several heuristic models involving destination specification and alternate allocation-location criteria [16, pp. 37–53].

In sum, many of the complex elements of distribution systems can be analyzed by simulation [60, pp. 65–75]. Simulation has the flexibility to incorporate specific factors, such as number of customers and customer location, as

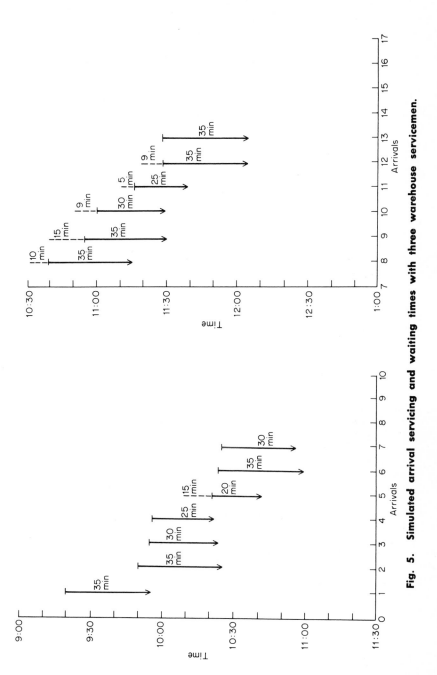

Fig. 5. Simulated arrival servicing and waiting times with three warehouse servicemen.

well as specific characteristics of warehouses, factories, transportation costs, and delivery requirements [27, pp. 62–69].

Marketing Mix.   Marketing-mix models are used to evaluate the impact of alternative marketing strategies on sales and profits.   A variety of business games, varying in complexity, are examples of this type of model.   Players of these games are usually involved in price setting, establishment of budgets for promotion, distribution cost analysis, budget allocations for research and product development, and overall evaluation of marketing plans and strategy. Carnegie-Mellon University's Marketing Analysis Training Exercise (MATE) is an example of a game incorporating the manipulation of elements of the marketing mix [13].   Consumer demand in the game is determined by repeated use of an equation for each time period under consideration.   When the total market demand for a product has been determined, it is then allocated among competing brands.   This allocation process depends on brand loyalty and brand shifting, the latter determined by the demand remaining in the market over and above loyal habitual repurchases of the market brands.

Marketing-strategy decisions of the competitors influence the loyalty and shifting patterns eventually developed in the model.   Pricing, advertising, product characteristics, and consumer preferences are among the variables utilized in the MATE game.

Another relative game is the Total Market Environment Simulation (TOMES) [3, pp. 47–60].   It synthesizes total demand from the sums of individual consumer demands in contrast with the aggregate method utilized in MATE.   In this game, consumers' attitudes and preferences are considered along with retailer preferences.

Institutional Applications

Total Market Structure.   Simulation models have been used to model the total market structure as an aid to management in marketing planning.   The Balderston and Hoggatt simulation of market interactions between manufacturers, wholesalers, retailers, and consumers in the lumber industry is an excellent example [5].

Perhaps the most detailed and successful simulation application of the total market process is the Amstutz and Claycamp model of the ethical drug market [11, pp. 113–150].   The microanalytic simulation approach used in this model was also successfully applied to models of the consumer-product market [2].

Retailing.   Uhr has developed an interesting simulation of a regional retail food chain which can be used to test alternative marketing strategies [65]. The model can be employed to simulate marketing activities of the supermarket chain for yearly periods.   It begins by calculating an initial sales estimate, modified to account for competitive reactions via Monte Carlo simulation. When expected sales are not achieved, promotional action, in the form of a home mailer, is initiated.   Costs of this action and the overall costs associated with the chain's operation are computed quarterly.   The quarterly profits are summed to derive the chain's final yearly profit level.

Consumer Behavior.   The heuristic model of consumer behavior developed by Howard and Sheth (Figure 6) is perhaps the most comprehensive model of its kind in the literature [33].   Howard and Sheth focus on the elements of repeat buying by presenting a theory which incorporates the dynamics of purchase behavior over time.   The model's theoretical roots are found in stimulus-response learning theory.   The basic view is that, given a drive (hunger) and the perception of a cue (advertising), the individual may make a response (purchase) which, if reinforced or rewarded, may lead to learning (repeat purchasing).

Farley and Ring tested the Howard-Sheth model with interesting results [23, pp. 427–438]. They cast the model in the form of a multiple-equation regression model for testing data on a grocery product in a specific market. It was

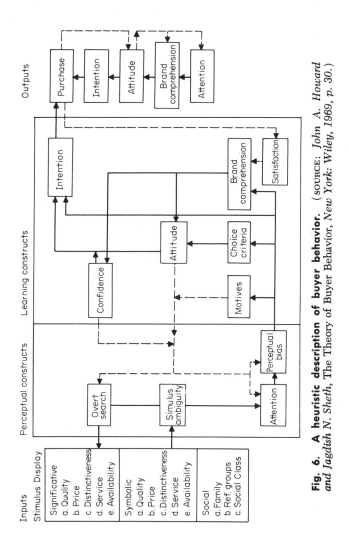

Fig. 6. A heuristic description of buyer behavior. (SOURCE: *John A. Howard and Jagdish N. Sheth*, The Theory of Buyer Behavior, *New York: Wiley, 1969, p. 30.*)

found that estimated structural parameters were generally consistent with the model's predictions, but some goodness-of-fit measures were weak. Perhaps these results allude to the fact that simulation procedures may yield greater validity to this model than quantitative analytical techniques.

Nicosia has also developed a comprehensive heuristic model of consumer behavior [51]. The consumer decision-making process in his model is based on a firm's introducing a new product. The model is a diagram of consumer behavior in the form of a flow chart representing a decision-making sequence similar to a complex computer program with feedback loops. Nicosia's model is designed so that it can be used experimentally with mathematical processes or with computer simulation.

CONCLUSIONS

State of the Art

Some important advantages of simulation as cited by several authorities include:

1.   After a simulation model has been adequately developed and tested, observations of the model can be used to derive and test new theories and hypotheses [48, p. 367].

2.   Simplifications and assumptions are not required for simulation to the extent that they are demanded for analytical solutions [66, p. 30].

3.   Simulation procedures can enhance the exploration of validity and implications of the marketer's insights into environmental factors. Talents among an organization's management team can be pooled and transcribed into a simulation that, it is hoped, will predict market outcomes [11, pp. 113–149].

4.   Marketing experimentation can be facilitated through simulation. It permits manipulation of data without recourse to actual field studies [66, p. 30].

5.   Simulation models can integrate historical research data and secondary data into meaningful statistical prediction tools.

6.   The nontechnical manager can understand the simulation process more easily than a complex, analytical mathematical model, and, in fact, less sophistication may be required to develop it [66].

7.   Simulation program languages, such as the General Purpose System Simulator (GPSS) and SIMSCRIPT, are available which can lower programming costs and are relatively easy to learn and apply. These special languages can also provide a conceptual view of a system or process which aids in developing simulation models.

8.   Simulation can be used to select the best solution techniques for analyzing marketing decisions [38, pp. 8–13].

On the other hand, there are several disadvantages involving simulation processes that should be noted:

1.   Realistic simulation processes are often time-consuming. The time requirement results from the repeated simulation runs necessary to study the behavior of the system under investigation. This problem is magnified by the inclusion of additional input variables [21, p. 362].

2.   The simulation process can be very expensive. Computer time, creative programmers and researchers, and data processors all cost money. The level of expenditures for models of social, political, and economic systems reported in a recent survey provides some indication of the magnitudes of these costs. Twenty projects were reported to have cost between $10,000 and $100,000, and 17 cost over $100,000. Some projects reported costs in excess of $2 million [1, pp. 64–65].

3.   The results of simulation models may be misinterpreted. Overzealous advocates may conclude that simulated outcomes are always more valid than

analytical results. This is definitely not the case. A simulation model should only be used where it is more efficient than an analytical technique [21].

4. It is often difficult to test simulation models. The numerous parameters may render it impossible to test all combinations of values proposed in the model. Sampling techniques may have to be used to select specific values for inclusion in sensitivity tests, with the hope that untested values will not cause erratic behavior of the model [11].

5. Determination of the validity of a simulation model is difficult. Subjective decisions involving the testing criteria for validity are often necessary, and they can yield results that are suspect [11].

Future Relevance to New Marketing Concepts

Among key factors relative to the future use of simulation in marketing will be the education of management to accept its results, and the education of the personnel required to produce these results. The complexity of problems facing the business firm of the future suggests the possibility of rising numbers of companies using operations research techniques, simulation, and management games. Thus, the men and women promoted into top executive jobs are likely to be those who are sufficiently familiar with these techniques to retain effective control in increasingly complex situations. As these highly trained individuals progress in their separate fields, many new applications of simulation to marketing and related fields can be expected.

One area certain to draw increased attention is marketing logistics. For example, a firm desiring to centralize its warehousing facilities could use simulation to provide information on refinements of the newly integrated system, to uncover major problems of the new system during the preliminary planning stages, and to demonstrate how the new system would work under various conditions. Such a simulation would consider empirical information on inventory levels and all unusual conditions such as stock shortages and facility waiting lines.

In product planning, simulation could be used to determine the payout time of the return on investment for various products. A computerized model relating selling prices, operating costs, sales revenue, plant and equipment investments, and working capital would be required. By altering the magnitude and rate of increase or decrease for key cost items, by shifting production volume relative to market demand and plant capacity, and by including or excluding improvements in production techniques, the feasibility of producing and marketing products under various assumed conditions could be measured.

The conceptual model by Barton may offer useful guidelines for predicting short-term sales, measuring the relative effectiveness of alternative test-market programs, and aiding in the allocation of promotional dollars [6, pp. 19–29]. The model seeks to identify the main variables affecting the sales of nondurable products, for example, nonbuyers, new buyers, new repeat buyers, and old repeat buyers. These variables are then structured conceptually for use in decision making in marketing management, and as a starting framework for a specific information-system design. Sufficient data to test this extensive model would involve combinations of consumer-panel data, survey research information, store audit, and experimentation. The cost of coordinating all these data might be prohibitive in some instances, but the model could serve as a framework for the future development of sales-prediction systems.

In the area of competitive gaming, promising uses of simulation may include the selection of marketing personnel. It should be possible, for example, to observe an individual's behavior under the stress of a game in which rapid decisions must be made in cooperation with other members of the game team. This type of information could provide insight into the participant's ability to react positively to the pressures of actual business decisions.

The continued development of simulations of consumer behavior may be of interest in the future. The bases for such models could include such inputs as known social norms, characteristics relative to class and group, and the probability of individual conformity. The ability to seek and find problem solutions relative to consumer needs should also be of importance.

Input-output analysis has been primarily used as an economic tool in the analysis of the gross national product [44]. Simulations of this process should prove useful in future estimates of firm and industry demand and in the interacting decision components of an organizational operating system.

Finally, as King [38, pp. 8–13] points out, methodological simulations may assist a business executive in comparing alternative models and techniques for describing and solving problems.

In conclusion, simulation's role in future marketing decisions should increase. Market simulators in the firm can be used to effectively model strategic or competitive strategies representing, among other things, physical-distribution systems, competition, the environment, the consumer, and the individual firm and its employees.

REFERENCES

1. Abt, C. C., et al., *Survey of the State of the Art: Social, Political, and Economic Models and Simulations,* Cambridge, Mass.: Abt Associates, 1965.
2. Amstutz, A. E., *Computer Simulation of Competitive Market Response,* Cambridge, Mass.: M.I.T., 1967.
3. Amstutz, A. E., and H. J. Claycamp, "The Total Market Environment Simulation," *Industrial Management Review,* vol. 5, Spring 1964.
4. Ashenhurst, R. L., "Computer Capabilities and Management Models," *Contributions to Scientific Research in Management,* Los Angeles: Western Data Processing Center, 1959.
5. Balderston, F., and A. Hoggatt, "Simulation of Marketing Processes," in Cateora and Richardson (eds.), *Readings in Marketing,* New York: Appleton-Century-Crofts, 1967.
6. Barton, S. G., "A Marketing Model for Short Term Prediction of Consumer Sales," *Journal of Marketing,* vol. 29, July 1965.
7. Bonini, C. P., *Simulation of Information and Decision Systems in the Firm,* Englewood Cliffs, N.J.: Prentice-Hall, 1963.
8. Bonini, C. P., R. K. Jaedicke, and H. M. Wagner (eds.), *Management Controls,* New York: McGraw-Hill, 1964.
9. Broadbent, S. R., "A Year's Experience of the LPE Media Model," Proceedings of the 8th Annual Conference of the Advertising Research Foundation, New York, Oct. 2, 1962.
10. Chorafas, D. N., *Systems and Simulation,* New York: Academic, 1965.
11. Claycamp, H. J., and A. E. Amstutz, "Simulation Techniques in the Analysis of Marketing Strategy," in F. M. Bass, C. W. King, and A. E. Pessemier (eds.), *Applications of the Sciences in Marketing Management,* New York: Wiley, 1968.
12. Cohen, K. J., *Computer Models in the Shoe, Leather, Hide Sequence,* Englewood Cliffs, N.J.: Prentice-Hall, 1960.
13. Cohen, K. J., W. R. Dill, A. A. Kuehn, and P. R. Winters, *The Carnegie Tech Management Game,* Homewood, Ill.: Irwin, 1964.
14. Conway, R. W., "Some Tactical Problems in Digital Simulation," *Management Science,* vol. 10, October 1963.

15. Conway, R. W., B. M. Johnson, and W. L. Maxwell, "Some Problems of Digital Systems Simulation," *Management Science*, vol. 6, October 1959.

16. Cooper, L., "Heuristic Methods for Location-Allocation Problems," *SIAM Review*, vol. 6, January 1964.

17. Cyert, R. M., and J. G. March, *A Behavioral Theory of the Firm*, Englewood Cliffs, N.J.: Prentice-Hall, 1963.

18. Dahl, O. J., and K. Hygaard, "SIMULA—An ALGOL-Based Simulation Language," *Communciations of the ACM*, vol. 9, September 1966.

19. Dawson, R. E., "Simulation in the Social Sciences," in Harold Guetzkow (ed.), *Simulation in Social Science: Readings*, Englewood Cliffs, N.J.: Prentice-Hall, 1962.

20. Day, R. L., "Simulation of Consumer Behavior," *The Southeastern Journal of Business*, April 1969, pp. 123–131.

21. Donnelly, J. H., and J. M. Ivancevich, *Analysis for Marketing Decisions*, Homewood, Ill.: Irwin, 1970.

22. Efron, R., and G. Gordon, "A General Purpose Digital Simulation and Examples of its Application; Part I—Description of the Simulator," *IBM Systems Journal*, vol. 3, no. 1, 1964.

23. Farley, J. U., and L. W. Ring, "An Empirical Test of the Howard-Sheth Model of Buyer Behavior," *Journal of Marketing Research*, vol. 7, November 1970.

24. Feldman, E., F. Lehrer, and T. L. Ray, "Warehouse Location under Continuous Economics of Scale," *Management Science*, vol. 12, May 1966.

25. Fishman, G. S., and P. J. Kiviat, *Spectral Analysis of Time Series Generated by Simulation Models*, Santa Monica, Calif.: The Rand Corporation, 1965.

26. Forrester, J., *Industrial Dynamics*, New York: Wiley, 1961.

27. Gerson, M. L., and R. B. Maffei, "Technical Characteristics of Distribution Simulators," *Management Science*, vol. 6, October 1963.

28. Greenlaw, P., "Marketing Simulation Problems and Prospects," in Martin Bell (ed.), *Marketing: A Maturing Discipline*, AMA Proceedings, Chicago: American Marketing Association, 1960.

29. Guetzkow, H. (ed.), *Simulation in Social Science: Readings*, Englewood Cliffs, N.J.: Prentice-Hall, 1962.

30. Hammersley, J. M., and D. C. Handscomb, *Monte Carlo Methods*, New York: Wiley, 1964.

31. Hespas, R. F., "Simulation as an Aid in Staffing a Customer Service Function," *Management Technology*, vol. 3, December 1963.

32. Hovland, C., "Computer Simulation of Thinking," in Harold Guetzkow (ed.), *Simulation in Social Science: Readings*, Englewood Cliffs, N.J.: Prentice-Hall, 1962.

33. Howard, J. A., and J. N. Sheth, *The Theory of Buyer Behavior*, New York: Wiley, 1969.

34. Jones, P. I., *The Thompson Medals and Awards for Media Research, 1965*, Kent, Conn.: Tombridge Printers, 1966.

35. Karush, W., *The Crescent Dictionary of Mathematics*, New York: MacMillan, 1962.

36. Kehl, W. B., "Techniques of Constructing a Market Simulator," in Martin Bell (ed.), *Marketing: A Maturing Discipline*, Chicago: American Marketing Association, 1960.

37. King, P., W. F. Massey, A. E. Amstutz, and G. B. Tallman, "The MIT Marketing Game," in Martin Bell (ed.), *Marketing: A Maturing Discipline*, AMA Proceedings, Chicago: American Marketing Association, 1960.

38. King, W. R., "Methodological Simulation in Marketing," *Journal of Marketing*, vol. 34, April 1970.

39. Kiviat, P. J., and A. Colker, *GASP—A General Activity Simulation Program*, Santa Monica, Calif.: The Rand Corporation, 1964.

40. Kotler, P., "The Competitive Marketing Simulator—A New Management Tool," *California Management Review*, vol. 7, Spring 1965.

41. Kotler, P., "Computer Strategies for New Product Marketing Over the Life Cycle," *Management Science*, vol. 8, December 1965.

42. Kotler, P., *Marketing Management, Analysis, Planning, and Control,* Englewood Cliffs, N.J.: Prentice-Hall, 1967.
43. Kuehn, A. A., and M. J. Hamburger, "A Heuristic Program for Locating Warehouse," *Management Science,* vol. 9, May–June, 1966.
44. Leontief, W. W., *Input-Output Economics,* New York: Oxford University Press, 1966.
45. Markowitz, H., B. Housner, and H. Karr, *SIMSCRIPT: A Simulation Programming Language,* Englewood Cliffs, N.J.: Prentice-Hall, 1963.
46. Mize, J. H., and J. G. Cox, *Essentials of Simulation,* Englewood Cliffs, N.J.: Prentice-Hall, 1968.
47. Morgenroth, W. M., "A Method for Understanding Price Determinants," *Journal of Marketing Research,* vol. 1, August 1964.
48. Morgenthaler, G. W., "The Theory and Application of Simulation in Operations Research," in Russell L. Ackoff (ed.), *Progress in Operations Research,* New York: Wiley, 1965.
49. Naylor, T., J. Balintfly, D. Burdick, and H. Chu, *Computer Simulation Techniques,* New York: Wiley, 1966.
50. Neilson, W. A., et al. (eds.), *Webster's New International Dictionary of the English Language,* 2d ed., Unabridged, Springfield, Mass.: Merriam, 1953.
51. Nicosia, F. M., *Consumer Decision Processes,* Englewood Cliffs, N.J.: Prentice-Hall, 1966.
52. Orcutt, G. H., M. Greenberger, J. Korbel, and A. M. Rivilin, *Macroanalysis of Social Economic Systems: A Simulation Study,* New York: Harper & Row, 1961.
53. Pessemier, E. A., *New Product Decisions: An Analytical Approach,* New York: McGraw-Hill, 1966.
54. Preston, L., *Studies in a Simulated Market,* Berkeley, Calif.: University of California Institute of Business and Economic Research, 1966.
55. Pugh, A. L., III, *Dynamo User's Manual,* Cambridge: M.I.T., 1963.
56. Rand Corporation, *A Million Random Digits with 100,000 Normal Deviates,* Glencoe, Ill.: Free Press, 1955.
57. Schlaifer, R., *Analysis of Decisions Under Uncertainty,* New York: McGraw-Hill, 1969.
58. Schmidt, J. W., and R. E. Taylor, *Simulation and Analysis of Industrial Systems,* Homewood, Ill.: Irwin, 197o.
59. Shubik, M., "Simulation and the Theory of the Firm," in *Contributions to Scientific Research in Management,* Los Angeles: Western Data Processing Center, 1959.
60. Shycon, H., and R. Maffei, "Simulation Tool for Better Distribution," *Harvard Business Review,* vol. 44, November–December, 1966.
61. Simulmatics Corporation, *Simulmatics Media Mix: General Description and Technical Description,* New York: The Simulmatics Corporation, 1962.
62. Stokes, C. J., and P. Mintz, "How Many Clerks on a Floor?" *Journal of Marketing Research,* vol. 2, November 1965.
63. Teichraew, D., and J. F. Lubin, "Computer Simulation—Discussion of the Technique and Comparison of Languages," *Communications of the ACM,* vol. 9, October 1966.
64. Tocher, K. D., *The Art of Simulation,* Princeton, N.J.: Von Nostrand, 1963.
65. Uhr, E. B., "Management of the Marketing Mix for a Regional Food Chain: A Simulation Study," unpublished doctoral dissertation, Troy, N.Y.: Rensselaer Polytechnic Institute, Graduate School of Business, 1969.
66. Weitz, H., "The Promise of Simulation in Marketing," *Journal of Marketing,* vol. 31, July 1967.

Part F

Model Building

Chapter 3

Stochastic Micro Models

ARNOLD E. AMSTUTZ *Decision Technology, Incorporated; Sloan School of Management, Massachusetts Institute of Technology, Cambridge, Massachusetts*

Models may be characterized by the functions they serve or the context in which they are used. They can be explicit as opposed to implicit, qualitative or quantitative, macro or micro, simple as opposed to complex, and descriptive or predictive. Other classifications have been given in Chapter 1 of this section.

An implicit model refers to an internalized concept of a process. When the process is described to others in detail sufficient to delineate its major aspects, the model becomes explicit. A qualitative model may be an explicit model, but the major aspects of the process have not been defined in terms that permit objective measurement or validation. In contrast, a model is quantitative if significant process characteristics are presented in a way that allows validation.

A macro model provides a broad, aggregate description of a process. It identifies major process segments and the most important interactions among those segments. A micro model is used when one must go beyond the aggregate level of macro description to adequately represent the process. It details the actions and reactions that make up relevant processes.

A model may be simple or complex, depending upon the way in which it describes a process. A simple model merely correlates two or three independent functions, whereas a complex model may encompass many variables and delineate their interactions. It is, of course, possible to have a complex total system built upon interacting simple-model segments.

If a model is to represent a real-world process, it should portray *that which is* rather than *that which should be*. Such models are descriptive. However, if models are to predict probable outcomes under specified conditions, they must be predictive as well as descriptive.

Stochastic micro models are most often explicit, quantitative, detailed, probabilistic representations of behavior or response. Market-oriented systems incorporating such models are designed to relate management actions to market reactions and may be used to evaluate alternative marketing policies and strategies.

This chapter discusses the development, testing, and validation of stochastic micro models. It outlines the nature of the development process and provides examples of conceptual structures and model formulations. Model testing and validation requirements are specified and various applications of micro model-based management systems are described.

THE FOCUS OF MICRO SYSTEM DEVELOPMENT

The first and foremost prerequisite of meaningful micro system development is that the model focus on a relevant and actionable process. The time and effort required to design and validate an accurate representation of detailed behavior can be justified only if the resultant product can contribute to more effective planning, decision making, or evaluation. Once a relevant and actionable process has been identified, the micro model builder must decide how he is going to view that process.

Three representative issues of micro model focus are discussed in this section. Specifically, consideration is given to (1) alternative probability formulations; (2) questions concerning descriptive versus normative representations; and (3) goals and organization structure as loci for representations of the executive's decision process. The structural attributes of micro model development are discussed in terms of general versus limited applicability and open versus closed systems.

Alternative Probability Formulations

A stochastic micro model will generally be concerned with a single phenomenon, such as the purchase of brand A, brand B, or no brand. The model builder usually states his understanding of this process in terms of the probability that various actions or states will occur, for example, the probability that a particular consumer will buy a specific brand. Probabilities may be considered to be constant; they may be formulated in terms of the outcomes of past probabilistic events as in a Markov chain model; or they may be derived from a representation of consumer experiences prior to the time of making the decision being modeled.

In the first probability formulation, the model builder excludes from his representation of the environment all factors influencing the decision. The decision probabilities are given and may be considered constant throughout the period to be encompassed by the model run. The model builder assumes that nothing that he or anyone else does will influence the process he is modeling.

In the second case, the model builder assumes that the probability of an individual's or a group's taking an action at one point can be determined by the outcome of prior decisions based on the same probability function. The various Markov models represent this conceptual focus. (See [8, pp. 2–10].)

In the third instance, the model builder derives a probabilistic statement about individual or group actions based on the behavior and response processes which, in his opinion, influence the decision of interest.

The model builder who relies on "judgmentally established" constant probabilities avoids serious micro model development. It is often argued that the manager or researcher can summarize his intuitive understanding in a single probability of event occurrence which is substantiated by clearly drawn word pictures. Process explication is an absolute prerequisite of systematic model development. Word pictures have much in common with their graphic counterparts in optical art, but a definitive perspective cannot be maintained with respect to them. Qualitative-model popularity may be largely attributable to illusive form. The verbal model builder certainly enjoys a substantial advantage in discussions with his quantitative colleagues. When faced with objections, he can reply ". . . in rather a scornful tone, 'when I use a word, it means just what I choose it to mean—neither more nor less' " [4, p. 94].

Descriptive versus Normative Models

The model builder may focus on the world as he perceives it or as he believes it should be. He should begin his model development with descriptive models showing (as said earlier) what *is* rather than what *should be*. However, once the behavior being modeled is thoroughly understood, the model builder may wish to consider the implications of alternative modes of behavior and response. Once he starts to evaluate these implications according to specified criteria, he is in the *normative model* building business.

Attempts to develop normative micro models without a descriptive model structure can produce significant problems. Once management acts on the basis of a particular normative model, neither management nor the researcher will ever know what would have happened if a different decision had been implemented. On the other hand, if management has developed a descriptive model of the environment in which action is being taken, it is possible to simulate the outcome that would be realized under different action conditions, and to evaluate the relative desirability of these outcomes, using selected criteria. It is thus reasonable to think of validating normative decision models by examining the outcomes realized through simulated application of alternative procedures.

There is, however, one small difficulty. The model builder intent on this approach must validate the basis of his validation procedure. He must first validate the descriptive environmental model. That is, his initial efforts must be reoriented toward descriptive model development and validation.

Goals versus Organization Structure

Micro model builders frequently view the management decision process in terms of goals set by top management which are then executed and/or modified by subordinates as they respond to higher management directives.

Models which describe management behavior as goal-seeking may be deceptive. The successful manager has usually learned to set "realistic" goals—goals he is confident of meeting. The model builder who selects this focus must assume that goals determine or measurably influence decision processes. In many instances, this assumption is invalid. Goals are frequently relevant only in retrospect. They merely determine the language of rationalization.

On the other hand, model builders may choose to define the management decision process through an organization-chart description of different executives' decision responsibilities. This approach provides an adequate starting point but it cannot be an end point. Once decision responsibility is established, the model builder must determine the executive's perception of the market environment and challenge him to describe the processes he is attempting to influence. It is important to distinguish between the executive's perception and his decisions, and to understand his perception of the environment before looking at his decision.

Once explicit, decision-oriented models are formulated, they are subject to testing and validation. Micro system development is an interactive process through which management and researcher work to refine and validate explicit models of those marketing processes which concern the executive. Models shared by the executive and researcher can be used to integrate existing data and identify new or revised data requirements.

Micro system development begins with management models but it must not stop with the initial formulations. Intuition and insight at the executive level provide a management perspective and ensure that subsequent analyses focus on actionable market processes.

STRUCTURAL ATTRIBUTES OF MICRO SYSTEM

General versus Limited Applicability

Many model builders indicate a concern for generalized or generalizable micro systems. A well-known marketing personality has commented that "[his research] aim . . . is to characterize how a 'typical' product manager might think through a particular problem facing product managers, and not to get at individual variations" [6, pp. 57–70].

Excessive concern with generalization can be detrimental to successful model development. Models designed for a particular management context may not be directly transferable. Is it realistic to attempt to support both research and management functions with the same system? The researcher's goals are inductive. He strives for broad applicability from a limited sample. Management's use of micro systems is deductive—narrowly focused on a particular problem.

In a broader sense, is it realistic to think in terms of generalized management systems applicable to many products, divisions, or companies? Each management group has unique requirements; its own perspective on the environment within and outside its area; its specific priorities; and an operating style that is the unique product of the group's personalities. Common micro sector models will appear in many systems since several groups may be concerned with the same or comparable markets. However, the interfaces linking these models to management will reflect each management's priorities and perspective.

Open versus Closed Systems

Most micro systems are based on open-, as opposed to closed-, loop structures. They are designed to respond to inputs from management and other market elements and to provide outputs to these elements. The design of interfaces linking these models to remaining marketing-system sectors is therefore of prime importance.

It is possible to develop closed macro systems made up of interactive micro sectors representing management and competitive actions, market responses, and management reactions. Such systems are being used to simulate competitive market interactions and to evaluate policies and strategies under assumed conditions [1].

MICRO MODEL DEVELOPMENT PROCESS

This section discusses the micro model development process and outlines a six-phase approach to the system development process. Management's requisite responsibilities in model development and system design are detailed and a relationship is drawn between effective management participation and successful system implementation.   If factors in the corporate environment limit or prohibit management involvement in micro model formulation, or if there is a lack of management understanding of the nature, implications, and limitations of the basic models, effective implementation of systems incorporating these models may be impossible.

The Importance of Management Involvement.   If micro model development is to provide management with more effective decision-making and planning capabilities, management must provide a focus for micro model design and make explicit its assumptions and perspectives regarding relevant model characteristics.   It is not likely, however, that managers will be technically oriented. Although vaguely familiar with basic quantitative techniques, they are apt to become uneasy with quantitative specification or evaluation.

Interaction between manager and would-be developer of a micro model often begins when management recognizes or feels that something is wrong.   The problem may be very specific, such as, "We're losing market share," or nothing more than a feeling, "We've got all kinds of numbers but really don't know what's going on in our market."   In either case, an approach to problem formulation and solution based on a micro model may introduce several potential difficulties.

Problem Definition.   In most instances, management initially defines a problem in vague and ambiguous "business terms."   However, if a behavioral model is to contribute to a problem solution, management must describe the problem in explicit terms, defining relevant factors and differentiating them from those considered irrelevant.

The importance of management involvement in quantitative problem specification cannot be overstated.   If management does not understand or agree with the conceptual structure of the problem, measurements which describe the problem environment cannot be developed.   If explicit, quantitative communication is not achieved, the model builder cannot possibly be sure that he is modeling the right behavior.

Explicit problem definition often reveals that various managers have different implicit conceptual models of the problem situation.   Making models explicit removes the ambiguities inherent in qualitative problem definition; the same words can mean different things to different people.   In such cases, the model builder must create, and then validate or reject, several behavioral representations.

Data Generation.   Once problems are explicitly defined, it is easier to identify data required for analysis or model testing.   Since data are often incomplete or were developed for other purposes, it may be necessary to generate new data to test hypotheses and/or provide estimates of model parameters. When management has developed system specifications, it supports research necessary to obtain estimates for model parameters.

Assumption Formulation.   It is sometimes necessary to go beyond available data and make assumptions regarding the behavior to be modeled.   If management has been involved in model development, its judgments will have been made explicit.   Without such explication, management perceptions may be ignored—with disastrous results.

Model Development.   During model development, management is exposed to and considers the implications of alternative model structures.   The manager should understand and agree with criteria used to choose among alternative functional representations.

System Evaluation.   If several micro models are to be combined in a system, total system performance must be evaluated after all micro models have been validated.   Performance criteria are established through joint management-specialist action which requires that management understand the conceptual structure and relationships associated with each micro model.

AN APPROACH TO MICRO MODEL DEVELOPMENT

The following approach to micro model development has been particularly successful in achieving management involvement in model design.   It is based on a policy management task force and an operating management project group.

The task force is composed of six to eight members of a company's top executive team who speak for the company in policy matters.   Their initial objective is to define the structure of the environment to be modeled—to identify (1) relevant elements and interactions within the environment; (2) planning and decision-making processes to be linked to the model; and (3) acceptable measures of behavior and responses to be encompassed by the model and monitored by later model-based systems.

The project group consists of company operating personnel who are concerned with micro model design and implementation.   This group is responsible for data organization and analysis, model design and validation, and detailed hardware, operating, and programming specifications.   At periodic intervals, the task force and the project group meet to evaluate progress and to verify conformance with task force objectives.

A Six-Phase Approach

An orderly approach to micro system development is achieved by dividing model design, development, and implementation into six phases.   Each phase encompasses specific objectives.   This approach ensures that progress is measured at planned intervals, and that energies and resources are not applied to subsequent phases until preceding objectives are met.

Phase I: The Project Plan.   In phase I, preliminary task force and project group personnel develop a detailed project plan.   In particular, they:

1. Establish preliminary planning and operating goals
2. Review alternative criteria for project, model, and system evaluation
3. Determine the scope and detail of Phase II investigations
4. Establish task force and project group memberships
5. Develop minimum and maximum time schedules and budgets for phases II through VI

Phase II: Environment Specification.   In phase II, the task force begins to identify major market elements and to develop a structure of the market process.   This structure provides a conceptual framework for later model design.   Specific objectives of this phase are to:

1. Identify major elements (individuals and institutions) within the company and market environments
2. Establish measures for monitoring significant interactions
3. Determine criteria for evaluating alternative model structures
4. Determine data requirements and availability, and set priorities for data collection
5. Specify functional characteristics of the management system incorporating the model, measures and evaluation criteria

Phase III: Management-oriented System Specification.   The third project phase produces explicit management-system specifications which establish:

1. Planning and decision procedures to be related to the model
2. The environment to be monitored

3. Models and measures to be used
4. Functions to be performed by the system
5. Criteria for evaluating system performance

Phase IV: Computer-oriented System Specification. The fourth phase produces a document of detailed system specifications to be implemented by programmers and system analysts. This document specifies:

1. System organization
2. Hardware and software requirements
3. Program structures
4. Measurement and data processing procedures
5. Management/system interfaces

Phase V: System Development. The ultimate product of phase V is an operating system meeting criteria defined in phases II through IV. Initially, a detailed schedule of personnel and facilities is drawn up. The remainder of phase activity is devoted to programming, testing, and evaluation.

Phase VI: System Implementation. In the final project phase, models and supporting systems are placed in operation. Support personnel are trained in operating procedures and management is familiarized with the specifics of system use. Procedures for continuous system review and modification are also established.

DEVELOPMENT OF A CONCEPTUAL STRUCTURE

Micro model development begins with the formulation of a conceptual structure through which the major elements of the market environment are identified. This section discusses the requirements of a conceptual framework, outlines the major elements to be encompassed by such a framework, and provides an example of conceptual structure development.

Requirements of a Conceptual Structure

Micro model development must be undertaken within a structure that relates the modeled behavior or response to management and competitive actions. A conceptual structure designed to serve this function must:

1. Identify a limited set of elements that can be described in detail sufficient to identify element subclasses and to represent changes in element status over time
2. Provide a mechanism for describing processes involving the elements—interactions between elements
3. Identify measurement points in the environment and provide for quantitative measurement of elements and processes

Major Elements of a Conceptual Structure. Although many different conceptual structures can be used, it is generally possible to reformulate them in terms of eight "active elements," three "elements of flow," and "three passive elements."

Eight Active Elements. The active elements in a marketing system are human and can originate and react to signals. The major ones included in most conceptual frameworks are (1) a producer, (2) his competitors, (3) distributors and wholesalers, (4) salesmen, (5) retailers, (6) consumers, (7) government, and (8) research agents. Each active element can be characterized by the inputs it receives, the input variations to which it is sensitive, the outputs it can generate, and the correlations, if any, between specific inputs and outputs.

Three Elements of Flow. The three elements of flow—product, information, and capital—are the channels through which active elements interact. Successful managements manipulate these factors in their attempts to achieve desired objectives.

Three Passive Elements. Passive elements are found in the channels through which elements of flow move. The three kinds are (1) time delays that affect the movement of elements of flow between active elements; (2) dissipators that reduce the magnitude of elements of flow transmitted between active elements; and (3) storage elements that accumulate backlogs of elements of flow.

AN EXAMPLE OF CONCEPTUAL STRUCTURE DEVELOPMENT

Since conceptual-framework definition is the first and perhaps most important step in micro model development, it may be useful to review how the management of a corporation producing a diversified line of food products established an explicit framework.

A task force, consisting of the president and other executives, and the planners and decision makers responsible for marketing policy and strategy, devoted approximately 10 days over an eight-month period to activities associated with phases II and III of the six-phase model-development process.

The first task force meeting opened with a series of questions. "How can we establish boundaries for this system? How much detail should it encompass? What factors should it include?" The vice president for production suggested that "It should certainly include our operation. After all, we make the product, it's a fine product, and . . . ."

After some discussion, the project coordinator drew a rectangle on a large sheet of paper and wrote "Producer." "Is there anything else we should include in the system?" he asked. "How about the distributors?" someone commented. "We make it. They distribute it." The project coordinator drew a second box connected to the first by a straight line and labeled it "Distributor." Here, someone suggested that the meeting had been called to define a micro analytic behavioral model but seemed to be spending time drawing boxes. The project coordinator asserted that the group was, in fact, making real progress toward model development. Already, they had identified two important elements of the action environment, the company and its distributors.

Four hours later, the group had produced the flow chart shown in Figure 1. Government, producer, competitors, distributors and their respective sales forces, retailers, and consumers were identified as major elements. Interactions among these elements were indicated by lines representing product and information flow. At a later stage, basic cash-flow relationships were also considered.

The first objective of this process was simply to identify a limited number of elements and interactions. Much remained to be done; much complexity was added later. The objective was not to deny complexity but to establish a realistic structure within which management could work with complexities in an orderly and systematic way. Once a conceptual structure had been established, attention was focused on processes associated with each interaction point. The group identified backlogs, delays, and transfer points at which the rates of product, information, or dollar flow could be measured.

Back at the task force meeting, one of the managers was anxious to "make things more realistic." He suggested that they start to identify key points in the distribution system.

"Those nice, neat black lines have been bothering me. They make things look too simple. Now let's take our manufacturing operation. Every time we get above a certain raw-material inventory level, our spoilage rate goes wild. We also have a problem with a packaged product. Can't move it fast enough. Keep getting spoilage. On the other hand, whenever we try to back off on production, the sales people start screaming about stockouts. The distributors have a real inventory-control problem, and most of the retailers don't even know what inventory control is.

"As far as the consumer is concerned," he went on, "we ought to be spending some of that advertising money to get the consumer to buy only when he is

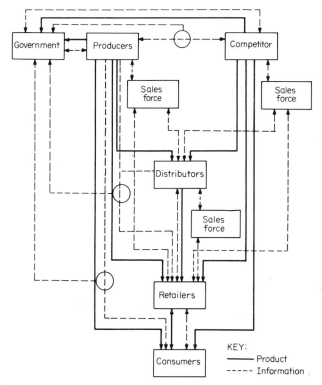

Fig. 1. A conceptual description of a company's environment.

ready to use. Some of our promotions have actually featured multiple-package deals, and I don't think the average customer gets through one container without a little mold starting to show up."

"The point is, these straight lines you're drawing just don't tell the whole story."

MICRO MODEL FORMULATION

Although micro models are generally developed to represent a single phenomenon, the nature of the representation may vary in its degree of complexity. This section discusses the issue of micro model complexity and presents an example of micro model development.

How Micro Is Micro?

Working within a conceptual framework, it is possible to develop micro models of varying degrees of detail.   One might construct a representation that is little more than two or three effectiveness functions correlating dollar inputs to unit or dollar sales.   Such a model provides information about the apparent historical correlation among variables that management can manipulate and sales. (See [11, pp. 152–186].)   However, it does not develop an understanding of how these variables influence sales.   It does not contain behavioral representations that can be validated.

To be useful, a micro model must state what is known and assumed about actions, reactions, and responses within the modeled environment.   Although a detailed behavioral representation is more complex than a simple micro model structure, it has the potential to provide a wealth of information that the more aggregate model cannot supply.   Since the former can be designed to encompass all behavior that management considers relevant, it can provide a structure for solving diverse consumer and industrial product-marketing problems [9, pp. 221–236].   Although a relatively aggregate model may generate correct answers at a point in time, it provides little or no insight into the reasons for these answers.

An Example of Micro Model Development

The micro model development process is best illustrated by returning to the food-products company example.   Working within the conceptual structure developed in the earlier meeting, the task force focused on factors influencing specific decisions and responses.   Management's intuitive understanding of market processes was converted into explicit and testable behavioral models. Relationships between inputs and observable behavior were formulated in terms which permitted model validation against available market data.   As an example, consider one consumer-decision point—the decision to shop.   The question to be answered was: Which management actions and characteristics of the marketplace influence a consumer to shop for a product?   The meeting discussion ran along the following lines.

"Well, people who think they could use the product—people who believe they have a need for the product—are most apt to go shopping.   It's a matter of perception.   People who have a high perceived need for the product will shop for it."

"Perceived need yields shopping.   Fine.   But how do you measure perceived needs?"

"We have been using 'buying-intentions' data.   We have interviewers going around asking people what they intend to purchase.   Someone who has a high perceived need is going to say that he intends to go shopping.   It doesn't make any difference whether he actually shops or not, it's his intention that we're concerned with."

"Assuming that we use this perceived-need concept, how do management actions affect an individual's perceived need?"

"Most of our advertising tells the consumer things he can do with our product—makes him aware of all the opportunities he has to use it.   This is a key idea.   The more opportunity the consumer has and is aware of, the more apt he is to think he needs the product.   Someone who is always giving cocktail parties has many more opportunities to use prepared hors d'oeuvres."

"Now wait a minute.   That's not really true.   There are quite a few folks around who have lots of opportunities to use our product. The problem is they have already had some of it and it turned green! And now they won't touch the stuff. Attitude is important here, too. We have to take into account how the customer feels about the product."

"We are forgetting something very basic. Someone who has already gone shopping and bought the product and has it in the refrigerator isn't going to want any more. We have to take into account the consumer's current supply of product."

"There is something else we forgot. There are many people around, probably the majority, who aren't even aware of the product. They don't know enough to know whether they like it or not."

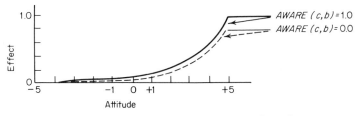

Fig. 2.   Effect of attitude on perceived need.

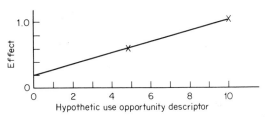

Fig. 3.   Effect of consumer use opportunity on perceived need.

An Example of Quantification

Management hypotheses regarding the decision to shop led to a qualitative concept of "perceived need," which, it was proposed, increases with (1) positive attitude toward the brand, (2) opportunity to use it, and (3) time since last purchase.

The project group then began working within the structure provided by the task force to refine and test these key behavioral assumptions.

The Effect of Attitude. By means of a modified Osgood scale, consumer orientation (attitude) toward a brand was measured by asking a respondent to rate the brand on an 11-point scale from +5 (strongly favor) to −5 (strongly dislike). The observed relationship between attitude and perceived need is shown in Figure 2.

Use Opportunity. Use opportunity was measured by the number of times, during the preceding quarter, the consumer used a brand within the given product class. This information was obtained by direct interview as well as diary maintenance. As Figure 3 illustrates, a linear association was established between use opportunity and perceived need.

Time since Purchase.   The time since purchase was measured in periods of average product line (one week).   This relationship is shown in Figure 4.

Income Stratification.   Initial attempts to validate the perceived-need concept showed that actual shopping behavior also depended on income.

By combining the three elements of perceived need with income stratification, the probability of shopping is represented by the function illustrated in Figure 5.

Given definition of the factors influencing the probability of purchase, it is necessary to consider the form of interaction between them.   For example, if a product is not available, the consumer cannot purchase it.   Therefore, product availability enters the formulation as a multiplier; when it is zero (indicating absence of product), it totally negates the effect of other factors.   Similarly,

Fig. 4.   Effect of time since purchase on perceived need.

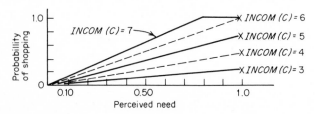

Fig. 5.   Probability of shopping as function of perceived need and income.

other interactions between purchase probability and price, salesman push, consumer attitude and awareness, and product availability can be expressed in a quantitative formulation [1, pp. 178–179].

MICRO MODEL TESTING AND VALIDATION

Tests of micro model-based systems are generally designed to evaluate either reliability or validity.   This section briefly defines reliability testing and describes in detail the various levels of validity testing.   The additional data requirements and evaluation procedures associated with model validation are outlined.

In testing reliability, one determines whether successive replications of a given model will reproduce within acceptable limits results obtained at one point in time.   Tests of validity are concerned with "truth."   Although reliability may be assessed using normal statistical techniques, there are no objective measures of truth.   Without objective measures, the researcher must turn to a subjective evaluation of the consistency of the model's performance with theory and prior knowledge.

Validity Testing

Tests of validity may be applied with varying degrees of rigor. When testing systems, five levels of validation may be distinguished: (1) viability, (2) stability, (3) consistency, (4) duplication of historical conditions, and (5) prediction of future states.

Tests of Viability. Tests of viability are concerned with a "[model's] ability . . . under plausible initial conditions and parameter settings, to generate behavior over time. . . . It does not require that equilibrium be achieved, but only that behavior should persist over a significant time interval [2, pp. 32–33]."

Tests of Stability. A second level of model validation tests the stability of modeled variables or processes known to be stable in the real-world environment.

Tests of Consistency. A third type of model validation is concerned with the consistency shown between model behavior and behavior observed in the real world. In essence, this is a test of "face validity—. . . (1) the extent to which the assumptions of a model agree with known facts, and (2) the internal consistency or 'deductive veracity' of the model. At least in the early stages this is usually the key test of a model; if it does not 'make sense,' development of a model is not likely to be pursued for long [3, p. 14]."

Sensitivity testing is one form of consistency evaluation. When conducting sensitivity tests, inputs to the model (or parameter values within the model structure) are varied between expected limits, and the response of the model is examined to determine whether system sensitivity is comparable to the observed sensitivity of the real-world environment.

Duplication of Historical Conditions. One of the more stringent tests of model validity focuses on the system's ability to duplicate behavior observed in the real world at a particular point in time. Tests of this ability require that the model be initialized with parameter values and population distributions equivalent to those in the actual environment at a particular time. Inputs duplicating those supplied to the real-world environment during the test period, for example, advertising, pricing, and competitors' product actions, are also supplied to the model. The model's validity is evaluated in terms of the correspondence between simulated and actual conditions.

Prediction of Future Conditions. From a system evaluation standpoint, the difference between historical simulation and future prediction is largely a matter of showmanship. From the management planner's point of view, the distinction is more substantive. In a properly conducted test, the system can duplicate all conditions of a future prediction. Beginning at the point of initialization, the system moves through time into the simulated future without access to information regarding the actual state of the real world at a comparable point in time. In historical simulation, the model is asked, "What happened when these conditions existed?" In predicting future response, the system is asked, "What would happen if these conditions were to exist?"

Data Requirements

Tests of validity require data describing real-world conditions in appropriate detail for evaluation. Much of the aggregate statistical data generated through traditional market research is inadequate as a reference for model validation. The validation of detailed functions within a micro model therefore often requires the generation of data at a sufficient level of detail to permit examination of relationships describing behavior at a micro level.

Establishing Functional Forms

Micro models are initially developed on the basis of theory and observation. The model builder theorizes that certain behavior may be expected from individuals exhibiting specified attributes. Although it may be easy to determine whether the attribute will increase or decrease the probability of action, validation of the relationship between the observed attribute and behavior requires data generation and analysis.

To return to the food-product example: Consumer attitude toward a brand was assumed to influence purchase probability. Attitude was thought to be positively correlated with purchase. To validate the hypothesized relationship, 888 consumers were interviewed. (See [1, p. 97].) Interview data were then analyzed to determine the proportion of consumers at each of the 11 brand-attitude levels (-5 to $+5$) who bought that brand on their most recent purchase. Table 1 summarizes the data generated on two frequently purchased items, a dairy product and a frozen food.

TABLE 1   Attitudes and Purchases among 888 Consumers of a Dairy Product and a Frozen Food

	Dairy product			Frozen food			
Attitude scale	Con- sumers expressing attitude	Pur- chasers	Per- cent	Con- sumers expressing attitude	Pur- chasers	Per- cent	Function effect*
+5	392	327	83	262	115	44	1.00
+4	51	31	60	54	21	39	.67
+3	111	50	45	98	25	26	.45
+2	51	17	33	51	6	12	.30
+1	59	15	25	72	9	12	.20
—	109	12	11	283	42	15	.13
−1	25	2	8	18	—	—	.10
−2	19	2	10	15	—	—	.08
−3	15	2	13	11	1	9	.05
−4	17	1	5	10	—	—	.03
−5	39	1	7	14	—	—	—
Total	888			888			

* This is a statistically derived estimate of the relationship between attitude and purchase of these two products.

Setting Parameter Values

Once functional forms are established, population parameters must be initialized to reflect the actual distribution of specified attributes among population members.

Initialization of Brand-Attitude Variables

Initial brand-attitude distributions can be established from data obtained while evaluating the effect of attitude on purchase. The proportion of the population with particular brand attitudes is a natural end-product of this interview procedure.   Population figures for the previously analyzed dairy product and frozen food are presented in Figure 6.

Decision and Response-Function Testing

The process used to examine the effect of attitude on purchase is indicative of the testing required to determine the impact of one factor entering a decision function.   Similar evaluations of multiple factors singly and in combination can be illustrated by returning to the previous food-product example.   Each of the formulations illustrated in Figures 2 through 5 were first validated following the procedures described in the section "An Example of Quantification."   Validation of a decision function made up of several micro relationships involves analysis of market data relating a measure of combined effect, for example, perceived need, to an action or response, such as probability of purchase.

The next level of testing determines whether the behavior exhibited by a single member of a modeled population is consistent with expectations based on data from the real world.

Simulated Population Behavior

The behavior of population groups within a simulation structure based on micro models is described by variables derived from simulated individual behavior.

Fig. 6.   Population distribution of attitude toward two brands.

Population output may be presented as the proportion of purchases allocated to each brand of product (brand shares), changes in population-attitude distributions toward brands, or changes in the perceived brand image for each brand held by a significant population segment.   (See [1, pp. 400–412].)

MICRO MODEL APPLICATIONS

Once a micro model has been validated, management must evaluate its applicability in specific environments or contexts.   If both a review of concepts on which the model is based and model performance indicate that it adequately represents the environment in question, several applications may be considered.

Testing Implicit Models

One of the first benefits of micro model development is management capability to refine its perceptions of its environment.   In reviewing alternative formulations and evaluating functions, model behavior, and total population performance, management can examine the implications of alternative behavioral assumptions, make explicit models, and refine previously implicit models on which its decision making and planning are based.

The "What If?" Question

Micro models can be combined to create a test market without memory in which management examines the implications of alternative policies and strategies. Whether introducing new products or considering marketing-program modifications, management may apply alternative strategies in the modeled environment and evaluate their implications under assumed competitive conditions.

The effectiveness of such pretesting depends not only on the model's accuracy but also on management's ability to predict probable competitive response to proposed actions. Management may find it profitable to examine the impact of the "best" and "worst" competitive-response patterns. In most instances, the "best" case assumes that competition will continue with programs developed prior to initiation of company actions, while the "worst" case is based on full competitor knowledge of the company's proposed program and combined action to thwart company efforts.

Performance Reference

Micro models provide a reference against which the progress of real-world operations can be measured. Given a model-based pretest, management can determine, by examining measures used in the model, whether a program is progressing as planned. If conditions producing satisfactory performance in the model-based test are encountered in the real world, it is assumed that final results will be comparable.

Information Systems Incorporating Stochastic Micro Models

Stochastic micro models may serve as the basic building blocks of market-oriented information systems. Data-gathering procedures are established to generate inputs describing the market's current state in terms of measures referenced in the model structure. Data files serve as the reference source for the information system and provide the historical data base for model initialization. Management can interrogate the data file for information on the current market and use the micro models to test proposed programs. Results obtained in the model environment are then transferred to the information system, which formats them for presentation to management. Management is thus able to evaluate the conditional results of proposed programs, using the same procedures and equipment employed to assess the current state of the market through interrogation.

Once policy and strategy have been finalized, the proposed plan is established as a reference and model-based measures are generated for use by a monitor program. As plans are implemented in the market environment, the monitor program compares actual measures of market performance with model-based measures indicating the expected results of planned implementation. Significant deviation from the plan becomes the criterion for monitor referral to management.

SUMMARY

This chapter has outlined the procedures followed in developing, testing, and validating stochastic micro models of market behavior. The processes of environmental description, conceptual structuring, and micro model formulation were discussed with reference to sample system structures. Methods of model testing and validation were examined and representative system applications were illustrated.

REFERENCES

1. Amstutz, Arnold E., *Computer Simulation of Competitive Market Response,* Cambridge, Mass.: M.I.T., 1967.
2. Balderston, F. E., and A. C. Hoggatt, *Simulation of Marketing Processes,* Berkeley: University of California, Institute of Business and Economic Research, 1962.
3. Buzzell, R. D., *Mathematical Models and Marketing Management,* Cambridge, Mass.: Harvard University Press, 1964.
4. Carroll, Lewis, *Alice Through the Looking Glass,* New York: Random House, 1946.
5. Churchman, C. W., "Reliability Models in the Social Sciences," in P. Langhoff (ed.), *Models, Measurement, and Marketing,* Englewood Cliffs, N.J.: Prentice-Hall, 1965, pp. 23–38.
6. Kotler, Philip, "Decision Processes in the Marketing Organization," in D. M. Slate and R. Ferber (eds.), *Systems: Research and Applications for Marketing,* Urbana: University of Illinois, Bureau of Economic and Business Research, April 1967.
7. Kuehn, A. A., "Complex Interactive Models," in R. E. Frank, A. A. Kuehn, and W. F. Massy (eds.), *Quantitative Techniques in Marketing Analysis,* Homewood, Ill.: Irwin, 1962, pp. 106–123.
8. Kuehn, A. A., "How Advertising Performance Depends on Other Marketing Factors," *Journal of Advertising Research,* vol. 2, March 1962.
9. Orcutt, G., "Views on Simulations and Models of Social Systems," in F. E. Balderston and A. C. Hoggatt (eds.), *Symposium on Simulation Models,* Cincinnati: South-Western Publishing Company, 1963.
10. Turing, A. M., "Computing Machinery and Intelligence," *MIND,* vol. 59, October 1950, pp. 433–460.
11. Weinberg, R. S., "Multiple Factor Break-Even Analysis: The Application of Operations Research Techniques to a Basic Problem of Management Planning and Control," *Operations Research,* vol. 4, April 1956.

Part F
Model Building

Chapter 4

Macroeconometric Modeling

JOHN U. FARLEY *Graduate School of Business, Columbia University, New York, New York*

Macroeconometric modeling, a newcomer in the market researcher's arsenal, promises breakthroughs in forecasting and in decision-oriented empirical analysis of marketing systems. A macroeconometric model is a model of an economic system or subsystem derived from simplification of some theory about how individuals in that system behave. The system, as shown in examples later, may be the market for a single brand or product, a sector of any economy, or an entire economy. The theory may involve maximization principles or it may be behavioral. The simplifications are usually aggregations, such as grouping demand conditions over buyers or grouping supply conditions over producers. When a manageable number of variables are configured in a manageable set of explicit functional relationships, parameters are estimated.

Macroeconometric models virtually always involve sets of equations, in contrast to the single-equation models discussed earlier. Multiple-equation models add an order of complication to statistical problems facing the market researcher (see Sec. II, Part E, Chap. 7), but they also help him circumvent a variety of problems which occur in marketing models. For example, single-equation regression models often have market share or sales as the dependent variable and advertising as an independent variable. However, if advertising budgeting rules are based on sales or expected sales, there is a modeling dilemma: Advertising is a function of sales and sales is also a function of advertising. Under these circumstances, which is the dependent variable if the model involves only one equation? Distribution and sales are similarly related, if salesmen base their sales-call strategies on very short-run sales potential; of course, sales-call decisions in turn affect sales. Some of the earliest macroeconometric models involved market decisions in which farmers based their planting on the expectation that prices prevailing in the last crop year would prevail again in the current year.   Again, because price is both the resultant and the cause of an output decision, it is both an independent and a dependent variable in a time series model.

Except for very special circumstances, the ambiguity about dependent and independent variables cannot be resolved in the framework of a single-equation model, but a set of equations can often handle the difficulty.   For example, one equation might involve sales as the explained variable and include advertising among the explanatory variables, while another equation might have advertising as the explained variable and lagged or expected sales among the explanatory variables.

The direct relationship to empirical analysis of marketing systems makes macroeconometric modeling a particularly attractive approach to a variety of marketing research and marketing systems problems.   This chapter examines how a macroeconometric model is put together, what its elements are, and why certain theories yield practical implications for modeling.   Some examples of marketing models are examined in detail, and the use of such models by a firm is described.

THE GENERAL FORM OF A MACROECONOMETRIC MODEL

Most macroeconometric models involve a set of simultaneous linear relationships of the following form:

$$Y_1 + \beta_{12}Y_2 + \ldots + \beta_{1n}Y_n + \gamma_{11}X_1 + \ldots + \gamma_{1k}X_k = U_1$$

$$\vdots \qquad\qquad \vdots \qquad\qquad\qquad \vdots \qquad\qquad (1a)$$

$$\beta_{n1}Y_1 + \beta_{n2}Y_2 + \ldots + Y_n + \gamma_{n1}X_1 + \ldots + \gamma_{nk}X_k = U_n$$

The linear form is generally used because of computational convenience, although nonlinear systems may sometimes be used, thanks to recent advances in numerical methods for the solution of nonlinear equations [3].   Even if certain relationships are nonlinear, they can often be linearized by transformation or approximated linearly about an equilibrium point [19].

The values of the observed variables in such a linear system are usually designated by Latin letters and the parameters by Greek letters.   The variables and the coefficients in the model are partitioned into two sets—endogenous and exogenous.   Endogenous variables (the Y's in Equation $(1a)$, with β's as coefficients) are variables whose values are determined by simultaneous interactions of the relationships of the model.   Values of the exogenous variables (the X's in $(1a)$, with the γ's as coefficients) are determined outside the system and are simply viewed as external data.   The U's are nonobservable random errors, usually assumed to have a multivariate normal distribution.   In general, errors occur only additively in the linear relationships.   The subscripts of the coefficients are also conventional, the first indicating the equation and the second the variable with which it is associated.   (β_{23} is thus in the second equation and is associated with the third endogenous variable, Y_3.)

Ordinarily, there is one equation for each endogenous variable.   Each equation, when examined separately, looks like a multiple-regression equation with one dependent variable and a set of explanatory variables which is a mixture of endogenous and exogenous variables.

The coefficients (the β's and γ's) are called the structural parameters of the system.   Estimating these parameters involves simultaneous-regression techniques, described in Sec. II, Part E, Chap. 7. Simultaneous equation models can be explicitly written out as Equation ($1a$) was, but the notation is clumsy and a matrix formulation is much more convenient [13]. Defining Y' and X' as column vectors of the endogenous and exogenous variables, and U's as a vector of random disturbances, the matrix equation representing the model in ($1a$) is:

$$BY' + \Gamma X' = u' \tag{1b}$$

B is the $n \times n$ matrix of coefficients of the n endogenous variables, and Γ is the $n \times k$ matrix of coefficients of the k exogenous variables. The entries in the matrices are the coefficients in Equation ($1a$).

$$B = \begin{bmatrix} 1 & \beta_{12} & \beta_{13} & \cdots & \beta_{1n} \\ \beta_{21} & 1 & & & \cdot \\ \cdot & \cdot & & & \cdot \\ \cdot & \cdot & & & \cdot \\ \beta_{n1} & \beta_{n2} & \cdots & \cdot & 1 \end{bmatrix} \quad \Gamma = \begin{bmatrix} \gamma_{11} & \cdots & \gamma_{1k} \\ \cdot & & \cdot \\ \cdot & & \cdot \\ \cdot & & \cdot \\ \gamma_{n1} & \cdots & \gamma_{nk} \end{bmatrix} \tag{1c}$$

Identification of parameters in the system, discussed in Sec. II, Part E, Chap. 7, requires that certain restrictions be placed on values in the B and Γ matrices; these restrictions usually involve some coefficients being set to zero, which is equivalent to excluding some variables from each equation. Otherwise, parameter estimation is, in principle, impossible.

Representing the system in matrix form, as in Equation ($1b$), has two benefits. First, it is easier to visualize interrelationships and to see how changes in values of one variable affect other elements of the system. Second, mathematical properties of these matrices are related both to whether the coefficients can be estimated at all and to proper methods for forecasting endogenous variables. As to estimation in principle, the identification problem is rather easy to handle in terms of matrix algebra and very inconvenient to handle otherwise.

For forecasting applications, the reduced-form equations are often useful. The reduced form, derived by multiplying Equation ($1b$) by the inverse of B, expresses each endogenous variable as a linear function of all the exogenous variables but no other endogenous variables. Thus:

$$Y_1 = \pi_{11}X_1 + \cdots + \pi_{1k}X_k + u_1{}^*$$
$$\vdots \qquad\qquad \vdots \tag{1d}$$
$$Y_n = \pi_{n1}X_1 + \cdots + \pi_{nk}X_k + u_n{}^*$$

is the reduced form of the set of equations in ($1a$). The coefficients of the reduced form are usually denoted as π, just as β and γ are used conventionally to denote the structural parameters of endogenous and exogenous variables. Notice that full specification of the model is needed before the reduced form can even be derived for any one of the endogenous variables.

The reduced form is useful for predicting or forecasting values of the endogenous variables. For a properly specified model, simple regressions of each of the endogenous variables on all the exogenous variables are then appropriate to forecast the endogenous variables, and are computationally simple. In general, forecasting with simple regressions on each of the structural equations in Equation ($1a$) is not appropriate, and parameters of the structural equations should be estimated with some of the more advanced techniques described in Sec. II, Part E, Chap. 7. It is obvious that models of this type necessarily require large-scale computer facilities for development and estimation. However, a growing set of sophisticated library computer routines [7], plus vastly increased speed and capacity of modern computers, help spare the latter-day model builder many of the headaches and time-consuming frustrations faced by the pioneers in building and fitting macroeconometric models.

EQUILIBRIUM THEORY AND MARKETING MODELS

Most macroeconometric models are based on an equilibrium theory of some type. The system is assumed to be at or near equilibrium, or to be moving in a more or less known way toward some equilibrium or steady state which it will reach if nothing in the system changes. A well-specified model also provides for the possibility that such changes might occur. For instance, the equilibrium is likely to shift if any important member of the system systematically changes some variable under his control—say, by changing the rules under which an advertising budget is set. It is clear that complex models such as Equation (1a) require something more than a set of ad hoc relationships as a basis for development, and the most convenient starting point is usually with general equilibrium analysis in economic theory.

General equilibrium theory deals with determining prices and outputs of market systems when each consumer attempts to get as much satisfaction as possible for his money and each producer of a factor of production attempts to get as much as possible for each unit [4]. The theory assumes implicitly that vast amounts of data about each element in the system are readily available to all other elements at virtually no cost. Demand schedules and supply schedules for factors and goods are involved, as are some market-clearing identities implied by the fact that the market is in equilibrium. Underlying the demand for goods are utility functions for each consumer, and underlying the demand for factors are production functions summarizing the output technology of firms. (A good review of equilibrium analysis is in [15], which also develops a simple model directly from general equilibrium theory.)

In this disaggregated form, however, general equilibrium theory is not very useful for empirical analysis of marketing systems. Even a small number of consumers, factor producers, and firms results in a very large set of equations, if each member of each population is considered separately. Since utility theory requires separate consideration of each unit, it has proved an almost useless approach to empirical demand analysis. Further, estimating demand functions for individual firms is usually not practical because of data limitations, computational burden, and the many overly restrictive assumptions required. However, by appropriate aggregation of subunits (over groups of consumers or over groups of firms in an industry, for example), the system can often be reduced so that it is manageable. Macroeconometric models usually deal with such aggregated units.

However, in actually setting up a model, aggregation is usually not enough; a number of pragmatic changes are required even though the model retains much of the flavor of equilibrium theory. The most common change is relaxing the oversimple treatment of market information, which is perfect and free in equilibrium theory. Instead, one of a variety of heuristic forecasting rules is usually built into a model. These rules allow members of the system to formulate expectations, particularly about price and output in future periods but sometimes also about investment levels, changes in market shares, and so on.

The most common approach is to model each member of a system as if the member expects the current situation to prevail in the short run—that is, that prices will remain constant within a limited decision horizon, that sales will continue about the same, and that similar conditions would not change.   When a new realization of the variable occurs (say a new market price develops), this new value is expected to prevail for a while.   This type of short-run behavior, called "static expectations" [16], is extremely useful and is sometimes behaviorally reasonable; applications are shown in some macroeconometric models discussed later.

Other modifications of equilibrium theory are also common.   Certain components of the system must sometimes be disregarded.   For example, it is often impossible to deal with both production and demand phenomena, so one side of the model is removed with simplifying assumptions.   Sometimes a full competitive equilibrium (no profit) assumption is replaced by another behavioral assumption, such as monopoly or use of satisficing decision rules by some or all members of the system.   These are also illustrated later.

In marketing applications, the equilibrium framework almost always requires two major modifications.   First, the economist's preoccupation with price as the sole market-clearing variable is insufficient in most applications for two reasons: (1) information production is almost always part of a marketing program, so a lack of, or need for, information exists [5]; and (2) other marketing decision variables—advertising, sales force effort, and so on—must appear with price as arguments of the demand functions for goods and, in some cases, for factors.

Second, the array of factors—usually limited to labor and capital in general equilibrium analysis—is too narrow, as advertising and sales-force effort are usually important factors of production in marketing models.   This latter complication often renders explicit formulation of production functions very complex, and production costs are usually modeled, instead, as if they were flat over broad ranges of outputs and inputs.   This assumption allows all quantities to be demand-determined, a very common and useful simplification for marketing models.

THREE MACROECONOMETRIC MARKETING MODELS

The three examples that follow illustrate many of the modeling techniques used in marketing applications of macroeconometric models.   The three models deal with three quite different types of market behavior, but they use similar modeling techniques.   Each is a partial analysis of a subsystem embedded in a larger economy.   Each attempts to model the interactions of marketing elements in the subsystem, and each involves an explicit statement of behavioral rules used by decision makers in the system.   The first is a time series model of the effect of advertising on sales of a brand of one product.   The second is a cross-sectional model of distribution and sales of a branded, nonadvertised product in Jamaica. The third is a time series model of price and output determination in the production and marketing of food products in the United States.

A Simultaneous-Equation Analysis of Sales and Advertising

A time series model of the relationships among sales and advertising of a given brand and of its competitors, developed by Bass and Parsons [2], involves three sets of variables:

1.   Sales and advertising of an existing brand, A, both of which are endogenous at any given point in time.   A model of this type might be developed to aid evaluation of the advertising program of this brand.

2.   Sales and advertising of all other brands in total, also endogenous at a given time.   The fortune of any one brand also depends on marketing activities of other brands.

3.   Sales and advertising of new brands, assumed exogenous during the period of introduction.   This is a convenient modeling artifact, since the advertising budget is well above that justified by the current sales rate during the introductory period.

Dividing a market into a "brand of interest" and an "all other" category is also a very useful modeling artifact, if the other brands can reasonably be thought of as homogeneous.   The model is smaller and more manageable than it would be if each brand were considered separately, and the data requirements are also much less severe.

Sales and the advertising decisions at a given point of time also depend on lagged sales and on lagged advertising decisions by both the producers of brand A and by their established competitors.   The endogenous variables, lagged one period, thus play the role of an exogenous variable as well.   Using lagged endogenous variables as exogenous is also a very common aspect of modeling to help solve certain statistical problems.   In addition, advertising budgeting rules of this type have been shown optimal under several reasonable types of supply and demand relationships [17].   Sales to all customers and advertising to all viewers are aggregated, so the model deals with average effectiveness of the marketing plan over any segments which might exist in the market [8].

More formally, the variables in the model are:

LIST OF VARIABLES
(all indexed for period t, in logs and defined in per capita terms)

Endogenous	*Exogenous*
Y_1 Sales of brand A	X_1 Sales of brand A in period $t - 1$
Y_2 Advertising of brand A	X_2 Advertising of brand A in period $t - 1$
Y_3 Sales of other established brands	
Y_4 Advertising of other established brands	X_3 Sales of other established brands in period $t - 1$
	X_4 Advertising of other established brands in period $t - 1$
	X_5 Sales of new brands
	X_6 Advertising of new brands
	$X_7, \ldots, X_{11}$ Bimonthly seasonal adjustment variables

The matrix of coefficients of the endogenous variables is:

$$
\begin{array}{cccc}
Variable & Y_1 & Y_2 & Y_3 & Y_4
\end{array}
$$

$$
B = \begin{bmatrix}
-1 & \beta_{12} & 0 & \beta_{14} \\
0 & -1 & 0 & 0 \\
0 & \beta_{32} & -1 & \beta_{34} \\
0 & 0 & 0 & -1
\end{bmatrix}
$$

Sales of brand A and of other brands depend both on A's and on other brands' advertising, whereas advertising decisions depend only on exogenous variables.

Since all variables are defined in logarithms and are at equilibrium values, the estimated values of β_{12} and β_{34} are estimated equilibrium advertising elasticities and can be used to examine relative effectiveness of A's advertising against that of other brands. Equilibrium elasticities, measures of marginal sales contributions of elements in the marketing program, are useful by-products of basing macroeconometric models on equilibrium theory.

The matrix of coefficients of the exogenous variables is:

$$
\begin{array}{cccccccc}
Variable & X_1 & X_2 & X_3 & X_4 & X_5 & X_6 \\
\end{array}
$$

$$
\Gamma = \begin{bmatrix}
\gamma_{11} & 0 & \gamma_{13} & 0 & \gamma_{15} & \gamma_{16} \\
\gamma_{21} & \gamma_{22} & \gamma_{23} & \gamma_{24} & 0 & 0 \\
\gamma_{31} & 0 & \gamma_{33} & 0 & \gamma_{35} & \gamma_{36} \\
\gamma_{41} & \gamma_{42} & \gamma_{43} & \gamma_{44} & 0 & 0
\end{bmatrix} \Gamma'
$$

(Γ', a matrix of coefficients for the seasonal factors, is unrelated to behavioral elements of the model.) Sales of established brands depend on lagged sales of all brands. Advertising decisions depend on both sales and advertising decisions in the previous period. The reduced form thus requires only current sales and advertising data, plus forecasts of new-brand introductions, to predict next period's sales and advertising levels for all established brands.

In addition to hypothesized signs and ranges on values of many of the coefficients in the system, the interrelationships among the endogenous variables provide a basis for testing a model of this type. A time path for movements of the endogenous variables is implied by certain relationships among the coefficients, providing predictions about the dynamic behavior of the model over time.

A Model of the Jamaican Distribution Structure

A model of the distribution for nonadvertised branded goods in Jamaica has been developed by Farley and Leavitt [10], based on behavioral forecasting and decision-making rules used by various members of the system. The behavioral assumptions, involving passive response to changes in market conditions and simple forecasting rules based on current sales levels, were established in exploratory research.

The model deals with decisions made by three parties in the structure (distributors, wholesalers, and retailers), and it also analyzes the forces generating retail sales. The model is cross-sectional and was developed to explain market variations over census areas in Jamaica. Cross-sectional multiple-equation models are much less common than time series models, but most principles of modeling and statistical analysis are the same in both cases.

The market activities are:

1. *Manufacturers and importers* decide whether to call on customers in an area with their own sales force or to deal through wholesalers. The likelihood of calling directly depends on the sales potential in the area (realized sales are used as a proxy for short-run expected sales) and on the cost of reaching the area (geographic distance from Kingston, where all sales forces are based, is used as a proxy for cost).

2. *Wholesalers* decide similarly whether to compete with other wholesalers in supplying a given store or whether to permit single-link, wholesaler-retailer

relationships over a broad range of products.   This decision is, again, based on area sales potential and costs of reaching retailers in an area.

3.   *Retailers* have two decisions—whether to stock a product at all and, given the decision to stock, whether to stock more than one brand.   Both decisions depend on local sales potential and on the intensity of merchandising by the manufacturers and by the wholesalers.

Finally, product-class sales depend on the retailers' decisions (distribution and width of lines carried) and on two basic determinants of demand—income and population.   The list of variables includes four endogenous variables related to activities of the three levels in the distribution system.   The fifth, sales, is the key link to the exogenous variables related to basic demand as well as marketing activities.   The exogenous variables are income, population, and the distance variables used as proxies for travel costs; all these are clearly determined outside the model.

LIST OF VARIABLES

Endogenous

Y_1 Index of distribution (percent of stores in an area stocking a product)

Y_2 Sales in units per month

Y_3 Proportion of retailers in an area contacted by importers and manufacturers

Y_4 Average number of wholesalers calling on retailers in an area

Y_5 Index of depth of brand assortment (average number of brands stocked by those retailers stocking the product)

Exogenous

X_1 Population in an area

X_2 Per capita income in an area

X_3 Distance to Kingston from the center of an area

X_4 Distance to nearest wholesale center from the center of an area

The model has five relationships:

$$Y_1 = f_1(Y_2, Y_3, Y_4)$$
$$Y_2 = f_2(Y_1, Y_5, X_1, X_2)$$
$$Y_3 = f_3(Y_2, X_3)$$
$$Y_4 = f_4(Y_2, X_4)$$
$$Y_5 = f_5(Y_2, Y_3, Y_4)$$

The model is designed to analyze the system for an individual product class, with all brands aggregated.   The matrices of coefficients of the endogenous and exogenous variables are, respectively,

		Variables								*Con-*	*Dependent*
Y_1	Y_2	Y_3	Y_4	Y_5		X_1	X_2	X_3	X_4	*stant*	*variable*
-1	β_{12}	β_{13}	β_{14}	0		0	0	0	0	γ_{51}	Distribution (Y_1)
β_{21}	-1	0	0	β_{25}		γ_{21}	γ_{22}	0	0	γ_{52}	Sales (Y_2)
0	β_{32}	-1	0	0		0	0	γ_{33}	0	γ_{53}	Manuf.-importer sales effort (Y_3)
0	β_{42}	0	-1	0		0	0	0	γ_{44}	γ_{54}	Wholesaler sales effort (Y_4)
0	β_{52}	β_{53}	β_{54}	-1		9	0	0	0	γ_{55}	Depth of brand stocking (Y_5)

$B =$ (first matrix) $\Gamma =$ (second matrix)

The second column in B shows the extent to which all the decision rules are oriented toward existing sales.   The underlying behavioral rules are thus a cross-sectional analog of static expectations, as all forecasting is done with rules which assume sales in the short run will continue at the present level. Sales also provide the link to the basic exogenous determinants of demand through the second equation. The first and fifth equations are rather peculiar because they include no exogenous variables; that is, retailers' decisions here depend on activities within the marketing system and are based on feedback of information through sales in the second equation.

Parameter estimation in this system ran into major difficulties which caused the major multiple-equation methods described in Sec. II, Part E, Chap. 7 (two-stage least squares, and limited- and full-information maximum-likelihood) to break down due to collinearity among the variables. The ordinary least-squares method produces estimates which are apparently robust with respect to many types of problems in simultaneous-equation systems, and it turned out to be the most satisfactory estimation procedure [9]. The model has been used to analyze relative effectiveness of alternative strategies to stimulate sales and distribution of certain unadvertised branded products [11].

A Model of Demand, Supply, and Prices for Food

A model of the aggregate United States food market, developed by Girschick and Haavelmo [12], is composed of five equations. The relationships are not formally derived from general equilibrium analysis, but they are nonetheless functions which are admissable under the theory [18]. The system is partial in the sense that it deals only with products, factors, and firms in the agricultural and food-production sectors. This model deals with much larger aggregates than either of the two models just discussed. The endogenous variables are per capita food consumption, per capita real income, per capita production of agricultural products, prices received by farmers, and retail food prices.

LIST OF VARIABLES

Endogenous	*Exogenous*
Y_1 Per capita food consumption	X_1 Prices received by farmers in the previous period ($Y_{4,\,t-1}$)
Y_2 Per capita real income	
Y_3 Production of agricultural products per capita	X_2 Per capital real investment
	X_3 Time trend ($X_t = t$)
Y_4 Prices received by farmers	X_4 Per capita income in the previous period ($Y_{2,\,t-1}$)
Y_5 Retail food price index	

Two of the exogenous variables are lagged values of the endogenous variables (lagged prices received by farmers is X_1 and lagged income is X_4). These variables are aggregated overall producers, consumers, and products, either by simple averaging (as with Y_1, Y_2, and X_2) or by a more complex index-number technique (as with Y_4 and Y_5).

The structural equations are:

$$Y_1 = \beta_{12}y_2 + \beta_{15}y_5 + \gamma_{13}X_3 + \gamma_{14}X_4 + \gamma_{10} \tag{2a}$$
$$Y_1 = \beta_{23}y_3 + \beta_{25}y_5 + \gamma_{23}X_3 + \gamma_{20} \tag{2b}$$
$$Y_2 = \gamma_{32}X_2 + \gamma_{34}X_4 + \gamma_{30} \tag{2c}$$
$$Y_3 = \beta_{44}Y_4 + \gamma_{41}X_1 + \gamma_{43}X_3 + \gamma_{40} \tag{2d}$$
$$Y_4 = \beta_{55}Y_5 + \gamma_{53}X_3 + \gamma_{50} \tag{2e}$$

This rather confusing version of the equations motivates using the matrices of coefficients instead of the system.

Variables										Corresponding equation number
Y_1	Y_2	Y_3	Y_4	Y_5	X_1	X_2	X_3	X_4	Constant	

$$\beta = \begin{bmatrix} -1 & \beta_{12} & 0 & 0 & \beta_{15} \\ -1 & 0 & \beta_{23} & 0 & \beta_{25} \\ 0 & -1 & 0 & 0 & 0 \\ 0 & 0 & -1 & \beta_{44} & 0 \\ 0 & 0 & 0 & -1 & \beta_{55} \end{bmatrix} \qquad \Gamma = \begin{bmatrix} 0 & 0 & \gamma_{13} & \gamma_{14} & \gamma_{10} \\ 0 & 0 & \gamma_{23} & 0 & \gamma_{20} \\ 0 & \gamma_{32} & 0 & \gamma_{34} & \gamma_{30} \\ \gamma_{41} & 0 & \gamma_{43} & 0 & \gamma_{40} \\ 0 & 0 & \gamma_{53} & 0 & \gamma_{50} \end{bmatrix}$$

Equation numbers (top to bottom): (2a), (2b), (2c), (2d), (2e).

The first equation, the market demand equation, makes consumption (Y_1) a function of prices (Y_5), income (Y_2), lagged income (X_4), a trend (X_3). This equation, like all others, also has a constant term. The second equation, the market supply equation, relates quantity supplied (Y_1) (which, at equilibrium, must equal the quantity demanded) to retail prices (Y_5), agricultural output (Y_3), and trend (X_3). The third equation, the income equation, makes income (Y_2) a function of lagged income (X_4) and investment (X_2). The fourth equation, the farmers' output equation, relates production (Y_3) to prices received (Y_4), prices received the previous year (X_1), and trend (X_3). The fifth equation is the derived demand equation for food by the commercial sector, relating prices farmers received (Y_4) to retail prices (Y_5) and time (X_3).

The notion of a "dependent variable" is arbitrary in a system such as this. Notice, for example, that retail prices (Y_5) do not appear as the predicted variable in any equation. In a multiple-equation system, any equation can be normalized so that any one of the endogenous variables appears without a coefficient (more precisely, with a coefficient of 1). The first two equations were simply normalized to make consumption (Y_1) play that role. Notice also that it is conventional to bring the normalized variable to the right side of Equations (2a) through (2e) before the matrices are set up, so that variable appears in the matrix with a coefficient of -1.

This model also illustrates some principles used frequently in developing dynamic models. Behavioral forecasting rules, albeit rather naïve, are built into the model. For example, in the fourth equation, the farmers' output decisions are related to price the previous year, which is used by farmers as part of the planning procedure for the current year. This is an element in the famed "cobweb" model from mathematical economics, in which output plans for the current period are based on realization of prices in the immediately previous period. Depending on certain relationships between supply and demand elasticities with respect to price, the system may be explosive in the sense that subsequent output decisions diverge in ever larger oscillations. Under other circumstances, the system may converge to a stable equilibrium, or it may oscillate stably among a small set of output decisions and price realizations. Since estimated demand and supply elasticities are implied by some estimated coefficients in the first, second, and fourth equations, a time path of price and output decisions is implied, providing a basis for empirical tests of the model in addition to the statistical tests described in Sec. II, Part E, Chap. 7.

For forecasting purposes, the reduced form is often useful. For example, one use of this model is to predict the index of prices received by farmers. The reduced-form equation to predict Y_4 is:

$$Y_4 = 4.51 + 0.649X_1 + 0.161X_2 - 0.078X_3 - 0.287X_4 \qquad (2f)$$

The endogenous variable, the price index, is expressed as a function of all the exogenous variables in that system, even though X_1, X_2, and X_4 did not appear explicitly in $(2e)$, the fifth structural equation in which the price index (Y_4) is the normalized endogenous variable.

MODELS FOR PLANNING AND ANALYSIS

Several large firms have developed macroeconometric models for internal use. These models, often large and complex, are based on the same principles as the smaller models just described. General Electric, one of the leaders in this area, uses models ranging in aggregation from total corporate performance to micro-macro models dealing with individual products. The development of corporate-level models, which has progressed over 10 years, involves two basic areas of application: (1) analysis of structure (and changes in structure), and (2) forecasts based on shifting exogenous variables and on alternative marketing strategies. Four models, differing in formulation and in level of aggregation, illustrate the range of macroeconometric analysis.

Aggregate Planning and Forecasting

A model projects those components of gross national product (GNP) which are particularly salient to developments in the many markets in which G.E. competes. The output of this macro model is used as input into a second model which projects the results of changes in the aggregate economic variables into the performance of G.E. operating divisions. This model provides short-run (one- and two-year) and long-run (five-year) forecasts.

Modified Input-Output Analysis

G.E. is one of 15 companies sponsoring a project at the University of Maryland [1] which continuously produces updated input-output tables for the United States. Input-output analysis is a relatively mechanical process, but G.E. uses a variation—the coefficients are themselves modified on advice of staff economists and behavioral scientists about changes in projected population, projected social and cultural patterns, and the like. Constraints are imposed to prevent explosive behavior (like that sometimes implied by cobweb models), and the model is used to predict changes in activity levels of various sectors in the economy. The input-output tables are more up to date than standard government tables. More important, the relatively mechanical implications of input-output (I/O) analysis are systematically modified with important economic and behavioral projections.

Models of Product Group Performance

A model of corporate operations deals with 10 product groups aggregated over the company's 150 decentralized profit centers. Sales, earnings, market shares, and investment levels are the key endogenous variables, and these are aggregated to project earnings and stock price. Exogenous variables are projected GNP components and indexes about the various markets in which the divisions compete. The model is used in simulations to evaluate potential product-market strategies for each product group, and also to examine time-path developments under different values of the exogenous variables.

Analysis of Product Performance

Some 200 variables describing various aspects of marketing and production related to 800 different products are catalogued regularly. The goal is to evaluate product performance for profit centers in terms of both investment requirements and market projections. The analysis requires substantial data reduction, using techniques such as those described earlier (Sec. II, Part E, Chap. 9).

All four types of model are used at the corporate level for periodic evaluation of short- and long-run plans for product groups, profit centers, and individual product managers. The more detailed models are used for periodic review and forecasting. They are also utilized for project analysis, especially involving decisions about significant expansion of production capacity in any market in which G.E. participates. Dr. Sydney Schoeffler, Manager, Long Range Plans Operation, Corporate Planning Operation, G.E., points out that the results of the models' analyses are in practice tempered with the experience of managers.

An interesting related development is that automated accounting systems in some of the operating units automatically produce input data for corporate level models, and they may also involve elaborate demand-projection models as well. The interface of macroeconometric modeling and marketing information systems is thus quite clear.

LARGE-SCALE MACROECONOMETRIC MODELS

A wider array of questions can be analyzed in full-system macroeconometric models which deal with less aggregated classes of products, consumers, firms, and government activities. Some models involving whole economies are extremely large and complex. One example is the quarterly model of the United States economy developed under the joint auspices of The Brookings Institution and the Social Science Research Council [6]. The original version of the model of the economy, which can be used for forecasting and policy analysis in many ways, took about six years to develop. Full-time staff, supplemented by part-time research assistants and temporary staff, continue work on data collection, on further development of the model, and on analysis of important policy questions. The temporary staff has included many famous names in econometrics, and grants totaling several hundred thousand dollars have been involved. Sections were developed by economists with experience in certain phases of economic activity, and linking the results from each section was itself a major undertaking. Provision has been made to prevent obsolescence through data revision and model modification.

The model deals with investment, consumption, price and wage determination, agriculture, foreign trade, and monetary and fiscal activities. It has about 500 variables, 50 accounting identities, and 300 equations. It is unlikely that any firm can or should underwrite development of such a large system for purposes of marketing analysis, but smaller models of sectors and firms, like those described in the last section, are quite feasible.

SUMMARY

Macroeconometric models provide a direct link to empirical work on interactive relationships in marketing systems. These interactions usually involve complex interrelationships among variables under management's control (advertising, price, sales-force effort, and so on) with variables determined outside the firm's control (income levels, demographic patterns, and the like). Among resultants of all these interactions are sales and profits—two variables of particular concern. Since many variables are both causers of, and caused by, other variables, a set of equations is almost always required to represent the system reasonably. Models range from those with a handful of equations and less than a dozen variables to those involving hundreds of equations and variables; they may deal with markets for single brands, for product classes, or for the output of an entire economy or sector. These models are based on implications of theories about how economic systems work, and are tempered with modifications which make the models empirically tractable and descriptively useful. Parameter estimation almost always poses problems such as those described in Sec. II, Part E, Chap. 7.

There are clear gains from turning to multiple-equation systems. For example, they buy the analyst out of the uncomfortable position of knowing that variables are jointly causal but being forced to designate (often arbitrarily) one variable as "the causer" and the others as "the caused." This allows more than one policy variable to be analyzed in the context of one model. Since several variables are usually under control of management (advertising *and* price *and* sales-force effort, for example), it is very difficult to build managerially useful normative models of a system limited to a single equation. In contrast, one macroeconometric model can be used to study individual phenomena as well as interactions among sectors—as with the manufacturer-retailer interaction in the Farley-Leavitt model and the interactions of brands' advertising-decision rules in the Bass-Parsons model. Models of this type thus provide key links to empirical work on problems in systems analysis.

REFERENCES

1. Almon, Clopper, *The American Economy to 1975, an Interindustry Forecast,* New York: Harper & Row, 1966.
2. Bass, Frank M., and Leonard G. Parsons, "Simultaneous-Equation Regression Analysis of Sales and Advertising," working paper, Lafayette, Ind.: Purdue University, Hermann Krannert School of Industrial Administration, 1968.
3. Bodkin, R. G., and L. R. Klein, "Non-Linear Estimation of Aggregate Production Functions," *Review of Economics and Statistics,* vol. 49, February 1967, pp. 28–44.
4. Cohen, Kalman J., and Richard M. Cyert, *Theory of the Firm,* Englewood Cliffs, N.J.: Prentice-Hall, 1965, pp. 168–170.
5. Dorfmann, Robert, and Peter D. Steiner, "Optimal Advertising and Optimal Quality," *American Economic Review,* vol. 44, December 1954, pp. 826–836.
6. Duesenberry, James S., Garry Fromm, Lawrence R. Klein, and Edwin Kuh, *The Brookings Quarterly Econometric Model of the United States,* Chicago: Rand McNally, 1962.
7. Eisenpress, Harry, *Forecasting by Econometric Systems,* Armonk, N.Y.: International Business Machines, 1963.
8. Farley, John U., "Analytical Approaches to Market Segmentation," working paper, New York: Columbia University, Graduate School of Business, 1968.
9. Farley, John U., "Estimating Structural Parameters in Marketing Systems: Theory and Application," in Charles Goodman (ed.), *Changing Perspectives in Marketing,* Chicago: American Marketing Association, 1968.
10. Farley, John U., and Harold J. Leavitt, "A Model of the Jamaican Distribution Structure for Branded Goods," *Journal of Marketing Research,* November 1968, pp. 362–368.
11. Farley, John U., and Harold J. Leavitt, "Private Sector Logistics in Population Control: A Case in Jamaica," *Demography,* vol. 5, December 1968.
12. Girschick, M. A., and T. Haavelmo, "Statistical Analysis of the Demand for Food," *Econometrica,* vol. 15, April 1947, pp. 79–100.

13. Johnston, John, *Econometric Methods*, New York: McGraw-Hill, 1970.
14. Jorgenson, Dale W., "Capital Theory and Investment Behavior," *American Economic Review*, vol. 53, May 1963, pp. 247–259.
15. Klein, L. R., *Economic Fluctuations in the United States*, Cowles Commission Monograph 11, New York: Wiley, 1950, p. 58.
16. Lucas, Robert E., "Adjustment Costs and the Theory of Supply," *Journal of Political Economy*, vol. 75, August 1967, pp. 321–334.
17. Nerlove, Marc, and Kenneth J. Arrow, "Optimal Advertising Under Dynamic Conditions," *Economica*, vol. 29, May 1962, pp. 129–142.
18. Russell, R. Robert, "The Empirical Evaluation of Some Theoretically Plausible Demand Functions," working paper, Cambridge, Mass.: Harvard University, Department of Economics, 1966.
19. Telser, L. G., "The Demand for Branded Goods as Estimated from Consumer Panel Data," *Review of Economics and Statistics*, vol. 44, August 1962, pp. 300–325.

Model Building

Chapter 5

Game Theory

WILLIAM LAZER *Graduate School of Business Administration, Michigan State University, East Lansing, Michigan*

GORDON D. THOMAS *Faculty of Commerce, University of Manitoba, Winnipeg, Canada*

THE CONCEPT AND ELEMENTS OF GAMES

Game theory refers to mathematical modeling that deals with competitive or conflict situations. It enables one to follow rather complex changes in reasoning and facilitates a logical study of the decision-making process under conflicting or competitive situations. The decision maker may be conceived of as an individual, a group, or an organization. The conflicting situation may result in diametrically opposed camps of action, in cooperation, or in both.

A game is merely a specified list of alternatives available to the players (competitors) and a list of the payoffs (consequences) that will occur in each situation. Games are comprised of acts or moves. For example, there are games having only one move, as when two players are involved in the single flip of a coin. Other, more interesting games, however, have many moves. This is the case with chess or checkers. In either instance, single or multiple moves, the games are equivalent conceptually and can be specified totally if the strategy each player will use in every instance is known. For once all the conceivable strategies have been determined, then, conceptually, the resulting payoffs can be specified and the moves detailed.

An example of a game-theory situation is that of two firms in a competitive advertising situation. Here, two marketing managers may control the advertising decisions and actions which, in turn, affect sales and profits of their respective companies. Each manager will choose an appropriate program with due regard to what he thinks his competitor is likely to do. The outcome, that is, sales, profits, or market share, for each company depends on the interaction of the strategies actually chosen—on the decisions made by both marketing managers.

The original work in game theory was done by John Von Neumann, whose first paper was published in 1928. Emile Borel [6] is also reported to have made important contributions in the 1920s. However, the most widely referenced original source is *Theory of Games and Economic Behavior*, by John Von Neumann and Oskar Morgenstern [17].

Illustration

Consider the following example of a hypothetical game-theory application. Two companies are competing for a market, and each can employ three marketing programs. Each company has alternative courses of action from which it must choose. Depending on the choices, each company stands to gain or lose. Thus, there is a specific result for each interaction, depending on the alternatives chosen. As a result of the program that company 1 chooses and the one that company 2 chooses, the respective market shares are determined.

These shares are depicted in the following game-theory matrix, which indicates the market share company 1 finally receives. For example, if company 2 selects marketing program X and company 1 selects marketing program B, then company 1 captures 61 percent of the market. Similarly, if company 1 selects C, and company 2 selects Z, then company 1 gets 42 percent of the market. The game-theory problem is what program each company should select to optimize its situation.[1]

PAYOFFS TO COMPANY 1 IN PERCENT OF MARKET

Company 1 marketing program	Company 2 marketing program		
	X	Y	Z
A	45%	52%	36%
B	61%	39%	54%
C	56%	51%	42%

Strategy

Game theory is concerned with scientifically determining and selecting the "best" strategy in a conflict situation. Selection of strategies in many parlor games and their selection in marketing-decision situations have many similarities. In a game, there are opposing players whose objectives are in conflict: they are out to beat their opponent. Business competitors are generally in effective opposition, and in some ways consumers' objectives conflict with those of the firm. In marketing decisions, opponents have some idea of the possible actions (or strategies) open to them and their competitors. With this

---

[1] The reader should not impart meaning to the strategies or numbers beyond the direct meaning mentioned in the illustration.

information, it may be possible to develop a payoff matrix for all players in much the same way one would in a poker or bridge game.

The payoff matrix gives the payoff for each player, or competitor, under all possible combinations of strategies. For example, in poker, which is basically a simple game insofar as possible strategies and potential payoffs are concerned, a payoff matrix is constructed only implicitly. For business decisions, which are infinitely more complex than poker, we also frequently use only an implicit formulation of a payoff matrix.

Thus, strategies anticipate all the conceivable situations that are likely to occur. They are based on an attempt to anticipate competitors' moves and to specify courses of action to take to counter them. Decision makers wish to find optimal strategies when possible. However, optimal strategies in marketing are at best difficult and usually impossible to establish.

Game-theory situations reflect psychological as well as economic aspects of decision making. For example, labor union negotiations, political situations, competition between firms and industries, or people playing poker all involve decision activities that may be viewed within the framework of game theory. They encompass psychological factors which, in marketing, are often very important.

Games involve decision makers with different objectives or goals. Yet, the resulting gains or losses accruing to each are intertwined. Thus, decision makers do not have complete control over others or over the outcomes of situations. The result is that game-theory problems are more than mere problems of simple maximization. Decision makers must consider the goals, attitudes, and likely moves and decisions of others whose actions will affect their goals and payoffs. "The decision maker in a game faces a cross-purposes optimization problem. He must adjust his plans not only to his own desires and abilities, but also to the desires and abilities of others" [16, p. 9].

CLASSIFICATION OF GAMES

Games may be classified on various bases. The most commonly used classifications are based on the number of participants, the nature of the conflict and the resulting payoffs, the method of representing the game situation, and the underlying conditions.

Number of Participants

One of the fundamental distinctions in game theory is the number of players or interests present in a game. A player need not be one individual. It can be a corporation, a union, or a group of individuals. It is a decision-making unit that selects actions. Games are usually classified on the basis of one, two, or n (more-than-two) persons.

One-person games are generally considered to be of limited relevance to marketing decision making because no conscious competitor exists. At most, the one-person game involves nature, and although nature may present difficulties to any particular player at one time or another, she is presumably impartial in the long run.

The significant difference between the two-person game and the n-person game is that the latter offers the possibility of coalition formation. A coalition may function to increase the certainty or the amount of the payoff, or both. Frequently a coalition of players may have a synergistic effect on their collective payoffs.

There is considerable difficulty in finding an acceptable explanation of how to predict which coalitions will form in a given situation. Von Neumann and Morgenstern, in developing their theory of the n-person game, provided a mathematical explanation. But several factors believed to be important in coalition formation were not considered and, for this reason, their explanation has not proven to be entirely satisfactory.

Another complicating variable introduced by the consideration of coalitions is that of side payments. These are extra payments made by the players to induce other players to join a coalition. The amount of side payment any player can expect depends on his expected payoff without joining a coalition, the value of his contributions to the coalition, the harm his opposition might cause the coalition were he not a member, and, of course, his bargaining skill.

A large body of literature in game theory is concerned with bargaining, with the process of determining a set of rules under which cooperative action will be taken by the parties concerned, and with the way in which the total payoff from cooperative action is distributed among the cooperating players. (See, for example, [3, 8, 9, and 12].)

The possibility of coalitions makes the determination of the optimal solution more difficult because their composition determines the outcome, and this composition is frequently indeterminate. However, the presence of coalitions tends to simplify the n-person game, for if sufficient coalitions and countercoalitions form, the game reverts to a two-person game, and the two-person game can more easily be solved with present concepts and states of knowledge.

The Nature of the Conflict

What is the relationship between the competitors and the payoff matrix? Games, like businesses, can be strictly competitive, strictly cooperative, or some combination of the two. In game theory, a strictly competitive relationship is one in which each player can gain only at the other's expense. What player A wins player B must lose (in a utility rather than a dollar sense). The interests of the players are diametrically opposed. What is best for one is worst for the other. Strictly competitive games are frequently called zero-sum games because the sum of the players' payoffs will equal zero under all possible combinations of strategy.

For illustration, let us envision a two-person zero-sum game. The two-person designation indicates there are two competitors—two companies or two organizations. The zero-sum component refers to the payoff, indicating what one competitor gains, another loses. The situation, therefore, is one of pure opposition. We can diagram this by presenting the following payoff matrix.

Each player has two possible actions. If A_1 and B_1 are chosen, A receives a payoff of 5 and B loses 5. Correspondingly, if A_2 and B_1 are selected, A receives a payoff of 3 and B receives a payoff of -3.

In any two-person zero-sum game, the payoffs to each player are identical numbers with different signs. What one player gives, the other must receive. Because of this, it is conventional for only player A's payoff to be listed in the payoff matrix.

In the preceding example, a complete payoff matrix need show only player A's payoff. As can be seen, in a zero-sum game the players cannot improve matters to their joint satisfaction by cooperating and inducing joint action. A strictly cooperative game, on the other hand, is one in which each player can gain the maximum payoff only by coordinating his activities with the action of the other player, whose returns are also maximized. The latter case would seem to be trivial, since we could assume that all players would wish to cooperate under these circumstances. This is true, and it *would* be trivial if the players could communicate freely and openly with one another. For several reasons, this may not be possible. Legal constraints exist in many forms of interfirm communication. There are many occasions when the interests of both competitors coincide, and the best solution is to coordinate actions. Advertising designed to develop the market by gaining product acceptance rather than merely brand acceptance might illustrate a marketing area in which the companies involved are not opposing one another.

Player A   Player B

		B_1		B_2
		-5		-4
A_1	$+5$		$+4 \cdot$	
		-3		-2
A_2	$+3$		$+2$	

Games not strictly competitive are referred to as non-zero sum. The non-zero sum game is conceptually similar to the zero-sum game, but it poses some additional operational problems. If two competitive salesmen have the following payoff matrix, what action will each take? The first figure in each parenthesis represents salesman 1's return, and the second, salesman 2's.

Salesman 1   Salesman 2

	A_2	B_2
A_1	(7, 7)	(6, 5)
B_1	(5, 4)	(5, 3)

If we assume that side payments or communication are not possible, salesman 1 can maximize his payoff by selecting A_1. But his position relative to salesman 2 is maximized by selecting act B_1. The objective of maximization assumed with the zero-sum game cannot, therefore, automatically be assumed for a non-zero-sum game.

There are many different situations in which cooperative and nonconstant sum games are involved. They lead to a consideration of power, threats, division of profits or sales, bargaining, bluffing, psychological phenomena, evaluation of strength. It is also conceivable that some competitors are in the game for the fun of it rather than for the spoils. Others may make decisions merely to improve their skills. However, in many marketing situations in which all companies are trying to win and their interests are opposed, it is reasonable to expect objectives to differ and competitors to be in conflict to some degree.

Games may be placed on a continuum with strictly competitive and strictly cooperative games as the anchors.[2]   Although most business decisions fall somewhere between these extremes, the basic relationship among players is primarily one of conflict rather than one of cooperation.

Underlying Conditions

Decisions may be made under conditions of certainty, risk, or uncertainty. The condition of certainty exists when there is only one possible outcome and it is known.   For example, if two people are playing stud poker and if player A has a straight and player B has J J 8 5 showing, the outcome is known with certainty: player A will win regardless of player B's hole card.

Risk exists when the outcome is "known" only in terms of probability.   In the previous example, if player A held two pairs, such as aces and fours, the probability that he would win would be one minus the probability that player B's hole card is another jack.

When the underlying condition is one of uncertainty, we have no probabilistic basis for estimating the outcome.   It is obvious that the distinction between conditions of risk and uncertainty is often unclear, for decision makers have some knowledge about most situations encountered.   It is very infrequent that marketing decision makers are completely ignorant about the range of payoffs or competitive strategies their actions will likely provoke.

The three conditions result in a problem's being a *decision problem under certainty* (DPUC), a *decision problem under risk* (DPUR), or a *decision problem under uncertainty* (DPUU).   In the literature of game theory, a DPUC is one in which nature (or chance) is not involved.   A DPUR is one in which nature (or chance) is involved and the laws of randomness are known.   A DPUU is one in which nature is involved in the game, but her strategy is unknown.

Although game-theory models tend to focus around DPUC, most business decisions involve chance elements and fall under the general categories of either DPUR or DPUU.   This is not to imply that the study of DPUC is not relevant or useful, at least conceptually, for business decision making.   The primary difference between DPUC and DPUR is that DPUC excludes one element, nature or chance, and is therefore more easily studied and understood and more readily generalizable to a variety of situations.

2 × M Games

Games can exists where one player has two strategies and the other has many strategies.   They are called 2 × M games, where M is any number greater than two.   Since their solution may be similar to the 2 × 2 games, the 2 × M games may frequently be reduced to the 2 × 2 games.   Once the games are reduced, a saddle-point mixed-strategy solution can more easily be determined.   Two-person zero-sum games are all soluble.   The mathematics of solutions of M × M games are more complex, but the logic is identical to that used in solving 2 × 2 games.

As it has developed, much of game theory has focused on the two-person zero-sum games under conditions of certainty or risk.   Much theoretical work has been done in other areas of game theory,[3] but the theory has not yet reached the stage of practical applicability.   It should be noted that the two-person zero-sum game is a very special game.   In a marketing situation, it

---

[2] This concept is generally attributed to Schelling.   For further discussion, see [15].
[3] The *Journal of Conflict Resolution* provides many such examples.

might have limited interest because it is not realistic.   Nevertheless, it is a useful vehicle for illustrating the theories.

In reality, there are usually more than two competitors involved in market situations, and the gains of one do not exactly compensate for the losses of the other.   In many situations it is profitable for both players or entities to cooperate.   Also, in marketing it is evident that by varying the elements of the marketing mix, the markets may be expanded and payoffs increased.   For example, by increasing advertising or altering prices, the market share, sales volume, or profitability can be altered.   Thus, the situation is not a simple game.   However, if we understand the essence of a two-person zero-sum game, the principles of game theory will become clear.

The following table summarizes the relationship between competitive game models and their areas of application.   It illustrates that, in the purest sense, most game models have only limited applicability to decision making in modern business organizations.   But pragmatically, many business decision problems can be modified or stated in a form such that game theory is relevant.

COMPETITIVE GAMES AND THEIR
APPLICATION TO MARKETING DECISION MAKING

Number of players	Nature in game		
	DPUC: Nature not in game	DPUR: Nature's strategy known	DPUU: Nature's strategy not known
1			
2		←———Most highly developed———→ game models	
n (3 or more)			Most marketing decisions ←————————————————→

THE DEVELOPMENT OF STRATEGIES

In normal business or military usage, *strategy* is the overall plan adopted to attain organizational objectives, and *tactics* are the modifications of strategy required by the unforeseen and unexpected.   In game-theory usage, a strategy is a plan covering all eventualities, a list of all possible actions which may be taken under a given set of circumstances.   Being complete, it is never necessary to modify it as a result of changing conditions or circumstances.   Thus, given the strategies, every possible reaction to an opponent's move has been predetermined.

A game's outcome depends on the strategies each player will use.   Players must think in terms of selecting their specific strategy, the counterstrategy that opponents might use, and the resulting payoffs.   In marketing terms, payoffs might deal with sales volume, profits, return on investment, or market share.   Payoffs, therefore, are merely the values each player attaches to the outcome that allocates resources in certain ways.

The fundamental argument underlying a two-person zero-sum game is as follows: Competitor A wants to do as well as possible.   However, he does not merely assume that competitor B will be overly generous to him.   In fact, he reviews each of his strategies from the opposite perspective—that his competitor is truly insightful, knowledgeable, and in essence is scrutinizing him carefully with full intent to "do him in." Under these conditions, A is concerned with how much he can win. He assumes that regardless of what strategy he selects, B will be so intelligent, so rational, and so well informed that he will make the best countermove. Thus B is a very malevolent competitor; and regardless of what A does, B will move to select the best strategy to offset it.

B makes a similar analysis from his vantage point. He, too, has great respect for his competitor A. He knows that A is knowledgeable, rational, and shrewd, and that A is scrutinizing him very carefully and will always make the best counterchoice. B wants to give A as little as possible—limit his sales, his profitability, his market share. In terms of the payoff matrix, B wants to operate so that A gets the least. When both players behave in this way, they arrive at what is known in game theory as the minimax solution.

The Minimax Criterion

To illustrate this criterion, consider a two-person zero-sum game with players A and B. Player A can choose either strategy 1 or strategy 2, designated A_1 and A_2. The resulting payoffs he receives are shown in the following matrix. They depend on whether player B chooses strategy B_1 or B_2. The payoff accruing to A for the intersection of A_1B_1 is 27; for A_1B_2, 6; for A_2B_1, 12; and for A_2B_2, 9, as the matrix indicates.

Player A	Player B	
	Strategy B_1	Strategy B_2
Strategy A_1	27	6
Strategy A_2	12	9

Thus, each player must choose between two alternatives. Player A will always receive some amount. The minimum he will get will be 6, the maximum, 27; and he wants to choose strategies to get as much as possible, the maximum. Player B has the opposite viewpoint. He will always pay and, therefore, wants to pay as little as possible. Thus, he would like a strategy that leads to the minimum payoff of 6. The question is, then, what should A do?

Obviously, in A's case he would like to get 27 as the payoff, and to do that, he would have to choose strategy A_1. However, to realize the payoff, he must hope that B reacts by choosing strategy B_1.

But, if B reasons that A is going after the big amount, then Player B will choose strategy B_2, which results in a payoff of only 6. But if B chooses B_2, then A would be better off choosing strategy A_2.

Through this kind of reasoning, we finally reach a situation in which neither A nor B will be willing to change his position. This will be A_2B_2. A will not change because when he does, B will only give up 6. Hence A is better off with strategy A_2. B does not want to change, because if he does, A is going to tag him for 12. Thus, it would appear that in this situation, there is an equilibrium point at which both seem to have reached an optimum position. There is no inducement for either player to move away from strategy A_2B_2.

A formal way of determining the equilibrium point, where one exists, has been formulated and is called the *minimax* or *maximin* solution. The payoffs for A are shown on the rows opposite each action, and for B, in the colums below each action. A's maximum payoff, given B's shrewdness, will be the maximum of the row minimums (or the maximin). B is striving for the lowest payoff to A, given A's shrewdness, which will be the minimum of the column maximums (or the minimax). When A's maximin equals B's minimax, an equilibrium or saddle point (to use the mathematical term) exists. This is illustrated where the maximin and the minimax both equal 9, and each player will select the act which provides that yield.

Player A	Player B		Row minimum
	B_1	B_2	
A_1	27	6	6
A_2	12	9	9
Column maximum	27	9	

In such simple situations, there is a pure, optimal strategy. The rational way to play this game is for each player to select the strategy giving him the best or greatest return under the worst possible conditions. The strategy is called the minimax or maximin strategy for the respective players. Given the minimax assumptions, a competitor can never obtain the maximum, the maximax. Thus, the minimax strategy is a pessimistic strategy. In real marketing situations, competitors are not so all-knowing and may not have the wherewithall to take advantage, in the best possible way, of any situation so as to inflict as much damage as possible on their competitors.

When the maximin and minimax are equal, the game has a *saddle point,* and each opponent should logically select the strategy that intersects at the saddle point. The value of the payoff associated with the saddle point of a two-person zero-sum game is termed the value of the game. How does one determine whether there is a saddle point? Each player examines his strategy from both his opponent's viewpoint and his own. He thus views the row minima and notes the largest of these, and the column maxima and notes the lowest of these. If they are equal, there is a saddle point.

Mixed Strategies

Given a set of available strategies, what options are available to the decision maker? He can adopt either one particular alternative and stick with it, or he can alternate on a probabilistic basis between two or more of these alternatives. The first case is called a *pure* strategy while the latter is termed a *mixed* strategy. Thus, a mixed strategy is made up of pure strategies and, as a super strategy, governs the selection of pure strategies.

Consider the following game with opponents A and B where the matrix gives A's payoffs.

Player A	Player B		Row minimum
	B_1	B_2	
A_1	12	24	12
A_2	20	16	16
Column maximum	20	24	

We have row minimums of 12 and 16 confronting A and column maximums of 20 and 24 confronting B. The maximin of the rows does not equal the minimax of the columns. Thus, no saddle point exists.

How do the players reach an equilibrium point? Look first at B's situation. B figures that A should on the average be able to get between 20 and 16 on a play. That is, A will be aware that he does not have to settle for 12 or 16. B knows that if he selects just one strategy or the other consistently (for example, if he chooses strategy B_1 all the time), A gains 20 each play; if he chooses strategy B_2 all the time, A gains 24 each play. B will reason that he is better off by mixing strategies—sometimes selecting strategy B_1 and sometimes selecting B_2. And he must select them in such a way that A will not know which strategy is being chosen. Thus, B arrives at a super strategy.

If A knows what strategy B will use, A will be able to clobber B. Security, therefore, is required. To maintain such security, we might let the selection of strategies depend entirely on random or chance events—for example, on a table of random numbers or the flip of a coin. B might choose to select B_1 whenever tails appear and B_2 whenever heads appear. If this strategy is used against A, then how much will B have to pay? About half the time he will have to pay 12 and half the time 24, or an expected payoff of 18.

The implicit reasoning used by B could have been stated formally. B wishes to select a probability p for act 1 and a probability $1 - p$ for act 2 such that the expected payoff is identical regardless of whether A selects A_1 or A_2. Let $E(B|A_1)$ and $E(B|A_2)$ be the expected payoffs of B, given A's act 1 and A's act 2, respectively.

Then

$$E(B|A_1) = 12\,(p) + 24\,(1 - p)$$
$$E(B|A_2) = 20\,(p) + 16\,(1 - p)$$

If we set

$$E(B|A_1) = E(B|A_2)$$

then

$$12\,(p) + 24\,(1 - p) = 20\,(p) + 16\,(1 - p)$$
$$p = 1/2 = .5$$

Therefore

$$1 - p = 1 - .5 = .5.$$

Minimum payoffs now become

$$E(B|A_1) = .5\,(12) + .5\,(24)$$
$$= 18$$

and

$$E(B|A_2) = .5\,(20) + .5\,(16)$$
$$= 18$$

While B is making these calculations, A is not idle. He too is trying to determine his optimum strategy, which, of course, will enable him to collect as much as possible from B. A calculates his probabilities in the same way.

$$E(A|B_1) = 12\,(p) + 20\,(1 - p)$$
$$E(A|B_2) = 24\,(p) + 16\,(1 - p)$$

If we set

$$E(A|B_1) = E(A|B_2)$$

then

$$12\,(p) + 20\,(1 - p) = 24\,(p) + 16\,(1 - p)$$
$$p = 4/16 = .25$$

Therefore, $1 - p = .75$.

$$E(A \mid B_1) = 12\,(.25) + 20\,(.75)$$
$$E(A \mid B_1) = 18$$
$$E(A \mid B_2) = 24\,(.25) + .75\,(16)$$
$$E(A \mid B_2) = 18$$

As before, with the pure strategy, the maximum of the row minimums (18) now equals the minimum of the column maximums, and we are once again in an equilibrium or saddle-point position. As long as A sticks to his prescribed strategy, there is no strategy B can adopt that will reduce his payment to A below the equilibrium expectation of 18. Similarly, as long as B continues to play his optimum strategy, there is no way that A can increase the payoff he receives beyond the expected value of 18. The use of mixed strategies is an important concept in game theory. It indicates that when no saddle point exists, it is best to mix strategies, and the rational selection on a particular play might depend on random choice.

The selection of mixed strategies is usually expressed in terms of odds. Thus, in our example we get selection A_1 versus A_2 at a ratio of 1 to 3, meaning that A selects strategy A_1 one time to every three times he selects strategy A_2. B selects B_1 and B_2 in the ratio of 1 to 1.

A mixed strategy, therefore, is a super or grand strategy which contains the original strategies as elements. The grand strategy governs the choice of pure strategies for a particular play. There is nothing unscientific about having strategy selection based on a probabilistic or chance mechanism [18]:

> ... All of the reasoning which you feel should go into it does go into it. It is injected when the problem is formulated, when the payoffs are assessed, and when the odds are computed which govern the choice of events and hence the choice of strategy. The chance device is thus an instrument of your will and not your master.

The minimax solution is extremely conservative. It assumes a zero-sum payoff matrix where one player is striving to minimize the payoff of the other. This conservatism is justified under these circumstances, but if acts of nature (or chance, or unknown conditions) are relevant, this approach has some weaknesses, for nature is not a consciously antagonistic opponent. For example, if the payoff matrix for actions A_1 and A_2 and states of nature S_1 and S_2 were as follows, the minimax solution for A would always be A_2.

A	S_1	S_2
A_1	0	100
A_2	1	1

This would be true regardless of how high the payoff for $A_1 S_2$ became. In addition, because of the conservative nature of the minimax solution, A would never be willing to pay for information which might show the true probabilities attached to each of the states of nature. In such situations, where risk or uncertainty is involved, it is intuitively obvious that the minimax criterion is inappropriate.

Other Decision Criteria

Several other decision criteria have been suggested or developed to deal with conditions of risk and uncertainty where the assumptions of the minimax solution are not believed to apply.

The *principle of insufficient reason* is based on the assumption that if knowledge of the true probabilities associated with the states of nature is unknown, it is reasonable to assume that all states have an equal probability of occurring.

The *Savage minimax regret* criterion has as its key variable the minimization of the amount of regret involved. "Regret" is the difference between the highest payoff a decision maker could have received had he been the wisest decision maker and the payoff actually received as a result of his choice, given the occurrence of a specific state of nature. It is the difference between "what is" and "what might have been." This criterion assumes that each player selects the strategy which will minimize his maximum possible regret.

Another criterion is the *Hurwicz criterion*. It refers to the development of a pessimism-optimism index for the decision maker. Here the psychological position of the decision maker is expressed in terms of a coefficient of optimism—a probability indicating the likelihood that the decision maker feels the optimum event has of occurring. Similarly, a coefficient of pessimism, a 1 minus the coefficient of optimism, is associated with the likelihood the "worst" event has of occurring. Then a weighted combination of the "best" and "worst" state of values can be calculated.

The use of *Bayesian* or *subjective probability* has also been suggested in selecting strategies, as explained in Sec. II, Part A, Chap. 3 and Sec. II, Part D, Chap. 1. Decision makers have insights and feelings about the likelihood of events happening. This knowledge, experience, and intuition should be used in assigning probability values to the occurrence of events.

Dominant Strategies

Game theory formally requires that all possible acts be considered in selecting a strategy for adoption. It is obvious that most business decisions involve a great many possible acts but considerably fewer reasonable ones. Williams suggests that all strategies be examined and "if one of his strategies is superior to another, *on a box by box basis*, then the former is *dominant*, and the latter should be eliminated from the matrix [18]." Only acts not dominated by other acts need normally be evaluated.

The difficulty in using domination as the criterion for reducing the number of possible actions is that the payoffs under all possible conditions must be determined before deciding whether an act is or is not dominant. This potential difficulty is overcome if we recognize that for most practical marketing decisions, all possible solutions are seldom considered. For the most part, we are content with a satisfactory payoff rather than with an insistence on the maximum possible return. This concept of "satisficing,"[4] as opposed to "optimizing," would appear to be realistic for most strategic decisions that are made in business.

A Dilemma[5]

There are situations where cooperation is desirable from the competitor's point of view, and where some of the game-theory "rules" do not seem to apply. A payoff matrix for the pricing policies of two gasoline service stations, which are, let us say, operating across the road from one another but without other competition, might illustrate such a situation. Their payoff matrix might be as follows:

[4] This concept is usually associated with J. G. March and H. A. Simon. See [11].
[5] This illustration is an adaptation of the "Prisoner's Dilemma," generally attributed to A. W. Tucker. See [18].

Pricing policy of gas station 1	Pricing policy of gas station 2	
	A_2 (maintain price)	B_2 (cut price)
A_1 (maintain price)	(6, 6)	(1, 8)
B_1 (cut price)	(8, 1)	(3, 3)

Examination of the matrix shows that for a given play, either station would benefit by cutting price. Station 1 can gain by cutting price, regardless of station 2's action, and vice versa, as its payoff for $B_1A_2 > A_1A_2$ and $B_1B_2 > A_1B_2$. Each station therefore has an incentive to cut price, and we would expect them to arrive at B_1B_2. But we can also see that the payoff at $A_1A_2 > B_1B_2$, and therefore both stations would prefer to be at A_1A_2 rather than B_1B_2. If both parties are familiar with the payoff matrix, communication (or collusion) is unnecessary for the stations to realize that they will be better off, both individually and collectively, if they both maintain the price.

What is required to reach A_1A_2 without collusion? First, mutual respect of abilities. Each player must recognize that the other player knows the payoff table and is aware of the long-run consequences of a price-cutting strategy. Second, both players must be willing to cooperate and must believe the other player is also willing to cooperate.

An unusual situation will frequently develop, for in this type of case, it pays to be (or act) uninformed about the consequences of price cutting. For if station 1 lapses occasionally and cuts price, it will benefit at the expense of station 2. The central question for station 1 is to determine how many lapses station 2 will tolerate before losing faith in the cooperative nature of its opponent. The temptation to communicate when this is possible and when one or both of the stations are (or pretend to be) uninformed is generally irresistible.

A great deal of study has been done on variations of this type of situation. One study of particular relevance to marketing decisions indicated that the likelihood of arriving at the cooperative intersection is inversely related to the number of noncooperative actions available [4].

GAME THEORY: APPLICATIONS IN MARKETING

How practical are game-theory models? Can they be applied to solve practical marketing problems? What confronts practitioners in using the models?

Conceptually, game-theory models have much to offer marketing practitioners. They stimulate decision makers to think of alternative strategies, of counterstrategies of competitors, of the consequences of each strategy, and of the likelihood of competitive decisions. They can take account of competitors' reactions and include the important psychological dimensions of competitive decisions.

Realistically, however, game-theory models have not been widely applied to solve marketing problems. Several difficulties confront the user. The initial problem is that of defining the game in real terms so that one can specify explicitly all the alternatives available to each player. The result is that one must simplify or remove the important influences of environments which are critical for marketing. It is difficult, if not impossible, to outline all the strategies a competitor might follow. Numerous possible courses of action are available to both a firm and its competitors.

The basic problem of measuring preferences is formidable. Where and how does one obtain the numbers in a payoff matrix? An assumption in applying game-theory concepts is that payoffs can be measured numerically. In practical marketing situations, this information cannot be derived. Payoffs cannot be measured with sufficient accuracy.

Game theory also assumes that the measurement of units is the same for all the boxes. In explicitly stating payoffs, they all must be expressed in dollars or some other common unit. If the payoffs do not represent homogeneous units, or cannot be so converted, formidable difficulties arise. For example, in marketing the payoffs not only might be sales volume or profits, which vary in value, but also might require the translation of equivalent values of image, reputation, or status.

Conceptually, therefore, the construction of an explicit game-theory matrix requires that payoffs be stated in terms of utilities rather than dollars or other absolute amounts. It is intuitively obvious that $10,000 in sales, or a 1 percent change in market share, will usually have greater utility to a firm with $100,000 total sales, or 5 percent market share, than the utility of the same absolute amount to a firm with $25 million sales, or a 75 percent market share. The payoff matrices of competitors are not stated explicitly. Thus, it is common to assign one's own utility preferences to the payoffs of competitors, which can create analytical problems.

Suppose the difficulty of measuring utilities or payoffs is overcome. Then how does one measure the impact of the interaction of competitor-opponent strategies? While the normalized form of the game-theory model summarizes all the details on strategies selected by competitors and opponents and their payoffs, and presents them very simply, developing such a model is at best a very complex activity involving a large number of assumptions about interactions. The empirical basis for such details is not available.

Another set of problems in applying game theory concerns the criteria to use. Game theory often adopts the posture that there is a way people ought to behave. "One refers to a mathematical morality, or at least frugality, which claims that the *sensible object of the player is to gain as much from the game as he can, safely, in the face of a skillful opponent who is pursuing an antithetical goal* [16, p. 23]."

This is usually termed the rational criterion. Thus, one adopts the strategy of choosing a criterion so that he can assure himself of winning at least a certain amount regardless of what his opponent does.

There is, in fact, a way to play every two-person game so that this criterion can be satisfied. The criterion, however, is conservative and attributes great knowledge and astuteness to one's competitors, which will probably not correspond with reality. Choosing criteria becomes even more complex when the payoffs may take one of several values and when the number of players is increased.

At this juncture, it seems highly unlikely that game theory will be used to solve many practical marketing problems. A few theoretical articles dealing with highly simplified situations are recorded in the literature, for example, [1] and [7]. More important, however, is the basic conceptualization of marketing problems that it offers in helping academicians and practitioners think through marketing situations. This makes an understanding of such models worthwhile.

REFERENCES

1. Bell, C. E., "The N Days of Christmas: A Model for Competitive Advertising over an Intensive Campaign," *Management Science*, vol. 14, May 1968.

2. Bierman, H., et al., *Quantitative Analysis for Business Decisions*, Homewood, Ill.: Irwin, 1965.
3. Deutsch, M., and R. M. Krause, "Studies of Interpersonal Bargaining," *Journal of Conflict Resolution*, vol. 6, March 1962.
4. Dolbear, F. T., et al., "Collusion in the Prisoner's Dilemma: Number of Strategies," *Journal of Conflict Resolution*, vol. 13, June 1969.
5. Dresher, M., *Games of Strategy: Theory and Applications*, Englewood Cliffs, N.J.: Prentice-Hall, 1964.
6. Frechet, M., "Emile Borel, Initiator of the Theory of Psychological Games and Its Application," *Econometrica*, vol. 21, January 1953.
7. Friedman, L., "Game Theory Models in the Allocation of Advertising Expenditures," *Operations Research*, vol. 6, September–October 1958.
8. Harsanyi, J. C., "Approaches to the Bargaining Problem," *Econometrica*, vol. 24, April 1956.
9. Harsanyi, J. C., "A Bargaining Model for the Cooperative N-Person Game," in A. W. Tucker and R. D. Luce (eds.), *Contributions to the Theory of Games*, Princeton, N.J.: Princeton University Press, 1959.
10. Luce, R. D., and H. Raiffa, *Games and Decisions: Introduction and Critical Survey*, New York: Wiley, 1957.
11. March, J. G., and H. A. Simon, *Organizations*, New York: Wiley, 1958.
12. Nash, J. F., "The Bargaining Problem," *Econometrica*, vol. 18, April 1950.
13. Rapaport, A., *Fights, Games and Debates*, Ann Arbor: University of Michigan Press, 1960.
14. Schelling, T. C., "Bargaining, Communication and Limited War," *Journal of Conflict Resolution*, vol. 11, March 1957.
15. Schelling, T. C., *The Strategy of Conflict*, New York: Oxford University Press, 1953.
16. Shubik, M. (ed.), *Game Theory and Related Approaches to Social Behavior*, New York: Wiley, 1964.
17. Von Neumann, J., and O. Morgenstern, *Theory of Games and Economic Behavior*, New York: Wiley, 1944.
18. Williams, J. D., *The Compleat Strategyst*, New York: McGraw-Hill, 1954.

Computer Techniques

Chapter 1

Computer Programs for Statistical Analysis

KENNETH M. WARWICK   *Grey Advertising, New York, New York*

INTRODUCTION

Marketing research is essentially an applied discipline which seeks practical answers to practical questions. The use of high-speed digital computers and sophisticated multivariate statistical techniques has not, in fact, altered this situation. Unfortunately, the rate at which the use of these techniques has proliferated has tended to obscure the practical approach alluded to in the first sentence, mainly because the availability of sophisticated computer programs has not been paralleled by an adequate understanding of their scope and limitations. This chapter aims to present these methods in a context which will enable the potential user to evaluate a specific computer program in relation to the practical requirements of the analytic problem which he faces.

Essentially, the philosophy underlying this discussion can be found in a series of papers by Tukey [302, 304], Tukey and Wilk [307], and Mosteller and Tukey [239]. The concept of data analysis put forward by Tukey suggests that the problem facing the market researcher is to extract some meaningful and relevant conclusions from his body of data, and that in achieving this goal, he should not be hamstrung by the specific mathematical models embodied in some statistical text, or by the availability of certain computer programs.

To be more specific, John Tukey [303] has commented as follows:

> Following a rule book for research seems to stimulate the attack on trivial problems. The great challenge is to teach investigators to formulate questions that have a chance of leading somewhere, not to be too tightly bound in the formulation by a preconceived model of research design. Only after the formulation

(but before empirical study) need there be attention to the procedures to be adopted for collecting and evaluating evidence—not right away changing the questions to fit a standard procedure, but (hopefully) selecting and/or adapting procedures which are suitable.

Also, Huber [152] observes that "there is no reason, except mathematical convenience, to impose linearity or unbiasedness."

In other words, although the primary purpose of this chapter is to review existing statistical computer programs, an earlier statement cannot be too strongly emphasized: The researcher's statistical methods should be dictated by the questions he is trying to answer and the nature of his empirical data, not by the availability of a specific computer program or the dogma of a specific statistical model. In this respect, the potential user of the techniques described here would be well advised to study carefully an article by Elashoff and Snow [85]. It provides an excellent illustration of the pitfalls awaiting any research worker who attempts to apply complex methods to his data in an uncritical fashion.

Thus, the objectives of this chapter are threefold: to provide a compilation of available computer programs which are of value in market research; to evaluate these computer programs in terms of their strengths and weaknesses as data-analytic devices; to briefly discuss some of the problems associated with statistical data processing; and to outline currently available solutions to these problems.

Within the compass of this chapter, it is not possible to give a detailed account of all the programs and systems of programs available to the market researcher. Instead, we shall try to develop a typology of programs which will serve to summarize the field. These will be characterized in terms of the level of sophistication—both statistical and programming—required for their use, and their relative flexibility as data-analytic tools.

TYPES OF COMPUTER PROGRAMS

Individual Programs

First, there are the individual computer programs which are self-contained entities designed to perform one specific function or technique. Typical examples are many of the programs distributed by the Marketing Science Institute, such as Kruskal's MDSCAL [188] or Young's TORSCA [335], both of which perform varieties of multidimensional scaling. The programs described in Cooley and Lohnes' book [61] for factor analysis, discriminant analysis, analysis of variance, and similar procedures are also of this type. (Also, see Veldman [311] or Hope [146].) This type of program requires little or no programming knowledge by the user. It simply involves completion of one or more control cards by the user to describe the options he wishes. However, it suffers from the disadvantage that the user is tied to the particular set of options provided by the program author. Unless he possesses some degree of programming skill, he will have considerable difficulty in modifying these programs for specific purposes of his own, not covered in the original program design. One further difficulty for the user is that programs of this type are usually written for a specific computer, and if they have to be transferred to a different computer, they may require a considerable amount of programming effort.

A vast number of individual computer programs, which cover the entire range of multivariate statistics, exist in this form, and the user is cautioned to examine each one he intends to use very carefully before applying it to his data. It is necessary to determine the specific computing algorithm used in each case, since different algorithms sometimes give different results. For example, Horst [148] has developed a program for the principal-components analysis of very large data matrices. However, under certain circumstances, and with certain data matrices, the results obtained with this program can be misleading, and do not agree with results obtained using other principal-components programs.[1]

Again, other programs require that the input data be in a specific format or of a certain type, and any deviation from this requirement renders the program useless. For example, many programs for the analysis of variance and covariance stipulate equal cell sizes and no missing observations—a situation rarely found in market research. Finally, some programs in fact produce downright erroneous results because of some oversight on the original programmer's part. This problem can be avoided by running several sets of test data through the program, for which independent results are known.

Packages of Computer Programs

A second level of available program is the program package, such as the BMD and BMDX Series (Dixon, [77] and [78]), Jones' Multivariate Statistical Analyzer [162], and the University of Miami Multivariate Statistical Programs (Clyde et al. [57]). Essentially, these are sets of individual statistical programs which have been drawn together into a package with a standardized format, but which remain as individual programs. The best known of these program packages is the BMD series, which has received a very wide circulation. Basically, the BMD series consists of a wide range of individual programs covering the majority of univariate and multivariate statistical techniques. They have the advantage of maintaining a standard format for control cards throughout the series, and are relatively easy for the unsophisticated user to handle. They suffer from the disadvantages that they have rigid requirements in terms of input format and options available to the user. To a large extent, little provision is made for handling missing data, and the available output options can be modified only with difficulty in many cases. In general, if one is satisfied with the output provided, these programs are highly satisfactory, but for many situations, they may be of little value.

The majority of large university computing centers have systems of statistical packages of this type, such as the University of Wisconsin's STATJOB system, or Illinois University's SSUPAC, or the University of Texas' EDSTAT system. However, to a very large extent, these systems are closely tied to the operating system under which they were developed, and transferring them to a new location is a problem of considerable magnitude.

In Milton and Nelder [235], there is a good deal of discussion about the development of higher-level systems of statistical programs. Basically, these systems are characterized by their use of a more natural, English-type language to describe statistical operations and by their file-handling capabilities, which permit the user to have a common data base and to move from one statistical procedure to another. This topic has been discussed in greater detail in a series of papers in applied statistics [109, 117, 246, and 247].

---

[1] Specifically, Horst's method depends upon partitioning the total correlation matrix into submatrices, which are analyzed separately and then recombined at a later stage in the procedure. Differing results may be obtained, depending on how the user decides to partition his original matrix (since it is left up to him to determine the partitions).

The outstanding examples of this type currently available are the DATATEXT system [65], SPSS [248], P-STAT [44], ASCOP [63], GENSTAT [245], OMNITAB [144], and DATMAN [256]. All these systems start with the concept of a basic data matrix and provide a language which can be used to manipulate elements in this matrix and perform a variety of statistical manipulations to it. For example, the DATATEXT system consists of an integrated set of programs [7] whose operations are entirely hidden from the user. He is provided with an English-type language, which can be used to describe the operations to be carried out on his original data matrix. If the user wishes to take the square root of the third column (variable) in his data matrix, he would write

° VAR(N) = SQRT X (3)

Here, the user is creating a new variable which is the square root of the third column in his original data matrix.

If he wished to develop a composite index derived from several of his original variables, he would write

° VAR(N) = (SUM X (6-10))/5.0

In this case, the user has created a new variable, which is the arithmetic mean of the sixth through the tenth columns of his original data matrix.

If he then wishes to perform some statistical computations with his modified data matrix, he would write statements such as

° COMPUTE FACTORS (1-20), ROOT = 1.0
° COMPUTE ANOVA (CITY WITHIN STATE), ANXIETY

The first instruction will perform a principal-components analysis on the first 20 columns of the data matrix, and will extract only as many components as have latent roots greater than, or equal to, 1.0. The second instruction will perform a nested analysis of variance, using the column labeled "ANXIETY" as the dependent variable, and the columns labeled "CITY" and "STATE" as the independent variables.

Systems of this type have many advantages in that they can handle large numbers of variables and provide extremely flexible recoding of the input data. They usually provide for missing observations and can perform a whole series of statistical operations within the context of a single run on the computer. Obviously, the user is limited by his skill in manipulating the control language, and he is tied down to the options currently available in the system. Also, complex systems of this type exact a price in increased machine time used, which can sometimes be an important consideration for the commercial user.

One disquieting feature of these systems is the relative ease with which the inexperienced user can request complex, multivariate statistical procedures without any real knowledge of what he is doing. Armor [7] gives an excellent description of the analysis of variance and covariance features available in DATATEXT, and there is no doubt that a considerable amount of both programming and statistical skill has gone into their design. However, there appears to be very little control over the user with respect to his applying these techniques in a completely inappropriate fashion.

In this respect, the AARDVARK system [142], a statistical system exclusively devoted to analysis of variance and covariance, shows some superiority. This language enables the user to specify in algebraic terms the specific statistical model he wishes to analyze and to specify the output he requires. For example,

IDENTIFICATION, COVARIANCE MODEL WITH 2 COVARIATES
MODEL, Y = A(I) + B(IJ) + C(K) + AC(IK) + C1 * X1 + C2**2 + E(IJK)
LIMITS, I = 2, J = 4, K = 3
ADJUSTED MEANS, A,B,C
END

This set of instructions informs the computer to perform a three-factor analysis of covariance, using two covariates, and specifies the number of levels within the three factors A, B, and C as $2 \times 4 \times 3$. It also requests that the means, adjusted for the covariates, be printed out for all three factors.

The AARDVARK system has been developed to the stage of handling both univariate and multivariate analysis of variance and covariance for both equal and unequal cell sizes [141]. It gives the user a very flexible approach to analysis of variance problems, enabling him to specify a variety of models and hypotheses. However, it does demand a certain level of statistical sophistication in the user, in that he is required to specify his model in the appropriate algebraic terms. This requirement should be contrasted with, for example, the BMD analysis of variance and covariance programs which require merely a cookbook knowledge of analysis of variance for their use.

Matrix Algebra Packages

Finally, at a much higher level of sophistication both in terms of statistics and programming, there exist several what have been termed matrix packages— IBM's STORM System [13], the IBM Scientific Subroutine Package, IBM MATLAN System [153], Bock and Peterson's matrix package [29], and Beaton's F4STAT System [18]. Basically, all these packages are sets of subroutines which perform various matrix operations ranging from matrix multiplication and transposition through more complex eigenvalue and eigenvector routines. Since all multivariate procedures can be expressed in terms of matrix algebra, these packages consist of building blocks which the sophisticated user can integrate to perform virtually any form of multivariate statistical analysis he desires.

Within this area, there are three types of packages. The Bock and Peterson matrix package [29] is an example of the simplest. Parenthetically, this particular matrix package has been extended and rewritten for both the IBM System/360 and the IBM 1130 [30].

The latter package (IBM 1130) is of especial value to those users who have access only to a small computer with limited core storage. It consists of a set of matrix operators in subroutine form, and the user is required to write his own program to integrate these subroutines for any given form of statistical analysis. At the next level, Beaton [18] has developed a set of specialized matrix operators specifically designed for statistical computation. For example, he has an SDP (sum direct products) operator, whose function is to compute the direct (Kronecker) product of the dummy variables for the main effects and interactions in an analysis of variance. However, again one is required to program these operators into an integrated system in order to have a functional program. A most sophisticated form of these matrix packages is IBM's MATLAN, which is essentially a matrix language in which one writes programs using matrices and vectors as the basic units or variables, as opposed to using single data points as one does in a language such as FORTRAN. The disadvantage of this system is that it requires some degree of programming skill to use MATLAN effectively, as the language structure is rather similar to that of an assembler language.

It is doubtful that this class of matrix packages will be of much value to the average market researcher unless he has access to a moderately competent computer programmer, or is one himself. Also, although these matrix operators give the user the advantage of extreme flexibility, in the majority of situations a program already exists to perform the required analysis. These packages are of considerable value, if one has the skills necessary to use them, in those situations where some unusual or unique analysis is required.

COMPUTATIONAL ALGORITHMS

An important consideration in the assessment of multivariate statistical programs is the choice of the specific computational algorithm implemented by the program author. In many cases, this choice is dictated by the particular machine being used or the programmer's level of knowledge and skill.

With regard to the choice of a particular algorithm, two considerations would seem to be important: (1) computational accuracy, and (2) computational efficiency. Although the desirability of an efficient and economical computer program is unquestionable, this factor should not be permitted to override the necessity for computational accuracy.

For example, Neely [244] examined the performance of several algorithms for computing means, standard deviations, and correlation coefficients. He discovered that some of the commonly used computing formulas produced rather large errors and that these errors can increase with an increase in sample size. The fact that inaccuracies can creep into the computation of relatively simple statistics, such as means and correlation coefficients, suggests that the problem of computational accuracy can be serious in the computation of much more complex algorithms, such as eigenvalues or determinants [341].

Longley [215] has studied the relative accuracy of several algorithms used in linear least-squares regression programs. He notes that some regression programs are simply adaptations of desk-calculator methods to the computer, and that routines such as the Doolittle method can produce inaccurate results on a digital computer due to the accumulation of round-off error. After testing several standard regression programs, which used a standard matrix inversion algorithm, Longley found that all the programs produced some degree of inaccuracy. When he compared the accuracy of these programs with a program using the Gram-Schmidt orthonormalization algorithm, he found that the latter algorithm produced a far higher degree of accuracy. (See [151].)

Moreover, it should be noted that Longley's study is not an isolated phenomenon. Many other studies of least-squares computer programs have been made, which indicate that gross numerical errors can occur in a wide variety of circumstances [45, 97, 100, 163, 220, 240, 315, 316, and 342]. On the positive side, a study by Bjorck and Golub [24] illustrates, however, that it is possible to develop accurate computational algorithms for least-squares problems.

Unfortunately, not too many statistical computer programs have been examined with the care exhibited by Longley. It is suggested that any user of multivariate statistical programs who may doubt the accuracy of their results should determine the specific algorithm used in his program. Some information can then be obtained as to the accuracy characteristics of any given algorithm by consulting a general text on numerical analysis, such as Kelly [178]. For specific problems such as matrix inversion, Westlake [322] gives an excellent discussion of the properties of all currently used algorithms. The basic point to keep in mind, however, is that error will occur using any algorithm; the important consideration is to know how much error is occurring. Golub [110],

Yohe [334], and Kuki and Ascoly [193] give excellent presentations of the problems associated with achieving accurate solutions from computer programs.

Although the average market researcher probably cannot devote the time, knowledge, and energy to thoroughly evaluate every computer program he uses in the manner just described, a new computer program should not be accepted at its face value. The user can run sets of test data, with known answers, and also seek consultation at his local computer center if he is still not satisfied with the program's performance.

THE PROBLEM OF MISSING DATA

In market research, missing data are an almost inevitable occurrence, and some rational method of dealing with the problem has to be developed. For many multivariate statistical programs, the solution is quite simple; these programs solve the problem by ignoring it. The documentation associated with this type of program usually states that the program automatically assumes no data are missing—the BMD Series adopts this strategy to a large extent—and if the user persists in running his data, the missing elements are set to a value of zero, which often produces some unusual answers. Another strategy adopted in some statistical programs, for example, in the University of Miami programs, is to drop the entire observation if data are missing for any variable. This solution is brutally effective in eliminating missing data, but can also result in the loss of a considerable portion of one's sample in the process.

From a statistical viewpoint, the problem of missing data for multivariate analysis is quite serious. Elashoff and Afifi [86, 87, 88] have provided a careful review of the literature on missing data in multivariate statistics. They suggest several methods of estimating the missing data, but restrict the use of these methods to situations in which the missing observations occur at random. This assumption can rarely be made in many market research situations. Horst [150] discusses the problem of missing observations for several nonrandom situations, and suggests a variety of solutions.

In those statistical computer programs which do attempt to deal with missing observations, the commonest solution has been to substitute the mean of the variable for the missing observation. In many situations, this solution can be quite satisfactory, although as the amount of missing data increases, or if the missing data are concentrated among a nonrandom subgroup of the sample, biased estimates can occur.

In substituting the mean of the distribution for those observations which are missing, it should be pointed out that this procedure has the effect of reducing the variance of the distribution and may also produce biased estimates for other parameters of the distribution. One method of avoiding this difficulty is through the use of a random number generator, which assigns other values of the distribution in a random fashion to the missing observations. A method used in market research to some extent, and which should be avoided, is the assignment of missing values to the mode of the distribution. Not only is this difficult to justify statistically, but also in many cases the distribution is multimodal, thus complicating the assignment problem.

Many multivariate statistical techniques involve the computation of the covariance or correlation matrix. One solution to the missing data problem in this case has been to compute the covariances or correlations only on the available pairs of observations in each vector. This obviously involves the computation of distinct sets of means and variances for each pair of variables, which for large correlation matrices can be slow and expensive. Moreover, correlation coefficients calculated in this manner may display considerable bias, the nature and extent of which may be extremely complex and difficult to formulate. Moreover, a correlation matrix calculated in this fashion can cause difficulties if it is then used as input to some multivariate procedure, such as factor analysis, since the possibility exists that such a matrix could have a negative determinant [296].

Basically, many of the statistical problems associated with missing observations in multivariate statistics remain unsolved, and this is reflected in the paucity of computer programs which attempt to deal with the problem in any but the most primitive fashion. In this respect, therefore, the market researcher is thrown back on his own judgment and knowledge of the data, in order to assess the possible effects of the missing observations on his proposed analysis. In the vast majority of cases, the expectation that there exists a computer program which will take this decision out of his hands is likely to remain unfulfilled.

However, Hartley and Hocking [138] have written a masterful review of the entire problem of dealing effectively with missing data. They state that they "make an attempt to provide what may be regarded as a simple taxonomy for the occurrence of incomplete data and propose a framework for coordinating the bewildering multitude of species of incompleteness. At the same time we will develop unified methods of analysis for at least certain species in our taxonomy." For the interested reader, this article is well worth close examination.

THE PROBLEM OF OUTLIERS

A related problem, also handled rather inadequately, if at all, by the majority of multivariate statistical programs, is the problem of *outliers* or wild observations. These may be the result of coding or keypunch errors, but they can seriously distort basic statistical measures, such as means and variances. The most effective way of avoiding outliers is probably careful editing and screening of the input data before submitting them to any form of statistical analysis [6]. However, if the market researcher wishes to be absolutely certain that no outliers exist in his data, a program, BMDX74, exists which will screen multivariate data for outliers by computing the Mahalanobis distance of each observation from the center of the distribution of the remaining cases [4].

If outliers do, in fact, exist in the data, Tukey [302] has suggested several methods of dealing with them without the necessity of dropping the outlying observations from the sample.

UNIVARIATE STATISTICAL METHODS

A great deal of the statistical data processing currently done by market researchers still involves relatively simple univariate or bivariate statistical procedures ranging from the calculation of means, medians, and modes, measures of dispersion, and standard errors, through the calculation of various measures of association between two variables; for example, the chi-squared statistic or the Pearson product-moment correlation coefficient and tests of statistical significance, such as t-tests and F-ratios.

In these areas, all the statistical packages—BMD, DATATEXT, SPSS, and so on—provide easy-to-use programs for the computation of these univariate statistics. Before using these programs, however, the researcher should check the program's ability to handle missing data, or whether there is any loss in accuracy when dealing with a large quantity of observations or with very large numbers. The smaller computers, such as the IBM 1130, place severe restrictions on the accuracy of many simple statistical calculations under some circumstances, for example, when dealing with large numbers. Also, in some cases, the actual algorithm used for computing a given statistic may be far from satisfactory, in terms of both speed and accuracy. Froemel [100] has tested three different programs for computing the tetrachoric correlation coefficient, and has demonstrated that one of the three methods is considerably more accurate and speedier than the others.

Another example of a potential problem relates to computer programs for computing the t-test for two independent samples. Some programs use an estimate of the variance derived from the combined samples, rather than calculate separate variance estimates for the two samples. If the situation arises in which the two samples have rather different variances, the use of a pooled variance estimate can produce misleading results.

In general, the major statistical packages can be used with little or no trouble as long as the user examines his data carefully and checks that they meet the assumptions required by the specific computer program.

CROSS-TABULATION PACKAGES

Possibly the bulk of the market research work involving the use of computers consists, for some researchers, of cross-tabulations. A profusion of cross-tabulation packages exists, all claiming to provide facilities to carry out any form of cross-tabulation that may be desired. The design of an effective and useful cross-tabulation system is an extremely complex task, and it is not possible within the context of this chapter to delve into all the intricacies of these packages.

Certain elementary checks can be made in evaluating a given cross-tabulation package.
1. Does it provide effective and appropriate data-editing facilities?
2. Does it have the ability to provide weighted tables using both fractional and integer weights?
3. Is it possible to use several levels of stratification, and to weight differentially within each of the strata?
4. Are the tables produced annotated adequately and legibly?
5. Has the package facilities for computing means, medians, standard deviations, and standard errors?
6. Can the package handle multipunched columns, such as are found in open-ended questions?
7. Is the program relatively easy to use in terms of writing up the tabulation requests?
8. Is the package economical to use?
It has been the writer's experience that no one has yet developed a cross-tabulation system which can meet all a user's requests all the time. Hence, in selecting a program, the user is best advised first to carefully examine the kinds of tabulations he is most likely to require and then to select the package which conforms most closely to those needs.

REGRESSION TECHNIQUES

One of the most commonly used multivariate statistical techniques in market research is multiple linear regression. Numerous computer programs exist in this area, but, as Longley [215] has pointed out, they are of very unequal value in terms of their computational accuracy, and great care must be taken in the selection of an appropriate program. Besides a large number of least-squares multiple linear regression programs, such as BMD03R (which, according to Longley, does not produce particularly accurate results, especially with almost singular correlation matrices), a profusion of programs exist for the computation of stepwise multiple linear regression, which involve forward, backward, and stepwise elimination or addition of independent variables to the regression equation. Draper and Smith [81] thoroughly discuss the merits and demerits of these various approaches to stepwise regression. Anyone contemplating the use of this type of program is recommended to examine the program carefully in the light of Draper and Smith's remarks, so that he may clearly understand the value of the particular program for his own analytical purposes. For example, a good one is RAPIER, by Sidik and Henry [284].

The most unsatisfactory feature of most stepwise regression programs is that they enter the independent variables in the order in which they contribute to increasing the multiple correlation coefficient. On many occasions, this can produce rather misleading results. For example, if two independent variables, with a moderate degree of intercorrelation, both correlate approximately to the same extent with the dependent variable, the independent variable with the marginally higher correlation will be entered first; consequently, the other independent variable will receive a considerably smaller beta weight when, in fact, both variables should receive approximately equal beta weights. It should be noted that this defect is a function of the method, not of the actual computer program. (See [254].)

A further difficulty with the majority of multiple linear regression programs —stepwise or not—is that they provide no effective safeguards against multicollinearity. This phenomenon occurs when the majority of the correlations between the independent variables are high (0.5 or greater) and results in the occurrence of unstable regression coefficients with high standard errors. Hamaker [131] discusses this problem in relation to stepwise multiple regression and demonstrates that the order in which the independent variables are entered into the regression equation is largely a chance phenomenon. If the user comes across a situation in which he suspects the existence of multicollinearity, the appropriate solution to the problem is to use a program, such as BMD01M, which calculates the regression equation on the principal components of the independent variables, which are, of course, uncorrelated, and then develops a back solution for the regression coefficients on the original variables [179].

A more recent development in the area of stepwise regression stems from the work of Mallows [222], Beale et al. [17], Furnival [101,] Garside [103, 104], and Gorman and Toman [114]. Starting from the assumption that currently available stepwise regression methods are, at best, unsatisfactory, and the further assumption that the computation of all possible subset combinations of the independent variables is computationally prohibitive for anything but very small numbers of independent variables, they have attempted to develop a computing algorithm which would assist the user in choosing the optimal subset of independent variables from his data. A computer program developed by Gorman and Toman and using this algorithm is distributed by IBM. This program provides convenient graphical displays by means of which alternative subset regression equations can be compared. This approach would seem to be the most desirable method currently available for choosing a subset of independent variables which optimally predict the dependent variable. (Also, see [194].)

The market researcher who is seriously interested in applying multiple regression techniques as an effective data-analytic device (in Tukey's sense of the term) should consult a book by Daniel and Wood [72]. In this book, the authors provide both the statistical and computational details for the optimal use of both linear and nonlinear regression techniques. The computer programs which they have developed in this area are probably the best available for the analysis of marketing data.

THE ANALYSIS OF VARIANCE AND COVARIANCE

In the area of analysis of variance and covariance, both univariate and multivariate, there are many computer programs of varying degrees of complexity and sophistication. At one end of the scale, there are the relatively unsophisticated programs for the analysis of balanced designs, both hierarchical and crossed, which are the computer equivalent of the cookbook designs and computational schemes found in many elementary statistical textbooks, such as Lindquist [206] and Edwards [84]. The BMD Series analysis of variance and covariance programs is largely of this type. In general, this type of program has a relatively rigid input format for the data and assumes equal cell sizes with no missing data. The programs have the advantage that they are relatively simple to use, and require of the user relatively little knowledge of the statistical basis for analysis of variance. Briefly, they possess all the advantages and disadvantages associated with cookbook techniques.

On the other hand, there exist extremely sophisticated computer programs, such as Hall and Cramer's MANOVA [57], the AARDVARK System [142], and Finn's [92] MULTIVARIANCE program. These are very general programs which have their computational and logical basis in the general linear hypothesis model [119]. Bock [27] has outlined the computational rationale behind this type of model. Finn's MULTIVARIANCE program is probably one of the most useful programs of this type. It will perform univariate and multivariate linear estimation and tests of hypotheses for any crossed and/or nested design, with or without covariates. The subclass observations can be equal, proportional, or unequal, and can, in fact, contain empty cells, which occur in the use of balanced and unbalanced, incomplete experimental designs. In these respects, the program is extremely flexible and will analyze practically any experimental design for which the linear model can be specified. However, the user pays a price for this great flexibility in that the correct use of the program for anything but the simplest of experimental designs requires that he thoroughly understand the logical basis of the general linear hypothesis model. This is necessary both for setting up the input parameters for the analysis of a specific design and for the correct evaluation of the input from the program.

Application of this program to designs in which there are disproportionate cell frequencies requires some care and foresight. To be specific, the case of an orthogonal (equal cell-size) design analysis of variance basically involves the additive partition of the total sum of squares among the various main effects and interactions. However, in the nonorthogonal case, this partitioning is not additive. As a result, great importance is placed on the order in which one extracts the main effects from the design, since different orderings will not necessarily give the same results. In this program, it is possible to reorder the effects and thus have results for multiple orderings. However, if the results of these multiple orderings are not independent, the calculation of error rates is hopelessly confused. It is therefore suggested that the user predetermine the order of importance of the main effects in terms of his research strategy, and extract the effects in this order.

It can be seen readily that while a program like MULTIVARIANCE can give tremendous flexibility in data analysis, numerous pitfalls exist in the analysis of nonorthogonal and incomplete designs, and that the successful use of any program of this type requires a certain statistical sophistication in the user. A similar type of program called MUDAID [6] has the additional advantage of handling irregular, and even unedited, input data. If the user wishes to edit his data, a two-pass system is used. After the first pass, the output can be screened carefully and edited, and the results of a second pass on the edited data can be used for interpretive purposes.

A third method for the analysis of experimental designs is exemplified in the work of Bottenberg and Ward [34] and Cohen [58]. Since the general linear hypothesis model also covers multiple-regression analysis, that is, both analysis of variance and multiple linear regression are computationally equivalent, experimental designs, with and without covariates, can be analyzed by means of standard multiple-regression programs [279]. The multiple-regression program developed by Jennings [159] is most suited for this form of analysis. Both Cohen and Jennings have stressed the great flexibility of least-squares multiple-regression analysis for testing hypotheses that are not normally examined in conventional analyses of variance and covariance.

So far, we have discussed three different methods for the analysis of experimental designs. The first method, characterized here as the cookbook method, takes into account the experimental design hierarchy of main effects and interactions, adjusting each effect for all other effects at an equal or lower level. The second type, the general linear hypothesis method, adjusts each effect, both main effects and interactions, for relationships to all other effects in the model. The third, or multiple-regression, method as described by Cohen [58] depends on an a priori ordering of all terms in the regression model and each effect is adjusted only for those preceding it in the ordering.

All these methods are "correct," but the user should be aware that each tests a different set of hypotheses and that these differences are not apparent in the usual analysis of variance tables. If the user has equal cell sizes, all three methods produce identical results. However, when one has disproportionate cell frequencies, the three methods can produce quite different results. The decision concerning which type of program to use then depends upon the questions being asked of the data. The standard experimental design approach [328] can be used when the data are in factorial form. In this case, the researcher wants to account for systematic variation in terms of simple, additive main effects, and merely tests the interactions to check for nonadditivity. The general linear hypothesis method can be used when one wishes to determine whether the main effects show differences above and beyond any significant interaction effects.

The third method, the multiple-regression approach, is most useful if a logical a priori ordering exists among the hypotheses to be tested, since each effect is adjusted only for those preceding it. This method has one distinct advantage in that the possibility that significant effects will cancel one another is minimized. A more detailed comparison of these methods can be found in Overall and Spiegel [250], Bargmann [14], and Mendenhall [232].

Finally, some comment should be made on the problem of covariate adjustment. Werts and Linn [320], Smith [288], and others have pointed out the dangers in making casual inferences after covariate adjustment of treatment means. Few of the available computer programs will reliably indicate when the assumptions underlying the analysis of covariance have been violated. Hence, great care must be taken in the interpretation of the results of such an analysis [214].

As Campbell [46] points out, "These techniques represent pathetic efforts to artificially reconstruct a zero pretest-treatment correlation by 'controlling for,' 'covarying,' or 'partialling out' the pretest correlation from the posttest. As many have demonstrated, . . . these statistical procedures are inappropriate to the task [p. 108]." However, since the measurement of "change" is of great importance in many marketing studies, the user of covariance techniques for this purpose would be well advised to read Cronbach and Furby's review of this topic [69].

PRINCIPAL-COMPONENT AND FACTOR-ANALYTIC TECHNIQUES

One of the most ubiquitous multivariate statistical techniques employed in market research goes under the rather vague label of *factor analysis*. Essentially, these techniques resolve themselves into a variety of methods for reducing a large number of variables into a much smaller number of dimensions, or factors, which can account for a reasonable proportion of the variance among the original variables. A vast number of such computer programs currently exist, with an almost infinite variety of options and variations. Once the user has satisfied himself that the specific program is computationally accurate and reasonably efficient, he is still left with a wide range of choices as to how he should factor his data matrix. He can choose from a straightforward principal-components analysis, or a principal-factor analysis with iterations on the communality estimates [132], or the more exotic models such as Rao's canonical factor-analysis model [258], or the Kaiser/Caffrey alpha-factor analysis [177], or Guttman's image covariance-factor analysis [128], or the mathematically more elegant maximum-likelihood models developed by Joreskog and Lawley [175].

Browne [40] has carried out an exhaustive evaluation of many of these methods and concludes that with the exception of the maximum-likelihood methods, there is very little difference among them. On the basis of his results, he recommends either a maximum-likelihood method or the Harman and Jones [133] MINRES technique. Derflinger [74] has developed computational algorithms for both the maximum-likelihood and the MINRES methods, which he claims are extremely efficient. However, Kaiser [176] still feels that his "Little Jiffy" method, essentially a principal-components solution with a normal Varimax rotation, produces quite satisfactory results in the majority of cases, with the possible exception of the situation where one is analyzing a relatively small number (less than 20) of variables [71].

Horst's *Factor Analysis of Data Matrices* [148] is a valuable source of the various mathematical methods underlying factor analysis, and it contains a set of ready-made computer programs for handling many factor-analytic problems. For example, it includes programs for factoring an incomplete correlation matrix, which is needed when the complete set of correlations between the variables is unobtainable.

Rotating the factor matrix to achieve simple structure and, it is hoped, meaning can usually be achieved using a Varimax rotation, but for those who prefer oblique rotations, the Promax method developed by Hendrickson and White [143] gives consistently good results and is economical with computer time.

Kaiser also recommends the Kaiser-Harris "orthoblique" method as giving satisfactory solutions [136, 176]. Eber [83] has developed a computer program for Cattell's Maxplane rotation, which also produces useful results.

As a footnote, McDonald [225, 226, 227] has developed a series of computer programs for nonlinear polynomial models of factor analysis, which he claims are useful for data which do not fit a linear model. Joreskog [172] has developed a method for the simultaneous factor analysis of several populations. Evans [89] gives an excellent exposition of the various methods available for comparing the results from different factor analyses in order to determine the degree of factorial similarity among them. (See also [52].)

In using any new factor-analysis program, it is advisable to check whether the program uses, for example, the Thurstone Box problem or Holzinger's 24 psychological variables. All necessary information on these can be found in Harman [132]. It is also advisable to check the running times on the computer because some programs are remarkably inefficient and can prove expensive for a large correlation matrix.

CLUSTER ANALYSIS

Since the publication of Sokal and Sneath's *Principles of Numerical Taxonomy* [290], there has been a veritable deluge of algorithms and computer programs designed to optimally cluster objects or people.

In market research, this development has been accelerated by the great interest in the concept of market segmentation, which has forced market researchers to find efficient and reliable methods of clustering large groups of consumers.

Ball [9] provides a comprehensive and critical review of the methods currently available. In finding one's way through this maze of algorithms, several considerations must be borne in mind: the sample size which can be handled by the program, the relative cost of running the program, and the kinds of data to be used as a basis for clustering. The most popular technique to date in market research studies has been a principal-component or Q-factor analysis of the original data matrix [148]. However, there is no logical reason to assume that it possesses any inherent superiority over other clustering methods. In fact, Ball [9] gives an example of three data sets which have identical means and covariance matrices, yet which are quite dissimilar in terms of their cluster structure. A technique such as Q-factor analysis would be unable to distinguish among these three data sets except where the data are normally distributed, which is not often the case with marketing research data.

Ball [8, 10], Ball and Friedman [11], and Friedman and Rubin [99] suggest several objective criteria for evaluating any given clustering algorithm. (See also [155].) These criteria are:

1. Computational complexity, which occurs in some of the highly iterative techniques, and can thus involve their users in considerable expense for computer time.

2. The memory requirements of the algorithm, which can seriously degrade the usefulness of an otherwise good algorithm either because its excessive memory requirements force the program to handle relatively small samples, or alternatively, if memory is extended by going out on disk or magnetic tape, because the costs of running large data matrices can be prohibitive. Those clustering algorithms which require the computation of the entire interperson similarity matrix suffer heavily in this respect.

3. Sample size, a cause of difficulties for those clustering algorithms which need to estimate the covariance matrix of the cluster variables. Allais [2] has

shown that small sample sizes relative to the size of the covariance matrix increase the probability of errors for predictions based on the covariance matrix.

4. The nature of the input data. Although it is difficult to be precise in this area, there is little doubt that the degree of structure originally present in the data should be a consideration in deciding on the most appropriate clustering technique.

5. The existence of some form of objective function which can be used to assess the efficiency of the clustering. For example, Ball's ISODATA algorithm or the Singleton-Kautz algorithm explicitly attempts to find that partitioning of the data which results in a minimum within-cluster variance.

Gower [116] gives a thorough discussion of similarity coefficients and how and where to use them. Williams and Lance [326] and Lance and Williams [195, 196, 197, 198, 200] provide an exhaustive review of clustering techniques used in numerical taxonomy and detail precisely the type of data structures most appropriate for each method. Cole [59] also contains an interesting survey of clustering methods currently used in numerical taxonomy. (Also see [151].)

Wishart [329] has developed a large, integrated package of programs for cluster analysis. This system is designed for the user who wishes to compare several different methods of clustering his data, using various objective criteria. This concept of "converging operations" enables the user to observe the effects of widely different techniques on his data, and can indicate whether the clusters remain invariant over different methods [115]. If they do not, the variations may throw a great deal of light on the structure of the data.

Possibly, the most thoroughly developed and tested clustering algorithm is Friedman and Rubin's Optimal Taxonomy program [99]. This technique enables the user to compare the partitioning of his data against several different objective criteria, and also, by means of an efficient hill-climbing algorithm, largely protects him against local minima in the development of clusters. Moreover, the authors of this program have attempted to integrate the clustering procedures with current multivariate statistical theory. The Friedman/Rubin algorithm is possibly one of the best clustering techniques currently—its only drawback being that clustering large data sets with many variables can make heavy demands on computer time and, ultimately, the user's pocketbook.

The Ball and Hall [12] and the Singleton-Kautz algorithms, both of which attempt to minimize the within-cluster variance, are excellent clustering techniques and are more parsimonious with machine time. The one criticism that might be leveled at these programs is the issue raised by Forgy [93], who advocates the development of "natural" clusters. He points out that the minimum variance algorithm will tend to produce dense spherical distributions of objects, and will have little success in creating good clusters, when the data are distributed in an irregular pattern in the sample space. In this respect, he raises the same issue as that put forward by Shepard and Carroll [282], who point out that severe nonlinearities in multivariate data can produce very strange results if linear methods are used. (See [207].)

Wolfe [333] has developed an objective method for clustering objects which avoids all the difficulties associated with other cluster analysis techniques. Wolfe's approach is to assume that the sample is drawn from a population distribution which is a mixture of distributions with known forms but unknown parameters. The cluster problem is then a matter of developing estimators for the parameters, along with associated tests of hypotheses. Thus, the parameters of each component distribution provide a description of that particular cluster. It can be seen that Wolfe has placed the clustering problem on a purely statistical and mathematical basis, so that his method bears a considerable resemblance to Lazarsfeld's latent structure analysis [201]. Wolfe has developed computational methods for estimating the parameters of mixtures of multivariate normal distributions, although it is obvious that this approach could be extended to other multivariate distributions. His current program can handle both equal and unequal covariance matrices. Wolf's approach is not expensive and can handle quite large sample sizes. The main disadvantages are that the estimators may not converge, and that the within-groups covariance matrix could turn out to be singular. In this respect, Wolfe's algorithm is sensitive to the structure of the input data.

A clustering algorithm developed by McRae [231] avoids most of the pitfalls associated with other cluster programs. McRae's MICKA program evolved out of the K-means approach developed by Macqueen [221]. The algorithm is similar to that of ISODATA [12]. MICKA adopted several of the objective criteria used in the Friedman/Rubin program to assess the effectiveness of the clustering. MICKA is also similar to Wolfe's algorithm [333] in some respects, as well as to the cluster program developed by Kendall [181] in England.

The MICKA program uses the same four objective criteria to evaluate the effectiveness of the clustering. Tests carried out on this program have demonstrated that its results are similar to those obtained by Friedman and Rubin [99].

Rohlf [265] has been concerned with the development of hierarchical clustering schemes or algorithms which are characterized by their ability to "adapt" to the possible kinds of variation found in natural clusters as they are being formed. Specific hypotheses about the shape of the clusters can be tested by setting up the appropriate algebraic model to describe a ring, or a parabola, or some other shape. Unfortunately, this type of method is likely to be extremely time-consuming on a computer, and is therefore restricted to relatively small samples.

Hartigan [137] has developed a set of clustering algorithms which differ from previous techniques in simultaneously clustering variables and respondents on a data matrix. He justifies this method on the grounds that the clusters obtained can be interpreted directly from the data matrix, rather than from some possibly arbitrary distance function. Computer programs for these algorithms are available in the BMD-P Series [79].

Tryon and Bailey [299, 300] have developed a system of computer programs called BC-TRY, which have been designed for clustering both variables and people via factor-analytic techniques. Essentially, the BC-TRY system is open to the same criticisms as any clustering algorithm based on covariance matrices with respect to the normality of their distributions.

Johnson [161] has developed an interesting nonmetric clustering algorithm, which is hierarchical in nature and is related to the earlier work of Ward [317] on hierarchical grouping, though Ward's method is metric in nature. The method operates on the basis of an interobject distance matrix, and possesses the advantage that it is able to form irregularly shaped clusters, thus meeting Forgy's objection to spherical clusters. However, it is limited in the number of objects that can be clustered, because of the necessity of computing a complete distance matrix between all pairs of objects.

Many other clustering algorithms exist and may be found in the references cited. Which method is "best" can only be answered with respect to a specific data matrix. However, it should be strongly emphasized that there is no "ideal" set of clusters, in the Platonic sense, in any given set of data. The clusters derived can only be evaluated in terms of their value to the user. In this respect, one should consider Bargmann and Graney's [16] distinction between *real clusters* and *virtual* clusters, using the analogy of "real" and "virtual" images in optics. They note, "Real clusters are simply clusters of points in the original space. Virtual clusters on the other hand are clusters of projections of points in a space of lower dimension than the original space." In this respect, many currently employed clustering techniques produce "virtual" clusters, which may, or may not, be an adequate representation of the "real" clusters.

MULTIDIMENSIONAL SCALING

Multidimensional scaling is currently undergoing a very high degree of development, and today's computer programs tend to become obsolete more rapidly in this area than in others.

Green and Carmone [123] have provided an excellent review of this whole area, so no attempt will be made here to go over the same ground in anywhere near the same detail.

The computer programs at present available stem from several sources. There are the Guttmann-Lingoes nonmetric series of programs [210], which have recently been rewritten for the IBM 360. Kruskal's MDSCAL program [187] has been extensively revised over the years and provides a very flexible method of analyzing similarities data [188]. The TORSCA program developed by Young [335] also is used extensively in multidimensional scaling applications. Finally, the series of programs developed by Carroll and Chang [49, 50] at Bell Telephone Laboratories provide good algorithms for multidimensional preference mapping.

Although all these programs have received considerable use in a variety of fields, the robustness of the algorithms underlying them is unknown to a large extent. Shepard, in an unpublished investigation of Kruskal's MDSCAL program, has explored the relative frequency of obtaining local minima. He found that it was about 40 percent, which is rather high. Klahr [183] has studied the stress values obtained with Kruskal's program using random data, and has demonstrated that it is possible to obtain apparent structure even when the actual input data were completely lacking in structure. Also, as Guttman [129] points out, "It is the task of experimental design—before the data are gathered—to ensure that enough points in space are observed, with sufficient spread, to reveal the basic lawfulness sought; a computing algorithm by itself need not always be able to compensate for deficiencies in the design of observations."

In other words, Shepard's *nonmetric breakthrough*, as it has been termed, does not give us something for nothing. These new multidimensional-scaling algorithms have proved of immense value to market researchers, but they have not done away with the problem of adequate definition of the research problem and a consideration of the appropriateness of the algorithm for the data being collected. Tversky [308] discusses this problem in relation to preference mapping and points out that the definition of preference used can markedly determine the outcome.

Roskam [268] and Young [337, 338] have studied the problem of designing an adequate computation algorithm for multidimensional scaling, and Lingoes and Roskam [213] have developed a new program, called MINISSA I, which they claim encompasses all the good features of both the Guttmann-Lingoes and the Kruskal approach. To date, however, the program has not been used extensively, so that it is not yet possible to say how much improvement has been achieved. However, on logical grounds, it would seem that MINISSA should produce superior results.

Moreover, a careful rereading of Torgerson [297] and Rao [260] would suggest that these nonmetric scaling methods may have been overvalued to some extent. With respect to the multidimensional scaling of similarities judgments, the more homely method of principal-components analysis would seem to give satisfactory results, and an inspection of the eigenvalues would give a more realistic feeling for the appropriate number of dimensions than the stress value used in nonmetric methods.

For example, Schonemann [277] has developed a metric, multidimensional, unfolding model which produces excellent results. It is computationally faster than the corresponding nonmetric methods, such as TORSCA or MDSCAL, and has the desirable feature of producing a set of residuals, that is, a comparison between the original data matrix and a matrix of distances developed from the reduced-rank solution. This enables the user both to obtain a much better estimate of the fit of his solution to the original data than the stress measure, and to pinpoint exactly where the lack of fit exists. However, it does not solve the problem that exists in all the conjoint measurement models of sometimes producing anti-ideal points instead of ideal points, so that one is required to reverse the signs of one of the sets of coefficients to create a meaningful map.

Bechtel [19, 20] has also developed some interesting metric models for analyzing preference data, which he claims will produce solutions to mapping preference structures more meaningfully than the nonmetric methods developed by Carroll and Chang [50]. Essentially, he suggests that nonmetric methods, such as Carroll's PREFMAP, work more successfully with perceptually simple stimuli, such as color preferences, whereas his metric methods are more realistic for cognitively complex stimuli such as brand preferences.

One other issue in multidimensional scaling which needs emphasis relates to the use of Kruskal's stress measure [187] as an index of the goodness-of-fit of any given solution. Young [339] points out that stress is far from a perfect measure of goodness-of-fit, but that it is the best available. Stress tends to overestimate the goodness-of-fit when too few points are used, or when there is error in the data, or when too many dimensions are extracted. Young has developed an index of metric determinancy which can be valuable in determining the best solution. Also, Capra [47] has developed an alternative measure of goodness-of-fit, V, which is related to Kendall's tau (rank-order correlation coefficient).

Sherman [283] discusses one problem that has been largely ignored by users of multidimensional-scaling programs, namely, the distance function used. The vast majority of studies are based on Euclidean distance measures (D^2) which, as Green and Carmone [123] point out, have the very desirable property of remaining invariant under any rotation. However, Sherman notes that the Euclidean distance function is only one special case of the Minkowski metric, in which the constant term is set equal to 2.0. He notes, however, that for any given set of data, several different values of this constant should be used in order to derive an optimal solution. He suggests that for perceptually simple stimuli, a Minkowski constant of 1.0 (the City Block metric) may be more useful, and that, where some of the stimulus attributes interact or dominate others, a value greater than 2.0 may be more successful.

DISCRIMINANT FUNCTION AND CANONICAL CORRELATION ANALYSIS

Two areas which have been ignored up to this point are multiple discriminant function analysis and canonical correlation analysis. One difficulty in these areas is the dearth of good computer programs.

In the case of multiple discriminant analysis, the user would be well advised to read Morrison [237] carefully before selecting his program.   In this article, Morrison points out many of the pitfalls associated with the use of this technique and makes suggestions on avoiding them.

Among the better programs is that developed at Northwestern University by Morrison and Art [238], and also the program developed by Cooley and Lohnes [61].   The BMD Series also contains an adequate program.   Bargmann [15] gives an excellent critical review of the usefulness of discriminant analysis. It is instructive to read his article in conjunction with Johnson's article [160] on potential applications of discriminant function analysis to market-segmentation studies.

As for canonical correlation, relatively few programs are generally available. Probably the most useful is described in Cooley and Lohnes [61].   This program is of considerable interest because it gives more than the usual type of output, including the actual canonical correlations.   Cooley and Lohnes point out that the canonical correlations themselves only indicate the degree of relationship between the two sets of variables.   They have developed a new coefficient, termed a redundancy coefficient, which they believe is more useful than the canonical correlation coefficient since it indicates the amount of actual overlap between the two sets of variables that is inherent in the first canonical variate as seen from one set of variables.   This new coefficient shows what proportion of variance in the canonical variate associated with the first set of variables is redundant to the variance in the canonical variate associated with the second set of variables.   The canonical correlation indicates only the amount of overlap, not whether the two canonical variates are important factors in their respective sets of variables.

THE ANALYSIS OF COVARIANCE STRUCTURES

Before leaving the area of multivariate statistical analysis, the statistically sophisticated reader may want to study the more generalized multivariate methods developed by Joreskog [170] and Bock and Bargmann [28].

Joreskog has developed a set of computer programs for the analysis of what he terms covariance structures.   The logical basis of his techniques lies in the fact that all multivariate statistical procedures ultimately rest on the computation of a covariance matrix among the set(s) of variables being analyzed.

Joreskog [166, 167] discusses a general mathematical model which assumes that the variables have a multivariate normal distribution.   The parameters associated with this model can be fixed, free, or constrained to be equal to other parameters.   The free and constrained parameters are estimated, using maximum-likelihood methods.   This permits the analyst to develop any specific model within this general model and to test the goodness-of-fit, using likelihood ratio techniques.

In allowing the user to specify his own statistical model, great generality and flexibility are achieved by imposing various specifications on the parameters of the general model.   Specific models which can be developed from this general model include first- and second-order factor analysis, the analysis of multitrait/ multimethod data, the analysis of growth curves and trend data, multidimensional judgment data, mixed- and random-effects ANOVA and MANOVA models, the analysis of multitest/multioccasion data, path analysis and the study of linear structural relationships, and the analysis of simplexes and circumplexes.   The interested user is referred to the series of articles by Joreskog [165 through 175] cited in the references for a detailed exposition of these techniques.

To conclude, an abbreviated coverage of various other areas of data analysis will be mentioned. The goal of the next few paragraphs will be to guide interested users to the appropriate sources for programs and theoretical material.

TIME SERIES ANALYSIS

The analysis of time series, including forecasting techniques, composes a vast literature. Excellent discussions of the problems involved in this area may be found in several sources. Brown [38] provides a thorough coverage of forecasting problems in a very practical fashion. Harris [134] and Jenkins and Watts [158] discuss the spectral analysis of time series. Box and Jenkins [35] give a detailed exposition of techniques for building autoregressive forecasting models.

Computer programs in spectral analysis have been revolutionized by the development of the Cooley-Tukey algorithm (the Fast Fourier Transform) which has made it possible to analyze large amounts of data economically [263]. Simpson [285] has developed a large package of computer programs for time series analysis. Unfortunately, they have been written in FORTRAN II for an IBM 7094 and will require modification for third-generation computers. Robinson [264] has compiled an excellent series of Fortran subroutines which can be used as building blocks for many time series applications. Salzman [274] describes a series of forecasting programs for exponential smoothing, regression, and the Census Bureau methods for seasonal adjustment. Also McLaughlin and Boyle [230] have developed a useful exponential smoothing program. Montgomery has worked out a forecast evaluation program (FORAC) which is available in a technical report from the Marketing Science Institute [32]. Lewis and Kelly [205] and Cox and Lewis [67] have evolved several techniques for what they term "a series of events." Green [122] has developed a program, SIMEMOD, which can be used for econometric forecasting and model-building.

NONPARAMETRIC STATISTICS

In the area of what might loosely be termed nonparametric statistics and miscellaneous techniques, several methods and computer programs are of potential value in the analysis of market research data.

Morris [236] has developed an integrated system of programs covering most forms of nonparametric statistical procedures. Before using the programs in this package, the user should consult Bradley [36] for a guide to the appropriateness of these nonparametric methods for his particular analytical problem.

However, before using any specific nonparametric technique, the user should consider Tukey's comment,

> Methods called "non-parametric" that do not make explicit use of a scale are occasionally useful, sometimes because they can show whether or not criticism is carping when it objects to particular analyses of particular sets of data, sometimes because they are handy and portable and contribute to our first-aid kit. For all their uses, such "order only" methods ought not to be taken as either standard or exhaustive [303, p. 87].

The AID and MCA programs, developed at the University of Michigan's Institute for Survey Research by Sonquist and Morgan [293] and Andrews et al. [5], can be used as valuable data-screening devices, especially with data which do not meet the requirements of interval scaling normally needed for more conventional methods, such as multiple linear regression. Sondquist [292] has written an excellent introduction to the use of these methods in data analysis.

CONTINGENCY TABLES

The analysis of contingency tables is closely allied to the analysis of the results of cross-tabulations in general. Kendall [180] points out:

> The problems of manifold classification in p dimensions are of three kinds: the pure problem of display so that one can look at the results as a whole; the problem of empty cells, or small frequencies, which are apt to arise on the edges of a table even for large samples; and perhaps the most difficult of all, a method of analysis which will bring out the various interrelationships among the classificatory variables.

Goodman [112] and Ku, Varner, and Kullback [192] have developed models for the analysis of multidimensional contingency tables. Ku and Kullback [191] have developed a computer program based on Kullback's information statistic. Lewis [204] has developed a different method based on fitting constants. Also several computer programs have been developed at the University of North Carolina for analyzing what have been termed linear categorical models. Essentially, these models are analogs of analysis of variance models for ordinal or categorical data. (See [3, 96, 124, and 184].) Cox [66] has written an excellent monograph on the analysis of binary data, which is relevant to these problems.

COMPUTER GRAPHIC AND SIMULATION TECHNIQUES

Two other areas of interest relevant to this chapter are computer graphics and computer simulation models. Ball [9] and Williams [325] give detailed surveys and analyses of the problems encountered in developing active computer graphics systems, especially with regard to those systems which interact with the personnel using them. These computer graphics systems will, in the future, enable the user to analyze his data interactively at a console, and make more feasible the kind of "data analysis" advocated by Tukey.

Computer simulation will be treated in much more detail in other chapters of this handbook. For some insight into the potential applications of simulation techniques for market research, see [113, 242, and 243].

In conclusion, it should be noted that this review has attempted merely to give an overview of the field; the reader will have to go to the references cited for more detailed information. For those readers who wish to brush up on their mathematics before plunging into the literature, two excellent introductory texts will fill in any mathematical gaps—Gemignani [105] and Graybill [120].

REFERENCES

1. Aaker, D. A., *Multivariate Analysis in Marketing: Theory and Application*, Belmont, Calif.: Wadsworth, 1971.
1a. Afifi, A., and A. Elashoff, "Missing Values in Multivariate Statistics. II. Point Estimation in Simple Linear Regression," *Journal of the American Statistical Association*, vol. 62, March 1967.
2. Allais, D. C., "The Selection of Measurements for Prediction," Report no. TR 6103-9, Palo Alto, Calif.: Stanford Electronics Laboratory, November 1964.
3. Allen, D. M., "An Iterative Weighted Least Squares Method for Analyzing

Categorical Data Having a Linear Model," unpublished manuscript, Lexington: University of Kentucky, 1969.
4. Anderson, T. W., *An Introduction to Multivariate Statistical Analysis*, New York: Wiley, 1958.
4a. Anderson, T. W., *The Statistical Analysis of Time Series*, New York: Wiley, 1971.
5. Andrews, F., J. Morgan, and J. Sonquist, *Multiple Classification Analysis*, Ann Arbor: University of Michigan, Institute for Survey Research, 1969.
6. Appelbaum, M., and R. Bargmann, "A FORTRAN II Program for MUDAID, Multivariate, Univariate and Discriminant Analysis of Irregular Data," Technical Report no. AD-669 696, Urbana: University of Illinois, December 1967.
7. Armor, D. J., "A Computer Language for the Analysis of Variance," *Proceedings of the Social Statistics Section of the American Statistical Association*, 1969.
8. Ball, G. H., "A Comparison of Some Cluster-seeking Techniques," Technical Report no. RADC-TR-66-514, Urbana: University of Illinois, November 1966.
9. Ball, G. H., and D. J. Hall, "Some Implications of Interactive Graphic Computer Systems for Data Analysis and Statistics," *Technometrics*, vol. 12, February 1970.
10. Ball, G. H., "Classification Analysis," Technical Note no. 5533, Stanford, Calif.: Stanford Research Institute, November 1970.
11. Ball, G. H., and H. Friedman, "On the Status of Applications of Clustering Techniques to Behavioral Sciences Data," *Proceedings of the American Statistical Association, Social Statistics*, vol. 34, 1968.
12. Ball, G. H., and D. Hall, "A Clustering Technique for Summarizing Multivariate Data," *Behavioral Science*, vol. 12, March 1967.
13. Bargmann, R. E., "A Statistician's Instructions to the Computer: A Report on a Statistical Computer Language," White Plains, N.Y.: *Proceedings of IBM Scientific Computing Symposium, October 1963*, 1965.
14. Bargmann, R. E., "A Survey of Appropriate Methods of Analysis of Factorial Designs," unpublished manuscript, Athens: University of Georgia, 1968.
15. Bargmann, R. E., "Exploratory Techniques Involving Artificial Variables," in P. Krishnaiah (ed.), *Multivariate Analysis—II*, New York: Academic, 1969.
16. Bargmann, R. E., and R. Graney, "An Algorithm for Testing and Identifying Virtual Clusters," Technical Report no. 42, Athens: University of Georgia, 1970.
17. Beale, E. M., M. G. Kendall, and D. W. Mann, "The Discarding of Variables in Multivariate Analysis," *Biometrika*, vol. 54, December 1967.
18. Beaton, A. E., "The Use of Special Matrix Operators in Statistical Calculus," Research Bulletin no. RB-64-51, Princeton, N.J.: Educational Testing Service, December 1964.
19. Bechtel, G. G., "An Inner Product Model for the Multi-dimensional Scaling of Symmetric Layouts," Research Bulletin no. RB-70-22, Princeton, N.J.: Educational Testing Service, 1970.
20. Bechtel, G. G., "A Covariance Analysis of Multiple Paired-Comparisons," *Psychometrika*, vol. 36, 1971.
21. Bechtel, G. G., "A Dual Scaling Analysis for Paired Compositions," *Psychometrika*, vol. 36, 1971.
22. Bechtel, G. G., L. Tucker, and Wei-Ching Chang, "Linear Multi-dimensional Scaling of Choice," Research Bulletin No. RB-69-73, Princeton, N.J.: Educational Testing Service, 1969.
22a. Bendat, J. S., and A. G. Piersol, *Random Data: Analysis and Measurement Procedures*, New York: Wiley, 1971.
23. Bhapkar, V. P., "On the Comparison of Percentages in Matched Samples," Technical Report no. 6, Lexington: University of Kentucky, Department of Statistics, August 1970.
24. Bjorck, A., and G. Golub, "ALGOL Programming Contribution No. 22: Iterative Refinement of Linear Least Square Solution by Householder Transformation," *Nordisk Tidskrift For Informations-Behandling*, vol. 7, 1967.
25. Bloxom, B., "Individual Differences in Multi-dimensional Scaling," Research Bulletin no. RB-68-45, Princeton, N.J.: Educational Testing Service, 1968.

26. Bock, R. D., "A Computer Program for Univariate and Multivariate Analysis of Variance," *Proceedings of the IBM Scientific Computing Symposium,* Armonk, N.Y.: International Business Machines, Inc., 1965.

27. Bock, R. D., "Programming Univariate and Multivariate Analysis of Variance," *Technometrics,* vol. 5, 1963.

28. Bock, R. D., and R. Bargmann, "Analysis of Covariance Structures," *Psychometrika,* vol. 31, 1966.

29. Bock, R. D., and A. Peterson, "Matrix Operation Subroutines for Statistical Computation," Research Memorandum no. 7, Chicago: The University of Chicago, Statistical Laboratory, January 1967.

30. Bock, R. D., and B. H. Repp, "ESL Matrix Operations Subroutines for the IBM 1130," Research Memorandum no. 10, Chicago: The University of Chicago, Education Statistics Laboratory, June 1970.

31. Bock, R. D., and B. H. Repp, "ESL Matrix Operations Subroutines for the IBM System/360 Computer," Research Memorandum no. RM-11, Chicago: The University of Chicago, Education Statistics Laboratory, August 1970.

32. Bond, R. O., and D. B. Montgomery, *FORAC MOD I: A Computer Program for Forecast Evaluation Statistics,* Boston: Marketing Science Institute, 1970.

33. Bonham-Carter, G., "FORTRAN IV Program for Q-Mode Cluster Analysis of Nonquantitative Data," Report no. 17, Lawrence: University of Kansas, State Geological Survey, 1967.

34. Bottenberg, R., and J. Ward, "Applied Multiple Linear Regression Analysis," Technical Report, Lackland Air Force Base, Tex.: USAF Personnel Laboratory, 1960.

35. Box, G. E., and G. Jenkins, *Time Series Analysis: Forecasting and Control,* San Francisco: Holden-Day, 1970.

36. Bradley, J., *Distribution-Free Statistical Tests,* Englewood Cliffs, N.J.: Prentice-Hall, 1968.

37. Brewer, M. B., W. D. Crano, and D. T. Campbell, "Testing a Single-Factor Model as an Alternative to the Misuse of Partial Correlations in Hypothesis-Testing Research," *Sociometry,* vol. 33, 1970.

38. Brown, R. G., *Smoothing, Forecasting and Prediction of Discrete Time Series,* Englewood Cliffs, N.J.: Prentice-Hall, 1963.

39. Browne, M. J., and H. O. Posten, "Statistical Analysis Using Statistically Oriented Matrix Language (STORM)," Research Report no. RC-1042, Armonk, N.Y.: International Business Machines, September 1963.

40. Browne, M. W., "A Comparison of Factor Analytic Techniques," *Psychometrika,* vol. 33, 1968.

41. Browne, M. W., "Precision of Prediction," Research Bulletin no. RB-69-69, Princeton, N.J.: Educational Testing Service, August 1969.

42. Browne, M. W., "A Critical Evaluation of Some Reduced-Rank Regression Procedures," Research Bulletin no. RB-70-21, Princeton, N.J.: Educational Testing Service, March 1970.

43. Buck, K. E., "SELMA Programmer's Reference Manual," Report no. 26, Institut Für Statik und Dynamik der Luft- und Raumfahrtkonstruktionen, Stuttgart, West Germany: University of Stuttgart, Aero-Space Computing Group, 1968.

44. Buhler, R., "P-STAT—An Evolving User-Oriented Language for Statistical Analysis of Social Science Data," Princeton, N.J.: Princeton University, Computer Center, 1966.

45. Cameron, J. M., "Some Examples of the Use of High Speed Computer in Statistics," in *Proceedings of the First Conference on the Design of Experiments in Army Research, Development and Testing,* no. 57-1, Washington: U.S. Department of the Army, Office of Ordnance Research, 1957.

46. Campbell, D. T., "Temporal Changes in Treatment-Effect Correlations: A Quasi-Experimental Model for Institutional Records and Longitudinal Studies," in *Proceedings of the 1970 Invitational Conference on Testing Problems,* Princeton, N.J.: Educational Testing Service, October 1970.

47. Capra, J. R., *A New Method of Multidimensional Scaling,* Washington: United States Naval Postgraduate School, June 1970.

48. Carroll, J. B., and G. F. Wilson, "An Interactive-Computer Program for the Johnson-Neyman Technique in the Case of Two Groups, Two Predictor Variables, and One Criterion Variable," Research Bulletin no. RB-69-68, Princeton: N.J.: Educational Testing Service, August 1969.

49. Carroll, J. D., "Individual Differences and Multidimensional Scaling," unpublished manuscript, Bell Telephone Laboratories, Murray Hill, N.J., 1969.

50. Carroll, J. D., and J. J. Chang, "Relating Preference Data to Multidimensional Scaling Solutions via a Generalization of Coombs Unfolding Model," paper presented at the Psychometric Society meetings, Madison, Wisc.: April 1967.

51. Carroll, J. D., and J. J. Chang, "Analysis of Individual Differences in Multidimensional Scaling via an N-way Generalization of 'Eckhart-Young' Decomposition," unpublished manuscript, Bell Telephone Laboratories, Murray Hill, N.J., 1969.

52. Cattell, R. B., "Isopodic and Equipotent Principles for Computing Factor Scores across Different Populations," *British Journal of Mathematical and Statistical Psychology,* vol. 23, May 1970.

53. Cattell, R. B., and M. Coulter, "Principles of Behavioral Taxonomy and the Mathematical Basis of the Taxonome Computer Program," *British Journal of Mathematical and Statistical Psychology,* vol. 19, May 1966.

54. Chambers, J. M., "Some General Aspects of Statistical Computing," *Applied Statistics,* vol. 16, no. 2, 1967.

55. Chambers, J. M., "Computers in Statistical Research: Simulation and Computer-aided Mathematics," *Technometrics,* vol. 12, February 1970.

56. Chernoff, H., "Metric Considerations in Cluster Analysis," Technical Report no. 67, Stanford, Calif.: Stanford University, Department of Statistics, September 1970.

57. Clyde, D., C. Cramer, and R. Sherin, "Multivariate Statistical Programs," Coral Gables, Fla.: University of Miami, Biometric Laboratory, 1966.

58. Cohen, J., "Multiple Regression as a General Data Analytic System," *Psychological Bulletin,* vol. 70, December 1968.

59. Cole, A. J., *Numerical Taxonomy,* New York: Academic, 1969.

60. Cooley, J. W., P. A. W. Lewis, and P. D. Welch, "The Fast Fourier Transform Algorithm and Its Applications," Research Report no. RC-1743, Armonk, N.Y.: International Business Machines, February 1967.

61. Cooley, W. W., and P. Lohnes, *Multivariate Data Analysis,* New York: Wiley, 1971.

62. Coombs, C., *A Theory of Data,* New York: Wiley, 1964.

63. Cooper, B. E., "ASCOP—A Statistical Computing Procedure," *Applied Statistics,* vol. 16, 1967.

63a. Cooper, L. G., "Metric Multidimensional Scaling and the Concept of Preference," working paper no. 163, Los Angeles: University of California, Western Management Science Institute, 1970.

64. Cooper, W. W., and G. Majone, "A Description and Some Suggested Extensions For Methods of Cluster Analysis," Research Report no. 162, Pittsburgh: Carnegie-Mellon University, Management Science Institute, March 1968.

65. Couch, A., "Datatext Manual," rev. ed., Cambridge, Mass.: Harvard University, Laboratory of Social Relations, 1971.

66. Cox, D. R., *Analysis of Binary Data,* London: Methuen, 1970.

67. Cox, D. R., and P. A. W. Lewis, *The Statistical Analysis of a Series of Events,* London: Methuen, 1966.

68. Craddock, J. M., and M. H. Freeman, "The METO Computer Language," *Applied Statistics,* vol. 16, no. 2, 1967.

68a. Cramer, E. M., "Significance Tests and Tests of Models in Multiple Regression," Report no. 93, Chapel Hill: University of North Carolina, L. L. Thurstone Psychometric Laboratory, 1971.

69. Cronbach, L. J., and L. Furby, "How Should We Measure 'Change'—or Should We?" *Psychological Bulletin,* vol. 74, July 1970.

70. Crow, B. A., "A Graph Theoretical Approach to Clustering," Modernization and Rapid Acculturation Project Technical Report no. 1, Lawrence: University of Kansas, October 1968.

71. Cureton, E. E., "Communality Estimation in Factor Analysis of Small Matrices," *Educational and Psychological Measurement*, vol. 31, Summer 1971.

71a. Dalenius, T. E., "Survey Sampling in a Computerized Environment," *Review of the International Statistical Institute*, vol. 39, 1971, pp. 11–13.

72. Daniel, C., and F. Wood, *Fitting Equations to Data*, New York: Wiley, 1971.

73. Delaney, F. C., and F. M. Speed, "GENHYP—a FORTRAN V Program for General Linear Hypothesis Testing," Technical Report, Houston, Tex.: Lockheed Electronics Company, May 1970.

73a. Dempster, A. P., "An Overview of Multivariate Data Analysis," *Journal of Multivariate Analysis*, vol. 1, 1971, pp. 316–346.

74. Derflinger, G., "Efficient Methods of Obtaining the MINRES and Maximum Likelihood Solutions in Factor Analysis," *Metrika*, vol. 14, nos. 2, 3, 1969.

75. Deuel, P., "A Survey of the ARIEL Programming Language," Technical Report no. 2, Berkeley: University of California, Ariel Consortium, March 1971.

76. Diehr, G. E., "An Investigation of Computational Algorithms for Aggregation Problems," working paper no. 155, Los Angeles: University of California, Western Management Science Institute, December 1969.

77. Dixon, W. J. (ed.), *Biomedical Computer Programs*, Los Angeles: University of California Press, 1968.

78. Dixon, W. J., *Biomedical Computer Programs—X-series Supplement*, Los Angeles: University of California Press, 1969.

79. Dixon, W. J., *Biomedical Computer Programs—P-series Supplement*, Los Angeles: University of California Press, 1970.

80. Dobson, G., L. Parker, and G. Rosbrook, "SSUPAC—Manual of Computer Programs for Statistical Analysis," Urbana: University of Illinois, Statistical Service Unit, 1964.

81. Draper, N., and H. Smith, *Applied Regression Analysis*, New York: Wiley, 1966.

82. Dunn, O. J., "Some Expected Values for Probabilities of Correct Classification in Discriminant Analysis," *Technometrics*, vol. 13, May 1971.

83. Eber, H. W., "Toward Oblique Simple Structure: A New Version of Cattell's Maxplane Rotation Program," *Multivariate Behavioral Research*, vol. 1, January 1966.

84. Edwards, A., *Experimental Design in Psychological Research*, New York: Holt, Rinehart & Winston, 1960.

85. Elashoff, J. D., and R. E. Snow, "A Case Study in Statistical Inference," Technical Report no. 15, Stanford, Calif.: Stanford University, School of Education, December 1970.

86. Elashoff, R. M., and A. A. Afifi, "Missing Values in Multivariate Statistics I—Review of the Literature," *Journal of the American Statistical Association*, vol. 61, September 1966.

87. Elashoff, R. M., and A. A. Afifi, "Missing Observations in Multivariate Statistics, III," *Journal of the American Statistical Association*, vol. 64, March 1969.

88. Elashoff, R. M., and A. A. Afifi, "Missing Observations in Multivariate Statistics, IV," *Journal of the American Statistical Association*, vol. 64, March 1969.

89. Evans, G. T., "Transformation of Factor Matrices to Achieve Congruence," unpublished manuscript, Toronto: Ontario Institute of Education, 1970.

90. Falkoff, A. D., and K. E. Iverson, "APL/360: User's Manual," Armonk, N.Y.: International Business Machines, 1968.

91. Feliciano, M., C. W. Nestor, N. B. Gove, and T. D. Calton, *Oak Ridge Data Evaluation and Analysis Language*, Oak Ridge, Tenn.: Oak Ridge National Laboratory, March 1970.

92. Finn, J. D., "A Generalized Univariate and Multivariate Analysis of Variance, Covariance and Regression Program," paper presented to SHARE, Houston, Texas, February 1968.

93. Forgy, E., "Evaluation of Several Methods for Detecting Sample Mixtures from Different N-Dimensional Populations," paper presented at American Psychological Association meeting, Los Angeles, September 1964.

94. Forrester, J., *Industrial Dynamics*, Cambridge, Mass.: M.I.T., 1968.

95. Forsythe, G. E., "Pitfalls in Computation, or Why a Math Book Isn't Enough,"

Technical Report no. CS 147, Stanford, Calif.: Stanford University, Computer Science Department, January 1970.

96. Forthofer, R., C. F. Starmer, and J. Grizzle, "A Program for the Analysis of Categorical Data by Linear Models," Institute of Statistics Mimeo Series no. 604, Chapel Hill: University of North Carolina, January 1969.

97. Freund, R. J., "A Warning of Round Off Errors in Regression," *The American Statistician*, vol. 17, December 1963.

98. Freund, R. J., and G. G. Early, "On the Interpretation of the Multivariate Analysis of Variance," paper presented at Biometric Society meeting, May 1970.

99. Friedman, H., and J. Rubin, "On Some Invariant Criteria for Grouping Data," *Journal of the American Statistical Association*, vol. 62, December 1967.

100. Froemel, E. C., "A Comparison of Computer Routines for the Calculation of the Tetrachoric Correlation Coefficient," *Psychometrika*, vol. 36, June 1971.

101. Furnival, G. M., "All Possible Regressions with Less Computation," *Technometrics*, vol. 13, May 1971.

102. Gabriel, M., "Special-Purpose Language for Least-Squares Fits," Report no. ANL-7495, Argonne National Laboratory, September 1968.

103. Garside, M. J., "The Best Subset in Multiple Regression Analysis," *Applied Statistics*, vol. 14, nos. 2, 3, 1965.

104. Garside, M. J., "Some Computational Procedures for the Best Subset Problems," *Journal of the Royal Statistical Society*, vol. 20, series C, 1971.

105. Gemignani, M. C., *Calculus and Statistics*, Reading, Mass.: Addison-Wesley, 1970.

106. Gleason, T. C., "A General Model for Non-Metric Multi-dimensional Scaling," Technical Report no. 67-3, Ann Arbor: University of Michigan, Mathematical Psychology Program, 1967.

107. Gleason, T. C., *Multi-Dimensional Scaling of Sociometric Data*, Ann Arbor: University of Michigan, Institute for Survey Research, 1969.

108. Gnanadesikan, R., and M. B. Wilk, "Data Analytic Methods in Multivariate Statistical Analysis," in P. Krishnaiah (ed.), *Multivariate Analysis*, vol. 2, New York: Academic, 1969.

109. Godfrey, M., "Operating System Considerations for Statistical Computing," *Journal of the Royal Statistical Society*, vol. 20, Series C, 1971.

110. Golub, G. H., "Matrix Decomposition and Statistical Calculations," in R. C. Milton and J. A. Nelder (eds.), *Statistical Computation*, New York: Academic, 1969.

111. Golub, G. H., and C. Reinsch, "Handbook Series: Linear Algebra Singular Value Decomposition and Least Squares Solutions," Technical Report no. CS 133, Stanford, Calif.: Stanford University, Computer Science Department, May 1969.

112. Goodman, L. A., "The Analysis of Multidimensional Contingency Tables: Stepwise Procedures and Direct Estimation Methods for Building Models for Multiple Classification," *Technometrics*, vol. 13, February 1971.

113. Gordon, G., *System Simulation*, Englewood Cliffs, N.J.: Prentice-Hall, 1969.

114. Gorman, G. W., and R. J. Toman, "Selection of Variables for Fitting Equations to Data," *Technometrics*, vol. 8, February 1966.

115. Gower, J. C., "Some Distance Properties of Latent Root and Vector Methods Used in Multivariate Analysis," *Biometrika*, vol. 53, December 1966.

116. Gower, J. C., "A General Coefficient of Similarity and Some of Its Properties," unpublished manuscript, Rothamsted, England: Rothamsted Experimental Station, 1969.

117. Gower, J. C., and I. D. Hill, "Internal Data Structures," *Journal of the Royal Statistical Society*, vol. 20, series C, 1971.

118. Gower, J. C., H. R. Simpson, and S. Martin, "A Statistical Programming Language," *Applied Statistics*, vol. 16, no. 2, 1967.

119. Graybill, F., *An Introduction to Linear Statistical Models*, vol. I, New York: McGraw-Hill, 1961.

120. Graybill, F., *An Introduction to Matrices with Applications in Statistics*, Belmont, Calif.: Wadsworth, 1969.

121. Green, B. F., "The Computer Revolution in Psychometrics," *Psychometrika*, vol. 31, 1966.

122. Green, R. R., "SIMEMOD: A General Purpose Computer Program to Simulate and Forecast with Econometric Models," Washington: U.S. Department of Commerce, July 1970.

123. Green, P. E., and F. J. Carmone, *Multidimensional Scaling and Related Techniques,* Boston: Allyn and Bacon, 1970.

124. Grizzle, J., C. Starmer, and G. Koch, "Analysis of Categorical Data by Linear Models," *Biometrics,* vol. 25, September 1969.

125. Gruvaeus, G. T., "A General Approach to Procrustes Pattern Rotation," *Psychometrika,* vol. 35, December 1970.

126. Gruvaeus, G. T., and K. G. Joreskog, "A Computer Program for Minimizing a Function of Several Variables," Research Bulletin no. RB-70-14, Princeton, N.J.: Educational Testing Service, 1970.

127. Guttman, L., "Image Theory for the Structure of Quantitative Variates," *Psychometrika,* vol. 18, December 1953.

128. Guttman, L., "Best Possible Systematic Estimates of Communality," *Psychometrika,* vol. 21, September 1956.

129. Guttman, L., "A General Non-Metric Technique for Finding the Smallest Coordinate Space for a Configuration of Points," *Psychometrika,* vol. 33, December 1968.

130. Hakstian, A. R., "A Comparative Evaluation of Several Prominent Methods of Oblique Factor Transformation," *Psychometrika,* vol. 36, June 1971.

131. Hamaker, H. C., "On Multiple Regression Analysis," *Statistica Neerlandica,* vol. 16, 1962.

132. Harman, H., *Modern Factor Analysis,* 2d ed., Chicago: The University of Chicago Press, 1967.

133. Harman, H., and W. Jones, "Factor Analysis by Minimizing Residuals," *Psychometrika,* vol. 31, September 1966.

134. Harris, B. (ed.), *Advanced Seminar on Spectral Analysis of Time Series,* New York: Wiley, 1967.

135. Harris, C. W., "Some Rao-Guttmann Relationships," *Psychometrika,* vol. 27, September 1962.

136. Harris, C. W., and H. F. Kaiser, "Oblique Factor and Analytic Solutions by Orthogonal Transformations," *Psychometrika,* vol. 29, December 1964.

137. Hartigan, J. A., "Clustering a Data Matrix," unpublished manuscript, New Haven, Conn.: Yale University, 1970.

138. Hartley, H. O., and R. R. Hocking, "Incomplete Data Analysis," invited address to the Institute of Mathematical Studies 1971 meeting, Penn State University, University Park, Pa.

139. Healy, M. J. R., and M. H. Westmacott, "Missing Values in Experiments Analyzed on Automatic Computers," *Applied Statistics,* vol. 5, November 1956.

140. Hemmerle, W. J., *Statistical Computations on a Digital Computer,* Waltham, Mass.: Blaisdell, 1967.

141. Hemmerle, W. J., and E. Carney, "An Algorithm for Multivariate Analysis of Covariance," in R. C. Milton and J. A. Nelder (eds.), *Statistical Computation,* New York: Academic, 1969.

142. Hemmerle, W. J., A. Johnson, R. Mensing, and J. Smith, "AARDVARK Reference Manual," Iowa City: University of Iowa, Statistical Laboratory, July, 1964.

143. Hendrickson, A., and P. White, "PROMAX: A Quick Method for Rotation to Oblique Simple Structure," *British Journal of Statistical Psychology,* vol. 17, May 1964.

144. Hilsenrath, J., G. Ziegler, C. Messina, P. Walsh, and R. Herbold, "OMNITAB— A Computer Program for Statistical and Numerical Analysis," National Bureau of Standards Handbook no. 101, Washington: U.S. Bureau of Standards, 1966.

145. Hocking, R. R., W. B. Smith, B. R. Waldron, and H. H. Oxspring, "Estimation of Parameters with Incomplete Data," Themis Optimization Research Program Technical Report no. 12, College Station: Texas A and M University, Institute of Statistics, 1969.

146. Hope, K., *Methods of Multivariate Analysis,* London: University of London Press, 1968.

147. Hope, K., "The Complete Analysis of a Data Matrix: Application and Interpretation," *British Journal of Psychiatry*, vol. 116, June 1970.
148. Horst, P., *Factor Analysis of Data Matrices*, New York: Holt, 1965.
149. Horst, P., "Measurement of Personality Dimensions, Parts I–IV," Technical Report no. Nonr-477(33), Washington: U.S. Office of Naval Research, May 1966.
150. Horst, P., "The Missing Data Matrix," Technical Report no. Nonr-477(33), Washington: U.S. Office of Naval Research, July 1967.
151. Householder, A. S., *The Theory of Matrices in Numerical Analysis*, New York: Blaisdell, 1964.
152. Huber, P. J., "Robust Statistics," unpublished manuscript, Zurich: Swiss Federal Institute of Technology, 1971.
153. International Business Machines Corporation, System/360 Matrix Language (MATLAN) (360A-CM-05X)—Program Description Manual, Armonk, N.Y.
154. International Business Machines Corporation, System 360/Scientific Subroutine Package (360A-CM-03X)—Version III Programmer's Manual, Armonk, N.Y.
155. Jackson, D. M., "The Stability of Classifications of Binary Attribute Data," *Classification Society Bulletin*, vol. 2, 1970.
156. Jackson, E. C., "Missing Values in Linear Multiple Discriminant Analysis," *Biometrics*, vol. 24, December 1968.
157. Jardine, N., and R. Sibson, *Mathematical Taxonomy*, New York: Wiley, 1971.
158. Jenkins, G. M., and D. G. Watts, *Spectral Analysis and Applications*, San Francisco: Holden-Day, 1968.
159. Jennings, E., "Fixed Effects Analysis of Variance by Regression Analysis," *Multivariate Behavioral Research*, vol. 2, January 1967.
160. Johnson, R. M., "Market Segmentation: A Strategic Management Tool," *Journal of Marketing Research*, vol. 8, February 1971.
161. Johnson, S., "Hierarchical Clustering Schemes," *Psychometrika*, vol. 32, September 1967.
162. Jones, K. J., *The Multivariate Statistical Analyzer*, Cambridge, Mass.: Harvard University Bookstore, 1964.
163. Jordan, T. L., "Experiments on Error Growth Asociated with Some Linear Least Squares Procedures," *Mathematics of Computation*, vol. 22, July 1968.
164. Joreskog, K. G., "UMFLA—Computer Program for Unrestricted Maximum Likelihood Factor Analysis," Research Memorandum no. RM-66-20, Princeton, N.J.: Educational Testing Service, August 1966.
165. Joreskog, K. G., "A General Approach to Confirmatory Maximum Likelihood Factor Analysis," Research Bulletin no. RB-67-48, Princeton, N.J.: Educational Testing Service, September 1967.
166. Joreskog, K. G., "A General Method for Analysis of Covariance Structures with Applications. I. Theory," Research Bulletin no. RB-69-46, Princeton, N.J.: Educational Testing Service, 1969.
167. Joreskog, K. G., "A General Method for Analysis of Covariance Structure with Applications. II. Applications," Research Bulletin no. RB-69-47, Princeton, N.J.: Educational Testing Service, 1969.
168. Joreskog, K. G., "Factoring with Multitest-Multioccasion Correlation Matrix," Research Bulletin no. RB-69-62, Princeton, N.J.: Educational Testing Service, 1969.
169. Joreskog, K. G., "Statistical Analysis of Sets of Congeneric Tests," Research Bulletin no. RB-69-97, Princeton, N.J.: Educational Testing Service, 1969.
170. Joreskog, K. G., "Estimation and Testing of Simplex Models," Research Bulletin no. RB-70-42, Princeton, N.J.: Educational Testing Service, 1970.
171. Joreskog, K. G., "A General Method for Estimating a Linear Structural Equation System," Research Bulletin no. RB-70-54, Princeton, N.J.: Educational Testing Service, 1970.
172. Joreskog, K. G., "Simultaneous Factor Analysis in Several Populations," Research Bulletin no. RB-70-61, Princeton, N.J.: Educational Testing Service, 1970.
173. Joreskog, K. G., and G. Gruvaeus, "RMFLA—Computer Program for Restricted

Maximum Likelihood Factor Analysis," Research Memorandum no. RM-67-21, Princeton, N.J.: Educational Testing Service, October 1967.
174. Joreskog, K. G., G. Gruvaeus, and M. van Thillo, "ACOVS: A General Computer Program for Analysis of Covariance Structures," Research Bulletin no. RB-70-15, Princeton, N.J.: Educational Testing Service, 1970.
175. Joreskog, K. G., and D. N. Lawley, "New Methods in Maximum Likelihood Factor Analysis," Research Bulletin no. RB-67-49, Princeton, N.J.: Educational Testing Service, September 1967.
176. Kaiser, H. F., "A Second-Generation Little Jiffy," *Psychometrika*, vol. 35, December 1970.
177. Kaiser, H. F., and J. Caffrey, "Alpha Factor Analysis," *Psychometrika*, vol. 30, March 1965.
178. Kelly, L. G., *Handbook of Numerical Methods and Applications*, Reading, Mass.: Addison-Wesley, 1967.
179. Kendall, M. G., *A Course in Multivariate Analysis*, London: Griffin, 1962.
180. Kendall, M. G., "On the Future of Statistics—A Second Look," *Journal of the Royal Statistical Society*, vol. 131, series A, 1968.
181. Kendall, M. G., "Cluster Analysis," unpublished manuscript, London: Scientific Control Systems, Ltd., July 1968.
182. Kennard, R. W., and L. A. Stone, "Computer Aided Design of Experiments," *Technometrics*, vol. II, 1969.
183. Klahr, D., "A Monte Carlo Investigation of the Statistical Significance of Kruskal's Non-Metric Scaling Procedure," *Psychometrika*, vol. 34, September 1969.
184. Koch, G. G., and D. W. Reinfurt, "The Analysis of Categorical Data from Mixed Models," *Biometrics*, vol. 27, March 1971.
185. Koerts, J., and A. P. Abrahamse, *On the Theory and Application of the General Linear Model*, Rotterdam: Rotterdam University Press, 1969.
186. Koopman, R. F., "Fitting a Multidimensional Component Model to Binary Data," Technical Report, Urbana: University of Illinois, Psychology Department, October 1968.
186a. Kramer, C. Y., *A First Course in Methods of Multivariate Analysis*, Blacksburg, Va.: Virginia Polytechnic Institute, 1972.
187. Kruskal, J. B., "Multidimensional Scaling by Optimizing Goodness of Fit to a Non-Metric Hypothesis," *Psychometrika*, vol. 29, March 1964.
188. Kruskal, J. B., "How to Use MDSCAL—a Program to Do Multidimensional Scaling and Multidimensional Unfolding," unpublished manuscript, Bell Telephone Laboratories, Murray Hill, N.J., 1968.
189. Kruskal, J. B., "Monotone Regression: Continuity and Differentiability Properties," *Psychometrika*, vol. 36, March 1971.
190. Kruskal, J. B., and F. Carmone, "MONANOVA—A FORTRAN IV Program for Monotone Analysis of Variance," unpublished manuscript, Bell Telephone Laboratories, Murray Hill, N.J., 1968.
191. Ku, H. H., and S. Kullback, "Interaction in Multidimensional Contingency Tables: An Information Theoretic Approach," *Journal of Research of the National Bureau of Standards*, vol. 72B, no. 3, 1968.
192. Ku, H. H., R. N. Varner, and S. Kullback, "On the Analysis of Multidimensional Contingency Tables," *Journal of the American Statistical Association*, vol. 66, 1971.
193. Kuki, H., and J. Ascoly, "FORTRAN—Extended Precision Library," *IBM Systems Journal*, vol. 10, no. 1, 1971.
194. LaMotte, L. R., and R. R. Hocking, "Computational Efficiency in the Selection of Regression Variables," *Technometrics*, vol. 12, February 1970.
195. Lance, G., and W. Williams, "Computer Programs for Hierarchical Polythetic Classification," *Computer Journal*, vol. 9, May 1966.
196. Lance, G., and W. Williams, "Mixed-Data Classificatory Programs: I. Agglomerative Systems," *Australian Computer Journal*, vol. I, 1967.

197. Lance, G., and W. Williams, "Mixed-Data Classificatory Programs: II. Divisive Systems," *Australian Computer Journal*, vol. I, 1967.

198. Lance, G., and W. Williams, "A General Theory of Classificatory Sorting Strategies: I. Hierarchical Systems," *Computer Journal*, vol. 9, February 1967.

199. Lance, G., and W. Williams, "Note on the Classification of Multi-Level Data," *Computer Journal*, vol. 9, February 1967.

200. Lance, G., and W. Williams, "A General Theory of Classificatory Sorting Strategies: II. Clustering Systems," *Computer Journal*, vol. 10, November 1967.

201. Lazarsfeld, P., and N. Henry, *Latent Structure Analysis*, Boston: Houghton Mifflin, 1968.

202. Lerman, I. C., "*Sur deux critères de la classification*," Report no. 20, Paris: Centre de Calcul, June 1967.

203. Lerman, I. C., "*Sur l'analyse des données prealable á une classification automatique*," Report no. 61, Paris: Centre de Calcul, March 1970.

203a. Levine, R. L., and J. E. Hunter, "Statistical and Psychometric Inference in Principal Component Analysis," *Multivariate Behavioral Research*, vol. 6, 1971, pp. 105–116.

204. Lewis, J. A., "A Program to Fit Constants to Multiway Tables of Quantitative and Quantal Data," *Applied Statistics*, vol. 17, no. 1, 1968.

205. Lewis, P. A. W., and T. C. Kelly, "A Computer Program for the Statistical Analysis of Series of Events," IBM Research Report no. RJ 362, Armonk, N.Y.: International Business Machines, November 1965.

206. Lindquist, E., *Design and Analysis of Experiments*, Boston: Houghton Mifflin, 1956.

207. Ling, R. F., "Cluster Analysis," Report no. AD-717 333, Springfield, Va.: National Technical Information Service, January 1971.

208. Lingoes, J. C., "An IBM 360/67 Program for Guttmann-Lingoes Conjoint Measurement—III," *Behavioral Science*, vol. 13, September 1968.

209. Lingoes, J. C., "The Rationale of the Guttmann-Lingoes Non-Metric Series: A Letter to Dr. Runkel," unpublished manuscript, Ann Arbor: University of Michigan, February 1968.

210. Lingoes, J. C., "An IBM 360/67 Program for Guttmann-Lingoes Smallest Space Analysis—SSAI," *Behavioral Science*, vol. 14, 1969.

211. Lingoes, J. C., "A General Survey of the Guttmann-Lingoes Non-Metric Program Series," paper presented to Seminar on Scaling and Measurement, University of California, Irvine, June 1969.

212. Lingoes, J. C., and T. Cooper, "PEP-I: A FORTRAN IV Program for Guttmann-Lingoes Nonmetric Probability Clustering," *Behavioral Science*, vol. 16, 1971.

213. Lingoes, J. C., and E. E. Roskam, "A Mathematical and Empirical Study of Two Multidimensional Scaling Algorithms," Technical Report no. MMPP-71-1, Ann Arbor: University of Michigan, Mathematical Psychology Program, 1971.

214. Linn, R. L., and C. E. Werts, "Assumptions in Making Causal Inferences from Part Correlations, Partial Correlations and Partial Regression Coefficients," Research Bulletin no. RB-69-6, Princeton, N.J.: Educational Testing Service, 1969.

215. Longley, J., "An Appraisal of Least Squares Programs for the Electronic Computer from the Point of View of the User," *Journal of the American Statistical Association*, vol. 62, September 1967.

216. Lord, F. M., "Estimation of Parameters from Incomplete Data," *Journal of the American Statistical Association*, vol. 50, September 1955.

217. Lord, F. M., "Large Sample Covariance Analysis when the Control Variable is Fallible," *Journal of the American Statistical Association*, vol. 55, June 1960.

218. Lord, F. M., "A Paradox in the Interpretation of Group Comparisons," *Psychological Bulletin*, vol. 68, November 1967.

219. Lorr, M., et al., "Conference on Cluster Analysis of Multivariate Data, New Orleans, Louisiana, Final Report," AD 653-722, Washington: U.S. Office of Naval Research, June 1967.

220. Macdonald, J. R., "Accelerated Convergence, Divergence, Iteration, Extrapolation, and Curve Fitting," *Journal of Applied Physics*, vol. 35, October 1964.

221. Macqueen, J., "Some Methods for Classification and Analysis of Multivariate

Observations," in *Fifth Berkeley Symposium on Statistics and Probability*, Berkeley: University of California Press, 1967.

222. Mallows, C. L., "Choosing a Subset Regression," unpublished manuscript, Murray Hill, N.J.: Bell Telephone Laboratories, 1968.

223. Mandel, J., "A New Analysis of Variance Model for Non-additive Data," *Technometrics*, vol. 13, February 1971.

223a. Marriott, F. H. C., "Practical Problems in a Method of Cluster Analysis," *Biometrics*, vol. 27, September 1971.

224. Mayer, L. S., "A Method of Cluster Analysis When There Exist Multiple Indicators of a Theoretic Concept," *Biometrics*, vol. 27, March 1971.

225. McDonald, R. P., "Some IBM 7090-7094 Programs for Non-Linear Factor Analysis," Research Memorandum no. RM-65-11, Princeton, N.J.: Educational Testing Service, August 1965.

226. McDonald, R. P., "Protean—a Comprehensive CDC 3200/3600 Program for Non-Linear Factor Analysis," Research Memorandum no. RM-67-26, Princeton: N.J.: Educational Testing Service, November 1967.

227. McDonald, R. P., "IBM 360/65 Programs for a Generalized Factor Analysis Based on Residual Covariance Matrices of Prescribed Structure," Research Memorandum no. RM-70-7, Princeton, N.J.: Educational Testing Service, April 1970.

228. McDonald, R. P., "The Theoretical Foundations of Principal Components Factor Analysis, Canonical Factor Analysis and Alpha Factor Analysis," *British Journal of Mathematical and Statistical Psychology*, vol. 23, May 1970.

229. McGee, V., "Multidimensional Scaling of N Sets of Similarity Measures: a Nonmetric Individual Differences Approach," *Multivariate Behavioral Research*, vol. 3, April 1968.

230. McLaughlin, R. L., and J. J. Boyle, *Short-term Forecasting—a New Computer Program*, no. 13, Chicago: American Marketing Association, 1968.

231. McRae, D., "MICKA: A FORTRAN IV Iterative K-Means Cluster Analysis Program," Preliminary Report, Chapel Hill: University of North Carolina, Psychometric Laboratory, January 1970.

232. Mendenhall, W., *Introduction to Linear Models and the Design and Analysis of Experiments*, Belmont, Calif.: Wadsworth, 1968.

233. Meyers, E. D., "Survey of Social Science Computer Systems," Technical Report, Hanover, N.H.: Dartmouth College, June 1969.

234. Miller, R. G., "Statistical Prediction by Discriminant Analysis," *Meteorological Monographs*, vol. 4, 1962.

235. Milton, R. C., and J. A. Nelder (eds.), *Statistical Computation*, New York: Academic, 1969.

236. Morris, J., "Non-Parametric Statistical System," Technical Report no. 40, East Lansing: Michigan State University, Computer Institute, 1967.

237. Morrison, D. G., "On the Interpretation of Discriminant Analysis," *Journal of Marketing Research*, vol. 6, May 1969.

238. Morrison, D. G., and R. Art, "A FORTRAN Program for Stepwise Multiple discriminant Analysis," Evanston, Ill.: Northwestern University, Vogelback Computing Center, 1967.

238a. Mosteller, F., "The Jackknife," *Review of the International Statistical Institute*, vol. 39, 1971, pp. 15–17.

239. Mosteller, F., and J. W. Tukey, "Data Analysis, including Statistics," in G. Lindzey and E. Aronson (eds.), *Handbook of Social Psychology*, 2d ed., vol. 2, Reading, Mass.: Addison-Wesley, 1968.

240. Muhonen, D. P., "An Experimental Comparison of Several Approaches to the Linear Least Squares Problem," Bendix Field Engineering Corporation Report TR-01-1004, November 1968.

241. Muller, M. E., "Computers as an Instrument of Data Analysis," *Technometrics*, vol. 12, May 1970.

241a. Myers, R. H., *Response Surface Methodology*, Boston: Allyn and Bacon, 1971.

242. Naylor, T. H., *Computer Simulation Experiments with Models of Economic Systems*, New York: Wiley, 1971.

243. Naylor, T. H., J. L. Balintfy, D. S. Burdick, and Kong Chu, *Computer Simulation Techniques*, New York: Wiley, 1968.

244. Neely, P., "Comparison of Several Algorithms for the Computation of Means, Standard Deviations and Correlation Coefficients," *Communications of the Association for Computing Machinery*, vol. 9, 1966.

245. Nelder, J. A., "General Statistical Program (GENSTAT), Version IV," Glen Osmond, South Australia: Waite Institute, Biometry Section, 1966.

246. Nelder, J. A., "Statistical Computing and Computer Languages," *Journal of the Royal Statistical Society*, vol. 20, series C, 1971.

247. Nelder, J. A., and B. E. Cooper, "Input/Output in Statistical Programs," *Journal of the Royal Statistical Society*, vol. 20, series C, 1971.

248. Nie, N., D. Bent, and C. Hull, *Statistical Package for the Social Sciences*, New York: McGraw-Hill, 1970.

249. Nygreen, G. T., "A FORTRAN IV Program for Density Cluster Analysis of Survey Research Data," Princeton, N.J.: Office for Survey Research, 1969.

249a. O'Neill, R., and G. B. Wetherill, "The Present State of Multiple Comparison Methods," *Journal of the Royal Statistical Society*, series B, vol. 33, 1971, pp. 218–250.

249b. Overall, J. E., and C. J. Klett, *Applied Multivariate Analysis*, New York: McGraw-Hill, 1972.

250. Overall, J., and D. Spiegel, "Concerning Least-Squares Analysis of Experimental Data," *Psychological Bulletin*, vol. 72, November 1969.

251. Peay, E. R., Jr., "Nonmetric Grouping: Clusters and Cliques," Technical Report no. 70-5, Ann Arbor: University of Michigan, Mathematical Psychological Program, 1970.

252. Pennell, R., "Additive Representations for Two-Dimensional Tables," Research Bulletin no. RB-70-29, Princeton, N.J.: Educational Testing Service, April 1970.

253. Plackett, R. L., "Multidimensional Contingency Tables: A Survey of Models and Methods," *Bulletin of the International Statistical Institute*, vol. 43, 1969.

254. Pope, P. T., and J. T. Webster, "The Use of an F-Statistic in Stepwise Regression Procedures," unpublished manuscript, 1970.

255. Potthoff, R., and S. N. Roy, "A Generalized MANOVA Model Useful Especially for Growth Curve Problems," *Biometrika*, vol. 51, nos. 3, 4, 1964.

256. Powers, J. R., "DATMAN—a Programming Language for Data-Manipulation and Statistical Analysis," Columbus, Ohio: Battelle Memorial Institute, October 1970.

256a. Press, S. J., *Applied Multivariate Analysis*, New York: Holt, 1972.

257. Raghavarao, D., *Constructions and Combinatorial Problems in the Design of Experiments*, New York: Wiley, 1971.

258. Rao, C. R., "Estimation and Tests of Significance in Factor Analysis," *Psychometrika*, vol. 20, June 1955.

259. Rao, C. R., "Analysis of Dispersion with Incomplete Observations on One of the Characters," *Journal of the Royal Statistical Society*, series B, vol. 18, 1956.

260. Rao, C. R., "The Use and Interpretation of Principal Component Analysis in Applied Research," *Sankhya:* series A, vol. 26, 1964.

261. Rao, C. R., "Cluster Analysis and Mathematical Programming," Management Sciences Research Report no. 183, Pittsburgh: Carnegie-Mellon University, October 1969.

262. Rice, C. E., and M. Lorr, "An Empirical Comparison of Typological Analysis Methods," AD-692 484, Washington: U.S. Office of Naval Research, August 1969.

263. Ritenour, R., "The Care and Feeding of the Fast Fourier Transform," Technical Report no. 1183-1446, UC32, Las Vegas, Nev.: EG and G, Inc., August 1969.

264. Robinson, E. A., *Multichannel Time Series Analysis with Digital Computer Programs*, San Francisco: Holden-Day, 1967.

265. Rohlf, F. J., "Adaptive Hierarchical Clustering Schemes," *Systematic Zoology*, vol. 19, 1970.

266. Rohlf, F. J., and D. R. Fisher, "Tests for Hierarchical Structure in Random Data Sets," *Systematic Zoology*, vol. 17, 1968.

267. Roskam, E. E., "Metric Analysis of Ordinal Data in Psychology," unpublished doctoral dissertation, University of Nijmegan, Holland, 1968.
268. Roskam, E. E., "A Comparison of Principles for Algorithm Construction in Non-Metric Scaling," Technical Report no. 69-2, Ann Arbor: University of Michigan, Mathematical Psychology Program, February 1969.
269. Roskam, E. E., "Data Theory and Algorithms for Non-Metric Scaling: Parts I and II," unpublished manuscript, University of Nijmegen, Holland, November 1969.
270. Roskam, E. E., "The Method of Triads for Non-Metric Multidimensional Scaling," Nederlands Tijdschrift voor Psychologie, vol. 25, 1970.
271. Roskam, E. E., and J. C. Lingoes, "MINISSA-I, a FORTRAN IV Program for the Smallest Space Analysis of Square Symmetric Matrices," Behavioral Science, vol. 14, 1969.
271a. Roy, S. N., R. Gnanadesikan, and J. N. Srivastava, Analysis and Design of Certain Quantitative Multiresponse Experiments, New York: Pergamon, 1971.
272. Rozeboom, W. W., "Scaling Theory and the Nature of Measurement," Synthese, vol. 16, 1966.
273. Rubin, H., "Decision Theoretic Approach to Some Multivariate Problems," in P. Krishnaiah (ed.), Multivariate Analysis—II, New York: Academic, 1969.
273a. Rummel, R. J., Applied Factor Analysis, Evanston, Ill.: Northwestern University Press, 1970.
274. Salzman, L., Computerized Economic Analysis, New York: McGraw-Hill, 1968.
275. Schatzoff, M., R. Tsao, and S. Feinberg, "Efficient Calculation of All Possible Regressions," Technometrics, vol. 10, November 1968.
276. Scheffe, H., The Analysis of Variance, New York: Wiley, 1959.
276a. Schlaifer, R., Computer Programs for Elementary Decision Analysis, Boston: Harvard University Press, 1971.
277. Schonemann, P. H., "On Metric Multidimensional Unfolding," Psychometrika, vol. 35, September 1970.
278. Schonemann, P. H., and R. M. Carroll, "Fitting One Matrix to Another under Choice of a Central Dilation and a Rigid Motion," Research Bulletin no. 69-78, Princeton, N.J.: Educational Testing Service, 1969.
279. Searle, S. R., Linear Models, New York: Wiley, 1971.
280. Searle, S. R., and W. H. Hansman, Matrix Algebra for Business and Economics, New York: Wiley, 1970.
281. Shepard, R. N., "Metric Structures in Ordinal Data," Journal of Mathematical Psychology, vol. 3, July 1966.
282. Shepard, R. N., and D. Carroll, "Parametric Mapping of Non-Linear Data Structures," in P. Krishnaiah (ed.), Multivariate Analysis, New York: Academic, 1966.
282a. Shepard, R. N., A. K. Romney, and S. B. Nerlove (eds.), Multidimensional Scaling: Theory and Applications in the Behavioral Sciences, vols. I, II, New York: Seminar Press, 1972.
283. Sherman, C. R., "Non-Metric Multi-Dimensional Scaling: The Role of the Minkowski Metric," Technical Report no. 72, Chapel Hill: University of North Carolina, Psychometric Laboratory, 1970.
284. Sidik, S. M., and B. Henry, "RAPIER—a FORTRAN IV Program for Multiple Linear Regression Analysis Providing Internally Evaluated Remodeling," Technical Note no. TN-D-5656, Washington: National Aeronautics and Space Administration, February 1970.
285. Simpson, S. M., Time Series Computations in FORTRAN and FAP, vol. I, A Program Library, Reading, Mass.: Addison-Wesley, 1966.
286. Smillie, K. W., "STATPACK2: An APL Statistical Package," Report no. 17, Edmonton, Can.: University of Alberta, Computer Center, February 1969.
287. Smith, C. F., "Properties of a Class of Objective Functions in Cluster Analysis," Technical Report no. 20, Project Themis, Gainsville: University of Florida, Systems Research Center, June 1969.
288. Smith, H. F., "Interpretation of Adjusted Treatment Means and Regressions in Analysis of Covariance," Biometrics, vol. 13, September 1957.

289. Snyder, F., "A Unique Variance Model for Three-Mode Factor Analysis," unpublished manuscript, Murray Hill, N.J.: Bell Telephone Laboratories, 1969.
290. Sokal, R., and P. Sneath, *Principles of Numerical Taxonomy*, San Francisco: Freeman, 1963.
291. Sonquist, J. A., "Recent Developments in Sequential Data Analysis Strategy," *Proceedings of the American Statistical Association, Social Statistics Section*, 1969.
292. Sonquist, J. A., *Multivariate Model Building*, Ann Arbor: University of Michigan, Institute for Survey Research, 1970.
293. Sonquist, J. A., and J. Morgan, *The Detection of Interaction Effects*, Ann Arbor: University of Michigan, Institute for Survey Research, 1964.
294. Spence, I., "Multidimensional Scaling: An Empirical and Theoretical Investigation," doctoral dissertation, Toronto: University of Toronto, 1970.
295. Symons, N. A., "Analysis of Variance Programs," SHARE Statistics Project Report, New Haven, Conn.: Yale University, June 1966.
296. Timm, N. H., "The Estimation of Variance-Covariance and Correlation Matrices from Incomplete Data," *Psychometrika*, vol. 35, 1970.
297. Torgerson, W. S., *Theory and Methods of Scaling*, New York: Wiley, 1958.
298. Trawinski, I. M., and R. Bargmann, "Maximum Likelihood Estimation with Incomplete Multivariate Data," *Annals of Mathematical Statistics*, vol. 35, June 1964.
299. Tryon, R. C., and D. E. Bailey, "The BC TRY Computer System of Cluster and Factor Analysis," *Multivariate Behavioral Research*, vol. 1, January 1966.
300. Tryon, R. C., and D. E. Bailey, *Cluster Analysis*, New York: McGraw-Hill, 1971.
301. Tucker, L. R., "Topics in Factor Analysis, II," AD 717-680, Urbana: University of Illinois, September 1970.
302. Tukey, J. W., "The Future of Data Analysis," *Annals of Mathematical Statistics*, vol. 33, March 1962.
303. Tukey, J. W., "Analyzing Data: Sanctification or Detective Work?" *American Psychologist*, vol. 24, February 1969.
304. Tukey, J. W., *Exploratory Data Analysis* (3 vols.), Reading, Mass.: Addison-Wesley, 1970.
305. Tukey, J. W., and J. Cornfield, "Average Values of Mean Squares in Factorials," *Annals of Mathematical Statistics*, vol. 27, June 1956.
306. Tukey, J. W., and B. F. Green, "Complex Analysis of Variance: General Problems," *Psychometrika*, vol. 25, December 1960.
307. Tukey, J. W., and M. B. Wilk, "Data Analysis and Statistics: Principles and Practice," unpublished manuscript, Bell Telephone Laboratories, Murray Hill, N.J., 1966.
308. Tversky, A., "Intransitivity of Preferences," *Psychological Review*, vol. 76, January 1969.
309. University of Michigan, OSIRIS/40, Institute for Survey Research Statistical Package, Ann Arbor, 1968.
310. van Thillo, M., and K. G. Joreskog, "SIFASP, a General Computer Program for Simultaneous Factor Analysis in Several Populations," Research Bulletin no. RB-70-62, Princeton, N.J.: Educational Testing Service, November 1970.
311. Veldman, D., *FORTRAN Programming for the Behavioral Sciences*, New York: Holt, 1967.
312. Wainer, H., "TALCAM, a Computer Program to Perform a Tucker Analysis of Learning Curves and More," Research Memorandum no. RM-68-4, Princeton, N.J.: Educational Testing Service, February 1968.
313. Wainer, H., "A Principal Components Analysis of Models and Men," Research Bulletin no. RB-68-29, Princeton, N.J.: Educational Testing Service, July 1968.
314. Walsh, J. E., "Computer Feasible Method for Handling Incomplete Data in Regression Analysis," *Journal of the Association for Computing Machinery*, vol. 8, April 1961.
315. Wampler, R. H., "An Evaluation of Linear Least Squares Computer Programs," *Journal of Research of the National Bureau of Standards*, vol. 73B, 1969.

316. Wampler, R. H., "A Report on the Accuracy of Some Widely Used Least Squares Computer Programs," *Journal of the American Statistical Asociation*, vol. 65, June 1970.

316a. Wang, M. D., and J. C. Stanley, "Differential Weighting: A Review of Methods and Empirical Studies," *Review of Educational Research*, vol. 40, December 1970, pp. 663–705.

317. Ward, J. H., *Hierarchical Grouping to Maximize Payoff*, WADD-TN-61-29, Wright Air Force Base, Texas, March 1961.

318. Ward, J. H., K. Hall, and J. Buchhorn, "PERSUB Reference Manual," Technical Report no. PRL-TR-67-3(II), Lackland Air Force Base, Texas, 1967.

318a. Warren, W. G., "Correlation or Regression: Bias or Precision," *Applied Statistics*, vol. 20, no. 2, 1971, pp. 148–164.

319. Watts, D. G. (ed.), *The Future of Statistics*, New York: Academic, 1968.

320. Werts, C. E., and R. L. Linn, "A Regression Model for Studying Growth," Research Bulletin no. RB-69-19, Princeton, N.J.: Educational Testing Service, 1969.

321. Werts, C. E., and R. L. Linn, "Considerations When Making Inferences within the Analysis of Covariance Model," Research Bulletin No. RB-69-28, Princeton: N.J.: Educational Testing Service, 1969.

322. Westlake, J. R., *Numerical Matrix Inversion and Solution of Linear Equations*, New York: Wiley, 1968.

323. Westley, G., and J. A. Watts, "The Computing Technology Center Numerical Analysis Library," CTC-39, Oak Ridge, Tenn.: Union Carbide Company, October 1970.

324. Williams, J. D., S. D. Harlow, A. Lindem, and D. Gab, "A Judgment Analysis Program for Clustering Similar Judgmental Systems," *Educational and Psychological Measurement*, vol. 30, Spring 1970.

325. Williams, R., "A Survey of Data Structures for Computer Graphic Systems," *Computing Surveys*, vol. 3, 1971.

326. Williams, W., and G. Lance, "Logic of Computer-based Intrinsic Classifications," *Nature*, vol. 207, July 10, 1965.

327. Wilkinson, J. H., *The Algebraic Eigenvalue Problem*, London: Oxford University Press, 1965.

328. Winer, B. J., *Statistical Principles in Experimental Design*, 2d ed., New York: McGraw-Hill, 1971.

329. Wishart, D., "CLUSTAN IA: A FORTRAN Program for Numerical Classification," St. Andrew's, Scotland: St. Andrew's University, Computing Laboratory, November 1969.

330. Wolfe, J. H., "Normix: Computational Methods for Estimating the Parameters of Multivariate Normal Mixtures of Distributions," Research Memorandum no. SRM-2, San Diego: U.S. Naval Personnel Research Activity, August 1967.

331. Wolfe, J. H., "NORMIX Program Documentation," Research Memorandum SRM 69-11, San Diego: U.S. Naval Personnel Research Activity, December 1968.

332. Wolfe, J. H., "NORMAP Program Documentation," Research Memorandum SRM 69-12, San Diego: U.S. Naval Personnel Research Activity, December 1968.

333. Wolfe, J. M., "Pattern clustering by multivariate clustering analysis," Research Memorandum SRM 69-17, San Diego: U.S. Naval Personnel Research Activity, March 1969.

334. Yohe, J. M., "Computer Programming for Accuracy," AD 674-459, Madison: University of Wisconsin, Mathematics Research Center, April 1968.

335. Young, F. W., "A FORTRAN IV Program for Non-Metric Multidimensional Scaling," Report no. 56, Chapel Hill: University of North Carolina, Psychometric Laboratory, 1968.

336. Young, F. W., "Polynomial Conjoint Analysis of Similarities: A Model for Constructing Polynomial Conjoint Measurement Algorithms," Report no. 74, Chapel Hill: University of North Carolina, Psychometric Laboratory, 1969.

337. Young, F. W., "Polynomial Conjoint Analysis of Similarities: Definitions for a Specific Algorithm," Report no. 76, Chapel Hill: University of North Carolina, Psychometric Laboratory, 1969.

338. Young, F. W., "Polynomial Conjoint Analysis of Similarities: Operations for a Specific Algorithm," Report no. 77, Chapel Hill: University of North Carolina, Psychometric Laboratory, 1969.

339. Young, F. W., "Non-Metric Multi-dimensional Scaling: Recovery of Metric Information," *Psychometrika,* vol. 35, December 1970.

340. Young, F. W., and M. I. Appelbaum, "Non-Metric Multidimensional Scaling: The Relationship of Several Methods," Report no. 71, Chapel Hill: University of North Carolina, Psychometric Laboratory, 1969.

341. Youngs, E. A., and E. M. Cramer, "Some Results Relevant to Choice of Sum and Sum-of-Product Algorithms," Report no. 58, Chapel Hill: University of North Carolina, Psychometric Laboratory, May 1968.

342. Zellner, A., and H. Thornber, "Computational Accuracy and Estimation of Simultaneous Equation Econometric Models," *Econometrica,* vol. 34, 1966.

Computer Techniques

Chapter 2

On-Line Computer Applications

DAVID B. MONTGOMERY   *Graduate School of Business, Stanford University, Stanford, California*

PROLOGUE

A Marketing Dialogue in 1988[1]

The year is 1988. The place is the office of the marketing manager of a medium-sized consumer products manufacturer. The participants in the following discussion are John, the marketing manager; Bill, the director of marketing science; Rod, Bill's assistant, who specializes in marketing research; and Scott, the sales manager for the company. The scene opens as Bill, Rod, and Scott enter John's office.

John: Good morning, gentlemen. What's on the agenda for this morning?

Bill: We want to take a look at the prospects for our new beef substitute.

John: What do we have on that new product?

Rod: We test-marketed it late in 1987 in four cities, so we have those data from last quarter.

John: Let's see how it did.

(All four gather around the remote console video display unit. John activates the console and requests it to display the sales results from the most recent test market. The system retrieves the data from random access storage and displays the information on the video device.)

John: That looks good! How does it compare to the first test?

(The console retrieves and displays the data from the first test on command from John.)

Rod: Let me check the significance of the sales increase of the most recent test over last year's test.

[1] Reproduced with permission from David B. Montgomery and Glen L. Urban, *Management Science in Marketing*, Prentice-Hall, Englewood Cliffs, N.J., 1969.

(Rod requests that the system test and display the likelihood that the sales increase could be a chance occurrence.)

Rod: Looks like a solid sales increase.

Bill: Good! How did the market respond to our change in price?

(Bill commands the system to display the graph of the price-quantity response based upon the most recent test data.)

John: Is that about what our other meat substitute products show?

(John calls for past price-quantity response graphs for similar products to be superimposed on the screen.)

John: Just as I suspected—this new product is a bit more responsive to price. What's the profit estimate?

(John calls for a profit estimate from the product planning model within the system.)

John: Hmm . . . $5,500,000. Looks good. Is that based upon the growth model I supplied to the model bank last week?

Bill: No. This is based upon the penetration progress other food substitutes have shown in the past as well as the information we have on the beef substitute from our test markets.

John: Let's see what mine would do.

(He reactivates the product planning model, this time using his growth model. The profit implications are displayed on the console.)

John: Well, my model predicts $5,000,000. That's close. Looks like my feelings are close to the statistical results.

Bill: Let's see if there's a better marketing strategy for this product. We must remember that these profit estimates are based on the preliminary plan we developed two weeks ago.

(Bill calls for the marketing mix generator to recommend a marketing program based upon the data and judgmental inputs which are available in the data bank's file on this product.)

Bill: There, we can increase profit by $700,000 if we allocate another sales call each week to the new product committees of the chain stores.

Scott: I don't think our salesmen will go along with that. They don't like to face those committees. The best I could do is convince them to make one additional call every other week.

John: What would happen in that case?

(The marketing mix generator is called with the new restriction on the number of calls.)

John: Well, the profit increase is still $500,000, so let's add that call policy recommendation to our marketing plan. I'm a little worried about our advertising appeals, though. Can we improve in that area?

Bill: Let's see what the response to advertising is.

(The video unit shows a graph of the predicted sales-advertising response function.)

Bill: If we changed from a taste appeal to a convenience appeal, what would the results be, John?

John: I think it would look like this.

(John takes a light pen and describes a new relationship on the video unit based upon his judgment of the effectiveness of the new appeal.)

Rod: Let me check something.

(Rod calls for a sample of past sales-advertising response curves of similar products using the convenience appeal.)

Rod: I think you are underestimating the response on the basis of past data.

John: Well, this product is different. How much would it cost for a test of this appeal?

(Rod calls a market research evaluation model from the console.)

Rod: It looks like a meaningful test would cost about $5,000.

Bill: Wait! Hadn't we better check to see if the differences between these two advertising response functions will lead to any differences in profit?

(The marketing mix model is called for each advertising function.)

Bill: Looks sensitive to the advertising response, all right.   There's a $900,000 difference in profit.

John: I wonder what risk we'd run if we made a decision to go national with the product right now.   What are the chances of a failure with this product as it stands if we include this morning's revisions to the marketing mix?

(A risk analysis model is called on the system.)

John: Looks like a 35 percent chance of failure.   Maybe we'd best run further tests in order to reduce the risk of failure.   What's next on the agenda this morning?

INTRODUCTION

The environment in which marketing decisions are made is undergoing dramatic change.   Marketing managers and market researchers of the future will be able to call on powerful information technology to assist them in evaluating and charting the course of a firm's marketing activities.   They will be able to store, retrieve, and manipulate data, using advanced data bank facilities. Models and statistical procedures will be readily available to assist the manager and market researcher in market analysis and in integrating judgments with the results of data analysis.   On-line computer applications will play a major role in the emergence of this new marketing-decision environment.

The prologue to this chapter illustrates what will become a commonplace decision setting for marketing by 1988.   The dialogue is not simply a "blue-sky" prediction of on-line applications.   Prototype systems and models for every element in the dialogue existed prior to 1970.   The dialogue simply presents an extrapolation and refinement of existing technology.   The realization of such on-line decision systems as the one depicted in the dialogue should augment a user's ability to think about and analyze his problems in much the same way as the industrial revolution multiplied man's muscle power.   The decade of the 1970s seems destined to become known as the information decade.

This chapter presents an introduction to on-line computer applications in marketing.   It begins with a brief, nontechnical discussion of on-line computer systems.   Attention then shifts to several operating examples of the application of on-line computers in marketing.   The third section outlines the benefits which accrue from interactive on-line systems.   The final section summarizes the discussion and presents concluding comments.

ON-LINE COMPUTER SYSTEMS

A basic on-line computer system consists of a central computer, file-storage facilities, and multiple remote terminals connected to the central computer via some telecommunications network.[2]   A schematic diagram of an on-line configuration is given in Figure 1.   These system elements will each be considered briefly in nontechnical terms.

Central Computer and File Storage

The central computer facility contains the principal hardware and software (programs) which enable the system to function.   The computer and its programs direct the search for data, the storage of data, and the updating of data in the files.   They interpret incoming messages from the terminals, act upon them, and transmit replies back to the terminals.   Furthermore, the central

[2] The author acknowledges the helpful comments of Professor H. Lucas of Stanford University on this section.

computer provides the system user with computational capability in the form of arithmetic and logical operations. The central computer hardware and software also serve to direct traffic when multiple users are active on the system, which is generally the case. They ensure that proper attention is paid to the computational needs of each user.

The central computer hardware contains the system's main memory, the highest-speed, but also the most costly, memory in the system. Because of its relatively high cost, the main computer memory is generally used only to store the systems programs as well as user programs and perhaps some user data, the last two being in main memory only during actual execution (running) of a user program. Most of the time, user programs and data will be stored in devices external to the main frame of the central computer.

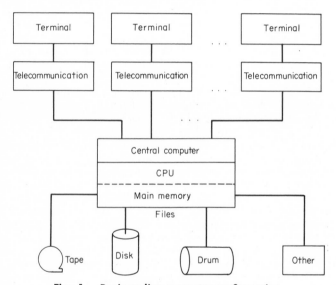

Fig. 1.   Basic on-line computer configuration.

External file-storage devices may be classified into two basic types: on-line and off-line. On-line devices are characterized by high transfer rates of user data and programs into the main computer memory, where they may be used. Although on-line devices are somewhat slower than main memory, they still provide a rapid transfer of stored data and programs into the system. It is this rapid transfer which makes these devices useful for on-line storage and use of data and programs. Another useful characteristic is that they generally provide random access within a user's files. Thus, a desired piece of information may be retrieved and brought into the main computer memory without scanning sequentially through a large mass of information in search of the required data. This saves vast amounts of time (and therefore expense) in on-line applications. The most popular on-line devices are random-access disk files and magnetic drums. The main factor against storing all data in on-line devices is that they are more costly than off-line file-storage methods.

Off-line file storage (including both user data and programs) is generally the least costly method of storage. Since off-line devices such as magnetic tapes, punched cards, and paper tapes provide sequential access to information, data and programs stored on such devices are read onto an on-line file-storage unit prior to on-line use. Since this "read in" operation consumes both computer time and calendar time, frequently used programs and data will often be left in on-line file storage.

The development of the removable disk pack has provided a file-storage method which has many of the advantages of both on-line and off-line storage. Data are stored on magnetic disk packs which can be readily inserted into a disk drive for on-line use. The user may thus have random access to his data without large time delays. However, the cost is lower than standard disk storage since the data are stored on relatively inexpensive removable disks, while the expensive hardware for reading and writing data on the disk may be used with many different disk packs.[3] Removable disk packs are an increasingly popular method for conveniently and economically providing file storage.

Telecommunications

Telecommunications facilities provide the linkage between the remote terminals and the central computer. The simplest such system is the use of ordinary voice-grade telephone lines for transmission between the terminals and the computer. The terminals may be connected to the telephone system either (1) directly, or (2) via an audio coupler. The direct connection involves wiring the terminal directly into a telephone. It has the advantage of a direct electrical connection between the terminal and the telecommunications system, but it has the disadvantage of fixing the terminal location.

Audio couplers, on the other hand, have made possible the development of portable terminals. The audio coupler functions by translating electrical signals from the terminal into coded "beeps" emitted into the mouthpiece of a telephone set. These beeps are converted into electrical signals by the telephone and are then transmitted to the computer. Similarly, electrical signals from the computer are translated into beeps emitted from the earpiece of the telephone set; these are then retranslated into electrical impulses to the terminal by the audio coupler. Use of an audio coupler makes any telephone a potential communications link between a terminal and the computer.

The use of regular dial-up telephone lines for telecommunications involves the regular area or long-distance telephone charges. Wide Area Telephone Service (WATS) lines are available to help reduce long-distance charges for heavily used connections. Leased lines are also available and varying degrees of line "conditioning" are possible in order to reduce transmission errors.

If a number of terminals are clustered in a given area and if the transmission distance to the central computer is great enough, economies may be achieved through use of a multiplexor or concentrator. In such a configuration, each terminal uses a line connected to the multiplexor which is located in the same geographical area as the terminals. The multiplexor then directs messages long distance to the computer over a high-speed, high-capacity leased line. Such a system enables the various users to afford a higher-grade data-transmission line, which offers reduced transmission errors in addition to the savings involved in the leased line.

Terminals

Terminals are the hardware which provide an interface or communications link between the user and an on-line system. Terminals may be categorized ac-

---

[3] Only one disk pack may be on a disk drive at one time.

cording to whether they are based on a typewriter or similar printing device (for example, a teletype) or on a video device such as a T.V.-like tube.

By far the most common type of terminal in use is the typewriter/Teletype. Such terminals have the advantages of producing hard copy, which may be referenced later, and of being reasonably inexpensive. One of their greatest drawbacks is their relative slowness as input/output devices.

Video systems, on the other hand, tend to be faster than the typewriter terminals in presenting information to the user. However, they are more costly and often do not provide for hard copy of information displayed on the video tube. Significant progress in both these areas seems likely during the 1970s.

The basic categorization of video terminals is between those which are capable of displaying only letters and numbers and those which, in addition, have the capacity to present graphical information. Graphical terminals tend to be more costly, but their ability to portray data and relationships graphically may be expected to have a significant impact on management use. Most managers seem to find that graphical relations communicate more clearly as well as more rapidly. In the next section, the impact of a graphical terminal at Westinghouse will be examined.

One of the most important terminal developments has been the portable terminal. This provides the user with tremendous flexibility as to where he may use the terminal. Portable terminals use audio couplers and telephones to communicate with a central computer. The usefulness of portability is easily illustrated. Suppose that a field salesman calls upon a customer and has a portable terminal with him. The customer may indicate a willingness to buy if he can be assured that the seller has the goods currently available and will initiate prompt delivery immediately. Using his portable terminal (which will probably have a built-in audio coupler) and the customer's telephone, the salesman may directly communicate with his company's central order-processing computer. The computer can verify the availability of the goods, type a verification back to the customer, and initiate the proceedings for prompt shipment and billing.

Furthermore, the portable terminal might well be used by the salesman in planning his calls in his territory. Lodish [7] has provided an experimental example of such use in actual practice. In any case, the portability of the terminal means that the salesman can utilize the computerized planning aids provided by the company whether he is in the office, on the road, or at home. Of course, similar advantages accrue to marketing managers and market researchers who may wish to utilize computer assistance in their respective tasks.

Summary

On-line systems are composed of remote terminals, telecommunications networks, a central computer, and file-storage devices. Such systems are designed to provide the user with rapid, convenient access to data and computer programs for analyzing data and problems.

MARKETING APPLICATIONS OF ON-LINE SYSTEMS

In Chapter 4 of Section I, the notions of marketing data banks, measurement-statistics banks, and model banks were developed along with certain design and organizational considerations. In this chapter, consideration will be given to the application of on-line computers in each of these areas of a balanced marketing information and decision system.

Before turning to a discussion of applications, it is well to distinguish between real-time and interactive systems and applications. *Real time* implies that data are absolutely current or that a decision must be made immediately. *Interactive* systems, on the other hand, merely imply immediate system response to either a question or a request for computation addressed to the system by the user. Often, in applications of interactive systems, data that are days, weeks, or even months old will be adequate. Similarly, a manager may want to utilize an interactive statistical or model-based analysis on a decision problem that does not require an instantaneous decision. The crucial need in such cases is that the on-line system provide immediate *response* to requests for information or analysis during a problem-solving session. This enables the user to browse through vast amounts of data, following up on suggestive leads. Further, when it comes to using statistical or model-based analysis, the user is free to compare a wide range of alternatives and to perform additional analysis based upon earlier results. Although much of this can, of course, be done with manual or batch-processing systems, experience seems to indicate that more analysis is likely to be performed, and more effectively, using an on-line system. On-line systems enable decision and analysis processes to proceed at speeds and with flexibility comparable to man's natural thought processes. Hence, the ready response of interactive on-line systems facilitates the user's natural problem-solving processes.

Data Bank Applications

IBM. Sales managers in IBM's Data Processing Division can interrogate a central data file via typewriter terminals in their offices [2]. The data in the file are current to within three or four days and relate to key-operating aspects of the firm's marketing effort. A manager using this system may request and receive a nearly immediate print out of such information as sales or rentals to date by product, customer type, and branch office; sales in relation to goals; or cross-classifications relating sales by product to customer type by branch office or other relevant factors. The user specifies that data file in which the required information is stored, the records he wants from those files, and the format in which he wants the output displayed.

Several features of this direct data-access system should be mentioned. Chapter 4 of Section I noted an example of "data browsing" and problem diagnosis which the IBM system facilitates. In addition, the system maintains a user profile for each manager. This enables the manager to tailor exception reports to his decision needs and style. For example, he could make the following request: "When sales are X percent below quota, let me know about it." He could then specify the X which reflects his needs, and that information will be stored in his user profile.

In addition, the system offers the opportunity to reduce the number of reports which the IBM manager receives on a regular basis. Prior to the installation of this system, one month's worth of these reports would make a pile five feet high [2]. Such bounty carried the danger that significant information would be buried in the pile of output. With the direct-access system, the managers know that they can retrieve the data when needed and can do so rapidly and conveniently. Consequently, they have less need for the bulky, inconvenient stack of reports which they previously received.

One final feature should be noted. The necessary updating of data in the data base did not put additional load on field personnel. All the data are a by-product of normal administrative processing.

Schenley. At Schenley, management has installed the Schenley Instant Market Reports (SIMR) system which provides executives with the ability for on-line retrieval and display of key marketing data [2]. The system differs from the IBM system in that the terminals are high-speed video terminals coupled with printers for hard copy. The SIMR system responds in seconds, in contrast to the many minutes or hours required in the previous system, which was a hybrid of computer and manual data retrieval. Using these video terminals, managers may request a wide variety of data (including cross-classifications) relating to current and past sales and inventory for any brand and package size (or combination) for each of 400 distributors. The president of Schenley's marketing subsidiary has succinctly expressed the impact of this on-line system:

> "We can get answers literally while we are still formulating the questions. Needed information is available so quickly that it helps us think [2]."

LANGUAGES FOR ON-LINE DATA RETRIEVAL AND ANALYSIS

In the previous examples, the user, generally a marketing manager, had direct on-line access to a data bank containing marketing information. The problem is how to provide the user with convenient, appropriate access. One solution, discussed in Chapter 4 of Section I, is to provide the user with a human buffer who operates very much like a librarian. In such an operation, the user requests a particular display of data which is then achieved through the intervention of a system operator. An alternative solution is to develop a general language that is easy to learn and use for on-line data retrieval and analysis. One of several such languages is MARKINF, developed by Mayer, Nugent, and Vollman [9].

Before illustrating the MARKINF language, it seems appropriate to examine certain desirable attributes of on-line data retrieval and display systems [9]:

1. *Inquiry capability.* Data must be retrievable via some sort of inquiry procedure which should have:
   a. *Simplicity,* so that nontechnical managers can readily use the system. For example, MARKINF has been used by marketing managers at all levels after about one-half hour of instruction.
   b. *Immediacy of response,* permitting the manager or market researcher to proceed with a sequential analysis procedure, testing hypotheses and requesting additional displays as the need becomes apparent.
2. *Analysis capability.* In addition to simple retrieval, the system should be able to perform certain logical and numerical operations on the data in order to prepare them for statistical or model-based analysis. Such capability will greatly enhance the utility of an on-line data bank.
3. *Evolutionary capability.* Systems must be readily adaptable to changing needs, since most viable marketing information systems are in a constant state of evolutionary development. Care must be taken to provide the system with the ability to adapt readily. As noted earlier [Sec. I, Chap. 4] modularity in system design generally provides for such capability with minimum cost and dislocation.

An important feature of MARKINF, especially from the standpoint of the nontechnical or occasional user, is that the program is self-documenting. That is, on the user's request the program itself will provide instruction in how to use the commands in the MARKINF language. Figure 2 illustrates a portion of the documentation which is available on request. The user first has the option to see a description of the MARKINF language. If he indicates his desire to see the description by typing YES, he learns, among other things, that data are specified by four identifiers: product (PROD), market (MKT), period

Fig. 2. MARKINF documentation.*

DO YOU WISH A DESCRIPTION OF MARKINF? <u>YES</u>†
                        DESCRIPTION OF MARKINF
        YOU ARE NOW USING 'MARKINF', A MARKETING INFORMATION
LANGUAGE. THIS LANGUAGE MAKES IT POSSIBLE TO RETRIEVE SALES
INFORMATION FROM THE DATA BASE PROVIDED BY 'SELLING AREAS—
MARKETING INC.'. THE DATA ARE PROVIDED FOR VARIOUS PRODUCTS
AND MARKETS FOR SEVERAL TIME PERIODS, AND ARE SPECIFIED BY
FOUR DATA IDENTIFIERS; PRODUCT (PROD), MARKET (MKT), PERIOD
(PER), AND FACT (FCT). THE LANGUAGE IS DESIGNED FOR USE IN
A CONVERSATIONAL MODE WITH THE USER RESPONDING TO QUESTIONS
AND QUESTION MARKS (?).
WOULD YOU LIKE A LIST OF MARKINF COMMANDS? <u>YES</u>†

WHAT'S	EQU	DIV	TREND	WRITENP
CALL	LIM	CUM	PROJECT	END
RET	ADD	AVE	SERIES	
PRT	SUB	GRAPH	MULTREG	
RETP	MPY	COR	WRITE	

WOULD YOU LIKE A DESCRIPTION OF THE COMMANDS? <u>YES</u>†
                           COMMANDS

COMMAND   DESCRIPTION
WHAT'S   ALLOWS USER TO INTERROGATE THE PRODUCT LIST
           TO LEARN EITHER NUMERIC CODE, OR MNEMONIC
           IDENTIFIERS.
           ? WHAT'S 'BETTY CROCKER POTATO BUDS 5 1/4 OZ
           12PK/ CASE'.   ℀
               THE PROGRAM WILL RESPOND WITH 'PROD (102)'
           TO THIS COMMAND.
           ? WHAT'S PROD (114)
               TO THIS, THE PROGRAM WILL RESPOND: BETTY
           CROCKER POTATO W ONION 5 1/4 OZ 12PK/CASE
CALL   ALLOWS EACH USER TO SPECIFY HIS OWN SET OF
           IDENTIFIERS FOR PRODUCTS AND FACTS. PRODUCT
           IDENTIFIERS WILL BE RETAINED, BUT FACT IDENTI—
           FIERS ARE RETAINED ONLY FOR ONE 'PRT' COMMAND.
           ? CALL PROD (102) 'BUDS' THIS COMMAND WOULD IN—
           STRUCT THE PROGRAM THEREAFTER TO REGARD THE
           TERM 'BUDS' AS EQUIVALENT TO '102' AS A
           PRODUCT IDENTIFIER FOR THIS PARTICULAR USER.
           ? CALL FCT ($VOL) 'MARKET SHARE'
           THIS COMMAND WOULD ALLOW THE FACT '$VOL' TO
           BE IDENTIFIED AS 'MARKET SHARE' IN A PRINT—
           OUT.
RET   RETRIEVES INFORMATION SPECIFIED BY THE FOUR IDENTI—
           FIERS, 'MKT', 'PROD', 'PER', AND 'FCT'.
           ? RET MKT (HOU); PROD (102); PER (14); FCT ($VOL)
           ? RET PROD (102; 103; 104); MKT (HOU; STL); FCT
           ($VOL; EQC); PER (11—14)
           THESE COMMANDS WOULD FETCH THE INDICATED DATA
           FROM THE DATA BASE FOR SUBSEQUENT MANIPULATION.
           IF PERFORMED SEQUENTIALLY, THE SECOND WOULD RE—
           PLACE DATA RETRIEVED BY THE FIRST.
PRT   PRINTS THE INFORMATION THAT HAS BEEN RETRIEVED.
           THE ORDER USED TO SPECIFY THE FOUR DATA IDENTI—
           FIERS DETERMINES THE WAY THE INFORMATION IS PRINTED.
           ? PRT PROD; MKT; FCT; PER
           THIS WILL CAUSE PREVIOUSLY RETRIEVED DATA TO BE
           PRINTED WITH PRODUCT AS THE MAJOR HEADING FOL—
           LOWED BY MARKET AS A SUB—HEADING. FACT NAMES
           WILL BE PRINTED ACROSS THE PAGE AND PERIOD NAMES
           DOWN THE PAGE. IF YOU HAD TYPED 'PRT', AND THEN
           A 'RETURN', THE DATA WOULD BE PRINTED OUT IN THE
           SAME FORMAT THAT WAS LAST SPECIFIED.

* Reproduced with permission from C. S. Mayer, C. E. Nugent, and T. E. Vollmann, "On-Line Data Retrieval and Analysis," in B. A. Morin (ed.), *Marketing in a Changing World*, Chicago: American Marketing Association, 1969.

† Underlined entries are typed by the user.

(PER), and fact (FCT). The latter refers to such items of interest as dollar volume ($VOL) or equivalent cases (EQC). The user next has an option to see a list of the 22 MARKINF commands.

Finally, if the user is new to the MARKINF language or if he has forgotten how to use some of the commands, he has the option to request a somewhat detailed description of them. Figure 2 illustrates the description given for four of the commands.

Notice throughout that the user is offered the instructions at his own discretion. Optional instructions are important as a design feature since (1) they meet the needs of the novice or the user who has forgotten how to use parts of the language, but (2) they provide an experienced user with an escape from the frustration of watching a terminal chattering out a long set of instructions which he already knows.

The use of the MARKINF language will be illustrated with the four commands—WHAT, CALL, RET, and PRT—which are detailed in Figure 2.[4] Suppose, for example, that a user wants to retrieve and print the dollar sales volume of 32-ounce "Crunchies" packed 24 to a case in the Philadelphia market for periods 10 to 14. If he doesn't know the product code for this brand/size combination, he may obtain the code from the program by responding to the first question mark with:

WHAT'S CRUNCHIES 32 OZ. 24PK/CASE

and the program would respond,

PROD (106)

The user now has the option to use the computer program code for "Crunchies" (that is, 106), or he may substitute a more convenient name by responding to the next question mark with:

CALL PROD (106) "CRUNCH"

The user may then refer to "CRUNCH" as the product code and the program will recognize this as PROD (106).

The user is now ready to retrieve and print the desired sales information by issuing the RET and PRT commands. The user types:

RET PROD (CRUNCH); MKT (PHIL); PER (10-14); FCT ($VOL)

and

PRT PROD; MKT; PER; FCT

in response to the next two question marks. These commands would cause the following results to be printed:

CRUNCH
PHIL

	10	11	12	13	14
$ VOL	1011	1051	1027	1074	1102

Note in the description of PRT in Figure 2 that the order in which the identifiers are given in the PRT command controls the format of the output. This example illustrates the simplicity and convenience of the MARKINF language.

---

[4] This discussion follows that of Mayer, Nugent, and Vollman [9].

Some of the other commands enable the user to perform more complex data retrieval, analysis, and display. For example, there is a command which will print out a graph. Other commands are available for performing calculations on the data. These include the ability to add, subtract, multiply, and divide. One command enables the user to accumulate the desired fact across two or more markets, products, or periods, and another automatically computes averages. Should the user require the retrieval only of data greater than (or less than) some particular value, the LIM command enables him to specify a desired limit and the system will then only retrieve data which fall in the desired range of values.

As was noted earlier, MARKINF is but one of many possible languages for on-line data retrieval and analysis. For example, Interactive Data Corporation has developed a system called MISTRESS which builds on IDC's First Financial Language, a language for on-line retrieval of financial information. MISTRESS, an acronym for "Marketing Information for Salesmen, Technical Representatives Especially Sales Statistics," provides the user with ready access to a wide variety of information concerning user accounts. Using MISTRESS, a manager can readily develop a series of commands which will retrieve and display the data he wants. Another example is Miller's DATANAL [10], which provides powerful data-management capability. However, its added power comes at a cost of increased complexity, so that it is likely to be used more by sophisticated market researchers than, say, by brand managers.

ON-LINE DATA BANKS

W. R. Simmons and Associates Research has cooperated in the development of an on-line retrieval and display program for their data service [13]. For many years Simmons data on consumer demographics, consumption patterns, media habits, and so on, have supplied valuable information to advertising decision makers and media planners relative to media-selection problems. The data are customarily supplied to users in the form of tabulated reports. However, users from time to time request special tabulations of the data. Prior to the new on-line system, termed the Interactive Market System or IMS, these special requests were serviced by runs on a batch-processing computer with 24- to 48-hour turnaround time. Under IMS, the user receives his answer in a matter of minutes rather than hours, and in his own offices. With the introduction of the rapid interactive turnaround, the user does not require 20-20 foresight concerning all the special tabulations he might want to examine. IMS now enables him to follow up on interesting leads and to adapt his tabulations as his analysis proceeds.

Marketing Control, Inc., also offers on-line access to marketing data banks and analysis [8]. In their World Data Bank they store hundreds of facts about more than 150 countries and nonsovereign areas. The data are gleaned from public sources, such as the United Nations, the Organization for Economic Cooperation and Development, and the *World Almanac,* and contain facts related to social, commercial, and political factors in each area. For example, the commercial data include statistics on consumer expenditures, media availability, and advertising expenditures; social data include economic, demographic, power, transportation, health, language, and religious statistics; political data relate to such areas as government, violence, security, and foreign affiliations. The on-line access to such data facilitates an unusually rapid and convenient use of such data resources in, for example, spotting sales and earnings opportunities abroad, monitoring market performance by country, grouping markets more meaningfully, and establishing marketing goals and priorities by country or region.

Some of the reports available from Marketing Control, Inc. include country profiles and country rankings. Suppose, for example, that a user company is contemplating entering the market in a particular country. In a matter of seconds, the system can print out an extensive profile of that country's current economy, demography, energy consumption, consumer purchases, media availability, advertising expenditures, and political factors. The user might, of course, want to compare the sales potential for his products across countries. The system enables the user to rank countries in terms of the data descriptors, including ratios, products, and sums and differences of the descriptors. For example, a user who produces consumer products might want to rank countries by expenditures in his product class or classes. Further, if the product is best sold by television, he may want to rank the countries by television receivers in use. He may then want a ranking of countries by the ratio of consumer expenditures to television sets in order to obtain a rough idea of the relative sales potential using T.V. All these data and analyses are available to the user in his own office within minutes.

Another firm offering on-line data access is Interactive Data Corporation. IDC offers subscribers access to voluminous amounts of economic and financial data of use in such areas as forecasting of economic conditions in a user's industry and customer-credit decisions. The data are stored in numerous files on a disk drive. For many data series, a user must pay an initial fee for access to the data as well as a variable usage cost. Hence, the system in effect often requires the user to purchase a "library card" before he is allowed use of the data. This mode of operation has the advantage of enabling syndicated data services to offer their data on IDC's interactive system while still maintaining their price structure. As a consequence, much of the data in IDC's system are not proprietary to IDC. Rather, it is a joint offering between IDC, which maintains the software systems (user-oriented retrieval languages and so on), and the data suppliers.

These examples demonstrate that on-line marketing data banks available to multiple subscribers are a current reality. It seems virtually certain that as the decade of the 1970s comes to a close, such data bank systems will have achieved a common place in the tool kit of the marketing manager and the market researcher. Their provision of a rapid, flexible, convenient access to vast amounts of data should lower some of the current barriers to effective market research in support of marketing decisions. Since such systems will likely be developed and marketed to numerous users by service organizations, scale economies in data collection, analysis, and computer software support should make them increasingly attractive.

Measurement-Statistics Bank Applications

Certain of the data- and judgment-based methods which should be incorporated in a measurement-statistics bank have already been outlined [Sec. I, Chap. 4]. Discussion here will focus upon a few examples of the use of such methods in an on-line system.

Marketing Control, Inc.'s Surprise Hunter exemplifies the combined use of data and judgment in marketing planning [8]. For each of 93 food, household, and toiletries products, the Surprise Hunter program provides a data bank of five-year projections of the sizes of those population groups most important to product sales. It is assumed that current purchase rates will prevail. Further, the program estimates the potential effect on sales of selected technological trends. These estimates are based on the processing of expert judgments concerning technological trends which may stimulate large sales changes.   The assumptions used by the experts are spelled out for each product in the *Surprise Hunter Workbook* so that a manager or market researcher may critically evaluate them.   The Surprise Hunter program and projections are available to users via remote-access, time-shared terminals.   The user of the system must specify the product he wishes to consider as well as the percent change in sales for that product over the next five years that will "surprise" him.   He then has the option to provide his own estimates of usage rates, technological impacts, *and their interactions*, or, alternatively, he may use the Surprise Hunter assumptions.   The computer program then prints out whether the assumptions result in a surprisingly large or small sales projection five years hence.   Further, the program shows which assumptions (including interactions) were most important in producing the surprise, and it notes whether the assumption was made by the user or the Surprise Hunter.   Using this program, the user can explore a wide variety of possible projections for his and other products in a matter of minutes.   This should increase his sensitivity to the key future trends over the next five years.

The World Data Bank, discussed in the previous section, enables the user to relate any descriptor variable to any other set of descriptor variables by multiple regression.   For example, if the user is interested in the relation between a country's food consumption and its media expenditures, the World Data Bank will provide summary statistical estimates of this relationship.

The convenience in statistical analysis provided by a well-designed on-line computer program can be illustrated, once again, by MARKINF.   Suppose a market researcher wants to correlate equivalent cases with dollar volume for periods 1 through 14 in St. Louis, Houston, and Boston.   This can be accomplished, using MARKINF, by simply typing the following two lines:

RET PROD (102); PER (1-14); MKT(STL; HOU; BOS); FCT ($VOL)
COR FCT (EQC)

The first line retrieves the proper data, a process which often is rather cumbersome and time-consuming in manual or batch-processing systems.   The second command initiates the statistical analysis which generates the following output:[5]

```
100% OF THE CHANGE IS EXPLAINED
DO YOU REQUIRE STATISTICAL DETAIL?   YES
NUMBER = 42        SLOPE = 0.113153
COEFFICIENT OF CORRELATION = 0.999311
ADJ INDEX OF DETERMINATION = 0.998587
MEAN OF X = 2164.79      OF Y = 250.119
Y-INTERCEPT = 5.16804
SUM-OF-SQUARES
                 TOTAL       4128889
                 MEAN        2.6275 E+6
                 SLOPE       1.49932 E+6
                 RESIDUAL    2069.36
STANDARD DEVIATIONS
                 X           1690.02
                 Y           191.362
                 ERROR       7.19263
                 Y-BAR       1.10955
                 SLOPE       6.64668 E−4
     F-RATIO FOR SLOPE = 28981.3
```

[5] From [10].

Notice that the user is given the option either to suppress or to print the statistical detail.

In addition to its correlation ability, MARKINF also provides multiple regression, trend analysis, and exponential smoothing forecasts. Miller's DATANAL provides an excellent statistical package (especially nonparametric statistics) for the somewhat more sophisticated analyst.

The Stanford Research Institute's PROMENADE system provides for on-line graphical analysis of data [1]. The system provides for more than two dimensional plots, and a user may use the program, in effect, to view his data from virtually any angle, even though it be a multidimensional scatter of points. The sophistication of PROMENADE does require that an expert system operator assist the analyst in using the system.

Model Bank Applications

Experience in the development and implementation of on-line models has led to the concept which Little [5] has labeled a *management decision calculus*. In this section, the concept will be defined and an outline given of desirable design features and the process of developing such an approach. Following this is a discussion of several on-line model applications.

A Decision Calculus. A decision calculus is a model-based set of procedures for processing judgments and data to assist a manager in his decision making. Little [5] suggests that a decision calculus should be:[6]

1. *Simple.* Only important phenomena and variables should be included. Users often generate considerable pressure to increase complexity and detail in a model. The model developers should resist this tendency until the users demonstrate an ability to handle the increased detail. Parsimonious inclusion of variables and phenomena promotes ease of communication between the model builders and the user as well as ease of understanding for the user.

2. *Robust.* The structure should constrain answers to a reasonable range of values. The model should be so designed as to make it difficult for implausible answers to result from inputs. Nothing will reduce a model's chances of successful implementation like a "stupid answer" in its early stages of use.

3. *Easy to control.* The user should be able to make the model respond in the way he wants it to. That is, he should be able to set inputs in order to obtain nearly any outputs.

    But doesn't this mean that a manager will then simply fudge the inputs until he gets the answer he wants? Two factors would seem to counter this problem: (1) Most managers seem honestly to want help with their decision problems and seem unlikely to abuse this ability and (2) their input assumptions are subject to review by others.

    Although one would like to have objective inputs throughout the model, this utopian state is infrequently realized in marketing. Marketing-decision problems will probably always involve a major amount of judgmental input for their solution. The decision calculus notion, then, is that if management judgment is to be an important component, the manager should be left in control. The model structure and its parameterization should represent the world as the manager sees it. If he is not in some sense in control, he will generally be reluctant to use the model. The key is to provide him with a decision aid, not a decision maker, which he will use.

4. *Adaptive.* It should be easy to alter the parameters and structure of the model as new information or insights become available. Again, this is the notion of systems evolution.

5. *Complete on important issues.* In counterpoint to simplicity, the model should be complete on important issues. The phenomena which the manager con-

[6] This discussion follows Little [5].

siders important must be capable of representation either explicitly in the model structure or implicitly as conditioning factors for specific parameter assumptions.

6. *Easy to communicate with.* The user should be able to change input assumptions readily and receive outputs rapidly. This will enable the manager to explore a broad range of alternatives and evaluate a wide variety of assumptions in using the model. It also enables a user to gain familiarity with, and confidence in, a model quickly during early stages of implementation or, say, when a new manager takes over a job. On-line computers and conversational programs make easy communication possible.

These desiderata for a decision calculus indicate that the focus is upon providing the user with a decision-relevant tool. In contrast to what the management scientist might traditionally try to build, a decision calculus model focuses on *decision relevance* and *implementation* rather than on elegance.

The following steps are involved in developing a decision calculus model:

1. *Determine the manager's "implicit model" of how the market works.* This is to assure that the model will be relevant and understandable to the manager. The process will take advantage of the manager's knowledge and experience, will educate the model builder, and will promote communication between the manager and the model builder. Another benefit is that this involves the manager in the model-building process so that the resultant model will be his model rather than something imposed upon him by the market research staff.

2. *Translate the manager's model into a formal structure.* The model should represent in the simplest fashion possible the critical variables and processes which the manager has identified as important. At this stage, one should seek to identify inconsistencies in the formulation and identify areas of incomplete and uncertain knowledge. This is likely to lead to an iterative recycling with step 1.

3. *Develop procedures for parameterizing the model.* Naturally, whenever relevant, objective data exist, they should be used. For those aspects of the model which require judgment, procedures must be developed which allow managers to quantify their judgments about market response. An important design issue at this stage is to phrase the questions relating to judgmental input in operational terms. For example, a manager may be able to make a reasonable judgment concerning the percent change in sales he would anticipate from a percent change in advertising, but he would probably have great difficulty in making a direct judgment of the advertising elasticity of his sales.

4. *Develop an interactive program.* Bring the model to the manager via an on-line, conversational computer program and a remote terminal.

Steps 1 through 3 are likely to be performed iteratively as a project progresses. They also involve the most time in development. In a successful application to sales-effort allocation across a multiproduct line, Montgomery, Silk, and Zaragoza [11] spent about ten weeks part-time on the first three steps and only about two weeks on the computer programming, again part-time.

ON-LINE MODELS

An important aspect of an on-line model is the development of an easy-to-use conversational program. An illustration of such a program is given in Figure 3 for ADBUDG I, a conversational model for advertising-budgeting decisions [5]. The user is first given the option to input new data or to reference data which he has previously inputted and saved in file storage. By typing "1," the user indicates that he wants to input new data and the program proceeds to request

Fig. 3. ADBUDG—An advertising budgeting model.

```
1 INPUT NEW DATA
2 USE SAVED DATA
ANS=1

TYPE NAME FOR BRAND
ANS=BRANDX

MARKET SHARE IN % AT CURRENT ADV. BUDGET
ANS=20

LATEST YEAR ADVERTISING BUDGET IN THOUSANDS OF DOLLARS
ANS=5000

WHAT MARKET SHARE WOULD YOU ESTIMATE
IF ADVERTISING WERE REDUCED TO ZERO?
ANS=10

WHAT MARKET SHARE WOULD YOU ESTIMATE
AT A SATURATION OF ADVERTISING?
ANS=30

IF THE ADVERTISING BUDGET WERE INCREASED 50 %,
WHAT WOULD YOU ESTIMATE TO BE THE MARKET SHARE?
ANS=24

GROSS PROFIT MARGIN OF OUR BRAND AS % OF SALES DOLLAR
ANS=45

LATEST YEARS INDUSTRY SALES IN THOUSANDS OF DOLLARS
ANS=20000

LATEST YEAR INDUSTRY ADVERTISING IN THOUSANDS OF DOLLARS
ANS=20000

INDUSTRY SALES IF ADVERTISING WERE REDUCED TO ZERO
ANS=100000

ESTIMATED INDUSTRY SALES IF ADVERTISING WERE INCREASED TO
SATURATION
ANS=175000

IF INDUSTRY ADVERTISING INCREASE 50 %
WHAT WOULD YOU ESTIMATE TO BE THE INDUSTRY SALES?
ANS=160000

1          SAVE DATA
2          CHANGE DATA
3          PRINT DATA
4          CALCULATE
5          RESTART
ANS=2

1          BRAND DATA
2          INDUSTRY DATA
3          CHANGES FINISHED
ANS=2

1          INDUSTRY ADV
2          MIN SALES
3          MAX SALES
4          SALES WITH INCREASED ADV
5          SALES WITH CURRENT ADV
6          NONE
ANS=5
```

Fig. 3. (Continued).

```
LATEST YEAR'S INDUSTRY SALES IN THOUSANDS OF DOLLARS
ANS=150000
1            BRAND DATA
2            INDUSTRY DATA
3            CHANGES FINISHED
ANS=3

1            SAVE DATA
2            CHANGE DATA
3            PRINT DATA
4            CALCULATE
5            RESTART
ANS=3

1            NAME BRANDX
2            SHARE 20.00
3            AD BUDGET 5000.
4            MIN SHARE 10.00
5            MAX SHARE 30.00
6            SHARE WITH INCREASE ADV 24.00
7            MARGIN 45.00

1            INDUSTRY ADV 20000.
2            MIN SALES 100000.
3            MAX SALES 175000.
4            SALES WITH INCREASED ADV 160000.
5            SALES WITH CURRENT ADV 150000.

1            SAVE DATA
2            CHANGE DATA
3            PRINT DATA
4            CALCULATE
5            RESTART

ANS=4

MIN. AD. BUDGET TO BE CONSIDERED IN THOUSANDS OF DOLLARS
ANS=4000

MAX. BUDGET TO BE CONSIDERED
ANS=7000

NUMBER OF INTERMEDIATE BUDGETS
ANS=11
```

	RESULTS FOR BRANDX		
AD BUDGET	SALES	CONT. TO	MARKET
(000)	(000)	PROFIT	SHARE
		(000)	
4000.	26302.	7836.	17.7%
4250.	27275.	8024.	18.3%
4500.	28218.	8198.	18.9%
4750.	29127.	8357.	19.5%
5000.	30000.	8500.	20.0%
5250.	30836.	8626.	20.5%
5500.	31635.	8736	21.0%
5750.	32398.	8829.	21.5%
6000.	33123.	8905.	21.9%
6250.	33813.	8966.	22.3%
6500.	34469.	9011.	22.7%
6705.	35092.	9041.	23.0%
7000.	35683.	9057.	23.4%

```
1            SAVE DATA
2            CHANGE DATA
3            PRINT DATA
4            CALCULATE
5            RESTART
TIME USED 0:0:03 IN 0:21:31
```

both historical data (for example, last year's advertising budget) and the manager's judgments (such as what the brand's market share would be one year hence if a saturation advertising compaign were run) with respect to both the brand and the industry in which the brand competes. After supplying the necessary inputs, the user is given the choice of saving these new data in file storage, changing one of the inputs, printing out a summary of the inputs, calculating results using the given inputs and the model structure, or restarting the input process.

At this point, the user in Figure 3 notices that he has erred in answering the question concerning last year's industry sales, so he types "2," which will allow him to selectively change his answer. Error-correction options are an important feature for convenient use. He first specifies the category of data he wishes to change (industry data) and then indicates that it is last year's sales that need to be changed. When the changes are complete, he is again given the option to save the data or to give some other instruction. At this point, he indicates that he wants to see a summary printout of the inputs. This gives him an opportunity to verify the inputs and provides him with a summary hard-copy record of the input assumptions he has made on this run of the model.

Since he is satisfied with the input, he now directs the program to use the input data to calculate sales, contribution to profits, and market share for the brand at different levels of the advertising budget. The user specifies the minimum and maximum budgets as well as the number of intermediate levels he wants to consider. The program then uses the inputs to establish parameters for functions relating sales and market share to advertising expenditures.

Once the calculated output is printed, the user may save the data for later, change one or more of his input assumptions, reprint the data, calculate results for a different range and number of budgets, or restart, perhaps with another brand. The terminal session illustrated in Figure 3 used only three seconds of computer time and involved the user's sitting at the terminal for two to three minutes.

The model just described is a vastly oversimplified one, initially developed to illustrate on-line models to managers. It has been used effectively for this purpose in a number of companies. (For example, see [11].) Little [5] has developed a much more comprehensive model, ADBUDG II, for actual use in decision making. ADBUDG II incorporates multiperiod effects including time lags in sales response, media efficiency, copy effectiveness, and a composite index of nonadvertising effects such as promotions, packaging, and competitive actions. In a yet more comprehensive model, BRANDAID, the nonadvertising effects are treated more explicitly. Other implemented conversational models include MEDIAC [6], a model for media selection, DETAILER [11], a model for allocation of sales effort across an ethical-drug product line, and CALLPLAN [7], a model to assist salesmen in planning their calling strategies.

One of the most advanced companies in the development of on-line marketing models and information systems has been Pillsbury. It has been reported that Pillsbury marketing managers have access to over 30 on-line models for assistance in the analysis of a wide variety of marketing problems [14].

As a case in point, consider the following on-line planning system. The user is first given the option to deal with one or more products or perhaps all products. Hence he can choose the appropriate level of aggregation for his problem. Once he has specified the product(s) he wants to consider, the program retrieves and prints out historical results for the past five years. It then automatically prints out a profit and loss statement for each of the next five years, based upon a projection of the historical results [4]. The user is then given the opportunity to change any of these historical projections, based upon his judgment. For example, suppose, for a product under consideration, that price dropped two years ago and has since remained at the lower level. The projection based upon historical trend would then indicate a steady decline in price over the planning period. If the manager believes that the price level will hold steady for the next five years, he may replace the historical projection with this assumption. At this stage, the manager must input his reference or base case in terms of price and expenditures on advertising and promotion, should he want to consider something different from historical trends. Once the base case is established, incorporating any changes the manager wishes to make in the projections, a base-case profit and loss statement is printed for each of the next five years.

The program now supplies the manager with a tool for exploring the possibility that alterations in the base levels of price, advertising, and promotion may lead to more desirable results. The effects of changes from the base case are assessed by means of a simple model structure which incorporates the mix effects of price, advertising, and promotion as well as time dependency representing cumulative and carry-over effects from previous marketing activities.

Perhaps the weakest link in the system is that the managers are asked to input the parameters of the response function directly. Since these parameters are essentially the sales elasticities with respect to the marketing variables, they are scarcely in operational terms. A better approach would be for the program to interrogate the manager for his judgment concerning the sales results which might be achieved under varying levels of each of the marketing variables. The program should then undertake the task of translating the manager's responses into the parameters required by the response function.

Once the response parameters have been supplied, the manager may use the program to compute and print out the profit and loss statement for any level of price, advertising, and promotion he wishes to study. After trying all the marketing alternatives he wants to consider for a given set of response parameters, he is given the option of trying a new set of response parameters.

Pillsbury managers may deal with the risk aspects of a five-year plan by calling for a risk profile. This program provides an assessment of the quartile distribution of sales and profits as well as an indication of the probability of a loss and the probability of missing a standard.

As a final example, consider the application of an on-line model and data display system to the problem of coordinating marketing and production at the washer and dryer division of Westinghouse [12]. The system used graphical display terminals and utilized the same data, models, and analytic approaches which had been in use before the graphical system was installed. Hence, the graphical system added nothing more nor less than the capacity for interactive graphical display of such items as forecasted and observed sales, production, and inventory by product over several time periods. Yet it changed the decision-making style drastically. Prior to the installation of the interactive graphical system, the three top managers who were charged with coordinating marketing and production would spend about three weeks of calendar time and six man-days to develop a plan. With the installation of the system, they could develop the plan in a single session at the interactive video console. Calendar time required to plan was reduced from three weeks to half a day, and the executive time commitment dropped from six man-days to one. Thus the interactive graphical capability released valuable executive time. Furthermore, it made the organization more responsive to planning errors, since the time required to correct a plan was dramatically reduced. It was also felt that decision making had improved as a result of the use of this system. This Westinghouse interactive graphics example illustrates the impact which on-line systems will have on management's decision-making processes.

Summary

On-line computers have had useful application in all phases of balanced marketing information and decision systems, as illustrated by these examples. The future seems certain to bring increasingly widespread use of on-line systems in marketing and marketing research.

ADVANTAGES OF INTERACTIVE ON-LINE SYSTEMS

Perhaps the major benefit from on-line systems is that they drastically reduce the barriers to systematic analysis of marketing problems. Analysis is often inhibited by the time-consuming and difficult process of data retrieval and data analysis. Further, systems oriented to batch processing make sequential analysis of problems a most arduous task. In such systems, the user is faced with either the need for 20-20 foresight as to what analyses he wishes to perform or the necessity to return sequentially to the batch system as he follows up on suggestive leads generated during prior analysis. Similar barriers exist when it comes to an examination of the sensitivity of a model or a statistical analysis to input assumptions. Lip service is given to sensitivity analysis, but all too often it is little practiced.

Manual or batch-oriented systems tend to be costly in both calendar time and user time. Calendar time is lost because of the often considerable turnaround time for jobs submitted to the corporate computer department. Delays are caused by the queue of jobs facing the computer, and they become especially acute at certain times of the month or year as the batch computer performs its necessary payroll, accounting, and financial reporting tasks. The backup can lead to frustrating, and at times devastating, delays in the solution of marketing problems. Management time may be lost through the user's need to refresh himself on the problem at hand once the batch-processing output is finally available. Furthermore, the manager's natural problem-solving processes are likely to be disrupted by the delays. Therefore, marketing managers tend to be discouraged from using more formal methods of analysis in solving their marketing problems. If analysis is useful, then severe opportunity losses may result because of these barriers to analysis.

Yet analysis promises to provide considerable returns to marketing management. Recall [from Sec. I, Chap. 4] the performance advantage that a simple competitive bidding model gave to R.C.A. [3]. It should be noted here that that bidding model is an interactive on-line model. Other planning examples would include the Pillsbury system [4], which combines financial reports with a structure relating marketing inputs to these financial results, and the MEDIAC media-selection model, which has been successfully implemented by media planners [6]. Furthermore, the time pressure in making future decisions often leaves the marketing manager with little time to analyze the antecedents of past success or failure. Since interpretation of the factors underlying former performance will have impact on judgments about the future, it seems imperative that marketing management, with the aid of market researchers, attempt to assess the effects of these factors.

On-line systems, by providing a rapid, easy-to-use, and flexible framework for analysis, have contributed greatly to the development of marketing information and decision systems. They have reduced the barriers to analysis in many situations in which it might otherwise not be undertaken. This is not, of course, to say that manual and batch-processing systems no longer have a role. Rather, it is to emphasize that interactive computer systems have provided a new dimension to marketing information and decision systems.

At the data bank level, on-line systems provide for convenient and timely data retrieval. As noted earlier [Sec. I, Chap. 4], this capability provides the manager with the opportunity for data browsing and sequential diagnosis of problems. This facilitates problem finding before standard methods would "flag" an emerging problem situation. It also provides the opportunity to reduce paper flow, as in the IBM system outlined earlier, by giving the user immediate, selective access to the data he requires.

For the measurement-statistics bank, on-line systems facilitate sequential analysis. This is especially helpful in exploratory phases of research and in giving statistical analysis support to the development of models. In making statistical analyses of relationships relatively easy, on-line systems should facilitate systematic learning from experience.

In the model bank, on-line computers have made conversational models, such as ADBUDG [5] and DETAILER [11], feasible. Thus managers are enabled to explore a broad range of alternatives, rather than a selected few, by delegating numerical drudgery to the computer while retaining for themselves what they do best—supplying judgment. Furthermore, on-line models make sensitivity analysis somewhat simpler. A special case of this is the way in which managers generally familiarize themselves with interactive models. They usually try a variety of alternative inputs and then examine the implied outputs to see if they make sense. In this way the potential user gets a "feeling" for how the model responds and thereby can assess for himself how much confidence he is willing to place in it.

The advent of on-line computers has given rise to the development of computer utilities. A computer utility rents time on its hardware and software systems to many users in reasonably small economic units. The user only pays for the service he uses plus some fixed fee for his terminal (if he rents one) and for his account with the utility. This means that small to medium-sized companies may now take advantage of advanced computer technology. On-line computer utilities have spawned yet another service, the model utility. In a model utility, an interactive model is made available to numerous users via a computer utility. Hence, companies of modest size may now have access to advanced marketing models. For example, MEDIAC is available as a model utility which can be used by small agencies [6]. Lastly, it should be pointed out that interactive on-line computers are extremely useful for editing and debugging computer programs, even those which will be used in a batch operation. The speed and convenience of on-line program editing are what made the development of the initial DETAILER program absorb only two weeks of part-time programming [11].

Although on-line computers offer many advantages, there are certain problems associated with their use. For example:

1. There is some tendency to use available on-line systems in instances where interaction offers little benefit. This is costly since computation and file storage on on-line systems are expensive relative to batch systems.

2. Access to the system from a terminal can be a problem during peak-load periods. The number of terminals an on-line system can handle simultaneously is limited. Consequently, during peak periods, a would-be user might well find that he cannot use the system because of its being full. Furthermore, even if he is able to get on the system, the fact that many users are currently on the system means that the response time is likely to be poor; that is, the user will have to wait a while for the system to respond.

3. Since the terminals in on-line systems are generally remote from the

central computer, transmission errors can become a problem. Although one can go to high-grade data lines and multiplexing, as discussed in an earlier section, transmission errors will likely remain as a source of frustration in the use of on-line systems.

4. Managers and other users exhibit some tendency not to think out a problem sufficiently when seated at a terminal. The question here is what happens to planning and judgment when the meter is running. The answer is to train personnel to shut off the terminal and spend some time thinking periodically during the planning process.

As a final note, it should be mentioned that documentation is crucial in such systems. Great care must be given to assuring that proper records will be kept concerning such things as what was done in a planning session and what code structures were used for data.

SUMMARY

This chapter has outlined the structure of on-line computer systems in nontechnical terms. It has then examined applications of on-line computers in data banks, measurement-statistics banks, and model banks. Finally, a brief look was taken at certain of the advantages of on-line systems.

REFERENCES

1. Ball, G. H., and D. J. Hall, "Some Implications of Interactive Graphic Computer Systems for Data Analysis and Statistics," *Technometrics*, vol. 12, February 1970.
2. Cox, D. F., and R. E. Good, "How to Build a Marketing Information System," *Harvard Business Review*, vol. 45, May–June 1967.
3. Edelman, F., "Art and Science of Competitive Bidding," *Harvard Business Review*, vol. 43, July–August 1965.
4. Eskin, G. J., and R. Dabbah, "Toward a Planning Oriented Marketing Information System," in B. A. Morin (ed.), *Marketing in a Changing World*, Chicago: American Marketing Association, 1969.
5. Little, J. D. C., "Models and Managers: The Concept of a Decision Calculus," *Management Science: Applications*, vol. 15, April 1970.
6. Little, J. D. C., and L. M. Lodish, "A Media Planning Calculus," *Operations Research*, vol. 17, January–February 1969.
7. Lodish, L. M., "CALLPLAN, an Interactive Salesman's Call Planning System," in D. B. Montgomery (ed.), *Management Science: Professional Issue—Marketing Management Models*, December 1971.
8. Marketing Control, Inc., "The World Data Bank" and "The Surprise Hunter," brochures, New York, 1970.
9. Mayer, C. S., C. E. Nugent, and T. E. Vollmann, "On-Line Data Retrieval and Analysis," in B. A. Morin (ed.), *Marketing in a Changing World*, Chicago: American Marketing Association, 1969.
10. Miller, J. R., "DATANAL: An Interpretive Language for On-Line Analysis of Empirical Data," working paper, Cambridge, Mass.: M.I.T., Sloan School of Management, 1967.
11. Montgomery, D. B., A. J. Silk, and C. C. Zaragoza, "A Multiproduct Sales Force Allocation Model," in D. B. Montgomery (ed.), *Management Science: Professional Issue—Marking Management Models*, vol. 18, December 1971.
12. Morton, M. S. S., "Interactive Visual Display Systems and Management Problem Solving," *Industrial Management Review*, vol. 9, Fall 1967.
13. Ness, D., and C. R. Sprague, "A Flexible System to Retrieve, Manipulate, and Display Information from a Stable, Questionnaire Oriented Data Base: Parts I, II, and III," working paper, Cambridge, Mass.: M.I.T., Sloan School of Management, 1970.
14. Sales Management, "Computerizing the Line Manager," vol. 102, April 1, 1969.

Section Three

Behavioral Science

Part A

Techniques

Chapter 1

General Concepts

IRVING CRESPI   *The Gallup Organization, Inc., Princeton, New Jersey*

INTRODUCTION

Marketing research is related to the behavioral sciences in a manner largely analogous to the relationship between engineering and the physical sciences. In both instances, the relationship is between a field seeking solution to action-oriented problems and a field whose endeavors focus on the acquisition of basic knowledge. Specifically, marketing researchers seek to obtain valid information bearing on people's behavior insofar as it relates to the solution of marketing problems.

Marketing can be understood as a process of interaction among producers, distributors, buyers, and users. That is, marketing is a process involving economic relationships between individuals and groups, the individuals differing in their personalities and motivations and the groups to which they belong differing in their organization and in the standards of behavior to which their members are expected to conform. Stated in these terms, marketing is a specific type of interactional process of the many types that behavioral scientists investigate, while marketing research is the action-oriented investigation of this process.

The goal of marketing research is to develop an understanding of the marketing process as it manifests itself in actual situations in order to guide one of the participants, namely, the marketer. Although a market researcher may not be particularly concerned with developing general theories of how and why people behave as they do, such theories can be directly relevant to the design of a marketing research project. Moreover, research methods that have been effective in testing these theories, albeit on altogether different types of behavior, are as applicable to the analysis of consumer behavior as to the analysis of any other form of behavior. Methods for analyzing how choices are made and acted on are as useful in the study of brand preference as in the study of occupational choice. Techniques for measuring communications effects are equally applicable to the study of propaganda, education, and advertising. Because of this, marketing researchers have been able to use profitably the theories and research methods developed by behavioral scientists.

To place the behavioral sciences within the framework of marketing research, this chapter starts with a brief historical sketch of the behavioral sciences' emergence which describes the content and methodological principles of the disciplines that comprise these sciences. With this foundation, the relevance of the behavioral sciences to marketing research is described by outlining the way borrowed research techniques and concepts have been used by marketing researchers. Finally, by way of review and summary, a classification of research methods is developed.

CONTENT AND METHODOLOGICAL PRINCIPLES OF THE BEHAVIORAL SCIENCES

The influence of the behavioral sciences on marketing research during the 1950s and 1960s has been both immediate and pervasive. During these two decades, a host of research techniques have been borrowed from psychologists and sociologists, and the methodological repertoire of marketing research has thus been considerably enriched. But the contribution of the behavioral sciences cannot be encompassed by cataloging research techniques. There is also a behavioral science viewpoint of man, a *style of research*, that has pervaded marketing research and, in the process, fundamentally changed it. *Marketing* researchers have acquired a way of looking at consumer behavior that leads to asking questions that would never have occurred to an earlier generation of *market* researchers. Hence, before discussing the specific ways in which behavioral sciences techniques have been adopted by marketing researchers, it is of value to outline the ingredients of this distinctive viewpoint.

Before the 1950s *behaviorism* referred to one of several competing intellectual traditions in the social sciences. By the mid-1960s, however, the term *behavioral science* had largely displaced the older concept of *social science*. Psychology, social psychology, and sociology had become virtually synonymous with behavioral science, while in the fields of political science, anthropology, and to a lesser degree economics, there were increasing numbers of behaviorists. This transition from social science to behavioral science is to some degree merely semantic, involving the substitution of a new name without any substantive change. However, it also reflects the triumph of a methodological orientation and, concomitantly, a theoretical one. The extent to which marketing research uses behavioral-science techniques consequently indicates the extent to which one of the many intellectual traditions in the social sciences has come to be regarded as relevant to marketing.

During the nineteenth century and well into the twentieth, as the social sciences were developing, considerable controversy focused on whether the physical sciences were an appropriate theoretical and methodological model for the social sciences. Those in the affirmative maintained that human behavior is interpretable in a "natural" causal form. That is, by systematic, empirical investigation it is possible to analyze and explain human behavior in terms of cause-effect relationships without recourse to metaphysical forces and processes. Man is part of the "natural" world, it was argued, and should be studied as part of it. The scientific investigation of man, the argument continues, requires adherence to the same rules of scientific research as apply to any of the natural sciences—physical, chemical, or biological.   The methodological problem facing the social sciences from this perspective was to invent techniques of observation and/or experimentation suitable to the study of man. ·

What Constitutes "Data" for the Social Scientist?

Solving this methodological problem involved varying difficulty for the many disciplines that constitute the social sciences, in large part because each faced different tasks in identifying what constitutes data suitable for scientific analysis.   For the economist, interested in such phenomena as supply and demand, price and wage, investment and capital formation, cycles of inflation and deflation, "factual information" usable as economic data was already in existence. Although the reliability of this information about the economy was often questionable, its meaning not always clear, and its coverage always scanty, economists had the advantage of starting with concepts that appeared to be naturally measurable.   The reason for this is that the existence of a monetary form of exchange makes it possible to apply "ratio scales" (the most rigorous kind of measurement of the type used in the physical sciences) to most, if not all, economic data.

Classical economics, taking for granted market organization, was not concerned with how such activity becomes organized.   Focusing on the measurement and analysis of the market as given, economists largely ignored questions about the roots of economic behavior.   Not until the beginning of the twentieth century did maverick economists like Thorstein Veblen attempt to analyze economic processes in terms of such motivational concepts as "conspicuous consumption," "pecuniary emulation," and "conspicuous leisure."   Most economists, however, continued to neglect the study of how "noneconomic" factors such as motivation and institutional forms influence the economy.   It is true that the development of econometrics, a wedding of mathematical models and statistics, generated interest in the application of mathematical models to market phenomena.   However, the models as constructed were intended for use with data (such as price) which are the *consequence* of economic behavior, not with data about economic behavior as such.   More recently, the use of behavioral data— for example, survey data on buying intentions—as input for forecasting models has interested some economists.

In contrast, sociologists, by definition, had to cope with the problem of how to deal objectively and empirically with such concepts as group, institution, community, cooperation, conflict, social control, social organization, social change, and status and role.   So difficult is this methodological problem that many concluded that sociology could not use mathematical models as espoused by some but instead must develop its own methodology involving the construction of conceptual models that could be understood subjectively.   Moreover, both the mathematical and conceptual schools faced the problem of what constituted sociological data as distinct from personal observation—however perceptive that observation might be.   Before sociologists could attempt to analyze cause-effect relationships, they had to develop methods for observing and recording sociological phenomena.

During the nineteenth century, a few areas of sociological interest proved to be comparatively amenable to objective, empirical methods, namely, those for which a statistical approach was suitable.   For example, demographers and analysts of deviant behavior found official statistics, such as those regarding births, deaths, crime, and suicide, a fruitful starting point.   Another and comparable nineteenth-century development was the compilation of family budgets as a means of analyzing family structure.   Most important of all was pioneering the "social survey" as a means of measuring social problems, such as poverty, during the last decades of the nineteenth century.

Thus, even while sociologists encountered serious difficulty in attempting to operationalize their conceptual framework, they were developing methods for compiling and analyzing statistical data that were, however imperfectly, related to their theoretical interests. At the risk of oversimplification, it can be said that these methods largely related to the question of measuring the evidence of behavioral forms in a way that could be validly related to group structures. In practice this meant the application of statistical theory to sample design and the analysis of survey data.

Comparable developments occurred during the nineteenth and early twentieth centuries in psychology. The mind-body controversy involved both theoretical and methodological issues. If psychological phenomena are essentially a manifestation of somatic (bodily) processes, the laboratory methods of neurologists provide an appropriate model for psychologists, for example, measurement of galvanic skin response and pupil dilation. If, on the other hand, the "mental" constitutes a different order of reality, new research techniques, such as introspection, would have to be developed. The question whether emotions are to be understood as subjective states of mind or as an aspect of physiological processes involving, for example, the endocrine glands illustrates this controversy. Similarly, intelligence could be defined either as a qualitative faculty or as the learning capability of an organism's nervous system. Whether it is possible to talk meaningfully about personality, perception, intelligence, motivation, learning, and remembering as psychic or somatic processes became a central concern of psychologists in their attempt to define what constitutes psychological data.

Those psychologists who adopted the experimental, laboratory method as their research model quickly became involved in problems of psychometrics, that is, how to measure somatic responses that could be considered "psychological." If one wants to deal experimentally, for example, with sensory processes, it is necessary to define whether, and in what sense, the sensations of weight, color, odor, pain, and so forth can be measured. The distinctiveness of ratio, interval, and ordinal measurements, and the limitations of each, became matters of central concern in such endeavors. Moreover, it was soon determined that sensations such as taste, color, heat, and odor varied as functions of both the individual's neurophysiological state and the total field of perception. This considerably complicates any attempt to measure perception objectively.

Defining intelligence operationally presents comparable problems, among which one of the most significant has been whether intelligence consists of a unitary learning capability or, alternatively, of several distinct factors which could be objectively defined by some appropriate statistical model, namely, factor analysis. Of equal significance has been the question of how to parcel out the effects of various influences on intelligence, such as genetically determined capability versus acquired abilities. Also central to much psychological research are the twin problems of the reliability of any measurement and techniques for controlling variables experimentally. Investigating how learning takes place, for example, took the form of experimentally varying the application of rewards and punishments in problem-solving situations—for example, discovering how to get past a barrier to food—and then applying statistical tests of significance to determine under which conditions learning occurs most effectively.

The interests of psychologists and sociologists converge with respect to (1) how individual behavior is patterned or conditioned by such factors as group membership and social values and (2) how patterns of group behavior emerge from the interaction of individuals.

Out of this convergence has developed the field of social psychology concerned with such issues as these: In what ways do the social roles that an individual plays—parent, teenager, religious communicant, housewife, wage earner, etc.—shape his personality? How do group memberships and values influence an individual's memory, perception, motivation, aspiration level, and judgment? How are characteristics of groups, such as morale, decision making, conflict, and leadership related to, for example, the satisfaction or frustration of individual motives? To what extent are social trends, such as the widespread adoption of new behavior patterns and changes in a society's basic value system, interpretable in terms of learning and/or psychodynamic theories of individual behavior?

Questions such as these presuppose that human behavior can best be analyzed as a dynamic process between individuals and their social environments. Thus one must know who are the "significant others," that is, persons whose affection and judgment are important to an individual, if he wants to understand his personality. Similarly, if one wants to understand how groups influence an individual's behavior, he must know his "reference groups," that is, the groups whose standards he adopts whether or not he actually is a member.

In investigating these questions, social psychologists have concentrated on the study of (1) personality as the socialization of the human organism and (2) group process as the interaction among individuals playing different roles. The analysis of motivation as a dynamic process whereby individuals learn more or less adequately to gratify their needs within a social setting has been important in such investigations. Thus the concept of "relative deprivation," that is, how deprived one feels relative to one's level of aspiration, has proved extremely useful in studying frustration. Similarly, the investigation of attitudes as an intervening variable—consisting of a system of beliefs, values, preferences, and feelings—between organism and society has been the focus of considerable research. For example, in group situations there is a strong tendency for individuals to adjust their perceptions of reality and their opinions to the group norm.

The methods used for investigating personality and group process, using either the conceptual framework of motivation or attitudes, have been borrowed from both psychologists and sociologists. From the former has come the interest in measurement and experimental control within laboratory settings, while from the latter has come the style of measurement in natural settings by means of the sample survey. From both has come a tendency to rely heavily on acquisition of attitudinal data, either through interviews or self-administered questionnaires. Although direct observation of behavior has been most typical of the psychological laboratory, social psychologists have drawn from both disciplines in developing techniques whereby an observer can code individual and group behavior directly in a manner analogous to coding a questionnaire.

Variations in Methodology in the Behavioral Sciences

The core behavioral sciences of sociology, psychology, and social psychology, in summary, are characterized by a common methodological orientation, namely, the invention of techniques for measuring and analyzing variations and consistencies in human behavior that can be analyzed objectively. It would be wrong, however, to conclude that there is any one method that can be considered *the* method of behavioral science. Behavioral scientists disagree among themselves on (1) the nature of social and psychological reality and (2) the extent to which this reality can be analyzed mathematically.

Illustrative of the controversy on the nature of social reality are the conflicting theoretical orientations underlying two techniques of attitude measurement: (1) Osgood's semantic differential and (2) Cantril's self-anchoring scale. The semantic differential was developed as a method for objectively defining "semantic space," that is, the dimensions of thought. Through factor analysis of semantic scale scores, Osgood defined three basic dimensions of thought—activity, evaluation, and strength. Using these three dimensions in combination with others that are also definable through factor analysis, Osgood concludes that any given concept occupies a unique position in the space delimited by these dimensions. Semantic space, consequently, is an "objective" reality in that it exists independent of the consciousness of any one person.

Cantril's self-anchoring scale, in contrast, requires a person to define what he means by some concept, for example, happiness, satisfaction, or life goals [5]. He then rates himself, his family, his country, and so forth in terms of his own definition using an appropriate scale device, such as an 11-rung ladder. The self-anchoring scale assumes that psychological reality exists in an individual's interpretation and evaluation of his sense perceptions. That is, rather than looking for an objective reality, it seeks to discover the "phenomenological reality" that emerges through an individual's transactions with his environment.

Independent of the issue of the nature of psychological and social reality is the question whether data can and must be organized quantitatively if they are to be analyzed objectively. As noted previously, the methodological tradition of these behavioral scientists, however, is the measurability of the phenomena they investigate. They take as axiomatic the adage that not until something has been measured is it known. Considerable ingenuity has characterized their efforts to obtain *some kind* of mathematical model, usually statistical, that could be used in their analysis.

For this reason, these behavioral scientists have been concerned with problems such as those attendant to the limitations of ordinal scaling methods. (Rating scales, paired comparisons, ranking, and summary scores are all types of ordinal scales.) These are the kinds of measurement most commonly used in the behavioral sciences. Since ordinal scales can only place the items being tested in rank order with no ability to determine the distance between ranks, the possibility of developing more rigorous scaling techniques that can measure distance (namely interval and ratio scales) has occupied the attention of many behavioral scientists. Similarly, application of sampling theory to the measurement of human populations required the invention of practical techniques which were at the same time theoretically acceptable. Finally, these behavioral scientists devoted much of their energy to applying analytical statistical models —for example, analysis of variance, correlation and regression analysis, factor analysis, and discriminant analysis—to the data obtained by their measuring devices.

In contrast are the far fewer behavioral scientists who, while adhering to the standards of objective empiricism, question the measurability of their subject matter. Scientific classification and analysis, in their view, can best be achieved by developing proper *conceptual* tools which, they contend, are more appropriate to the study of human behavior than are the alleged "concoctions" of the quantifiers. Conceptualized, nonquantified models of human behavior are applied, as rigorously as possible, to the analysis of observed, reported, or recorded behavior. In psychology, Freudian theory typifies this approach [1, 2]. Thus, the psychoanalytically oriented researcher applies "psychodynamic" concepts, such as projection, sublimation, repression, oral masochism, and reaction formation, to place his data in meaningful relation to each other.

A sociological counterpart is "verstende" theory, whose most noted representative is Max Weber. He used "ideal type" concepts such as life style, charisma, the Protestant ethic, and instrumental versus traditional action to analyze specific forms of social behavior, such as capitalism [4]. Though in the minority, behavioral scientists who challenge the meaningfulness of quantified measurements have been important in the development of behavioral theories and methods. Most notably, quantitatively oriented behavioral scientists have borrowed heavily from the conceptualists in setting goals for their research and in interpreting the meaning of the quantified output, for example, of a factor analysis.

RELEVANCE OF BEHAVIORAL SCIENCES TO MARKETING RESEARCH

The behavioral sciences have made a dual contribution to marketing research. First, the research techniques pioneered by psychologists, social psychologists, and sociologists have been widely adopted by marketing researchers. Second, many concepts and theories of the behavioral sciences have been directly relevant to the kinds of questions marketing researchers seek to answer.

Methodological Contributions

The scientific description and analysis of human behavior require the development of valid and reliable methods for recording behavior and for identifying causal influences on that behavior. Illustrative of the kinds of techniques that behavioral scientists have pioneered are the use of personal documents such as diaries, the measurement of attitudes in sample surveys, group discussions, measurements of sensory perception (for example, with the tachistoscope), experiments designed to measure communications effects, tests that identify personality types and dynamics, and the recording and coding of direct observation of behavior in real-life situations.

There is no one rationale behind these various techniques, but they do have in common the intent to record, as objectively as possible, relevant facts about human behavior. This has meant, first, not relying on the naïve reports of an untrained observer or of the respondent himself. Instead, behavioral scientists have sought methods for systematically gathering observations or reports of behavior in a way that enables the analyst to test their validity and reliability. In some cases this has meant the development of question styles and recording forms that make it easy for a person to report accurately his behavior, thoughts, and feelings. In other cases, this has meant devising techniques for coding observed or recorded behavior that uncover relationships not readily apparent to the unskilled analyst. In still others, it has been necessary to invent techniques that can reveal aspects of one's behavior that are difficult to articulate or unknown to oneself.

When applied to marketing research, these techniques facilitate the accurate description and analysis of consumer behavior. Of most direct significance to marketing research are methods developed for investigating attitudes, measuring preferences, and obtaining information not reliably accessible through direct questioning. Methods developed for measuring attitudes and preferences include the use of rating scales, ranking, paired and multiple comparisons, and so forth. These can be used to compare preferences between such things as brands, products, and advertising copy.

Techniques for measuring how consumers perceive (1) a brand's qualities (brand image), (2) the kind of people who purchase that brand (user image), and (3) the kind of company that manufactures it (corporate image) that have been used in marketing research also derive from the behavioral sciences. These techniques normally involve measuring techniques such as rating scales, rankings, or paired comparisons as applied to a set of adjectives and phrases that denote qualities known or thought to be of significance.

Illustrative of this is a study designed to test consumer preferences among a set of patterns that were being considered by a manufacturer of kitchenware. The study design involved measuring reactions in three ways:

1. A 10-point rating scale, from +5 to −5, was used by respondents to indicate the degree of liking or disliking for each test pattern.

2. Test patterns were grouped into sets of three, each set consisting of similar patterns, and respondents selected the one pattern they liked best from each set.

3. A list of adjectives was prepared, and respondents were asked to select those adjectives they felt applied to each pattern.

When results of the test were later compared with actual sales, the top-scoring patterns were those which achieved the highest sales while the low-scoring patterns fared poorly. The manufacturer has adopted this testing procedure to select new patterns in preference to his earlier reliance on the judgment of salesmen and department store buyers.

Considerable success has been reported in measuring *summary attitudes* that correlate highly with purchasing behavior. Summary attitude, meaning *behavioral intention*, is in effect a summing up of all the influences, attitudinal and motivational, on the individual. In marketing research, this typically has been done by using some kind of rating scale requiring the consumer to indicate the likelihood that she will buy some particular product or brand. Stapel [23] reported a series of studies in which such measurements of buying intentions correlated well with subsequent behavior. For example, among those who rated themselves as "certainly will buy" a T.V. rediffusion service, 64 percent did so by the year's end; while among those who rated themselves "certainly not," only 5 percent did so.

Nevertheless, identifying *specific* factors that correlate with purchasing behavior has proved to be a much more difficult problem. That is, although it has become possible to measure reasonably accurately the attitudinal *outcome* of causal influences on behavior, attempts to measure the weight or contribution of each of these influences have been far less successful.

Multivariate analytical methods, allowing isolation and then interrelation of attitudinal, motivational, and other personality variables, have been used for this purpose. Most attempts to relate such variables to purchasing behavior are interesting more in terms of their future promise than their current performance. Massy, Frank, and Lodahl [21], after an intensive analysis of the interrelations among personality traits, socioeconomic status, and purchasing behavior (using factor analysis and multiple regression), were able to achieve only weak predictive measurements.

The problem of obtaining information not accessible to direct questioning occurs frequently in marketing research. A variety of factors, such as limited insight, inability to articulate, emotional connotations, and prestige, sometimes generates vague and misleading answers when direct questioning is used. Projective methods derived largely from clinical psychology have proved useful in such situations. These methods avoid asking respondents direct questions on their feelings and beliefs. Instead, they provide stimuli that, apparently unrelated to the research objectives, evoke reactions that provide insight into underlying causal influences.

Theoretical Contributions

Useful as these technical innovations have been, the theoretical influence of the behavioral sciences on marketing research has had the greatest significance. Behavioral science theory identifies variables and processes of relevance to marketing problems that would otherwise be at best imperfectly recognized. For example, sociologists interested in social stratification have provided an alternative to the inadequacy of analyzing consumer behavior solely in terms of income. Social strata which differ in their life-styles, and thus their buying behavior, can be identified only by taking into account the joint influences of income, education, occupation, and residential neighborhood. SES (socio-economic status) indices have been constructed by sociologists such as Lloyd Warner and August Hollingshead for just this purpose [11, 12].

Similarly, chronological age is an imperfect correlate of buying behavior as compared with life cycle data. That is, it is often more useful for a marketing manager to know that one woman has been married six years and has two children and that another is engaged to be married than to know only that the former is 26 years old and the latter 28 years old. The analytical value of demographic data is greatly enhanced when they are treated not merely as "objective" information but as *indicators of the social roles that people play*. For this, it is necessary to define *social roles as multidimensional* rather than in terms of a single dimension such as age or sex.

The *belief systems and values of individuals* constitute another type of variable relevant to many marketing problems. These may be used in two distinct but complementary ways. Consumer beliefs about what makes a good product can differ considerably. Furthermore, evaluations of a brand's closeness to the ideal can vary, if for no other reason than that definitions of what an ideal product would be like often vary considerably. One type of analysis maps consumer beliefs about desirable product qualities and then determines where specific brands are positioned on this map. This could help define the best advertising strategy for an established brand; it could also identify "unoccupied" positions on the map and thus give direction to new-product development. Alternatively, by categorizing consumers according to their belief systems, the market could be segmented in a manner analogous to segmentation by SES or by life cycle. The possibility that holders of different beliefs buy different brands could then be investigated.

In either case, research strategy is predicated on the principle that it is not sufficient to take product qualities as objective facts, identifiable through laboratory analysis. It is the *perception of these qualities* in relation to antecedent beliefs and values that is crucial.

Personality characteristics and motivations constitute a third set of variables that may be valuable in analyzing consumer behavior. Correct analysis of motivational influences can help identify effective themes to use in advertising, fruitful lines for new-product development, and new approaches to merchandising. By segmenting markets in terms of motivational factors, the possibility that brand preference is a result of these factors can be investigated. Even when this is not so, the determination of what the effective motives for product use are can be of practical value.

For example, a motivational study of the confectionery products market investigated the relative significance of such motives as hunger, "fun," controlling one's weight, and self-indulgent pleasure at various age levels. The data were analyzed in terms of the conflicting influences of rewards (physiological need and psychological gratifications) and costs (deleterious effects on health and feelings of guilt). This analysis indicated the need for different advertising and distribution strategies for the preteen, teen-age, and adult markets.

A final theoretical contribution of the behavioral sciences to marketing research is in the study of purchase behavior dynamics. The act of purchasing a brand is best understood as part of a process that occurs on several levels, psychological and sociological. Three observations will suffice to illustrate this point. First, deciding to buy a food product and then selecting a specific brand involves such factors as the allocation of responsibility within a family for budgeting, performance of household chores and child care, as well as the conciliation of possibly conflicting preferences. It is seldom that one person makes the complete purchase decision; more often, *making a decision is a process in which each family member plays a somewhat different role.* The housewife plays a central role in this process. The possibility of her making autonomous decisions is ever present, but there are always limits to this imposed by her responsibilities to other family members. Rather than being *the* decision maker for her family, the typical housewife plays a "gatekeeper" role in a family's food purchasing decisions. For this reason, it is far more useful to define the nature and scope of influence of each family member on purchase decisions than to ask the unitary question, "Who makes the decision?"

Second, the beliefs, preferences, feelings, and values that each family member brings to the decision-making process are subject to change. There is a dynamic interaction between attitudes and behavior, the consequence of conflicting influences. Choosing often requires selection among alternatives each of which has positive and negative elements: preferred product qualities, pricing, economic risks, uncertainty about the fulfillment of promised benefits, and so forth. Reactions to advertising messages and point-of-purchase displays, as well as willingness to experiment with new products and intensity of brand loyalty, cannot be correctly analyzed unless they are considered as part of an *ongoing process of conflict resolution.* Measurements of purchase intentions can be misleading if account is not taken of the dynamics of consumer behavior and attitudes.

Third, the effect of "personal influence" in the secondary transmission of advertising, as well as in exchange of personal experience, can be of major significance in purchase decisions. A housewife's beliefs and evaluations about a brand consequently derive not only from her direct experience and direct exposure to advertising but also from what she has gleaned from communications *via her friends and family.* Advertising is only one kind of communication, and its effect is often strongly conditioned by the extent and manner in which its content enters into the total flow of communications to which a housewife is exposed. Identifying innovators and other kinds of opinion leaders and measuring their contribution to a housewife's purchase decisions can enhance the ability of a research design to make predictive measurements [20].

Powerful as the theoretical and methodological innovations of the behavioral sciences may be, their uncritical application can lead to serious error. Such errors can occur both at the level of measurement and of analysis. At the measurement level, the limitations of ordinal scaling techniques (such as rating scales and rankings) and the pitfalls of the paired comparison method must be recognized if research findings are not to be overinterpreted. Subsequent chapters in this section are concerned with such considerations.

At the analytical level, extreme caution must be exercised since the sources of possible error are less obvious. Hypothesizing that motivations for product use and corporate image are determinants of brand preference is a useful research strategy. For some products and brands this is indeed the case, but not necessarily for all. Illustrative of this is the result of a multiple regression analysis of the relation between four types of attitudinal measurements and preference for a beverage brand. The attitudinal measurements were:

1. User image, as measured by the association of 12 kinds of persons with proclivity to buy the specified brand.

2. Corporate image, as measured by the association of seven characteristics with the manufacturer.

3. Ideal product image, as measured by nine semantic differential scales of product qualities.

4. Brand image, as measured by the same semantic differential scales used to measure ideal product image.

A multiple regression of each of these four types of attitude measurements with likelihood of buying brand X showed:

1. There was no correlation between ideal product image and likelihood of buying brand X.

2. Two of the brand-image scales explained about 38 percent of the variance of measured likelihood of buying brand X (the multiple regression coefficient, R, was 0.62).

3. One corporate-image trait and one user-image trait contributed slightly to the analysis (increasing R to 0.67).

4. None of the other items increased R significantly.

Thus of the 37 variables that were hypothesized as likely to have a significant relation with purchasing behavior, only two did so. Even such a result must be treated with caution, and only after it is confirmed by replication of the original study can one be confident that these two variables in fact predict brand preference to a significant degree.

Market segmentation, using either sociological or psychological variables, also requires caution. It is deceptively simple in the computer age to create indexes of social status or to generate, through factor analysis, types of personality. Moreover, since brand preferences are not uniform, it can be expected that some correlation between brand preferences and some index of social status or some personality typology will be found. What is less certain is that these correlations will be any higher than what might be obtained by less sophisticated techniques or that the *causally significant* variables have been defined.

REVIEW AND SUMMARY

Behavioral scientists investigate human behavior at three levels—the individual, the interactional, and the group. At the *individual level*, the unit of measurement is the person considered as an acting organism. His relations with other people are treated as part of the environment to which he reacts. This is the psychological level of analysis, concerned with learning, perception, and motivation. At the *group level* of analysis, the unit of measurement is the collectivity of persons considered in terms of their commonly determined behavior. Individual differences are treated as part of the input of stimuli to the group.

This is the sociological level of analysis, concerned with group structures and processes, institutional organization, and social change. Intermediate between these is the interactional level of analysis, at which the unit of measurement is the relationship between the individual and his social environment. Individual differences and collective uniformities are examined in terms of the processes that connect them to each other. This is the social-psychological level of analysis, concerned with attitudes, communication, and role playing.

The kinds of data collected by different types of behavioral scientists crosscut these three levels. This is indicative of the fact that the difference between these levels of analysis is not that they examine totally different phenomena but that they analyze the same phenomena from alternative perspectives.

Three types of behavioral science data can be defined:

1. Behavioral, consisting of direct observation or reports of activities

2. Attitudinal, usually in the form of verbal reports on beliefs, feelings, values, and intentions

3. Psychodynamic, consisting of information about an individual derived from tests designed to tap dynamic processes not otherwise apparent to an outside observer and about which individuals are unwilling or unable to report.

There are two levels of measurement, direct and analytical. At the *direct* level, three types of measurement can be distinguished. One is the *sample survey*, in which the incidence of behavior, beliefs, feelings, and so forth are measured through such instruments as questionnaires and diaries. Another type of measurement is the *experiment,* in which variations in behavior and/or verbal expressions are related to the controlled manipulation of specified stimuli. Third is the *clinical interview,* which investigates how an individual handles the problem of satisfying his often conflicting inner desires and feelings.

At the *analytical* level, data obtained through direct measurement are processed to develop second- and third-order measurements. For example, multivariate scales may be constructed by applying appropriate statistical models to data obtained through direct measurement. It is also possible to analyze clinical data conceptually to develop complex models of the dynamic relationships among motives.

The following chapters deal with selected research techniques that have been widely adopted by marketing researchers from the behavioral sciences and do not attempt a comprehensive coverage of the total research repertoire. Although the techniques described can be used at the individual, group, and interactional level of analysis, most marketing researchers tend to use them only at the individual and interactional levels. The scaling techniques described are used to obtain attitudinal data, as are the methods of measuring preference. These techniques can be used both in survey and experimental designs. Psychodynamic data can be obtained through use of projective tests, most typically in a clinical interview but also in sample surveys. Finally, methods for recording behavior, typically in some type of sample survey, are described.

REFERENCES

General Theory

1. Hall, C. S., and G. Lindzey, *Theories of Personality,* New York: Wiley, 1957.
2. Koch, S., ed., *Psychology, A Study of a Science,* New York: McGraw Hill, 1958, 3 vols.
3. Lindzey, G., ed., *Handbook of Social Psychology,* Cambridge: Addison-Wesley, 1954, 2 vols.
4. Parsons, T., E. Shils, D. Naegele, and J. R. Pitts, eds., *Theories of Society,* New York: Free Press, 1969, 2 vols.

Special Theories

5. Cantril, H., *The Pattern of Human Concerns,* New Brunswick: Rutgers University Press, 1965, chaps. 1–3.

6. Fishbein, M., ed., *Readings in Attitude Theory and Measurement,* New York: Wiley, 1967.
7. Hare, A. P., *Handbook of Small Group Research,* New York: Free Press, 1962.
8. McClelland, D., *The Achieving Society,* Princeton: Van Nostrand, 1961.
9. Rokeach, M., *Beliefs, Attitudes and Values,* San Francisco: Jossey-Bass, 1968.

Methodology

10. Hyman, H. H., *Interviewing In Social Research,* Chicago: University of Chicago Press, 1954.
11. Festinger L., and D. Katz, *Research Methods in the Behavioral Sciences,* New York: Holt, 1966.
12. Goode, W. J., and P. K. Hatt, *Methods in Social Research,* New York: McGraw-Hill, 1952.
13. Lazarsfeld, P. F., and M. Rosenberg, *The Language of Social Research,* Chicago: The Free Press, 1955.
14. Selltiz, C., M. Jahoda, M. Deutsch, and S. W. Cook, *Research Methods in Social Relations,* New York: Holt, 1965.
15. Stouffer, S. A., L. Guttman, E. A. Suchman, P. F. Lazarsfeld, S. A. Star, and J. A. Clausen, *Measurement and Prediction,* Princeton: Princeton University Press, 1950.

Behavioral Science and Marketing Research

16. Foote, N. N., *Household Decision Making,* New York: New York University Press, 1961.
17. Glock, C. Y., and F. M. Nicosia, "The Consumer," in P. F. Lazarsfeld, W. H. Sewell, and H. L. Wilensky, eds., *The Uses of Sociology,* New York: Basic Books, 1967.
18. Juster, F. T., *Anticipations and Purchases: An Analysis of Consumer Behavior,* Princeton: Princeton University Press, 1964.
19. Katona, G., *The Powerful Consumer,* New York: McGraw-Hill, 1960.
20. Katz, E., and P. L. Lazarsfeld, *Personal Influence,* Chicago: Free Press, 1955.
21. Massy, W. F., R. E. Frank, and T. M. Lodahl, *Purchasing Behavior and Personal Attributes,* Philadelphia: University of Pennsylvania Press, 1968.
22. Morgan, J. N., "Contributions of Survey Research to Economics," in Charles Y. Glock, ed., *Survey Research in the Social Sciences,* New York: Russel Sage, 1967.
23. Stapel, J., "Predictive Attitudes," in L. Adler and I. Crespi, eds., *Attitude Research on the Rocks,* Chicago: American Marketing Association, 1968.

Part A

Techniques

Chapter 2

The Measurement of Beliefs and Attitudes

G. DAVID HUGHES *Graduate School of Business and Public Administration, Cornell University, Ithaca, New York*

THE NEED FOR INSTRUMENTS TO MEASURE ATTITUDES

Motivations for buying a product or service in an affluent society are not limited to an individual's physical needs (food, shelter, and clothing) or his ability to buy the product (price and income); they include also his social-psychological needs, which are reflected in his attitudes toward himself and his environment. The marketing concept, therefore, must be extended to include measures of attributes when searching for unmet needs. Product segmentation must be along attitudinal dimensions as well as demographic and economic dimensions. A prerequisite to developing product and promotional strategies that will meet social-psychological needs is the development of instruments to measure attitudes and their components.

Definition of Terms

An attitude is a state of potential behavior toward an attribute of an object. If the attribute seems to fill an individual's need, he will have a favorable attitude toward it; which means he will be inclined to act favorably toward it. The degree of favorability is determined by the potency of the attribute for fulfilling the need [57]. A measure of the degree of favorability or unfavorability is called attitude valence or simply an attitude.

An individual's overall attitude toward an object is determined by his attitudes toward each attribute of the object and the importance of each attribute to his decision process. The importance of the attribute is frequently referred to as attribute salience or simply salience. To measure an individual's attitude toward brands, it is necessary to identify the attributes of the generic product that are salient to his decision and then measure his attitude toward each brand along these attributes.

An attribute is a property of a good or service that fulfills a physical, social, or psychological need. An individual does not buy a food product but rather a bundle of attributes such as taste, sustenance, convenience, and social acceptability. Each person will weight these attributes according to his personal value system and the decision environment. Weights will vary across decision environments. For instance, hamburger may be socially acceptable for a family dinner but unacceptable for guests.

An overall attitude toward a brand may be measured as a subjective probability of buying the brand. This probability is a function of attitudes and salience. One form of expressing the functional relationship is an additive-linear model [35], such as the following:

$$Pr_b = \sum_{i=1}^{n} S_i A_{bi}$$

where Pr_b is the subjective probability of buying brand b, S_i is the salience of attribute i, A_{bi} is the attitude of brand b along attribute i, and there are n attributes. S_i may be measured directly or estimated using multiple regression techniques.

An attitude toward a brand may be dissected into belief and value components [21, p. 394]. A belief is the likelihood that brand b contains attribute i. A value is a perception of whether attribute i is desirable. Values are learned from culture, reference groups, education, and commercial promotions. An attitude toward a brand of toothpaste, for example, may be determined by the belief that it contains a decay preventive ingredient, the belief that it is priced reasonably, the perceived value of possessing sound teeth, and the value of being economical. Brand attitude may be expressed as follows:

$$A_b = \sum_{i=1}^{n} B_{bi} a_i$$

where A_b is the overall attitude toward the object, B_{bi} is the belief that brand b contains attribute i, and a_i is the evaluation of attribute i.

To summarize, an overall attitude toward a brand of a product is determined by the salience of the attributes in the generic product—for example, toothpaste—and the evaluation of the brand along each attribute. This evaluation is the attitude toward the brand attribute. An attitude may be divided into belief and value components. Values may range from enduring cultural values that are slow to change, through less enduring life-styles, to short-duration values such as fads. When a person receives information about a brand, he processes the information according to his value system. The outcome of this processing is his attitude toward the brand.

The terms as defined are consistent with definitions by marketers and social psychologists. Beliefs, attitudes, and probability of buying carry the same meaning as cognitive, affective, and conative as defined by Lavidge and Steiner [40]. Social psychologists refer to these as three components of an overall attitude—beliefs, feelings, and response tendencies [39]. The definitions in this discussion are refinements of these earlier definitions in that they reflect new knowledge of the relationships among these components in overall attitude formation, specifically the role of values in attitude formation and the role of salience in the formation of subjective probabilities of behaving.

Marketing Strategies Based on Attitudes

Brand strategies may be based on measures of overall image, the components of brand image (attribute salience and attitude valence), or the components of attitude valence (beliefs and values). Market segmentation by the salience of attributes is common among toothpaste brands. One brand will be directed toward parents who weigh heavily the attribute of decay prevention. Another brand will be identified with the segment that regards social acceptability as the most important attribute. A third brand may be directed toward the segment which is concerned only with price.

Promotional strategies attempt to alter buyers' beliefs about a brand's possessing an attribute or to alter their attitude valence toward the brand. For example, some gasoline advertisements attempt to alter beliefs—the likelihood that a brand is lead-free. Other promotions are concerned largely with altering attitudes toward a brand with regard to its ability to clean an engine or give maximum mileage.

Strategies may be based also on values. Lunn [41, 42] has shown that basic values such as traditionalism, experimentalism, and sociability explain buying behavior for a labor-saving household product better than demographic variables. Values may be reflected in life-styles that cause some persons to be early adopters of new products.

Attitudes are not limited to brand image strategies; they are central to models of buyer behavior. [For examples, see 2, 16, 30, 47.] The most frequent use of attitude measurement in marketing management, however, is concerned with brand image and related strategies.

IDENTIFYING SALIENT ATTRIBUTES[1]

To measure an attitude toward a product or service the salient attributes of the object must be identified; because it is the attributes that are evaluated by a buyer, not the object itself. Salient attributes for a detergent, for instance, may include cleansing power, sudsing level, whiteness, and freshness of odor. For frozen orange juice they may be taste/flavor, price, texture, nutritional value, and packaging. For toilet tissue, texture, color, price, package size, and strength are the salient attributes [6].

The techniques used to identify attributes may be classified according to their degree of structure. Unstructured methods include depth interviews and projective techniques. The repertory grid method is partially structured. Structured techniques include sophisticated statistical routines. After the salient attributes have been identified, the next step is to measure the subject's belief that a brand possesses an attribute or his evaluation of a brand along the attribute.

Unstructured Techniques

Unstructured procedures for identifying relevant psychological attributes of a marketing good or service have been borrowed directly from psychology. During the 1950s these procedures were known in marketing as motivation research techniques [19]. Today they are a standard tool in researchers' kits [10].

---

[1] This discussion abstracts from Chaps. 5 through 7 of Hughes [33].

Depth Interviews

Depth interviews are conducted by highly trained interviewers who probe in depth the respondents' thoughts relevant to the attitude object. Respondents may be asked to describe their attitudes when using or shopping for a good. Respondents are interviewed either on an individual basis or in a group. In the latter case, other members of the group provide stimuli which elicit an individual's thoughts. Research by Payne [52] suggests that group interviews may not be as efficient as their enthusiasts suggest.

Projective Techniques

Projective techniques are vague or incomplete stimuli which the respondent is required to complete. In the process of completion it is thought that he reveals attitude dimensions that could not be elicited by direct questions because either the attitude was located in the subconscious, was unstructured and could not be verbalized, or could not be reported because it was socially unacceptable. Two projective techniques used frequently in marketing research are the sentence-completion test and the cartoon technique, as described in Part A, Chapter 5 of this section.

A Partially Structured Technique—Repertory Grid

The repertory grid method requires the respondent to compare objects along dimensions that he selects. The interviewing procedure is briefly as follows: (1) the subject culls from a pack of cards those brands with which he is totally unfamiliar, (2) three cards are selected randomly from the familiar brands, (3) the respondent is asked "to think of a way in which any two of the three are similar to each other and different from the third" [22, p. 165]. Having identified a dimension, the respondent is asked to rate the remaining brands along this dimension. This rating may be a simple paired comparison, a ranking, or a rating along a scale. In Table 1 the ratings are paired comparisons, with a plus sign indicating similar products. Three more brands are selected randomly and the procedure is repeated. The process is continued until the respondent exhausts his dimensions, 18 per respondent on the average. Generally, only 40 interviews are required to identify all the relevant dimensions.

The responses are summarized as a matrix or grid in which the rows are attitude dimensions, the columns are brands (or test products, packages, advertisements, etc.), and the cell entries are attitude measurements. The grid may be analyzed using matrix algebra or less sophisticated techniques. Competitive products may be identified by comparing the columns. For instance, brands 8 and 11 are competitive. A duplication of dimensions is detected by comparing rows: dimensions 2 and 9, "give as a present" and "expensive," are nearly synonymous.

The grid technique is thought to be superior to unstructured methods in two respects. First, the respondent identifies the dimensions, thereby removing the interviewer bias or the researcher's misinterpretation. Second, the dimensions are named by the respondent in his own terms. When these terms are used in an attitude questionnaire they may convey more meaning for other respondents than terms selected by the researcher.

Structured Techniques

Unstructured and partially structured techniques require the researcher or the respondent to identify the salient attributes. Structured techniques use statistical methods for this identification. Four techniques used frequently in marketing for attribute identification include the Automatic Interaction Detection (AID) model, factor analysis, cluster analysis, and nonmetric multidimensional scaling as discussed in Section II, Part E of this handbook.[2]   The AID technique identifies the characteristics of those market segments with the highest probability of buying a product or a brand, for example, see [4].

Included in attribute identification are the tasks of data reduction and classifying objects (persons or brands) into homogeneous groups.   Factor analysis performs the first task and cluster analysis performs the second.   In a data matrix where objects are along rows and variables are in columns, cluster analysis reduces the number of rows and factor analysis reduces the number of columns with little loss of information.   (See Part II, Section E, Chapter 8.)

TABLE 1   A Repertory Grid of Twelve Brands of Confectioneries

Dimension	Brand											
	1	2	3	4	5	6	7	8	9	10	11	12
1. Luxurious—ordinary	⊕	O	⊕			+		+	+		+	
2. Give as present—buy for myself	+			O	⊕	⊕		+	+		+	
3. Hard centers—soft centers	+		+		+		⊕	O	⊕			
4. Eaten by younger people—eaten by older people		+		+		+	+			⊕	⊕	O
5. Established brand—new brand	O				⊕	+		+	⊕		+	+
6. Wide appeal—limited appeal		⊕	+	+		O	+			⊕		+
7. Would eat at home—would eat at theater			⊕	⊕	+		+		+		O	+
8. More bitter taste—less bitter taste	⊕				+	+	⊕	+		+		O
9. Expensive—inexpensive	+	O			⊕	+		⊕	+		+	

Key: Crosses mean brands are similar.
       Circles indicate the three brands compared initially.
SOURCE: [22, p. 166]

In practice a combination of multivariate techniques is used.   For instance, Morgan and Purnell [44] used factor analysis to identify the relevant dimensions that describe British voters, multiple regression to test the ability of these dimensions to predict voting intentions, and cluster analysis to identify the dimensions of a new political party intended to meet the needs of the electorate not well served by the present parties.   They also used cluster analysis to locate gaps in respondents' perception of available beverages.   Green and Carmone [24] used this analysis to classify 102 computer models according to their performance characteristics.

Mapping objects into space according to respondents' attitudes is not new. The semantic differential scale was developed in experiments that located concepts in three-dimensional space to reflect the meaning that respondents gave to them [50].   This mapping assumed that the attitude measures formed an

[2] The discussion is limited to techniques which identify attributes.   Techniques for estimating predictive equations, such as multiple regression, discriminant analysis, and multiple classification analysis [3], are frequently used in a stepwise fashion for attribute identification.   For an overview of multivariate techniques, see [23].

interval scale. Furthermore, the dimensions were identified by the researcher before the measurements were made. Nonmetric methods of multidimensional scaling (see the following chapter) in one operation identify dimensions and place objects in n-dimensional space without requiring interval data.

Nonmetric scaling techniques are appropriate when the scale of measurement yields more than rank-order data but less than interval data. This intermediate scale is known as an ordered metric. The distinction can be illustrated with an example from horseracing. We have rank-order data when we are told that our horse came in fourth. If we are told it was a distant fourth, we have more information and an ordered metric scale. If we learn that it was fourth by five lengths, we have an interval scale because we know the intervals between rankings. A nominal scale of measurement is less than a ranking. It is merely the naming of a classification, for example, brown horses.

The structured techniques of attribute identification require data input, which requires consideration of the scale of measurement necessary for each technique and the instruments for making the necessary measurements. These two considerations will be discussed briefly as they apply to the techniques for attribute identification.

The measurement requirements for the AID model are minimal. The independent variables can be as low as a nominal scale of measurement. The dependent variable must be an interval scale of measurement. When the dependent variable is nominal, such as bought–did-not-buy, it can be converted into an interval scale by computing the proportion of the sample who bought or did not buy.

Factor analysis is a metric technique that requires data which form an interval scale. It has been customary to use factor analysis on attitudinal data, under the assumption that instruments to measure attitudes form interval scales. Nonmetric cluster analysis and nonmetric multidimensional scaling were developed because this assumption is generally unwarranted.

The attitudinal data input to nonmetric multidimensional scaling algorithms is of two types—similarities and preference data. Preference data imply choice behavior. For instance, preference data are generated when a respondent chooses a brand in a brand-comparison study. Similarities data are generated when a respondent compares brands according to their similarities and differences without regard to preferences or probabilities of buying. Similarities measures are useful when developing new products or identifying competitors of present products.

INSTRUMENTS TO MEASURE BELIEFS

Once salient attributes have been identified, the next step is to measure respondents' beliefs that a brand possesses these attributes. The problem may be stated in marketing terms with the following example: Do consumers believe that brand A toothpaste has characteristics that prevent tooth decay and brighten teeth? In marketing, instruments for measuring beliefs have been limited, until very recently, to measures of awareness. These measures are very coarse because they measure only two probability states, 0.0 (unawareness) and 1.0 (awareness).

Measures of awareness are frequently used in marketing to measure the effect of a promotional campaign or to locate areas where additional promotion is necessary. Awareness is generally easy to measure in marketing because it is a conscious state and because there is generally little social risk in reporting awareness of a product attribute.

Awareness is measured with aided and unaided recall techniques.   An unaided recall question is as follows:

> Please list the first four services that come to mind when you think of the Old Ezra Bank.
> 1. _____   3. _____
> 2. _____   4. _____

The unaided recall method tends to yield a more valid measure of awareness because it requires more thought by the respondent.   By comparison, the following aided recall question requires little deliberation by the respondent:

> Please check all of those services performed by the Old Ezra Bank.
> _____ Checking account   _____ Mortgage
> _____ Savings account   _____ Trust department
> _____ Safe deposit box   _____ Utility payments
> _____ Auto loan   _____ Other (please explain)

The aided method tends to inflate claims of awareness.

The principal advantage of measures of awareness is their low cost.   They can be adapted easily to mail or telephone survey techniques, which tend to be lower in cost than personal interview methods.   A disadvantage of these techniques is that they are only remotely related to action tendencies and therefore tend to be poor explainers or predictors of buying behavior.

Measures of awareness could be made finer by asking respondents to state the subjective probability that a service or product characteristic exists.   For instance:

> Using a scale of 0 to 100, indicate the probability that the Old Ezra Bank performs the following services, 0 meaning no probability and 100 meaning you are certain that service is provided.
> _____ Checking accounts
> _____ Utility payments
> _____ Safe deposit boxes

Beliefs can be measured also with techniques used to measure attitudes, such as the Thurstone, the Likert, and the semantic differential scales [21], described in the next section.

INSTRUMENTS TO MEASURE ATTITUDES

Marketing problems are frequently solved at the preliminary investigation stage, which includes identification of salient attributes in the buying decision.   If the problem is not solved at this stage, the researcher may find it necessary to increase sample size so that he can measure attitudes in many market segments. He may also want to use more precise measuring instruments.   These more specialized techniques reduce costs by (1) permitting the use of mail and telephone surveys instead of personal interviews and laboratory settings, (2) simplifying the coding and punching of data for analysis, and (3) using more powerful statistical analyses generally available on computers.   Selection of an appropriate method requires understanding of the features and limitations of the instruments commonly used in marketing research to measure attitudes and action tendencies.

The Thurstone Equal-appearing Interval Scale

The Thurstone equal-appearing interval scale is an early attempt to measure psychological stimuli [64].   The basic task was the measurement of distances between psychological stimuli. The original Thurstone equal-appearing interval technique required 300 judges to array 200 statements along an attitude dimension divided into 11 equal parts. Later methods reduced the required number of judges and statements. The goal of this effort was 22 statements whose scale values were distributed evenly along an 11-point scale. A scale value was the median of the scores assigned by the judges. Statements with narrow interquartile ranges were used to reflect agreement among judges.

A very abbreviated Thurstone scale follows:

Please check the statement that best describes your opinion of each bank.

Bank A	Bank B		
_____	_____	Would prefer not to do business with this bank	(1.1)
_____	_____	Not eager to please	(2.7)
_____	_____	Not a dynamic organization	(4.2)
_____	_____	Neither good nor bad	(5.5)
_____	_____	Has more good points than bad	(7.2)
_____	_____	A bank with good character	(8.4)
_____	_____	A reliable bank	(9.6)
_____	_____	The only bank I will do business with	(10.7)

The values of the respondent's attitudes toward bank A and bank B are 8.4 and 4.2, respectively. The scale values shown in parentheses do not appear in the questionnaire. Instructions and methods of scoring vary. Some researchers require respondents to check 3 statements out of 22 and use the median as the score.

Even though many shortcut techniques have been developed for the creation of a Thurstone scale [15], considerable time and effort are required, which makes the method expensive. In addition, scales which require considerable reading are disliked by respondents [31]. Therefore, the Thurstone scale is generally not recommended for use in marketing research.

The Semantic Differential

The semantic differential scale [50], with almost as many variations as there are researchers, has been used widely in marketing research. It consists essentially of pairs of antonyms (adjectives or phrases) with cues spaced in between. Cues may be numerical, graphic, verbal, or some combination. The methods for presenting them to subjects also vary. They generally are presented in a questionnaire, but they have been presented also in a booklet, with each scale on a separate page [67]; as spokes on a wheel [9]; and by a computer in a computer-controlled experiment where a random-number generator assigned the items to the subjects randomly to avoid the order effect [35]. One variation, known as the Stapel scale, placed a single adjective in the center with a negative progression of numbers on one side and a positive progression on the other [11].

The bipolar nature of these scales conforms to the basic concept of motivation, that of the attraction to or repulsion from an object [28, pp. 456–457]. To be correct, the scales as generally used in marketing research should be called bipolar scales; they are not used to measure *changes* in the *meaning* of an object as projected in three-dimensional space, the original intent of the semantic differential [50].

When developing a semantic differential scale, several factors must be considered: (1) whether cues should be balanced or unbalanced; (2) the type of cue—numerical, graphic, verbal, or some combination; (3) the number of cues to use; (4) whether the scale should be the forced- or nonforced-choice variety;

and (5) the selection of antonyms. Examples of each of these points will help to guide the decision.

Balanced and Unbalanced Scales

A scale is balanced when it has an equal number of cues on either side of the indifferent cue. For example, the following verbal scale is balanced:

How would you describe the Old Ezra Bank?
_____ Very progressive
_____ Progressive
_____ Moderately progressive
_____ Neither progressive nor conservative
_____ Moderately conservative
_____ Conservative
_____ Very conservative

Subjects who use extreme values on a scale produce a distribution of responses that is truncated by the end of the scale rather than the statistically desirable normal distribution around the mean attitude. To eliminate *end piling*, an unbalanced scale is used. More cues are added to the end of the scale where the piling is likely to occur, thereby stretching the distribution of responses along the attitude dimension. The following scale is heavily unbalanced on the favorable end of the scale:

What is your reaction to bank charge cards?
_____ Enthusiastic
_____ Extremely favorable
_____ Very favorable
_____ Favorable
_____ Fair
_____ Poor

Type of Cue

The cues may be verbal, numerical, graphic, or some combination. In its original form the semantic differential was in the following graphic manner [50]:

Friendly _____:_____:_____:_____:_____:_____:_____ Unfriendly

Respondents were instructed to place an X on the line that represented their attitude.

Numerical and verbal cues are frequently combined, thereby eliminating the need to code the questionnaire for data processing and clarifying the intent of the scale for the respondent. For example:

Please evaluate the performance of Federated Airlines by circling the number that represents your evaluation.

	Very good		*Fair*		*Very poor*	
Airport counter service	6	5	4	3	2	1
Convenient flight connections	6	5	4	3	2	1
Prompt baggage delivery	6	5	4	3	2	1

The number circled can be read directly by the keypunch operator or an optical scanner. The verbal cues and the direction of the numbers convey the intent of the scale to the respondent. The balanced and unbalanced scales in the previous section represent pure verbal cues.

Number of Cues

The number of cues used between antonyms depends on the type of respondent, the research environment, and the nature of the analysis. Generally, the more intelligent respondent can scale more cues meaningfully if the environment is favorable. An example of an unfavorable environment is a long interview with a busy doctor. An example of a favorable environment is a short questionnaire (with a reward for completion) mailed to farmers during the winter.

The analysis determines if the scale should be fine or coarse, that is, with many or few cues. If chi-square tests are sufficient, for instance, two or three cues will be adequate. If an interval is assumed, a finer scale is necessary to use parametric statistics. From a statistical point of view, the more cues the better; but it is unlikely that a respondent utilizes more than eight cues and too many cues may irritate him. If the measurement of changes in attitudes is the goal of the study, a fine scale is needed [31]. Reliability increases as the number of cues are increased, but Nunnally [48] reports that increases in reliability tend to level off at 7, and after 11 cues there is little gain in adding more. Similarly, Green and Rao [26] concluded that little additional information was gained beyond 6 points on the scale.

Some researchers prefer an even number of cues to eliminate a midpoint in the scale, thereby forcing the lazy respondent off the center to either a favorable or unfavorable attitude. The airline questions just shown have an even number of cues.

Forced and Nonforced Scales

A respondent cannot honestly report an attitude when he is not aware of the object or the dimension of the object in question. When a large portion of the sample lacks awareness, some provision must be made for distinguishing between the respondent's state of awareness and his attitude valence. In its original form, the semantic differential instructed the respondent to check the midpoint of the scale when he was unaware of the object or if he thought that the dimension was irrelevant [50]. It has been shown that this forcing of an attitude where one does not exist confounds unawareness and indifference (the scale midpoint). The confounding, in turn, distorts measures of central tendency and variance [32]. A better approach is to use a nonforced-choice scale such as the following:

How does Federal Airlines compare with other airlines? Please circle the number that represents your evaluation or circle "Can't say."

Better than other airlines		Equal to other airlines		Worse than other airlines		Can't say
6	5	4	3	2	1	0

Respondents who cannot make a comparison because they have not flown on other airlines can now be distinguished from respondents who have a valid opinion.

Some bipolar adjectives may be developed simply by adding *un* or *in*, for example, favorable-unfavorable and convenient-inconvenient. Other adjectives require elaborate techniques such as factor analysis to determine if the respondents consider the adjectives bipolar. Osgood, Suci, and Tannenbaum [50] used factor analysis to select bipolar adjectives such as beautiful-ugly, strong-weak, and sharp-dull, which represent the dimensions of "evaluative, potency, and activity" respectively.

Measuring Attribute Salience

Most scaling techniques attempt to measure the valence of an attitude, that is, the degree of favorability. The semantic differential is appearing with greater frequency as a means of also measuring the salience of an attribute. The airline study provides an example:

> If you could choose among several airlines serving the same airports, what factors would you consider important to the choice of an airline? Please score the importance of each of the following items by circling the appropriate number. (For example, if the item is one of your most important reasons for selecting an airline, circle Number 6; if it is of no importance, circle Number 1, etc.)

	Most important					Least important
Airport counter service	6	5	4	3	2	1
Convenient flight connections	6	5	4	3	2	1
Prompt baggage delivery	6	5	4	3	2	1

Because only one antonym pair is used, this method is more like a graded checklist than a semantic differential.

Other techniques for measuring salience should be considered when the respondents are likely to give invalid direct responses to the importance of attitudes, such as attitudes of social or personal values. Nonmetric multidimensional scaling techniques for measuring salience have been developed by Carroll [8] and Rao [54]. Multiple regression yields beta coefficients that are estimates of respondents' attitude salience when the dependent variable is buying behavior and the independent variables are attitude valences [34].[3]

The Q-Sort Technique

The applications and limitations of the Q-sort technique to marketing research can be understood best by examining the purpose for which the method was developed in psychology.[4] The Q sort is generally used in psychology to compare different responses within the same person rather than to compare responses among many persons, as is the usual case in psychometrics. The Q sort is used as a means for measuring the effectiveness of treatment in psychotherapy. Using the Q sort, the patient reports his self-image and his ideal image before and after treatment. Correlation between these two images increases as the patient responds favorably to treatment. The application in marketing is obvious. Respondents are asked to report their images of their ideal brands, specified brands, and their present brand.

The Q-sort rating task is essentially an efficient rank-ordering procedure. Subjects are given a large number of attributes (50 to 150) and are instructed to array them along a scale. Clinical patients are given many statements such as "submissive," "conscientious," "efficient," and "just" with instructions to array them along a scale marked "least like—most like myself." The cards are then shuffled and the patient is instructed to array the cards along a scale

---

[3] For a discussion of additional methods, see Lunn [42].

[4] For a detailed description of the development of the technique, see Mowrer [45]. Briefer discussions with examples may be found in Kerlinger [38, pp. 581–599] and Nunnally [48, pp. 544–558]. A review of applications is provided by Wittenborn [43]. For applications to advertising, see Schlinger [58].

designated "least like—most like the ideal person." In marketing research the statements describe the characteristics of a product. For example, respondents could be asked to compare automobile brands using adjectives such as "stylish," "comfortable," "economical," and "safe," with instructions to array them along the continuum "least like—most like the ideal car."

The Q-sort procedure permits the use of more items and is faster and less tedious for subjects than the ranking or paired-comparison procedures. Nunnally [48, p. 546] notes that it is difficult to use more than 50 attributes with the ranking procedure, but 100 attributes are generally used with the Q-sort method. Paired comparisons of 50 attributes would be extremely tedious for subjects because judgment of each pair requires 5,225 comparisons. Nunnally reports that the use of 50 items with the Q-sort technique requires about 30 minutes while a complete ranking requires more than an hour.

To facilitate statistical analysis, the subject is forced to conform to quotas at each point in the scale so as to yield a normal distribution. Nunnally [48] suggests the following quotas for 100 stimuli:

Scale number	0	1	2	3	4	5	6	7	8	9	10
Quota		2	4	8	12	14	20	14	12	8	4	2

The subject is generally instructed to work from the most favorable to the least favorable end of the scale.

The Q sort has two advantages. It requires less time and effort than ranking and paired comparison methods and therefore is less costly. The technique may give more precise comparative measures than rating techniques because it requires subjects to make comparative responses [48, pp. 555–556].

While the Q sort is faster than ranking, it is slower than rating methods. Nunnally reports that subjects can make 100 ratings in less than half the time required to Q sort 100 attributes. A final limitation of this method is that it requires at least a personal interview and generally a laboratory experimental design, thereby increasing costs.

The Summated (Likert) Scale

A summated scale contains many statements relevant to the object, but generally no attempt is made to scale the items along an attitude dimension as is the case with the Thurstone scale [15, 60]. Instead, each respondent indicates how strongly he agrees or disagrees with each statement. The statements vary in their degree of favorability or unfavorability toward the attitude object. The attitude score is the sum of the weights assigned to the cues. An example of the Likert scale will clarify these points.

> The following sentences describe the Old Ezra Bank. If you strongly agree with the statement, underscore "Strongly agree," if you are uncertain, underscore "Uncertain," etc.
> 1. The Old Ezra Bank is a solid institution.

Strongly agree	Agree	Uncertain	Disagree	Strongly disagree
(5)	(4)	(3)	(2)	(1)

> 2. This bank is progressive.

Strongly agree	Agree	Uncertain	Disagree	Strongly disagree
(5)	(4)	(3)	(2)	(1)

3. This bank may be considered old fashioned.

Strongly agree	Agree	Uncertain	Disagree	Strongly disagree
(1)	(2)	(3)	(4)	(5)

The weights, in parentheses here, are not shown on the questionnaire. The sequence of numbers in the third statement has been reversed so that scores will be consistent. In this case higher numbers indicate a more favorable image of the bank.

The score of these three items is 9, which has no meaning unless it is compared with scores of other respondents. The primary criticism of the summated scale is that a total does not reflect a unique attitude since the total can be derived in many different ways. For example, a score of 9 could mean that uncertainty was underlined on each scale or that the attitude pattern was strongly disagree (1), strongly agree (5), and uncertain (3). Each pattern reflects a different attitude, but the total score does not reflect these differences.

Scales like the Likert are frequently used in marketing without summated scoring by treating each item as a scale. Thus, in the above example there would be three scales, not one. Another method for making the score represent a unique attitude is to scale the statements using Thurstone's procedures. The score is then a sum of the products of the Likert and the Thurstone scale values [15, pp. 201–219].

The Cumulative (Guttman) Scale

The cumulative scale is like a summated scale in that a respondent agrees or disagrees with each statement. But there is one important difference: there is no attempt to relate statements in the summated scale, while in a cumulative scale the statements are rank-ordered. Thus, in the latter sense, a respondent who agreed with statement 3, for example, might be hypothesized to agree also with statements 1 and 2. The Bogardus social-distance scale [7] is a cumulative scale. The Guttman scalogram method for determining if statements form a unidimensional scale yields a cumulative scale.[5]

An abbreviated version of the Guttman technique will serve to illustrate the cumulative scale. Four to six statements in random order are given to subjects who are instructed to check those statements with which they agree. The responses are then analyzed, using methods described by Guttman, to rank the statements in increasing order of favorability. Statements form a perfect unidimensional scale when a respondent's score permits reproduction of all his responses. For example, assume that respondents A, B, and C agreed with five statements in the following pattern:

A	B	C	Statement
x	x	x	1. As good as any other bank
x	x		2. Neither a good nor bad bank
		x	3. A friendly bank
		x	4. A greatly respected bank
			5. The only bank for me
(2)	(3)	(4)	(Scores)

The knowledge that the scores of A and B are 2 and 3 respectively permits the researcher to reproduce their responses perfectly. Respondent C "erred" by fail-

---

[5] For a discussion of scalogram analysis, criticisms, and citations, see [15, pp. 172–200], [28, pp. 460–462], and [60, pp. 370–377].

ing to agree with statement 2. In the terminology of scalogram analysis, these items have 93 percent reproducibility ($1 - \frac{1}{15}$). For a scale to be accepted as unidimensional, Guttman specified reproducibility of at least 90 percent.

Of all the unidimensional techniques, only the Guttman method tests for unidimensionality. The technique is rarely used in marketing research, however, for one or more of the following reasons. First, construction of just one scale requires considerable time and effort. Since most marketing problems require the measurement of attitudes along many dimensions, the construction of a questionnaire would be very expensive. In addition, response may be reduced by the fact that respondents must evaluate every sentence. Second, there is considerable risk in using the scalogram method because the scale is formed after the data are collected and not prejudged, as with the Thurstone technique. Thus if acceptable levels of reproducibility cannot be achieved, the data are useless. The statements could be prejudged, as with the Thurstone method, but this would increase the cost of building a scale.

Paired-Comparison Techniques

The paired-comparison method can be used to measure attitudes on many occasions. The most common applications include brand preference studies, pretesting advertisements, and similarities measures in multidimensional scaling [25].

The paired-comparison technique generally instructs the respondents to consider two stimuli—for example, new food products—and report a preference according to some dimension such as taste, consistency, and so forth. Each subject compares all possible pairs of n stimuli, that is, $n(n-1)/2$. Thus, 5 stimuli would require each subject to make 10 comparisons according to a single dimension. If a comparison by two dimensions were required, 20 paired comparisons would be necessary.

The psychological distance between two stimuli, S_i and S_j, is based on a normal curve transformation of the proportion of respondents who judge S_i greater than S_j. This transformation has been established in Thurstone's law of comparative judgment.[6] In brief, an interval scale is derived from paired comparisons in the following manner. The number of respondents selecting one stimulus over another is cast in an n by n matrix. These frequencies are then converted into proportions in which the main diagonal in the matrix of proportions has approximately 0.5 in each cell. That is to say, if S_i were compared with S_i, approximately half the respondents would report that S_i was greater and half the respondents would report that S_i was less than S_i, which is to say that they are equal. All other cell entries will be greater or less than 0.5, thereby reflecting a perceived psychological distance between two stimuli. This matrix of proportions is converted to a Z matrix in which the cell entries are the normal deviates, Z corresponding to the deviation of the proportion from 0.5. Thus the main diagonal will be approximately 0, signifying that the psychological distance between S_i and S_i is zero. Entries below the diagonal will carry minus signs, indicating a proportion less than 0.5. The mean of each column is the scale value of the stimulus. The difference between any two scale values is the psychological distance between two stimuli.

The advantages of the paired-comparison method are twofold: (1) analysis can establish an interval scale which permits the use of more powerful statistics and (2) the task assigned to the respondent is a simple one, the comparison of

---

[6] For a detailed description see [15, pp. 20–29], [28, pp. 154–168], and [27, pp. 194–198].

two stimuli. The disadvantages include the computational effort required to scale the stimuli and respondent fatigue. If the number of stimuli and of attitude dimensions is large, respondents must make numerous paired comparisons. Respondent fatigue may bias the results.

The Rank-Order Method

The rank-order method requires the respondent to rank stimuli along an attitude dimension in a manner similar to the Q sort and the Thurstone judging process except that there is only one stimulus in each category. It shares the advantage of the paired-comparison method by forcing observers to discriminate among all items, but it avoids errors in transitivity that occur with paired comparisons; for example, a subject reports $S_i > S_j$ and $S_j > S_k$, but he reports that $S_i < S_k$. Another advantage is that ranking is faster than the comparison of pairs. For example, a respondent can rank 10 items more quickly than he can judge 45 pairs, that is, $10(10 - 1)/2 = 45$.

Respondents may be required to rank actual advertisements or package designs, in which case an interviewer or a laboratory is required so that the stimuli may be handled physically. But ranking may be used also in a printed questionnaire. Assume that a respondent is ranking possible names for a new product. The names would be printed on a questionnaire and he would be instructed to put 1 beside his first choice, 2 beside his second choice, and so on.

The simplest method for scoring rank-order data is to compute the median rank given to the stimulus by a group of respondents. The statistics appropriate to ordinal scales may be used to compare the rankings assigned by different groups.

Numerous methods have been developed to compute higher-order scales from ranked data, but the discussion will be limited to two techniques—the normalized-rank and the comparative-judgment approaches.[7] The normalized-rank method assumes that the frequency distribution of ranks will be normally distributed and that each stimulus will occupy the same area under the curve. If there are 10 stimuli, each will occupy 10 percent of the area. The scale boundaries can be determined by using a table of normal curves. Stimuli are assigned to each scale interval according to the rank order established by the respondents.

A more defensible method, according to Guilford [28, pp. 183–186], is the comparative-judgment approach. Comparative data can be derived from rank data. For example, given three stimuli ranked in decreasing order of preference, S_i, S_j, and S_k, these may be converted to paired comparisons where $S_i > S_j$, $S_j > S_k$, and $S_i > S_k$. These paired comparisons may be scored using Thurstone's law of comparative judgment. Guilford [28, p. 182] shows that other simpler methods give comparable results with considerably less effort.

The Constant-Sum Scale

The constant-sum scale [28, 66] is gaining popularity in marketing research. This scale requires the respondent to divide a constant sum, generally 10 or 100, among two or more stimuli. For example, a constant-sum scale for three brands of a product may appear as follows:

> Divide 100 points between each of the following pairs of brands according to your preference for the brands.

[7] For a discussion and examples of these and other methods of scaling from rank data, see [28, pp. 178–195].

1. Brand A   60   Brand B   40
2. Brand B   70   Brand C   30
3. Brand A   90   Brand C   10

Or the three brands may be presented together, as follows:

> Divide 100 points among each of the following brands according to your preference for the brands.
>
> Brand A   50   Brand B   30   Brand C   20

The first format is similar to the paired comparison method and the second is like the rank-order technique. Guilford [28, p. 220] reports that subjects prefer the two-stimuli arrangement. The constant-sum scale may be used also with one brand or an "ideal brand" as a standard, thus:

> Divide 100 points between the following pairs of brands according to your preference for the brands.
>
> Ideal brand _____   Brand A _____
> Ideal brand _____   Brand B _____
> Ideal brand _____   Brand C _____

Assuming the constant-sum scale yields interval measures, the data can be transformed into an interval scale by averaging all the points assigned to a brand. This transformation is expressed algebraically as:

$$S_i = \sum_{i=1}^{n} S_{ic}/n(n-1)/2$$

where S_i is the interval scale value of brand i, S_{ic} is the score of brand i during comparison c, and n is the number of brands being compared. The number of brand i comparisons, c, will equal $(n-1)$. Applying this equation to the paired comparisons of brands A, B, and C as shown above, we find the interval scale value of brand A is 50, B is 36⅔, and C is 13⅓.[8]

A similarity between the two-stimuli constant-sum scale and indifference theory, as described in economics, should be noted. A respondent who is asked to assign points to two stimuli is, in effect, placing himself on a continuum between these stimuli at a point that represents his attitude. This decision process seems to be very similar to the task assigned to the consumer who is required to report his indifference point between quantities of two goods. Thus, at this point, economic theory and psychological theory converge.[9]

The constant-sum scale requires a large number of comparisons and, like the paired-comparison method, may fatigue respondents. In addition, the scoring technique requires more work than a rating-scale technique, such as the semantic differential, but not as much as the scoring of paired comparisons. The advantage of the technique is that it provides more information than the paired-comparison technique.

---

[8] For methods of ratio scoring, see [28, pp. 214–220] and [66]. If one assumes that a ratio scale of measurement is formed, the geometric mean, not the arithmetic mean, should be used as a measure of central tendency.

[9] For an early discussion, see Thurstone [65]. Myers and Roberts [46] have used ratio scales and indifference maps to show preferences for clothing patterns and the desired sex and number of children.

UNIDIMENSIONAL OR MULTIDIMENSIONAL ANALYSIS?

Unidimensional and multidimensional analyses use the same measurement techniques but with different tasks assigned to the respondent. The paired-comparison technique provides an example. For unidimensional analysis, the respondent compares objects. For multidimensional analysis, the respondent compares the distances between objects by reporting pairs of objects that are most similar to other pairs. Thus the task and method of analysis, not the measurement technique, determine dimensionality.

Which is preferable, unidimensional or multidimensional analysis? There is no easy answer. Multidimensional analysis was introduced into attitude measurement techniques about twenty years after unidimensional methods were developed. Multidimensional analysis has become more feasible during the last ten years as computer developments have permitted more sophisticated techniques. Because it is newer and more sophisticated, there is a tendency to think that it is better. The choice of analysis depends on the nature of the problem being researched and the complexity of the respondents' judgment processes.

Why should multidimensional analysis be used? This question is easier to answer. Persons use more than one dimension to make judgments even though they are instructed to place a concept along a single dimension. The stimulus, color, provides an example. It is a complex stimulus because it is composed of light waves with three physical dimensions: amplitude, frequency, and complexity. Multidimensional analysis has revealed that people organize color stimuli according to three subjective dimensions: brightness, hue, and saturation. The objective and subjective dimensions are highly correlated. Persons' final judgments of color similarities are combinations of the subjective dimensions [59, p. 170]. Multidimensional analysis describes a complex judgment process by identifying (1) the number of dimensions required to reproduce the original similarity judgments with minimal error, (2) a ranking of objects along each dimension (valence), and (3) the salience of these dimensions in the judgment process.

INSTRUMENTS TO MEASURE ACTION TENDENCIES

During the third stage of information processing, the individual organizes his attitudes into a cluster, weighting each attitude according to its perceived importance, that is, its salience. This cluster is his action tendency, his overall attraction to or repulsion from the attitude object. In marketing research this tendency to act is measured by the individual's subjective probability of buying, of visiting the dealer, of seeking additional information, of buying a substitute good, and so forth.

Measures of buying expectations for durable goods interest economists because these expenditures represent a large share of total consumer expenditures. To provide data for economic planning, the U.S. Bureau of the Census quarterly collects from a sample of households their buying expectations for automobiles and many household durables. Prior to July 1966, buying *intentions* were measured with the following cues: No, Don't know, Maybe, Yes—probably, and Yes—definitely.[10] After this date, buying *expectations* were

[10] This type of scale continues to be used in many surveys. See, for example, Katona et al. [37]. The weakness of this scale lies in its treatment of respondents with a low purchase probability as nonintenders, that is, zero probability, thereby excluding them from analysis. For a discussion and related citations, see Ferber [18].

measured using the following scale of subjective probabilities with verbal cues [67]:

100   Absolutely certain
 90
 80   Strong possibility
 70
 60
 50
 40
 30
 20   Slight possibility
 10
  0   Absolutely no chance

There is some evidence that too many adjective cues "reduce the accuracy of probability judgments" [36]. These probabilities tend to underestimate subsequent automobile purchases. The mean probability has been less than 65 percent of the actual purchase rate during a subsequent six-month period. Despite this downward bias, 76 percent of the variance in subsequent automobile purchases was associated with the variance in purchase probability and a dummy variable to reflect supply shortages caused by strikes.

Probabilities can be used in forecasting despite the bias if there is a stable relationship between these probabilities and subsequent purchases [67]. Thus, buying expectations can be a useful variable in short-range forecasts of durable goods purchases.

CRITERIA FOR SELECTING INSTRUMENTS

The selection of instruments to measure attitudes depends on (1) the stage and size of the research project; (2) the data requirements of the statistical analysis necessary to answer the marketing problem; (3) theoretical characteristics of the instrument—validity, reliability, and sensitivity; and (4) the costs of developing and implementing the instrument.

Stage and Size of the Project

Unstructured techniques are appropriate during the early stages of research, such as problem formulation and attribute identification. These techniques may be appropriate for gathering data when the project is small (fewer than 100 respondents). As the sample size increases, the greater costs of analyzing unstructured responses must be weighed against the cost of developing and testing a more structured instrument.

Statistical Analysis

A more structured instrument permits the use of more powerful statistical methods which reduce the sample size, thereby reducing the cost of gathering data. Therefore the measuring instruments must be selected in conjunction with the definition of the marketing problem and the methods required to solve the problem [33, Chap. 7]. Statistical techniques appropriate to each scale of measurement are summarized in Table 2. Note that the number of defining relations (column 2) between the object being measured and the number system increases as the scale of measurement moves from a nominal to a ratio scale. An instrument that yields an interval scale of measurement, for example, provides more information than an instrument that yields only a nominal scale. This additional information permits the use of more powerful

TABLE 2 Statistical Methods Appropriate to Scales of Measurement

Scale (1)	Defining relations (2)	Examples (3)	Appropriate statistical measures of				
			Centrality (4)	Dispersion (5)	Association or correlation (6)	Significance (7)
Nominal...	(1) Equivalence	Numbers on football player's jerseys Assignment of type or model numbers to classes	Mode	Information, H	Contingency correlation coefficients	Chi square
Ordinal....	(1) Equivalence (2) Greater than (rank-order)	Hardness of minerals Street numbers Grades of leather, lumber, wool, etc. Intelligence test raw scores	Median	Percentiles	Rank-order correlation Spearman r_s Kendall Tau Kendall W	Sign test Runs test Mann–Whitney U test
Interval....	(1) Equivalence (2) Greater than (3) Known intervals (additivity)	Temperature (Fahrenheit) Position in space Time (calendar)	Arithmetic mean	Standard deviation Average deviation	Product-moment correlation Correlation ratio	t test F test
Ratio......	(1) Equivalence (2) Greater than (3) Known intervals (4) Known ratio of any two scale values (known origin)	Numerosity Length, density, work time intervals, etc. Temperature (Rankine or Kelvin) Loudness (sones) Brightness (brils)	Geometric mean Harmonic mean	Percent variation Coefficient of variation		

SOURCES: from S. S. Stevens, "Measurement, Psychophysics, and Utility," in C. West Churchman and Philburn Ratoosh, eds., *Measurement: Definition and Theories*, New York: Wiley, 1959; and [62, p. 30].

statistical techniques (columns 4 through 7). To use a statistical technique less powerful than the instrument permits has the effect of discarding valuable information. Conversely, using a technique more powerful than the instrument permits assumes information into the analysis and may produce an erroneous conclusion and an incorrect course of action.

The researcher may work from the desired statistical technique to the scale of measurement required (Table 2) and then from the measurement scale to the appropriate instruments for identifying attributes (Table 3) and for meas-

TABLE 3   Summary of Techniques for Identifying Salient Attributes*

Approach (1)	Procedure for		
	Naming salient attributes (2)	Evaluating the object (3)	Measurement scale (4)
Unstructured: Depth interviews and projective techniques.............	Analyst	Decision of analyst	Nominal
Partial structured: Repertory grid.............	Respondent	Matrix of attributes and brands	Nominal (or ordinal if brands are ranked)
Structured: Dyad, triad, or a ranking of similarities (or preferences)....	Analyst	Computer algorithm for multidimensional scaling	Ordered metric
Any attitude-measurement technique.................	Automatic Interaction Detection algorithm	Not evaluated	Nominal to interval (depending on the measurement technique)

* To identify the problem, for use with more structural instruments, to identify needs not met by present products, to create promotional themes, and to identify competition.

uring attitudes (Table 4). He may also start with the marketing problem (see footnotes in Tables 3 and 4), select the appropriate instrument (column 1 in Tables 3 and 4), determine the measurement scale (column 4 in Tables 3 and 4), and then turn to Table 2 for the appropriate statistical method. To illustrate the first approach, if the analysis requires the F test, the instrument must generate interval data (Table 2). Appropriate instruments may be the Q sort, the Likert scale (if standardized), paired comparisons, rank-order methods (if scored appropriately), and the constant-sum scale (Table 4). If, however, he starts with the problem of identifying salient attributes using unstructured techniques (Table 3), his analysis is limited to statistical techniques appropriate to nominal scales of measurement, such as the mode and the chi-square test (Table 2).

TABLE 4 Summary of Techniques for Measuring Attitudes*

Instrument (1)	Procedure for		Measurement scale (4)
	Identifying salient attributes (2)	Determining the attitude score (3)	
1. Thurstone equal-appearing interval scale........	Preliminary investigation	a. Compute median or arithmetic mean scale value of sentences selected by subject b. Method of successive intervals [15, pp. 120–147]	Ordinal
2. Semantic differential scale........	Preliminary investigation	Compute medians or arithmetic means	Ordinal
3. Q sort........	Preliminary investigation	Methods, which are controversial [60, p. 379], include tests of significant difference, correlation, factor analysis, and successive-interval scoring	Ordinal or interval
4. Summated (Likert) scale........	Item analysis of pretest scores	Sum of respondent's scores relative to distribution of a defined group or standardized T scores [15, pp. 158–159]	Ordinal or interval (if scores are standardized to T scores)
5. Cumulative (Guttman) scale........	Scalogram analysis	Highest item scored	Ordinal
6. Paired comparisons........	Preliminary investigation	Thurstone's law of comparative judgment, location of zero point [28, pp. 171–173]	Interval
7. Rank order........	Preliminary investigation	a. Compute median b. Normalize or law of comparative judgment	Ordinal or interval
8. Constant-sum scales........		Arithmetic mean	Interval
Probability scale†........		Multidimensional	Interval

* To measure needs, to measure corporate and brand images, to pretest advertisements, and to measure promotional effectiveness.

† To estimate the probability of buying a product or brand and to estimate the probability of visiting a dealer.

Theoretical Criteria

The requirements of statistical analysis narrow the choice but do not select a specific instrument. Theoretical criteria that must be considered include validity, reliability, and sensitivity.

Validity. An instrument is valid when it measures what it is supposed to measure; but since attitudes are elusive, attitude-scale validation is difficult. *Predictive* validity correlates observed behavior with that which was predicted from attitude measures. When attitudes and behavior are measured at a point in time, correlations yield *concurrent* validity. *Content* validity is a subjective judgment of the relevance of an item to a scale. The Thurstone judging procedure, for example, tends to establish content validity. *Construct* validity is established by correlating an attitude measure with measures of different attitudes or personality dimensions.

Clinical psychologists of the late 1930s and marketing researchers of the early 1950s thought that projective techniques gave more valid measures of attitudes than structured methods. Maher, Watt, and Campbell observed that this conclusion was derived more from a knowledge of the imperfections of structured techniques than any demonstrated superiority of projective ones. There are few such comparative tests. To meet this deficiency, these researchers compared the unstructured sentence-completion method with the structured attitude-scale method. They reported that the "tests were found to validate each other quite satisfactorily" and that the structured tests were slightly better in differentiating among the respondents [69, p. 287].

Reliability. A measuring instrument is reliable when it gives consistent results over time. There are three methods of estimating the reliability of attitude scales. *Test-retest* reliability correlates the attitudes of a group measured with the same scale at two different times. *Equivalent-form* reliability correlates the attitudes of a group measured with two scales considered equivalent. *Split-half* reliability correlates attitudes measured by half of the items in a scale with attitudes measured by the other half of the items. The last two methods measure internal, not temporal, consistency and therefore are not true measures of reliability.[11]

Validity and reliability refer to specific scales, not to the techniques for building them. Thus we cannot generalize that one technique produces more valid or reliable scales than another method. Many standardized scales have been developed by social psychologists for measuring attitudes toward social concepts. Estimates of reliability and validity are provided to aid in their selection [55, 61]. Unfortunately for marketing researchers, standardized scales are not possible due to the lack of standardized marketing problems. Practitioners should, however, develop measures of validity and reliability so that their scales can be improved [1, 5].

Sensitivity. The sensitivity of a scale is important in marketing because of the attempts to measure the effect of promotional effort by measuring changes in attitudes. A more sensitive measure is needed to measure change. In scaling this means adding more items to the scale. If the scale is verbal, such as the Thurstone or Guttman scale, an increase in items increases respondents' fatigue and reduces their cooperation.

---

[11] The discussion of reliability and validity follows that of Shaw and Wright [61. pp. 16–20].

Practical Criteria—Costs of Developing and Implementing the Techniques

Unstructured Techniques. Cost comparisons of unstructured techniques are at best very subjective because of the scarcity of experiments comparing techniques. The marketing literature reflects conflicting opinions and evidence. For instance, Hess [29] concluded that group interviews have great promise in marketing research. Payne [53], in contrast, concluded that 25 tape-recorded individual interviews yielded the same results as 10 recorded group interviews (four or five persons to a group), costs were about equal, and tapes from the individual interviews were easier to analyze.

The important criterion when selecting among subjective techniques is the useful content that each generates. Payne [52] compared depth probing and reason-why questions and found that the depth approach increased the verbiage but increased the content only about a sixth.

The selection of open-end questions or cartoon pictures as projective techniques seems to depend on the nature of the attitude being measured. Engel and Wales [17] found that the techniques gave similar results during a personal interview when there was no social risk in holding an attitude. When a social risk was involved, the techniques appeared to measure different types of attitudes—private or public ones. After comparing open and closed questions, Dohrenwend concluded that open questions were less efficient and that "there is no evidence that open questions possess the advantage of being more productive of depth" [13, p. 183].

Dohrenwend [13] and Payne [52] emphasize the importance of using unstructured methods to identify dimensions, to develop structured questions, to establish a range of answers, and to provide quotations for the final report. The elimination of all unstructured questions in the final questionnaire, however, requires extensive preliminary investigation and numerous pretests of the final questionnaire. In practice, the researcher must choose between the expense and delay in refining a questionnaire and the expense and delay in analyzing unstructured questions. If the questionnaire will be used many times and if the sample is large, effort spent in developing a structured questionnaire will be offset by savings in analysis. Conversely, the final questionnaire can be less structured when the marketing problem does not warrant large expenditures of money or time, when the survey will not be repeated, and when the sample is small.

Structured Techniques. The editing and coding costs for structured instruments are lower than those for unstructured methods, but the development costs are higher. These development costs include the selection of cues that are unambiguous to respondents. Procedures for selecting unambiguous cues vary among techniques. The Thurstone procedure is expensive because it requires 100 or more judges to evaluate hundreds of statements to form just one scale. These costs are a major reason why Thurstone scales are not used often in marketing research. Factor analysis is used to identify cues for the semantic differential and item analysis for the Likert scale. The cost per cue tends to be less with these scaling instruments.

Respondents' preferences for scaling techniques influence the cost of research through nonresponse, uncompleted questionnaires, and longer interviews. Respondents do not like highly verbal scales such as the Thurstone scale. Their preference is for rating-type scales [31].

The field costs associated with a measuring instrument depend on the conditions required to administer the instrument. The Q sort, for instance, may require a laboratory setting or at least a trained interviewer. The semantic differential and Likert scales can be used in a low-cost mail survey.

LIMITATIONS OF ATTITUDE MEASUREMENTS

Most of the present applications of scaling devices may be classified as descriptive or diagnostic. Scaling devices are used to describe the needs of a market with the hope of identifying untapped market segments for present and new products. The more common applications are diagnostic. Why is a brand doing poorly? Where do we need more promotion? Was the promotional effort effective? Diagnostic studies compare the attitudes of a test group of respondents with certain benchmark attitudes. A benchmark may be the attitudes of respondents who have recently purchased the product, it may be respondents' attitudes toward a successful product, for example [14], their attitudes toward the "ideal" product, or their attitudes at some previous point in time. Smith [63] provides an example of the use of benchmarks to direct promotional effort at General Motors. In this case the concepts that need promotion are identified by comparing the attitudes of respondents who would consider a brand with the attitudes of those who would not. While benchmarks are useful, they are a poor substitute for a model that describes the relationship between attitudes and buying behavior. Thus, the utility of the measures is limited by the lack of models.

The main criticism of attitude scales, their inability to predict behavior [20, 51, 56], tends to be misplaced. Inability to predict stems less from the limitations of scaling devices than from the lack of a model of behavior that reflects the role of attitudes in the decision process. We do not have models that describe relationships among changes in behavior, attitudes, group membership, roles, and value systems. "The concept attitude is still in a surprisingly crude state of formulation considering its widespread use" [12, p. 30].

Attitudes toward objects are measured without considering the influence of environment during the measurement and during the decision process. Measures tend to concentrate on the dimensions of the product or service being sold with insufficient attention to measuring the dimensions of an individual's need, thereby ignoring the fact that motivation consists of one's perception of his needs and goals. Thus, a prerequisite to a well-designed marketing research questionnaire is an understanding of the consumer's decision environment.

NEW DIRECTIONS

Trends in attitudinal research are toward multidimensionality, multivariate non-metric analysis, more complete models of the decision process, and more efficient means for testing hypotheses and developing new models. Needed are models that are more than single attitudinal equations. More complete systems of equations will relate buying behavior to demographic, economic, social, and psychological variables. Also needed are models that relate the many dimensions of behavior. At the present time behavior is regarded in isolated forms— buying, visiting a dealer, reading ads, talking to friends—which are actually related forms of behavior. Furthermore, behavior is defined in unidimensional terms. More powerful insights will be possible when attitudes can be mapped into multidimensional behavior.

SUMMARY

Motivations for buying are not limited to physical needs but include social-psychological needs which are reflected in an individual's attitudes toward himself and his environment. Motivation includes also an individual's evaluation of the alternative means for meeting these needs. These evaluations are attitudes—learned predispositions to act. An attitude is learned because it is the product of information and an individual's value system. His value system is learned from his culture, reference groups, education, and commercial sources such as advertising.

An individual does not buy a product; he buys those attributes of the product that will meet his needs. To understand buying motivation, therefore, those attributes which are salient to his buying decision must be identified. His attitudes toward alternatives, such as brands, are comparisons along these attributes. Attributes are identified using unstructured techniques (depth interviews and projective techniques), partially structured techniques (the repertory grid), and structured techniques (the Automatic Interaction Detection algorithm, factor analysis, cluster analysis, and nonmetric multidimensional scaling).

An attitude has two components—beliefs and values. Advertising researchers frequently use measures of beliefs to identify areas where additional promotion is needed. Beliefs may be measured as a dichotomy (awareness-unawareness) or along a probability continuum. Aided and unaided techniques are used to measure beliefs.

Instruments for measuring attitudes have been borrowed from social psychology. These include the Thurstone scale, the semantic differential, the Q sort, the Likert scale, the Guttman scale, the paired-comparison technique, rank-order methods, and the constant-sum scale. The semantic differential has been the most frequently used scale in marketing research.

An overall attitude to an object, such as a brand, may be expressed as a subjective probability of buying the brand. This probability is a function of the salience of the generic attributes and attitudes toward the brand attributes. Subjective probabilities of behavior—for example, buying or visiting a dealer—are measured along scales using verbal, numerical, or verbal-numerical cues. The trend has been toward numerical cues.

The final selection of an attitude instrument depends on the stage and size of the research project, the statistical techniques to be used during analysis, theoretical characteristics of the instrument, and the costs of developing and implementing the instrument. Generalizations about each of these criteria are difficult in marketing because of the lack of standardized problems and the confidentiality of the research.

The main limitation of attitude research has been its emphasis on describing attitudes rather than predicting behavior. The inability to predict behavior from measures of attitudes may be traced to the lack of models that describe the role of attitudes in behavior. Attitude research is moving toward the development of more complete models of behavior.

REFERENCES

1. Abrams, J., "An Evaluation of Alternative Rating Devices for Consumer Research," *Journal of Marketing Research*, vol. 3, May 1966, pp. 189–193.
2. Andreasen, A. R., "Attitudes and Customer Behavior: A Decision Model," in L. E.

Preston, ed., *New Research in Marketing*, Berkeley: Institute of Business and Economic Research, University of California, 1965, pp. 1–16.

3. Andrews, M., N. Morgan, and A. Sonquist, *Multiple Classification Analysis*, Ann Arbor, Mich.: Survey Research Center, The University of Michigan, p. 967.

4. Assael, H., "Segmenting Markets by Group Purchasing Behavior: An Application of the AID Technique," *Journal of Marketing Research*, vol. 7, 1970, pp. 153–158.

5. Axelrod, J. N., "Attitude Measures that Predict Purchase," *Journal of Advertising Research*, vol. 8, March 1968, pp. 3–17.

6. Bass, F. M., and W. W. Talarzyk, "A Study of Attitude Theory and Brand Preference," Working Paper no. 252, West Lafayette, Ind.: Institute for Research in the Behavioral, Economic, and Management Sciences, Purdue University, July 1969, p. 8.

7. Bogardus, E. S., "Measuring Social Distances," *Journal of Applied Sociology*, vol. 9, 1925, pp. 299–308; reprinted in Martin Fishbein, ed., *Readings in Attitude Theory and Measurement*, New York: Wiley, 1967, pp. 71–76.

8. Carroll, J. D., "Individual Differences and Multidimensional Scaling," 1969, mimeographed.

9. Cohen, B., and M. Houston, "Some Alternatives to a Five-point Likert Scale"; paper read at a workshop on attitude research and consumer behavior, Urbana, Ill.: University of Illinois, December 5, 1970.

10. Collins, L., and C. Montgomery, "Whatever Happened to Motivation Research? End of the Messianic Hope," *Journal of the Market Research Society*, vol. 12, January 1970, pp. 1–11.

11. Crespi, I., "Use of a Scaling Technique in Surveys," *Journal of Marketing*, vol. 25, July 1961, pp. 69–72.

12. DeFleur, M. L., and F. R. Westie, "Attitude as a Scientific Concept," *Social Forces*, vol. 42, October 1963, p. 30.

13. Dohrenwend, B. S., "Some Effects of Open and Closed Questions on Respondents' Answers," *Human Organization*, vol. 24, Summer 1965, p. 183.

14. Downing, J. A., "A Study of Brand Images, An Experimental Approach to Attitude Measurement," *Attitude Scaling*, Publication no. 4, The Market Research Society, London: The Oakwood Press, 1960, pp. 57–67.

15. Edwards, A. L., *Techniques of Attitude Scale Construction*, New York: Appleton-Century-Crofts, 1957.

16. Engel, F., D. T. Kollat, D. Blackwell, *Consumer Behavior*, New York: Holt, 1968.

17. ———, and H. G. Wales, "Spoken versus Pictured Questions on Taboo Topics," *Journal of Advertising Research*, vol. 2, March 1962, p. 17.

18. Ferber, R., "Anticipations Statistics and Consumer Behavior," *The American Statistician*, vol. 20, October 1966, pp. 20–24.

19. ———, and H. G. Wales, eds., *Motivation and Market Behavior*, Homewood, Ill.: Irwin, 1958.

20. Festinger, L., "Behavior Support for Opinion Change," *Public Opinion Quarterly*, vol. 27, Fall 1964, pp. 404–417.

21. Fishbein, M., "A Behavior Theory Approach to the Relations between Beliefs about an Object and the Attitude toward the Object," M. Fishbein, ed., *Readings in Attitude Theory and Measurement*, New York: Wiley, 1967, pp. 394–396.

22. Frost, W. A. K., and R. L. Braine, "The Application of the Repertory Grid Technique to Problems in Market Research," *Commentary*, vol. 9, July 1967, pp. 161–175.

23. Gatty, R., "Multivariate Analysis for Marketing Research," *Applied Statistics*, vol. 15, 1966, pp. 151–172.

24. Green, P. E., and F. J. Carmone, "The Performance of the Computer Market: A Multivariate Approach," *Economics and Business Bulletin*, vol. 21, 1968, pp. 1–11.

25. ———, and F. J. Carmone, *Multidimensional Scaling and Related Techniques in Marketing Analysis*, Boston: Allyn and Bacon, 1970.

26. ———, and V. R. Rao, "Rating Scales and Information Recovery—How Many

Scales and Response Categories to Use?" *Journal of Marketing*, vol. 34, July 1970.

27. ———, and D. S. Tull, *Research for Marketing Decisions*, Englewood Cliffs, N.J.: Prentice-Hall, 1966.

28. Guilford, J. P., *Psychometric Methods*, New York: McGraw-Hill, 1954.

29. Hess, J. M., "Group Interviewing," in R. L. King, ed., *Proceedings of the American Marketing Association*, Chicago: American Marketing Association, 1968, pp. 193–196.

30. Howard, J. A., and J. N. Sheth, *The Theory of Buyer Behavior*, New York: Wiley, 1969.

31. Hughes, G. D., "Selecting Scales to Measure Attitude Changes," *Journal of Marketing Research*, vol. 4, February 1967, pp. 85–87.

32. ———, "Some Confounding Effects of Forced-Choice Scales," *Journal of Marketing Research*, vol. 6, May 1969, pp. 223–226.

33. ———, *Attitude Measurement for Marketing Strategies*, Glenview, Ill.: Scott, Foresman, 1971.

34. ———, and J. L. Guerrero, "Testing Cognitive Models through Computer-controlled Experiments," paper delivered at the meeting of the Association for Consumer Research, Amherst, Mass., August 28, 1970.

35. ———, and P. A. Naert, "A Computer-controlled Experiment in Consumer Behavior," *Journal of Business*, vol. 43, July 1970, pp. 354–720.

36. Juster, F. T., *Consumer Buying Intentions and Purchase Probability*, National Bureau of Economic Research, occasional paper.

37. Katona, G., W. Dunkelberg, J. Schmiedeskamp, and F. Stafford, *1968 Survey of Consumer Finances*, Ann Arbor, Mich.: Survey Research Center, Institute for Social Research, The University of Michigan, 1969.

38. Kerlinger, F. N., *Foundations of Behavioral Research*, New York: Holt, 1965, pp. 539–553.

39. Krech, D., S. Crutchfield, and E. L. Ballachey, *Individual in Society*, New York: McGraw-Hill, 1962.

40. Lavidge, R. J., and G. A. Steiner, "A Model for Predictive Measurements of Advertising Effectiveness," *Journal of Marketing*, vol. 25, October 1961, pp. 59–62.

41. Lunn, J. A., "Empirical Techniques in Consumer Research," in Denis Pym, ed., *Industrial Society*, Baltimore: Penguin, 1968, pp. 401–425.

42. ———, "Prospectives in Attitude Research: Methods and Applications," *Journal of the Market Research Society*, vol. 11, 1969, pp. 201–213.

43. Maher, B. A., N. Watt, and D. T. Campbell, "Comparative Validity of Two Projective and Two Structured Attitude Tests in a Prison Population," *Journal of Applied Psychology*, vol. 44, August 1960, pp. 284–288.

44. Morgan, N., and J. Purnell, "Isolating Openings for New Products in a Multidimensional Space," *Journal of the Market Research Society*, vol. 11, July 1969, pp. 255–260.

45. Mowrer, O. H., "Q-Technique—Description, History, and Critique," *Psychotherapy: Theory and Research*, New York: Ronald, 1953.

46. Myers, G. C., and J. M. Roberts, "A Technique for Measuring Preferential Family Size and Composition," *Eugenics Quarterly*, vol. 15, September 1968, pp. 164–172.

47. Nicosia, F. M., *Consumer Decision Processes*, Englewood Cliffs, N.J.: Prentice-Hall, 1966.

48. Nunnally, J., *Psychometric Theory*, New York: McGraw-Hill, 1967.

49. Osgood, C., and P. Tannenbaum, "The Principle of Congruity in the Prediction of Attitude Changes," *Psychological Review*, vol. 62, 1955, pp. 42–55.

50. ———, Suci, and P. Tannenbaum, *The Measurement of Meaning*, Urbana, Ill.: University of Illinois Press, 1970.

51. Palda, K. S., "The Hypothesis of a Hierarchy of Effects: A Partial Evaluation," *Journal of Marketing Research*, vol. 3, February 1966, pp. 13–24.

52. Payne, S. L., "Are Open-ended Questions Worth the Effort?" *Journal of Marketing Research*, vol. 2, November 1965, p. 418.

53. ———, "Return to Quantification," in L. Adler and I. Crespi, eds., *Attitude Research at Sea*, Chicago: American Marketing Association, 1966, pp. 85–91.
54. Rao, V. R., *The Salience of Price in the Perception and Evaluation of Product Quality*, unpublished dissertation, University of Pennsylvania, 1970.
55. Robinson, J. P., and P. R. Shaver, *Measures of Social Psychological Attitudes*, Ann Arbor, Mich.: Institute for Social Research, The University of Michigan, 1969.
56. Rokeach, M., "Attitude Change and Behavioral Change," *Public Opinion Quarterly*, vol. 30, 1967, pp. 529–550.
57. Rosenberg, M. J., "Cognitive Structure and Attitudinal Affect," *Journal of Abnormal and Social Psychology*, vol. 53, 1956, pp. 367–372; reprinted in Fishbein, [21], pp. 325–331.
58. Schlinger, M. J., "Cues on Q-technique," *Journal of Advertising Research*, vol. 9, September 1969, pp. 53–60.
59. Schroder, H. M., M. J. Driver, and S. Streufert, *Human Information Processing*, New York: Holt, 1967.
60. Selltiz, C., M. Jahoda, M. Deutsch, and S. W. Cook, *Research Methods in Social Relations*, New York: Holt, 1959.
61. Shaw, M. E., and J. M. Wright, *Scales for the Measurement of Attitudes*, New York: McGraw-Hill, 1967.
62. Siegel, S., *Nonparametric Statistics for the Behavioral Sciences*, New York: McGraw-Hill, 1956.
63. Smith, G., "How GM Measures Ad Effectiveness," *Printers' Ink*, May 14, 1965, pp. 28ff.
64. Thurstone, L. L., "The Indifference Function," *Journal of Social Psychology*, vol. 2, 1931, pp. 139–167; reprinted in L. L. Thurstone, *The Measurement of Values*, Chicago: University of Chicago Press, 1959, pp. 123–144.
65. ———, "Law of Comparative Judgment," *Psychological Review*, vol. 34, 1927, pp. 273–286.
66. Torgerson, W. S., *Theory and Methods of Scaling*, New York: Wiley, 1960.
67. U.S. Bureau of the Census, *Consumer Buying Indicators: Recent Purchases of Cars and Other Durables and Expectations to Buy during the Months Ahead, Survey Data through 1969*, Current Population Reports, series P-65, no. 25, March 1969, p. 6.
68. Weiss, E. H., and Company, *A Manual on the Use of the Semantic Differential in Advertising and Product Testing*, Chicago: E. H. Weiss and Company, December 1955, mimeographed, p. 5.
69. Wittenborn, J. R., "Contributions and Current Status of Q Methodology," *Psychological Bulletin*, vol. 58, March 1961, pp. 132–142.

Part A

Techniques

Chapter 3

Multidimensional Scaling[1]

MARSHALL G. GREENBERG *National Analysts, Inc., Philadelphia, Pennsylvania*

PAUL E. GREEN *Wharton School, University of Pennsylvania, Philadelphia, Pennsylvania*

INTRODUCTION

The flourishing interest in market segmentation during the past decade among manufacturers and marketers of consumer products has produced a demand for the application of new quantitative techniques in analyzing consumers' perceptions of products. The research specialist who was formerly asked "Should this product be evaluated in a pair-comparison test or a monadic test?" is now being asked to provide new perspectives regarding the answers to such questions as these:

1. What are the most salient product attributes in this category?
2. Is my brand positioned where I want it to be?
3. What specific changes in product formulation or marketing strategy would be required to move it towards its intended position?
4. Has the position of my brand changed significantly of late?
5. Where are the new-product opportunities in this category?

Questions such as these have prompted researchers to examine quantitative techniques by which products could be studied and evaluated, not in isolation or in pairs but in the context of the broader market in which they are competing. Multidimensional scaling techniques have shown increasing promise of being relevant and practical in such studies.

---

[1] Much of the work reported in this chapter was conducted while the first author was with The Procter & Gamble Company.

This chapter is intended to convey a conceptual, rather than a statistical, understanding of multidimensional scaling techniques. The versatility and usefulness of these techniques are illustrated in a variety of applications selected to demonstrate the breadth of data collection procedures, analytic approaches, and content areas which have been employed. The emphasis throughout is upon the behavioral assumptions and their relationships to the underlying mathematical models. These relationships are, of course, critical to the successful application of any mathematical model to the analysis of real problems.

MEASUREMENT THEORY

Before introducing multidimensional scaling, a brief introduction to measurement theory is in order.[2]

In its broadest context, measurement consists of the assignment of one set of entities, usually mathematical entities or numbers, to another set of entities, usually empirical phenomena or objects. The researcher attempts to structure such assignments so that basic relationships among the mathematical entities represent relationships among the empirical entities. If the correspondence holds well enough to be useful, the known properties of the mathematical system can serve as a model for describing the empirical system.

Ordinal Scales

In marketing research studies, people are frequently asked to *order* objects or concepts according to some criterion. For example, they may be asked to state whether ice cream A has more, less, or the same amount of chocolate as ice cream B. They may be asked to rank order several ice cream samples with respect to chocolatiness. Such data are collected in a variety of studies dealing with buyer perceptions, attitudes, beliefs, and preferences. When a set of n objects is ranked, we usually assign the integers 1, 2, 3, . . . , n to these objects in a manner which preserves the ranking relationship. However, we could assign a sequence of numbers such as 1, 4, 5, 10, 12, . . . , n, and we would still preserve the ranking relationship as long as the numbers were monotonically increasing. Furthermore, all the information about the relationships among the objects (that is, their rank order) would be preserved. When the numbers assigned to objects are intended to represent only order relationships, the data are said to be *ordinally* scaled.

Interval Scales

Sometimes numbers are assigned to objects to represent not only the order of the objects but also the size of the *difference* between objects on some criterion. In such cases the difference between the two objects reflects not only which object has more of a property but also how *much* more as measured in some appropriate unit. When numbers are assigned in this manner, the resultant scale is called an *interval* scale. If an interval scale is obtained, then equal differences (intervals) between the scale values of objects will reflect equal empirical differences between the corresponding objects.

Ratio Scales

If numbers are assigned at the level of an interval scale and, in addition, one can establish a unique zero point or natural origin, the scale is called a *ratio*

---

[2] For a more detailed introduction to the technical literature, Chap. 2 in Coombs, Dawes, and Tversky [3] is highly recommended.

scale. Ratio scales exist for such physical properties as height, weight, length, and so forth but are seldom achieved in the measurement of consumer behavior. However, for purposes of statistical analysis, ratio scales are seldom required. Most tests assume only interval-scaled data[3] and many tests have been developed to deal with ordinal data [23].

Permissible Transformations

Another way of looking at the differences among ordinal, interval, and ratio scales is in terms of their uniqueness under certain types of transformations. Ordinal scales are unique up to a (strictly) monotonic increasing transformation, as shown in Figure 1a.

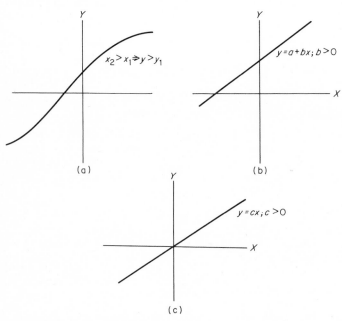

Fig. 1 Permissible transformation by scale type. (a) Monotonic; (b) linear; (c) proportionate.

Any transformation which preserves rank order (monotonicity) is appropriate; that is, any order preserving transformation of the original scale is just as good a representation of the empirical relationships as the original scale.

Permissible transformations of interval scales are constrained to be linear; that is,

$$y = a + bx; b > 0$$

Figure 1b illustrates this type of function. A conventional illustration of interval scaling is temperature, as measured on the centigrade or Fahrenheit scales. Each scale represents a linear transformation of the other.

---

[3] See Green and Tull [8], Chap. 7.

Ratio scales are unique up to a positive proportionate transformation; that is, we are allowed to change only the unit of measurement.

$$y = cx; c > 0$$

Figure 1c illustrates this case. The transformation is constrained to pass through the origin as exemplified by the conversion of feet to inches. While we would like to be able to measure various classes of psychological and social phenomena on ratio scales, such possibilities are rare. Fortunately, interval-scale measurements are usually sufficiently "strong" for various marketing research purposes and policy objectives as well.

Ordered Metric Scales

While ordinal, interval, and ratio scales represent the more familiar types,[4] a less common scale of particular significance to multidimensional scaling is the *ordered metric*. An ordered metric scale is one in which all possible intervals between pairs of scale positions can be ranked. To illustrate, suppose we have ordered five objects, A, B, C, D, and E, along a continuum. Also, assume that we can order all 10 interpoint distances $\overline{AB}$, $\overline{AC}$, ..., $\overline{DE}$ of the five objects taken two at a time. The scale is still an ordinal scale, but with additional information ranking the *distances* separating pairs of points. In the limit (by adding more and more points on the continuum whose end points are A and E), we will obtain an interval scale.

While a single ordering of objects which differ in only one aspect provides no basis for developing a stronger representation of the data (for example, an interval scale), it turns out that orderings of *pairs* of points, or interpoint "distances," imply more information about the positions of the points than might be first imagined. Similarly, several orderings (not all of which are the same) of a set of objects by *different* respondents can provide metric (interval-scaled or stronger) information about interrelationships among objects and people in terms of the whole set of data.

These are both illustrations of conjoint measurement [18]. An outcome or event is conjoint if it represents a combination of two or more elements. A response to relationships involving pairs of objects is conjoint, as is a response to a pair of items involving a person and an object. If we can establish an order relation on such pairs, *we may be able to upgrade the data to some stronger form of scale.* Such is the major objective of nonmetric multidimensional scaling.

THE NATURE OF MULTIDIMENSIONAL SCALING

Multidimensional scaling (MS) comprises a body of techniques for representing geometrically the locations and interrelationships among a set of points. Given information about a set of interpoint distances, MS techniques attempt to locate the points in a space of one or more dimensions such as to best summarize or represent the information contained in the interpoint distances. The distances in the solution space should optimally reflect the distances contained in the input data. Most of the important issues in multidimensional stimulus scaling can be readily illustrated by considering the analysis of some data for which the solution is known. The example here, previously pre-

---

[4] Some authors, for example, S. S. Stevens [26], include nominal classifications as a type of scale. Such scales are unique only up to a permutation transformation; the numbers serve only as individual (or perhaps class) labels.

TABLE 1 Intercity Road Mileages

City name	City number	1	2	3	4	5	6	7	8	9	10	11	12	13
								Column						
Bismarck	1	0												
Boston	2	1,852	0											
Denver	3	689	1,984	0										
Detroit	4	1,131	716	1,287	0									
Miami	5	2,210	1,552	2,081	1,401	0								
New Orleans	6	1,617	1,575	1,285	1,091	879	0							
Phoenix	7	1,515	2,679	826	2,031	2,369	1,533	0						
St. Louis	8	987	1,165	866	157	1,226	694	1,514	0					
San Antonio	9	1,391	2,059	938	1,437	1,419	559	985	934	0				
San Francisco	10	1,652	3,180	1,273	2,459	3,095	2,270	790	2,128	1,775	0			
Seattle	11	1,268	3,108	1,372	2,387	3,436	2,636	1,548	2,220	2,224	853	0		
Washington, D.C.	12	1,547	441	1,631	515	1,104	1,114	2,326	807	1,636	2,863	2,803	0	
New York	13	1,691	216	1,851	667	1,330	1,325	2,459	966	1,962	3,025	2,904	225	0

sented by Greenberg [9] and by Neidell [20], has proved particularly useful in explaining multidimensional scaling to nontechnical management.

The Road-Map Problem—An Illustrative Example

In this example, we employed a set of imperfect data for which the exact solution is known. The stimuli to be scaled were 13 cities distributed across the United States. As measures of the interpoint distances between the 78 pairs of cities, we used the intercity road mileages taken from an atlas. Certain distances reflect the necessity of detours around the Great Lakes, mountains, and so on, and consequently the data matrix shown in Table 1 may be viewed as containing true straight-line distances upon which has been superimposed a degree of systematic and random error (not unlike real market research data).

Kruskal's MDSCAL program [15, 16, 17] was employed to analyze the data.[5] The program contains a nonmetric algorithm which attempts to position the cities in such a manner that their interpoint distances are rank ordered the same as the input data. (For a more detailed description of the algorithm, see the following chapter.) The program was instructed to find the best solutions in three, two, and one dimensions, respectively.

Stress = 0.160

Fig. 2. **One-dimensional solution for cities.**

The best-fitting solution in one dimension is shown in Figure 2. The value of stress = 0.16 indicates that the best solution is rather poor, although the projections of the cities on an east-west dimension are reasonably representative of reality. The poor fit, of course, arises from the fact that such pairs as Boston-Miami, Bismarck-Denver, and Seattle-San Francisco are relatively close. Their separation requires an additional dimension.

The best two-dimensional solution is shown in Figure 3. Now the fit is excellent, as indicated by an extremely low value for stress = 0.009.[6] The best three-dimensional solution provides no appreciable improvement.

The orientation of the solution in Figure 3 illustrates an issue which will be seen to be of great importance in the analysis of marketing data—the rotation problem. Obviously, the computer cannot distinguish north from south or east from west! Since Euclidean distances are invariant under the rotation and reflection of axes, these operations were performed to produce Figure 4, which presents a more familiar solution and superimposes it upon an actual map of the United States, showing the precise locations of the 13 cities.

It should be noted that much of the lack of fit can be attributed to imperfec-

---

[5] Our version of this program was modified to include a rational starting configuration. We used a variation of the factor analysis procedure employed in the TORSCA program.

[6] Our program was controlled to stop when stress ≤0.01, even though minor improvements in the solution might have been made with further iterations.

tions in the input data.   The city locations are quite well constrained by the attempt to reproduce the rank order of the mileages in the solution space.   Increasing the number of cities studied would reduce the average error between the actual and derived locations.

The rotation and interpretation problems can perhaps be clarified in the context of the above example.   Suppose it were not known that the input data were intercity road mileages but only that they represented some measure of proximity which could be a perceived similarity or dissimilarity between cities based upon demographic characteristics, climate variables, and so on.   Suppose

Fig. 3.   Two-dimensional solution for cities.

also that, for each city, data had been collected on a number of attributes, including not only latitude and longitude but also such characteristics as population, altitude above sea level, per capita income, and mean rainful.   By attempting to correlate such data with the coordinates of the cities on the axes in the solution space under various rotations, a rotation that produced extremely high correlations with the latitude and longitude variables would eventually be discovered.   Presumably, correlations with the other variables examined would be much lower.   A means of labeling or interpreting the axes is frequently of great importance, as multidimensional scaling is usually applied in a context where the determinants of the input data are not precisely known.

Nonmetric versus Metric Approaches to Multidimensional Scaling

We now generalize from the road map example to consider any m by m matrix of interpoint distances.   In attempting to construct a space containing m

points such that the $m(m-1)/2$ interpoint distances reflect the input data, a number of approaches have been suggested.

The Metric Approach   Metric analyses attempt to utilize all the information in the data in obtaining a solution.   Young and Householder [30] solved the problem for a set of "true" distances.   If the data reflect exact distances between real objects in an r-dimensional space, their solution will reproduce the set of interpoint distances.   However, since real data of any interest are fallible and contain errors of measurement, both random and systematic, alternative procedures were needed.   Two approaches to fitting fallible data have been suggested by Torgerson [27] and Messick and Abelson [19].   These methods are described in some detail by Torgerson [28] and will not be outlined here.

Fig. 4.   Two-dimensional solution for cities rotated and reflected.

They treat the input as interval scale data and solve for the additive constant which minimizes the dimensionality of the solution space.

The Nonmetric Approach.   Nonmetric analyses, previously studied by Coombs [3] and his colleagues Bennett and Hays [1], came into prominence during the 1960s when methods were discovered for using high-speed computers to generate metric solutions for ordinal input data.   Shepard [21, 22] and Kruskal [15, 16] were pioneers in this effort.   The nonmetric multidimensional scaling programs seek a representation of points in a space of minimum dimensionality such that the rank order of the interpoint distances in the solution space maximally corresponds to that of the data.   This is achieved by requiring only that the distances in the solution be monotone with the input data.   (For a more detailed description of this approach, see the following chapter.)   The techniques which have received the widest distribution and use are Kruskal's MDSCAL [15], the Guttman Lingoes series [11], and TORSCA [29].   These programs differ somewhat in the algorithms employed for solving the problem, criteria for goodness of fit, starting configurations, plotting subroutines, and so forth, and each is characterized by a unique set of strengths and weaknesses for a particular type of problem—see Spaeth and Guthery [24].

Interpretation of the Solution

In the broadest sense, MS enables one to study the perceptual structure of a set of stimuli and the cognitive processes underlying the development of this structure. Psychologists, for example, employ MS techniques in an effort to scale psychophysical stimuli and to determine appropriate labels for the dimensions along which these stimuli vary.

In the investigation of a product category, it is frequently misleading to depend upon consumers to "truthfully" tell us what are the most salient dimensions or which product attributes are the primary determinants in their purchase decisions. There is a strong tendency for people to give socially acceptable or function-oriented responses in an attempt to appear highly rational. The automobile purchaser says he is concerned with performance and economy, not status. The toothpaste purchaser says she is looking primarily for decay prevention, whitening, and brightening, not flavor. MS provides a mechanism for determining the truly salient attributes without forcing the judge to appear irrational.

One of the most powerful and useful properties of MS techniques is the lack of necessity in the data collection process to specify to the judge the attributes along which he is to compare the brands. One may simply obtain judgments of similarity among the brands under investigation in the hope that the most salient attributes will be revealed in the ultimate structure obtained from the analysis. Considering the road-map example discussed earlier, the fact that the data represent Euclidean distances (although distorted) between cities is revealed in the *solution*. It need not have been known a priori that latitude and longitude were the determinants of the data. Often, however, it is helpful to have the stimuli evaluated on a number of different attributes in order to provide confirmation for the ultimate interpretation of the map obtained from the MS procedure.

ANALYSIS OF LAUNDRY DETERGENTS—AN APPLICATION

We proceed now to consider an application of MS to the mapping of a consumer product. Our purpose is to develop a geometric representation of a product category such that products positioned near one another are perceived as similar and products positioned far apart are perceived as dissimilar. The primary input data for this analysis will consist of some measures of perceived similarity between pairs of products. From these data, we will hope to (1) construct a "map" which summarizes the similarity relationships and (2) determine which product attributes are most salient in consumers' perceptions of the category. The particular MS analysis employed will be a nonmetric one using the modified MDSCAL program just discussed.

During the past several years, a number of studies have been conducted at Procter & Gamble in an attempt to analyze the packaged soap and detergent category. The studies reported here were conducted prior to the introduction of enzyme presoak products and enzyme additives. Three investigations are briefly summarized in the following subsections.

The Northeastern Study

This study investigated the relationships among eight detergent brands as perceived by 206 women in a metropolitan area in upstate New York during July 1967. Input data were collected by asking each woman to rate each of the 28 pairs of brands on a three-point scale ranging from high to low similarity.

Values of 1, 2, and 3 were assigned to these ratings and summed across all women to generate the input data for the analysis in the form of an 8 by 8 matrix of perceived similarities.[7] A two-dimensional solution was generated and is depicted in Figure 5.

The particular rotation shown was selected partly on the basis of additional data which had been collected from the women in order to determine their perceptions of the brands on a number of product attributes. In addition to making the similarities judgments, women had evaluated the brands on such attributes as suds, strength, suitability for delicate fabrics, harshness, and cleaning power. From their data, the eight brands were scaled on each of these five

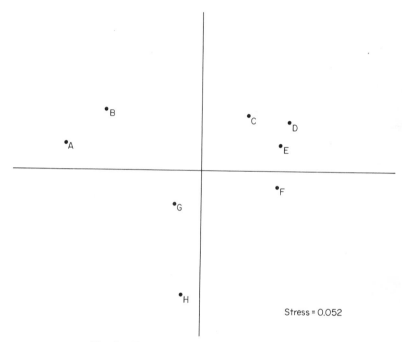

Fig. 5. Detergent map—Northeastern study.

attributes. After obtaining the original MS solution, an attempt was made to find a rotation which would produce high correlations between the coordinate axes of the solution and two of the attribute scales. The rotation in Figure 5 was the best we could find. The loadings on the horizontal axis produced a product-moment correlation of $r = .971$ with the suds scale. The other four attributes were highly intercorrelated among themselves, and all correlated well with the vertical axis, the highest value being $r = .931$ for harshness.

Positioning of the products within the framework of these two attributes was supported by knowledge of the performance characteristics of the brands, by additional information about consumers' perceptions derived from usage and

[7] Actually, the data were weighted before summing in order to give equal representation to users of each of the brands and to an "all others" category. The desirability of such a weighting depends upon the purposes of the study.

attitude studies, and by familiarity with their advertising campaigns. However, since this was one of the first studies of its type, it was decided to replicate in another city three months later. A metropolitan area in the Southwest was chosen.

The Southwestern Study

The same eight brands were investigated using a questionnaire identical with that employed in the New York study. Analyzing the data from 354 women in the same manner yielded the two-dimensional solution shown in Figure 6. Comparing this with Figure 5, it can be seen that the basic configuration and

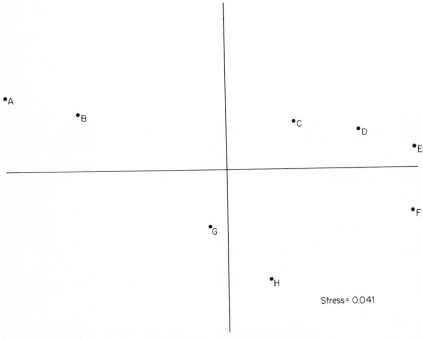

Fig. 6.   Detergent map—Southwestern study.

its structure were unaltered. Except for the fact that brand A moved higher on the vertical dimension, the relative projections of all brands on each axis remained unchanged. This time, the correlation between the horizontal axis and the suds scale was $r = .964$ and the correlation between loadings on the vertical axis and the harshness scale was $r = .845$.

A supplementary study was conducted among an additional 105 women. After completing the set of similarity judgments, these women did not rate the products on the five attributes studied. Instead they were asked to state, for each pair of brands rated as "highly similar," in what way the brands were most alike. Two classes of comments were found most often: (1) comments on suds and (2) comments on effectiveness. This was quite consistent with the high correlations found in the basic studies relating the attribute data to the axes of the solution space. Few comments were found, for example, related to things like color, odor, price, or package, indicating that in the original questionnaires the most salient attributes had not been overlooked.

The Attitude Study

An additional analysis was performed upon some data which were already in hand. During the first six months of 1967, attitudes toward 12 laundry detergents had been measured in a large sample of cities across the United States. As part of a summary analysis, we had available data on favorable and unfavorable comment levels on each of the brands on 19 different product attributes. From these data were extracted the figures on the 8 brands included in

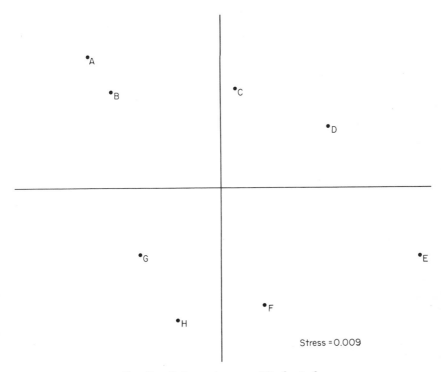

Fig. 7.   Detergent map—attitude study.

the studies just reported. Similarity indices were constructed for each of the 28 pairs of brands by correlating the percentages of people commenting unfavorably on each attribute.[8] A high value of r indicated that a pair of brands tended to receive relatively high and low levels of unfavorable comments on the same attributes. The 28 correlation coefficients were treated as indexes of similarity and analyzed with the MDSCAL program as in the earlier studies. The two-dimensional solution is shown in Figure 7.

In this solution, the correlation between loadings on the horizontal axis and level of comments on "Too Much Suds" (normalized to remove brand popu-

---

[8] Only the data on unfavorable comments were used because they appeared to provide better discrimination and were less affected by overall brand popularity than the data on favorable comments.

larity effects) was $r = .990$. The vertical axis had correlations greater than .90 with comments on bleaching, heavy soil removal, and fabric damage. The three clusters, (A, B), (C, D, E, F), and (G, H), are less well defined than in the maps for the previous two studies. In particular, brands E and F have moved somewhat lower on the vertical axis and F has moved closer to H. Yet many of the properties of the earlier solutions remain intact. This is particularly encouraging, since the method of data collection was so vastly different from that employed in the studies using direct judgments of similarities as input.

In the attitude study, the derived similarity indexes might have reflected distortion to the extent that the 19 attributes employed included many which were not perceived as salient by the women who performed the similarities judgments. That so little distortion was obtained is most encouraging and may reflect the possibility that most of the variance in levels of comments was associated with those same kinds of attributes found to be salient in the work employing direct similarities judgments.

Some Comments

The results from the three studies briefly reported above could easily be characterized in terms of their differences or in terms of their mutual support. While the differences are worthy of recognition, it is the similarities which appear to be more impressive.

The data collected in each of the studies reflect temporal and geographical differences as well as the usual sampling errors. In dealing with a heavily advertised product category such as laundry detergents, in which perceptions are constantly shifting and in which regional differences in perceptions are present, the tendency toward stability and reproducibility of a category map is most encouraging.

It should be noted that the methods of data collection employed in the first two studies reflect a different philosophy from that employed in the attitude study. In collecting judged similarities data, one does not specify in any way the attributes upon which the woman is to base her judgments. It is hoped that the configuration which summarizes the similarities data will facilitate the *inference* of the salient product attributes.

This approach would seem particularly valuable when studying product categories for which it is unlikely that people can or will verbalize what is really important to them. In the attitude study, an attempt was made to derive an index of perceived similarity between pairs of brands by combining everything said about the brands on a large number of product attributes thought to be salient on an a priori basis. That these two approaches yielded similar input matrices, solutions, and interpretations is the strongest kind of cross-validation one could offer for the hypothesis that there exists a basic perceptual structuring of the brands that is relatively stable across temporal, geographical, and experimental variables. Still further support is offered for the interpretation methods by the results of the supplementary study in the Southwest, in which women explained their similarities judgments in a manner not inconsistent with the inferences made from the major studies.

ADDITIONAL APPLICATIONS

The analyses of laundry detergents reported in the previous section represent a single application of multidimensional scaling to the mapping of a nondurable consumer good. Many studies have investigated other types of stimuli, employed alternate analytic techniques, and used different methods of data collection. A few of these approaches are briefly reviewed here in order to indicate the versatility of multidimensional scaling approaches and their rapidly increasing influence upon research during the past few years. Several such studies are described in the next chapter, and will not be discussed here.

Analysis of Graduate Business Schools

Green, Carmone, and Robinson [5, 6] report a study in which they attempted to scale students' perceptions of six graduate business schools: Carnegie Institute of Technology, Chicago, Harvard, M.I.T., Stanford, and Wharton. The data were obtained from first-year graduate students at the Wharton School, using three different methods of data collection to measure the perceived similarities among schools. One group of 50 students, presented with all possible

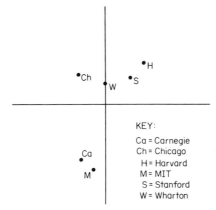

Fig. 8. Two-dimensional solution for business schools. (*From Green, Carmone, and Robinson, 1968*)

triads of the schools, judged for each triad which pair of schools was most similar and which was least similar. Another group, presented with each school in turn as an anchor, was required to rate the others on a 0 to 10 scale of decreasing similarity from the anchor. Still a third sample received a semantic differential type of questionnaire on which each school was evaluated on 31 sets of bipolar adjectives.

Methods for converting the raw data from the triad and anchor techniques to yield rank orderings of the 15 interstimulus similarities are discussed in Coombs [2]. The semantic differential data were subjected to a principal component analysis and Euclidean distances between schools were calculated in a reduced space.

All three of the 15 by 15 similarities matrices were analyzed using Kruskal's MDSCAL program. Figure 8 illustrates the configuration for the solution derived from the triad data. The other two configurations were remarkably similar.

The authors labeled the vertical dimension as "quantitative-qualitative" and the horizontal dimension as reflecting the overall "prestige" of the schools. These interpretations were strongly supported by supplementary attribute data collected at the same time the similarities data were obtained.

Normally, a configuration of six points in a two-space derived by nonmetric multidimensional scaling techniques might be subjected to serious questions of stability and reliability. However, the use of three independent samples, each presented with a different form of questionnaire for collecting the data, adds considerable credence to the results obtained.

Scaling of Political Figures

Johnson [12] presented a case for the use of metric techniques in multidimensional scaling and employed multiple discriminant analysis to scale 14 political

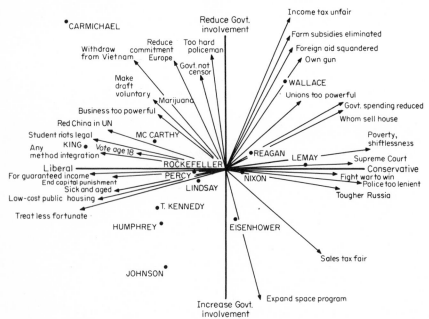

Fig. 9.   Two-dimensional space for key political figures.   (*From Johnson, 1969*)

figures, all of whom were prominent on the national scene during 1967 and 1968.

A questionnaire sent to 1,000 members of a mail panel asked respondents to indicate their amount of agreement with each of 35 political statements and to describe their perceptions of two of the 14 political figures' stands on the statements. The statements dealt with Vietnam, law and order, welfare, and other issues which were current.

A discriminant analysis produced the two-dimensional space depicted in Figure 9 which accounted for 86 percent of the variance among images of the political figures. The labels assigned to the horizontal and vertical axes were as shown. Furthermore, the mean ratings of the figures on each of the 35 attributes are reflected by a vector representation. Each vector is positioned by its loadings on the two discriminant dimensions. These vectors make explicit the types of changes in stance on political issues which would be required to move the position of a political figure in the perceptual space.

Other Applications

Combinations and variations of the techniques described so far have been employed in a number of contexts. Green and Maheshwari [7] found 10 common stocks to be embedded in a two-space which appeared to be characterized by "perceived risk" and "perceived growth." They also mapped eight popular magazines and found the resulting two dimensions to resemble "sophisticated-unsophisticated" and "fiction-nonfiction." Klahr [14] derived a four-dimensional space to characterize admissions officers' perceptions of student applicants. Green and Carmone [4] summarized the scaling of a set of 11 automobiles in a space whose dimensions were labeled as "luxuriousness" and "sportiness." Other studies reported in master's theses, working papers, and meetings of professional societies indicate that MS techniques have been employed with considerable success in mapping T.V. commercials, beer, coffee, cigarettes, toothpaste, and a host of other consumer products.

PREFERENCE SPACES

While a multidimensional stimulus space may be useful to marketers, such maps could be of even greater value if they contained people locations as well as product locations. A class of multidimensional scaling techniques has been developed which attempts to construct joint spaces containing both stimulus points and ideal points. An ideal point represents that combination of stimulus attributes which would be maximally desirable to the individual represented by the point.

Given the distribution of ideal points throughout a product space, it is usually assumed that an individual's preferences for products will be inversely proportional to their distances from his ideal point. The theory of joint space construction and analysis is presented in Coombs [2], although most of the computer algorithms for dealing with the problem have been developed since the publication of Coombs's book.

A detailed description of joint space analysis is beyond the scope of this chapter. Several of the nonmetric techniques for constructing such spaces from preference data are discussed in the following chapter. The value of joint spaces or preference spaces lies in their potential for describing and predicting the demand for existing products or new-product introductions. Those products positioned nearest to regions containing high densities of ideal points should attract a relatively high demand. New product opportunities should exist where there are "holes" in the product space containing clusters of ideal points. A product introduction in such a region should cause the consumers with those ideal points to shift their brand choices from their present brand (remote from their point of maximum satisfaction) to the new brand.

One can formulate product development and marketing problems in a concise but admittedly oversimplified manner using the notation of a joint space. Within this framework there are basically two approaches, which may be used singly or in combination, to increase the demand for a product. The first approach is to reposition the product, either through formulation changes or through advertising, so that it is the point of minimum distance from the greatest number of ideal points. This maximizes the number of "first-place votes" the brand should receive. A second approach is to leave the image of the product unchanged and to attempt to move people's ideal points closer to it. The latter approach is probably the more difficult and costly of the two but may be necessary in instances where the product image is inherently well defined and not readily subject to modification.

SUMMARY AND CONCLUSIONS

It appears that multidimensional scaling techniques offer great potential for assisting marketing managers in systematically analyzing their problems and aiding them in the formulation of solutions.

The development of high-speed computers with large storage capacities has led to a proliferation of new and versatile techniques for solving MS problems. The techniques, like factor analysis, are seductive in their ease of use and in the apparent simplicity and rationality of the results they produce. For the most part, the statistical properties of MS solutions are unknown, although some guidelines are presented by the work of Stenson and Knoll [25] and Klahr [14]. For these reasons, it is suggested that the potential user of MS techniques be thoroughly acquainted with the general theory and the specific properties of the analytic procedure or computer program employed.

The development of MS techniques and applications appears to occupy a rather unique role among researchers today. There is probably no area in which so much work has been carried out on many different fronts but in which such a relatively small portion of the work has found its way into formal communication channels of the profession. Much of the research and development work has been communicated through the informal circulation of computer programs, working papers, and personal correspondence. This situation will improve with time, but until it does, the technology will not achieve the wide distribution and use necessary to fully develop its potential.

REFERENCES

1. Bennett, J. F., and W. L. Hays, "Multidimensional Unfolding: Determining the Dimensionality of Ranked Preference Data," *Psychometrika*, vol. 25, 1960.
2. Coombs, C. H., *A Theory of Data*, New York: Wiley, 1964.
3. ———, R. M. Dawes, and A. Tversky, *Mathematical Psychology*. Englewood Cliffs, N.J.: Prentice-Hall, 1966.
4. Green, P. E., and F. J. Carmone, "Multidimensional Scaling: An Introduction and Comparison of Nonmetric Unfolding Techniques," *Journal of Marketing Research*, vol. 6, 1969.
5. ———, F. J. Carmone, and P. J. Robinson, "Analysis of Marketing Behavior Using Nonmetric Scaling and Related Techniques," Interim Technical Monograph, Marketing Science Institute, 1968.
6. ———, F. J. Carmone, and P. J. Robinson, "Nonmetric Scaling Methods: An Exposition and Overview," *Wharton Quarterly*, vol. 2, 1968.
7. ———, and A. Maheshwari, "Common Stock Perception and Preference: An Application of Multidimensional Scaling," *Journal of Business*, vol. 42.
8. ———, and D. S. Tull, *Research for Marketing Decisions*, Englewood Cliffs, N.J.: Prentice-Hall, 1966.
9. Greenberg, M. G., "A Variety of Approaches to Nonmetric Multidimensional Scaling," *Paper presented at the Sixteenth International Meeting of The Institute of Management Sciences*, 1969.
10. ———, "Some Applications of Nonmetric Multidimensional Scaling," *Proceedings of the 129th Annual Meeting of the American Statistical Association*, 1969.
11. Guttman, L., "A General Nonmetric Technique for Finding the Smallest Coordinate Space for a Configuration of Points," *Psychometrika*, vol. 33, 1968.
12. Johnson, R. M., "Relationships Between Product Attributes and Preferential Choice Behavior," *Proceedings of the 129th Annual Meeting of the American Statistical Association*, 1969.
13. Klahr, D., "A Monte Carlo Investigation of the Statistical Significance of Kruskal's Nonmetric Scaling Procedure," *Psychometrika*, vol. 34, 1969.
14. ———, "Decision Making in a Complex Environment: The Use of Similarity Judgments to Predict Preferences," *Management Science*, vol. 15, 1969.

15. Kruskal, J. B., "Multidimensional Scaling by Optimizing Goodness of Fit to a Nonmetric Hypothesis," *Psychometrika*, vol. 29, 1964.

16. ———, "Nonmetric Multidimensional Scaling: A Numerical Method," *Psychometrika*, vol. 29, 1964.

17. ———, "How to Use MDSCAL, a Program to Do Multidimensional Scaling and Multidimensional Unfolding" (Version 4 and 4M of MDSCAL, all in FORTRAN IV), Bell Telephone Laboratories, Murray Hill, N.J., March 1968 (mimeographed).

18. Luce, R. D., and J. W. Tukey, "Simultaneous Conjoint Measurement: A New Type of Fundamental Measurement," *Journal of Mathematical Psychology*, vol. 1, 1964.

19. Messick, S. J., and R. P. Abelson, "The Additive Constant Problem in Multidimensional Scaling," *Psychometrika*, vol. 21, 1956.

20. Neidell, L. A., "The Use of Nonmetric Multidimensional Scaling in Marketing Analysis," *Journal of Marketing*, vol. 33, 1969.

21. Shepard, R. N., "The Analysis of Proximities: Multidimensional Scaling with an Unknown Distance Function, Part I," *Psychometrika*, vol. 27, 1962.

22. ———, "The Analysis of Proximities: Multidimensional Scaling with an Unknown Distance Function, Part II," *Psychometrika*, vol. 27, 1962.

23. Siegel, S., *Nonparametric Statistics*, New York: McGraw-Hill, 1956.

24. Spaeth, H. J., and S. B. Guthery, "The Use of the Monotone Criterion in Multidimensional Scaling" (Submitted for Publication).

25. Stenson, H. H., and R. L. Knoll, "Goodness of Fit for Random Rankings in Kruskal's Nonmetric Scaling Procedure," *Psychological Bulletin*, vol. 71, 1969.

26. Stevens, S. S., "Mathematics, Measurement and Psychophysics," in Stevens, S. S., ed., *Handbook of Experimental Psychology*, New York: Wiley, 1951.

27. Torgerson, W. S., "Multidimensional Scaling: I. Theory and Method," *Psychometrika*, vol. 17, 1952.

28. ———, *Theory and Methods of Scaling*, New York: Wiley, 1960.

29. Young, F. W., and W. S. Torgerson, "TORSCA, a FORTRAN IV Program for Shepard-Kruskal Multidimensional Scaling Analysis," *Behavioral Science*, vol. 12, 1967.

30. Young, G., and A. S. Householder, "Discussion of a Set of Points in Terms of Their Mutual Distances," *Psychometrika*, vol. 3, 1938.

Chapter 4

Ordinal Methods
in Multidimensional Scaling
and Data Analysis

PAUL E. GREEN *Wharton School, University of Pennsylvania, Philadelphia, Pennsylvania*

MARSHALL G. GREENBERG[1] *National Analysts, Inc., Philadelphia, Pennsylvania*

Multidimensional scaling methods, considered generally, attempt to represent certain types of data as relations on points in a multidimensional space. The dimensions of the space are assumed to represent properties by which the objects (stimuli) are compared. As we shall see, the stimuli may be real—for example, brands of toothpaste, corporate names, advertisements—or hypothetical—for example, an "ideal" stimulus [6] which possesses a particular combination of property levels that the respondent would prefer to any other combination.

DISTANCE FUNCTIONS AND CONFIGURATION RECOVERY

As mentioned in the preceding chapter, the key concept underlying nonmetric multidimensional scaling is the ordered metric scale, consisting of a rank order on all interpoint "distances." Before showing the application of nonmetric

[1] The authors extend their appreciation to Arun Maheshwari, of the University of Pennsylvania, who performed most of the computer runs associated with the presentation of this chapter. Support for this project was, in part, provided by the Marketing Science Institute.

methods to the analysis of perception and preference data, it should be instructive to demonstrate the characteristics of these methods in the context of artificial data.   In this way the reader can get some idea of how well the methods work on data of known characteristics.

Figure 1 shows an illustrative two-dimensional plot of the initials A.M.   Each of the 35 points tracing out the initials can be characterized by a coordinate value on each of the two axes.   Suppose we were to compute interpoint dis-

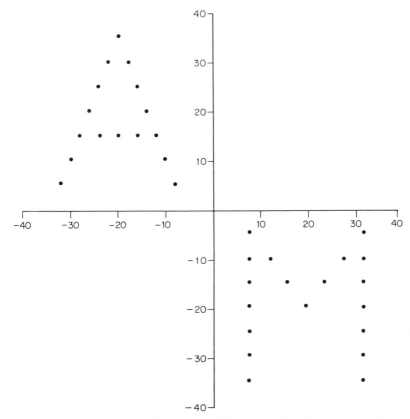

Fig. 1.   Synthetic data utilized in multidimensional scaling computations.

tances between each pair of points according to the Euclidean distance formula[2]

$$d_{ij} = [(x_{i1} - x_{j1})^2 + (x_{i2} - x_{j2})^2]^{1/2}$$

where x_{ik}, x_{jk} represent projections of points i and j on axis k $(k = 1, 2)$.

[2] This formula is generalized to r dimensions as:

$$d_{ij} = \left[\sum_{k=1}^{r} (x_{ik} - x_{jk})^2 \right]^{\frac{1}{2}}$$

For example, if $x_{i1} = 2$, $x_{j1} = 3$, $x_{i2} = 4$, $x_{j2} = 5$, $x_{i3} = 1$, $x_{j3} = 3$, then $d_{ij} = [(2 - 3)^2 + (4 - 5)^2 + (1 - 3)^2]^{\frac{1}{2}} = \sqrt{6}$

If this were done, we obtain 595 interpoint distances. Now suppose we discard all of this computed information except the distance ranks. Can the configuration of Figure 1 be satisfactorily recovered from *rank-order* data alone?

Figure 2 shows that it can, albeit with a different orientation than originally appeared. The left-hand panel shows a plot of the configuration resulting from the TORSCA multidimensional scaling program [39], while the right-hand panel shows a plot of the results obtained from a similar type of program, Kruskal's M-D-SCAL-IV program [23]. We note that in both cases the original configuration is recovered from only the rank order of the 595 distances.

When we say "recovered" we mean that a configuration is obtained which is (virtually) unique up to a similarity transformation—translation of the origin, rotation about the origin, reflection, and uniform stretching or compressing of the axes. None of these operations will affect the rank order of the interpoint distances which, after all, is what we are trying to preserve.

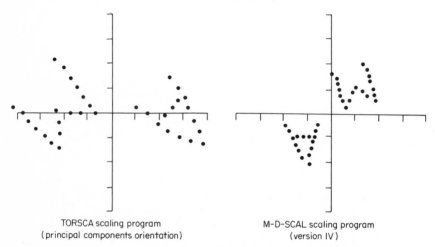

TORSCA scaling program   M-D-SCAL scaling program
(principal components orientation)   (version IV)

Fig. 2.   Results of multidimensional scaling of ranked distance data.

If the degree of recovery of the known configuration seems rather remarkable, the reason is easily explained. Recall that we started out with the ranks of 595 distances. Each inequality provides, in quite dilute form, some information. To portray 35 points uniquely in two dimensions we need only 70 numbers—two coordinate values for each point. What happens is that, with a large number of inequalities relative to the number of values needed to specify a configuration, the inequalities restrict the movement of the points markedly. For example, changing the position of only one point changes its distances with the remaining 34 points; thus, if a configuration is found whose distance ranks exactly correspond to the input data ranks, chances are that a point cannot be moved much without violating at least one of the inequalities in the input data.

Such intuitive arguments have been supported more rigorously by Shepard [33] and other developers of the methodology. With as few as 12 points (positioned in two dimensions), Shepard found virtually perfect recovery, in terms of interpoint distance correlations, from rank-order input alone.

Conversion of ordered metric data to ratio-scaled distances (the axis projections representing interval scales with common unit) can also be accomplished under conditions where the interpoint distances are subject to moderate amounts of "noise." Figure 3 shows the TORSCA program output for the preceding illustration for a case in which the original distances were "distorted" by the addition of random error before obtaining their ranks. In the left-hand panel of the chart, the error term was drawn from a normal distribution with mean zero and a standard deviation equal to 0.1 of the mean interpoint distance. While recovery is not as accurate as those recoveries shown in Figure 2, the reconstructed configuration is still quite similar to the original. In the right-hand panel of Figure 3 the standard deviation was 0.3 of the mean interpoint distance of the original configuration. Here the recovery is not good, since many of the original values have been changed by virtue of the large amount of added random error.

In summary, the scaling programs appear to perform quite well in the recovery of error-free, synthetic data from rank-order information alone. We now turn to a brief discussion of their historical development.

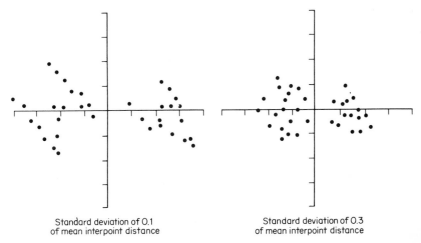

Standard deviation of 0.1
of mean interpoint distance

Standard deviation of 0.3
of mean interpoint distance

Fig. 3.   Results of scaling "noised" configuration (TORSCA Scaling Program).

The Development of Nonmetric Scaling

The history of ordinal methods of multidimensional scaling is short; the first conceptual paper and computer program by Roger Shepard [34] appeared in 1962. Since that time, however, progress in algorithm development has been rapid. Some appreciation for the versatility of these methods might be gained by contrasting them with precursor approaches: (1) fully metric and (2) fully nonmetric, multidimensional scaling.

Fully metric methods, as the name suggests, require ratio-scaled distances to begin with. The principal task of these techniques (which utilize a factor analytic approach) is, given a set of interpoint distances, to find the dimensionality and configuration of points whose distances closely match the numerical input values (up to a proportionality transformation) when both are converted to inner products. Fully metric methods go back to 1938 and are based on a set of theorems proved by Young and Householder [40]. In general, such methods—since they are based on the linear factor model—will require higher dimensionality of solution if the relationship between input data and output distances is nonlinear (but still monotonic). Early multidimensional scaling work by Richardson [30], Klingberg [21], and Torgerson [37] used this type of approach.

Fully nonmetric methods do not assume more than a rank order of the input "distances." The objective of this class of methods is to find a metric space of low dimensionality and the rank order (in the multidimensional case) of each point on each dimension in turn that satisfy certain order relations in the input data. Thus one does *not* obtain the configuration but only the rank order of stimulus projections. These methods were originally developed by Coombs [7] and Bennett and Hays [1]. While the techniques require only nonmetric (ordinal) input data, unfortunately in the multidimensional case they also yield nonmetric output.

Nonmetric methods would appear to combine the best of both previous approaches—ordinal input and metric output. Given only a rank order of distance data, the objective of these approaches is to find a configuration whose rank order of (asymptotically) ratio-scaled distances best reproduces the original input ranks. One tries to do this in the lowest dimensionality which produces a close enough ordinal fit. As already demonstrated, with a sufficient number of points the solution is virtually unique (up to a similarity transform).

A PILOT APPLICATION OF NONMETRIC SCALING

As motivation for the ensuing discussion, let us assume that a group of 17 housewives were asked to make numerical judgments about the subjective similarities of the following set of 10 breakfast food items:

1. Ham, eggs, and home fries	6. Eggs
2. Pancakes and sausage	7. Lox and bagels
3. Instant breakfast	8. Bacon and eggs
4. Pastry and/or toast	9. Cold cereal
5. Hot cereal	10. Fruit dish

Such judgments could be obtained by having each housewife rate each of the 45 distinct pairs of the 10 items on an 11-point "thermometer" scale ranging from 1—almost identical, to 11—completely different. (We discuss various methods of collecting similarities judgments a bit later on.)

Suppose we first direct our attention to the whole group of respondents. Table 1 shows the ranks of the averaged dissimilarity ratings of the 17 respondents.[3] For the moment, let us assume that all respondents see the breakfast food world in the same way. Moreover, we assume that the numerical values of averaged similarities shown in Table 1 are no more strongly scaled than rank order. Lower ranks indicate similar pairs and high ranks indicate dissimilar pairs of breakfast foods.

The objective of nonmetric multidimensional scaling is to convert such ranked dissimilarity data—representing an ordered metric scale—into a configuration in some space of reasonably low dimensionality whose interpoint distances are ratio-scaled. That is, we would like to find a pictorial representation of the 10 breakfast foods whose interpoint distance ranks reproduce the psychological distance ranks of the data shown in Table 1.

Notice, then, that we are assuming that *subjective* expressions of the comparative similarity of pairs of stimuli (in this case, breakfast foods) can be modeled by the mathematical expression of distance. Thus, two points (breakfast foods) which are close together in a respondent's "cognitive map" will be

---

[3] These data were drawn, with permission, from data collected by the first author's graduate student, R. F. Seamans [32].

TABLE 1 Ranks of Average Subject's Dissimilarities—Breakfast Foods

Dissimilarity rank	Stimulus number									
	1	2	3	4	5	6	7	8	9	10
1	0.0	2.000	45.000	30.000	16.000	5.000	21.000	1.000	31.000	40.000
2	2.000	0.0	43.000	32.000	18.000	6.000	24.000	3.000	28.000	42.000
3	45.000	43.000	0.0	17.000	22.000	33.000	35.000	41.000	8.000	9.000
4	30.000	32.000	17.000	0.0	25.000	38.000	14.000	44.000	10.000	15.000
5	16.000	18.000	22.000	25.000	0.0	7.000	29.000	11.000	13.000	27.000
6	5.000	6.000	33.000	38.000	7.000	0.0	20.000	4.000	19.000	36.000
7	21.000	24.000	35.000	14.000	29.000	20.000	0.0	26.000	23.000	37.000
8	1.000	3.000	41.000	44.000	11.000	4.000	26.000	0.0	34.000	39.000
9	31.000	28.000	8.000	10.000	13.000	19.000	23.000	34.000	0.0	12.000
10	40.000	42.000	9.000	15.000	27.000	36.000	37.000	39.000	12.000	0.0

viewed as more similar than two points farther apart. Put rather simply, such is the psychological basis of the scaling model: in making similarity judgments, subjects are assumed to be responding as though they could tell for each pair of pairs which pair is more dissimilar (exhibits a larger psychological distance).

While more will be said later about the implied psychological theory of multidimensional scaling, let us now concentrate on the purely mechanical problem of representing the data of Table 1 as relations on a set of points in a metric space.

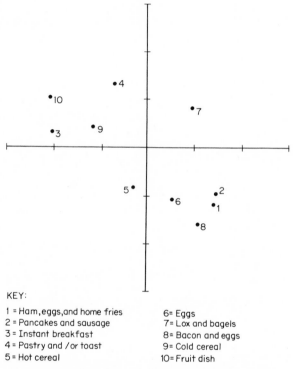

KEY:

1 = Ham,eggs,and home fries	6= Eggs
2 = Pancakes and sausage	7= Lox and bagels
3 = Instant breakfast	8= Bacon and eggs
4 = Pastry and /or toast	9= Cold cereal
5 = Hot cereal	10= Fruit dish

Fig. 4.   Two-space scaling solution of breakfast food items.

Figure 4 shows a plot of the 10 points in Euclidean two-space. Forgetting for the moment how Figure 4 was obtained, suppose we were to compute the interpoint distances between all the pairs of points in the chart, again using the Euclidean distance formula:

$$d_{ij} = [(x_{i1} - x_{j1})^2 + (x_{i2} - x_{j2})^2]^{1/2}$$

If this were done, the rank order of these interpoint distances would agree closely with the rank order of the input data; as a matter of fact, in this case the Spearman rank order correlation is 0.96, indicating a good fit in two dimensions.

The TORSCA nonmetric scaling program was used illustratively to find the two-space configuration shown in Figure 4. While we do not go into the mathematical details underlying this program, a technical appendix to this chapter explains how the program works.

Like factor analytic techniques, multidimensional scaling methods do not provide "labels" for the dimensions. *Interpretation* of the configuration must be done judgmentally, using, where feasible, responses provided by the respondent regarding the criteria he used in making dissimilarity judgments. In this case a tentative label for the horizontal axis appears to be "degree of nutrition"; but other labels—"heartiness" or "caloricness"—might serve as well. The vertical axis is even more difficult to interpret. Based on an analysis of subjects' responses after the similarity judgments were obtained in this study, one might suppose that "ease of preparation" could represent a candidate label. However, the fact of the matter is that solution interpretation represents one of the major problems in multidimensional scaling. (We discuss some approaches to this problem in the concluding section of the chapter.)

Including the Preference Data

The same group of 17 housewives were also asked to rate the 10 breakfast food items in terms of preference. A thermometer scale, with scale values ranging from 1—highly liked, to 11—highly disliked, was used in this phase of the study. Table 2 shows the preference ratings for each of the 17 respondents.

Suppose we were to try to represent the preference data in the same space in which the stimulus configuration of Figure 4 appears. Clearly, certain assumptions underlie such a representation. The basic assumption involves the concept of *ideal point*. As described by Coombs [6], an ideal point is a hypothetical stimulus (which may or may not correspond to a real stimulus) which possesses that particular combination of stimulus property levels which would be preferred to all other combinations.

In terms of the configuration of Figure 4, a person's ideal point represents that combination of "nutrition" and "ease of preparation" which would be preferred to all other combinations. As Coombs originally formulated the concept, he assumed that preference would decline monotonically with the distance of each real stimulus (the breakfast food items) from the ideal point location. That is, real stimuli nearer the ideal point would be preferred to those farther away from the ideal.

What we observe, however, is each respondent's preference data for real stimuli. The problem is to locate a subject's ideal point such that the order of the distances of real stimuli from the located ideal point closely matches the observed preference order.

We assume, then, that the perceptual dimensions by which stimuli are compared are also arguments of the preference function. We further assume that interperson perceptions of the stimuli are homogeneous and that the preference function is monotonically and symmetrically declining from the point of maximum utility.

Carroll and Chang's generalization of the Coombsian formulation relaxes some of these assumptions [5]. The metric version of their generalization assumes that utility is linearly related to the weighted squared distance of the real stimuli from the ideal. While their formulation permits one to apply models of increasing flexibility, the particular model used here is the Coombsian model of equal weighting for each subject, but *after* the perceptual space has been rotated and differentially stretched to best accommodate the preference data of the average subject.

TABLE 2 Individual Preference Ratings—Breakfast Foods

Individual preference	Stimulus number									
	1	2	3	4	5	6	7	8	9	10
1	11.0	11.0	11.0	4.0	11.0	1.0	11.0	4.0	1.0	11.0
2	3.0	5.0	11.0	11.0	5.0	2.0	11.0	1.0	5.0	7.0
3	1.0	7.0	11.0	4.0	11.0	5.0	11.0	2.0	11.0	11.0
4	10.0	8.0	11.0	4.0	8.0	2.0	11.0	2.0	3.0	8.0
5	4.0	3.0	11.0	3.0	10.0	1.0	5.0	1.0	4.0	11.0
6	7.0	4.0	11.0	8.0	11.0	4.0	11.0	3.0	1.0	11.0
7	3.0	7.0	11.0	2.0	11.0	3.0	11.0	3.0	3.0	9.0
8	11.0	11.0	11.0	11.0	3.0	1.0	11.0	1.0	5.0	5.0
9	5.0	3.0	11.0	6.0	10.0	2.0	11.0	1.0	11.0	1.0
10	11.0	7.0	11.0	4.0	11.0	2.0	3.0	2.0	11.0	9.0
11	11.0	11.0	2.0	5.0	3.0	1.0	11.0	11.0	10.0	2.0
12	9.0	10.0	9.0	1.0	11.0	9.0	11.0	8.0	11.0	11.0
13	4.0	2.0	11.0	11.0	6.0	4.0	11.0	3.0	2.0	11.0
14	1.0	3.0	11.0	11.0	4.0	4.0	11.0	1.0	10.0	1.0
15	10.0	8.0	11.0	6.0	1.0	4.0	11.0	2.0	2.0	11.0
16	7.0	7.0	11.0	9.0	6.0	5.0	3.0	2.0	2.0	10.0
17	11.0	8.0	11.0	6.0	10.0	2.0	11.0	1.0	10.0	2.0
Average	7.0	6.8	10.4	6.2	7.8	3.1	9.7	2.8	6.0	7.7

Figure 5 shows the stimulus configuration and ideal point positions of 14 of the 17 subjects whose preference data are shown in Table 2.[4] Also shown is the ideal point position of the average subject. We first notice that the stimulus configuration displays a new orientation from that shown in Figure 4. Inclusion of the preference data has resulted in a rotated and differentially stretched stimulus configuration. We might interpret this difference in the two configurations as the result of difference *saliences* that the perceptual dimensions take on in the context of preference (as well as orientation differences).

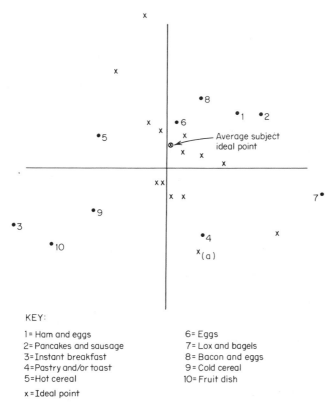

KEY:

1 = Ham and eggs	6 = Eggs
2 = Pancakes and sausage	7 = Lox and bagels
3 = Instant breakfast	8 = Bacon and eggs
4 = Pastry and/or toast	9 = Cold cereal
5 = Hot cereal	10 = Fruit dish
x = Ideal point	

Fig. 5.   Joint-space configuration of stimuli and ideal points.

We further note that the ideal points show quite a bit of scatter about the average. Since in the formulation used here preference decreases with increases in squared distance from the ideal point, we observe that egg dishes and hot cereal are nearest the ideal point of the average subject. Instant breakfast, the fruit dish, and lox and bagels are quite far from the average subject's ideal point. On the other hand, for the ideal point labeled *a*, plotted in the lower right-hand quadrant, we see that pastry or toast is most preferred

---

[4] The ideal of three of the subjects, numbers 11, 14, and 16, plotted outside the range of the data; as such they appear better represented by a vector model. See J. D. Carroll and J. J. Chang [5].

while instant breakfast is least preferred. Thus the model is able to accommodate rather disparate differences in preference rankings.

For this particular set of data the model's fit was not outstanding. While the correlation between squared distance from the ideal point and the average subject's preference ratings was 0.88, this degree of fit is misleading; the correlation coefficients of 9 of the 17 subjects were below 0.70. More important is the fact that the data are pilot study results, meant only to be illustrative of this approach. Even at that, however, we notice the disparity in ideal point locations, a reflection of heterogeneity in the original preference data. The implications of this are of interest to market segmentation, a topic to be discussed later.

OTHER APPROACHES TO THE SCALING OF PREFERENCE DATA

Although we shall not go into the matter deeply, it should be mentioned that other approaches are available for the multidimensional scaling of preference data. In the Carroll-Chang model we noted that input to the program consisted of *both* a perceptual configuration (obtained from the analysis of similarities data) and preference data for the same stimuli. The objective was to locate ideal points in the (possibly rotated and differentially stretched) stimulus configuration which was obtained from the prior analysis of similarities data.

Other, somewhat "bootstrapping" approaches are available for obtaining a joint space of stimuli and ideal points. These approaches are generally classed under the heading of "unfolding," a concept proposed by Coombs [6]. Their objective is this: given only a set of preference data of a group of N respondents for a common set of n stimuli, to find a configuration of $N + n$ points such that certain interpoint distance ranks are closely monotone with the original rank orders. As such, one attempts to obtain both a stimulus configuration and a set of ideal point positions *from preference data alone*.

Returning to the preference data shown in Table 2, the TORSCA program, as employed in unfolding, assumes that any entry can be compared with any other entry in terms of rank order. As such, interpersonal comparisons of utility are implied by this procedure.

Kruskal's M-D-SCAL-IV program does not require such a stringent assumption, however. This approach merely requires that the rank order of stimuli from each ideal point be maintained *within* row. But in this case fewer constraints are available for fixing the positions of the points.

In order to illustrate these approaches most simply, both were applied to the synthetic data of Figure 1. This time, however, we pretended that the points representing letter A were stimuli and those representing letter M were ideal points in a common space. In the TORSCA run we computed the interpoint distances of each of the points in A from each of the points in M. These 304 interpoint distances were ranked and submitted to the program. In the M-D-SCAL-IV run, however, input ranks of the 16 points comprising the letter A were compared only *within* each of the 19 rows comprising the letter M.

The left-hand portion of Figure 6, summarizing the TORSCA program results, shows the effect on recovery of fewer constraints available for fixing the configuration (see the left-hand portion of Figure 2 for contrast). For ease of interpretation, the points comprising the letter A have been connected by a light line, while those comprising the letter M have been joined by a heavy line. We note some distortion in both letters, indicating that a reduction in rank information involving 595 distances to 304 distances provides less determinancy in the solution.

The effect is even more pronounced in the right-hand portion of the figure. While the letter A appears to be recovered quite well, the letter M (representing the 19 ideal points) is quite distorted compared to the recovery achieved in the right-hand panel of Figure 2. This is not surprising in view of the fact that no *direct* constraints are placed on ideal point location in the M-D-SCAL-IV application. However, the assumption of interutility comparisons is not required in this model either, which seems more realistic in applied research. In this case, then, ideal points might more appropriately be construed as *regions* insofar as the model's ability to portray their positions accurately is concerned.

In summary, unfolding approaches can be used to construct joint-space configurations from preference data alone. As would be surmised, however, the reduction in the number of nonmetric constraints takes its toll in our ability to recover synthetic data configurations by means of these procedures.[5] Similar limitations would apply to applications involving real data.

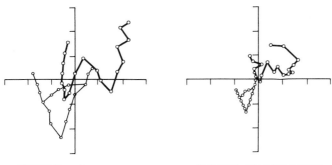

TORSCA 9 scaling program   M-D-SCAL-IV scaling program

Fig. 6.   Unfolding solutions applied to synthetic data of Fig. 2.

POTENTIAL MARKETING APPLICATIONS OF ORDINAL MULTIDIMENSIONAL SCALING

Our description of nonmetric multidimensional scaling methods has been, by necessity, brief and incomplete. As was indicated earlier, the recency of these techniques suggests that much testing—with synthetic and real data—will be required before their potential contributions to marketing research can be intelligently evaluated. Potential applications must therefore be described quite speculatively and tenuously at this point.

Of course, it is not hard to imagine a variety of possible applications, and the first author, along with Carmone and Robinson, has already done so [12]. For purposes of this chapter only, two potential applications, market segmentation and product life-cycle analysis, will be mentioned.

In market segmentation we are usually interested in how various groups of buyers respond differently to various marketing efforts—product, price, packaging, promotion, distribution, and so forth. From the point of view of nonmetric scaling, a market segment can be characterized as a buying group who both perceive and evaluate the entities of a product or supplier class similarly. In terms of this theory, their perceptual maps would be similar and they would occupy similar ideal point positions as derived from the preference data.

---

[5] For other disadvantages of this class of procedures, see P. E. Green and F. J. Carmone [9].

Methods are available—albeit still to be refined—for partitioning respondents according to various points of view [38] regarding a common set of stimuli, that is, the saliency of various properties of the brands or suppliers of service which underlie their similarity judgments. Procedures are also available for clustering subjects [13] according to commonality of ideal point position and salience weights applied to the dimensions in the context of preference.

From the standpoint of marketing policy, the problem would be to move a firm's brand (or service) toward clusters of ideal points or perhaps to move the ideal points toward the firm's brand. Further, it may be possible to change the salience of dimensions—or even membership of the segments themselves—or the bases (axes of the perceptual and evaluative space) by which brands are perceived. But virtually nothing is known at this point about the feasibility of this procedure and, for the time being, it might be best described as primarily a conceptual approach to the problem of market segmentation.

In product (or service) *life-cycle analysis,* our concern is with the behavior over time of various aspects of brands or services. Past research in this area has emphasized various types of empirical curve-fitting procedures to time-series data.

In our view, an alternative approach would be to characterize components of a product or service class in a type of performance space where the points are subscripted by time period. Changes in technology could be represented as movements of points along performance dimensions, including the possibility of adding or deleting dimensions. By means of this approach one might analyze not only general movements of all entities in performance space but also the interrelationships among specific brands or suppliers of service through time. An analysis of the computer market suggests that the approach is feasible [10].

Clearly, a wide variety of potential applications seem possible, including new product development [36], brand switching research, advertising evaluation, and the like. Moreover, as will be discussed in the next section, ordinal methods can be utilized as general multivariate techniques in which at least some of the data are only rank ordered.

ORDINAL APPROACHES TO MULTIVARIATE DATA ANALYSIS

Nonmetric models can also be used as ordinal analogs to multivariate statistical techniques.[6] In this type of application the data need not consist of similarities or preferences at all.

Historically, nonmetric methods were first developed for data matrices which were *not* partitioned in advance into criterion versus predictor subsets. These models, dealing with nonmetric factor analysis, are discussed first, followed by a description of methods utilizing partitioned matrices.

Nonpartitioned Matrices

In the typical application of metric principal component analysis (R technique), one starts with an N by n data matrix representing interval scaled values of each of N objects on each of n variables. One then finds orthogonal linear combinations of the n columns which account for as much variance as possible in the original data set. The values of these linear combinations, usually called component scores, are then correlated with the original variables, leading to a set of variable-by-component loadings.

In nonmetric analogues to principal component factor analysis, we assume only that the N objects are ranked by each of the n variables in turn. Instead

[6] This section is drawn from P. E. Green and V. R. Rao [16].

of reproducing various types of scalar products—for example, correlation coefficients—most nonmetric factoring approaches attempt to represent the data in one of three ways:

1. Find sets of N points and n vector directions in a space of low dimensionality such that the rank order of projections of each of the N points on each of the n vectors most closely matches all the original rankings.

2. Find two sets of points $(N + n)$ in a space of low dimensionality such that the rank order of each of the N objects from each of the n ordering variables most closely matches all of the original rankings.

3. Find one set of points $(N$ or n, but not both$)$ in a space of low dimensionality such that the rank order of interpoint distances most closely matches the inverse rank order of a set of association coefficients (for example, Spearman rank correlations) derived from the original data matrix.

Computer algorithms which utilize the first approach are represented by the procedures of Shepard and Kruskal [35] and the linear model of Roskam [31]. These analogs to factor analytic models—point-vector models—assume that the values of each ordering variable (vector) are monotone with the saturation of object i on dimension k.

Computer algorithms utilizing the second approach, a two-set point representation, include Kruskal's M-D-SCAL-IV program [23] and Guttman and Lingoes' SSAR [26] and CM-III [25] programs. The M-D-SCAL-IV and SSAR-II approaches utilize a distance representation. That is, a reduced space is found with two sets of points, object and variable, referred to common orthogonal axes. The objective is to find a configuration whose ranks of interpoint distances are closely monotone with the original ranks of objects as ordered by variables. If the model is appropriate, however, one *derives* object-object and variable-variable distances, although these do not enter directly as monotone constraints in the solution process.

Guttman and Lingoes' SSAR-III and SSAR-IV procedures differ from the above in that both rows and columns can serve as monotone constraints in the former procedure (the solution being achieved by averaging row and column results at each iteration) and communalities are computed in the latter. As such, these procedures upgrade the assumption underlying the data by assuming interobject comparability. Their CM-III program entails the finding of monotone transforms of each column which maximize the average correlation among all pairs of variables. It can be used as a preliminary transformation device prior to conducting a metric factor analysis on a set of data originally consisting only of ranks of objects by each ordering variable.

A number of computer algorithms can utilize the third approach which obtains a *single* set of points—objects or variables but not both—whose ranks of interpoint distances in a space of low dimensionality are closely monotone with either an N by N or n by n symmetric matrix of nonmetric association measures. Again, inter-object comparability is assumed if an N by N matrix is used. Kruskal's M-D-SCAL-IV program, Young and Torgerson's TORSCA program [39], Guttman and Lingoes' SSA program [27], or McGee's scaling program [28] can all be utilized for this purpose.

Nonmetric factoring programs, considered generically, typically lead to spatial representations of lower dimensionality than their metric counterparts, particularly if the relationship between interpoint distances and input data is highly nonlinear but still monotonic.

Matrices Partitioned by Prior Judgment

In many applied problems the researcher exercises prior judgment in partitioning the columns of the matrix into criterion and predictor sets. Such judgments underlie the techniques of multiple regression, discriminant analysis, canonical correlation, and univariate and multivariate analysis of variance. We next describe nonmetric analogues to these procedures.

Monotone Multiple Regression

In the typical application of multiple regression, all variables are assumed to be interval-scaled. Variations of this approach stipulate that one or more of the predictors are dummy (zero-one) variables. Let us now assume that the criterion variable is rank-ordered while the predictor set is interval-scaled (or possibly consists in part of zero-one variables). A general approach to this problem is to employ monotone multiple regression.

In monotone regression, a series of linear regressions are performed on a set of criterion values which are constrained to be monotone with the original criterion ranks. At each iteration, the transformed criterion values are chosen to be as close as possible to the computed values of the previous iteration (after first treating the criterion values as metric), subject to being monotone with values of the original criterion variable. Carroll and Chang [4] have incorporated this approach, as has Kruskal [22]. In the case where *all* variables are only rank-ordered, Guttman and Lingoes' CMII program [25] appears to be the only approach which is operational currently.

Discriminant Analysis and Canonical Correlation

Since discriminant analysis (either two-group or multiple-group) can be viewed as a special case of canonical correlation, we treat both these techniques together in this section. Unfortunately no fully satisfactory approach has yet been developed as a nonmetric analogue. One rather ad hoc procedure entails a sequential approach, assuming the predictor set of variables are all ordinal scaled and the criterion set is either ordinal scaled or, in the case of discriminant analysis, consists of m-1 dummy variables for m exclusive and exhaustive classes.

Commenting first on the former conditions, one could do the following:

1. For the criterion and predictor sets, separately refer the objects to orthogonal axes in reduced space such that the ranks of interpoint distances in the reduced space are closely monotone with nonmetric coefficients summarizing with each of the two N by N interobject matrices.

2. Perform a metric canonical correlation on the two N by k and N by k' sets of coordinates in the reduced spaces.

A major problem of this approach is loss of information about the importance of the original variables in contributing to the canonical correlation between the two sets of (reduced space) coordinates.

In the case of m-way discriminant analysis, only the predictor set of ordinal scaled variables would be referred to reduced space coordinates. One would then perform a conventional discriminant analysis using the reduced space coordinates as the predictor set. The same deficiency noted in the preceding paragraph is relevant here.

It should be mentioned, however, that direct approaches to the problem have been suggested by Carroll [3] and de Leeuw [8]; neither algorithm has been programmed as yet, however.

Univariate and Multivariate Analysis of Variance

Univariate analysis of variance can be viewed as a special case of multiple regression (and hence canonical correlation) where the predictor set consists of dummy variables and the criterion variable is assumed to be interval-scaled. If the criterion variable is only ordinal-scaled, the procedures described under the label "monotone regression" can also be used here. Also, J. C. Lingoes considers this problem in his CM-I program [25].

Multivariate analysis of variance can be portrayed (formally) as a special case of canonical correlation where the predictor set again consists of dummy variables and the criterion set is assumed to be interval-scaled. If the criterion set is only ordinal-scaled, the objects can be referred to reduced space coordinates. Then either a metric canonical correlation or multivariate analysis of variance can be performed, and interval scaled covariates can be handled as well. The limitations of this sequential approach have already been described.

Summary Considerations in Nonmetric Multivariate Analysis

From the foregoing comments, it is evident that nonmetric analogues to linear multivariate models *already* exist. It is probable that many refinements to present procedures will appear in the future. Still one might ask, even in their current stage of development, if such procedures provide advantages over the linear models. Unfortunately little research has been conducted on the robustness of linear models to departures from linearity. The research that has been conducted in the context of factor analysis suggests that departures from linearity lead to extra (artifact) dimensions when one uses linear models, although the configurations obtained by each procedure in the *appropriate* dimensionality can be quite similar. Analogously, Green and Rao [16] found that departures from monotonicity produce extra (artifact) dimensions if monotone methods are used.

Matched against the above advantage of nonlinear models are special problems of: (1) uniqueness of solution, (2) degeneracy, and (3) local minima which are associated with nonmetric models. Thus it may be pragmatically useful to analyze data using *both* metric and nonmetric approaches. This tandem approach produces comparative results and also provides safeguards against some of the special problems associated with the application of nonmetric techniques.

CURRENT PROBLEMS IN NONMETRIC SCALING AND FUTURE RESEARCH OPPORTUNITIES

While the field of nonmetric scaling appears provocative enough to justify serious study, many problems requiring concerted research effort remain. The past few years have witnessed a high degree of activity on algorithmic development with comparatively few applications of the methodology. While no exhaustive listing of empirical problems is attempted here, some of the problems encountered in pilot applications of the techniques are described in the hope that interested marketing researchers will devote effort toward their resolution.

Data Collection Methods

One of the problems in the application of ordinal scaling methods concerns appropriate methods for the collection of similarities data. A variety of such procedures are available—triads, n-dimensional rank order, rating scales, pair comparisons of pairs, monadic ratings with subsequent computation of pairwise distance functions, and the like.[7] All these procedures ultimately are concerned with developing a rank order of pairs.

---

[7] For a description of a variety of such methods, see W. S. Torgerson [37] and C. H. Coombs [6].

For relatively small numbers of stimuli (say, 12 or less), such procedures can be used without incurring undue respondent fatigue or boredom. But for larger numbers of stimuli the procedures become unwieldly, since the number of distinct pairs of n items increases as $\frac{1}{2}(n)(n-1)$.

Several approaches to the problem of handling large stimulus sets (for example, $n > 12$) can be mentioned. If the researcher is willing to pool data over respondents, various types of subjective grouping can be used, either with or without an anchor item. Green, Carmone, and Fox [11] utilized one such procedure and developed a stimulus configuration for 38 stimuli (T.V. shows) using a method due to Johnson [20].

A second approach to the problem is to use a core set of stimuli for each subject and subsets of new stimuli which are not common over subjects. Stimulus configurations are developed for subsets of subjects whose perception is common over the core set by a type of "interlocking" procedure [14]. This procedure has the advantage of permitting the development of several points of view in which data are aggregated only over those subjects who demonstrate commonality of perception over the core set of stimuli.

A third approach, which still requires the pooling of data over subjects, is based on balanced incomplete block designs [19] in which each stimulus appears an equal number of times and each pair of stimuli also appears an equal number of times across subjects. Still another procedure is to use subjective grouping in a hierarchical fashion in which subjects are asked to combine clusters at various prespecified levels after the stimuli have been originally grouped subjectively into as many clusters as the subject desires. While not fully tested as yet, this procedure would seem capable of developing stimulus configurations for individual subjects (assuming metric techniques are used).

Finally, some mention should be made of the possibility of designing pairwise data collection procedures involving missing comparisons. With large numbers of stimuli it is usually the case that a high degree of "overdeterminism" of the solution exists. Moreover, most of the nonmetric scaling programs are capable of handling missing data. The problem concerns which and how many comparisons to omit.

Relatively little systematic examination of alternative methods for obtaining similarities data has been conducted thus far. Moreover, a variety of alternatives—and little information about their similarity of results—exist with respect to the collection of preference data as well.

Configuration Invariance

Another problem for research in scaling methods concerns the stability of scaling solutions over (1) alternative data collection methods, (2) alternative instructions or scenarios under which judgments are to be elicited, (3) changes in the composition of the stimulus set, (4) people at a given point in time, and (5) a given person at different points in time.

It is the contention of the authors that both similarity and preference judgments are conditioned by context. Indeed, it is possible to imagine a reference or "superconfiguration" of a set of stimuli which undergoes various transformations based on utility concepts. That is, the dimensions which are evoked for similarity judgments would seem to be related to such teleological considerations as product use, the buyer's current inventory of brands, and the like.

Some investigation has been made of configuration invariance over changes in the composition of the stimulus set [17], but such work is at a very early stage of development. Insofar as marketing applications are concerned, little is known about the sensitivity of either similarities or preference judgments to "change agent" stimuli, at least within the context of multidimensional scaling methodology.

Configuration Interpretation

A third problem area for future research involves the development and test of procedures for interpreting multidimensional scaling solutions, that is, the dimension labeling problem. In the past the usual procedure has involved the researcher's use of subjective expertise about the stimulus set along with information obtained from the subject's postinterview responses to open-ended questions about the criteria which he believed he used.

Somewhat more defensible procedures can be suggested, however. For example, after similarities judgments are obtained on an "overall" (unstructured) basis, the subject may be asked to give similarities judgments according to prespecified attributes. These attributes would be hypothesized by the experimenter as being salient in the overall similarity judgments. Procedures are available for finding rotations in the overall space whose projections are most congruent with the hypothesized dimensions [29].[8]

Another possibility for developing relevant constructs is to use a type of repertory grid technique in which subjects are asked to respond to the prototypical question: "In which way are two of these three stimuli alike and different from the third?" Stimuli can then be rated according to the constructs evoked by the subjects and rotations of the overall space can be made which yield maximally congruent projections which the candidate constructs. Canonical correlation appears particularly useful in this regard if one desires to "match" configuration dimensions with the best linear combination of "constructs."

Clearly, if multidimensional scaling procedures are to reach operational significance in various aspects of marketing planning, alternative approaches to the interpretation of spatial dimensions must be developed and tested.

Other Problems

The preceding research areas hardly exhaust the classes of problems which require further study. Alternative approaches to the identification of respondents' perceptual points of view, the problem of scaling "bundles" of stimuli versus individual entities, nonstationary models of perceptual judgments, and the whole problem of statistical inference are illustrative of areas for future investigation.

CONCLUSIONS

In this chapter we have tried to present an overview of ordinal methods of multidimensional scaling and the potential usefulness of this methodology in the measurement of buyer perception and preference. While it is easy to imagine a variety of future applications, it is equally easy to enumerate the many significant problems which remain for future investigation.

It is hoped that this chapter has served a dual purpose: (1) to acquaint the marketing researcher with the rudiments of the methodology and (2) to caution him concerning many of the fundamental problems still to be resolved. We cannot overemphasize the second objective. Computer programs for multi-

---

[8] Also, for a description of a procedure that leads to a unique orientation of the space, see J. D. Carroll and J. J. Chang [4].

dimensional scaling are being widely disseminated—it is inevitable that abuses of this methodology will take place. While the potential application of these methods to marketing behavior is exciting to contemplate, responsible use of these problems will require a sizable intellectual commitment on the part of applications researchers. It is one thing to "turn the handle" and observe the reams of computer output—it is quite another to understand what the computer program is doing and why.

APPENDIX

Computational Aspects of Multidimensional Scaling

In this technical appendix we discuss briefly some of the computational features of multidimensional scaling algorithms.[9] For illustrative purposes we concentrate on only one of these computer programs, Young and Torgerson's TORSCA program [39], as representative of these procedures.

For expository purposes assume that we have a set of ranked pairs δ_{ij}, where $i = 1, 2, \ldots, n - 1$ and $j = 2, 3, \ldots, n$. We can call the δ_{ij} proximities, or psychological distances. Our objective is to find a configuration $X = x_1, x_2, \ldots, x_n$ consisting of n vectors in the space of r dimensions. The coordinates of a given vector x_i can be specified as:

$$x_i = (x_{i1}, x_{i2}, \ldots, x_{ir})$$

For each x_i, x_j in X we may compute a distance d_{ij}. If X is a "good" configuration in that the ranks of its distances d_{ij} reproduce the input ranks δ_{ij}, then that configuration should be "final" or close thereto for representing the δ_{ij}.

The appropriate numbers (they may not be distances) which *are* perfectly monotone with the δ_{ij} can be denoted as $\hat{d}_{ij}$. The TORSCA algorithm considers, then, relationships among the three sets:

1. The δ_{ij}—the input data ranks
2. The d_{ij}—computed distances between all pairs of points
3. The $\hat{d}_{ij}$—a set of ratio scaled numbers, chosen to be as *close to their respective* d_{ij} *as possible* subject to being monotone with the δ_{ij}. That is, $\hat{d}_{ij} \leq \hat{d}_{kl}$ whenever $\delta_{ij} < \delta_{kl}$.

All these algorithms must then consider two problems: (1) the development of an index of goodness of fit by which one can tell if the configuration X is an appropriate one for representing the input data δ_{ij} and (2) a procedure for moving the points x_i, x_j to some "better" configuration if the current index of fit is poor.

Index of Fit. Most all of the nonmetric scaling algorithms provide an index of fit which represents some variant of Kruskal's stress measure [24].

$$\sqrt{\dfrac{\sum\limits_{i \neq j}^{n} (d_{ij} - \hat{d}_{ij})^2}{\sum\limits_{i \neq j}^{n} d_{ij}^2}}$$

The numerator of this index consists of the sum of squares of the discrepancies between each computed d_{ij} for some configuration X and a set of numbers

---

[9] This section is drawn, with permission, from P. E. Green and D. S. Tull [18].

$\hat{d}_{ij}$ chosen to be as close to their respective d_{ij} as possible subject to being monotone with the original δ_{ij}'s. If the d_{ij} equal their $\hat{d}_{ij}$ counterparts, the numerator of the expression becomes zero and hence stress is also zero, indicating a perfect fit.

The denominator of the expression is merely a normalizing value, computed to allow comparisons of the fit measure across different dimensionalities since, in general, the d_{ij} will increase with increasing dimensionality. More recent versions of the stress formula [23] place the quantity:

$$\sum_{i \neq j}^{n} (d_{ij} - \bar{d})^2$$

(where $\bar{d}$ equals the mean distance) in the denominator. While there are theoretical advantages ascribed to this second formulation, in practice both versions of the formula are used.

Suppose, however, that the stress S of a particular configuration is high; that is, the monotonic fit is poor. The next feature of these algorithms consists of finding a new configuration X' whose ranks of interpoint distances are more closely monotone to the original δ_{ij} than the previously ranked distances.

Improving the Configuration. Assume now that we wish to move the points around such that their distance ranks are closer to the input data ranks than those found in the previous configuration. In particular, consider a specific point i and its relationship to each of the points j in turn. We would like to move point i so as to decrease its average discrepancy between the distances d_{ij} and the numbers $\hat{d}_{ij}$, the latter set numbers being monotone with the δ_{ij}.

If d_{ij} is larger than $\hat{d}_{ij}$, we could move point i toward point j by an amount which is proportional to the size of the discrepancy. Conversely, if $\hat{d}_{ij}$ is larger than d_{ij}, point i is to be moved away from point j by an amount proportional to the discrepancy. However, ordinarily we would not like to do this in just one step since we may "overcorrect" in so doing. Suppose we let α represent the coefficient of proportionality ($0 \leq \alpha \leq 1$) or step size. (Often α is set at 0.2.)

To find a new coordinate $x'_{ia(j)}$ for point i on axis a, as related to point j, we can use the formula:

$$x'_{ia(j)} = x_{ia(j)} + \alpha \left(1 - \frac{\hat{d}_{ij}}{d_{ij}}\right)(x_{ja} - x_{ia})$$

This formula will move point i in the appropriate direction with respect to point j, but we must consider all other points insofar as their effect on point i is concerned.

To do this we merely use the expression

$$x'_{ia} = x_{ia} + \frac{\alpha}{n-1} \sum_{\substack{j=1 \\ i \neq j}}^{n} \left(1 - \frac{\hat{d}_{ij}}{d_{ij}}\right)(x_{ja} - x_{ia})$$

Note that we move point i along axis a in such a way as to take into account the discrepancies involving all other points. This is, of course, done for all points in all dimensions.

The procedure can be summarized, then, as involving the following steps:

1. For a given dimensionality, select some initial configuration X_0.

2. Compute d_{ij} between the vectors x_i, x_j of the configuration X_0 and also compute $\hat{d}_{ij}$, chosen to be as close as possible to the original d_{ij}, subject to being monotone with the δ_{ij} (input data).

3. Evaluate the fit measure S, the stress of the configuration.

4. If $S > \varepsilon$ (a "stopping" value) find a new configuration X_1 whose ranks of the d_{ij} are closer to the δ_{ij}.

5. Repeat the process until successive configurations X_0, X_1, X_2, . . . , X_p converge such that S is satisfactorily "small."

6. Repeat the above process in the next lower dimensionality, and so on.

7. Choose the lowest dimensionality for which S is satisfactorily "small."

Although specific fit measures and procedures for moving the points differ among the various algorithms, they all seem to be based on the above, rather straightforward concepts.

Specific Features of the TORSCA Program. The TORSCA program displays a number of features which should be mentioned in passing.

1. The initial configuration X_0 is obtained by factor analytic methods and hence is a type of fully metric method. However, since points are *then* moved by nonmetric criteria, the complete method is of a nonmetric variety.

2. Latest versions of the program permit solutions in any type of Minkowski metric, including, of course, the Euclidean and city-block metrics as special cases.

3. The program possesses a "passive cell" feature which enables the researcher to scale input data which display missing entries. This feature also permits a variety of analyses to be performed when all δ_{ij} are not comparable.

4. The program provides a history of the computation, configuration plots, and "Shepard" diagrams which are scatter plots of the δ_{ij} versus, in turn, the d_{ij} and $\hat{d}_{ij}$. These scatter plots show the particular type of monotonic function which links the solution with the original input data.

5. Optional printout includes the d_{ij} and the $\hat{d}_{ij}$ expressed in tabular form.

6. Depending upon computer size, up to 60 points can be scaled in up to 10 dimensions.

The program has several options for terminating the iterative process. For the problem whose results are summarized in Figure 2, the program required less than one minute (on an IBM 360/65 computer) to perform 25 iterations and all subsequent steps for scaling the data in two dimensions.

REFERENCES

1. Bennett, J. F., and W. L. Hays, "Multidimensional Unfolding: Determining the Dimensionality of Ranked Preference Data," *Psychometrika*, vol. 25, 1960.
2. Carroll, J. D., "Individual Differences and Multidimensional Scaling," Murray Hill, N.J.: Bell Telephone Laboratories, 1969, multilithed report.
3. ———, personal communication, October 1968.
4. ———, and J. J. Chang, "Analysis of Individual Differences in Multidimensional Scaling via an N-way Generalization of 'Eckart-Young' Decomposition," paper presented at the spring meeting of the Psychometric Society, Princeton, N.J., April 1969.
5. ———, and J. J. Chang, "Relating Preferences Data to Multidimensional Scaling Solutions via a Generalization of Coombs' Unfolding Model," Murray Hill, N.J.: Bell Telephone Laboratories, 1967, multilithed report.
6. Coombs, C. H., *A Theory of Data*, New York: Wiley, 1964.
7. ———, "Psychological Scaling Without a Unit of Measurement," *Psychological Review*, vol. 57, 1950.
8. de Leeuw, J., personal communication, November 1969.

9. Green, P. E., and F. J. Carmone, *Multidimensional Scaling and Related Techniques in Marketing Analysis*, Boston: Allyn and Bacon, 1970.
10. ———, and F. J. Carmone, "The Performance Structure of the Computer Market: A Multivariate Approach," *Economic and Business Bulletin*, vol. 21, 1968.
11. ———, F. J. Carmone, and L. B. Fox, "Television Program Similarities: An Application of Subjective Clustering," *Journal of Market Research Society*, vol. 11, 1969.
12. ———, F. J. Carmone, and P. J. Robinson, "Nonmetric Scaling Methods: An Exposition and Overview," *Wharton Quarterly*, vol. 2, Winter-Spring 1968.
13. ———, R. E. Frank, and P. J. Robinson, "Cluster Analysis in Test Market Selection," *Management Science*, vol. 13, April 1967.
14. ———, A. Maheshwari, and V. R. Rao, "Dimensional Interpretation and Configuration Invariance in Multidimensional Scaling: An Empirical Study," *Multivariate Behavioral Research*, vol. 6, 1969.
15. ———, and V. R. Rao, "Nonmetric Approaches to Multivariate Analysis in Marketing," working paper, University of Pennsylvania, December 1969.
16. ———, and V. R. Rao, "A Note on the Sensitivity of Multidimensional Scaling Solutions to Departures from Monotonicity," working paper, University of Pennsylvania, 1969.
17. ———, and V. R. Rao, "Configuration Invariance in Multidimensional Scaling: An Empirical Study," *Proceedings of the AMA Cincinnati Conference*, August 1969.
18. ———, and D. S. Tull, *Research for Marketing Decisions*, Englewood Cliffs, N.J.: Prentice-Hall, 1969.
19. Gulliksen, H., and L. R. Tucker, "A General Procedure for Obtaining Paired Comparisons from Multiple Rank Orders," *Psychometrika*, vol. 26, June 1961.
20. Johnson, S. C., "Nonmetric Clustering," Murray Hill, N.J.: Bell Telephone Laboratories, 1968, multilithed report.
21. Klingberg, F. L., "Studies in Measurement of the Relations among Sovereign States," *Psychometrika*, vol. 6, December 1941.
22. Kruskal, J. B., "Analysis of Factorial Experiments by Estimating Monotone Transformations of the Data," *Journal of the Royal Statistical Society*, vol. 27, 1965.
23. ———, "How to Use M-D-SCAL, A Program to Do Multidimensional Scaling and Multidimensional Unfolding (Version 4 of M-D-SCAL, March 1968, all in FORTRAN IV)," Murray Hill, N.J.: Bell Telephone Laboratories, 1968.
24. ———, "Multidimensional Scaling by Optimizing Goodness of Fit to a Nonmetric Hypothesis," *Psychometrika*, vol. 29, 1964.
25. Lingoes, J. C., "An IBM Program for Guttman-Lingoes Conjoint Measurement," CMIII, *Behavioral Science*, vol. 13, 1968.
26. ———, "An IBM Program for Guttman-Lingoes Smallest Space Analysis," RI-RIV, *Behavioral Science*, vols. 11 and 12, 1966–1967.
27. ———, "An IBM Program for Guttman-Lingoes Smallest Space Analysis," SSA I-IV, *Behavioral Science*, vols. 10 and 11, 1965–1966.
28. McGee, V. E., "The Multidimensional Scaling of 'Elastic Differences,'" *British Journal of Mathematical and Statistical Psychology*, vol. 19, 1966.
29. Miller, J. E., R. N. Shepard, and J. J. Chang, "An Analytical Approach to the Interpretation of Multidimensional Scaling Solutions," *American Psychologist*, vol. 19, 1964.
30. Richardson, M. W., "Multidimensional Psychophysics," *Psychological Bulletin*, vol. 35, 1938.
31. Roskam, E. E. C. I., "Metric Analysis of Ordinal Data in Psychology," doctoral dissertation, University of Leiden, Holland, 1968.
32. Seamans, R. F., "Breakfast Food Perception and Preference: An Application of Multidimensional Scaling," unpublished MBA Thesis, Wharton School of Finance and Commerce, University of Pennsylvania, 1968.
33. Shepard, R. N., "Metric Structures in Ordinal Data," *Journal of Mathematical Psychology*, vol. 3, 1966.
34. ———, "The Analysis of Proximities: Multidimensional Scaling with an Unknown Distance Function," Part One, *Psychometrika*, vol. 27, 1962.

35. ———, and J. B. Kruskal, "Nonmetric Methods for Scaling and for Factor Analysis," *American Psychologist*, vol. 19, 1964.
36. Stefflre, V. J., "Market Structure Studies: New Products for Old Markets and New Markets (Foreign) for Old Products," in F. M. Bass, C. W. King, and E. A. Pessemier, eds., *Application of the Sciences in Marketing Management*, New York: Wiley, 1968.
37. Torgerson, W. S., *Theory and Methods of Scaling*, New York: Wiley, 1960.
38. Tucker, L. R., and S. Messick, "An Individual Differences Model for Multidimensional Scaling," *Psychometrika*, vol. 28, 1963.
39. Young, F. W., and W. S. Torgerson, "TORSCA, a FORTRAN IV Program for Shepard-Kruskal Multidimensional Scaling Analysis," *Behavioral Science*, vol. 12, 1967.
40. Young, G., and A. S. Householder, "Discussion of a Set of Points in Terms of Their Mutual Distances," *Psychometrika*, vol. 3, March 1938.

Part A
Techniques

Chapter 5

Projective Methods

HAROLD H. KASSARJIAN[1] *Graduate School of Business Administration, University of California, Los Angeles, California*

Since World War II various projective methods of personality assessment in clinical psychology have gained increasing acceptance and use. Their use in marketing research, as well as in attitude and opinion measurement, however, has been sporadic and often marked by controversy. Their fate has depended on the day's current fad and the dynamics of motivation research. This chapter presents and examines psychology's basic theoretical foundations from which the use of projective techniques has evolved and the role and potential contributions of projective techniques to marketing research and market analysis.

Much marketing research knowledge comes from consumer responses to a yes-no kind of question or a similarly restricted response situation affording the subject little freedom of choice. Projective techniques, however, allow greater latitude of consumer response. The respondent is presented cartoons, ink blots, or other ambiguous stimuli—situations in which the researcher has no preconceived notions or categorizations of what the responses will be—and the subject has full freedom to react as he wishes. Modifications of some of the basic psychological tools or techniques—such as sentence completion tests, word association tests, the picture frustration test, and the thematic apperception test—have been used with varying degrees of success and researcher competence. They will be discussed briefly later in this chapter. The questions of reliability and validity, also to be examined, dominate the use of projective methods, whether on the psychologist's couch or the researcher's clipboard. Finally, the use of any indirect kind of questioning by an attitude and opinion researcher involves ethical questions, such as the propriety of deception and misuse of tools.

[1] The author is indebted to Waltraud M. Kassarjian, E. Laird Landon, Jr., and Philip J. Schreiner for critical evaluation of an earlier draft.

THEORETICAL FOUNDATIONS

The term *projection*, from which projective techniques derive their title, was first used psychologically by Sigmund Freud. In psychoanalytic theory, projection is an ego defense mechanism similar to rationalization, repression, reaction formation, regression, and so on through which the ego tries to master the dangers, threats, and anxieties that beset the person by denying, falsifying, or distorting "reality." The individual, by using projection defensively, attempts to relieve his anxiety by attributing its causation to the external world [5]. According to Freud [15, p. 857]:

> The projection of inner perceptions to the outside is a primitive mechanism which, for instance, also influences our sense-perceptions, so that it normally has the greatest share in shaping our outer world. . . . Even inner perceptions of ideational and emotional processes are projected outwardly, like sense-perceptions, and are used to shape the outer world. . . .

Whether of a psychoanalytic orientation or not, most clinical psychologists would agree that the process of projection is at least partially unconscious, that it serves as a defense against unconscious drives, tends to reduce personal tension, and results in attributing to the outer world impulses, feelings, ideas, and attitudes held by the individual [12a].

In short, when an individual is presented with ambiguous stimuli about which he is asked to find meaning and make interpretations and under conditions in which the examiner's intent is not made clear, he will interpret the material in a manner that will reflect his own personality or need-value system.

From a slightly different route, the social psychologist has also been historically interested in the influence of the need-value-attitude systems of the individual on his behavior patterns and his perception of the outer world [25].

Selective perception, originally coined "the new look in perception," is the belief that the individual's needs, motivations, and experiences modify or screen out the various meanings received from stimuli in the external world such that he perceives what he wants to perceive. For example, in a classic study, Hastorf and Cantril presented a football game analysis as perceived by opposing fans. The football contest between two Ivy League teams, Dartmouth and Princeton, was unusually rough and charged with emotion. As might have been expected, the fans of these two teams, sitting in the same stadium on the same Saturday afternoon, saw two different games. Hastorf and Cantril write [18]:

> The data indicate that there is no such thing as a game existing out there in its own right which people merely observe. The game exists for a person and is experienced by him only in so far as certain happenings have significance in terms of his purpose. Of all the occurrences going on in the environment, a person selects those that have some significance for him from his own ego-centric position in the total matrix.

Hence, one way to measure personality is to present the subject with a series of ambiguous stimuli (material that allows for varied interpretation), ask him to organize the stimuli into a meaningful context, to tell a story, complete a sentence, or in some other way interpret the stimuli, and then consider his response a reflection of the need-value system. This is the development of projective techniques in clinical psychology and in marketing research— ambiguous stimuli to be interpreted by subjects from their own particular and individual frames of reference.

THE ROLE OF PROJECTIVE TECHNIQUES IN MARKETING ANALYSIS

The raison d'être of the introduction of projective techniques into marketing is that they elicit responses that the subject will not or cannot otherwise give. Both proponents and opponents of projective tools seem to feel that, at times, the direct questioning methods and the public opinion surveys have failed to meet the demands placed on them.[2]   Despite the increasing sophistication of and refinements in interviewing, data processing, and sampling, the fact that the respondent may intentionally or unintentionally completely misunderstand, misinterpret, or mislead the researcher is a basic deficiency in the direct questioning technique, at least from the market researcher's limited point of view. Often the issues put to the respondent are unimportant to him—whether he prefers the packaging of Crest or Colgate toothpaste—and hence his opinions are not always solidified.   Or if the issue under question is important to him, he may not be willing to disclose certain opinions although he may appear most cooperative throughout the interview.   If pressed by the interviewer who is instructed to probe, he may express attitudes, feelings, or opinions that he does not in fact possess [13].

The purpose of projective techniques, then, is to provide a tool that will, it is hoped, increase the validity of the attitude measure by disguising its purpose.   For example, in an early study of the use of projective techniques in marketing, Mason Haire tried to discover what factors determined the attitudes of housewives toward instant coffee [16].   Subjects were asked, "Do you use instant coffee?"   (If no) "What do you dislike about it?"   The bulk of the unfavorable responses fell into the general area "I don't like the flavor."   This is such a simple answer to a complex question that Haire suspected it was a stereotyped response to get rid of the interviewer and perhaps conceal other motives.

Hence he developed a projective or disguised technique to uncover any underlying motives.   Two shopping lists were prepared which included such items as "bunch of carrots, 2 pounds of potatoes, two loaves of Wonder bread," and so forth.   The two lists were identical except that one list contained the item, "one pound Maxwell House coffee (drip grind)," and the other, "Nescafé instant coffee."   Subjects were asked to read one or the other shopping list and characterize the woman who bought these particular groceries.   The woman buying the instant coffee was described as lazy, failing to plan schedules and household purchases well, not a good wife, and not thrifty.   The Maxwell House purchaser was described as thrifty, a good wife, not lazy, and a good planner.

Clearly the Nescafé and Maxwell House users were perceived differently by the housewives (at least in 1950).   A reasonable inference drawn from the data is that the perceptions reflected differences in attitudes toward instant coffee and the role of the housewife—attitudes that were not measured in the directed questioning in which taste emerged as the basic variable.

Levels of Consciousness

For various reasons a respondent who may be perfectly aware of his actual feelings and opinions is often unwilling to express them either to a stranger interviewing him or even a close friend.   Group norms, social pressures, feelings of privacy, and learned social graces may account for some of the distortions.   The need to preserve one's self-concept or ego, the need not to appear

[2] An excellent discussion of problems associated with direct questioning can be found in [39].

ignorant, or lack of introspective ability may contribute to invalid answers. For example, in the past two decades anti-Semitic attitudes were not to be expressed freely in public. A person voting for a fringe right-wing political candidate "to keep the Jew in his place" may be perfectly aware of his reasoning and yet not express it to a dark-haired, olive-complexioned interviewer. In fact, if he sees himself as an educated and enlightened American, he may well not express it to a blond, "Aryan" interviewer or neighbor either.

Also, there may be certain types of consumers who, although perfectly willing to discuss their attitudes and needs, may be unable to do so. Lacking the right words, concepts, or ideas, they may be unable to verbalize their feelings and thus may appear confused.

Conscious Level of Awareness. Despite these difficulties, however, a respondent is usually free and willing to express himself on many topics. Depending on the interview's content, the individual is perfectly aware of what he is saying. He makes assumptions about how the researcher will react and accept his views, and neither his self-concept, his privacy, nor his standing in the eyes of others is threatened. Much marketing and attitude and opinion research today is directed at compiling data at this conscious level. The direct questioning, questions that ask for yes-no responses, the open-ended probing interview, the "depth" interview at the doorstep, and perhaps even some projective techniques such as sentence completion and word association in the hands of a nonprofessional are tapping this kind of information.

Undoubtedly many existing attitudes, values, and opinions can be expressed validly. Which soap do you prefer? What brand of socks or candy do you most often buy? Which of two noncontroversial candidates will you vote for? But an answer to the question, "Why did you buy, vote, or prefer?" of course, may not be as easy to verbalize or state validly. Further, questions such as: "Have you recently purchased sanitary napkins? Prophylactics? Hard liquor? Drugs for syphilis, skin disorders, or anxiety?" may elicit a response but not necessarily an accurate one.

Semiconscious Level. On a continuum of awareness levels, a second broad category and overlapping concept is that of a semiconscious area. The psychologically sophisticated and introspective individual may occasionally have flashes of partial insight into his motivations. The employee who slams the front door and screams at his children on return from work may be able to admit to himself or even others, under the right conditions, that his behavior was caused by his anger at his employer. Direct questioning about why one subscribes to the air-mail edition of *The New York Times* may easily lead to answers relating to the quality of the newspaper, although it may also be possible under certain conditions to elicit motives such as the need to feel important or intellectual, to impress colleagues or superiors, to play one-upmanship at cocktail parties, or to compensate for feelings of inferiority.

The values, emotional drives, and motivations residing at this level of consciousness are disguised to the outer world by rationalizations, intellectualization, and other ego defenses. The aggressive impulses or inferiority feelings that may have led to the purchase of an expensive sports car are accounted for by the "great deal" he got from the salesman, the rickety condition of his previous car, the importance of impressing his own customers and clients, and, of course, the fact that it is a tax write-off.

In the hands of a trained psychologist this level of consciousness can be explored. The various projective techniques discussed in the next section in most cases have been designed to tap the semiconscious level.

Unconscious Level. At the deepest level of consciousness the basic drives and demands of the individual are completely hidden from him and available only after many hours of psychological or psychoanalytic interviewing. Psychoanalytically oriented theoreticians claim that the conflicts and drives at this level lead to psychosis, alcoholism, and various other mental disorders [14]. In the field of marketing, perhaps some behavior of certain consumers may be related to motivations stemming from the unconscious level. Perhaps one can claim that the excessive use of cosmetics by males may be related to latent homosexuality or that the reckless driving at high speeds of a sports car is related to a death wish stemming from guilt over oedipal feelings. And perhaps under certain conditions it is possible to discover these underlying drives in any given individual; nevertheless, they are of little significance or value to the marketing researcher.

Projective techniques alone, used by a $2-an-hour interviewer, appear inadequate. Even if it were possible to gather such information on a valid basis, one is hard-pressed to imagine the marketing strategy required to peddle, say, body talc packaged in the phallic shape of a sinuous serpent with an extended tongue to appeal to a specific market segment.

If projective tests are to be used validly, the best we can expect to do with them is to tap, at the conscious level, respondents' need-value systems which they may be unwilling or unable to express or perhaps the semiconscious motivation about which the individual has little immediate awareness.

SELECTED PROJECTIVE TECHNIQUES

Error-Choice

Based on the concept that a person's attitudes are related to selective perception and selective recall, Kenneth Hammond developed the error-choice technique of attitude measurement [17]. The method uses an "information" test which, for every item, forces the respondent to choose between two alternative answers, each of which is factually wrong, indeterminable, or controversial.

The test situation provokes the subject to select "facts" from memory and direction of the error is measured as an indication of the respondent's attitudes. A sample question might be, "Average weekly wage of the war worker in 1945 was (a) $37, (b) $57." Here the facts were determinable, and the alternative answers were equidistant from the truth in opposite directions. A second type of question is, "Russia's removal of heavy industry from Austria was (a) legal, (b) illegal." In this case the facts are indeterminable and controversial.

In the original instrument these types of questions were interspersed with straight informational items for which the true answer was an alternative. Hammond's research indicates that the technique appears to be valid and reliable and that respondents were unable to perceive the fact that it was actually an attitude test measuring their values towards labor and Soviet Russia.

Irvin Weschler successfully used this technique to measure attitudes in the field of labor relations [40]. Union members and students classifying themselves as prolabor scored high in the prolabor direction as measured by the test, while management representatives and students declaring themselves as promanagement scored low. Labor mediators of high ability as judged by their colleagues tended to score in the neutral zone on the test, while those of low ability scored either in the promanagement or prolabor end of the scale [11].

The technique has not been extensively used in marketing, but one can easily imagine a multitude of topics that would be amenable to the error-choice method. Women's attitudes towards cigar smoking, male use of perfumes and hair sprays, attitudes toward big business, image studies, and so forth are potential candidates. Although the technique does not necessarily deserve the term *projective* in the usual psychological sense, it is clearly a potentially very useful indirect method of attitude measurement, especially for those topics which one hesitates to discuss in public. And perhaps it does tap some semiconscious needs and values in that both selective perception and selective retention are important causal agents.

Word Association

This particular method has long been known and used both in clinical psychology and marketing. It was first used in 1880 by Wilhelm Wundt, the father of experimental psychology, and extensively used in marketing by James Vicary after World War II. A series of words is presented to the respondent; mixed among many neutral stimuli such as water, carrot, tree, and house are the critical words, such as instant coffee, Pillsbury cake mix, and premium beer. The subject is asked to respond with the very first word that comes to his mind. Hence, to a word like "cake mix" the response may be "easy," "high quality," or "lousy homemaker."

In responding to key stimuli a subject may often show embarrassment, laugh anxiously, bow his head, or take considerably longer to respond. In a psychological interview this kind of response gives extremely important cues indicating to the examiner that perhaps these areas do concern the patient and should be examined later [31]. Unfortunately, in a marketing research type interview at the doorstep, such important cues are often missed as the interviewer rushes through the schedule. Nevertheless, the technique has been widely used in marketing in such areas as trade-name recognition, effects of advertising slogans, taboo topics, and effects of promotions. For example, George Smith reports a study in which just two stimulus words were used—Doeskin and Kleenex. The former drew a decidedly larger number of replies such as "soft," "softness," and "downy," suggesting that the concept of softness is built into the Doeskin trade name—an important feature in selling cleansing tissue [9].

The word association technique with its long, respectable history shows promise in marketing research when used properly. Content analyses of the associated words can lead to numerous hypotheses to be tested later.

Sentence Completion

An alternative to the word association method but seemingly tapping similar variables is the sentence completion test developed by Payne in the 1930s. It appears to overcome some of the weaknesses of the word association technique in that single-word responses are often difficult to analyze, and it reduces the multiplicity of associations evoked by a single word. It is better able to suggest the subject's attitudes and feelings.

The objective of the technique is to present the subject with an incomplete and ambiguous sentence that he is to complete. The respondent is free to use his imagination and experiences. Sample sentences from psychological forms are:

> When people push me around ＿＿＿＿.
> I get angry when ＿＿＿＿.
> My mother ＿＿＿＿.
> I worry over ＿＿＿＿.
> I become disgusted with ＿＿＿＿.

The literature in psychology indicates that when responses to such questions are compared with known biographical data and case history material, the technique will evoke data often difficult to elicit in a short interview and will indicate differences in personalities [12]. The test is usually not timed and has the advantage of being administrable to large groups.

In the marketing literature (this technique has been heavily used by motivation researchers), the question is typically stated either in the first person singular ("I never _____," "When I think of beer _____") or in the third person ("The average person considers television _____," "Most people feel that men who use cologne _____"). The results, taken alone, are perhaps not valid enough to serve as a base for major decisions, but clearly the test offers a measure of the respondent's need-value system and, when corroborated with other data, can lead to meaningful results.

In one study, Kassarjian and Cohen asked 179 smokers who believed cigarettes to be a health hazard why they continued to smoke. The majority gave responses such as, "Pleasure is more important than health," "Moderation is O.K.," "I like to smoke." One gets the impression that smokers are not dissatisfied with their lot. However, in a portion of the study involving sentence-completion tests, smokers responded to the question, "People who never smoke are _____," with comments such as "better off," "happier," "smarter," "wiser, more informed." To the question, "Teenagers who smoke are _____," smokers responded with, "foolish," "crazy," "uninformed," "stupid," "showing off," "immature," "wrong."

Clearly, the impression one gets from the sentence completion test is that smokers are anxious, uncomfortable, dissonant, and dissatisfied with their habit. This is quite different from the results of a probed open-end question. This finding was further supported in other phases of the study, indicating that it is probably the more valid of the findings [20].

Rosenzweig Picture Frustration Test

First published in 1945 by Rosenzweig [34], the original instrument consists of 24 pictures resembling incomplete cartoons with standardized norms measuring reactions to frustration [35]. Each picture contains two figures, the one on the left saying something or describing a situation that frustrates the person on the right. The frustrated person has a blank balloon above his head, and both characters wear expressionless faces.

For example, in one figure a waiter is serving food to a female patron with the comment, "I'm sorry but the cook didn't do this the way you ordered it." The customer has a blank balloon pointing at her. In another example an automobile driver is apologizing to a pedestrian for having splashed the latter's clothing. Or two men are sitting on chairs with one saying, "You were telling me about something that was bothering you. What was the problem?" The second person has a blank balloon over his head.

The subject is asked to fill in the balloons, that is, to project his own need-value system into the incident. For instance, on reactions to the scene in which the automobile driver is apologizing to the pedestrian, responses might range from, "Thanks for apologizing" and "Very thoughtful for you to have stopped," to "People like you should be locked up" and "Why don't you watch where you're going."

In the marketing research literature, this type of picture-completion technique has been used widely, perhaps because of its ease of adaptability to a wide variety of situations from product-preference studies and measurement of brand recognition to talking about self-derogatory attitudes and taboo topics.

The technique also seems to facilitate rapport, since interviewees seem to enjoy working with pictures, and both the client and marketing researcher seem to be enamored of its somewhat exotic characteristics, which are, however, not so exotic that it cannot be easily understood.

Finally, its wide usage is perhaps related to the belief that since it is somewhat exotic it therefore must be yielding information that cannot be obtained by more direct questioning techniques. For example, in one study [21] one of the balloon pictures consisted of a woman in a housedress asking a man in a business suit, "What about serving soup tonight?" Although in combination with responses to other pictures the reactions were quite revealing, one can only wonder if similar results could not have been obtained more simply by asking the housewife, "What does your husband think about serving soup?"

However, if the researcher is trying to uncover semiconscious motives, attitudes towards taboo topics or topics that the respondent will not or cannot discuss, the method may be appropriate [9]. Zober reports a study in which a milk company was having trouble with sales and was convinced that it had a poor reputation. The sales force reported that they could not compete successfully because their milk was considered to be low in butterfat and unclean. The responses to balloon picture tests indicated, however, that among other things the children exerted considerable pressure toward the purchase of brands of milk that were advertised on children's programs. The conclusion of the study was that the company did not have an unfavorable reputation but rather needed to change its marketing mix [43].

Like all projective techniques, a critical aspect of the picture frustration test is one of interpretation. The results by themselves lead, at least, to hypotheses to be confirmed or rejected by other techniques, including direct questioning, open-ended probes and the use of other projective methods such as sentence completion or the Thematic Apperception Test.

Thematic Apperception Test (TAT)

Perhaps the most widely used projective technique both in clinical psychology and marketing research is the TAT. First mentioned in the literature by Morgan and Murrary [28], it has been extensively developed by Henry Murray starting in 1938 [29]. The original test consists of 30 cards on which are printed pictures selected from paintings and drawings. The respondent is asked to make up a story about each picture: what the picture is about, what has happened, what will happen in the future, what each character is like, and what he is thinking or feeling.

The theory behind the technique is that when stories are constructed around ambiguous pictorial stimuli, the individual organizes the material around his personal experiences, his hopes and aspirations, and his conscious and semiconscious need system. It is theorized that the stories will reflect unconscious impulses, conflicts, attitudes, and personality structure, and that these can be interpreted by a highly trained and skilled artisan. The test materials have been standardized in the psychological literature, and some of the best-quality research in projective techniques is based on the TAT technique.

As with the previously mentioned projective methods, the stimuli usually cannot be used directly as presented in the psychological literature. Pictures are changed or modified to fit the particular marketing problem under study. Perhaps the TAT allows the greatest flexibility of the projective tests in marketing research. The pictures can be modified to fit most kinds of marketing problems ranging from image and preference studies to basic underlying consumer attitudes. An example of the various levels of responses elicited can best be seen in the following protocol. The stimulus consisted of a woman equidistant from two storefronts, one labeled *bank* and the other *store*.

> She wants to spend rather than save but she knows she had better save. If it was a dress shop, she would be saying, I'd sure like to buy that dress, but I'd better go to the bank! (What do you think she will do?) Probably go to the bank. I know in my case if I had the money, I'd go to the bank. I always go there first and then to the stores. (Why will she do that?) That's how I overcome temptation.
>
> She doesn't know whether to save it or spend it. (What do you think she is saying to herself?) Do I need the dress or should I save it for a rainy day? If it was me I'd put it in the bank. Hesitating because she doesn't know whether to spend the money or bank it . . . (What will she do?) She's going to spend it. (Why?) Well I would say women are more apt to spend money. A woman has less ability to resist temptation [9].

Undoubtedly these responses are biographical, and yet to a direct question as to whether windfall income should be saved or spent, the response from this subject would probably have indicated and been coded as "save."

Similarly Rogers and Beal [32] attempted to secure information from Iowa farm operators on such topics as weed spray, fertilizer, antibiotic feeds, miracle fabrics, and so forth. The respondents did not object to demographic questions regarding such things as income, age, and so on. However, when questioning turned to the "reference groups" influential in the adoption process, responses to direct questions were vague and evasive, and the respondent often showed embarrassment. Rural people apparently viewed these questions as violating socially accepted limits. TAT type pictures were later presented to the original respondents. The use of pictures increased rapport and elicited the kind of information sought by the researchers, including many negative attitudes they were unable to learn by the usual type of survey.

The flexibility and breadth of the TAT have been recognized by social scientists as having utility in the study of persons in cultures other than our own [24], in studies of institutions [38], and in studies of social roles [19]. All in all, the TAT is an appropriate aid to the study of any system of human interaction, whether it be of a psychological or sociological nature or one of consumer behavior, attitudes toward products and brands, images of institutions, or numerous other facets of marketing as long as it is administered by trained and skilled technicians.

Rorschach Test

Competing with and perhaps exceeding the TAT as the most heavily used and most researched projective instrument in clinical psychology is the Rorschach ink blot test. The instrument consists of ten ink blots developed by Hermann Rorschach and published in 1921 in a major contribution to personality measurement [33]. The subject is asked to look at each card (ink blot) for as long as he wishes and tell what he sees. Beck [12] and Klopfer [22] have developed extensive and complex scoring methods using such criteria as the number of responses made, part of the blot used, use of white spaces, reactions to the fact that some cards use more than one color ink, whether movement is perceived, texture, shading, and so on. Many psychologists believe that the Rorschach is able to reveal much deeper levels of the unconscious than other available projective instruments, and the published research papers number well into the hundreds.

In marketing research this particular instrument, so dear to the hearts of psychologists, has not been used much. Perhaps the major reason is the extensive training required in its proper interpretation and the fact that most researchers and clients do not understand the tool nor the protocols. A response to a blot such as, "This looks like an ape sitting on a big stump. He seems to be quivering and looks frightened," has little meaning or face validity to a marketer attempting to peddle soap flakes, toothpaste, or an electric knife. The sentence completion or balloon picture tests appear to have much more useful or understandable responses. To the trained interpreter, of course, a series of such responses may have a great deal of meaning regarding the individual's basic personality and need-value structure.

Indeed, the avoidance of this instrument by marketing research is not completely illogical. If the Rorschach is really revealing the deeper layers of the unconscious—forces that lead to suicide, rape, psychosis, or assassination—it may be folly to expect that these same forces lead to the selection of Marlboro cigarettes over Salem or Pillsbury cake mix over Gold Medal flour.

This criticism, of course, is just as relevant to the use of all projective methods as originally developed by psychologists. But for the previous instruments, the marketing researcher has been able to modify the stimulus such that it at least has the appearance of face validity. It is unlikely that ink blots can be sufficiently modified to channel the respondent to discuss his attitudes toward Sunkist Oranges, Cannon Towels, or Perfect Circle Piston Rings.

Other Techniques

The psychologist, in his attempt to measure validly the individual's attitudinal and personality characteristics, has developed numerous other creative and original projective techniques. Many have been used for very specific purposes, for example, the Blacky test is used primarily to measure the libidinal impulses from Freudian theory, and the Bender visual motor gestalt test for differential diagnosis of brain damage. Others such as the four picture test, draw a person, make a picture story test, and role playing have wider applications but as yet have not made major inroads in marketing. Still others, such as the Szondi test, have fallen into disuse or have not yet been fully accepted or developed, as is true of graphology and finger painting.[3] Undoubtedly many of these are perfectly adaptable to marketing research, while others must suffer the same fate as the Rorschach. Unfortunately, in recent years, and concurrent with the lessening of the motivation research fad, careful and scientifically controlled studies in the use of these less-known instruments have not been multitudinous.

Two other methods, the semidirective depth interview and the group interview, are often classified with projective techniques in the marketing literature. In the depth interview the interviewer is armed with general questions and the subject is encouraged to talk. Its purpose is primarily to facilitate expression of attitudes and motivations of which the respondent is perfectly aware but which he is, perhaps, unable to divulge in the usual yes-no type of direct questioning. Rapport may also be facilitated, so that feelings may be expressed which ordinarily are inappropriate at a stranger's doorstep.

In the group interview, several respondents are interviewed in a group situation. Its purpose is to create an atmosphere in which information can be gleaned that might not be possible without the social support of other respondents. However, under no conditions can either of these interviewing tech-

---

[3] A description of many of these techniques can be found in [12a] or [2]. Recently, graphology has stimulated several articles in marketing research. See [27] and [30].

niques be considered projective. Unlike the psychiatrist's couch, they do not provide conditions under which semiconscious or unconscious motivations emerge, nor are interviewers ordinarily trained to perceive or note cues to underlying personality structure. Basically this type of interview is merely a discussion among two or more people about a specific topic and not a projective device, despite its usefulness as an information collection technique.

RELIABILITY AND VALIDITY

The value of any instrument—whether it be a doorstep interviewing schedule, the semantic differential or other attitude and opinion measuring devices, or a projective technique—is directly dependent on the validity and reliability of the gathered data, as noted in Section 3, Part A, Chapter 2.

Test *reliability* refers to the information's stability. For example, in temporal reliability the technique must yield data that are stable over time. If a sample of subjects is tested and then retested, say one month later, the responses over time must be similar and highly correlated. Obviously, the individual's basic need-value system, his underlying motivations, are long-enduring. If the test responses are affected by what was eaten for breakfast or the color of the respondent's dress, the instrument is unreliable and the data generally are unusable.

Another form of reliability is that of test stability; namely, is the instrument measuring *consistently* what it purports to measure? Typically this is indicated by a split-half method. The responses to the various items are randomly divided into two parts and the degree of correlation is measured. For example, if on half of the TAT cards specific personality characteristics seem to emerge, they should also emerge on the second half of the cards. If not, the meaningfulness of the generalization is seriously jeopardized.

A final form of reliability crucially important to any projective device is coder or interpreter reliability. Obviously, if data can be interpreted in a significantly different manner by two equally competent interpreters or are scored with significantly different results, the instrument is questionable.

Much research has been conducted on the reliability of standardized projective devices. For example, in a Sanford and Rosenstock study [37] which tested the Rosenzweig picture frustration test as an attitude measuring device, the coder reliability on 30 protocols produced correlation coefficients ranging from .91 to .95, indeed respectable figures. The instrument's test-retest reliability coefficients ranged from .54 to .81. With other instruments the reliability often falls below .50. Usually test-retest reliability results below .80 should be questioned.

Reviewing the general state of the art at this point, dozens of studies in the psychological literature indicate adequate levels of reliability for the carefully developed and standardized projective methods often used by psychologists. On the other hand, one can find an equal number of studies suggesting that these instruments do not reach an acceptable level of reliability.

Turning to projective techniques as modified by marketing researchers, the paucity of available studies that examine the reliability of these modified devices, or for that matter the usual direct questioning techniques, is overwhelming. Obviously either the reliability of instruments used by marketing researchers little concerns them or the client or such studies have been conducted but both researcher and client disregard their social responsibility to the profession by hoarding such data in proprietary files long after competitive advantage has ceased to exist.

Once reliability is established, one can consider *validity*, the degree to which the instrument is measuring what it purports to measure. That is, if the projective devices purport to measure underlying motivations or need-value systems, how well are they actually measuring this basic substructure of the individual? Or, at another level, if a standard direct question asks the respondent's opinion about a specific subject, how accurately is the question measuring the subject's true opinion?

Again, in the psychological literature there are tens of dozens of studies on validity of projective techniques. For example, Sanford finds that the average correlation between needs as expressed on the TAT and overt behavior is .11 [36]. Korner, however, reports that themes or fantasies reflected in TAT stories were the same as those revealed in a series of play interviews and several symptomatic acts [23]. Sanford found that results of the Rosenzweig picture frustration test correlated with paper-and-pencil tests measuring the same variables at a most acceptable level [37].

Using the usual experimental and statistical techniques available to the researcher, the validity of the psychological tests cannot be easily determined. The literature is replete with experimental studies in which psychologists are unable to predict individuals' behavior from projective protocols showing poor correlations with other instruments or are unable to determine the individual's personality structure without corroborating data. On the other hand, there are as many studies that indicate the tools' validity.

Hence one must ask, "validity for what?" The instruments were not developed nor intended to predict behavior experimentally nor to generalize statistically to populations. The core purpose of the projective test is to serve the psychologist or psychiatrist as a diagnostic aid in determining the individual's underlying motivational drives and the powerful forces that brought him to the clinician's office in the first place. Its advantages include saving time and diagnosing the difficulty without many hours of psychological or psychoanalytic interviewing. Used by a highly trained, experienced master psychologist, the projective tests can be immeasurably helpful. Armed with several batteries of tests, some interviews, and a comprehensive case history, the diagnosis and interpretation of the data can be viewed as a masterful display of art, if not exactly a science.

When one turns to marketing research, unlike clinical psychology, one finds very few validation studies, perhaps for the same reason that reliability studies are not published. One finds, rather than standardized instruments, tools created or modified for a particular project; hence even the weak validity and reliability studies in the literature cannot serve as a foundation. One finds problems not related to schizophrenia or incest or a massive inability to cope with the environment, but rather extremely low-intensity forces that determine the purchase of Mobil gasoline rather than Standard, the use of cologne rather than aftershave lotion, or the voting preference toward one of two equally bland, uninspiring, and uninteresting city councilmen. One finds not hundreds of master psychologists or trained practitioners at work in marketing research, but at the most a few dozen.

One further problem plagues the marketing researcher. The clinician is concerned about a single individual, a population of one, but the marketing researcher is of necessity concerned with sampling. From typically a small and perhaps an unrepresentative sample the researcher must often generalize to a population of potential users or buyers. Little wonder the techniques have been heavily criticized!

In all, however, much of the criticism of projective techniques may as well be aimed at the more conventional methods of public opinion and attitude scaling in marketing research. Little experimental evidence on reliability and validity exists for either methodology outside of voting studies. And the simpler projective devices are not only technically feasible in marketing research but have obviously been successful in obtaining information unavailable through more conventional procedures. Further, sufficient evidence exists that uncensored answers can be elicited at the doorstep—answers which may prove to be at least as reliable and valid as answers to direct questions.

The purpose of the projective techniques is the measurement of the underlying need-value system of the individual, his personality, his motivation—data the individual will not or cannot give to an interviewer at the doorstep. To ask when it is appropriate to use projective techniques in marketing research is identical to asking when it is appropriate to measure the underlying personality system of the respondent.

Robert J. Williams presents the following illustrative example [42]. Imagine that you have just observed a cat walk to a bowl of water and take a drink. We might ask, "why did the cat drink water?" A reasonable answer might be, "Because it was thirsty." But how do we know that the cat was thirsty? Because he drank the water? And why did he drink the water? Because he was thirsty?

To avoid this circularity we might add the following information about the animal: prior to his appearance here he had been deprived of water for 24 hours. Now the circularity is broken. "Why did the cat drink?" "Because he was thirsty." "Why was he thirsty?" "Because of 24-hour water deprivation, the antecedent condition."

Obviously in marketing research we are in most cases capable of researching either water consumption; the antecedent conditions such as advertising; or the intervening variables of thirst, motivation, attitudes, beliefs, or personality. Projective techniques are generally inappropriate if one is attempting to measure water consumption, voting behavior, or market share and usually inappropriate if one is attempting to measure the antecedent conditions, primarily because very seldom is the marketing or advertising researcher interested in the conditions such as having been weaned too early, fear of an authoritarian father, or a conditioned aversion to snakes. However he may very well be interested in measuring such antecedent conditions as advertising, "cents off," couponing, or promotion. Again under these latter conditions projective techniques are probably inappropriate. A survey or experimental approach would be more logical and perhaps more accurate with representative samples, sophisticated statistical technology and knowledge of content, and provision for interviewer and coding biases.

If, however, the research inquiry is concerned with beliefs, values, motivation, personality, or other aspects relating to the individual, his unique cognitions, and his behavior, projective techniques can make a significant contribution. With well-trained interviewers and analysts and if representative sampling is not an important criterion, a great deal of information could be made available to the advertising and marketing manager by proper application of these tools. Unfortunately, the problems of sampling and interpretation can seldom be ignored and overcome.

It is evident that the greatest contribution of projective techniques is that they supplement and verify intuition in the generation of hypotheses. Hypotheses as to why the consumer behaves as he does, why he buys or does not buy, why he is influenced or not influenced, can emerge from the protocols— hypotheses that later must be tested and verified by experimental techniques, panel studies, and survey research on representative samples with carefully designed procedures.

THE QUESTION OF ETHICS

In marketing, fewer competent researchers of projective methods exist than researchers claiming the capability of conducting such studies. This is a most important problem facing the decision maker. In the decision-making process, bad information is obviously far inferior to no information. However, the researcher often faces the dilemma in which the client organization is uninterested in the quality or scientific validity of the data and is instead using the research organization as either a mediator or ally in internal arguments between advertiser and advertising agency, between the marketing department and line executives, or between the president and his wife.

A second difficulty is the misuse of tools and presentation and interpretation of the results of research involving projective techniques. There are various pressures on both the seller and purchaser of research to circumvent strict scientific methodology; the purchaser demanding too much at too low a price and the seller promising more than the parameters of his capability will allow. Pressures exist on both parties to confuse hypotheses with conclusions and intuition with facts.

Perhaps the foremost ethical problem in using projective techniques in marketing research is protecting the individual's privacy. The researcher, if not the client, must be primarily concerned with his subjects' interests and their basic right not to reveal unwittingly attitudes, values, or personality characteristics possibly harmful to their social, economic or psychological well-being.[4] The patient on the psychiatrist's couch has knowingly and willfully foregone this right. The respondent to a public opinion interviewer at the doorstep preserves his basic inalienable right to mislead, confuse, or lie to an interviewer if he feels it is in his best interest to do so. With projective techniques, once he agrees to participate, he may have unwittingly forfeited that right. Using projective techniques in marketing research involves deception, and the respondent loses his ability to be dishonest, at least psychologically. The ethical dilemma, hence, is based on the researcher's right to investigate without full disclosure of his purpose, as discussed further in Section I, Chapter 9.

CONCLUSION

Projective methods have existed for approximately half a century and have been marketing researchers' tools for two decades. As an indirect technique for measuring an individual's personality characteristics, underlying motivations, and basic value structure, they have proved to be at least theoretically suitable [41].

The ultimate measure of any technique's usefulness, of course, depends on whether it can deliver what it promises. Unfortunately at this stage of development the strict reliability and validity of the methods are unknown. Scientifically they must be rated as equivocal, and yet administered by a skilled artisan, they cannot be rated short of enticing.

Compared with the traditional techniques of direct questioning and attitude scaling, the projective tools clearly show the potential for superiority in drawing out attitudes, needs, and drives that the respondent is either unwilling to

---

[4] For a recent discussion of the law of privacy, see [26].

disclose or unable to discuss since he himself may be unaware of his underlying motivations. Herein lies the ethical dilemma—the right of any man to investigate the inner being of any other man for his own purposes without explicit approval.

REFERENCES

Selective Bibliography

1. Advertising Research Foundation, Committee on Motivation Research, *A Bibliography of Theory and Research Techniques in the Field of Human Motivation,* New York: Advertising Research Foundation, 1956.
2. Anderson, H. H., and G. L. Anderson, *An Introduction to Projective Techniques,* New York: Prentice-Hall, 1951.
3. Bruner, J. S., "Social Psychology and Perception," in E. E. Maccoby, T. M. Newcomb, and E. L. Hartley, eds., *Readings in Social Psychology,* New York: Holt, 1958.
4. Ferber, R., and H. G. Wales, eds., *Motivation and Market Behavior,* Homewood, Ill.: Irwin, 1958.
5. Hall, C. S., *Primer of Freudian Psychology,* New York: New American Library, 1954.
6. ———, and G. Lindzey, *Theories of Personality,* New York: Wiley, 1957.
7. Krech, D., R. S. Crutchfield, and E. L. Ballachey, *Individual in Society,* New York: McGraw-Hill, 1962.
8. Newman, J. W., *Motivation Research and Marketing Management,* Boston: Harvard University Graduate School of Business Administration, Division of Research, 1957.
9. Smith, G. H., *Motivation Research in Advertising and Marketing,* New York: McGraw-Hill, 1954.
10. Wales, H. G., and R. Ferber, *A Basic Bibliography on Marketing Research,* Chicago: American Marketing Association, 1963.
11. Weschler, I. R., "Problems in the Use of Indirect Methods of Attitude Measurements," *Public Opinion Quarterly,* vol. 15, Spring 1951.

Other References

12. Beck, S. J., *Rorschach's Test,* New York: Grune & Stratton, 1944 and 1949, 2 vols.
12a. Bell, J. E., *Projective Techniques,* New York: Longman's, 1948.
13. Cobliner, W. G., "On the Place of Projective Tests in Opinion and Attitude Surveys," *International Journal of Opinion and Attitude Research,* vol. 5, Winter 1951.
14. Fenichel, O., *The Psychoanalytic Theory of Neurosis,* New York: Norton, 1945.
15. Freud, S., in A. A. Brill, ed., *Basic Writings of Sigmund Freud,* New York: Random House, 1938; as quoted in J. E. Bell, *Projective Techniques,* New York: Longmans, 1948.
16. Haire, M., "Projective Techniques in Marketing Research," *Journal of Marketing,* vol. 14, no. 5, April 1950.
17. Hammond, K. R., "Measuring Attitudes by Error Choice: An Indirect Method," *Journal of Abnormal and Social Psychology,* vol. 43, 1958.
18. Hastorf, A. H., and H. Cantril, "They Saw a Game: A Case Study," *Journal of Abnormal and Social Psychology,* vol. 40, 1954.
19. Henry, W. A., "The Business Executive: The Psychodynamics of a Social Role," *American Journal of Sociology,* vol. 54, January 1949.
20. Kassarjian, H. H., and J. B. Cohen, "Cognitive Dissonance and Consumer Behavior: Reactions to the Surgeon General's Report on Smoking and Health," *California Management Review,* vol. 8, Fall 1965.
21. ———, unpublished study using picture completion method, University of California at Los Angeles, 1963.

22. Klopfer, B., and D. M. Kelley, *The Rorschach Technique*, New York: World, 1942, and later editions.
23. Korner, A. F., "Theoretical Limitations Concerning the Scope and Limitations of Projective Techniques," *Journal of Abnormal and Social Psychology*, vol. 45, October 1950.
24. Lessa, W. A., and M. Spiegelman, *Ulithian Personality as Seen Through Ethnological Materials and Thematic Test Analysis*, Berkeley: University of California Press, 1954.
25. Levine, R., I. Chein, and G. Murphy, "The Relationship of the Intensity of Need to the Amount of Perceptual Distortion, A Preliminary Report," *Journal of Psychology*, vol. 13, 1942.
26. Mayer, C. S., and C. A. White, "The Law of Privacy and Marketing Research," *Journal of Marketing*, vol. 33, April 1969.
27. McNeal, J. U., "Graphology: A New Marketing Research Technique," *Journal of Marketing Research*, vol. 4, November 1967.
28. Morgan, C. D., and H. A. Murray, "A Method for Investigating Phantasies, The Thematic Apperception Test," *Archives of Neurological Psychiatry*, vol. 34, 1935.
29. Murray, H. A., *Explorations in Personality*, New York: Oxford University Press, 1938.
30. Myers, J. H., "More on Graphology and Marketing: An Empirical Validation of Marketing Graphology," *Journal of Marketing Research*, vol. 6, February 1969.
31. Rapaport, D., M. Gill, and R. Schafer, *Diagnostic Psychological Testing: The Theory, Statistical Evaluation and Diagnostic Applications of a Battery of Tests*, vol. II, Chicago: Year Book, 1946.
32. Rogers, E. M., and G. M. Beal, "Projective Techniques in Interviewing Farmers," *Journal of Marketing*, vol. 23, October 1958.
33. Rorschach, H., *Psychodiagnostik: Methodik und Ergebnisse eines Wahrnemungsdiagnostischen Experiments Deutenlassen von Zufallsformen*, Bern: Ernst Bircher, 1921. In English, *Psychodiagnostics, A Diagnosis Test Based on Perception*, translated by P. Lemkau and B. Kronenburg, Bern: Huber, 1942; New York: Grune & Stratton, 1942.
34. Rosenzweig, S., "The Picture Association Method and Its Application in a Study of Reactions to Frustration," *Journal of Personality*, vol. 14, 1945.
35. ——— et al., "Scoring Samples for the Rosenzweig Picture Frustration Study," *Journal of Psychology*, vol. 21, 1946.
36. Sanford, F. H., "The Use of a Projective Device in Attitude Surveying," *Public Opinion Quarterly*, vol. 14, Winter 1950–1951.
37. ———, and I. M. Rosenstock, "Projective Techniques on the Doorstep," *Journal of Abnormal and Social Psychology*, vol. 47, January 1952.
38. Warner, W. L., and W. A. Henry, "The Radio Day Time Serial: A Symbolic Analysis," *Genetic Psychology Monographs*, vol. 37, 1948.
39. Webb, E. J., D. T. Campbell, R. D. Schwartz, and L. Sechrest, *Unobtrusive Measures: Non-Reactive Research in the Social Sciences*, Chicago: Rand McNally, 1966.
40. Weschler, I. R., "The Personal Factor in Labor Mediations," *Personnel Psychology*, vol. 3, Summer 1950.
41. ———, and R. E. Bernberg, "Indirect Methods of Attitude Measurement," *International Journal of Opinion and Attitude Research*, vol. 4, Summer 1950.
42. Williams, R. J., "Is It True What They Say About Motivation Research?" *Journal of Marketing*, vol. 22, October 1957.
43. Zober, M., "Some Projective Techniques Applied to Marketing Research," *Journal of Marketing*, vol. 20, January 1956.

Part A

Techniques

Chapter 6

Measuring Preferences

RALPH L. DAY *Graduate School of Business, Indiana University, Bloomington, Indiana*

Clear and accurate indications of preferences are typically difficult to obtain. The data of preference measurement are necessarily in the form of judgments or opinions about the desirability of various alternatives available to the respondent. The usual difficulties of obtaining information are complicated further by the fact that preference judgments are relative rather than absolute assessments. Deriving the overall pattern of preferences from a set of relative judgments typically requires a large number of comparisons. As a result, the design of preference studies frequently taxes both the conceptual skills of the researcher and the subject's powers of evaluation.

In this chapter emphasis will be placed on the particular problems of measurement and research design which are encountered in preference research. Discussions of the strategy of preference testing are provided in the applications section of this handbook, especially in the chapter on product testing [Section IV, Part A, Chapter 2]. Discussions of the general problems of research design and analysis are also provided elsewhere in the handbook. Emphasis in this chapter will be placed on the measurement of preference for sets of objects which can be treated as unidimensional. Discussions of the methods of multidimensional scaling were covered in Chapters 3 and 4 of this part.

After discussing the meanings of preference which are relevant to marketing research, alternative models of choice behavior will be discussed and the various methods of collecting preference data will be described. Particular emphasis will be placed throughout the chapter on the need for careful design of preference studies in order to obtain accurate and unambiguous information for the use of marketing management.

THE NATURE OF PREFERENCES

The process by which the individual develops preferences and bases his behavior on them is a highly complex and poorly understood aspect of human behavior. While preferences are generally regarded as part of the psychological makeup of the individual, they are also influenced by physiological factors [17] and various social and environmental influences [15]. The complexity of preference suggests that the marketing researcher should be unusually cautious in designing preference studies and evaluating their results. There is a constant danger that preference tests will produce useless or misleading results. Precisely worded reports of measurements on vaguely defined variables or findings stated in terms of an ambiguous criterion are likely unless the preference researcher can precisely define what he is attempting to measure and fully understands the measurement problems he is likely to encounter.

This section will consider some alternative ways of viewing preference and will discuss the need for operational definitions of preference. Later sections will consider measurement problems and their implications for the design and analysis of preference studies.

Although an individual's preference for one item relative to another appears to be a common-sense notion, preferences are subject to a number of different interpretations which can have an important influence on the design and interpretation of research. Three basic views or interpretations of preference will be discussed: simple categorical notions of preference, preferences as attitudes, and preferences as evaluations of the utility to be derived from alternatives.

Categorical Models of Preference

Much of the work in preference measurement appears to have been based on the simplest possible notion of preference. Preference for one object rather than another has been treated as an intrinsic attribute of the individual which is reflected in his behavior in preference tests. An expression of preference for one item rather than another thus provides a basis for classifying subjects neatly into a set of categories related to the objects being tested. Much of the literature of preference measurement and product testing appears to be based on a simple categorization of subjects. Many studies make no reference to underlying models of any sort, but the categorization of subjects makes it clear that such a model is implicit. In some reports of preference research, the use of a categorical model is explicitly stated [9].

The Three-State Model. In the simplest of categorical models, the individual is assumed to be in one of three states relative to the preference object or objects. In the evaluation of a pair of items A and B, the three states are "prefer A to B," "prefer B to A," and "no preference." This model is strictly categorical and there is no recognition of the degree of preference within categories. Categorical models are inherently situation-specific since the category in which an individual is placed depends specifically on the properties of the particular object or objects being evaluated. Categorical models of preference are usually defined deterministically so that a person who likes or prefers an item on one trial must like or prefer that item on every trial.

When testing is limited to independent comparisons of pairs of test items in situations where indications of the direction of preferences are all that is required, the use of this model may cause the researcher no difficulties. In more complex circumstances, the application of this model frequently yields confusing results. For example, suppose that a blind paired-comparison test is repeated with the same subjects and same items. The typical result is that many individuals will change their preference indication from one item to the other.

Suppose, for example, that a researcher conducts a paired-comparison test with 200 subjects and finds that 100 prefer item A and 100 prefer item B. If he stops there and concludes that the two products are equally good, this model of choice behavior would seem satisfactory. Let us suppose, however, that the hypothetical researcher decides to repeat the test to confirm its reliability, and his overall results were again 100 choosing A and 100 choosing B. Suppose further that the researcher found that the 100 choosing A on the second trial was composed of 60 who chose A on the first trial and 40 who chose B on the first trial. Similarly, of those preferring B on the second trial, 60 had preferred B and 40 had preferred A on the first trial. Given the categorical model of preference, the researcher must conclude that 40 percent of his subjects behaved in a totally inconsistent and perverse manner.

While this example is hypothetical, actual occurrences of similar nature are not at all unusual. In a repeat forced-choice paired-comparison test conducted by the author with 253 subjects, it was found that 37.2 percent (94 subjects) reversed their choices in the second test. The literature of product testing is filled with similar examples of preference test results which are not consistent with the three-state categorical model of preference.

A Four-State Model.   Some researchers who have recognized that the three-state model is unsatisfactory have concluded that the problem stems from the inability of subjects to tell the difference between test items. Placed in a test situation which strongly suggests that they should be able to recognize differences and express a preference, the nondiscriminators are believed to make arbitrary choices even in tests which provide them with an escape in the form of a "no preference" answer. The erratic behavior of the nondiscriminators is thus thought to be the source of apparent inconsistencies in preference tests. The four-state model simply adds a category, the nondiscriminators, to the three preference categories.

If one accepts this four-state model, the problem of obtaining consistent and reliable behavior from subjects in preference tests appears to be simple. One must first screen out the nondiscriminators. Then he may proceed to test only those subjects who are perfectly consistent and reliable in preference tests. This seems so obvious that many researchers have devised means of screening out nondiscriminators and then have proceeded to conduct preference tests with no concern for further checks of consistency and reliability.

The tricky problem in designing research based on the four-state model is identifying the nondiscriminators. It appears that nondiscriminators often behave as if they could discriminate and frequently report that they detect differences and have preferences. One researcher has broken down nondiscriminators into those who recognize that they cannot discriminate and "pseudodiscriminators" who report preference judgments [10].

The most common approach to screening out the nondiscriminators is to conduct tests which offer the subject an opportunity to behave in an inconsistent manner. Those who behave inconsistently in a test situation are assumed to be unable to discriminate and are dropped from further testing. Those who remain in the test panel are typically assumed to be reliable discriminators.

Probably the most frequently used test for screening out nondiscriminators is the triangle or triad test. In the triangle test, the subject is given three items of which two are identical. If he correctly identifies the item which is different, he is classified as a discriminator and a useful subject for preference tests.

If he indicates that one of the two identical items is the different one, he is classified as a nondiscriminator and usually is dropped from the test panel.

A variation of the triangle test is to give the subject the three items and ask him to rank them from best to worst. If he ranks one of the two identical items as the best and one as the worst, he is considered to be unable to discriminate and is dropped from the test panel. A different method of screening is to give each subject a blind paired-comparison test and then repeat the test under circumstances which suggest that the second pair is not the same as the first. Subjects who give a different preference judgment in the second test are deemed nondiscriminators.

Given the assumptions of the four-state categorical model, the triangle test and the repeat paired-comparison test should logically eliminate only nondiscriminators because the discriminators can always be expected to discriminate. In addition, some of the nondiscriminators who recognize that they cannot tell the difference can be expected to report this. Thus inconsistent behavior should be expected only from the nondiscriminators who are either unaware that they cannot tell the difference or who intentionally fake a response.

If such pseudodiscriminators simply guess, one can predict their behavior in discrimination tests on an expected value basis. In the triangle test, the expectation is that one-third of the nondiscriminators taking the test will correctly identify the different item by chance. In a repeat paired comparison of items A and B, the expectation is that one-fourth of the guessers will choose A on both trials, one-fourth will choose B on both trials, and one-half will choose one then the other. Thus one-half the guessers can be expected to appear to be consistent. In the "best to worst ranking" version of the triangle test, the expectation is that two-thirds of the guessing nondiscriminators will appear to be discriminators by pure chance.

If those who can tell a difference are always able to discriminate and from one-third to two-thirds of those who cannot tell a difference can appear to be discriminators by chance, one would expect discrimination tests to result in high indications of discrimination ability. To the discomfiture of those who like to think of preference in deterministic, categorical terms, results of discrimination tests do not bear out the expectations of the four-state categorical model. The following results are not atypical:

> In a study conducted among a cross section of 2,267 users of a certain product class, a triad discrimination test was used early in the initial interview. Respondents were given three samples (two the same, one different) and asked to try the three and indicate the different one. The results follow for that "discrimination" test on selection of the different product.
>
> | | |
> |---|---|
> | The different product | 31% |
> | The same product (Sample A) | 27 |
> | The same product (Sample B) | 23 |
> | Don't know; couldn't tell | 19 |
>
> One in five admitted that they could not pick the different product. The balance divided into almost equal thirds on which was the different product with the truly different product receiving only slightly more votes than each of the two identical products. It should be noted that the two products were both well known, nationally advertised products that, according to both taste experts and consumer-image studies, were at *opposite* ends of the taste spectrum. In other words, the differences between the two products was not subtle enough to represent a minor variation but was as great as what exists in the marketplace. Yet, the 2,267 people demonstrated practically no discrimination in the triad test [21].

When the repeat paired-comparison test is used to identify nondiscriminators, results are similar.   In a series of studies using the repeat paired-comparison test, Greenberg and Collins [13] found that the proportion of nondiscriminators ranges around 50 percent (Table 1).   Recall that if all members of a panel are merely guessing, the expectation is that 50 percent of the panel would guess the same item twice.

TABLE 1   Consistency in Double Preference Test of Two Beers (A versus B)

Test II	Test I			
	Preferred A (percent)	Preferred B (percent)	No preference (percent)	Total (percent)
Preferred A.................	24	23	2	49
Preferred B.................	20	21	2	43
No preference...............	2	3	3	8
Total.....................	46	47	7	100

SOURCE: [13, p. 78]

Following up on the repeat paired-comparison test, Greenberg had the discriminators take a triangle test with the same brands, and then he repeated the triangle test.   The results (Table 2) show that those isolated as potential discriminators in the repeat paired-comparison test showed discrimination ability in the triangle test only slightly better than the expected level of apparent discrimination by nondiscriminating guessers.

TABLE 2   Discrimination Test among Potential Discriminators in Double Preference Test*

Result of discrimination test	Potential discriminators in preference tests† (percent)	Discrimination expected by chance (percent)
Correct discrimination in both tests..............	16	11
Correct once, incorrect once....................	45	44
Incorrect discrimination in both tests............	39	45
Total..	100	100
Number......................................	270	

* Note: Chi-square test yields only borderline significance at the .05 confidence level.
† Consistent in two tests.
SOURCE: [13, p. 79]

While the notion of screening out the nondiscriminators with a simple test in order to conduct preference tests with only those who are consistent discriminators is appealing, the evidence is overwhelming that it just does not work.   Experience suggests that if one uses rigorous screening procedures such as several repetitions of the triangle or paired tests or a combination of them, eventually all but a very small part of the sample will be eliminated and any notion that the sample is representative of a total population will be destroyed.

After a single repetition of the "best to least" triangle test, Gruber and Lindberg had eliminated 51 percent of their sample as "insensitive and not reliable" [14]. In Greenberg's study, only 16 percent of the 48 percent of the original panel who were consistent in the repeat paired test made the correct discrimination in the repeat triangle test. In other words, less than 8 percent of Greenberg's original panel could be retained if all those who had made inconsistent or incorrect choices were to be screened out as nondiscriminators [13].

One possible conclusion to be drawn from the failure of efforts to screen out nondiscriminators is that in general people are simply unable to recognize differences in products and thus reveal their preferences in testing situations. While this may very well be a reasonable description of the situation when test items are virtually identical, there is much evidence to indicate that even in test panels which show much inconsistent behavior the proportions of the total panel preferring the various test items tend to remain stable in repeat tests. The stability of preference indications *in the aggregate* suggests that deterministic categorical models are inadequate, not that preference tests are useless.

Probabilistic Discrimination and Preference.   The lack of a flexible conceptual framework for viewing choice behavior in preference tests has been a serious impediment to progress in the development of preference testing methods. Realistic models must allow for consumers to behave probabilistically in preference tests. The human choice process is simply too complex to be usefully modeled in a simple deterministic fashion. While deterministic models may provide useful approximations of consumer behavior in some situations, their use in designing and interpreting preference tests is highly suspect.

Fundamental to the notion of probabilistic responses in preference tests is the concept of probabilistic discrimination. The ability to detect differences among a set of alternatives would appear to be a necessary condition for making preference judgments about the alternatives. It is less clear that one should consider this as a distinct two-stage process in which a discrimination is first made and recognized before a preference judgment is made, as implied by discrimination screening. One might well take the position that too little is known about how individuals process information and make decisions to justify treating discrimination and choice as disjoint processes. Whether or not one views discrimination as a distinct process, consumer behavior in pure discrimination tests as well as in preference tests suggests that discrimination is a probabilistic process for practically all consumers.

The notion of probabilistic discrimination has a long history in the literature of psychophysics. Figure 1 shows a psychometric function fitted to data obtained when subjects were asked to indicate which of two weights was the heavier. It can be seen that the probability that a variable weight will be judged as the heavier is very high when in fact it is much heavier than the fixed weight, that it becomes pure chance when the two weights are equal, and that it declines toward zero as the variable weight is made much lighter than the fixed weight.

The discrimination aspect of the subject's task in a preference test is analogous to the weight-lifting experiment. Suppose that, in a test of consumers' preferences for differing levels of saltiness in margarines, two samples are prepared to be identical except for the amount of salt. A subject would have a high probability of recognizing which is saltier if there is much more salt in one than the other, but he would have a probability of recognizing the saltier item close to .5 if the amounts of salt were almost the same.

Since one would expect the ability to recognize the difference in saltiness to vary over individuals, the probability of making a correct discrimination at any actual difference level would be expected to vary over a population. Some individuals might have probabilities of making a correct discrimination of only slightly more than .5 even when the difference in salt content is rather large, while others might have high probabilities of making the correct choice even when the difference in salt content is small. Few if any individuals would be expected to be completely devoid of the ability to detect differences in the salt content of margarine and thus be nondiscriminators in an absolute sense.

If discrimination is probabilistic, the outcomes of preference tests are necessarily probabilistic. Whether the discrimination is made prior to a preference judgment or as an integral part of it, the dependence of preference judgments

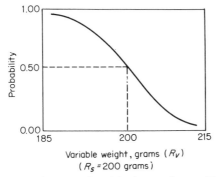

Fig. 1. A psychometric function for lifted weights. (*Based on materials contained in J. P. Guilford, Psychometric Methods, McGraw-Hill, 1936.*)

on the outcome of the probabilistic discrimination process ensures that there is a random element in the preference process. If an individual likes salty margarine, his choice between two samples will depend on the one he "recognizes" as the saltier rather than the one which in fact contains more salt. While the recognition of a difference, whether right or wrong or real or fancied, is necessary for a preference judgment to be made, recognition of a difference does not imply the existence of a preference. A subject might recognize that one of two margarine samples is a bit saltier than he likes while the other is a bit less salty than he likes and thus have no preference as between the two. The notion of ideal point, discussed later in this chapter, provides a useful conceptual framework for understanding choice behavior in preference tests.

Summary. This section has sought to demonstrate that simple deterministic models of preference behavior are inadequate for the design and analysis of preference tests. In particular, it has been suggested that categorizing subjects as those who always discriminate and those who never discriminate is not likely to be fruitful. Efforts to screen out the nondiscriminators do not appear to work and tend to confuse the major issues of preference measurement.

Preferences and Attitudes

Even if the measurement problems mentioned above could be overcome, the simple categorization of consumers still would not be satisfactory for most purposes. Information on the strength or degree of preference is frequently as important as knowledge of the existence of preferences. In searching for a more useful concept of preference, researchers have turned to the methods of attitude measurement. A variety of methods have been developed by behavioral scientists to measure the direction and strength of attitudes and beliefs. Attitudes are generally described in terms of the *direction* and *degree* of liking or disliking, agreement or disagreement, approval or disapproval, or other feelings about the attitude object. The use of attitude measurement in preference research is based on the belief that measurements of consumers' feelings about products or brands can be used to predict their preferences. If a consumer's attitude toward item X is more favorable than his attitude toward item Y, it seems logical to predict that he will express a preference for X.

There are a number of approaches to the definition of attitudes in the behavioral science literature. No attempt will be made here to precisely define attitudes. For marketing research purposes it is usually adequate to define attitudes as tendencies or predispositions to respond in a particular way to some object or set of objects. Attitudes are typically described by a single numerical index which states the strength of the subject's feelings. Some of the best-known methods of attitude scaling have been used in preference measurement. These include Thurstone's method of equal-appearing intervals, Guttman's scalogram method, Likert's summated scale, Osgood's semantic differential, and more recently the work of Bass and Talarzyk based on Fishbein's model of attitudes. However, the first attitude scale to be used widely in preference research still appears to be the most frequently used scaling method in preference research. It is the simple like-dislike or *hedonic* scale. Space does not permit a discussion of all the methods of attitude scaling which have been employed in preference research, so discussion will be limited to three approaches which appear to be of considerable current interest; the hedonic scale, the semantic differential, and the Bass and Talarzyk method.

The Hedonic Scale. The simplest form of attitude scale still appears to be the most popular in preference research. The hedonic scale provides for the direct expression by the subject of his degree of liking or disliking of an object. It is extremely flexible and can be designed to allow as many levels of possible response as desired. Some of the early preference research using the hedonic scale presented the scale in the form of a thermometer with a range of a hundred points. In recent work it is more common to find five-, seven-, nine-, or eleven-point scales with a verbal description of each point. The following nine-point scale is an example:

Like extremely	———	$(+4)$ or	(9)
Like very much	———	$(+3)$	(8)
Like moderately	———	$(+2)$	(7)
Like slightly	———	$(+1)$	(6)
Neither like nor dislike	———	(0)	(5)
Dislike slightly	———	(-1)	(4)
Dislike moderately	———	(-2)	(3)
Dislike very much	———	(-3)	(2)
Dislike extremely	———	(-4)	(1)

Hedonic scales have been used in a variety of arrangements. Some researchers prefer to have lines graphically depicting a continuum in addition to the phrases. Some favor a horizontal arrangement and some a vertical arrangement. There does not appear to be any evidence in the literature of preference research to suggest that either the number of steps chosen or the geometrical arrangement of the scale is critical to the results obtained.

The wide appeal of the hedonic scale seems to be based primarily on two factors: the ease of use for the subjects and the fact that it directly provides numerical results. The expression of feelings of liking or disliking in general is not difficult for subjects, and the provision of numbers and descriptive phrases makes their choice of a specific response relatively easy. For the researcher, the scale provides precoded responses which appear to be very easy to analyze.

Criticisms of the hedonic scale center on the analysis of the subjects' responses. Preference researchers have generally treated hedonic scale data as interval scale data and have computed means, standard deviations, and product moment correlation coefficients. The application of statistical techniques to hedonic scale data requires the assumption that the points on the scale are equally spaced on an underlying psychological continuum which holds across the members of the population being sampled. Such an assumption is regarded as highly suspect by many behavioral scientists, who feel that a set of relative statements on the degree to which an individual likes or dislikes an item can at most be regarded as reflecting a rank ordering.

Even when the verbal statements related to scale positions are selected through psychometric techniques such as Thurstone's method of equal-appearing intervals, the assumption that an interval scale has been found remains suspect. More cautious preference researchers feel constrained to restrict themselves to the identification of modes and medians and the use of such statistics as chi square and rank correlation which assume either nominal or ordinally scaled data.

The Semantic Differential. A form of attitude scale which has found considerable use in preference studies is the semantic differential scale developed by Osgood and his associates [20]. Semantic differential scales are defined by a pair of adjectives. The original work by Osgood was related to pairs of words thought to represent the opposite extremes of some quality possessed by an object. The subject chooses some point between the polar extremes which reflects his feelings about the object. Implicit in the construction of such scales is the assumption that midway between the pole words is a point of neutrality, and that it is possible to establish steps of equal width to divide up the continuum. Once established, semantic differential scales are treated as if they yield interval data, although there are no procedures required to establish either that a semantic differential reflects a scalable quality or that the steps on the instrument do in fact reflect equal steps on a psychological continuum.

Many marketing researchers who have utilized the semantic differential have relaxed the requirement that the word pair establishing a scale consist of polar opposites. One form of modification is to identify the scale with some quality of the object. Rather than simply applying a *good–bad* scale to a preference object, scales are used such as *good flavor–bad flavor, good aroma–bad aroma,* or *good appearance–bad appearance.* Such scales in a sense still represent polar extremes but are semantically more complicated than the original pair of simple pole words and thus might not appear to be as comparable across subjects. Further violence to the initial concept of simple pole words has been done by making use of pairs of descriptive phrases which could hardly be construed to be polar extremes such as *distinctive flavor–ordinary flavor, watery looking–not watery looking,* or *really refreshing–not really refreshing.*

The semantic differential scale has traditionally been used in instruments made up of a large number of individual scales which are related to a single object. The results have typically been analyzed by factor analysis to identify apparent dimensions of the subjects' "image" of the object. In other cases sets of profiles of choices over the various steps on the different scales have been utilized for comparative analysis of different brands or test versions of products. In general, the semantic differential has been used more as a tool for describing brand images and attitudes toward specific attributes than as a method of predicting overall preferences for particular brands or proposed products [8].

Attitude Formula.   An interesting application of attitude scales to predicting preference choices has been reported by Bass and Talarzyk. The subjects rate given brands on several attributes on a scale ranging from *very satisfactory* to *very unsatisfactory*. In the Bass and Talarzyk study, a five-point scale was used to obtain evaluations on five attributes for each brand. Each respondent then was asked to rank-order the five attributes according to their importance in the purchase decision. The evaluations and the weights are combined according to a formula derived from the theoretical work of Fishbein:

$$A_o = \sum_{i=1}^{n} B_i a_i$$

where A_o = the attitude score for object o
B_i = a weighting of the importance of a belief about the attribute x_i to the evaluation of o
a_i = the evaluation of the attribute x_i on a rating scale
n = the number of attributes considered

This formula provides an attitude score for each of several brands of a product class. The attitude scores are then ordered to provide a prediction of the subject's preference ordering of the brands.

Bass and Talarzyk studied several product classes including toothpaste, orange juice, toilet paper, and brassieres. They compared the orderings of the attitude scores with the subject's preference orderings. They found that "If a brand is predicted to be the first choice of a consumer on the basis of attitude scores, the brand will actually be ranked first or second with probabilities which vary from .75 to .90 depending on the product category and the tie rule." Two rules were used for breaking ties in attitude scores: random assignment or assignment according to relative market shares. The latter rule yielded better predictions. Bass and Talarzyk concluded that attitude scores derived from a formula such as the one they used are useful predictors of preference orderings [2].

While the Bass and Talarzyk study does seem to support the usefulness of attitude scores in predicting preferences, it can hardly be regarded as a definitive study. Data on both preference orderings and for the attitude formula were obtained by mail questionnaires; and the possibility that the reporting of attitudes influenced the reporting of preferences, or vice versa, cannot be ruled out. Nevertheless, the authors do seem justified in feeling that further work on this approach is warranted.

Summary.   Attittude scaling methods provide a means of easily obtaining evaluations by individuals of products or other attitude objects relevant to marketing. However, preference judgments necessarily involve two or more objects which are in some sense alternatives. Thus the formation of preferences implies comparative evaluation leading to the assessment of the relative attractiveness or desirability of the alternatives. In general, the methods of attitude measurement have been designed to measure feelings about single attitude objects and do not appear to be well suited for the direct measurement of preferences with respect to a number of alternatives which must be considered simultaneously. On the other hand, attitude scaling methods have been successfully used to increase understanding of the attributes which contribute to overall preference, and some preliminary efforts in predicting preference by attitude scaling have had promising results.

Preference and Utility

The foregoing sections have discussed the conceptual problems which occur in using simple categorical models of preference and have briefly mentioned some of the difficulties of treating preferences as attitudes. This section will consider preference judgments as reflections of the utility of the alternatives being considered.

The notion of choices based on assessments of the utility of the alternatives being considered reflects the efforts of behavioral scientists to develop more useful concepts of preference. Theories of utility provide both a rationale for the choice process and an approach to measuring preferences. The basic appeals of utility theory to preference researchers are that it leads to the quantification of preference information and provides a conceptual structure for relating sets of preference objects to each other and to individuals. Thus, utility theory offers a more general and more highly structured approach to preference analysis than simple categorical models and a more direct and potentially more precise approach than afforded by the methods of attitude measurement.

Utility Theories. A variety of theories of utility have been developed in economics, psychology, and the management sciences. The literature of utility theory is now so extensive that even a summary of the major approaches is beyond the scope of this chapter. A useful review of utility theory has been presented elsewhere by Fishburn [11]. Only some of the basic notions will be presented here in order to provide a framework for treating preferences as reflections of the utility of alternatives.

The basic ingredients of a utility theory are a set of items which are the objects of preferences and the individual's preference-indifference relations with these items. A particular utility theory is a set of internally consistent postulates and assumptions about the individual's preference-indifference relationships on a set of alternatives and the predictions of behavior which can be deduced from them. A fundamental assumption of any utility theory is *connectivity*; all items in the set are connected (related) to each other by the preference-indifference relations. Two additional assumptions, *consistency* and *transitivity*, are usually made. Consistency at some point in time means that an individual who prefers A to B cannot prefer B to A or be indifferent as between A and B. Transitivity means that if A is preferred to B (has more utility than B) and B is preferred to C (has more utility than C), then A must be preferred to C (have more utility than C). In the theory of consumer economics, the consistency and transitivity assumptions are said to establish the *rationality* of the consumer.

The assumptions of connectivity, consistency, and transitivity are sufficient to establish a rank ordering of a set of items from the least preferred (one that provides the least utility) to the most preferred (one that provides the most utility). In other words, these three basic assumptions are adequate to generate an ordinal scale of utility for an individual with reference to a set of objects. Major issues in the development of utility theory have been whether it is possible to derive utility scales with interval or ratio scale properties and whether it is possible to make interpersonal utility comparisons. While the theoretical issues are very complex and perhaps unresolvable, there has been a recent tendency among marketing researchers and management scientists to accept assumptions which allow the assignment of metric properties to utility scales and the assignment of individuals to locations on common metric scales or to points in multidimensional metric spaces.

Ideal Point. Whatever its measurement properties, a utility scale assigns numbers to a set of preference objects. While one of the objects in a set is usually assigned a higher level utility than any other, none of the items in a set necessarily represents the one item of all possible items which offers the highest possible level of utility for the individual. For example, suppose a utility scale is developed for champagnes from the preference judgments of an individual. All champagnes available for him to test can be positioned on the scale but no individual could test every type and vintage of champagne in existence. The place on the scale which would belong to the champagne he would judge the best of all possible champagnes is called the *ideal point.* The concept of ideal point provides the basis for locating the individual as well as the objects of preference on a utility scale.

The concept of ideal point has been closely associated with the work of Clyde Coombs and his "unfolding theory" [4]. Coombs' unidimensional scaling model consists of a joint scale (J scale) on which both the stimulus objects and the subject's ideal point are located. The preference ordering of the objects by the subject is viewed as the process of *folding* the J scale at the ideal point to form the individual's scale (I scale). The estimation approach is to collect the preference orderings of a sample of individuals and to *unfold* these to recover the underlying J scale.

The unfolding model and the associated measurement methods for both the unidimensional case and multidimensional unfolding are described by Coombs [4] and will be discussed here. Recent efforts concentrating on the "recovery" of multidimensional product spaces and the location of individuals' ideal points in these spaces are discussed in other chapters. Efforts to estimate the distribution of ideal points in previously defined spaces by fitting stochastic models to preference data have been reported by Kuehn and Day [16] and Day [6, 5] and will be discussed here.

The concept of the individual's ideal point on a scale is very useful in interpreting preference as a reflection of the individual's utility function. The ideal point can be viewed as the highest point on the utility function, so that any movement away from the ideal point will mean a reduction in utility. If the consumer of champagne is primarily influenced by the dryness of a fine champagne, his utility function over a dryness scale might be as shown in Figure 2. While neither brand A nor brand B is very close to the individual's ideal point, brand A offers more utility and is the one that the individual could be expected to rank first. If other aspects of champagnes are important to the individual and are recognized in his utility function, then a multidimensional utility function (surface) would be required to describe his utility. If, for example, the "fruitiness" of the champagne is an important determinant of the utility of a champagne, the individual's utility could be described as a surface in a three-dimensional space, and the ideal point would represent the optimal combination of the dryness and degree of fruitiness of a champagne.

Stochastic Preference and Utility. If preference is viewed as a deterministic process, an individual's behavior in preference tests is assumed to be precisely determined by the location of his ideal point with respect to the levels of product attributes. For example, the individual whose utility curve is depicted in Figure 2 would always recognize that brand A is closer to his ideal point than B, and that B is closer than C, and thus he would always rank-order the items A, B, and C and would always choose A over B, A over C, and B over C in paired comparison tests. As discussed earlier, actual choice behavior frequently fails to show the consistency that would support such a deterministic interpretation of behavior.

Three approaches within the utility theory framework may be taken to modeling choice behavior as a probabilistic process. First, one can assume deterministic perception of the attributes of the objects (perfect discrimination) and view the ideal point as subject to random variation. Second, one could assume probabilistic discrimination and deterministic utility assessment given the individual's perception of the objects. In other words, one could assume discriminal error in evaluating the alternatives while assuming complete stability of the ideal point. Third, one could assume that both dis-

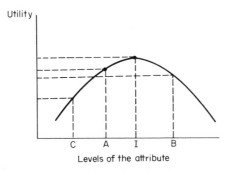

Fig. 2.   Hypothetical utility function.

crimination and the ideal point of the utility function are subject to random variation.

While each of these approaches can provide a theoretical explanation for observed inconsistencies in preference tests, the first is of questionable value. Its assumption of perfect discrimination is immediately placed in question by massive evidence of the probabilistic nature of discrimination. The second approach avoids this objection and is theoretically appealing, especially that the utility function and ideal point are stable aspects of the individual's makeup and not subject to random variation. This model of choice behavior would appear to be a useful conceptual framework for the design and analysis of preference tests. However, the third approach, which relaxes the assumption that the individual has perfect ability to judge utility, might be considered as the most realistic.

The notion of variation in both the perception of stimuli and in the location of the ideal point is demonstrated in Figure 3. The case of probabilistic discrimination and deterministic utility (stable ideal point) is shown in Figure 3*a* and the case of both probabilistic discrimination and probabilistic utility is shown in Figure 3*b*. The distributions of the values for the objects R, S, and T perceived by the individual are shown in both 3*a* and 3*b*. In 3*b* a distribution curve depicting variation in the ideal point is also shown.

Note in Figure 3*a* that the overlap of the dispersion around objects S and T makes it possible for the subject to perceive the value of S to be at the extreme right side of its distribution, shown by s, and the value of T to be at the left side of its "true" value, shown by t, with the result that, on this particular testing occasion, the subject will have perceived S to be to the right of T rather than the actual situation. This would result in a preference indication for T over S, which would appear inconsistent when compared with the more frequent case in which S is recognized as the item providing greater utility.

If the ideal point varies as shown by the distribution around the ideal point in Figure 3b, it would be possible in the case shown for the "correct" preference judgment to be reported in spite of the reversed perception of the two objects. If the ideal point were evaluated by the subject as being at i in the diagram, given the perceptions of s and t, S would be reported as preferred over T. Note that even with the fairly diffuse distributions around the objects shown in Figure 3, one could expect the great majority of preference judgments to reflect the correct relationships between the objects and the individual's ideal

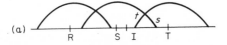

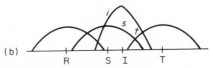

Fig. 3. The notion of variation in both the perception of stimuli and in the location of the ideal point. (*a*) Variable stimuli and fixed ideal point; (*b*) variable stimuli and variable ideal point.

point. Thus in a stochastic (expected value) sense, one obtains consistent and reliable results in preference tests, although the individual would occasionally make such apparently inconsistent choices as choosing T over S after having chosen S over T in previous trials.

The degree of consistency of observed behavior will depend largely on (1) the degree of difference among the objects with respect to the important attribute, (2) the degree of discriminal dispersion around the attribute levels of the objects, and (3) the stability of the individual's utility function. In the extreme case where the objects are very close together on the attribute scale (very similar), discriminal dispersion is large, and the ideal point is relatively unstable, one can expect the results of preference tests to contain much "noise." Conversely, when the differences among objects are large, discriminal dispersion is low, and the ideal point is very stable, one can expect a high degree of consistency in preference test behavior. Experience in preference testing suggests that one or more of the sources of noise is almost always present to a considerable degree when test circumstances are at all realistic.

The recognition of random variation in the results of preference tests requires restatement of the assumptions of utility theory in stochastic terms. In a deterministic sense, consistency means always repeating the same choice given the same alternatives. In a probabilistic sense, consistency would seem to mean the existence of a choice pattern which could not be attributed to pure guesswork. For example, stochastic consistency in a series of choices in a paired-comparison test would mean a significantly larger number of choices for one of the items than could be attributed to chance variation if no differences were being perceived. Stochastic transitivity can be defined in a somewhat more precise manner. Letting (AB) mean that A is preferred to B, Coombs has defined three levels of stochastic transitivity as follows:

Weak stochastic transitivity: If $P(AB) \geq .5$ and $P(BC) \geq .5$, then $P(AC) \geq .5$

Moderate stochastic transitivity: If $P(AB) \geq .5$ and $P(BC) \geq .5$, then $P(AC)$ is at least as large as the *smaller* of the first two probabilities.

Strong stochastic probability: If $P(AB) \geq .5$, and $P(BC) \geq .5$, then $P(AC)$ is at least as large as the larger of the first two probabilities.

Coombs has suggested that the condition to be expected when conducting preference research is moderate stochastic transitivity [4, p. 106].

Summary. This section has sought to demonstrate that utility theory provides a useful conceptual structure for preference measurement. The notion of the ideal point on the individual's preference function and the concept of a joint scale of individuals and products (or a joint space in multidimensional cases) was described as a more useful conceptual framework for describing behavior in preference tests than those offered by simple categorical models or the concepts of attitude measurement. For more realistic interpretations of actual choice behavior in preference tests, stochastic models were suggested.

COLLECTION OF PREFERENCE DATA

Data which are useful in the measurement of preferences may be collected in many different ways, casual or formal. Merchants derive information about their customers' preferences for styles, colors, or other features of their merchandise by simply noting the items which sell and those which do not. Brand share analysis and brand rating services also provide information which is to some extent a reflection of preferences. Concern here will be restricted to the problem of collecting data as a part of formal marketing research activities.

A number of factors are important in the choice of the appropriate data-collection methods to meet any specific need for preference information. A major factor is the nature of the preference objects themselves. Different methods may be required depending on whether the objects are real or abstract, existing items or prototypes, established brands or new products, and similar considerations. Methods will also differ according to the model of choice behavior employed by the researcher and the methods of analysis to be used. Consideration will be given to the form of the objects, the alternative methods of presenting the objects to subjects, problems of selecting subjects, and choices with regard to the testing environment.

The Preference Objects

Since preference is a relative concept, any preference study requires at least two objects for comparison. While the nature of the objects is sometimes prescribed by the circumstances, specification of the nature of the test objects is often a part of the study design. This section considers the issue of "real" versus abstract objects, "blind" versus identified objects, and the degrees of difference to be incorporated in the objects.

Real or Abstract Objects. Preference judgments can be obtained with respect to verbalized concepts, pictorial representations, mockups or physical models, or samples of the items as they exist in the real world. The degree of corre- spondence of the objects used in preference tests with real-world items can vary widely depending on the situation. In the early stages of the development of new ideas for products or marketing tools, useful information can be ob- tained by testing the concept in abstract form.

For example, in the days when all appliances were "white goods," the con- cept of colored kitchen appliances could have been tested at several stages. At one extreme is the testing of simple verbalized concepts such as "yellow stove" and "Robin's egg blue stove" against the concept of "white stove." The other extreme is the testing of complete production models of colored appliances. In between in abstractness is testing artists' renditions of colored appliances or testing with small models. Which level to use, or what succession of steps to take through the stages of concreteness, is a matter for judgment of the predic- tive power of tests of various alternatives relative to costs.

When preferences for objects depend largely on psychological dimensions rather than physiological factors, abstract representations may serve as useful test objects. However, when subtle physical aspects such as the touch or taste of an object are important, physical versions of the real thing are usually called for.

Blind or Identified. The items in a test situation can be presented to sub- jects with identification such as descriptive labels or brand names, or such iden- tification can be concealed. When some means of identification must be visible to the subject, code names, numbers, or psychologically neutral symbols may be used. If the primary concern is to measure the intrinsic features or aspects of the objects, the objects are best tested "blind." Otherwise, prefer- ence judgments will tend to be a mixture of the subject's reaction to the name and to the object itself. In fact, experience suggests that extreme care is necessary in the selection of identifying marks in order to avoid extraneous influences from the symbols.

If it is desired to test preferences for the "total impact" of the test item and its brand name or other identification, identified tests may be useful. How- ever, such tests pose the question of how much influence on preferences is due to the object and how much to the name. Identified and blind tests of branded items can be run with separate samples as a means of isolating the influence of brand image from the influence of the physical products them- selves. Thus it would be possible to develop simultaneous measures of blind preference share, brand preference share, and sales share.

Degree of Difference. When the test items are very similar, the problem of discrimination in preference tests becomes very severe. Preferences are of necessity very weak and may be obscured by "noise." When the objective is to obtain preference judgments of a set of existing objects, there may actually be relatively little difference among the items and one must be prepared to accept such an outcome. However, in test situations where one has some con- trol over the design of the objects, care should be taken to ensure that detect- able differences are incorporated.

If primary concern is with preferences for the alternative levels of a single attribute, one should take care not to introduce offsetting or confounding dif- ferences in other variables. Items with minor differences on several attributes may generate such weak indications of preference that the results are incon- clusive. While "single stimulus" studies with highly artificial objects may overcome this problem, they typically are of little practical value. Careful design of preference experiments is needed to make sure that the alternatives provide a choice situation in which the objects are really different on one or more dimensions but not in such an exaggerated or artificial way as to destroy the usefulness of the results.

The Testing Situation

Items may be presented to respondents in preference tests in a variety of ways: singly, in pairs, in small groups, or all together. Which method to use depends on several factors, such as the degree of difference in the items, the difficulty of evaluation, the desired degree of realism in the testing situation, and the form of the input data required in the analysis of the results. Much discussion has taken place in the literature of preference testing with respect to the relative merits of the major alternatives—the *monadic* test, the method of *paired comparisons*, and the *rank ordering* of the entire set of alternatives.

Monadic Tests. The practice of giving a respondent a single item to evaluate in isolation from the other alternatives is called monadic testing. In its simplest form, a particular subject tests only the one item and evaluates it on some form of rating scale. Each object of a set is tested by a separate sample of respondents and inferences about preferences are made only in an aggregative way. Advocates of the monadic test maintain that it is more realistic than direct comparison tests, which create a test situation unlike the situation in which the product is normally used. A widely used form of the monadic test is the "placement" of samples of new products in the homes of consumers. The item is used in the home in the normal way, after which the appropriate member of the household fills out a rating form. Inferences are made by comparing the patterns of responses across the samples of consumers using the various versions of the product.

A variation of the monadic test is called the comparative monadic. The individual tests a single item as before, but after an appropriate lapse of time he tests a different item from the set of alternatives. The presumption of the comparative monadic test is that the individual compares each item to his ideal conceptualization of the product rather than to the other items he has tested at a different point in time.

The major claim of superiority for the monadic test is based on the reduction of the artificiality of the test situation. For example, it is reasoned that the housewife does not form her preferences for competing food products by cooking samples of each and making direct comparisons. Thus she cannot be expected to react to multiple items in a test situation in a "normal" way. Critics of monadic testing point out that "testing effects" cannot be completely eliminated even when a single item is tested and argue that any gain in realism in use is typically offset by loss of control over extraneous variables. Perhaps a more salient criticism is the expensive nature of monadic testing relative to direct-comparison methods. If the true monadic test is used, a separate representative sample of the population is required for each item in the set. In the comparative monadic test a single sample may be used, but a replication of the test must be carried out for each item.

Several studies have found that monadic testing tends to be less sensitive than comparative methods [13, 3]. On theoretical grounds, one can question if monadic testing is truly preference testing, since it provides only a measure of the respondent's attitude toward an item rather than a direct judgment of preference with reference to other items in the set.

Direct Comparisons. Direct judgment methods involve the presentation of two or more items to the respondent at the same time and require an overt choice. The most widely used form of the direct-comparison test is the paired comparison. The paired-comparison test may require a "forced choice" of one of the items or may allow a neutral or "no preference" choice. Paired comparisons can be used for isolated tests of single pairs of items but are more frequently used for pairwise testing of a set of preference objects. Some analytical methods for preference evaluation such as the Thurstone comparative-judgment method require the "round robin" testing of all possible unique pairs of a set of test objects, as described in Chapter 2 of this part.

Advocates of the paired-comparison method claim that it offers better control over the test situation by placing the comparison of two items together in time and under identical circumstances. Since the respondent deals with only two items at a time, the need for remembering and sorting out impressions of objects is minimized, as are fatigue and opportunities for confusion. A problem sometimes encountered in using paired comparisons is that the order of testing influences the outcome. Order bias has been noted to be in favor of the first item in some studies, in favor of the second item in other studies, and not present in still other studies. The author's experience has suggested that order bias is a function of the degree of difference in the items [7]. In any event, the effects of order bias can be controlled by randomization of the testing order.

Another frequently used method of direct-comparison preference testing is the method of rank order. The respondent is given a set of objects and is instructed to place them in order with respect to his degree of preference. This method has the advantage of being a relatively simple way to obtain preference judgments for an entire set of objects. Subjects use or examine each of the objects to make a preference evaluation and then arrange them in ascending or descending order of preference. Although a seemingly simple procedure, rank ordering of a set of objects creates a very complex choice situation, especially when the number of objects is large. The respondent has to collect and store information about each of the objects and make a large number of comparisons in order to place them in rank order. This tends to lead to fatigue and confusion. Banks [1] has reported that respondents become confused when asked to rank-order more than four items.

A modification of the rank ordering method for use when the number of items, n, is large is called the *rank k of n* method. Rather than rank all of a large number of items, each respondent is given a smaller number, typically three or four items, to rank-order. Some additional discussion of the kinds of preference tests will be given in the section on analysis of test results.

Respondents and Environment

Before considering some of the problems of selecting respondents and designing test circumstances, preference testing should be distinguished from the two related concepts of discrimination of differences and evaluation of quality by experts. The difference between discrimination and preference was previously discussed. It was pointed out that while the discrimination of differences is implicit in preference judgments, the conscious recognition of differences on specific attributes is not only unnecessary for preference evaluation but is likely to introduce extraneous influences. While quality evaluation by expert judges or tasters can provide valuable information for marketing management, quality evaluations are not preference judgments and frequently are not good predictors of consumer preferences. For example, the quality judgments of expert wine tasters might reflect the preferences of gourmet wine lovers but not of the general wine buying public.

Sampling. The problems of drawing samples for preference testing are basically the same as those encountered in survey research in general. The major difference results from the need to present the objects to the respondents for their consideration. When the items are abstract verbal concepts, it is usually possible to incorporate them in the questionnaire. More frequently the presentation of test items and the recording of evaluations are separate steps. When the items can be incorporated in the questionnaire, or presented graphically, or are simple and small, it is frequently possible to conduct preference research by mail. On the other hand, respondents are sometimes brought to a testing room or laboratory where special facilities are available for handling complex or perishable items. However, the bulk of preference testing lends itself to the personal interview form of survey research.

Organizations which do a lot of preference testing frequently find it convenient to recruit and maintain continuous panels rather than draw a new sample for each occasion. This is especially appealing when the research is done in the laboratory. However, the panel approach seems rather hazardous for preference research. In addition to the usual problems arising from self-selection and attrition, the problems of testing effects and learning would appear to be acute. The panel members may quickly become "expert testers" and no longer be representative of the general population.

Environmental Conditions. Whether or not a continuous panel is used, the choice between testing in the home, in other natural settings, or in a laboratory must be made. The major advantages claimed for testing in the home are realism in the circumstances surrounding the use of the items and the relative ease of obtaining a representative sample. For many classes of objects and forms of testing, however, greater realism in the home may be questionable. If testing procedures such as paired comparisons or rank ordering are used, the degree of artificiality would appear to be about the same whether carried out in the home or in a laboratory. For monadic testing of a single item which normally involves preparation and use in the home, testing in the home may be advantageous. However, unsupervised use of test items in the home virtually eliminates any control of the situation, and extraneous factors may bias the results. Lack of control over the testing situation is particularly acute with a mail study.

The maximum degree of control can be obtained when testing is carried out in special facilities designed for the purpose. Each respondent evaluates the items under comparable conditions free of distractions and extraneous influences. The uniformity of test items themselves often can be better controlled in a laboratory. When the test items are food products, for example, the uniformity of temperature, time since preparation, and other factors which might influence choices can be controlled. On the other hand, the laboratory environment creates an artificial situation and the results of laboratory tests may not have external validity. Although this question has not been extensively researched, one study found that there was general agreement between results obtained in a laboratory setting and those obtained in the respondents' homes [19]. Another disadvantage of laboratory testing is the difficulty involved in inducing a representative sample of consumers to come to the laboratory. This typically involves considerable extra expense and may introduce sampling errors as the result of self-selection.

Summary. The manner of selecting respondents and the testing environment for preference research depends on a number of factors, including the nature of the items, the form of the test chosen by the researcher, and the importance of control over the testing circumstances. Other issues such as the importance of the results and the differences in cost of the various approaches also influence the choice of a sampling plan and the place of testing.

ANALYSIS AND INTERPRETATION

The need for an organizing conceptual structure in the design and analysis of preference studies has been stressed throughout this chapter. It has been suggested that although simple categorical models and some of the methods of attitude measurement can be useful in particular circumstances, a more general and precise approach to preference measurement can be built on utility theory. It has been further suggested that preference testing under realistic conditions usually requires a probabilistic interpretation of choice behavior. After first considering the traditional methods of statistical analysis of preference test results, this section will discuss the application of complex models and will consider two methods, Coombs's unfolding theory and preference distribution analysis, in some detail.

Statistical Tests.   Preference tests usually are performed with probability samples, and it is generally appropriate to apply statistical tests to the results in a formal test of the null hypothesis that observed indications of preference are the result of sampling variations. In situations where there are a few unique alternative items, the decision problem is unique and nonrecurring, and the objective is to determine which if any of the objects is preferred to the others, simple test designs are usually adequate and standard statistical tests are appropriate. However, even in situations of this nature, it is necessary to look beyond the outcome of the significance test and interpret the results in a broader framework. In many situations the objectives of preference tests are more complex than the identification of a most preferred item, and in such cases more complex forms of analysis are required.

A test reported by Allan Greenberg provides an example of a simple preference study and illustrates the limitations of significance tests [12]. Two competitive brands of matzo crackers were tested for overall preference using three different test procedures: a monadic test using a five-point like-dislike scale, a comparative monadic test using the same scale on both occasions, and a paired-comparison test with "no preference" answers permitted. Greenberg applied a chi-square test to the results and found no significant difference in overall preference. However, as is usually the case, the meaning of this result was not obvious. Were the two items perceived as identical so that the reported results were merely "noise" resulting from pure guesswork? Were the two items equally good (or equally bad)? Or were the items perceived as different by most of the subjects who were about equally split in their judgments of which was best?

To interpret this result, Greenberg looked to other sources of information in the circumstances and data of the study. He rejected the notion that the items were perceived as identical, because there were clearly discernible differences in the appearance and taste of the items, primarily as a result of the fact that one cracker contained seeds and the other did not. Also, he found that when he partitioned his panel into Jewish and non-Jewish consumers, there was a significant difference in reported preferences.

Other aspects of the situation also tend to support the explanation that there were differences but preference was about equal. Other studies have suggested that when differences are very minor or nonexistent, there tends to be a high level of "no preference" answers in paired-comparison tests, a high percentage of reversals in repeat tests, and a high degree of order bias [7]. In the Greenberg study the reversal rate in the repeat test was 31 percent, the rate of "no preference" choices was 5 percent, and order bias was significant at the .02 level. Together, these results tend to suggest that the two matzo crackers were perceived as different by most respondents but not dramatically so, and that they were preferred by roughly equal segments of the sample.

Statistical tests of the difference in preference across a large number of items are used in much the same way as in the two-item test. The choice of a technique is somewhat more complex, depending on the way in which samples are submitted and data are collected and on the scale properties the researcher attributes to the data. A survey of techniques for the statistical analysis of preference tests has been reported by Marquardt [18]. Whatever their form, statistical tests are used to test the null hypothesis of no difference in preferences. Whether or not the test leads to the rejection of the null hypothesis, the researcher must look to his test circumstances and data to interpret the results. The following sections will consider two approaches to the analysis of preferences which attempt to test for the existence of an underlying preference structure rather than testing the hypothesis of no difference in preferences.

Coombs' Unfolding Theory

Undoubtedly the most elegant and logically precise system yet developed for dealing with preferential choice data is a part of Coombs' "theory of data" [4]. Coombs provides an organizing framework for designing and interpreting preference tests by postulating a joint scale or space containing both items and individuals as points. From this conceptual framework he has developed an algorithm for "unfolding" preferential choice data to reconstruct the scale or space which generated it. The model underlying the unfolding technique will be briefly described and its use in the design and analysis of preference tests will be discussed.

Coombs' theory has been developed from the point of view of psychological scaling. This is reflected in his following statement:

> The problems the psychologist may be interested in include those of discovering whether a common latent attribute may be underlying the preferences of individuals among the alternatives, measuring such an attribute, determining the degree to which such an attribute exists, or determining for what subpopulations such an attribute exists [4, p. 81].

Thus the existence of a latent attribute is essentially a hypothesis which the unfolding technique tests. In other words, if a population has a basically similar conception of a set of objects and can array them on a scale which is the same for all members of the population and if individuals can relate themselves to unique positions on the "latent attributes" and express preferences which accurately reflect their positions, the unfolding technique can "recover" the scale and position both the individuals and the objects on it. The individual's position on the scale is customarily interpreted as the ideal point on his utility function, so that his preference ordering of the objects reflects his utility appraisals of the objects.

The basic assumptions of Coombs' theory of preferential choice can be stated as follows: (1) Each item in a set of objects to be evaluated can be represented as a point on a scale; (2) an individual can also be represented as a point on the same scale, called the J scale; (3) the individual will place the items in preference order according to their absolute distances from his ideal point, the nearest item being the most preferred; and (4) the individual's preference ordering, called his I scale, reflects the J scale folded at his ideal point.

The data collected in a preference study are in the form of complete preference orderings of the objects, the I scales. Thus the analytical problem is how to unfold the I scales to obtain the common J scale which generated them and in so doing to position the individuals on the scale. The process of folding the J scale to obtain the I scale is demonstrated in Figure 4. A description of the computational procedure involved in recovering the J scale for a set of objects is beyond the scope of this chapter. However, a property of the I scales which aids in the recovery of the J scale is the necessity that an I scale must have one of the end points of the J scale as one of its end points. Further relationships can be deduced from the assumptions of the model, and any set of data which strictly meets the model's assumptions can be easily unfolded. However, the typical preference test does not produce data likely to meet any strict set of assumptions. Thus it is usually necessary in applying unfolding theory to replicate the study several times over each individual to obtain data which will meet the requirements in a probabilistic sense.

An application of unfolding theory to the analysis of preference test results has been reported by Taylor [22]. Preferences for the level of sugar in coffee were measured. Taylor replicated the test three times, twice obtaining a complete preference ordering of the five test items and once obtaining hedonic scale ratings which were used to impute a preference ordering. From the three preference orderings for each subject, a stochastically dominant preference ordering was obtained and used as the I scale of the individual. Taylor found that 128 of the 140 subjects were able to generate a stochastically dominant I scale which could be used to recover a J scale at the ordinal level. He reported that 122 subjects generated I scales which allowed the recovery of a partially ordered metric scale.

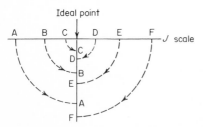

Fig. 4.   Illustration of unfolding. An I scale preference ordering C D B E A F, obtained by folding a J scale.

In summary, unfolding theory offers a sophisticated model of preference behavior which requires stringent assumptions. The model and its computational procedure provide the basis of testing the hypothesis that the model fits the data. When such a fit occurs, the unfolding technique provides results with very appealing properties. It can return a scale with ordered metric properties and reveal the weightings of the population over this scale. As further testing of the method reveals classes of items which meet the assumptions of unfolding theory reasonably well, it may become a valuable approach for the design and analysis of preference tests.

Preference Distribution Model

Another model which provides an organizing structure for designing preference studies and a computational technique for measuring preferences is the preference distribution model developed by Kuehn and Day [16, 6]. As in Coombs' unfolding technique, the model assumes an underlying continuum related to a dominant attribute (or structure of attributes in the multidimensional case) upon which both objects and individuals can be located. Both models are based on utility theory and assume an individual utility function which specifies the ideal point and utility level of the objects of the set (product class) being considered.

The preference distribution model is different from the Coombs model in several important ways. The most fundamental difference is that preference distribution analysis does not extract a scale from the data but begins with a scale which has been hypothesized as the result of knowledge of the nature of the objects or the findings of previous research. The test items are selected or designed to have known levels of the dominant attribute. The set of test items spanning the continuum are preference tested and the results are used to estimate the distribution of individuals' ideal levels over the scale.

An application of the preference distribution model was a study of preferences for different levels of cocoa solids in chocolate ice cream [5, 6]. The range of feasible levels was established in consultation with experts in the manufacture of ice cream after a review of previous preference research on ice cream. The scale was centered on the "commercial normal" level, and five batches containing levels ranging from 60 to 140 percent of the normal level were carefully prepared. All attributes other than the level of cocoa solids were carefully controlled for uniformity across the test items.

All possible unique pairs of the items were tested in blind forced-choice paired-comparison tests and the data were analyzed to obtain the weightings of respondents over the five levels. It was found that the modal level of preference in the sampled population appeared to be somewhat lower than the "normal" level and preferences seemed to be more diffuse than had been anticipated.

The preference distribution model is built around the forced-choice paired-comparison test and reflects the probabilistic nature of choice behavior. It relates the individual's choices in a paired-comparison test to the distances between the two items on the scale and his ideal point. The effect of these distances is a function of a parameter which reflects the degree of difficulty respondents experience in making choices in the test situation. The equation which expresses the expected outcome of a particular paired test, $E(P_{jk})$, as a function of the test levels, difficulty parameter, and the proportions of the sample with ideal levels at each of the various steps on the scale is as follows:

$$E(P_{jk}) = \sum_{i=i}^{n} \frac{d^{|j-i|}}{d^{|j-i|} + d^{|k-i|}} \cdot x_i$$

where d = the difficulty parameter estimated for this particular product class

x_i = the proportion of the population at each step on the scale ($i = 1, 2, \ldots, n$)

j = the point on the scale represented by the lower item of the pair ($j = 1, 2, \ldots, n - 1$)

k = the point on the scale represented by the higher item of the pair ($j = 2, 3, \ldots, n$)

n = the number of points on the scale

For each paired test the values of j and k will be known and the value of the proportion preferring item j to item k will be observed. The system of equations is solved to obtain estimates of the values of the x_i and d. The values of the x_i provide estimates of the proportions in the population which prefer each of the levels of the attribute and the value of d gives information on the level of "noise" in the choice process.

At their present stage of development, neither the unfolding technique nor the preference distribution model are immediately applicable to a wide range of preference testing problems.   However, they do provide interesting examples of methods which provide an organizing framework for preference studies. Further development of these and the related multidimensional scaling models offers considerable promise for increasing the quality and usefulness of preference research.

SUMMARY

This chapter has considered the complex problems of designing, executing, and interpreting preference tests.   It has stressed the probabilistic nature of behavior in preference tests, pointing out the need for models and measurement techniques which can produce useful information in spite of the "noise" which is typically encountered.   Alternative models of choice behavior were described and the application of utility theory, particularly the notion of ideal points, was stressed.   Alternative approaches to data collection were discussed with emphasis on monadic, paired-comparison, and ranking methods.   Various statistical tests and formal models for the analysis and interpretation of test results were discussed.   It was suggested that comprehensive models such as the unfolding technique and the preference distribution model are forerunners of sophisticated new techniques for the design and analysis of preference tests.

REFERENCES

1. Banks, S., *Experimentation in Marketing*, New York: McGraw-Hill, 1965.
2. Bass, F. M., and W. Wayne Talarzyk, "A Study of Attitude Theory and Brand Preference," Chicago: American Marketing Association 1969 Fall Conference Proceedings, 1970.
3. Bengston, R., and H. Brenner, "Product Test Results Using Three Different Methodologies," *Journal of Marketing Research*, vol. 1, November 1964.
4. Coombs, C. H., *A Theory of Data*, New York: Wiley, 1964.
5. Day, R. L., "Systematic Paired Comparisons in Preference Analysis," *Journal of Marketing Research*, vol. 2, November 1965.
6. ———, "Simulation of Consumer Preference," *Journal of Advertising Research*, vol. 5, September 1965.
7. ———, "Position Bias in Paired Product Tests," *Journal of Marketing Research*, vol. 6, February 1969.
8. Eastlack, J. O., Jr., "Consumer Flavor Preference Factors in Food Product Design," *Journal of Marketing Research*, vol. 1, February 1964.
9. Ferris, G. E., "The K-Visit Method of Consumer Testing," *Biometrics*, vol. 14, March 1958.
10. ———, "A New Model in Consumer Testing," *Food Research*, vol. 25, 1960.
11. Fishburn, P. C., "Utility Theory," *Management Science*, vol. 14, January 1968.
12. Greenberg, A., "Paired Comparisons vs. Monadic Tests," *Journal of Advertising Research*, vol. 3, December 1963.
13. ———, and Sy Collins, "Paired Comparison Product Tests: Some Food for Thought," *Journal of Marketing Research*, vol. 3, February 1966.
14. Gruber, A., and Barbara Lindberg, "Sensitivity, Reliability, and Consumer Taste Testing," *Journal of Marketing Research*, vol. 3, August 1966.
15. Krugman, H. E., and E. L. Hartley, "The Learning of Tastes," *Public Opinion Quarterly*, vol. 24, Winter 1960.
16. Kuehn, A. A., and R. L. Day, "Strategy of Product Quality," *Harvard Business Review*, November–December 1962.
17. Arthur D. Little, Inc., *Flavor Research and Food Acceptance*, New York: Reinhold, 1958.

18. Marquardt, R. A., "An Evaluation of the Methods Used in Designing and Analyzing Consumer Preference Studies," unpublished doctoral dissertation, Michigan State University, 1964.
19. Miller, P. G., J. H. Nair, and A. J. Harriman, "A Household and Laboratory Type of Panel for Testing Consumer Preferences," *Food Technology*, vol. 9, 1955.
20. Osgood, C. E., G. J. Suci, and P. H. Tannenbaum, *The Measurement of Meaning*, Urbana, Ill.: University of Illinois Press, 1957.
21. Roper, B. W., "Sensitivity, Reliability, and Consumer Taste Testing: Some 'Rights' and 'Wrongs,'" *Journal of Marketing Research*, vol. 6, February 1969.
22. Taylor, J. R., "Unfolding Theory Applied to Market Segmentation," *Journal of Advertising Research*, vol. 9, December 1969.

Chapter 7

Measuring Purchase Behavior

ROBERT W. PRATT, JR. *General Electric Company, Louisville, Kentucky*

A number of research techniques available for measuring product and/or brand preferences have been discussed in previous chapters. In general, use of resources to establish or enhance preference is justified only to the extent that the preference or predisposition is eventually manifested in purchase behavior; thus purchase behavior is itself the single most important measure of preference.

What types of information about purchase behavior are required by marketing management? In virtually all instances, the most fundamental need is for an up-to-date description of what end-consumers are buying. In a single small retail store, procedures for meeting this requirement are frequently unstructured. Simply dealing with customers and keeping an eye on inventories may be sufficient. As marketing systems increase in scope, however, there tends to be a corresponding increase in the complexity and cost of alternatives available for obtaining timely descriptive information. One purpose of this chapter is to discuss ways in which descriptive data about purchase behavior can be obtained.

But descriptive data, at best, offer only an accurate overview of recent history. They provide a picture of what has already taken place. To formulate marketing strategy that will have the greatest possible impact on future buying behavior, management must be provided with insight into the influences, or combinations of influences, that underlie behavior reflected in descriptive statistics. A fundamental question is, "*Why* do people behave as they do?" To answer this type of question, research must go beyond description to explanation. Hence, a second purpose of this chapter is to discuss explanatory research techniques as they pertain to understanding purchase behavior.

Before reading a discussion of measurement techniques, however, the reader should be familiar with what is being measured. What is meant by *purchase behavior*? What fundamental characteristics of this type of behavior must be taken into account in the formulation of a research design? A useful framework for answering these questions, as well as for considering specific research techniques, is provided by a brief conceptualization of the nature of a purchase transaction. Accordingly, the chapter opens with this topic.

CHARACTERISTICS OF A PURCHASE TRANSACTION

A purchase transaction may be thought of in terms of four primary sets of characteristics:

1. Characteristics of the customer or buying unit
2. Characteristics of the product or service being purchased

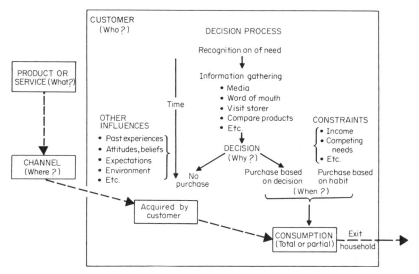

Fig. 1. Purchase transaction. *For more details of decision process, see Fig. 2.*

3. Characteristics of the channel by which goods or services reach end customers

4. Characteristics of the larger environment in which the transaction takes place

These characteristics are represented graphically in Figure 1. Superimposed on the diagram are five generic questions (Who? What? When? Where? and Why?), each of which can be associated with one of the four characteristics. As demonstrated throughout this chapter, virtually every question about purchase behavior can be associated with one or more of these questions.

Further, while the five questions are frequently examined independently, they may also be combined or "linked" to study interrelationships among product, channel, customer, and environment. For example, one may ask "Who buys what, where, when, and why?" Translated to a specific example, "What factors or characteristics best describe purchasers (who) of Timex watches (what) in jewelry stores (where)? What are the seasonal patterns, both aggregate and among these characteristics (when)? What factors motivate or cause buyers to make the combination of decisions—for example, brand, price, store type—that they do (why)?" An ability to *link* information about product, customer and channel is necessary to answer many marketing questions; the research process by which linkages are achieved will be discussed later.

THE NATURE OF PURCHASE BEHAVIOR: WHAT IS BEING MEASURED?

In its simplest form, purchase behavior is simply the act of making a purchase —the exchange of goods or services for cash or a promise to pay. Knowledge about the exchange itself is an important input to marketing decisions. Perhaps more important, however, is knowledge about the process by which a consumer decides to enter into the exchange. As indicated in Figure 1, a purchase transaction may be either (1) the end result of a decision process or (2) the manifestation of a habit. An understanding of the distinction between these two modes of behavior is essential to any discussion of measurement.

Purchase Decisions

Decisions are best thought of as the end result of a complex process.[1] In order to discuss measurement techniques that can be applied to gain understanding of this type of problem-solving behavior, it is useful to expand the "decision process" portion of Figure 1 (center of "Customer" box). This is accomplished in Figure 2. A brief discussion of the diagramed steps follows; each step is keyed to the chart.[2] Figure 2 is a monumental oversimplification of the manner in which decisions are actually reached; each of the four major "steps" shown, however, will serve as background for the consideration of selected research techniques. While product purchases are used for illustrative purposes, this discussion applies equally to purchase of services.

Predispositions. As a rule, prior to entering into a decision process, a person will hold certain beliefs, assumptions, prejudices, attitudes, feelings, and expectations about at least some of the alternatives. These will be held with varying degrees of intensity and clarity; in some cases they will be reinforcing, in other cases they will be contradictory. The net influence of these variables will result in a predisposition to behave in a certain way. Each predisposition represents the net result of what is often a complex matrix of influences and interactions that have their roots in past learning and experience.

Allocation of Available Resources. Before a product is purchased, it must compete successfully against alternative expenditures of available resources. The process by which available income is allocated among alternatives will vary greatly among households, and within a single household will vary in accordance with both (1) the composition of the total set of alternatives under consideration, and (2) the process or system by which that particular household makes decisions.[3] These processes cannot be easily understood using available empirical techniques. In an insightful article which reports results from two pilot studies of husband-wife planning and the subsequent impact of these plans on economic decisions, Morgan states that "studies of the decision

---

[1] For examples of models of this process, see [2, p. 12]; also [15, Chap. 6].

[2] These steps are outlined here to provide a brief introduction to the types of events that, singly or in combination, precede a purchase decision. No attempt is made to provide an exhaustive summary of published material relating to choice processes.

[3] For a general discussion of the process by which households allocate resources, see [1, especially Chap. 6].

process involving real decisions in real families are so difficult that they have not been seriously tried" [13, pp. 113–121].

Information Gathering. Prior to making a purchase, choices must be made among alternative manufacturers, brands, and stores. These choices, and the influences and events precipitating them, constitute what is frequently labeled *shopping* or the *shopping process.* Although the specific manner in which individuals and families approach shopping will vary greatly, the shopping process frequently involves gathering new information, including information

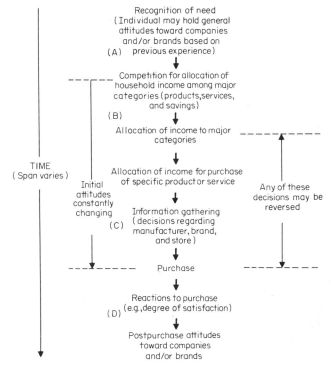

Fig. 2. Paradigm of the decision process. *(Modified from a chart that first appeared in R. W. Pratt, Jr., "Consumer Behavior: Some Psychological Aspects," in George Schwartz, ed.,* Science in Marketing, *New York, Wiley, 1965, p. 131.)*

obtained from media of all kinds, discussions with family and friends, discussions with salesmen, and so on. Although *information gathering* is listed in only one location in Figure 2, information may impinge on the decision process at any point. Indeed, information gathering often precedes recognition of need.

Decision and Postdecision Reactions. Each new information input may lead to a decision or it may lead to the reversal of a previous decision.[4] At that point in time at which a final decision is reached—whether the decision is to purchase or not to purchase—the particular process in question has been

---

[4] In complex models of the decision process, impact of new information is frequently conceptualized in the form of "feedback" loops.

terminated. If a purchase is made, the individual or family purchasing the product will have various reactions which are often expressed in terms of feelings of satisfaction and/or dissatisfaction. These feelings will be weighed, in one way or another, in the formulation or reformulation of the initial set of general attitudes held toward the company manufacturing the product and/or the brand. In turn, this new set of attitudes represents the prepurchase position of the individual or household prior to undertaking a subsequent purchase. It should also be noted that any new learning completed during the decision process, coupled with postpurchase experience, may result in a new set of attitudes toward companies and brands associated with products that were considered but *not* purchased.

Establishing Habits

Virtually all purchase behavior is motivated in the sense that it is instigated by needs internal to an individual and directed toward goals that are expected to satisfy these needs. The basic challenge to marketing is to offer a product or service that will serve as a goal toward which need-oriented behavior can be directed. If a purchase does satisfy the need, an incentive is established for repeating the purchase when the same need recurs; the initial decision has been reinforced. Continuous reinforcement of a particular mode of behavior underlies the formulation of habits.

Habitual Behavior

Habits, then, are response patterns that have become automatic to given stimuli. Virtually all buying behavior is habitual. Habit is particularly prevalent in the acquisition of frequently purchased products, such as food. The general reasons for this are not hard to pinpoint. Once a housewife has considered alternatives and arrived at a decision that, for example, a particular brand of soap will best satisfy her family's requirements, it is not necessary for her to reconsider this decision each time soap is purchased. Indeed, it would be next to impossible to make a decision about each item placed in the shopping cart on every visit to a grocery store. Katona has summarized the essential nature of habits exceedingly well [10, p. 139]:

> The basic principle of one form of behavior is repetition. The strength of a habit depends on the frequency of its repetition, as well as on its recency, and on the degree of resultant success or satisfaction. In this area it is correct to say that the best way to know what a man will do is to know what he did the last time in the same situation. Habits, once established, are fairly inflexible. To be sure . . . habits can be broken. But when we behave habitually it is not because we have made a choice or decision. Habits tend to be carried out quite automatically, without being influenced by motives or attitudes.

Breaking Habits

Habits are generally broken in one of two ways. First, the automatic response pattern may cease to gratify the need. This usually comes about because the basic need is altered in some way,[5] but it may also occur because the buyer finds an alternative response that is more gratifying. For competitive products

[5] Frequently as a result of over-time changes in the characteristics of the buying unit. For example, families move, the composition of families changes, incomes go up or down, individuals marry or get divorced, and the interests and activities of family members change, as do procedures for family decision making.

with short repurchases cycles, such as soap or cereal, two principal tasks of promotional efforts are intended (1) to ensure that consumers presently purchasing a competitor's product are provided with a rationale for reconsidering their previous brand decision and (2) to reinforce, at the same time, earlier decisions of those consumers making up one's own brand franchise. Efforts in this area may take the form of a new packaging design, a reduced price, more intensive advertising, and so on.

Conditions Associated with Decision Making

Although most buying behavior is habitual, it is possible to identify general conditions under which a consumer will tend to consider alternatives and make a genuine decision. Katona has identified six such characteristics, each associated with either the item purchased or the purchase situation [11, pp. 289–290]. These are listed here, the first four followed by brief additional notations that relate the quote to material presented earlier in this chapter.

1. "Expenditures which are subjectively thought to be major and which are fairly rare. Many of these expenditures are large (e.g., a house or, in many but not all cases, a car, etc.), but some may be small and yet of great importance to the buyer (as, for instance, a dress or a present for a specified occasion)." This category includes products with long repurchase cycles and/or purchases for which conditions necessary for the establishment of habits are not present.

2. "Unsatisfactory past experience, especially disappointment of expectations." In other words, the product or service failed to gratify the need for which it was purchased.

3. "Some (by no means all) purchases of new products or the first purchase of a product." These purchases would represent a *possible* first step in the sequence of events necessary for establishment of habitual behavior.

4. "Awareness of a difference between one's customary behavior and that of the group to which one belongs or an important reference group." The basic need is altered.

5. "Impact of strong new stimuli or precipitating circumstances; these stimuli may consist of general news (threat of war, inflation, etc.) or of news regarding specific products, which may be transmitted by advertisers."

6. "Certain personality characteristics, often associated with education."

Recapitulation

A purchase transaction can be conceptualized in terms of characteristics of product (or service), channel, customer, and environment. The act of purchasing most frequently results from habit; alternatively, a purchase may represent the culmination of a decision process. This process may be characterized both by a time dimension and by a series of intermediate events. Prior to entering into a decision process, many people will hold definite predispositions toward one or more alternatives, and these predispositions may be expected to exert some influence on ultimate purchase behavior. However, as a potential customer proceeds through the process, a multitude of influences impinge on the ultimate decision. Many of these influences result in new learning.

The remainder of this chapter is devoted to a discussion of sources of information about purchase behavior, including both primary and secondary data. Major portions of the text, especially sections concerned with measurement techniques, rely importantly on the material just presented.

SOURCES OF INFORMATION ABOUT PURCHASE BEHAVIOR

As products move through production and distribution to end consumers, a wide assortment of information becomes available about each step in the flow. This section concentrates on information that describes or explains the purchase behavior of end-consumers; that is, information about the purchase transaction that immediately precedes consumption. Material is presented using the general framework developed earlier and reflected in Figures 1 and 2. Opening paragraphs review descriptive data that can be used to answer the "what," "when," "where," and "who" type questions. Emphasis then shifts to a discussion of research techniques that seek to explain the "why" of buying behavior. The chapter concludes by commenting both on approaches to linking information in all five areas and on the value of continuous information systems for measuring purchase behavior.

Wherever possible, the text is restricted to discussions of specific *types* of information as opposed to specific sources. Individual references to commercial marketing research firms, trade associations, government agencies, and other organizations that generate data are held to a minimum because there are enormous year-to-year changes in both availability and alternative sources of any one type of data. Also, the more general sources are covered in Section II, Part A, Chapter 2.

Information About WHAT Is Being Bought

This chapter opened by emphasizing management's basic need for current information about the purchasing patterns of end consumers. For a specific product, this would include information about industry sales, market share by brand and/or other major product characteristics (for example, size of package for nondurables or model number for durables), price paid, and so on. Descriptive information of this type may be obtained from either seller or buyer or both. Following is a listing of types of information that are widely used.

Trade Association Reports. Most industries have trade associations that assemble and report a wide assortment of statistical information. A typical example is reports on current levels of factory shipments.[6] Each participating company reports its shipments and receives in return a summary report showing total industry volume plus its own percentage share of that volume. Competitors' shares are not reported. Frequently, these same aggregate data are reported in industry trade publications. Figures for nonparticipating companies are imputed. Validity depends on both (1) the accuracy of data submitted and (2) the percentage of total industry sales represented by participants.

Retail Audits. A sample of retail outlets is selected and visited at periodic intervals by trained auditors who record information on inventories and sales. For a product or product class, a typical report will present descriptive information showing total sales by brand, retail inventory and stock turnover data, and selling prices. Audit results are usually examined by available characteristics of the audited stores—for example, store type, volume, region of country, city size. Although available for many products, audits have been most successful in the food and drug areas; recently, however, viable services have been developed for clothing and even gasoline.

[6] The extent to which factory shipment data can be used to estimate retail sales depends on elapsed time between shipment and final purchase as well as availability of up-to-date information about inventory levels. In general, shipment data *do not* provide an accurate picture of retail activity.

For any audit, cooperation of sampled stores is vital. For this reason, most participants are compensated with cash, research findings, or both. Nonetheless, accurate audit data have been difficult to obtain for many products, including most consumer durables. Consider, for example, the appliance area, where efforts to complete representative audits have come up against two major stumbling blocks. The first problem has been lack of cooperation from a significant proportion of sampled stores. Many vertically integrated national chains that feature their own private brands, as well as many large department store chains, have refused to cooperate with in-store audits conducted by outside firms. Second, many smaller stores either do not maintain complete records or refuse to open their records to outsiders. Appliances are frequently ordered at one store and shipped from another store or from a central warehouse. When this happens, it becomes extremely difficult to trace the flow of merchandise through the particular outlet sampled for study.

Dealer Intelligence and Attitude Reports. In situations where formal audits are not feasible, frequently it is possible to interview a representative sample of dealers (in person or by telephone) at periodic intervals in order to provide a quick barometer of sales and inventory trends, expectations regarding short-term prospects, and attitudes toward such factors as competitive lines, specific features, sales programs, service and pricing policies, and so on. While this information cannot be quantified or projected in any statistical sense, it does provide meaningful indicators of retail climate. This type of report is used for a wide assortment of consumer durables.

"Hot Model" Reports. So called "hot model" reports are used most often as either a supplement to or substitute for audits. They were first developed and sold by a large audit firm. Reports are designed to tell a manufacturer which models of a product are the current best sellers. Data are obtained by telephoning a representative sample of stores and asking a salesman on the floor to report brand, model number, and price paid for the most recent units sold, usually the last two. Results are weighted using some measure of sales volume for each store and, within limits of the sample design, are examined using store characteristics like those listed under "Retail Audits," as just noted. One limitation of this approach is that the purchase transaction must involve a salesman; it is not surprising, then, that most successful applications have been for relatively expensive durables.

Retail Observation Reports. Valuable information can be obtained about characteristics of a given store or a sample of stores by visiting the premises to observe and/or ask questions. Location and physical attributes of stores can be assessed together with characteristics of competitive displays. For instance, it is possible to evaluate the comparative size and diversity of floor displays for various makes and product lines. Direct questions can be asked to determine product knowledge and sales techniques of store personnel.

Consumer Expenditure Surveys. These studies are based on direct collection of data from end consumers. While tremendous variations exist among both research objectives and research designs, respondents are generally asked to provide a substantial amount of information about each expenditure being studied; questions asked frequently include brand or make purchased, specific product characteristics, quantity purchased, price paid, where purchased, who purchased, whether credit was used, and much more.[7] (As will be made clear

---

[7] For a comprehensive review of methodology and content of many of these studies, see [16].

shortly, information of this type can be relevant to any or all of the five question types listed in Figure 1.)

Research techniques used in consumer expenditure surveys include detailed personal interviews,[8] telephone interviews, self-enumeration forms (for example, purchase diaries), reinterviews with the same individuals or buying units at two or more points in time, as well as *combinations* of the above survey methodologies and others not discussed here. Some expenditure studies are completed only once, others are repeated at periodic intervals, and still others are conducted on a continuous basis. As Pearl points out, "Unlike most other technical fields of similar complexity, there appears to be relatively little standardization of approach in survey methodology even where the objectives of different investigations are virtually identical" [16, p. 10]. Advantages and disadvantages inherent to most survey research techniques are discussed at length elsewhere in this handbook.

Information About WHERE and WHEN Purchases are Made

It should be made clear, first, that information about both where and when purchases are made can be obtained from each of the data sources just discussed. There are, however, additional comments specific to each of these areas that deserve mention.

Where Are Purchases Made? In addition to information sources already mentioned, in situations *where names and addresses of retail outlets are available*, a great deal of information specific to the named stores can be obtained from secondary sources. Consider this sampling of information available from Dun & Bradstreet:

1. Standard Industrial Classification (SIC) Code—a widely used classification scheme prepared by the Bureau of the Budget
2. Net worth
3. Year business was started
4. Dun & Bradstreet financial rating
5. Whether financial rating has changed in last year (if so, nature of change)
6. Total annual sales
7. Number of employees
8. Number of retail outlets
9. Dollar value of inventory
10. Percent of total sales made for cash
11. Whether (named) store is branch or headquarters

These items of information can, in turn, be used to calculate various ratios that are useful for analytical purposes. For example:

1. Inventory turnover rate (ratio of total annual sales to dollar value of inventory)
2. Sales per net worth (a rough measure of efficiency with which invested capital is being utilized)
3. Sales per employee (a rough measure of efficiency with which personnel are being utilized)

Furthermore, ratios like these can be combined. "Discount" type stores, for instance, are generally identified by high inventory turnover rates and high sales per employee. Any of these variables can be used singly or in combination to study a group of retail outlets. More often, they are linked with other

---

[8] The Bureau of Labor Statistics of the U.S. Department of Labor has conducted in-home interviews lasting up to eight hours each.

available information to study questions like, "What are the characteristics of stores in which various types of products are sold?"

When Are Purchases Made? Questions pertaining to seasonal and secular sales patterns should be viewed at two levels. First, management needs a picture of the aggregate over-time sales pattern for a product, particularly for products that exhibit extreme seasonal sales fluctuations, such as room air conditioners and products primarily purchased as Christmas gifts. Aggregate sales patterns can be established using trade association data, retail audits, and results from consumer surveys that are either repeated periodically or conducted on a continuous basis.

A somewhat more subtle information requirement is inherent in the fact that, for many products, the *composition* of markets also exhibits seasonal variation. Characteristics of buyers and reasons for purchase may change substantially from season to season. Using as examples specific seasonal changes in consumer attitudes and behavior as regards photographic supplies and watches, Haley and Gatty have concluded that "seasonal changes may bring variations in the proportions of men and women buyers, of gift and non-gift purchases, and of goods moving through different distribution channels—with all that means for advertising, promotion and other sales tactics" [6, p. 65]. For purposes of understanding the composition of seasonal buying, Haley and Gatty strongly argue for continuous information systems as opposed to traditional one-shot surveys.

Information about WHO Is Buying

With few exceptions, *information necessary to describe buyers must be obtained directly from the buyers themselves.* This is usually accomplished with in-home interviews using any of the large number of available survey research techniques described in Part II of this handbook. Examples of other possible sources of buyer information include (1) appliance purchase record cards, (2) credit applications, and (3) in-store interviews. In some instances, analysis of aggregate census data may provide insights into characteristics of a served market, particularly if geographic market boundaries can be approximated (for example, the area served by a small neighborhood grocery store or, possibly, by a branch bank).

Information About WHY People Buy

An understanding of the inner conditions that motivate buying behavior is a must if one expects to formulate marketing programs that actually have an impact on behavior. While it is useful to track gains and losses in market shares using descriptive data in order to allocate resources in a way that will *change* the trends in a favorable direction, it is essential to know what *caused* the purchase behavior reflected in the aggregate statistics. Are people purchasing in response to price, package design or product configuration, shelf or store location, brand or store reputation, or some combination of these and other factors? Answering questions like these is the most difficult research assignment in the area of purchase behavior. How is "why" research accomplished?

Understanding Habitual Behavior. One frequently used approach to determining why a particular purchase transaction took place is to ask the buyer a direct question. "What are the major reasons you decided to purchase the (product or brand) you did?" More times than not, unfortunately, results from this type of retrospective questioning are badly misleading. The principal reason for failure can be traced to the fact that most purchasing behavior is habitual, and a respondent simply cannot answer a "why" question for a transaction that results from habit.   Bucklin and Carman offer a succinct statement of the problem [3, p. 4]:[9]

> The facts are that often these purchases have been repeated for such a long period of time and have become so much a matter of habit that the respondent cannot evoke the real reason for a particular brand or store choice nor what led her to adopt her present habit pattern.   The closer a good lies to the "convenience" end of the product classification spectrum, the harder it is for the consumer to be conscious of her reasons for choosing a particular brand.

Thus the researcher must contend with an apparent paradox: respondents cannot be expected to provide meaningful answers to "why" questions about habitual behavior, yet most buying behavior is habitual.

How, then, does one design research to get at the real reasons underlying habitual behavior?   There are two general research strategies available.   The first is to force respondents who have established habitual buying patterns to again consider alternatives and make a decision, that is, to repeat the decision-making process.   The second is to locate for research purposes a group of respondents who are actually going through the decision process.   One approach to implementing the first stategy is this [3]:

> ...the researcher must first measure the consumer's attitude toward the brands in a particular product group; second, disturb the consumer's environment and brand choices; and third, study the process through which the consumer develops new brand attitudes.   Thus, the researcher uses some disturbance in the consumer's life to trigger the entire decision-making process and, thereby, tries to identify and measure all the interacting cause and effect relationships involved in the decision process and the formulation of attitudes.

The essential element in both these strategies is that *the "why" of habitual behavior is not researched directly*.   Rather, an understanding of both the formulation and termination of habitual buying patterns is gained by studying the decision processes by which habits are established or broken; there is no viable alternative.   *Hence all "why" research is focused on decision processes.*

Understanding Decision Processes.   A decision process may be characterized by a time dimension and by a series of intermediate events (see Figures 1 and 2 and the accompanying text).   In Figure 2, intermediate events are grouped into four broad categories: predispositions, allocation of available resources, information gathering, and decisions and postdecision reactions.   In general, research designed to contribute to an understanding of reasons underlying decisions can either focus on specific intermediate events or treat the total process as a single entity.[10]   Depending on the specific questions to be

---

[9] Bucklin and Carman use such diverse examples as bread, milk, services of a parking lot, automobiles, automobile insurance, magazine subscriptions, and fertilizer.

[10] A complete analysis of the influences underlying any one purchase decision is an exercise in futility.   The absurdity of attempting to research the *initiating* cause of a particular action has been aptly expressed by Krech and Crutchfield in the following paragraph:

"Explanations may frequently deteriorate into an endless search for the 'ultimate' or 'first' cause.   If it can be said that Mr. Arbuthnot seeks membership in the country club because he sees it as a goal of social approval, it is then asked why he seeks that goal.   If it is answered that this goal has arisen because of a need for personal security, it is then asked why that feeling of insecurity arose.   If it is answered that the feeling of personal insecurity has arisen because of a socially embarrassing speech defect that Mr. Arbuthnot has acquired, it is then asked why that speech defect.   The

answered, every research technique discussed in this handbook becomes a potential candidate for application. Longitudinal research techniques, however, are particularly well suited to gaining insights into the nature of over-time change processes that involve learning. To understand why this is true, it will be useful to discuss one concept from psychology; namely, intervening variables.

As stated earlier, an understanding of the inner conditions that motivate buying behavior is necessary to formulate marketing programs that will influence behavior. These "inner conditions" are referred to by psychologists as "intervening variables" (Figure 3). They are postulated to function within an individual; that is, they are a part of the inward, psychic experience of each individual. As noted in Figure 3, intervening variables provide the psychological framework within which perceived environmental stimuli, including all elements of a marketing program, are organized and interpreted. This orga-

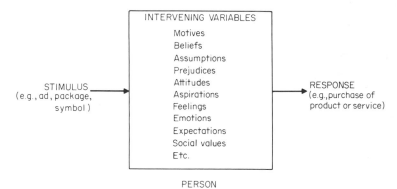

Fig. 3.   Psychological framework for interpreting environmental stimuli.

nization and interpretation ("cognition"), in turn, leads to overt behavior. Psychologists further point out that the structure of intervening variables within a psychological frame is constantly changing through time as a result of new learning and experience.

How does this concept relate to the issue of understanding decisions? Consider the first category of "intermediate events" shown in Figure 2—predispositions. Note that every predisposition listed as an example in the text is also included among the list of intervening variables shown in Figure 3. The perceptual theory based on intervening variables holds that *marketing activities, no matter how effective they may appear to be, never have a direct influence on purchase behavior.* Rather, marketing activities have an impact on variables internal to the potential buyer; whether or not he decides to buy depends on the manner in which he *perceives* the external events. Thus, if a sufficient number of potential buyers perceive a price reduction as offering a short-term bargain, sales are likely to increase. On the other hand, if a price

---

answer may be that the speech defect was a defense against a precocious younger brother. Thus, at this stage, we are to understand that Mr. Arbuthnot seeks membership in the country club because his younger brother was precocious! But why stop here? The analysis can go as far as the ingenuity of the theorist will carry him, without ever really reaching the ultimate, or first cause."

reduction is perceived as the first of a number of expected reductions, sales are likely to decrease.

If the structure of intervening variables remained constant over time, the challenge to research would be to determine relationships between key variables (for example, attitudes and the particular behavior one wished to influence), and then to use this knowledge to structure marketing programs that would influence these variables in ways that would trigger the desired buying behavior. However, the structure of intervening variables is constantly changing through time as a result of new learning and experience. The response to a given advertisement may be quite different at two points in time. The difference occurs because the mix of intervening variables is in some unspecified way different at the times of exposure.

Within the context of Figure 2, initial predispositions are altered by all information-gathering activities as well as by procedures used to allocate resources. Whether the decision process is terminated by a purchase or by a decision not to buy, individuals will emerge from the process with a somewhat altered set of attitudes and feelings. These will represent initial "predispositions" if the individual is confronted with the same decision at some future time.

In order to understand the "why" of purchase behavior, then, one must identify relevant variables, measure over-time changes in these variables, and finally quantify relationships between measured changes and behavior. Knowledge gained from this type of research provides a basis for formulating marketing programs that will have maximum influence on behavior. The sum of these leads to an essential question, "How can over-time change best be measured empirically?"

Longitudinal Research. Longitudinal research techniques are uniquely suited to the study of change. In its simplest form, a longitudinal design requires that each respondent be asked the identical question at two or more points in time. This approach permits structuring of *turnover tables*; hence the term *turnover analysis* is frequently used.[11]

The nature of turnover analysis can be most easily demonstrated by considering a dichotomous characteristic that is measured at two points in time. Table 1 shows a hypothetical turnover table giving answers to a brand attitude question asked during two interviews with the same respondents. Note first the similarity in totals from each interview. These findings are comparable to those that would be forthcoming from two independent cross-sectional surveys. But the interior cells of the table provide information that cannot be derived from cross-sectional research. They show that only 45 percent of all respondents gave the same answer on both interviews. Furthermore, attitudes of 25 percent of all respondents changed from favorable to unfavorable between interviews, and attitudes of 30 percent of all respondents moved in the opposite direction—from unfavorable to favorable.

Table 1 both documents a high level of instability in brand attitudes and defines change groups for further analysis. Brand buying behavior could be analyzed for those whose attitudes worsened and results compared to findings from a similar analysis for those whose attitudes improved. This would provide some insight into the *effects of attitude change* on brand buying behavior. No other empirical technique will accomplish this particular research task.

Because the sequence of stages in a decision process may often involve

---

[11] For a more detailed discussion of this technique, see Section II, Part B, Chapter 10.

TABLE 1   Example of a Turnover Table: Brand Attitudes at Two Points in Time

Attitude at time 1	Attitude at time 2		Total, time 1 (percent)
	Favorable (percent)	Unfavorable (percent)	
Favorable........................	35*	25‡	60
Unfavorable......................	30§	10†	40
Total, time 2...................	65	35	100

* Attitudes favorable at both interviews.
† Attitudes unfavorable at both interviews.
‡ Attitudes worsened between interviews.
§ Attitudes improved between interviews.

learning, changes in attitudes, allocation of decision roles within a family, and rationalization after purchase, it is impossible for an individual to accurately report psychological variables—for example, any of the intervening variables listed in Figure 3—as they existed at various points in the decision process. Longitudinal research improves the quality of data by vastly reducing reliance on memory.

LINKING INFORMATION ABOUT PURCHASE BEHAVIOR

Figure 1 highlighted the importance of being able to combine or link information about product, channel, customer, and environment in a meaningful way; that is, to ask the question, "Who acquires what, where, when, and why?" *Information is linked by means of a common sampling frame.* When such a frame is present, it becomes possible to study interrelationships among any combination of the characteristics discussed in this chapter. Thus, variables obtained from the same source—for example, in-home interviews with house-wives—can be combined in any way the analyst desires. Characteristics of housewives that report buying in department stores might be analyzed using store characteristics furnished by these same housewives.

If respondents are asked to provide the names and addresses of stores, how-ever, additional information—for example, the type of Dun & Bradstreet data outlined earlier—can be obtained independently and linked to the information about buyers. One could, for example, study characteristics of women who buy in stores having high inventory turnover rates *and* high sales per employee —data that cannot be furnished by the housewives themselves.

When a common sampling frame is not present, linkages cannot be made. For example, whether one-time or part of a continuous information system, the typical retail audit describes only the flow of products through channels. It does not indicate who is buying what type of product in the various outlets. Nor do audits indicate why decisions are made to purchase particular types of goods in particular types of outlets.

CONTINUOUS INFORMATION SYSTEMS

Variables that influence or are influenced by purchase behavior have dynamic qualities that cannot be ignored. To account for these variables on a system-atic basis requires frequent information feedback from the marketplace. In an increasing number of companies, required feedback is being generated by a continuous information system. The essential reason for using continuous measurement systems is that many of the key variables that influence purchase behavior, whether intervening or a part of the external environment, are subject to relatively abrupt change. Hence, to make knowledge of these variables *operationally useful*, the market analyst must move from traditional one-time cross-sectional studies (sometimes repeated periodically) to some form of continuous system. To generalize further, if it is true that purchase behavior is influenced significantly by variables that are subject to rapid change, then rapid and continuous measurement of these variables is essential to marketing planning.

Haley and Gatty have listed a number of specific advantages inherent in continuous consumer information systems [6, p. 69]. Their list includes these items:

1. Changes in market conditions can be spotted quickly, and any necessary actions can be taken.
2. The impact of changing national moods and social conditions can be seen, and marketing policies can be adjusted accordingly.
3. Advertising and promotion can be planned so that they fit market trends.
4. New product launchings can be timed more precisely so that they coincide with appropriate market conditions.

The advantages of continuous information systems vis-à-vis traditional one-time studies are so numerous that such systems are likely to emerge over time as the single most widely used type of research design, as discussed in Section II, Part G, Chapter 2.

CONCLUDING COMMENTS

At this writing, most research on purchase behavior is descriptive and is concerned with the "what," "where," "when," and "who" type questions; further, these questions are frequently treated separately. Explanatory research directed toward the "why" question tends to focus on only one or a limited number of the intermediate events or processes outlined in this chapter. Research designed to gain sufficient understanding of the dynamics of purchase decisions so that findings can be applied by management to the solution of day-to-day operating problems remains a frontier area in marketing.

Despite extensive empirical work, useful insights into the complexities of the total process have been few and far between. Yet research in this area must and will be continued. A detailed understanding of the dynamics of consumer demand, the resultant changes made by manufacturers and sellers to adjust to this demand, and the actions which effectively influence consumer decision processes will become increasingly necessary to the formulation of effective marketing programs. The application of longitudinal techniques on a continuous basis seems to offer the most effective empirical approach for gaining knowledge of the type required.

REFERENCES

1. Alderson, W., *Marketing Behavior and Executive Action*, Homewood, Ill.: Irwin, 1957.
2. Andreasen, A. R., "Attitudes and Customer Behavior: A Decision Model," in Lee E. Preston, ed., *New Research in Marketing*, Berkeley: The Institute of Business and Economic Research, 1966.

3. Bucklin, L. P., and J. M. Carman, *The Design of Consumer Research Panels: Conception and Administration of the Berkeley Food Panel*, Berkeley, Calif.: University of California Institute of Business and Economic Research, 1967.

4. Engel, J. F., D. T. Kollat, and R. D. Blackwell, *Consumer Behavior*, New York: Holt, 1968.

5. Foote, N. N., ed., *Household Decision-Making*, New York: New York University Press, 1961.

6. Haley, R. I., and R. Gatty, "Monitor Your Market Continuously," *Harvard Business Review*, vol. 46, no. 3, May–June 1968.

7. Howard, J. A., *Marketing: Executive and Buyer Behavior*, New York: Columbia University Press, 1963.

8. Howard, J. A., and J. N. Sheth, *The Theory of Buyer Behavior*, New York: Wiley, 1969.

9. Katona, G., *Psychological Analysis of Economic Behavior*, New York: McGraw-Hill, 1951.

10. ———, *The Powerful Consumer*, New York: McGraw-Hill, 1960.

11. ———, *The Mass Consumption Society*, New York: McGraw-Hill, 1964.

12. Krech, D., and R. Crutchfield, *Theory and Problems of Social Psychology*, New York: McGraw-Hill, 1948.

13. Morgan, J. N., "Some Pilot Studies of Communication and Consensus in the Family," *Public Opinion Quarterly*, vol. 32, Spring 1968.

14. Newman, J. W., *Motivation Research in Marketing Management*, Boston: Harvard University Graduate School of Business Administration, Division of Research, 1957.

15. Nicosia, F. M., *Consumer Decision Processes: Marketing and Advertising Implications*, Englewood Cliffs, N.J.: Prentice-Hall, 1966.

16. Pearl, R. N., *Methodology of Consumer Expenditure Surveys*, Washington: U.S. Bureau of the Census, Working Paper no. 27, 1968.

17. Smith, G. H., *Motivation Research in Advertising and Marketing*, New York: McGraw-Hill, 1954.

Part B

Theories

Chapter 1

Cognitive Dissonance

M. VENKATESAN[1] *School of Business Administration, University of Iowa, Iowa City, Iowa*

No theory in social psychology has generated so much research and had so much impact as the theory of cognitive dissonance proposed by Festinger [15]. While its impact has been great, as one reviewer has observed, it continues to generate "more hostility than any other one approach" [28, p. 492]. Research studies in marketing have not been untouched.

Our interest in this theory stems particularly from our needs for a nomothetic approach, that is, one explaining what most people do most of the time. Second, the simple postulates of the theory and the provocative hypotheses it generates have resulted in more research than from those of any other theory in social psychology. Such massive research has provided a multitude of examples of experimental situations, experimental designs, and intricate experimental manipulations, all of which have relevance for research in marketing. In general, the popularity of this theory in marketing is due to its applicability to a wide range of research areas and also to its generality and simplicity.

This chapter will review the major approaches to cognitive consistency, including cognitive dissonance; provide a brief explanation of the theory of cognitive dissonance; and indicate the nature of empirical support for those major aspects of the theory with implications for marketing. Empirical support both

[1] I want to thank Professor Ivan Ross, University of Minnesota, for his provocative discussions and insightful comments on cognitive dissonance. I also wish to thank Professors Gordon Haaland, University of New Hampshire, Robert Mittelstaedt, University of Missouri, and Richard Cardozo, University of Minnesota, for their helpful comments.

from the psychological and marketing literature is reviewed.[2] Subsequent sections deal with the uses and misuses of this theory in marketing and make suggestions for its potential use. The chapter concludes with a look at the advantages and shortcomings of the theory.

CONSISTENCY THEORIES AND COGNITIVE DISSONANCE[3]

Cognitive dissonance concerns dynamic intrapersonal cognition processes and the relationships between cognitions[4] and behavior. Its main appeal is the core notion that an individual strives for psychological consistency in his beliefs, attitudes, and actions. As McGuire [27] has observed, this theoretical notion of "consistency" has a long past but a short history.

In its historical perspective, cognitive dissonance is one of the three major formulations of cognitive consistency theories. The other two are known as structural balance theory [18] and the congruity principle [30]. The consistency theories generally assume that an individual tries to minimize the internal inconsistency among his cognitions, interpersonal relations, and behavior, and that the existence of such inconsistency in the individual gives rise to pressures to reduce or eliminate it. Festinger's theory of cognitive dissonance [15] encompasses a wider range of situations and is more general than the other two formulations. Thus, to fully appreciate the theoretical formulations of cognitive dissonance, a short review of the other two major approaches is necessary.

BALANCE THEORY

The balance theory, or the concept of structural balance, was proposed by Heider [18], who was concerned with perception of individuals, ideas, and concepts. Since his analysis concerned interpersonal perception, it was limited to two individuals (designated as A and B) and to one object (an impersonal entity, labeled X). In this three-element structure, the interest centered on finding the organization of relations among A, B, and X in A's cognitive structure. "In the case of three entities, a *balanced* state exists if all three relations are positive in all respects or if two are negative and one positive" [36, p. 283]. Thus, relations among the three elements in the structure are either "balanced" or "unbalanced."

In Figure 1, A and B are individuals and X is a brand of a product. Thus, if A likes (or dislikes) B, A likes (dislikes) X, and B likes (dislikes) X, a balanced state is obtained. The theory proposed that when a structure is in a state of imbalance, such a state produces tension and therefore there is a tendency to change it to restore balance. Empirical support for the balanced state comes from studies in which the pleasantness of hypothetical situations was rated and from experiments on interpersonal attitudes. Thus Zajonc [37, p. 353] noted that "20 years after the original statement of the balance prin-

---

[2] Not all the studies reviewed—only the "classical" or most representative—are included in the section dealing with empirical support. For a complete bibliography of all the studies, the reader may wish to refer to a comprehensive reference such as that by Margulis and Songer [26].

[3] The sources for the discussions and critical evaluations of the cognitive consistency theories and the theory of cognitive dissonance are McGuire [27], Aronson [2], and Zajonc [37]. The reader may wish to refer to these sources for amplification.

[4] Cognitions are defined as "any knowledge, opinions, or belief about the environment, about oneself, or about one's behavior" [15, p. 3].

ciple was made, practically no research on balance has gone beyond attempts to demonstrate the validity of the basic definition."

CONGRUITY PRINCIPLE

The second major approach of cognitive consistency, in chronological order, is known as the congruity principle, whose proponents are Osgood and Tannenbaum [30]. Their principle deals specifically with the problem of direction of attitude change and thus can be viewed as a special case of balance [35]. There are again three elements to this theory, namely, a source, a concept or an object, and an assertion made by the source about the concept (object). In the marketing context, the paradigm of congruity can be viewed as relating what sources say about objects and the effect of these assertions on audience and attitude towards objects.

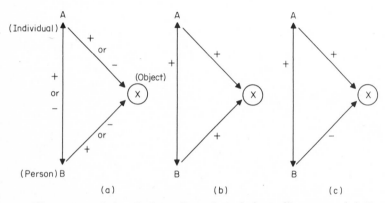

Fig. 1.   Illustration of the "balanced" and "unbalanced" states. (*a*) Possible relations among elements; (*b*) "balanced" state; (*c*) "unbalanced" state.

"The paradigm of congruity is that of an individual who is confronted with an assertion regarding a particular matter about which he believes and feels in a certain way, made by a person toward whom he also has some attitude" [36, p. 287]. In the marketing context one can view this paradigm as involving an assertion by a source about an object and the effect of these assertions on the individual—particularly on his attitude towards objects.

To illustrate, the source can be television commercials, the object can be a product, and the individual buyer can be assumed to have some attitude toward the product and toward the television commercials in general (Figure 2). Thus, if one knows the evaluations of two of these three elements, one can predict the change in attitude following the introduction of the third element.

The principle states that such a change occurs in the direction of increased congruity. Accordingly, when a person's attitudes toward the source and the object are similar (or dissimilar) and the attitudes implied by the assertion are positive (negative), a state of congruency exists among the three elements. However, a negative assertion in the former case or a positive assertion in the latter case gives rise to a state of incongruency and leads to reevaluation of the source and of the object (concept). Such a reevaluation tends to be in the direction of establishing increased congruity among the elements. Thus, the congruity formulation takes into account the varying magnitudes in evaluation, and it can also predict the magnitude and direction of changes.

While much empirical evidence supports the congruity principle and while its formulation in quantitative terms allowed for precise predictions, it has fallen far short of its promise in precise numerical predictions of the extent and direction of attitude change [37].

WHAT IS COGNITIVE DISSONANCE?

In 1957, Festinger [15] proposed the theory of cognitive dissonance as another formulation in the area of cognitive consistency. The theory of cognitive dissonance is incredibly simple in its formulation. Stripped of all verbiage, it states that all situations are not optimal. Therefore man, as a rationalizing animal, strives for consistency—consistency within himself.

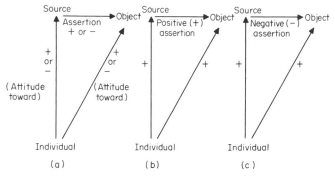

Fig. 2. Illustration of congruity and incongruity relations. (a) Possible relations among elements; (b) congruity relations; (c) incongruity relations.

The statement of the theory is not elegant. It asserts that whenever two *relevant cognitions* do not "fit," this leads to psychological inconsistency within the individual. This occurrence is called dissonance, which is viewed as a noxious or unpleasant state. In the presence of this psychological discomfort, the individual will attempt to reduce this dissonance and bring the relations between the two dissonant cognitions into consonance.

Several points need elaboration if we are to understand cognitive dissonance and appreciate its place among the "consistency theories." First, contrary to common misconceptions and misuses, Festinger's formulation is aimed at explaining the dynamic cognitive processes within the individual after he has made a decision. In short, its domain is the situation confronting the individual after he has been engaged in some decision-making process.

Second, the theory does not relate to just any two cognitions. It implies that the two dissonant cognitions are relevant cognitions and that they interact with each other. As indicated in Figure 3, dissonance could arise only if the two cognitions, for one reason or another, do not fit. Such a situation would arise only if the two cognitions in question interact, and they interact only if they are relevant. This "nonfitting relation" is formally stated by Festinger [15, p. 13] as follows: "These two elements (*cognition*) are in a dissonant relation if, considering these two alone, the obverse (*opposite*) of one element would follow from the other.   To state it a bit more formally, x and y are dissonant if not-x follows from y."[5]

Third, while the balance theory and congruity principle generated specific and direct experimental predictions, the theory of cognitive dissonance does not, generally, make specific predictions.   While the former two approaches are restrictive in the areas to which they can be applied, cognitive dissonance theory applies to a wide range of human behavior.   Its heuristic value lies in its simplicity.   Aronson [2] points out that this very simplicity is at once its great strength and its serious weakness.   While the core of this theory[6] is clear and has generated many hypotheses unique to it—that is, they could not have been derived from any other theory—its weakness lies in the impossibility of making predictions based on its "fringes."   While the shortcomings of this approach will be considered later, suffice it to point out that the dissonance theory is a major, all-encompassing formulation in the cognitive consistency area.

So far, we have only considered the theoretical formulation of the dissonance theory.   Two questions are relevant: (1) is dissonance likely to occur, and (2) what does one do when he gets there?   In response to the first question,

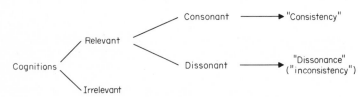

Fig. 3.   Relationships among cognitions.

Festinger [15] pointed out that there is a fairly wide variety of situations in which dissonance seems to be nearly unavoidable.   Specifically, where a decision must be taken, some dissonance is almost unavoidable, since the cognition of the action taken and the opinions (knowledge) which may point to a different action may not be fitting.   Again, Festinger [15] pointed out some of the obvious situations giving rise to dissonance, such as logical inconsistency, inconsistency with cultural mores, and past experience.

With regard to the second question, the answer is that cognitive dissonance is an antecedent condition, which leads to activity oriented toward its reduction or elimination.   Stated differently, the presence of cognitive dissonance will lead to pressures to reduce the dissonance.   Reduction or elimination of dissonance is achieved by changing existing cognitions or adding new ones.   If either of these two avenues cannot be used, then behavior "favoring consonance will be recruited.   Seeking new information is an example of such behavior" [37, p. 361].   Within these two broad categories there are multiple modes of reducing dissonance; generally, an individual can reduce his dissonance in one or more ways.

In summary, it is seen that the theory of cognitive dissonance proposed that when "nonfitting" relations exist among cognitions, this gives rise to dissonance,

---

[5] Italics added for emphasis.

[6] Core is indicated as "situations in which the self-concept or other firm expectancies are involved—and in which most people share the same self-concepts or other firm expectancies" [2, p. 25].

a psychologically inconsistent state, which is uncomfortable to the individual and therefore leads to activities to reduce such psychological discomfort.

EMPIRICAL EVIDENCE ON DISSONANCE THEORY

Dissonance theory has generated an enormous amount of research in social psychology. The findings can be classified in several major categories of interest to social psychologists. Since our interest is in the usefulness and application of this theory to marketing, no exhaustive review of the empirical work on dissonance theory will be made here. Four major aspects appear relevant for marketing: (1) postdecision, postchoice dissonance; (2) compliance and attitude change; (3) selective exposure to information; and (4) effort, expectation, and dissonance.

An example often used by Festinger [15] and others to illustrate cognitive dissonance deals with the habitual smoker and the knowledge that cigarette smoking causes cancer. The explanation goes something like this: Since the cognition that he continues to smoke is dissonant with the knowledge (cognition) that cigarette smoking is injurious to his health, he should experience dissonance. There are several ways that our habitual smoker can reduce this dissonance: by discontinuing the habit, by derogating the evidence relating cancer and cigarette smoking, or by convincing himself that there are worse ways of dying, and so on.

This habitual smoker has been researched. In a study, Kassarjian and Cohen [24] set out to find the habitual smoker after publication of the Surgeon General's report. Their findings indicate, for this classical example, the rationalizing aspects of the cigarette smokers in the face of dissonant information. They conclude [24, p. 63] that

> as inconsistent as smoking must seem to the logical analyst who realizes that the smoker is aware of the published reports on its potential health hazard, the behavior of the smoker is not irrational to himself. With rare exceptions, the confirmed smoker appears to be behaving consistently with his belief system by continuing to smoke. He has justified its rationality either by dissociating his responsibility over the decision; by denying, distorting, misperceiving or minimizing the degree of health hazard involved; and/or by selectively drawing out new cognitions and new information that will reduce the inconsistency of his behavior and achieve consonance in his own cognitive world.

Dissonance studies differentiate between high and low cognitive dissonance. This is because all dissonant relations cannot be equal in magnitude. Festinger [15] pointed out the need to distinguish degrees of dissonance. Though no precise specification of what determines the magnitude of dissonance is available, the following factors are indicated by Festinger [15] as important in its determination: (1) importance of the decision, (2) importance of each of the cognitive elements, (3) ratio of dissonant to consonant elements, and (4) cognitive overlap.[7] The original dissonance formulation has been updated by addition of such features as commitment to a choice or course of action and volition or free choice. See Brehm and Cohen [5] and Festinger [17].

Postdecision Dissonance

Dissonance, being a postdecision phenomenon, concerns the consequences of making a choice. A decision in a free-choice situation implies that it will be

[7] Cognitive overlap as termed by Festinger [15] refers to "similarity" and "dissimilarity" aspects of two alternatives. High cognitive overlap implies more similarity and low cognitive overlap indicates that the two things are "qualitatively different."

followed by dissonance, since the choice was made from among alternatives. The alternatives can be viewed as possessing desirable (positive) and undesirable (negative) attributes. Each alternative is attractive by itself and each one, considered alone, has several attractive features which might lead to its selection. Thus, choosing one from several alternatives involves giving up the desirable features of the rejected alternatives and accepting the unattractive features of the chosen alternative. According to the theory, cognition of the negative attributes of the chosen alternative is dissonant with the cognition that the attractive features of the unchosen alternative(s) are given up by not choosing it. In such a situation, dissonance may be reduced by changing or revoking the decision. In many cases revoking a decision is not possible or involves heavy costs. Changing or reversing the decision simply transfers these features. The remaining avenue is to reevaluate the attractiveness of the alternatives.

The pioneering study in this area was conducted by Brehm [4]. In his study, subjects evaluated eight articles. Subsequently they were to choose between two of them and then rate each of the articles again. Thus, the attractiveness of the articles was measured both before and after the choice. This study clearly supported dissonance theory and found that, after the choice, the chosen alternative increased in attractiveness and the unchosen alternatives decreased in attractiveness—a greater spreading of the alternatives. Several other studies [5, 26] have found similar results.

The number of alternatives considered and cognitive overlap or similarity of alternatives are related to choice situations. As the number of alternatives among which to choose increases, there will be greater conflict before the decision and consequently the dissonance will be greater after choice making. If alternatives are more similar (qualitatively), the implication is that the individual is not giving up a whole lot in making his choice. Thus he should experience less dissonance after considering similar alternatives than dissimilar alternatives. Studies [5] indicate that (1) dissonance increases with the number of alternatives among which the individual has to make a choice and (2) dissonance increases as the dissimilarity between the alternatives increases. These studies generally employ the same methodology-paradigm as that of Brehm [4], namely, pre- and postevaluation of attractiveness and a choice situation.

Research in marketing confirms the occurrence of postchoice dissonance and attempts to reduce it by spreading the chosen and unchosen alternatives. Anderson [1] found pressure to reevaluate the chosen and unchosen alternatives. Such pressures increased as the number of alternatives being considered for the choice situation rose from two to four. Besides two- and four-alternative situations, his design involved conflict and preference conditions. With a minor exception, his results were in the predicted direction. The two conflict situations produced more significant dissonance arousal and reduction than the two preference situations.

LoSciuto and Perloff [25] found that their subjects, when given a choice between two similarly attractive record albums, experienced dissonance. The reduction attempt followed the expected pattern, that is, reranking the chosen album as more desirable than the unchosen, which was reranked as undesirable. An additional hypothesis of this study deals with continued attempts at dissonance reduction over time. For this purpose, their subjects reranked the alternatives again (after postdecision rating) after one week. After this interval, their subjects were still trying to reduce dissonance.

Holloway [19], in a study which included, besides the usual choice situation, several dissonance-producing factors, found a statistically significant change between pre- and postratings and the usual "spreading apart" effects. He also found partial support for a modified hypothesis for the cognitive overlap factor.

Sheth [34] showed that for the same set of alternatives, both his student subjects and adult housewives exhibited remarkable similarity in their postdecision dissonance-reduction behavior. This study also supported the dissonance theory derivation that a high-conflict choice situation creates greater dissonance than a low-conflict situation.

From the review presented here, it can safely be concluded that, both in the behavioral literature and in the marketing literature, one finds evidence for the postdecision dissonance phenomenon, and it is affected by the number of alternatives and the similarity-dissimilarity characteristics of the alternatives. One major consequence of dissonance has been observed to be not only the reevaluation of the chosen and unchosen alternatives but also the spreading apart effects, that is, the chosen alternative is valued more (increased in desirability and so on) and the unchosen alternative is valued less.

While the experimental studies of postdecision dissonance in social psychological literature were concerned only with this phenomenon, research studies in marketing have attempted to expand this approach to repeat purchasing behavior, such as brand loyalty. Mittelstaedt [29], in an interesting and ingenious extension of the dissonance derivation to the brand loyalty phenomenon, points out that the greater the postchoice dissonance after the first purchase, the greater will be the individual's attitude change. Therefore the greater will be the increase in the probability of his purchasing the same brand again. In addition, since dissonance should tend to increase with the number of unchosen alternatives, Mittelstaedt reasons that brand loyalty for all brands would increase as the number of brands increases. In his experiment, besides the usual choice situation, he introduced a second choice situation. As predicted by his hypothesis, subjects tended to repeat the choice made on the previous trial. His results suggest that, using the dissonance approach, it may be possible to predict decision situations that might lead to repeat purchases.

Cohen and Goldberg [9] point out that differential prior information about brands must be taken into account in predicting cognitive reevaluation of alternatives. An experimental study by Sheth [33] attempted to assess the impact of brand preference and past familiarity with the product in the arousal and reduction of dissonance in a choice situation. With an ingenious design, he was able to show not only that the usual reevaluation in terms of increasing the attractiveness of the chosen alternative and decreasing the attractiveness of the unchosen alternative takes place but also that prior brand preference affects the magnitude of dissonance. The hypothesis relevant to past familiarity was not supported.

Compliance and Attitude Change

Corollary to the postdecision situation is the insufficient justification for behavioral commitment and its consequences. This area of compliant behavior and attitude change has received considerable attention. In situations involving overt acts, seldom can the action be revoked. Dissonance theory under these circumstances would predict that the individual will tend to convince himself by accepting and favoring his act. Festinger [15] postulated that the best way to obtain private attitude change would be to offer just enough reward (or punishment) to elicit overt compliance. Several studies in this area have used insufficient reward or justification as inducement for compliant behavior. They have generally found that low inducement as opposed to high inducement produces greater dissonance for having engaged in the act, and the subjects tended to reduce dissonance by changing their attitude toward the act. The low inducements in these studies ranged from 5 cents to $1.

While these predictions of attitude change by dissonance theory have resulted in considerable controversy in the literature, the empirical evidence suggests interesting applications of this paradigm. Though there are interesting speculations in the marketing literature about attitude change following behavioral change, particularly with small inducements (such as samples, coupons, and so forth), there is virtually no empirical evidence at this time.

Selective Exposure to Information

Postdecisional information seeking, particularly to add a consonant cognition, has received much attention in the social psychology literature, since it is one manifestation of the pressure to reduce post decision dissonance. The theory postulates that the individual will tend to actively seek information which he knows will be favorable and will tend to avoid nonsupportive (dissonance producing) information.

The first study [11] to examine this phenomenon reasoned that recent purchasers of a new automobile should experience dissonance and that they would tend to read the advertisements about the car they had just bought and to avoid reading about cars they had considered but did not buy. The former prediction from dissonance theory was supported, but this study did not find avoidance of reading ads for other cars. In fact, they read as many ads about the cars they had considered as they read about other cars. As Festinger [17] admits, the results were equivocal.

At least three other studies [see 37] corroborate this evidence and fail to find any evidence of avoidance of nonsupportive information. One explanation advocated for such findings is that the alternatives that had been considered but rejected were more desirable than the ones not considered at all. Such explanations do not seem plausible. Virtually no experimental study (with the exception of one) has demonstrated avoidance of discrepant nonsupportive information. As Zajonc [37] pointed out, many of the experimental studies in this area suffer from the confounding of certain variables with the degree or level of dissonance.

In an experiment [6] to clarify this area further, usefulness of information was experimentally manipulated. Here, it was found that in general individuals prefer to read supportive information and that there was a preference for nonsupportive (negative) information if it was useful. Besides usefulness, two other factors are seen to be related to postdecision information seeking: amount of confidence of the individual and commitment.

Marketing literature in this area is sparse. Engel [12] attempted to replicate the advertising readership study, reported earlier, of the new owners of an automobile. This study was concerned with new owners of Chevrolets and their readership of specially placed Chevrolet ads subsequent to purchase of and exposure to four advertisements for automobiles, including the one for Chevrolet. While the study found that owners had exposed themselves to the dealer's Chevrolet ad (with price), the data taken as a whole did not support the dissonance prediction.

A more recent study [20] attempted to assess the effectiveness of posttransaction messages, sent (deliberately) from a retailer to recent purchasers, in reducing postdecision dissonance. In partial support of the hypothesis, the study found that the posttransaction letter helped to reduce dissonance. The information provided was not sought by the purchasers. Indeed, telephone information tended to increase dissonance.

Strictly speaking, this last study does not relate to selectivity hypotheses regarding information seeking that can be generated by the dissonance theory. But even in this broad area of supportive information, the findings are equivocal in the marketing literature, just as they are in social psychology.

Effort, Expectation, and Dissonance

One possibility for greater dissonance when the choice situation involves two close alternatives is suggested by Jones and Gerard [22] as involving greater effort. Extending this reasoning further, this can be seen as the other side of the coin of insufficient justification, discussed earlier. That is, if a person expends a good deal of effort to acquire something or join a group and so forth, any knowledge that the object is of less value (than expected) or that the group itself is not attractive will be dissonant with the expended effort. Thus the dissonance theory will suggest that the attractiveness of the goal object will be heightened by the effort expended [22, p. 223].

The classical study in this area deals with severity of initiation to join a discussion group. The results indicated that those subjects who experienced severe initiation showed greater attraction to a (banal) discussion than those who had had the "mild" initiation or than noninitiated groups. This effort-justification hypothesis has received additional experimental evidence.

A problem more similar to postdecision dissonance is that of disconfirmation of expectancy. "If an individual develops an expectancy about a given outcome only to discover that what he expects fails to materialize, he suffers a *disconfirmed* expectancy" [37, p. 378]. An expectancy that is disconfirmed, being an unpleasant experience according to dissonance theory, should produce dissonance. Of course, the greater the expectation that is disconfirmed, the greater should be the resulting dissonance.

Some experimental [37] evidence supports such hypotheses. In one experiment, for some subjects the expectancy was confirmed in a task involving subjects' performance and for others their expectancies were disconfirmed. In the latter group, considerably more changes in evaluations (task performance) were observed for the former group.

Some attempts to replicate the general findings in this area have been successful. However, Zajonc [37, pp. 380–381] concluded that the dissonance hypothesis in this area is probably true in its general form because "the reason why disconfirmed expectancy produces dissonance is that the cognition that the individual has prepared himself for a given event psychologically and perhaps otherwise, is in conflict with the cognition that the event has failed to materialize. Thus the more investment there is in initial preparation, the greater should be post decision dissonance."

In marketing literature, only a single study has so far been concerned with effort and expectation, and the hypotheses of this were based, in part, on the dissonance formulation. In this laboratory study by Cardozo [7], the purpose was to investigate the relationships between effort and expectation and the evaluation of a product in a simulated shopping situation. The results indicated that the expenditure of high effort produced a more favorable evaluation of the product than use of little effort. The results also indicated that (particularly negative) disconfirmation of (high) expectancy produced an unfavorable reaction toward the product under evaluation.

USES AND MISUSES IN MARKETING

It was stated earlier that the theory of cognitive dissonance has a wide range of application by its simple formulation. As a theory in social psychology, it has dealt with areas of human behavior.   Thus the usefulness of this theory in marketing relates to consumer behavior as an aspect of human behavior.

The theory of cognitive dissonance has stimulated considerable research in consumer behavior.   As is evident from the summaries in the last section, the major thrust of dissonance research in marketing concerns situations involving postdecision dissonance after a choice among products and the reduction of dissonance by spreading the alternatives.   These findings corroborate theoretical findings and have yielded insight into this phase of postpurchase behavior. However, studies investigating active seeking of consonant information are rather sparse.   Only one study investigated the provocative hypothesis that comes from dissonance in the area of effort and expectation.

In general, the research studies in consumer behavior have tried to research the postdecision area with the help of dissonance formulation.   The real usefulness of dissonance formulation can be seen in the repetitive decision areas, where the works of Mittelstaedt [29], Sheth [33], and Cohen [9] are already focusing on the issues of familiarity, brand loyalty, and dissonance reduction. This seems to be a fruitful avenue of research, for the implications these issues portend are enormous.

Misuse of dissonance formulations in marketing studies has arisen from lack of understanding of experimentation and the role of experimental evidence as well as overeagerness to specify practical applications and implications for marketers.   Writers admonish their readers by saying that relating behavioral science concepts such as dissonance to consumer behavior and making assumptions about their practical implications must be carefully done, as wholesale borrowing from the behavioral sciences cannot help our understanding.   Yet on the basis of findings or lack of them in a single study, wholesale practical implications or lack of them are suggested for marketers.   At best, findings in these studies are verifications of postdecision phenomena in consumer decision making and can be regarded as the beginnings of experimental evidence of testable propositions.   As Festinger observed, the perspective of basic research is 50 to 100 years, and it is as difficult as the original research to undertake "additional research to apply the basic contentless theory to some specific context" [16, p. 90].   Therefore, additional systematic research via experimental evidence is needed before implications for marketers can be specified.

Most researchers who have attempted to relate some aspect of cognitive dissonance to the consumer behavior area have conducted a single study, with no follow-up studies.   In the absence of systematic research in areas of applications,[8] dissonance research in the marketing literature does not support their assertion of practical implications and is in some cases absurd.[9]   Misuse of

[8] Only Holloway [19] and his group [1, 7, 19, 29] have studied different aspects of cognitive dissonance theory which are relevant to consumer behavior.   All these are experimental studies.   The single study researchers, with two exceptions, have only attempted to replicate.   These studies have not considered different aspects of the theory, nor did they involve a wide range of relevant variables.

[9] An illustration will perhaps make this point clear.   One major implication that has been pointed out is that specific advertising ought to be tailored for the recent purchaser.   The relevant questions are how would "dissonance-reducing" ads be different from the regular ads; and how would one reach this "dissonant" market segment selectively?   Part of the problem stems from a desire to spell out specific marketing implications, many of which seem premature and without sufficient empirical support.   Another problem relates to some studies which have failed to support the predictions based on dissonance theory.   Here it seems that such researchers may have experienced dissonance, and they seem to have reduced it by questioning the relevance (or some similar comments) of the theory for their practical realms!

research, then, comes from not realizing that dissonance theory and its applications are more relevant for understanding consumer behavior qua consumer than for aiding marketing management.

The second area of the theory's "misuse" stems from a lack of precisely understanding it. Some researchers in social psychology have misunderstood the theory and consequently view it as nothing but conflict theory. Similarly, some researchers in marketing are also confused about these two theories and complain that dissonance theory does not permit any formulations about the processes before the decision [32]. As Aronson [2] has clearly pointed out, dissonance theory is anything but conflict theory.

Another misunderstanding stems largely from some researchers' inability to distinguish between the forest (attitude theory) and the trees (dissonance theory). Consequently, they treat dissonance theory as if it were a theory of attitudes; which *it is not*. It relates to only a small domain of attitude, namely, attitude change.

Some misunderstanding of the theory has been due to lack of understanding that magnitude of dissonance is a hypothetical construct [38]. Some state they have measured it directly through some questionnaire [3, 20] and others point out the need for direct measurement of dissonance [13, 14]. If it is really and truly a hypothetical construct (or an intervening variable as some [8] have suggested), it is not *possible* to directly measure dissonance. If these studies had actually measured it (they have not), it would no longer be a hypothetical construct! If it is a motivational state, as Festinger's assumption would indicate, one can no more measure this drive directly than he can any other drive.

Dissonance as a construct is related to some specified independent and dependent conceptual variables and some not unambiguous rules of correspondence, which have permitted specific operations and manipulations in these experiments [38]. The added difficulty for researchers in the applied areas is that there are no rules linking the conceptual dependent variables to behavior.

A related criticism, which has also been applied to some of the experimental literature in psychology, is that some researchers have taken a cavalier approach to experimentation [37]. Such criticism equally applies to researchers in marketing [31].

POTENTIAL USEFULNESS IN MARKETING

As indicated earlier, the theory of cognitive dissonance, like any other behavioral concept, is useful for the study and understanding of consumer qua consumer. It is difficult to make precise theoretical predictions because of conceptual ambiguities still present and because the theory itself concerns psychological inconsistency. Therefore, it is difficult to specify precisely on an a priori basis under what conditions dissonance is likely to arise. As Aronson has observed, "Even a knowledge of the kinds of situations in which dissonance *can* occur is not always useful in determining whether dissonance *does* occur" [2, p. 9].

Moreover, the formulation of the theory itself concerns only two cognitions, which are seldom taken by themselves in most everyday situations confronted by consumers. Their prior experience, brand loyalty, social support, and other underlying cognitions that are relevant and which may tend to neutralize any dissonance arousal are all important and should be taken into consideration. The core of the theory has considerable empirical support; however, at the "fringes" the dissonance formulations have been ambiguous and the results equivocal. Under these circumstances, the situations we encounter in marketing have to be carefully analyzed, and ingenious designs and creative modifications of the dissonance predictions to suit our needs are of vital interest. Holloway's [19] hypothesis on cognitive overlap and his experimental design to ascertain interactions between several factors deemed to affect dissonance illustrate the types of modifications and extensions which may be necessary to apply the theory to "practical" problems.

A criticism leveled against this study is that it was a laboratory experiment; hence it is not "real" and not dealing with "real life" situations. Such criticisms evince lack of knowledge about laboratory methods. To get unequivocal findings in any area, including dissonance, controlled experimentation is essential. If our concern is to *understand* the consumer's cognitive processes, lack of realism in the experimental situation does not imply lack of relevance. The question then is one of internal validity, not its *range of validity* across all marketing situations.

This question of laboratory experimentation is also relevant for our suggestions of creative modifications, since much of the empirical support for dissonance theory has come from laboratory experiments in social psychology where alternate ways of effective dissonance reduction were blocked. Most of the experimental situations were such that subjects' prior experience and other factors did not materially affect the experimental outcome. Such cannot be the case for long if our interest is in "applied" areas. The multimodes of dissonance reduction should be of prime interest. What conditions give rise to dissonance are as important as what modes and combinations are used by consumers to reduce such dissonance in specified situations. Experimental research in actual settings can uncover some of these modes. A related problem that should be investigated is the duration during which dissonance persists in the individual and the time interval it takes to reduce dissonance.

Studies of dissonance in marketing should also be concerned with questions of inducement, disconfirmation of expectancy, effort and satisfaction, and the like. They have direct and clear implications for the behavior of consumers and the practical application areas—such as trials, samples, cents-off coupons, advertising claims, and the like. The use of a dissonance approach was suggested for a new classification of goods [23]. No empirical study has yet been attempted for this purpose, nor are there attempts to systematically investigate product categories and associated purchasing characteristics likely to be dissonance-producing.

It would appear that individual difference variables, such as personality, self-esteem, confidence, uncertainty, and factors affecting the level of tolerance of dissonance, should be of more interest to application-oriented researchers. Cannon [6] has found that self-confidence is related to dissonance reduction through selective exposure to new information. Dissonance formulations have generally assumed high self-concepts or other firm expectancies for the individuals [2].

The only marketing study which has investigated the relationships between self-confidence and persuasibility upon consumer's postdecision dissonance has found no association between the customer's persuasibility and this experience of dissonance [3]. However, when controlled for the self-confidence of the customers, the study found significant relations between persuasibility and dissonance. To conclude, these variables need our attention because our interest is in understanding behavior in the marketplace and some of these variables have been seen to be related to aspects of predecision behavior.

PREDECISION COGNITIVE PROCESS

The situations indicated in the last section for potential dissonance theory applications pose a peculiar problem. Since predecisional factors are very likely to be related to dissonance reduction in many situations involving consumer decision making, some understanding of the cognitive processes underlying the predecision phases is essential. Conflict theory may be highly relevant but, as McGuire [27] has observed, dissonance theorists seem a little ahead in this area. Since our interest is in the cognitive processes of the entire decision-making sequence—from evaluation of alternatives, ordering of preferences, decision, postdecisional feedback, effect of feedbacks on reevaluation of decision, of rejected alternatives, and finally of further behavior—the behavior sequence through these stages should be the focus. Since taking a more "general" look at dissonance theory may be more fruitful for marketing, some attention is paid to the cognitive phase of the predecision process.

The studies by Jecker [21] and Davidson and Kiesler [10] indicated that during the predecision phase, the individual is oriented toward impartial evaluation of the alternatives. Therefore, during this period, he is engaged in continual search for and evaluation of information. No biasing influence nor noticeable divergence of alternatives takes place during the predecision period. A related finding indicated that "the more a person has thought over the relevant details before dissonance is aroused, the more rapidly does dissonance reduction proceed after the dissonance has been introduced" [17, p. 153].

The point made by Festinger [17] is that only after a decision is there a decisive change in the psychological situation for the individual. He further points out that simply making a decision does not result in the onset of dissonance, but when a definite commitment is present, dissonance will occur and affect cognitions. In short, there is a difference between a statement of preference and a decision. "The world, in a sense, has been changed by the decision—consequences follow and commitment exists. Dissonance reduction can now be expected to occur" [17, p. 156].

ADVANTAGES AND SHORTCOMINGS

The theory of cognitive dissonance is a more general theoretical formulation, less restrictive, and flexible. The balance theory and the congruity principle are limited in their applications. The theory of cognitive dissonance extends the "cognitive consistency" notion to a multitude of diverse areas of behavior. It has generated impressive research in social psychology, provided intriguing hypotheses for many areas of application, and employed a variety of ingenious, imaginative, and engaging designs and experimental manipulations. New findings have led to incorporation of new components in the theoretical formulations. Replicated experimental findings have reduced other plausible explanations and reliability continues to be strengthened.

In particular, the dissonance formulations have revolutionized our thinking about attitude and behavior and about cognitions and behavior [38]. Attitude and attitude change are in the center of many marketing phenomena, and thus the usefulness of the theory for further research in marketing has never been in doubt. "If we accept the statement that the value of a theory resides both in the magnitude of testable reductions generated from it and the extent and diversity of the phenomena that it can explain, then, by these criteria, dissonance theory appears to be a good theory" [35, p. 208].

Many shortcomings relate to methodological problems [8] of experimental design, operationalization, manipulations, and measurements. Aronson [2] has so aptly pointed out that the methodological problems are not peculiar to this area of research, nor even to social psychology, and it is no fault of the theory. In fact, some of these methodological weaknesses have been unearthed because of the massive research generated by this theory.

Some shortcomings are obvious: (1) no two postdecisional situations have involved the same alternatives; (2) different attitude measures have been employed, and no standardized means has been used to induce subjects to make counter attitudinal statements; and (3) no standardized experimental manipulation procedure has been available [37].

In summary, dissonance theory has both advantages and shortcomings, the former outweighing the latter.

> The theory of cognitive dissonance is much more complicated than it was thought to be ten years ago. A good deal of research has been done since 1957. Many of the problems which were specified early have been solved; many new problems have been unearthed, some of which remain to be solved. Hopefully, future research will lead to the emergence of still new problems, which will lead to still more research, which will continue to yield an increased understanding of human behavior. I guess that is what science is all about. In their critique of five years of dissonance theory, Chapanis and Chapanis concluded with the pronouncement "not proven." Happily, after ten years, it is still not proven; all the theory ever does is generate research [2, pp. 26–27].

APPLICATIONS TO PRACTICAL PROBLEMS IN MARKETING

As pointed out in earlier sections, while further research is needed in many areas of marketing applications for cognitive dissonance theory, there are obvious applications of this theory to marketing operations. Since purchase of any product or service by consumers and industrial buyers generally involves choices among alternatives, the dissonance theory with all its ramifications for postdecisional behavior becomes relevant to postpurchase behavior. Specifically, the relation of the experiencing of dissonance to the number of alternatives considered, the attributes perceived by the decision makers to be relevant, and the distinct and different modes or avenues utilized to reduce the dissonance experienced are of vital interest to marketers. Such knowledge would aid in providing the types of postpurchase services, warranties, and the kinds of informational aids to be provided by the firm.

It was seen that from a dissonance standpoint brand loyalty can be viewed in the following way: choice of a brand—postchoice dissonance after first purchase—attitude change—increased probability of purchasing the same brand. It was also seen that prior brand preference affected the magnitude of dissonance experienced. These findings suggest direct applications for introduction of new brands, their acceptance by consumers, and the strategies to be followed by the firms.

The findings that disconfirmation of expectancy produced an unfavorable reaction toward the product has obvious implications for advertising claims.

Contrary to traditional findings with respect to rewards, dissonance formulations imply that small rewards or inducements, such as coupons, cents off, and the like, would be more effective than large inducements. A moot question to marketers is whether attitude change precedes or follows buying behavior. Dissonance theory findings reviewed earlier would imply that small inducements, such as samples and trials, may lead to attitude change after the consumer has used the sample.

While the theoretical findings do seem to have applications for some of the practical problems of a firm's marketing operations, the methodological contributions of research in cognitive dissonance to marketing research cannot be overlooked. Experimental manipulations in dissonance research have attempted to ingeniously separate the several phases of the decision process, such as the evaluation of alternatives in the predecision period and in the various postdecision phases. The sheer massiveness of research studies in the dissonance area has provided innumerable experimental situations which can be replicated with minor modifications and substitutions, reflecting real-life choice situations in the marketplace.

For example, the intricate and ingenious manipulations employed in the choice-making (experimental) situations in dissonance studies can be used, with minor modifications, to choices made among products, brands, and services in the marketplace. We could successfully use these situations in a number of field studies in marketing which, although maybe lacking in rigor and control, are likely to produce a wealth of information.

CONCLUSIONS

Cognitive dissonance as a major theoretical contribution has made an indelible impact in social psychology. Its theoretical formulations have found diverse areas of application, including marketing. Our review indicates sufficient evidence that dissonance formulations in marketing are applicable, and there are clear indications of great potential for applying this theory to major aspects of postdecision behavior in marketing. The shortcomings are not the faults of the theory but are methodological problems, which are intertwined with the state of the research technology.

The major contribution of dissonance theory to marketing is that it has treated man as a distinct phenomenon. Consumer behavior, which is a major aspect of human behavior, is an area where the theory's usefulness is apparent for gaining understanding and insights.

REFERENCES

1. Anderson, L. K., J. R. Taylor, and R. J. Holloway, "The Consumer and His Alternatives: An Experimental Approach," *Journal of Marketing Research*, vol. 3, February 1966.
2. Aronson, E., "Dissonance Theory: Progress and Problems," in Robert P. Abelson and others, eds., *Theories of Cognitive Consistency: A Sourcebook*, Chicago: Rand McNally, 1968.
3. Bell, G. D., "The Automobile Buyer after the Purchase," *Journal of Marketing*, vol. 31, July 1967.
4. Brehm, J. W., "Postdecision Changes in the Desirability of Alternatives," *Journal of Abnormal and Social Psychology*, vol. 52, May 1956.
5. ————, and A. R. Cohen, *Explorations in Cognitive Dissonance*, New York: Wiley, 1962.
6. Cannon, L. K., "Self-confidence and Selective Exposure to Information," in L. Festinger, ed., *Conflict, Decision and Dissonance*, Stanford: Stanford University Press, 1964.
7. Cardozo, R. N., "An Experimental Study of Consumer Effort, Expectation, and Satisfaction," *Journal of Marketing Research*, vol. 2, August 1965.
8. Chapanis, N., and A. Chapanis, "Cognitive Dissonance: Five Years Later," *Psychological Bulletin*, vol. 61, January 1964.
9. Cohen, J. B., and M. E. Goldberg, "Factors Relevant to the Adequacy of the Dissonance Model in Post-Decision Product Evaluation." (Mimeographed.)
10. Davidson, J. R., and S. B. Kiesler, "Cognitive Behavior Before and After Decision," in L. Festinger, ed., *Conflict, Decision and Dissonance*, Stanford: Stanford University Press, 1964.
11. Ehrlich, D., I. Guttman, P. Schonback, and J. Mills, "Post Decision Exposure to

Relevant Information," *Journal of Abnormal and Social Psychology,* vol. 54, January 1957.

12. Engel, J. F., "The Psychological Consequences of a Major Purchase Decision," in W. S. Decker, ed., *Marketing in Transition,* Chicago: American Marketing Association, 1963.

13. ———, and M. L. Light, "The Role of Psychological Commitment in Consumer Behavior: An Evaluation of the Theory of Cognitive Dissonance," in F. M. Bass, C. W. King, and E. A. Pessemier, eds., *Application of the Sciences in Marketing Management,* New York: Wiley, 1968.

14. ———, D. T. Kollat, and R. D. Blackwell, *Consumer Behavior,* New York: Holt, 1968.

15. Festinger, L., *A Theory of Cognitive Dissonance,* Stanford: Stanford University Press, 1957.

16. ———, "Some Theoretical Foundations for Advertising Research," in "Management Challenges and Research Responses," *Proceedings of the Sixth Annual Conference of the Advertising Research Foundation,* New York, 1960.

17. ———, *Conflict, Decision and Dissonance,* Stanford: Stanford University Press, 1964.

18. Heider, F., *The Psychology of Interpersonal Relations,* New York: Wiley, 1958.

19. Holloway, R. J., "An Experiment on Consumer Dissonance," *Journal of Marketing,* vol. 31, January 1967.

20. Hunt, S. D., "Post-transaction Communications and Dissonance Reduction," *Journal of Marketing,* vol. 34, July 1970.

21. Jecker, J. D., "The Cognitive Effects of Conflict and Dissonance," in L. Festinger, *Conflict, Decision and Dissonance,* Stanford: Stanford University Press, 1964.

22. Jones, E. E., and H. B. Gerard, *Foundations of Social Psychology,* New York: Wiley, 1967.

23. Kaish, S., "Cognitive Dissonance and the Classification of Consumer Goods," *Journal of Marketing,* vol. 31, October 1967.

24. Kassarjian, H. H., and Joel B. Cohen, "Cognitive Dissonance and Consumer Behavior," *California Management Review,* vol. 8, Fall 1965.

25. LoSciuto, L. A., and R. Perloff, "Influence of Product Preference on Dissonance Reduction," *Journal of Marketing Research,* vol. 4, August 1967.

26. Margulis, S. T., and E. Songer, "Cognitive Dissonance: A Bibliography of Its First Decade," *Psychological Reports,* vol. 24, June 1969.

27. McGuire, W. J., "The Current Status of Cognitive Consistency Theories," in Shel Feldman, ed., *Cognitive Consistency,* New York: Academic Press, 1966.

28. ———, "Attitudes and Opinions," *Annual Review of Psychology,* vol. 17, 1966.

29. Mittelstaedt, R., "A Dissonance Approach to Repeat Purchasing Behavior," *Journal of Marketing Research,* vol. 6, November 1969.

30. Osgood, C. E., and P. H. Tannenbaum, "The Principle of Congruity in the Prediction of Attitude Change," *Psychological Review,* vol. 62, January 1955.

31. Oshikawa, S., "The Theory of Cognitive Dissonance and Experimental Research," *Journal of Marketing Research,* vol. 5, November 1968.

32. ———, "Consumer Pre-Decision Conflict and Post-Decision Dissonance," *Behavioral Science,* vol. 15, March 1970.

33. Sheth, J. N., "Cognitive Dissonance, Brand Preference and Product Familiarity," in J. Arndt, ed., *Insights into Consumer Behavior,* Boston: Allyn and Bacon, 1968.

34. ———, "Are There Differences in Dissonance Reduction Behavior between Students and Housewives?" *Journal of Marketing Research,* vol. 7, May 1970.

35. Silverman, I., "In Defense of Dissonance Theory: Reply to Chapanis and Chapanis," *Psychological Bulletin,* vol. 62, September 1964.

36. Zajonc, R. B., "The Concepts of Balance, Congruity, and Dissonance," *Public Opinion Quarterly,* vol. 24, Summer 1960.

37. ———, "Cognitive Theories in Social Psychology," in G. Lindzey and E. Aronson, eds., *The Handbook of Social Psychology,* 2d ed., Reading, Mass.: Addison-Wesley, 1968, vol. 1.

38. Zimbardo, P., and E. B. Ebberson, *Influencing Attitudes and Changing Behavior,* Reading, Mass.: Addison-Wesley, 1969.

Theories

Chapter 2

Small-Group Theory

ALVIN J. SILK *Sloan School of Management, Massachusetts Institue of Technology, Cambridge, Massachusetts*

HARRY DAVIS *Graduate School of Business, University of Chicago, Chicago, Illinois*

This chapter is concerned with the application of behavioral science knowledge about small groups to the study of marketing phenomena.   Our purpose is twofold: first, to introduce the reader to small group theories and research by indicating what behavioral scientists working in this area have studied and how; and second, to illustrate how this knowledge can be used in marketing.

Accomplishing these two objectives poses a formidable problem.   A truly massive quantity of literature is available on small group processes.   In compiling his *Handbook of Small Group Research* over a decade ago, Hare [48] cited almost fourteen hundred references and estimated that articles were appearing at a rate of two hundred a year.   Groups are a pervasive element in marketing systems, and much in this vast storehouse of material is potentially relevant to understanding marketing behavior.

In order to examine in some depth both the promise and limitations associated with the use of small group concepts in marketing research and still confine the discussion to a manageable length, we have chosen to focus on two problem areas where small group research has been shown to have operational significance: family decision making, and personal selling.   Family purchasing decisions illustrate a problem area where virtually all small group concepts and measurement techniques can be applied.   The relationship between a salesman and customer, on the other hand, lends itself to study by a smaller number of concepts and techniques.   Other types of marketing behavior where small group processes are important include industrial or organizational purchasing and the diffusion of innovations, but these topics are covered in other chapters and hence are not considered in detail here.

SMALL GROUP THEORY

Groups are an important focus for study simply because an individual's behavior is influenced by other people. A person's preference for particular foods or certain fashions is influenced to a large extent by what others say is good or appropriate. The transportation needs of a family may require a man to forego the pleasure of a sports car for the practicality of a station wagon. A computer salesman supplies information to a prospect and in turn gets a contract.

While these examples are obvious descriptions of everyday behavior, not so obvious are the dynamics of social influence in specific situations. Social scientists have attempted to identify whether an individual's behavior is subject to social influence. In cases where it is, they have tried to identify which group(s) or individuals will exert influence, in what direction, and over what range of behavior. Generally, the social scientist's interest stops at this point; his objective is to define and explain the process of group influence. The marketing practitioner must take still another step and determine how best to use this knowledge.

A person can be influenced by several kinds of groups, only one of which will be discussed in this chapter.[1] At one extreme are groups that people belong to because they happen to be male or female, married or not married, young or old, high status or low status. Behavior is influenced in these societal groups because roles appropriate to each of these positions have been internalized. For example, husbands may pay the bills because of expectations about the male's competence in financial affairs; a teen-ager may develop particular tastes in music as a way of identifying with the youth culture. Nonmembership groups can also influence behavior if one wants to join—a good example being the activities of people who are upwardly mobile. In an attempt to gain entrance into a higher class, they will emulate the life-style of those who are already members, whether it involves changing political parties, driving a different make of car, or drinking wine rather than beer with dinner. The term *group* is also used in the sociological literature to refer to more formal associations, such as an orchestra or football team.

The focus of this chapter is on social influence within small face-to-face groups. While both societal and primary groups influence a person's behavior and determine how satisfied he will be with his achievements, the small group has at least two additional characteristics. First, group members interact with each other. Second, they have expectations or norms about what appropriate behavior and attitudes are. When these norms center around one individual and specify his rights and responsibilities, they define a role. Group norms along with the network of communication that link members together determine the nature of group influence over the individual.

In the following sections we will briefly discuss these three important aspects of small groups: (1) interpersonal influence, (2) norms, and (3) communication. It should be noted that this discussion is by no means a comprehensive review of small group theory. All research dealing with group productivity and member satisfaction has been excluded since it has little obvious relevance

---

[1] The word *group* is commonly used in a statistical sense, as, for example, when respondents are grouped together on various demographic characteristics. Since these groupings usually do not possess a "consciousness-of-kind" [11] and hence do not have any direct influence on the individual, they have been excluded from this discussion.

to marketing.[2] Also, small group literature is not without its share of competing (and often untested) theories as well as measures with unknown reliability and validity. For example, the strongly reactive nature of the laboratory and reliance on college students for subjects pose real problems in generalizing findings to marketing behavior. One must resist the temptation to overestimate the relevance of small group research to marketing problems and to underestimate the ease of translating and applying this research.

Interpersonal Influence. That groups exert influence on their members should not be a revelation to even the most casual observer of social life. Expressions of personal preferences are often modified as a result of group pressures to conform. An individual's level of aspiration is influenced by group standards or norms. Groups can influence individual decisions by providing information or by suggesting additional criteria. The real question, therefore, is not whether groups influence a person's values, attitudes, and behavior, but rather how this takes place. Why is it, for example, that individuals accept influence from others? How much influence? Over what range of decisions and activities or in what circumstances can influence be observed?

Social psychologists have found it useful to distinguish between "informational" and "normative" motives for accepting social influence [20]. In the former, members of a group influence each other in establishing a common frame of reference—a social counterpart to objective reality. Sherif's [84] classic study using the autokinetic effect illustrates how a group norm becomes a standard by which individuals judge subsequent events. The more unstructured a stimulus situation (as would be the case with art, fashion, or social customs), the more influence of the group in providing a frame of reference for the individual.

Normative social influence, on the other hand, is based upon an individual's desire to conform to the expectations of the group. A good example of this can be seen in Asch's [3] experiment in which a subject was asked to make judgments about the length of a line in the face of unanimous and erroneous judgments from other group members. The degree of conformity was found to be related to the clarity of the stimulus, whether or not the "opposition" was unanimous, the size of the group, and personality characteristics of the subject. Some of those who yielded to group pressures did so simply because they were unwilling to appear different from other group members. Unlike the case of informational influence, these subjects conformed to group pressure in full knowledge that their judgment was incorrect.

These two motives refer only to the person being influenced. It is also necessary to consider the related question of the group's ability to satisfy an individual's needs. French and Raven [42] have proposed a widely quoted typology which specifies several bases for social influence.

Reward power occurs when a person (P) believes that some person (O) or group will reward him for conformity. What constitutes a reward is varied and could include, for example, instrumental services such as advice or social acceptance. O's decision to give or withold rewards can influence P's behavior simply because rewards, as valued resources, are desired by others. In much the same way, *coercive power* can affect P's behavior, since punishments, as "negative rewards," are avoided by others. The amount of influence exerted is dependent on the number and magnitude of rewards and punishments controlled by O as well as P's assessment of the probability of being rewarded for

---

[2] Of course, such work is relevant to problems of marketing management involving organizational considerations. See [71].

conformity or punished for deviance. Necessary prerequisites for the exercise of reward and coercive power are (1) knowledge of what rewards and punishments are meaningful to P and (2) the opportunity for surveillance by O.

In the case of *referent power,* surveillance is unnecessary, since P accepts influence based upon his desire to identify with an attractive group or person. Unlike the situation with reward and coercive power in which interaction serves only as a means of gaining rewards or avoiding punishments, O's power is based on the "rewardingness" of the interaction itself.

Surveillance is also unnecessary in the exercise of *legitimate power.* People tend to share definitions about appropriate attitudes, behavior, or values for various societal and organizational roles—for example, men, women, husbands, wives, teachers, business executives, foremen, or army sergeants. These definitions are learned and internalized through socialization and are reinforced by a variety of social controls. Legitimate power is based on internalized values in which P legitimatizes O's right to influence P as well as P's obligation to accept this influence. A wife, for example, may accept her husband's decision regarding a new car because she considers it appropriate for men to make such decisions.

Whereas legitimate power rests upon role expectations that are external to the social relationship, *expert power* occurs when one group member has skills considered by others instrumental to their needs. These skills are a source of power since they give one the ability to control rewards and punishments. To rely upon a hi-fi "buff" prior to making such a purchase may make good sense if one is interested in obtaining a good buy. An individual's competence becomes manifest through direct observation of P's past success in dealing with tasks or as a result of expectations of competence about various classes of actors such as teachers, politicians, or women.

Closely related is *informational power.* This takes place when a person (O) or group supplies information to another person (P) that results in a change in attitudes or behavior. Any change is socially independent of O since he simply transmits information—as, for example, when a teacher gives the right answer to a mathematics problem or a politician introduces new information about a controversial issue. Power is based upon the content of the information communicated; the communicator is not directly relevant to any resulting change in attitudes or behavior.

Having these resources is a necessary but not sufficient determinant of social power. Only if a person is dependent upon a group's or person's resources for satisfying his needs will influence be exerted. Thus the possession of resources determines the range of *potential* influence over other group members, while the evaluation of these resources in terms of individual needs and group goals defines *actual* influence. How dependent a person becomes is a function of: (1) judgments whether the group is providing outcomes that are unavailable or better than those attainable elsewhere [71, 90] and (2) individual characteristics such as level of aspiration [53].

These comments regarding interpersonal influence have at least two important implications for marketing research. First, it is necessary to view the flow of influence as a two-way street—dependent both upon O's resources and P's needs. Discussions of personal selling and word-of-mouth advertising often ignore this fact. Many studies have looked for personality or demographic correlates of good salesmen and opinion leaders. The results to date have been largely inconclusive, possibly because little attention is paid to characteristics of those influenced or to the relationship between the influencer and the influencee.[3]   Only under the very unrealistic assumption that people subject to influence have needs of similar kind and magnitude would these "one-sided" studies of interpersonal influence be justified.   The same orientation also characterizes many studies of opinion leadership, as evidenced by measures which emphasize leader-initiated as opposed to follower-initiated influence [86].

A second implication of this discussion for marketing relates to the multiple bases of interpersonal influence.   People can influence others to buy or use a particular product for various reasons.   In one case someone might simply communicate information seen in an advertisement.   Someone else might exert influence because he considers himself (or is considered by others) to be an expert.   Still another person might be able to coerce someone into buying a new product.   Knowing whether influence takes place or not is not sufficient.   If marketers are to understand how word-of-mouth advertising works [2] or the range of an opinion leader's influence [75], these alternative bases of social power must be made explicit and measured.

Norms.   Groups develop shared expectations about what is appropriate behavior for members of that group.   These expectations or norms often refer to a single individual and thereby constitute his role in the group.   A family may agree it is appropriate for the wife to do the shopping, the husband to bargain for a lower price with an automobile salesman, and for the children to defer to their parents in deciding where to vacation.   A computer salesman may adopt a low-pressure approach because he believes this is what customers expect.   Or a purchasing agent may pay close attention to corporate policy regarding which decisions he can make without consulting others.

Second, norms relate to the kinds of behavior expected of all group members.   Bible salesmen, for example, usually develop standards about how many sales constitute a good day's performance.   Neighbors who entertain each other for dinner will tend to establish norms about how much drinking is appropriate and how elaborate the menu should be.

Norms also exist for attitudes.   Many of the seemingly personal attitudes that people hold about such things as the desirability of buying goods on credit, preferences for particular foods, or the reputation of certain retailers are formed and reinforced through group interaction.   Whatever the object of a group norm (the individual, group, or objects in the external world), members will be rewarded when they conform to these expectations and punished when they deviate.

In defining the kind of influence norms can have on an individual, it is useful to distinguish among several structural characteristics.[4]   The intensity of a norm, that is, the extent to which conforming or deviant behavior is rewarded or punished, is perhaps the most obvious of these characteristics.   Within any group there will be some kinds of behavior, typically in areas of vital concern to the group's interest, where feelings run very high.   A salesman who drinks on the job or a wife who greatly exceeds her monthly budget are both examples of behavior that is likely to be regulated.   On the other hand, when an individual's behavior is not or is only marginally relevant to the group's purpose, the intensity of norms will be low.   A child's respect for parental authority will usually be governed more by group expectations than will his preferences for breakfast cereal.

A second characteristic—crystallization—refers to the amount of agreement

---

[3] For an example of an exception to this statement, see [60].

[4] This discussion is based on a scheme developed by Jackson [55].

which exists among group members regarding a given area of behavior. Crystallization is high when members agree in their expectations and low when they disagree. Finally, the range of behavior regulated by norms differs among groups. We would expect norms within families not only to cover many areas of behavior but also to be high in both intensity and crystallization. Thus, a buying committee may have well-developed norms defining each member's responsibility in choosing suppliers but no expectations for members' behavior in other realms.

Much of the discussion and research on group norms has focused on two questions: (1) what function do norms serve for the group and the individual, and (2) what factors determine the extent to which an individual will conform to these norms?

On the first question, norms are instrumental to a group in achieving its goals. Uniformity of attitudes is often a prerequisite for group action. Certainly if a sales organization is to develop workable plans, the members must agree on the company's objectives and policies. A family is more likely to accomplish all the work associated with buying and furnishing a home if the husband and wife assume responsibility for certain decisions and tasks. These rules become the sources of pressure toward uniformity because they are viewed as helping the group reach its objectives. Group norms also serve to maintain the group. Attending conventions or sales meetings is often a requirement for membership in formal organizations. Accepted traditions such as Sunday dinner with the in-laws or the Thursday night poker game serve the same function in less formal groups.

The norms of primary groups, as reference groups, also have important consequences for the individual. In the first place, norms serve a comparison function; that is, they are standards against which one can judge his behavior and attitudes. Some reference point is necessary because of the absence of any empirical test for many social attitudes. How, for example, can one objectively determine whether preferences for double-breasted suits and Danish modern furniture are "right"? As Festinger, Schachter, and Back explain in their classic study of the Westgate housing project:

> There are not usually compelling facts which can unequivocally settle the question of which attitude is wrong and which is right in connection with social opinions and attitudes as there are in the case of what might be called "facts." ... The "reality" which settles the question in the case of social attitudes and opinions is the degree to which others with whom one is in communication are believed to share these same attitudes and opinions [40, pp. 168–169].

If people value a group, its norms are likely to provide meanings for the many objects or situations requiring a social reality. Norms also protect individuals from efforts of others to influence them, since groups provide strong social support for particular behaviors and attitudes. A person is more likely to withstand criticism for his "radical" ideas about fashion if he belongs to a group or lives in a community where the same clothes are worn by others.

A third function of group norms for the individual is an instrumental one when conformity is a prerequisite for joining or staying in a group that one finds attractive. Newcomb's study [78, pp. 420–430] of Bennington undergraduates showed that most well-accepted students tended to adopt liberal political attitudes even though many had conservative backgrounds. Conformity to norms in this case served less as a standard for individual judgments and more for receiving rewards from others.

A second topic for research has been the extent to which individuals conform to group norms. The Asch-type experiment, discussed earlier, has consistently shown that people sometimes conform to the opinions of others even when they realize they are going against their own perceptions [3]. Several factors seem to influence the degree to which an individual will conform, including such things as the composition of the group, aspects of the situation, and individual differences. At the risk of oversimplifying, let us briefly summarize what is known about each.

The nature of the group itself affects the strength of pressures on individuals to conform. As the size of the group increases, up to a point, so does the amount of conformity [3, 44]. A large majority having similar norms apparently offers a more convincing definition of reality to the individual than one or two people.[5] Closely related is the amount of agreement within the group, that is, the extent to which norms are crystallized. When unanimity is broken by one member, the pressure on another individual to conform is dramatically decreased. Another group characteristic related to conformity is the expertise and status of the members. The more someone feels that the majority knows a great deal about the topic under discussion or the more he views the majority as high in prestige, the more he will value their opinion and adopt it as his own.

Characteristics of the situation are also relevant to conformity. As already noted, groups will influence behavior in some areas but not in others. Rather than assuming that behavior is subject to group norms simply because one belongs to a group, it is, therefore, important to determine to what extent group influence is operating in specific situations.

Another factor is the extent to which a person must "go on record" as deviating from group norms. Not surprisingly, it has been shown that conformity is greater when a group member must publicly state his preferences or reveal his behavior [39]. If group members cannot find out how another member feels or acts, that member takes little or no risk in deviating from group norms. This behavior can be observed in a housewife's selection of brands. When the specific brand will not be visible to others (for example, instant coffee), reference group influence is weak. When the brand is socially conspicuous, as in the case of cigarettes or beer, reference group influence is high [12].

A final factor about the situation, and one of great significance to marketing, is the complexity or ambiguity of the object. Generally, the more difficult the judgment, the greater will be the influence of other group members on a person's "own" judgment. Since product evaluation is often ambiguous (for example, in fashion) or complex (for example, in buying a new car), consumers undoubtedly rely upon informational social influence.

Characteristics of the group and the situation seem to have the same effect across individuals. A third determination of conformity is found within the individual. Although research on this variable is sparse and inconsistent, a few generalizations have emerged. Women conform more than men [92], presumably because of differences in culturally defined roles. Intelligence and self-confidence vary inversely with the amount of conformity [22]. Both imply certain task-related skills that an individual brings to a group—skills that are often useful in achieving group objectives or reducing uncertainty.

Communication. The factors discussed up to this point have been rather

---

[5] Continuing to add group members to the majority rapidly reaches a point of diminishing returns once more than a few group members have unanimously stated a position. In fact, larger groups are more likely to have subgroups, with the possibility of norm conflict and less conformity to the larger group.

static. Only to the extent that people communicate or interact with each other will interpersonal influence take place.

If one observes a group from the outside, a particular *form* of communication is apparent. Some people talk a great deal; others say very little. In addition, certain channels or networks are used more extensively than others. Leaders, for example, generally say more and communicate more freely than other group members. If one listens to the *content* of what is said, he will discover that it also differs among the members.[6] Much of what is said in a problem-solving group is task-oriented; that is, communication is instrumental to "getting the job done." Another type of communication, however, is directed toward the solution of social-emotional problems that arise during task behavior. It is of great interest that regularities in the form and content of communication can be observed across a wide range of groups—including those that are large or small, composed of strangers or friends, or involved in solving a wide variety of problems. Each of these two dimensions of communication is discussed separately.

Perhaps the most visible component of form is a group's communication network. The purchase of an automobile, for example, may involve considerable discussion between husband and wife and limited communication with the children. The more experienced members of a buying committee are likely to direct and receive more communication than other committee members, while opinion leaders typically have access to more people than do their followers.

Several factors, including some of those just discussed, can influence a group's communication network. If some person has particular resources (for example, competence or social contacts) that are useful to the group in satisfying its goals, he will likely assume a more central position in that structure. Doctors in a drug study [21] who were centrally located in their ties to local doctors were more committed to the profession as measured by visits to out-of-town medical meetings, readership of professional journals, and knowledge of medical developments in other communities.

The content of specific roles often includes certain "rights" about who can talk to whom, as in a formal organization where the vice president typically has access to more people within the organization than the director of marketing research. Communication networks have also been shown to depend upon additional factors such as the size of the group, the relation of members in physical space, and the amount of time available for completing a task [49].

The type of communication network has a major impact on the way in which a group functions. Studies have consistently shown that the more central a person is within a group's network—that is, the more access he has to all others in the group—the greater his satisfaction [6, 62]. The efficiency with which tasks are performed is also associated with the communication structure, although the specific relationship seems to depend on such things as the kind of task to be performed and members' prior experience with solving problems as well as the location and quality of information available. A person who controls communication within a group tends to become the leader. Finally, a number of studies [19, 64] have demonstrated that the more freedom members have to talk, the more effective are attempts to change individual attitudes or group norms.

Describing a group's communication network only tells us who speaks to whom. A second dimension of the form of communication is amount—both in terms of the total amount and its distribution among group members. The latter has a rather direct relationship to influence, since the most active member in

---

[6] The distinction between form and content was first set forth by Hare [48].

terms of communication generally becomes the group leader. Active participation is dependent to a large extent on one's location within a group, but it is also true that a person can increase his influence simply by talking more [7]. While the relative rates of communication are indicative of a person's influence within a group, the total amount of communication is a good measure of a group's influence over its members. Cohesive groups, those composed of people who like to be together, have higher rates of interaction. This provides more opportunities to influence members' attitudes and behavior and increases the pressure on individual members to conform to group norms.

As noted earlier, information about the form of communication—network and rate—will not suffice to explain the nature of group interaction. Analysis of the content of that communication must also be undertaken.

Just as group members differ in the amount of talking they do, so they differ in what they talk about. The purchase of life insurance, for example, may find a husband deeply involved with the salesman in negotiating the most coverage for the least money. At the same time, his wife may interject comments designed, perhaps unconsciously, to reduce some of the tension generated by this exchange. Several participants at a regional sales meeting may spend most of their time informing the others about company sales patterns, competition, or the reaction of consumers to a new product; others may focus on formulating plans for the next sales period; and still others will try to deal with the tensions and conflicts that arise during the meeting.

The task of analyzing what is said within a group is obviously more difficult than simply recording who talks to whom and for how long. Fortunately, a number of category systems have been devised by social psychologists that enable an observer to describe a complex communication in terms of a relatively small number of categories. In the most widely used of these, the Bales Interaction Analysis [4], each communication act (usually a sentence) is placed by Bales into one of 12 categories: shows solidarity or antagonism; tension or tension release; agreement or disagreement; and gives or asks for information, opinions, or suggestions. For example, consider the following interchange:

> Consumer A: I think I will buy a used station wagon (gives opinion).
> Consumer B: You're silly to do that (shows antagonism).
> Consumer A: Why (asks for information)?
> Consumer B: Because my cousin bought one that was a lemon (gives information).
> Consumer C: But the one I bought for my wife has been very dependable (shows disagreement).
> Consumer A: Well then, how should I go about finding a good one (asks for suggestion)?

Six of the Bales categories constitute social-emotional behavior—the three positive reactions of agreement, solidarity, and tension release along with the negative reactions of disagreement, antagonism, and tension. The remaining six categories describe task behavior—giving and asking for information, opinions, and suggestions.

Analyses of small group interaction have demonstrated a marked difference in what is said by the two most active members. One person engages primarily in communication designed to move the group toward its goal. He gives many suggestions and opinions as well as communicating negative reactions toward other group members ("let's get going," "that's irrelevant," or "you're being unrealistic"). The other active member tries to keep the group running smoothly. He asks questions frequently and makes supportive statements such as "that's a good idea," "you did a good job," or "it's fun to work together."

The latter role is generally referred to as that of the socioemotional leader and the former as that of the task leader.

When groups begin to interact with no prior differentiation of roles, which members will eventually assume these two leadership roles is likely to depend upon certain personality traits, the possession of relevant problem-solving skills, or both. In other groups, leadership behavior may be built into culturally defined roles, as in the family where husbands tend to be more task-oriented than wives and wives more emotionally oriented than husbands.

Our discussion up to this point has considered only the verbal component of communication. Indeed, the Bales Interaction Analysis is designed specifically to score overt behavior and to ignore other nonverbal messages that are exchanged between members. Yet it is clear that nonverbal communication cannot be overlooked if one is to understand how influence works. A housewife, for example, may be more influenced by seeing a new chair in a neighbor's living room than by any verbal effort of that neighbor to influence her. Certainly many a wife has learned more about her husband's attitude toward buying new carpeting from his facial expression or from what he did *not* say than from what he did say. Salesmen rely heavily on the nonverbal feedback from prospects to alter their sales presentation.

While these more subtle aspects of communication pose serious measurement problems relative to those involving verbal interaction, efforts need to be made to collect such data. In marketing applications where the primary interest centers on ongoing groups (for example, the family, neighborhood or kinship groups, and organizations) rather than on one-time laboratory groups, the importance of nonverbal communication is likely to be great. To the extent that a group has been interacting over a period of time, roles and norms tend to become well-defined, thereby requiring less verbal communication to achieve the group's objectives and maintain satisfaction among the members. When communication does take place, nonverbal messages will often suffice.

Having discussed those individual and group characteristics that help to explain interpersonal influence, we will now examine their application in two problem areas of interest to marketers—family decision making and personal selling.

THE FAMILY AS A SMALL GROUP

References to the family in the study of consumer behavior are infrequent. This apparent disregard for the family is surprising, since the fundamental unit for the study of demand is often a family unit as opposed to an individual. Major items of consumer spending such as food, shelter, and transportation are often jointly "consumed." Even preferences for products individually consumed are likely to be influenced by feedback from other family members. What limited discussions and data are found suggest two very different orientations.

On the one hand are economic studies that view the family as a consumption unit.[7] Research in this tradition has considered such questions as what percent of disposable income will be spent; what percent of spendable income will be allocated to various disbursement categories such as clothing, food, or shelter; and how income and demographic characteristics affect expenditure patterns between families.

---

[7] For a comprehensive review article on household spending behavior, see Ferber [37].

There are virtually no ties between this research and small group theory since the "family" in this literature displays none of the characteristics of a small group described earlier. In the first place, the research is largely concerned with family consumption in aggregate terms. As Ferber notes, many economists purposely avoid investigating the consumption function for individual families because "the importance of erratic factors is so great for individual households as to obscure more basic relationships" [37, p. 20]. Whether relationships uncovered for groups of households are equally appropriate to the individual family unit is questionable, and it is, furthermore, likely that predictions about consumption within individual families requre an understanding of these so-called "erratic" factors.

Second, the way in which income is typically measured (that is, total family or household disposable income) involves some seemingly unrealistic assumptions about family behavior. For example, it assumes that the family spends its incomes as a family unit—an assumption requiring either a dictator or unanimous committee. The measurement of family income also overlooks the impact of number and sources.

In the main, economists would not predict any differences in consumption behavior between families in which either the husband or wife was sole provider and those in which both spouses contributed equally as long as total family income was the same. The family in this literature thus bears a striking resemblance to the economist's model of an individual consumer.

A second orientation, and one having a much closer tie to the small group literature, is to view the family as a decision-making unit. Some of these studies have described the allocation of decision-making responsibility between husband and wife; others have examined the division of labor between family members [70, 83, 96]. Given the commercial nature of much of this research, these studies have tended to concentrate on decision making about particular product categories—automobiles, appliances, liquor, and supermarket purchases. Marketing strategies require information about the relative participation of men versus women in various purchase decisions as a basis for selecting advertising media and appeals.

Whether because of this commercial orientation or the frequent disregard for explicit theory which characterizes much research in marketing, these studies as a whole contribute little to our understanding of the family as a small group. As in the case of economics literature discussed earlier, researchers seem to retain their long-held preoccupation with individual rather than group behavior.

For example, the Fawcett study [70] found that husbands decide about what make of automobile to buy in 61 percent of the families. Hsuband and wife were found to make this decision together in another 38 percent, while the wife decided in the remaining 1 percent of the families. The following conclusion is drawn: "The husband, as the family 'authority' on mechanical matters, decides upon the make of the new family car" [p. 59]. But notice that this conclusion as a directive for advertising could be very misleading if husband-wife influence is related to income, geographic location, life cycle, or other social or demographic characteristics. One could conceive of the extreme case in which a firm's (or brand's) market segment was composed entirely of couples who made this decision jointly. To appeal only to husbands in this case would clearly be ill-advised.

Researchers have made few attempts to employ concepts central to small group theory, and what illustrations can be found often reveal extreme oversimplifications. As a case in point, generalizations about the roles of wife, husband, and children are often made without regard to the specific decisions and activities being investigated or to such family characteristics as the life cycle or social class. Discussions based upon these absolute views of family roles have yielded a number of apparent contradictions, especially whether the husband's (or wife's) influence is increasing or decreasing. One marketing text describes the growing *involvement of women* in family decisions [8]. These authors ascribe the wife's increasing influence to her gainful employment outside the home and related advancements in political and social status. According to the authors, the implications of this change are clear:

> Today, marketing executives think of the housewife as the family producing agent.... It is generally recognized that women exert a profound influence in the purchase of much merchandise even though the actual buying may be done by men. Merchandise must appeal to women, publicity must be adapted to their motivation, and the place of sale must be adjusted to their needs, whims and fancies [8, pp. 66–67].

Other marketing textbooks, however, describe a seemingly opposite trend— the *growing involvement of men* in family decisions. For example, Phillips and Duncan [80] observe that a rising percentage of purchases are now made by the husband alone or by the husband and wife jointly. The reasons include weekend and evening shopping hours at many retail outlets and the increasing use in the home of mechanical products whose purchase requires the mechanical expertise of the male.

> Although the figures still emphasize the importance of women as buyers, they also indicate that many retailers must appeal to both men and women. Neither the manufacturer nor the middleman can overlook the implications found in the growing importance of men as buyers . . . [80, p. 68].

The implication for marketing strategies is directly opposite to that reached by the previous authors.

Although a few marketing researchers have studied the family as a small group, a few developments in recent years deserve discussion. One area concerns the study of husband and wife roles in consumer decision making, another the study of product-related communication within families.

Marital Roles in Consumer Behavior. In the previous section on small group theory we defined roles as expectations or norms that center around a position within the group. The study of the family lends itself particularly well to role analysis, given the regularities often associated with the roles of husband, wife, and children. In contrast to the somewhat more fluid role definitions characteristic of other social groups, family roles (including prescriptions about task responsibility, power, and attitudes) are learned during childhood socialization and reinforced over time by a variety of societal controls.

Sociologists frequently employ two "ideal" types as a means of classifying families along a continuum from "tradition-bound" to "companionship." Those holding a traditional definition of marital roles are characterized by large authority differences between husband and wife (as well as between parents and children) and a highly differentiated division of labor. A sharp distinction is made between concepts of masculinity and femininity. A democratic or companionship definition of roles, on the other hand, prescribes a high degree of joint participation in tasks and decisions.

In a traditional ideology, the distribution of authority within the family is built into the roles themselves and one gains power by ascription rather than achievement. The husband's influence in major family decisions is based upon members' acceptance of culturally defined norms (that is, legitimate power) rather than upon any particular decision-making resources controlled by the husband. When a couple holds companionship norms, on the other hand, the personal resources of family members become an important base for social influence. A husband may help his wife prepare dinner each night because he likes to cook and spend time with her. His wife may learn how to play golf so that they can spend more of their leisure time together. In both examples, companionship norms reinforce these behaviors by legitimating the right of each spouse to do whatever he or she wishes in the pursuit of "togetherness."

If families within a culture conform to either of these two ideologies, predictions can easily be made about which spouse has various task- and decision-making responsibilities. In the first place, roles would be differentiated along a small number of dimensions. Assuming a unidimensional structure, families could then be classified simply as "patriarchal" or "companionship." Or, a researcher might assume two power hierarchies by making a distinction between "instrumental" and "expressive" roles [79] or between "policy" and "routine" decisions [35].

In either case predictions about roles in consumer decisions would be straightforward. Under a traditional ideology, for example, we would expect husband dominance in important decisions such as the choice of housing, the purchase of automobiles, life insurance, or major appliances as well as in decisions about the family's financial management. Brand decisions about most household products, being "routine," are properly delegated to the wife as homemaker. Conformity to either ideology also implies a small variance in marital roles across families. That is, decisions made by a husband in one family would be much the same as those made by other husbands. Information about the role (rather than about the person who occupies it) is sufficient to predict "who decides."

Unfortunately for ease of prediction, the few studies that have investigated the dimensionality of marital roles and the uniformity of these roles across families suggest a more complex structure than that implicit in either "ideal" type. Davis [28] studied the relative influence of husbands and wives in 12 automobile and furniture purchase decisions. Using a clustering technique to group decisions together in terms of their similarities on relative influence, two bases for role differentiation were apparent. The first was the product itself—decision roles in the purchase of an automobile were not related to decision roles in the purchase of furniture. Simply stated, knowing the roles played by a husband and wife in buying a car provides little or no information about who makes furniture purchase decisions in the same family.

The study also showed that roles were differentiated on the basis of the type of decision. Within each product category, relative influence in "product-selection" decisions (what model, make and color to buy) was unrelated to relative influence in "allocation" or "scheduling" decisions (how much to spend and when to buy the car). Although this research needs to be replicated using a larger and more representative sample and with extension to other product categories, the evidence suggests that family authority roles in consumer decisions are more differentiated than the undimensional or bidimensional structures hypothesized by many sociologists.

Another study [29] casts doubt on the uniformity of husband-wife roles when considered across families for the same purchase. A sample of 211 French-speaking, Catholic families living in and around the city of Quebec, Canada, provided information about the relative influence of husband and wife in seven automobile purchase decisions—when and where to purchase the car, how much money to spend, and what make, model, color, and accessories to buy.

Although one might have anticipated husband dominance in all (or certainly most) of these decisions given the traditional culture of the area studied, the data showed considerable variability between the "husband decided" and the "we both decided" categories. Families fell about evenly into these two categories for several of the decisions. None of the decisions could be satisfactorily described as husband-dominated or joint. Even for the most highly skewed decision (that is, what color of automobile to buy), such a statement would be incorrect for over 20 percent of the couples.

Interestingly, analysis of the factors accounting for differences in relative influence among families showed situational rather than person- or family-related characteristics to be most important. Wives had more influence in buying the family car when they had a driver's license, drove the car as much as their husbands, shopped for the car with their husbands, and perceived themselves as being competent to make such decisions. Of the many family-related characteristics described by sociologists [27], only three were found to be significant predictors of relative influence—socioeconomic status, family size, and the family's orientation to the wife's relatives.

This finding illustrates the limitations of behavioral science concepts when applied to marketing research. Real-world applications require the marketing researcher to employ whatever factors (family or situational) account for differences in decision-making influence for specific products. The sociologist, given his use of questions about purchasing decisions only as a proxy measure of authority, has not developed an adequate framework to explain how the requirements of tasks or decisions influence roles. Small group research is therefore just a starting point for those interested in predicting influence for specific products.

A pilot study by Jaffe and Senft [56] is one of the few attempts to apply sociological theory to the explication of husband-wife roles in purchasing decisions. Jaffe and Senft hypothesize that household consumption requires several roles at different points in time. Throughout the decision process, someone must gather information via people and the media. One person plays the role of the initiator—suggesting the need for a new product purchase. Several roles are evident at the purchase phase: (1) suggester of brand requirements within a product class (for example, type or style), (2) suggester of brand, (3) the budgeter—the one who specifies an acceptable price level, (4) the shopper, and (5) the purchaser.

At the consumption phase someone may convert the product into usable form; someone else may actually consume the product and evaluate the extent to which it satisfies the needs. Finally, someone serves as process validator—evaluating what was either right or wrong about the decision process and suggesting whether it should be changed the next time. Jaffe and Senft document the variability of husband-wife roles at different stages in the consumption process by analyzing in-depth purchase histories for several convenience foods, household items, and appliances.

Although this framework has received little attention by marketers, it does have at least two important implications for the study of family purchase decisions. In the first place, the study demonstrates that roles are remarkably multidimensional even for routine purchasing decisions. In the case of coffee, for example, the percentage of husbands who actually purchased coffee (29 percent) was considerably less than the percentage who initiated the purchase or who suggested a particular brand (41 percent). In the same way, a relatively small percentage (16 percent) of husbands initiated the purchase of pet food, yet 40 percent of the husbands suggested what brand of pet food to buy.

Thus it seems to make little sense to talk about how much influence the husband has in a product category; the correct reference is his influence in particular subdecisions leading to the purchase.

Second, each family purchase is viewed as a complex series of activities (including search behavior, evaluation, decision making, and consumption) taking place over time. Viewing purchase decisions as part of the larger problem of consumption management avoids the now common practice of oversimplifying how decisions are made. Consider, for example, a number of families who report that the "wife decided" about what new piece of furniture to buy. In some of these families the wife decides because the husband is not interested. Decisions regarding the home may have been delegated to the wife. Another group of these families discuss furniture prior to the time that the wife decides what piece to buy. Still another group disagree about what furniture to buy. If wives "win," they have (in a sense) made the decision.

All these examples yield the same results in terms of a straightforward question about who made the decision. Yet it is clear that the authority relationship and the resulting implication for marketing communication differ between the three. The framework proposed by Jaffe and Senft is responsive to these subtleties in decision processes.

A quite different application of data about marital roles is seen in the lifestyle research of Wells and Tigert [94]. Wanting to find out more about product or brand users than is provided by the usual demographic profile, they assembled a large number of questions on activities, attitudes, interests, values, needs, and opinions. A number of these relate to actual role performance within the family—"I spend a lot of time with the children talking about their activities, friends, and problems," or "I take care of the money and pay the bills." Other questions measure the extent to which the respondent (usually the housewife) agrees with traditional or companionship definitions of marital roles—"A woman's place is in the home," "The father should be the boss in the house," or "Men should not do the dishes." Such information is of value to marketers (particularly copywriters) since it describes the consumer in ways that suggest specific advertising appeals.

Communication within the Family. Knowing the roles that people occupy in a family tells us more about the potential for social influence than it does about what actually takes place. As our earlier discussion of communication suggested, the particular form and content of what is said are crucial for understanding how decisions are made. Available research on this topic is very sparse. What few studies are relevant focus on one of the following three questions: (1) To what extent are brand preferences known and similar within families? (2) To what extent are specific product requests made by husbands or wives? and (3) What is the nature of communication during joint purchasing decisions?

Representative of studies directed toward the first of these questions is Coulson's [24] pilot research on wives' awareness of the brand preferences of other family members. Awareness was found to vary a great deal by product class. Housewives were more aware of family preferences when the brand name was clearly visible in use (for example, beer, cigarettes, deodorant, candy bars, chewing gum, and cold cereals), less aware when the brand was not visible (for example, canned peas and spaghetti), and even less aware when there was a substantial change in the product prior to use (for example, cake mix or margarine).

Related to the same question are two studies by Nowland and Company for *Life* magazine [33, 34]. Questionnaires were administered separately to husbands and wives to ascertain their brand preferences for 15 food items. A pantry check was then made to determine which brands had actually been purchased and were in the home at the time of the interview. When husbands and wives agreed about their preferred brand, it was in the kitchen an average of 86 percent of the time. When couples disagreed, the brand preferred by the wife was in the kitchen on the average of only 53 percent of the time. In addition, the nonconsensus families were twice as likely to purchase store and special-price labels.

Unfortunately, these studies tell us very little about the nature of product-related communication within families since the measures of both awareness and consensus do not require any information about whether husbands and wives discussed brands or when these discussions took place. In the case of the two Nowland studies, for example, it is possible that husbands' responses to questions about brand preferences are actually measures of brand awareness under the following kinds of logic: (1) "I know what brands my wife buys since I see them on the table and in the cupboards" or (2) "I have seen ads for instant coffee on T.V. and it's a good thing to have preferences when filling out questionnaires." To the extent that these reasons operate, it makes little sense to match husbands' and wives' responses. Consensus could imply discussion, no discussion, real preferences, or no preferences!

A study of 936 housewives conducted for the National Opinion Polls Limited [76] illustrates research addressed to the question about specific product or brand requests. Data were obtained from wives about whether their husbands asked them to buy specific brands, and if so, whether these requests were honored. The percentage of husbands who asked their wives to buy particular brands ranged from a low of 8 percent in the case of desserts to a high of 18 to 20 percent in the case of cheese, pickles, cereals, meat, toothpaste, and biscuits. The study showed that over half the housewives did in fact buy what their husbands requested.

A much higher estimate of the husband's influence in the purchase of many of these same packaged goods is reported in a study by Learner Marketing Research and Development for *Life* magazine [30]. Data about the frequency, recency, and importance of the husband's brand comments for specific products were obtained from both spouses in 1,005 families. Among users, the percentage of wives who reported that their husband's brand comments were very important to them in making brand decisions ranged from 26 percent for peanut butter to 98 percent for dog food. Other products for which a majority of wives considered their husbands' comments important included soft drinks, headache remedies, cereal, beer, and shampoo. Husbands consistently rated lower the importance of their own brand comments (ranging from 6 to 25 percentage points).[8]

Studies investigating the nature of family communication during purchasing decisions are virtually nonexistent. Kenkel [59] has made use of the Bales Interaction Analysis to study marital and family roles in simulated problem-solving sessions—typically involving the allocation of money received by the family as a gift. He argues that the kind of information obtained from inter-

---

[8] It is possible that question bias accounts for some of the discrepancy between the Learner and N.O.P. studies. For example, what woman who considers herself to be a good wife would want to admit that her husband's brand comments are not important to her? In the same way, husbands who view themselves as being responsible for important decisions (either real or imagined) may not admit that they are concerned with the choice of such "mundane" things as brands of peanut butter and shampoo.

action studies (for example, who suggests ideas, has information about alternatives, and leads the discussion) would be more useful to advertisers than knowing only who made the decision or the actual purchase.

Another discussion of family interaction is contained in a paper by Sheth [85]. He argues that when disagreements arise during joint buying decisions due to differences in evaluative beliefs or buying motives, couples can use several means of resolving conflict. Perhaps the most common is problem solving in which differences of opinion about the details of a purchase (for example, what color or model of automobile to select) lead one or more family members to search for additional information. Sometimes conflict can be resolved by persuasion—the attempt to convince someone of the inconsistencies in his reasoning. Sheth uses the example of families trying to dissuade a husband from buying a new car at a time when the family is already heavily in debt.

Bargaining represents a third means of conflict resolution. Employing notions of distributive justice or equity, a husband may be "allowed" to go on a fishing trip with the boys in return for letting his wife buy a new dress. Sheth describes politics as a final strategy whereby coalitions are formed (for example, the wife and children against the husband) to force one member to conform. Systematic research to study these four alternative strategies in the context of family purchasing decisions has yet to be undertaken.

Discussion. There is little doubt that a better understanding of family purchasing decisions would be helpful to marketing practitioners. Media could be selected more efficiently if buyers had a better idea of which household members to reach with that message. This information could guide the creation and testing of copy. And the validity of attitude surveys and product tests depends on whether the right respondent has been studied. As a way of dealing with some of these issues, we suggested small group theory and research. Unfortunately, an examination of the marketing literature shows that few such applications have been made. Family roles are often viewed in overly simplistic terms in the face of contrary evidence showing a good deal of differentiation by type of decision and activity. There has been very little attention given to the interrelationship between roles and decision processes.

Further developments in the study of family decision behavior can benefit from small group theory and research in at least four important ways.

1. Purchase influence within the family should be viewed in a larger framework than role theory. Empirical research has shown that the roles of husband and wife are variable across families and that predictions based on cultural stereotypes about these roles are likely to be inaccurate for any given purchase situation. Legitimate power, to use the French and Raven [42] terminology, is at best a partial determinant of decision-making influence. Other bases of social power frequently studied in the laboratory—competence, information, attraction, the ability to reward or punish—need to be incorporated.

2. Small group research has shown that relevant aspects of the situation have a major impact on the influence exerted by group members. In terms of family purchasing decisions, this means that careful attention must be paid to characteristics of the product and of the situation surrounding its purchase. We would hypothesize, for example, that joint purchase decisions are positively related to such product characteristics as economic and social importance, risk, use by several family members, and visibility during consumption. Factors surrounding the purchase, such as who does the shopping or the amount of time pressure, are also likely to influence decision making.

3. Small group researchers frequently use behavioral measures to assess interpersonal influence—who talks the most, gives suggestions, or engages in

socioemotional activities. In contrast, much of the existing research on purchasing influence makes the implicit assumption that people can accurately report "who decides." But this assumption overlooks the often invisible nature of social influence. Even if a wife, for example, wanted to tell someone how she chose a new brand of T.V. dinner, she would probably find it difficult. One way around the problem is to lean more heavily on behavioral measures as additional indicators of influence. Information about who within the family shopped, was exposed to media advertising, or talked with the neighbors exemplifies such measures. Such questions have two major advantages. Respondents can more readily and accurately answer questions about "who did something" than they can about "who decided to buy something." In addition, behavioral measures serve as a criterion in deciding which measures of purchase influence are performing well—that is, are predictive.

4. Finally, the laboratory experiment, which characterizes much small group research, should be used more extensively. We described earlier how little is known about the process of decision making within families, the emphasis having been on group structure rather than interaction. Laboratory experiments using real families may offer a relatively cheap way of obtaining the kind of data necessary for understanding how family purchase decisions are made.

PERSONAL SELLING

Selling as Interpersonal Interaction

A criticism sometimes made of behavioral science research is that after cutting through the specialized lingo and complex methodology, one finds, in barely recognizable form, little more than an affirmation of what was already "obvious" to everyone—mere "truisms, platitudes, and tautologies."[9]

The observation that the most fundamental aspect of personal selling is the "interaction" between a prospect and a salesman may well appear as yet another example of befuddling the commonplace with fancy verbiage. While it may seem self-evident that selling involves interaction, such a description implies a somewhat different view of the selling process than that generally stressed in the vast literature of this field. More important, empirical studies of personal selling as interaction have begun to appear which offer some fresh insights of practical significance into thorny issues of long standing.

The Customer-Salesman Dyad. The person primarily responsible for stimulating current interest in salesman-prospect interaction is Franklin B. Evans. Examining a sampling of the abundant and diverse writings of practitioners on the subject of selling, Evans points out that "invariably these deal with only the salesman's point of view" [31, p. 76]. The customer is certainly not ignored in these conventional writings, but the emphasis is, understandably, on how to sell, and the typical discussion places the customer, at least implicitly, in a somewhat passive role. In prescribing such things as the personal characteristics required of the "successful" salesman, means of diagnosing and adapting to customers' needs, persuasive techniques, and so on, salesmanship authorities naturally focus on how the salesman's behavior affects the outcome of a sales contact. As a consequence, analysis of the influence of the prospect on the process tends to be neglected.

A similar imbalance characterizes most past empirical research on personal

[9] See, for example, Henry [52]. For an opposing view on this issue, see Lazarsfeld [61].

selling, which is also voluminous. As Miner has observed, "There is little question but what the salesman is one of the most extensively studied men in the business world" [74, p. 6]. The focus of attention has been on the prediction of some measure of salesman performance from information about his background and a variety of personality, interest, and ability factors measured by psychological testing instruments.[10]

The results of these attempts to discover criteria useful for recruiting and selecting salesmen have been mixed—sizable correlations have been reported for certain sales occupations while in numerous other studies, few of which are published, no meaningful relationships have been found [88].

Even for its limited purpose of aiding in making personnel decisions, the value of this work remains highly controversial and, as noted by others [74], it has contributed very little to our *understanding* of why or how a salesman becomes effective. In attempting to predict sales performance, this research has concentrated almost entirely on the characteristics of salesmen and has failed to take explicit account of who the salesman interacts with in attempting to make a sale.[11]

The assumption tacitly made is that differences among salesmen with respect to the types of prospects they contact are minimal and that hence variations in performance must be due to differences among the salesmen themselves. As we shall discuss shortly, such an assumption seems tenuous for many if not for most types of selling.

In contrast, Evans argues that the unit of analysis in personal selling research should not be the salesman alone but rather the interaction dyad—the salesman-prospect pair involved in a sales encounter.

> ... the sale (or no sale) is the result of the particular interaction situation, the face-to-face contact of the given salesman and his prospect. The result of the contact depends not on the characteristics of either party alone but how the two parties view and react to each other [32, p. 25].

Interpersonal Attraction. Given such an orientation, what can behavioral science suggest about the nature of a prospect-salesman interaction and the chance of a sale being made? One source of relevant ideas is research on "interpersonal attraction" [10]. The general question motivating work by social psychologists and sociologists in this area is this: Why is a person attracted by certain individuals and repelled by others?

Considerable evidence suggests that the answer lies in how "similar" the two individuals are. It has been repeatedly demonstrated in a long list of both experimental and correlational studies of such phenomena as friendship formation, mate selection, and survey interviewing that a strong positive relationship exists between interpersonal similarity and liking [12]. Various dimensions of similarity have been investigated, including background characteristics, attitudes, interest, values, and personality. That similarity leads to liking can be derived from several theoretical propositions such as those involving models of

---

[10] For a recent review of some of this work, see [23].

[11] One method for evaluating salesmen reported to be highly successful many years ago was a mechanical device (the "interaction chronograph") which recorded the time pattern of responses of a subject as he interacted with an observer in a standardized interview. Measurements obtained in this fashion were found to correlate highly with sales of department store and industrial sales personnel [17, 18]. Interestingly, the interaction chronograph was viewed as a method for measuring personality characteristics.

cognitive consistency [51, 77], and social exchange [53, 90], but most emphasize the notion that interacting with others who are similar to oneself or agree with oneself provides rewards or need satisfaction.[12]

Salesman-Customer Similarity.   Drawing upon these ideas, Evans hypothesized that "the more similar the parties in the dyad are, the more likely a favorable outcome, a sale" [31, p. 78].

Evans tested this hypothesis on life insurance selling.[13]   The latter was chosen because it represented an area where the salesman (rather than the product offering and/or other promotion) appeared to be the critical factor in whether a sale is made.   A group of 86 experienced male agents were selected from three insurance firms.   From records of all the face-to-face contacts they made during a 4-week period, a random sample of 168 sold and 183 unsold prospects was chosen.   Personal interviews were conducted with the sample on the average of 11 weeks after the date of the salesman's visit.   Care was taken to minimize the chance of respondents' making a connection between the sales call and the interview.

Sold and unsold prospects responded to a questionnaire which covered the following classes of variables: attitudes and knowledge of life insurance and life insurance salesmen in general; attitudes and perceptions of the "last" insurance agent who had called on them; management of personal finances; demographic, background, and physical characteristics; and personality needs.   Essentially the same instruments were administered to the salesmen except that the agents rated themselves on scales similar to those prospects had used to describe the salesmen who had contacted them.

In general, the results supported the similarity hypothesis: the insurance agents were found to be more alike to the sold than to the unsold prospects. Evans demonstrated that whether a prospect would buy insurance from a particular agent could *not* be predicted in any straightforward manner solely on the basis of knowledge of the prospect's attitudinal, personality, and demographic characteristics.   As groups, the sold and unsold prospects were essentially similar in all individual respects.   However, when the three groups were compared to one another, the salesmen appeared to be more like the sold prospects than the unsolds.

To illustrate, the difference in mean ages between the salesmen and sold prospects was 1.2 years while that for the salesmen and unsold prospects was 2.5 years.   The same pattern of results manifested itself when similar comparisons were made over a wide range of variables ranging from background and physical characteristics through personality needs.   Furthermore, "objective" measures of the variables indicated not only that the salesmen were more similar to the sold than the unsold prospects but also that the sold prospects tended to *perceive* the salesmen as more like themselves than the unsolds did.

The basic notion underlying Evans' research was that the more a prospect likes a salesman, the greater the chance that the latter will be able to influence the former.   These notions indicated that the probability of a sale occurring was related to salesman-prospect similarity.   In addition, Evans also investigated the intervening variable, liking.   As expected, sold prospects evaluated the salesmen more favorably than did the unsolds.

---

[12] Extensive reviews of various aspects of this literature are available.   See [13, 15, 66; 68, especially pp. 496–509; 72, especially pp. 621–637].

[13] Only a brief preliminary account of this work has appeared in the literature [31]. An extensive report of the study's details and results are found in a lengthy monograph not yet published [32].   We have relied on the latter source.

The successful salesman is seen by sold prospects as (1) an expert in insurance, (2) similar to themselves in outlook and situation, (3) as a person they'd like to know better, and (4) interested in them personally, not just as a source of revenue [32, p. xii].

The sold and unsold prospects held a common negative stereotype of the "typical" insurance salesman as aggressive, fast-talking and untrustworthy. However, the two groups did not share the same view of the particular agents who had contacted them. Compared to the unsolds, the ratings of the particular salesmen by sold prospects were more positive and closer to the salesmen's own evaluations of themselves. This would suggest that salesman-prospect similarity facilitated the development of a friendly, relaxed interaction.

Inasmuch as Evans' study is basically a correlational one utilizing data obtained *after* the salesman-prospect contact had taken place, whether the sold prospects' greater liking of the salesmen preceded or followed the sale cannot be determined. Clearly, the similarity-attraction hypothesis would suggest that liking was the antecedent condition and the occurrence of the sale the consequence. On the other hand, for a variety of reasons one would expect prospects to evaluate a salesman from whom they had bought an insurance policy more positively than one from whom they had declined to buy. For example, individuals tend to like persons who have influenced them [68, p. 276].

A related question about causal priorities might also be raised concerning the relationship Evans observed between *perceived* prospect-salesman similarity and the occurrence of a sale. Although it has been frequently demonstrated experimentally that similarity leads to interpersonal liking, there is also a large body of evidence that persons tend to perceive others whom they like as similar to themselves [68, pp. 290ff]. Thus an association between perceived similarity and attraction could reflect causation in either direction. However, Evans found that not only did the sold prospects *perceive* the salesmen to be more similar to themselves than the unsolds but in fact they actually were more similar when compared with respect to such "objective" enduring attributes as physical and personality characteristics, which would remain unchanged before and after the sales transaction.

If one accepts the basic notion that salesman-prospect similarity affects the likelihood of a sale, the practical question that comes to mind is this: With respect to what attributes is similarity critical? Two additional studies have been reported which support Evans's views and are relevant to this question.

Another study of life insurance selling, by Gadel [43], suggests that age may be a key factor. An analysis of some 22,000 policies revealed that agents' sales tended to be concentrated among persons in the same age group as themselves. This concentration was greatest for young agents and tended to decrease with years of experience.

If salesman-prospect similarity affects sales success, salesmen are likely to develop an awareness of this condition. To the extent that insurance agents have some latitude in choosing prospects, one would expect them to seek out prospects similar to themselves. Clearly, their ability to do so is limited by what they can ascertain about a prospect *before* making a sales contact. Given the ways agents learn about prospects initially, it is probably easier to obtain a rough indication of the prospect's age and use that as a screening criterion rather than attempt to assess other personal characteristics. Of course, agents may well use more than one criterion.

A different aspect of customer-salesman similarity was investigated by Tosi [91] in a study of middleman selling. Here attention was focused on the extent to which customer and salesman share the same conception of the salesman's role. A group of 40 wholesale drug salesmen and 103 retail pharmacists whom the former contacted regularly were asked to indicate their perceptions of the "ideal" and "actual" behavior of salesmen on a set of predetermined scales. Difference between the salesman's and customer's responses on the "ideal" scales were taken as a measure of "role consensus"—the extent to which the salesman and customer agreed as to what the salesman's behavior *should* be. Discrepancies between the ideal and actual ratings by either the salesman or the customer were used as indicators of "expectation level"—the degree to which the salesman's actual behavior was perceived to differ from that which was considered desirable.

Tosi hypothesized that both role consensus and expectation level would be related to sales performance, the latter measured by (1) the share of a given customer's business placed with the salesman's firm and (2) the number of *other* suppliers also serving the customer. Contrary to the first hypothesis, no statistically significant relationship was found between role consensus and either measure of sales success. However, the buyers' expectations *were* related to the number of suppliers they purchased from but not to the share of business the salesmen obtained.[14] That is, the less the discrepancy between a buyer's conception of the "ideal" behavior of a salesman and his perception of how the particular salesman conducted himself, the fewer other suppliers the customer tended to deal with. Thus it appeared that agreement between the customer and salesman as to how the salesman *ought* to behave did not have any bearing upon the latter's effectiveness, but the closer the salesman came to meeting the customer's expectation regarding how he should function, the fewer were the number of his competitors.

Selling Strategies. The studies of Evans, Gadel, and Tosi just described dealt primarily with the relationship between salesman-prospect similarity and sales performance. All three were correlational investigations based on data obtained after sales contacts had been made. As such, they were not well suited to uncovering much about exactly what transpired between the salesman and prospect. The interpersonal attraction theory referred to here would suggest that salesman-prospect similarity is conducive to an amicable exchange between the two parties, thereby making it more likely that the salesman influences the prospect to buy.

Willett and Pennington [95] made a detailed study of customer-salesman interactions occurring in retail stores in connection with the purchase of certain appliances. The interactions were tape-recorded in a seemingly unobtrusive way and content-analyzed using the Bales Interaction Analysis [4]. Comparisons were drawn between "successful" and "unsuccessful" transactions involving 132 customers and 14 salesmen. The interactions that resulted in immediate purchases appeared to be characterized by more suggestion-seeking and giving and fewer displays of negative feelings than those interactions that did not culminate in a purchase. Although salesman-customer similarity was not examined, these data provide evidence that interactions preceding a sale tend to be friendlier, more free-flowing exchanges than those which do not produce a purchase.

From a managerial standpoint, the important question about sales interactions is how the salesman's behavior affects the outcome. What can the salesman do to shape the course along which an interaction proceeds? Are certain

---

[14] The salesmen's expectation level was also significantly related to the number of suppliers, but in a nonlinear manner.

selling strategies and techniques more effective than others? Consider the following problem: In selling paint to customers, who will be more successful—the salesman who appears to be more knowledgeable about using paint or one whom customers perceive as having about the same amount of experience (or lack thereof) as themselves?

At first glance, most would probably opt for the prediction favoring the salesman who appeared more knowledgeable than his customers. Besides its common-sense appeal, this proposition finds support in numerous experimental studies of communications source credibility which have demonstrated that the effectiveness of a given message in changing attitudes varies according to the expertise attributed to the source of the message [54, Chapter 2].

However, application of the salesman-customer similarity hypothesis, discussed earlier, to this situation leads to just the opposite prediction! The amount of experience a salesman claims to have had with the product could affect the customer's perception of their similarity. For the typical consumer who is only an occasional painter, the more painting the salesman indicates he personally has done, the less similar he will appear to the novice buyer and hence the less influence the salesman will have with the buyer.

The efficacy of these two competing factors, salesman expertise and customer-salesman similarity, was investigated in a field experiment by Brock [14]. Over a five-month period two part-time salesmen in the paint department of a retail store attempted to influence customers to purchase paint at a different price level than that which they initially selected. After a consumer indicated that he wished to buy a given amount of some variety of paint at a particular price, the salesman tried to alter his choice by delivering one of two predetermined appeals. Half the time the salesmen represented themselves as being similar to customers by emphasizing that the magnitude of their own recent paint consumption was the same as the amount being purchased by the customer. For the other half of the cases the dissimilar or "expert" condition was applied by having the salesmen portray themselves as having just used 20 times the quantity of paint the consumer planned to buy. Attempts were made to influence some customers to buy at higher prices and others at lower prices than they originally intended.

The results indicated that similarity was more important than expertise. While the dissimilar salesman was presumably perceived as more knowledgeable about the paint, he was less effective than the salesman who identified his own paint consumption as being similar to that of his customers. The differential effectiveness of the two approaches held for attempts to persuade consumers to buy higher- as well as lower-priced paints.

Central to the view of selling as interpersonal interaction is the proposition that the more a prospect likes a salesman, the greater the influence that the salesman will have on the prospect. This would imply that an ingratiating tone should be an effective selling tactic. Farley and Swinth [36] performed an experiment bearing on this matter, in their case to compare the impact of two different sales messages for a roll-up yardstick. One message, dubbed the "product pitch," emphasized a description and demonstration of the product's features. The other, a "personal pitch," featured a favorable personal discussion of the customer's role and stressed how the product was compatible with it.

A group of 87 females served as subjects—about a third were undergraduates and the remainder were housewives. After hearing one of the presentations, subjects chose between the product and an equivalent sum of money (75 cents) and then rated the product and the salesman on a number of scales.

The percentage choosing the yardstick over the money was slightly greater for the group hearing the personal than the product pitch. However, the difference was not statistically significant.

Paradoxically, subjects exposed to the product pitch evaluated both the product and the salesman more positively than those receiving the personal pitch. Regardless of which sales presentation they heard, those selecting the product had more favorable attitudes toward the product and the salesman than those who chose the money.

Here again, the design of the study did not permit the direction of causal relations between attitudes and choice to be untangled. As Farley and Swinth note, the results suggest that an effective sales appeal alters the buyer's perception of the attractiveness of the product and the salesman. Hence, *both* considerations require attention in designing sales messages.

Implications.   Applying the core idea of interpersonal attraction to selling suggests that the greater the similarity between a salesman and a prospect, the more the prospect will like the salesman and, therefore, the greater the salesman's influence. While the number of investigations available is limited and various methodological questions can be raised about them, significant relationships between several aspects of customer-salesman similarity and buying have been reported with considerable regularity. Much remains to be learned about why and under what conditions this relationship occurs. For example, it would be useful to consider how not only similarity but also complementarity between salesmen and customers is related to sales success. While the old adage that "birds of a feather flock together" seems plausible enough, is there not also something to that other often repeated maxim about "opposites attracting"?

In pursuing such questions the available behavioral literature should prove useful as a source of ideas for conditional propositions which can be tested so as to refine our knowledge about where a certain relationship does or does not hold. A theory of interpersonal *congruency* has been proposed which suggests that under certain circumstances attraction will be facilitated by dissimilarities as well as similarities [72, pp. 629–631].

Research has scarcely begun on the question of how and to what extent the salesman can influence and/or control the direction a sales interaction takes. Nonetheless, Brock's provocative experiment dealing with customer-salesman similarity with respect to product experience is indicative of how a nonobvious relationship involving an important control variable suggested by the similarity-attraction hypothesis can be studied in a natural sales setting.

An intriguing question raised by Brock's study is this: In what types of selling situations will it be more effective to stress salesman-customer differences rather than similarities with respect to product expertise? Here again, the behavioral literature can offer some relevant insights. Recently a review has appeared which attempts to integrate research on interpersonal similarity and attraction with that bearing on source credibility and attitude change [87].

Having discussed research on sales interactions, it is appropriate to consider practical implications. This work is relevant to several aspects of sales force management.

1. *Sales Force Recruitment, Selection and Manpower Planning.* Evans has pointed out that the notion that the outcome of a sales contact depends on customer-prospect similarity casts doubt on the usefulness of much practice in salesman recruitment and selection aimed at identifying a successful "sales type" [32]. If a firm's potential customers are appreciably more heterogeneous than its sales force, it may be effectively excluding itself from penetrating cer-

tain market segments. Gadel [43] has described how simple models of the size and composition of a sales force can be structured for manpower planning purposes to assure that the sales force will be matched to the markets they serve with respect to key characteristics.

2. *Sales Training.* Training for salesmen should focus on helping them develop the special skills they require to be effective in interacting with prospects [93]. For example, familiarity with existing knowledge about how we develop perceptions of others might enable salesmen to discriminate better among prospects. That there is much room for improvement in this area is suggested by data reported by Granbois and Willett [46]. They found that salesmen failed to perceive as ready to buy 69 percent of appliance shoppers who had previously indicated that they had definite purchasing plans. Salesmen might be taught more reliable procedures for identifying the prospect status of shoppers.

3. *Allocating Salesmen to Customers.* Evans has made a number of suggestions as to how a closer match between the characteristics of salesmen and prospects might be effected in the life insurance field. For example, a salesman who uncovers a prospect unlike himself could turn over the lead to another salesman who is more similar to the prospect and would have a better chance of making the sale. The notion that salesmen should be "compatible" with the customers they serve is certainly not new [88], but knowledge of what dimensions of similarity and differences are critical in particular types of selling might lead to improved matchings.

The research reviewed here was primarily concerned with customer-salesman interaction and sales performance. We next consider some work in which selling is viewed as a *process* of influence and an attempt is made to apply behavioral knowledge about this phenomenon to problems of personal selling.

Selling as Interpersonal Influence

Influencing others via verbal communications is the salesman's basic stock in trade. At the same time, the study of communication and persuasion has long represented one of the major areas of interest to social psychologists.[15] In light of this, one might expect to find that the large body of behavioral science theory and research on this subject would have found considerable use in dealing with problems of personal selling. While general discussions of "selling as communication" are readily available [93] and so-called "principles of persuasion" are sometimes presented in sales training programs [1], the diligent reader of the marketing literature would be hard pressed to find any extensive list of systematic applications of such knowledge to issues of real concern to practitioners in the field of personal selling.

Rather than belaboring the reasons for this state of affairs, we prefer to accentuate the positive. Fortunately, some examples of the productive utilization of behavioral science research on influence processes are available. Examination of some of this work illustrates what behavioral scientists have to say about persuasion and how these ideas can be brought to bear on selling problems.

Using Group Pressure to Overcome Buyer Resistance. The most sophisticated and creative application of behavioral research on influence processes to personal selling that has come to our attention is a program developed by Jacoba

---

[15] A number of short, highly readable accounts of this research are available. See [9, 57, 97]. Undoubtedly, the best and most complete review of the field is McGuire [73].

Varela, a consultant in Uruguay.[16]   The selling problem tackled was that faced by an upholstery firm in marketing fabrics to retailers.   The firm's sales objectives conflicted with the established buying habits of both consumers and retailers.   The product being promoted was ready-made curtains.   Traditionally, however, Uruguayan housewives had their curtains custom made.   The firm's efforts to sell retailers in the fall also ran contrary to the latter's customary practice of selecting new fabrics only in the spring.   Furthermore, economic conditions were extremely adverse.   Severe inflation had led to stringent government policies to curb consumer spending.

To deal with this difficult set of circumstances, Varela designed an elaborate and extensive selling program based on concepts and propositions borrowed from social psychological research on influence.   A few aspects of this work can be described here.

One phase of Varela's program made use of the results of Asch's classic experiments on group pressure and conformity referred to earlier [3].   Such an experiment would surely seem to be a prime candidate for the "interesting but irrelevant" category as far as suggesting anything applicable to personal selling.   The subjects (college undergraduates), setting (artificial and highly controlled), and task (judging line length) bear little resemblance to selling curtains.   Yet the sales situation was skillfully manipulated so that it essentially became a simulation of Asch's laboratory setting.   Rather than have the company's salesmen sell the retailers in their stores, prospective buyers were invited to the company's offices.

Buyers came in small groups.   In the firm's own showroom, various facilities could be used which enabled the product line to be presented far more effectively than would have been possible in the retailers' stores.   As an item was being presented, the salesman made an assessment of how favorably impressed each of the prospective buyers was with the product.   The salesmen had been trained to scan buyers' facial expressions and look for other cues that might reflect evaluations of the product.   The buyer appearing most favorable was then asked for his opinion of the product and encouraged to explain why his reaction was positive.   By this process the buyer was led to commit himself gradually and finally asked to place an order.

In the meantime, the salesmen had been on the alert, watching how other buyers were reacting.   The buyer identified as being next most positive was asked to express his views and the whole process was repeated.   Thus the salesmen proceeded from the most to the least positive buyer and thereby took advantage of the opportunity of bringing to bear on those initially unfavorable the pressure of their peers with more positive attitudes.   In line with Asch's experimental results, a large percentage of resistant buyers are reported to have been successfully converted by this approach.

What has just been described represents only one phase of a much larger problem developed by Varela which involved the ingenious use of numerous facets of social psychological knowledge about influence.   For example, attention was given to the nontrivial persuasive task of convincing the retailer to come to the firm's showroom in the first place.   To reduce opposition, an approach referred to as the "foot-in-the-door technique" was used.

Freedman and Fraser [41] demonstrated in two field experiments that once a person has carried out a small request, he is more likely to comply with a larger one.   Hence, before inviting the retailers to the showroom, Varela had the

[16] This discussion is based on descriptions of Varela's work given in [38; 97, pp. 114–122].

salesmen ask the retailers to display a small sign in their stores. If they agreed to this small favor, when the salesman returned a week later he asked them to come to the showroom. Having once made a small commitment to the salesman, the retailers were more likely to take the next, larger step on the path leading to a sale that had been carefully laid by Varela.

The last phase of the selling strategy was aimed at developing long-run loyalty. Techniques suggested by research on "immunizing" persons against counterpersuasion [73, pp. 258–265] were employed in an effort to reduce the retailers' susceptibility to the promotion of competitors. From all indications, the total campaign developed by Varela was highly successful. Large sales increases were realized despite unfavorable economic conditions.

The Influence of Company Reputation on Salesman Effectiveness. An example of a somewhat different use of research on communication and influence processes may be found in Levitt's experimental study of the role of company reputation in industrial selling [63]. The basic issue was whether evaluations of a new product by those involved in the purchase decision process of industrial organizations are influenced by their general attitudes toward the producing firm. Industrial marketers have long debated the value of expenditures on such activities as media campaigns undertaken to build a favorable corporate image. One rationale sometimes put forth in support of such programs is that they make buyers more receptive to the firm's salesmen. Implementing the elaborate kind of experimental design needed to measure such an effect would be extremely difficult in an industrial market—especially in the absence of a model of the process that would determine what effects to look for.

Levitt developed a framework for analyzing this problem using concepts suggested by communications research on the influence of source credibility on communications effectiveness [5]. He then carried out a laboratory experiment which enabled him to achieve the degree of control required to study the problem.

As noted in the earlier discussion of salesman-customer similarity, the same message tends to produce more attitude change when it is ascribed to a source of high rather than low credibility. Competence and trustworthiness are the components of credibility that have been manipulated in these studies [73, pp. 182–187]. Levitt suggests that the effectiveness of an industrial salesman will be influenced by the general opinion buyers hold of the firm he represents (its reputation), much in the same way that source credibility affects the impact of an impersonal communication. In the parlance of communications research, the salesman is the communicator, the presentation he delivers is the message, and the firm for whom he sells is the source.

A second factor considered by Levitt was the quality of the salesman's presentation. He was interested, for example, in whether a high-quality sales presentation by a salesman from a lesser-known firm could be as effective as a lesser-quality sales promotion made by a salesman from a better-known firm.

The final factor examined was the recipient of the sales effort. Levitt reasoned that persons in various management roles who became involved in the purchase decision process (purchasing agents and technical personnel) would evaluate a new product from different frames of reference and hence might be differentially affected by a given message from a given source. Thus the overall impact of the salesman was hypothesized to be dependent upon the source he represents (company reputation), the quality of his sales presentation, and the type of audience he deals with (technical versus purchasing personnel).

The experimental test involved exposing subjects to one of four versions of a 10-minute filmed sales presentation for a fictitious but plausible new product (a paint ingredient). In one version the salesman gave a careful, professional ("good") presentation while in the other the same salesman delivered a less polished ("poor") presentation. Company reputation was manipulated by varying the name of the firm which the salesman was identified as representing.

A group of 113 practicing purchasing agents and 130 engineers and scientists participated in the experiment. Immediately after viewing the film and again five weeks later, subjects filled out a questionnaire which asked, among other things, (1) whether they would recommend the product be given further consideration in their organizations and (2) whether they would favor adoption of the product.

The expected effects of company reputation and quality of the sales presentation were observed with regard to the willingness of both the purchasing agents and the technical personnel to recommend the product to others. However, for the riskier choice of whether to adopt the product, the pattern of results was more complex. The intriguing finding that emerged was that company reputation influenced the propensity of technical personnel to adopt the product but *not* that of the purchasing agents.

The principal implication would seem to be that a seller's reputation makes a difference to a salesman in getting a favorable first hearing for a new product with both purchasing and technical personnel; but when it comes to making an actual purchase decision, the advantage of a good reputation only obtains with technical personnel.

Discussion. These examples illustrate two ways in which behavioral research on influence processes can be useful in dealing with selling problems. Levitt's study represents the kind of application which results in a better understanding of a previously ill-structured problem. The findings bearing on the differential responsiveness of the purchasing and technical personnel are examples of the kind of suggestive new insights which such efforts may produce.

In Varela's work, we saw an application of a different order. There behavioral concepts were used to develop specific, operational selling procedures that apparently worked. This type of immediate and direct application rarely occurs. In assessing the applicability of behavioral science research findings to practical problems, a question frequently asked is whether the results produced in the comfort and control of a psychological laboratory can be extrapolated to the complexity of the real world. Perhaps the lesson worth remembering from Varela's work is that we should also consider what opportunities there may be to arrange our real-world problem situation so that it begins to resemble the laboratory setting where our knowledge is more certain.

CONCLUSIONS

In the beginning of this chapter, we attempted to convey what the term *small group* means to behavioral scientists and to indicate how they have approached the subject. Attention was focused on the kinds of structural properties and processes with which behavioral-science research on small groups has been concerned. We described how interpersonal influence depended on both the resources controlled by the influencer and the needs of the influencee.

The multiple bases of social power were also discussed. Two components of small groups were then reviewed. The first of these—norms—relates to shared expectations about the appropriate behavior for each individual and for all group members. When norms relate to things in the outside world, they serve as a social support for individual attitudes. A second component—communication—was discussed in terms of both form (who talks to whom) and content (who says what).

Following this overview of the small group field, we examined how such knowledge has been used in marketing. Two areas of application were discussed at some length: family purchase decision making and personal selling. Viewing the family as a small group, we saw how concepts borrowed from sociological research have been used to analyze and investigate the relative influence of husband and wife in purchase decisions. The available research indicates that the answer to this seemingly straightforward question is quite complex: It depends on several factors—the product, the particular stage in the decision process, and certain characteristics of husbands and wives.

The immediate implication seems to be that of discouraging marketing strategies based upon gross generalizations about which spouse decides. Developing more positive recommendations, such as some type of segmentation strategies based upon family influence types, will require much additional work in the areas of modeling, data collection, and analysis in order to evaluate the practical feasibility of different approaches.

The discussion of personal selling indicated the possibility of bringing knowledge about small group processes more directly to bear on specific operating problems in marketing. Research on interpersonal similarity and attraction suggested a set of variables and relationships that not only appear relevant to understanding variability in the salesman's performance but also have some immediate implications for policies with respect to the selection, training, and allocation of salesmen. Examples were also given where concepts borrowed from social-psychological research on influence processes had been used to analyze problems pertaining to selling strategies and to develop operational methods for solving them.

For what types of operating problems is small group research relevant? In the broadest sense, it is useful to marketing in those situations where the particular behavior or outcome of interest involves group processes. Simply recognizing that the appropriate unit of analysis is a group rather than an individual, or a complex influence process rather than a socially isolated purchase decision, can be of substantial help in formulating marketing strategies.

For example, we earlier stressed the importance of viewing the family as the relevant decision-making and consumption unit for many consumer goods. This is particularly critical when questions of market segmentation are being considered. Often attempts have been made to relate measures of purchasing behavior, which in fact reflect family activity, to information about the attitudes and characteristics of individual family members. Failure to maintain consistency in this regard is probably one of the major reasons for the disappointing results produced by so much of this work.

These considerations are also germane to industrial marketing. Here again, the typical emphasis has been on determining who in a customer's organization "influences" and who "decides" purchases. As has been the case in the consumer field, little systematic attention has been paid to the multidimensional nature of industrial purchase decision making or to the dynamics of the process.

Finally, the area perhaps most amenable to small group analysis is that of personal selling. Interpersonal interaction and influence are the very essence of selling, and these are processes on which behavioral scientists have focused their attention in studying small groups. The previous discussion attempted to show how a small portion of this work could be used to deal with a variety of selling and sales force management problems, including manpower planning, recruitment, selection, allocation, and the development of specific selling methods.

How can the real potential of this research be realized in marketing? While small group theory offers marketers a certain amount of material that is potentially useful to them, the utilization of such knowledge is not a simple task. As a first step, marketing research studies need to incorporate small group research considerations on a continuing basis.

In order to accomplish this successfully, marketing researchers must recognize two critical ingredients. The first are the skills and knowledge of what Guetzkow refers to as a "social engineer or middleman"—"someone who knows how to transform basic knowledge into usable forms" [47, p. 77]. An unusual combination of talents is needed to perform this role effectively. On the one hand, such a person must have the training and background that give him a firm grasp of a broad range of behavioral-science subject matter. On the other hand, he must be of both a creative and practical bent if he is to be able to interact with management personnel and identify their problems.

The other element needed is the kind of problem-oriented, programmatic approach to applying behavioral science notions to real-world problems which Ray has proposed with reference to advertising [81]. To assure relevance, the starting point is a search for applicable behavioral-science knowledge. The key variables of the problem must be identified in theoretical terms and a model selected which interrelates them. Insofar as possible, the latter should take the form of conditional propositions (or "microtheoretical notions")—statements which not only describe relationships between variables but also specify qualifying or limiting conditions. Following that stage comes empirical testing and estimation, and this involves a gradual movement from highly controlled (or laboratory) to more natural (or field) research settings.

The final steps are prediction, implementation, and monitoring of results. Difficulties encountered at any stage require a recycling of activities. By such a systematic approach one hopes to avoid the failures and disappointments which plague efforts to transfer knowledge from the realm of behavioral science to the real world.

Most of the applications described in this chapter (with the exception of Varela's work) represent efforts at the beginning or middle stages of Ray's scheme. The task ahead is to carry forward through the subsequent stages those promising ideas that appear to have some practical payoff.

REFERENCES

1. Andelson, R. P., "Harnessing Engineers and Scientists to the Sales Effort," in John S. Wright and Jack L. Goldstucker, eds., "New Ideas for Successful Marketing," *Proceedings of the June 1966 Conference of the American Marketing Association*, Chicago: American Marketing Association, 1967, pp. 204–215.
2. Arndt, Joan, *Word of Mouth Advertising*, New York: Advertising Research Foundation, 1967.
3. Asch, S. E., "Effects of Group Pressure upon the Modification and Distortion of Judgments," in [69, pp. 174–183].
4. Bales, Robert F., "A Set of Categories for the Analysis of Small Group Interactions," *American Sociological Review*, vol. 15, April 1950, pp. 257–263.
5. Bauer, Raymond A., "Source Effect and Persuasibility: A New Look" in [25, pp. 559–578].
6. Bavelas, A., "Communication Patterns in Task-Oriented Groups," *Journal of the Acoustical Society of America*, vol. 22, 1950, pp. 725–730.
7. ———, A. H. Hastorf, A. E. Gross, and W. R. Kite, "Experiments on the Altera-

tion of Group Structure," *Journal of Experimental Social Psychology,* vol. 1, 1965, pp. 55–70.

8. Beckman, T. N., and W. R. Davidson, *Marketing,* 7th ed., New York: Ronald, 1962.
9. Bem, Daryl J., *Beliefs, Attitudes, and Human Affairs,* Belmont, Calif.: Brooks/Cole, 1970.
10. Berscheid, Ellen, and Elaine H. Walster, *Interpersonal Attraction,* Reading, Mass.: Addison-Wesley, 1969.
11. Bierstedt, Robert, "The Sociology of Majorities," *American Sociological Review,* vol. 13, 1948, pp. 700–710.
12. Bourne, Francis S., "Group Influence in Marketing and Public Relations," in Rensis Likert and Samuel P. Hayes, Jr., eds., *Some Applications of Behavioral Research,* Paris: Unesco, 1957, pp. 207–257.
13. Bramel, Dana, "Interpersonal Attraction, Hostility, and Perception" in Judson Mills, ed., *Experimental Social Psychology,* New York: Macmillan, 1969, pp. 1–120.
14. Brock, Timothy C., "Communicator-Recipient Similarity and Decision Change," *Journal of Personality and Social Psychology,* vol. 1, June, 1965, pp. 650–654.
15. Byrne, Donn, "Attitudes and Attraction," in Leonard Berkowitz, ed., *Advances in Experimental Social Psychology,* vol. 4, New York: Academic Press, 1969, pp. 35–89.
16. Cartwright, Dorwin, and Alvin Zander, *Group Dynamics,* 3d ed., New York: Harper and Row, 1968.
17. Chapple, Eliot D., and Gordon Donald, Jr., "An Evaluation of Department Store Sales People by the Interaction Chronograph," *Journal of Marketing,* vol. 12, October 1947, pp. 173–185.
18. Chapple, Eliot D., "The Interaction Chronograph: Its Evolution and Present Applications," *Personnel,* vol. 25, January 1949, pp. 295–307.
19. Coch, Lester, and John R. P. French, "Overcoming Resistance to Change," in G. E. Swanson, T. M. Newcomb, and E. L. Hartley, eds., *Readings in Social Psychology,* rev. ed., New York: Holt, 1952, pp. 474–491.
20. Cohen, A. R., *Attitude Change and Social Influence,* New York: Basic Books, 1964.
21. Coleman, J. S., E. Katz, and H. Menzel, *Medical Innovation,* Indianapolis: Bobbs-Merrill, 1966.
22. Coleman, J. F., R. R. Blake, and J. S. Mouton, "Task Difficulty and Conformity Pressures," *Journal of Abnormal and Social Psychology,* vol. 57, 1958, pp. 120–122.
23. Cotham, James C. III, "Selecting Salesmen: Approaches and Problems," *MSU Business Topics,* vol. 18, Winter 1970, pp. 64–72.
24. Coulson, J. S., "Buying Decisions within the Family and the Consumer-Brand Relationship," in Joseph W. Newman, ed., *On Knowing the Consumer,* New York: Wiley, pp. 59–66.
25. Cox, Donald F., ed., *Risk Taking and Information Handling in Consumer Behavior,* Division of Research, Graduate School of Business Administration, Boston: Harvard University Press, 1967.
26. Crane, Lauren E., "The Salesman's Role in Household Decision-Making," in L. G. Smith, ed., "Reflections on Progress in Marketing," *Winter, 1964 Conference Proceedings,* Chicago: American Marketing Association, 1965, pp. 184–196.
27. Davis, Harry L., "Marital Roles: An Inventory of Propositions," unpublished M.A. thesis, Northwestern University, 1969.
28. ———, "Dimensions of Marital Roles in Consumer Decision Making," *Journal of Marketing Research,* vol. 7, May 1970, pp. 168–177.
29. ———, "Determinants of Marital Roles in Consumer Purchase Decisions," unpublished working paper, October 1970.
30. *Dynamics of Household Brand Decision Making,* conducted for *Life* Marketing Research by Learner Marketing Research and Development, November 1967.
31. Evans, Franklin B., "Selling as a Dyadic Relationship," *American Behavioral Scientist,* vol. 6, May 1963, pp. 76–79.

32. ———, *Dyadic Interaction in Selling: A New Approach,* unpublished monograph, Graduate School of Business, University of Chicago, 1964.

33. *Family Participation and Influence in Shopping and Brand Selection,* conducted for *Life* Marketing Research by Nowland and Company, Inc., 1964.

34. *Family Participation and Influence in Shopping and Brand Selection: Phase II,* conducted for *Life* Marketing Research by Nowland and Company, Inc., 1965.

35. Farber, Bernard, *A Study of Dependence and Decision Making in Marriage,* unpubished Doctoral dissertation, University of Chicago, September 1949.

36. Farley, John U., and Robert L. Swinth, "Effects of Choice and Sales Message on Customer-Salesman Interaction," *Journal of Applied Psychology,* vol. 51, April 1967, pp. 107–110.

37. Ferber, Robert, "Research on Household Behavior," *American Economic Review,* vol. 52, 1962, pp. 19–63.

38. Festinger, Leon, "The Application of Behavioral Science Knowledge," paper presented at the Sloan School of Management, Cambridge, Mass.: M.I.T., Fall 1968.

39. ———, and Elliot Aronson, "Arousal and Reduction of Dissonance in Social Contexts," in [16, pp. 125–136].

40. Festinger, Leon, S. Schachter, and K. Back, *Social Pressures in Informal Groups,* New York: Harper, 1950.

41. Freedman, Johnathan L., and Scott C. Fraser, "Compliance Without Pressure: The Foot-in-the-Door Technique," *Journal of Personality and Social Psychology,* vol. 4, August 1966, pp. 195–202.

42. French, John R. P., and Bertram Raven, "The Bases of Social Power," in D. Cartwright, ed., *Studies in Social Power,* Ann Arbor, Mich.: University of Michigan, 1959.

43. Gadel, M. S., "Concentration by Salesmen on Congenial Prospects," *Journal of Marketing,* vol. 28, April 1964, pp. 64–66.

44. Gerard, H. B., R. A. Whilhelmy, E. S. Connolley, "Conformity and Group Size," *Journal of Personality and Social Psychology,* vol. 8, 1968, pp. 79–82.

45. Greenberg, Allan, "Is Communications Research Worthwhile?" *Journal of Marketing,* vol. 31, January 1967, pp. 48–50.

46. Granbois, Donald H., and Ronald P. Willett, "Patterns of Conflicting Perceptions Among Channel Members," in L. George Smith, ed., "Reflections on Progress in Marketing," *Proceedings of the Winter 1964 Conference of the American Marketing Association,* Chicago: American Marketing Association, 1965, pp. 86–100.

47. Guetzkow, Harold, "Conversion Barriers in Using the Social Sciences," *Administrative Science Quarterly,* vol. 4, June 1959, pp. 68–81.

48. Hare, A. Paul, *Handbook of Small Group Research,* New York: Free Press, 1962.

49. ———, and Robert F. Bales, "Seating Position and Small Group Interaction," in [50, pp. 427–433].

50. ———, E. F. Borgatta, and R. F. Bales, *Small Groups,* rev. ed., New York: Knopf, 1965.

51. Heider, Fritz, *The Psychology of Interpersonal Relations,* New York: Wiley, 1958.

52. Henry, Jules, Review of *Human Behavior: An Inventory of Scientific Findings,* by Bernard Berelson and Gary A. Steiner, *Scientific American,* vol. 211, July 1964, pp. 129ff.

53. Homans, George C., *Social Behavior: Its Elementary Forms,* New York: Harcourt, Brace & World, 1961.

54. Hovland, Carl I., Irving L. Janis, and Harold H. Kelley, *Communication and Persuasion,* New Haven, Conn.: Yale University Press, 1953.

55. Jackson, Jay M., "The Dynamics of Instructional Groups: Socio-Psychological Aspects of Teaching and Learning," in M. B. Henry, ed., *Yearbook of the National Society for the Study of Education,* Chicago: University of Chicago Press, 1960.

56. Jaffe, L. J., and H. Senft, "The Roles of Husbands and Wives in Purchasing Decisions," in Lee Adler and Irving Crespi, eds., *Attitude Research at Sea,* Chicago: American Marketing Association, 1966.

57. Karlins, Marvin, and Herbert I. Abelson, *Persuasion,* 2d ed., New York: Springer, 1970.

58. Katz, Elihu, and Paul F. Lazarsfeld, *Personal Influence*, Chicago: Free Press, 1955.
59. Kenkel, William F., "Family Interaction in Decision Making on Spending," in Nelson Foote, ed., *Household Decision Making*, New York: New York University Press, pp. 140–164.
60. King, Charles W., and John O. Summers, "Dynamics of Interpersonal Communication: The Interaction Dyad," in [25, pp. 240–264].
61. Lazarsfeld, Paul F., "The American Soldier: An Expository Review," *Public Opinion Quarterly*, vol. 13, Fall 1949, pp. 377–404.
62. Leavitt, Harold J., "Some Effects of Certain Communication Patterns on Group Performance," *Journal of Abnormal and Social Psychology*, vol. 46, 1951, pp. 38–50.
63. Levitt, Theodore, *Industrial Purchasing Behavior*, Boston: Harvard University, Division of Research, Graduate School of Business Administration, 1965.
64. Lewin, Kurt, "Group Decision and Social Change," in G. E. Swanson, T. M. Newcomb, and E. L. Hartley, *Readings in Social Psychology*, rev. ed., New York: Holt, 1952, pp. 459–473.
65. Lindzey, Gardner, and Elliot Aronson, ed., *Handbook of Social Psychology*, 2d ed., Reading, Mass.: Addison-Wesley, 1968–1969.
66. ———, and Donn Byrne, "Measurement of Social Choice and Interpersonal Attractiveness," in [65, vol. 2, pp. 452–525].
67. Lombard, George F., *Behavior in a Selling Group*, Boston: Harvard University, Division of Research, Graduate School of Business Administration, 1955.
68. Lott, Albert J., and Bernice E. Lott, "Group Cohesiveness as Interpersonal Attractiveness: A Review of Relationships with Antecedent and Consequent Variables," *Psychological Bulletin*, vol. 64, October 1965, pp. 259–309.
69. Maccoby, Eleanor E., Theodore M. Newcomb, and Eugene Hartley, eds., *Readings in Social Psychology*, 3d ed., New York: Holt, 1958.
70. *Male vs. Female Influence on the Purchase of Selected Products as Revealed by an Exploratory Depth Interview Study with Husbands and Wives*, New York: Fawcett Publications, 1958.
71. March, James, and Herbert A. Simon, *Organizations*, New York: Wiley, 1958.
72. Marlow, David, and Kenneth J. Gergen, "Personality and Social Interaction," in [65, vol. 3, pp. 590–665].
73. McGuire, William J., "The Nature of Attitudes and Attitude Change," in [65, vol. 3, pp. 136–314].
74. Miner, John B., "Personality and Ability Factors in Sales Performance," *Journal of Applied Psychology*, vol. 46, February 1962, pp. 6–13.
75. Montgomery, David B., and Alvin J. Silk, "Patterns of Overlap in Opinion Leadership and Interest for Selected Categories of Purchasing Activity," in Phillip R. McDonald, ed., "Marketing Involvement in Society and the Economy," *Proceedings of the Fall 1969 Conference*, Chicago: American Marketing Association, 1970, pp. 377–386.
76. National Opinion Polls Grocery Shopping Survey, National Opinion Polls, Ltd., 1967.
77. Newcomb, Theodore M., "An Approach to the Study of Communicative Acts," *Psychological Review*, vol. 60, November 1953, pp. 393–404.
78. ———, "Attitude Development as a Function of Reference Groups," in [69, pp. 265–275].
79. Parsons, Talcott, and Robert F. Bales, *Family Socialization and Interaction Process*, Chicago: Free Press, 1955.
80. Phillips, C. F., and D. J. Duncan, *Marketing: Principles and Methods*, 5th ed., Homewood, Ill.: Irwin, 1964.
81. Ray, Michael L., "The Present and Potential Linkages between the Microtheoretical Notions of Behavioral Science and the Problems of Advertising: A Proposal for a Research System," in Harry L. Davis and Alvin J. Silk, eds., *Behavioral and Management Science in Marketing*, New York: Ronald, in press.
82. Robertson, Thomas S., *New Product Diffusion*, New York: Holt, Rinehart, Winston, 1971.

83. Sharp, Harry, and Paul Mott, "Consumer Decisions in the Metropolitan Family," *Journal of Marketing,* vol. 21, October 1956, pp. 149–156.
84. Sherif, M., *The Psychology of Social Norms,* New York: Harper, 1936.
85. Sheth, Jagdish N., "A Theory of Family Buying Decisions," paper presented to the American Psychological Association, September 1970.
86. Silk, Alvin J., "Response Set and the Measurement of Self-Designated Opinion Leadership," *Public Opinion Quarterly,* vol. 35, Fall 1971.
87. Simons, Herbert W., Nancy N. Berkowitz, and R. John Moyer, "Similarity, Credibility, and Attitude Change: A Review and A Theory," *Psychological Bulletin,* vol. 73, January 1970, pp. 1–16.
88. Stevens, S. N., "The Application of Social Science Findings to Selling and the Salesman," in *Aspects of Modern Management,* New York, 1958, pp. 85–94.
89. Taguiri, Renato, "Person Perception," in [65, vol. 3, pp. 395–449].
90. Thibaut, John W., and Harold H. Kelley, *The Social Psychology of Groups,* New York: Wiley, 1959.
91. Tosi, Henry L., "The Effects of Expectation Levels and Role Consensus on the Buyer-Seller Dyad," *Journal of Business,* vol. 39, October 1966, pp. 516–529.
92. Tuddenham, R. D., "The Influence of a Distorted Group Norm upon Individual Judgment," *Journal of Psychology, vol.* 46, 1958, pp. 243–251.
93. Webster, Frederick E., Jr., "Interpersonal Communication and Salesman Effectiveness," *Journal of Marketing,* vol. 32, July 1968, pp. 7–13.
94. Wells, William D., and Douglas Tigert, "Activities, Interests, and Opinions," *Journal of Advertising Research,* vol. 11, August 1971, pp. 27–35.
95. Willett, Ronald P., and Allan L. Pennington, "Customer and Salesman: The Anatomy of Choice and Influence in a Retail Setting," in Raymond M. Haas, ed., "Science, Technology, and Marketing," *Proceedings of Fall 1966 Conference of the American Marketing Association,* Chicago: American Marketing Association, 1967, pp. 598–616.
96. Wolgast, Elizabeth H., "Do Husbands or Wives Make the Purchasing Decisions?" *Journal of Marketing,* vol. 23, October 1958, pp. 151–158.
97. Zimbardo, Philip, and Ebbe E. Ebbeson, *Influencing Attitudes and Changing Behavior,* Reading, Mass.: Addison-Wesley, 1969.

Part B
Theories

Chapter 3
Diffusion of Innovation

C. MERLE CRAWFORD *Graduate School of Business Administration, University of Michigan, Ann Arbor, Michigan*

Perhaps no marketing research has received as much attention, money, and experimentation in recent years as that on new products, though the graveyard of new-product failures proves we have a long way to go. As tricky as predicting new-product sales and profit success is, however, one phase of new-product research is increasingly proving of value—that concerning the measuring of success (or failure) of a product during its early period on the market.

This research embodies the concepts of diffusion of innovation: hypothesizing a pattern of market acceptance of a new product, building a promotional program based on this pattern, measuring actual market acceptance upon introduction, and setting forth immediately upon remedial action programs designed to correct for any unwanted deviations from the target pattern. In this chapter will be presented the current thinking relative to the various patterns or structures that commonly are found, some considerations relative to the research techniques used, and some managerial implications from the body of relevant theory. There are also some strong cautions, since the techniques are unquestionably still in the development stage.

INNOVATION

The concepts of innovation and its diffusion have come from a diversity of nonmarketing sources, including anthropology, rural sociology, recreation, education, health, and science. On a highly generalized plane they include the following: First, there must be an innovation. Second, every individual who ultimately becomes a user or practitioner of the innovation goes through various steps en route to his destination. Third, this individual pattern is not entirely unconnected—most persons have interfaces with others, and innovation diffuses itself throughout the total audience in some detectable fashion.

Definition. An innovation is an idea perceived as new by the individual. Although this focus on the individual introduces some problems (boiling water is obviously not a new idea, and persons moving to a new city see old established stores as "new"), for most marketers it is quite adequate.

It should be noted, however, that a genuinely new product is an innovation only so long as consumers *see* it as being different. If they miss the "point," they feel there is no innovation and thus abort the adoption process. Likewise, at the other extreme, a successful promotional program may significantly alter the perceived characteristics of a product and thus move it into a new adoption cycle even though it may have been on the market for years. Product improvements, if significant, may also result in innovations as far as consumers are concerned. So the concepts of innovation and diffusion seem to be widely applicable in marketing efforts today.

Further clarification of the concept of innovation can be found in Rogers [8], where he describes the traits an innovation usually has (relative advantage, compatibility, complexity, divisibility, and communicability), and in Robertson [7], where innovations are classified as "continuous" (the least disruptive), "dynamically continuous" (more disruptive, such as new segments of existing markets), and "discontinuous" (the most disruptive, constituting entirely new product markets). Practitioners, however, need only be aware of newness in the minds of customers as a signal that the basic technology of diffusion is applicable. Refinements along these lines should be undertaken only after considerable experience with the basics.

THE ADOPTION PROCESS

Although the idea of diffusion (for example, the spreading of a rumor) is applicable to marketing, the most valuable contribution has come from the adoption process as an individual activity. How does an individual move from complete ignorance on a new product to where he is consuming it at what the marketer calls an ideal rate? What constitutes the researchable behavior pattern?

Stages in the Adoption Process. Every researcher in this field seems to have developed his own paradigm for the set of stages an individual goes through en route to total acceptance of an innovation, but a good one to start with is the one most commonly used [8]. First, there must be *awareness,* awareness of something about the innovation. Some marketers have simply used brand awareness, either at the recall level or the recognition level. Others have insisted that nothing can follow unless the consumer becomes aware of at least one attribute of a product which makes it different and thus an innovation.

In any case, a person becoming aware of an innovation reaches that state with incomplete knowledge of it. He is merely aware that it exists, and to move further down the adoption process he must enter the *interest stage,* during which he will seek or at least receive additional information about the innovation. The nature of this stage varies, of course, according to the innovation; for high-risk, complex innovations there may be a lengthy or intensive search for further information, but for inexpensive food preparations virtually no information beyond that on the package may be required for a "test." This particular stage is quite difficult to isolate. Most marketing research today combines it with the awareness stage or, better yet, with the next step in the process—*evaluation.*

As soon as his interest generates additional information, the consumer begins to evaluate it—to see how the purchase of the particular new product would fit his situation. Again, research has failed to penetrate this particular stage—we know it goes on, with varying degree of activity and intensity varying principally with the factors of risk and reward, but efforts to isolate the activity have usually failed. So current research tends to focus on the result of evaluation: trial purchase or delay. This decision introduces the *trial stage*, a go no-go decision, and to the extent possible it is on a miniature or limited-scale basis.

Obviously, quickly consumed repeat-purchase items fit the model well, since a housewife can easily try a new detergent product. But major commitments, such as cars, appliances, or homes, force the decision maker to skip the trial stage completely unless he takes advantage of sellers' attempts to create a trial situation with such offers as the 10-day free trial. Even with low-cost items, any trial beyond the first purchase is difficult to define. Sooner or later, if he is to become an adopter, the consumer reaches a mental state which holds that the trial was successful; the new purchase pattern will be continued indefinitely. This is *adoption*, the final stage in the process.

For practical purposes, most marketing researchers use a simple three-step substitute: awareness, trial, and adoption. Each must be carefully defined and adhered to consistently if research experience over time is to have value. The following definitions are typical:

Aware. The consumer claims to have heard of a product when asked. (This can be either recall or recognition, and false awareness can easily be screened out.)

Trial. The consumer has purchased the item under study. It is best to omit trial use of free samples or free products obtained from other persons in the market, since the purpose of this stage of research is to measure the degree of the consumer's conviction.

Adoption. There is no single standard for this phase, but researchers use (1) repeat purchase, (2) several additional purchases, or (3) respondent statement to the effect that the trial has been successful and continued use is intended. Again, the definition is not as important as is continued use of one particular definition.

Adopter Categories. The fact that consumers move through the adoption process at different rates of speed gives a second fruitful dimension to the analysis. Specifically, most researchers use the following categories based on what is felt to be a nearly "normal" distribution, even though an unbelievable array of names has been developed for them; it is also known that these categories are merely segments of a continuum, comparable to social class categories.

1. *Innovators.* Also frequently called tastemakers, this group consists of those few (sometimes rigidly defined as the first 2½ or 5 percent) who are the first to adopt an innovation.

2. *Early Adopters.* Also frequently called the early minority, these are the ones who by definition are not the earliest to try a new product but are still quite definitely ahead of the majority. Constituting perhaps 10 to 12 percent of the total, they give a new product its initial sales thrust.

3. *Early Majority.* Members of this group, comprising perhaps one-third of the total market, are the key to substantial market success. They usually are more deliberate, desiring to benefit from the experience of those who are more venturesome and who represent some form of "authority" or "expertness."

4. *Late Majority.* Comprising yet another third, these people are skeptical

latecomers who typically require considerable persuasion.   They will also abandon the innovation quicker than will early adopters.

5. *Laggards.* These are the remaining 10 to 15 percent who are the last to adopt. This particular term is unfortunate since it implies a criticism, but it is the most widely used term for this category. Until recently, it has not been studied in depth [10].

Of these five categories, marketers are most interested in the first two, the innovators and early adopters, partly because they provide the initial sales volume but principally because of the conviction that persons in the early groups either actively or passively influence the decisions of those in the later groups.

Marketers would like to know the particular characteristics of those persons who will be the first to use each specific new product, but for various reasons this seems virtually impossible. (Recent attempts which give some hope are Bernhardt [1b], Painter and Pinegar [5b], and Peterson [6a]; they cover an industrial process, women's clothing, and life insurance.) In general, the following characteristics seem to predominate:

Venturesomeness. The willingness and desire to be daring, to try the new and different in many areas of activity. "Sticks his neck out." Deviates from social group norms.

Social Integration. The person who has frequent and extensive contact with others in his "area," be it work, neighborhood, social life, or whatever.

Cosmopolitanness. The personal point of view that extends beyond the immediate neighborhood or community. Interest in world affairs, travel, reading.

Social Mobility. The characteristic of upward movement on the social scale. Successful young executive types.

Privilegedness. Usually defined as being better off financially than others in his group. Thus the person has less to lose if the innovation he experiments with fails and costs him money. Tends to reflect attitude toward money as much as possession of money.

Except for personality variations, these classifications might best be summarized by saying that early adopters have some reasons for wanting to use the new (to impress others, for example), have the resources or standing which negate the usual drawbacks to having tried something that didn't work, and have the basic spirit of the adventurer. They are willing to violate the adage "Be not the first to try the new nor the last to abandon the old."

Summary. Each individual in a market, if presented with an innovation, enters upon a rather systematic process of reacting to that innovation. He becomes aware of it, he becomes interested in it, he evaluates it, he tries it, and he then adopts it. Of course, at any of these stages he may voluntarily or involuntarily push an "abort" button and leave the process, thus becoming a nonadopter.

Additionally, we have seen that this process may move at various rates of speed, with the result that some persons in a market become adopters early, some at average speed, and some late. Sales result from a combination of the two factors—progress through process and speed of progress. It is now possible to discuss the research techniques applicable to this problem.

RESEARCH TECHNIQUES

Many of the basic techniques discussed elsewhere in this book are applicable here, since the need is for information of particular characteristics, gathered at certain time and cost restraints, and analyzed in such a way as to yield meaningful and valuable marketing management insights. However, there are some aspects of innovation research that deserve special mention.

Relatives versus Absolutes. As indicated earlier, much is yet to be learned about the nature of innovation adoption. So much so, in fact, that a single diffusion of innovation study, independently undertaken by a given firm, will probably prove disappointing. For instance, one of the first tasks in such a study is to define awareness; when does a person become aware of innovation? This is not an absolute phenomenon like catching the measles. A person may have heard of a product but forgotten it; he may remember upon being reminded; he may remember voluntarily when asked; he may actually volunteer that he knows; or he may already have moved to the second stage.

When did he become "aware"? Who in a given market are aware now? One researcher might study a given innovation at time x and find 30 percent "aware," and another researcher using a different definition may find an entirely different percentage at the same time. Who is correct? Only an arbitrary standard can provide the answer.

What then should be done? The best answer is to use relative measurements rather than absolutes. Thus if one can find meaningful benchmark studies by others in his given market situation, he can use the same definitions and simply draw meaning from his data by comparing them to the other studies. Most commonly, however, he should simply undertake diffusion studies on a continuing basis, using the same definitions in all studies, and build his own base for interpretation. Thus a 30 percent awareness figure may mean nothing alone; but if it is five points higher than on previous innovations studied, it begins to acquire meaning.

Exactly the same thinking applies to other definitional problems. When is a person classified as seeking information, what is evaluation, what constitutes a trial, and, perhaps most important of all, what must he do to become an "adopter"?

Speed. Most innovation diffusion research has value as it discovers (1) problems that are developing in the rate of factory shipments before they become obvious and (2) opportunities that can still be capitalized upon. Thus speed is usually essential, leading to the use of research techniques—the telephone, for example—that lend themselves to fast return of data from the field. Speed also requires that procedures be set up to provide rapid and automatic tabulation of data as they arrive. Routine information handling procedures are not appropriate in diffusion research.

Need for Planning. As is evident from the need for speed, this type of research must be thoroughly planned and arranged before the new-product introduction. Thus, working from past studies, the researcher (1) defines the process of adoption that he sees pertinent to the particular new product, (2) defines the individual terms involved, (3) selects the several steps in the overall process that he feels are critical to his firm's marketing decisions and that are researchable, (4) determines the specific research techniques that will be incorporated in the plan, and (5) structures the field procedures or retains the outside research firm appropriate to the data needs.

Good innovation technique demands that the field research start before the product is introduced; in this way, one can learn of nondeliberate distortions of memory (such as brand awareness that always seems to occur even though a brand has not yet been introduced) and the other appropriate benchmark facts. This is simply in line with the earlier thought that relative data are more meaningful than absolute data, and changes from the status quo (whatever it may be) provide the basis for interpretation. Going to the field prior to actual introduction also guarantees that there will be a flow of data pertinent to the new product *immediately* upon introduction. This is the critical period for most new-product marketing programs.

There is another reason for thorough and early planning of field research. The same theory of adoption that has been developed for the buyer (or consumer) can be applied to the various levels of the trade, a research opportunity often overlooked. Retailers too must become aware of the new product, they must evaluate it, they must try it in the sense of at least a temporary stock, they must find that it works in the sense of moving at an acceptable rate, and they must adopt it in the sense of deciding to keep it as a regular item in their line. Since adoption in the trade sense inevitably is intertwined with the stocking and promoting of competitive products, it is readily apparent why premarketing research is necessary to provide a platform for data interpretation.

Objectives.   Stemming from the idea that relative data provide the most meaningful research results, a given piece of field data (for example, 22 percent of consumers are "aware") begins to give managerial direction when it can be compared with benchmark or goal figures. If on similar new-product introductions a firm usually has had at least 40 percent awareness at this particular time, the situation demands attention. But, even more important, if the marketing team has said they need 40 percent on this specific product at this time, then the need for immediate action is apparent.

The adoption process is a movement through predetermined stages of action, and successful marketing of new products demands that enough customers move through that process with sufficient speed to generate the required level of sales. If customers do not move rapidly enough through the process, appropriate remedial action is necessary immediately. There is no time during a product's life when remedial boosts of firepower will do as much for the product as when it is new—when the people moving through the adoption process have a degree of forward momentum. A year later, new interest and action have virtually ceased and remedial expenditures meet high stationary inertia.

Moreover, research has shown that there is no one predictable stage in the adoption process where potential buyers typically falter. They may fail on awareness, they may misfire on evaluation, they may try but not repeat, and so on. In fact, the essence of research contribution from the entire theory of innovation adoption and diffusion is that research must be established to study the *process* step-by-step, not just the outcome of the process. Marketing strategists must likewise anticipate potential problems at each stage and prepare separate remedial action plans for any reasonably likely problem. To actuate any one of these remedial plans, they need a "signal," which in turn requires that the adoption process be measured against predetermined objectives set by the marketing planners as meaningful benchmarks of acceptable progress, as is discussed by Crawford [2].

APPLICATIONS OF ADOPTION/DIFFUSION THEORY

The theory of innovation adoption is new enough that marketers are still finding additional uses for it. At the moment, several are getting the most attention, but they are by no means exclusive.

Direction of Promotional Effort.   Any politician, student protest leader, or military commander could quickly cite the principal application of diffusion theory to marketing: If one knows the particular individuals who are most likely to adopt an innovation first, he can direct his principal effort to them and thus economize on his total outlay of effort.

Similarly, the marketer who seeks to establish a given innovation knows there are certain influential persons, or at least early adopters, whom he needs first. The other adoptions should follow much more easily after that.

Thus, by identifying who these persons may be, he can (1) develop a promotional theme or concept that particularly appeals to them and (2) direct this promotional theme through media which optimize the reaching of these particular individuals. He cannot deal with specific individuals, of course, so he attempts to determine innovator "potential" by various demographic and psychographic characteristics. Thus he is interested in what were referred to earlier as characteristics associated with early adopters—venturesomeness, social mobility, and the like. Although these generalizations seem widely applicable, they must be applied carefully. In particular marketing situations, other characteristics may override the generalized ones in significance.

Multiple Marketing Mix. Just as one promotional strategy and the promotional mix of "change agents" may be the most appropriate to those persons designated as "influential," so too are marketers finding that diffusion of innovation theory suggests the need for different strategies (especially mixes of effort) as potential consumers move through the adoption process.

Thus, for instance, mass media or mailed samples may be particularly good for encouraging awareness of a new packaged good; personal contact and in-store displays may be best for providing information during the evaluation stage; samples or combination offers may be best at stimulating trial; word-of-mouth may be best to assist in posttrial evaluation, and mass media may be best for encouraging continued use on the part of a person who has completed a successful trial.

If information can be secured on each class of adopter (innovators, early adopters, and so on), the marketing team is in a position to think of a changing blend of promotional strategy or mix of tools. In the beginning the blend favors awareness pressures on early adopters, then it switches to awareness pressures on early majority and trial pressure on the early adopters and so on, adding awareness pressures for each successive group and moving each earlier group over one notch on the adoption scale.

Early Predictions of Sales. If the adoption process is regular and predictable and if the researchers have been able to predetermine it, marketing management can predict eventual outcomes early in the marketing process and adjust their efforts accordingly. A slow start would indicate the need for new boosts of marketing power. A fast start might indicate an opportunity to expand the original financial commitment. An extremely disappointing result after a quick rejuvenation effort might suggest forgetting the whole thing while part of the budget can still be salvaged.

Until recent years, marketers have had to make such judgments with no precise knowledge of the "standard" curves. Even knowing the standard curve was not enough unless each part of it could be divided into proportions of persons in the various stages of the adoption process. Inadequate sales at Month two probably means the new product is not capturing its expected share of business among the early adopters, but research should also be prepared to tell whether the trouble is awareness, evaluation, early trial, or what. Poor sales may be the result of failure to move any particular adopter category through the adoption process.

Thus, the marketing research department should, at the time of a product's introduction, predict the source of company business by adopter category and by stage in the adoption process for each category. This would be a compilation of the objectives referred to earlier, and would serve as the doctor's wall chart for assessing the future of the new product as its market acceptance unfolds.

This requires that the researcher do essentially what doctors, floriculturalists, and other scientists have done—gather data on actual new-product introductions (including marketing effort, environment, and sales results) and seek in these data clues of regularity. Published reports of research by others are helpful, especially for constructing hypotheses to be tested in specific situations.

Currently advocated are sales curves with slopes determined by formula. Some have used the standard S curve, some a simple constant percentage increase, some a curve based on a mathematical extension of previous sales (with or without exponential smoothing). The important point is that the curve should have a rationale—a logic against which market progress can be measured.

A good example of this application of diffusion can be found in Crawford [2]. He studied the introduction of several new products and developed "trajectories" (expected curves for awareness, trial, adoption, and so on). These were then applied to new products, one of which was discussed in detail in the report cited and for which selected figures are shown here in Figure 1. This product was promoted to general practicing dentists and to prosthodontic dentists, and the principal concerns of marketing management were that there be awareness and trial usage of the product. Additional interests centered on trade stocking, requests for a patient instruction booklet, and the resulting factory sales.

The graphs show clearly that after only 10 weeks a critical problem had developed; general-practice dentists were aborting the innovative process. Moreover, the data showed where the aborting was taking place—on awareness. Although actual awareness (and trial) by prosthodontic dentists was meeting established goals (trajectories), such was by no means the case with the general-practice dentists, and there was no evidence of expected short-term improvement.

As a result, marketing management was able to apply the particular remedial effort needed, since they had determined which market segment was aborting and at which specific phase of the adoption process.

Other Applications. The theory of diffusion of innovation defines innovation as *anything* new—not just products. Thus new promotional themes can be measured (and extended by a curve of forecasted adoption) in the same way. Retail chains can use the theory in setting probable sales curves for new outlets opened [4]. New techniques of product or customer service can be treated as innovations, as can product improvements, new media, and new geographical markets.

LIMITATIONS

Diffusion-of-innovation theory is no exception to the generalization that marketing research rarely benefits from perfect tools of measurement and prediction. In fact, this particular area of research is remarkably plagued with problems, and anyone attempting to use the ideas in this chapter must be aware of major cautions.

Defining and Measuring Adopter Categories. Although it appears simple to define awareness, evaluation, trial, adoption, and the like, only one of the steps in the adoption process—trial—can be defined in such a way as to permit accurate and consistent measurement. Other definitions tend to be quite arbitrary and pragmatic—chosen for their researchability more than their rationale. Thus, for example, one common questioning technique is "Have you heard of a product called X?" A yes answer qualifies the respondent as aware. But aware of what? The brand? Some generic classification for the product? The product's actual physical characteristics? Its key difference from other,

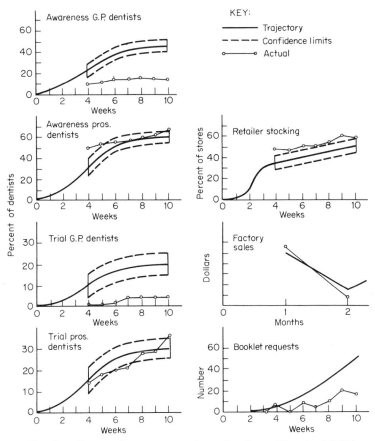

Fig. 1. Case study on new-product adoption. *(Crawford [2].)*

similar products? How much knowledge should constitute awareness? The same criticisms apply to the other steps in the process.

Influence in the Diffusion Process. At this time, no marketer can assume that his innovators or early adopters will influence the majorities to join in adopting the innovation under study. Certainly the theory is sound—innovators, by their personalities or by their standing in the community, should be able to influence others, even unintentionally. But the specific lines of influence have not been ascertained. By overdirecting marketing effort to the early-innovator class, marketing management can end up with high penetration in a tiny segment of the market.

Except under near-laboratory conditions, consumers cannot trace inputs from other individuals let alone assess their power of influence. Any research plan predicated upon early adopters having an influence upon later adopters is shaky indeed [1].

Poor Research. Many companies are active in innovation research. Unfortunately their results are rarely published, so one who undertakes to do research in this area must turn to the new studies which have been published. They suffer several weaknesses.

Small Samples. The high cost of adoption/diffusion research has forced most published studies to rely upon inadequate samples, so their conclusions must be challenged. Most published research has yielded nothing more than hypotheses.

Ex Post versus Ex Ante. If firm X is preparing to market new product Y, innovation research requires that the probable early users of the product be identified so that marketing effort may be directed to them especially. Unfortunately, although it is relatively simple to determine later who the early adopters actually were, determining them in advance is extremely difficult. Research reports appearing in the journals may dissect innovator characteristics in great depth without making clear that the identification came after the fact. Trying to make the estimations prior to marketing requires the transfer of experience from some other product or company to the new one, a dangerous procedure.

Little Replication. Research findings can be generalized only when a given study has been replicated by others. Since the study of innovation is new, most findings are still speculative. Though substantiating research will no doubt be forthcoming, any marketer undertaking innovation research is still a pioneer.

Data Obsolescence. Unfortunately, the greatest weakness in this type of research will probably always be present. It concerns the fact that any model of innovation is pertinent only as long as the market conditions existing during its development do not change significantly. Thus a given firm may carefully research several new-product introductions, discover the adoption process applicable to its market, measure the customary diffusion parameters, and conclude with a highly accurate generalization of what should happen on the next introduction, only to find that some other innovation (for example, a new firm entering the market or an institutional change in the trade structure) effectively destroys the environment in which backlog data were acquired. The old adage that nothing stands still in marketing is particularly applicable to any situation where one attempts to predict the future by using the past as a model. Bass [1a] formulated a generalized mathematical growth model in 1969, and Nevers [5a] later reported successful tests of it in four diverse product areas.

SUMMARY

This chapter has attempted to spell out the fundamentals of what is known about the applications of diffusion and innovation theory to marketing. Key terms have been defined and the integrating process has been explained. In addition, it has been shown that the ideas of innovation, taken from allied social sciences, have widespread application in the marketing of new products. However, there are special cautions in the use of these techniques, stemming partly from special research data needs and partly from a shortage of published research reports on successful applications.

BIBLIOGRAPHY

1. Arndt, J., "Role of Product-Related Conversations in the Diffusion of a New Product," *Journal of Marketing Research*, vol. 4, August 1967, pp. 291–295.
1a. Bass, F. M., "A New Product Growth Model for Consumer Durables," *Management Science*, vol. 15, January 1969.
1b. Bernhardt, I., "Diffusion of Catalytic Techniques Through a Population of Medium Size Petroleum Refining Firms," *Journal of Industrial Economics*, vol. 19, November 1970.
2. Crawford, C. M., "The Trajectory Theory of Goal Setting for New Products," *Journal of Marketing Research*, vol. 3, May 1966, pp. 117–125.
3. Engel, J. F., D. T. Kollat, and R. D. Blackwell, *Consumer Behavior*, New York: Holt, 1968.
4. Kelly, R. F., "Estimating Ultimate Performance Levels of New Retail Outlets," *Journal of Marketing Research*, vol. 4, February 1967, pp. 13–19.
5. King, C. W., "The Innovator in the Fashion Adoption Process," *Reflections on Progress in Marketing*, American Marketing Association, 1965, pp. 324–339.
5a. Nevers, J. V., "Extensions of a New Product Growth Model," *Sloan Management Review*, vol. 13, Winter 1972.
5b. Painter, J. J., and M. L. Pinegar, "Post-High Teens and Fashion Innovation," *Journal of Marketing Research*, vol. 8, August 1971.
6. Pessemier, E. A., P. C. Burger, and D. J. Tigert, "Can New Product Buyers Be Identified?" *Journal of Marketing Research*, vol. 4, November 1967, pp. 349–354.
6a. Peterson, R. A., "Speed of Marketing Innovations in a Service Industry," *Journal of Business*, vol. 45, October 1972.
7. Robertson, T. S., "The Process of Innovation and the Diffusion of Innovation," *Journal of Marketing*, vol. 31, no. 1, pp. 14–19, January 1967.
8. Rogers, E. M., *Diffusion of Innovations*, New York: Fress Press, 1962.
9. *The Adoption of New Products*, Ann Arbor, Mich.: Foundation for Research on Human Behavior, 1959.
10. Uhl, Kenneth, Roman Andrus, and Lance Paulsen, "How Are Lagards Different? An Empirical Inquiry," *Journal of Marketing Research*, vol. 7, February 1970, pp. 51–54.

Section Four

Major Areas of Application

New-Product Development and Introduction

Chapter 1

Estimating Market Potential

WILLIAM R. KING *Graduate School of Business, University of Pittsburgh, Pittsburgh, Pennsylvania*

The term *market potential* is one which has an intuitive appeal to anyone with a concern for marketing. Like many such marketing terms, however, it is subject to a variety of interpretations. Often, for instance, the term is confused with *sales potential*. Indeed, Cowan [4] has described nine different interpretations of the term *market potential*, at least one of which is that usually thought of as *sales potential*.

Before presuming to define *market potential*, we must be assured that we have a common understanding of the more basic term—*market*. *A market is a group of potential customers who have something in common.* The term is often applied in referring to geographical markets, for example, the Pittsburgh market—in which the common element is the location of the consumers' residences, and to age groups—for example, the "under twenty-five" market.

In this context, the most useful way of thinking of market potential is as *the total amount of a product or product class which would be sold to a market in a specified time period and under a given set of conditions.*[1] The "conditions" referred to in this definition include such *uncontrollable* environmental and competitive factors as the political situation, government actions, technological levels, and general economic conditions as well as the *controllable* aspects of total marketing effort, such as advertising and promotional levels, product characteristics, and the intensity of distribution.

DETERMINATION OF MARKET POTENTIALS

Although the market potential concept is equally applicable to existing products and new products, this chapter treats only *the determination of market potentials for new products.*

---

[1] "Sales potential," on the other hand, is the proportion of the market potential which a given company expects to obtain.

In the context of an overall plan for the introduction of a new product, market potential analysis plays a complementary role to consumer reaction tests, market tests, test marketing, and other forms of evaluation and assessment. Although some of these allied techniques can be used to revise initial assessments of market potential, they require that the product already be developed. In this chapter, we concentrate on the predevelopmental assessment of market potential, that is, on the assessment of market potential for new product *ideas*.

In this context, market potentials are, at best, elusive creatures, for they have no existence outside the minds of the analysts and managers who create them. Since no product history is available to serve as a basis for the assessment of a new product's potential, the process is typically an unnerving and enlightening experience. Because of the idiosyncratic nature of most new products, there is no standardized step-by-step procedure which can be applied to the assessment of a new product's market potential. Each instance is unique, and while there are basic methodologies which can be brought to bear, each requires that the analyst be thoughtful, creative, and imaginative.

The Importance of Market Potentials

Market potentials are among the most important, most pervasively used, and most error-prone inputs to a wide variety of marketing decisions. Their pervasiveness is readily apparent. In addition to their crucially important role in the evaluation of new products, market potentials are essential to the marketing manager in dealing effectively with such diverse problems as the establishment of sales territories, the assignment of sales personnel to territories, the establishment of sales quotas, the determination of distribution channels, the location of physical distribution facilities, the allocation of advertising and other promotional expenditures, the development of sales incentive compensation plans, and the assessment of the effectiveness of marketing effort. Indeed, if one reviewed the treatment given to the major decision areas of marketing management in virtually any text,[2] he would be unable to find a single decision area which does not directly presume a knowledge of market potentials.

In specific areas of marketing concern such as new-product decisions, much of the literature emphasizes the way in which market potentials can be manipulated in order to arrive at "optimal" decisions.[3] In few of these instances is the importance of having accurate potentials emphasized when, in fact, good product selection decisions are undoubtedly more dependent on the quality of the estimate of market potential than they are on any other element.

The errors and problems involved in current practices for establishing market potentials are illustrated by Konopa [15, p. 26], who indicates that "faulty estimates of market potential" and related factors accounted for the overwhelming majority of the new-product failures which were reported in a survey of "Fortune 500" corporations.

Models in Market Potential Assessment

Since the process of assessing market potentials is both fraught with difficulties and tailored to suit the individual product situation, it is necessarily at least as artistic as it is scientific. However much the process thus depends on the creativity and ingenuity of the analyst, it is not dependent on mysticism, nor even is it much dependent on luck.

The process of establishing potentials should begin with the recognition that

[2] For instance, see King [13] or Howard [10].
[3] See, for example, Pessemier [18] and King [13, Chap. 5].

an explicit model will be required. That this is indeed a requirement can be easily recognized if one thinks of himself as being in the familiar situation of a retail manager who must assess the sales potential of a product or product line sold in his store. In doing so, he might try to begin by listing the factors and data which he would "require" to make such an assessment—for example, population and age distributions, income statistics, volumes of other retail locations, and so on. In doing so, he would probably make a long list of relevant factors. Then he would realize that, to assess a potential, he must put these factors together in some logical way.

The relationship that he would eventually develop to put the relevant factors together is his *model,* and for the sake of efficiency, *he might just as well have started out with the model and then obtained the data necessary to exercise it.* To perform the data collection first is both inefficient (since much of the data will go unused) and ineffective (since a profusion of data may lead to confusion in model development).

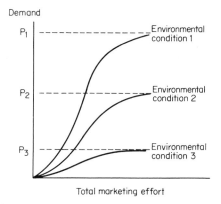

Fig. 1

Of course, this does not imply that the model need be irrevocably specified in advance. Sometimes the exigencies of time and data unavailabilities may require that an initial market potential model be altered so that an "answer" can be realistically achieved. Almost inevitably, the analyst learns as he attempts to implement his initial model, and in so doing he is able to develop a better model. To cling to a prespecified model in such instances would be foolhardy, but no more so than it would be to make the common mistake of starting out without a specific tentative model which can serve as a guide for learning and data collection.

Market Potentials and Demand Concepts

The concept of demand is an important aspect of economic analysis. Traditional economic demand theory is useful as a basis for conceptualizing market potential and, to a limited degree, for assessing it.

A simplistic view of demand and market potential is shown in Figure 1. There, demand for a given product, time period, and market segment is displayed in terms of its relationship to total marketing effort for several different environmental conditions. In interpreting this figure, one should recognize that demand is not a single value; rather, it is dependent on the controllables which make up the total marketing effort (for example, advertising expenditures). Thus the demand level is different for different levels of this *controllable determinant*—total marketing effort. It also depends on *uncontrollable determinants* such as government policies and general economic conditions, which are described as environmental conditions in Figure 1. Thus different curves are needed to describe the demand relation for different sets of environmental conditions.

The levels respectively indicated as P_1, P_2, and P_3 in Figure 1 indicate market potentials for the various environmental conditions, that is, the *maximum* level of demand which can be achieved through marketing efforts in the specified environment.

Market Potential Determination—Theory and Practice

The need for an explicit model to use in assessing market potential and the demand relationships of Figure 1 makes it clear that the basic concept for assessing a market potential involves *the development of a model which relates demand to its determinants*.

A Basic Assumption. However valid this conceptual demand model approach may be, market analysts often find it necessary to make simplifying assumptions which make the potential assessment problem more tractable.

For instance, *market potential is most frequently viewed as a demand level resulting from a specified level of marketing effort* rather than as a maximum level of demand. In other words, since the relationship of Figure 1 is unknown and complex, the analyst may think of himself as occupying a specified point on the horizontal axis (a specified level of total marketing effort), and he may therefore view his task as one of assessing the demand level *for that assumed level of marketing effort*. He can then base his assessment solely on uncontrollable determinants, with the controllable determinants assumed to be fixed at prescribed levels.

Of course, if the analyst chooses to think of the fixed level of marketing effort as being the level which will result in the greatest sales, he is indeed assessing market potential in the sense described in Figure 1. If not, he is not really assessing "true" market potential but rather a measurable quantity which he believes to be "realistic," that is, a point on one of the curves in Figure 1 rather than the top of the curve. In some instances, it is indeed almost necessary that he do this, since he probably has no historical basis for relating various levels of total marketing effort to demand.

Two Approaches. The analyst has a choice between two general approaches to the determination of market potential. Often, however, one of these approaches is prescribed for him by the use to which the potential is to be put, the unavailability of data, or some other constraint.

The most direct of these two approaches involves the estimation of *absolute levels of potential for various market segments*—either in terms of physical units of a product or in terms of revenue dollars. In the case of geographical markets, this means that the potential of each city or county (or whatever geographical unit is being used) would be directly assessed in terms of physical units or dollars. Then, aggregate potentials can be developed simply by summing over the various market segments.

The other major approach involves the assessment of an overall potential for a total market—for example, the United States—and its subsequent disaggregation into potentials for the various market segments based on the relative relationship of each segment to the total market.

The direct approach is generally preferable but more difficult to implement because of data restrictions for the various market segments. Both approaches will be illustrated in the models to be discussed.

Controlling the Results. One of the important implications of the concessions to practicality made in assessing market potentials is the clear indication that *the numbers developed as estimates of potential are subject to error.* That they are error-prone does not make them any less useful; it merely means that they should be treated with skepticism.

There are several ways in which the uncertainty associated with the market potential estimates may be subjected to formal scrutiny.

First, interval estimates may be developed rather than point estimates. In other words, a *range of values* may be quoted as the market potential rather than a single numerical value. Such a market potential range can be developed by using ranges of values for the independent variables of the model. For example, if market potential is to be assessed using the distribution of family expenditures as one of the components of the model, it may be desirable to use several alternative values of "percent of family expenditures in product class" which vary over some prescribed range. The use of such a range is an explicit recognition of our less than certain knowledge of this quantity. Since we are uncertain, we may use a range of *likely* values which, in turn, translates itself into a range of market-potential estimates.

Another way of treating the question of uncertainty is in terms of *sensitivity analysis.*[4] After we have developed a point estimate of market potential, we ask, "How much would this estimate change if we altered one of the quantities which went into calculating it by one unit?" In some cases, we will find that the estimate is relatively insensitive to changes in the quantity in question, that is, that these changes lead to relatively small changes in the potential estimate. In such an instance, we feel much more comfortable with our uncertainty about the quantity, since it matters relatively little. If, on the other hand, we discover that the market potential estimate is relatively sensitive to one of the quantities which went into calculating it, we know where attention should be given to reducing uncertainty, as by collecting more information concerning the quantity in question.

A more sophisticated use of sensitivity analysis focuses on the *sensitivity of the decision* in which the market potential is being used rather than on the sensitivity of the potential estimate itself. If, for example, the market potential is being used to compare two alternative product ideas, the question may be phrased as: "How much would this factor have to change in order to lead to a different decision?" This level of sensitivity analysis recognizes that a wide range of market potentials (and hence a wide range of values of the factor used to determine potentials) may lead to the same conclusion—for example, "Product A is better than product B." Since the manager is usually concerned more that he make the "right" decision than that he have an accurate market potential estimate, it is logical that the influence of changes in these quantities on the decision itself should be investigated.

As in all sensitivity analyses, if a wide range of values for the quantity in question leads to the same conclusion about the two products, the manager would be relatively confident about his selection *even though he may not be at all confident about the precise market-potential value which went into his choice.* If only a narrow range of the quantity is associated with a particular conclusion, he is much less confident and would probably choose to investigate his uncertainty further.

[4] This approach is discussed more extensively in King [13, Chap. 3].

In these ways, the analyst can retain control of the potentials which he has created rather than allowing them to control him. Too often, when no healthy skepticism has been developed and no indications of uncertainty are appended, market potentials become "cast in concrete" as they are used in organizational decision making. With such controls, analysts and managers recognize some of the limitations of the market potentials they are using, and they are thereby more likely to use them rationally and with care.

MARKET POTENTIALS FOR CONSUMER PRODUCTS

Since consumer and industrial markets have traditionally been thought of as different entities, we shall here adhere to the practice of discussing them separately by first taking up the establishment of potentials for consumer products. We shall find that the approaches taken in the consumer and industrial situations are similar in concept if not in detail, so that the subsequent discussion of assessing industrial product market potentials can be abbreviated.

Basic Income and Expenditure Model

A classic market potential model is one which relates market potential to *income levels* and *expenditure patterns*. The basic assumption of the income and expenditure model is that the consuming unit (for example, the family) can consume only what its income permits, at least in the long run. Further, there is a good deal of evidence to suggest that families of similar size, composition, and income level do tend to distribute their consumption expenditures similarly among the various major categories—food, clothing, housing, and so on (see [20]).

The income and expenditure model involves four simple steps:
1. Specification of *market segments*
2. Determination of the number of *consuming units* in each segment
3. Application of *expenditure data* to market segments
4. *Aggregation of potentials* for market segments

For instance, market segments may be defined and categorized on both geographic and income level bases. Thus the analyst might consider the Allegheny County market as classified by income level as "under $3,000," "$3,000–$4,999," and so on.[5] Having defined the various market segments, the analyst must determine the number of consuming units—families, households, and so on—in each segment for the period of interest.[6] This enables him to apply consumer expenditure data to each segment and then to sum the resulting potentials to obtain aggregate potentials for metropolitan areas, states, and other levels.

This procedure is illustrated in Table 1 using hypothetical data.[7]

The overall expenditure of $531,248 in the product category for this county

---

[5] *Sales Management*'s annual "Survey of Buying Power" contains such relative data. Other income data for Standard Metropolitan Statistical Areas (SMSAs) are made by the Department of Commerce (Bureau of Economic Analysis) and published in the May issue of the *Survey of Current Business*. For a fee, the Bureau of Economic Analysis will make available similar data at the county level (also refer to May issues of the *Survey of Current Business*).

[6] Potential sources of data are *Sales Management*, the Rand-McNally *Commercial Atlas and Marketing Guide*, and the Census Bureau's *County and City Data Book*. Sources such as the Rand-McNally guide contain *projections* of population for metropolitan areas for 1985.

[7] These data are similar to those in [20, report no. 237-93, supplement 3, part A].

TABLE 1   Market Potential in County A

After-tax income	Number of families	Average annual expenditure on product category	Annual expenditure on product category
Under $1,000............	47	$ 14	$ 658
$1,000–1,999............	167	5	835
2,000–2,999............	238	10	2,380
3,000–3,999............	466	20	9,320
4,000–4,999............	2,427	26	63,102
5,000–5,999............	5,900	39	230,100
6,000–7,499............	1,263	59	74,517
7,500–9,999............	1,004	83	83,332
10,000–14,999.........	228	183	41,724
15,000 and over........	64	395	25,280
Total county potential for product category...			$531,248

can then be summed with similar figures for other counties to arrive at an assessment of potential for multicounty markets, states, or the nation.

This basic model can be applied in a myriad of variations to suit particular products and situations. The basic consuming unit may be varied—individuals, households, families, and so forth. The segments may be subdivided further, for example, into income, family size, *and* geographic categories. The available historical data may be updated for the time period in question on the basis of time trends in expenditure patterns for various product categories.[8] If the methods used in the collection of available information are in question or if it is deemed necessary to update available data on a basis other than that of simple trends, other refinements can be made in the basic model, since its essence lies in reliance on the determinant income and expenditure patterns rather than in the particular measures which may be used.

Income Market Index Model

If expenditure data are not available for the market segments of concern and if income is deemed to be a desirable measure for "environmental" influences on market potential, an *income market index* approach can be used.

Any market index is a measure of the *relative* potential of a market segment. Usually, the assessment is relative to the total market.[9] In the case of the income market index, the assessment is in terms of the income level of the market.

Since the income market index is a relative measure, its use illustrates the second major approach to assessing market potentials discussed earlier, that is, the assessment of an overall potential and its subsequent disaggregation into potentials for the various market segments. Such an approach would be appropriate, for example, if data for a particular product were available which would permit an overall national potential to be assessed but data were not available to build up segment potentials as in the previous model.

The procedure for developing an index is:

[8] Such as those contained in [20].

[9] See [21] for a description of the methods used to develop the data reported in [20].

1. Specification of market segments (for example, relevant income groups by geographic area)
2. Determination of the number of consuming units in each segment
3. Calculation of the index
4. Application of index to overall market potential assessment

Suppose that a firm feels that the sole market for a new product is the "$10,000 and over" cash income group. The income market index for a specified geographic area would simply be the ratio of the number of consuming units of this income group in the total market.[10] This ratio could then be applied to an overall market potential to determine a potential assessment for the area.

For example, if the overall national potential is $11 million and an area contains 3.5 per cent of the "$10,000 and over" consuming unit population, the market's potential would be assessed to be $11,000,000 (0.035) = $385,000.

The same approach can be used if more than one income group makes up the market for the product. If surveys or other evidence indicate that the relative importance of various income groups is disparate, they may be *weighted* in calculating an income index. For example, if an area contains 3.5 per cent of a consumer group which is rated twice as significant as a consumer group whose representation in the market makes up 5 per cent of the nation's consumer group population, the potential would be:

$$\$11,000,000 \left[\frac{0.035(2) + 0.05(1)}{3} \right] = \$440,000$$

One of the principal advantages of this model as well as of the income-expenditure model lies in their consideration of market segments which are in part defined according to income. Aggregate income statistics for an entire geographic market often fail to depict *differences in the distribution of income* among various income groups. And if such differences are important, as they would be if the potential market were concentrated in a small proportion of the various income groups, aggregate income data can be very misleading. When the market is segmented according to income categories, such differences can be given their due consideration.

Other Index Models[11]

The index approach previously illustrated for an income market index can be applied using any market indicator or combination of market indicators. The basic assumptions underlying index models are that

1. Market factors can be determined which indicate the relative buying power of the market segments for the product in question.
2. Measures of these market factors can be determined.
3. The relative importance of the market factors can be assessed.
4. An overall market potential can be independently established.

Three general varieties of market factors are often thought of as related to the market potential for a consumer product—*consuming units, income,* and a *willingness to spend.* We have already discussed several measures appropriate to the "consuming units" factor (population, number of households, number of families). The measures appropriate to the "income" factor may be disposable income, cash income, or after-tax income. A relative "willingness to spend"

---

[10] *Sales Management's* annual "Survey of Buying Power" contains such data.

[11] See Crisp [5, Chap. 5] or Hummel [11, Chap. 11] for examples of other index models.

may be characterized by actual expenditures by the market segment for a product, product class, or general sales category. Frequently, for example, "retail sales" or "shopping goods sales" are used as measures of this factor.

The determination of the appropriate market factors to include in an index can be performed subjectively or objectively using other similar products as standards. For instance, "population" is a market factor which has been found to be appropriate for many low-priced staples. Appropriateness can be objectively determined by observing whether a market index based on population closely parallels the proportion of the total sales of selected low-priced staple products in various markets. In this same fashion, "income" has been shown to be an appropriate market factor for many luxury products.

Buying Power Indexes. When more than one market factor is to be incorporated into an index, the relative importance of the various factors is usually independently assessed. For instance, one well-known and widely used index which involves three general market factors is *Sales Management's* Buying Power Index.[12] The index (BPI) is calculated for a market using the formula:

$$\text{BPI} = \frac{5x + 3y + 2z}{10}$$

where x = market's proportion of "U.S. effective buying income"[13]

y = market's proportion of "U.S. retail sales"

z = market's proportion of "U.S. population"

The BPI has been found to be useful in determining relative potentials for mass products sold at popular prices. For products which do not fall into this category, other similar indexes can be developed. For example, some consumer products have been shown to be more closely related to the manufacturing volume of a given geographical area than to retail sales in that area. If this is the case, an index using "value added by manufactures" instead of "retail sales" might well be appropriate.[14]

Other measures of the "willingness to buy" market factor which are also commonly used in place of "retail sales" in developing market indexes—for example, "office equipment sales"—might be used for products where this is more logically related than is "retail sales." Other definitions of the "consuming units" factor may also be appropriate to use. An auto manufacturer might see the "under-30 male" group as the primary market for a new low-priced sports car. Hence, he might consider this group as his "consuming units." (Indeed, such a manufacturer might also use "new car registrations" as indicative of the "willingness to buy" factor.[15]) If several consumer groups are identified as relevant, they too may be weighted in the manner discussed for income groups in the preceding paragraphs entitled "Income Market Index Model."

The Critical Assumptions. The index-model assumptions that market factors can be determined and measured are usually less critical than are the assumptions concerning the determination of an overall potential and the determination of relative factor weights.

---

[12] See *Sales Management's* annual "Survey of Buying Power."

[13] "Effective Buying Income" is personal income minus federal, state, and local taxes. It is generally equivalent to the measure called "disposable personal income" by the federal government.

[14] See Rand McNally's *Commercial Atlas and Marketing Guide* for a discussion of this approach.

[15] Such data are available for local markets from sources such as university-based bureaus of business research.

The assumption that a total potential can be independently developed obviously directly affects most uses to which the indexes may be put. The assumption that the relative importance of the various factors can be independently assessed is also a crucial one, since any index depends directly on the weights chosen to reflect this relative importance. (In the BPI the weights are 5, 3, and 2 for "income," "retail sales," and "population" respectively.)

These weights may be determined objectively from past data or subjectively using judgment. They may be objectively determined through multiple regression analyses[16] of past data or simply by finding weights which "worked" in the past. Often, experienced people "know" relationships among the factors as they relate to a particular product. For instance, in the case of high-priced products, "income" is known to be relatively more important than "number of consuming units." For low-priced products, the converse is true. Such knowledge can lead to the subjective development of rational weights for the factors in a specific situation.

In any case, the analyst should recognize any arbitrariness which is involved in the determination of the weights and *act to prevent it from unduly influencing the actions on which the market potentials bear.* For instance, the analyst may use the approaches discussed earlier by developing ranges of market potential estimates based on alternative "reasonable" sets of weights or by conducting an analysis of the sensitivity of the result (either the potential estimate itself or the action to which it leads) to changes in the weights.

Sales Models

The most significant difference between the assessment of market potentials for new products and existing products lies in the absence of historical sales information for new products. However, the need for new-product market potentials, their complexity, and the lure of available "hard" sales data often lead the market analyst to question whether any new product is "really new."[17]

The assumption that there are no truly new products may be valid if one views the product as a means of satisfying needs rather than as a physical entity, for a product would either have had to result from a basic change in nature or a change in human needs to be truly new in this sense. Indeed, many new products actually do represent rather direct *evolutions* of existing products.

If the product whose potential is to be assessed is one of these varieties, historical sales data can be used in developing indexes or in assessing absolute market potentials. The most common situation involves the use of total industry sales as an index of the market potential for a yet unmarketed product.

Of course, other kinds of sales measures may also be used. Sales data may be available for similar products or for products for which the new product is a direct substitute. If the product directly evolves from another, sales data from the ancestor product may be used. In the instance where the new product is a substitute for one or more existing products, the *rate of displacement* becomes of paramount importance.[18]

If historical sales data for an appropriate product or product class are available for use as an index, the methods of Section IV, Part B, Chapters 1 to 4 or Section II, Part E may be applied.[19]

---

[16] See Sec. II, Part E, Chaps. 4 and 5.
[17] See Howard [10, Chap. 5] or Britton [3] for discussion of this point.
[18] See Dean [6, p. 174] for a discussion of this approach.
[19] Also see Sec. IV, Part F.

Survey-based Models

Survey-based approaches to the determination of market potentials fall into two general categories—those in which the ultimate consumer is queried and those in which "experts" are asked to provide information for developing potentials.

Consumer Surveys.[20]   The consumer survey approach is based on the simple assumption that decisions to purchase new products are made by people who can and will relate their intention or at least their willingness to purchase the product. Further, since most consumer products have such a large number of potential consumers, it would be prohibitively costly to query each concerning the product in question. As a result, the second basic assumption of survey models is that a *sample* can be used to estimate the potential for a total market (population).

Thus, consumer surveys usually involve the direct querying—by written questionnaire or verbally—of a sample of consumers selected from the potential consuming population. Obviously, one of the great problems in this approach is the difficulty of adequately describing a new product to the consumer. If the product is already in development, mock-ups or prototypes may be examined by the consumer; but if not, descriptive literature and verbal descriptions must suffice.

Such surveys may be conducted using one's own staff or professionals. However, many bad experiences using nonprofessionals in questionnaire development and interviewing over a wide range of companies have demonstrated to marketers that professional help is essential in structuring surveys, designing samples, and in conducting interviews or administering questionnaires.

Alternatively, published surveys may be used. For example, surveys are conducted on a regular basis by the U.S. Bureau of the Census, the National Industrial Conference Board, McGraw-Hill, and the Survey Research Center of the University of Michigan.

Once survey data are available, the market potential is developed by using sample statistics to draw inferences concerning the total market population. This may be accomplished using simple methods of inferential statistics.[21]

Expert Opinion.   Another "survey" approach which may be used to assess market potential involves the use of expert opinion. Rather than interviewing consumers, the analyst may interview experts who he believes possess a subjective basis for estimating market potential. For example, a sales manager who has spent his career with a product class should have the judgment, intuition, and experience which would lend itself to estimating the market potential for such a product.

If market potentials are developed from such "questionnaires" through the use of a process which has three important characteristics, good results are often achieved. The three characteristics are:

1. The obtaining of judgments for a range of possible values on a probability basis
2. The application of "the expected value" concept to the probability assessment
3. The obtaining of judgments from a number of experts and their subsequent aggregation into a single joint assessment

The obtaining of judgments on a probability basis involves the specification of *subjective probabilities*[22]—degrees of belief—for a range of possible market

[20] See Sec. II, Parts B and C.
[21] See Sec. II, Part D.
[22] See Sec. II, Part C, Chap. 3.

potentials. For instance, the expert might be asked to assign probabilities (decimal quantities summing to one) to the market potentials for 100,000, 110,000, 120,000, and 130,000 units. Since these figures would be stated only after initial "ballpark" assessments were discussed, the expert might be able to say that the 110,000 figure was twice as likely as any of the other three. He would therefore be imputing probabilities as follows:

Market potential	Probability
100,000	.20
110,000	.40
120,000	.20
130,000	.20

The expected-value concept is then used to condense this series of estimates into a single number. (The expected value is analogous to the arithmetic average.) In this case the expected value (EV) is $EV = 100,000 \ (.20) + 110,000 \ (.40) + 120,000 \ (.20) + 130,000 \ (.20)$, or 114,000 units. This figure could then be used as the individual expert's opinion of market potential.

This assessment may be combined with other similar assessments obtained from other experts to assure that no single individual biases the overall assessment. A simple average may be taken across the individuals; or the various experts' opinions may be weighted according to past biases, position in the organization, degree of expertise, or some other relevant measure. For example, if the assessment of the above expert were to be weighted at three times that of another whose expected value was 128,000, the overall market potential would be calculated as

$$\frac{114,000 \ (3) + 128,000 \ (1)}{4} = 117,500$$

MARKET POTENTIALS FOR INDUSTRIAL PRODUCTS

The problems and methods for determining market potentials for industrial products are not structurally different from those encountered in analyzing consumer products. The basic relevant differences encountered in industrial marketing are the size and nature of the total market and market segments and the different indicators of the demand determinants which must be used.

Basic Industrial Market Potential Models

Survey, sales, and index models may all be used for industrial products. Since the customers of industrial marketing are themselves business firms, the number of different customers is usually different by an order of magnitude on more than the number of customers for a consumer product. This raises the possibility of a *census survey*[23] rather than a sample survey and of simple sales trend analysis[24] rather than the use of more sophisticated sales models which presume the use of a probability sample.

Surveys which ask *buyer's intentions* are of more use in industrial marketing than in consumer marketing since purchases are presumably made on a more rationally planned basis according to objective criteria. This means that the industrial buyer's intentions may "mean more" than do consumers' intentions.[25]

With index models, the indicators used for demand determinants in the in-

---

[23] See Sec. II, Part B, Chap. 1.
[24] See Sec. II, Part E, Chap. 1.
[25] See National Bureau of Economic Research [16].

dustrial case are generally such things as number of employees, number of plants, value added by manufacture, expenditure on plant and equipment, value of materials consumed, value of electrical energy consumed, or shipments.[26] These indicators may be given relative weights and treated in analogous ways to those factors discussed in the development of indexes for consumer products.

If market segments are to be utilized in any of these models, industry categories may provide a basis for their determination. Those categories defined by SIC codes[27] are the most commonly used.

An Exception

One structural difference between industrial and consumer markets which is not accounted for in any of the applications of these basic models is the fact that *industrial customers are not final consumers;* they buy and sell from and to each other. This is clearly not the case in the consumer sector and it creates certain difficulties.

The primary difficulty is that in identifying the potential for a product based on future projections of a given industry, one is omitting the additional demand generated by *changes in the demand of customers of that industry.* Thus, if industry A sells to industry B, changes in demand *by* A must reflect changes in demand *on* A by B. Simple projections usually do not account for such interactions.

Input-output models—which are based on the *flow* of goods and services through the various sectors and industries in the national economy—may be used to take account of the complex relationships and interdependencies among industries. These models are discussed in [Section IV, Part D, Chapter 3].

EXISTING PRODUCTS

The determination of market potentials would not superficially appear to be important for existing products. If a product is already being sold, what need is there for market research on sales potentials? It would appear that the "hard" sales information which is lacking for new products is available to supplant potentials.

The answer is straightforward. Many of the uses to which market potentials can be put—establishing sales territories, allocating sales personnel to territories, and so on—implicitly assume a "steady state" condition. Many products, particularly those that have been marketed for only a short time, have exhibited only transient sales behavior. Their sales levels may be little indicative of the underlying potential of the market.

Obviously, the marketing manager might prefer to make such crucial "permanent" decisions as the establishment of sales territories and the assignment of salesmen on the basis of something more than transient sales performance. If this is the case, he will undoubtedly find the market potential techniques of this chapter to be useful.

Other special situations can call for the use of market potential techniques. For example, if sales are known by one geographic distribution, say by regions,

---

[26] See U.S. Census of Manufacturers (Census Bureau), Rand-McNally *Commercial Atlas and Marketing Guide, Survey of Current Business* (Census Bureau), *Annual Survey of Manufacturers* (Census Bureau), *County Business Pattern* (Census Bureau), *Statistical Abstract of the United States* (Census Bureau), *Sales Management's* annual "Survey of Industrial Buying Power," the journal *Industrial Marketing,* and various industry and trade association publications. Also see Frank [8].

[27] Standard Industrial Classification. This is a numerical system used to classify industries. See Sec. IV, Part D, Chap. 3.

but market assessments are needed in terms of different geographic entities, say metropolitan areas, market potential assessment techniques may be applied. Bass [2] has provided a regression approach for such situations.

SUMMARY

Market potentials are among the most elusive and important measures related to marketing decisions. As such, assessments of market potential should be treated as critical measures which are to be viewed with a healthy skepticism. Emphasis should be at least as much on methods for dealing with uncertainty and for controlling the potential errors in assessments as with the basic estimation methods themselves.

REFERENCES

1. Abrams, J., "Reducing the Risk of New Product Marketing Strategies Testing," *Journal of Marketing Research,* May 1969, pp. 216–220.
2. Bass, M., "Decomposable Regression Models in the Analysis of Market Potentials," Herman C. Krannert Graduate School of Industrial Administration, Purdue University, paper no. 239, March 1969.
3. Britton, H., "Directories and Census Data in Establishing New Product Potentials or First Things First," chap. 25 in AMA [9].
4. Cowan, D. R. G., "Market Potentials and Marketing Management," in J. C. Halterman and T. W. Meloan [9], pp. 1–3.
5. Crisp, R. D., *Sales Planning and Control,* New York: McGraw-Hill, 1961.
6. Dean, *Managerial Economics,* Englewood Cliffs, N.J.: Prentice Hall, 1951.
7. Enrick, N. L., *Market and Sales Forecasting,* San Francisco: Chandler, 1969.
8. Frank, N. D., *Market Analysis,* New York: The Scarecrow Press, 1964.
9. Halterman, J. C., and T. W. Meloan, eds., *Proceedings of the Seminar on Market Potentials and the Use of Census Data,* Chicago: American Marketing Association, 1958.
10. Howard, John A., *Marketing Management: Analysis and Decision,* Homewood, Ill.: Irwin, 1957.
11. Hummel, Francis E., *Market and Sales Potentials,* New York: Ronald, 1961.
12. Hummel, F. E., "Principles and Techniques for Establishing Potentials for New Industrial Products," chap. 26 in AMA [9].
13. King, W. R., *Quantitative Analysis for Marketing Management,* New York: McGraw-Hill, 1967.
14. Kline, C. H., "The Strategy of Product Policy," *Harvard Business Review,* July–August 1955, pp. 91–100.
15. Konopa, L. J., *New Products: Assessing Commercial Potential,* New York: American Management Association, Inc., 1966.
16. National Bureau of Economic Research, *The Quality and Economic Significance of Anticipations Data,* Princeton, N.J.: Princeton University Press, 1960.
17. O'Meara, J. T., Jr., "Selecting Profitable Products," *Harvard Business Review,* January–February 1966, pp. 83–89.
18. Pessemier, E. A., *New Product Decisions: An Analytic Approach,* New York: McGraw-Hill, 1966.
19. Richman, B., "A Rating Scale for Product Innovation," *Business Horizons,* Summer 1962, pp. 37–42.
20. U.S. Bureau of Labor Statistics, *Survey of Consumer Expenditures, 1960–61,* Research Report 237-1, 1966.
21. U.S. Bureau of Labor Statistics, *Handbook of Methods for Surveys and Studies,* Bulletin 1458, 1966, chap. 8.
22. Warshaw, M. P., and G. P. Murphy, eds., *New Product Planning for Changing Markets,* Bureau of Business Research, Graduate School of Business Administration.
23. Wilson, A., *The Assessment of Industrial Markets,* London: Hutchinson, 1968.

New-Product Development and Introduction

Chapter 2

Product Testing

DAVID K. HARDIN *Market Facts, Inc., Chicago, Illinois*

INTRODUCTION

A major role of market research lies in product testing. Product testing has always been a basic part of a complete marketing information or research system. It is basically aimed at providing management with meaningful feedback on the probable acceptance of their products by the marketplace. Few research users are without systematic product testing budgets and procedures.

The importance of product testing to management varies according to the type of product class involved. For example, product testing can be critical to high-turnover grocery and drug products where the repurchase cycle is short, for example, every month or so. For these product classes, product performance can dynamically affect the loyalty and, therefore, the short-term sales of the product.

Among the more durable products, product performance may or may not play a critical role. For example, in automobile-make loyalty studies, it has become very clear that the number of product problems encountered by a car buyer dramatically affects his brand loyalty when he buys his next car. And word-of-mouth comments about product quality have effects that go well beyond measured results.

On the other hand, in the case of highly durable products, such as ranges or automatic washing machines, product performance is sometimes not as critical an issue. There is a fairly low level of brand loyalty on products which are generally replaced every 10 to 12 years. Because of the technical changes made during the intervening period, brand loyalty generated by product performance seems to play a minor role.

Product quality does seem to have an increasing role in durable goods because of growing consumerism.   There is a real need to protect the manufacturer from government incursion on the grounds of product performance.   The view is growing that product performance must measure up to the product promise or even implied promise in the advertising and promotion.   Otherwise the manufacturer seems to face an implied breach of contract, even if only a moral contract.   Thus product performance is rising in importance.   Product performance and its relationship to consumer expectations play a critical role in the successful long-term life of a particular brand.

In a marketing research sense, product testing tends to be restricted to the low-cost, short-life products.   It is virtually impossible for a manufacturer to product test a new car, since by the time the car has been made in sufficient volume, it must be marketed just in terms of tooling and production costs.

While it is not wise to generalize too much, there is a relationship between the needs for product testing and the nature of the market involved.   Some of the key variables that call for product testing consideration are shown at the left of this tabulation:

RELEVANCE OF PRODUCT TESTING TO MANAGEMENT

New brand	*Established brand*
Large sales volume	Small sales volume
Short purchase cycle	Long purchase cycle
Highly competitive product class	Noncompetitive product class
Considerable brand differentiation	Little brand differentiation
Physical attributes important to consumer	Physical attributes not important to consumer

SHOULD A COMPANY DO PRODUCT TESTING?

There are a number of fairly objective criteria which one can apply to the decision as to whether a substantial investment in product testing development and procedures is justified.   Basically, product testing is valid and desirable when the following conditions tend to exist:

1.   *There is a high level of uncertainty among decision makers about the appeal of the proposed product formulation or design.*   Where management is unanimous or virtually unanimous in the decision to make a change or to market a new product, product testing is of little value—it will seldom change management's mind.   Where there is some uncertainty or disagreement among the decision makers, then product testing can often dynamically resolve the uncertainties in favor of the prudent financial decision.

2.   *There is a high financial risk involved in being wrong.*   Where the decision to make the product involves an extremely high financial or marketing cost, product testing can clearly be a profitable action.   It is easy to see that a $5,000 product test which substantially reduces the risk of being wrong on a $1 million decision should be undertaken without further discussion.   On the other hand, a $5,000 product test involving a $25,000 risk is far less likely to be justifiable.

3.   *Physical product performance is critical to long-term consumer acceptance.*   There are many product classes where the actual performance of the product is not critical to its acceptance or success.   Examples would include high-fashion women's clothing, certain children's toys, proprietary drug products which rely on psychology rather than physical performance for their acceptance, and items in a product class which lacks competition.

4. *The effectiveness of competitive brands or makes is low.* Refinements available through sophisticated product testing may well lack justification if the competitive environment is such that the cost of the improvements is not justified by a significant change in market performance. Sales volume of Polaroid film is probably not dynamically affected by quality issues.

An observation of product testing behavior by various industries reveals substantial clustering. In other words, if one major industry is committed to product testing, the others are generally also committed to some extent. Where product testing is not done by leading companies in an industry, it is seldom done by other companies in the same industry. This is not to say that some form of product testing or evaluation does not offer significant competitive advantage to the company operating in an industry which has never discovered it. It can give such a company a unique edge which redounds substantially in terms of ultimate profitability.

THE ROLE OF PRODUCT TESTING

Product testing has many roles. The proper research of a product idea or execution depends upon the nature of the marketing decision involved. Some of the roles of product testing include the following:

1. *The evaluation of new-product ideas and prototypes.* Increasingly, new products are not so much based on really innovative new-product ideas as they are on some alteration in form, content, or marketing strategy for a new brand in an existing product class. Few truly new products have been evolved in this onrushing new-product revolution. Xerography might be one; the Polaroid camera and freeze-dried coffee might be others. But for every truly innovative and successful new product, there are a dozen successful new products involving only variations in form, concept, or marketing strategy.

One of the best ways of evaluating a new product *idea* is to incorporate the product idea test in a product test. When management can prepare adequate numbers of test products which embody this concept, a combination of concept and product tests can be undertaken.

Simply stated, the product and concept test is a measure of the market value of both the product idea and its performance as a product in the marketplace. Is it perceived by the market as an interesting and appealing product? Does it offer competitive advantages over existing products? Is it seen as filling a regular need—replacing an existing, regularly used product?

Should the concept be widely accepted, then the second question centers around the product execution itself. Does the product really fit the concept? Is it an adequate representation of the promise implied in the concept? When tried, does it increase or diminish the tester's enthusiasm for the product idea and for getting involved with the product?

In a sense, product concept and usage tests can provide substantially marketable information. For example, to state it simply, one of the following four results will be obtained from a concept product test. Each suggests a further course of management action.

Findings are seldom this clear, but general directions will be provided. Bad products will be dropped and good ideas continued. When possible, the product concept and usage test can be critical to avoiding serious financial loss or uncovering substantial profit potentials.

A good example of the value of this kind of test will be found in the marketing history of the ready-to-eat cereals with freeze-dried fruits introduced in the sixties. These products had strong early acceptance but quickly faded. The

Research finding	*Marketing action*
High concept acceptance; low product performance.	Additional physical product; development or lab work is needed and should be undertaken.
Low concept acceptance; high product performance.	Reexamine the marketing strategy being considered and the current positioning of the product which may have a better potential in a different context.
Low concept acceptance; low product performance.	Abandon the product idea.
High product acceptance; high product performance.	Proceed with positive marketing action.

idea was simply more appealing than the execution—good concept, inadequate product.

2. *Separating long-run potential winners from appealing bad items— extended use testing.* The developer of the innovative product faces a basic concern: Is this going to be a fad or does it have a long-term future? Costly manufacturing and marketing investment decisions ride on getting the right answer to this question.

One kind of product test that can make the answer easier is the extended use test. This involves (*a*) leaving the respondents far more product than they used in the short run and then measuring usage rates or (*b*) constantly replenishing the consumer's needs to determine long-run usage patterns and rates.

The *extended use test* will generally require that all the (major) brands in this product class be made available along with the new one being tested. The test must meet as many of these requirements as possible:

a. Be as close to market conditions as possible—that is, "sell" the product, don't give it away.

b. Have as little use bias for the new product as possible. Use a control group if necessary.

c. Provide adequate safeguards to ensure accurate usage measurement.

d. Run the test as long as possible to be sure that equilibrium is met.

There is no rule of thumb for the length of an extended use test. However, it should go through at least three purchase cycles. The goal is to produce equilibrium. For example, in Figure 1, usage rates measured to Point A did not identify the winner (X) or the loser (Y). A test to Point B did achieve that goal.

3. *Evaluating the need for changes in product formulation.* This is the basic ingredient in an ongoing product testing program. Tastes change, and the company that does not recognize these changes soon finds its product obsoleted by competitors. Moreover, marketing efficiency and the return on advertising investment are closely related to the extent to which attractive and current product formulations are offered to the market. Advertising which is selling a product with limited acceptance is costly, since it is constantly called on to replace the dissatisfied customers.

Many products have subtly but steadily altered their nature over the past decade or two. Graham crackers have steadily become far sweeter and saltine crackers have become far thinner. The automobile has evolved to a much lower silhouette and considerably more horsepower. Only an alert, evaluation-oriented management can stay ahead of the trend by making the forward leap that becomes necessary as tastes change.

For this kind of product testing, it is critically important that systematic evaluation techniques and ground rules be established and that regular trend lines be created. Changing tastes can be readily measured if careful attention is paid to maintaining the same technique or using split run tests when techniques are improved.

The testing of product formulation changes or alternative physical properties requires careful consideration of the management strategy involved. For example, the correct testing procedures when one is considering a lower-cost product formulation may be vastly different from that required when one is considering a change which will not affect costs and is, therefore, aimed at marketing improvement.

When a change that could substantially reduce the product cost is considered, management may well prefer to determine whether the change is one that is *perceptible* by the consumer rather than whether this change creates a product which is preferred to the one it replaces. If a cost reduction of a significant magnitude, such as 10 percent or more, is being considered, management might well be willing to make the change even though direct product preferences favor the old product by a ratio as high as three or four to one. The willingness to make the change would hinge on the fact that only 6 percent of the consumers could notice the change or were aware of the change in the normal marketing environment.

On the other hand, a product change which is costless or which involves somewhat greater costs should produce not only adequate levels of recognition but also significant improvements in product preferences for the brand being changed over leading competitive brands.

For example, in a measure of a consumer paper product class, a significant cost reduction in a major brand's manufacturing process was being considered.

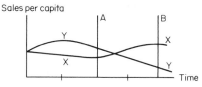

Fig. 1. How usage rates may vary over time.

When blind-tested in pairs, the old product outperformed the new, lower-cost product by a ratio of 71 to 29. A look at these data alone would have caused management to reject the notion of saving the money.

However, a more subtle product testing technique which involved the application of product sampling rather than any kind of testing suggestion revealed that only one consumer in twenty had even noticed or felt there was any difference between the two products. Thus, management could safely proceed with the cost reduction even though flying in the face of reduced, forced consumer preferences.

4. *Product testing for market segmentation.* Increasingly, as markets proliferate and as product classes grow to maturity, they support increasing numbers of brands or makes. With multiple-brand product classes comes the opportunity for market segmentation strategy. Basically, market segmentation today means the recognition of varying sets of product needs by different groups of consumers.

The toothpaste market has been traditionally viewed as a costly and highly competitive product class into which one would not venture lightly. Traditionally, toothpastes have been sold with the two basic appeals of decay prevention and breath or mouth freshener. By discovering a major untapped market segment or need group, several successful new toothpastes have been recently introduced. The need reached was based on the cosmetic aspects of toothpaste—a bright smile and the sex appeal which goes with it. Obviously, a toothpaste aimed at a market segment requiring a sexy smile may have far different physical product requirements than one aimed at a market seeking diminished decay levels. Thus, segmented marketing requires careful attention to the products offered to the segments at which one is focusing the brand.

Basically, product testing in a segmented market should restrict or at least focus the testing of the product on the market segment at which it is to be aimed later. The more clearly this segment can be defined, the more efficient and valid the product testing results will be. In other words, it is not essential that one's product outperform competitive products on an across-the-board basis in the market—it is only essential that product performance be adequate or superior within the segment one has decided to attack. Increasingly, product testing is being focused on market segments.

5. *Using product testing to evolve packaging or marketing strategies.* Often a product test is the most effective device for determining the real performance of a new package or a new advertising strategy. For example, if one is thinking of changing or modernizing a label, the most valid test of the effectiveness of the old versus the new label may be a *product* test. Respondents are given the packages with new and old labels containing identical formulations.

The normal form of such a test is *not* to test the old against the new—this is too artificial and lacks the essential subtlety. Instead, two matched groups are each given, say, three brands to test—the test brand and two leading competitors. But one group gets the new label and one gets the old. The results might be as follows:

Group	Percent preferring product		
	Test brand	Competitor X	Competitor Y
A (new label)................	42	18	40
B (old label)................	31	26	43

Winner: New label by 9%, significant at 2σ (95% confidence level)
Action: Move to market or market test the new label.

Packaging changes should enhance *product* acceptance, *not* package appeal. By measuring *product appeal,* an indirect and more meaningful measure of the package contribution to the product image can be obtained without the consumer's knowledge. This kind of subtlety is often essential in package testing. Overt questioning or attitude measures focused on packaging may produce not only invalid but even misleading results as the consumers try to "judge" the more esthetic, cultural, and prestigious aspects of the package design rather than responding in a real way to the marketing appeals which would cause them to purchase.

Similarly, a product test can be objectively used in evaluating alternative advertising strategies, as in packaging. The various advertising strategies are embodied in the product test through concept descriptions with the implication that different products are being tested. Since the products tested are identical, the responses can honestly be attributed to the kinds of appeals generated for the product or brand by the advertising concept.

6. *Product testing when the product cannot be made for testing.* Very often, it is impractical to consider a product test as a part of the evaluation program for a new product or a changed product. A classic example would be the

new car models, where one would have to tool up for product testing prior to launching the product. In this case, can any kind of product testing be useful? Pictures, scale models, and full-size prototypes have often provided extremely valuable information in terms of ultimate customer acceptance of the product. A critical issue is that the market research test involve a valid portrayal of those product attributes which are vital to the purchase decisions to be made by consumers. If a car's styling is critical to purchase levels, then a prototype which portrays the styling can provide adequate product information—though it is only a Fiberglas shell. On the other hand, if the way the washing machine whitens really dirty clothes is critical to its acceptance, a style test of the alternative washing machine models is not overly useful.

When testable prototypes are available but very expensive, useful information can be provided by small group sessions or by sequenced in-home tests. In a sequenced test, several households may use the same prototype in a series.

PRODUCT TESTING METHODOLOGY

There are many ways to test products. The goal of the product tester should be to find that method or technique which produces the desired information (at an acceptable risk level) for the lowest cost and in the shortest time. When selecting the proper methods and techniques, *total* costs—inside and outside—should be included. Inside costs, such as formulation and management involvement, should be added to the outside testing service charges—something which is seldom done. Often, the outside test charges are a fraction of the total cost, especially in terms of management time and resources. While it is not possible to build a manual of testing techniques, it is important to consider all the options when planning a product test or system.

1. *Alternative product testing techniques.* One product testing decision centers on whether to use expert or average consumers in a product test. In general, the earlier the product formulation stage, the more appropriate is the use of experts—for example, trained taste panels. As the product moves into market planning, consumer tests using typical samples of potential users are required for valid information.

The sampling technique involved may be any one of several. Perhaps the most commonly used are:

a. Personal, in-home product placements and testing procedures
b. Clinics or central location tests
c. Controlled mail-panel tests
d. Some combination of techniques, such as personal placements with telephone evaluation interviews

Personal placements are most costly, mail-panel or central location testing least costly. Whether the product requires in-home usage or standard trial under normal circumstances, mail-panel technology is often desirable if the product is mailable. The mail panel offers an effective, highly dispersed sample. Moreover, it provides legitimate concept and product data in contrast to personal interviews.

An article in the *Journal of Marketing Research* [1] suggests the validity of mail panels in contrast to the more expensive personal interviews. To quote from that article:

Market Facts, Inc., recently evaluated a number of new product ideas shown to respondents using colored photographs. Few, if any, technological production problems for the products being considered had been solved before the research. However, several new products (in limited distribution) were also included.

TABLE 1 Weighted Averages and Ranking of Products

Product	Overall opinion				Taste appeal				Ease of preparation[a]				Appropriateness for friends			
	Personal		CMP[b]		Personal		CMP[b]		Personal		CMP[b]		Personal		CMP[b]	
	Avg.	Rank	Avg.	Rank	Avg.	Rank	Avg.	Rank	Avg.	Rank	Avg.	Rank	Avg.	Rank	Avg.	Rank
A	2.19	4	2.69	4	1.89	4	2.51	4	3.83	2	3.93	2	2.05	4	2.12	4
B	2.44	2	2.76	3	2.45	2	2.68	3	3.70	3	3.91	3	2.46	2	2.55	2
C	3.06	1	3.49	1	3.01	1	3.43	1	...	...	...	...	3.02	1	3.22	1
D	2.33	3	2.88	2	1.96	3	2.77	2	3.87	1	4.06	1	2.21	3	2.54	3
Number of respondents	363		733		363		733		363		733		363		733	

[a] Product C was not evaluated on ease of preparation.
[b] Consumer Mail Panels.

Early sales results for these products were highly favorable, and these products served as a control or reference frame.

The objective of the research was to aid in determining which, if any, new product ideas merited additional technological development. Personal, face-to-face data collection and a symmetrical rating scale maximized comparability with other research projects.

Four products were also studied using Consumer Mail Panels, a controlled mail panel of respondents. The research costs of controlled mail panel studies are lower than the costs of personal, face-to-face interviewing.

The four products in colored prints were evaluated by controlled mail panel members with a replication of the questionnaire and rating devices used in the personal phase. The four products were also evaluated by another sample of panel members using an asymmetrical rather than a symmetrical rating scale.

Thus, the same four products were evaluated by three samples of respondents. One sample evaluated the four products in a personal, face-to-face situation. Another sample evaluated the products with data collection from a controlled mail panel of respondents. The same questionnaire and rating devices were used in samples one and two. A third sample, also drawn from a controlled mail panel of respondents, evaluated products using an asymmetrical rating scale.

The objective of this research was to determine the differences, if any, between reactions:

1. from controlled mail panel members
2. from respondents interviewed face to face
3. from using alternative rating devices.

RESULTS

Attribute Ratings

Each product was evaluated on specific attributes or characteristics using the same symmetrical scale. Some of the attributes were overall opinion, taste appeal, ease of preparation, and apropriateness for friends. Thus, each respondent in the control panel sample and face-to-face samples considered the same attributes of the products using the same eleven-point symmetrical scale.

There are many methods of analyzing the frequency distribution of responses. One of the most common methods involves assigning equal interval weights to each point of the distribution and then computing a weighted average score. What differences are there between the average scores obtained?

There is a statistically significant difference* in the absolute average reported for the two types of data collection methods (Table 1). The weighted averages from the controlled mail panel sample are about .3 higher than the weighted averages from face-to-face interviews. However, despite the difference in absolute average ratings, the two methods yield similar information in terms of relative or ranking evaluations. For example, Product C is rated highest on overall appeal, taste appeal, and appropriateness for friends regardleass of data collection method. Product A is rated lowest on the same attributes.

Central location studies are required when the need is to offer the product in a prepared form under expert supervision—for example, a prepared soup taste test.

---

* The *t* values for the differences between the mean ratings of overall opinion by mail panel and personal interview are:

Product	t value
A	3.676
B	2.554
C	4.056
D	4.457

All differences are significant at the .01 level or more. Source is [1, pp. 104–6].

Test requirement	Appropriate method		
	Personal placement in homes	Mail panel placement	Central location test
High sample dispersion.............		X	
Broad sample representativeness......	X	X	
Controlled serving conditions........			X
High-speed results..................	X		X
Difficult instructions...............	X		
Open-end responses.................	X		X

2. *Sample size considerations.* The sample size should be only as large as necessary to provide the desired level of confidence about the expected differences in the data. Most product tests settle for 90 percent levels of confidence or less. Estimates of the sample sizes required for the two most common comparisons—comparing statistics in the same sample and different samples—are shown in Table 2.

TABLE 2   Expected Accuracy of Percentages at 90 percent Level of Confidence

Sample size	Single samples, observed percentage			Different samples, average of two observed percentages		
	10% 90%	30% 70%	50% 50%	10% 90%	30% 70%	50% 50%
100	4.9	7.5	8.2	7.0	10.7	11.6
200	3.5	5.3	5.8	4.9	7.5	8.2
500	2.2	3.4	3.7	3.1	4.8	5.2
1,000	1.6	2.4	2.6	2.2	3.4	3.7
2,000	1.1	1.7	1.8	1.6	2.4	2.6

The following examples illustrate how to estimate accuracy levels from this table:

1. Assume that 500 respondents product tested two chocolate cake mixes and that cake A was preferred by 50 percent, cake B was preferred by 30 percent, and 20 percent had no preference. Is mix A preferred by a significantly larger proportion of the testers? The left-hand side of the table shows a 3.7 percent confidence interval at the 50 percent level so the preference level for mix A can be described as 50 percent ± 3.7 percent; or 46.3 percent to 53.7 percent of the people prefer it. Similarly, mix B is preferred by 30 percent ± 3.4 percent, or from 26.6 to 33.4 percent. Since 46.3 percent is greater than 33.4 percent, one can conclude that A is significantly better liked than B.

2. Assume that two individual-concept test samples of 200 respondents each produced an acceptance level of 63 percent for product concept A and 70 percent for product concept B. Is B significantly more acceptable than A? The right-hand side of the table shows that a difference of 7.5 percent is required for significance for statistics at about 30 or 70 percent (in this case

$(63 + 70)/2 = 66.5)$. The actual difference is $70 - 63$ or 7 percent. So, the difference is almost but not quite significant at the 90 percent confidence level.

A second determinant of sample size is the size of important subgroups to be analyzed. If it is anticipated that certain key groups in the data will need to stand on their own feet statistically, for example, heavy users of the product class, current users of own brand, and so on, then the sample should be based on the accuracy requirements of the smallest of the subgroups.

3. *Development of product alternatives.* Every product class has a number of physical characteristics that can be reasonably well defined. For example, if a manufacturer were contemplating marketing a new soft drink, he would be concerned with characteristics that would determine the final composition of his product: the taste, the odor, the nutritional values, the calorie level, the color, the carbonation level, and so on.

Since the manufacturer's product may assume any given variation on each of these characteristics, it is obvious that the number of different products that he could develop is virtually infinite. As a result, it is customary for the manufacturer to select from this large number of possible varieties two or three variations. From these, one is eventually selected as being the most desirable.

It could certainly be argued that this first phase, that of developing a limited number of product alternatives, is the most crucial step of all. *However successful the second phase (of selecting the one product alternative to be marketed), this final selection can be only as good as the best of the two or three alternatives that were tested.*

In developing any product—whether new or existing—the manufacturer must decide first *which particular attributes of the product he should include or change.* In many cases, it is simply not feasible to change all aspects of the product. Furthermore, there may be a *critical relationship between various product attributes;* that is, the manufacturer may not be able to change one attribute without affecting other characteristics of the product.

The manufacturer has a number of criteria he might use in deciding which attributes he might change. We would expect him to be genuinely concerned with the *general importance* of each attribute to consumers, both in causing them to use the product class in general and in differentiating between brands, and we would think the manufacturer would be very much interested in the specific weaknesses of his product in the eyes of various segments of the consuming public.

There are a number of approaches that measure not only *what* product attributes are important to the consumer but also *how* important these attributes are in determining product or brand selection.

One method calls for a series of attributes to be scaled or rated by the consumer. The procedure involves several distinct steps:

1. Determining which attributes or characteristics should be submitted to the consumer for scaling
2. Developing the appropriate measurement techniques
3. Administering the scale to consumers
4. Checking the reliability of the scaling
5. Ascertaining the importance of the attributes in the consumer's product selection

These are some of the sources which can be mined for determination of product attributes to be studied in product testing:

1. The manufacturer's knowledge and experience in the product field. Any systematic research should be preceded by discussion with the manufacturer's

technical and marketing staff to determine what the product was designed to do and what its major competitive advantages or disadvantages are.

2. Current and past advertising for the product as well as for competitive products. A content analysis of the advertising claims—explicit or implicit—for products in this class will often provide important clues for consideration.

3. The researchers' own experiences with consumer attitudes toward similar products. These will often suggest avenues of exploration which have been ignored by the manufacturer or advertiser.

4. Intensive preliminary depth interviews with consumers. A constant concern of the product planner is that his laboratory criteria on given attributes may not coincide with the consumer's. Depth interviewing is very helpful in suggesting not only the specific characteristics that are important but also the ways in which consumers formulate opinions of various products on these given characteristics.

A complete evaluation of product research methodology would involve consideration of a large number of specific, detailed product testing questions which could well cover the entire field of experimental design. Let us restrict our attention to one or two critical areas:

1. *The single paired-comparison concept* in which *one* product alternative is tested against another or against *one* other competitive product.

2. *The validity of consumer preferences* under conventional product testing methods in which the consumer is cognizant of the test situation and compares the alternative products on a side-by-side basis.

One very common product testing approach is to test one product alternative against another. Frequently, the results one gets from such a comparison are ambiguous and may lead one to choose the wrong product. This is especially likely when the marketing implications of a product test have not been considered fully.

Let us assume that a paired-comparison test of two product alternatives has been conducted and that 75 percent of the participants prefer product alternative A and 25 percent prefer product B. These findings are ambiguous to the extent that some members of the management group might well contend that product B (25 percent preferring) should be selected because, among other reasons, it is different from other products currently on the market and would enjoy an exclusive share of one segment of the market.

If a marketing research technique uncovers findings which can lead almost as easily to one course of action as to another, then the role of the research has clearly not been defined.

Using our general criterion of validity (the relationship between the marketing environment in which the product is sold and the product test situation), a single paired comparison does not meet the criterion. In the real market, product alternative A does not compete with product alternative B, but rather with competitive products C, D, E, F, and G.

Therefore a more logical approach to the problem of deciding between experimental product alternative A and product alternative B is to measure consumer preferences for each of them against the field of competitive products and to determine which one of them stands up better against the field. Such a judgment may be made, for instance, on the basis of several pairwise comparisons.

Data exemplifying the results of such comparisons are shown in the following tabulation. These data would seem to reveal clearly that the experimental product B should be preferred over product A.

However, even this type of comparison may be inadequate, since it cannot predict how well each of the products A or B might do against future competition other than C or D.

Product being compared	Percent preferring experimental	
	Product A	Product B
Existing product C........	47	58
Existing product D.......	50	55

L. L. Thurstone, a pioneer in the field of psychometrics, has used a concept that he refers to as "discriminal dispersion" to show how the validity of this kind of comparison for predicting the behavior of a product in a competitive market may be improved.

To illustrate this concept, let us use the data in the preceding table. Product A was preferred by 47 percent over product C, while product B was preferred by 58 percent over product C.

Even though one might feel inclined to select product B over product A, we still don't know how each of these products will behave in the presence of competition other than products C or D. Additional data on the strength of preference for products A and B over C will enable us to predict much better how each of these products will behave in a competitive market.

One could argue on the basis of the following data that, despite the seemingly greater preference for product B, the alternative product A would actually stand up much better in a competitive market. This argument would be based on the reasonable assumption that the group which shows a very weak preference for the product would be more easily swayed than the group which shows a very strong preference. On this basis, one might expect the 40 percent who "very much" prefer A to C will stay with product A against other competition, whereas the apparent majority for product B is made up very largely of the 30 percent whose preference is actually quite weak.

Response	This percent testing:	
	A and C	B and C
Prefer product A or B (total)...	47	58
Very much................	40	14
Somewhat................	10	10
A little...................	3	30
No preference (total)..........	20	30
Prefer product C (total).......	33	12
A little...................	13	9
Somewhat................	5	2
Very much................	15	1

In general terms, Thurstone propounded the idea that the *dispersion of intensity of preferences* toward the product alternative has a crucial bearing on how well the product will be accepted when it is competing with other brands.

A product in which the dispersion is high (both liked and disliked a great deal by a substantial number of consumers) could well be the first choice in a competitive market situation of many more consumers than a product whose discriminal dispersion is low (where everybody liked it to about the same extent) *even though the average attitude toward the two products is the same.*

While this whole area justifies a great deal of experimental research, even a cursory appraisal indicates that product test comparisons should meet these two requirements:

1. The product alternatives should probably not be tested solely against each other or *one* competitive brand, but rather against *groups* of products currently available.

2. Product testing should incorporate scales that precisely measure the *intensity* of the consumer's feelings on the various products. Without this information, it is not possible to learn the discriminal dispersion which, in turn, has a marked effect on the likely acceptance of the product.

INDUSTRIAL PRODUCT TESTING

Because product testing today is concentrated among consumer products companies, little mention has been made of industrial product evaluation and tests. To some extent, the same techniques apply while the practice is very different. For example, institutional food product tests along the lines of consumer products are becoming commonplace. The key issue is still the one of relating the effects of the findings to the level of risk and the cost of being wrong.

SUMMARY

Product testing is one of the classic forms of marketing research. It is one of the most useful marketing research techniques available to management. Because it tends to be unambiguous, it is often used and acted upon.

The future growth of useful product testing lies in its applicability to the more sophisticated aspects of market segmentation and new-product development. It is in these areas that product testing is just beginning to scratch the surface. By integrating product testing systems into management analyses and decision models, the future of product testing programs is clearly assured.

REFERENCES

1. Abrams, J., "Reducing the Risk of New Product Marketing Strategies Testing," *Journal of Marketing Research,* vol. 6, May 1969.
2. Biel, A. L., American Management Association Seminar on Test Marketing Speech, New York: November 16–18, 1966.
3. Eastlack, J. O., Jr., ed., "New Product Development," American Marketing Association, Marketing for Executives Series no. 13.
4. Hanan, M., "Concept Advertising," *American Management Association Bulletin* 37, 1963.
5. Market Facts, Inc., *Product Research Methodology, A Critical Review Based on Experimentation with Alternative Methods,* Chicago: April 1957.
6. Warshaw, M. P., and G. P. Murphy, eds., *New Product Planning for Changing Markets,* Ann Arbor, Mich.: University of Michigan Business Papers, no. 47.

New-Product Development and Introduction

Chapter 3

Market Testing: Using the Marketplace as a Laboratory

ALVIN A. ACHENBAUM   *J. Walter Thompson Company, New York*

It seems incredible that at this stage of marketing's development so basic a question as the purpose of market testing—or test marketing, as it is often called—is still a subject of controversy.[1] But while market testing as a tool of marketing is almost universally accepted, it is far from being universally understood or from being effectively utilized. Yet a clear understanding of what can be expected from market tests is more than desirable; it is essential if we are to avoid misusing the tool and if we are to develop techniques of value in marketing management.

This chapter seeks to clarify the meaning of market testing, to indicate its specific commercial functions, and to suggest how market tests can be best designed and used now and, one hopes, more fruitfully in the future. Let us begin by placing market testing in its proper perspective as a commercial research tool.

THE ROLE OF COMMERCIAL RESEARCH

There is common agreement that the key function of commercial research is to help business reduce its risk, whether in marketing existing products or in in-

---

[1] These two terms are so often used interchangeably that to make a distinction between them would be artificial to say the least. Yet they both make sense. *Market testing*, which I prefer, suggests the concept of using the market as a place to test a proposed marketing decision. *Test marketing*, on the other hand, puts more emphasis on the marketing rather than testing in the marketplace, although the latter is evidently implied.

vesting in new ones. One way that commercial research can do this is by predicting the consequences of alternative courses of action.

In the case of product or advertising-copy tests, for example, where the alternatives available are tangible, the predictive nature of the test is clear-cut. The ability of this kind of research to reduce risk depends solely on the validity of the theoretical framework upon which the results are obtained; that is, whether the evaluative criterion is meaningfully related to sales or its counterpart, brand usage, and whether the test procedure reliably measures that criterion.

Yet many marketers are disinclined to rely on product and advertising-copy test results because they seem remote from the actual market. Marketers often feel that there is an interdependence between the various elements in the marketing mix which can only be uncovered in the marketplace itself. For precisely this reason, market testing has long been one of marketing management's favorite commercial research tools for, unlike product and advertising-copy tests, it has been considered the most realistic means of testing a proposed marketing decision. Furthermore, by market testing, marketers feel that anticipated actions can be tested on a small scale to determine whether they are sound before taking such actions on a more expensive large scale. Considering the tremendous risks in making large-scale marketing mistakes, small wonder that this tool has been so popular.

Yet while there is general agreement on this *ultimate* function of market testing—the reduction of commercial risk—one need only be exposed to a diverse group of marketing people to learn how little agreement exists on what a market test is and how it is best used in fulfilling this function.

DEFINITION OF MARKET TESTING

To the research-oriented person, the term *market test* has a rather precise meaning. To him, *it is a controlled experiment, done in a limited but carefully selected part of the marketplace, whose aim is to predict the sales or profit consequences, either in absolute or relative terms, of one or more proposed marketing actions.* It is essentially the use of the marketplace as a laboratory and of a direct sales measurement which differentiates this test from other types of market research.

At the other extreme, *market testing* has the very loose meaning of merely *trying something out* in the marketplace. This meaning is commonly held by, although hardly limited to, the self-made businessman. A substantial number of entrepreneurs have established successful businesses built to a large extent on this process of *trying something out.* The proprietors of these businesses often had an idea, pragmatically tried it out in a market or two, succeeded, and went on to succeed on a larger scale, either regionally or nationally. Needless to say, those that followed this simple approach on a small scale but failed when they went national are not pushing it very hard. We therefore do not hear much about the unsuccessful side of this approach. Like stock market investors, we only hear from the winners.

Of course, between the two extremes of *scientific testing* and *trying something out,* there is room for many different degrees of experimentation. Often, the choice of a market test design between the two extremes is largely governed by the purse strings. Yet, no matter what choice is made, one thing is common to all such tests: the results are used as if they were predictive. Unfortunately, evidence keeps popping up which reveals that market tests done in a traditional manner have another thing in common: predictively, they are not working very well.

This was abundantly clear as far back as 1963. Quoting from a speech made by the author, *Television Age* reported:

> A check of the combined experience of Grey Advertising's media, marketing, and research personnel revealed a paucity, if not complete absence, of any single success in the usage of market tests for the evaluation of media patterns. Moreover, discussions held with others who have undertaken market tests for this purpose have suggested that we are not unusual in our undistinguished record in this area. The fact is that in no case have we ever seen a media/market test which yielded conclusive results which clearly and logically led to a definite media conclusion [1].

Later, in 1965, after making a rather comprehensive review of the field, *Printer's Ink—Consumer Advertising* reported:

> Although the whole area has gained in sophistication in recent years, there still remains a sizable number of men who scoff at market testing.
> "We have never had a successful test market project," says the marketing chief of a large company: Why? "We never got clear answers. We never got accurate predictions on sales and profits."
> Leaders of the marketing research community themselves are among the first to admit this. Says Bart Panitierre, GF Corporate Marketing Research Director, "Life would be wonderfully simple if the so-called national sales picture were one smooth canvas. It's not. It's really a mosaic—a rather uneven one—made up of hundreds of local markets each having a different shape and color. Test markets are only sample chips. Their results are difficult to project now to a national pattern, though the better the choice of sample chips, the better the odds on an accurate projection—providing, of course, you play fair in handling the chips and running the market tests."
> One research director—Arthur Koponen—then at Colgate-Palmolive said, "Projectivity is a myth." [18]

Nothing has changed since 1965. While companies have continued to do various types of market testing, they are experiencing much the same results as always.

Many of these failures are traceable to confusion about the technique and its consequent misuse. Fortunately, the problems are gaining recognition. Yet if we are to develop market testing to its full extent, we must understand it clearly —its uses and how well it works for each use.

USES OF MARKET TESTING

No matter which kind of market test is used—the more precise scientific test or the looser, pragmatic trial-and-error one—we can distinguish two fundamental types, each type serving a more or less unique function:

1. The first serves what we might call the *managerial control function*. It permits a company to gain needed information or experience before going into something on a large scale.

2. The second serves what we might call the *predictive research function*. This, like any other decision-oriented method, is supposed to indicate whether an action should or should not be taken.

Both functions deserve review in detail, for the first can and does play a critical role in sound marketing management. While not concerned with prediction, its use can certainly reduce risk. Besides, it may well represent the most important use of market testing today.   The second is the traditional purpose of market testing.   Yet as we shall see, its value largely depends on whether we can truly design and implement predictive tests.

Market Testing as a Managerial Control Tool

Many managements, faced with a new product or a new process, are often apprehensive—as they should be—about converting their operation to it on a full scale.   Everyone recognizes the risks of doing so.   For one thing, it is difficult to anticipate all the problems associated with a change.   Things occur which cannot be visualized in advance.   Then there is the matter of training. Rarely can one be effective or efficient without some experience.   And finally, there is the question of being sure that it (if not the whole operation, then at least some of its more important individual parts) will work.   Considerations such as these make some kind of experimentation or exploration worth doing. A parallel from manufacturing may help to clarify the use of market testing as a managerial control tool.

It has long been the practice of manufacturers to set up a pilot plant or operation before building the final factory [19].   It is usually not the function of a pilot plant to predict precisely what will happen in the large-scale plant. It is taken for granted that the final operation will be different from the pilot one, since size almost always has an independent effect on outcomes.   Plants are run by people, and personal relationships change with the size of the operation.   As operations become bigger, new elements must be added to permit the operation to work without friction.   Although restricted in scope, the pilot plant still serves management in many ways:

1.   By allowing it to check out specific elements in the operation to see how they work

2.   By permitting it to discover and iron out unanticipated difficulties

3.   By providing it with valuable experience while the risks are small

4.   By giving it a chance to observe the operational team, to see how its members work together

5.   By offering it some measure of the costs involved

In brief, it gives management some basis for going ahead, for avoiding many of the pitfalls on the way to success.

While not predictive, a pilot plant can reduce risk.   For example, say the management of a company learns that when two operations are placed in juxtaposition in a pilot plant, the operators of one become terribly unhappy and, as a consequence, are less productive.   Based on such a finding, future alteration costs could be avoided by changing the location of the operations before building the actual plant.   Or, say in building a pilot operation, management learns that there is considerable spillage in a particular operation.   Obviously much can be saved by correcting the problem before building the final plant.

A market test can serve this very same function.   Very often, if it does nothing else, it can more than justify its cost by merely *serving as a pilot operation for the large-scale marketing activity*.   This is particularly true for marketing new products and new brands.   Certainly where completely new products are concerned—ones not familiar to consumers—there is reason for management apprehension.   But even with new brands in established categories, where innovations may be slight or where the product is new only to the company, there is reason for caution.   National marketing is a risky business.   There are, for example, many physical problems—of handling, shelf life, breakage, storage, stocking, and shipping—which can turn into costly mistakes if not carefully worked out in advance.   Take the case of the prominent manufacturer who tested facial tissue in a smaller, more compact box than his regular one. Fortunately, one of his test markets was in the South. The dampness in that area made it clear that the box was inadequate for its purposes. After being on the shelf for one month, many of these boxes exploded at the seams because the tissues absorbed more moisture than the box would allow.

Think of the cost if the marketer went directly national with the new box. Or think what would have happened if it were only product tested and not permitted to sit on shelves for a month or so. Yet until the product is actually sold in the marketplace in a normal manner, it is difficult to anticipate such problems.

Then there are the marketing problems of alternative executions in packaging, in product form, in advertising, in promotion, and in price. Often, without being in the market, research on these elements cannot be done effectively. For example, with some products, it is virtually impossible to test the product unless it is obtained through the distribution system. Frozen food is a good case in point. Because of the way retailers handle this product, *blind* product tests would not be fair unless all the products involved were stored similarly. This would not be possible unless the product were put on the market.

Then there is the problem of simply learning the ropes—of finding out firsthand the difficulties of getting distribution, of learning from experience the real price structure, of producing a new commercial, of seeing the actual operation in action. Until one enters the market, such problems cannot be attacked with any degree of confidence. Yet many of these problems can be mitigated with a pilot introduction in one or more markets—with a miniature marketing operation. Obviously, such a pilot introduction should be planned and handled as much as possible like the real thing, for only then is it possible to expose difficulties.

Finally, there is the matter of not having enough merchandise to supply more than a limited introduction. Often a company has the productive capacity to start only a local or regional operation immediately. Under such circumstances, it makes sense to go from market to market, checking progress along the way.

But let us not be under any illusions about market testing used this way. Its purpose is to help improve the *mechanics* of the marketing operation, to find out if unanticipated problems in fact exist, to constantly improve one's approach while doing the job on a limited scale. Its purpose is *not* to predict whether a product will be a success or a failure nationally.

Thus when market testing is used for managerial control purposes, we need not worry about developing elaborate experimental designs and conducting store audits for projecting sales. To do so is a waste of money, time, and effort. Instead, we should use these pilot introductions to gain experience, to ferret out problems that need correction, and to do the kind of research that will help develop a sound marketing program. The choice of markets—number used, size, and location—is more a matter of convenience than scientific selection. At most, one wants more than one market and considerable geographic dispersal, for only in this way can one be sure of testing under the varying circumstances eventually faced in national marketing.

Market Testing as a Predictive Research Tool

While market testing may be both a useful and a desirable managerial control tool, most tests are treated as though they were designed for prediction. The fact that market testing has failed to live up to its potential as a predictive tool has not deterred many from using it in this fashion.

Essentially, market testing has been used as a predictive device in two broad and quite dissimilar situations, (1) the introduction of a new product or brand and (2) the evaluation of alternative marketing variables.

Actually, the methodological requirements for both uses of test marketing are almost identical, with one major exception—testing alternative variables requires a control group. Yet there are other distinctions which should be covered before we get into method.

Market Testing New Products or Brands.   In its most widely accepted use, market testing *is considered the predictive aspect of a new product or new brand introduction,* where management not only expects to learn something about how its new product or brand will perform in the marketplace but also hopes to predict the outcome of a national introduction by first testing the introduction in a small area.   In this case, management considers the whole marketing mix as a single variable which is to be tested, although it often does not think this way.

Needless to say, a number of different new-product situations face a company, and each of these calls for different testing requirements.

The New-Product Category Where There Are No Direct Substitutes.   In this case, not only is the company devoid of experience with the product category but it is difficult to rely on the experience of others even if available.

In the consumer goods areas, there are very few such situations.   Almost every product that can be developed has some kind of substitute.   For example, even if someone developed a hair restorer, he would have to consider toupees as a substitute, although not necessarily a desirable one.

In reality, very few new consumer products have been developed in recent years.   Most new food products are merely convenient substitutes for the homemade thing.   Most toiletries have been around for too long a time in one form or another to be considered really new.   Probably, the most recent so-called new-product success in this field has been the female vaginal spray deodorant.   Yet it is truly only a substitute for the older liquid douche, which has been in existence from time immemorial.

Obviously, for new-product categories, particularly where substitutes are not that similar, the key to product success is consumer acceptability—will it satisfy an overt or latent need better than what is currently available?   While product tests and consumer surveys have been used to determine this, they are not predictive since there usually are no standards against which to measure the results.   For this reason market testing is usually required.   Not only can it serve as a pilot operation but, if done properly, it can permit other forms of research as well as attempt to yield a predictive market result.

The New Brand of an Existing Product Category.   This is the most common situation.   In reality, in consumer marketing most so-called new products are nothing more than new brands.   But even in this case there are a number of different possibilities.

On one continuum, there is the matter of differentiation; some brands are real innovations, that is, quite different from others in the category, either in the way they are made, in the way they are used, or in the needs they can gratify.   Others can be "me-toos," identical in almost every way except perhaps for the way they are positioned competitively or the way they are sold.   Since close substitutes of the new brand are available, much valuable product research can be done prior to market introduction.   Certainly some form of blind product testing is desirable to ascertain if the innovation is more acceptable than or at least on a parity with competitive brands.   Too often, marketers use market testing to do what can be done better and cheaper with consumer product testing.

Even with so-called parity brands, where positioning may be crucial, market testing may not be called for immediately. Certainly much can be learned from copy testing to see whether a position is being clearly communicated and whether it has persuasive leverage with the consumer before going to the expense of a market test. But when all this is done and the results are still favorable, a market test may eventually be called for, particularly if the innovation requires a higher price or some different method of shelving, packaging, or distribution.

The other continuum is experience with the product category. Obviously, a marketer with great experience with the brand would be foolish to test market if he is sure from product tests and copy tests that his product is at least on a parity with competition and his copy is understood and persuasive. If no major difference in the marketing mix is involved, a market test will not reveal anything not already learned from other research. On the other hand, marketers often use market tests because they are afraid to make a decision; they use them either as security blankets or as post facto excuses in case something goes wrong.

Yet a situation in this case may call for a market test. Many times, a marketer has no way of knowing whether his new proposition will pay in terms of the promotional investment he has in mind. A market test—again only if done right—will help predict the consequences. Unfortunately, most payouts for highly promoted items are set for three years. It is, therefore, difficult to make a payout prediction unless a test is run for the full three years, a highly unlikely proposition to say the least.

Recycling an Existing Brand. Some marketers consider a major repositioning or repackaging of a brand or some improvement in an existing brand a basis for market testing before going national. However, unless the change is dramatic or at least readily discernible by the consumer, there would appear little reason for market testing.

For product improvements, it might be enough to do some large-scale blind product testing. Of course, if the established brand is a success and if the difference could produce major market changes, it might be advisable to market test. But again, unless done correctly, the anticipation of a prediction will not be forthcoming.

While the aforementioned situations essentially deal with market tests of an entire marketing mix, some marketers try to test more than one marketing mix in introducing a new product. In so doing, they are in essence also incorporating the design imperatives of testing alternative variables, which in one very important respect changes the ground rules—it requires some control area. On the other hand, in total marketing-mix introductions, no control group of markets is necessary. In that case the marketer attempts to get market measurements which can be projected to the total universe. Once this is done, he then ascertains if it is economically feasible to go ahead on a broader scale.

Testing Alternative Marketing Variables. Market testing's other predictive use is *to evaluate alternative individual marketing variables, strategies, or patterns.* Here we are not concerned with measuring the effect of the total marketing mix but rather a single variable of that mix or, as is often the case, one variable versus another, usually the one in use. For example, market tests are often used to determine the extent to which a new media pattern is better than an existing one, or one distribution method more effective than another, or a higher advertising budget more profitable than a lower one. Obviously, any subdecisions of these variables are also susceptible to test. One might choose to learn whether night television expenditures produce more sales than the same expenditures in day television.

Almost any marketing variable—a broad issue or a minor one—is amenable to testing, although it may be more difficult to measure the effect of a minor variable. The issue is not what can be tested but how one can design a predictive test. Yet in some situations the variable to be tested cannot be isolated in the test design. A good example is the addition of a new medium to an advertising media schedule—say magazines to an existing television buy. This perforce is a dual variable since it involves not only the new medium but also the amount of money to be spent. Since the two variables cannot be separated, one can never test the incremental value of adding to a different medium.

There are also instances where one cannot practically set up a real test, where what is wanted nationally cannot be done in a local area. This was once true for magazines, when one could not buy regional or local circulation. Even today, network television can be used in test market situations only by paying an expensive penalty. It therefore becomes extremely difficult to test variations of network television.

Finally, one may want to test more than one variable—or a variable on some continuum. These are all possible theoretically, although whether a predictable result can be achieved will depend on the test design.

This, of course, is not to say that everything is worthy of test. Most marketing variables are amenable to testing, but the real issues deal with the design of the test—how to design one that can predict a national outcome, whether it is worth the cost, and whether one is exposing oneself to other problems.

DESIGN METHODOLOGY

Designing a market test so that it predicts a national outcome is not as simple as most marketers would seem to believe. In some ways, it is the most complex problem in research today. The devil we are fighting is market variation. Yet in designing market tests, little attention has been given, at least until lately, to the variation inherent in the American marketplace. While it is generally recognized that a large number of variables can affect sales performance —variables such as price availability, competition, weather, economic conditions, and so forth—it is often tacitly assumed in market testing that if these variables are ignored, they will not cause any trouble. Or, to be more precise, it is assumed that these variables are randomly distributed and that the effect of each will cancel out in the total.

But prediction is at best an optimistic hope with any research method. To assume it can be achieved without a carefully developed methodology is wishful thinking. As with any laboratory experiment, three methodological conditions must be met:

1. The experiment or test must be *representative of the whole,* at least to the degree that one wishes to quantitatively project the relationship of the small area to the larger one. This is not merely a matter of spatial representativeness. It is also a matter of choosing a representative time period and of doing what one eventually hopes to do in the larger universe.

2. The test must be *carefully controlled.* One must do what is planned and keep extraneous variables from contaminating the test. This is particularly important in testing alternative variables where a control group against which the new element can be compared is necessary. In other words, the variation intrinsic to the test must be controllable either directly by what is done or indirectly through some statistical procedure. Unless this is done, we do not know whether the results are engendered by the test variable or by extraneous, often unknown factors operating in the market.

3. The test must be *accurately measured.* This is a much more complex

issue than usually contemplated. For one thing, which type of sales measure should be used—factory shipments, wholesale sales, retail sales, usage, and so forth? Even after accepting a measurement criterion, there is the matter of projecting it to the total. There are many methods for doing this and they often yield different answers. There is also the issue of the base period against which the comparison is to be made, and again there are various approaches.

These are not minor problems. Each can have a major impact on the projectability of the test. Each must, therefore, be thoroughly understood if we are to comprehend their role in prediction, to recognize the pitfalls of market testing, and to overcome the difficulty of designing predictable market experiments.

Test Representativeness

Achieving representativeness in a market test experiment is perhaps the most critical aspect of predictability, particularly in testing a new-product introduction. As indicated, there are a number of elements to representativeness.

1. There is the matter of choosing a sample of markets, both in terms of the number and their dispersion, that are truly reflective of the total universe involved—usually the continental United States. In reality, the sampling problem in the market test experiment is no different from that in most research. The sample must be large and random enough to reflect the heterogeneity of the universe being measured. As in any sampling problem, the more heterogeneous the population, the bigger the sample required.

Obviously, if the country were truly homogeneous, one city or market anywhere would do. Traditionally, this is what was done. In new-product introductions, one market would often be deemed adequate. Even in tests of an alternative variable, only one market would be used for injecting the test variable. The results would then be compared to the rest of the United States on the assumption that the sample city was typical of the country as a whole.

Unfortunately for market testers, the United States is not homogeneous. There are, in fact, vast regional and city size differences which reflect differences in climate, ethnic composition, work force mix, and so on. These differences affect consumer behavior in countless ways, and they also affect the way goods are distributed and promotion is communicated. This heterogeneity led many market tests to go awry. Before long, those with experience recognized the need to do things differently. At first, there were attempts to increase the size of the sample, either by increasing the number of markets or increasing the size of the individual test area. Typically, three or four test cities were used or some larger area, like a sales region or Nielsen area, was chosen. Some would even use an area as large as New England or the West Coast. While these larger areas were often 6 to 10 pecent of the United States, they were not truly representative, so that the problem was really not eliminated.

Another approach was to match the test area with the control area. This was usually done on the basis of demographic information—income, home ownership, age distribution, share of market, and so on. Yet it soon became abundantly clear that even matching would not do.

It was in reality not a matter of which city or cities were chosen, for there is no such thing as a small group of cities or a large region being representative of the United States. Nothing has been more detrimental to the development of sound test-market design than the publication in our trade press of lists of cities widely used in market tests. It was as if use of these cities made them representative of the United States.

A number of years ago, in some work for one of our company's clients, we learned how variable the marketplace was. In three cases covering three different brands, we found the following variance (at the two-sigma level as a percentage of sales) to exist in our market test areas.[2] As can be seen, it took four markets representing over 3 percent of the United States to reduce the variation to a minimum of 16.8 percent.

		Study B	
Number of markets	Study A (percent)	Brand 1 (percent)	Brand 2 (percent)
1	65.6	. . .	. . .
2	43.4	43.6	33.8
3	31.2	28.2	25.6
4	. . .	24.8	16.8

Gold's paper reported on some of this work and revealed the magnitude of the variation in the marketplace for the first time [20]. For those who expect payout estimates to be accurate within a few percentage points, these data are truly frightening. For example, he found that if one area was selected, the standard deviation of the market share was 32.8 percent. If two areas were selected, it dropped to 21.7 percent. And if three areas were used, the standard deviation was reduced to 15.6 percent.

These figures may not seem too shocking. Yet in interpreting them, several things should be kept in mind. First is the statistical consideration: a range of one standard deviation around the test-area market share will include the national share only two times in three. Thus there is a good chance that the true share will not be in the ranges indicated in his experiment. Second, the areas used in these tests were substantially larger than those used in normal market tests. In fact, each of the areas used averaged about 3 percent of the United States, not the 9 percent necessary to get the variation down to a reasonable level.

Furthermore, the tests were fairly extensive. Seven products were investigated by Gold in each of the six separate trading areas. He found that the between-product variation was less than the between-market variation in almost every case.

In addition, no attempt was made to project test results into the future. The ranges of error cited deal only with the extension of test-area findings to the country as a whole for the same time period in which tests were conducted. Certainly if a year had passed before the accuracy of test-area results was assessed, the ranges of error around the test-market estimates would have been substantially larger. And what would be the case once competition recognized the introduction and did something about it? Would that not add to the variability? Nor did the method of projection matter; no one approach did the job better than any other. Thus the problem was in the basic sample size, which is most disconcerting.

Similar results were found in the United Kingdom using the same form of analysis as ours and Gold's. Treasure examined two brands and found that, in one case, seven times out of fifteen the error was ±15 percent and in the other case ±15 percent in fourteen projections out of fifteen [42]. Kraushar also reported a similar result [28].

[2] These examples were for two clients of Grey Advertising, Inc.

2. There is the question of a representative time period. The marketplace is not static. It changes not only with respect to season but also changes over time in terms of market communications, competitive responses, and so on. For example, once a competitor knows that a market is being used to test a new product or an important marketing variable, he may react in a number of ways. He can obviously ignore it until the test marketer goes national and then react. This, of course, could easily distort the prediction, particularly if his reaction is effective. Or he might try to distort the test by some immediate, gross action in the test market itself. This is often done deliberately so that the test marketer cannot make an accurate prediction, usually with the hope that the new product or test alternative will be killed. Finally, the competitor can react normally to find out for himself what to expect. In any case, unless the test is run long enough to see what will happen, it can hardly be a reflection of what is to come.

Traditional tests were usually run for a year. But as so often happens, the marketer will either launch his new product prematurely if all is going according to expectations or abort the test prematurely by taking some expedient action in marketing his established products.

However, more and more marketers are realizing the necessity of covering all the situations that time will allow in a market test—seasonal fluctuations, communication cycles, and competitive reactions. They are also recognizing that unless a test is run for a substantial time, they will not be giving consumers enough time to buy the product again. Because sales efforts are not effective immediately, the sales curve at the beginning of a test market usually represents only the initial trial of a product. After a while, depending on the use rate of the product, the sales curve begins to reflect continued trial plus repeat purchases. As so many packaged goods marketers have learned to their sorrow, until they know what proportion of the consumers will buy the brand again, they do not have an accurate picture of possible future sales.

3. There is the matter of keeping the test variable representative of future reality. The purpose of a predictive test is to see if what is done in the small will work in the large. The most amusing misuse of this concept is the so-called *vitality test,* where the marketer decides to force distribution beyond what he hopes to get on a national scale and promotes at a level which is usually uneconomic. The assumption here is that because it is often hard to get a measurement, one should force one. If perchance one fails, clearly the idea is a failure. Unfortunately, a positive result does not indicate feasibility. It is almost as if these tests were designed to kill off bad ideas rather than to determine good ones. Needless to say, the vitality test is totally irrelevant if prediction is our aim.

Accordingly, good test-market practice would suggest translating every anticipated national action as realistically as possible in the test market. Thus distribution should be obtained exactly as desired normally. Nothing special should be done to get the product into stores. Moreover, all promotion and advertising budgets should be economically realistic. Prices and discount structure should also be as planned nationally.

Some have suggested adjusting the test-market results to account for lack of representativeness. Unfortunately, to date there has been no meaningful way to make these adjustments after the fact. Representation must be built into the design from the very beginning.

Test Control

Probably nothing can disrupt a market test from being predictive more than extraneous noise. No matter how carefully we control test inputs (often called the endogenous variables), unless the exogenous variables are kept under control, prediction is virtually impossible.

Test control is of particular importance in testing alternative variables. This is not to say that controlling variables is unnecessary in testing new-product introductions. As we pointed out, it is a problem there too. Yet any test of two or more marketing alternatives almost automatically implies the need for *comparing* two or more markets as well as the need for projecting from them. Even in those cases where we are not concerned with the magnitude of differences, where we only need to choose between two alternatives—is one action better than another—controlling variation can be critical in the decision.

Traditionally, variation has been dealt with in one of three ways: by ignoring it, by attempting to match markets, or by using the statistical principles of experimental design. None of these has proved especially effective to date, although the latter offers some hope. Obviously, ignoring the influences of the exogenous factors is ludicrous. Too many elements can affect sales, and sometimes small, unexpected changes can destroy the results of market experiments. Marketers have not given enough attention to the effect of nondeliberate competitive actions and acts of God, actions not usually distributed evenly across geographical areas. No other explanation can be found for the strange results of some tests. For example, how else can one rationalize sales declines where promotional effort is increased and upturns where promotional effort is reduced? This, unfortunately, has not been an unusual experience to those involved in market tests.

The second approach—matching markets—is usually impractical. Attempting to match markets on as few as 4 variables (it is easy to list 20 which might be pertinent) can exhaust a list of even 200 markets. Besides, one really does not know in advance the truly pertinent variables for matching purposes. What may seem relevant could easily play no part in the sales of a product. But even elaborate matching schemes have proved ineffectual. As long as the selection system is not random, it will not, theoretically, yield the desired result.

Even the third approach—the use of sophisticated experimental designs—is not an automatic guarantee of success. Three or four markets do not permit true randomization. As already pointed out, markets in the United States are much too different from each other for three or four to be representative of the whole. Moreover, what does one do about the truly unique ones like New York, Chicago, and Los Angeles? Thus, test results often show a high level of random variation, and statistical significance of any but tremendous differences in performance is difficult to detect. Yet, of the three approaches, randomization must remain our best hope.

Unfortunately, experience with market testing in predicting the results of alternative marketing strategies has been negative. One major advertiser known for test marketing reported that in none of 180 tests during a six-year period did he obtain a conclusive result. The normal variations of the marketplace were too great to isolate the effects of any but the grossest variables when a few markets were used. Moreover, since the differences between any two markets are great, conclusive results are hard to obtain even when tests are run under relatively ideal conditions.

Test Measurement

No matter how well one designs an experiment and controls its implementation, without a relevant and accurate measurement of the test market, one will fail to predict what will happen in the larger universe. Test-market measurement and projection present complex problems.

One problem is the measurement criterion—the so-called dependent variable.

By definition, the measurement criterion is some reflection of sales, of which there are many—manufacturer sales, wholesale sales, or retail sales. The two latter measures usually must be obtained from special audits, such as Nielsen, Sales-area Markets, Inc., or some tailor-made survey of retail outlets.

Sometimes share-of-market measures can be obtained from which sales can then be calculated. This approach also requires some special auditing procedure. Some advocate consumer usage data derived from consumer surveys or panels. It is only from such surveys or panels that the distinction between trial and repeat usage, which is often necessary to make accurate projections about the future, can be made. Moreover, some products are sold in outlets not covered by syndicated audits. An accurate prediction requires covering their sales too, and survey data are often the only way to do so.

While sales are almost always accepted as the ultimate measure of market results, many marketers believe they are inadequate for predicting future success. Some favor measuring distribution—that is, how many stores carry the product—shelf facings, and average store inventory. The latter is important if one is to estimate pipeline as opposed to regular sales. These measures are usually very useful since there is much variation in all these numbers.

Moreover, there are situations—particularly in testing a single marketing variable—where sales are not the most accurate criterion of the effect of a variable. For example, in testing two different media alternatives, some researchers believe that differences in brand or advertising awareness are more pertinent criteria of effectiveness than sales. From a diagnostic point of view, they are probably correct, but if market tests are to be truly meaningful, they must eventually be translated into sales.

Finally, a good case can be made—especially when we are concerned with the economic feasibility of a new-product introduction—for using anticipated profits as the basic criterion of test effectiveness. To do this obviously requires sales (revenue) estimates and accurate cost figures. While manufacturers' sales were traditionally considered good enough, most sophisticated market testers now recognize the need for a complete set of measurements. Too much is at stake to rely on one criterion of market success.

The second issue in measurement is the choice of base period against which the measurements are to be made. Normally there are two choices—comparing the results to the same time period one year before or to the last previous time period before the test began. Because seasonal factors are almost always present, the best practice is to use the same period of the previous year. Needless to say, this requires substantial back data. Moreover, even this practice does not take into account longer trend values. If product-category sales are trending up or down at a somewhat inordinate rate, one must almost always choose a control area to take this trend into account; the difference between the test area and the control area prior to injection of the test variable must be discounted from results during the test period.

Finally, consideration must be given to the method of projecting the measurement criterion to the larger universe. These methods of projection vary from those that are very simple to those that are quite complex. Five basic techniques have been isolated by Davis [11].

1. *Projection of brand share:* This method involves taking a brand-share figure in the test market and applying the same figure to the larger universe by multiplying it by the known national product category sales level. This is sometimes called the buying index method of projection. A refinement of the method is to project period by period. In this way, brand development is taken into consideration.

2. *Projection of sales per head:* Here one calculates actual sales (retail

sales, it is hoped) per capita and multiplies it by the known population of the larger area. This method assumes an accurate measure of population in the test area as well as the larger universe. It also assumes that the rate of usage for the population in the test area also obtains in the larger universe.

3. *Projection of purchasing power:* Since there are many product categories whose distribution by area is not directly proportional to population, projection by sales per head is not too accurate. For this reason, many test marketers prefer some other measure which they believe is more reflective of the product category's sales. This is often necessary because the absolute measure of product sales in the test market may not be accurate.

In this case, some index of purchasing power—*Sales Management* magazine's BPI (Buying Power Index) is a good example—such as disposable personal income or retail sales is used, and one multiplies the reciprocal of the proportion of purchasing power in the test area over purchasing power in the nation by absolute sales in the test area to obtain the national estimate.

4. *Projection using a known brand:* Many times a company is selling a brand similar to the one it is market testing. Rather than using the absolute figures found in the test market, it may use the ratio of test-market sales of its test brand to the test-market sales of its established brand. This ratio is then multiplied by the total factory sales of the nontest brand. This permits the manufacturer to eliminate possible errors in projection resulting from distribution channels. However, the technique makes no sense if there is no meaningful relationship between the two brands.

5. *Projection using market segments:* This is probably the most complex approach, although it offers the best hope for accuracy. Essentially, the method involves getting either brand share, per capita sales, or retail turnover rates by subunits or segments within the market for which data are also available in the larger universe. For example, given sales per capita by income levels or age groups in the test area, one can multiply these figures by the known sizes of these same groups nationally and then sum the total. The same technique applies to retail sales per store by different store sizes in the test area. These per-store rates are then multiplied by the number of stores in each category nationally and summed.

It is difficult to say which of these different projection methods is best, since they often yield somewhat different results. Two approaches to making a choice are worth considering. The first is using as many methods as possible. If the results are similar, there is some reason to be more optimistic about the prediction. An average of the methods may yield the most likely result. The other alternative is to "backcast" as many methods as possible to see which replicates the past best and to use that one for forecasting the future.

Cost and Other Considerations

Cost has always been a major consideration in the design and implementation of market tests. While comprehensive statistics on the subject are not available, most market tests—even erstwhile predictive ones—are run on a shoestring. The number of markets is usually few and their individual size small. Yet almost nothing in the literature compares the costs of various size tests with the costs of a wrong decision that results from being misled by the test.

A number of factors affect the cost of a market test. The two most important are the cost of marketing for advertising, personal selling, and promotion and the cost of measurement. Obviously, the more markets used and the greater their dispersion, the greater the cost of marketing. This is also the case with measurement, particularly where special audits and surveys are required.

There are also other costs. In new-product introductions, there is the cost of producing the merchandise—much of which may never get sold—inefficiently, and the cost of administering the test. The latter represents the opportunity costs involved in spending management's time on the market test as opposed to spending it in running the established business.

Too often, in determining the size of a market test, most emphasis is on the cost of measurement. A company would be wise to balance its cost—not undermeasuring in order to save a little money compared to spending large outlays for production or administration.

The size and scope of a market test should be determined by comparing the risk of not testing against the risk of not getting a decisive result. Davis has done some interesting work on this matter [11]. He suggests that much can be done by preanalyses of the probabilities of success and failure. In doing so, one must consider not only out-of-pocket expenditures but pull-out costs as well—the net loss if one must abort a test prematurely.

But there is a philosophical issue here which needs discussion. Considering how difficult and expensive it is to obtain a decisive result, are we truly approaching market testing in the correct manner? Would we not be better off testing fewer products more accurately than testing a great many with little chance of success? It would seem wiser to spend more money in screening products by doing situation analyses and by conducting need/satisfaction studies, product tests, and copy tests before subjecting a product to market test. Many ideas and products would never reach a market test if this were done, but when they did succeed, a company would be able to afford a larger-scale operation, one which might at least offer some probability of projectability.

With regard to alternative variables, it is a rare marketing variable other than a major change in advertising or promotion budget that is worth the cost of a well-executed market test. Yet, if one is called for, the change should at least be large enough so that the effects will overcome the "noise" in the marketplace. Again, one should consider fewer tests in the hope of doing them better.

Another major issue that usually arises in market testing is *confidentiality*— letting the competition know too far in advance what is contemplated. To some degree, if the plan is easy to copy and of great prima facie value, competition may well try to reach the marketplace first. But if such is the case, why market test at all? If the idea is so manifestly good, should not the originating company see its intrinsic value? If so, this is probably the place for a "preemptive" limited introduction—one so large to have the advantage of being first but small enough to reduce the risk of going national all at once.

On the other hand, if the idea is not that good, why would a competitor want to copy it? Besides, does it not make sense to induce the competition to react, to follow into the market to see what will happen? Obviously, the most desirable situation is one where response is realistic.

Any way this issue is viewed, it should not prevent market testing for fear of competitive reaction. In fact, if competitors stay out, a projectable result is less likely. Probably the silliest thing is to try to distort someone else's test. If anything, the most intelligent response is to compete in a realistic manner and to track the results.

DESIGNING PREDICTIVE MARKET TESTS

Despite all the failure, predictive market testing still remains a desirable objective. The question is how this is to be done.

Following more or less traditional lines based on what has been covered so far, a projectable test requires adhering to sound principles of representativeness, control, and measurement.

Representativeness.   To achieve test representativeness, we must first and foremost pick a large enough set of markets. Anything less than 20 percent of the entire United States will not reduce the variance within the marketplace enough to achieve meaningfully precise predictions. To do this would no doubt create serious difficulties, the least of which might be cost. In cases where new production facilities might be involved, this may not be feasible at all.

Second, the markets should be randomly dispersed. It might be wise to stratify the universe regionally first and then choose individual markets within each region. This will at least assure adequate sample dispersion. Again, there are problems. It is often very difficult to move merchandise through the distribution channels in this way. To do it for the test product separately may be impractical. Yet a big advantage to a 20 percent test that should not be ignored is that it acts as a preemptive introduction. No competitor can foul up a test based on so large a part of the United States. And while 20 percent of the country may seem large, it is still a long distance from a national investment.

Third, it is imperative to run the test for at least a year before any kind of go no-go decision. It is a rare product that has no seasonal pattern. Moreover, we must always make sure that the repeat-purchase situation is fully accounted in our sales curve. If the manufacturer would only recognize that many of his costs are self-liquidating—after all, he is selling some product—he might not be so reluctant to run the test for a proper length of time. (If his sales are not even close to what he expected, he obviously did not do enough preresearch. If there is one point worth taking away from this chapter, it is that market tests should be undertaken only when there is strong reason, from other research, to believe that the product will succeed in the marketplace.)

If the results after a year are favorable and suggest further roll out, it is advisable to continue to test beyond the first year. Much can still be learned. While the market test will lose much predictability under new circumstances, it can still act as an important pilot operation and testing ground. Some recent techniques suggest that prediction of success or failure can be made before a year has expired. The methods essentially match the growth curve of the new product with those of previously tested successful products, the assumption being that successful products follow a basic sales curve. While this may be the case, not every marketer is blessed with previous experience from which comparisons can be made.

Moreover, there is the question of the validity of the assumption. Maybe like products do follow such a curve, but what about disparate ones? How do we know in advance?

These comments apply mostly to new product or brand introductions but also to the testing of alternative variables. In the latter case, need for a control group merely complicates the matter, but if two 20 percent areas of the country are required for a predictive test, we must question whether it is really worth doing. There is reason to doubt whether traditional testing techniques make sense. Anything less than 20 percent of the country is not likely to produce measurable results. Thus, if we are to face the reality of the situation, predictive market tests of alternative variables may not be possible using traditional techniques.

Control.   To be properly controlled, a market test must relate not only to what is eventually contemplated but also to what is implemented. Constant surveillance and discipline are a necessity throughout the test period. This may require designing a specific set of control procedures before the test. The key is to track all variables, including competitive activity, and to guard against taking expedient action which could destroy the test.

Control is more crucial in testing alternative variables. A control group must be identical with the test area and should be chosen in an identical way. It should also be as large and as randomly dispersed as the test area. Moreover, considering that it will take a large area to test a variable, it would be wise to test only one variable at a time. Measuring more than one element may easily complicate matters.

Measurement. As a minimum, all market tests must include a measure of retail or consumer sales. But to make the most of a test market, other measures are desirable. Perhaps the ideal would be retail store audits and a consumer tracking study covering brand usage, repeat purchase, and attitudes toward brands. From this, one should be able at least to measure revenue results. If cost figures are recorded and translated to reflect national indexes, profit payouts would be possible and most useful too.

But to make the necessary projections, it is wise to use at least one year's back data as the base. By backcasting some of the usual projecting techniques, better estimating procedures can be deduced. If a few techniques work well, use the average; it will tend to yield the most likely estimate.

Needless to say, following the aforementioned prescriptions would lead to expensive market tests. No doubt compromise will be necessary. The more compromise, however, the less likely it is that the test will remain projectable. One then wonders if following traditional lines is the productive way for the future. Perhaps some radical departure is indicated.

NEW APPROACHES TO MARKET TEST DESIGN

So far, only two truly novel approaches to market test design have been developed which meet the criteria of projectability and which may still be practical. Since they have not been widely used, it is difficult to say that they will work. Yet they do offer hope. In addition, there is a third approach which, while not predictive of the total, may still be worthy of consideration for new-product introductions because it reduces risk without a national introduction.

The Checkerboard Design Test[3]

Conceptually, this method is simple; it is in a sense a practical extension of the grid approach to sampling populations. Without going into details here, it requires, (1) dividing the universe into two or more (preferably no more than five) equal but randomly selected groups of markets; (2) injecting basically opposite or different marketing patterns in each group of markets (in a continuum if more than two); and (3) measuring sales results in each using special tabulations of a readily available national survey or syndicated retail auditing service. Standard television areas (there are 192 well-defined, relatively mutually exclusive ones in the United States) are the basic market areas.

For example, a typical advertising expenditure test using the checkerboard design would be handled in the following way:

1. First, all 192 television markets would be arrayed from the biggest to the smallest (by population) in each of the seven Nielsen regions.

---

[3] This technique was developed jointly by the author, Harold Miller, and Lawrence Deckinger while at Grey Advertising in 1965. See [27].

2. Using a random starting point, the markets in each Nielsen area would be divided into, say, three equal parts on a random basis. Tabulation of sales and market share for all major brands in the product category would be obtained on an a priori basis to test projectability.

3. A different magnitude of advertising expenditure would be injected into each group of markets—say 80 percent of the current level into group A, 100 percent into group B, and 120 percent of current level into group C.

4. Three complete national media plans at each expenditure level would be developed. Spot television, newspapers, and local magazines would be used to produce the variations over the basic national underlay. Each plan would be implemented for a year and would be started simultaneously in each market.

5. Special checkerboard tabulations of sales and share of market would be obtained for each group of markets from Nielsen's regular syndicated service on a bimonthly basis. The previous year's data would be used as a base.

6. A comparison of the sales results in the three different market groups would be tracked bimonthly over the year to ascertain which budget yielded the best result.

On logic alone, the assets of the checkerboard test design would appear to be great; in almost every way it overcomes the basic shortcomings of traditional market tests. First, it comes as close as possible to being a representative test. Certainly with a two- or three-group test it is inconceivable that each group alone would not come extremely close to being representative of the nation. The sample is not only large but systematically dispersed in a random fashion. Moreover, it can be run for as long as necessary to cover seasonal variations. In addition, by its very size, the design requires the test variable to be used in a typical fashion.

Unlike the traditional market test, the checkerboard test is easy to control. Nothing need be done other than carefully implementing the plan. The random nature of the sample is theoretically designed to eliminate the effect of extraneous variables. With such a broad variety of markets in each test group, unique influences are unlikely to affect the results, nor could a competitor easily figure out how to distort it.

In terms of measurement, nothing could be easier for a company already receiving syndicated sales data or doing standard tracking studies. No supplemental samples are required, only special tabulations of the same random groups. Nor can it be criticized as impractical. It is flexible enough to implement broadly. It is even unlikely that marketing exigencies could upset the test. There are almost no measurement costs; only the cost of special tabulations.

A problem does, however, exist—risk—though in many cases it is more apparent than real. Obviously a test over such a broad area of the country does entail taking a big chance. Nevertheless, for many variables, this is an unreal risk. For example, consider the three-group expenditure test previously mentioned. No advertiser knows if his current level of expenditure is best. Yet if an advertiser tested the three alternatives, his sales might suffer if one of the other alternatives were unsound. However, he might also obtain better results, and the good ones might well largely offset the bad. Since the advertiser would be tracking on a bimonthly basis, any big deviation could easily be spotted and the test terminated if the change deleteriously affected sales.

The checkerboard design has wide application. It can be used for all types of advertising expenditure and media tests where the variations can be handled locally—spot broadcasts, major magazines, supplements, outdoor advertising, and newspapers. It can be used to test different creative strategies, distribution systems, promotions, prices, and personal selling approaches as long as the marketer can control these locally.   It can also be used to test new-product introductions, although it is vulnerable to many of the cost and practical problems associated with large-scale, dispersed, traditional market tests.

Unfortunately, the technique has not been widely used.   Yet the results of five experiments, done by clients of one major advertising agency, are known. In the first test, three different rates of expenditure were used—one 25 percent above the national rate, one at the national rate, and one 25 percent below the rate.   After a year's time, no significant differences in sales performance were observed among the three areas.

Three of the tests were all of extra spending; the proportion by which the budgets were increased was approximately 90 percent, 45 percent, and 40 percent, respectively.   The similarity in the patterns of results was remarkable.   In all cases, the greatest effect was obtained in the first bimonthly sales period following the budget increase.   Thereafter, there was a gradual diminution in the impact of the added weight.   Yet the cumulative effects remained positive in all three tests and statistically significant in two of the three.   In only one case did the incremental advertising pay for itself.

The final case concerned two alternative theories of geographical budget allocation—spending money in so-called high brand development markets versus spending where brand sales were increasing at an above average rate. The test results indicated that greater sales could be achieved in those markets where brand sales were accelerating.

In all of these cases, less than the 20 percent minimum checkerboard was used.   While preanalysis indicated this would reduce the predictability of the tests, there was no doubt that if the tests had been done on a grander scale, the results would have been cleaner.

Interestingly enough, in one of the tests where a preanalysis of the sales data was made on four brands, the variance between the national figures and test area figures was 7.0, 6.8, 1.8, and 3.2 percent at the two-sigma level.   This was considerably lower than the figures obtained in the traditional market tests reported earlier in the chapter.

The Marketing Model Design

A marketing model normally attempts to describe the process by which a market operates and how, by manipulating the factors which determine the process (such as advertising, price, distribution, and so on), a company can affect the final level of sales and profitability.   Such a model will not merely reveal the relationship of the factors in the process but also indicate the magnitude of each factors' influence.   These factors can then be expressed in some form of mathematical equation [9].

In a sense, a model, if good, should allow one to change one variable and ascertain the net effect based on how the others will react.   Knowing this permits the use of marketing models in two ways as market testing techniques. One is to obtain pretest data from the marketplace and use them in a computer simulation of the model.   A number of these are in use and all cannot be listed here.   Yet one developed by the Hendry Corporation is worth mentioning.   It basically depends upon the theory that changes in marketing variables will have differential effects depending upon the brand distribution in the particular market and changes in that distribution over short periods of time.   Thus if one knows the brand share from the marketplace and how it changes between two points in time, one may presumably predict the change in brand share as a result of a change in some marketing variable.

Needless to say, such a prediction, if accurate, is a breakthrough in marketing experimentation. Recent work by Erhenberg also suggests that it works [17a]. The second approach is one developed by E. J. Davis. He suggests using a traditional test market, but instead of using the raw data as results, he injects the results into a marketing model. In doing so, the known changes in the test market on all variables in the model are also applied to the model for the industry, thereby adjusting them in accordance with the known national model. The adjusted results are then projected to national levels. A recent experiment in Great Britain would suggest that this technique also offers great possibilities [12].

Needless to say, if either of these techniques works, many of the practical problems which have plagued market testing would be obviated. They, therefore, deserve further exploration and experimentation. They certainly offer greater hope than the traditional market tests which remain so prevalent even in the face of continued failure.

Preemptive Limited Introductions

This approach, one may quibble, is not projectable. Yet, it has experimental merit beyond the pilot-test concept for introducing a new brand. It essentially involves picking the top five markets—New York, Los Angeles, Chicago, Philadelphia, and Boston in the United States (they represent approximately 25 percent of the total population)—and introducing the new brand in them. Since they are large and broadly dispersed, they can give a strong indication whether the brand will succeed economically, for the fact is that no basic product can be a national success unless it does well in these five markets. Moreover, if it is economical, one can then expand into the next 20 markets, representing slightly more than 25 percent of the United States, and so on until national distribution is achieved.

The point is simple. The initial risk is only 25 percent of going national. While large, it is still much smaller than going national. Yet it is a preemptive move, easy to measure, and probably capable of control.

OTHER APPROACHES TO MARKET TESTING

One cannot review market testing methodology without discussing other suggested approaches, some of which do not seem very promising.

Mini-Market Tests

Perhaps the most widely heralded recent approach is the mini-market test. Essentially, a mini-market test is conducted in a very small area. Its popularity relates to new-product introduction. It is not seriously suggested for testing alternative marketing variables.

The major reason for its popularity would appear to be its low cost and the speed with which results can be obtained. In a way, the idea developed as an outgrowth of inflation and of the poor results from traditional tests. There seems to be an assumption among those who use mini-market tests that the way to new-product success is to roll the dice often; in that way a winner is bound to show up sooner or later. Evidently, the theory goes, many cheaper tests— no matter how ridiculous their design—are better than a few good ones, since a good product will eventually show through.

Yet in light of what we have said about designing a predictive market test, one would have to consider mini-market testing unadulterated nonsense. It cannot possibly have predictive capability except by pure coincidence. It is not representative in any way, being limited to one market, nor is a mini-market test typical of reality. Although many measures are usually obtained, it is hard to see how such tests can project to the United States, considering the sample they start with. One can conclude, using the design framework discussed so far, that mini-market testing is an excuse for real testing; like so much in research, some are more concerned with cost and speed irrespective of utility.

In-Store Tests

This is also a form of market testing, being done in the marketplace. It is almost always used for measuring an alternative marketing variable rather than a new-product introduction—usually for testing a revised package or a different price on an established brand.

When this is done well, the stores within a market are usually randomly split into two groups, with one approach put into one group and the other approach into the second group. To eliminate extraneous differences between the two groups from distorting the test, the variables are crossed over every month. To really work, tests must be carefully controlled. (See Section IV, Part E, Chapter 3.)

Most of the time, the tests are made in one market or at most in a few markets. The assumption is that the between-city variation is less than the within-city variation. If so, the test may yield a decisive result, particularly when properly handled. It has been used effectively for checking whether a variable which does not need advertising or promotion (some action outside the store) is uneconomic. If in-store tests were done in a number of places and if similar results were obtained, one could feel more secure in moving forward on a larger scale even if the results were not perfectly projectable. Yet, because its value is only where an in-store variable is testable, its usefulness is limited.

CATV/Ad Labs

The use of CATV (Community Antenna Television) for market testing began when split cables were installed in a city in such a way that two randomly matched groups could be reached by television. The ad lab is similar (the only recent one was begun by the *Milwaukee Journal*) in that the media are controlled within a city so that two matched groups can be contacted differently.

In the CATV approach, since the matching is home to home, distribution is not controlled. Measurements have to be by consumer panels or surveys. The ad lab, on the other hand, uses randomized areas; their distribution is controlled, although there may be some overlap. Thus, sales can be measured in the stores as well. In both cases, these tests can be of only two alternatives at any one time.

Like the in-store test, the assumption—particularly where only one city is involved, which has been the case so far—is that the within-city variation is greater than the between-city variation. There is a question of the validity of this assumption with respect to promotion. Evidence to date would suggest that the between-city variation is high.

In any case, both have limited value, being usable for testing advertising variables only. Yet the CATV idea should not be discarded too quickly. Currently, less than 12 percent of households are tied to a CATV system, and these usually in small markets. However, someday CATV systems may cover most of the United States. When they do, representativeness may be possible. Since they offer tremendous control of media, they could be an excellent market testing vehicle.

A FEW FINAL POINTS

Before summarizing, three additional points are worth mentioning. First, what has been discussed applies essentially to consumer products. Industrial product markets are usually not geographically dispersed or defined. Thus it is almost always impossible to use the market as a laboratory. Of course, to the degree that analogous situations might be found, the same principles of test design would still apply.

Second, it should not be inferred that the type of test one designs or uses is an either-or proposition. There may be reason to use the marketplace for pilot testing and to continue with such a test even when a bigger, predictive test is possible. Each type of use has its own design imperatives.

Finally, it is hoped that the desirability of more basic market research prior to test marketing was clearly communicated. Too much emphasis—both in time and money—is placed on market testing and too little on premarket test research. If more premarket test research were done, fewer market tests would be necessary, therefore permitting companies to do better market tests when required.

SUMMARY

There are basically two market testing functions—*managerial control* and *prediction*. Before a market test is conducted, it must be decided which function the test is to perform.

Marketing testing is an extremely valuable tool when used for managerial control. It can do for marketing what a pilot plant does for manufacturing—determining where problems exist and permitting other forms of research. In this way it can perform magnificently in reducing business risk. In using market testing for pilot purposes, there is no need for systematic market selection procedures or elaborate auditing systems. It must be recognized, however, that this is clearly a trial-and-error procedure from which no meaningful market prediction can be made. It therefore has no value for testing alternative marketing variables. Misuse of such a test is bound to lead to managerial unhappiness if national action is based on its results.

On the other hand, traditional marketing testing of one or two markets—used either for projecting the results of new-product introductions or for testing alternative marketing variables—has not lived up to expectations when used as a predictive tool. Serious problems of obtaining representativeness, maintaining control, and developing adequate measurement impair the ability of this tool to overcome variation inherent in the marketplace. Nor have the traditional solutions of increasing the number or size of markets, limiting the number of variables tested, or using more measurements done much in enhancing the projectability of these tests.

The problem appears to be one of design, not application, since market tests of one kind or another can be used to test just about anything. While substantially larger, randomly dispersed samples of markets may yield better results, the cost of doing so may be economically impractical. It would, therefore, seem that more radical departures are necessary.

Two seem to offer some hope: the checkerboard test design and experimental marketing models. Neither is costly. Yet they require sophisticated understanding of the theory of markets and therefore are presumed risky. While not tested widely, initial results suggest a greater degree of conclusiveness and a reduction in the variance of a prediction. In addition, for new product launches, using the preemptive limited introduction as an alternative method of market entry may reduce risk yet permit a basis for deciding whether to expand operations.

Other approaches to market testing—mini-market tests and CATV/ad lab tests—at the moment are not valid substitutes for predictive market testing. Mini-market testing meets none of the criteria for a predictive testing tool. While CATV offers longer-term hope, availability of split cable facilities is so limited that representativeness cannot be assured, which is also the case in the ad lab approach. On the other hand, in-store testing is of value in limited situations, although its projectability to the national scene may be wanting.

Based on our experience with market testing, we must conclude that the time has come for industry to seriously experiment with the more radical approaches of this research tool. Until test designs can take into account the heterogeneity of the marketplace, our ability to project results will continue to be minimal. Therefore, until the necessary experimentation is done, market testing's value will be as a managerial control tool and not as a reliable, predictive research tool. It would be a shame to relegate the marketplace as a laboratory to such a limited role.

REFERENCES

1. Achenbaum, A. A., "The Purpose of Market Testing," *Proceedings of the Forty-seventh National Conference of the American Marketing Association,* Chicago, June 1964.
2. Appel, V., "Multi-market Testing: A Practical Method for Choosing Between Media Alternatives," *Commentary, Journal of the Market Research Society,* vol. 7, April 1965.
3. Appelbaum, W., and R. F. Spears, "Controlled Experimentation in Marketing Research," *Journal of Marketing,* vol. 14, January 1950.
4. "Are You Using the Right Test Market?" *Printers' Ink,* May 20, 1953.
5. Banks, S., *Experimentation in Marketing,* New York: McGraw-Hill, 1965.
6. ———, "Implementation of Test Marketing," *Proceedings of the Forty-seventh National Conference of the American Marketing Association,* Chicago, June 1964.
7. Benson, P. H., and F. R. Pilgrim, "Testing Less Desirable Product Possibilities," *Journal of Marketing,* vol. 26, July 1961.
8. Bradley, E. C., "Seven Basic Steps in Planning Test Marketing of New Consumer Package Goods Product," *Advertising Age,* August 22, 1960.
9. Buzzell, R. D., *Mathematical Models and Marketing Management,* Cambridge, Mass.: Harvard University Press, 1965.
10. Christopher, M., *A Cluster-Analysis of Towns in England and Wales According to Their Suitability for Test Market Locations,* Bradford, England: University of Bradford Management Centre, 1969.
11. Davis, E. J., *Experimental Marketing,* London: New Company, 1970.
12. ———, "Test Marketing: An Examination of Sales Patterns Found during Forty-Four Recent Tests," in *Research in Marketing,* Seventh Annual Conference, Market Research Society, 1964.
13. Enright, E. J., "Market Testing in Canada," *Business Quarterly,* vol. 28, September–October 1958.
14. ———, "Market Testing in Canada," *Business Quarterly,* vol. 28, Spring 1963.
15. ———, "Testing the Market," *Business Quarterly,* vol. 26, Spring 1961.
16. Ewin, D. W., "Pilot Operations and Test Marketing," in *Effective Marketing Action,* New York: Harper, 1958.
17. Ehrenberg, A. S. C., "On Matching and Experimental Design," *Proceedings of 6th Annual Market Research Society,* Eastbourne, 1963.
17a. ———, "Predicting the Performance of New Brands," *Journal of Advertising Research,* vol. 11, December 1971.

18. Ford, K., "Management Guide: Test Marketing," *Printers' Ink*, August 27, 1965.
19. Fry, J. N., "Testing the Market," *The Business Quarterly*, vol. 26, Spring 1961.
20. Gold, J., "Testing Test Market Predictions," *Journal of Marketing Research*, vol. 1, August 1964.
21. Green, P. E., R. E. Frank, and P. J. Robinson, "Cluster Analysis in Test Market Selection," *Management Science*, vol. 13, April 1967.
22. Green, P. E., and D. S. Tull, *Research for Marketing Decisions*, Englewood Cliffs, N.J.: Prentice-Hall, 1971.
23. Groome, H. C., Jr., "Take the Risks Out of Test Marketing," *Sales Management*, April 17, 1964.
24. Hardin, D. K., "Tomorrow's Test Market—The Controlled Store Measurement," *Food Product Development*, December–January 1971.
25. Hilton, P., "Ten Ways to Cut Your Risk When Test-Marketing," *Sales Management*, September 1, 1953.
26. "How New-Product Test Cities are Selected," *Printers' Ink*, September 25, 1959.
27. Kroeger, A., "Test Marketing: The Concept and How It Is Unique," *Media/Scope*, December 1966.
28. Kraushar, P. M., *New Products and Diversification*, London: Business Book Ltd., 1969.
29. Ladik, F., L. Kent, and P. C. Nahl, "Test Marketing of New Consumer Products," *Journal of Marketing*, vol. 24, April 1960.
30. Lipstein, B., "Tests for Test Marketing," *Harvard Business Review*, March–April 1961.
31. Lipstein, B., "The Design of Test Marketing Experiments," *Proceedings of the Forty-seventh National Conference of the American Marketing Association*, Chicago, June 1964.
32. Nielsen, A. C. Jr., "Eight Pitfalls in Market-Testing New Products," *The Management Review*, February 1958.
33. "Piloting the Test Market," *Modern Packaging*, October 1961.
34. "Portrait of a Top Test Market: Milwaukee," *Printers' Ink*, August 10, 1962.
35. "Seven Steps in Planning Test Marketing of a Consumer Package Goods Product," *Advertising Age*, August 22, 1960.
36. "Test Marketing Goes Truly National," *Sales Management*, November 10, 1958.
37. "Test Marketing: The New Horizons," *Printers' Ink*, April 12, 1963.
38. "Testing: Big Business Across the Country," *Printers' Ink*, October 4, 1957.
39. "Testing Your Way to More Profit," *Advertising Age*, August 22, 1960.
40. "Test Marketing: Solid Sales Tool or Waste of Money," *Sales Management*, January 5, 1962.
41. "The Nation's Top Test Markets and How They're Used," *Sales Management*, January 5, 1962.
42. Treasure, J., address to Marketing Society, England, 1964.
43. Weiss, E. B., "Trials and Tribulations of Test Marketing," *Advertising Age*, January 16, 1961.
44. "Why Good Products Fail in Test Markets," *Printers' Ink*, April 13, 1962.
45. Wills, G., and Hayhurst, R., "Test Marketing: How Can We Improve Practice?" *Twelfth Annual Conference Papers, Market Research Society*, England, 1969.

Sales Analysis and Forecasting

Chapter 1

Sales Forecasting

ROBERT L. McLAUGHLIN *Scovill Manufacturing Company, Waterbury, Connecticut*

The sales forecast should be one of the company's most important documents. Unfortunately it rarely measures up to this distinction, even though it is quite possible to efficiently plan for future events by means of careful forecasting. In this chapter we will examine means of organizing the sales forecasting function. We will also examine the three most common forecasts made in corporations: (1) the short-term operating forecast, (2) the annual budget forecast, and (3) the long-term capacity forecast.

ORGANIZING THE SALES FORECAST

At the outset it must be stressed categorically that unless the general manager and his important department heads fully support the forecasts, they will have little stature. Indeed, the general manager, if practicable, should give final approval to all forecasts before they are issued.

The Need for Consensus. The forecasting program should not be wholly identified with a single personality. It should be coordinated by one man (most properly, the marketing research manager), but it must have the active participation of such key people as sales managers and production managers. Consensus here is vital, because if the key people who manage the business do not take the forecasts seriously, they will not be of any real value.

A good plan is for the marketing research manager to analyze the economic, industry, and company environment and then hold a conference with one representative each from (1) sales and (2) production. Such a three-man conference can be held for each major product line. The results of these conferences are brought together into a single forecasting document which is brought to the top marketing director for discussion and approval. The marketing director and his marketing research manager should then meet with the general manager for final approval, possibly in company with the purchasing director. Such a system brings together a consensus of the critical people.

The Official Forecast. There should be only one official forecast of sales. If various departments make their own forecasts because they do not agree with the official one, the result is not only lack of coordination but management chaos. Although a method should be developed for revising the forecast when it needs revising, it should at all times be the official planning device of the enterprise, with the full authority of the general manager behind it.

Market Demand versus Production. The sales forecast should be oriented toward market demand. An exception is when the business operates at capacity. Under conditions of full capacity, the sales forecast tends to become a "documentation of capacity production rates." But under "normal" conditions (which we might generalize as peacetime), business tends to operate at less than full capacity. This is because American companies—for purposes of flexibility and growth—tend to build more capacity than they generally need. When the firm is operating at less than capacity, then market demand should be constantly measured by means of a sales forecast. And this forecast should represent the single document for guiding operating decisions.

THE SHORT-TERM OPERATING FORECAST

The short-term operating forecast should be the principal guide in running the business in its daily operations. It should be frequently revised, in most cases monthly, but even then with intramonth reviews. Production schedules should be set by it, raw material purchases guided by it, inventories controlled by it, and cash flows forecasted by it.

The operating forecast is usually in terms of monthly figures, although they can be weekly or quarterly. The general practice is to forecast units, then convert to dollars. The extent to which the forecast is broken down into separate product classes can only be determined within the specific business. Usually though, the sales forecast deals with general product lines. Because its accent is on broad market demand, it should not become too burdened down with the details of thousands of items, sizes, and colors. Production scheduling should do this, following the sales forecast for general guidance.

Underlying Business Conditions. The drift of general business is one of the most difficult things to grasp, and its effect on the specific business is even more tenuous. Still, in order to run a business well, we must constantly try to predict what will happen to our business as a result of the behavior of the economy in general.

The Trend. The long-term secular trend is rarely significant in the short-term operating forecast, because the trend rarely causes a series to vary much over a short period of time. (It is, of course, highly important in the long-term capital forecast.)

The Cycle. The cycle is important in the operating forecast, and the further we get from the present, the more important it becomes. The cycle is the thing within a series that induces us to say "business is good lately" or "business is bad." The cycle might better be called something like demand energy, a force in the marketplace that signals producers to either increase or decrease production. For example, retailers may overstock an item. When it does not move as expected, the retailers (by not reordering) "signal" the manufacturers to reduce production. Most of our recessions since World War II have been described as "inventory recessions," periods when retailers are signaling manufacturers to lower production until supply comes down to meet demand. This demand energy is the cycle. It is a phenomenon that all businessmen intuitively monitor.

The cycle is extremely difficult to forecast. Although the pattern of this demand energy is *recurrent*, unfortunately it is not *periodic*. Since it does not have a periodically repetitive character, it is extremely arduous to develop reliable patterns of its behavior.

The Seasonal Pattern. Most businesses have some kind of seasonal pattern, causing volume to change from month to month or season to season. Seasonal fluctuations recur at the same time each year and are frequently linked in some way to the weather (air conditioners, skis, and so on). Seasonality is crucial in short-term forecasts because it can cause volume to change strikingly from one month to the next.

It is of great importance to study the seasonal pattern of the business that is being forecast. It is particularly important to understand the rationale behind the pattern. If one cannot develop a thorough understanding of why the pattern exists, look out. It may be spurious and cannot be relied upon as a basis for forecasts. In evaluating the rationale of the seasonal pattern, also check the series from year to year. If a long period of less than capacity operation precedes a period when you operate at capacity, it may be that the carefully developed seasonal factors will not work. If, for example, November tended to be low prior to Vietnam and then the company began to operate at capacity, there is serious question whether volume would fall off in that month under the conditions of full capacity.

One of the major problems with mathematically derived seasonal factors is introducing them into the day-to-day operations of the business. Managers rarely understand them and do not like to work with things they do not understand. It is useful to consider seasonally adjusted data in terms of two separate functions: (1) to report on recent trends and (2) for forecasting future volumes. A seasonally adjusted series can be extremely helpful in magnifying underlying trends which otherwise might not be clear. The same type of data, however, can be very confusing to management when used for forecasts. Therefore seasonally adjusted data can be used for the first function, but it is not wise to issue *forecasts* in this form. In dealing with future magnitudes, management personnel are accustomed to think in terms of real data, machine time, and so on.

Calendar Variations. The calendar also causes volume to change from one month to the next, not because economic conditions vary but simply because there are more or less days in which "the store is open." The number of days included within the accounting period obviously affects volume and therefore must be considered when forecasting. Often seasonality and workdays are lumped together when analyzing seasonality, but this is not wise. Workdays or trading days are a very measurable entity, since we know how many there are long in advance. Their impact should be evaluated and considered independently from the much more subtle "seasonal" pattern.

Irregular Gyrations. The trend, cycle, season, and calendar all cause volume to change from period to period. Often these four factors will account for a very substantial portion of the total change in the product line. But *some* change is always taking place for still other reasons. It is necessary, therefore, to have a fifth category representing all change not accounted for by the other four. It is, in effect, the "all other" category.

Such fluctuations are generally called irregular. These effects can be a strike, a major machine breakdown, or a fire; the most common to a business-man is a price change. When a company announces on January 1 that it will raise prices in a couple of weeks, January sales can easily become a flood. But this windfall can cause later sales in February and March to be low, for obvious reasons. An inevitable law of compensation sets in. Irregular gyrations are virtually impossible to anticipate and consequently most forecasters do not attempt to forecast them.

Computer Help. There are two computer programs that are widely used in short-term forecasting of corporate sales. One is the well-known seasonal adjustment program of the U.S. Census Bureau. This program (often called the X-11 program) is very popular in evaluating the history of any product line. By using it, an analyst can learn much about the product line's cyclical behavior, its seasonal pattern, and its irregular fluctuations. It is a must for the sales forecaster, and is the subject of Section II, Part E, Chapter 2 of this handbook.

The other computer program is used as an "updater" to the Census Bureau's program. It is called FORAN II and was published in 1968 by the American Marketing Association [6]. This computer program was designed to help an analyst evaluate a time series each month. Its objective is to help the analyst forecast the next few months.

THE MEDIUM-TERM BUDGET FORECAST

Just about every organization must have a budget forecast for the following calendar year. This includes corporations, governments, and private agencies. It is a traditional practice in the United States and elsewhere to prepare budgets every fall. This is a particularly difficult assignment for the sales forecaster because budgets are greatly affected (1) by the business cycle, which is extremely difficult to forecast so long in advance, and (2) by inside "political" considerations that inevitably affect all organizations. Still, forecast we must and the sales forecaster must do the best he can to help guide his management toward an optimum plan for the ensuing year.

Forecast versus Plan. The forecaster must take the future state of the national economy into consideration when making the annual budget forecast. There is a whole round of economic forecasting conferences each fall in which the economy in the coming year is discussed. In addition, there are thousands of articles in newspapers and magazines in which the state of the economy is reviewed. The forecaster, having considered the state of the general economy, goes on to his industry. By using the Census Bureau's seasonal adjustment program, it is possible to develop a good picture of the behavior of the specific industry in relation to changes in the general business cycle. Having deductively evaluated the economy and then the industry, the forecaster goes on to his own company's market share. From the market share, he produces a forecast of sales.

At this point, subjective considerations enter. The forecasts of the economy and the industry can be done with considerable objectivity, but almost always there are special considerations when the company sales forecast is begun. It is quite possible to forecast a rise in sales in the face of a forecasted decline in industry sales by simply planning an aggressive increase in market share. Bringing off the increase may be difficult, but forecasting it is easily accomplished by optimistic sales departments.

The three-phase economy-industry-company forecasting process generally starts with forecasts of the first two, which actually become the instruments of planning the company program. It is often very difficult to call the *company* part of the process a forecast or a plan.   Ultimately, the process must result in some kind of plan of action, reaching to top management for final approval.

The Budget Forecast.   More and more frequently, the annual budget forecast is becoming an extension of the short-term operating forecast.   A good practice is to issue a monthly sales forecast showing the months of the current year as well as those of the following year.   In such a scheme, three basic parts are always visible: (1) actual data for those months that are already history; (2) the short-term operating forecast covering three to five months after the latest actual month, which is reviewed with considerable scrutiny each month and which gets close supervision of the key management personnel; (3) the remainder of the twenty-four-month period, which carries through the following year for which budgets must eventually be developed.

With such a device, management at all times during the current year has some idea of what the next year will be like.   As the current year moves toward the fall, the budget forecast for the following year gradually "hardens" into a final budget.

Econometrics.   One of the great new forecasting tools to be developed in recent years is the econometric model, a device built basically on regression analysis.   The principal idea is to develop equations representing relationships between the national economic accounts as reported quarterly in the *Survey of Current Business* and the industry of which the company is a part.   Most corporations do not have so large an economic staff that they can build econometric models of the United States economy.   Consequently they must rely on such outside models as the Wharton School Model or the Michigan Model.   The former is at the University of Pennsylvania and the latter is at the University of Michigan.   Both these models are quarterly and are available to the public for a subscription fee.

Timing Relationships.   When using an econometric model of the United States economy as a device for forecasting one's own industry, the idea is to develop regression equations with one's industry's quarterly series as the dependent variable.   The independent variables are those forecasted by the econometric model.   Having established equations for producing forecasts of the industry, the analyst assumes that the forecasts of the econometric model are correct.   These forecasted variables become the independent variables in his equations.   Throughout such analyses, the forecaster tries to develop timing relationships among the variables.

Although one cannot get much help from regression equations in the early months of a forecast, they become more and more valuable to the forecaster after this period.   In the short-term operating forecast, a large dosage of judgment must be brought into the analysis because so much happens in the very short term that is nonsystematic.   Regression equations imply the very notion of systematic relationship.   In the very short term, such relationships are constantly upset by exogenous factors like huge military orders, sudden price changes, and inventory policy alterations.   But beyond a certain time, the most acute manager cannot call upon his judgment to help; and using econometrics to pick up the burden has great promise.   Even though the econometric model will not always be accurate, the alternatives to this technique seem to be even less promising.

Computer Help.   The very nature of an econometric model, with all its calculations and complex relationships, implies the necessity of a computer.   Whether the user subscribes to an econometric model of the United States economy or builds his own model, the computer is imperative.   In order to establish relationships among variables, multiple regression techniques must be used, and this would be extremely time-consuming without a computer. Several very fine multiple regression computer programs have been developed in recent years, as discussed by Warwick in Section II, Part G, Chapter 1, and most computer companies will provide them to their customers.

THE LONG-TERM CAPACITY FORECAST

All businesses—and especially large businesses—require long-term forecasts for planning new plant and equipment expenditures. Often these forecasts are made on a routine basis in the fall, when budgets are being prepared. These long-term capacity forecasts are for 5, 10, or 20 years, depending on the life cycle of the equipment that is being considered for installation. The data are usually in yearly time units, and such forecasts are generally made in "real" terms, that is, with no attempt to predict inflation.

Two basic kinds of problems emerge in analyzing the long term, those involving (1) businesses that are still in the rising phases of the S curve, not yet having reached saturation, and (2) those that are at the upper ends of the S curve. The former are generally characterized as growth businesses, while those which have thoroughly penetrated the marketplace are characterized as mature businesses. Forecasting the two is quite different. Therefore they are taken up separately.

Forecasting Growth Products. A growth product is here defined as a product or service which has not yet fully penetrated the marketplace. The electric car is a growth product. Most people would say that it has a future, perhaps a great future, but at the moment it has a very tiny share of the overall auto market. Its penetration of the market is extremely small. But it will more than likely rise. Eventually it will reach a penetration level, relative to the internal combustion engine, that will be its own. Right now it is well-nigh impossible to know what the ultimate level will be. Only time will tell. This is a growth product, because it has not yet reached its optimal penetration. Full penetration—whatever it may be in the specific market—is akin to "saturation." This is the point at which a product or service can no longer grow by either taking from a substitute or creating its own new demand. After this point of saturation, the continued growth of the product or service must come from the replacement market and the natural growth (increase in population, households, and so on) of the market itself.

Saturation Analysis. For those products or services that have not yet reached their full penetration level, we must first estimate what this level could be *now* if the market were fully exploited. For example, for electric knives, the question is how many households there are and what percentage of these represent realistic potential right now, given the price of the product. This is a critical estimate, for without such a beginning it is extremely difficult to estimate anything else. If, after a survey, it is estimated that saturation could be 80 percent of the households and there are now 50 million of them, then the estimate is that 40 million households could use them. This becomes the *present potential market.*

The Ultimate Potential. Given a decision respecting the penetration level (80 percent), we must next forecast the number of households to the year that management has requested the forecast to go. Let us say it is a 10-year forecast. By using the Census Bureau's estimates of future population and households, let us say that we find the number of households at 60 million 10 years hence. At 80 percent saturation, we can then say that the *ultimate market potential* in the tenth year will be 48 million knives. We have now done two things: (1) we have estimated the logical saturation as 80 percent of the households and (2) we have set the ultimate market at the tenth year, at which time there will be 60 million households.

The S Curve. We must now go back and estimate what percentage of the ultimate number of households presently are using electric knives. If industry figures indicate that, since the introduction of electric knives, there have been a total of 10 million sold, then the *ultimate market potential* is presently 20.8 percent saturated (10 ÷ 48). The analyst must now determine the cumulative totals of electric knives in use at the end of each year since their introduction. These quantities can be quickly converted to percentage saturations by dividing by the ultimate 48 million. Once these figures are derived, they should be plotted on probability paper.

In using probability paper, the analyst can put the years on the bottom scale running from the first year in which the electric knife was introduced through the tenth year beyond the most recent *actual* year. In the graph, the tenth year out into the future is assigned a point at 80 percent—the saturation expected at the end of that time period. In the early years, the actual derived percentages are plotted. If everything is "on schedule," this line of the early years ought to reach near the 80 percent mark in the tenth year. If there is a "normal" S curve developing in the earlier years, this fact should result in a relatively straight line on the probability paper.

In Figure 1, we see a classic before and after look at an actual case study the writer made in 1953 while at General Electric's two-way radio department. At the time of the study, we conducted a census of radios in use on American railroads. This figure is equivalent to point A in the figure. We did not know at that time the actual year-by-year growth in radios between 1948 and 1952. But such radios must be licensed by the Federal Communications Commission, and we did investigate the number of radios licensed by year. Through a careful analysis of the number of diesel engines and cabooses that were expected to be in operation by 1964, the year in which dieselization was expected to be completed, we started our estimate of the *ultimate market potential.* By plotting cumulative licenses as a percentage of the *ultimate potential,* we developed the straight dashed line in the graph from 1948 to 1952 and then extrapolated it through 1964 at point B. It came to 82 percent saturation, the amount of saturation that would take place by the completion of dieselization given that the pace through 1952 continued. The dashed line became the guide for the yearly estimates.

Many years later, by a fortunate surprise, the Association of American Railroads began to make statistics available on the use of railroad radios. In fact a whole history was developed. This made it possible to evaluate the 12-year forecast made in 1953. The historical evaluation was made in the mid-1960s. Knowing the actual number of diesels and cabooses in service during the year 1964, we knew then the *ultimate market potential.* The solid line in the figure shows actual saturation year by year. It was never quite on target, but on the average through the 12 years, the saturation estimate was extremely accurate. The reason for the gap in the early years to the left of point A is that it took time for the railroads to install radios to fill their licenses, since licenses actually provided for more radios than were actually installed. As the years went by this gap gradually closed.

Keep in mind that the straight dashed line of saturation on the probability paper would actually be in the form of an S curve if plotted on regular arithmetic paper. The convenience of probability paper is that it enables the analyst to manipulate his data using straight lines rather than curved ones. But—

at this point, remember—we have only evaluated the new user. We now proceed to investigate the replacement market.

The Replacement Market.   In order to evaluate the replacement market, a study must be made of the product's life cycle.   Products are generally re-

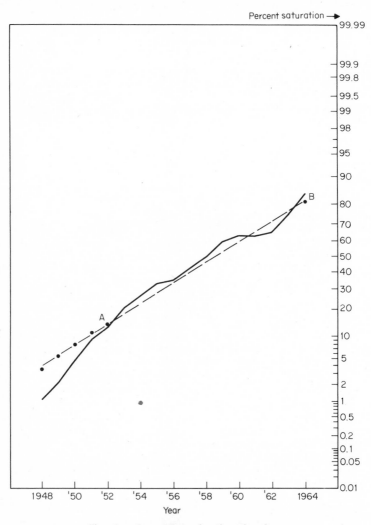

Fig. 1.   Saturation of railroad radios.

placed either by wearing out (including those destroyed accidentally) or by obsolescence. With established products, it is possible to estimate the life cycle in the field; but with new products the cycle must be estimated by laboratory techniques.

When a new product comes on the market, it almost immediately begins to be replaced. Some are broken; others survive long years. But in general, a product's life cycle can be depicted in the form of a frequency distribution. To take a highly simplified example, if the life cycle is five years and the median life is three years, there will be a percentage for each year, with the highest percentage in the third year (see Figure 2). Before and after that year the percentages will decrease, but the total of the percentages for all five years will be 100 percent or very close to it.

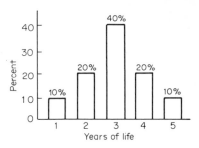

Fig. 2.   Product life cycle.

With the percentage life cycle calculated for the product, it is easy to determine the number of units "ending" their lives in each year after they are sold. Given 1,200,000 units sold in 1973, we can estimate the number that will be replaced in each future year by multiplying 1973 sales volume five times, by the percentages shown in Figure 2. Although a lot of arithmetic is involved, each year's sales can thus be broken down into future years' replacements. (See Table 1.)

Each column in Table 1 represents the number replaced in future years, and each vertical column totals the same amount as was sold as original equipment. By adding across, we can estimate the annual replacement market, and this must be added to the original equipment sold to new households. In this way, the total annual market for a growth product can be forecasted for the long term.

Forecasting Mature Products. Although the more exciting forecasting assignments are those in the growth area, most long-term forecasting assignments are for known products, services, and commodities that are past their sharp S curve phases. Their growth comes from increases in population, households, businesses, and services. Their penetration, though not static, is relatively stable, rising high and low in response to the competitive conditions prevailing. Copper yields to aluminum, which in turn yields to plastics. And so the battle of penetration goes on, with one material or product rising and falling in relation to its competitors.

TABLE 1   Calculating the Replacement Market (Thousands of Units)

Year replaced	1973	1974	1975	1976	1977	19xx	Replacement market	Original equipment	Total market
1974	120						120	1,500	1,620
1975	240	150					390	1,600	1,990
1976	480	300	160				940	1,900	2,840
1977	240	600	320	190			1,350	2,100	3,450
1978	120	300	640	380	210		1,650	2,100	3,750
1979		150	320	760	420		Etc.	Etc.	Etc.
1980			160	380	840				
1981				190	420				
1982					210				
Etc.									
Original equipment	1,200	1,500	1,600	1,900	2,100	Etc.			

The Full-Capacity Case.   The easiest type of long-run forecast is that which assumes full capacity. Some fortunate companies simply operate at capacity, selling all they can produce. If they produce too much, they just lower the price until they have sold the output from their capacity—whatever that may be. This is obviously an easy forecasting problem. But even here, if we say that the product or service has a growth rate, some effort must be made to forecast its continuance. Will the past rate of growth continue into the future? Will the rate increase? Decrease?

The Logarithmic Trend.   The principal forecasting technique for developing long-term forecasts of the mature industry is logarithmic trend projection. Such a trend contains equal *percentage* change from period to period (being different from the arithmetic trend which has equal absolute *values* from period to period). This trend is a straight line when drawn on semilog paper. By far the most difficult problem is selecting the proper historical span of years for extrapolation into the future. If the slope is wrong, it can compound into an enormous error many years out, thus causing the company to provide too much or too little capacity.

Choice of Span.   The technical rule is that the span of years included in the historical period should be longer than a single business cycle. It would cause a gross distortion if the first year were a recession year and the final year a peak, since such a choice of initial and terminal years would produce too high a growth rate. This could lead a company into a serious overcapacity problem. The opposite choice of a peak year first, with recession year last, will yield too low a growth rate.

Be wary of extreme beginnings or endings. If the first year is a recession, end in a recession; if the first year is a peak, end in a peak. However, even the formal business cycle does not guarantee foolproof selection. The years 1958 and 1967 were both low years, and a case can be made for using them as initial and terminal years, but two problems come to mind. First, 1958 has been designated a recession year, and by post-World War II standards a rather serious one, while 1967 was not considered a recession year, even though it had many of the characteristics of a recession. Such a selection of initial and terminal years can cause the trend slope to be too high. Second, the ending years (the late 1950s) of the Eisenhower administration are considered by economists to be a period of low growth, sometimes called stagnation. On the other hand, 1967 was the peak of the Vietnam War, and wars are always a stimulant to an economy. So we have a long 10-year period starting low and ending high, even though we have selected our initial and terminal years by following the technical rules.

Length of Span.   Probably the best way to choose the span is first to draw the series on semilog paper using annual data. If at all possible, get data back to World War II. The longer the span, the better the analysis. A long period like this can enable the analyst to look for past structural changes in the trend that might not be expected to continue in the future. For example, from the end of World War II through the middle 1960s, copper water tube exhibited the classical early phases of the S curve. In the late 1950s and early 1960s, the rate of growth was very high, but since then it has flattened out.

During the same period the housing industry did not exhibit a very high rate of growth, nowhere near that of copper water tube. The fact is that during the period of sharp growth, copper water tube was penetrating the plumbing market, which had been dominated by galvanized iron. By the middle 1960s, copper's penetration was probably approaching 90 percent. The very high growth rate of the past cannot reasonably be hoped for in the future because the penetration level has probably been maximized. Plotting the data back to 1946 enables an analyst to see this.

The Penetration Problem. Often in mature industries, there will be a give and take among like products and services. This is the substitution phenomenon that affects a product's penetration level. In the materials industries there is a constant "war of materials." Stainless steel replaces a copper part, which in turn is replaced by a plastic part. The materials war tends to be related, as one might expect, to price. When copper gets scarce, its price goes up, thereby making a substitute more attractive. The loss of copper markets produces an oversupply of copper, which lowers its price, thereby making it attractive once again.

This interplay of substitution in many markets (domestic autos versus imports, aluminum home siding versus wood, wax paper versus plastic film, air versus rail passenger transport, and so on) causes extreme difficulty in evaluating long-term trends. An industry or product can decline for several years and then stage a comeback for another period of years. The latter phase of sharp growth can induce a forecaster to forecast the sharp growth to continue, whereas the period of sharp growth could simply mark the industry's recovery.

This is a good reason for graphing the data over a long period of years—the more the better. It enables the analyst to see the behavior of the business in various phases of many business cycles, under conditions of differing national growth, war and peace, inflation and deflation, secular exuberance and secular stagnation.

Computer Help. Most computer companies make logarithmic trend programs available to their customers. In addition, there are now econometric models for long-term forecasting. Input-output models will become more useful for long-term forecasts, particularly where technological change is a consideration. One of the most promising new long-term forecasting models begins with a long-term growth-rate projection of the industry and ends with the company's discounted cash flow from the investments required to maintain the company's market share. The various input factors into the model have Monte Carlo simulations for measuring the risks. The model is heavily influenced by the long-term forecast of the industry.

SUMMARY

Sales forecasting is becoming a more and more important function in the modern corporation, partly because our abilities in this area are improving and because the large corporation is leaning more toward formal planning. In this chapter we have discussed how a modern forecasting effort should be organized to take advantage of the new mathematical techniques of systematic analysis while in no way overlooking the very important elements of judgment that can be contributed by key members of management.

The new statistical approaches are improving with great speed, essentially due to the computer. Consequently, sales forecasting is one of the more dynamic fields of business. Many new approaches will become feasible in future years and the progressive corporation is well advised to stay close to the state of the art. Improved techniques will help the company in the game of strategy in the marketplace and the successes will be significant.

REFERENCES

1. Brennan, M. J., *Preface to Econometrics,* Cincinnati: South-Western Publishing Company, Incorporated, 1967.

2. Brown, R. G., *Statistical Forecasting for Inventory Control*, New York: McGraw-Hill, 1959.
3. Evans, M. K., and L. R. Klein, *The Wharton Econometric Forecasting Model*, Philadelphia: Wharton School of Finance and Commerce, University of Pennsylvania, 1968.
4. Hertz, D. B., "Risk Analysis in Capital Investments," *Harvard Business Review*, January–February 1964.
5. McLaughlin, R. L., *Time Series Forecasting*, Chicago: American Marketing Association, 1962.
6. ———, and J. Boyle, *Short-term Forecasting*, Chicago: American Marketing Association, 1968.
7. Murdick, R. G., and A. E. Schaefer, *Sales Forecasting for Lower Costs and Higher Profits*, Englewood Cliffs, N.J.: Prentice-Hall, 1967.
8. Reichard, R. S., *Practical Techniques of Sales Forecasting*, New York: McGraw-Hill, 1966.
9. Winters, P. R., "Forecasting Sales by Exponentially Weighted Moving Averages," *Management Science*, vol. 6, April 1960.

Part B

Sales Analysis and Forecasting

Chapter 2

Predicting Sales of a New Product

ROBERT F. KELLY *Commerce and Business Administration, University of British Columbia, Vancouver, Canada*

INTRODUCTION

The purpose of this chapter is to review the methods that are or might be used to predict sales of a new product. *Method*, in this context, includes information sources as well as specific prediction techniques. Most of the methods described have been developed in a consumer products context, but except where noted, they may also be applied to new industrial products.

Two assumptions underlie the discussion on predicting sales of new products. First, the product is "given." That is, additional product development is not seen as an objective of the prediction process. And second, "newness" in a product is a function of customer perception. Thus, central heating systems are new in Scotland and diodes are not new to manufacturers in the United States electronics industries.[1]

A minimum of technical jargon and mathematical notation is used in this chapter. An attempt is made to describe the conceptual basis of some fairly sophisticated prediction techniques, but the reader is referred to the source for a description of the necessary details.

Initially, attention is given to a formulation of the problems of prediction. This is followed by a consideration of the sources and the nature of information required to predict sales levels of new products. Then various prediction techniques and their most promising areas of application are described. The chap-

---

[1] This definition of a new product is consistent with diffusion of innovations theory. See Sec. III, Part B, Chap. 3.

ter concludes with a discussion of the limitations of the various prediction methods.

It is important to note before proceeding that there is no one best prediction technique for all products on all occasions. Nor is it possible to provide the reader with a cookbook approach to the selection and application of prediction techniques. Some attention is given both to the selection and the application problems, but the success of any attempt at new-product sales prediction still rests in large measure on the judgment and knowledge of markets possessed by those who have the responsibility for predictions.

NATURE OF PREDICTION PROBLEMS

The first step in predicting market response to any new product is to define, as precisely as possible, the nature of the prediction problem. Variables that must be considered in this process include (1) the nature of the product, (2) the nature of the prospective purchasers, and (3) the nature of competition. These factors are discussed in some detail below.

The Nature of the New Product

Different new products present different prediction problems. Some of the more important factors that must be considered when one develops a prediction procedure for a given new product are:[2]

1. Degree of "newness" of a new product
2. Frequency of purchase
3. Average size of purchase
4. Relative economic/social advantage over product(s) it is expected to replace
5. Divisibility
6. Communicability
7. Complexity
8. Compatibility

Degree of Newness. A new brand in an established product class represents a very different (and much simpler) prediction problem than a new brand of a product class with which consumers are not familiar. In the former instance, it is possible to benefit from previous introductions of new brands in that product class—that is, analogies—to a significant degree. Purchase rates, purchase quantities, degrees of brand loyalty, consumer attitudes toward new brands, consumer responses toward various promotional strategies employed to support previous new brand introductions, and so on all can be determined. Such information at least establishes a "ballpark" within which sales of the new brand in question can be expected to reside.

Where a new product with which customers are not at all familiar is being introduced, the problems of prediction are formidable. Empirical information must be generated from a prospect population that has no notion of the intended use characteristics of the new product; no established acceptability of the new product from a functional, economic, or social point of view; and no incentive to develop such notions or attitudes in the absence of artificial test conditions. Furthermore, it is extremely difficult to identify analogous product introductions (although this should always be attempted).

In general, the newer the new product, the more difficult the prediction

---

[2] Items 4 through 8 are discussed in some detail in the diffusion literature. See Sec. III, Part B, Chap. 3; also Rogers [16].

problem and the more imperative the development of an imaginative prediction procedure. Some insight may be provided by the paragraphs that follow on procedures that are particularly appropriate to the new brand/new product case.

Frequency of Purchase. The expected frequency of purchase—that is, the repurchase cycle—for a new product must be established both to identify appropriate prediction techniques and to establish sales estimates for the product in question. If the new product is frequently repurchased, it may be possible to make use of test-market or early general-market returns to predict sales levels for the new product. Techniques for extrapolating early sales data are described toward the end of the chapter.

If a new product is expected to be purchased only once or infrequently by a given customer—for example, color television—repurchase rates are of little short-run strategic interest to those responsible for sales predictions. Emphasis must be placed instead on the expected extent and rate of market penetration, that is, initial purchases.

Average Size of Purchase. The expected average size of individual purchases is of significant importance in predicting sales levels of some new products. Obviously, information on estimated average quantity purchased must be combined with estimated frequency of purchase and the overall number of purchases expected to derive sales estimates. Nearly all prediction techniques except those covering high-unit-value, one-shot purchases require an information input covering estimated average size of individual purchases; and even those require breakdowns along price and/or model lines.

Perceived Economic/Social Advantages of a New Product. Knowledge of prospective customer reactions to a new product is obviously essential to the sales prediction task. The greater the perceived advantages of the new product, the greater the magnitude of customer response to that product. Perceived advantage should be determined from a social as well as a functional and/or economic point of view. This suggests the necessity for caution when using data on perceived advantage from consumer test panels or other laboratory-type sources. One must attempt to determine whether, within the context of a market, social endorsement is important to a product's success. As a general rule, the more visible or conspicuous a product, the more necessary social endorsement becomes.

The Perceived Divisibility of a Product. *Divisibility* refers to the extent to which a new product may be tried or sampled before an adoption commitment is made. Most low-unit-value, frequently repurchased items are divisible in this sense. It is very easy to try a new brand of cigarettes, for example. If the new brand does not satisfy the trier, he can go back to his old brand with little sense of loss. A new automobile is not divisible. One must either make a purchase and live with the consequences or make no purchase at all. The more divisible a new product, the greater the level of penetration (initial purchases) one may expect and the less significance one should attach to the rate of first purchase in projecting sales levels for subsequent periods.

The Communicability of a New Product. Communicability reflects the ease with which the nature and advantages of a new product can be gotten across to consumers—usually via the mass media. It is not always easy to judge the communicability of a new product. For example, the first brand of freeze-dried instant coffee introduced on any significant scale (Maxim) did not yield the high initial purchases and rates of repurchase expected because it proved extremely difficult to inform customers how the product should be used to realize its very tangible advantages over conventional instant coffees. That difficulty had not been anticipated and consequently early sales estimates were overly optimistic.

Perceived Complexity of a New Product.   New-product complexity, like communicability, must be assessed from the consumer's point of view.   Maxim turned out to be a "complex" product because people had to change their established use patterns to properly appreciate it.   Color television, although much more complex in a technical sense, is not perceived as complex by consumers because they have only to turn a knob, as they were accustomed to doing with their black-and-white sets, to appreciate the qualities of a color set. The more complex a new product is perceived to be, the more prolonged the time over which first purchases will occur.   Where problems like that cited for Maxim are encountered, complexity may also slow the rate of repurchase in the short run.

Perceived Compatibility of a New Product.   *Compatibility* refers to both the ease with which consumers fit a new product into established consumption patterns and the extent to which a new product is seen as socially acceptable within a given market context.   The importance of social compatibility has already been mentioned; use compatibility is equally important.   One should expect consumers to change established consumption patterns not for the convenience of a marketing organization but because a new product has decided advantages over its more established competition.   Where changes in consumer behavior are implicit in a new-product introduction, one must, as with complexity, expect a relatively slow initial purchase pattern.

The Nature of Prospective Purchasers

A new product, like any other mechanism for social change, spreads throughout a population over time through the influence of mass-media communication, interpersonal communication, and as an outgrowth of observation and emulation.   This process is described in detail in the diffusion of innovations literature (and in Section II, Part B, Chapter 3) and need not be repeated here.[3] A few factors about the nature of new-product purchases derived from diffusion research are directly relevant to this chapter, however, and since they underlie most new-product prediction techniques, a bit of redundancy seems justified.

Independent of the nature of a new product or the extent to which it is ultimately purchased, the pattern of initial purchases for that product will resemble the purchase patterns for previous new products introduced in that market. Figure 1 indicates the general shape of new-product initial purchase curves. The extent of initial purchases is often referred to as *penetration*.   The significance of the uniformity between penetration curves is that the relationship between the magnitude of purchases during any given time period t and any other time period t_1 is likely to be about the same, regardless how well (in an absolute sense) the product is received in the marketplace.   The constant relationship between penetration levels for a new product at various points in time suggests that the same social process is repeated with each new product that appears on the market.   And if the same pattern is observed, it is highly likely that individual consumer behavior is relatively uniform with respect to each new-product introduction.

These deductions are confirmed by empirical studies of new-product adoption patterns.   These studies also indicate that people who purchase immedi-

---

[3] For a comprehensive description of diffusion concepts applied specifically to marketing problems, see King [7].

ately after a product is introduced can be distinguished from later purchasers by a number of measurable attributes. Furthermore, the reactions to a new product of these consistently early purchasers influence, positively or negatively, the reactions of later prospective purchasers. Appropriately, early purchasers are called *influentials;* later purchasers are called *the early majority,* the *later majority,* or *laggards.* Obviously, the more one knows about the characteristics of these various consumer groups and the manner in which they make initial purchase decisions, the easier the prediction of new-product sales will become.

Study of consumer roles in new-product adoptions leaves much to be determined at the present time. It is clear, however, that information should be sought prior to introduction concerning (1) the attitudes of influentials toward new products; (2) the proportions of heavy users, light users, and nonusers in the appropriate product category; and (3) the proportions of brand loyals and switchers in the target market (the latter are usually highly price-conscious). Once a product has been introduced either to test markets or to the general

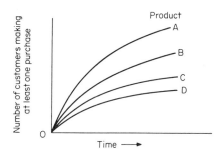

Fig. 1.   New-product initial purchase curves.

market, one should also seek information on (1) new purchase versus repeat purchase, (2) the average size of purchases, and (3) trial purchase versus committed purchase, all classified according to the time at which they occurred. The reasons for acquiring consumer data of this character will become apparent when specific prediction techniques are described.

Nature of Competition

The new product is usually either a modification of existing brands of a product or a direct substitution for some other established product class. In either instance there will likely be a reaction by competition to a new-product introduction. Such a reaction must be considered both in the selection of appropriate prediction methods and in the prediction process per se.

The nature of competitive reaction can often be anticipated on the basis of reactions to previous new-product introductions. In most instances one can expect increased spending for advertising, more "dealing," and an overall effort to offset the impact of an introductory promotional program for the new product. (In addition, it is inevitable that competitors will be "reading" consumer reaction to a new product through audits and special surveys.) Predictions for a new product should be made under a range of assumptions about the impact of competitors' actions.

Some competitive reactions cannot be anticipated. This holds particularly when a test market (an integral part of some prediction procedures) or a market-by-market introduction is concerned. Most readers have undoubtedly heard of companies that have spent extraordinary amounts, far out of proportion to what they *could* spend on a national scale, to confound an introductory campaign. While one cannot anticipate such action, it is possible to set up prediction procedures that preclude competitors both from "reading" and from sabotaging a test set up to produce information on consumer response to a new product. This will be discussed further in the next section. With such a procedure, one can have some confidence in long-term sales forecasts for new products, even if competitors do shake up a market in the period immediately after introduction.

SOURCES OF INFORMATION FOR PREDICTING SALES OF NEW PRODUCTS

Since conventional sources of information for prediction purposes are described elsewhere in this book, discussion here will center largely on the type of data one may reasonably hope to obtain from those sources.[4] Among the sources that may be considered in this context are:
1. Analogous new product introductions
2. Surveys
3. Consumer juries
4. Consumer panels
5. Test markets

Just as there is no one optimum prediction technique, there is no one source of information inherently superior to others. Judgment on what sources of data to employ must be a function of the product and the market under consideration.

Analogous New-Product Introductions

The basic question to be resolved before using analogies as a source of information for new-product sales predictions is the extent to which the product(s) and the market(s) used as models are like the new product and its market(s). Consideration must also be given to similarities and differences in the promotional programs of the product in question.

To what extent, for example, was Crest like Gleem? Should Procter & Gamble have based their estimates of consumer response to Crest on how consumers responded to Gleem? The two products were presumably directed toward the same general market; they were to be used in the same manner for *nearly* the same purposes (Crest apparently had more decay-preventive capacity); the same marketing organization would be employed to distribute and promote them; and so on. So it would appear that P & G's experiences in introducing Gleem could have been used as a means of estimating response to Crest. There *were* differences (particularly in the competitive climate) that should have been anticipated and accounted for, of course. But it is much easier to estimate the influence of differences in two reasonably analogous situations than it is to be totally without a frame of reference.

Analogies available as a basis for prediction are not often as close as the Gleem-Crest example just cited. As long as the difference is well-defined and provisions are made for these differences in the prediction process, however, analogous new-product introductions can be a valuable source of information for prediction purposes.

A company that proposes to employ analogies as an information source

---

[4] Compare with Sec. IV, Part A, Chap. 3; also Sec. II, Part B, Chap. 10.

should monitor its own introductions and those of companies having similar product lines for the following types of information:
1. Number, size, and rate of initial purchases
2. Number, size, and rate of repurchases, all by time period
3. Amount and character of promotional support provided the new product
4. Nature and extent of competitive response to the new-product introduction
5. Purchaser breakdowns according to heavy versus light purchasers, trial versus committed purchasers, new market entries versus brand shifters, and by demographic characteristics

Note also that analogies may be the basis for prediction techniques as well as prediction information. Many of the mathematical and/or computer market simulations used for new-product sales predictions were developed from analogies.

Surveys as a Source of Information for Sales Predictions. The extent to which surveys may be used to generate useful information for new-product sales predictions obviously depends upon the extent of the knowledge individual prospects have of the product in question. If the new product is a new brand of an established product, consumers may express attitudes toward existing brands, brand-switching, prices, the degree of "match" between existing brands and their ideal, rates and magnitude of purchases in the product class, and so on. Such information undoubtedly will facilitate an assessment of consumer reaction to the new brand. The same will hold true in industrial markets where prospective buyers are well informed and new-product attributes can be described in explicit terms.

Conversely, surveys are unlikely to be useful for prediction where a product represents a significant departure from those with which prospective users have had experience. This would also seem to hold true in some industrial markets. When IBM introduced the first widely adopted general-purpose computer (the 650), they were unable to obtain useful reactions from prospects in advance of the first installations. IBM acknowledged they did not know whether they would sell five or five hundred units. Actually they sold several times their most optimistic estimate.

Surveys may be very useful for new-product sales predictions based on feedback from the period immediately after introduction. By surveying early purchasers and their reactions to a new product, it may be possible to extrapolate sales levels for subsequent periods with a significant degree of accuracy. The basis for this statement was discussed earlier in connection with the nature of prospective purchasers. The types of data one should attempt to obtain from such surveys are the same as those listed for analogies.

Consumer Juries

Consumer juries appear to have limited value for producing prediction information. Aside from the artificial context in which jury members are expected to react to a new product, such groups are rarely representative of the population for which the new product is intended. One suspects that juries are much more useful at a prior stage when a product is still in its developmental phase. Nevertheless, information on the relative appeal of the new product in comparison to the products it is designed to replace might be obtained from a consumer jury. Also, consumer types who represent particularly promising prospects might be identified from consumer juries. Such information would have value both for prediction purposes and in planning an introductory promotional program.

Consumer Panels

Many of the relatively advanced prediction techniques make use of consumer panel data. The most important attribute of consumer panels is the opportunity they provide for observation of the purchasing patterns of *individual* panel members over time. Thus, information on timing of purchases, brand preferences, brand loyalty, usage rates, places of purchase, and so on for relatively large numbers of people who are ostensibly representative of some general population group can be obtained. This information may relate to analogous new-product introductions in the recent past or to the early stages of introduction of a new product for which predictions are being prepared.

Information on individual purchasing behavior makes possible statements of conditional probabilities for various future acts. One may, for example, determine the probability of at least one purchase of a new brand given (1) a history of brand shifting or (2) brand loyalty. The range of possible statements of the sort just illustrated is extensive. In the final analysis, such statements are the basic mechanism of prediction.

The most important shortcoming of panels as a source of prediction information should be noted: Panel data are valid only as long as the panel represents the population for which a new product is intended. Critics of panel data claim that since panel membership is voluntary and some people refuse to participate, panels cannot be truly representative—even if the demographic attributes of the panel perfectly match those of the population as a whole. Of course it is possible, even if the alleged differences in personality did exist between panel members and nonpanel members, that they would not affect either group's purchasing behavior with respect to a given product.

Another criticism of panel data more worthy of concern is the lack of reliability of individual purchase data, either because of oversight or imperfect recall. While panel members are ordinarily instructed to record every purchase immediately after purchase, they undoubtedly forget. And if they are at all representative of the general population, they also distort and dissemble.

Panel data should be employed for prediction purposes with these possible shortcomings in mind. Wherever possible, one should seek other sources of information for confirmation, even when the panel data appear complete.

Tests Markets

Test markets can represent a valuable source of information useful in predicting new-product sales levels. The major advantage of test-market information is that it is produced in a "natural" market environment. The artificial constraints necessary for the implementation of alternative data gathering techniques are not required.

One may obtain purchase levels, market-share data, competitive behavior, and impact on sales of the new product from test markets. If surveys are employed in conjunction with test-market introduction, it is possible to gain insight on individual purchasing behavior—for example, repurchase patterns—as well.

Data from test markets are available to anyone interested—including competitors; that is a major disadvantage of test marketing. Furthermore, competitors may directly distort test-market data through their own promotional activity. When that occurs, it is unlikely that the data will be of value in predicting sales for the general market. Finally, if the product is really new, test marketing permits competition to get started that much earlier in developing their own brands of the new product. Because of this strategic disadvantage, the use of test markets should be minimized *if their primary purpose is to produce data for sales predictions.*

An Alternative Approach

Kuehn [9] has described a method for acquiring prediction data on food products that combines features of consumer panels and test markets while avoiding major disadvantages of both.   The members of a panel agreed to purchase all their groceries from a home delivery service (provided at no cost).   Inducements to members, in addition to free home delivery, included double trading stamps, cash rebates where lower prices on some items might have been available locally, and the opportunity to purchase products (including the test products) not available in the local market.   Obviously, a complete record of the purchases of each member (insofar as they abided by their agreement) was assured—offsetting one major objection to conventional panel data.   Furthermore, because the new products are not generally available, competitors had no means of "reading" or directly interfering with test results.

By this method, the manufacturer obtained initial and repeat purchase information from "matched halves" of the panel that was useful for evaluating alternative product forms, packages, prices, and advertising copy as well as for prediction purposes.

Some Concluding Comments on Information Sources

It should now be apparent that a number of sources of information may be employed in predicting new-product sales levels.   The character and validity of the information are much more important than the source(s) from which it is obtained.

Among the types of information most likely to be useful during the prediction process are:

1.   Initial and repeat purchases classified by the time period during which they occur

2.   Character of the purchase cycle

3.   Size of purchases

4.   Socioeconomic characteristics of early purchasers and other distinguishable consumer groups

5.   Classification of new-product purchasers by whether they are new market entries or brand shifters; brand loyal or fickle; heavy, moderate, or light users; according to the degree of satisfaction they express toward the new product, and so on

Where analogies are employed (and they are often the only detailed information source prior to the introduction of a new product), differences between the anticipated introduction and the analogous introductions should be spelled out explicitly and an assessment should be made of the significance of those differences in arriving at estimates of new-product sales.

Once a product has been introduced, emphasis should shift from analogies to the test market or general market involved, but essentially the same sort of information should be recorded.   The basic problem with the use of early sales data for prediction derives from possible differences in the test market(s) and the general market and/or competitive conditions the new product is likely to encounter.

TECHNIQUES FOR PREDICTING NEW-PRODUCT SALES LEVELS

There is no set of procedures or formulas that provide valid sales predictions automatically.   The information input to any prediction procedure is more important than the procedure itself. The basic values derived from any prediction procedure may come from enhanced understanding of one's market and of one's new product rather than from reliable sales forecasts for that product. These reservations notwithstanding, sales predictions must be made for a variety of obvious reasons. And there are prediction techniques that appear to offer a substantially better chance for valid sales predictions than a sales manager's "best judgment." The simplest techniques are well-documented elsewhere—for example, build-up of territory-by-territory sales forecasts by salesmen—and will not be discussed here. Instead, attention will be focused on the concepts underlying three rather complex prediction techniques with which researchers have recently been concerned. These are:

1. Growth-curve prediction models
2. Stochastic process models
3. Computer simulations

Growth-Curve Models for New-Product Sales Predictions[5]

Growth-curve models are based on the concept, mentioned earlier, that adoptions of new products follow similar patterns regardless of the nature of the product or the duration of a given product's life cycle. That general pattern was illustrated in Figure 1.

The curves in Figure 1 represent initial purchases only and are generally called penetration curves. Such a curve has been expressed mathematically as a geometric straight line—that is, a curve that approaches some ceiling at a constant rate over time.[6] It follows, then, that if one can identify two or more points on that curve, the other points can be deduced from the general properties of the curve. Or, expressed in operational terms, if the level of initial purchase of a new product is known (or can be predicted with accuracy) at the end of any two periods, the level of initial purchases, or penetration, can be predicted with some degree of confidence for all periods.

For products likely to be purchased only once or very infrequently by any given customer, penetration data are sufficient to predict new-product sales levels. Where frequently repurchased products are concerned, one must employ additional analysis to determine the probability of repeat purchases. Thus, through the use of data on early sales, or sales in a test market, or through analogy, one must develop statements of the following form: "Given that a customer has made $n - 1$ purchases of a product A, the probability that that customer will make an nth purchase of product A is ———."

This is accomplished through the construction of depth-of-repeat-purchase curves and an evaluation of the relationship between the first repeat purchase curve and the penetration curve, the second repeat purchase curve and the first repeat purchase curve, and so on. Thus sales predictions for a new product that one expects to frequently be repurchased are made for each period through totaling initial purchases, first repeat purchases, second repeat purchases, and so on to n repeat purchases expected during the period in question.

Obviously, growth-curve models can only be applied when some knowledge of sales levels for a new product exists. This is not so much a limitation as one might initially suspect. Most new products can be test marketed or at least

---

[5] This discussion is taken largely from a previous paper by the author. See Kelly [6].

[6] See Kelly [6] or Fourt and Woodlock [5] for a description of the mathematical properties of the penetration curve. Both articles also provide detailed descriptions of how the model is applied to empirical data.

introduced on a market-by-market basis.   Many new products are so similar to previous introductions that analogous data exist before the new product reaches the market.   The data specified in the section on sources of information can just as reliably be employed with growth-curve models as with any other prediction technique.

However, there are important limitations to the application of growth-curve models.   First, it is assumed in using this method that no substantial changes in competitive conditions will occur during the period for which a prediction is made.   Such an assumption is clearly unjustified for other than the short run in most markets.   Second, it is assumed that the probability of an early first purchaser making a repeat purchase is the same as for a later first purchaser.   A number of studies (and the whole of the diffusion literature) suggest that this assumption is not justified.

Frank Bass [2] has developed a model for predicting new-product sales that somewhat offsets the second limitation associated with the growth-curve model. He distinguishes between early buyers and later buyers.   Early buyers are defined as those who first purchase a new product during that product's "dynamic phase" when personal communication and new-product interest are high. Later buyers are those who first purchase after new-product interest is essentially depleted.   The latter group enters the market at a leisurely and relatively constant rate, that is, at a constant percentage of remaining potential later first purchasers.   Early buyers, by way of contrast, have a very dynamic first purchase pattern.   They enter the market according to an exponential pattern such that the number of purchases in any given period is a function of the number of purchases in preceding periods.

Thus Bass (and a number of other authors) see "early buyers" and "later buyers" as distinct consumer populations that exhibit different purchase patterns.   His prediction model, in effect, determines separately the probabilities of initial purchase and repurchase for each group, then sums them to arrive at overall sales forecasts for a new product.

Parfitt and Collins [14] have developed a method for predicting new-product brand-share positions from consumer panel data.[7]   Their technique, conceptually similar to the Fourt and Woodlock approach described at the beginning of this section, is simpler than the Bass method yet also makes provision for differences in early and later buyers and for heavy, average, and light users.

The Parfitt-Collins technique requires a separate calculation of (1) penetration (using a standard growth-curve model), (2) repeat-purchasing rate over time (using continuous panel data), and (3) a buying rate index that indicates the intensity of use for the customer group in question as contrasted with customers for the product category in question.   Multiplication of those three factors yields the ultimate market share prediction for the product in question. Thus a new product estimated to eventually reach 34 percent of the customers in a product class, where a 25 percent repurchase rate is observed among those panel members who purchase the new product at least once and who use the product 1.20 as much as the general market for the product class, would be estimated to settle down to a market share of 10.2 percent ($34 \times 25 \times 1.2$).

The Parfitt-Collins model is appealing, in particular because it has been thoroughly tested against empirical data in a variety of consumer product categories.   The model has a number of additional refinements that cannot be de-

[7] See also Lawrence [10] for a means of estimating repurchase rates from continuous panel data.

scribed in this limited space but that should prove valuable to practitioners who wish to employ the technique.

Stochastic Process Models to Predict New-Product Sales

Massy [12] has developed a model for predicting new-product sales levels that represents a significant improvement on the original growth-curve concept. He refers to his model as a stochastic evolutionary adoption model (STEAM) for new products. STEAM is designed to be used with consumer panel data for both diagnostic and forecasting purposes. Its application is largely limited to frequently repurchased consumer products. The Massy technique is made up of a "primary model" that reflects the purchasing patterns of individual households at given points in time, a set of "secondary models" that describe how the parameters of the primary model vary for different household types, and a "composite probability law" that describes the aggregation of individual household adoptions.

In essence the STEAM primary model is based upon a vector of probabilities that expresses the likelihood of next purchase for each brand of a product class (including the new brand) by a given household. The STEAM secondary models provide parameters concerning (1) the length of time between purchases (which may vary over time), (2) differences in household purchase rates (these too may vary over time), (3) learning effects from purchase of the new brand of a product, (4) time of conversion to the new brand, and (5) depth of repeat purchase by some given point in time. These parameters could conceivably be applied in a different degree to each of several distinct household types (market segments).

The Massy model, unlike the models described in the preceding sections, does not separate the procedures associated with initial and with repeat purchases (although depth of repeat purchases is a factor in the model). Information inputs for the STEAM models are essentially the same as for the Fourt and Woodlock and the Bass models, however, and the information outputs, because of STEAM's greater flexibility and comprehensiveness, appear more likely to yield a reliable sales forecast than its predecessors for many frequently repurchased consumer products.

Computer Simulations for Predicting New-Product Sales

A number of researchers have developed computer simulations that provide new-product sales predictions. They differ from one another in detail, but conceptually they are quite similar.[8] A principal quality of most computer simulation models is an ability to vary marketing-mix factors and competitive reactions to determine the likely impact of such changes on sales of a new product without compromising one's actual market position.

One such model, called DEMON (see Learner, [11]), attempts to relate controllable marketing variables to sales through the following set of postulates. Advertising dollars influence, in turn, gross rating points, reach and frequency, and advertising awareness. Awareness, along with promotion and distribution, determine trial rate. Usage rates—that is, sales levels—are a function of trial rates and price. One must therefore provide DEMON with a description of the functional relationship between awareness and trial (derived through em-

---

[8] Montgomery and Urban [13] provide an excellent description of computer simulations that may be employed to predict sales levels for new products. The discussion that follows draws heavily on that source.

pirical investigation, presumably) along with inputs covering the various factors linking trial to usage.

Amstutz [1] carried the concepts implicit in the DEMON model one step further by developing process-type models that represented the functional effects of each market segment for a given product type. The computational complexities of the Amstutz simulation are such, however, that one may consider only a few alternative marketing strategies.

A means around the dilemma Amstutz faced is provided by considering each demand variable as an independent factor in an aggregate formulation of the demand equation. The simplest application of such an approach suggests that sales levels are linearly related to each demand variable. Urban [17] has described a model called SPRINTER in which general nonlinear or discontinuous functions may be formulated. "Response functions" are described that relate some absolute change in the value of a variable to changes in the quantity sold. One could presumably develop response functions for each major demand variable (from test markets, panels, analogous market introductions) and, through aggregation, produce sales-level predictions under a variety of alternative marketing strategies.

CONCLUDING COMMENTS

Those seeking *the* technique for predicting sales levels for new products will undoubtedly be frustrated by the substantive content of this chapter. There is no sure-fire prediction technique and, even if there were, it would still be wholly dependent upon an accurate and complete information input. Information is the key to valid predictions of new-product sales levels and justifies devoting more attention to sources of information than to information processing techniques.

For those who wish to know about a given prediction technique in detail, references are provided in the bibliography that follows. Pessemier [15] considers the full range of problems associated with new products. Topics in his book range from where the responsibility for new-product decisions should reside within an organization to the bases on which decisions on marketing, test marketing, or dropping a product should depend. He considers not only how predictions of new product sales may be generated but the uses to be made of such information in seeking to fulfill the overall objectives of a firm as well. In summary, Pessemier has placed the problems of predicting new-product sales in a perspective not possible in this limited space.

REFERENCES

1. Amstutz, A. E., *Computer Simulation of Competitive Market Response*, Cambridge, Mass.: M.I.T. Press, 1967.
2. Bass, F. M., "A New Product Growth Model for Consumer Durables," *Management Science: Theory*, January 1969.
3. Burger, P. C., F. M. Bass, and E. A. Pessemier, "Forecasting New Product Sales: The Timing of First Purchase," paper no. 204, West Lafayette, Ind.: Purdue University, Institute for Research in the Behavioral, Economic, and Management Sciences, Graduate School of Industrial Management, February 1968.
4. Day, G. S., "Using Attitude Change Measures to Evaluate New Product Introductions," *Journal of Marketing Research*, November 1970.
5. Fourt, L., and J. Woodlock, "Early Prediction of Market Success for New Grocery Products," *Journal of Marketing*, October 1960.

6. Kelly, R. F., "Estimating Ultimate Performance Levels of Retail Outlets," *Journal of Marketing Research,* February 1967.
7. King, C. W., "Adoption and Diffusion Research in Marketing: An Overview," in R. M. Haas, ed., *Science, Technology and Marketing,* Chicago: American Marketing Association, Fall 1966.
8. Kotler, P., "Competitive Strategies for New Product Marketing Over the Life-Cycle," *Management Science,* December 1965.
9. Kuehn, A. A., "Measurement of Consumer Dynamics in New Product Evaluations and Market Tests," in J. Arndt, ed., *Insights Into Consumer Behavior,* Boston: Allyn & Bacon, 1968.
10. Lawrence, R. J., "Patterns of Buyer Behavior: Time for a New Approach?" *Journal of Marketing Research,* vol. 6, May 1969.
11. Learner, D. B., "DEMON New Product Planning: A Case History," in F. E. Webster, ed., *New Directions in Marketing,* Chicago: American Marketing Association, 1965.
12. Massy, W. F., "A Dynamic Model for Monitoring New Product Adoption," Working Paper No. 95, Palo Alto, Calif.: Stanford University, Graduate School of Business, March 1966.
13. Montgomery, D. B., and G. L. Urban, *Management Science in Marketing,* Englewood Cliffs, N.J.: Prentice-Hall, 1969.
14. Parfitt, J. H., and B J. K. Collins, "The Use of Consumer Panels for Brand-Share Predictions," *Journal of Marketing Research,* May 1968.
15. Pessemier, E. A., *New Product Decisions: An Analytical Approach,* New York: McGraw-Hill, 1966.
16. Rogers, E. M., *Diffusion of Innovations,* New York: Free Press, 1962.
17. Urban, G. L., "SPRINTER: A Tool for New Product Decision-Making," *Industrial Management Review,* Spring 1967.

Part B

Sales Analysis
and Forecasting

Chapter 3

Estimating Market Potential:
Established Products

DAN E. SCHENDEL *Krannert Graduate School of Industrial Administration, Purdue University, Lafayette, Indiana*

INTRODUCTION

One of the most difficult aspects of allocating marketing effort between geographic markets, products, or components of the marketing mix is determining how much is to be gained from a given market, or from a particular product, or in response to one or more elements of the marketing mix. Without some knowledge of the demand response possible, the decision to allocate marketing effort and dollars must be made blindly and probably inefficiently.

It is precisely the engineering concept of efficiency, input related to output, that is central to the concept of market potential and its value to marketing decisions. Properly defined and used, market potential represents the maximum demand response to be gained from a particular market. As such, it is the benchmark or criterion against which marketing efforts are measured and evaluated, and it is also an important element of the criteria used to allocate marketing efforts.

For example, knowledge of the market potential of a sales territory permits the sales manager to decide how many salesmen to commit to that territory and, later, to control and evaluate those salesmen's efforts. Used by the overall marketing manager, the same territorial market potential, when grouped and compared with other territorial potentials, can be used in a planning sense to allocate territories among sales districts and to determine promotional funds to be used in each. Such territorial market potentials, singly or aggregated, can also be used in a control sense to evaluate district sales managers' performances, the returns on marketing funds invested in sales territories, or whether more effort is needed in one territory and less in another.

As a criterion for allocation decisions and general market planning, then, the concept of market potential plays a useful and significant role, as it also does for the control and evaluation function that marketing managers must perform.

This chapter will first develop and define the concept of market potential for established or what might be called "old" products. Here, products will be defined in their broadest sense to include services and service institutions. The usefulness of the market potential concept, as well as examples of how the concept can be used by marketing management, will then be developed. Next is a discussion of the methods that can be used to estimate market potential, the advantages and disadvantages of the methods, and how a particular method might be chosen in practice. This will be followed by a section devoted to means of improving estimates. Finally, a concluding section will summarize the major features of this chapter.

MARKET POTENTIAL DEFINED

The definition that follows is the one used throughout this chapter. It captures the essential features of many such definitions that exist in the marketing literature.

> Market potential is the *maximum demand response* possible for a given *group of customers* within a well-defined *geographic area* for a given *product or service* over a specified *period of time* under well-defined *competitive* and *environmental conditions*.

Ponderous as this definition appears, every phrase is essential to the concept to be developed here. The key phrases underlined are worth examining in detail.

Maximum Demand Response

Demand response, and therefore market potential, is measured in two basic ways: (1) units of product or service or (2) dollar sales. These two measures, while intimately connected by price, cannot be regarded as interchangeable in all cases. For example, it may be relatively simple to determine the numbers or units of pleasure boats registered each year, but it is much more difficult to determine the dollar value associated with new registrations, because retail price paid is not recorded. Hence assumptions are frequently required to translate units into dollars.

Maximum demand response is a function of the assumptions and forecasts that must be made about environmental conditions and competitive marketing programs. To these forecasts and assumptions must be added the firm's own market plans and programs. With these expected conditions in mind, it is possible to estimate maximum demand response. It should be apparent, however, that the maximum demand response is not a unique amount but acts as a variable itself. It is dependent upon variables a particular firm controls as well as variables it does not control. As assumptions and optimism of forecasts change, so will the maximum demand response. While a unique outcome for market potential is lacking for most products and services, this does not destroy the concept's usefulness as a meaningful boundary condition on ultimate demand.

Customer Groups

Another key condition upon which the concept of market potential depends is a definition of the set of relevant consumers of the product or service. In the strictest sense, the term *consumer* is misleading, suggesting as it does a proved buyer. To be accurate, *potential consumer* is the term needed here, for the concern is with maximum expected demand and not proved sales and buyers. Of more importance than this qualification, however, is the need to define sets of potential consumers carefully. Frequently, markets are defined only in terms of geographic boundaries. While useful and necessary and probably the most obvious means of defining mutually exclusive market subsets, geography is not the only or even always the most important means of consumer differentiation.

Much current research in marketing is based upon the importance of customer groupings in market segments. Such segments are based not only upon standard demographic characteristics but also upon psychological and sociopsychological characteristics of individuals, families, and other consuming and purchasing groups. By defining subsets of potential customers in terms of nongeographic variables and in terms of variables influencing purchase behavior, the marketing manager can obtain market potential measures for buying segments more naturally aligned with marketing variables he controls and about which he must make decisions.

Depending, then, upon which particular customer group is of interest, market potential measures will vary. For example, for the denim jeans manufacturer it would be useful to know the market potential for jeans used by adults as work clothes and teen-agers as casual dress. These two market segments respond to different motivations and are probably reached most effectively by different marketing programs and trade channels.

Geographic Area

Segmenting customers by geographic area, as just noted, is not the only means of breaking total demand into segments. It is worth special mention and specific inclusion in the definition of market potential, however, because of the uses made of the potential concept. It is the easiest manner in which to obtain mutually exclusive subsets of customers that are conformable both to market information and data and to management's problems, for example, in the assignment and control of field sales personnel. Easy aggregation of potentials is permitted by the simple assurance that subsets are geographically disjoint.

The distinction between geographic units used as managerial planning and control units versus units looked at in a product usage sense is at the very heart of the market segmentation problem. The matching of usage segments with planning and control segments is of utmost importance to marketing decision making and profitable marketing programs. Careful definition of geographic areas with this basic managerial problem of matching in mind goes a long way in determining just how useful market potential measures will be.

Product or Service

This chapter is concerned with established products and services. While the data and methods developed here differ somewhat from those useful to new products and services (see Section IV, Part A, Chapter 1), the concept of market potential applies equally to old and new.

It is necessary to be cautious about how a given product or service is defined whenever marketing strategy and programs are being developed. It is necessary to understand the full range of products that can fulfill a particular consumer need. For example, a butter manufacturer could not think of his product's market potential without thinking of margarine. In general, substitute products with a high cross-elasticity of demand must be viewed as the product class for which potential estimates are to be made.

Not only existing but also potential substitutes for the product or service should be considered. Long range, for example, it would be foolish for airline firms to discount the inroads that the videotelephone may have on business travel.

The variability that can exist for the demand for products with luxury characteristics versus the demand stability for necessary products and services influences strongly the entire methodology appropriate to estimating market potential. For this reason care must be taken in defining the product or service and in understanding its role in the economy.

Time Period

Specification of the time period for which the potential estimate is to be made is usually felt necessary. It avoids expressing potential in rate-of-purchase terms and focuses attention on short- and long-range considerations. Because potential measures are used typically as an integral part of planning procedures, the time period is usually selected to conform to planning periods, both long and short range, already used by the firm.

Environmental and Competitive Conditions

As already noted, maximum demand response is critically dependent upon general exogenous environmental conditions, such as the state of the economy, levels of disposable personal and discretionary income, tax levels, and similar factors. It is also critically dependent upon the actions of competitors offering products in the product class under consideration.

Clearly, these uncontrollable elements must be forecast and assumptions made about them before market potential can be determined. For example, where primary demand for a product is not fully developed, that is, where a product class is in an early part of its life cycle, it is necessary to know the level of competitive advertising and promotional programs and, in turn, to forecast the growth impact of total industry promotional programs.

Contrast to Sales Potential

It should be noted that market potential is being developed here for a product class. It could also be developed for a particular *brand* or *firm*. Some refer to the latter notion of market potential as sales potential, the share of industry or product-class market potential that appears available to a brand or a firm. As such, sales potential is akin to a sales forecast, although here too some prefer to distinguish between sales potentials and sales forecasts. The sales forecast typically is a point estimate of what future sales *will* be, while sales potential represents a boundary condition, what it *might* be in an idealized sense. In the latter sense, sales potential is to a firm what market potential is to an industry or product class: both represent maximum demand response and are boundary conditions.

USES OF MARKET POTENTIAL

This section discusses some of the major uses of market potential measures in planning and control problems encountered by the marketing manager. The role of potential measures in marketing information systems will also be examined.

Marketing Management

The hallmark of modern marketing management is the development of profitable marketing plans and programs for the products and services offered by the firm. The most basic decision in market planning is the allocation of marketing dollars and effort to the various elements of the marketing mix. A vital data input to marketing-mix decisions is the potential profit or return to be achieved per dollar invested in each of the mix variables. Market potential measures can play a central role in profit determination and therefore in market planning as well, because they define the opportunities open to the firm.

Marketing plans and the goals set in them can be used to identify exceptions to plans. A marketing control system set to be triggered by these exceptions can set in motion corrective action for any weaknesses so isolated.

Product Decisions. Market potential estimates coupled with market-share goals determine sales potentials for a given brand or product line. By comparing actual sales and sales forecasts to sales and market potentials, the marketing manager can learn how a particular brand is doing relative to its competition. Where weaknesses are indicated, steps can be taken to redesign the product or product line, improve distribution methods, increase promotion, enter new markets, undertake further technical development to update the product, improve production facilities, cut costs, or undertake still other measures to improve the product's market position.

Pricing Decisions. The degree to which the product class or industry has penetrated a given market segment is identified by comparing actual industry sales with a measure of market potential. Where penetration is low, this may indicate an opportunity to find a segment protected from price competition and one that has sales and profit growth opportunities. Where penetration is high, further gains may be possible only in market-share increases. In these instances, competitors must lose share. In either case—for further market penetration or greater market share—price elasticity of the product is the key to whether lowered price can be a tool for expansion. By comparing market share and market penetration across sales territories and competitive products, it may be possible to isolate instances where pricing decisions have been faulty.

Channel Decisions. Because they are so closely related to geographic segments, market potential measures are suited to channel decisions. Weaknesses in market coverage and in elements of channels can be identified by comparing market potential and actual sales. Without the outside benchmark of market potential, some growth in sales could be mistaken for satisfactory coverage.

Potential measures are of value in facility location decisions. Where to add plant capacity, how much to add, where to place a sales office or warehouse— these are examples of location decisions that can be aided by knowledge of potential.

Promotion Decisions. The marketing decision area facilitated most by potential data is that involving promotion decisions. Market potential measures can be of significant help both in advertising and in the management of the field selling force, the two major components of the promotion variable.

The natural alignment of geographic segments and their market potentials with promotion decisions explains the usefulness of the concept. Both advertising and sales management decisions rest heavily upon the concept of geographic market segments. Field sales, in particular, are typically organized around rather small geographic territories, the aggregate of which make up the total geographic market. These small geographic territories, often called sales territories, form the basic planning and control units for marketing operations.

The formation of sales territories is customarily done on the basis of equal market potential. The reasons for this are many, but one of the major ones is to assure that the revenue and profit to be derived from a sales territory will exceed the basic cost of coverage of the territory. Another major reason is to ensure that sales incentive programs, sales quotas, and other tools of sales management are common across all basic geographic planning and control units. Periodic review and realignment of sales territories to ensure approximately equal market potential are a common practice in field sales management.

The allocation of promotional effort to sales territories is usually done on the basis of market potential. However, these allocations should not be uniform across territories even where market potentials are uniform. The sales potential of a given firm is a much better basis for allocation decisions, because territories will vary as to the particular market share any given competing product or firm can achieve. Some territories will contain well-entrenched regional competitors that are difficult to dislodge.

For example, national brands of beer are in competition with local beers, some very strong, some on the wane. Across territories, depending upon the strength of the local brand, sales potential for the national brand will vary. Where a strong local competitor has captured and maintains a larger than average market share, the national brand would be well advised to spend fewer promotional dollars and shift attention to territories where weaker regional competitors exist.

Once territorial sales potentials are determined, it is possible to allocate salesmen and advertising budgets or generally determine the level of marketing effort to be assigned to the basic control unit or to aggregations of them.

The field sales manager can find many control uses for market potential data on the geographic territory he manages. Sales quotas and sales incentive and compensation programs, in which market potential plays a role, represent means of controlling salesmen's efforts: where they spend their time; how effective the selling effort is by individual salesmen, groups of salesmen, product line, or season; or where sales training gaps exist among salesmen or supervisory personnel. To the field sales manager, market potential data are a key element of the measure of effectiveness he must use to evaluate his organization's efforts.

Information Systems and the Role of Market Potential

With the development of large-scale electronic computing machinery and cheaper, more efficient memory banks and data retrieval systems will come growth in the use of formal informations systems, both by general management and functional managers—marketing management included, as discussed in Part I, Chapters 3 and 4.

As management and marketing information systems grow to include both data and decision models to process the data, provision should be made to include market potential measures for all market segments of management interest. These data are as important to marketing management as sales potential measures or indeed even sales forecasts.

The sales forecast is essential to planning decisions, both long and short range. While it can be made independently of potential estimates, any forecasting system that does not include a measure of the market opportunity available provides no means of evaluating the sales forecast and the marketing decisions which underlie the programs intended to realize the forecast. Because it is a key to effectiveness and efficiency, market and sales potential measures should be central elements of any information system.

METHODS OF ESTIMATING MARKET POTENTIAL

A number of problems must be understood in estimating market potential. This section will first discuss these problems, then the available classes of estimating methods will be taken up, and finally their advantages and disadvantages will be examined.

Major Problems

Product and Market Definition. The necessity for careful definition of both product and markets has already been stressed. Care should be extended to ensure that markets are broken into geographical subsets consistent with the basic planning and control units in use by the firm. The units chosen must be selected with a view to the planned uses of market potential measures. Usually, this means aggregation or disaggregation across geographic units by products and product lines. For example, it would be useless to estimate market potential for a geographic unit that was not consistent with the units used for sales territories.

Data Sources. Sales territories should not be formed independently of the availability of sales and other data of interest for the geographic unit chosen. Especially where reliance must be placed on secondary data sources, close attention must be paid to the definition of the territory covered by the basic planning and control unit.

This conformability problem, matching data availability and basic geographic sales territories, is not a trivial one. Most published data sources are segmented by political and not economic boundaries. The Standard Metropolitan Statistical Area (SMSA) definition is one notable exception to this. The unit boundaries most meaningful for a firm's markets may not conform to political boundaries. Great care should be taken to ensure that geographical boundaries are set to conform to political boundaries to the greatest extent possible. By so doing, problems in using secondary data sources will be minimized. If primary data sources are to be used, the conformability problem is less serious.

Frequency of Estimates. The frequency with which estimates of market potential are to be made and the time period to be covered by the estimate are determined by the short-range planning period used by the firm. One year is common. Long-range planning periods usually do not exceed three to five years. Estimates of potential need to be made for the longer planning period also. These are usually updated anually.

Accuracy Required and Costs of Estimates. The accuracy required of the potential estimate depends upon the use to which it is put. Where sunk costs will be incurred, as with plant expansion and new facilities construction, more accurate estimates are required. If it is possible to easily recover from an inaccurate estimate, as with salesmen assignments to territories, less accurate forecasts are necessary.

The time, funds, and personnel made available to estimate potentials will influence the accuracy that is possible. While it is not always possible to achieve greater accuracy, it comes only with higher costs in terms of time, dollars, and manpower. Greater accuracy also usually requires more sophisticated methodology and almost certainly better data inputs.

What Is Measured? The distinction between sales forecasts for a firm or the industry, sales potential, and market potential should be understood. Only if a market is saturated can the industry sales forecast be considered equivalent to market potential. This condition can exist for mature, established products. More likely though, the industry sales forecast will be some amount less than the market potential and so will the sales forecast be less than a firm's sales potential.

Unless care is exercised in interpretation and initial construction of estimating methods which rely on historical data, the result may be an estimate of future sales and not market or even sales potential.

Methods Available

Estimates of market potential can be made by a number of individual methods. Those to be suggested here can be grouped into six categories: (1) judgment methods, (2) survey methods, (3) test or experimental methods, (4) correlation methods, (5) time-series methods, and (6) input-output methods.

Some of these methods rest on statistical methodology explained elsewhere, and the reader is referred to the chapters devoted to detailed procedures and theory. Emphasis here will be given to the applications of such methodologies to estimating market potentials.

Judgment Methods. All methods used to estimate market potential use judgment as an important ingredient. Someone must supply the basic assumptions about environmental conditions and competitive behavior. In this way judgment enters the picture. Also, judgment is ultimately used to accept or reject the result of any particular method used to estimate market potential.

It is not uncommon to have salesmen supply data about the accounts or territory they are assigned to cover. Sales forecasts are often made this way, especially for industrial products that are technical in nature. Other experts are often used—sometimes independently, sometimes in combination with others—to determine market potential for a territory, industry, or product line. In any case, it is common to aggregate the territorial potential estimates made by individuals to determine total market potential.

To assure some degree of standardization, salesmen or other experts should be supplied with a standard form and general procedure to follow in making estimates. An example of this is to list all accounts actively served by a salesman, asking him to fill out total needs of the account, the share the firm might be expected to receive under the assumed degree of effort, and to do this across time. Such a form could be improved by asking for a range of estimates. In this way the possible variance in potential can be determined. The standardized forms can then be used to aggregate market potentials. Some way must be found to make estimates for accounts not served by the firm and for potential customers.

One of the major advantages of judgment methods is that they are easily understood. They are low in cost and do not usually require extra manpower, using as typically they do existing salesmen or sales managers.

Judgment methods have several disadvantages. Humans differ widely in their perceptions of events. As a result, wide variance in estimates is possible from territory to territory. The uses to be made of the estimates will affect the type of estimate made. If the uses are not uniform across territories, it is unlikely that the estimates across territories will be uniformly made.

This method is most useful for highly technical products, where there are few customers, where there is a high degree of demand stability, and where costs need to be minimized. It is most likely to be used for industrial goods.

Survey Methods. Survey methods are characterized by customer contact with the intention of identifying that customer's future product needs. Where a complete census of actual and potential customers is possible, this method results directly in the market potential estimate. Where a sample of actual and potential customers is surveyed, an extension of the results is required to determine the potential estimate.

All the problems of field survey techniques apply to this means of estimating market potential. (See Section II, Part B, Techniques.) The first major problem to be solved is to obtain a listing of actual and potential customers (a sampling frame). From this listing, a complete census can be made or a sample drawn. The sample may be based on judgment or, preferably, on probability sampling. In either case, however, the result will be no better than the frame or listing developed. If incomplete, a true census cannot be obtained or, if a sample is to be drawn, sampling error may result. Where high accuracy is necessary, great care must be taken in the development of the sample frame.

Actual customer accounts already being serviced are one major data input for development of the frame. Where many accounts are served, this is no easy task unless the firm's information system already uses computer listings of accounts. Even more difficult is ensuring that the frame contains actual customers not now served by the firm as well as potential customers not now buying the product class under consideration. Here, trade association listings may be a valuable source of information, as are such listings as *Thomas' Register of Manufacturers*.

Once the sample frame is obtained, an instrument must be designed for collection of data; the survey personnel must be trained in the use of the instrument to ensure uniform application across industry users and geography; the information must be checked for quality, encoded and tabulated; and finally, estimates must be made on the basis of samples drawn. While this can be stated very simply, much time and effort are required to design and physically administer the survey.

Survey methods, whether complete census or sample survey in nature, can be highly accurate when properly used. Inasmuch as they go directly to the consumer for his intentions to purchase, they do not depend upon historical data and thus are more likely to detect abrupt changes in market conditions. Used in conjunction with statistical sampling methodology, estimates of likely error are possible. Survey methods can be used equally well for both industrial and consumer products.

However, this methodology can be costly in both dollars and time, though sample surveys can lower the cost (a census is efficient only where there are relatively few customers). Surveys of buyer intentions require extensive development of survey instruments. Also, considerable difficulty can be encountered in developing a sample that is complete. Careful training of field personnel is important if uniformity and consistency of results are to be ensured. These methods are cumbersome where customers represent many different industries and are widespread geographically.

Surveys of buyer intentions are useful where a product has few customers. With proper questionnaire design, it is possible to identify how intentions would vary with changing economic conditions and alternative environmental conditions. In this way, survey methods permit a form of sensitivity analysis to be used. Where historical perspective is lacking, as would be the case for products early in their life cycle, survey methods may be useful. They are also useful where demand is unstable and likely to change dramatically from period to period.

Survey methods can serve as inputs to more complex methods of estimating market potential. Inasmuch as they survey *intentions* to purchase, they can also be used in connection with methods based on past buying histories. Through the use of survey methods, historically based methods can be checked for turning points or major changes that the historical purchase records may not reflect.

Test or Experimental Methods. Although test-market methods are not used as much for established products as they are for new products, there are two circumstances where market potential estimates may be facilitated by test-market concepts. The first and most obvious condition is where the old product is to enter a new market, such as a foreign market. Purchase behavior may be different enough in the new market to warrant test conditions.

The second circumstance occurs where an experiment is undertaken to identify an optimal or at least more satisfactory marketing mix. Conditions exist for established products where such experiments could be readily undertaken. For example, in market segments where a product has not performed, experiments could be undertaken to improve the marketing program. Certain products that are good performers in some regions but not in others are natural candidates for such experimental programs.

This method leads to actual purchases and revenues. It provides a measure of what people will do under conditions which simulate actual purchase conditions. It is a very useful method for estimating the sales potential of new markets or the sales potential that may result from new marketing approaches. If market potential is to be explored, idealized marketing programs would be required. The cost of such programs is difficult to sustain in the entire market. This method requires no historical data. Their generally higher costs can be substantially lowered or even more than offset by revenues generated.

On the other hand, such test programs are difficult to design and they can be very costly. Conditions must be controlled in the test so that the results can be interpreted as sales potential or market potential.

Such programs are useful where a product line needs to be refurbished and new marketing approaches undertaken. Frequent purchase conditions are necessary, and this means that consumer products would be the most likely candidates for this method.

Correlation Methods. These methods are widely used to estimate geographic market potentials and have application to market potential estimates for other types of nongeographic market segments as well. Their basic feature is the relationship of sales to some other variable or set of variables—that is, the correlation of one variable with one or more other variables.

It is desirable to have the dependent variable or potential related to one or more causal independent variables. For example, the market potential for children's shoe sizes worn by five-year-olds is causally related to the number of children five years of age. No one would argue that the sale of aspirin to parents was related causally to the sales of children's shoes, even though there might be a high correlation between the two variables. Causality and correlation are not the same thing. Good practice dictates that causal links be sought, so that the underlying demand structure can be understood.

To highlight the notion of causality and its importance and to introduce relative versus absolute measures of potential, three subclasses of the correlation methods will be discussed here: (1) market index methods, (2) regression methodology, and (3) statistical demand analysis. Market index methods have received much attention in the market potential literature and for that reason alone warrant attention. They permit introduction of relative versus absolute measures of market potential.

Statistical demand analysis is based on extensive work in the field of econometrics and combines institutional considerations as well as statistical and economic theory. Its most useful feature is that it demands that attention be paid to causality. Since its functional form is usually estimated by regression methods, these latter methods in turn deserve separate mention. All three subclasses are based on the notion of correlation, however, and should not be regarded as separate methods.

The *market-index method* is reported in the literature as one of the most widely used techniques in estimating potential. The essential feature of such indexes is that they provide an ordering of market segments in terms of potential; that is, the index measures the importance of a market segment relative to all other segments.

Such an ordering can be used in two ways. First, the index, which may be regarded as a proportion, can be used to allocate total market potential to each segment. Presumably, an absolute measure of market potential would be available. Second, the index can be used to allocate marketing resources, such as advertising or salesmen, directly without determining potential. There are many applications to allocation of marketing resources where only this relative measure of potential is required.

An example of a well-known market index is the one *Sales Management* magazine annually publishes in its June Survey of Buying Power issue. For each county, this issue lists a so-called buying power index which is in fact a multiple factor index for counties of the United States. The resultant index is made up of three factors: population, which is given a weight of two in the calculation; effective buying income, given a weight of five; and retail sales, given a weight of three.

There are several ways in which such an index can be constructed. A published index such as *Sales Management* magazine's Buying Power Index can be used directly or with some modification. The index could be constructed from scratch for a specific use. , Where this is done, the basic problem is to (1) determine the independent variables (or factors) that are correlated to potential, (2) define the dependent variable (or potential), and (3) find estimates of the functional relationship between dependent and independent variables.

The identification of independent variables correlated with the dependent variables should be based on institutional and theoretical considerations. The desirable properties that the independent variables should have is that (1) they have a causal relationship to the dependent variable, (2) they be readily available in published form, (3) they remain consistent over time, (4) they conform with the basic planning and control units in use by the firm, and (5) there be uniform purchase behavior across the basic planning and control units.

Concepts and theory underlying *statistical demand analysis* can be of aid in the selection of independent variables. It is beyond the scope of this chapter to review the extensive literature of this complex field, but use of its concepts can help ensure that causality enters the relationship that is ultimately determined. Not only considerations taken from the extensive development of demand theory but also statistical considerations will enter.

For example, economic theory holds that price is fundamental to the quantity of a product sold. In the estimation of a demand relationship by means of regression methodology, as in Section II, Part E, Chapter 3, the price variable must enter the relationship in a statistically significant sense, but it also must enter with the proper algebraic sign in accordance with underlying theoretical considerations. In this general way, theoretical constraints of both an economic and statistical nature help ensure that causality is present.

Definition of the dependent variable, that is, a measure of potential in terms of historical data, is needed for statistical methods such as regression methodology. This represents a considerable problem because as market potential is defined here, it represents a conditional or theoretical maximum. Unless the product class is mature and saturation has occurred, industry sales cannot be used as a substitute for market potential.

Where relative estimates of potential for market segments are all that is needed, it may be justifiable to use industry sales data for the dependent variables and to assume correlation between industry sales and market potential. If this is done, an assumption is implicitly made that there are no gaps in the development of potential across all segments. Another possibility for deriving a data series is to use a market segment for which saturation has occurred, either because of especially contrived experimental marketing programs or for other special reasons. The relationship for this segment can then be extended across all segments, again with a homogeneity assumption implicit in the extension.

The estimates of the functional form of the relationship between dependent and independent variables in a demand analysis is most often made by *regression methods*. Note that regression analysis per se does not require nor imply that there be a cause-effect relationship among independent and dependent variables. It merely is a technique which permits consistent estimates of the relationship (see Section II, Part E, Chapters 3, 5, and 7).

Regression analysis requires historical data. The extent of the history depends upon whether cross-sectional or time-series data are to be used. Where uniformity exists across basic planning and control units, cross-sectional data can be utilized. Where units differ, as they may for certain types of market segmentation, time-series data may be more desirable.

Conformability of the data, both for dependent and independent variables, is a difficult problem, especially since it is typical to use multivariate regression relationships and secondary data sources for the independent variables. Of course, secondary data sources cannot be controlled and frequently require that geographic segments conform in some manner to political subdivisions.

Several caveats must be noted in the use of regression methodology to estimate potentials where the underlying demand structure—that is, causality—is to be reflected in the relationship estimated. For example, the independent variables chosen, in addition to having sufficient numbers of observations, should be independent of one another. If two or more are highly correlated with one another, only one should be retained. This general problem, termed the multicolinearity problem, can give unsatisfactory and misleading estimates. Also, residuals should not be autocorrelated. Where these are found, further independent variables should be sought. For a more thorough treatment of these problems and others, as well as the theory of multiple regression methods, see Section II, Part E, especially Chapters 3 and 7.

Among the advantages of regression analysis is that it provides a means of scientifically evaluating a proposed relationship between measures of potential and one or more independent variables. The functional relationship makes possible an estimation of the probable error that is likely in the estimate made utilizing the relationship.

Once a functional relationship has been estimated, it can be used as long as it appears stable. To the degree that causality is reflected in the relationship, a better understanding of the basic structure underlying demand can be gained. This understanding can, in turn, be used to forecast basic turning points in demand and to indicate those variables that management must control to maximize sales. The functional relationship permits the "What if?" question to be asked. By changing values of the independent variables, the effect of such changes on the dependent variable can be determined. This process, known as sensitivity analysis, can provide broader understanding and a sounder basis for market planning.

By estimating a relationship for basic planning and control units, it is possible to find an index factor which can order the units in terms of their potential. Such ordering gives a relative rather than an absolute measure of potential. This relative measure may be applied directly to the allocation of marketing resources. Such an ordering can also be used to apportion a total market potential estimate.

Correlation methods can be misunderstood and can lead to misuses if unqualified personnel apply them indiscriminately. They require historical data matched to the basic planning and control segments used by the firm. Acquiring adequate data sufficient to meet both theoretical economic and statistical assumptions as well as data that conform to needs can be costly.

On balance, correlation methods are preferred methods for estimating market potential. They permit replication, scientific evaluation, and have the capacity to reflect cause and effect—all very desirable properties.

Time-Series Methods. Another group of methods used to estimate market potentials is based solely on the notion that past sales or potentials are a predictor of future sales or potentials. Where there is a high degree of stability in demand, using only past history can be a very effective means of forecasting.

If consumption of a product per capita is stable, as may be the case for table salt, extrapolation of past sales may be adequate. Naturally, correlation methods relating table salt sales to population could also be used. At the opposite extreme are products whose sales are highly variable, such as voting machines, pleasure boats, or paper corrugating machines. Between these extremes are many products whose sales, while they appear somewhat erratic when plotted against time, also show some degree of regularity. Here such time-series techniques as moving averages and exponential smoothing are of value in estimating potentials.

For many products it is often possible to discern three separate patterns: (1) trend, (2) cyclical, and (3) seasonal. A fourth component is necessary to accommodate the residue or random events reflected in the time series. Techniques exist for identifying each of these four elements of a time series. (See Section II, Part E, Chapters 1 and 2.)

The trend component usually reflects the growth in potential due to such factors as population, increases in efficiency, and improvement in technology. The cyclical factor reflects the wavelike portion of the series and is often associated with macrochanges in the economy. Housing starts and raw materials sales, for example, show cyclical behavior. The third factor reflects the seasonal variations evidenced by some products.

Knowledge of these three components, coupled with judgments of factors affecting each of them, can be used to arrive at estimates of market potential.

Time-series methods have the advantage of being relatively easily understood. They do not depend upon large amounts of data, although they do require a sales history of the product. This is an advantage where there are conformability problems for possible independent variables.

A good deal of computation is required to break down a time-series relationship. Where computing equipment is readily available, this problem is not serious. Since the method can only reflect what has happened, it cannot be expected to adequately predict changes due to new causes. As such it is most useful where demand is reasonably stable and continues to react to the same underlying variables. These methods cannot reflect structural change in the same manner as would a relationship on regression methods.

Input/Output. Input-output analysis is a technique with great promise for estimating market potentials. An input-output table for the United States economy for 1963, produced by the U.S. Department of Commerce, interrelates the sales of 383 different industries. This input-output table involved collecting and processing a colossal amount of data. The use of such a table is described in Chapter 3, Part D, of this section.

With the use of such a table (there are in fact three basic tables), it is possible to forecast industry-by-industry consumption of a given industry's output and thus to have an estimate of potential by consuming industry segments. These, in turn, must be related to basic planning and control units used by the firm. Since the method simultaneously adjusts the economy and considers all the interrelationships, it has great appeal in principle. In practice, the tables are not extensive enough as yet to give sufficient refinement for many product lines.

This methodology is not well developed, but it can be expected to expand in usefulness. It has the advantage of simultaneously covering all industries a product might serve. As such it can reflect structural changes, although current tables do not take a dynamic approach to technological changes. Sensitivity analysis is possible with this methodology.

With only 383 industries, some product classes will be hidden by their grouping with other products. Moreover, a given firm may not match the industry exactly. The method gives a national forecast only; regional tables have not been developed. The tables are frequently criticized for being old, for the lag between data collection and published tables has been quite long. Technological changes are said to occur much more rapidly than is reflected in the lag, which for the most recent table was six years.

Summary. Table 1 summarizes the strengths and weaknesses of the major methods of estimating market potential discussed in this section. Eight important considerations in selecting and describing a method are shown.

METHODS OF IMPROVING ESTIMATES

Inasmuch as potential estimates are used repeatedly over time, any method selected for use in estimating market potential should be evaluated and improved with subsequent use. Also, at any given time a more accurate assessment of market potential may be required. This section suggests means of improving estimates of market potential.

Use of More than One Method

A means of assessing and improving the accuracy of an estimate is to use more than one method to independently determine potential. For example, it would be well to check the results of a regression estimate with a census or sample survey of several sales territories. With proper selection of widely varying territories, some evaluation of the regression results could be made. In a similar fashion, certain experimental marketing programs could be undertaken to do the same thing. Where divergence occurs in the multiple estimates, judgment must determine which should be used.

Sequential Estimates

Because estimates are made over time, it is possible to review previous forecasts with actual results. In the case of potential, it must be measured against actual sales history for the product class. At a minimum, the potential estimate should never be less than sales for the product class. By comparing past estimates with actual results, a pattern may develop. This pattern can then be used to correct forecasts. For example, if salesmen were used in the forecasting process, the records of each could be observed. For those who consistently, say, underestimated potentials in their assigned territory, a correction factor could be devised to improve the estimate.

TABLE 1 Characteristics of Estimation Methods

Factor	Judgment	Survey	Test or experimental	Correlation	Time series	Input-Output
Accuracy	Variable	Can be very accurate when properly done	Can be very accurate if test is representative	These methods can be very accurate, especially regression and statistical demand analysis	Can be accurate where demand patterns are stable	If underlying technology has not changed, this method can be accurate, especially where many industries are involved
Sensitivity analysis	Difficult to be consistent if more than one person is involved	If survey instrument is properly constructed, sensitivity analysis is possible; not very flexible	Properly designed experiments can give sensitivity information	Easily possible with the regression and statistical demand methods	Parameters can be changed; some limitations, especially for changes in demand structure	Some limitations, but it has the advantage of determining simultaneous effects on many industries
Data requirements	Variable, but not great	Data are generated by this technique	Data are generated by this technique	Data demands can be very heavy, especially for independent variables	Only historical sales or potential data are required	Self-contained in the tables
Conformability	Minimizes conformability problems	No problem if sample frame is properly constructed	If the market is properly chosen, this is no problem	This method creates a considerable problem in securing conformable data sets unless the basic sales territory is defined in terms of political subdivisions	This can be a problem for time-series estimates of market potential; sales forecasts do not have this problem	As currently used, this method provides a national estimate; other techniques, such as the index method, must be used to allocate potential to territories

4-95

TABLE 1 Characteristics of Estimation Methods (Continued)

Factor	Judgment	Survey	Test or experimental	Correlation	Time series	Input-Output
Product type	Useful across all types	Most useful where there are a limited number of buyers	Most useful for items that are purchased frequently and widely consumed	Useful across all product classes	Useful across all product classes	Most useful for industrial products with little brand differentiation and where many industries are served
Causal relationship	No way to measure assumptions that are made	Causal relationship measured through intentions to purchase	Because actual purchase measures are obtained, causal structure is generally measured	Statistical demand analysis should provide analysis of demand structure; other correlation methods need not provide causal relationships	Only that reflected in the historical series	Not made explicit, but they underlie the construction of the tables
Demand stability	Good where demand trend is stable	Well suited to cases of demand instability	Useful for new markets as well as new products	These methods are well suited to cases of demand instability	Less useful where demand is unstable	Can perform well where unstable demand conditions exist
Cost	Low	Low where few customers; sample survey can help reduce costs	Expensive, but revenues generated can offset costs	Initial estimates can be costly; successive use of the function estimated will lower per-use cost	Low once methodology is established	Initial high costs can be offset where many industries must be covered

Similar correction factors could be devised for other methods, including time-series and correlation methods, so long as the error pattern was consistent. Of course, where a quantitative method is being used, a consistent pattern of under- or overestimating is itself a clue that some important causal factor is missing and that the relationship should be reestimated.

Life-Cycle Patterns

It is well known that products typically exhibit a life-cycle pattern which can usually be represented by an S-shaped curve. Knowledge of where a product lies in its life cycle can give boundary conditions for estimates made by other methods. In addition, knowledge of such life cycles can have other planning uses in marketing management. Estimates of market potential should, over time, trace out such life cycles.

Behavioral Factors

Because potential estimates are used to judge performance, care must be taken to ensure that the human aspects of the estimating procedure are uncolored by the subsequent uses of the estimates. Where judgment enters the estimating process, incentive systems can be installed to encourage accurate estimates. Since judgment cannot be eliminated from the estimating process, good management practice demands that judgment biased by the control uses of the estimate be eliminated. If this is not done, the planning uses of the estimate will be less effective.

Information Input

None of the methods for estimating market potential can go beyond the quality of the input data. Better information systems for collecting and cleaning data have an important role to play in improving estimates. Better data inputs are especially desirable for methods such as regression analysis, time-series analysis, and input-output methods, where the functional form rests in large measure on the quality of the historical data.

Longer time series, more data series, and the ability to store and efficiently retrieve them are also ways in which the quality of estimates can be improved. These "administrative" data matters are very important because such things as missing observations and greater length of history can do much to improve the estimates obtained by most quantitatively based techniques.

Better Methods

Which of the six classes of methods discussed is best depends upon a number of general conditions. It is possible to say that methods which tend to eliminate arbitrary judgment and which reflect causality can deliver a more accurate and useful estimate. Certainly a method such as regression analysis is to be preferred in most instances to mere guesses and extrapolations by a host of busy, untrained salesmen, if for no other reason than that the weaknesses in the regression method can be evaluated. Of course, quantitatively based methods are more easily replicated. In general, use of better estimating methodology is another way in which the quality and accuracy of estimates can be improved.

SUMMARY

This chapter has discussed the general problems and methodology related to the estimation of potentials, both for the total market and for the firm. The distinction between market opportunity, as measured by market potentials, and sales forecasts (expected sales for a firm) is an important one . The definition of *market potential* given is intended to reflect the market's ability to absorb a product class under carefully stated conditions. As such, market potential is a boundary on maximum demand and in a sense represents all that could be achieved.

The principal use of potentials is to provide both a benchmark against which actual performance can be measured and to act as one of the criteria in allocation decisions involving marketing effort. Hence, measures of potential find managerial uses both in planning and control decisions.

Six classes of methods for estimating potentials were discussed: (1) judgment, (2) survey, (3) test and experimental, (4) correlation, (5) time series, and (6) input-output. In general, no one of these methods is best suited to all situations. Their strengths and weaknesses were discussed in terms of the general problem of selecting a method.

The most important means of improving the estimates of market potential rest in improving the data inputs and in using what may be more costly methods, preferably methods grounded in economic and statistical theory.

BIBLIOGRAPHY

Bass, F. M., "Decomposable Regression Models in the Analysis of Market Potentials," *Management Science*, vol. 17, April 1971.

Brion, J. M., *Corporate Marketing Planning*, New York: Wiley, 1967.

Brown, R. G., *Smoothing, Forecasting and Prediction*, Englewood Cliffs, N.J.: Prentice-Hall, 1963.

———, *Statistical Forecasting for Inventory Control*, New York: McGraw-Hill, 1959.

Cowan, D. R. G., *Sales Analysis from the Management Standpoint*, Ann Arbor, Mich.: Wolverine Publications, 1967.

Davis, K. R., and F. E. Webster, Jr., *Sales Force Management*, New York: Ronald, 1968.

Frey, A. E., ed., *Marketing Handbook*, New York: Ronald, 1965.

Halterman, J. C., and T. W. Meloan, "Market Potentials and Use of Census Data," *Seminar on Market Potentials and the Use of Census Data*, American Marketing Association, 1958.

Hummel, F., *Market and Sales Potentials*, New York: Ronald, 1961.

Kotler, P., *Marketing Management*, Englewood Cliffs, N.J.: Prentice-Hall, 1967.

Peterson, E. H., "The Meaning and Use of Sales Potentials," in *Aspects of Modern Marketing*, American Management Association, report no. 15, 1958.

Uhl, K. P., and B. Schoner, *Marketing Research*, New York: Wiley, 1969.

Winters, P. R., "Forecasting Sales by Exponentially Weighted Moving Averages," *Management Science*, vol. 6, April 1960.

Sales Analysis and Forecasting

Chapter 4

The Design of Market Segmentation Studies

RONALD E. FRANK *Department of Marketing, University of Pennsylvania, Philadelphia, Pennsylvania*

INTRODUCTION

Market segmentation has been a hot topic for the last 10 years. It is on the verge of getting even hotter. The field of marketing is in the early stages of witnessing a virtual revolution in the nature and conduct of research pertaining to this problem area. These changes stem from an increased sophistication in our understanding of the logic underlying the strategy of market segmentation; from a burgeoning stock of published research on the topic; from changes in our way of conceiving of the determinants of human behavior; and from changes in the stock of quantitative methods available for dealing with the measurement and analysis problems posed by the aforementioned changes.

The content of this chapter draws on knowledge of (1) the problem of market segmentation and (2) the field of marketing research. Its primary objective, however, is not to present a treatise on either of the two topics in and of themselves. Instead, it is to indicate the relationship between one's formulation of the segmentation problem and one's choice of research design (especially as it relates to the selection of appropriate quantitative techniques).

The following paragraphs contain a discussion of the logic underlying the strategy of market segmentation. Next is presented an example of the type of research that is typically done as a basis for evaluating whether a given basis for segmentation is indeed desirable.

The Strategy of Market Segmentation

The strategy of market segmentation is defined as the development and pursuit of different marketing programs by the same firm for essentially the same product but for different subsets of customers within the overall market. The choice of segmentation as a strategy is usually predicated on the assumption that the market for a particular product is composed of segments of customers with somewhat different needs and wants. If the nature of these differences can be determined, then it may be possible to develop a marketing program for each that corresponds to its requirements.

For example, a carbonated beverage manufacturer may choose to develop products and/or change appeals on existing products in order to disproportionately appeal to a given segment of the market—for example, 7-Up's efforts to appeal to the youth market [12]. Still another attempt at market segmentation is the practice of many manufacturers to aim their promotion disproportionately at the heavy buyers of a product category or brand by choosing media that have a particularly strong appeal to these groups.

Marketing management is faced with two crucial questions with respect to segmentation:

1. To what extent should a firm pursue a strategy of market segmentation?

2. If the market is to be segmented, upon what basis (or bases) should it be done?

It is normal to answer the first question in the affirmative if it can be shown that, on the average, certain segments (groups) of people buy more of the product under consideration than do other groups.

These customer segments are usually classified in terms of socioeconomic, life-cycle, or locational characteristics, although other dimensions such as personality variables may also be used. Groups for which the *average purchase rate* is high are identified as "target" market segments. Presumably, if average purchase rates were equal among all groups of a product's customers, segmentation would not be a profitable strategy.

An Ilustration

Frank, Douglas, and Polli [6] report a study of the relationship between household demographic and socioeconomic characteristics and brand loyalty for grocery products. Their analysis is based on *Chicago Tribune* panel data for 1961. The authors obtained a complete purchase history for 491 households for each of 44 product categories. The categories ranged from food products (such as regular coffee, carbonated beverages, margarine, and peanut butter) to household products (such as liquid detergents, scouring cleansers, toilet tissues, and food wrappers).

Separate multiple regression analyses were conducted for each of the product categories. The dependent variable was the proportion of purchases devoted to the most frequently bought brand in 1961, while the independent variables were 14 socioeconomic and demographic characteristics.

Because *cross-sectional studies* such as the Frank, Douglas, and Polli investigation (hereafter referred to as the FDP study) are by far the most common type of design used in market segmentation research, the next section of this chapter discusses the changes occurring in the design of this type of investigation. This is followed by a section on the role of longitudinal analysis (studies over time) in market segmentation research.

CROSS-SECTIONAL STUDIES

The design of cross-sectional market segmentation studies has been a subject of controversy for some time. Most of the issues which receive attention relate to the researcher's choice of variables as candidates for predicting and/or understanding household purchasing behavior. For example, there is a considerable amount of debate about the relative merits of demographic, socioeconomic, and various psychological characteristics as predictors of purchasing behavior. Similar questions have been raised as to the usefulness of such constructs as social class, life cycle, and life-style. The issues underlying questions concerning the nature and content of the independent variables are discussed in this section.

The emphasis on the side of the independent variables is overdone. Many of the same issues that are recognized as problems in the context of the independent variables are also present in the case of the dependent variables (household purchasing characteristics) which are commonly used in market segmentation investigations. First are discussed the issues involved in the measurement of household purchasing behavior. This is followed by a discussion of the changes occurring on (1) specification of the independent variables and (2) the way in which they are assumed to be related to purchasing behavior.

Dependent Variable Specification

Two basic issues are inherent in the way one approaches the problem of classifying customers based on their purchasing behavior, namely:

1. Is the particular aspect of purchasing behavior—for example, brand loyalty—a unidimensional or a multidimensional phenomenon?

2. Does the researcher have sufficient confidence in his prior judgment of the most appropriate way of classifying customers based on their purchasing behavior?

Unidimensional versus Multidimensional Phenomena. Much of the behavior we are interested in studying is a complex of many factors, that is, it is *multidimensional* in character. We often sidestep this complexity by picking some unidimensional attribute which we assume is an indicant of the more complex phenomena we seek to understand. For example, in studies of household brand loyalty one often finds such variables as (1) the proportion of purchases spent on the most frequently purchased brand (as used in the FDP study) or (2) the proportion spent on the brand of central interest to the researcher, used to measure the degree of brand loyalty.

For many purposes, however, these measures may be too limited a measure of loyalty in that they fail to come close to a full description of a rather complex phenomenon. Customers do not typically buy a single brand or even two brands. Many households will purchase three, four, or five brands of a particular product. In addition, the subset of brands chosen for consumption will vary from household to household.

If brand loyalty is looked upon as involving not only the number of brands a household buys but also the proportion of purchases made for each of them, as well as their identity, it is clear that simple unidimensional measures of brand loyalty cannot serve as adequate bases for the cross-sectional classification of households. Instead, what is needed is a more complex classification system, that is, a *multidimensional classification system* for classifying households into groups buying similar "bundles" of brands.

The argument favoring the use of multidimensional classification systems can be extended to a number of aspects of purchasing behavior in addition to brand loyalty, such as store loyalty and total consumption.

The change from a unidimensional to a multidimensional view of brand loyalty typically involves a shift from the use of multiple regression procedures (as the multivariate technique for measuring the degree of association between a set of independent variables and brand loyalty) to n-way multiple discriminant analysis.

Regression procedures are based, in part, on the assumption that the dependent variable is either interval- or ratio-scaled, whereas n-way discriminant analysis requires that the dependent variable be either ordinally or nominally scaled. Many unidimensional measures of brand loyalty (such as the percent spent on brand most often purchased) are interval- or ratio-scaled. In contrast, multidimensional classification systems are more often than not only nominally scaled or, at best, ordinally scaled.

A priori versus Natural Classification Systems. The use of an a priori classification system implies the existence of a "hunch," a highly developed body of theory and/or past research that indicates how best to classify a set of objects (in the case of the FDP study the objects are households) for the purpose of further study. For example, if one were to conduct an investigation of household brand loyalty in the cereal market, one might establish a category of households that were primarily purchasers of sugar coated cereals, another that had a disproportionate concentration of its purchases on high-energy cereals, and so on. Such a classification might be based on some a priori judgment as to the nature of the different brand bundles to which households would be likely to be attracted in a particular product category. The principal advantage of an a priori system of classification is that the researcher is less apt to be led astray by purely spurious classification systems that might arise if "the data were permitted to speak for themselves"; as is the case to a considerably greater degree when one makes use of "natural" procedures for developing a classification system.

One disadvantage of the a priori approach is that one's prior convictions can act more as a set of blinders than as a guide to further study and understanding. In addition, regardless of the complexity of reality, human beings find it difficult to classify objects by more than two or three characteristics at a time. If reality requires greater complexity—that is, a more elaborate multidimensional classification scheme—we are severely constrained by our own conceptual limitations.

Suppose, for example, one wanted to study the clusters of brands that different households consume. How would he proceed? All possible combinations of brands could be computed and then the households could be sorted into their respective classes. But this approach involves a few problems. How many combinations are there in a market with only 12 brands? There are well over 4 million if one adds up the number of partitions resulting from grouping 12 brands into two clusters, and so on. If this were not bad enough, one may want to measure the similarity of brand purchasing behavior not just in terms of the combination of brands but also in terms of the relative proportion of dollar outlays spent on each brand.

The problem of developing multidimensional classification systems where the number of characteristics (for example, brands) is relatively great is not unique to brand loyalty, let alone to the field of marketing. In recent years a new class of quantitative procedures has been developed in biology which consists of a set of numerical procedures for classifying objects. The label given to this approach is *numerical taxonomy.*[1]

In a sense, taxonomic procedures may be called *preclassification techniques, since their purpose is to describe the natural groupings that occur in large masses*

[1] For a detailed overview of taxonomic methods, see [5, pp. 83–94].

of data. From these natural groupings (or clusters), the researcher can sometimes develop the requisite conceptual framework for classification.

Taxonomic procedures can be used as the basis for forming clusters of households whose purchase requirements over the principal brands in a product category are similar within a cluster and dissimilar between clusters. The resulting categories of households can in turn be used as the nominally scaled dependent variable in an n-way multiple discriminant analysis in which the independent variables would be whatever measured characteristics—for example, socioeconomic or psychological—were hypothesized to be correlated with the observed differences in the bundles of brands purchased by each household category.

Independent Variable Specifications

There are three principal issues which reflect ongoing changes in the nature of the specification of independent variables for segmentation studies, namely:

1. What should be the *content coverage* of the independent variables, for example, socioeconomic versus psychological characteristics?

2. Given that a set of measures are taken on a set of respondents, what is the most parsimonious and meaningful way in which they can be utilized for further analysis? That is, *can the measured characteristics themselves be classified* in some fashion so as to simplify the analysis without losing essential information about each respondent?

3. Given a parsimonious and meaningful set of measures, what is the value of developing a *multidimensional classification system of the households or respondents* based on the independent variables? As will be shown, the use of such a classification system as a basis for *predicting* some aspect of purchasing behavior (such as brand loyalty or total consumption) implicitly assumes the existence of high-order interactions or nonlinearities with respect to the relationship between the dependent and independent variables.

Content. The results of cross-sectional studies almost without exception indicate that there is at best only a modest degree of association between demographic, socioeconomic, and/or personality characteristics and selected aspects of household purchasing behavior such as total consumption, brand loyalty, and deal-proneness. For example, in the FDP study cited previously, the average proportion of variation in household brand loyalty associated with demographic and socioeconomic characteristics across all 44 products included in their investigation is only 12 percent.[2]

If demographic, socioeconomic, and general personality characteristics are not important determinants of household buying behavior, what variables are likely to make a difference? To answer this question one needs to keep in mind three other pieces of information: (1) that most measures of household purchasing behavior have high reliability—that is, high temporal stability,[3] [9]; (2) though they are reliable, our measures of household buying behavior nonetheless have relatively low correlation from one product to the next [13] (for example, knowing a person's brand loyalty in one product provides virtually no information as to the level of loyalty he will exhibit toward another product); (3) demographic, socioeconomic, and general personality measures are *general* measures of a household's or an individual's state. That is, they are measures which are "common denominators" of (which stay constant

---

[2] For a more comprehensive review of previous research, see [4, pp. 39–68].
[3] See [9, pp. 35–39].

across) his behavior regardless of the nature of the problem or situation with which he is faced.

The presence of high reliability supports the notion that a large component of household buying behavior is systematic in nature and potentially amenable to understanding and prediction. In spite of this fact, demographic, socioeconomic, and personality characteristics have low correlations with buying behavior. The low intercorrelation of purchasing behavior across products can provide some insight into this anomaly. The more stable household purchasing behavior is from one product to the next, the more importance can be potentially attached to the aforementioned enduring characteristics.

The logic of this argument leads to the conclusion that one of the most fruitful directions for future research dealing with the problem of segment delineation *is the study of psychological and sociological characteristics which are idiosyncratic to both the consumer and the product and not to the consumer alone.* For example, in a study of breakfast cereals, rather than measure a person's personality using some general-purpose test, one might take measurements of the subject's attitude toward breakfast as a meal and/or his attitude toward nutrition in the context of breakfast.

One should not infer from the aforementioned discussion that socioeconomic and demographic characteristics are to be relegated to the trash can. First, there are some products and brands for which these characteristics are reasonably good segment identifiers. In addition, there may well be interactions between socioeconomic-demographic characteristics and psychological-sociological characteristics; for example, the association of one's attitudes toward breakfast as a meal with his choice of cereal brands may depend on his education, family size and composition, and so on. At present applied work in segmentation research is in the midst of struggling with developing adequate measures of psychological-sociological characteristics. The study of their interactions with socioeconomic-demographic characteristics has yet to begin.

Variable Classification. Virtually all market segmentation studies require the development of a "paper-and-pencil" test aimed at measuring whatever of the respondents' characteristics—for example, demographic, socioeconomic, psychological, or sociological—are hypothesized to be of importance in predicting cross-sectional differences in buying behavior. Given the present state of the art, there are severe limitations on our knowledge of (1) the dimensions that should be measured and (2) how best to measure them. Both of these limitations tend to lead to relatively lengthy questionnaires.

For example, suppose one were to develop a questionnaire aimed at measuring the determinants of household purchasing behavior with respect to new grocery products. One might hypothesize that such dimensions as the degree of a person's urbanness, group participation, and self-confidence as to meal preparation would be positively associated with new grocery product acceptance.

For each of the aforementioned dimensions (hypothesized constructs) there is a marked lack of knowledge as to the best paper-and-pencil questions to be used for their measurement. Typically this leads to building into a questionnaire (at least initially) several questions that the analyst hypothesizes are apt to be measures of the same dimension. For example, several possible measures of a respondent's urbanness might be (1) the number of trips greater than 100 miles in length in the last year, (2) the number and breadth of subject matter of the books read in the same time period, (3) the diversity of types of people who are considered acquaintances—for example, doctors, plumbers, religious figures, and so on. In most segmentation studies both the number of dimensions (hypothetical constructs) and the number of ways in which they might be measured are substantially greater than in the preceding illustration. To further complicate the matter, there is often a fair degree of uncertainty as to (1) the way in which the various dimensions (based on the researcher's a priori judgments) are related to each other and (2) whether the various measures of a given dimension do in fact appear to measure the same thing.

In dealing with measurement problems, the researcher is faced with the same issues as were discussed in the preceding section on dependent variable specification, namely, whether to use (1) unidimensional versus multidimensional procedures and (2) a priori versus natural procedures as a basis for classification. In this context, however, the *classification* problem is the inverse of the one previously discussed. In the previous illustration, *households* were grouped based on the similarity of their *measurements* (in the example, purchases of brands). The problem facing the researcher in this context involves the classification of the *measurements* based on the similarity of their scores over households.

The same taxonomic procedures that are appropriate for one problem are also appropriate for the other. To date, the most frequently used procedure for this purpose is R-type factor analysis. R-type factor analysis (which is only one type of taxonomic technique that could be used in this context) focuses on a given set of measurements taken over respondents and, in effect, asks the question: Can the information contained in the original variables be summarized in a smaller number of new variables?[4]

In other words, taxonomic procedures such as factor analysis can be used as a partial basis for determining:

1. Whether or not a series of paper-and-pencil measures that were chosen to measure the same dimension are in fact highly correlated with each other over respondents. (This is simply another way of saying that the original variables can in fact be summarized into a smaller number of variables without the loss of much information.)

2. The degree to which a series of dimensions (based on the researcher's a priori judgment) are correlated with each other.

This type of analysis can serve two important functions, namely: (1) to help interpret what the paper-and-pencil measures really measure and (2) to help choose a subset of variables or summary measures—for example, factor scores for inclusion in subsequent analysis of the relationship between the independent variables and purchasing behavior.

Respondent Classification. One of the current vogues in marketing research is not only to use taxonomic procedures to classify measured characteristics but also, once this is done, to take the resulting summary measures and group respondents (whether they be households or individuals) together who have similar *profiles* of scores over the measured characteristics. Stated another way, numerical taxonomic procedures are used to develop natural (as opposed to a priori) *multidimensional* classification systems of the respondents. The most frequently used procedure for this purpose is Q-type factor analysis. At present there is often a mystical quality attributed to the outcome of this type of analysis. Phrases such as "life-styles" or "overall psychological orientation" are used as though the words themselves explained the meaningfulness of this approach. The purpose of this discussion is to make the assumptions *implicit* in this approach *explicit*.

---

[4] For a more detailed discussion of the application of factor analysis, see [10, pp. 291–307].

Presumably the principal motivation for developing natural multidimensional classifications of respondents is based on the belief that such a classification system will improve one's ability to predict household purchasing behavior. The assumptions that are implicit in this type of analysis are (1) that natural classification procedures for developing household types are apt to be superior to the a priori conventions which currently are accepted in practice (for example, social class and life cycle) and (2) that high-order interactions and/or nonlinearities are present in the relationships between the dependent and independent variables.

The issues surrounding the first of the assumptions are the same as those previously discussed under the heading of dependent variable specification and therefore will not be repeated. However, the second set of assumptions are idiosyncratic to this topic and therefore are discussed in the following paragraphs.

Suppose, for example, that we were attempting to develop a model of the relationship between a household's consumption of alcoholic beverages (A_i) and three independent variables, namely, income, education, and home ownership.

One such model might be as follows:

$$A_i = \alpha + \beta_1 I_i + \beta_2 E_i + \beta_3 H_i + \epsilon_i \qquad (1)$$

where A_i = total dollar expenditure of ith household for alcoholic beverages during time period of study

I_i = total household income

E_i = the number of years of formal education for head of household

H_i = dummy variable which takes value of 1 if household owns own home and value of 0 otherwise

ϵ_i = error term

If appropriate data were collected and analyzed using multiple regression procedures, the resulting estimates of β_1, β_2, and β_3 would represent the estimated effect of a one unit change in the magnitude in each of the three respective independent variables. Though this model contains a number of assumptions, two of them are of particular interest, namely: (1) that the relationships between the independent variables and the dependent variable are linear and (2) that the effect of any one independent variable is not a function of one or more of the independent variables—that is, that no interactions are present.

Suppose, however, that the analyst suspects that nonlinearities or interactions might be present. How might he proceed? One way to test for the presence of nonlinearities and interactions simultaneously would be to do as follows. He might partition each of the variables into several categories. For example, income might be divided into three categories, say, under $6,000, $6,000 to $10,000, and over $10,000. Education might also be divided into three categories: (1) completed high school or less, (2) some college, (3) completed undergraduate training or more. Home ownership is already split into two categories.

Next a series of 18 dummy variables could be created—one for each combination of the aforementioned categories (3 income times 3 education times 2 home ownership). A given household's score would take a value of 1 for one of the variables and 0 for the other 17. For example, if a household had an income of under $6,000, had some college, and owned its own home, it would be coded 1 for the dummy variable representing this combination of income, education, and home ownership and 0 for all remaining variables. The resulting model would look like this:[5]

$$A_i = \alpha + \beta_1 X_{1i} + \beta_2 X_{2i} + \sum_{j=3}^{18} \beta_j X_{ji} + \epsilon_i \qquad (2)$$

Under what conditions will this model do a better job of predicting alcoholic beverage consumption than the preceding model? First, the division of the income and education variables into a series of dummy variables implies that the resulting regression model will fit whether the relationships are linear or nonlinear. *Therefore the presence of any nonlinearities will result in this model outperforming the first model in its ability to predict.* Second, by coding the variables so that each one represents a *group* of households with a different combination of income, education, and home ownership, the effects of each of these three dimensions is free to vary as a function of the level of the other. For example, three of the estimates for income will be conditional on household heads having completed high school or less and renting. Another three estimates of the effect of income will be for households with some college who rent their homes, and so on. *Stated another way, this model will also outperform the first model if there are interactions present between the effects of any one of these three dimensions and the levels of the others.*

By now the reader may be wondering what this discussion has to do with using taxonomic procedures to group households into "natural" categories based on a set of independent variables. It has a great deal to do with it. In the second model the variables amount to an *a priori* system for grouping households in three dimensions. *The variables themselves represent 18 household groups.*

Why not settle for a priori judgment alone? Suppose there were 10, 20, or more variables. If one suspected that *higher-order* interactions were present (interactions involve the interrelationships of a substantial number of independent variables at once), how would he proceed to pick and choose which ones are the most appropriate?

One way to proceed would be to use Q-type factor analysis based on either the original variables or factors scores computed from an R-type factor analysis. The purpose of the Q-type analysis would be to group households together whose profile of scores over variables are "similar." These household groups can in turn be used as the basis for defining variables in a regression model, just as were the 18 household groups based on income, education, and home ownership. Suppose, for example, 5 groups were formed as a result of a Q-type analysis. The resulting model would look like this:

$$A_i = \alpha + \sum_{j=1}^{5} B_j X_{ji} + \epsilon_i \qquad (3)$$

where the 5 X_{ji}s would be dummy variables coded in the same fashion as were the 18 groups discussed in the previous example.

Not only are the coding conventions similar, but much more important is the fact that the assumptions built into this model are also similar to those inherent

---

[5] In practice, the full set of variables would not be included for estimation purposes as by definition there would be high multicolinearity. However, this point is not germane to the issue under discussion.

in the regression model with 18 variables representing group membership. If either of these models outperforms Equation (1), it will be due to the presence of high-order interactions and/or nonlinearities.

Stated in this fashion, much of the "mystical" character of the people-typing fad disappears. Not only does it disappear, but the aforementioned discussions point the way to appropriate procedures for testing these aforementioned assumptions. One can simply compare the results of the first model, Equation (1), with those based on the use of dummy variables to represent group membership as defined by the results of some taxonomic procedure such as Q-type factor analysis.

LONGITUDINAL STUDIES

Reorientation of the Problem

Management needs a criterion for determining the extent to which segmenting its market will place it in a more beneficial position than treating the market as a homogeneous entity. Should differences *in the average level of demand* from segment to segment (which are the criteria used in cross-sectional investigations) be used as the only or even the most important criterion? Presumably a firm desires to achieve increased profits via segmentation. Under what conditions can these be obtained?

If the incremental costs of serving different customers in a market are the same, then there is only one condition under which a firm can achieve greater profitability via market segmentation: different groups of customers must have different responses to changes in the firm's marketing program.

In other words, one crucial criterion for determining the desirability of segmenting a market along any particular dimension is whether the different submarkets have different elasticities with respect to the price and promotional policies of a firm.[6] An elasticity is simply a summary measure that relates a percentage change in quantity demanded to the associated percentage change in some causal variable such as price.

Where there are differences in the incremental costs involved in serving customers in the different submarkets, these cost differences should be matched against the effects of price and promotion upon demand in order to arrive at a criterion for judging the desirability of market segmentation. The treatment of costs in market segmentation is beyond the scope of this paper; the important point for our purposes is that, whether costs are equal or not, the degree to which the demand elasticities in the various submarkets are different from one another remains a crucial criterion for market segmentation.[7]

In spite of the clear need for information about the demand elasticities of various submarkets, existing published research contains little information on this point.

Most studies provide data *on the average level of consumption* of different groups of customers. As previously stated, analysis is often based on the classification of customers by socioeconomic status, life cycle, location, and/or personality characteristics.

While these results are interesting and useful, our previous discussion has

[6] For a more detailed statement of the logic underlying this point, see [11, pp. 179–188] and [7, pp. 608–615].

[7] For a discussion of the relationship between costs and promotional sensitivities, see [1].

shown that measures of the *level* of consumption for a given submarket are not the crucial criteria for determining whether the market can be segmented fruitfully. What management needs to know is whether customers belonging to the upper class have a different set of price and promotional elasticities for the firm's products than do customers in the lower class, or whether customers with a dominant personality tend to have different elasticities than those with a different personality profile.

Implications for Research Design

Acceptance of the criterion of *differential response to policy variables* implies a considerably different class of research designs than those which are appropriate for the analysis of cross-sectional differences in *average level of demand*. Investigations aimed at measuring differential response to policy variables by market segment require combining cross-section with time-series data. One illustration of such a study is reported by Frank and Massy.[8] The investigation is based on a branded, frequently purchased food product bought by a high percentage of households in the United States. The data consist of measures of customer purchasing behavior for one major metropolitan area over a 101-week period. The analysis is focused on the response of market share to changes in pricing, dealing, and retail advertising of one particular brand (hereafter referred to as brand M) as well as that of competing brands.

Purchases of the product occur at the rate of several a month for many users. The product is sold through supermarkets and receives a significant amount of promotion at both the manufacturer and retailer levels. Two sets of data were used in the analysis:

1. The purchase records of several hundred households who were members of the Market Research Corporation of America's consumer panel.

2. A sample of retail advertising lineage for the product covering every brand in the market. The sample includes approximately 90 percent of the food lineage placed in the market during the 101-week period of the investigation.

Seven different household characteristics were used as the basis for defining customer segments. They were (1) total consumption of the product, (2) a measure of brand loyalty, (3) income, (4) household size, (5) wife's age, (6) wife's employment status, and (7) wife's education. Separate analyses were conducted for each of the seven characteristics. In each case the sample of household was divided into two groups on the basis of their relative standing on the characteristic being investigated. For example, all families who earned more than $6,000 a year were assigned to the high-income group and, conversely, families earning equal to or less than $6,000 were assigned to the low-income group.

For each group, weekly time series were computed of M's market share, its price relative to the prices of competing brands, the magnitude of its dealing relative to other brands, the extent of its dealing coverage, and the magnitude of its retail advertising as well as that of competitors. Using econometric techniques (based on multiple regression analysis), these two sets of time series were used as the basis for estimating the current and long-run effects on weekly market share for M of the changes in pricing, dealing, and retail advertising activity of both M and its competitors.

[8] The most comprehensive statement of the project's design and results appears in [3, pp. 147–225]; two articles have been published reporting on an earlier stage of the project development: [8, pp. 171–185] and [2, pp. 186–199].

This example only serves to illustrate one approach to the design of research for measuring differential response across customer segments. Depending on the nature of the problem faced by a given firm, it may well be preferable to measure differential response to policy variables other than those treated in this investigation. Or it may be preferable to base the analysis on the results of an experiment as opposed to a time-series analysis. What is important, however, is that the study be designed to yield direct measures of the response of demand by customer segment to whatever changes in the firm's promotional program are deemed appropriate.

Variable Specifications. In the aforementioned Frank-Massy investigation, the independent variables include not only household characteristics such as income and family size but also policy variables such as price and advertising. The implicit assumption leading to this design is that the *effects* of the policy variables on market share *interact* with the *level* of the household characteristics—for example, that the effect of variation in price on market share is different for high- as opposed to low-income households. Looked at in this way, there are two principal steps involved in the specification of the independent variables: (1) household characteristics specification and (2) policy variable specification.

The problems involved in the specification of household characteristics for this type of segmentation study are virtually the same as those involved in cross-sectional studies, namely: (1) content questions—for example, the choice of demographic, socioeconomic, and/or psychographic characteristics, (2) the use of unidimensional versus multidimensional household classification data, and (3) the use of a priori versus natural procedures for delineating customer segments.

The issues implicit in the specification of policy are of the same logical character as those pertaining to the household characteristics and therefore will not be repeated.

Whether one uses sales of a given brand, market share, or anything else, the problems of dependent variable specification are reasonably straightforward in this type of analysis.

The construction of longitudinal segmentation studies usually involves combining several different methodologies. For example, classification procedures such as factor analysis might be used to (1) group the household characteristics to be used in the analysis (in order to eliminate redundancy or to facilitate interpretation) and/or (2) to group the households in order to establish multidimensional customer segments. Once the segments are established, single or multiple equation regression procedures might then be used as the primary analytical technique to estimate the effects on sales of the policy variables included in the study.

CONCLUSIONS

Whether one discusses the specification of dependent or independent variables, cross-sectional or longitudinal investigations, at every step in the design and execution of segmentation studies quantitative methods have a potentially important role to play. This, as has been shown, arises in part from the nature of the problem itself as well as the limitations of the human mind in tracing out the logical implications inherent in such a complex problem area.

In the opinion of the author, the changes in the design of segmentation studies represent a step forward in the evolution of segmentation research for three reasons:

1. The increased use of quantitative methods (along with the computer, without which they would be impossible to use effectively) puts even more pressure on the researcher to think through the specification of both the measurements to be taken and their interrelationships. Failure to do so, in the age of the computer, can easily result in "numerical indigestion." Without a computer the researcher has a fighting chance to be able to interpret numbers and give direction to future analysis before the next set of calculations can be completed. With the computer the researcher is the loser unless he takes more time than most of us are used to for *thinking* in advance of number gathering and manipulation.

2. The techniques are capable of handling the calculation burden imposed by reasonably complex models of buyer behavior (models which admit a wide range of variables as well as relationships which are nonlinear and interactive in nature).

3. The techniques constitute a vastly improved set of procedures for testing alternative models of customer buying behavior than we heretofore have tended to use.

REFERENCES

1. Baumol, W. J., and C. H. Sevin, "Marketing Costs and Mathematical Programming," *Harvard Business Review,* September–October 1957.
2. Frank, R. E., and W. F. Massy, "Market Segmentation and the Effectiveness of a Brand's Price and Dealing Policies," *Journal of Business,* vol. 8, April 1965.
3. ———, and W. F. Massy, "Effect of Short-Term Promotional Strategy in Selected Market Segments," in P. J. Robinson, ed., *Promotional Decisions Using Mathematical Models,* Boston: Allyn and Bacon, 1967.
4. ———, "Market Segmentation Research: Findings and Implications," in F. Bass et al., ed., *Applications of the Sciences to Marketing Management,* New York: Wiley, 1968.
5. ———, and P. E. Green, "Numerical Taxonomy in Marketing," *Journal of Marketing Research,* vol. 5, February 1968.
6. ———, S. P. Douglas, and R. E. Polli, "Household Correlates of 'Brand Loyalty' for Grocery Products," *Journal of Business,* April 1968.
7. Boulding, K. E., *Economic Analysis,* New York: Harper, 1955.
8. Massy, W. F., and R. E. Frank, "Short-Term Price and Dealing Effects in Selected Market Segments," *Journal of Marketing Research,* vol. 2, May 1965.
9. ———, R. E. Frank, and R. M. Lodahl, *Purchasing Behavior and Personal Attributes,* Philadelphia: University of Pennsylvania Press, 1968.
10. ———, "Applying Factor Analysis to a Specific Marketing Problem," in S. Greyser, ed., *Toward Scientific Marketing,* Chicago: American Marketing Association, December 1969.
11. Robinson, J., *The Economics of Imperfect Competition,* London: Macmillan, 1954.
12. "7-Up Bids for Youth with a Negative Pitch," *Business Week,* February 15, 1969.
13. Wind, Y., and R. E. Frank, "Interproduct Household Loyalty to Brands," mimeographed, Philadelphia: University of Pennsylvania, Wharton School, February 1969.

Part C
Advertising Research

Chapter 1

Audience Measurement Techniques

CLARK SCHILLER *TIME Magazine, New York, New York*

All decisions by the advertiser on selection of media are normally aimed at obtaining the greatest sales volume per dollar expenditure. However, in the absence of exact data expressing the sales power per media dollar, the advertiser makes his own estimates about sales power. Outside of the mail order business, no advertiser possesses data directly related to sales per media dollar. Therefore most advertisers estimate the relative sales effectiveness by indirect methods. They try to collect data on as many media characteristics as possible which may contribute to sales effectiveness for their specific products. From these data they develop an estimate of the most probable sales effectiveness.

One type of data an advertiser has for evaluating a medium's potential advertising value is an estimate of the number of people exposed to a given issue, time segment, or telecast. This estimate is referred to as the medium's total audience or average audience. It is the purpose of this chapter to discuss the audience measurement techniques currently practiced by the research community insofar as these methods relate to magazines, newspapers, radio, and television.

Two alternatives are available for defining the members of the audience of any medium. The first alternative defines a member of the audience by means of some objective criterion; the second does so by means of a respondent's self-appraisal. Whenever the first alternative is used, some criterion invariably must be established—a decision has to be made defining the minimum behavior any individual must engage in to qualify as a member of the audience. All audience techniques involving some objective criterion except one set the qualification for audience membership at the level of minimum exposure. The exception is the technique that estimates audience by means of an electronic device.

Establishing the criterion for audience membership simply as exposure or nonexposure means, for example, that the reader of one editorial item counts the same as the reader of all editorial items. Defining a member of the audience according to the respondent's self-evaluation may mean that some people who would qualify by some objective criterion would not consider themselves as exposed to the medium. The converse is also possible.

MAGAZINES

Each of the techniques currently practiced to determine magazine audiences can be broadly classified as either a *recognition* or *unaided recall* method. Recognition methods define a reader according to some objective criterion, whereas the unaided recall methods define a reader according to his self-appraisal. The basic requirement of a recognition method is that the respondent is given some sort of visual stimuli before he is questioned about prior readership of a particular issue. Unaided recall methods offer the respondent no stimuli for recall of previous readership behavior other than the questioning procedure itself. In addition, the respondent is not asked about behavior regarding a particular issue but rather is queried about readership during some time period. Statistical theory is then applied to these responses to estimate average issue audience.

Recognition methods	*Unaided recall methods*
1. Editorial interest technique	1. Frequency technique
2. Cover technique	2. Recent reading technique

Editorial Interest Technique

In the 1930s and early 1940s, magazine audiences were determined by a questioning procedure which simply asked people to look through the issue and point out the pages they remembered. A person was counted as a reader if he remembered seeing any editorial page. These audiences were then adjusted to discount mistaken readership claims. To do this, separate interviews were conducted with prepublished issues to estimate the amount of overclaimed readership, and this was then applied to a formula devised by Darrell B. Lucas to adjust the postpublished issue audience.

In ensuing studies, the procedure for adjusting mistaken readership claims was modified by counting a person as a reader of the issue only if he remembered seeing a specified number of pages in the issue. It was reasoned that people who remember seeing fewer than the specified number of pages were overclaiming and therefore should be omitted from the audience. The number of pages required to be remembered was varied for different magazines. This was done in an effort to equalize the number of people omitted from the audience by the *number of pages remembered* technique and the *prepublished* method. Periodic check studies conducted with prepublished issues were done to update the specified number of pages an individual had to remember before being counted as a reader.

The *specified number of pages remembered* procedure was later modified to the *editorial items remembered* concept. The editorial items remembered concept counted complete articles or stories as units rather than individual pages.

In 1946, a new readership questioning approach was developed to correct readership overclaiming at the source as opposed to correcting it at the tabulating stage. The respondent was asked to go through the issue and, on each editorial item, was asked whether it looked interesting and whether this was the first time he had seen it. At the end of the issue, the respondent was also asked, as a check, whether he had read the issue before. This was done to substantiate any prior claims based on individual items. To count in the issue's audience, a respondent had to report having seen the issue before and having seen at least one editorial item. Experimentation with prepublished issues showed considerably less overclaiming than with preceding methods, and it was decided to discontinue the correction factor interviews.

In 1949, *Life* magazine together with the Alfred Politz organization embarked on a vigorous program to further improve the accuracy of audience measurement. Politz reasoned that although the use of interest in the appearance of editorial items was an excellent way of getting previous readership, the manner in which it was applied created additional problems; that is, the respondent catches on to the readership purpose of the interview when he is asked to report on previous readership. This in itself destroys an objective of the interest questioning by putting a psychological premium on prior issue reading. Further, by the responses on the first few items, the respondent feels already committed to being a reader or nonreader of the issue under study and to give a consistent answer when later asked about the issue as a whole. In other words, he is often unwilling to back down on the committal when later asked about the issue as a whole, even if his later inspection leads him to doubt whether he saw this particular item or any item in the issue before.

Politz further reasoned that the way to solve these problems was to have the respondent inspect the complete editorial contents of the issue *before* being asked to state whether he previously looked into it and not commit himself while inspecting the issue. Also, it should appear to the respondent that whether he had seen the issue before or not is just one aspect of the survey and not its primary concern. Prior to conducting a final study with the *editorial interest* technique, a small experiment among 225 individuals was conducted employing the newly developed questioning procedure with a prepublished issue. In this study only one person, or less than ½ percent of the 225 respondents, claimed prior readership of the prepublished issue.

Studies employing the editorial interest method—or the *through-the-book* method as it is also known—define the audience of an issue as the number of people exposed to any of that issue's editorial contents. No specified amount of reading is required to qualify an audience member other than the minimum of having looked into the issue at all and thus having seen or read at least one item.

This minimum requirement does not imply that all or most see only one or a few items. The definition of issue audience as those people who saw or read any of the issue's editorial contents draws the simplest and least arbitrary boundary between exposure and nonexposure to the issue.

The Simmons syndicated service procedure deviates from inspection of the complete editorial contents by displaying only 10 items to the respondent. Since the Simmons study covers approximately 60 magazine issues in an interview, the sheer weight of complete issues would make it impossible for the interviewer to carry the interviewing kit from interview to interview. Hence Simmons limits display to only 10 editorial items. The effects on audience estimates of this deviation from the tested procedure are unknown.

The first magazine question screens respondents who had not looked into any issue of the particular magazine for a long period of time: "We're interested in knowing the kinds of magazines you may have looked into during the last six or seven months, either at home or anywhere outside your home. Did

you happen to look into any copy of ——— (magazine) in the last six or seven months?"
The magazine logo is then shown to the respondent. This question is asked about all magazines being studied. Respondents who are certain they did not look into any copy of a particular magazine in the last six or seven months are classified as not having looked into the specific recent issue and are asked no further questions about that magazine.

The remaining respondents are asked to examine the editorial contents of the magazine being studied. In multimagazine studies, the order of asking about each magazine is generally rotated from interview to interview to avoid positional bias. The following question gets the respondent to examine the issue without suggesting or revealing the actual purpose of determining whether he had looked into that issue before: "While I leaf quickly through this issue of . . . (magazine), please stop me if we come to an item that looks especially interesting."

During display of the issue's contents, the interviewer uses one or the other of two formalized comments to discourage or discount premature commitments. If the respondent states that he hasn't seen some item or the issue before, the interviewer comments, "We're just as interested in your opinions whether you've seen this before or not." If the respondent reports he has seen some item or the issue before, the interviewer comments, "Suppose this were the first time you had seen it; does this item look especially interesting?" One or two uses of these comments is usually sufficient to get the respondent to report only his present interest in items and to keep him from committing himself in advance on possibly insufficient evidence.

After the respondent has inspected the issue, if he had made any previous claim of having seen an item or the issue before, a third standard comment is used to caution him against confusing items in the issue he just examined with similar items seen elsewhere: "As you know, similar items can appear in different magazines, newspapers, or on television. Just to keep the record straight, let me ask you . . . ." Then, the crucial readership question is asked of all respondents who examined the issue: "Now that we've been through the whole issue, are you sure whether or not you happened to look into this issue before?" Only those respondents who answer in the "certain affirmative" are counted as members of the issue's audience.

The number of editorial items which a person must examine in the interview before he can be sure whether or not he had looked into the issue before is unknown and varies from person to person. That is why the standard editorial interest audience technique shows substantially all the editorial material before asking the respondent whether he had looked into the issue before and prevents him from making premature commitments based on only one or a few of the issue's editorial items. The questioning on what items look interesting provides a reason for complete display of the issue and avoids focusing attention on the real objective until the respondent has full evidence for his decision. Finally, the emphasis on editorial opinions, the comments on the importance of these opinions regardless whether the issue was seen before, and the wording of the final question all contribute to removing the understandable tendency of some respondents to report what they consider usual or desirable behavior rather than actual behavior with respect to the particular issue studied.

By rotating the issues studied during the field period, estimates of the average issue audience can be made. The life of a copy of a particular issue of a magazine can last for an indefinite length of time. As long as a copy is "alive" it can generate new readers. However, for purposes of audience research, which studies particular issues, magazines are considered to have an active issue life. In practice, the active issue life of weeklies is 5.0 weeks, biweeklies 6.0 weeks, and monthlies approximately 10.7 weeks.

Cover Technique

The *cover* technique uses the cover of an issue, instead of the issue's editorial contents, for purposes of respondent recognition—that is, to determine whether he read the issue. In this technique no screening question is used; all respondents are shown every issue cover under study and are questioned about their readership of each issue. The Starch/Hooper organization employs this technique and claims that it has several important features:

It provides clear and simple identification of a specific issue about which the respondent is being asked to declare his readership status.
It provides a uniform basis for all magazines for the purpose of respondents' readership declarations. This basis is independent of the kinds of editorial items in the issue and the number of such items and therefore does not favor some types of publications over others where there may be differences in distinctiveness or quantity of editorial content.
Ease of administering the questioning procedure by the interviewer assures a high degree of adherence to the method. The interviewer is not tempted to seek shortcuts in order to maintain rapport.
The time required in obtaining readership information for a large number of publications is rather short and therefore there is small risk of inaccuracy of responses due to boredom of respondents or unwillingness to cooperate fully.[1]

Each respondent is questioned as follows: "Now I'm going to show you some magazine covers. As you look at each cover, will you please tell me if you, yourself, have looked into or read that particular issue, either at home or elsewhere?" The interviewer then displays the magazine cover and asks, "Did you read or look into this particular issue of . . . (magazine)?" The order of asking about magazines is rotated in a manner which gives all magazines an equal chance of being asked about in each position. Starch/Hooper studies examine about 80 magazines in an interview.

Critics of the cover technique claim that the display of only the cover can lead to confusion on the part of the respondent, who may make erroneous claims about readership. For example, it often happens that newsmagazines have the same subject on their respective covers. This is also true for women's magazines. Not long ago there was a short period of time when Jackie Kennedy Onassis was the cover subject on over 50 magazine issues. Some magazines, like the *Reader's Digest,* have covers which are difficult to distinguish from issue to issue. Many people feel that display of only the cover is not enough of an aid to recognition, especially to the infrequent reader.

Frequency Technique

The *frequency* technique, as a procedure for estimating average issue audiences, has been popularized by the Brand Rating Index organization. Brand Rating Index uses the technique in a self-administered questionnaire; that is, a questionnaire which the respondent fills out without the aid of an interviewer. This method, however, can be adapted so that the information can be collected

[1] Starch/Hooper *1970 Media Study* [17].

by means of personal face-to-face interviews, via the telephone, or in mail surveys. The Brand Rating Index questionnaire is personally placed by an interviewer, and the respondent fills it out at his own convenience. The Brand Rating Index service studies about 91 magazines.

Brand Rating Index has termed their procedure the *filter-recall* method. In their method, there is no rotation in the order of asking about magazines. Magazines published weekly are asked about first, followed by the biweekly magazines and then the monthly magazines. Due to the fact that many Sunday newspapers include a separate television program booklet, a separate question, following the weekly magazine question, is asked about *TV Guide*. The objective of this separate question is to eliminate any confusion that may exist between *TV Guide* and the newspaper television program booklets.

The questioning procedure for weeklies is as follows:

Below is a list of magazines that are put out once a week. Next to each magazine, please check the box that describes how many different issues of the magazine, if any, you personally have read or looked into in the last four weeks. This includes all issues of the magazine that you have looked into in the last four weeks, even if they came out some time ago, and you just got around to reading them in the last four weeks.

IF YOU DO NOT READ THE MAGAZINE CHECK THE FIRST BOX. IF YOU READ THE MAGAZINE NOW AND THEN, BUT HAVE NOT READ ANY IN THE LAST FOUR WEEKS, CHECK THE NEXT BOX. IF YOU HAVE READ THE MAGAZINE IN THE LAST FOUR WEEKS, CHECK THE BOX THAT TELLS HOW MANY ISSUES YOU HAVE READ OR LOOKED INTO IN THE LAST FOUR WEEKS.

TABLE 1   Example of Frequency Response Questionnaire Form

	Did Not Read Magazine	Read Now And Then But Not In Last 4 Weeks	In The Last 4 Weeks, I Read: 1 Issue	2 Issues	3 Issues	4 Issues
Magazine A	☐	☐	☐	☐	☐	☐
Magazine B	☐	☐	☐	☐	☐	☐
etc.						

The questioning procedure for biweeklies and monthlies is identical to that used for weeklies except the frame of reference is eight weeks for biweeklies and four months for monthlies.

In tabulating the average issue audience, each respondent is assigned a measure of probability with regard to his reading behavior of each magazine studied. This probability of reading is either 4/4, 3/4, 2/4, 1/4, or 0 depending upon whether the respondent read 4, 3, 2, 1, or 0 issues of the magazine during the stated period. In other words, the average issue audience is comprised of all individuals who read 4 issues, 3/4 of the individuals who read 3 issues, 1/2 of the individuals who read 2 issues, and 1/4 of the individuals who read 1 issue.

Whereas the editorial interest and the cover methods make an assumption regarding the active life of an issue, the frequency technique does not. It is conceivable that a person might have read a year-old issue during the stated time period. Since the frequency technique counts a reader regardless of the age of the issue he read, this method should produce larger audience estimates than the editorial interest or cover methods.

Critics of the frequency technique point out what they consider to be two major problems with the technique. First, they claim since no memory aid is given to the respondent, his ability to recall accurately his reading behavior during a long time period is somewhat dubious. Many people may have looked into more than four issues during the stated time period, and they may be confused by the questionnaire which only allows recording of reading up to four issues. The respondent may also be confused whether the week in which the questionnaire is filled out counts as one of the four or eight weeks. If it does, is there a difference in the frame of reference for someone filling it out on Monday as opposed to a person doing so on Saturday? Even if the respondent is not confused and is able to perform prodigious feats of memory, the technique for magazines contains a statistical bias.

Magazines, because they are space media, may be read over several days spread over several weeks. By definition, a person counts only once in the audience, regardless of the number of days or weeks he reads the issue. The four-week, eight-week, or four-month time period for a given respondent actually represents a random sample of one consecutive four-week, one consecutive eight-week, or one consecutive four-month period of all possible such periods. Respondents interviewed in the first week of the field period are statistically equivalent to those interviewed the second week, the third week, and so on.

Now let us examine a person with respect to his reading behavior of magazine A.

Week 1	Week 2	Week 3	Week 4	Week 5	Week 6
Read issue I	Read issue I	Did not read	Did not read	Did not read	Did not read

When the person is interviewed in week 5, he reports he read 1 out of 4 issues of magazine A and thereby qualifies to come into its audience with a 1/4 probability. When this person (actually his statistical counterpart) is interviewed in week 6, he also reports he read 1 out of 4 issues of magazine A; and he too qualifies to come into its audience with a 1/4 probability. What has happened is that the frequency technique counts multiple readings of the same issue as audience insofar as they occur in different weeks for weekly magazines, different two-week periods for biweeklies, and different months for monthlies. Due to the counting of the particular type of multiple reading, the frequency technique should generate larger audience estimates than the recognition methods, which study particular issues and count a reader only once regardless of the number of days or weeks he read the issue.

Comparing Editorial Interest versus Frequency Method

In 1967 *Life* magazine sponsored a study, in consultation with the Advertising Research Foundation, to compare audience estimates established by the editorial interest method versus the frequency method. This study was conducted by Alfred Politz Media Studies and was entitled *An Experimental Study Comparing Magazine Audiences as Determined by Two Questioning Procedures*. The major findings of that study were that across all six weekly/biweekly magazines studied, the frequency estimate of audience exceeded the editorial interest estimate of audience by an absolute margin of 1.3 percentage points (18.1 percent versus 16.8 percent) and a relative margin of 7.7 percent. The chances are less than 1 in 39 that the margin of difference is due to chance sampling variation only.

Across all eight monthly publications studied, the frequency estimate of audience exceeded the editorial interest estimate by an absolute margin of 2.7 percentage points (23.4 percent versus 20.7 percent) and a relative margin of 13.1 percent. The chances are less than 1 in 1,000 that the margin of difference is due to chance sampling variation only.

The relative margin by which frequency estimates of audience exceeded editorial interest estimates of audience was almost twice as great for the monthlies (15.3 percent) as for the weeklies/biweeklies (7.7 percent). The chances are less than 1 in 17 that these differential margins are due to chance sampling variation only.

Another important finding was the range of 2 to 40 percent in the relative amount that the frequency estimates exceeded the editorial interest estimate.

Another unaided recall measurement recently has been popularized by Target Group Index (TGI). This method is commonly referred to as the *recent reading* technique. Target Group Index uses the technique in a self-administered questionnaire. As in the "frequency" method, the "recent reading" technique can be accomplished by other forms of data collection. Target Group Index covers over 120 magazines in a given interview.

The recent reading questioning procedure determines for weekly magazines readership of any issue in the previous week, for biweeklies readership of any issue in the previous two weeks, and for monthlies readership of any issue in the month before the interview. In other words, the technique establishes whether any reading has occurred during the publishing interval of the magazine. A positive response classifies the respondent as a reader of the "average issue."

Target Group Index does not rotate the order of asking about magazines. It first studies weeklies, then biweeklies, followed by monthlies. Within each group the magazines are arranged alphabetically. Critics of the recent reading technique use arguments similar to those about the frequency method to point out the weaknesses in the procedure. Those who favor the technique point out the simplicity of administering the interview and the economics of the total study. However, it is important to note that the repetition of the questioning procedure may lead to respondent boredom and fatigue, especially considering that television program data and newspaper readership are collected in the same interview. As Table 2 points out, Target Group Index uses the frequency method to provide the input to estimate the reach and frequency of multi-issue campaigns.

NEWSPAPERS

Audiences of weekly newspapers are generally estimated by the editorial interest or frequency technique. When the editorial interest method is employed, the newspaper is studied at an average age of 2.5 weeks. The preparation of the issue displayed to the respondent for purposes of recognition is slightly different than that of magazines. This difference arises from the makeup of the newspaper, insofar as it contains many more pages containing both editorial and advertising material.

Audiences of weekday editions of daily newspapers are generally estimated by the *yesterday reading* technique, a specialized extension of the *recent reading* method. Use of the editorial interest technique to measure audiences of daily weekday newspapers is virtually impossible because most newspapers have different editions on a given day. The interviewer might be displaying the early edition and the respondent might have been exposed to the late edition, which had a different headline or a different first page or contained

TABLE 2

Question 1

Weekly	Have You Looked At Any Copy in The Past Week?		Where Did You Read It?		If You Have How Much Did You Look At?			
	Yes	No	Home	Outside	About 1/4	About 1/2	About 3/4	Almost All
Magazine A								
Magazine B								
.								
.								
.								

Question 2

Weekly	About How Many Issues Do You Look At In An Average Month?				
	Less Than One	One	Two	Three	Four
Magazine A					
Magazine B					
.					
.					
.					

coverage of late sports. The frequency technique has been employed in many audience studies of weekday daily newspapers.

A weekday daily newspaper is considered to have a life of one day. Therefore determining how many people read on a given day is synonymous with the average issue audience.

The yesterday reading technique is a self-appraisal method. If a person has read a specific paper on a specific day, then to whatever extent the person considers himself a reader, the method accepts him as such. (This is, of course, true of the frequency technique.) The shortcoming of this definition is that it provides many opportunities for respondents to rationalize. People tend to overclaim reading newspapers which carry high intellectual prestige and to understate reading of newspapers with low intellectual prestige. By means of a few psychological devices, these under- and overstatements based on rationalization can be prevented.

The first question in the procedure, "Have you looked into or seen a copy of . . . (newspaper) in the last seven days?" allows the respondent to "blow off steam" and makes it easy for him to give a yes answer. The next audience question, "Not counting today, when was the last time you looked into a copy of a weekday edition of . . . (newspaper)?" by the way it is structured, also tends to eliminate rationalizations. By saying "not counting today," the respondent may reply, "I read it today (prestige), but not counting this I read it three days ago." Only people who say "yesterday" are counted as members of the audience.

The yesterday reading technique puts certain restrictions on how the day's interviewing is conducted and on the sample design. Since "yesterday" must be a day on which the newspaper is published, interviewing should only be conducted on Tuesday through Saturday. Probability sampling designs may specify a sample of individuals in *time* as well as in space (geographic). The *not at home* plan is a probability procedure for drawing a sample in *time:* each individual's probability of selection is proportional to his frequency of being at home. A callback plan seeks to make each individual's probability of selection in *time* equal to one (unity). This is accomplished by making repeat (usually up to six) attempts to secure an interview with the individual. Studies which, for reason of response accuracy, limit each individual recall of activities to "yesterday" must use a not at home plan. To avoid bias in the measurements of yesterday behavior, the interview calls must be randomly timed. For example, consider the case of a person who reads a newspaper on Monday, is out of town on Tuesday—the designated day of interview, and is home for interview on Wednesday. When interviewed on a callback plan on Wednesday about his yesterday reading, he is a nonreader; whereas in a not at home plan, he would have been accounted for in an unbiased manner. Syndicated services which presently measure audiences of newspapers with the yesterday reading technique employ callback plans.

The nature of the questioning procedure for the yesterday reading technique is such that data collection may be accomplished either by personal face-to-face interviews, or via the telephone. By spreading the interview equally over many days, the audience estimates generated are labeled average issue audience. Interviewing equal numbers of respondents each day is important, especially if there are big variations in the day-to-day circulation of the newspaper.

Estimates of weekend or Sunday newspapers are made with the frequency technique or with an unaided recall procedure similar in nature to the yesterday method. Again, a screening question is used to avoid putting pressure on the respondent and the readership question is a version of "Just thinking about last Sunday's ———— (newspaper), did you happen to look into or read any part of it?"

TELEVISION

Although it is possible to estimate television or radio audiences by a recognition method using a playback of the telecast or time segment, this procedure is very impractical. Therefore all techniques (except the electronic one) that measure television and radio audiences are some form of unaided recall method. Since telecasts and time segments generate their audiences during a specific time period, it is possible to control the interval between behavior and interview in an effort to reduce respondent memory failures.

Yesterday Viewing Technique

Execution of the yesterday technique to determine viewing or nonviewing may be done by means of personal face-to-face interviews or via the telephone. Essentially the same questioning procedure employed for newspapers is used for television programs. Practically speaking, the only difference between the two is a longer interview for television because there are many more television programs on a day than newspapers. Also, many studies attempt to estimate not only the audience of a given telecast but its quarter-hour by quarter-hour components. The screening question or the aid to recall question in the procedure generally is: "Just thinking about yesterday, from the time you woke up until the time you finished breakfast, did you happen to look at or watch any television?" After helping the respondent reconstruct yesterday, questions then are asked about viewing specific programs and time periods.

Roster Recall

The yesterday technique, while providing the minimum recall period between behavior and interview, restricts the number of different telecasts (only those on yesterday) for which viewing behavior may be obtained from a given respondent.

This means that to obtain equally reliable estimates, in the statistical sense, for telecasts on each of the seven days of the week, the yesterday technique requires seven times more interviews than when the same person reports viewing behavior for an entire week of telecasts. In addition, the yesterday technique, since the respondent is questioned only about a given day, does not permit estimates of duplication of audience between programs on different days of the week.

To overcome these two problems, many studies employ an audience technique known as *roster recall*. This technique, self-appraisal in nature, asks the respondent to recall viewing behavior for the previous seven days. Programs are arranged according to day of the week and the respondent is asked about yesterday, the day before yesterday, and so on. Although the response error is unknown, it probably increases as the period of time between day of behavior and day of interview increases. To avoid this kind of positioning bias, interviews are conducted every day of the week to ensure that, on the average, the interval between behavior and interview is equal for all days of the week. Due to the length of the interval between behavior and recall, it is very difficult to estimate quarter-hour audiences by the roster recall method.

Frequency Technique

The statistical problems inherent in the frequency technique applied to magazines are not present when it is used to estimate television audiences. This is because television is a time medium. Since a given telecast appears in only one time period, exposure to that telecast must, by definition, be the first exposure. In terms of statistical theory, audience estimates according to the frequency technique are considered to be unbiased. Again, due to the interval between behavior and interview, there is a problem with response memory failures when the frequency technique attempts to estimate quarter-hour by quarter-hour television audiences.

Coincidental Method

Since all the viewing of an average minute of a telecast occurs in a given minute, it is possible to estimate this audience by coincidental observations, that is, observations coinciding with a given point in time. Coincidental observations may either be conducted by personal face-to-face interviews or via the telephone. In this technique, households or people not at home are counted as not viewing. Actually, the measurement is a recall method since it asks people about behavior which took place the instant the doorbell was rung or the instant the telephone was rung.

Generally, the questioning sequence starts with a television ownership question followed by whether the set or sets were on, which channel was turned to, and who was in the room watching. Since the measurement refers to only one point in time (average minute) of a given telecast, very large samples are needed if the object is to provide audience estimates of many different telecasts. The estimates from "coincidental" measurements only provide average minute audience and not total telecast audience, that is, all or any part of the telecast. Average minute audience is a more stringent measurement than average telecast audience. For example, suppose there are four viewers of telecast A, an hour program, each of the people viewing it exactly 30 minutes. The average telecast audience is 4.0 and the average minute audience is 120 minutes divided by total telecast minutes or 2.0 people.

Audimeter[2]

The Audimeter could be considered as a continuous coincidental measurement. The Audimeter is an electronic device attached to a television set which automatically records, on a continuous basis, television set tunings. Since the device automatically records the channel tuned, the measurements derived from its recording are inherently free of response error insofar as questioning of respondents is not necessary to determine viewing behavior. While audience estimates are not in terms of people, this procedure does produce audience estimates based on television sets tuned and households. Both average minute and average telecast audience estimates may be provided from this technique. In addition, since the device is installed on a given set for a long period of time, duplicated and cumulative audience estimates can easily be tabulated. In another sense, the Audimeter can be considered a diary method, since it keeps a continuous record of set tunings.

For economic reasons, Audimeters must be employed in a continuing panel operation. Inherent in any panel operation are advantages and disadvantages. A panel's principal advantages are cost savings, its ability to provide trend information, and its ability to provide a multiple of possible combinations of data for analytical purposes. Its disadvantages stem from the possibility that the people who accept panel membership may be different in their demographic characteristics and life-style from those people who refused to become panel members. In addition, panel members may be "conditioned," that is, they change their behavior because of panel membership. See Section II, Part B, Chapter 10 for a further discussion of these questions.

Diary Method

The *diary* method involves either a household record or an individual record. If a household record is used, one member—generally the female head—is designated as the person who is supposed to record the viewing behavior of other household members. This may prove difficult. An individual or personal record is one in which the designated respondent records his own viewing activity. Since a diary is probably not filled out at the exact time of behavior, many people feel it is a recall method.

[2] Reg. U.S. Pat. Off., A. C. Nielsen.

The diary or record format itself may be a key element in obtaining accurate reporting by respondents. Diaries are generally structured by day parts—for example, morning—and by quarter-hours within day parts. The diary should contain ample room for clear reporting and should contain reminders of the definition that the study employs as viewing. Adequate space should also be provided for recording nonviewing for each time period studied. This accomplishes two things: first, it distinguishes between nonviewing and nonreporting and, second, it attempts to avoid exaggeration by letting the respondent know that both viewing and nonviewing are important.

Diaries may be placed with the respondent either personally by an interviewer or via the mail. Personal placement is preferred since it yields considerably higher rates of cooperation and it permits personal instruction on how to maintain the diary. To avoid conditioning or artificial changes in respondent behavior that may occur at the beginning of the record-keeping period, it is a good idea not to include the first day or two in the tabulations. To ensure maximum cooperation and to stimulate accurate recordings, several contacts should be made with the respondent during the record-keeping period.

Then length of time a respondent keeps the diary varies from study to study and is a function of costs and the kinds of data desired. Some studies require that respondents keep a diary for only one day and other studies have been known to have a respondent keep a diary for several years. Most studies employing a diary technique involve a panel operation and therefore take on a panel's advantages and disadvantages. The diary method estimates average telecast audiences. Duplication and cumulation data are also obtained by the diary method.

RADIO

All the techniques employed to estimate telecast audiences can be employed to measure radio audiences. The Audimeter, although not now in use for radio, was originally devised for radio and later adapted for television. Generally, the measurement units for radio are time segments, for example 9 to 9:15 A.M. However, recent studies have been done where the unit of measurement was network programs. Because of the fractionalization of radio, that is, the availability of a large number of stations to listen to in a given area, large samples are generally required to obtain reliable estimates.

Coincidental measurements, including the Audimeter, are impractical since a large portion of radio listening occurs out of the home, especially during driving time and summer beach days. For this reason, coincidental measurements would severely underestimate total listening.

ACCUMULATIVE AND REPEAT AUDIENCES

Until now we have been discussing the concept of average audience defined as the number of people exposed to all or any part of a particular issue, time segment, or telecast. The audiences reached by a series of issues, time segments, or telecasts of a medium build up as the number of issues, time segments, or telecasts increases. For example, suppose that one issue of a magazine reaches 1 million people and that a second issue also reaches 1 million people. (In fact, every issue reaches 1 million people or every issue is the average issue.) The question then is how many people are reached by two issues of the magazine? Two extreme situations are possible:

1. The *same* 1 million persons are reached by both issues.

2. The persons reached by the second issue are completely *different* from the persons reached by the first issue.

In the first situation, the number of different persons reached by the two issues is 1 million—the same as the number reached by one issue. Each person is a "repeat." Each person reached was exposed twice to the magazine, since he was reached by both issues.

In the second situation, the number of different persons reached by two issues is 2 million—the 1 million reached by issue one and the 1 million different people reached by issue two. In this case there are no repeats. The audience of a single or average issue was 1 million, but the accumulative audience of two issues was 2 million since all new persons were added by the second issue.

In reality, of course, the true situation lies somewhere between the two extremes just mentioned. Some of the persons reached by issue one would also be reached by issue two. It is important for the advertiser to know how many persons reached by one issue, time segment, or telecast are also reached by a second, third, fourth, and so on. He must know whether a medium makes repeat impressions on the same people or whether succeeding issues, time segments, or telecasts accumulate new audiences.

Consider a more realistic situation of hypothetical media A and B. Both, let us say, reach the same number of people—1 million—with issue one. Then, by definition, both also reach 1 million people with issue two. However, here is the difference: The accumulative audience of medium A is 1.8 million and the accumulative audience of medium B is 1.2 million. A has more accumulation than B. However, medium A has a repeat audience of 200,000 and medium B has 800,000; that is, B has more repetition than A.

From these examples, it is evident that two media with the same number of people with an average issue, time segment, or telecast can have very different accumulative and very different repeat audiences. Conversely, two media which reach a different number of people with an average issue, time segment, or telecast may reach the same accumulative or the same repeat audiences. Many other combinations are possible and, in addition, both repetition and accumulation continue as the number of issues, time segments, or telecasts increases.

Duplication

In a sense there are two kinds of duplication. First, as previously discussed, there is the intraduplication pattern of a particular medium—for example, the duplication or repetition existing between different issues of the same publication. This type of duplication is expressed as accumulative and repeat audiences. The second kind of duplication is the intermedia duplication, or the duplication that exists between different media vehicles. This type of duplication is expressed as the net unduplicated audience of a combination of media.

To illustrate intermedia duplication, let us consider hypothetical media A and B. Medium A reaches 1 million people with an average or single issue. Medium B reaches 800,000 people with an average or single issue. The chart shows the duplicated and the net unduplicated audiences obtained by combining an average issue of each medium.

Thus 200,000 of 1 million readers of an average issue of Medium A also read an average issue of medium B. Conversely, 200,000 readers of an average issue of medium B also read an average issue of medium A. The 200,000 readers of both are termed the average issue duplicated audience of medium A and medium B. The 800,000 readers of A who do not read B and the 600,000

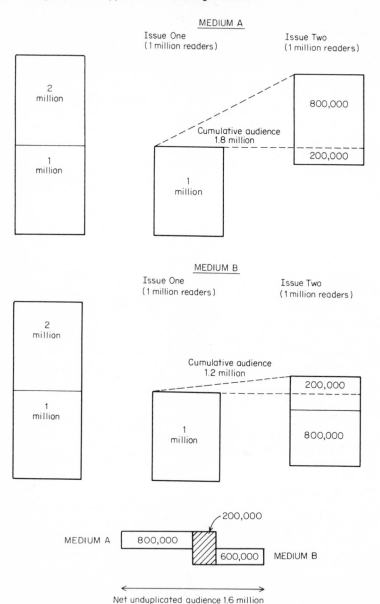

readers of B who do not read A are termed the "exclusive" audience of the respective media.   The 1,600,000 readers who read either A or B or both are termed the net unduplicated audience.

STATISTICAL PROCEDURES FOR ESTIMATING AUDIENCES

To illustrate how estimates of various types of audiences are made statistically, let us again use hypothetical medium A and medium B and the reading behavior of five people with these media.   In the following table, R means that the person read the issue and NR means the person did not read the issue.

TABLE 3   Average Issue Audience for Media A and B*

Medium A	Person					Total
	A	B	C	D	E	
Issue one........	R	R	NR	NR	NR	2R
Issue two........	R	NR	NR	NR	NR	1R
Issue three......	R	NR	R	NR	NR	2R
Issue four.......	R	R	R	R	NR	4R
Total..........	4R	2R	2R	1R	...	9R

Medium B	Person					Total
	A	B	C	D	E	
Issue one........	NR	R	NR	NR	NR	1R
Issue two........	NR	R	R	NR	NR	2R
Issue three......	NR	NR	R	NR	NR	1R
Issue four.......	R	NR	R	NR	NR	2R
Total..........	1R	2R	3R	...	...	6R

* The average issue audience of medium A could be obtained by summing the audience of each issue and dividing by four: $(2 + 1 + 2 + 4)/4 = 2.25$. For medium B the same calculation can be done: $(1 + 2 + 1 + 2)/4 = 1.50$.

Another and simpler method of estimating average issue audience is to assign each respondent a probability according to the number of issues he read out of the number studied and to include that person in the average issue audience according to that probability.   (In essence, it is these probabilities that the frequency technique attempts to determine.)   Now let us examine our five people on this basis (Table 4):

TABLE 4   Probability of Reading Media A and B

Person	Medium A	Medium B
A	4/4	1/4
B	2/4	2/4
C	2/4	3/4
D	1/4	0/4
E	0/4	0/4

Summing the reading probabilities for A and B, we determine that the average issue audience is 2.25 and 1.50 respectively.   In this same example, the cumulative audience, which is defined as the number of people exposed to at least one issue in a series of issues, is 4.00 for medium A and 3.00 for medium

B.   Remember, the cumulative audience counts each reader equally, regardless of the number of issues to which he was exposed.

The repeat audience, which is actually a frequency distribution, is defined as the number of people exposed to a stated number of issues out of the number studied.

TABLE 5   Estimation of Repeat Audience

Exposed to exactly	Medium A	Medium B
0 out of 4 issues. . .	1, person E	2, persons D and E
1 out of 4 issues. . .	1, person D	1, person A
2 out of 4 issues. . .	2, persons B and C	1, person B
3 out of 4 issues. . .	0	1, person C
4 out of 4 issues. . .	1, person A	0

The average number of issues a reader is exposed to in a series of issues is obtained by dividing the cumulative audience by the average issue audience. This statistic is often referred to as the average frequency. For medium A the average frequency is 4.00/2.25 or 2.22 and for medium B the average frequency is 3.00/1.50 or 2.00.

Another statistic often used by media analysts is gross audience of a series of issues. The gross audience is defined as the sum of the average issue audiences in the series. In the previous examples, the gross audience of medium A is (2.25) × (4) or 9.00 and the gross audience of medium B is (1.50) × (4) or 6.00.

The net unduplicated audience (defined as the number of people exposed to at least one of a combination of media) of one issue of medium A and one issue of medium B could be obtained by calculating the average of the results produced by all possible combinations of issues of the respective media. Since each person was interviewed on four issues of medium A and four issues of medium B, there are 16 possible combinations of one issue of each medium for each person. This tabulating procedure can prove very tedious, so instead we do it by means of probabilities.

The probability that a given person is in the net unduplicated audience of one issue of a combination of media is equal to 1.00 minus the product of the probability that he is *not* in the audience of average issue of the respective media. For example, person C has a 2/4 chance of being in the average issue audience of medium A and a 3/4 chance of being in the average issue audience of medium B. Therefore the probability that he is in the net unduplicated audience of one issue of A and one issue of B is 1.00 − (2/4 × 1/4) or 14/16. Similarly, this probability is 16/16 for person A, 12/16 for person B, 4/16 for person D, and 0/16 for person E.

The number of people in a one issue net unduplicated audience of medium A and medium B is 2.88, which is more than either medium by itself but less than the gross of the combination (3.75). The net unduplicated audience also generates repeat audiences—people exposed to both issues and people exposed to one or the other medium.

Estimates of cumulative audiences of less than the observed data and levels of net unduplicated audiences within the observed data can be made according to the laws of probabilities. Cumulative and net unduplicated audiences beyond the observed data require some mathematical model. At the present time, the most popular models are the Metheringham method and the beta distribution method [6].

ESTIMATING AUDIENCE DUPLICATION

Television

In a 1969 paper, Goodhardt and Ehrenberg presented a mathematical method for estimating the net unduplicated audiences of pairs of telecasts when such estimates are not available from the collected data. Evidence on the reliability of their procedure comes from data analyzed for telecasts appearing on different days of the week in two-channel markets. The underlying basis for their model rests on the principle that the duplicated audience, r_{st}, for two telecasts s and t on different days of the week can be estimated from the ratings r_s and r_t for the two telecasts. Accordingly, $r_{st} = Kr_s r_t$, where K is a constant for all telecast pairs on the two days on the two channels under investigation. Actually, K is an empirical average correction factor determined by comparing the observed duplication and the unadjusted estimated duplication:

$$K = 100 \left(\frac{E_{rst}}{E_r E_{rst}} \right)$$

where E_{rst} is the sum of the observed duplications and E_{rs} and E_{rt} are the sum of the ratings or gross rating points on the two days.

Interestingly, Goodhardt and Ehrenberg found that for telecasts of different channels, K, for all practical purposes, was approximately 1.00. They concluded, therefore, that the chances of viewing telecasts on different days of the week on different channels are generally independent of program content and that the amount of duplication is a function of program size. On the other hand, their analyses found that K for telecasts on different days of the week on the same channel was larger than 1.00. From this finding, they concluded that there is, to a small degree, channel loyalty. Although their paper does not suggest reasons for channel loyalty, part of this loyalty may be a function of the clarity of video reception among channels in a given market.

Magazines

The first published model for projecting audiences beyond the observed data was presented by Alfred Politz Research in a study, sponsored by *Life* magazine in 1953, entitled *A Study of Four Media*. The projection model estimated audiences of seven to thirteen issues based on observed data of one to six issues.

In 1962, J. M. Agostini published a method for estimating the accumulative audience on n issues of a magazine, knowing only the average issue and the accumulative audience of two issues. Agostini's model essentially handles only a single vehicle.

Subsequently, Richard A. Metheringham suggested two models, a single vehicle and a multimedia model. The single vehicle model involves the beta distribution, which has repeatedly reproduced observed data. Essentially, the multimedia model, by an averaging process, combines all media in the analysis and treats them as a single vehicle, using the mathematics of the beta distribution. This multimedia model tends to overstate reach (cumulative audience) and understate average frequency. Furthermore, the model provides a smooth frequency distribution which does not look like the curve of observed data.

These models led to the development of various models commonly referred to as multivariate beta models. These models, while restricted to analyses of only five to six vehicles, yield close approximations of observed data. Related to mathematical models, though not strictly considered as such, is the area of simulation. A pioneer in this field was the now defunct Simulmatics Corp. In this area, Jerome D. Greene has recently suggested an approach termed *personal probability*. In this approach each person is randomly assigned a personal probability for each medium by frequency class. This assignment is controlled so that across the entire sample the probabilities distribute exactly as the computed distributions from which they are chosen. Calculations of reach and frequency are generated then by the binomial distribution.

It must be noted that the observed data against which all models have been compared were collected in the 1950s. Media behavior in the 1950s does not necessarily reflect current media behavior. Hence, data provided by projective models may be leading the media analyst astray.

SUMMARY

As is evident, there are various methods, even within the structure of a single study, of estimating audiences of media. The direct comparability of these estimates for purposes of intermedia evaluations is a matter of judgment on the part of the media analyst. It can be argued that on the basis of audience, magazines are unduly penalized when compared to other media. The basis for this argument is that magazines, because they are space media, can provide repeat exposures for a single advertising insertion to the same reader. These repeat exposures, which are provided without repeat payment, are valuable to the advertiser. Repeat exposures occur not only over the course of several days of reading but also within a given day of reading. Newspapers have the latter benefit but not the former, and the advertiser is required to pay for both these types of repeat exposure in radio and television.

The comparability of audience estimates generated by the same technique for different vehicles within a given media form is also a matter of judgment. Since no requirement is placed on the amount of reading that must take place before an individual qualifies as a member of the audience, is a reader equal to another reader? For example, it has been demonstrated that primary readers, readers in households that subscribe to or bought the magazine at the newsstand, retain more of the advertising, take more action with the advertising, and, in general, are more involved with the medium than pass-along readers. Similar evidence exists about the in-home readers versus out-of-home readers.

Is the cover-to-cover reader, whose behavior and attitude are different from the skimmer reader, worth more to the advertiser? Is a magazine whose average issue audience comprises a greater concentration of regular readers, that is, those readers who have the greatest rapport with the magazine, worth more to the advertiser than a magazine which has less concentration of this type of reader?

Evaluation of the validity and reliability of audience estimates cannot be done solely on the technique employed to generate these estimates but must also be done in the context of other factors related to the survey design. These factors include sample design and selection, sample execution, length of interview and how it might affect responses, completion rate and whether the sample represents the population, training of interviewers, coding and editing procedures, methods of accounting for nonresponses, tabulating methods, and sampling error or tolerances. The analyst must evaluate the entire survey in order to judge the validity of its findings.

Another judgment the analyst must make is whether the advertising value is different for an individual when he is exposed to a series of advertising messages in a given medium as opposed to when he is exposed to the same series in several media. In other words, are the two kinds of duplication, intermedium and intramedium, equivalent in advertising value? Is the ability to retrieve the impact of the previous exposure to advertising campaigns enhanced when the present exposure takes place in the same environment (medium) as the previous exposures?

To be sure, audience is only one characteristic of a medium. Other information is needed to evaluate the medium which offers the greatest likelihood of return on investment.

REFERENCES

1. Agostini, J. M., "Analysis of Magazine Accumulative Audience," *Journal of Advertising Research*, vol. 2, December 1962.

1a. American Market Research Bureau, *Target Group Index Plan*, New York: American Market Research Bureau, 1972.

2. Brand Rating Research Corp., *1970 Basic Report on Heaviness of Use of Products and Demographic Characteristics of Adult Men with Different Levels of Exposures to Major Media Types*, New York: Brand Rating Research Corp., 1970.

3. Green, J. D., "Personal Media Probabilities," *Journal of Advertising Research*, vol. 10, October 1970.

4. Goodhardt, G. J., and Ehrenberg, A. S. C., "Duplication of Television Viewing between and within Channels," *Journal of Marketing Research*, vol. 6, May 1969.

5. Lucas, D. B., and Britt, S. H., *Advertising Psychology and Research*, New York: McGraw-Hill, 1950.

6. Metheringham, R. A., "Measuring the Net Cumulative Coverage of a Print Campaign," *Journal of Advertising Research*, vol. 4, December 1964.

7. A. C. Nielsen Company, *Nielsen Television Index, Technical Appendix*, New York: A. C. Nielsen Company, 1970.

8. Alfred Politz Research Inc., *A Study of Four Media, Their Accumulative and Repeat Audiences*, New York: Time, Inc., 1953.

9. ———, *Life Study of Consumer Expenditures*, New York: Time, Inc., 1958.

10. ———, *The Audiences and Advertising Page Exposures of Twelve Magazines*, New York: Politz Media Service, 1966.

11. ———, *Characteristics of Readers and Non-Readers of the New York Mirror*, New York: The New York Mirror, 1951.

12. ———, *A Study of the Accumulative Audience of Life*, New York: Time, Inc., 1950.

13. Schreiber, R. J., "The Metheringham Method for Media Mix: An Evaluation," *Journal of Advertising Research*, vol. 9, June 1969.

14. ———, "Probability Assignment for the Simulation of Media Reach and Frequency," *Journal of Advertising Research*, vol. 8, June 1968.

15. Simmons, W. R., & Associates Research, Inc., *Selective Markets and the Media Reaching Them—1970 Reach and Frequency Report, Technical Appendix*, New York: W. R. Simmons and Associates Research, Inc., 1970.

16. Simmons, W. R., & Associates Research, Inc., *Selective Markets and the Media Reaching Them, 1970 Demographic Report Technical Appendix*, New York: W. R. Simmons and Associates Research, Inc., 1970.

17. Starch/Hooper, *1970 Media Study, Technical Appendix*, New York: Series 1, Report 1, Daniel Starch & Staff Inc./C. E. Hooper Inc., 1970.

Advertising Research

Chapter 2

Copy Testing

CORNELIUS DuBOIS *Consultant; Advertising Research Foundation, New York, New York*

Since the problems of testing advertising copy and the techniques for doing it are similar to the problems and the techniques discussed throughout this handbook, this chapter shuns the duplication of effort that would result from detailed descriptions. Instead it seeks to place copy testing in a perspective both of advertising and of research, to provide a framework for looking at methods, and to present a rationale for choosing among them.

BEFORE THERE IS ANYTHING TO TEST

It has been all too fashionable for too many years to debate the question of copy research versus creative judgment. Yet the true question is not of the either-or variety but a *how* type of question—that is, not whether the advertiser should rely on either research or creative judgment but how research can be used to help creative judgment (remembering that copy research includes much that must precede copy testing).

Indeed the first, and perhaps most important, contribution of research to copy is made before copy appears on paper. This contribution is the collection and interpretation of basic facts on which a sound copy strategy can be based —not just a compilation of facts but an interpretive summary of them which can help our understanding in four fundamental areas.

First, we must fully understand the facts about the product we are selling. We must define what the product is physically; what it is designed to do for people; how it works; how it compares physically and functionally with its competitors; how it is sized, priced, packaged; and what the trends and developments in the area of product progress are, both for our client's brand and for competitors.

Second, we must completely understand the market. We need to know and understand the people to whom we are selling. How many are there? Who are they? Where are they? What is the difference, if any, between those who use much of the product and those who use only a little? What is our market share for this product, our competitive situation in the home as well as over the counter? Emphasis is needed on the people using our own brand—their numbers, their characteristics, their locations, how they use the product.

In characterizing people, we will, of course, be concerned with such standard descriptive labels as their ages, incomes, education levels. Ideally, we attempt to define personality characteristics of our users. And remembering that the marketplace is constantly changing, we must keep track of trends and developments.

The third major area requiring understanding also has to do with people, in this case with their attitudes and motivations. Here, the first thing we need to know is the direct interaction between people and our product. We need to know how they perceive its benefits; how they see its differences from other brands. We need to know their satisfactions and dissatisfactions and loyalties for our brand and for competitors. We need to know people's direct reasons for using or not using our brand or product, and we need to be able to draw at least reasonable inferences about our brand's psychological benefits and potential emotional appeals. Here too, we need to know what trends and developments have been occurring in brand reputations and images, what impact new products and new developments have on consumer attitudes.

Fourth is the advertising environment in which we compete. We need to know what competitors are claiming, with what weight and through what media. Unless we are dealing with a totally new brand, we need to review every now and then our own past budgets, media emphasis, and copy emphasis. We must understand the taboos, the restrictions, and the mandatory inclusions that apply to this particular brand. We need to review whatever evidence we have of the effectiveness or ineffectiveness of our own and of our competitors' past advertising.

With understanding of our product, of our market, of the mental or emotional interaction of product and people, and of the advertising environment, the agency can define the problems and opportunities, establish advertising objectives, and build the specifications for advertising strategy. Then what?

Sometimes it will be clear that there is only one probably productive direction for the copy. Usually there are several directions. The research department may be called upon to test them and retest them until, ideally, the agency arrives at one strong idea (which may or may not be a direct selling argument).

In this continuing search for knowledge, the ideal situation is one in which the researcher and the copywriter work closely together, each stimulating the other with hypotheses and facts, with generalizations and further questions.

In this context and in this ideal situation, copy testing is a positive help. During the testing of rough or semifinished ideas, there is no real conflict between the writer and the researchers—or between agency and client for that matter. It is only later, when it becomes necessary to test the execution of the agency's ads, that toes begin to hurt—whether stepped on or not.

Some copywriters have been conditioned by experience to look on copy tests as the obscene daubing of a beautiful ad with queer numbers or the strangling of an infant idea with chains of statistics. Yet agency management and client management both need evaluation of the advertising as assurance that advertising dollars are being spent effectively.

Sometimes, but not always, such assurance can be provided by market testing. Sometimes it requires research on ads that are already running and sometimes the reassurance of pretesting.

At these stages of more formal testing there is the least agreement on methodology among researchers. There are literally scores of techniques available to the copy tester, some good for one purpose, some good for another, none of them foolproof. He must choose with caution.

SOME ANCIENT HISTORY

Before we look at methods now in use, it would be wise to inject a bit of perspective.

I am indebted to Roger Barton (whose memory began long before he was born) for evidence that attempts to provide really valid pretests of advertising are not as new as some of us like to think. In his files are references back to 1896, when Harlow Gale of the University of Minnesota tried to measure the relative values of illustration and text in advertising. No doubt a still longer memory and a still more voluminous file could pick up references before that.

Before World War I, H. I. Hollingsworth and E. K. Strong had been busy devising what they called the Order-of-Merit test, more commonly called a consumer jury test today. They recognized the same pitfalls in their method that people point out nowadays.

Before the market crash of 1929, Daniel Starch had expanded the method; Walter Mann and staff were actively promoting it; and S. H. Giellerup, Kenneth Groesbeck, and others were crusading for more ad testing to remove guesswork. Dr. Starch again and Harold Rudolph were separately analyzing the responses to mail order advertising (correspondence schools, insurance companies, and others), in a search for universal truths that would say whether big ads were better than little ones, right-hand pages better than left-hand ones, big pictures better than small ones, and so on.

Before the Depression was over, John Caples had established the value of the newspaper split run for testing specific headline appeals and selling ideas; Starch and Gallup separately had developed a recognition method of testing ads for their reading and noting or attention and interest values; Stanton and Lazarsfeld had developed their Program Analyzer gadget for studying the interest value of programs and commercials on the radio; and Horace Schwerin of NBC, L. M. Clark and C. E. Hooper, and many others were actively developing methods in various directions. Even the eye-movement camera, heralded as something new in the late 1960s, was being used in the 1930s at Purdue University to try to spot those elements in an ad or an illustration that captured and held attention.

A bow must be made even to the Townsend brothers, who proclaimed that advertisements succeeded or failed according to how many of their magical 27 points were embodied in the copy and layout. For them, a pretest consisted of submitting an advertisement for diagnosis and scoring.

As far back as 1930, Kenneth Groesbeck of H. K. McCann Co. was proclaiming that pretests under "laboratory" conditions were not enough, that pretests of sales effect were also important and could be made productively by matching two groups of towns, using one group as a control and the other as test market for the new advertising. Groesbeck emphasized the need for several markets of each kind to avoid the pitfalls of outside or undue influence. Of all the early practitioners, only Gerard Lambert could afford to do his testing in one town with one other as a control. He owned the agency, and since he also controlled the client, he could forbid the sales manager to have any of his men enter the test or control town or correspond with dealers during the period of the test.

The world of the pioneers has changed. Most of the pioneers in copy testing, most of those who succeeded in establishing syndicated services for copy research, concentrated their early efforts on just one technique or at the most two. Even those who have made reputations based on one technique must now deal with a multiplicity of techniques—too many of them.

A SCHEME FOR CLASSIFYING TECHNIQUES

There are so many different copy test methods, so many variants of each, that an unclassified listing of them would be confusing and hence useless. It makes sense to classify the methods on two dimensions, as was done several years ago by the research directors of Foote, Cone & Belding and undoubtedly by others as well. The following array of methods, with permission, adapts the FCB system of classification.

In one dimension, methods can be classified according to the stages of advertising development, as follows:

1. Testing basic themes, ideas, appeals
2. Testing elements of advertisements such as headlines, pictures, jingles, story sequences
3. Pretesting whole ads in rough or finished form
4. Pretesting the effect of repetition to simulate a campaign

The foregoing are done in the laboratory, in overt tests or under analog conditions that try to simulate the real world. But there are two more stages of development at which testing is pertinent:

5. Posttesting single ads in their normal media
6. Posttesting whole campaigns in normal media

At each of these six stages of testing, there is another dimension which reflects what we are trying to find out.

1. To assess the ad (or element, or idea) for its attention value, interest value, or arousal
2. To test the materials for communication of their intended messages
3. To test them for their effect on consumer attitudes
4. To test them for their effect on purchasing behavior

This yields $6 \times 4 = 24$ different cells, in many of which we can choose among a large number of methods or variants. For every method mentioned in what follows, the reader will think of one or two that are omitted. And for every broad description of method, the reader may think of several variants depending on applications of the technique. No attempt is made in the following discussion to give detailed instructions on how to apply any of the techniques. In most cases, one sentence is enough to convey the essence of a method.

PRETESTING BASIC THEMES, IDEAS, APPEALS

The purpose of these early tests is to assist in deciding which of given alternative appeals the advertising should make. For example, for an automobile ad, the choice may lie between horsepower and gasoline mileage. In theme testing we are trying to find out what the advertising should say rather than specifically how to say it. Themes and ideas are presented to the consumer usually in simplified form, often as a brief statement on a file card.

It is admittedly hard to divorce the theme from its expression. Theme and idea tests are often applied before a copy platform has been finally established. They can be unnecessary if the background research has been thoroughly done, but even there it may sometimes be necessary to test two or more versions of a basic theme.

This is as good a place as any to mention one of the great hazards in copy tests of all kinds. All too often we are testing things that can produce only small differences. Yet it is the nature of advertising in the United States that a very small difference in percentages can make a very big dollar difference in such a big marketplace. The copy researcher and his principal should agree ahead of time how big a difference between themes or between elements, ads, or campaigns will be required in the marketplace and how big or how small a difference in test conditions the agency and client will recognize as grounds for making a decision.

The pretesting of themes should always be approached with an awareness that some kinds of themes and ideas will never test well in this form. There is always a risk here and in other forms of testing that the test process itself will kill the best idea. It is important also to remember that different ways of expressing the same idea may be too subtle for preliminary testing.

Here are some of the tests used for this type of pretest, classified by the purpose of the pretest.

Pretesting for Attention, Interest, Arousal

Curiosity Tests. The respondent is shown various theme statements ostensibly representing different brands of the product, or even different products, and is then asked on which he would like more information. This method assumes that the differences in curiosity correspond to differences in interest and attention without at any point asking the respondent, "Which looks more interesting to you?" or "Which do you think would interest more people?" A pitfall is that the respondent may ask for information because something is not clear or because something about another statement seems already so familiar as not to need more information.

Focus Group Interviewing. The theme ideas are presented on a screen or on cards to a small group of consumers in someone's home or in a specially built laboratory room. A professional moderator then tries to bring out which of several themes is more interesting and why.

Projective Questioning. Respondents singly or in groups are shown a statement and asked to describe the people to whom this product or idea would appeal. This method is in that fuzzy borderline between a consumer jury test in which people become "experts" and projective questioning in which they reveal their thoughts by talking about somebody else.

Physiological Measurement Devices. For a long time it has been known that the human nervous system responds in many nonvoluntary ways, and many attempts have been made to measure them. The psychogalvanometer or lie detector, measuring arousal in terms of the sweat glands, is one way. Pupil dilation is another, based on experiments showing that the pupil dilates and contracts in reaction to many other things besides light and dark. Other work has been done with blood flow and pulse rate and even with electro-encephalograms (which seem to measure something when transducers are wired to the skulls of monkeys but are hardly practical with housewives). The eye camera photographs quick involuntary movements of the eyes from one part of an ad to another.

All the physiological methods using the eye, the blood, the sweat, the heart, and so on are probably nonprojectable. They are affected by novelty, by shock, and by the mental work of absorbing something new, working out a problem, or reading something difficult. Their measures of arousal are not necessarily measures of interest.

Pretesting for Communication

Quick Recall Tests. There is some utility in exposing people to themes, ideas, and appeals on cards and then asking for playback if we are trying to ascertain whether an idea is misinterpreted. This should probably be considered also a measure of interest, and it verges on the element testing stage since the playback can depend as much on the exact phrasing of the stimulus as on the underlying idea.

Pretesting for Effect on Attitudes. There are several possible acceptable and useful methods here, but since they all correspond closely to methods used for concept testing in product development, they will be mentioned only briefly.

Theme-labeled Product-Use Test. Consumers are asked to use two products with different labels and asked to express their product preference. However, the contents of the two packages are identical. This trades on the well-known phenomenon that taste is in the mind as well as in the palate, that sense reactions are influenced by ideas as well as by the chemistry or physical attributes of the product. As an example, when two identical cans of beer, differently labeled, were used in an ostensible taste test, a sizable majority thought they detected a real difference—one-sidedly in favor of one of the beers.

Theme-identified Product-Choice Test. Consumers are shown a pair of cards which contain two of the themes to be studied and asked to choose which of the two products they would like to receive as a free sample.

Neither of the two foregoing methods should be used to test a new theme against a well-known one.

Product Attribute Questioning. Consumers are shown lists of possible product attributes and asked to put together those they consider desirable for an ideal product of this type. Alternatively, each attribute can be scaled for desirability.

Sample versus Cash. A less acceptable alternative is to show (either in personal interview or by mail) just one theme statement and ask people whether they would rather receive a free sample of that product or a given sum of money. This method should not be used unless prior experiments are conducted to determine the sensitivity point—what sum of money is too large and what sum is too little. If respondents are accustomed to trying new products and have been recruited in a panel for such purposes, they will too often choose a product regardless of its apparent merits unless the cash reward is substantial.

Pretesting for Effect on Purchasing

In-Store Tests. Display cards or tape recorders are used to tell the product story in simplest form at selected retail stores. Results are then determined by actual sales or by special coupons.

ELEMENT TESTING

Pretesting of elements of advertising is designed to help decide how basic ideas should be presented. The elements can be studied in the context of a complete advertisement, which may or may not be finished and which may or may not be a current or actual planned ad. For print ad purposes, an element can be tested in the context of a layout with only the element to be tested shown clearly. Or sometimes an element such as a headline or a picture can be taken out of context entirely and exposed by itself.

For T.V., the video can be shown without any sound and the audio without any sight, as the Gallup organization has done at its Mirror of America in order to make sure that the two major elements are telling the same story. In a commercial, a moot element or part of a commercial can be shown by itself in a few seconds, before the rest of the commercial has been produced. There is also a test of storyboards as a means of pretesting the *sequence* of the story, which is in itself an element.

The different tests can once again be classified by the purpose of the pretest.

Pretesting for Attention, Interest, Arousal

Element-Curiosity Test. Similar to the theme-curiosity test already described, this test is conducted by presenting to the respondent an advertising layout in which only the moot element, a headline or a picture, is openly exposed, everything else being covered by flaps. When two such ads are shown to the respondent, the criterion is which flaps the respondent lifts first.

Physiological Measuring Devices. Those already described under the heading of theme testing apply even more here.

Split-Run Tests, Buried Offer Tests. If the *text* of an ad or the gestalt of a storyboard is at stake, one handy device is the newspaper split run in which a free offer or a 10-cent offer is buried at the end of each version of the copy. Or the offer can be buried in a standard block of copy under a series of different headlines being tested, in which case different response rates are attributed to the extent to which the headline interested people in reading the ad.

Pretesting for Communication

Element Recall Test. This is really a kind of show and tell in which the respondent is exposed briefly to the elements under study and questioned about what he recalls and what it means. The respondent is shown what purports to be an advertisement with parts of it blanked out. She may be shown a headline, an illustration, or both. She is then asked questions about the product as she would visualize it, to describe it from the elements she has seen. As an alternative, she may be asked what else she would say about the product to complete the ad that begins with this headline and/or illustration (this being one case where treating the respondent as an expert can be justifiable).

Common to all element tests is the necessity for a controlled experiment situation. Except in the group interviewing or show-tell situations, the validity of an element test depends on having one group of people exposed to one version and a second group to another version or to none at all.

Word-Association Tests. Sometimes an element is not a whole headline but two or three words or even just one. The test follows the usual staccato procedure of getting the respondent's first one-word reaction to each word that is presented to him. ("What one word do you think of first when I say the word bread? . . . knife? . . . octane? . . .") The word or phrase being tested is buried in a longer list. Usually, if the respondent is unable to give a one-word reaction quickly, the investigator goes on to the next test word. As a variant, it is possible to accept a delayed reaction—making note of the length of the delay.

A word-association test of this general sort can be used in conjunction with one of the physiological measurement devices to get not only association but amount of arousal.. It can be conducted after exposure to test materials. It can also be useful with no exposure at all unless carried to the extreme typified by one researcher who told a pineapple canner that he had unearthed his real sales problem: the word *pineapple* itself made some people think of hand grenades.

Other Projective Tests. Another standard method applied after exposure to advertising elements is the sentence-completion test. People can also be asked to look at a proposed illustration and tell a story about the product or the situation, as discussed in Section III, Part A, Chapter 5.

Pretesting for Effect on Attitudes

Element-labeled Product-Use Test. This is the same as the theme-labeled product-use test already described except that the variation in the product packages is an advertising headline or an advertising illustration.

Element-identified Product-Choice Test. This is the same as the theme-identified product-choice test.

Physiological Tests. We mention them here as a caveat. Pupil dilation in response to pistol shots, scenes of slaughter, and so on casts doubt on the theory expressed by some that dilation means desire. The physiological devices should be limited to their primary role as measurements of arousal.

Pretesting for Effect on Purchasing

Store Advertising Tests. These can be carried further with element tests than with theme tests. Headlines or pictures can be shown in counter displays or can be exposed to people in vans outside the store. Measurement of the effect of varied elements can be assessed by coupon redemptions.

Split runs. For many kinds of products, the traditional newspaper split run as used by John Caples and others can be used to measure the effects of headlines or other elements on orders for the product. Some papers offer geographic splits: the *Milwaukee Journal* has a balanced checkerboard pattern based on newsboy delivery routes; the Des Moines papers offer a balanced three-way split; others cover large geographic units, similar to the regional editions of magazines. Still other papers offer an alternate-copy split.

LATER STAGES

By this time it should be clear that more variables are involved than the stage of development and the ad function to be tested. As we consider more developed ads, let us examine some of these other variables: the means of achieving a test exposure, the measurement devices or tools to be used, and the research design to be employed.

Procedures for Exposing Test Commercials

Laboratory Exposures. This heading includes pupillography, measures of blood flow and pulse, and other measures of autonomic reactions while watching a commercial. We are almost automatically limited to very small samples or else to atypical samples.

To some researchers laboratory exposures mean focused group interview sessions at which about six to ten consumers see an ad, often a very rough one, and discuss it with a moderator while a copywriter, listening and watching through a two-way mirror, may rewrite the ad while the discussion is going on.

The Special T.V. Theater. Typified by Schwerin and Audience Studies, Inc., this has the advantage that a large number of people can be exposed at one sitting and that conditions of exposure can be controlled. Sample composition, however, cannot be controlled so well. There is also the influence of people in the theater on each other and the fact that one theater showing cannot represent geographic variations—which may be sizable.

Portable Projectors Taken into the Home. This is at the other extreme. Sample composition can be controlled (at least in theory). The test can be done in several cities during the same week. Conditions, however, are just as artificial as in the theater, although personal interactions are missing. However, the method is expensive and creates interviewing problems because of the equipment.

A Van. Here people can be exposed singly or in very small groups in a vehicle that can travel from one place to another and hence provide some degree of sampling control. Probably the van is best used at supermarkets in connection with some kind of coupon redemption or other means of measuring immediate sales effect. The method does require an investment and is certainly not a natural exposure.

Commercials Played inside the Store. This sounds wonderful, but the trancelike state of customers who are walking supermarket aisles seems to block such stimuli.

On the Air, with Induced Viewing. This means contacting people ahead of time and asking them to watch certain programs. The natural exposure medium thus becomes a good deal less natural. It might be more natural if people are asked for opinions over a period of a few days with special attention to three or four different shows, one of which is the one we care about. To keep this test under control, it is wise to ask half the people to watch something else at that time.

On the Air, Induced by T.V. Itself. In this case there is no advance contact with potential viewers, but special programs are plugged on the air ahead of time.

On the Air, No Inducement at All. This is the ideal, but it can lead to mammoth samples.

On the Air with Viewing Withheld by Statistical Control. This was accomplished in the *Milwaukee Journal* laboratory which could "mute" a T.V. signal in half the homes that comprised its measurement panel.

On the Air via Cablevision Split. Though some people have used induced viewing, CATV is best used when the viewers are not aware of a test or of any special circumstances and when the CATV system is equipped with a means of sending two signals simultaneously on the same channel, each to half the subscribers in an area. Facilities for doing this are available. Market Facts has such a system in Maryland; Adtel in West Virginia. Foote, Cone & Belding is building a multitown system in the Far West.

On the Air, with Exposure Controlled by the Buyer. This involves buying simultaneous minutes on all the channels available to a town, a tricky buying problem and always subject to Murphy's law—if anything can possibly go wrong, it will.

Procedures for Exposing Test Print Ads

Nearly all these procedures have been covered in preceding sections, so they will only be listed here.

Laboratory exposures.

Theater screen. This successfully exposes a headline and illustration, but exposure of text is moot.

Portfolios taken into the home.

Single ad exposed in the home or in an intercept situation.

A van.

Single-ad mailings.

Store displays.

Dummy magazine left by an interviewer or mailed.

Binding test ads in selected subscriber copies of certain magazines.

Newspaper split runs.

Controlled checkerboard placement of ads in patterns of markets via newspapers or selected editions of magazines. Full run.

Measuring Instruments

Almost every device for measuring human response is potentially at the service of the copy researcher. As a reminder we can mention the laboratory instruments for measuring eye movement, pupil dilation, blood flow, pulse, and sweat. There are also the objective remote measurements of behavior: audited sales, warehouse withdrawals, and coupon counting.

The gamut of interview methods includes the following:

Focused Group Interviews. Valuable for diagnostics but never for estimates of numbers.

Consumer Purchase Diaries. Theoretically useful for tracking purchases of many products over a period of time in relation to controlled exposures, but there are drawbacks not only of expense but of incompleteness and guesswork.

T.V. Viewing Diaries. The same comments hold as for purchase diaries except that the diary can be used as a means of soliciting opinions of shows viewed and as a means of asking for special opinions of certain shows and hence intensifying exposure to that extent. They are useful for copy tests only in connection with some separate measure of attitude toward brands or behavior.

Self-administered Questionnaires. These are either mailed to homes in selected areas or delivered by interviewers.

Personal Interviewing. These are done in depth or unstructured. They are limited in affordable size.

Structured Personal Interviews. This is the normal thing when affordable.

Card-sort Personal Interviews. These are useful when much information is needed per person.

Telephone Interviewing. This is the norm these days, especially with WATS lines.

Pushbutton Recording. Instantaneous electronic recording of the votes for or against something put on the air; this is horrifying politically, perhaps useful commercially.

The assumption underlying each of these interview methods is that we need to study attitudes and behavior within a group of people exposed. But the problem can be approached from the other direction: what were the exposures last night or last week within a group of purchasers? The simplest way to do this is to station interviewers in the store and ask anybody buying toilet soap about T.V. exposures at certain hours the previous evening or about yesterday's paper or a current magazine. This could be applied in the case of simultaneous commercials in multitown designs or with cablevision splits.

Research Designs

Some tests are so simple one would hardly dignify their formats by calling them designs. However, often a more sophisticated plan is vital, such as one of the following.

Test Group versus a Control Group. The assumption here is that people measured just after exposure are different, to the extent that the exposure influenced them and only to this extent, from a nonexposure control group measured at the same time. This requires large samples and considerable precision. The design can be improved when more than one client is testing at the same time, as follows:

Two clients, two samples:

Client	Sample 1	Sample 2
I	Expose	Control
II	Control	Expose

Three clients, each testing two ads, three samples:

Client	Sample 1	Sample 2	Sample 3
I	Ad A	Ad B	Control
II	Ad B	Control	Ad A
III	Control	Ad A	Ad B

Pre-Post Interviews, Same Respondents. This design makes it possible to (1) measure changes with small samples and (2) separate the holding and the generating effects. The chief disadvantage with interviewing the same people is that the first interview can influence the second; hence the second interview often should be made only after a lapse of at least two or three months. This design is most appropriate for testing campaigns rather than single ads.

Pre-Post Interviews, Different People. This can measure the net changes from exposure without knowing who changed from what position or in what direction. It requires much larger samples and great precision in matching.

Criss-Cross Design. All sample members are interviewed twice, but on different subjects. This design has an advantage over the pre-post method with different people in that one can select from the first interview those people actually exposed to a program or publication, thus getting a preexposure brand measurement of an exposed group. As usually operated, however, this is done with samples too small to produce useful figures and does not show holding or generating effects.

The design can be described schematically as follows:

Stage	Sample 1	Sample 2
Premeasure	Attitude, product A	Attitude, product B
Exposure	A and B	A and B
Postmeasure	Which viewed? Attitude, product B	Which viewed? Attitude, product A

Single Postexposure Interview with Preequivalent. Here the key question is "what brand will you probably buy next time you buy toilet soap?" or some other next-purchase question. A little later in the interview (not before), the respondent is asked, "Last time you bought toilet soap, what brand was it?" Thus the changes can be measured in a single interview, both questions usually being asked unaided. A change from last purchase to current can also be found via coupon redemptions if special coupons are used in the store and redeemed by interviewers. The act of redeeming constitutes current purchase; only the previous purchase must be ascertained by questioning.

PRETESTING COMPLETE ADS

The focus here is on the pretesting of complete ads (crude, quasifinished, or final) before they appear in their normal media. The testing of complete ads in a publication or on the air is discussed under another heading.

In this prepublication stage of testing complete ads, reliance is usually placed on portfolios rather than actual publications and on portable projectors or theater projection rather than broadcast media. Publications can, however, be simulated, as Dr. Gallup started doing years ago at Young & Rubicam with his *Impact* magazine. And arrangements can be made for tipping in advertisements in sample copies in certain communities, as Eric Marder has done with *Ladies Home Journal* and other publications.

Pretesting for Attention, Interest

Laboratory Test. Several of the methods already discussed apply here as well—focused group interviews, the various physiological measurements of arousal, the eye camera, and so on. Two other methods are also worth mentioning.

Schwerin Research has a device which shows the video parts of two commercials simultaneously. The people watching can listen to only one of them, and they can switch back and forth between them. Relative interest of the two is determined by how much they listen to each commercial.

ARBOR (Associates for Research in Behavior) has a pedal device (Compad) whereby the commercial fades away unless the respondent keeps pushing the pedal. It takes a little work to see the whole commercial, and interest is judged by how much pedal work a person puts in.

U-bottom Test. A sometimes sensitive portfolio or projector test is to place the test ad or commercial in the middle of a sequence of five or more ads, expose all the ads without pause, and then ask the respondent to name the brands advertised or to describe the ad. The normal U-shaped curve works against the middle or test ad. If ad A scores better than another ad for the same brand in the same sequence, it is judged more interesting.

Pretesting for Communication

Portfolio Recall Tests. To illustrate how artificial the classification of methods can be, this portfolio recall test is a communication *and* attitude change test. Ads are exposed in a portfolio containing not only one or two test ads for different brands but also some nontest ads as control or even competing ads. Before exposure, certain questions are asked about product preferences and past use of brands. After exposure and usually after a set of recall questions that can include the extraneous ads as diversions, the product preference and brand preference questions are repeated either in the identical form or somewhat differently. Attitude can be a single overall preference, or it can be an expression of beliefs about specific product values. A portfolio recall test can be used without the attitude change feature simply by having people leaf through a portfolio of advertisements and then (with the portfolio closed) play back what they remember.

Portable Projector Recall Test. Measurements here are the same as for portfolio tests, but the exposure is provided through a portable projector taken into the home or used in a van. Commercials for one, two, or three brands can be shown by themselves or buried in a kinescope of a T.V. program.

Playback Test. These can be conducted with a single ad or a single commercial when all we want to know is how much of the advertisement the respondents can play back shortly after having seen or read it.

Dummy Magazine Recall Test. Some advertising agencies, for example, Young & Rubicam, have a standard pseudomagazine into which they can insert test advertisements. The magazine can be mailed to people or hand-delivered by interviewers. Questioning is usually delayed long enough to allow for at least a simulation of normal reading behavior. This is the technique used by Gallup & Robinson for its pretest service, run as an adjunct of its regular "proved name registration" test.

Direct Mail Recall Test. Here the exposure is applied through the mail and questioning, ostensibly not connected with the mailing, follows over the phone a little later asking what people remember about advertising for this type of product. Gradually the questioning begins to focus on the particular ad that had been mailed. At the time of receiving it, the respondent would not know that any test was underway.

Pretesting for Effect on Attitudes

Consumer Jury Test. In this ancient method, respondents are shown two or more ads for the same brand and asked which is the better. The theory is that their judgments of the ads reflect the relative favorability toward the product which the ads induced. Sometimes people are asked which ad they think would persuade other people to try the product—with the assumption that people cannot impute attitudes to others except as a reflection of their own unconscious reactions.

This sounds simple but is actually tricky. Nowadays few researchers would use this method as a means of scoring ads. But as a conversation stimulator this approach can be useful in the search for diagnostic clues on where an ad might need strengthening.

Product-Choice Test. In product-choice tests as administered by the two major organizations offering services in this area, large audiences are assembled in a theater to watch a test television program or a movie. They also see commercials. Before any exposure, a lottery is conducted offering a sizable supply of whatever brand the respondent chooses from a list of brands flashed on the screen in the product categories about to be tested and sometimes in other categories as well. After exposure to the commercials, the product-choice lotteries are conducted again. Measurement then consists of the shifts of brand choice from preexposure to postexposure. The two organizations are Schwerin Research and Audience Studies, Inc.

Variants of the product-choice test can be conducted in the home or in vans among individuals or very small groups.

In other attitude-change studies, the attitude after exposure is compared with the attitudes of a control group that has not been exposed, the assumption being that the control group represents attitudes just before exposure. (For this and other pertinent designs, see the preceding section.)

Ad-associated Product-Use Test. This is similar to the theme-labeled product-use test except that two complete ads with dummy names are used with two dummy packages of the same product.

Ad-identified Product-Preference Test. This is similar to the theme-identified product-preference test.

Pretesting for Effect on Purchasing

Store Coupon Test. As practiced by TeleResearch and by others, this method consists of inviting people into a van in a shopping center parking lot, exposing them to ads or commercials (among other things), and then giving them a set of coupons to redeem—immediately—at that particular store.

Usually the coupons are good for any one of a certain list of brands of a product category. The respondent receives several such coupons for product categories in which she has seen a commercial as well as categories for which she was a control with no exposure. Evaluation of a commercial is by counting the coupons redeemed for each specific brand, the name of which must be written on the coupon.

Direct Mail Brand Purchasing Test. Print ads are mailed to people who are later telephoned and asked questions about recent and current brand use. The theory is that if the ad worked, there will be more users among those receiving the ad than among those not receiving.

Pretesting Campaigns

The fact that there are practically no techniques listed under this heading indicates one of the current needs of the advertising business: a more valid means of simulating the campaign effect.

Much, however, can be done in a test-market situation, as more appropriately discussed under the heading of posttesting.

Pretesting for Attention, Interest, Arousal. At best what can be done under laboratory conditions is to see if a second, third, or seventh exposure to an advertisement produces the same reactions as the first. However, this is cumbersome and scarcely practical.

Pretesting for Communication

Extended Direct Mail Test. A large sample of people receives a series of advertisements in one campaign through the mail. Some of them are telephoned after the first mailing, some after the second, some after the third, and so on, to ascertain what they can play back from this brand's advertising.

Pretesting for Effect on Attitudes

Direct Mail Simulation. This is the same as the test just described, but the questions asked at each stage relate to brand preference.

Pretesting for Effect on Purchasing. It seems appropriate here to mention the *Milwaukee Journal* advertising laboratory. It is possible through the *Milwaukee Journal*'s use of newspaper splits in a checkerboard division of the market to run a campaign in half the market but not the other half. Here and in Des Moines, the newspaper furnishes the exposure pattern; the advertiser provides his own research.

There is also the growing number of services offering the capability of campaign testing on a split or comparative basis via cable television. Both in CATV and in the *Milwaukee Journal* operation, it is possible to control the exposures over a period of time. This is not possible in ordinary split runs where the receipt of one campaign or another by an individual is a new random split for each insertion.

POSTTESTING SINGLE ADS

The distinction between this group of tests and those previously discussed is that we now deal with advertisements that are not only completed but that are appearing in their intended media. If exposure for these tests is entirely normal, usually unforced in any way, respondents are not aware that any test is in progress until they are asked questions, maybe long after the exposure.

Although exposure is normal, it can be controlled in several ways. An exposed versus controlled situation can be achieved by taking one group of cities for a test ad and another group for no ad at all, or an ABC scheme can be applied with three groups of cities. Attempts to split television exposures within a city by buying simultaneous commercials on two or three different stations have theoretical advantages but often practical difficulties. In print, in magazines, with the increasing availability of regional or even local editions, there are numerous possibilities for valid geographic splits provided enough different markets are used.

The criss-cross design (noted earlier) is also appropriate. In this method, and in most others used for on-air testing or in-publication testing of anything beyond attention and communication, large samples are required since differences are usually small.

Posttesting for Attention, Interest, Arousal

Syndicated Readership Studies. By far the most prevalent method for studying the noting and reading of printed ads is that developed long ago independently by Gallup and Starch. The latter is still using this recognition technique. The Starch service provides the reading and noting figures for all the ads above a certain size in selected magazines, newspapers, and trade papers. Some variants of the method have been applied by Roy Eastman in business papers, by Mills Shepherd in business and industrial papers, and by Carl Nelson in newspapers.

Independent Readership Studies. These can be conducted by anybody at considerably greater cost per ad. Both in syndicated and in independent readership studies, there is usually no control group. Data on the noting and reading of a particular ad are compared with norms or averages for similar ads in the recent past.

Keyed Nonproduct Offers. Many newspapers offer an alternate copy split which enables an advertiser to use two different advertisements or two versions of an advertisement at the same time and thereby to test interest in the two on the basis of how many people respond to a buried offer toward the end of the copy.

T.V. Viewing Studies. Tests designed to get at the attention and interest value of an individual commercial just after it has been on the air, or next day, are usually oriented also toward communication or attitude change. Indeed, it is in the nature of on-air or in-publication exposures that any variation in measurements of recall or attitude effect must contain the variations due to attention and interest.

Posttesting for Communication

Advertising Recall Studies. Both Gallup & Robinson and Burke offer standardized measurements of advertising recall for print and for television. The usual procedure is to call or visit a day after the exposure has presumably occurred. People are qualified as readers of X magazine or as viewers of programs by one series of questions, and then they are asked to see whether they can, in the Gallup & Robinson term, "prove" that they saw certain advertisements by playing back what was in them. Results are used to measure both the attention value and communication value of the ad or commercial.

Day-after recall studies can be conducted independently. There also are the Starch reader impression or viewer impression services operated partly in conjunction with the reading and noting studies.

Posttesting for Effect on Attitudes.

On the theory (noted later) that attitude change can be not only bigger but more measurable than purchase change resulting from a single ad, a number of people have attempted to secure more or less immediate measurement of attitude change effect resulting from one exposure on the air or in a publication. Many failed because there were insufficient funds for adequate sampling.

Posttesting for Effect on Purchasing

Mail-Order Results.   Certain advertisers can do this well.   For others it is irrelevant.   However, it is a rare ad for any product sold at retail that can be measured in terms of single-ad sales result by mail.

POSTTESTING CAMPAIGNS

The next chapter in this handbook is devoted to measuring advertising effectiveness, which is almost synonymous with posttesting campaigns.   Here, therefore, only a couple of highlights are presented, albeit important ones.

Posttesting for Interest and Communication.   Some kinds of tests previously discussed really reflect a campaign result although they are ostensibly based on single ads.   Recognition recall scores of advertisements will rise as repeated similar ads become more familiar, although the operators of syndicated services try to control this factor.   But after a campaign has run a long time the scores may reach a plateau.

Recognition Test.   L. M. Clark used to mask all names and trademarks and ask people whether they remembered the ad and whose ad it was.   If a campaign was consistent in format the scores usually rose up to a point.   The Poster Appraisal Service does this with color photos of billboards.   D. B. Lucas demonstrated the campaign effect while seeking a means of deflating the recognition scores.   He obtained advance copies of magazines, conducted a recognition interview before the normal delivery date, and found just about as many people claiming they saw a Campbell Soup ad as he later found when he interviewed people about the same issue after it appeared.

Identification Studies.   People have had success with repeated questioning at intervals along the lines of "What soap advertiser says . . . ?" or "What cold capsule contains tiny time pills?" or "What does the . . . say in its commercials?" or (visually) "Whose trademarks or signature is this?"

Posttesting for Effect on Attitudes and Purchasing

Brand Trend Studies.   There is no need to use a national cross section for all campaign tests and no need to shun a test-market design just because the brand is marketed nationally.   One set of test markets can be given special treatment, another set can receive the regular national effort.   Both sets can be measured at intervals using methods that produce data on brand awareness, brand attitude, brand use before and during the campaign.   We can then study the results in relation to the amount of pressure exerted and the nature of the copy run between measurements.   With luck, a meaningful relation between campaign exposure and attitude change can be derived.   However, other influences may intervene.

One device for ensuring reliable results is to use repeat interviewing of the same people, thus enabling the researcher to spot attitude changes that occurred over a period of time among people who were already favorable or who were not favorable originally and among people who were already users and those who were nonusers.   Similarly, the effects on use can be examined within attitude groups.

Store Audits.   These data can be analyzed in relation to advertising potentially exposed during a period—provided the test runs long enough in a large enough set of markets.

Coupon Redemptions.   Usually analyses of special coupon returns from mailings at intervals to random subdivisions of a list can give some indication whether buying behavior is being influenced.

Withdrawal Method. One way to find out how well an advertising campaign is working is to withdraw it entirely from portions of the market and then to apply any of the three methods just mentioned to these portions and to the remainder. It is a rare client, however, who will dare to test his advertising copy by withdrawing it.

HOW, THEN, DO YOU CHOOSE?

The foregoing listing of methods presents only 54 entries out of hundreds of possibilities. Each can be executed in any of several designs and with any of several measuring instruments. It has been the aim of this chapter not to describe all possible methods but to point out the multiplicity available and to provide a framework for choice.

To Test or Not to Test

But before choosing a method, pause a moment and consider whether to use any method at all.

Do not test everything—not by any means. One does not need numbers to reject an ad that is in bad taste or too strident, irrelevant, or tinged with the unethical. Some things are far too small to test with the instruments available to us. Some things are too big and basic to test; some are too nebulous to test, and some are so obvious that they do not require testing.

Copy testing has both its real uses and its real imperfections. It can help us to uncover the flaws and weaknesses that might spoil a good ad yet fail to reveal, in the test situation, the strength that a good ad will have in the marketplace.

The Role of Theory

In choosing a method, be sure it is well adapted to the stage of development of the materials being tested and to the criteria on which a decision will be based (that is the reason for the classification scheme in this chapter). And perhaps above all, test ads in the light of some underlying theory, some basic understanding of what advertising is and does.

What the Experts Say

To help elucidate this matter of choice and the role of theory in it, this writer wrote the 39 active fellow members of the Copy Research Council (a limited-membership group of researchers and writers in New York) asking three questions:

1. What hypothesis or theory about how advertising works do you try to keep in mind when planning tests of advertising copy?

2. In your mind, what method of testing serves you best according to that theory of how advertising works?

3. What is the one biggest problem you face in connection with copy-test phases of your work?

The answers illustrated that theory and method do indeed go together in the minds of most of the 23 who replied. As to theory, one man talked in terms of advertising that makes a direct sale, two said that advertising's function is just to communicate major relevant sales points, one was so long-winded that his theory could not be clearly perceived, one said he was skeptical of all theories and believed in measuring only what can be measured, while 18 (or 78 percent of those replying) subscribed in one way or another to the theory that advertising worked by building and fortifying an attitude or set of attitudes that sooner or later increase the probability of a purchase. Awareness, interest arousal, or communication were also mentioned by 13 of the 18 as the means by which advertising achieves its attitude effect.

Several men, however, pointed out that the effects of a single ad are both small and ephemeral. Some used this fact to justify their statements that while they *want* to measure changes in attitude under natural conditions, they feel forced to do it under controlled and hybrid conditions.

If the men answering this informal questionnaire could choose just one method by consensus, it would be one that includes a measure of attitude. Yet several reject the idea of just one method: there are too many variables in advertising research to allow them to ignore the variables in solutions.

Their own problems fall into these patterns:

1. *Size:* Incremental effects of advertising are too small to measure with small samples.

2. *Dollars:* Money is seldom forthcoming for a test of adequate size.

3. *Rigidity:* Clients too often insist on a pet or standard method.

4. *Timidity:* Clients and account executives often demand one magical figure that makes their decisions automatic.

5. *Validity:* Too much of what we do has never been validated due to problems 1, 2, 3, and 4.

Several also pointed to the need for using two or more methods in tandem, one to measure persuasiveness-if-people-pay-attention, another to measure attention or interest. And some commented on the need both for comparative scores and for qualitative or diagnostic data to explain the scores.

That was quite a few seasons ago. The problems existed long before that and will probably continue to exist. But theories change; each new one (if it's any good) includes rather than negates the best previous theories. The progression of emphasis from interest to communication to attitude change is a demonstration of constant enlargement. And as this book goes to press, theory is enlarging again, stressing the premeasurement of sales effects. The facilities for measurement are already emerging, and the methods of using these facilities will follow *inevitably.* Ten years from now—maybe less—someone will have to revise this chapter, but it will still be necessary to conclude it this way:

When we test, we try to avoid deluding ourselves that there is a magic method that can produce one magic figure with which to evaluate an ad. For many test situations we have to use a variety of measurements, always with regard for their limitations. If we know what we are measuring and what our methods can and cannot do, we can obtain figures on the interest, communication, and (above all) persuasiveness of an ad.

The copy test that merely produces scores, that merely produces figures on attention, playback, or persuasiveness or all three, is only partly useful. To be fully useful the copy test must contribute also to basic copy research, to development of the next ad or the next campaign, to confirming the basic strategy or redefining it.

There is no available copy testing method that can substitute for more basic research, no copy testing method that can by itself provide the information needed for next year's planning.

Since keeping score on the ads cannot do this job alone, copy testing as such must be viewed as a part—an important part, but only a part—of our continuing research on the product in the marketplace: what the product does for people and how people react to the product.

BIBLIOGRAPHY

Adler, L., Allan Greenberg, and D. B. Lucas, "What Big Agency Men Think of Copy Testing Methods," *Journal of Marketing Research*, vol. 2, November 1965.

Advertising Research Foundation, Inc., *Copy Testing*, New York: Ronald, 1939.

———, *Copy Testing: Annotated Bibliography*, New York: Advertising Research Foundation, Inc., 1972.

———, *The Feasibility of Establishing a CATV Advertising Laboratory*, New York: Advertising Research Foundation, Inc., 1967.

———, *A Study of Printed Advertising Rating Methods*, VVI-5, New York: Advertising Research Foundation, Inc., 1956 (out of print).

———, almost any issue of *Journal of Advertising Research* since 1960.

———, *Proceedings*, annual conferences, New York: Advertising Research Foundation, Inc.

Borden, N. H., and C. S. Lovekin, *A Test of the Consumer Jury Method of Ranking Advertisements*, Cambridge, Mass.: Harvard University Press, 1935.

Caples, J., *Tested Advertising Methods*, rev. ed., New York: Harper, 1947.

———, "How to Test Your Copy," *Advertising Handbook*, Englewood Cliffs, N.J.: Prentice-Hall, 1950.

Firth, L. E., *Testing Advertisements*, New York: McGraw-Hill, 1934.

Greenberg, A., "Copy Research," *Handbook of Advertising Management*, New York: McGraw-Hill, 1970.

Haskins, J. B., *How to Evaluate Mass Communications*, New York: Advertising Research Foundation, Inc., 1968.

Hovland, C. O., A. A. Lunisdaine, and F. D. Sheffield, *Experiments on Mass Communication*, Princeton, N.J.: Princeton University Press, 1950.

Hyman, H. H., *Survey Design and Analysis: Principles, Cases and Procedures*, Chicago: Free Press, 1955.

Lucas, D. B., and S. H. Britt, *Advertising Psychology and Research*, New York: McGraw-Hill, 1950.

Marketing Science Institute, *Advertising Measurement and Decision-Making*, Boston: Allyn and Bacon, 1968.

Stouffer, A., et al., *Measurement and Prediction*, Princeton, N.J.: Princeton University Press, 1950.

Wolfe, H. D., J. K. Brown, S. H. Greenberg, and G. C. Thompson, *Studies in Business Policy, No. 109, Pretesting Advertising*, New York: The Conference Board, 1963.

Part C
Advertising Research

Chapter 3

Measuring Advertising Effectiveness

ROGER M. JOHNSON *Roger Johnson & Associates, Inc., Pasadena, California*

Advertising is a major channel of communication between marketers and their publics. For many it is *the* major channel. While there are many purposes for advertising, the immediate as well as the ultimate goal usually is contribution to sales and profits.

Measurements of advertising effectiveness help management to maximize the contributions that advertising can make. These measurements may be taken before an advertisement, direct mail piece, or commercial is created; at the time of initial creation in rough or semifinished form; after it has been put into finished form but before it is run; or at various times during or after the course of its exposure in media forms. The definition of effectiveness varies with what is being measured and when measurement is made.

For most advertising the eventual measure of effectiveness is frequently tied to sales produced per dollar spent. However, before advertising can make its contribution to the overall sales effort, certain communication objectives must be met. The eventual buyer must have been exposed to the advertising, it must have communicated a message, and it must have motivated or conditioned the buyer, either consciously or unconsciously, to want to purchase. The effectiveness of the advertising in achieving these communication objectives will regulate its sales effectiveness.

Effectiveness measurements may be based on a single advertisement, on a campaign, or on a sequence of campaigns. They may be taken at a single point in time or compiled over short or extended periods of time.

Measurements may be qualitative, quantitative, or a combination of both. They may be taken during the normal course of advertising or under experimental or artificial conditions. They may measure the medium, the message, or both.

WHY MEASURE ADVERTISING EFFECTIVENESS?

When a marketer hires a salesman, he expects results. The salesman is held accountable for producing those results.

Advertising is a salesman and should be held accountable. If the effectiveness of advertising is not measured, the efficiency and efficacy of the dollars expended for advertising cannot be calculated. The marketer then cannot benefit from any meaningful advertising accountability system and full advantage probably will not be realized from contributions that advertising can make to sales and profits. One may employ advertising as a defensive rather than an offensive weapon—by spending for advertising simply because the competition does.

Regardless of the size of the advertising budget, if advertising is ineffective, money is being spent that could be more profitably used elsewhere. Some marketers, especially those with limited advertising budgets, feel they cannot afford the cost for research to find this out. In actuality they cannot afford the cost of *not* finding it out.

Most unmeasured advertising is probably effective to varying degrees and in one way or another. However, well-planned and conducted research can be an important aid in pinpointing areas needing improvement. In many cases, if sales effectiveness of advertising is increased, even if only by a small amount, short- and long-range sales gains can be substantial. Without the guidance measurement can provide, the same mistakes that limit effectiveness of current advertising will be repeated over and over again in the future.

Advertising May Aid Competition. Some advertising is not only nonproductive for the marketer but benefits his competition. One company ran a full-page four-color advertisement for its new fruit juice drink in a major newspaper. Unaided recall for the advertisement on the day after the ad ran was impressive. About one-third of the issue readers reported having seen the advertisement and the majority of these could recall one or more points from the ad about the product. The only problem was that about eight out of ten readers credited the ad to a leading competitor!

Using a slogan or theme that closely resembles one that has been preempted by a competitor can make dollars spent for advertising more effective for the competitor than for the advertiser. Use of company names, initials, or symbols that remind readers or viewers of a competitor can have the same effect.

The author is continually reminded of CBS when NBC identifies itself on television by tracing the letters in reverse order—starting with the C, continuing with the B and finishing with the N.

Launching a campaign when the brand is not on the shelves, or when it is improperly displayed, can have a salutory effect on product movement—but for the competition and not the brand.

Sales Measurements Can Have Limitations. Some marketers do not employ measurement methods involving research because they believe their sales records are measure enough. This can be a realistic viewpoint where advertising is the dominant contributor to sales, where sales response is immediate, and where internal and external variables that can affect sales are held constant or are unimportant.

For most marketers, however, reliance on sales records as the sole measure of advertising effectiveness can have a number of limitations. The actual measure of advertising effectiveness *cannot* be sales produced per dollar spent since advertising does not work alone.

1. When advertising is only one part of the marketing mix it is difficult,

and often impossible, to isolate (unless controlled testing is used) the relative contributions of each of the elements comprising the mix. If sales are stagnating, advertising may be the scapegoat when the sales force is the real culprit.

2. National advertisers using multiple media simultaneously often find it impossible to associate changes in sales or in brand share with any single medium. Changes could have occurred because of the particular combination of media or the sheer weight of impressions afforded by the combination. Perhaps one medium effected the majority of the change while the others contributed little.

3. There is usually a lag between the appearance of advertising and the sales resulting from that advertising. For some product categories (such as automobiles or slow-moving items like Tabasco sauce) the time lag can be pronounced. In such cases the effect of a single advertisement, commercial, or campaign is not easy to isolate.

4. Most advertising requires continuity and building upon strength for maximum effectiveness. Sales response may start slowly and then build rapidly some time later. Before the build, sales records are unrevealing. The advertising effort may be starting to gain momentum or it may not. The distinction cannot be made.

5. From his sales records, a marketer selling through middlemen normally has no way of knowing the rate of current product movement into the hands of consumers. There can be considerable filling of pipelines before it is discovered that the brand is dying on the shelves because of ineffective advertising.

6. Sales volume for the product category as a whole may be changing. Unless the advertiser knows this, changes in his own sales may be erroneously attributed to advertising.

7. Competitive activities and many other intervening variables of the marketplace have a pronounced influence on sales. Using only sales records, there is often no way to isolate accurately the influence of advertising from the other variables that are operating to affect sales.

Sales records cannot talk. For most advertisers they cannot reveal why the product was bought, who bought it (or, in the case of some industrial advertisers, who made the buying decision), whether buyers were new customers or repeats, or whether advertising really played any role at all in the decision to purchase.

The Case for Pretesting. The cost of preparing advertisements or commercials is usually small compared to media costs, and the cost of developing rough or semifinished versions is often much less than that of producing a finished ad or commercial. While either rough or finished versions can be used in pretesting, use of preliminary versions saves on production costs if changes are indicated and enables the testing of multiple approaches at less cost than if finished alternative versions were used. Findings from tests made with preliminary versions can be highly predictive of the performance that will be achieved by finished counterparts.

If only posttesting (measurement taken after the advertising has run) is used, the advertising budget will be partially or entirely committed before the marketer can assess the effectiveness of his expenditure. Pretesting is, at the very least, sound insurance against outlays for advertising that are less effective than they could be.

Budgets Can Be Set More Realistically. At any given time, the level of advertising expenditure required to attain a specified marketing goal is regulated by such factors as:

The economic or political climate

The life-cycle stage of the brand or product category

The nature of the product category itself

The degree of existing brand loyalty for the brand or for competitive brands

The company's current market position, share of market, or brand advantages

The nature and level of competitive advertising and marketing efforts

The cost of media for reaching selective audiences

The magnitude of the marketing goal

The role identified for the advertising in achieving the overall marketing goal

The absolute and relative effectiveness (compared to competition) of the company's advertising

It is an economic axiom that a company's profits will increase when incremental revenue exceeds incremental costs. Increases in advertising expenditure levels will not usually be justifiable if incremental advertising produces sales or gains in brand awareness or share of market at a rate that is less than that required to warrant the expenditure.

This is commonly the case when a particular brand holds a dominant share of market. It has been found that some advertisers overspend, from the standpoint of profits, to add hard-to-achieve incremental share points. More commonly, however, advertising budgets are set too low to permit the continuity and frequency that are necessary for full impact.

Measurements of effectiveness of a marketer's advertising and of the advertising of his competitors are essential to value judgments relating to expenditure levels. Such assessments are integral components of the various simulation or other predictive mathematical models that have been devised to aid in intelligent determination of the probable effects on sales or profits of variations in levels of advertising expenditures.

DEFINING GOALS FOR MEASUREMENT

Establishing goals for measurements of advertising helps to make research more productive, more efficient, and—in some instances—less expensive. Measurement goals are easier to set if a marketer has carefully defined goals for his advertising. The two are closely interrelated.

Measurement Goals Relate to Advertising Goals. One goal of advertising might be to deliver messages to targeted subsegments of the public. These subsegments could be categorized by demographics, psychographics, product or brand buying and consumption patterns, geography, life-styles, and so on. The measurement goal then would be the production of readings on results achieved by advertising among the targeted subsegment or segments.

For many products, a minority of users account for the majority of the sales. If advertising is targeted to heavy users of the brand or product category, measurements should be based upon this segment. If the majority of the heavy users live in rural areas, measurements taken in a large city are limited in usefulness and likely to be misleading.

If the primary intent of advertising is to implant brand awareness, the immediate goal for measurement should not relate except as a by-product to the level of the sales that are produced by the advertising. An example would be a new-product advertiser whose initial advertising is aimed at making the buying public aware of his existence. After awareness has been implanted, his measurement goals would shift progressively to persuasion, motivation, and purchase.

Anticipating the degree of change that advertising is intended to produce will, in many instances, regulate the cost of research. Generally, the larger the expected change, the smaller the sample that is required. Estimating the extent of exposure advertising is likely to receive may also regulate the size of sample required and the corresponding research costs. For example, if quantification of copy point recall is the goal for measurement, a relatively small sample will be needed if all respondents have been exposed to the advertising. If only 5 percent have been exposed, the sample to locate them will have to be 20 times as large to obtain the same quantitative precision.

The degree of precision required for decision making is an important consideration. Measurements *can* be either more or less precise than they need be. If they are less precise than required, the danger of acting on them is apparent. If they are more precise than needed, research moneys are not being used to full advantage. Anticipation of the degree of precision required for decision making will avoid unwarranted expenditures for research.

For example, the agreed upon goal for an advertisement might be to register a particular brand benefit among a majority of those exposed. A relatively small sample can determine whether this goal has been achieved. If it should be found with good statistical accuracy that only between 10 and 20 percent are aware of the brand benefit, that finding is sufficient. The advertising did not accomplish its goal. A much larger sample to find out the *precise* percentage who are aware would in no way affect the conclusion.

Measurement Methods Relate to Advertising Goals. A goal for advertising can be immediate, short-term, long-term, a combination or all three. Although there is considerable overlap in the measurement methods available, especially in those for measuring achievement of short-term goals, the time span of the goal will tend to dictate the method or combination of methods selected.

Immediate Goals. Mail order advertisers, retail advertisers, correspondence schools, and classified advertisers typically are oriented toward rapid, direct response. Promotional advertising also falls into this category.

Usual measurement methods include orders, inquiries, coupon redemptions, sales checks, and so on.

Short-Term Goals. Most national marketers do not expect immediate results from advertising in terms of product sales. Nor are they satisfied if advertising works too slowly. Their goal is usually short-term sales production.

Measurement of a series of progressive stages preceding and following sales is often an objective. Measurement may relate one or a combination of these successive stages. A marketer of an established, well-known, and accepted product is likely to be much more concerned with measurements of the later stages. A new-product marketer is likely to be concerned with measurement of each of the stages, moving from measures of product and brand awareness on through to repeat buying. These successive stages can be categorized as:

Product and/or brand awareness
Recognition of benefits
Predisposition to purchase
Motivation to purchase
Actual purchase
Reinforcement of satisfaction with purchase
Repeat buying

Measurements taken during the earliest stages are usually derived from surveys to measure recall of an advertisement, commercial, outdoor poster, or of an entire campaign in a single medium or combination of media.

Most researchers agree that recall measurements during these earliest stages are useful. The higher the recall (or awareness) scores, the more *likely* it is that the advertising is productive. Certainly if no one is consciously aware of the advertising, the product, or the benefits, it is fairly safe to bet, even if some subliminal or unconscious recognition is achieved, that the advertising is not productive.

Measurement of the next two stages has created considerable controversy concerning methodology. Some researchers believe that direct attitudinal questioning will measure predisposition and motivation to purchase. Others believe that respondents are motivated for reasons that are locked in their unconscious or subconscious minds. Proponents of this school of research utilize depth interviews and projective techniques to attempt to unlock the unconscious motivations that they believe are controlling factors in measuring the motivating power of advertising. Yet another group of researchers look to physiological or uncontrolled response measurements for the answers. These researchers contend that answers volunteered by respondents concerning reactions may be unreliable.

The fifth stage, actual purchase, is the only criterion that some marketers and researchers will accept as valid evidence of the effectiveness of advertising. They observe that favorable attitudes, reactions, or even motivations do not guarantee purchase. Methods have been devised to simulate purchase situations following exposure to advertising—especially in the area of television-commercial testing. Other techniques involve taking advertisements and commercials to shopping centers and measuring consumer purchase patterns through coupon redemptions (or other means) following exposure to advertising.

The last two stages, although important goals for advertising and measurement, are not focal points for advertising research. Since they relate to product satisfaction, they are more frequently measured by product or marketing research. It is recognized, however, that the seventh stage is an important factor in readership of advertising. Buyers of brand X are more likely than are buyers of other brands to read advertising for brand X following their purchase. This is particularly true for product categories where a large purchase price is involved. Buyers of a particular brand read that brand's advertising following purchase to reinforce, or justify, to themselves the wisdom of their purchase.

Long-Term Goals. If a goal for measurement is long-term, the kind of advertising being measured is frequently of the institutional or goodwill variety. Messages are low key, sometimes indirect, and tend to be repeated over a long period of time. The advertising most often promotes the company rather than the individual products of that company.

Measurement of the effect of this type of campaign is often accomplished by successive readings spaced over months and even years. Measurement may be concerned with awareness, but it often assesses changes in respondent attitudes toward the company or shifts in opinions relating to the company image. Although direct-question survey research is most commonly used, depth interviewing and projective methods are also employed.

In some instances advertising is directed toward one audience with the purpose of actually or additionally influencing another group. For example, unless distribution is assured, a new-product marketer may select his media and set his budget in accordance with retailers' requirements for taking on the product. Some advertising is placed in general business publications with the primary intent of influencing that part of the audience comprising the investment community.

In such cases, indirect as well as direct goals must be clearly defined and the relative importance of both established. Advertising that succeeds in accomplishing its indirect goal, even though less effective than it might be for its ostensible purpose, is not necessarily a failure. Measurement of effectiveness must take both primary and secondary aims into account.

Regardless of the goal of the advertising, the more precise and realistic its definition, the more meaningful and useful the measurement is likely to be. A goal of "We want to increase brand awareness among rural prospects by 10 percent during the next six months" is far superior to "We want to increase brand awareness." The parameters for measurement have been defined. These parameters then regulate method, cost, sample composition, precision of measurements required, and so on.

It is important, however, in defining goals, to distinguish between advertising goals and marketing goals. A marketing goal must include *all* the elements of a marketing mix. Advertising is a single element in this mix, and its contribution to achievement of the marketing goal must be defined. If it is not, measurements of effectiveness of advertising may in reality be measurements of effectiveness or lack of effectiveness of the overall marketing effort.

MEASUREMENT METHODS

Methods used to measure the effects of advertising fall roughly into six groups. These groups are not mutually exclusive for measurement purposes. They may be employed in sequence to provide a measurement, or they may be employed in combination.

Voluntary response measures
Involuntary response measures
Psychological measures
Mechanical aids
Objective measures
Controlled tests

Voluntary Response Measurements. This is the traditional, most commonly used measurement method. Questions are asked of respondents and answers are volunteered.

Interviews can be made in the homes of respondents, in their offices, on the street, in shopping centers, in other public places, and so on. They can also be made by telephone, by mail, or with groups of people assembled in a single location. These various methods of interviewing respondents are not necessarily interchangeable. For example, telephone interviews cannot be used if exhibits or props are required. Shopping center interviews are impractical or unreliable if the questionnaire is too long.

Surveys to obtain volunteered response to advertising often include measures of:

Awareness—What share of the targeted audience is aware of the advertising?

Brand Identification—How many of those aware can correctly name the brand or the advertiser?

Where Seen/Heard—What media or medium contributed to the awareness?

Frequency of Exposure—Was the advertising seen just once, a few times, or many times?

Recall—What can be remembered about what was seen or heard?

Attitudes—What are the reactions to the advertising or to components? Did the advertising change or affect attitudes toward the product, the brand, or the advertiser?

New Information—Was anything new learned?

Importance—Was there anything particularly important about what was seen or heard?

Confusion/Disbelief—Was there anything that was difficult to understand, confusing, unbelievable, or exaggerated?

Purchase Influence—How convincing or persuasive is the advertising in causing respondents to want to try or buy the product?

If respondents are shown actual advertisements or commercials to stimulate recall, an "aided" measurement form is being used.

In the print field, the majority of services furnishing voluntary response measurements rely almost entirely upon aided recall. Measurements are usually in terms of scores that indicate the number of readers who saw a particular advertisement, read half or more, or associated the ad with the advertiser at the time of original reading. This type of measurement is limited because of the opportunity for honest confusion. The respondent may have seen the ad in another place, he may have seen the same ad previously, he may have seen a similar ad in the campaign that makes him think that he saw this ad and so on.

Unaided recall measures are also used. Respondents must rely on their memories for recall of advertising in a particular issue of a magazine. Recall may be aided to the extent of asking the respondent for recall of advertising for a specific product category or for an individual brand.

Voluntary response measurements frequently utilize scaling to indicate the intensity with which an opinion or attitude is held. Scales are also used to measure, for example, the degree to which a respondent believes a company is big or small based upon impressions gained from the advertising.

In pretesting advertising, to avoid favorable bias, respondents are frequently exposed to competitive approaches (often by reducing finished competitive advertisements to rough form for comparability with test versions) as well as the test versions. When two or more advertisements are shown simultaneously to evoke comparative response, the technique for measurement is referred to as paired-comparison testing. A principal limitation of this method is that an artificial situation is created. Consumers do not normally see competitive advertisements simultaneously, or if they do, they do not make the effort to differentiate between them (exceptions occur when purchase is contemplated but no decision as to the brand or product to purchase has been made).

Group interviews, or focused group sessions, are used to obtain qualitative insights into the effectiveness or probable effectiveness of advertisements or commercials. Groups are typically small and usually consist of targeted prospects for the product or products advertised. Discussion between participants is encouraged. A limitation of these sessions is that unusually vocal participants may dominate others. For diagnostic purposes, this limitation can be partially overcome by use of self-administered questionnaires prior to group discussion.

Before-and-after studies are another form of voluntary response measurement. In this case measurements of awareness, attitudes, purchase habits, and so on are taken before the advertising begins and the same measurements are repeated (usually among a different but matched group) following or during the advertising campaign.

Involuntary Response Measurements. A number of different devices are used to measure physiological response to advertising stimuli. Proponents of these devices claim the advantage of measurement of uncontrolled response. They believe that, at least in certain situations or for certain products, respondents may not give truthful answers to questions. This doubt exists particularly in situations where the truthful answer would be or could be construed to be derogatory to the respondent.

Early devices had the defect that there was no way of knowing whether a blip in the instrument reading was a positive or negative response. More sophisticated devices now make this distinction. However, precise cataloging of emotions that cause response is difficult. A complicating interpretation is that any given advertising stimulus normally contains multiple elements. Readings may relate to reactions to any one of these elements. To clarify interpretation of readings produced by instruments, volunteered response measures (interviews taken after instrument readings) are frequently used.

Psychological Measures. Proponents of psychological measures contend that direct questioning of buyers of a product is unlikely to yield a valid measure of the importance played by advertising in the buying decision. They also fault direct questioning for yielding at best, in their opinion, superficial response relating to reactions, attitudes, predispositions, or motivations.

The basic premise is that people act or react "off the top of the head" or for unconscious and subconscious reasons. The objective of psychological research is to allow respondents to reveal their unconscious motivations through projection or introspection.

Projective devices include sentence completion tests, word association tests, thematic apperception tests, and balloon tests. Introspective methods are typified by the in-depth interview. Small samples are the rule, and findings are qualitative rather than quantitative. The usefulness of these methods is highly dependent upon test design, the skill of the interviewer, and the ability of the interpreter to analyze the findings impartially and correctly.

Mechanical Aids. There are optical devices that track eye movement as a test subject reads an advertisement. The object is to evaluate the influence of layout, positioning, and relative dominance of illustrations or of headlines or similar material on the manner in which an advertisement is scanned or read.

Another device attempts to obtain a nonverbal measurement of the degree of interest a test subject has in a particular advertisement. The subject first views the advertisement with benefit of little illumination. If he is interested in seeing it better he can pump a foot pedal to increase the light intensity. The premise is that the more he pumps, the more interested he is in seeing or reading the advertisement.

The tachistoscope is widely used as an aid to measurement. This device is similar to a slide projector but is capable of extremely rapid exposures. It has been used to test outdoor poster recognition and comprehension by exposing viewers for only fractional seconds to each test poster. It has also been used at speeds that simulate a reader flipping through a magazine to measure the extent messages are communicated or attention is captured.

In television commercial testing, a dial-twisting device is sometimes used to correlate positive, negative, and neutral reactions with segments or short parts of a particular commercial.

Measurement methods that rely upon mechanical aids for response have the limitation of artificiality in the testing situation. Test subjects are abnormally conscious that they are being measured. This same limitation applies to other methods in varying degrees but is particularly acute where mechanical aids are used, as noted in the preceding chapter.

Objective Measurements. Objective measures may or may not be objective in the strict sense of the word. *Objective* in this context describes measures of *actions taken* as a result of exposure to advertising. Two of the primary objective measures used in advertising research are advertising response measurements and sales measurements.

Advertising Response Measurements. The number of inquiries generated by offers made in advertising is a frequently used form of advertising response measurement. An offer may be the entire subject of an advertisement; it may be prominently featured as a part of the advertisement (with or without a coupon); or it may be made within the body of the text. If the offer is a part of the body copy and in the same type face and style, it is referred to as a "hidden" or "buried" offer.

The advantage of a buried offer is that to discover it the reader must have become involved in the ad. Where offers are prominently featured or where they are listed on "bingo cards," the reader may have been attracted by the offer rather than by the advertisement.

Most marketers realize that an offer must be related to the product to serve as a basis for measurement. Even if it is so related, however, an inquiry may constitute unqualified response in the sense that the inquirer is not a prospect for the product advertised.

Another form of advertising response measurement is the rate of redemption of price discount coupons printed as a part of an advertisement. For established brands, product movement is usually the goal; but for new products or brands, coupon redemption rates can be used to aid assessment of the effectiveness of various copy approaches or media.

Sales Measurements. Many methods for measuring advertising effectiveness include sales or purchases of the brand and product category as a part of the overall measurement.

A good illustration is supplied in the test marketing of new products. In addition to measurements of brand awareness, attitudes, intentions to purchase or repurchase, and so on, actual sales or purchases are monitored. Measurement methods include company sales records, store audits, time sampling, warehouse withdrawals, and consumer diary panels. Testing usually involves multiple cities and geographic areas. Objectives may be to measure the relative effectiveness of:

Different media forms or combinations
Different advertising approaches
Varying expenditure levels
Varying frequency of exposure patterns
Different promotional approaches
Varying combinations of advertising and promotions

Measurements of this kind provide important input for construction of mathematical models. Marketers of established products may use test marketing for this purpose. Properly conducted tests allow marketers to experiment on a small scale. However, since it is advisable to measure the effect of a single variable in at least several markets, test marketing can be expensive. If the test variables are, for example, radio versus television, six markets (three for each medium) would be required. If it is desired to test the effectiveness of two campaign approaches in connection with each medium, twelve markets are needed. In addition, it is often advisable to use three more markets as controls—to receive neither the radio nor the television campaigns.

Findings from test marketing can be clouded for many reasons—strikes, unusual competitive activities, weather, out-of-stock conditions, and so on. Use of three markets for each test variable reduces the probability that uncontrolled variables will completely obscure findings (variables affecting results in one market but not present in the other two) but does not rule it out. To avoid this risk, some marketers use simulation models to substitute for test marketing. However, obtaining reliable and discriminating input for these models is often difficult and much of the input must be derived from surveys or testing, as noted in the three chapters in Part A of this section.

Some research organizations use purchase or simulated purchase measurements in an attempt to get closer to an objective measure of the sales effectiveness of advertising. One such method resembles a lottery, and the prize is a large quantity of a particular brand that has been predesignated by the winner. Participants designate brands (usually a single brand per product category but including several product categories) they would want should they win. At two times during their stay at the central location where the test is being conducted, participants make their brand selections (upon arriving at the location and prior to exposure to advertising and then following exposure to advertising for a brand in each of the product categories).

The extent to which participants alter their brand choices in favor of the advertised brand from preexposure to postexposure is the measurement used to evaluate the effectiveness of each advertisement or commercial. Normally, to reduce the artificiality of the testing situation, diversion is provided by inclusion of a television program or editorial material in addition to the advertising. Normative data (averages derived from previous tests involving the brand or product category) are required to interpret the significance of the magnitude of the pre-to-post change. In addition to the change measure, self-administered questionnaires are frequently used to obtain qualitative insights into why changes occurred. Mechanical aids, physiological measures, and group discussions may also be incorporated.

Another method exposes shoppers to an advertisement or commercial shortly before or at the time of their shopping trip and measures (by recontact at a later time, by coupon redemptions and so on) the extent to which brands exposed were purchased. Interpretation is usually based on normative data and an awareness (or control) of variables such as in-store activities, competitive advertising and other efforts that may affect the results.

Simulated purchase methods are limited by the artificiality of the created purchase situation. As with other methods that use normative bases, reliability is often questionable unless changes are pronounced or samples are large.

Controlled Tests. In essence, all research is controlled testing in one way or another. Control in this context, however, relates to testing that eliminates variables of time, place, positioning, and so on that may affect the purity of findings when one advertisement or commercial is measured against another in its natural environment—placed in a circulation copy of a magazine or run on television.

An alternate issue split run in a newspaper or magazine is an example. The size of the advertisement is the same and the position within the publication is identical. The only difference is that reader A sees one version of the advertisement and reader B another.

Another is the use of cable television to expose, in the identical time slot and on the same station, one commercial to half the audience and another to the other half.

Control of variables in this manner permits accurate measurements of differences in effectiveness of each version. Artificiality of exposure, a limitation for most other methods that employ controlled exposure, is not a limitation of this method.

PROBLEMS IN MEASUREMENT

Advertising never operates in a vacuum. Competitive efforts, external variables, and the overall marketing effort of a company must be considered in assessing effectiveness of advertising. When these variables cannot be identified, problems exist. In some cases variables can be identified, but their effects cannot be measured except at prohibitive cost.

Other factors often operate to blur assessments of advertising. Four of the more important follow:

Residual effects of prior advertising cannot be eliminated.

Certain brands and product categories are slow to respond to variations in expenditure levels or campaign approaches.

Use of multiple media generates interaction.

The influence of a single medium can be obscured in a mix of media.

In the real world, where variables are complex and interrelated, exact measurements of advertising effectiveness are rarely attainable. This is not to say, however, that testing should be disregarded in situations where findings cannot be completely definitive. If measurements are thoughtfully combined and intelligently assessed, their value is unquestionable. Through their use, a company can profit most fully from advertising's contribution to its total marketing thrust.

MEASUREMENT METHODS COMMONLY USED IN VARIOUS SITUATIONS

Selection of a particular measurement method depends upon the entity being measured and the purposes of the advertising. However, given the entity and the purposes, a variety of methods can usually be used, singly or in combination, to accomplish the objectives.

This summary describes measurement methods most commonly used in situations the reader is most likely to encounter or have questions about.

Situation. How can we determine, before advertisements are created, which advertising concepts or appeals are most likely to be effective?

Measurement Methods. Promising concepts are first developed into short copy sentences or paragraphs. Psychological marketing research frequently precedes concept formulation. If this has not been done, depth interviews and projective techniques are useful to avoid superficiality of response.

After potentially effective or persuasive concepts have been identified and formulated, the relative effectiveness of each can be measured by opinion surveys or group discussions. These methods are used to measure communication and to obtain rankings of concepts in terms of importance, believability, attitude changes, persuasiveness, and so on.

Situation. How can we assess the probable effectiveness of one or more rough or semifinished advertisements or commercials?

Measurement Methods. The most commonly used techniques are:

Opinion surveys exposing rough versions to respondents to evaluate communication, layout, recall after forced exposure, attitude shifts, persuasiveness, and so on

Paired comparison tests that elicit choices between alternate versions, roughly rendered competitive approaches versus test approaches, and so on

Portfolio testing for print ads in near-finished form

Group discussion sessions with ranking on self-administered questionnaires, followed by discussion

Involuntary response measures, mechanical aids, or simulated sales measures, especially if volunteered response is suspected to be subject to inaccuracies

Situation. How do we learn the probable effectiveness of a finished version prior to launching the full-scale media program?

Measurement Methods. The process is the same as that used for testing rough or semifinished versions. However, finished advertisements or commercials may also be tested after they have run or been aired on a small scale in just one or a few market areas (or circulation zones). Cable television or, if available, split runs in print may be employed. Results can be measured by before and after:

Surveys to establish exposure, recall, brand identification, attitudes, persuasiveness, motivation, purchase, intent to purchase, and so on

Sales measurements

Advertising response measures

Situation. How can the effects of an advertising campaign be measured?

Measurement Methods. The methods just described for limited testing of finished advertisements or commercials are also the most commonly used for campaign testing or for measuring the effects of an advertisement or commercial during and after full-scale exposure in media. The marketer can also avail himself of various readership and brand-related advertising exposure studies to assess certain aspects of effectiveness.

Whatever methods are used, before-during-after measurements are usually a must. Exceptions include direct response evaluations provided by coupon redemptions, orders by mail, inquiries, and so on.

Situation. How can we tell if our campaign has worn out?

Measurement Methods. In some instances advertisers change ads or campaigns too slowly. More frequently, however, they change too quickly. Some correspondence schools, for example, have run the same advertisement for years with scarcely diminished effectiveness. The trick is in knowing when advertising (assumed to have been effective) should be changed. Commonly used research methods to assess obsolescence include periodic measurements obtained by:

Direct response measures

Opinion surveys or group sessions, usually involving paired comparisons with new test versions or competitive advertisements.

Sales measurements

Simulated sales measures utilizing past performance normative data

Situation. How can we measure the relative effectiveness of various media or of varying expenditure levels?

Measurement Methods. Circulation and audience measurements can supply quantitative likelihood-of-exposure measures. Readership studies and brand-related exposure studies can provide some bases for comparisons. Opinion surveys to associate purchase attribution to individual media or mediums are commonly used but are notoriously unreliable in certain instances. Test marketing has been the dominant indicator used to supply these measurements. Where variables are controlled, such as confusion between media forms, opinion surveys and sales measurements are usually relied upon as measurement yardsticks.

Mathematical models have attracted much interest as a possible tool to predict the effectiveness of variant advertising patterns. However, it is vitally important that models have enough accuracy, comparability, and flexibility of input data to accommodate variables in the marketplace, product category, relative effectiveness of advertising messages in various media, relevant definitions of exposure, and so on.

A Word of Caution. For any measurements taken in the marketplace before, during, or after advertising has run, whether under test or actual conditions, all variables—competitive efforts, other external influences, and the overall marketing goals and efforts of the company itself—must be identified, considered, and understood for their effects before intelligent assessment of the contributions of advertising can be made.

BIBLIOGRAPHY

Konrad, Evelyn, and Rod Erickson, *Marketing Research, a Management Overview,* New York: American Management Association, 1966.

Lucas, Darrell Blaine, and Steuart Henderson Britt, *Measuring Advertising Effectiveness,* New York: McGraw-Hill, 1963.

Mayer, Martin, *The Intelligent Man's Guide to Sales Measures of Advertising,* Advertising Research Foundation, 1965.

Measuring Advertising Results, Studies in Business Policy, no. 102, New York: National Industrial Conference Board, 1962.

Wheatley, John J., *Measuring Advertising Effectiveness,* American Marketing Association, Homewood, Ill.: Irwin, 1969.

Part C
Advertising Research

Chapter 4

Determining Advertising Budgets

CHARLES YANG   *Hakuhodo Incorporated, Tokyo, Japan*

INTRODUCTION

Advertising budget appropriation methods are traditionally classified into three major categories: the subjective approach, the ratio approach, and the task approach.[1]   The *subjective method* of budgeting relies largely on an executive's judgment and experience, either intuitive or systematic.   On the most rudimentary level, an executive depends entirely on his intuition in setting aside a portion of the marketing costs for advertising.   On a more advanced level, heuristic rules that represent successful judgment and experience are developed and programmed for routine use.   The chief characteristic of the subjective approach is lack of objective rationality, both theoretical and empirical.

The *ratio method* calls for setting an advertising budget with a fixed or variable ratio of a predetermined base.   The base figure is most often the volume of anticipated sales.   Occasionally, a ratio is applied to past sales or profits or even the amount of money spent on advertising in the previous year.   There has been a trend to replace the fixed-ratio method with variable ratios which reflect changing market conditions or different stages in the product life cycle.

The *task method* requires an executive to set an advertising budget to achieve predetermined objectives.   This method can be regarded as an outgrowth of management by objectives.   The marketing activities of a company are coordinated by the objectives of all its subdivisions, of which advertising is one.   Once marketing goals are finalized, they are translated into detailed advertising objectives.   The advertising budget is then set to obtain these objectives.   The

---

[1] A survey in 1967 by the National Industrial Conference Board of 267 senior marketing executives also revealed that these three methods were prevalent in the minds of executives [3].

contemporary way of determining the advertising budget under this method, however, incorporates the systems concept, whereby not only objectives but also inputs and outputs are coordinated and integrated into a system of marketing operations. It calls for an optimum mix of marketing inputs of which the advertising budget is one part.

While the traditional task method tends to be functional—that is, the fulfillment of the objectives given to the advertising section—the contemporary approach requires that an advertising program be evaluated and determined in the context of total optimization. With adequate hardware and software support, a marketing executive can now evaluate the probable outcomes of various advertising strategies in conjunction with other marketing factors in order to achieve the best marketing input mix. This permits him to determine the size of advertising appropriations with a greater degree of accuracy as well as flexibility. Hence, total optimization and predictive capability characterize the modern approach to setting advertising budgets under the task method.

Many executives mistakenly believe that advertising budget setting began with the subjective method, progressed to the ratio method, and finally moved on to the task method. In practice, all three techniques experienced somewhat parallel growth in business operations. This simultaneous development is due to the growing popularity in recent years of the interdisciplinary treatment of advertising problems, particularly a combination of behavioral science, quantitative methods, and the marketing approach. This trend has opened up a wide range of theoretical and technical possibilities for the development of different budget appropriation models growing out of the three basic approaches.

Since many techniques are often interwoven, it has become considerably more difficult to classify advertising budget appropriation methods into definite groups. Nevertheless, there is a definite advantage in reviewing the various approaches on the basis of their orientation and in light of their historical origin in order to provide executives with a clear perspective of the current state of budget determination. Table 1 summarizes the traditional techniques and their contemporary counterparts for the three basic approaches. Since it is not possible to review all the techniques that have been advanced, we have included only those which are considered representative.

TABLE 1   Classification of Advertising Budget Appropriation Methods

Method	Subjective approach	Ratio approach	Task approach
Traditional	Intuitive method	Fixed ratio methods: 1. Percent of sales 2. Percent of Profits 3. Percent increase from previous year's budget	Objective methods: 1. Sales or market share objective *a.* Nonexperimental (Weinberg) *b.* Experimental (McNiven) 2. Communication objectives (Yang)
Contemporary	Heuristic simulation	Variable ratio method (Friedman)	Systems method: Dual budget appropriation model (Yang)

NOTE: Names in parentheses indicate the authors of the representative models cited in this chapter.

Our discussion will center mainly on the contemporary techniques with special attention given to the task approach, the most popular of the three basic approaches in modern management.

THE SUBJECTIVE APPROACH

Traditional Methods

The subjective approach covers a wide spectrum of probable appropriation methods, ranging from personal intuition to a highly sophisticated heuristic simulation that quantifies the decision-making process of successful executives.

On the most elementary level, the decision maker relies on his own intuition and learned experience with a notable lack of formal allocation program either in terms of theory or empirical evidence. In the past, such decision making was largely influenced by the company's profits and the personal preference of the executive. As the approach advanced, more research data were incorporated into decision making, although still without formal decision rules. It is this lack of established decision rules—not the lack of research data—which distinguishes this approach from the others. Thus it is entirely possible that the decision maker may employ one subjectively determined rule one year and a totally unrelated rule the following year should the previously employed rule fail to yield desired results. This trial-and-error process characterizes the traditional subjective method.

Heuristic Simulation

The attempt to eliminate this trial-and-error process by systematizing and programming the decision rules of more successful decision makers resulted in the contemporary method of heuristic simulation. What goes into the decision programs, however, remains subjective and without logical support. The method differs from the traditional in that decision rules which have proved successful in the past are used and can be employed with greater confidence, although there is no assurance they will continue to operate effectively in the future.

Heuristic simulation, then, is the programming of rules of thumb employed by the experts who have been successful in advertising budget appropriation. Such decision rules can be in either verbal or quantitative terms and may also be programmed for computer simulation. Most of the heuristic models in advertising have thus far been developed to deal with the problem of budget allocation between different markets rather than with the task of budget determination.[2] The same procedure used in these models, however, can be applied

[2] Perhaps the best-known heuristic model for advertising budget allocation is that reported in Green and Tull's book involving allocation of the advertising budget for different users' markets for synthetic fibers. Green and Tull's model involves allocation of advertising expenditures among various end users for synthetic fibers. Based on detailed conversations with the appropriate advertising personnel, they constructed a model which appeared to incorporate the various considerations which the executives felt to be important. The model is then expressed in a mathematical equation as follows [7, pp. 427–430 passim]:

$$A_i = \frac{A_T E_i \left[\bar{F} k_i \dfrac{S_i}{F_i} + \dfrac{F_i}{F} (1 - k_i) (P_i - S_i) \right]^{1/2}}{\sum\limits_{i=1}^{N} E_i \left[\bar{F} k_i \dfrac{S_i}{F} + \dfrac{F_i}{F} (1 - k_i) (P_i - S_i) \right]^{1/2}}$$

(Footnote continued on next page)

to budget setting. The usual approach in developing a heuristic budget determination model is to first interview key personnel within the company who are responsible for budget setting or, in the case of academic researchers, to interview these key people at various companies. The factors that are *judged* as important in budget determination by these executives are then extracted for modeling. The decision process is then described either in a mathematical model or a flow diagram that incorporates the extracted variables.

The value of such a heuristic model is primarily to show the decision makers the implication of their *judgments*. If the model has operated successfully in the past, it might be used as a first approximation to actual allocations. The decision maker, of course, is free to modify the decision process should special considerations arise which are not encompassed by the model. Departures from the model serve as a check on the decision maker's consistency and force him to explicate the reasons for the departures.

THE RATIO APPROACH

Fixed-Ratio Method

A 1967 survey by the National Industrial Conference Board found the widespread application of the ratio approach among many companies [3]. Simplicity rather than rationality is the main attraction of this approach. This is particularly true of the fixed-ratio method. When this method is employed, the advertising budget is commonly established as a percentage of the sales volume. Occasionally, however, cases can be found where a company may use profits as the base figure. Of those companies using the fixed-ratio method in the NICB survey, relatively few indicated that the amount allocated to advertising in their companies is expressed as "so much per unit of product expected to be sold." Overwhelmingly, the base figure is the sales volume, particularly the volume of anticipated sales. The typical procedure is to apply a predetermined ratio, often in use for a number of years, to the sales volume projected for the period that the advertising budget will cover.

The sophistication of the fixed-ratio method varies in accordance with two factors: the way in which the ratio is determined and the accuracy of sales forecasting. The ratio can be determined arbitrarily by the executive in charge, or it may be based on the average for the industry. In some cases, analytical techniques (such as regression analysis and market experiments to be

---

where A_1 = advertising dollars to be allocated to the ith market
E_i = margin of dollars per pound for ith market
A_T = total advertising dollars available for allocation
$k_i = \dfrac{\text{current sales level for } i\text{th in pounds}}{\text{target sales level in } i\text{th in pounds}}$
F_i = sensitivity to the firm's advertising factor for the ith market expressed as a rating from 1 (very insensitive) to 100 (very sensitive)
  These factors were derived from the judgmental estimates of the advertising executives
F = average sensitivity to advertising for all markets under consideration
P_i = annual potential sales to the ith market (total market size, in pounds)
S_i = current annual sales to the ith market (in pounds)
N = number of markets in allocation group
Two other heuristic models are reported by Marschner involving budget allocation at Guardian Oil Company and King's Crown Coffee [9].

discussed under the task approach) are applied to discover the most effective rate of spending. The use of more advanced techniques in setting a ratio, however, does not basically alter the nature of the ratio approach. It is still distinguished from the task approach in that the decision maker implicitly assumes the company's goals to remain invariant in the short run and that changes in market conditions can be ignored so that the appropriate ratio as derived from an analysis works effectively, at least in the short run. Under the task approach, the decision maker relaxes such assumptions and gears budget setting to reflect current market conditions and to achieve the changing objectives that advertising must assume from year to year.

Some companies apply a fixed rate of increase over the previous year's budget. The rate is repeated year after year unless there is a specific reason to change it. The ratio often reflects both the rate of growth in sales and the rising trend of media costs. When sales growth is at a fixed rate and if due allowance is made for rising media costs, this type of fixed-ratio method can work even better than one that uses sales as the base figure because the latter method can result in a decline in the real rate of expenditures in the face of rising media costs.

In spite of its obvious lack of optimization capability in markets where marketing factors vary significantly year after year, the fixed-ratio method should achieve a condition of near optimization if and when the following conditions are met: (1) the ratio is determined through adequate analysis, (2) the advertising elasticity remains stable over a number of years, and (3) due allowance is made for the rising costs of advertising, particularly media costs.

The Variable-Ratio Method—The Friedman Model

Between the fixed-ratio method and the task method lies the variable-ratio method. Here the emphasis is still on setting a ratio in advance, again often as a percentage of anticipated sales. The ratio, however, is allowed to vary in a set pattern that anticipates changes in the advertising elasticity during the various stages of the product's life cycle. Perhaps the most advanced treatment of the variable-ratio approach is the model proposed by Lawrence Friedman [6].

In the Friedman model, the advertising budget is divided into two parts: consumer-oriented advertising budget and trade-oriented advertising budget.[3] Each part is then expressed in terms of advertising-to-sales ratio which varies from stage to stage in the life cycle of a product. In essence, the ratio is governed by the volume of sales and the rate of change in sales at any given stage. Thus

$$\frac{A_t}{S_t} = k_1 + k_2\left(\frac{dS_t/S_t}{dt}\right) = \text{the advertising budget as a percentage of sales}$$

As the total budget is divided into two parts, the ratios for the two component parts become

$$\frac{C_t}{S_t} = k_1 + k_2\left(\frac{dT/T}{dt}\right) = \text{the consumer-oriented advertising budget as a percentage of sales}$$

$$\frac{P_t}{S_t} = k_2\left(\frac{dD/D}{dt}\right) = \text{the trade-oriented advertising budget as a percentage of sales}$$

[3] Friedman [6] dealt with the marketing budget which may, for our purpose, be treated as all-inclusive of advertising expenditures in order to facilitate explanation.

where A_t = the advertising budget for the time period t
        S_t = the volume of sales for the time period t
        C_t = the consumer-oriented advertising budget (Note: M_t in Fried-
            man's equations has been replaced by C_t)
        P_t = the trade-oriented advertising budget
        T = the average turnover per store or sales divided by distribution
        D = distribution of a product in the time period t as expressed in
            terms of an overall index of product availability
  k_1, k_2 = constants

The preceding three equations can be described verbally as follows:[4]

$$\frac{\text{Advertising budget}}{\text{Total sales}} = k_1 + k_2 \text{ (percentage increase in sales)}$$

$$\frac{\text{Consumer-oriented budget}}{\text{Total sales}} = k_1 + k_2 \text{ (percentage growth in turnover)}$$

$$\frac{\text{Trade-oriented budget}}{\text{Total sales}} = k_2 \text{ (percentage growth in distribution)}$$

The coefficient k_1 is essentially related to the desired profit level of the product under normal circumstances. The coefficient k_2 is related to the investment management is willing to make in a growing product.

Seven inferences can be drawn from the above system of allocation:

1. New products should have a large proportion of the sales dollar allocated to marketing since sales are growing at the fastest rate.

2. The distribution-oriented expenditure (P_t), as a fraction of the marketing budget, will be greatest for new products since distribution is growing fastest.

3. When turnover is increasing at a high rate, it is a good idea to increase consumer-oriented expenditures.

4. The advertising for a new product should not start until some distribution is available. Both turnover and sales are zero.

5. A product showing declining sales trends will very likely get no trade-oriented budget and very little consumer-oriented budget. In general, the

---

[4] Mathematical derivations of these equations are as follows [6]: The policy equation is first set as $A_t = k_1 S_t + k_2(dS_t/dt)$. Next, the advertising budget is divided into consumer-oriented expenditure and trade-oriented expenditure, $A_t = C_t + P_t$. Since the volume of sales during a given time period t is the product of the extent of distribution and turnover rate, $S_T = D_t T_t$, the rate of increase in sales is

$$\frac{dS_t}{dt} = D_t\left[\frac{dT_t}{dt}\right] + T_t\left[\frac{dD_t}{dt}\right]$$

Incorporating this into the policy equation, we have

$$A_t = k_1 S_t + k_2 D_t\left[\frac{dT_t}{dt}\right] + k_2 T_t\left[\frac{dD_t}{dt}\right]$$

Dividing this budget into two parts, it becomes

$$C_t = k_1 S_t + k_2 D_t\left[\frac{dT_t}{dt}\right]$$

$$P_t = k_2 T_t\left[\frac{dD_t}{dt}\right]$$

allocation principles suggest that funds be allocated to those elements of marketing in an uptrend.   If followed rigorously, these principles undoubtedly would save a lot of money which has been allocated to "repair jobs" . . . and second, third, or even fourth tries at saving a dying product.

6.   The allocation of trade-oriented budgets to individual product items can follow the same principles.   Product items growing in distribution get the greatest "trade" activity.   Items declining in distribution get no trade activity or promotions.

7.   The coefficients k_1 and k_2 are very important in this model and control the overall level of the marketing budget.   They should be based upon top management marketing decisions.

In order to develop a budgeting plan, one must start with a management philosophy on k_1 and k_2.   Then, one must have a sales forecast by product and item.   It is very desirable to indicate how the sales forecast will be achieved; that is, one should forecast whether the sales change is coming from changes in turnover or distribution.   To the extent that analysis or controlled testing can determine causal relationships, it should be included as part of the budgeting decisions.

Budget forecasting is iterative because by this procedure forecasts result in marketing budgets, which, in turn, affect sales and lead to new forecasts. Friedman suggested the following seven-step procedure:

1.   Management determines values of k_1 and k_2.   The former, k_1, is the normal ratio of advertising to sales that management believes the company must spend in order to maintain the desired level of profit, say 5 percent of sales. The latter, k_2, indicates how much of the additional revenues management wishes to invest in advertising in order to achieve a higher level of sales.   For example, if the marginal profit is 40 percent (marginal production costs are 60 percent of sales) and management wishes to spend the entire portion of the marginal profit on advertising, then $k_2 = 0.40$.

2.   A sales forecast is made by product and item.   This should be an annual forecast for budgeting purposes.   In some cases, this can be a simple continuation of trend.   In other cases, there may be specific reasons for forecasting changes in trend.

3.   Advertising budget guidelines are developed by pack and by product.

4.   Promotion and advertising plans are developed.   They do not necessarily have to follow the budget guidelines but should have specific reasons for major deviations.

5.   An official forecast is made using the advertising plans developed.

6.   The theoretical advertising budgets are recalculated.

7.   Major deviations from the guidelines are reviewed and final changes incorporated as necessary.

The latest development in the variable-ratio method is the use of the adaptive concept suggested by John D. C. Little and P. T. Fitzroy [4 and 8, respectively].   The basic premise is that the parameter of a function relating advertising response to budget inputs varies from time to time as the market environment changes and that the ratio of advertising to sales should be adjusted accordingly.   To detect changes in the market environment, Little suggested introduction of a monitoring device, which is a small-scale market experiment to be run on a continuing basis.   Information from the experiment is then incorporated into the past year's experience when determining the new ratio for the coming year.   How much weight the new information carries in the computation of a new ratio depends on the accuracy of the information as evaluated by Bayesian criteria.

For large advertisers, the adaptive concept will undoubtedly play an increasingly important role in advertising budget appropriation for years to come. How successful its implementation will be among medium-size and small advertisers, however, must wait for the discovery of less expensive monitoring devices.

THE TASK APPROACH

Management by objectives is the guiding principle of the task approach to advertising budget allocation where the essential first step is to establish objectives. The general practice is for the manager to develop detailed advertising objectives on the basis of marketing objectives. Broadly speaking, these advertising objectives may be either sales-oriented, communication-oriented, or a combination of both. Sales-oriented advertising objectives usually place primary emphasis on the direct relationship between sales or market share and the level of advertising spending. This relationship is often supported by a set of advertising strategies that can be employed to attain the established goal. To discover the true relationship between sales or market share and advertising then becomes the crucial step in the planning process.

There are two basic methods that can be used to uncover such a relationship: nonexperimental and experimental methods. Regression analysis which utilizes historical data on sales and advertising expenditures is by far the most popular nonexperimental method used by advertisers. The technique permits a decision maker to set an advertising budget to achieve a given objective, based on the revealed functional relationship between the volume of sales and the level of advertising spending. Such a relationship may also be expressed in terms of market share vis-à-vis the level of advertising spending or market share versus advertising share (as in Weinberg's model to be discussed).

The experimental method of discovering the relationship between sales and advertising has one basic advantage over the regression method in that the causal relationship between the two variables can more easily be determined, thus affording the decision maker a more accurate means of determining an optimum level of advertising spending. The method, however, is considerably more expensive than the nonexperimental regression method.

Many advertisers, particularly those oriented toward the behavioral sciences and communications theory, prefer to link advertising with communications objectives rather than with sales or market share. Their argument is that the direct relationship between sales or market share and advertising is difficult to establish because of the influence of many other marketing variables. It is, therefore, more appropriate to translate the sales goal into a communications objective before allocating the advertising budget. For example, in one of Westinghouse Corporation's advertising campaigns for its new extra-high voltage (EHV) transmission equipment, the communications objective is expressed as "to increase association with Apple Grove activity in EHV from the present level of 28 percent to 53 percent among management and engineering personnel in the transmission segment of major electric utilities" [11].

Whatever objective is used, the functional relationship must be established between the level of advertising appropriation and the expected output, that is, sales, market share, or communications factor. Work on the advertising/ sales relationship has been relatively abundant while studies of the advertising/ communication relationship have been less frequent. Instead of reviewing all the major works in the field, we shall discuss three typical examples: two (Weinberg and Du Pont) showing the method of establishing the advertising/

sales (or market share) relationship and one showing the advertising/communication link (Yang). All three models have been developed for the purpose of advertising budget appropriation.

Sales or Market Share Objective

Nonexperimental Method: The Weinberg Model. The Weinberg model attempts to give a practical solution to budget setting given a market share objective. It employs the regression method to analyze the interrelationship between changes in the company's share of market and its advertising exchange rate. This relationship provides the basis for developing an optimum level of advertising budget under a given market share objective. The following is a summary description of the model [12].

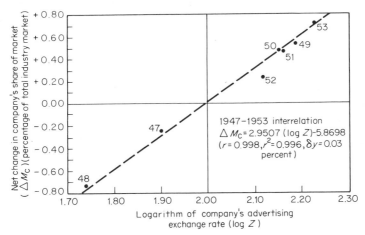

Exhibit 1. The company's share of the market—exchange rate relation. (SOURCE: Robert Weinberg, "Developing an Advertising Planning Procedure—An Econometric Approach," How Much to Spend for Advertising? Association of National Advertisers, Inc., p. 50.)

The company's share of the market is first related to the company's advertising exchange rate using the historical data. The company's advertising exchange rate is defined as the ratio between the company's advertising expenditure per dollar of sales and that of the residual industry. In essence, it is intended to represent the relative strength of the company's advertising program and implicitly assumes that the advertising impact per dollar is the same for all the companies in the industry. In Weinberg's example, net change in the company's share of the market (ΔM) is related to the logarithm of the company's advertising exchange rate ($\log Z$). Mathematically stated, $\Delta M = b \log Z - a$. The data given for the case (see Exhibit 1), for example, yields the following equation: $\Delta M = 2.9507 \log Z - 5.8698$.

Once the relationship has been established, the following steps are taken to determine the level of advertising spending for the coming year:

Step 1: Determine the company's advertising objective in terms of its intended share of market for the coming year, say 20.8 percent. Subtract this from this year's market share, say 20.0 percent. This yields a desired change in the market share (ΔM) of 0.8 percent.

Step 2.   Forecast total industry sales for the coming year, say $257.3 million in this example.   With the desired share of market for the company of 20.8 percent, total industry sales are divided into $53.5 million for the company and $203.8 million for the rest of the industry.

Step 3.   Forecast the total advertising volume of all the other companies in the industry (the residual industry)—for example, $11.90 million for the coming year.

Step 4.   Compute advertising spending per dollar of sales for the residual industry by dividing the estimated advertising expenditures for the residual industry ($11.90 million) into the estimated volume of sales for these companies ($203.8 million).   The ratio in this case is 0.0584.

Step 5.   Compute the exchange rate that is required to achieve the established advertising objective.   In this case, 0.8 (percent) = 2.9507 log Z − 5.8698.   Hence, Z = 182.1 (percent).

Step 6.   Compute advertising expenditures per dollar of sales needed by the company to achieve its objective by multiplying the advertising expenditure per dollar of sales of the residual industry by the required exchange rate. That is, 0.0584 × 1.821 = 0.1063.

Step 7.   The company's advertising budget for the coming year is a product of the forecasted sales of the company and the needed advertising outlay per dollar of sales.   In this example, $53.5 million × 0.1063 = $5.69 million.

The ability to relate the size of advertising budget to the planned objective (market share in this case) has made this model particularly appealing to practitioners, notwithstanding the difficulty of forecasting accurately industry sales and the volume of competitors' advertising expenditures.   However, it must be noted that the model deals exclusively with the effect of the relative advertising intensity on the company's share without giving sufficient attention to the level of sales as a probable factor that may influence the relationship.

Sales or Market Share Objective

Experimental Method: Du Pont Case.   The Weinberg nonexperimental method often takes the causality structure as given, since a regression analysis measures only covariation, not cause and effect.[5]   It is this weakness that has led some researchers and executives to turn to the experimental method.   The basic feature of a market experiment is for a decision maker to manipulate advertising inputs in such a way as to discover the true effects of advertising while controlling the effects of other market variables.[6]   This procedure enables the decision maker to know with greater confidence how different levels of advertising outlay may affect the company's sales or profits.   The most profitable level of spending is then determined.   Du Pont's case is perhaps the best illustration of how the experimental method is applied to advertising budget setting.   The objective in this case was to choose the level of advertising expenditures that maximizes operative earnings.   A brief summary of the case is given here [10].

Du Pont's management was interested in assessing the value of its advertising strategy for Teflon.   It was believed that by generating adequate consumer demand for cookware coated with Teflon, the company would encourage the manufacturers to apply this product to their cookware.

---

[5] In addition to its inability to clarify the cause-effect relationship, the validity of regression analyses may also be reduced by problems of autocorrelation and spurious correlation.

[6] For a comprehensive discussion of different experimental designs see [Sec. II, Part E, Chap. 12, and Sec. IV, Part E, Chap. 3]; also [1].

The problem was, "How much advertising was required for a product of this sort which was a genuine innovation and had no direct competition?" Daytime television was clearly the most appropriate medium for introduction of this product and no other media were tested, at least at this stage.

A test-market study was designed which varied the advertising level from zero through $1 million. Twelve test markets were used, and the results are shown in Exhibits 2 and 3.

There was no difference between "no advertising" and $500,000, but a significant sales effect occurred at the $1 million level. This was clearly a profitable level of expenditure and the product was introduced nationally at this level.

	Fall		
	No. adv.	$ ½ MM	$ 1 MM
No. adv.	XX	X	X
Winter $½MM	X	XX	X
$1 MM	X	X	XX

	Fall		
	No. adv.	$ ½ MM	$ 1 MM
No. adv.	25	26	32
Winter $½MM	29	29	35
$ 1 MM	49	53	70

Exhibit 2.   Experimental design. (SOURCE: Malcolm A. McNiven, "Choosing the Most Profitable Level of Advertising: A Case Study," How Much to Spend for Advertising? Association of National Advertisers, Inc., p. 91.)

Exhibit 3.   Winter results in units per thousand households. (SOURCE: Malcolm A. McNiven, "Choosing the Most Profitable Level of Advertising: A Case Study," How Much to Spend for Advertising? Association of National Advertisers, Inc., p. 91.)

Although it was known that the $1 million level was profitable, it was not necessarily the optimum level in terms of sales growth and operative earnings. Another experiment (Table 2) was set up to test higher levels of advertising.

TABLE 2   Experimental Design—Measurement Periods

Advertising treatment	Spring 1964	Fall 1964
Present national level . . .	National probability sample of 2,000 housewives	National probability sample of 2,000 housewives
Increased level	Samples of 1,000 housewives in each of five markets	Samples of 750 housewives in each of same five markets plus one new market

SOURCE: Malcolm A. McNiven, "Choosing the Most Profitable Level of Advertising: A Case Study," How Much to Spend for Advertising? Association of National Advertisers, Inc., p. 92.

A national sample of housewives served as a control group to reflect normal growth at Du Pont's current national level of advertising. A group of test markets was selected and the rate of advertising expenditures was increased to a higher level. This was done during the spring and fall of 1964. The increased level affected the Teflon-coated cookware sales markedly (Exhibit 4). There is clearly an effect of the increased advertising level. This difference could not have occurred by chance. By analyzing the unit sales required to produce adequate profits with which to pay for the advertising, the increase which would be necessary to break even on the increased advertising level was found. Any increase beyond that would represent increased profits.

Advertising research data indicated that the odds were at least 20 to 1 that the increased advertising would return more than it was costing. On the basis of these very favorable odds, management approved the recommendation of the increased budget level for 1965. At that time, however, the question was raised, "How much is *really* enough?" Consequently, a multilevel experiment to test higher levels of advertising was designed in an effort to find the expenditure range within which the best level lay.

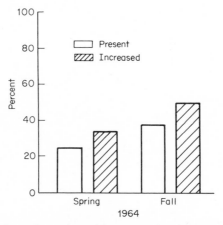

Exhibit 4. Proportion of total cookware purchasers who purchased Teflon-coated cookware by advertising treatment. (SOURCE: *Malcolm A. McNiven, "Choosing the Most Profitable Level of Advertising: A Case Study,"* How Much to Spend for Advertising? *Association of National Advertisers, Inc., p. 92.*)

This study involved 20 test markets in which much higher levels were tested. In addition, print media along with television were tested. The results of this study found that extremely high levels of advertising did not move enough additional cookware to pay for the advertising costs in a short-run period. The effects of these different advertising levels on operative earnings are shown in Exhibit 5.

Note that operative earnings fall below the break-even point at low budget levels, as was found in the first experiment. It then increases dramatically as advertising is added but, after passing the optimum, falls sharply until one is in a loss position. The only difficulty is in determining the scale of the horizontal axis which represents the advertising budget level (presumably spent in the best media with the best copy).

It is a management decision at which point within the profitable area one should advertise. The optimum point is that at which one gets back the most per dollar. However, the point at the right of the optimum, just before operative earnings reach break even, is the point at which one's marginal profit is still greater than zero and advertising would still be returning more than it cost. However, there is naturally some amount of error in these estimates, so that by moving to the point of maximum marginal profit one is running the risk of possibly being in the loss area.

The point Du Pont selected was slightly to the right of the optimum, but not to the point where advertising was returning the last additional dollar of profit. Since this relationship will not remain constant over time, testing of higher and lower levels from time to time must be carried out to be sure that the company is still within the band of profitability.

The payoff from the market experiment in the Du Pont case has proved to be quite handsome despite its high cost. As more executives come to realize the advantages of market experiments and as better cost-saving designs are made available, this technique of advertising budget appropriation should gain in popularity.

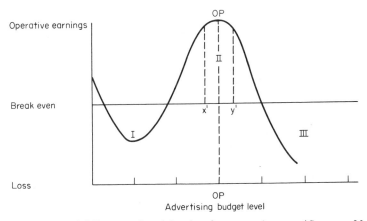

Exhibit 5. Effect of different advertising levels on earnings. (SOURCE: *Malcolm A. McNiven, "Choosing the Most Profitable Level of Advertising: A Case Study," How Much to Spend for Advertising? Association of National Advertisers, Inc., p. 93.*)

Communications Objective

While many marketing executives are convinced that the use of sales or market share or even profit as an objective is more realistic and meaningful when determining the advertising budget, there is a definite advantage in adopting a communication objective as the intervening variable, particularly when advertising is not the dominant part of the marketing effort. In such a case, the advertising manager may wish to set an advertising budget on the basis of the communication objective(s) to be attained.

Although it is not impossible theoretically to establish the functional relationship between the level of advertising outlay and the degree of communication impact the target population receives from the advertising program, researchers have not been particularly successful on this point. The main reason appears to be that variation in media selection tends to be too large to render the relationship stable. In other words, the same advertising budget can buy several different media combinations and schedules having different degrees of advertising impact. It is because of this difficulty that the author prefers an indirect approach, relating the objective to the response function and then to the best media schedule for which the size of budget is determined.[7]

The following steps outline this system of allocation:

1. An advertising manager first determines a communication objective(s)—for example, awareness, knowledge, and so on—to be achieved during the coming year.

2. Estimate the response function that relates the level of exposure to the established communication objective. This response function also sets the basic advertising strategy for the company.

3. Find the media schedule which best achieves the objective at minimum cost.

4. The cost of the selected media schedule together with costs of producing copies and commercials and other related expenses form the budget for the coming year.

Turning to the Westinghouse case mentioned earlier, suppose the company's advertising campaign calls for an increase in the number of engineers who can associate Westinghouse with the Apple Grove project for EHV equipment from 500,000 to 780,000 engineers. A budget must be set to achieve this communi-

Number of exposures	Response index
0	10 %
1	31 %
2	46 %
3	56 %
4	63 %
5	69 %

cation objective. Obviously, several media schedules can satisfy this objective, but there is usually only one schedule which can be bought at minimum cost. To search for such a schedule, it is necessary for the planner to know how the target population responds to advertising. This is termed a response function.

A response function relates the expected impact from the advertising copy to the number of exposures. It can be represented by a response index having different values for different levels of exposure. For example, if the function has a convex shape that shows diminishing returns for higher levels of exposure and is represented by a geometric function of the form $R = 0.10 + 0.70 (1 - 0.7^S)$, where R is the response value and S the number of exposures, the response index for the first five levels of exposure clearly suggests that advertising impact is subject to profound diminishing returns and that the planner would be well advised to choose a media schedule which is highly reach-oriented. In other words, he should not go for a schedule with heavy repetitive exposures.

How such functions can be derived is, of course, of paramount importance. The planner can do this with a statistical estimation method, using historical or experimental data, or he can combine his judgment with whatever evidence is available [2].

In analyzing most of the response functions that have been published, the geometric function is by far the dominant form. In such a case it becomes possible for the planner to estimate the entire response schedule with only the

[7] For a comprehensive discussion of this approach, see [13, Chaps. 7 and 8].

knowledge of the extent of contribution to be expected from the initial exposure and the level of ultimate saturation. Returning to the Westinghouse example, suppose the planner is fairly sure that the response function is of the geometric form and fits the general equation $R_S = a + g\ (1 - r^s)$, where R is the response value for S number of exposures, a the impact without any exposures, g the saturation level, $r = 1 - f$ where f is the impact of the initial exposure, and s is the number of exposures. He can estimate these values as follows:

1.   What is the percentage of people who would acquire the necessary communication impact (understanding the advertising message, for example) even if they have not been exposed to the ad at all?

If the answer is 10 percent, then $a = 0.10$.

2.   What is the maximum percentage of people who will acquire the necessary impact if they have been exposed to the ad for an infinite number of times?

If the answer is 80 percent for the saturation level, then $h = 0.80$ and the range $g = h - a = 0.80 - 0.10 = 0.70$.

3.   Taking g as the maximum contribution that can be expected from the program, how much of g would be accounted for by the first exposure? In other words, what percent of this total contribution is to be expected from the first impact?

If the answer is 30 percent, then $f = 0.30$ and $r = 1 - f = 1.0 - 0.3 = 0.7$.

This estimation procedure yields $a = 0.10$, $g = 0.70$, $r = 0.10$, and a response function, $R_S = 0.10 + 0.70\ (1 - 0.10^s)$.[8]

After obtaining the response function, the decision maker must find a media schedule that can yield the best results in terms of the established objective and at minimum cost. This may be done by an iteration procedure, as follows:

1.   Start with a one-vehicle schedule with the lowest cost per thousand that satisfies the objective.

2.   Substitute the marginal unit one by one with the vehicle having the second-lowest cost per thousand while maintaining the same level of output until no further saving in costs is possible.

3.   Move on to the next vehicle. The process terminates when no further cost reduction is feasible.

Numerically, the first step will yield, for example, a frequency distribution of the kind shown in Table 3, which is then applied to the response index to yield the expected output.

TABLE 3   Media Schedule: Five Issues of Business Week; Cost—$100,000

Number of exposures	Number of engineers reached by the schedule		Response index, percent	Response value, engineers who have the needed knowledge
0	300,000	×	10	30,000
1	100,000	×	31	31,000
2	200,000	×	46	92,000
3	300,000	×	56	168,000
4	400,000	×	63	252,000
5	300,000	×	69	207,000
				780,000

[8] For a detailed discussion of this estimation procedure, see [13, Chap. 8].

The second step involves substituting one unit of the magazine with the next-best magazine or vehicle option to see if cost reduction is possible. The process is repeated as long as additional gain can be made from either the same vehicle or another vehicle.

With the data bases currently available, particularly W. R. Simmons, computation of the reach and frequency schedule for any combination of vehicles can be obtained with relative ease, although different advertisers may prefer different computation procedures.[9]

When the best schedule has been selected, the production costs for advertising copies and commercials plus other related expenses are added to media costs to determine the size of the advertising budget needed for the coming year.

The Systems Approach: A Dual Advertising Budget Appropriation System

The traditional task approach tends to treat advertising appropriations on a functional basis. That is, the task is to optimize the payoff from the advertising program, with other marketing variables being treated independently. The result is often less than ideal from the point of view of the company's entire operation. The systems approach to budget setting attempts to overcome this weakness by crossing the functional boundaries of advertising into other areas. It becomes necessary, therefore, for a marketing manager to introduce other variables directly into the appropriation system. One such system is proposed here; it may be called a dual advertising budget appropriation system, which utilizes the concept of industrial dynamics and incorporates production costs into the appropriation system.

The use of industrial dynamics in advertising operations was first proposed by Jay W. Forrester [5]. His model emphasizes delayed responses and the importance of the feedback mechanism in a marketing system. This concept has been developed into a more workable form by the author with a view toward practical budget setting procedures.

Three basic features characterize this dual appropriation system: (1) The advertising budget should be established to optimize the company's profits over the course of a business cycle, taking into account the alternative costs of not spending on advertising. (2) The advertising budget should be divided into two parts—a regular budget and a contingency budget. The first is to achieve long-run objectives while the second is for short-term objectives. (3) Budget setting should be treated as a system capable of predicting the probable course of business fluctuations and of detecting the impact of advertising on marketing performance.

In determining the regular portion of the budget, the advertising manager is required to specify the task to be accomplished during the coming year in light of long-run objectives. This should be expressed in terms of sales or indirectly in terms of market share. Since production capacity is generally planned for operation in a normal year on a long-run basis, the advertising objective can be set to achieve this level of operation. Ideally then, the anticipated volume of sales in a normal year should be equal to or only slightly below or above the production capacity, so that capacity wastes are minimized. Hence the usual task method is sufficient for determining the regular portion of the advertising budget.

---

[9] There are two popularly used methods for computation of the reach and frequency schedule of a media schedule—the beta function method and the Metheringham method. For a discussion of these two methods, see [13, Chap. 7].

A recession, however, poses a problem for companies with recession-sensitive products, not only because of a loss in sales but also because of the resulting rise in undercapacity costs associated with underutilization of plant capacity, as well as shut-down and start-up costs. It is worthwhile, therefore, for a company in this situation to consider additional spending on advertising in order to lessen the impact of a recession. That is, if marginal gains from advertising can more than offset the resulting undercapacity wastes which would have been present in the absence of such spending, then a contingency budget should be allocated to serve as a recession buffer.

Two decisions need to be made in budgeting a contingency fund: the size and timing of spending. The basic principle for the first decision is that contingency money should be spent up to the point where the marginal gain is equal to the marginal outlay. The concept of industrial dynamics governs the timing of spending.

The use of the following heuristic rules is recommended for determining the size of a contingency fund.

1. Forecast expected monthly sales for the coming year, taking into account probable fluctuations in business (sales forecast).

2. Estimate expected monthly losses in sales due to recession in terms of deviations from full-capacity production.

3. Estimate monthly opportunity losses in profits due to lower level of sales and estimated plant shutdown and start-up costs.

4. Determine monthly contingency spending in proportion to the volume of sales short of the full-capacity production. This is done by first estimating the effectiveness of the contingency funds. The size of budget is then computed to minimize under-capacity costs as computed in step 2.

5. Add the contingency budget to the regular budget to arrive at the total budget for the coming year.

The second decision is "When should the contingency fund be spent?" The contingency fund, if not properly spent, could aggravate rather than moderate fluctuations in sales, thereby enlarging over- and undercapacity wastes. Because of the time lag involved in generating advertising effects, a higher-order feedback system must be developed for this operation. That is, for the system to be effective it must have predictive ability, so that the contingency fund can be used in time to moderate a forthcoming downturn. The minimum length of lead time required for such an adjustment depends on the structures of the production and distribution systems, as Exhibit 6 illustrates.

This hypothetical case shows that it takes two weeks before a temporary campaign reaches consumers, who will then take another two weeks to make purchasing decisions. Assuming a constant inventory level throughout the distribution system, retailers will have to replenish inventory by placing an additional order, which takes one week to reach wholesalers. They, in turn, need another week to place orders with the manufacturer. The length of time needed to process orders from a factory warehouse to a factory takes another 0.5 week. In total, it takes 6.5 weeks from the time the decision is made to use the contingency fund to the moment when additional production actually takes place. This means that a temporary advertising campaign must have a minimum lead time of 6.5 weeks to yield maximum effect. Hence, the predictors should be designed to give this minimum lead time.

If properly designed and executed, a temporary advertising campaign can reduce the size of fluctuation in sales as shown in Exhibit 7, where the advertising campaign gets under way 6.5 weeks in advance of the downturn. It also ends ahead of the subsequent upturn by the same length of time. The amount

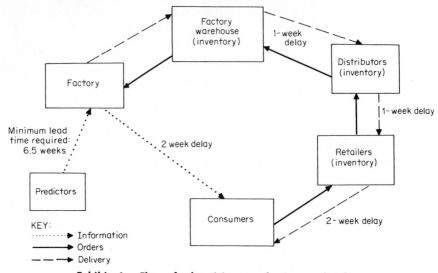

Exhibit 6.   Flow of advertising, purchasing, and orders.

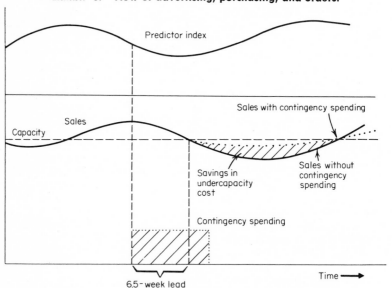

Exhibit 7.   The effect of contingency spending on sales.

of savings realized is equal to the shaded area under the sales trend times the per-unit undercapacity cost.

As can be readily observed, how well this model works depends on the system's capability to diagnose changes in the system environment and predict the directions of these changes. The feedback system that contains this ability to predict and adjust is shown in Exhibit 8, which determines the timing and the size of spending in the contingency fund in accordance with changes in the external conditions and the variation in the rate of advertising outputs.

The following example illustrates the above budget setting procedure. Assume (1) that a manufacturer of television sets plans to achieve a sales goal of $240 million for the coming year under normal economic conditions and that the company must spend $12 million in advertising to achieve this goal; (2) that the product has an income elasticity of 3, meaning that sales will decline by 3 percent for each percentage drop in consumer income; (3) that the marginal efficiency of advertising is assumed to be 20, that is, each additional dollar of the regular budget can generate $20 in sales; and (4) that a lag of two months is needed before advertising takes effect. Under the above assumptions, a recession of the magnitude of 10 percent at trough and five months in duration will cause a loss of as much as $6 million in sales per month at the lowest point. The undercapacity costs, including the foregone

Exhibit 8   Dual Advertising Budget Appropriation System

Output: Sales
Input: Regular budget (fixed) and contingency budget (variable)
System Structure:
  1. Predictor: Prediction equations for economic forecast, competitive behavior, consumer behavior, and other marketing dynamics.
  2. Receptor: Receives the outputs of the predictor and transmits them to the memory bank.
  3. Memory bank:
      a. Stores and analyzes feedback information and input data from the receptor.
      b. Estimates the effects of changes in the volume of sales on the capacity conditions of the production and distribution systems.
      c. Determines the rate of adjustment needed in advertising spending.
  4. Effector: Effectuates a change in flexible budget to achieve required outputs.

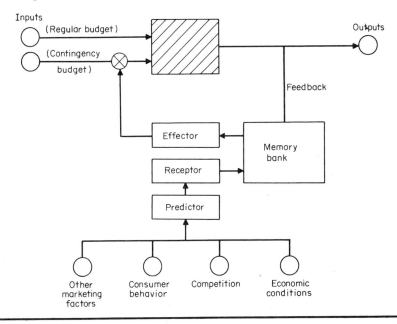

profit, are estimated at 20 cents per dollar of sales. The results from advertising spending on the regular basis and without a contingency fund are shown in Table 4.

If, for example, the effectiveness of the contingency budget is 70 percent of the regular budget or $E_c = 0.70\ E_r$, one additional dollar of contingency spending can generate only $14 in sales rather than $20 as with the regular budget. Since each dollar of contingency spending brings in $14 in sales, which would save the company $2.8 in undercapacity costs including the foregone profit, it is profitable for the company to allocate a contingency fund in order to bring production to full-capacity level. To determine the monthly contingency spending, it is necessary to multiply the monthly cyclical deviations by k, which is 0.0143. Thus the contingency spending for the first month

TABLE 4   Spending the Regular Budget

Month	Advertising expenditures (regular budget)	Production capacity	Estimated volume of sales	Under-capacity	Undercapacity costs
1	$1	$20	$24		
2	1	20	22		
3	1	20	20		
4	1	20	18	$2	$0.4
5	1	20	16	4	0.8
6	1	20	14	6	1.2
7	1	20	16	4	0.8
8	1	20	18	2	0.4
9	1	20	20		
10	1	20	22		
11	1	20	24		
12	1	20	26		
	$12				$3.6

NOTE: All figures in millions of dollars.

TABLE 5   Spending the Regular and Contingency Budgets

Month	Regular budget	Contingency budget	Expected sales	Under-capacity
1	$1		$24	$0
2	1	$0.143	20	0
3	1	0.286	20	0
4	1	0.429	20	0
5	1	0.286	20	0
6	1	0.143	20	0
7	1		20	0
8	1		20	0
9	1		20	0
10	1		22	0
11	1		24	0
12	1		26	0
	$12	$1.287		

NOTE: All figures in millions of dollars

TABLE 6 Evaluation of Advertising Budget Appropriation Methods

Method	Advantages	Disadvantages	Applicable situation
Subjective approach: Intuitive method	Very little, but with sufficient data and experience permits capable executive to capitalize on his good judgment promptly and with flexibility.	No theoretical or empirical rationale; formal rules not established; trial-and-error process.	Advertiser with a small budget; when direct selling plays a dominant role in marketing and advertising a supplementary role.
Heuristic method	Rules are formally established; can work well under stable market conditions when rules formed by capable executive; executive required to explain deviation from established rules; capable of simulating a decision-making process.	No theoretical or analytical base; no assurance that the established rules will remain effective when market conditions change.	Medium or large advertiser with successful appropriation experience or with executives of high caliber in a complex market situation where analysis of interrelationships between market variables does not lend itself to analytical optimization.
Ratio approach: Fixed-ratio method	Simplicity; effective when appropriate ratio is applied to a product with constant growth rate; easy to use in multiple products situation.	Inflexible; cannot accommodate changes in market conditions and competitive situations; unable to maintain proper spending level when media costs are rising quickly.	Company with a long-life product with stable growth rate and relatively insensitive to changes in market conditions; also when competitive situation is stable; company with good forecasting capability and sufficient research data to determine the ratio.
Variable-ratio method	More realistic than fixed ratio; able to accommodate to changes in market conditions and changing stages in the product life cycle.	If ratio is not carefully established, error can compound; less capable of adjusting to short-run changes in market conditions than task method.	A product with an intermediate range of life cycle; change in ratio can be systematically regulated in advance or adjusted through adaptive process.
Objective approach: Sales objective: nonexperimental method	Able to adjust to short-run changes from year to year; able to integrate and coordinate the advertising functions with other functions of the company.	The cause-effect relationship may be difficult to establish or may be misleading; not applicable to new product which lacks historical data.	A medium or large advertiser who needs to gear advertising strategy to short-run objectives; where market conditions require flexibility in advertising spending; with a large

TABLE 6 Evaluation of Advertising Budget Appropriation Methods (Continued)

Method	Advantages	Disadvantages	Applicable situation
			advertising budget relative to other marketing expenditures so that sales-advertising relationship can be more easily established; when sufficient data are available to establish the advertising-sales relationship.
Sales objective: experimental method	Able to identify true cause-effect relationship; able to net out the effect of advertising from the total marketing action.	Expensive and generally time-consuming.	For large, nondurable goods advertiser with sufficient funds to conduct market experiments; where the sales-advertising relationship is expected to remain fairly stable for the intermediate range.
Communications objective method	Able to relate advertising expenditures to more immediate objectives where the advertising-sales relationship is difficult to establish; tighter control over how money should be spent on media when such selection can cause significant difference in performance.	Difficult to assess the true contribution of advertising to sales if the communication-sales relationship is not known; requires a fairly complex simulation.	A medium or large advertiser, particularly of durable goods or of services, where advertising is important but not dominant force in marketing and when task to be accomplished can be best expressed in terms of communication variables; when different media schedules are likely to create a significant variation in the final payoff.
Systems method	Capable of integrating advertising with other operations for profit maximization; effective use of feedback mechanism.	Difficult to apply without sufficient data and system capability; requires joint decision making among different departments.	A large advertiser with sufficient computer software and hardware support; where product is sensitive to changes in market conditions; requires management sophistication with predictive capability of market; where joint effort between advertising and other operations is crucial.

of recession is determined as $-k(d) = -0.0143 \, (-10) = \$0.143$. Since there is a two-month period before contingency fund expenditures take effect, monthly contingency outlays must be allocated sufficiently in advance to allow for this time lag. When the contingency budget is added to the regular budget, the results are as shown in Table 5.

Using the contingency fund has yielded a saving of \$2.313 million, the difference between the saving from the undercapacity costs (\$3.6 million) and the contingency expenditures (\$1.287 million). The required budget for the coming year is then the sum of the regular budget and the contingency budget, or \$13.287 million.

CONCLUSION

This review of various budget appropriation techniques suggests considerable overlap among the three basic approaches. In actual practice some advertisers draw on more than one method in determining their budgets or employ different methods for different product lines.

Which method should be adopted depends on the size of the company, the type of product, and its management capability. A large firm, for example, marketing a product with an intermediate product life in rapidly changing market conditions, may need a complex simulation-based system that calls for a large volume of input data; on the other hand, a very small advertiser marketing producers' goods in a steadily growing market may require only a simple ratio method.

Table 6 summarizes the advantages and disadvantages of each method and suggests situations under which each can best be utilized.

REFERENCES

1. Banks, Seymour, *Experimentation in Marketing*, New York: McGraw-Hill, 1965.
2. Broadbent, S. R., and S. Segnit, "Response Functions in Media Planning," *The Thomson Medals and Awards for Advertising Research*, 1967.
3. *The Conference Board Record*, National Industrial Conference Board, March 1968.
4. Fitzroy, P. T., "An Adaptive Model for Promotional Decision Making," Philadelphia: Marketing Science Institute, Special Report, 1967.
5. Forrester, Jay W., *Industrial Dynamics*, Cambridge, Mass.: M.I.T., 1961.
6. Friedman, Lawrence, "Allocating Marketing Expenditures—A Budget Forecasting Procedure," Cambridge, Mass.: Marketing Science Institute, working paper, 1970.
7. Green, Paul E., and Donald S. Tull, *Research for Marketing Decisions*, Englewood Cliffs, N.J.: Prentice-Hall, 1966.
8. Little, John D. C., "A Model of Adaptive Control of Promotional Spending," *Operations Research*, vol. 14, November 1966.
9. Marschner, Donald C., "Theory versus Practice in Allocating Advertising Money," *The Journal of Business*, vol. 40, July 1967.
10. McNiven, Malcolm A., "Choosing the Most Profitable Level of Advertising: A Case Study," *How Much to Spend for Advertising?* Association of National Advertisers, Inc., 1969.
11. Sands, Saul S., "Setting Advertising Objectives," New York: National Industrial Conference Board, *Business Policy Study no. 118*, 1966.
12. Weinberg, Robert S., "Developing an Advertising Planning Procedure—An Econometric Approach," *How Much to Spend for Advertising?* Association of National Advertisers, Inc., 1969.
13. Yang, Charles Y., *Management of Media Programs*, New York: Harper (forthcoming).

Advertising Research

Chapter 5

Advertising Media Selection

DENNIS H. GENSCH *Graduate School of Business Administration, Carnegie-Mellon University, Pittsburgh, Pennsylvania*

Prior to selecting media schedules, it is assumed the advertiser has determined the content of his advertising message and can identify the target population.

Selection of the most effective television shows, radio programs, magazines, newspapers, and other media vehicles to convey a message to a target population has always been more involved than simply selecting the set of media vehicles with the lowest cost per thousand. Other factors to be considered are the editorial climate of the vehicle, its prestige, the visual and/or audio qualities in relation to the requirements of the product message, interactions between vehicles, and the social environment in which the audience reads or views the vehicles. The major types of media vehicles are:

1. Television
   a. Network
   b. Spot
2. Magazines
   a. Consumer
   b. Industrial
   c. Technical and professional journals
3. Radio
   a. Network
   b. Spot
4. Newspapers
5. Outdoor (billboards)
6. Direct mail
7. Transit advertising
8. Novelties (skywriting)
9. Point of purchase

Current media research effort is directed primarily at analyzing the first four types of vehicles just listed. Therefore the remainder of this chapter will concentrate on these four media types.

Due to differences in products, message appeals, target populations, geographic distribution networks, size of advertising budgets, and competitive environments, there is no "best" set of criteria or rules to follow in selecting the most "cost efficient" set of media vehicles. Rather, what the media scheduler needs is some *system* for interrelating the objective data with the subjective judgments that he feels are most appropriate to the circumstances of his particular situation. Greater use of computers in advertising has increased the volume of objective data available as well as the number of quantitative models. Quantitative models using linear programming, dynamic programming, iteration, heuristic programming, and simulation have been designed to select media schedules.

These models are basically systems for selecting media schedules in which certain functional relationships between the relevant variables are postulated. Relevant variables are usually called media weights; that is, the relevant factors that give one media vehicle more or less weight in relation to other available vehicles. An evaluation and comparison of these models are given by Gensch [11].

Preliminary analysis can greatly reduce the number of alternatives evaluated by the quantitative model. The media planner can usually specify the types of media that should be considered on the basis of (1) distribution system for product, (2) target population, (3) budget size, and (4) characteristics of the product. For example, it is of limited value to advertise heavily in geographic areas in which the product is not sold or in which few members of the target population live. Thus for a local or regional product national television and magazines may be excluded from consideration. A product may have characteristics that must be seen to be understood, so radio might be eliminated.

Besides eliminating certain types of media from consideration, the initial screening can also eliminate specific media vehicles unavailable to the advertiser. There is little sense in evaluating *Gunsmoke* as a vehicle if it is known that present sponsors plan to continue.

Following this initial screening, the complex problem of picking the best set of media vehicles from acceptable and available choices must be faced. Factors used to adjust a simple cost-per-thousand ranking of vehicles can be grouped into five categories:

1. Target population weights
2. Vehicle appropriateness weights
3. Commercial exposure weights
4. Commercial effectiveness weights
5. Cumulative frequency weights

In the opinion of this author, weights that attempt to attribute change of attitude or sales increases directly to specific commercials are presently of little value to media schedulers. Attitude change is primarily a function of copy; thus if the same copy is used, selection of media vehicles should not be affected by these weights. Furthermore, is it realistic to believe a person's attitude has really changed due to one advertising exposure? The Schwerin (pre-post) method of measuring attitude changes caused by television commercials has been severely criticized with respect to technique and meaningfulness [4, 8, 9].

Weights that attribute sales directly to advertising are usually gross oversimplifications of the real world. Purchase decisions are not a sole function of advertising. Many other variables, such as product price, product quality,

TABLE 1 Individual Weighting System

Individual	Variable 1 College education			Variable 2 Child 30 months			Variable 3 Aggressiveness			Individual's value weight			
	Weight	Scale	VI	Weight	Scale	V2	Weight	Scale	V3	V1	V2	V3	Weight
1	3	1.00	3.00	10	1.00	10	5	0.20	1.0	3.0	10.0	1.0	30.0
2	3	0.01	0.03	10	1.00	10	5	0.80	4.0	0.03	10.0	4.0	1.2
3	3	1.00	3.00	10	0.01	0.1	5	0.50	2.5	3.0	0.1	2.5	0.75
4	3	0.50	1.50	10	0.01	0.1	5	0.60	3.0	1.5	0.1	3.0	0.45

availability, actions by competitors, peer-group evaluation of product, present cash position, and so on interact with advertising to determine purchase. To ignore the actions of these other variables seems unrealistic.

Because of the number of influences found within each category, it is possible to use a number of quantitative weighting schemes to arrive at the one value to represent a particular media weight. This chapter will not go into the many variations of these weighting systems except to say that when the influences within a category are independent of each other, an additive relationship is in order. When the influences are interdependent, then a multiplicative relationship such as a geometric average is recommended.

Each of the five categories just listed will be reviewed and current possibilities in the areas mentioned.

Target Population Weights

The advertiser usually considers certain members of the mass audience to be of greater importance to him than other members. Advertising has been designed for and will have greater effect upon a certain subset of the total audience. This target population may be identified and valued on the basis of past purchasing activity, socioeconomic variables, or personality traits.

The target population can sometimes be defined on the basis of a single attribute. For example, denture adhesive advertisers may define their target population as only those people who wear dentures. A simple 1 or 0 value can be attached to each individual in the vehicle's audience. Throughout this chapter, weights will be assigned on an individual rather than aggregate basis.

Most target populations are not determined on the basis of only one attribute. Many target populations are valued over a one-variable spectrum such as past purchase behavior. A manufacturer of canned dog food might assign the following weights on the basis of past purchase behavior and dog ownership:

Weight	Category
1.00	Purchased 30 cans of dog food in the last month
0.60	Purchased 15 cans
0.40	Purchased 10 cans
0.20	Purchased 5 cans
0.10	Purchased 0 cans but own dog
0.01	Purchased 0 cans but do not own dog

These weights attempt to reflect the purchasing potential as well as the past purchasing record of each individual. It is hoped that light users can be encouraged to increase purchases; thus weighting is not in direct proportion to past purchases.

Individuals can be identified on the basis of socioeconomic variables, past purchasing, and personality traits. Assume potential customers are identified by some combination of these variables. For example, assume a new form of baby food is the product. The potential customer is defined as female (college education) with youngest child less than 30 months of age, the mother possessing traits of aggressiveness and venturesomeness.

To the advertiser, some variables are more important than others; also many variables can be present in various strengths or degrees. Thus variables must be weighted on both an inter and intra basis. Table 1 shows this weighting scheme for three variables in the baby food example.

The weight indicates the importance of one variable in relation to another. The scale indicates the degree to which the particular individual possesses each variable.   The 0.01 value is used in place of 0 so that each individual will have a positive value.   Some minimum positive value is desirable when combining the individual weights with other systems of weights.   This approach is fine when the variables and weights are known.   Unfortunately, most of the time the advertiser is not sure what the most relevant variables are, much less what the relative importance of each variable is.   Through research techniques, the advertiser can identify these variables and their relative importance.   Multiple regression analysis and factor analysis are methods of identifying variables which appear to be significant.   One can even get a crude weighting system from these approaches.   Multiple discriminant analysis can reduce the multidimensional system with a continuous dependent variable to a multidimensional system in which the dependent variable is dichotomous.   In other words, individuals are rated either as potential customers or not.   They are weighted 1 or 0 depending on whether they are customers or not.   This removes the relative differences in potential.

Another approach is to estimate the relative importance of various individuals to the advertiser.   A cluster analysis technique [13] could be used to determine the set of variables which seem important.   Using cluster analysis or factor analysis as a first step, one could rank order the variables.   Then, various nonmetric scaling methods could be employed to change the ranking from ordinal (first, second, and so on) into cardinal (1, 2, 3.6, and so on) scales [10].

Given the information obtained from these methods, the advertiser might build a model that attempts to explain interactions between these relevant variables.   Based upon this approach, each individual in the target population could be weighted in terms of his probable response to the ad and his purchase potential.

Vehicle Appropriateness Weights

Most professional advertising experts have taken the position that media vehicles are much more than passive conductors of messages.   There is an interrelationship between the vehicle and the advertising message it delivers to an audience.   This "rub-off" effect of the vehicle can make substantial negative or positive contributions to the advertising effectiveness of the message.   After some controversy on this point with Seymour Banks, Alfred Politz verbalized the prevailing attitude in his introduction to the well-publicized *Reader's Digest–Saturday Evening Post* exposure study [22].

> Exposure is entirely the responsibility of the medium though the medium's function goes beyond that—into the mood it creates in its readers, viewers, or listeners, their confidence in the medium and other benefits the medium delivers for its advertising content.   These other benefits are not measured in this study, which confines itself to exposure.

This belief that vehicles have carryover effects which influence the effectiveness of its ads has been documented in studies related to magazines, radio, and television.

Winick used an accordion method of paired comparisons in testing how the same advertisement might be perceived in the context of two different magazines.   Magazines X and Y were directly competitive.   In magazine X, the advertisements were significantly *better liked* (chi square = 22.6, $p < 0.01$), *more believable* (chi square = 73, $p < 0.01$) and *better recalled* (chi square = 6.3, p between 0.01 and 0.02).   From this and further research Winick [33] concluded "Where advertising is placed—its vehicle—affects recall of its message, rating of its sponsor, and return of its coupon."

A 1957 radio study [33] concluded:

Listeners pay more attention to these CBS Radio stations than to the leading independents. Listeners distinguish between stations—regard these CBS Radio stations more favorably than the leading independents. Listeners believe these CBS Radio stations more than the leading independents—both their programs and their advertising. It seems it's a matter of authority.

Television studies conducted in Britain and the United States indicate that the programs affect the audiences' response to commercials. Nuttall of the London Press Exchange observed [22]:

We also establish that the interest of viewers in the programs they watched considerably affected their attention to commercials. This was reflected both in the lower levels of activity during commercials of viewers to programs of high interest relative to programs of low interest, and also in the greater ability of these viewers to correctly identify advertisements that had appeared.

Barclay, Doub, and McMurtrey concluded that during the daytime, certain programs had a more positive affect on commercials [2], saying "In the daytime serial programs generated somewhat more recall and especially, attentiveness than other specific program types. Situation comedies fared least well. At night major program types differed relatively little."

Research performed by Crane tends to support this conclusion. Crane observed that women were significantly more affected than men by the media vehicle in making judgments about commercials [7].

Once it is accepted that the media vehicle affects advertising effectiveness, the media schedule must weight the number of exposures generated per vehicle by the factors that make one exposure in vehicle A more effective than one exposure in vehicle B. The following factors may affect the media vehicle appropriateness weight:

1. Editorial climate
2. Product fit
3. Technical capabilities
4. Competitive advertising strategy
5. Target population receptiveness
6. Product distribution system

These considerations are not implied to be affecting each advertising message. As products, target populations, and advertising messages differ, various factors can influence the appropriateness of each media vehicle. It is up to the media scheduler to decide the relevance and importance of each factor in relation to his particular advertising message.

The effect of any stimulus is influenced by the environment in which the stimulus is presented. Thus the *editorial climate* or environment can produce a more or less suitable setting for the advertisement. Some of the authority or believability of the publication affects the advertisement. Generally readers select magazines, newspapers, television news, and discussion shows that reinforce their present views. For this reason editorial climate is usually considered a positive factor as it puts the reader in an accepting frame of mind. The editorial climate is primarily associated with the general "honesty," "authority," "timeliness," and "believability" of the vehicle in handling political and social issues.

Some vehicles are assumed to have more knowledge and authority on certain products. For example, a power drill manufacturer might prefer that a reader see his ad in *Popular Mechanics* rather than *Playboy*. A manufacturer of men's slacks might feel *Playboy* is viewed as having more knowledge and expertise on men's fashions than *Popular Mechanics*. This is one way of fitting the product to the available vehicles.

Vehicles may be more fitting for a particular product because of their "mood" or "prestige." Products that have built an exclusive quality image, such as brands of women's perfumes or men's colognes, may use "status consciousness" as an appeal. Exclusive or high-prestige vehicles such as *The New Yorker* may be preferred to high circulation mass media vehicles, in which a product is apparently recommended for everyone.

Technical capabilities such as quality of paper, brightness of color, and quality of sound vary from one media vehicle to another, making some vehicles more suitable for certain types of copy format.

Competitive strategy considerations may make some media vehicles more desirable than others. If the competition is spending heavily on prime-time television, a decision may be made to go very lightly in this area and instead try to dominate the magazines used by the target audience. It is also important to consider how different the product's appeal, copy, and format are from the type of ads anticipated to be in the same issue. Uniqueness or difference enables an ad to stand out and be remembered. This author, while working for an advertising agency, was involved in tests to determine the degree to which use of color affected the attitude rating and recall score of an ad. It was interesting to note that if a black-and-white ad was inserted near the end of a sequence of 20 color ads, this black-and-white ad received good attitude ratings and excellent recall scores. The same black-and-white ad viewed in a sequence of 10 color and 10 black-and-white ads ranked below average in attitude ratings and recall scores.

The *social context* in which a media vehicle is viewed or read can make a difference. Some advertisements might want the entire family together for its presentation. This would mean evening television would be more desirable than daytime television or magazines and newspapers, which are usually read separately by the individual members of the family. An advertiser might wish to reach the housewife when she is relaxed. This would mean that T.V. programs would be weighted in relation to the time of day at which they are on.

Certain programs are thought to fit various products and target audiences. Depth interviews reported by Campbell-Ewald suggest that men's products are best advertised on Westerns whereas food products do best on situation comedies [5]. Schwerin [24] reports that food commercials fit well with situation comedies but do poorly in a mystery, adventure, or Western context. Analgesics do well both in adult Westerns and situation comedies. A problem with this type of research is that viewers do not always put programs into the same general categories as do researchers.

Distribution systems for many products are not uniform throughout the country. Therefore, vehicles with the highest ratings or circulation in areas where the product has the strongest distribution should receive higher weights. Sometimes it is also desirable to give higher weights to the media vehicles that wholesalers and retailers in the distribution system feel are particularly good. This does not mean that the distributors' favorite vehicles are superior to other vehicles. But it might be of value to have the retailer feel the manufacturer is doing the best job he can in supporting the product.

Commercial Exposure Weights

There are really two separate systems of commercial weights. The first set attempts, given the number of vehicle exposures, to predict the number of commercial exposures. The second set of commercial weights is more concerned with the perception of the ad given that exposure has occurred.

The concepts of exposure and perception are really quite different. An exposure is simply the opportunity to perceive. Perception means that some cognitive action has been taken by the individual. Although exposure and perception are clearly two different concepts, they are often treated as one in both weighting systems used by advertising models and by media research studies concerning press advertisements. We will attempt to keep these concepts separate and discuss first research relating to commercial exposure. This research estimates the probability that an individual will be exposed to the advertising message given that he is exposed to the media vehicle.

A number of studies have focused on the attention individuals give to television commercials. Nuttall found that, among British housewives, the proportion of women reported as viewers of a program when they were in fact not present in the viewing room during part of the commercial varied from 34 to 19 percent [22].

Nuttall summarized his findings as follows:

> Not in room..............24%
> Not sitting................10%
> Viewing other............36%
> Viewing only............30%

This indicates that of the housewives classified as viewers of the program, only about 30 percent were solely viewing during the commercial, 70 percent being engaged in some other activity as well.

The pattern of viewing changed throughout the evening. The proportion of women program viewers absent from the room during commercials grew from 13 percent in the early evening to 28 percent by peak time; it then fell again to 17 percent in the latter part of the evening. The proportion of men viewers absent from the room during the commercials was somewhat smaller than that of housewives, falling from about 20 percent at 7 P.M. to about 10 percent by 8:30 P.M.

One of the conclusions from this study was that a considerably larger number of people are absent during breaks than during programs. This, of course, has implications for spot T.V. versus program sponsored T.V.

Research findings in the United States are quite similar to the British findings. The study conducted by Barclay, Doub, and McMurtrey reports "in 49% of the network-tuned homes, the housewife reported being in the room at commercial exposure time" [2]. Steiner reported that only 47 percent of the in-home audience watches all or almost all of an average network commercial [26].

In the United States, the "island" commercial (which occurs within a program) receives more attention than a "clutter" commercial [32]. Clutter is defined as those commercials which occur near the beginning or end of a program and are closely preceded or followed by spot commercials, station identification, public service announcements, and so on.

Steiner found that while the number of people actually getting up and leaving the room more than doubled when comparing 20-second commercials to 60-second or 120-second commercials, as the length of the commercial increased, interestingly, the percentage of people who paid *full* attention to the commercial increased [26]. Steiner explained this finding by observing that the longer a commercial, the more likely it is to follow programming rather than another commercial. As commercials increase in length from 20 to 120 seconds, full attention just before the commercial shows a steady climb from 51.8 to 80.3 percent. Since it is easier to maintain a viewer's attention than to reattract this attention once it is lost, it probably does make some difference if a commercial follows programming rather than another commercial.

Most of the research in evaluating newspaper and magazine advertisements uses some form of recall or recognition measure. This means that the individual must have *perceived* and *remembered* the ad in addition to being exposed. Thus most of the press research will be discussed under the next heading, which deals with perception.

The three methods of measuring press exposure without regard to perception are glue-sealed issues (an individual must break a thin glue seal in order to look at each page), fingerprint tests, and eye camera tests. While glue-sealed issues and fingerprint tests clearly show the exact pages examined by a reader, they do not guarantee that the smaller ads on the page were observed. Eye camera tests reveal the exact eye patterns a viewer's vision followed over a page.

These three tests are not regularly used because they are costly and time-consuming in relating to the information they provide. The laboratory environment associated with the eye camera, in which the subject must hold his head in a fixed, rigid position to enable the camera to stay focused on his eye while he reads the ads, is unnatural and creates a viewing pattern quite different from the pattern the subject would follow if he were casually browsing through the magazine in his home.

Commercial Perception Weights

Given that an individual is exposed to a commercial message, what is the probability he will consciously perceive the message? People can have "open eyes in front of a television set" without really seeing or hearing what is being advertised. The person is thinking about something else; his mind is not consciously open to the product message. Thus a set of commercial weights used to predict perception is often used in conjunction with commercial exposure weights.

The methods most commonly used to measure perception are recall and recognition. Recognition tests consist of showing a subject a magazine and asking him if he can pick out the ads he recognizes from his previous reading of the magazine. Unaided recall asks the subject to list the ads he recalls having seen in a previous issue of a magazine. Aided recall provides the subject with some clues as to what the advertisements were. Both of these tests determine not only whether the subject *actually perceived* the ad but also whether the subject *consciously remembers* what he perceived.

Therefore, when interpreting findings such as Garfinkle and Greenberg's observation that illustrations substantially increase recall scores, one should ask whether this is because the illustrations increase the depth of perception or because illustrations are easier to remember than printed copy [14].

The following four variables are most often used to predict the probability of perception of print advertisements:

1. Length of ad
2. Use of color
3. Position of ad
4. Thickness of issue

What advantages do various page sizes have? Troldahl and Jones looked at four factors affecting the probability of getting a newspaper ad "seen" [28]. The factors of page size and type of product advertised were found to be highly significant and explained 60 percent of the variation in readership. Page size alone explained some 40 percent. The other two factors, ratio of illustration size to copy space and number of items included, had little effect on whether or not the tested ads were seen. Daniel Starch, who has conducted continuing studies of newspaper reading since 1932, reports that [25]:

> Readership as a rule is directly proportional to the size of the advertisement with this exception: A full page attracts not quite twice as many readers as a half-page ad, and a two-page ad attracts not quite twice as many readers as a full page. Also, spectacular, or multi-page advertisements will attract a smaller total reader audience than the same number of pages issued as separate one-page ads at suitable intervals.

In an attempt to provide a simple heuristic rule for use in mathematical models, functional relationships between page size and exposures have been suggested. The best-known of these relationships is the "square root" rule. The rule was first used by Lee and Burkhart in their heuristic model for advertising media selection [17]. The concept is that the change in attention is equal to the square root of the multiple by which one changes the page size; for example, if 100 people observe a quarter-page ad, 200 people are expected to observe a full-page ad.

There is little reported research to validate this rule. Most researchers take the position that a strict functional relationship between one of the several variables affecting exposure without regard to the influences of the other variables is convenient but naïve. Alan Donnahoe of the *Richmond Times-Dispatch* and *News Leader* has used Starch data and the square root law to calculate reading at various linage levels by men and by women for each of 20 different product categories. Donnahoe concluded [30]:

> ... just as products differ in innate interest, so do they also differ in incremental gain in readership with increase in ad size. . . . In the case of alcoholic beverages, for example, doubling of space size produces an average gain of 30 per cent in men readers and 14 per cent in women readers. In beer advertising, the comparable gains are 47 and 106 per cent. If a choice is to be made between large-space advertising and small-space times greater frequency, these data suggest that a beer manufacturer should select the former and a liquor distiller the latter alternative.

The conclusion that relative page size affects the exposure probability in a positive but not directly proportional ratio is supported by most of the research on magazine page size.

Daniel Starch [25] reported that

> Detailed results of three years' study based upon inquiries from 8,200 advertisements in national magazines disclosed that if returns from full pages were pegged at 100, half-page advertisements bring returns equal to around 60, and quarter pages produce returns equal to around 33.

In a 1957 study by the J. Walter Thompson agency, the effect of page size was reported to affect exposure probabilities more than the use of color. This report [27] stated that

> ... in terms of cost against added readership, four-color spreads are not so efficient as pages. They generally add about 50 per cent more readership at double the cost. . . . since female ad-noting for a page is usually higher than male, spreads increase female readership on the average by only one-third.

Next to page size, the variable most often considered is the use of color in an advertisement. Assael, Kofron, and Burgi analyzed 1,379 advertisements which appeared in *Iron Age* by a multiple regression technique which included an iterative heuristic to form subgroups. They found the key characteristics, in order of importance, to be three- or 4-color, inserts, coated stock, spread, color with illustration, and bleed pages [1].

The position of the ad within the vehicle has been studied from time to time. It is clear that covers and turnout spreads clearly give higher exposures than other pages. The evidence on left- versus right-hand exposure seems inconclusive. The top is generally felt to be superior to the bottom of a page for a fractional page ad. While the buyer can specify cover and spreads (by paying a premium), he usually has little control over the left versus right or top versus bottom positioning of his ad. The publisher usually decides this relatively independent of the buyers.

The thickness of the vehicle has some effect upon the exposure. Starch attempted to estimate the effect of thickness by counting the number of inquiries generated by each advertisement. His conclusion was that "Within the range up to 200 pages, the effect of thickness of issue is moderate. For larger issues, the decline in inquiries becomes more rapid" [25].

The conclusion seems reasonable that, as the size of the vehicle increases, there is a point at which readers will no longer read each page. The method of using inquiries as a measure of exposure or perception is questionable. Some types of ads clearly do not lead nor are they intended to lead to inquiries. Readers of specific vehicles may have different degrees of willingness to make inquiries. Thus the inquiry counting could be measuring different target populations' propensity to inquiry rather than exposures.

Unpublished surveys by a number of advertising agencies come to the same conclusion. As magazine page count passes the 175-page mark, a sharp decline in the recognition scores per advertisement starts to take place. Again, while the conclusion seems reasonable, it could be explained by the fact that people being interviewed just get tired of the interview and start to plead ignorance of ads in order to terminate the interview.

The results for newspapers are much the same. Carter reported that in a newspaper study, ads in thin issues received higher recall scores and reading time per page decreased as the number of pages increased [6].

Anyone wishing to determine commercial exposure weights from the type of regression analysis used in most of the studies just mentioned should be aware of two major limitations.

First, there is clear evidence of considerable *interaction* among the variables mentioned above. Assael, Kofron, and Burgi reported that having over a half page of illustrated area was the most important independent variable used to predict recognition of an advertisement when all the advertisements studied were four-color ads. Yet the half-page illustration ranked as only the fifth most important when the ads were all black and white. The gestalt psychologist would argue that the probability of exposure and the depth of perception are not determined by adding up component weights of the advertisement; rather, the ad must be viewed in its entirety and in the environment in which it is expected to appear before a meaningful commercial exposure weight can be assigned. It can be argued that the key factor determining the probability of commercial exposure is the uniqueness of the ad in relation to the other ads being carried by the media vehicle.

Second, there is evidence to indicate that the probability of advertising exposure is determined by the product being advertised rather than aspects of ad format. People who are interested in specific products will search out these product messages regardless of whether the message is presented in a full-page four-color ad or in a quarter-page black-and-white one. Buchanan reports that interest in the product significantly affects recall of magazine ads but not recall of television commercials [3]. Wells reports that recall scores are related to product interest [29]. Crane found that men's like-dislike rating of television commercials was primarily determined by product rather than program context and commercial type [7]. Troldahl and Jones found the product advertised to be significant in predicting rating scores [28].

Thus it would seem that weighting advertisements on the basis of particular features possessed by the advertisements may provide a starting point, but judgment must be used in adjusting these weights to fit the product being advertised and to estimate the uniqueness of the ad in relation to the expected environment of competing advertisements.

The British use the *Gallup-Robinson Report* and Americans use the *Starch Advertisement Readership Report* as syndicated sources providing current data on commercial perception. The Starch readership studies employ a recognition method. After an individual indicates he has read a particular issue, the interviewer pages through the issue with the reader and attempts to estimate the reader's degree of perception and memory associated with each ad in the issue. Readers are placed into four categories:

Non-Reader:	A person who did not remember having previously seen the advertisement in the issue being studied.
"Noted" Reader:	A person who remembered having previously seen the advertisement in the issue being studied.
"Seen-Associated" Reader:	A person who not only "Noted" the advertisement but also saw or read some part of it which clearly indicates the brand or advertiser.
"Read Most" Reader:	A person who read half or more of the written material in the ad.

Users of this data should be aware of the limitations of the Starch study. Sample sizes range from 100 to 150 per sex per issue. With this small sample size, chance variations in sampling could be expected to cause variations of over 20 points at the 1 percent level of significance, thus making it risky to rate one over another on the basis of these numbers. Also there is the carryover effect of national advertisements seen in other magazines and media vehicles. It is difficult for people to remember in exactly which issue they saw a well-known ad. In defense of Starch it must be remembered that in 1955 the Committee on Printed Advertising Rating Methods (PARM) of the Advertising Research Foundation duplicated both the Starch and Gallup and Robinson studies for one issue of *Life* magazine. The independent and extensive research conducted by PARM indicated that both Starch and Gallup and Robinson provided reasonably accurate results [25].

There is no syndicated service that rates the levels of perception achieved by each television commercial. Advertising agencies often check the levels of perception for specific commercials using telephone interviews and aided recall techniques. These studies are conducted for specific clients and usually are not published.

Cumulative Frequency Weights

Does the tenth exposure to the same ad have the same effect upon the viewer as the first exposure? Most advertising professionals would answer no, yet they would be hard pressed to indicate what the precise relationship is. Very little empirical research has been performed in measuring the cumulative effect of advertising.

An example of a weighted frequency distribution is given in Table 2.

TABLE 2   A Weighted Frequency Distribution

Frequency	Frequency weight
1	0.30
2	0.40
3	0.50
4	0.80
5	1.00
6	1.00
7	0.90
8	0.80
9	0.80
10	0.80

The exposures are all weighted in relation to the number of exposures the advertiser judges necessary for the particular product message and target population under consideration. In this example, the rationale for the weighting is that the first three exposures in and of themselves will tend to be lost in the swirl of competing messages and stimuli. The fifth and sixth exposures are the ones that register with the individuals. The seventh to tenth exposures have value as they repeat and remind individuals of the message. This weighting system would call for a campaign that would aim at getting most of the individuals exposed at least six times. In terms of *estimated effectiveness* per dollar, it appears better to deviate on the high side than on the low side.

The objectives of *repetition* and *coverage* are the dominant variables in estimating the weighted frequency distribution. These variables are modified by the five other factors discussed later in this section.

Zielske supervised a study at Foote, Cone, and Belding in 1959 on this topic and little has been done since. In Zielske's study two groups of randomly selected women were mailed an advertisement for an ingredient food product. The first group received an ad every week; the second received an ad every four weeks. Recall of the advertising was measured by telephone interviewing throughout the year. The results of this campaign are shown in the graph in Figure 1 [34].

The curve for thirteen exposures at four-week intervals has a saw-toothed shape, since there was forgetting of the advertising between exposures in this schedule. Actually, there is also some forgetting between exposures in the weekly schedule, but one week was the smallest unit of time measured in the study.

If recall is accepted as a valid criterion for measuring advertising effectiveness, it is clear that the relative value of the thirteenth exposure in relation to the first exposure is dependent on the time interval between exposures. Also advertising is quickly forgotten if the consumer is not continuously exposed; and as the number of exposures to advertising increases, the rate at which it is forgotten decreases. These conclusions are consistent with the psychological literature on learning theory.

The literature on learning theory suggests that the following factors significantly affect the rate at which a given advertisement is recalled:
1. Clarity of organization
2. Present interest in product
3. Present attitude set
4. Memory differences
5. Personality differences in relation to copy appeal

The qualities of advertising copy that most significantly affect the speed at which an ad will be learned and remembered are the *meaningfulness* of the material and the way it is *organized*. Many advertisers and copywriters talk of how attractive the advertisement is, yet research by this author indicates that if a person perceives an ad as meaningful, he tends to rate the ad as attractive.

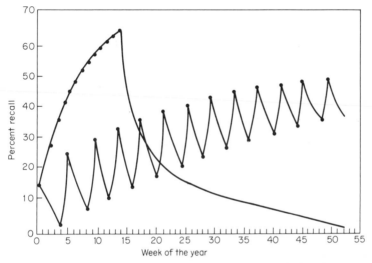

Fig. 1.   Recall in relation to time and exposure frequency.

Meaningfulness is a function of the receiver as well as copy, whereas organization is a direct function of the ad copy. Information theory suggests that meaningful or well-organized material is learned more rapidly because it requires that we learn less. Miller and Selfridge point out that when the material is not organized for us, we have to learn both the pattern (or organization) and the content, whereas when the material is well organized, one merely fits the new information into a known pattern [20]. Clarity of organization is probably more important in ad commercial learning than in other learning situations such as classroom learning. This is because most adults simply do not make a strong conscious effort to learn commercials. If the message is unclear or disorganized, the tendency is to disregard the ad and move to some other stimuli attracting one's attention. Krugman calls this process "learning without involvement" [16].

What factors influence an individual's perception of meaningfulness? One is his present interest in the product being advertised. Interest in the product is usually highest in two groups. First, there are people who feel the product could satisfy one of their needs and look to ads on that product for information and encouragement as a prelude to possible purchase. The second group are those people who have recently purchased the product and are now looking for reassurances that they have purchased the correct brand and/or that purchase of the given product is a highly desirable act—cognitive dissonance. See Section III, Part B, Chapter 1.

Messages sympathetic to a person's present set of attitudes are learned much quicker than messages that challenge existing attitudes. Levine and Murphy have demonstrated this in tests measuring the speed of learning two types of prose material, one consistent and the other inconsistent with the attitudes of the learner [18]. Their results show it took longer to learn material inconsistent with one's attitude, and later on this unacceptable material was more rapidly forgotten. People seem to consciously or subconsciously screen out messages that would lead to the tensions of resolving internal doubts and conflicts. The more integrated a given attitude is into a person's value system and self-perception, the more difficult it is to get a conflicting stimulus past the person's self-screening defenses.

If memory tests such as recall and recognition are used, different learning curves can be expected because of the variance in the memory capacities of the individuals. Havland, Janis, and Kelley point out that personality traits will affect the learning response rate for particular types of appeals [15]. The authors argue that personality factors influence an individual's susceptibility to persuasion or attitude change. They have devised and tested a series of propositions dealing primarily with personality factors related to intelligence, motivation, and emotion. If it is possible to break the target population into subgroups on the basis of these personality traits, it would be interesting to establish a weighted cumulative frequency distribution on the basis of the group's estimated *susceptibility to persuasion* for the particular advertising message being considered.

Estimation of the relative effect of each repetition of the same advertisement is a difficult problem upon which to generate meaningful empirical data. The estimated effect of cumulative exposures is further complicated when more than one medium is used. Do exposures to the same message on television, on radio, in newspapers, or in magazines have the same effect? If not, should television precede magazine exposures? Exactly how do the different types of exposures interact in and affect the learning and forgetting rates?

It is quite clear that due to the lack of empirical research in determining and measuring the variables determining the cumulative effectiveness of advertising, subjective judgments will have to be used in determining the appropriate weighted distributions.

Combining the Weights

There are only two basic alternatives in combining sets of weights. An additive relationship should be used if the weights are felt to be independent of each other. A multiplicative relationship should be used when it is felt that there is interaction between the variables.

As an example, consider the following data used in predicting the impact upon a young male of an advertisement for a new household tool. The three variables under consideration are the type of magazine used, size of the ad, and use of color in the ad. Assume costs and all other variables are equal.

Strategy	Media vehicle	Length	Color
1	0.9	0.3	0.2
2	0.4	0.5	0.6

Strategy 1 calls for a half-page black-and-white ad to be placed in *Popular Mechanics*. Strategy 2 calls for a full-page four-color ad to be placed in *Reader's Digest*. The values listed here reflect the media scheduler's individual judgments concerning the three variables (probably based more upon subjective feelings than empirical evidence). He feels that an identical exposure in *Popular Mechanics* is worth more than two exposures in *Look*. This might be because *Popular Mechanics* is viewed as being more "believable," having more expertise in recommending household tools than the more general-purpose magazine *Reader's Digest*. The preferences for greater length and the use of color are self-evident.

Now which strategy should be selected? If the media scheduler regards each variable as independent of the others—that is, if the use of color does not change the relative differences between page size weights or media vehicle appropriateness weights—he should add the weights together. Thus strategy 2 is slightly preferred (1.5 to 1.4).

If he feels that the use of color interacts with the page size but not the appropriateness of the vehicle, he might multiply the color weight by the page size weight and then add this product to the vehicle appropriateness weight. This would lead to the selection of strategy 1: $0.9 + (0.3 \times 0.2) = 0.96$ versus $0.4 + (0.6 \times 0.5) = 0.7$.

If he feels the page size and use of color affect the relative vehicle appropriateness, he might multiply all three values together. This would lead to the selection of strategy 2: $0.9 \times 0.3 \times 0.2 = 0.054$ versus $0.4 \times 0.5 \times 0.6 = 0.12$.

There are infinitely many variations on the basic additive and multiplicative combinations to use. A harmonic average might be substituted for straight multiplication. Yet underlying any formula for combining the variables are the concepts of independence and interdependence, which are basically additive and multiplicative relationships respectively. (For an actual example of how these sets of weights are combined within a quantitative model, see [12].)

This is only one method for combining the sets of weights. The decision system used by the media scheduler for combining the various sets of weights is often influenced by the type of analytical model being used, for example, a linear programming combination rather than a multiplicative combination of weights for a given formulation of the problem. To extensively review the alternative methods of combining sets of weights is to review the structures of the many analytical media selections, a review beyond the scope of this chapter.

CONCLUSION

A number of factors beside cost per thousand should be evaluated in selecting media schedules. More recent advertising media research has concentrated upon the development of quantitative models to use in fitting the data and judgments together. However, when one examines the quality of the data presently available, it is doubtful if the decision maker has accurate or meaningful measures of the variables he wishes to consider in selecting media. Furthermore, little is known concerning the interactions between the relevant variables. There is a lack of empirical research upon which to postulate the functional relationships between the variables.

Since a model is only as good as its basic data, the most useful and significant research in the field of advertising media selection, at this point in time, will be to measure and define the interactions between the key variables rather than to further refine the quantitative structures of the basic models.

REFERENCES

1. Assael, H., J. Kofron, and W. Burgi, "Advertising Performance as a Function of Print Ad Characteristics," *Journal of Advertising Research*, vol. 7, no. 2, June 1967.
2. Barclay, W., R. Doub, and L. McMurtrey, "Recall of TV Commercials by Time and Program Slot," *Journal of Advertising Research*, vol. 5, no. 2, June 1965.
3. Buchanan, D. I., "How Interest in the Product Affects Recall: Print Ads vs. Commercials," *Journal of Advertising Research*, vol. 4, no. 1, March 1964.
4. Buzzell, R. D., M. Kolin, and M. P. Murphy, "Television Commercial Test Scores and Short-Term Changes in Market Shares," *Journal of Marketing Research*, vol. 2, August 1965.
5. Campbell-Ewald Company, *The Television Viewer—His Tastes, Interests, and Attitudes*, Detroit: Campbell-Ewald Company, 1961.
6. Carter, D. E., "Newspaper Advertising Readership: Thick vs. Thin Issues," *Journal of Advertising Research*, vol. 8, no. 3, September 1968.
7. Crane, L., "How Product, Appeal, and Program Affect Attitudes toward Commercials," *Journal of Advertising Research*, vol. 4, no. 1, March 1964.
8. Fothergill, J. E., and A. S. C. Ehrenberg, "The Schwerin Analysis of Advertising Effectiveness," *Journal of Marketing Research*, vol. 2, August 1965.
9. ————, "Concluding Comments on the Schwerin Analysis of Advertising Effectiveness," *Journal of Marketing Research*, vol. 2, November 1965.
10. Frank, R., and P. Green, "Numerical Taxonomy in Marketing Analysis: A Review Article," *Journal of Marketing Research*, vol. 5, February 1968.
11. Gensch, D. H., "Computer Models in Advertising Media Selection," *Journal of Marketing Research*, vol. 5, November 1968.
12. ————, "A Computer Simulation Model for Selecting Advertising Schedules," *Journal of Marketing Research*, vol. 6, May 1969.
13. Green, P., R. Frank, and P. Robinson, "Cluster Analysis in Test Market Selection," *Management Science*, vol. 13, no. 8, April 1967.
14. Greenberg, A., and N. Garfinkle, "Visual Material and Recall of Magazine Articles," *Journal of Advertising Research*, vol. 3, no. 2, June 1963.
15. Havland, C. I., I. L. Janis, and H. H. Kelley, *Communication and Persuasion: Psychological Studies of Opinion Change*, New Haven, Conn.: Yale University Press, 1953.
16. Krugman, H. E., "The Impact of Television Advertising: Learning Without Involvement," *Public Opinion Quarterly*, vol. 29, Fall 1965.
17. Lee, A. M., and A. J. Burkhart, "Some Optimization Problems in Advertising Media Planning," *Operational Research Quarterly*, vol. 11, September 1960.
18. Levine, J. M., and G. Murphy, "The Learning and Forgetting of Controversial Material," *Journal of Abnormal and Social Psychology*, vol. 38, October 1943.
19. Lucas, D. B., "The ABC's of ARF's PARM," *Journal of Marketing*, July 1960.
20. Miller, G. A., and J. Selfridge, "Verbal Context and the Recall of Meaningful Material," *American Journal of Psychology*, vol. 63, April 1950.
21. Motivation Analysis, Inc., *Mike & Mike—Are Not Alike—Different!* New York: CBS Radio Inc., 1957.
22. Nuttall, C. G. F., "TV Commercial Audiences in the United Kingdom," *Journal of Advertising Research*, vol. 2, no. 3, September 1962.
23. Politz, A., Media Studies, *Ad Page Exposure in 4 Magazines*. New York: The Reader's Digest Association, Inc., and The Curtis Publishing Company, 1960.
24. Schwerin Research Corporation, "Program-Commercial Compatibility," *Schwerin Research Corporation Bulletin*, vol. 8, no. 8, August 1960.
25. Starch, D., "How Thickness of Issue, Seasons, Affect Inquiries," *Media/Scope*, February 1959.
26. Steiner, G. A., "The People Look at Commercials: A Study of Audience Behavior," *Journal of Business*, vol. 39, April 1966.
27. Thompson, J. W., "Report on Magazines as an Advertising Medium," *Advertising Age*, May 5, 1958.

28. Troldahl, V., and R. Jones, "Predictors of Newspaper Advertising Readership," *Journal of Advertising Research,* vol. 5, no. 1, March 1965.
29. Wells, W. D., "Recognition, Recall, and Rating Scales," *Journal of Advertising Research,* vol. 4, no. 3, September 1964.
30. "What Is Best Size for a Newspaper Ad?" *Media/Scope,* July 1965.
31. "What Is Best Size for a Magazine Ad?" *Media/Scope,* October 1965.
32. Wheatley, J. J., "Influence of Commercial's Length and Position," *Journal of Marketing Research,* vol. 5, May 1968.
33. Winick, C., "Three Measures of the Advertising Value of Media Content," *Journal of Advertising Research,* vol. 2, no. 2, June 1962.
34. Zielske, H. A., "The Remembering and Forgetting of Advertising," *Journal of Marketing,* January 1959.

Chapter 6

Corporate Image Studies

JOSEPH C. BEVIS *Consultant, Stuart, Florida*

THE CORPORATE IMAGE CONCEPT

A company's image is the net result of all the experiences, impressions, feelings, and knowledge that people have about a company. To a greater or smaller degree, everything a company is, has, does, or says affects its image.

Every person, every day, deals with many people, things, and events. In order to deal meaningfully with each one, he must sort and arrange, either consciously or unconsciously, the many impressions—positive, negative, and neutral—that are part of each experience. Each person has his own unique way of assimilating and sorting these impressions and of reacting to them. Thus different persons can and do evolve different images of the same company, person, or thing.

This image principle functions in all aspects of people's lives. Their images of themselves, their families, their jobs, world events, and so on are continually developing and changing. In the same way, people's images of corporations go through a steady process of development and change.

Research has shown that images help to shape people's behavior toward companies. Whether a person's image of a company is positive or negative, strong or weak, detailed or generalized will influence his predisposition to buy the company's products, pay attention to and believe its communications, speak favorably of it to others, listen to its point of view in controversies, seek a career in the company, purchase or recommend its stock, and so on.

Naturally, the extent to which such a predisposition will be a controlling factor in an individual's behavior will vary from situation to situation. For example, a stronger and more favorable image of company A may not be sufficient to induce a customer to wait a month for delivery of one of company A's products if a comparable product manufactured by company B (whose image may be somewhat weaker or less favorable) is on the dealer's shelf today. Nevertheless, the important point is that, other things being equal, a favorable image can exert influence in the right direction for a company.

IMAGE RESEARCH IN PERSPECTIVE

A company's image should not be regarded as something separate and distinct from other ideas people hold. In effect, the image of a company occupies the center or core of a series of interrelated attitude constructs which can affect the image and are in turn influenced by the image. These are outlined in the following:

Attitudes toward Large Companies or Business in General. As important elements of the nation's economic and social environment, large companies are inevitably affected by events and trends beyond their immediate control. The reputation of any major corporation is not an isolated phenomenon shaped only by factors within the company's influence. People's attitudes toward an individual company are determined not only by what the company itself does but also by their attitudes toward the industry of which the company is a part. Perhaps even more important, people's attitudes toward individual companies are strongly influenced by their attitudes toward large companies generally and their views regarding the roles of business, government, and the individual in society.

Attitudes toward the Industry of Which the Company Is a Part. People's attitudes toward major industries help provide a context within which to evaluate attitudes toward specific companies within those industries. For example, a member of a relatively familiar and well-liked industry such as the food industry tends to be in an essentially more favorable reputational position than a company in an industry that is not very well known or very well regarded, for example, the coal mining or tobacco industries.

Familiarity with or Knowledge of the Company and Its Competitors. Widespread familiarity with a company, beyond a minimal level of recognition or awareness, is a necessary precondition to, but not a guarantee of, the formation of widespread favorable attitudes toward it. Familiarity is the foundation of attitudes. The nature and content of the familiarity will, of course, affect the nature of the attitudes. As a general rule, the extent of a person's familiarity with a company will have some influence on the likelihood of his using or recommending the company's products, applying for a job with the company, believing the company's communications, considering purchase of its stock, and so on.

There are wide variations in familiarity and favorability toward companies within most industries. Table 1 shows variations in familiarity with leading chemical companies.

In building a strong corporate image, a basic problem facing many leading corporations is low public awareness.

Even companies with widely distributed products sometimes lack the public visibility to give them a well-defined corporate reputation. The prescription drug industry is an example of one that has promoted company reputation and products mainly among a selected audience—in this case, doctors. Thus, as Table 2 shows, drug firms are generally well known to physicians who prescribe their products but little known to the people who use the products.

Two points worth observing in Table 2 are that (1) there is a wide range in familiarity with the four companies, particularly among the public where the "never heard" proportion ranges from 24 to 55 percent, and (2) there is no relationship between physicians' familiarity and that of the public. The reason some prescription drug companies have gained visibility among the general public is that they have branded consumer products, while the less well-known drug companies typically do not enjoy this type of consumer exposure.

Overall Favorability toward the Company and Its Competitors. This is a basic measure of a company's overall reputation. The data collected through questions dealing with favorability help in analyzing the company's image in

TABLE 1   Familiarity Comparisons: Chemical Companies

Company	Total public	
	Have heard of, percent	Know very well, fair amount, percent
A	92	39
B	85	25
C	80	28
D	65	11
E	48	11
Five-company average	74	23

TABLE 2   Familiarity Comparisons: Prescription Drug Companies

Company	Audience	Know well or fairly well, percent	Know little or almost nothing, percent	Never heard of company, percent
A	Physicians	81	19	0
	General public	17	28	55
B	Physicians	75	25	0
	General public	32	41	27
C	Physicians	72	28	0
	General public	24	36	40
D	Physicians	67	33	0
	General public	31	45	24

detail and in determining what causes this image to be favorable or unfavorable.

Specific Impressions of the Company, Both Favorable and Unfavorable. A company's image can be measured fairly precisely in both its broad and specific aspects. Analysis of a company's image in terms of its strengths and weaknesses can help management in deciding where to place emphasis in communicating with the general public or with special publics. For different publics, various aspects of a company's image differ in importance. Security analysts, for example, are most interested in the management and profitability of a company, while the general public is more concerned with the company's products and its dealings with customers. Thus the facets of an image covered in a research project vary with the objective of the research, and the "public" to be studied.

The Process of Image Formation and Change. It is important that image research be action-oriented. It should measure not only the "what" but also the "why" insofar as possible. In addition to finding out how well a company is known and what the specific elements of its reputation are, it is helpful if elements like the following are covered:

1. The process by which people obtain information about the company and how their impressions are formed. For example, have members of the public been exposed to the company's television programming or other promotional efforts? Have stockholders read the company's annual report? Do employees rely primarily on the grapevine or on formal sources of communication in forming their image of the company they work for?

2. Why people have specific favorable and unfavorable impressions of the company. Here, we give people a chance to tell us in their own words why they feel the way they do toward a company.

3. In what respects changes have taken place over time in the company's image. This requires measuring a company's reputation on a regular basis to observe change in the specific aspects of its image.

It is also important in most circumstances to recognize and understand the differences in images between different publics and between different segments of each public studied. This requires sufficiently large samples to make the data for each segment meaningful.

In analyzing the company's image, differences between various *demographic* subgroups (men versus women, blacks versus whites, customers versus noncustomers, and so on) should, of course, be evaluated. Equally important, however, the data should be examined in terms of *psychographic* variables, such as people's attitudes toward big business in general, their degree of favorability toward the company being studied, and the extent of their knowledge about the company and its activities.

IMAGE RESEARCH TECHNIQUES

Many different techniques are used in corporate image research, and many different types of studies could be included under the general heading of corporate image research. Small-scale, exploratory studies are frequently used to develop hypotheses which will later be tested in larger-scale studies. These qualitative studies employ probing depth interviews, and results are often reported merely in the form of respondents' comments.

Even in larger-scale studies, the researcher often begins with a relatively unstructured interviewing instrument, since each individual's image of a company is a complex and loosely structured whole. While depth interviews are valuable for developmental purposes, however, it is not feasible to continue with a completely unstructured interview approach if definitive image data are needed. People differ in their ability to articulate their images of companies, even with the assistance of skillful interviewer probing. The costs of administration and the problems involved in analysis and quantification of unstructured interviews are well known. It is particularly difficult to compare the results of one such survey with a later one (possibly done with different interviewers and different coders) and obtain any reliable picture of image change.

In the quantification stage, a variety of techniques can be used to obtain a detailed image of the company or companies being studied. To some degree, the technique used depends upon the purpose of the study, the budget available, how much time is available in the interview, and how much detail is desired.

Familiarity and favorability measurement can be based on individual ratings of the company, card sorting, selection of company names from a list ("Which of these do you feel most informed about?"), and so on.

A number of approaches can be also taken to measure a corporate image. The approach selected depends on the number of companies studied in the project, the detail desired, and the time available in the interview.

To measure a corporation's image, one method is to get people to rate individual attributes in terms of how well they feel the company does on each. Another method is the semantic differential approach, in which opposing qualities are put on opposite ends of a scale and respondents designate which points in the scale they feel apply to the company. At Opinion Research Corporation, we have found that a third method, the image profile, is usually the most productive. The reputation profile combines many of the advantages of unstructured and structured personal interview procedures while embracing as few as possible of the limitations of either.

The following discussion describes how Opinion Research Corporation measures corporate images in large-scale studies among the general public.

A list of statements or ideas concerning large companies in all their relevant aspects is compiled from depth interviews and from testimony about companies accumulated in previous studies. The statements are screened and pretested. The final list may include as many as 50 statements. These appear on a card (sequence rotated), and the respondent chooses the ones which fit his own impressions of the company in question.

The item-list procedure permits the respondent to range through his experiences and react selectively to statements about the company, much as in an unstructured interview situation. The respondent's attention is not forced to a given item, nor is a yes-no response encouraged where the item may be irrelevant for him. Instead, he is given a list and is told to look for statements that fit his ideas about a given company. This approach helps to bring together inner feelings about a company with statements on the item list. Those items that connect with the respondent's views about the company in question are the ones that he selects as descriptive of his image, and irrelevant ideas or those that do not square with his image are left unselected.

The item-list approach includes attributes of the structured interview in that various aspects of corporate reputation are presented in a uniform way for all respondents. Data processing and quantification are straightforward operations which can be readily communicated to those who will apply the research results. Factor analysis can be used to show how various reputational attributes are grouped in people's minds.

The relative score achieved by each image item among the survey public provides valuable information to corporate management. It permits comparison with previous results (utilizing the same measurement techniques), with similar results for other companies, and with norms or averages for a number of companies. Because trend measures are often important, the study needs to be controlled carefully (including sampling, question and item rotation, consistency of techniques from one survey to another, and so on).

The following observations, based on Opinion Research Corporation's experience in many corporate image studies, may be useful in analyzing and interpreting corporate image data from the general public:

1. An image item which is selected by more than 40 percent of the public represents an extremely strong element of a company's reputation and is one that is quite firmly established.

2. An image item selected by 20 to 40 percent of the public may be re-

garded as a stronger-than-average element in a company's reputation, particularly for companies that serve mainly industrial markets.

3. An image item selected by 10 to 20 percent of the public is a significant part of a company's image but in most cases not a very strong or important one.

4. Ideas about a company which are found among fewer than 10 percent of the public contribute relatively little to feelings about the company.

5. Low scores on favorable-image items do not necessarily mean that people are critical or unfavorable toward a company on that point. Rather, infrequent selection of a favorable item is more likely to mean that the particular idea in question does not set the company apart from other companies in the respondent's mind or else is an idea on which he has little or no basis for evaluating the company.

6. These prior points refer to favorable or neutral ideas about companies. Unfavorable items are usually selected by smaller proportions of those surveyed, so an unfavorable item mentioned by 10 percent or more of the public can be considered significant criticism of a company and should be a matter of management concern.

In addition to measuring the specific components of the image profile, it is often desirable to measure the relative *importance* of each component in the individual's evaluation of the company and, also, to obtain a measure of the degree to which there are perceived differences among companies on these points. In gaining a marketing advantage over its competitors, it can be important for a company to know which are the most important criteria to a consumer in appraising companies and on which points companies are felt to differ substantially from each other. These are the points to emphasize in marketing and advertising strategy, since they offer the greatest "leverage" in gaining a competitive advantage.

Table 3 shows selected image findings on nine leading companies compiled from a recent corporate image study. The data are grouped into various factors resulting from factor analysis. For each item, the average percent of selection and the nine-company range are shown.

Note that

1. The product image usually is strongest. For most companies, this is the chief point of contact with the public. There are exceptions, of course.

2. Companies usually achieve less recognition in the other areas of corporate reputation.

3. It requires extraordinary effort to get credit for some specific attributes such as those that relate to the company's role as an employer or to its sense of social responsibility.

Managements are frequently concerned about possible negative characteristics in their public image. Often such fears are groundless. Results for the nine companies shown in Table 3 show the pattern that is usually found. Note, however, that in some instances sizable proportions of the public do have negative feelings toward individual companies.

CASE HISTORIES OF CORPORATE IMAGE RESEARCH

Following are some case histories in each of the subject areas mentioned at the start of this chapter.

Brand Image Research

There is considerable variability in the image influences that determine the brand commitment of the consumer; each product field differs in the criteria

TABLE 3   Examples of Corporate Image Findings among the General Public

	Percent selecting items	
Test item	Nine-company average	Nine-company range
Product:		
Average score (4 items)............................	29	20–40
Sample item:		
Their products are of the highest quality...............	31	19–45
Corporate leadership:		
Average score (5 items)............................	23	16–35
Sample item:		
A fast-growing and expanding company................	29	17–42
Customer relations:		
Average score (5 items)............................	18	9–36
Sample item:		
Treat customers fairly on complaints..................	16	5–49
Ethics:		
Average score (5 items)............................	13	10–18
Sample item:		
Live up to their guarantees and promises..............	16	9–34
Social responsibility:		
Average score (5 items)............................	7	5–15
Sample item:		
Have good relations with communities where they operate..	15	8–32
Employee relations:		
Average score (5 items)............................	15	8–34
Sample item:		
A good company to work for.........................	20	10–42
Miscellaneous items:		
Average score (7 items)............................	21	13–33
Sample item:		
One of the best companies to own stock in..............	19	7–39
Negative items:		
Average score (14 items)............................	4	2–10
Sample items:		
Their prices are too high............................	10	4–19
Pollute the air or water............................	6	1–18

that consumers use to compare brands.   In conducting research to determine the effect of corporate image on brand commitment, one tries to determine the image of the company that stands behind the brand as differentiated from the companies that provide other brands.   For example, the research seeks to measure the importance of such ideas as "The company that makes brand Z breakfast cereals is constantly doing research to improve its products" or "Brand C insulating glass is made by a company with very helpful architectural representatives."

Table 4 shows findings on some of the corporate image characteristics consumers associate with four different marketers of cereals.   Note, for example, that while company A is considered a recognized leader in the dry cereal industry, company C is better known for coming out with new or improved products.   On another point, only 6 percent of consumers associate company D with cereals intended mostly for children.   Thus, company D's image is such that it would be at a relative disadvantage compared with the other three companies in introducing a new product primarily for children. Company A, on the other hand, is thought by 30 percent of the public to advertise mostly to children, and this factor should help it in a campaign for a new cereal aimed at children. These examples show that there are wide variations in the public's image of the four different companies, and these variations have definite marketing and advertising implications.

TABLE 4   Selected Corporate Image Characteristics of Four Cereal Marketers

Characteristic	Company	Consumers, percent
The recognized leader	A	42
in the dry cereal	B	20
industry	C	12
	D	8
They are always com-	A	33
ing out with new or	B	21
improved products	C	37
	D	15
They advertise mostly	A	30
to children	B	25
	C	12
	D	6

Product Compatibility Research

This type of study determines whether a new product is compatible with a company's existing image. Whether it is or not, different brand names are often used so that these names will not be identified with the company. Where it is, the company can use the corporate name to help sell the product.

The research in product compatibility testing seeks to determine the relative "fit" of various new products with the dominant elements of the existing brand or corporate images. One technique used is a card-sorting procedure: respondents are asked to sort cards bearing the names of types of products into boxes labeled "excellent," "good," "fair," or "poor" (or some other scaling of quality) according to how good they think the product would be if it were put out by X company or under the X brand name. From this type of test, products can be analyzed on a continuous scale from relatively high compatibility to relatively low compatibility.

Analysis of the results can give a company a reliable guide on what product fields are most compatible with its brand or company name, what types of products would gain from use of the name and what types would not, what types of products would conflict with or dilute the established brand image. Thus the research helps in deciding which advertising strategy is appropriate for a new product.

The new products that are compatible with an established corporate name may not be those that management expects. Consumers judge product compatibility from a personal point of view that may differ drastically from that of the manufacturer. In developing and marketing products under an established brand name, the manufacturer may reason that he should stick to the manufacturing processes and types of end products that seem most compatible with what *he* believes to be his image—be it in the field of disposable paper products, snack foods, or precision equipment, for example.

The consumer, on the other hand, may see other products as equally compatible with the manufacturer's image, even though they are unrelated to the manufacturer's traditional line. For example, the manufacturer of snack foods may find that the consumer readily accepts him as a potential marketer of beverages and perhaps such other leisure time products as party favors or games.

In one example, a manufacturer had a well-established image for its line of closely related products, all bearing the same brand name. It had developed a new product line that, in blind consumer tests, was found to be superior. The decision to be faced was how closely to link the new product with the established name.

1. Would the established name help the new product, even though it was in a somewhat different field and required entirely different manufacturing skills?

2. Would the product class image of the new product conflict with or dilute the already established and highly favorable image of the company?

3. What effects would the new product, if closely associated with the established name, have on the corporate image of the company (which was closely associated with the brand name)?

Research showed that the company was extremely well known and well thought of—even more so than potential competitors in the new product's class. The details of the corporate image did not conflict with diversification beyond the established product field.

Product compatibility testing showed that the new product was in a product class that would be quite compatible with the established name. (The research also showed that many product classes requiring manufacturing skills very similar to those called for by the established products would be decidedly *incompatible* with the established name.)

Subsequent to the research, the company introduced the new product, linking it closely with the established name. It rapidly became successful.

Name and Trademark Research

Corporate image research helps determine:
1. if a company's current name or trademark is compatible with its image
2. if a proposed new name or trademark will be compatible with the company's present image (or desired future image).

In one situation, Opinion Research Corporation was asked to provide the management of a relatively small company with information that would assist it in its decision on what the company's future name should be. Management was planning to inaugurate a broad-scale corporate identity program in which the company's name would be more prominently displayed than previously on the company's products, packages, advertisements, stationery, and so on. The basic decision facing management was whether the company's name should be changed or should remain the same.

Because existing familiarity with a name can obviously affect people's reactions, we concentrated the research among people who were unfamiliar with either the current or the proposed name in order to make our findings as objective as possible. Our findings on the impressions conveyed by the two names showed that:

1. Both in general and on a number of specific issues, the *current* name suggested a favorable series of ideas to people, even when they were not familiar with the company. The name suggested a well-established, reputable company which turned out high-quality products and cared about its customers. The current name was much more successful in this respect than the proposed name.

2. The *proposed* name tended to suggest to people a small new company which was more likely to be in an industrial or technical field than a producer of consumer goods.

3. In terms of people's overall reactions to the two names, the proposed name produced fewer positive and more negative reactions on a number of specific issues.

Table 5 illustrates our findings in detail. To obtain the data, we gave respondents a list of ideas or impressions and asked for their opinion as to which name seemed to give them more of each impression. On most points, the present name was superior, although on some points there was not much difference. This kind of research, of course, measures people's "top-of-the-head" reaction and deals with opinions which are rather vague and not firmly held. Nevertheless, the idea content of a company name can have material influence on that company's success in the marketplace.

TABLE 5   Reactions to Present versus Proposed Company Name

Test item	Present name, percent	Proposed name, percent	Can't choose, percent
Current name selected by a majority:			
Pleasant-sounding............................	83	4	13
Large company.............................	77	18	5
Cares about its customers.....................	64	11	25
A name which can be used with nearly any kind of product................................	63	17	20
Proposed name selected by a majority:			
New, unknown company......................	10	58	32
Small company.............................	14	52	34
No majority for either name:			
Scientific, research-minded company.............	40	41	19
Silly or ridiculous...........................	2	22	76

On the basis of the research, the company decided to retain its present name and use that name in its new corporate identity program. Not only was the company spared the major expense of a corporate name change; it also avoided a mistake in terms of the probable undesirable effect the new name would have had on the company's reputation.

Financial and Stockholder Research

The financial community's view of a company's image is important because, through their decisions and recommendations, analysts can have substantial influence over the market valuation of a company's securities. Image research in this area measures not only what analysts think of a company, its management, and its investment appeal but also how well it is communicating with them. Another group among whom a company's image is important is stockholders, particularly during proxy fights, takeover bids, and merger discussions. The stockholders' image may be the deciding factor at such times.

In 1962 and again in 1967, Opinion Research Corporation conducted personal interviews among a sample of 100 major institutional stockholders of a large company. Between these two studies, the company had improved its operating performance substantially. It had also renovated its communications program. It increased both the quantity of information and the quality of its publications. Its 1967 annual report received the highest rating in the industry by financial analysts. As a result, the image of the company among this important public improved in just about every area.

The Opinion Research Corporation report concluded: "Obviously, improved operating results by the company play the most important part in stockholders' improved image of the company; but the importance of communications in keeping stockholders informed of the company's progress cannot be overstated."

Table 6 shows a few examples of how the image improved during this five-year period.

TABLE 6   Examples of Changes in Corporate Image Items among Institutional Stockholders of a Major Corporation

| | Institutional stockholders | |
Test item	1962, percent	1967, percent
Management:		
A profits-minded management	33	76
A fast-growing and expanding company	1	28
Plant, organization:		
An efficient, low-cost operation	28	56
Too much capacity	15	1
Products, research:		
High-quality products or services	49	53
Marketing:		
Well-planned sales, distribution, and branch setup	15	35

Community Relations Research

Companies conduct research in local communities to determine their standing as a present or potential employer, to measure local goodwill that the company can draw upon in the event of controversies such as strikes, and to determine needs or problems within the community and how the company can best lend its assistance.

Opinion Research Corporation periodically conducts research for a large corporation in communities where it is a major employer. The company uses this research to correct any weaknesses in its relations with these local communities. Table 7 shows a few examples of how the company was able to improve its image in one community in a three-year period.

Corporate Advertising

As part of Opinion Research Corporation's biennial image project, we often include evaluations of the effectiveness of corporate advertising programs among the public. Because we conduct this project on a biennial basis, ORC

TABLE 7   Community Image of Leading Employer

Test item	First survey, percent	Current survey, percent
Favorable ideas:		
Company is community-minded.................	66	75
Outstanding on job safety......................	44	62
Pays its employees very well....................	51	61
Unfavorable ideas		
Known for frequent layoffs......................	24	12
Has a lot of labor trouble.......................	22	9
Takes little interest in the community.............	7	8

is also able to gauge the impact of reductions or increases in a corporate advertising budget. One company, for example, recently initiated sponsorship of a television series in which its corporate advertisements sought to increase public recognition of the company and its products. About a year following the program's beginning, we investigated its impact on the company's reputation.

About three members of the public in ten said they had remembered seeing the company's program one or more times "in the last six months." Analysis of reported viewership data suggested that the program had had rather broad appeal among all segments of the public.

The study's key findings were then analyzed in terms of people's stated exposure to the company's program. As Table 8 shows, self-identified viewers of the program reported a higher level of familiarity with the company than nonviewers and were also more favorable than nonviewers. Similarly, on a number of important characteristics, the company's image was considerably stronger among viewers than nonviewers. (Examination of other data from the study suggested that the sizable differences between viewers and nonviewers could not be attributed simply to greater sophistication or higher educational levels on the part of viewers.) ORC's report to the company therefore concluded: "This study offers persuasive evidence that the program has contributed to gains in the company's reputation. The kinds of ideas the company has been seeking to communicate about itself through the program seem to be registering with people."

A later study showed that, according to people's own testimony, television represented one of the main sources of information about the company. Fully

TABLE 8   Familiarity, Favorability, and Image: Viewers versus Nonviewers of Company Television Program

Test item	Viewers, percent	Non-viewers, percent	Points difference
Know company very or fairly well...............	38	23	+15
Very or mostly favorable toward company.........	76	56	+20
Key image items:			
Have done a lot to make life easier or better......	52	29	+23
Continually developing new or improved products..	49	31	+18
Have interesting advertising.....................	28	16	+12
Show an interest in people as well as profits.......	19	13	+6

half of those who knew the company said television advertising or television programs sponsored by the company had been the chief way they had formed impressions of the company.

Quite obviously, changes in a major corporation's image over time are the result of many different factors, and advertising is only one of these. Nevertheless, carefully conducted trend studies in some instances can give a good approximation of the effect of specific elements of a corporate communications program on a company's total public reputation.

CONCLUSION

Briefly, this chapter has suggested that a company's corporate image bears an important relationship to the company's overall success in the marketplace, in plant communities, among financial influentials, with its own employees, and in other situations. The corporate image is subject to fairly precise measurement, which can be used to show changes in the company's image over time and which may on occasion indicate why these changes are taking place.

Corporate image research can be used by management to help arrive at decisions relating to many different aspects of advertising and communications, and a number of examples of this have been shown.

Finally, corporate image research is in a continuing state of evolution and improvement. As the sophistication of management, the public, and researchers increases, better and more effective techniques for conducting corporate image research will undoubtedly be needed—and developed.

Part D

Industrial Marketing

Chapter 1

The Industrial Buying Decision Process

CHARLES W. FARIS *The Boston Consulting Group, Inc., Boston, Massachusetts*

Marketing Strategy

Developing and implementing an effective marketing strategy require analyzing and matching three separate but closely interrelated factors:

Customer requirements in the market segments of interest

The marketer's own competitive strengths and weaknesses

The strengths and weaknesses of major competitors in the segments of interest

The buying decision process is important because it is a key factor in market segmentation. And market segmentation is a logical starting point in strategy development. A market segment is a group of actual or potential customers who meet two criteria:

All members of the segment have the same value system and priorities with respect to the particular product and/or service offering.

The marketer's cost of serving each customer in the segment is approximately the same.

Although methods of market segmentation are discussed in Section IV, Part B, Chapter 4, in view of their importance to industrial marketing, it seems desirable to discuss them further in this more specific context in this chapter.

By itself, market segmentation is merely a way of analyzing, describing, and classifying customers. The process has operational value when it is undertaken as part of the strategy development process. The fundamental initial question is: "What is it about potential customers and their requirements that really makes a difference as far as the sale of my product is concerned?" Answers to the question are developed through the process of research and analysis known as market segmentation.

Implicitly or explicitly, all marketers segment their customers. At the least, they segment according to the information and data they use for operating and planning purposes. The difficulty is that the categories typically used—SIC codes, annual purchase volume, distribution channels, or geographic location—are typically not the critical ones as far as the development of a marketing strategy is concerned.

For example, a leading paper mill had been segmenting its business along conventional lines: merchant versus direct, type and grade of paper ordered, geographic location, and so forth. The company was losing market share and had not been able to determine why. A marketing research study showed that the really critical bases for segmentation lay in the printer's buying decision requirements in several different buying situations:

1. Many jobs were routine, repetitive, and highly predictable. Here the printer wanted to minimize the price paid and time and effort he devoted to the purchase, even though the dollar value of the purchases was high.

2. Some jobs were sold because he could deliver to the customer before his competitors could. Here delivery was the critical factor.

3. In submitting a sealed bid on a large job, the price the printer paid for his paper relative to the prices his competitors paid for the same paper was critical.

4. Some jobs were sold because of a particular attribute of the paper the printer was using. Here technical assistance was the key factor.

The mill, of course, had long known that price, delivery, reliability and technical assistance were important to the printer. But it had not explicitly taken into account that the relative importance of these factors varied considerably from one paper buying decision to another. It had been, in effect, averaging out the services it provided across all the buying decisions. The analysis made it possible to tailor the package of services more closely to the requirements of the particular buying situation. This resulted in *lower total distribution costs*, improved responsiveness, lower prices on many items, and a much strengthened competitive position.

This is not always so, for in some instances the tailoring process can lead to excessive segment costs that exceed the benefits of segmenting; but it is an alternative to be considered.

Nature of Consumer Requirements

Most marketers are aware of the fact that customer requirements—what he needs and wants and the relative importance of the various factors—will be different in different buying situations. In practice, however, too many follow the policy of averaging the elements of the marketing mix across all customers and all buying situations of a given customer, leaving it to the individual salesman to provide, within certain limits, the flexibility required in any particular buying situation. But a growing body of evidence suggests that total costs can be lowered and competitive position improved by an explicit study of the buying decision process within customer organizations, followed by a formal adjustment of the marketing strategy tailored to the requirements of the customer in any given buying situation.

Conventional wisdom says that segments are best drawn along company or organizational lines. These companies or plants or operations are in one segment, and those "organizational entities" are in another segment. The distinction between organizational units is assumed to be rather clear cut. The Dallas plant of Dioxide Furthburners, Inc., is either in segment A or in segment B. Implicitly, the marketer realizes that some of Dioxide Furthburners' purchases really fit into segment B. But records are kept—and more importantly, the customer company is handled—as though all its purchases from the seller were essentially the same. How well the individual adjustments ("fine tuning") are made depends upon what the individual salesman has learned rather than upon what the marketing company itself has learned.

The thesis of this chapter is that relative competitive performance and total profitability can be significantly improved by the marketer who explicitly thinks through and organizes his marketing effort around what he already knows implicitly:

1. Probably no two purchases in any given company will ever be exactly alike. Each purchase is different.

2. At the same time, there will be a few general patterns of behavior and customer needs and wants which will hold in the great bulk of the individual purchases. Pareto's law (that 20 percent of the customers usually account for 80 percent of the business) will apply here as elsewhere.

3. Across different companies buying the same goods and services, the same general patterns can be observed, although the proportions or "mix" may vary greatly from customer to customer.

4. The most relevant way to segment is according to these basic behavior patterns or buying situations rather than around customers, applications, or geographic locations per se.

5. Depending upon the size and frequency of purchases, it may or may not be economical to organize the sales force along buying situation lines. At higher organizational levels (region, corporate), it becomes progressively more feasible to organize backup support for the salesforce along buying situation lines. As marketing management learns to think and to segment and collect information along these lines, the organization learns and it becomes much easier to translate the experiences of the "best" salesmen to all the other salesmen.

While simple in concept, segmenting according to buying behavior patterns is difficult in execution. It requires that the marketer understand the customer's needs and wants and buying behavior patterns better than does the customer himself.

The customer's perceived needs and wants are obviously important. But this is true in a negative rather than a positive fashion—failure to convince the customer that he is getting what he thinks he wants will kill the sale. But typically the basic segmentation should probably not be on the basis of the customer's perceived needs. The marketer must be sensitive to these, of course. But real success is more likely to accrue to the marketer who understands the customer's true needs better than does the customer himself and can convince him of it.

The point, then, is that within each customer organization there will be a handful of basically different buying situations or buying decision patterns which account for the overwhelming majority of that company's purchases of the goods and services of interest to the marketer. In most cases, the first level of explicit segmentation should start with these buying situations and not with the company, its applications, or its geographic location.

At the risk of oversimplifying, it may be said that all customer requirements can be considered to fall into the following categories:

purchase price

total economics of the product in use

performance relative to expectations
availability, including the logistics of distribution
assurance—risk factor
assistance—technical, application, information
There are probably few situations where all these factors are not of some importance to the buyers. But it is their relative importance in any given situation that is critical for the marketer. The question is not "Which of these is important?" but "What is the relative importance of each of these factors in the particular buying situation?" Then the total marketing effort can be adapted to emphasize the one or two critical factors. This approach is likely to lead to improved competitive position (more units sold) and lower total costs (more profit per unit).

There are defensive as well as offensive strategic reasons for adapting the marketing effort to recognize more precisely the basic requirements of each segment in any particular buying situation. To illustrate the point, consider the situation currently facing the leading producer of a consumable industrial supply item used across a wide range of industries. The company's situation may be illustrated as follows:

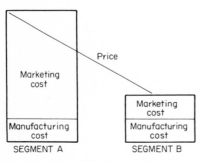

Fig. 1

Not surprisingly, the marketer found that what it costs him to serve a customer varies greatly. Some customers are highly profitable while others are clearly unprofitable. A quantity-price schedule is in effect, but it does not accurately reflect the cost differences to the company. Clearly, the company is "average costing." Large customers are subsidizing small ones.

Prices do not accurately reflect either costs or the price-service trade-off preferences of the large accounts. The situation was further complicated because salesmen, seeing the significantly higher margins received on small accounts, tended to believe that this business was the more profitable and so concentrated on getting more of it.

Several small competitors had been quite successful in stealing away the large customers' use of the high-volume items. These new entrants had segmented the total market, analyzed the requirements of large customers, and were providing products at lower prices and lower costs to the high-volume accounts. This left the large producer with the worst of both worlds. He was losing his highly profitable customers (by dollar, not gross margin, measures), and being left with the high-cost, low-profitability customers. This might have been avoided had the company taken the initiative by segmenting the total market along lines suggested by the customer's buying decision process and basic requirements.

The relative importance of the elements which comprise the customer's total requirements (purchase price, total economies of the product in use, performance relative to expectations, availability, assurance, and assistance) will obviously vary greatly according to the particular situation. Some of the more important variables which will influence the relative importance of these factors include:

1. Overall economies of the buyer's business and buyer's type of operation (assembly, job shop, continuous process, service versus manufacturing, high versus low volume, and so on)

2. How the product or service purchased fits into the buyer's procurement and "production" operations
3. The nature of competition in the buyer's business
4. The nature of competition in the seller's business (what customers are used to receiving)

The Buying Decision Process

The buying decision process may be considered as a set of eight more or less sequential and distinct phases. The outcome of each phase is highly dependent on the outcome of the previous phases, so that the final decision is more of a "creeping commitment" to a particular course of action than it is a series of independent decisions. The phases are highly interrelated. Decisions made in one phase not only depend on the outcome of the past phase but strongly influence the outcome of succeeding phases. Indeed, the entire process may be visualized as starting with a large number of alternatives which are gradually narrowed down until only one remains. It is not possible to point to one phase and say "this is where the decision was made." Rather, the entire process must be considered as an entity.

The buying decision process consists of the following phases:
1. Anticipation or recognition of a problem or need and a general idea of the direction in which the solution is likely to lie
2. A general determination of the characteristics and quantity of the needed item
3. A more specific description of the characteristics and quantity of the needed item
4. The search for, and qualification of, potential solutions or suppliers
5. The acquisition and analysis of proposals for solving the problem
6. The evaluation of the proposals and the selection of one or more suppliers
7. The determination of an order routine
8. Performance feedback and evaluation

In a logical sense, it may be said that there is a sequential flow of phases or activities. In practice, two or more phases may take place concurrently. This would be the case, for example, when the buyer and the seller work closely together to develop a new product or a new application. Similarly, the phases are not mutually exclusive. It is almost always difficult—and probably pointless—to attempt to determine exactly where one phase ends and another begins.

Nor is the relative importance of each phase equal, either in a particular buying situation or in comparing several buying situations. Source qualification, for example, will be critical in some cases, less important in others, and virtually automatic in others. The importance of each phase depends primarily upon the relevant past experience, as they see it, of the people involved in the process. When, for example, those involved have little relevant experience, the early problem definition phases will tend to be the critical ones. On the other hand, when a commonly used item is being rebought, the later proposal evaluation and supplier selection phases may be the only ones to which time is devoted—the earlier phases having been resolved on comparable earlier decisions.

Similarly, the fact that the procurement process has begun is no guarantee that it will proceed, step-by-step, from its inception to the purchase of an item. The process may be stopped at any time by someone directly involved or by a veto from a higher organizational level. The process may be proceeding smoothly when a sudden redefinition of the basic problem occurs, stalling, halting, or recycling the entire decision-making process.

Buying Situations

Essentially, there are three types of buying situations. They may be defined in terms of three variables:

Relevant past experience, as they perceive it, of the decision makers

Information needs

Effort devoted to seeking and considering different alternative solutions

The buying situation may be referred to as *new task, routine rebuy,* and *modified rebuy.* Their characteristics are described below:

New Task—Problem or requirement where the buyers' experience is low, thus causing them to devote considerable effort and attention to finding the "best" solution subject to certain organizational and personal constraints. This also means that they seek a great deal of information in making the decision and believe that the time, effort, and money devoted to seeking out and evaluating alternatives is well spent.

Routine Rebuy—Buyers' relevant experience is high, thus causing them to believe that they already know enough to make a good decision. Hence, information needs are low—perhaps no more than a telephone call to check on current prices and delivery dates. Similarly, buyers believe that the results of seeking and evaluating new alternatives are not likely to be worth the time and effort.

Modified Rebuy—Like the routine rebuy in many respects. The need is likely to be a continuing or recurring one, so that the buyers' experience factor is high. It differs from the routine rebuy in that the buyers seek to deroutinize what is normally handled in a routine fashion. They believe that benefits of investigating new alternatives are likely to exceed the costs involved. Information needs are medium, as new answers to old problems are sought. In practice, the modified rebuy tends to occur as a periodic exception to what is normally handled as a straight rebuy. For a variety of reasons, organizations find it advisable to periodically deroutinize and reassess their normal procurement routine, even if they wind up buying from the same suppliers as before.

The distinguishing characteristics of the buying situations may be summarized in the following exhibit.

Buying Influences

A buying influence is anyone who becomes involved—directly or indirectly—in the problem solving or decision making activities which constitute the procurement process. The roles and the relative importance of the buying influences will vary greatly, of course.

TABLE 1   Different Buying Situations and Their Characteristics

	Characteristic		
Buying situation	Buyers' relevant experience	Information needs	Resources devoted to considering alternatives
New buy.............	Low	High	High
Routine rebuy..........	High	Low	Low
Modified rebuy.........	Medium to high	Medium	Medium

A given individual can become involved in a buying situation for one of two reasons:

1. He has an organizational stake in the outcome (the production manager of a tractor company would probably be involved in the company's buying decision to switch from steel to fiber glass fenders; a purchasing agent is partially evaluated on the basis of how much money he saves the company as a result of his buying practices).

2. He is a source of information considered relevant by those with organizational responsibility (metallurgical engineers in the advanced engineering group would probably be involved in a jet aircraft engine maker's decision to switch from a forging to a casting for a particular component).

The perspective of any given buying influence will be a function of his total personality, including his past experience and his present organizational function within the buying company.

The best source of analysis concerning the human factors is probably a book on psychology. A number of observations can, however, be made here about the organizational influences on the buying decision process. The functional perspective has the following effects on the buying influence's interest in the buying process:

Marketing—Marketing men look at the procurement process as a way of enhancing the salability of their own products. This tends to cause them to favor parts and components made by "name" suppliers in those cases where the part retains its identity in the product the market sells. Marketing is also likely to have pricing responsibility and so is interested in ensuring that the items purchased are inexpensive enough that a targeted selling price can be achieved. Since they bear most of the brunt of customer complaints, marketing men place a high value on the reliability of the items used.

Manufacturing—Production men are interested in maximizing production volume, minimizing problems or delays, and reducing production costs. They want to buy items that make the manufacturing job efficient, simple, and trouble-free. Especially in dynamic businesses, manufacturing men tend to be relatively progressive, continually seeking out and testing new products and processes which enable them to operate more efficiently.

Engineering—Design and development people are typically responsible for the proper operation of the company's products. They establish operating specifications and make sure that the product meets them. This tends to make them conservative. What is known and has worked in the past is usually preferable to a new and therefore risky item. In practice, there is often considerable overlap with the production people, although it is probably no great oversimplification to say that engineers and marketers are concerned with "this is what we can do." Engineers usually have the final authority on technical matters within their organizations. Their selections tend to be written into the specs, thus becoming locked in in many cases. They also tend to have strong images of the relative capabilities of various suppliers and to be highly influenced by these images. Well-known "name" suppliers are preferred, since their selection allows the engineer to pass on to the name supplier much of the responsibility for the proper operation of the final product.

Research and Development—Especially in high-technology and dynamic businesses, R&D men can be powerful, if often informal, buying influences. Because of their detailed knowledge of particular fields (metallurgy, chemicals, and so on) and suppliers, their inputs into the buying process are often solicited.

General Management—In most situations, top operating management does not become actively involved in the buying decision process. These decisions, with two exceptions, are delegated to others in the organization. For some products, such as an executive jet airplane or a new headquarters building, top management may play a major, personal role in the buying decision process. Top management is also likely to be heavily involved where it is known in advance that the decision will significantly affect the company's general direction and its freedom of choice in the future. This would be the case if a major new plant, process, or product were being considered or in other *new task* buying situations where the outcome of the decision will strongly influence the company's ability to act in the future. Except in these situations, top management, if involved at all, is likely to act as reviewing or confirming authority and likely to exercise its power only in a negative sense—it may veto decisions made elsewhere in the organization.

Purchasing—The purchasing agent is basically the overseer of the more routine procurements. In any organization, there is a need to routinize the buying process as much as possible. As the company's buying experience on a particular product increases, it needs less new information to make its decisions. It becomes less and less economical to devote substantial amounts of effort to seeking and considering alternative solutions. The purchasing agent is responsible for handling and routinizing the procurement process for those items where buying experience is high. He is evaluated primarily on the basis of reducing the costs of items purchased and of assuring reliable and uninterrupted deliveries of those items.

Marketing Implications

Any marketer may be said to be selling to both *new buy* and *rebuy* situations. The relative proportion will vary with the life cycle of the product and the application. In a rapidly growing business, the marketer may find that a significant part of his sales effort is devoted to new-buy situations. In stable, mature businesses, *new buys* will occur only rarely.

In new-buy situations, the early phases of the procurement process are critical: seeking the general area of the problem solution and determining the general characteristics and specifications of the needed item. Problem recognition is largely internal to the using department, but it can be anticipated and perhaps triggered by an aggressive marketer. The sooner in the process the marketer gets involved, the better his chances are of having his product become the "solution" to the problem.

The new buys are important to the marketer far beyond the actual dollar volume of business they generate since they tend to set the pattern for a series of routine purchases in the future. Since the nature of the selling effort may involve a high degree of creativity and applications engineering effort and since the key buying influences are likely to be at fairly high organizational efforts, the marketer should consider using some of his own technical and middle-management people as part of a sales team. The marketer has a unique opportunity to use the *new buy* to invest in future business, and he should therefore treat the situation as such.

In rebuys, the "in" supplier should seek to build and strengthen his relationship with the customer. He seeks to routinize the purchase as much as possible, to increase his share of the customer's business, and to collect information relating to potential changes in the nature of the customer's requirements.

Where he is an "out" supplier, the marketer typically instructs his salesmen to continue to call in hopes of getting in. Expressed another way, he seeks to deroutinize the procurement process; to get it handled as a *modified* instead of a *routine rebuy*. Experience suggests that a cost benefit analysis of continuing to make regular calls on companies that are not now customers is likely to be clearly uneconomic.   Further, this tends to raise the marketer's total cost, thus further decreasing his probability of getting new customers and increasing the chances that someone will be able to sell his existing customers at lower prices.

The relationship between users and suppliers tends to be much stronger than many people realize.   In selling many types of standardized products, a new supplier is likely to get in only if an existing supplier makes a series of fairly serious mistakes and does not do an adequate job of making good on those mistakes.   Also, buyers tend to be more tolerant of long-time suppliers' errors than they are of the comparable mistakes of newer suppliers.   Even when buyers see a margin of superiority for a new supplier's offer, they are likely to remain with existing suppliers unless they are convinced that the margin is great enough to offset the costs and risks associated from changing a satisfactory working routine.

Why would a buyer elect to remain with a supplier of a less attractive product or service?   For one thing, the buyer is not likely to see the same degrees of superiority that the marketer sees.   And any change in suppliers or products involves both *costs* and *risks*.   Buyers do not jump for every superior product or service because they believe that the costs and risks associated with making the change outweigh the potential advantages which the change might bring. A known quantity is often preferred to promises of better things to come.   A job of the out supplier is to convince the buyers that the risks of sticking with the existing goods or service exceed the risks of changing.

Any salesman who survives for more than a short time becomes intuitively aware of these things, and he adapts his presentation and behavior to this perception of what the buyers' needs are in each individual situation.   An advantage of the buying situation analysis is that it makes the experience and learning of the "best" salesmen more easily and fully understandable to the "worst" salesmen.

It is worth emphasizing that all buying involves uncertainty, whether it is done by a housewife or by the president of a billion-dollar company.   In an organizational setting, there are two types of risks: organizational risk and personal risk.   Being human, buyers try to minimize both types of risks, whether they are company presidents, purchasing agents, engineering managers, or shop foremen.

In many cases, the personal risk reduction is more important to the buying influencer than the organizational risk.   "It is better to eliminate the personal risk of my actions even if the organizational risk is increased," says the selector of a machine tool, "because I can't be faulted for an inferior product selection if the supplier is recognized as having the highest reputation for quality and largest market share.   If I choose them, it's *their* fault, not mine, if something goes wrong."

Risk minimization leads to conservatism, so that the known supplier is usually preferred to the unknown one even if the unknown supplier has a more potentially attractive offer.   There is a great deal of inertia in any organization, and that inertia favors existing suppliers.

Summary

The essence of marketing strategy is to consistently outperform competitors. Strategy development depends on an analysis of three separate but interrelated factors: customer requirements and priorities in the market segments of interest, an objective appraisal of the competitive strengths and weaknesses of the marketer, and the relative strengths and weaknesses of his major competitors.

The first step in strategy development is to segment the total heterogeneous market into smaller homogeneous groups called segments. Markets can be segmented along many different lines. No one method of segmenting is inherently better or worse than any other method. It depends on how the insights and information provided by the segmentation process are to be used. It is often useful to segment the total market along several different lines.

Markets are typically segmented along conventional lines—customer, application, location—because that is how it has been done in the past and how data are easiest to collect. Experience suggests that segmentation according to the various buying situations that arise in customer companies—in addition to whatever other means of segmentation the marketer has found useful—can help the marketer in a number of important ways. It forces him to analyze the customer's business as a whole, causing him to realize that the customer's world does not necessarily revolve around the marketer's product. In the process of understanding the customer's business as a total system, the seller may end up with a better understanding of the dynamics and interrelationships of the various parts that the customer himself has.

Marketing competition is a matter of relative strengths and weaknesses, not absolutes. The marketer who understands the customer's business and the buying situations or behavior patterns that arise in customer organizations, and who tailors his marketing and selling effort to explicitly focus on the different needs and wants in each major buying situation, typically finds that he has gained a significant advantage relative to his competitors.

There are three fundamentally different buying situations—*new task, routine rebuy,* and *modified rebuy.* They are distinguished according to three variables:

Relevant past experience of the buying decision makers

Information needs

Effort devoted to seeking out and considering different alternative solutions

By understanding how much and what level of each is involved in each buying situation of his potential customers, the marketer can tailor his effort accordingly.

BIBLIOGRAPHY

Customer Requirements

Bullen, H. J., "New Competitive Selling Weapon—Physical Distribution Management," *Sales Management*, vol. 94, May 7, 1965.

Christian, R. C., "A Checklist for New Industrial Products," *Journal of Marketing,* vol. 24, July 1959.

————, "Three-Step Method to Better Distribution Channel Analyses," *Journal of Marketing*, vol. 33, October 1969.

Cook, P. W., Jr., "Fact and Fancy in Identical Bids," *Harvard Business Review*, vol. 41, January–February 1963.

Day, C., "Service: the 'Something Extra' in Industrial Selling," *Sales Management,* vol. 92, May 15, 1964.

Edelman, F., "Art & Science of Competitive Bidding," *Harvard Business Review,* vol. 43, July–August 1965.

Magee, J. F., "Logistics of Distribution," *Harvard Business Review*, vol. 38, July–August 1960.

Simon, L. S., "Measuring the Market Impact of Technical Service," *Journal of Marketing Research,* vol. 2, February 1965.

Stewart, W. M., "Physical Distribution: Key to Improved Volume and Profits," *Journal of Marketing*, vol. 29, January 1965.

The Buying Situation

Alijian, G. W. (ed.), Purchasing Handbook, New York: McGraw-Hill, 1958.
Colton, R. R., Industrial Purchasing: Principles & Practices, Columbus, Ohio: Merrill, 1962.
England, W. B., Procurement: Principles & Cases, 4th ed., Homewood, Ill.: Irwin, 1962.
Heinritz, S. F., and Farrell, P. V., Purchasing Principles and Applications, 4th ed., Englewood Cliffs, N.J.: Prentice-Hall, 1965.
Lusardi, F. R., Purchasing for Industry, New York: National Industrial Conference Board, Studies in Business Policy, no. 33, 1948.
Robinson, P. J., and C. W. Faris, Industrial Buying and Creative Marketing, Marketing Science Institute Series, Boston: Allyn and Bacon, 1969.

The Buyer Decision Process

General

Thain, D. H., C. B. Johnston, and D. S. R. Leighton, How Industry Buys: With Conclusions and Recommendations on Marketing to Industry, sponsored by the Business Newspapers Association of Canada and the Canadian chapters of the National Advertisers Association, 1959.
U.S. News & World Report, How Business Buys, Sections II, III. Washington, D.C.: United States News Publishing Corp., 1957.

Identifying Buying Influences

Harding, M., "Who Really Makes the Purchasing Decision?" Industrial Marketing, vol. 57, September 1966.
"Helping Salesmen Identify Points of Buying Influence," Industrial Marketing, vol. 47, May 1962.
Kernan, J. B., and M. S. Sommers, "The Behavior Matrix—A Closer Look at the Industrial Buyer," Business Horizons, vol. 9, Summer 1966.
Walsh, C. E., "Reaching Those Hidden Buying Influences," Industrial Marketing, vol. 46, October 1961.

Human Factors as Determinants of Buying Decisions

General Personality of Buyer

Blumenthal, L., "The Hidden Influences on Buying," The American Salesman, vol. 4, August 1959.
Copeland, M. T., "Buying Motives for Industrial Goods," in Principles of Merchandising, Chicago: A. W. Shaw Co., 1924.
Dichter, E., "The Human Being in the Job of Buying," The American Salesman, vol. 4, January 1959.
Duncan, D. J., "What Motivates Business Buyers," Harvard Business Review, vol. 18, Summer 1940.
Levitt, T., Industrial Purchasing Behavior: A Study of Communication Effects, Boston: Harvard Business School, Division of Research, 1965.
Robertson, G. M., "Motives in Industrial Buying," AMA Proceedings, Summer 1960.

Effects of Organization and the Buyer's Personality

Perlmutter, I., "Purchasing and Motivations," Purchasing, vol. 55, July 1, 1963.

Organizational Influences on the Buying Decision Process

Liston, S., "Engineers Need the P.A.'s Help," Purchasing, vol. 54, March 25, 1963.
"Purchasing & Engineering: Can They Work Together?" Purchasing, vol. 55, August 12, 1963.
Strauss, G., "Tactics of Lateral Relationship: The Purchasing Agent," Administrative Science Quarterly, vol. 7, September 1962.

Part D

Industrial Marketing

Chapter 2

Sales Territory Analysis

EDWIN C. GREIF   *Department of Business Administration, University of Vermont, Burlington, Vermont*

Design of sales territories is of special significance for the firm and its salesmen. Since the construction of the sales territory indicates the appropriate work load for the salesman in terms of quantity and the type of work expected of him, certain determinations must be made.   These determinations include analysis of what each territory represents and the type of salesman best suited to serve its particular needs.   It is essentially a matching of the right man to the appropriate sales territory.

This chapter, in an effort to provide an improved guide to more effective construction of sales territories, will consider the following subjects: the criteria essential to effective construction of individual territories; measurement of sales potential in the particular territory; establishment of territorial boundaries; determination of quotas and other types of stimulus plans; degree of supervision warranted to assure performance; and evaluation of the sales territory.

CONSTRUCTION OF INDIVIDUAL SALES TERRITORIES: CRITERIA

The carefully designed sales territory is its own reward.   The salesman's time can be more productively used since his routine and coverage lend themselves to more effective supervision.   Each territory is assured of more careful study and better sales plans result since these will be based on a knowledge of sales potential as well as the numbers, types, and buying power of customers located therein.   The many factors that affect a salesman's effectiveness also can be more accurately appraised.

Thought in the design provides more equal opportunities for salesmen, allows for better comparison of men, and indicates competitive challenges and other factors that assure more intensive exploitation. It provides assurance that individual salesmen in a territory will have approximately the same population, outlets, and income potential and ensures appropriate call frequencies.

This approach should provide answers to the several basic questions just mentioned. The following design criteria enter into the development procedure.

Design Criteria

1. Does the territorial assignment provide equality in task and sales potential? Management judgment must be exercised since the sales task may vary despite statistical analysis that may indicate equal potential. Thus the commission form of compensation requires that a particular territory provide the diligent salesman with a satisfactory income level.

2. Does the territorial assignment assure thorough coverage of the market? All prospective customers of sufficient potential, although they may represent businesses of different types and sizes, should receive the attention and service warranted by the account. Contrary to what should logically be expected, salesmen have a marked propensity for directing more attention and time to the smaller rather than the larger accounts.

3. Does the territorial assignment provide the salesman with a definite responsibility? The territorial assignment can provide this specifically, especially when quota assignments are set.

4. Does the territorial assignment use marketing areas rather than political units as its base? Customers buy where appropriate, convenient, and favorable sources of supply are located. The search for goods and services is hardly restricted by political boundaries such as state, county, and city lines. To illustrate, wholesale and trading area units should be used if salesmen are engaged in selling to wholesalers and retailers. This also facilitates analysis and assists in a more effective direction of sales effort.

5. Does the territorial assignment improve management's ability to evaluate sales performance? Armed with information on potential demand in a given territory, management can use this to assess the salesman's actual performance. Management can, through proper territorial assignment, not only compare territory against territory but it can also determine *trends*. Opportunity equalization efforts can, however, produce other problems that will shortly be considered.

6. Does the territorial assignment ensure improved distribution expense accounting? Sales experience in the field can be more readily secured through territorial assignment. In turn, this provides for a greater standardization of factors which contribute to an improved budgeting and cost accounting.

7. Does the territorial assignment avoid duplication and improve customer relations? Proper territorial assignment will reduce useless travel and other related and costly activities. Of greatest importance, better customer relations with respect to orderly call procedures and service should result. Customer turnover through competitive retaliatory action should be reduced.

HOW SALES TERRITORIES ARE ESTABLISHED

Increased sales costs and missed sales opportunities are the penalties for establishment of sales territories not premised on scientific method. Added to this is the constant need for adjustments in sales territory determinations based on the many expansions and contractions that can take place because of changes in market conditions [24, p. 705].

As a basic concept, manpower should be spread over the market in relation to potential demand. . . . While . . . studies indicate the basic pattern for the distribution of sales effort, the pattern must be modified for any particular company. For instance, the basic pattern will be similar for all manufacturers of office equipment; or consumer durables; but this factor does *not* mean that all companies in each of these industries will have identical sales territories. There are *no* ready-made sales territories acceptable for all concerns. The problem is to secure an index of potentiality as a general guide for the distribution of effort, and then to permit other factors—some of general significance, some pertinent to only one company's operation—to bear upon the actual selection and later revision of sales territories. . . . Study of the market becomes necessary; but initially there is no question of adjusting one salesman's territory to others. Later, if expansion takes place and the markets are cultivated intensively, all the problems of sales territory determination appear. More effective planning then becomes necessary.

Procedures

In any procedure to establish sales territories, the aim is always to ensure adequate market cultivation. To accomplish this the firm must consider two factors: *its market* and *the work load for salesmen.*

Two philosophies on proper size present perplexing problems. Should we strive to develop territories of equal potential or resolve the problem by equal work load? Territories of equal potential sit well with salesmen and, from the firm's viewpoint, indicate (the) differences of effort or ability by the individuals assigned. The theory is that the salesman will thus be motivated to maximize his selling effort. The difficulty is that territories vary in density so that unsalaried men in the larger and less dense territory earn less income— unless an unusually superior effort is directed to the sales task.

There are, however, two ways to overcome the difficulty just outlined: One is to provide higher compensation in the larger and less dense territories, which of course results in lower profits for the firm; the other possibility is to staff the better territories with better men based on ability and seniority. The problem here is one of transfer, since it affects customer relationships and transfer expenses for both firm and salesman involved.

But what about resolving the problem through our other alternative— equalizing the work loads of the salesmen? Once again we face a problem. Sales potentials in territories vary. While salesmen who are on straight salary are not in difficulty, those who are not totally on straight salary may find the situation otherwise, because territories vary in their desirability.

Is there any way around this problem? Again, there are two ways out of the dilemma: We can lower compensation rates where the territory has a higher sales potential or, again here, the man of superior ability or greater seniority will be assigned to the higher-potential territory.

A guide to action is what so many companies are seeking: they try to combine the principles of sales potential and equalized work load.

Determining a Basic Territory

As indicated earlier, political lines alone cannot be used to establish sales territories. Territories should be built on sound methodology to ensure equal opportunity for the new firm and, for the established firm, to ensure excellent coverage and sound control. No one procedure offers the answer. In one situation salesmen may sell more than one product line in their specific territory, while in others salesmen may sell many or especially complex products in a given territory with several men in a particular territory—a sales force oriented on product lines.

The latter can be best illustrated by companies that sell thousands of products, that produce unrelated lines, or whose products are particularly complex. Again, several principles of sales-force structure will be combined in situations where companies distribute a wide variety of products in a large geographical area for various types of customers [18, p. 71–77; 31, p. 10; 33, p. 7–13].

A METHOD FOR SETTING UP A TERRITORY

This method should assist in the establishment of a new sales territory and also help to adjust territories long established, often arbitrarily and on a basis of expediency, to meet new market conditions more effectively.

Step 1: Determine the territorial unit on the basis of sales potential.

Step 2: Determine the workload of the salesman and the indicated sales call patterns.

Step 3: Determine regularly through analysis of conditions those factors that can change the territorial unit.

Step 1: The Territorial Unit

It is not a sound practice—as was already mentioned—to use cities, counties, and states as political units in the design of sales territories where salesmen will be selling to wholesalers and retailers. Sales territories should be established by *marketing areas* on the basis of customer buying habits.

A practical way to accomplish this objective is to build the territory by joining several smaller units on the basis of geography—these areas should be adjoining, have the appropriate transportation facilities, and maintain the common characteristics of the adjoining areas. The idea is to develop a territory of the desired potential and/or work load.

To do this, information must be secured on sales by states, counties, metropolitan centers, or trade areas. As an illustration, estimates of retail sales may be found in the "Survey of Buying Power" published by *Sales Management;* and data for certain products and product groups may be obtained from the decennial census as well as from the Department of Commerce, trade associations, and others. From such information we can develop some idea of past sales by territorial units if we can assume *our* sales will be the same, an assumption that may require upward or downward revision.

For consumer goods, the U.S. Department of Commerce annual estimates of personal income (by geographic areas and major cities) as well as the estimates of the annual *Sales Management* Buying Power Index (by counties, metropolitan areas, and principal cities) may provide indexes of potential demand. Then on the basis of past experience and competitive conditions, the firm estimates the percentages of potential sales in each territorial unit.

For industrial products, rather than estimating area potentials by breaking down estimates of total sales, estimates of individual salesmen in dollars or physical units can be combined to yield a sales forecast for the company. Armed with a knowledge of total sales and trends and the company's hoped for sales, a basis is set up for defining or adjusting a sales territory.

When we then do is combine enough of an adjacent city or cities, county or counties, trade area or areas so that the potential of the territory is sufficient to support a salesman. In some cases, based on customer density and potential demand, several city blocks might constitute a territory; in other situations, a single city or county; and, in still others, several cities, counties or states might be required.

One source [30] suggests the *buildup* method, a method particularly suited for manufacturers of consumer products or those products where intensive distribution is wanted. The procedure is as follows:
1. Determine the number, location, and size distribution of customers
2. Determine desirable call patterns (number and frequency)
3. Determine number of accounts to assign each salesman
4. Draw territorial boundary lines

For manufacturers of industrial products or where degrees of selective distribution are wanted, the *breakdown* method can be used:
1. Determine sales potential
2. Determine volume expected from each salesman
3. Determine number of territories needed
4. Tentatively establish territories
5. Modify basic territories

Step 2:   Determination of Work Load and Sales Call Patterns

Territorial design is meaningful only when we relate the elements that influence work load to the sales territory. To illustrate, the type of product can have a considerable influence on the sales job. A product with a slow rate of turnover and slow repeat sales requires many fewer calls by salesmen than a high-turnover product with a constant repeat-sale business. The job itself may have great effects on the call pattern: If the territory, for instance, requires missionary work as part of the sales job (as compared to the territory where there is only a selling job to do), the pattern will allow for less calls unless two salesmen are in the territory—one for missionary work and the other for selling.

Obviously the situation is quite different if one sells through a wholesale distributor or endeavors to sell direct. Forms of transportation and the type used may alter things, since the question here is always how the man can reach more accounts more efficiently and inexpensively.

Additional Influences. Whether the product is in the pioneering, competitive, or retentive stage is important. A product in the retentive stage will permit the individual salesman to work a smaller territory since it will usually provide a sufficient volume of business to assure satisfactory income. The opposite is true with a new product or where the company is seeking penetration in a new area.

The degree of market coverage and the competition also condition the work load relationship to territorial design. Mass distribution calls for *smaller* territories; selective or exclusive distribution permits *larger* territories. Similarly, with a severe competitive program that seeks to overcome competition, the odds are that the territorial assignments will be smaller. The danger in this last-mentioned situation is that profits will be compromised. The alternative? Combine adjacent territories and endeavor to secure orders only from the better accounts.

Differences in abilities of salesmen and variations in sales potentials of territories are also serious considerations. For this reason Kotler [12, pp. 515, 516] indicates the need for care in the assignment of salesmen: ". . . better salesmen should be assigned the better territories in a rough rather than an exact way. Assignments should reflect man-territory interactions and not just the average ability of salesmen and the average potential of territories."

Interestingly, the particular sales territory and the conditions in it, the sales potential, and the work load may all be equal but still some accommodations and reapportionments may be required, since salesmen differ in age, initiative, knowledge, physical condition, and personality, among other things.

Sales Call Patterns and Routing. The better the effort in the original establishment of the territory, the easier it is to arrange routing for the salesman. Call rate and frequency having been established, what remains is to establish the routes themselves. The more advanced company uses mathematical analysis and the computer to ensure optimum time use and/or minimum travel costs.

Routings will depend on two prime considerations. First is the location of accounts that shape the territory. These shapes may include triangle, circle, wedge, straight line, or hopscotch. The second consideration relates to the transportation facilities available: auto, air, train, or bus. These relate to the three major problems involved in maximizing the salesman's use of time: traveling, waiting, and selling. An economical solution is achieved by reducing the travel and waiting periods and maximizing the time for selling.

However, there are those who object to routing, claiming that it produces a lack of flexibility required for territorial coverage and that it compromises the better and higher-caliber salesmen. Still, for sales situations calling for regular call frequencies and routine service activities of the account, there is much to be said for routing.

Sales Call Patterns. In addition to earlier comments on sales call patterns, it is appropriate to consider the determination of the correct number of salesmen to employ. Semlow [28, pp. 126–132] advocates use of data based on sales experience. Relationships are established between the share of the total potential available in the various territories and the sales that have been secured from the territory. There are numerous weaknesses and assumptions, however, in Semlow's method.

Perhaps a better approach is to consider the number of customers in a particular territory and then estimate how many salesmen are needed to call on and service them. One such formula is [5, pp. 233–235]:

$$S = \frac{E_1 + E_2 \cdots + E_N}{e} + \frac{E_{P1} \cdots E_{PN}}{e_p}$$

where S = salesmen needed (number)
E_1 = sales effort to direct toward established customer class 1 (call frequencies and time length based on dollar volume and companies' individual experiences with accounts over time)
E_i = sales effort for ith established customer class
E_p = sales effort for prospective customers
e = time availability per year per salesman to call on established customers
e_p = time available to call on prospective customers per salesman per year

Each E_i is a function of the number of customers in each potential class, the travel time between customers, the best call frequency, and the time which should be spent in selling and service within the customer's establishment in view of the potential volume available. The major problem is to determine how sales are likely to respond to call rate variations for each customer as well as the relationship between sales and the time spent with the customer in selling and service work on each call.

To illustrate, let us restrict the example to E_1 to E_N, the established customers. Owing to the varying needs of established customers and the difficulties of servicing the accounts, we can assume that $E_1 \neq E_2$, and so on; that is, salesmen will have to spend more time servicing some customers than others.

Let us further assume four established customers—C_1, C_2, C_3, and C_4. The time the firm feels it must devote to each customer per week is estimated as follows:

$E_1 = 10$—number of hours per week spent on C_1
$E_2 = 5$—number of hours per week spent on C_2
$E_3 = 5$—number of hours per week spent on C_3
$E_4 = 20$—number of hours per week spent on C_4

We will also assume that a salesman can spend 40 hours per week servicing accounts. The number of salesmen then needed to service established accounts is:

$$S = \frac{E_1 + E_2 + E_3 + E_4}{40} = \frac{10 + 5 + 5 + 20}{40} = 1$$

Alternatively, if we assume a salesman can spend only 20 hours per week servicing accounts (the remaining 20 hours spent on administrative tasks), then S is 2.

Step 3: Revision of Sales Territories

To establish a new territory or territories is one thing. In contrast, it is very hard to change existing sales territories. Great care should therefore be directed to any changes because performance and morale are involved. Nevertheless, appropriate changes and adaptations to changing conditions *should* be made.

What are some of the reasons that recommend change in a particular situation? Included would be rising selling costs, distribution channel changes, unprofitable accounts, selling cost reduction possibilities, the overloading of salesmen—or their underloading, incomplete market coverage, neglect through skimming, poor use of time by men, and the fact that the capabilities of salesmen were not adjusted to territories.

Besides these reasons that relate to salesmen, some territories from their inception may have lacked clear boundaries or have been too large for proper coverage. Perhaps the salesmen did not observe territorial boundaries. Possibly customer groupings were not made correctly or attempts were made to have the salesman canvass too much territory.

Revising sales territories is *a continuous problem*. To do this job effectively requires overall statistical information supplemented by detailed information from salesmen and customers. Such information also provides assistance in setting quotas, bonuses, and general compensation plans and incentives, to which our attention is now directed.

Application of the three steps is illustrated by the case of the M Chemical Production Company, which wanted an improved territorial design to provide the following [33, pp. 7–13]: regular and efficient field sales service; clear definition of customer assignment and territorial lines; a balance between territories of travel; a method of determining the number of salesmen that would maximize the sales department's profit contribution; and, finally, a basis for a sound salesman's compensation plan.

First a five-class customer breakdown by size in dollars was made (the large-quantity customers to be serviced differently from those in the medium range):

Class	Yearly gross dollar sales
1	Over $100,000
2	$25,001 to $100,000
3	$5,001 to $25,000
4	$1,001 to $5,000
5	$0 to $1,000

Next, a theoretical call frequency for each class was developed at a national sales meeting.

Class	Yearly dollar sales	Average calls per year
1	Over $100,000	20
2	$25,000 to $100,000	14
3	$5,000 to $25,000	9
4	$1,000 to $5,000	3
5	$0 to $1,000	1

Experience had shown the company that as a customer grows larger, the number of sales calls does not grow in direct proportion to the increase in dollar sales. It had also found that the relationship between customer size and sales calls was linear when these two factors were plotted on semilog paper, as shown in Figure 1.

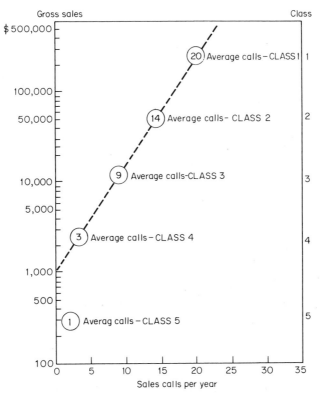

Fig. 1. Sales calls per year versus gross dollar sales for consolidated chemical company.

Total work load for the company was then developed by multiplying the call frequencies by the number of accounts in any class, as follows:

Class	Calls per year	Number of accounts	Total calls per year by class
1	20	18	360
2	14	70	980
3	9	120	1,080
4	3	180	540
5	1	612	612
		1,000	3,572

It then becomes necessary to determine how many salesmen were needed to complete 3,572 calls per year. Company statistics indicated the number of working days, nonselling time (sales meetings, sick leave, laboratory training, and so on), number of calls per day by salesman and by territory as well as variation in call capacity between urban and rural territories. The company determined that an average salesman could make 750 calls per year.

Hence the company needed at least 5 salesmen (3,572 calls divided by 750) to make the 3,572 calls with the 1,000 present customers.

Now that the company knew the number of salesmen required, it could develop the territories. To do this, each of the company's 1,000 customers was assigned a yearly call frequency consistent with his dollar volume of contributed business. M's call frequency was then summarized by city, county, and state. Since experience had shown that county summaries were the most convenient base, these were accumulated until the total call frequencies approximated 750 calls per year per man.

Additional study of the company's resulting call frequencies by county indicated that call concentration was in metropolitan and/or industrial areas. Since the large metropolitan areas generally had more calls than any one man could serve, they were cut into pie-shaped sections.

COMPENSATION PLANS

Sound compensation plans assure the direction of selling efforts that are fruitful and maximize the effectiveness of the individual salesmen. A good plan results in greater returns for both company and salesman.

The company wants a plan that salesmen will feel is fair. It would also prefer that the plan provide stimulation for strong sales effort and entail reasonable administrative expense. The plan selected must give cognition to the type of salesman required, what he is expected to do, and the intensity of *sales* effort desired. The *optimal mix of marketing effort* in terms of market programming theory and mathematical analysis is well described by John A. Howard [6, pp. 475–479].

From the salesman's standpoint, a plan is desired that provides better income for better performance, one that rewards for ability and experience. Usually he also wants some base income, paid regularly, to assure a minimum income.

The Elements of Compensation

There are four basic parts—at most—that make up a compensation plan: the fixed part, the variable part, the expense allowance part, and the fringe benefit part. It is not necessary for all parts to be included in every plan; this is determined by individual firm selling conditions. Generally speaking, there is a 70–30 scale—70 percent fixed and 30 percent for other elements. The particular plan has to be modified in light of the numerous problems that face each individual company.

The Basic Compensation Plans

In essence there are three plans: straight salary, straight commission, and a combination of salary and commissions. Each plan has its advantages and its limitations both from the firm's and the individual salesman's point of view.

Straight Salary Plan. This plan provides management with the following advantages: simplicity of administration (lower administration costs); more disciplined control over salesmen (less resistance to performance of other than selling activity); and it often simplifies morale problems.

Added to this *incentive weakness,* however (propensity to do an *average* job), there are these additional limitations from the firm's viewpoint: it does not distinguish between ability and initiative among salesmen (unless evaluations are frequent and skillful); disagreements often occur that affect morale (raises for cost of living, and so on); and changing economic conditions (hard to adjust to these) may produce serious problems. However, capable and diligent administration can overcome many of these limitations.

Freed from financial uncertainty, the salesman likes this plan, which is also easy to understand. He has added confidence, particularly as a new recruit, since the company is literally underwriting his sales experience.

On the other hand, salesmen often feel—especially the better men—that they carry the less diligent men and that the disadvantages the firm suffers with the plan are the same for the more accomplished performer.

This type of compensation plan is used in selling situations that require technical and/or engineering advice, where much missionary work or sales promotion work is required, and in the more routine types of selling, for example, driver-salesmen and order-takers found in wholesaling and manufacturing.

Straight Commission Plan. For the firm, this plan, under appropriate conditions, also has numerous advantages. First and foremost, men are paid on a productivity basis (sales volume only is rewarded); maximum incentive is provided (sales volume emphasis); management has control over selling cost (sales volume determines cost—traveling and miscellaneous expenses excluded); added stimulation can be given (commission rates can be changed to stimulate sale of higher-profit items).

Again there are certain limitations: the firm has more limited control over its men—they are primarily interested in receiving orders and not only will resist various types of requests but believe that their accounts are their own private grounds. The low-margin items are often pushed and prices are often cut to effect sales. Administration and auditing costs are naturally higher than with the straight salary plan. The company must also decide the base on which the commissions are due. This may be total sales, shipments, payments, gross margins, or the like.

For the salesman, this plan provides a genuine incentive (the more one works, the more one receives), and individual abilities are highlighted and rewarded (the strong do not carry the weak). The disadvantages for the salesman are little security (much depends on economic conditions), and morale may be impaired (sales obstruction may not relate to the man himself).

A variation of the straight commission plan is the drawing account. By this method periodic withdrawals are made against an account. The idea works like a straight salary. Some firms prefer the "guaranteed" drawing account.

Since overdraws do not have to be paid back with this latter form, salesmen are not tempted to leave when overdrawn.

Combination of Salary and Commission. To secure the advantages and to minimize the disadvantages of the previously described compensation systems, the great majority of firms use the combination salary and commission plan.

The prime advantage is stimulation for better and greater effort and yet control over the salesman's activities. The plan, in addition, provides both an element of income security for the salesman and also financial incentive. Better adjustment to business conditions also results, which means positive effects on the morale of the staff.

On the other hand, once again there are problems to be considered. The incentive part of the plan must be carefully decided. An incentive portion that is too strong may well result in selling-related activities; if this portion is too low, the desired extra effort is lost. Note should also be made of possible administrative difficulties, since salesmen may have trouble understanding the details of a possibly complicated compensation plan.

The Bonus as an Incentive

A bonus, in contrast to a commission that varies in payment with the commission base, is used to accomplish a specific sales task; it is a reward for the salesman who accomplishes results in excess of originally set minimums.

A combination plan results if this bonus is used with straight salary; used with straight commission, there is the advantage of added control of the salesman; used with salary and commission, it is a part of incentive income. A principal problem with the bonus is to have the salesmen believe it has been developed in an equitable manner.

The bonus in relation to the establishment of quotas is discussed further in the section on quotas.

Fringe Benefits

Any discussion of compensation plans includes attention to the fringe benefit aspect. Today, salesmen have a share in practically all the fringe benefits given other company employees. Insurance, retirement provisions, vacations, medical care, and the like are significant morale factors. In effect fringe benefits are additional compensation for the salesmen.

Setting Quotas for Incentive Compensation

The quota is the essential ingredient that determines the success of any bonus plan. It should be fairly set so that, with appropriate effort on the salesman's part, it can be attained. Only then will the bonus provide genuine incentive for the salesman. Quotas must therefore not be guesses, as is all too frequently the case. Accurate market potential estimates for the given industry under question must be made and the same accuracy is needed by the company in estimating its own sales potential.

To avoid arbitrary estimates of quotas, the following elements should be regularly considered:

1. Market potential
2. Sales potential
3. Estimates by distributors and dealers
4. Estimates by company salesmen
5. Productive capacity of firms
6. Sales costs (advertising and sales promotion)
7. Types of product or products
8. Ability of salesmen

9. Surveys of buyer intentions
10. Environmental conditions

The basic procedures for determining forecasts—given knowledge of product uses and probable uses—are the *unit forecast procedure* or direct evaluation method and the *overall forecast procedure* or the index method. The unit forecast procedure is used usually for high-unit-value industrial items; the overall forecast procedure for companies that sell to a large number of small-quantity buyers who are widely scattered. While the overall forecast procedure may be applied for both industrial and consumers' goods, it is the only sound method for consumers' goods since the individual buying units are so small.

The overall forecast method results in a market forecast which is broken down to a company forecast. Finally, the company forecast is divided territorially into quotas. Actually the same thing is done when a unit forecast procedure is used: we go from market forecast to company forecast to divisions on the basis of territory and then quotas.

The overall forecast procedure illustrated here takes us through five steps, while the classification of index methods provides a schematic arrangement of the various index methods available [24].

OVERALL FORECAST PROCEDURE

This method of forecasting is more pertinent to companies which sell to a large number of widely scattered customers, each of which buys in relatively small quantities. There are five steps in this procedure:

1. A forecast of business conditions
2. A forecast of the effects of the predicted business conditions on the demand for the product of an entire industry
3. A forecast of what part of industry sales will be made by the company in question
4. Preparation or selection of an index to subdivide the company's anticipated sales into sales for smaller geographical units
5. The application of the chosen index to the company total to determine the quota for each territorial unit

CLASSIFICATION OF INDEX METHODS

The following classification indicates the various index methods that may be used to subdivide actual or anticipated sales of a company by geographic units. In effect, decision must be made by the use of an index based on a single fac-

Single-factor index methods	Sales and purchase data	Company sales Noncompeting product sales Magazine circulation Census data on sales in retail outlets Individual product sales Individual product purchases Consumer expenditure data
	Product-in-use data	
	Corollary data Objective factors data	
Multiple-factor index methods	Arbitrary factors or percentage average method Multiple correlation method	

tor or on one that combines two or more factors. The choice of method depends to a large extent on what data are available and on their reliability.

The measurements needed for market planning—which includes sales analysis, sales forecasting, predicting of sales of a new product, and estimates of market potential—were covered in earlier chapters. The thrust of the remainder of this section is therefore directed to additional qualitative considerations.

Estimates by Middlemen, Wholesalers, and Dealers

Sales forecasts and sales quotas can be aided by opinions of buyers such as middlemen, wholesalers, and dealers. This statement is, however, subject to certain reservations: first, attention must be given to securing careful estimates; second, observations should be based on a broad outlook of business conditions in the area; and finally, any estimates should reflect objectivity without effort to secure personal advantage.

Astute salesmen and sales managers, through experience, have learned to assess the quality of their customers. Strength characteristics and weaknesses are known. Yet purchasing agents and industrial buyers may not want to reveal planned purchases. Buying expectations are also based on business conditions at the time. However, barring unexpected changes in business conditions, substantial assistance can be obtained by this method. Industrial buyers are therefore frequently surveyed about planned plant, material, and equipment purchases.

Potential purchasing by buyers of major consumer durables such as automobiles, appliances, and furniture and housing can be gauged by intentions and attitudes data, as are collected by various commercial sources. However, these indicators may be unstable because they are subject to personal factors and changes in business conditions.

Retailers are in a position to pulse sales activity and can be sensitive to customer buying attitudes and general conditions in the trade area served by them. Wholesalers in turn monitor the retailers whom they serve and become in turn centralized sources of information.

Estimates by Company Salesmen

Company salesmen can be and are used to prepare sales forecasts for the coming year on both national and local territorial estimates. To encourage objective and more careful estimating measures, companies offer incentives. Salesmen are given an opportunity to compare their forecast with actual sales and, later, with forecasts of their colleagues. Certainly the salesman is in a position, probably the best of all, to observe trends and provide information on customers, products, and the general conditions in his case.

To be carefully considered are the bases that the salesman may bring to his forecast. To keep his sales quota lower, he may submit conservative estimates of period sales. This can be corrected, however, by finding what percentage of sales he had in the previous year (based on his forecast) and taking a weighted average error in the last of several periods. The correction factor is then applied to the new forecast.

Also to be considered in evaluating the salesman's forecast of sales is his capacity to grasp and sense the "big picture" in business conditions and in his company. Finally, one must be alert to the salesman who gets "carried away," projects a high estimate, and then becomes discouraged in efforts to reach it.

Advertising and Sales Promotion Costs

Proper coordination of advertising and sales promotion activities with those of the salesman can have pronounced influence on sales forecasts and sales quotas.

The potential effects of extensive national and local advertising efforts are substantial. Point-of-sale advertising at the dealer level contributes additional impact. Cooperative advertising plans for distributors and dealers add up to expectations of increased sales. By the same token, the reverse procedure would probably adversely affect future sales estimates.

An additional influence of advertising and sales promotion is their ability to pave the way for salesmen's calls and appointments with buyers and dealers of the particular product and service. Direct mail sales promotion activities can be used to relieve salesmen from calling on unprofitable accounts.

Type of Product

Sound forecasts also require, almost before anything else, a careful knowledge of the product and how it relates to prospects and customers. The single or variety uses of the product become the basis for measurement. Knowledge of products enables estimates to be made for the development and expansion of markets.

What the company does in product improvement and differentiation— whether the company is a follower or leader; how effective the company's decision on product lines is—what to drop and what to add, and finally how astute it is in meeting product competition through product change will have substantial effects on future demand and on the quota potential for salesmen in general.

To help achieve better control of salesmen's performance, standards of performance are instituted. To do this requires a total understanding of the specific sales job and what the particular firm wishes to accomplish. Also required is a knowledge of the company's market and the potential prospects and customers to be served in it. Finally, the factors necessary for implementation must be included.

To provide sales performance comparisons with sales potential and resultant net profits, numerous quantitative performance standards are regularly used by different companies: some use quotas, already discussed in other sections of this chapter, such as selling expense to sales volume ratios (not recommended for use alone in performance evaluation). Territorial net profit and share-of-market analysis are also commonly used, as discussed earlier. Call frequency ratios are useful (Hauk [5] writes about an experiment on salesmen, call patterns, and sales), as are order call ratios and calls per day plus the average cost and order size of the individual order. Another article on personal selling provides information on an experiment that measured the effects of various variables on sales performance [15, pp. 140–156].

Qualitative performance measurements are secured with the aid of numerically scored and nonnumerically scored merit rating systems.[1]

Information to control salesmen is secured through a variety of salesmen's reports that include call reports, route reports, expenses, new accounts, lost sale and complaint reports, and general information summaries. The objective in the development of a report system for control purposes is to delineate the number needed and the amount of information necessary.

Supervision is aided further through personal contact meetings with salesmen and through conventions, correspondence, reports, manuals, sales bulletins, and—the most recent development—taped newsletters for use with cassette players to help keep salesmen up to date on feature product news, sales techniques, industry developments, and other matters.

Finally, attention must be accorded to the computer and computer centers

---

[1] For an excellent description of various merit rating systems, see [17].

that provide the sales executive with a high level of sophistication in achieving the previously described problem solutions. Through cooperation with other departments, such as accounting, much information can become available not only on billing but also on sales, product, and inventory control.

Discretion, however, must be exercised in data collection. Instead of printing huge quantities of data, listings of those activities below the desired standards or below the average of other activities may be compiled, such as salesmen failing to achieve quotas; sales activities exceeding budgeted expenses; markets in which the company is losing competitive position; customers with declining purchases; and product lines which have slow sales movement, declining profit margins or both [11, pp. 9–10].

Use of the computer also extends to the *field manager* and his salesmen. The field manager will need not only a people orientation but also an information orientation. William Lazer states the case well [13, p. 71]:

> To date, the regional (or district) manager's job has been mainly managing the sales force. He has been people oriented. While this will continue to be important, in the future he will also have to be a manager of information concerning his territory, the effectiveness of his sales force, and the relationships between the various variables of marketing. The manager will be more of a planner and director than the salesman he commonly is today. His job will become more like the manager of an experimental process, whereby he is continually gathering information and revising his estimates.

The computer will assist in developing work loads of salesmen based on account demands, helping him to respond to account gains and losses, file activities, and other manpower planning activities. More facts will be available to assist the field manager in his evaluations of salesmen's performances.

Many companies also have computer centers that provide automatic ordering opportunities for customers. All the customer need do is to follow the automatic ordering procedure, punching the order on a console teleprocessing station linked to the central computer. Immediately the central computer goes to work examining inventory availability and customer credit. It prepares requisite shipping orders and retains the information in its memory bank.

CONCLUSION

This chapter was concerned with the coordination of the selling function with marketing activities. The emphasis was on the elements related to the development of territories and the achievement of goals. The importance of logical design of sales territories and their relation to market coverage, service, costs, coordination, and finally supervision and evaluation were highlighted. Compensation as a prime source for motivation of salesmen was described.

The various subjects included owe their presence to one simple fact: they should assist the salesman in performing his job more effectively and provide the company with additional assurance that it will meet the challenge of company objectives in marketing more economically, efficiently, and profitably.

REFERENCES

1. "A Useful Policy Guide," *Industrial Marketing*, vol. 47, January 1962.
2. Day, R. L., and P. D. Bennett, "Should Salesmen's Compensation be Geared to Profits?" *Journal of Marketing*, vol. 25, October 1962.
3. Dixon, W. R., "Redetermining the Size of the Sales Force," in *Changing Perspec-*

tives in Marketing Management, Ann Arbor, Mich.: Michigan Business Papers, no. 37, Bureau of Business Research, University of Michigan, 1962.

4. Farley, J. U., "An Optimal Plan for Salesmen's Compensation," *Journal of Marketing Research,* vol. 1, May 1964.
5. Hauk, J. A., "Research in Personal Selling," in G. Schwartz, ed., *Science in Marketing,* New York: Wiley, 1965.
6. Howard, J. A., *Marketing Management: Analysis and Planning,* rev. ed., Homewood, Ill.: Irwin, 1963.
7. Huff, D. L., "Defining and Estimating a Trading Area," *Journal of Marketing,* vol. 28, July 1964.
8. Juster, F. T., *Anticipation and Purchases,* General Series, no. 79, Princeton, N.J.: Princeton University Press, 1964.
9. Karg, R. L., and G. L. Thompson, "A Heuristic Approach to Solving Traveling Salesman Problems," *Management Science,* vol. 10, January 1964.
10. Katona, G., *The Powerful Consumer,* New York: McGraw-Hill, 1960.
11. Kelley, T. C., Jr., "The Marketing-Accounting Partnership in Business," *Journal of Marketing,* vol. 30, July 1966.
12. Kotler, P., *Marketing Management: Analysis, Planning, and Control,* Englewood Cliffs, N.J.: Prentice-Hall, 1967.
13. Lazer, W., "The Computer in Marketing—Part II," *Sales Management,* March 15, 1969.
14. Little, J. D. C., K. G. Murty, D. W. Sweeney, and C. Karel, "An Algorithm for the Traveling Salesman Problem," *Operations Research,* November–December 1963.
15. Magee, J. F., "Determining the Optimum Allocation of Expenditures for Promotional Effort with Operations Research Methods," in F. M. Bass, ed., *The Frontiers of Marketing Thought and Science,* Chicago: American Marketing Association, 1958.
16. McBurney, W. J., Jr., *Goal Setting and Planning at the District Sales Level,* American Management Association Research Study no. 61, 1963.
17. *Measuring Salesmen's Performance,* Studies in Business Policy no. 114, New York: National Industrial Conference Board, Inc., 1965.
18. Meilstrup, S. S., "Redesigning Sales Territories: A Case Study," in *Changing Perspectives in Marketing Management,* Ann Arbor, Mich.: Michigan Business Papers, no. 37, Bureau of Business Research, University of Michigan, 1962.
19. National Industrial Conference Board, Inc., *Compensating Field Sales Representatives,* Studies in Personnel Policy, no. 202, New York, 1966.
20. ———, *How to Stimulate Salesmen to Better Selling,* Experiences in Marketing Management, no. 4, New York, 1963.
21. ———, *Incentives for Salesmen,* Experiences in Marketing Management, no. 14, New York, 1967.
22. ———, *Motivating the Older Salesman,* Experiences in Marketing, no. 5, New York, 1964.
23. "Pensions and Profit Sharing," *Merchandising Week,* September 26, 1966.
24. Phelps, M. D., and J. H. Westing, *Marketing Management,* 3d ed., Homewood, Ill.: Irwin, 1968.
25. Rehmus, F. P., and H. M. Wagner, "Applying Linear Programming to Your Pay Structure," *Business Horizons,* vol. 6, Winter 1963.
26. Research Institute of America, *Sales Compensation Practices,* New York, 1965.
27. Risley, G., "A Basic Guide to Setting Quotas," in M. Alexander and E. M. Mazze, eds., *Sales Management: Theory and Practice,* New York: Pitman, 1965.
28. Semlow, W. J., "How Many Salesmen Do You Need?" *Harvard Business Review,* vol. 37, May–June 1959.
29. Smyth, R. C., "Financial Incentives for Salesmen," *Harvard Business Review,* vol. 46, January–February 1968.
30. Stanton, W. J., and R. H. Burkirk, *Management of the Sales Force,* 3d ed., Homewood, Ill.: Irwin, 1969.
31. Stickney, R. W., "Deploying Multi-Line Salesmen," *Harvard Business Review,* vol. 38, March–April 1960.

32. "Survey of Buying Power," published annually in May issue of *Sales Management*.
33. Talley, W. J., Jr., "How to Design Sales Territories," *Journal of Marketing*, vol. 25, January 1961.
34. "3 or 4 Pre-Sale Calls?" *Industrial Marketing*, vol. 46, July 1961.
35. Vizza, R. F., *Improving Salesmen's Use of Time*, prepared under the Director of the Research Committee, New York: Sales Executives Club of New York, 1962.
36. Webster, F. E., Jr., "Rationalizing Salesmen's Compensation Plans," *Journal of Marketing*, vol. 30, January 1966.
37. "When and How to Split a Salesman's Territory," *Industrial Marketing*, vol. 47, December 1962.

Part D

Industrial Marketing

Chapter 3

Forecasting with Input-Output

PHILIP J. BOURQUE   *School of Business Administration, University of Washington, Seattle, Washington*

Input-output, or interindustry relations analysis, is a technique of quantitative analysis of the linkages which bind together the activities of industries in a complex interrelated economy.   In recent years economists have made increasing use of input-output as a model for economic forecasting, and since the procedure focuses upon purchases-sales relationships among industries, it has particular application in forecasting industrial sales.

In a highly diversified economy characterized by industrial specialization in the provision of goods and services to meet the wants of consumers, production takes place in stages.   Direct consumer sales represent only a portion of the sales of many industries and are completely absent in the sales of others. Many producers are so remote from consumer markets that a direct analysis of consumer demand tells us little about the industrial markets of the preceding stages in production.   Only after a circuitous route of processing and exchange does the output of many establishments satisfy consumer wants.   In sales forecasting, then, it is important to predict industrial market demands as an indirect function of the demands of final users.

Input-output is a technique for analyzing the chain reaction as demands of final users set in motion activities among industries directly or indirectly affected.   It can translate the implications of a forecast of GNP and its components into the purchases and sales among industries to produce that GNP or "bill" of final demand.   It is also an information system that provides a framework for organizing large amounts of relevant data describing the flows of goods and services among participants in the economic process.   Since Wassily Leontief of Harvard University pioneered its development, the input-output methodology is often called a Leontief model.

THE INPUT-OUTPUT ACCOUNTING FRAMEWORK

Before discussing the forecasting uses of input-output, we should consider the information contained in the accounting framework of the model. Our discussion runs in terms of an *interindustry* input-output model, but the techniques to be described are applicable to the study of other types of interdependencies and have predictive implications as long as the feedbacks among units can be posited as occurring in a necessary or behaviorally fixed pattern.

The accounting framework of input-output specifies the relationship between the output of industries, measured in dollars, and its disposition. The output of any industry may be traced to the markets in which it is sold. That portion of the output of an industry sold to another industry for further processing is called intermediate product, for it is used by the purchasers as a current input in their production processes. The output of an industry not sold to industry as current input is by definition sold to final demand. Final demand is conventionally defined for input-output purposes in the same way as in the GNP accounts to include the spending of consumers, government, investors (capital formation and net inventory accumulation), and sales to export markets. This definition of final demand has the advantage of relating industrial output to the GNP accounting framework. But the definitions of final sales and intermediate sales may be varied, and in principle the distinction separates those areas of activity in which the investigator believes he can successfully establish the existence of invariance between input and output from those for which he cannot. In the language of econometrics, intermediate transactions are the endogenous variables of the system while the final demand components are exogenous.

The flows of goods and services among industries and between industries and final users may be notationally described:

Let X_i = the sales of any industry, $i = 1, \ldots, n$ industries

 x_{ij} = the sales of the ith industry to jth industrial user, $j = 1 \ldots n$ industries

 Y_i = the sales to consumers, investors, government, exports

Then

$$X_i = x_{i1} + x_{i2} + \cdots + x_{in} + Y_i \tag{1}$$

which is a balance equation that defines the output of any industry as equal to the sum of the sales it makes to all industrial customers and to all final users.

A balance equation may be written for each industry so that a system of equations is created which is called a transactions matrix:

$$
\begin{array}{lllll}
Output & Intermediate\ Demands & Final\ Demand & \\
X_1 & = & x_{11} + x_{12} + \cdots + x_{1n} & + & Y_1 \\
X_2 & = & x_{21} + x_{22} + \cdots + x_{2n} & + & Y_2 \\
\multicolumn{5}{c}{\cdots\cdots\cdots\cdots\cdots\cdots\cdots\cdots\cdots\cdots\cdots\cdots\cdots\cdots\cdots} \\
X_n & = & x_{n1} + x_{n2} + \cdots + x_{nn} & + & Y_n
\end{array} \tag{2}
$$

Each of the row variables on the right side of each equation of the matrix, after values have been estimated for them, describes the value of the output of the ith industry sold to each jth industry customer (x_{ij}s) or sold to final users (Y_is). Each sale is also a purchase, so the columns of the intermediate sector show how much the jth industry demanded as current input from each supplier. Since the transactions matrix describes the sales-purchase network in a selected period, it is an "input-output" table. Entries in the table may be estimated either by measuring the inputs purchased by each industry from each of the others or by measuring the distribution of the output of each industry to others (a row versus a column approach). The conceptual and empirical problems of quantifying this matrix are quite involved, but benchmark input-output tables are available for the United States for the years 1947, 1958, and 1963.[1]

These accounts of industrial flows are useful in marketing analysis. Comparisons of successive tables show the changing importance of markets over time. An individual producer, by comparing his sales patterns with those of his industry, can appraise the extent to which he shares in supplying the input requirements of various industrial and final markets for his product. By reading down the column for his industry, he can compare his purchases (costs) with those of his competitors.

Several caveats are important in analyzing input-output tables of the kind just described. One is that the definition of *industries* consolidates establishments producing different products, and hence the mix of output of the input-output industry may be different from that of a particular firm. Mix differences also mean that the inputs used by a particular business may be different from those of the input-output industry. After all, industries are pragmatically identified as establishments producing "related" products or using "similar" processes; this means that industry statistics conceal a good deal of heterogeneity among the establishments which compose it. In making interpretations from input-output tables, one should carefully consider the conventions for valuation and classification—a practice appropriate in the interpretation of any accounting framework.

INPUT-OUTPUT COEFFICIENTS

The discussion thus far has been limited to the framework for tracing the actual flows of goods and services among industries. Having determined the historical network of interindustry transaction, how can we use this pattern to forecast future levels of industry activity? More specifically, what determines the values X_i and x_{ij}?

Economic theory offers a hypothesis to explain the relation between the purchases by industry j from industry i. The magnitude of x_{ij} depends on the level of output of the jth industry. Increases or decreases in the output of an industry are to be accompanied by increases or decreases in the various current inputs absorbed by the industry. This proposition is merely a statement of the "law of costs," which states that larger outputs require more inputs and may be described generally as follows:

$$x_{ij} = F(X_j) \qquad (3)$$

This form does not specify the exact character of the relationship. The law of costs requires merely that this relationship be restricted to make the function a monotonically increasing one. Under these conditions the ratio of x_{ij} to X_j

---

[1] The dimensions of United States tables vary in size. The 1947 table was prepared for approximately 450 industries but published in collapsed versions of 210 and 50 sectors. The 1958 table was initially published with 82 sectors, with some additional detail published separately. The 1963 table has nearly 370 industries, with an 82-sector version comparable to the 1958 table.

need not be constant. It is usual, however, to write this relationship in a more restricted form, namely:

$$x_{ij} = a_{ij} X_j \tag{4}$$

where a_{ij} is a constant coefficient of production termed a flow coefficient. It implies a linear, homogeneous relationship between the output of an industry and the various industrial supplies and services the industry must purchase to produce output. This form of production coefficient is not a theoretically valid generalization but an approximation. Its chief appeal lies in its simplicity both for estimation and in subsequent computations. It is important to note that this linear relationship is not a necessary condition for the use of input-output and need not be adhered to if a variable rather than a constant coefficient of production is important enough to warrant additional complications.

Substituting Equation (4) into Equation (1) yields

$$X_i = a_{i1} X_1 + a_{i2} X_2 + \cdots + a_{in} X_n + Y_i \tag{5}$$

Each of the a_{ij} values is estimated from past ratios of x_{ij}/X_j. A complete set of flow coefficients for an input-output model of n industries forms a square matrix as follows:

$$\begin{vmatrix} a_{11}, a_{12}, \ldots, a_{1n} \\ a_{21}, a_{22}, \ldots, a_{2n} \\ \cdot \quad \cdot \quad \cdot \\ \cdot \quad \cdot \quad \cdot \\ \cdot \quad \cdot \quad \cdot \\ a_{n1}, a_{n2}, \ldots, a_{nn} \end{vmatrix}$$

in which each column describes the cents' worth of each kind of material, energy, and service required from other industries by a given industry per dollar of its output. In Leontief's terms, each column describes the "menu" or "recipe" followed by that industry when it buys goods and services to be used as operating inputs in producing a dollar's worth of output.

Can the matrix of flow coefficients, derived from past experience, be used to forecast the input requirements of industry for some future period? This depends upon its stability over time. Practitioners of input-output view the coefficients matrix as primarily determined by the technological structure of production. Since technology changes but slowly over time, they argue, the flow coefficients will have a degree of stability useful for forecasting purposes.

If the pattern of inputs required by industry to produce output exhibits strong elements of stability, observations from recent experience may be used to infer the distribution of procurement for some interval of time beyond that of the observations. Coupled with the assumption that the distribution of inputs is not significantly affected by the level of output, the coefficient matrix becomes a constant useful for prediction [6].

> In other words, and in rather oversimplified form, a basic concept of input-output approach is that in many cases the pattern of goods and services needed to carry on a given productive activity is identifiable through empirical research, exhibits strong elements of stability, and hence is useful for a variety of analytical purposes.

By treating flow coefficients $(a_{ij}s)$ as independent structural parameters in the system of Equations (5), the substitution effects due to relative price changes are ruled out. Since all current inputs are assumed to be utilized in fixed proportions regardless of variations which may take place in their relative prices, the model may be considered theoretically deficient.

Leontief argues that the importance of substitution due to changes in relative prices has been exaggerated in production economics. In his view, the degree of complementarity among inputs is so high that even the wide variation in their relative prices could affect the combination of inputs that would be used only slightly. Moreover, insofar as relative price changes are important to particular industries, such changes themselves are in large part the consequences of technological changes. That is, changes in the technology of production alter the industrial demand for inputs and through this impact upon markets lead to relative price variations. If this is so, it is more the coefficient structure of production which determines prices than prices determining the coefficient structure. However, the issue is not a matter of basic theory but a matter of emphasis; the assumption of fixed coefficients within a given technology is used as a pragmatic simplification.

Since the coefficients that express the input structure of industries are taken from observations of past experience, to what extent can that experience be projected into the future? The assumption that technology changes but slowly over time has uncertain appeal. Innovations reported in production processes in both the popular and engineering literature and the obvious development of new products certainly lend the impression that the pace of technological advance is very rapid indeed. However, technological change within a nation has not yet been subjected to the kind of independent measurement which would make possible an evaluation of this assumption. Even when remarkable new innovations in production appear, they are introduced marginally, and the carryover of existing techniques is likely to dominate an industry's input pattern for some time. Indeed, the empirical investigations conducted to determine input-output coefficients are increasing our knowledge of the technological structure of industry, and the pattern of change over time is the subject of current research by several investigators.[2]

How long it takes before an input-output table becomes outmoded is difficult to say since this depends upon the purposes to which it is put and the precision expected. It has been suggested that input-output tables have a useful life of up to a decade from their date of construction, and it is always possible to alter historical coefficients where new information indicates these have changed. Engineering studies and operating cost projections for new or proposed plants are sometimes available to advance the input coefficients into the period of projection.

The development of the flow coefficient matrix is central to the input-output concept because it sets the behavioral pattern for translating the implications of a set of final demands (Y's) into levels of industry activity (X's) required to achieve those final demands. Consider Equation (5). This says the level of output of the ith industry depends upon the levels of output of each of its industrial customers (X_js), these customers' dependence upon the ith industry for inputs ($a_{ij}s$), and the levels of final demand for the ith product (Y_i). Since there are as many equations of the form shown in Equation (5) as there

---

[2] Comparison of coefficient matrices over time or between countries is a method for quantifying the notion of technological change.

are industries $(i = 1, 2, \ldots, n)$, the production levels of each of these industries is determinate. In other words, given a column vector of n final demands and the matrix of flow coefficients, the X_i terms may be solved simultaneously.

The economic significance of the calculation is that both the direct and indirect production requirements implied by any level of final demand are solved. For example, if the demand for automobiles changes by \$1, the coefficient column for automobiles describes the direct inputs the automobile industry needs in order to increase its deliveries to final users by that amount. Its purchases of steel, glass, paper, paints, electrical parts, fuel, and so forth are described by its column in the coefficient matrix. Suppliers of these products, in order to make deliveries to the automobile industry, must purchase inputs from other industries, whose amounts per dollar of their sales likewise are described by their column coefficients. These suppliers in turn place orders with other suppliers.

The demands upon the outputs of each industry to support the production of a dollar's worth of automobiles may be accumulated to show how much production must take place in each industry to supply the automobile industry, its suppliers, their suppliers' suppliers, and so on. This computation is analogous to the Keynesian income multiplier which measures the effects of changes in respending for consumption upon income; but in the input-output framework, the respending effects for inputs are accumulated and it is the output (or sales) of each industry which is measured.

A more convenient way, certainly more compact, of representing a system of input-output equations is in vector and matrix notation. Let X represent a vector of outputs whose values are to be determined for each of n industries, Y represent a vector of final demands, and A the matrix of flow coefficients. Then

$$X = AX + Y \tag{6}$$

which states that the outputs of different industries depend upon the demands for inputs by industry and by final users. Since the A matrix is a given constant and the Y vector is independently determined, the solution of the X vector is obtained as follows:

$$X - AX = Y \tag{7a}$$
$$(I - A) X = Y \tag{7b}$$

where I is an identity matrix which bears the relationship in matrix algebra which the number 1 holds in ordinary numbers. Dividing both sides by $(I - A)$ we obtain:

$$X = \left(\frac{I}{I - A}\right) Y \quad \text{or} \quad X = (I - A)^{-1} Y \tag{7c}$$

The expression $(I - A)^{-1}$ is called the inverse matrix. Such a table constitutes the focus of an input-output study for impact analysis since it indicates both the direct and indirect effects upon the output of *every* industry per dollar's worth of final demand for the output of any *one* industry. It is a table of industrial output multipliers.

The preceding discussion of the input-output tables has been abstract. As a more concrete expression of these ideas, portions of the 1963 input-output tables for the United States are reproduced from the *Survey of Current Business* (November 1969) in Tables 1, 2, and 3. Table 1, the Interindustry Transactions Table, corresponds to the AX matrix. It shows the dollar flows

TABLE 1 Interindustry Transactions, 1963 [In Millions of Dollars at Producers' Prices]

For the distribution of output of an industry, read the row for that industry.

For the composition of inputs to an industry, read the column for that industry.

Industry No.		1 Livestock and livestock products	2 Other agricultural products	3 Forestry and fishery products	4 Agricultural, forestry and fishery services	5 Iron and ferroalloy ores mining	6 Nonferrous metal ores mining	7 Coal mining	8 Crude petroleum and natural gas	9 Stone and clay mining and quarrying	10 Chemical and fertilizer mineral mining	11 New construction	12 Maintenance and repair construction	13 Ordnance and accessories
1	Livestock and livestock products	4,750	1,819	117	192							323		
2	Other agricultural products	7,897	769	117	550								(*)	
3	Forestry and fishery products			35								3	(*)	
4	Agricultural, forestry and fishery services	445	1,053	74										
5	Iron and ferroalloy ores mining					55	1			(*)	1			
6	Nonferrous metal ores mining					25	263	(*)	(*)	5	(*)			
7	Coal mining					5	1	410	(*)	5	1			1
8	Crude petroleum and natural gas								297					
9	Stone and clay mining and quarrying	1	85		(*)	5	(*)	1		17	5	478	259	
10	Chemical and fertilizer mineral mining		35				6	(*)		1	31			
11	New construction													
12	Maintenance and repair construction	200	367			1	7	14	379	11	3	17	7	6
13	Ordnance and accessories											5	3	161
14	Food and kindred products	3,554	2	44	34					(*)	(*)	26		
15	Tobacco manufactures													
16	Broad and narrow fabrics, yarn and thread mills	9	9							(*)	(*)	31	(*)	(*)
17	Miscellaneous textile goods and floor coverings		29	62	41				2			124	3	
18	Apparel											29	13	4
19	Miscellaneous fabricated textile products	17	43	1		2			(*)	(*)			(*)	
20	Lumber and wood products, except containers	2	2				10	17				3,553	723	16
21	Wooden containers		97		14									5
22	Household furniture											342	4	(*)
23	Other furniture and fixtures											184	71	2
24	Paper and allied products, except containers	12	1	(*)	(*)	(*)	(*)	1	2	6	2	208	(*)	3
25	Paperboard containers and boxes	2	3		86	(*)	(*)					4		7
26	Printing and publishing	5	9	(*)	(*)	(*)	(*)	(*)		(*)	(*)	2	1	1
27	Chemicals and selected chemical products	57	1,424					38	101	34	20	201	54	16
28	Plastics and synthetic materials		1	2	1	21	56			(*)		1	(*)	1

4-253

TABLE 1 Interindustry Transactions, 1963 [In Millions of Dollars at Producers' Prices] (Continued)

For the distribution of output of an industry, read the row for that industry.

For the composition of inputs to an industry, read the column for that industry.

Column headings:
1. Livestock and livestock products
2. Other agricultural products
3. Forestry and fishery products
4. Agricultural, forestry and fishery services
5. Iron and ferroalloy ores mining
6. Nonferrous metal ores mining
7. Coal mining
8. Crude petroleum and natural gas
9. Stone and clay mining and quarrying
10. Chemical and fertilizer mineral mining
11. New construction
12. Maintenance and repair construction
13. Ordnance and accessories

Industry No.	Industry	1	2	3	4	5	6	7	8	9	10	11	12	13
29	Drugs, cleaning and toilet preparations	83		(*)	(*)	(*)	(*)	(*)	(*)	(*)	(*)	2	(*)	1
30	Paints and allied products		954	4	(*)	(*)	(*)	(*)	5	(*)	(*)	308	859	(*)
31	Petroleum refining and related industries	170	114	34	3	11	7	23	64	52	6	1,119	540	13
32	Rubber and miscellaneous plastics products	29		1	(*)	7	10	33	16	70	2	487	139	103
33	Leather tanning and industrial leather products													
34	Footwear and other leather products	7		(*)	3				(*)	(*)	(*)	1	(*)	(*)
35	Glass and glass products	5		(*)				(*)				81	(*)	(*)
36	Stone and clay products	1			(*)	4	2	3		116	(*)	5,813	93	
37	Primary iron and steel manufacturing		39	(*)		21	27	3	41	28	14	2,125	410	149
38	Primary nonferrous metal manufacturing	1	1	(*)		1	(*)	39	30	2	2	1,244	317	193
39	Metal containers	8	13	21				(*)					209	
40	Heating, plumbing and structural metal products					(*)	2		18	2	1	6,159	569	10
41	Stampings, screw machine products and bolts	25	31									112	19	35
42	Other fabricated metal products	21		15	132	1				4	1	975	269	35
43	Engines and turbines					1	4	12	13	4	1	26	1	3
44	Farm machinery and equipment	5	229			8	11	36	16	37	5	2	71	
45	Construction, mining and oil field machinery					24	30	85	25	48	16	238	96	(*)
46	Materials handling machinery and equipment					(*)	3	1		16	4	257	(*)	3
47	Metalworking machinery and equipment					1	1	5				11		1
48	Special industry machinery and equipment													22
49	General industrial machinery and equipment						1	2	25	23	2	210	43	1
50	Machine shop products	3		(*)		(*)	32	11	(*)	8	2	12	1	20
51	Office, computing and accounting machines			(*)	(*)	(*)						404	116	13
52	Service industry machines		7		(*)							337	56	10
53	Electric industrial equipment and apparatus					(*)	1	7	82	7	5	184	99	25
54	Household appliances													5
55	Electric lighting and wiring equipment	1	1	36	(*)	(*)	1	11	(*)	1	1	1,123	183	46
56	Radio, television and communication equipment						(*)		4			79	20	281
57	Electronic components and accessories						(*)		15			1	1	106

	C1	C2	C3	C4	C5	C6	C7	C8	C9	C10	C11	C12	C13
58 Miscellaneous electrical machinery, equipment and supplies	6	25		(*)	2	(*)	1	1	1	(*)	37	10	18
59 Motor vehicles and equipment	7	14	(*)	(*)	1	(*)	8	3	15	1	36	14	1
60 Aircraft and parts	(*)						9	4				(*)	1,868
61 Other transportation equipment		4	21	1							4	(*)	17
62 Scientific and controlling instruments											208	70	40
63 Optical, ophthalmic and photographic equipment											4	(*)	53
64 Miscellaneous manufacturing	2	2					(*)	(*)	(*)	(*)	89	77	1
65 Transportation and warehousing	606	308	44	26	126	30	46	281	34	39	2,143	490	28
66 Communications; except radio and T.V. broadcasting	52	83			1	2	4	9	1	3	180	79	52
67 Radio and T.V. broadcasting	96	204	(*)	1	27	41	65	141	62	36	205	90	26
68 Electric, gas, water and sanitary services	870	843	56	42	21	28	58	145	54	14	5,453	1,702	93
69 Wholesale and retail trade	156	315	3	6	7	25	28	94	29	6	401	161	27
70 Finance and insurance	289	2,020		41	111	42	73	2,246	45	11	307	134	30
71 Real estate and rental													10
72 Hotels; personal and repair services except auto.	139	836	1	(*)	33	14	28	108	22	6	2,959	281	110
73 Business services	76	161	7	1	1	2	8	42	19	1	235	101	9
75 Automobile repair and services													
76 Amusements													
77 Medical, educational services and nonprofit organizations	181	13		1	1	1	5	5	(*)	2	57	24	8
78 Federal Government enterprises	(*)	4	(*)	(*)			2	5	(*)	2	18	8	10
79 State and local government enterprises	2	1	(*)	(*)	1	1	3	5	2	1	28	10	(*)
80A Directly allocated imports	2	214			423	213	1	3					
80B Transferred imports	174	221	428	16	3	7	2	1,046	108	88	359	154	18
81 Business travel, entertainment and gifts	18	32	18		3	7	11	67	11	2	17	7	49
82 Office supplies	1	1	(*)	(*)	(*)	(*)	1	5	1	(*)	38		10
83 Scrap, used and secondhand goods		5	5		5	5	1	5	5				
84 Government industry													
85 Rest of the world industry													
86 Household industry													
87 Inventory valuation adjustment													
I. Intermediate inputs, total	19,992	12,437	1,153	1,190	954	893	1,097	5,338	901	336	39,629	8,663	3,777
VA. Value added	6,692	14,830	598	582	475	625	1,540	6,926	1,123	360	25,890	11,132	2,525
T. Total	26,684	27,266	1,751	1,772	1,429	1,519	2,637	12,265	2,024	696	65,519	19,794	6,302
TR. Transfers[1]	210	261	709	560	565	237	3	1,365	258	116			1,589

* Less than $500,000.

[1] Entry in each column represents the sum of the value of transferred imports at domestic port value and the value of the secondary output of other industries which has been transferred to the industry named at the head of the column.

[2] The detailed entries reflect gross exports of goods and services from each producing industry. Imports in total are shown as negative entries in this column on rows 80A and 80B. Therefore, the sum of the column equals the GNP component "net exports of goods and services."

TABLE 2   Direct Requirements per Dollar of Gross Output, 1963 [Producers' Prices]

For the composition of inputs to an industry, read the column for that industry. Industry No.	Livestock and livestock products	Other agricultural products	Forestry and fishery products	Agricultural, forestry and fishery services	Iron and ferroalloy ores mining	Nonferrous metal ores mining	Coal mining	Crude petroleum and natural gas	Stone and clay mining and quarrying	Chemical and fertilizer mineral mining	New construction
	1	2	3	4	5	6	7	8	9	10	11
1 Livestock and livestock products	0.17800	0.06673	0.06687	0.10823							
2 Other agricultural products	.29596	.02819	.06665	.31040							0.00493
3 Forestry and fishery products	.01667		.01992								.00005
4 Agricultural, forestry and fishery services		.03863	.04243								
5 Iron and ferroalloy ores mining					0.03840	0.00089	0.00004		0.00002	0.00215	
6 Nonferrous metal ores mining	.00021	.00002			.01782	.17332	.00010	0.00002	.00225	.00013	
7 Coal mining					.00361	.00090	.15561	(*)	.00227	.00087	
8 Crude petroleum and natural gas	.00006							.02418			
9 Stone and clay mining and quarrying		.00311		(*)	.00339	.00029	.00026		.00860	.00772	.00729
10 Chemical and fertilizer mineral mining		.00129				.00408	.00001		.00072	.04442	
11 New construction	.00750				.00060	.00491	.00549	.03093	.00543	.00394	
12 Maintenance and repair construction		.01344									.00027
13 Ordnance and accessories											.00008
14 Food and kindred products	.13319	.00008	.02529	.01933						.00010	.00040
15 Tobacco manufactures									.00007		
16 Broad and narrow fabrics, yarn and thread mills	.00035	.00034	.03536	.02296	.00001	.00019			.00006	.00043	.00047
17 Miscellaneous textile goods and floor coverings		.00106			(*)	.00010	(*)	.00017			.00189
18 Apparel	.00065					.00001					.00044
19 Miscellaneous fabricated textile products		.00158									.00011
20 Lumber and wood products, except containers	.00008	.00008	.00072	.00798	.00169	.00651	.00636	.00001	.00002	.00043	.05424
21 Wooden containers		.00355									.00523
22 Household furniture											.00281
23 Other furniture and fixtures											.00317
24 Paper and allied products, except containers	.00044	.00004	.00022	.00003	.00015	.00026	.00038	.00014	.00287	.00289	.00007
25 Paperboard containers and boxes	.00006	.00011	.04877								

#	Industry											
26	Printing and publishing	.00018	.00032	.00020	.00001	.00002	.00005	.00002	.00003	.00004	.00005	.00003
27	Chemicals and selected chemical products	.00213	.05224	.00091	.00051	.01487	.03669	.01443	.00822	.01688	.02871	.00807
28	Plastics and synthetic materials	.00310		(*)	(*)	(*)	.00009	(*)		.00011	.00025	.00002
29	Drugs, cleaning and toilet preparations			.00252	(*)	(*)	.00001	(*)		.00001	.00002	.00003
30	Paints and allied products						.00001		.00037	.00001		.00469
31	Petroleum refining and related industries	.00636	.03499	.01959	.00195	.00737	.00462	.00868	.00524	.02550	.00823	.01079
32	Rubber and miscellaneous plastics products	.00109	.00419	.00059	.00004	.00473	.00641	.01233	.00128	.03455	.00250	.00743
33	Leather tanning and industrial leather products	.00027			.00156							.00001
34	Footwear and other leather products	.00020		(*)		(*)	.00001	(*)		.00001	.00001	.00001
35	Glass and glass products											.00123
36	Stone and clay products	.00005	.00143	.00028	(*)	.00251	.00112	.00119	.00333	.05715	.00065	.08872
37	Primary iron and steel manufacturing	.00003	.00003			.01493	.01777	.01486	.00243	.01362	.01974	.03244
38	Primary nonferrous metal manufacturing	.00029	.00046			.00102	.00025	.00003		.00116	.00287	.01898
39	Metal containers			.01216								
40	Heating, plumbing and structural metal products					.00022	.00099		.00150	.00084	.00080	.09400
41	Stampings, screw machine products and bolts	.00093		.00861	.07439							.00171
42	Other fabricated metal products	.00077	.00115			.00091	.00249	.00466	.00107	.00220	.00099	.01488
43	Engines and turbines	.00020	.00840			.00585	.00719	.01355	.00129	.01838	.00663	.00040
44	Farm machinery and equipment											.00002
45	Construction, mining and oil field machinery					.01674	.01954	.03210	.00200	.02354	.02341	.00364
46	Materials handling machinery and equipment					.00015	.00228	.00022		.00792	.00636	.00393
47	Metalworking machinery and equipment					.00083	.00037	.00172				.00017
48	Special industry machinery and equipment											
49	General industrial machinery and equipment	.00011	.00024	.00025	.00001	.00016	.00048	.00079	.00200	.01130	.00240	.00320
50	Machine shop products			.00011		.00014	.02082	.00425	.00003	.00378	.00248	.00018
51	Office, computing and accounting machines											
52	Service industry machines											.00617
53	Electric industrial equipment and apparatus					.00004	.00043	.00279	.00666	.00367	.00693	.00515
54	Household appliances											.00280
55	Electric lighting and wiring equipment	.00003	.00005	.00001	.00001	.00013	.00040	.00419	.00002	.00051	.00137	.01715
56	Radio, television and communication equipment					.00004	.00013		.00033			.00121
57	Electronic components and accessories						(*)		.00119			.00002
58	Miscellaneous electrical machinery, equipment and supplies				.00001							
59	Motor vehicles and equipment	.00022	.00093	.00105	.00003	.00017	.00018	.00030	.00007	.00069	.00020	.00056
60	Aircraft and parts	.00025	.00051	.00022	.00022	.00156	.00155	.00301	.00027	.00724	.00143	.00056

TABLE 2 Direct Requirements per Dollar of Gross Output, 1963 [Producers' Prices] (Continued)

Industry No.	For the composition of inputs to an industry, read the column for that industry.	Live-stock and livestock products (1)	Other agricultural products (2)	Forestry and fishery products (3)	Agricultural, forestry and fishery services (4)	Iron and ferroalloy ores mining (5)	Non-ferrous metal ores mining (6)	Coal mining (7)	Crude petroleum and natural gas (8)	Stone and clay mining and quarrying (9)	Chemical and fertilizer mineral mining (10)	New construction (11)
61	Other transportation equipment	(*)	.00016	.01184		.00006	.00122	.00337		.00006	.00044	.00007
62	Scientific and controlling instruments			.00040		.00025	.00033		.00036			.00317
63	Optical, ophthalmic and photographic equipment	.00006	.00007	.00012	(*)	.00001	.00067	(*)	(*)	.00002	.00003	.00007
64	Miscellaneous manufacturing	.02272	.01131	.02517	.01445	.08811	.01947	.01760	.02293	.01661	.05592	.00136
65	Transportation and warehousing	.00196	.00303			.00091	.00115	.00134	.00070	.00030	.00402	.03271
66	Communications; except radio and T.V. broadcasting											.00275
67	Radio and T.V. broadcasting											
68	Electric, gas, water and sanitary services	.00360	.00749	.00009	.00045	.01868	.02687	.02469	.01148	.03054	.05155	.00313
69	Wholesale and retail trade	.03260	.03090	.03215	.02382	.01502	.01827	.02199	.01180	.02669	.02059	.08323
70	Finance and insurance	.00583	.01155	.00188	.00322	.00476	.01637	.01076	.00763	.01423	.00832	.00612
71	Real estate and rental	.01082	.07407		.02324	.07753	.02748	.02769	.18312	.02212	.01622	.00469
72	Hotels; personal and repair services exc. auto											
73	Business services	.00519	.03068	.00038	.00092	.02282	.00923	.01080	.00881	.01070	.00882	.04516
75	Automobile repair and services	.00285	.00589	.00387	.00051	.00073	.00151	.00293	.00343	.00032	.00137	.00358
76	Amusements											
77	Medical, educational services and nonprofit organizations	.00677	.00047	.00018	.00017	.00054	.00068	.00077	.00039	.00019	.00262	.00087
78	Federal government enterprises	.00015	.00015	.00017	.00003	.00080	.00082	.00068	.00043	.00050	.00230	.00028
79	State and local government enterprises	.00002	.00003		.00006	.00040	.00057	.00024	.00026	.00112	.00122	.00043
80	Gross imports of goods and services	.00659	.01594	.24437		.29580	.14007	.00083	.38531	.05336	.12564	
81	Business travel, entertainment and gifts	.00066	.00117	.01002	.00904	.00231	.00453	.00409	.00544	.00533	.00274	.00547
82	Office supplies	.00003	.00003	.00025	.00023	.00023	.00030	.00041	.00041	.00041	.00032	.00026
83	Scrap, used and secondhand goods			.00309		.00037	.00344	.00033		.00233	.00145	.00059
VA.	Value added	.25080	.54388	.34163	.32835	.33257	.41171	.58412	.56475	.55470	.51735	.39516
T	Total	1.00000	1.00000	1.00000	1.00000	1.00000	1.00000	1.00000	1.00000	1.00000	1.00000	1.00000

* Less than 0.000005. NOTE.—Detail may not add due to rounding.

SOURCE: U.S. Department of Commerce, Office of Business Economics.

TABLE 3 Total Requirements (Direct and Indirect) per Dollar of Delivery to Final Demand, 1963 [Producers' Prices]

Each entry represents the output required, directly and indirectly, from the industry named at the beginning of the row for each dollar of delivery to final demand by the industry named at the head of the column.

Industry No.	Industry	Livestock and livestock products (1)	Other agricultural products (2)	Forestry and fishery products (3)	Agricultural, forestry and fishery services (4)	Iron and ferroalloy ores mining (5)	Nonferrous metal ores mining (6)	Coal mining (7)	Crude petroleum and natural gas (8)	Stone and clay mining and quarrying (9)	Chemical and fertilizer mineral mining (10)
1	Livestock and livestock products	1.31963	0.10112	0.11907	0.18536	0.000291	0.00268	0.00239	0.00483	0.00253	0.00193
2	Other agricultural products	.43481	1.07832	.12999	.39019	.00331	.00314	.00285	.00639	.00286	.00222
3	Forestry and fishery products	.00141	.00073	1.02000	.00130	.00048	.00134	.00124	.00038	.00038	.00037
4	Agricultural, forestry and fishery services	.03898	.04347	.05041	1.01832	.00028	.00020	.00027	.00042	.00024	.00019
5	Iron and ferroalloy ores mining	.00074	.00090	.00111	.00153	1.04173	.00375	.00242	.00063	.00233	.00470
6	Nonferrous metal ores mining	.00063	.00091	.00083	.00143	.02314	1.21088	.00113	.00051	.00396	.00151
7	Coal mining	.00182	.00156	.00120	.00187	.00653	.00433	1.18698	.00113	.00630	.00472
8	Crude petroleum and natural gas	.01799	.02576	.01660	.01405	.01089	.01089	.01162	1.03246	.02066	.01430
9	Stone and clay mining and quarrying	.00245	.00460	.00107	.00225	.00447	.00135	.00120	.00142	1.01508	.00900
10	Chemical and fertilizer mineral mining	.00180	.00373	.00081	.00174	.00090	.00701	.00090	.00050	.00202	1.04780
11	New construction	.02803	.02957	.00964	.01835	.01665	.01670	.01643	.05321	.01650	.01616
12	Maintenance and repair construction	.00008	.00007	.00009	.00015	.00012	.00016	.00023	.00011	.00026	.00018
13	Ordnance and accessories	.21689	.02195	.05810	.06081	.00406	.00560	.00466	.00484	.00550	.00442
14	Food and kindred products	.00021	.00020	.00042	.00043	.00019	.00029	.00026	.00027	.00040	.00020
15	Tobacco manufactures										
16	Broad and narrow fabrics, yarn and thread mills	.00313	.00340	.01341	.00975	.00084	.00152	.00139	.00068	.00279	.00149
17	Miscellaneous textile goods and floor coverings	.00290	.00326	.04164	.02729	.00062	.00095	.00119	.00055	.00239	.00056
18	Apparel	.00064	.00047	.00091	.00099	.00035	.00048	.00047	.00034	.00064	.00039
19	Miscellaneous fabricated textile products	.00228	.00227	.00261	.00195	.00019	.00026	.00028	.00015	.00056	.00021
20	Lumber and wood products, except containers	.00485	.00562	.00319	.01094	.00468	.01367	.01318	.00365	.00326	.00304
21	Wooden containers	.00229	.00444	.00106	.01007	.00009	.00016	.00015	.00009	.00016	.00010
22	Household furniture	.00010	.00009	.00021	.00027	.00006	.00010	.00012	.00006	.00009	.00006
23	Other furniture and fixtures	.00006	.00006	.00006	.00012	.00004	.00005	.00005	.00004	.00006	.00005
24	Paper and allied products, except containers	.01327	.00861	.00856	.03399	.00166	.00571	.00540	.00384	.01086	.00812
25	Paperboard containers and boxes	.00776	.00459	.00615	.05617	.00119	.00181	.00183	.00097	.00280	.00152

TABLE 3 Total Requirements (Direct and Indirect) per Dollar of Delivery to Final Demand, 1963 [Producers' Prices] (Continued)

Indus-try No.	Each entry represents the output required, directly and indirectly, from the industry named at the beginning of the row for each dollar of delivery to final demand by the industry named at the head of the column.	Livestock and livestock products 1	Other agricultural products 2	Forestry and fishery products 3	Agricultural, forestry and fishery services 4	Iron and ferroalloy ores mining 5	Nonferrous metal ores mining 6	Coal mining 7	Crude petroleum and natural gas 8	Stone and clay mining and quarrying 9	Chemical and fertilizer mineral mining 10
26	Printing and publishing	.01370	.01342	.00678	.01021	.00976	.00764	.00753	.00646	.00814	.00669
27	Chemicals and selected chemical products	.03981	.07688	.02055	.03908	.02566	.06130	.02855	.01544	.03461	.04297
28	Plastics and synthetic materials	.00390	.00448	.01021	.00877	.00263	.00428	.00494	.00176	.01020	.00281
29	Drugs, cleaning and toilet preparations	.00646	.00227	.00164	.00225	.00000	.00143	.00095	.00078	.00136	.00140
30	Paints and allied products	.00197	.00207	.00412	.00200	.00117	.00147	.00145	.00305	.00154	.00132
31	Petroleum refining and related industries	.03544	.05210	.03428	.02758	.01822	.01563	.01827	.01308	.03688	.01929
32	Rubber and miscellaneous plastics products	.00706	.00757	.00553	.00694	.00797	.01105	.01863	.00343	.04126	.00008
33	Leather tanning and industrial leather products	.00020	.00016	.00012	.00052	.00007	.00010	.00010	.00000	.00010	.00008
34	Footwear and other leather products	.00054	.00020	.00026	.00193	.00009	.00012	.00012	.00010	.00017	.00009
35	Glass and glass products	.00328	.00078	.00195	.00135	.00040	.00053	.00073	.00064	.00076	.00050
36	Stone and clay products	.00270	.00389	.00223	.00309	.00460	.00370	.00375	.00593	.06772	.00302
37	Primary iron and steel manufacturing	.01035	.00951	.01917	.02613	.03139	.04617	.04418	.01031	.04014	.04263
38	Primary nonferrous metal manufacturing	.00471	.00535	.00891	.01509	.00672	.01011	.00983	.00470	.01212	.01258
39	Metal containers	.00620	.00228	.01458	.00271	.00057	.00097	.00065	.00058	.00087	.00076
40	Heating, plumbing and structural metal products	.00122	.00128	.00137	.00154	.00131	.00262	.00165	.00354	.00258	.00216
41	Stampings, screw machine products and bolts	.00299	.00134	.00231	.00294	.00143	.00224	.00285	.00097	.00319	.00201
42	Other fabricated metal products	.00759	.00730	.01625	.08295	.00404	.00779	.01049	.00358	.00817	.00514
43	Engines and turbines	.00072	.00104	.00083	.00070	.00816	.01101	.01956	.00195	.02223	.00945
44	Farm machinery and equipment	.00433	.00978	.00139	.00373	.00075	.00095	.00139	.00027	.00113	.00094
45	Construction, mining and oil field machinery	.00052	.00070	.00039	.00074	.01941	.02570	.04052	.00267	.02671	.02684
46	Materials handling machinery and equipment	.00032	.00037	.00022	.00045	.00065	.00352	.00094	.00042	.00034	.00770
47	Metalworking machinery and equipment	.00068	.00078	.00104	.00187	.00260	.00394	.00559	.00076	.00864	.00252
48	Special industry machinery and equipment	.00083	.00111	.00076	.00130	.00065	.00116	.00090	.00053	.00118	.00094
49	General industrial machinery and equipment	.00118	.00180	.00173	.00186	.00286	.00462	.00627	.00322	.01734	.00080
50	Machine shop products	.00087	.00107	.00082	.00094	.00177	.02967	.00750	.00050	.00666	.00443

No.	Industry										
51	Office, computing and accounting machines	.00058	.00067	.00034	.00062	.00058	.00050	.00057	.00044	.00061	.00046
52	Service industry machines	.00045	.00049	.00035	.00056	.00039	.00046	.00051	.00062	.00072	.00051
53	Electric industrial equipment and apparatus	.00109	.00129	.00212	.00164	.00159	.00296	.00613	.00845	.00701	.01005
54	Household appliances	.00041	.00043	.00058	.00071	.00035	.00048	.00062	.00069	.00072	.00056
55	Electric lighting and wiring equipment	.00062	.00062	.02199	.00057	.00060	.00102	.00568	.00084	.00126	.00209
56	Radio, television and communication equipment	.00052	.00052	.00061	.00070	.00066	.00099	.00106	.00102	.00125	.00084
57	Electronic components and accessories	.00042	.00041	.00072	.00053	.00048	.00079	.00076	.00193	.00089	.00080
58	Miscellaneous electrical machinery, equipment and supplies	.00137	.00168	.00249	.00111	.00097	.00115	.00160	.00053	.00213	.00111
59	Motor vehicles and equipment	.00311	.00302	.00285	.00301	.00504	.00585	.00921	.00204	.01567	.00552
60	Aircraft and parts	.00071	.00051	.00081	.00132	.00134	.00135	.00166	.00058	.00186	.00131
61	Other transportation equipment	.00067	.00062	.01371	.00069	.00126	.00248	.00535	.00051	.00110	.00157
62	Scientific and controlling instruments	.00059	.00049	.00102	.00001	.00077	.00139	.00087	.00103	.00104	.00075
63	Optical, ophthalmic and photographic equipment	.00063	.00061	.00040	.00058	.00048	.00046	.00046	.00040	.00053	.00040
64	Miscellaneous manufacturing	.00159	.00158	.00169	.00208	.00112	.00209	.00124	.00104	.00167	.00102
65	Transportation and warehousing	.05962	.03203	.05176	.04894	.11195	.04261	.03795	.03689	.04034	.07874
66	Communications; except radio and T.V. broadcasting	.00910	.00793	.00390	.00621	.00504	.00544	.00531	.00384	.00479	.00801
67	Radio and T.V. broadcasting	.00271	.00316	.00117	.00199	.00234	.00163	.00165	.00139	.00176	.00143
68	Electric, gas, water and sanitary services	.02165	.02173	.01031	.01695	.03317	.05121	.04521	.02054	.05182	.07696
69	Wholesale and retail trade	.08091	.05503	.05991	.06494	.03059	.03814	.04167	.02735	.04712	.03670
70	Finance and insurance	.02567	.02563	.01168	.02038	.01610	.03172	.02278	.02097	.02611	.01822
71	Real estate and rental	.06725	.10152	.02556	.07187	.09030	.04684	.04565	.20300	.03873	.03058
72	Hotels; personal and repair services except auto	.00236	.00182	.00263	.00305	.00157	.00194	.00181	.00200	.00212	.00146
73	Business services	.04330	.05064	.01877	.03180	.03737	.02606	.02645	.02192	.02814	.02286
75	Automobile repair and services	.00951	.00885	.00715	.00582	.00375	.00382	.00539	.00543	.01180	.00396
76	Amusements	.00145	.00164	.00094	.00136	.00128	.00101	.00100	.00117	.00107	.00083
77	Medical, educational services and nonprofit organizations[1]	.01012	.00200	.00147	.00231	.00129	.00168	.00164	.00118	.00106	.00344
78	Federal government enterprises	.00384	.00358	.00224	.00323	.00375	.00417	.00367	.00303	.00376	.00567
79	State and local government enterprises	.00555	.00497	.00348	.00455	.00859	.00917	.00785	.00571	.00977	.01383
80	Gross imports of goods and services	.03454	.03137	.27063	.02899	.32309	.18303	.01286	.09393	.06975	.14571
81	Business travel, entertainment and gifts	.00727	.00058	.01470	.01505	.00633	.00998	.00905	.00868	.01066	.00695
82	Office supplies	.00134	.00113	.00163	.00136	.00114	.00151	.00145	.00123	.00157	.00129

* Less than 0.000005.

1 To remove a source of instability in the measurement of total requirements per dollar delivery to final demand, the Commodity Credit Corporation has been excluded from this industry. The excluded inputs to the CCC from the specified industries are: Industry 2, $636 million; Industry 14, $214 million; Industry 16, $15 million; Industry 65, $642 million; Industry 69, $24 million; and value added,—$1,531 million.

from each industry to each user. Reading across the rows shows the markets in which the output of the industry named at the left is sold. Reading down the column reveals the inputs purchased by the industries listed at the top (exclusive of capital expenditures). Only the first 13 columns are shown because of space limitations; readers are referred to source documents for complete tables.

The A matrix or input coefficient structure is shown in Table 2, Direct Requirements per Dollar of Gross Output, 1963. The columns of this table indicate the cents' worth of input per dollar of its output required by each industry from each supplier shown in the rows. These entries show the percentage distribution of production costs per dollar of output; together with value added (which includes wages, rents, interest, profit before taxes, and depreciation), these outlays account for 100 percent of revenue. Sellers can easily see the relative importance of their output to each industry in the economy by reading across the appropriate row.

The total requirements (direct and indirect) are shown in Table 3; this is the inverse table, the equivalent of the expression $(I - A)^{-1}$. It is used for impact analysis; the figures in a column indicate the output required, both directly or indirectly, from the industries shown at the left for each dollar of output sold to final demand by an industry designated at the head of the column. Reading across a row indicates how much output is required of the industry named at the left per dollar of output sold to final demand by the industries designated at the top of the table, taking into account all supporting transactions.[3]

Similar tables have been constructed for 1958 and 1947 for the United States, and it is expected that tables will be prepared in the future at five-year intervals. Input-output tables are available for a number of areas within the United States and in many other countries as well [2, 18].

INDUSTRIAL MULTIPLIERS AND KEYNESIAN INCOME MULTIPLIERS

The Leontief input-output model bears a formal resemblance to the Keynesian model of income determination. While both models are capable of expansion to introduce additional variables, their basic properties bear striking similarity. Expressing the Keynesian model in its usual simplified form, letting Z represent government plus investment expenditures, and using S to represent a vector of internal transactions in the Leontief model, we obtain:

	Leontief input-output	*Keynesian national income*
Definitional equation	$X = S + Y$	$Y = C + Z$
Behavioral relation	$S = AX$	$C = MPC\,(Y)$
Reduced form	$X = (I - A)^{-1}Y$	$Y = (1 - MPC)^{-1}Z$

The Keynesian model is directed toward the determination of the level of aggregate final demand, given autonomous investment and government ex-

---

[3] The diagonal elements are greater than one for two reasons: (1) Specialization within an industry grouping leads to transactions among establishments within the same categories. (2) Some output of a given industry is needed by its suppliers to provide inputs to that industry. For example, the livestock industry must produce $1.32 of output in order to deliver $1 to final demands because (1) it takes calves to produce cows, and cows to produce calves; (2) it takes food to produce livestock, but it also takes livestock to produce food. These feedbacks mean the livestock industry must supply its suppliers if it is to provide output to final demand.

penditures; the Leontief model translates the implications of a given level of final demand for industrial production. The behavioral relationships of Keynesian economics turn mainly on a fixed psychological relationship between consumption and income. In the Leontief model, the posited behavior is a fixed technical relationship between intermediate inputs and industrial output. The multiplier relationship of the Keynesian model runs in terms of the multiple increase in final demand (via consumption) associated with autonomous income; the multiplier relationship of the Leontief model is the multiple increase in industrial output (via intermediate input) generated by any sale to final demand.

Since a Keynesian income-expenditure model provides a technique for determining the level of final demand while the Leontief input-output model provides a way of determining the implications of that level of final demand upon industrial output, the complementary features of the two models should be apparent.

There are, of course, differences between the two models. The usual version of the Keynesian model is highly aggregative, while an input-output model is disaggregated by industry. The units of measurement in the Keynesian system are stated in terms of net expenditure (GNP), while those of the input-output system measure gross shipments (sales). By means of an input-output system, the Y values of the Keynesian system, which represent net final demand, can be translated into gross industrial shipments. Because of the industrially disaggregated character of the input-output model, it employs a system of equations usually expressed by matrix algebra; the Keynesian model can usually be expressed in a few equations. In order to restate a final demand obtained from a GNP forecast in terms capable of being used in an input-output model, aggregate demand must be divided according to delivering industry. That is, GNP projections must be converted into a vector showing the distribution of total expenditures according to producing industries (the equivalents of Y_1, Y_2, ..., Y_n).

The relationships between the national income determination model and the input-output model may be sketched graphically:

$$X = AX + Y \qquad\qquad Y = MPC \cdot Y + Z$$

The arrows indicate the direction of the spending flows, with the loop between X and AX and between Y and $MPC \cdot Y$ representing the feedbacks associated with the input-output inverse and the investment-income multiplier respectively.

USE OF INPUT-OUTPUT IN IMPACT ANALYSIS

One of the basic uses of input-output, certainly to this time the most frequent application, has been to make appraisals of the industrial impact of changes in final demands. The simplest impact analysis can be made directly by reading the computed inverse—the $(I - A)^{-1}$ matrix—since each column of this matrix describes the direct and indirect output changes required of each of the industries in the economy per unit change in final demand for the output of any given industry. From the OBE 1963 tables we find that the automobile industry purchases about \$250 of paper to produce \$1 million of motor vehicles; but the paper industry will be called upon to produce \$10,440 of output per million dollars' worth of motor vehicles in order to supply auto manufacturers, other producers who supply the automobile manufacturers, or those who supply their suppliers, and so on. Furthermore, one also can ascertain from the inverse table that, per dollar, it takes less paper to produce airplanes and more to support the production of food. Paper manufacturing firms can size up the implications of shifting demands in seemingly distant and unrelated markets to determine what it means in terms of how much paper will be needed in total and by using industry. Each industry can learn a great deal about its markets by a careful scrutiny of the tables.

More elaborate computations, requiring the use of a computer, make it possible to assess the impact of changing technology in one industry upon the demand for output of others. A paper container manufacturer, for example, may be interested in estimating how deeply a trend toward utilizing metal containers (by food processors, tobacco manufacturers, or other industries) will cut into demand for paper containers. The A matrix may be altered to reflect an unexpected substitution in which inputs of one kind are being displaced by another and an alternative inverse matrix computed. These inverses are then compared to contrast the total requirements for paper containers under one technology with those under an alternate.

The Economic Impact of Disarmament

An interesting and illuminating application of input-output to forecasting the industrial consequences of a transfer of national expenditures from military to civilian purchases has been made by Leontief and Hoffenberg [10]. They ask: If the level of government defense expenditure were reduced, and some other category of final demand increased by the same amount, what would happen to the output and employment in different industries? Since the shopping list of the Defense Department is quite different from that of the housewife, conversion from serving military to civilian markets creates substantial shifts in the levels of output required of different industries.

In order to evaluate both the direct and indirect industrial consequences of alternative spending packages (Y vectors), each bill of final demand—military, investment, consumption, exports—is expressed in amounts directly spent for particular goods per $100 million of each alternative. Each bill of final demand is then multiplied by the inverse matrix to obtain estimates of the dollar flows required directly or indirectly by each industry in order to produce each final demand alternative. The differences between the inverse weighted by a $100 million military package and the inverse weighted by each alternative civilian-type use of $100 million show the net industrial effect of a change in that amount of spending from military to each set of civilian demands.[4]

The net effects per $100 million of expenditure are emphasized because virtually every industry, directly or indirectly, is affected by a shift in final demands—but each package of final demands affects them in different degrees. A table of differences indicates that a cutback of military spending reduces the demand for the products of some industries by a smaller amount than the induced rise in demand for their products caused by an offsetting expenditure for nonmilitary purposes raises it. In the case of apparel and textile mill products, for instance, a shift of $100 million of military spending to nonmilitary government spending or to residential construction would lead to a net decrease in demand for that industry's output. A shift to investment would have negligible effects. A shift to either personal consumption expenditure or exports would increase demand for apparel and textile mill products by much more than the decreases in demand associated with the reduction in military spend-

---

[4] That is $(I - A)^{-1}Y' - (I - A)^{-1}Y'' = X' - X''$, where Y' is the military spending vector and Y'' is an alternative. Then X' and X'' are the output vectors under each condition.

ing. The net changes in output and employment in apparel and textiles as spending shifts from military to some other forms of final demand are illustrated in Table 4.

TABLE 4   Net Change of Output and Employment in Apparel and Textile Mill Products Industry by a Shift in Final Demand from a $100 Million Military Procurement Package to an Alternative

Alternative demands which could be served	Net change in output (thousands of dollars)	Net change in employment (man-years)
Government, nonmilitary.....................	−300	−20
Residential construction.....................	−100	−14
Personal consumption.......................	7,700	572
Business investment........................	nil	−6
Exports (except military)...................	7,400	416
Exports to India (nonfood).................	8,500	473

SOURCE: *Scientific American*, April 1961, p. 52.

The implications of disarmament for industrial output can be readily seen from this type of analysis. It is important to understand that these predictions take account of the indirect as well as the direct industrial requirements needed to produce each bill of final demand. Simply looking at the direct military and alternative demands will not provide a measure of impact on an industry since the largest buyers served by industry are often other industries. Even though final demands constitute the raison d'être of production, the means for their fulfillment are indirect.

INPUT-OUTPUT PROJECTIONS

Perspectives on the growth and composition of the American economy in future years are essential in evaluating prospective market trends. But broad aggregates, such as forecasts of GNP, employment, and population, conceal the crosscurrents of change which underlie the process of growth. Furthermore, for marketing and various other planning purposes we would like to know not only how much the nation will produce but also the kinds of goods which will be consumed; not only how many people will be employed but also what type of work they will be doing. Now, it should be apparent that there is a connection between the distribution of consumers' expenditures and the rates of production and employment in industries. As noted earlier, input-output is a device for translating final demands into their consequences for industrial output. Thus input-output constitutes a bridge between the rather aggregative GNP-type forecasting framework usually employed in making projections of output and the disaggregation needed in order to trace its implications to detailed activities. Two comprehensive studies of industrial growth are taken as illustrative of the application of input-output in forecasting.

The Interagency Growth Study

Projections 1970 was a study prepared by the U.S. Bureau of Labor Statistics of the potential demand, interindustry relationships, and employment in the United States under alternative growth rate assumptions [16]. In basic outline, projections were initially made of the growth of the labor force, hours of work, and productivity to 1970. Given alternative assumptions concerning unemployment rates, these elements determine the GNP or potential output. The mix of final demand for this potential output is then estimated for each of the major demand components of GNP; this involves extensive analysis of consumer, investor, and government spending. The composition of spending, broken down into expenditures on the products of 86 supplying industries, is then projected on the basis of past trends and other factors. These studies provide a basic projection of final demand as a vector for forecasting industry activity.

The projected total final demand vector, Y, is then multiplied by a projected inverse matrix $(I - A)^{-1}$ for 1970 to obtain X, projected levels of industry activity. Because of the emphasis of the study upon manpower, the inverse in this projection model is expressed in labor equivalents required by each industry from other industries per billion dollars of final demand. Thus the forecast variable in the model $X = (I - A)^{-1}Y$ is the level of employment in each industry required to produce the level and composition of projected 1970 final demand. As the reader may surmise, supporting studies were required to take into account changes in techniques of production, productivity changes, and other factors influencing the direct employment requirements by each industry.

It is not appropriate here to discuss the substantive results of *Projections 1970*, but its implications for market forecasting are important. Of major significance is the linking of projections of industrial activity to final sales so that intermediate transactions are determined. While *Projections 1970* is primarily oriented toward an analysis of the industrial distribution of employment, it is rather easy to adjust it to a dollar flows basis which shows how much industries would sell to or buy from each other. From these projections the relative growth of each market served by each industry can be calculated. Further, it should be noted that the projections of spending by consumers, investors, government, and each industrial sector are specified in unusual detail. This feature will be especially helpful to market forecasters who have found the familiar GNP expenditures categories far too broad for most commercial purposes. Of course, neither emphasis on causal interdependencies nor disaggregation by themselves guarantee a projection; but the framework within which these have been made provides a significant advance in forecasting technique.

The Almon Model

Professor Clopper Almon, Jr., at the Maryland Research Center, has been making projections of American economic growth by means of an input-output model. His projections for 1975 have been published, and they have been extended annually through 1980. The Almon models have somewhat more dynamic properties than the Interagency Growth Model discussed earlier, and, because consumer and investment spending as well as interindustry activities are mutually interdependent, the system is essentially an integration of a dynamic Keynesian demand model and the Leontief input-output model. In Professor Almon's words [1]:

… the keynote of the system is that it builds checks and balances into the forecasts, assuring a fivefold *consistency* between:
1. The sales projected for an industry and the purchases of its products by all its customers;
2. The output of an industry and the materials it purchases and the labor it employs;
3. The growth of each industry's sales and its capital investment;

4. Consumers' after-tax income and their spending on the products of each industry;

5. Total employment and the expected future labor force.

The Almon model is discussed by reference to the schematic diagram shown in Figure 1, which is not an exact representation of his system but conveys its broad features. Government spending, exports, and those components of consumption and investment functions which are related neither to income nor output are exogenous; these are independently forecast either by assumption or from past trends. This demand (G, E, Z) vector gives rise to direct demand for industry output, $X_1, \ldots, X_n$. To produce these outputs, industries purchase from suppliers in successive rounds (in amounts as shown by the inverse).

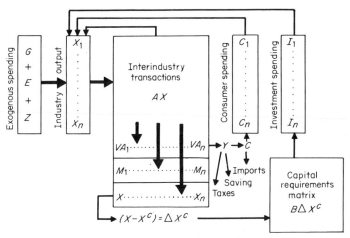

Fig. 1. Diagrammatic representation of interindustry model. This is a partially closed, dynamic interindustry model. Exogenous expenditures create a demand for industry output, generating interindustry transactions and value added (GNP); incomes affect the level of consumer spending, creating further demand for industry output. If output levels of industry exceed X^c, capacity output, then ΔX^c, desired increments in capacity, create investment demand by amounts and kinds indicated by the capital requirements matrix.

Industrial output gives rise not only to interindustry transactions but also to payments to factors of production or value added (VA_i). Leakages in the form of imports (M_i), taxes, and savings take place, but the income generated affects spending by consumers. Their response to income changes depends upon disaggregated marginal propensities to consume outputs produced in different industries so that consumer demands for industrial output rise but not strictly proportional to the income of consumers. Consumer spending leads to a higher level of interindustry transactions, income, and consumption in a familiar output-multiplier and income-multiplier fashion.

At the same time, another feedback relationship is also at work. Changes in the level of industry demand may require increases in productive capacity if demand presses on capacity. Thus, either simultaneously or with some lag, each industry responds to increased demand for its output by requiring more capital inputs as well as current inputs. The amount of capital additions required depends upon capital requirements per unit of capacity change. These are described by a matrix of capital coefficients which shows the amount of investment goods required by each industry from each producer of capital for each unit of change in its capacity. In this way, changes in industrial output generate additional demands for output from industry in the form of capital goods. This is depicted by the arrow from the investment vector to the output vector. This, of course, now has further effects on both consumption and investment. Hence, the consumption sector and the investment sector are internally dependent upon income and output, as in the Hicksian-type multiplier-accelerator model.

What limits the system so that a forecast for a particular year is unique? The ceiling which fixes the level of industrial output, personal income, consumption, and investment expenditure is the available labor force. By tying labor requirement coefficients (adjusted for productivity change) to output, the full-employment income level is fixed by fiscal policy (government spending, tax rates).

The especially interesting features of this model for forecasting are (1) the linking of a dynamic income-expenditure model to an input-output system so that industry-level activity results from the analysis; (2) the disaggregation of industrial and final demands which permits introduction into the analysis of large amounts of detailed factual information as well as particularized behavioral relationships; and (3) the opportunity the model gives for incorporating new information or positing varying situations whose implications may be explored.

Among its drawbacks—aside from quantitative problems related to data accuracy—are problems of incomplete or incorrect specifications of behavioral relationships and the large number of side forecasts which are necessary inputs into the system. For short-term projections, the coefficient structure should be time-phased to reflect the lags which are necessarily entailed in the linkages. Adjustments for price changes are exogenously determined where considered at all. It must be recognized that a good deal of judgment and side calculations are required to make the models operational. Indeed, input-output models demand that their users bring to them both much data analysis and many causal linkages, and they therefore serve to remind us of our limited knowledge while organizing that which we possess. Certainly the Almon model is a daring attempt to construct a quantified and detailed model of the inner workings of the economy which provides a more coherent picture of the whole economy than we have ever had before.

Applications of Input-Output at the Firm Level

From a practical viewpoint, input-output forecasts provide individual industries with estimates of their probable future growth, of the industrial markets which account for that growth, and of the inputs each industry will require from others if that growth is to be achieved. While it is traditional for a company's projections to be prepared in the light of its own industry's probable growth, many business firms are not a part of a single industry but produce products classified in several industrial categories. Moreover, because of market specialization, a given firm may selectively service certain types of users or users in certain regions. It then becomes necessary for such companies to split input-output industries into subcategories that engage their special interests.

The absence of highly detailed industrial sectors has been one of the recurring criticisms of input-output by company economists. In part, this criticism has been met by the detailed 1963 input-output study prepared by the Office of Business Economics. For even greater detail, it is possible to relate the industrial sectors of input-output to product components by using commodity information available in census reports.[5]

Another way of adapting input-output tables to the needs of a particular firm has been suggested by Tiebout. In essence, he says that a firm can better use interindustry tables by inserting itself as a separate row in the available tables. The marketing department of a firm can estimate its own sales to the sectors specified in the input-output study, and from this it can calculate how much each industry requires from it per dollar of output. Other row coefficients are appropriately adjusted to accommodate the company row. The firm may also insert itself as an additional column in the coefficient matrix simply by entering its own cost experience. A new inverse is then computed as a basis for individual company input-output forecasting.

If an added conditional assumption is made in the enlarged inverse to the effect that the individual firm will hold a stipulated relative share as a supplier in each of the markets in which it sells, the company can estimate how much it should produce as changes take place in final demand and how each market it serves will change [18].[6] Simulations may be run which assume different degrees of market penetration or combinations of market shares that are needed to assure a specified growth in total sales.

A rather novel use of input-output has been developed by a company particularly concerned about the ability of its suppliers to meet delivery schedules. Initially the analysis was made by finding out the union contract expiration dates of its direct suppliers. Then, in order to catch strike threats in earlier stages of the production chain, the inverse table was used to determine important backup industries, and collective bargaining difficulties were appraised at still earlier stages. In this way, the firm was forewarned not only of work stoppages which might directly affect its own suppliers but stoppages in earlier stages which might indirectly affect its suppliers' ability to meet commitments.

It has been suggested that input-output be applied to internal operations of companies that have a number of interrelated divisions. Hubbell and Ekey have designed a variant of the Leontief model in which intracompany transactions are projected by substituting "departments" for the usual industrial sectors [9]. Several companies are experimenting with this type of model for use in facilities planning, budgeting, and in manpower planning.

Concluding Comment

Input-output focuses upon the interdependence of industrial activity. Its most promising feature is as a technique for analyzing the productive process as a complete economic system. Since many variables not specified directly in the model are functionally related to industrial activity, its value is enhanced by its capacity to be related to a number of decision problems. It can, with assumptions far less heroic than those of some time-worn methods, be useful as a part of the forecaster's tool kit. But it is not a forecaster's panacea. Input-output rests on simplified assumptions concerning economic behavior. This means its utility in any particular application must be evaluated in the light of the compromises with reality which make the system quantitatively workable.

[5] As an illustration see the discussion in *Sales Management,* November 5, 1965.

[6] Tiebout suggests only a desk calculator is necessary provided an original inverse is available, but full advantage of "inserting yourself" into the matrix is gained by rather conventional input-output computer programs.

REFERENCES

1. Almon, C., Jr., *The American Economy to 1975—An Interindustry Forecast,* New York: Harper, 1966.
2. Bourque, P. J., and M. Cox, *An Inventory of Regional Input-Output Studies in the United States,* Seattle: University of Washington Graduate School of Business Administration, 1970.
3. Carter, A., "Changes in the Structure of the American Economy, 1947 to 1958 and 1962," *The Review of Economics and Statistics,* vol. 49, May 1967.
4. Chenery, H. B., and P. G. Clark, *Interindustry Economics,* New York: Wiley, 1962.
5. Evans, W. D., and M. Hoffenberg, "The Interindustry Relations Study for 1957," *The Review of Economics and Statistics,* vol. 54, May 1952.
6. ———, and M. Hoffenberg, "The Nature and Uses of Interindustry Data and Methods," *Input-Output: An Appraisal, Studies in Income and Wealth,* vol. 18, Princeton University Press, 1955.
7. Goldman, M. R., M. L. Marimont, and B. H. Vaccara, "The Interindustry Structure of the United States," *Survey of Current Business,* vol. 44, November 1964.
8. ———, M. L. Marimont, and B. H. Vaccara, "The Transactions Table of the 1958 Input-Output Study and Revised Direct and Total Requirements Data," *Survey of Current Business,* vol. 45, September 1965.
9. Hubbell, J. P., and Ekey, D. C., "The Application of Input-Output Theory to Industrial Planning and Forecasting," *The Journal of Industrial Engineering,* vol. 14, January–February 1963.
10. Leontief, W. W., and M. Hoffenberg, "The Economics of Disarmament," *Scientific American,* vol. 204, April 1961.
11. ———, *The Structure of the American Economy 1919–1939,* New York: Oxford University Press, 1951.
12. ———, and others, *Studies in the Structure of the American Economy,* New York: Oxford University Press, 1953.
13. ———, "The Structure of the U.S. Economy: 1963," *Survey of Current Business,* vol. 49, November 1969.
14. National Economics Division, "Input-Output Structure of the U.S. Economy: 1963," *Survey of Current Business,* vol. 49, November 1969.
15. Office of Business Economics, "Input-Output Structure of the U.S. Economy: 1963," vols. 1–3, a supplement to the *Survey of Current Business,* 1969.
16. *Projections 1970—Interindustry Relationships—Potential Demand-Employment,* U.S. Department of Labor, Bureau of Labor Statistics, Bulletin no. 1536, 1966.
17. Taskier, C. E., *Input-Output Bibliography,* United Nations Statistical Papers, series M, no. 39, 1964, 1967.
18. Tiebout, C. M., "Input-Output and the Firm: A Technique for Using National and Regional Tables," *The Review of Economics and Statistics,* vol. 44, May 1967.
19. Vaccara, B. H., "Changes Over Time in Input-Output Coefficients for the United States," in *Applications of Input-Output Analysis,* vol. 2, North Holland Publishing Co., 1970.

Industrial Marketing

Chapter 4

Distribution Channels

LOUIS P. BUCKLIN *Institute of Business and Economic Research, University of California, Berkeley, California*

INTRODUCTION

A channel of distribution comprises the set of firms through which a product flows in the process of moving from the point of production to the point of consumption. In the marketing of industrial goods, consumption occurs after the product is sold either to a manufacturer (where it is used or incorporated as a component of some more complex item) or to an institution—for example, a hospital, university, or government agency (where it is employed in the production of the services). The industrial goods channel, in other words, is the mechanism which links the specialized units of production in an economy. As specialization is a necessary requirement for material progress in a society, the cost and efficiency of industrial channels are critical to the translation of the benefits inherent in this process to the improvement of living standards.

In a highly developed society, the constituents of any finished good typically move through a number of industrial channels, each linked sequentially to the other. In such *vertical marketing systems,* the constituent materials may be sold many times. In a painstaking study of the flow of building material products to the point of use in home construction, the wood in certain types of millwork was found to have passed through 20 transactions with up to 33 different business agencies participating in some way. Contrarily, some basic commodities, such as sand and quarried stone, were subjected to but one transaction and moved through only two agencies [9]. The distinction reflects the adaptation of channel organizations to different requirements for both processing and distribution, adaptations necessitated by the pressures of competition to attain the most efficient route.

Within a competitive economy, then, the channel sequence is one derived neither randomly nor from the pleasures of man's mind. Rather, it emerges from the basic economic conditions and organizational capabilities that dictate the minimal-cost route, given the services desired by the industrial buyers and the prices they are willing to pay for such services. The role of marketing research is to ascertain the nature of these services and the costs of employing alternative types of channels to provide them.

To the marketing executive, the purposes behind this research are threefold. The most basic concern is to choose, from the many routes to the industrial buyer, that particular one (or group) that the firm's product line is to follow. Because channel choices typically involve the use of specialized resources and the long-term investment in trade relationships, incorrect decisions on the best route are not easily reversible. Capital investment in channels is often of a "sunk" nature and not easily convertible from one system to another. Insofar as changes in market conditions can turn the appropriate decision of yesteryear into a nightmare of red ink in the future, decisions to continue or buttress the firm's position in a channel must be based upon forecasts of a long-range nature. The task of research is to clarify and continuously update the wisdom of specific channel choices.

On the second level, channel decisions involve the allocation of resources. Channel activities are usually the joint undertaking of a number of firms. Allocation is determining the kinds of activities to be performed and the particular firm that is to be responsible. These decisions both complement and, to a great extent, overlap the firm's own marketing-mix decisions. Insofar as historic patterns for the type and division of responsibility for different activities may or may not be optimal, regular review, in which marketing research should play a vital role, is required.

At the third and last level, the marketing executive has concern for the operating efficiency of each of the activities performed in the system, whether undertaken under his direct responsibility or under the supervision of associated firms. Weakness in performance may be due to the internal failure of management of any firm in the channel to control these functions. It may also be due to the ineffectual coordination of channel work among the several firms involved. The measurement and evaluation of performance of these activities through marketing research are the third role that this function should play.

However, analysis and research for each of these three roles must proceed from a conceptual framework explaining how these systems are structured and the rationale for different patterns of organization. To provide background, we will, in this chapter, first present a qualitative model of channel organization. This will provide the perspective for the consideration of a simple quantitative decision model reflecting the industrial goods manufacturer's problems of channel choice and management.

CHANNEL MODELS, QUALITATIVE AND QUANTITATIVE

The system of distribution employed for any product may be considered in terms of two dimensions, vertical and horizontal.

The Vertical Dimension

The vertical dimension of a distributive system is defined by the route that title to product takes in its movement from production to the industrial buyer. Each such route is a distinct channel and is measured by the number of firms (or alternatively, establishments) which sequentially act to negotiate the sale or purchase of the product. Routes with similar unit strings belong to the same channel type.

As shown in Figure 1, several different types of channels are to be found in industrial marketing. A two-level type includes only the producer and the industrial buyer. The three-level type might encompass, additionally, an industrial distributor. The four-level type could include both the industrial distributor and a manufacturer's representative. Channels with additional levels are to be found in the industrial market, but not with great frequency.

For any given product, distribution is likely to be accomplished through a system containing channels that vary in length (number of levels). While the predominant type may consist of but two levels, this seldom precludes the existence of longer forms. Moreover, over time, change may be in either direc-

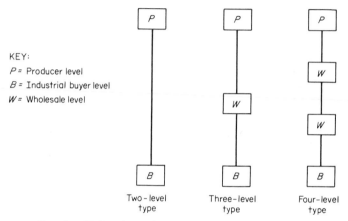

KEY:
P = Producer level
B = Industrial buyer level
W = Wholesale level

Two - level type   Three - level type   Four - level type

Fig. 1. Major channel types in industrial marketing.

tion. While it is commonly thought that channels have tended to shorten in industrialized economies, one study has shown that the number of levels of industrial channels has increased in the United States in the post-World War II period. This result occurred because of changes in the composition of industrial products and the markets to which they are sold [5]. Another study of industrial channels for equipment, machinery, and supplies found that all but 22.3 percent of these products traveled through routes in which some kind of independent middleman was employed [11].

The Horizontal Dimension

The horizontal dimension of a distributive system lies across that of the vertical. It is measured by the number and kinds of firms operating upon each of the levels in a given channel type. For example, a three-level channel type for some industrial good might encompass several hundred industrial middlemen. As just noted, these middlemen might be merchant wholesalers or they could include agent wholesalers as well. The distinction lies in the holding of ownership to goods, a function which the merchant performs but the agent does not.

If the levels in the channel were being enumerated on an establishment basis, we might also find manufacturer sales branches or offices in the three-level type channel. Such establishments may operate in lieu of independent middlemen and are typically included in the study of distributive system structure.

These three basic categories—merchant, agent, and manufacturer branch— also serve to classify intermediaries operating on the interior levels of channels of all lengths. Additional subcategories within each of the three basic groups are defined upon the basis of other functions performed, such as inventory, the specific product line carried, or the breadth of the product line carried [21]. These distinctions affect the operating costs and the kind of marketing services they can provide. They represent a second means (in addition to adjustments in the number of levels) whereby channels adapt to specific product attributes and environmental conditions. They also provide a basis for distinguishing among channels of the same type (length).

Rationale for Channels with Different Dimensions

The factors which influence the organization of the two dimensions of the channel are related to the savings that can be secured from the large-scale movement and storage of product *and* the degree of disorganization occurring in messages as they pass from level to level. These factors relate, in turn, to the physical characteristics of the product and its technological complexity, the state of the art in logistics and communication, and the heterogeneity in firm size and product line at the producing and using levels.

As to the movement of goods, where both producer and user are capable of dealing in large lot sizes, the per unit cost of marketing goods in a two-level channel will usually be relatively low. Under the opposite set of conditions, two-level channels will usually generate high physical distribution costs. Additional levels are required to concentrate the flows from a variety of producers into assortments of sufficient size to qualify for the transport savings inherent in moving goods in volume. While this concentration, and the subsequent dispersion, of products necessitates additional handling activities in the sequence (as opposed to what is found in direct channels), the costs incurred are offset by savings in transport, particularly where the distances are long or where customers are calling for fast delivery.

In the transmission of messages about products, two subfactors are working. There is a savings in the cost per message unit where additional channel levels concentrate and disperse goods, as each message can encompass more product units. On the other hand, these additional links will also tend to distort messages that must pass from the producer to the industrial buyer and vice versa. Hence longer channels will be found to be suitable for products which require simple messages. More complex products will find shorter channels more suitable.

This tendency for the quality of information to deteriorate in channels is also a function of the type of concentration and dispersion process employed by the middleman. In particular, as the number of competing and different types of products handled by a middleman grows, the clarity of the channel communication link between the producer and user diminishes. The consequence is that where products are complex, middleman agencies will tend to be more specialized by product line.

Heterogeneity along the horizontal dimension of the distributive system reflects parallel heterogeneity among firms at the producing and using levels. Variations in producer and user-firm size, assortments of products used, and distances from each other spawn middlemen types adapted to particular circumstance. The degree of buying expertise on the part of the user, as reflected in his need for information, creates another basis for variation among middlemen types.

1.   The smaller the scale in which goods are produced and/or bought, the greater is the number of levels in the channel.

2.   The greater the distance between the producers and users, the greater is the number of levels in the channel.

3.   The greater the technicality of information, quantity necessary, and need for producer-user feedback, the fewer are the levels of the channel and the more specialized the middlemen.

4.   Heterogeneity in the producing and using levels is reflected in the diversity of middlemen and the variance in channel lengths within the system.

The Decision Model

These generalizations serve as the basis for defining the nature of the research problem facing the firm seeking to ascertain the type of channel that it should employ and how the set of channels should be managed.   This problem may be divided into the following parts:

1.   Defining the nature of the cost functions for alternative channel types

2.   Defining the nature of the revenue opportunities for alternative channel types

    a.   From the perspective of the number of customers reached by each

    b.   From the perspective of the extent of information impairment incurred by each

3.   Defining the nature of the factors that control the costs of product and information flows within a chosen channel so that these may be managed with optimal efficiency

These issues may be expressed in the framework of a simple optimization model.   The revenues to be derived from the use of the ith channel, R_i, are a function of the degree of marketing effort the firm puts into that channel:

$$R_i = f(a_{ij}I_{ij}) \qquad j = 1, \ldots, w \tag{1}$$

where the I_{ij} represent the w different types of marketing inputs that the firm can put into the channel and a_{ij} the revenue generated per unit of input.   The latter includes personal selling, sales promotion, sales service, and discounts offered.

The costs of the same channel, C_i, are a function of the same set of inputs:

$$C_i = g(b_{ij}I_{ij}) \qquad j = 1, \ldots, w \tag{2}$$

where the b_{ij} represent the unit costs of each type of input.

The intent of the firm is to maximize its profits by allocating its w types of resources to the n channel type alternatives that it perceives to be available to it.   Specifically, this involves:

$$\max \pi = \sum_{i=1}^{n} \left(R_i - C_i \right) \tag{3}$$

The research task is to identify these costs and revenues to enable the firm to select the particular channel types or combination of channels that will permit achievement of its objectives.

RESEARCH PROGRAMS

In the initial stages of a study program on channels, exploratory research may usefully be conducted to define the n channel alternatives that the firm should consider.   This would include both the investigation of existing sequences as well as those that might be developed *de novo*. In some instances, where alternatives are limited and the differences among them rather substantial, exploratory research may be sufficient to resolve the issue of the type of channel that the firm should join.

Goals of the exploratory research should include the following:

1. Estimates of the product volume moving through each channel type and the composition of that volume

2. The market segments, if any, served by each channel type

3. Changes in product volume occurring over time in each channel type

4. The extent to which entry into any channel type is blocked by prior commitments between manufacturers and middlemen

5. Typical middleman margins and/or commissions

6. The competitive advantage of each channel type for each market segment

7. The relative importance of product-oriented factors (for example, special features or quality) versus middlemen-oriented factors (for example, rapid delivery, ease of purchasing) as an element in industrial buyer behavior

8. The stability of prices over time within and between channel types

9. The bargaining power of middlemen in each channel type

10. The locus of channel control—the point in the sequence from which directions (if any) emanate to coordinate activities of the channel as a whole—for each type.

Sufficient information on most if not all of these issues may be obtained through secondary sources and personal interviews with small samples of middlemen and industrial purchasing agents.

Secondary sources of major importance are trade journals and publications by industry trade associations. Such organizations frequently take polls to determine the number of firms at the various levels in the channel system, the volume of product they sell, and their typical costs and profits. The *U.S. Census of Business*, taken every four or five years by the Bureau of the Census, provides additional information of value on these topics.

Speculation as to the kinds of feasible channel types not yet to be found in the distributive system may proceed from a functional approach to channel organization. Fundamentally, each institution or establishment in a channel represents a point from which a cluster of activities (that is, storage, transportation, ownership, and negotiation) are managed. Conceiving of the channel as a sequence of these activities or functional acts, we may define the cost of operating each (and the factors upon which this depends) and experiment with rearranging these acts in different patterns. Experimentation of this order, which could be programmed into a computer, may result in the definition of channel types which offer the prospect of either dramatically lower costs or improved customer service [15].

Research on Distribution Channel Costs

Once the range of channel alternatives to be considered is completed from the exploratory studies, more formal plans to evaluate the profitability potential for each commence. Procedures depend upon the extent to which the firm possesses data from historic dealings with the different channels upon which the analyst may draw.

The availability of internal data permits the use of distribution cost accounting methodology to provide the necessary cost inputs to the study [17]. Distribution cost accounting is a technique which allocates the firm's expenses to those centers of its marketing activities which control or influence these charges. This is opposed to older methodologies which typically recorded firm expenses in so-called "natural" accounts—that is, rent, utilities, salaries, taxes, and so on.

As applied to channels, distribution cost procedures allocate all expenses incurred directly in the operation of each type of system that the firm employs to that type. Such costs might include all salesman expense, service charges, warehouse or branch office, and transportation. Costs not specifically attributable to any channel may be indirectly allocated in two ways. Expenses which are directly incurred in behalf of different products, such as central warehousing, advertising, brand management, and so on, may be allocated to separate accounts. Charges in each may then be reallocated by channel according to the proportion of each product sold.

Expenditures which cannot be handled in this manner are initially placed in "functional" accounts. These accounts are associated with the performance of a specific activity or work center, such as order processing. Into such an account would be placed the salaries of the clerical and managerial employees, the equipment used, and pro rata shares of utilities, building costs, and so on. Examination of the operation of this center leads to the development of bases for reallocating its costs to either channels, products, or customers. Such a basis might be the number of orders written or the number of order lines. To the extent that the best basis of allocation relates to products or customers, a final allocation to channels would again be made on the basis of use.

The end result is a cost function and expanded form of Equation (2):

$$C_i = a_i + b_{i1}I_{i1} + b_{i2}I_{i2} + b_{i3}I_{i3}, + \cdots + b_{iw}I_{iw} \qquad (4)$$

where a_i is the sum of the fixed expense allocated to channel i (this could usefully be divided into two components, avoidable and unavoidable) and the b_{ij} are the variable costs for each of the types of market effort and for the product itself. In the case of the product category, a number of subcoefficients might be defined, b_{ijk}, to separately reflect the cost of delivery of the product, product cost itself, and the discounts off list selling price allowed to middlemen.

Where the firm has no firsthand experience in the use of a specific type of channel, two alternatives remain. Information of the kind required by Equation (4) may be gained through experimental use of the unfamiliar channels. Such experiments are possible where the firm operates in a large number of semiautonomous trading areas. Several of these may be chosen as sites for the experiments. Ideally such choices should be representative of the entire range of market conditions that the firm faces. In actual practice, however, there are numerous objections to this where the firm has an ongoing operation. The experiments tend to disturb sales in existing channels and to frighten or worry distributors. They may also prove to be exceedingly expensive to administer.

As a result, resort must usually be made to engineering studies and the derivation of synthetic cost curves. This requires that the firm clearly specify, in each of the channels it wishes to investigate, the total set of activities to be performed. Once a detailed listing of this type is developed, either from the exploratory research already undertaken or extensions thereof, the channels are divided according to the level of responsibility which the firm will bear for their cost: full, partial, or none. For those falling in the first and second categories, performance criteria must be established and engineering studies of expense patterns launched. For physical handling, upper boundaries on costs may be derived through consultation with tariffs of transportation agencies and/or fees of public warehouses (services of the latter are surprisingly broad). For communication costs, estimates of sales force size must proceed from the number and complexity of calls required and charges for salesman time and backup facilities.

Costs for which the firm may bear partial responsibility are cooperative promotional activities, warranties, service, price-level guarantees, and product returns. Informal discussions with management personnel from several of the types of agencies concerned will be helpful in pinpointing the nature of the shared responsibility and the estimation of potential liability under a variety of market circumstances.

The result of these efforts may be usefully expressed in a function comparable to that of Equation (4). To the extent that uncertainty exists for some of the coefficients and for the quantity of the resources that must be applied, the researchers may express this in the form of standard errors for both the b_{ij} and the I_{ij}.

Minimization of Channel Cost Coefficients

Whether derived from internal records or outside data gathering, the b_{ij} coefficients of Equation (4) are based upon existing patterns for the processing of channel work. Implicitly one assumes that they are based upon the most efficient methods. Considerable research, however, may be required to verify such an assumption.

In this context, research in the logistics of distribution is most advanced. We may exemplify this by research focused upon the number of warehouses that the firm maintains (at some level of a channel) to service some specific channel. The issue is how and to what extent variations in the number of these warehouses will affect the firm's cost of delivering goods to its customers. Study of this requires separating the costs of warehousing from the costs of transportation and examination of their separate patterns.

For example, warehouse costs are sensitive, on a per-unit basis, to the volume of product handled. In general, there are substantial savings on higher volumes. These derive from the opportunities in the specialization of labor and in the mechanization of the process. There also may be savings in administrative and overhead costs, smaller units requiring virtually as many administrative personnel as larger and being more expensive to build on a square footage basis.

This view is expressed in Figure 2, where warehouse costs are expressed as W. The vertical axis measures the average unit cost for moving the product to the customer. The horizontal axis defines the number of warehouses. The total number of product units shipped is held constant. This means that as additional warehouses are added, the volume of product shipped through each declines. Hence costs rise.

On the other hand, transportation costs may be substantially reduced by an increase. If we assume that the warehouse delivers to customers who buy in relatively small lots, then a larger number of warehouses will reduce the average distance that goods must be shipped in this expensive manner. The savings incurred are shown by the curve labeled T in Figure 2. As the average distance declines, the rate of savings secured diminished sharply as the proportion of costs incurred in handling rises compared to those involved in actually moving the goods.

The task of marketing research is to identify these cost functions and to estimate the number of warehouses which will minimize the total logistics cost curve, $T + W$. Such estimates may require again the construction of synthetic cost curves. One study, using data obtained from company records, employed the following equation to express the issue [3]:

$$C = a + b/KA + c/A \tag{5}$$

where C was the cost per dollar's worth of goods distributed, a, b, and c were coefficients derived from the data, A the area covered in square miles by the typical warehouse, and K the dollar volume of goods sold per square mile of territory. The optimal territory per warehouse was derived by taking the derivative of C with respect to A, setting this equal to zero (where C will be minimized), and solving for A. Given the total size of the territory, the appropriate number of warehouses can then be determined.

A similar approach might be developed for testing the value of altering the number of competing wholesalers on the second level of some three- (possibly four-) level channel being used by the firm for a change in the size of each wholesaler's trading area. A wholesaler's willingness to accept lower discounts in exchange for a wider territory depends upon his estimate of the profits obtainable from an increased flow of product through his warehouse. To the

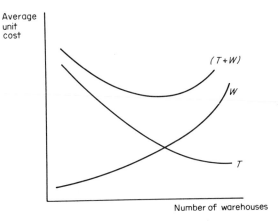

Average unit cost

$(T+W)$

W

T

Number of warehouses

Fig. 2.   Effect of changes in the number of warehouses on logistics cost.

extent that competitive conditions make margin adjustments difficult, trade-off negotiations may focus upon the level of support provided distributors for service or promotional activities.

In both this and the previous example, the assumption of no change in total sales as a result of changes in the number of warehouses (or distributors) is implicit. To the extent that this is invalid due to concomitant changes in the delivery time likely to accompany such shifts, constraints on the delivery time (or other critical factor) may have to be added to the evaluative model.

Analysis of Channel Revenues

At this point, necessary cost data for each channel the firm wishes to consider may be assumed to be assembled. Ideally, these should be in the form of the price coefficients, b_{ij}, of Equation (3) and the quantity of promotional input required, I_{ij}. From these figures, average costs of operating within each channel at different volume levels may be computed. The comparison of these cost curves for alternative channels may lead immediately to the exclusion of several that are obviously not tenable.

For the remainder, management may choose to make some rough forecasts, from the data gathered in the exploratory research and from judgment, of the volume obtainable through each. Given the strength of management conviction as to these estimates and its capacity to absorb risk, the problem of channel choice may be solved at this point. However, where the range of profit estimates is wide and overlaps for two or more of the channels under consideration, more formal methods of revenue estimation may be required.

Before discussing the kinds of approaches to improved estimates, the contribution that additional information on revenues by channel may provide should be evaluated relative to the cost of undertaking the additional research. This consideration requires the calculation of the opportunity loss that would occur from the choice of one channel as opposed to the other through Bayesian analysis and comparison with the cost of improving the decision through research, as discussed in Section II, Part A, Chapter 3. Instances where the cost of additional research looms larger than the opportunity loss indicate that the channel choice should be made at this point. Given, however, that channel decisions tend to affect revenues over a long period of time, discounted revenue flows must be used in computing opportunity loss. Under such conditions, it is difficult to imagine circumstances where firms engaged in fairly substantial operations would fail to elect further investigation [1].

Two principal means are available to assess potential revenues where data are not available internally. The first is survey research, the second experimentation. In the case of surveys, two types of subjects must be considered; the industrial buying organizations and the industrial middlemen. In both instances, it will be necessary to define the universe and devise a sampling plan for securing information from representative elements.

The primary task of the industrial buyer survey is to sharpen the company estimates of the market potential in each channel type and determine how this is distributed among different market segments. Toward this end, questions should be designed to probe the following issues with respect to each of the products the firm sells:

1. The channel sources employed by the industrial buyer and the extent of use of each; degree of satisfaction with each

2. The number and organizational position of personnel of the industrial buying institution who influence the purchase of the product

3. The degree of technical knowledge and expertise among buyer personnel who will influence the purchase

4. The degree of buyer in-house product operating and service capability

5. The number of product units typically contracted for at a given time, the number of units per shipment, and the frequency of contract letting or purchasing

6. The assortment of products, including the seller's product, which is purchased on a given order

7. The basis of choice among suppliers employing similar types of channels, as, for example, among industrial wholesalers

8. The degree of awareness of alternative manufacturing sources of supply and the extent of search through channels for the products of these firms

9. The degree of variability in purchasing patterns, units shipped, delivery time, special parts and orders, and importance of special services

10. The preferred method of product delivery and delivery time sensitivity

From questions 1 and 5, we obtain estimates of channel market potential. Cross tabulation of the answers obtained from question 1 with the remaining nine provides insight as to the extent to which each channel type serves an exclusive market segment.

Thus question 1 would serve as the basis for classifying industrial buyers into groups preferring different channel types. The remaining nine variables may then be evaluated for cumulative explanatory power. Cross classification and discriminant analysis provide the basis for evaluating and extending the four generalizations about channel usage developed earlier in this chapter.

The primary task of the middleman survey is to assess the share of the market potential in each channel type that the producer might be expected to obtain. Specific issues to be considered are:

1. Awareness of supplier sources of supply and the image that they hold for each.

2. Basis of choice for current supplier(s)—for example, width of product line, services offered, price, product quality, and degree of satisfaction with each.

3. Rationale as to the number of suppliers (for products being sold by the firm instituting the survey), the types of promotional support provided, and completeness of inventories stocked for each.

4. The total range of products carried, the lines of primary importance, and the potential or existing sales of the specific line sold by the firm.

5. The market segment or segments covered.

6. The degree and intensity of market coverage as determined by the size of sales force and frequency of call.

7. Technical capability of the sales force. Mode of organization, that is, product, customer type, area. Extent of engineering backup for salesmen. Depth of industrial buyer personnel covered.

8. Trading area coverage.

9. State of physical facilities, equipment, procedures, capital.

10. The importance of exclusive distribution rights to the supplier's product line and its relation to promotional practices.

The results from a survey of this type may be used to evaluate the quality of distributors in a given type of a channel and the likelihood that the producer could recruit distributors at any quality level for its line. *Quality* refers to the fact that middlemen in any channel are by no means homogeneous. Specific middlemen will not only be more suitable for the producer but will have the organizational capacity of doing a better job. Questions 4 to 9 are intended to enable the producer to rank middlemen along this quality continuum and to estimate the proportion of the market held by each point of the range.

Questions 1 to 3 and 10 relate to the probability that the firm could recruit distributors and to the standing it would hold in the interests of the middleman. When the answers to this issue are cross tabulated by the quality rating of the middleman, the producer will obtain a measure of the extent to which he would be likely to be able to recruit at any given level, which in turn will determine the share of channel market potential he could expect to obtain.

While survey research of this kind offers a refined basis for making estimates of the potential from alternative types of channels, uncertainty may yet remain. The alternative is to experiment with potential channels to develop a historical perspective upon which management may find itself psychologically able to place greater reliance. Unfortunately, however, not all circumstances warrant either this approach or such reliance. Uncertainties will still remain.

As discussed under costs, companies with wide territorial distribution may find some sectors which they are willing to devote to experimentation. However, if such experimentation is not carried out over the full range of competitive circumstances which the firm faces (for fear of dislocating current marketing efforts), the results may not be projectable to the whole. Companies starting out *de novo* are in the best position to develop an experimental design which has better promise of reliability.

Even here, however, certain cautions are warranted. To the extent that middlemen are included in any experiment and are aware of the project, promotional efforts made on behalf of the product may not be representative of those that may be made in the long run. Further, the full potential of a channel type may not be obtained in a short period of time. The time lags associated with marketing effort in these instances may be painfully long. Expenditures may often be of the sunk cost variety and the firm may, in some instances, find it costly to withdraw from a given system.

Hence, while experimentation is likely to provide invaluable information on the extent to which the firm can work readily with any given type of channel, the revenue estimates may be much less reliable than those of operating costs. They should be supplemented by other data.

Management of the Going Channel

Another broad area for research in channels is on continuing improvement in the efficiencies of those systems in which the producer is currently engaged. Our concern to this point has been to select one or more channels from among many. Here, it is to improve the performance of those to which commitments have already been made.

The nature of the problem may be expressed with regard to the mathematical notation of Equations (1) and (2). One major issue lies with the allocation that the firm will make of its resources among the various I_{ij}. Essentially this is the marketing mix problem as it exists in conjunction with the operation of the channel. A second major issue has regard to the b_{ij} coefficients. These coefficients represent the sensitivity of the other firms in the channel to the efforts of the producer to influence their behavior. As such, they reflect the effectiveness of the producer's channel programming.

With regard to the first issue of effort allocation, the employment of experimental methodology (through the deliberate variation in patterns of marketing expense) may prove to be particularly useful in evaluating alternative strategies. Some care must be exerted to avoid strategies which could lead to extraordinarily poor results, such as dramatic reduction in effort allocation or increases in price. Aside from this concern, there are few reasons why systematic testing of different expenditure patterns should not be a regular part of the producer's channel research activities.

Existing historical data may also be studied through multivariate analysis. Particularly useful results may be obtained by instituting data collection procedures to gather information on marketing effort expended in each of the trading areas where the producer's products are being sold. Indeed, the simple organization of the firm's statistical processing activities to gather such data and their review may provide eye-opening results, particularly where information about the promotional and other marketing efforts of distributors is included. It is odd that so few firms collect data in this fashion.

Once such information is available, along with estimates of market potential in each territory, the extent of association between the firm's efforts and results may be begun. In general, through inadvertence or historical accident, the patterns of marketing effort applied in each territory are different. Cross classification of performance by territory with each pattern provides insight on the impact each pattern is having. Multiple regression analysis provides a more sophisticated basis to measure the influence of each of the variables and to evaluate their overall explanatory power [19].

As just noted, the second major issue in the management of a channel's operation deals with the sensitivity of middlemen to the firm's marketing efforts. The firm may discover the optimal allocation of marketing expenditures but be unable to produce desirable performance because of poor implementation of programs. A major area for research, then, lies in the assessment of the factors which determine middleman sensitivity to the producer's activities [18].

In researching this area, three types of failures have been observed:
1. Communication breakdown
2. Program irrelevance
3. Program conflict

Communication breakdown occurs because of use of terms and constructs which are part of the world of one channel member but not the other. Distributor organizations, for the most part, tend to be relatively small firms manned and directed by personnel whose training has come principally from the marketplace. Contrarily, personnel in manufacturing, particularly at the staff marketing level, have received much of their training in academic atmospheres where problem solving is studied in a more abstract manner and terminology has become esoteric. The result is that marketing programs relevant to the entire channel are not translated into language which is meaningful to all members. Efficiency is impaired in direct proportion to this failure.

Program irrelevance occurs where marketing strategies devised at one level have little meaning to the goals and need of the firms at another. Such irrelevance may occur where a manufacturer fails to show how his program will influence a distributor's operation. Manufacturer strategies are often constructed on a national or regional basis without direct regard for their impact upon individual sectors. Yet this is where the distributor exists, and unless he can be shown how special promotions will affect his customers in specific terms, he is likely to have little interest and cooperation will be minimal.

Program irrelevance may also occur when there is a lack of awareness of distributor goals and needs at the manufacturing level. It can be easily assumed by the manufacturer that distributor objectives toward profits, growth, and long-term existence are parallel to his. In many cases this is true. In others, however, major differences may be found. The distributor has a local community commitment, his needs may be satisfied at profit levels below the optimal, and he may be unable to make long-term projections because of retirement plans. The distributor may also have commitments to middlemen trade groups which limit his willingness to compete in certain ways. More specifically, the manufacturer's goals are those of a corporate body; the middleman's are likely to be highly personal. Plans based upon the interests of one, as a consequence, may be meaningless to the other.

The final issue of program conflict occurs when planning on the part of one member of the channel results in strategies perceived by another to operate to his disadvantage. While it is unlikely that the pattern by which a manufacturer prefers to allocate his marketing effort could ever be fully congruent with the one that would best satisfy the distributor, divergencies of a substantial nature result in ineffective program implementation. Efforts by manufacturers to force distributors to adhere to undesired strategies, through threat of franchise cancellation for example, often lead to greater problems over the long run through lost efficiency and opposing power plays through distributor trade association activity.

Conflict within the system occurs where the manufacturer of a particular brand employs different channel types which compete for the same market segment. Antagonisms are particularly apt to be sharp where distributors perceive that the manufacturers systematically reserve the best customers for themselves. Disputes may also occur over the timing and handling of new products, the phasing out of old, warranty provisions, returns for products damaged in transit or of substandard quality, the handling of cooperative advertising expenditures, and over the methods by which the manufacturer may attempt to exert control over distributors—for example, sales goals, inventory policy, capital investment, sales force organization, and level of promotional effort.

All these issues suggest the need for a continuing research program to monitor the degree of conflict and effectiveness of communication between the members of a channel. While personnel involved in industrial distribution channels have close relationships with the management of these organizations and should be in a position to identify deteriorating conditions, the existence of ill will and lack of cooperation has been persistently observed. It appears likely that pressures placed directly upon sales personnel working with distributors may not only contribute to the conflict potential but restrict the quantity and quality of information top management receives about field conditions. Moreover, to the extent that feedback to higher management levels does occur, it is rarely complete or usefully organized.

Formal research programs, then, are required to monitor the condition of the firm's relationship with distributors and to identify points of discontent and lack of interest. Both cross-sectional and longitudinal type designs may be useful to detect trends and to evaluate the impact of possible problems upon sales volume and the manufacturer's long-run position within the channel. These may also be broadened to monitor the continuing market share that each channel type holds and the firm's standing in that channel. While the manufacturer may infrequently alter his channel, research of this nature is useful to signal future changes in distribution patterns and to allow management ample time to make the necessary changes.

REFERENCES

1. Alderson, W., and P. E. Green, *Planning and Problem Solving in Marketing,* Homewood, Ill.: Irwin, 1964, chaps. 5, 11.
2. Balderston, F. E., and A. C. Hoggatt, *Simulation of Market Processes,* Berkeley: Institute of Business and Economic Research, University of California, 1962.
3. Bowman, E. H., and J. B. Stewart, "A Model for Scale of Operations," *Journal of Marketing,* vol. 20, January 1956.
4. Brion, J. M., *Marketing through the Wholesaler/Distributor Channel,* Chicago: American Marketing Association, 1965.
5. Bucklin, L. P., *Competition and Evaluation in the Distributive Trades in the United States,* Englewood Cliffs, N.J.: Prentice Hall, 1972, chap. 6.
6. Bucklin, L. P., ed., *Vertical Marketing Systems,* Glenview, Ill.: Scott, Foresman, 1970.
7. Christian, R. C., "Industrial Marketing: Three Step Method to Better Distribution Channel Analysis," *Journal of Marketing,* vol. 23, October 1958.
8. Clewett, R. M., ed., *Marketing Channels for Manufactured Products,* Homewood, Ill.: Irwin, 1954.
9. Cox, R., and C. S. Goodman, "Marketing of Housebuilding Materials," *Journal of Marketing,* vol. 21, July 1956.
10. Davidson, W. R., "Channels of Distribution—One Aspect of Marketing Strategy," *Business Horizons,* vol. 4, February 1961.
11. Diamond, W. M., *Distribution Channels for Industrial Goods,* Columbus, Ohio: Bureau of Business Research, Ohio State University, 1964.
12. Kreisberg, L., "Occupational Controls Among Steel Distributors," *American Journal of Sociology,* vol. 61, November 1955.
12a. Longman, D. R., and M. Schiff, *Practical Distribution Cost Accounting,* Homewood, Ill.: Irwin, 1955.

13. Mallen, B., ed., *The Marketing Channel: A Conceptual Viewpoint,* New York: Wiley, 1965.
14. McCammon, B. C., Jr., and R. W. Little, "Marketing Channels: Analytical Systems and Approaches," in George Schwartz, ed., *Science in Marketing,* New York: Wiley, 1965.
15. McCarthy, E. J., and R. J. Williams, "Simulation of Production-Marketing Channels," in R. M. Hass, ed., *Science, Technology, and Marketing,* Chicago: American Marketing Association, 1967, pp. 335–346.
16. McFarland, S. W., "The Marketing Position of Industrial Distributors," *Journal of Marketing,* vol. 17, April 1953.
17. See, for example, Sevin, C. H., *Marketing Productivity Analysis,* New York: McGraw-Hill, 1965.
18. Stern, L. W., ed., *Distribution Channels: Behavioral Dimensions,* Boston: Houghton Mifflin, 1969.
19. Sturdivant, F. D., et al., *Managerial Analysis in Marketing,* Glenview, Ill.: Scott, Foresman, 1970, pp. 633–635.
20. Thompson, D. N., *Contractual Marketing Systems,* Lexington, Mass.: Heath-Lexington, 1971.
21. U.S. Bureau of the Census, *Census of Business,* 1963.
22. Warshaw, M. R., *Effective Selling through Wholesalers,* Ann Arbor, Mich.: Bureau of Business Research, The University of Michigan, 1961.

Part D

Industrial Marketing

Chapter 5

The Art of Price Forecasting

GEORGE B. HEGEMAN *Arthur D. Little, Inc., Cambridge, Massachusetts*

INTRODUCTION

Price forecasts are used every day in management decisions about marketing strategy, new investments, budgeting, and raw material purchasing. Most of these forecasts are based on the intuitive judgment of marketing management, even though economic theory has given us a scientific basis for price forecasting. Unfortunately, in order to develop a price forecast, we must first have appropriate supply and demand curves. Such curves simply have never been developed for most products, and they are viewed as abstract academic concepts by almost every businessman. This is so because the word *demand* summarizes all the complexities in the marketplace and *supply* encompasses all the internal activities of the various producers. As a result, the task of developing supply and demand curves has been viewed as too formidable by most producers.

A variety of techniques have been developed to deal with the problems of supply, demand, and prices and to help reduce the risk and uncertainty in management decisions. Though the different approaches vary considerably in their sophistication, no one of them has universal application; each must be considered in the light of its own advantages and limitations with respect to the specific need.

Price forecasting is still an art rather than a science. Success depends as much on the talent of the practitioner as it does on the merits of the tools available. Nonetheless, some useful tools have been developed, and the skilled user can make significant reductions in the inherent risks of price forecasting. Despite the large number of uncertain factors at work in the marketplace, there appears to be sufficient rational behavior within most market environments to make price forecasting a reasonable endeavor. In fact, the choice is seldom whether or not to forecast; it is usually whether to forecast systematically or intuitively. Virtually all business planning requires that the price and volume forecasts be made and that confidence be placed in the values or range of values chosen as the forecast.

PRICE FORECASTING TECHNIQUES

Basically, there are three approaches to forecasting price: inertial, inductive, and deductive.

Inertial. Inertial forecasts are statistical projections based on historical data. They include price exclusion charts, cost and experience curves, and conventional statistical forecasts based on time-series and correlation analysis. Using a wide variety of mathematical techniques to extrapolate past history, inertial forecasts can usually be developed rapidly. Because of the generally accepted thesis that the "past is prologue," forecasts based on historical statistics have considerable credibility with many people.

Inductive. Inductive forecasts take the inertial forecast as a base and adjust the projections on the basis of management knowledge and experience. This is a common approach of market research as it modifies statistical forecasts on the basis of knowledge about the current and future environment.

Deductive. Deductive forecasts use current data and decision rules about alternatives to develop an independent long-range forecast. The deductive approach takes into account the unique characteristics of an industry and requires an intimate knowledge of the business.

In developing a price forecasting model, one must consider the trade-off between the cost of the forecast and the cost of error. The least expensive methods are inertial forecasts, which may provide useful insight into long-range price trends without the expense of delving into the cause and effect relationships within the market environment. Inductive and deductive forecasts are more sophisticated forecasts, reflecting the relationships between a large number of variables, and thus are more expensive. They often use a mathematical model, the form of which—for example, correlation, linear programming, or simulation—gives a totally different dimension to the problem of establishing the required input and evaluating the output.

Inertial Forecasts

The Price Exclusion Chart. The price exclusion chart is a simple first step toward gaining insight about the future price for a specific product. This approach permits one to say that a given level of demand for a product competing with many other items in a major market area can probably be reached only if the product sells at or below a given price. The exclusion chart is totally empirical and depends upon the availability of information on a large number of products for a given end-use market.

A typical price exclusion chart (Figure 1) is constructed by plotting data on price and production for a large number of products used in a single market. The U.S. Tariff Commission provides such data annually for synthetic organic chemicals. A chart should be prepared for each year for each end use by plotting price versus production volume on a semilog scale. It is then possible to draw a line so that nearly every point falls below the line. The area above the line is termed the exclusion area and all points are below and typically to the left of the line as shown. Since the exclusion charts are empirical, the more years that this relationship can be shown to hold, the greater the faith

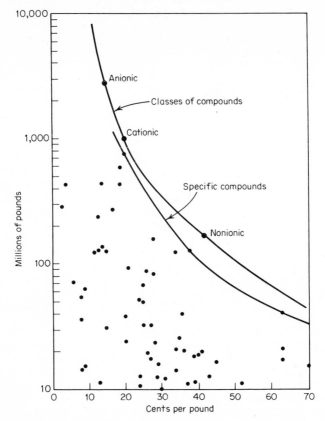

Fig. 1.   Price exclusion curve, surface-active agents—1969.   (*Arthur D. Little, Inc., based on* U.S. Production and Sale of Surface-Active Agents, *U.S. Tariff Commission, June 1971.*)

that can be placed in its accuracy. In the chemical market area, using data from the Tariff Commission, exclusion charts have been found successful in the areas of medicinals, flavor and perfume materials, plasticizers, surface-active agents, and pesticides. This approach has been unsuccessful for some other product groups such as dyes and organic pigments where only specific chemicals are applicable in a given end use and hence premiums can be obtained for their performance [1]. While a price exclusion chart will not forecast the price of a specific product, it does supply some indication of the price limits within which a product could achieve different levels of sales volume within a major market area.

Cost and Experience Curves. A second and equally straightforward method of gaining guidance on the future price of a specific product is through the use of cost and experience curves [1]. In this approach a historical plot of cumulative production volume and cost should show that costs have declined by some characteristic amount each time accumulated production has doubled. For most products, the characteristic decline is 20 to 30 percent in constant dollars for each doubling of accumulated production. This decline appears to continue regardless of the rate of growth of production. Because of the highly competitive environment for most products, prices tend to decline in the same pattern as costs as long as the relationship between competitors is stable. According to the work done to date in this area, if prices do not parallel costs in this manner, it usually means the market leader is holding an umbrella over the market; when the cost-profit relationship shows a high level of profitability, the entrance of new producers typically creates a rapid fall in price until cost and price are back in line. Figure 2 shows the outlines of a typical stable price-cost relationship and of an unstable pattern. If one is able to ascertain the future periods of price stability and instability, it then becomes possible to forecast the price over an extended period of time. If one can assume a long-term stable relationship between prices and costs, then clearly the experience curves provide an inexpensive approach to price forecasting.

Statistical Price Forecasting. Where prices move in a steady cycle, it is probably efficient to use time-series or correlation analysis to identify seasonal factors and to show the existence of these trends in the price forecast. Once identified, the seasonal factors can be of considerable assistance in policy decisions about inventories in anticipation of price changes. The establishment of lead-lag relationships is also important in developing short-term price forecasts in order to detect as rapidly as possible the likelihood of price shifts. Commodity price forecasting through chart analysis, trend following, and volume and open-interest analysis are well-established techniques used by commodity speculators [5]. Several computer price forecasting models based on statistical time-series and correlation analysis have been developed in the process industry, particularly for chemicals and forest products. Weyerhaeuser has reported considerable success in the use of these models for short-term forecasting [7]. A chemical price forecasting equation had also been proposed [8].

In many cases, when price forecasting covers only short periods ahead, supply can be ignored as a constraint. In such cases a clear understanding of demand-price relationships can be useful in understanding future prices [3]. One way to develop these data is to undertake a controlled market test. If this is practical, the product demand curve can be developed empirically. Other methods include consumer questionnaires or correlation analysis. For agricultural commodities, correlation analysis of the relation of sales to price has been widely used [11].

The key assumption in all statistical forecasts is that what will happen in the future is guided only by what has happened in the past. Because technology is moving so rapidly and economic, political, and social change are ever-

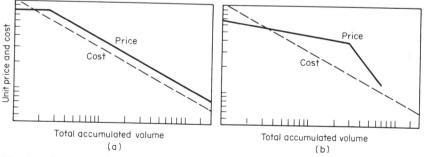

Fig. 2. Cost-price experience curves. (*a*) Typical stable pattern; (*b*) typical unstable pattern. (Perspectives on Experience, *The Boston Consulting Group, June 1968.*)

present, this type of forecasting is generally most effective for a one- to two-year period where the inertia and traditions of the past can still hold sway. Beyond this, the magnitude of the pressures from major changes in the environment tends to negate the validity of such forecasts. Since the weakness of purely statistical forecasts is that they, in effect, say that history will be repeated, they are seldom accepted as the sole basis for strategic planning and decision making.

Inductive Forecasts

Managers who are unwilling to base decisions on a mechanical forecast derived from past data typically rely on a hybrid forecast which combines the subjective judgments of management with the statistical forecast of the economist. This inductive type of forecasting relies heavily on intuitive judgment and is the most widely used approach to price forecasting.

An interesting example of the inductive type of price forecast is contained in a 1966 Arthur D. Little, Inc. (ADL) report prepared to project the likely cost and availability of naphtha in Western Europe [6]. The analytical portion of this project involved the development of a linear programming (LP) model of the European refining industry. In such LP models, price forecasts are typically inputs, but the models can provide an analysis of how the value of one product shifts over a wide range of demand when the prices and demands of all other products remain constant. By using the LP as a simulation to test the sensitivity of the market, ADL was able to gain some insight as to how the cost and therefore the price of naphtha would change in the future at different levels of demand. (See Figure 3.) Various surveys and statistical forecasts provided background for the demand estimates, but ADL's evaluation of the market suggested a range of demand in 1970 which was at or below the critical point in the cost curve where prices would increase sharply if demand were to reach these levels. Supply was not considered a constraint in these simulation runs, though the variation in naphtha production from different sources of crude was evaluated.

At the time of publication, the ADL report was particularly controversial because the major oil companies believed future naphtha demand would be significantly higher and therefore naphtha prices would reflect the higher valuation on the demand curve. Thus, despite the analytical work of estimating future naphtha prices, the conclusions of this study rested on a judgment regarding the scope of future demand. Clearly, the choice of a price forecast was a judgment decision superimposed over an analytical solution of demand-cost relationships.

A similar type of linear programming model has been used to estimate the value of commercial aircraft using varying estimates of future air traffic. In this study [9] the time horizon of the forecast was limited to three years because the supply was assumed to be the number of aircraft on hand and on order at the time of the study. The LP then allocated routes to the most efficient planes available and determined the price of the aircraft from the discounted value of the income stream that could be generated over time. In this case the volume of traffic involved was a judgment forecast and the most sensitive variable affecting the price forecast.

Deductive Forecasts

Deductive forecasts, a totally different type of forecasting system, are based on behavioral simulation models. These forecasts start with current industry data, decision rules about how different competitors act, and the judgment of management regarding future trends in all aspects of the business. The behavioral simulation model takes into account judgments, attitudes, and decision rules regarding future action that have an important bearing on how a competitive market evolves.

Simulation models for evaluating the outlook for new ventures have been under development by a variety of companies. These so-called venture simulations usually focus on profitability as the primary output, with a variety of assumptions regarding future price imposed on the model to test overall sensitivity to price changes. However, modifications of these same simulators using criteria regarding expected profitability can convert these venture simulations into price forecasting models.

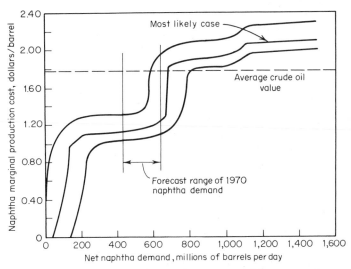

Fig. 3.   Projected marginal naphtha production costs for western Europe, 1970. (*Arthur D. Little, Inc.*)

Du Pont has given some details on its work with venture simulators which it has developed for a number of products [3], and Arthur D. Little has reviewed some of its work with regard to both venture simulation and price forecasting [6]. These reports indicate that a model which defines the cause and effect relationships within a market environment can produce quite different results than normal forecasting techniques. Typically, other approaches yield a specific price at some future point in time, leaving to management's imagination the question of how the price arrived at that level and what can be expected to happen in the intervening years. A simulation, which incorporates decision rules on each of the key cause and effect relationships, produces a history of the price forecast showing why and how the price moved over time. The focus of attention is not on what the price may be in ten years but on what intervening price cycles the industry will experience.

The most important new concept in this type of forecast is the incorporation of decision rules in the model structure. The decision rules cover all aspects of the business from production costs and inventory control to market share and new investment planning. With each decision rule is a set of constraints which define the limits within which the model can operate without invoking a decision for change.   Along with decision rules come the critical time delays required to implement the decisions.   Management knowledge and understanding about future events and trends are also incorporated.

The use of decision rules in the forecasting process is the key to developing a supply forecast, an area which is typically ignored in other types of price forecasts.   While industry capacity can be forecast with some degree of reliability for one to two years ahead based on announced plant expansions, it is essential to gain some insight into capacity cycles further in the future.   This is accomplished by forcing the model to follow the general guidelines or decision rules of the industry regarding new investment and by making sure that when projected profits look especially attractive, there is an occasional new producer entering the market to upset the best laid plans of existing producers.

A price forecasting model must also consider the relationship between price and demand, or price elasticity.   The model also includes operating rate and cost-profit relationships, producer market share and pricing policies, and the effect of inventory on price.   A flow sheet for a price forecasting model already in use in the plastics industry is shown in Figure 4.   This model includes several major producer groups and different grades of material.   Perhaps the most

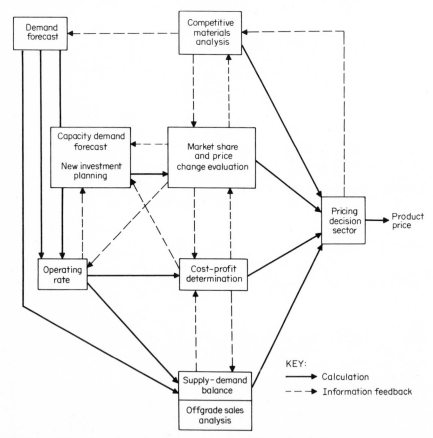

Fig. 4.   Flow chart for price forecasting model based on behavioral simulation. (*Arthur D. Little, Inc.*)

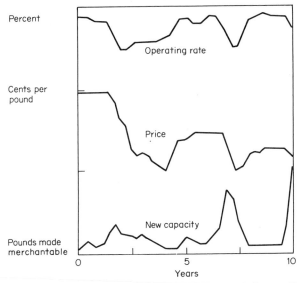

Fig. 5.   Simulation price forecasting model output.   (*Arthur D. Little, Inc.*)

striking feature of the flow chart is the heavy dependence of the model on information feedback systems. This type of model is based on the assumption that changes in the system at a given point in time affect subsequent decisions; thus, when given appropriate guidelines for response to change, the model is capable of continuing to project the course of events over an extended period of time. (See Figure 5.)

Most product prices are the result of a balance in the forces at work within the market environment. Therefore the price forecasting model must simulate as realistically as possible the development and dissipation of each of these forces over time. The impact that these forces have on the environment is counterbalanced by the reaction of customers, competitors, and competitive materials suppliers. Thus it is also necessary to incorporate decision rules covering competitive response mechanisms and to assure feedback of these reactions within the model as the demand and price forecasts proceed through time.

Deductive models which explore the cause and effect relationships within the marketplace in such extensive detail are obviously far more costly than the inertial or inductive approaches to price forecasting. Since price forecasting is really still an art rather than a science, the use of a deductive model is probably relevant only to those major products upon which a company's future depends. Then, the research required to support the analysis of cause and effect relationships serves an educational function as well as providing a price forecast. For less significant products, the inertial or inductive forecasts are clearly quicker and more economical.

Benefits of Better Forecasts

If more realistic price forecasts are possible, there are many implications for management. Most important is the improved payoff in better decisions regarding marketing strategy. Knowing when to initiate price changes, hold the line, or follow suit can substantially reduce the risks in dealing with customers during a very sensitive period in supplier-customer relations. A knowledge of pricing trends for various product lines also suggests the most appropriate balance of marketing effort for each product. For example, with a product that is expected to fall in price and then to recover in several years, it may be desirable to reduce the current selling effort and emphasize research in the short term, in order to have the best product available when prices recover. Conversely, a product in a rising price and profit trend could undoubtedly benefit from a more effective selling effort immediately.

Other areas which can be affected by improved price forecasting are budgeting and raw material purchasing. Clearly, a better view of product prices will enhance the accuracy of future sales budgets, while an understanding of raw material pricing will provide an appreciation of changing production costs. Raw material price forecasting also suggests the potential for inventory savings resulting from judicious purchasing patterns.

Perhaps the most important implication for management in improved price forecasting lies in the area of investment decisions. Here long-range price forecasts based on intuition have often been the cause of poor investment decisions. If a more thorough and rational approach to developing a price forecast can reduce the risk associated with major capital commitments, the costs involved in developing a deductive forecast may well be worthwhile. In addition, improved insight into future prices may permit a company to break the normal industry investment and price cycles and achieve a more balanced growth in profits. In fact, the well-timed countercyclical investment which comes on stream just when prices are rising provides the greatest payoff to efforts to improve price forecasting capabilities.

REFERENCES

1. Boston Consulting Group, Inc., *Perspectives on Experience*, 1968.
2. Dean, J., *Managerial Economics*, Englewood Cliffs, N.J.: Prentice Hall, 1951.
3. "DuPont's 'answer machine,' " *Business Week*, December 20, 1969.
4. Hegeman, G. B., "The Computer and Forecasting of Market Demand and Prices," Symposium on Chemical Marketing—The Challenge of the Seventies, American Chemical Society, September 11, 1968.
5. Jiles, H., ed., *Guide to Commodity Price Forecasting*, Commodity Research Bureau, Inc., April 1967.
6. Little, Arthur D., Inc., *The Outlook for Naphtha in Europe to 1970*, report to The Dow Chemical Company and Union Carbide Corporation, July 1966.
7. Massey, D. J., and J. H. Black, "Predicting Chemical Prices," *Chemical and Engineering News*, October 20, 1969.
8. "Mathematical Model Becomes Marketing Tool," *Chemical and Engineering News*, January 2, 1967.
9. Parkany, J., "Price Forecasting—A Part of Sales Forecasting," New York: National Industrial Conference Board meeting, October 17, 1968.
10. Sobotka and Schnabel, "Linear Programming as a Device for Predicting Market Value: Prices of Used Commercial Aircraft, 1959–65," *Symposium on Methods to Forecast Prices*, American Chemical Society Division of Chemical Marketing and Economics, Miami Beach, Fla., April 1967.
11. Spencer, M. H., C. G. Clark, and P. W. Hoguet, *Business and Economic Forecasting—An Econometric Approach*, Homewood, Ill.: Irwin, 1961, chap. 5.
12. Zabel, H. W., "Use of the Exclusion Chart to Forecast Price," *Symposium on Methods to Forecast Prices*, American Chemical Society Division of Chemical Marketing and Economics, Miami Beach, Fla., April 1967.

Industrial Marketing

Chapter 6

Marketing Image Studies

BRUCE M. BARE *Arthur D. Little, Inc., Cambridge, Massachusetts*

A marketing image study is an analysis of how the total marketing effort of each of a group of suppliers influences buying decisions in a given market. It is to industrial marketing what consumer research is to consumer marketing. As noted in Section IV, Part C, Chapter 6 in connection with advertising research, the successful marketing image study gives management a clear reading of the impact of its marketing programs, comparing that impact with those of major competitors. It thus reduces the normal uncertainties of marketing planning and directs the way to improvements in sales and profits. Knowing whether the market share of a given company is increasing—or decreasing—is not enough. One must also know (1) what specific factors are influencing the results, (2) how the marketing environment is changing, and (3) what changes in the company's organization or marketing programs can favorably influence its market share.

Necessary for such a study in the industrial field is knowledge of which individuals in the buying organization significantly influence the purchase decision and which buying influences lead to that decision. In most cases this precludes using a structured, written questionnaire to obtain the required data. More generally it requires in-depth interviews under circumstances conducive to open discussion.

The successful marketing image study does the following:

1. It introduces a thorough and orderly analytical thought process to marketing problems that, because of their subjective nature, are frequently thought to resist analysis

2. It is based on feedback from several persons in various influential roles in their respective companies

3. It measures competitors by the same standards as those used for the subject company

4. It includes pertinent, current, factual knowledge of both supplier and customer industries

5. It is based on information obtained in an objective climate enhanced by candid discussion

6. It provides rigorously examined results and conclusions owing survival to fact, not conjecture or assumption

VALUE OF A MARKETING IMAGE STUDY

Of what value is the marketing image study and how can it best be used? When marketing management has available a statement of its company's image (how it appears to various customer groups and how it compares with competitors), what is done with it?

The real value of marketing image analysis is that it provides the marketing manager with an objective assessment of his company's standing—in the eyes of his customers—relative to his competitors'. Knowing this, he can plan short- and long-range strategy with greater certainty than he could before. He can set specific objectives to improve his marketing efforts, reinforcing the weaker parts of his present strategy and taking even greater advantage of the stronger.

For example, the study may have uncovered specific problems associated with salesmen, the product line, quality control, or delivery. The company's management can meet reasonably straightforward situations by obvious actions such as training or transferring a salesman, adding selected new products to the line, installing a statistical quality control system, or acquiring selected warehouse sites. They represent "fine tuning" of the marketing effort based on fresh, objective information.

Other problems—or opportunities—uncovered by the study can form the basis for long-term shifts in the marketing effort. For instance, there may be an opportunity to improve the product form (say from granules to spheres), making the product easier to use. This may not be new information; it may even have been reported occasionally by salesmen without resultant action. However, the marketing image study may actually function as an unintended dividend, pretesting the idea by allowing various customers to assess its real potential importance.

A longer-range response may be required if the problem is a poor image resulting from inadequate participation in industry technical activities. As a result the supplier is viewed as having only a casual commitment to the customer industry. It may be appropriate in considering such information to shift research and development spending to support the necessary changes.

The technical service laboratories may have a reputation for slow or ineffective response to customer needs. This would require reviewing the ways in which technical service is brought to the customer as well as the size and orientation of the company's present technical service effort. Frequently a marketing image study can put distortions of competitors' strengths, skills, or weaknesses into proper perspective. A company may be trying hard to obtain additional business by concentrating on sales and technical service efforts when, in reality, new business cannot be obtained in that way. A study can often identify such a situation, thus allowing the company's efforts to be channeled more usefully.

For example, a supplier may feel it is disadvantageous to compete with another supplier having an impressive research facility. To attempt a similar facility may be economically impractical. But the marketing image study may show that the supplier initiating the study is already providing valued technical service at the point of sale, and doubling the impact of such service will generate unexpected rewards. The marketing image study often permits the expanded use of proved strengths rather than imitation of a competitor's.

A longer-term and perhaps potentially more useful result of the marketing image analysis is that it provides an opportunity for making and then testing fundamental changes in both people and operating philosophy. By subsequently reexamining the marketing image, the impact and value of those changes may be determined. This technique is only beginning to be used, but it offers the marketing manager maximum strategy advantages.

The concept is similar to that of a controlled experiment in which a situation is measured, a known change is made, and the situation is remeasured later to identify and interpret the results. Of course a truly controlled experiment is not possible in the marketplace. Nonetheless, one can develop valuable insights into the effect of marketing change with this technique under certain conditions. For example, the marketing changes made by the initiating company must be substantial compared with the normal practices of its own company and competitors. Furthermore, using the same investigating group for both studies may be essential to obtain valid readings of differences and change.

PREREQUISITES FOR A SUCCESSFUL STUDY

There are six prerequisites for successful analysis of a marketing image.

1. *Supplier Anonymity.* To assure objectivity, the identity of the company initiating the market image study must remain unknown to the person being interviewed. The interviewer discusses the various marketing approaches of the leading companies, differentiating among the approaches and evaluating them without the respondent knowing which company the interviewer represents.

2. *Objective interviewer.* The interviewer should not be an employee of the company initiating the study, but he should have access to those in the buying company who control or influence the purchase and sufficient rapport to ensure free and easy discussion.

3. *Security within the initiating company.* The number of individuals in the initiating company who know that a study is in progress should be limited —another measure to preserve anonymity. Frequently, customers pressure representatives of the initiating company to learn whether their employer is interested in the study.

4. *Standing of the initiating company.* A company must be an important factor in the market if its image is to be compared with those of major competitors. Otherwise its marketing activities may not be mentioned enough during the interviews. If the initiating company is obscure, the interviewer can theoretically stimulate response by a specific reference to that supplier. To do so, however, may well lead the respondent to identify the named company as the initiating company with resultant loss of objectivity.

5. *Safeguarding confidential information.* The respondent should have assurance that confidential information he gives the interviewer will not be linked to him or his company.

6. *Knowledgeable analyst.* The analyst should understand the market well enough to appreciate the relevance of particular buying influences to that market and the company roles usually associated with the buying decision. These are frequently individuals in purchasing, manufacturing, engineering, research, and general management.

FACTORS INFLUENCING A MARKETING IMAGE

Although its salesmen may be the most visible factor in establishing a company's marketing image, many individuals and the company's policies contribute significantly to that image. Among the most important are the following:

Technical Resources. The technical resources include the company's efforts in new-product development, applications research, and technical service.

The Salesman. The salesman influences his company's marketing image by his knowledge of the product line, his familiarity with the market, his appreciation of the customer, his problem-solving abilities, and his usefulness to those making the purchasing decision. A successful salesman typically stands out from his competitors in one or more of several ways. He has (1) solved a customer problem in times of crisis, (2) rendered a service by assuming a portion of his customer's work, (3) brought about cost or performance improvements in his customer's operations that the customer had been unable to do himself, or (4) developed a close friendship with key individuals in the customer's organization. Such contributions by salesmen—since they do contribute to the marketing image—must be evaluated.

Tradition. In many buyer-seller relationships, the original influences, which may have been technical, social, or the result of some special service, are forgotten over time. Then the relationship persists as a traditional one. Tradition is a real influence often overlooked by the marketing image analyst.

Breadth of Product Line. Purchasers may select suppliers with broad product lines either because they find it more convenient to place multiple-product orders or because they can realize economies from mixed truckload, carload, or tank car shipments.

Geography. The proximity of a manufacturing plant, a warehouse, a salesman's location, or a supplier's technical support may have a profound influence on the purchasing decision. When shipments are f.o.b. manufacturing plant without freight equalization, the influence may be economic. This is also true if the plant or warehouse location permits inventory reduction.

Reciprocity. Because of the constant threat of federal government action, the assurance that reciprocity is a significant buying influence may be difficult to develop. Determining the influence of reciprocity, frequently referred to as trade relations, is made even more complex when the relationship is indirect—that is, when the buying company, A, applies pressure on the supplier, B, to purchase B's product requirements from company C, which company then becomes (or remains) a customer of A. Situations like these demand that the interviewer be a third party and the respondent organization be unidentified.

Management Contact. The relationships between managements frequently represent a significant buying influence. The seemingly casual, annual visit by the chief executive of the supplier to his important customers may be the key factor contributing to the purchase decision—and to the supplier's marketing image.

Corporate Reputation. Many purchasers are flattered by the attention given them by the industry leader. This is particularly true when the buying company is small and the supplier's lead over his competition is significant. A sense of security may influence the buyer in this relationship.

Delivery. The capability of delivering goods on time and in good condition is frequently more important than geographic advantage. A purchaser may even find a small supplier more responsive to these needs and favor it with increasing orders.

Quality Control. The importance of maintaining quality and product uniformity within and among shipments can hardly be overstressed as a primary buying influence. Other criteria become more important, however, when most competitors are equally competent in maintaining quality control.

Competitive Aspects. It may seem almost axiomatic to assume that a company prefers to purchase from suppliers that are not competitors. However, in a commercial environment characterized by diversification and conglomerate industry, this buying influence is more likely to be overemphasized than underemphasized by the unskilled analyst.

Price. The most obvious of all buying influences, price, may also be the most transitory. Furthermore, it may seem so obvious to the marketing image analyst that more significant influences are missed. The ramifications of price may be complex. For example, the price advantage may appear to be an extra service or extra quality benefit to the uninitiated when it actually translates to a price advantage.

Entertainment. Entertaining customers may include acts as subtle as an invitation to lunch when both parties know each other well or as obvious as expensive gifts or vacations at company-owned resorts. In some markets, that which is acceptable or contributes to a favorable image may differ greatly from that which does the same in another market. Hence the use of entertainment in various forms may contribute either favorably or unfavorably to the supplier's image.

Advertising and Promotion. In industrial marketing, unlike consumer marketing, the influence of advertising, promotional literature, and other informational or promotional devices such as models and exhibits may be the most difficult to measure for contribution to the buyer-seller relationship, even though the objective of such use may be the definition or creation of marketing image.

Many factors influence a marketing image, and some are more important than others. The list primarily indicates the complexity of the factors that motivate the buying decision. To the degree that they characterize the supplier's activities, the analyst can develop the supplier marketing image for a product, market, or geographic area.

THE FIELD INVESTIGATION

Discovering the key buying influences that characterize the market and the ways in which each of a group of major competitors use those influences is the purpose of the field investigation part of a marketing image study. This requires a skilled analyst to visit personally a predetermined sample of the companies comprising the market, a sample that is chosen with regard to the geographic balance desired and that includes both customers and noncustomers of the supplier whose image is sought. Because the image relates the marketing effectiveness of the supplier of primary concern to the images of major competitors, the well-designed and well-executed marketing image study portrays the image of each major competitor separately.

Differences in emphasis result largely from the perspective and facts developed. That is, the marketing image study does not seek the image of one supplier but the images of competitive suppliers, all of which are interrelated. For example, there is limited value in describing a company as one with a record of prompt deliveries from local warehouses. Its record must be compared with that of competitive suppliers. If all major competitors have equivalent records, the image of the initiating company will be quite different than if only half the major competitors are so recognized. We might say, then, that a more descriptive term for an industrial marketing image study would be the study of relative marketing images of major competitors.

The field investigation requires not only establishing a suitable test group of customer and noncustomer accounts but identifying those individuals in each company who wield the most influence on purchasing decisions. The chief executive may make that decision in some companies. In others it may be made in the purchasing department, often the third echelon from the top. Research and development or engineering personnel may have a critical voice. The decision may be made by a mill superintendent without headquarters' interference, or it may be imposed by headquarters. In any event the field interviewer must determine the key individuals and include them in the interviews. Their testimony will provide critical insights that a single interview in a company may never reveal.

The Interview

Although it may be possible to obtain some elements of a marketing image from a structured mail questionnaire, the odds against it are too great to warrant using it for the type of study discussed here. Furthermore, even a structured questionnaire personally delivered has limited opportunity for developing in the respondent the unusual insights necessary for optimum differentiation of marketing strategies and capabilities of a group of competitive suppliers.

The optimum environment occurs when the interviewer (1) knows the respondent and his organization, (2) understands the nature and technology of his business, (3) is trusted by the respondent to guard the discussion's confidential elements, and (4) can keep the initiating company unidentified through most or all of the interview. Even with such an optimum environment, the value of simple, direct answers to questions is limited. The in-depth interview providing the respondent with adequate opportunity to express subtle nuances of meaning is of maximum benefit. Frequently it is not what the respondent says but what he means that is important. For this reason a degree of understanding and confidence between interviewer and respondent must be established if less obvious factors are to be probed and developed.

Direct questions can quickly put the situation in perspective, although it may be inappropriate to ask them initially. To learn which suppliers are preferred, it is necessary to know which of the group of competitive companies are selling to the respondent company. The direct question of which suppliers are significant and what their shares are may not only be rebuffed but may result in guarded future responses. An initial question on which of the competitive companies call regularly or appear most interested in developing the account may lead more casually to a discussion of suppliers than a direct question. Correlation of the more responsive suppliers with shares of business will often develop subsequently. Whether such basic information is gained directly or indirectly depends on the interview's environment and the familiarity of the parties involved.

To learn subsequently the real reasons for supplier preference is closer to the study's purpose. To ask the respondent on what basis suppliers are chosen by his company often results in platitudes about quality, price, and service. Therefore, it may be better to inquire about changes in supplier pattern that have occurred over the years—a discussion that may lead to insights about the *real* reasons why such changes have occurred. It is the interviewer's skill and experience that develop ultimate recognition of these real reasons.

It may be extremely important to learn how competitive salesmen differ on capability and impact. To ask which suppliers have the best sales representatives frequently prompts the useless response that all are good. To lead the conversation to the subject of competitive salesmen by asking which companies have changed salesmen most frequently may be more successful because it is relatively noncontroversial. The desired inputs will, one hopes, be derived piece by piece with further discussion.

Thus each interview may follow a different pattern. With some respondents it becomes apparent that almost any direct question will receive a direct, meaningful response. It is more probable, however, that maximum information will be achieved through an unstructured, in-depth discussion of many facets of the competitive environment. The skilled interviewer quickly learns with experience the most fruitful opening questions for a specific study and the most effective routes to their amplification. However, the basic environment, previously described, for a successful exchange must exist if much is to be accomplished. It is unreasonable to expect candor from the respondent when this is unwarranted. Therefore it is important to have both the environmental conditions and the kinds of questions that nourish candor which, when even incomplete, permits well-founded deductions.

All this discussion of individual interviews relates only to the basic inputs from the work involved in the study. Of equal importance is their eventual analysis, which develops the patterns of the different marketing images of a group of competitors. It usually requires multiple interviews to determine the pattern of competitive suppliers of a single respondent company. It is the patterns of groups of respondent companies—for example, geographic groups or market groups—that translate into the marketing images of the suppliers thereto.

EXAMPLES OF MARKETING IMAGE STUDIES

The following examples of values derived from marketing image studies may serve to clarify their use:

Case A

The management of one of a half dozen major suppliers of a line of chemicals to paper mills suspected that its field salesmen were making less progress in developing new accounts than competitive salesmen and that market share was static even though sales were growing at a rate commensurate with the growth of the paper industry. A consultant organization was employed which had good rapport with paper companies and had served several major paper producers; it actually had more than a casual acquaintance with mill production and technical personnel.

Through a series of meetings with these mill production and technical personnel, it was possible to learn differences in the sales approach of salesmen from a series of selected companies, including the supplier with the problem. This was done without disclosing which company initiated the investigation; in fact, this anonymity was essential to the respondents' objectivity.

The investigation developed a detailed profile of the full marketing approach with which each supplier dealt with the market. It indicated that although much basic purchasing policy may be formulated at paper company headquarters, in many companies considerable authority resides at the mill level to choose among approved suppliers on the basis of local conditions—for example, grades of pulp used and types of paper produced. It was learned that mill operating and technical personnel use the product suggestions of salesmen when they are known through experience to be practical. Some chemical suppliers took advantage of this by hiring salesmen with paper mill experience.

The company which instigated the investigation, however, chose its chemical salesmen for all markets on a well-organized basis, selecting personable young men with technical degrees in chemistry or chemical engineering and providing them with a year's training course in the appropriate company laboratory. Its salesmen for the paper industry received excellent training in the applications of its chemicals used in paper production. However, this training did not establish the same bond of familiarity with the mill personnel as the experience of competitive salesmen who had actual mill experience.

Able to compare its image with competition and relate that image to its program for procurement and training of salesmen, the supplier company revised its policy for selecting paper chemical salesmen without changing its general policies for other markets. In time it achieved the mill rapport necessary for increased market penetration.

Case B

The management of a supplier of machinery to plants manufacturing synthetic rubber was the recognized leader in its field. However, from the three or four plants in one of its territories it was not achieving the expected volume of new orders. The district sales manager had a proven record of success in other districts.

A competent consultant was selected, a company having done considerable technical and organizational work for the rubber industry, including manufacturers of synthetic rubber. Anonymously and objectively, several interviews were conducted with purchasing, engineering, manufacturing, and general management personnel who determined the suppliers from whom equipment was ordered. It was learned how this purchasing pattern had changed over the past two-year period, why some previous suppliers were used less frequently, and what strengths new suppliers exhibited.

As a result of the interviews it became clear that one of the companies—actually the acknowledged leader—was losing its position because of the subjective feeling of operational management that this supplier was less responsive to service requests than it had been. The negative aspects were never serious enough to develop into formal complaints. The problem was viewed as one of degree, and the feelings involved were too subjective to document when the supplier inquired why he was not given some orders.

With this image of the problem as viewed by the buying organizations, the machinery company pinpointed as the cause of the problem certain district office relationships, specifically those between the sales and service departments. The trouble was isolated as a personality problem. By transferring one individual to another district, the situation was corrected.

This case emphasizes the reluctance of many organizations to disclose minor subjective problems to the supplier, even though these same problems relate importantly to the buying decision. To an impartial, trusted third party, such elements of each supplier's image can be disclosed, particularly when the respondents' names are not given and remain confidential.

Retail Research

Chapter 1

Consumer Images of Retail Institutions

ROBERT G. WYCKHAM *Simon Fraser University, British Columbia, Canada*

Current management and research interest in the influence of consumers' attitudes and images in store selection and rejection is based on much historical precedent. At the turn of this century, Scott [25] investigated the psychological factors influencing consumer patronage behavior. In an early issue of the *Journal of Retailing*, Kenneth Collins argued that because every store has an "individuality that distinguishes it from its competitors," it must devise strategy "to get its individuality across to some portion of the buying public" [4, p. 10]. Somewhat later Edwards and Howard [6, p. 162] encouraged retailers to use institutional advertising to create an exciting store personality, dramatize its position in the community, and build confidence in its merchandise and services. More recently, the renowned Texas retailer Stanley Marcus expressed the thoughts of many retail executives about their own institutions when he said that Nieman-Marcus is a "state of mind, not just a store" [18, p. 185]. It is this state of mind, or retail image, that will be pursued here.

In this chapter retail images will be discussed in reference to four questions:

1. Given that management is concerned with its image, how can that image be measured?

2. Based on awareness of the current image, operational reality, and corporate objectives, what image do store executives want consumers to hold?

3. In what ways can the present image be changed to concur with the desired image?

4. What long-run strategy and measurement steps are necessary to assure a measure of control over the retail institution's image?

RETAIL IMAGE MEASUREMENT

Image measurement must be based on some implicit or explicit model of consumer behavior and the part played by images in that behavior. To this end, a simple notion of consumer decision making espoused by a number of marketing scientists and a model of image creation, maintenance, and change will be discussed in this section.

Consumer decision making may be described as a process of matching self-images with the images of relevant market objects: brands, products, manufacturers, or retailers. Where there is some degree of congruence of the individual's self-image and his image of a market object, the evidence indicates that positive behavior toward that object will result [7, 20, 29]. In other words, consumers tend to patronize those stores which they feel are somewhat like themselves.

Acceptance of the premise of this model by the retailer researcher necessitates measurement of consumers' images of the store and measurement of consumers' self-images. Or, alternatively, it may necessitate segmenting the consumer population into groups by demographic characteristics or patronage practices based on differences in images of the retail institution. The model also points out the uncomfortable fact that images are individual phenomena and must be aggregated by the marketing scientist to form *the* image of a particular store.

A consumer's image of a store is the summation of his attitudes towards various aspects of that store. It is necessary, therefore, to discuss the factors influencing the development of these attitudes. Figure 1 depicts the process of attitude formation and the resultant image (defined as a constellation of attitudes). Attitude and image formation take place within and are affected by the physiological, sociological, and psychological environments. Within these environments the individual's perception, motivation, interpersonal response traits, and concept of self interact to form attitude toward various dimensions of the attitude object. These attitudes in turn affect the person's perception, motivation, interpersonal response traits, and self-concept. The summation of all relevant attitudes is termed the image of the object, in this case the image of a retail institution.

This paradigm is based on the literature of attitudes in psychology and sociology. Sherif wrote that "The first stage in attitude formation . . . is the perceptual stage" [26, p. 5]. Perception is the process of organizing the sensory data by which the individual gives meaning to objects, persons, and situations. Research by social scientists of many disciplines has shown the impact of social and individual factors on perception. For example, perceptual differences attributed to status in the family [28], social class membership [21], and education [23] have been reported. A person's behavior is directed by what he perceives his world to be, but why he acts in a particular fashion depends on his motivation. Needs, the internal component of motivation, arouse, direct, and integrate behavior. Incentives, or goals, are external and influence the direction of behavior. Interpersonal response traits are influenced by the individual's self-concept and interact with perception and motivation in the formation of attitudes [15, p. 104]. These interpersonal reactions are akin to the concept of self. Both are socially derived. But while self-concept denotes the totality of an individual's evaluation of himself, interpersonal traits describe the person's tendencies to respond to others in characteristic ways.

The interaction of these four psychological processes results in what Allport describes as an attitude: "a mental . . . state of readiness, organized through experience, exerting a directive . . . influence upon the individual's response to all objects and situations with which it is related" [1]. It is the aggregation of these attitudes formed by an individual's experience (real, vicarious, or imagined) with the multitude of facets of a retail institution that is defined here as his image of that store.

Retail Image Dimensions. In order, therefore, to measure the image of a retail institution, it is necessary to identify and aggregate the relevant consumer attitudes. Numerous studies have reported on the factors influencing consumer attitudes toward stores in terms of shopping practices [24] and in terms of store characteristics [2, p. 10; 3, pp. 113–114; 12, p. 83]. Perhaps the most lucid presentation is Fisk's "Conceptual Model" [9], in which he summarizes store qualities as cognitive dimensions of a store image (see Table 1). These dimensions may be used to identify relevant attitudes and assist in the development of a measurement instrument.

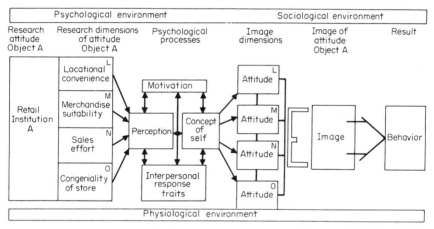

Fig. 1.   Image development.   (*Adapted from Wyckham [29], p. 334.*)

Measuring Image Components. Attitude, the image component, is a hypothetical or latent variable rather than an immediately observable variable, and so it must be inferred from behavior. Measures of attitudes are derived by reasoning from the subject's reports of his beliefs, feelings, and behavior; from observed overt behavior; from interpretations of ambiguous material; from task performance; and from physiological reactions [5].

The six principal scaling methods for attitude measurement are (1) the Thurstone technique of equal appearing intervals; (2) the Likert method of summated ratings; (3) the Bogardus social distance scale; (4) the Guttman process of cumulative scaling; (5) Edwards and Kilpatrick's scale discrimination technique; and (6) Osgood's semantic differential. [See Section III, Part A, Chapters 2 and 5.]

From published reports it appears that most researchers of retail corporate images have used some variation on the semantic differential or adjective checklist techniques. It is not the purpose of this chapter to discuss in detail the various attitude-image measuring methods. However, the following should serve as a guide in selecting an appropriate measurement device:

1.   An image measure should provide a "quick, efficient means of obtaining

in a readily quantifiable form, and for large samples, the direction and intensity of opinions and attitudes" [22].

2. The device chosen should allow analysis of all the dimensions of the image [22].

3. A measurement technique must yield reliable data, that is, results which are dependable, accurate, and relatively free from errors of measurement [14, pp. 429–443].

4. In analyzing the validity of an instrument, three questions should be asked. Does it measure what it purports to measure? Has the predictive validity of the test been checked against some predetermined outcome? Can the differences in individual test scores be explained by accepted theory [14, pp. 444–462]?

TABLE 1   Department Store Image

Cognitive dimension	Determinant
1. Locational convenience	(1) access routes, (2) traffic barriers, (3) traveling time, (4) parking availability
2. Merchandise suitability	(1) number of brands stocked, (2) quality of lines, (3) breadth of assortment, (4) depth of assortment, (5) number of outstanding departments in the store
3. Value for price	(1) price of a particular item in a particular store, (2) price of same item in another store, (3) price of same item in substitute store, (4) trading stamps and discounts
4. Sales effort and store services	(1) courtesy of sales clerks, (2) helpfulness of sales-clerks, (3) reliability and usefulness of advertising, (4) billing procedures, (5) adequacy of credit arrangements, (6) delivery promptness and care, (7) eating facilities
5. Congeniality	(1) store layout, (2) store decor, (3) merchandise displays, (4) class of customers, (5) store traffic and congestion
6. Posttransaction satisfaction	(1) satisfaction with goods in use, (2) satisfaction with returns and adjustments, (3) satisfaction with price paid, (4) satisfaction with accessibility to store

5. For a variety of reasons, subjects may be inclined to be deceptive or to rationalize their responses to attitude measures [1, p. 836]. The popularity of indirect and disguised techniques has resulted in part from this.

6. Researchers may obtain from subjects answers which purport to be attitudes but which are really only responses to the measuring instrument [15, p. 176]. Some students of image measurement advise that, in order to avoid stereotyped responses, data be obtained only from respondents who are familiar with the attitude object.

7. Forcing attitude structures into scales may result in unnatural or unrealistic descriptions. Factor analysis should be used in developing and pretesting attitude scales to ensure their meaningfulness.

8. Haley's outline of the advantages of attitude scaling [11] provides a means of assessing the characteristics of other measurement techniques:

   a. The quasi-game situation encourages respondent participation.

   b. Many items may be evaluated quickly, thus reducing subject fatigue.

   c. The influence of respondent articulateness is minimized.

d.   Uniformity of stimulus produces reliable results.

e.   Interviewer bias is controlled.

f.   Precoding of answers ensures correct classification of results and quick and easy tabulation.

REALITY AND CORPORATE OBJECTIVES

The term *image* conjures up a variety of meanings.   Some may consider the image of a retail corporation to be an artificial veil created by advertising and public relations, a screen set up to hide the real people, products, and services of the store.   The purpose of this veil is to deceive the consuming public into believing that the store is different than it really is.   It is assumed that, because the store's image is relatively stable, various activities detrimental to the public's interest can be carried on behind this image with impunity.

The retail image may also be interpreted to be akin to a rosy glow which, while not obscuring reality, tends to create an illusion of quality and warmth. This rosy glow, it is argued, provides an atmosphere within which consumers are happy to be overcharged, to overlook the inadequacies of sales personnel, and to forgive delivery and billing errors easily.   Management is under no pressure, therefore, to adjust store operations to fit consumer wants, because the image assuages any customer unhappiness.

Another description of a retail image would indicate that it is a reflection of reality; the result of personal exposure to the multitude of factors which make up a retail institution.   It is the individual's interpretation of product quality, store congeniality, product return policies, and advertising messages.   It is influenced by the kinds of people he sees as the store's customers and is affected by the opinions of friends and relatives.   The operational reality of the store, in the long run, must be compatible with the consumer's image, or he will change his image.   Executive action on image matters, therefore, must be related to changes in the way the store attempts to satisfy consumer demands.

There is, no doubt, some truth in all these views of the retail image.   In the short run it is usually possible to delude some portion of the consuming public. Activities at this extreme make interesting if repulsive reading in newspapers and Better Business Bureau reports.

It is also feasible to create an atmosphere which assists the shopper to believe what he or she wants to believe.   Out-of-towners are frequently amazed at the inadequacies of "the best store in town."   They are not burdened with what Martineau has called the "halo effect" which imparts attributes to the store which are not wholly real.   This may in part be due to the stability of images which are slow to adjust to new realities.   But adjust they do, as is evidenced by the numbers of retail executives concerned with retaining customer patronage in a changing market situation.

Retail image problems are compounded by the high degree of consumer intimacy with and awareness of the institution.   Unlike the manufacturer whose primary contact with the consuming public is through products and advertising, the retailer relates directly to the consumer through physical premises, employees, products, and services.   Thus, customers develop personal images of retail institutions based on firsthand experience.

The first step in image analysis for the retailer who has a picture of how the public perceives his institution is an investigation of corporate objectives and store operations.   It is highly likely that differences will be found in the way that various store executives interpret corporate objectives.   This may result in operating practices which foster image confusion.   For example, the merchandising vice president may be oriented toward buying and displaying a quality array of products while the director of advertising may emphasize price in promoting those goods. Studies by Social Research, Inc., tend to support this contention [17]. Conflicting activities within the store may result in an image which lacks "sharp definition" and restricts market penetration. Unclear imagery may also hinder the development of customer loyalty by promoting a tendency for consumers to shift from store to store [13].

The problems of image confusion are especially serious for the retail institution with a number of outlets each designed to appeal to different market segments. Members of each of these market segments have different needs and expectations which must be taken into consideration in planning the retail institution, its products, decor, and services. These operational realities plus the differences in each outlet's customer population will mean a multiplicity of images. Heidingsfield has suggested that a potential solution to this problem lies in development of a corporate image with which each of the outlet images has a degree of compatibility [13]. Decentralization of outlet management and the dynamics of the marketplace will make image confusion a continuing problem for retail management.

A second step in retail image and analysis involves a comparison of the images of the store held by company executives with those held by the consumer population. Martineau says that "In virtually every area we have studied, we find the biggest discrepancies imaginable between what the company thinks of itself—the image it believes it is presenting to the public—and the way the customer actually sees it" [18, p. 174]. A lack of common understanding of the image of the business will make decisions about what the store image ought to be even more difficult.

Perceptual Market Segmentation. Having established the degree of compatibility among the images held by store executives and those held by the overall consumer population, the next step in image analysis is comparison of the images held by differing market segments. A large number of surveys and experiments have produced evidence to support the following:

1. Consumers in different social classes hold differing images of particular stores [2, p. 11; 12, p. 79; 16, p. 4]. Gardner, however, disagrees: "The image of a . . . [store] . . . does not vary from group to group . . ." [10, p. 147]. This position is supported in part by a study by Lazer and Wyckham which indicated a communality of images among all social classes for one of three test department stores [16]. Most students of images, however, would support Martineau's contention that "there is no such thing as a store image with equal appeal . . . for all social classes" [19, p. 50].

2. Differentiable images of particular department stores may or may not be held by consumers at different stages of the family life cycle. Collazzo argued that consumers' attitudes are affected by life-cycle stage [3, p. 66]. Wyckham, however, reported that little difference could be found among images held at various stages except where comparisons among nonadjacent stages were made [29, p. 336].

3. Comparisons of retail images held by white and nonwhite consumers tend to show differences in images of particular stores [29, p. 336]. These differences, however, tend not to be as great as the variability among social classes.

4. Little difference has been found in retail image comparisons between sexes [29, p. 36].

5. Consumers who like to shop hold favorably different images of individual stores compared to consumers who do not like to shop. It is not known whether the shopping attitude affects the image of the store or vice versa [29].

6.   Image comparisons among consumers who like to shop alone and those who like to have company while shopping indicate little differentiability of retail images [29].   This finding is significant in view of the high proportion of shopping done by husbands and wives together [27].

7.   Comparisons among consumers whose friends support their beliefs about a particular store with those whose friends do not support their beliefs result in differences on some image dimensions [29].

8.   Loyal store customers have favorably different images compared to occasional customers and noncustomers [12, p. 79; 20, p. 53; 29, p. 336].

9.   Regular readers of a store's advertisements have more favorable images than those who sometimes or never read the ads [2, 29].

10.   Consumers' store image differences do not appear to be associated with shopping recency, location of shopping within the store (regular versus basement merchandise), or payment method (cash versus credit) [29].

A final step in image analysis suggested by Mindak [22, p. 30] is the comparison of the aggregate consumer image and/or images held by various market segments with a hypothetical "ideal" store.   This has the advantage of providing an indication of the direction and distance the retail institution must travel in order to achieve a degree of perfection in the eyes of consumers.   The effect of the use of the notion of the ideal store may simply be to invoke a comparison with the store perceived as best in the consumer's experience.   This in itself would be advantageous.

It may be argued, however, that because the individual store is attempting to create a distinct personality for itself, comparisons with the ideal are not useful.   Corporate objectives may not be compatible with the ideal.   For example, there may be a significant difference between the image of the store and the image of the ideal store on the depth of product lines.   This may simply reflect a definite policy of management.

CHANGING THE RETAIL IMAGE

It is obvious from the discussion to this point that the major component of any image-change process must be adjustment of operating practices to conform with the desired image.   Although the trade papers are replete with image-change success stories, there is little research evidence to support their contentions.   The notion that changes of advertising theme, company name, interior decor, or corporate logo individually and in and of themselves can make substantial changes in the consumers' image of the store is dangerous.   It masks the real problem; the problem of providing the total package of need satisfiers demanded by consumers in a way which is congruent with their expectations.

The researcher of retail images must go beyond the simple descriptive phase of portraying what the store image is.   The question of why the image is as it is must be attacked.   Those factors which are most important in the development of consumers' images must be discovered.   This may require adjustment of what are believed to be the critical components of the store's need-satisfier mix in order to point out those which have the greatest influence on the consumers' perception of the institution.   The vast literature of consumer behavior in retail situations can assist in this search.

At this point in the image-change process, management may be forced to make a trade-off.   It has been pointed out here that various consumer segments hold varying images of a particular store.   On the basis of this it may be assumed that, individually, consumers respond to the same stimulus (the store's package of need satisfiers) in different ways. Hence, a change in the makeup of the store's need-satisfier mix may result in widely differing effects among various consumer groups. This may necessitate a decision to trade off a more favorable image response from one group of consumers for a less favorable image response from another group. The "symbols of extremely high fashion and upper class atmosphere are literally warning the middle-income and lower-income woman that she will be out of place here, that the other customers and certainly the clerks will make her feel altogether uncomfortable" [18, p. 175]. It is important, therefore, to consider both positive and negative results in designing an image change program.

The use of promotion devices as the primary factor in changing retail images has been questioned here. It is important, however, to recognize the vital role played by mass and face-to-face communications in image creation and maintenance. Informing consumers, especially noncustomers, through advertising of adjustments in the store's operating procedures increases awareness and is the first step in image change. This contention is supported by research results reported previously which indicate that loyal customers and regular readers of a store's advertisements hold more favorable images than occasional customers and noncustomers or than those who read advertisements irregularly.

Advertising is also the first stage in the multistep flow of information through opinion leaders, followers, and reference groups which affects face-to-face communication. The importance of interpersonal communication is evidenced by the more favorable store images held by consumers whose friends agree with their image of the store.

Martineau has argued forcibly that retailers pay too little attention to the nonverbal flows of information which influence the way that consumers see the store [18, p. 175]. The media, the design and style of copy, the promotion themes, and the use of color are symbols which tell the consumer much about the store. This can be seen in the results of a Social Research, Inc., study which showed that women who judged a store only by its advertisements (with identification omitted) described it almost identically with women who knew the store [18, p. 175].

LONG-RUN IMAGE STRATEGY

By its very nature, the retail image program must be long-run in design and execution. There is a great deal of evidence that attitudes tend to be static, to resist change, and to change in tiny adjustments over considerable time [1]. This suggests that any attempt to change the image of a retail institution will likely be expensive (although there is conflicting evidence) [18, pp. 178–179] and require a long-run strategy of operational change and promotion consistent with the desired image.

A major decision point in developing an image strategy results from the conflict of store differentiation and market segmentation. It has been pointed out in this chapter that a distinctive image is a necessary component of a successful store. There is much research showing that consumers do distinguish among stores on the basis of image [3, p. 1; 24, Chapter 7; 29, p. 335]. Particular actions, then, are necessary for the individual retailer to differentiate his store from those of his competitors.

Decisions on store differentiation must be rationalized with those concerning market segmentation. It has been shown that consumers' images differ depending on their membership in various demographic and shopping practice groups. How and where store differentiation image strategy conflicts with actions designed to develop appeals to various market segments is a topic worthy of management concern and research emphasis.

To digress, in designing image strategy it is worth considering Evans' suggestion to create a somewhat ambiguous image in order to allow consumers to read into the image what they want. He based this on his research which indicated no evidence of strong images attracting particular types of people [8]. To accept this strategy is to ignore the basis of the image (operational reality) and to abandon whatever small degree of control is obtainable through promotion.

A necessary ingredient in the long-run image program is a continual monitoring of the store's image. This is consistent with the notion of image change as a process of tiny steps over an extended period. It is also in agreement with the systems concept of the firm which indicates the necessity of continuous feedback of environmental information.

It appears from the literature that, in large part, image studies are considered special research problems and are designed and executed to fit particular needs at a point in time. Some commercial research firms do offer continuous image data gathering and analysis, but acceptance has not been widespread. Implementation of continuous image monitoring offers the obvious advantage of a moving picture of the store's image over time. A measure of the firm's success in meeting its image objectives is provided. Image changes over time can be associated with actions and events at points in the period. It is probable that average costs per unit input of information will be lower, that refinements in image measurement and analysis will be obtained, and that decisions made on image data will be more consistent and oriented to the long term.

REFERENCES

1. Allport, G. W., "Attitudes," in Carl Murchison, ed., A Handbook of Social Psychology, Worcester, Mass.: Clark University Press, 1935.
2. Arons, L., "Does T.V. Viewing Influence Store Image and Shopping Frequency?" Journal of Retailing, vol. 37, Fall 1961.
3. Collazzo, C. J., Jr., Consumer Attitudes and Frustrations in Shopping, New York: National Retail Merchants Association, 1963.
4. Collins, K., "Institutional Advertising," Journal of Retailing, vol. 3, April 1927.
5. Cook, S. W., and C. Selltiz, "A Multiple-Indicator Approach to Attitude Measurement," Psychological Bulletin, vol. 62, July 1964.
6. Edwards, C. M., Jr., and W. H. Howard, Retail Advertising and Sales Promotion, Englewood Cliffs, N.J.: Prentice Hall, 1936.
7. Engel, J. F., "Motivation Research—Magic or Menace?" Michigan Business Review, vol. 13, March 1961.
8. Evans, F. B., "Psychological and Objective Factors in the Prediction of Brand Choice: Ford versus Chevrolet," Journal of Business, vol. 32, October 1959.
9. Fisk, G., "A Conceptual Model for Studying Consumer Image," Journal of Retailing, vol. 37, Winter 1961–1962.
10. Gardner, B. B., "Behavioral Sciences as Related to Image Building," in F. E. Webster, Jr., ed., New Directions in Marketing, Chicago: American Marketing Association, 1965.
11. Haley, R. I., "New Insights into Attitude Measurement," in F. E. Webster, Jr., ed., New Directions in Marketing, Chicago: American Marketing Association, 1965.
12. Harris, L. M., and Mass Observation, Ltd., Buyers Market: How to Prepare for the New Era in Marketing, London: Business Publications, Ltd., 1963.
13. Heidingsfield, M. S., "Building the Image—An Essential Marketing Stratagem," in F. E. Webster, Jr., ed., New Directions in Marketing, Chicago: American Marketing Association, 1965.

14. Kerlinger, F. N., *Foundations of Behavioral Research*, New York: Holt, 1965.
15. Krech, D., R. S. Crutchfield, and E. L. Ballachy, *Individual in Society*, New York: McGraw-Hill, 1962.
16. Lazer, W., and R. G. Wyckham, "Perceptual Segmentation of Department Store Markets," *Journal of Retailing*, vol. 45, Summer 1969.
17. McCann, C. B., *Women and Department Store Newspaper Advertising*, Chicago: Social Research, Inc., 1964.
18. Martineau, P., *Motivation in Advertising*, New York: McGraw-Hill, 1957.
19. ———, "The Personality of the Department Store," *Harvard Business Review*, vol. 36, January–February 1958.
20. ———, "Sharper Focus for the Corporate Image," *Harvard Business Review*, vol. 36, November–December 1958.
21. ———, "Social Class and Spending Behavior," *Journal of Marketing*, vol. 23, 1958.
22. Mindak, W. A., "Fitting the Semantic Differential to Marketing Problems," *Journal of Marketing*, vol. 25, April 1961.
23. Munn, H. L., "Brand Perception as Related to Age, Income and Education," *Journal of Marketing*, vol. 24, January 1960.
24. Rich, S. U., *Shopping Behavior of Department Store Customers*, Boston: Harvard University, Graduate School of Business, Division of Research, 1963.
25. Scott, W. D., *The Theory of Advertising*, Boston: Small Maynard and Company, 1904.
26. Sherif, M., "A Study of Some Social Factors in Perception," *Archives of Psychology*, vol. 187, July 1935.
27. *The Sixth Du Pont Consumer Buying Habits Study*, E. I. duPont de Nemours & Co., Inc.
28. Wolgast, E., "Do Husbands or Wives Make the Purchasing Decisions?" *Journal of Marketing*, vol. 23, October 1958.
29. Wyckham, R. G., "Aggregate Department Store Images: Social and Experiential Factors," in Reed Moyer, ed., *Changing Marketing Systems*, Chicago: American Marketing Association, 1967.

Part E
Retail Research

Chapter 2

Determining Store Trade Areas

WILLIAM APPLEBAUM and **HOWARD L. GREEN** *Nova University, Fort Lauderdale, Florida,* and *Howard L. Green & Associates, Inc., Bloomfield Hills, Michigan.*

The purpose of this[1] chapter is twofold. First, it reviews the principles upon which the analysis of retail trade areas is based. And second, the chapter describes techniques used to study retail trade areas.

THE THEORETICAL FOUNDATION—FACTORS WHICH CREATE TRADE AREAS

A store's or shopping district's trade area is the geographic area from which the retailer draws its customers. The theory of trade areas has been stated many times under a variety of names—Reilly's law, gravity models, central place theory, Huff's laws, and so on. The basic premise of each of these formulations, however, can be summarized as follows: The consumer will tend to shop at the first intervening retail opportunity (from the point of trip origin) that provides merchandising equivalent to his expectations.

Let us examine this statement to determine what it implies. First, since most shopping trips originate at home and the customer tends to travel the least distance to purchase the desired merchandise, a store or shopping district will tend to obtain as its customers those people who live nearby rather than those who live at greater distances. For example, if all supermarkets were to appeal equally to all consumers and their stores were distributed equally over an area, then each store's trade area would be roughly the same hexagonal shape, with the trade-area boundaries of each equidistant between the two

---

[1] The authors acknowledge the assistance of Herbert J. Harlton, associate in the marketing research and consulting firm of Howard L. Green & Associates, Inc., Bloomfield Hills, Michigan.

stores. The sales of each store would differ only because of the number of people in each trade area.

Despite this theoretical uniformity, however, actual store trade areas do differ. The factors which create these distortions are fourfold:

1. Each store differs in its merchandising appeal.

2. Each consumer, because of economic and demographic differences, differs in what he or she wants from a store.

3. Accessibility to each store differs to some extent, making some stores physically easier to get to than others.

4. The size of the trade area of those stores located in retail shopping districts will vary depending on the size of that shopping district.

Let us explain these differences further. First, all stores differ in their merchandising appeal because each retailer attempts to attract customers to his store. The techniques he uses may be wider variety, a more attractive facility, more imaginative sales promotion, lower prices, greater service, or any combination of factors. To the extent that the merchant is successful, he will create a desire on the part of the customer to shop at his store. If to do so a customer may have to bypass other, more convenient stores, a distortion in the trade area—in this case an enlargement of the area—is created.

A second distortion in the size or shape of a store's trade area is created by the economic and demographic composition of the area's residents. Poor people, for instance, are less mobile because they possess fewer automobiles per family. So, while they may desire to shop at a more attractive but more distant store, they may lack the mobility to get there. Hence, for them the first intervening opportunity may be the neighborhood store within walking distance.

Unequal accessibility is another distorting influence upon trade area. As an example, while downtown shopping may offer the greater assortments, traffic congestion and the lack of free parking may divert the shopper to a regional shopping center instead. Another such cause of trade-area distortion may be a narrow surface street which, while it may be a short and direct route to a department store, is so congested that the shopper is unwilling to use it. Hence she makes a longer trip along an uncongested expressway to another department store.

Finally, the size of the store or the size of the shopping district in which the store is located may create distortions in its trade area. A very large store with a number of unique departments—for example, gourmet section, special fashion goods, a large shoe selection—can draw customers past other similar stores because this store offers something superior to the others. Similarly, the agglomeration of stores or store departments, which together create greater drawing power, can be a distorting influence on trade area.

To recapitulate, trade-area analysis theory is simple to state and provides guidelines of uniformity for the purposes of analysis. However, there are distortions to the size and shape of the store's trade area and to the store's penetration of it that require identification; the quantification of these distortions and the evaluation of their relevance make trade-area analysis the fascinating study it is.

THE MEASUREMENT OF A TRADE AREA

The study of the trade area of a shopping district or of an individual store within that shopping district is the application of theory to the practical business problem of determining the boundaries of the geographic area from which customers are attracted and, in the case of the individual store, evaluating the degree of market penetration in that area. Essentially, trade-area boundaries can be determined in two ways—empirically and theoretically. The empirical method is, however, more accurate and is the only one from which further measurements of penetration can be made. The theoretical techniques lend themselves primarily to the determination of trade-area boundaries (whether of a shopping district or of an individual store within that shopping district). When further analyses of market penetration are required, it is first necessary to determine the store's trade-area boundaries empirically.

The theoretical techniques of trade-area measurements will be discussed first.

Theoretical Methods

There are several techniques by which the trade area boundaries of a region, town, shopping district or individual store can be determined. Two of them— driving time and retail gravitation—are discussed here.

Driving Time. One frequently used technique for estimating a retail trade area, regardless of the size of the retail center, is to measure driving time from the retail center. For example, if it is known that the average customer of a particular retail center will be willing to spend 10 minutes driving to that center, the center's trade area can be determined by estimating how many miles can be covered in 10 minutes. This measurement can be made either by actual driving or by assuming an average speed.

The weaknesses of this method are twofold. First, it implies that one knows how far customers would be willing to travel. This may be difficult to determine. Second, by assuming that people will patronize a store primarily because of the driving time required to get there, it ignores other, more important reasons people patronize certain stores—for example, greater merchandise selection, no nearby alternative, ethnic appeal, and so on. In summary, this technique may be useful to indicate the approximate configuration of a trade area but not to delineate its actual boundaries.

Retail Gravity Models. The most quantitative of the theoretical methods of trade-area determination is the construction of a gravitational model. This technique overcomes some of the weaknesses of the driving-time technique.

An adaptation of Reilly's law of retail gravitation holds that a retail district in competition with another neighboring retail district attracts customers from a rural area in direct proportion to the size of its retail facilities and in inverse proportion to the square of the driving-time distance.

As an example, in estimating the food store trade area of town N, the following facts were used: (1) town N has 25,000 square feet of food store selling area, (2) town O has 50,000 square feet, (3) town P has 25,000 square feet, and (4) town Q has 75,000 feet. Additionally, the time-distance from town N to town O is 70 minutes (7 units), from town N to town P, 23 minutes (2.3 units), from town N to town Q, 60 minutes (6 units). These facts are depicted in Figure 1. The formula that is employed to determine the breaking point in trade between town N and the surrounding three towns is, as applied to town O:

$$x = \frac{\text{total driving time from town N to town O}}{1 + \sqrt{\dfrac{\text{selling area of town O}}{\text{selling area of town N}}}} \tag{1}$$

In this case, x represents the driving time outward from town N. Thus:

$$x = \frac{7 \text{ driving-time units}}{1 + \sqrt{\dfrac{50{,}000}{25{,}000}}}$$

$$= 2.9$$

The boundary line between town N and town O is therefore 2.9 units or 29 minutes from town N. By the same formula, the line extends 11 minutes in the direction of town P and 21 minutes in the direction of town Q. This formula simply affixes the point at which the boundary is to be drawn—that is, the breaking point where trade is evenly divided.

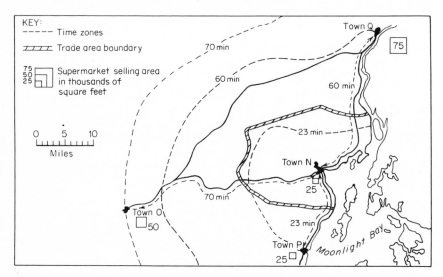

Fig. 1.   **Boundary of a trade area according to the law of retail gravitation.**

The theory of gravity models suffers from several shortcomings. Its greatest weakness is that, in quantifying only distance and size, it ignores the major reason people shop at a given store—merchandising.[2] A second shortcoming is that it is extremely difficult to employ such gravitational models in metropolitan areas. This is because competition is found in so many different directions and at so many different levels of intensity. Also, driving-time distinctions may be only a matter of moments. Under these circumstances, the boundaries of trade areas for specific stores have to be determined individually, generally through an actual "spotting" of customers.

Empirical Method—Customer Spotting

Simply stated, the empirical method of trade-area analysis consists of first determining where a store's customers live, spotting this information on a map, and then quantitatively evaluating the store's trade area.

[2] It should be noted that there have been numerous attempts to incorporate a merchandising variable into gravity models. All, however, suffer the same weakness—quantification of such an intangible factor varies from analysis to analysis, as it is based largely on subjective judgment.

Obtaining Customers' Addresses.   There are a number of sources from which customers' addresses can be obtained.   Two common sources are sales slips and charge accounts.   Other sources are coupons issued in connection with prize drawings at store openings or other promotions, contest entry blanks, delivery receipts, and mailing list.   Yet another source is a parking lot survey to obtain customers' license plate numbers (which can generally be translated into addresses using data supplied by the state department of motor vehicles).

All these methods share two common drawbacks, however.   First, none yields truly representative samples because they tend to draw more heavily from some customer segments than from others.   For example, using charge accounts excludes cash customers, using car license plates excludes those who do not drive to the store, and so on.   Second, the only data these sources yield are customer addresses.   Nonetheless, these sources are useful when in-store customer interviewing (discussed in the following paragraph) is not feasible.

The method which draws the most representative customer sample and also provides an opportunity for the researcher to obtain any other customer information he deems important is the in-store customer interview.   In this method trained interviewers administer a prepared questionnaire to a representative sample of customers while they are in the store.   In this way one can obtain data that indicate not only where customers live but also their demographics and their likes and dislikes about the store.

The proper selection of interviewing days and times and the proper training of interviewers virtually assure the selection of a representative sample.

For supermarkets, it has been found practical to obtain one customer interview per $100 of weekly sales; such sampling is sufficient to adequately delineate the trade area [2, p. 127].   Other store types may require a higher or lower ratio depending on the amount of their average sale.

Careful selection of the actual days and times during which interviews are to be conducted is critical to assure a representative sample.   For most studies the interviewing of customers can be conducted in a one-week period.

Care should be exercised, however, to select as typical a week as possible.   Holiday shopping periods and weeks when the store is running promotions should be avoided because during these times the store's trade area may be distorted.   Typically, it is not necessary to interview for an entire week to obtain a representative sample.   In supermarkets and in general merchandise department stores, for example, over half a store's business generally occurs on Thursday, Friday, and Saturday, and interviews conducted during these days are more likely to yield a representative sample.

It is equally important to interview during all hours the store is open, as its trade area may vary by time of day.   For example, during the day a disproportionate share of the store's customers may be people employed in the immediate area.

It is absolutely necessary to select randomly the customers who are to be interviewed.   To avoid bias in the sample, interviewers should not be allowed to choose the customers they interview.   The interviewer should be given a fixed interviewing schedule.   For example, when there are checkouts (as in a supermarket or discount department store), interviewers should be positioned at each checkout lane and instructed to interview every nth customer (a number predetermined to yield the desired sample size).   When there are too many checkouts, interviewers should be instructed to take a predetermined number of customers from a given line before moving on to another line.   The formalization of the customer-interviewer selection procedure assures that the sample of customers will be as random as possible.

Spotting Customers' Residences. Once the customers' addresses have been determined, they next need to be plotted on a map. This plotting should be done on a large, clear street map of the area which is cross-indexed to show all streets. Also useful for determining the exact location of an address are street guides because they show, by address number, the nearest cross street.

Before spotting, the location of the store should accurately be marked on the map and concentric mile rings should be drawn around it. These rings should represent distances from the site that are known or believed to be significant. For most location types these concentric rings should be drawn out from 3 to 5

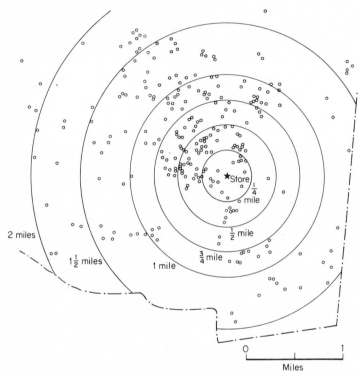

Fig. 2.   Customer spotting map.   Each dot represents a customer.

miles; however, in more densely populated areas, they can be drawn out to only 2 miles; and in rural, sparsely populated areas, they should extend out often as far as 10 miles. In addition, if more detailed analysis is desired, the area around the store may be divided into quadrants (northeast, southeast, southwest, and northwest) and census-tract boundaries may be transposed onto the map.

Once the map has been prepared, each customer's home address should be located on it by a dot. The customer's street can be found by using the map's cross index; the street guide may then be used to locate the nearest cross street. As each survey address is spotted, its distance (and, if desired, its direction and census tract) should be recorded on the questionnaire to facilitate later cross tabulations with the data contained thereon. A completed spotting map is shown in Figure 2.

When all the customers are spotted in this way, the number of dots in each zone and/or geographic segment should be counted and the proportion this represents of the total calculated. These proportions, the store's "drawing power," have been calculated in Table 1 as an example.

TABLE 1   Customers within 5-Mile Trade Area

Mile zone	Number of spotted customers	Drawing power (proportion of total, percent)
0–1	175	35
1–2	125	25
2–3	100	20
3–4	50	10
4–5	25	5
Beyond 5 miles	25	5
Total	500	100

This table and the completed spotting map show quantitatively and graphically the geographic distribution of customers around the store—this is the store's trade area. The techniques by which this trade area can be analyzed are discussed in the next section.

Customers do not always have to be physically "spotted" to determine a store's trade area. For example, when a store has an extremely large trade area—for example, all of a large city—or when accuracy is not a crucial factor, customers may be tabulated according to zip code areas or municipalities. The use of such large areas, however, reduces geographic precision and the reliability of the findings; consequently it is not recommended as a standard practice.

Interpretation. After the store's customers have been spotted, their distribution can be compared with the population distribution and analyzed to determine what effect competition, accessibility, and travel barriers have on the shape and boundaries of the store's trade area and the level of its penetration within that trade area.

It will be noted that the spotted customers are very dense in some sections of the trade area, thinner in other sections, very thin in still other parts of the trade area, and altogether lacking in some sections. The density of this distribution needs to be analyzed—both visually and quantitatively—to determine the relationship with other factors.

Visual comparison of the customer spotting map with a population-distribution/land-use map (such as the one shown in Figure 3) gives a rough indication whether the density of the spotted customers is proportionate to the density of population throughout the store's trade area. Further examination of the city's business centers, major roads, and natural and man-made barriers (bodies of water, cemeteries, parks, and so on) makes possible an interpretation of the size, shape, and character of the store's trade area and gives the analyst a feel for the market. This feel is important in the quantitative evaluation of market penetration.

The first step in the quantitative evaluation of a store's trade area is the calculation of the sales coming to the store from each geographic segment of the trade area.

The sales being made to residents of an area can be determined directly from the previous spotting data. It has been established that a store's drawing power (the proportion of customer transactions coming from a given area as indicated by the spotting) is equivalent to the proportion of the store's sales dollars coming from that same area [2, p. 127]. Hence if, as our spotting showed, 35 percent of the spotted customers come from the first mile zone, then 35 percent of the store's sales volume (weekly, monthly, or annual) also comes from this area. From this information the store's per capita sales and market share—two measures of trade-area penetration—can be calculated.

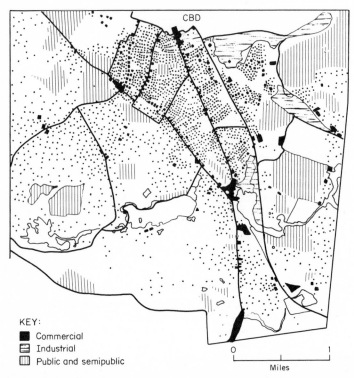

Fig. 3. **Population distribution and land-use map.** Each dot represents 25 people. CBD is city business district.

Per capita sales is an index number used to evaluate the store's penetration in the various segments of its trade area. It represents the *average* dollar amount each person in the trade area spends in the store in a given period (week, month, or year). Hence, the per capita sales in a given geographic market segment can be determined by dividing the sales which are made to residents of that area by the number of people living in that same area (as determined from the population-distribution/land-use map).

Market share is another measure of a store's trade-area penetration. A store's market share of a given segment of its trade area indicates how well that store is performing in that segment relative to its competition. Market share is calculated by dividing the store's sales in each geographic segment of its trade area by the total expenditures made by residents of that segment on merchandise the store sells. The latter figure can be determined from a number of sources. For example, the U.S. Bureau of Labor Statistics estimates that in Chicago a four-person family with an intermediate budget spent $2,325 for food in 1969, or $581 per person.

Table 2 shows by mile zone, for the store in the previous example, drawing power, annual sales volume, population, annual per capita sales, and market share.

TABLE 2   Per Capita Sales and Market Share by Mile Zone

Mile zone	Drawing power proportion of customers, percent	Annual sales volume (000)	Population	Per capita sales	Market share, percent
0–1	35	$1,225	20,000	$61.25	10.5
1–2	25	875	24,000	36.46	6.3
2–3	20	700	31,200	22.44	3.9
3–4	10	350	26,000	13.46	2.3
4–5	5	175	29,400	5.95	1.0
0–5 miles	95	3,325	130,600	25.46	4.4
Beyond 5 miles	5	175			
Total	100	$3,500			

The per capita sales estimates and market shares should be examined to determine where significant variations exist. Normally, as in our example, the per capita sales and market share figures are expected to be largest in the first concentric circle and then to become progressively lower in succeeding circles.

When market penetration is not evenly distributed, several factors should be examined to determine why. The first factor which should be examined is geographic: Is there an intervening natural barrier to traffic, or are the road patterns leading to the stores unfavorable?

Another major factor is competition. A strong competitor or one located in an interceptive position can sharply affect a store's performance. Another factor is different ethnic or income groups in a particular area. All these factors should be examined by the analyst in evaluating the store's performance, as such knowledge is quite useful in solving location problems.

Use of Findings. When the store characteristics, market factors, consumer shopping behavior, and sales are statistically quantified and related as described in the previous sections, this record of experience becomes an "analogue"—a benchmark for reference. Given these analogues, a retailer is much better equipped to solve problems, which heretofore were solved by "educated" guessing. For example, should a retailer find that he is not covering certain sections of a city with his established stores, he can, using these analogues to estimate potential sales, evaluate the advisability of opening an additional store there.

The sales of this proposed store can be estimated by referring to the research department's files[3] to locate an analogous situation and then applying these

[3] The research department should conduct trade-area studies for each of its stores and have the findings readily accessible.

data to the new location. For example, suppose a discount chain wishes to open a new unit at a site in a section of the city in which it does not yet have a store. Examination of the area discloses that it is made up of younger families with higher incomes. Further, there are only two competing discount stores within the proposed store's trade area—one immediately across the street from the site, the other a mile away. The researcher, in looking through his files of trade-area studies, finds that his company has stores in two similar shopping centers in other sections of town. Both these units have the same competitors as would this new unit; however, they are not located at the same proximity.

The experienced analyst can, by examining the analogs for these stores and comparing them with the facts he has about the new site, synthesize a third set of drawing power and per capita sales figures predicting the new store's performance. These per capita sales figures, when multiplied by their respective population estimates, will yield an estimate of the sales that the new unit should achieve. These estimates can then be "plugged into" a pro forma income statement to determine the profitability of the new unit. Knowing the proposed unit's sales and profitability, the analyst can then evaluate the advisability of opening it.

In addition to using this information generated from trade-area analysis for store location decisions, retailers can also apply these data to planning and evaluating their advertising programs. A detailed knowledge of a store's trade area is valuable to any intelligent advertising program. If a competitor threatens to encroach upon a part of the trade area of an established store, the operator can consider the possible effect upon his business and take measures to concentrate his advertising efforts in those sections where the damage is likely to occur.

Similarly, if it is found that some part of a store's trade area is well populated but contributes few customers, that particular section may justify intensive circularization to bring more customers from it to the store. Knowledge of a store's trade area may point to the desirability of advertising in a weekly community newspaper in large metropolitan cities, or it may suggest the advisability of eliminating such advertising.

CONCLUSION

The science of trade-area analysis is relatively young. Although scattered attempts were made to evaluate retail sites as early as the turn of the century, it was not until the 1930s and 40s that the principles of marketing geography, statistics, economics, and the behavioral sciences were combined and brought to bear upon the problems of store locations. Today trade-area analysis—in spite of its newness—is a technique whereby retail locational errors can be kept at an absolute minimum. This is very important to the modern mass merchandiser because, with tight money and the high costs associated with the opening of new stores, he can ill afford to open units that will produce an insufficient return on their investment.

BIBLIOGRAPHY

Applebaum, W., *Guide to Store Location Research,* sponsored by Super Market Institute, Inc., Reading, Mass.: Addison-Wesley, 1968.
———, "Methods for Determining Store Trade Areas, Market Penetration, and Potential Sales," *Journal of Marketing Research,* vol. 3, May 1966.

————, "How to Measure the Value of a Trading Area," *Chain Store Age*, November 1940.

————, and S. B. Cohen, "Store Trading Areas in a Changing Market," *Journal of Retailing*, vol. 37, Fall 1961.

————, "The Dynamics of Store Trading Areas and Market Equilibrium," *Annals of the Association of American Geographers*, vol. 51, 1961.

————, "Trading Area Networks and Problems of Store Saturation," *Journal of Retailing*, vol. 37, Winter 1961–1962.

————, and R. F. Spears, "How to Measure a Trading Area," *Chain Store Age*, January 1951.

Berry, B. L. L., *Geography of Market Centers and Retail Distribution*, Englewood Cliffs, N.J.: Prentice-Hall, 1967.

Converse, P. D., "New Laws of Retail Gravitation," *Journal of Marketing*, vol. 14, October 1949.

Duddy, E. A., and D. A. Revzan, "Market Areas of the Retail Market," in *Marketing: An Institutional Approach*, 2d ed., New York: McGraw-Hill, 1953, chap. 23.

Green, H. L., "Hinterland Boundaries of New York City and Boston in Southern New England," *Economic Geography*, vol. 31, October 1955.

————, "Planning a National Retail Growth Program," *Economic Geography*, vol. 37, January 1961.

Huff, D. L., "A Probabilistic Analysis of Shopping Center Trade Areas," *Land Economics*, vol. 39, February 1963.

————, "Defining and Estimating a Trading Area," *Journal of Marketing*, vol. 28, July 1964.

————, and J. W. Haggerty, *Determination of Intra-Urban Retail Trade Areas*, Los Angeles: Real Estate Research Program, University of California, 1962.

Reilly, W. J., *Methods for the Study of Retail Relationships*, Studies in Marketing, no. 4, Austin, Texas: Bureau of Business Research, University of Texas, 1959— (reprint of original 1929 edition).

————, *The Law of Retail Gravitation*, New York: W. J. Reilly, Inc., 1931.

Revzan, D. A., *A Geography of Marketing: Integrative Statement*, Berkeley: The Schools of Business Administration, University of California, 1968.

Chapter 3

Measuring the Effects
of Store Promotions

PETER L. HENDERSON and WILLIAM S. HOOFNAGLE *Marketing Economics Division, U.S. Department of Agriculture, Washington, D.C.*

What are the objectives of store promotion as contrasted with other forms of promotion? Except for gaining entrance to a market segment, store promotions are generally aimed at generating immediate or direct sales or a greater market share, in contrast to building goodwill, improved image, change of attitudes, and so on. Any one or a combination of the latter could be objectives of advertising, publicity, and public relations activities. The use of store promotions in product introduction and market penetration cannot be ignored, since consumers must be enticed or persuaded to make an initial purchase of a product. Also, sufficient movement or rate of purchase must be attained to make it profitable for retailers to stock it. Moreover, store promotions of this kind are usually supported with media advertising. Store promotions can also be part of overall promotional programs, coordinated with advertising and other promotional inputs.

These are some of the apparent objectives of store promotions. There are doubtless others, such as new-store openings. In any event, the method used for measuring the promotion's effects is determined by the objective. Methodological procedures appropriate for determining the relative sales effectiveness of point-of-purchase advertising materials are obviously inappropriate for appraising the effectiveness of promotions for a new-store opening. In the first instance, a controlled rotational experiment might be used, whereas the rotational aspect of this procedure would preclude its use for new-store openings, since a store can be opened only once.

The objective also dictates, if not in total then at least to some degree, the kind of data required to determine the effect of store promotions. For example, data needs for new-product introductions involve not only sales data during and after the promotional phase to estimate potential sales levels but also additional data on consumers' use of the product, satisfaction, and similar reactions for use in (1) improving the product and/or (2) follow-up advertising and promotional appeals.

Data sources can be generally classified under the following broad categories: manufacturers' or processors' record of shipments, retail store sales, and data obtained directly from consumers. Sales or movement data from the manufacturer and retail store levels can be obtained from audits of records or at the retail level by observation and recording of customer purchases. Collection of data from consumers may be accomplished through surveys, observation of purchases, and consumer panels using a continuous diary reporting system. Each source and method of collecting data has unique advantages and disadvantages, as covered in Section II, Parts B and C. Therefore reference here will be made only to major considerations applicable to designing research to measure response to store promotions.

Audits of firms' records are probably the least costly means of collecting data and are subject only to counting errors. Sales data collected in retail outlets before, during, and after store promotions accurately reflect changes in sales levels and market share. If such data are collected for a sufficient period after a store promotion, they can serve as a general index of consumers' relative acceptance or tolerance of the product. These data, however, provide information on sales only. They do not provide any information on consumers' uses, attitudes, opinions, and other reactions to the product or the retailers' reaction to the promotion.

Data to provide insights on such qualitative variables must be obtained from consumer and trade sources through personal interviews or mail questionnaires. Survey data also provide evidence of changes in sales level. The chief advantage of this method is the wide array of pertinent information on product and/ or activity obtainable from a cross section of consumers or tradesmen in a relatively short time period. Moreover, if samples are properly drawn, projection can be made for the entire universe. However, it must be pointed out that survey data are not subject only to the same mechanical errors of audits of store sales, but also to biases which arise from several sources—for example, conscious or unconscious prejudices of interviewer or respondent, a poorly framed questionnaire, nonrandom sample selection, dishonest interviewers, "yea saying" and "nay saying" respondents, and so on [9]. The critical problem concerning such errors is the lack of a measure of their magnitude.

Consumer panels may be used to collect data on volume purchased, prices, frequency and purchase size, and so on, as well as consumers' reaction to products. Continuous reporting panels also make it possible to detect changes in purchase rates over time. The panel method of collecting data involves the establishment and maintenance of representative samples over time. Generally, panel data are subject to the same errors associated with data collected by one-time surveys. However, for a continuous panel, it is possible to reconcile the panel purchase data with other sources of sales data and to obtain reliable estimates of the bias. Moreover, the magnitude of such errors tends to be constant from one reporting period to another to the extent that the same questionnaire is used with the same respondents. Thus, bias errors have little if any effect on measures of changes in sales levels, attitudes, opinions, and so on associated with some promotion. (See Section II, Part B, Chapter 10.)

Most often, measuring the effects of store promotion involves the sales response or consumers' response (purchases, attitudes, reactions, and so forth) to some special promotional activity or stimuli free of the effects of other influences present in the marketing system. The promotional stimuli may apply to the entire store, to broad product categories, or to a single product. In any event, other influences must be controlled, equalized, or measured to obtain reliable estimates of the effect of the promotional activity.

Some variables influencing sales, such as display, size and location, prices, variety, and/or number of competing products, can be controlled. Other variables cannot be controlled, and each of these may exert an equal or greater effect on sales than the variables that can be controlled or the ones being measured. Important variables in this category include:

1. Income levels and consumers' ethnic background, which vary from store to store

2. Consumers' expendable income, which varies from week to week because of cycling of payrolls, installment payments, utility bills, and so on

3. Seasonal and holiday influences on purchase and consumption patterns of consumers

4. Variations in numbers of customers patronizing individual stores

Fortunately for the researcher, most of these are highly correlated with individual stores and/or time. Thus one can design tests to equalize, and measure, the influence of uncontrollable variables by using statistical procedures of replicating and stratifying on the basis of stores (markets) and time periods. However, for valid results one must adhere to assumptions underlying the statistical techniques used in assigning the promotional techniques being evaluated to stores and time period. Usually, statistical techniques for analyzing data include analysis of variance, analysis of covariance, and regression analysis. The assumptions underlying these analyses are covered in standard statistical texts, articles in statistical journals, and papers presented to professional societies [3, 6, 15]. Descriptions and explanations are generally couched in technical terms but are easily understood by researchers with limited statistical training. Therefore, when possible, procedures will be described and explained here in nontechnical terms. Readers are also advised to consult Section II, Part E, Chapter 10 in connection with this material.

CONTROLLED EXPERIMENTS

Controlled experiments or market tests range from simple before, during and after, and paired-comparison tests involving only a few experimental units (stores) to complex experimental designs. The latter designs were developed by biological and physical scientists to equalize and measure the effect of extraneous sources of variation on variables undergoing test. For example, in field tests to determine the relative yields of different varieties of wheat, corn, oats, and so on, the researcher can control such variables as amount of fertilizer applied, number of plants per square foot, and so forth.

He can also replicate the experiment over different soil types and general climatic conditions. But, if the basic fertility of the soil in the experimental plot varied from one side to the other, as illustrated in Figure 1, it would be necessary to subdivide the main plot and assign the varieties to the subplots in a manner that would equalize the difference in basic soil fertility. If the test includes three varieties (one of which can be a control variety), the researcher could divide the plot into three equal plots, as indicated by the dotted lines, and assign one variety to each plot. This arrangement corresponds to the simple before, during, and after market test.

This design is simple and easy to execute. However, it does have several weaknesses or disadvantages; namely, it must be assumed that the three plots (or time periods for market test) have equal effects on the response of items undergoing test and that all sources of variation have been controlled or equalized except the variables undergoing test. That is, any differences found among test items are real differences free from error, including sample errors. Moreover, with this design there is no basis for estimating sampling errors or chance variation in response measurement.

This design can be effectively used for screening tests in field trials using experimental plots on which homogeneity trials have been conducted and estimates of the magnitude of expected experimental errors are available. However, in market tests this design has limited value since the influence of variables undergoing tests is inseparably entwined with the effects of time or markets (subplots or strata in the design). Also, extraneous environmental factors affecting the influence of these stratified variables are more numerous than those encountered in laboratory or field experiments and are subject to wider and more varied directions of change.

Illustrative of the difficulty in using this design in market research is a study conducted by the U.S. Department of Agriculture to appraise the short-run effects of promotion on sales of lamb in Sacramento, California [8]. The promotional campaign was sponsored by the American Sheep Producers Council during the spring of 1956. The promotion included consumer advertising in local newspapers, radio and television, and point-of-purchase (POP) display material in stores to draw attention to lamb displays. The theme of the advertising and POP materials emphasized menu suggestions for various lamb cuts—chops, legs, crown roast, and so on. The research techniques consisted of obtaining data on lamb sales and on other variables thought to affect lamb sales from a stratified random sample of 57 retail food stores during three time periods of equal lengths *before*, *during*, and *after* promotion. Data obtained included price of lamb, quantity of lamb sold, display space allotted to lamb and other meats, availability of lamb, use of in-store display material, and limited data on the price of other red meats and poultry. Lamb sales (price, quantity, and value) were determined by audits of store records. The data on the remaining variables were obtained by observations in each store.

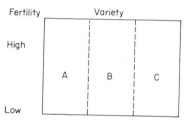

Fig. 1. Fertility level of soil in experimental plot varying in one direction.

The only appreciable changes that occurred from the prepromotion to the promotion period among the variables studied were in the composite retail price of lamb, availability of lamb, and the display space devoted to lamb. The average composite retail price of lamb was 59 cents per pound during the prepromotion period and 68 cents per pound during the promotion and postpromotion periods, a 15 percent increase. The corresponding decrease in display space was about 10 percent.

Lamb sales declined in the sample stores about 20 percent during the promotion and postpromotion periods (Table 1). Since the sales effect of the changes in display space, availability, and price of lamb were entangled with the promotion effects during the promotion and postpromotion periods and data were not available to estimate the effects of these variables on sample stores sales, it was impossible to determine whether the promotion influenced sales.

TABLE 1   Index of Retail Prices, Display Space, Quantity of Lamb Available, and Lamb Sales during Prepromotion, Promotion, and Postpromotion Periods, 57 Retail Food Stores, Sacramento, California, 1956*

	Quantity			
Period	Retail price	Display space	Available in stores	Lamb sales, volume
Prepromotion............	100	100	100	100
Promotion..............	115	90	85	79
Postpromotion............	115	90	85	78

*Index based on prepromotion period = 100.

RANDOMIZED COMPLETE BLOCKS DESIGN

The researcher can improve the design illustrated in Figure 1 by subdividing the subplots as shown in Figure 2; that is, the experimental plot is subdivided into nine subplots. He can then randomly assign the three test varieties to each of the main subplots or blocks. This arrangement is called the randomized complete block design. It ensures that each of the varieties will be replicated under each level of soil fertility when variability is in only one direction.

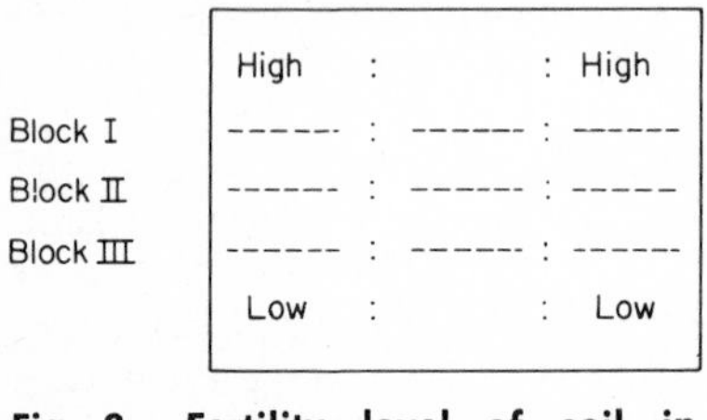

Fig. 2. Fertility level of soil in experimental plot varying in one direction, subdivided into subplots.

Analysis of variance procedures can also be used to separate the variation in yield response into the following components: between blocks, between test items, and experimental error.[1] The latter is an unbiased estimate of sampling errors or chance variation and can be used in appropriate statistical tests to determine whether differences in treatment (test items) means are significant, that is, whether the probability of obtaining such differences from chance variation is so low or remote that it is more likely the difference between treatment means is associated with treatments.[2]

This design's unique feature is that each block is a complete replication of a test. Therefore each block must be subdivided into as many subplots as there are treatments. But the researcher is not restricted on the number of complete blocks or replications. This allows him to plan the number of replications for optimum precision. If properly designed, the matched store or matched market research technique used in marketing research is, in essence, application of the randomized complete block design. That is, stores or markets are combined into homogeneous groups or blocks and randomly assigned to treatments. Ideally, matching should be based on equal sales level of the product under-

[1] For computational procedures, see [16].
[2] *Treatments* refer to items undergoing test and will be used in that sense hereafter.

going test for stated time periods corresponding to the length of time a store promotion is to be conducted. The number of stores to be matched for each block would depend on the number of promotional techniques being evaluated.

Care in selecting and grouping test stores or test markets cannot be overemphasized, because the normal sales performance of the groupings must conform to the assumptions underlying the analysis of variance. See Section II, Part E, Chapter 10, also [1, 4, 16].

Expressed algebraically, the model for analysis of variance (including assumptions) is

$$y_i = u + a_i + e_i$$

where y_i = an observation.

u = the true mean of all observations.

a_i = constant terms associated with block, rows, and columns, stratified in design and treatments randomly assigned to strata. The sum of the a_is equals zero.

e_i = experimental errors that are independently and normally distributed with mean zero and a common variance.

For the randomized complete block design, the model is

$$Y_{ij} = U + B_i + T_m + e_{ig}$$

where y_{ij}, u, and e_{ij} = values defined above

B_i = the constant effect of the ith block

T_j = the constant effect of the jth treatment

The constants for block and treatment effects are calculated by subtracting algebraically the overall mean from individual block or treatment means. Thus the sum of the B_is as well as that of the T_js equals zero.

These assumptions, applications, and analyses can be illustrated by a hypothetical market experiment.

Assume that

1. Sixteen stores have been grouped into four homogeneous groups, or blocks, of four stores each.

2. The overall mean (u) or sales per store for the promotion period is 250 units.

3. Block effects are $B_1 = +20$, $B_2 = -5$, $B_3 = +10$, and $B_4 = -25$ (that is, average sales per store for stores in each of the blocks are greater or less than the overall average by the number of units specified).

4. The corresponding effects of treatments designated A, B, C, and D are $A = -20$, $B = +17$, $C = -15$, and $D = +18$.

5. Experimental error, $e_{ij} = 5$ units.

Note that the experimental error term e_{ij} is either positive or negative. Thus, in calculating expected values from the preceding assumed values, 5 units are randomly added to or subtracted from each observation. As a result of this random assignment, the deviation of block and treatment means from the overall mean may or may not coincide with the values assumed for block and treatment effects. However, the maximum differences between such deviations and assumed effects will not exceed 5 units, since the means will only deviate from assumed values by the average of the net additions or subtractions over all calculated observations for each treatment or block. For example, if 5 units were added to each of four observations for treatment A, the mean of A would be increased 5 units, $(4 \times 5)/4$.

Substituting the assumed values in the model,

$$Y_{ij} = U + B_i + T_j \pm e_{ij}$$

the results would appear as shown in Table 2a if the e_{ij} are completely balanced within treatments and blocks. Table 2b shows possible results with random assignment of the e_{ij} term.

TABLE 2a   Illustration of Randomized Complete Block Experimental Design to Appraise Sales Effect of Store Promotion with Assumed Data for Sales Response, Random Variation ±5 Units Balanced within Treatments and Blocks

Block	Store				Block		Deviation from overall mean
	1	2	3	4	Total	Mean	
I	(A) 245	(C) 250	(D) 293	(B) 292	1,080	270	+20
II	(C) 235	(B) 257	(D) 268	(A) 220	980	245	−5
III	(D) 273	(A) 245	(B) 272	(C) 250	1,040	260	+10
IV	(B) 247	(A) 210	(C) 205	(D) 238	900	225	−25
	Grand total and mean				4,000	250	

Item	Treatment			
	A	B	C	D
Total..............	920	1,068	940	1,072
Means.............	230	267	235	268
Deviation from overall mean.....	−20	+17	−15	+18

TABLE 2b   Illustration of Randomized Complete Block Experimental Design to Appraise Sales Effect of Store Promotion with Assumed Data for Sales Response, Random Variation ±5 Units not Balanced within Treatments and Blocks

Block	Store				Block		Deviation from overall mean
	1	2	3	4	Total	Mean	
I	(A) 255+	(C) 260+	(D) 283−	(B) 282−	1,080	270	+20
II	(C) 225−	(B) 267+	(D) 258−	(A) 230+	980	245	−5
III	(D) 273−	(A) 245+	(B) 272−	(C) 250+	1,040	260	+10
IV	(B) 247	(A) 210+	(C) 205−	(D) 238−	900	225	−25
	Grand total and mean				4,000	250	

Item	Treatment			
	A	B	C	D
Total..............	940	1,068	940	1,052
Means.............	235	267	235	263
Deviation from overall mean.....	−15	+17	−15	+13

Note that the deviations of the treatment means (estimates of treatment effects) from the overall mean do not coincide with the assumed treatment effects used to calculate Table 2b. This resulted from randomly assigning the e_{ij} term, ± 5. However, the treatment means and deviations were within 5 units of the assumed or expected values. This illustrates two of the assumptions underlying the analysis of variance; that is, (1) the Y_{ij} have a common variance σ^2 and (2) the Y_{ij} are distributed in a multivariate normal distribution. The observations also show that the effects of the constant terms stratified in the design are additive.

The practical significance of these assumptions is that stores should be carefully selected and grouped to satisfy the assumption that the block effect is constant over all stores within each block. This is most critical in using the randomized complete block design, since the effects of treatments are confounded or entwined with those of individual stores. Moreover, if the stores are not approximately the same in all respects affecting sales response to treatments, the results would be invalid because the treatment response would not be independent of individual stores. For example, if the ethnic background of one store's customers was such that the sales response to treatments would be different from the response in other stores in the block, results would be biased even though the basic sales level was the same.

Remember that treatment effects are confounded with, and cannot be separated from, sampling units (stores) in a randomized complete block design. In such cases, the experiment must be replicated over homogeneous groups of such stores to estimate relative sales response for each group.

Examining the analysis of variance for a randomized complete block design should increase the understanding of the assumptions underlying this analysis, as given in Table 3.

TABLE 3   Analysis of Variance for a Randomized Complete Block Design

Source of variation	Degrees of freedom	Sum of squares	Mean square	Expected mean square
Total.........	$bt - 1$	Σy^2		
Between:				
Blocks.......	$b - 1$	Byy	$Byy/(b - 1)$	$\sigma^2 + [t/(b - 1) \sum\limits_{i=1}^{b} B_i^2]$
Treatments..	$t - 1$	Tyy	$Tyy/(t - 1)$	$\sigma^2 + [b/(t - 1) \sum\limits_{j=1}^{t} T_j^2]$
Experimental error........	$(b - 1)(t - 1)$	Eyy	$Eyy/(b - 1)(t - 1)$	σ^2

The symbols in Table 3 are as follows:
b = the number of blocks
t = the number of treatments
Σy^2 = the sum of squared deviations of individual observations from overall mean
Byy = the sum of squared deviations of block means from overall mean
Tyy = the sum of squared deviations of treatment means from overall mean
Eyy = the residual or unexplained sum of squared deviations from the overall mean, that is, total SS − block SS − treatment SS

$\Sigma B_i{}^2 =$ the sum of squared deviations of the true block means from true mean

$\Sigma T_j{}^2 =$ the sum of squared deviations of the true treatment means from true mean

$\sigma^2 =$ the true variance or chance variation within treatments and/or blocks

First, it can be seen that the expected mean square of experimental error is the common variance σ^2. This is the first term in the expected mean square for the variation between block treatment means, with the second term representing the squared deviation of true block or treatment means from the overall mean corrected for the number of independent replications of blocks or treatments.[3] The assumption that the e_{ij} are independently and normally distributed with mean zero and a common variance σ^2 is the basis for F and other tests to determine significant differences between means. In this respect, it is apparent that if the second term in the expected mean square for treatments is

zero (this can be true only if the $\sum_{j=1}^{t} T^2 = 0$, and this can be true only when

$$T_1 = T_2 = \cdots = T_n, \text{ since } \sum_{j=1}^{t} T^2 = \text{sum of squared deviations from overall}$$

means), the ratio of mean square treatment to mean square error will always equal 1.[4]

The mean squares calculated from observed data are unbiased estimates of corresponding expected mean squares when the assumptions for analysis of variance are met. It is interesting to compare the mean square obtained from the assumed data (Table 2) with expected mean squares based on the assumed true constants and variances (Table 4). These values do not agree in all instances because the assumed term for the common variance, 5, was deliberately assigned randomly, without regard to the restriction that this variance was common to both block and treatment, to introduce the concept of sampling errors which may vary from experiment to experiment (sample to sample).

One may reasonably ask what the implication of these assumptions is to the

TABLE 4   Analysis of Variance of Assumed Data for Randomized Complete Block Design

Source of variation	Degrees of freedom	Sum of squares	Mean square F	Expected mean square F
Total....................	11	9,714		
Between blocks............	2	5,000	2,500	2,525
Between treatments........	3	4,447	1,482	1,228
Experimental error.........	6	267	44	25

[3] The number of independent replications can best be explained by example. If we have five homogeneous stores grouped within each block and randomly assign five treatments to the five stores, the treatment assigned last is fixed; it cannot be assigned to any of the other stores. In this sense independence is synonymous with degrees of freedom.

[4] Tabular values of F are based on the probability, .01, .05, and so on, of obtaining stated ratios from sampling errors with stated degrees of freedom for numerators and denominators used in calculating ratios from sample data.

market researcher wanting to use a biometric design to economize on time, experimental units, and so on to attain optimum precision in research results. He must simply exercise the same care and discretion in grouping experimental units into homogeneous units as that exercised in stratified random sampling procedures. This usually means some knowledge or prior research to determine the inherent variation associated with sampling units.

Latin Square Experimental Design

As noted in Section II, Part E, Chapter 10, the Latin square design differs from the randomized complete block design in that environmental or outside sources of variation can be controlled in two directions instead of one, as illustrated in Figure 3.

	Column		
Row	1	2	3
1	High A	B	Medium C
2	B	C	A
3	C Medium	A	B Low

Fig. 3. Illustration of Latin square design to equalize variation in two directions on experimental treatments.

This design is especially useful in market research since environmental influences outside the researcher's control are usually two-dimensional, that is, associated with different sales levels between stores or markets as well as variation in sales over stated time periods. Some influences outside the researcher's control but highly correlated with individual stores and specified time periods were discussed previously. In particular, one must be careful in grouping stores into squares to ensure that stores *have* a constant effect over all periods and that time has a constant effect over all stores, as shown in Figure 4.

In this figure, it is apparent that influences of stores and time are equalized on treatments. However, if stores do not have the same sales pattern over preselected time periods, as shown in Figure 5, the influence of these variables is

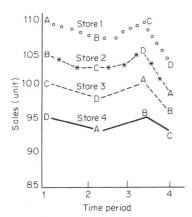

Fig. 4. Constant period-to-period sales variation among stores and constant between store levels of sales among time periods and treatments.

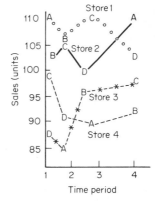

Fig. 5. Nonconstant period-to-period sales variation among stores and nonconstant between store levels of sales among time periods and treatments.

confounded with treatment effect and results are not valid. Thus, it can be seen that treatment C appears during peak sales periods in all stores except one; treatments A and B are fairly well balanced between high and low periods; while treatment D appears in low sales periods in all stores except one. Obviously, test results under such conditions would be biased in favor of treatment C and unfavorable to treatment D.

It is not always possible to group experimental units so that sales will fall in the perfect pattern shown in Figure 4. However, every effort should be made to approximate this pattern. In some cases where period-to-period variation within stores is proportionate to the average sales level of each store, the data may be indexed or converted to logarithms to conform to the assumptions underlying the analysis of variance, as will be illustrated later.

Measurement of promotional techniques involving media advertising in conjunction with other promotional devices precludes using stores within a single city or market as sampling units because media advertising for one treatment would overflow other treatments. Thus, cities must be used as the main sampling units to exercise control over media messages reaching consumers.

The model for this design is as follows:

$$Y_{ijk} = U + c_i + P_j + T_k \pm e_{ijk}$$

It is similar to that for the double changeover design described in the following section. It differs in only one respect—the T_k term, constant for treatment effects, is subdivided into two components, direct and residual effects, in the double changeover design. Because of the similarity of the models and analytical procedures, an illustration of this design will not be given.

Double Changeover Design

In experiments in which treatments are applied sequentially to the same experimental unit (animal, field plot, store, city, and so on), the effect of certain treatments may continue after application of the treatment is discontinued. That is, a given treatment's effect may be influenced by the carryover of the treatment preceding it in sequence. This is critical in planning research to appraise the impact of promotion designed to generate not only an immediate sales response but also repeat purchases for a longer period of time.

One way to eliminate the carryover influence of previous treatments is to insert rest periods between promotion periods. In this way treatment effects are freed of most residual effects of previous treatments. It is not always possible or desirable to use such rest periods because of the cost involved and timeliness of results. An alternative is to use an experimental design that yields a measurement of both residual and direct effects of treatments and the adjustment of direct effects for residual effects and vice versa. Cochran et al. developed such a design, the double changeover experimental design, and the accompanying analysis to measure the response in milk production to various rations fed to dairy cows in 1941 [5]. It was later adapted and applied to market research problems by Henderson [10] as cited by Federer [7].

The design is a special linking of orthogonal Latin squares in which the sequence of treatments is reversed so that residual influences of treatments on subsequent treatments in sequences are balanced (Figure 6).

Note that the treatment sequence in square 1 follows the cycle $A \rightarrow B \rightarrow C \rightarrow A$; whereas in square 2, the cycle of treatments is exactly opposite, $A \rightarrow C \rightarrow B \rightarrow A$.

It can be assumed that treatments during the first period have no residual effect, or any residual effects would be equal if all experimental units were treated alike before the experiment. The residual effects are designated by lowercase letters of the previous period in subsequent time periods. The effective number of replicates for estimating residual effects, however, is less than for direct effects, and in no case is a treatment's residual influence carried over to itself.

Lucas pointed out that with this design residual effects are partially confounded with items in the design as well as being positively correlated with direct effects [13]. By introducing a single new feature to the double changeover design, Lucas found that the covariance between direct and residual effects could be eliminated and the variance of direct and residual effects could be more nearly equalized [14]. This is accomplished by replicating the treatments appearing in the third time period during a fourth time period (Figure 7). Note from the lowercase letters used to denote residual effects that such effects are balanced in the extra period double changeover design as contrasted to the previous design.

Henderson et al. used this improved changeover design together with covariance and multiple regression to evaluate the influence of two campaign themes

Time period	Latin square 1: market			Latin square 2: market		
	1	2	3	4	5	6
I	A	B	C	A	B	C
II	B(a)	C(b)	A(c)	C(a)	A(b)	B(c)
III	C(b)	A(c)	B(a)	B(c)	C(a)	A(b)

Fig. 6.   Double changeover design.

Time period	Latin square 1: market			Latin square 2: market		
	1	2	3	4	5	6
I	A	B	C	A	B	C
II	Ba	Cb	Ac	Ca	Ab	Bc
III	Cb	Ac	Ba	Bc	Ca	Ab
IV	Cc	Aa	Bb	Bb	Cc	Aa

Fig. 7.   Extra period double changeover design.

and related merchandising practices employed by food stores on apple sales [11] and to appraise the impact of varying levels of advertising on sales of fluid milk [12].

The model for this design is

$$Y_{ijk} = U + C_i R_j + T_k + (T_k - 1) + e_{ijk}$$

It differs from the model for the Latin square design in only one respect—the term $T_k - 1$, the fixed constant for residual effects of treatments. The other symbols in the model are defined as follows:

Y_{ijk} = sales in ith city, jth time period, kth treatment, $k - 1$ treatment in previous time period

U = average sales of overall observations

C_i = a fixed constant representing effect of ith city

R_j = a fixed constant representing effect of jth time period

T_k = a fixed constant representing direct effect of kth treatment

$T_k - 1$ = a fixed constant representing carryover effect of prior treatment in sequence

e_{ijk} = random and unexplained variation in sales

The study, conducted in cooperation with the American Dairy Association, will be discussed to illustrate this design.

The association's promotional expenditures at the time of the study averaged about 2 cents per capita annually for its national program. However, producer groups in certain markets supported supplemental programs which raised the expenditure level from 4 to 6 cents per capita annually. The association felt

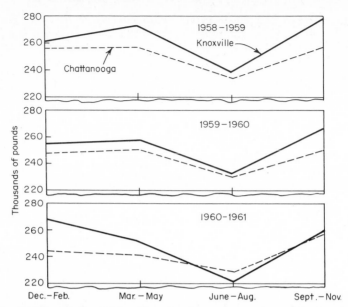

Fig. 8. Average daily fluid milk sales by quarters for selected milk order markets 1958 to 1959 through 1960 to 1961. (*U.S. Department of Agriculture, Economic Research Service.*)

that increases in expenditure of 15 and 30 cents per capita annually above current levels would sufficiently increase advertising intensity to have an impact on consumers and produce a measurable response.

Other criteria for designing the study included (1) application of the intensified promotion to fluid or class I milk only; (2) detection of 2 percent differences between treatment means at the 0.05 level of significance;[5] (3) detection and measurement of any residual or carryover influence of intensified promotion, since the important question to be answered was permanent effects—immediate plus residual; and (4) application of findings to all markets in which the association was active.

The second requirement was perhaps the most critical, since measuring sales changes or differences with such precision is a formidable task. However, a series of historical data published monthly for federal and state milk order markets were available which could be analyzed to determine the inherent sources of variation in fluid milk sales and the feasibility of conducting the study.[6]

These data were analyzed to determine the primary sources of sales variations. Initially a graphic analysis was made of the monthly sales data covering a five-year period for approximately forty markets in which the association had programs. These analyses indicated that the major sales variation could be associated with two factors—differences in sales levels between markets and seasonal patterns of consumption within markets, as illustrated in Figure 8.

[5] The reason for such precision was the relative stability in annual per capita consumption of fluid milk and the low elasticity of demand with respect to price and income.

[6] Data for each market included total hundredweight of producer milk received and the use by end product, butterfat content, and class I and class II prices received by producers.

This suggested the necessity of designing the study with some controls in allocating promotional expenditures among test markets to (1) equalize the effect of these factors on the level of advertising tested or (2) isolate and quantify the effects of these factors so that adjustments could be made in sales data obtained for various levels of promotional investments. Several alternatives were available to satisfy these requirements, such as multiple regression analysis, matched markets, a combination of matched markets and multiple regression, and use of Latin square experimental design or some variation of it.

Statistical analysis of the data revealing the number of replications necessary for the desired degree of precision precluded using the matched market and multiple regression approaches.

If the data satisfy assumptions underlying the analysis of variance, the Latin square design is well suited for problems in which two factors not directly under the researcher's control account for major sources of variation in sales. Randomly assigning test treatments to test markets and time periods according to the design's restriction—that each treatment appears only once in each market and time period—equalizes the constant influences associated with the markets and time periods.

As noted earlier, three levels of promotional investments were of interest to the association—present levels, and 15 and 30 cents above the present level—hereafter denoted by capital letters A, B, and C, respectively. Figure 9 illustrates that all expenditure levels are subject to any peculiarities affecting sales that are associated with a particular market or time period for milk consumption; in other words, no level of investment enjoys an advantage or handicap because of the market or time period in which it happened to be tested [14].

Like the Latin square design, the assumption underlying the analysis of variance must be satisfied if this design is used. Therefore we used graphic analysis to compare and match markets with similar seasonal patterns and long-term sales trends to check that the effect of time was constant among test markets or that market differences were constant over different time periods. These comparisons revealed that most markets had similar sales patterns (Figures 10a and b), but seasonal patterns of some markets subject to major population shifts were different.

For example, markets containing resort areas had higher sales during summer months than those without (Figure 10c). The markets with similar sales patterns were further grouped by average monthly sales. These groupings were necessarily broad since each market's average daily sales were largely a function of population, but this helped to minimize differences in sales levels between cities within squares and to maximize differences between squares.

The graphic analysis of historic sales data also revealed that seasonal variation among cities was proportional to the mean level of annual sales. Thus it was necessary to convert data to logs to satisfy the analysis of variance assumption of additivity.

Time period	Square 1			Square 2		
	Chatt.	Knox.	Roch.	Clksbg.	S.F.	N.V.
I	A	B	C	A	B	C
II	B(a)	C(b)	A(c)	C(a)	A(b)	B(c)
III	C(b)	A(c)	B(a)	B(c)	C(a)	A(b)
IV	C(c)	A(a)	B(b)	B(b)	C(c)	A(a)

Fig. 9. Extra period double changeover experimental design for allocating promotional investments to markets and time periods.

The next step was to assign markets to the design and analyze sales data to determine the magnitude and range of normal sales variation (experimental errors) without intensified advertising.[7]   However, it was necessary to determine the length of experimental time periods before conducting the uniformity trials.   This was an important decision, since experience has shown that the total sales response to promotional campaigns frequently lags, but the anticipated increase in sales must be obtained within a definite time period for added

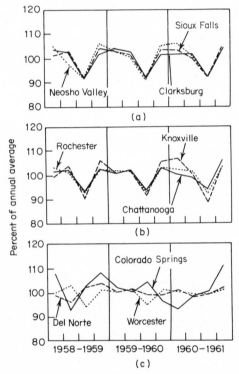

Fig. 10.   Fluid milk sales in nine cities, by quarter.   (*a*) Sioux Falls, Clarksburg, and Neosho Valley; (*b*) Chattanooga, Knoxville, and Rochester; (*c*) Colorado Springs, Worcester, and Del Norte. (*U.S. Department of Agriculture, Economic Research Service.*)

revenue from sales to equal the investment or to return a profit on it.   Thus, we calculated the maximum time period to be six months.

Several uniformity trials were run with different combinations of selected markets.   Differences among treatments were nonexistent in all cases, as shown in Table 5.   The magnitude of the standard error of difference between treatment was less than ½ percent of the means.   Applying these statistics in multiple *t* tests, least significant difference (*lsd*) and most significant difference (*msd*) tests showed that treatment differences of even less than 2 percent could be

---

[7] This is in effect the same as a uniformity test in field experiments, that is, all plots are treated uniformly in all respects.

detected at the 0.01 significance level.[8]   On the basis of these findings, we felt a 2 percent change in sales could be measured.

Also, from these analyses, three alternative markets were selected for each column of the design that would satisfy the criteria specified for the study. The six markets selected were Chattanooga and Knoxville, Tennessee; Rochester, New York; Clarksburg, West Virginia; Sioux Falls, South Dakota; and Neosho Valley, Missouri and Kansas (Figure 9). Table 5 shows the analysis of variance of historical sales data (in logs) for these markets. Note that markets and time periods were the statistically significant sources of variation in milk sales. These factors together accounted for practically all variation—over 99 percent. Treatment differences were not significant, which was expected since these are uniformity data. Unexplained or random variation as reflected in the error term was only 0.1 percent of the total variation.

TABLE 5   Analysis of Variance of Fluid Milk Sales in Six Markets, Uniformity Data, March 1959–February 1961*

Source of variation	Sum of squares	Degrees of freedom	Mean square	F	Percent of total variation
Total.................	1.635895	23			100
Between squares.......	1.172811	1	1.172811	4,927.78	71.7–7
Periods within squares..	0.006734	6	0.001122	4.71	0.4–4
Between periods.......	0.006460	(3)	0.002153	9.05	
Periods × squares.....	0.000274	(3)	0.000091	0.38	
Markets within squares.	0.454376	4	0.113594	477.29	27.8–8
Treatment—direct.....	0.000045	2	0.000023	0.10	0.0–0
Carryover............	0.000025	2	0.000013	0.05	0.0–0
Error................	0.001904	8	0.000238		0.1–1

* Original data converted into logs.   Coefficient of variation = 0.5 percent.

These markets also provided a cross section of population and economic conditions. For example, annual per capita consumption of whole and skim milk varied among markets from 243 pounds to 368 pounds. Per capital income varied from about \$1,900 to \$2,700. Unemployment rates varied from under 2 percent to as much as 9 percent. Thus when the expenditure levels were rotated over each market, they were subjected to a broad cross section of economic conditions.

It was hypothesized that (1) such factors as local retailer merchandising support would be directly affected by the promotional levels under actual marketing conditions and would, therefore, be part of the experimental treatment; but (2) such factors as per capita disposable income, level of unemployment,

[8] The least significant difference test is the difference required between two treatment means to reject the null hypothesis that the treatment means are equal at the .05 probability level. The *msd* test is the difference required between treatment means to reject the null hypothesis of no difference at the .01 probability level. That is, the probability of rejecting the null hypothesis when no difference actually exists is 5 percent and 1 percent, respectively, for the two sets. The computational procedures are simple and straightforward. Thus, the *lsd* (.05) is the product of the standard error of the difference between means and the tabular value of t at the 5 percent level for the number of degrees of freedom associated with the standard error of the means.

and general price level would be independent of the experimental treatments.

Thus, besides monthly sales data obtained for the milk order markets, supplementary data were obtained to determine whether significant relationships existed among any of the factors and milk consumption during the experiment. Analyses of these data would provide a basis for adjusting sales data for any significant changes in these factors. However, analysis of variance revealed that no significant variations occurred among the promotion levels tested except those hypothesized to be part of the treatment for any of these factors.

Analysis of Observed Sales Data.   Treatment effects on sales are divided into two parts—direct effect and carryover effect. The first is the immediate response to promotion, while the second represents the response to the treatment that carried over into the next six-month period.

The analysis of variance of the sales data (Table 6) shows a significant difference among treatments. It is interesting to compare the mean squares from the uniformity data *and* from the actual experiment itself. The major differences are for treatment effects (direct and residual) and experimental error. A possible explanation for the *reduction* of experimental error is the greater care taken in auditing sales data during the experimental period.

TABLE 6   Analysis of Variance of Fluid Milk Sales in Six Markets during Promotion, March 1963–February 1965*

Source of variation	Sum of squares	Degrees of freedom	Mean square	F values	Expected mean square
Total.................	1.724089	23			
Between squares.........	1.295240	1	1.295240		1.172811
Periods within squares....	0.006473	6	0.001079		0.001122
Between periods.........	0.006347	(3)	0.002116		0.002153
Periods × squares......	0.000126	(3)	0.000042	1.1	0.000091
Markets within squares...	0.420878	4	0.105220		0.113594
Between markets........	0.226032	(2)	0.113016		
Treatment, direct........	0.000772	2	0.000386	10.16	0.000023
Carryover..............	0.000419	2	0.000210	5.53	
Error..................	0.000307	8	0.000038		0.000238

* Data converted to logs.

The results of the two-year market test are summarized in Tables 7 and 8. Table 7 gives the physical increase in average daily sales attributed to the additional promotional investments, while Table 8 compares the net added revenue generated by the intensified promotion with the added promotional expenditures. The net added revenue was calculated by multiplying the weighted average price differential between class I price and class II price by the total increase in sales associated with intensified promotion.[9] That is, total sales increase is daily sales increase multiplied by the number of days the increased promotion was in effect.

As a further check on the results' accuracy, sales for each market, time period, and treatment were predicted by fitting the coefficients derived from

[9] Class I price applies to milk used for fluid consumption; class II price applies to milk used in manufacturing products. The increase in volume associated with promotion was transferred from class II to class I use.

the analysis to the statistical model, $Y_{ijk} = U + C_i + R_j + T_k + T_{k-1} + e_{ijk}$, and comparing the actual or observed sales to the predicted values. The greatest variation of actual sales from predicted sales did not exceed 2 percent and, in most cases, was less than ½ percent. The estimated standard error of the difference between treatment means was approximately 1 percent at the .01 probability level.

Consumer surveys conducted concurrently with this controlled market test revealed that the increased sales were from new customers attracted by the intensified promotion. Data obtained from the surveys on consumers' demo-

TABLE 7   Estimates of Sales Response to Three Levels of Promotional Expenditures for Fluid Milk in Six Markets, March 1963–February 1965

Effect	*Normal promo-tion** Sales per day (000 lb)	*Medium promotion* Sales per day (000 lb)	Increase over normal (000 lb)	Percent	*Heavy promotion* Sales per day (000 lb)	Increase over normal (000 lb)	Percent
Direct effect...	288	296	8‡	2.8	298	10§	3.5
Carryover.....	...	5	5†	1.7	7	7‡	2.4
Combined effect........	288	301	13§	4.5	305	17§	5.9

* Adjusted to zero carryover for normal.
† Significant at 5 percent level.
‡ Significant at 2 percent level.
§ Significant at 0.5 percent level.

TABLE 8   Costs and Returns of Promotion in Six Markets, March 1963–February 1965

Level of promotion	Cost of promotion	Added income	Net returns
Medium....................	$237,350	$398,580	$161,050
Heavy......................	436,363	521,220	84,907

graphic characteristics also provided information helpful to the association in planning future programs and directing promotional activities.

FACTORIAL EXPERIMENTS

A factorial experiment in itself is not considered an experimental design. Any of the experimental designs discussed previously and others may be used for the factorial experiment in which the effects of two or more factors are investigated simultaneously. The choice of treatments determines whether the experiment is factorial. The treatments consist of all combinations possible from the factors being investigated.

Since sales promotions most often involve combinations of several different promotional techniques, the advantage of factorial experiments in investigating sales response to alternative promotional strategies is obvious. One can determine whether the sales response to different levels of one factor (technique) is the same over all levels of other factors being investigated, that is, if the response to different levels of, say, factor A is independent of the influence of different levels of factor B.

This approach also makes it possible to determine if response to different levels of one factor is related to the level of a second or third factor. For example, in an experiment in which three levels of factor A and four levels of factor B are being investigated, results might show that average response to factor A was greatest for level three over all levels of factor B; but the maximum response for various combinations of different levels of factors A and B was for the first level of A and the fourth level of B. The statistical term for this is *interaction*.

Analysis of variance procedures provide a means of determining whether responses to different levels of factors being investigated are independent or related. Thus, through carefully planned and executed experiments, the optimum combination of promotional inputs for maximizing sales response can be determined.

Illustrative of the use of factorial experiments is a study conducted by the U.S. Department of Agriculture with the National Broiler Council [2]. The study's objective was to determine the sales influence of offering (1) an additional broiler cut—a quarter—to broiler displays in food stores and (2) methods of providing recipe materials at point of purchase.

The test was conducted over a six-week period in Dayton and Columbus, Ohio. In each city, six supermarkets were selected from a single retail organization to ensure identical pricing, merchandising, and advertising practices among the test stores. A Latin square design was used to assign the treatments (combinations of test factors) to stores and time period in each city, as shown in Table 9.

TABLE 9   Experimental Design Used to Test Effect of Cutting Methods and Recipe Information on Broiler Sales, Columbus and Dayton, Ohio, August–October 1962*

Week	Dayton stores						Columbus stores					
	1	2	3	4	5	6	7	8	9	10	11	12
1	B_1	B_0	B_2	A_1	A_2	A_0	A_0	A_2	A_1	B_2	B_0	B_1
2	A_1	A_2	A_0	B_1	B_0	B_2	B_0	B_1	B_2	A_2	A_1	A_0
3	A_2	A_0	A_1	B_0	B_2	B_1	A_1	A_0	A_2	B_1	B_2	B_0
4	B_2	B_1	B_0	A_0	A_1	A_2	A_2	A_1	A_0	B_0	B_1	B_2
5	A_0	A_1	A_2	B_2	B_1	B_0	B_2	B_0	B_1	A_0	A_2	A_1
6	B_0	B_2	B_1	A_2	A_0	A_1	B_1	B_2	B_0	A_1	A_0	A_2

* A—Whole, whole cut up, and parts
B—Whole, whole cut up, parts, and quarters
0—No recipe material
1—Recipe label on package
2—Recipe leaflet

Analysis of variance of the sales data (Table 10) revealed that the sales response to the number of cuts offered in displays was independent of the presence of method of offering recipe materials, as indicated by the nonsignificant F ratio for cutting multiplied by recipe interaction.

It was also found that sales response to the offering of recipe information (whether on a label attached to the package or a leaflet displayed in holders

TABLE 10   Analysis of Variance of Significance of Effects of Stores, Time Periods, Cutting Methods, and Recipes on Broiler Sales in 12 Supermarkets, Columbus and Dayton, Ohio

Source	Degrees of freedom	Sum of squares	Mean square	F ratio
Cities...............	1	6,911,142	6,911,142	15.7*
Stores within cities.........	10	16,552,066	1,655,207	3.8*
Weeks within cities........	10	91,087,254	9,108,725	20.7*
Treatments within cities.....	(10)	6,017.701	601,770	1.4
Treatments..............	(5)	3,887,344	777,469	1.8
Cutting.................	1	1,698,632	1,698,632	3.9†
Recipe..................	2	546,920	273,460	0.6
Cutting × recipe..........	2	1,641,792	820,896	1.9
Treatments × cities........	5	2,130,357	426,071	1.0
Error....................	40	17,643,690	441,092	
Total..................	71	138,211,853		

* Significant at the .01 probability level.
† Significant at the .05 probability level.

attached to broiler displays) compared with offering none was no greater than could be expected from chance variation in sale.   Adding the quarter cut to broiler displays increased broiler sales approximately 16 percent, an increase significant at the .05 probability level.   In reality the sales increase associated with offering the added quarter cuts in broiler displays could be attributed to two factors—a greater variety or choice of cuts offered and an increase in size of display, since it was necessary to enlarge broiler displays to accommodate the added quarter cuts.

SUMMARY

The examples given illustrate the experience gained in conducting marketing experiments related to the advertising and promotion of agricultural products. Specifically:
1.   Reliability and precision of results are primarily dependent on the proper planning and design of the research.
2.   Carefully planned and executed experiments will provide relative sales response to alternative promotional inputs such as levels of investments, various advertising and promotional techniques, promotional themes, and so on.
3.   But such efforts will not provide insights into sources of sales unless supported by data obtained from tradesmen and consumers.
4.   Sales results of various alternatives are relative to each other rather than precise estimates that can be applied per se.

REFERENCES

1. Banks, S., *Experimentation in Marketing*, New York: McGraw-Hill, 1965.
2. Brown, S. E., "Increasing Broiler Sales through Offering an Additional Cut and Recipe Materials," ERS-127, U.S. Department of Agriculture, 1963.
3. Cochran, W. G., "Some Consequences when Assumptions for Analysis of Variance Are Not Satisfied," *Biometrics*, vol. 3, March 1947.
4. ———, and G. M. Cox, *Experimental Designs*, New York: Wiley, 1950.
5. ———, K. M. Autrey, and C. Y. Cannon, "A Double Changeover Design for Dairy Cattle Feeding Experiments," *Journal of Dairy Science*, vol. 24, November 1941.

6. Eisenhart, C., "The Assumptions Underlying the Analysis of Variance," *Biometrics*, vol. 3, March 1947.
7. Federer, W. T., *Experimental Designs*, New York: Macmillan, 1955.
8. Grubbs, V. D., W. E. Clement, and J. S. Hunter, "Results of a Promotional Campaign for Lamb in Sacramento, Calif.," Market Research Report 200, Agricultural Marketing Service, U.S. Department of Agriculture, October 1957.
9. Hansen, M. H., W. N. Hurwitz, and W. G. Madow, *Sample Survey Methods and Theory*, New York: Wiley, seventh printing, 1966 (vol. 1, chap. 1).
10. Henderson, P. L., "Application of the Double Changeover Design to Measure Carryover Effects of Treatments in Controlled Experiments," *Methods of Research in Marketing*, Ithaca, N.Y.: Cornell University, 1952.
11. ———, J. F. Hind, and S. E. Brown, "Sales Effect of Two Campaign Themes," *Journal of Advertising Research*, vol. 1, December 1961.
12. ———, "Measuring Effects of Varying Levels of Advertising Investments on Sales of Fluid Milk" and "Market Experimentation for Measurement of Advertising and Promotion Effectiveness," *Proceedings of the Business and Economic Statistics Section, American Statistical Association*, 1965, 1966.
13. Lucas, H. L., "Techniques in Animal Science Research" and "Design in Animal Science Research," *Proc. Auburn Conf. on Stat. Applied to Res. in Soc. Sci., Plant Sci., and Animal Sci.*, 1948.
14. ———, "Extra-period Latin Square Changeover Design," *Journal of Dairy Science*, vol. 40, March 1957.
15. Ostle, B., *Statistics in Research*, Ames, Iowa: Iowa State College Press, 2d ed., 1964.
16. Snedecor, G. W., and W. G. Cochran, *Statistical Methods*, Ames, Iowa: Iowa State College Press, 6th ed., 1967.

International Marketing

Chapter 1

Organization of International Marketing Research

A. GRAEME CRANCH *Russell International Marketing Services, Ltd., London, England*

INTRODUCTION

Today more and more countries—from the wealthiest to the most recently "developing"—emphasize the need for selling more of their products abroad. Even in the more sophisticated industrialized countries, most manufacturers give attention to the systematic definition of their home market and the precise catering to its needs.

When it comes to international marketing however, their standards fall short. There is a tendency to regard "abroad" as an extension of the home market. Because it is almost always less profitable, the marketing operation tends to be less well attended to and certainly not in the necessary depth. This is of course a generalization. But it is true remarkably often and means that before considering any international research, it is first necessary to ensure that management has the right *attitude of mind* to undertake that research. Complete humility toward the unknown is essential. So too is the absolute denial of the all too prevalent opinion that methods found successful at home can automatically be introduced abroad.

This is why most manufacturers are bad exporters and their researchers (who ought to be dispassionate observers) are often equally shortsighted. And finally, in this background to research thinking, it is a fair generalization in the field of consumer products that wherever a user can afford to pay for what he needs, in all but the poorest countries today he can be supplied very largely from national or nearby international manufacturers. These comments apply equally to firms of all sizes, whether already operating abroad and wishing to extend their activities or whether considering foreign trading for the first time.

BASIC PROCEDURES AND ORGANIZATIONAL REQUIREMENTS

Marketing research undertaken abroad essentially follows the same mental discipline and procedural development as research for the home market. The instruments used may be cruder but the methods of use are much the same. The major stages at which research is mainly used in international marketing are as follows:

1. *Broad assessment of potential markets, undertaken "at home."* A short-listing procedure based upon published information and subjective evaluation of known or readily ascertained economic and political influences.

2. *Market evaluation in depth, undertaken at home and abroad.* A more intensive examination, including on-the-spot study of selected markets, to produce a priority list for the likely value to the manufacturer for his existing or modified products for each selected country. Research is here designed to enable go no-go decisions by management for trading in the market concerned. It will therefore include product suitability studies, likely growth opportunities, pricing problems, and promotional requirements.

When foreign trade is already undertaken, this kind of evaluative research can show whether to investigate intensification of existing markets or opening of new ones, especially in putting sales into time perspective by bringing out rising or falling market share.

3. *Measurement under launching conditions, undertaken abroad.* Pre-search is highly desirable to measure essential marketing factors when the product is launched in a new area, especially if it takes place under test-marketing or similarly limited conditions. Studies involved here will cover user acceptability under open purchase conditions, achievement in distribution penetration, trade acceptance, and repurchasing. These studies clearly must be made on the spot. Their intensity will depend upon the rate of purchase within the product group concerned.

4. *Measurement of continued selling under competitive conditions.* Here the research requirements are precisely the same as when selling at home, but the emphasis on any one marketing aspect or factor to be studied will vary enormously between markets. Although research will be used to compare one market's results with another, the actual form of research in each may have to differ to allow for national characteristics.

Head Office Staff Requirements

These are broad outlines only. They apply particularly to consumer products but also, in lesser degree (as with marketing at home), to industrial goods. Their intensity of application will vary between product groups and according to the importance of the individual product within the total market. Small or medium-sized home manufacturers can be very important overseas. Even the giant corporations are minuscule or nonexistent in some markets. For this reason it is inadvisable to specify the head or central office requirements for international research.

What is essential, however, is that regardless of the relative size of international activities, there must be an executive wholly responsible for planning and coordinating international research. This executive should preferably be separate from those responsible for home research. Experience suggests that parallel functioning, supported by the maximum exchange of marketing data, is the best under today's conditions. It is fair to add that as trading conditions become more standardized across national borders, this dichotomy between home and abroad will eventually disappear.

Some large corporations go further and set up their head office for foreign business in a foreign country. There is probably more justification for this action in research than in any other branch of the marketing function.

The staff infrastructure also will depend upon the extent of the corporation's intended foreign activities. The key criterion is usually the amount of traveling away from home that is likely to be required. There is relatively little executive work to be undertaken at the head office. Total staff can be very small. Both the senior executive and his staff must be highly professional or they are not worth having. Their function is basically supervisory. They must at all costs be mobile. They must be xenophilic and truly understanding of all the trading anomalies, inconsistencies, and nuances found in foreign countries. A head office research executive of a company with widely spread international business will spend some 50 percent of his time abroad. That clearly calls for mental qualities unlike those required for research at home.

Axiomatic in this is the complete integration of activities of the researcher within the corporation's marketing planning. It has long been fashionable for market researchers to live in some isolation from other marketing functions. But separate operation does not mean noncommunication. In international research this can happen even more easily than in home trade. The result is expensive but unusable research. Some international corporations therefore make the executive finally responsible a kind of marketing planner, with assistants to undertaken the practical functions under the marketing umbrella.

RESEARCH IN ACTION—MARKET ASSESSMENT

Before considering any marketing research abroad, the head office research executive should go back to first base. Although the information he will need for foreign trading is much the same as for selling in his own country, he must take no step for granted. Let him first consider, therefore, the headings under which information—that is, research—is needed. These will apply particularly for a product proposing to enter a market. But it is just as advisable to check them at intervals for products already established in a foreign market to ensure that such products are not losing to competition or wasting time in a dying market.

For any product seeking sales abroad, the following information is needed at one stage or another in planning the attack on any market.

1. Existing and potential sales within the product group that is under review

2. Competitive products catering to the existing market and their relative consumer acceptability

3. Likely opportunities for the product to enter into the market, and the fitness of the product (packaging, pricing, quality, feasibility) for those opportunities

4. Distribution facilities and their special characteristics for various sections of the trade

5. How best to promote the sales of the product under the foreign conditions, not only in the media but also in the advertising approach and message adopted

This list may seem naïve to an established manufacturer. That is what is meant by going back to first base. And it is equally necessary to do this whether the products under review be consumer or industrial. Moreover, one overriding item for investigation may upset all the others. This is the regrettable extension of governmental and political interference, both by tariff and by nontariff policy, to the freedom of international trade.

The collection of data at this basic stage in examining markets abroad, whether new or already existing, is commonly called *desk research*, because it can largely be undertaken at the head office from published material supplemented by similar material obtained from abroad by correspondence. Published information is improving rapidly in quantity, quality, and scope. Governments of all leading countries publish production data. Many include sales data on major product groups. Import and export figures vary in quality but are readily available, particularly from the major countries, whose figures can be used by extraction to provide indications of trading conditions in less well-documented countries. So too can the consular reports, which major countries issue gratis or at low cost. Intergovernmental sources such as United Nations, GATT, and the Organization for Economic Cooperation and Development add their published statistics, more particularly of raw materials [1, 2]. There are also many publications by trade associations, chambers of commerce [3], and internationally known publishers available free or at low cost.

Finally, there is a host of subscription publications from major research organizations, like the Economist Intelligence Unit, which augment the rapidly increasing corpus of publicly available marketing data. Statistics are slowly being standardized. It is usually possible to secure sufficiently accurate comparisons of basic marketing data (demographic, socioeconomic, consumption, housing, wages, and so on) for the most likely countries for foreign trading activities.

Essentially, this is the work of the international head office research staff. The larger the existing or planned international operation, the greater the justification for permanent analytical researchers. The mental requirements for this work are a readiness to appreciate the *background* to overseas data; an understanding of the interpretation of statistics which will be provided on varying bases and different methods of calculation; and an acceptance that things are different "over there," not necessarily worse than at home, but different. (This point cannot be made too often.) In other words a purely statistical, library-oriented approach is not enough. The *reasons for differences* in the statistics are more important in marketing planning than the statistics themselves.

The qualitative variations in published information become increasingly important where developing countries are concerned. Here factual data are usually limited in extent. In their place comes the need to know how local habits affect the potential use of a product. These habits are often well written up, so that the researcher can acquire background color for his bare statistics.

Setting up a good library is an essential for desk research. Alternatively—but this is possible only in certain major cities and centers of research—access to a good library will provide for the smaller organization. This library should have a background of statistical material about countries in general as well as specialist data about the product group with which the manufacturer is concerned. The American Marketing Association's bibliography series provides a useful start to the building up of an appropriate library.

Smaller organizations, faced with these problems for less immediate financial return, can be daunted by the prospects. However, the detailed work involved can be contracted out to market research agencies on an ad hoc fee basis. This facility can well be used, for less frequently involved markets or countries, to supplement the more readily obtained data from major countries. But management must ensure that the work is done and to the highest appropriate standards.

RESEARCH IN ACTION—FIELDWORK

Desk research is a first basic step. It can answer simple questions, more often than not of a go no-go nature. For positive action, however, fieldwork in the countries under review is necessary, as the following case history shows.

A food manufacturer was exporting in varying degree in most European markets. Preliminary desk research suggested that the manufacturer should concentrate on growth prospects, reflecting changing disposable incomes, rather than on established selling areas. All European countries were then studied afresh using only published information, including consular reports. Several countries already produced their own popular versions of the product in large quantities. At first sight those countries with lowest current usage or product penetration offered most immediate export gains.

Further study of consumer habits with the cooperation of research agencies in the countries concerned, however, revealed that high consumption was restricted to a very limited section of the community. In the mass-producing countries, a consistent and strong demand had been built up. This, in turn, created a taste for variety, so that these countries also showed reasonable imports.

The three largest (by consumption) markets were then selected for the next stage of research—product acceptance, distribution facilities, and so forth. These studies eliminated one country. The remaining two were chosen for development, but with different intensity based upon the research findings. But neither country would have been chosen by hunch or by the first research results. In this case, research showed a way in, and in doing so it indicated the marketing strategy (sell on quality at a premium price) and discovered an unexpected advertising and sales promotion approach (enjoy variety by using an entirely different, imported product).

In this particular instance, the classical procedure of international market research was followed. All desk research was undertaken in the home country from source data available there. The researcher then personally visited the three short-listed countries and initiated three more detailed—but still informal—studies by local research agencies. Finally, in two countries, consumer research on a formal basis was undertaken by local agencies with questionnaires and plans prepared at home but translated into the local languages. Special questions appropriate to each country were added on the recommendation of the local researchers. The briefing throughout was in the presence of head-office executives.

Executive Interviewing. Apart from showing the standard progression from one stage to another, this example brings out the integral part played by executive interviewing in good international research. A head office executive should always attend any major briefing before fieldwork. His task is to interpret the central research plan in terms of local conditions and idiom. This can be done only if that executive knows the country at least as far as the product group is concerned. He should have been around the trade, the industry, and the private homes to learn at first hand the immediate reactions to his particular problem. This time-consuming chore is often brushed aside—and the chances are that the briefing will suffer, with the resultant research good in itself but off tune for the problem in hand. "Time spent in reconnaissance is seldom wasted." So the researchers say in justifying the principle of market research. But it applies equally forcibly to those planning fieldwork in a foreign country.

It may well be that this experience of a market will have been obtained at the earlier general assessment stage or when studying other product groups. It cannot be stressed too strongly however that—no matter when this experience is gathered—it is of vital importance in international research.

RESEARCH IN ACTION—TECHNIQUES AVAILABLE

When the time comes to undertake the kind of research abroad that an international researcher is accustomed to having in his own country, he will find that, broadly speaking, he can have almost everything carried out that he is likely to require. Personal interviewing facilities are now available in every major country of the Western world [5]. They can also be provided, but with far less efficiency, in several developing countries.

It is not appropriate to comment here upon the relative efficiency of individual countries. Many of the industrialized countries have market research associations to encourage the technical development of research and to safeguard the ethical standards of its practitioners. In "newer" countries, numbers are still insufficient to warrant self-support, so researchers group together with other disciplines to form marketing associations. The frequent meetings of these groups at international conferences and seminars to discuss sophisticated topics in marketing and research are a constant means of raising the general level of research practice. Indeed, it is fair to say that wherever sophisticated *marketing* is required the necessary *research* can support it. Where marketing methods are more primitive, research is equally primitive—or virtually nonexistent.

The best researchers in all countries undoubtedly know technically far more than they are usually called upon to use. It is, however, pointless to ask more of an informant than he is in a position to answer. International research is therefore relatively basic; the questions straightforward and very direct, especially if more than one area is to be covered by a survey. Experience has taught that each country is best taken as a separate entity, with the research appropriate to itself but well-controlled within an international brief. It is almost certain that any multinational study will involve different social customs, languages, ways of life, and moral and social outlooks. To insist on identical questioning except on the very simplest of factual questions would put a survey into a straitjacket and produce material of little marketing application.

For this reason, researchers must modify their techniques to suit the needs. Visual aids become important for illiterate informants; psychology takes a different, more positive, turn; and husbands often insist on being interviewed rather than their wives. Therefore major psychological changes are necessary. Group interviewing has been most beneficial to researchers throughout the world and has become commonplace. (In some countries, like India, it has tended to become a social occasion, but not necessarily any the worse for that.) It is likely that quick interviews, "church hall" tests and their more sophisticated version of "workshop tests," will become a similar worldwide development. At present, however, they are mainly limited to the United States and the United Kingdom. They are spreading slowly into Europe.

For personal interviewing in the developed countries, all research organizations—whether in the United States or anywhere else—follow the same basic fieldwork practice. In the case of consumer research, part-time interviewers

—mostly women—are usually used. They are supervised to a lesser rather than a greater degree, checked for honesty rather more than accuracy, and trained very well in a few countries (particularly Great Britain). Fieldwork planning is in theory similarly standardized. In practice, local conditions impose variations. Probability samples are infrequent except in the United Kingdom, Holland, and Sweden. Most other countries accept well-interlocked quota sampling or alternatively the various modifications of truly random sampling which have been particularly well developed in some European countries. Basic data for quota or probability planning are improving but are still very inadequate in the developing nations. As a simple example, definitions of a *family* or *household* vary enormously.

In the less developed countries, considerable simplifications have to be made. Interviewers often have to be men (and to be prepared to risk bodily attack). Supervision needs to be much more direct and greater in extent. Western executive control becomes desirable and often imperative. The complications of language add to fieldwork problems, particularly when it comes to seeking any reasoning behind the informants' behavior or choice.

Understandably therefore, there is much greater use of executive interviewing among much smaller samples of reasonably typical informants in these countries in place of a more systematized sample survey. This applies particularly where the buying public for the product under review is very limited and usually found only in one or two major cities. A true sample survey can then be unnecessarily costly and would achieve no more useful and usable information than skilled executives can produce more economically and quickly.

Techniques using other than face-to-face interviewing are less easy to apply outside the United States. *Mail interviewing* is rather discredited but can be used under controlled conditions—particularly for specialist top-level or industrialist interviewing—in some developed countries, but the problem of the non-respondents deters serious researchers. *The telephone* is rarely used, its incidence being too atypical and its owners not yet accustomed to its use as a selling device let alone as an interviewing one.

Retailer interviewing is undertaken in most countries. So too is *medical and professional interviewing*, although this is increasingly difficult in the more sophisticated countries. *Retail audits* are now commonplace; *consumer* panels are less so but are slowly extending; *advertising research* is increasing more rapidly. It is more highly developed than anywhere in the world in Great Britain, where press readership and T.V. audience surveys set a standard to which other nations are rather slowly aspiring. Readership still tends to be confused with circulation, and the T.V. set is still a focal point for large mobile audiences in many, even European countries.

The use of audience survey techniques depends upon the sophistication of the business community. But national researchers at least know about these techniques, practice some of them regularly, and can usually arrange for others to be undertaken, if need be, on a temporary basis.

One technique justifies separate mention: the *omnibus survey*. Such surveys are readily available in most European countries. In Britain, for example, there is a wide choice of many, both general and specialized. Thanks to their development by the large research organizations, these surveys are now on offer in many countries, both developed and less developed. They provide a particularly convenient device to the international researcher in the early stages of his inquiry. They can supply factual support for an otherwise subjective assessment of a market. Moreover, where a product is not intended for deep penetration into a market, the limited information from an omnibus survey is more than likely to be adequate for the purpose and much more economical than a major sample inquiry.

There are various—and usually obvious—reasons for the inadequacies in international fieldwork and interviewing techniques. Underlying them all is the respondents' universal fear, except in Britain and in perhaps one or two Anglo-Saxon countries, that any "evidence" will be passed on either to the police or to the equally distrusted tax man. But to mention problems and inadequacies is not to say they cannot be overcome. Indeed, international research consists rather of a series of hurdles to be traversed—over, under, or through. Confronted with a task, the practice is to see how it would be tackled under ideal or completely free conditions and then to modify sophisticated techniques according to local customs and interviewer facilities. Ironically, the latter are often better than expected because, in almost all countries of the world outside the very richest, a large body of intelligent middle-class citizens need subsidiary income. They—and the older students—provide a remarkably good corpus of interviewers.

The overriding problem is that there are not enough fully trained people operating full time in marketing research. Exceptions to this statement are the United States, Great Britain, and perhaps three or four Western European countries. Elsewhere work—and the justification of capital investment in brains and manpower—is gradually increasing, and every year brings higher standards. But the obvious conclusions that can be drawn from this necessarily simplified description of world research conditions lead to the key to the planning of fieldwork for international research. To succeed, such research must comply with the following criteria:

1. The research briefing must be prepared by a senior executive with a thorough appreciation of the problems in the countries concerned.

2. There must first be a clear sorting out of all unnecessary or possibly confusing elements in order to simplify the interviewing.

3. The executive should ideally conduct at least part of the preliminary planning on the spot in each country concerned.

4. If that is not possible, he must know the country and his advisers there well enough to assess each preparatory step accurately.

5. Transference of centrally produced plans into fieldwork action requires detailed examination for appropriateness; translation not merely into the idiom but into the equivalent local meaning; and the use of fieldwork planning, sampling, and interviewing techniques that will produce *usable* answers, not merely answers to a series of questions.

6. To accomplish this, local research organizations in the country are essential. But quality varies, so a knowledge of the abilities and facilities of local research agencies is equally essential.

Fieldwork for Industrial Marketing Research. This can be undertaken in a limited number of countries. Organizations specializing in such work are not found to any degree outside North America, certain countries in Western Europe, Japan, and Australia. There is no doubt, however, that interest and activity in industrial market research are growing rapidly. It is no longer sufficient to say that the principles are the same as for consumer products. Today those principles are being put into practice.

The comparatively recently formed European Association for Industrial Marketing Research (EVAF) is growing very rapidly. Its success is already encouraging developments in other countries, particularly Australia. Where adequate local fieldwork facilities exist, industrial researchers can follow the same procedure as their consumer colleagues. But fieldwork outside this very small number of countries must be undertaken by the head office researcher himself with his own staff or local representative or teams of specialist researchers must be sent out from the sophisticated countries. Industrial market research often has the advantage of a well-defined universe, relatively small and contactable directly. But this simplification emphasizes in turn the ever greater importance here of on-the-spot investigation by fully trained executive personnel.

Indeed, this is even more strongly brought out by the kind of inquiry which mostly faces the industrial market researcher. In consumer research the emphasis is more often than not on specific activities within the marketing chain. In industrial research information is more likely to be required on a wider scale. In fact it comes closer to the requirements of a marketing *planner* rather than to those of a researcher. It includes in its sphere of influence studies on product planning, chain of distribution, pricing policy, sales policy and selling methods, sales promotion and advertising, servicing of products, warehousing policy, and spare parts backup.

Clearly interviewing important informants on these very specialized subjects is no job for unqualified interviewers. Where the sample is relatively small, therefore, there is a natural tendency to use executives from the manufacturing company. No matter who does the interviewing, however, he will everywhere come up against the same basic problem: who in a buying organization is the decision maker in the purchase of industrial goods?

To some extent this answer tends to be easier outside the few major industrialized countries because channels of communication tend to be centralized in the hands of a small number of executives whose support is essential for any order placing. It is the task of the industrial market researcher in international surveys to ensure that his interviews get through to these vital informants.

Experiments are being made with mail surveys once the key informants in a company have been located. Such surveys have obvious economic advantages, especially where much traveling is involved. But the problems of nonresponse or even of misunderstanding of the import of questions have potentially disastrous consequences. Nothing can really be said to replace the personal interview, particularly when it comes to assessing the implications of the information that has been gathered.

METHODS OF ORGANIZING MARKET RESEARCH ABROAD

There are several ways of having research undertaken. A manufacturer operating in many countries will almost certainly avail himself at some time or another of all of them. In simple terms, research can be produced by:

1. The manufacturer's own staff (from head office and/or local offices) making executive interviews through local trade sources.

2. Making use of local research organizations wherever they exist in the countries concerned, under the direct control of the manufacturer's own head office staff.

3. Appointing a research consultant or agency to plan, commission, and supervise the research wherever it is required. (In this case the consultant or agency replaces the manufacturer's own staff in the procedure. This method is particularly useful to organizations not wishing to build up large head office departments for which fieldwork is not continuous. The consultant or central research agency need not be located in the manufacturer's own country.)

4. Use of the relatively few global chains of research organizations with affiliates in most major countries, the work again being organized through one of those affiliates as the "lead" agency. (This is a refinement of 3.)

There is no order of preference for those alternative methods of organization. Choice turns on the economics of size of operations, convenience, communication, and—above all—cost-effectiveness. Certain generalizations may be made:

1. It is always *desirable*—as has just been inferred—that the manufacturer should have at least a small department responsible for his market research abroad. The extent to which that department undertakes either desk research, preliminary fieldwork, or active control of surveys depends entirely on the volume of work and upon the countries concerned.

2. It is *essential* that the manufacturer's own executive should visit countries abroad to see for himself how research can be undertaken in each. This need not mean that he should visit each country for every survey. But he must be able to assess fieldwork results before he can interpret them.

3. Experienced market research executives with knowledge of conditions in several countries are very rare, usually heavily involved, and not easily weaned away from their current employment. However, they cannot be in two places at once. Further, small inquiries are just as time-consuming and involve just as heavy a transportation commitment as do larger inquiries, especially when countries new to the manufacturer's experience are involved.

4. There is a very strong case to be made, therefore, for a combination of small central office staff plus maximized use of "outside" research facilities. This case is even stronger when manufacturers are entering international trading for the first time on a major scale.

Research Consultants. There is a small but growing number of experienced researchers now acting as consultants on the international scale. Their appointment by a manufacturer can be

1. *On a continuing basis,* whereby for a retainer fee they are available to give immediate advice and act, in effect, as a member of the central office team even though living in another country

2. *On an ad hoc basis,* employed only as required, for example, to assist in new countries where the manufacturer has neither staff nor experience

The justification for these consultants is their independence. They are not involved financially in any fieldwork organization and can therefore recommend whichever is best suited for the work in hand. They tend to have fewer clients and therefore claim greater mobility to supervise on-site inquiries and to give closer personal attention at all times. This has greater importance for inquiries in countries where honesty in fieldwork is at a premium or where illiteracy makes communication difficult. Their appointment should not increase the cost of any survey because it would be their responsibility to safeguard the manufacturer against unnecessary costs and overcharging. Their advantage in this respect lies in keeping the size of inquiries down to a pragmatic rather than an academic level.

The consultants' role in selecting the right research agency for the job in hand replaces to a large degree the modern practice of contracting out research projects. It is arguable whether this practice is sound under any circumstances, increasing though it may be in the United States. But in international research it can readily become irrational when truly comparable alternatives are not available. Clearly more than one potential agency should always be considered if such a choice exists. Clearly also, costs must be taken into account. But in international research other factors—particularly honesty, efficiency, and accuracy—are of greater importance; and the greatest of these is honesty.

Research Agencies.   These are of three kinds:

1.   *Independent market researchers* operating in one country alone, able to undertake most kinds of research but usually with particular interest in certain fields.

2.   *Members of international research chains* which operate similarly to independents (since they are mostly financially self-contained in each country) but have linking arrangements which facilitate international control from one "lead" country.

3.   *Research divisions of advertising agencies.*   In certain countries, especially where research facilities are scarce, the major advertising agencies undertake research organized through internal departments or subsidiary companies which can have the same advantage as the chain organizations of offering centralized control through the "lead" agency.   It is not necessary to use the advertising agency concerned for any promotional work, although for obvious reasons this is customary.

Whichever of these three choices is employed, the end result should be the same.   In a growing number of countries all these research agencies are grouping together into national associations, working to a common code of standards and ethics.   Nearly all such associations are members of the International Marketing Federation, and individual researchers are themselves also members of international professional bodies.   All these activities help to improve the technical level of competence in countries.   The manufacturer's concern therefore is to ensure that those whom he employs are the best for his task.   Hence advice can be useful from either an independent consultant, an international advertising agency (if he employs one), or from his research agency in his home territory (if it is experienced in international work).

Reference Centers.   These exist round the world to help in this task.   Major international bodies like the International Marketing Federation, the European Society for Opinion and Marketing Research (ESOMAR), and the European Association for Industrial Marketing (EVAF) all provide on request names of members able to undertake research.   Each of these bodies has close liaison with national associations.

Additionally, the (British) Market Research Society published in January 1969 an *International Directory of Market Research Organizations.*   The booklet provides for the first time as complete a list as possible on a worldwide basis. Names, addresses, telephone numbers, processing facilities, and services offered are included for no fewer than 38 countries in addition to the United States and the United Kingdom.   Addresses for reference to these bodies are given at the end of this chapter.

Research in a Consortium.   Several efforts have been made—without conspicuous success—to undertake research in some form of group operation with other sponsoring bodies or companies.   In theory, this idea is irreproachable. In practice, it fails because no two firms have precisely the same aims for research, or, if they have, they do not wish to share the results.   Governments, however, tend to encourage efforts of cooperative research, and sometimes manufacturers can certainly undertake their initial investigation of a market under such sponsorship.

Among the national agencies actively supporting fieldwork in this way are the Japanese Export Trade Research Organisation (JETRO) and the British National Export Council (BNEC).   Some countries also support "piggyback" research whereby a small firm uses the research and staff facilities of larger, noncompetitive firms with an international setup. Again theoretically sound, these schemes involve obvious practical difficulties and proven successes are rare. All these examples—using government support in some degree—depend on research being conducted in selected areas beneficial to the governments concerned. Two-way research encouragement is still in its infancy.

Danger Points in Research Organization. Emphasis has been laid several times on the necessity for on-the-spot study and control. There is no substitute for this. Local color, experience, and practice are essential. But it is wrong to leave too much to the local operator who claims, most often rightly, that he knows more about his own country than any foreigner does. What he usually does not know, however, is the way the foreigner wishes his work to be done for comparability with other countries. International research sponsors are therefore advised against too much reliance on the local man "who knows best."

Similarly, however, they are advised against imposing too rigid methods or procedures purely in the name of comparability. The biggest danger here lies in a centrally designed plan which does not allow for national variations in seemingly similar circumstances. A breakfast food survey, for example, faces a different context in every country. Semantics provide a major hurdle, not merely in drafting questions but also in the psychological background to an inquiry. Where the way of life differs greatly, multinational studies should concentrate on the broad aspects of the problem, not upon details. These latter should be considered only in individual studies of selected nations.

It is items of practical experience like these which only go to emphasize the cardinal elements of international research organization. It is fitting, therefore, to close by summarizing them:

1. Think globally, never in terms of the home country.

2. By all means use home experience, but expect at all times to have to bend it to suit national differences resulting from language, way of life, or social and economic development.

3. Do not overlook the very considerable amount of information available "at home" for desk research and preliminary sorting out of priorities.

4. Always *control* activities abroad but do not *dictate* procedures.

5. Use expert advice. Be prepared to pay for it. It will save money in other directions.

6. Check personally by on-the-spot examination.

7. Chose as national collaborators those best equipped to handle the enquiry. They will not necessarily be those most easily contacted at home.

8. Take advantage of national facilities. In some cases they will—for various reasons—be better than those that are available at home.

Following this procedure will not ensure success. But at least the procedure will deserve it—and be more likely to achieve it.

REFERENCES

1. *Export Marketing Research*, GATT International Trade Center, Geneva, May 1967.
2. *The Compilation of Basic Information on Export Markets*, GATT International Trade Center, Geneva, 1968.
3. *How Marketing Research Can Help Developing Countries in Increasing Their Trade and Export Marketing Research*, International Chamber of Commerce, Paris, November 1966 (two brochures containing useful case histories).
4. MARKET RESEARCH ORGANIZATIONS AROUND THE WORLD
   No organization has yet succeeded in producing a comprehensive list of agencies,

firms, institutes, or consultants capable of undertaking market research in the major countries of the world. The most informative, but far from complete, is the *International Directory of Market Research Organizations*, published by the Market Research Society, 51 Charles Street, London W1. All firms listed include essential data on their claimed facilities, and the completeness is marred only by the inability of firms to provide the data requested by the publishers. It is recommended as the best worldwide directory and contains no paid advertising or pressurized entries.

For Europe only, the *ESOMAR Handbook* is published annually by the Secretariat, Raadhuisstraat 15, Amsterdam, Netherlands. This handbook also contains information on facilities offered and specialist techniques employed in some 23 countries but is confined to organizations represented by members of the Society.

There are now four international associations and national associations in no less than 32 countries. The latter are usually closely linked with one or more of the international associations to ensure regular exchange of ideas, communications, and educational facilities. For information about research organizations in any of these countries, it is best to write to the secretariat addresses of the national societies listed below. They do not recommend individual firms but do provide lists of qualified organizations from which a choice can be made.

INTERNATIONAL ORGANIZATIONS

International Marketing Federation
General Secretary: A. van Goch
                 Parkstraat 18
                 The Hague
                 Netherlands

World Association for Public Opinion Research
Secretary-Treasurer: P. Hastings
                      Roper Public Opinion Research Center
                      Williams College
                      Williamstown
                      Massachusetts

ESOMAR—European Society for Opinion and Marketing Research
Secretary General: Ms. F. Monti
                  Raadhuisstraat 15
                  Amsterdam
                  Netherlands

EVAF—European Association for Industrial Marketing Research
Secretariat: Mrs. Boyd Stevenson
             39-40 St. James's Place
             London SW1
             United Kingdom

NATIONAL ASSOCIATIONS

Argentina
Sociedad Argentina de Marketing
Avenida Belgrano 1670, 5 Piso,
  Buenos Aires
Australia
Marketing Research Society of
  Australia
c/o Dr. Arthur Meadows,
  8 Beauty Point Road
Mosman, New South Wales
Austria
Verband Marktforscher Osterreichs
c/o Henkel Austria,
  Erdbergstrasse 29, A-1030
  Vienna

Belgium
Belgian Market Research Association
Chaussée de Wavre 16,
  1050 Brussels
Belgian Management and Marketing
  Association
5 Place du Champs de Mars,
  1050 Brussels
Brazil
Associação dos Directores de Vendas
  do Brasil
Alameda Santos 2326, São Paulo
Czechoslovakia
Czechoslovak Marketing Association
Smetanovo Nabrezi 26, Prague 1

Denmark
Association of Market Research
Organizations in Denmark—
AMROD
Lindevangs Alle 14,
2000 Copenhagen
Danish Market Research Association
c/o Masius Reklamebureau A/S,
Halmtorvet 20
1700 Copenhagen
Finland
Finnish Marketing Association
Runeberginkatu 22-24, Helsinki 12
Finnish Marketing Research Society
c/o Suomen BP Oy, Nikonkatu 8,
Helsinki 10
Suomen Myynti—Marketing
Research Section
c/o Mrs. Sirpa Saarikivi,
IFH Research International Oy
Keskukatu 3, Helsinki 10
France
ADETEM—Association nationale
pour le Développement des
Techniques de Marketing,
30 rue d'Astorg, 75 Paris 8ème
Germany
ADM—Arbeitskreis Deutscher
Marktforschungsinstitute e.v.
Altkönigstrasse 2,
6231 Schwalbach am Taunus
BVM—German Market Research
Association
Eulenkamp 14, 2000 Hamburg 70
Greece
GMA—Institute of Marketing
6 Philellinon Street, Athens 118
Hellenic Marketing Association
c/o 57 Acadimias Street, Athens
Hungary
Hungarian Committee for Marketing
V. Kossuth Lajos ter 6-8, Budapest
India
Indian Marketing Association
PO Box 1015, Bombay 1
Ireland
Marketing Society of Ireland
19 and 20 Upper Pembroke Street,
Dublin 2
Israel
Israel Marketing Association
Leon Recanti Graduate School of
Business Administration
Ramat-Aviv, Tel-Aviv
Italy
Associazione Italiana per gli Studi
di Marketing
Via Olmetto 3, Milano

Japan
Japan Marketing Association
Ginza Studio Building
16-7, 2-chome, Ginza Chuo-ku,
Tokyo
Korea
Korean Marketing Association
PO Box 3774, Seoul
Mexico
Mexican Marketing Association
PO Box 20-350, Mexico 20 D.F.
Netherlands
Nederlands Instituut voor Marketing
Parkstraat 18, Den Haag
Nederlandse Vereniging van
Marktonderzoekers
Organisatie-Bureau Wissenraet NV
Van Eeghenstraat 86, Amsterdam
1007
New Zealand
Market Research Society of
New Zealand
PO Box 2147, Wellington
Norway
Norwegian Marketing Research
Society
c/o Marketing Assistanse A/S
Tronheimsveien 135, Oslo 5
Pakistan
Marketing Association of Pakistan
23 Zaibunnisa Street, PO Box 7438,
Karachi 3
Portugal
Sociedade Portuguesa de
Commercialização—Marketing
Avenida Elias Garcia 172, 2 Esq,
Lisboa 1
Rumania
Rumanian Marketing Association
12 Republicii Boulevard
Bucharest
South Africa
South African Market Research
Association
PO Box 10483, Johannesburg
Spain
Asociación Española de Marketing
Avenida de Calvo Sotelo 29, Madrid
Asociación Española de Estudios
de Mercado y de Opinión
c/o Apartado 12.170, Barcelona 6
Sweden
Swedish M—Gruppen
Fladerstigen 7, 13671 Handen
Switzerland
GFM—Schweizerische Gesellschaft
für Marktforschung
Dorfstrasse 29, 8037 Zurich

GREM—Groupement Romand
pour l'Etude du Marché
et du Marketing
Bellefontaine 18, 1001 Lausanne
Thailand
Marketing Association of Thailand
c/o Thailand Management
Development and Productivity
Center
6 Rama Road, Bangkok
United Kingdom
Association of Market Survey
Organisations
c/o Victory House, 99-101 Regent
Street, London W1R 8DH
Industrial Marketing Research
Association
28 Bore Street, Lichfield,
Staffordshire
Market Research Society
51 Charles Street, London W1X 7PA
United States
American Marketing Association
222 S. Riverside Plaza,
Chicago, Illinois 60606
Yugoslavia
Yugoslav Marketing Association
Makanceva 16, 41000 Zagreb

Note: The above addresses are the latest reported mid-1973. In several countries, addresses change with the election of officers. Correspondents should, however, contact the above in the first instance.

International Marketing

Chapter 2

Problems of Cross-cultural Research

S. WATSON DUNN   *Department of Advertising, University of Illinois at Urbana-Champaign, Illinois*

The average business firm—regardless where it is located—devotes surprisingly little attention to the markets its executives normally know least about—its foreign markets.   One study of 30 large United States corporations, for example, indicated that only a handful were conducting or having their agencies or research firms conduct what could reasonably be called "cross-cultural" or "international" research [6].   Many foreign operations fail primarily because the international marketer did not research his market before he ventured into the foreign area with a major financial commitment.

Yoshino points out that there is "a perceptibly inflexible attitude among . . . firms . . . toward devising an appropriate entry strategy. . . .   Frequently an entry is determined *prior* to market investigation" [21].   He describes the case of a United States manufacturer of electronic products who concluded on the basis of cost comparisons that the potential profit in some Asian markets justified establishing a beachhead there as soon as possible.   The venture was a failure mainly because many relevant market factors were neglected.

In one case known to this author, a large American manufacturer of farm machinery rushed into establishment of a manufacturing and marketing subsidiary in Western Europe primarily on the recommendation of the firm's distributor in that country.   The market for the type of machine produced by the factory turned out to be far less than the company anticipated, and the operation was phased out at considerable loss after four years.

In this chapter we shall concentrate on those problems which are most likely to cause the cross-cultural researcher serious difficulty.   Much is sometimes made of the difference among the terms, *cross-cultural, international, comparative,* and *multinational* research, but these differences need not concern us here since the operational problems are much the same in each. Nor do we need to discuss in detail the tools and techniques of cross-cultural research, since these are not generally different from those one would use in domestic marketing research. It is instead the environment in which the tools are used that varies from country to country and most often causes difficulties. The researcher need not devise new methods of research, but he must develop the ability to adapt his tried and tested techniques to strange and often frustrating environments. Though he will be searching for the same general types of information (for example, channels, distribution facilities, advertising media coverage and characteristics, and relative effectiveness of alternative strategies), he will find the information more difficult to ferret out than in the domestic market, and he is likely to have more serious doubts as to its accuracy.

The following problems of cross-cultural research will be treated in this chapter: communication, particularly with research personnel and respondents; organization of the research operation; collection of data; sampling; utilizing the proper resources; research costs; and analysis and interpretation of research findings.

COMMUNICATION

The problem of communication in cross-cultural research has many dimensions. It involves, for example, finding out whether the questions used in one country mean the same thing to respondents in another. It involves also communicating to research personnel in various countries and making sure instructions are perfectly clear to them. Research personnel, like respondents, have a tendency to say politely that they understand instructions when they really do not. The slowness of communicating with foreign research personnel and the leisurely pace at which some foreign interviews progress can become quite frustrating to an American marketing executive who fancies himself an efficient person.

For example, the author conducted a series of field studies in France and Egypt. In France it took two sessions of about an hour each to train the interviewers; in Egypt the same sort of training consumed three two-hour sessions. The average interview in France consumed 38 minutes; a similar interview in Egypt took well over an hour.

Communication problems are due partly, of course, to differences in language. In India one will find 14 different "official" languages and a very low level of literacy among the population. Furthermore, most of these languages are unfamiliar to the Western researcher who may be at home only in English, French, or German. The researcher must decide whether the information is worth the time, trouble, and expense of adapting the questionnaire and instructions into each of these languages. Even small countries are multilingual. Switzerland has three major languages and Belgium two.

There are wide variations in language usage within a single language block. Most Americans who have been in England know that an elevator there is a "lift" and that a can of beans is a "tin" of beans. They may not, however, be so aware of the vast differences between the spoken and written Spanish of Puerto Rico as compared with that of Chile, or between the spoken French of eastern Canada as compared with that of France.

Commonly used terms can also be a source of trouble. Alfred Boote of Pepsico points out that the term *soft drink* often has a different meaning in foreign markets. He found that the term often excluded noncarbonated products which competed just as strongly as carbonated ones in some of the primary market segments [1]. For example, consumer surveys in Japan showed that the rough equivalent of the expression *soft drink* included traditional fruit and cider drinks. In America these were not considered direct competitors because some of them did not exist or were classified under another product definition. When the United States meaning of soft drink was used in Japan, the answers to questions were misleading and the company's competitive position appeared to be far stronger than it really was. Also, the marketers were blinded to certain alternative advertising and marketing strategies.

A common and often satisfactory approach to ironing out communication problems in questionnaires is to have the translated version of an advertising theme, a questionnaire, or instructions to interviewers translated back into English by someone who has not seen the original. For example, Pepsi-Cola management wanted to use in Hong Kong a successful Australian theme line, "Baby, It's Cold Inside," an obvious play on an old American pop song, "Baby, It's Cold Outside." When the Cantonese version of this was translated back into English it became "Small Mosquito, on the Inside It Is Very Cold." In colloquial Cantonese, "Small Mosquito" is the accepted expression for referring to a very young child or baby, but the intended meaning had been lost.

The order in which questions are asked and the congruence of the questionnaire may have a good deal to do both with comprehension and establishing rapport with respondents. As Hall points out, "The placing of a [story's] climax varies all over the world" [11, p. 122]. A perfectly natural and understandable order in one country is confusing in another, and in some languages and cultures order is of no particular importance. Certain wordings may be incongruous in some cultures and perfectly acceptable in others. For example, in some we would prefer a rather formal wording in questionnaires; in others, a friendlier approach might be more appropriate. In some, metaphors are congruous, in others they may obscure the meaning.

ORGANIZATION

If the international operation of a company is centralized, the research operation is ordinarily centralized also. For example, in General Foods the executive responsible for research is situated in the firm's headquarters in Rye, New York. In Beatrice Foods, however, there is practically no centralized control from the firm's headquarters, since each overseas subsidiary has almost complete autonomy in research as well as in its other activities. Instead of trying to coordinate the marketing activities (including research), the management expects merely that the various subsidiaries report on the projects in progress and on results of projects which are completed.

In general, as a company becomes internationalized, it will tend to centralize the coordination and guidance, if not the operational control, of its research operation. The top management of a company should have available certain information on the firm's marketing activities in various markets of the world. Also, centralization allows greater specialization by researchers. A firm might, for example, employ specialists in electronic data processing or psychological testing at a central headquarters, while it would not be economic to employ them at a foreign office. Or the firm might have researchers who work full time on a particular project in all markets or who work on all projects involving a certain geographical area. As research becomes more technical and specialized, firms may have even more reason to consider centralizing the research operation.

The job of the international research coordinator or director is a complex one. He must keep track of the problems in each foreign market if he is to make recommendations on which should be supported and which should be postponed or canceled. The dilemma of the international research head is well summarized by T. Edward Gavin of Cyanamid International [10]:

> The organization of the international research function presents a whole series of problems beyond those that we encounter operating a research department in the domestic area. How do you manage personnel 3,000 to 10,000 miles away? To whom do they report? Who designs their research plans? How do you check on their work? Who administers supervision and what degree of guidance can the international research manager give on a regular basis? Beyond these points, how do we determine which studies should be undertaken if we market a series of products in 80 to 100 countries? If you are a multi-line company, such as Cyanamid, how do you staff and implement research on a wide variety of products—from those of rapid turnover, low-price consumer items to ethical pharmaceuticals and on to chemical specialties, bulk chemicals and building products? Add to this wide variety of products which may require some market research attention, the lack of homogeneity among your markets and you will see we are faced with problems which are considerably different from those encountered in running a department in the United States.

Mr. Gavin suggests a combination of utilizing people in the home office, internationally oriented research firms, personnel from the domestic research departments, and participation in multiclient studies as possible solutions. He suggests further that a small group be maintained in the home office and that personnel be added as needed in the major market areas.

Prior to having personnel in the foreign markets, a firm can borrow experienced research personnel and have them travel. If the domestic research expert is sent to a particular market, he can enlist the aid of the sales personnel, distributors, and the firm's advertising agency. If the firm has no personnel in a particular market which is to be researched, it is probably best to call on the services of an international research firm which has an office or strong affiliate in that country.

Among the principal considerations in deciding how much centralization of the research function is needed are the uses to which the information will be put by the firm's top management, the importance of international operations as compared with domestic, and the stage of development of the corporate organization. For example, a firm that is exporting its product and has done little in the way of developing subsidiaries or joint ventures around the world and the company which is truly global in managerial outlook will both need a continuous flow of information.

COLLECTION OF DATA

Some researchers, accustomed to the comparative ease of obtaining respondent cooperation in the United States, have been surprised at the difficulties they have encountered in other countries. This is partly due to the state of the art of interviewing. Since consumer research has become a major function of business in the United States, one can find a corps of good interviewers in almost any part of the United States. The chances are these people will have various kinds of interviewing experience and will be able to collect information with only a minimum of supervision. This is simply not true in most other countries.

Certain cultural factors also influence the collection of information. For example, many cultures place a high value on one's privacy, and people of such cultures tend to resent any questions which appear to violate it. Respondents in many countries feel—as do some in the United States—that questions about one's income, one's religious beliefs, or one's feeling toward a particular country are overly nosy. In some cases, people feel that information about income may be used against them by the tax collector. In totalitarian states people are understandably reluctant to provide any information they think might be used against them by the government.

In some cultures it is not proper to ask a housewife for certain information without the presence of her husband. And in such cases the husband will do most of the answering, apparently on the basis that he knows better than his wife what her attitude is toward certain products or services. In some cultures it is difficult to gain cooperation from businessmen accustomed to running a tight ship and keeping all disclosures to their workers, their government, their stockholders, and even their trade associations to a minimum.

Those methods of overcoming respondent noncooperation that work in the United States are worth trying in other countries. For example, respondents almost everywhere are impressed by assurances that the information is to be treated confidentially, that no data will be reported by name, and that cooperation will help businessmen serve them better. Respondent cooperation has been improved in France through a series of cinema commercials which point out, in a lighthearted manner, how much fun and how flattering it is to be interviewed in a survey. These also point out that cooperation helps respondents receive the products and services that will serve them best.

In some areas of the world, cooperation is better if certain amenities are observed. This may consist of having a cup of coffee or tea with the respondent; it may consist of leading up to the topic of the survey through indirection; or it may consist of making sure that an appointment is made ahead of time for the interview.

The problems of collecting data are well illustrated by the "mysterious girls" incident which took place in Hong Kong in late 1967 [1]. Four leading, conservative Chinese papers carried headlines such as this one: "A Group of Mysterious Girls Questioning People's Opinions on Living. . . . It Looks as if Hong Kong Communists Have Some New Ideas." The next day the English-language *South China Morning Post* attempted to stifle the controversy with the headline "Mystery of Strange Interviews Solved." This story explained that the "mysterious girls" were not Communist agents but were employed by a market research organization and were simply collecting information for commercial purposes. Two days later the secretary of the Market Research Society of Hong Kong issued a statement—carried by several neutral papers—explaining research objectives and urging continued cooperation of the public with survey interviewers. A day or so later the leftist daily *New Evening Post* ran a story whose headline, translated, read "After the Mysterious Girls Had Nowhere to Hide, the British Royal Hong Kong Research Organization Tries to Cover Themselves and Use a Society's Name to Deny." It was charged that the government had used this society to "carry out an extensive research to collect data in order to obstruct our compatriots in Hong Kong and Kowloon to practice Chairman Mao's ideas."

In order to avoid becoming involved in political controversies such as this in sensitive areas of the world, Mr. Boote recommends that researchers take precautionary measures—such as issuing valid credentials to interviewers, clearing the survey with appropriate government agencies before fieldwork begins, and making sure questions are not phrased so ambiguously that they may have political implications.

In a survey in the Middle East, supervised by the author, one male respondent who fell within the sample turned out to be a government official who was highly suspicious of the survey, particularly so when he heard it had American sponsorship. However, he did not complain about the interview until it was completed and the interviewer was about to leave. He then threatened to have her arrested. She reported this to the native supervisor who telephoned the respondent immediately to assure him the survey had government approval and he (the supervisor) offered to come to the respondent's house to discuss the survey in person. This pacified the irate respondent.

In the developing countries it is almost impossible to collect data by telephone. Few persons have phones. In some countries this is a result of general poverty, in some the result of very high cost of installation, in others the result of long delays for installation. In many cases the persons who answer—particularly women—are suspicious of strangers on the phone.

Mail surveys also present serious problems. In some cases this is a result of a low literacy rate. In many parts of the world the postal service is poor and many letters—even those which go first class—are delivered after a long delay or not at all. In some cultures people do not believe in writing replies which will be read by a stranger. In many cases, of course, cooperation in mail surveys can be improved by making sure the questionnaire is quite satisfactory.

Researchers should be very careful not to force a standard interview schedule or questionnaire upon all markets before it has been checked in each market. To achieve cross-cultural comparability, it is often necessary to make substantial changes in a questionnaire. Not only the wording but also the order of questions may cause trouble in collecting information.

SAMPLING

The scarcity of details on the universe being sampled makes it somewhat difficult to draw a sample in many parts of the world. If the researcher cannot find current and reliable lists, sampling becomes more complex and less reliable. In many countries telephone directories, street directories, city directories, census tract and block data, and detailed information on the social and economic characteristics of the universe are available. In some, however, no such information is obtainable and the researcher will have to make his own estimates. In some parts of the world street maps are simply not available, and if they are, they can often be hopelessly out of date. Selection of blocks on a probability basis is often not feasible. Without block statistics it is not possible to draw blocks proportionate to the population.

Sampling within blocks is often difficult also because houses in many areas of the world—particularly in the Middle East—are not numbered or otherwise identified. Even the concept of "dwelling unit" is a hazy one when many families live in the same dwelling.

If satisfactory statistics on which to base a probability sample are not available, the researcher will have to use his ingenuity. In one such case a government agency in the Middle East wanted to find out what socioeconomic groups in a given city were more apt to watch broadcasts from the government-owned television station [2]. Only a map of the city was available. The research director divided the city into a large number of areas that he felt were about equal in population. Using probability techniques, he selected 50 of these. In each of the 50, interviewers were instructed to contact a given number of men and women over 16 years of age. A second round of interviews was planned in case data for a particular group were too sparse for analysis.

Boyd, Frank, Massy, and Zoheir point out that such difficulties "make it relatively easy to rationalize the use of convenience sampling. . . . Even quota sampling, i.e., non-probability sampling in which interviewing quotas are established for various kinds of respondents, is not typically possible because of the lack of needed secondary data."

In some cases it is not economical to use random samples. Lucy Webster mentions the case of a survey in five Western European countries where either random or quota sampling might have been used. In four of these, random sampling could have been accomplished from readily available lists, but in the fifth it would have been necessary to buy a special list at a very high price. Consequently, the quota method was chosen for the fifth country since previous experience had shown that it could produce acceptably correct and meaningful results comparable with results obtained by random sampling in other countries [20].

RESOURCES AND SOURCES

Primary

In such areas as the United States, Western Europe, Australia, and Japan, the international marketer can find a variety of resources readily available. However, in Africa and many parts of Asia, it is still difficult to conduct multination studies which are comparable, even though there are often sound, effective local agencies capable of providing a wide range and scope of research service. In the Iron Curtain countries, the economic system has emphasized production rather than marketing, and consequently marketing research activities still receive low priority [16].

There are few parts of the world where a marketer cannot find a research organization or two or at least a person who offers to provide such services as the collecting, processing, analyzing, and interpreting of research data. These include specialized economic and marketing research organizations, many of which are affiliates of some international organization like International Research Associates. On the other hand, some international research firms such as A. C. Nielsen have wholly owned subsidiaries in countries where they operate. Other firms which often provide research service include research departments of advertising agencies; management consultants; certain large accounting firms; publishers of books, periodicals, magazines, or newspapers which have a research department; and certain international law firms whose services to clients include information on such legal questions as taxation, organizational structure, and regulation of copy claims.

Although universities outside the United States are not as likely as their United States counterparts to have a bureau of business research or a survey research center, many professors around the world are experienced administrators of research projects and can be called on for help. In some cases they can draw on marketing or psychology students as trained interviewers.

American marketers sometimes disparage foreign research organizations, partly because the United States has more such firms than other countries and partly because the average United States corporation, advertising agency, or advertising medium tends to have a sizable research department. Some researchers have pointed out, however, that quantity does not always connote superior quality.   For example, David Hardin, board chairman of Market Facts, Inc., maintains that European marketing research is "much more professionalized" than American [12].   He adds, however, that "they're not as problem-solving oriented as we are.   What it boils down to is European brainpower versus American efficiency.   We spend more time selling research—they spend more time thinking about it."

Anyone wanting to hire a research agency would be well advised to consult one of the many directories of research agencies.   One standard source is *Bradford's Directory of Marketing Research Agencies and Management Consultants in the United States and the World* [3].   This directory lists and describes the services offered by more than 350 agencies around the world.

Such periodicals as *Journal of Marketing, Journal of Marketing Research, Advertising Age, International Advertiser, Marketing/Communications,* and *Journal of Advertising Research* accept advertisements from research firms and include articles written by the executives of various research organizations. The United States Department of Commerce has published an annotated list of advertising and marketing research agencies which provide international service.

Secondary

Secondary sources should always be evaluated prior to making a primary study. It is particularly important to check them in the case of cross-cultural research, where primary research is likely to be complicated and expensive and to be full of unknowns.   Sometimes secondary data can be collected on a fairly regular basis as a guide to deciding at what point a particular market justifies a primary study.   Among the major secondary sources for cross-cultural studies are the following:

Supranational Government Organizations.   Among these are the United Nations, United Nations Education and Scientific Organization, Organization for Economic Cooperation and Development, the European Economic Community, the European Free Trade Association, the General Agreement on Trade and Tariffs, the European Coal and Steel Community, the International Bank for Reconstruction and Development, the International Monetary Fund, and the World Health Organization.   Most of these maintain an office in New York, Washington, or some other world center.

National Governments.   Most national governments have a variety of agencies and bureaus which publish information of interest to international marketers.   In the United States, for example, helpful information might be gleaned from publications of the Department of Commerce, Department of State, Department of Agriculture, Department of Labor, Treasury Department, Federal Trade Commission, Tariff Commission, Agency for International Development, United States Information Agency, and the Export-Import Bank.   The Department of Commerce is especially helpful in that it maintains offices around the United States as well as in major countries of the world.   The commercial attaché's office in most embassies is a prime source of information regarding the country in which the embassy is located.

Financial Institutions.   Commercial banks and investment firms involved in international business have departments which keep much helpful information on hand.   Some, such as Chase Manhattan Bank, publish statistics and articles on markets around the world on a continuing basis.

Trade Associations.   Trade associations and professional groups are becoming increasingly interested in international marketing and most are making an effort to pull together statistics of interest to their members. The International Chamber of Commerce, headquartered in Paris, has associate private business member groups all over the world. Its general objective is to encourage trade among nations, and it collects information which fits in with this objective. The Chamber of Commerce of the United States and its various associate chambers of commerce around the country are also active in encouraging foreign trade. The Chamber's publication, *Foreign Commerce Handbook,* is a compendium of information on governmental, business, and professional organizations involved in international trade; sources of information on international trade; and articles and books on international trade.

Advertising Media. Those media which sell space in the international field tend to make surveys they think will enhance that medium in the eyes of potential space or time buyers. However, this fact should not blind international marketers to the fact that much useful information is collected by these media. For example, the publication *The European Common Market and Great Britain,* by *Reader's Digest,* contains a wealth of information on the buying habits and attitudes of Western Europeans which is not available in any other form.

Research Firms. Some secondary data are released by international firms from time to time. For example, A. C. Nielsen will include some information gleaned by its offices around the world in the *Nielsen Researcher* and its other publications.

Trade and Technical Media. Perhaps the most important secondary source of all is the wealth of material published in trade, technical, and business publications around the world. It is often a laborious task to track down articles on a given subject, but the results are often well worth the effort. In the United States the task is greatly simplified through the *Business Publications Index,* which indexes on a regular basis the major United States business publications.

Although a wealth of cross-cultural data from secondary sources is available, there are difficulties in putting it to use. For one thing, much more information is available on the developed than the underdeveloped countries. Also it is difficult to make comparisons from one area to another where different bases were used for reporting or where explanatory footnotes which interpret the data are lacking.

COSTS OF RESEARCH

A common mistake in making up research budgets is to equate the costs of research in various areas of the world with general wage and salary levels in those areas. For example, one might expect that a survey in a country where wages and salaries are roughly half those of the United States would cost about half that in the United States. In practice it is likely to cost just as much or perhaps a little more in spite of the wage differential. Savings in hourly wages for interviewers or supervisors are likely to be balanced by such items as travel costs (gasoline, for example, is much more expensive in most countries than in the United States), costs of sending supervisory personnel from the home office, costs of supplies (the paper on which questionnaires are printed is quite expensive in many areas), and the inefficiency of operating a survey many miles from the home office.

Ideally costs should be related as closely as possible to the value of the information collected. In practice, it is difficult to put an exact figure on expected value, and at best it is a subjective figure. One must decide whether the decision which is to be based (either entirely or in part) on this information is sufficiently important to justify the cost. For some foreign markets, the potential is so small that a major research expenditure is probably not justified. For larger or rapidly developing markets, a substantial expenditure may well be justified.

ANALYSIS OF DATA

Among the problems likely to cause trouble in analyzing cross-cultural data are questionable or inadequate data and lack of comparability.

Some of the influences that cause data to be distorted have already been covered in this chapter. Many of these are cultural, since culture and tradition can influence not only willingness to give information but also the accuracy and amount of information. Consequently it is always dangerous to accept information at face value. Whether one is analyzing data on people's attitudes, media circulation figures, or information on buying habits, he should remember that people do not necessarily tell the whole truth to interviewers.

Lack of satisfactory data is likely to be a particularly thorny problem to one analyzing data from underdeveloped countries. Many factors contribute to this situation: too few trained research personnel, lack of careful supervision, poor government data, and poor communications among others. Moyer suggests that researchers resort to certain shortcut methods to overcome, at least to some extent, the lack of data [16]. Among those he suggests as particularly appropriate for less-developed areas are deduction by analogy, analysis of import substitution, analysis of elasticities, and the use of regression analysis.

Most analysts hope for comparable data in multicountry studies, but they often question whether the data collected are really comparable. Lucy Webster suggests that sameness of method of collection by no means assures comparable data for analysis [20]. She suggests that data are comparable if we have used the most *efficient* rather than the *same* method of collection in each country. She alleges that we need not worry whether the data were collected by the same method in each country, but that we should, instead, determine whether they have the same degree of reliability.

If the local alternative methods are all equally good, one may as well use the same methods in one or more countries. If, on the other hand, they may lead to some bias, one might deliberately choose different methods to check whether and how potential biases operate.

Hess and Cateora suggest that the research analyst "should be either a national or should be advised by someone who can accurately appraise the data collected in light of the local environment, thereby helping to validate secondary as well as primary data" [13, p. 398]. Whether he is a national or a foreigner, he must somehow combine a healthy dose of skepticism with considerable resourcefulness and imagination if he is to be a good analyst.

SUMMARY

As a firm becomes more committed to foreign marketing, the cost of failure increases and research becomes more necessary. Cross-cultural research, however, involves several problems not normally encountered—at least in the same form—in domestic research. Among the most troublesome is communicating with research personnel and with respondents in the various countries in which one is conducting research. These difficulties are due partly to language and partly to cultural barriers of all sorts. Careful testing of the questionnaires and instructions and back translation where possible are among the best methods of overcoming communication difficulties.

Another thorny problem is deciding how the research organization will be set up. To what extent will it be centralized? How can the research director operate efficiently in managing research personnel around the world and in making sure the research design is followed? A combination of centralization and decentralization appears to be the best answer. Among the considerations determining how much one should centralize the operation are the extent to which local personnel can be utilized, the probable use of information gained, the importance of the international operation to the firm, and the stage of development of the corporate organization.

Collection of data is another problem that may cause serious trouble. This stems partly from the lack of skilled interviewers in many parts of the world, partly from cultural traits that discourage giving information to strangers or casual acquaintances, and partly from poor construction of interview schedules or questionnaires. With telephone or mail surveys, it is particularly difficult to elicit satisfactory respondent cooperation.

Sampling is particularly troublesome in countries where lists and statistics for drawing probability samples are lacking. In some cases it is just not economical to use random samples. Resources vary substantially from country to country, although there are few where they are completely lacking. In most developed countries there are many research organizations and facilities to draw on. In the case of secondary data there is a wide variety of sources, but it is sometimes difficult to make use of it—especially in comparing countries—since a disproportionate amount comes from the better developed countries and since explanatory notes are often missing.

Costs should be related as closely as possible to the value of the information to be gathered. However, it is a mistake to assume one can make a low-cost survey in a low-wage country, because this is not usually the case. Among the problems that cause trouble in analyzing cross-cultural data are the poor quality of the data and the lack of comparable data.

REFERENCES

1. Boote, A. S., "Cultural Myopia," talk delivered to the International Marketing Group, American Marketing Association, New York, May 1, 1969.
2. Boyd, H. W., Jr., R. E. Frank, W. F. Massy, and M. Zoheir, "On the Use of Marketing Research in the Emerging Economies," *Journal of Marketing Research*, vol. 1, November 1964.
3. Bradford, E. S., *Bradford's Directory of Marketing Research Agencies and Management Consultants in the United States and the World*, 11th ed., Middleburg, Va.: Ernest Bradford, 1968.
4. Carson, D., *International Marketing: Comparative Systems Approach*, New York: Wiley, 1967, part II.
5. Dunn, S. W., "The Case Study Approach in Cross-Cultural Research," *Journal of Marketing Research*, vol. 3, February 1966.
6. ———, "Cross-Cultural Research by U.S. Corporations," *Journalism Quarterly*, Summer 1965.
7. Edwards, A. R., "Organizing for International Market Information," in S. W. Dunn, ed., *International Handbook of Advertising*, New York: McGraw-Hill, 1964.
8. Fayerweater, J., "Practical Guides to Collecting International Advertising Information," in S. W. Dunn, ed., *International Handbook of Advertising*, New York: McGraw-Hill, 1964.

9. ———, *International Marketing*, Englewood Cliffs, N.J.: Prentice-Hall, 1965, chaps. 1–4.
10. Gavin, T. E., "Reducing the Marketing Research Job to Manageable Proportions," speech presented at Annual Marketing Conference, National Industrial Conference Board, New York, October 21, 1965.
11. Hall, E. T., *The Silent Language*, New York: Fawcett, 1963.
12. "Hardin Calls European Research More Sophisticated Than American," *Advertising Age*, June 22, 1964.
13. Hess, J. M., and P. R. Cateora, *International Marketing*, Homewood, Ill.: Irwin, 1966, chap. 13.
14. Leighton, D. S. R., *International Marketing: Text and Cases*, New York: McGraw-Hill, 1966, chap. 5.
15. Lorimor, E. S., and S. W. Dunn, "Reference Groups, Congruity Theory and Cross-Cultural Persuasion," *Journal of Communication*, vol. 18, December 1968.
16. Moyer, R., "International Market Analysis," *Journal of Marketing Research*, vol. 5, November 1968.
17. Ryans, J. K., and J. C. Baker, *World Marketing: A Multinational Approach*, New York: Wiley, 1967, part V.
18. Sommers, M. S., and J. B. Kernan, eds., *Comparative Marketing Systems*, New York: Appleton-Century-Crofts, 1968, part I.
19. Thomas, M. J., *International Marketing Management*, Boston: Houghton Mifflin, 1969, part IV.
20. Webster, L., "Comparability in Multi-Country Surveys," *Journal of Advertising Research*, vol. 6, December 1966.
21. Yoshino, M. Y., "Marketing Orientation in International Business," *Business Horizons*, Summer 1965.

International Marketing

Chapter 3

Market Opportunities across National Boundaries

HARPER W. BOYD, JR. *Graduate School of Business, Stanford University, Stanford, California*

As more and more firms turn to marketing their products outside their national boundaries, realistic ranking of the potentials of countries for profitable absorption of a company's products becomes an increasingly acute problem. At first thought, the problem might seem to be solvable by merely extending the methods used to measure domestic potential by geographical units. But international market analysis differs substantially from domestic market analysis because the heterogeneity of countries makes it difficult to generalize; each country is almost a unique case. Further, each of the over 100 countries making up the "world" usually represents only a small potential both now and in the future. This relatively low potential inhibits the spending of funds required to obtain the data needed to determine the present and future size of the market.

These problems are particularly relevant in the "developing" countries. Western European countries (with the exception of Spain and Portugal), Canada, South Africa, Australia, and Japan tend to have reasonably adequate data on which to base estimates of potential, and the value of the data warrants the cost of undertaking a detailed study. "Developing" countries obviously do not possess data with these characteristics; further, their futures are more uncertain. Precisely these difficulties make international market analysis a serious challenge.

This chapter focuses on estimating market potentials for either a product or a group of related products on a country-by-country basis. Conceptually and methodologically, the problem is similar to that of domestic market analysis, which represents an extension of market segmentation. In the international as well as the domestic situation, the meaning of *potential* must be carefully considered. It may be defined as "sales opportunities for a product or a service per some specified time period given *certain conditions.*" It is the *conditional* aspects of the measurement which must be given detailed attention.

The importance of this becomes abundantly clear in the following type of question: "What will be the demand for fertilizer in India *if* the government of India subsidizes its purchase by farmers?" The conditionals often come in series. For example, "What will be the demand for a high-protein food in Indonesia *if* the government restricts the local consumption of rice (to permit more to be exported) and *if* the consumer price is not subsidized?" As always, unless the conditions or assumptions underlying the meaning and measurement of potential have specificity—as well as reality—the derived statistics will have little significance.

Effective demand or potential is, of course, a function of several variables which are difficult to measure under the best of conditions. This is particularly the case with those developing nations in which the actions of governments are hard to predict. And products which are deeply embedded in either the social or technological cultures pose additional problems. But the reasoning is still clear because it can be logically argued that isolating and measuring the demand variables over time will lead to a better estimate of the return on investment as well as the extent of risk involved. This chapter has no intention of going this far in the discussion, but an awareness of the direct linkage between the measurement of potential and returns on investment (ROIs) is important.

Neither is it the purpose of this chapter to recount the obvious problems inevitably associated with the derivation of potentials by country. Rather, what will be attempted is a constructive statement which will help to "solve" the problem. In the ensuing discussion, the same format will be employed as that utilized to estimate domestic potential by geographical units. This may oversimplify the discussion somewhat, but at least it will follow a familiar line of presentation. This means that attention will be paid to such subject areas as product definition (including role), segmentation by countries, segmentation within country, measurement methods, and general data sources. The latter are contained in Appendix A, and each major source is briefly annotated.

The reader will observe that certain assumptions are being made about his familiarity with the setting of potentials. Familiarity with the concept, its operational usefulness to the firm, and the major alternative ways that potential can be measured is indeed assumed. (Those not familiar with it are advised to consult Part A, Chapter 1 of this section.)

PRODUCT DEFINITION AND ROLE

The starting point in any attempt to measure potential must be a definition or itemization of the product(s) involved. This classification is acute *across* national boundaries, because a product in one culture is obviously *not* always the same product in another. Its role—or roles—often differs substantially, and the factors affecting its demand may vary even more. Unless much is known about how the product is perceived locally and what part it plays in the indigenous consumption system(s), it will be difficult to predict demand.

An important beginning point in attempting to define the product is to deal with generic use. Thus, the end uses to which the product can be applied and the needs the end use is attempting to satisfy should be indicated by country and category of country. Admittedly, this requires knowledge of local cultures, but to do otherwise runs the risk that product perception may be biased with respect to the country being studied. Several examples come quickly to mind.

1. *Refrigerators.* In the United States, the average housewife uses this product to accomplish four types of food cooling: (1) to store frozen foods, (2) to preserve perishables for several days, (3) to cool certain bottled or canned beverages, and (4) to house certain semiperishables such as margarine. In other countries—including European ones—the housewife uses a refrigerator to keep a small amount of perishables cool for a short time and to store leftovers. In the United States, refrigerators of 10 to 12 cubic feet are the rule; elsewhere, the average size tends to be more like 6 cubic feet [13].

2. *Lamps.* A survey among housewives in Mexico revealed that most bought a lamp as a decorative item—one to enhance their homes. In the United States, a combination of decorativeness *and* functional utility is sought [3].

3. *Automobiles.* In countries such as those of Scandinavia, the car is a strictly utilitarian object with emphasis on reliability and economy. In the more affluent countries, like the United States and West Germany, greater individuality in car owning is stressed. The desire is for high-quality, almost custom-tailored vehicles [11].

In addition to looking at generic use, one must view the product as part of some consumption system. By this is meant that the product belongs to a set of interrelated parts. The total system exists to satisfy a basic need, and no part of it can be understood without comprehending the aspect of wholeness. It may be helpful to regard a consumption system as a series of steps which embrace one or more products plus different actions by the user(s) relative to solving a problem. This solving of a problem or goal directedness is critical, because a failure to understand the nature of the goal and the standards set by the consumer to determine the expertness with which the goals are accomplished will inevitably result in a misunderstanding of the system *as well as the role of the product of interest.*

The emerging countries have been too prone to "borrow" products for local manufacturers which have been developed for use in the consumption systems of the more affluent nations. This often means that scarce resources are committed to the production of items which do not readily fit the local scene. The status derived from the use of foreign products frequently covers up the mistake. If the product could be specially designed to fit local needs, its potential could be substantially affected.

> Take, for example, the production of bicycles in India. Almost without exception bikes produced in India are carbon copies of those which have been developed for use in societies in which the streets are well paved, sidewalks are present, the temperature varies significantly, it frequently rains, the main user is likely to be a child or a teenager, service stations and tire-repair outlets are plentiful, spare parts can be obtained easily, and so on. Needless to say, almost none of these environmental conditions prevails in a country like India where the user is apt to be a mature male who uses his bike for transportation of self as well as, frequently, nonhuman objects. It is difficult to believe that a different potential would not exist if a bicycle were built specifically for local use which at least had sturdier wheels, solid rubber tires, a stronger frame, and a seat which would not rot out from continuous and long exposure to rain and sun.

At the very least, knowledge of consumption systems will—or should—reveal whether a present product is compatible within presently employed systems. Clearly, a packaged detergent is not usable if the family washing is done by hand in running water or a community washing pool. A frequent problem with mechanical products is that no repair service is locally available, which thereby necessitates the establishment of another part of the system to accommodate the sale of the product.

SEGMENTATION BY COUNTRIES

Heilbroner has pointed out that most Americans concerned with the problems of other countries make the mistake of thinking of "Americanization" as the solution [16]. This view inevitably leads some business executives to believe "that history will repeat itself and that the institutions and organizations appropriate for developed countries today will be equally appropriate for underdeveloped countries tomorrow. . . . If such a pattern exists, the task of writers on marketing in underdeveloped regions is relatively simple; it is merely to apply the marketing organizations and techniques of the most economically advanced countries, with appropriate lags, to all less advanced countries" [10]. Under such conditions, one could locate countries in a given stage of development and, with hindsight, proceed to make estimates regarding their present and future potentials for certain products.

As attractive as this assumption of a norm of development may be, it probably does not exist [10]. But even so, some international market analysts find value in attempting to set up a scheme of classification that will cluster those countries which appear to be in the same stage of economic development. Leander reports a situation in which an executive in a food manufacturing company

> . . . read a summary article about Rostow's theory and deliberately set out to see how it applied to his international business. He collected data on market indicators and on performance of major products in foreign markets. The markets were grouped according to the level of development concept. From this analysis he discovered a significant relationship between the types of product sold and the level of economic development. At the time of this study he was undertaking a similar analysis for other product lines and was much encouraged by the results. He believed that this approach would be helpful in developing a model of product mix appropriate to various levels of development. The model could be used as a guideline in changing the product mix in a given country as it moves from one stage of development to another [20].

Another way of clustering countries is by trade blocs such as the European Economic Community (EEC), the European Free Trade Association, the Latin American Free Trade area, and the Central American Common Market. Each of these "common" markets has different objectives and regulations, but all seek to combine several national states into larger markets to facilitate the development of larger production units which will obtain economies of scale. It is obvious that such groupings can be thought of as large or master segments and the individual states as subsegments.[1]

Depending on the rules and regulations of the group, an international marketer might or might not feel it necessary to analyze the markets of the individual countries involved in such blocs. Such a decision would also hinge on the purpose of his analysis. For trade blocs, the relative size of the various national members, the differences in their cultures and levels of economic wellbeing, and even their potential stability more often than not require the analysis of individual markets. This appears to be true with respect to all the trade areas with the possible exception of the Central American Common Market, composed of such small states as Costa Rica, Guatemala, Nicaragua, Honduras, and El Salvador. Great heterogeneity usually characterizes these trade blocs,

---

[1] For an interesting discussion of the similarities and dissimilarities of the EEC consumer, see [18].

for example, Holland versus Germany; Portugal versus Sweden; and Chile versus Mexico. But the study of trade blocs qua blocs helps to determine the potential available in making a choice, for example, between entering by licensing or by building a manufacturing plant.

Cluster Analysis

This type of analysis has as its objective the grouping of objects (countries) into subsets containing similar objects. Thus, cluster analysis is the process by which segments are derived. The problem is essentially one of finding a classification scheme which will yield maximum homogeneity *within* each group (or segment) and maximum heterogeneity *between* groups. The criteria for the clustering in our case would be expected behavior at some point in time regarding the purchase of a given product type. If we could successfully cluster countries on such a basis, we could obtain measures of relative potential as well as indications of what countries should receive similar marketing efforts.

Cluster analysis is a complex subject since there are many ways by which groupings can be effected. In recent years considerable interest has been expressed by marketing analysts in this procedure because of the growing awareness of the importance of market segmentation. Some use has even been made of numerical taxonomy, a technique developed by biologists to classify objects.[2]

An illustration of the use of cluster analysis with respect to classifying like countries is provided by Sherbini, who used 12 environmental and societal characteristics within 5 levels of development. Clearly he assumed that behavior was multidimensional![3] His selected characteristics and their descriptive attributes were as follows:

  I. Environmental Factors
    1. Total population
    2. Population density
    3. Annual percentage rate of increase in population
    4. Percentage of population of working age (15–64)
    5. Literacy: literate percentage of population aged 15 and over
    6. Agricultural population as a percentage of total population
    7. Urbanization: percentage of population in cities over 20,000 population
    8. Primacy: population of the primate city as a percentage of the total population of the four largest cities
  II. Societal Factors
    9. Ethnic diversity: number of ethnic groups which amount to 1 percent of the population or more
    10. Religious homogeneity and identification
        Homogeneous—75 percent of the population with one religion
    11. Racial homogeneity and identification
        Homogeneous—90 percent of the population belonging to one racial stock
    12. Linguistic homogeneity: percentage of the adult population which speaks a common language
        Homogeneous—a common language spoken by at least 85 percent of the adult population

In abbreviated form, Sherbini's findings by development level were as follows:

[2] For an excellent discussion of the various techniques which can be used to cluster objects, see [14, pp. 83–93].

[3] This section is based on A. A. Sherbini, "Classifying and Comparing Countries," in [28, pp. 57–90]. For a discussion of the concepts involved in comparative marketing, see [1; 9, pp. 59–63].

I. *Most Highly Developed Countries*, e.g., the United Kingdom, West Germany, Belgium, the United States, France, Canada, Sweden, Netherlands, Italy, and Australia. All have a very high literacy rate and relatively high urbanization. None has an overwhelmingly predominant metropolis. Almost all have a very large measure of cultural homogeneity and possess a dominant language.

II. *Developed Countries*, e.g., Finland, South Africa, Ireland, Mexico, Portugal, Israel, and Brazil. These countries do not possess a single common attribute. Most are highly literate, highly urbanized, not densely populated, and not overwhelmingly agricultural. They show wide variances in population increase. Most have a dominant language and are heterogeneous in religion and race.

III. *Semideveloped Countries*, e.g., Lebanon, Greece, U.A.R., Turkey, Colombia, Peru, India, and Iraq. A majority of these countries are literate, have a predominantly agricultural population with a high annual population increase, possess a low working age/dependency ratio, and a dominant language, race, and religion. They vary substantially in population size.

IV. *Underdeveloped Countries*, e.g., Tunisia, Ghana, Syria, Bolivia, Iran, and Indonesia. Most of these countries contain largely illiterate rural (agricultural) populations, have high annual rates of population increase, and are reasonably homogeneous with respect to race and religion. They vary a great deal in size of population.

V. *Very Underdeveloped Countries*, e.g., Nigeria, Burma, Thailand, Sudan, Jordan, Mali, Haiti, Liberia, and Ethiopia. The size of population in these countries varies widely, but almost all have a low population density. Most have a high dependency ratio and a high population rate increase. There is considerable heterogeneity in race, religion, and language.

Sherbini's work reveals considerable diversity among regions. Organizing multinational operations largely on the basis of geography is therefore questionable. Cultural attributes other than geographic proximity surely should also be considered in setting up administrative units.

By implication, Sherbini's method of clustering countries is similar to the corollary data method, which typically uses a multiple factor index. This is a frequently used technique for estimating market potentials. A multiple factor index assumes—and quite rightly—that several variables affect the sales of a given product group in a given market and that these factors should be represented in the index. In practice, it is extremely hard to identify these factors, to obtain a measure of each, and to determine their relative importance. There is the inevitable problem of validating the appropriateness of the final index. Does it, in fact, represent the relative market potential for a product?[4]

Sherbini's procedure could easily be modified to include or exclude factors as desired by the analyst, assuming the availability of reliable data. Also, the relative weights assigned to the individual factors could be altered to suit the analyst. It should be noted that conceptually, at least, any attempt to cluster countries will, one hopes, do more than to "predict" relative potential. If successful, it will also reveal likenesses which would imply that similar marketing methods could be applied to the "related" countries. To what extent the environmental and cultural factors used by Sherbini to develop the clusters do in fact accomplish this is not known. In its present form, the Sherbini procedure is not useful for measuring potential because it does not quantify the factors and does not assign a numerical value to individual countries on either a gross or a per capita basis [28].

No mention has yet been made of the laws (including monetary restrictions) which various countries employ either to discourage or to encourage trade with or direct investment by other countries. Nor has any account been made of a

---

[4] For a more thorough discussion of multiple factor indexes, see [17].

measure of present and future political stability of individual countries. These factors are obviously of greater importance in the measurement of realistic potential than any others. Because of variations among countries as well as in the complexity of the factors, it is not possible to discuss them in this chapter. It would seem, however, that before any attempt is made to study countries from the point of view of market potential, they should be ranked on the basis of their political stability and legal "openness."

SEGMENTATION WITHIN COUNTRY

As noted earlier, it is extremely difficult to obtain an absolute or relative measure of potential at the national or country level, let alone *within* a country. Ideally, this should be accomplished through a direct measurement—for example, of industry sales—by geographic units. This is only possible for some frequently purchased products in certain of the more industrialized nations. Import statistics are of importance for certain industrial products, but only where little or no domestic production is involved and where the import classification system is sufficiently precise so as not to mask the character of the product being measured. Further, import statistics are not always reliable. Even where data of this type are available, they are not broken down as to use or consumption by areas within the country.

Our concern, therefore, is with indirect measurements that will enable us to segment the relevant population, to measure the relative worth of the segments, and then to distribute it geographically. Market segmentation is the process by which a firm classifies its prospective customers (the market) into a number of subgroups (segments). By this definition, we are saying that the market lacks homogeneity in its response to desire for a given product as well as to a firm's marketing effort. For our purpose, the following conditions must be met if market segmentation is to be operational:

1. The identification and categorization of actual or potential buyers into mutually exclusive groups that have high intragroup homogeneity with respect to responses to the product(s) in question.

2. The identification of characteristics of the members of the segment which makes quantifying the worth of individual segments possible.

3. The distribution of the results of the two preceding steps within the country being studied.

There are five major ways of segmenting—by geography, culture, demographic characteristics, socioeconomic descriptors, and behavior and/or behavioral predispositions, for example, attitudes. The first four "methods" require the analyst to *infer* differences in behavior on a classification scheme which *ascribes* behavior. Because of the problem of space, only the more generalizable principles affecting the five methods will be discussed.

A question of considerable importance is the extent to which the methods to be discussed can be quantified within a given country. Suffice it to say at this point that, generally speaking, data on each of the characteristics to be discussed can be obtained with sufficient reliability to make the segmentation scheme feasible.

Geography

Most countries are divided into regions or areas which are sufficiently homogeneous to warrant consideration as segments. Often these regions are historical and reflect racial differences. This is certainly the case with Spain, where [22]:

Madrid is the commercial hub of the central and western parts of the country. Barcelona, considered to be the leading industrial and commercial city of Spain, is also an important Mediterranean port. It is the gateway to the "Costa Brava" and is the distribution point for the northeastern provinces—the region known as Cataluña.

The central Mediterranean coastal area, the Levant, is served from Valencia, a port, the center of the citrus industry, and the third ranking commercial city in Spain. The southern provinces, which make up Andalusia, hinge on the fourth largest commercial city, Seville. Balboa, located on the northern coast in an area of heavy industry and La Coruña (in Galicia) are the leading commercial centers in the northern part of the country.

In many emerging countries, because of the traditional aspects of their societies, "regions" have high internal homogeneity and there is great heterogeneity among them. Such countries as Nigeria, India, the United Arab Republic, and Thailand come quickly to mind in this respect. In the more industrially mature economies, the concept of regionalism comes into focus because of the concentration of certain industries—for example, Italy, Yugoslavia, West Germany, and France.

Culture

For multinational firms, cultural grouping is an obvious and important way of segmenting. By *culture* is meant "the abstracted nonbiological conditions of human life—'artifacts, sociofacts, and mentifacts'" [2]. Culture thus has a significant effect on how individuals behave, especially in dealing with problems common to the group. All cultures consist of regularized ways of behaving both explicitly and implicitly, and these are apt to vary substantially. All people must eat to live, but what is eaten is determined largely by cultural preferences.

Fashion is distinctly linked to culture. Fashions are quick to respond to and reflect all changes in the fundamental ideas and beliefs of the culture. Thus, in our society, changing attitudes toward modesty are quickly revealed in the fashions of the day. But this is not true in the more traditional societies [19, 27, 29].

Actual values clearly affect social order through statutes and the differentiation of roles by age, sex, and social class. Culture ascribes certain behavior to individuals of a certain sex, class or occupation, and age. The more traditional the society, the more pronounced are the benefits and penalties attached to being of a certain sex, class, or age.

Demographic Variables

Age runs a predictable course. On the basis of the age distribution of the population as of a given date, reasonably reliable predictions can be made about the size of age groups of the future. Because age is correlated with key events *and* biological functions, it is often used as a basis for segmentation. The purchase and use of many products obviously vary by age groups. In the emerging nations, it is not uncommon to find that half the population is under 20 years of age, indeed, under 15 years of age. Such an age distribution has an important effect on the consumption of certain products and services, especially those having to do with health and education. It is also important that in such countries old age is viewed with great respect and the role of the child (as well as woman) is prescribed in considerable detail [23]. Reliable statistics are available on age distributions within most countries.

Income is an important basis for segmentation within a country because effective demand depends upon the availability of money to support desire.

Further, the amount of income also affects the types of goods that will be purchased. Too often, analysts pay attention to per capita income instead of studying income distribution. It is true, of course, that incomes in other countries are typically much smaller than those in the United States. But certain costs are frequently lower than those in the United States—for example, the low rents charged in state or cooperative housing units in Yugoslavia. While income statistics are not as easy to come by as those for age distribution, they are relatively common.

Language and dialects are additional bases for segmenting. Some countries have one central language but numerous local idioms. This is true in Spain, where the regional language is Catalan around Barcelona and Basque in the north [22]. In India, there are "fifty-one dialects spoken by one or more million people each. No one language is spoken by more than about 50 million of the almost 400 million population. Only about 15 percent of the population is literate in any language" [31].

Education is yet another important variable for segmentation, and its importance varies more than perhaps most other variables by the product or service under investigation. Educational attainment is increasing rapidly throughout the world, and data on it are usually available in considerable detail in most countries.

The distribution of the population by city size can be an important basis for segmentation, since those families living on a farm or in small towns or villages are often thought to be less monied, less well educated, more tradition-oriented, and more resistant to change. In many of the emerging countries, such individuals are either out of the monetary sector of the economy or, at best, spend most of their income on food, kerosene, and textiles. Rural households buy staples, such as grain and cloth, and process such staples within the home [4]. Population distribution data by city size are ordinarily obtainable.

Socioeconomic Variables

Every society has its status groupings, and from these emerges a social class system which serves to maintain barriers between people with different status rankings.[5] People tend to associate most with people whom they regard as their "equals," that is, those who possess similar values and attitudes. Carman, after making a detailed study of the applicability of the social class concept to marketing, concluded that it was a valuable basis for segmenting the consumer market into reasonably homogeneous parts [7].

The best evidence suggests that social classes exist in all societies and that the boundary lines between them tend to be more severe in the less developed countries than in the more industrialized nations. The evidence also suggests that the social values and attitudes held by members of the different classes are roughly similar across national boundaries, although, clearly, the ways in which these social values are expressed in consumption differ substantially.

As might be expected, the middle class is relatively small (but growing) in most of the emerging countries. Hassan El Saaty estimated that in Egypt the middle class contained 18.8 percent of the population and was growing due mainly to the land reform laws and increased employment by the government. He estimated that the upper class constituted 1.2 percent and the lower class 80 percent of the total population.[6]

---

[5] For a detailed discussion of social class, including its measurement, see [30; 8, pp. 171–184; 21, pp. 146–160].

[6] As reported in [4].

A study in Managua, the capital of Nicaragua, used principles of the theory of social classes as the basis for studying food purchasing habits. An attempt was made to relate the purchasing of goods with a low markup (for example, meat, rice, cereals, beans, and dairy products) versus those with a high markup (for example, canned foods, household items, and liquors) to various social classes. In this study, it was found that the upper-middle and middle-middle classes accounted for about 70 percent of the sales of a local supermarket and an even higher share of the gross margin [3].

In trying to assess the changing nature of the European consumer, Groves and Trotman employ a segmentation scheme which has some relation to social class theory. They advocate the use of two segments [15]:

> The first is smaller, faster growing, and contains the cosmopolitan elite who cross national and language borders frequently and who accept standardized products and advertising appeals which are the same throughout Europe. The other segment is composed of a much larger number of people who stay in their own localities and can usually only be reached with appeals and products tailored to their particular habits, tastes, customs, and other cultural mores. Much evidence points to the fact that the "cosmopolite" market segment is homogeneous on a pan-European scale, and that its members, who are not distinguished from others solely on the basis of higher incomes, gradually influence the other to adopt their own way of life. The great majority of the latter have never had the good fortune to enjoy much discretionary time or income and have never seen the opportunity to get rich even in a small way.

This indicates a belief in certain "principles" having to do with the diffusion of innovations. Generally speaking, this concept holds that individuals with certain characteristics are apt to adopt an innovation before others do. Earlier adopters are thought to be younger, possess higher social status, have a more favorable financial position, and have a different type of mental ability than late adopters [26]. In the marketing of relatively new products or ideas, the "market" is or can be segmented through time on the basis of these characteristics. Generalizations regarding the characteristics of the adopter categories are roughly true across national lines.

Use Behavior and Predispositions

A common way of segmenting has to do with use behavior—for example, heavy versus light users. If, indeed, heavy buyers of a product class have different characteristics than light buyers, then information exists by which different actions can be taken—for example, the selection of different media. There seems to be some question whether such differences exist with respect to consumer goods [25]. But similar data for industrial goods are obviously important because of the ease of identifying the particular account and of taking appropriate action.

To obtain use behavior or predispositional—for example, attitudinal—data typically requires either the availability of survey data or the resources to accomplish the same. Survey use behavior data are available in only a few countries (for example, the Atwood consumer panel in England); they are difficult and expensive to obtain elsewhere. Despite what was considered to be a thorough search of the literature, the author was not able to locate examples of attitudinal research that dealt with attitudes toward salient product characteristics and which could, therefore, be cited as a means for segmentation.

Marketing research of a high caliber is practiced in the Western European countries, Canada, Australia, and Japan. Competent technicians with adequate experience are available in these countries. Further, the environments for conducting surveys at the household level are similar to that of the United States. But such is not the case in most of the emerging countries. Not only is there a shortage of trained personnel, but their lack of experience in attempting to provide relevant data which can be used in the decision process is severe. Further, the environment in which surveys are attempted is relatively hostile. Thus, block maps from which to draw samples are often nonexistent, poor transportation frequently makes the use of a dispersed sample difficult, data collection by telephone and mail is almost impossible, the refusal to cooperate, and the number of languages or dialects used all make the marketing research function a difficult one to implement with any precision.[7]

This section has focused on the more important bases for segmentation *within* countries. It was not intended to be all-inclusive, and the reader will easily think of other bases by which such segmentation can be accomplished. What is important is that much of the data required for determining potentials by certain groupings are often available from local data sources.

DATA METHODS

This section inevitably duplicates, to some extent, previous sections. Even so, it is thought desirable to present a brief statement of estimating methods per se.

One method for estimating market potentials both between and within countries involves the use of direct data—for example, data dealing with the actual product or service of interest. Total anticipated sales in units and dollar equivalents for some specified future year is one type of direct data. Such data, especially when the country has used the product for some years, have high relevance because they "give the composite experience of the entire industry and take into account not only the characteristics of the individual markets (population, income, buying habits, and so on), but the past sales efforts of the firms comprising the industry" [6].

Availability of such sales data varies substantially by country and by product. Typically, more are obtainable in the more industrialized countries than in the emerging countries, but data are usually available only for the total country; that is, data by areas within a country are difficult to come by. Further, the more the product in question is produced locally, the more difficult it is to get reliable data; because if imports are large, import statistics (though of doubtful validity in some cases) are often available. One problem in using import data is the product groupings employed. These often are so general or broad as to mask the sales of a particular product. Also, the groupings are not constant between countries.

For certain consumer products, there are continuous data sources outside the United States which report product group sales and even brand shares at fairly frequent intervals. The A. C. Nielsen store audit service is available on a country-by-country basis throughout most of Europe as well as in Canada and Australia. A number of consumer panels also exist in these countries, although they are not as widespread as store audits. From a variety of sources, direct data can be obtained on the production of certain industrial and consumer products because of taxes, licenses, and government ownership.

It is impossible in the space available to cite sources to which the reader can refer to check the availability—and reliability—of direct data by country.

---

[7] For a further discussion of the problems associated with doing survey work in the emerging countries, see [5, pp. 20–23].

Suffice it to say here that more such data are available than might be thought, although by no means a great deal. Any search for such data should include the U.S. Department of Commerce, the applicable consuls where accessible, large domestic banks with worldwide operations, large indigenous banks, local media, the statistical offices of such regional organizations as the O.E.C.D., and the United Nations.

Some indication of present sales can, of course, be garnered through marketing research. The difficulty here is that trend data cannot be obtained, the data collection cost is normally high and time-consuming, and, in some countries, it is hard to get accurate measurements.

Where direct data are not available, corollary data may be used. Such a method is based on the idea that if one data series is highly related to another, it can be used as a surrogate for the first. Thus, the sales of one product—for example, gasoline—may be used to indicate the sales of another product—for example, tires. The relationship is most apt to be satisfactory when the two products have a closely related demand either on a derived or complementary basis. It is possible, as noted earlier, to use such statistics as those having to do with population, income, and retail sales as corollary data.

Multiple Factor Indexes

This method, by definition, calls for a combination of several factors to develop an index to measure a product's potential. Basically the index measures the potential indirectly and only on a relative basis. The analyst preparing the index typically uses his judgment of what factors to use as well as how much weight to assign each. Where specific data are scarce, general factors such as population, retail sales, and income may be combined to obtain an index for consumer products similar to that of *Sales Management*. Erickson constructed such an index for Brazil which purported to measure the potential for consumer goods by each of Brazil's 21 states [12].

The J. Walter Thompson advertising agency has constructed a general multiple factor index for Western European markets. It uses nine factors—population, population density, value of imports, value of exports, personal consumption, expenditures, number of cars, number of radios, and number of telephones. All factors are weighted equally and each country is ranked on the basis of the gross values of the factors as well as their per capita values.

Multiple regression analysis is often used to make the multiple factor method more objective by determining the relative importance of alternative factors and the weights to be assigned to each. One difficulty here is that a substitute value has to be found for the dependent variable (sales potential) because this is not known, and yet without it the estimate of the regression equation cannot be obtained. Moyer suggests that this problem can often be overcome by "analogy, i.e., by studying the relationship between gross economic indicators and demand for a specific commodity for countries with *both* kinds of data. We then transfer this relationship by analogy to the less developed country where, more than likely, only the gross economic indicators are available" [24].

Demand Patterns and Income Elasticity Measures

Moyer also suggests the use of industrial growth patterns to obtain relative measurements of consumption patterns. He argues that knowing manufacturing production trends is important because they reflect stages of economic growth. These, in turn, indicate certain import patterns. Thus, as industrialization proceeds, demand for fuel, capital equipment, transportation vehicles, and raw materials increases. Further, industrialization ordinarily leads to higher incomes which, in turn, lead to greater demand for consumer durables.

Moyer has developed certain income elasticity measures for a number of both industrial and consumer items. These were calculated on a time series *and* a cross-section basis using a model which includes measures of domestic production, imports, exports, domestic final use, intermediate use, total supply, total demand, and income changes. He uses these elasticity measurements to estimate import substitution elasticities which measure the responsiveness of imports to changes in domestic variables such as income [24]. Any attempt to estimate elasticities should take into account the country's development plan, which may deliberately call for a change in the amount of imported goods relative to total supply.

SUMMARY AND CONCLUSIONS

The purpose of this chapter has been to describe briefly the various ways by which market opportunities between and within countries can be measured. Because of the relative uniqueness of each of the countries in the world, it is difficult to treat the problem of measurement or at least to do so in detail. This is particularly true with the emerging countries which are most dissimilar to the United States.

Caution was advised in defining the product of interest before trying to estimate its potential, because product role varies substantially across national boundaries. The need to understand the indigenous consumption system applicable to the product in question was also stressed, since this too affects potential.

Country groupings can be accomplished in a number of ways. The purpose of such an exercise is both to reveal commonality with respect to the use of similar marketing methods and to indicate categories of relative potential. A multiple factor index using environmental and societal variables would likely be the device used to effect such groupings, although validation of the index would prove difficult.

Segmentation within a country typically requires the use of indirect measures, since rarely are industry sales data available, especially by areas within the country. Generally speaking, statistics are available which can be helpful in dividing up the within-country potential on the basis of such demographic variables as age, income, language, education, and city size. (See the appendix to this chapter for a listing of some general sources of such data.) Product usage and attitudinal data require the use of market surveys, which are difficult to implement in the less developed countries.

The methods used to estimate potential both within and between countries are similar to those currently used by market analysts in the United States. They include direct data, corollary data, multiple factor indexes, multiple regression analysis, and survey data. The direct data method, since it is based on sales, is the best way—the most realistic way—of estimating both absolute and relative potential *provided* the analyst does not want an estimate derived from a set of sales determinants, which are essentially different from those which have existed in the past. The use of sales data has the additional advantage of making possible, where desirable, the computation of market share data which can serve as performance indicators.

Corollary data methods, by definition, use related data to estimate potential and hence suffer in their being "once removed" from direct measures. Often a number of factors are combined, in which case there is not only the question of correlation of the factors used with actual potential but also the matter of how the individual factors are weighted in the index. Multiple regression methods tend to be less subjective, but again there is the problem of validating the results. Surveys represent a way of collecting the desired data and have the advantage of enabling the analyst to collect those data thought to be most pertinent to the problem at hand. They are, however, expensive and difficult to execute in most emerging countries.

REFERENCES

1. Bartels, R., "Are Domestic and International Marketing Dissimilar?" *Journal of Marketing,* July 1968.
2. Berelson, B., and G. A. Steiner, *Human Behavior,* New York: Harcourt, Brace & World, 1964.
3. Boyd, H. W., Jr., et al., *Marketing Management: Cases from the Emerging Countries,* Reading, Mass.: Addison-Wesley, 1966.
4. ———, A. A. el-Sherbini, and A. F. Sherif, "Channels of Distribution for Consumer Goods in Egypt," *Journal of Marketing,* October 1961.
5. ———, R. E. Frank, W. F. Massy, and M. Zoheir, "On the Use of Marketing Research in the Emerging Countries," *Journal of Marketing Research,* November 1964.
6. ———, and R. L. Westfall, *Marketing Research,* Homewood, Ill.: Irwin, 1964.
7. Carman, J. M., *The Application of Social Class in Market Segmentation,* Berkeley, Calif.: Institute of Business and Economic Research, University of California, 1965.
8. Coleman, R. P., "The Significance of Social Stratification in Selling," in Martin L. Bell, ed., *Proceedings of the 43rd National Conference of the American Marketing Association,* Chicago: American Marketing Association, 1960.
9. Cundiff, E. W., "Concepts in Comparative Retailing," *Journal of Marketing,* January 1965.
10. Currie, L., "Marketing Organization for Underdeveloped Countries," in R. Moyer and S. C. Hollander, eds., *Markets and Marketing in Developing Economies,* Homewood, Ill.: Irwin, 1968.
11. Dichter, E., "The World Consumer," *Harvard Business Review,* July–August 1962.
12. Erickson, L. G., "Analyzing Brazilian Consumer Markets," *Business Topics,* Summer 1963.
13. Fayerweather, J., *International Marketing,* Englewood Cliffs, N.J.: Prentice-Hall, 1965.
14. Frank, R. E., and P. E. Green, "Numerical Taxonomy in Marketing Analysis: A Review Article," *Journal of Marketing Research,* February 1968.
15. Groves, J., and E. Trotman, "A New Look at European Marketing," *European Business,* January 1968.
16. Heilbroner, R. L., *The Great Ascent,* New York: Harper & Row, 1963.
17. Hummel, F. E., *Market and Sales Potentials,* New York: Ronald, 1961.
18. Kuhlmeijer, H. J., "Market Integration in Europe," Manchester, England: Manchester Historical Society, April 12, 1967.
19. Kunkel, J. H., "Values and Behavior in Economic Development," *Economic Development and Cultural Change,* vol. 13, April 1965.
20. Leander, B., ed., *Comparative Analysis for International Marketing,* Boston: Allyn and Bacon, 1967.
21. Levy, S. J., "Social Class and Consumer Behavior," in J. W. Newman, ed., *Knowing the Consumer,* New York: Wiley, 1966.
22. Lewis, E. H., "Marketing in Spain," *Journal of Marketing,* October 1964.
23. Moore, W. E., and M. M. Tumin, "Some Social Functions of Ignorance," *American Sociological Review,* December 1949.
24. Moyer, R., "International Market Analysis," *Journal of Marketing Research,* November 1968.

25. Rich, D. M., "Limitations of Current Approaches to Understanding Brand Buying Behavior," in J. W. Newman, ed., *Knowing the Consumer*, New York: Wiley, 1966.
26. Rogers, E. M., *Diffusion of Innovations*, New York: Free Press, 1964.
27. Sapir, E., "Fashion," *Encyclopedia of the Social Sciences*, vol. 6, New York: Macmillan, 1937.
28. Sherbini, A. A. el-, "Classifying and Comparing Countries," in B. Leander, ed., *Comparative Analysis for International Marketing*, Boston: Allyn & Bacon, 1967.
29. Sommers, M. S., and J. B. Kervaa, "Why Products Flourish Here, Fizzle There," *Columbia Journal of World Business*, March–April 1967.
30. Warner, W. L., M. Meeker, and K. Wells, *Social Class in America*, Chicago: Science Research Associates, 1949.
31. Westfall, R. L., and H. W. Boyd, Jr., "Marketing in India," *Journal of Marketing*, October 1960.

APPENDIX: SOME GENERAL SOURCES

The following list is a representative sampling of the many valuable sources available which pertain to the subject of this chapter:

American Marketing Association, New York Chapter, *International Directory of Marketing Research Houses and Services*, 11th ed., 1973.

Andersen, I. G., ed., *Marketing and Management: A World Register of Organisations*, Beckenham, England: CBD Research Ltd., 1969.

Angel, Juvenal L., comp., *Directory of American Firms Operating in Foreign Countries*, 7th ed., New York: World Trade Academy Press, 1969.

———, *Directory of Foreign Firms Operating in the United States*, New York: World Trade Academy Press, 1971.

———, *Directory of International Agencies*, New York: Simon & Schuster, 1970.

———, *The Handbook of International Business and Investment Facts and Information Sources*, New York: Simon & Schuster, 1967.

———, *International Marketing Guide for Technical, Management and Other Consultants*, New York: World Trade Academy Press, 1971.

———, ed., *International Reference Handbook of Services, Organizations, Diplomatic Representation, Marketing, and Advertising Channels*, 4th ed., New York: World Trade Academy Press, 1965.

———, *Looking for Employment in Foreign Countries Reference Handbook*, 6th ed., New York: World Trade Academy Press, 1972.

Bureau of Domestic Commerce, U.S. Department of Commerce, *Marketing Information Guide*, Washington, D.C.: Bureau of Domestic Commerce, U.S. Department of Commerce. Monthly. Includes international marketing.

Bureau of International Commerce, U.S. Department of Commerce. *Checklist of International Business Publications*, Washington, D.C.: Bureau of International Commerce, U.S. Department of Commerce, June 1971.

———, *International Marketing Information Service*, Washington, D.C.: Bureau of International Commerce, U.S. Department of Commerce. Irregular series. Since 1969.

———, *Overseas Business Reports*, Washington, D.C.: Bureau of International Commerce, U.S. Department of Commerce. Irregular series. Includes profiles of specific foreign markets as well as studies of market factors in specific foreign markets.

———, *World Trade Information Service*, Washington, D.C.: Bureau of International Commerce, U.S. Department of Commerce. Irregular series.

Bureau of International Commerce, Commercial Intelligence Division, U.S. Department of Commerce, *Trade Lists of Foreign Business Firms*, Washington, D.C.: Published triennially. 1,000 separate lists by product and by country.

Chamber of Commerce of the United States, *Foreign Commerce Handbook: Basic Information and a Guide to Sources*, 16th ed., Washington, D.C.: 1967.

———, *Guide to Foreign Information Sources*, rev. ed., Washington, D.C.: 1962.

Croner, Ulrich H. E., comp. and ed., *Trade Directories of the World: Always Up To Date*, Queens Village, N.Y.: Croner Publications, 1970.

Croner, Ulrich H. E., comp., and Kurt J. Guggenheimer, ed., *Croner's Reference Book for World Traders: Always Up To Date,* Queens Village, N.Y.: Croner Publications. Monthly amendments. 2 vols.

Development Centre, OECD, *Catalogue of Social and Economic Development Research Institutes and Programmes,* 3d ed., OECD, Paris: 1970.

Dun & Bradstreet, *1971 Exporters' Encyclopaedia: Complete Export Guide,* 66th ed., New York: Dun & Bradstreet, 1971. Annual.

Funk and Scott Index International, Cleveland: Predicasts, Inc. Monthly. Foreign business information by subject, country, and company.

Gallatin Annual of International Business, New York: American Heritage, 1965 and after. *Gallatin Letter* updates information biweekly.

International Advertising Association, U.K. Chapter, *Concise Guide to International Markets,* 2d ed., London: 1969. Publication of the 3d ed. expected in 1973 or 1974.

International Research Associates, New York: *Tenth IAA Survey around the World* (1970), New York: 1972.

International Trade Centre, UNCTAD, GATT, *Market Surveys by Products and Countries: Analytical Bibliography,* Geneva: 1969.

———, *World Directory of Industry and Trade Associations,* Geneva: 1970.

Manufacturers Hanover Trust Co., International Division, New York: *Exporter's Handbook.* Annual.

Market Research Society, The, *International Directory of Market Research Organisations,* 2d ed., London: 1972.

Mulvihill, Donald F., comp., *Domestic Marketing Systems Abroad: An Annotated Bibliography,* 2d ed., Kent, Ohio: Kent State University Press, 1967.

National Register Publishing Co., *Standard Directory of Advertising Agencies:* no. 166. Skokie, Ill.: National Register Publishing Co., 1972. Includes foreign agencies.

Price Waterhouse & Co., *Information Guides for Those Doing Business outside the United States.* Looseleaf. Kept up-to-date with supplements.

Rehman, I., comp. and ed., *Directory of World Chambers of Commerce and Trade Associations,* 2d ed., Karachi: Overseas Publisher, 1971.

Sandeau, Georges, ed., *International Bibliography of Marketing and Distribution,* 4th ed., New York: Bowker, 1971.

Wasserman, Paul, Eleanor Allen, and Charlotte Georgi, eds., *Statistics Sources: A Subject Guide to Data on Industrial, Business, Social, Educational, Financial, and Other Topics for the United States and Selected Foreign Countries,* 3d ed., Detroit: Gale Research Co., 1971.

Index